A

# Dictionary of the Bible

DEALING WITH ITS

LANGUAGE, LITERATURE, AND CONTENTS

*INCLUDING THE BIBLICAL THEOLOGY*

EDITED BY

JAMES HASTINGS, M.A., D.D.

WITH THE ASSISTANCE OF

JOHN A. SELBIE, M.A., D.D.

*EXTRA VOLUME*

CONTAINING ARTICLES, INDEXES, AND MAPS

NEW YORK
CHARLES SCRIBNER'S SONS
EDINBURGH: T. & T. CLARK
1904

# PREFACE



This Extra Volume of the Dictionary of the Bible contains thirty-seven Articles, six Indexes, and four Maps. A word will be sufficient on each of these parts of its Contents.

## I. The Articles

Those who have kept in touch with the study of the Bible in recent years will understand why it has been found necessary to prepare an Extra Volume. Discoveries have been made which have an important bearing on the interpretation of both the Old Testament and the New. It is enough to name the three articles which stand first in the alphabetical list given below—Agrapha, Apocryphal Gospels, and Code of Ḫammurabi. A Dictionary of the Bible cannot ignore such discoveries. But they do not form part of the Contents of the Bible; nor do they deal directly with its Language or its Literature; so that they are not likely to be looked for in the alphabetical order of words in the Dictionary. The best way seemed to be to gather them into an Extra Volume.

Other articles will be found in this volume, for reasons which will be readily understood and appreciated. Some of them, like the article on the Sermon on the Mount, with which the volume opens, might have taken their place in the alphabetical order of the Dictionary. But they have not usually been so included, and it was felt that the Extra Volume would give more prominence to their special character and importance.

## II. The Indexes

The Indexes have been prepared with great care. They are full, and yet it will be found that every item in them has been carefully selected and described.

The Index of Texts contains all the passages of Scripture upon which there is any note of consequence in the Dictionary; and, again, the most important notes are distinguished by their authors' names. Further, it sometimes happens that a text is quoted in support or illustration of some argument: when such a quotation throws significant light upon the text itself, it is included in the Index.

The Index of Subjects contains the titles of all the articles in the Dictionary, including the Extra Volume. It also refers to a great many other topics which are dealt with in the course of the work. When the subject of an article comes up for treatment in other places, and a reference is made to these places, then the *first* reference in the Index is always to the article itself. Thus—Ithamar, ii. 519[a]; i. 6[b]; ii. 123[a]; iv. 89[b]—the second volume is mentioned before the first because in it falls the article under its own title; there is also some account of Ithamar in the article on Abiathar in vol. i. p. 6[b], as well as in the other places noted. When the article is of some length the name of the author is given. His name is not repeated under the same heading, so that references without a name attached are to be ascribed to the first author mentioned.

The *cross-references* in the Index of Subjects are always to other parts of the Index itself. Words which occur only in the Apocrypha are marked 'Ap.' or 'Apoc.': as Dabria (Ap.).

## III. The Maps

The maps are intended to illustrate the articles on Roads and Travel. These articles will be of great service to the student of either Testament, and the maps will add to the value of the articles. But they have been prepared so as to be complete maps of the countries they cover, the Roads which are marked on them being additional to the information which such maps usually contain. They have been prepared under the direct supervision of Professor Buhl (for the Old Testament) and Professor Ramsay (for the New), who have spared no pains to make them accurate and up to date.

And now the work on this Dictionary of the Bible is at an end. The Editor has been assisted by the same friends as before and with the same readiness, and he heartily thanks them all. He is also grateful for the way in which the four volumes already published have been received.

# AUTHORS OF ARTICLES IN THE EXTRA VOLUME

| | |
|---|---|
| BARTLET, Professor J. VERNON | Didache. |
| BEBB, Principal LLEWELLYN J. M. | Continental Versions. |
| BENNETT, Professor W. H. | Wages. |
| BLOMFIELD, Rear-Admiral R. M. | Ships and Boats. |
| BUHL, Professor FRANTS | New Testament Times. |
| ,, ,, ,, | Roads and Travel in the Old Testament. |
| DRUMMOND, Principal J. | Philo. |
| FAIRWEATHER, Rev. W. | Development of Doctrine in the Apocryphal Period |
| FARNELL, Dr. L. R. | Worship of Apollo. |
| GARVIE, Professor A. E. | Revelation. |
| HARRIS, Dr. J. RENDEL | Sibylline Oracles. |
| JASTROW, Professor MORRIS | Races of the Old Testament. |
| ,, ,, ,, | Religion of Babylonia and Assyria. |
| JOHNS, Rev. C. H. W. | Code of Ḫammurabi. |
| KAUTZSCH, Professor EMIL | Religion of Israel. |
| KENYON, Dr. F. G. | Papyri. |
| KÖNIG, Professor ED. | Samaritan Pentateuch. |
| ,, ,, ,, | Style of Scripture. |
| ,, ,, ,, | Symbols and Symbolical Actions. |
| LUPTON, Dr. J. H. | English Versions. |
| MCCURDY, Professor J. F. | Semites. |
| MENZIES, Professor ALLAN | Gospel according to the Hebrews. |
| MURRAY, Dr. J. O. F. | Textual Criticism of the New Testament. |
| RAMSAY, Professor W. M. | Numbers, Hours, Years, and Dates. |
| ,, ,, ,, | Religion of Greece and Asia Minor. |
| ,, ,, ,, | Roads and Travel in the New Testament. |
| REDPATH, Dr. H. A. | Concordances. |
| ROPES, Professor J. HARDY | Agrapha. |
| SCHECHTER, Dr. S. | Talmud. |
| SCHÜRER, Professor E. | Diaspora. |
| SCOTT, Professor H. M. | Trinity. |
| STANTON, Professor V. H. | Theocracy. |
| STENNING, JOHN F. | Diatessaron. |
| TASKER, Professor J. G. | Apocryphal Gospels. |
| THACKERAY, H. ST. JOHN | Josephus. |
| TURNER, CUTHBERT H. | Greek Patristic Commentaries on the Pauline Epistles. |
| VOTAW, Professor CLYDE W. | Sermon on the Mount. |
| WIEDEMANN, Professor A. | Religion of Egypt. |

# ALPHABETICAL LIST OF ARTICLES IN THE EXTRA VOLUME

| Page. | Title of Article. | Author's Name. |
|---|---|---|
| 337 | THEOCRACY . . . . . . . . | Rev. VINCENT HENRY STANTON, M.A., D.D., Fellow of Trinity College, and Ely Professor of Divinity in the University of Cambridge. |
| 308 | TRINITY . . . . . . . . . | Rev. HUGH M. SCOTT, D.D., Professor of Ecclesiastical History in the Chicago Theological Seminary. |
| 236 | VERSIONS (ENGLISH) . . . . . | J. H. LUPTON, D.D., formerly Surmaster of St. Paul's School, London. |
| 357 | WAGES . . . . . . . . . | Rev. WM. HENRY BENNETT, M.A., Litt.D., D.D., Professor of Old Testament Exegesis in Hackney and New Colleges, London; sometime Fellow of St. John's College, Cambridge. |
| 143 | WORSHIP OF APOLLO . . . . . | LEWIS RICHARD FARNELL, M.A., Litt.D., Fellow and Senior Tutor, Exeter College, Oxford. |

# MAPS AND INDEXES IN THE EXTRA VOLUME

## MAPS



## INDEXES

# LIST OF ABBREVIATIONS

## I. General

Alex. = Alexandrian.
Apoc. = Apocalypse.
Apocr. = Apocrypha.
Aq. = Aquila.
Arab. = Arabic.
Aram. = Aramaic.
Assyr. = Assyrian.
Bab. = Babylonian.
c. = *circa*, about.
Can. = Canaanite.
cf. = compare.
ct. = contrast.
D = Deuteronomist.
E = Elohist.
edd. = editions or editors.
Egyp. = Egyptian.
Eng. = English.
Eth. = Ethiopic.
f. = and following verse or page: as Ac $10^{34f.}$
ff. = and following verses or pages: as Mt $11^{28ff.}$
Gr. = Greek.
H = Law of Holiness.
Heb. = Hebrew.
Hel. = Hellenistic.
Hex. = Hexateuch.
Isr. = Israelite.
J = Jahwist.
J″ = Jehovah.
Jerus. = Jerusalem.
Jos. = Josephus.
LXX = Septuagint.
MSS = Manuscripts.
MT = Massoretic Text.
n. = note.
NT = New Testament.
Onk. = Onkelos.
OT = Old Testament.
P = Priestly Narrative.
Pal. = Palestine, Palestinian.
Pent. = Pentateuch.
Pers. = Persian.
Phil. = Philistine.
Phœn. = Phœnician.
Pr. Bk. = Prayer Book.
R = Redactor.
Rom. = Roman.
Sam. = Samaritan.
Sem. = Semitic.
Sept. = Septuagint.
Sin. = Sinaitic.
Symm. = Symmachus.
Syr. = Syriac.
Talm. = Talmud.
Targ. = Targum.
Theod. = Theodotion.
TR = Textus Receptus.
tr. = translate or translation.
VSS = Versions.
Vulg. = Vulgate.
WH = Westcott and Hort's text.

## II. Books of the Bible

### *Old Testament.*

Gn = Genesis.
Ex = Exodus.
Lv = Leviticus.
Nu = Numbers.
Dt = Deuteronomy.
Jos = Joshua.
Jg = Judges.
Ru = Ruth.
1 S, 2 S = 1 and 2 Samuel.
1 K, 2 K = 1 and 2 Kings.
1 Ch, 2 Ch = 1 and 2 Chronicles.
Ezr = Ezra.
Neh = Nehemiah.
Est = Esther.
Job.
Ps = Psalms.
Pr = Proverbs.
Ec = Ecclesiastes.
Ca = Canticles.
Is = Isaiah.
Jer = Jeremiah.
La = Lamentations.
Ezk = Ezekiel.
Dn = Daniel.
Hos = Hosea.
Jl = Joel.
Am = Amos.
Ob = Obadiah.
Jon = Jonah.
Mic = Micah.
Nah = Nahum.
Hab = Habakkuk.
Zeph = Zephaniah.
Hag = Haggai.
Zec = Zechariah.
Mal = Malachi.

### *Apocrypha.*

1 Es, 2 Es = 1 and 2 Esdras.
To = Tobit.
Jth = Judith.
Ad. Est = Additions to Esther.
Wis = Wisdom.
Sir = Sirach or Ecclesiasticus.
Bar = Baruch.
Three = Song of the Three Children.
Sus = Susanna.
Bel = Bel and the Dragon.
Pr. Man = Prayer of Manasses.
1 Mac, 2 Mac = 1 and 2 Maccabees.

### *New Testament.*

Mt = Matthew.
Mk = Mark.
Lk = Luke.
Jn = John.
Ac = Acts.
Ro = Romans.
1 Co, 2 Co = 1 and 2 Corinthians.
Gal = Galatians.
Eph = Ephesians.
Ph = Philippians.
Col = Colossians.
1 Th, 2 Th = 1 and 2 Thessalonians.
1 Ti, 2 Ti = 1 and 2 Timothy.
Tit = Titus.
Philem = Philemon.
He = Hebrews.
Ja = James.
1 P, 2 P = 1 and 2 Peter.
1 Jn, 2 Jn, 3 Jn = 1, 2, and 3 John.
Jude.
Rev = Revelation.

## III. English Versions

Wyc. = Wyclif's Bible (NT *c.* 1380, OT *c.* 1382, Purvey's Revision *c.* 1388).
Tind. = Tindale's NT 1526 and 1534, Pent. 1530.
Cov. = Coverdale's Bible 1535.
Matt. or Rog. = Matthew's (*i.e.* prob. Rogers') Bible 1537.
Cran. or Great = Cranmer's 'Great' Bible 1539.
Tav. = Taverner's Bible 1539.
Gen. = Geneva NT 1557, Bible 1560.
Bish. = Bishops' Bible 1568.
Tom. = Tomson's NT 1576.
Rhem. = Rhemish NT 1582.
Dou. = Douay OT 1609.
AV = Authorized Version 1611.
AVm = Authorized Version margin.
RV = Revised Version NT 1881, OT 1885.
RVm = Revised Version margin.
EV = Auth. and Rev. Versions.

## IV. For the Literature

*AHT* = Ancient Hebrew Tradition.
*AJSL* = American Journal of Sem. Lang. and Literature.
*AJTh* = American Journal of Theology.
*AT* = Altes Testament.
*BL* = Bampton Lecture.
*BM* = British Museum.
*BRP* = Biblical Researches in Palestine.
*CIG* = Corpus Inscriptionum Græcarum.
*CIL* = Corpus Inscriptionum Latinarum.
*CIS* = Corpus Inscriptionum Semiticarum.
*COT* = Cuneiform Inscriptions and the OT.
*DB* = Dictionary of the Bible.
*EHH* = Early History of the Hebrews.
*GAP* = Geographie des alten Palästina.
*GGA* = Göttingische Gelehrte Anzeigen.
*GGN* = Nachrichten der königl. Gesellschaft der Wissenschaften zu Göttingen.
*GJV* = Geschichte des Jüdischen Volkes.
*GVI* = Geschichte des Volkes Israel.
*HCM* = Higher Criticism and the Monuments.
*HE* = Historia Ecclesiastica.
*HGHL* = Historical Geog. of Holy Land.
*HI* = History of Israel.
*HJP* = History of the Jewish People.
*HPM* = History, Prophecy, and the Monuments.
*HPN* = Hebrew Proper Names.
*IJG* = Israelitische und Jüdische Geschichte.
*JBL* = Journal of Biblical Literature.
*JDTh* = Jahrbücher für deutsche Theologie.
*JQR* = Jewish Quarterly Review.
*JRAS* = Journal of the Royal Asiatic Society.
*JRL* = Jewish Religious Life after the Exile.
*JThSt* = Journal of Theological Studies.
*KAT* = Die Keilinschriften und das Alte Test.
*KGF* = Keilinschriften u. Geschichtsforschung.
*KIB* = Keilinschriftliche Bibliothek.
*LCBl* = Literarisches Centralblatt.
*LOT* = Introd. to the Literature of the Old Test.
*NHWB* = Neuhebräisches Wörterbuch.
*NTZG* = Neutestamentliche Zeitgeschichte.
*ON* = Otium Norvicense.
*OP* = Origin of the Psalter.
*OTJC* = The Old Test. in the Jewish Church.
*PB* = Polychrome Bible.
*PEF* = Palestine Exploration Fund.
*PEFSt* = Quarterly Statement of the same.
*PSBA* = Proceedings of Soc. of Bibl. Archæology
*PRE* = Real-Encyclopädie für protest. Theologie und Kirche.
*QPB* = Queen's Printers' Bible.
*RB* = Revue Biblique.
*REJ* = Revue des Études Juives.
*RP* = Records of the Past.
*RS* = Religion of the Semites.
*SBOT* = Sacred Books of Old Test.
*SK* = Studien und Kritiken.
*SP* = Sinai and Palestine.
*SWP* = Memoirs of the Survey of W. Palestine.
*ThL* or *ThLZ* = Theol. Literaturzeitung.
*ThT* = Theol. Tijdschrift.
*TS* = Texts and Studies.
*TSBA* = Transactions of Soc. of Bibl. Archæology.
*TU* = Texte und Untersuchungen.
*WAI* = Western Asiatic Inscriptions.
*WZKM* = Wiener Zeitschrift für Kunde des Morgenlandes.
*ZA* = Zeitschrift für Assyriologie.
*ZAW* or *ZATW* = Zeitschrift für die Alttest. Wissenschaft.
*ZDMG* = Zeitschrift der Deutschen Morgenländischen Gesellschaft.
*ZDPV* = Zeitschrift des Deutschen Palästina-Vereins.
*ZKSF* = Zeitschrift für Keilschriftforschung.
*ZKW* = Zeitschrift für kirchliche Wissenschaft.
*ZNTW* = Zeitschrift für die Neutest. Wissenschaft.

**A small superior number designates the particular edition of the work referred to: as *KAT*$^{2}$, *LOT*$^{6}$.**

# DICTIONARY OF THE BIBLE

## EXTRA VOLUME

### SERMON ON THE MOUNT.—



The message of Jesus to men contained in the Sermon on the Mount can be essentially understood, and is valid and useful, apart from the historical, literary, and exegetical questions concerning it which are now receiving so much attention, and which tend to overshadow the real significance and power of His teaching. There are problems still unsolved regarding the origin and transmission of the discourse, problems also regarding the interpretation and application of some of its utterances; but the truth, the preaching, and the living of the Gospel have not to wait upon the results of such investigations. The words of Jesus in this Sermon present an ideal of human life, founded upon religious truth and ethical principles, which has been and is intuitively recognized as the highest standard of life yet conceived, or even as the ultimate standard to which mankind can and must attain. They need not so much to be explained by men as to be appreciated, accepted, and lived by them. A sufficient understanding of the Sermon was not meant to be the possession of the few only. In this teaching Jesus aimed at being universally intelligible; and He was so, for through the Christian centuries the kind of life which He here describes has been the guiding star of civilization. If misconceptions as to the origin and interpretation of the discourse have at times arisen, out of imperfect historical knowledge and limited ethical and spiritual insight, these will gradually disappear before a better knowledge and a clearer vision.

i. *ORIGIN AND TRANSMISSION.*—The historical and literary criticism of the Gospels, which has attracted the labours of many eminent scholars in the past three generations, is by no means finished. Yet some important conclusions have been reached regarding the origin and preservation of the NT records of Jesus' life. To this field of investigation belong the introductory questions concerning the Sermon on the Mount. Was there, in fact, such a discourse? If so, what were the circumstances of its delivery? How were the accounts of the discourse affected by the processes of transmission and translation? And what is the condition of the text of the discourse as we now have it?

1. HISTORICITY OF THE DISCOURSE.—It is the prevailing opinion among NT scholars that in Mt 5–7 we have an account of a discourse actually delivered by Jesus, the theme and substance of which are here preserved.* It is entirely consistent with this view, and is by the majority held in conjunction with it, that the account as it stands in the First Gospel is not coextensive with the discourse originally given by Jesus. Probably not all of the Sermon is contained in Matthew's report, but only excerpts or a digest; for there is no reason to think that means were at hand for reporting the discourse *verbatim* and entire; Jesus seems not to have cared that His discourses should be so preserved; He was accustomed to teach the people *at length* when a multitude was with Him,† while the matter given in Matthew could easily be spoken in twenty minutes; and one would think it faulty pedagogical method to present a series of striking sayings, full of meaning and difficult for the hearers offhand to grasp, without connecting with each germinal saying a more explicit and concrete teaching to illustrate and apply it.

Conversely also, the Matthæan report of the Sermon probably contains some matter which did not form a part of the original discourse. Certain sections of Mt 5–7 are less evidently connected

* So Origen, Augustine, Chrysostom, Luther, Tholuck, Meyer, Keim, Achelis, Edersheim, Godet, Bruce, Broadus, Kübel, Nösgen, Feine, Steinmeyer, Wendt, Sanday, Plummer, B. Weiss, H. Weiss, Grawert, Burkitt, Bartlet, Bacon, and many others.

† See Mk $4^{1f.}$ $^{35}$ $6^{34f.}$

than the others with the specific theme of the Sermon and its development, *e.g.* $5^{25. 26. 31. 32}$ $6^{7-15}$ $7^{6. 7-11. 22f.}$. With regard to these and other passages the possibility of their belonging to the actual Sermon cannot be denied, but the probability is felt by most scholars to be against some or all of them. This view is strongly confirmed by the fact that we find parallels to these sections elsewhere in the Gospels, in other settings which in some cases commend themselves as original. It is difficult to conceive that Luke, or any one else, would break up a discourse of Jesus which had been handed down so fully as in Mt 5–7 and scatter the fragments as in the Third Gospel.* And, finally, it has become recognized that the First Gospel arranges its teaching material into topical groups;† all of the four Gospels exhibit the results of this process, but the First Gospel more than the others.

There have been, and are to-day, a number of eminent scholars who regard the Sermon as a compilation throughout, holding that no such discourse was really delivered by Jesus, and that the alleged occasion of it was a well-meant fiction of tradition or of the Evangelists.* According to this hypothesis, the material grouped under the title of a mountain discourse to His disciples came from various occasions in the ministry which were no longer remembered. The compilation was made for the practical use of the early Christians, to furnish them with a manual of Christian conduct.† But this is to press the theory of compilation to an extreme. It is not an impossible view, and would not entail serious consequences, since it does not deny the authenticity of the sayings; but it must be counted less probable. The examination of the great teaching masses in Matthew seems to show that the briefer sayings were generally grouped with the historical remains of some great discourses, whose approximate position in the ministry and whose circumstances were not wholly forgotten. The main portion of the Sermon, contained in Mt $5^{3}$–$6^{18}$, is (with the exception of certain verses) so closely woven as theme and exposition that it cannot well be denied historical unity and occasion. Jesus must logically have given such teaching as the Sermon presents, in the earlier Galilæan ministry to which the Gospels assign this teaching; and we know that He was accustomed to speak long and connectedly to His hearers. It is therefore probable enough that at least this much of a digest of one of Jesus' most important and impressive discourses should have been preserved.

2. Circumstances of its Delivery. — The occasion on which the Sermon was given appears to be clearly indicated by Lk $6^{12-20}$, which makes it follow closely upon the appointment of the twelve apostles.‡ The Gospel of Matthew agrees with that of Luke in locating the Sermon on the Mount in the first half of Jesus' ministry in Galilee, although Matthew places it somewhat nearer to the beginning of that period.§ There is good

* See Heinrici, *Bergpredigt*, i. 49 f. It is obviously true that Jesus taught the same truths and principles on various occasions to different individuals, and in doing so may have at times repeated some of His sayings in quite the same, or nearly the same, words. Such repetition may *sometimes* serve to explain the several forms in which similar sayings have been handed down. But it cannot be used as a universal resolvent of the mass of variations. This stock argument of the apologetic harmonists proceeds upon the assumption that Jesus' words *must* have been transmitted in every case precisely as He uttered them. But the assumption is unwarranted, and the phenomena of variation abundantly and decisively disprove it. Nearly all NT scholars now agree that the differences which appear in parallel passages of our Gospels are due chiefly to the vicissitudes of transmission and translation. The Gospel teaching did not consist of a set of formulæ, to be learned and repeated *verbatim*.

† See Godet, *Collection of the Four Gospels, and the Gospel of Matthew*, p. 131 ff.; Wendt, *Lehre Jesu*, i. 52, 84, 106, 185; Wernle, *Synopt. Frage*, pp. 61–80; Weizsäcker, *Apost. Zeitalter*², pp. 369–393 [Eng. tr. ii. 33–62]; Jülicher, *Einleitung i. d. NT*, p. 195: Heinrici, *Bergpredigt*, i. 8 f.; B. Weiss, *Meyer-Komm. ü. d. Mattevgm. in loc.*; H. Holtzmann, *Hand-Comm. ü. d. Synoptiker, in loc.* The discourses of Mt 5–7. 10. 13. 18. 23. 24. 25 are compilations in the sense that to the historical nucleus of each discourse there has been joined some matter upon the same or a kindred subject which originally belonged to other historical connexions. Thus Mt 10 contains as a nucleus some instruction which Jesus gave the Twelve when He sent them out on their trial mission ($10^{5-15}$); but to this section there has been added material from another occasion ($10^{16-42}$, esp. $^{17-23}$), when Jesus in the latter part of His ministry was preparing His disciples for the work they must do after His departure. The first Christians found it practically convenient to have the mission teaching grouped together. Mt 13 contains a collection of Jesus' parables upon the nature and development of the kingdom of God. The collection is not found in the corresponding passages Mk 4 and Lk 8. It is quite unlikely that Jesus would make up a discourse of these seven parables (Mt $13^{1-9. 24-30. 31f. 33. 44. 45f. 47-50}$). If the disciples did not understand the first parable until it was explained to them privately (Mk $4^{10}$), it would be of little use to add six others no more intelligible. But the chapter itself, by the two breaks at v.$^{10}$ and vv.$^{34-36}$, shows that it is a compilation; vv.$^{3. 53}$, which *seem* to make all that intervenes a connected discourse, is the editorial device for giving unity and vividness to the teaching. It is probable that the parable of the Sower was given on some occasion (vv.$^{1-3}$) in Jesus' Galilæan ministry, accompanied by explicit teaching along the same line. On other occasions the other parables were given: then, their original setting having been lost, all seven were topically grouped by the early Christians for practical instruction. Mt 18 contains a collection of teachings from various occasions, grouped about the nucleus of an original discourse (cf. Mk $9^{33-50}$) concerning the relations and duties of the Twelve and the community life of the first disciples. Mt 23 is a collection of sayings from different parts of the ministry (cf. Mk $12^{38-40}$, Lk $11^{37-52}$ $13^{34f.}$ $20^{45-47}$), in which Jesus condemned certain acts and characteristics of the Pharisees. The nucleus is apparently in vv.$^{1-12}$; seven woes (the complete number) are here grouped together as were the seven parables of ch. 13. Mt 24 exhibits the same topical arrangement of material (cf. Lk $12^{39-46}$ $17^{22-37}$ 21). And in Mt 21. 22 and 25 appear similar compilations of related teaching. It is probable that the author of the present Gospel of Matthew found this material grouped in this way, although he may have carried the process farther, and have unified these groups by editorial retouching. If, then, the First Gospel has several discourses, consisting in each case of the nucleus of some original sermon augmented by kindred material from other occasions, it becomes quite probable that the discourse in Mt 5–7 is of a similar construction. The added matter is just as valuable and trustworthy as the nucleus matter, being equally the authentic utterances of Jesus.

* So Calvin, Baur, Neander, Bleek, Pott, Semler, Strauss, Kuinöl, Wieseler, H. Holtzmann, Weizsäcker, Jülicher, Heinrici, Ibbeken, Hawkins, Schmiedel.

† Weizsäcker, *Apost. Zeitalter*² (1892), p. 380 f. [Eng. tr. ii. 46 f.]: 'The discourse, as Matthew has adopted it, was in fact a kind of code, but such as originated in and was designed for the Church. . . . The nucleus consists of a few long main sections, $5^{21-48}$ $6^{1-18. 19-34}$. . . . The commandments in these three sections together form a sort of primer, which was, however, first composed by the combination of these didactic pieces, whose original independence is at once apparent from the parallel sections of Luke's Gospel. . . . The evangelist put on an introduction, $5^{3-12. 13-16}$, and an appendix, $7^{1-29}$, to fit the whole to the historical situation which he gave it.' H. Holtzmann, *Hand-Comm. ü. d. Synoptiker*, p. 99: 'Probably the discourse was constructed by the evangelist himself out of written and oral sources, with the primary purpose of furnishing an order of life for the new Church.' Heinrici, *Bergpredigt*, i. 39: 'The Sermon on the Mount of Matthew seems to be a free composition of a speech of Jesus from certain genuine sayings of His, which were in part already grouped together, in part in circulation as single sayings.' Similarly Jülicher, *Einleitung i. d. NT*³ (1901), p. 232; Hawkins, *Horæ Synopticæ* (1899), pp. 131–135; Schmiedel, *Encyc. Bibl.* vol. ii. col. 1886.

‡ The corresponding passage in Mark is $3^{13-19}$, but the Sermon is not found at that point nor elsewhere in the Second Gospel. There is no indication at Mk $3^{19}$ that a discourse followed historically.

§ Too much has often been made of the difference between Matthew and Luke regarding the position to which the Sermon is assigned by each. Matthew places after the Sermon, in chs. 8. 9. $12^{1-21}$, some matter which Luke places before the Sermon in $4^{31}$–$6^{11}$; but this section contains only incidents, miracles, and brief teachings, which, even if they are all in their proper places in Luke (and Mark, which corresponds), would not require more than a few weeks of time. Matthew does not record the appointment of the Twelve, but first mentions them as apostles in ch. 10 in connexion with their mission. Nor does Matthew represent the Sermon as Jesus' *first* teaching, since he distinctly relates before the discourse ($4^{23f.}$) that 'Jesus went about in all Galilee, teaching in their synagogues, and preaching the gospel of the kingdom, and healing all manner of disease and all manner of sickness among the people. And the report of him went forth into all Syria' (*i.e.* throughout Jewish territory). The earlier work and teaching are compressed rather than ignored, and the words are given more prominence than the deeds. A compilation of representative teaching by Jesus in chs. 5–7 is followed by a compilation of representative deeds of Jesus in chs. 8. 9.

reason to think that they are sufficiently correct. The contents of the discourse, as clearly as its position in the Gospels, mark it as a part of His Galilæan teaching,—not, indeed, the first instruction Jesus gave, but of the kind fitted for receptive hearers who had gained some acquaintance with Him, and had by skilful preparation on His part become ready for a general presentation of His religio-ethical ideas. To find Jesus giving one of His most significant discourses in connexion with the appointment of the twelve apostles is altogether what one might expect. That appointment was a great event in His ministry. It marked the stage when His popular success required Him to choose and train some men to assist Him in His work (Mk 3[14]); and it behoved Him also, since the storm of opposition was gathering on the horizon (Mk 2[1]–3[6], cf. Mt 23[29-39]), to prepare these men to carry forward His work after He should lay down His life at Jerusalem.

The Sermon is not, however, addressed exclusively or specifically to the newly-appointed apostles. It contains no trace of esoteric teaching. There is no portion of the discourse which does not pertain equally to all of Jesus' followers, present and future. The internal evidence of the Sermon, therefore, sustains the correctness of the Evangelists' statements (Mt 7[28. 29], Lk 7[1]) that Jesus spoke directly and inclusively to the people who thronged Him at this time.* The multitude was a *disciple* multitude in the sense that many were professed followers of Jesus, many were contemplating discipleship, and all were favourably disposed towards Him, listening with interest to His teaching. The Sermon contains no direct polemic against opponents, but an appeal to all to adopt and to attain a higher type of righteousness than that which was conventionally taught them by the scribes.

The exact time, *i.e.* the year, month, and day, at which the Sermon was given cannot be determined. There is no agreement among scholars as to either the duration or the calendar dates of Jesus' public ministry.† But on any chronological hypothesis the discourse stands about half-way between the beginning of Jesus' public work and His crucifixion.

The Sermon was spoken in Galilee, the scene of the main ministry of Jesus (cf. Mt 4[23-25], Lk 6[17]). If there is an indication in Mt 8[5], Lk 7[1] that the place of the event was near Capernaum, the precise locality would not even then be defined, since the site of Capernaum itself is in dispute. The mountain referred to in Mt 5[1] 8[1], Lk 6[12] is not named and cannot be identified.‡ We may suppose, however, that the scene of the Sermon was in the region to the west of the lake, not far distant from the thickly-populated shore.

3. Transmission and Translation.—We seem to have in Mt 5–7, Lk 6[20-49] two accounts of the Sermon; they differ somewhat in setting, verbal expression, and content, but are nevertheless essentially one discourse.* Both Gospels assign the Sermon to the earlier Galilæan ministry. The circumstances of the discourse are similar—the mountain, the representative multitude, the healings, the address to disciples. The theme of the discourse is the same in each—the true righteousness. The development of the theme is similar—a characterization of this righteousness, with specific teaching as to how it is to affect thought and conduct, and an exhortation to men to live in this way. Each account begins with the Beatitudes, and closes with the injunction to *do* God's will as revealed in Jesus' teaching, enforced by the parable of the Two House-builders. And, finally, nearly the whole of Luke's discourse is contained in Matthew's.

* That the discourse was addressed to the multitude is the view of Achelis, Bleek, Bruce, Godet, Meyer, Nösgen, and others. That it was addressed to close disciples, but overheard by the multitude to whom it did not directly pertain, is held by Tholuck, B. Weiss, Grawert, and others. Burton and Bacon maintain that the discourse was spoken only to an inner circle of followers. But these hypotheses presuppose a sharper line between disciples (Mt 5[1], Lk 6[20]) and general followers of Jesus than Jesus Himself indicates in the Sermon, or than can otherwise be made out at this stage of the public ministry. The use of the second personal form by Luke cannot be adduced as evidence that Jesus was speaking only to a close circle of disciples; it was equally applicable to a large company. Matthew's account also has the second personal form after 5[3-10]. Yet both Evangelists have statements (Mt 5[1] 7[28], Lk 6[19] 7[1]) to the effect that Jesus addressed His teaching to the multitudes at this time; and it is not clear that these statements are mere literary features, without historical value. The discourse contains positively nothing to indicate that Jesus was speaking only to a small, inner circle of His followers.

† See artt. Chronology of NT, vol. i., and Jesus Christ, vol. ii.; also art. 'Chronology of NT' in *Encyclopædia Biblica*, vol. i.; and Literature cited in connexion.

‡ Four views are now current concerning this 'mountain': (1) Latin tradition identifies it with *Karn Ḥaṭṭin*; the theory is accepted by Stanley (*SP* p. 368 f.), and also by Plummer and H. Weiss. This Latin tradition did not arise until the 13th cent., and is quite unknown to the Eastern Church, so that it cannot have been more than a plausible guess. The location and features of *Karn Ḥaṭṭin* correspond sufficiently well with the history; but there are a number of other hills along the western shore of the lake which are also suitable (Robinson, *BRP* iii. 487). (2) Some specific mountain is referred to, and was known to the early Christians as the scene of the discourse, but its identity became lost from the Gospel tradition. So Tholuck, Meyer, Keil, Kübel, Achelis, Andrews. (3) The phrase τὸ ὄρος designates not a particular hill or mountain peak, but the range of tableland rising to the west of the Sea of Galilee; and the site of the event is not more specifically designated. The Jews used three leading terms to distinguish the surface features of their territory—'mountain,' 'plain,' and 'valley': of these designations the first is understood to have referred to the tableland, whether broken into isolated peaks or not (cf. Gn 19[17. 19. 30] 31[23. 25] 36[8. 9], Mt 14[23] 15[29], Mk 6[46], Lk 9[28], Jn 6[3]). Therefore τὸ ὄρος would in any particular instance refer to the high land—whether tableland or peak—in the vicinity of the event. This view also leaves the site of the Sermon undetermined. So Bleek, Robinson, Ebrard, Thomson, Edersheim, Broadus, Bruce, Nösgen, Stewart, B. Weiss, Bacon. (4) Those who regard the Sermon as a mosaic only, resting upon no particular discourse, but made up of material gathered from many connexions (see names in footnote above), perforce look upon 'the mountain' as a part of the artificial scenery which the compiler of the Sermon arranged about it to give verisimilitude to the whole. Of these four views one may adopt the second or the third, but between these two it is difficult to choose.

The accounts in Mt 5[1] 8[1], Lk 6[12. 17], which describe the setting of the Sermon, both make mention of the mountain, but are not in agreement concerning it. Matthew locates the entire scene upon the mountain; Jesus and His disciples ascend it, apparently by His deliberate choice, to speak and to hear the Sermon; when it is finished they descend. According to the Third Gospel, Jesus goes up the mountain to spend the night in solitary prayer (cf. Lk 9[28], Jn 6[3. 15]); when it is day He calls His disciples to Him, and appoints the Twelve; afterwards He comes down from the mountain to the multitude which had gathered on a level place below, where He heals many, and later delivers the discourse. The well-meant harmonistic efforts expended upon these passages do not seem convincing. But the discrepancy is neither sufficient to remove the datum of a mountain in connexion with the discourse, nor, in face of strong evidence for their identity, to force the conclusion that the reports of Matthew and Luke represent two separate and distinct discourses with different settings.

* This is the almost unanimous opinion of scholars: Tatian (*Diatessaron*), Origen, Jerome, Chrysostom, Euthymius, Theophylact, Luther, Calvin, Maldonatus, Meyer, Bengel, Neander, Schleiermacher, Stier, Ewald, Wieseler, Keim, Keil, Köstlin, Robinson, Ellicott, Schneckenburger, Hilgenfeld, Edersheim, Godet, Tholuck, Tischendorf, Achelis, Andrews, Beyschlag, Broadus, Farrar, Feine, Schanz, Sanday, Steinmeyer, Sieffert, de Wette, Wendt, H. Weiss, B. Weiss, Bruce, Burton, Heinrici, H. Holtzmann, Ibbeken, Jülicher, Kübel, Nösgen, Wernle, Bacon, and many others. The theory of two separate discourses was advocated for apologetic purposes by Augustine, and, following him, by St. Gregory and certain minor Rom. Cath. writers, as, recently, Azibert (*Revue Biblique*, 1894). A few modern Protestant writers also have taken this view, as Greswell, Lange, Plumptre, and, most recently, Plummer (*Comm. on Luke* [1896], p. 177).

The arrangement of the material in Tatian's *Diatessaron* (see Hill, *Earliest Life of Christ, being the Diatessaron of Tatian* [1894], pp. 73–84), which combines the Matthew and Luke accounts, is thus: Mt 5[1a] Lk 6[13b-17] [Mk 3[14. 15]] Mt 5[2]=Lk 6[20a] Mt 5[3-10] Lk 6[22a] Mt 5[11b. 12] Lk 6[24-27a] Mt 5[14-16] [Mk 4[22. 23]] Mt 5[17-25a] [Lk 12[58b]] Mt 5[25c-42] Lk 6[30b. 31] Mt 5[43-46a] Lk 6[32b-36] Mt 5[47. 48] Mt 6[1-8] [Lk 11[1b. 2a]] Mt 6[9b-18] [Lk 12[32. 33a]] Mt 6[19-23] [Lk 11[35. 36]] Mt 6[24-27] [Lk 12[26]] Mt 6[28b-31] [Lk 12[29b]] Mt 6[32-34] Mt 7[1]= Lk 6[37b] Lk 6[38] [Mk 4[24b. 25]] Lk 6[39-42] Mt 7[6] [Lk 11[5-13]] Mt 7[12-16a] Lk 6[44] Mt 7[17. 18] Lk 6[45] Mt 7[19-23] Lk 6[47. 48a] Mt 7[25–81].

The relation of the contents of the two accounts can be shown in a table :—

| | | | | | |
|---|---|---|---|---|---|
| Mt $5^{3}$ | = | Lk $6^{20}$ | Mt $7^{1.\,2}$ | = | Lk $6^{37.\,38b}$ |
| $5^{4.\,6}$ | = | $6^{21}$ | $7^{3-5}$ | = | $6^{41.\,42}$ |
| $5^{11.\,12}$ | = | $6^{22.\,23}$ | $7^{12}$ | = | $6^{31}$ |
| $5^{39.\,40.\,42}$ | = | $6^{29.\,30}$ | $7^{16.\,17}$ | = | $6^{43.\,44}$ |
| $5^{44-48}$ | = | $6^{27.\,28.\,32-36}$ | $7^{21}$ | = | $6^{46}$ |
| $6^{1-34}$ has no parallel in Lk $6^{20-49}$ | | | $7^{24-27}$ | = | $6^{47-49}$ |

Matthew's account has 107 verses, Luke's account 29. Of Luke's 29 verses, 23½ find a parallel in the Matthæan account, where they are arranged as 26 verses. There is no parallel in Mt 5–7 for Lk $6^{24-26.\,38a.\,39.\,40.\,45}$.* Of Matthew's remaining 81 verses, 34 find a parallel in Luke outside of ch. 6 (in chs. 11–14. 16) † as follows : ‡—

| | | | | | |
|---|---|---|---|---|---|
| Mt $5^{13}$ | = | Lk $14^{34.\,35}$ | Mt $6^{22.\,23}$ | = | Lk $11^{34-36}$ |
| $5^{15}$ | = | $11^{33}$ ($8^{16}$) | $6^{24}$ | = | $16^{13}$ |
| $5^{18}$ | = | $16^{17}$ | $6^{25-33}$ | = | $12^{22-31}$ |
| $5^{25.\,26}$ | = | $12^{58.\,59}$ | $7^{7-11}$ | = | $11^{9-13}$ |
| $5^{32}$ | = | $16^{18}$ | $7^{13.\,14}$ | = | $13^{24}$ |
| $6^{9-13}$ | = | $11^{2-4}$ | $7^{23}$ | = | $13^{27}$ |
| $6^{19-21}$ | = | $12^{33.\,34}$ | | | |

This leaves 47 verses of the Matthæan discourse which have no parallel in the Third Gospel : Mt $5^{5.\,7-10.\,14.\,16.\,17.\,19-24.\,27-31.\,33-38.\,41.\,43}$ $6^{1-8.\,14-18.\,34}$ $7^{6.\,15.\,18-20.\,22}$. That is, four-ninths of the Sermon in Matthew is peculiar to that Gospel.§

These phenomena of the comparative contents of the two accounts of the Sermon present a complex and difficult problem, and compel one to investigate the history of this discourse from the time of its utterance until it took its present two-fold form in our First and Third Gospels.

Another important feature of these two reports of the Sermon, and one which must be investigated in conjunction with the problem of content, is the remarkable variation in wording—in the literary expression of the same ideas. Sometimes this variation is slight, as in : ‖—

| Mt $7^{2b}$. | Lk $6^{38b}$. |
|---|---|
| καὶ ἐν ᾧ μέτρῳ μετρεῖτε μετρηθήσεται ὑμῖν. | ᾧ γὰρ μέτρῳ μετρεῖτε ἀντιμετρηθήσεται ὑμῖν. |

| Mt $7^{3-5}$. | Lk $6^{41.\,42}$. |
|---|---|
| 3 τί δὲ βλέπεις τὸ κάρφος τὸ ἐν τῷ ὀφθαλμῷ τοῦ ἀδελφοῦ σου, τὴν δὲ ἐν τῷ σῷ ὀφθαλμῷ δοκὸν οὐ κατανοεῖς; 4 ἢ πῶς ἐρεῖς τῷ ἀδελφῷ σου Ἄφες ἐκβάλω τὸ κάρφος ἐκ τοῦ ὀφθαλμοῦ σου, καὶ ἰδοὺ ἡ δοκὸς ἐν τῷ ὀφθαλμῷ σοῦ; 5 ὑποκριτά, ἔκβαλε πρῶτον ἐκ τοῦ ὀφθαλμοῦ σοῦ τὴν δοκόν, καὶ τότε διαβλέψεις ἐκβαλεῖν τὸ κάρφος ἐκ τοῦ ὀφθαλμοῦ τοῦ ἀδελφοῦ σου. | 41 τί δὲ βλέπεις τὸ κάρφος τὸ ἐν τῷ ὀφθαλμῷ τοῦ ἀδελφοῦ σου, τὴν δὲ δοκὸν τὴν ἐν τῷ ἰδίῳ ὀφθαλμῷ οὐ κατανοεῖς; 42 πῶς δύνασαι λέγειν τῷ ἀδελφῷ σου Ἀδελφέ, ἄφες ἐκβάλω τὸ κάρφος τὸ ἐν τῷ ὀφθαλμῷ σου, αὐτὸς τὴν ἐν τῷ ὀφθαλμῷ σοῦ δοκὸν οὐ βλέπων; ὑποκριτά, ἔκβαλε πρῶτον τὴν δοκὸν ἐκ τοῦ ὀφθαλμοῦ σοῦ, καὶ τότε διαβλέψεις τὸ κάρφος τὸ ἐν τῷ ὀφθαλμῷ τοῦ ἀδελφοῦ σου ἐκβαλεῖν. |

Similarly compare Mt $6^{24}$ = Lk $16^{13}$ and Mt $7^{7.\,8}$ = Lk $11^{9.\,10}$. In these four passages there is almost complete verbal agreement—not quite, however—which must be explained. And the four sayings are widely scattered in Luke as compared with Matthew.

But such close verbal agreement is exceptional. In all the other parallel passages the variation in literary form is great, as in :—

| Mt $5^{39.\,40}$. | Lk $6^{29}$. |
|---|---|
| 39 Ἐγὼ δὲ λέγω ὑμῖν μὴ ἀντιστῆναι τῷ πονηρῷ· ἀλλ' ὅστις σε ῥαπίζει εἰς τὴν δεξιὰν σιαγόνα [σου], στρέψον αὐτῷ καὶ τὴν ἄλλην· 40 καὶ τῷ θέλοντί σοι κριθῆναι καὶ τὸν χιτῶνά σου λαβεῖν, ἄφες αὐτῷ καὶ τὸ ἱμάτιον. | τῷ τύπτοντί σε ἐπὶ τὴν σιαγόνα πάρεχε καὶ τὴν ἄλλην, καὶ ἀπὸ τοῦ αἴροντός σου τὸ ἱμάτιον καὶ τὸν χιτῶνα μὴ κωλύσῃς. |

| Mt $7^{12}$. | Lk $6^{31}$. |
|---|---|
| Πάντα οὖν ὅσα ἐὰν θέλητε ἵνα ποιῶσιν ὑμῖν οἱ ἄνθρωποι, οὕτως καὶ ὑμεῖς ποιεῖτε αὐτοῖς· οὗτος γάρ ἐστιν ὁ νόμος καὶ οἱ προφῆται. | καὶ καθὼς θέλετε ἵνα ποιῶσιν ὑμῖν οἱ ἄνθρωποι, ποιεῖτε αὐτοῖς ὁμοίως. |

| Mt $7^{24-27}$. | Lk $6^{47-49}$. |
|---|---|
| 24 Πᾶς οὖν ὅστις ἀκούει μου τοὺς λόγους [τούτους] καὶ ποιεῖ αὐτούς, ὁμοιωθήσεται ἀνδρὶ φρονίμῳ, ὅστις ᾠκοδόμησεν αὐτοῦ τὴν οἰκίαν ἐπὶ τὴν πέτραν. 25 καὶ κατέβη ἡ βροχὴ καὶ ἦλθαν οἱ ποταμοὶ καὶ ἔπνευσαν οἱ ἄνεμοι καὶ προσέπεσαν τῇ οἰκίᾳ ἐκείνῃ, καὶ οὐκ ἔπεσεν, τεθεμελίωτο γὰρ ἐπὶ τὴν πέτραν. 26 καὶ πᾶς ὁ ἀκούων μου τοὺς λόγους τούτους καὶ μὴ ποιῶν αὐτοὺς ὁμοιωθήσεται ἀνδρὶ μωρῷ, ὅστις ᾠκοδόμησεν αὐτοῦ τὴν οἰκίαν ἐπὶ τὴν ἄμμον. 27 καὶ κατέβη ἡ βροχὴ καὶ ἦλθαν οἱ ποταμοὶ καὶ ἔπνευσαν οἱ ἄνεμοι καὶ προσέκοψαν τῇ οἰκίᾳ ἐκείνῃ, καὶ ἔπεσεν, καὶ ἦν ἡ πτῶσις αὐτῆς μεγάλη. | 47 Πᾶς ὁ ἐρχόμενος πρός με καὶ ἀκούων μου τῶν λόγων καὶ ποιῶν αὐτούς, ὑποδείξω ὑμῖν τίνι ἐστὶν ὅμοιος· 48 ὅμοιός ἐστιν ἀνθρώπῳ οἰκοδομοῦντι οἰκίαν, ὃς ἔσκαψεν καὶ ἐβάθυνεν καὶ ἔθηκεν θεμέλιον ἐπὶ τὴν πέτραν· πλημμύρης δὲ γενομένης προσέρηξεν ὁ ποταμὸς τῇ οἰκίᾳ ἐκείνῃ, καὶ οὐκ ἴσχυσεν σαλεῦσαι αὐτὴν διὰ τὸ καλῶς οἰκοδομῆσθαι αὐτήν. 49 ὁ δὲ ἀκούσας καὶ μὴ ποιήσας ὅμοιός ἐστιν ἀνθρώπῳ οἰκοδομήσαντι οἰκίαν ἐπὶ τὴν γῆν χωρὶς θεμελίου, ᾗ προσέρηξεν ὁ ποταμός, καὶ εὐθὺς συνέπεσεν, καὶ ἐγένετο τὸ ῥῆγμα τῆς οἰκίας ἐκείνης μέγα. |

Similarly compare Mt $5^{44.\,45}$ = Lk $6^{35}$, Mt $7^{1.\,2a}$ = Lk $6^{37}$, Mt $7^{16.\,17}$ = Lk $6^{43.\,44}$; and also Mt $5^{15}$ = Lk $11^{33}$, Mt $5^{18}$ = Lk $16^{17}$, Mt $5^{25.\,26}$ = Lk $12^{58.\,59}$, Mt $6^{19-21}$ = Lk $12^{33.\,34}$, Mt $6^{25-33}$ = Lk $12^{22-31}$.

In some passages the wording of Matthew is so

* But there are parallels for two or three of these passages elsewhere in Matthew, thus : Lk $6^{39}$ = Mt $15^{14b}$, Lk $6^{45}$ = Mt $12^{35}$; and with Lk $6^{40a}$ compare Mt $10^{24}$ (Jn $13^{16}$ $15^{20a}$).

† These chapters belong to the somewhat clearly marked middle third of Luke's Gospel ($10^{25}$–$18^{34}$), which consists mainly of discourse material. It is commonly known as the 'Peræan section,' because its position in this book is between the final departure of Jesus from Galilee (Lk $9^{51}$–$10^{20}$) and His public entrance into Jerusalem (Lk $18^{35}$–$19^{46}$). During this period Jesus perhaps spent some days or weeks in Peræa (Mt $19^{1}$ = Mk $10^{1}$, Lk $13^{31}$, Jn $10^{40}$), and some of the material in Lk 10–18 may belong to that period, as $12^{1-12.\,35-59}$ $13^{1-9.\,22-30.\,31-35}$ $17^{20-37}$ $18^{1-8}$. But the main contents of these chapters (Lk $11^{1-36}$ $12^{13-34}$ $13^{10-21}$ 14. 15. 16. $17^{1-10}$ $18^{9-34}$) quite surely belong to the Galilæan ministry, because (1) this is indicated by various allusions in the chapters themselves, *e.g.* $11^{29-32}$ (cf. Mt $12^{39-42}$), $13^{10.\,17.\,18-21}$ (cf. Mt $13^{31.\,32}$), $14^{25-35}$; (2) the subject of most of this teaching is more suitable to that period ; (3) it is altogether unlikely that Jesus would have left so large and so important a portion of His general teaching till the last weeks of His ministry. Luke had for these chapters (10–18) a special source, probably a document of some extent, which contained most valuable teaching ; but the settings of the teaching had been largely lost, and he therefore put these passages, with other unattached material from the *Logia* and other sources, into this middle, mixed section of his book,—in fact, what else could he do? The material was too important to omit, and he was too conscientious a historical author to create scenes for the several pieces.

‡ In the case of three of these passages there are parallels in Mark also : Mt $5^{13}$ = Mk $9^{50}$ = Lk $14^{34.\,35}$, Mt $5^{15}$ = Mk $4^{21}$ = Lk $11^{33}$ (and $8^{16}$), Mt $5^{32}$ = Mk $10^{11}$ = Lk $16^{18}$. There is but one sentence which is put by both Matthew and Luke into the Sermon that has a parallel in Mark, namely, Mt $7^{2b}$ = Mk $4^{24b}$ = Lk $6^{38c}$; and this saying is of the gnomic type, so that it may have been repeated on various occasions by Jesus. Consequently one is inclined to say that the portion of the Sermon common to Matthew and Luke is not found in Mark. And of the matter in Matthew's Sermon which is found in Luke outside of the Sermon, or not found in Luke at all, Mark has parallels perhaps for five verses,—the three just indicated, and the two named in the following footnote,—so that the Second Gospel scarcely knows of this teaching material which the First and Third Gospels make so prominent.

§ Except, perhaps, Mt $5^{29.\,30}$ = Mk $9^{43.\,47}$, Mt $6^{14.\,15}$ = Mk $11^{25}$. It is worth observing that three passages of the Matthew Sermon have parallels within the First Gospel itself : Mt $5^{29.\,30}$ = Mt $18^{8.\,9}$, Mt $5^{32}$ = Mt $19^{9}$, Mt $7^{18}$ = Mt $12^{33}$.

‖ The Greek text here used is that of Westcott and Hort.

different from that of Luke that a difference even of the thought results, or seems to result :—

| Mt $5^{3.\,4.\,6}$. | Lk $6^{20.\,21}$. |
|---|---|
| 3 Μακάριοι οἱ πτωχοὶ τῷ πνεύματι, ὅτι αὐτῶν ἐστὶν ἡ βασιλεία τῶν οὐρανῶν. | 20 Μακάριοι οἱ πτωχοί, ὅτι ὑμετέρα ἐστὶν ἡ βασιλεία τοῦ θεοῦ. |
| 4 μακάριοι οἱ πενθοῦντες, ὅτι αὐτοὶ παρακληθήσονται. | 21b μακάριοι οἱ κλαίοντες νῦν, ὅτι γελάσετε. |
| 6 μακάριοι οἱ πεινῶντες καὶ διψῶντες τὴν δικαιοσύνην, ὅτι αὐτοὶ χορτασθήσονται. | 21a μακάριοι οἱ πεινῶντες νῦν, ὅτι χορτασθήσεσθε. |
| **Mt $5^{48}$.** | **Lk $6^{36}$.** |
| Εσεσθε οὖν ὑμεῖς τέλειοι ὡς ὁ πατὴρ ὑμῶν ὁ οὐράνιος τέλειός ἐστιν. | Γίνεσθε οἰκτίρμονες καθὼς ὁ πατὴρ ὑμῶν οἰκτίρμων ἐστίν. |
| **Mt $6^{9-13}$.** | **Lk $11^{2-4}$.** |
| 9 Πάτερ ἡμῶν ὁ ἐν τοῖς οὐρανοῖς· | 2 Πάτερ, |
| ἁγιασθήτω τὸ ὄνομά σου, | ἁγιασθήτω τὸ ὄνομά σου· |
| 10 ἐλθάτω ἡ βασιλεία σου, | ἐλθάτω ἡ βασιλεία σου· |
| γενηθήτω τὸ θέλημά σου, ὡς ἐν οὐρανῷ καὶ ἐπὶ γῆς· | |
| 11 τὸν ἄρτον ἡμῶν τὸν ἐπιούσιον δὸς ἡμῖν σήμερον· | 3 τὸν ἄρτον ἡμῶν τὸν ἐπιούσιον δίδου ἡμῖν τὸ καθ' ἡμέραν· |
| 12 καὶ ἄφες ἡμῖν τὰ ὀφειλήματα ἡμῶν, ὡς καὶ ἡμεῖς ἀφήκαμεν τοῖς ὀφειλέταις ἡμῶν· | 4 καὶ ἄφες ἡμῖν τὰς ἁμαρτίας ἡμῶν, καὶ γὰρ αὐτοὶ ἀφίομεν παντὶ ὀφείλοντι ἡμῖν· |
| 13 καὶ μὴ εἰσενέγκῃς ἡμᾶς εἰς πειρασμόν, ἀλλὰ ῥῦσαι ἡμᾶς ἀπὸ τοῦ πονηροῦ. | καὶ μὴ εἰσενέγκῃς ἡμᾶς εἰς πειρασμόν. |

Similarly compare Mt $5^{32}$ = Lk $16^{18}$ (= Mk $10^{11}$ = Mt $19^{9}$) and Mt $7^{11}$ = Lk $11^{13}$. The corresponding context or setting of each pair of these parallel sayings, or as regards the Lord's Prayer the nature of the case (see below, ii. 4 *h* (2)), indicates that however variant the words have become in transmission, they started from the same utterances of Jesus. The parallel records run the entire gamut of variation from close verbal similarity to wide verbal divergence, and in a few cases even to difference of idea itself.

Now the explanation of these striking phenomena of content, form, and substance in the Sermon of Matthew and Luke is to be found in the history of the transmission of this material during the years *c.* 29–85 A.D. This section of history is one part of the great 'Synoptic problem.'* While many elements of this problem are still in dispute, certain fundamental facts pertaining to it now seem well established.

(1) Jesus habitually taught in Aramaic, not in Greek.† The thorough and deliberate discussion of this question seems to have reached a settled conclusion.‡ We were all eager to believe that these very Greek words of our Gospels came directly from Jesus' lips; yet historical investigation shows that they are but a translation from the original utterances. While the theories of Resch, Marshall, Dalman, Blass, E. A. Abbott, and others as to a primitive Aramaic or Hebrew Gospel are uncertain, it is clear that the Memorabilia of Jesus were originally and for some years in the Aramaic language. The Aramaic vocabulary, syntax, and influence can everywhere be seen through the Greek of the Gospels, like the earlier text in a palimpsest manuscript.

(2) Jesus' more important teachings were marked and remembered from the time they were spoken. It is not too much to suppose that He impressed certain teachings—not their form, but their substance—upon His disciples. From day to day, therefore, during Jesus' public ministry, His followers were gathering and pondering His utterances, holding them in memory and repeating them to one another nearly or quite in Jesus' own words. After His death and resurrection His followers treasured these sayings of their Master's, studied them, preached them, and faithfully taught them to all who came into the Christian brotherhood (cf. Ac $2^{42}$). The story of Jesus' life, His deeds and His words, was the guide of every individual Christian, of every Christian community, and of the entire Christian movement. What He had taught was the staple matter of all Christian instruction and worship, and was everywhere regarded as the norm of Christianity. And of all that Jesus had taught there was nothing more prominent, vital, and practical—indeed nothing more generally revered and used—than the teaching contained in the Sermon on the Mount.

(3) It is also certain that, for years after Jesus had given His teaching, it was circulated and transmitted by word of mouth. Jesus Himself wrote nothing, nor did His disciples until long after. Both these facts were due to the Jewish custom of the time. The teaching of the Rabbis in Jesus' day was entirely oral—only their sacred books, the Old Testament, might be written; therefore the pupils of the Rabbis heard and memorized their teaching. Out of this custom arose a special qualification for, and efficiency in, oral instruction and oral transmission among the Jews. To men of this nation and country Jesus' sayings were given, and by them preserved. It cannot, of course, be supposed that Jesus insisted upon *forms of words*; He was neither a literalist nor a verbalist. Therefore His disciples did not place undue emphasis upon the *ipsissima verba* of His teaching. But so perfectly worded were the most significant of His shorter sayings—many of which can be seen in this discourse—that they would persist in their original form. For the remainder of the teaching an exact verbal transmission was unlikely, and the evidence shows that it did not so happen.

(4) After fifteen or twenty years (*c.* 45–50 A.D.) Christianity began to reach out into the great Roman world by the labours of the Apostle Paul and many others; and it became necessary to translate the Gospel story into Greek, since the non-Palestinian Jews and the Gentiles did not know Aramaic—the language in which the story had arisen, and had thus far been handed down. That this translation took place 50–80 A.D. is proved by our present Greek Gospels and the early disappearance of all Aramaic Gospel documents. Now there is every reason to think that this translation of the Memorabilia of Jesus was a *process* rather than an act. The data do not permit us to think of one formal, authoritative translation, comprising the whole Gospel story, and passing directly into the use of all the Greek-speaking Christians. Rather there were numerous persons in various places and at different times who translated portions—the *same* as well as different portions—of the story from the Aramaic into Greek. These individual and fragmentary translations were characterized by various degrees of literalness, differing vocabulary and syntax, loss of original colouring, obscuration of shades of meaning, interpretative modifications and expansions, varying success in reproducing the original ideas, and some adaptation of the sayings (by way of selection, arrangement, and altered expression) to the practical needs of the Churches for whom the respective translations happened to be made. Then these various translations, at first located at the chief centres of the Christian movement, passed into general circulation, and acted and reacted upon each other, mixing the phenomena of the several translations. The features just described can all of them be traced in our two Gospel records of the Sermon on the Mount.

(5) It is now generally understood * that, after fifteen or twenty years of circulating and transmitting the utterances of Jesus by word of mouth, the Gospel Memorabilia were gradually put into writing. We have in Eusebius (*HE* iii. 39. 16) the important testimony of Papias, which is regarded by most scholars as trustworthy, that the Apostle Matthew composed (συνετάξατο, *al.* συνεγράψατο, cf. Lk $1^{1}$ ἀνατάξασθαι) a collection of the sayings (Λόγια) of Jesus, in the Hebrew (*i.e.* the Aramaic?) language. If Papias' statement, and the common interpretation of it as a written account, are correct, then we have a distinct witness that there was a written record of Jesus' teaching, which we may assign to *c.* 50 A.D. That it was in Aramaic(?) shows an adoption of writing, even by the Palestinian Christians, as a

* In the extensive and highly important literature upon this subject is to be sought the presentation and treatment of the matters outlined in the following paragraphs. See the art. GOSPELS, vol. ii., and literature there cited; also art. 'Gospels' by Sanday in Smith's *DB*², and by E. A. Abbott and Schmiedel in *Encyclopædia Biblica*, vol. ii.; also Wernle, *Synopt. Frage* (1899); Wendt, *Lehre Jesu*, 1 Th. (1886); B. Weiss, *Matthäusevangelium* (1876); H. Holtzmann, *Synopt. Evangelien* (1863); Weizsäcker, *Untersuchungen ü. d. evangelische Geschichte* (1864, 2nd ed. 1901); Wright, *Composition of the Four Gospels* (1890); Hawkins, *Horæ Synopticæ* (1899); Burkitt, *Two Lectures on the Gospels* (1901).

† It is not unlikely that Jesus knew some Greek, for many Greek-speaking Gentiles lived in Galilee, and that language must have been used not a little in such a hive of commerce as Capernaum was. Jesus' work, however, was exclusively among the Jews, and there is no conclusive evidence that He knew or spoke Greek at all; even His trial before Pilate cannot prove this, as Pilate must have been accustomed to use an interpreter in treating with the Sanhedrin. See O. Holtzmann, *Leben Jesu* (1901), p. 22.

‡ That Jesus taught in Greek has been ably argued by Roberts (*Greek the Language of Christ and His Apostles*, 1888) and by T. K. Abbott (*Essays chiefly on the Original Texts of the OT and NT*, 1891, ch. 5). The contrary, that Jesus taught in Aramaic, has been shown by Neubauer, *Studia Biblica*, i. 39–74 (1885); A. Meyer, *Jesu Muttersprache* (1896); Zahn, *Einleitung i. d. NT*, i. 1–51 (1897); Dalman, *Worte Jesu*, i. 1–72 (1898): see also art. LANGUAGE OF THE NEW TESTAMENT, vol. iii.

* Although there still remain a few earnest advocates of an exclusively oral tradition.

means of collecting, circulating, and preserving the Memorabilia of Jesus. But whether Papias' statement is correct or incorrect, it is practically certain that when the Gentiles received the story of Jesus they committed it to writing, for they were not accustomed to the oral transmission of extended material. This change of oral to written records was informal, unauthorized, and gradual, like the translation already described. But it is probable that soon after 50 A.D. there were many written portions of the Gospel Memorabilia in existence and use. These documents then grew in number and extent until after twenty to fifty years our canonical Gospels absorbed them and became recognized as the final records of Jesus' ministry (cf. Lk 1[1-4]). There are also indications that the oral tradition continued along with the written tradition through the whole period until our Gospels were composed (and indeed afterwards also), and furnished a larger or smaller amount of the material which went into them.

The history here sketched of the transmission of the entire Gospel story is at the same time the history of the transmission of the Sermon on the Mount, which was one of the most valuable sections of the Memorabilia of Jesus. The whole process has left its marks upon our two accounts of the Sermon, for to it are to be attributed in the main the difference of setting, content, arrangement, variety of literary expression, and divergence of thought. But the fundamental agreement of the two accounts, which shows them to be reports of the same historical discourse, has not been seriously obscured in transmission.

When one attempts to trace more in detail the particular history of the Sermon on the Mount during the years c. 29–85 A.D., one comes upon many perplexing problems about which at present there is no agreement. Opinions ventured in this sphere can only be tentative and modest.

(1) It seems probable that the Matthæan *Logia* was used in a Greek form, indeed in differing Greek forms, by both the First and the Third Evangelists.* If the same Greek form of the *Logia* was used by both, the one or the other (or perhaps both) has introduced a remarkable series of changes in content, arrangement, and wording which it would be difficult to explain. A much more probable supposition is that the Matthæan *Logia* was *variously translated into Greek*,† in whole or in part, by different persons and in several localities: then these complete or fragmentary translations had each its own history for about 30 years, during which they experienced the vicissitudes of transmission. When the First and Third Evangelists came to prepare their Gospels in c. 80–85 A.D. there were in circulation and use these various Greek forms of the Matthæan *Logia*. The two authors adopted different forms, according to the usage of the locality in which each wrote, or, less likely, according to their judgment of which form was best historically.

(2) In addition to this basal *Logian* source of both our accounts of the Sermon, there were probably other lines of transmission of the discourse in both oral and written tradition. Many disciples had heard the Sermon when Jesus gave it, and for years afterwards had told of it. There must thus have grown up variant reports—one used in one church or circle of churches, and another in another. These further reports also are likely to have been handed down, and some of them may well have come under the notice of the two Evangelists in composing their Gospels.* How much influence such outside sources had upon their reports it would be difficult to determine—perhaps it was considerable.

(3) We need to allow for a fair amount of editorial selection, arrangement, adaptation, and revision on the part of our two authors. Luke (1[1-4]) has given us important information concerning his material, purpose, and method; and the First Evangelist probably wrote under similar conditions. As they gathered their sources, they found themselves in possession of three classes of sayings from Jesus—(*a*) brief sayings still joined to specific events of His ministry, and which they could in part arrange in their right order; (*b*) the remains

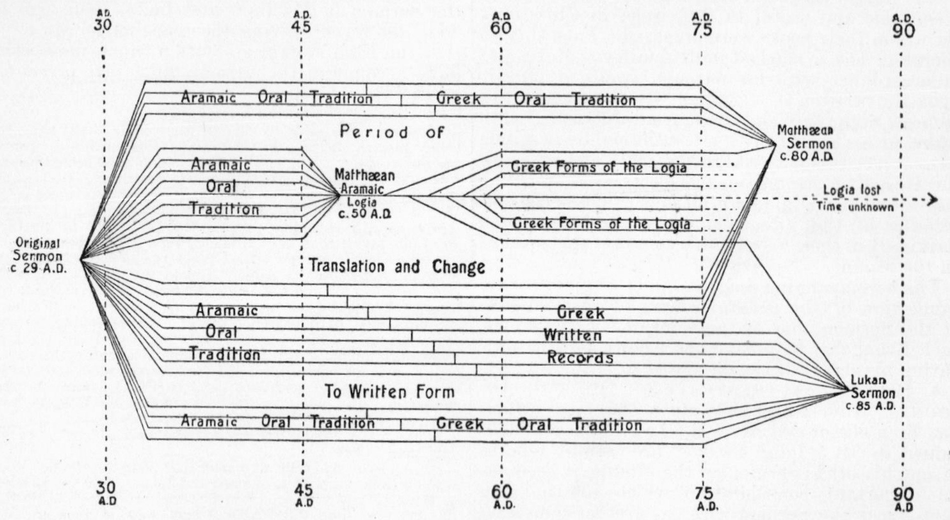


Diagram to Illustrate the Transmission of the Sermon on the Mount.

* See Wendt, *Lehre Jesu*, i. 52, 53; Jülicher, *Einleitung i. d. NT*[3], p. 219; Wernle, *Synopt. Frage*, pp. 79, 80; Hawkins, *Horæ Synopticæ* (1899), pp. 88–92; J. Weiss, *Predigt Jesu vom Reiche Gottes*[2] (1900), pp. 179–182. That the same Greek form of the *Logia* was used by both the First and Third Evangelists is maintained by O. Holtzmann, *Leben Jesu* (1901), pp. 22–24.

† See Feine, *Jahrb. f. Protest. Theologie*, 1885, p. 1 ff.

* The First Gospel of our NT Canon is neither the Matthæan *Logia* itself, which was in Aramaic (Eusebius, *HE* iii. 39. 16), nor is it an immediate translation of that *Logia*, since it does not contain the inevitable indications of a translated work. The Greek Gospel of Matthew is rather a combination of the *Logia* in some mediate Greek form with the Gospel of Mark, plus the addition of various portions and characteristics which did not belong to either of the original books. However, because it substantially incorporated the *Logia*, it continued to bear the Apostle's name. The author of the enlarged Greek edition of the original Matthew work is unknown. On this matter see the works on NT Introduction by B. Weiss, H. Holtzmann, Jülicher, Zahn, Salmon, and others; also Commentaries on the Gospel of Matthew.

of certain of Jesus' greatest discourses, containing the theme and some of the essential matter belonging thereto; these also could generally be assigned to their proper places in the history; (*c*) small sections of teaching or single sayings, the original connexion of which was no longer known; these would be inserted here and there in the narrative without particular attachment, or would be associated with the nuclei of the great discourses wherever the subject of the one was similar to that of the other. Such compilation would produce the phenomena of extraneous material which we find in both accounts of the Sermon, as well as in other discourse sections of both Gospels. When the material of his Gospel had been arranged satisfactorily by the author, it remained for him to adjust the several parts to each other, to smooth over the joints by his literary skill, and in various ways to give the book a unity and finish such as an author would desire for his work.

(4) In view of the fact that the Gospels were written for the *practical* use of the Christians in their life and worship, the Evangelists felt at liberty to make such a selection and presentation of the Gospel facts and teachings as would be most acceptable and useful to the circles of Christians for whom their books were prepared. Each Gospel therefore has a marked individuality. Matthew, in accordance with his purpose, dwells at length upon the relation of Jesus and His message to the Hebrew Scriptures and the current Judaism. But Luke, or his source, with a Gentile public in mind, passes over this material in the main and presents the Gospel in its universal aspects as a spiritual and altruistic religion for all men. These characteristics of the First and Third Gospels appear strikingly in their respective accounts of the Sermon on the Mount.

The accompanying diagram aims at giving some suggestion of the general course of transmission of the Sermon, and of the kind of sources which each Evangelist may have had before him in preparing his report of the discourse.

4. RELATIVE AUTHENTICITY OF THE TWO ACCOUNTS.—Proceeding now upon the view which has been elaborated, that the two discourses contained in Mt 5–7 and Lk $6^{20-49}$ are variant reports of one historical Sermon on the Mount, it becomes an important consideration which of the two reproduces the Sermon with the greater completeness and accuracy. The question is as to their *relative* excellence, for the phenomena of the accounts and the vicissitudes of transmission show that neither the First nor the Third Gospel has *perfectly* reproduced the content and wording of the original discourse.

In content, Matthew has much more than Luke of that material which is commonly recognized as having been an essential portion of the Sermon, namely, Mt $5^{3-48}$ $6^{1-7. 16-18}$; compare with this Lk $6^{20-23. 27-36}$. Luke or his source omitted most of this section, apparently on the ground that it was inapplicable to the Gentiles, for whom the account was prepared.* This omission was perhaps justifiable for the practical purpose of a Gospel, although innumerable Gentiles ever since Luke's day have preferred the Sermon of the First Gospel, as we now do; but however that may be, from a historical point of view such an extensive omission could leave only a seriously incomplete account of the discourse. The further section of the Matthæan discourse ($6^{19-34}$) may or may not have been a part of the historical Sermon; opinion is quite evenly divided upon this point, and there seems no conclusive evidence either way. The fact that Luke places this material in $12^{22-31}$, where it has a topical connexion with what precedes it ($12^{13-21}$), suggests another occasion, although that occasion is not chronologically located by Luke. On the other hand, if the theme of the Sermon is found in the Beatitudes rather than in the verses Mt $5^{17-20}$, this passage, which inculcates devotion to the Kingdom and trust in God, is germane, and marks the discourse as more than an anti-Pharisaic manifesto. For the present, at least, one may prefer to regard this section as belonging to the Sermon. In this case Luke's account of the Sermon, which contains nothing of this portion, is again strikingly incomplete.* The final section of the Matthæan discourse ($7^{1-27}$) has been preserved with some fulness by Luke ($6^{37-49}$), varying less than the two preceding sections from the Matthæan account. It will appear farther on, that in both the Matthæan and Lukan reports there are some brief extraneous passages which cannot have been in the original Sermon, such as Mt $5^{25. 26. 31. 32}$ $6^{7-15}$ $7^{6-11. 22. 23}$, Lk $6^{23-26. 38a. 39. 40. 45}$. But in this kind of variation the two reports have both expanded the historical discourse. Considering the relative contents of the Sermon in Matthew and Luke, there can be no doubt (even waiving the question of Mt $6^{19-34}$) that the First Gospel presents a much more complete account of the Sermon than that presented by the Third Gospel.†

* So B. Weiss, *Meyer-Komm. ü. d. Mattevgm.* p. 163; Wendt, *Lehre Jesu*, i. 58; Plummer, *Comm. on Luke*, p. 183; Wernle, *Synopt. Frage*, p. 62; Bacon, *Sermon on the Mount* (1902), pp. 36–39; and most other scholars.

* It seems impossible to suppose that Luke could have had before him the Sermon in the form in which it now appears in the First Gospel. This is also the opinion of Wernle (*Synopt. Frage*, p. 80), Bartlet (art. MATTHEW in vol. iii.), O. Holtzmann, (*Leben Jesu*, 1901, p. 21), and of Heinrici (*Bergpredigt*, i. 10). Heinrici says the two reports of Matthew and Luke 'are reconstructions of a discourse restored independently by Matthew and Luke rather than in dependence upon one another or upon the same written source.' The Evangelists have re-worked their material, but that alone cannot explain the phenomena of the two accounts. Would Luke have deliberately broken up a collection of teachings so usefully grouped as in the Matthæan accounts, and have scattered them so unreasonably through seven chapters of his own work? On the other hand, the First Evangelist might, so far as the Sermon is concerned, have had Luke's account before him. His own report was surely better than Luke's, and so would not be altered into conformity with the latter. The general phenomena of the two Gospels, however, are against this particular interrelation, and the prevailing opinion assigns Matthew's Gospel to a somewhat earlier date than Luke's.

† It is a somewhat difficult matter to explain the absence of the Sermon from the Gospels of Mark and John. The only parallels in Mark to any of the Sermon material are Mk $4^{21. 24}$ $9^{43. 47. 50}$ $10^{11}$ $11^{25}$; in John, $13^{16}$ ($15^{20}$). And these sayings are only *possible* parallels, *i.e.* they need not have come into the Gospel of Mark from accounts of the Sermon. The opinion of Ewald, H. Holtzmann, Keim, and Wittichen, that Mark originally contained the Sermon, but that it has disappeared from the canonical work, cannot be accepted. Feine (*Jahrb. f. Protest. Theologie*, 1885, p. 4), is right in holding that Mark did not use the sources which, containing variant accounts of the discourse, were used by Matthew and Luke independently. It seems quite certain, however, that Mark could not have been ignorant of the Sermon. If that discourse did not appear in his sources, oral and written, it must have been because he voluntarily limited those sources. The Sermon was altogether too highly valued and too widely used in the Apostolic age to have escaped any careful compiler of the Gospel Memorabilia. This would be esp. true of Mark, who, if common opinion is correct, had an ultimate Petrine base for much of his material. Is it imaginable that Peter did not give the Sermon a prominent place in his teaching? Surely Mark must have known the Sermon. Why, then, did he omit it from his Gospel? A plausible explanation, which may be the true one, is this:—

When Mark wrote his Gospel, about 65–70 A.D., the Matthæan *Logia* (in various Greek forms) was in general use; this *Logia* passed over the narrative material of the story of Jesus, and consisted mainly of a collection of Jesus' discourses and shorter sayings; it included the Sermon, although in what precise form it is very difficult to determine—probably not that in which it appears in either of our canonical Gospels. Now Mark's Gospel, in striking contrast, reports mainly the acts and events of Jesus' public ministry, giving much less attention to the teaching (the longest sections of discourse material are in $2^{18-22}$ $3^{23-30}$ $4^{1-32}$ $6^{8-13}$ $7^{6-23}$ $8^{34-38}$ $9^{1. 39-50}$ $10^{24-31. 38-45}$ $11^{23-25}$ 12. 13). Perhaps Mark wished to put into more complete and permanent transmission that other side of the Gospel story which was neglected in the *Logia*. If so, it was unnecessary for him to repeat the Sermon and certain other discourse elements of that work, since he wrote to complete the

In wording, a like verdict of superior excellence falls to the Gospel of Matthew. Since both Gospels contain the discourse in Greek, therefore in translation we cannot find in either of them the *ipsissima verba* of Jesus (except for the few Aramaic words transliterated, as in Mt $5^{22}$). But when we ask which Gospel has more accurately transmuted into Greek the ideas that Jesus expressed in Aramaic, which has more faithfully interpreted His meaning in this teaching, there are many indications that Matthew gives the better record. A complete study of the parallels in the two accounts of the Sermon shows that in almost every instance there is a greater authenticity in the Matthæan account; of this a few illustrations will suffice. (1) The first Beatitude is variously worded (Mt $5^{3}$ *μακάριοι οἱ πτωχοὶ τῷ πνεύματι*; Lk $6^{20}$ *μακάριοι οἱ πτωχοί*). It is perhaps true that the Lukan form corresponds more nearly to the Aramaic utterance of Jesus, which may not have had a term corresponding to Matthew's *τῷ πνεύματι*; the important consideration, however, is as to the idea rather than the form. In the Lukan Beatitude, material poverty is intended, as is shown conclusively by the converse woe in $6^{24}$ *οὐαὶ ὑμῖν τοῖς πλουσίοις* (woe could not be pronounced upon those who were spiritually rich). But in the Matthæan Beatitude the ambiguous term *πτωχοί*—corresponding to the OT עֲנָוִים (Ps $69^{33}$, Is $61^{1}$) and אֶבְיוֹנִים (Ps $109^{16}$, Is $14^{30}$), and standing in the LXX for those Hebrew words (see art. POOR in vol. iv.), with a primary moral and spiritual import—is made explicit for the moral and spiritual signification by the addition of the phrase *τῷ πνεύματι*, to protect the Beatitude from the material interpretation which had made its impress upon Luke's source. Thus Matthew has preserved Jesus' original meaning of the first Beatitude (perhaps at the expense of its form); of course it is the meaning rather than the form that is of value. (2) In Mt $5^{43-48}$ = Lk $6^{32-36}$ there are many indications of the secondary character of Luke's material: Mt $5^{43}$ does not appear; the idea of lending (Lk $6^{34.35}$) is a disturbing importation; instead of *τελῶναι* Luke has *ἁμαρτωλοί*; Mt $5^{45a}$ is given in a non-Jewish form—*ἔσεσθε υἱοὶ Ὑψίστου* instead of *ὅπως γένησθε υἱοὶ τοῦ πατρὸς ὑμῶν τοῦ ἐν οὐρανοῖς*; Mt $5^{45b}$ does not appear, nor the term *οἱ ἐθνικοί* of Mt $5^{47}$; and the reminiscence of Dt $18^{13}$ in Mt $5^{48}$ *ἔσεσθε . . . τέλειοι* is replaced by a non-Jewish and much weaker *γίνεσθε οἰκτίρμονες*. That is to say, Luke's account lacks the Palestinian setting, the local colour, the Jewish phrases, and the OT allusions, besides introducing an extraneous practical element. (3) A similar practical addition or expansion of Mt $7^{2b}$ may be seen in Lk $6^{38a}$; a true teaching, but foreign to the context. Similarly Lk $6^{45}$. (4) In the Mt $7^{12}$ and Lk $6^{31}$ forms of the 'Golden Rule' (quoted above), the Matthæan wording approves itself as being a better reproduction of what we may understand Jesus to have said; the Matthæan phrase *οὗτος γάρ ἐστιν ὁ νόμος καὶ οἱ προφῆται* is absent from the Lukan account on the constant principle of expunging Jewish elements. (5) The same principle explains the significant difference of wording in Mt $7^{21}$ (*οὐ πᾶς ὁ λέγων μοι Κύριε κύριε εἰσελεύσεται εἰς τὴν βασιλείαν τῶν οὐρανῶν, ἀλλ' ὁ ποιῶν τὸ θέλημα τοῦ πατρός μου τοῦ ἐν τοῖς οὐρανοῖς*) = Lk $6^{46}$ (*τί δέ με καλεῖτε Κύριε κύριε, καὶ οὐ ποιεῖτε ἃ λέγω*;). (6) It is obvious in a comparison of the Matthæan and Lukan accounts (quoted above) of the closing parable of the Sermon that the Palestinian colour and the vivid picturesqueness of the story as given in the First Gospel do not appear in the commonplace, secondary expressions of the Third. (7) To these six illustrations from the parallel reports of the Sermon must be added the twofold account of the Lord's Prayer (Mt $6^{9-13}$ = Lk $11^{2-4}$), which is discussed below (under ii. 4 *h*), and most strikingly shows the relative merits of the Matthæan and Lukan reports of Jesus' teaching. It is not to be denied that the Matthæan form may be somewhat expanded from the original Aramaic; but this has to do with form rather than with substance, and the expansion is in the interest of the true interpretation of the Prayer. Here, also, we note (see the two accounts quoted above) the absence from Luke of the Jewish phrases which speak of God as in heaven, and of His 'will' as supreme. The comprehensive and deeply ethical and spiritual term *ὀφειλήματα* of Matthew is replaced in Luke by the conventional term *ἁμαρτίας*. And the petition for deliverance from evil, a characteristically Jewish conception, is expunged.

It cannot be doubted that the strong Jewish element and Palestinian colour of Matthew's discourse actually pervaded Jesus' teaching as originally given. Jesus was a Jew, and spoke to Jews only; His language and His ideas were therefore Jewish and adapted to Jews. There is no room for a theory that this feature was a subsequent artificial transfusion of Judaism into the teaching of Jesus. But it is easy to see how just this feature was eliminated from His teaching in the course of the Gentile mission. The Gentiles neither understood nor liked the Jews, with their peculiar notions and exclusive ways. In order, therefore, to make the Gospel acceptable to them, the Christian missionaries thought it necessary to *universalize* the language of Jesus. This has clearly been done in the case of Luke's account of the Sermon, possibly by himself,* but more likely by a long process of elimination, through which the material had passed on the Gentile field whence Luke drew his sources for the Third Gospel. It is possible that portions of the original Sermon which were too strongly Jewish to remain in that position found their way into Luke's Gospel apart from that discourse, and with the Jewish colouring removed. Perhaps this is the explanation of the variant position of Mt $6^{19-34}$ = Lk $12^{22-31}$, since the same kind of elimination of the Jewish element is apparent here, *e.g.* *τὰ πετεινὰ τοῦ οὐρανοῦ* is replaced by *τοὺς κόρακας*; *ὁ πατὴρ ὑμῶν ὁ οὐράνιος* is replaced by *ὁ θεός*, note the peculiar addition in Lk $12^{26}$; *τὰ ἔθνη* is replaced by *πάντα τὰ ἔθνη τοῦ κόσμου* (a clear

current record of Christ's life, not to produce a new Gospel which should antiquate and supersede the *Logia*. This appears also in the fact that the present Greek Matthew combines probably the Matthæan *Logia* with the Gospel of Mark (plus some additional matter) into a quite extensive account of the life of Christ. What makes this theory somewhat unsatisfactory is the fact that no small amount of Jesus' sayings actually contained in Mark's Gospel was in all probability present in the *Logia*, *e.g.* Mk $4^{1-20}$ $8^{34-38}$ $9^{1.39-50}$ 12; but perhaps an explanation for this can be found. At any rate, the problem of Mark's omission of the Sermon cannot yet be considered solved.

As for the absence of the Sermon from the Gospel of John, the entire character of that book offers a probable reason for its omission. The author has distinctly chosen not to reproduce Synoptic material, but to make a Gospel with different contents, and setting forth Gospel truth in a different way. That he passes over the Sermon is, therefore, not at all due to his ignorance of the discourse, but to his motive, according to which he passes over *all* the Synoptic discourses (Mt 5-7. 10. 13. 18. 21-25, Lk 6. 10-21), and most of the narrative matter as well. Nor did he, in passing by all this, wish his readers to regard that part of the Gospel story as unhistorical or unessential. He chose to treat a particular phase of Christ's life and personality—what he probably considered the highest phase. This Gospel was designed to illumine, not to supersede, the others.

* Bacon, *Sermon on the Mount* (1902), p. 109 f., says: 'It was indeed, from the standpoint of the historian of Jesus' life and teaching, a disastrous, almost incredible mutilation to leave out, as our Third Evangelist has done, all the negative side of the teaching, and give nothing but the commandment of ministering love toward all. We can scarcely understand that the five great interpretative antitheses of the new law of conduct toward men *versus* the old [Mt $5^{21-48}$], and the three corresponding antitheses on duty toward God [Mt $6^{1-18}$], could have been dropped in one form of even the oral tradition'; but the Third Evangelist has done this in order to 'concentrate the teaching upon the simple affirmation of the law of love.'

alteration to remove the disparaging reference to the Gentiles' love for material wealth and power); again, the absence of ὁ οὐράνιος in Lk 12[30]; and the absence of τὴν δικαιοσύνην αὐτοῦ (a technical Jewish term) from Lk 12[31]. There would seem, therefore, to be no room for question that, historically considered, the Sermon as given by Matthew is of much greater authenticity than the Sermon of Luke, since it has better preserved the actual contents of the historical discourse, its theme and development, its Jewish elements, its Palestinian colour, and the true interpretation of its sayings; and, in addition to these merits, the Matthæan account has a Greek style of higher literary skill and finish. In this preference for the Matthæan report of the Sermon nearly all scholars are now agreed.*

But this relative superiority of the account in the First Gospel does not mean its *absolute* authenticity. This account is still but a series of excerpts from the historical Sermon, marred by the incidents of long transmission, showing the inevitable effects of the process of translation, and containing certain passages which originally belonged to other occasions (see below). Even in some cases we are uncertain whether the ideas themselves of Jesus are not misrepresented by the wording of Mt 5–7. Two instances about which there has been much dispute may be mentioned. In Mt 5[18. 19] the peculiar tone of Jewish literalness has led many scholars to postulate a Judaistic-Christian colouring of Jesus' words in these verses, since they seem quite foreign to His anti-literal utterances and spirit. Every explanation of them as coming in just this sense from Jesus is beset with difficulties, and fails to satisfy completely (see under ii. 4*c*). Again, in Mt 5[32] we find a most significant addition to the teaching of Jesus concerning divorce. This saying probably belongs to the occasion with which it is associated in Mt 19[3-12], where it is repeated. In both the Matthæan instances we have the exceptive phrase παρεκτὸς λόγου πορνείας (μὴ ἐπὶ πορνείᾳ), which is not found in the other Synoptic parallels, Mk 10[11], Lk 16[18]. A serious question is involved concerning the permissibility of divorce. The phrase is rejected as a later interpolation by many of the best modern scholars (see under ii. 4*d*).

But if we cannot think of the Sermon in Matthew as presenting an absolutely authentic account of that historical discourse, we may yet feel much certainty that it contains many essential teachings from that discourse with substantial trustworthiness. In the Evangelists' reports of the Sermon we have not complete historical accuracy, but practical adequacy.

5. Present Text of the Discourse.—The text of the Sermon as it finally took form in the First and Third Gospels has come down to us through the centuries with less variation than might have been expected; it is in excellent condition. The number of variations is not many hundred, and few of them are of special importance. The Textus Receptus of the 16th cent. (and therefore the AV of 1611 A.D.), compared with the text given us by the great uncials of the 4th–6th cents., shows here as elsewhere numerous elements of assimilation, emendation, revision, and variation; but these have been excluded in the critical texts of the modern editors, Westcott and Hort, Tischendorf, the English Revisers, and others. The most conspicuous changes are the dropping out of words and phrases which have been imported into the text of one Gospel to assimilate its readings to the text of the other, and the literary 'improvements' which the scribes have introduced. The variations which are of importance for interpretation will be treated in their respective places below.

ii. *Interpretation.*—All study of the origin and transmission of the Sermon on the Mount is but a preparation for its interpretation, just as all study of its interpretation is but a preparation for its practice. Both lines of preparation are essential if the teaching is to be understood historically and comprehensively, and is to be applied truly and thoroughly. Surely the untrained English reader can find through the Sermon the spiritual assurance and strength which he needs, and an ideal of life which can determine his conduct in the limited sphere in which he thinks and acts; the gospel is for all, and essentially intelligible to all, rather than the exclusive possession of the educated few (as is the case with intellectual systems of theology, philosophy, ethics, and the like). But when the Sermon is used—as it can and should be used—to illumine the great problems of religion, of morals, and of society, every resource of spiritual capacity, mental ability, and the acquisition of learning should be brought to bear upon this supreme teaching of Christ, in order that it may exert its due and proper influence upon the world.

1. Popular, Gnomic, and Figurative Style.—Interpretation must take full account of the literary style in which Jesus chose to express Himself. That style, as seen in the Sermon on the Mount and throughout the Synoptic Gospels, was distinctly popular and Oriental. Too often Jesus' teaching has been handled as though it were a systematic, scientific treatise on theology and ethics, whose expressions were fittingly to be subjected to laboratory test, each element to be exactly determined by finely-graduated measuring-rod or delicate weighing-scales. No greater mistake could be made, and the results so obtained must be hopelessly incorrect and perverse. Microscopic analysis is a radically wrong process to be applied to Jesus' teachings. For He chose to deal with the masses, and His ideas were expressed in language which they could hear and consider. If at times He disputed with the learned men of His nation, and in doing so in part adopted their dialectical method (see the Johannine discourses), still this was not His main interest or His chief field of work. The common people were open-minded and receptive: to them, therefore, He addressed His teaching. It was to the Galilæans that He gave Himself and His message, while in Jerusalem and elsewhere He had to defend both against the hostile leaders.

As He taught the multitudes, in their synagogues, upon the highways, along the seashore, and on the hillsides of Galilee, He put His religious truths and ethical principles into concrete popular sayings, contrasting His ideal of life in many simple ways with the conventional notions and practices, and illustrating His teaching from the ordinary avocations, experiences, and environment of His hearers.* Entirely free from scholasticism and intellectualism, He did not tell the how and why of things, nor present scientific definitions, nor deal in abstractions; but with Divine wisdom and skill He taught those things

* The constant preference shown by H. Holtzmann, Wendt, and a few others for the Lukan account of the Sermon as against that of Matthew is, in view of these considerations, a mistake. It is not a true historical criticism to eliminate from the records of Jesus' teaching as much as possible of the characteristic Jewish element, or to give the place of honour to the briefer and more fragmentary of two parallel accounts.

* One reading should be given to the Sermon in Mt 5–7 with no other intent than to note Jesus' remarkably fine and abundant allusions to things around Him—religious practices, ethical conceptions, commerce, industries, agriculture, animals, plants, home life, house furnishings, civic institutions, social customs, the conduct of men, human needs, fortune, and misfortune. His observation and appreciation of everything was unequalled, and the relative valuation which He placed upon things was the true norm of all subsequent judgment. No poet—not even Shakespeare—has seen so clearly, felt so truly, or pictured so perfectly the hearts and lives of men.

which it is essential for all men to know. The religious facts and truths which He presented form the foundation of Christian theology, and His instruction concerning human conduct must lie at the root of any true system of ethics; but He did not teach these subjects in the manner of the ancient or modern schools. He put His ideas in such a way as to make His knowledge universal. He spoke with a simplicity, insight, and fervour which would appeal to all serious listeners.

It was a part of Jesus' method to use all kinds of *figurative* language. That was natural to Him as an Oriental, and by no other means could He have reached the Orientals who formed His audiences. Similes, metaphors, all kinds of illustrations, parables, hyperbolical expressions, were constantly upon His lips.* We have constantly to be on our guard against interpreting literally what He has spoken figuratively.† The Sermon presents the true righteousness, the ideal human life, popularly and practically portrayed and enjoined. To treat this teaching as scientific ethics is to produce confusion. But to draw from it the essential principles of ethics is to find light and peace for mankind.

Many of Jesus' utterances, especially in this discourse, are of the gnomic type in poetic form—a style so effective in the Wisdom literature of the OT and Apocrypha. The wise men of Hebrew history, particularly after the Babylonian exile, put into this attractive literary dress their crystallization of experience, their philosophy of life, their instruction for conduct and practical affairs. This was a favourite style of teaching with the Jews—a fact that was at once the cause and the motive for Jesus' adoption of it. As a literary mode of expression, Jesus used the gnome, as He used the parable, with consummate art.‡ Even the translation of these sayings into a radically different language has not destroyed their literary finish, rhythm, and symmetry, *e.g.* the Beatitudes, the Lord's Prayer, and many other passages in Mt 5–7. The simplicity, lucidity, and energy of Jesus' utterances mask the art with which they were fashioned. Not that we are to conceive of Jesus as *labouring* over His literary productions to bring them to perfection, but that ideal thought intuitively found ideal expression. Jesus' supreme interest was assuredly not in mere letters, but in the truth He taught. Yet this included the vital lodgment of the truth in the minds and hearts of men, and to this end the language in which He clothed His teaching was of great importance. The uniqueness of Jesus manifests itself in the ability to present His teaching acceptably and effectively, as well as in His perfect insight into the truth itself.

* Metaphorically, Jesus calls the disciples the salt of the earth and the light of the world (Mt $5^{13.\,14}$). Symbolically, He commands the plucking out of the right eye ($5^{29}$). Figuratively, He speaks of the mote and beam ($7^{3-5}$), of the pearls before swine ($7^{6}$), of the narrow way ($7^{13.\,14}$), of the false prophets ($7^{15}$), of the tree and its fruits ($7^{16-20}$). He gives the parable of the Two House-builders ($7^{24-27}$). And most difficult of all to interpret correctly, we have His hyperbolical utterances, in which He says more than He means, setting forth a principle rather than a rule of conduct, and leaving its application to the judgment of men. Such are the four famous 'non-resistance' injunctions ($5^{39-42}$), and the sayings concerning the secrecy of benevolence ($6^{3}$), prayer in the closet only ($6^{6}$), anxiety for the necessaries of life ($6^{25.\,34}$), answers to prayer ($7^{7\text{ff.}}$), and the 'Golden Rule' ($7^{12}$).

† See Wendt, *Lehre Jesu*, ii. 74–112; Tholuck, *Bergrede*[5], p. 169 ff. [Eng. tr. p. 165 f.].

‡ See Heinrici, *Bergpredigt*, i. 19–26; Kent, *Wise Men of Ancient Israel*[2] (1899), pp. 176–201; Briggs, 'The Wisdom of Jesus the Messiah' in *Expository Times*, 1897, viii. 393–8, 452–5, 492–6, ix. 69–75. Dr. Briggs says: 'Jesus put His wisdom in this poetic form for the reason that Wisdom had been given in the artistic form of gnomic poetry for centuries, and was so used in His time. If He was to use such Wisdom, He must use its forms. Jesus uses its stereotyped forms, and uses them with such extraordinary freshness, fertility, and vigour that His Wisdom transcends all others in its artistic expression' (viii. 395).

But not only was Jesus the true successor of the OT sage. The Hebrew prophets also gave their messages in remarkably fine literary form, as in the Psalms, Isaiah, and Amos. And the prophetic utterances of Jesus, too, were clothed in language full of beauty, fire, and force. Indeed, Jesus was more a prophet than a sage.* He taught not so much as a philosopher of this life; rather, as a seer who has a vision of a higher life which is to be produced in men. Jesus' earnestness and tempered zeal in His teaching were more persuasive and searching than the fervour of any preceding prophet of truth and righteousness. In the Sermon on the Mount He showed men the ideal life, but that was not all—He strenuously urged them to attain it. They must forthwith *do* the will of God which He had made plain to them (Mt $7^{21-27}$). Active love, self-denial, and service He fixed as absolute requirements for those who would be members of the kingdom of God. In these utterances the voice of the true prophet is heard proclaiming God's will and demanding that 'justice roll down as waters, and righteousness as an everflowing stream' (Am $5^{24}$). Jesus was both wise man and prophet, but greater than either and greater than both; and never greater than in the Sermon on the Mount, where He immeasurably surpassed every lawgiver, seer, and sage. It is with this supreme appreciation of Jesus and His teaching that one should enter upon the specific interpretation of His words in Mt 5–7 and the Lukan parallels.

2. Effect of the Translation into Greek.—In view of the fact that we have Jesus' words only in a translation (the original of which has probably passed out of existence), it will be always a wise proceeding to attempt to reproduce the Aramaic form of the words of Jesus which have come down to us only in Greek. By this process, even though success in it can be only partial, an atmosphere for interpretation is obtained, and shades of meaning are disclosed which would otherwise escape us. Unless we get back into the Semitic world to which Jesus belonged and in which He worked, we can never completely understand Him or His teaching. It is therefore a proper and useful undertaking upon which a number of excellent scholars are now engaged,† to restore by conjecture the original Aramaic of Jesus' words. Some of the results already reached are of importance, and still greater things may be expected of it in the future. It is likely that to some extent the variant vocabulary in the Greek of parallel Gospel passages can be explained as the result of translation, a single Aramaic term being represented in the several translations by two or more synonymous Greek words.

A thorough study of the Septuagint in close comparison with the Hebrew text, showing how translators actually put Hebrew into Greek, gives a valuable insight into method, and furnishes criteria for judging of the Aramaic original behind the Greek of our Gospels. Various degrees of literal and free rendering of the Aramaic can be seen in our two accounts of the Sermon on the Mount. Sometimes the translators have been unable to find exact Greek equivalents for the Aramaic words; sometimes they have imperfectly comprehended, and therefore have failed exactly to reproduce, the Semitic ideas; sometimes they

* See this view defended by J. Weiss, *Predigt Jesu vom Reiche Gottes*[2] (1900), pp. 53–57, against Wellhausen, *Israelitische u. Jüdische Geschichte*[3] (1897), ch. 24.

† See Resch, *Logia Jesu* (1898), who endeavours to reconstruct in Hebrew the Matthæan *Logia*, which he regards as the primary source for the material of the Synoptic Gospels; suggestive for this study is his reconstruction of the Sermon on the Mount, pp. 19–29. Further, Marshall, artt. in *Expositor* (1891–2); Dalman, *Worte Jesu*, i. (1898); E. A. Abbott, *Clue: A Guide through Greek to Hebrew Scripture* (1900); Nestle, *SK* (1896).

have placed a current interpretation upon Jesus' sayings; sometimes they have expanded the sayings as they put them into Greek to remove ambiguity, or to improve the literary form. These and other inevitable phenomena of translation appear in this discourse of the First and Third Gospels, and must be adequately dealt with in an exposition of its contents.

3. Theme of the Discourse and its Development.—It is the unanimous opinion of all students of the Sermon on the Mount (whether they regard its contents as original or compiled), that the discourse as it appears in Mt 5–7 and Lk $6^{20-49}$ has a real unity, presenting a definite theme and developing it logically and effectively. If an actual discourse of Jesus constitutes the nucleus of these accounts, the unity of the Sermon is original with Jesus, notwithstanding the presence of certain extraneous material in the Gospel reports. But, even on the supposition that there was no historical Sermon, still the unity of this discourse in Matthew and Luke remains, and is to be attributed to the sources used by the Evangelists, or to the Evangelists themselves. We have seen good reason, however, for holding that the Sermon, as it comes down to us, rests upon a real event and contains excerpts from a great discourse of Jesus, whose theme and development are here preserved. What the theme is must be carefully considered. There are differing shades of opinion and various statements on this point. The crucial question seems to be: Is the theme of the discourse to be found in the Beatitudes (Mt $5^{3-12}$= Lk $6^{20-23}$) or in the verses about the fulfilment of the Law (Mt $5^{17-20}$)?

If the theme lies in Mt $5^{17-20}$, as is maintained by some,* several conclusions must follow. (1) The Beatitudes, given both in Matthew and in Luke as the beginning of the discourse, are extraneous matter brought in from some other connexion, or are merely introductory, containing no essential element of the discourse. (2) The account in Luke omits the very verses of the discourse which contain the theme, since Mt $5^{17-20}$ has no parallel in Lk $6^{20-49}$; yet Luke's discourse *has* a theme, and an excellent one, in the promulgation of a perfect life of patience, trust, love, service, and obedience. (3) To find the theme in Mt $5^{17-20}$ is to make the discourse an apologetical one, in which Jesus was defending Himself against the charge of destroying the OT Law. What follows, however, in $5^{21-48}$ is not at all in accordance with this conception, for Jesus' teaching in these verses abrogates the OT Law in some points, and in other points supersedes it by a higher ideal of thought and conduct; in other words, He is here showing how little rather than how much He has in common with that legal system—He criticises rather than defends it. (4) Or, the theme in Mt $5^{17-20}$ may call for a polemical discourse in condemnation of the perverse Pharisaic interpretation of the OT Law. But the occasion of this discourse did not suggest or make appropriate a polemic against Pharisaic conceptions any more than a defence of Himself against Pharisaic charges. If we can trust Luke to have given us the substantially correct setting of the Sermon, it was an address to the Galilæan multitude who followed Jesus, eager to hear His words, well disposed towards Him, and many of them already His professed disciples. Jesus had just formally chosen twelve men to assist Him in His work, which was now assuming the character and proportions of a new religious movement. At this juncture a discourse of a *negative* quality, apologetical or polemical, would have been unsuitable and unwise. The occasion called for a positive, comprehensive setting forth of what this new religious movement aimed to accomplish, for what it practically stood. (5) Finally, to take the theme from Mt $5^{17-20}$ makes it impossible to find any place in the discourse for the greater part of the material contained in Mt 5–7, since the great sections $5^{3-16}$ $6^{19-34}$ $7^{1-27}$ have no logical relation to a defence against the charge of destroying the OT Law, or a polemic against the Pharisaic interpretation of it.

These considerations point strongly towards another theme for the Sermon. Where should one look for that theme but in the first section, in the Beatitudes themselves? They present the ideal life in character and conduct, the true righteousness over against current shallow and perverse conceptions of righteousness. This, then, is the true theme of the Sermon on the Mount, because: (1) It stands, where the theme should, at the head of the discourse. (2) It is the theme which both Matthew and Luke fix for the discourse, and the only theme which is common to both accounts of the Sermon.* (3) This theme *includes* the section about the Law, Mt $5^{17-20}$, with the Jewish allusions contained in its logical development in $5^{21-48}$ $6^{1-18}$, as one of several elements in the discourse, which therefore Luke or his source can omit without radically changing the thought of the Sermon. In this feature of the section the ideal life of Jesus' conception is painted against the background of the Pharisaic conception; and not with an apologetical or polemical purpose, but as an effective mode of positive instruction. When the Gospel story was shorn of this local colouring to make it suitable for the Gentiles, the essential, universal elements of the teaching were extracted and used; compare Lk $6^{27-36}$ with Mt $5^{21-48}$. (4) This theme is appropriate to the occasion described by Luke. There is abundant probability that Jesus, at some middle point in the Galilæan ministry, after careful preparation of the people, and to a general company of His followers, would undertake to set forth somewhat specifically and comprehensively the kind of men and women for whom the kingdom of God called; what it meant in actual life to become a member of that kingdom; the kind of righteousness which God required as contrasted with the current scribal teaching. This would be a definite theme for a great discourse. It would logically involve a characterization of ideal character and conduct; a comparison of this ideal with the ideal commonly held among them; some illustrations of how this ideal character and conduct would manifest themselves in one's attitude towards God, self, and fellow-men; and, lastly, earnest injunctions to the actual attainment of this ideal. This is what we have in the Sermon on the Mount. And there is in the public ministry of Jesus no occasion so suitable for just such a discourse as that of the appoint ent of the apostles, with which event Luke associates the Sermon.

Certain scholars hold that this general theme of the ideal life, or the true righteousness, unifies the whole contents of Mt 5–7 so that *every verse* finds a place in its development. On this view the Sermon contains no extraneous material, is in no degree a compilation, but, on the contrary, came from Jesus exactly in its present contents and arrangement.† It does not need to be said that we should all like to think of the Sermon in this way, if it were possible. But in the judgment of

* H. Holtzmann, Ibbeken, B. Weiss, Wendt.

* Luke's form of the Beatitudes does not show this as clearly as Matthew's, but the subsequent material of Luke's discourse leaves no doubt that the original import of them was the same as of those of the First Gospel. On other grounds also it appears that the Lukan interpretation of the Beatitudes (placed upon them probably not by the Evangelist but by his source) is seriously misconceived.

† So Stier, Morison, Keil, Kübel, Steinmeyer, H. Weiss, Broadus, Grawert.

the great majority of NT scholars * two facts are decisive against this hypothesis. (1) Particular verses in the two accounts have no logical connexion with the theme of the discourse and its development, *e.g.* Mt $5^{25. 26. 31. 32}$ $6^{7-15}$ $7^{6-11. 22. 23}$, Lk $6^{24-26. 38a. 39. 40. 45}$. It does not meet the point to reply that, since the Gospel reports contain only excerpts from the Sermon, abrupt transitions are to be expected. That is true, as we may see at Mt $5^{12. 16. 48}$ $6^{18. 34}$, Lk $6^{26. 31. 42}$. But in these cases it is possible to discover a thought relation in the contiguous sections, although the sections are not smoothly joined to one another. In the former class of passages, however, it is difficult to see any logical relation to the theme and discourse as a whole. If now it be said that thought connexion need not exist throughout the contents, this is to attribute to Jesus a mosaic of sayings instead of a discourse, which seems very unlikely. (2) The second fact to be mentioned is still more certain. Most of the material in Matthew which appears to be extraneous to the discourse has parallels in Luke's Gospel *outside* of his Sermon (see table of parallel passages above). Now, if Matthew has right places for these verses, Luke has wrong ones. But can it be considered probable that the Sermon should have been preserved so complete as Matthew's account in one line of transmission, and should have become so disintegrated as Luke's account in another? Would not Luke, who had 'traced the course of all things accurately from the first' (Lk $1^{3}$), have discovered and obtained for his book this far superior account of the Sermon? Again, the original historical setting of some of these extraneous passages in Mt 5–7 is fixed by Luke as not in the Sermon but elsewhere. The Lord's Prayer is shown by Lk $11^{1-4}$ to have been given by Jesus on another occasion in response to a specific request from His disciples. The true place of the divorce teaching (Mt $5^{31. 32}$) is established by Matthew's own Gospel, in Mt $19^{3-9}$ = Mk $10^{2-12}$, where it is germane to the occasion, while in the Sermon it interrupts the movement of the discourse.† Similarly, the parable of the blind guiding the blind, Lk $6^{39}$, belongs more likely to the position assigned it in Mt $15^{14}$.

There are, then, some passages in Mt 5–7 and Lk $6^{20-49}$ which did not historically form a part of the Sermon on the Mount, but which by a process of compilation (either in transmission or as the work of the Evangelists) have become associated with it. But one cannot be sure just how much extraneous matter is present in these reports, and the question is more difficult in Matthew than in Luke. There is much difference of opinion as to the amount of compilation, even among those who are best qualified to judge. It may be best to indicate three grades of the material: that which probably belonged to the original discourse, that about which there is uncertainty (accompanied by an interrogation-point in the table), and that which must be considered foreign addition (marked by enclosing brackets). The table that follows is intended to show the general opinion of scholars rather than any individual opinion.

| | | | |
|---|---|---|---|
| Mt $5^{3. 4. 6. 11. 12}$ | =Lk $6^{20-23}$ | Mt [$5^{25. 26}$] | |
| ? $5^{5. 7. 8. 9. 10}$ | | $5^{27. 28}$ | |
| | [$6^{24-26}$] | ? $5^{29. 30}$ | |
| ? $5^{13-16}$ | | [$5^{31. 32}$] | |
| $5^{17-24}$ | | $5^{33-48}$ | =Lk $6^{27-30. 32-36}$ |
| Mt $6^{1-6}$ | | Mt ? $7^{12}$ | =Lk ? $6^{31}$ |
| [$6^{7-15}$] | | ? $7^{13-15}$ | |
| $6^{16-18}$ | | ? $7^{16-20}$ = | ? $6^{43. 44}$ |
| ? $6^{19-34}$ | | | [$6^{45}$] |
| $7^{1-5}$ | =Lk $6^{37. 38b. 41. 42}$ | $7^{21}$ = | $6^{46}$ |
| | [$6^{38a. 39. 40}$] | [$7^{22. 23}$] | |
| [$7^{6-11}$] | | $7^{24-27}$ = | $6^{47-49}$ |

* Calvin, Baur, Strauss, Neander, Tholuck, Wieseler, Kuinöl, Bleek, Keim, Weizsäcker, Godet, Meyer, Bruce, H. Holtzmann, Nösgen, Achelis, Wendt, B. Weiss, Ibbeken, Wernle, Jülicher, Heinrici, Sanday, Bartlet, Bacon, and many others.

† The parallel passage in Luke is at $16^{18}$, but this verse and the preceding one are both unattached in this position, which indicates that they are dislocated; $16^{17}$ belongs to the original Sermon, but this determines nothing for $16^{18}$, which stands in no logical relation to it.

In a problem so important as this of the theme and content of the Sermon on the Mount, attention must be given to the opinions of many scholars. A brief conspectus of these opinions follows, arranged in two groups: those who hold that the discourse of Mt 5–7 is a perfect and original whole, and those who regard as extraneous a smaller or larger portion of these chapters.

Morison thinks Mt 5–7 a complete unit, given by Jesus to 'the constantly increasing multitude of such as took Him to be the long promised Messiah, and who wished to be instructed by Him as to what they should do in connection with the inauguration and establishment of His kingdom' (*Comm. on Matthew*, new ed. 1884, p. 57).—Broadus maintains that the discourse was given exactly as in the First Gospel, and that in it Jesus 'sets forth the characteristics of those who are to be subjects of this reign [of heaven] and share the privileges connected with it, and urges upon them various duties. In particular He clearly exhibits the relation of His teachings to the moral law, in order to correct any notion that He proposed to set the law aside, or to relax its rigour, when, on the contrary, He came to inculcate not merely an external, but a deeply spiritual morality' (*Comm. on Matthew*, 1886, pp. 83, 84).—Steinmeyer assumes that the Sermon as it appears in Matthew 'came from Jesus in this order and in these words . . . Righteousness is the glittering thread which clearly runs through the whole discourse from the beginning to the end; this is the idea which constitutes its unity' (*Die Rede des Herrn auf dem Berge*, 1885, pp. 10, 20). He makes a threefold division of the contents: the longing for righteousness, ch. 5; the striving for righteousness, ch. 6; the attainment of righteousness, ch. 7.*—Hugo Weiss also defends the integrity of Matthew's discourse, and considers it as 'a necessary strand in the development of the Messianic movement. . . . [It contains] a characterization of the Messianic kingdom and of the duties of its members against a background of Jewish and Gentile conceptions of the world, teaching and practice' (*Die Bergpredigt Christi*, 1892, pp. 2, 3).—Nösgen theoretically admits the possibility of the presence of some extraneous verses in Mt 5–7, but he does not as a matter of fact discover any. He thinks that in the discourse Jesus, as the fulfiller of the Law and the Prophets, aims to set forth the moral conditions of obtaining membership in the Messianic kingdom which is at hand (*Das Evangelium nach Matthäus*², 1897, p. 54).—Plummer holds that Luke's Sermon is a different one from Matthew's, though Luke has dropped out of his account the long section Mt $5^{17}$–$6^{18}$ as inapplicable to his readers. And as to the theme, 'the main point in Matthew is the contrast between the legal righteousness and the true righteousness; † in Luke the main point is that true righteousness is love' (*Comm. on Luke*, 1896, p. 183).—Grawert is the latest defender of the complete unity of Mt 5–7 (*Die Bergpredigt nach Matthäus*, 1900). The proof of this integrity is developed on a new line: the Beatitudes as given by Matthew constitute the key to the whole discourse, each Beatitude corresponding to a particular section of these chapters and forming its epitome. He thinks that for this reason the Beatitudes must have stood originally at the close of the Sermon instead of at the beginning, so that Mt $5^{13-16}$ was the proper prologue to the Sermon (pp. 5–8). The eight Beatitudes as they now stand in Matthew are in inverse order as compared with the material of the discourse, thus: $5^{10}=5^{11-16}$, $5^{9}=5^{17-26}$, $5^{8}=5^{27-37}$, $5^{7}=5^{38-48}$, $5^{6}=6^{1-34}$, $5^{5}=7^{1. 2}$, $5^{4}=7^{3-5(6)}$, $5^{3}=7^{7-11}$ (p. 66). The purpose of the Sermon was 'the consolidation of the disciple-group. By this we mean the inner and outer separation of the disciples from their former Jewish past, and the establishment of their new position on the basis of their relation to the Lord, and in their actual outer connexion with Him as His followers and future messengers of the Kingdom of Heaven' (p. 18). But the discourse has a double character, for it also 'indicates the point at which Jesus steps forth from His former reserve with respect to the ever-increasing hostility of the Pharisees and scribes, and engages in open war against them' (p. 18). It was this that made the picking out and the union of the disciples a necessity. The occasion of the Sermon, as of the appointment of the Twelve with which it was immediately connected, was the daily increasing labours of the Pharisees against

* Steinmeyer's analysis is entirely formal—it does not characterize the material. The whole treatment is shallow, uncritical, and disappointing.

† From Plummer's view of Luke's discourse it seems fair to conclude that he would hold Matthew's discourse to be practically original as it stands. If so, this statement of the theme of Mt 5–7 is unsatisfactory, since the Jewish contrast appears only in $5^{17-48}$ $6^{1-6. 16-18}$ $7^{1-5}$, less than one-half of the whole Sermon. But this conception of the Sermon is also shown to be inadequate by the fact that it lacks the breadth, point, and positiveness which the circumstances of the Sermon on the Mount required.

Jesus and their persecution of His followers, which called out a public manifesto from Jesus and a positive resistance (p. 33). He makes five divisions of the Sermon: $5^{17-37}$ $5^{38-48}$ $6^{1-18}$ $6^{19-34}$ $7^{1-11}$; the introduction is $5^{11-16}$, and the conclusion $7^{12-27}$, while the Beatitudes $5^{3-10}$ form a *résumé* of the whole teaching.*

The compilation view, which sees in the discourses of Matthew and Luke a larger or smaller quantity of extraneous sayings, is held by the great majority of scholars, who can be represented here by quotations from but a few. Some members of this class have the same large idea of the theme of the Sermon on the Mount as the seven just named. Godet (*Collection of the Four Gospels, and the Gospel of Matthew*, 1899, p. 135) says that 'the report of this discourse in Matthew is a work of a composite order, in which have been combined many heterogeneous elements; but this does not deny that there was really a great discourse of Jesus.' The passages which he thinks belonged originally to other connexions are Mt $5^{7-12. 25. 26. 29-32}$ $6^{7-15. 19-34}$ $7^{(6). 7-14. 21-23}$ (pp. 132-134). The purpose of the Sermon was 'the installation of the true people of God on the earth by the proclamation of the only righteousness conformable to the holy nature of God, which should characterize the true members of His people, in opposition to the formal righteousness inculcated by the traditional teaching and the example of the doctors. This righteousness, far from being contrary to the law, is the very fulfilment of it, since the meaning of the law has been falsified by those who call themselves its interpreters' (p. 135).—B. Weiss (*Meyer-Komm. ü. d. Mattevgm.* 1898) holds that a primitive *Logian* account of the Sermon was essentially shortened by Luke but largely expanded by Matthew. 'If we remove the additions of our Evangelist, we get the form of an original discourse which may well be substantially the Sermon of Jesus, by reason of its unity of thought, its certain prologue $5^{1-12}$ and epilogue $7^{13-27}$, its highly important theme $5^{17-20}$, with the exposition in twice three antitheses against the scribal interpretation of the law $5^{21f. 27f. 31f. 33-37. 38-42. 43-48}$; also in twice three antitheses against the practices of the Pharisees $6^{1-4. 5f. 16-18}$ $7^{1f. 3-5. 12}$, with their genuine reflexion of the conditions of the time' (p. 163). Therefore the extraneous matter in the Matthæan account is $5^{13-16. 23-26. 29. 30}$ $6^{7-15. 19-34}$ $7^{6-11}$. In the discourse 'clearly the opposition to the prevailing teaching of the law and the Pharisaic practice of righteousness form the leading point of view and historical motive' (p. 164).—Tholuck (*Die Bergrede Christi*[5], 1872 [Eng. tr. from ed.[4], 1860]) thinks that there is some indication of compilation, as perhaps Mt $5^{25. 26. 29. 30}$ $6^{7-15}$ $7^{1-11}$ (p. 22), but hesitates to pronounce against any specific passages; he defends the Matthæan position of the Lord's Prayer $6^{7-15}$ and of the important section $6^{19-34}$. Jesus' purpose in the Sermon was 'to exhibit Himself as the fulfiller of the law, and to enunciate the Magna Charta of His new kingdom.† . . . To exhibit the new economy of the kingdom of God as the truest fulfilment of the old; in this the condemnation of the superficial religion of Pharisaic Judaism was of course implied' (pp. 14, 15). The Sermon must have contained throughout a strictly progressive train of thought, but this disappears in Mt $6^{19}$–$7^{11}$ by the fault of the Evangelist.—Bruce (*Expositor's Greek Testament*, vol. i. 1897) presents a novel theory: the material in Mt 5–7 is a literary assemblage of various teachings given during a period of instruction. It is supposed that the Beatitudes were given on one day, teaching concerning prayer on another day, warning against covetousness on a third day, and so forth. 'As these chapters stand, the various parts cohere and sympathize wonderfully, so as to present the appearance of a unity' (pp. 94, 95).—Achelis (*Die Bergpredigt*, 1875) holds that 'the speech of Mt 5–7 is to be regarded as a work of compilation, in which the genuine Sermon of Jesus was combined with sections from other discourses into a new unity' (p. 491). The portion Mt $5^{3}$–$6^{18}$ is the actual nucleus of the Sermon, and $7^{13-27}$ was the actual close; but the entire portion $6^{19}$–$7^{12}$ consists of extraneous matter brought in here from other connexions (p. 400). In this great discourse Jesus 'set before His disciples the norm and the essence of the righteousness of the Kingdom of Heaven' (p. 321).—Wendt (*Die Lehre Jesu*, vol. i. 1886) regards the speech as in part a compilation, the foreign passages being Mt $5^{13-16. 25. 27. 29b. 30}$ $6^{7-15. 19-34}$ $7^{6-11. 19. 20. 22. 23}$.—Feine (*Jahrb. f. Protest. Theologie*, 1885, pp. 1–85) holds firmly to a historical discourse, and regards the Matthew account as the more authentic, but separates as extraneous matter Mt $5^{11-16. 18f. 23-26. 29-32}$ $6^{7-15. 19-34}$ $7^{6-11. 13f. 19f. 22f.}$ (p. 84). The theme of the Sermon is the true righteousness as against the current Pharisaic conception and practice of righteousness (p. 35).—Bacon (*Sermon on the Mount*, 1902) argues stoutly for an actual discourse of Jesus, and defends the account of the First Gospel as the more complete. The portions which did not originally belong to the Sermon are Mt $5^{5. 7-10. 13-16. 18. 23-26. 29f.}$ $6^{7-15. 19-34}$ $7^{6-11. 13-17. 19-23}$. He calls the Sermon 'the discourse on the Higher Righteousness' (p. x), and thinks it 'worthy to be called the new Torah of the Kingdom of God' (p. 35).

H. Holtzmann (*Hand-Comm. u. d. Synoptiker*[2], 1892) thinks the speech is a work of compilation *in toto* by the Evangelist, whose aim was to furnish an order of life for the new Church (p. 99). The theme of the entire discourse is in his opinion to be found in Mt $5^{17-20}$ (p. 103).—Weizsäcker (*Apost. Zeitalter*[2], 1891) also regards the Sermon as a collection by the Evangelist of passages adapted to the instruction of the primitive Church (p. 378 f.).—Heinrici (*Die Bergpredigt*, vol. i. 1900) similarly views Matthew's discourse as a free composition from scattered authentic sayings (pp. 10, 39). As to the theme of the Sermon, 'the whole appears as the Magna Charta of true discipleship to Jesus' (p. 13).—Ibbeken (*Die Bergpredigt Jesu*[2], 1890) offers a striking view which calls for careful consideration. According to him, the First Gospel was designed throughout to show a close parallelism between the events of Israel's history and the events of Jesus' life, as may be seen in the Evangelist's treatment of the Infancy Narrative (chs. 1. 2), the Baptism (ch. 3), and the Temptation (ch. 4). Then when the author comes to the Sermon (chs. 5–7) he provides for Jesus a multitude explicitly described ($4^{25}$) as representative of all the Hebrew territory, drawing significantly the parallelism between the giving of the Law on Sinai and the second giving of the Law by Jesus on 'the mount of Beatitudes' (cf. Mt $5^{1}$ $7^{28}$ with Ex $19^{3}$ $24^{9. 13}$). The contents and arrangement of the Sermon also correspond, Ibbeken thinks, with the Sinai law-giving. There are four chief sections of the Matthæan account: $5^{3-48}$ concerning ethical perfection (the Beatitudes corresponding to the Ten Commandments), $6^{1-18}$ concerning piety, $6^{19-34}$ concerning the highest good, $7^{1-12}$ concerning the judging of members of the Kingdom of Heaven; then follows an epilogue $7^{13-27}$ containing earnest warnings and admonitions to faithful obedience to this new law (pp. 1–11). He declines to decide whether this parallelism between the old and the new law-giving was drawn by Jesus Himself or only by the Evangelist: 'however many may be the grounds for thinking that the speech was first put together out of the Matthæan Aramaic *Logia* by the author of the First Gospel, the *possibility* remains that Jesus Himself gave the discourse in this form and on this occasion. . . . It seems to me to be unnecessary for the understanding of the Sermon to determine whether Jesus Himself actually gave it in this form, at this time and place, or whether the material of it was first gathered together by Matthew out of scattered single sayings and arranged in this way' (pp. 5, 6).*

But granting, as seems necessary, that the Sermon on the Mount, as it comes down to us in twofold form, is in some degree a compilation, though with the nucleus of a historical discourse, it is yet possible to recognize that the material as it stands in Matthew and Luke has a kind of unity, by the consonance of all Jesus' religious-ethical teaching, and by the intelligent grouping of the additional matter within the framework of the actual address. And considering that in those sections of the discourse which are original we have mere excerpts from the whole, only a small part of all that Jesus said in that epoch-making discourse, we can still feel confident that in these verses the theme of the Sermon is before us, and many of the essential ideas—a sufficient number to show the main development of the theme by Jesus. If an

* Grawert's theory is composed of two parts which are not interdependent. (1) His analysis of the discourse, parcelling out a number of verses to each Beatitude as its epitome, is artificial and reaches absurdity when it is forced to make 'Blessed are they that mourn' ($5^{4}$) the epitome of the saying about the mote and the beam ($7^{3-5}$). Certainly the Beatitudes contain the essential ideas of the Sermon, which are developed, made concrete, and illustrated by the teaching which follows. But no such absolute connexion between the Beatitudes and the contents of the discourse can be shown as shall guarantee that *every verse* of Mt 5–7 was a part of the original Sermon. Not only this, but he has entirely ignored the phenomena of Luke's parallel account and the distribution of much of Matthew's discourse through chs. 10–14. 16 of the Third Gospel. (2) The conception which Grawert has of the theme, occasion, and purpose of the Sermon might as readily be held in conjunction with a mild compilation theory, and unquestionably contains a great deal of truth. The main objection to it is that it presses to an extreme the idea of the Pharisaic opposition to Jesus and His followers *at this stage* of the ministry, and postulates a much sharper separation between the Christian and the Jewish adherents than was then at all probable.

† A similar view concerning the theme of the Sermon is held by Baur, Neander, Delitzsch, Ebrard, Ewald, Meyer, Köstlin, and Hilgenfeld.

* Logically, however, Ibbeken is driven to a belief in the entire compilation of the Matthæan discourse, and he seems to acknowledge this on p. 5. It is impossible to agree with him that it makes no difference for the interpretation of the Sermon whether the parallelism is from Jesus or from the Evangelist. But his observation is a true one, often noted (see H. Holtzmann, *op. cit.* p. 99; Godet, *op. cit.* p. 131), that the First Evangelist delights in arranging parallels between the events of Hebrew history and the events of Jesus' life. In this interest and occupation he probably represented a large school of primitive Jewish Christians. It is quite likely that he and they found deep significance in comparing the law-giving by Moses with that by Christ. There is clearly an important truth in the parallelism; Jesus came to create a second great epoch as Moses had created a first, and He gave to men a Gospel which superseded the legal system (see Bacon, *Sermon on the Mount*, pp. 8 f., 26, 36). But the artificial and dramatic devices for indicating the parallelism, which Ibbeken supposes, are hardly to be attributed to Jesus, and it is even doubtful whether the Evangelist intended them to be implied in his narrative. The circumstances and description of the giving of the Sermon are fairly simple and have verisimilitude.

*analysis* of the Sermon on the Mount is, properly speaking, excluded by the facts just mentioned, we can at least construct an outline of the discourse as given to us by the Evangelists.*

THE SERMON ON THE MOUNT

AS RECORDED BY MATTHEW AND LUKE.

Theme: The Ideal Life:† Its Characteristics, Mission, and Outworkings, and the Duty of attaining it.

*A*. The Ideal Life described, Mt $5^{1-16}$, Lk $6^{20-26}$.
 (*a*) its characteristics, Mt $5^{1-12}$, Lk $6^{20-26}$.
 (*b*) its mission, Mt $5^{13-16}$.
*B*. Its Relation to the Earlier Hebrew Ideal, Mt $5^{17-20}$.
*C*. The Outworkings of the Ideal Life, Mt $5^{21}$–$7^{12}$, Lk $6^{27-42}$.
 (*a*) in deeds and motives, Mt $5^{21-48}$, Lk $6^{27-30.\ 32-36}$.
 (*b*) in real religious worship, Mt $6^{1-18}$.
 (*c*) in trust and self-devotion, Mt $6^{19-34}$.
 (*d*) in treatment of others, Mt $7^{1-12}$, Lk $6^{31.\ 37-42}$.
*D*. The Duty of living the Ideal Life, Mt $7^{13-27}$, Lk $6^{43-49}$.

4. THE CHIEF PROBLEMS OF INTERPRETATION.—It is an interesting evidence of the relativity of language, and of the large subjective element in all interpretation, that Jesus' words in the Sermon have been variously understood in the Christian centuries. Men have found in them what they were prepared to find, by reason of their political ideas, their social environment, their philosophical theories, their theological beliefs, their moral character, and their spiritual aspirations. Nor can we hope to escape similar contemporary influences when we attempt an interpretation. But in three important respects the expositor of to-day is in a more favourable position than his predecessors for getting at the true interpretation of Jesus' teaching: (1) the prolonged, able, and thorough historical investigation of the four Gospels during the 19th cent. has given us a new knowledge and wisdom in determining the origin and the first meaning of Jesus' words; (2) the present high development of the science of ethics—both individual and social ethics—has enabled us as never before to understand and to appreciate Jesus' teaching in the Sermon; (3) the modern change of emphasis from a Christianity of right belief to a Christianity of right character and right social service has brought us nearer to Christ, and has made us both able and willing to learn from Him.

Space here permits only a brief, general treatment of the interpretation of the material contained in Mt 5–7, Lk $6^{20-49}$.

*a. The Beatitudes.*—Mt $5^{3-12}$ = Lk $6^{20-23\ (24-26)}$. In a discourse whose one purpose was to describe and to enjoin the true righteousness, it was altogether appropriate that the Divine ideal for men should be characterized at the outset. Jesus presented this ideal in a most significant way; not in a reenactment of the Ten Commandments of Moses—which His people for centuries had regarded as embodying the will of God for man; nor in a new table of commandments to take the place of the old: but in a series of sayings which pronounce the highest blessings upon those who aspire to the best kind of life. 'Blessed are the poor in spirit,

* The entire material of Mt 5–7 and Lk $6^{20-49}$ is included in this outline, since the passages regarded by the present writer as extraneous would not, if removed, essentially alter what is here given. That Mt $5^{25.\ 26.\ 31.\ 32}$ $6^{7-15}$ $7^{6-11.\ 22.\ 23}$, Lk $6^{24-26.\ 38a.\ 39.\ 40.\ 45}$ can be best explained as belonging originally to other connexions seems quite clear; but Mt $5^{13-16.\ 29.\ 30}$ $6^{19-34}$ $7^{12-20}$, Lk $6^{31.\ 43.\ 44}$ are here left uncertain.

† Or, The True Righteousness. The former phrase is given the preference here because 'righteousness' (δικαιοσύνη) is a technical term of theology, and is seldom used outside of the vocabulary of religion. In Jesus' day also it was a technical Jewish term. While it occurs five times in Matthew's account of the Sermon ($5^{6.\ 10.\ 20}$ $6^{1.\ 33}$), it is wholly absent from Luke's account. Nor does it appear in Luke's Gospel except at $1^{75}$, nor in John except at $16^{8.\ 10}$; and in Mark not at all. This indicates that the term was largely displaced among Gentile Christians by the non-technical terms 'love' (ἀγάπη) and 'mercy' (ἔλεος). St. Paul's constant use of the term (δικαιοσύνη) continued its theological designation.

the mourners, the meek, those who hunger and thirst after righteousness, the merciful, the pure in heart, the peacemakers, those who are persecuted for righteousness' sake.'

This beatitude type of utterance was not new upon Jesus' lips, for it appears abundantly in the OT.* But Jesus made the Beatitude His own (as He made the Parable His own), and constantly used it as a mode of expression which carried the idea of love rather than of exaction, the idea of persuasion rather than of force, the idea of God's blessing and assistance to His children whom He tenderly leads and exalts.† When in the 5th cent. B.C. the legal element in the Hebrew Scriptures had become the chief interest of the nation, there followed logically the dominance of the legal idea of God, according to which He was an austere lawgiver and judge, demanding under severe penalties an exact obedience to His statutes, regarding men as slaves to be driven to their tasks or to be punished if they failed. The higher conception of God which is expressed in the Psalms and the Prophetical Writings was for centuries sadly obscured by this supremacy of legalism. It fell to Jesus, as one part of His mission, to restore the former better idea of God as a loving Father who cares for, comforts, guides, and blesses His children.‡

When, therefore, Jesus sets at the beginning of the Sermon these Beatitudes, He does so with the profound intention of revealing at once the spirit and the substance of the Gospel. Man is not made subservient to an external law forced upon him from without, but is made responsive to a creative light and power within. The criterion by which God judges him is not primarily a standard of external performance, but a standard of internal purpose and aspiration, of which external performance is in due time a necessary outworking. This fact is seen in the Beatitudes, whose description of the ideal of human life pertains to the fundamental nature of a person and concerns all men equally. Jesus furnishes here a universal ideal and a universal criterion. Not only did He describe the ideal in words; He also illustrated it in His own life.§ According to Jesus' teaching

* See particularly Ps $41^{1}$ $65^{4}$ $84^{5-7}$ $89^{15}$ $119^{1.\ 2}$ $128^{1.\ 2}$, Pr $8^{32.\ 34}$, Is $30^{18}$ $32^{20}$ $56^{2}$, Dn $12^{12}$; also 1 S $26^{25}$, 1 K $8^{15}$, Ps $28^{6}$ $68^{19}$ $72^{18.\ 19}$ $118^{26}$, Jer $17^{7}$. The idea 'Blessed' is expressed in the Hebrew OT (see also Sir $14^{1.\ 2.\ 20}$ $25^{8.\ 9}$ $26^{1}$ $28^{19}$ $48^{11}$ $50^{28}$) by two different words, אַשְׁרֵי and בָּרוּךְ. The former is a noun in construct case from the root אָשַׁר meaning 'to go straight, to advance, to prosper.' אַשְׁרֵי is in OT usage nearly confined to the Psalms, where it appears nineteen times (elsewhere seven times). It is always rendered in the LXX by μακάριος, which in classical meaning was quite akin to this Hebrew word (see Heinrici, *Bergpredigt*, i. 27). בָּרוּךְ, Qal pass. ptcp. of בָּרַךְ meaning 'to bless' occurs fifteen times in the Psalms, and frequently (twenty-two times) elsewhere. It is always rendered in the LXX by εὐλογητός or εὐλογημένος, never by μακάριος. In the Psalms without exception, and predominantly elsewhere, it is used with reference to God as the object of the blessing, 'Blessed be the Lord God of Israel.' The NT uses both μακάριος and εὐλογητός (-μένος), and after the prevailing practice of the LXX, for μακάριος is used of men and εὐλογητός (-μένος) of God as recipient. אַשְׁרֵי denotes a status of true well-being, due to right thoughts and right conduct, the harmony of a man with his God. בָּרוּךְ when referring to men as recipients denotes some special blessing bestowed by God and coming upon one from without. It is a fair inference from these data that Jesus used אַשְׁרֵי rather than בָּרוּךְ, and the Greek translators of His words did well to follow the LXX in rendering this by μακάριος. The point is of some importance for determining the exact meaning of Jesus when He uses thi term in His Beatitudes. In the 'Blessings and Cursings' of Dt 27. 28 the terms are בָּרוּךְ and אָרוּר, rendered in the LXX by εὐλογημένος and ἐπικατάρατος. The Greek word for 'Woe' in the Woe passages of the Gospels is οὐαί.

† 'Like as a father pitieth his children, so the Lord pitieth them that fear him,' Ps $103^{13}$. See also Dt $8^{5}$ $32^{6}$, Is $1^{2}$ $63^{16}$, Mal $1^{6}$ $2^{10}$.

‡ Cf. especially Wendt, *Lehre Jesu*, ii. 139–160 (Eng. tr. i. 184–209); G. B. Stevens, *Bibl. Theol. of the NT*, pp. 65–75.

§ Gore, *Sermon on the Mount*, pp. 15, 16: 'The character which we here find described [in the Beatitudes] is beyond all

and example, a man's success or failure is to be judged not by the amount of money he can accumulate, or by the amount of social distinction he can command, or by the extent of his intellectual or official achievements; but rather by the essential character which he fashions within himself, and by the service which he renders to his fellow-men. In the Beatitudes Jesus calls men away from the superficial tests and standards which so commonly prevail, to a criterion which concerns the real nature of man, is equally just to all, and stands in relation not alone to the few years of a man's present existence, but to the whole of his eternal career. In no respect was the Judaism of Jesus' day more perverse, and perhaps in no respect has error been more perpetuated, than in the maintenance of superficial tests of righteousness and of success (cf. Lk $18^{9-14}$, the parable of the Pharisee and the Publican). The Gospel of Christ was, in the 1st cent. A.D., the rebuke and the correction of this condition; and that Gospel needs, as much now as then, to be established in the world. In no words of Jesus has His essential teaching concerning the ideal of humanity been so simply and clearly epitomized as in the Beatitudes of Mt $5^{3-12}$. The man, woman, or child who sincerely, persistently aspires and strives to attain to the character and to perform the service described in the Beatitudes, will not fail of Christianity either in knowledge or achievement.*

Whether all the Beatitudes which now appear in Mt $5^{3-12}$ originally stood at the beginning of the Sermon cannot be affirmed with certainty. The fact that the parallel section in Lk $6^{20-23}$ presents but four Beatitudes, suggests that the four additional Beatitudes in Matthew (the meek, merciful, pure in heart, peacemakers) may not have belonged historically to this connexion, but possibly were a part of the composite material which came later to be associated with the historical nucleus of the Sermon.† Even on this theory these four Beatitudes would be authentic utterances of Jesus. And since on many occasions He used the beatitude form of expression, the theory is by no means impossible that the eight Beatitudes of Matthew are a compilation. Yet there are good reasons for the contrary opinion, that they constitute an original unit: (1) the absence of four of the eight Beatitudes from the Lukan account can be explained as a part of the drastic treatment which Luke's material had received in course of transmission. The materialistic import which has been forced upon the four Beatitudes in Lk $6^{20-23}$ gives evidence of such treatment. Since the other four Beatitudes of Mt $5^{5.7-9}$ will by no means admit of a materialistic interpretation, it is not improbable that for this reason they dropped out of the narrative in that line of transmission. (2) The Third Gospel has not in any connexion recorded these four Matthæan Beatitudes; neither does the Second Gospel have them. So that as the First Gospel has them only in this connexion, no other setting is suggested for them. (3) Their truth is quite too searching and sublime to allow us to regard them as a later creation. They must have come from Jesus. And He must have given them in some significant connexion, such as the Sermon. (4) These four Beatitudes are necessary to the connexion in which they stand in Mt $5^{3-12}$, since without them the ideal of life which the Beatitudes seem designed to characterize would be essentially incomplete and ineffective. If, as has been argued above, the Beatitudes of Matthew present the theme of the Sermon, and in a way epitomize all that the following discourse contains, one cannot well suppose that the four Beatitudes found only in the Matthæan account were absent from the original group.

As to the number of Beatitudes in Mt $5^{3-12}$ there is difference of opinion. It is customary to count them as either seven or eight, and prevailingly the latter.* Of the first seven, in vv.$^{3-9}$, there is little question: the disagreement relates to the enumeration of vv.$^{10-12}$, whether they should be counted into the group at all; or if counted, whether they contain more than one additional Beatitude. The occurrence of the word 'Blessed' (μακάριος) is not generally regarded as determining the number of the Beatitudes, for it appears nine times (vv.$^{3-11}$); instead, the enumeration is by subject-matter—since vv.$^{10-12}$ all treat of persecution for righteousness' sake, they are counted as one Beatitude.† Then is the teaching concerning persecution for righteousness' sake to be classed with the preceding seven ideas as fundamental to ideal manhood, so that these verses present an eighth Beatitude? Such classification seems preferable, and it is strongly supported by the fact that Luke also gives this teaching concerning persecution in his account as the closing Beatitude. Exact correspondence of idea and form among the eight Beatitudes is not to be required.

The order in which the eight Beatitudes of Mt $5^{3-12}$ stand in relation to one another does not appear to be a closely wrought one, such that any other arrangement would have been illogical. They do not seem to present an ascending, climactic order.‡ Nos. 1 and 4 pertain to the longing for God and righteousness, Nos. 2 and 8 pertain to patient endurance and spiritual growth under affliction and persecution, Nos. 3, 5, 6, 7 pertain to the outworkings in character and service of the internal righteousness. The desire for righteousness, of course, precedes the achievement of righteousness, so that Nos. 1 and 4 should precede Nos. 5, 6, 7; but logically the place of Nos. 2 and 3 seems to be after No. 4. This transposition is made in Luke's account, where the two Beatitudes of desire ($6^{20.21a}$) precede the other two ($6^{21b.22.23}$). If this order of the Beatitudes has the semblance of originality, it may be that Matthew's Beatitudes were rearranged in transmission. It scarcely seems necessary,

question nothing else than our Lord's own character put into words, the human character of our Lord corresponding always in flawless perfection with the teaching which He gave. Here are two reasons why our Lord's teaching is capable of universal and individual application: (1) because it is not made up of detailed commandments, but is the description of a character which, in its principles, can be apprehended and embodied in all circumstances; (2) because it is not only a description in words, but a description set side by side with a living example.'

* Harnack, *Das Wesen des Christentums*, 1901, p. 47 [Eng. tr. p. 74], says: 'Should we be threatened with doubts as to what He [Jesus] meant, we must steep ourselves again and again in the Beatitudes of the Sermon on the Mount. They contain His ethics and His religion, united at the root, and freed from all external and particularistic elements.'

† So Resch, Wendt, H. Holtzmann, Adeney (*Expositor*, 5th ser. vol. ii.), O. Holtzmann (*Leben Jesu*, 1901, p. 186 f.), and Bacon (*Sermon on the Mount*, p. 129). J. Weiss (*Predigt Jesu*², pp. 127, 187) excludes the three Beatitudes of Mt $5^{7-9}$. Klöpper, *Zeitschr. f. wiss. Theol.* 1894, thinks that the eight Beatitudes were originally scattered through the Sermon, but were collected and placed at the beginning by the First Evangelist; an improbable supposition.

* The number of Beatitudes is counted as seven by Ewald, Hilgenfeld, Köstlin, Lange, Meyer, Nösgen, Steinmeyer, B. Weiss. The arguments for this view are that Mt $5^{10-12}$ does not really co-ordinate with vv.$^{3-11}$ to make an eighth Beatitude, that Matthew has an intentional parallel to his Beatitudes in the seven Woes of ch. 23, and that probability is in favour of the sacred and frequent number seven being used instead of eight. Bacon (*Sermon on the Mount*, p. 127) counts seven Beatitudes by regarding Mt. $5^{5}$ as a marginal gloss interpolated from Ps $37^{11}$. The Beatitudes are counted as eight by Achelis, Bleek, Feine, Hahn, Heinrici, Ibbeken (although he holds that they correspond closely to the Ten Commandments), Keil, Keim, Kübel, Tholuck, H. Weiss, Weizsäcker, and many others. Delitzsch (*Neue Untersuchungen*, p. 76) enumerated them as ten, to complete their parallelism with the Ten Commandments; but this view has found little acceptance.

† Since v.$^{10}$ and vv.$^{11.12}$ have a common theme and are actual duplicates, it may be that the one or the other passage is not original in this connexion. The Beatitudes had originally a short form, and were probably of about equal length. Given one of these passages at this point, the other might easily have become topically associated with it. That this has happened is further suggested by the fact that while v.$^{10}$ is given in the third personal form, like the other Beatitudes in Matthew, vv.$^{11.12}$ are given in the second personal form, like the Beatitudes of Luke. Achelis and B. Weiss, however, regard all three verses as original, saying that at v.$^{11}$ Jesus turns to speak directly to His disciples. Whether, on the former theory, v.$^{10}$ would be the extraneous passage or vv.$^{11.12}$ (so Feine, Hilgenfeld, Weizsäcker, J. Weiss), it is difficult to decide. H. Holtzmann thinks all three verses foreign to the connexion. But the unity of the eight Beatitudes is not affected by the question of duplicate material in these verses.

‡ Most commentators endeavour to show a special meaning and significance in the Matthæan arrangement of the several Beatitudes. Tholuck, *Bergrede*⁵, p. 56 f. (Eng. tr. p. 64 f.): 'These eight Beatitudes are arranged in an ethical order. The first four are of a negative character. They express the state of spiritual desire which belongs to the indispensable conditions of participation in the Kingdom of God. The next three following are positive: they set forth what attributes of character are required in the members of that Kingdom. The eighth shows how the world will treat the members of the Kingdom.' However, 'the progression among the qualities pronounced blessed is not to be regarded as of such a nature that each stage excludes the rest; or that, in advancing to another, the former are left behind.' Achelis, *Bergpredigt*, pp. 73–75, classifies the first four Beatitudes as pertaining to the desire for salvation, the second four as pertaining to the possession of it; he further subclassifies them also. H. Weiss, *Bergpredigt*, pp. 9, 23, regards the first four as passive, the second four as active. Feine, *Jahrb. f. Protest. Theol.* 1885, thinks the eight Beatitudes make four neatly-fitting pairs. Ibbeken, *Bergpredigt*², p. 19, says that the effort to find a close logical order in the Beatitudes as they stand has been unsuccessful. Heinrici, *Bergpredigt*, i. 28, thinks that if they had been arranged logically, according to their inner relation, the order would have been Nos. 1, 4, 6, 3, 5, 7, 2, 8. It is scarcely necessary to say that the idea that in their present arrangement the Beatitudes indicate the several consecutive stages of normal Christian growth is a purely fanciful one.

however, to suppose that Jesus insisted upon a particular succession of them.*

Of much more importance is the question whether Matthew or Luke presents the more authentic form of the Beatitudes. The difference between them is of two kinds: (1) Luke gives the Beatitudes in the second person, in the form of direct address; while Matthew has them in the third person, in the form of a general statement (see a similar phenomenon in Mt $3^{17}$ = Lk $3^{22}$). An examination of Jesus' other Beatitudes recorded elsewhere in the Gospels indicates that He used both forms, and apparently without preference for either. The OT Beatitudes are in the third personal form. But since Matthew agrees with Luke in giving the remainder of the discourse (from $5^{11}$ onwards) in the second person, some scholars hold that the Beatitudes themselves were originally of this form.† On the other hand, a change to the second person in the Lukan account might arise from the materialistic interpretation which has been cast over the Beatitudes and Woes in this Gospel. The change would make the Beatitudes personal and specific to his hearers, instead of general and universal as in Matthew. (2) The wording of the same Beatitudes is in some respects strikingly different in the two accounts. Concerning the first Beatitude (as suggested above, i. 4), it seems probable that Matthew's form of it, while conveying more explicitly Jesus' meaning, has been expanded in transmission by the addition of τῷ πνεύματι, the original Aramaic form of the utterance being shorter, as in Luke.‡ The fourth Beatitude (Luke's second) presents a somewhat similar case; when Matthew says, 'Blessed are they that hunger and thirst after righteousness,' it is possible or even probable that Jesus' words were shorter (as suggested by the Lukan form) by the implication rather than the expression of the idea contained in τὴν δικαιοσύνην, perhaps also of that contained in the διψῶντες. These words, too, may have been added to prevent a materialistic misinterpretation. Since the idea of hungering spiritually was common in the OT, Jesus may have used the οἱ πεινῶντες alone with that meaning, the additions being made later to remove all ambiguity. In the second Beatitude (Luke's third) the πενθοῦντες of Matthew and the κλαίοντες of Luke are probably two varying Greek words employed to translate one Aramaic word; the former is the better in this context, since it carries a deeper, finer meaning. The double occurrence of νῦν in Lk $6^{21}$ is an obvious importation. In regard to the eighth Beatitude (Luke's fourth), concerning patient endurance and spiritual growth under persecution, one notices that Luke has no parallel to the first of the two duplicate forms in which Mt $5^{10}$ gives it; instead, Lk $6^{22.23}$ = Mt $5^{11.12}$. A comparison of these passages shows general thought agreement, but much difference in wording; nor can there be any doubt that the Lukan form of the Beatitude is secondary (consider especially $6^{22b.23b}$).

The Gospel of Luke contains, in addition to its four Beatitudes and in immediate sequence upon them, four corresponding Woes. With these Woes an increasing difficulty has been felt; many scholars have come to regard them either as so modified in transmission that they no longer represent Jesus' spirit, or as a free traditional expansion of the four Beatitudes, and therefore unauthentic. Four chief objections are made to them: (1) These Woes find no parallel in the Matthæan account, nor elsewhere in any of the Gospels. Jesus used the Woe type of expression (cf. Mt $11^{21}$ $18^{7}$ $23^{13-36}$, Lk $10^{11-15}$ $11^{37-52}$) against those who had long and deliberately refused Him and His message; but these four Woes of Lk $6^{24-26}$ are found only in this passage. If Jesus gave them at this time, they have failed to be preserved in the longer and better of the two reports of the discourse which have come down to us. (2) These Woes have a crass material import. Each of the four Woes gives the converse of each of the four Beatitudes, in the same order, and fixes upon them a materialistic sense. 'Blessed are ye poor!' conversely, 'Woe unto you that are rich!'; therefore only economic poverty and wealth are meant, since spiritual riches cannot be deprecated. 'Blessed are ye that hunger now!' conversely, 'Woe unto you, ye that are full now!'; therefore the 'hungry' are those in physical need of food, for the spiritually 'full' are not doomed to eternal spiritual privation. Also the third and fourth Woes are harsh in their terms, shallow and external in their conceptions. The exaltation of material poverty and distress which thus appears in Luke's Beatitudes and Woes can be seen also in other parts of his Gospel (see the account of the rich young man, Lk $18^{18-30}$; the parable of the Rich Fool, Lk $12^{16-21.33}$; the parable of Dives and Lazarus, Lk $16^{19-31}$, cf. $1^{53}$).* The Evangelist probably is not responsible for these views; rather they had already impressed themselves upon the material which constituted the sources for his Gospel. They represent a strong sentiment in the first century, which grew out of a false contempt for the earthly life and an exaggeration of Jesus' teaching about riches. (3) These Woes are out of character with Jesus. He never condemned wealth as such; what He condemned was that a man should permit wealth to be his supreme purpose and his master. On this subject Jesus taught much, and with profound insight into the true relation of men with things; from Him we must learn the real aim of living and the proper use of the material world about us.† It is difficult, if not impossible, to bring the tone and import of these Woes into accord with Jesus' spirit, conceptions, and method. (4) These Woes are inappropriate to the Sermon. This discourse was given to a large company of people who had been attracted to Jesus by His words and His works; many of them were His professed followers, all of them were well disposed towards Him. The occasion was not suitable for violent language and condemnatory pronouncements. Jesus used the Woe type of utterance for His final judgments against those who rejected their Messiah; but here He is in the midst of His Galilæan ministry, the people hear Him gladly, and the enmity of His opponents has not yet reached its final stage. In view of these four considerations, the full authenticity of the four Woes in Lk $6^{24-26}$ must be counted an open historical question. If they are not authentic as they stand, they may represent in a modified form actual Woes spoken by Jesus in another connexion during the closing months of His work. Or, if they cannot be attributed to Jesus at all, they will be explained as free expansion in transmission, due to a desire to intensify the teaching against earthly goods. The verses may then have been constructed on the pattern of the 'Blessings and Cursings' of the Old Covenant (Dt 27. 28), or still more likely on the pattern of the great Prophetic utterance (Is 5). Such an expansion should not be charged to Luke himself, but to the line of tradition from which he drew his material.‡

The blessedness which Jesus in His Beatitudes affirms of men who attain to the character and perform the service therein described, belongs both to the present and to the future. In one aspect it is eschatological: the endless future of such men is assured as one of perfect happiness, glory, and communion with God. Since Jewish hopes and expectations were largely eschatological, Jesus met them on this ground. But the blessedness which Jesus promised belonged also, and primarily, to the present life; in His teaching Jesus constantly kept the present life clearly and strongly to the front. Jesus' Beatitudes, just as the Beatitudes of the

* The reversal of the order of the second and third Beatitudes of Matthew which is found in Codex D, 33, Syr cur and a few other early text witnesses, was adopted into the text by Lachmann, Tischendorf, and Tregelles; Achelis approves it, and H. Holtzmann thinks it may be the true reading. It is rejected, however, by Tholuck, Westcott and Hort, Nestle, and B. Weiss. The transposition may have been due to the close OT association of the two ideas of 'poor' and 'meek' (the LXX renders the Hebrew עֲנָוִים by both πτωχοί Ps $69^{33}$ and πραεῖς Ps $37^{11}$); or it may have been merely fortuitous.

† Similarly Wendt, *Lehre Jesu*, i. 56; Bacon, *Sermon on the Mount*, p. 126.

‡ So Klöpper, *Zeitschr. f. wiss. Theol.* 1894; Kabisch, *SK*, 1896; J. Weiss, *Predigt Jesu*², p. 182 f.; Schmiedel, *Encycl. Bibl.* vol. ii. col. 1855; Heinrici, *Bergpredigt*, i. 29, who says: 'An effort to exclude all misinterpretation is seen in the phrases of closer definition, τῷ πνεύματι (v.³), τὴν δικαιοσύνην (v.⁶), τῇ καρδίᾳ (v.⁸), and ἕνεκεν δικαιοσύνης (v.¹⁰). These additions mar the parallelism. They cannot be explained except as expansions of the original made in the process of translating Jesus' words into Greek.' Similarly Bacon, *op. cit.* p. 127 f. The preservation of the precise meaning of the Beatitudes was of the first importance, and to Greek-speaking Christians they would not have been quite clear in their original brevity, for they would not have understood the terms 'poor' and 'hungry' to have a meaning primarily spiritual. The addition of these phrases removed all ambiguity.

* For this view see Campbell, *Critical Studies in St. Luke's Gospel* (1891), ch. 2; Rogge, *Der irdische Besitz im NT* (1897), pp. 9–68; Peabody, *Jesus Christ and the Social Question* (1901), pp. 190–201; Schmiedel in *Encycl. Bibl.* vol. ii. col. 1841; Cone, *Rich and Poor in the NT* (1902), pp. 118–142; and J. Weiss, *Predigt Jesu vom Reiche Gottes*² (1900), p. 182 f., who says: 'There can no longer be any doubt that Luke [in his Beatitudes] aims to draw a sharp contrast between the different external social conditions; his Beatitudes contain nothing of an ethical or religious element.'

† Mathews, *Social Teaching of Jesus*, ch. 6; Peabody, *op. cit.* ch. 4; Rogge, *op. cit.* pp. 1–68.

‡ The authenticity of the Woes in Lk $6^{24-26}$ is defended by Wendt, *Lehre Jesu*, ii. 168 f.; Bacon, *Sermon on the Mount*, p. 126; O. Holtzmann, *Leben Jesu*, p. 187; and by Plummer, *Comm. on Luke*, p. 181 f., who says: 'There is no evidence that these were not part of the original discourse. Assuming that Matthew and Luke report the same discourse, Matthew may have omitted them. But they may have been spoken on some other occasion.' On the other hand, many reject them. Tholuck, *Bergrede*⁵, p. 54 (Eng. tr. p. 62): 'Unquestionably, these Woes must be regarded as an expansion of the thought by the recorder of the narrative.' H. Holtzmann, *Synoptiker*, p. 102: 'The Woes of Luke were constructed for the purpose of strengthening and explaining [the Beatitudes] according to the model of Dt $27^{15-26}$, Is $5^{8-23}$, and not without a remembrance of Jer $5^{31}$, Mic $2^{11}$.' Similarly B. Weiss, Feine (*Jahrb. f. Protest. Theol.* 1885, p. 15 f.), Wernle (*Synoptische Frage*, p. 62), Schleiermacher, Strauss. F. H. Woods, *Expos. Times*, 1893, p. 256, says: The first Christians 'aimed at giving the general sense rather than the exact words. We can easily understand, *e.g.*, an early preacher so repeating the Beatitudes as to give them in what may be called a negative as well as a positive form; especially when by so doing he would be making a more exact parallel between the blessings and cursings of the old law and the blessings and cursings of the new law. Such a modification of Christ's language might arise in course of time quite unconsciously, when we remember how often so striking a portion of our Lord's teaching must have been repeated to catechumens.'

Psalms, have to do first of all with present well-being. The term *μακάριος* appears in this connexion, as always,* to refer to that condition of true well-being which results from committing one's self wholly to God, with the purpose of living according to His will; it connotes also the effect produced by this status, namely, the peace and joy arising from the consciousness of God's approval and blessing, and the feeling that one's present and future well-being is assured. The conception of blessedness in Mt $5^{3-12}$ is not essentially different from that which the OT at its best had already presented, but Jesus perfected and exalted the idea of blessedness, setting it before men with a new attractiveness and power. That Jesus' Beatitudes re-echo the highest ideals and promises of the Psalms and of the Prophets has been frequently and truly noted; both the conceptions and the phrases stand in the closest relation to the OT. In the Beatitudes, as everywhere in His teaching, Jesus was building upon the foundation of the Hebrew religion, fulfilling it, *i.e.* perfecting it and establishing it.

The Beatitudes consist each of two phrases: the one expresses the condition, the other the result; the one states the character or service to be attained, the other the blessedness of attaining it. In neither portion of the sayings are the phrases used by Jesus new ones; on the contrary, they are taken up by Him from the OT and current Jewish terminology, and turned to good account in His own teaching, receiving from Him a larger, higher import. Thus the phrases the 'poor,' the 'mourners,' the 'meek,' the 'hungering and thirsting,' the 'merciful,' the 'pure in heart,' the 'peacemakers,' the 'persecuted,' are staple conceptions and terms of the OT and of the Judaism of Jesus' day. And the same thing is true of those ideas and phrases which constitute the second members of the Beatitudes, the 'Kingdom of Heaven,' the 'comfort of the afflicted,' the 'entering into possession of the earth,' the 'satisfaction of longing for righteousness and truth,' the 'seeing God,' and the 'becoming sons of God.'† Jesus' use of OT and current religious terminology served to form an essential connexion between His hearers and Himself; but He did not use it as a mere matter of expedience, a pedagogical device to gain the attention and confidence of His hearers; rather He used it because He found an essential unity between His own ideas and those of the Hebrew prophets. These phrases in their highest meaning were rooted in fundamental spiritual needs, realities, and aspirations such as Jesus came to satisfy, to proclaim, and to fulfil.

The Beatitudes present each a special idea, but they are not mutually exclusive. An organic unity binds them all together, and they interlace with one another. Like so many facets of a diamond, they present the ideal life in eight different aspects, they indicate the several characteristics which make up the whole. The specific meaning of each of the Beatitudes must be carefully determined, in order that we may apprehend correctly the ideal of Jesus for men which they embody.

(1) 'Blessed are the poor in spirit: for theirs is the kingdom of heaven.'‡ The phrase 'the poor' (*πτωχοί* = עֲנִיִּים and אֶבְיוֹנִים) was a current one among the Jews, arising in the OT period and bearing a somewhat technical meaning (see art. POOR in vol. iv.). It designated that class, generally in humble circumstances, who lived the higher life, fixing their thought upon God and seeking His spiritual blessings, instead of living in a worldly way, to accumulate property and to attain social distinction and political power; they were in the world, but not of it; they were the faithful and righteous ones whom God could approve and bless.* It seems probable, since Jesus in the Beatitudes has taken up many current Jewish phrases to put upon them His own interpretation, that He here used the phrase 'the poor' in the sense of, and with regard to, the current conception of it. In that case the words 'in spirit,' which in Matthew are associated with the phrase, but not in Luke, may be an expansion of the original utterance made in the Greek for the purpose of protecting Jesus' words from a material misinterpretation.† The *τῷ πνεύματι* would, then, although a later addition, preserve the original meaning of Jesus; as it stands, it limits *οἱ πτωχοί* (not *μακάριοι*) as a phrase of closer definition,‡ like 'the pure in heart' of Mt $5^{8}$ and the 'lowly in heart' of Mt $11^{29}$; cf. also Mk $8^{12}$, 1 Co $7^{34}$. It fixes the sphere in which the poverty is predicated. Jesus means, not that spiritual poverty is in itself a good thing, but that the man who has a deep sense of his spiritual deficiency and dependence upon God will turn to Him, and will then receive the spiritual blessings which he needs. Therefore the phrase 'the poor in spirit' designates an internal rather than an external condition, a moral and spiritual rather than an economic status.§

* See the discussion of the term in the footnote * on p. 14[b].

† Tholuck, *Bergrede*[5], p. 59 (Eng. tr. p. 66): 'There can be no doubt—and this should be carefully noted—that all the ideas which meet us here in the Sermon on the Mount, those of the Kingdom of God, the righteousness of that Kingdom, the poor in spirit, the pure in heart, seeing God, etc., were no new ideas, but well-known ones, of which Christ only revealed the deepest meaning.' The passages of the OT in which these ideas are found will be indicated below.

‡ Mt $5^{3}$ *μακάριοι οἱ πτωχοὶ τῷ πνεύματι, ὅτι αὐτῶν ἐστιν ἡ βασιλεία τῶν οὐρανῶν*; Lk $6^{20}$ *μακάριοι οἱ πτωχοί, ὅτι ὑμετέρα ἐστὶν ἡ βασιλεία τοῦ θεοῦ.* The Gospel of Matthew usually, though not always, employs the phrase *ἡ βασιλεία τῶν οὐρανῶν*, while all the other Gospels and the other books of the NT use *ἡ βασιλεία τοῦ θεοῦ*. Did Jesus use both phrases in their Aramaic equivalents? If so, did the two phrases mean different things? Or was only one of the phrases used by Jesus, the other being of a different origin? If so, which was Jesus' phrase? These questions have been variously answered. The majority of scholars, however, are of the opinion that the two phrases are identical in meaning, that Jesus was accustomed to use both of them, and that His more frequent term was 'the Kingdom of God.' (See esp. O. Holtzmann, *Leben Jesu*, pp. 124–126). The other phrase, 'the Kingdom of Heaven,' is to be explained as arising out of the fallacious reverence for the name of God which characterized the Jewish people and led them to use circumlocutions instead of speaking the name itself. Jesus, however, did not share this superstitious regard for the name of God; on the contrary, he spoke of God constantly. The First Gospel adopted the phrase, 'the Kingdom of Heaven,' which probably was in general use among Jewish Christians, in order to be more acceptable to the Jewish readers for whom it was intended. On the other hand, in the Second and Third Gospels, and elsewhere, the phrase 'the Kingdom of God' occurs, since this universal use of terms was more acceptable to the great body of Gentile Christians for whom and among whom most of our NT books were written.

* So Ps $9^{12.18}$ $10^{2.9.12}$ $12^{5}$ $40^{17}$ $69^{29}$ $72^{2.4.12.13}$ $82^{2-4}$ $86^{1}$ $109^{22}$ $113^{7}$, Is $61^{1}$ (cf. Lk $4^{18}$) $66^{2}$. See Achelis, *Bergpredigt*, p. 7 f.; Kabisch, *SK*, 1896; Klöpper, *Zeitschr. f. wiss. Theol.* 1894; Wellhausen, *Israelitische u. Jüdische Geschichte*[3], 1897, ch. 15; Rahlfs, עָנִי *und* עָנָו *in den Psalmen*, 1892; J. Weiss, *Predigt Jesu vom Reiche Gottes*[2], 1900, pp. 183–185; Driver, art. POOR in vol. iv., who argues for Rahlfs' distinction between עָנִי (poor, needy) and עָנָו (humble towards God).

† It is obvious that when Jesus' words came into the hands of the Gentiles, who were not familiar with the history, literature, ideas, and religious terminology of the Jews, there would be great danger of His words being misunderstood. The first Beatitude, for instance, was likely to be misinterpreted, because the term 'poor' was used by the Gentiles only in a material sense, not with an ethico-religious content. It was therefore necessary to add the words 'in spirit,' in order that Jesus' meaning might not be misunderstood. Modern English usage of the term 'poor' is also economic instead of religious, and therefore we also need the words 'in spirit' to guard against misinterpretation.

‡ So H. Holtzmann, Ibbeken, Kabisch, Klöpper, Tholuck, B. Weiss. The *πνεύματι* does not refer to the Holy Spirit, as maintained by Achelis (*Bergpredigt*, p. 5); so that the phrase 'the poor in spirit' does not mean 'the poor through the Holy Spirit,' nor 'the poor by the Holy Spirit,' nor 'the poor in the possession of the Holy Spirit.' Rather, the *πνεύματι* refers to the spiritual nature of the man himself.

§ So the best of the ancient commentators, Origen, Chrysostom, Augustine, Theophylact, and nearly all modern scholars. Tholuck, *Bergrede*[5], p. 63 f. (Eng. tr. p. 70 f.): 'a consciousness of poverty in the blessings of salvation. . . . The idea of

This is in accordance with the tone of the whole group of Beatitudes, for they present an ideal of character and service in its essential elements; while external conditions, the possession or lack of property, are not essential. The Beatitudes and Woes, as given by Luke, speak only of material want and misery;* but that is a perversion of Jesus' teaching as recorded in Matthew. It is intelligible how the more spiritual teaching might have been coarsened in transmission, under the influence of strongly held false theories concerning a man's relation to the material world, to the form which Luke derived from his sources; but how could the reverse have happened? Who could subsequently have perfected Jesus' teaching by creating the lofty spiritual conceptions contained in Mt $5^{3-12}$?*

Jesus wished to establish, as the first principle of the better life, that true well-being is not reckoned in earthly goods, or obtained by them; on the contrary, ideal manhood and womanhood come through complete self-committal to God, drawing from Him our spiritual sustenance, making His will our will, and finding in His supreme purpose the only object of our lives. Of such men, and of such alone, can it be said that the Kingdom of God is theirs. He would turn men away from the customary material standard of well-being to the pursuit of the highest good, where one's external conditions become a matter of comparative indifference. Those are blessed who, instead of being self-seeking and self-sufficient, strive earnestly for that communion and co-operation with God which will enable them to realize the highest type of character and to perform the highest kind of service. The conditions of possessing the Kingdom are not external but internal, not material but spiritual. Poor and rich may alike possess it. The poor have it, not as a reward or a recompense for their poverty, but because they set their hearts on things which are above; and the rich have the Kingdom for the same reason, inasmuch as they use their material possessions for the spread of righteousness, truth, joy, and peace.

The second clauses of the Beatitudes respectively express the results of realizing the character or performing the service described in the first clauses. They are promised blessings which correspond to current longings, and are worded in the fixed phrases by which those longings had of old found expression. These blessings, although varied in form, are kindred in meaning; they promise not so much a number of different things, as they convey the idea in various ways that the entire good of which God is the creator and provider will come to those who sincerely seek it in the way He appoints.† 'The Kingdom of God' was a phrase which had long been used to express all conceivable good, to sum up the longings of the devout souls of Israel. Jesus therefore tells them how they may obtain all their desire. And the possession of the Kingdom is not a thing of the far distant future, but of the immediate present: 'theirs is the Kingdom of Heaven.' The Kingdom of God, while it has its consummation in the future, was an existing reality when Jesus spoke; and its blessings were available at once for those who would comply with the conditions of receiving them.‡

(2) 'Blessed are they that mourn: for they shall be comforted.'§ Here, also, Jesus has taken up an OT phrase, which may be seen in Is $61^{1-3}$ ('to

physical poverty is here carried over into the sphere of poverty of spirit, . . . those poor are pronounced blessed who are sensible of their spiritual poverty.' Kabisch, *SK*, 1896, says that the τῷ πνεύματι is added 'in order to remove the poverty into the realm of the religious sense.' Klöpper, *Zeitschr. f. wiss. Theol.* 1894, holds that there is no reference in the Beatitude of Matthew to the poor in social position; rather they are the poor in spiritual things, those who in opposition to the wise and understanding (Mt $11^{25}$) are characterized as 'babes' or 'little children' (Mt $18^{3}$); dissatisfied with the traditional wisdom of the scribes, they long for direct Divine instruction. J. Weiss, *Predigt Jesu vom Reiche Gottes*², 1900, pp. 130–132: 'They are called "poor" . . . not because they have no money, but because, as the עַם הָאָרֶץ, they have no religious, and therefore no social, standing. They do not belong to the righteous, pious class, but are shunned by them like the lepers. . . . They could not and would not conform to the conventional standard of piety. But what was to hinder them from pouring out their heart before their God in their inner chamber? They live as children of God in a true simplicity, naïve and unassuming, without great joy over their condition; because it has been so deeply impressed upon them that they never can attain the true righteousness according to the Pharisaic ideal. . . . They do not realize that they already have, what is precious in God's sight, τὸ πραῢ καὶ ἡσύχιον πνεῦμα (1 P $3^{4}$). They do not see that God, in his mysterious wisdom, has chosen to pass by the wise and the learned in order to reveal salvation to just such νήπιοι as they (cf. Lk $10^{21}$, Mt $18^{1-4}$).'—It is true that a materialistic interpretation of the first Beatitude prevailed in the early and middle Christian centuries, whereby voluntary poverty was pronounced blessed; and this view is still taken by Roman Catholic commentators, as Hugo Weiss, *Bergpredigt*, p. 10. The Lukan form of the Beatitudes arose out of and gave a foundation for this false attitude towards material things. But the whole notion of asceticism is wrong: Jesus neither taught nor practised it; He did not regard material poverty and physical misery as in themselves meritorious. It cannot be said that the poorer men are, the better they are; not even when the poverty is voluntary. Jesus did not require the abandonment of wealth, except in specific cases where it formed an insuperable obstacle to spiritual well-being; what He did require was the supremacy of the spiritual life and the right use of material things.

* So O. Holtzmann, *Leben Jesu*, 1901, p. 186 f. Similarly Plummer, *Comm. on Luke*, p. 179: 'In the four [Beatitudes] that Luke gives, the more spiritual words which occur in Matthew are omitted, and the blessings are assigned to more external conditions. Actual poverty, sorrow, and hunger are declared to be blessed (as being opportunities for the exercise of internal virtues); and this doctrine is emphasized by the corresponding Woes pronounced upon wealth, jollity, and fulness of bread (as being sources of temptation).' Here the materialistic tone of the Lukan Beatitudes is recognized, but the writer has avoided the problem of adjusting the two accounts of the Beatitudes to each other by regarding them as two distinct utterances on different occasions; this is to ignore the facts and data of the Synoptic problem. Wendt, *Lehre Jesu*, ii. 167 f., thinks that the economic poor are meant: 'Because this salvation of eternal life offers an incomparably rich return for all troubles of the earthly life, Jesus can at the beginning of His discourse concerning the true righteousness pronounce blessed the poor, the hungry, the mourning, the persecuted, because of their future participation in the heavenly blessedness of the Kingdom of God. His meaning here is not that in earthly poverty and unhappiness as such lies the ground for their longing for the future salvation of the Kingdom of God; still less in the following Woes against the rich, the satisfied, the laughing, and the praised, does He present earthly happiness as in itself the ground for the future loss of salvation. He intends only to affirm with the greatest emphasis that all future salvation is the single true and full salvation, in comparison with which the earthly unhappiness is insignificant and earthly happiness is not really such. Consequently he declares that those very persons who from the world's point of view are counted miserable are the truly happy ones because of the part which awaits them in that future salvation.' Wendt holds that the Lukan form of the Beatitudes, together with the Woes, is authentic as against the Matthew report, and can therefore give this interpretation; but if the Beatitudes of Matthew are the more authentic report, then Jesus' teaching at this point must be understood as presented by them—and they give a very different set of ideas. Kabisch, *SK*, 1896, interprets: 'Blessed are those who have freed their minds from the earthly wealth: for theirs is instead the heavenly wealth. . . . The absence of earthly goods and happiness is placed in the foreground, here [in Matthew] as in Luke; but not as there that accidental poverty must be blessed, only that voluntary, quiet and meek poverty will be blessed. . . . I regard the Lukan form [of the first Beatitude] as the more original, but at the same time hold that the First Evangelist in his added phrase has come nearer to the actual meaning of Jesus than the Third Evangelist, who with Ebionitic tendency has interpreted the words of the Lord which lent themselves to this apparent condemnation of all material possessions, as well as other words concerning the Kingdom, in a similar way.'

* Yet O. Holtzmann, *Leben Jesu* (1901), p. 186 f., holds that just this change was made.

† So Kabisch, *SK*, 1896; Ibbeken, *Bergpredigt*², p. 19. Tholuck, *Bergrede*⁵, p. 57 (Eng. tr. p. 64), says: 'If we consider the substance of the several promises, we shall find that they are all essentially identical, and that the difference is merely rhetorical; formally, they correspond to the thing desired or possessed, but each of them really comprises all spiritual blessings.'

‡ Upon the meaning and use of the term 'Kingdom of God' in Jesus' teaching, see esp. Wendt, *Lehre Jesu*, ii. 293–328.

§ Mt $5^{4}$ μακάριοι οἱ πενθοῦντες, ὅτι αὐτοὶ παρακληθήσονται; Lk $6^{21b}$ μακάριοι οἱ κλαίοντες νῦν, ὅτι γελάσετε. The Lukan form is secondary, and its harsh, superficial tone is unsatisfactory. Compare with it Ja $4^{9}$.

comfort all that mourn,' אֲבֵלִים) and Ps $126^{5.6}$. The term 'mourning' (πενθοῦντες) is so general a one that it is difficult to determine precisely its scope. The early commentators inclined to regard it as the sorrow of penitence for sin (cf. 2 Co $1^{4}$ $7^{10}$), while others think of it as the sorrow which comes from afflictions, adversities, and persecutions.* There seems no sufficient reason why the term should not be understood here in the inclusive sense, to designate all those experiences of life—internal or external, physical, mental, or spiritual,—which bring sadness and sorrow to men. The world is full of mourning; no one escapes the anguish of pain, disappointment, bereavement, and conflict with sin. And men have always longed for a better day, when this mourning shall be no more. It was one element of the Messianic hope that with the advent of that glorious Divine Kingdom complete comfort and consolation for the world's sorrows would be given to God's faithful ones, Is $61^{2}$; cf. Lk $2^{25}$ $4^{18}$. Jesus gave the assurance that this hope would be realized. The Apocalyptist has repeated with thrilling joy the promise: 'And he shall wipe away every tear from their eyes; and death shall be no more; neither shall there be mourning, nor crying, nor pain any more: the first things are passed away' (Rev $21^{4}$).

Although the promise of comfort is in the Beatitude expressed in the future tense, its bestowment is not to be regarded as exclusively eschatological. As the Kingdom was present among men at the time when Jesus spoke these words, so the comfort of the Kingdom was already a present reality and available to all. Not that all mourning was then to cease,—that stage belongs to the future consummation of the Kingdom,—but that Jesus brought a true consolation for all sorrow, in the knowledge that God is a loving Father who does all things well, and that all men, like the Son Himself, are perfected through suffering (He $5^{8}$ $12^{3-11}$). Rest and peace came to the world in and through Christ (Mt $11^{28.29}$, Jn $14^{1.27}$ $16^{33}$).

(3) 'Blessed are the meek: for they shall inherit the earth.'† The idea is that of Ps $37^{11}$ 'the meek shall inherit the earth,'‡ and the LXX renders עֲנָוִים by πραεῖς. Meekness is an OT ideal, and is closely related to that of the 'poor,' which Jesus had already taken up in the first Beatitude. This same Hebrew word is rendered in the English VSS now by the one word, now by the other; also אֶבְיוֹנִים, commonly translated 'poor,' is sometimes translated 'meek' (cf. Is $61^{1}$ in RV text and margin, and see Lk $4^{18}$). In Is $66^{2}$ the term עָנִי is associated with נְכֵה־רוּחַ and חָרֵד עַל־דְּבָרִי, where the three ideas seem closely akin: 'To this man will I look, to him that is poor and of a contrite spirit, and that trembleth at my word.' Cf. also Ps $25^{9-13}$, Pr $16^{19}$. The OT conception of meekness seems therefore to concern a man's attitude towards God rather than towards other men. The opposite of this meekness is pride and arrogance towards God, and such men He will bring to nought, Ps $75^{4-7}$ $94^{2-4}$. It is primarily His attitude towards God which Jesus has in mind when He says, 'Take my yoke upon you, and learn of me; for I am meek and lowly in heart: and ye shall find rest unto your souls' (Mt $11^{29}$). And the 'meek' who in the third Beatitude are pronounced blessed are those who live in trustful submission to God, seeking to know and to do His will; humility rather than self-assumption and pride characterizes them. Compare also the parable of the Pharisee and the Publican, Lk $18^{9-14}$. They become a part of the great world, and are fellow-labourers with God in His great purposes, instead of being ends in themselves and isolated elements in the Divine system. They do not thereby lose their identity and their importance; instead, by complete self-committal to God, they find the perfect realization of themselves, and achieve a personality of greatest influence in the universe.

A necessary outworking of this meekness towards God is a quality of gentleness, forgiveness, and self-abnegation in a man's relations to his fellow-men. This is the conception which St. Paul seems to have had of the meekness of Jesus, 2 Co $10^{1}$ (cf. also Eph $4^{2}$, Ja $3^{17}$, 1 P $3^{4}$); and it is the meaning which the earlier interpreters found in this Beatitude, since they paid more heed to the classical Greek usage of πραεῖς than to the Hebrew conception of עָנִי. The Greeks had scarcely an idea of that humility of man towards God which formed so true and striking an element in the religion of Israel.

When Jesus promised that the meek 'shall inherit the earth,' He adopted the popular phrase of the Hebrew covenant conception, which was then in use among the more deeply religious as a symbolic expression to denote all those good things which were to come with the Messianic kingdom.* The material and ephemeral elements of this hope Jesus passed by; but the spiritual content of it, the inspiring expectation that God would triumph over the world in the persons of His faithful and obedient servants among men, He reaffirmed. Nor did Jesus conceive that this supremacy of the meek on the earth would be solely eschatological and catastrophic; quite the reverse, for the growth of the Kingdom was to be gradual (Mk $4^{26-32}$), and the dominance of the world by meekness and humility is progressively realized. Men of such character become increasingly influential and successful; the Divine ideal is making its way among men. Every passing year marks real advance towards the supremacy of the people of God.†

(4) 'Blessed are they that hunger and thirst after righteousness: for they shall be filled.'‡ The

* For the former view, Clem. Alex., Chrysostom, Jerome, and recently Achelis; for the latter view, Augustine, Luther, Calvin, and recently Ibbeken. B. Weiss holds that it is impossible to tell whether the one or the other idea is intended or both. Tholuck, *Bergrede*[5], p. 73 (Eng. tr. p. 79), says: 'The mourning spoken of is the sorrow of penitence immediately flowing from a felt poverty of spirit. . . . This penitential grief is not, however, to be regarded as confined to the period of conversion, but ought to be viewed as a continuous condition of the soul.'

† Mt $5^{5}$ μακάριοι οἱ πραεῖς, ὅτι αὐτοὶ κληρονομήσουσιν τὴν γῆν. Luke has no parallel.

‡ Bacon, *Sermon on the Mount*, pp. 116, 127, holds that this Beatitude was not given by Jesus, but 'is a mere scribal gloss, a marginal addition from Ps $37^{11}$, which has crept in after v.[3] in some manuscripts, after v.[4] in others.' This is a possible, but not a likely, hypothesis.

* The phrase יָרַשׁ אֶת־הָאָרֶץ arose in a literal sense, with reference to the inheritance of the Promised Land of Canaan by the Israelites; cf. Gn $15^{7}$, Dt $4^{38}$, Jos $14^{9}$. After the Israelites had come into possession of Canaan, the conception was enlarged, and the phrase became figuratively used to designate an anticipated material, moral and spiritual supremacy of the people of God on the earth, as in Ps 37, esp. vv.[9. 11], already quoted, and in Ps $25^{9-13}$ 'The meek will he guide in judgment, and the meek will he teach his way. . . . His soul shall dwell at ease, and his seed shall inherit the land.' See also Is $60^{21}$, Dn $7^{27}$; and in the NT the idea can be seen in Mt $25^{34}$, Mk $12^{7}$, Ro $4^{13}$, Gal $3^{18}$, Rev $5^{9.10}$.

† Tholuck, *Bergrede*, p. 78 (Eng. tr. p. 83): 'In this promise humility and meekness are by him pronounced to be the truly world-conquering principle, with reference to their ultimate victory in the history of the future.' B. Weiss thinks this idea lies very remote from the passage, and describes the meek as 'those quiet sufferers who, trusting in God, bear, without bitterness or a feeling of revenge, the abuse of those who afflict and persecute them. The painful consciousness of their own shortcomings makes them humble when they are treated unjustly by others.' Certainly this teaching is germane to Jesus (Mt $5^{39}$), but it comes under the eighth Beatitude rather than under the third.

‡ Mt $5^{6}$ μακάριοι οἱ πεινῶντες καὶ διψῶντες τὴν δικαιοσύνην, ὅτι αὐτοὶ χορτασθήσονται. Lk $6^{21a}$ μακάριοι οἱ πεινῶντες νῦν, ὅτι χορτασθήσεσθε. It may be that the original saying was shorter than that which appears in Matthew's Greek form, the τὴν δικ. or even καὶ διψ. τὴν δικ. being possibly an expansion; but it seems sufficiently clear that in any case the Matthew account preserves the true idea, and that the material tone of Luke's Beatitude (compare his corresponding Woe, $6^{25}$) is a later perversion of Jesus' utterance.

terms 'hunger' and 'thirst,' representing the fundamental physical necessities, had been of old used symbolically to denote intense spiritual longing, cf. Is 49$^{10}$ 55$^{1.2}$ 65$^{13}$, Am 8$^{11}$, Ps 34$^{9.10}$ 42$^{1}$ (and in the NT see Jn 6$^{35}$ 7$^{37}$, Rev 22$^{1.2}$); χορτάζομαι also was used figuratively of spiritual supply, Ps 17$^{15}$ 107$^{9}$. Of the meaning of this Beatitude there can be no doubt. The righteousness which men are to seek is that righteousness which the entire Sermon is designed to elucidate and to enjoin. Those who earnestly desire it are pronounced blessed, because it is theirs; every one who sincerely wills to have righteousness obtains it (Rev 22$^{17}$). Righteousness was the technical Jewish term to connote that quality and quantity of character and conduct which God requires of men, and which it is the one aim of life to attain. It was Jesus' mission to correct and to perfect men's conception of righteousness, and to inspire them to its actual realization. In this Beatitude He speaks of the blessedness of those who long for righteousness, while in the other Beatitudes and throughout the discourse He shows them what true righteousness is, and how it is to be obtained. Since righteousness consists in right character and service, it cannot be externally bestowed,* but must be achieved, by each individual, with the help of God through Christ. And its achievement is a process of growth into the likeness of our Divine Example. It is the glory of the Gospel that to every desirous soul is promised the attainment of God's ideal for him and membership in the eternal Kingdom of the sons of God.

(5) 'Blessed are the merciful: for they shall obtain mercy.'† It is probably by intention that this Beatitude stands immediately after the one concerning righteousness, for in both OT and NT the two ideas of righteousness and mercy are correlative:‡ Mic 6$^{8}$ 'He hath showed thee, O man, what is good; and what doth the Lord require of thee, but to do justly, and to love mercy, and to walk humbly with thy God?' (cf. also Ps 18$^{24-26}$, Is 58$^{1-11}$); Mt 23$^{23}$ 'Woe unto you, scribes and Pharisees, hypocrites! for ye tithe mint and anise and cummin, and have left undone the weightier matters of the law, judgment [*i.e.* justice §], and mercy, and faith.' There is no righteousness without mercy, whether of God or man. One of the most frequent OT ideas is that God is merciful towards men, and one of its most frequent injunctions is that men must be likewise merciful towards one another. Jesus re-established both teachings, and gave them great prominence in His instruction. Mercy is twofold: subjective and objective. Subjectively, mercy requires that a man shall be loving and forgiving towards all; not revengeful nor cherishing ill-will; not thinking evil of others (Mt 18$^{21-35}$, 1 Co 13$^{4-7}$, Eph 4$^{32}$). Objectively, mercy requires that a man shall show deep, inexhaustible sympathy with all his fellows, manifesting itself in unremitting, helpful service, and in a loving considerateness towards all (Mt 5$^{43-48}$ 9$^{10-13}$ 12$^{7}$ 25$^{31-46}$, Lk 10$^{25-37}$ 16$^{19-31}$, Ro 12$^{9-21}$, Gal 5$^{22.23}$, Col 3$^{12-14}$, 1 Jn 3$^{14-18}$). It is striking that in the Beatitudes no specific mention is made of *love*, although love (towards God and man) is proclaimed by Jesus as the sum of all duty (Mt 22$^{34-40}$, cf. Ro 13$^{8-10}$, Gal 5$^{14}$). And farther on in the Sermon, at Mt 5$^{43-48}$, the duty of love is explicitly taught. But the fact is, that although the term 'love' does not appear in the Beatitudes, yet the idea of love underlies every one of them. Roughly grouped, the first four concern love to God, the last four love to men. All that the eight Beatitudes contain is but an application of the principle of love to the most important aspects of life, formulating more specifically what love requires in the essential experience and relations of human existence.

The mercy of God precedes the mercy of men, and is its prototype. Inasmuch as God is merciful towards men, He rightly requires that men shall be merciful towards one another. In the parable of the Unmerciful Servant this is most impressively taught, Mt 18$^{21-35}$. And as the last verse of the passage sets forth, unless men show mercy in their relations to each other, God cannot ultimately deal mercifully with them; cf. also Mt 6$^{12-15}$, Mk 11$^{25}$, Eph 4$^{32}$, Ja 2$^{13}$. This is not retaliation on God's part. If it seems severe, it is yet a necessary provision to the end that love may triumph in His world. If love is to transform all and to reign supreme, then what is unloving must disappear.

(6) 'Blessed are the pure in heart: for they shall see God.'* The phrase 'pure in heart' occurs in Ps 73$^{1}$ (בָּרֵי לֵבָב, LXX τοῖς εὐθέσι τῇ καρδίᾳ) and in Ps 24$^{4}$ (בַּר לֵבָב, LXX καθαρὸς τῇ καρδίᾳ); cf. also Ps 51$^{10}$. In the NT the phrase is only twice used (1 Ti 1$^{5}$, 2 Ti 2$^{22}$), although the thought is all-pervasive. The term καρδία, corresponding to the Hebrew לֵב and in the NT deriving its signification therefrom, denotes the essential personality, the inner central self, where all feeling, thought, and action originate.† In its dative form here it indicates the sphere in which the purity is predicated, like τῷ πνεύματι in the first Beatitude. By 'purity of heart' is meant that profound sincerity and uprightness of thought and feeling which produces an honest, clean, holy life in all its elements and relations. It does not need to be said that this condition of things can exist only where the individual is committed, body and soul, to the love and obedience of God, and regards all men as his brethren and himself as a sacred trust. Jesus has in mind the superficial standards of goodness which prevailed in His day. The rich young man had kept all the commandments from his youth, and yet his heart was set upon his material possessions (Mk 10$^{17-31}$); the Pharisees outwardly appeared righteous unto men, but within they were full of hypocrisy and iniquity (Mt 23$^{25-28}$). Against such shallow, false conceptions of right living, Jesus most emphatically sets the duty of real righteousness, of purifying the fountain of a man's life in order that what flows from it may indeed be pure.

That the 'pure in heart' 'shall see God' is an

* Neither in this passage nor elsewhere does Jesus use the term 'righteousness' in the forensic sense to which St. Paul gave currency. That God does, in His love and mercy, pardon and receive every man who in and through Christ sets himself seriously towards the Divine ideal, is abundantly taught by Jesus; but He does not use this term to denote that idea. So nearly all commentators. Achelis, *Bergpredigt*, p. 22: 'The words indicate that high degree of longing which rests upon the certainty that the object of the longing is essential to life, that without it life would become death. Righteousness is the object of such desire; what is meant by it is that moral condition which is in accordance with God's will.' B. Weiss defines the righteousness here referred to as that 'righteousness which corresponds to the norm of the Divine will, the highest good of every true Israelite, upon the possession of which depends the certainty of God's good pleasure and the participation in all the promises. The Kingdom of God proclaimed by Jesus offers men this good in an abundance which will satisfy all longings, bring full contentment, and fill them with righteousness. For in the Kingdom of God, and only there,—though there with the greatest of certainty,—will the ideal of righteousness be actually realized.'

† Mt 5$^{7}$ μακάριοι οἱ ἐλεήμονες, ὅτι αὐτοὶ ἐλεηθήσονται. Luke has no parallel.

‡ So closely connected are the two ideas that the Heb. צְדָקָה, which more commonly should be and is represented in the LXX by δικαιοσύνη, is at times translated by ἐλεημοσύνη; cf. Dt 6$^{25}$ 24$^{13}$, Ps 24$^{5}$ 33$^{5}$ 103$^{6}$, Is 1$^{27}$. In the Sermon passage Mt 6$^{1}$ ἐλεημοσύνην appears as a variant reading of δικαιοσύνην; the former, however, is not strongly attested (EL against ℵBD), and is accepted by few scholars.

§ So H. Holtzmann, B. Weiss, Wendt; cf. Ps 33$^{5}$.

* Mt 5$^{8}$ μακάριοι οἱ καθαροὶ τῇ καρδίᾳ, ὅτι αὐτοὶ τὸν θεὸν ὄψονται. Luke has no parallel.

† See Wendt, *Lehre Jesu*, ii. 116–121; Cremer, *Bibl.-Theol Wörterbuch*$^{7}$ (1892), *in loc.*; art. HEART in vol. ii.

essential result of their character, not a mere unrelated reward for their goodness. Nor is this seeing of God a solely eschatological event; for, while the perfect vision of Him belongs to the future, there is a present vision which increases day by day with the growth of the pure in heart. Seeing God is, of course, not a physical process, but a spiritual one; it is to enter into full communion with Him, to be spiritually in His immediate presence and to be at rest there, to share directly His favour, joy, and blessings. The phrase to 'see God' arose in ancient Hebrew usage out of the fact that men counted it a supreme privilege to come into the presence of an earthly king (1 K $10^{8}$, Est $1^{14}$); * how much more would it mean to come into the presence of the King of kings! The hope of such a vision of God grew with the development of the Hebrew religious conceptions, and became the rapturous aspiration of the OT saints (Ps $11^{7}$ 'the upright shall behold his face'; $17^{15}$ 'As for me, I shall behold thy face in righteousness; I shall be satisfied, when I awake, with thy likeness'). In the NT also the aspiration, now become a certainty, reappears (1 Jn $3^{2}$ 'we shall see him even as he is'; He $12^{14}$, Rev $22^{4}$); the veil of the temple has been rent in twain (Mt $27^{51}$), for in and through Christ men have immediate access to God. This standing in the very presence of God, this direct communion with Him and direct responsibility to Him, is more than a theological theory—it is an actual and essential fact of the utmost practical significance. God is not an absentee ruler, who can be dealt with only through intermediaries; on the contrary, those who love Him live in His presence, rest in His care, receive His blessings, and participate in His joy.

(7) 'Blessed are the peacemakers: for they shall be called sons of God.'† The term *εἰρηνοποιός* occurs in the LXX form of Pr $10^{10}$, and the thought is present also in Pr $12^{20}$. But 'peace' was not so common an OT idea as those dealt with in the previous Beatitudes. Some have maintained that the meaning of *εἰρην.* in this passage is exclusively passive, *i.e.* 'peaceable.' But the mass of interpreters find a larger meaning, which includes this while containing also an active element—to make peace.‡ Certainly Jesus' idea here is comprehensive; He has in mind to commend and to inculcate the spread of peace—all kinds of peace—among men (cf. He $12^{14}$, Ja $3^{18}$). In this He is the great leader and example, Mt $11^{29}$, Jn $14^{27}$ (the paradox, Mt $10^{34}$), Eph $2^{13\text{-}18}$, Col $1^{20}$ $3^{15}$; for God is the God of Peace, Ro $15^{13}$, 2 Co $13^{11}$, Ph $4^{7.9}$, 1 Th $5^{23}$, He $13^{20}$, who sent peace to the earth in Christ, Lk $2^{13.14}$. Peace between God and men was proclaimed by Jesus, and peace between men and their fellow-men was enjoined. Peace therefore is the Christian ideal. Individual composure and social harmony are to be brought about by the concentration of all interests and forces on the achievement of the individual and social ideal as taught by Christ, and by the realization, within one's self and among all, of those Divine principles of concord and co-operation through which alone true peace can be obtained.

The peacemakers 'shall be called sons of God' because in this essential characteristic they are like Him, the God of Peace. The fact that the article does not accompany the *υἱοί* signifies that the designation is to be understood qualitatively. This idea of sonship as consisting in moral resemblance is of Hebrew origin, and is found in both Testaments; cf. esp. Mt $5^{45}$, Rev $21^{7}$. The expression 'called' sons of God is also a Hebraism, found frequently in the Book of Isaiah; its special function here seems to be to emphasize the fact of sonship (cf. Mt $5^{19}$, 1 Jn $3^{1}$) as something not only true, but recognized to be true.

(8) 'Blessed are they that have been persecuted for righteousness' sake: for theirs is the kingdom of heaven. Blessed are ye when men shall reproach you, and persecute you, and say all manner of evil against you falsely, for my sake. Rejoice and be exceeding glad, for great is your reward in heaven: for so persecuted they the prophets which were before you.' * Although the essence and purpose of the gospel was peace, nevertheless those who enjoyed and endeavoured to spread this peace in the world would incur reproach and abuse from their fellow-men. The OT does not supply passages similar in form to this Beatitude, but the Hebrews had no lack of experience in persecution for righteousness' sake, and the conception is developed with marvellous insight and feeling in Is 40–66. In the NT it is an ever-present idea—the sufferings of the OT saints are recalled (He $11^{33\text{-}40}$), Jesus lives and dies a martyr to this principle, He predicted persecution for His followers (Mt $5^{10\text{-}12}$, Jn $16^{2}$), and this persecution actually befell them (Jn $9^{22}$, Ac $5^{41}$ $8^{1\text{-}3}$, 1 P $3^{14}$ $4^{14\text{-}16}$). The primitive Christians bravely endured and faithfully preached when they were despised, ostracized, punished, and maliciously slandered.†

* On the 'vision of God' as held by Philo, see Schürer, *Geschichte d. Jüdischen Volkes*[3] (1898), vol. iii. p. 561.

† Mt $5^{9}$ *μακάριοι οἱ εἰρηνοποιοί, ὅτι [αὐτοὶ] υἱοὶ θεοῦ κληθήσονται.* Luke has no parallel.

‡ For the passive sense only, Grotius, Socinus, Wetstein, and recently Ibbeken, *Bergpredigt*[2], p. 43. For an active meaning also, Luther, Meyer, Tholuck, Bleek, Achelis, H. Holtzmann, B. Weiss, and the RV. Others incorrectly regard the 'peace' mentioned as that obtained by the atoning work of Christ; so Chrysostom, Stier.

* Mt $5^{10\text{-}12}$ *μακάριοι οἱ δεδιωγμένοι ἕνεκεν δικαιοσύνης, ὅτι αὐτῶν ἐστιν ἡ βασιλεία τῶν οὐρανῶν. μακάριοί ἐστε ὅταν ὀνειδίσωσιν ὑμᾶς καὶ διώξωσιν καὶ εἴπωσιν πᾶν πονηρὸν καθ' ὑμῶν ψευδόμενοι ἕνεκεν ἐμοῦ. χαίρετε καὶ ἀγαλλιᾶσθε, ὅτι ὁ μισθὸς ὑμῶν πολὺς ἐν τοῖς οὐρανοῖς· οὕτως γὰρ ἐδίωξαν τοὺς προφήτας τοὺς πρὸ ὑμῶν.* Lk $6^{22.23}$ *μακάριοί ἐστε ὅταν μισήσωσιν ὑμᾶς οἱ ἄνθρωποι, καὶ ὅταν ἀφορίσωσιν ὑμᾶς καὶ ὀνειδίσωσιν καὶ ἐκβάλωσιν τὸ ὄνομα ὑμῶν ὡς πονηρὸν ἕνεκα τοῦ υἱοῦ τοῦ ἀνθρώπου. χάρητε ἐν ἐκείνῃ τῇ ἡμέρᾳ καὶ σκιρτήσατε· ἰδοὺ γὰρ ὁ μισθὸς ὑμῶν πολὺς ἐν τῷ οὐρανῷ· κατὰ τὰ αὐτὰ γὰρ ἐποίουν τοῖς προφήταις οἱ πατέρες αὐτῶν.* With regard to these two reports of what must be regarded as a single utterance, two things are to be said: (1) the corresponding Lukan Beatitude $6^{22.23}$ is parallel not to Mt $5^{10}$, but to Mt $5^{11.12}$. It is suggested above that $5^{10}$ and $5^{11.12}$ may be duplicates, the one or the other passage appearing here through the process of compilation. Since one feature of the Beatitudes was their brief, striking form (like the Ten Commandments of the OT), the original eighth Beatitude must have contained few words, and $5^{10}$ is closely parallel in form to the preceding seven Beatitudes; both of which things favour its originality. In Luke also the last Beatitude is very long compared with the others. Perhaps, therefore, Mt $5^{11.12}$ and Lk $6^{22.23}$ are varying words from one historical saying, introduced here by a transmitting or editorial hand because of their close similarity in thought to that of the eighth Beatitude. Or another view would be that Mt $5^{11.12}$ is an expansion of the idea contained in Mt $5^{10}$ by Jesus Himself (or possibly by some subsequent Christian teacher when the persecutions actually came upon the Christians); for the essential thought of the three verses is the same, the general conception of persecution in v.[10] being expanded in vv.[11. 12] into the specific ideas of verbal abuse, hostile acts, and false reports. (2) The Lukan form of this Beatitude is in several respects secondary in character, *i.e.* it shows greater departure than Matthew's from the probable original form of the utterance. These modifications arose out of a freer handling in transmission, a partial conformity to the new Gentile field in which the material circulated, and a greater yielding to the influence of the actual events of persecution in the Apostolic age. The term *μισήσωσιν* is used in a characteristic Lukan way, cf. Lk $14^{26}$ $16^{13}$ $21^{17}$. The *ἐκβάλωσιν τὸ ὄνομα ὑμῶν ὡς πονηρόν*, as also the *ἀφώρισεν*, refer to the excommunication of the Christians as heretics from the synagogues and other Jewish relationships—things which actually happened, but which the Matthæan passage does not specifically predict. The *ἕνεκεν ἐμοῦ* of Matthew is more original than the *ἕνεκα τοῦ υἱοῦ τοῦ ἀνθρώπου* of Luke. Lk $6^{23}$, first clause, seems modified. And Lk $6^{23}$, last clause, shows various secondary elements, due to the denationalizing of the material. These phenomena are constant throughout Luke's Gospel as compared with Matthew's.

† The *ψευδόμενοι* of Mt $5^{11}$ is attested by ℵBCE and the majority of witnesses; it is omitted by D and certain other witnesses of the 'Western' text. The word is therefore commonly accepted here. But if the new claims for the 'Western' type of text have good foundation, it is not impossible that this *ψευδόμενοι* is, in the terminology of Westcott-Hort, a 'Western non-interpolation.' Jesus, of course, implied the thought which

And in this conduct they were richly blessed—not by the persecutions, but through them; for Jesus, of course, did not mean that persecutions are essential to the development of the ideal life, but only that, where outward circumstances are such as to induce them, they are blessed who steadfastly and joyfully glorify the Gospel. The ἕνεκεν δικαιοσύνης of Mt $5^{10}$ and the ἕνεκεν ἐμοῦ of the following verse are synonymous. The persecutions which would afflict Jesus' disciples were to be met in carrying forward the work which He had begun; if they lived as He lived, and taught as He taught, they would experience the same treatment as He had received (Jn $7^{7}$ $15^{18.\,19}$ $17^{14}$). Had He not been a true successor of the OT prophets in suffering for righteousness' sake (Mt $5^{12}$ $23^{29-39}$)? With the advancing centuries the kind of persecution directed against Christianity has changed, and the amount has lessened; but Christian people can never expect to be free from misinterpretation, ridicule, and abuse until all men become devoted to the righteousness and truth for which Christianity stands. And this Beatitude promises the highest blessings to those who in trust, patience, and forgiveness uphold the Gospel, and allow the persecution to fulfil its own true mission in their lives and in the Church (He $12^{5-11}$).

These promised highest blessings are denoted here by the term 'the Kingdom of Heaven,' so that in the eighth Beatitude Jesus has returned to the promise which accompanied the first Beatitude. This conception of the Kingdom of Heaven is the inclusive one, since it comprises all conceivable good and brings absolute well-being. The phrase 'great is your reward in heaven,' which appears in Mt $5^{12}$=Lk $6^{23}$, is practically one in meaning with that of Mt $5^{10}$ 'for theirs is the Kingdom of Heaven.'* The term 'reward' (μισθός) was taken over into the Gospel from the commercial, *quid pro quo* terminology of legal Judaism; its legalistic designation had therefore to disappear, and now it was a term to express those gracious spiritual blessings which are at hand and in store for the true children of God. In this Beatitude, then, is promised 'the Kingdom of Heaven' and 'great reward,' but not the Kingdom of Heaven *plus* some additional reward, since the Kingdom itself contains all the good which men can receive.

*b. The World Mission.*—Mt $5^{13-16}$ (cf. Lk $11^{33}$ $14^{34.\,35}$).† The connexion of these verses with those which precede is close. Men of such character and conduct as Mt $5^{3-9}$ has described will assuredly meet with opposition and calumny, Mt $5^{10-12}$; but they must not on this account go into hiding—rather must they stand forth, endure persecution, and uphold the Gospel standard in the world, Mt $5^{13-16}$. Salt is a preservative element, light is a life-giving one;‡ both were current figurative terms for spiritual realities. Men who appreciate the Divine ideal of life which Jesus has presented in the Beatitudes, and who strive to attain it, are God's chosen instruments for the realization of His purpose in the world. They are to live and to work among men, where their character and their deeds may exert their full, true influence. The Christian is not permitted either to withdraw himself from the world, or to live an isolated, unprofessed religious life in the world. He must not only himself be good and do good; he must also help others into the appreciation and the attainment of the same ideal. Salvation is not merely individual; it is social as well. Until Christians do the most and the best they can with themselves and for all others, they are not faithful to the mission which Jesus has laid upon all of His followers, and the consummation of God's Kingdom is in so far delayed.

*c. Relation to the Old Testament.*—Mt $5^{17-20}$ (cf. Lk $16^{17}$). The logical relation of these verses to what precedes is clear: Jesus has set forth the new Gospel norm of life ($5^{3-12}$), and has enjoined His followers to live this life openly before the world ($5^{13-16}$); now He proceeds to show the relation of this new Gospel norm to the Hebrew norm of life which in the OT had come down through the centuries and now held the field among His countrymen. Since Jesus' ideal differed so much from the current scribal standard (as any one could see), the question easily arose—not only among His opponents, the religious leaders of the day, but also among those who 'heard him gladly'—whether this revelation of God's will by Jesus was a wholly new revelation superseding that made by Moses and the Prophets. Jesus gave the answer to this question when He said, 'Think not that I came to destroy the law or the prophets: I came not to destroy, but to fulfil.'*

it contains, but it was quite superfluous to express it, and its expression disturbs the proper emphasis in the saying. The word is much more likely to have been added later (as a practically useful expansion) than to have been excluded.

* On the NT term 'reward' see B. Weiss, *Bibl. Theologie des NT*[6] (1895), § 32; Tholuck, *Bergrede*[5], pp. 99–101 [Eng. tr. p. 101 f.]; Achelis, *Bergpredigt*, pp. 52–55.

† This section is regarded as not belonging to the original Sermon by Feine, H. Holtzmann, B. Weiss, Wendt, Bartlet, Bacon; it is defended by Achelis, Meyer, Tholuck, and most commentators. If the theme of the discourse is comprehensive, as maintained above, these verses supply a logical and useful portion of the whole treatment given it.

‡ The exact function of salt which Jesus had here in mind is somewhat uncertain: was it its quality to save from decay, as in 2 K $2^{19.\,20}$ (so Meyer, B. Weiss), or its quality as a pleasing condiment, as in Job $6^{6}$, Col $4^{6}$ (so Bleek, H. Holtzmann), or its ritual function as developed in the ancient sacrificial system, cf. Mk $9^{49.\,50}$ (so Achelis, Keil, Tholuck, *Bergrede*[5], pp. 102–106 [Eng. tr. pp. 105–109])? The second of these views is perhaps too shallow for this passage, and the third too complex, too erudite; it seems a simpler and stronger utterance when the salt is conceived in its fundamental property of a preservative. The other metaphor, light, is one of the most common religious expressions, cf. esp. Is $42^{6}$ $49^{6}$ $60^{1.\,2}$, Jn $1^{4.\,5.\,9}$ $8^{12}$ $12^{35.\,46}$, Eph $5^{8}$. Ph $2^{15}$, 1 Th $5^{5}$. The phrase of v.[16] τὸ φῶς ὑμῶν, means either 'the light which is intrusted to you,' viz. the Gospel (so H. Holtzmann, B. Weiss), or 'the light which you are,' as in v.[14].

* Mt $5^{17}$ μὴ νομίσητε ὅτι ἦλθον καταλῦσαι τὸν νόμον ἢ τοὺς προφήτας· οὐκ ἦλθον καταλῦσαι ἀλλὰ πληρῶσαι. The customary phrase, ὁ νόμος καὶ οἱ προφῆται, is a phrase which arises from the Jewish designation of the OT literature, the νόμος designating the first five books, the προφῆται the remainder; while the whole phrase denotes the OT in its entirety and its unity. It is noticeable that in Mt $5^{17}$ we have the disjunctive particle ἤ instead of the usual καί in this phrase. The variation is probably intentional, introduced in order to suggest that the Law and the Prophets were distinct portions of the OT, and that a different attitude might be assumed by the same person towards the two divisions—He might abrogate either one without the other, but He wishes to abrogate neither (so Tholuck, Meyer, Ibbeken, Bruce, Wendt, B. Weiss).

While Jesus mentions 'the Prophets' in $5^{17}$, He does not again refer to them throughout the whole following section, $5^{18-48}$. All that He goes on to say pertains to the Law; He does not present any similar illustrations of how the teaching of the Prophets is to be perfected. This silence concerning the Prophets is explained in different ways. Achelis (*Bergpredigt*, p. 79) thinks that if what He said was true of the Law, that He came not to destroy but to fulfil, *a fortiori* it was true of the Prophets. The more common explanation is that He passed by the Prophets in the remainder of His teaching at this point because He was much more in accord with them, and because the contemporaneous religious teachers paid so little attention to the Prophets that He did not come seriously into conflict with them concerning the prophetic teaching. Recently Professor Briggs (*Expos. Times*, viii. 398) has argued that Mt $5^{17}$ as given by Jesus stood, 'Think not that I came to destroy the law: I came not to destroy but to fulfil,' for 'the Evangelist added "the Prophets" in order to make the statement refer to the whole OT. This addition destroys the measure of the line, and has nothing in the context of this discourse or in the experience of Jesus to justify it. He was constantly charged with violating the Law, but nowhere with destroying the Prophets.' Bacon takes a similar view (*Sermon on the Mount*, pp. 87, 176). This hypothesis is worthy of consideration. The words ἢ τοὺς προφήτας might easily have been introduced subsequently to round out the original utterance of Jesus, for of course He did come to fulfil both Law and Prophets; even though on this historical occasion He had spoken only of the Law, His attitude towards which was liable to be misunderstood and needed careful explanation. The material contained in the First Gospel has perhaps been retouched at several points to show Jesus as the fulfiller of the entire OT, and especially of the Prophets; the

Jesus' constant warfare during His ministry was not so much against the OT standard of life in itself as against the interpretation of the OT standard which was held and taught in His day. For hundreds of years the priests and scribes had been busily engaged with the legal literature of their religion. These labours had resulted in an elaboration and externalization of the Law; so that when Jesus came the current Jewish teaching was in some respects extremely perverse: (1) it largely ignored the Prophetic portion of the OT, which was the very soul of the Hebrew history and Bible; (2) it exalted legalism until Judaism had become a system of precepts for the performance of an innumerable series of great and small duties which few could know and none could fully obey; (3) it so externalized the Law that religion came to consist chiefly in the observance of minute ceremonial performances, while the internal, spontaneous, and genuinely spiritual elements of the Law were neglected or ignored. Against this scribal abuse of the OT, Jesus had on many occasions to assert himself, and He did so with vehemence. He would not keep their fasts (Mk $2^{18}$); He would not observe the Sabbath according to their code (Mt $12^{1-14}$, Mk $2^{23}$–$3^{6}$, Jn $5^{16-18}$); He denounced, with a true prophetic insight and indignation, their whole legislation regarding the ceremonially clean and unclean (Mt $15^{1-20}$, Mk $7^{1-23}$, cf. Is $1^{10-17}$, Mic $6^{6-8}$); He continually associated with the sinful and the despised who did not keep the Law, in order to do them good (Mk $2^{16.17}$). Such an attitude on Jesus' part towards the teaching of the scribes and Pharisees was involved in His introduction of a higher standard. In this attitude He was not, in fact, opposing the OT; rather, He was defending it against the false interpretation which had become current. Nevertheless, and quite naturally, the Jewish leaders identified their conception of the OT with the OT itself—how could they be mistaken about it? Therefore Jesus was a traitor to the religion, the history, and the literature of the race; He richly merited a traitor's death. It seemed to them logical and conclusive, because in their bigotry they regarded their own ideas and interpretations as heaven-penetrating and infallible. To be sure, Jesus' teaching went much deeper than the mere removal of the rubbish which had accumulated about the OT during the preceding centuries; His work did not consist solely in re-establishing the OT as it came from the hands of its makers. But had the Jews been true to the OT in the breadth and height of its teaching, they would have welcomed Jesus instead of rejecting Him; they would have been prepared to appreciate and to receive the fuller revelation of God's will which He brought into the world.

That His Gospel was a fuller revelation, Jesus made abundantly plain. He did not re-enact the Ten Commandments, but only re-established the principles which underlay them (Mt $22^{34-40}$). He abrogated such provisions and implications of the Law as were adapted only to the earlier stages of civilization, thus: mere external conformity to statutes regarding moral conduct, Mt $5^{21-24.27.28}$; divorce, $5^{31.32}$; the use of oaths, $5^{33-37}$; the practice of retaliation, $5^{38-40}$; the pride of race, which made men despise other nations, $5^{43-48}$. In these matters, which He dealt with as specimen cases, Jesus revealed an attitude, a method, and certain principles which He intended to be applied to the OT throughout.* He did not repudiate the past, He did not even break with the best which the past had produced; He only developed and perfected the high ideal of life which had found embodiment in the Hebrew Bible. He did not set the seal of absolute duty and truth upon all that the lawgivers and prophets had taught, but He took up and reaffirmed the essential ethical principles and religious ideas which the Hebrew lawgivers had endeavoured to formulate and the Hebrew prophets had endeavoured to instil into the lives of men. That Jesus regarded His own revelation of the will of God as immeasurably superior to that contained in the OT is most strikingly expressed when He says, 'Verily I say unto you, Among them that are born of women there hath not arisen a greater than John the Baptist; yet he that is but little in the kingdom of heaven is greater than he' (Mt $11^{11}$, cf. also Mt $13^{17}$). To the same effect is Mk $2^{21.22}$ 'No man seweth a piece of undressed cloth on an old garment; else that which should fill it up taketh from it, the new from the old, and a worse rent is made. And no man putteth new wine into old wine-skins; else the wine will burst the skins, and the wine perisheth, and the skins.' Full of a similar meaning, also, is Jesus' parabolic statement in Mt $13^{52}$ 'Every scribe who hath been made a disciple to the kingdom of heaven is like unto a man that is a householder, which bringeth forth out of his treasure things new and old.'†

When, therefore, Jesus says, 'I came not to destroy, but to fulfil' (Mt $5^{17}$), He places in our hands the key to His relation to the OT,‡ and bids us see the continuity of God's purpose among men, the eternity of right and truth, and the absolute certainty that the Divine ideal is to develop and triumph in the world. In these words is comprised all that Jesus was, and did, and taught; they describe His mission. And He felt Himself competent to perform this mighty work, this manifestation of God to men, because He knew Himself to be chosen by God and qualified by Him for the conveyance of this revelation. Since He was superior to all previous revealers of God, He was capable of passing judgment upon their teachings; He was appointed to pronounce what elements in those teachings were of permanent and what of transient value. And it was also His mission to unify, to perfect, and to establish the whole sum of religious and ethical ideas among men. For this service He had the

phrase 'the law and the prophets' is a favourite one in Matthew, compare $7^{12}$ with Lk $6^{31}$; $22^{40}$ with Mk $12^{31}$, Lk $10^{28}$. But to this argument it may be replied that the Gospels of Mark and Luke, being written for use among the Gentiles, incorporated tradition from which many of the distinctly Jewish elements and phrases actually employed by Jesus had been removed in the interest of a universal Gospel.

* Jesus attacked existing ideas, practices, and institutions only to the extent absolutely necessary for the establishment of His gospel. Many of the evils and wrongs of society He did not attempt to correct, many of the current misconceptions He left for subsequent teachers to remove. His purpose was to transform mankind, not to produce a social or political revolution, and He saw most truly that this transformation was a process for which abundant time must be allowed (Mt $13^{24-33}$, Mk $4^{26-29}$). His work was not destructive but constructive, not negative but positive, as all true work for the world is. Progress involves the putting aside of old bottles for new, the correction of false ideas and practices, the clearing away of spurious accretions, the defeat of those who counsel stagnation; but no one who follows Jesus' example in advancing the Kingdom will labour exclusively, or even primarily, to overthrow the false; rather will he lovingly and trustfully devote himself to the establishment of what is true. There is a radical difference between a critical and a helpful attitude in one's work for the world.

† On the interpretation of Mt $13^{52}$ see particularly Wendt, *Lehre Jesu*, ii. 349.

‡ St. Paul's conception of the relation between the Law and the Gospel is the same as that of Jesus, as may be seen in the Epistles to the Romans and Galatians. In Ro $3^{31}$ St. Paul claims not to annul but to establish the Law; not in form and letter, but in substance and spirit. This is to acknowledge the great law of progress, or development, in the universe. An acorn fulfils its mission not by remaining an acorn, but by growing into an oak. A child fulfils its mission not by remaining a child, but by becoming a man. So the OT Law was fulfilled and established not by continuing in literal force when men were ready for something better, but by becoming in due time through Christ a perfected revelation (cf. Gal $4^{4.5}$), adapted to the higher needs and possibilities of mankind. On the attitude of Jesus and St. Paul towards the Law, see esp. art. LAW IN THE NT in vol. iii.

Divine ideal within Himself, and needed no external criterion.

So that there seems no room for a difference of opinion as to what Jesus meant by saying that He came to 'fulfil' the Law and the Prophets. He could not have meant that He would secure the literal accomplishment of everything hoped for and promised in the OT, as though the OT simply presented a programme which it was His mission to carry out. Nor could He have meant that He would secure the complete, literal observance and performance of all that is commanded in the Law and the Prophets. He neither did nor attempted to do the one thing or the other. If His Jewish hearers might at first understand Him to promise that in 'fulfilling' the Law and the Prophets He would reaffirm their authority, and render and secure absolute obedience thereto, He yet explicitly and emphatically provided against such a misconstruction of His words by what He immediately adds in vv.$^{18-48}$. Jesus could only have meant that He came to 'fulfil' the Law and the Prophets by first perfecting them and then accomplishing them.*

In accordance with this view of Jesus' thought in Mt $5^{17}$ must be interpreted His words in Mt $5^{18.19}$. The former, v.$^{18}$, seems to say: I affirm most emphatically that to the end of time † the OT Law, and every portion of that Law, shall remain and shall be actually and completely realized. The latter, v.$^{19}$, seems to say: The minute observance and inculcation of this OT Law, in every statute and in every detail, is literally and strictly required of every member of the Kingdom of Heaven.‡ Now neither of these statements could have been made by Jesus; they are diametrically opposed to both His teaching and His practice. The OT Law, as a system and as a code, He distinctly set aside, to supersede it with a Gospel dispensation. It was the spirit, not the letter, of the Law which Jesus approved and continued; the high conceptions of God and man and the noble principles of moral obligation which are taught in the OT, Jesus reaffirmed as true and perpetuated for ever. Do these verses then contain some inconsistent elements, or can their apparent inconsistencies be explained away? The commentators have commonly been satisfied with thinking that these difficult statements in vv.$^{18.19}$ could in some manner be harmonized with Jesus' other teaching and His general attitude towards the OT. Some have attempted to show how the Law in every branch and in all its minutiæ was fulfilled in Christ;* others have maintained that Jesus had reference to the Law only on its ethical side and in general, the ceremonial and predictive elements in the Law being passed over; † and still others, having regard to Jesus' frequent use of hyperbolical language, have held that these verses contain hyperbolical statements, the hyperbole being used not to deceive, but to impress the truth he wished to convey.‡ But an increasing number of scholars have come

* This is now the generally accepted interpretation. Tholuck, *Bergrede*[5], pp. 124, 126 [Eng. tr. pp. 125, 127]: 'So Christ has come to perfect, to fill up with religious knowledge and life, all that in the OT revelation existed only in outline. . . . That the fulfilling was merely an external supplementing or improvement of the Law cannot be admitted' (see Tholuck's entire discussion of Mt $5^{17}$, pp. 113–131 [Eng. tr. pp. 115–131]). Bruce, *Expositor's Greek Testament*, i. 104: 'He brings in a law of the spirit which cancels the law of the letter, a kingdom which realizes the prophetic ideals while setting aside the crude details of their conception of the Messianic time.' B. Weiss, *Meyer-Komm. ü. d. Mattevgm.* p. 102: 'He comes not at all to undo or to abrogate; his mission is a positive one, to provide a new [revelation of the will of God], in which he will bring to perfection all God's revelations and plans of salvation.' Feine, *Jahrb. f. Protest. Theol.* 1885: 'Thus he says that no essential difference exists between the OT revelation and his message of the Kingdom, but that there is a close continuity between them; true religion, presented as an ideal in the OT, is now realized, and the Gospel is the fulfilment of the OT prophecy.' Wendt, *Lehre Jesu*, ii. 338 f.: 'He would say that he recognizes in the Law and the Prophets a true revelation of the will of God, and consequently he does not feel called upon to annul its value for others. But at the same time he would affirm that he could not leave just as it stood the presentation given by the Law and the Prophets of this earlier revelation of God's will, and that he would not explain and confirm that revelation in the detailed manner of the scribal teaching; but that instead he would perfect that revelation, so that the OT presentation of the will of God would find its ideal expression' (see Wendt's entire discussion, pp. 333–351). Similarly also Luther, Meyer, Hilgenfeld, Achelis, Bacon, and many others. H. Holtzmann, *Comm. ü. d. Synoptiker*, p. 104, says, concerning Mt $5^{17}$: 'It is open to question whether during the public life of Jesus so radical an interpretation of His mission could have been formulated, either in the positive sense (cf. Ro $10^{4}$) or in the negative sense.'

† The phrase ἕως ἂν παρέλθῃ ὁ οὐρανὸς καὶ ἡ γῆ does not define a *terminus ad quem*, but means 'for ever,' in the sense that He has no pronouncement to make as to a time when the Law shall be no longer valid. So Luther, Calvin, Meyer, Tholuck, Ibbeken, Bruce, B. Weiss; a contrary opinion by Achelis, *Bergpredigt*, p. 84, and Lechler, *SK* 1854. The former view is supported also by the parallel saying in Lk $16^{17}$ εὐκοπώτερον δέ ἐστιν τὸν οὐρανὸν καὶ τὴν γῆν παρελθεῖν ἢ τοῦ νόμου μίαν κεραίαν πεσεῖν (on this passage and its relation to Mt $5^{18}$ see esp. Feine, *Jahrb. f. Protest. Theol.* 1885, pp. 31–35). B. Weiss, *Meyer-Komm. ü. d. Mattevgm.* p. 104, says that in the phrase 'till heaven and earth pass away' Jesus 'does not indicate a point after which the Law shall no longer be in existence, but [this] is only a popular expression (cf. Job $14^{12}$) for the permanent authority of the Law. Since Jesus is speaking of what shall take place in the present world-era, he states that the Law can never pass away. But of a continuation of the Law beyond the last world-catastrophe, as referred to in Mt $24^{35}$, nothing is here said.' The second phrase ἕως ἂν πάντα γένηται is parallel to the ἕως ἂν παρέλθῃ ὁ οὐρανὸς καὶ ἡ γῆ, and in meaning can only be synonymous with it.

‡ Concerning the interpretation of the phrase ὃς ἐὰν οὖν λύσῃ μίαν τῶν ἐντολῶν τούτων τῶν ἐλαχίστων, B. Weiss, *Meyer-Komm. ü. d. Mattevgm.* p. 105, says: 'The phrase "one of the least of these commandments" refers not to the Pharisaic distinction between small and great commands; since Jesus has in v.$^{18}$ denied that there was any such distinction in fact, the reference can only be to such commands as seem less important to superficial observation. But these also stand in real organic union with the ideal contents of the whole.' On the contrary, Achelis, *Bergpredigt*, p. 91: 'It is Jesus himself who here makes the distinction between great and small commandments, and in so far he recognized the Pharisaic (later rabbinic) distinction which was the object of their ardent efforts in spite of their tendency to regard unessential things as essential.' The difficulty of regarding the words of this verse as coming from Jesus in just their present form is great. He did make a distinction in values and obligations, cf. Mt $23^{23}$ 'Woe unto you, ye scribes and Pharisees, hypocrites! for ye tithe mint and anise and cummin, and have left undone the weightier matters of the law, judgment, and mercy, and faith: but these ye ought to have done, and not to have left the other undone'; see also Mt $22^{37-40}$.

* See particularly Tholuck, *Bergrede*[5], pp. 142–146 [Eng. tr. pp. 141-144], who holds that 'more than the moral law is included here, as the expression ἰῶτα ἓν ἢ μία κεραία shows; while v.$^{19}$ indicates that the fulfilment here spoken of extends to all the ἐντολαί. To limit the meaning of the verse to the ethical law is accordingly inadmissible. . . . The Redeemer can have spoken of the necessity of a fulfilment of the ritual law only in its pedagogical and typical symbolical character.' This fulfilment was accomplished 'in His own sacrificial death, in which the shadowy outline of the OT sacrifices was filled up, and their idea realized (He $10^{1}$).' Similarly, 'the idea of the theocracy is realized in the Church; of the priesthood, in the Christian people; the passover, in the Lord's Supper; circumcision, in baptism; the command to avoid the dead and the ceremonially unclean, in avoiding the morally dead and unclean,' etc.

† Achelis, *Bergpredigt*, p. 78 f.: 'The reference here is not to the Law in respect of its typical prophetic element (*e.g.* the law of sacrifice), nor to the Prophets in respect of their predictions concerning the Messianic future; but to the Law and the Prophets in so far as they, corresponding to the new demands and promises of Jesus in the first section of the Sermon, embrace the codified demands and promises current in Israel.' Ibbeken, *Bergpredigt*[2], pp. 54, 56: 'That he is thinking here (v.$^{18}$) especially of the Ten Commandments, which in the Hebrew original had a very much shorter form than in the modern translations, is evident when he says that not a jot or tittle shall pass away; of these short commands at least, not the smallest part could be taken away. . . . The whole difficulty which is felt in this verse (v.$^{19}$) arises from taking the expression "the law and the prophets" too literally, as though Jesus had intended to say that not the slightest detail of the Mosaic law, including the ritual law, should pass away. If he meant this, then his later life and especially his attitude toward the Sabbath law were entirely inconsistent with his words. But the phrase "the law and the prophets" is to be understood here in a much narrower sense, as signifying only the existing legal order of the common moral life, an interpretation which is placed beyond doubt by the repetition of this phrase in Mt $7^{12}$. For if he can say, "All things therefore whatsoever ye would that men should do unto you, even so do ye also unto them: for this is the law and the prophets," then it cannot be denied that in $5^{18}$ he refers only to those commands of the law by means of which the legal order of the common society of men is maintained.' Burton and Mathews, *Constructive Studies in the Life of Christ*, p. 101 f.: 'It is evidently the moral teachings of both Law and Prophets that Jesus is speaking of, not the predictions. . . . Jesus declares his devotion to the Law, and its permanence in the new Kingdom. This Jesus could do, although he disregarded or disapproved certain statutes of the Law (for example, respecting fasting, Mk $2^{19.20}$; clean and unclean meats, Mk $7^{17-19}$; and divorce, Mt $19^{7-9}$), because he identified the Law with its great principle of love (Mt $7^{12}$ $22^{37-40}$). This was to him *the Law and the Prophets*, and individual statutes were of value and of permanent authority only in so far as they embodied and expressed this central principle. This was just the opposite position from that which the Pharisees took. They gave all heed to the statutes as authoritative in themselves, and lost sight of the principles. Hence the conflict between them and Jesus.'

‡ The figurative language should therefore be interpreted qualitatively, not quantitatively. So apparently, though not

to question the precise authenticity of the utterances as they stand reported in Mt $5^{18.19}$.* The wording of them presents the rabbinical conception of the Law as eternally and literally valid;† the formulæ used are those of the rabbinical phraseology. The statements themselves are too likely to be misunderstood and to mislead the hearers. The hyperbole is too much in the direction of the literalism which He was strenuously opposing.

It is not necessary to suppose, nor is it at all probable, that Mt $5^{18.19}$ was a free composition of a subsequent period. The two verses seem to have a real nucleus of something said by Jesus on this occasion. But a certain Jewish-Christian colouring they may have received in transmission. Jesus may well have used some strong expressions in this connexion, for the purpose of affirming the Divine character and the essential correctness of the OT revelation, and of impressing the duty of members of the Kingdom which He was establishing to recognize and preserve the truth thus intrusted to them. And these words of Jesus, already more conservative than He was accustomed to use in His general teaching, may, through the processes of transmission and translation, have taken on a still more conservative tone than He had given them. When it is remembered that for 15 or 20 years after Jesus' death the primitive disciples had no other conception of the OT than that it was literally and completely in force, Jesus' teaching being only supplementary thereto, it is not difficult to see how these words which dealt with that matter assumed a form and interpretation in accordance with the disciples' conceptions of the relation of the New to the Old Dispensation. In such a transformation of Jesus' words and meaning there would be no intention to misrepresent Him, but rather a conscious purpose to make more definite what they at that time conceived Him to have meant by these utterances. What these verses now say is inconsistent with Jesus' other teaching and with His practice regarding the OT Law; but it is consistent with the primitive Apostolic teaching and practice of the Law, which maintained the former Jewish position, ignoring for a time that constant and significant portion of Jesus' teaching and conduct which was against the literal authority and the permanent observance of the OT.

In the following verse, Mt $5^{20}$, we are again on firm ground. Jesus assures His hearers that the current conception and attainment of righteousness, as taught and practised by the scribes and Pharisees, was entirely insufficient—not enough to admit one to the Kingdom of Heaven.‡ Instead, therefore, of abrogating or diminishing religious requirements, as they charged against Him, He was, in fact, demanding of men a great deal more than they demanded, with all their boasted devotion to the Law. What the character of the Pharisees' righteousness was can be seen in Mt $23^{1-33}$, Lk $11^{37-52}$ $16^{14.15.19-31}$ $18^{9-14}$; their painful shallowness and perversity, in comparison with what they would have been had they lived faithful to the OT teaching, need not here be described. In vv.$^{17-19}$ Jesus has explained the relation of His Gospel norm to that of the Law and the Prophets. In v.$^{20}$ He has contrasted His ideal standard of life with that of the Pharisees. And now in the verses which follow, vv.$^{21-48}$, He illustrates how both the OT and the Pharisaic norms fall short of that Divine ideal for men which He has come to establish in the world. As generally enumerated, these illustrations are six in number, concerning: (1) anger, vv.$^{21-26}$; (2) social purity, vv.$^{27-30}$; (3) divorce, vv.$^{31.32}$; (4) oaths, vv.$^{33-37}$; (5) retaliation, vv$^{38-42}$; (6) love for all, vv.$^{43-48}$. They illuminate the field of social relations between men by showing what principles are to determine their feelings and their conduct towards one another. These principles we may for convenience designate as the principle of inner righteousness, the principle of unselfishness and forgiveness, and the principle of universal love; although the first comprises really the second and third also.

*d. Inner Righteousness.*—Mt $5^{21-37}$ (cf. Lk $12^{58.59}$ $16^{18}$). The essential difference between the OT system and the Gospel is that between an external code forced upon one from without and an internal life which first develops character and then manifests itself in conduct. The OT Law told what a man must do and must not do, mainly the latter; although it contemplated right motives, it did not generally formulate them or effect them. A man might 'keep all the commandments from his youth up,' and yet lack some essential element of righteousness (Mk $10^{17-22}$). If it is true that for the childhood of the race an external system of conduct is alone suitable and possible, if a child must be dealt with on the basis of precepts until knowledge, judgment, and conscience qualify him for a basis of principles, the reason for the radical difference between the OT and the NT becomes clear: they belong to different stages of human development. And St. Paul is right in saying that 'when the fulness of time came, God sent forth his Son' (Gal $4^{4}$). The OT was really and properly superseded by the Gospel, which enjoined life by principle, internal as well as external righteousness, true character as well as good conduct, right thinking and right feeling as the source of all that one is and does.

Consequently, Jesus in His teaching, recorded in these vv.$^{21-48}$, does not need to distinguish between the OT and the scribal interpretation or elaboration of it, because His teaching supersedes both * and furnishes the one true and sufficient guide to life. The scribes and Pharisees, to be sure, misunderstood the Law and neglected the Prophets, whereby their religious ideas and practices fell far short of the OT standard. Sometimes Jesus tried to make His contemporaries realize this; cf. Mt $15^{3.6}$, Jn $5^{45}$. But Jesus did not reenact the Hebrew Bible, even though it was better than Pharisaism. It was His mission to perfect the Law and the Prophets. He therefore let the OT stand as a monument of previous Divine revelation and earlier human development, giving in its stead

clearly, B. Weiss, *Meyer-Komm. ü. d. Mattevgm.* p. 104: the jot and tittle 'signify in the concrete-plastic form of Jesus' expression every part of the Law, however small. . . . That Jesus has in mind here only the moral law, not the ceremonial law, is an untenable view. He includes the whole Law, and contemplates an antitypical fulfilment of the ceremonial element in it.' With Weiss agree Tholuck, Achelis, Feine, H. Holtzmann, and others, that a distinction of moral and ceremonial portions in the Law, which could be separately and might be differently viewed, is an entirely modern one, unrecognized by Jesus and His contemporaries.

* So Baur, Strauss, Keim, Wittichen, Köstlin, Weizsäcker, Hilgenfeld, Feine, H. Holtzmann, Schmiedel. Holtzmann, *Comm. ü. d. Synoptiker*, p. 106, regards the three verses, vv.$^{17-19}$, as an answer of the Evangelist to the Pauline anti-legalism. Feine, *Jahrb. f. Protest. Theol.* 1885, pp. 26–35, argues at length that vv.$^{18.19}$ cannot be authentic, but must be Jewish-Christian additions. Bacon, *Sermon on the Mount*, pp. 133–138, rejects v.$^{18}$, but thinks that v.$^{19}$ can be explained here as it stands.

† The Jews of Jesus' day conceived the Law to be the Divinely revealed will of Jehovah, made known to Moses for the permanent guidance of the people; it could not therefore change or pass away. So Tholuck, H. Holtzmann, B. Weiss (against Meyer, who on the basis of Jer $31^{31}$ thought that the Jews looked for a new law). See also Bar $4^{1}$, To $1^{6}$; Philo, *Vita Mosis*, ii. 656; Josephus, *contra Apionem*, ii. 38. *Bereshith R.* 10. 1 reads: 'Everything has its end, the heaven and earth have their end; only one thing is excepted which has no end, and that is the Law.' *Shemoth R.* 6: 'Not a letter shall be abolished from the Law for ever.' *Midrash Ḳoheleth*, 71. 4: '[The Law] shall remain in perpetuity for ever and ever.'

‡ It is difficult to understand how the words of Mt $23^{2.3}$ can be authentic just as they stand. How could Jesus command the people to render complete obedience to the teachings of the scribes and Pharisees ('All things whatsoever they bid you, these do and observe')? Their teaching was certainly better than their practice, but both were essentially defective and perverse. Jesus characterized the scribes and Pharisees as 'blind,' Mt $13^{13}$ $23^{17.19}$; His whole mission was concerned with the establishment of an anti-Pharisaic ideal of belief and conduct. So that we seem to have in Mt $23^{2.3}$, as in Mt $5^{18.19}$, a certain false colouring of Jesus' language, the modification of His words in transmission to express an ultra-conservative Jewish-Christian conception.

* This is the only possible view, notwithstanding Tholuck's elaborate argument, *Bergrede*[5], pp. 156–164 [Eng. tr. pp. 154–159], to prove that Jesus did not offer any 'correction of the Mosaic Law,' as He taught only that 'the righteousness of His disciples must go beyond—*not the Mosaic Law, but the legal religion of its representatives*' (his italics). That the righteousness of His disciples must exceed the righteousness of the scribes and Pharisees, Jesus has distinctly said in Mt $5^{20}$; but that their righteousness need not exceed that commanded by the Mosaic Law, is a statement which Jesus is not reported to have made. Nor could He have consistently so taught, since He came to fulfil the OT, not by re-enacting it but by perfecting it—which is Tholuck's own view when he is interpreting Mt $5^{17}$.

a fuller and better revelation adapted to a higher stage of the world's progress. Now and then Jesus had occasion to attest the absolute truth and permanent value of much which the OT contained; but these things He regarded as true and valuable, not because He found them in the OT, but because He knew of Himself that they were so. He set up an ideal of religious belief and conduct which was not put together out of the OT (however many resemblances there may have been), or dependent upon the OT for its truth and authority, but was His own creation, resting on the separate foundation of His own immediate perception of Divine truth and human duty. Jesus was not a mere restorer of a former revelation, but a new authority in the field of religion and ethics, the bearer of a new revelation of God to men. This is the explanation of His words, 'But I say unto you' (vv.$^{22. 28. 32. 34. 39. 44}$). And this is what the people recognized when they testified that 'he taught them as one having authority, and not as the scribes' (Mt $7^{29}$).

Jesus' ideal of human brotherhood is first illustrated by an exposition of the principle which lay behind the Sixth Commandment, 'Thou shalt not kill.' In this Commandment the act of murder was explicitly forbidden, and the Jews conscientiously abstained from murder; they kept the letter of the precept. But there existed also the spirit of the Commandment, the principle on which it was founded, that brethren should not hate one another; for it was out of hatred that murder came. Since the Commandment did not explicitly forbid hatred, men had allowed themselves to cherish anger, hatred, and contempt against others without regarding themselves as disobedient to the Law. Jesus set over against this notion the emphatic teaching that all feelings of anger and hate are in themselves sinful, whether or not they take effect in acts of violence; they fall under the condemnation and punishment of God, since His Kingdom cannot fully come until all men love one another.* And for that reason He adds in vv.$^{23. 24}$ that no act of worship, however sacred (such as they understood the offerings in the temple to be*), was acceptable to God when the formal worshipper cherished ill-will against any fellow-man. The real brotherhood is a paramount religious obligation.

It is doubtful whether vv.$^{25. 26}$ are original in this connexion.† Neither does the setting of the parallel passage in Lk $12^{58. 59}$ seem to be the historical one. The saying is figurative, and may be interpreted in either of two ways: (1) it may teach that a man must put away all hatred of others, and be brotherly towards them, in order that he may be qualified to receive God's forgiveness, so Mt $5^7$ $6^{14. 15}$ $18^{21-35}$, Lk $7^{36-50}$; or (2) it may teach that such banishment of ill-will is a matter of common prudence, in order that a man may get on well in his social relations (this in addition to the truth already stated in vv.$^{21-24}$ that the putting away of hatred was also a Divine command to men).‡ Either interpretation contains truth, and has a general bearing upon the subject here under discussion in the Sermon.

The second illustration which Jesus uses, vv.$^{27. 28}$, for inculcating true righteousness in human relations is the Seventh Commandment (Ex $20^{14}$, Dt $5^{18}$). This statute forbade the violation of the marriage union. It was supplemented by the Tenth Commandment (Ex $20^{17}$, Dt $5^{21}$), which forbade a man to desire another's wife. The two commands together went far towards preserving the peace and purity of the home. Jesus, however, set His own teaching in sharp contrast with even this high teaching of the Seventh Commandment, forbidding a man to look with lustful eyes upon a woman. His demand exceeds that of the OT in two respects: (1) it insists not only upon abstention from the act, but upon the repression of all wrong thought and desire (in this going much deeper than even the Tenth Commandment); (2) it forbids impure thoughts and desires on the part of any one. For while γυναῖκα and ἐμοίχευσεν (v.$^{28}$) might be taken in a limited sense as referring only to those who are married, it is inconceivable that Jesus could have given a different standard for the unmarried; and it is altogether probable that, in setting out the principle and ideal of social purity, He had in mind the whole society in which this principle and ideal must be realized. A narrow interpretation, which would limit His teaching exclusively to what would be wrong for a married man to do or think, would be contrary to Jesus' method and intention. Social purity is an equal obligation of men and women, of married and unmarried. And Jesus clearly had in mind to establish by this teaching the absolute necessity for the Kingdom of pure social thought and conduct on the part of every member.§

* With οὐ φονεύσεις (v.$^{21}$) compare LXX of Ex $20^{13}$, Dt $5^{17}$. ἠκούσατε (v.$^{24}$) refers to the reading and exposition of the OT in the synagogues. τοῖς ἀρχαίοις (v.$^{21}$) is a dative of indirect object, as nearly all scholars (against Ewald, Keim) now hold= 'to the ancients,' *i.e.* to those who first received the Mosaic Law (so Bleek, Tholuck, Achelis), or to both those who first received it and also subsequent generations (so B. Weiss). κρίσει (v.$^{21}$) refers to the official trial and condemnation of the murderer by the appropriate Jewish court; the punishment was death, Ex $21^{12}$, Lv $24^{17}$, Dt $17^{8-12}$. ὀργιζόμενος (v.$^{22}$) does not include or deny 'righteous indignation,' which has its proper place, cf. Mt $3^7$, Mk $3^5$, Eph $4^{26}$. εἰκῆ, which is read in v.$^{22}$ by Text. Recept., is not found in אB, and is rejected by modern editors and commentators as a superfluous and weakening expansion. ἀδελφῷ (v.$^{22}$) means any and every person, as in $5^{24}$ $7^{3. 4. 5}$ $18^{15. 21}$. The threefold characterization of hatred and punishment in v.$^{22}$ seems to be cumulative: anger unexpressed, anger expressing itself in contemptuous epithet (ῥακά= רֵיקָא), and anger expressing itself in a term which implies at once lack of sense, character, and piety (μωρέ= נָבָל 1 S $25^{25}$, Ps $14^1$, or מוֹרֶה Nu $20^{24}$, Dt $21^{18-21}$); while the κρίσει refers to the local Jewish courts (Dt $16^{18}$, Mt $10^{17}$), the συνεδρίῳ to the supreme SANHEDRIN in Jerusalem, and the τὴν γέενναν τοῦ πυρός to the Divine judgment and its consequences. It is important to consider, however, that Jesus has used this triple, cumulative form of expression, not for the purpose of distinguishing grades of guilt in hatred, or of indicating how nicely punishment is meted out in accordance with desert, but to make as emphatic as possible His teaching that all hatred is sinful and destructive, for which reason it can have no place among the members of God's Kingdom. So that the detailed interpretation of Mt $5^{22}$ is more a matter of historical interest than of practical importance. Bacon, *Sermon on the Mount*, pp. 88 f., 139, 177, adopts the reconstruction of v.$^{22f.}$ which was advocated by Peters (*Journal of Bib. Lit.* 1892), according to which he would read the passage: 'Ye have heard that it was said to the ancients, Thou shalt not kill, and whosoever killeth shall be amenable to judgment. But I say unto you, Whosoever is angry with his brother shall be amenable to judgment. [Moreover, it was said,] Whosoever shall call his brother scoundrel shall be amenable to the court. [But I say unto you,] Whosoever calleth him simpleton shall be amenable to the hell of fire.'

* Jesus in speaking to Jews appealed, no doubt often (cf. Mt $6^{5. 17}$ $7^{15}$ $10^{41}$ $18^{17}$), to their reverence for the temple with its sacrificial system, and to their many religious ideas and customs. In doing so He did not signify that He shared all these ideas and practices with them. Jesus is not reported by the Gospels as ever offering a sacrifice or otherwise taking part in the customary temple worship (cf. Mt $12^{6. 7}$); He went to the temple, but only to teach. Had the contrary been the case, the First Gospel could hardly have failed to tell of it, because this Gospel is interested to show how close Jesus brought Himself to the Jews of His day.

† They are regarded as compiled material by Neander, Wittichen, Feine, Godet, H. Holtzmann, Wendt, B. Weiss, Bacon; while all these scholars except Godet and Wendt regard vv.$^{23. 24}$ as also extraneous to the Sermon.

‡ For the former view, Jerome, Calvin, Luther, Bengel, and others; for the latter view, Chrysostom, Tholuck, Achelis, H. Holtzmann, B. Weiss, and others.

§ Jesus is not here attempting to define the relative sinfulness of lust and the performance of lust; it would be a perverse and false inference that the former is as bad as the latter, for the lustful look does not produce the fearful consequences which follow the lustful act. What Jesus means is, that the entertaining of impure thought and desire is in itself a heinous sin, quite as bad as men commonly supposed adultery itself to be.

The logical relation of vv.$^{29.30}$ to the two preceding verses is not close, which has led some scholars to regard them as extraneous matter in this discourse. There are parallel sayings in Mt $18^{8.9}$, Mk $9^{43.47}$, but in both these places also the passage seems to be only partially relevant. The words are figurative and hyperbolical. Jesus means to say with great emphasis that no effort and no sacrifice * are to be considered too great for a man in his struggle to master his lower nature and to secure the supremacy of his higher, better self. Until a man brings his body into subjection to his spirit, he fails both individually and socially of what God requires of him (cf. 1 Co $6^{13-20}$, Gal $5^{16-24}$).

The teaching concerning divorce, contained in vv.$^{31.32}$, appears also in connexion with a specific historical occasion in Mt $19^{3-9}$=Mk $10^{1-12}$, while the Lukan parallel $16^{18}$ is entirely unconnected. Not a few modern scholars have come to regard the later Matthæan setting as the original one, explaining $5^{31.32}$ as an importation into the Sermon for the purpose of bringing Jesus' teaching about divorce into immediate connexion with His general ethical discourse, and also to place side by side what He taught concerning the closely related subjects of adultery and divorce.† This seems the more probable view, but the teaching is the same whether given in the Sermon on the Mount or under some other circumstances. Divorce was a subject of discussion in Jesus' day. The two rabbinical schools headed by Shammai and Hillel, interpreting Dt $24^{1.2}$,‡ promulgated different opinions concerning the proper grounds of divorce: the former school was more strict, allowing divorce only in case of adultery and other serious moral offences; the latter school allowed divorce on almost any pretext which the husband might indicate. Remarriage after divorce was considered proper by both schools.§ It was therefore a matter of lively interest what attitude towards divorce would be assumed by the new Teacher, who was independent of both Hillel and Shammai, and had had no rabbinical training. The Pharisees undertook to discover Jesus' position by their question: 'Is it lawful for a man to put away his wife?' (so Mk $10^2$, while Mt $19^3$ adds 'for every cause'). Jesus in reply (Mk $10^{3.4}$) first directs their attention (if Mark's order is to be followed instead of Matthew's) to the OT teaching on the subject contained in Dt $24^{1.2}$, where divorce and remarriage are allowed for good cause, the divorce being testified by a formal document. But then He goes on to show (Mk $10^{5-9}$) that this permission of divorce was only a concession to a low moral stage of the people, that the Divine ideal of marriage as revealed in Gn $2^{23.24}$ was an inseparable union of man and wife, both spiritually and physically.‖ This ideal conception of marriage Jesus now solemnly reaffirms and promulgates as His own teaching.

According to Mk $10^{10-12}$ (cf. Mt $19^{9-12}$) Jesus subsequently spoke further on the subject in private to His disciples, forbidding remarriage after divorce. This would be a corollary of His previous statement, for separation might not prevent ultimate realization of the marriage ideal between the husband and the wife, while remarriage would effectually prevent such a realization. Much uncertainty, however, exists as to just what Jesus said about remarriage.* The parallel passages to Mk $10^{10-12}$, which appear in Mt $5^{32}$ $19^9$, Lk $16^{18}$, are in serious disagreement, and there is also difficulty in determining the best textual reading in some places. These variations indicate an agitation of the subject of divorce among the primitive Christians, and an attempt to formulate Jesus' ideal of marriage into practical rules of conduct for specific cases. The words of Jesus on remarriage, so variously reported, reflect the different views on the subject which were current among the Christians while our Gospels were in process of formation.

The fact seems to be, that Jesus in His teaching concerning marriage is dealing with the principle and the ideal of marriage, rather than enacting legal statutes in regard to it. The whole treatment of His words as marriage *legislation*, which began with His disciples and has continued to the present day, is a mistake, and has led to confusion, hardship, contradiction, and strife. Jesus here, as always, was setting forth the will of God for men in revealing the purpose and the Divine conception of the institution of marriage. He therefore establishes the ideal of marriage as a perfect, permanent union in body and spirit, and enjoins

* The words are not to be understood literally, as though Jesus enjoined the mutilation of the body. Lust would not be removed by the destruction of the physical eye or hand. Nor do the eye and hand stand for specific kinds of evil desire. These concrete figurative utterances, as so frequently in Jesus' teaching, have only a general purpose to fix and impress one idea of moral duty.

† So Bleek, Olshausen, Köstlin, Godet, Feine, Ibbeken, H. Holtzmann. That the words belong to the Sermon is held by Meyer, Achelis, B. Weiss, Wendt, Bacon, and many others.

‡ In Dt $24^{1.2}$ we read: 'When a man taketh a wife, and marrieth her, then it shall be, if she find no favour in his eyes, because he hath found some unseemly thing in her, that he shall write her a bill of divorcement, and give it in her hand, and send her out of his house. And when she is departed out of his house, she may go and be another man's wife.'

§ On the Jewish marriage laws and practice see Josephus, *Ant.* IV. viii. 23; *Vita*, § 76. Also cf. Wünsche, *Erläuterung der Evangelien*, pp. 52–57; Edersheim, *Life and Times of Jesus the Messiah*, i. 352–354, ii. 332–334; Tholuck, *Bergrede*$^5$, pp. 227–234 [Eng. tr. pp. 217-221]; and art. MARRIAGE in vol. iii.

‖ Tholuck, *Bergrede*$^5$, p. 239 [Eng. tr. p. 225], thus states the biblical idea of marriage: 'Marriage is a Divine institution, having for its aim to bring man and woman to an indissoluble unity of body and spirit, that they may thus mutually complement each other, and lay the foundation of a family.'

* In Mt $5^{32}$ $19^9$ there is a striking addition to the words of Jesus as recorded in Mk $10^{11}$, Lk $16^{18}$; cf. also 1 Co $7^{10.11}$. This exceptive phrase παρεκτὸς λόγου πορνείας or μὴ ἐπὶ πορνείᾳ is taken to mean that in the case of adultery Jesus explicitly permitted the divorce and remarriage of the innocent party. But this Matthæan addition falls under suspicion for four reasons: (1) the Matthæan account $19^{3-9}$, with which $5^{31.32}$ is probably to be associated, is distinctly secondary and divergent from that of Mk $10^{1-12}$; (2) this exceptive phrase is significantly absent from the accounts in Mark, Luke, and Paul; (3) the exception is of a statutory nature, while Jesus is establishing the principle and the ideal of marriage; (4) in accordance with Jesus' general teaching, adultery is not *in itself* a sufficient ground for divorce. Consequently, the opinion is becoming strongly supported that these words of the Matthew passages are a mollifying interpretation put upon Jesus' teaching by a generation or group of Christians who took His words as a new marriage legislation, and regarded the statute as intolerably severe (so Bleek, de Wette, Schneckenburger, Bruce, Heinrici, H. Weiss, H. Holtzmann, Wendt, Schmiedel, Bacon). In this case Mark and Luke unite in preserving Jesus' actual words, which laid down a principle and not a statute, leaving the application of this principle, as of others, to be worked out according to the possibilities of the circumstances in any given instance (cf. Mal $2^{14-16}$). Similarly Bacon (*Sermon on the Mount*, pp. 117, 177 f.). Other scholars hold that the exceptive phrase in Matthew is an interpolation, but only states explicitly what was already implied as true in the nature of the case, that the act of adultery actually destroys the marriage union and is the divorce, instead of being merely a proper ground of divorce (so Meyer, Tholuck, E. Haupt, B. Weiss). But adultery cannot be *in itself* a proper ground for divorce on Gospel principles. In a case of adultery, divorce might be necessary if the offending party persisted in this evil conduct, wilfully regardless of all moral sense and duty. Suppose, however, that after the wrong had been done, the guilty party became truly repentant, and resolved upon a right life henceforth? The Gospel requires mercy rather than justice, love rather than revenge; forgiveness, patience, and long-suffering. The prophet Hosea, in his trying marriage relation, had discovered the Divine principle involved in such cases, and had recognized that in dealing lovingly and forgivingly with a wayward wife he was following God's own method with His wayward children; cf. also Jer $3^{1-15}$. Jesus most impressively taught that love, gentleness, and forgiveness were to characterize the true Christian, even in a case of adultery; for He said to the adulteress: 'Neither do I condemn thee; go, sin no more.' Such teaching seemed to the early Church quite too lenient, so that this incident with its teaching failed to find a place in the Gospels until the 2nd cent., and then not a suitable one. Jesus' treatment of this woman has been lost sight of in the interpretation of His words concerning divorce. The hard spirit of vengeance has ruled men's thoughts rather than the forgiving spirit of love.

all the married to strive for the attainment of this ideal. He did not enter into the casuistry of the matter, but fixed the principle. How far in actual ecclesiastic or civic legislation, at any given period or place, the ideal can be practically formulated and demanded, He left for the decision of those upon whom the administration of such matters devolved. Marriage and divorce regulations, upon which the welfare of society so largely depends, must embody the Divine ideal to the fullest extent made possible by the stage of spiritual, moral, and social progress concerned. And Christian people must never fail to apply to themselves this Divine marriage ideal; however low the current conception of marriage may be, or whatever laxity the civic laws may permit, the disciples of Christ can never conduct themselves according to any standard but that set by Him. Not that they must regard His teaching as statutory and divorce as never permissible; but that the act of divorce would be a confession of complete failure to attain His ideal, so that the highest degree of effort, patience, endurance, and self-sacrifice should be used in order to accomplish the permanence and the perfection of a marriage union when undertaken. In addition, Christian people must uphold Jesus' marriage ideal in the world, striving by every means to secure its increasing recognition and realization in society at large. For only in these ways can the Kingdom of God fully come.

The next subject dealt with in the Sermon is the use of Oaths (Mt $5^{33-37}$). The oath or vow was a frequent type of expression in all antiquity, and its use has diminished little with the passing of centuries. In its origin the oath was a solemn religious act, in which God—or some object sacred to Him or through Him—was invoked as a witness of the truth of an utterance or the sincerity of a promise, and as an avenger of falsehood and of non-fulfilment of the promise. The use of the oath and vow is recognized and approved in the OT (cf. Ex $22^{11}$, Dt $6^{13}$ $10^{20}$, Ps $63^{11}$, Is $45^{23}$, Jer $4^{2}$, and He $6^{13-18}$), and the commands concerning them look towards the preservation of their religious character and solemn function. This was the intent of the Third Commandment, 'Thou shalt not take the name of the Lord thy God in vain' (Ex $20^{7}$, Dt $5^{11}$), in which all misuse of the oath is forbidden, as where an oath is taken thoughtlessly or maliciously, or to cover falsehood.* In the same tenor are Lv $19^{12}$ 'Ye shall not swear by my name falsely, so that thou profane the name of thy God,' and Nu $30^{2}$ 'When a man voweth a vow unto the Lord, or sweareth an oath to bind his soul with a bond, he shall not break his word; he shall do according to all that proceedeth out of his mouth.'† The form of Jesus' expression in Mt $5^{33}$ takes up the substance, though not the exact form, of these OT teachings. The Jews of Jesus' day made most extravagant use of the oath, both in frequency and in variety; some oaths were regarded as binding and some as not binding, the difference of form being purely technical.‡

Christ denounced this casuistry as perverse in the extreme (Mt $23^{16-22}$). And in this passage of the Sermon He has the intention of sweeping away the whole system of oaths as resting upon a false theory, namely, that a man might use two qualities of statement: one with the oath, which pledged him to truth or fulfilment; and one without the oath, which required neither truth nor fulfilment. As against this double-dealing and authorization of falsehood, Jesus demands that a man shall speak only the truth, and implies that an oath is not only unnecessary, but harmful. This interpretation of Mt $5^{33-37}$ is that of the early Fathers and of the majority of modern commentators.* We find the same teaching, with close similarity of words, in Ja $5^{12}$ 'But above all things, my brethren, swear not, neither by the heaven, nor by the earth, nor by any other oath: but let your yea be yea, and your nay, nay; that ye fall not under judgment.' That Jesus submitted to the high priest's oath at His trial (Mt $26^{63.64}$), as a matter of the moment's necessity, is in no way against this interpretation.† Jesus forbids oaths not as statutory legislation, so that the taking of an oath is sinful; but in principle, on the ground that a man is accountable to God for every utterance (Mt $12^{34-37}$). He sets forth the ideal of truthfulness which is to be striven for and ultimately accomplished. A Christian can have no need of an oath. If in the present stage of civilization oaths are still necessary for civic purposes, then Christians must seek to establish a higher standard of honesty in speech, according to which a man's simple word will be the best possible guarantee of the truth and performance of what he says.

*e. Unselfishness and Forgiveness.*—Mt $5^{38-42}$ = Lk $6^{29.30}$. The OT Law did, in fact, provide that punishment should be in degree and kind, 'an eye for an eye, and a tooth for a tooth'; thus we read in Ex $21^{23-25}$ 'Thou shalt give life for life, eye for eye, tooth for tooth, hand for hand, foot for foot, burning for burning, wound for wound, stripe for stripe'; as also Lv $24^{17-21}$, Dt $19^{16-21}$.‡ This *lex talionis* was understood to apply to all relations of men. And not only that, for God Himself was believed to be retributive in His punishment, so that when men could not themselves execute the just penalty God could be appealed to for visiting retribution upon one's enemies; cf. Dt $23^{3-6}$ $25^{17-19}$, Ps $35^{1-8}$ $41^{10.11}$ $58^{6-11}$ $68^{1.2}$ $69^{22-28}$ $78^{20.21.60-66}$ $109^{6-15}$, Jer $17^{18}$ $18^{23}$, La $3^{64-66}$. This primitive conception and type of justice was probably required, at least in principle, by the conditions of the earliest civilization to which it ministered. When the modes of punishment subsequently changed, and penalties were executed no longer in kind but in some suitable equivalent, it still remained true that the punishment was meant to be retributive and equal to the crime. It is only in modern times that there has come in a new conception of punishment, according to which society is to be protected, not by avenging the wrong in kind or degree, but by reforming the evil-doer. This higher type of justice, based upon the principle of forbearance and helpfulness, also found recognition in Israel. The deeply spiritual saw that God's action was in love, mercy, and forgiveness, and they plead for a like principle of treatment among men; so Lv $19^{18}$ 'Thou shalt not take vengeance, nor bear any grudge against the children of thy people'; Dt $32^{35}$ 'Vengeance is mine, and recompense,' *i.e.* God's; Pr $20^{22}$ 'Say not, I will recompense evil: wait on the Lord, and he shall save thee'; cf.

* On the interpretation of the Third Commandment, see Coffin, *Journal of Bib. Lit.* 1900, pp. 166–188; art. DECALOGUE in vol. i.

† See, further, Lv $5^{4}$, Nu $30^{1-16}$, Dt $23^{21-23}$, Jg $11^{29-39}$, Jer $7^{9}$, Ezk $17^{18}$, Zec $5^{3.4}$ $8^{17}$, Mal $3^{5}$.

‡ See Wünsche, *Erläuterung der Evangelien*, pp. 57–60, 288–292; Edersheim, *Life and Times of Jesus the Messiah*, ii. 17–21.

* So Justin, Irenæus, Clement Alex., Origen, Jerome, Augustine; of our own day, Meyer, Achelis, Bruce, B. Weiss, H. Weiss, and others; see esp. Wendt, *Lehre Jesu*, ii. 210–213 [Eng. tr. i. 269–273]. For the view that Jesus did not forbid all oaths, but only their misuse, thereby simply re-establishing the OT teaching, may be cited Luther, Calvin, Bengel, Stier, Ewald, Keim, Tholuck. H. Holtzmann holds that Mt $5^{33-37}$ is intended to forbid all oaths, but attributes this tone to the Essenic tendencies of the First Evangelist rather than to Jesus, whose purpose was only to rebuke the profusion and casuistry of the Pharisaic practice.

† St. Paul's use of the oath, 2 Co $1^{23}$ $11^{31}$, Ro $1^{9}$, Gal $1^{20}$, 1 Th $2^{5}$, and elsewhere, is simply a continuation of the OT and Jewish custom in its best use; the primitive Christians in this, as in many other respects, failed to rise at once to the appreciation and attainment of Jesus' ideal.

‡ Similarly the Ḫammurabi Code (*c.* 2250 B.C.), Nos. 196, 200.

also 2 K $6^{21-23}$, La $3^{27-30}$. But the love of retaliation, the zeal for executing vengeance, and the passion for seeing strict justice done without delay, held the field in both OT and NT times. And consequently, when Jesus came, He found little of the true spirit and service of brotherhood.

Against this false and hateful temper of men Jesus set His principle of unselfishness and forgiveness, following out the higher conception presented in the OT, and requiring that by this principle all men shall determine all their conduct towards one another. In order to make His meaning more explicit and clear, Jesus used four concrete illustrations (Mt $5^{39-42}$), in them suggesting what kind of conduct would result from living by this principle. The illustrations, of course, are figurative, and are to be interpreted not literally but in their main idea.* A man is not to be thinking constantly of his own *rights*, as though the chief aim of his life was to avenge injustices and slights towards himself (v.$^{39}$); he must be willing to endure wrongs, to sacrifice his feelings and his possessions, in order to avoid trouble with others (v.$^{40}$); he must be ready to labour freely and unselfishly for the good of others, without expecting recompense (v.$^{41}$); he is not to be of a grasping, penurious disposition—rather he is to assist others in every reasonable way (v.$^{42}$).†

In this principle of forgiving love and unselfish service lies the essence of Jesus' ethical teaching;‡ it has been well called 'the secret of Jesus.'§ On this principle God acts towards men, and on this principle men must act towards one another. Jesus not only taught this standard of life, but He realized it in His ministry and in His death, thereby becoming the perfect example of human love and service. These are the qualities which make true brotherhood. One cannot for a moment suppose that Jesus, in setting forth this principle as the supreme guide in men's dealings with one another, had the intention of overthrowing the civic laws which society requires for its preservation and welfare; any such interpretation would reduce His sayings to absurdity. What He purposed was to make men recognize the wretchedness of a standard of conduct which rests upon the ideas of revenge and retaliation, of for ever insisting upon one's rights and one's dignity, of working only for one's self and never for others, of getting as much and giving as little as possible. Civic laws and private practice must accept this teaching of Jesus and embody it, not necessarily in the same way, but to the same end.*

* In Jn $18^{22.23}$ it can be seen that Jesus did not have in mind literal non-resistance, since He did not Himself practise it. That certain individuals (most recently Tolstoi) and sects (Anabaptists, Mennonites, Quakers) have taken these sayings literally, as statutes to be obeyed, is not to the credit either of their knowledge of the teaching of Jesus or of their own common-sense. Such literalism is the perversion of Jesus' method and intent, and is one of the worst enemies of the Gospel, for it holds up the teaching of Jesus to the ridicule of all sane, thinking men.

† In v.$^{39}$ the τῷ πονηρῷ cannot be the Evil One (as thought by Chrysostom and Theophylact), for Jesus would have him for ever resisted; it might be regarded as a neuter noun, referring to evil in general (so Augustine, Luther, Calvin, Ewald, Achelis, Kübel); but probably the evil man is meant who offers the indignities and demands described; cf. πονηρούς in v.$^{45}$ and Lk $6^{35.45}$ (so H. Holtzmann, Nösgen, B. Weiss). The δεξιὰν σιαγόνα of Mt $5^{39}$ is altered in Lk $6^{29}$ to simply τὴν σιαγόνα, since the first blow would naturally be given by the right hand upon the left cheek. In v.$^{40}$ κριθῆναι means to bring a legal action against one (cf. 1 Co $6^{1}$), in order to secure property of some kind from him. The χιτών (כְּתֹנֶת) was the common Oriental under-garment worn next the body, while the ἱμάτιον (שִׂמְלָה, בֶּגֶד) was the more costly and elegant tunic or over-garment (cf. art. Dress); that is, if a man attempts to get from you by law a little property, give him much in order to avoid quarrel and litigation with him. In the Luke parallel ($6^{29}$) the idea of a lawsuit is replaced by that of a personal assault, in which case the outer garment would first be taken, after which the inner garment was to be offered. In v.$^{41}$ the ἀγγαρεύσει (cf. B. Weiss, *Meyer-Komm. ü. d. Mattevgm. in loc.*) refers to official impressment for temporary service, a common practice in that day (Mt $27^{32}$); Jesus uses it as a figure to teach that men must assist others by generously given and willing service. Luke does not have this verse, perhaps because it was liable to be misunderstood as literally referring to legal requisitions instead of figuratively to all social relations. In v.$^{42}$ is added a fourth illustration which, because it is somewhat loosely joined to the preceding, and out of deference to the number 3, has been regarded by some scholars (Ewald, H. Holtzmann, Köstlin, Wittichen) as a remaining fragment of a separate section of this discourse, treating of the interpretation of the Eighth Commandment; they would therefore insert between v.$^{41}$ and v.$^{42}$ something like this, drawn from Ex $20^{15}$, Dt $5^{19}$ $24^{12.13}$ ἠκούσατε, ὅτι ἐρρέθη· οὐ κλέψεις, ἀποδώσεις δὲ τὸ ἱμάτιον τῷ πτωχῷ· ἐγὼ δὲ λέγω ὑμῖν· τῷ αἰτοῦντι, etc. This explanation of v.$^{42}$ has not, however, found general acceptance, being specifically rejected by Tholuck, Meyer, Feine, B. Weiss, and others; Luke has the saying in the same connexion as Matthew, and it joins well enough, logically, to vv.$^{38-41}$. The verse does not refer, at least directly, to the lending of money without requiring the payment of interest (so Feine, on the basis of Ex $22^{25-27}$, Lv $25^{37}$, Dt $15^{7}$ $23^{20}$, against Tholuck, B. Weiss).

‡ See esp. Harnack, *Das Wesen des Christentums*, 1901, pp. 45-47 [Eng. tr. pp. 70-74].

§ Matt. Arnold, *Literature and Dogma*, p. 181 f. See also Mt $26^{49-54}$, Mk $8^{31-37}$, Lk $9^{54.55}$, and cf. Is $50^{6}$ $53^{1-12}$. St. Paul also teaches with great emphasis the same forgiving and self-sacrificing principle of life (Ro $12^{17-21}$, 1 Co $6^{1-8}$, 1 Th $5^{15}$; cf. also 1 P $3^{9}$).

* Similarly Bacon, *Sermon on the Mount*, pp. 109-114: 'The Sermon is not legislative, as our First Evangelist seems to regard it, but prophetic. It does not enact, but interprets. It does not lay down rules, but opens up principles. . . . Matthew, as we have seen, is quite absorbed in the relation of the new *Torah* to the old. So much so that he fails to appreciate that his material is not really a series of new enactments, but in reality, just as Luke perceives, a simple application to the situation of that one principle which Jesus elsewhere enunciates more briefly; and not then as enacting something new, but as explaining the old [Mt $22^{35-40}$].' Mt $5^{21-48}$ gives 'illustrations of the one *principle* which Jesus saw in "all the Law and the Prophets," and saw as well in all nature and history, that the divine calling is to ministering love and service—that and that alone.' Thayer, *Journal of Bibl. Lit.* 1900, p. 149: 'Jesus is not intent on giving precepts, but would lay emphasis on principles. The distinction between the two is most important. A precept is a direction respecting a given action; it is definite, precise, specific, fitting and belonging to particular cases. A principle, on the other hand, is comprehensive and fundamental; it prescribes, not particular actions, but a course of conduct. . . . A precept bids him do, a principle trains him to be; and so begets that inwardness and continuity which are essential to character.' B. Weiss, *Meyer-Komm. ü. d. Mattevgm. in loc.*: 'Jesus explains that His will, as He would have it fulfilled in the Kingdom of God, demands the forbearing, self-forgetful love which renounces all standing on one's rights and desire for retaliation. Jesus illustrates the general principle by concrete examples, which are not to be understood as literal commands to be obeyed, but as setting forth a general standard according to the main idea contained in them.' Tholuck, *Bergrede*$^{5}$, p. 291 [Eng. tr. pp. 269, 270]: 'The commands in vv.$^{39-42}$ are to be regarded as only concrete illustrations of the state of mind and heart required. . . . It is only the spirit of revenge that our Lord condemns, and therefore it is not inconsistent with His command to seek the protection of the law.' Burton and Mathews, *Constructive Studies in the Life of Christ*, p. 105: 'Some have undertaken to apply such sayings as "Resist not him that is evil," and "Give to him that asketh of thee," literally as fixed rules. But this is utterly to misinterpret Jesus. This whole discourse is a criticism of the Pharisees for making morality consist in a literal keeping of the rules of the OT. It is impossible to suppose that it simply imposes a new set of rules. Others, feeling that a literal obedience to these rules is impossible, if not also harmful, give up all attempt to obey the teachings of this discourse. Both are wrong. [Jesus teaches here] the *principle*, which we ought always to strive to follow. The single precepts are intended to correct the selfishness and narrowness that Jesus saw about Him, and to point out some of the ways in which the principle may be applied. They, too, are to be obeyed, always in spirit, and in letter when such an obedience is consistent with the principle. If a man would follow Jesus, he must not resist an enemy in a spirit of revenge; nor should he refuse to give to a beggar from a selfish motive. If he resist or withhold, he must do so because love, regard for the highest well-being of society in general, requires it.' Plummer, *Comm. on Luke*, p. 185: 'The four precepts here given ($6^{29.30}$) are startling. It is impossible for either governments or individuals to keep them. A State which endeavoured to shape its policy in exact accordance with them would soon cease to exist; and if individuals acted in strict obedience to them, society would be reduced to anarchy. Violence, robbery, and shameless exaction would be supreme. The inference is that *they are not precepts, but illustrations of principles*. They are in the form of rules; but as they cannot be kept as rules, we are compelled to look beyond the letter to the spirit which they embody. If Christ had given precepts which could be kept literally, we might easily have rested content with observing the letter, and have never penetrated to the spirit. What is the spirit? Among other things, this: that resistance of evil and refusal to part with our property must never be a personal matter; so far as we are concerned,

*f. Universal Love.*—Mt $5^{43-48}$ = Lk $6^{27.\ 28.\ 32-36}$. When Jesus begins this sixth paragraph illustrative of His statements in Mt $5^{17-20}$ with the words 'Ye have heard that it was said, Thou shalt love thy neighbour and hate thine enemy,' He is not quoting precisely any OT or extra-biblical utterance on record (cf. Sir $18^{13}$). The clause 'Thou shalt love thy neighbour' is found in Lv $19^{18}$ 'Thou shalt not take vengeance, nor bear any grudge against the children of thy people, but thou shalt love thy neighbour as thyself.' But the further clause, 'and hate thine enemy,' while not appearing in that form, is really implied in the words 'the children of thy people,' which fixes a national limitation upon the teaching in the Leviticus passage. There was on the part of the Hebrews a profound contempt and disregard of other nationalities (cf. Dt $23^{3-6}$ $25^{17-19}$, the Book of Jonah, esp. $3^{10}$–$4^{11}$). So that the phrase 'hate thine enemy' justly characterized the prevailing OT conception of social duty (in spite of occasional efforts towards a larger idea, Ex $23^{4.\ 5}$), the 'enemy' signifying any foreigner who did not enter into Hebrew practices, and the 'hatred' signifying their superior disdain for other peoples. The same hatred towards all Gentiles was felt by the stricter Jews of Jesus' day; and the Pharisaic pride and exclusiveness went so far as to include in the sphere of their hatred the lower classes among the Jews themselves who did not satisfactorily observe the Law (Jn $7^{49}$ 'This multitude which knoweth not the law are accursed').

When Jesus sets over against this national bigotry and caste spirit His own teaching, Mt $5^{44}$ 'Love your enemies, and pray for them that persecute you,' the term 'enemies' is to be understood in the most comprehensive and general sense of all who do not feel and act lovingly towards one. It no longer means 'foreigners,' for Jesus has removed all national barriers, making all men brethren (cf. Ac $17^{26}$). To the primitive Christians the outstanding class of 'enemies' were those referred to by Jesus as their persecutors for the cause of Christ, as also in Mt $5^{10-12}$. Jesus wishes to establish the principle of a universal love which would unite all men in a complete human brotherhood.* Every man is to love every other man, and to serve him so far as it lies in his power, with reasonable regard to all his duties. Barriers, castes, classes, distinctions of all kinds are removed, so that love and service are to be all-inclusive. When the scribe propounded to Jesus the question, 'Who is my neighbour?' He replied with the parable of the Good Samaritan (Lk $10^{25-37}$), in which He set forth clearly and impressively that the 'neighbour' whom one is to love 'as himself' is any one and every one. And this love which Jesus enjoins is not to be of the self-seeking kind which is common in the world. There may be no real love, He says, in the exchanges of attention and courtesy which men are accustomed to make with one another, for it may proceed on a commercial, *quid pro quo* basis. The Gospel demands a different kind of relation between men which is not self-seeking, does not ask how much will be given in return, is bestowed freely without thought of recompense. And here appears the close logical relation between these verses and vv.$^{38-42}$, for vv.$^{43-48}$ carry forward to complete expression the thought which underlies the previous words.†

This kind of love, all-embracing, unremitting, realizing itself in both feeling and conduct, has its origin and perfect manifestation in God,‡ who cares for all men, however they treat Him. He sets the example of universal love and service, which Jesus reveals in His words and deeds. And men by following this example in their relations to one another become the 'sons' of God (Mt $5^{45}$), because in essential respects they feel and act like Him. The sonship thus spoken of is a moral sonship, which is attained by choosing to be and do what is right, rather than a genetic sonship, which is inherent because God has made men in His own

we must be willing to suffer still more and to surrender still more. It is right to withstand and even to punish those who injure us; but in order to correct them and to protect society, not because of any personal animus. It is right also to withhold our possessions from those who without good reason ask for them; but in order to check idleness and effrontery, not because we are too fond of our possessions to part with them. So far as our personal feeling goes, we ought to be ready to offer the other cheek, and to give without desire of recovery whatever is demanded or taken from us. Love knows no limits but those which love itself imposes. When love resists or refuses, it is because compliance would be a violation of love, not because it would involve loss or suffering.' Gore, *Sermon on the Mount*, p. 103 f.: 'We may truly say that the Sermon gives us a social law for Christians. That is true in this sense: the Sermon gives us principles of action which every Christian must apply and reapply in his social conduct. But just because it embodies motives and principles and does not give legal enactments, it must appeal in the first instance to the individual, to his heart and conscience; and it is only as the character thus formed must set itself to remodel social life on a fresh basis, that the Sermon can become a social law for Christians. You cannot take any one of its prescriptions and apply it as a social law at once. You cannot take the maxim, "If a man smite thee on the one cheek, turn to him the other also," or, "If a man take away thy coat, let him have thy cloak also," and make it obligatory on Christians as a rule of external conduct, without upsetting the whole basis of society, and without ignoring a contrary maxim which our Lord gives us in another connexion. But each of the maxims can be taken to the heart and conscience of the individual, to become a principle of each man's own character and conduct, and then to reappear, retranslated into social action, according to the wisdom of the time, or the wisdom of the man, or the wisdom of the Church.'

It is difficult to understand how Dr. Sanday (art. JESUS CHRIST, vol. ii. p. 621) can say: 'The ethical ideal of Christianity is the ideal of a Church. It does not follow that it is also the ideal of the State. If we are to say the truth, we must admit that parts of it would become impracticable if they were transferred from the individual standing alone to governments or individuals representing society.' A similar view was advocated by the Bishop of Peterborough in the *Fortnightly Review*, Jan. 1890. This misconception of Jesus' teaching seems to arise out of a confusion of principles with precepts. Social ethics and individual ethics cannot rest upon different *principles*; but the principles of ethics will call for different outworkings in concrete cases of their application—and this will be as true for individuals as for society. The people acting collectively through their governing officials (the State) are required to act according to precisely the same ethical standard as when they are acting individually; namely, they are bound to obey the principles of forgiving kindness to all (Mt $5^{21-24}$), of moral purity ($5^{27\text{f.}}$), of protection of marriage ($5^{31\text{f.}}$), of honesty in speech ($5^{33-37}$), of an absence of the revengeful spirit ($5^{39}$), of long-suffering ($5^{40}$), of helpfulness ($5^{41}$), of generosity ($5^{42}$), and of an all-embracing love ($5^{43-48}$). Can any one think that the State is not bound so to act?

* For the Biblical teaching concerning love, see esp. art. LOVE in vol. iii.

† Lk $6^{27.\ 28.\ 32-36}$ has a different order of the contents from that of Mt $5^{43-48}$; if the Matthæan material were arranged in the same order, the verses would stand: (43). 44 (39-42 $7^{12}$). 46. 47. 45. 48; and Lk $6^{34.\ 35a}$ is an addition or expansion for which Matthew has no parallel. It is not easy to determine which order is the more likely to have been original. The striking differences in the wording of the passages, however, indicate beyond a doubt that Luke's account is secondary, with much verbal modification: thus in vv.$^{27.\ 28}$ expansions appear; in v.$^{32}$ *χάρις* is found instead of *μισθός* as in Mt $5^{46}$, a manifest dropping of a Jewish for a Gentile or universal term (though Luke has *μισθός* at $6^{35}$); in the same and following verses, and for the same reason, Luke twice has *ἁμαρτωλοί*, once instead of *οἱ τελῶναι*, once instead of *οἱ ἐθνικοί*; in v.$^{33}$ Luke has *ἀγαθοποιῆτε* instead of Matthew's *ἀσπάσησθε*, a Jewish custom; in v.$^{35}$ Luke has *υἱοὶ Ὑψίστου* instead of Matthew's clearly more original *υἱοὶ τοῦ πατρὸς ὑμῶν τοῦ ἐν οὐρανοῖς*; in the same verse Luke reduces the fine Jewish words about God's making the sun rise and the rain fall to a commonplace Gentile phrase, *χρηστός ἐστιν ἐπὶ τοὺς ἀχαρίστους καὶ πονηρούς*; in v.$^{36}$ Luke changes the imperatival future form *ἔσεσθε*, common in the LXX through the influence of the Hebrew, and occasionally found in the NT (*e.g.* Mt $5^{43}$ $6^{5}$ $22^{37-39}$), to a better Greek form, the imperative *γίνεσθε*; he has also the less Jewish and less lofty *οἰκτίρμονες* instead of Matthew's significant *τέλειοι*; and again he has only *ὁ πατὴρ ὑμῶν* instead of Matthew's *ὁ πατὴρ ὑμῶν ὁ οὐράνιος*. These numerous and important variations in the two accounts of these verses leave no room for doubt that Matthew's form is much nearer to the historical words spoken by Jesus, and that the Third Gospel contains material which had undergone wide verbal divergence, partly perhaps in Luke's own hands, but mainly in the earlier Gentile transmission.

‡ So in the Johannine writings frequently, Jn $3^{16}$, 1 Jn $4^{8.\ 10.\ 19}$; cf. also Ro $5^{5-8}$.

image (Gn 1$^{26}$).* Jesus therefore commands men to be perfect in love as God is perfect in love,† setting before them an absolute ideal of social goodness; not that the ideal is at once attainable, but that towards its realization every man—and all men together—must strive, and in God's providence this striving will ultimately achieve success.

*g. Religious Worship.*—Mt 6$^{1-6. 16-18}$ (no parallel in Lk).‡ The connexion of these verses with the historical Sermon cannot well be doubted; they follow in logical consecution upon the material contained in Mt 5$^{3-48}$, illustrating the true righteousness still further and on another side. The ideal life which was characterized in vv.$^{3-12}$, enjoined in vv.$^{13-20}$, and illustrated with regard to character and service in vv.$^{21-48}$, is further illustrated in these verses with regard to religious worship. Almsgiving, prayer, and fasting were, in the estimation of the Jews, three of the chief elements of religion, and received a disproportionate attention; while the three performances, really so different in importance, were regarded as about equally necessary and useful.§ In v.$^{1}$, which forms an introduction to the group, Jesus gives the key to the interpretation of the whole: * He does not pronounce against the acts themselves, but against the spirit and purpose which too often animated the doing of them. Religious worship, such as almsgiving (which the Jews rightly considered an act of worship), prayer and fasting, must never be performed ostentatiously, with the intent of securing a reputation for piety. It was mainly the proud, hypocritical Pharisees who were guilty of such motives in their worship; but the multitude of common people to whom Jesus was now speaking had been brought up to believe implicitly in the teaching and practice of the Pharisees, and were therefore in great danger of being corrupted by the Pharisaic example of ostentation, worldliness, and deceit.

Jesus will therefore warn them against these specific errors of their religious leaders, and in contrast exhibit the character of true religious worship. The three acts of almsgiving (vv.$^{2-4}$), prayer (vv.$^{5. 6}$), and fasting (vv.$^{16-18}$) are treated in a parallel way, the same thing being said of each in almost the same language. When they give money in the synagogues, or upon other occasions, for charitable objects, it is to be contributed solely for the benefit of others, with no purpose of obtaining a reputation of generosity for themselves (cf. Ac 5$^{1-11}$). Against almsgiving in itself He does not speak, but only of the motive behind it. The giving of money to assist others is, in fact, an act of worship to God, and a necessary element of all true righteousness. But such giving must be quietly done, without providing or even wishing that others may know of the fact or the amount, in order that one may receive credit therefor.† So also when men pray, as pray they must, their prayers are to be a genuine communing with God, instead of being designed to win the praise of men for a superior piety.‡ To counterfeit true spiritual communion with God is an intolerable profanation of religion. Jesus, of course, has no thought of forbidding prayer in public, but He will have only sincere prayers made, whether in public or private. And if they fast, as they were accustomed to do regularly and often, they are to observe the fast as a simple humiliation before God, not forced upon others for the purpose of gaining credit for exceptional devoutness.§ On another occasion

* On this sonship see Wendt, *Lehre Jesu*, ii. 145 f. In using the term 'Father' for expressing most completely His conception of God, Jesus thinks of the *family* as most characteristic of the relation between God and men. In the family the sons may be either true or false to their relation to their father; if they love, honour, and obey him they realize their sonship—they are sons indeed; if they disrespect him, disgrace him, and disregard his will they are not sons in the moral sense, for they repudiate their sonship. But the actual genetic sonship is none the less a fact, even if the sons will not acknowledge and exalt it. So in the relation of men to God; they do not in reality *become* His sons any more than He *becomes* their Father; this mutual essential relation exists from the first, for all men are His sons, and He is the Father of all. But the NT use of the term 'son' is generally a moral one, and those only are designated 'sons' who honour and realize their sonship. This does not deny the genetic, spiritual sonship, however, which the NT also teaches.

† The words of Jesus, 'ye shall be perfect,' can have only the imperative force, as in Lk 6$^{36}$ (so Meyer, H. Holtzmann, B. Weiss, H. Weiss, Wendt, Blass, and nearly all); cf. Burton, *Moods and Tenses in NT Greek*, § 67. The whole v.$^{48}$ is made up from OT language; *e.g.* Lv 19$^{2}$ (LXX) reads, ἅγιοι ἔσεσθε, ὅτι ἅγιός εἰμι ἐγὼ κύριος ὁ θεὸς ὑμῶν; cf. also Lv 11$^{44}$, 1 P 1$^{15}$; and Dt 18$^{13}$ (LXX) reads, τέλειος ἔσῃ ἐνάντιον κυρίου τοῦ θεοῦ σου. But the thought of these similar OT passages, as their contexts show, is of levitical purity and national separateness, and it is therefore superficial as compared with the deep meaning which Jesus puts into the words. In Mt 5$^{48}$ we have the closing verse of the short section vv.$^{43-48}$ concerning universal love (so Achelis, Bruce, Heinrici, H. Holtzmann, Tholuck, B. Weiss), not a general summary conclusion of the whole section vv.$^{21-48}$ (so Burton, Ibbeken, H. Weiss). The τέλειος refers only to perfection in love, not to the whole series of attributes which constitute the perfection of God in the theological sense, or to the comprehensive idea of human perfection. This love which Jesus establishes as the principle of the ideal life, to be felt and acted upon by every man towards every other man, cannot be understood as condoning the sins or imperfections in the character and service of others, but insists upon viewing men not as they are but as they may be and should be, and upon rendering them every assistance of sympathy, counsel, and help towards the attainment of the Divine ideal. It is thus that God has dealt with men, and we are to do likewise for one another.

‡ The account of the Sermon in Luke does not contain this section, probably for the same reason that no parallel appears for Mt 5$^{17-37}$, namely, because these passages are so saturated with Jewish phraseology, ideas, and customs as to be difficult of understanding for Gentile readers (so Feine, Wendt). Here also, as there, it is more likely that Luke's sources did not contain these sections than that Luke himself excised them.

§ The giving of alms was held to be a primary duty and a means of salvation, as seen already in the Apocrypha, To 4$^{7-11}$ 12$^{8-10}$ 14$^{9-12}$, Sir 4$^{1. 2}$ 7$^{10}$, cf. also Ps 41$^{1}$, Is 58$^{7. 10}$, Dn 4$^{27}$; there are also many striking Rabbinic sayings concerning the merit of almsgiving (see art. ALMSGIVING in vol. i.; Weber, *Jüdische Theologie*, pp. 285–288; Wünsche, *Erläuterung der Evangelien*, on Mt 6$^{1-4}$). The Greek word in use for the alms is ἐλεημοσύνη (the motive employed by metonomy for the thing), as here in v.$^{2}$, representing, perhaps, צְדָקָה; since this Heb. word meant primarily 'righteousness,' it came about that δικαιοσύνη might also have this special meaning, but that is not the sense in which δικ. is used here in v.$^{1}$ (the textual variant at this point, ἐλεημοσύνη, is improbable on both external and internal evidence). Prayer was offered by the Jews thrice daily, at 9 A.M., at 12 noon, and at 3 P.M. (cf. Ac 3$^{1}$), and on three days in the week the people went to the synagogue for prayer. Liturgicai forms of prayer were in use (cf. Lk 11$^{2}$, and Mishna, tractate *Berakhoth*), and they were recited at the proper time wherever one might be. Fasting was prescribed by the OT for the Day of Atonement (Lv 16$^{29-34}$), and was practised on other occasions also (Ex 34$^{28}$, 1 S 7$^{6}$, 2 S 12$^{16}$, Jer 36$^{9}$, Dn 10$^{3}$). The prophets sometimes spoke against it (Is 58$^{3-8}$, Jer 14$^{12}$, Zec 7$^{5}$), but it was a prevailing usage throughout the Hebrew history, cf. Jth 6$^{8}$, To 12$^{8}$. In the NT also the Pharisee is represented as boasting in his prayer, 'I fast twice in the week' (Lk 18$^{12}$), and the frequent fasts are mentioned in Mt 9$^{14}$ (cf. art. FASTING in vol. i.). It is noticeable that Jesus has not joined with these three outstanding acts of Jewish worship the observance of the Sabbath, which stood in somewhat the same prominence; but elsewhere He dealt with that subject also (Mk 2$^{23-28}$), and on a similar principle.

* δικαιοσύνη is to be understood here in a comprehensive sense; it is a repetition of the δικ. of v.$^{20}$, now to be illustrated in acts of religious worship, and embraces alike almsgiving, prayer, and fasting.

† In v.$^{2}$ σαλπίσῃς is a figurative term signifying ostentation. ὑποκριταί refers to the Pharisees; they were hypocrites because they wore a mask of piety over their selfish lives; cf. also Mt 23$^{5-7}$. συναγωγαῖς, ῥύμαις indicate that almsgiving was a part of the regular synagogue services, but that alms were also given upon the streets to those in need. The ἀμὴν λέγω ὑμῖν puts a special emphasis upon the fact that this almsgiving, when done out of vanity, had no real merit; cf. Lk 6$^{24}$. In v.$^{3}$ the phrase, 'let not thy left hand know what thy right hand doeth,' is quite surely a current Semitic proverb to express secrecy.

‡ In v.$^{5}$ ἔσεσθε is an imperatival future, as in Mt 5$^{48}$; the parallel verb in v.$^{2}$ is an imperatival subjunctive, and in v.$^{6}$ an imperative, the meaning being quite the same in each. The γωνίαις τῶν πλατειῶν were the four corners of street intersections, which were chosen as the most conspicuous place for the ostentatious prayers. ἑστῶτες indicates that prayers were customarily offered in a standing posture. The ταμεῖον, or, more frequently in the NT, ὑπερῷον, was the upper room of an Oriental house used for guests or for retirement to pray; see Ac 1$^{13}$ 9$^{37. 39}$ 20$^{8}$. With the language of v.$^{6a}$ compare 2 K 4$^{33}$, Is 26$^{20}$.

§ In v.$^{16}$ σκυθρωποί and ἀφανίζουσιν τὰ πρόσωπα refer to neglect of the customary care for the head, the unwashed face and

Jesus removed all obligation from His followers to observe the Pharisaic system of fasts, or to practise fasting except as it was the personal and spontaneous expression of inner feeling (cf. Mk $2^{18-22}$). Here He teaches that when one fasts it must be a genuinely religious performance, free from all ostentation and selfish motives.

It is true, Jesus says, that those who turn these acts of religious worship to selfish account do secure their object; 'they have their reward' in the false reputation for generosity and piety which for a time they can win. But they cannot win God's approval, or secure any spiritual blessings. These things, which alone are worth while, belong only to those whose worship is sincere, who give and pray and fast with pure unselfish motives, for the good they can do their fellow-men and for their own spiritual growth. And the principle which Jesus here sets forth for these three acts of religious worship is to apply to every kind of religious observance. Sacred things are never to be turned to worldly account; everything we do in the name of religion, and for the sake of religion, must be untarnished by self-seeking ends and unholy purposes.*

*h. The Lord's Prayer.*—Mt $6^{7-15}$=Lk $11^{1-4}$. No words of Jesus which have come down to us are of greater significance or usefulness to mankind than this Prayer, which He taught His disciples, indicating as it does the true foundation, the true spirit, and the true substance of all prayer, prayer being our communion with God. A consideration of the Lord's Prayer will involve the following points: (1) the historical occasion on which the Prayer was given; (2) the original form of the Prayer as taught by Jesus; (3) the genetic relations of this Prayer to the OT, to Jewish prayers, and to the life of Christ; (4) the analysis and interpretation of its contents; (5) the right use of the Prayer.

(1) There is no portion of the Sermon as given by Matthew (chs. 5–7) which is so obviously an addition to the historical discourse as the section $6^{7-15}$ containing the Lord's Prayer. That these verses are extraneous matter, introduced here by the process of compilation, is now maintained by many scholars.† This fact appears in several ways: (*a*) Lk $11^1$ explicitly states that Jesus gave the Prayer to His disciples in response to an expressed wish on their part for a form of prayer, such as John the Baptist had given his disciples (the Jews were accustomed to many liturgical prayers). This statement, while it might be a mere literary setting of the Third Gospel, is probably a historical datum; and if historical, it points to another occasion than the Sermon for the presentation of the Prayer. (*b*) The precise time when the Prayer was given is not fixed by Luke, but it is assigned in a general way to the Peræan period, after the close of the Galilæan ministry. This is perhaps too late a position, since it was the example of John the Baptist's disciples which led Jesus' disciples to ask Him for a prayer; but this influence of John's upon Jesus' disciples is more likely to have been exercised before John's death, which came during Jesus' work in Galilee (Mk $6^{14-29}$). If, then, the Lord's Prayer was given earlier than the Sermon, it would not have been given again as new teaching in that discourse; and if later, then it can stand in the Sermon only as a result of subsequent compilation. What seems to have happened is, that the original occasion of the giving of the Prayer was remembered (Lk $11^1$), but the exact time at which it was given was forgotten; consequently each Evangelist, or his source, introduced the Prayer into his narrative where it was deemed suitable. (*c*) The Prayer, where it stands in the Sermon, clearly interrupts the movement of the discourse, and destroys the unity of the section into which it has been inserted. This is true not only of the Prayer, vv.$^{9-13}$, but also of the two verses preceding, vv.$^{7.8}$, and of the two verses following, vv.$^{14.15}$. The whole passage, vv.$^{7-15}$, does not pertain directly to the subject which Jesus is presenting in vv.$^{1-6.16-18}$, namely, the sin of ostentation and hypocrisy in acts of religious worship; and it mars the symmetry of Jesus' three illustrations about almsgiving, vv.$^{2-4}$; prayer, vv.$^{5.6}$; and fasting, vv.$^{16-18}$. Nevertheless, it is quite intelligible how these verses $^{7-15}$ were brought into this connexion by the compiling process. The Sermon was one of Jesus' most important discourses, and during the Apostolic age it was everywhere in use as a practical digest of His teaching. As the Sermon already contained some instruction about prayer, and the teaching on the same subject in vv.$^{7-15}$ was separated from its historical position, it came easily into association with vv.$^{5.6}$, where—although it was an extraneous element—it added to the completeness of the prayer instruction.

(2) It is in the highest degree improbable that the Lord's Prayer was given on two separate occasions—once in the Sermon in the form which Matthew reports, and again under other circumstances and in a different form as reported by Luke.* This would have been unnecessary; but still more, each of the two Gospels supposes that it reports the one and only giving of the Prayer. On the theory of repetition, why did Jesus present the Prayer in two forms so very different from each other? Having once given it in the fuller, smoother form of Mt $6^{9-13}$, why should He subsequently repeat it in the shorter, cruder form of Lk $11^{2-4}$? The reason for the postulation of two deliveries of the Lord's Prayer is the unwillingness of certain scholars to admit that Jesus' words could be so variantly transmitted (see the two Greek forms of the Prayer quoted in parallel columns on p. 5). Certainly it is not to be thought that Luke, with the Matthæan form of the Prayer before him, deliberately cut it down and changed it to the form contained in his Gospel; or that Matthew, with the Lukan form of the Prayer before him, deliberately enlarged and altered it into the form which the First Gospel presents. But the two forms may well be the respective results of two independent lines and processes of transmission. The Prayer as given by Jesus in Aramaic was briefly worded, as we may assume from the nature of the language and the Jewish custom, as well as from the original Hebrew 'Ten Words' and the Beatitudes. It is therefore not unlikely that the form of the Prayer given by Matthew is somewhat longer than the historical Aramaic form, for the purpose of producing a more perfect Greek

dishevelled hair being an Oriental sign of grief and abasement, cf. 2 S $12^{20}$, Is $61^3$, Dn $10^3$, 1 Mac $3^{47}$; that this is what is meant is seen in v.$^{17f.}$, where Jesus bids them give no external sign of their fasting.

* No one would seriously attempt to put these commands of Jesus into practice as precepts to be literally obeyed, so that all charity should be unorganized, and all prayers be absolutely private. Here, again, as in ch. 5, Jesus is dealing with principles only, and His illustrations are to be considered as illuminating the principles rather than as fixing statutes for literal observance.

† So Calvin, Strauss, Neander, Schleiermacher, Bleek, de Wette, Olshausen, Ewald, Ebrard, Meyer, Hanne, Godet, Kamphausen, Page, Feine, Sieffert, Bruce, Chase, Kübel, Weizsäcker, Wendt, H. Holtzmann, Bartlet, Heinrici, B. Weiss, Baljon, Nestle, Bacon. The Matthæan position of the Prayer is regarded as historical by Tholuck, Keil, Morison, Broadus, Achelis, Steinmeyer, H. Weiss, Nösgen, Plummer, Grawert, it being the opinion of most of them that the Lukan position is also historical, and therefore that the Prayer was given on two separate occasions by Jesus. Tholuck is undecided whether to prefer Matthew's position for the Prayer, or to hold that it was repeated.

* Yet this is maintained by Achelis, *Bergpredigt*, p. 297; Chase, *Lord's Prayer in the Early Church* (1891), p. 11, and by some others. Against this view, see Page, *Expositor*, 3rd ser. vol. vii. p. 433 ff.

translation. But in the main the differences which appear in the accounts of Matthew and Luke are due to the influences of independent translation from the Aramaic, and of handing down in practical Church use through fifty years of time. Neither account can be supposed to furnish a literal equivalent of the Prayer precisely as worded by Christ for His disciples.* Consequently it becomes a matter of importance to discover which of the two Gospel reports contains the more exact reproduction of the historical Prayer. The Church, with striking unanimity, from the 1st cent. to the present, has testified to the greater fidelity, dignity, and usableness of the recension in Mt 6$^{9-13}$; and this choice, as respects both quantity and quality, has been confirmed by the great majority of scholars.†

In order to consider in detail the differences which exist between the two accounts of the Lord's Prayer, it is necessary to make the comparison on the basis of the modern critical texts of the NT, such as Tischendorf's eighth edition and Westcott and Hort's text (with which the RV closely agrees). One notices first the exclusion of the doxology to the Prayer contained in the TR at Mt 6$^{13}$ (and familiar to us through the AV): *ὅτι σοῦ ἐστιν ἡ βασιλεία καὶ ἡ δύναμις καὶ ἡ δόξα εἰς τοὺς αἰῶνας· ἀμήν.* This ending of the Prayer is not given in Luke, and the external evidence against its genuineness in Matthew is conclusive; so that its authenticity is no longer supposed.‡ It grew up gradually in the 2nd cent. as a product of the Jewish custom of doxologies and responses, continued in the public services of the Christian Church; see esp. 1 Ch 29$^{11-13}$. The earliest mention of the liturgical use of the Prayer is in the *Teaching of the Twelve Apostles*, viii. 3, where the repetition of it three times daily is enjoined; and there is abundant Patristic evidence that this liturgical use rapidly increased. Readily, therefore, this doxology, which came to be used always at the close of the Prayer, found its way into the later exemplars of the NT text; and the fact that it appears in conjunction with Mt 6$^{9-13}$ instead of Lk 11$^{2-4}$ shows that it was the Matthæan form of the Prayer which the early Church adopted for its liturgy. The doxology is found in many of the secondary uncials, but is absent from ℵBD, the earlier versions, and the Patristic witnesses of the 2nd and 3rd cents. generally. Again, in numerous secondary and late witnesses of the text the fragmentary Lukan account of the Prayer is filled out and modified by the introduction of some or all of the elements peculiar to the Matthæan account; but these are manifest assimilations, and therefore have no textual standing in the Third Gospel.

Taking Mt 6$^{9-13}$ and Lk 11$^{2-4}$ thus according to the best Greek text, it appears that, after the address which is common to both, the Lukan account has five petitions, while the Matthæan account has six (or seven). The five parallel petitions are: (1) Hallowed be Thy name, (2) Thy Kingdom come, (3) Give us our daily bread, (4) Forgive us our debts (sins), and (5) Bring us not into temptation. To these Matthew adds, between (2) and (3), 'Thy will be done, as in heaven, so on earth,' which is clearly a new petition, and after (5) he adds, 'but deliver us from evil,' which may be a separate petition, but is more likely a fuller, reverse wording of the 'bring us not into temptation.'* Are these two additional clauses in Matthew authentic portions of the Lord's Prayer? The only denial of their authenticity has come from the few modern scholars who hold to the relative originality of the Lukan account here and elsewhere as against the longer Matthæan account, which they think was expanded and supplemented in transmission.† But Matthew's third petition, 'Thy will be done, as in heaven, so on earth,' brings into the Prayer one of Jesus' essential ideas and constant phrases (cf. Mt 7$^{21}$ 12$^{50}$ 26$^{39.42}$, Jn 4$^{34}$ 6$^{38}$); it is necessary to the literary structure of the Prayer, since it forms the third member of the first triplet of petitions; and while in a general way the same thought is expressed in the clause 'Thy kingdom come,' the Prayer needs this more definite statement of *how* the kingdom must be realized, what *men* must do to make the Kingdom come. It is not difficult to see why this petition was excluded from the Lukan form of the Prayer: the source from which Luke drew his account had passed through a Gentile line of transmission, in the course of which a large part of the characteristically Jewish element in the Gospel story was eliminated, as a detriment to the spread of the Gospel among the Gentiles. Its omission is therefore parallel to the omission of Mt 5$^{17-37}$, and much other material, from the Third Gospel.‡ With regard to Matthew's other addition to the Lord's Prayer, the enlargement of the sixth petition by conjoining the phrase 'but deliver us from evil,' there is less argument for its authenticity; but its absence from Luke is readily explained in the manner just described, it is a characteristic Jewish conception entirely suitable to Jesus' thought and expression, and it fits in with the literary structure of the second triplet of petitions, since without it the sixth petition would not correspond in structure with the other two.

The phenomena of the parallelism in the wording of the several clauses which Matthew and Luke have in common are striking. The thought and the language of the two accounts agree precisely in the first, second, and sixth petitions (except that in the sixth Luke does not have the phrase *ἀλλὰ ῥῦσαι ἡμᾶς ἀπὸ τοῦ πονηροῦ*).§ The third petition Luke

* It has been sufficiently argued above, under i. 3, that the entire phenomena of the primitive transmission of the Gospel material require us to recognize extensive verbal variation and occasional thought modification, such as appear in these parallel reports, throughout the narratives of the four Evangelists. There is a striking similarity between the Matthæan and Lukan accounts of the Beatitudes and their two accounts of the Lord's Prayer, and judgments arrived at concerning the features and merits of the one pair will be found to hold in general for the other pair also; the chief differences between the two forms of the Beatitudes and the two forms of the Lord's Prayer are due to similar causes operating on both.

† So Tholuck, Meyer, Feine, Bruce, H. Weiss, Plummer, B. Weiss, and many others; those also who think that Jesus gave the Prayer in two forms hold, almost without exception, that the form in Matthew is to be preferred. The modern scholars who regard the Lukan report as the more authentic (Bleek, Kamphausen, H. Holtzmann, Wendt, Bacon), seem to follow too rigid and exclusive a theory of literary criticism.

‡ See Westcott and Hort, *New Testament in Greek*, vol. ii. Appendix; Scrivener, *Introd. to the Criticism of the New Testament*$^{4}$, vol. ii. pp. 323–325; Chase, *Lord's Prayer in the Early Church*, pp. 168–176.

* Augustine (*Enchirid.* 116) regarded this phrase as a separate petition, making seven in all, and this became the standard Roman Catholic interpretation: it was adopted also by Luther, and is continued by Lutheran commentators. Among modern scholars there are many who accept this—some on traditional grounds (Kübel, Nösgen, H. Weiss), others on critical grounds (Bleek, Hilgenfeld, Ibbeken, Chase, v. d. Goltz). That the petitions are but six in number was held by Origen and Chrysostom, was adopted by Calvin, and has had the support in recent years of Tholuck (apparently), Bengel, Olshausen, Keim, Kuinöl, Meyer, Achelis, Feine, Hatch, Plummer, B. Weiss, Bruce, Hort, Nestle, and others.

† So Bleek, Kamphausen, H. Holtzmann, Wendt, Bacon.

‡ Feine, *Jahrb. f. Protest. Theol.* 1885, thinks that Luke omitted the third petition because he considered that its idea was already contained in the first and second petitions, so that it was simply redundant. This is also the view of Kamphausen, *Das Gebet des Herrn*, p. 67. H. Holtzmann, *Hand-Comm. ü. d. Synoptiker*, *in loc.*, regards Luke's five petitions as original, designed to be counted on the fingers of one hand. O. Holtzmann, *Leben Jesu* (1901), p. 203, also maintains that the short form of Luke is original.

§ The presence of this phrase in the text of Lk 11$^{4}$ in ACD and some other witnesses is to be explained as the result of a process of text assimilation with the Matthæan reading; it does not appear in ℵBL, the more important versions, or the earlier Patristic writings. Similar cases are the insertion in Lk 11$^{2}$ of

does not have. In the remaining two petitions, the fourth and fifth, we find approximately the same ideas and words, but with some variation: thus the δὸς ἡμῖν σήμερον of Mt $6^{11}$ is paralleled in Lk $11^{3}$ by δίδου ἡμῖν τὸ καθ' ἡμέραν, the latter being an attempt to generalize and simplify the former; the τὰ ὀφειλήματα of Mt $6^{12}$ is paralleled in Lk $11^{4}$ by τὰς ἁμαρτίας, the latter being the substitution of an easy, well-known word for one full of significance but less common—that this substitution took place can be inferred from the τῷ ὀφείλοντι in the adjoined clause; and in the same petition the ὡς καὶ of Mt $6^{12}$ is paralleled in Lk $11^{4}$ by καὶ γάρ, which also is an obvious attempt to remove the possibility of a false *quid pro quo* interpretation. Very interesting also is the difference in the two accounts of the address of the Prayer; Lk $11^{2}$ gives only one word, Πάτερ, while Mt $6^{9}$ gives Πάτερ ἡμῶν ὁ ἐν τοῖς οὐρανοῖς. It is, of course, possible that the Lukan report is correct, but it certainly seems too familiar and abrupt for this solemn, lofty prayer; while Matthew's two attributives seem logical and important. The ἡμῶν indicates that the Prayer is a universal one for all who will pray to God. The ὁ ἐν τοῖς οὐρανοῖς is an OT conception (cf. Ps $2^{4}$ $115^{3}$) which Jesus used (see passages below), because it was a customary Jewish expression full of religious meaning.* Its usual, though not entire, absence from Luke is best explained as due to the process already described by which the characteristic Jewish element was largely eliminated from the sources of the Third Gospel. In all these parallel passages, therefore, where Matthew and Luke give different readings for the clauses of the Prayer, the report of Matthew commends itself as possessed of a greater authenticity.† This confirms by historical tests the strong preference of the Church for the longer form of the Prayer as given in the First Gospel, a preference which rested primarily on spiritual and practical tests.

(3) When Jesus would condense His teaching into seven concise phrases (the address is an essential part of the Prayer), containing in Aramaic not fifty words, it became necessary for Him to embody His chief ideas about God and men in comprehensive phrases whose significance was already well understood by His followers. To introduce new phrases and new conceptions would have been to confuse those whom He wished to instruct. Consequently, the language and the ideas of the Lord's Prayer are closely related to the OT, where essential truth about God, and about the duty of men towards Him and towards one another, had in many respects been reached. Jesus' general teaching to His disciples previous to the giving of this Prayer had made known to them what He would have them understand by these OT conceptions and phrases.

Naturally, we find in Jewish prayers of a time contemporaneous with Jesus some phrases which are similar to those in the Lord's Prayer. Such parallels have been pointed out for the address and first two petitions; for the remaining four clauses there are no real parallels, although there are expressions with a certain similarity.‡ Some of these Jewish prayer-formulas are subsequent in origin to the 1st cent. A.D., and may well have been influenced by the Christian Prayer. But there is no reason why Jewish prayers of Jesus' own time should not have contained some of the essential religious ideas which Jesus reaffirms, and in language which the OT had already made sacred. Such parallelisms furnish no proper basis for an attack upon the originality and authority of Jesus. His work was not to make a clean sweep of all existing religious conceptions and phraseology, as though the world had never had any vision of God, or truth, or goodness, or right; on the contrary, He came to show that the OT revelation was, in its best thought and teaching, a true, Divine revelation, which He would exalt and perfect (Mt $5^{17}$, cf. He $1^{1.2}$). Jesus was not 'original' in the sense that He created a wholly new fabric of religious ideas, or introduced a wholly new set of religious terms; that kind of originality was made impossible by the fact that God was already in His world. Jesus' originality—and the term is not misapplied—consisted in His Divine ability to separate the true from the false, the permanent from the transient, the perfect from the imperfect; and then to carry forward the whole circle of ideas and practices to their ideal expression. The work of an artist is not to manufacture his paints, but to produce with them a perfect picture. Jesus' mission was to clarify and to perfect religious truth, to show the unity and perspective of its many elements, and to transform humanity by revealing the nature, the beauty, and the necessity of the ideal life.

One observes also with interest how the Lord's Prayer embodies the experiences of Jesus in His own personal and official life. His teaching grows out of and expresses His own religious perceptions and realizations, so that there is a vital unity, an instructive correspondence, between this Prayer and His experience.* He finds God to be His Father and their Father, the common Father of all, to whom prayer is to be addressed. He lives and works that God may be revered, that His Kingdom may come, and that His will may be perfectly done by men. He has experienced the truth that God cares for the physical needs of men, and it is their privilege to trust Him for these things. He knows and teaches that men are sinful, needing God's forgiveness; they also must show a forgiving spirit towards one another. He has Himself passed through severe temptations, praying for deliverance from them (cf. Mk $14^{36.38}$, Mt $4^{1-11}$).† In giving this ideal Prayer to His disciples, Jesus does not necessarily imply that His experience is in no respect different from theirs, *e.g.* that there is no uniqueness in His relation to God, or in His character and career as regards sin. But He does mean that He has shared humanity with them, has lived through its experiences, has found the way to attain the human ideal, and will declare to them in His words and in Himself the secret of the true life.

(4) An analysis of the Lord's Prayer, accepting the Matthæan form as practically authentic, discloses a well-considered literary structure: there are seven clauses in all, the first containing the address, followed by two groups of petitions, three in each. Regard, therefore, is had to the sacred

Matthew's γενηθήτω τὸ θέλημά σου ὡς ἐν οὐρανῷ καὶ ἐπὶ γῆς (so ℵACD against BL, versions, and quotations), and ἡμῶν ὁ ἐν τοῖς οὐρανοῖς (so ACD against ℵBL, versions, and quotations). Modern text-critical authorities are agreed that these passages are interpolations in the Lukan text.

* Compare the later Jewish prayer-formula, אָבִינוּ שֶׁבַּשָּׁמַיִם; see Achelis, *Bergpredigt*, p. 229; Lightfoot, *Hor. Heb.* p. 299.

† See Page, *Expositor*, 3rd ser. vol. vii. pp. 433–440; Plummer, art. LORD'S PRAYER in vol. iii.

‡ On this point see the older works of Möller, Augusti, Wetstein, Lightfoot, and Schöttgen; also, Achelis, *Bergpredigt*, p. 238 f.; B. Weiss, *Meyer-Komm. ü. d. Mattevgm.* p. 138; Plummer, art. LORD'S PRAYER in vol. iii.; Nestle, art. 'Lord's Prayer' in *Encycl. Bibl.* iii. 2821; Taylor, *Sayings of the Jewish Fathers*² (1900), pp. 124–130; Dalman, *Worte Jesu*, i. 299–306; v. d. Goltz, *Das Gebet in der ältesten Christenheit* (1901), pp. 40–42.

* See v. d. Goltz, *op. cit.* pp. 1–53; Burton, 'The Personal Religion of Jesus' in *Biblical World*, vol. xiv. (1899), pp. 394–403.

† Chase, *Lord's Prayer in the Early Church* (1901), p. 104 f., notes, but exaggerates, the relation of the Lord's Prayer to the personal experiences of Jesus.

numbers 3 and 7, for the purpose of moulding perfectly the literary form of the Prayer.* The first group of petitions pertains to God—'Thy name,' 'Thy kingdom,' 'Thy will.' They express the most profound and comprehensive aspiration of men, that God may be all in all. Only when this is the supreme desire, can one offer the three petitions of the second group, which pertain to the needs of the individual life—'our daily bread,' 'our debts,' 'deliverance from temptation.' The several clauses would have been, in the original Aramaic, shorter and more nearly uniform in length than appears in a Greek translation. One cannot be certain whether the 'as in heaven, so on earth,' which follows the third petition, pertains to that alone, or equally to all the three petitions of the group.†

The address of the Prayer (Πάτερ ἡμῶν ὁ ἐν τοῖς οὐρανοῖς) introduces the term 'Father,' which was Jesus' prevailing and characteristic designation for God. It signified God's supremacy, authority, and power, but at the same time His love, patience, and care for men. The OT also has the term, but in the national sense, denoting God's relation to His covenant people; later there grew up the individual consciousness, and God came to be thought of as a personal Father to the worshipper.‡ Jesus was accustomed to use this title for God in various ways: § often without any limiting attributive except the article, often also with a limiting 'my' or 'your'; but it is only in this passage, Mt $6^{9}$, that Jesus is reported to have used the attributive 'our.' One might therefore infer that this 'our' is an unauthentic liturgical addition; but this inference is neither necessary nor satisfactory. 'Our Father' is a significant address, indicating at once the ground and the motive of prayer to Him, as well as the brotherhood of men under a common Father; the 'our' contributes an important element, therefore, to the address, and the occasion of its use is great enough to call for a special expression. It may be that the phrase 'Our Father' was oftener upon Jesus' lips than our Gospel records now show; the widening gulf which the disciples fixed between their ascended Lord and themselves might tend to the disuse of phrases which indicated that 'it behoved him in all things to be made like unto his brethren' (He $2^{17}$). The second attributive to the Πάτερ in the clause of address, 'who art in heaven,' is a truly OT and Jewish phrase, which Jesus quite surely adopted and employed.* It expresses the transcendent position and character of God. In the pre-scientific age it was natural to assign God to a particular locality; the distant sky above the heads of men was logically chosen. But this local conception gradually retired before a growing sense of God's spiritual nature and omnipresence. With Jesus the phrase was a useful one (and we still find it so) to denote the separateness of God from men, His supermundane attributes, His absolute power and authority, His infinite character and qualities. Since the phrase meant these important things to the Jewish people of His day, and it was desirable that they should be in the mind of him who would pray to God, Jesus might well attach these words to His title of address in His model Prayer.†

The first petition (ἁγιασθήτω τὸ ὄνομά σου)‡ expresses the devout wish of the worshipper in view of what, according to the address of the Prayer, he conceives God to be, namely, that God may be fully recognized, honoured, and revered by all. The English word 'hallow' is no longer in common use; it meant to 'treat as holy,' to revere. Thus it was a proper translation of ἁγιάζειν (Lat. *sanctificare*), which, together with δοξάζειν, was employed in the LXX to render the Hebrew forms הִקְדִּישׁ and קִדֵּשׁ.§ Calvin, Kamphausen, and some others have understood that 'the name' in this petition was to be taken in the sense of the Third Commandment, which forbade the misuse of, and disrespect to, the title of God (so also Mt $5^{33-37}$). This interpretation is true as far as it goes, but it is too restricted for so comprehensive a prayer as this. Rather, 'the name' is to be understood here in the Oriental sense, as a periphrasis for the Person Himself, as though it were said, 'May God receive due reverence.' To the Hebrew 'the name' stood for what the individual was who bore the name. God's name designated Him as He had made Himself known to men.‖ Therefore the petition prays that God may be perfectly acknowledged by all men, so that all that He is and does may receive due honour, and that men may commit themselves to Him as their Father (cf. Ro $14^{11}$, Eph $3^{14-19}$).

The second petition (ἐλθάτω ἡ βασιλεία σου)¶ ex-

* It is not to be said that the artistic literary structure of the Prayer is unworthy of Jesus, and must therefore be attributed to the Evangelist. On the contrary, Jesus designedly presented much of His teaching in metre and rhythm (see above, ii. 1). His marvellous literary power was exercised not for art's sake, but to make art serve the highest well-being of men; for ideal thought cannot fulfil its whole mission until it is ideally expressed. On the logical relation of the petitions, see Plummer, art. LORD'S PRAYER in vol. iii.

† Tholuck, *Bergrede*[5], p. 350 [Eng. tr. p. 328], notes that there are three elements which make up the address clause of the Prayer, and three elements which make up the doxology that came to be used at its close.

‡ For the national sense cf. Dt $1^{31}$ $8^{5}$ $32^{6}$, Ps $68^{5}$ $89^{26}$ $103^{13}$, Is $1^{2}$ $9^{6}$ $63^{16}$ $64^{8}$, Jer $3^{4.19}$, Hos $11^{1}$, Mal $1^{6}$ $2^{10}$; for the individual sense, Wis $2^{16}$ $14^{3}$, Sir $23^{1.4}$, To $13^{4}$, 3 Mac $6^{3.8}$.

§ In the Gospel of Matthew the term 'Father' is frequent, and is generally accompanied by either 'my' or 'your' ('thy') in about equal proportion. The term occurs rarely in the Gospel of Mark. In the Gospel of Luke, also, there are relatively few instances of it. But the Fourth Gospel has it abundantly in the discourse sections, often with 'my,' but in the main only with the article, 'the Father.' A comparison of the occurrence of the term in parallel Synoptic passages raises the question as to how much confidence is to be placed upon the precise attributive reported in connexion with the title, or upon the occurrence of the title itself: thus in the group Mt $26^{39}$ = Mk $14^{36}$ = Lk $22^{42}$ we find 'O my Father,' 'Abba, Father' (the Aramaic word with its translation), and 'Father,' respectively; in Mt $5^{45}$ = Lk $6^{35}$, Mt $10^{29}$ = Lk $12^{6}$, Mt $10^{33}$ = Lk $12^{9}$, the First Gospel has 'Father,' while the Third Gospel has 'Most High' and 'God'; in Mt $12^{50}$ = Mk $3^{35}$ = Lk $8^{21}$ the First Gospel has 'my Father which is in heaven,' while the Second and Third Gospels have simply 'God'; in Mt $20^{23}$ = Mk $10^{40}$ the Second Gospel strikingly lacks the words 'of my Father.' It seems probable that Jesus constantly used the title 'Father,' as the First and Fourth Gospels record; but that it had been largely suppressed or altered in the sources of the Second and Third Gospels, again for the reason that it was a characteristically Jewish designation.

* This is shown by the frequent occurrence of the phrase in the First Gospel, *e.g.* Mt $5^{16.45.48}$ $6^{1.14.26.32}$ $7^{11.21}$ $10^{32.33}$ $12^{50}$ $15^{13}$ $16^{17}$ $18^{10.14.19.35}$ $23^{9}$; cf. also Mk $11^{25.26}$, Lk $11^{13}$; its almost total absence from the Second and Third Gospels is another feature of the universalization of this material. For Jewish usage see *'Abôth* v. 30; *Sôṭā* ix. 15; *Yômā* viii. 9; and Dalman, *Worte Jesu*, i. 150–159, 299–306. Wendt, *Lehre Jesu*, i. 62 f., can hardly be right in holding that this phrase is an addition in the Matthew passages, not to be attributed to Jesus.

† Whether the Prayer was originally given in Aramaic or Hebrew has been discussed, but without a certain conclusion. Chase is sure it was in Aramaic; see, further, Taylor, *Sayings of the Jewish Fathers*[2] (1897), p. 176 f.

‡ Compare the parallel clause in the Jewish synagogal prayer *Ḳaddish*: 'Magnificetur et sanctificetur nomen eius magnum in mundo' (Maimonides' translation); see Achelis, *Bergpredigt*, p. 238 f.

§ See Ex $20^{8}$, Lv $21^{8}$ $22^{32}$, Nu $20^{12}$, Dt $32^{51}$, Is $29^{23}$, Ezk $36^{23}$; and in the NT, 1 P $3^{15}$.

‖ See Ps $5^{11}$ $9^{10}$, Pr $18^{10}$. So the peculiar phrase (still in religious use) 'for his name's sake,' Ps $23^{3}$ $25^{11}$ $31^{3}$ $79^{9}$; cf. Achelis, *Bergpredigt*, pp. 240–243.

¶ Compare here, also, the *Ḳaddish* parallel: 'Regnare faciat regnum suum.' Marcion, in his Lukan form of the Lord's Prayer, read as the second petition, not what we have here, but δὸς ἡμῖν τὸ ἅγιον πνεῦμα, or another form of the same, ἐλθέτω τὸ ἅγιον πνεῦμά σου πρὸς ἡμᾶς. The same thought in a more expanded form was known, as a feature of Luke's text, to Gregory of Nyssa and Maximus the Confessor; thus: ἐλθέτω τὸ ἅγιον πνεῦμά σου ἐφ' ἡμᾶς καὶ καθαρισάτω ἡμᾶς (cf. Westcott and Hort, *New Testament in Greek*, vol. ii. Appx.; Nestle, in *Encycl. Bibl.* iii. 2818). This petition for the Holy Spirit cannot be authentic in this connexion, for it has small attestation, is not suitable to the context, and is obviously a drastic substitution to bring into the Prayer a specific request for the Holy

presses the wonderful Messianic Hope of the Hebrews; it was in substance the prayer which for centuries Israel had addressed to God.* Jesus bade them continue this prayer for the coming of the Kingdom of God, but taught them the true conception of what that Kingdom was, and how it was to be accomplished. The Kingdom of God was Jesus' constant and all-inclusive term to denote the individual and social good which would come to men when they would trust themselves to God's guidance and conform themselves to His ideal (Mt $6^{33}$ = Lk $12^{31}$). In Jesus' conception the coming of the Kingdom was a process, a development through successive stages with a final consummation (Mk $4^{26-32}$). He established the Kingdom among men (Lk $17^{20.21}$), His followers were to carry it forward (Mt $28^{19.20}$), and in due time He would bring about its complete realization (Mt 24. 25).† Our prayer, therefore, must be that God in His wisdom, power, and love may hasten the growth among men of righteousness, mercy, and peace; that the principles of the Gospel may prevail in individuals and in society as a whole, that humanity may become transformed into the likeness of Him who revealed to them the Divine ideal of God for His children.

The third petition (γενηθήτω τὸ θέλημά σου, ὡς ἐν οὐρανῷ καὶ ἐπὶ γῆς) was needed in the Prayer to guard the second petition against misinterpretation. It had become a prevalent misconception that the coming of God's Kingdom depended after all upon Himself, and that when He should choose to do so He could by His omnipotence bring that Kingdom into complete existence; so men had importuned God to become loving and forgiving towards them, and to grant to them the blessings which out of dissatisfaction or neglect He was withholding from them. Jesus makes that idea impossible when He gives this third petition, teaching that God's will must be absolutely done by all.‡ To do God's will, to accomplish His work, was the one purpose of Jesus' own life (Mt $26^{39.42}$, Jn $4^{34}$ $6^{38}$ $12^{27}$ $17^{4}$), and He enjoined it upon all as the one comprehensive human obligation (Mt $7^{21}$, Jn $7^{17}$). Men must therefore co-operate with God in the realization of the Kingdom by making themselves, with God's help, what they should be, and by bringing in the true brotherhood of universal love and service.

The fourth petition § pertains to the physical needs of men, upon which the spiritual life is dependent during this earthly stage of existence.* The conditions under which we live are created by God, He has full knowledge of them (Mt $6^{8.25-32}$), and He stands ready to supply what is necessary to human well-being (Mt $5^{45}$ $6^{33}$ $7^{11}$). This providential bestowal comes, of course, not as a pure gratuity, but as a return for the honest, energetic labour of men. The 'bread' which is asked for in this Prayer is meant in the wider sense as referring to all necessary food; and by implication it certainly includes all those things which are essential to physical welfare. The petition contemplates only a simple, frugal life, enjoining trustfulness and contentment therein. In other words, the idea of the Prayer is that men are to ask God confidently for what they need; but only for what they really need, and only as they need it. The disciples of Jesus are to live trustfully in the present and for the present, without anxious concern as to the future (Mt $6^{34}$). About this general interpretation of the fourth petition there can be no question. A difficulty exists, however, as to the precise force of ἐπιούσιον; since it is a *hapaxlegomenon*, we cannot determine its usage from other contexts; the Greek word most like it is περιούσιος, which appears first in the LXX. Recent scholars are largely in agreement that the word is derived somewhat irregularly from ἐπί + εἶναι in a fem. ptcp. form, signifying 'being unto,' 'pertaining to'; so that the prayer would be, 'Give us to-day the bread which pertains (to this day),' *i.e.* just so much as is needed for to-day to meet one's physical requirements (cf. Ja $2^{15.16}$).†

Spirit which Jesus had included only by implication. The prominence given to the Holy Spirit in the Apostolic age has left its impress upon the Lukan account of Jesus' words; cf. Mt $7^{11}$ = Lk $11^{13}$, Mt $11^{25}$ = Lk $10^{21}$, also Mt $10^{20}$ = Lk $12^{12}$.

* See art. MESSIAH in vol. iii.; *Encycl. Bibl.*, art. 'Messiah'; also Goodspeed, *Israel's Messianic Hope* (1900).

† See art. KINGDOM OF GOD in vol. ii.; also Wendt, *Lehre Jesu*, ii. 293–325. The verbal form ἐλθάτω does not favour the idea that the coming of the Kingdom is continuous; which part of the verb was used in the original Aramaic can only be matter of conjecture—one would suppose a jussive imperfect, and this would have presented no difficulty. At any rate, this petition must be interpreted in the light of Jesus' entire teaching concerning the Kingdom. The Greek aorist here may be due to the idea held by all Christians in the Apostolic age, that the return of Christ was imminent, and that with His return He would bring the catastrophic consummation; this passage would then be one of a number in the Gospels which received an eschatological colouring in transmission, on account of the failure of the disciples to take completely Jesus' view of the nature and coming of the Kingdom.

‡ The conception that God's will is already perfectly done in heaven, by the angelic host, is at the same time an assurance and a model for the full realization of His will on earth among men. The angels are frequently mentioned both in the OT (Ps $91^{11}$ $103^{20}$) and in the NT (Mt $18^{10}$ $24^{36}$ $26^{53}$, Mk $8^{38}$ $12^{25}$ $13^{27.32}$, Lk $12^{8.9}$ $15^{10}$ $16^{22}$, Jn $1^{51}$, He $1^{4-14}$ $12^{22.23}$); on the Jewish angelology see art. ANGEL in vol. i.; *Encycl. Bibl.*, art. 'Angel'; also Edersheim, *Life and Times of Jesus the Messiah*, vol. ii. Appx.; Wendt, *Lehre Jesu*, ii. pp. 121–126.

§ Mt $6^{11}$ τὸν ἄρτον ἡμῶν τὸν ἐπιούσιον δὸς ἡμῖν σήμερον; Lk $11^{3}$ τὸν ἄρτον ἡμῶν τὸν ἐπιούσιον δίδου ἡμῖν τὸ καθ' ἡμέραν. It is striking that the strange word ἐπιούσιον, which is found nowhere in all Greek literature outside of this passage (so Origen, *de Orat.* 27), should appear in both of these widely divergent accounts of the Lord's Prayer. The fact can be explained only by the hypothesis that these two Greek forms of the Prayer must have had a literary relation to one another in some stage of their transmission.

* Taylor, *Sayings of the Jewish Fathers*², p. 125, thinks that this petition contains an allusion to the giving of the manna, Ex $16^{4}$; cf. Ps $78^{24f.}$, Wis $16^{27f.}$, Jn $6^{32}$.

† So Achelis, *Bergpredigt*, pp. 265–271; H. Holtzmann, *Hand-Comm. ü. d. Synoptiker*, p. 116; Kamphausen, *Das Gebet des Herrn*, p. 97 ff.; Leo Meyer in Kuhn's *Zeitschr. f. vergleich. Sprachforschung*, vii. 401 ff. (though he afterwards withdrew this opinion, in *Nachrichten d. kgl. Gesellschaft der Wissenschaften zu Göttingen*, 1886, p. 245 ff.); Tholuck, *Bergrede*⁵, pp. 375–385 [Eng. tr. 341–353]; B. Weiss, *Meyer-Komm. ü. d. Mattevgm.* p. 135 f.; Wendt, *Lehre Jesu*, ii. 239 f.; Taylor, *op. cit.* pp. 125–127, 178–186, 190 f.; as also Ewald, Nösgen, Bassett, and many others. A list of the older literature upon the subject may be seen in Tholuck, *loc. cit.* Other interpretations of the passage are: (1) that the derivation of ἐπιούσιον is from ἐπί + the noun οὐσία, which in philosophical usage signified 'subsistence,' 'existence'; therefore the petition would read, 'Give us to-day our bread for subsistence,' *i.e.* that bread which serves to maintain our physical existence. So Cremer, *Bibl.-Theol. Wörterbuch*⁷, *in loc.*; also Origen, Chrysostom, Theophylact, Maldonatus, Bleek, Keil, Kuinöl, Kübel. This conception, however, seems forced, and too technically philosophical; nor is there any certain parallel instance of such a usage of οὐσία. It differs from the view adopted above in stating the end of the giving instead of the measure, for what purpose the bread is asked rather than the quantity of bread asked for. (2) That the derivation of ἐπιούσιον is from ἐπί + ἰέναι, and that with it is understood in sense a ἡμέρα (cf. Ac $16^{11}$ ἐπιούσῃ, $23^{11}$, Pr $27^{1}$ LXX); it then means 'the coming day,' and the petition says, 'Give us to-day our bread for to-morrow.' So Lightfoot, *Fresh Revision of English N.T.*³ (1891), Appx. I.; Schmiedel in Winer's *Grammatik d. NTlichen Sprachidioms*⁸ (1894), pp. 136–138; also Grotius, Wetstein, Bengel, Fritzsche, Winer, Gore, Bruce, Meyer, Marshall, O. Holtzmann, and RVm. The difficulty with this temporal interpretation of ἐπιούσιον is that it contradicts the very idea of the petition as intended by Jesus: instead of having men pray for to-morrow's food, He would have them pray for to-day and trust for to-morrow. No other meaning can be derived from the passage Mt $6^{25-34}$, ending with the words, 'Be not therefore anxious for the morrow; for the morrow will be anxious for itself. Sufficient unto the day is the evil thereof.' This temporal interpretation also throws an incongruous meaning into the Lukan form of the prayer, 'Give us every day the bread for the next day'; that would be a mechanical kind of Providence. (3) That the 'bread' for which this petition asks is to be understood spiritually, at least in its primary reference. This was the favourite interpretation among the Fathers of the early Christian centuries; it arose easily from the figurative use of 'bread' in Jn $6^{48-58}$, and was suitable to the allegorical mode of the time. Augustine held the 'bread' to refer to three things, in an ascending scale of significance: (*a*) physically, actual food; (*b*) intellectually, the word of Christ; (*c*) spiritually, the Lord's Supper. For the

As περιούσιος means 'beyond what is necessary,' so ἐπιούσιον means 'exactly what is necessary.' This is the conception of supply which we find in Pr 30$^{8}$ 'Feed me with the food that is needful for me.' There are similar Targumic and Talmudic expressions. The wording of the petition as given by Matthew is a specific request for a single occasion, understanding that the Prayer will be repeated as frequently as need arises, presumably each day;* while Luke's wording presents a general request for a constant supply: it would seem clear that the Matthæan form is of greater authenticity.

The fifth petition† concerns the present religious status of the man in relation to God. The worshipper is to measure himself against the Divine ideal of the highest, fullest self-development, and of complete love and service to God and one's fellow-men. He is to observe how far he has failed to meet the obligations placed upon him by God, and why he has failed to meet them. When a man has made this inventory of his physical, moral, and spiritual status, with a sincere repentance for all his transgressions and shortcomings, and with a supreme purpose to achieve the Divine ideal for men, he is ready to ask God's forgiveness in the words of this petition. Holding that God's will is the only law of life, and that His Kingdom is the only end of life, the worshipper needs God's forgiveness for his spiritual comfort and inspiration, in order that he may start anew each day towards the achievement of the ideal. It is in this fundamental and comprehensive sense that the term ὀφειλήματα is figuratively employed in this petition, including everything that we should be and do towards God, our fellow-men, and ourselves.* The second clause contains an explicit condition of this Prayer, that men must feel and exercise the same spirit of forgiveness towards one another which they wish God to show towards themselves. Jesus places these words in the petition, in order that men may be face to face with this condition whenever they pray to God for their own forgiveness. This principle of love as the basis of all human and Divine relations is a constant teaching of Jesus, and furnishes the key to the Sermon on the Mount, cf. esp. Mt 5$^{7. 23f. 43-48}$; it is also most impressively set forth in the teaching and parable of Mt 18$^{21-35}$. In the Lord's Prayer as recorded by Matthew this idea is further strengthened by the two added verses, 6$^{14. 15}$, with which Mk 11$^{25}$ may be compared.† It is not to be understood that the ὡς καί which introduces Matthew's second clause signifies a *quid pro quo* kind of forgiveness on God's part, as though God forgave men only in a measure proportionate to their own forgiveness. The words might have this force (as in Mt 20$^{14}$, Rev 18$^{6}$), but it is not the only meaning for them (cf. Mt 18$^{33}$). Such a commercial idea is inconsistent with the method of God as abundantly shown in Jesus' teaching. God is in amount more loving and forgiving than men can be, but He requires that men also shall be loving and forgiving.‡

The sixth petition,§ which closes the Lord's Prayer, provides for the moral and spiritual welfare of the individual in the future. As the fifth petition sought forgiveness for past failures to do God's will, so the sixth petition seeks His protection from future failures. The worshipper, conscious of his own weakness, puts his dependence upon God. He prays for deliverance from those situations in life where he will be liable to yield

spiritual meaning also stood Tertullian, Cyprian, Cyril of Jerusalem, Athanasius, Ambrose, and Jerome; and in modern times Delitzsch, Olshausen, Stier, M'Clellan. (4) That the ἐπιούσιον has a temporal signification referring merely to the day of the prayer. So the RV, 'Give us this day our daily bread,' and this is the wording in common use in Christendom to-day, made so by the popular translations of the Bible. It is redundant in expression, and its only merit is simplicity; for it lacks the profound meaning which inheres in the ἐπιούσιον as interpreted in the text above. Lately this view has been again defended by Nestle (*ZNTW*, 1900, pp. 250-252; *Encycl. Bibl.* iii. 2819 f.) on the basis of the reading אֲמִינָא (=continual), which is found in Syr cur at Mt 6$^{11}$ and Lk 11$^{3}$, and in Syr sin at Lk 11$^{3}$, the Matthæan section being wanting; also in the Syriac *Acts of Thomas* (ed. Wright, p. 313). This אמין is said to be the regular Syriac word for the translation of the Heb. תָּמִיד; and Nestle has learned that a Jewish translation of the First Gospel into Hebrew, made in the 16th cent., rendered the ἐπιούσιον by תָּמִיד. He supposes, therefore, that the Greek ἐπιούσιον in the Lord's Prayer represents an original לֶחֶם הַתָּמִיד, and says that the translation 'our daily bread' is the best English translation of the Greek text. The difficulty with this interpretation is twofold: (*a*) it gives a purely tautological rendering, which is unlikely to have been original; (*b*) it altogether fails to account for the presence in the Greek text of this strange word ἐπιούσιον, which seems to have been created to express an intricate thought for which no current Greek word was suitable; but if the thought was so simple as 'continual' or 'daily,' there were several common expressions at hand to use (*e.g.* the τὸ καθ' ἡμέραν of Lk 11$^{3}$ 19$^{47}$), and the LXX had already employed such (cf. Ex 5$^{13}$ 16$^{5}$, Nu 4$^{16}$, Ps 67$^{20}$, Dn 1$^{5}$, 1 Mac 6$^{57}$ 8$^{15}$); while the early Syriac reading may well be nothing more than a simplification of a difficult expression whose exact meaning had not been clearly conveyed by the ἐπιούσιον, and which in the circle of the translator was no longer understood. Chase, *Lord's Prayer in the Early Church* (1891), pp. 44–53, holds that the original form of the petition was, 'Give us our (or, the) bread of the day,' and suggests that the newly coined word ἐπιούσιον was later interpolated to meet liturgical exigencies in connexion with the use of the Lord's Prayer in the evening. With this reading the Prayer could be used in the morning, and would ask bread for that same day; or it could be used at night, and would ask bread for the morrow; however, the σήμερον so replaced did not in fact disappear, but remained in the text as a confusing redundancy. Chase's view is accepted by v. d. Goltz, *Das Gebet in der ältesten Christenheit* (1901), p. 49 f.

* B. Weiss, *op. cit.* p. 136, holds that the σήμερον in the Matthew form of the petition is a subsequent addition, bearing witness to the fact that the Prayer was assigned to daily use in the early Christian liturgy. That the Prayer was used daily, or oftener, in the earlier part of the 2nd cent., is established by the *Teaching of the Twelve Apostles* (viii. 3), and other witnesses; but it does not follow that the σήμερον of Mt 6$^{11}$ is merely a product of that practice. There is no inherent reason why Jesus should not Himself have given the corresponding Aramaic word in this connexion. The Prayer was given to the disciples for regular use, because they wished some set form of prayer to recite in the common liturgical manner of the Jews (cf. Lk 11$^{1}$). The 'day' was a natural and convenient period of time (cf. Mt 6$^{34}$) for the repetition of the Prayer. Why should not Jesus have arranged the wording on that basis?

† Mt 6$^{12}$ καὶ ἄφες ἡμῖν τὰ ὀφειλήματα ἡμῶν, ὡς καὶ ἡμεῖς ἀφήκαμεν τοῖς ὀφειλέταις ἡμῶν. Lk 11$^{4a}$ καὶ ἄφες ἡμῖν τὰς ἁμαρτίας ἡμῶν, καὶ γὰρ αὐτοὶ ἀφίομεν παντὶ ὀφείλοντι ἡμῖν.

* In classical Greek, ὀφειλήματα was used generally of financial debts, and it was probably to avoid this ambiguity that Lk 11$^{4}$ reads ἁμαρτίας instead (originally Luke's account must have had ὀφειλήματα like Matthew's, as is seen by the ὀφείλοντι in the second clause; so Chase, *Lord's Prayer in the Early Church* (1891), p. 55, and Page, *Expositor*, 3rd ser. vol. vii. p. 437). But ὀφείλημα (and its kindred forms) is a frequent NT word for moral and spiritual obligation (Lk 17$^{10}$, Jn 13$^{14}$, Ro 15$^{1. 27}$, Gal 5$^{3}$), although used also in the money sense (Mt 18$^{28}$, Lk 7$^{41}$ 16$^{5}$, Ph $^{18}$). Luke's ἁμαρτίας lacks the Aramaic colour, the strength and the comprehensiveness of the ὀφειλήματα. In the EV also the word 'debts' gives a deeper meaning when rightly understood than the word 'sins,' since the latter term tends in popular usage to signify only positive, flagrant wickedness. And still less satisfactory is the word 'trespasses,' given currency in this petition by the Episcopal Prayer-Book (apparently from Tindale [? by reading 'trespasses' from v.$^{14f.}$ into v.$^{12}$]); for it is not a proper translation of either ὀφειλήματα or ἁμαρτίας, and is the most limited in its scope of the three English words.

† Mt 6$^{14. 15}$ has apparently found its way into the Sermon through its previous connexion with the Lord's Prayer. Whether it had its place historically in that connexion is uncertain. Mk 11$^{25}$ has a different setting for the passage, but one due to topical association rather than to original position. There is nothing unlikely in the hypothesis that Jesus, after giving the Prayer, spoke in explanation of it, and that this fragment was a part thereof. In these two verses, as in Mk 11$^{25}$, παραπτώματα is used instead of ὀφειλήματα or ἁμαρτίας.

‡ Luke's variant, καὶ γάρ, is distinctly intended to remove the possible misinterpretation that God forgives a man just to the extent that the man forgives others. But the Matthæan wording gives evidence of being a closer translation from the Aramaic. Another instance of Lukan modification is his ἀφίομεν in this clause instead of Matthew's ἀφήκαμεν, to give the petition a general character instead of the specific import of the original Prayer. It was noted that in the fourth petition changes were made for the same purpose, Luke having δίδου instead of δός, and τὸ καθ' ἡμέραν instead of σήμερον.

§ Mt 6$^{13}$ καὶ μὴ εἰσενέγκῃς ἡμᾶς εἰς πειρασμόν, ἀλλὰ ῥῦσαι ἡμᾶς ἀπὸ τοῦ πονηροῦ. Lk 11$^{4b}$ καὶ μὴ εἰσενέγκῃς ἡμᾶς εἰς πειρασμόν. The first clause is the same in both accounts, while the second clause does not appear in Luke (see above).

to wrong or false influences. But inasmuch as men must undergo trials, and in them work out their own character and service, Jesus gives to this petition a second clause, which provides against necessary trials by asking for strength to come through them safely. We may then paraphrase the sixth petition of the Prayer in this way: 'Spare us as much as possible from all trials in which there is danger that we shall fail to do Thy will; but, so far as we must meet trials, give us the strength necessary to withstand the temptations to evil which are involved in them.'* It thus becomes clear that the second clause of the petition, 'but deliver us from evil,' is not a separate, seventh petition, but an essential element in the sixth, pertaining to those trials from which God cannot and should not deliver us. In them we pray Him to preserve us from falling. The 'evil' which is meant is, of course, moral and spiritual transgression or failure of doing God's will; and the context therefore makes it improbable that the τοῦ πονηροῦ should have been intended to refer concretely to the devil in person.† The term πειρασμός is used with a wide range in the NT, having both a neutral meaning (=trial) and a bad meaning (=malicious temptation).‡ Only in the former, neutral sense can God be spoken of as 'tempting' men, *i.e.* bringing them into situations which test their character and thus promote their growth. Such trials involve a possible lapse into evil, and must cause anxiety and apprehension; so that men may well fear them and pray for deliverance from them. Jesus said to His disciples, 'Watch and pray, that ye enter not into temptation: the spirit indeed is willing, but the flesh is weak' (Mk $14^{38}$, cf. Ja $1^{13f.}$). But, since God brings these trials for the individual's good, He will never allow the tried person to fall into evil if he will commit himself wholly to God's guidance and care through the experience (cf. 1 Co $10^{13}$, He $2^{18}$ $4^{15f.}$, Ja $1^{2-4.\ 12f.}$, 1 P $1^{6f.}$).

(5) The Lord's Prayer is thus seen to be an epitome of Jesus' teaching; it contains the essential ideas of God and human duty, expressed in the briefest, simplest, and most impressive words. The vital truths of the Gospel are presented in such a way that any and every man can grasp them, and can see them in their right perspective and relations.* Since the Prayer was intended for universal use, its meaning must be readily intelligible to all; it must be not intricate, but simple of interpretation. And the Lord's Prayer is adapted to every kind of Christian use. It is designed for repetition as it stands, both in private and in public devotions. It is also a pattern prayer, after which all prayer to God should be modelled. Here we learn what things are to be prayed for, how God's glory, Kingdom, and will take precedence of the individual's affairs, and in what spirit all prayer is to be made. The religious practice of Jesus' day too often regarded the virtue of a prayer as consisting in its recital, and measured its value by its length or repetition (cf. Ac $19^{34}$). The Gospel of Matthew ($6^{7f.}$) has preserved in connexion with the Lord's Prayer some words of Jesus which were directed against this abuse. Since God knows what things are necessary for men, He does not need to be informed of them; and since He is a loving Father who cares for His children, He does not have to be importuned to give His blessings. These facts do not make prayer useless; on the contrary, real prayer is possible only on the basis of them. God never wished the empty repetition of prayer formulæ, which is a waste of time and strength; and it was an entire misconception of Him that He had to be coaxed into goodwill towards men, or solicited to supply their needs. Prayer, in Jesus' conception, is the loving, obedient and trustful communion of men with their Heavenly Father. It brings men comfort, joy, and peace; it reassures and strengthens them in all their labours and experiences; it brings them to know only God's will in their lives, and to seek only its full realization. As we learn to know God in the words and face of Christ, we pray more instead of less; prayer becomes a privilege instead of a duty. Indeed, to the true Christian, prayer is the atmosphere in which he lives. Instead of occasional periods or moments of prayer, the whole life becomes a prayer, so that we walk and talk with God. Into this perfect communion with God the Lord's Prayer leads us, voicing all our aspirations and petitions, when we come to appreciate its full significance.†

* Jesus' Gethsemane experience illuminates the words of this petition (cf. Mt $26^{36-46}$, esp. v.$^{39}$). The Saviour is here face to face with the bitterest trial of His life; the attitude of the Jewish nation towards Him has come to be that of fixed and final rejection; the chosen people are ready to repudiate their Messiah with a violent death, and so to fail of fulfilling their Divine mission to the world (cf. Mt $23^{37.\ 38}$). Jesus in the garden feels that He cannot endure this; He is in agony that God should seem to allow it, and prays that He may be spared this trial—that there may be some other outcome of the situation; nevertheless, He has no other desire than that God's will should be done. The prayer of Jesus was answered not by a removal of the trial, but by a Divine reassurance, and an impartation of strength for its endurance (cf. Lk $22^{43f.}$, which gives an essentially correct idea, even if textually uncertain). One may also compare St. Paul's experience when he three times prayed for the removal of his 'thorn in the flesh'; God's reply to him was, 'My grace is sufficient for thee; for power is made perfect in weakness' (2 Co $12^{8.\ 9}$; cf. also 1 Co $10^{12}$).

† The objection to taking the τοῦ πονηροῦ as a masculine (with Tertullian, Cyprian, Origen, Chrysostom, Theophylact, Calvin, Erasmus, Bengel, Meyer, Olshausen, Ebrard, Fritzsche, Hanne, Gore, H. Holtzmann, Lightfoot, Thayer, Plummer, Chase, v. d. Goltz, Nestle, and the RV) does not lie in the fact that the phrase could not be so used, for there are a number of clear NT cases where ὁ πονηρός refers concretely to the devil (cf. Mt $13^{19.\ 38}$, Eph $6^{16}$, 1 Jn $2^{13f.}$ $3^{12}$ $5^{18}$); nor in the meaning of the collocation ῥύεσθαι ἀπό τινος, which is used of both persons (Ro $15^{31}$) and things (2 Ti $4^{18}$); nor in an avoidance by Jesus of the current Jewish conception and terminology regarding the personal devil (cf Mt $4^{10}$ $12^{27}$ $13^{38f.}$, Lk $10^{18}$, Jn $8^{44}$), for, so far as we can discover, He did not give any new teaching on this point (cf. Wendt, *Lehre Jesu*, ii. 121–126). The objection lies rather in the thought of the petition itself, which cannot be, 'Bring us not into trial, but deliver us from the devil,' since this destroys all connexion between the two clauses, though the ἀλλά demands a connexion; nor, 'Bring us not into the temptation of the devil, but deliver us from the devil,' which is improbable tautology. So that some ancient and many modern scholars interpret the τοῦ πονηροῦ as a neuter (Augustine, Luther, Stier, Ewald, Keil, Nösgen, Tholuck, Alford, Burgon, Cook, M'Clellan, Achelis, Ibbeken, B. Weiss, Taylor, and others). This neuter use of τὸ πονηρόν to denote all moral and spiritual evil may be seen in Mt $5^{37}$, Lk $6^{45}$, Jn $17^{15}$, Ro $12^{9}$, 2 Th $3^{3}$, 1 Jn $5^{19}$ (the RV is probably wrong in translating most of these as masculines); cf. also 2 Ti $4^{18}$. On πονηρός -όν see Cremer, *Bibl.-Theol. Wörterbuch*⁷, *in loc.*; Achelis, *Bergpredigt*, pp. 286–289; letters in the *Guardian* by Lightfoot (Sept. 7, 14, 21) and Cook (May 21, Nov. 26) (Lightfoot's letters appear in *Fresh Revision of the English N.T.*$^{3}$, 1891, Appx. II.); Chase, *Lord's Prayer in the Early Church* (1891), pp. 85–167; Hatch, *Essays in Biblical Greek* (1889), pp. 77–82. Taylor, *Sayings of the Jewish Fathers*$^{2}$ (1897), pp. 37, 64, 128–130, 147–150, 191 f., takes the τοῦ πονηροῦ as referring to the יֵצֶר הָרָע, man's evil nature (Gn $8^{21}$ 'the imagination of man's heart is evil from his youth,' cf. Ja $1^{13-15}$); see also Porter, 'The Yeçer Ha-ra',' in *Yale Biblical and Semitic Studies* (1901), pp. 93–156.

‡ On the NT usage of πειρασμός, see Cremer, *Bibl.-Theol. Wörterbuch*$^{7}$, *in loc.*; Tholuck, *Bergrede*$^{5}$, pp. 394-401 [Eng. tr. pp. 357–362]; Achelis, *Bergpredigt*, pp. 280–284; Mayor, *Comm. on James*, 1892, pp. 175–183.

* Similarly Harnack, *Das Wesen des Christentums*, 1901, p. 42 [Eng. tr. p. 65]: 'There is nothing in the Gospels that tells us more certainly what the Gospel is, and what sort of disposition and temper it produces, than the Lord's Prayer. With this Prayer we ought also to confront all those who disparage the Gospel as an ascetic or ecstatic or sociological pronouncement. It shows the Gospel to be the Fatherhood of God applied to the whole of life; to be an inner union with God's will and God's Kingdom, and a joyous certainty of the possession of eternal blessings and protection from evil.'

† Further, on the Lord's Prayer, see Kamphausen, *Das Gebet des Herrn* (1866); Chase, *The Lord's Prayer in the Early Church* (1891); Tholuck, *Bergrede*$^{5}$, pp. 346–408 [Eng. tr. pp. 315–369]; Achelis, *Bergpredigt*, pp. 225–305; J. Hanne, *Jahrb. f. deutsche Theol.* 1866; Haffner, *Das Gebet des Herrn* (1880); G. Hoffmann, *De Oratione Domini* (1884); Rieger, *Das Gebet des Herrn* (1901); Wendt, *Lehre Jesu*, ii. 238–245; Plummer,

*i. Devotion to the Kingdom.*—Mt $6^{19-34}$ (cf. Lk $12^{33.34}$ $11^{34-36}$ $16^{13}$ $12^{22-31}$). Nearly all of those scholars who regard the Sermon in the First Gospel as a composite production in whole or in part, look upon this section as extraneous to the original discourse, being brought in here from some other historical connexion.* Two arguments against its present position are offered: (*a*) the subject-matter of the section is thought by many to be remote from the theme of Mt $5^{17}$–$6^{18}$; and (*b*) this material is found scattered in the Gospel of Luke, none of it appearing in his parallel discourse ($6^{20-49}$). To the first argument it may be replied (see above, ii. 3) that the theme of the Sermon does not lie in Mt $5^{17-20}$, but is more general, pertaining to the true nature and duty of righteousness. So that Mt $5^{17}$–$6^{18}$, while containing the longest section of the reported discourse, is by no means to be regarded as the only original matter in Matthew's account. There is an abrupt transition, to be sure, between Mt $6^{18}$ and $6^{19}$; but this abruptness may be due to the fact that we have only extracts or a digest of the historical Sermon. Moreover, the teaching contained in Mt $6^{19-34}$ would seem to be germane—indeed essential—to a setting forth of the true righteousness; the ideal life must be free from material aims, divided efforts, and distracting anxieties. The second argument presents a greater difficulty, for Luke's arrangement of this material in other connexions must be explained. Concerning this it may be said that the Lukan Sermon had received severe treatment in transmission, as already frequently noted; perhaps the exclusion of this section was a part of that process. Also, that the position assigned to this material in the Third Gospel is surely not historical; it appears in the so-called 'Peræan section,' but such teaching as this belonged in all probability to the Galilæan ministry. Further, the Lukan settings of these verses show either no contextual relations, or only literary ones; they are not associated with specific, distinct events. Therefore, while the question must be counted an open one whether Mt $6^{19-34}$ belonged to the historical Sermon, good reasons are at hand for treating the section as original in this connexion.

The passage has a real unity of thought, to the effect that there is but one aim in life. This aim is the complete realization of the Kingdom of God, in which every man attains that character and performs that service which God requires. The idea thus finds its general statement in Mt $6^{33}$ 'Seek ye first his kingdom, and his righteousness; and all these things shall be added unto you.'† As Jesus had been teaching in Mt $5^{21-48}$ how the Divine ideal for men was to be worked out in the sphere of individual and social ethics, and in Mt $6^{1-18}$ in the sphere of religious worship, so in Mt $6^{19-34}$ He sets forth how this ideal demands an exclusive devotion to spiritual things—not that material things are to be ignored, but they are to be used only that they may contribute to the highest well-being of humanity. This teaching is developed in three paragraphs of the section vv.$^{19-21}$ vv.$^{22-24}$ vv.$^{25-34}$,* presenting three distinct phases of the subject of duty as regards earthly things: the one comprehensive aim of life must be spiritual, there must be no division of interests, and there must be no anxiety about the incidental things.

According to the teaching of vv.$^{19-21}$,† a man is not to devote himself to an accumulation of wealth for its own sake, or for selfish use. His time is not to be occupied with transient labours, social trivialities, vain displays, and empty talk. 'To lay up treasure in heaven' is to be and to do those things which are pleasing to God, to live nobly, purely, and helpfully. Jesus condemned in the strongest language the kind of life which seeks, first of all, for the gratification of greed and selfish ambition. When a certain man asked Jesus to assist him in securing some property, he rebuked him, and said to His hearers, 'Take heed, and keep yourselves from all covetousness; for a man's life consisteth not in the abundance of the things which he possesseth.' And He gave the significant parable of the Rich Fool, who must leave all his wealth at his death, adding, 'So is he that layeth up treasure for himself, and is not rich toward God' (Lk $12^{13-21}$). To make material things the chief end of life is to reverse the true relation of body and spirit. Immortal spirit is the permanent, ultimate thing for which our lives are to be lived. The possession or the accumulation of wealth is not forbidden by Jesus (see above, ii. 4*a*), but He insists that wealth is a means, never an end; and that wealth must be conscientiously used for the highest good, or it becomes a curse to its owner (cf. Mk $10^{17-22}$, Lk $16^{1-9}$).‡ The right Christian attitude is not a despising of riches, but a true valuation and employment of them for human well-being. The ascetic life, the frivolous life, the indolent life, are

art. LORD'S PRAYER in vol. iii.; Nestle, art. 'Lord's Prayer' in *Encyclopædia Biblica*, vol. iii.; v. d. Goltz, *Das Gebet in der ältesten Christenheit* (1901), pp. 35–53; Maurice, *Sermons on the Lord's Prayer* (1870); Boardman, *Studies in the Model Prayer* (1879); Newman Hall, *The Lord's Prayer*² (1889). Also, the Patristic treatment of the Prayer by Tertullian (*de Oratione*), Cyprian (*de Oratione Dominica*), and Origen (περὶ Εὐχῆς).

* So Feine, Godet, H. Holtzmann, B. Weiss, Wendt, Heinrici, Bacon, and others. Its Matthæan position is defended by Tholuck, Meyer, Keil, Morison, Broadus, Steinmeyer, H. Weiss, Nösgen, Grawert. Achelis regards the section as original here, with the exception of vv.$^{20.21.24}$; and other partition theories are offered.

† Mt $6^{33}$ ζητεῖτε δὲ πρῶτον τὴν βασιλείαν καὶ τὴν δικαιοσύνην αὐτοῦ, καὶ ταῦτα πάντα προστεθήσεται ὑμῖν. Lk $12^{31}$ πλὴν ζητεῖτε τὴν βασιλείαν αὐτοῦ, καὶ ταῦτα προστεθήσεται ὑμῖν. There is much textual variation as respects the wording of the Matthæan verse. It is difficult to determine the precise original form of this saying of Jesus. Bruce thinks it was simply 'Seek ye his kingdom,' all else in the present Greek forms being expansion for purposes of interpretation; but it seems probable that the second clause was also given, as bringing the saying more closely into relation with its context. The πλήν which introduces the Lukan form is an idiosyncrasy of the Third Gospel (cf. Lk $6^{24.35}$ *et al.*). Matthew's πάντα, in the second clause, is likely to have been an expansion. The πρῶτον of Matthew may belong to the original saying. On this supposition it cannot be understood to mean that there are two things to be sought for, one before the other; it is to be interpreted, not numerically, but qualitatively—there is just one thing to live for, the Kingdom; and the necessaries of physical existence should be trusted to God's providence. The πρῶτον has then disappeared from the Lukan form, perhaps because of its ambiguity and consequent danger of being misunderstood. Whether the historical saying had 'the kingdom,' or 'his kingdom,' or 'the kingdom of God,' all of which are attested, can only be matter of conjecture, and is unimportant. Lastly, Luke does not have the τὴν δικαιοσύνην which is given in this saying by Matthew (whose αὐτοῦ probably limits also the βασιλείαν as in RV). Perhaps it was dropped from the Lukan sources because it was a technical Jewish term; it has been noted above that δικαιοσύνη does not appear in Luke's Sermon, and in his Gospel only at $1^{75}$. Or, its presence in Mt $6^{33}$ may be due to an expansion of the original saying, making a closer verbal connexion of the verse with the Sermon in Matthew (cf. $5^{6.10.20}$ $6^{1}$). This would be a probable explanation of its presence on the theory that Mt $6^{19-34}$ has been imported into the Sermon in the course of transmission. But the τὴν δικαιοσύνην may also be original in this saying. If so, the 'righteousness' referred to is that actual perfect character and conduct on the part of men with which this whole discourse is concerned (so Tholuck, Achelis, B. Weiss); not a righteousness which God imparts to the believer (Meyer, Ibbeken), nor the righteousness of faith according to the Pauline forensic sense. It is thus the righteousness which God requires, that complete conformity to His will which brings in the consummated Kingdom of God.

* Feine thinks that vv.$^{22-24}$ are interpolated into this passage from another connexion; Achelis thinks the same of vv.$^{20.21.24}$, and B. Weiss of v.$^{22f.}$. These are possible views, but there is not much to substantiate them. Matthew's setting for these verses is as good as Luke's, or even better.

† Lk $12^{33f.}$ has the same thought, but the wording is characteristically different—the 'Sell that ye have and give alms' is a feature of the Third Gospel's exaltation of poverty, as in the Beatitudes and Woes ($6^{20-26}$). It is striking that the two accounts are in almost exact agreement on the essential utterance, 'Where your treasure is, there will your heart be also.' So Paul in Col $3^{2}$.

‡ See Wendt, *Lehre Jesu*, ii. 163-168.

all alike wrong; no less wrong than the life of worldly pride and ambition. Poverty is not righteousness, nor is it even meritorious; men must be provident and self-supporting. The accumulation of material goods, when not carried on by dishonesty, oppression, or disregard of others' needs and rights, may minister to the highest welfare of one's fellow-men.

Still more specifically does Jesus say, in vv.$^{22-24}$,* that the Kingdom must be an exclusive aim. Using the physical eye, which illuminates the body, as a figure (cf. Ps 119$^{18}$, Mk 8$^{18}$, Lk 24$^{31}$), He says that the spiritual discernment must be kept clear in order that one may not go astray from the path of highest duty. A divided aim, which endeavours to combine spiritual and material interests, is impossible; one cannot strive for spiritual goods part of the time, and for earthly goods the other part. Special moments of lofty aspiration, of unselfishness, of generosity, come to almost every one; but in Jesus' thought these things will become habitual and supreme in the true Christian. Everything must be made subordinate and contributory to the attainment of righteousness and the realization of the Kingdom.

But what of our material needs—food, clothing, and shelter, means and opportunities for mental and spiritual growth? Must not life be largely a struggle for these earthly, transient things? To this fundamental problem of human existence Jesus gives an explicit answer in vv.$^{25-34}$.† It is that God knows these needs of men, and wills to provide for them (v.$^{32f.}$): men should depend upon and trust Him for those things necessary to life. If the Heavenly Father cares for the birds and the flowers, He will certainly care for His higher human creatures. Men, therefore, must not be anxious about these things; they must live trustingly for to-day, leaving to-morrow to God (v.$^{34}$). And so in the Lord's Prayer He taught them to pray, 'Give us this day the bread suited to our need.' Here again Jesus is setting forth a principle of life, not laying down a precept to be literally applied. No one could suppose Him to advocate a purely hand-to-mouth existence, like that of the animals; the higher well-being of the individual or the race could not be accomplished by such a manner of living. Common-sense supplies the interpretation that Jesus contemplates labour, prudence, and forethought for necessary material things; in general God provides, not the things themselves without effort on men's part, but the way by which with effort men can secure what they need. And it is no life of ease and luxury to which God calls us, but a working, frugal life. What Jesus wishes is that in it we should be free from the distraction and anxiety which come to those who will not put themselves wholly into God's hands and trust Him for everything. Each day as it comes is to be dealt with in the present, leaving the future with God: if we do our best to-day, God will take care of to-morrow (cf. Ro 8$^{28}$). Why should it not be so? God has a great purpose in the world, which men are to help Him to accomplish; assuredly, He will care for and assist those who accept their task and sincerely strive to perform it.

*j. The Treatment of Others.*—Mt. 7$^{1-12}$=Lk 6$^{31.37-42}$ (cf. Lk 11$^{9-13}$). The main idea of this passage lies in vv.$^{1-5.12}$ (vv.$^{6.7-11}$ belonged originally to other connexions), and pertains to the right attitude and conduct towards our fellow-men. The verses, therefore, form a fourth section in Jesus' exposition of the true righteousness, co-ordinate with sections 5$^{21-48}$ 6$^{1-18}$ 6$^{19-34}$. Their teaching is twofold: men are not to be of a censorious disposition towards one another (vv.$^{1-5}$), and they are to show the same respect, kindness, and helpfulness to others which they themselves would like to receive (v.$^{12}$). The two teachings contained in vv.$^{6.7-11}$ are also of interest and importance, but they interrupt the sequence of thought in the Sermon. It is the view of many scholars that the 'Golden Rule' in v.$^{12}$ follows logically upon vv.$^{1-5}$, and not only finishes this section, but in a way forms a closing utterance for the body of the discourse from 5$^{21}$ onward, 7$^{13-27}$ being in the nature of a hortatory conclusion.*

Mt 7$^{1-5}$ finds its parallel in Lk 6$^{37-42}$, the two accounts showing the usual amount of similarity and variation.† While the Lukan context gives a somewhat different aspect to the teaching, the substance is the same. Jesus is here setting forth an essential principle of all true righteousness, on the recognition and practice of which depends the realization of the individual and social ideal. This principle requires that men shall not be critical, fault-finding, and flaw-picking in thought or conduct towards one another. The only right attitude is a full, penitent recognition of one's own weak-

* The Lukan parallels 11$^{34-36}$ 16$^{13}$ again have the same thought as the Matthæan passage, but with much variation; except that in the verse about the 'two masters' there is a remarkable verbal agreement. The word 'mammon' is a transliteration from the Aramaic מָמוֹנָא, and signifies here the riches which have become an idol to be worshipped and served.

† Lk 12$^{22-31}$ furnishes a parallel for Mt 6$^{25-33}$, but not for v.$^{34}$, which is found only here in the Gospels; there are good reasons for thinking that this verse belonged originally to the connexion in which it here appears. The phenomena of the parallel passages are as usual: striking likeness in certain clauses, but many important additions, omissions, and variations. Luke's account has obviously undergone adaptation for Gentile use, as seen in his 'ravens' where Matthew has 'the birds of the heaven,' 'God' and 'Father' where Matthew has 'heavenly Father,' 'nations of the world' where Matthew has 'nations'; and instead of Matthew's 'Be not anxious saying, What shall we eat?' Luke's account reads, 'Seek not what ye shall eat . . . neither be ye of doubtful mind.' The word ἡλικίαν in Mt 6$^{27}$ is capable of two different interpretations, and commentators are divided between them. The RV translates, 'Which of you by being anxious [*i.e.* by giving the matter intense, anxious thought] can add one cubit to his stature?' Since this is the clear meaning of the word where it is found elsewhere in this Gospel, Lk 2$^{52}$ 19$^{3}$, it has been so understood here by the Vulgate, Chrysostom, Augustine, Luther, Calvin, Bengel, Fritzsche, and others. But the cubit was 18 inches or more, which makes this interpretation seem highly improbable, as a very small amount in proportion to the whole is intended in this context. The word may mean 'age' (RVm); and it was not uncommon to think of life in terms of linear measure (cf. Ps 39$^{5}$ 'Behold, thou hast made my days as handbreadths'; also Jn 9$^{21.23}$, He 11$^{11}$). So that this is the meaning understood by Bleek, Tholuck, Meyer, Achelis, Feine, H. Weiss, Ibbeken, Thayer, B. Weiss, and most modern scholars.

* So Neander, Meyer, Kuinöl, Feine, H. Weiss, H. Holtzmann, B. Weiss, and others. Tholuck and Achelis regard v.$^{12}$ as extraneous material in the Sermon, holding that it was probably the closing epitome of some other discourse; similarly Godet. But in Luke also the verse is given in the Sermon, which—together with the fact that logically it is entirely suitable thereto—makes a strong presumptive case that this was its historical connexion. The position in the Sermon which the verse has received in Luke (6$^{31}$, as though it stood at Mt 5$^{42}$ instead of 7$^{12}$) is preferred by Bleek, Wendt, and Bacon, but such a displacement in the Matthæan account is not likely.

† In Mt 7$^{1.2a}$=Lk 6$^{37}$ we find a similar difference to that in Mt 6$^{12}$=Lk 11$^{4}$, the Lukan form avoiding the measure for measure idea which can be read into the Matthæan words; although both accounts strikingly agree in reporting the statement, 'With what measure ye mete, it shall be measured unto you' (Mt 7$^{2b}$=Lk 6$^{38b}$, cf. also Mk 4$^{24}$), a mode of treatment which can be predicated of God only in a qualitative sense, not quantitatively. Lk 6$^{37}$ is in an expanded form, containing three clauses in synonymous parallelism, for the purpose of emphasis: Mt 7$^{1.2a}$ produces the emphasis, but in a somewhat different way. But Lk 6$^{38a}$ is surely an extraneous element in the Lukan account, an authentic and valuable teaching of Jesus regarding generosity coming from some other occasion than the Sermon. The figurative illustration of the particle in the eye, Mt 7$^{3-5}$=Lk 6$^{41f.}$, is given in almost complete verbal agreement by the two reports (see them quoted above, under i. 3). Foreign also to the Sermon is Lk 6$^{39.40}$. The first verse has its parallel in Mt 15$^{14}$, which is probably its true context, referring to the Pharisees; the second verse has a partial parallel in Mt 10$^{24}$ (cf. Jn 13$^{16}$), and seems logically related there, but the saying may also have been spoken at some other time more in the Lukan form. With this teaching of Jesus about judgment may be compared Hillel's saying, 'Judge not thy neighbour until thou comest into his place.'

nesses, limitations, failures, and transgressions, such as will keep a man humble, make him sympathetic for others, ready to overlook their faults, and to see their virtues. The duty of the Christian is to measure himself against the standard which Christ has set, and to judge himself severely with respect to his shortcomings, instead of making his own religious ideas and practices the criterion by which he judges and condemns others. A man is a 'hypocrite' (v.$^{5}$) when, professing a desire to increase goodness in the world, he assumes a censorious attitude towards the faults of others rather than undertakes the improvement of himself first. In the background of this teaching stands the proud, self-righteous Pharisee, with his odious contempt for all who were less punctilious than himself (cf. Mt $23^{4. 23f. 27f.}$, Lk $18^{9-14}$, Jn $7^{47-49}$). Jesus does not mean, of course, that the character and conduct of men should never be matter of criticism by their fellows; this would be to remove one of the most important aids to uprightness in practical experience. In the affairs of life it often becomes necessary for us to judge others, both privately and publicly. Jesus recognizes this fact when He says also in this same discourse, 'By their fruits ye shall know them' ($7^{16}$, cf. Mt $18^{15-17}$). But the teaching, 'Judge not that ye be not judged,' pertains to that unloving, critical attitude of mind and heart which picks out and magnifies the faults, failures, and inconsistencies of others. This is not the spirit of human brotherhood, and the man who has it cannot himself anticipate a loving, forgiving treatment of himself by God.* It is not that God deals with men on a *quid pro quo* basis—that is not to be understood here any more than in the fifth petition of the Lord's Prayer (see above). But the man who does not come to love his fellow-men, and to treat them accordingly, can have no place in a heavenly Kingdom where love is supreme, and where ultimately it will be perfectly realized.

Mt $7^{6}$ presents a saying which is found only in this Gospel, and which stands in the Sermon only as a result of the compiling process.† It enjoins prudence and good judgment in the dissemination of the Gospel. Truth is sacred, and it must be carefully dealt with. There are wrong times as well as right times for trying to assist others religiously. The Gospel is to be offered only to the receptive, under suitable circumstances, else it will receive rebuff and indignity at unappreciative hands. The dogs and the swine, in the East the most despised of animals (cf. Mt $15^{26}$, Lk $15^{15f.}$, Ph $3^{2}$, 2 P $2^{22}$), are used here to typify those men, whether Gentiles or Jews, who are devoted wholly to material things, and are indifferent to the higher spiritual realm for which God created them. The parallelism in this verse is for no other purpose than to make the teaching impressive, a literary method of which the Sermon contains numerous instances.

* It was thought by Augustine, Fritzsche, Kuinöl, and de Wette, that the return judgment of which this passage speaks is rendered by men, *i.e.* other men will judge you and measure back to you exactly as you judge and measure. This, however, can hardly be the meaning: it rather refers to the judgment of God upon men, both in the future Day of Judgment and in His present treatment of them; so the modern commentators generally.

† So Neander, Bleek, Tholuck (?), Kuinöl, Godet, Achelis, Feine, Wendt, B. Weiss, Bacon, and others. It is the view of Köstlin, Feine, Hilgenfeld, and H. Holtzmann, that this verse as it now appears is Judaized, to make it a polemic against the heathen (cf. above on Mt $5^{18f.}$); reference is made to the *Teaching of the Twelve Apostles*, ix. 5, which reads, 'But let no one eat or drink of your Eucharist except those who have been baptized into the name of the Lord. This was what the Lord referred to when He said "Give not that which is holy unto the dogs."' Ibbeken thinks the verse refers to the use by Christians of heathen tribunals, as in 1 Co $6^{1-4}$. Neither of these views is required to explain this teaching, which has an excellent general sense and import.

In Mt $7^{7-11}$=Lk $11^{9-13}$ we have another section extraneous to the historical discourse, whose presence here seems fortuitous, since it stands in no topical association with its context.* The teaching herein contained is that God is ready and willing to give all His blessings to men, since He is a loving Father who provides—better than any human parent†—for His children. Men, therefore, are to feel free to pray to Him for all things. The thought is similar to that set forth in Mt $6^{25-34}$; but there the attention was fixed upon the physical necessities, while here the thought is of all kinds of blessings, spiritual not less than material. The injunction to pray is thrice repeated, 'ask—seek—knock,' without difference of meaning in the several clauses, in order to produce great emphasis. Jesus promises absolutely that our prayers shall be answered by God; the obvious and necessary conditions can be easily supplied from His other teaching. Thus, all prayer must be made with the intent and in the spirit of the Lord's Prayer (Mt $6^{9-13}$), for the sole purpose of the Kingdom (Mt $6^{33}$), and with full submission to God's will (Mt $26^{39. 42}$). Our petitions must permit God to answer them in the way which He knows to be best, and our trust in His wisdom, power, and love must be complete.

Mt $7^{12}$=Lk $6^{31}$, as already noted, closes this section of the Sermon, and in some sense constitutes the capstone of the whole discourse. The οὖν which introduces the verse (mistakenly dropped from ℵ*L) seems to mark this general relation. Matthew gives the saying in a fuller, more rounded form than Luke,‡ and adds the clause, 'for this is the law and the prophets.'§ The idea contained

* So Achelis, Feine, Godet, B. Weiss, Wendt, Bacon, and others. Futile efforts have been made by Chrysostom, Augustine, Luther, Stier, and Tholuck to find a logical relation of these verses to the verses which precede them. Feine, Weizsäcker, H. Holtzmann, and B. Weiss think that Luke has the original setting for the paragraph, which may be true; but it is also possible that in both Gospels this material is detached. In Luke, at any rate, it has received a topical association. A comparison of the two accounts shows practical identity of the first two verses in each: the second two verses in each account vary, but have the same thought; and Luke adds a third clause about the 'egg and the scorpion' (v.$^{12}$), perhaps to balance the threefold 'ask, seek, knock.' The last verse of each account (Mt $7^{11}$=Lk $11^{13}$) is quite the same, with two significant exceptions: (*a*) instead of Matthew's ἀγαθά Luke has πνεῦμα ἅγιον, which Tholuck, Achelis, and even Steinmeyer regard as a gloss, due to the prominence which the Holy Spirit, as the personification of all good things, attained in primitive Christian thought; (*b*) instead of Matthew's ὁ πατὴρ ὑμῶν ὁ ἐν τοῖς οὐρανοῖς, Luke has ὁ πατὴρ ὁ ἐξ οὐρανοῦ, a peculiar expression of which various explanations are given; see Feine, *Jahrb. f. Protest. Theol.* 1885, p. 74; Achelis, *Bergpredigt*, p. 386; H. Holtzmann, *Hand-Comm. ü. d. Synoptiker*, p. 125. The Lukan reading as it stands cannot be original. Some text-witnesses delete the second ὁ, but this is only a makeshift. Perhaps the ἐξ οὐρανοῦ came in under the influence of the πνεῦμα ἅγιον, to indicate the place from which the Spirit was given; and then, subsequently, the ἐξ οὐρανοῦ was imperfectly turned to account in connexion with the ὁ πατήρ.

† The phrase, 'if ye then, being evil' (πονηροί), contrasts men, in their imperfect, selfish, and sinful lives, with God, who is perfect in love and holiness. The argument is *a minore ad majus*: if limited love provides some good things, how much more will absolute love provide?

‡ Mt $7^{12}$ πάντα οὖν ὅσα ἐὰν θέλητε ἵνα ποιῶσιν ὑμῖν οἱ ἄνθρωποι, οὕτως καὶ ὑμεῖς ποιεῖτε αὐτοῖς· οὗτος γάρ ἐστιν ὁ νόμος καὶ οἱ προφῆται. Lk $6^{31}$ καὶ καθὼς θέλετε ἵνα ποιῶσιν ὑμῖν οἱ ἄνθρωποι, ποιεῖτε αὐτοῖς ὁμοίως. It would be difficult to explain these two divergent forms as coming from a common Greek original; perhaps they represent two lines of transmission, arising from two different translations into Greek of the same brief Aramaic utterance. It is noticeable that in this verse, as in the Beatitudes, the Lord's Prayer, and other portions of the discourse, Matthew gives the sayings of Jesus in a fuller, finer literary form, which in every instance has commended itself to the Christian Church as the better expression of Jesus' thought and spirit.

§ Luke's source did not contain this clause, perhaps for the usual reason that it was too Jewish. The case is the same in Lk $10^{25-28}$=Mt $22^{33-40}$=Mk $12^{28-31}$, where Matthew's clause, 'On these two commandments hangeth the whole law and the prophets,' is entirely absent from Luke's account, and in Mark's account is differently worded, 'There is none other commandment greater than these.' It is not unlikely, therefore, that in this passage, as in many others, the more Jewish First Gospel

in this teaching is closely related to that of 'loving one's neighbour as one's self'; this idea was already formulated in the OT (Lv $19^{18}$), and was pronounced by Jesus to be one of the two great commandments comprehending all human duty (Mt $22^{38-40}$). St. Paul also followed his Master in the same teaching (Gal $5^{14}$). Our verse has come to be known as the 'Golden Rule,' which marks the high place that it holds in the Gospel teaching. What it presents, however, is not a precept for literal application everywhere, but a principle for the determination of social conduct. It inculcates a spirit which men are to cultivate towards one another.* Jesus wishes by means of it to correct the mood of selfishness and contempt which obstructs the realization of a true human brotherhood. Men are prone to use their fellow-men as *tools* for their own comfort, advancement, or pleasure. Kant gave perfect expression to the higher idea when he wrote, 'So act as to treat humanity, whether in your own person or in that of another, in every case as an end, never as a means only.' It is still the rule rather than the exception that those men who, by reason of their wealth, social rank, or public office, are in a position to command others, abuse them by ignoring their personality, disregarding their rights, appropriating the fruits of their labour, withholding from them opportunities for attaining higher manhood, and in other ways treating them like machines or slaves. This condition of present society is essentially un-Christian, and is to be counteracted and transformed by the Gospel. For this achievement the 'Golden Rule' can be exceedingly useful, when applied as a principle, with the aid of a well-trained judgment and a consecrated common-sense. Let each man respect the individuality and observe the rights of every other man, let him honour and treat every other man as he in their places would wish to be honoured and treated, let him give such sympathy and assistance to others as he would himself like to receive. In this manner the 'Golden Rule' will be fulfilled.†

*k. The Duty of Righteousness.*—Mt $7^{13-27}$=Lk $6^{43-49}$ (cf. Lk $13^{24.27}$). The discourse which has set forth the Divine ideal of life, closes with strong exhortation for its attainment. Jesus solemnly enjoins the duty of righteousness. It is a strenuous undertaking, in which men must follow only trustworthy guides. And this righteousness does not consist in mere profession, but in actually being and doing what God wills.

It must remain a matter of doubt whether the two verses, Mt $7^{13.14}$, belonged originally to the Sermon. The thought presented by them has no topical connexion with $7^{1-12}$, but, on the view that $7^{13-27}$ is a concluding hortatory section, such a relation could not be required; while this thought is entirely suitable to a portion of the discourse setting forth the duty of righteousness. The only serious argument against the Matthæan position of the verses is that Luke seems to have them in another and an original setting, $13^{23.24}$; perhaps it can be maintained in reply that these passages are not parallel, but belong to different occasions, and are rightly placed in each of the Gospels.* That the gospel demands are lofty, severe, and exclusive, so that to become a member of the Kingdom requires complete self-commitment and an unceasing struggle to attain the ideal, is what Jesus teaches in these verses. The 'small gate' and the 'narrow way' forcibly express this idea. The figure is perhaps drawn from the Oriental city, to which the Kingdom of God is sometimes likened (cf. He $11^{10}$ $12^{22}$, Rev $21^{2}$). The 'gate' signifies one's entrance into the Kingdom as present, and the 'way' signifies his earnest life thereafter.† Jesus' statement that 'few will find their way into the kingdom' is perhaps best explained out of the circumstances of His ministry, instead of being taken eschatologically as in Luke. It would then refer to the small number of real followers whom Jesus had secured as a result of His work—a fact which must have impressed the disciples, and for which they may well have sought an explanation from Him. His reply was thus along the line of His teaching about the growth of the Kingdom (Mt 13), that time was required to achieve numbers and maturity.‡ The parallel saying in Lk $13^{24}$, which is made by its context (vv.$^{25-30}$) to refer to the number of persons ultimately to be saved, states—not that the whole number will be small, which

has better preserved the original saying of Jesus. Of course it cannot be denied as a possibility that the clause in Mt $7^{12}$ stands there as the product of an apologetic Judaistic retouching (as in Mt $5^{18f.}$), or by misplacement, or through liturgical usage. As for the meaning of Jesus' words in this connexion, the Golden Rule 'is the law and the prophets' in the sense that it states the principle on which the Law and the Prophets tried to build up a real human brotherhood (cf. Ro $13^{9f.}$, Gal $5^{14}$). This is true, even though the Law and the Prophets did not fully accomplish their purpose, or even perfectly grasp the ideal towards which they were working. Jesus would emphasize the fact of the continuity of revelation, showing how the Divine ideal had preceded Himself in the world, and that the OT history and teaching were inspired by the same God and with essentially the same truth as constituted His own revelation. It is thus with deliberate intention that He closes the body of His discourse with this statement, which connects significantly with the words used to introduce the main argument, 'Think not that I came to destroy the law or the prophets: I came not to destroy, but to fulfil' (Mt $5^{17}$).

* See esp. O. Holtzmann, *Leben Jesu* (1901), p. 189.

† Sayings similar to this of Mt $7^{12}$ are found in pre-Christian and post-Christian Jewish writings, and also among Greek, Roman, and Oriental peoples, showing that this principle of life was not first formulated, or exclusively formulated, by Jesus. This does not impugn Jesus' originality or authority, but indicates that truth and the desire for goodness are innate in man (cf. Ac $17^{22-31}$). Jesus, however, so changed the wording of this principle as to give it a new force and sphere, for He stated it—not negatively, as it everywhere else appears—but *positively*, insisting upon that loving service to others which is peculiar to the Gospel. Legalism says, 'Thou shalt not' do this and that—a system of repression; the Gospel of Life says, 'Thou shalt' do countless good and helpful things—a system of development. The difference is like that between the false and the true child-nurture: the false method says constantly, 'Don't do this, don't do that'; the true method fills the child's mind with lovely and useful things to do, so that the child will grow in goodness and service. Jewish forms of the Golden Rule may be seen in To $4^{15}$ 'That which thou hatest, do to no one'; also in the saying attributed to Hillel, 'What thou hatest thyself, that do not thou to another: this is the whole of the law, all the rest is only comment upon it' (Bab. *Shab.* f. 31. 1). The non-Jewish forms are numerous; Isocrates wrote, "Α πάσχοντες ὑφ' ἑτέρων ὀργίζεσθε, ταῦτα τοῖς ἄλλοις μὴ ποιεῖτε; the Stoic maxim was, 'Quod tibi fieri non vis, alteri ne feceris'; and in Confucius we read, 'Do not to others what you would not wish done to yourself' (Legge, *Chinese Classics*, i. 191 f.). Other parallels have been collected by Wünsche and Wetstein. See literature cited in Taylor, *Sayings of the Jewish Fathers*[2] (1897), p. 142 f.

* This is the view of Neander, Tholuck, Achelis, and all who defend the unity of Matthew's discourse; while Mt $7^{13.14}$ is regarded as material extraneous to the Sermon by Feine, Godet, B. Weiss, and others. A comparison of the Matthæan and Lukan passages shows that Matthew as usual has the longer and more literary form, while Luke gives much the same idea in briefer form and different words. In the former the figures are the 'gate' and the 'way,' in the latter it is the 'door.' The final clause of each passage is strikingly varied: Matthew reads, καὶ ὀλίγοι εἰσὶν οἱ εὑρίσκοντες αὐτήν, while Luke reads, ὅτι πολλοί, λέγω ὑμῖν, ζητήσουσιν εἰσελθεῖν καὶ οὐκ ἰσχύουσιν. According to Luke, the statement was made by Jesus in reply to a specific request from some one, 'Lord, are they few that be saved?' and after the close of the Galilæan ministry when Jesus was journeying to Jerusalem. Then what follows in the Lukan account ($13^{25-30}$) makes this question refer to the Final Judgment. But in Matthew the saying does not appear to be eschatological; nor does the statement that 'there are few who find the narrow way' appear suitable to the Sermon, since at this time Jesus' ministry was meeting with large success—much more suitable would it have been after the disappointed withdrawal of the Galilæan multitude, when in sorrowful isolation and rejection Jesus was going up to Jerusalem for the cross. Luke's position of the saying may therefore be better than that of the First Gospel, while the original form and intent of the saying may have been better preserved by Matthew.

† ὅτι is read at the beginning of v.[14] by nearly all modern editors and commentators, on the authority of ℵB and other important witnesses. τί, which is preferred by Lachmann, Tregelles, Meyer, and Achelis, has strong secondary attestation.

‡ Similarly Tholuck, Achelis, and others.

could not be true on any possible view of Jesus' teaching or of the world—but that 'many will fail.' If the saying is authentic in this form (it may have become modified when an eschatological meaning was read into it), Jesus is more likely to have intended it as a practical admonition than as an omniscient disclosure of the outcome of the Final Judgment. It is worthy of note that we find in Mt $7^{14}$ the significant term ζωή to denote the full, blessed existence which comes to him who does God's will. This word, so common in the Gospel of John ($1^{4}$ $3^{15f. 36}$ $5^{24. 26. 29}$ $6^{27. 33. 35. 51}$ $10^{10}$ *et al.*) occurs but rarely in this sense in the Synoptic Gospels (cf. Mt $19^{16}$).

The next paragraph in the Sermon, as it appears in Mt $7^{15-20}$ = Lk $6^{43-45}$, quite surely belongs as a whole to the historical discourse.* Since it is the duty of all men to attain righteousness, it becomes a matter of the utmost importance that men shall choose true teachers who will teach them what true righteousness is, and how it is to be attained. The false teachers† against whom He warns them are all those morally blind and unworthy individuals who assume to guide men into the Kingdom of God. Outstanding representatives of this class were those scribes and Pharisees of Jesus' day whom He described in the severe language of Mt 23; doubtless He had them in mind—blind guides (Mt $15^{14}$) and hypocrites, unfit for the task which they performed of teaching the people religion.‡ If this was the explicit and primary reference of Jesus' saying in v.$^{15}$, there is no reason why it should not implicitly refer to other incompetent and bad teachers such as appeared in the early years of Christianity. Any one who assumes to teach religion and morals without himself living the upright life comes within that class against which Jesus here gives warning. And whether they are bad or good, false or true teachers, can be known by their 'fruits,' *i.e.* by their character and their service. If they manifest the 'fruit of the Spirit' as St. Paul describes it in Gal $5^{22-26}$, they will be trustworthy teachers and guides.§

That Jesus has in mind the practical manifestation of righteousness in thought and conduct is proved by the verse which immediately follows this paragraph, Mt $7^{21}$, in which He says that only those persons shall enter the Kingdom of Heaven who *do* God's will. Jesus neither here nor elsewhere put the emphasis upon creed apart from character, which the Church has done from the 2nd cent. until our own. His aim was to make individual men and a human brotherhood, not a system of theology. Love, mercy, and peace, purity, trust, and helpfulness, were the tests of goodness which Jesus established (Mt $5^{3}$–$7^{12}$ $25^{31-46}$). Inasmuch as He came for the express purpose of making God's will known, and in His words, deeds, and character did make God's will manifest to men, He can only mean that men must do and be what He has thus taught them. Luke's form of the saying $6^{46}$ is therefore equivalent to Matthew's, although so differently worded.* As was seen in considering the third petition of the Lord's Prayer, 'Thy will be done' (Mt $6^{10}$), the will of God is the one thing to be accomplished; for this Jesus lived (Jn $6^{38}$), and for this He would have us live (Mt $12^{50}$ $21^{28-31}$). His statement that only such shall 'enter the Kingdom of Heaven' seems to be an intentional echo and return to the words of Mt $5^{20}$.

The following two verses, Mt $7^{22. 23}$, stand here in all probability as a result of compilation. Luke gives them in another connexion, which appears original ($13^{26f.}$); and since they refer to the Last Judgment, they belong, with Jesus' other eschatological teaching, to the closing months of His ministry. One needs only to consider carefully the time, circumstances, audience, and purpose of the Sermon to see that these verses present an idea, and sound a note, which do not belong to this occasion and discourse.† Nevertheless, they contain authentic teaching of Jesus, and teaching of profound meaning. The thought is analogous to that of Mt $7^{21}$ in affirming that nothing shall admit to the Kingdom but the actual attainment of righteousness (cf. Lk $10^{20}$). The profession of Christianity, the preaching of Christianity, even the production of some good results for the Christian cause, shall not in themselves alone secure salvation, for the criterion of judgment in the great Judgment Day shall be a genuine realization of God's will in and through one's self. And Luke adds ($13^{28-30}$), what is germane to this connexion, that 'there are last which shall be first, and there are first which shall be last' (cf. Mt $8^{11f.}$ $19^{30}$); *i.e.* some who, like the Pharisees of Jesus' day, had had a great reputation for piety, and had been looked upon as models of righteousness, shall be shown to have been selfish, vain, and hypocritical, unworthy to enter the Kingdom of God; while other obscure and once despised persons shall find a welcome there (cf. Lk $18^{9-14}$).‡

And, finally, the duty of righteousness is most

* For v.$^{15}$ there is no parallel in Luke, but there is no reason to question its authenticity, and it is not foreign to this connexion. For v.$^{19}$ also there is no parallel in Luke; it may be a verbal reproduction of Mt $3^{10}$, perhaps imported into this context in transmission because of the similarity of the figure and the theme, cf. Mt $15^{13}$, Jn $15^{2. 6}$ (so Feine, Wendt, and others). Again, v.$^{20}$ is a repetition of v.$^{16a}$, perhaps therefore a subsequent expansion, resumptive of the main thought after the interpolation of v.$^{19}$. And, finally, Lk $6^{45}$ is clearly extraneous to the Sermon, having perhaps its historical setting at Mt $12^{34f.}$ (so Feine against Wendt). The original portion of this paragraph may thus have been Mt $7^{15-18}$ = Lk $6^{43f.}$. The two reports have the same idea in the same figure, but are peculiarly variant in manner of expression; it is not likely that they started from a common Greek translation.

† The term 'prophet' in both OT and NT denotes primarily the teacher of religious truth and duty, and has no other import in this passage.

‡ So Tholuck, Achelis, Feine, Ibbeken, B. Weiss. The figure of wolves and sheep was a common one among a pastoral people (cf. Is $11^{6}$ $65^{25}$, Mt $10^{16}$, Jn $10^{12}$, Ac $20^{29}$), but only here in the Bible is found the idea of the wolf in sheep's clothing, as in Æsop's *Fables*.

§ There was never any justification for the Roman Catholic view, adopted by Calvin and sometimes promulgated even by Luther, that the καρποί in these verses signified primarily, indeed exclusively, sound doctrines. It is, of course, true that those who teach false doctrines cannot be safe guides, but the Bible rightly interpreted is the criterion of sound doctrines, not the pronouncements of any ecclesiastical organization past, present, or future.

* Mt $7^{21}$ Οὐ πᾶς ὁ λέγων μοι Κύριε κύριε εἰσελεύσεται εἰς τὴν βασιλείαν τῶν οὐρανῶν, ἀλλ' ὁ ποιῶν τὸ θέλημα τοῦ πατρός μου τοῦ ἐν τοῖς οὐρανοῖς. Lk $6^{46}$ Τί δέ με καλεῖτε Κύριε κύριε, καὶ οὐ ποιεῖτε ἃ λέγω;

† So Feine, Godet, Ibbeken, Weizsäcker, Wendt, and others. The parallel sayings, Mt $7^{22f.}$ = Lk $13^{26f.}$, give the same idea, with wide divergence of expression. It may be true, as Ibbeken thinks, that the three acts named in Mt $7^{22}$ sound improbable on Jesus' lips (certainly they are foreign to the Sermon), and they may therefore reflect the experiences of the Apostolic age. But Lk $13^{26}$ 'We did eat and drink in thy presence, and thou didst teach in our streets,' is also not without difficulty, because so insipid and un-Jewish. The better explanation is that the Matthæan verses are authentic, but belong to the close of the ministry; while Lk $13^{26}$ has been universalized. In the second verse of each passage, Mt $7^{23}$ = Lk $13^{27}$, there is identity of thought, with some variation of language. The phrase, 'Depart from me, ye that work iniquity,' is a quotation from Ps $6^{8}$ (cf. Mt $13^{31f.}$ $25^{41}$); its two Greek forms here, ἀποχωρεῖτε ἀπ' ἐμοῦ οἱ ἐργαζόμενοι τὴν ἀνομίαν (Mt.) and ἀπόστητε ἀπ' ἐμοῦ, πάντες ἐργάται ἀδικίας (Lk.), present an interesting minute problem of translation and transmission.

‡ Mt $7^{21-23}$ has a value also for determining the Christological conceptions of the Synoptic Gospels. See particularly Schlatter in *Greifswalder Studien* (1895), pp. 83–105. This passage is only one of a number where Jesus appears as claiming the Divine prerogative of Judge at the Final Judgment (Mt $25^{31-46}$ $10^{32f.}$ $11^{27-30}$, Mk $8^{38}$, Lk $20^{18}$; cf. Jn $5^{27}$ $12^{48}$, Ac $17^{31}$, Ro $2^{16}$, 2 Co $5^{10}$), a function appropriate to the Messiah. It would require a radical treatment of the Gospel narratives to explain this idea of Jesus as Judge as an exaggerated Apostolic appreciation of Him. The uniqueness of Christ in mission, person, teaching, and career—in other words, His Divinity—cannot well be denied by a serious historical interpretation of the Gospels; and when this uniqueness is recognized, it is not difficult to admit Jesus' office as Judge.

impressively set forth at the close of the whole discourse by the parable of the Two House-builders (Mt $7^{24-27}$ = Lk $6^{47-49}$).* That this piece belongs to the Sermon, and forms its remarkable conclusion (as the οὖν in v.[24] suggests), can be considered certain. The parable follows logically upon v.[21], enlarging and enforcing the teaching therein. It is a saying of tremendous strength. The life which Jesus has depicted in the Sermon as the ideal life is wonderfully beautiful, inspiring, and attractive to every sincere soul. But men were likely to recognize and to reverence this ideal without achieving it, since that is the earnest and arduous labour of a lifetime. Hence Jesus meets them with the solemn affirmation that the duty of actually doing what He teaches is imperative; that it shall be of no avail for them to have listened to His words, if they do not straightway go and live the life which as God's will He has described to them.

5. THE RELATION OF THE SERMON ON THE MOUNT TO JESUS' TEACHING AS A WHOLE.—The teaching contained in the Sermon on the Mount was given in the middle portion of Jesus' Galilæan ministry, when enthusiastic multitudes were hearing Him and many followers attended Him. It was in this period that He gave the general teaching about the Kingdom of God—what it consisted in, what it brought to men, what it required of men, what relation He Himself sustained to it, and what its future was to be. The Sermon is an epitome of this general teaching, condensing the whole into a brief statement and exposition of the ideal of life, given for the practical purpose of a simple guide to right thought and conduct. It showed the multitude what He as a teacher of religion had to present as truth and duty, with which they could readily contrast their own and the current ideals.

Jesus confined His teaching entirely to the religio-ethical field; and in this field He dealt with essential truths, facts, and principles rather than with the speculative mysteries of the universe or with the casuistry of ethics. Consequently, He taught again and again the same things, to different persons, under different circumstances, and in different ways and lights. A close organic relation unites all Jesus' teachings, each involving the other, and all together illuminating the path of human existence. The Gospel was so brief and simple that it had not to be committed to writing like the philosophy and the ethics of the schools. Common men could comprehend and communicate Jesus' teaching. His was a universal message which all could grasp; it presented an ideal to which all could aspire and attain.

As has been abundantly seen, the Sermon on the Mount sets forth Jesus' conception of what men should be and do as members of the Kingdom which He came to establish in the world (not as a new movement entirely, but as giving higher content and greater impulse to a movement which God had inaugurated with the very creation of the human race). The true righteousness is determined by God; as He is the source of all life, so it is He who determines what that life shall be. Ethical obligations rest therefore upon religious truths. The ideal of a man's life is to be derived from God, and for its realization he is responsible to God. The aim of man's life is to achieve that personal character and service which fulfil the true manhood, after the pattern of Christ, and to advance as far as possible the real brotherhood of all men as sons of the one common Heavenly Father. The Kingdom of God in its Divine aspect is the purpose, love, and power of God which determine and accomplish this ideal condition; in its human collective aspect it is the company of those who have earnestly set about the realization, in themselves and among men, of this Divine ideal. So that Jesus can sum up all duty, individual and social, in the one injunction to 'Seek supremely the kingdom of God, and the righteousness which he wills' (Mt $6^{33}$, Lk $12^{31}$; cf. Mt $22^{34-40}$). And this righteousness is primarily an internal characteristic; it is apprehended *within* the man. The religio-ethical ideal which God implants in every human heart must be heeded by each man, and his life must become conformed to it. Created by God in His own image, men must attain to God-likeness; and this attainment is, first of all, the recognition of and obedience to the ideal of life which God furnishes in the soul, moved and guided by the teaching and example of Jesus. Those persons will achieve perfect self-realization who enter into complete communion with God, hearing His voice, and doing His will as revealed within themselves and in and through Christ.

The absolute assurance of Jesus that He can reveal the will of God to men, and that this is His mission in the world, is a guarantee of the trustworthiness of His teaching. If the Sermon on the Mount contains few explicit statements concerning the person of Christ such as abound in the Fourth Gospel, it is none the less true that the implications of the discourse are equally high. The Divine personality, knowledge, and authority of Jesus are the foundation on which the discourse rests. The passages, Mt $5^{11.17}$ $7^{21-23}$, only state what all the teaching involves, that He who speaks these words is 'the Son of God' in the highest sense, sustaining to Him a unique relation, and rendering to men a unique service. The value of the Sermon cannot therefore be overestimated, and the historical study or critical treatment of this material should never dominate or obscure the fact that this teaching is a Divine revelation of the will of God for men which is forthwith to be accomplished upon the earth.

LITERATURE.—For the quotations from, and allusions to, the Sermon on the Mount in the extra-canonical Christian literature of the first three centuries, see esp. Resch, *Aussercanonische Paralleltexte z. d. Evangelien*, Teil 1 (1893), pp. 62–114; Teil 2 (1895), pp. 62–106. For ideas and expressions akin to those of the Sermon on the Mount in Rabbinic literature, see Weber, *Jüdische Theologie*[2] (1897); Wünsche, *Neue Beiträge z. Erläuterung d. Evangelien aus Talmud u. Midrasch* (1878); Dalman, *Die Worte Jesu*, Bd. 1 (1898) [Eng. tr. 1902].

From the Patristic period the only specific separate treatment of the Sermon on the Mount is by Augustine, *de Sermone Domini in Monte* (*Op.*, ed. Bened. vol. iii.) [Eng. tr. in 'Nicene and Post-Nicene Fathers,' pp. 63]; it is an important work of interpretation, containing much that is of permanent value. Elsewhere in his writings Augustine dealt further with the Sermon, presenting in some respects different views. Trench collected all this material and prepared a digest of it, which he published under the title, *Exposition of the Sermon on the Mount, drawn from the Writings of St. Augustine* (3rd ed. rev. 1869). Useful also are the interpretations of Origen, *Comm. on Matthew* (*Op.*, ed. Lommatzsch, vols. iii. iv.); Jerome, *Comm. on Matthew* (*Op.*, ed. Vallarsi, vol. vii.); Chrysostom, *Homilies on Matthew* (*Op.*, ed. Montfaucon, vol. vii.); Hilarius Pictaviensis, *Comm. on Matthew* (*Op.*, ed. Oberthür, vol. vii.); the work of the Auctor *Operis Imperfecti*; and the very brief matter in the *Comm. on the Four Gospels* by Theophylact and Euthymius Zigabenus.

From the Reformation period the important interpretation by Luther is first to be named, *Comm. on Matthew* (*Works*, ed. Walch, vol. vii.); and after him, Calvin in his *Harmony of Matthew, Mark, and Luke* (*Works*, ed. 1835–1838, vols. i. ii.). The three Roman Catholic works of most value are the *Comm. on the Four Gospels* by Maldonatus, Jansenius, and Cornelius a Lapide. The extensive but unimportant post-Reformation literature can be seen in full in Tholuck, *Die Bergrede Christi*[5], pp. 30–40 [Eng. tr. pp. 41–49].

The Modern period has provided many works upon the Sermon on the Mount, some of them of great value. The standard work upon the subject for the past seventy years has been that of Tholuck, *Die Bergrede Christi* (1st ed. 1833; 5th

* See the text of both passages quoted above under i. 3. The Lukan form of the parable is conspicuously secondary in character; the Jewish phraseology is largely removed, and the description is generalized so as to be adapted to any locality. Matthew, on the other hand, gives a faithful picture of the conditions of house-building in the wadis of Galilee. Again, also, the literary superiority belongs to the First Gospel.

ed. Gotha, 1872, pp. 484 [Eng. tr. from 4th Germ. ed., Edinburgh, 1860, pp. 443]), and this still remains the most valuable volume on the Sermon, although a portion of the contents is now antiquated. Next in extent and importance is the equally elaborate work of Achelis, *Die Bergpredigt* (Bielefeld, 1875, pp. 492). Other works of scientific character, but smaller dimensions, are: Feine, 'Die Texte der Bergpredigt bei Matthäus u. bei Lukas,' in *Jahrbücher für Protestantische Theologie*, 1885, pp. 1-85; Steinmeyer, *Die Rede des Herrn auf dem Berge* (Berlin, 1885, pp. 156); Ibbeken, *Die Bergpredigt Jesus* (2nd ed., Einbeck, 1890, pp. 216); Hugo Weiss (Rom. Cath.), *Die Bergpredigt Christi* (Freiburg, 1892, pp. 111); Grawert, *Die Bergpredigt nach Matthäus* (Marburg, 1900, pp. 77); Heinrici, *Die Bergpredigt, quellenkritisch untersucht* (Leipzig, 1900, pp. 81), and a second part dealing with the interpretation is promised; Bacon, *Sermon on the Mount* (New York, 1902, pp. 258).—Homiletic treatments of the Sermon are numerous in German, French, and English. An anonymous work, *Die Bergpredigt* (Gütersloh, 1881, pp. 48); Grüllich, *Die Bergpredigt des Herrn Jesu Christi* (Meissen, 1886, pp. 148); Harnisch, *Die Bergpredigt des Herrn* (Breslau, 1901, pp. 35); Kaiser, *Die Bergpredigt des Herrn* (Leipzig, 1901), pp. 521; Monneron, *Le Sermon sur la Montagne* (Lausanne, 1889, pp. 412); J. B. Bousset, *Le Sermon sur la Montagne* (Paris, 1900, pp. 150 [Eng. tr., New York, 1900, pp. 144]). The best English work is by C. Gore, *The Sermon on the Mount* (London, 1896, pp. 218); it contains much, however, that is only of local ecclesiastical interest; further, W. B. Carpenter, *The Great Charter of Christ* (London, 1895, pp. 300). Of special importance are the works of B. Weiss, *Meyer-Kommentar über das Matthäusevangelium* (Göttingen, 1898), and of H. Holtzmann, *Hand-Commentar über die Synoptiker* (3rd ed., Freiburg, 1900); other commentaries upon Matthew (Meyer, Morison, Keil, Broadus, Kübel, Bruce, *et al.*), Luke (Godet, Plummer), and both Matthew and Luke (Bengel, Bleek, Olshausen, Ewald, Fritzsche, Kuinöl, Nösgen, *et. al.*) are of varying usefulness.

Literature upon special portions and aspects of the Sermon has been cited in the footnotes. C. W. Votaw.

## NEW TESTAMENT TIMES.—

Introduction.
i. Distribution of the Jewish Population in the Holy Land.
ii. Languages.
iii. Political Constitution.
iv. Social Conditions.
v. Parties.
vi. Education and Culture.
vii. Art and Literature.
viii. The Jews of the Diaspora.
Literature.

The Advent of Christ falls within the penultimate period of that era of Israelitish history which begins with the Return of the Jews from Babylon (B.C. 538) and ends with the Fall of Jerusalem (A.D. 70). From both an external and an internal point of view, this era marks a far-reaching transformation of the conditions of Jewish life. At the outset, Judæa, which was not quite the same in extent as the ancient kingdom of Judah, forms a small province of the Persian, and afterwards of the Greek Empire. The population, at first scanty and poor, gradually increases, and, under the orderly arrangements of the Law, attains to a certain measure of prosperity. But internal party-strife consumes its strength, and, under Antiochus Epiphanes, reaches such a height that this Seleucid monarch, in the pride of his Greek culture, but with political shortsightedness, forms the resolution of entirely rooting out the proper Jewish religion. This period of extreme danger is unexpectedly followed by a brilliant revival of the Jewish State, which recalls the flourishing period of pre-exilic history, and which struck the people themselves in this light. The nation shakes itself free from the foreign yoke, and the Hasmonæan princes not only become high priests, but finally assume the title of 'king.' This glory, however, is of short duration, and the Jewish people are rudely awakened from their dream. The internal dissensions that followed the death of queen Alexandra, hasten the intervention of the Romans, and lead to the conquest of Jerusalem by Pompey (B.C. 63). The Romans do not, however, destroy the Jewish State, but allow it to continue under a variety of changing forms, until at last the perpetual discontent of the Jews leads to the outbreak of the desperate war for freedom, which issued in the destruction of the State and the Temple.

From the spiritual point of view, this period marks the development of *Judaism* in opposition to the national life and the religion of the pre-exilic period. The deeper foundation of this is found in the remarkable recasting which the Jewish spirit underwent during the Exile. Nowhere else in the history of mankind is there an instance of a people being transformed in so wonderful and radical a fashion as the Jews in the course of their captivity in Babylon. They left Babylon a body whose true life lay not in the actual state of things, but in future expectations and in a world of cultus-notions created out of recollections of the past. To the actual world they sought to accommodate themselves upon certain abstract principles, and, when this attempt failed, they withdrew entirely into that spiritual world which was constructed wholly according to those dogmatic principles. They found their support in the Messianic expectation, for the sake of which they submitted to the burdensome prescriptions of the Law, which were intended to shield them from the heathen impurity of the world, and thereby render them worthy to hail the advent of the Messianic glory. Yet it is not to be overlooked, in this connexion, that the noblest spirits in the Jewish community, especially during the earlier periods of the post-exilic era, filled those outward forms with a rich inward content. There still survived in them the pure prophetic spirit, and the ideas created by men like Jeremiah and Deutero-Isaiah; nay, the writings which emanated from this period, such as the Psalms and the Book of Job, touch us almost more nearly than the writings of those prophets, because the ideas contained in them have found simpler expression and are less closely bound up with the historical form. But the conditions under which the Jews lived seldom permitted a lengthened enjoyment of this contemplative life. Not only were they disturbed in their rest by contact with the heathen world, but even amongst themselves there were men of a different disposition, whose recollections turned rather to their pre-exilic forefathers, and who, with a stronger sense of actualities, plunged vigorously into the relations of life, and sought to help themselves. Between them and the 'quiet in the land' there grew up an ever-increasing opposition, which may be regarded as the moving factor in the post-exilic history. Through these conflicts with opposition without and within, not only was the stricter Judaism disturbed, but it was driven also to the discussion of the great religious problems and to new developments. The fruits of these spiritual struggles may be seen in the entirely new conception of the state of man after death and in the transformation of the Messianic hope, which in the Apocalyptic literature seeks to free itself from national limitations and takes a start in the direction of universalism. It may be safely concluded that, in this movement, contact with foreign forms of thought was not without importance—primarily contact with Parsism, secondarily with the Greek world.

i. Distribution of the Jewish Population in the Holy Land.—Leaving out of account meanwhile those Israelites who were scattered in various lands, the Jewish population was at first confined to *Judæa* proper, from which the Israelites derived their now universally current appellation (Gr. Ἰουδαῖοι, Germ. 'Juden,' Eng. 'Jews'). The land taken possession of by the returning exiles was considerably smaller in the southern direction than in pre-exilic times. Whereas formerly Beersheba was regarded as the southern limit, the part of Judæa that lay to the south had been taken possession of during the Exile by the Edomites, and the post-exilic community was at first far too weak to drive back the intruders.* The boundary between this New-Edom and Judæa was formed in the 2nd cent. B.C. by the town of Beth-ẓur, and this was, in all probability, approximately the division between the respective territories also at an earlier period. According to Neh 6[2], the original N.W. boundary appears to have been the Plain of Ono (*bik'ath 'Onō*, probably the modern *Kefr-'ânâ*). But at a later period the Samaritans, who lived at constant feud with the Jews, must have got possession of three places inhabited by Jews, namely Lydda, Ramathaim, and Aphærema (1 Mac 11[34]). In the Maccabæan period, however, Judæa underwent considerable expansion. The three places just named were taken from the Samaritans and restored to the Jews as early as the time of Jonathan. Afterwards the boundary was extended still farther to the north, for, according to Josephus (*BJ* III. iii. 5; *Ant.* XIV. iii. 4), the N. boundary of Judæa ran by Borkaos (prob. the modern *Berkît*) in the hill-country and Koreæ (now *Ḳurâwa*) in the Jordan Valley. The country in the south inhabited by the Edomites, which now bore the name *Idumæa*, was conquered by John Hyrcanus. As it was originally Israelitish land, the inhabitants were compelled to adopt the Law and submit to circumcision. Accordingly, from that time onwards (in conformity with the prescription of Dt 23[8f.]), they were regarded as Jews, although they continue to be called Idumæans. That they also regarded themselves as genuine Jews is evident, for instance, from the words attributed to them by Josephus (*BJ* IV. iv. 4, τῶν πατρίων ἱερῶν . . . τῆς κοινῆς πατρίδος), but of course their foreign origin could not be wholly forgotten.† On the other hand, in the cities on the Mediterranean coast, which had only transitory periods of subjection to the Jews, the population was preponderatingly heathen, although considerable Jewish minorities existed in them. Only in Joppa (*Jaffa*) were the Jews in the majority, this city having continued after the death of Herod to be united with Judæa. During the war for freedom it played, accordingly, a prominent part, and had to be twice captured by the Romans (Jos. *Ant.* VII. xi. 4; *BJ* II. xviii. 10, III. ix. 2).

To the north of Judæa lay *Samaria*, which stretched as far as the Plain of Jezreel. The population of this district sprang partly from the ancient Israelites, but had received a strong intermixture through the heathen peoples who were settled here by the Assyrian conquerors (cf. 2 K 17[24ff.]). In course of time these heathen elements were absorbed by the Israelitish remnants, but the ill-will shown by the Samaritans towards the returning Jews kept the latter from ever forgetting the impure origin of their northern neighbours. Matters came to an open breach when the Samaritans built a temple of their own upon Mt. Gerizim, and thus renounced all connexion with the community at Jerusalem. It is true that they, equally with the Jews, acknowledged the Law, but the breach remained irreparable, and the Samaritans continued excluded from the further development of Judaism. The contempt of the Jews which found vent in the nickname 'Cuthæans' (Jos. *Ant.* IX. xiv. 3, XI. iv. 4, and in the Talmud), and which finds very sharp expression on the part even of the otherwise mild Ben Sira (Sir 50[25f.] 'Two nations my soul abhorreth, and *the third is no people*: the inhabitants of Seir and Philistia, and *the foolish nation that dwelleth in Sichem*'), was repaid by the Samaritans with bitter hate. This manifested itself at times in the form of attacks upon the pilgrims journeying to Jerusalem, who, in consequence, frequently preferred to take the long roundabout way by the east of the Jordan (Lk 9[52], Mk 10[1]; Jos. *Ant.* XX. vi. 1). The destruction of the Gerizim temple by John Hyrcanus made no change in these relations, but rather embittered the feelings of the Samaritans still more.

As to *Galilee*, we learn from 1 Mac 5 that in the course of the post-exilic period Jews had settled in it, but that during the first half of the 2nd cent. B.C. these were still so few that they could not hold their own against the heathen population, and were consequently brought by Simon to Jerusalem. It was not until the time of Aristobulus I., as Schürer (*GJV*[3] i. 275 f.) was the first to prove, that this portion of the land and its inhabitants, regarding whose nationality we have unfortunately no more precise information, were compelled on the same ground as the Idumæans to adopt the Law (Jos. *Ant.* XIII. xi. 3). It is extremely probable, however, that there were further settlements of Jews of purer birth in these fertile districts, so that they became more completely Judaized. It is characteristic in this respect that Judith (8[19]) speaks of 'our fathers,' *i.e.* the ancient Israelites. At the time of Christ the land of Galilee was essentially Jewish, and had its Pharisees and scribes (Lk 7[36], Mt 8[19]), as well as its synagogues (Mt 12[9], Lk 4[16] 7[5]). The designation 'half-Jews' is never applied to the Galilæans as it is to the Idumæans.* It may be added that the Judaizing of Galilee embraced only the southern portion of it, for Ḳedesh, lying to the west of Lake Ḥûleh, marked the boundary between the land inhabited by Jews and the territory of the Tyrians.†

A similar condition of things prevailed also in the country to the *east of the Jordan*. Here, too, there had been numerous settlements of Jews, who, however, were so hard pressed by the heathen that Judas Maccabæus brought them to Jerusalem (1 Mac 5[45]). But at a later period the middle portion of the trans-Jordanic tract was conquered by Alexander Jannæus, and the Law imposed upon its inhabitants for the same reason as in the case of the Idumæans (cf. Jos. *Ant.* XIII. xv. 4). As the boundaries of *Peræa* (עֵבֶר הַיַּרְדֵּן), the district inhabited by the Jews, Josephus gives: Pella on the north, Philadelphia on the east, and Machærus on the south. Considerable tracts, however, of the trans-Jordanic country belonged to the Hellenistic cities, which were specially numerous here, and in which the Jews constituted only a minority. Also in the northern portion (Batanæa, Gaulanitis, Auranitis, and Trachonitis) the population was half-heathen half-Jewish (Jos. *BJ* III. iii. 5 f.). But the Jewish element was strengthened by the Babylonian Jews whom Herod transplanted here in order to combat the plague of robbers (Jos. *Ant.* XVII. ii. 13).

The task which, since the time of Ezra, had been assigned to strict Jews—the task of maintaining a complete isolation from the heathen world—was thus an extremely difficult one; for not only were they surrounded on all sides by the heathen, but Hellenistic cities intruded as *enclaves* in the midst of the Jewish country itself. Moreover,

* On Neh 11[25ff.] cf. now, above all, E. Meyer, *Entstehung des Judentums*, 106 f., 114 ff.

† Josephus says of Herod that, as an Idumæan, he was only half a Jew (*Ant.* XIV. xii. 2). On the other hand, when Agrippa I. once felt hurt by the epithet 'foreigner' in Dt 17[15], the people, whom he had gained over by his friendly offices, cried out, 'Thou art our brother' (Meg. *Sôtâ* vii. 8).

* Quite remarkable is the severe judgment on Galilee attributed to Joḥanan b. Zaccai (Jerus. *Shabbath* 15*d*): 'Galilee, Galilee, thou hatest the Law, therefore thou shalt yet find employment among robbers.'

† Cf. Buhl, *GAP* 72.

the rapid development of commerce brought the Jews into close contact with foreigners, while, finally, the foreign rule naturally introduced many non-Jewish elements into the land. The attractive influence which Greek culture exercised over the Jews is shown by the history of events immediately preceding the Maccabæan era; and even the Hasmonæans who originally came forward to oppose the ethnicizing of the Jews, were afterwards increasingly attracted by Hellenism, so that Aristobulus I. actually received the surname of Φιλέλλην ('friend of the Greeks'). Herod the Great, too, in spite of his essentially barbarian nature, sought to pose as a patron of Greek culture, surrounded himself with Greek orators and writers, had his sons educated at Rome, and made his appearance as a pure Greek in the Hellenistic cities that were subject to him. Nay, even in Jerusalem, to the scandal of the Jews, he caused theatres, circuses, and other Greek buildings to be erected. The same course was pursued by his successors. Tiberias, for instance, was a city with a perfectly pronounced Greek stamp, which may account for the fact that Jesus never visited it. The maintaining of Jewish uniqueness unimpaired was, we repeat, a very difficult task; much more difficult in Palestine than for the Jews of the Diaspora, who found themselves in unequivocal opposition to their environment.

ii. LANGUAGES.—The language of the Jews who returned to Palestine from Babylon was *Old Hebrew.* But even during the Persian domination *Aramaic*, which was then the language of commerce and diplomacy, began to force its way among the Jews as with the neighbouring peoples. The earliest traces of this are found in the extracts in the Book of Ezra drawn from an Aramaic historical writing. The Book of Daniel, composed in the 2nd cent. B.C., is written partly in Aramaic. At the time of Christ the ordinary speech of the people had come to be Aramaic, as is evident not only from the New Testament, but from various cultus terms used by Josephus, and from statements contained in the older Jewish literature. The necessary consequence of this change was the custom of having the passages of Scripture which were read in the synagogue followed by an Aramaic translation—a custom which the Mishna presupposes as an ancient inheritance. The Aramaic spoken by the Jews was a dialect of the Western Aramaic, the pronunciation of which, moreover, differed somewhat in different parts of the country, varying again amongst the Samaritans as compared with the Jews.*

The Old Hebrew language yielded, however, only gradually to the Aramaic idiom, and, before it disappeared, it developed a final species, the so-called *New Hebrew.* Even after men had begun to write in Aramaic, Hebrew writings were still composed; *e.g.* the Book of Chronicles (*c.* 300 B.C.), the Book of Sirach (not long after 200), various Psalms belonging to the Maccabæan period, and the Book of Ecclesiastes. The Hasmonæan rulers, who above all laboured for a national reawakening, favoured the ancient speech, as the Hebrew legends on their coins show; and the First Book of Maccabees was unquestionably written in Hebrew. But the last remark applies also to the Psalms of Solomon, which emanated from the middle of the last century B.C., and to the Apocalypses of Baruch and Ezra, composed after the Fall of Jerusalem. Later still, Hebrew continued to be for long the language of teachers of the Law, so that the Mishna (2nd cent. A.D.) is composed in New Hebrew. It was only after the date last named that Hebrew ceased to be a living language, and subsequently played the same rôle as Latin did in the Middle Ages. See, further, Driver, *LOT*[6] 503 ff.

Along with the idioms just discussed, we have to take into account, for NT times, also the *Greek* language. The factors we noticed as favouring the introduction of Greek culture paved the way also for the language of Greece. The clearest evidence of this is afforded by the very numerous Greek words adopted into the languages of the Jews. A few of these are found even in the Book of Daniel, notably such as are names of musical instruments (Driver, *l.c.* 501). In all probability אפריון of Ca 3[9] must also be considered Greek (=φορεῖον), and perhaps we should assign to the same category some other terms in the Song of Songs (*l.c.* 449 n.). In the Book of Ecclesiastes, again, we have Heb. renderings of Gr. forms of expression, such as עָשׂוֹת טוֹב=εὖ πράττειν, תַּחַת הַשֶּׁמֶשׁ=ὑφ' ἡλίῳ, etc. In the post-Biblical literature we encounter a large number of Greek loan-words, especially in the domain of political administration, or of commerce, or of public institutions.* It is characteristic, further, that, whereas on some of the later coins of the Hasmonæans we find Hebrew legends side by side with the Greek, the coins of the Herod family bear only Greek inscriptions. It may be held as certain that every Jew who made any claim to higher culture, and therefore in particular every one who was brought into contact with the court, understood and spoke Greek. Traders also must be assumed to have had a certain acquaintance with this tongue. And those Jews who lived in the immediate vicinity of districts where Greek was spoken would doubtless acquire the habit from their youth of using the Greek as well as the Aramaic language. But how far it was customary elsewhere to learn Greek, and how far the knowledge of this language had penetrated among the general body of the people, cannot be determined with certainty. According to *Sôṭā* ix. 14, during the war with Quietus [so read instead of 'with Titus'] in 115–117, it was forbidden that any one should teach his son Greek. From this we may infer that until then this had been a usual practice even within strict circles. It was also an important circumstance that Jerusalem, upon the occasion of the great festivals, was the rallying-point not only of the Palestinian Jews, but of those whose homes were in all other lands. Only a very small proportion of the latter can have been acquainted with Hebrew or Aramaic. And at times some of these, instead of returning to their homes, would settle in Jerusalem. It may also be supposed that the choice of the Alexandrian Jew, Boethus, to be high priest would draw a number of Alexandrians to Jerusalem (cf. Jos. *Ant.* XV. ix. 3). Special synagogues were built at Jerusalem for the use of those foreigners who did not understand the language of the country (Ac 6[9]; Tos. *Megilla* iii. 6). Proselytes also would come from other lands to settle in Jerusalem. In this way some knowledge of Greek may be presumed to have been diffused in Judæa as well. In Jn 12[20ff.] we hear of Greeks ("Ελληνες, *i.e.* either Jews of the Diaspora [?] or proselytes) who asked Philip to introduce them to Jesus—a circumstance which implies that this disciple at least understood Greek. That the same was the case with Jesus Himself cannot be

* Cf. Mt 26[73]; Dalman, *Grammatik des jüd.-pal. Aramäisch*, 43 ff., *Die Worte Jesu*, i. 64.

* As examples may be cited: אפרכא *ἔπαρχος*, בולי *βουλή*, סנהדרין *συνέδριον*, קטיגור *κατήγωρ*, פרוזבול *προσβολή*, קפילא *κάπηλος*, טימי *τιμή*, קטאלפטא *κατὰ λεπτά*, פנדקין *πανδοκεῖον*, בלני *βαλανεῖον*, דימוסין *δημόσιον*. Less numerous are the Latin loan-words, the majority of which, moreover, came in through the Greek: *e.g.* דיקומני *decumani*, דיסקיפילינה *disciplina*. Cf. S. Krauss, *Griechische und Lateinische Lehnwörter im Talmud, Midrasch und Targum*, 1–2 (1898–99).

proved with complete certainty from His conversations with Pilate, for the services of an interpreter may have been utilized, although this is not expressly mentioned in the narrative. We may compare the occasion when Josephus (*BJ* V. ix. 2) represents Titus as delivering an address to the people of Jerusalem, although we learn afterwards (VI. ii. 5) that on such occasions he availed himself of the help of Josephus as interpreter. From the last cited passage it is evident, at all events, that the mass of the people in the Jewish capital did not understand Greek.*

iii. POLITICAL CONSTITUTION.—The Greek rule, under which the Jews were brought by Alexander the Great, did not in general press very heavily upon subject peoples, who were left in the enjoyment of no small measure of self-government. The foreign domination confined itself mainly to the taxation of the provinces. So high, however, were these taxes at times, and such was the rapacity of some of those entrusted with the collecting of them, that there was scope here for oppression enough. In the Ptolemaic period Josephus (*Ant.* XII. iv. 3) tells us that the imposts were farmed out to the highest bidder, who could then claim military aid in recovering them. In the Seleucid period, on the other hand, the taxes were collected by officers of the king (1 Mac 1[29]). The internal administration, however, was in the hands of the native authorities, which meant for the Jews that henceforward, as before, they were governed by the high priest and the council associated with him (γερουσία, Jos. *Ant.* XII. iii. 3).† This council was originally an assembly of the heads of families (Neh 5[17]); but, after the high priest obtained the right of presiding over it, it came to be composed increasingly of members of the temple aristocracy (see art. SANHEDRIN in vol. iv.). The succession of legitimate high priests (the 'anointed' of Dn 9[23f.]) was violently interrupted under Antiochus Epiphanes. But after the Hasmonæans by their valour and address had raised the Jewish people to the rank of a Power that had to be reckoned with politically, the Syrian king nominated Jonathan high priest, and thus ruler of the nation of the Jews. The grateful people afterwards handed over this dignity to the last of the Maccabee brothers as a hereditary prerogative: he was to take charge of the sanctuary, appoint the officials, etc., and in his name all instruments were to be executed (1 Mac 14[41ff.]). Through the conquests which the Hasmonæans succeeded in making, the sphere of authority of the high priests (or, as they soon came to call themselves, kings) and of the Sanhedrin was materially enlarged. An important epoch for the internal administration was the reign of queen Alexandra, under whom the *Pharisees* succeeded in gaining a footing in the Sanhedrin and an influence upon the legislation.

The independence of the country was brought to a sudden end by the conquests of Pompey. The Jews were henceforward under the Roman domination. The extent of the land was materially diminished by Pompey's withdrawing the numerous Hellenistic cities from Jewish rule. On the other hand, he left to Hyrcanus, as high priest, a certain measure of political authority, so that the conditions were practically the same as those that existed immediately before the war for freedom. But in the year 57 B.C. Gabinius deprived Hyrcanus of all political rule by dividing the whole country into five districts, whose principal cities stood in direct subordination to the Romans (Jos. *Ant.* XIV. v. 4; *BJ* I. viii. 5). Cæsar, however, in 47 restored to Hyrcanus his former power and gave him the title of 'ethnarch.' But the real ruler was not the weak Hyrcanus, but the crafty Idumæan Antipater, who was made Procurator of Judæa, and who succeeded in having his sons Phasael and Herod appointed *strategoi* of Jerusalem and Galilee. After the death of Antipater (B.C. 43), Antony named the two brothers 'tetrarchs,' a step whereby Hyrcanus was once more deprived of all secular power and became merely an ecclesiastical prince. The attack made by the Hasmonæan Antigonus, with the aid of the Parthians, cost Hyrcanus and Phasael their offices, but Herod escaped to Rome, where he was nominated king of the Jews. It was not until the year 37 that he succeeded in conquering his kingdom, but from that date onwards he reigned undisturbed till his death. His position was that of a *rex socius.* Such a king was entrusted with rule only personally: after his death it was left open to the Emperor to decide as to the future lot of the particular country. For this reason Herod required the permission of the Emperor to put his own son to death. Nor could a *rex socius* wage war on his own initiative or conclude treaties, and, if the Romans were engaged in war, he had to furnish auxiliary troops. His right to coin money was restricted, and included only coins of small value. Otherwise he was an independent ruler, levied the various imposts of the country, was the supreme judge within his own land, and could execute capital sentences. Alongside of Herod there was still the Sanhedrin, but its authority was now, of course, very limited. The high priest was its president, but the setting up of an independent kingly authority had practically stripped this office of all significance. The high priests were appointed and deposed by Herod in the most arbitrary fashion—a course of procedure quite contrary to the Law, which intended this office to be held for life and to be hereditary.

After the death of Herod, his kingdom was divided into three portions. Philip received, with the rank of tetrarch, the northern trans-Jordanic territory, over which he ruled till his death, in A.D. 37. Herod Antipas, likewise as tetrarch, had Galilee and Peræa assigned to him, but was deposed in 37. Archelaus had been destined to rule as tetrarch over Judæa and Samaria, but as early as the year 6 the Emperor deprived him of his land, which he united more closely with the Roman Empire. It was, however, subject only indirectly to the Imperial legate in Syria, having a governor of its own, a Roman *Procurator* (ἐπίτροπος, ἡγεμών) chosen from the knightly body, who attended to the administration except when any very special necessity called for the action of the legate. The Procurator resided at Cæsarea on the seacoast; but on the occasion of the great festivals, when the mood of the people was always most turbulent, he came to Jerusalem, where he took up his residence in the former palace of Herod on the west side of the city. The largest Roman garrison was stationed at Cæsarea; but smaller bodies of troops were quartered in various towns throughout the land—amongst others in Jerusalem, where they had their barracks in the temple citadel of Antonia. The troops consisted entirely of non-Jews, the Jewish population being, it would appear, exempt from military service.* The taxes were now assigned to the Imperial

* Cf. Schürer, *GJV*³ ii. 18 ff., 63 ff.; Zahn, *Einleit. ins NT*, i. 1–51; Delitzsch, *Saat auf Hoffnung*, 1874, p. 185 ff.; Kautzsch, *Gramm. des bibl. Aram.* 4 ff.; Neubauer, *Studia Biblica*, Oxford, 1885, p. 39 ff.; Dalman, *Gramm. des jüd.-pal. Aram.* 344 ff., *Die Worte Jesu*, i. 1 ff., 63 ff.; Büchler, *Die Priester und der Kultus*, 1895, p. 61 ff.; A. Meyer, *Jesu Muttersprache*, 1896; T. K. Abbott, *Essays chiefly on the Original Texts of the Old and New Testament*, 1891, p. 129 ff.

† Büchler (*Die Tobiaden und Oniaden*, 1899) and H. Winckler (*Orient. Ltzg.* iii. 87 ff.) maintain that the pre-Maccabæan high priests had no political power; but their arguments are artificial and not convincing.

* Cf. Schürer, *GJV*³ i. 460.

*fiscus*, and were levied by the Procurator, the highest financial official, who in this work availed himself of the aid of the various *communes*. The duties, on the other hand, were farmed out at a fixed sum to private officials (*publicani*).* Both these 'publicans' and their subordinates were often of Jewish extraction (cf. *e.g.* Lk 19[1ff.]); on account of the inordinate greed and dishonesty that frequently characterized them, they were greatly hated and despised ('publicans and sinners,' Mt 9[10f.] *et al.*). The taxation was probably connected with the division of the country into eleven toparchies, each with its capital. The Roman taxation of Judæa after the deposition of Archelaus led also in the year 7 to the visit of the legate Quirinius, for the purpose of having the inhabitants assessed.† Finally, the Procurator was the highest judicial authority in the land, and had to attend to all important lawsuits; in particular, no capital sentence could be executed without being confirmed by him. In such cases he had sometimes associated with him a council made up of Romans (συμβούλιον, Ac 25[12]). In other respects the country enjoyed the right of self-government, which was exercised, as formerly, by the high priest and the Sanhedrin. Josephus (*Ant.* XX. 10) puts the matter very well when he says that the Jews, after they had had a monarchical, had now again an aristocratic constitution. But one essential and characteristic change was that the high priest was now appointed by the Roman Procurator. This condition of things underwent no interruption except when Agrippa I., under the title of king, gathered the whole land for a short time (41–44) under his sway. During this period the same arrangements were followed as under Herod the Great; the high priest, for instance, being appointed by the king. After Agrippa's death, not only Judæa, but the whole country of the Jews (with the exception of the districts to the east of the Jordan and in the north, which were assigned to Agrippa II.), came directly under the Roman sway. The constitution was now quite the same as in Judæa prior to Agrippa I., except that the Romans handed over the right of nominating the high priest first to Herod of Chalcis (44–48) and then to Agrippa II. The regular order of things came to an end with the outbreak of the final war for freedom. The land was divided into various districts, each under a ruler invested with dictatorial authority. But this organization gave way before the advance of the Romans. The last high priest, Phannias, was chosen by lot by the Zealots. He was a man of humble extraction, who had lived all his life in the country, so that he understood nothing of the office (Jos. *BJ* IV. iii. 8). After the Fall of Jerusalem, the relative independence of the Jews was gone for ever. The high priests disappeared along with the temple, and the Sanhedrin along with them. Henceforward the cohesion of the Jews was dependent solely upon those spiritual factors which lent such invincible strength to the Jews of the Diaspora and had been the real life-principle even of the Palestinian Jews—the Law and the Messianic hope.

From the foregoing sketch it will be evident that the whole of the properly Jewish administration throughout the period in question was concentrated in the high priest and the Sanhedrin (γερουσία, later συνέδριον, hence סנהדרין). The sway exercised by these authorities underwent change, however, in the course of time. It reached its culminating point under the Hasmonæans, when the high priest had become the ruler of an independent State. It was weakest under Herod, who left little room for other authorities beside him (cf. Jos. *Ant.* XIV. ix. 4). Those periods during which the Jews were under foreign rulers marked the normal stage of the power of these institutions. Originally, the jurisdiction of the high priest and the Sanhedrin extended only to Judæa. It was otherwise when the Hasmonæans enlarged the boundaries of the country, and it continued to be so during the following periods. But upon the partition of the land after the death of Herod, Judæa became once more the sphere of jurisdiction, the Samaritans being, of course, subject only to the Romans and not to the Jews, while in the other parts of the country the tetrarchs were the judicial heads (cf. Jos. *Ant.* XVIII. iv. 6, and the expression ἐπὶ ἡγεμόνας καὶ βασιλεῖς in Mt 10[18]).

As to the functions of the *Sanhedrin*, there are a number of allusions which enable us to form a pretty clear conception. In conjunction with the high priest it was the representative of the nation to foreign nations and princes (1 Mac 11[23] 12[3] 13[36]). It decided on measures for the fortification and defence of the land (1 Mac 12[35]; Jos. *BJ* IV. iv. 3; cf. Jth 4[8]). It granted dispensation in the matter of the sacred dues (Jth 11[14]), and made arrangements for the organization of the *personnel* of the temple (Jos. *Ant.* XX. ix. 6). But, above all, it was the supreme court of justice, all important cases being brought before it, and the decision lying with it when the inferior courts were not agreed (cf. Mt 5[22], Ac 4[15] 5[21] 6[12] 22[30], and the story of the Passion). In the earlier period no sentence of death could be carried out without the approval of the Sanhedrin (Jos. *Ant.* XIV. v. 3); but Herod, in order to make the Sanhedrin more pliable to his will, caused a number of its members to be put to death (*ib.* XIV. v. 4); and when at a later period he appealed to this court, his action would appear to have been more *pro forma* (*ib.* XV. vi. 2). Under the direct rule of the Romans, the Sanhedrin lost, as was noted above, the right of condemning to death (Jn 18[31]; cf. Jos. *Ant.* XX. ix. 1, and Jerus. *Sanhedrin* i. 1). As long as the Jewish State subsisted, the head of the Sanhedrin was the high priest. This is clear from the concurrent testimonies of the NT and Josephus. The statements of the Talmud on this subject are based upon later theories, and cannot be brought either in whole or in part into harmony with the reality. Thus the high priest had, at all times, a certain juridical and also political authority in addition to the functions he exercised in connexion with the cultus. Even in later times the members of the Sanhedrin were chosen by preference from the leading priestly families, a special fondness being shown for those who had held the office of high priest. But, as has already been said, the Pharisees succeeded, under queen Alexandra, in making their way into the Sanhedrin, and in maintaining their position there, a minority though they were, in the times that followed.

iv. SOCIAL CONDITIONS.—The principal occupation of the Jews in the time of Christ, as in the earlier periods, was *agriculture*, with which cattle-breeding was generally combined. The Letter of Aristeas (107 ff.) properly emphasizes the fact that in Palestine the right relation was established between town and country, the land being fertile, yet in need of diligent culture, and thus requiring a dense population settled upon it, so that the great cities did not flourish here, as elsewhere, at the expense of the country population. 'The land,' says the author, 'is thickly planted with olives, covered with fields of grain and leguminous plants, rich in wine and honey; the other fruits and the dates cannot be numbered, while cattle of

* Cf. Schürer, *GJV*[3] ii. 181 f.

† Jos. *Ant.* XVIII. i. 1. On Lk 2[1-5] cf., above all, Schürer, *l.c.* i. 508 ff.

all kinds are there in abundance, as well as rich pasture land for them.' Especially fruitful was Galilee, where Jesus spent most of His life, and from which He borrowed the numerous country scenes that we encounter in His parables. A great many people found employment on the larger estates, there being numerous servants, maids, and officials of all kinds attached to the service of a single house (cf. Lk $12^{42}$ $16^{1}$).* *Fishing* was a leading occupation in Galilee, being prosecuted in the teeming waters of the Lake of Gennesareth. We find allusions to this both in the Gospel narratives and in the words of Jesus (Mt $13^{47ff.}$, Lk $5^{10}$; cf. also the reference in Mt $7^{9f.}$ to bread and *fish*, corresponding to bread and *flesh* elsewhere). After the Jews, under the Hasmonæans, gained access to the sea, they began to prosecute fishing in it as well. A variety of preparations were made from the fish that were caught, and these again played their part as articles of commerce.† See, further, art. FISHING in vol. ii. *Hunting* is said in the Talmud to have been prosecuted by some for a livelihood; the abundance of game in Palestine is shown by the history of Herod, who was an enthusiastic sportsman.‡

An important source of income in post-exilic times was that derived from the work of the different *artisans*. Of the industry of some (builders, engravers, smiths, potters) we have a graphic picture in Sir 38; that of others is illustrated by the Talmudic writings.§ Ben Sira recognizes their importance (without them is no city built, and if they sojourn in a strange land, they need not hunger), but he considers them excluded from all higher spheres of activity, such, for instance, as the public service (v.$^{33f.}$). The later scribes held a sounder opinion on this subject, many of them, indeed, supporting themselves by manual labour.‖

*Commerce* took a great stride in the Greek period. Particularly after the Jews came into possession of Joppa and other seaport towns, they began to imitate zealously the example of their brethren of the Diaspora, and to take their share in the trade of the world. Palestine was favourably situated in this respect. Ancient caravan roads led through Galilee and Samaria to the coast, where the wares were shipped; Arab caravans brought the treasures of S. Arabia to the southern part of the land, from which they could in like manner be exported to the West. See, further, art. ROADS AND TRAVEL (IN OT), below, p. 369 f. The products of the fertile land, such as oil, grain, wine, flax, formed articles of export, which were exchanged for the products of Egypt and the Mediterranean lands. The Jews began to undertake long journeys by sea in order to enter into commercial relations with foreigners (Ps $107^{23ff.}$, Pr $7^{19f.}$, Sir $43^{24}$). In Palestine there were both merchant princes and petty traders (Sir $26^{29}$). The connexion between home-born and foreign Jews led also to a commencement being made in Palestine with those financial transactions for which the Jews of the Diaspora had developed such a turn, having found in Babylon an excellent training school.¶ Since such a condition of things was quite unknown to the traditional Law, and its enactments were felt to be hampering, Hillel devised the so-called '*prosbole*-rule,' whereby the legal prescription as to the cancelling of all debts every seven years was practically annulled (see, on this and on the Deuteronomic regulations as to the remission or suspension of debts, Driver, *Deut.* 178 ff.). The method of taking security was regulated very precisely, as the Talmudic writings show (cf. the Lexicons, *s.v.* אחריות). There were forms in which the names had merely to be inserted. According to Josephus (*BJ* II. xvii. 6), the bonds signed by debtors were kept in the public archives. As to the estimation in which mercantile occupations were held, Ben Sira speaks as disparagingly as he does of artisans. But at a later period things were otherwise, and both priests and teachers of the Law engaged in trade. For instance, Josephus (*Ant.* XX. ix. 2) tells us that the high priest Ananias was a great man of business; cf. Tos. *Tĕrûmôth*, where we read of the shop of a priest. We may also recall in this connexion the parables which Jesus borrows from commercial life (*e.g.* Mt $13^{45f.}$) The Essenes alone abjured on principle all contact with trade. See, further, art. TRADE in vol. iv. The increasing intercourse for trade purposes led, moreover, to other branches of industry. Thus *inns* sprang up along the much frequented roads, where the hosts had their charges for attending to travellers (cf. Lk $10^{34f.}$). The 'publicans' also, to whom the taxes were farmed out by the Romans or the native princes, were indebted to the growing commercial intercourse for their livelihood and for the wealth which they so often acquired.

How far the civil officials—the military do not come into consideration for reasons indicated above—received payment cannot be made out with certainty. In many cases their office may be assumed to have been an honorary one. This would be the case, for instance, with the elders of the community, the judges, the members of the Sanhedrin, etc. But, upon the generally accepted principle that the labourer is worthy of his hire,* it may probably be inferred that, if not the rulers of the synagogue and the collectors of alms (גבאי צדקה), yet at least the synagogue attendants (חזני הכנסת) had a salary. The same would probably hold good of the numerous officials attached to the court, who would be paid by the king. When we pass to the case of the priests and temple officials, we have precise information to go upon. The incomes of these were very considerable, and they increased with the increasing population and the growing wealth. The Levites were entitled to a tenth of the whole produce of the land, and had then to hand over a tenth of this to the priests (Nu $18^{25f.}$). Other dues besides, of all kinds and in some instances very considerable in amount, fell to the priests. In peaceful times all this was exactly regulated; for what Josephus (*Ant.* XX. viii. 8) relates of the high priests, that they sent their servants to the threshing-floors to seize the portion of the grain due to the priests, belongs to the latest period in the history of the Jewish State, when all legal relations were dissolved. Admittance to the priesthood or to the Levitical body was open to none but those who belonged to the tribe of Levi, and the members of the privileged caste watched over their prerogative with the utmost vigilance. Not only the priests in Palestine, but even the members of priestly families who lived in foreign lands, drew up exact genealogies whose correctness was examined at Jerusalem (Jos. *Vita*, 1; *c. Apion.* i. 7). In the matter of the revenues, however, account had to be taken merely of the priests who

* Cf., further, Vogelstein, *Die Landwirtschaft in Palästina*, 1894.

† Herzfeld, *Handelsgesch.* 105 f.

‡ *Ib.* 103. Cf. also art. HUNTING in vol. ii.

§ Delitzsch, *Handwerkerleben zur Zeit Jesu*, 1875; Rieger, *Versuch einer Technologie und Terminologie der Handwerke in der Mischna*, 1894.

‖ The characteristic saying of Simon b. Zoma, that when he looked on the crowd of humanity he felt impelled to thank God because He had formed them all to serve Him (*i.e.* to execute all His purposes), has reference not to the favoured body of the Wise, but to the division of labour amongst men (Jerus. *Berakhoth* 13*a*).

¶ It is very significant that To $1^{13}$ represents Achiacharus as 'purveyor' (ἀγοραστής) of a foreign king.

* Mt $10^{10}$, 1 Co $9^{7ff.}$. A man engaged to accompany one on a journey received, according to To $5^{15}$, not only travelling expenses but wages, and a present after the journey was ended.

lived in the Holy Land, who were divided into twenty-four classes, of which each had to officiate for a single week, but as a rule only twice a year. Quite a number of priests lived constantly in Jerusalem, but there were also some who had their home in other towns of Judæa, or even in Galilee. According to the calculations, somewhat doubtful, indeed, of Büchler (*Die Priester und der Kultus im letzten Jahrzehnte des Jerus. Tempels*, 48 ff.), the total number of priests in the last days of Jewish history amounted to about 20,000, of whom some 5000 lived in Jerusalem.

Of payment of *teachers* there is no mention. According to *Shabbath* i. 3, it was the synagogue attendants that gave elementary instruction to children on the Sabbath. These would receive at most a salary for attending to their duties in general. In any case, the teachers of the Law and the scribes did not live by their work of teaching; on the contrary, if they were without means, they pursued some handicraft, or even engaged in trade, in order to gain a livelihood.—That *physicians* received a fee when their services were over is plain from such passages as Sir 38$^{2}$, and Midrash *'Ekhā* on La 1$^{5}$.

The class of free citizens included also the *day-labourers*, who owned no land, and had no fixed employment, but hired out their labour daily (cf. the picturesque description in the parable of Mt 20$^{1ff.}$). When, not long before the outbreak of the war for freedom, the temple was at last finished, Josephus (*Ant.* XX. ix. 7) tells us that more than 18,000 labourers were thrown out of work, that it was resolved to utilize the treasure of the temple in order to procure employment for them, and that they received their wages even if they had wrought only a single hour. See also art. WAGES, below, p. 358.

Quite different was the standing of the *slaves* proper, who enjoyed no personal freedom. Even Jews might fall into this condition, if, for instance, they could not pay their debts (cf. Mt 18$^{25}$), or had been guilty of theft. The Law, however, contained a series of enactments (see full discussion of these in Driver, *Deut.* 181 ff.) by which the slavery of a Jew had a time limit imposed upon it. By means of the combining method of exegesis, this period was shortened still more, namely when the year of Jubilee happened to fall within the six years' period of service.* But, as the year of Jubilee was not really observed, this enactment could have no practical consequence. On the other hand, the later teachers of the Law laid it down that a Jewish girl was to serve as a slave only till she reached the age of puberty.† It may further be assumed that, as the prosperity of the people increased, such cases would always be more rare, and that poor Jews would be saved from this fate by the ready benevolence of the people, coupled with the organized methods for the relief of the poor (the third tenth every three years, and the collecting of alms in the synagogues). The majority of slaves were, accordingly, without doubt, foreigners acquired by purchase.‡ See, further, art. SERVANT in vol. iv.

When we compare the condition of the Jews immediately after the Exile with that which prevailed in the time of Christ, a very important difference, as was above remarked, presents itself. Instead of the small, poverty-stricken population of Nehemiah's day, we see a numerous people, which with energy and industry can turn to good account the many sources of wealth that abound in their land. In spite of their longing for Messianic times, in spite of the unreality of their world of ideas, they displayed in real life much adroitness and a remarkable turn for business, so that their position had come to be one of great material well-being. The clearest evidence of their extraordinary energy is afforded by the circumstance that, although they were very heavily burdened with taxes, they were not reduced to poverty, but on the contrary continued to increase in wealth. The dues they had to pay were partly sacred and partly secular. The former were based upon the enactments of the Priests' Code (esp. Lv 2$^{3}$ 6$^{16-18}$ [Heb. $^{9-11}$] 7$^{32-34}$, Nu 18$^{8-28}$), with which certain prescriptions from Deuteronomy (14$^{22-29}$ 18$^{1-8}$)* were combined. The principal due was the Levites' tenth of all the produce of the soil, in the paying of which the most painful exactness was shown by strict Jews (cf. Mt 23$^{23}$). But before the tithing of the produce of the soil there was a twofold due deducted: the first-fruits of the 'seven kinds' (see Schürer, *GJV*$^{3}$ ii. 249), viz. barley, wheat, grapes, figs, pomegranates, olives, and honey; and the *tĕrûmā*, which was not exactly measured, but was understood to be the fiftieth part (see Schürer, *l.c.* 249 f.) of all the fruit of field and tree. From the products which were then tithed there was taken (in addition to the tenth part paid to the priestly tribe) a *second* tenth,† which, however, was destined, along with the tenth of cattle (Lv 27$^{32f.}$), for sacrificial feasts. But every three years a *third* tenth (the מעשׂר עני, the 'poor-tithe,' according to the Rabb. interpretation of Dt 14$^{28f.}$; but see Driver, *l.c.* 170 n.) was deducted for the benefit of the poor. Further, the firstlings of all animals that might be offered in sacrifice were claimed as a due, while a sum of money had to be paid for firstborn children and the firstlings of unclean animals (Nu 18$^{15-17}$); not to speak of a firstlings' cake (the *ḥallā*) of coarse flour (Nu 15$^{20f.}$, cf. Ro 11$^{16}$), and a part of the wool at the first shearing (Dt 18$^{4}$). Lastly, there were various occasional offerings that required to be brought. The annual temple poll-tax (Ex 30$^{14f.}$, Mt 17$^{24}$), on the other hand, was not high (half a shekel for every adult male), and could not be felt except by the very poorest. See more fully, on the subject of this paragraph, Schürer, *GJV*$^{3}$ ii. 243–262 [*HJP* II. i. 230–254].

In addition to these very considerable dues,‡ there were the secular taxes. After the Jews were freed from the Greek domination, which, from a financial point of view, was very burdensome, requiring a third part of grain and half the produce of fruit trees to be paid, the taxes passed to the Hasmonæans.§ When Herod afterwards became king, he obtained command of all the secular taxes of the country. According to Josephus (*Ant.* XV. ix. 1), these consisted mainly in the rendering of a certain proportion of the produce of the land, besides which the king levied a market toll on all that was sold in Jerusalem (*ib.* XVII. viii. 4). Herod's whole revenue, according to *Ant.* XVII. xi. 4 (with which, indeed, *BJ* II. vi. 3 does not agree), amounted to more than 900 talents (=£369,000) a year. The Jews complained bitterly of the amount of the taxes laid

* Jos. *Ant.* IV. viii. 28; cf. Saalschütz, *Mosaisches Recht*, 713.

† Saalschütz, *l.c.* 817.

‡ With these foreign slaves they had generally, according to the Talmud, a great deal of trouble; cf. Zadok Kahn, *L'esclavage selon la Bible et le Talmud*, 1867, p. 173 f. For an earlier period, cf. Sir 33$^{24ff.}$.

* On the irreconcilable conflict between these codes in certain particulars, see Driver, *Deut.* 169 f., 218 ff.

† Following the Rabb. interpretation of Dt 14$^{22-27}$, which held the tithe here prescribed to be distinct from, and in addition to, the tithe of Nu 18$^{21-28}$; but see Driver, *l.c.* 169 f.; Schürer, *l.c.* 246; and art. TITHE in vol. iv. p. 730.

‡ In the Sabbatical years all dues based upon the produce of the soil would of course be dispensed with (cf. Jos. *Ant.* XVII. xi. 6).

§ Regarding their system of taxing we know nothing except the few details contained in Josephus (*Ant.* XVII. x. 6; cf. Schürer, *GJV*$^{3}$ i. 345). The people felt the taxation of Herod to be heavy in comparison with what had gone before (Jos. *ib.* XVII. xi. 2).

upon them, and alleged that it was only by bribing the king himself and his tax-collectors that it was possible to save oneself from injustice (*Ant.* XVII. xi. 2, cf. viii. 4). But of course we are not to lend too much credit to these complaints, especially as we learn that, after the great famine, Herod voluntarily granted the people remission of a third of the taxes (*Ant.* XV. x. 4). Herod's successors no doubt organized the matter of taxation upon the same lines as himself. Herod Antipas, who derived from his territories an annual revenue of 200 talents, had customs officials stationed on the frontiers (Mt 9[9]), to levy duties on imports and possibly also on exports. Agrippa, too, who for a short time had the whole land under his sway, would probably utilize the system of his predecessor. But during his reign not only was the market toll at Jerusalem abolished (see below), but the king, who was anxious to gain the affections of the Jews, remitted also the duty upon the houses of the capital (*Ant.* XIX. vi. 3). During the period that intervened between the deposition of Archelaus and the accession of Agrippa I., Judæa,* and, after Agrippa's death, the whole country, was taxed by the Romans, and the revenues passed into the Imperial *fiscus* (cf. Mt 22[21]). The taxes proper were levied by the Procurator, the commercial imposts were farmed out to private officials. The taxes consisted partly of a proportion of the produce of the soil, which was paid either in kind or in money, but they included also a poll-tax, which was levied even on women and slaves.† Vitellius remitted to the Jews the market toll that had to be paid at Jerusalem (*Ant.* XVIII. iv. 3); but in spite of this the taxes were very high, and were felt by the people to be extremely oppressive (Tac. *Ann.* ii. 42).

Taking all these dues together, we see that the material resources of this little nation were drawn upon to an extraordinary degree, and that none but a very energetic and temperately living people could have borne such burdens, and upon the whole even prospered under them. From the social point of view, the Jews must be reckoned among the more fortunate nations. As long as the foreign yoke was not too heavy and their religious susceptibilities were not offended, there prevailed amongst them a considerable degree of contentment and a healthy enjoyment of life (Sir 14[11. 14]), which at times might rise to hearty rejoicing, as we see, for instance, in the Song of Songs and the noisy celebration of the Feast of Tabernacles. No doubt there were social extremes, the one of wealth and luxury, the other of grinding poverty (cf. the parable of Dives and Lazarus), but the majority belonged to neither of these classes, and in peaceful times led a temperate and generally contented life.

v. PARTIES.—If the Jewish people was thus free from sharp social contrasts, there were opposing elements of another kind amongst them, which consumed their strength in the most dangerous fashion, and whose conflicts are the moving factors of the whole post-exilic history, until at last they brought about the destruction of the nation. The essential principle of this opposition is of a religious character, social and political principles play only a subordinate rôle in it.

What in pre-exilic times had been the wealthy secular nobility, became after the Exile the temple aristocracy: a privileged class to which a number of quite diverse circumstances gave a marked superiority. We have seen how, in consequence of the growing prosperity of the nation, the priests necessarily came into the possession of great wealth. At the same time the condition of things involved the passing of the relics of independence which were left to the Jews, into the hands of the high priest and his priestly coadjutors. In this way they were brought to interest themselves in actual politics, and thus were gradually forced into opposition to the strict party, whose ideal was complete political passivity and a confident expectation of Divine intervention. There were thus developed opposite religious principles, which by constant friction were always brought into sharper contrast. The 'pious' could not avoid looking upon their opponents with the same eyes as those with which the prophets had regarded the secular nobility of their day. The rich aristocracy were thought of as the ungodly, who believed not in God's help but in political devices often of a desperate nature; they were the unrighteous, who used their wealth and their influence with foreign nations to inflict all kinds of damage upon their opponents, the strict party. At the same time it would be a serious misunderstanding to reduce this opposition to a mechanical system, and to suppose, for instance, that all the priests belonged to the broader party. That there were even high priests who sympathized with the stricter tendency is sufficiently proved by the instance of Simon the Just, whose memory is still glorified in the later Pharisaic literature; and among the ordinary priests there were many who belonged to the 'pious.' Jewish history shows also that, among the priests who politically occupied the standpoint of the secular school, there were earnest men who were prepared to lose their life rather than neglect the duties assigned to them in connexion with the cultus (Jos. *Ant.* XIV. iv. 3). It would be equally wrong to suppose that the strict party represented an opposition to the temple cultus because this was in the hands of the temple aristocracy. That it was not so may be shown from the way in which Ben Sira, who himself belonged to the stricter school, exhorts his readers to honour the priests and to pay them their appointed dues (Sir 7[29ff.]). The correct view is simply that in the ranks of the temple aristocracy there was a party prepared to sacrifice the sacred uniqueness of Israel for the sake of worldly advantages, and that this disposition was so strongly developed that its representatives could not but appear to the strict school in the light of apostates.

The name under which in later times the adherents of the secular party meet us is *Sadducees*, properly members of the Jerusalem priesthood (from *Zadok*, 1 K 1[8], Ezk 40[46]). In opposition to them the *Pharisees* stand for the most uncompromising representatives of the stricter tendency. The name means properly 'those who *separate* themselves,' who keep at a distance from the ordinary unclean life and from all unclean persons (in contrast to the *'am hā-'āreẓ*, the common people, who were indifferent in matters of Levitical purity, etc.).

It was the elevation of the Maccabees that was responsible for the above-described opposition becoming a chronic malady. The Maccabees were originally allies of the stricter school, but, after they attained to the supreme power, they slipped over to the views of the temple aristocracy and thus came into conflict with the Pharisees. Above all, it was repugnant to the strict party that the Hasmonæans should confuse and corrupt the Messianic hopes. It is evident from the so-called First Book of Maccabees that the adherents of the Hasmonæan princes believed that these hopes had found a fulfilment in the persons of the latter. After they had conquered the whole land and assumed the royal title, it did indeed look as if

* The Samaritans, who also came under the Roman sway, were relieved, according to *Ant.* XVII. xi. 4, of a third of the taxes, because they had taken no part in the revolt.

† Cf., further, Schürer, *GJV*[3] i. 511.

the old Davidic kingdom had been raised up once more. The condemnation of this desecration of the Davidic throne and the sacred hopes meets us in the Psalms of Solomon ($17^{4ff.}$) and in a passage in the Book of Enoch (chs. 94 ff.); cf. also Assump. Mos. $6^{1ff.}$. The overthrow of the Maccabæan house cleared the air. The Sadducees were completely subjected under Herod, and had lost all influence. Under the Roman domination, the high priest, and with him the Sadducees, regained greater political importance (see above, p. 48), but they no longer played the principal part. When the war for freedom broke out, they sought at first to stifle the movement, and then, when they failed in this, to guide it. But the waves now ran so high that they quickly swept away this time-worn and enfeebled party. See, further, art. SADDUCEES in vol. iv.

The development of *Pharisaism* was very materially shaped by the Maccabæan period. Opposition to the Hasmonæans brought out its one-sided tendencies to the full, especially when, under Alexander Jannæus, things went so far as a civil war, in which the Pharisees were at first victorious, but afterwards beaten and cruelly punished. But it was a momentous circumstance that immediately thereafter, under queen Alexandra, they gained political power. They forced their way into the Sanhedrin, carried a number of their laws, and thus tasted the sweets of rule. Thereby their less estimable qualities were developed, and there arose among them those Pharisees with whom we make acquaintance in the Gospels. With them the external flourished at the expense of the internal; beneath their numerous religious exercises, such as fasting, ablutions, prayer, almsgiving, there was often concealed an impure, ambitious, haughty disposition, whose end and aim was to lord it over the crowd. Their renunciation of all interest in foreign politics was abundantly compensated by the influence they exercised over the people—an influence to which even the Sadducees had to bend (Jos. *Ant.* XVIII. i. 4). It may be added that it is not only the New Testament that describes the Pharisees in this way. The Assumption of Moses contains a passage ($7^{3ff.}$) of precisely similar import, which also refers without doubt to the Pharisees.* Of course there were exceptions among them, as we learn even from the New Testament; and the Psalms of Solomon, which emanated from Pharisaic circles, still contain much of the pure and noble piety which we encounter in the canonical Psalms. See, further, art. PHARISEES in vol. iii.

While the sharp opposition between the Sadducees and the Pharisees receded somewhat after the overthrow of the Hasmonæans, there grew up within Pharisaism itself opposing influences, which were destined to be still more dangerous to the life of the people. Although the Pharisees otherwise were identified with the quiet and passive waiting for the time of the Messiah, the enrolment of the Jewish people by Quirinius (see above, p. 49[a]) gave birth to a new party, which in other respects agreed with the Pharisees, but regarded the struggle for freedom and the casting-off of the Roman yoke as a sacred duty. The founders of this party of *Zealots* (קנאין) were a man of Galilee, named Judas, and a Pharisee, Sadduk (cf. Jos. *Ant.* XVIII. i. 4). From the ranks of these patriots there came, during the last decades before the war for freedom, the utterly ruthless *Sicarii*, who, armed with a short dagger (*sica*), mingled with the crowd, especially on the great feast days, and selected their victims alike from among foreigners and from their fellow-countrymen (Jos. *Ant.* XX. viii. 10; *BJ* II. xvii. 6, etc.; Ac $21^{38}$). Against wild offshoots like these the more sober-minded of the Pharisees came forward, and were thus at times led to go hand in hand with the Sadducees.

The theological points of difference between the Sadducees and the Pharisees, upon which Josephus lays so much stress, are merely particular illustrations of the above-described deeper contrasts. The spiritual development which had taken place in the stricter circles since the time of Antiochus Epiphanes, and the new conceptions which had been thus reached, were not shared by the Sadducees, who held conservatively to ancient tradition. Hence they rejected and ridiculed the doctrine of a resurrection — a circumstance from which we may infer that they did not accept the Book of Daniel.* In general, the present possessed more significance for them than the hope of Israel, which was the life-principle of the stricter party. Similar was the state of things with their rejection of the belief in spirits and angels. In the circles of the 'pious' there had also been a very pronounced development of the notions regarding these, which had its roots, indeed, in the earlier OT writings, but yet was so peculiarly influenced, partly by foreign conceptions, that strict conservatives were bound to reject it, especially if, like the Sadducees, they had positivist tendencies. When the Sadducees, again, laid stress upon the freedom of the will, this was connected with their political leanings as above described: in their polemic they would have in view not only the passivity of the 'pious,' but also the growing disposition to transfer the real sphere of history to the angel-world, and to convert history into a conflict between good and evil spirits, of which human history was only a reflexion. As to legal enactments, the Sadducees held strictly to the Law, and rejected the oral Torah of the Pharisees. It is, no doubt, also in this connexion that the controverted points mentioned in the Jewish literature come in, but these give no clear picture of the root-principle of the opposition.

The third, 'philosophical,' party, mentioned by Josephus generally along with the Pharisees and the Sadducees, namely the *Essenes*, belonged to an entirely different world. This was a small ascetic sect, permeated with mysticism, and holding some extremely strange notions, the origin of which is still an unsolved problem. From a social point of view, the community of goods was the most characteristic feature of their organization. They employed themselves in agriculture and various handicrafts, but would have absolutely nothing to do with commerce. At least the majority of them renounced marriage. They acknowledged the temple, and sent votive gifts to it, but rejected entirely animal sacrifice. They held the Law in very high esteem. They believed in the immortality of the soul, but did not teach the resurrection of the body, because they regarded connexion with the body as a species of bondage for the soul. The doctrine of angels played a great part in their system. Among their many peculiar customs, those which express a veneration for the sun are the most notable, because they show most clearly that we cannot completely account for this sect from Judaism itself. What is genuinely Jewish in their opinions and customs comes nearest to Pharisaism, but the differences are too great for Essenism to be set down as a degenerate offshoot from it. This small, peaceful body never probably had very much weight. See, further, art. ESSENES in vol. i.

* The authority followed by Josephus in *Ant.* XVII. ii. 4 knows of the Pharisees as εἰς τὸ πολεμεῖν καὶ βλάπτειν ἐπηρμένοι.

* Cf. Mt $22^{23ff.}$. On the question to what extent the Sadducees recognized the Torah alone as Holy Scripture, as several of the Church Fathers assert, see Schürer, *GJV*[3] ii. 411 ff.

vi. Education and Culture.—Regarding the education of Jewish children we have only scanty information. According to the Bab. Talmud (*Bābā bathrā*, 21*a*), Joshua b. Gamaliel (probably the high priest who held office A.D. 63–65) appointed teachers for boys in every province and every city, and children were brought to these when they were six or seven years of age. According to *Shabbath* i. 3, the synagogue attendant (*ḥazzān*) was required on Sabbath to teach children to read. Josephus (*c. Apion.* i. 12) and Philo (ed. Mangey, ii. 577) speak as if it was customary for the Jews, even as children, to learn the Law. But this can refer only to the circle of the scribes and the educated classes, and not to the mass of the people. For if children learned in the boys' school to read the Law, and if this accomplishment was general, it would have been superfluous to have the Hebrew text translated into Aramaic at the synagogue service (see above, p. 47[a]). The latter custom was manifestly due to the circumstance that the common people no longer understood Hebrew. When, therefore, Jesus, the carpenter's son (Mt 13[55]), was able to read and expound the Bible text (Lk 4[16ff.]), this would naturally strike the people as something unusual and excite their wonder. But it is impossible to decide with certainty how large the circles were that possessed rolls of the Law (1 Mac 1[56f.]). As little are we informed as to the number that were able to write, although it is evident that the growth of commerce and the increasing pursuit of a business life must have contributed largely to the spread of this accomplishment (Lk 16[6]). There is no mention of any regular instruction of girls, a branch of education which was not enjoined in the Law.*

The higher education consisted in the stricter circles of a deeper study of the Law, especially the special enactments that had been orally transmitted. The student selected some eminent legal expert as his teacher. Thus, for instance, the two famous exegetes Judas and Matthias were very popular teachers of youth at the time of Herod the Great (Jos. *Ant.* XVII. vi. 2); the disciples of Hillel and Shammai formed two well-defined schools of interpreters of the Law. St. Paul studied at Jerusalem under Gamaliel (Ac 22[3]), etc. After his course of instruction was complete, the disciple was reckoned among the Wise (חֲכָמִים), as opposed to the unlearned (הֶדְיוֹט, *i.e.* the Gr. *ἰδιώτης*).† Yet the detailed statements contained in the Talmudic writings as to the instruction in these higher schools (בָּתֵּי הַמִּדְרָשׁ), and as to the organization of teachers and pupils, are not to be transferred *simpliciter* to the time of Christ, for without doubt the conditions subsequent to the destruction of the State must have influenced the development of things.‡

But there were other circles in which the higher education had a somewhat different character, inclining more towards the worldly culture of the time, as was the case in great measure with the Hellenistic Jews. As a matter of course, it was the nobility and the courtiers that favoured this culture. A good example of such an education presents itself in the person of Josephus, a scion of the leading temple aristocracy, related on his mother's side to the Hasmonæan royal family. According to his own account (*Vita*, 2 f.), he commenced even as a child to read the Law, and speedily made such progress that, when a boy of fourteen, he used to be consulted by the leading priests on points of interpretation of the Law. At the age of sixteen he began to study carefully the tenets and maxims of the three sects—the Sadducees, the Pharisees, and the Essenes; nay, he even lived for three years with a rigid ascetic in the desert, in order to put also this conception of life to the proof. When nineteen years old he decided to cast in his lot with the Pharisaic party, but he studied, further, the Greek language and literature. He had such a command of Greek that in his twenty-sixth year he was able to travel to Rome, where he obtained access to the Empress, who treated him with great consideration. He tells us, however, regarding his attainments in Greek, that, while he had made a thorough study of the language, his Jewish usages had hampered him in acquiring an exact pronunciation of it. 'It is not our way to accord any great appreciation to those who have learned many languages . . . for this is an accomplishment of which slaves are as capable as freemen. But those alone are regarded as wise who thoroughly understand the laws, and can expound the Holy Scriptures' (*Ant.* XX. xii. 2). That Josephus had difficulty, further, in the use of Greek in writing, is evident from the circumstance that, in preparing his history of the Jewish war, he availed himself of the help of colleagues who were proficient in Greek (*c. Apion.* i. 9). But he not only devoted himself to the study of the language, but, as his writings show, had read a very considerable number of Greek authors, besides being acquainted in some measure with Greek philosophy. Here, then, we see how, in the case of a Palestinian Jew of good family, a strictly Jewish education might be combined with a Hellenizing tendency.*

As to the ordinary stage of culture among the Jews, this was in general conditioned by their acknowledged dependence upon the Holy Scriptures. Here lay hidden all the treasures of wisdom for those who knew how to dig them up. While the Hellenistic Jews were under the influence of Greek philosophy, and made frequent attempts to discover in the Scriptures the ideas of foreign wisdom, the native exegesis was based essentially upon the text itself, whose many secrets it was sought to penetrate by an acuteness which displayed itself in the form of ingenious combinations of passages of Scripture. Nothing had any value whose presence could not be demonstrated in the Law and in the Scriptures. And yet the world of ideas in which these men moved was not so completely uninfluenced by foreign culture as they themselves may have imagined. Several centuries of contact with Parsism had not passed without leaving clear traces.† As little were the Palestinian Jews able to shut themselves off from the influence of the Greek spirit, by whose effects they were everywhere surrounded, and whose traces may be largely observed in the Palestinian Midrash.‡ Yet all this worked quietly and unconsciously, and did not lead to any essential transformation of the Palestinian culture.

As far as a knowledge of *history* was concerned, there was naturally a disposition to abide by the information contained in the Bible; whereas there were only broken reminiscences of the events of the post-Biblical period. In this respect, indeed,

* Later Jews deduced from the word 'sons' in Dt 11[19] that the Law did not require the instruction of daughters (Bacher, *Die Agada der Tannaiten*, ii. 372).

† On the other hand, the phrase עַם הָאָרֶץ 'people of the land' is used in opposition to *Pharisees*, who were not all scribes.

‡ Cf. Weber, *Jüd. Theologie*[2], 1897, p. 125 ff.

* On the other hand, when Rabbi Ishmael was asked whether it was allowable to learn Greek wisdom along with the Law, he replied (in allusion to the words 'by day and by night,' Jos 1[8], Ps 1[2] etc.): 'Only if thou canst find a time which is neither day nor night' (Bacher, *Die Agada der Tannaiten*, i. 262).

† Cf. E. Stave, *Ueber den Einfluss des Parsismus auf das Judentum*, 1898; also the art. Zoroastrianism by J. H. Moulton in vol. iv. The Babylonian influence contended for, especially by Gunkel, is still somewhat problematical, and its extent is in any case not yet demonstrated.

‡ Cf. Freudenthal, *Hellenistiche Studien*, 1875, p. 66 ff.; Siegfried, *Philo von Alexandrien*, 283 ff.

a man like Josephus forms an exception, but he is likewise an exception among his Palestinian fellow-countrymen, and his great work on the history of Israel was intended not for Jews but for the rest of the world.*

Of an acquaintance with *natural science* we can scarcely speak. The Book of Enoch, it is true, occupies itself in detail with cosmological and astronomical secrets, and shows, amidst a multitude of fantastic notions, a knowledge of the twelve signs of the zodiac, the regular phases of the moon, the solar and lunar years, perhaps the 8-year cycle of the Greeks, the four intercalary days, and it contains also some geographical allusions (chs. 72 ff.). But this must be viewed as peculiar to a few writers, and not as the standard of the prevailing culture. At all events, in a letter of R. Gamaliel II.† the intercalating of 30 days into the current year is justified on the ground that the lambs are still small, and the crops not yet ripe. On the 30th day of each month the Sanhedrin met, and, if it was then announced to it that the moon-crescent was visible, the day was marked as holy, so that the preceding month had only 29 days counted to it. If the day was cloudy, the new moon was not reckoned to commence till the following day.‡ Geographical knowledge was enlarged by the journeys of Jewish merchants, but yet was in general superficial and vague.§

*Medicine* was upon a primitive basis. The mild and sensible Ben Sira exhorts his readers not to despise the physician's help, since the Lord has created medicines out of the earth, which the apothecary knows how to mix and the physician how to apply (Sir 38[1ff.]). The healing powers of the various hot springs of Palestine had been discovered, and they were largely taken advantage of (Jos. *Vita*, 16; *Ant.* XVII. vi. 5). But the conception of diseases was still essentially a purely religious, or, in most instances, a superstitious one, so that in the treatment of them all kinds of magical methods took a prominent place. In general, the belief in magic played no mean rôle amongst the Jews, although it was forbidden in the Law. This was a sphere in which the Law was powerless to control the notions of men.‖ See art. MAGIC in vol. iii.

It was only in the sphere of *religion* that the standard of popular education was high, and it was regarded as extremely important to see that this should be so. While the cultus was essentially the concern of the priests, there had been for long established all over the land synagogues, where religious instruction was attended to and the people acquired an acquaintance with the holy Scriptures (Ac 15[21]). The synagogue building (בֵּית הַכְּנֶסֶת, *συναγωγή* or *προσευχή*) contained a press where the sacred writings were kept, and an elevated place where the reader stood. The service was introduced by repeating the passages Dt 6[4-9. 11. 13-21], Nu 15[37-41]; then came a prayer spoken by a member of the congregation, to the accompaniment of the 'Amen' and other responses by the people. This was followed by the lesson from the Law, which was read by several members, preferably priests or Levites, and translated into Aramaic, verse by verse, by an interpreter (מְתוּרְגְּמָן). Next came the reading of a section from the Prophets, which was translated in the same way (Lk 4[17], Ac 13[15]). To this reading there was attached a sermon, during the delivery of which the speaker was accustomed to sit, whereas the readers stood (Lk 4[20ff.]). The service closed with the benediction (Nu 6[22ff.]), which was pronounced by a priest. The principal service was that of Sabbath forenoon, but there were less elaborate services also on Sabbath afternoon and on some week days. Lastly, Divine service was celebrated on all feast days. In this way those of the people who felt that they formed a community had abundant opportunity given them of making acquaintance with the Scriptures and of receiving instruction and edification. It is worthy of note how in this matter there is a retrocession of any privileged class, the service being of quite a democratical character. Even if a preference was given to priests in the reading of the Scriptures, this function could be discharged by others as well, while the delivery of the address was open to any member of the congregation, or any qualified visitor who happened to be present (see art. SYNAGOGUE, vol. iv. p. 641[b]).

The above account of things applies, properly speaking, only to the men. But if we would have a complete picture of the stage of culture among the Jews, we must face the question of how it stood with the women. There is a want of historical data here, but certain characteristic features come out. For instance, we learn from Josephus (*Ant.* XVII. ii. 4) that the Pharisees exercised great influence over women, a circumstance which proves that the latter felt an interest in party questions and themselves took sides. Thus even queen Alexandra allowed herself, contrary to all the traditions of the Hasmonæans, to be guided by the Pharisees. The Gospels show us how deep was the religious interest on the part of women, and how receptive they were to the teaching of Jesus. On the other hand, evidence of the slender culture of women is afforded by the circumstance that it was they especially that devoted themselves to magical arts, so that even women of noble birth were at times accused of sorcery.*

vii. ART AND LITERATURE.—With the Jews the first place among the fine arts is held by *music*, because this had entered into the service of religion. The temple musicians formed a guild, in which the technique and the understanding of the numerous technical expressions were hereditary, not being communicated to outsiders—a circumstance which explains why these expressions, when they occur in the Psalms, especially in their titles, were unintelligible to the Greek translators of the LXX.† The members of this guild, who were not at first (Ezr 10[23f.], Neh 7[1. 73]) reckoned among the Levites, had been by the time of the Chronicler (1 Ch 6[33-47]) included in this class of temple officials, and shortly before the destruction of the State they obtained, by the aid of Agrippa II., the right of wearing the same linen garments as the priests—an innovation which, according to Josephus (*Ant.* XX. ix. 6), contributed to bring about the punishment of the people. The pieces that were sung were the Psalms of the Old Testament. The whole of these were not, indeed, adapted to this purpose (*e.g.* Ps 119), but in the case of a large proportion of them there is ancient testimony to their liturgical use. The Psalms were sung by the official singers, the people struck in only with certain responses. The singing was accompanied by harps, zithers, flutes, and cymbals, although, unfortunately, we are not informed as to the exact form of procedure either with the singing or the instrumental accompaniment.

* How inconsiderable were the historical recollections in the Rabbinical literature is shown in Dérenbourg's *Essai sur l'histoire, etc. de la Palestine*, 1867.

† To be found in Dalman's *Aramäische Dialektproben*, 1896, p. 3.

‡ It was not until about 200 years after the destruction of Jerusalem that the Jews began to fix the new moon on astronomical grounds. See Riehm, *HWB* ii. 1094, and cf. art. NEW MOON in vol. iii. p. 522[b], and TIME in vol. iv. p. 764[a].

§ Cf. Neubauer, *Géographie du Talmud*, 289 ff.

‖ To 11[7]; Jos. *Ant.* VIII. ii. 5; L. Blau, *Das altjüdische Zauberwesen*, 1898; Schürer, *GJV*[3] iii. 294 ff.

* Blau, *Das altjüdische Zauberwesen*, 23 ff.

† Cf. Jacob in *ZATW* xvi. (1896) 171.

The trumpets blown by the priests would not belong to the orchestra proper, but would serve simply to mark fixed points in the service. How early the liturgical system was developed may be inferred partly from the statements of the Chronicler and partly from the very graphic description in Sir 50. But the Psalms were sung also outside the temple, especially at the Paschal meal in private houses (Mt 26[30]). Alongside of this sacred music there was also a secular species, which was used especially to accompany the popular dance (Mt 11[17]). The Israelites, in fact, had always been a music-loving people, with whom this exercise was resorted to on all occasions either of rejoicing or of mourning. The height to which popular poetry had risen among them is evident above all from the Song of Songs, which points back to the songs sung at wedding celebrations.

On the other hand, the *plastic arts* were completely forbidden to the Jews, in so far at least as they had to do with the representation of any living creature. When Pilate on one occasion, forgetting the consideration for Jewish scruples usually shown by the Procurators, caused standards emblazoned with pictures of the Emperor to be brought to Jerusalem, the popular feeling was so violently excited that after a while he ordered the offensive emblems to be removed (Jos. *Ant.* XVIII. iii. 1). The golden eagle which Herod had placed over one of the gates of the temple was an abomination to strict Jews, and a number of fanatics, upon the occasion of a false report of the king's death, tore it down—an act for which they were themselves punished with death (*ib.* XVII. vi. 2). Those of high rank, indeed, set themselves above the strict custom in such matters. The Hasmonæan queen Alexandra caused portraits of her children, Aristobulus and Mariamne, to be painted and sent to Antony (*ib.* XV. ii. 6). Agrippa I. had statues made of his daughters (*Ant.* XIX. xix. 1). In the non-Jewish cities both Herod and his successors played the part in general of decided patrons of Greek art. In Cæsarea on the coast, and in other towns, they caused temples and theatres to be erected. Nay, Jerusalem itself did not escape, for Herod had a theatre and a hippodrome constructed in it, to the great offence of the strict Jews. The same course was pursued by Herod Antipas at Tiberias, which assumed quite the stamp of a Greek city (see above, p. 47[a]). The Jews thus made acquaintance with Greek architecture mainly as an element in heathen civilization, and on this account the splendid pile of temple buildings at Jerusalem was not an unmixed source of joy to the strict party. That there were some Jews, however, who availed themselves of this art is shown by the sepulchral monuments in the Ḳidron valley, one of which, according to the inscription, belonged to a priestly family.

The Jewish *literature* that has come down to us from this period, with the single exception of the historical works of Josephus,* is composed in the interest of religion. Shortly before the Maccabæan era, the Book of Sirach, a collection of rules of conduct and *Hokhma* teachings, was written. From the Maccabee period itself we have the Book of Daniel, some of the canonical Psalms, and probably also the Book of Ecclesiastes, the beast-vision in the Book of Enoch (chs. 83–90), the First Book of Maccabees (*c.* 100 B.C.), the strongly anti-Hasmonæan passage Enoch 91–105, while the Psalms of Solomon belong to the time of the overthrow of the Hasmonæans. The rest of the Book of Enoch is also possibly all pre-Christian. The Assumption of Moses appears to have been composed shortly after the death of Herod the Great. On the other hand, neither of the two extremely important Apocalypses of Baruch and Ezra was composed till after the destruction of the Jewish State—that of Ezra under Domitian (A.D. 81–96), that of Baruch apparently somewhat earlier. There are, further, the legends of Tobit and Judith, the Book of Jubilees (a midrashic recension of Genesis), and the Martyrdom of Isaiah, which cannot be dated with certainty, but all belong to the period under consideration.

As regards the estimation in which this literature was held at the time, some writings, namely Daniel, Ecclesiastes, and the 'Maccabæan' Psalms, were received into the Canon of the Pharisees, which afterwards became the only authoritative one. The Book of Sirach was not, indeed, canonized, but enjoyed high esteem, and is not infrequently cited by the Talmudic teachers, so that even the original Hebrew text of this work survived, and has recently been recovered in large part. See art. SIRACH in vol. iv. The Psalms of Solomon emanated, beyond doubt, from the heart of the Pharisaic circle, and so frequently remind us of the canonical Psalms that it is a matter of surprise that their original text has completely disappeared. The rest of this literature, on the other hand, was afterwards disavowed by Palestinian Judaism, and hence we make acquaintance with it only in translations which circulated in Hellenistic circles. It is difficult on this account to say how these writings, above all the apocalyptic portions of them, were regarded at the time by the proper representatives of Judaism. The Apocalypse of Ezra itself claims to be a work of mystery to be read only by the initiated.* And the same is true, no doubt, in part of the other Apocalypses, with their many secrets.† On the other hand, they not only obtained currency among the Hellenistic Jews, but their world of thought comes in contact on the one side with the New Testament, and on the other, in spite of essential differences, with the late Jewish literature, in such an unmistakable fashion as to show that they must have been widely read. Even if it should be held that these coincidences are due, not to direct use of these writings, but to a common world of thought, with which the people were familiar and on which the literature in question also shows its dependence, our view of the then existing Judaism would have to be modified all the same; for then we should have to employ for its reconstruction not only the characteristic features of the official Torah study, in conjunction with the survival of the pure and inward spirit of the OT in some circles, but also the mystical sphere of ideas, with its descriptions of the world beyond and its numerous attempts to burst the barrier created by the national limitations of Judaism. Here we have a difficult task, but one that is of extreme importance for the correct appreciation of Christianity, and for the accomplishment of which the necessary preparations have only been commenced.‡

viii. THE JEWS OF THE DIASPORA.—As long as the existence of the post-exilic Jewish State in Palestine continued, the Jewish communities of the Diaspora were thrown into the shade by it. Nevertheless, developments and transformations took place amongst these, which were of the greatest significance both for Judaism itself and

* The historical work of Josephus' contemporary, Justus of Tiberias, is lost.

* 2 Es 12[37f.] 'Write all this in a book, and put it in a secret place, and teach the wise of thy people, of whom thou art sure that they are able to comprehend and keep these secrets.'

† The Assumption of Moses appears to have originated in Zealot circles.

‡ Cf., among others, Dalman, *Worte Jesu*, 1898 [Eng. tr. 1902]; Wellhausen, *Skizzen und Vorarbeiten*, vi. 225 ff.; Baldensperger, *Das Judentum als Vorstufe des Christentums*, 1900.

for Christianity. At the time of Christ there were Jewish communities in every considerable town of the world. Originally, the Jews had been forcibly transported to foreign lands: by the Assyrians and Babylonians to the Euphrates districts, by Artaxerxes Ochus to Hyrcania, etc.; or they had taken their flight abroad from fear of their enemies: so, for instance, those Jews who fled to Egypt after the murder of Gedaliah (2 K $25^{26}$, Jer $41^{17ff.}$). But afterwards they migrated, in ever-increasing numbers, to various countries and settled there, partly, it may be, because they were dissatisfied with the conditions at home, partly because great material advantages were offered them in foreign parts. The chief centres were the Euphrates districts, Syria, and Egypt;* but there were also many Jews settled in the other Mediterranean lands, and it may be presumed that in NT times there was a large Jewish community in Rome. Of all the cities inhabited by Jews the most important was Alexandria, for here they were not only so numerous that two of the five districts of the city were called 'the Jewish,' but they came into contact here especially with the Hellenistic world of thought, and allowed themselves to be strongly influenced by it.

An essential factor in the life of the Jews of the Diaspora was the free exercise of their religion, which was allowed them in the time of the *Diadochi* and under the Roman domination. Things went best with them in places where they lived as an independent body with State recognition, whereas, in those lands or cities where they simply enjoyed equal rights of citizenship with others, they readily came into collision and conflict with the heathen population. Amongst their privileges must be reckoned also the possession of a jurisdiction and a coinage of their own. The latter in particular was of importance, for thus alone were they in a position to pay the poll-tax to Jerusalem. On other points the constitution and organization of Jewish communities differed in different countries.

The religious instruction of the Jews of the Diaspora was based, like that at home, upon the regular service of the synagogue, there being one or more synagogues wherever Jews were settled. In Hellenistic circles the Septuagint played the same part as the Hebrew text in the mother country, being without doubt used in the reading of the Scriptures, as acquaintance with Hebrew must have been rare on the part of Jews living abroad. See, further, art. DIASPORA in the present volume, p. 91 ff.

The Jewish-Hellenistic literature, owing not only to its being written in the Greek language, but to its being more or less interpenetrated with the Greek spirit, and its use of the Greek literary forms, has a different stamp from the Palestinian. Leaving out of account the Alexandrian expansions of some books of the OT, we may classify this literature under the three heads of History, Poetry, and Philosophy.

A number of writers treated the ancient Jewish *history* in a modernizing fashion, in order thereby to claim for it the interest of the foreign world of readers. In addition to some fragments, of which those of Eupolemus, owing to their peculiar syncretism, are the most notable, we have to mention here especially the *Antiquities* of Josephus, a work which for the reasons mentioned above must be assigned to the Hellenistic rather than to the Palestinian literature. Other authors made the immediate past the subject of their narratives. Thus the so-called Second Book of Maccabees is an extract from the extensive work of Jason of Cyrene on the Maccabæan rising. The most valuable of these writings is Josephus' account (*BJ*) of the great revolt of the Jews against the Romans, to which are attached certain portions of his autobiography. An ill-natured attack upon the Jews led Josephus, further, to compose an apologetic work (*c. Apion.*), having for its aim to exhibit the high antiquity of Judaism. To the class of literary forgeries belongs the so-called Letter of Aristeas, in which a Jewish author makes a heathen relate the story of the origin of the Septuagint. The same is the case with a 'tendency' recension of a work on the Jews by Hecatæus, the reviser of which put forth his composition under the name of the Greek historian.

As regards the employment of *poetry*, we have, first of all, the remarkable attempts to transfer the forms of the epos and the drama to the realm of Jewish history. There are, for instance, fragments of an epic presentation of the history of Jerusalem by a Philo, and a drama by an Ezekiel, whose subject is the Exodus. To the same category belong also the verses put by Jewish poets into the mouth of the ancient oracle-giving Sibyls, and which mark the apocalyptic tendency that was so prominent in Palestinian, but less so in Hellenistic, circles. See below, p. 66 ff.

Most important of all are the writings which are more or less influenced by Greek *philosophy*. The only independent Jewish thinker is Philo, who plays no unimportant rôle in the history of philosophy. The others assume an eclectic attitude towards the various Greek schools, and aim only at bringing their ideas into harmony with those of Judaism, several of them seeking at the same time to justify their dependence on Greek thinkers by maintaining that the latter originally borrowed from the Mosaic Law. The principal expedient to which these authors resort in order to harmonize the heterogeneous elements, is the allegorical interpretation of the Law and the Jewish history.* To this category belong the writings of Aristobulus (2nd cent. B.C.), of which only fragments are extant; the Stoicizing work on the authority of reason (the so-called Fourth Book of Maccabees); and the writings of Philo. A transition to this species of literature is exhibited by the Book of the Wisdom of Solomon, which, in spite of Gr. influence, still reminds us strongly of the Pal. *Hokhma* literature. Cf., further, artt. WISDOM in vol. iv., and PHILO, below, p. 197 ff.

LITERATURE (in addition to works on the history of Israel or of the Jews).—Schneckenburger, *Vorlesungen über neutest. Zeitgeschichte*, 1862; Hausrath, *Neutest. Zeitgeschichte*[2], 1873–77 [3rd ed. 1879 (Bd. i.)]; Wellhausen, *Die Pharisäer und Sadducäer*, 1874; Raphall, *Post-biblical History of the Jews*, 1856; Stapfer, *La Palestine au temps de Jésus-Christ*, 1885, *Les idées religieuses en Palestine à l'époque de Jésus-Christ*[2], 1878; Baumgarten, 'Der national-jüdische Hintergrund der neutest. Geschichte' (in *JDTh*, 1864–65); Wieseler, 'Beiträge zur neutest. Zeitgeschichte' (in *SK*, 1875); Langen, *Das Judenthum in Palästina zur Zeit Christi*, 1866; Edersheim, *The Life and Times of Jesus the Messiah*, 2 vols., 1883; Schürer, *GJV*[3], 3 vols. and Index vol., 1898-1902 [Eng. tr. (*HJP*) from 2nd ed.]; Holtzmann, *Neutest. Zeitgeschichte*, 1895. For a fuller Bibliography the reader may consult the work of Schürer.

FRANTS BUHL.

**TALMUD.**—The *Talmud* (תַּלְמוּד), meaning a 'teaching,' an 'inference,' or a 'doctrine,' is a term commonly applied to a collection of works embodying the Oral Law—תּוֹרָה שֶׁבְּעַל פֶּה, lit. 'the Torah by mouth'—handed down to the Jews by way of Tradition, in contradistinction to the Written Law—תּוֹרָה שֶׁבִּכְתָב, lit. 'the Torah in writing.' The origin of this Tradition is unknown: the common view of the mediæval authorities, claiming the same Mosaic authorship and high antiquity for it as for the Scriptures, is uncritical. But, as it is closely connected with the history and development of the

* Philo estimates the number of Jews in Egypt at about a million (ed. Mangey, ii. 523).

* An interesting attempt to demonstrate the reasonableness of the laws about food is found in the Letter of Aristeas, 142 ff.

hermeneutics of the Scriptures, its commencement may safely be dated back to the exilic period in which was first established the institution of the Synagogue, whose main function consisted in teaching and interpreting the word of God. The Hebrew term for 'interpretation' is *Midrāsh* (מִדְרָשׁ, cf. 2 Ch 13[22]); and this term, like the Rab. term *Ḳabbālā* (קַבָּלָה, matter received by way of Tradition), which includes the Prophets and the Hagiographa, may likewise, perhaps, be applied to certain portions of the canonical writings, *e.g.* Chronicles. The prominent feature of the *Midrāsh*, however, as an instrument for enlarging upon and expanding the word of the Scriptures, is best discernible in the ancient Rab. productions, which, in spite of some hyperbolical expressions, provoked by heat of controversy, never seriously aspired to the dignity of Scripture. As a consequence, they for the most part properly kept apart text and interpretation, and thus clearly showed the process of expansion. The results gained by this method varied in their character with the nature of the Scripture passages, according as they were legal and ritual, or spiritual and homiletical. The former classes are comprised under the name *Hălākhā* (הֲלָכָה), signifying guidance, a rule of practice, a legal decision; and the term extends also to the usages, customs (*Minhāgîm* מִנְהָגִים), ordinances (*Tĕḳānôth* תְּקָנוֹת), and decrees (*Gĕzērôth* גְּזֵירוֹת), for which there is little or no authority in the Scriptures. The latter (spiritual and homiletical) are classified under the term *Haggādā* (הַגָּדָה, Aram. אַגָּדָה),* meaning a tale, a narrative, an explanation, a homily; and the term includes also the gnomic lore of the Rabbis, as well as stories and legends bearing upon the lives of post-biblical Jewish saints. Such topics as astronomy and astrology, medicine and magic, theosophy and mysticism, and similar subjects, falling mostly under the heading of folk-lore, pass as a rule also under the name of *Haggādā*.

The schools active in this work of the interpretation and expansion of the Scriptures extend over many centuries, and are known under various designations, each designation marking in succession a different period.

i. The *Sôphĕrîm* (סוֹפְרִים), 'Scribes,' commencing with Ezra and going down to the Maccabæan period (450–100). Scarcely anything is known of their literary activity; the term 'Words of the *Sôphĕrîm*' (דִּבְרֵי סוֹפְרִים) is used indifferently by the Rabbis of *Hălākhôth* dating from various ages, and implying in most cases not the *authorship* of, but the *authority* for, certain given statements. Less vague are the Rab. references to the 'Men of the Great Assembly' (אַנְשֵׁי כְנֶסֶת הַגְּדוֹלָה) and 'their Remnant' (שִׁירֵי א׳ כנס׳ ה׳), thought by some scholars to be identical with the *Sôphĕrîm*, or at least to have formed the executive of the latter.† To these are attributed not only certain sayings, suggestive, among other things, of their teaching activity (as 'Raise many disciples,' M. '*Ābôth* i. 1), but also many ordinances and decrees, the most important of which are those bearing upon the arrangement and the completion of the Canon of the OT, the reading of the Law on certain days of the week, the fixing of the daily prayers (probably in six benedictions now embodied in the so-called Eighteen Benedictions, שְׁמֹנֶה עֶשְׂרֵה), and the introduction of the saying of grace after meals. The custom of pouring libations of water at the Feast of Tabernacles, and going in procession round the altar with branches of willow trees, declared by some Rabbis to have been introduced by the prophets, as well as the so-called 'Laws unto Moses from Mount Sinai' (amounting to the number of forty-three, more than a third of which refer to the preparation of the phylacteries), may also have dated from those *ṣopheric* times, remoteness of assigned date pointing, as a rule, to the pre-Maccabæan period.*

ii. The *Zûgôth* (זוגות; Gr. ζυγόν), 'Pairs,' a name given to the leading teachers that flourished between the Maccabæan and the Herodian period (*c.* 150–30). Five such 'Pairs' are recorded in the Rab. literature, extending over 5 generations, and succeeding each other in the following order: 1. Joṣe b. Joezer of Ẓereda and Joṣe b. Johanan of Jerusalem; 2. Joshua b. Peraḥya and Nittai of Arbela; 3. Jehuda b. Ṭabbai and Shim'on b. Shetaḥ; 4. Shema'ya and 'Abṭalyon; 5. Hillel and Shammai.† According to tradition each 'Pair' represents the heads of the Sanhedrin of their age, the one whose name occurs first in the list serving in the capacity of *Nāsî* (נָשִׂיא), 'Prince *or* President' of the Sanhedrin, the other in that of '*Ab Bêth Dîn* (אַב בֵּית דִּין), 'Father of the House of Judgment,' or 'Vice-President.' This tradition is contested by many modern scholars as incompatible with the statements of Josephus and of the New Testament, according to which the high priest for the time being was *ex officio* the president of the Sanhedrin. But, whatever their particular function and title were, the existence of the 'Pairs' as the heads of a religious corporation to which the large bulk of the nation belonged, and which thus formed an important factor in the development of the Oral Law, cannot well be doubted.‡ To them are attributed not only various *Haggadic* sayings (M. '*Ābôth* i. 4–15), but also *Halakhic* statements as well as certain ordinances and decrees. It was under the first 'Pair' (also called '*Eshkôlôth* אֶשְׁכּוֹלוֹת [? identical with the Gr. σχολή], a title that disappears with them) that, according to the testimony of the Rabbis, the first difference of opinion regarding the performance of certain religious practices occurred between the sages. The *Hălākhôth* attributed to Joṣe b. Joezer, the first named of this 'Pair,' as well as the ordinances and decrees ascribed to him and to his colleague of the first 'Pair,' were apparently composed in his age, the language of the *Hălākhôth* (Aramaic [M.

* See Bacher in *JQR* iv. 406 ff.

† See Weiss, *Dor Dor W'Dorshow*, i. p. 54; Kuenen in his essay, 'Über die Männer der grossen Synagoge' (occupying pp. 125–160 of the *Gesammelte Abhandlungen zur Biblischen Wissenschaft von A. Kuenen*, Freiburg and Leipzig, 1894), contests the existence of such an assembly (cf. also art. SYNAGOGUE [THE GREAT] in vol. iv., and the Literature cited at the end of that article); whilst D. Hoffmann (*Magazin für die Wissenschaft des Judentums*, x. 45 ff.) and S. Krauss (*JQR* x. 347 ff.) try to refute his argument. On the whole, the present writer is inclined to admit that there is an element of truth in this tradition regarding the Great Assembly. The Judaism which emerges suddenly after this nebulous period is essentially a product of the Synagogue. It is hard to see how it could ever have thriven under the care of the historical priests or the cosmopolitan *Ṣôphēr* of the moderns; and such a Synagogue would most naturally have developed under the auspices of an authority which acted in conformity with the spirit of the ordinances, decrees, and teachings attributed by the Rabbis to the men of the Great Assembly.

* See Weiss, *ib.* p. 66. The high priest Simon the Just (probably Simon I., *c.* 300 B.C.) is supposed to have belonged to this Remnant, but the saying recorded in his name is really *ṣopheric* in its character: 'On three things the world is stayed: on the Torah, and on the Worship, and on the bestowal of Kindnesses' (M. '*Ābôth* i. 2). Of his successor (2nd in the *ṣopheric* line), whose name Antigonos of Sokho shows already a marked Hellenistic influence, only the following saying is known: 'Be not as slaves that minister to the lord with a view to receive reward, but be as slaves that minister to the master without a view to receive reward' (M. '*Ābôth* i. 3). This saying, which has a certain Stoic savour about it, is supposed to have given rise to two heretical sects.

† See C. Taylor, *Sayings of the Jewish Fathers*[2], p. 14, note 9, for the chronology.

‡ For Literature on this point, see Schürer, *GJV*[3] ii. p. 188 ff. Of special importance are Kuenen, *l.c.* pp. 49–81; Hoffmann, *Die Präsidentur im Synedrium Mag.* v. 1878, pp. 94–99; and Jelski, *Die innere Einrichtung des grossen Synedrion*, etc. Wellhausen's *Die Pharisäer und Sadducäer* must be taken with great caution, as his command of the Rabbinic sources is imperfect.

*'Edûyyôth* viii. 4]) and the subject of the ordinances and decrees (Levitical purity) being both signs of antiquity. Shim'on b. Shetaḥ of the third 'Pair' is credited with having introduced several important reforms in various religious departments, whilst Shema'ya and 'Abṭalyon were called the 'Great Ones of the Generation' and the 'Great Interpreters' (דַּרְשָׁנִים גְּדוֹלִים). The most important 'Pair,' however, are Hillel (the Elder) and Shammai (the Elder), in whose names more *Hălākhôth* are recorded than of any other 'Pair'; they were also the founders of two great schools (*Beth Shammai*, *Beth Hillel*, בֵּית שַׁמַּאי, בֵּית הִלֵּל, 'the House *or* School of Shammai' and 'the House of Hillel') which continued the work of their masters for some generations. Hillel, a native of Babylon and (according to tradition) a descendant of the house of David, was particularly famous for his meekness and humble-mindedness. Among other things he is reported to have said, 'Be of the disciples of Aaron, loving peace and pursuing peace, loving thy fellow-creatures, and drawing them near to the Torah' (M. *'Abôth* i. 12); whilst he also taught to a heathen, seeking admission into Judaism, 'What is hateful to thyself do not to thy fellow-man; this is the whole Torah, the rest is only commentary' (*Shabbath* 30*b*). Shammai's saying was, 'Make thy Torah a fixed thing, say little and do much, and receive every man with a cheerful countenance' (M. *'Abôth* i. 15); but he was not particularly famous for his gentle temper. The most marked feature about these two leaders is their activity as interpreters of the Law and their application of the results of this interpretation to practice. Thus Shammai presses the words עַד רִדְתָּהּ ('until it be subdued,' Dt 20[20]) to mean that the act of subduing a hostile place must not be interrupted even on account of any religious consideration, and thus he permits the continuing of a battle even on Sabbath (*Shabbath* 19*a*). Hillel, by subjecting the term בְּמוֹעֲדוֹ ('in its season,' Nu 9[2]) to the interpretatory 'rule of analogy,' inferred from it the *Hălākhā* that the duty of sacrificing the Paschal lamb overrules all consideration of Sabbath, when the 14th of Nisan falls on the 7th day of the week (*Pĕsāḥîm* 66*a*).* Indeed it was Hillel who first framed the Rules of Interpretation, seven in number (Introduction to the *Tôrath Kōhănîm*), and which developed later into thirteen and more.

iii. The *Tannaim* (תַּנָּאִים), 'Teachers,' the name given to the authorities living during the first two centuries of the Christian era (*c.* 10–200), commencing with the schools of Shammai and Hillel and terminating with R. Jehuda the Patriarch, a great-grandson of Hillel. The period of the *Tannaim*, most of whom bear the title *Rabbi* (רַבִּי 'my Master,' but losing later its pronominal signification) or (more rarely) *Rabban* (רַבָּן 'Master'), may conveniently be divided into four successive generations, the principal men of which are—

*First Generation* (10–80).—The 'schools of Shammai and Hillel,' comprising many teachers whose names have not come down to us. The underlying principle dividing these schools on many important points is not known; but on the whole the school of Shammai may perhaps be characterized as staunch conservatives in their adherence to Tradition, who allowed little room for the play of interpretation, and were as a rule very rigorous in their decisions; whilst the school of Hillel, already described by the old Rabbis as 'pleasing and meek,' were more inclined to compromise in their teaching, greatly given to the developing of the *Midrash*, and in general less severe in their *Halakhic* dicta. The most important of those known by name are Rabban Gamaliel the Elder, and Rabban Johanan b. Zakkai, both of the school of Hillel. Gamaliel, a son (some say a grandson) of Hillel, is known for various reforms introduced by him, as well as for the part he took in the trial of the Apostle Paul (Ac 5[34-39]); whilst Johanan was equally famous as one of the leaders of the peace party in the war against the Romans (66–70), and as the founder of the Academy of Jamnia, which became the centre of Jewish life and thought after the destruction of the temple.

*Second Generation* (90–130).—Rabban Gamaliel II., President of the Academy of Jamnia after the death of R. Johanan [having been rather autocratic in the treatment of his colleagues he was removed from his office for a time, but soon after restored to it]; R. 'Eliezer b. Jaḳob I., who was considered a great authority in traditions regarding the structure and the arrangement of the service in the temple; R. 'Eliezer b. Hyrkanos, a brother-in-law of R. Gamaliel, and the head of a school in Lydda [though a disciple of R. Johanan b. Zakkai, of the school of Hillel, he cherished Shammaitic principles, which fact brought him into collision with the majority of his colleagues, and subsequently led to his excommunication]: R. Jehoshua b. Ḥananya, likewise a disciple of R. Johanan b. Zakkai, but unlike his colleague, R. 'Eliezer, with whom he had many controversies, of a humble and submissive disposition; R. 'Eliezer b. 'Azarya, who derived his pedigree from Ezra the Scribe, and who obtained the office of President of the Academy of Jamnia when R. Gamaliel was deposed. To the younger teachers of this generation belong R. Ṭarphon, of the school of Shammai (?), who had attended the service in the temple; R. Jose of Galilee, who had controversies with R. Ṭarphon and other *Tannaim*; R. Ishmael b. 'Elisha, best known for his thirteen Rules of Interpretation (see above). Together with other members of the Sanhedrin he emigrated from Jamnia to Usha, where he founded a school called after his name, to which various *Midrashim* are attributed. R. 'Akiba b. Joseph, a disciple of several older teachers of this generation, was master of most of the distinguished Rabbis of the next generation, and not less famous for his skill in systematizing the content of tradition than for his ingenious methods of interpretation, which enabled him to find a basis for all the enactments of the Oral Law in the Scriptures. This fact, together with the circumstance of his patriotic zeal and his martyr death in the Hadrianic persecutions (*c.* 130), made him the most famous of the *Tannaim*. To this generation belong also the older disciples of R. 'Akiba—Shim'on b. 'Azai and Shim'on b. Zoma—best known for their moralizing sayings and mystical tendencies (in the direction of a Jewish gnosis) which they shared with their master, but from which, unlike the latter, they did not escape without injury. 'The one gazed (into the chambers of heaven) and died, and the other gazed and was not in his mind.' Their contemporary 'Elisha b. 'Abuyah, also called 'Aḥer (the Other One), was less happy than these, for he 'gazed' and 'cut the branches,' that is, became an apostate.

*Third Generation* (130–160).—The disciples of R. Ishmael, of whom only two are known by their names (R. Joshia and R. Jonathan), whilst the others are usually quoted as 'the Tanna of the school' of R. Ishmael. The younger disciples of R. 'Akiba are R. Meir, who continued the systematizing labours of his master, and is thus supposed to have laid the foundation of a Mishna; R. Jehuda b. 'Ilai, who is called 'the first of the Speakers'; R. Shim'on b. Yoḥai, of whom R. 'Akiba said, 'Be satisfied that I and thy Maker

* For the historical and theological significance of this method of interpretation, see Chwolson, *Das letzte Passamahl Christi und der Tag seines Todes* (St. Petersburg, 1892), p. 20 ff.

know thy powers'; R. Nehemiah, to whom, as to the two last-mentioned Rabbis, various *Tannaitic* compilations are attributed; R.'Eleazar b. Shamua, round whom the greatest number of disciples gathered, and R. Joṣe b. Ḥalaphta, to whom the book *Ṣeder 'Olam* (סֵדֶר עוֹלָם), containing a chronology of events and personages in the Bible, is attributed. Abba Shaul, compiler of a Mishna, and the Patriarch R. Shim'on II. b. Gamaliel II., are also included in the third generation.

*Fourth Generation* (160–220).—R. Nathan Habbabhli, who emigrated from Babylon to Palestine, and there held under the last-mentioned Patriarch an office in the Sanhedrin the nature of which is not quite known; Symmachos, the disciple of R. Meir, and a great authority in matters of civil law; and various other *Tannaim*, sons and disciples of the authorities of the preceding generation. The most important among them is the Patriarch R. Jehuda Hannasi, also called *Rabbênû hakḳādôsh* (רַבֵּינוּ הַקָּדוֹשׁ), 'Our Master, the Saint,' but more frequently *Rabbi*, 'the Master,' without adding his name. He was the son of the Patriarch R. Shim'on II., and the disciple of R. Shim'on b. Yoḥai, and of R. 'Eleazar b. Shamua; he presided over the Sanhedrin, which during this generation was, as it would seem, a migratory body, shifting from place to place, from Usha to Beth-shearim, and thence to Sepphoris and Tiberias. This R. Jehuda is said to have maintained friendly relations with the Roman authorities of Palestine at that period. This fact, as well as the circumstances of his noble birth, great wealth, official position, saintly character, and his mastery of the contents of the Oral Law, gave him an authority over his contemporaries never enjoyed by any other *Tanna*, and gathered round him a band of distinguished disciples and colleagues which rendered possible his work as compiler and codifier of the Mishna.*

The literary productions of all these generations of *Tannaim*, as well as of their predecessors the 'Pairs' and the *Ṣôphĕrîm*, both in *Hălākhā* and in *Haggādā*, are, as far as they have been preserved, embodied in the following collections.

The **Mishna** מִשְׁנָה† (from שָׁנָה), meaning a 'teaching,' a 'repetition,' is a designation most appropriate for a work generally looked upon as the main depository of the contents of the Oral Law, which (in contradistinction to מִקְרָא, reading matter, or the Scriptures) could be acquired only by means of constant repetition. This work, compiled (apart from some later additions) by R. Jehuda the Patriarch, is divided into 6 Orders (שִׁשָּׁה סְדָרִים=ש"ס), each of which contains several *Maṣṣikhtôth* (מַסֶּכְתּוֹת, sing. מַסֶּכֶת (Aram. מַסֶּכְתָּא), derived from נָסַךְ, meaning 'to weave'; cf. the Latin *textus*), or 'texts' (but more commonly called 'tractates'), whilst each tractate is divided into *Pĕrāḳîm* (פְּרָקִים, sing. פֶּרֶק), 'joints' or 'sections,' each of which, in its turn, consists of so many *Hălākhôth* (in the sense of paragraphs). The number of the tractates is 63 (or, in another enumeration, 60), bearing the following titles, which are suggestive more or less of their varied contents, though extraneous matter that is in no way indicated by the title is everywhere introduced:—

I. ZĔRĀ'ÎM, זְרָעִים, 'Seeds.'

1. *Bĕrākhôth*, בְּרָכוֹת 'Benedictions,' treating of laws and regulations relating to the liturgy. 9 chapters.
2. *Pē'ā*, פֵּאָה 'Corner,' treating of the laws relating to the corner of the field and the forgotten sheaves, etc., to be left for the poor (Lv $19^{9}$, Dt $24^{19.21}$). 8 chapters.
3. *Dammai*, דְּמַּי (also דְּמָאי) the 'Doubtful,' respecting corn and other productions of the earth, of which it is doubtful whether the prescribed tithes had been paid. 7 chapters.
4. *Kil'ayîm*, כִּלְאַיִם 'Mixtures,' *i.e.* mixtures of seeds, animals, and materials for cloth, prohibited by the Scriptures (Lv $19^{19}$, Dt $22^{9\text{-}11}$). 9 chapters.
5. *Shĕbî'ith*, שְׁבִיעִית the 'Sabbatical year' (Ex $23^{11}$, Lv $25^{1\text{ff.}}$, Dt $15^{1\text{ff.}}$). 10 chapters.
6. *Tĕrûmôth*, תְּרוּמוֹת 'Heave-Offerings,' for the priest (Nu $18^{8\text{ff.}}$ and Dt $18^{4}$). 5 chapters.
7. *Ma'ăsĕrôth*, מַעַשְׂרוֹת 'Tithes' (Nu $18^{21\text{ff.}}$). 5 chapters.
8. *Ma'ăsēr Shēni*, מַעֲשֵׂר שֵׁנִי 'Second Tithe' (Dt $14^{22\text{ff.}}$). 5 chapters.
9. *Ḥallā*, חַלָּה the 'Dough,' a portion thereof to be given to the priest (Nu $15^{18\text{ff.}}$). 4 chapters.
10. *'Orlā*, עָרְלָה 'Uncircumcised,' fruits of the tree during the first three years (Lv $19^{23\text{ff.}}$). 3 chapters.
11. *Bikkûrim*, בִּכּוּרִים 'First Fruits,' brought to the temple (Dt $26^{1\text{ff.}}$, Ex $23^{19}$). 3 chapters.

II. MÔ'ĔD, מוֹעֵד 'Season.'

1. *Shabbath*, שַׁבָּת 'Sabbath,' laws relating to it, mainly prohibitions of work (Ex $20^{10}$ etc.). 24 chapters.
2. *'Ērûbin*, עֵירוּבִין 'Amalgamations' or ideal combinations of localities with the purpose of extending the Sabbath boundary, as well as laws as to the Sabbath day's journey. 10 chapters.
3. *Pĕsāḥim*, פְּסָחִים 'Passovers,' laws relating to them (Ex $12^{1\text{ff.}}$, Lv $23^{4}$, Nu $9^{1\text{ff.}}$). 10 chapters.
4. *Shĕḳālîm*, שְׁקָלִים 'Shekels,' collected for the temple (Ex $30^{12\text{ff.}}$, Neh $10^{33}$), and the various objects for which they were spent; including lists of the higher officials of the temple. 8 chapters.
5. *Yômā*, יוֹמָא 'The Day' (also *Yôm Hakkippûrîm*, יוֹם הַכִּפּוּרִים 'The day of Atonement'), treating of the service in the temple on that day, and of the laws relating to fasting (Lv $16^{1\text{ff.}}$). 8 chapters.
6. *Ṣukkā*, סֻכָּה 'Booth' or 'Tabernacle,' respecting the laws on dwelling in booths for seven days, and other observances during this feast (Lv $23^{34\text{ff.}}$, Nu $29^{12\text{ff.}}$). 8 chapters.
7. *Bêẓā*, בֵּיצָה 'Egg' (so called after the first words with which the tractate begins, but also termed *Yôm Ṭôb*, יוֹם טוֹב 'Feast'), enumerating the different kinds of work permitted or prohibited on festivals (Ex $12^{16}$). 5 chapters.
8. *Rôsh Hashshānā*, רֹאשׁ הַשָּׁנָה 'New Year,' dealing with questions relating to the calendar, but chiefly with the laws to be observed on the first of the 7th month (*Tishri*), the civil New Year of the Jews (see Lv $23^{24}$, Nu $29^{1\text{ff.}}$). 4 chapters.
9. *Ta'ănith*, תַּעֲנִית 'Fast,' respecting the laws observed and the order of the liturgy on such days. 4 chapters.
10. *Mĕgillā*, מְגִלָּה 'Roll' of Esther, relating to the laws to be observed on the feast of *Purim*. 4 chapters.
11. *Mô'ēd Ḳāton*, מוֹעֵד קָטָן 'Minor Feast' (also called מַשְׁקִין, the first word of the tractate), *i.e.* the laws relating to the days intervening between the first and last days of the feast of Passover and that of Tabernacles. 4 chapters.
12. *Ḥăgîgā*, חֲגִיגָה 'Feast-Offering,' treating of the duty of pilgrimage to Jerusalem and the sort of sacrifices to be brought on such occasions (see Ex $23^{17}$ and Dt $16^{16}$), as well as of laws regarding the degrees of defilement (against which the pilgrims are cautioned). 3 chapters.

III. NĀSHÎM, נָשִׁים 'Women.'

1. *Yĕbāmôth*, יְבָמוֹת 'Levirate Marriages' (Dt $25^{5\text{ff.}}$), and the forbidden degrees in marriage (Lv 18, etc.). 16 chapters.
2. *Kĕthûbôth*, כְּתוּבוֹת 'Marriage Deeds and Marriage Settlements' (see Ex $22^{16}$). 13 chapters.
3. *Nĕdārîm*, נְדָרִים 'Vows,' and their annulment (Nu $30^{3\text{ff.}}$). 11 chapters.
4. *Nāzîr*, נָזִיר 'Nazirite' (Nu $6^{2\text{ff.}}$). 9 chapters.
5. *Ṣôṭā*, סוֹטָה 'The Suspected Woman' (Nu $5^{12\text{ff.}}$). 9 chapters.
6. *Giṭṭîn*, גִּטִּין 'Letters of Divorce' (Dt $24^{1\text{ff.}}$). 9 chapters.
7. *Ḳiddûshîn*, קִדּוּשִׁין 'Betrothals.' 4 chapters.

IV. NĔZÎḲÎN, נְזִיקִין 'Damages.'

1–3. *Bābā Ḳammā*, בָּבָא קַמָּא 'First Gate'; *Bābā Mĕẓi'a*,

* Some authorities number five generations of *Tannaim*. For the purpose of brevity, we have accepted the plan of those who have condensed them into four. For the same reason, we have confined ourselves to the most important *Tannaim*, omitting many who deserve mention. Compare H. Strack's excellent monograph *Einleitung in den Thalmud*², p. 76ff., and his bibliography appended to each *Tanna*. The references there given include those to Bacher's works, which are the most important contributions to the subject in any language other than Hebrew.

† St. const. מִשְׁנַת. The Patristic δευτέρωσις (see references in Schürer, *l.c.* i. p. 88, n. 1) speaks for מִשְׁנָה (second to the Torah), st. const. מִשְׁנַה. Both explanations are represented in Rab. literature. Cf. *Arukh Completum*, *s.v.* משנה.

מְצִיעָא בָּבָא 'Second Gate'; *Bābā Bathrā*, בָּבָא בַּתְרָא 'Last Gate.' These formed in ancient times only one tractate, bearing the same title as the whole order, מסכת נזיקין 'Tractate of Damages,' divided into three sections, each section consisting of 10 chapters. These three treat of (1) damages and injuries caused by man and beasts for which he is responsible (see Ex $21^{18ff.}$ $22^{5ff.}$); (2) of laws concerning lost property, trusts, the prohibition of usury and similar matters, duties towards hired labourers, etc. (see Ex $22^{6ff.}$ $23^{3.4}$, Lv $19^{13}$ $25^{14.36}$, Dt $23^{20.25}$ and $24^{14}$); (3) laws relating to the different ways of taking possession of various kinds of property, the right of pre-emption, definition of certain terms used in contracts and oral transactions, order of inheritance (see Nu $27^{6ff.}$), etc.

4. 5. *Ṣanhedrin*, סַנְהֶדְרִין (10 chapters), and *Makkôth*, מַכּוֹת 'Stripes' (3 chapters), also forming in ancient times one tractate. The former treats of the constitution of the various courts of justice and their modes of procedure, the examination of witnesses, and the four kinds of capital punishment for grave crimes, as well as of the punishment consisting in being excluded from eternal life, etc. etc. The latter deals with offences for which the infliction of 39 stripes is prescribed (Dt $25^{2ff.}$), with false witnesses (Dt $19^{16ff.}$), and the laws relating to the cities of refuge (Nu $35^{10ff.}$, Dt $19^{2ff.}$).

6. *Shĕbhû'ôth*, שְׁבוּעוֹת 'Oaths,' taken in private or administered by the court (Lv $5^{1.4}$). 6 chapters.

7. *'Edûyyôth*, עֵדֻיּוֹת 'Evidences,' containing a collection of laws and decisions gathered from the statements made by distinguished authorities. 8 chapters.

8. *'Ăbôdā Zārā*, עֲבוֹדָה זָרָה 'Idolatry,' regarding the treatment of idols and their worshippers (Dt $4^{25ff.}$). 5 chapters.

9. *'Ābôth*, אָבוֹת 'Fathers' (of Jewish tradition), containing mostly ethical sayings and maxims of the *Tannaim*. 5 chapters.

10. *Hôrāyôth*, הוֹרָיוֹת 'Decisions' (wrong ones) given by the authorities, treating of the sacrifices to be brought if the public acted in accordance with such erroneous teachings (Lv $4^{1ff.}$). 3 chapters.

V. Ḳodāshîm, קָדָשִׁים 'Sacred' things.

1. *Zĕbāḥîm*, זְבָחִים 'Sacrifices' (also called שְׁחִיטַת קָדָשִׁים and קָרְבָּנוֹת), treating of the laws relating to the various modes of offerings, the sprinkling of the blood, the burning of the fat pieces or of whole animals, etc. (Lv $1^{1ff.}$). 12 chapters.

2. *Mĕnāḥôth*, מְנָחוֹת 'Meat-Offerings,' including also the laws regarding libations (Lv $2^{5ff.}$ etc., Nu $15^{3ff.}$) 12 chapters.

3. *Ḥullîn*, חֻלִּין (also שְׁחִיטַת חוּלִין) 'Things Secular,' regarding the mode of killing animals and birds for ordinary use, as well as the various diseases disqualifying them from being eaten, and many other dietary laws. 12 chapters.

4. *Bĕkhôrôth*, בְּכוֹרוֹת 'Firstborn,' of men and animals (Ex $13^{2.12ff.}$ etc.), including also the laws regarding the tithes of animals (Lv $27^{26.32ff.}$). 9 chapters.

5. *'Ărākhîn*, עֲרָכִין 'Valuations,' of persons and things dedicated to the temple (Lv $27^{2ff.}$), also including some laws relating to the year of Jubilee (Lv $25^{15ff.}$). 9 chapters.

6. *Tĕmûrā*, תְּמוּרָה 'Change,' the laws bearing on cases of substituting a secular animal for one already dedicated to the altar (Lv $27^{9.33}$). 7 chapters.

7. *Kĕrîthôth*, כְּרִיתוֹת 'Excisions,' treating of sins subject to the punishment of 'the soul being cut off' (Gn $17^{14}$, Ex $12^{15}$ etc. etc.). 6 chapters.

8. *Mĕ'îlā*, מְעִילָה 'Trespass,' treating of sacrilege committed by secularizing things belonging to the temple or to the altar (Lv $5^{15ff.}$). 8 chapters.

9. *Tāmîd*, תָּמִיד 'Continual' sacrifice, describing the temple service in connexion with this daily sacrifice (Ex $29^{38ff.}$, Nu $28^{3ff.}$). 7 chapters.

10. *Middôth*, מִדּוֹת 'Measurements,' of the temple, describing its courts, halls, chambers, and gates, etc. etc. 5 chapters.

11. *Ḳinnîm*, קִנִּים 'Nests,' of birds, or pairs of doves brought as sacrifice by the poor (Lv $1^{14ff.}$ $5^{7ff.}$). 3 chapters.

VI. Ṭohărôth, טְהָרוֹת 'Purifications.'

1. *Kēlîm*, כֵּלִים 'Vessels,' furniture, garments, and all kinds of utensils subject to Levitical impurity (Lv $11^{32}$). 30 chapters.

2. *'Ōhālôth*, אֹהָלוֹת 'Tents' and habitations as conductors of Levitical impurity (Nu $19^{14ff.}$). 18 chapters.

3. *Nĕgā'îm*, נְגָעִים 'Leprosy,' in all its various degrees (Lv 13–14). 14 chapters.

4. *Pārā*, פָּרָה 'Red Heifer,' the use made of its ashes for the purpose of purification (Nu $19^{2ff.}$). 12 chapters.

5. *Ṭohărôth*, טְהָרוֹת 'Purifications,' used euphemistically for טומאות 'deflements' of all sorts and their various degrees. 10 chapters.

6. *Mikwā'ôth*, מִקְוָאוֹת 'Wells' and cisterns to be used as means of ritual purification (Lv $15^{11.12}$ etc. etc.). 10 chapters.

7. *Niddā*, נִדָּה the 'Menstruous,' the Levitical impurity attaching to women under certain physical conditions (Lv $15^{19ff.}$). 10 chapters.

8. *Makhshîrîn*, מַכְשִׁירִין 'Preparers,' respecting the conditions under which certain articles became (by coming in contact with liquids) prepared for eventual defilement (Lv $11^{37ff.}$). 6 chapters.

9. *Zābîm*, זָבִים 'Persons afflicted with running issues,' the impurity arising thereof (Lv $15^{2ff.}$). 5 chapters.

10. *Ṭĕbûl Yôm*, טְבוּל יוֹם 'Immersed during the day,' *i.e.* the condition of a person who had taken the ritual bath prescribed but has still to wait for sunset to be considered as quite pure (see Lv $22^{6.7}$). 4 chapters.

11. *Yādayim*, יָדַיִם 'Hands,' respecting the ritual impurity attaching to them (according to the Oral Law), and the mode of cleansing them by pouring water over them. 4 chapters.

12. *'Ukẓîn*, עוּקְצִין 'Stalks,' how far they are considered a part of the fruit so as to convey impurity when touched by anything unclean. 3 chapters.

The idiom in which the Mishna is compiled is the New Hebrew, interspersed with occasional Greek and Latin words; its diction is fluent and easy when not disfigured, as all works coming to us from antiquity are, by interpolations and textual corruptions. The date of its compilation may be fixed about A.D. 220. This was undertaken and accomplished by R. Jehuda the Patriarch, not with the purpose of providing the nation with a legal code, but with the intention of furnishing them with a sort of thesaurus, incorporating such portions of the traditional lore as he considered most important. Hence the ground for his including in the work the opinions of the minority (*e.g.* of the school of Shammai), which only in a few exceptional cases were accepted as a norm for practice. A preliminary acquaintance with the contents of the Scriptures bearing upon the topic expounded by tradition is always assumed; so that, *e.g.*, the tractate *Sukkā* commences: 'A booth (the interior of which is) higher than 20 cubits is disqualified,' thus premising the duty of living in booths for seven days according to Lv $23^{42}$. In many cases even a knowledge of the institutions established by the Oral Law is presupposed. Hence such a statement as that with which the Mishna commences: 'When do they begin to read the *Shĕma'* in the evening (*i.e.* the 3 paragraphs in the Scriptures, Dt $6^{4-9}$ $11^{13-21}$, and Nu $15^{37-41}$, the first paragraph of which begins with the word *Shĕma'* שְׁמַע)? From the time the priests (in the case of defilement) come back (from their ritual baths) to eat their heave-offering' (*i.e.* after sunset, see Lv $22^{4-7}$). The duty or the custom of daily reading the *Shĕma'* is thus assumed as something generally known though not mentioned in the Scriptures.

The works after which R. Jehuda modelled his compilation and the sources upon which he drew were probably the older Mishna collections, the first composition of which was, as there is good reason to believe, begun by the first successors of Shammai and Hillel, then compiled by R. 'Akiba, and continued by his disciple R. Meir, who enriched it by additions of the later *Tannaim*. This Mishna became the groundwork of that of R. Jehuda, apart from various other collections of a similar kind (*e.g.* the Mishna of Abba Shaul), which were equally known to the compiler and utilized by him.* The strata of these older compositions are still in many places discernible, either by their style and phraseology or by the nature of their contents. An instance of the former is the passage illustrating the prohibition against transporting things on Sabbath from a space belonging to a private individual to that constituting a part

* For this 'higher criticism' of the Mishna, see Dr. Lewy, 'Über einige Fragmente aus der M. des Abba Saul' in *Zweiter Bericht über die Hochschule für die W. d. J. in Berlin*, 1876, and Dr. D. Hoffmann, *Die erste Mischna* (Berlin, 1882).

of the public property. This commences יְצִיאוֹת הַשַּׁבָּת (M. *Shabbath* i. 1), instead of הוֹצָאוֹת הש׳, through which the Scripture expression אַל יֵצֵא (Ex 16[29]) is still visible, and thus points to a time when the *Hălākhā* was still in its early stage, forming a sort of paraphrase of Scripture, not a set of abstract laws. As an instance of the latter, it is sufficient to refer here to the historical description of the procession in which the sacrifice of the first-fruits was brought to the temple (Ex. 23[19]), concerning which we read in M. *Bikkûrîm* iii. 4: 'The pipe was playing before them (the pilgrims) until they arrived at the temple mountain, when even Agrippa the king would take the basket (containing the first-fruits) on his shoulders, stepping forward till he reached the courts; then the Levites spoke in song (chanted), "I will extol thee, O Lord, for thou hast lifted me up"' (Ps 30[2]). The mention of Agrippa (probably Agrippa I., *c.* 40) points to a contemporary document, since a Rabbi of a later period would, for the sake of emphasis, have named some biblical potentate (*e.g.* Solomon), not a mere Herodian prince.* This is only a specimen of many other portions of the Mishna, which contain lengthy descriptions of the sacrificial service on certain occasions, or give accounts of the architecture of the temple, its administration (including lists of the names of the higher officials), and its economy; whilst others furnish us with records of actual transactions of the Sanhedrin, the procedure of the courts, and the various methods of execution. All these bear the stamp of their own age, and testify to the early date of their composition.

The question whether R. Jehuda, besides compiling, actually wrote down the Mishna, is still a controverted point amongst modern scholars, as it was nearly a thousand years ago between the Franco-German and the Spanish authorities. The balance of evidence is still about equal on each side. Three things, however, seem to be certain. First, there existed a law or custom, dating from ancient times, prohibiting the writing down of the contents of Tradition, though the Scripture support for this custom (Bab. Talm. *Tĕmûrā* 14*b* and parallel passages) was not advanced till a comparatively late period (end of the 2nd cent.). Ample evidence of this fact is afforded by the traditional term, 'Torah by mouth,' as well as the various mnemotechnical aids to be found in the Mishna (*e.g. Megilla* i. 4-11, אין בין) and the homage paid to those who invented them (see Jerus. *Shĕķālîm* 48*c*, regarding the grouping of *Hălākhôth* in numbers, and *Aboth d' R. Nathan* 18, respecting R. 'Akiba's arranging of the Torah in links). Second, the prohibition did not extend to books of a *Haggadic* character (סִיפְרֵי דאַגָּדְתָּא), of which we know that they both circulated among, and were read by, the Rabbis. Under *Haggādā* was included also the gnomic literature—as, for instance, the Wisdom of Ben Ṣira, which both the *Tannaim* and the *'Amoraim*, as well as the authorities of a later period, the *Geonim* (*e.g.* R. Saadya), knew in the Hebrew original, and were constantly quoting, and of which fragments covering nearly two-thirds of the book have now been found after a disappearance of nearly 700 years. Third, the prohibition was often disregarded, even in cases of *Hălākhā*, as in the case of the *Mĕgillath Ta'ănîth* (מְגִילַּת תַּעֲנִית), containing a list of certain days in the year on which no fast could be declared, or the *Mĕgillath Ṣammānîn* (מְגִילַּת סַמָּנִין), 'the Roll of Spices,' treating of the preparation of the incense (Ex 30[34ff.]) in the tabernacle and the temple (Jerus. *Shĕķālîm* 49*a*).

Owing to the great authority of R. Jehuda the Patriarch, his compilation became the *Mishna κατ' ἐξοχήν*, a sort of canonical collection of the teachings of the *Tannaim*, forming the text-book of the students of the Oral Law, round which centred all the comments, discussions, and the additional matter produced by the succeeding generations. The other collections, likewise confined to the teachings of the *Tannaim*, but composed in schools not presided over by the Patriarch, pass under the name either of מִשְׁנָה הַחִיצוֹנָה *Mishna Haḥîẓônā* (more frequently the Aram. בָּרַיְיתָא *Băraithā*), 'the external Mishna,' or *Tôṣephtā* (תּוֹסֶפְתָּא), 'addition' (to the Mishna). No treatise representing the 'external Mishna' has come down to us, but many hundreds of quotations from such external Mishnas are scattered over the two Talmuds, mostly introduced by such phrases as תָּנוּ רַבָּנָן ('our Masters taught'), or תַּנְיָא ('it is taught'), or תנא and תָּנֵי ('he taught'). But we possess a work, bearing the name *Tôṣephtā*, corresponding with the arrangement of the Mishna, and dealing with the same subjects. It shows marks of different ages; and, whilst it embodies portions coming from collections preceding our Mishna, it presupposes the knowledge of the latter, whilst in some places it even affords comments and explanations taken from the *Gemara* and recast in the New Hebrew style of the Mishna. It is thus safe to assume that the date of its final redaction falls in the later age of the *'Amoraim*, though its composition may have been initiated by R. Ḥiya and R. Hoshaya the disciples of R. Jehuda, to whom tradition attributes such a work undertaken in imitation of the *Tôṣephtā* of R. Nehemia, who is credited with having collected 'additions' to the Mishna of R. 'Akiba. To this class of works also belong the so-called Minor Tractates bearing the following titles:—*Aboth d' R. Nathan* (אָבוֹת דר׳ נָתָן), a sort of *Tôṣephtā* and *Midrash* to the tractate *'Ābôth*, existing in two recensions;* *Maṣṣekheth Ṣôphĕrîm* (מַסֶּכֶת סוֹפְרִים),† 'Scribes,' dealing with the laws relating to the writing of the Scriptures. The text is in a bad condition, the interpolations and additions (on the Jewish liturgy, etc.) almost obliterating the original plan of the work, and it should be studied in connexion with the tractates *Ṣepher Tôrā*, *Mĕzûzā* (laws relating to the writing of certain verses from the Scriptures and to fixing them on the door-posts, see Dt 6[9]), and *Tĕphillîn* (Phylacteries), edited by Kirchheim; *Maṣṣekheth Sĕmāhôth* (מַסֶּכֶת שְׂמָחוֹת 'Joys'),‡ a euphemistic title for laws and customs connected with mourning—of which we have also a shorter recension ed. by C. M. Horwitz under the title מַסֶּכֶת שְׂמָחוֹת זוטרתי ('Tractate Joys, the Minor'); *Maṣṣekheth Kallā* (מַסֶּכֶת כַּלָּה 'Bride'), laws of chastity to be observed in conjugal life; *Maṣekheth Derekh 'Ereẓ* (מַסֶּכֶת דֶּרֶךְ אֶרֶץ), 'Manners' and behaviour of the different classes of society on various occasions. The tractate exists in two recensions, a longer (רַבָּה) and a shorter one (זוטא). The latter, dealing almost exclusively with the rules of life prescribed for the 'disciples of the wise,' is of a very spiritual nature. Lastly, we have to note here the other tractates ed. by Kirchheim, including, besides those mentioned above, the tractates dealing with the laws relating to *Ẓîẓîth* (צִיצִית), 'Fringes' (Nu 15[38]); *'Ăbādim* (עֲבָדִים), 'Slaves'; *Kûthîm* (כּוּתִים), 'Samaritans'; and *Gērîm* (גֵּרִים), 'Proselytes.'

The works recorded thus far, though containing occasional hermeneutical elements, convey, owing to their scantiness and the long intervals at which they occur, but a faint idea of the interpretatory

* See Hoffmann, *l.c.* p. 15; but cf. also A. Büchler, *Die Priester und der Cultus in den letzten Jahrzehnten des Jerusalemischen Tempels* (Wien, 1895), p. 10.

* See S. Schechter's introduction to his edition of *Aboth d' R. Nathan*, Vienna, 1878.

† See Dr. Joel Müller's introduction to his edition of the *Masechet Soferim*.

‡ See N. Brüll, 'Die Talmudischen Tractate über Trauer um Verstorbene' (*Jahrbücher der Jüd. Litt.* pp. 1-57).

work of the *Tannaim*. For this we must turn to the earlier *Midrash*, which has come down to us in the following works:—the *Mĕkhiltā* (מְכִילְתָּא), 'Measure' on a portion of Exodus; the *Ṣiphrê* (סִפְרֵי), 'the Books' on portions of Numbers and the whole of Deuteronomy, both *Midrashim* emanating from the school of Ishmael; and the *Siphrā* (סִפְרָא) or *Tôrath Kôhănîm* (תּוֹרַת כֹּהֲנִים), 'The Book' or 'The Law of the Priests' on Leviticus, a product of the school of R. 'Aḳiba. Besides these fairly complete works we also possess fragments of a *Mĕkhiltā* of R. Shim'on b. Yoḥai on Exodus, and of a small *Ṣiphrā* (סִפְרָא זוּטָא) on Numbers, both originating in the school of R. 'Aḳiba; and of a *Mĕkhiltā* on Deuteronomy, coming from the school of R. Ishmael.* The exegetical system of the Rabbis, forming the basis of the *Midrash*, grew with the rise of the new schools, the seven hermeneutical rules of Hillel having been developed by R. Ishmael into thirteen, and expanded (particularly as regards their application in the department of *Haggādā*) by R. Eliezer, the son of R. Joṣe of Galilee, into thirty-two or thirty-three rules; whilst rules of interpretation of other distinguished Rabbis are also mentioned. The practical object of the *Midrash* was the deduction of new *Hălākhôth* from the Scriptures, or the finding of a 'support' (אַסְמַכְתָּא) for the old ones. It is very difficult to determine in which cases the *Midrash* preceded the *Hălākhā*, and in which the *Hălākhā* preceded the *Midrash*, but it may be safely assumed that in most cases where the interpretation of the Rabbis is forced and far-fetched the *Hălākhā* was first handed down by tradition as an ancient usage or custom, and the Biblical 'support' was invoked only to give it the weight of Scripture authority. Here are one or two instances, which, given in the language of the Rabbis, may convey some idea of the vivid style of the *Midrash*—

'R. Ishmael, R. 'Eliezer b. 'Aẓarya, and R. 'Aḳiba were walking on the high-road, and Levi Hassadar and R. Ishmael the son of R. 'Eliezer b. 'Aẓarya were walking behind them. And then the following question was put before them, "Whence is it to be inferred that danger of life 'removes' the Sabbath?" . . . R. Jose of Galilee answered, "It is written, BUT (אַךְ) *my Sabbaths ye shall keep* (Ex $31^{13}$); the (limiting particle) אַךְ teaches, there are Sabbaths which thou keepest, others which thou 'removest' (the latter in cases of danger of life)." R. Shim'on b. Manasya says, "Behold Scripture says, *And ye shall keep the Sabbaths, for it is holy unto* YOU (*ib.* v.$^{14}$), the Sabbath is given to you (with stress on the word לָכֶם) to desecrate in case of need, but thou art not given to the Sabbath"' (*Mĕkhiltā, ad loc.*). Other Rabbis base this *Hălākhā* on the logical principle of *à fortiori* (קַל וָחוֹמֶר, one of the hermeneutical rules of Hillel), but none disputes the *Hălākhā* in itself, which had evidently the authority of ages. Another instance is the interpretation of Ex $21^{24}$ (cf. Lv $24^{20}$): '*Eye for eye*, that is, money (amounting to the value of the eye). Thou sayest money, perhaps it means the real eye (*i.e.* that his eye should be blinded in retaliation for the organ which he has destroyed). R. Eliezer said, "It is written, *And he that killeth a beast he shall restore, and he that killeth a man shall be put to death* (Lv $24^{21}$). The Scripture has thus put together damages caused to a man and those caused to a beast. As the latter may be atoned for by paying (the damages), so can also the former (except in cases of murder) be punished with money"' (*Siphrā Lev. ad loc.*; *Mĕkhiltā ad loc.*; *Bābā Ḳammā*, 83*b*). This argument, called הֶקֵּשׁ (analogy of matter), is in direct opposition to the literal sense of the Scriptures, which implies the *jus talionis* in unmistakable terms; but it was only meant to lend some biblical sanction to a *Hălākhā* that had been a controverted point between the Sadducees and the Pharisees for centuries before. It is different, when we read, for instance, with regard to the law, *And the land shall keep Sabbath to the Lord* (Lv $25^{2}$): 'One might think that it is also forbidden to dig pits, canals, and caves (this being a disturbance of the land) in the sabbatical year, therefore we have an inference to say, *Thou shalt neither sow thy field nor prune thy vineyard* (*ib.* v.$^{4}$), proving that it is only work connected with vineyard and field that is forbidden.' In instances like this, where the interpretation has nothing forced or strange about it, it would not be risky to assume that the *Hălākhā* was the outcome of the *Midrash*. But it is not such mere practical questions that have produced the vast *Midrash* literature. A great portion of it is simple commentary, though sometimes reproduced in that vivid dialogue style which makes it appear *Midrash*-like. *E.g. And ye shall take a bunch of hyssop and shall dip it in the blood that is* בַּסַּף (Ex $12^{22}$), on which the *Mĕkhiltā* (*ad loc.*) has the following comment: 'The Scriptures tell us that he carves out a hole on the side of the threshold over which he kills (the passover lamb); for סַף means simply the threshold, as it is said, *In their setting of their thresholds by my threshold* (סִפָּם אֶת־סִפִּי Ezk $43^{8}$, cf. LXX and Vulg.). This is the opinion of R. Ishmael. R. 'Aḳiba says סַף means nothing else but a vessel, as it is said, *the bowls* (סִפִּים), *the snuffers, the basins'* (1 K $7^{50}$, cf. Aram. versions and commentaries). Another example may be taken from the expression וְיִנָּזְרוּ *from the holy things of the children of Israel* (Lv $22^{2}$) on which the *Ṣiphrā* comments: 'נְזִירָה (a noun, derived from וינזרו) means nothing else but separation. And so he says *which separateth himself from me* וְיִנָּזֵר (Ezk $14^{7}$), and he says again, *They separated backwards* (נָזֹרוּ Is $1^{4}$).' Such instances of mere פְּשָׁט (simple meaning) could be cited by hundreds, and it is not impossible that many more were omitted by the scribes, who considered such renderings of words and definitions of terms as universally known through the medium of the various versions, and hence not sufficiently important to be copied.* In the *Haggadic* portions of the *Midrash* the elements of simple exegesis are less prominent—a fact which is easily explained by their subjective character. Sometimes the interpreter or preacher is so deeply convinced of the truth of the lesson he has to teach that he feels no compunction in interweaving it with biblical texts, and putting it into the mouth of a biblical hero. Thus we read in the *Ṣiphrā* with reference to Lv $9^{6}$ *This is the thing which the Lord commands ye shall do*: 'Moses said unto Israel, *Do* remove the *evil desire* (יֵצֶר הָרָע) from your hearts. Be all in awe and of one counsel to worship before the Omnipresent. As he is the Sole One in the world, so shall your service be single-hearted, as it is said, *Circumcise* the foreskin *of your heart, for the Lord your God is the God of gods and the Lord of lords* (Dt $10^{16.17}$), and *then the glory of the Lord shall appear unto you* (Lv $9^{6}$).' The thought expressed in this interpretation is that the manifestation of the Divine glory is the reward for the fulfilment of a commandment, and is sure to occur whenever Israel accomplishes the laws of the Torah in true devotion and single-heartedness of spirit. Occasion-

* See on these *Midrashim*: I. H. Weiss' Introduction to his edition of the *Sifra* (Vienna, 1862); M. Friedmann's Introduction to his edition of the *Mĕkhiltā* (Vienna, 1870); Dr. Lewy, *Ein Wort über die 'Mechilta des R. Simon'* (Breslau, 1889); and Dr. D. Hoffmann, *Zur Einleitung in die halachischen Midraschim* (Berlin, 1886–87).

* See Friedmann's *Introduction to the Mekhilta*, p. lxxvi, and Dr. L. Dobschütz' brochure, *Die einfache Bibelexegese der Tannaim* (Breslau, 1893).

ally the preacher in his enthusiasm leaves the text altogether and rushes off into a sort of hymn, as, for instance (Ex 15[1]), *I will praise God*, on which the *Mĕkhiltâ* (*ad loc.*):—'I will give praise to God that he is mighty . . . that he is wealthy . . . that he is wise . . . that he is merciful . . . that he is a judge . . . that he is faithful.' Each attribute is followed by a proof from Scripture, and the whole is a paraphrase of 1 Ch 29[11. 12]. The constant citing of parallel passages by way of illustration is a main feature of the *Midrash*, *e.g.* *Ṣiphrê* on Nu 15[39] '*And ye shall not seek after your own heart and your own eyes* עֵינֵיכֶם : By this latter is meant adultery, as it is said, And *Samson said to his father*, *Get* her for me, for she is pleasing to *my eyes*' (בְּעֵינָי Jg 14[3]). Again, Dt 6[5] 'And thou shalt love the Lord thy God with *all thy heart and all thy soul*,' where the *Ṣiphrê* adds by way of comment: 'Even if he should take away thy soul. And so he (the Psalmist, 44[22]), *Yea, for thy sake are we killed all the day long*.' The great exegetical principle was, 'The words of the Torah are poor (or deficient) in one place but rich in another, as it is said, *She is like the merchant's ship; she bringeth her food from afar*' (Pr 31[14]; Jerus. Talm. *Rôsh Hashshānā* 58*d*).

iv. The *'Amoraim* אֲמוֹרָאִים 'Speakers,' 'Interpreters'; a designation commonly applied to the authorities who flourished 220–500, and whose main activity consisted in expounding the Mishna. The seats of learning were no longer confined to Palestine, great schools having arisen, as in the time of the *Tannaim*, in various places in Babylonia, destined even to overshadow the former. The Babylonian teachers (who received ordination) bear as a rule the title *Rab* (רַב) in contradistinction to their Palestinian brethren who were called *Rabbi* (רַבִּי). The most important among the *'Amoraim* are the following:—

*First Generation* (220–280).—(*a*) *Palestine:* R. Jannai, of whom we have a saying in the Mishna; R. Ḥiya and R. Hoshaya Rabba, the supposed compilers of the *Tôsĕphtâ* (see above); R. Joshua b. Levi, the subject of many legends, to whom various mystical treatises (descriptions of paradise and hell, etc.) are attributed; R. Joḥanan (b. Nappaḥa) of Sepphoris and Tiberias, disciple of R. Judah and the most prominent teacher in Palestine during the 3rd cent., and his brother-in-law R. Shim'on b. Lakish. (*b*) *Babylon:* Abba Arikha ('Long Abba'), commonly cited by his title Rab. He 'went up' (from Babylon) to Palestine together with his uncle R. Ḥiya (mentioned above) to study under R. Jehuda, and on his return founded at Sura the school over which he presided; Samuel ירחינאה (the astronomer), a relative of Rab, and, like him, a disciple of R. Judah (though he did not receive ordination from him). He became head of the school in Nehardea.

*Second Generation* (280–300).—(*a*) *Palestine:* R. Eleazar b. Pedath, R. Simlai, R. Aṣṣi (also Iṣṣi and R. Ammi) (also Immi), and R. 'Abuha. The first four emigrated to Palestine from Babylon; whilst R. 'Abuha, who was a native of Palestine, taught in Cæsarea, where he often had controversies with Christian teachers. The famous *Haggadist* R. Shamuel b. Naḥmani also belongs to this generation. (*b*) *Babylon:* R. Huna (Sura), R. Jehuda (b. Jeheṣkel), founder of the school of Pumbeditha; R. Ḥiṣda, R. Shesheth, founder of a school in Shilhi. All these were disciples of Rab and Shamuel, or of one of them.

*Third Generation* (320–370).—This period marks the decay of the schools in Palestine, a consequence of the religious persecutions inaugurated under the reign of Constantine. (*a*) *Palestine:* Jeremia, R. Jona, and R. Joṣê. (*b*) *Babylon:* Rabbah (רַבָּה) b. Naḥmani (Pumbeditha), famous for his dialectical skill and called 'the mountain-mover'; his colleague R. Joṣeph, a great authority on Targum, whose wide acquaintance with all branches of the Law brought him the title of 'Sinai'; their pupils 'Abayi and Raba (רָבָא), both famous for the ingenious methods exemplified in their controversies scattered all over the Bab. Talmud; R. Papa, founder of a school in Nares.

*Fourth Generation* (375–427).—(*a*) *Palestine:* R. Shamuel (b. Joṣe b. R. Bun); (*b*) *Babylon:* R. Ashi (Sura); R. Kahana II. (Pumbeditha), and Amemar (Nehardea). The former is credited with having begun the compilation of the Bab. Talmud.

*Fifth Generation* (427–500).—*Babylon:* Mar bar R. Ashi; Rubbina (contraction of Rab Abina (Sura)), and R. Tosphaa (Pumbeditha). The two latter were greatly instrumental in accomplishing the work commenced by R. Ashi, finishing the compilation of the Bab. Talmud, and reducing it to writing.

The literary productions of these two schools are largely embodied in the two Talmuds bearing the title of their native countries: (*A*) **Palestinian Talmud** called the Talmud of Jerusalem, ת׳ יְרוּשַׁלְמִי, which is also more correctly called (since there were no schools in Jerusalem after the destruction of the temple) ת׳ אֶרֶץ יִשְׂרָאֵל ת׳ רמערבא and גְּמָרָא דִּבְנֵי מַעַרְבָא 'the Talmud of (the children of) the Land of Israel,' 'the Talmud (or the *Gemara*) of (the people of) the West.' (*B*) The **Babylonian Talmud** ת׳ בַּבְלִי, which (though only occurring once) was also known under the title of ת׳ אַנְשֵׁי מִזְרח 'the Talmud of the people of the East.'* The main object of the Talmuds is the interpretation of the Mishna, tracing its sources, giving its reasons, explaining obscure passages, as well as real or seeming contradictions, by the aid of parallel passages in the 'external Mishnas,' and illustrating its matter and expanding its contents (especially in the branches of civil law) by giving such cases as life and altered circumstances were constantly furnishing. It is perhaps in this latter quality that the text of the Talmud proper as distinguished from the Mishna is called *Gĕmārā* גְּמָרָא, meaning, according to some authorities, 'Supplement' or Complement to the Mishna.† The Talmuds differ in various minor respects. Thus, the non-Hebrew portions of the Jerus. Talmud are composed in the West Aram. dialect, whilst those of the Bab. Talmud are written in an East Aram. idiom, closely related to the Syr. and still more akin to the Mandaic language. The style of the Jerus. Talmud is more concise, its discussions less diffuse, than those of the Bab. Talmud. The former is altogether free from the casuistic and lengthy discourses on imaginary cases which form a special feature of the productions of the Eastern Rabbis. It should, however, be remarked that, so far as dialect and diction are concerned, the Bab. Talmud is not always uniform, there being various tractates, such as *Nĕdārîm*, *Nāzîr*, *Tĕmûrā Mĕ'îlā*, and *Kĕrîthôth*, which betray certain grammatical forms and peculiarities of style, reminding us in some places of the diction of the Talmud of Jerusalem. Apart from the main object as described, the text of the Mishna serves sometimes (particularly in the Bab. Talmud) as a mere peg on which to fasten matter having hardly any connexion with the contents of the latter. *E.g.*

* See *JQR* ix. 120.

† Neither the Jerus. nor the Bab. Talm. extends over all the 60 (or 63) tractates of the Mishna. The Jerus. Talm. has *Gĕmārā* to the first four orders of the Mishna and to three chapters in the tractate *Niddā* in the sixth order; but in the second order there is missing the *Gĕmārā* to the last four chapters of the tractate *Shabbath*, to the third chapter of the tractate *Makkôth*, and in the fourth order to the tractates *'Ābôth* and *'Ēdûyyôth*. The Bab. Talm. has *Gĕmārā* as follows: in the first order to tractate *Bĕrākhôth* only; in the second order, tractate *Shĕḳālîm* is omitted; in the fourth order, tractates *'Ābôth* and *'Ēdûyyôth* are omitted; in the fifth order, tractates *Middôth* and *Ḳinnîm* are omitted; in the sixth order, *Gĕmārā* to tractate *Niddā* alone.

the lines in Mishna tractate *Giṭṭîn*, 'that the laws regarding the σικάριοι (a name under which certain leaders of the Zealot bands were known) did not apply to the land of Judæa,' are followed in the Bab. Talmud by a legendary account of the wars preceding the destruction of the second temple, and various incidents connected with it, extending over more than 5 folio pages (55*b*–58*a*). Again in the tractate *Bābā Bathrā*, the accidental remark in the Mishna, that a volume (or roll) containing the Scriptures inherited by two or more brothers must not be divided among them by cutting it up into its constituent books even when the parties agree to this, provokes in the *Gĕmārā* (of the Bab. Talmud) a discussion relating to the arrangement of the Canon of the OT, its rise, and the dates at which the various books included in it were composed, accompanied by a long discourse on the particular nature of the Book of Job, the character and date of its hero, together with a few remarks on other biblical personages, which covers nearly 8 folio pages (13*b*–17*a*). This process of inserting matter but slightly connected with the text is at times carried further by adding to the inserted matter other topics having a similar slight connexion with it. As an instance of this process we may regard the following. Mishna *Bĕrākhôth*, ch. ix. 1, runs, 'He who sees a place in which miracles were performed for the sake of Israel says, Praised be he who wrought miracles for our fathers in this place.' By way of illustration the *Gĕmārā* (Bab. Talm. *ib.* 54*a*) cites an 'external Mishna' in which it is taught that 'He who sees the crossings of the Red Sea (*i.e.* the place at which the Jews crossed the Red Sea, Ex 14[22]), or the crossings of the Jordan (Jos 3[14ff.]) . . . is bound to give thanks and praise to the Omnipresent' (*Mākôm*). The last words suggest a quotation of R. Jehuda in the name of Rab, adding to the number of those who are under the obligation to give thanks, also the four cases enumerated in Ps 107 (people returning from a sea voyage, coming back from a journey through the desert, recovering from a serious illness, or released from prison, 54*b*). This statement is followed by several other sayings (54*b*, 55*a*) which have no other connexion with the preceding matter than identity of authorship, all being cited in the name of Rab. One of these citations is to the effect that for three things man should in particular pray to God (who alone can grant them): 'a good king, a good year, and a good *dream*' (55*b*); but the last word again suggests a new train of thought on the subject of dreams, their interpretation and fulfilment, which forms the theme of the next 6 folio pages (55*a*–57*b*). Owing to these sudden and violent changes from subject to subject, the style of the Talmud becomes very uncertain and rather rambling;* but, on the other hand, it is this very circumstance that keeps the 'sea of the Talmud' in constant motion, relieving it from the monotony and tedious repetition so peculiar to the majority of theological works dating from those early ages. Indeed, owing to this facility for dragging in whatever interested the compilers or the scribes, the Talmud almost loses the character of a work of divinity, and assumes more the character of an encyclopædia, reproducing the knowledge of the Rabbis during the first five centuries on all possible subjects, whether secular or religious. This is, as already indicated, particularly the case with the Bab. Talmud, the *Haggādā* of which is very discursive and rich in all sorts of folk-lore. It must, however, be borne in mind that the authorities in whose names the strangest stories are sometimes communicated are often Rabbis from Palestine, whose sayings and statements were as much studied and discussed in the East as they were in the West.

v. The *Ṣaborai* סְבוֹרָאֵי 'Explainers' or 'Meditators' (upon the words of their predecessors), whose activity is supposed to have extended over the whole of the 6th century. The most important among them are Rabbah Joṣe (Pumbeditha) and R. 'Aḥai (of Be Ḥathim), who flourished about the beginning of the 6th cent., and probably shared largely in the compilation work of the last of the '*Amoraim*; and R. Giza (Sura) and R. Simona (Pumbeditha), who belonged to the middle of the same century. The activity of the *Ṣaborai*, about whose lives we know little, consisted mainly in commenting upon the Talmud by means of explanatory speeches, and contributing to it some additional controversies marked by peculiarity of style and by absence of the names of those engaged in the dialogue, as well as by insertion of final decisions upon the differing opinions of their predecessors.* The school of the *Ṣaborai* is peculiar to Babylon, there being no corresponding class of teachers in Palestine. Nor is there any reliable tradition, regarding the compilation of the Jerus. Talmud, by whom it was accomplished, and when it was undertaken. Maimonides' statement, that R. Joḥanan composed the Jerus. Talmud, can, since this work contains quantities of matter dating from a much later period, mean only that by the aid of the schools he founded, this Rabbi was largely instrumental in giving rise to a work embodying the teachings of the later Western authorities. But in consequence of religious persecutions and political disturbances the decay of the schools set in too early to permit even such comparative completeness and finish as are to be found in the Bab. Talmud, which is itself far from perfection in this respect. Indeed the abruptness of the discussions of the Pal. Talmud, the frequent absence of formulæ introducing quotations or marking the beginning of the treatment of a fresh subject or the conclusion of an old one, as well as the meagreness of its matter where the analogy of the Bab. Talmud would suggest the greatest fulness, and the fact that it has no *Gĕmārā* at all on the 5th order (sacrifices), which is so strongly represented in the Bab. Talmud,†—all these circumstances convey the impression that the Jerus. Talmud was never submitted to a real conscious compilation with the object of presenting posterity with a completed work. What was reduced to writing does not give us a work carried out after a preconcerted plan, but rather represents a series of jottings answering to the needs of the various individual writers, and largely intended to strengthen the memory. And thus lacking the authority enjoyed by the Mishna and the Bab. Talmud, which were the products of the great centres of learning, the Jerus. Talmud was, for a long time at least, not elevated to the rank of a national work, and it is therefore easy to understand how such portions of it as had not much bearing upon actual practice were permitted to disappear. Altogether, the people of Palestine were, as an old Rabbi said, 'sick with oppression,'

* It is this discursiveness which makes a proper translation of the Talmud almost impossible: see M. Friedmann's brochure, דבר על אודות התלמוד, Vienna, 1895 (Heb.)

* On all these points see N. Brüll's essay, 'Die Entstehungsgeschichte des bab. T. als Schriftwerkes'; and Weiss, as above, vol. iii. p. 208ff., and vol. iv. p. 1ff.

† The question whether the Jerus. Talmud ever had *Gĕmārā* to the fifth order is best discussed in the *Hehalutz* . . . by Osias H. Schorr, who on excellent grounds maintains that such a *Gĕmārā* must have existed. But it must be stated that hitherto, not even in the Cairo collections, which have restored to us so many lost works, has a single line turned up to confirm Schorr's hypothesis. About the peculiarities of the fourth order, see I. Lewy, *Interpretation des 1. Abschnittes des paläst. Talmud-Traktats Nesikin* (Breslau, 1895), p. 20; but compare also the references to the other authorities there given. This essay is the best piece of work yet done on the redaction of the Jerus. Talmud.

and had no time to spare for the niceties of the *Hălākhā*, 'and did not listen to the words of Talmud (in the narrower sense of discussing the legal portions of it) and the Mishna.' The deeper was their devotion to the *Haggādā*, which gave them 'words of blessing and consolation.' This will account for the copiousness of the *Haggadic* literature, which reached its highest development during the period of the *'Amoraim*. This literature is embodied in the *Midrashim* to various books of the OT as well as in certain independent *Haggadic* treatises, the contents of which, though possibly compiled at a later age, are made up of the homilies and moralizing exhortations given in the names of the same Palestinian Rabbis who figure as authorities in the two Talmuds. They, however, form a literature by themselves, never having served as sources or factors of the Talmud, though they are sometimes useful as parallel passages to the *Haggadic* portions of the latter. They thus do not fall within the scope of this article. It is, however, only fair to warn the theologian that though he may dispense, *e.g.*, with the *Pĕsiḳtā* (collection of homilies mainly based on the *Haphṭārôth*) or the Midrash *Shîr Hashshîrîm* (allegoric interpretations of the Song of Songs) in his study of the Talmud, he cannot do so safely in his study of the Rabbi, whose performance of his prophetic office is seen to best advantage in such moralizing works as those of which the *Haggadic* pieces just mentioned are a fair specimen.

LITERATURE (omitting mostly such books as have already been referred to in the notes).—EDITIONS: There are very few critical editions of the ancient Rabbinical literature, though new reprints are constantly appearing. The following, however, deserve special notice:—*Mishna*, Naples, 1492, ed. pr.; *Mishna . . . Latinitate donavit* . . . J. Surenhusius, Amstelod., 1698; *The Mishna, edited from a unique MS*, by W. H. Lowe, Cambridge, 1883; *Mishnayoth: Hebräischer Text mit Punktation, Deutscher Übersetzung*, von A. Samter, Berlin, 1887 (not yet finished). Most editions have, as a rule, the commentaries of 'Obadya di Bertinoro and of Yom Ṭob Lipman Heller (תוספות יום טוב), or the commentary of Maimonides (not as frequently as the two former). As useful editions for students, the tractates edited by Strack may be recommended. *Toṣephta*, edited by Zuckermandel (after MSS), Pasewalk, 1880. *Jerus. Talmud*, Venice, 1523, ed. pr., Krotoschin, 1866, and Zitomir, 1860–67. This last edition has several commentaries. Of single tractates there have appeared, among others, *Bĕrākhôth*, *Pē'ā*, and *Dĕmā'î*, with the commentary *Ahabath Zion*, by Z. Frankel, and a part of *Bābā Kammā* with a commentary by I. Lewy. *Bab. Talmud*, Venice, 1520, with the commentaries of R. Solomon b. Isaac, and the *Glosses* of the Franco-German Rabbis called *Toṣaphoth* (Additions). The last and best edition of the Talmud is that which appeared in Wilna, 1880–86, 25 vols. The *Variæ lectiones in Mischnam et in Talmud Babylonicum*, by Raph. Rabbinowicz, consisting of 16 vols., and extending over a large part of the Bab. Talmud, is a most important work for the critical study of the Talmud. Also to be consulted is the work קונטרס למלאות הסרונות השם, Königsberg, 1860, restoring the words and passages omitted or corrupted by the censors. Of single tractates we have only to notice here the *Tract. Makkoth*, ed. Friedmann, Wien, 1888.*

INTRODUCTORY AND BIBLIOGRAPHICAL: N. Krochmal מורה נבוכי הזמן, Lemberg, 1851 (Heb.); L. Zunz, *Die Gottesdienstlichen Vorträge der Juden*², Frankfurt-a.-M. 1892; M. Steinschneider, *Jewish Literature*, §§ 1–7, London, 1857; Z. Frankel, דרכי המשנה, *Hodegetica in Mischnam* . . . Lipsiæ, 1859 (Heb.); by the same, מבוא הירושלמי, *Introductio in Talmud Hierosolomitanum*, Breslau, 1870 (Heb.); Graetz, *Geschichte der Juden*, vols. 3 and 4 (Germ.); Dérenbourg, *Essai sur l'histoire et la géographie de la Palestine d'après les Thalmud et les autres sources rabbiniques* (Paris, 1867); I. H. Weiss, דור דור ודורשיו *Zur Geschichte der Jüdischen Tradition*, vols. 1–3; Strack, *Einleitung in den Thalmud*, Leipzig, 1894; M. Mielziner, *Introduction to the Talmud*, Cincinnati, 1894; Schürer, *GJV*², i. § 3 E, Leipzig, 1890 (Germ.). For popular accounts see E. Deutsch, *The Talmud*, Philadelphia, 1896; A. Darmesteter, *The Talmud*, Philadelphia, 1897.

DICTIONARIES AND GRAMMARS: Nathan b. Yeḥiel (of the 11th cent.), ספר הערוך, 1480, ed. pr. This work was last edited or rather incorporated in the *Arukh Completum . . . auctore Nathane filio Jechielis . . . corrigit explevit critice* Alex. Kohut, 8 vols., Wien, 1878–92; Joh. Buxtorf, *Lexicon Chaldaicum Talmudicum et Rabbinicum*, Basel, 1640; Jacob Levy, *Neuhebräisches und chaldäisches Wörterbuch über die Talmudim und Midraschim*, Leipzig, 1876; M. Jastrow, *Dictionary of the Targumim, the Talmud Babli and Jerushalmi*, London and New York, 1886; Sam. Krauss, *Griechische und lateinische Lehnwörter im Talmud, Midrasch, und Targum* . . . Berlin, 1898; W. Bacher, *Die älteste Terminologie der jüdischen Schriftauslegung: Ein Wörterbuch der bibelexegetischen Kunstsprache der Tannaiten*, Leipzig, 1899; H. L. Strack and C. Siegfried, *Lehrbuch der Neuhebräischen Sprache* . . . Karlsruhe and Leipzig, 1884; A. Geiger, *Lehr- und Lesebuch der Sprache der Mishnah*, Breslau, 1845 (Germ.); I. H. Weiss, משפט לשון המשנה, Wien, 1865 (Heb.); G. Dalman, *Grammatik des Jüdisch-Palästinischen Aramäisch*, Leipzig, 1894 (Germ.); S. D. Luzzatto, *Elementi grammaticali del . . . dialetto Talmudico Babilonese*, Padua, 1865 (Ital.), of which a Germ. tr. was prepared by M. S. Krüger, and was published in Breslau, 1873; Levias, *Grammar of the Bab. Talm.*, Cincinnati, 1900.

The attempts towards translating the Talmud are many and various. A full account of them will be found in Dr. Erich Bischoff's *Kritische Geschichte der Thalmud-Übersetzungen aller Zeiten und Zungen*, Frankfurt-a.-M. 1899 (Germ.). The present writer can, however, recommend only the following books: On the Mishna see above. On *Minor tractates: Masecheth Sopherim*, by J. Müller, Leipzig, 1878; *Derech Erez Suta*, by A. Iawrogy, Königsberg, 1885. Jerus. Talm.: A. Wünsche, *Der jerusalemische Talmud in seinen haggadischen Bestandtheilen ins Deutsche übertragen*, Zürich, 1880. Bab. Talm.: *A Translation of the treatise Chagigah*, by A. W. Streane, 1891; *Tractate Baba Mezia mit deutscher Übersetzung* . . . by A. Samter, Berlin, 1876; *Der Bab. Talmud in seinen Hagadischen Bestandtheilen wortgetreu übersetzt*, by Wünsche, 1888. The student would do well to consult always, when reading a *Haggadic* text, the following standard works by W. Bacher: *Die Agada der Babylonischen Amoräer*, Strassburg, 1879; *Die Agada der Tannaiten*, Strassburg, 1884; *Die Agada der Palästinischen Amoräer*, Strassburg, 1892.

S. SCHECHTER.

* A good bibliographical account of the various reprints of the Bab. Talmud is to be found in Rabbinowicz's מאמר על הדפסת התלמוד, München, 1877, whilst a short list of the various MSS in the different libraries is given by Strack in his *Einleitung*, p. 70 ff. It should, however, be noted that the last 20 years have brought to light many Talmudical pieces, not known to any bibliographer. They are stil awaiting description. Mr. Elkan N. Adler's library (London) is especially rich in early prints not known to Rabbinowicz; whilst the Cambridge collections, both in the possession of the University Library and in that of Mrs. Lewis and Mrs. Gibson (now in Westminster College), contain many MSS fragments of the Bab. and Pal. Talmuds of the highest critical value.

**SIBYLLINE ORACLES.**—The collection of Jewish and Christian poems which pass under the name of the Sibyl covers in its time of production a period of many centuries, reaching back into at least the 2nd cent. B.C., and coming down (when its latest developments are included) far into the Middle Ages. When we take further into account that, even in its first Jewish and Christian forms, Sibyllism was merely an attempt to transplant a feature of literature that was centuries old, and already effete in the pagan world, it will be seen that it constitutes a very important element in historical theology, and one which has had every influence upon the mind of man that could be secured for it by the exercise of authority (operating through the State as in Roman life, or through great names as in the case of the Christian Church), supported as that authority was by the natural love of the secret and mysterious which characterizes the major part of men in all periods of human history.

The original Sibyl is very nearly the equivalent of 'prophetess' in the Gr. and Rom. world; the derivation of her name from an assumed combination of Σιὸς (for Θεὸς) and βουλή (in a form βυλλά) goes back to Varro (cf. Lact. *Div. Inst.* i. 6); and, although it may be (and probably is) invalid philologically, it is sufficient evidence of the character assigned to the persons known as Sibyls, who had the knowledge (as it was supposed) of the Divine will in the fatalistic sense, and were in the habit of recording the fiats of that Divine will in various oracular and prophetic ways. Accordingly, they could be consulted, either in some special *antrum* or grotto, or through an inspection of such prophecies as they had committed to writing. Now, according to the ancients, there were a number of such Sibyls, known sometimes by actual names, and sometimes by the places where they prophesied, as the Chaldæan,

Erythræan, Delphic, etc. But for practical purposes the one that exercised the commanding influence over the Christian Church to which we have alluded above is the Cumæan Sibyl. It is necessary to bear in mind that this commanding influence is merely a case of survival from the Roman State religion. And the question for the student of the Sib. Oracles as we have them extant, is as to the extent of the survival. It can be tested under the heads of (1) the language, (2) the form, (3) the matter of the ancient and the more modern oracles.

The Rom. tradition affirmed that these oracles had originally been offered by a certain Sibyl to a certain Roman king (say Tarquinius Superbus), but at an excessive price; the price being refused, she departed and destroyed a certain part of her books, and returned to offer the remainder at the original price; and, after this process had been repeated a certain number of times, the king was sufficiently interested to buy the remainder, which thus became in the Roman government a State deposit of information concerning the future, placed under the control of the augurs or *viri quindecemvirales*, and to be consulted in time of exigency.

There is no need to spend time in criticising the details of such a story, which is merely an attempt to find a venerable origin for a Roman practice; for it is certain that the Roman government had such books of Sib. oracles, which they from time to time augmented or retrenched by various editorial processes. What is important to remember is—(i.) that these oracles were for the most part, perhaps wholly, in Greek; (ii.) that they were in hexameter verse, probably with the literary devices of alphabetic and acrostic writing; (iii.) that they were concerned *inter alia* with the fortunes of the world at large and of the empire, the ages of the universe, and the collapse and rejuvenescence thereof. The first of these points, and, in part, the second, may best be illustrated by references to an actual oracle which has come down to us, preserved by Phlegon, *de Mirabil.* c. 10, apparently from a Roman writer, Sextus Carminius, and dated in the year A.V.C. 629 (=B.C. 124). It relates to the birth of a hermaphrodite, which the oracle alludes to in the words—

καὶ τοί ποτε φημὶ γυναῖκα
Ἀνδρόγυνον τέξεσθαι ἔχοντά περ' ἄρσενα πάντα
Νηπίαχαι θ' ὅσα θηλύτεραι φαίνουσι γυναῖκες.

Obviously, the oracle was made to suit the portent, and it was composed in hexameters. At this time, then, we know the method of formation of the oracles, and that the collection was subject to accretion or modification. They were written, as all later oracles and books of oracles, in the religious metre and language of Homer. Moreover, on examination it will be found that the oracle is acrostic, and apparently based upon an earlier acrostic which has been used, which was itself metrical. The books were therefore treated as *sortes* by the augurs, but handled with freedom in secret so as to adjust the prophecies to the needs of the time. That they contained some scheme of the ages of the world and of the ἀποκατάστασις πάντων, is clear from Virgil's

'Ultima Cumæi venit iam carminis ætas;
Magnus ab integro sæclorum nascitur ordo.'
(*Eclog.* iv. 4),

and a number of similar considerations.

All of these features are abundantly illustrated in the Jewish and Christian Sib. books. It was necessary that they should be if the world was to swallow the literary deception that was being practised upon it.

It must not be supposed that such a gigantic and long-continued fraud could have been carried on without meeting with criticism from a people as acute and polished as the Greeks. While it is certain that almost all the Fathers of the Church were firm believers in the inspiration of the Sibyls (for we need not doubt the honesty of Justin and Clement, of Tertullian, of Lactantius, and a host of others, though it is equally clear that the deceived must have been near of kin to the deceivers), it was not possible that such keen wits as Lucian and Celsus should come under the spell. They saw at once that the Christians were making oracles to suit their own propaganda, and were quick to proclaim the fact; and Lucian, in particular, himself turned Sibyllist in order to tell in mock heroics the fortunes of Peregrinus and of Alexander of Abonoteichos. This extant criticism and ridicule must have been widely extended. We can trace from the successive Sibyllists themselves the objections which they had to meet. One, of necessity, was the dependence of the Sibyl upon Homer, for Sibyllism is closely related to Centoism, and borrows lines and expressions freely from Homer. It was necessary, therefore, for the assumed Sibyl to explain that the borrowing was really on the side of that thief Homer. Accordingly, the Sibyl herself attacks the supposed later poet in the following lines—

καί τις ψευδογράφος πρέσβυς βροτὸς ἔσσεται αὖτις
ψευδόπατρις· δύσει δὲ φάος ἐν ὀπῇσιν ἑῇσιν
. . . . . .
. . . ἐπέων γὰρ ἐμῶν μέτρων τε κρατήσει.
(*Orac. Sib.* iii. 419 ff.);

and this judgment is endorsed by Tatian, who in his tract *Against the Greeks*, § 41, maintains the superior date of the Sibyl to Homer. A closer examination, however, of the oracles reveals that Homer is not the only writer pilfered; there is a constant coincidence with fragments of Orphic hymns, which would certainly be much more pronounced if we were not limited in our comparison to the few fragments that have been conserved of this branch of literature. Now, it is worth noticing that Clement of Alexandria (the best read of all the early Fathers in the matter of Greek literature) expressly declares that the Sibyl is earlier than *Orpheus*; while, to quote another author of nearly the same date, Tertullian will have it that the Sibyl is older than *all other literature* (cf. Tert. *adv. Nationes*, ii. 12). It is clear from these testimonies that there had been from the first a critical dispute over the antiquity of the supposed Sibylline verses; at all events, the anti-Homeric strain in the Sibyl which we have quoted above occurs in verses which Alexandre assigns to the time of Antoninus Pius, and the writers who endorse the sentiment belong very nearly to the same period. And before this time there must have been an active Sibylline propaganda carried on by the early Christians, most of whom were deceived and some of them deceivers.

Something of a similar kind to this contest between Homer and the Sibyl and Orpheus and the Sibyl for priority, appears to have taken place at a later date in regard to Virgil. We have already pointed out that the acquaintance of Virgil with Sibylline oracles may be assumed. It does not follow that these oracles have anything to do with the extant collection; rather they seem to be the Roman collection, which Virgil must have known by report, and perhaps by actual study of published or unpublished portions. Now it has been shown by Dechent (*Ueber das erste, zweite und elfte Buch der Sib. Weissagungen*, 1873) that the eleventh book of the Oracles has coincidences of language with Virgil. The Sibyl describes, for example, the flight of Æneas from Troy in ll. 144 ff., which begin—

> ἄρξει δ' ἐκ γενεῆς τε καὶ αἵματος Ἀσσαράκοιο
> παῖς κλυτὸς ἡρώων, κρατερός τε καὶ ἄλκιμος ἀνήρ,

which may be compared with

> 'Romulus, Assaraci quem sanguinis Ilia mater
> Educet' (Virg. *Æn.* vi. 779).

After describing the person and fortunes of Æneas, the writer proceeds to explain that her verses will be stolen by a later poet, much in the same language as we noted in Bk. iii. for Homer—

> καί τις πρέσβυς ἀνὴρ σοφὸς ἔσσεται αὖτις ἀοιδός
>
> . . . . . .
>
> τοῖσιν ἐμοῖσι λόγοις μέτροις ἐπέεσσι κρατήσας·
> αὐτὸς γάρ, πρώτιστος ἐμὰς βίβλους ἀναπλώσει
> καὶ κρύψει μετὰ ταῦτα.

But here we must, in view of the coincidences in language between the Sibyl and the *Æneid*, understand Virgil and not Homer as the supposed thief. Obviously, the Sibyllist, who is so anxious to be prior to Virgil, must have written a good while after Virgil, as is also shown by the reference to Virgil as hiding the oracles. Alexandre refers this part of the oracles to the year A.D. 267; and it is interesting to observe that, not long after that date, the emperor Constantine in his oration to the Nicene Fathers invokes the authority of the Sibyl, and suggests the dependence of Virgil upon her writings, quoting Virgil for convenience in a Greek rendering. It is reasonable, therefore, to suppose that the question of relative priority between Virgil and the Sibyl belongs to this period of time.

It is to be noted, however, that the earliest of all the books of oracles does not seem to have encountered any such hostile reception. Parts of what is now edited as the third book, ll. 97–294, 491–fin., are assigned by Alexandre to the year 166 B.C. It is not decided whether the production of these verses was due to some active inquiry which was being made at the time after extant oracles, which search might easily have led to the fabrication of them by some learned Alexandrian Jew, or whether it is only one more example, to be added to many belonging to this time, of the transference of the text of the LXX into Gr. verse. Whatever may be the reason, it is certain that the versified story of the destruction of the tower of Babel, with the poetic expansion that it was accomplished by the agency of mighty winds, was accepted as a fresh historical authority by contemporaries (Abydenus, Polyhistor, and, following them, Josephus), and as confirming the accuracy of the biblical record from which it is derived, by Clement of Alexandria and Eusebius. So that it does not appear that the earliest Jewish portions of the Sibylline books provoked the same hostility as those which are later and definitely Christian. They appear to have met with an unquestioning acceptance.

It will be convenient to set down here the dates which have been assigned to the extant books. Our first scheme is that of Alexandre, whose *Excursus ad Sibyllinos Libros* is the storehouse of material for all who wish to have a thorough knowledge of the subject. According to him—

Bk. iii. ll. 97–294 and 489–fin. is a Jewish work, written in Egypt in the year 166 or 165 B.C.

Bk. iv., the oldest of the Christian Sibyllines, was written in Asia in the 1st cent. A.D. under Titus or Domitian.

The Prooemium to the collection (a fragment preserved by Theophilus of Antioch) and Bk. viii. ll. 217–429, are probably by the same Christian hand, and written in the beginning of the 2nd cent. under Trajan or Hadrian.

Bk. viii. ll. 1–217, written by a Christian of a millenarian type, in Egypt in the reign of Antoninus Pius.

Bk. iii. ll. 295–488 and Bk. v. are Judæo-Christian, and were written in Egypt in the reign of Antoninus Pius.

Bks. vi. and vii. are Christian (?heretical), and written in the reign of Alexander Severus, about A.D. 234.

Bk. viii. ll. 430–fin., by Christian hands in the middle of the 3rd cent.

Bks. i. ii. and iii. ll. 1–96, by Christian hands, in Asia in the middle of the 3rd cent.

Bks. xi. xii. xiii. xiv., Judæo-Christian, written in Egypt about the year 267 A.D.

With this scheme of Alexandre may be compared that propounded by Ewald. According to Ewald (*Abhandlung über Entstehung Inhalt und Werth der Sib. Bücher*, Göttingen, 1858) we have—

Bk. iii. ll. 97–828, about B.C. 124.
Bk. iv., about A.D. 80.
Bk. v. ll. 52–530, about A.D. 80.
Bks. v. ll. 1–51, vi. vii., in A.D. 138.
Bk. viii. ll. 1–360, about A.D. 211.
[Bk. viii. ll. 361–500, Ewald declares to be non-Sibylline.]
Bks. i. ii. iii. ll. 1–96, about A.D. 300.
Bks. xi. xii. xiii. xiv., much later: Ewald imagines references to the emperor Odenatus and to the rise of Islam!

Further discussions of dates of the whole or parts of the different books may be found in Friedlieb, *Orac. Sibyll.* (Leipzig, 1852), or Bleek (*Theol. Zeitschrift*, Berlin, 1819), or Dechent (see above). The different judgments arrived at by these writers would probably be rectified by a closer study of the whole body of Sibylline literature. So far, the best guide is Alexandre, whose *Excursus* is a monument of patiently accumulated facts.

Editions of the Sibylline Oracles.—The first published portion of the Sibyllines was the famous acrostic, Ἰησοῦς Χριστός, Θεοῦ υἱός, Σωτήρ, which was printed by Aldus. The first ed. was due to Xystus Betuleus (Sixtus Birken) at Basel in 1545. It contained the first eight books. The second (Lat.) ed. was issued from the same printing-house (John Oporinus) in the following year. The third (Gr.-Lat.) appeared at Basel in 1555. The fourth ed. (that of Opsopœus = Koch) appeared at Paris in 1599, three years after the death of the editor. In 1817 the collection was expanded by Cardinal Mai's discovery of the Books xi.–xiv., which were printed first in his *Scriptorum vet. nova collectio*, vol. iii. pt. 3. Of more modern edd. the ones in common use are those of Friedlieb (Leipzig, 1852), Alexandre (Paris, 1860), and Rzach. Of these, the last, published at Prague in 1891, is by far the best for the text; it contains no excursus, but has a brief critical preface, and a most valuable appendix exhibiting the dependence of the Sibyllines on Homer, Hesiod, the Orphic hymns, etc. With the text of Rzach and the excursus of Alexandre, the student can find out almost all that is known of the Sibyllines. It is necessary to add a final caution with regard to the quotation of the books. There is a fluctuation in their numbering on the part of the editors, due to the imperfection of the series. The last four books, for example, are numbered ix. x. xi. and xii. by Friedlieb.

[Since the writing of the foregoing article, Geffcken's tract, entitled *Komposition und Entstehungszeit der Oracula Sibyllina*, has appeared, to which the student is referred for the latest view of the subject.] J. Rendel Harris.

**SAMARITAN PENTATEUCH.**—i. Historical connexion between the Samaritans and the Pentateuch.—The Samaritans are a mixed race, sprung from the remnants of the ten tribes which lost their independence in B.C. 722, and from the foreign colonists who were settled by the Assyrian kings in Central Palestine. Hence the question arises whether the Pentateuch was already known to the subjects of the Kingdom of the Ten Tribes. It might be supposed that this question must be answered in the negative, for the single reason that the Jahweh cultus introduced by Jeroboam I. (1 K $12^{28}$) deviated to so large an extent from the Law. This argument, however, is not absolutely decisive, for even the kingdom of Judah, *e.g.* under Ahaz (2 K $16^{3}$) and Manasseh ($21^{2ff.}$), witnessed frequent and serious departures from the legitimate religion. But there is at least one valid ground for the conclusion that the Pentateuch was first accepted by the Samaritans after the Exile. Why was their request to be allowed to take part in the building of the second temple (Ezr $4^{1ff.}$) refused by the heads of the Jerusalem community (v.$^{3}$)? Very probably because the Jews were aware that the Samaritans did not as yet possess the Law-book. It is hard to suppose that, otherwise, they would have been met with this refusal. Further, one who, like the present writer, regards the modern criticism of the Pentateuch as essentially correct, has a second decisive reason for adopting the above view. Or does the very existence of the Samaritan Pentateuch present an obstacle to the conclusion at which most representatives of modern Pentateuchal criticism have arrived, namely, that the sources of the Pentateuch were united by Ezra into the one stream which we see in our Pentateuch? At the present day there is scarcely any longer a single writer who would claim that the Samaritan Pentateuch supplies any argument against the critical position. No such claim is made, for instance, by C. F. Keil in his *Einleitung in d. AT*, 1873, § 204, or by Ed. Rupprecht in *Des Rätsels Lösung*, II. i. (1896) p. 196 f., or by the Roman Catholic Fr. Kaulen in his *Einleitung in die Heilige Schrift*, 1892, § 194.

How long after Ezra's time it was when the Samaritans accepted the Pentateuch is uncertain. They may have already done so at the time that Nehemiah, upon the occasion of his second visit to Jerusalem (B.C. 433), expelled the son of Joiada, the high priest, who had married a daughter of the Samaritan prince Sanballat (Neh $13^{28}$). For there was hostility between the Jews and the Samaritans even at a much later period, although the latter had adopted the Law. But the view that appears to be most probable is that the above-mentioned son of the high priest induced the Samaritans both to accept the Pentateuch and to build a temple of their own upon Mt. Gerizim. It is well known that Josephus (*Ant.* XI. viii. 2) relates how Manasseh, son of the high priest Ἰαδδοῦς, and son-in-law of the Samaritan prince Σαναβαλλάτης, fled to the Samaritans in the time of the Persian king Darius Codomannus. But here, in all probability, we have simply a chronological error, for later writers were weak in their knowledge of the chronology of the post-exilic period. For instance, in To $1^{18-21}$ the years 701–681 are compressed into πεντήκοντα or τεσσαράκοντα ἡμέραι (Fritzsche, *Libri apocryphi*, pp. 110, 113), and in *Seder 'olam rabba* 30 it is said that the rule of the Persians after the building of the second temple lasted only 34 years (see, further, art. by the present writer in *Expos. Times*, x. [1899] p. 257). Nor are there wanting in the post-Biblical tradition indications pointing to the fact that it was near the time of Ezra that the Samaritans accepted the Pentateuch. For instance, in Bab. Talm. (*Sanhed.* 21*b*) we read: 'The Torah was originally revealed in the Hebrew character and in the holy [*i.e.* Hebrew] language, the second time in the Assyrian character and in the Aramaic language, and Israel chose the Assyrian character and the holy language, whereas it gave over the Hebrew character and the Aramaic language to the ἰδιῶται.'* This second revelation of the Law which is here presupposed, has in view the activity which, according to other passages of the tradition, Ezra displayed with reference to the Pentateuch. For instance, in Bab. Talm. (*Ṣukkā* 20*a*) it is said: 'The Torah was forgotten by the Israelites until Ezra came from Babylon and restored it' (other passages are translated in König's *Einleit. in d. AT*, p. 241 f.). Nor is there anything inexplicable in the circumstance that the Samaritans, about the year B.C. 433, accepted no part of the OT but the Pentateuch, for even the Jews exalted the Torah above the other parts of the OT. The Mishna enacts in *Megillā* iii. 1: 'If one sells books (*i.e.* parts of the OT other than the Pentateuch), he may take a Torah in exchange; but if one sells a Torah he may not take other books in exchange' (many further testimonies to this later appreciation of the Torah above the rest of the OT will be found in König's *Einleit.* p. 455 f.).

Later notices of the actual existence of the Samaritan Pentateuch are found in the Talmud (cf. Zach. Frankel, *Ueber den Einfluss der palästinischen Exegese auf die alexandr. Hermeneutik*, p. 243), in Origen (whose *Hexapla* reads on the margin of Nu $13^{1}$ ἃ καὶ αὐτὰ ἐκ τοῦ τῶν Σαμαρειτῶν ἑβραϊκοῦ μετεβάλομεν), and in Jerome (*Prologus galeatus*: 'Samaritani Pentateuchum totidem literis scriptitant, figuris tantum et apicibus discrepantes'). But about the year A.D. 1600 not even a scholar like Scaliger (*De emendatione temporum*, lib. 7) was aware whether there were copies of the Samaritan Pentateuch in existence in the East. At last, in the year 1616 Piedro della Valle purchased a complete manuscript of this Pentateuch from the Samaritans at Damascus. Between the years 1620 and 1630 Ussher collected in the East six copies of it. Since then many codices of this work have been collated; cf. de Rossi, *Variae lectiones VT*, 1784–88, vol. i. p. CLV f.; Rosen, *ZDMG*, 1864, p. 582 ff.; Abr. Harkavy, *Katalog der Samaritan. Pentateuchcodices in St. Petersburg*, 1874. The Samaritan Pentateuch was first *printed*, under the superintendence of Joh. Morinus, in the Paris Polyglott (1645). A second impression appeared in the London Polyglott (1657). It was published, transcribed in the square character, by Blayney at Oxford in 1790. Its peculiarities are also set forth in a separate column of Kennicott's *Vetus Test. heb. cum variis lectionibus* (Oxonii, 1776–80), and in H. Petermann's extremely interesting work, *Versuch einer hebräischen Formenlehre nach der Aussprache der heutigen Samaritaner*, 1868, pp. 219–326. In the latter will be found also a transcription of the whole of the Book of Genesis, as Amram, the then high priest of the Samaritan community at Nâblûs, dictated it to Petermann (pp. 161–218).

ii. COMPARISON BETWEEN THE SAMARITAN-HEBREW AND THE JEWISH-HEBREW PENTATEUCH.—(*a*) *The character of the MSS, and the method of dividing the text.*—The Samaritan manuscripts, like the majority of the Jewish ones, are of parchment or paper; the Samaritans likewise preferred the roll form for use in Divine worship. The Samaritan MSS want the vowel signs and the accents, which are employed in the Jewish Pentateuch. In lieu of these they exhibit the following signs: a point separates each word from the next; two points, similar to the colon in modern languages, mark off smaller and larger paragraphs (Kohn, *Zur Sprache, Litt., u. Dogmatik d. Samaritaner*, p. 1 f.). The whole Pentateuch is divided by the Samaritans into sections which they call קצין (*ḳaẓîn*). Of these they reckon in the Pentateuch 966 (Hupfeld, *ZDMG*, 1867, p. 20), while the Jews are accustomed to count in the Torah 379 close and 290 open *parashas* (cf. König, *Einleit.* p. 463).

(*b*) *Linguistic* differences. The *vowel letters* are much more frequently employed in the Samaritan than in the MT. Even *shĕwā* is many times indicated by ו or י: for instance, אוניות, a form which the MT first exhibits in 2 Ch $8^{18}$, is written by the Samaritan in Dt $28^{68}$, or גישורי is read for גְּשׁוּרִי in Dt $3^{14}$. The orthography which the MT favours, especially in the earlier parts of the OT, agrees still oftener with that found on the Jewish coins. But the Samaritan Pentateuch thus reflects the latest stage of development reached by Hebrew orthography within the OT, and in a great many instances goes even beyond this. In the matter of *pronouns*, the unusual forms are regularly changed into the usual ones. For instance, הוא, which in the Pentateuch (Gn $2^{12}$ etc.) stands for the later היא 195 times, and which is altered in the MT *only in the margin*, is replaced by היא in the Samaritan *in the text*. The form נַחְנוּ, which is permitted in the MT, is changed in the Samaritan into אנחנו (Gn $42^{11}$, Ex $16^{7f.}$, Nu $32^{32}$). As to the conjugation of *verbs*, the lightened form of the imperfect, the so-called jussive, is almost always changed into the ordinary form: וַיָּשָׁב (Gn $32^{1}$) is replaced by וישוב (read by the high priest Amram as *uyeshôv*); יֵרָא ($41^{33}$) by יראה (*yere'i*); וָאֵרֶא ($31^{10}$ $41^{22}$) by ואראה (*wêre'i*).—In the declension of *nouns*, the endings in *-ô* and *-î*, which, in spite of J. Barth (*ZDMG*, 1899, p. 598), are to be considered relics of the old case-endings, are almost uniformly dropped: חַיְתוֹ appears as חית in Gn $1^{24}$ (בנו of Nu $23^{18}$ $24^{3.15}$ is left unaltered); גנבתי as גנובת (*genuwat*) in Gn $31^{39}$; and אֵימָתָה as אימה in Ex $15^{16}$. In the construction of nouns, many of the marks are obliterated which point to a *nomen generis* being of common gender: *e.g.* נער 'young

* The view of L. Blau, expressed in his programme 'Zur Einleitung in die heil. Schrift,' 1894, p. 74, that the term ἰδιῶται here does not refer to the Samaritans, will not hold its ground.

maiden' (Gn $24^{14.16.28.55.57}$ $34^{3.12}$, Dt $22^{15-29}$ [except v.$^{19}$]), which the Massoretes altered *only in the margin*, is changed into נערה (*nâra*) *in the text* of the Samaritan (cf. Gesenius, *de Pentateuchi Samaritani origine*, etc. p. 28 ff.). The solitary occurrence of מֵ which the present writer (*Lehrgeb.* ii. 293) has been able to discover before the article in the Pentateuch is מֵהָעוֹף of Gn $6^{20}$, and this disappears in the מן העוף (*min a'ôph*) of the Samaritan.—In the *lexical* sphere, the following differences are worthy of note: ילד 'beget' is replaced by the form that became usual in later times, הוליד, in Gn $10^8$ and $22^{23}$. The verb נגח, which is used in Ex $21^{28.29.31.32.36}$ of the 'pushing' of an ox, is replaced by the more familiar verb הכה 'strike.'—Differences of a *syntactical* or *stylistic* kind are the following: the sentence הלבן מאה ש.ה יִוָּלֵד (MT of Gn $17^{17}$ 'shall a child be born to one who is a hundred years old?' LXX εἰ τῷ ἑκατονταετεῖ γενήσεται υἱός;) is in perfect agreement with the Hebrew linguistic usage as this appears in Gn $4^{18}$ etc. But the Samaritan has missed this construction, and substituted the easier *alben maat shena ulêd* (אוליד), 'shall I at the age of a hundred years beget a child?' In the MT of Gn $7^2$ the formula אִישׁ וְאִשְׁתּוֹ appears alongside of the synonymous pair of words זָכָר וּנְקֵבָה (v.$^3$). This variety of expression disappears in the Samaritan, which uses the latter formula in *both* verses. The asyndetic עֵץ (Gn $1^{11}$), אַל ($3^{16}$), הנפלים ($6^4$), תמים (v.$^9$), are changed into ועץ etc., and greater clearness is thus obtained.—Under the same heading may be ranged certain phenomena of *diction*, due to the Aramaic dialect, which afterwards became naturalized among the Samaritans. For instance, we find הררט for אררט (Gn $8^4$), נבחים for גבהים ($7^{19}$), עכר for חמר 'wine' (Dt $32^{14}$). The gutturals are thus very frequently interchanged, because to the Samaritan copyist, accustomed to the Aramaic dialect, they had lost their distinctive phonetic values. To the same cause are due such forms as that of the pronoun אתי (Gn $12^{11.13}$ $24^{47.60}$) and אתין ($31^6$), or of צחקתי (for צחקת Gn $18^{15}$), the infinitive לאוכרה (for לזכר $9^{16}$), etc. (cf. Gesenius, *l.c.* p. 53 ff.).

(*c*) *Material* differences: (α) many passages are altered or supplemented from parallel passages. For instance, לא אעשה of Gn $18^{29f.}$ is replaced in the Samaritan by לא אשחית *lâ ashît*, after vv.$^{28.31f.}$. The servant of Moses is called in the MT sometimes הוֹשֵׁעַ (Nu $13^{8.16}$, Dt $32^{44}$), and sometimes יהוש(ו)ע (Ex $17^{9f.13f.}$ $24^3$ etc.), but the Samaritan writes the latter form even in the three passages in which the change of *Hoshea* into *Jehoshua* is recorded, so that we read in Nu $13^{16}$ 'and Moses called Jehoshua, the son of Nun, Jehoshua'! Again, in Gn $11^{11-26}$ the formula is regularly added, 'and all the years of . . . were . . . years, and he died,' which is derived from the parallel genealogy ($5^{5ff.}$). In $17^{14a}$ 'on the eighth day' is read in harmony with the parallel passage. After $30^{36}$ we find a long addition, which is borrowed from $31^{13}$. Specially striking is the following series of passages: Ex $6^9$ (cf. $14^{12}$) $7^{18}$ (cf. vv.$^{16-18}$) $7^{29}$ (cf. vv.$^{26-28}$) $8^{19}$ (cf. vv.$^{16-19}$) $9^{5.19}$ $10^2$ $11^3$ (cf. $4^{22f.}$) $18^{25}$ (cf. Dt $1^{9-18}$) $20^{17}$ (cf. Dt $27^{2\ 5-7}$) $20^{21}$ (cf. Dt $5^{26.28}$ $18^{18-22}$ $5^{27f.}$) $39^{21}$, Nu $4^{14}$ $10^{10}$ $12^{16}$ $13^{33}$ $20^{13}$ $21^{11f.20}$ $27^{23}$ $31^{20}$, Dt $2^7$ $5^{18}$ $10^7$. The remarkable circumstance about all these passages is that in every instance where it is recorded that Moses said or did something, this is always preceded by a statement in so many words that it was a Divine command that he should act so, and, wherever a Divine command is recorded, this is repeated in the same terms when we are told that Moses fulfilled it. This is a carrying to the extreme of that pleonastic form of expression which may be observed also in certain portions of the Jewish-Hebrew Pentateuch (cf. König, *Stilistik*, etc. pp. 169, 172, 176). That the above passages in the Samaritan Pentateuch are of secondary origin is sufficiently evident from the circumstance that its text there has not the support of a single ancient witness.—(β) There are differences due to a religious or other like interest. The statement in Gn $2^{2a}$ וַיְכַל אֱלֹהִים בַּיּוֹם הַשְּׁבִיעִי וגו', 'and God declared all his work finished (see König, *Syntax*, § 95*b*) on the *seventh* day' was not understood, and so the seventh was changed into the *sixth* day (Sam. *beyôm eshshishshi*). The number 430 years, during which the Hebrews sojourned in Egypt, according to the MT of Ex $12^{40}$, appeared to be too large, and hence the expression בארץ כנען 'in the land of Canaan' was inserted before the words 'in the land of Egypt.' (By the way, the MT of Ex $12^{40}$ is shown by Ezk $4^{5f.}$ to have been the text in existence at the time of the prophet, for the 390 + 40 years of Ezk $4^{5f.}$ are nothing else than a reflexion of the 430 years of the Egyptian bondage of Israel). Again, the plural predicate with which אלהים 'God' is coupled in Gn $20^{13}$ $31^{53}$ $35^7$ and Ex $22^8$, is changed into a singular, in order to avoid the appearance of polytheism (Kohn, *de Samaritano Pentateucho*, p. 22).—Another group is formed by the following passages.—The statement in Ex $24^{11}$ ויחזו 'and they beheld (*sc.* God),' is replaced by ויאחזו 'and they cleaved to (God),' the idea being that the Deity must have been strictly invisible. The conception of God was thus transcendentalized. In obedience to the same motive, so-called intermediary beings are introduced between God and man, אלהים ('God') being replaced by מלאך אלהים ('an angel of God') in Nu $22^{20}$ $23^4$, and יהוה by מלאך יהוה in vv.$^{5.16}$. Conversely, המלאך ('the angel') is once, Gn $48^{16}$, changed into המלך ('the king'), in order to avoid attributing to the angel what God Himself had accomplished, namely, the deliverance of Jacob. The Samaritans showed themselves in other instances as well very jealous for the character of God. From this motive they changed the words 'take all the heads of the people and hang them up' (Nu $25^{4f.}$) into 'command that they slay the men who attached themselves to Baal-peor,' the command as it runs in the MT appearing to involve an injustice on the part of God. To the same category belongs the substitution of 'hero (גבור) of war' for 'man (אִישׁ) of war,' as a designation of God in Ex $15^3$.—Yet another group of differences have for their aim the securing of the æsthetic purity of the Law. The Samaritans, for instance, have not only taken into the text those marginal readings which the Jewish Massoretes adopted for æsthetic reasons (Dt $28^{30}$), but have replaced the term מבשיו 'his secrets' ($25^{11}$) by בשרו 'his flesh.'—Finally, it was upon national grounds that the name עֵיבָל ('Ebal) was exchanged for גריזים (Gerizim) in Dt $27^4$. It has been shown, notably by Verschuir (in No. iii. of his *Dissertationes philologicæ-exegeticæ*, 1773), that the context demands the building of the altar nowhere but upon Mt. 'Ebal. God is presented especially as witness to the oath and as avenger of any breach of it ($29^{12.14.19}$), and accordingly we look both for the building of the altar as a symbol of the Divine presence, and for the offering of sacrifice by the people, upon *that* mountain from which the curse was proclaimed ($27^{13}$). After the Samaritans, moved probably by $27^{12}$ where Gerizim is named as the mount of blessing, had built their temple upon this mountain to the south of Shechem, they would be led naturally enough to introduce the name Gerizim in v.$^4$. The Jews, on the other hand, had no interest to substitute the name 'Ebal for the name Gerizim, for the point that concerned them was not whether Gerizim or 'Ebal was to have the preference, but whether the hegemony belonged to Gerizim or to Zion (Jn $4^{20}$).

In view of all these differences between the

Jewish-Hebrew and the Samaritan-Hebrew Pentateuch, there can be no doubt that what the Samaritans possess is a *later* form of the Pentateuch. Whether we look at the groups dealing with linguistic differences or at those connected with the subject-matter, the indications point to a *late* period. A sufficient evidence of this is supplied by the Jewish *marginal* readings which are taken by the Samaritans into the *text* itself, but the same conclusion follows equally from the theological peculiarities of the Samaritan Pentateuch which have been mentioned above. For the same transcendentalizing of the conception of God is met with also in the later writings of the Jews: *e.g.* the statement 'and God was grieved' (Gn $6^{6}$) is replaced in the Targum of Onḳelos by 'and He commanded by His מימרא (*word*) to destroy their energies according to His will.'

iii. RELATION OF THE SAMARITAN PENTATEUCH TO THE HELLENISTIC (*i.e.* THE SEPTUAGINT).—(*a*) Both these forms of the Pentateuch agree in many details of form. For instance, both, differing in this from the MT, have an 'and' before 'tree' in Gn $1^{11}$ (MT עֵץ, Sam. *weẓ*, LXX *καὶ ξύλον*). The case is the same in $3^{16}$ (אֶל־הָאִשָּׁה *wel a'ishsha*, *καὶ τῇ γυναικί*), $6^{4}$ (הנפלים *wannephilem*, *οἱ δὲ γίγαντες*), and $6^{15.\,19}$. Again, both have in common some considerable deviations from the MT. In Gn $2^{2}$ the LXX, like the Samaritan, has replaced 'on the seventh day' by 'on the sixth day' (*τῇ ἡμέρᾳ τῇ ἕκτῃ*). Instead of the strange order 'earth and heaven' which the MT exhibits in Gn $2^{4b}$, the other two forms of the Pentateuch have the more usual succession of the two words (*shamêm waareẓ*, *τὸν οὐρανὸν καὶ τὴν γῆν*). Both supplement the words of Cain in $4^{8}$ by 'let us go into the field' (*nelaka ashshadi*, *διέλθωμεν εἰς τὸ πεδίον*). Both interpolate into the MT of Ex $12^{40}$ the words 'in the land of Canaan,' but, while the Samaritan has this addition *before*, the LXX has it *after*, the words 'in the land of Egypt.' Finally, the Samaritan and the LXX agree in some of the expansions of the MT which are derived from parallel passages. For instance, in Gn $1^{14}$ there is the addition 'to give light upon the earth' (*la'êr al aareẓ*, *εἰς φαῦσιν ἐπὶ τῆς γῆς*), and in $11^{8}$ 'and the tower' (*wit ammegdal*, *καὶ τὸν πύργον*) is added.

(*b*) Differences between the Samaritan and the LXX. As regards the use of 'and,' the LXX agrees with the MT in Gn $6^{9}$ (צדיק תמים, *δίκαιος τέλειος*, against Sam. *ẓadêḳ utamem*). The LXX prefers asyndesis in *τὸν Σήμ, τὸν Χάμ, τὸν Ἰάφεθ*, as against the syndesis of the MT ('Shem, Ḥam, *and* Japheth') and the polysyndesis of the Samaritan (*it Shem wit Am wit Yephet*). In $2^{25}$ the האדם of the MT and the ὁ Ἀδάμ of the LXX agree, but the Samaritan has the anarthrous אדם (*adam*), whereas in $3^{20}$ the article is wanting alike in the Samaritan (*adam*) and the LXX (Ἀδάμ). In $3^{3}$ the MT and the LXX have the simple expression 'the tree,' but the Samaritan reads 'this tree' (*a'iẓ azze*). The LXX has different numbers from the Samaritan in the genealogies of Gn $5^{3\text{ff.}}$ and $11^{10\text{ff.}}$. Finally, in the sphere of religion, the Samaritan Pentateuch has retained the Divine name Jahweh in its *text*, only that the Samaritans read for it *Shema* (Petermann, *l.c.* p. 162), which means 'the name' *κατ' ἐξοχήν*. This use of the expression 'the name' has the foundation already laid for it in Lv $24^{11}$, and makes its appearance for the first time in the Mishna in the words 'Let him offer a short prayer, saying, Help, O name (הַשֵּׁם), thy people the remnant of Israel' (*Bĕrākhôth* iv. 4). The Greek Jew has already replaced in his *text* the most holy Name יהוה (*Jahweh*) by the expression 'the LORD' (ὁ κύριος) which the Hebrew Jews placed in the *margin*. But, on the other hand, the Greek Jew has retained the term 'God' in Nu $22^{20}$ and $23^{4}$ (ὁ θεός), whereas the Samaritan has introduced the expression 'angel of God,' thus raising the Deity above any intercourse with man.

iv. SOURCE OF THE PECULIARITIES OF THE SAMARITAN PENTATEUCH. — Four principal suggestions have been made to account for these peculiarities.

(*a*) May not the features in which the Samaritan and the Greek Pentateuch agree with one another, and differ from the Jewish-Hebrew Pentateuch, be traceable directly to certain views and aims of later scribism? This is not only possible, but is even positively favoured by the circumstance that the relation of the Samaritan and the Greek to the Jewish Pentateuch is a mixture of agreement and difference. Let us look at two examples. The later scribes held that אדם in Gn $2^{20\text{ff.}}$ is not the *nomen appellativum*, 'man,' but the proper name 'Adam.' This common opinion, however, found expression in various ways. The Hebrew-Jewish Massoretes pronounced, in $2^{20}$ $3^{17.\,21}$ *le-adam*, *i.e.* without the article, because this was possible in these three passages without alteration of the *text*, which in the other two passages ($2^{25}$ $3^{20}$) would have had to be altered to get rid of the article. The Greek Jew likewise retains the article in $2^{25}$ (ὁ Ἀδάμ) and drops it only in $3^{20}$. But the Samaritan in *both* these passages has introduced the anarthrous word אדם (*adam*) into the text. Again, the view that the 430 years of Ex $12^{40}$ included Israel's sojourn in Canaan *and* Egypt, finds expression in *different* ways in the Samaritan and in the LXX.

(*b*) Is it more likely that the readings wherein the Samaritan and the LXX agree in differing from the MT were found in older Hebrew codices? (Abr. Geiger, *Urschrift u. Uebersetzungen*, p. 99 f.; de Wette-Schrader, *Einleit.* p. 98; Vatke, *Einleit.* p. 109). There are traces, of course, of Jewish-Hebrew MSS whose text deviates in some points from the MT. For instance, the tract *Ṣôphĕrîm* (vi. 4) relates that 'Three books were found in the forecourt (בעזרה): in one was found written הוא eleven times, and in two היא eleven times, and the two were declared to be right, and the one was left out of account.' That is to say, a manuscript was discovered in the forecourt of the temple in which the personal pronoun of the 3rd pers. sing. was expressed by הוא not only in the well-known 195 passages, but also in the other eleven passages of the Pentateuch, where that pronoun occurs. Yet this is but a weak support for the view that at one time a Jewish-Hebrew MS of the Pentateuch contained the peculiarities wherein the Samaritan and the LXX differ from the MT. Or may it be supposed that a Jewish-Hebrew MS of this kind took its rise amongst the Hellenistic Jews in Egypt? (Riehm, *Einleit.* ii. 446). At all events, the accounts we have of the origin of the LXX know nothing of Egyptian MSS of the Heb. Pentateuch which formed the basis of the Greek translation.

(*c*) Or are we to hold that the Samaritan Pentateuch was subsequently corrected from the Greek? (Ed. Böhl, *Die alttest. Citate im NT*, p. 171). This view cannot be set down as absolutely impossible, but it raises new and difficult questions. Was there once a Greek Pentateuch, which was simply copied by the Samaritans? There is no evidence for this, nor is it likely. On the other hand, if the present text of the LXX was used by the Samaritans for correcting their Pentateuch, why did they adopt only a portion of the peculiarities of the LXX?

(*d*) The same difficulties arise if we assume that it was a Samaritan-Hebrew codex (Eichhorn, *Einleit.* ii. 641 f.) or a Samaritan-Greek codex (Kohn, *Samaritanische Studien*, p. 38 ff.) that was translated at Alexandria. For, in the first place, tradition knows nothing of this. Secondly, it is not in the least likely that as early as the 3rd cent. B.C., when the so-called Septuagint version of the Pentateuch originated, so many Samaritans had adopted the Greek language that a Greek translation of the Pentateuch would have been executed for their use. It is true there are 43 Greek passages which are marked by Origen as τὸ Σαμαρειτικόν (Field, *Origenis Hexaplorum quæ supersunt*, p. lxxxii ff.). It is also certain that these passages are relics of a complete Greek translation of the Pentateuch (Kohn, 'Das Samareitikon' in *Monatsschrift f. Gesch. u. Wissensch. d. Judenthums*, 1894, pp. 1–7, 49–67), which was prepared for the use of Samaritans living in Greek-speaking countries. For we are told that Symmachus put forward his Greek translation in opposition to a Greek translation which was current among the Samaritans (Epiphanius, *de Ponderibus et Mensuris*, c. 16). But there is not the slightest probability that this Greek translation was older than the LXX.

When all these considerations are taken into account, the first of the views enumerated above remains the most probable, namely, that the greater part of the differences which show themselves between the MT and the Samaritan Pentateuch, grew up through the influence of later currents of thought, just as is the case with the majority of the differences between the MT and the LXX.

We see the influence of later hermeneutics and theology continuing to work in another form which the Pentateuch assumed among the Samaritans, and which must not be confused with the Samaritan

Pentateuch hitherto spoken of. When the W. Aramaic dialect had inundated also Central Palestine, the Samaritan-Hebrew Pentateuch was *translated* into this new country dialect of the Samaritans. Thus originated the Samaritan Pentateuch-*Targum*, which, according to the tradition of the Samaritans, dates from the 1st cent. B.C., and is attributed to a priest, Nathanael, but which is more correctly derived, with Kautzsch (*PRE*[2] xiii. p. 350), from the 2nd cent. A.D. This translation was first printed in the Paris (1645) and London (1657) Polyglotts, and the text given there was transcribed in the square character by Brüll (*Das Samaritanische Targum*, 1873–75). After fresh comparison with many MSS, it was published by H. Petermann under the very misleading title *Pentateuchus Samaritanus* (1872–91). The Oxford *Fragments of a Samaritan Targum*, published by Nutt in 1874, have also been used by Petermann in restoring the text of Leviticus and Numbers, as well as the St. Petersburg Fragments published by Kohn in 1876, which are made use of in the 5th part, which embraces Deuteronomy. 'But there are more variants than appear in Petermann-Vollers,' says P. Kahle in his *Textkritische und lexicalische Bemerkungen zum samaritan. Pentateuchtargum* (1898), pp. 8, 11, etc. On the character of this Targum the reader may now compare, above all, the thoroughgoing article of Kohn in *ZDMG*, 1893, pp. 626–97. Kahle (*l.c.* p. 8) remarks that in the Targum 'the Hebrew-Samaritan text is rendered slavishly, word for word.' Yet the transcendentalizing of the Divine and the glorification of Moses show themselves in a still higher degree here than in the Sam. Pentateuch itself.

After the Mohammedan conquest of Palestine (A.D. 637), when Arabic was becoming more and more the medium of intercourse employed by the Samaritans, Abu Sa'îd in the 11th cent. translated the Pentateuch into Arabic. (The books of Genesis, Exodus, and Leviticus in this translation have been edited by A. Kuenen, 1851–54). The so-called Barberini Triglott, a MS which was deposited in the Barberini Library at Rome, exhibits in three columns the Samaritan-Hebrew text, the Samaritan-Aramaic, and the Samaritan-Arabic versions.

ED. KÖNIG.

**RACES OF THE OLD TESTAMENT.**—*Scope and Definition.*—It is essential to the proper treatment of a subject to determine first of all its scope. In the broad sense of the term, the races of the OT include all the peoples that are mentioned within that promiscuous compilation representing a large number of distinctive works and embracing the remains of a literature which covers a period of almost one thousand years of intellectual activity. The character of this literature, as thus defined, makes it natural that the geographical horizon of the OT writers should be practically coextensive with the then existing ethnological knowledge. By actual contact the Hebrews are brought into relationship with the entire group of nations settled around the Mediterranean, as well as with many inland groups to the north, east, south, and south-west of the land which became the home of the Hebrews *par excellence*. The early traditions and the legendary accounts of periods and personages lying beyond the confines of trustworthy knowledge, increase this number by many races of which little more than the names have been preserved. To give an exhaustive account, therefore, of the races of the OT would involve writing a treatise on ancient ethnology.

On the other hand, as ordinarily understood, the races of the OT include primarily those peoples only which stand in close contiguity to the central group in the scene of OT history—the Hebrews themselves; and here, again, a further twofold division suggests itself, viz. between those which belong to the more immediate ethnic group of which the Hebrews form a part, and those which lie outside of these limits. Confining ourselves in the main to a discussion of the theme in the narrower sense, it will meet our purposes best to treat it under these two aspects.

i. THE HEBREWS AND SEMITES.—The group historically known as the Hebrews, and forming the confederation of tribes to which the name Bĕnê Israel is given in the OT, forms part of a larger group known as the SEMITES. By virtue of this relationship, and in consequence of the geographical distribution of the other branches of the Semites, it is to the Semitic family that the races most prominently mentioned in the OT belong. The term Semite is used both in an ethnological and in a linguistic sense. As originally employed by J. G. Eichhorn* at the close of the 18th century, it embraced the peoples grouped in Gn 10 as the 'sons of Shem.' Since, however, it has been ascertained that the peoples thus grouped do not belong to one race or even to allied races, the ethnological application of the term has been modified to designate a race distinguished by the following features: dolichocephalic skulls; curly and abundant hair; slightly wavy or straight strong beard, the colour predominantly black; prominent nose, straight or aquiline; oval face.†

It must, however, be borne in mind that the pure type is comparatively rare. At an exceedingly remote period the mixture of Semites with Ḥamites and Aryans began, so that except in the less accessible regions of central Arabia it is doubtful whether pure Semites exist at all. So pronounced has this mixture been that some investigators regard the Semites as the product of two races—a blonde and a dark race; but the introduction of such a division is confusing. The mixture has not been with one race but with many races, and hence it is but natural that a variety of types should have been produced. The preponderating type, however, being dark, it is legitimate to conclude that the latter represents the original stock, and that the 'blonde' Semites furnish the proof precisely of that admixture which we know from other sources actually took place.

Where the original home of the Semites lay is a matter of dispute, and will probably never be settled to the satisfaction of all scholars. The drift of scholarly opinion, after vacillating between southern Babylonia, the eastern confines of Africa, southern Arabia, and the interior of the Arabian peninsula, is now in favour of the latter region.‡ It is, at all events, in central Arabia that the purest Semitic type is still found, and, so far as known, it was invariably from the interior of Arabia that the Semitic hordes poured forth to the north-east and north-west and south to establish cultured States or to assimilate the culture which they already found existing.

It is in this way that we may account for the greatest of Semitic States—that of BABYLONIA and ASSYRIA in the Euphrates Valley and along the banks of the Tigris. The course of culture in Mesopotamia is from south to north, and this fact is in itself an important indication that the Semites who took possession of Babylonia came

* *Hist.-Kritische Einleit. in das AT* (Leipzig, 1780), p. 45.

† See, *e.g.*, Brinton, *Races and Peoples* (New York, 1890), p. 134.

‡ For recent discussions of the various theories, see Nöldeke, *Die semitischen Sprachen* (Leipzig, 1887), and his article 'Semitic Languages' in *Encyc. Brit.*[9]; also Brinton and Jastrow, *The Cradle of the Semites* (Philadelphia, 1891), where further references will be found; and more recently G. A. Barton, *A Sketch of Semitic Origins* (New York, 1902), ch. i.

from a district lying to the south of Babylonia. The Babylonians and Assyrians thus form a distinct branch of the Semites, though at the same time furnishing an illustration of the admixture with other races upon which we have dwelt. The Euphrates Valley appears to have been from time immemorial a gathering-place of various nations, and, in passing, it may be noted that the Biblical legend of the confusion of tongues (Gn 11), which significantly takes place in Babylonia, appears to be based upon a dim recollection of this circumstance. So far as present indications go, the Semites upon coming to the Euphrates Valley already found a culture in existence which, however, they so thoroughly assimilated, and on which at the same time they impressed the stamp of their peculiar personality to such an extent, as to make it substantially a Semitic product. Indeed, the presence of this earlier culture was probably the attraction which led to the Semitic invasion from the interior of Arabia, just as at a later date the Semitic civilization of the Euphrates attracted other Semitic hordes towards making a northern movement from this same region. It is among these hordes, pouring out of the steppes of Arabia, and proceeding in the direction of the Euphrates Valley, that we are to seek for the ancestors of the Hebrews.

The sociological process which began thousands of years ago is still going on at the present time, where nomadic groups, attracted by the opportunities of spoil, continue to skirt the regions of culture in the East, with the result that a certain proportion of them are permanently gained for the cause of civilization, and settle in culture centres.* The Biblical tradition which goes back to settlements on the Euphrates—Ur and Ḥarran (Gn 11[28-31])—finds an explanation in such a movement. Forming part of a nomadic invasion, the Hebrews were among those who, allured by the attractions of Babylonian culture, made settlements of a more permanent character along the Euphrates, first at Ur and later farther north at Ḥarran. That, however, these settlements did not involve casting aside nomadic habits altogether, is shown by the Biblical tradition which records a movement of Hebrews from Ur to Ḥarran and thence by the northern route into Palestine. The presence of an Eliezer clan of Damascus in close affiliation with Abraham (Gn 15[2]) and his band, points to a temporary settlement at Damascus on the route to the west. Once on the west of the Jordan, the Hebrews continue their semi-nomadic habits for several centuries, and it is not until the 11th cent. that this stage in their career is definitely closed.

These movements of the Hebrews, as recorded in a blurred, and yet for that reason not altogether unhistorical tradition, suggest, as already pointed out, the manner in which southern Mesopotamia became a thoroughly Semitic State, the invading Semites absorbing the old culture (whatever that was, and whatsoever its origin may have been), and giving a new direction to the further intellectual, social, and religious development of the Euphrates Valley. This parallel also indicates—what is more important for our purposes—a common origin for the Semites who obtained possession of Babylonia and those who, after moving up and down the western outskirts of Babylonia, entered Palestine. The testimony of language bears out this supposition, for the relationship between Hebrew and Babylonian is such as to warrant our concluding in favour of the descent of the two peoples from one common branch to which the name 'Aramæan' may be given.

It is both interesting and significant to find that tradition preserves the appropriateness of this designation. On a solemn occasion, when the Hebrew, appearing before Jahweh, is to recall his past, a formula is introduced in which he refers to his ancestor as 'a stray (אֹבֵד) Aramæan' (Dt 26[5]).

1. The ARAMÆAN branch of the Semites thus assumes large dimensions. Besides the Babylonians and Assyrians and Hebrews, it includes the Semites who settled in Syria as well as the groups of Moabites and Ammonites settled on the east side of the Jordan, while the Phœnicians settled on the Mediterranean coast constitute another Aramæan division or offshoot. Of the relationship existing between Hebrews and Babylonians we have already spoken. *When* the early contact in the Euphrates district began, of which Biblical tradition preserves a faint recollection, it is impossible to say; nor must it be supposed that the Hebrews at the time of their forward movement from interior Arabia were sharply differentiated from the promiscuous groups of Semites who participated in the movement.

By virtue of the relationship existing between Hebrew and the various Aramaic dialects, particularly between Hebrew and Aramaic in its oldest form,* we are justified in thus placing the group subsequently distinguished as a conglomeration of clans, from which the Hebrews trace their descent, in the same category with that large and somewhat indefinite branch of Semites which we have already designated as Aramæan. While the relationship between Hebrews and Babylonian-Assyrians was never entirely broken off, political or commercial associations being maintained with but short interruptions between Mesopotamia and Palestine from the time of the permanent settlement of the Hebrews to the west of the Jordan, down to the destruction of the two Hebrew kingdoms in the 8th and 6th cents. respectively, this relationship was not so close as that which was maintained between the Hebrews on the one hand, and the Moabites, Ammonites, Edomites, Ishmaelites (or Arabs), Phœnicians, and other subdivisions of the great Aramæan branch, on the other. Among the races occurring in the OT, it is these which occupy the most prominent place in Hebrew history. It seems desirable, therefore, to dwell upon them in greater detail.

The tradition recorded in Gn 19[30-38] which ascribes the origin of the MOABITES and AMMONITES to an act of incest committed by Lot with his two daughters, simply reflects the hostility between these two nations and the Hebrews. To throw discredit upon an opponent's ancestry is a favourite method in Arabic poetry of expressing one's contempt and inveterate hatred. More significant, as pointing to the close bond between these three groups, is the circumstance that Abraham and Lot are represented as uncle and nephew. Interpreted historically, this relationship points to a clan or group of clans exercising supremacy over another group or sending forth this group as an offshoot. The character of the Abraham-Lot cycle of stories points to the latter contingency. The separation of Lot from Abraham (Gn 13) is decisive in this respect. It is the form in which tradition records the recollection that one group is an offshoot of a larger one. The quarrel between Abraham's 'men' and the followers of Lot is the common occurrence among nomads. They separate into little groups, and, as these groups grow, rivalry ensues, leading to further separation. We are therefore justified in concluding that Moabites and Ammonites were at one time not differentiated from the Hebrews, or rather that all three belonged to a single group, whatever the

* See Lady Anne Blunt, *The Bedouin Tribes of the Euphrates* (London, 1879), especially chs. xxiii. and xxiv.

* *e.g.* the inscriptions of Teima (*c.* 6th cent. B.C.) and the inscriptions of Zinjerli (8th cent. B.C.).

name of that group may have been. That there were other clans or tribes arising from that general group is quite certain, and, as this body of Aramæan tribes moved northwards from the Euphrates Valley and settled to the east and west of the Jordan, they were joined on the road by others. It is not necessary for all the members of the group to have come into Palestine at one time. On the contrary, it is more likely that, owing to circumstances beyond our knowledge, it was a series of waves of emigration that led Aramæan groups away from the Euphrates and by a devious northern route towards lands farther to the west. The Hebrews, Moabites, and Ammonites were carried along by these waves; and, whatever the order in which they came, the motives leading them to the west were the same in all. Language again comes to our aid in confirming this theory of the intimate bond uniting Hebrews to Moabites and Ammonites. The Moabite Stone (see vol. iii. p. 404 ff.), found in 1868 at Dibon, the capital of Moab, and recording the deeds of Mesha, king of Moab (*c.* 850 B.C.), proves that Hebrew and Moabitish differ from one another as much as and no more than the dialect of northern Germany differs from the speech of southern Germany, while the proper names of Ammonitish rulers and gods in the OT, in default of Ammonite records which have not yet been found, indicate that Hebrew and Ammonitish stood in the same close relationship to one another. That the political relations continued to be hostile from the first differentiation of the three groups, is the natural outcome of conditions which still characterize the districts once occupied by the Moabites and Ammonites.

The case is somewhat different with the EDOMITES. The fact that they do not enter upon the scene until after the Hebrews had crossed the Jordan is significant. The process of differentiation had progressed sufficiently to single out of the Aramæan branch the Hebrews as a distinct subdivision. If tradition is to be trusted, the continuation of this same process which led to the separation of the Abraham and Lot clans, further divided the Hebrews into two subdivisions, one represented by Isaac—Jacob—Israel, the other by Ishmael—Esau—Edom. The double line of tradition, however, complicates the situation considerably. Ishmael and Isaac as 'sons' of Abraham are paralleled by Esau and Jacob as 'sons' of Isaac. To conclude that the Abrahamitic group first separated into two subdivisions, Isaac and Ishmael, and that subsequently another differentiation took place between Esau and Jacob as branches of the Isaac group, seems tempting; but this simple solution of the problem encounters some obstacles. The ISHMAELITES, according to Biblical tradition, are identified with the large body of tribes in central northern Arabia, and the Arabs themselves have accepted this tradition; but the unequal proportion between the two, the Hebrews representing a well-defined group of comparatively small extent, while the Ishmaelites assume the dimensions of a branch of the Semites as extensive and as undefined as the 'Aramæans,' raises the suspicion that the Biblical tradition in this instance is not of popular origin, or at all events not wholly popular, but due to a 'learned' theory which attempted to account for the close racial and the no less close linguistic affinities between Hebrews and Arabs. The theory is naturally interpreted in the OT with due allowance for national pride, so that, while Ishmael is conceded to be the older son of Abraham (Gn $16^{15}$), Isaac is the favourite one ($22^{2}$). While, again, the tradition is forced to make the concession to historical fact in predicting for Ishmael a large progeny (Gn $16^{10}$–$17^{20}$), and otherwise admitting Elohim's partiality for Ishmael (*e.g.* $17^{18}$),—witness the act of circumcision which admits him into the covenant with Elohim ($17^{23-26}$), and Ishmael's miraculous deliverance ($21^{13-20}$),—the general aim of the tradition is to play off Isaac against Ishmael. This is consciously done, and in a manner quite different from the naïve way in which in other instances popular tradition is given a literary form. If in addition it be borne in mind that, in the actual history of the Hebrews, Ishmaelites play no part, it seems plausible to conclude that the Ishmaelitic current in the OT tradition is not of popular origin. The Ishmaelites do not dwell in Palestine or in the immediately adjacent districts, and popular tradition takes no interest in groups of peoples with which it has nothing to do. At most, Ishmael's being driven away from the domain set aside for Isaac may recall a settlement in Palestine prior to the advent of the Hebrews; but even this element of historical sediment in the tradition is doubtful, and it seems more plausible to assume that the separation of Isaac and Ishmael is a 'doublet' suggested either by Lot's separation from Abraham or Jacob's separation from Esau, the story itself being introduced to account for the ethnic relationship between Hebrews and Arabs. As such it has its value and, in a certain sense of the word, its justification.

2. The ARABS represent the second great branch into which the Semites may be divided, and as further subdivisions of this branch we may distinguish (1) the Arabs of central and northern Arabia; (2) the Arabs of southern Arabia; (3) the offshoot of the latter in Africa—notably in Abyssinia; (4) the offshoots in modern times of the Arabs of northern and central Arabia in (*a*) Egypt and the N. African coast, (*b*) Palestine and Syria, (*c*) India and the Malay Archipelago.

So far as the OT is concerned, we are interested only in the first two subdivisions. The culture of the Arab branch of the Semites begins in the south — in southern Arabia and in Abyssinia. Which of these is the original and which the offshoot is a question which a number of years ago could have been answered without hesitation in favour of the former, but which now is an open one. During the past two decades, inscriptions have been found in Yemen and in Abyssinia revealing the existence of several important kingdoms in southern Arabia, and indicating both here and on the opposite African coast a noteworthy degree of culture, the age of which is at least fifteen hundred years before our era, and which may turn out to be considerably older.

If the theory which places the home of the Semites in central Arabia be accepted, the probabilities are that, corresponding to a northern movement, there was a tendency for certain groups of Semites to spread towards the south; and if the culture in the south was actually established by them in this way, it would also be natural to suppose that this culture was carried by emigrants from Yemen to Abyssinia. However that may be, the language of southern Arabia, known as Himyaritic,—subdivided into a number of dialects, — and that of Abyssinia, known as Ethiopic, prove a close connexion between the groups inhabiting this district. It is interesting to note that southern Arabia and Abyssinia are mentioned in the famous description of the rivers of Paradise (Gn $2^{11-13}$); for, whatever the origin of the name *Ḥavilah* is, there is little doubt that some district of Arabia is meant,* while the land of *Cush* is, to the writer of Gn 2, Ethiopia.

The historical relations between Hebrews and the Arabs of southern Arabia appear to have been entirely of a commercial character, and these

* Glaser, *Skizze der Geschichte und Geographie Arabiens* (Berlin, 1890), ii. 323-326.

seem to have been confined to the short period of political glory which tradition associates with the reign of Solomon. This commercial intercourse between southern Arabia and Palestine gave rise to the 'Midrashic' tale of the queen of Sheba's visit to Solomon (1 K $10^{1-10}$), to which the Arabs have added as supplement Solomon's visit to Yemen.* The Arabs have also retained the recollection of the twofold division of the branch, and, in the genealogical lists prepared with such infinite care by the genealogists, one branch—the northern—is traced back to Adnan, and the other—the southern—to Kahtan.

The Ethiopians were well known to the Hebrews, and the prophets are fond of introducing allusions to them into their orations (*e.g.* Is $18^1$, Jer $46^9$, Ezk $29^{10}$ $30^4$ etc., Nah $3^9$, Zeph $3^{10}$), although *Cush* does not always stand for Ethiopia.

Coming back to the tradition in Genesis which divides the Hebrews after Isaac into two divisions—Jacob-Israel and Esau-Edom—there can scarcely be any doubt that we have here again a case of a popular tradition and perfectly reliable, in so far as it points to a common origin for the Hebrews and the Edomites. While the Moabites and the Ammonites remained east of the Jordan and the Hebrews moved to the west, the Edomites eventually established themselves to the south and south-east of the Hebrews; though, retaining their nomadic habits of life and nomadic fierceness of manner, they frequently made incursions into the territory of their neighbours. The form of the Biblical tradition would also indicate that the Edomites formed part of the 'Aramæan' emigration that entered the lands to the east of the Jordan in a series of migratory waves, coming by the northern route from the Euphrates district. Jacob and Esau are represented as twin sons of the Isaac and Rebekah clans. The marriage between Isaac and Rebekah, interpreted historically, means that a branch of the Abrahamitic group formed an alliance with another group which, in continuation of the western movement that brought Abraham and Lot to the west, prompted other Aramæan groups to follow the example. Rebekah coming from 'Aram-naharaim' to join the Hebrew group is a proof for the theory above maintained, that the stream of 'Aramæan' emigration to the west continued steadily for an indefinite period, and perhaps never ceased entirely. Alliances between small groups are common among the nomads to this day; but the result is generally that after a time a separation again takes place, not necessarily between the same groups, but in the next generation or two, by which time the growth of the united group has been such as to engender rivalries among the members.

In the case of Jacob and Esau there is another reason for the separation, and one of no small historical moment. It was natural that some at least of the Aramæan hordes, attracted to the Euphrates district by the culture existing there, should have been influenced by the example of this culture to take a forward step in civilization. We may safely set down Babylonian culture as an important factor in bringing about the division of the Semitic nomads into two classes—those of the fiercer grade retaining their nomadic habits unchanged, dependent upon hunting and plunder for their sustenance; and the higher grade, softer in manner, wandering about, followed by their flocks, and continuing nomadic habits chiefly for the sake of the latter and because of the necessity of seeking proper pasturage at the various seasons of the year. Those groups of the Aramæan branch which became differentiated as Hebrews, Moabites, and Ammonites, attain the higher grade at the time of their entrance into western lands or shortly thereafter, while the Edomites represent a subdivision which either relapses into the fiercer state—a not uncommon experience—or was, for some reason or other, prevented from taking the step forwards which eventually leads to the agricultural stage, and with this the complete laying aside of nomadic habits. Jacob, described as 'a tent dweller' (Gn $25^{27}$), represents the nomad on the road to culture, and is contrasted with Esau the hunter—the Bedawî proper* (*ib.*). A hint of impending change in social conditions is already furnished by the tradition associated with Abraham and Isaac of digging wells (Gn $26^{14-33}$) for the needs of the extensive herds of sheep and cattle which they acquired (v.[14]). This being the case, it is not easy to account for the close association of the two groups, Jacob and Esau, representing such different levels of culture, and why there should be, in the case of one of the subdivisions of the Hebrew group, a reversion to the ruder nomadic type. Such, however, is evidently the case, and the Edomites, tracing back their descent to the Esau clan, represent a branch of the Hebrews that remained in a lower stage of culture, while the other steadily advanced till the agricultural stage was reached. The bond between the Israelites and the Edomites appears to have been much closer than that between the Hebrews and any other subdivisions. The rivalry, too, appears to have been keener. There is not merely hatred between Jacob and Esau, but the former adroitly dispossesses the latter, drives him away from his inheritance back almost to the desert, where he takes up much the same sort of life as that led by the Semites before coming into touch with culture at all. Still, the recollection that Israel and Edom are brothers is preserved in the popular mind in quite a different manner from that in which Ishmael and Isaac are so spoken of. A late psalmist (Ps $137^7$) still denounces the treachery of Edom at the time of the downfall of the Southern kingdom as particularly reprehensible, because, as a brother, he should have come to the rescue instead of helping to the downfall of Judah. It lies, of course, outside the province of this article to consider the details of the relationship between Israel and Edom. For our purpose it is sufficient to specify in this general way the relationship existing between the Hebrews and the various subdivisions of the Aramæan and Arabic branches of Semites.

Two other branches of the Arabic group which appear prominently among the races of the OT are the Amaleḳites and the Midianites. The tradition recorded in Gn $36^{12}$ traces the AMALEḲITES back to Esau. Like the Edomites, they represent the fiercer type of the Bedawîn. Their first encounter with the Hebrews takes place during the period when the latter themselves are still in the nomadic stage. The rivalry between the two must have been bitter indeed, since the hatred of the Hebrews towards the Amaleḳites not only survives to a late period, but is inculcated in the Pentateuch as a religious duty (Dt $25^{17-19}$). While originally the name of an Arab tribe settled around Ḳadesh, the term seems to have come to be applied to roaming bands of marauders in general. It is in this way probably that we are to account for the presence of Amaleḳites not only at Rephidim (Ex $17^{8-16}$), but as far north as Mt. Ephraim (Jg $12^{15}$, cf. $5^{14}$). Indeed the Hebrews are molested by Amaleḳites as late as the days of Saul (1 S $15^{1-9}$), and it was left for David to drive them

* Weil, *Biblische Legenden der Musselmänner* (Frankfort, 1845), pp. 245-275.

* The Arabic word *bedwij* signifies the 'one outside,' and is therefore the equivalent of the Hebrew phrase 'man of the field' (Gn $25^{27}$).

finally back to their desert haunts (1 S $30^{1-20}$). The Ḳenites and Ḳenizzites settled around Ḥebron are set down as branches of the Amaleḳites who joined the federation of the Bĕnê Israel, and this defection must have intensified the hatred of the Amaleḳites for Israel, and led to atrocities and barbarous treatment of captives on the part of the Amaleḳites, the recollection of which survived among the Hebrews to a late day.

The application of the name *Amaleḳ* to Bedawîn in general finds a parallel in the still more indefinite manner in which the term *Midian* is used by some OT writers. That the MIDIANITES also belong to the Arabic group of Semites is sufficiently shown by their settlement around Mt. Sinai, where we first find them (Ex $2^{15.17}$) described as shepherds. They were evidently regarded as already, in the days of Moses, belonging to the milder class of Bedawîn—the nomad on the road to culture; and yet subsequently, in the period of the Judges, the Midianites are in alliance with the Amaleḳites (Jg $6^{3}$). In genuine Bedawîn fashion they pounce down upon the Hebrews, who had now become agriculturists, and rob them of their flocks and belongings. At this time they are scarcely to be distinguished from the Amaleḳites; and the two groups become synonymous with the marauding bands of Bedawîn, belonging in reality to a vast number of different tribes who constantly threaten the existence of the cultured States of Palestine.

3. There is still one branch of the Semites to be considered which receives prominent mention among the races of the OT—the PHŒNICIANS. If we were to be guided by the testimony of language alone, the settlers along the northern Mediterranean coast certainly belong to the same branch as Hebrews, Moabites, Ammonites, and Edomites; but the totally different social conditions prevailing in Phœnicia, and the unique rôle played by the Phœnicians in history as merchants and seamen, suggest that another factor is at work here. The theory has been advanced and met with considerable favour, that the Phœnicians were not the original settlers of the coastland of Syria, but came there from their homes, which were originally on the southern coast of Asia Minor, or, as some are inclined to believe, at the mouth of the Persian Gulf. There is, however, not sufficient material to settle so delicate a problem. There is no indication that the population along the Syrian coast represents a mixture of Semites with other races, and our knowledge of Phœnician antiquities is too meagre—and what there is does not reach far enough back—to enable us to specify the historical relationship existing between the Phœnicians and other subdivisions of the Aramæan branch. As long as no evidence to the contrary is forthcoming, we must continue to place the Phœnicians in the same category with Hebrews, Moabites, etc.; and, assuming that they formed part of the general movement of 'Aramæan' groups from Arabia, they became differentiated after settling along the coastland, where they may already have found a seafaring population, whom they gradually dispossessed, just as the Hebrews upon entering Palestine found the country settled by a population whom they in turn drove out.

The relationship between Hebrews and Phœnicians was, again, chiefly commercial, just as between Hebrews and Yemenites. Commercial intercourse led to political alliances; and at one time, in consequence of such an alliance,—in the days of Ahab,—there was danger of the Phœnician cult becoming a serious rival to the national Jahweh worship.

The Phœnicians lead us to consider another group, which entered into far closer relations with the Hebrews than almost any other, and which, among the races of the OT, occupies a peculiarly prominent and significant place—the CANAANITES. The OT usage of 'Canaan' is not consistent, being sometimes employed to include all of Palestine proper, Phœnicia, and even lands to the east of the Jordan, and at times restricted to Palestine. It is therefore not easy to determine the precise extent of Canaanitish settlements. From the fact that 'Canaanite' comes to be synonymous with the merchant of Phœnicia (Is $23^{8}$, Ezk $17^{4}$, Pr $31^{24}$), we may certainly conclude that the Phœnicians were regarded as Canaanites, and the further use of the term as a designation of the pre-Israelitish inhabitants of Palestine is an indication of a close relationship between some sections at least of those peoples whom the Hebrews dispossessed and the Phœnicians. But at this point certainty ends. The Canaanite is frequently introduced in the OT in connexion with a number of other groups—the Amorites, Ḥittites, Perizzites, Ḥivvites, and Jebuṣites (*e.g.* Ex $34^{11}$), to which elsewhere the Girgashites are added (*e.g.* Gn $15^{20.21}$ *). It is quite clear from the way in which these peoples are grouped,—sometimes five being mentioned, sometimes seven, at times only two—Canaanite and Perizzite (*e.g.* Gn $13^{7}$ $34^{30}$),—that they were no longer sharply differentiated in the minds of the writers. Taken together, they constitute the inhabitants of Palestine whom the Hebrews encountered when they attempted to conquer the country; but the survival of the term 'Canaan' as the name for the district, and 'Canaanite' as a general designation for the earlier inhabitants, points to Canaanites as forming the most powerful, and probably also the most prominent, part of the population. It may well be that some of those mentioned in the above conglomeration—notably the Perizzites and Girgashites—were merely subdivisions of the Canaanites that for a time acquired an independent position, but afterwards were again absorbed into the general body of Canaanites. At all events, it is plausible to assume that the interior of Palestine was occupied for an indefinite period, prior to the advent of the Hebrews, by groups of Semites more or less closely related to one another of which the Canaanites became the most prominent.

These Canaanites belonging to the same branches as the Semitic settlers in Phœnicia, the question of their origin is involved in the problem as to the origin of the Phœnicians. Adopting again the general theory above advanced, we may assume a movement similar to that which brought the Hebrews to Palestine to have taken place at a much earlier date. What Hebrew tradition assigns to the days of Abraham appears, then, to have been only a repetition of much earlier events. The Phœnicians and the Palestinian Canaanites would thus represent a subdivision of the Aramæan branch that moved along the Euphrates, and finally passed over by the northern route towards western lands, some settling along the coast and others pushing into the interior.

In the course of time these groups took a step forwards in culture, and became agriculturists. Their villages developed into towns, while those groups living on the coast were lured to seafaring careers.

It was the Canaanites—to use the general name—whom the Hebrews, upon entering Palestine, found in possession, and the wars with them continued for many generations, until finally the Hebrews obtained the upper hand. This contact with the Canaanites forms a most important factor in Hebrew history. By that power of attraction which the higher culture possesses for those of an inferior grade, the Hebrews were

* 'Rephaim' in this verse is an explanatory gloss.

prompted to make the attempt to secure for themselves the towns and cultivated lands to the west of the Jordan. The success of their efforts is followed by the permanent abandonment of nomadic habits, and instead of sheep raisers they become and remain for subsequent centuries tillers of the soil. From a religious point of view, the contact with the Canaanites was also fraught, with important consequences. The national deity, Jahweh, originally associated with the sojourn of the people in the wilderness,—the nomadic period of their existence,—becomes the protecting deity of the fields, and the people do not hesitate to call Jahweh by the name which the Canaanites applied to their field deities — Baal. For a time the amalgamation of the Jahweh and the Canaanitish Baal cult seemed imminent, when a 'national' reaction takes place, and, under the lead of jealous Jahweh-worshippers, the attempt is made to drive the Baal priests with the Baal rites out of the country, just as the worshippers of Baal had been forced out of their possessions. For all that, Jahweh absorbs some of the traits of Baal, and it is not until several centuries later—when Jahweh Himself was on the point of becoming a deity singled out from all others by the ethical character attributed to Him—that the last traces of the old Canaanitish cults also disappear.

How far back the arrival of the Canaanites in Palestine is to be dated is a question which cannot be answered with any degree of certainty. It is safe to assume an interval of several centuries between this event and the movement of Hebrew tribes from the Euphrates Valley towards western lands. The earliest occurrence of the name is in the Tel el-Amarna tablets, dating from *c.* 1400 B.C., in which we find the name Canaan under the form *Kinaḫi*, but limited in its application to the seacoast, and more properly the northern seacoast, *i.e.* Phœnicia. But, at whatever date we fix the entrance of the Canaanites, even they do not appear to have been the first Semitic group that settled in Palestine. Of the groups mentioned so frequently with the Canaanites in the OT—the Perizzites, Ḥittites, Ḥivvites, Amorites, Girgashites, and Jebusites—we know unfortunately very little, with the exception of the Ḥittites and the Amorites. The Perizzites and the Girgashites, it has been pointed out, may have been subdivisions of Canaanites, and yet from the way in which, in two places (Gn $13^{7}$ $34^{30}$), Canaanites and Perizzites are put side by side as comprising all Palestine, one might be tempted to conclude that the Perizzites represented an independent group, which was at one time coequal in importance with the Canaanites. It seems even more certain that the Jebusites and Ḥivvites had no direct connexion with the Canaanites. Taking this in connexion with the circumstance that in the Tel el-Amarna tablets the term Canaan does not include Palestine proper, it is more than probable that some of the groups mentioned with the Canaanites represent still other settlers. In a notable passage (Gn $15^{19}$) three additional groups—Ḳenites, Ḳenizzites, and Ḳadmonites—are spoken of as occupying the territory later claimed by the Hebrews. That these groups are Semitic is sufficiently indicated by their names, the last mentioned of which, the 'Easterners,' still contains a trace of the district whence they came.

At the period of the Hebrew conquest of Palestine we no longer hear of these groups. They appear ere this to have been driven to the south by the all-powerful Canaanites, and subsequently to the west by the Hebrews. It is quite natural that the traditions regarding these earlier movements should be dimmed. There was no reason why the Hebrews or the Hebrew writers should have been sufficiently interested to preserve any distinct recollection. Their relations were primarily with the Canaanites. The importance of the latter in the eyes of the Hebrews is revealed in the earlier form of the story of the distribution of mankind as furnished in Gn $9^{25-27}$, which makes Canaan, Shem, and Japheth the progenitors of the human race; and, on the other hand, the hatred of these rivals of the Hebrews crops out in this same chapter which connects Canaan with Ḥam — the 'accursed' son of Noah (v.$^{25}$).

ii. RACES OF DOUBTFUL ORIGIN. — A peculiar position is occupied by the Amorites and the Ḥittites. The AMORITES are found throughout northern Palestine as early at least as the 12th century B.C., when we encounter the name *Amurru* (or *Amurra*) in cuneiform inscriptions. So prominent do they become that they furnish to the Babylonian and Assyrian chroniclers the name for the entire district of northern and southern Palestine, and there are indications that the Hebrews, too, at one time gave to the term Amorite an extensive application. In the so-called Elohistic document, 'land of the Amorite' is used in this way.* These Amorites must accordingly have turned to the south, and, indeed, when the Hebrews entered Palestine, they found their way blocked by a large powerful kingdom on the east of the Jordan (see AMORITES in vol. i.). The remarkable statement of Ezekiel ($16^{3.45}$), that the 'mother' of Jerusalem was a Ḥittite, and the 'father' an Amorite, points also to the early presence of Amorites on the west of Jordan. To assume, however, that 'Canaanites' and 'Amorites' are synonymous terms representing one and the same population, is not justified. In the Tel el-Amarna tablets the 'Amurru' land is frequently mentioned and always designates the interior of Palestine, though more particularly the northern section; but the name may be carried back still farther. In Babylonian legal documents of the period, *c.* 2300 B.C., a town Amurru occurs, situated in Babylonia. If we are to conclude from this that the Amorites also came from the Euphrates Valley, we should have still another instance of the movement which brought such various groups of Semites to the west. A more important conclusion that appears to be warranted, is that the Amorites would thus turn out to be settlers in Palestine earlier than the Canaanites, and that the latter represent the group which finally obtains the ascendency and retains it until the appearance of the Hebrews. That with the conquest of the land by the Canaanites, the Amorites do not disappear, any more than the Ḥivvites, Jebusites, and other groups, is quite natural, seeing that when the Hebrews conquered the Canaanites the old inhabitants were dispossessed, but, by the express testimony of OT writers, not driven out (Ex $23^{29.30}$, Jg $1^{21.27-36}$).

The question has been raised, notably by Sayce (*Races of the Old Testament*, p. 110), whether the Amorites and other groups of the pre-Israelitish inhabitants were Semites. Much stress has been laid upon the representation of Amorites on Egyptian monuments where they are depicted with yellow skin, blue eyes, red eyebrows and beard, and light but also black hair (W. M. Flinders Petrie, *Racial Types from Egypt*, London, 1887). The Egyptian artists, however, were not always consistent in their drawings, and more particularly in their colourings, as Sayce himself is forced to admit (*l.c.* 113, 114). Too much importance, therefore, must not be attached to the colouring of the racial types on the Egyptian monuments. Anxiety to produce a pleasing or startling effect was a factor which interfered

* See Steinthal, *Zeits. f. Völkerpsychologie*, 12, 267, and Ed. Meyer, *ZATW* i. 122.

seriously with ethnographical accuracy. But, apart from the colouring, there are no such decided distinctions between Amorites and Judæans on Egyptian monuments as to warrant the supposition that the two belonged to different races or even to different branches of the Semites; and to account for this, as Sayce would have us do, by assuming that up to comparatively so late a period as the days of Rehoboam the population of southern Judæa was still largely Amoritic (*l.c.* p 112), is simply building a further argument upon a mere supposition. The term Amorite, moreover, has a Semitic sound and appearance, and until better evidence to the contrary is forthcoming we may group them with the same race as the later settlers of Palestine. The Amorites were a warlike people, living in walled towns. The recollection of their prowess survived to a late date, and they became to subsequent generations the giants of olden days. It has become customary in consequence to identify the Amorites with the ANAḲIM, REPHAIM, EMIM, and ZAMZUMMIM, or to regard these as so many subdivisions of the Amorites. It is true that the Rephaim and Anaḳim are occasionally spoken of in the OT as though they were identical with Amorites, but this is due to the fact that 'Rephaim' and 'Anakim' (cf. *e.g.* Dt $2^{11.20}$ $3^{11.13}$) are used as generic terms for a powerful race, and no longer as specific designations of any particular group. This, however, does not imply that there were no groups known as Rephaim and Anakim respectively, but that they belong to such a remote past as to become mere names to later generations; and since strength and gigantic stature are invariably ascribed by a later generation to remote ancestors,—in part, no doubt, justifiably ascribed, —we may only conclude from the way in which these terms are used that no definite traditions about these groups have survived. As for Emim and Zamzummim (possibly identical with the Zuzim of Gn $14^{5}$), they are merely the names of the ancient population of Moab and Ammon respectively (Dt $2^{11}$ and $^{20}$). While it is no longer possible to specify the extent of the territory of the Rephaim and Anaḳim, so much appears tolerably certain that these groups, with the Emim and Zamzummim, constitute the oldest inhabitants of Palestine and the district to the east of the Jordan known to us —preceding the Amorites but afterwards commingled through the faintness of tradition with Amorites, just as Amorites in time are not sharply distinguished from Canaanites, and just as the groups Ḥivvites, Perizzites, etc., come to be viewed in some strata of tradition as subdivisions of Canaanites.

If we are to seek for a *non-Semitic* race in Palestine at all, we must go back beyond the Amorites to the nebulous Rephaim, Anaḳim, Emim, and Zamzummim. There are some reasons for actually supposing the pre-Amoritic settlers to have been of a different race, which was gradually subdued by the Amorites both to the east and west of Jordan; but the thesis is one which in the present state of our knowledge cannot be proved with certainty, though the fact of the existence of an early non-Semitic population in certain portions of Palestine has now been established by ethnological evidence (see Alex. Macalister in *PEFSt*, Oct. 1902, pp. 353–356).

With even greater assurance than in the case of the Amorites, has it been maintained that the ḤITTITES belong to a non-Semitic race. The problem in this instance is even more complicated, in consequence of the vague and indefinite usage of the term. We find a group of Ḥittites in the south around Ḥebron carried back by tradition to the days of Abraham (Gn $23^{5.7.10}$ etc.). These Ḥittites are also in alliance with Edomites, and in the days of David we encounter Ḥittites in his army (2 S 11, cf. 1 S $26^{6}$). The Egyptian and Assyrian monuments, however, reveal the existence of Ḥittite settlements in the north along the Orontes as early as the 15th cent. B.C., and these gave the mighty Assyrian rulers a great deal of trouble before they were finally subdued towards the end of the 8th century. The term appears to include a variety of groups which extend northward and westward of the Amorites to the southern and western crests of Asia Minor as well as far into the interior. These northern Ḥittites do not seem to have anything more in common with those of the south than the name. How this is to be accounted for is an unsolved problem. While the northern Ḥittites have left numerous monuments containing sculptures and inscriptions, those in the south do not appear to have even reached the stage of culture which produces art and literature. From the Egyptian monuments we catch glimpses of the Ḥittite physiognomy, and, to judge from these, the Ḥittites were not a Semitic race; and yet too much stress must not be laid upon these representations. Certainly, we have no sound reason for supposing those of the south to belong to any other race than the Semites. The rather close relations between them and the Hebrews and the Edomites would point to ethnic affinity; and if there is any connexion between the Ḥittites of the south and those of the north, we may at most assume that the latter became mixed with the non-Semitic population without losing Semitic traits altogether.

iii. NON-SEMITIC AND MIXED RACES.—1. But, while a doubt thus remains as to the ethnic character of the Ḥittites, there is no question as to the non-Semitic character of a group with which the Hebrews from a certain period came into close though always hostile contact — the PHILISTINES. There is no reason to question the tradition which makes them come from CAPHTOR (Am $9^{7}$, Dt $2^{3}$, Jer $47^{4}$); and, while the problems connected with the identification of Caphtor have not been entirely solved, still all the indications point towards Crete, and scholars are now pretty generally agreed in regarding the Philistines as pirates belonging to some branch of the Aryan stock, who, attracted perhaps, as were the Hebrews, by the fertile lands of Palestine, forced their way into the Canaanitish settlements, and succeeded in obtaining the supremacy in the entire 'Shephēlah,' where they established a number of petty kingdoms. Almost immediately after they entered Palestine, hostilities between Hebrews and Philistines began, and, long after the Canaanites were subdued, the Hebrews still had to contend against the armies of the Philistines. In the days of David their opposition was broken, and, though after the death of Solomon they regained their independence, it was but a shadow of the old power that remained. The interference of Assyria in Palestinian affairs dispelled even this shadow.

We have thus passed in rapid review the large variety of groups in Palestine and adjacent districts with which the Hebrews came into political or commercial contact, and who occupy a more or less prominent place among the races of the OT.

2. Passing beyond the narrower bounds, and yet not leaving Semitic settlements altogether, we have first to deal with the EGYPTIANS. Like Babylonia, Egypt, by virtue of its flourishing culture, proved an attractive magnet which drew the nomads of the Sinai peninsula and adjacent districts to frequent sallies against the outlying Egyptian cities, and, as in the case of the Aramæan advances along the banks of the Euphrates, the higher culture prompted groups now and then to a forward step which led to the partial abandonment of the life commensurate with the Bedawîn stage of culture. Egypt, accessible both from the north and

the south, on several occasions fell a prey to invaders who managed to obtain control of the political fortunes of the country. The monuments at Beni Hassan depict most graphically an invasion of foreigners, who are none other than the Semites, entering Egypt, and, as we learn from various sources, gradually becoming powerful factions in certain of the Egyptian districts. The Hyksos dynasty is an illustration of the power which foreigners managed to obtain in Egypt; and whoever may be intended by the Pharaoh under whom Joseph, according to Biblical tradition, rose to eminence, his presence marks the success of one of the Semitic invasions of Egypt. The groups that primarily came to Egypt naturally belonged to the Arabic branch of the Semites, but these were not infrequently joined by those coming from southern and central Palestine, who formed part of the Aramæan movement from the Euphrates Valley towards the west. The higher class of nomads, who were prompted to change their location with a view to securing pasturage for their flocks, would find themselves specially attracted to Egypt in those periods, not infrequent in Palestine, when the insufficiency of rain during the wintry season is sure to be followed by a drought and scarcity of food. It was such an occurrence that led some of the tribes which afterwards formed the confederation of the Israelites to pass down to Egypt, and their numbers, as appears from the form of the narrative in Exodus, were from time to time reinforced by others. In that sense we are to interpret the story which tells of Simeon and Benjamin being kept in Egypt as hostages before the others joined them there, which means simply that certain tribes reached Egypt earlier than others. The narrative in Genesis ($46^{8-27}$) makes all the 'twelve' tribes proceed to Egypt, but we can hardly expect a reliable tradition on such a question of detail. So accustomed are the writers of a later age to regard the federation of the twelve tribes as a unit, that they project this union into the remote past, though without historical warrant for doing so. The OT writers, viewing history from the point of view of later theorists, cannot conceive of less than twelve tribes at any time, and suppose that necessarily these tribes clung to one another. We are permitted to assume that certain Hebrew groups left their Palestinian settlements to seek better pastures in Egypt, but to go further and bring all twelve tribes into the district of the Nile is unhistorical, for the sufficient reason that the federation did not exist at this time except in the mind of the OT narrator, who is so fond of genealogies, and attaches such importance to them that he is inclined to place, in a remote past, facts and factors which really belong to a much later age. It is not surprising, in view of the location of Egypt, thus open to invasion from two sides, that its population was of a mixed character. If one may judge from the language of Egypt, the substratum of which has now been ascertained to be Semitic,* the basis of the population is likewise Semitic; but both language and people are largely mixed with 'Ḥamitic' elements, more particularly Libyan. This element in the course of time appears to obtain the mastery, despite the frequent Semitic immigrations into Egypt, and to such an extent indeed that both the people and the language retain but few Semitic traits.

3. Of the BABYLONIANS we have already had occasion to speak. In the Euphrates Valley, likewise, a mixture of races appears to have taken place at a remote period; but here the situation is just the reverse of what we have found in Egypt, inasmuch as it is the Semitic element which obtains the supremacy to such an extent as to give to the Babylonian culture, from the earliest period revealed to us by historical inscriptions, a purely Semitic character. But the Egyptians and Babylonians (and subsequently the Assyrians) agree in this respect, that their relations to the Hebrews continue, with but few interruptions, throughout the period of the political existence of the latter. Before the counter movement of Hebrew tribes and other Semitic groups* from Egypt back to the Arabian peninsula takes place, Egyptian rulers enter into close relationship with Palestine, Phœnicia, and Syria. The Tel el-Amarna tablets, so frequently mentioned in the course of this article, are the evidence of this uninterrupted intercourse in the 15th cent. before our era. The establishment of a Hebrew confederacy in Palestine exposes the Hebrews to constant danger of being absorbed either by the rulers of the Nile or by the ambitious lords of the Euphrates Valley and the Tigris. The political history of the two Hebrew kingdoms is largely taken up with the endeavour to steer clear of this danger—an endeavour that ends in failure.

iv. THE TENTH CHAPTER OF GENESIS.—The races hitherto discussed are the ones which play a part in the historical events unfolded in the OT narratives, but they are far from exhausting the races whose existence is recorded in the pages of the OT. The geographical horizon of the OT is remarkable for its wide extent, and indeed there are but few races—*e.g.* the Chinese and Japanese—which are left out of account in the famous *tenth chapter of Genesis*, which forms our principal source for a survey of the races of the OT in the wider sense, as including all those *known* to the Hebrews, or, more correctly speaking, to Hebrew writers, whether these races had anything to do with Hebrew history or not. The chapter itself in its present form is the result of considerable editing, involving more particularly the dovetailing of two documents, one of which is commonly assigned by modern scholars to the Jahwistic history, the other to the Priestly Code. The composition of the former of these documents is placed in the 9th cent., the latter shortly after the end of the exilic period; but how much earlier the traditions are, and the knowledge upon which the chapter is based, it is quite impossible to say. Apart from some additions in the list of the descendants of Shem, the chapter may be viewed as representing the geographical knowledge of a group of Hebrew writers in the 8th and 7th cent. B.C. The absence of any direct reference to *Persia* is an indication that even the post-exilic compiler took as his point of view conditions existing previous to his own day. In forming an estimate of the chapter, it should, however, be borne in mind that the traditions embodied therein are of a scholastic and not a popular character, and that, while there are no substantial reasons for assuming that the writers had before them geographical lists written in cuneiform or Egyptian characters from which they transcribed their data, the grouping of the races and nations of the world is distinctly the work of Hebrew schoolmen who are guided by learned and not by popular tradition. This is manifest already in Gn 9, the closing verses of which beginning with v.[18] should be studied in connexion with ch. 10.

The *three groups* into which the human race is divided do not represent a popular point of view. A people's geographical horizon—its *tout le monde*—is limited by its political and social interests. The three sons of Noah in the popular form of the tradition are not the broad subdivisions of mankind, but three subdivisions within the groups in which the Hebrews were more particu-

* See Erman's article in *ZDMG* xlvi. pp. 93–129, and Hommel in the *Beiträge zur Assyriologie*, ii. 342–358.

* Ex $12^{38}$ speaks of the 'mixed multitude' which left Egypt at the same time as the Hebrews.

larly interested: (*a*) Shem, by which the Hebrews themselves are meant; (*b*) Canaan, the predecessors and hated rivals of the Hebrews in Palestine; (*c*) Japheth, originally designating probably the people of Phœnicia,* with perhaps the adjacent island of Cyprus. These are the three sons of Noah in the original form of the famous blessing and curse (Gn 9[25-28]). In the scholastic recasting of the popular tradition, the three sons of Noah become the progenitors of the human race. SHEM is taken as an extensive term to include a group of peoples who were regarded as ethnically close to the Hebrews, JAPHETH is similarly extended to embrace a large group of races to the north of the Hebrews, while *Canaan* is replaced by ḤAM, who is viewed as the progenitor of the group of races to the south of Israel as well as of others who were particularly hostile to the Hebrews. Interpreted in this way, it is manifest that we must not seek for a purely scientific division of the races known to the OT writers, but one in which science is linked to national prejudices and preferences. With these preliminary remarks we may pass to an analysis of this remarkable document, so far as scholarship has succeeded in interpreting it. The suggestion has already been thrown out that the grouping of peoples in the chapter in question is *geographical* rather than ethnic or linguistic, though it may at once be added that the geographical principle is not consistently carried out. The clearest section is that referring to the sons of Japheth (vv.[2-5]), the core of which belongs to the post-exilic writers.

1. The *Japhethites* represent groups and races lying to the north of Palestine. Of the 'sons' of Japheth, namely, Gomer, Magog, Madai, Javan, Tubal, Meshech, and Tiraṣ, the majority have been identified. GOMER is the equivalent of the Gimirrai frequently referred to in the inscriptions of Assyrian kings, and represents a promiscuous group of peoples who, forced across the Black Sea by Scythian hordes pressing upon them, settled in Cappadocia. In the early part of the 7th cent. we find these Gimirrai in conflict with Assyria and Lydia, and shortly after the middle of that century they are driven still farther to the east. MADAI is Media, JAVAN represents the Ionians, while TUBAL and MESHECH are found in juxtaposition in the Assyrian inscriptions under the forms Tabal and Muski; and the location of these groups may with certainty be fixed in central Asia Minor. There remain only Magog and Tiraṣ. Outside of the occurrence of MAGOG here (and in 1 Ch 1[5], which is copied from Gn 10[2]) the name is found twice in Ezekiel (38[2] and 39[6]). In the former of these passages it is a gloss to Gog, indicating the identity of Gog and Magog in the mind of the annotator; while in the second passage the LXX has 'Gog,' which the Hebrew text also exhibits in Ezk 38[14. 16. 18] and 39[1]. In view of this, it seems reasonable to suppose that Magog is a slip for Gog, the M being superinduced perhaps by the M of the following Madai. The error, once introduced, was carried over into Ezekiel, once as a variant, and in the second case as an actual reading instead of Gog. From the passages in Ezekiel the views connected with Gog may be clearly deduced. The name is a collective one, for a whole series of peoples coming from the north, and threatening at one time, during the 7th cent., to engulf the Semitic world much as the Goths and Vandals threatened the Roman empire. The danger was averted, but so great was the terror inspired by the northern hordes that Gog survived to a late period as the symbol of wickedness and evil power—a pre-Christian Antichrist. The identification of TIRAṢ is not certain. The view of Ed. Meyer (*Gesch. d. Alterthums*, i. p. 260), which associates Tiraṣ with the Turusha, a seafaring nation mentioned in the Egyptian inscriptions of the 13th cent., and whom the Greeks reckon to the Pelasgians, has been generally accepted; but recently W. Max Müller (*Orient. Lit.-Zeitung*, 15th Aug. 1900, col. 290) prefers to regard Tiraṣ as a doublet—a variant of Tarshish mentioned in v.[4], and to identify both with Turs, *i.e.* the land of the Tyrsenians or Italy.

As subdivisions of Gomer, there are mentioned Ashkenaz, Riphath, and Togarmah. The passage in Jer 51[27], where ASHKENAZ is placed in juxtaposition with Minni and Ararat, is conclusive for placing the Ashkenazites in western Armenia, while the occurrence of a personage Ascanios as a leader of the Phrygians and Mysians in the *Iliad* (ii. 862 and xiii. 79) has, together with some other evidence (see ASHKENAZ in vol. i.), led some scholars to fix upon the Phrygians as the group more particularly denoted. For the location of RIPHATH there are no certain data, while TOGARMAH appears to be some part of Armenia, whence horses and mules were exported to the markets of Tyre (Ezk 38[6]).

As of Gomer, so of Ionia, a number of subdivisions are noted—Elishah, Tarshish, Kittim, and Dodanim. It has become customary to identify ELISHAH with Hellas; but since W. Max Müller has shown satisfactorily that Alashia, occurring in the Tel el-Amarna tablets, is the ancient name for Cyprus, it seems natural to connect Elishah with this term (*Or. Lit.-Zeit.*, 15th Aug. 1900, col. 288). TARSHISH has commonly been identified with the Phœnician colony Tartessus in southern Spain; KITTIM with Cyprus, in view of the town Citium; and DODANIM, for which the LXX as well as the parallel passage (1 Ch 1[7]) has 'Rodanim,' with Rhodes. There are, however, serious objections against all these identifications. One can hardly suppose that a writer would jump in this wild fashion from Hellas to Spain, then back to Cyprus, and then on to Rhodes. The very frequent references to Tarshish—no fewer than twenty-five times in the OT—make it certain that an intelligent reader knew where to look for it. But while there was *one* Tarshish, whose location was well known, which probably lay in Spain, it does not follow that 'Tarshish' in all passages refers to this place. There is significance in the juxtaposition with Pul (probably an error for Puṭ, or Punt) and Lydia in Is 66[19]. This suggests another Tarshish adjacent to Asia Minor; and, while in many if not most of the passages the location in Spain suits the context, in Gn 10 and in some other instances we do not appear to be justified in going so far to the west. Whether Kiṭṭim is really the city of Citium in Cyprus has been questioned by both Winckler and Müller (see *Or. Lit.-Zeit.*, 15th Aug. 1900, *ib.*). If Dodanim is really a corrupt reading for Rodanim, the identification with Rhodes may be admitted, but we cannot be certain that the LXX reading and the one in 1 Chron. do not represent an intentional change with a view of suggesting this identification. All therefore that can be said with regard to Elishah, Tarshish, Kittim, and Dodanim is that we must probably seek for them among the larger islands of the Mediterranean and Ægean Sea—preferably among those adjacent to the southern and western coasts of Asia Minor. On this assumption we can understand the reference in v.[5] to the 'islands of the nations,' which appears to be a convenient manner of designating the minor islands of this region. The groupings of these four names is based on a tradition which regards the people meant as offshoots of Ionia on the Asia Minor coast. It does not, of course, follow that 'the sons of Japheth' represent necessarily subdivisions of the Aryan race. As already pointed out, the

* The expression 'dwelling in the tents of Shem' (9[27]) points to a land adjacent to Palestine.

writer of Gn 10 has but vague notions regarding racial affinities of nations, whereas his geographical views are quite clear and definite. Still it so happens that Asia Minor, from the western coast far into the interior, was at an early date the seat of Aryan settlements, and in the 7th cent. the greater portion of the population belonged in all probability to the Aryan group of races.

2. The '*sons of Ḥam*,' as the second division, embrace the races of the south, so far as known to the Hebrews, CUSH being Ethiopia, MIẒRAIM the equivalent of Egypt, while the evidence which identifies PUṬ with Libya—so already Josephus—is still the most satisfactory available. At the same time, it would appear from the passage in Is 66[19] (above referred to) as well as from other evidence (see Winckler, *Altor. Forschungen*, i. p. 513, note), that there was another country, Puṭ, situated near Lydia, and designating probably some island or group of islands in the Ægean Sea. In most of the passages in the prophetical books in which Puṭ is mentioned, it is this region and not the Puṭ of Gn 10[6] which is meant. The introduction of CANAAN at this point and the grouping with the 'Ḥamites' is not to be taken as an indication that in the mind of the writer the Canaanites came from the south. The mention is due to the hostility which existed between the Hebrews and Canaanites, and which prompted the writer, in obedience to popular prejudices, to place the Canaanites with the 'accursed' race. The same spirit is responsible for the insertion (vv.[8-12]), which places the *Babylonians* and *Assyrians*—whose ultimate control of Palestine was already imminent at the time when the section was written—also with the sons of the 'accursed' son of Noah, though it is possible that the confusion of Cush=Ethiopia with the Cossæans (a people to the north-east of Babylonia), may have been a factor also in bringing about this result. As offshoots of Cush, there are mentioned Ṣeba, Ḥavîlah, Ṣabtah, Raamah, Ṣabteca, and as offshoots of Raamah again, Sheba and Dedan. Of these seven districts, Ḥavîlah and Sheba and Dedan can be fixed with sufficient definiteness to form starting-points for the general determination of the rest. ḤAVÎLAH is certainly some district in Arabia—probably on the western coast,—SHEBA is a portion of southern Arabia, while DEDAN, to judge from the juxtaposition with Tema in central Arabia (Jer 25[23], Ezk 25[13]), must be sought in the interior of Arabia, extending considerably towards the north. The remaining names appear likewise to have been designations for other portions of the Arabian peninsula, more particularly the western and south-western sections. Unless we assume that the tradition is utterly without foundation, we must perforce conclude that Cushites settled in large numbers on the western coast of Arabia from the southern extremity to a point considerably north. Similarly, in the subdivisions of Egypt (vv.[13. 14]) the certainty that the LEHABIM are Libyans, and that PATHROS is Upper Egypt, justifies the conclusion that the NAPHTUḤIM and CASLUḤIM are to be sought in northern Africa, even though the precise identification is still doubtful. The introduction of the *Philistines* in v.[14] is, without much question, a gloss which has been inserted into the text at the wrong place. It would come appropriately after the mention of the CAPHTORIM,—*i.e.* probably Cretans (see above),—and the gloss itself, which connects the Philistines with Caphtor, rests upon the traditions embodied in such passages as Dt 2-[3], Jer 47[4], Am 9[7]. There, again, the bitter hostility between the Hebrews and the Philistines appears to have been the factor which prompted the association of the Cretans and Philistines with the descendants of Ḥamites.



As offshoots of the Canaanites a large number of groups are mentioned, most of which are known to us from the actual relations existing at one time or the other between them and the Hebrews. Such are the Jebuṣites, Amorites, Girgashites, and Ḥittites, while the situation of Ẓidon, Simyra, Ḥamath, and Arvad is perfectly definite. The other groups, ARḲITES and ṢINITES, therefore belong to this same region between the Phœnician coast and eastern Syria. How unimportant, in the mind of the writer, ethnological affinity is may be judged from the introduction of the ḤITTITES in the form of a gloss in v.[15] and as an offshoot of Canaan. Whatever and wherever the Ḥittites were, they certainly were not closely allied to Canaanites. The name itself designates, as already intimated, a promiscuous group of peoples whose settlements at one time covered a good portion of the interior of Asia Minor, whose culture and general character have little in common with Canaanites. The importance of the Ḥittite settlements in Syria adjacent to the territory covered by Canaanitish groups has led to the mention of Ḥeth, by the side of Ẓidon, as an offshoot of Canaan. It thus appears that the second group—the Ḥamites—represents a greater mixture of totally distinct races than we encountered in the case of the Japhethites. Ḥamites, Semites, Aryans, and Turanians are thrown together without any scruples.

3. The remainder of the chapter, vv.[21-32], is taken up with the favoured group—the *Shemites*. It is evident from a superficial survey of the list that it cannot originally have belonged to the preceding enrolment of nations. One and the same writer would not have placed Assyria with Cushites (v.[11]), and a few verses later on made Assyria an offshoot of Shem (v.[22]). Nor is it conceivable that in one part of a document the Lydians should have been placed with Egypt (v.[13]) and in another with Aram (v.[22]). Again (vv.[28. 29]), we encounter Sheba and Ḥavilah among the sons of Shem, whereas in v.[7] they are grouped with Cushites. Quite peculiar to this third section of the chapter is also the long genealogical chain—Arpachshad, Shelah, Eber, Peleg, and Joḳtan,—whereas, in the case of the Japhethites and Ḥamites, at most a double chain is furnished. The longer chain, in the case of the Shemites, suggests a relationship between this section of the tenth chapter and such a chain as is found in the eleventh chapter. Here as a matter of fact we have the 'doublet' of our section, for vv.[10-26] present a genealogical table of Shemites introduced as a preface to the narrative of Abraham. Comparing these two lists, it will be found that the Shemites in the narrower sense consist of two branches which meet in the series Arpachshad, Shelah, Eber. With the latter the division begins, the Abrahamitic group tracing descent to PELEG, one of the sons of Eber, while the other branch starts with another son, JOḲTAN. In Gn 10[26-29] the subdivisions of Joḳtan are given, and the section thus complements the genealogical chain of the Pelegites in the 11th chapter. There is no difficulty in determining the region where the writer places these two branches of Shemites, or, more strictly speaking, Eberites. The descendants of Peleg are represented by the Aramæan settlements along the Euphrates with the gradual extension of these groups into the district to both sides of the Jordan, while the Joḳtanites represent those who passed on to the south and west of Arabia. The situation of Sheba and Ḥavilah has already been referred to. ḤAẒARMAVETH is identical with Ḥadramaut along the southern coast; and HADORAM, UZAL, OBAL, and the rest must likewise be sought in the region of Yemen. Only in the case of the mysterious OPHIR is it possible

that the writer intends to have us take a leap over to the African coast (see Peters, *Das Land Ophir*, 1902, who has made out a strong case for locating Ophir in the district near the Zambesi river in southern Africa). Roughly speaking, the twofold division of the Shemites corresponds to the customary division of Arabia into Yemen and Sham (or Syria), the 'right' and the 'left' land, or, as it was mistranslated by Latin writers, Arabia *Felix* and Arabia *Infelix*. Gn $10^{21}$, where Shem is referred to as the 'father' of all 'the sons of Eber,' reveals the real sentiment underlying the genealogical lists of vv.$^{24-29}$ and $11^{10-26}$. The two branches—the Pelegites and Joḳtanites—comprise those groups which, in his opinion, are genuine Shemites, the only Shemites worth speaking of according to his view, though perhaps not the only ones he knew of. The inclusion of south Arabian tribes is rather significant, and strengthens the thesis maintained at the beginning of this article, which makes central Arabia the starting-point for Semitic emigration in two directions. However this may be, it would appear that a later writer, not satisfied with this narrow scope given to the Shemites, saw fit to add as separate subdivisions Elam, Assyria, Lud, and Aram, embracing what he considered *the Mesopotamian branch* of the Shemites, Elam being to the east of Mesopotamia, Assyria the general term for Mesopotamia itself, Aram the designation for the district to the west of Assyria, while LUD (following upon Arpachshad) is one of the puzzles in the chapter. The identification with Lydia is out of the question. That it may be some textual error—*we-Lud* being superinduced by the *Arpachshad yalad* of v.$^{24}$—is not impossible. If, however, the reading be accepted as correct, the most natural suggestion would be to place Lud to the north or north-east of Mesopotamia. The attempts to identify ARPACHSHAD have hitherto failed. Even Cheyne's proposal (*ZATW* xvii. (1897) 190) to separate the term into two words, ארף (*'Arap*=Arapcha) and כשד (*Kashed*=Chaldæa), which is the most plausible of the many suggestions offered, does not commend itself; and it would appear, indeed, that Arpachshad is no more a district than Sheba, Eber, or Peleg, but in reality only the name preserved by tradition of some ancient group to which the Eberites traced their descent. If this be so, the name is out of place in v.$^{22}$, and has either been introduced by the writer, whose chief aim it was to add Elam, Assyria, and Aram as a Mesopotamian branch of Shemites to the south Arabian and Syriac-Palestinian branches, or has in reality been brought in by an error, וארפכשד ולוד (v.$^{22}$) being a 'doublet' of וארפכשד ילד (v.$^{23}$). At all events, it appears to be clear that Elam, Assyria, and Aram represent a third Shemitic branch added by some writer to the original twofold division. Of the subdivisions of Aram—Uẓ, Ḥul, Gether, and Mash—Uẓ, though not definitely marked off, is the region of Ḥauran, extending, however, considerably to the south; MASH (for which 1 Ch $1^{17}$ has *Meshech*) may be identical with the Mons Masius between Armenia and Mesopotamia, while ḤUL and GETHER are altogether obscure, and it would be idle to hazard any conjectures at present.

The addition of Aram narrows still further the scope of the Pelegites, who are thus practically confined to the groups of Hebrews in Palestine and their neighbours directly to the east of the Jordan. The omission of Babylonia in this addition of a Mesopotamian branch is an index to the age of the writer who added it. Not, indeed, that we are to conclude that he belongs to the period when the supremacy of Assyria over the south was so undisputed as to justify the application of 'Assyria' to the northern and southern Mesopotamian districts, for, as a matter of fact, the distinction between Babylonia and Assyria was at all times maintained. The omission is intentional, and similarly the inclusion of Elam among the descendants of Noah's favourite son is also dwelt upon with intent. There can be little doubt that *Elam* is merely another designation for Persia in the mind of the writer. The reign of Cyrus, with whom brighter times for the Judæan exiles set in, was a sufficient reason for glorifying Persia at the expense of Babylonia. The writer was willing to permit the hated Babylon to be founded by a descendant of Ḥam, but Persia belongs to the favoured race; and Assyria, which for more than a century had been merely a name without substance, could also be magnanimously included, since consistency demanded that the country adjacent to Persia should belong to the same group. The writer, however, takes his revenge upon Babylonia, ignoring the name entirely and substituting that of her own hated rival Assyria. We are therefore brought down to the end of the Exile for the *addition* of the Mesopotamian branch of the sons of Shem. Once more we observe that ethnic affinity is an unimportant factor in the grouping—geographical proximity counts first, and natural preferences and dislikes second. Still, in the case of the 'sons of Shem' as in that of the Japhethites, it so happens that all those enumerated go together ethnically. With the exception of the *Elamites*, who are Aryans, the members of all three branches of Shemites are also to be grouped as subdivisions of a single race, only that it must be borne in mind that not all the subdivisions are enumerated; and that some which unquestionably belong here, *e.g.* the Canaanites with their numerous branches, are to be found in the Ḥamitic division, while some of those in the Japhethite group, not yet definitely identified, may likewise turn out to be members of the Shemitic race. See also following article.

In this survey, necessarily defective, of the important tenth chapter of Genesis, the chief aim has been to present the view taken of the races of the ancient world by a Hebrew writer, or, more exactly, by Hebrew writers. Two features stand out prominently in this view—firstly, the breadth of the writers' horizon; secondly, their indifference to the ethnic relationships among the peoples grouped together. The main factors in determining this group are, again, two—(1) geographical affinity, and (2) natural dislikes. It is the combination of these two factors that leads to many of the inconsistencies in the grouping that we have noted. The writers are not merely interested in those races with which the Hebrews have come in contact, but extend their view to those which stand outside of this limit, and yet they do not pass farther than Elam and Armenia in the east; the western limits are the islands of the Mediterranean adjacent to the southern and western coasts of Asia Minor; they take in all of northern Africa, and embrace Arabia from the extreme south up to the mountains of Syria. The aim of the writers being to include all mankind, the limitations of the chapter fairly represent the bounds of historical knowledge at the time of composition. The races of the OT in the larger sense, and as revealed by this chapter, cover the civilized States grouped around the Mediterranean, the Red Sea, and the Persian Gulf, together with the less cultured races and tribes of this district. While the tenth chapter of Genesis occupies a unique place in the OT by virtue of the large number of races and peoples enumerated, yet the prophets furnish the proof that the knowledge evidenced by this chapter was not exceptional. A trait of the great prophets is their fondness for including in their view many other nations besides the people whom they addressed.

The Book of Amos opens (chs. 1. 2) with a series of denunciations of a variety of districts: Damascus, Gaza, Tyre, Edom, Ammon, Moab being introduced as a means of heightening the dramatic effect when Judah and Israel are reached. Isaiah (chs. 13–23), Jeremiah (46–51), and Ezekiel (21–32 and 38. 39) similarly have a series of 'oracles' directed against nations near to and remote from the Hebrews, and in addition to this they incidentally introduce many others by way of illustration to their arguments. So, *e.g.*, Ezk 38 is a miniature reproduction of Gn 10. The prophet enumerates in the course of his oration Gog, Meshech, Tubal (v.[2]), Persia, Ethiopia (Cush), Put (v.[5]), Gomer, Togarmah (v.[6]), Sheba, Dedan, Tarshish (v.[13]). Elsewhere (ch. 27) we encounter Tyre (v.[3]), Zidon, Arvad (v.[8]), Persia, Lud, and Put (v.[10]), Javan, Tubal, Meshech, Togarmah, Dedan, Aram (vv.[10-16]), Arabia, Sheba, Raamah, Eden, Assyria (vv.[22-23]). Through these references, the explanation of the races mentioned in Gn 10 is considerably advanced, though new problems are also presented by the mention of nations not otherwise known. So in the two chapters of Ezekiel under consideration we encounter for the first time Persia, Arabia, and also Eden.* The omission of Persia in the Genesis list (though referred to probably in the supplemental mention of Elam) has already been commented upon. In the case of ARABIA, it is the name rather than the race that is new; while EDEN—corresponding, perhaps, to *Bit-Adini* in cuneiform literature and occurring with ḤARAN and CANNEH (probably an error for Calneh)—is covered in Genesis by Assyria and Babylonia.

More important, however, than the variation in nomenclature and the additions, to be gathered from the prophetical orations, to the ethnological phases of the OT, is the circumstance that the prophets in question should have an acquaintance with so many races. The prophets would not have referred to these many nations had they not been certain of being understood by the people to whom they address themselves. From this point of view, the prophetical books reveal the existence of an international intercourse in ancient times on a much larger scale than is ordinarily supposed. The tenth chapter of Genesis is an illustration of this general acquaintance with the races of a considerable section of the ancient world; and while the list rests in part on a theoretical basis, and is prepared for a scholastic purpose, yet it cannot be doubted, in view of the evidence furnished by the prophetical books, that a majority of the peoples there mentioned are races with which, either politically or commercially, the Hebrews came into direct contact.

In this way the treatment of the races of the OT resolves itself, after all, into a consideration mainly of those associated with the Hebrews. While, therefore, the distinction made at the beginning of this article may be maintained [(*a*) the subdivisions of the Semitic race and of the pre-Israelitish inhabitants of Palestine, (*b*) the non-Semitic and mixed races with whom the contact was less constant and in many cases less close where it did exist], the races introduced from the purely theoretical point of view form a comparatively small minority. To be sure, the underlying principle of the chief source for the larger view of OT ethnology which divides the whole of mankind into three divisions is deprived by modern ethnological investigation of its scientific value. The races enumerated under each one of these divisions do not, as we have seen, necessarily form a homogeneous group. The distribution being controlled largely by the geographical factor, it was not to be expected that this should be the case, quite apart from the fact that an ancient writer could hardly be expected to have the ethnological attainments required for such a method of grouping. As a conspectus, however, of races known to the Hebrews, largely through contact and in part through learned tradition, the tenth chapter of Genesis not only retains its intrinsic value, but serves as an indispensable aid in supplementing the ethnological material, furnished incidentally by the narrative which follows the remarkable history of the Hebrews, from the early time of the departure of the first group from the Euphrates Valley through the nomadic period, with its frequent changes of residence, on to the conquest of Palestine and the growth of the federation of Hebrew tribes into a nation in the full sense of the word, with a distinct political organization, down to the political decline and fall of this people, which survived in a strange way even the loss of national independence.

* Gebal, Damascus, and Ḥelbon also occur in ch. 27, but as names merely of cities, and need not therefore be taken into consideration. So Zidon (27[8]) is covered by Canaan and by Tyre in Gn 10.

LITERATURE.—Sayce, *The Races of the Old Testament*, London, 1891, also 'White Race of Ancient Palestine' (*Expositor*, July, 1888); Nöldeke, *Die semitischen Sprachen* Leipzig, 1887, see also his art. 'Semitic Languages' in *Encyc. Brit.*[9]; Chwolson, *Die semitischen Völker*, Berlin, 1872; Renan, *Hist. générale et système comparé des langues sémit.*[5], Paris, 1878; Hommel, *Die semitischen Völker und Sprachen*, Leipzig, 1883; W. M. Flinders Petrie, *Racial Types from Egypt* (London, 1887); G. A. Barton, *A Sketch of Semitic Origins* (New York, 1902); Brinton and Jastrow, *The Cradle of the Semites* (Phil. 1891); A. Knobel, *Die Völkertafel der Genesis* (Giessen, 1850); de Goeje, 'Het tiende Hoofdstuck van Genesis (*ThT* iv. (1870) 241 ff.); Merx, art. 'Voelkertafel' in Schenkel's *Bibellexicon* [bibliographical references]; Glaser, *Skizze der Geschichte und Geographie Arabiens* (Berlin, 1890), chs. xxiv.–xxxi.; E. Schrader, *Keilinschriften und Geschichtsforschung* (Giessen, 1878), *COT* (2 vols. London, 1885–88), *KAT*[3], pt. i. 'Gesch. u. Geogr.' by H. Winckler (Berlin, 1902); Fried. Delitzsch, *Wo Lag das Paradies?* (Leipzig, 1881); Commentaries on Gn 10 by Dillmann, Delitzsch, Holzinger, Strack, Ball, Gunkel; and the introductory chapters to the *History of the Hebrews* by Ewald, Guthe, Stade, Piepenbring, etc.; compare also the identifications in Rabbinical literature of the nations mentioned in Gn 10 as put together by Neubauer, *La géographie du Talmud*, Paris, 1868, pp. 421–424; Epstein, 'Les Chamites de la Table Ethnographique selon le pseudo-Jonathan' (*REJ* xxiv. 82–98); S. Krauss, 'Die Biblische Völkertafel in Talmud, Midrasch, and Targum' (*Monatsschrift f. d. Wissenschaft des Judenthums*, xxxix. [two articles]), 'Zur Zahl der biblischen Völkerschaften' (*ZATW* xx. [1900], pp. 38–43); see also the separate articles on the different races mentioned in this article.

MORRIS JASTROW, JR.

**SEMITES.**—The term *Semite* (*Shemite*), forming the adjective *Semitic* (*Shemitic*), is derived from the patriarch **Shem,** who in the Bk. of Genesis is named as the ancestor of most of the peoples known to ethnologists and now popularly designated as 'Semites.' The account of Shem and his descendants in Gn 10 is partly genealogical and partly geographical, and does not exactly correspond to a scientific classification. Hence we take the family tree of Genesis as the starting-point of our inquiry rather than as an exhaustive summary. None the less, any description or discussion of the Semites as a whole must have chiefly a biblical interest, and that for two main reasons. In the first place, the actors in and makers of Bible history were Semites, who did their deeds and said their say within the Semitic realm. Further, the truth of God, as it is revealed in the Bible, was not merely conveyed to the world through an outward Semitic channel; it was moulded in Semitic minds, coloured by the genius of Semitic speech, and put to the proof for the education of the world in Semitic hearts and lives. It is perhaps enough in this connexion to remind the reader that Moses, David, Elijah, Amos, Hosea, Isaiah, Jeremiah, St. John, St. Paul, and the Son of Man Himself, were Semites. The religious and moral significance of the race thus indicated may be further illustrated by citing the fact that Tiglath-pileser, Nebuchadrezzar, and Hannibal are the only Semites of the pre-Christian time whose names stand for world-moving achievements outside the realm of religion and morals.

The principal list of the descendants of Shem appears in Gn $10^{21-30}$. This whole table proceeds from one source, J, except that, according to the critics, v.[22], which gives a list of the sons of Shem, belongs to P. These immediate descendants are Elam, Asshur, Arpachshad, Lud, and Aram. Of these names the third and fourth are unfortunately obscure, and it would be unprofitable to discuss here the various explanations that have been offered. *Lud* is generally supposed to stand for Lydia; but the reason for such an enormous interval of separation from the other Semitic peoples is far to seek. Possibly this brief word (לוּד from לַד) very early underwent some change, and does not represent the original. It is almost certain that this is the case with *Arpachshad*, since the latter half of the word is the stem of *Kasdîm* (but see p. 82[a]), the Heb. word for *Chaldæans*, who lived in Lower Babylonia. The whole word, thus assumed to be modified in MT, would naturally stand for a portion of the territory to the N.W. of the Persian Gulf.* The first in the list, *Elam*, though historically non-Semitic, must have had many Semitic immigrants. *Asshur* is the well-known people and country of Assyria. The last named of the sons of Shem is *Aram*, that is, the Aramæans. The sons of Aram are next enumerated (v.[23]). Thereafter the interest is concentrated upon the progeny of Arpachshad. His grandson is *Eber*, who is not only the ancestor of the Hebrews, as is fully detailed by P in ch. 11, but also of the Arabs ($10^{26-30}$). We may now attempt a present-day view of the descendants of Shem, referring to any of the lists of Genesis as occasion demands, and thus working back from the known facts of modern research instead of attempting to work downward from the indistinct hints of tradition.

i. Classification of the Semites.—The surest token of racial affinity is ordinarily the possession of a common language or of closely related idioms. It is not an infallible test; for it may happen that through inherent weakness or stress of fortune a tribe or a nation may be absorbed by another, and lose its own form of speech. On the other hand, it very rarely happens that a race predominant in numbers or political influence loses its language and adopts that of an inferior or degenerating race. Hence, while even the exclusive use, by a large community, of a given language or dialect does not necessarily indicate that the race is unmixed, it may be reasonably held that the predominating racial element in that community originally spoke the current language. Again, as regards the degrees of relationship between kindred peoples, it should be remembered that the most valid kind of linguistic evidence is that afforded by the common possession of grammatical or structural elements, and of terms for the most fundamental ideas and the most indispensable or rudimentary arts and appliances of life. These simple and elementary working principles are far-reaching in their application, and will need to be taken into account in all that is said, either as to the original Semitic race and its language, or as to any of the derivative races and their languages or dialects.

On the evidence of language and of historical distribution combined, these peoples are made to fall into two great divisions, the *Northern* and the *Southern* Semites. Roughly speaking, the Southern branch of the family had its permanent and proper home in the peninsula of Arabia; while the Northern division was included in the region bounded on the N. by the modern Kurdistan, on the W. by the Mediterranean, and on the E. by modern Persia. We have, however, except from linguistic induction, no indication of a time when either the Northern or the Southern division formed by itself a homogeneous whole, much less of the presumptive earlier stage when all Semites together were comprised in a single community. On the contrary, our earliest archæological evidence reveals to us these regions as occupied by several families or groups more or less nearly related. Thus, while Arabia has long been known as the home of a single people, though of many tribes, speaking a common language, the earlier record is of peoples speaking and writing distinct though closely related languages. Similarly, the Northern division, as far back as we can see through the mists of antiquity, is found to be made up of distinct families. A tentative comprehensive grouping may be made as follows:—

| | |
|---|---|
| Southern Semites | Northern Arabians.<br>Sabæans.<br>(Abyssinians). |
| Northern Semites | Babylonians and Assyrians.<br>Aramæans.<br>Canaanites.<br>(Hebrews). |

The above classification would describe the distribution of the Semites as a race during that period of ancient history when they were the ruling power of the world, roughly speaking from B.C. 2000 to B.C. 500. It should be added that the hypothesis of a Southern branch is surer than that of a distinct Northern group, and that some scholars (as Hommel and Zimmern) prefer to assume an East-Semitic division—Assyro-Babylonian, and a West-Semitic—Aramæan, Canaanite, Arabo-Abyssinian. It is, indeed, so difficult to unify the Assyrian, the Aramaic, and the Canaanitic languages, that if we were to use linguistic data alone, it would, for working purposes, be allowable to assume these four separate units: Assyro-Babylonian, Aramæan, Canaanite, and Arabo-Abyssinian.

(*A*) *Southern Semites*.—(*a*) *Northern Arabians*.—The term 'Arab,' which at present connotes the only survivors on any large scale of the Semitic races, was originally of very restricted significance. Ancient usage confines it to a comparatively small district in the north of the peninsula E. of Palestine, extending sometimes over the centre of the Syro-Arabian desert. In this sense the word is used in the Assyr. inscriptions, in OT (*e.g.* 2 Ch $17^{11}$ $21^{16}$ $22^{1}$ $26^{7}$, Is $13^{20}$ $21^{13}$, Jer $3^{2}$ $25^{24}$, Neh $2^{19}$, Ezk $27^{21}$), as well as in the lately discovered Minæan inscriptions. It was not till shortly before the Christian era that it was enlarged so far as to include the whole of the peninsula.* Besides the 'Arabs,' there were several other important ancient communities in N. Arabia. Most of these are embraced under the names of the descendants of Ḳeṭurah ('the incense-bearer'), and of Ishmael, in Gn 25 and 1 Ch $1^{29-33}$. We may cite as of historical fame Midian, the northern Sheba (cf. Job $1^{15}$), Dedan, Asshur (Gn $25^{3.18}$), Nebaioth, Ḳedar, Dumah, Massa (cf. Pr $30^{1}$ $31^{1}$), Tema, and Jeṭur. The general distinction between Ḳeṭurah and Ishmael is that the latter stretched farther to the

* Some such people seems necessary here, since Arpachshad is indicated as the ancestor of Aramæans and Arabs alike, and the region in question is their natural dividing-point. Moreover, it was peopled also by Semites from the earliest known period. Confirmation of this view is afforded by the fact that, according to v.[25], Peleg, 'in whose days the earth was divided,' was a descendant of Arpachshad, while the reference to the dividing of the earth points to Babylonia as the place of his residence, according to $11^{2-9}$, which is also the production of J.

* This extension came about largely through the fact that the original 'Arabs' were the most important tribe living in the neighbourhood of the Greek and Roman possessions in Syria and Mesopotamia. The classical writers use the name not only in the narrower but also in the wider sense, *e.g.* Herod. iii. 107.

east and south. According to Gn 25[18], the tents of Ishmael were pitched as far east as Ḥavîlah on the south-west border of Babylonia (Gn 2[11]). In the west, however, their several routes intersected and their pasture-grounds were contiguous. Dumah (Is 21[11]) and Massa, Ishmaelites, lay in the path of the Ḳeṭurites, Midian, Dedan, and Asshur. But these by no means exhaust the category of N. Arabians. We must fairly include those of the 'Edomites' who are historically and locally Arabs. Thus not only Teman but Amaleḳ is reckoned to Edom in Gn 36[11-18]. Furthermore, towards the east side of the desert is the great tribe or country of Mash, which with Uẓ, the home of Job in the west, is allotted to the Aramæans in Gn 10[23], though, according to Gn 36[28], the latter is given to the Ḥorite Edomites. The explanation of the anomaly comes from the important fact that the Aramæans, who, as a rule, did not wander in ancient times far from the valley of the Euphrates, stretched out in certain regions favourable to pasturage, to mix and mingle with the more purely nomadic tribes of the desert.

(*b*) *Ṣabæans.*—We call the ancient inhabitants of S.W. Arabia Ṣabæans, because this people created the most powerful and extensive kingdom of all that region. Many other tribes, however, sometimes their subjects, also flourished. Among these were the Katabanians, directly north of Aden, and the Himyarites to the east. The latter were so important that scholars formerly called the ancient S.W. Arabians generally by their name. Recent researches, however, which have disclosed elaborate architectural remains, and brought to Europe hundreds of inscriptions, the work of Sabæans, more than confirm the ancient fame of Sheba, and vindicate its claim, not only to a wide commerce and a productive soil, but to an influential empire as well.* A branch of the same people formed a less known nation, whose recently found inscriptions have suddenly brought it into great prominence—the Minæans. The proper home of this people was the west coast of Arabia between Yemen and Mecca. That they were not identical with the Ṣabæans proper is abundantly proved. Their language is, in fact, a distinct dialect of the S. Arabian or 'Ṣabæan.' Their inscriptions are found over a very wide range of the west country, from the heart of Yemen itself to the very borders of Palestine. Their abundance, as well as the contents of some of them, show that both regions alike were then subject to them. That was, however, before the rise of the Ṣabæan power, and therefore long before the Christian era. They are possibly alluded to in 1 Ch 4[41], 2 Ch 26[7], where the word employed (מְעוּנִים) reminds us of the original name *Ma'īn*. See, further, art. SHEBA in vol. iv.

(*c*) *Abyssinians.*—This term is more appropriate than the current 'Ethiopians,' since that is the proper designation of the people of the Nile Valley above the First Cataract, in other words the biblical Cushites. That is to say, the Ethiopians are an African race, while the Abyssinians are fundamentally Semitic. At a very early date, far earlier than is generally supposed, a migration from S.W. Arabia, of a people closely akin to the Ṣabæans and Minæans, was made over the narrow sea to the cooler and healthier region of the Abyss. highlands. Here they developed a community which long remained uninfluenced by African elements, and cherished close relations with the Arabian mother-land. Its principal seat was Aksum, the centre of a powerful monarchy, which at length, in the 4th cent. A.D., conquered, and for a time held, Yemen and W. Arabia.* The Abyssinians have long since ceased to be a pure Semitic race or to speak a pure Semitic idiom; though 'Ethiopic,' as their language is called, is still their sacred tongue; and the Semitic type is still unmistakable in a large section of the population.

The attempt thus made to bring the Southern Semites under distinct groupings is only approximately successful. Besides the tribes already enumerated, many others are found, particularly in the S.E. and E. of Arabia, which, though Semites, have at least no permanent historical association with any of the groups. Very interesting, however, is the tabulation in Gn 10[26-30], which brings the most prominent of these remaining communities under one category. Thus, among the sons of Joḳṭan son of Eber, we find, along with Ḥaẓarmaveth, the modern Ḥadramaut, or the coastland east of Yemen, also Sheba and, to our surprise, OPHIR and ḤAVÎLAH. Unfortunately, the remaining nine tribes or localities cannot as yet be absolutely identified. But inasmuch as Ophir is almost certainly to be found on the E. coast of Arabia, and Ḥavîlah S.W. of Babylonia (but see above, p. 81[a]), the presumption is that they represent families intermediate between these remotely separated districts. In brief, the summation seems to point to a close connexion between the N.E., E., S., and S.W. inhabitants of ancient Arabia. Furthermore, the brotherhood of Joḳṭan and Eber, the father of Peleg and grandson of Arpachshad, points to a tradition of kinship between the ancient Babylonians and the remotest S. Arabians. These are matters deserving serious attention.

(*B*) *THE NORTHERN SEMITES.*—Of far more importance to the Bible student than the Arabians and Abyssinians is the Northern branch of the Semitic family. Fortunately, it is also not very difficult to indicate the several divisions of the Northern Semites, and their local distribution. Taking them up in the order of their primary settlements from east to west, we have first to do with those dwelling by the lower waters of the Euphrates and Tigris.

(*a*) *Babylonians and Assyrians.*—In that region which Gn 2 describes as the cradle of the human race, lived a people whose history, traced not simply in their language, but also in their architectural remains, and even in their literary monuments, goes back to a period far beyond any other known to men. We call this people summarily *Babylonian*, from the name of the great historical capital. But Babylon or Babel did not come into prominence till about B.C. 2250. We have to regard the whole surrounding country as having been, for centuries and even millenniums before that era, divided up among a number of city-States, having a longer or shorter history of narrower or wider dominion. These communities we have also to consider essentially Semitic. The hypothesis of a so-called 'Sumerian' civilization and 'Sumerian' language, preceding the rise of the Semites, is in its current form the result of hasty and superficial theorizing, and the present writer is convinced that it will have to be essentially modified. As neighbours to the Semites, and more or less mingling with them from time to time, were a foreign people, probably more than one people, who contributed some important elements to their mythology and civic life, with corresponding terms to their language. Who they were and whence

* Its ancient capital was Ma'rib, though San'ā, three days' journey to the west, was a city of greater renown, and is the present capital of Yemen. Thus the Ṣabæan kingdom long comprised the whole of Tihāma, the S.W. coastland of Arabia. It also extended itself far both to the east and north.

* That they were separated from the Minæans and Ṣabæans at a very remote period is proved by the fact that their language, though more akin to the Ṣabæan than is the Arabic, is yet quite distinct from the former, whose written characters it borrowed, while it is also much less closely related to the Ṣabæan than is the Minæan dialect.

they came cannot as yet be said. Possibly they were of a race akin to the Elamites across the Tigris, or to the Kassites of the highlands to the north of Elam. The name 'Sumerian' as applied to them is, in any case, a misnomer; and the supposed Sumerian language is possibly only the Semitic Babylonian, or 'Assyrian,' written according to a system developed alongside of the popular syllabic from the original ideographic, and preserving the essential features of the latter. There are, it is true, many phenomena of this peculiar idiom which such an hypothesis does not explain. On the other hand, no one has yet succeeded in constructing a reasonable or consistent grammar of the supposed language, though good material is abundant. Until this is done, the Semitic has a right of possession, precarious though it may be. Many invasions of Babylonian territory were made by non-Semitic peoples from the most ancient times, especially Elamites and Kassites, but the language, the religion, both State and popular, and the civilization as a whole, remained always essentially Semitic down to the time of Cyrus and the Persians. Distinctive of the Babylonians, although adopted by other people, was their mode of writing in wedge-like characters, which, however, is far from representing the original ideographs. Distinctive of them especially were their culture, their inventive genius, their intellectual enterprise and love of knowledge. They were thus not only prominent among the Semites, but were also the most influential of all the peoples of antiquity, except the Hebrews, Greeks, and Romans. Indeed, when we consider their early development among the races of men, and the indirect influence of their genuine ideas, we may regard them fairly enough as the primary intellectual movers of the world.

*The Assyrians* were of the same race as the Babylonians, and in all probability an offshoot from them. The name is derived from the city of *Asshur*, which was founded at an unknown early date on the west of the Tigris just above its confluence with the Lower Zab, which formed the normal southern boundary of the kingdom of Assyria. The Assyrians used the Bab. language in its purity. Indeed we usually call this language 'Assyrian,' because it was principally from the monuments of Assyria, and not from those of Babylonia, that our knowledge of it was first obtained, towards the middle of the 19th century. Unlike Babylonia, which contained many large cities, Assyria proper had but few, the principal being Nineveh and the surrounding fortresses. The Assyrians had virtually the same institutions as the Babylonians, with many of the same deities, and the same modes of worship. They were inferior to them in intellectual enterprise and culture, but superior in the military art, and in capacity for organization. They would appear, moreover, to have suffered less from the irruptions of outsiders, and therefore to have preserved, on the whole, a more purely Semitic racial type. It should be remarked, however, that the biblical lists make out the Assyrians and a portion of the Babylonians to have been of Cushite descent (Gn 10[8-12]), perhaps in view of the mixture of races that had gone on in Babylonia (but cf. also p. 81[a]). According to the same account (v.[11]), Assyria was settled from Babylonia. See, further, artt. ASSYRIA and BABYLONIA in vol. i.

(*b*) *The Aramæans.*—The second great division of the Northern Semites, the biblical 'Aram,' had as its proper home a much larger range of country than any of the others. Within historical times the Aramæans had their settlements at various points on both sides of the Lower Tigris, to the west of the Lower Euphrates, in Mesopotamia, and in Syria south as far as Palestine. Indeed it is impossible to say with certainty what was their original centre. They seem to have been equally at home herding cattle for the markets of Babylon, driving caravans along the Euphrates, or holding bazaars in the crowded cities of Ḥarran and Damascus. A partial explanation of their ubiquity and versatility is found in their genius for trade and commerce. They were *par excellence* the travellers and negotiators of the ancient East. What the Phœnicians achieved by sea, they with almost equal enterprise and persistence attained on the land. To them was largely due the commercial and intellectual interchange between Babylonia and Assyria on the one hand, and the western States, particularly Phœnicia, on the other. They had their trading posts even in Asia Minor, through which the Greek cities appear to have obtained much of their knowledge of letters and the liberal arts.

It is possible to make certain restrictions of the general fact of the wide extension of the Aramæans. Until the 12th cent. B.C. they are not found in large settlements west of the Euphrates, though doubtless many isolated expeditions had from time to time crossed the River. They appeared in great numbers, with huge herds of cattle, upon the grazing grounds within reach of the Bab. cities. They also formed numerous settlements on the upper middle course of the Euphrates, especially on the left bank, and between that river and the Chabor. Here was Mesopotamia proper, the Aram-naharaim (or 'Aram of the two Rivers') of OT. Here also was Ḥarran, a city of enormous antiquity, held in historical times principally by Aramæans. After the fall of the Ḥittite dominion in Syria, Aram. immigration hither went on apace, and Carchemish, Arpad, Aleppo, Ḥamath, Zobah, and, last and greatest of all, Damascus, were colonized and enriched by them. In the time of David (*c.* 1000 B.C.) they are found firmly planted in Syria (2 S 8). From the 10th to the 8th cent. B.C. decisive importance attached to the rôle of the 'Aramæans of Damascus' (the 'Syrians' of EV). But their westward career did not end with the political decay of Damascus. By the 3rd cent. B.C. Palestine, which politically had become in succession Babylonian, Egyptian, Assyrian, Neo-Babylonian, Persian, and Greek, spoke popularly an Aram. idiom. After the rise of Christianity and the complete destruction of the Jewish State, the Jewish church perpetuated one dialect of Aramaic and the Christian Semites another. The Euphrates was the general dividing-line between W. and E. Aramaic, just as it had for many centuries parted the two main divisions into which the Aram. race had fallen. The vitality of Aramaism is attested by the fact that, while the popular dialects of Syria and Mesopotamia soon yielded to Arabic after the establishment of Islam in the 7th cent. A.D., Syriac, the principal E. Aramaic dialect, flourished as a literary language till the 13th cent., long after all traces of Aram. political influence had completely disappeared. See, further, art. ARAM in vol. i.

(*c*) *Canaanites.*—For want of a better term, we give this name to the pre-Hebrew inhabitants of Palestine and Phœnicia, with their descendants. We class them as Semitic by reason of their language, their civil institutions, and their religion, all of which reveal the purest type of Semitism. It is true that the Phœnicians of the coastland differed surprisingly from the inhabitants of the interior in their pursuits and mental habits. But common to both are 'the language of Canaan' (Is 19[18]), and analogous forms of Baal-worship. As to their place of departure from the common camping-ground of the Semites we are again left to the widest sort of inference.* Of interest is the question as to the direction from which the Canaanites came into their historical abiding-place. The answer is: from the north or east; for if they had come from the south they would have spoken Arabic, or some dialect of South Semitic nearly akin to Arabic. That they were not the primitive inhabitants of Palestine is clear from the Bible statements as well as other evidence. We may for convenience call the earlier residents 'Amorites,' a people whose antiquity may be inferred from the name 'Land of the Amorites,' given to the country in the remotest times by the Babylonians. The Amorites were possibly not Semitic. The most significant fact about them is that there is no indication that they ever occupied the lower coastland, though they had settlements on both sides of the Jordan. They survived as a community longest in the east, where they were finally absorbed by Moabites, Ammonites, and the invading Hebrews.

The most striking feature of the civic and social life of the Canaanites was their residence in small city-States, independent of each other, and only confederated, if at all, under stress of common danger. This tendency to mutual repulsion was exhibited even among the Phœn. cities, which, however, partly on account of their foreign colonizing experience, became more disposed towards voluntary federation. The pursuits of the two branches of the Canaanites were not more dissimilar than their fortunes. While those of the interior remained isolated, exclusive, and comparatively uncultured, those of the coastland became the most cosmopolitan, and, in a material sense, the most directly serviceable to mankind of all their race. While the one did not survive for more than a generation or two the Heb. occupation of Canaan, the other, in the political world yet not of it, utilizing and subsidizing the great world-powers in the form of tribute-giving, following their own way to opulence and commercial supremacy, survived not only the Heb. monarchy, but the Assyr., the Bab., the Pers., and even the Macedonian empire, succumbing at last to the Roman alone.

It may be added that the various tribes mentioned in the Hexateuch as inhabiting Palestine are in all probability merely local subdivisions of the Canaanites, and not co-ordinate independent races. An exception is made of the ḤITTITES by those who hold them to have been immigrants from Syria, where they preceded the Aramæans. It is a matter of surprise that in Gn 10 the Canaanites, as well as the people of Middle Babylonia, are associated with the people of Upper and Lower Egypt (Cush and Miẓraim). The explanation, probably, is that the Egyptians are partly of Semitic origin, and that there existed in Palestine, as well as in Babylonia, from very remote times, a population supposed to be akin to the Egyptians, with whom the later inhabitants mingled. The PHILISTINES were probably a non-Semitic people, possibly from the island of Crete, whose settlement in Palestine was made not earlier than the 14th or 13th cent. B.C.

(*d*) *The Hebrews.*—By this name we have to understand, not Israel alone, but all the Hebraic peoples, including as well the Edomites proper, the Moabites and Ammonites, whom the traditions of Israel with good reason claim as kindred. Their larger affiliations are not easy to make out. At least Israel and Moab spoke 'Hebrew.' But this was the language of Canaan; and they may have acquired it by immigration, just as the Edomites learned Arabic. Our best guide is the biblical record, according to which Abraham, their common ancestor, of the line of Arpachshad, Eber, and Peleg, came from Ur of the Chaldees, in the west of the Lower Euphrates. This implies Bab. kinship. But as belonging to a family of shepherds he was likely to have Aram. associations, since Aramæans abounded in all the neighbouring pasture-grounds. It is in accordance with this hypothesis that we find him sojourning in Ḥarran, the great Aram. settlement in Mesopotamia. His kindred there were always reckoned as Aramæans; and the immediate ancestor of the Israelites, though born and reared in Canaan, is called a 'stray Aramæan' (Dt 26[5]). But none of the Semites show such a racial admixture as do the children of Israel. Primarily of Bab. affinity, their association with the Babylonians is attested by the common traditions of these two most highly endowed branches of the Semitic race. The residence in Egypt did not add any new elements to the already acquired Aramæan. Nor does it seem probable that all of the Hebrews of Canaan joined in the migration to Egypt with the family of Jacob. But both before and after the permanent settlement in Canaan large accessions were made of Arab. derivation (Ḳenites and others), while we have also to take account of the absorption of much of the Can. population after the conquest. It was therefore not till shortly before the founding of the monarchy that the people of Israel assumed that fixity of racial type popularly known as 'Hebrew.' What kept the community together through endless vicissitudes of fortune, what still gives Israel even now a bond of spiritual unity, is not purity of race, but steadfastness of faith in J″, the old-time God of Israel. At the same time it is manifest that, so far as descent is concerned, the Hebrews must be taken only secondarily as one of the divisions of the Northern Semites.

ii. HISTORY OF THE SEMITES.—It appears, therefore, that we have to reckon with four primary branches of the Semitic stock: Arabians (and Sabæans) in the south; Babylonians, Aramæans, Canaanites in the north. From the Southern branch the Abyssinians are a secondary offshoot; from the Northern, the Hebrews. When we seek for the original home of this oldest of civilized races we are pointed to a region in N. Arabia, probably not far from the Lower Euphrates. The Semitic civilization is essentially of nomadic origin. N. Arabia is the geographical centre of the race. It is much more likely to have peopled the surrounding highlands than to have been peopled from them. The Arabic language is upon the whole nearest the primitive Sem. speech, as it is by far the oldest and purest of all living tongues, and its speakers in Arabia belong to the oldest and purest of races. Again, the Egyp. language has an important Sem. admixture; and it must have been from Arabia that this element was derived. We assume that the Northern Semites—Babylonians, Aramæans, Canaanites—lived long together apart from the Arabs, who tended always to the centre of the desert.*

The order of divergence seems to have been as follows:—The ancestors of all the Semites remained in their desert home for an indefinitely long period before the decisive separation took place. Very early, however, apparently even before the Sem. language was fully developed, a section of the tribes leavened the N. African population

* As to their places of settlement on the west coastland it is noteworthy that the Phœn. maritime cities extend to the north of Lebanon, while the Canaanites of the interior are not found to a certainty anywhere except south of that mountain range. The opportunities of trading by sea perhaps account for this local divergence.

* The first of all the Semites to form fixed settlements were the Babylonians. Since the 'Hebrew' language shows on the whole closer phonetic relations with the 'Assyrian' than does the Aramaic, it follows that the speakers of the former, or the Canaanites, must have lived longer together with the speakers of the latter, or the Babylonians, than did the Aramæans.

with a strong and persistent Sem. element. It is not yet certain whether the transit was made across the Isthmus or over the lower entrance of the Red Sea. Recent discoveries of remains of primitive Egyptians in Upper Egypt seem to point to the latter route. Possibly there was a very early movement of Semites along E. and S. Arabia, from which came the African migration. This must have preceded the Sabæan development. Next, the tribes representing the Northern Semites moved northwards, not yet attaining to fixed settlements, or at least not to life in cities. From these the Aramæans branched off as northern nomads. The ancestors of the Babylonians and Canaanites still held together for a time, while yet civic life and government were unknown. Next came the settlement of the Babylonians between the Lower Euphrates and Tigris, where they found an inferior alien population, which they subdued or absorbed. The Canaanites, parting from them, moved westward across the wilderness till they reached the highlands of Palestine and the sea. The Phœn. tradition that the fathers of the family came from the shores of the Persian Gulf, may perhaps be an authentic reminiscence of this memorable movement. It was not till many ages later that the Hebraic clans made a similar and still more fateful migration to the Land of Promise. A long residence of all the Arabian tribes upon the oases of the central desert preceded the departure of the S. Arabians and their gradual occupation of the coast of the Red Sea and the Ocean. Still another interval elapsed before a migration took place over the sea to Abyssinia.

Some faint conception of the antiquity of the Sem. race may be gained from a consideration of its oldest literary monuments. We now have access to specimens of the language of the Babylonians as it was written between 5000 and 4000 B.C. It there presents an aspect differing not at all from that which it exhibits over three millenniums later. That is to say, it is a language showing signs of advanced phonetic degeneration, separated by a decisive stage of phonological and structural change from the Heb., still more from the Aram., and more again by an enormous interval from the South Sem. dialects. How many thousands of years we have thus to add to what we may call the historical period, as above indicated, cannot be said. Backward beyond that period we have still to take into account the ages that intervened between the Sem. migration into Africa and the separation of the South and the North.

For biblical study the history of the *Southern Semites* is of comparatively little significance. The interests of the OT centre in Palestine; and it was not till long after the Christian era that the life and thought of our race were affected by any decisive movement from the south. The Arabs played no part in the world's history till the time of Islam. But it would be a mistake to exclude, on that account, Arabia entirely from our historical survey. In the first place, S. Arabia was in the earliest known times a region of much greater importance than it was during the later period of Israel's history. It would appear that wide stretches of grazing land were occupied by great tribal confederations, some of which at certain periods at least assumed the dignity of kingdoms. In very remote times also the mineral productions of gold and precious stones were more abundant and valuable than they are now. The Bab. inscriptions bear testimony that in the fourth millennium B.C. the liveliest intercourse was maintained, and that by overland routes, between Babylonia and E. and W. Arabia,—and it would even appear that Arabs at one time obtained control of Babylonia. On the other hand, Gn 14 mentions what was apparently no exceptional instance of an expedition from Babylonia in the 23rd cent. B.C. to the peninsula of Sinai. In the next place, we learn from the recently discovered Minæan inscriptions that this people had established a flourishing trade and even a kingdom of their own on the west coast of Arabia before the rise of the kindred kingdom of Sheba, that is to say, before the time of Solomon, and that with the aid of writing they had attained to a fairly high degree of civilization. Lastly, it must be remembered that many Hebrews resided for a whole generation in Arabia, that thence its population was perpetually recruited, and that the biblical literature makes great account of the wisdom, piety, and patriarchal simplicity of various tribes of the Arabian borderland.

Outwardly considered, the Bible story of the career of Israel is an episode in the history of the *Northern Semitic* communities. That history begins with the first Sem. settlements in Babylonia. Here agriculture was first practised with large and rich results. Thereupon followed trade by river, sea, and land in days when Zidon and Tyre were still untenanted rocks, and the fertilizing waters of the Nile still flowed to the sea through an uncultivated waste. Cities one after another were built, cities famous in tradition and history, each the centre of a little kingdom, each with its own patron deity, its own temple and priesthood, and its own priest-king, such as were Akkad, and Sippar, and Nippur, and Erech. In these days—perhaps as early as 6000 years B.C.—Ur of the Chaldees and the no less renowned Eridu were unknown, ancient as they are; for the waters of the Persian Gulf then rolled over their future sites.

The next stage was that in which individual cities began to extend their dominion widely and to form little empires of their own. One city after another thus arose to power, until there came to be a few independent kingdoms instead of many. These, however, could not all survive in the rivalries and ambitions of that time and country, and so there came to be two dominant centres, the one in Northern and the other in Southern Babylonia. About B.C. 4000 we find Akkad in the north aiming at dominion, not only over Southern Babylonia, but over the most productive regions of Arabia and Syria, as far as the Mediterranean. This, however, we have reason to believe, was not the first great 'empire.' It is only the first that is fairly well known as yet. The centre of authority was also sometimes in the south, where, among the monarchies of B.C. 3000 and onwards, Ur of the Chaldees occupies a prominent place. The term of this alternating dominion lasted very long. In the 23rd cent. B.C. the rule was broken by an invasion of the Elamites, of whose subsequent domination Gn 14 gives a partial record. Not long thereafter the city of Babylon came to the front, and was made the capital of a united Babylonia, a position which was never abdicated till the close of the Sem. régime. But foreign rule was not at an end. After a lengthy period of native control, Kassites from the eastern highlands broke in upon Babylonia and held sovereign sway from the 18th to the 13th century. This is the period of the political decadence of Babylonia, due not merely to the domination of a foreign dynasty, but to the rivalry of a kindred nationality. For the result of the gradual rise of Assyria was that Babylonia played no world-moving rôle till its revival under the Chaldæan dynasty at the close of the 7th century B.C.

The early history of Assyria is obscure. Beginning very early with the growth of the city of Asshur, it gradually extended northward, mainly on the east of the Tigris, till it touched on the mountains of Kurdistan. The kingdom proper was never very large, but the race had a genius for war, and more capacity for government than any of the other ancient Semites. Its steadily cherished purpose was to secure the dominion in W. Asia already claimed by Babylonia, and to enlarge it till it should embrace the world. It took many centuries to reach the summit of power; but the idea was at length in a measure realized. By far the most important incident in this process of Assyr. extension was the prolonged and bitter strife with Babylonia, ending in the total subjugation of that venerable empire.

Bible students are concerned primarily with the people of Revelation, and secondarily with the actors in the events that prepared the way for that people and determined their providential destiny. From these points of view we are able to look at the history of the N. Semites as one great connected series of events co-operating towards the making and the discipline of Israel. In this 'increasing purpose' each one of the great divisions of the N. Semites played an important part. The home of Israel was to be in the West-land, more particularly in Palestine. This region from the remotest known times was of special interest to the inhabitants of the East. Thither came from the East the Can. immigrants. Thither followed them in course of time the slower-moving Aramæans. Thither came the Hebrews themselves, also from the farther East, as to a land of promise. Thither, before and after the earliest and latest of these permanent emigrants, came the all-dominating Babylonians, for conquest and still more for exploration and for self-enrichment. Normally, until the 16th cent. B.C., the whole of the West-land was under the sway of Babylonia. And when its political control was relinquished, its intellectual influence remained, so that near the close of the 15th cent. the Bab. language and its cuneiform writing were the international means of communication between the remotest regions. Even letters from Mesopotamia, Syria, Phœnicia, and Palestine, not to speak of Assyria and Babylonia itself, were written therein to the court of Egypt, 300 miles up the Nile. This state of things at length passed away, because Babylonia and Assyria spent their force upon one another, and thus both alike lost their hold upon the West.

It was in this period, which we may fairly call exceptional in the history of ancient W. Asia, that the opportunity for independent action came to the peoples of the western coastland. It was then also that the Egyptians, who in their whole history never successfully interposed in Asia, except when the Babylonians or Assyrians were enfeebled or quiescent, essayed to conquer Palestine and Syria. It was in this period, too, that the Hittites arose to power in Northern and Central Syria, and contended long and bitterly for supremacy with the invaders from over the Isthmus. Within the same limits of time, Israel, emerging from the obscurity and shame of Egypt, began to play its rôle in Palestine. Then was enacted the earlier half of its unique history, including its conquest and absorption of one branch of the Canaanite race, and its 'brotherly covenant' (Am 1[9]) with the other, and culminating in its greatest external power and splendour under David and Solomon. Then also were formed the settlements in Syria of the Aramæans, which became so fateful for Israel in its 'hundred years' war,' in its cruel suffering, and its moral and spiritual chastening after its own internal dismemberment.

But the Bab. idea of Western dominion, inherited by Assyria, was at length realized. Assyria was the first of Sem. nations to learn how to govern as well as to subdue the territory of its rivals. After intermittent attempts at conquests, progress westward was surely made and maintained from the 9th cent. onwards till the middle of the 7th. The Aramæans were crushed; and Israel, repressed for a time, arose again to prosperity under Jeroboam II. and Uzziah. But its 'day' also came at last. N. Israel was obliterated and added to the realm of Assyria, while Judah was made an Assyr. vassal. Till near the close of the 7th cent. B.C. Assyria remained the undisputed mistress of W. Asia, not simply controlling the other Sem. communities, but making most of them an administrative portion of her own empire. Thus it came to pass that the individuality of the various communities was gradually destroyed, that one was distinguished from the other less by racial connexion than by traditional usages and spoken language. Ethnical terms were generalized, so that Western seafaring men and merchants came to be known as 'Phœnicians' or 'Canaanites,' inland traders and travellers as 'Aramæans,' and at a later date also learned men and astrologers as 'Chaldæans.' The general revolution of which this phraseology is a symptom was immensely accelerated by the irruptions of northern barbarians, Kimmerians, and Scythians, which took place during the later years of the Assyr. dominion. The same influx of foreigners hastened the fall of Assyria, which was in any case inevitable, on account of the impossibility of holding together for ever a multitude of petty communities by centralized force alone.

But when Nineveh fell, in B.C. 607, its ruin was utilized by new exponents of the ancient Bab. spirit, the Chaldæans from the shores of the Persian Gulf. Combined with them, and foremost in the attack upon Nineveh, were the Aryan Medes—a people new to dominion, but the precursors of a movement which was to put an end to the rôle of the N. Semites. In the partition which followed the conquest, the Chaldæans retained the proper Sem. domain, while the Medes claimed the highlands to the east and north. The régime of the Chaldæans was stern and strenuous, though not so cruel as that of the Assyrians. Egypt, which had been subdued and then given up by the later Assyr. empire, made a futile attempt, during the brief interregnum, to occupy Syria and Palestine. It was thrust out by Nebuchadrezzar the Chaldæan. Egypt itself was in due time visited and disciplined within its own domain. The kingdom of Judah, removed from Egyp. control, was put under bond to the Chaldæans. Repeated revolts brought about at last the destruction of Jerus. and the kingdom, and the exile of the people.

But internal decline effected a decay of the Chaldæan empire almost as swift as that of the Assyrian. A round seventy years limited its duration. *Its* destruction also was accelerated by an Aryan power. Cyrus the Persian, beginning his career as the head of a little province of Media, had become lord of the vast Median dominion, the conqueror of Lydia, and the ruler of a territory stretching from the Indus to the Ægean Sea. Babylon fell to him in the summer of 539, and with its transfer into Aryan hands the political sway of the N. Semites was for ever ended.

The rule of Cyrus was tolerant and humane. Under it the principle of delegated power, unknown to the Semitic rulers, was put in force. Under the comparatively genial sway of the Persians, many of the old Sem. communities, Bab., Aram., Can. (Phœn.), and Heb., continued to exist, and some of them to flourish. The Aram. people, in small communities, survived in greatest numbers, and taught their language to most of the old N. Semitic realm. But Jerusalem and Tyre were long the most outstanding representatives of the Sem. genius. Surviving longest as centres of influence, they recalled to the world the ancient power of the Sem. mind and spirit. The one handed over to Europe the method as well as the example of a world-wide commerce. The other, in the more potent and more enduring realm of religion, continued to verify and to publish the essential truth about God and man and duty.

It was, above all, in this region of thought and feeling that the Semites did their work for humanity. In their front we place the community of *Israel*, with all its feebleness and insignificance. It was under the vassalage to Assyria and Babylonia that the prophets and poets of Israel uttered those words which form the most precious legacy of all ancient time. And it was after the national life had been finally extinguished that the ancient Church abjured false gods for ever, and first realized the idea of local and individual worship apart from the central sanctuary. Thus was prepared the way for that final epoch, when He who was not only a Semite and a Hebrew but the Son of Man, did away with ritual, priesthood, and caste, and erected His temple in the heart of humanity. Thus a greater service was done for the world by the most potent of the forces of Semitism under political disability and decline, than any which had been wrought by the mightiest of Semitic empires in the days of their power and pride.

iii. Characteristics of the Semites.—It has been stated above that the Sem. civilization is essentially of nomadic origin. We may go further, and assert that the character of the people was vitally affected by their early habitual mode of life. Probably no race in the world's history has had such a prolonged experience of tribalism as a preparation for its wider active career among the nations. The general sketch already given of the early history of the Semites may give some indication of the conditions of their life in those distant ages. The inland Arabs of the present day present the nearest surviving analogy, changed though the type has been from the ancient prototype. A better representation, though still far from adequate, is afforded by the picture which the Arabian historians and poets have drawn of the manners and pursuits of their countrymen in the centuries before Islam: the migrations of their tribes, their alliances, their feuds, their forays and raids, their revenges, their stormy passions, their loves and hates, their swift growth and decline, their superstitions, their monotonous activity, their impulsive energy. But the correct estimate, as nearly as it may be reached, can be gained only by the use of the imagination, trained in the inductions of prehistoric archæology. By a process of reduction and elimination we may arrive at an approximate view of primitive Semitic society.

We must not imagine the Semites shortly before their separation as one large community swayed by a common leader, obeying common laws, and inspired by common memories. We have rather to think of a multitude of small communities, some of them scarcely more than parasitic unorganized hordes, speaking various closely related dialects, constantly intermingling with and modifying one another, and ranging over a vast extent of wilderness land. Hunting still engrossed the attention of many of the tribesmen, though immense herds of cattle were the property of others. They had learned something of the practical uses of metals, especially of copper and iron, besides gold, silver, and several precious stones. The various tools and weapons essential to the business of hunters and shepherds are also represented by words common to the several derivative languages. They were close observers of animals, wild and domesticated, and of various species of plants. They would even appear to have employed some rude form of writing, though none which was later developed into a general system. Their common vocabulary is naturally deficient in legal terms; for their only law was usage and prescription, and their only court that of the family or tribal chiefs. On the other hand, the religious habit and consciousness had found copious expression.

The reciprocal antagonism of a multitude of tribes, so long maintained in spite of frequent alliances and absorptions, and guarded by the tribal badges of social and religious usage, had its most marked result in the permanent political character of the later Sem. communities. Mutual repulsion, even between the States most closely allied by blood or common interest, was universal, and was scarcely ever overcome, even after prolonged forcible amalgamation. City-kingdoms became the rule in all fixed settlements—an institution which was essentially tribal chiefdom made permanent and hereditary. This type of government was scarcely modified, even in the most highly organized States; there intervened no real substantial authority between the king and any of his subjects. Even Israel, which exceptionally began its settled career as a tribal confederation, reverted inevitably to the normal Sem. type of government. After the establishment of the kingdom, Israel was reduced to 'Ephraim,' and Samaria became the synonym of either, while Jerusalem ere long became the virtual surrogate of Judah.

Of absolutely immeasurable importance to the world were the intellectual and moral character and temper of the ancient Semites. Long-continued intense activity, within a wide yet monotonous and secluded territory, was the habit of this unique people. Such a habit of necessity produces men eager, impulsive, and intense, but narrow and unimaginative. Such were the prehistoric Semites, and such the Semites of history. Religious, for the most part, rather than moral; patient, resolute, enduring, brave, serious; faithful to friends, implacable towards foes,—they have borne the stamp of tribalism all through their history. With little breadth of imagination, or range of invention, or intellectual or moral sympathy, they have given to literature scarcely anything dramatic or epic. But their ardour and passion, their religious and patriotic fervour, have inspired a lyrical poetry unequalled or unsurpassed. Intensely subjective, they have little spontaneous interest in experimental science and the pictorial arts. Incapable of wide speculation, they have had no genuine philosophy of their own; but, wholly practical in their views and modes of life, they have attained to the highest eminence in gnomic wisdom. Their faculty of surviving in strange conditions and surroundings, and of arousing themselves from chronic inactivity to almost superhuman daring and enterprise, seems to be the manifestation of a reserve power potentially acquired through ages of undaunted persistence under hard conditions. Not looking far around them, they have at times seen all the farther beyond and above them. And when it has been given them to see straight and clear, they have beheld 'unspeakable things, which it is not possible for a man to utter.' But they are apt to see only one thing at a time, and so in their judgments of men and things they are exclusive, partial, and extreme. When they perceive the principal part of a thing, it is conceived of and described as standing for the whole. In their mental pictures there is but little combining of elements, or shading or perspective. In their vocabulary there are few qualifying or restrictive terms. In their view of the universe they refer everything to direct supernatural agency. Hence they leave little scope to the individual human will, and a circumscribed choice of action to themselves. They know of but two types of government, the one a development of the other: the patriarchal and the absolute monarchical. They follow but few occupations, and their work is divided among hereditary guilds. For the like fundamental reason, they are quite limited in their view of human merits and allotments; men are to them either absolutely good or absolutely bad; and their destiny is to be either beatific or hopelessly wretched. With such mental and moral qualities, they have been, according to the light which they have seen and the course to which they have been driven, the most beneficent or the most noxious of our species. There are two consummate forms and modes of Sem. faith and practice—Judaism and Mohammedanism. The one, with all its inevitable limitations, was incomparably the greatest gift of God to the world in ancient times. The other, in spite of the truth which it has appropriated, is one of the greatest evils of the world's later days, one of the most perverse and malignant, one of the most perplexing and disheartening.

LITERATURE.—On possible relations between the Semites and other races, see Benfey, *Verhält. d. ägypt. Sprache z. semit. Sprachstamm* (1844); Friedr. Delitzsch, *Indogerm.-Semit. Wurzelverwandtschaft* (1873); McCurdy, *Aryo-Semitic Speech* (1881); Brugsch, *Hierogl.-demot. Wörterb.* (1867), Introduction. On the question of the original seat of the Semites and their classification, essays have been written by von Kremer, Guidi, and Hommel in favour of the theory of a migration from the N.E.; by Sprenger, Schrader, and de Goeje approving of the view that Arabia was the starting-place. See the summation in favour of the latter hypothesis in Wright, *Compar. Gramm. of Sem. Languages* (1890), p. 5 ff.; and comp. Nöldeke, art. 'Semitic Languages,' in *Encyc. Brit.*[9] Hommel's latest classification, as based on language, may be found in *AHT* (1897). The genius and character of the Semites are discussed in Hommel, *Die semit. Völker und Sprachen* (1883), p. 21 ff., where the views of Renan, Ewald, Chwolson, Grau, and Sprenger are also cited and criticised. On the religion of the Semites, see W. R. Smith, *RS*; Baudissin, *Studien zur sem. Religionsgeschichte*; and Baethgen, *Beiträge z. sem. Religionsgeschichte*. For the history of the Semites, see Max Duncker, *Hist. of Antiquity* (tr. from the German [1879], vols. i.–iii.); Meyer, *Gesch. des Alterthums* (1884), vol. i.; Maspero, *Hist. anc. des peuples de l'Orient*; Lenormant, *Hist. anc. de l'Orient*; G. Rawlinson, *The Five Great Monarchies of the Ancient Eastern World*; Sayce, *The Ancient Empires of the East*; McCurdy, *HPM*. See also artt. ASSYRIA and BABYLONIA in vol. i. and in the *Encyc. Bibl.*, and the Literature there referred to; and add on the Sumerian question, Weissbach, *Die sumer. Frage* (1898).

J. F. McCURDY.

**DIASPORA.**—

Introduction.

i. Extent of the Diaspora: in (1) the Euphrates districts; (2) Syria; (3) Arabia; (4) Asia Minor; (5) Egypt; (6) Cyrenaica; (7) North Africa; (8) Macedonia and Greece; (9) Rome; (10) the rest of Italy, and Spain, Gaul, Germany.

ii. Organization of the communities: certain features common to them everywhere; differences as to (1) the *name* of the community, (2) the *officials*. Constitution of the Jewish communities akin to that of the Greek communes.

iii. Toleration and recognition by the State anthorities. Three forms of political existence: (1) as a colony of foreigners (κατοικία); (2) as private societies or 'unions'; (3) as more or less independent corporations alongside the communal bodies. Toleration of the Jewish cultus a main essential. Right of administering their own funds, and jurisdiction over their own members. The question of military service. The cult of the Emperor; advantage of the Jews in this matter over the Christians. Varying attitude of different Emperors towards the Jews.

iv. Rights of citizenship, and social standing. Citizenship possessed by the Jews especially in recently founded cities like Alexandria and Antioch, or in those whose constitution had been reorganized like the cities of Western Asia Minor. In such instances the Jews formed a φυλή by themselves. Many Jews enjoyed even *Roman* citizenship. Social standing of the Jews. The offices of *alabarch* and 'head physician.'

v. Religious and intellectual life. Danger of syncretism and philosophic indifference. The Synagogue a safeguard. The *Greek* language used in the Synagogue services. The temple at Leontopolis. Payment of dues to the temple at Jerusalem. Pilgrimages to the festivals. Greek influences. Pædagogic part played by the Diaspora in relation to Christianity.

Literature.

Amongst the causes that contributed to the rapid spread of Christianity during the Apostolic and post-Apostolic periods, one of the most important was the circumstance that Judaism was already dispersed as a powerful force throughout the whole extent of the Roman Empire, nay even beyond it. Everywhere the preachers of the gospel found Jewish communities, which furnished them with the starting-point for their proclamation of the advent of the Messiah. And, even if their success was not very marked within the pale of the communities themselves, it must be assumed to have been all the greater in the circles of 'God-fearing' Gentiles, who in many places had attached themselves as an appendage to the community of Jews. Through these circles being won over by the Jewish propaganda to a worship that was monotheistic and determined by ethical interests, the soil was loosened for the seed of the gospel to be scattered on it.

The enormous extent of the Jewish Diaspora in comparison with the petty mother country presents an enigma to historical inquiry which it is unable to solve with certainty. In any case, various factors must have co-operated to bring about the result in question. In the time of the Assyrians and the Chaldæans forcible deportations to the Euphrates districts took place, and a process of the same kind was repeated even in the Persian period, under Artaxerxes Ochus. At the beginning of the Greek period the rulers sought, in the interests of the consolidation of their dominions, to effect the greatest possible intermixture of populations, and with a view to this they incited and favoured general migrations, by guaranteeing certain privileges and by other means. Pressure from above and the prospect of gain, in particular the interests of trade, combined to produce an ebbing and flowing of the peoples scattered over the wide dominions of the Diadochi. It is to this period that we ought presumably to assign a large proportion of those Jewish migrations, whose occurrence we can only infer from their results in the Roman period. But all this is hardly sufficient to account fully for the fact before us. Is it possible that the small community, which under Ezra and Nehemiah organized itself around Jerusalem, and which even about the year B.C. 200 had not spread beyond the territory of Judæa (in the narrower sense), should have produced merely by natural increase the many thousands, nay millions, who at the latest in the 1st cent. A.D. are found scattered over the whole world? This is highly improbable. We are thus compelled to suppose that it was not only to migration and natural reproduction, but also to numerous conversions during the Greek period, that Judaism owed its wide diffusion over the whole world, and the great number of adherents whose existence we can prove in general with complete certainty, although we cannot give the actual figures.

In the present article we shall describe (1) the extent of the dispersion of the Jews; (2) the organization of the communities; (3) the measure in which they enjoyed toleration and recognition by the State; (4) the share of the Jews in citizenship; (5) their religious and intellectual life in general.

i. EXTENT OF THE DIASPORA.—We have general testimony to the wide dispersion of the Jewish people, commencing with the middle of the 2nd cent. B.C. In the Third Book of the *Sibylline Oracles*, composed probably about B.C. 140, it is said that 'every land and every sea is filled with them' (*Orac. Sibyll.* iii. 271, πᾶσα δὲ γαῖα σέθεν πλήρης καὶ πᾶσα θάλασσα). In the time of Sulla we are told by Strabo that the Jewish people had already 'come into every city; and one cannot readily find any place in the world which has not received this tribe and been taken possession of by it' (*ap.* Jos. *Ant.* XIV. vii. 2). According to Josephus, there is 'no people in the world without a fragment of us' (*BJ* II. xvi. 4 [Niese, § 398]: οὐ γὰρ ἔστιν ἐπὶ τῆς οἰκουμένης δῆμος ὁ μὴ μοῖραν ἡμετέραν ἔχων). The fullest details are found in the survey given by Philo in the letter of Agrippa to Caligula (*Legatio ad Gaium*, § 36 [ed. Mangey, ii. 587]): 'Jerusalem is the metropolis not only of Judæa, but of most countries. This is owing to the colonies which on suitable occasions she has sent to the neighbouring lands of Egypt, Phœnicia, Syria, Cœle-Syria; to the remoter Pamphylia, Cilicia, most parts of Asia, as far as Bithynia; and to the farthest corners of Pontus, as well as to Europe, Thessaly, Bœotia, Macedonia, Aetolia, Attica, Argos, Corinth, to the most and the fairest parts of the Peloponnesus. And not only is the mainland covered with Jewish settlements, but also the principal islands: Eubœa, Cyprus, Crete. I leave unnamed the lands beyond the Euphrates, for, with the exception of a small portion, all this district, including Babylon and the satrapies that embrace the fertile territory lying around, has Jewish inhabitants.' We are not able to test the correctness of this testimony in every detail. But the more our knowledge is enlarged by new discoveries, the more do we find the accuracy of the above description established. Coming now to particulars, the following are the most important testimonies:—

1. *THE EUPHRATES DISTRICTS.*—The earliest Diaspora of the Jews is that found in these regions (Assyria, Media, Babylonia). Large masses were deported by the Assyrians from the kingdom of the Ten Tribes, and by the Chaldæans from the kingdom of Judah. The Assyrians settled those whom they had carried away 'in Halah and in Habor by the river of Gozan, and in the cities of the Medes' (2 K $17^{6}$ $18^{11}$), *i.e.* in the northern part of the region watered by the Euphrates, to the west of Nineveh (see the articles on the various localities just named). The Chaldæans brought their captives to the region of Babylon. It is true that large companies of the Judahites and Benjamites who had been carried to Babylon, afterwards returned to their native land and founded a new community there. But there was no such thing as a complete return of the Babylonian exiles. Still less was this the case with the members of the Ten Tribes deported by the Assyrians. Practically, the whole of these remained in foreign parts. This is not only implied in the biblical narrative, which knows nothing of a return on their part, but is expressly testified to by later writers (Jos. *Ant.* XI. v. 2: αἱ δὲ δέκα φυλαὶ πέραν εἰσὶν Εὐφράτου ἕως δεῦρο, μυριάδες ἄπειροι καὶ ἀριθμῷ γνωσθῆναι μὴ δυνάμεναι; cf. 4 Ezr $13^{39\text{-}47}$; Origen, *Epist. ad Africanum*, § 14; Commodian, *Carmen Apologet.* 936–939). As late as the time of R. 'Akiba, the Rabbis continued to dispute whether the Ten Tribes would ever return or not (Mishna, *Sanhedrin*, x. 3 *fin.*; tradition vacillates regarding the authorities who supported the different views [see Bacher, *Die Agada der Tannaiten*, i. 143 f.]).

A fresh deportation was carried out by Artaxerxes Ochus, who about the year B.C. 350 transported Jewish prisoners to *Hyrcania* (Euseb. *Chron.*, ed. Schoene, ii. 112, ad ann. Abr. 1657; Orosius, iii. 7), probably because they had taken part in the revolt of the Phœnicians against the Persian sway.

All these Israelites who lived in the Euphrates districts maintained communication with the mother country, and, as the centuries ran their course, took their share in its religious development. Instead of being absorbed by the surrounding heathenism (as one would naturally have expected), they rather advanced in the direction of proper, strict, legal Judaism. And to such an extent did their numbers increase that in the Roman period they were counted by millions; and thus, even from a political point of view, constituted a power with which the Romans had to reckon, seeing that their settlements lay on the border of [down to the time of Trajan chiefly outside] the sphere of Roman authority. P. Petronius, the legate of Syria, considered it dangerous in the year A.D. 40 to provoke them to a hostile disposition towards Rome (Philo, *Legatio ad Gaium*, § 31 [ed. Mangey, ii. 578]). Trajan in his advance against the Parthians was exposed to a real danger by the revolt of the Mesopotamian Jews which threatened his rear. It is not probable that these millions (μυριάδες ἄπειροι) of Jewish inhabitants were simply descendants of the former exiles. We must rather think of a successful propaganda among the surrounding heathen. This propaganda, too, must have been directed from Judæa, for the population of which we are speaking was Jewish in the sense of Pharisaism, as is evident from the forms of activity displayed by its religious life (pilgrimages to the feasts, sending of dues to the temple, etc.; see, on this, below). The main stock, however, was certainly composed of the ancient exiles, for in the Roman period we find the Jewish population most thickly settled in the very spots to which the Assyrians and the Chaldæans once transported their prisoners. Josephus names, as their two principal cities, Nehardea (Νέερδα, Νάαρδα) and Nisibis (*Ant.* XVIII. ix. 1 and 9 *fin.*). The former of these was in Babylonia; the latter on the Mygdonius, a tributary of the Chaboras (Ḥabor), in the centre of the localities named in 2 K $17^{6}$ $18^{11}$. Around Nehardea were thus grouped the descendants of the tribes of Judah and Benjamin; around Nisibis, the descendants of the Ten Tribes.

It may be further mentioned that, in the time of Tiberius, two brothers, Asinæus and Anilæus, founded in the neighbourhood of Nehardea a robber State, which, owing to the weakness of the Parthian monarchy, maintained its existence for several decades (Jos. *Ant.* XVIII. ix.).—In the time of Claudius the royal house of Adiabene (Izates, his mother Helena, and his brother Monobazus) adopted the Jewish faith, and proved its attachment by keeping up intimate relations with Jerusalem, by establishing various foundations there, and by taking part with the Jews in their great war with the Romans under Nero and Vespasian (Jos. *Ant.* XX. ii.–iv.; *BJ* II. xix. 2, IV. ix. 11, V. ii. 2, iii. 3, iv. 2, vi. 1, VI. vi. 3, 4).

2. *SYRIA.*—This is characterized by Josephus as the country which, on account of its proximity to Palestine, had the largest percentage of Jewish inhabitants, these being specially numerous in the capital, Antioch (*BJ* VIII. iii. 3: τὸ γὰρ Ἰουδαίων γένος πολὺ μὲν κατὰ πᾶσαν τὴν οἰκουμένην παρέσπαρται τοῖς ἐπιχωρίοις, **πλεῖστον δὲ τῇ Συρίᾳ** κατὰ τὴν γειτνίασιν ἀναμεμιγμένον **ἐξαιρέτως ἐπὶ τῆς Ἀντιοχείας** ἦν πολὺ διὰ τὸ τῆς πόλεως μέγεθος). At Antioch the Jews enjoyed the rights of citizenship, they had a splendid synagogue, and carried on a zealous and successful propaganda among the heathen population (Jos. *l.c.*). It is true that by all this they drew upon themselves the hatred of the pagan inhabitants. Regarding the state of things in most of the other towns of Syria we know nothing very definite. But Philo states that there are

'great numbers of Jews in every city of Asia and Syria' (*Legatio ad Gaium*, § 33 [ed. Mangey, ii. 582]: Ἰουδαῖοι καθ' ἑκάστην πόλιν εἰσὶ παμπληθεῖς Ἀσίας τε καὶ Συρίας). For Damascus exact figures are given by Josephus, who, however, contradicts himself on this point. In one passage he states that, at the outbreak of the great war in the year A.D. 66, there were 10,500 [so Niese's text of *BJ* II. xx. 2; according to another reading, 10,000] Jews massacred at Damascus. In another passage (*BJ* VII. viii. 7 [Niese, § 368]) he gives, instead of this number, '18,000, with women and children.' According to the first cited passage (*BJ* II. xx. 2), the women of Damascus were almost all devoted to the Jewish religion (τὰς γυναῖκας ἁπάσας πλὴν ὀλίγων ὑπηγμένας τῇ Ἰουδαικῇ θρησκείᾳ).

3. *SOUTH ARABIA.*—At what date Judaism reached this quarter is unknown, but it was strongly diffused there from the 4th cent. A.D. at the latest. When, under Constantius, attempts were made to extend Christianity in that quarter, these had to contend with Jewish opposition (Philostorgius, iii. iv.). At the beginning of the 6th cent. a Jewish king reigned there. Owing to his persecution of the Christians, he was dethroned by the Christian king of Abyssinia (see Fell, 'Die Christenverfolgung in Südarabien,' etc., in *ZDMG* XXXV. [1881] 1–74. Against Halévy, who argued that the king in question was not a Jew but an Arian, see Duchesne in *REJ* xx. [1890] 220–224).

4. *ASIA MINOR.*—Here we have numerous testimonies, and are able to demonstrate the presence of Jews in almost every quarter. They were most thickly settled in Phrygia and Lydia, and we know further how they came there. Antiochus the Great transplanted two thousand Jewish families from Mesopotamia and Babylonia to Lydia and Phrygia, because he considered them more loyal subjects than the Lydians and Phrygians, who were inclined to revolt (Jos. *Ant.* XII. iii. 4). While these Babylonian Jews peopled the inland provinces of Asia Minor, others were attracted by trade interests to the towns on the coast. An indirect evidence of the early appearance of the Jews in Asia Minor may be discovered also in 1 Mac 15[15-24]. According to this passage, the Romans in the year B.C. 139 simultaneously despatched to a number of kings a letter in identical terms, charging them to refrain from showing any hostility towards the Jews. From this it may be inferred that Jews were already to be found in all the places there named. Of States and cities in Asia Minor the following are mentioned: the kingdoms of Pergamum and Cappadocia; the district of Caria, with the cities of Myndos, Halicarnassus, and Cnidos; Pamphylia, with the city of Side; Lycia, with the city of Phaselis; and, finally, Sampsame, *i.e.* the Samsun of later Arab geographers, or Amisus in Pontus, to the east of Sinope. These various districts and cities were in the year B.C. 139 politically independent, and are therefore named separately beside the great kingdoms of Pergamum and Cappadocia.

As showing the great numbers and the prosperity of the Jews of Asia Minor about the middle of the 1st cent. B.C., we have, on the one hand, the numerous acts in their favour during the closing years (B.C. 50–40) of the Roman Republic (collected by Josephus in *Ant.* XIV. x.); and, on the other hand, the remarkable passage in Cicero, *pro Flacco*, 28, in which he gives precise details as to the circumstances under which quantities of Jewish money, intended to be sent from Asia Minor to Jerusalem, were confiscated by the governor Flaccus (B.C. 62–61). The whole passage reads thus: 'Quum aurum Judæorum nomine quotannis ex Italia et ex omnibus provinciis Hierosolyma exportari soleret, Flaccus sanxit edicto ne ex Asia exportari liceret. . . . Ubi ergo crimen est? quoniam quidem furtum nusquam reprehendis, edictum probas, judicatum fateris, quæsitum et prolatum palam non negas, actum esse per viros primarios res ipsa declarat: *Apameæ* manifesto deprehensum, ante pedes prætoris in foro expensum esse auri pondo centum paullo minus per Sex. Cæsium, equitem Romanum, castissimum hominem atque integerrimum; *Laodiceæ* viginti pondo paullo amplius per hunc L. Peducæum, judicem nostrum; *Adramyttii* per Cn. Domitium, legatum; *Pergami* non multum.' If we add to these general testimonies other special ones, particularly those of the inscriptions, we obtain for the Jews in Asia Minor the following data (commencing with the N.W.):—

**a.** *Adramyttium* and *Pergamum:* the above testimony of Cicero.

**b.** *Phokæa:* an inscription (*REJ* xii. [1886] 236–242=*Bulletin de corresp. hellén.* x. [1886] 327–335): Τάτιον Στράτωνος τοῦ Ἐνπέδωνος τὸν οἶκον καὶ τὸν περίβολον τοῦ ὑπαίθρου κατασκευάσασα ἐκ τῶ[ν ἰδ]ίων ἐχαρίσατο τ[οῖς Ἰο]υδαίοις. Ἡ συναγωγὴ ἐ[τείμη]σεν τῶν Ἰουδαίων Τάτιον Σ[τράτ]ωνος τοῦ Ἐνπέδωνος χρυσῷ στεφάνῳ καὶ προεδρίᾳ.

**c.** *Magnesia* on Mt. Sipylus: a Jewish tomb-inscription (*REJ* x. [1885] 76).

**d.** *Smyrna:* an inscription from the time of Hadrian, with a list of those who had made presents to the city, among them οἱ ποτὲ Ἰουδαῖοι (*CIG* 3148). The Jews played a prominent part in connexion with the death of Polycarp (*Martyr. Polyc.* 12–13, 17–18; *Vita Polycarpi auctore Pionio*, ed. Duchesne, 1881; cf. also Reinach, *REJ* xi. 235–238). There is, further, this inscription from the 3rd cent. A.D. (*REJ* vii. [1883] 161–166): Ῥουφεῖνα Ἰουδαῖα ἀρχισυνάγωγος κατεσκεύασεν τὸ ἐνσόριον τοῖς ἀπελευθέροις καὶ θρέμασιν μηδενὸς ἄλου ἐξουσίαν ἔχοντος θάψαι τινά, εἰ δέ τις τολμήσει, δώσει τῷ ἱερωτάτῳ ταμείῳ δηνάρια ͵αφ καὶ τῷ ἔθνει τῶν Ἰουδαίων δηνάρια ͵α. Ταύτης τῆς ἐπιγραφῆς τὸ ἀντίγραφον ἀποκεῖται εἰς τὸ ἀρχεῖον.

**e.** *Sardis:* three official documents quoted by Josephus—**1.** A despatch of L. Antonius to the authorities of Sardis (B.C. 50, 49), permitting the Jews to refer their disputes for decision to their own tribunals, even when they are Roman citizens (*Ant.* XIV. x. 17). **2.** A popular resolution of the city of Sardis, guaranteeing to the Jews the undisturbed exercise of their religion (*Ant.* XIV. x. 24). **3.** A despatch of C. Norbanus Flaccus, from the time of Augustus, to the authorities of Sardis, reminding them afresh of the religious freedom of the Jews (*Ant.* XVI. vi. 6).

**f.** *Hypaepa*, to the south of Sardis: an inscription of *c.* 200 A.D., containing only the two words Ἰουδαίων νεωτέρων (*REJ* x. 74 f.).

**g.** *Ephesus:* the granting of the city franchise to the Jews, probably as early as the reorganizing of the city constitution by Antiochus II. Theos (B.C. 261–246). Numerous official documents are quoted by Josephus, particularly those dating from the years B.C. 49–42, according to which the Jews living in Ephesus were exempted from military service even when they possessed the Roman citizenship (*Ant.* XIV. x. 11–13, 16, 19, 25. During the years named the Roman citizens in Asia Minor were called out for military service). Under Augustus the authorities of Ephesus were repeatedly reminded that the Jews were not to be interfered with in sending the sacred money to Jerusalem (Philo, *Legatio ad Gaium*, § 40; Jos. *Ant.* XVI. vi. 4, 7). Their synagogue is mentioned in Ac 18[19. 26] 19[8]. In a late tomb-inscription we meet with a Jewish ἀρχίατρος (*Ancient Greek Inscriptions in the British Museum*, iii. 2, No. 677). The 'head physicians' were appointed by the city, and enjoyed immunity from all burdens.

**h.** *Tralles:* incidental mention in a despatch from the Laodiceans (Jos. *Ant.* XIV. x. 20).

**i.** *Caria:* see, in general, 1 Mac 15[23], and cf. also the above remarks.

**j.** *Miletus:* a despatch of the proconsul to the city authorities, bearing on the religious freedom of the Jews (*Ant.* XIV. x. 21).

**k.** *Jasus*, to the south of Miletus: an inscription from the middle of the 2nd cent. B.C., according to which one Νικήτας Ἰάσονος Ἱεροσολυμίτης gave a money contribution in support of the festival of the *Dionysia* (Le Bas et Waddington, *Inscr.* iii. No. 294 = *REJ* x. 76). It is not impossible that Jason, the father of this Niketas, is to be identified with the high priest of this name who lived in the Maccabæan period. Support of heathen festivals by Jews was not unknown at that time even in Palestine.

**l.** *Myndos:* a tomb-inscription from the beginning of the Byzantine period (*REJ* xlii. 1–4).

**m.** *Halicarnassus:* a popular resolution regarding the religious freedom of the Jews (Jos. *Ant.* XIV. x. 23).

**n.** *Phrygia:* see Ramsay, *Cities and Bishoprics of Phrygia*, vol. i. pt. ii. (1897) pp. 667–676.

**o.** *Laodicea:* see Cicero, *pro Flacco*, 28; also a despatch of the authorities to the proconsul C. Rabirius, in which they disclaim any intention of interfering with the religious freedom of the Jews (*Ant.* XIV. x. 20).

**p.** *Hierapolis:* three Jewish inscriptions published in *Jahrbuch des deutschen archäol. Instituts*, ivth Ergänzungsheft (= *Alterthümer von Hierapolis*, herausg. von Humann, Cichorius, Judeich, Winter), 1898. We give extracts, showing the most important points—**1.** No. 69 a tomb-inscription, closing with the threat of a penalty: εἰ δὲ μή, ἀποτείσει τῷ λαῷ τὸν (*sic*) Ἰουδαί[ω]ν προστε[ί]μου ὀν[όμ]ατι δηνάρια χείλια. **2.** No. 212 a tomb-inscription ending thus: εἰ δὲ ἔτι ἕτερος κηδεύσει, δώσει τῇ κατοικίᾳ τῶν ἐν Ἱεραπόλει κατοικούντων Ἰουδαίων προστείμου (δηνάρια) (.) καὶ τῷ ἐκζητήσαντι (δηνάρια) (δισχίλια). ἀντίγραφον ἀπετέθη ἐν τῷ ἀρχίῳ τῶν Ἰουδαίων. **3.** No. 342 (= Ramsay, *Cities and Bishoprics of Phrygia*, i. 545) tomb-inscription of a certain Publius Ælius Glykon, who bequeathed to the managing body of the guild of purple-dyers (τῇ σεμνοτάτῃ προεδρίᾳ τῶν πορφυραβάφων) a capital fund, the interest of which was to be applied yearly, ἐν τῇ ἑορτῇ τῶν ἀζύμων, to the decorating of his tomb. He bequeathed likewise to the directorate of another guild (τῷ συνεδρίῳ τῶν καιροδαπιστῶν) a sum to be applied to the same purpose, ἐν τῇ ἑορτῇ πεντηκο[στῆς]. The whole of the members of these guilds must, accordingly, have been, if not exactly Jews, at least well disposed to Judaism (cf. Ramsay, *Expositor* of Feb. 1902, pp. 98–100).

**q.** *Apamea:* Cicero, *pro Flacco*, 28 (see above); also a tomb-inscription (*ap.* Ramsay, *Cities and Bishoprics of Phrygia*, i. 538) ending thus: εἰ δέ τις ἐπιτηδεύσι, τὸν νόμον οἶδεν τῶν Εἰουδέων. The 'law of the Jews' cannot here be the Mosaic law, but a legal ordinance, recognized by the State, imposing a penalty on any harm done to Jewish tombs. The strength of Jewish influence at Apamea can be gauged from the circumstance that at the beginning of the 3rd cent. A.D. coins were struck by the city authorities (!) having upon them figures of *Noah* and his wife descending from the ark, and bearing the legend ΝΩΕ (fullest description of these coins in Madden, *Numismatic Chronicle*, 1866, pp. 173–219, pl. vi.; cf. also the Catalogue of the Collection Waddington in the *Revue Numismatique*, 1898, p. 397 f., Nos. 5723, 5730, 5731). Apamea thus claimed to be the spot where Noah's ark was stranded. This claim, which is known also from other sources, is connected in some way with the name of the city, Ἀπάμεια Κιβωτός, for κιβωτός is the biblical term for the ark of Noah. It may have been just this appellation of the city that led to the localizing of the Noah-legend. That this localizing is to be traced to Jewish influence, has been shown especially by Babelon ('La tradition phrygienne du déluge' in *Revue de l'histoire des religions*, xxiii. [1891] 174–183). Not only the Noah- but also the Enoch-legend reached Phrygia by means of the Jews; for the Phrygian Ἀννακός or Νάννακος, who lived over 300 years, and after whose death the great Flood came, is certainly no other than the biblical Enoch (he is called Ἀννακός by Stephanus Byzant. *s.v.* Ἰκόνιον; but Νάννακος by Zenobius, *Proverb.* vi. 10, and Suidas, *Lex. s.v.* Νάννακος).

**r.** *Akmonia:* an inscription in honour of a number of synagogue officials who had restored 'the synagogue built by Julia Severa' (τὸν κατασκευασθέντα οἶκον ὑπὸ Ἰουλίας Σεουήρας . . . ἐπεσκεύασαν, see Ramsay, *Revue des études anciennes*, iii. [1901] 272 [an earlier copy in *Cities and Bishoprics of Phrygia*, i. 649 f.]). It closes thus: οὕστινας καὶ ἡ συναγωγὴ ἐτείμησεν ὅπλῳ ἐπιχρύσῳ διά τε τὴν ἐνάρετον αὐτῶν [βί]ωσιν καὶ τὴν πρὸς τὴν συναγωγὴν εὔνοιάν τε καὶ σπουδήν. This inscription shows us to what influence Judaism had attained in the highest circles of society; for the Julia Severa who is named as the builder of the synagogue is known to us from coins and inscriptions (Ramsay, *Cities and Bishoprics of Phrygia*, i. 637, 647) as a noble lady of Akmonia in the time of Nero (*Prosopographia imperii Romani*, iii. 224 f., *s.v.* 'Servenius'; also coins in the Collection Waddington, *Revue Numismatique*, 1898, p. 384, Nos. 5488, 5490, 5494). Since she was at the same time high priestess of the cult of the Emperor, she cannot indeed have been a Jewess.

**s.** *Antioch of Pisidia:* a Jewish synagogue mentioned in Ac 13[14].

**t.** *Lycia* and the city of *Phaselis:* see 1 Mac 15[23], with the above remarks on that passage.

**u.** *Korykos* in Lycia: a tomb-inscription of late date (*REJ* x. 76).

**v.** *Tlos* in Lycia: a tomb-inscription from somewhere about the end of the 1st cent. A.D. (*Eranos Vindobonensis*, 1893, pp. 99–102). According to it, the ἡρῷον (sepulchral monument) was erected by a certain Ptolemæus for himself and his son Ptolemæus ὑπὲρ ἀρχοντείας τελουμένας παρ' ἡμεῖν Ἰουδαίοις, ὥστε αὐτὸ εἶναι πάντων τῶν Ἰουδαίων καὶ μηδένα ἐξὸν εἶναι ἕτερον τεθῆναι ἐν αὐτῷ. ἐὰν δέ τις εὑρεθείη τινὰ τιθῶν ὀφειλέσει Τλωέων τῷ δήμῳ [the conclusion is wanting].

**w.** *Pamphylia* and the city of *Side:* see 1 Mac 15[23] and the general testimony of Philo (see above, p. 92[a]), also Ac 2[10].

**x.** *Cilicia:* see likewise Philo, *l.c.* Since, according to Ac 6[9], Cilician Jews lived in Jerusalem in somewhat large numbers, the Diaspora in Cilicia must have been very considerable. Tarsus, the capital of Cilicia, was, as is well known, the birthplace of the Apostle Paul (Ac 9[11] 21[39] 22[3]). One Ιουδας υιος Ιοση Ταρσευς is mentioned on a tomb-inscription of Jope (Euting, *Sitzungsberichte der Berliner Akademie*, 1885, p. 686). In the 4th cent. A.D. the Jewish patriarch caused the dues to be collected '*in every city of Cilicia*' from the resident Jews (Epiphanius, *Hær.* xxx. 11: **ἀπὸ ἑκάστης πόλεως τῆς Κιλικείας** τὰ ἐπιδέκατα καὶ τὰς ἀπαρχὰς παρὰ τῶν ἐν τῇ ἐπαρχίᾳ Ἰουδαίων εἰσέπραττεν).

**y.** *Korykos* in Cilicia: a Jewish sarcophagus with inscription (*Denkschriften der Wiener Akademie*, Phil.-Hist. Classe, Bd. xliv. [1896] p. 68).

**z.** *Iconium* in Lycaonia: a Jewish synagogue mentioned in Ac 14[1]; on inscriptions there, cf. art. GALATIA in vol. ii. p. 88[b].

**aa.** *Galatia:* testimonies here very scanty, for there are none in Jos. *Ant.* XVI. vi. 2 (the closing remark that the edict of Augustus in favour of the

Jews was to be set up at *Ancyra* is based upon a false reading: the MSS have αργυρη). A tomb-inscription from Galatia will be found in *Bulletin de corresp. hellén.* vii. 24 (=*REJ* x. 77). The inscription *CIG* 4129 was found in the neighbourhood of Dorylæum, not therefore in Galatia. Cf., in general, art. GALATIA in vol. ii. p. 85[b].

**bb.** *Cappadocia:* 1 Mac 15[22] (despatch from the Romans to king Ariarathes) is sufficient to justify the assumption that Jews were settled there. Cf. also Ac 2[9]; Mishna, *Kethuboth*, xiii. 11; Neubauer, *Géog. du Talmud*, pp. 317–319; tomb-inscriptions of Cappadocian Jews at Jope, in *PEFSt.* 1893, p. 290, and 1900, pp. 118, 122. In the Jerusalem Talmud we meet with three Jewish scholars from Cappadocia (R. Judan, R. Jannai, R. Samuel); see Krauss, *Griech. und lat. Lehnwörter im Talmud*, ii. [1899] 558; Bacher, *Die Agada der paläst. Amoräer*, iii. [1899] 106, 749.

**cc.** *Bithynia* and *Pontus:* the general testimony of Philo (*Legatio ad Gaium*, § 36, ἄχρι Βιθυνίας καὶ τῶν τοῦ Πόντου μυχῶν); a Bithynian tomb-inscription of late date (*REJ* xxvi. 167–171). On Sampsame (1 Mac 15[23])=Amisus in Pontus, see above, p. 93[a]. From Pontus came both the Aquilas, the companion of St. Paul (Ac 18[2]), and the author of a Gr. translation of the Old Testament. Cf. also Ac 2[9].

**dd.** *Pantikapæum* in the Crimea: two inscriptions of great interest (Latyschev, *Inscriptiones antiquæ oræ septentrionalis Ponti Euxini*, ii., Nos. 52, 53 [better texts here than in *CIG* 2114[bb], 2114[b]]), one of which is dated from the year A.D. 81. Both contain deeds relating to the manumission of slaves of Jewish owners. At the close it is noted that the Jewish community 'took part in superintending' this legal instrument, *i.e.* shared the responsibility for its correct execution (συνεπιτροπεούσης δὲ καὶ τῆς συναγωγῆς τῶν Ἰουδαίων). Thus even in that remote region there was in the 1st cent. A.D. an organized Jewish community.

5. *EGYPT.*—If even in Syria and Asia Minor the Jewish population was a numerous one, this was pre-eminently the case in Egypt. Here, moreover, the Jews came to play an important part in the history of civilization; for, thanks to their favourable social position, they were able to adopt in large measure the Greek culture, and thus became the principal representatives of the Jewish-Greek form of thought. The emigration of larger masses of Jews to Egypt must undoubtedly be held to have first taken place in the Greek period. But sporadic migrations or even forcible transplantings happened earlier than this. Soon after the destruction of Jerusalem by Nebuchadrezzar (B.C. 586), a large company of Jews, from fear of the Chaldæans, and in spite of the protests of the prophet Jeremiah, took their departure to Egypt (Jer 42. 43; for the motive see Jer 41). They settled in various parts, at Migdol, Tahpanhes, Noph, and Pathros (Jer 44[1]). But we do not know whether their descendants maintained their existence here as Jews. —Pseudo-Aristeas speaks of two transplantings of Jewish settlers to Egypt prior to the time of Ptolemy Lagi: one in the time of the Persians, and one much earlier, under Psammetichus, who in his expedition to Ethiopia is said to have had even Jewish soldiers in his army (*Aristeæ Epist.*, ed. Wendland, § 13: ἤδη μὲν καὶ πρότερον ἱκανῶν εἰσεληλυθότων σὺν τῷ Πέρσῃ καὶ πρὸ τούτων ἑτέρων συμμαχιῶν ἐξαπεσταλμένων πρὸς τὸν τῶν Αἰθιόπων βασιλέα μάχεσθαι σὺν Ψαμμητίχῳ. The king last named is probably Psammetichus II. [B.C. 594–589], who undertook a campaign against Ethiopia. That amongst others there were Semitic mercenaries in his army, we know from the inscriptions of Abu-Simbel [on which cf. the Literature cited in Pauly-Wissowa's *RE*, art. 'Abu-Simbel']. The Jewish migration to Egypt in the time of the Persians is not regarded by pseudo-Aristeas as a voluntary one; cf. § 35, ed. Wendland). See also 'Additional Note' at end of this article.

Whether as early as the time of Alexander the Great any considerable numbers of Jews migrated to Egypt, we know not. But we may trust the statement of Josephus, that, at the founding of Alexandria by the monarch just named, Jewish settlers were from the first incorporated among the citizens (*BJ* II. xviii. 7, *c. Apion.* ii. 4). Confirmation of this is supplied by the decree of the emperor Claudius (*ap.* Jos. *Ant.* XIX. v. 2), according to which the Jews in Alexandria were settled there from the very first (τοῖς πρώτοις εὐθὺ καιροῖς) along with the Alexandrians. Larger masses appear to have first come to Egypt under Ptolemy Lagi. According to pseudo-Hecatæus, we are to think in this instance of voluntary migrations (Jos. *c. Apion.* i. 22 [Niese, § 194]: οὐκ ὀλίγαι δὲ καὶ μετὰ τὸν Ἀλεξάνδρου θάνατον εἰς Αἴγυπτον καὶ Φοινίκην μετέστησαν διὰ τὴν ἐν Συρίᾳ στάσιν, cf. § 186). According to pseudo-Aristeas, on the other hand, Ptolemy Lagi transplanted Jewish prisoners in large numbers to Egypt. The details of his narrative belong, indeed, to the realm of romance. Ptolemy, we are told, carried captive to Egypt 100,000 Jews. Of these he armed 30,000 able-bodied men, whom he employed to do garrison duty in the fortresses of the country (§ 13: ἀφ' ὧν ὡσεὶ τρεῖς μυριάδας καθοπλίσας ἀνδρῶν ἐκλεκτῶν εἰς τὴν χώραν κατῴκισεν ἐν τοῖς φρουρίοις). The old men, the children, and the women, he is said to have handed over as slaves to his soldiers, on demand, as compensation for their services (*Aristeæ Epist.*, ed. Wendland, §§ 12–14, cf. 35–36). Afterwards Ptolemy Philadelphus is stated to have procured the freedom of all these Jewish slaves by paying to the owners twenty drachmæ per slave (§§ 15–27, 37). Since Josephus, in relating the same narrative (*c. Apion.* ii. 4 [Niese, §§ 44–47], *Ant.* XII. i.), simply reproduces the account of pseudo-Aristeas [in the first cited passage this is self-apparent, and in the other at least probable], the latter is our only witness. But, in spite of the romantic character of the narrative in question, this much at least is credible, that Ptolemy Lagi brought Jewish prisoners to Egypt and set them to garrison duty in the fortresses. For the fact that Ptolemy Lagi took Jerusalem by storm is unimpeachably vouched for by Agatharchides (Jos. *c. Apion.* i. 22 [Niese, §§ 209–211], *Ant.* XII. i.; cf. Appian, *Syr.* 50). And the employment of Jews for garrison work in strongholds is confirmed by the circumstance that at a still later period we hear of a 'Jews' camp' (Ἰουδαίων στρατόπεδον, *castra Judæorum*) in various places (see further, on this, below).

At Alexandria, in the time of the Diadochi, a special quarter, separated from the rest of the city, was assigned to the Jews, 'in order that they might be able to live a purer life by mixing less with foreigners' (Jos. *BJ* II. xviii. 7; from *c. Apion.* ii. 4 it might appear as if this quarter had already been assigned to the Jews by Alexander the Great, but, according to the manifestly more exact account in *BJ* II. xviii. 7, this was first done by the Diadochi; cf. also Strabo *ap.* Jos. *Ant.* XIV. vii. 2). This Jewish quarter stretched along the harbourless strand in the neighbourhood of the royal palace (*c. Apion.* ii. 4 [Niese, § 33]: πρὸς ἀλίμενον θάλασσαν, § 36 πρὸς τοῖς βασιλικοῖς), to the east, therefore, of the promontory of Lochias on the north-east of the city. The separation came afterwards, indeed, not to be strictly maintained, for Philo tells us that not a few Jews had their dwelling-places scattered about in the other quarters of the city. But even in Philo's time two of the five city-divisions were called 'the Jewish,' because they were predominantly inhabited by Jews (Philo, *in Flaccum*, § 8 [ed. Mangey, ii. 525]). We learn from this that *the Jews constituted something like two-fifths of the population of Alexandria.* According to Josephus, the fourth city-division was inhabited by Jews (*BJ* II. xviii. 8: τὸ καλούμενον Δέλτα, the city-divisions being named after the first five letters of the alphabet).

*The total number of Jews in Egypt is reckoned by Philo in his own time at about a million* (*in Flaccum*, § 6 [ed. Mangey, ii. 523]). He remarks in this connexion that they had their dwellings 'as far as the borders of Ethiopia' (μέχρι τῶν ὁρίων Αἰθιοπίας). This general statement is confirmed by many special testimonies, of which the following are the most important:—

**a.** *Lower Egypt.* To the east of the Delta, in the nome of Heliopolis (and near to Leontopolis, which must not, however, be confounded with the better known Leontopolis situated much farther to the north), lay the Jewish temple (formerly a temple of Bubastis), which owed its origin to the Jewish high priest Onias in the time of Ptolemy Philometor (Jos. *Ant.* XIII. iii. 2: ἐν Λεόντων πόλει τοῦ Ἡλιοπολίτου; see more fully, regarding this temple, below, p. 107[b]). The region was known as ἡ Ὀνίου χώρα (*Ant.* XIV. viii. 1, *BJ* I. ix. 4). With this we should probably connect the 'vicus Judæorum' mentioned in the *Itinerarium Antonini* (ed. Parthey et Pinder, p. 75). But the 'castra Judæorum' mentioned in the *Notitia Dignitatum Orientis* (ed. Böcking, i. 69) is presumably different, although also situated in the same neighbourhood. At the spot where, according to the statement of distances given in the *Itiner. Anton.*, the 'vicus Judæorum' should be sought, there is still a *Tell el-Jehudiyeh*, in proximity to which a temple of Bubastis had once stood. Another *Tell el-Jehudiyeh*, which, according to Naville, has 'quite the appearance of a fortress,' lies farther south (see Naville, *Seventh Memoir of the Egypt. Explor. Fund*, London, 1890). We should probably identify the first named *Tell el-Jehudiyeh* [not, as Naville, the more southern one] with the building of Onias, and the other with the 'castra Judæorum.' While these places lay to the east of the Delta, Josephus in his account of Cæsar mentions an Ἰουδαίων στρατόπεδον, which, from the context of the narrative, must have lain to the west of it (*Ant.* XIV. viii. 2, *BJ* I. ix. 4). It cannot therefore be the same as the 'castra Judæorum' mentioned in the *Notitia Dignitatum.* The existence of various 'Jews' camps' is readily intelligible in the light of the statements quoted above from pseudo-Aristeas. Likewise in the Delta, in its southern portion, lies Athribis, where, according to an inscription of the Ptolemaic period found there, a certain Ptolemæus, son of Epikydes, chief of the police, acting in conjunction with the resident Jews, built a synagogue to the most high God (Πτολεμαῖος Ἐπικύδου ὁ ἐπιστάτης τῶν φυλακιτῶν καὶ οἱ ἐν Ἀθρίβει Ἰουδαῖοι τὴν προσευχὴν θεῷ ὑψίστῳ, *REJ* xvii. 235–238 = *Bulletin de corresp. hellén.* xiii. 178–182).

**b.** *Middle Egypt.* The more recent papyrus 'finds' have furnished information regarding the early settlement of Jews in Middle Egypt. According to a document of the 3rd cent. B.C. discovered in the nome of Arsinoë (the modern Fayum), there had to be paid for the possession of slaves in the village of Psenyris a duty εις τα αποδοχια της κωμης παρα των Ιουδαιων και των Ελληνων (*The Flinders Petrie Papyri*, ed. by Mahaffy, pt. i. 1891, p. 43). In another, belonging to the same region and dating from 238–237 B.C., we meet with a [παρεπ]ιδημος ος και συριστι Ιωναθας [καλειται] (*op. cit.* pt. ii. 1893, p. 23). Towards the end of the 2nd cent. B.C. a προσευχὴ Ἰουδαίων is mentioned at Arsinoë (*Tebtunis Papyri*, ed. by Grenfell, Hunt, and Smyly, pt. i. 1902, No. 86). At Oxyrhynchus, south of Arsinoë, documents have been found of the Roman Imperial period, in which a 'Jews' lane' (αμφοδος Ιουδαικη) is mentioned (*The Oxyrhynchus Papyri*, ed. by Grenfell and Hunt, pt. i. 1898, No. 100; pt. ii. 1899, No. 335).

**c.** *Upper Egypt.* Here there were Jews settled as early as the time of Jeremiah, for the Pathros of Jer 44[1] is Upper Egypt. A great many tax-receipts from the 2nd cent. B.C., written upon clay tablets (*ostraca*), have been found in the neighbourhood of Thebes. Among the names of the tax-collectors who grant such discharges there are many which are undoubtedly Jewish: *e.g.* Ιωσηπος Αβδιου, Ιωσηπιος, Σαμβαταιος Αβιηλου, Σαμβαθαιος Σολλουμιος, Σιμων Ιαζαρου, Σιμων Αβιηλου (see the collection in Wilcken, *Griechische Ostraka*, vol. i. 1899, p. 523 f.). A papyrus emanating from the same time and place contains a fragment of a letter, from which we learn that a Jew, named Δανοουλος, had failed of his engagement to make delivery of a horse (Grenfell, *An Alexandrian Erotic Fragment*, 1896, p. 75). On tax-receipts of the time of Trajan we repeatedly encounter the name of one Αντωνιος Μαλχαιος who had charge of the harbour dues (?; ὁρμοφυλακία) at Syene, on the southern border of Upper Egypt (Wilcken, *Griechische Ostraka*, ii. Nos. 302–304, cf. i. p. 273). As general evidence of the diffusion of the Jews 'as far as the borders of Ethiopia,' we have the above cited testimony of Philo. The great extent of their numbers in the Thebaid is best shown by the circumstance that in the time of Trajan they rose in arms here, as in the rest of Egypt, against the non-Jewish inhabitants (Euseb. *Chron.*, ed. Schoene, ii. 164 f.).*

6. *CYRENAICA.*—Here too the Jewish Diaspora was present in force. Even Ptolemy Lagi is said to have sent Jewish colonists thither (Jos. *c. Apion.* ii. 4 [Niese, § 44]). The Roman despatch of 1 Mac 15[23] presupposes the presence of Jewish inhabitants in Cyrene. According to Strabo, the population of the latter city in the time of Sulla fell into four classes: citizens, farmers, *metoikoi*, Jews (Strabo *ap.* Jos. *Ant.* XIV. vii. 2: τέτταρες δ' ἦσαν ἐν τῇ πόλει τῶν Κυρηναίων, ἥ τε τῶν πολιτῶν καὶ ἡ τῶν γεωργῶν, τρίτη δ' ἡ τῶν μετοίκων, τετάρτη δ' ἡ τῶν Ἰουδαίων). At that time the Jews already played a prominent part in the disturbances which Lucullus, on the occasion of his incidental presence, had to allay (Strabo, *l.c.*). A Jewish πολίτευμα in the city of Berenike in Cyrenaica is brought to our knowledge by a lengthy inscription (*CIG* 5361; see more fully, below § ii.). Augustus and Agrippa took measures in favour of the Jews of Cyrene (Jos. *Ant.* XVI. vi. 1, 5). We have a number of testimonies in the NT to the presence of Jews in Cyrenaica: Mt 27[32], Mk 15[21], Lk 23[26] (Simon the Cyrenian); Ac 2[10] (Cyrenians present at Jerusalem at the Feast of Pentecost); 6[9] (a synagogue of the Cyrenians at Jerusalem); 11[20] (Cyrenians come from Jerusalem to Antioch); 13[1] (Lucius of Cyrene a prominent member of the church at Antioch). In the time of Vespasian the Jewish *sicarii* also found adherents among their co-religionists in Cyrene (Jos. *BJ* VIII. xi.; *Vita*, 76). The great rising of the Jews in Cyrenaica in the time of Trajan was marked by terrible violence (Dio Cass. lxviii. 32; Euseb. *HE* iv. 2).

7. *NORTH AFRICA.*—Here we can demonstrate the presence of Jews, during the Roman period,

* The diffusion of Semites throughout Egypt in the earlier Ptolemaic period is witnessed to also by a papyrus probably of the year B.C. 240–239, in which a *major-domo* makes a return of the *personnel* of his house for taxation purposes. He enumerates amongst others the γεωργοὶ μισθῷ Χαζαρος Ραγεσοβααλ Ιεαβ Κρατερος Σιταλκες Ματανβααλ (Wilcken, *Griechische Ostraka*, i. 436, and also the correction on p. 823). But the Semites here named may be Phœnicians or Philistines equally well with Jews. For Phœnician inscriptions in Egypt, see *CIS* i. Nos. 97–113; *Répertoire d'épigraphie sémitique*, i. 1901, Nos. 1–4.

from the border of Cyrenaica to the extreme west (cf., especially, Monceaux, 'Les colonies juives dans l'Afrique Romaine' in *REJ* xliv. [1902] 1–28). We do not know when or how they came there. But, as the neighbouring Cyrenaica was largely settled by Jews as early as the Ptolemaic period, the colonization of Africa will also have begun then, at least that of proconsular Africa, and later that of Numidia and Mauretania.

**a.** *Proconsular Africa.* At Carthage there has been discovered an extensive Jewish cemetery, containing more than 100 vaults, each with from 15 to 17 *loculi.* Its Jewish character is shown by the frequent portrayal of the seven-branched candlestick (see Delattre, *Gamart ou la nécropole juive de Carthage*, Lyon, 1895; for Latin inscriptions from this cemetery, see *CIL* viii. Suppl. Nos. 14097–14114). The work *adv. Judæos*, attributed to Tertullian, presupposes the presence of Jews in Carthage. At Hammâm-Lif, not far from Carthage, the foundations of a synagogue of the Roman period have been discovered, upon the mosaic floor of which there are Jewish inscriptions in the Latin language (Renan, *Revue archéol.*, trois. Série, i. [1883] 157–163, iii. [1884] 273–275, plates vii–xi; Kaufmann, *REJ* xiii. [1886] 45–61; Reinach, *ib.* 217–223; *CIL* viii. Suppl. No. 12457). At Oea in Tripolis the Christian bishop in the time of Augustine consulted the Jews there about a passage in Jerome's new translation of the Bible (Augustine, *Epist.* lxxi. 3, 5). On the Peutinger Table there is mention of a place in the same neighbourhood, called 'Judæorum Augusti.'

**b.** *Numidia.* The presence of Jews at Hippo is evident from Augustine, *Serm.* cxcvi. 4. At Cirta there are Latin inscriptions (*CIL* viii. Nos. 7150, 7155, 7530 [cf. Add. p. 965], 7710).

**c.** *Mauretania.* At Sitifis there are Latin inscriptions (*CIL* viii. Nos. 8423, 8499). At Tipasa there was a Jewish synagogue, at Cæsarea the house of a Jewish 'ruler of the synagogue' is mentioned (see the evidence from processes against martyrs in Monceaux, *REJ* xliv. 8). Even in the extreme west of Mauretania, at Volubilis, a Hebrew inscription, probably of the Roman period, has been found (Berger, *Bulletin archéol. du comité des travaux historiques*, 1892, pp. 64–66, pl. xiii).

8. *MACEDONIA AND GREECE.*—The most important testimony is that of Philo, or of the letter of Agrippa to Caligula which he quotes (see above, p. 92[a]). Thessaly, Bœotia, Macedonia, Ætolia, Attica, Argos, Corinth, and, finally, *τὰ πλεῖστα καὶ ἄριστα* **Πελοποννήσου,** are named by him as countries where Jews dwell. If we compare this general statement with the meagre special testimonies that are available, we see how full of *lacunæ* our information is. Interesting dates are furnished by two manumission-deeds from Delphi. In the one a certain Atisidas gives their liberty to three Jewish female slaves (*σώματα γυναικεῖα τρία αἷς ὀνόματα Ἀντιγόνα τὸ γένος Ἰουδαίαν καὶ τὰς θυγατέρας αὐτᾶς Θεοδώραν καὶ Δωροθέαν*); in the other the subject of manumission is described as *σῶμα ἀνδρεῖον ᾧ ὄνομα Ἰουδαῖος τὸ γένος Ἰουδαῖον* (*Sammlung der griechischen Dialekt-Inschriften*, herausg. von Collitz, Bd. ii. Heft 3–5 [1892–1896], Nos. 1722, 2029). Since these documents belong to the first half of the 2nd cent. B.C., we have to do in all probability with prisoners of war of the Maccabæan period who had been sold into slavery in Greece. From 1 Mac 15$^{23}$ it is evident that at the same date there were Jews also in Sparta and Sicyon. In the time of St. Paul there were Jewish synagogues at Philippi, Thessalonica, Berœa, Athens, Corinth (Ac 16$^{2ff.}$ 17$^{1.10.17}$ 18$^{4.7}$). For Jewish-Greek inscriptions at Athens, see *CIAttic.* iii. 2, Nos. 3545, 3546, 3547; at Patræ, *CIG* 9896; in Laconia and Thessalonica, *REJ* x. 77 f.; at Mantinea, *REJ* xxxiv. 148.

In the great islands of Eubœa, Cyprus, and Crete the Jews were very numerous. All three are named by Philo in the letter of Agrippa (see above). For Cyprus, cf. also 1 Mac 15$^{23}$, Ac 4$^{36}$ 11$^{20}$ 13$^{4ff.}$; Jos. *Ant.* XIII. x. 4. In the time of Trajan the Jews in Cyprus massacred thousands of the non-Jewish population and devastated the capital, Salamis. For this they were completely rooted out of the island (Dio Cass. lxviii. 32; Euseb. *Chron.*, ed. Schoene, ii. 164 f.). For Crete, cf. 1 Mac 15$^{23}$ (Gortyna); Jos. *Ant.* XVIII. xii. 1, *BJ* II. vii. 1, *Vita*, 76.

Of the other islands there is mention in 1 Mac 15$^{23}$ of Delos, Samos, Cos, and Rhodes. The three last named were off the coast of Caria. The settlement of Jews in them would thus be connected with their settlement in Caria. At Cos, as early as the time of Mithridates, we hear of great sums of Jewish money being carried off by that monarch (Jos. *Ant.* XIV. vii. 2: *τὰ τῶν Ἰουδαίων ὀκτακόσια τάλαντα*). Rhodes was in the first half of the 1st cent. B.C. the home of two prominent authors who wrote against the Jews, viz. Posidonius and Apollonius Molon (both combated by Josephus in his work *c. Apion.*). In the time of Tiberius a grammarian named Diogenes lived there, whose habit it was to hold disputations only on the Sabbath day (Sueton. *Tiber.* 32). Delos, owing to its political and commercial importance during the Greek period, was a meeting-point for Oriental traders. That Jews with a Greek education were settled there about B.C. 100 at the latest, is shown by two Greek inscriptions emanating from the island of Rheneia (the burying-place of the inhabitants of Delos). The two inscriptions in question are of an imprecatory order, invoking Divine vengeance on the unknown murderers of two maidens. The prayers are unquestionably Jewish; the inscriptions are shown by the character of the writing to be not later than the end of the 2nd or the beginning of the 1st cent. B.C. (cf., on these interesting inscriptions, Deissmann, *Philologus*, lxi. [1902] 252–265). Acts in favour of the Jews of Delos, belonging to the time of Cæsar, are quoted by Josephus in *Ant.* XIV. x. 8 and 14. We have evidence, further, of the presence of Jews at Paros (Jos. *Ant.* XIV. x. 8), Melos (*Ant.* XVII. xii. 1; *BJ* II. vii. 1), and Ægina (*CIG* 9894).

9. *ROME.*—When we pass to Italy, we find that Rome in particular was the home of a Jewish community which could be counted by thousands. According to Valerius Maximus (I. iii. 2), Jews were expelled from Rome by the prætor Hispalus as early as the year B.C. 139, in consequence of their attempts at proselytizing (the passage, which has not survived in the original, reads thus, as extracted by Nepotianus: 'Judæos quoque, qui Romanis tradere sacra sua conati erant, idem Hispalus urbe exterminavit'; or, as given by Paris: 'Idem Judæos, qui Sabazi Jovis cultu Romanos inficere mores conati erant, repetere domos suas coegit' [Sabazius is a Phrygian divinity; there is here manifestly a confusion with Σαβαώθ = Heb. צְבָאוֹת *Ẓĕbā'ôth*]). Since, according to 1 Mac 14$^{24}$ 15$^{15-24}$, at that very time (B.C. 140–139) a Jewish embassy was sent to Rome by the high priest Simon, it would appear as if the propaganda referred to had been the work of parties in the train of this embassy (not the work of the members themselves).

The earliest witness to the existence of a Jewish colony in Italy (*i.e.* probably in Rome) is Cicero, *pro Flacco*, 28, from whom we learn that already in the time of Flaccus (*i.e.* B.C. 62–61) Italy was one of the places from which Jewish money was wont to be sent to Jerusalem. It was just then that the Jewish community at Rome received a large reinforcement through those of their countrymen whom Pompey brought there as prisoners of war (B.C. 61). The latter were sold as slaves, but were soon afterwards set at liberty, as they proved an awkward possession to their masters (Philo, *Legatio ad Gaium*, § 23 [ed. Mangey, ii. 568]). There were many Jews in the audience when Cicero delivered his speech in defence of Flaccus, in the year B.C. 59 (Cicero, *l.c.*). On the death of Cæsar, their great protector, a multitude of Jews continued their lamentations for whole nights beside his funeral pyre (Sueton. *Cæsar*, 84). In the time of Augustus the Jews were already counted by thousands; we are told that a Jewish deputation, which came to Rome after the death of Herod, was joined on its arrival by 8000 Jews (Jos. *Ant.* XVII. xi. 1; *BJ* II. vi. 1). By the time of Tiberius repressive measures had begun. A resolution of the Senate was passed in the year A.D. 19, whereby all the Jews in Rome capable of bearing arms were deported to Sardinia to perform military service there, while the rest were banished from the city (Jos. *Ant.* XVIII. iii. 5; Sueton. *Tiber.* 36; Tac. *Annal.* ii. 85; the last named speaks of banishment from *Italy*). This measure was inspired mainly by Sejanus; after the fall of the latter, in A.D. 31, Tiberius once more adopted a friendly policy towards the Jews (Philo, *Legatio ad Gaium*, § 24 [ed. Mangey, ii. 569]). We may therefore suppose that he granted them permission to return to the city. In any case, they had once more gathered in Rome at the time of Claudius, for he, too, made an attempt to expel them from the city. Suetonius tells us that this step was taken owing to the violent tumults 'impulsore Chresto' [*i.e.* occasioned by the preaching of Christ]. But the edict of banishment, issued probably in the year 49, was not enforced, but restricted simply to a prohibiting of any assembling on the part of the Jews (a decree of expulsion is spoken of in Ac 18[2] and by Sueton. *Claud.* 25; but, according to Dio Cass. lx. 6, Claudius, owing to the difficulty of carrying it into effect, contented himself with withdrawing from the Jews the right of assembly [ἐκέλευσε μὴ συναθροίζεσθαι]. The year 49 is given as the date by Orosius [VII. vi. 15], who appeals, incorrectly indeed, to Josephus). Since the prohibition of assembling was equivalent to a prohibition of worship, the existence of the Jews in Rome was seriously endangered. But they succeeded, we know not how, in surviving even this crisis as well as many later ones, for, as Dio Cassius (xxxvii. 17) sums up their history, 'though often oppressed, they always exhibited the most vigorous power of growth.' Educated Roman society looked down on them with contempt. The satirists, Horace, Persius, Martial, Juvenal, made them the butt of their wit (cf. Hausrath, *Neutest. Zeitgeschichte*[2], iii. 383–392). Yet they constituted a factor of no little importance in public life. Even at the Imperial court they entered into manifold relations, whether as slaves or as officials of higher rank. The Jewish societies of the Αὐγουστήσιοι and the Ἀγριππήσιοι (see, on these, below, § ii.) were in all probability societies formed of placemen of Augustus and Agrippa. The empress Livia had a Jewish slave, Akme (Jos. *Ant.* XVII. v. 7; *BJ* I. xxxii. 6, xxxiii. 7). The emperor Claudius had friendly relations with Alexander [*var. lect.* Lysimachus], the Jewish alabarch of Alexandria, who had served his mother Antonia as minister of finance (Jos *Ant.* XIX. v. 1). At the court of Nero we find a Jewish actor, Alityrus (Jos. *Vita*, 3). Poppæa herself is spoken of as θεοσεβής, and she was always ready to lend her aid in obtaining a favourable response from the emperor to petitions brought to him by Jews (Jos. *Ant.* XX. viii. 11; *Vita*, 3).

The dwellings of the Jews were situated at first and predominantly in the division of the city across the Tiber, which they occupied entirely in the time of Augustus (Philo, *Legatio ad Gaium*, § 23 [ed. Mangey, ii. 568]: τὴν πέραν τοῦ Τιβέρεως ποταμοῦ μεγάλην τῆς Ῥώμης ἀποτομήν, ἣν οὐκ ἠγνόει κατεχομένην καὶ οἰκουμένην πρὸς Ἰουδαίων). But at a later period they spread into other divisions of the city as well. We find them in the Campus Martius and in the very midst of the Roman business world, namely, in the Subura (see below, § ii.). Juvenal makes the jocular assertion that the sacred grove of Egeria before the Porta Capena was let to Jews and swarmed with Jewish beggars (*Sat.* iii. 12–16). As to the internal organization of the communities and the stage of culture they had reached, we derive information from the numerous tomb-inscriptions, composed for the most part in bad Greek but also in Latin, which have been found in the subterranean burying-places before the gates of Rome. These belong to somewhere between the 2nd and 4th cent. A.D. The Greek tomb-inscriptions known up to about fifty years ago are collected in *CIG* iv. Nos. 9901–9926. They emanate probably for the most part from a cemetery before the Porta Portuensis which was discovered in 1602, but whose site is now unknown. Rich materials were supplied by the cemetery discovered some forty years ago in the Vigna Randanini on the Via Appia (cf. Garrucci, *Cimitero degli antichi Ebrei scoperto recentemente in Vigna Randanini*, Roma, 1862; also the same author's *Dissertazioni archeologiche di vario argomento*, vol. ii. Roma, 1865, pp. 150–192). Since then some other cemeteries have been discovered, but these do not contain many inscriptions. Five inscriptions from a cemetery in Porto are given, from communications of de Rossi, by Derenbourg in *Mélanges Renier*, 1887, pp. 437–441. For some Latin ones, see *CIL* vi. Nos. 29756–29763. A complete collection of all the Jewish-Greek and Latin tomb-inscriptions at Rome known down to 1896 is given by Vogelstein-Rieger in *Geschichte der Juden in Rom*, i. [1896] 459–483. See also Berliner, *Geschichte der Juden in Rom*, i. [1893].

10. *THE REST OF ITALY, AND SPAIN, GAUL, GERMANY.*—The presence of Jews in these localities is not for the most part demonstrable before the period of the later empire. Relative antiquity belongs to the Jewish community at Puteoli (Dikæarchia), the principal port for the trade between Italy and the East. In addition to Phœnicians and other Orientals we meet here with Jews as well, at the latest about the beginning of the Christian era (Jos. *Ant.* XVII. xii. 1; *BJ* II. vii. 1). But even in a petty town like Pompeii their presence is demonstrable at the date of the destruction of the place, A.D. 79. The names 'Sodoma' and 'Gomora' are scratched on the wall of a house; and not only 'Maria,' which might be the feminine of Marius, but 'Martha,' occurs. The following also are found on earthen vessels: 'mur[ia] cast[a],' and 'gar[um] cast[um] *or* cast[imoniale],' with which cf. Pliny, *HN* xxxi. 95 (Mau, *Pompeji in Leben und Kunst*, 1900, p. 15 f.).

In the period of the later empire the Jews were specially numerous in *Southern Italy* (see Neubauer, 'The Early Settlement of the Jews in Southern Italy' in *JQR* iv. [1892] 606–625). In Apulia and Calabria during the 4th cent. there were many places where the communal offices could not be properly filled, because the Jewish inhabitants declined to accept them (see the decree of the emperors Arcadius and Honorius [A.D. 398] in *Codex Theodosianus*, XII. i. 158). At Venosa (Venusia in Apulia, the birthplace of Horace) a Jewish catacomb has been discovered, with numerous inscriptions in Greek, Latin, and Hebrew, belonging to somewhere about the 6th cent. A.D.

(Ascoli, *Iscrizioni inedite o mal note greche latine ebraiche di antichi sepolcri giudaici del Napolitano*, Torino, 1880; *CIL* ix. Nos. 6195–6241). During this later period we meet with Jews also at Tarentum, Capua, and Naples, as well as in all the principal towns (Syracuse, Palermo, Messina, Agrigentum) of Sicily.—They do not appear to have been quite so thickly settled in *Northern Italy*. Yet we find them here too in most of the larger towns (Ravenna, Aquileia, Bologna, Brescia, Milan, Genoa).

For the other provinces of the West, *Spain, Gaul, Germany*, the testimonies likewise commence about the 4th cent. A.D. As it does not fall within the scope of the present article to examine all these in detail, we would refer the reader to Friedländer, *Darstellungen aus der Sittengeschichte Roms*, iii. [1871] 511 f.; the same author's *de Judæorum Coloniis*, Königsberg, 1876; and, above all, Th. Reinach, art. 'Judæi' in Daremberg-Saglio's *Dictionnaire des Antiquités grecques et romaines*.

ii. ORGANIZATION OF THE COMMUNITIES.—Everywhere where Jews lived together in any number, they organized themselves into societies, with a view to maintaining their uniqueness, safeguarding their interests, and practising their worship. It is certain that this organization was not everywhere the same. Differences in regard to the possession of political rights, differences in the degree of authority they were allowed to exercise, differences in the stage of culture in the various places where Jews lived, brought with them differences also in the internal organization. Where they formed an imposing political power, the constitution was different from what it was in instances where they formed only petty, modest, private societies. Nevertheless, there are certain common features that run through almost the whole body of the immense Jewish Diaspora. We can prove both these points from a variety of examples, although in many instances we are unable to pursue the details.

We know practically nothing about the constitution of the Jewish communities in the *Euphrates districts* in pre-Talmudic times. Our survey must thus confine itself to the communities within the sphere of the Roman sway.

At *Alexandria* the Jews, owing to their large numbers and their political influence, found themselves in a peculiarly favourable situation. Although they possessed the rights of citizens (see below, § iv.), they constituted a State within a State. Not only had they their own residential quarters, as mentioned above, but they formed an almost independent community, with a kind of monarchical head. Their constitution is thus described by Strabo (*ap.* Jos. *Ant.* XIV. vii. 2): 'But there is also an ethnarch at their head, who rules the people and dispenses justice, and sees that obligations are fulfilled and statutes observed, like the archon of an independent State' (καθίσταται δὲ καὶ ἐθνάρχης αὐτῶν, ὃς διοικεῖ τε τὸ ἔθνος καὶ διαιτᾷ κρίσεις καὶ συμβολαίων ἐπιμελεῖται καὶ προσταγμάτων, ὡς ἂν πολιτείας ἄρχων αὐτοτελοῦς). The maintaining of this independence was materially facilitated during the Imperial period by the circumstance that, from the last of the Ptolemies down to Septimius Severus, Alexandria, unlike nearly all Hellenistic towns, had no city Senate (Spartian, *Severus*, 17; Dio Cassius, li. 17). In the time of Augustus a certain modification of the condition of things appears to have taken place. It is, indeed, noted in the decree of the emperor Claudius (*ap.* Jos. *Ant.* XIX. v. 2) that even Augustus, after the death of the ethnarch who held office during the administration of Aquila [10–11 A.D., see *Ephemeris Epigraphica*, vii. 448 (=*CIL* iii. Suppl. No. 12046)], 'did not prevent the appointment of ethnarchs' (καὶ καθ' ὃν καιρὸν Ἀκύλας ἦν ἐν Ἀλεξανδρείᾳ, τελευτήσαντος τοῦ τῶν Ἰουδαίων ἐθνάρχου, τὸν Σεβαστὸν μὴ κεκωλυκέναι ἐθνάρχας γίγνεσθαι). But the whole object of Claudius in this decree is to insist that even under Augustus the political rights and the religious freedom of the Jews in Alexandria had not been diminished. This is not at all irreconcilable with a certain modification of the internal constitution. But we are expressly told by Philo that such a modification was introduced by Augustus. His statement is to the effect that, when the Jewish *genarch* died, Magius Maximus, who was on the point of undertaking for the second time the office of administrator of Egypt, received instructions from Augustus that a *gerusia* was to be appointed to manage the affairs of the Jews (*in Flaccum*, § 10 [ed. Mangey, ii. 527 f.]: τῆς ἡμετέρας γερουσίας, ἣν ὁ σωτὴρ καὶ εὐεργέτης Σεβαστὸς ἐπιμελησομένην τῶν Ἰουδαικῶν εἵλετο, μετὰ τὴν τοῦ γενάρχου τελευτήν, διὰ τῶν πρὸς Μάγνον Μάξιμον ἐντολῶν, μέλλοντα πάλιν ἐπ' Αἰγύπτου καὶ τῆς χώρας ἐπιτροπεύειν [the traditional Μάγνον of the MSS is incorrect, the name was *Magius* Maximus, see *CIL* ix. No. 1125]). Accordingly, we may probably suppose that the difference between this later and the earlier organization consisted in the substitution of a *gerusia* for the monarchical authority of the ethnarch, or in the setting up of a *gerusia* side by side with him. In favour of the latter supposition it can be urged that the decree of Claudius appears to presuppose the continued existence of ethnarchs even after the interposition of Augustus. At the same time, it is also possible that Claudius only means to say in general that the Jews still continued to have their own superiors (ἐθνάρχαι). The γερουσία and the ἄρχοντες at its head are further mentioned by Philo several times in the same context (§ 10 [ed. Mangey, ii. 528]: τῶν ἀπὸ τῆς γερουσίας τρεῖς ἄνδρες; *ib.* μεταπεμψαμένῳ πρότερον τοὺς ἡμετέρους ἄρχοντας; *ib.* p. 528 f. τοὺς ἄρχοντας, τὴν γερουσίαν; *ib.* § 14 [p. 534] τῶν μὲν ἀρχόντων). Josephus mentions the πρωτεύοντες τῆς γερουσίας (*BJ* VII. x. 1). According to the principal passage of Philo (§ 10 [ed. Mangey, ii. 527 f.]), Flaccus caused thirty-eight members of the *gerusia* to be dragged into the theatre and scourged there. The whole number was, accordingly, greater than this; it may have been seventy, after the model of the Sanhedrin at Jerusalem. In any case the ἄρχοντες were not the whole body of the γερουσία, but only its committee of management. This is clear not only from the statements of Philo, but from the standing usage of the Greek word.*—A widely diffused error is the identification of the Egyptian *alabarch* with the Jewish *ethnarch*. The first named office was a purely civil one, although, of course, it was repeatedly held by Jews of note (see below, § iv.).

* In the above account no regard is paid to a passage in the Letter of Aristeas, which, if its terms were more precise, would supply us with information regarding the organization of the Alexandrian Jews about the year B.C. 200. The passage (*Aristeæ Epist.*, ed. Wendland, § 310) reads: στάντες οἱ ἱερεῖς καὶ τῶν ἑρμηνέων οἱ πρεσβύτεροι καὶ τῶν ἀπὸ τοῦ πολιτεύματος οἵ τε ἡγούμενοι τοῦ πλήθους εἶπον (this, which is the text of our MSS, is reproduced exactly in Euseb. *Præp. Evang.* VIII. v. 6; Jos. *Ant.* XII. ii. 13 [ed. Niese, § 108] gives a free summary of the contents of the passage). Since there is no sufficient reason for deleting the τε before ἡγούμενοι, there are four classes mentioned: (1) the priests, (2) the elders of the interpreters, (3) the elders of the πολίτευμα of the Jews, (4) the ἡγούμενοι τοῦ πλήθους (cf. the explanation of Wendland in *Festschrift für Joh. Vahlen*, 1900, p. 128). The last two classes answer to the γερουσία and the ἄρχοντες as organized by Augustus. It would thus appear as if the organization in those early times had been similar to what it again became subsequent to the time of Augustus, whereas in the intervening period it had more of a monarchical form. There is, indeed, nothing strange in a modification of the constitution having taken place more than once in the course of three centuries. But the statement of pseudo-Aristeas is too vague to build certain conclusions upon.

When we take a survey of what we know otherwise about the constitution of the communities of the Diaspora, certain common features show themselves amidst many local differences.

1. One point in which a difference shows itself concerns *the name for the community*. In so far as the latter forms an independent political corporation, it is called **πολίτευμα.** This term, however, is found only in the case of Alexandria (*Aristeæ Epist.* § 310), and of Berenike in Cyrenaica. In the latter instance the word occurs in a decree set up by the Jewish community in honour of the Roman governor, M. Tittius (*CIG* 5361; see facsimile in Roschach's Catalogue of the Museum of Toulouse [where the inscription now is], *Musée de Toulouse, Catalogue des Antiquités*, 1865, No. 225): ἔδοξε τοῖς ἄρχουσι καὶ τῷ πολιτεύματι τῶν ἐν Βερενίκῃ Ἰουδαίων. The names of the ἄρχοντες who stood at the head of the πολίτευμα are given at the beginning of the decree; there are nine of them. (On the use of πολίτευμα in a similar sense, see Perdrizet, 'Le πολίτευμα des Cauniens à Sidon' in *Revue archéol.*, trois. Série, xxxv. [1899] 42–48; and Wendland, *Aristeæ Epist.*, Index, *s.v.*).

In most towns the Jews formed at first a colony of foreigners side by side with the body of citizens. This is the condition implied in the expressions **κατοικία** (inscription at Hierapolis: δώσει τῇ κατοικίᾳ τῶν ἐν Ἱεραπόλει κατοικούντων Ἰουδαίων; cf. Ramsay, *Expositor*, Feb. 1902, p. 96 f.), **λαός** (inscription at Hierapolis: ἀποτείσει τῷ λαῷ τῶν Ἰουδαίων), **ἔθνος** (inscription at Smyrna: δώσει τῷ ἔθνει τῶν Ἰουδαίων).* These various designations all express the fact that the Jews belonged to a foreign nation, and in Greek towns were counted non-citizens.

The commonest designation, however, especially in later times, is **συναγωγή.** In Greek usage this word occurs only in the sense of 'assembly,' 'festal gathering.' Thus, for instance, *c* 200 B.C., in the so-called Testament of Epikteta (*CIG* 2448 = *Inscriptiones Græcæ insularum maris Ægæi*, fasc. iii. No. 330), the society which is to attend to the hero-cult instituted by Epikteta is called τὸ κοινόν, but the annual gathering of the society συναγωγά (col. iv. line 23 f. τὰν δὲ συναγωγὰν . . . γίνεσθαι ἐμ μηνὶ Δελφινίῳ ἐν τῷ μουσείῳ καθ' ἕκαστον ἔτος ἁμέρας τρεῖς). But in Jewish usage συναγωγή stands for the community as a corporation (in the LXX it mostly represents עֵדָה; see art. CONGREGATION in vol. i.). This term has the most general sense, and hence could be retained even when the Jews through Greek culture and participation in the rights of citizenship had become assimilated to the rest of the inhabitants. They then formed a 'society' for the protection of their religious interests. We can adduce instances of the use of συναγωγή in this sense from inscriptions in Asia as well as at Rome. So, for instance, in Asia: at Phokæa (ἡ συναγωγὴ ἐτείμησεν τῶν Ἰουδαίων Τάτιον Στράτωνος), Akmonia in Phrygia (οὓς τινας καὶ ἡ συναγωγὴ ἐτείμησεν), Pantikapæum (συνεπιτροπεούσης δὲ καὶ τῆς συναγωγῆς τῶν Ἰουδαίων).

At *Rome* the Jews were not, as at Alexandria, organized as a single great corporation, such a thing being apparently not tolerated by the authorities. They had, on the contrary, to content themselves with the more modest position of a number of small private societies. Each society had its special name. The following names are preserved in the inscriptions: **1.** συναγωγὴ Αὐγουστησίων (*CIG* 9902, 9903 = Fiorelli, *Catalogo del Museo Nazionale di Napoli: Iscrizioni latine*, Nos. 1956, 1960; *CIL* vi. No. 29757; *REJ* xlii. 4). **2.** συναγωγὴ Ἀγριππησίων (*CIG* 9907). **3.** 'Synagoga Bolumni' (*CIL* vi. No. 29756). These three societies are named after prominent persons [Bolumnus is = Volumnus], whether for the reason that the members were in the service of these men (cf. Ph 4[22] οἱ ἐκ τῆς Καίσαρος οἰκίας), or because the latter were the patrons of the societies. Since we meet with Ἀγριππήσιοι as well as Αὐγουστήσιοι side by side, the reference is doubtless to the first Augustus and his friend Agrippa. The name assumed by the societies would be retained even after the death of their patrons. Other societies take their name from the quarter of the city of Rome in which their members lived, namely, — **4.** The Καμπήσιοι, called after the Campus Martius (*CIG* 9905 [more correctly in Garrucci, *Dissertazioni*, ii. 188, No. 4]; also Garrucci, *l.c.* ii. 161, No. 10; *CIL* vi. No. 29756 'mater synagogarum Campi et Bolumni'). **5.** The Σιβουρήσιοι, named from the Subura, one of the most frequented quarters in Rome, a centre of trade and business life (*CIG* 6447 = Fiorelli, *Catalogo*, No. 1954). The following additional synagogues are also known:—**6.** A συναγωγὴ Αἰβρέων, presumably that of the Hebrew-speaking Jews (*CIG* 9909; *Mélanges Renier*, 1887, p. 439 = Kaibel, *Inscr. Gr. Sicil. et Ital.*, No. 945). **7.** A συναγωγὴ Ἐλαίας, named after the symbol of the olive tree (*CIG* 9904; de Rossi, *Bullettino di archeol. crist.* v. p. 16). **8.** At Porto a συναγωγὴ τῶν Καρκαρησίων, which derived its name from the occupation of its members, who were *calcarienses*, 'lime-burners' (*Mélanges Renier*, 440; and in *CIG* 9906 we should in all probability read not Καμπησίων but Καλκαρησίων [see Garrucci, *Cimitero*, 38 f.]).

An isolated occurrence of another designation for the Jewish corporation of a city has yet to be mentioned, namely, the '*Universitas* Judæorum qui in Antiochensium civitate constituti sunt.' This is found in an Imperial statute of the year A.D. 213 (*Codex Justin.* I. ix. 1).

2. A pretty extensive uniformity appears to have prevailed in the matter of the organization and titles of the *officials* of the community. Almost everywhere we have evidence that the managing committee bore the name **ἄρχοντες. 1.** For Alexandria we have to refer to the above-cited passages from Philo. **2.** For Berenike in Cyrenaica see in like manner the above-mentioned inscription, according to which there were nine ἄρχοντες at the head of the Jewish πολίτευμα. **3.** At Antioch a Jewish ἄρχων is incidentally mentioned by Josephus (*BJ* VII. iii. 3). **4.** At Tlos in Lycia the office of Jewish archon (ἀρχοντεία) is referred to in an inscription (see above). **5.** For North Africa we have the testimony of Tertullian, who names quite generally, amongst other Jewish offices, that of ἄρχων (*de Corona*, 9: 'Quis denique patriarches, quis prophetes, quis levites aut sacerdos aut *archon*, quis vel postea apostolus aut evangelizator aut episcopus invenitur coronatus?'). It is therefore extremely probable that the archon mentioned in a Latin inscription in Utica is a Jewish one (*CIL* viii. No. 1205, also Addenda, p. 931). **6.** In Italy, too, the title appears to have been in general use. In a Homily for the birthday of St. John (printed among the works of Chrysostom in editions prior to that of Montfaucon, *e.g.* ed. Paris, t. ii., 1687), which takes account of the conditions of Italy in the time of the later empire, it is made a matter of reproach to the Jews that, in opposition to the law of God, they begin the year, not in spring but in the month of September: 'mensem Septembrem ipsum novum annum nuncupant, *quo et mense magistratus sibi designant, quos Archontas vocant.*' When we turn to the Jewish inscriptions of Italy we meet with the title at Capua (*CIL* x. No. 3905 'Alfius Juda arcon arcosynagogus'), at Porto near Rome (Kaibel, *Inscr. Gr. Sicil. et Ital.*, No. 949 Κλαύδιος Ἰωσῆς ἄρχων), and with special frequency at Rome itself (*CIG* 9906, 6447, 6337;

* In the case of the inscriptions that have been already quoted in § i. we give here only the references.

Garrucci, *Cimitero*, 35, 51, 61, 67, also the same author's *Dissertazioni*, ii. 158, No. 4, 164, Nos. 15, 16, 17, 18; de Rossi, *Bullettino*, v. 16).—At Rome each of the societies, it is certain, had its own archons. They were elected, according to the Homily just named, annually in the month of September. There might be re-election (δὶς ἄρχων, *CIG* 9910; Garrucci, *Cimitero*, 47); nay, it would appear as if an archon might be elected for life, for this is the probable meaning of the repeatedly recurring διὰ βίου (*CIL* x. No. 1893 'Ti. Claudius Philippus dia viu et gerusiarches'; *CIG* 9907 Ζώσιμος διὰ βίου συναγωγῆς 'Αγριππησίων). Cf., in general, Wesseling, *De Judæorum archontibus ad inscriptionem Berenicensem*, 1738; Schürer, *Die Gemeindeverfassung der Juden in Rom in der Kaiserzeit nach den Inschriften dargestellt*, 1879.

It is only for Italy that the presence of the title **γερουσιάρχης** or **γερουσιάρχων** is demonstrable. The first of these forms is found in the tomb-inscriptions at Rome (*CIG* 9902=Fiorelli, *Catalogo*, No. 1956; Garrucci, *Cimitero*, 51, 62, 69, *Dissertazioni*, ii. 183, No. 27) and in the neighbourhood of Naples (*CIL* x. No. 1893); the other occurs at Venosa (*CIL* ix. Nos. 6213, 6221). The title can have no other meaning than 'president of the *gerusia*.' We thus learn from it, what without this evidence might have been assumed, that the communities had not only ἄρχοντες but also a γερουσία. The fact that, in spite of this, the title πρεσβύτερος nowhere occurs in the numerous tomb-inscriptions at Rome, is instructive. The elders were not officials in the proper sense, they were the confidential advisers of the community. Hence πρεσβύτερος was not a title. It is not till a very late period that we find it so employed (*e.g.* at Venosa, and that even in the case of women, *CIL* ix. Nos. 6209, 6226, 6230, cf. also *Codex Theodosianus*, XVI. viii. 2, 13, 14).

The office of **ἀρχισυνάγωγος** (EV 'ruler of the synagogue') was quite generally established. We can prove its existence for all the leading spheres of the Jewish Diaspora. **1.** Egypt (Hadrian's alleged letter to Servianus *ap.* Vopiscus, *Vita Saturnini*, 8). **2.** Asia Minor: Antioch in Pisidia (Ac 13[15]), Cilicia (Epiphan. *Hær.* xxx. 11), Smyrna (inscription in *REJ* vii. 161 f.), Myndos in Caria (*REJ* xlii. 1–4), Akmonia in Phrygia (see above, p. 94[a], for inscription; in this instance an ἀρχισυνάγωγος διὰ βίου). **3.** Greece: Corinth (Ac 18[8. 17]), Ægina (*CIG* 9894). **4.** Italy: Rome (*CIG* 9906; Garrucci, *Cimitero*, 67), Capua (*CIL* x. No. 3905), Venosa (*CIL* ix. Nos. 6201, 6205, 6232), Brescia (Kaibel, *Inscr. Gr. Sicil. et Ital.*, No. 2304). **5.** Africa: Hammâm-Lif near Carthage (inscription on the mosaic pavement of the synagogue), Cæsarea in Mauretania (*Acta Marcianæ*, iv. 1; *REJ* xliv. 8). **6.** The Roman empire in general (*Codex Theodosianus*, XVI. viii. 4, 13, 14).

The duty of the ἀρχισυνάγωγος was to take charge of the public worship. Since there was no official preacher in Jewish communities, any qualified member of the congregation being permitted to read the Scripture lessons or deliver an address or lead in prayer, it was necessary to have an official to direct and watch over the exercise of this freedom by the members. This was the ἀρχισυνάγωγος (Heb. רֹאשׁ הַכְּנֶסֶת). He had to fix on the reader of the lessons and the leader in prayer, and to invite competent persons to address the congregation (Ac 13[15]). To him fell the general duty of seeing that nothing unseemly took place in the synagogue (Lk 13[14]), and he had doubtless to take care also that the synagogue buildings were kept in proper repair. He belonged to the number of the ἄρχοντες of the community, but his office was a more special one than that of the ἄρχοντες in general; hence the two offices are named side by side as distinct (*CIG* 9906; Garrucci, *Cimitero*, 67; *CIL* x. No. 3905; Ac 14[2] [according to the text of D: οἱ δὲ **ἀρχισυνάγωγοι** τῶν 'Ιουδαίων καὶ οἱ **ἄρχοντες** τῆς συναγωγῆς]). Since we meet with a γερουσιάρχης side by side with the ἀρχισυνάγωγος in the tomb-inscriptions of Rome and Venosa, those two offices also are to be regarded as distinct. That is to say, the ἀρχισυνάγωγος was not, as such, at the same time the head and president of the γερουσία. It is quite possible, however, that outside Italy [it is only in this country that we hear of a γερουσιάρχης] both offices were united in one person.

Finally, we encounter pretty frequently in the inscriptions the titles *pater synagogæ* and *mater synagogæ*:—πατὴρ συναγωγῆς (*CIG* 9904, 9905, 9908, 9909; Garrucci, *Cimitero*, 52, *Dissertazioni*, ii. 161, No. 10; *Mélanges Renier*, 440); 'pater synagogæ' (*CIL* viii. No. 8499; *Codex Theodosianus*, XVI. viii. 4); πατὴρ τῶν 'Εβρέων (*Mélanges Renier*, 439=Kaibel, *Inscr. Gr. Sicil. et Ital.*, No. 945); πατὴρ τοῦ στέματος (*CIG* 9897); πατὴρ λαοῦ διὰ βίου (*REJ* xxxiv. 148); 'pater,' without any addition (Garrucci, *Dissertazioni*, ii. 164, No. 18; *CIL* ix. Nos. 6220, 6221); 'mater synagogæ' (*CIL* v. No. 4411, vi. No. 29756). The very circumstance that the title is found in the feminine as well as the masculine form, makes it probable that it does not stand for a communal *office*, strictly so called. Nor are we to understand it of the patron of the community; it was simply a title of honour given to aged members who had deserved well of the community (cf. the statement of ages in *CIG* 9904 ἔτων ἑκατῶν (*sic*) δέκα, and *CIL* vi. No. 29756 'quæ bixit an. lxxxvi. meses vi.').

The employment of the terms ἄρχοντες and γερουσία shows that the constitution of the Jews in the Diaspora *was based on the communal constitution of the Greek cities*. There are other traces besides this of the strong influence exercised by this model upon the external arrangements of the Jewish communities. Like the Greek communes, the Jewish communities honoured deserving men and women by the bestowal of a wreath and of the *proedria*. Thus the community of Phokæa honoured a woman who had taken upon herself the cost of building the synagogue, χρυσῷ στεφάνῳ καὶ προεδρίᾳ (see above, § i.). The Jewish *strategos* Chelkias was likewise honoured with a golden wreath (*Archiv für Papyrusforschung*, i. [1900] 48–56; *REJ* xl. [1900] 50–54). The community of Berenike resolved regarding the Roman governor, who had shown himself friendly to the Jews, στεφανοῦν ὀνομαστὶ καθ' ἑκάστην σύνοδον καὶ νουμηνίαν στεφάνῳ ἐλαΐνῳ καὶ λημνίσκῳ (*CIG* 5361). At Alexandria honorific decrees and gifts of this kind, including also such as related to the emperors, were exhibited in the vestibules of the synagogues (Philo, *in Flaccum*, § 7 [ed. Mangey, ii. 524]). Hence Philo complains that, when the synagogues were wrecked by the Alexandrian mob, 'even the shields and golden wreaths and steles and inscriptions in honour of the emperors' perished in the general destruction (*Legatio ad Gaium*, § 20 [ed. Mangey, ii. 565]: καὶ σιωπῶ τὰς συγκαθαιρεθείσας καὶ συμπρησθείσας τῶν αὐτοκρατόρων τιμὰς ἀσπίδων καὶ στεφάνων ἐπιχρύσων καὶ στηλῶν καὶ ἐπιγραφῶν).

The influence of Greek processes of law shows itself in the Jewish legal instruments affecting manumission of slaves, found at Pantikapæum (Latyschev, *Inscriptiones antiquæ oræ septentr. Ponti Euxini*, Nos. 52, 53).—In Asia Minor there was a widely recognized right to exact a money penalty for the unauthorized use of a grave. Hence in a multitude of tomb-inscriptions we find a warning against such an act, with a specification of the fine that would be incurred. Penal cautions of this kind, couched exactly in the terms usual in other quarters, may be read also on Jewish tombs at Smyrna, Hierapolis in Phrygia, Tlos in Lycia, Korykos in Cilicia (see above, § i.). The fines are to be paid either to the Imperial *fiscus* or to the Jewish community (τῷ ἔθνει τῶν Ἰουδαίων [at Smyrna], τῷ λαῷ τῶν Ἰουδαίων, τῇ κατοικίᾳ τῶν Ἰουδαίων [at Hierapolis]), or to both.—To Greek influence should probably be attributed also the bestowal of titles and honorary offices upon women. In Greek communes and societies we encounter women with such titles as πρύτανις, στεφανηφόρος, γυμνασίαρχος, ἀγωνοθέτις, δεκάπρωτος; so amongst the Jews we have ἀρχισυνάγωγος (at Smyrna [*REJ* vii. 161 ff.], and Myndos in Caria [*REJ* xlii. 1–4]), πρεσβυτέρα, and 'mater synagogæ' (see above).

But, in spite of this extensive adoption of Greek forms, the influence of Greece upon the Jewish communities must not be exaggerated. Not only their religion, but even their civil law was retained by them as far as possible. Everywhere they laid the greatest stress upon justice being administered in the bosom of Jewish communities κατὰ τοὺς πατρίους νόμους (Jos. *Ant.* XIV. x. 17). And this jurisdiction of their own was to a large extent conceded to them by the heathen authorities.

iii. Toleration and Recognition by the State Authorities.—The framework of political rights into which the Jewish communities had to fit themselves, varied in different places and at different times. We may distinguish some three forms under which the communities in the Diaspora attained to a political existence; and all three have more or less numerous analogues.

1. The nearest analogy is that of the *settlements of foreigners*, especially Orientals, in the great trading cities of the Græco-Roman world. In all the great seaports of the Mediterranean, during the era of Hellenism we meet with Egyptian, Phœnician, Syrian traders, who not only carry on their business in passing, but are permanently settled there in greater or smaller numbers, and have formed themselves into close corporations for the defence of their common interests. They built their temples, maintained their religious service, and supported one another in their material interests. Settlements of this kind are known to us from inscriptions, particularly at Athens (Egyptians, Κιτιεῖς from Cyprus, Sidonians), Delos (Tyrians, Berytenses, Egyptians), Puteoli (Tyrians, Berytenses). The members of the corporation lived in the city as strangers (non-citizens), but their society enjoyed toleration and recognition from the State authorities. To this class belonged, without any doubt, the oldest settlements of the Jews in many places. They formed a κατοικία, *i.e.* a colony of foreigners, separate from the political commune.

2. Another analogy is presented by the *private societies* which existed in enormous numbers and in a great variety of forms throughout the whole of the Græco-Roman world. Religious or commercial interests, or both together, led in ancient as in later times to the forming of a great many 'unions' (θίασοι, ἔρανοι, *collegia*), which had their own administration of funds, and exercised a certain discipline over their members. In looking after their own affairs they occupied an independent position in relation to the political commune similar to that of the colonies of foreigners just described, but were distinguished from them by the circumstance that (at least as a rule and for the most part) they consisted of natives, whether citizens and freedmen, or non-citizens and slaves. To this class belong most of the Jewish communities in later times. For the more the Jews became assimilated to their surroundings, the more they passed from the position of foreigners to that of homeborn, particularly in instances where they possessed the rights of citizenship. With all this, however, they appear as a rule to have retained a certain position of isolation, for the amount of jurisdiction which, with the consent of the city authorities, they exercised within their own circle was, so far as we know, for the most part greater than was conceded to other religious or trades unions.*

3. A third analogue to the communities of the Jewish Diaspora is seen in the *corporations of Greeks and Romans in non-Greek or non-Roman countries*. The Greeks, in view of the wide diffusion of Hellenism, had less occasion for forming such corporations. These were much commoner where Romans were concerned. As the ruling nation, the Romans outside Italy everywhere laid claim to a unique position. They were subject neither to taxation by the communes nor to the jurisdiction of the city authorities, but formed independent bodies alongside of the communal societies of the particular cities in which they lived. Examples of this kind are to be met with in great numbers throughout the whole extent of the Roman Empire (Mommsen, *CIL* iii. Suppl. p. 1306, on No. 7240; Mitteis, *Reichsrecht und Volksrecht in den östlichen Provinzen des römischen Kaiserreichs*, 1891, pp. 143–158). It is with this entirely independent position which these associations held in or rather alongside the communes, that we may compare the position of the Jews in Alexandria and in the city of Cyrene as described by Strabo (*ap.* Jos. *Ant.* XIV. vii. 2). For here they were not subject, as would appear, to the rule of the communal authorities, but constituted an independent corporation side by side with the rest of the body of citizens. Their independence thus went beyond what was enjoyed by the first two classes above described.

A uniform presupposition in all these political regulations was *State toleration of the Jewish cultus*. This was enjoyed by the communes almost everywhere and at most periods of time. In the empires of the Ptolemies and the Seleucids the religious freedom of the Jews was a matter of course. But the early Ptolemies and Seleucids also conferred important political rights upon their Jewish subjects (see below, § iv.).† Antiochus the Great protected the cultus at Jerusalem by royal statutes (Jos. *Ant.* XII. iii. 3, 4). [The genuineness of these is, indeed, disputed (see Büchler, *Die Tobiaden und die Oniaden*, 1899, pp. 143–171; Willrich, *Judaica*, 1900, pp. 48 f., 58–60), but on what appear to the present writer insufficient grounds. The genuineness is held, amongst others, by Ed. Meyer, *Die Entstehung des Judenthums*, 1896, pp. 66, 68]. The persecution of the

* Mommsen (*Histor. Zeitschrift*, lxiv. [1890] 421–426) has contended that it was only down to the fall of Jerusalem that the Jews were regarded as a people (*gens*, ἔθνος), and that after that event 'the place of the privileged *nation* was taken by the privileged *confession*.' That is to say, in the earlier period political privileges had been accorded to all who were Jews by birth, and to them alone, whereas in the later they belonged to all who professed the Jewish religion, and to them alone. But, in the opinion of the present writer, this is pushing an observation which is correct in itself to far too sharp a point, when an actual juristic formula is thus arrived at. Even during the period of the late empire the Jews were still in many instances regarded as a 'people' (the inscription of Smyrna τῷ ἔθνει τῶν Ἰουδαίων dates at the earliest from the 3rd cent. A.D., and even the inscriptions of Hierapolis must be placed subsequent to A.D. 70). And it was just the later emperors who sought to prevent the 'confession' from being extended beyond the circle of the Jewish nation; that is to say, they granted privileges only to the people, and not to the confession. Mommsen's view, however, will be found correct to this extent, that the Jews, as time went on, advanced more and more from the first of the above two classes to the second.

† Cf., on the friendly disposition of the early Ptolemies to the Jews, in general, Jos. *c. Apion.* ii. 4, 5.—A Ptolemy once actually granted the right of asylum to a Jewish *proseuche* (*CIL* iii. Suppl. No. 6583 Βασιλεὺς Πτολεμαῖος Εὐεργέτης τὴν προσευχὴν ἄσυλον. The monarch referred to is probably Ptolemy III., for had it been Euergetes II. = Ptolemy VII., we should have expected his consort to be named along with him).

Jews by Antiochus Epiphanes was quite an exceptional phenomenon. Pre-eminent as a friend of the Jews was Ptolemy VI. (Philometor), who even permitted a Jewish temple to be built in Egypt (see below, § v.). The hostile attitude to the Jews assumed by Ptolemy VII. (Physcon) was due, not to their religious but their political partisanship (Jos. *c. Apion.* ii. 5).

The free exercise of their religion was expressly allowed to the Jews also by the Roman legislation, which safeguarded it from any attempts at suppression by the Greek communes. It was especially to Cæsar and Augustus that the Jews were indebted for their formal recognition in the Roman Empire. A whole series of acts have been preserved for us by Josephus (*Ant.* XIV. x., XVI. vi.), partly resolutions of the Senate, partly edicts of Cæsar and Augustus, partly those of Roman officials or of communal authorities of the same date. These all have the same purpose, namely, to secure for the Jews the free exercise of their religion and the maintenance of their privileges (cf., on these acts, especially the investigation of Mendelssohn in *Acta Societatis Phil. Lips.*, ed. Ritschelius, v. [1875] 87–288; also *Theol. Literaturzeitung*, 1876, cols. 390–396; Niese in *Hermes*, xi. [1876] 466–488). While Cæsar prohibited in general all *collegia* except those that had existed from remote antiquity, the Jewish communities were expressly excluded from this prohibition (Jos. *Ant.* XIV. x. 8: *καὶ γὰρ Γάιος Καῖσαρ ὁ ἡμέτερος στρατηγὸς καὶ ὕπατος ἐν τῷ διατάγματι κωλύων θιάσους συνάγεσθαι κατὰ πόλιν* **μόνους τούτους οὐκ ἐκώλυσεν** *οὔτε χρημάτων συνεισφέρειν οὔτε σύνδειπνα ποιεῖν*). We find, for instance, a Roman official appealing to this decree in warning the authorities of Paros not to interfere with the Jews in the practice of their religious observances (Jos. *l.c.*). It is likewise to the influence of Cæsar that we should probably trace the four decrees quoted by Josephus, *Ant.* XIV. x. 20–24. The object, direct or indirect, of all of them is to guarantee to the Jews of Asia Minor (Laodicea, Miletus, Halicarnassus, Sardis) the unimpeded exercise of their religion. After Cæsar's death, the two contending parties vied with one another in maintaining the privileges of the Jews. On the one hand, Dolabella, the partisan of Antony, who made himself master of Asia Minor in the year B.C. 43, confirmed to the Jews the exemption from military service and the religious freedom granted them by former governors (*Ant.* XIV. x. 11, 12). On the other hand, M. Junius Brutus, who in the spring of the year 42 was making warlike preparations in Asia Minor against Antony and Octavianus, persuaded the Ephesians to adopt a resolution that the Jews were not to be interfered with in their observance of the Sabbath and their other religious practices (*Ant.* XIV. x. 25).

All this had the effect of bringing about a legal standing, in virtue of which *Judaism was a 'religio licita' throughout the whole of the Roman Empire* (Tertull. *Apolog.* 21, 'insignissima religio, certe licita' [the expression, by the way, is not a technical one in Roman law, which speaks of '*collegia* licita']). That, amongst others, the Jews in the city of Rome enjoyed this legal standing, is specially testified by Philo for the time of Augustus (*Legatio ad Gaium*, § 23 [ed. Mangey, ii. 568 f.]). It is true, however, that down to the 2nd cent. A.D. foreign *sacra* could be practised only outside the 'pomerium.'

The State recognition of the Jewish communities is essentially connected with two important concessions: *the right of administering their own funds, and jurisdiction over their own members.* The former of these had a special importance, owing to the collecting and transmitting of the dues paid to the temple at Jerusalem. The governor Flaccus, a contemporary of Cicero, had interfered with this (Cic. *in Flaccum*, 28; see the text of the passage quoted above, § i.). The communal authorities of Asia likewise appear, even after the edicts of Cæsar's time and in spite of these, to have continued to act in a similar way. The decrees of the time of Augustus accordingly bear chiefly upon this point. As Augustus permitted the export of sums of money from Rome itself (Philo, *Legatio ad Gaium*, § 23 [ed. Mangey, ii. 568 f.]), it was impressed upon the communes of Asia Minor and Cyrene that in this matter they must put no obstacle in the way of the Jews (Jos. *Ant.* XVI. vi. 2–7; Philo, *Legatio ad Gaium*, § 40 [ed. Mangey, ii. 592]).

Of equal importance for the Jewish communities was *the possession of a jurisdiction of their own.* Since the Mosaic law has regard not only to the performance of the cultus but also to the relations of civil life, placing the latter under the control of a Divine law, it was intolerable to the Jewish conscience that Jews should be judged by any code of laws but their own. Wherever the Jews came they brought their own system of law with them, and executed justice, according to its standard, in the case of their fellow-members. It may be regarded as probable that the employment of their own code in *civil processes* was everywhere sanctioned by the State authorities, in so far, that is to say, as complaints of Jews against one another were concerned. Not only must this have self-evidently been the case at Alexandria, but it is witnessed to also for Asia Minor by a despatch of Lucius Antonius (governor of the Province of Asia, B.C. 50–49) to the authorities of Sardis (Jos. *Ant.* XIV. x. 17: *Ἰουδαῖοι πολῖται ἡμέτεροι προσελθόντες μοι ἐπέδειξαν αὑτοὺς σύνοδον ἔχειν ἰδίαν κατὰ τοὺς πατρίους νόμους ἀπ' ἀρχῆς καὶ τόπον ἴδιον, ἐν ᾧ τά τε πράγματα καὶ τὰς πρὸς ἀλλήλους ἀντιλογίας κρίνουσιν· τοῦτό τε αἰτησαμένοις ἵν' ἐξῇ ποιεῖν αὐτοῖς, τηρῆσαι καὶ ἐπιτρέψαι ἔκρινα*). The terms of this despatch show that even those Jews who possessed the Roman citizenship (*πολῖται ἡμέτεροι*), and as Roman citizens could have sought redress before the *conventus civium Romanorum*, preferred to bring their disputes before the Jewish tribunal (*σύνοδος*, *conventus*) for decision. Even in the legislation of the later Imperial period, this Jewish jurisdiction continued to be recognized in civil cases (*Codex Theodosianus*, II. i. 10 [Decree of the emperors Arcadius and Honorius of the year 398]: 'Sane si qui per compromissum, ad similitudinem arbitrorum, apud Judæos vel patriarchas ex consensu partium in civili duntaxat negotio putaverint litigandum, sortiri eorum judicium jure publico non vetentur: eorum etiam sententias provinciarum judices exsequantur, tamquam ex sententia cognitoris arbitri fuerint attributi').

A jurisdiction of their own in *criminal cases*, in the complete sense of the expression, was certainly not conceded to the Jews in most places. On the other hand, not only do we meet with undoubted instances of the exercise of a *correctional police authority* (see Mommsen, *Zeitschrift für die Neutest. Wissenschaft*, ii. [1901] 88 f.), but this would even appear to have been permitted by the State authorities. It is from this point of view that we are to understand how Saul of Tarsus applied to the Sanhedrin at Jerusalem for full powers to punish Jewish Christians living outside Palestine (Ac $9^2$ $22^{19}$ $26^{11}$). He himself was afterwards as a Christian scourged five times by the Jews (2 Co $11^{24}$); in these instances we are certainly to think, not of Palestinian but of foreign Jewish communities. At Corinth the proconsul Gallio leaves it to the Jews to proceed against St. Paul according to their own judgment, for he himself will not act as judge when an offence against the Jewish religion is concerned (Ac 18[12-16]).

In addition to the freedom of initiative secured for the Jews in the instances we have just described, the Roman toleration paid a very large regard to their religious sensibilities. One chief difficulty concerned the question of *military service*. Such service was quite impossible for a Jew in a non-Jewish army, for on the Sabbath day he might neither bear arms nor march more than 2000 cubits. This question became a specially practical one when, on the outbreak of the civil war between Cæsar and Pompey in the year B.C. 49, the party of Pompey commenced the enrolment of troops on a large scale all over the East. In the Province of Asia alone the consul Lentulus raised two legions of Roman citizens (Cæsar, *Bell. Civ.* iii. 4). Amongst these were included the resident Jews who possessed the Roman citizenship. At their own request, however, Lentulus exempted them from military service, and gave his conscription agents everywhere instructions to the same effect (Jos. *Ant.* XIV. x. 13, 14, 16, 18, 19). Six years later (B.C. 43) Dolabella, with express appeal to the earlier edicts, confirmed the privilege of ἀστρατεία to the same Jews (*Ant.* XIV. x. 11, 12). Further privileges enjoyed by the Jews were the following :—**1.** By a statute of Augustus they were exempted from citation before a court on the Sabbath day (*Ant.* XVI. vi. 2, 4). **2.** If a public payment of money or delivery of corn fell on a Sabbath, the Jews were to receive their share on the following day (Philo, *Legatio ad Gaium*, § 23 [ed. Mangey, ii. 569]). **3.** Instead of the oil furnished by the communes, the use of which was forbidden to the Jews, they received a money equivalent (Jos. *Ant.* XII. iii. 1).

The whole political standing above described was never in later times essentially and permanently altered. The measures taken by Tiberius against the Roman Jews affected only the city of Rome. The great question of the *cult of the Emperor*, which afterwards became the main occasion of the bloody persecutions of the Christians, led in the case of the Jews to a merely transitory and local persecution. Augustus and Tiberius were, indeed, gratified when the provincials voluntarily offered them divine honours after the Greek fashion, but they did not demand that this should be done. Caligula was the first to make such a demand universally. Since the Jews on account of their religion could not comply with it, a bloody persecution began at Alexandria, due at first to the anti-Jewish mob, but afterwards carried on by the governor himself. But Claudius hastened to issue an edict of toleration by which all the rights and privileges of the Jews were restored (Jos. *Ant.* XIX. v. 2–3). No subsequent attempt was ever made to compel the Jews to take part in the cult of the Emperor. It came to be regarded as an ancient privilege that they were exempt from this. They had thus the advantage over the Christians in that their privileges had been long established before the cult of the Emperor became the State religion, and was demanded of subjects as a test of loyalty. While the Christians had to atone by bloody martyrdom for their refusal to sacrifice to the Emperor, no such demand was ever made upon the Jews.

It is true, indeed, that certain vacillations in their attitude to the Jews are found on the part of the Emperors. Claudius himself felt compelled to take measures against the Jews in the city of Rome. But these were local, and were not thoroughly carried out. The great war of Vespasian and the destruction of the temple at Jerusalem led, in the case of the Jews of the Diaspora, to the result that the former temple tax of two drachmæ had now to be paid to the temple of Jupiter Capitolinus (Jos. *BJ* VII. vi. 6; Dio Cassius, lxvi. 7). This must certainly have been repugnant to the feelings of the Jews. But their religious freedom was not otherwise interfered with by Vespasian. Their political rights were even expressly protected by him, for instance in Alexandria and Antioch (*Ant.* XII. iii. 1, *BJ* VII. v. 2). Domitian exacted the two drachmæ tax with the utmost rigour (Sueton. *Domit.* 12), and inflicted severe penalties on any Romans who passed over to Judaism (Dio Cass. lxvii. 14). But the existing rights of the Jews were not annulled. Under Nerva a milder condition of things was inaugurated, in so far as he forbade any one to be accused for 'living in the Jewish manner' (Dio Cass. lxviii. 1). By this order the 'calumnia fisci Judaici,' *i.e.* accusations laid by informers in the interests of the Jewish *fiscus*, was abolished (cf. coins inscribed 'calumnia fisci Judaici sublata').

A violent shock to the existing condition of things was given by the great Jewish revolts under Trajan and Hadrian. The latter was due, not wholly but partially, to Hadrian's *prohibition of circumcision* (Spartian, *Hadrian.* 14). This prohibition, so far as we can learn, was quite a general one, issued on grounds of humanity, and not specially directed against the Jews. But the carrying out of such a decree would have been tantamount to a destruction of real legal Judaism. Hadrian's immediate successor, Antoninus Pius, however, while he retained the prohibition in other instances, once more granted the Jews permission to circumcise their children (*Digest.* xlviii. 8, 11 pr.). Similarly, Septimius Severus forbade only the formal passing over to Judaism (Spartian, *Sept. Sev.* 17). Of Alexander Severus we are expressly told that he 'Judæis privilegia reservavit' (Lamprid. *Alex. Sev.* 22). The policy of the Christian Emperors was not always the same, but in general was directed towards preventing the spread of Judaism, without annulling its existing rights.

iv. RIGHTS OF CITIZENSHIP, AND SOCIAL STANDING.—It has already been remarked above that the Jews as a rule, at least in pre-Christian times, lived in Greek cities as *foreign settlers*, like the Egyptians, Phœnicians, or Syrians. That is to say, they were *not citizens*, and had no share in the management of municipal affairs. But there were not a few towns where they possessed the citizenship. This was the case especially in such cities as had been newly founded, or whose constitution had been reorganized during the Greek period. To the category of the recently founded belong pre-eminently the two capitals of the empires of the Ptolemies and the Seleucids, namely, Alexandria and Antioch.

At *Alexandria* the Jews, we are assured by Josephus, were placed by Alexander the Great on a footing of equality with the Macedonians from the very first founding of the city (*c. Apion.* ii. 4: εἰς κατοίκησιν δὲ αὐτοῖς ἔδωκεν τόπον Ἀλέξανδρος καὶ ἴσης παρὰ τοῖς Μακεδόσι τιμῆς ἐπέτυχον . . . καὶ μέχρι νῦν αὐτῶν ἡ φυλὴ τὴν προσηγορίαν εἶχεν Μακεδόνες). In another passage Josephus asserts that Alexander, by way of rewarding them for their services against the Egyptians, gave them equal rights with the Hellenes, and that the Diadochi further permitted them to call themselves Macedonians (*BJ* II. xviii. 7: Ἀλέξανδρος . . . ἔδωκεν τὸ μετοικεῖν κατὰ τὴν πόλιν ἐξ ἰσοτιμίας [*var. lect.* ἰσουμοίρας, probably a corruption of ἰσομοιρίας] πρὸς τοὺς Ἕλληνας. διέμεινεν δ᾽ αὐτοῖς ἡ τιμὴ καὶ παρὰ τῶν διαδόχων, οἳ . . . καὶ χρηματίζειν ἐπέτρεψαν Μακεδόνας). In the decree of the emperor Claudius, quoted by Josephus (*Ant.* XIX. v. 2), it is said that the Jews had been settled side by side with the Alexandrians from the first, and that they had obtained equal political rights 'from the kings' (ἴσης πολιτείας παρὰ τῶν βασιλέων τετευχότας). These rights were expressly confirmed to them by Cæsar. A brass pillar set up by the latter in Alexandria proclaimed that the Jews were Alexandrian citizens (*Ant.* XIV. x. 1, *c. Apion.* ii. 4). Philo likewise notes that the Jews had the legal standing of Ἀλεξανδρεῖς and not that of the Αἰγύπτιοι (*in Flaccum*, § 10 [ed. Mangey, ii. 528]). The annulment of their rights during the persecution under Flaccus was merely temporary, for Claudius soon hastened to restore their ancient privileges (*Ant.* XIX. v. 2). Even after the great war of A.D. 70 the petition of the Alexandrians, that the Jews should be deprived of the citizenship, was not granted (*Ant.* XII. iii. 1).

A similar condition of things prevailed at *Antioch.* Here, too, from the founding of the city by Seleucus I. (Nikator), the Jews had received the same rights of citizenship as the Macedonians and Hellenes (*Ant.* XII. iii. 1: Σέλευκος ὁ Νικάτωρ ἐν αἷς ἔκτισεν πόλεσιν ἐν τῇ Ἀσίᾳ καὶ τῇ κάτω Συρίᾳ καὶ ἐν αὐτῇ τῇ μητροπόλει Ἀντιοχείᾳ πολιτείας αὐτοὺς ἠξίωσεν καὶ τοῖς ἐνοικισθεῖσιν ἰσοτίμους ἀπέφηνεν Μακεδόσιν καὶ Ἕλλησιν, ὡς τὴν πολιτείαν ταύτην ἔτι καὶ νῦν διαμένειν; and to a similar effect *c. Apion.* ii. 4 [Niese, § 39]). In this city also their privileges were set forth on brass tablets (*BJ* VII. v. 2 [Niese, § 110]). In one passage Josephus expresses himself as if these rights were first conferred upon them by the successors of Antiochus Epiphanes (*BJ* VII. iii. 3). But probably he is thinking of a restoration of their privileges after the period of persecution under Epiphanes. When in the time of Vespasian the Antiochenes begged that the Jews might be expelled from the city or deprived of their privileges, this petition was refused as in the case of the similar application of the Alexandrians (*BJ* VII. v. 2 [Niese, §§ 108–111], *Ant.* XII. iii. 1).

According to the above-cited passage (*Ant.* XII. iii. 1), Seleucus I. (Nikator) granted the rights of citizenship to the Jews, and placed them on a footing of equality with the Macedonians and Hellenes, not only at Antioch, but in all the cities founded by him in Asia and Syria. The number of these cities was very considerable (Appian, *Syr.* 57). Even if the statement of Josephus does not justify the conclusion that there were Jewish settlers in *all* of them, this must have been the case with no inconsiderable proportion.

In all the above instances equality of rights on the part of the Jews was based upon the recent foundation of the cities during the Greek period. In the older cities, if Jews came to settle, they could not obtain the citizenship. There was one contingency, however, which made this possible, namely, if the political constitution of the city came to be organized afresh. Such recastings of their constitution took place frequently at the commencement of the Greek period in the cities of Western Asia Minor. Alexander the Great himself overthrew the oligarchical governments that prevailed there, and replaced them by democratical constitutions (Arrian, I. xviii. 2). This was followed by a series of fluctuating forms in the troubled times of the Diadochi. The definite restoration of autonomy and democracy in the cities of the Ionian coast was essentially the work of Antiochus II. (Theos), B.C. 261–246 (Jos. *Ant.* XII. iii. 2: τῶν γὰρ Ἰώνων κινηθέντων ἐπ' αὐτοὺς [*scil.* τοὺς Ἰουδαίους] καὶ δεομένων τοῦ Ἀγρίππου, ἵνα τῆς πολιτείας, **ἣν αὐτοῖς ἔδωκεν Ἀντίοχος** ὁ Σελεύκου υἱωνὸς ὁ παρὰ τοῖς Ἕλλησιν **θεὸς** λεγόμενος, μόνοι μετέλθωσιν, κ.τ.λ. This general testimony of Josephus, according to which Antiochus II. bestowed their πολιτεία on the Ionians, is confirmed by a number of special inscriptional testimonies). It is probable that at this time of the political reorganization of the cities in Western Asia Minor the Jews amongst others received the rights of citizenship. It is wrong, indeed, to refer the αὐτοῖς in the above quotation to the Jews; it really stands for the Ionians. But the context of the passage makes it probable that at the same time with the Ionians the Jews also obtained the citizenship, and that in the time of Agrippa the non-Jewish inhabitants demanded the sole possession of this for themselves (so also Ramsay, *Expositor*, Feb. 1902, pp. 92–95). At all events, in the time of Josephus the Jews in *Ephesus and in the rest of Ionia* possessed the rights of citizens (*c. Apion.* ii. 4 [Niese, § 39]: οἱ ἐν Ἐφέσῳ καὶ κατὰ τὴν ἄλλην Ἰωνίαν τοῖς αὐθιγενέσι πολίταις ὁμωνυμοῦσιν, τοῦτο παρασχόντων αὐτοῖς τῶν διαδόχων). Incidentally we learn that they enjoyed the citizenship in Sardis also (*Ant.* XIV. x. 24), and even outside Asia Minor, at Cyrene (*ib.* XVI. vi. 1).

Wherever the Jews had the rights of citizenship, they must in their totality have formed a φυλή by themselves. For the citizens of Greek towns were divided into φυλαί, which also practised their own special religious cults. On the latter ground it is inconceivable that an individual Jew, if he desired to remain a Jew at all and to adhere to his religion, could hold the citizenship in a Greek town (attention has been called to this point especially by Ramsay, *Expositor*, Jan. 1902, pp. 22–29). Only where a considerable number of Jews formed a φυλή of their own, on the same footing as the other φυλαί, could they be citizens. If then St. Paul was a citizen of Tarsus (Ac 21[39]), we must conclude that the Jews in general who were settled there possessed the citizenship. Ramsay (*l.c.* pp. 29–33) suggests that they may have obtained it on the occasion of the rearranging of the constitution of the city by Antiochus IV. about the year B.C. 170. This appears, however, very improbable in view of the hostility of Antiochus to the Jews.

Even when the Jews formed a φυλή of their own, they found themselves, as citizens of a Greek town, in *a self-contradictory position.* They had to take their part in municipal business. But this included, amongst other things, the care of the native religious cults, a duty towards which the Jews were compelled to maintain a uniformly passive relation. And this passivity was a constant ground of complaint on the part of their heathen fellow-citizens. If they desired to be citizens, they must also honour the gods of the city. Such was the demand made by the representatives of the Ionian cities when they brought their complaint against the Jews before Agrippa (*Ant.* XII. iii. 2: ἀξιούντων, εἰ συγγενεῖς εἰσιν αὐτοῖς Ἰουδαῖοι, σέβεσθαι τοὺς αὐτῶν θεούς). The same view was taken everywhere in the Greek cities. Hence it is quite intelligible that the Jews should have been most exposed to the dislike, nay the hatred and persecution, of the heathen inhabitants just in those places where they possessed the citizenship. So it was, for instance, at Alexandria (*BJ* II. xviii. 7, persecution under Caligula), Antioch (*BJ* VII. iii. 3–4, v. 2), the cities of the Ionian coast (*Ant.* XII. iii. 2); and the same was the case at Cæsarea in Palestine, where they had obtained, through Herod the Great, the ἰσοπολιτεία (*Ant.* XX. viii. 7, 9, *BJ* II. xiii. 7, xiv. 4–5, xviii. 1). Everywhere it was only the superior authority of the Roman *imperium* that protected them in the enjoyment of the privileges that were recognized as belonging to them.

In addition to the local franchise, not a few of the Jews of the Diaspora possessed also the *Roman citizenship.* At Rome many of them had the degree of citizenship enjoyed by freedmen (*libertini*), for a large proportion of the community was made up of the descendants of those prisoners of war who were brought to Rome by Pompey and sold as slaves, but afterwards manumitted (Philo, *Legatio ad Gaium*, § 23 [ed. Mangey, ii. 568 f.]). This citizenship was, indeed, not a complete but a limited one (Mommsen, *Römisches Staatsrecht*, iii. 1, 420–457).—In Asia many Jews would appear to have been possessed of Roman citizenship: so, for instance, at Ephesus (*Ant.* XIV. x. 13, 16, 19), Sardis (*ib.* 17), Delos (*ib.* 14), in general (*ib.* 18). Hence it is not surprising to find St. Paul also in possession of it (Ac $16^{37ff.}$ $22^{25\text{-}29}$ $23^{27}$). We are not, indeed, aware how the Jews attained to this rank.

The advantages which accompanied the possession of Roman citizenship were very considerable. The possessor was exempt from degrading punishments such as scourging (Ac $16^{37ff.}$ $22^{25ff.}$) and crucifixion. He had also the right not only to appeal to the Emperor against a judgment that had been pronounced, but to 'call upon' the Emperor at the very commencement of the process and at every stage of it, *i.e.* to demand that the examination should be conducted at Rome, and judgment given by the Emperor himself (Ac $25^{10ff.\ 21}$ $26^{32}$; cf. Mommsen in *Ztschr. f. Neutest. Wissenschaft*, ii. [1901] 90–66). Of one important right the Jews made no use. While they were entitled as Roman citizens to bring civil processes before the special tribunals consisting of Roman citizens, which were found everywhere in the provinces, they preferred to have them decided by the courts belonging to their own communities (*Ant.* XIV. x. 17).

The *social standing* of the Jews must have varied greatly in different places. They appear to have been most favourably situated in Egypt, especially at Alexandria. Owing to their prosperity and culture they here played an important rôle in public life, and under some of the Ptolemies they even rose to high offices in the State. Ptolemy VI. (Philometor) and his consort Cleopatra 'entrusted their whole empire to Jews, and the commanders of the whole army were the Jews Onias and Dositheus' (Jos. *c. Apion.* ii. 5). Another Cleopatra, the daughter of the royal pair above named, likewise appointed two Jews, Chelkias and Ananias, to the chief command of her army in the war against her son Ptolemy Lathyrus (*Ant.* XIII. x. 4, xiii. 1–2).* In an inscription at Athribis there is mention of a Ptolemy, ἐπιστάτης τῶν φυλακιτῶν (chief of police), who, in conjunction with the Jewish community, built the synagogue of the place (see above, p. 96[a]). Although it does not necessarily follow from this that he was a Jew, the probability, in view of analogous cases, is in favour of such having been the case. The Ἀντωνιος Μαλχαιος who in the time of Trajan held the ὁρμοφυλακία at Syene (see above, p. 96[b]), *may* also have been a non-Jewish Semite, but ought in all probability to be regarded as a Jew. We may also remind the reader of the above (p. 96[b]) mentioned Jewish tax-collectors in the Thebaid during the earlier Ptolemaic period.

During the Roman period several Jews of noble birth and wealth held the office of *alabarch*. So, for instance, Alexander, the brother of the philosopher Philo (Jos. *Ant.* XVIII. vi. 3, viii. 1, XIX. v. 1, XX. v. 2), and a certain Demetrius (XX. vii. 3). The view that the *alabarch* was the head of the Jewish community is certainly wrong. He is in all probability identical with the ἀραβάρχης, whose office was that of chief superintendent of customs on the Arabian frontier, *i.e.* on the east side of the Nile. (A 'vectigal Arabarchiæ per Ægyptum atque Augustamnicam constitutum' is mentioned in the *Codex Justin.* IV. lxi. 9; an inscription found at Koptos contains a tariff fixing 'how much is to be raised by those who farm the ἀποστόλιον [?] at Koptos under the *arabarchy*'; see the text of this inscription in *Bulletin de corresp. hellénique*, xx. [1896] 174–176; on the office of the *alabarch* in general, see the Literature in Schürer, *GJV*[3] iii. 88 f., and add Wilcken, *Griechische Ostraka*, i. [1899] 347–351). Perhaps it is the office of the *alabarch* that is in view when Josephus says that the Romans 'continued (to the Jews of Alexandria) the position of trust given them by the kings, namely, the watching of the river' (*c. Apion.* ii. 5 *fin.*: 'maximam vero eis fidem olim a regibus datam conservaverunt, id est fluminis custodiam totiusque custodiæ' [the last word is certainly corrupt]). The 'watching of the river' refers to watching it in the interests of levying customs. In any case the *alabarch* was not an official of the Jewish community, but a man who held a prominent place in civil life.—Tiberius Alexander, a son of the alabarch Alexander, even reached the highest grades of a Roman military career, although at the expense of renouncing his ancestral religion.

Outside Egypt the Jews do not appear to have anywhere gained so influential a footing. Yet instances are not wanting elsewhere of their rising to positions of prominence. In Jerusalem at the outbreak of the war of A.D. 66 there were Jews holding the rank of Roman knights (Jos. *BJ* II. xiv. 9). At Ephesus and Venosa we meet in tomb-inscriptions with Jewish 'head physicians' (ἀρχίατροι; see *Ancient Greek Inscriptions in the British Museum*, iii. 2, No. 677; Ascoli, *Iscrizioni inedite o mal note*, 1880, No. 10). These were appointed by the city, and are thus to be regarded as municipal officials. In Italy the Jews from the time of Septimius Severus were admitted to the city offices (*Digest.* L. ii. 3: 'Eis qui Judaicam superstitionem sequuntur, divi Severus et Antoninus honores adipisci permiserunt').

V. RELIGIOUS AND INTELLECTUAL LIFE. — In spite of all its contact with Greek surroundings, the Jewish people preserved its religious uniqueness in a surprising fashion. The effects of the Maccabæan rising manifestly extended also to the Diaspora. As in the mother country at the time of Antiochus Epiphanes there was in aristocratic circles an inclination towards Hellenism even in religious matters, so in the city of Jasus in Caria we hear about the same time of a Νικήτας Ἰάσονος Ἱεροσολυμίτης who contributed money to support the festival of the *Dionysia* (see above, p. 94[a]). But the Maccabæan rising removed the danger of a wholesale syncretistic amalgamation of Judaism with Hellenistic heathenism. Instances of this last phenomenon do, indeed, occur. The Jewish Hellenist Artapanus considered that he was glorifying Judaism by representing the patriarchs and Moses as not only the creators of all secular culture, but the founders of the Egyptian religious cults in the sense in which Artapanus himself understood these (see the fragments of his writings in Euseb. *Præp. Evang.* ix. 18, 23, 27). In the temple of Pan at Apollonopolis Magna in Upper Egypt two Jews recorded their thanks to 'the god' for an act of deliverance (*CIG* 4838[c]). In a professed letter of Hadrian it is even said in general that in Egypt all the Jewish ἀρχισυνάγωγοι are 'astrologers, *haruspices*, and quacks' (Vopisc. *Vita Saturnini*, c. 8, in the 'Scriptores Historiæ Augustæ': 'Nemo illic archisynagogus Judæorum, nemo Samarites,

* Chelkias and Ananias were the sons of the high priest Onias IV., the founder of the temple of Leontopolis.—A Greek inscription, now in the Berlin Museum, contains a fragment of a decree in honour of a certain *Chelkias* or, as is more probable, his son. All that has survived of the name is the genitive Χελκίου. The subject honoured was στρατηγός, and received as a mark of distinction a golden wreath (see Willrich, *Archiv für Papyrusforschung*, i. [1900] 48–56). It is possible, but not certain, that this Chelkias is identical with the one mentioned by Josephus.

nemo Christianorum presbyter non mathematicus, non haruspex, non aliptes'). Side by side with syncretistic mixture we find also philosophic indifference to the literal sense of the Law. There were Jews with an education in philosophy who, on the basis of the allegorical interpretation of Scripture, regarded the higher, philosophical, or ethical sense of the commandments as the only one of value, and neglected the observation of the literal sense (Philo, *de Migratione Abrahami*, § 16 [ed. Mangey, i. 450]: *εἰσὶ γάρ τινες οἳ τοὺς ῥητοὺς νόμους σύμβολα νοητῶν πραγμάτων ὑπολαμβάνοντες τὰ μὲν ἄγαν ἠκρίβωσαν, τῶν δὲ ῥᾳθύμως ὠλιγώρησαν*). It may be also assumed in general that the observance of the Law on the part of Greek Judaism did not attain to the rigour and preciseness of the Pharisaic party in Palestine. Greek culture formed a heavy counter-weight to the latter. Nevertheless, the Judaism of the Diaspora asserted itself in the main along the same lines as in Palestine. Syncretistic movements and philosophic indifference never gained the upper hand. The leaders of the communities took care that even in the Diaspora the religious life was regulated by the standard of the Law of Moses. Any one who seriously broke off from the latter was expelled from the community. Even a philosopher like Philo complains of the depreciation and neglect of the literal sense mentioned by him in the above quotation. With all his skill in the allegorical interpretation, he yet maintained the binding character of the literal sense, nay he attempted to show that all commands, even those relating to ceremonial purity and to food, are based upon reason and nature.

One principal agency in maintaining the ancestral faith was found in *the regular gatherings in the synagogue on the Sabbath.* It is beyond question that these were held also in the Diaspora in every instance where a community had been organized. According to Philo, 'On the Sabbath day in all cities thousands of houses of instruction are opened, in which understanding and self-restraint and ability and justice and all virtues are taught' (*de Septenario*, § 6 [ed. Mangey, ii. 232]). The apostle Paul, in the course of his journeys in Asia Minor and Greece, found Jewish synagogues everywhere, *e.g.* at Antioch in Pisidia (Ac $13^{14}$), Iconium ($14^{1}$), Philippi ($16^{2.3}$), Ephesus ($18^{19.26}$ $19^{8}$), Thessalonica ($17^{1}$), Berœa ($17^{10}$), Athens ($17^{17}$), Corinth ($18^{4.7}$). In the larger cities there were more than one synagogue; at Alexandria there were a great many (Philo, *Legatio ad Gaium*, § 20 [ed. Mangey, ii. 565]: *πολλαὶ δέ εἰσι καθ' ἕκαστον τμῆμα τῆς πόλεως*).

The *language* used in the synagogue service was undoubtedly as a rule *Greek.* The Church Fathers expressly testify that the Greek Bible was used in the synagogues (Justin, *Apol.* i. 31, *Dial. c. Tryph.* 72; Tertull. *Apol.* 18; Pseudo-Justin, *Cohort. ad Græc.* 13). The Old Testament is familiar to St. Paul in the LXX translation only. It is not therefore likely that the Hebrew and Greek texts were used both together. The prayers and the address were also, it may be regarded as certain, in Greek, for in every instance where this language prevailed the Jews adopted it as their mother tongue. This is shown above all by the tomb-inscriptions. The early period at which the language of the LXX began to exercise a commanding influence on liturgical forms, and especially on the language of prayer, has been recently shown by the above (p. $97^{b}$) mentioned imprecatory inscriptions of the island of Rheneia near Delos. These should be dated, in the opinion of epigraphic experts, not later than about B.C. 100. They are couched quite in the style of the LXX (*ἐπικαλοῦμαι καὶ ἀξιῶ τὸν θεὸν τὸν ὕψιστον, τὸν κύριον τῶν πνευμάτων καὶ πάσης σαρκός . . . κύριε ὁ πάντα ἐφορῶν καὶ οἱ ἄνγελοι θεοῦ, ᾧ πᾶσα ψυχὴ ἐν τῇ σήμερον ἡμέραι ταπεινοῦται μεθ' ἱκετείας*). Even the Palestinian Rabbis could not avoid sanctioning the writing of the Scriptures in Greek and the uttering of prayers in the same language. The exceptions not covered by this permission are very trifling (*Mĕgillā*, i. 8; *Ṣôṭā*, vii. 1, 2). For the ordinary prayers (*Shĕma'*, *Shĕmōneh 'Esreh*, and blessing at meals) the employment of any language is expressly sanctioned.

No *sacrificial cultus* was legal, after the Deuteronomic reformation, outside Jerusalem. In spite of this, such a cultus was practised in Egypt for more than two centuries. The occasion of its establishment was the deposition of the ancient high priestly family during the general upheaval under Antiochus Epiphanes. The high priest's son, Onias, having no prospect of gaining his ancestral office at Jerusalem, came to Egypt in the time of Antiochus V. (Eupator) (B.C. 164–162). Here he received a cordial welcome from Ptolemy VI. (Philometor) and his consort Cleopatra. The king placed at his disposal an ancient ruined temple at Leontopolis in the nome of Heliopolis, which had formerly been a sanctuary of the *ἀγρία Βούβαστις*.* This was converted by Onias into a Jewish sanctuary, modelled after the temple at Jerusalem, but smaller and plainer, and with a number of deviations in details. Since there were already priests on the spot in sufficient numbers, a formal Jewish temple-cultus was established, which continued uninterrupted from that date (*c.* B.C. 160) until, after the destruction of Jerusalem, the temple of Leontopolis was also closed by the Romans in the year A.D. 73 (see, in general, Jos. *Ant.* XII. ix. 7, XIII. iii. 1–3, x. 4, XX. x. 3; *BJ* I. i. 1, VII. x. 2–4; *Orac. Sibyll.* v. 429–511). It is true that this cultus was never regarded by the teachers of the Law in Palestine as justifiable, and that the sacrifices offered in the Egyptian temple had only a very limited degree of validity attributed to them (Mishna, *Mĕnāḥôth*, xiii. 10). Nay, even the Egyptian Jews themselves were not satisfied with their own cultus, but kept up their connexion with Jerusalem. They performed the pilgrimages to that city like all other Jews (Philo, *de Providentia*, quoted in Euseb. *Præp. Evang.* viii. 14, 64, ed. Gaisford), and their priests, when they married, always had the genealogy of their wives verified at Jerusalem (Jos. *c. Apion.* i. 7).

Amongst the most important obligations which the Law imposed upon the Jews was that of paying *the manifold dues to the priests and to the temple at Jerusalem*: firstfruits, heave-offering, tithe, firstlings, dues in connexion with baking and killing, offerings on divers occasions, and finally the two drachmæ tax. So far as a due levied on the products of the soil of the *Holy Land* was concerned (firstfruits, heave-offering, tithe), the Jews of the Diaspora were, as a matter of course, exempt. But there remained still enough of performances to which even a Jew living far from Jerusalem was bound, if he meant to be true to his religion. If the dues could not, owing to distance, be paid in kind, they had to

* Its situation is most precisely defined in Jos. *Ant.* XIII. iii. 2: *τὸ ἐν Λεόντων πόλει τοῦ Ἡλιοπολίτου ἱερὸν συμπεπτωκὸς . . . προσαγορευόμενον δὲ τῆς ἀγρίας Βουβάστεως.* In other passages Josephus says merely that the temple was situated 'in the nome of Heliopolis' (*Ant.* XII. ix. 7, XIII. x. 4, XX. x. 3; *BJ* I. i. 1, VII. x. 3). We have to do, then, not with the better-known Leontopolis, which formed a nome of its own, but with another, which was included in the nome of Heliopolis. The latter lay on the east side of the Delta. In this neighbourhood there are still two mounds, each bearing the name *Tell el-Jehudiyeh* (see Naville, 'The Mound of the Jew and the City of Onias' in *Seventh Memoir of the Egypt. Explor. Fund*, 1890). One of the two will be identical with the foundation of Onias. Naville fixes upon the one farthest south, on account of its being nearer to Heliopolis. The more northern one, however, seems to the present writer the likelier site, because there are evidences of the Bubastis cult at it. See also above, p. $96^{a}$.

be converted into money. All these obligations were, so far as we know, punctiliously and zealously discharged by the far scattered Diaspora. The result of this was the accumulation of immense stores of wealth at the central sanctuary. Josephus (*Ant.* XIV. vii. 2) expressly accounts for these by pointing to the great extent of the Diaspora. Philo gives a detailed account of the collecting and delivery of the money (*de Monarchia*, ii. 3 [ed. Mangey, ii. 224]): 'The temple derives its revenue not merely from a few pieces of land, but from other and much more copious sources, which can never be destroyed. For so long as the human race endures, the temple's sources of revenue will also continue, since their permanence is bound up with that of the whole world. For it is prescribed that all Jews over twenty years of age shall pay annual dues. . . . But, as might be expected in the case of so numerous a people, the dues amount to an enormous sum. *In almost every city there is a receiving office for the sacred funds, into which the dues are paid. And at fixed times men of noble birth are entrusted with the conveyance of the money to Jerusalem.* The noblest are chosen in every city, in order that the hope of every Jew may be transmitted unimpaired. For the hope of the pious is based upon the regular payment of the dues.' In the Euphrates districts the principal treasuries were in the cities of Nisibis and Nehardea. In these the money was first collected and thence transmitted to Jerusalem at a fixed time, many thousands taking charge of its conveyance, in order to protect the sacred treasure from the plundering attacks of the Parthians (Jos. *Ant.* XVIII. ix. 1).

The transmission of such large sums to Jerusalem repeatedly gave rise to collisions with the Roman and municipal authorities. Flaccus, during his administration of the Province of Asia, prevented the money being sent, and municipal authorities were constantly inclined to do the same. But the Roman legislation subsequent to the time of Cæsar protected the religious liberty of the Jews in this as in other matters (see above, p. 103). After the destruction of the temple, the payment of sacred dues necessarily underwent transformation. The two drachmæ tax was converted into a Roman tax; other dues which depended upon the continued existence of the temple could not, in the nature of things, be paid any longer. But even under these circumstances the Jewish people, by voluntary self-taxation, continued to assert their unity. A new central authority, the Patriarchate, was created, to which at least a portion of the prescribed sacred dues was paid every year. The collecting of these was now accomplished by deputies of the Patriarchate, the so-called *apostoli*.

The principal means of maintaining an exchange of thought between the mother country and the Diaspora, and of furthering and maintaining a close fellowship between the two, was found in the frequent *festival pilgrimages* made by Jews from all parts of the world to Jerusalem. 'Many thousands from many thousand cities journeyed to the temple at every festival, some by land and some by sea, from east and west, from north and south' (Philo, *de Monarchia*, ii. 1 [ed. Mangey, ii. 223]). The number of Jews ordinarily present at Jerusalem at the feasts is reckoned by Josephus at 2,700,000, a number which, indeed, also includes the permanent population of Jerusalem (*BJ* VI. ix. 3).

While the Jews scattered all over the world thus held fast to the religion of their fathers, and that in the legal form it had received through the Restoration under Ezra, they had become in other respects *Greeks*. Greek culture asserted its supremacy in a decisive fashion here, as elsewhere. In Asia Minor, Greece, Egypt, Cyrenaica, nay even at Rome, Greek was the mother tongue of the Jews. All the relics of writing that have come down to us from the Diaspora during the last centuries B.C. and the first centuries A.D. are in Greek. This is true especially of the tomb-inscriptions, whose evidence is of importance because they are concerned not only with the rich and noble, but with the poor and humble (see above, § i., for the most important materials under this head). These tomb-inscriptions are at the same time a faithful mirror of the stage of culture that prevailed in the communities. The Greek of the tomb-inscriptions at Rome is barbarous, and shows, what might otherwise have been supposed, that the Jews here remained for the most part at a low social level. In other places the inscriptions of various kinds that have survived reveal a higher degree of culture.

It was in *Egypt* that the Jews most thoroughly assimilated the Greek culture. Here, as is shown by the case of Philo, they read the Greek poets and philosophers; Homer, Sophocles, and Euripides; Plato, Aristotle, and Zeno. All this could not, as a matter of course, be without far-reaching influence upon their whole intellectual life. Their conception of the world and of life, in spite of their adherence to legal Judaism, was powerfully influenced in its contents by Greek culture. The literature produced by Hellenistic, especially Alexandrian, Judaism is, in consequence, of an extremely varied character. It serves, on the one hand, religious ends, the defence and propagation of Judaism (Apologetics and Propaganda); and, on the other hand, it follows Greek models in History, Poetry, and Philosophy. So far as poetical art is concerned, it was indeed somewhat meagrely represented. The extant fragments of Greek dramas and Greek epics treating of biblical subjects can scarcely be said to be marked by any high poetic strain (see the fragments of a drama treating of the story of the Exodus from Egypt by the tragedian Ezekiel *ap.* Euseb. *Præp. Evang.* ix. 28, 29; and the fragments of an epic on the history of Jerusalem by the elder Philo *ap.* Euseb. *ib.* ix. 20, 24, 37). In philosophy, however, the Jews made very notable achievements. Greek philosophy had indeed advanced far on the way towards monotheism. It had also, as represented by many of its teachers, an ethical cast. Hence the Jews discovered here many elements which were capable of assimilation by them. These they adopted with remarkable powers of adaptation; and in this way, by combining the religious world-conception of the Old Testament with the philosophic world-conception of the Greeks, they created a new unique philosophy of religion which was as much Jewish as Greek. A clear picture of this is given us by the writings of the Alexandrian Philo, which have come down to us in great numbers.

The adoption of Greek culture enabled the Jews again for their part to exercise an influence on their heathen environments. From all that we know, they carried on a vigorous and successful propaganda. Those whom they gained over were either formally received into the communities by circumcision, or they attached themselves to them in a loose form 'as God-fearing' (σεβόμενοι, φοβούμενοι τὸν θεόν), forming a kind of appendage to the communities (see art. PROSELYTE in vol. iv.). This Jewish propaganda served in great measure as a preliminary to Christianity. In general the Jewish Diaspora, as was remarked at the beginning of the present article, paved the way along which the first preachers of the gospel went forth into the world, and in many ways laid the foundation of the rapid success of their preaching.

[*Additional Note* to § i. (5).—The early settlement of Jews in Alexandria is confirmed also by an inscription, discovered in 1902 in the neighbourhood of Alexandria, which reads thus: Ὑπὲρ βασιλέως Πτολεμαίου καὶ βασιλίσσης Βερενίκης ἀδελφῆς καὶ γυναικὸς καὶ τῶν τέκνων τὴν προσευχὴν ὁ Ἰουδαῖοι (see *REJ* xlv. [1902] p. 162). The inscription refers in all probability to Ptolemy III. Euergetes (247–222 B.C.)].

LITERATURE.—Remond, *Versuch einer Gesch. der Ausbreit. des Judenthums von Cyrus bis auf den gänzlichen Untergang des Jüdischen Staats*, Leipzig, 1789; Gieseler, *Lehrbuch der Kirchengeschichte*, Bd. i. Abth. 1 (4 Aufl. 1844), p. 53 ff.; Winer, *RWB*², art. 'Exil' (i. 357-360), and 'Zerstreuung' (ii. 727–730), also the articles on particular cities, *e.g.* 'Alexandria,' 'Antiochia,' 'Cyrene,' 'Rom,' etc.; J. G. Müller, art. 'Alexandrinische Juden' in Herzog's *RE*¹ i. [1854] 235-239; Reuss, art. 'Hellenisten,' *ib.*¹ v. 701–705, ²v. 738-741; Lutterbeck, *Die Neutest. Lehrbegriffe*, i. [1852] 99–120; Frankel, 'Die Diaspora zur Zeit des zweiten Tempels' in *Monatsschr. für Gesch. und Wissensch. des Judenthums*, 1853, pp. 409–429, 449–463, also the same author's art. 'Die Juden unter den ersten römischen Kaisern,' *ib.* 1854, pp. 401–413, 439–450; Jost, *Gesch. der Israeliten*, ii. 239-344, *Gesch. des Judenthums und seiner Secten*, i. 336 ff., 344-361, 367–379; Herzfeld, *Gesch. des Volkes Jisrael*, iii. 425–579, *Handelsgeschichte der Juden des Alterthums*, 1879; Grätz, *Gesch. der Juden*⁴, iii. [1888] 24–49; Champagny, *Rome et la Judée au temps de la chute de Néron*, i. [Paris, 1865] 107–154; Ewald, *Gesch. des Volkes Israel*, iv. 305 ff., v. 108 ff., vi. 396 ff.; Holtzmann in Weber-Holtzmann's *Gesch. des Volkes Israel*, ii. 38–52, 253–273; Hausrath, *Neutest. Zeitgeschichte*², ii. 91–145, iii. 383-392; Neubauer, *La Géographie du Talmud*, 1868, pp. 289–419; Friedländer, *Darstellungen aus der Sittengesch. Roms*, iii. [1871] 504–517, also 'de Judæorum Coloniis,' Regimonti Pr., 1876 [Progr.]; Deutsch, art. 'Dispersion' in Kitto's *Cyclopædia of Biblical Literature*; Westcott, art. 'Dispersion' in Smith's *DB*²; Weizsäcker, art. 'Zerstreuung' in Schenkel's *Bibellexicon*, v. 712–716; Hindekoper, *Judaism at Rome* B.C. 76 *to* A.D. 140, New York, 1876 (cf. *Theol. Literaturzeitung*, 1877, col. 163); Hamburger, *RE für Bibel und Talmud*, Abth. ii. (1883), arts. 'Zehn Stämme,' 'Zerstreuung,' also 'Alexandria,' 'Antiochia,' 'Rom,' etc., further, art. 'Ausbreitung des Judenthums' in Supplementbd. iii. [1892] 9–24; Mommsen, *Röm. Gesch.* v. [1885] 489–499; Pressel, *Die Zerstreuung des Volkes Israel*, 1889; Renan, *Histoire du peuple d'Israel*, v. [1893] 221–247; M. Friedländer, *Das Judenthum in der vorchristlichen griechischen Welt*, 1897; Reinach, art. 'Judæi' in Daremberg-Saglio's *Dictionnaire des Antiquités grecques et romaines*; Schürer, *GJV*³, iii. [1898] 1-102 [*HJP*, II. ii. 219-327], where a number of points are discussed in fuller detail.

E. SCHÜRER.

## RELIGION OF GREECE AND ASIA MINOR.—

Introduction.

*A.* PRIMITIVE ANATOLIAN AND PRE-HELLENIC RELIGION.

I. Sacred Stones and other Inanimate Objects: (1) stones, pillars, columns, etc.; (2) thrones; (3) weapons; (4) wooden posts.

II. Sacred Trees.

III. Sacred Animals: (1) animals as parts of the god; (2) the bull; (3) the goat; (4) the sheep; (5) the horse; (6) the swine; (7) the bee; (8) the sacredness of domesticated animals; (9) domesticated animals as sacrifice; (10) the lion, the stag; (11) the serpent; (12) sacredness of wild animals.

IV. Sacred Places: (1) mountains; (2) sacred caves and mountain glens; (3) sacred springs and lakes; (4) development of the sacred place into a religious centre or *Hieron*; (5) sacred places in the religion of Greece.

V. Relation of the original *aniconic* religion to image-worship: (1) coexistence of the two kinds of worship; (2) votive images and representations of the Deity; (3) shrines (*naoi*).

VI. The Divine in human form and character: (1) the Great Mother; (2) the growth of mythology as the story of the Great Mother; (3) myths of the goddess and the god; (4) the birth and death of the Divine nature.

VII. Ritual and Ceremonial: (1) the origin of ritual; (2) the Mysteries; (3) nature of the Mysteries; (4) the character of the Phrygian and the Greek Mysteries; (5) the growth of ritual; (6) purification; (7) confession; (8) approaching the Deity; (9) priests; (10) *hieroi*.

VIII. Influence on Society and Life: (1) marriage; (2) *hierodouloi*; (3) women guards; (4) self-mutilation; (5) burial; (6) brotherhoods and guilds; (7) government and administration; (8) household *protegés*; (9) religious influences on social conditions.

IX. History and Chronology: (1) development of the Anatolian Religion in history; (2) local diversity in Anatolian Religion; (3) chronology

*B.* THE HELLENIC RELIGION.

I. Early Greek Religion.

II. Greek Religion and Greek Law.

III. The Elements of Hellenic Religion.

IV. The Growth of Hellenic Religion: (1) continuity of development; (2) growth of mythology; (3) polytheism and the Hellenic unity; (4) formation of the Hellenic Pantheon; (5) the Hellenic Religion an ideal; (6) theory of the Hellenic Pantheon; (7) moralization of the Hellenic gods; (8) the Daimones and the Divine in the physical world; (9) restrictions on the nature of the gods; (10) State gods and gods within the State; (11) extension of the worship of a god; (12) State recognition of the Pan-Hellenic Religion; (13) the Hellenic Religion a part of the City-State; (14) the Hellenic conception of piety.

V. The Hellenic classification of deities as Olympian and Chthonian: (1) Hellenism and the thought of death; (2) the Olympian and the Chthonian gods.

VI. The Religion of Apollo and the Delphic Oracle (L. R. F.).

*C.* LATER DEVELOPMENT OF RELIGION IN THE GREEK WORLD.

I. Religion in Literature and Philosophy.

II. The attitude of St. Paul to Greek Philosophy.

III. Degradation of the Hellenic Religion: (1) foreign influence; (2) susceptibility to foreign religious influence; (3) manner in which foreign religion entered Greece; (4) itinerant priests; (5) magic; (6) the worship of living men as deities.

IV. Religion of the Græco-Asiatic cities.

V. Decay and death of the Hellenic Religion.

Literature.

The religion of the Greek peoples and of the races which lay between Hellas and the strictly Oriental nations, in communication with both, influencing and influenced by both, is a subject which can hardly be omitted in a survey of the religions which came into immediate relation to Christianity in the earliest stage of its history; and yet it is a subject which at the present time is hardly susceptible of adequate treatment within narrow space. The antiquities of the most notable Hellenic cults have been much investigated, though not always in a very intelligent fashion or with a proper conception of the religious bearing of the details so carefully and laboriously collected. Hence the religious ideas and conceptions entertained by the various tribes of Greece, often differing widely from one another, have hardly been sufficiently observed and studied in their gradual evolution; and, in fact, evidence is so scanty in regard to most of them, that it is doubtful if the attempt could be successful.

If the religion of the strictly Greek tribes is still very obscure, much more is this the case with what may be called the half-Greek peoples* of Asia Minor. This is a subject still almost unstudied, or studied occasionally, in a haphazard way, partially, and as a sort of appendix to the religion of Greece proper. This way of entering on the study, under the bias and colouring influence of Greek prepossession, is, we believe, injurious, and has caused much misapprehension. One should rather begin the study of Greek religion from Asia Minor, both as being more primitive in many of its forms, and as having sent into Greece a series of religious waves which strongly affected that country. At a later period the Greek influence returned over Asia Minor, and overran it in a superficial way; but this new period in religion was broadly different, and easily distinguishable from the older and truly Anatolian period. It is necessary to begin afresh in that country, to collect and classify and value the religious facts, and on this basis to give an account of the religion of the peoples; but that is a great work, which is far too large for the narrow limits of an article. Probably the most useful way at present will be to state as simply and clearly as possible the views which the writer is disposed to hold, avoiding disputation and argument, and therefore making little reference to discrepant views, except where such reference is the shortest way of stating the subject clearly. This gives unavoidably an appearance of dogmatism, which the writer can only apologize for as the necessary result of the attempt to make the subject clear in small space: if the views of others were stated, either the article would become a confusing congeries of irreconcilable theories, or it would grow too large in estimating and discussing

* On the meaning which we attach to this term 'half-Greek,' see the following paragraph.

other views. It is also necessary to explain that the writer's views are founded on a far from complete survey of the facts, and are liable to correction, doubtless, in many details, if the opportunity should ever be granted him of writing a complete account of Anatolian religion; but the general principles are the result of more than twenty years of interest and occasional study, and are not likely to be much changed by further thought.*

The phrase 'half-Greek races' is not used in an ethnological sense in this article. It does not imply a mixture of Greek and non-Greek blood in any race. It is employed to indicate a gradual shading off of character, as one proceeds from Greece proper towards the East. The view which we take is that even the tribes of Greece proper were far from uniform in blood and stock. The Hellenic idea and civilization which those tribes evolved was far too many-sided to arise among a homogeneous nation: there were combined in its composition a great variety of characteristics contributed by various tribes of very diverse character, nursed and matured amid the peculiar circumstances of the seas and lands that touch and mingle in south-eastern Europe and Asia Minor. The lands that border on the Ægean Sea were pre-eminently the nursing home of Hellenism, and the further we go from it the more faint and evanescent become the traces of the Greek spirit. Hellenism is only partially a racial fact; it denotes also a general type of intellectual and political development, of industrial education and artistic achievement.

The point of view from which we start may be stated in outline as follows. (1) The religion of the Anatolian race or races, in its origin, was to a considerable extent an idealized presentation of the actual life of the time, exhibiting a Divine model and authorization for the existing customs and institutions in family and society and the State as a whole.

(2) Their religion was the authority for the laws and rules on which rested their industry and agriculture and general well-being. Perhaps it originally taught those rules to a simple people, in which case the knowledge embodied in them probably belonged at one time to the priests alone. Certainly, the sanction for the rules was religious: the violation of them was punished by the Divine power through sickness, whether disease of any part of the body or the general indefinite fact of fever, which was considered to be a consuming of the body and strength by Divine fire.

(3) The Divine power was the ruler of the people, acting through its visible representatives, namely, the kings or priests: there is every probability that the king was the priest: the priest-kings or priest-dynasts are a most characteristic feature of Anatolia.

This is obviously the religion of a comparatively civilized people, not of a barbarous race. And it must be distinctly understood from the outset that we are not investigating the origin of the religious forms which are described in the following pages: we are attempting to understand clearly and state precisely the religious ideas of a population, possessing an ordered system of government of a peculiar and well-marked character, surrounded by many equipments and devices and implements of an artificial and developed character, practising both agriculture and a very highly developed system of treating domesticated animals and adapting them to the benefit of mankind.

* In the *Cities and Bishoprics of Phrygia*, i. and ii., the present writer was groping his way to the views now expressed in part A. A considerable portion of part B was written in 1879-81, and needed hardly any change to adapt it to the writer's present views. In view of recent theories it should be added that the view here advocated, as to the way in which pre-Hellenic religion developed into Hellenic, remains practically unchanged since 1881, but the name 'Pelasgian' was not used in that old sketch of the subject.

A question of extreme interest and importance is, how far any signs of progress and development can be observed in the religion which we are studying. It may be doubted whether there can be detected anything in the way of growth from within, of elevation of the religious idea and of the moral standard in the application of religion to life, such as is the most striking feature in the history of Hebrew religion. On the whole, the history is one of deterioration and degradation rather than one of elevation. Any improvement that does take place seems rather attributable to, and fully explained by, the meeting of different races with different religious ideas corresponding to their differing social and family organization; and is probably not caused by any mind working from within the religion, unfolding and vitalizing the germs of truth which it contained, and burning away the envelope and accretion of accidental idolatrous forms that clung to it. We use intentionally these last words, for it will appear that the fundamental and essential idea in the Anatolian religion is not strictly idolatrous, and that the development in polytheism and image-worship was gradual, and was external and accidental rather than natural and necessary.

A. *PRIMITIVE ANATOLIAN AND PRE-HELLENIC RELIGION.*—In treating this subject, reference must often be made to primitive Greek, or, as it may be called, Pelasgian worship (anticipating part B, §§ I, II), which illustrates the Anatolian religion so remarkably as to demonstrate that some intimate relation once existed between them. We must here simply assume the relationship without inquiring into its nature.

I. SACRED STONES AND OTHER INANIMATE OBJECTS.—As a preliminary, we may ask what traces of the worship of inanimate things can be observed in Asia Minor or Greece, and what is the idea involved in this worship? Many examples are known of such things being regarded with deep religious veneration.

(1) *Stones, Pillars, Columns*, etc.—A rude and shapeless stone, which had fallen from heaven (διοπετής), doubtless a meteorite, existed originally at Pessinus, and was brought to Rome about B.C. 204; it is a type of many other similar stones at Orchomenos, Thespiæ, Synnada, Adada, etc. Many of these stones had some approximate regularity of shape, sometimes perhaps accidental, in other cases distinctly due to human workmanship. Such were the conical or roughly pyramidal stones in the temples at Paphos (of Aphrodite), Perga (Artemis), Delphi (Apollo), etc.: obelisks, columns, and stones of a distinctly tetragonal shape are indicated in many other cases: above all other gods in Greece such stones or pillars were connected with Hermes, and called *Hermaia* or *Hermai*.*

It admits of no doubt that many sacred stones had primarily a purpose in family life or social or political organization. Boundary stones or *termini* were erected by mutual agreement between disputants, and were consecrated by every religious sanction known at the time, by ceremonial, and by a curse on the violator or remover; and the belief indubitably was that the ceremonies of erection and consecration had caused Divine power and life to take up its abode in the stone: this Divine power demanded worship in recognition and propitiation, and was able and ready to punish neglect or violation. The *terminus* was valueless

* μεθόριον στησάμενοι τὸ Ἑρμαῖον (Polyænus, *Strat.* vi. 24); τὸ Ἑρμαῖον ἐς ὃ Μεσσηνίοις καὶ Μεγαλοπολίταις εἰσὶν ὅροι (Pausanias, viii. 34. 6). These *Hermaia* were columns, or heaps of stones, or single stones. A useful collection of ancient authorities will be found in Mr. M. W. de Visser's treatise, *de Græcorum diis non referentibus humanam speciem*, Leyden, 1900.

unless it was respected and inviolate: human need was urgent that it should be respected, but mere human power was unable to make it so: accordingly, the Divine power was invoked to supply the deficiency, and by proper rites was brought down and caused to dwell in the pillar or the stone. One of the ceremonies proper to the cult of such sacred stones was the pouring of oil on them; and in general a similar ceremonial to that described in § II was practised. Similarly, in a house any peculiarly important bearing member, a central pillar or roof-tree, was placed under Divine protection by invoking the Divine power to reside in it.

In all cases there is but one method and one principle. The more urgent man's need is, and the more important for his life and well-being any stone or erection is, the more does it become necessary to make the Divine power take up its abode in the stone. In other words, the stone becomes a *Beth-el*, or 'House of God'; the pillar embodies the god Hermes.

The subject in its bearing on early Greek religion has been admirably treated by Mr. A. J. Evans in an elaborate paper on 'Mycenæan Tree and Pillar Cult' (*Journ. of Hell. Stud.* 1901, pp. 99–203), which will henceforth be regarded as fundamental in this department, though it will doubtless receive development and improvement and correction in details from both the author and others. The preceding remarks will show why the objection recently raised against Mr. Evans' theory in *Journ. of Hell. Stud.* 1901, pp. 268–275, cannot weigh with us: the objection is that many of his examples of 'sacred pillars' are obviously structural members, and need not therefore be considered to have any religious purpose: we, however, hold that the structural importance produced the sacred character of the 'pillar.' The sacredness of rude purposeless stones was perhaps due to 'false analogy,' that fruitful agency in thought, and should be regarded as not primitive, but cases of degradation.

Probably no one could doubt that the rude meteoric stone was worshipped because it had fallen from heaven, and was obviously and unmistakably a mark and sign and example of Divine activity and power. Similarly, it seems beyond doubt that the boundary stone, or the supporting member of the family home and roof, is made into a dwelling-place of Divine power, in order that human needs may be satisfied by Divine aid. The same principle of interpretation must be applied in many other cases where the stone was neither in itself an object useful to man, nor marked by its natural character and origin as Divine. It was often urgently necessary to protect a locality for the common use of men, and this was done in a similar way by setting up one or more sacred stones in it; but in such cases the sacred stone was an addition, and not an integral part of the structure or equipment.

In a town it was urgently required that the street, the common property and a necessary convenience for all, should be inviolate and properly kept and respected by the dwellers or passers-by. The common need was guaranteed by the sacred *Hermai* or pillars, which were made the residence of Divine power by charming it into them through the proper rites; and misdemeanour in the street or encroachment on it was thus constituted a disrespect of the divinity, and punished by him.

In a more developed state of society, roads leading from city to city were probably put under Divine protection in a similar way; and the sacred stones were commonly made useful to human requirements by having distances engraved on them, thus becoming milestones.* But such stones

* Curtius, *Gesch. des griech. Wegebaus.*

generally belonged to a more advanced stage of thought, when men refused to consider a stone the abode of Divine power. On the Roman Imperial roads they were dedicated to the Emperor, and thus placed under the guardianship of the Imperial god incarnate in human form on the earth. The god and the stone are in this stage separated in thought, but the stone remains sacred in a new way as the property of the god.

A meeting of three roads or streets, as an important point, was placed under the guardianship of the Divine power. When the anthropomorphic tendency had become strong, the Divine guardian of the triple crossing was represented as the goddess (under the name Hekate in Greece) with three faces, looking to the three ways (just as in Italy the god protecting the archway and the door was represented with two faces looking in the two directions). But before the anthropomorphic idea had gained full strength, there was doubtless some other way of symbolizing the Divine guardianship of the meeting of the ways; and the suggestion seems obvious that the symbol was the *triskeles*, three human legs and feet, diverging from a common centre, and typifying the walking of men along the three ways which radiated from the meeting-place (*compitum*). Little is known with regard to this form of cultus, except in Rome, where the feast of the *Compitalia* was an important part of the city-religion; but few will doubt that, as streets and roads became important, a cultus corresponding to the *Compitalia* developed in primitive Anatolia. In the coinage of Anatolia the *triskeles* is almost entirely confined to the cities least affected by Hellenic culture, in Pisidia, Isauria, and early or inner Lycia. Moreover, the epithets τρικάρανος, τετρακάρανος, applied to Hekate-Selene, are doubtless to be understood as applying to the goddess who guards the *trivium* or the *quadrivium*.*

It may therefore be reasonably maintained that in many other places, where we know only that in primitive thought a stone was regarded as sacred and made the object of worship in the Greek world, the fundamental character was the same. The stone was worshipped as home and symbol and proof of Divine power—a power able and ready to respond to human needs. See also below, (2), and § IV (1).

As Greek thought developed in the direction of anthropomorphism and polytheism, there arose an opinion that the old sacred stone was either a representation and image of a god, the rudest beginning of a statue, or an altar dedicated to the god. Such views seem not to be original and genuine religious conceptions, but merely philosophic interpretations by which more developed thought tried to bring primitive religious facts into conformity with itself. Thus the pillars, mentioned above, in streets and open places, which were originally called *agyiai* or *agyieis*, were regarded as altars or representations of a Deity, sometimes Helios, sometimes Dionysos, but most commonly Apollo; and *Agyieus* was then usually regarded as an epithet of Apollo. The Greeks themselves hesitated whether to call the pillars altars or statues of Apollo, a sure proof that neither description was complete and true. The pillars or stones in open places and gymnasia, by roads, at boundaries, originally and commonly styled *Hermai*, *i.e.* embodiments of Hermes, came to be regarded rather as statues of Hermes, and were developed accordingly in art, as we shall see in the ensuing paragraph.

The institution of sacred stones was modified by another influence. Art was engaged in the service

* See *Hermes*, iv. p. 64; Ramsay, *Hist. Com. on Galatians* p. 219.

of the anthropomorphic tendency in religion, and wrought out ideal expression in human form of the various gods: the types of gods and goddesses were elaborated, and distinguished from one another, in the ruder stage to a considerable extent by symbols and equipments, but in the more developed and perfected stage by the varying artistic expression of the idealized conception of each deity as an individual character. Alongside of this rapid progress in the artistic presentation of different types of Divine character as different personal gods in human form, there was another line of development, through which the sacred pillars (which still continued to be erected in numbers during this more developed period) were made to assume more resemblance to the human form. The top of the pillar was carved into a bust, and parts of the body were indicated on the sides: such figures were commonly called *Hermai*, and Greek art developed the type at a later time in various ways, making the busts portraits of real human persons. In all such cases art takes the view that the pillar is a rude statue of some deity or hero, and makes additions or modifications to bring out this character more clearly.

The epithet of meteoric stones, διοπετής, was sometimes transferred to certain very archaic statues, about which the legend grew that they had fallen from heaven: such was the case with the rude figure of barely human form in which Artemis of Ephesus was represented (Ac $19^{35}$). The nature of those rude old idols will be more fully considered in § III (1) and § V (1).

(2) *Thrones.*—The ancients mention many stones in Greece which were said to derive their sacred character from having been the seat of deities or heroes (who in these cases may usually be regarded as deities degenerated in popular legend). Such were the Agelastos Petra at Eleusis (or at Athens) on which Demeter sat sorrowing for her lost Kora,* or, as another legend said, where Theseus sat before descending to Hades; the chair of Manto at Thebes, the stone of Telamon at Salamis, etc. The bed of Actæon at Platæa and various other stones may be classed with these. The Omphalos at Delphi is often represented with Apollo sitting on it.

In Asia Minor there are examples of rocks cut to the rough form of a seat. The 'Throne of Pelops' in Sipylus beside Magnesia (Pausanias, v. 13. 7) is probably to be identified with the rock-cutting, forming a sort of broad seat, or platform with a back, on the highest point of an early rock citadel on the slope of Sipylus, about 4 or 5 miles east of Magnesia.

Dr. Reichel has elaborated these facts into a theory of Throne-worship: viz., that the Divine nature, not yet represented in personal human form, was symbolized by the throne or seat, which was regarded as an indication of its presence.

Some of Dr. Reichel's examples of Divine thrones rest on his own far-fetched and almost certainly erroneous explanations; † in other cases the recorded story about a Divine or heroic throne may be only a later popular explanation of an older religious fact, no longer understood. But whether that aspect of his theory is only pressed too far and applied to unsuitable cases, or whether it is wholly erroneous, there is, at any rate, another and a true side to his theory. He is right in his view that before the period of images and image-worship we must admit the existence of an imageless worship in the Ægean lands and Asia Minor generally: a Divine power invisible to man was approached and adored; it was felt in the phenomena of the world, in the growth and life and productivity of nature; its presence and power were symbolized and envisaged to its worshippers in various ways, but the symbols were not considered as images or likenesses of that Divine nature, but rather as its home or residence, or as an effect and exemplification of its power. The statement of Nicol. Dam. *Synag. fr.* 19 (p. 148), and Stobæus, *Serm.* xlii. p. 292, that the Phrygians did not swear or exact from another an oath (by any god), probably has some reference to this belief in a Divine nature without images.* On this topic see further, § V (1).

Dr. Reichel has erred, as we believe, only in the direction in which he has developed a correct observation. It was not the seat or throne of the formless and invisible Divine nature that was in the beginning worshipped; for the very idea of a seat already involves the attribution of something like form and personality to the power which needs and uses a seat. The fundamental idea was that of the home and abode, or the origin of Divine power. Out of this springs all the symbolism and all the earlier phenomena of Anatolian religious observances. The sacred stone or the sacred tree is the home of the Divine nature: the cave among the wild mountains, the simple shrine, are easy developments of the same idea.†

(3) *Weapons.*—Other inanimate objects besides stones were made the object of worship. The Alani, a rude barbarian tribe south-east of the Black Sea, are said to have worshipped a naked *sword*, which they fixed for the occasion in the ground. This might be disregarded as a savage custom which had come in from Central Asia, were it not that one of the reliefs—among the most important, to judge from its size—portrayed on the walls of the *adytum* before the eyes of the initiated at Boghaz-Keui (Pteria probably), east of the Halys,‡ represents a gigantic sword stuck in the ground, with only the hilt and a small part of the blade protruding. The hilt in itself is evidently a symbol or representative of Divine power, composed of two pairs of animals, evidently lions, surmounted by a human head wearing the tall pointed hat characteristic of the supreme god. It is therefore not open to doubt that the custom of the Alani in the 4th cent. after Christ was the same as the ancient Anatolian custom. We see clearly that the sword was regarded not as a god in and for itself, but as a symbol of a vague pervading Divine power. That power resides mainly in the hilt, not in the blade, and is moulded not altogether unlike the human form, and yet differing essentially from it, full of the terror and strength of savage nature embodied in the four lions, but human-headed.

If some tribes worshipped the sword, others regarded the *battle-axe* as sacred. The difference obviously arises from difference of warlike custom: the weapon to which the tribe trusted especially in battle was esteemed by it the home of the Divine strength by which they conquered and hoped to conquer. In Caria and in Crete the axe appears as a Divine symbol. We may confidently assume that it was made the object of a special cult, like the Sword-god among the Alani. Though this is not exactly proved definitely by the evidence, yet the importance of the Carian name *Labrys* (*bipennis*, 'battle-axe') in Carian religion leaves little doubt on the point: Labranda was one of the chief centres of the worship of the Carian god, who was actually called *Labraundos*,§ and one of

* A similar stone and legend probably existed in Asia Minor; and a Christian form was given to it later; see *Journ. of Hell. Stud.* 1882, p. 349.

† See A. J. Evans in *Journ. of Hell. Stud.* 1901, p. 189; Fritze in *Rhein. Museum*, 1900, p. 588.

* The Pontic oath by Men Pharnakes (Strabo, p. 557) is later (cf. p. 128); but see Roscher, *Selene*, p. 122.

† On the shrine see § V (3); on the sacred cave, § IV (2).

‡ See Perrot, *Histoire de l'Art dans l'Antiquité*, iv. pp. 642, 647; Chantre, *Voyage en Cappadoce*, gives the latest account.

§ Hellenized as *Zeus Labraundos*.

the Kouretes in Carian mythology was Labrandos.* But, even more unmistakably than the sword, the axe was a symbol of a Divine power felt as lying behind it and expressing itself through it, and not as a power or a terror in itself. The god carrying the battle-axe on his shoulder is one of the most familiar and widely diffused symbols in east Lydian and west Phrygian coinage.†

We notice that the worship of the axe belongs to the Carians, a people who beyond doubt were an immigrant race; and we shall see among them some examples of divergence from the Anatolian type of religion (see § VI (2)). The worship of the axe must be regarded as also a divergence from that type; and, in accordance with the principle stated at the beginning of the article, this divergence is to be attributed to the character of the Carian race. In the same way the worship of the sword, though traceable in the religion of the central plateau in the earliest period known to us, is probably a development out of the original Anatolian type due to pressure from the east and north-east. The east Anatolian type of cultus is of a much more bellicose type than the central Anatolian (see § IX (2)), and the reason indubitably lies in the rough and warlike character of the tribes on that side, such as the Kardouchoi, modern Kurds, etc.

(4) *Wooden posts.*—A rude wooden post was sometimes worshipped in a way similar to the more common sacred stone. The Divinity at Samos was originally symbolized by a wooden plank; and in the more anthropomorphic development, when the Divinity had come to be thought of as the goddess Hera, this plank was called the earliest statue of her. Many other similar stumps of wood experienced the same development in anthropomorphic thought.

In origin some, and probably most, of those sacred stumps or planks were holy trees, decayed and dead; ‡ and they strictly fall under § II. But in other cases the original was a wooden pillar or column, the support of a chamber or house, and falls under the class described above, § I (1); this was clearly the case with the Dionysos Kadmos at Thebes, described by Pausanias, ix. 12. 4 (which de Visser, p. 88, has aptly illustrated from Diod. Sic. I. xxiii. 4).

II. SACRED TREES.—The worship of sacred trees is one of the most widely spread religious phenomena in the early Greek world. The ancient Homeric hymn to the Aphrodite of the Troad (264–272) mentions that the life of the mountain nymphs, who shall nurse the goddess's son, is associated with the life of the sacred trees, which man may not cut down; and that, when a tree withers and dies, the nymph dies with it. The oaks of Dodona were Divine, and the sound of the motion of their branches was the voice of the god declaring his will and revealing the future to men. The bay tree of Apollo, the olive of Athena, and many others, had doubtless the same origin. In later time the popular legend often attached itself to such trees, that they had been planted by some hero or Divine figure (so with two oaks at Heraclea in Pontus), or in some other fashion they were involved in his life-history (a frequent form being that the god or hero or heroine had been suspended from the tree).§

The worship of the tree was conducted on precisely the same plan as that of the image in later times. It was clothed, crowned, adorned;* processions were made to it, sacrifices were burnt to it, and meat-offerings laid before it. People prayed to it and kissed it (Ov. *Met.* vii. 631). It was impious to go beneath it without the proper rites (Ov. *Fast.* iv. 749). It was wrong to pass it without some token of respect (Apul. *Flor.* 1). The fall of a holy tree was a very bad omen; and in Rome on such an occasion an *exauguratio* was performed, as there had originally been an *inauguratio* (Plin. *HN* xv. 20).

Dedication of the *hair* has always been the greatest sign of devotion to any deity; boys dedicated their hair on entering manhood, brides before marriage, married women at the birth of a child; and in Delos it was customary for boys and bridal couples to dedicate their hair under the olive tree that grew on the grave of Hyperoche and Laodice.

The sacred tree was the pledge of the presence and favour of the god, and on it therefore depended the prosperity of the family, tribe, or State which worshipped it. Such belief is seen in reference to the fig tree in the Roman forum,† or the olive in the Acropolis at Athens; and when the latter put forth a new shoot after the burning of the city by the Persians, the people knew that the safety of the city was assured. A piece of the sacred tree was a pledge of security to the Argo and to the fleet of Æneas (*Æn.* ix. 92). The fate of Megara depended on an olive tree (Plin. *HN* xvi. 72).

The tree, then, was on earth the embodiment or the home of Divine life; and the life of man in some forms of belief was connected with a tree during his earthly existence and passed into it at his death. Like the gods, men are often said to be born from trees. Hesiod's third race of men were born from ash trees, and Meleager's life depended on a piece of wood. Ares was born from Hera and a plant (see below, § VI (2)). Talos and Adonis were born from trees. Most instructive are the cases in which the tree is said to have grown out of the hero's grave. Such was the plane tree on the tomb of Amycus in Bithynia: Amycus had opposed and fought with all strangers; and if any part of his tree was taken on board a ship, there ensued constant quarrelling, until his influence was got rid of by throwing away the bough. Here the tree is evidently the embodiment of the spirit of the dead person. There was generally a fountain beside the tree, as at Dodona and Aulis.

Moreover, transformation into a tree was equivalent to translation to the company of the gods: and the tree became then a sacred pledge for posterity, the prototype of the later hero-chapel. The plants and trees which grew on the grave were the life of the buried human being. Phemonoe, the first Pythia, foretold that from her dead body would spring herbs which would give to animals that ate them the power of showing the future by the state of their entrails. Thus she would live on with men. And, similarly, the plants on graves made a connexion between the deceased and this world: an Athenian law (Ael. *Var. Hist.* 5. 17) punished with death any one who cut a holm-oak growing in a sepulchral ground (*heroon*). From this sprung the later custom of planting gardens in cemeteries. Many passages in literature allude to the sympathy between the dead man and the trees or plants on his grave. On that of Protesilaus grew plane trees, whose twigs pointed towards Troy, and whose leaves fell sooner than those of any tree around.‡

The belief in holy trees has lasted, probably unbroken, in Anatolia through Christian times down

* The Carian local names *Laryma* and *Lôryma* (both bishoprics) may be connected (through an intermediate form *Lavryma*); also *Lobrine*, a title of Cybele at Cyzicus.

† See list in Head's *Catalogue of Coins Br. Mus.: Lydia*, p. cxxviii.

‡ Examples in great number are alluded to by Maximus Tyrius, viii. 1 (de Visser, p. 88).

§ The oaks at Heraclea, Plin. *HN*, xvi. 89. On the whole subject Boetticher, *Baumkultus*, is fundamental; but Mannhardt and many other writers must be consulted.

* Theocr. xviii. 45.

† Pliny, *HN* xv. 20, 77.

‡ See also Paus. x. 5. 4; Persius, i. 39; Propertius, iv. 5. 1, 73.

to the present day. In the *Acta* of St. Philetærus* a grove of tall cypress trees at a place in Mysia called Poketos, on the road from Nicæa and the Rhyndacus to Cyzicus, is mentioned as the chief seat of local pagan rites in the 4th cent.; the reference probably proves that the grove existed or was still remembered when the *Acta*, a late composition but embodying a real local tradition, took form. An inscription of Sandal (Satala in the Lydian Katakekaumene) mentions the punishment inflicted in the form of disease by the gods Sabazios and Anaitis Artemis on a man who had cut their trees; and the Mohammedans still believe that disease will afflict any one who cuts the trees on a neighbouring hillock.† Sacred trees were hung with garlands, just as at the present day rags and scraps of garments are tied by Mohammedans to sacred trees in many parts of Asia Minor, though this practice is not in accordance with the spirit or the rules of their religion.

The veneration of the sacred tree or grove evidently implies the idea that the tree is an embodiment of the Divine life and power, and that he who maltreats the tree injures the Divinity that lives in the tree. At the same time, the utilitarian element also entered here, for the belief protects and safeguards the interests of men, or their deep feelings of respect for the dead. The trees beside a village were useful to its population, or they were sentinels keeping watch over the grave of the dead. The worshippers of the Divine power ornament the tree in which that power is manifested with garlands, or with small representations of the power in some of its manifestations: and out of the latter custom, through growing religious degeneration, springs the legend that some hero (connected with, sometimes a mere impersonation of, the Divinity) has been suspended from the tree, as Marsyas from the plane near Celænæ in Phrygia, or Helena from the plane at Sparta (Paus. iii. 19. 10; Theoc. 18, 43).

III. SACRED ANIMALS.—That various animals had some religious awe attached to them in early Greek and Anatolian religion is well known; but the nature and real meaning of this awe are far from certain. No branch of our subject is more obscure than this; and in none are so many wild and vague statements and such mixture of ideas current.

The question of sacred animals is always liable to be mixed up with the question of Totemism. There are, indubitably, certain facts in the religious ceremonial and symbolism of the Greek peoples which can be most easily and naturally explained as survivals of Totemism. But we cannot think that Totemism held any place in Greek or Anatolian religion as it presents itself to our study. Similarly, the black stone of the Kaaba in Mecca is an old fetish, the veneration of which has survived in Mohammedanism; but fetishism is not really an influence in, or part of, Mohammedanism. Many survivals of pagan rites and symbols are apparent in the developed Hebrew worship, but they did not touch its essence or affect its development except to be successively eliminated from it. Similarly, the survivals of Totemistic forms in the Greek world do not affect our study of its religion, though they are of extreme interest to the archæological investigator. The religious ideas of the tribes and races, whose contact and intercourse produced the form of thought, religion, and civilization which we call Hellenism, were raised above the level of Totemism; and even the earliest Greek thought did not understand those survivals in a Totemistic way, but put a new, and historically incorrect, interpretation on them in popular legend.

* *Acta Sanctorum*, 19th May, p. 324.

† Μουσεῖον καὶ Βιβλ. τῆς Εὐαγγ. Σχολῆς, Smyrna, 1880, p. 164.

Also, the form of religious thought in which the sacred animal was regarded and worshipped as being actually a god incarnate is not characteristic of Anatolia. The nearest approach to that idea is in the Ephesian religion of Artemis (7), where the goddess was the queen bee; but there is no proof that any actual bee was worshipped. The explanations of sacrificial rites as being cases in which celebrants kill and eat the sacred animal as the body of their god, are not admissible, except perhaps in some borrowed rites of external origin.

We may, with some confidence, lay down the general principle (which we shall find confirmed in several instances and contradicted in none), that the sacred animals of Anatolian religion are regarded in relation to a more generalized conception of the Divine power, which lies behind them and finds expression through them. Hence they are often represented in the rude symbolism of primitive Anatolian art as associated with, or employed in, the service of some deity or Divine figure, who is an embodiment of that higher Divine power.

(1) *Animals as parts of the god.* — The most typical appearance of animals in this way is as bearers or supporters or companions or components of gods. A god or goddess is often shown in rude Anatolian cult-representations as standing on an animal or bird: that is the case with a god, presumably Sandon or Baal-Tarz (Hellenized as *Zeus Tarsios*), represented on coins of Tarsus, with several deities on the religious sculptures in the *adytum* at Boghaz-Keui, and with various small works of art in bronze or on seals or in other forms. The Horseman-god described below, (5), perhaps belongs to this class.*

In other cases the figure of a god has a rough resemblance to the human form, but is composed of one or more animal forms, supporting a human head, or in an Egyptianizing type the head is that of a beast or bird, but the body is human (as in some figures at Boghaz-Keui, or the Black Demeter with the head of a horse at Phigalia in Arcadia).

To this class belong the representations of Cybele with her lions, or of Artemis with her stags. In those cases the earliest known types show the Deity with a form in which nothing is human except the head and perhaps the arms: the rest of the figure is a mere shapeless non-human mass or stump. The animals stand on each side of this central figure. In one case Cybele's lions rest their forepaws on her shoulders.† Greek art took these ancient native types and developed them freely, making the figures of the goddesses entirely human, giving beauty and dignity to them, seating Cybele on a throne with her symbols (*patera* and *tympanon*) in her hands, representing Artemis after the type of the Greek hunting goddess, and introducing some dramatic motive in their relation to the accompanying animals: the goddess plays with the animals or caresses one of them with her hand. Sometimes the lion reclines in Cybele's lap like a pet dog. See also § V (3).

In such representations it is clear that the original religious conception did not regard the Deity as of human form. There is sufficient resemblance to suggest at first sight the human form; but at the second glance the differences are seen to be very marked. The types arose, as we shall see, in the way of votive offerings. The worshipper offered to the Divine power some rude representation of itself, laying this on or near the stone, or

* G. F. Hill, *Catalogue of Coins Brit. Mus.: Cilicia*, p. 178; Perrot, *Histoire de l'Art dans l'Antiq.* iv. pp. 637–40, 646, 772, etc. See also § I (3).

† *Journal of Hell. Studies*, 1884, p. 245 and plate.

hanging it from the tree, which was considered to be the home of the Divinity. The representation rudely embodied the vague, unformed conception entertained by the worshippers: the Divine power was not wholly unlike human, but it was different, and contained the strength and swiftness or the teeming productive power of various animals.

The conception of the *Satyr*, a half-human half-bestial form, belongs originally to Asia Minor, and was developed, first in Ionian, and then in general Greek art. The more strictly Greek conceptions of Thessalian Centaur and Arcadian Pan are fundamentally the same in character. The Satyr-type varies between human mixed with horse and human mixed with goat, while the Centaur is only of the first kind and Pan only of the second. Silenus is a similar idea, of Anatolian origin probably, but developed in art more on the human side. The idea in all these figures is that of rude, free, natural life, untrained, unfettered by conventions and ideas of merely human origin; this life of nature is the spontaneous expression of the Divine life, and comes nearer to the Divine nature than men can approach, but also it has a distinct human side, and can come more easily into relations with mankind than the Divine nature can. Men can by stealth catch and force to their will * the Satyr and Silenus, who are thus intermediaries between the Divine and the human. On the other hand, those figures are the companions and servants and associates of the god Dionysos, a deity of marked Anatolian character. In another respect they are a means of mediating between the Divine nature and mankind: 'they took them wives of all that they chose' (Gn $6^2$). Now the idea lies deep in the Anatolian religion, as we shall see, that man has come from God and goes back to him at death; and evidently this relation between Satyrs or Sileni and human women is one of the grotesque developments by degradation of that idea; see below on the serpent (11).

(2) The *bull* often appears in surroundings which show his religious significance: in one case he seems to be standing on an altar, as an object of worship to the human figures looking towards him.† The very frequent employment of a bull's head on sepulchral and other steles and on sarcophagi at a later period evidently originated in the sacred character of the animal, and had at first an apotropaic purpose (the Divine power protecting the grave), but became purely conventional and ornamental in the lapse of time. But even in the above-mentioned case, where the bull is the object of worship, a glance at the figure is sufficient to show that he is worshipped as a symbol: he represents and embodies the generative power of nature: there lies behind him the Divine power of growth and life, which he expresses: in this character he played a part in the Phrygian Mysteries.‡

(3) The *goat*, which is mentioned as sacred in the worship of Leto and Lairbenos, § and doubtless generally, was associated with Dionysos, a deity of markedly Anatolian character. At Laodicea on the Lycus the goat appears as a companion of the god Aseis (identified with the Greek Zeus, and treated as an epithet of Zeus), who lays his hands on the horns of a goat standing beside him. In Greek art there is known a type showing Aphrodite riding on a goat, which may probably be an artistic development of an old schema showing a deity standing on a goat. Such also is a late Anatolian type showing Men sitting or riding on a goat.

The goat and the ox are evidently the animals characteristic of a pastoral people on the great plains of central Asia Minor; and the fact that they were so useful must have helped to give them their sacred character. Countless herds of goats are still a feature of the great plains of the central plateau.

Like the bull, the sacred goat is doubtless to be understood as the male animal, the embodiment and representative of the productive Divine power regarded on the active side. The Divine nature, as we shall see, was regarded in Anatolia sometimes as complete and sexless, but more frequently as divided into two Divine beings, male and female; and in the latter case the life of nature is pictured in the cultus as the mutual relations of the Divine pair, the god and the goddess.

(4) The *sheep* was a third animal of great importance on the pasture-land of the plateau; and there is evidence that it was sacred. The sheep was worshipped by the Samians, and was closely connected with the worship of Hermes. Milchhöfer in *Archäolog. Zeitung*, 1883, p. 263, quotes examples of the occurrence of the ram as a figure on graves in Phrygia and Armenia.

The sacred sheep is to be understood as the ram. He stands in the same relation to Hermes as the goat does to Dionysos. It is a ram that appears on the Anatolian and Armenian tombs.

(5) The *horse* must be regarded as a sacred animal (as might be expected), on account of the widely-spread representations of the Horseman-god. No Divine figure is so common in the later hieratic art of Asia Minor as this deity. He occurs on the coins of many cities in Lydia and West Phrygia, and on rock reliefs as well as on votive steles in the Pisidian hill-country; these are almost all of the Roman period, but the type is certainly much older. In many cases the Horseman-god is a hero, *i.e.* the deified form of a dead man (regarded as identified with the god, § VIII (5)), and the type must in those cases be regarded as sepulchral. Hence the horse-head, which appears in many sepulchral reliefs in Attica, may be taken as a symbolic indication of the same type, the part standing for the whole. In those reliefs the deified dead is usually represented as a seated figure of heroic size, and the horse-head in an upper corner of the relief indicates in brief the type of the Horseman-god, which is another form of the dead man's new heroized nature. The horse was probably imported into Anatolia, and belongs to a later period than bull, sheep, and goat.

(6) The *swine*.—Most difficult and obscure are the questions connected with the swine. There is good evidence to show that the swine was sacred in the Anatolian religion. In Crete, which was in strong religious sympathy with Asia Minor, the swine was sacred, and played an important part in the Mysteries and the birth of Zeus. At the Eleusinian Mysteries, which were influenced both from Crete and from Asia Minor, the swine constituted the most efficacious and purificatory sacrifice; the Greek purification for murder or homicide involved the sacrifice of a swine, and the Lydian ceremony is said by Herodotus (i. 35) to have been identical with the Greek (which may be taken as proof that the rite was carried from Anatolia to Greece). In Lycia a swine is represented on the Harpy Tomb, under the chair on which sits the heroized or deified dead. Small pigs of terra-cotta or porcelain have been found in Lydian graves.* The older and general Phrygian custom had at least no horror of swine.†

* Xenophon, *Anab.* i. 2, and many other places.

† Perrot, p. 668 f.; cf. p. 672.

‡ Ταῦρος δράκοντος καὶ πατὴρ ταύρου δράκων, 'the god-bull is father of the god-serpent, and the serpent of the bull,' was a formula of the Phrygian Mysteries (Clemens Alex. *Protrept.* ii.).

§ See Roscher's *Lexikon der gr. u. röm. Mythologie*, *s.v.* 'Lairbenos' (Drexler), and Ramsay, *Cities and Bish. of Phrygia*, i. p. 138 f. See also below, (8).

* Ramsay, *Histor. Geog. of Asia Minor*, p. 32.

† *Ib.* p. 32.

But this Anatolian custom was interfered with by a new influence, namely, the Semitic (or perhaps we ought to say simply the Jewish) and Egyptian abhorrence for the swine.* This ruled, at least in later time, at the Pontic Komana, where a swine might not be brought into the city, much less into the sacred precinct or temple of the goddess.

Here we are brought in view of two opposing and irreconcilable ideas; and our view is, in all such cases, that these contradictory ideas originate from different races (or, in the case of Jewish religion, from the influence of a new step in development). The attempt has been made to interpret the abhorrence and loathing of the swine as arising naturally out of the extreme awe and fear with which it was regarded on account of its high supernatural powers; but, on such a principle, anything can be evolved out of anything. There are two opposite conceptions of the swine.

According to the one, the swine is a sacred and purifying animal; it is in close relation with the Divine nature, and the human worshipper uses it to cleanse himself so that he may be fitted to come into relation with the Deity—sacrificed as the Eleusinian and Eteocretan prelude to initiation or marriage [identical rites, § VIII (1)]; not eaten except after sacrifice (see (8), (9), and Ath. 376).

According to the other conception, the swine must not be brought near the Deity nor permitted even to approach his neighbourhood, any one who has touched a swine is unclean, any one who habitually comes in contact with swine is a permanent outcast. We refuse to consider that these two opposing views have a common origin: they belong to two irreconcilable modes of thought. The abhorrence of the swine we explain on grounds of health: in a hot country the flesh of the swine is not wholesome, and in the development of thought and religion in Egypt and in Palestine this was observed and constituted into a religious law for the benefit of man.

It is said that the Egyptians once a year sacrificed a swine to the moon and Osiris, and ate its flesh; and in Is 66[17] we hear of Jews who met secretly to eat the flesh of swine and mice as a religious rite. But these are natural examples of the persistence of the old religious facts in secret or on some exceptional occasion: the new and higher religious idea cannot wholly extirpate the ancient idea: the old superstition has a hold on the souls of men, and usually something is conceded to it. Only, the Hebrew prophets would concede nothing, but insisted on the absolute and utter abolition of the old superstition: that is one of the numberless points of distinction between Hebrew religion and all other ancient religions which competed with it.

The principle laid down in the preceding paragraph is one of great importance in our subject. In the religious history of the Greek tribes we observe numerous cases in which the religious idea of one tribe overpowers that of another when the two tribes come together. But a religious fact rarely, if ever, dies utterly: though the weaker, it produces some effect on the stronger, and one of the commonest effects was that a secret and mysterious performance of the submerged religious ritual was permitted at long intervals.† Thus human sacrifice seems to have been allowed to continue in rare acts of ritual, many centuries after the general feeling of the Greek tribes had condemned the idea of sacrificing a human being. Another way in which the submerged religion maintained itself was in the superstitions of the lowest and least educated classes, and in rites which were rejected as magical and irreligious by the higher thought of the people.

The rules of impurity connected with the swine are also a subject of great difficulty; and here again the difficulty seems due to the interlacing and intermixture of different religious ideas, no one of which has made itself absolutely supreme. Thus, for example, the statement is sometimes made that the worshippers of the Lycian and Anatolian god Men Tyrannos abstained from swine's flesh; yet the swine was intimately connected with the Divine power in Lycia (as we have seen).

Out of these facts a very elaborate theory that men abstained from the sacred animal as being holy can be spun. But the abstaining from swine's flesh in the ritual of Men Tyrannos was merely a very brief temporary act of purificatory preparation, as is obvious from the context,* and did not amount to a permanent rule of avoidance, such as obtained in Egypt and Palestine. The rules of preparatory purification in the later period (our authority belongs to the time of the empire) were much influenced by analogy; and this case proves nothing as to the real and original theory ruling in the worship of Men Tyrannos.

The abstinence from swine's flesh, said to have been practised at Pessinus in Phrygia, was, perhaps, a much more serious and real fact. It would hardly have been mentioned by Pausanias had it been a mere act of brief occasional purification: he records it, evidently, as standing in marked contrast to the ordinary usage of Western Anatolia (of which he was a native, and whose people he had chiefly in view as his readers). The custom of Pessinus is to be explained as due to Semitic influence gradually spreading westwards over Asia Minor.

The sacred character of the swine in early Anatolian and Greek ritual was due, beyond all doubt, to its being considered as a symbol and representative of the Great Mother. It was the domesticated sow, with her teeming litters of young, that suggested its holy character. Thus the holiness was founded on similar grounds to that of the bull or cow and the sheep and the goat: the animals which were most useful to man were esteemed sacred, as the gifts of God. There can hardly be any doubt that the method of domesticating and caring for these animals was considered to have been revealed by the god, who continues to be their patron, and whose beneficent power towards man is manifested in them: see (8).

The *wild boar*, which is sometimes connected in mythology with the Divine nature, would derive his sacredness from a different cause, for he must be classed with the wild animals which are impersonations of the Divine strength and swiftness and might: see (10).

(7) *The bee.*—Most instructive of all in regard to the Divine nature is the bee. The bee was the sacred symbol at Ephesus, *i.e.* the bee was the type of the goddess. A large body of subordinate priestesses connected with her worship were called *melissai*, the working bees; and a body of officials (who were originally of priestly character) † were called *essenes.* Now there was a mistake, common in Greece, with regard to the sex of bees; the queen bee was thought to be a male, and called *essen* or βασιλεύς. But, when we look at the Ephesian cult, we find that it was founded on

* See Wiedemann, *Herodot's Zweit'es Buch*, p. 85. Origen, *c. Cels.* v. 49, speaks of the Egyptian priests alone as refraining, which implies a relaxation of usage.

† See below, § VII (2).

* The authority is a pair of almost identical inscriptions frequently published: Dittenberger, *Sylloge*, No. 379, *CIA* iii. 73, 74; Foucart, *Assoc. Relig.* p. 219. The worshipper must purify himself ἀπὸ σκίρδων καὶ χοιρέων καὶ γυναικός, but the purification was a matter of a day, and after washing from head to foot the worshipper could enter the god's presence the same day: the eating of garlic and swine's flesh, like the third fact, is implied to be the habitual and ordinary way of life of the worshippers.

† See, *e.g.*, Pausanias, viii. 13, 1.

a true knowledge. The goddess was the queen bee; and her image makes this plain. Her body has only the slightest resemblance to a human body, but has the outline of the body of a bee. What are ordinarily called *mammæ* on her body are not so, for no nipple is indicated: they really represent eggs, and the mass of the body is simply a great ovary or skin filled with ova. The goddess is literally indicated as the one great mother of all life in the community. The *essenes* are the male bees or drones, who do no work. The *melissai* are the female and working bees, in whom the sexual character is undeveloped (see § VI (3)). The resemblance between the constitution of the swarm or community of bees and that of the primitive Anatolian community, as described in § VIII (3), (7), is striking.

The resemblance is even more striking in respect of the life-history of the Mother-Goddess and of the queen bee; but this will be treated in § VI (3). Taking this in conjunction with the preceding remarks about the Divine power and life under the bee form, we see clearly that the place of the bee in the cultus implies such knowledge of its habits as would be impossible without careful observation and intelligent methods of treatment. This is merely one example of the wisdom and skill applied to the utilization and domestication of animals in the ancient Anatolian theocratic system. The arts of domestication were rooted in religion. The remarkable practice of self-mutilation as a religious act, characteristic of Phrygian worship (§ VIII (4)), seems clearly to have originated from the rule (divinely given, as was supposed) of mutilating in the same way oxen and other domesticated animals, and from the natural mutilation of the bee (§ VI (3)).

(8) *The sacredness attaching to domesticated animals.*—It is obvious that the sacred character of the animals which have hitherto been mentioned rests ultimately on their domestication and their usefulness to man. This suggests that some of the arts of domestication may have originated on the great Anatolian plateau, where the conditions are exceedingly favourable,* and where the existing traces show that a large population and great cities were found where now for many centuries only a very sparse sprinkling of nomads and a certain number of small villages have existed. That a high degree of skill was reached in the domestication of animals is also certain. Valuable breeds of animals were artificially produced by intelligent cross-breeding. Of these the Angora goat still survives; and the secret of its breeding is still carefully treasured and concealed.† That the secret of preserving the purity of the wool lies in breeding is pointed out elsewhere,‡ on the authority of practical experience; and the natural probability of this explanation (which has never been mentioned elsewhere) is admitted as obvious by some high authorities to whom it has been mentioned. But the breed of the Colossian sheep with its glossy violet fleece, and the glossy black-fleeced sheep of Laodicea, have entirely disappeared; and the reason is that those artificial breeds were through carelessness allowed to degenerate.§

(9) *Domesticated animals as sacrifice.*—No doubt need be entertained, though the fact cannot be definitely demonstrated by extant evidence, that the life of all domesticated animals was sacred. Their existence was so important to man that it

* See art. on 'Geographical Conditions determining History and Religion' in the *Geographical Journal*, Sept. 1902, p. 272: see also below, (12).

† We cannot accept the view advocated by some distinguished German writers, that the Angora goat was introduced from Central Asia, and is a naturally distinct species.

‡ Ramsay, *Impressions of Turkey*, p. 272 ff.

§ *Impressions of Turkey, loc. cit.*

must be guaranteed and protected by the strongest religious sanctions. To slay the ox or the sheep or the goat or the swine was an act of impiety. Among the Phrygians it was a capital crime to slay an ox used in ploughing.*

Yet there can be equally little doubt both that the flesh of the animals was wanted as food and that they were needed as offerings in sacrifice. Here two religious laws come into collision with one another. A quaint and evidently very archaic ceremony, which was preserved among the people of Athens (a race characteristically autochthonous and Pelasgian), illustrates the way in which the difficulty was met. The ox for sacrifice was selected by a sort of chance, the one being taken which first came forward out of a herd to eat the corn scattered on the altar near which the animals were driven. The ox thus selected was slain for the sacrifice; but the ministers who slew it with axe and knife fled, and in their absence the weapons which had killed the sacred animal were tried and condemned, and punished for sacrilege by being thrown into the sea. The flesh of the ox was eaten; its skin was stuffed with straw, and the stuffed animal was harnessed to a plough.†

The character of the ceremony, as an expiation of the apparent crime of slaying the sacred animal, is clear. The god, in his kindness to man, has shown how the guilt may be avoided or diverted, and the flesh of the animal can be enjoyed by man without suffering the due penalty. The name of the sacrifice, τὰ Βουφόνια, 'the ceremonies connected with the slaying of the ox,'‡ makes the meaning of the whole clear. Probably, in the origin, the killing of an ox (not a common act in agricultural life), perhaps even the killing of any sacred animal, was always accompanied with that elaborate ceremonial, and made a religious act. The ox was induced to commit an act of impiety in eating the sacred barley and wheat on the altar; any guilt involved in slaying him was visited on the murdering weapon; and, finally, the pretence was gone through that the ox was still ready to be used for its ordinary agricultural work.

The attempt has been made to explain the *Bouphonia* as the slaying in the harvest season of the ox which represents the spirit of vegetation: the ox, as the Divine being who constitutes the life of the crop, is supposed to be slain at the harvest (as Lityerses in Phrygia was slain by the sickles of the reapers). This attempt is supported by an incorrect interpretation of the word *Bouphonia*, as 'the slaying of the ox.' The explanation is forced and unsatisfactory, and may be considered as an example of the extreme to which excellent scholars are sometimes led in trying to adapt a theory, which furnishes the correct explanation of many usages, to other usages which it does not suit.

A Phrygian inscription throws some light on this subject. The goat is there mentioned as sacred. A certain person confesses to have sinned because he had eaten the flesh of the goat, though the animal had not been offered as a sacrifice with the proper ceremonial: he atones for the sin, and acknowledges the justice of the penalty with which the god has visited him.§

* Nic. Damasc. in Dindorf, *Hist. Græc. Min.* i. p. 148.

† The accounts of the ceremony vary a little as regards details: see Mr. J. G. Frazer's *Golden Bough*[2], vol. ii. p. 294 f.

‡ This sense of the plural is typical and common: Διὸς γοναί, 'the circumstances connected with the birth of Zeus,' and so on. A false interpretation of the word Βουφόνια is alluded to in the next paragraph.

§ See *Cities and Bishoprics of Phrygia*, i. pp. 138, 150. The present writer has there adopted an explanation suggested to him by Prof. Robertson Smith, which would take the crime to consist in eating goats' flesh at all. But it is more probable that the crime lay in eating it without first offering the animal in sacrifice. Either of the two different senses given to ἄθυτος in the two explanations is grammatically possible.

(10) The *lion*, which is so often associated with Cybele, is also found in art as the supporter on which a deity stands. Like the bull, and doubtless for the same reason, the lion was taken as a common ornament on tombstones—originally with a protective meaning, later as a mere conventional figure—especially in Phrygia and Pisidia.* Similarly, the *stag* was the regular accompaniment of Artemis, and appears carrying a deity on an early Anatolian seal.†

There can be no doubt that the sacredness of these two animals, the lion and the stag, springs from their being the most typical representatives of wild natural life in its strength and its swiftness. These two typical wild animals are connected intimately and characteristically with the Divine nature as female, *i.e.* with Cybele or Artemis. That side of the Divine nature bulked far more largely in old Anatolian religion than the male side.‡ The Great Goddess, the All-Mother, plays a much more characteristic and commanding part than the god, who is often pictured as her attendant, and as secondary to her. The life of nature is commonly represented as female. The spirits of the trees and mountains, the lakes and forests, are the Nymphs, described often as if they led a sexless, separate existence, though there are not wanting examples of the other conception, which brings them into association with the Satyrs or Sileni and makes the reproduction of the life of nature spring from the relations between the male and the female divinities.

Accordingly, it is a pair of lionesses, not of lions, that appear on the most ancient Phrygian Lion-Tombs and on the Gateway at Mycenæ. But the sex is not always emphasized; and artistic considerations probably contributed to determine the ultimate preference for lions and stags, so that these were regularly represented as companions even of the goddesses Cybele and Artemis: the mane and the horns made the male animals more picturesque and striking types.

But in none of these cases is there any universal rule of sex. If the male Divinity is symbolized by the ram or he-goat, there are certain to be some cases in which the female Divinity must be represented by the female animal in order to carry out the mythological tale or the cult-act. These less usual and less typical instances, which need not be quoted in detail, do not really interfere with the general rule of sex which has been stated.

(11) The *serpent*, however, was pre-eminently the sacred animal in Anatolian and Greek religion. It dwells in the bosom of the earth, the Great Mother. It appears and disappears in a mysterious way. In many Greek temples, and especially in the temple of Athena Polias on the Acropolis at Athens, a sacred serpent dwelt: it was fed by the priests, and considered to be a sort of embodiment or guarantee of the Divine presence in the temple. This idea, however, was below the religious level of the highest Greek literature, in which it does not make much appearance; but it played a great part in popular belief and superstition, as well as in actual ritual. Especially, a serpent with large cheeks, called *pareias*, which was believed to be friendly to man and hostile to dangerous serpents, was considered holy, and used in the ritual of the Mysteries. In the sacred drama enacted in the Mysteries the god in the form of a serpent became father of the god-bull by Kora or Persephone his daughter (see the quotation in note to § III (2)); and the initiated fondled a *pareias* serpent in imitation of this.* Hence the idea that human life is of Divine origin took the form, in regard to some special heroes, (*e.g.* Alexander the Great) that a serpent was their father.

The idea that the serpent is a representative of the Divine life appears in various forms: a serpent was intimately associated with, and almost the embodiment to human eyes of, Æsculapius or Asklepios, of Sabazios, of Zeus Meilichios, and in general of most heroic and dæmonic conceptions, and of the departed dead. Naturally, the animal, which often took up its residence in graves, was regarded by popular superstition as the embodied spirit of the dead; and, when a serpent took possession of any grave in this way, there was a general tendency to regard the person there buried as being peculiarly active and efficacious, *i.e.* as a hero.† The dead man, again, has become identified with the Divine nature; and the serpent therefore is peculiarly representative of the Divine nature in its Chthonian aspect, *i.e.* as connected with the world of death. The Agathos Daimon, a Chthonian power, associated with the earth and the riches of the earth, is represented by a serpent (sometimes with a human head). See B, § V.

The worship of the god-serpent at Hierapolis and Laodicea in the Lycus valley‡ has played some part in the formation of Christian legend: the sacred serpent is there called the Echidna, and is described as the powerful enemy of St. John and St. Philip.

The belief in the sacredness of the serpent was practically disregarded by the majority of Greeks in the classical period, and despised as a superstition unworthy of an educated person; but some peculiarly sacred serpents, such as that of Athena Polias, retained a hold on general opinion. Ælian mentions that, of all the Peloponnesian Greeks, only the Argives refrained from killing serpents.

(12) *Sacredness of wild animals.*—Obviously, there is not the slightest appearance that the sacredness of the above-mentioned wild animals in this early religion was founded on dread of their power, and anxiety to propitiate them. The facts as stated are absolutely opposed to that opinion. Moreover, in the region of Asia Minor which we take to be the centre and origin of its religious ideas, the great central plateau, wild animals can hardly have been a serious danger within historical times. The country is open, and there is such total absence of cover§ that beasts of prey cannot have existed in any numbers. The Austrian traveller Sarre quotes the statement of Von Moltke, that the great plains are the most perfectly level known in the world. As a rule, they are and have been for thousands of years so bare and, apart from human work and provision, so unproductive, that little wild life, and none of the greater savage animals, could be supported in them. In such a level country deer would be a difficult prey; and when human skill wrought out some irrigation, found water, where it was not accessible on the surface, by sinking very deep wells, and introduced great herds of domesticated animals, the wild beasts which were able to prey on sheep or oxen

* For Phrygia, see *Journal of Hellenic Studies*, 1882, etc. For Pisidia, see Sterrett, *Wolfe Expedition*, pp. 91–93. The present writer has seen many other Pisidian or Isaurian examples. Rohde (*Psyche*, p. 679) thinks that the lion was used as denoting the fourth grade in Mithraic initiation, and Cumont (*Monum. relat. au Cult de Mithras*, p. 173) inclines to agree with him. This cannot be correct. It leaves the sex out of account: see the two following paragraphs.

† Perrot, *op. cit.* iv. p. 772.

‡ See below, § VI.

* Σαβαζίων γοῦν μυστηρίων σύμβολον τοῖς μυουμένοις ὁ διὰ κόλπου θεός· δράκων δέ ἐστιν οὗτος, διελκόμενος τοῦ κόλπου τῶν τελουμένων (Clemens Alex. *Protrept.* ii. 16; cf. Arnobius, v. 21; Foucart, *Les Associations Religieuses*).

† Strictly, every dead man was a hero; but such ones were heroes *par excellence*.

‡ Ramsay, *Cities and Bishoprics of Phrygia*, i. pp. 51, 87.

§ The central plains were known as *Axylon*, the treeless region, two centuries before Christ, in the first glimpse of them that the records permit; and other considerations show that this state had existed for a long time previously.

or goats could shelter themselves only in the broken ground of the surrounding mountains,* and in some of the isolated mountain peaks of the plateau (for others of those plateau mountains are singularly bare and shelterless). Thus the greater beasts of prey must have been from a very remote period few, and regarded in practical life as an object of the chase and of sport to the rulers and the nobles (in whatever form nobles existed); and it is probable that this condition of things fostered the tendency to regard them as sacred by some sort of religious substitute for a game law.

Again, serpents are neither very numerous nor at all dangerous. Various quite harmless species occur in moderate abundance, and a few are said to be venomous, but death from the bite of a serpent is practically unknown in the country. Yet the scantiness of the population in recent centuries, and the small extent of agriculture, have given full opportunity for wild life to increase to its natural limits.

Accordingly, for a period of four thousand years or more, wild animals in the plateau must probably have derived their sacredness from other considerations than the terror and danger that they caused; and the evidence of religious facts is clear that the origin lay in their noble qualities of strength and swiftness, and in their association with the Divine nature living free in the wild and mountainous districts. See also above, (10).

IV. SACRED PLACES.—(1) *Mountains.*—If a stone could be holy, much more could a great rock or a mountain be regarded as the home or the embodiment of the Divine power.† Mount Argæus, the lofty mountain which towers above Cæsarea in Cappadocia to the height of nearly 13,000 feet, was regarded as a god or as an image of the god, and by it men took a solemn oath: on the coins of Cæsarea it is the regular type, taking the place which the image of a god occupies in most coins of Hellenic or Hellenized cities. On coins of Prostanna in Pisidia, Mount Viaros is represented in a similar way, and it, too, was evidently regarded by the people who dwelt near it as the holy mountain. The identification proposed in the *Historical Geography of Asia Minor* (p. 407) for Mt. Viaros rests chiefly ‡ on a certain similarity in the situation of the lofty peak, which towers over Egerdir and the great lake called by the ancients Limnai, to Argæus rising out of the level Cappadocian plateau.

Then in general it is probable or certain that the Great God was adored on the tops of other mountains. An example from another Cappadocian hill is proved by an inscription found on the summit.§ The lofty mountain, now called Hassan Dagh, 10,000 feet high, north-west from Tyana, seems to have borne the same name, *Argæus*, as the Cæsarean mountain; and in that case it probably had a similar sacred character. The Bithynians worshipped Zeus under the names of Papas ('father') and Attis ‖ on the tops of mountains.

In the rock-temple at Boghaz-Keui, one of the figures, evidently a personage of great importance on account of his size,¶ is represented as standing, or rather striding, with his feet on the summits of two mountains. The Divine nature rests on the mountains, and is at home on their summits, just as, in other representations on the walls of the same natural temple, several deities stand on their own sacred animals.* Again, in that same rock-temple, several of the sacred animals stand with their feet placed on the top of high squared pedestals; and the so-called 'Niobe' on Mt. Sipylus, which is beyond doubt an image of the goddess Cybele, sits with her feet resting on two similar pedestals.† Those pedestals are probably to be interpreted as holy pillars (such as those at Gnossos in Crete, pictured in Mr. Evans' article, *Journal of Hellenic Studies*, 1901, p. 110). The present writer formerly interpreted them as mountains;‡ but in the art as practised at Boghaz-Keui the type of the sacred mountain was rounded in form and broken in outline, and it seems hardly permissible to suppose that two types so different were employed there simultaneously to indicate the same conception.

The truth may indeed probably be that the sacred stone when unshaped and rude derived its holiness, in some cases, from being regarded as representative of the sacred mountain, the part standing for the whole (just as the bull's head stands for the god-bull, § III (2)), or the miniature for the vast reality. The *omphalos*, on which Apollo sits or stands, would then be a sort of miniature of the mountain which is his Divine abode.

It seems, at any rate, beyond doubt that originally any great mountain, such as Mt. Argæus, was considered sacred, because on it there rested a vague formless Divine presence and power, whose might dominated the country round. This becomes all the more clear when one considers the sacred caves: see the following paragraph.

(2) *Sacred caves and mountain glens.*—Many sacred caves are known: as, for example, Steunos, the cave of Cybele, near Aizani, described by Mr. J. G. C. Anderson in *Annual of British Sch. Ath.*, 1897–8, p. 56; the cave of Leto or Cybele, beside Hierapolis, described in *Cities and Bishoprics of Phrygia*, i. p. 89; the cave of Zeus on Mt. Dicte in Crete, recently excavated by Mr. Hogarth; etc. All these are caves in the mountains, lonely, far from cities, full of the impressiveness and religious awe of wild and majestic nature. Along with caves in the stricter sense we may class deep gorges and glens among the mountains, in which holy places of Anatolia were often situated. They are roofed with the sky, instead of with a covering of rock.

In those caves and gorges the Divine power was not worshipped in any visible embodiment. The human mind was impressed by the vague formless presence of the Divine nature in such solitary places, and went there to worship. So, in modern times, at the head of the deep romantic gorge of Ibriz, where the great springs of the river of Cybistra-Heraclea flow forth from the rock in surroundings of impressive grandeur, the rude peasants from the neighbouring village come and tie a rag to the tree by the great fountain; and, if you ask the reason why they do so, they reply in simple phrase, '*Dede var*,' which is the nearest approach their untrained thought and scanty words can make to expressing their sense of present Divine power.§ In ancient times men had the same thought, that the Divine power was clearly manifested for the benefit of man at Ibriz; and they expressed it similarly by votive offerings, as

* The present writer has there seen bears and boars often; panthers and leopards are reported to exist.

† *ὄρος Καππαδόκαις καὶ θεὸς καὶ ὅρκος καὶ ἄγαλμα* (Max. Tyr. viii. 8); graves on hill-tops, Puchstein, *Reisen in Kl.* p. 228.

‡ The order of Hierocles and the established identification of surrounding cities place Prostanna somewhere there.

§ Ramsay, in *Bull. Corresp. Hell.* 1883, p. 322.

‖ Surely *Attis* must mean 'king' or 'prince.'

¶ Perrot, *Histoire de l'Art*, iv. p. 639.

* See above, § III: the figures are shown in Perrot, *Histoire*, iv. p. 637.

† *Journal of Hell. Stud.* 1882, p. 39.

‡ As quoted in the previous note.

§ *Dede* doubtless means originally 'ancestor': it is the name applied to those heroized personages worshipped in the *Turbes* common all over the country: the *Turbe* always contains or is built above the grave of the *Dede*, who is sometimes a known historical figure, sometimes a mythical personage, sometimes one whose very name has been forgotten, and who is simply 'the *Dede*.' See below, § VIII (5).

we may be sure. But they expressed it also in more civilized and artistic ways; and above all other forms they expressed it in a great rock sculpture, showing the god presenting his gifts of corn and wine to the king of the land. The river makes this part of the dry Lycaonian plain into a garden; and the god has given the river, making it flow forth from his holy mountain at the head of that deep gorge, which is like a vast cave open to the sky. The king is dressed in gorgeous embroidered robes: the god wears a peasant's dress, for he is the impersonation of the toiling cultivator, who by patience and faith adapts nature to the benefit of man. Nowhere is the spirit of Anatolian religion expressed so unmistakably as at Ibriz. In the words in which St. Paul appealed to a simple audience of Lycaonians, the fountains of Ibriz are a witness to the Divine power, that it did good and gave men fruitful seasons, filling their hearts with food and gladness (Ac 14[17]). The speaker knew his audience, and caught the exact tone of religious feeling that sounded in their hearts.

The rock-temple at Boghaz-Keui, which has been so often mentioned above, was of this class. A mile away from the great city, up a gorge in the side of a rocky hill, two chambers with vertical walls cut in the rocks (the human hand having assisted the natural formation of the recesses), entirely open to the sky, and connected by a narrow passage, leading from one to the other, constitute the temple and place of worship.

To the same class belonged the great Cappadocian sanctuary of Komana, in a glen of the Anti-Taurus, where the river Sarus flows in its winding channel deep down among the lofty mountains. To the same class, too, belonged one of the holy places of Ephesus. Besides the familiar and famous home of the Ephesian Artemis, which lay out in the open plain near the city and close to the isolated holy hill near the middle of the Cayster valley, there was another seat of her worship in a glen among the mountains that bound the valley on the south. This more sequestered place retained its sanctity alongside of the more famous temple. The account given of it has been transformed by adaptation to the later Greek mythology of Artemis; and the true old Anatolian aspect can only be guessed at. But there the birth of the goddess had occurred: there an annual festival and assembly (*panegyris*) was celebrated: there were both an ancient temple with archaic images and a later temple with Greek statues: there an association of Kouretes, evidently a society meeting in the worship of the goddess,* called by an ancient Anatolian and Cretan name, had its centre and celebrated certain mystic rites. And when the religion of Ephesus had been changed to a Christian form, the city had not merely the Church of St. John beside the great temple in the plain and the church called Maria in the city (where the Council of A.D. 431 was held): † there was also a holy place of the Mother of God among the mountains on the south of the plain (to which the Greeks of the district continued to make an annual pilgrimage down to the present day, calling the place Panagia Kapulu, the Virgin of the Door).‡

(3) *Sacred springs and lakes.*—In the holy place of Ibriz we have found that the awe attaching to glens amid the mountains was inseparable from the similar religious emotion suggested by bountiful springs. In that thirsty country the most fertile soil without water is a desert; but if water is given or brought it becomes a garden. A fountain, then, was the gift of God; and the modern name applied to such great springs, *Huda-verdi* ('God hath given'), is probably a mere Turkish version of an ancient Anatolian expression. A fine spring* which rises in the undulating plain on the east side of Lake Caralis (Bey Sheher), and flows down to the lake, is overhung by a series of ancient sculptures of obviously religious character, which are carved on the side of a small chamber built at the edge of the springs, so that the water seems to run out from under the huge stones of which the nearest wall of the chamber is built.

The fountain was the gift of God. The belief is distinctly different from the Greek idea of the Naiad nymph who lives in and gives life to the spring; and yet the two ideas readily pass into one another. The Greek mind was filled with the sense of joy and life that the spring suggests; the spring was the life of a god; and the life of the spring in the Greek anthropomorphic imagination was pictured as a Divine maiden, human in form and character and emotions, but eternal and ever young. The Anatolian mind regarded the spring as Divine, because given by God, and at the same time it was conceived as the home and embodiment of Divine life, the proper object of worship, the mother of the life of the fields which derive their fertility from its waters, and ultimately, too, the mother of the heroes and men who are born beside it and fed from its produce. This last idea appears still in its earlier form in *Iliad*, ii. 865, where the Lydian chiefs are the sons 'to whom the Gygæan lake gave birth.' But from this it is an easy step to the Greek idea of the Naiad; and we see that the step has been taken in *Iliad*, vi. 22, where the Naiad nymphs in the Troad bear two noble sons to the hero ox-herd. The ultimate cause of sacredness, viz. purity and use to man, appears in the Italian prohibition of bathing in sacred springs or the sources of aqueducts (Plin. *Ep.* viii. 8. 20. 5; Tac. *Ann.* xiv. 22; Sen. *Ep.* 41).

When the spring was of hot or medicinal water, its beneficent qualities and God-given origin were equally or even more conspicuous. Many such springs are known to have been the scene of a special worship, and doubtless all were so. The Divine power was clearly seen in them.

(4) *Development of the sacred place into a religious centre or Hieron.*—Naturally, some of the sacred places became much more famous and important than others. The circumstances that produced such fame and importance belong to the history of each individual locality. It was the needs, the numbers, and the nature of the surrounding population that made some shrines greater than others. Holy places in very secluded situations could hardly become very important as religious centres, though devotees often visited them and made offerings. The great *Hiera* were usually connected with some centre of population, where the primitive form of theocratic government and the needs of the ritual (on which see § VIII (7) and § VII (9)) caused the growth of a large establishment, whose influence became recognized far beyond the immediate circle of its original worshippers. Such, for example, were the Pontic and the Cappadocian Komana, the Galatian Pessinus, the two *Hiera* of the Cappadocian Zeus at Venasa and at Tyana, the *Hieron* of the Milyadic Zeus or Sabazios, mentioned by Ælius Aristides (which is certainly the one that is described in considerable detail in the writer's *Cities and Bishoprics of Phrygia*, i. ch. ix., though the identification is not there mentioned), the *Hieron* of Leto and Lairbenos at Dionysopolis and Hierapolis (*ib.* ch. iv.), and many others.

* See *Cities and Bishoprics of Phrygia*, i. p. 96 ff.; ii. pp. 359, 630 f.; below, § VIII (6).

† ἐν τῃ ἁγιωτάτῃ ἐκκλησίᾳ τῇ καλουμένῃ Μαρίᾳ: see above, vol. i. p. 725.

‡ The Roman Catholics of Smyrna have taken up this place during the last ten years, calling it the house where the Virgin lived after St. John brought her to reside at Ephesus.

* Eflatun Bunar, 'Plato's Spring': *Hist. Geogr. As. Min.* p. 39.

It is not the case, however, that those great *Hiera* were later in growth than the cities beside which or in which they were situated. In many cases it was the *Hieron* which caused the city to grow by attracting population. But a large population required a suitable home, and the town where people should dwell could in many cases not be situated exactly at the holy place, and must be placed at some distance. At Ephesus it is highly probable that the place among the mountains on the south of the valley where the goddess was believed to have been born, and where *Mysteria* were regularly performed, was the true old holy place; but the *Hieron* grew in the open valley, beside an isolated hill, which formed a convenient centre for the growing population.

(5) *Sacred places in the religion of Greece.*—It is obvious how entirely pre-Hellenic this religion was, so far as we have yet described it, and how entirely unlike it was to the religion that we are familiar with as Greek. Not a single feature which we regard as characteristically Hellenic is apparent in it. And yet, to everything that we have described, parallels can be cited from religious foundations in the strictly Greek lands. Behind Greek religion proper there lies, far away back, that old aniconic worship in mountain solitudes and mysterious caves, or on mountain tops, like that of Hera on Mount Ocha in Eubœa, or of Zeus on Mount Lycæus in Arcadia; and the most barbarous of the rude symbolic images of Anatolia, compounded of parts of animals, are not more absolutely un-Hellenic than the Arcadian horse-headed Demeter. That early religion of the Greek lands seems to have been the religion of the aboriginal race who elaborated the Mycenæan civilization of Crete and the Ægean Islands, and, above all, of the Argolic valley and other parts of the West Ægean coastland, the people whom Prof. W. Ridgeway would identify as Pelasgian. On this ancient foundation the religion of later and more artistic Greece was gradually built up: see below, B, § I.

V. Relation of the original aniconic Religion to Image-Worship. — (1) *Coexistence of the two kinds of worship.*—We have spoken of that primitive religion as aniconic, as reverencing the Divine nature without giving it any definite form; and yet we have been forced often to speak of the rude images in which that primitive conception of the Deity was expressed. The truth seems to be that the inconsistency, in which we find ourselves involved, lies in the religion from the beginning. Probably it was at no time absolutely aniconic and impersonal: doubtless there was always in the popular conceptions a deep-seated and unconquerable tendency to give form to the Divine nature, to regard it as envisaged in something like human or animal form. The anthropomorphic side alone was steadily developed in the growth of Hellenism. In the Anatolian religion the aniconic side and the barbaric bestial envisagement both continued strong and important, until they were forced into the background by the invasion of the formed and completed Hellenic civilization, with its philosophic scepticism about the old religion in theory and its anthropomorphic orthodoxy in practice. But even then those native characteristics were far from being extirpated. They persisted in the form of superstitious and secret mysterious rites, and, for the most part, even the educated tolerated them and accorded a moderate amount of recognition to them.

Again, even in the latest period, when image-worship was apparently universal, the old, vague, impersonal conception of the Divine nature was not extirpated, but remained still vigorous. No inconsistency was felt between the aniconic and the iconic personal idea. All the stages in this long process of development could perfectly well exist at the same time. Two or three centuries after Christ, it is evident from many inscriptions that the popular mind often thought of and spoke about 'the God,' or 'the just God,' or 'the pious and just God,' as the vague, formless Divine power. The people were all acquainted with and reverenced both the purely human representations of the Greek religious art and the barbarous symbolic images of primitive Anatolian worship. But still their mind was also occupied with a mysterious power behind them.

Similarly, we must recognize that from the earliest stage the germs of image-worship and anthropomorphism were not wanting.

(2) *Votive images and representations of the Deity.*—The need for some outward and material representation of religious conceptions seems to have been felt especially in approaching the Divine nature with prayers and vows, and in making acknowledgment of and expiation for neglect or disobedience. The worshippers came to the holy place, cave or grove or mountain or spring or stone, and they desired to leave there either some token of their reverence or some reminder of their own person and their own needs, or perhaps both. In proof of their reverence they dedicated offerings, either the sacred emblems and symbols of the Divine power, *e.g.* axes to the god with the axe in the Dictæan cave of Crete, or representations of the home and nature of the Deity. The most characteristic of those representations were the shrines (*ναοί*), on which see below, (3). Further, in evidence of their gratitude when they paid their vow, or of their penitence when they atoned for some neglect of the Divine will and power, they often left representations of themselves as they had been aided by the god, or of the part of the body in which they had suffered punishment, just as the modern peasant ties a rag from his clothing on a sacred tree beside the old sacred fountain.

(3) *Shrines* (*naoi*). — Most typical among the votive offerings of Anatolian religion are the shrines or *naoi*, which filled so large a place in the practical elaboration of Artemis-worship in Ephesus. The *naoi* of Artemis are described at some length in vol. i. p. 606. Here we have only to allude to the origin of this representation. We seem to find the oldest known form of the *naos* in the colossal figure of the so-called Niobe in Mt. Sipylus, which is indubitably an image of the goddess (whether Cybele or Artemis, two names of the one ultimate Divine nature), and which is probably the ancient statue of the Mother-Goddess described by Pausanias as the work of Broteas. This image we take to be rather a votive representation than intended as a cultus-statue. Its conspicuous situation in a perpendicular rock at the top of a very steep slope seems to prove its votive character: it is a token of the piety of the dedicator, not an image set up to be the object of worship for others, though doubtless some cultus would be established here by the dedicator as part of his pious act.

Other very archaic examples of the same character are probably the Cybele between her lions at Arslan-Kaya,* and the little figure of the goddess on the outside of the wall of the Midas city.†

The thought which the dedicator desired to express was that of the Mother-Goddess in her sacred cave; he imagined her as of vaguely-human form, for she to whom man owes his birth cannot be wholly unlike the human form: he tried to give her the accompaniments and emblems suited to express her power or her chosen ritual, lions or *tympanon*. This primitive idea, worked on the

* *Journal of Hellenic Studies*, 1884, p. 245.
† *Ib.* 1882, p. 42.

rocks, was developed in numberless small votive works in terra-cotta or marble or silver; and many examples of those in the cheaper materials are found at most of the seats of Anatolian worship. See also vol. i. p. 606.

VI. The Divine in Human Form and Character.—If various animals seemed suitable expressions or embodiments of the might of the Divine nature, the human analogy most of all affected the mind, and commended itself as proper to convey some idea of the Godhead. That the anthropomorphic tendency existed from the beginning alongside of other forms of expression which have been described, seems indubitable (just as the aniconic idea has been traced as surviving even in the most developed iconic period); and it has given rise to far the largest mass of myth.

(1) *The Great Mother.*—The characteristic which specially distinguishes the Anatolian religion is its conception of the Divine Being as the mother, not the father, of mankind. This feature runs through the social system and the history of the land. Strong traces of *Mutterrecht* have been observed and collected by several writers. Even in the Græco-Roman period, when those traces had almost disappeared from the cities owing to the spread of Greek manners, women magistrates are very frequently alluded to.

The life of man was conceived in that old religion as coming from the Great Mother: the heroes of the land were described as the sons of the goddess, and at death they returned to the mother who bore them. The god, the male element in the Divine nature, was conceived as a secondary figure to the Great Mother; he was recognized as only an incidental and subsidiary actor in the drama of nature and of life, while the permanent feature of the Divine nature is its motherhood, as the kindly protecting and teaching power. In later development, under the influence of external conditions and foreign immigration, more importance (especially in the exoteric cult) was attached to the god: see § VIII (7).

That conception of the Divine power was prompted and strengthened by the physical character of the land. The great plateau, where the religion had its ancient home, was separated from the sea by broad and lofty mountain walls (and it is on the sea that the sense of personality and individual initiative are most encouraged); and its character tends to discourage the sense of personal power, and to impress on the mind the insignificance of man, and his absolute dependence on the Divine power.* But the Divine was kind, lavish of good gifts in rain and useful winds and fountains of water and everything that was needed; but all those good things required skill and work and obedience to the divinely taught methods, in order to take advantage of them. Disobedience to the Divine commands meant ruin and unproductiveness. Obedience was the prime necessity. With patience and observance the children of the earth found that the Divine power was a protecting, watchful, and kind mother.

That character is permanently impressed on the history of the land and the people; not vigour and initiative, but receptivity and impressibility, swayed the spirit of the people, breathed through the atmosphere that surrounded them, and marks their fate throughout history; † and this spirit can be seen as a continuous force, barely perceptible at any moment, yet powerful in the long-run, acting on every new people, and subtly influencing every new religion that came into the land. Thus, for example, the earliest trace of the high veneration of the Virgin Mary in the Christian religion is in a Phrygian inscription of the 2nd cent.; and the earliest example of a holy place consecrated to the Mother of God as already almost a Divine personality is at Ephesus, where her home among the mountains * is probably as old as the Council of Ephesus, A.D. 431.

In regard to the nature of the Goddess-Mother, it is unnecessary to repeat what has been said in vol. i. p. 605 on the nature of Diana: that whole article may be assumed here.

(2) *The growth of mythology as the story of the life of the Great Mother.*—The Great Mother, evidently, was often imagined simply as the Divine guardian and protecting mother, without any distinctly sexual character being thought of. But her character as the mother could not be separated from the sexual idea in the popular mind; and, naturally, it is on this side that most of the mythology and dramatic action connected with the Divine story originates. The mystery of life, the succession of child to parent and of crop to seed, the growth of plant and tree and animal and man, lay deep in the minds of the primitive Anatolian people or peoples. They regarded all these phenomena as manifestations of the same ultimate Divine power. The custom of killing a human being in the field that his life may pass into the coming crop and make it grow well, is clearly implied in the legend of Lityerses at Celænæ. Similarly, the life of the tree is the life of the Dryad or Nymph. Each form can pass into the others, if the suitable situation occurs.

The life of nature begins anew every spring. This process is the life of the Great Mother: her child is born every year. Sometimes this birth was imagined as originating through her own innate power; she combined, as it were, the male and the female principle in herself. In Caria and in Cyprus this took the grotesque form that the supreme god was bisexual, and some repulsive legends were founded on this barbarous idea. These are probably not strictly Anatolian: they are distortions of the original thought, for a male deity imagined as endowed with some bisexual characteristics does not explain the continuance and perpetuation of the life of nature. They probably arose among immigrant peoples, like the Carians, whose national character substituted a god for a mother-goddess as the supreme conception of Divinity.

Certainly, that bisexual idea was on the whole rejected in the development of Anatolian religious symbolism; and little mythology was founded on it. More common is the idea that the Great Mother conceives through the influence of some flower or fruit, or in some other non-sexual way, as in the birth of Attis at Pessinus.† Not unrelated to this is the already mentioned idea that the god-serpent was the father of the Divine child.

But far more characteristic and widespread, and more simple and natural, is it to describe the Divine life more exactly according to the analogy of the natural world. The Divine nature is then imagined as divided between the two sexes; there is the god and the goddess, and the process of the Divine life evolves itself in the reciprocal action of the Divine pair and the birth of a new offspring: thus we find that the God-Father, the Goddess-Mother, and the Son (Dionysos, Sabazios, etc.) or the Daughter (Kora, etc.), are all assumed as essential to the drama of Divine life in numerous cults and myths.

While we cannot penetrate, in the dearth of

* See the art. on 'Geographical Conditions determining History and Religion in Asia Minor' in the *Geographical Journal*, Sept. 1902, where the subject is more fully treated.

† See the art. in the *Geographical Journal*, as in previous note.

* See above, § IV (2). † Pausanias, vii. 17.

evidence, to the earliest forms of these sacred myths and of the cult usages with which they are connected, it seems only reasonable to suppose that they began in a simple and self-consistent form. The view which forces itself on us is that the drama of the Divine life was at first understood and presented to the worshippers in some single and definite form at a time, and not in a confused mixture of different forms. In this ancient ritual the goddess is generally the important and essential figure, while the god is an adjunct needed for the proper development of her life, who passes out of notice when he has fulfilled his part in the drama; and in many cases the union of the two is described as a crime against some law, or actually as an act of fraud or violence even of the most abominable character, which sometimes entails punishment even unto death.

(3) *Myths of the goddess and the god.*—Sometimes the union of the goddess and the god is pictured under the forms of agriculture, as of Demeter with Iasion 'in the thrice-ploughed fallow field.' Thus the goddess bears the Divine child; but Iasion is slain by the thunderbolt; for a life must be given in primitive ritual that the crop may acquire the power to grow. This cult myth (ἱερὸς λόγος) is connected with the Samothracian Mysteries and with Crete, two ancient centres of the primitive population, which we may now call Pelasgian, using the same name that the Greeks used, though modern scholars long ridiculed it.

Most important and most instructive as to the nature of the Anatolian religion is the idea, described above in § III (7), that the Divine power and the Divine life are revealed in the nature of the bee. As we have seen, the form of the Ephesian goddess (a form not restricted to Ephesus, but widely prevalent in Lydian and Phrygian cities) is modelled far more closely on the shape of the bee than of the woman. Now, the life of the queen bee (as described in the *Encyclopædia Britannica*[9], whose account may be given more shortly in the following terms) is the best explanation of the Attis legend. As regards reproduction, the opinion was once maintained that the queen bee was in herself sufficient without any male bee, or that the male principle was conveyed to the queen without her coming into contact with a male. But it has been clearly proved that the queen comes into relation with a male bee while taking a flight in the air; and if she does not find a mate within three weeks of her birth the power of intercourse seems to become lost. In the intercourse the male is robbed of the organs concerned; and thus mutilated is left to perish on the ground. His existence seems to have no object apart from the queen bee, and he fulfils no other function and no other duty in life. This description applies with striking exactness to the relation between the Mother-Goddess and the god, who (as we have seen) exists merely to be her consort, and is quite an insignificant personage apart from his relation to her. We must here anticipate what is said in later sections as to the character and original importance of the Goddess-Mother, and as to the growth of the dignity of the god in historic development, in order to bring out the bee nature in her life-history. The god consorted with the goddess by stealth and violence: the goddess was angry at the outrage: she mutilated the assailant, or caused him to be mutilated (*exsectis virilibus semivirum tradidit*). Even the false but not unnatural opinions about the impregnation of the queen bee have obvious analogies in the myths about the Mother-Goddess.

The myths riot in variations on this ugly theme, and we need not allude to them, except in so far as they are necessary for understanding the facts. The god, though mutilated, must still be living in perfect form, for the life of nature (whose annual bloom he represents) is renewed in perfection every year; and accordingly the myth sometimes tells that the penalty was inflicted vicariously, ἀποσπάσας ὁ Ζεὺς τοῦ κριοῦ τοὺς διδύμους φέρων ἐν μέσοις ἔρριψε τοῖς κόλποις τῆς Δηοῦς, τιμωρίαν ψευδῆ τῆς βιαίας συμπλοκῆς ἐκτιννύων, where there is an obvious reference to the treatment which the sacred instructions prescribe for domesticated animals.* Further, purely fanciful developments in Greek myth produced such tales as that the goddess was a lover of the god, and mutilated him in jealousy, or that the mutilation was intended to compel and enforce chastity. Such tales are absolutely opposed to the original Anatolian idea, which is intended to account for the fruitfulness and new life of nature. The subject offered a good opening for attack to the Christian polemical writers, Clemens Alexandrinus, Firmicus Maternus, Arnobius, etc.; and they are our best authorities. The accounts which they give, hideous as they are and concentrating attention only on the evils, must be accepted as correctly stating facts: it would have ruined their effect if they had not been recognized as true statement of facts. Moreover, they are corroborated in various details by pagan authorities; and as a whole they bear the unmistakable stamp of truth, but not the whole truth.

The myths in their older form, as distinguished from the fanciful variations, are obviously in the closest relation to the ritual: they are simply descriptions of the drama as represented in the sacred rites.

At other times the union of the two Divine natures is pictured after the animal world: Demeter as the mare meets the horse Zeus, Pasiphae became the cow, and so on. Popular and poetic imagination, which sported in the most licentious fashion with all those myths of the Divine unions, worked out this class of tales especially with the most diabolical and repulsive ingenuity; and it is in the degraded conception of the Divine nature implied in these abominable fantastic developments that the Christians who inveighed against the pagan religion found their most telling weapons. The mythology that grew around this subject would in itself make a large subject; but, though it possesses considerable interest as bearing on history and social customs, it has little value from a religious point of view.

These exaggerated and really distorted myths did not remain mere tales. They reacted on the ritual, which grew and elaborated itself and took in new elements in the lapse of time. But in this process of elaboration there was no real religious development, but simply degradation.

(4) *The birth and death of the Divine nature.*—The mystery of birth is matched by the mystery of death, and the one occupied the mind of the primitive Anatolian peoples as much as the other. Death was regarded and imagined by them under similar illustrative forms drawn from external nature; and the Divine nature, which is the model and prototype of all the activity of man, was seen living and dying in the life of trees and plants, of grass and corn. The recurring death of nature, the bright and beautiful luxuriance of spring cut off in its prime by the sun of summer, the joy and warmth of the summer alternating with the coldness and darkness of the long severe winter on the Anatolian plateau, the light of day transformed into the deadness of night, furnished a series of expressions of the same principle; and mythology and cult are full of them. In numberless local varieties the same truth is expressed: the young hero is slain in the pride of life and the joy of his

* See above, § III (7 f.).

art: Marsyas the sweet rustic musician vies with the god, and is by the god hung up on the plane tree and flayed: Hylas is drowned in the fountain by the nymph who longs for him and takes him away to herself from the earth: the twelve children of Niobe are all slain by the wrath and arrows of the god: Achilles must die young, and his grave was shown at various seats of his worship, in Elis, in the Troad, on the south Russian coasts. The eternal contradiction repeats itself: the life of nature is slain, yet reappears: it is slain by the Divine power, yet it is in itself the embodiment of the Divine power: the god slays the god: on this, mythology plays in endless variations of the same tale.

With this obvious fact of the death of nature, its birth is equally obviously connected. The life of nature never ends: it dies only to be born, different and yet the same. Men mourn for the dead god, and immediately their mourning is turned to joy, for the god is reborn. The mourning over Attis in the Phrygian worship of Cybele was succeeded by the *Hilaria*, as the lamentation for Adonis or 'Thammuz yearly wounded' in Syria was followed by the rejoicing over his rejuvenation.

With this subject the largest and the most valuable class of myths is connected; but the few examples which have been quoted above must suffice.

VII. Ritual and Ceremonial.—We have spoken of the growth of mythology before speaking of the ritual in which the Anatolian religious ideas sought to express themselves. This order must not be taken as implying the opinion that myth is, either logically or chronologically, prior to ritual. On the contrary, ritual comes first, and myth is secondary: myth grows around the rite, and explains it or justifies it or enlarges it to the popular mind. But myth begins from the very origin of ritual, and there was probably never a time when rite existed free from myth. The human mind must from the beginning describe and think about and imagine to itself the reason and nature of the religious rite; and its thought and fancy and description express themselves as myth. But the ritual has perished, while fragments of the mythology have been preserved; and it is through the myths, compared with some rare pieces of evidence about the rites, that we penetrate back to the ritual.

(1) *The origin of ritual.*—The ritual of the Anatolian religion is very imperfectly known. So far as we are able to discover, it is founded entirely on the idea that the Divine nature is the model according to which human life must be arranged. The god, or rather the Goddess-Mother, is the teacher, protector, corrector, and guide for an obedient family of children. What they ought to do is to imitate the Divine life and practise the divinely revealed methods. The ritual is the whole body of Divine teaching. The sacrifice, as the method whereby man can approach and seek help from Divine power, has been revealed by God; so the god was at the beginning the first priest, and the ritual is the repetition before successive generations of mankind of the original life of the Divine beings. The successive priests in the cultus were each of them representative for the time being of the god; each wore the dress and insignia, and even bore the name of the god.

In accordance with this principle various reliefs are to be explained, in which the representation is grouped in different zones: in the upper zone the Divine figures appear in their own proper circle of circumstances; in the lower zone the Divine figures appear as brought into relations with mankind, their worshippers, and, *e.g.*, as teaching men the method of sacrifice and offering. One of the best examples has been published by an old traveller, Wagener, in his *Inscr. rec. en Asie Mineure*, pl. i. It is still in existence, and will be republished in the proper chapter of the *Cities and Bishoprics of Phrygia*, iii.

According to our view, then, the Anatolian religious ritual was a representation or repetition of the stages and actions of the Divine life. The important stages in human life were embraced therein; and human individuals made their lives right and holy by performing their actions after the Divine plan.

This is a large subject. It is as wide as the life of the ancient Anatolian races, and in its full breadth it would have to include the progress of history and the march of conquerors and of immigration, for all those events affected and modified ritual. Here we touch on a few details only. Fortunately, circumstances favoured the preservation, throughout the dominance of paganism, of an important part of the primitive ritual under the form of *Mysteria* in many of its original seats, not merely in Anatolia, but also in Attica, Samothrace, etc. The primitive forms were not, indeed, kept pure, but were adulterated by many additions; but still they remained; and if we had a complete knowledge of the *Mysteria*, we could go far to recover the primitive forms. It is necessary here to treat together the Anatolian and the Greek Mysteries, anticipating part B.

(2) *The Mysteries.*—The ancient ritual of the Greek or Pelasgian tribes was overlaid but not destroyed by later religious forms of more 'Hellenic' character. In mythology this is expressed by tales of the conquest of the old deities by younger gods, Kronos or Saturn by Zeus or Jupiter, Marsyas by Apollo, etc. In such cases the old religion, though conquered, is not extirpated, but only submerged. It takes a long time, and much education, to eradicate a religion from the popular heart: the hearts of the educated and privileged classes are more easily changed. When the new religion stands on a distinctly higher platform than the old, or is of an uncompromising nature, the ancient beliefs persist in some such form as magic and witchcraft and rites proscribed as unhallowed and evil, and the older gods are stigmatized as devils: see B, §§ I, V; C, § III (5).

But in this case the new religion was not uncompromising, but singularly accommodating in type. Its spirit was polytheistic and eclectic in the highest degree. It had little objection to a pair or a score or a hundred of additional gods, old or new. Where laws existed in the Greek cities forbidding the introduction of 'new gods,' the intention was rather political than religious: the dread was lest anything should be introduced that would disturb the delicate equilibrium of Hellenic city-constitution, and especially anything that would prove self-assertive or bigoted, and would tend to subvert the established city religion, which formed an essential element of the city-constitution, and was to a great extent political in character: see B, § IV (14).

Accordingly, the old forms persisted in the form of Mysteries, sanctioned by the State as ancient and holy, yet distinctly regarded as a survival not quite in keeping with the true Hellenic religion. The old gods were still considered and reverenced as gods, admitted as members of the Hellenic Pantheon; and though Zeus was nominally the supreme god, yet in some ways the old gods whom he had dethroned were esteemed more holy and more efficacious than he. The name *Mysteria*, which was given to the ancient rites, was indicative of an element of secrecy, and a certain uncanny character, as of ideas which were not to be admitted as part of ordinary life.

What, then, were the Mysteries? In what lay their essential character? Before trying to answer this question we must point out that, though there is in the general view a distinct separation between Mysteries and the cults of the properly Hellenic gods, yet in practice and in detail they pass into one another, so that it is impossible in some cases to say what category certain rites fall under. But there is a general type characterizing all the cults called Mysteries; and, as we shall see, the great Mysteries were in Roman times developed so as to be even more strikingly similar to one another. The Mysteries of the Anatolian religion may be conveniently summed up under the name Phrygian Mysteries, as they are commonly called by the ancient writers; but they were celebrated far beyond the bounds of Phrygia. The name *Mysteria* was, doubtless, given to them in Asia Minor rather from their analogy to the *Mysteria* of Greece proper; and not because they were considered there so mystic and separate from ordinary religion as they were in Greece proper. In the cities of Asia Minor, however, the Greek or Hellenic views of religion became steadily more effective; and as those views grew stronger, the native religion was more and more felt to be of the nature of *Mysteria*.

(3) *Nature of the Mysteries.*—In the Anatolian religion, either originally or at some stage in its history (whether through contact with some other race or through some other educational influence), the idea of the recurring death and new birth of the natural world—regarded, of course, as the annual death and rebirth of the Divine life—was combined with the fact of the sequence of generations in human life. The same sequence must exist in the Divine nature, for the Divine nature is the counterpart and prototype of the human in all stages of its history. The Divine parents and the Divine child correspond to the human. The drama of this Divine life was set before the worshippers in the Mysteries.

But again in the Divine life, as we see it in the annual life of nature, the father is the son, the mother reappears as the daughter: it is never possible to draw any definite line of division between them: the Divine child replaces the parent, different and yet the same. If that is the case with the Divine, the same must be the case in human life. The stream of human life goes on continuously, changing yet permanent; and death is only a moment in the succession. Here the idea of immortality and a life of man wider than the limits of the material world is touched.

Obviously, an important aspect of religion is here introduced. Human life is regarded as permanent and everlasting, like the Divine life of nature; and the religion of the grave is the foundation of the entire religion [see also § VIII (5)]. That man when he dies becomes a god, was considered already in the 4th cent. B.C. to be part of the teaching conveyed in the Mysteries, as is shown in the curious metrical inscriptions engraved on plates of gold which have been found in graves of South Italy and Crete, and which belong to that and the following centuries. There the deification is considered to be the result of initiation; but in the primitive religion, when all men were religious and the Mysteries were the religion of the whole people and not restricted to some chosen *mystæ*, the dead all went back to the god from whom they came. In a very ingenious paper, S. Reinach has discovered the mystic formula uttered by the initiated—'a kid I have fallen into the milk,' which conveyed in symbolic terms the same meaning as the words which the goddess of the world of death seems to have addressed to the initiated dead who came before her—'thou hast become a god instead of a man,' or 'thou shalt be a god instead of a mortal.'*

It is certain that the pagan apologists, defending the established religion and attacking the Christian, found this philosophic meaning in the ritual of the Mysteries, in which that early religion still lived on. That this meaning was implicit in the ritual from the beginning seems fairly certain. That it was understood by some persons is probable, and that some development of the ritual was made at some time or times to give more emphasis to the meaning is also probable. Not merely people in general, but also some of the most educated among the Greeks, believed in the salutary effect of the Eleusinian Mysteries; and this salutary effect is expressly connected with the future world.† Advantages in the world of death (or of life) are said to be gained by those who are initiated; and those advantages are not the result of the mere ritual observance. The initiated are said to grow better; and salvation in the future life is said by Isocrates to be gained both by the initiated and by all who live a pious and just life (*Symm.* xii. 266).

But this effect of the Mysteries was not attained or helped by any formal instruction. It was dependent entirely on the intense interest and eager contemplation of the initiated, and the strong impression produced on their minds. The ceremonies at Eleusis took place at night, after a considerable period of preparation and purification: the purification consisted mainly in ritualistic acts, but not entirely so, for probably some stress was laid on the condition that the initiated must be pure in heart and not conscious of having committed any crime: they were, certainly, left to judge for themselves of their own moral purity, and the best ancient pagan conception of purity was consistent with habitual disregard of some of the elementary moral rules of the Christian and of the Hebrew religion. But the principle of moral purity was admitted, even though only in a very defective and poor form; and that was a great thing, at least in comparison with the general character of ancient paganism.

After this preparation, and when in a state of high expectancy, the initiated were admitted to see the drama of the Divine life: the words spoken in the drama were few, and concerned only with the action: the mystic objects were simple in character: the most holy and crowning act at Eleusis was the ear of corn mowed down silently. But there was a belief ready in the minds of the spectators that certain truths were enigmatically expressed in the action, though, as the ancient writers say, a philosophic training and a reverent religious frame of mind were required to comprehend them.‡

The details of the Mystic drama set before the worshippers cannot here be described. A very

* That the kid is here the mystic form of Dionysos, as the God-Son in the Divine nature, is generally recognized: see S. Reinach, *Rev. Arch.*, Sept. 1901, p. 205 (though we cannot go with him beyond what we have adopted from him in the text above). The Phrygian Zeus Galaktinos, or Galaktios, may be brought into comparison (*Histor. Geogr. As. Min.* p. 235, and A. Körte, *Beilage zum Vorlesungsverzeichniss*, Greifswald, 1902, p. 30): he is the god of the pastoral people of the great plains and the grassy hills of Phrygia.

† Plato, *Phædr.* p. 250, *Epinomis*, p. 986; Isocr. *Paneg.* vi. p. 59, § 28; Pindar, *fr.* 96 (H.); Soph. *fr.* 719 (Dind.); Crinagoras in *Anthol.* ii. 332 (Jac.); Diodorus Sic. *Hist.* v. 49; Cicero, *de Legg.* ii. 14; Andocides, *de Myst.* § 31; Sopater, *Diær. Zetem.* p. 121 in Walz, *Rhet. Græc.*; Theon. Smyrn. *Mathem.* i. p. 18 (Bull); Strabo, p. 467 f.; Philostr. *Vit. Apoll.* i. 15, 17; Herod. viii. 65; and many other passages (see Lobeck, *Aglaoph.* i. p. 67 ff., etc.; Lenormant in *Contemp. Review*, Sept. 1880, p. 429 ff., and in Daremberg-Saglio's *Dict. Antiq.* ii. p. 579 ff. etc.).

‡ See Aristotle, quoted by Synesius, *Orat.* p. 48, ed. Petau; Galen, *de Us. Part.* vii. 14 (ed. Kuhn); Plut. *Defect. Orac.* 22, etc.: see preceding note.

brief description is given, in vol. iii. p. 467, of the ceremonial of the Eleusinian Mysteries; and in the last few paragraphs we have had those Mysteries chiefly in mind.

(4) *The character of the Phrygian and the Greek Mysteries.*—Probably there was not a wide difference even in the beginning, and still less in later times, between the Eleusinian and the Phrygian Mysteries as regards actual ritual: many ceremonies were probably common to both, and in both there was much that was disgusting and repulsive. Yet the Phrygian Mysteries are described as abominable and immoral by the older Greek writers, even by those who praise and admire the Eleusinian: the former were believed to ruin and degrade a Greek city, but the latter to save and ennoble it. The difference lay not simply in the fact that some repulsive ceremonies are quoted by the Christians as peculiar to the Phrygian Mysteries; for much of what remains in Clemens' description of the Eleusinian is equally detestable. The real superiority of the Eleusinian over the Phrygian Mysteries lay, first, in a certain difference of spirit, as the Greek sense of order and measure and art undoubtedly gave a harmony and artistic character to their version of the Oriental forms; and, secondly, in the fact that, as known in Greece proper, the Phrygian Mysteries were introduced by slaves and foreigners, and participated in by the superstitious and the ignorant: they were celebrated for money by strolling priests, and any one who paid a fee was initiated without preparation except some ritual acts: there was no solemnity in the surroundings, and no dignity in the ceremonial, but all was vulgar and sordid. A very few persons, also, might observe that the slight requirement of moral purity made at Eleusis had become a mere phrase in those street celebrations, and that advantages in the future world were promised in return for mere participation in those vulgar rites. But that observation was probably beyond the ordinary range of even the educated Greeks.

As regards the many disgusting details against which the Christian writers direct their polemic, the admirers of the Mysteries might defend them by arguing* that religion places us face to face with the actual facts of life, and that, when the mind is exalted and ennobled by intense religious feeling, it is able to contemplate with pure insight phenomena of nature and life in which the vulgar mind sees nothing but grossness. They would point out that the language of religion may be and ought to be plainer and more direct than the language of common life. These arguments are weighty; but one has only to read the undeniable accounts given by Clemens, Arnobius, etc., to see how insufficient they are to palliate the ugliness of the ritual.

In primitive thought the direct and simple expression of the facts of life would need no apology and no explanation. The feature of the Mysteries that needs and is incapable of apology is that, as known to us in later time, they are not simple and direct: they are elaborate and artificial products of diseased religion. They stand before us as the culmination of a long development; and the development has been a depravation, not an elevation, of a ritual which had at first been naïve and direct in its simple rudeness.

(5) *The growth of ritual.*—The process of growth in ritual went on in two ways.

(*a*) In the meeting of two different races their respective religions affected one another. Doubtless, the one generally swamped and submerged the other; but the apparent victor was not unaffected in the process. An indubitable example is seen in the Lydian Katakekaumene, otherwise called Mæonia. Here an old Mæonian or Lydian population was mixed with a body of colonists introduced by the Persian kings five centuries B.C.; and in the Roman inscriptions six or seven hundred years later the goddess is called Artemis Anaitis, the first name being her ordinary title in Lydian cities, and the second being Persian. In other Lydian cities, where the same mixture of population took place, the goddess is called Artemis Persike, in which the same religious mixture is even more clearly expressed. In cultus, obscure as that subject always is, it is certain that the fire-worship and Magian priests of the Persians were thus introduced into those Lydian cities.*

(*b*) There was often a conscious and deliberate elaboration of forms and ritual by the priesthood. This enlargement of the ceremonial was the result of an attempt to adapt the established religion to popular taste, and was accomplished chiefly by introducing rites that had proved fashionable. The Mysteries celebrated at different religious centres competed with one another in attractiveness, for there was much to gain from a great concourse of worshippers in any city. Hence all of them adapted to their own purposes elements which seemed to be effective in others; and thus a marked similarity of character between the rites of Eleusis, Samothrace, and Anatolia came to exist. Sometimes, at least, new priests were added along with the new ceremonies. These ceremonies were often derived from or influenced by the growth of mythology, and they seem (so far as the scanty evidence justifies an opinion) to have generally tended to obscure any healthy religious idea that lay in the ritual, and to have increased the ugly and repulsive element.

The older forms of religion are the simpler, but it is not probable that any form was ever absolutely simple. There is a certain tendency in human nature to mingle forms, and to see the Divine idea under several aspects. Just as in early literary expression metaphors are often mixed, so in primitive thought different envisagements of the Divine power arise simultaneously, and these pass into one another without the inconsistency being felt. Still, it is beyond question that, when we get any of these religious ideas at an early stage, it has a simpler form and embodies a single process, though the accompanying religious myth may express the process in a way that involves some inconsistency in details. This ancient form is markedly and unmistakably different from the elaborate and artificial ritual of later times.

Especially, the elaborate dramas of the later Mysteries, as played before the initiated in the Roman Imperial period, are obviously composed by a process of syncretism out of various inharmonious and inconsistent cults. In the story enacted in the Eleusinian Mysteries, as described by Clemens Alexandrinus, there are traces so obviously Phrygian, that many modern scholars have regarded his whole description as applying to the Phrygian Mysteries alone. But Clemens distinctly implies that he is describing the Eleusinian Mysteries, and he illustrates his description and his invective by quoting other details, saying that these are taken from the Phrygian Mysteries. The explanation of these facts, undoubtedly, must be that the later Eleusinian Mysteries had been influenced by the Phrygian Mysteries.

That details from various sources were united in those later Mysteries is shown by their composite character: there is not merely the fundamental element, the story of the Divine father and mother

* The following sentences are slightly modified from the writer's article 'Mysteries' in the *Encyclopædia Britannica*[9].

* Pausanias, v. 27. 6, VII. 6. 6; the name Artemis Persike is found often on coins of Hierocæsarea in Lydia. See also Head, *Catalogue of Coins, Brit. Mus.: Lydia*, pp. lviii–lxvi and 111 ff.

and the birth of the child: there are several such stories interlocked in one another: the god-bull, the god-ram, the god-serpent, appear in different details, and pass into each other in kaleidoscopic fashion. There is here an original germ and a series of successive additions due to the reception of new religious forms and ideas, which were incorporated in the growing ceremonial.

(6) *Purification.*—This subject has been alluded to in § III (6), where the later rules of ceremonial purity are mentioned. But there can be no doubt that certain practices of purification were prescribed in the original Anatolian ritual. The Greek purificatory rules for homicides were identical with the Lydian;* and, as the Lydian cannot be supposed to be derived from the Greek, we must here see an example of the influence which throughout ancient times was exerted by Anatolian religion on Greek. In these and in the preparation for the Mysteries the swine was the cleansing animal.

The ceremonial of purification after homicide carries the inquirer back to a very primitive stage. As the ritual was common to Greece and Lydia (and doubtless Phrygia also, as is probable though unattested), we may presume that the early Greek ideas connected with it are true of Anatolia also. Now, one of the rites of the Dionysiac festival *Anthesteria* was called 'the Cans' (Χόες), because every celebrant drank out of a separate can; and the myth explained that Demophon, son of Theseus, instituted the custom when Orestes came to Athens unpurified: wishing to receive him hospitably, yet not to let an impure person drink out of the same cup as the pure worshippers, the king ordered that every person should drink from his own can separately, and proposed a prize to the best drinker. Here the rite of competition and prize-giving to an individual victor is Hellenic, and belongs to the later development (B, § III). But other elements in the ceremony point to an early date; the chief rite was the marriage of the representative woman or queen among the people (the wife of the Archon Basileus) to the god; and the idea was also associated with this day that it was accursed, for the dead arose on it and must be propitiated. Here again the idea of connecting evil omen and a curse with the dead is Hellenic and late (see B, § V); but the association of the rising from the dead with the Divine marriage is primitive and original. Similarly, we may regard the horror against a homicide partaking of the common cup as a thoroughly primitive idea; he must be purified before taking part in that sacred ceremony of civilized man, the drinking of the common cup. But the application of this to the rite of 'the Cans' is late, and probably founded on a misconception. In the marriage of the risen god and the queen, as an annual rite to ensure wealth and increase to the land (which at that season, 12th February, was being prepared for the coming year's crop and harvest), the common cup was partaken of only by the bridal pair [see § VIII (1)]; and the people in general rejoice separately as individual spectators of the holy rite.

The distinction between the unity and close relationship implied by the ritualistic drinking from the common cup and the separateness implied by drinking from separate cups is a noteworthy feature; and explicit emphasis was probably placed on it in the ceremony; but the details are unknown. Similarly, in the Christian Sacrament the Saviour laid emphasis on the breaking and distribution from one loaf, in contrast to the use in ordinary Oriental meals of a loaf for each guest (see 1 Co $10^{16f.}$). See further, § VIII (1) and (6).

The most important fact for us in purification is that it implies some germs of a conception of sin which has to be atoned for before the worshipper may approach the Divine power. Breaking an oath and refusal to restore money entrusted to one's care entail impurity; and the Divine anger punishes any one who approaches the sanctuary without expiating such a crime. It is, however, true that impurity equally results from offence against purely ceremonial rules, and that the conception of sin and expiation which is revealed in the evidence on this subject is of a very humble kind; but there was at least a germ capable of higher development, though there is little or no sign that any development ever took place, except perhaps to some small extent through the contact with and resistance to Christianity.

Guilt and impurity entailed punishment. The punishment seems to have been inflicted in some cases independently of any disrespect to the Deity due to entering the holy place in a state of impurity. The sin results directly, and without the sinner entering the sanctuary, in punishment at the hand of the god or goddess, who therefore must sometimes have been conceived as on the watch to punish sin. Here again there is the germ of higher moral conceptions.*

But the utilitarian element which is so clear in many features of the primitive Anatolian religion can be distinctly traced also in the rules of purification. The Goddess-Mother was the teacher and guide of her people from their birth till she received them back to her in death. The ablutions which she required from them were an excellent sanitary precaution; and if the whole system of purificatory rules were known to us, this side would probably be much more obvious and incontestable.

(7) *Confession.*—A remarkable and important fact in connexion with impurity and sin was that the process of expiation seems to have involved (whether obligatorily or voluntarily, we cannot be sure; but probably obligatorily) a public confession. Sense of guilt was brought home to the individual by some punishment, generally disease (fever, in which the unseen Divine fire consumes the strength and the life, was recognized as the most characteristic expression† of Divine wrath). Thereupon the sinner confessed, acknowledged the power, and appeased the anger of the god or goddess, and was cured and forgiven. Finally, as a warning to others, the confession, the punishment, and the absolution were engraved often on a stele and deposited in the sanctuary.‡ See also below, C, § III (4).

(8) *Approaching the Deity.*—Apart from prescribed ritual, the worshipper came voluntarily to the god or goddess for three purposes: (*a*) to pray for good for himself or his family; this was called εὐχή in Greek, and the prayer was necessarily accompanied by giving, or by a promise to give, something in return to the Deity, if the desire was granted: thus εὐχή (in Latin, *votum*) involved both prayer and sacrifice or vow: it was a sort of bargain with the Divine power; (*b*) to imprecate evil on one's enemies (ἀρά, κατάρα, ἐπαρά): this was really a variety of the former, for ἀρά strictly means 'prayer'; but in the development of Greek religion it was commonly and almost invariably addressed to the powers of the old régime, who had become mysterious, occult, and uncanny, and passed more and more into the sphere of magic. The vow in this case fell into disuse, for the occult powers were not gratified by public gifts, but by the mere recognition of their

* Herod. i. 31.

* See papers on 'The Early Church and the Pagan Ritual' in the *Expository Times*, 1898–99 (vol. x.), especially p. 108 f.

† This is shown most clearly in the curses engraved on leaden tablets, in which the wrath of the Deity is invoked against any enemy or false friend; it is usually the Divine fire which is invoked to destroy the fever-struck wretch.

‡ On this subject see *op. cit.* in footnote * above.

efficaciousness: the mere approaching them in the proper ritual and method enabled the worshipper to call them into action on his side, and he could as it were compel them to act by addressing them by the proper formulæ (which thus acquired a magic character); but some kind of sacrifice was an invariable part of the ritual.* (c) To invoke the Deity as a witness of what they were about to say or had said (ὅρκος). This, again, was strictly a variety of the previous class, for the *horkos* was simply an imprecation of evil on oneself in case one were speaking falsely. The person swears by the Deity whom he invokes as a witness, and who is his *horkos*; and, as the form was very ancient, the object sworn by might be an animal or a stone, as the primitive embodiment or home of Divine power: such was the old Cretan oath associated with the name of Rhadamanthus (though the Scholiast on Aristoph. *Av.* 520 speaks as if Rhadamanthus were the inventor of such milder forms of oath, as by the dog, the goose, the ram, etc.): such also was the sacred Latin oath, *per Jovem lapidem.* An oath, as being really a prayer to the Deity, was properly accompanied by a sacrifice.

In all such cases the prayer or oath is binding on the descendants or representatives of him who has invoked the Deity, and the consequences may fall on them even generations later. It was not uncommon to bring the children to the place where the oath was taken, and thus make them explicitly and publicly parties to the act and sharers in its consequences.

These voluntary and occasional acts, which persisted alongside of the stated ritual, were older than, and gave rise to, ritual. The asking of help from the god in difficulties or troubles was as old as the idea of a god; for in the Anatolian belief the god was the helper and teacher. The way in which he was efficaciously approached naturally came gradually to be stereotyped as ritual, and was regarded as revealed by the god, who was in this way his own first priest, and teacher of his own rites.

(9) *Priests.*—The original idea which gave rise to the Anatolian priesthood has become clear in the preceding investigation. The priest is the bearer of the Divine knowledge; he can teach men how to approach and propitiate the Divine power. This knowledge was originally taught by the Divine Being personally to men; in other words, the god is the first priest, performing as an example to his successors the due ceremonies. The idea of a Divine revelation, through which man becomes aware of the nature and will of God, is here present in a very crude and rude form; and it is hardly possible to distinguish how far this rudeness is the real primitive simplicity of a very early stage, when thought is hardly separated from the sensuous accompaniments through which it is suggested to men, and how far it may be imparted by degeneration, *i.e.* by the stereotyping of primitive sensuous forms, and the loss of the germ of thought implicated in those forms.

While the priest in this ancient stage of religion possesses the knowledge and imparts it to the worshippers, he is not considered to be necessary in himself. The worshipper, whether a private individual who approaches the Deity on behalf of himself and his family, or an official or magistrate who acts on behalf of the State or body which he represents, needs no intermediary between himself and the god. Provided he can perform fully and correctly his part in the transaction,† the Deity is satisfied and must respond. The priest or helper is needed only to keep the worshipper right, to guard him against errors, and to help him to understand the way in which the Deity replies or conveys information; in other words, the helping priest merely acts as instructor, while the worshipper plays the part of priest-officiator, and performs the series of acts which the god himself originally did as an example to mankind who come after him.

In this stage there is not, in the strict sense, any priest or any sacerdotal order or caste, though naturally the Divine knowledge would tend to be handed down from father to son. Priests in the strictest sense begin only when a person permanently assumes the place of the god's representative, and plays the part of the god regularly in the ritual as it was rehearsed at the proper intervals before a body of worshippers. The priest in this fuller sense was connected with and helped the growth of an anthropomorphic conception of the Deity. He was the representative on earth of the god as the priestess was of the goddess; and the two played their parts year after year in the Divine drama, which constituted the most important part of the growing body of ritual.

The priest who represented the god wore his dress,* and in some cases, probably in most, assumed his name. In Pessinus, for example, the chief priest was called Atis, as is shown by inscriptions of the 2nd cent. B.C.; and undoubtedly this was simply the name of the god variously spelt Attis or Atys or Ates, and was assumed as an official title, implying that the office was ἱερώνυμος, *i.e.* the bearer lost his individual name and assumed a hieratic name when he entered on office.

In Asia Minor the succession to the priesthood was, in all probability, hereditary (according to some principle of inheritance not as yet determined) in early times. Where the Greek element entered sufficiently strongly, this principle was usually altered; some more democratic principle of succession was substituted; and sometimes life-tenure was changed to tenure for a period of four years, or more frequently of one year, or occasionally even of a shorter period. In some of the more thoroughly Greek cities of the coast, such as Erythræ, the priesthoods of the numberless deities were put up to auction by the State, and sold to the highest bidder. But wherever an early or a more purely Anatolian and less Hellenized condition can be traced, the great priesthoods seem to be for life, and to be connected with certain families.

The number of priests, in this fuller sense, tended to increase from various causes, and to become a sacerdotal order. The possession of knowledge of the Divine law was a powerful engine, for the body of ritual was steadily growing in volume, and any mistake in it would have nullified its effect. Attention was entirely concentrated on details, and the spirit seems to have been wholly lost. But the knowledge of the multitudinous details required study and teaching; and this caused the formation of a priestly caste or order, in which the tradition was handed down. The power of that order rested on the inaccessibility and difficulty of their lore, and on the ignorance of the worshippers; and hence there was every temptation to keep up that ignorance, to multiply details of cultus and make the knowledge of it harder, and to create a bar of separation between the priestly order and the people. But no details are known, though the general principle may be confidently assumed.

Moreover, as the great religious centres or *Hiera* grew into importance (see § IV (4), above), they required a permanent staff of priests and ministers,

* This second purpose frequently passed into the sphere of magic: see C, § III (4).

† ἐμπορικὴ ἄρα τις εἴη τέχνη ἡ ὁσιότης: Plato, *Euth.* 14 E.

* See *Cities and Bish. of Phrygia*, i. pp. 56, 103, 110.

in order that the increasing number of persons who frequented them might always find help and counsel. In turn the increase of the permanent staff at the great *Hiera* tended to foster the growth of the established ritual. Instead of merely aiding the individual worshipper to perform one single act of the Divine action which suited his special circumstances at the moment, the priests of each *Hieron* on stated occasions set the whole Divine drama before the eyes of bodies of worshippers. While this more elaborate ceremonial had its justification in producing a certain good effect on the spectators, and in imparting ideas to them, yet there was the strongest temptation for the permanent priests to refrain from emphasizing this aspect of the ceremonial, and to elaborate the spectacular side in the way described above. In the simpler Anatolian system of society this strengthened their power (§ VIII (7), below); and in the developed Hellenic system it added to the wealth and influence of the *Hieron* by attracting immense crowds to the great festivals accompanying the annual (or in rare cases biennial) ceremonies.

Thus there was, necessarily, a large establishment maintained at the principal religious centres: see § IV (4). Besides the great priesthoods there were required large numbers of inferior priests, *ministri* and *ministræ*, to perform the details of the cultus (see § II, above) and prophecy and give attention to the worshippers and the offerings; also *hierodouloi*, of whom there were many thousands at the greatest *Hiera*. The *hierodouloi* had become serfs or slaves attached to the *Hieron* in various ways, and were protected and governed by the theocratic administration of the *Hieron*: on the female *hierodouloi*, see § VIII (2), below. Finally, there was a class of persons called *hieroi*: see next § (10).

It is clearly established by numerous cases, that, in later times at least, there was a college of priests in every religious centre in Anatolia. This college was a hierarchy, with distinct gradation of authority and allotted duties. At Pessinus a priest is described as occupying the fifth or tenth place in order of rank; and in other cases where the evidence shows only that there was a chief and various subordinate priests, we may probably assume from the analogy of Pessinus that strict gradation extended throughout the college. Every religious act was probably the work of the priests as a body (though the chief priest would be the leader); and this furnishes some argument in favour of the Bezan reading ἱερεῖς in Ac 14[13], where Prof. Blass condemns that reading on the incorrect ground that there was only one priest for each temple.

(10) *Hieroi.*—This class of persons, mentioned at Ephesus and many other religious centres, and evidently very numerous, have been much discussed, with varying results, by many modern writers. Their status is very obscure. The opinion advocated in the writer's *Cities and Bishoprics of Phrygia*, i. 147 f., is that the *hieroi* are merely a modification of the non-Hellenic institution of the *hierodouloi* under the influence of Hellenic institutions and spirit. The *hierodouloi* were serfs, but not slaves; whereas the Greek law knew only the grand distinction between freemen and slaves. The peculiar relation of the *hierodouloi* to the *Hieron* gave a power to the latter which was alien to the Hellenic spirit; and the old *hierodouloi* seem to have been transformed in the Hellenized cities into an inferior order of the city population, distinct alike from citizens and from resident strangers and from freedmen. The relation of the *hieroi* to the *Hieron*, and their service at the *Hieron*, seem to have been more a voluntary matter; and violation of it was left to be dealt with by the god; it was not enforced as a rule by legal action.

VIII. Influence on Society and Life.—It is a necessary part of our task to observe the bearing of this religion and ritual on social life; but this subject is too obscure to justify any general statements of a very positive kind; and only a very few details can here be mentioned.

(1) *Marriage.*—There is unmistakable evidence that a marriage ceremony of a religious nature existed, and that this ceremony stood in close relation to a part of the ritual of the Mysteries. In fact, the marriage was, as it were, a reproduction by the bride and bridegroom of a scene from the Divine life, *i.e.* from the mystic drama. The formula, 'I escaped evil: I found better,' * was repeated by the celebrant who was initiated in the Phrygian Mysteries; and the same formula was pronounced as part of the Athenian marriage ceremony. Another formula, 'I have drunk from the *kymbalon*,' † was pronounced by the initiated; and drinking from the same cup has been proved to have formed part of a ceremony performed in the temple by the betrothed pair. ‡ It is distinctly stated by a grammarian that the marriage ceremony took the form of celebrating the 'Holy Marriage' in honour of the Divine pair.§ At marriages in Athens certain instruction was imparted to the contracting pair by the priestesses of Demeter and Athena.

The ritual of the Mysteries as reported to us does not contain, it is true, any idea of marriage between the goddess and the god, but on the contrary presents a series of incidents of violence and deceit; and, as we have seen, the whole story is taken straight from the life of nature as seen in animals and crops. Undoubtedly, the suggestion from these incidents would seem to be that the Divine life, which is to form the model and exemplar for mankind, was of that rude and savage kind. But it must be remembered that our information comes from opponents whose object was only to paint the horrors, and not to give a fair judgment of the ritual as a whole. While we must admit the truth of everything they say, we must add what they have omitted; and in all probability they have omitted the reconciliation and the exhibition of the progress of life to a higher level through the influence of religion. That some such exhibition formed part of the Mysteries is made practically certain by certain allusions among the pagan authorities. The formula, 'I escaped evil: I found better,' implies it. So does the whole tone of the defence which the ancients give of the Mysteries. We suppose that the idea of legal union and of marriage formed part of this exhibition and improvement.

Diels, *Sibyllinische Blätter*, p. 48, has observed that part of the marriage ritual was almost identical with the purificatory ceremonies practised in the Mysteries (compare also S. Reinach's ingenious paper, *Rev. Archéol.*, Sept. 1901, p. 210): the connexion was suggested tentatively in the present writer's *Hist. Com. on Galatians*, p. 90; and it may now be regarded as proved.

It is an extremely important fact that the human marriage ceremony was thus celebrated by forms

* ἔφυγον κακόν· εὗρον ἄμεινον (Demosth. *de Cor.* 259).

† ἐκ κυμβάλου πέπωκα: Firmicus, *de Err. Prof. Relig.* 18.

‡ The proof is given in the present writer's *Historical Com. on the Epistle to the Galatians*, pp. 88–91, and is here strengthened by details there omitted.

§ οἱ γαμοῦντες ποιοῦσι τῷ Διῒ καὶ τῇ Ἥρᾳ ἱεροὺς γάμους: *Lex. Rhetor.* p. 670 Porson, p. 345 Nauck. The grammarian probably did not correctly apprehend the nature of this fact, which he must have got from a good authority. Usener in *Rhein. Mus.* xxx. p. 227, assumes that the reference is to the Athenian 'Holy Marriage,' a festival well known at Athens. But the *Hieros Gamos* was known elsewhere, and the true meaning of the grammarian's words is certainly as stated in the text above.

taken from the Mysteries; and the conclusion must be that the human pair repeat the action in the way in which the god and goddess first performed and consecrated it, and that, in fact, they play the parts of the god and goddess in the sacred drama. This single example is, as we may be sure, typical of a whole series of actions. We have seen also that some, probably all, domesticated animals, intended to be eaten, were slain and sacrificed according to an elaborate ritual (§ III (9)); and we may accept as highly probable the general principle that all the important acts of life were regarded as religious ceremonies, which must be performed in the proper fashion, as inaugurated by the god or goddess and taught by them to men. Every important stage in life was modelled on what the goddess or the Divine pair had done, and thus each stage was consecrated by a sort of sacrament. The subject is both wide and obscure: see below, Nos. (5) and (6).

There are, however, many difficulties connected with the question of Anatolian marriage which must first be noticed briefly.

The practice of marriage between such near relations as father and daughter, mother and son, brother and sister, is often described as common in Asia Minor. This disregard of the common restrictions on marriage is mentioned usually as characteristic of tribes or persons, called *Magusæi*, immigrant from Persia, and diffused over Cappadocia, Phrygia, and Galatia, who retained during the Christian period their mysterious ritual, worshipped fire, refrained from slaying animals (though they employed other people to kill the animals which they required for food).* But we must be struck with the fact that, except as regards the worship of fire, we know that all the characteristics attributed to the Magusæi are clearly marked in the Anatolian ritual. The mystic ritual of the Divine life consisted of a series of incestuous unions. The slaying of an animal for food was an impious act, and the impiety was punished in the ritual (§ III (9)), though the animal slain was eaten. Basil, who is one of our authorities about the Magusæi, describes marriage by capture as practised and not harshly judged by ordinary opinion in his own time.† Now, marriage by violence is characteristic of the mystic drama.

(2) *Hierodouloi.* — In this connexion another social fact must be noted, viz. ceremonial prostitution of the female *hierodouloi* or slaves of the sanctuary. This custom is known to have been widely practised at the great centres of Anatolian religion. Strabo mentions it at Komana and other Eastern centres. In the West it was characteristic of Lydia generally;‡ and the women who contributed to build the grave of Alyattes were only employing in a sacred purpose the money which belonged to the goddess. This duty was originally or theoretically incumbent on all unmarried women for a season; but how far it was practically acted on by people in general we have no means of determining. During the Græco-Roman period it seems (so far as the scanty evidence permits any judgment) to have been carried into effect by women of ordinary society only in exceptional cases, on account of some special vow or some Divine command (given in dream or oracle). But, even in the most educated period and society, the custom, though doubtless regarded as a mark of superstition and devotion to an un-Hellenic cult, was recognized and practised in some cases as one of the duties of religion by women who apparently returned to their ordinary place in society after their term of service.* Apart from these devotees, the custom was practised in later times by large numbers of women, slaves of the *Hieron*, as a permanent way of life.

* Eusebius, *Præp. Evang.* vi. pp. 275, 279 (Viger); Basil Cæs. *Epist.* 258: see an article (by the present writer) in the *Quarterly Review*, vol. 186, No. 372, p. 425.

† *Quarterly Review*, No. 372, p. 426; Basil, *Epist.* 270.

‡ In Phrygia, compare, for example, a Roman inscription (erected by a native of Pisidian Antioch), interpreted and printed correctly in *Histor. Com. on Epistle to the Galatians*, p. 201 (incorrect in Kaibel, *Inscrip. Græc. Ital.* etc., No. 933, and elsewhere), with Strabo, p. 577.

It might fairly be disputed whether that custom belonged to the original Anatolian religion, or was part of the accretion which gathered round it in the course of its development. Evidence does not exist to warrant a decided opinion; but the custom probably belongs to a more 'advanced' and artificial state of society than the primitive Anatolian, and is to be ranked as belonging only to its development.† This forms part of the ground on which rests our opinion that no trace of elevation can be observed in the history of that religion, but that its development is simply a degradation. The custom is, undoubtedly, not in keeping with the simple type which we attribute to primitive Anatolia, and seems incongruous with the institutions described in the following section. If we are right in this opinion, then the custom would have to be regarded as one of the instances of Oriental influence (like the horror of the swine in § III (6)), due to immigration from the East and long subjection to a succession of Asiatic monarchies. It is certainly an old-established part of the religion, going back to the earliest days of Oriental influence; but we believe it is possible to go back on fairly reliable evidence to an older stage in the history, when the women *hierodouloi* were of a different character, viz. guardians of the goddess and of her worshippers.

(3) *Women guards.*—The myth of Herakles and the Lydian queen Omphale, in which the woman wears the hero's arms, while he sits and spins under her command, takes us back to the primitive type of society which is described in a series of early Anatolian legends of the Amazons. Omphale and Herakles are obviously types of the Great Goddess and her companion or attendant god; and we remember that the Lydian kings for five centuries boasted to be descendants (*i.e.* representatives in orderly succession) of the first priest-king Herakles. The tale of the hero Achilles dressed as a woman and spinning in the family of Lykomedes is another example of the way in which Greek fancy worked up that primitive custom: Achilles is a hero of the north coast of Asia Minor and of some points on the Greek coast.

The Great Goddess, the protecting and guarding mother of her people, had her attendant women. These were armed as warriors, and were called Amazons in Greek legend, where fantastic characteristics are assigned to them.‡ But that a real foundation lies under those fanciful tales is certain. We can dimly descry in primitive history the Amazons, the servants of the native Anatolian goddess, contending, on the banks of the Sangarios, against the immigrant Phryges from Europe, among whom Priam fought as a young leader of the Western tribe.§

The women servants of the goddess are to be considered as resembling her in part of her character as her active and armed *ministræ*. In Ephesus they were the *melissai* or working bees, while the

* See Ramsay, *Church in Rom. Emp.* p. 397 f.; *Hist. Com. on Galatians*, pp. 40, 201.

† The present writer formerly erred in considering it to be a relic of the primitive stage in Anatolian religion; the orderly analysis of that religion, above given, shows that it belongs to its degradation. Marriage was the original rule, though with barbarous usages: promiscuity belongs to the stage of deterioration.

‡ It is an interesting illustration of the view stated in § III (7) and § VI (3), that the modern discoverer of the sex of the working bees, Dr. Warder, called them 'true Amazons.'

§ *Iliad*, iii. 184-190.

goddess was the queen bee. The sexual side of the *melissai*, alike in the bee and the priestess, is not developed: the *ministræ* therefore must have been young, and their term of service was part of their education. Evidence has perished as regards the women servants of the goddess; but in all probability at the conclusion of their term of service they passed into ordinary society, and in the ceremonial of marriage went through the ceremonies above described, imitating the actions and fate of the goddess. The opinion stated by the present writer, that a number of those armed servants of the goddess are portrayed on the wall of the rock-sanctuary at Boghaz-Keui,* has not been adopted by recent scholars; but the argument against it—the failure of any indication of the female form in the breast—has no force in view of the character of the *ministræ* as active guards, in whom the sexual type is so slightly developed as to be imperceptible in their fully draped and armed forms.

In the primitive Anatolian period the women *ministræ* must be taken to have been real guardians of the goddess and agents of her government (which she exercised through her priest-king), true Amazons or armed warriors. But history changed: the plateau became a subject land; society, manners, and needs altered, and the *ministræ* necessarily lost their original character. During this change we may believe that their development into the slaves of the sanctuary, as we see them in the more developed period, occurred. There was an element in the old *ministræ*, hinted at in legend, which could be intensified and systematized so as to transform them into the later *hierodouloi*; but the primitive element was essentially different from the organized savagery of the time of the degradation, (2).

(4) *Self-mutilation.*—The most remarkable example of the way in which the individual man imitated in his acts the life of the Deity, was in the practice of mutilation. The fate of the god, the consort of the Great Goddess, had hallowed the act; and it was familiar to all as part of the treatment prescribed by the Divine regulations for domesticated animals. Not merely was it practised on occasion of great religious festivals as a part of the ritual, not merely was it almost certainly the prescribed and necessary condition, originally, for the priest who represented the god in the ritual; it was also often performed on themselves by individuals in a state of religious excitement, induced by some crisis of their own life or of the country in which they lived. On the origin of this ceremony, see § III (7).

This act was alien to the character of Hellenic civilization and religion; and was always regarded with horror and contempt by the Greek spirit as the crowning proof of the barbarity and vulgarity of Anatolian superstition, as in the *Attis* of Catullus (which follows a Greek model).

(5) *Burial.*—In a religion which taught, explicitly or implicitly, that men are children of the Goddess-Mother, and at death return to the mother who bore them, it is natural that great sanctity should be attached to graves and sepulchral rites. In fact the religion of the grave is the religion of the household, and lies at the foundation of religion in general. The dead man, as heroized or deified, was represented under the form of the Deity, and one of the commonest later types was the Horseman-god, § III (5).

This is an exceedingly wide subject; and more can be learned about it than about any other department of Anatolian religion. The principal points may here be briefly stated. See also § IX (1).

The grave was conceived as the house or home of the deceased; and the word οἶκος is sometimes applied to it in epitaphs. But, inasmuch as the dead man is now part of the Divine nature, more frequently the grave is conceived as his temple. His right to the sole possession of it was guarded with jealous care, for, if any unauthorized corpse gains entrance, this intruder will share in the offerings and honours of the temple, and thus in the godhead of the deceased (for the dead man's godhead consists practically in the cultus and offerings paid to him; a god unworshipped is a dead god). It is noteworthy that the sepulchral inscriptions guard far more carefully against intrusion than against mere injury done to the tomb: injury can readily be repaired, but intrusion, if once successful, is hardly reparable.*

Then the making of the grave and the erection of a tombstone was a dedication to the Deity; and the epitaph on the grave was expressed often in the form of a prayer (and, of course, a vow accompanying it) to the Deity with whom the dead person was identified. Even when a person, during his lifetime, prepared his own grave, he expressed the epitaph in the form of a prayer and dedication to the Deity.† It was a duty which one owed to God to make a grave.

Thus every Phrygian grave was also a shrine or temple. Accordingly, there is no force in the argument, which many writers have employed, that such a monument as the famous sculptured rock which bears the dedication 'to king Midas' (ΜΙΔΑΙ ϜΑΝΑΚΤΕΙ) was a cult-shrine, and therefore cannot have been a sepulchral monument. In truth it was both. Similarly, some of the tumuli in the Phrygian land have probably a utilitarian purpose, being intended to serve as watch-towers and road-marks. But they were, in all probability, also sepulchral. It was desired to give them permanent sanctity, and this end was attained by the grave inside, with the religion attached to it. Probably it is not too bold to lay down the general principle that the sanctity of a locality was generally, in the primitive Anatolian system, confirmed by the awe attaching to the grave-temple. That principle remains to a large extent in force still. Sacred places are numerous all over the country; and in almost every one the sacredness is confirmed by, or founded on, the awe attaching to the supposed grave of some saint or hero. The fact that the grave is often demonstrably fictitious (as when the hero is a mere myth, or has several graves in different places) shows how strongly the need for a grave in every holy place is still felt by the Anatolian mind. The primitive custom in Greece of burying in the house, consecrated and guarded the family home.‡

The essential parts of the grave-monument were an altar and a door; and the two typical forms of gravestone in later Phrygia were developments of the altar and of the door. The former at least retained the name, and is called 'the altar' in numberless inscriptions. On this altar-tombstone there is sometimes engraved, apart from the epitaph (and even on a different side from it), the word 'door' (θύρα); and this custom obviously

* *Journal of R. Asiatic Society*, 1883, p. 14 f.: the relief is reproduced by Perrot, *Histoire de l'Art*, iv. p. 643.

* *Cities and Bishoprics of Phrygia*, i. pp. 99 f., 348 (n. 24).

† These statements, made at first in explanation of the identity in form, appearance, and general character between grave-monuments and stones recording a prayer and vow or dedication, were controverted by Prof. A. Körte; but he has since published a stone whose inscription is purely a dedication to the god, except that at the end the dedicator adds the sepulchral form καὶ ἑαυτῷ ζῶν, proving beyond question that the dedicatory stone was at the same time the gravestone over his intended tomb. We are now agreed that this custom was characteristically Phrygian; but the present writer sees far more examples of it than Prof. Körte admits.

‡ See above, § IV (2); also Ramsay, 'Permanent Attachment of Religious Veneration to Special Sites in Asia Minor,' published in *Transactions of the Oriental Congress at London*, 1892, p. 381.

arises from the feeling that a door was essential and must be indicated, even if only by a word. We have already seen that, in later grave-monuments, members which originally had a meaning were indicated by some part of their original form, and became mere conventional ornament. We may suppose that the door was simply an essential part of the house or temple in which the dead god dwelt, while the altar was necessary for the living worshippers to lay their offerings on.*

It was probably on the worship of the dead that the worship of Divine personal beings was built up. The dead parent links the family with the Divine nature. Any inexplicable misfortune or mischance was often attributed by the Greeks to some neglect of this cult, and expiated by special attention to the dead. Among the Greeks the special sacrifice to the dead hero took place on his birthday, and was called γενέσια or γενέθλια quite as often as νεκύσια. Among Christians, on the contrary, the day of death of a martyr was celebrated as his *dies natalis*, birth into his true life.

The cult of the dead was therefore of prime importance, and this applies as much to Greece as to Anatolia. Here, too, the gods had set the example, which was to be followed in the case of men. The grave of Zeus, the grave of Achilles, and so on, formed an integral part of the equipment of their worship. The worship of the heroes, *i.e.* the Divine dead, bulked far more largely in Greek life and religion than would appear from a superficial survey of the literature. This is partly due to the fact that the cult of the dead was part of the half-submerged archaic religion, believed in by all, but not made prominent in public life. But even in the literature it is often evident, and must always be understood as the substratum on which all social life rests.

(6) *Brotherhoods and guilds.*—If the ritual of the Mysteries was used as a sort of sacrament to consecrate or give the Divine sanction to marriage and the other important steps in the family life of man, so that the family was united and constituted and maintained by Divine law, the same seems to have been the case in the formation of associations and unions wider than the family. Such groups played a highly important part in Anatolian society. Originally, in the simplest form of primitive society, there was probably only the one wider group, the village, united in the religion of the central sanctuary or *Hieron* [see (7)]. The ritual of the Mysteries (to use the later Greek name anachronistically) constituted the bond to hold the village together. All were brothers, because all knew in the mystic ritual that they were the children of the Great Mother.

But as life and society became more complex, as towns became too large for a common bond of ritual to hold them (while no common municipal bond existed, such as the Greek city offered), groups of persons with common interests and pursuits were formed, some as trade guilds, some for other purposes. They are known under many names, Boukoloi, Korybantes, Hymnodoi, Satyroi, etc.,† but all were united in a common ritual; and an essential part of this lay in the common meal and the cup of which all partook. There can be no doubt that the ceremonial was similar to that of the Mysteries, and was of the nature of a sacrament or religious consecration of the common tie, and yet no direct evidence can be given, or is likely ever to be found. But the indirect evidence seems conclusive: the most general name for the members of any association is *symbiotai* ('those who live in association'), but the term *symmystai* is occasionally used as an equivalent;* and this term seems conclusive, for it is inexplicable unless the *symbiotai* were united by the tie of the common mystic ritual.

The unity of the brotherhood or society was consecrated, therefore, by the common meal and the common cup from which all drank: this was the ritual of the Mysteries, according to the formula, 'I ate from the *tympanon*: I drank from the *kymbalon*'; where the names of the sacred instruments of the Mother-Goddess are given to the common dish and the common cup. The Christian idea of breaking a common loaf was perhaps peculiar to Christianity, and due to the direct institution of the Founder: the common meal of the pagan societies probably followed the usual practice of simple Oriental meals, in which each guest has his own loaf, though all eat from a common dish. But that eating from one loaf implies brotherhood is an old idea.

(7) *Government and administration.*—The form of social organization which, in the historical period, was characteristic of Anatolia was the village-system,† which is often contrasted with the highly articulated and self-governing municipality (πόλις) of the Hellenes. The people dwelt in groups of houses called villages: at the head of each village was a *komarch*, who represented it to the supreme authority, which in the strict Anatolian system was the priesthood of the neighbouring temple (ἱερόν) as representative of the Divine power in human form. The government was in theory a theocracy: in practice the priest (usually hereditary, according to some uncertain system of inheritance) or priest-dynast was autocratic, as speaking in the name of the Deity. One restriction of his power lay in the fact that intimation of the Divine will was often conveyed to worshippers in dreams; but even in this case the interpretation of the dream usually required aid from the priesthood. 'Beyond this there was no education, and no State, and probably little or no formal law.'‡

In what relation this system, as we find it later in practical working, stood to the primitive Anatolian system is uncertain. It shows obvious traces of development, in that the mother has become less prominent, and the male element more important. This line of development was inevitable. Immigrant races were usually insufficiently provided with women; and armed conquerors must certainly have consisted mainly of men. The conquering race, therefore, must take wives from the conquered race; and the social position of women necessarily deteriorated when the conquering caste was mainly men, and the women for the most part belonged to the subjugated people. In the earliest period there can be little or no doubt that theocracy was the ruling system; but the way in which it was worked, and the exact position of women in the priesthood, remain uncertain. Further, we know that there were in early Anatolia imperial systems and great monarchies; but what was the relation in which they stood to the theocracy is obscure. We may be confident that the Herakleid dynasty in Lydia ruled as priest-kings, each new king representing the god Herakles, consort of the Great Goddess (as we see in the myth of Herakles and Omphale);

* *Journal of Hellenic Studies*, 1884, p. 253; *Cities and Bishoprics of Phrygia*, i. p. 99 f., ii. pp. 367, 395.

† *Cities and Bishoprics of Phrygia*, i. p. 96 ff., ii. pp. 359, 630. See also the following note, and (among other places) *Athen. Mittheil.* 1899, p. 179 f., where the priest of Dionysos Kathegemon is head of a list of Boukoloi.

* οἱ συμβιωταὶ καὶ συμμυσταί, where the two names are embraced under the common article, and thus identified: see Ziebarth, *Griech. Vereinswesen*, pp. 52, 206. The subject is treated more fully in *Histor. Com. on Corinthians*, § xxxi. ff., in the *Expositor*, Dec. 1900.

† ᾠκεῖτο κωμηδὸν is the expression of Strabo.

‡ *Histor. Com. on Galatians*, p. 40.

and it is probable that the inheritance passed in the female line, and the king reigned as consort of the heiress.* The natural inference that the same practice existed in the ancient empire of the central plateau, whose chief city was at Boghaz-Keui, and in the later kingdom of Tyana, is valueless, while we have no information as to the relation of this chief priest-king to the priests of the many sacred centres throughout the land (each of which was, presumably, a small theocracy for its surrounding village or villages). The supposition that the empire consisted of a loose aggregate of separate theocracies would not account for the great size and imperial character of the city at Boghaz-Keui; and we are at present reduced to mere conjecture; but evidence is likely to be discovered, when the hieroglyphic inscriptions of the country are deciphered.

(8) *Household protegés.*—A class of persons who are called in documents of the Roman period by various names, *alumni*, θρεπτοί, θρέμματα, θρεπτά, are frequently mentioned in Asia Minor. In the Roman period they are identified almost completely with foundlings, *i.e.* infants exposed by their parents and brought up as a speculation by strangers with a view to selling them for profit: such foundlings were not peculiar to Asia Minor, but known generally over the Empire, and rescripts relating to them were issued by Vespasian, Titus, and Domitian for the province of Achaia, and by Trajan for Bithynia,† and their status and rights formed a frequent subject for Imperial legislation. But in the inscriptions of Asia Minor these *protegés* are mentioned so frequently in epitaphs as to prove clearly that under that name is included also some class of persons peculiarly characteristic of the country. They are generally mentioned immediately after the children, and are sometimes distinguished from and mentioned before slaves, so that it is hardly possible to regard them as *vernæ*, slaves born and brought up in the household, although we would not deny that the term possibly may sometimes have that signification. This class is at present of quite unknown character and origin, but probably it takes us back to a primitive custom — some Anatolian institution similar to, yet distinct from, the Roman *clientela*. In a Bithynian inscription, a husband and wife and their protectress (θρέψασα ἡμῶν used as a noun) have a common tomb: all three have the same *nomen*, which the two θρέμματα must have received from the protectress; but the two were not the children of the protectress either by nature or adoption, for they were free to marry one another. The inscription, No. 36, in *Cities and Bish. of Phrygia*, shows a case in which a child had been exposed in accordance with a dream and brought up by another person, and yet the parents retain some rights over him. The tie uniting the *protegé* and the protector was evidently a close and sacred one; but the subject is one for further investigation, and nothing positive can yet be laid down with regard to it.

(9) *Religious influences on social conditions.*—While immigration, war, and conquest are favourable to the male sex, it may conversely be assumed that the high position of women and the influence exercised by, and respect paid to, the mother in the primitive Anatolian system, imply the long continuance of a peaceful condition amid a settled and, so to say, autochthonous people, such that the importance of motherly care in promoting social development had full opportunity to make itself thoroughly appreciated.

In our brief survey of the prominent features of the primitive Anatolian religion, it has become clear that this religion was originally a consecration of the rules and practices which were useful and almost necessary in actual life. While it cannot be proved in detail, yet all the evidence points to the conclusion, that in this religion the life of a simple community was ordered and prescribed from birth to death in a series of religious formulæ for personal conduct, personal purity, relation to others in the family and the community, management of the household and of agriculture and farm economy. A great deal which, in recent times, has ceased to be familiar to the poorest and the least educated classes was, in that early time, enforced on all as obligatory religious ceremonial. In modern times this growing ignorance of the fundamental principles on which comfort, propriety, and happiness in life depend, is felt to be a serious danger alike among the most civilized peoples, and in the less civilized Christian nations like the Russian. It cannot be denied that the tendency of the Christian Church to concentrate teaching on theoretical dogma and Church ritual, and to lose hold on the practical household life of the people, has contributed to spread this ignorance by gradually allowing the ancient stock of practical household wisdom to fall into oblivion, and sometimes even actively discouraging it as involved with superstition.

We have laid little stress on the barbarous elements in the Anatolian cultus, but have omitted them or passed them over lightly. Partly this is due to the fact that in many cases they seem to result from degradation of the primitive religion, due to the influence of foreign conquerors and immigrants, and accompanied by a probable deterioration of the original people. In other cases the barbarous elements are original, and correspond to the equipments and surroundings of primitive Anatolian society: these might profitably be investigated with a view to acquiring a better idea of that society, but time and wide knowledge on the part of the investigator are required.

The failure to develop the higher side of the Anatolian religion is doubtless due to many causes. The country was on the highway of armies, and the uncertainty and suffering consequent thereon were unfavourable to orderly development, while the best and most spirited element in the people was most exposed to extermination under the successive foreign conquerors. Nothing is more destructive to the highest qualities of human nature than the presence of an entirely uncertain and capricious, yet serious and ever dreaded, danger. In the succession of military conquerors the intermixture of foreign religious elements was often brought about in the worst way, viz. through the instrumentality of a rude, brutal, uneducated, and therefore superstitious Oriental soldiery, which had received not even military discipline.

The unquestioned and absolute domination of a priesthood was also unfavourable to development. The element of prophecy, in the sense of becoming sensitive to the Divine will and interpreting it with reference to contemporary events, was recognized, but seems to have been kept entirely under the control of the official priesthood. Moreover, the succession of priests in Anatolia was largely or altogether hereditary (according to unknown rules of inheritance): this increased the cast-iron and unprogressive nature of priestly rule. If, as seems probable, the chief priest in early times had to be a eunuch, that must have further debased the character of the priesthood. Thus there was no opportunity for the growing wisdom of the national mind to declare itself, since the nation outside the priesthood seems to have been given over to ignorance and practical slavery; or, rather, there was

* The evidence is collected by Gelzer in *Rhein. Museum*, xxxv. p. 519 ff. (cf. xxx. p. 5).

† Pliny, *Ep. ad Traj.* 65, 66; *Cities and Bish.* ii. p. 546.

probably no nation and no national life, but merely a congeries of villages.

IX. History and Chronology.—(1) *Development of the Anatolian Religion in history.* — It would be impossible in this place to treat even in outline the development of the Anatolian religion. The development was different in every region, varying according to the diverse historical vicissitudes and succession of immigrants and conquerors in each; and the subject would thus be a very complicated one. Moreover, as regards no single region has even any attempt been made to collect and classify the extremely scanty evidence. We can merely quote a very few examples of the process.

In north-eastern Phrygia the Gauls settled during the 3rd cent. B.C. They found there the ancient Phrygian worship of Cybele and Attis. In many instances we can prove that the Gauls adopted the religion of the land, in accordance with the ancient belief that every land has its own deities, whose power is supreme there (cf. 2 K 17[26]). The religious types on the Galatian coins are entirely either Phrygian or Græco-Roman, the latter character coming in later. The marriage ceremony in the one recorded instance was of the Anatolian type:* this instance belongs to the family of a chief probably of the 2nd cent. B.C., and the noble families were doubtless more ready to change their religious customs than the common people; but Gaulish tribes would follow their chiefs.

It is, however, beyond doubt that the Gauls introduced some modification into the old worship. The Gallic spirit and temper undoubtedly made some impression on the character of Phrygo-Galatic religion. For example, we know that at Pessinus, one of the chief centres, where the spirit of the ancient religion continued dominant and little affected by Hellenism until the latter half of the first century after Christ, an arrangement was made about B.C. 160, whereby half of the places in the college of priests were appropriated to the Gauls and half left to the old priestly families.† We can, however, say little with any confidence about the Celtic element in the Phrygo-Galatic religion. That the Gauls retained the use of the Celtic language as late as the 4th cent. after Christ is certain, but how far they imposed it on the old Phrygian subject-population is uncertain.

But, when we go further back in the history of Phrygia, we find that the Phrygians themselves were immigrants from Europe, who adopted the religion of the native population. The Mother-Goddess was seated in the land before the Phrygians entered it; and mythology retained the memory of the contest between the immigrants and the old religion with its women-guards, the Amazons.‡ The Phrygian conquerors adopted the worship of Cybele, probably imposing their own language on the mixed population. But there is no trace in mythology that the women-guards were retained in the Phrygian system; and we may probably attribute to this crisis the strengthening of the male element in the Divine idea, and the introduction of the worship of the God-Thunderer (Hellenized as *Zeus Bronton*) or the God-on-the-Car, *Benni* or *Benneus*,§ into the Phrygian worship.

On the other hand, a special mode of burial was retained among the priests of the Phrygian land, evidently the old priestly usage. They were placed upright on a rock,‖ whereas in the rock-graves that remain in the country of the Phrygian kings this custom was evidently not followed.

In these two cases we have types of what must have occurred in the many conquests of parts of the country by immigrant races. There was no attempt to exterminate or expatriate the old people and religion. The conquerors took part of the land—sometimes one-third was recognized as the proper proportion—and shared in the established religion along with the ancient worshippers; but they affected the cultus more or less, and imparted to it some part of their own nature.

(2) *Local diversity in Anatolian Religion.* — While we have necessarily directed attention mainly to the common character of religion over the whole of Asia Minor, it must be clearly understood that this community of character was not complete, but that there were great local diversities, which cannot here be properly estimated. For example, the East Anatolian religion of the warlike goddess at Komana, who was identified by the Romans with Bellona, shows a marked diversity from the true Anatolian type; but this is probably to be attributed to racial difference. More warlike and barbarous tribes pressed in from the east of the Euphrates (see § I (3), above), and superinduced a new stratum of religious ideas and rites which belonged to their own tribal character. Similarly, in southern Thrace the Orphic ritual shows a character approximating on one side to the Phrygian, but also revealing clearly a different racial character, viz. that of more barbarous tribes accustomed to eat raw flesh, and giving to this custom a place and a consecration in their religion. This, however, is a large subject.

(3) *Chronology.* — As to the age to which we are carried back before we reach the primitive Anatolian worship in its uncontaminated form, it is not possible to make any positive estimate. The earliest stage in its development that is attested by external evidence is probably found in the subjects portrayed in the rock-sculptures of Boghaz-Keui, which are commonly dated somewhere in the second millennium before Christ. But there we are already face to face with a stage of contamination with the religion and cultus of a people from the east or north-east (perhaps in some degree also from the south-east)—a people who superimpose a new and incongruous stratum of religious, social, and governing ideas on the primitive forms.

Nor is it certain by any means that the Boghaz-Keui stratum was the first stage superimposed on the primitive religious foundation. Those sculptures are of such a highly complex character that they have as yet resisted all attempts at a complete solution; and none of the attempts at a partial explanation has commanded general approbation among scholars. For practical purposes the sculptures are still a mere riddle; and hence we have been unable in this study to make any use, except in a few superficial details, of these earliest and most elaborate religious records of Anatolia. But the very fact that they are so complicated and obscure furnishes probably a sufficient proof that they are not the records of a simple cultus, but of one which had already passed through a complex process of development and contamination.

Thus we are reduced to the study of the development from the inside — a method always unsatisfactory, because subjective and liable to become fanciful, but specially unsatisfactory on the chronological side, for only contact with external facts gives any marks of time. In the development we are struck with the tenacity with which primitive characteristics were retained, readily distinguishable from the added elements; and the primitive character seems autochthonous,

* See the following footnote.

† On this point and on the whole subject, see a fuller discussion in *Histor. Com. on Galatians*, pp. 66 f., 86 ff., 131 ff.

‡ *Iliad*, iii. 184-190: see above, § VIII (3).

§ *Journal of Hellenic Studies*, 1882, p. 123; 1887, p. 511 f.

‖ Nic. Damasc. in Dindorf, *Hist. Græc. Min.* i. p. 152: presumably the corpse was put in a pit in the rock.

springing from the land, stimulated by its atmosphere, and imposing its character in some degree, more or less, on every new people or religion that entered the land.

The character of the plateau marks it out as an early home of human culture. The soil is fertile, the country is level and little exposed to dangerous animals, and in certain districts, where water is naturally abundant, cereals are naturally produced in sufficient quantity to furnish regular food to an early race of men. The art of agriculture was there taught almost by Nature herself, who thus revealed herself as mother and teacher of her people. The art of irrigation was also taught there by the same kindly mother: in some places it is so easy that the life-giving stream, flowing from a great heaven-sent spring (§ IV (3)), seems to invite men to divert and distribute its waters. The art, when once begun, was readily extended, and a country, which is now almost entirely uncultivated, and part of which is loosely indicated on Kiepert's map as *désert salé*, is shown by the remains to have supported many towns and cities in early times.* Step by step, and precept upon precept, the Goddess-Mother, the Thesmophoros of the Bœotian plain and the Athenian plain (see B, § II), educated her people; and showed them how to make the best of the useful animals, swine, ox, sheep, and goat, and later also of the horse, by proper nurture and careful treatment and breeding. The history of the education which she gave remains for us in that Anatolian religion of which some faint outline has been traced in the preceding pages.

If our view is correct, it is obvious that in a better knowledge of the Anatolian worship lies the key to an extremely early stage of human development; and that this religion has to be compared with the most primitive stages of the known ancient religions of the east Mediterranean lands. As a rule, even the most ancient Semitic cults are known to us chiefly in a considerably developed stage; and the Anatolian religion takes us behind them. In that land true religious development was arrested by causes at which we might guess; and the primitive revelation of the Mother-Goddess found no prophets and seers to carry it to completion: see § VIII (9).

B. *THE HELLENIC RELIGION.*—In studying the development of thought in the strictly Greek lands, we are inevitably carried back to an ancient form of religion there prevalent, which presented a marked similarity to the simple primitive Anatolian cultus. The extent and the limits of the similarity cannot be determined with our present knowledge. But everywhere, in attempting to comprehend the developed Hellenic religion, one finds that it rests on this substratum of deep religious feeling, which sometimes was hardly articulate, and in that case was often rather looked down upon as superstition and δεισιδαιμονία (Ac 17[22]) by the more educated and philosophic minds.

I. EARLY GREEK RELIGION.—Frequent references occur in Herodotus to an older Greek or Pelasgian religion different in character from the religion of which he conceived Homer and Hesiod to be the organizers (ii. 53). Arcadia he believed to contain more of the Pelasgian character than any other part of Greece. Precisely in Arcadia and the adjoining parts of the Peloponnesus, the strongest traces of such a pre-Hellenic religion are shown in the description of Pausanias. According to Herodotus (ii. 53), the gods of that old religion had no names and no images. The meaning of this statement is that statues (ἀγάλματα) in the later sense were not used. Symbols of various kinds, however, existed in greater number and variety perhaps in Arcadia than in other parts of Greece; but Herodotus, who was speaking of the anthropomorphizing tendency in religion, would not call those rude and non-human embodiments ἀγάλματα. Epithets of a more general character were attached to these gods, but not proper individual names: among these epithets we may reckon 'the Great God or Gods' (θεὸς μέγιστος, θεοὶ μέγιστοι), 'the Pure Gods' (θεοὶ καθαροί), 'the Good God or Genius' (ἀγαθὸς θεός or δαίμων), as well as 'the Propitiated Gods' (θεοὶ μειλίχιοι), 'the Revered Ones' (Σεμναί), 'the Kings' (ἄνακτες).

In this religion the worship of the Earth-Goddess appears in various aspects. She is sometimes the physical conception, but more generally is conceived in a more moral aspect, as the orderly harmonious march of physical phenomena, under such epithets as Themis, Harmonia, etc. This order is an avenging power that punishes all offence against itself: it is then Praxidike, Adrasteia, Nemesis, etc. It is also connected with happiness, wealth, and prosperity, and the goddess is then Tyche, Chryse, etc. The goddess is often accompanied by a male genius or deity, described as her husband or brother or attendant or child. He appears as the ἀγαθὸς δαίμων, the protecting hero, or the genius of fertilizing power.

Traces of this religion may be found in most parts of Greece: in Attica, in Bœotia, and the Northern islands, as well as in the Peloponnesus. The goddess is akin in nature to the Italian *Bona Dea*. It is a pre-Hellenic religion, but it has much of the Greek spirit about it. The deities have in many cases as much of moral as of physical character; Themis becomes a Hellenic conception. The relation of such older forms of belief to the true Hellenic religion is well given by Æschylus (*Eumen.* 1 ff.) in his history of the oracle at Delphi, where the gradual change from the first Gaia to the latest Apollo is clearly shown. No conflict is there said to take place, but the older religion merges in and is recognized by the later, so that the purely physical conception of the Earth (*Gaia*) is moralized and harmonized into Themis, and Themis is elevated into the highest Hellenic type, Phœbus Apollo, through the intermediate stage Phœbe, who is evidently a mere device to facilitate the transition in sex, as the god Phœbus inherits in right of his sister Phœbe. On the other hand, Æschylus (*Agamemnon*, 178 ff.) describes the relation of the Hellenic Zeus to the older dynasty as that of a conqueror and almost a destroyer.

These passages are important as showing that the Greeks always retained the recollection of a certain succession and development in religion, and occasionally they connect it—and in our view rightly—with the succession of races in Greece, where the later conquered without destroying the older.

The development of the Earth-Goddess into Themis was exactly paralleled by that of the older Demeter into Demeter *Thesmophoros*, 'the introducer of *thesmoi*' (θεσμοί, 'ordinances'), who is known chiefly in Bœotia, the plain of Athens, and Paros. The agricultural idea lies at the bottom of her chief festival at the time of the autumn ploughing and sowing. But that fundamental reference was merged in another idea, viz. the analogy between the continuation of the human family and the operations of agriculture.* The goddess Thesmo-

* The 'nomadization' of Asia Minor has been the chief cause of the present desolation: see *Impressions of Turkey*, p. 103, and the paper already quoted in *Geographical Journal*, Sept. 1902.

* Cf. Soph. *Œdip. Tyr.* 1497; Æsch. *Sept.* 753; Eurip. *Phœn.* 18, etc.; also the old Attic legal formula ἐπ' ἀρότῳ παίδων γνησίων. See A, § VI (2), (3).

phoros founded and presided over social order, family life, the functions of women, and the birth of children; marriage was the chief *thesmos*,* and the priestess Thesmophoros gave some instructions to newly married couples. A Hellenic touch lies in the custom of giving prizes to the most beautiful women in Arcadia, and apparently also at Thermopylæ.† Here two great Hellenic ideas, love of beauty and liking for the competitive principle, are united in the developed form of the rites; but the goddess whose festival was thus honoured was Eleusinia and not the more primitive Thesmophoros.

The resemblance of this Demeter Thesmophoros to the outlines of the Anatolian Mother-Goddess, as it has been traced in the earlier part of this article, is too obvious to need any words; and Herodotus points out (ii. 171) that the *Thesmophoria* rites were formerly practised by the Pelasgian women of the Peloponnesus, but perished when the Dorians conquered the country, except in Arcadia, where the primitive population and ritual remained. Moreover, the worship of the goddess Thesmophoros was confined to women (which markedly distinguishes her worship from that of the Eleusinian Demeter), and swine were sacrificed to her by throwing them alive into holes in the ground. These are very primitive characteristics, and show that the cult of this goddess had not been developed so much as that of the Eleusinian goddess, who is in the myth marked as an immigrant with a long history of growth out of her Pelasgian germ.

Pausanias is sometimes inclined to identify those earlier conceptions with Hellenic deities. He feels that 'the Good God' must be Zeus;‡ but about the nature of the two *Anaktes* he expresses doubt, which proves that he was struck by some marked difference between them and the two Dioscuri. In short, the Greeks felt that those gods whom they counted older, and sometimes called Pelasgian, were different from their own gods, and yet closely related to them. The succession is sometimes described as the inheritance of child from parent, sometimes as the acquisition by victor from vanquished and even exiled gods. Those old deities were not in harmony with the later Hellenic gods; there belonged to the older a graver, sterner, and more solemn character; yet there were implicit in them the germs of the double Hellenic conception of Olympian and Chthonian deities, on which see § V, below.

The conservatism with which, as a rule, the old cult-ideas were preserved in Greece and allowed a certain scope alongside of the later, give great historical importance to the study of Greek religion. Often the institutions of a bygone age retained a religious existence long after they had disappeared from actual society.

II. Greek Religion and Greek Law.—That early religion was practically coextensive with the whole circle of public and private life. Religion was the only sanction which originally existed to enforce a custom or strengthen an institution; religion impressed these on the people by constituting them into solemn rites binding on all. When in the development of the Hellenic system political institutions grew and law became a power, the legal sanction to some extent replaced the religious sanction.

One by one the various branches of duty between members of the State were taken into the circle of law. In earlier times this was often done under the advice and approval of the oracles (especially the Delphic). One set of duties after another was formulated as a branch of public law sanctioned by stated punishments and penalties. In various cases the old form was continued alongside of the later, and the offender against a law was not merely punished legally, but was also formally cursed, *i.e.* handed over to the punishing care of Heaven. The Court of Areopagus in Athens well exemplifies the gradual transformation of the religious into the legal sanction, with the religious forms persisting to some extent alongside of the legal.

But the old sanction in its primitive form continued to reign in the circle of family duties and rights, the duty of children to parents and of the younger to the older, the right of children to protection and care at the hands of their parents, of the poor to the charity of the richer, and of the stranger to hospitality. It was the *Erinnyes*, the old vague conception of the avenging power of nature, older almost than the conception of personal gods, who punished any infraction of those duties and rights.* Here a conception akin to the primitive one reigned in the developed Hellenic thought. The *Erinnyes* of the father, of children, of the poor, protected their rights and punished the violator; in other words, punishment was left to Divine action, and rarely interfered with by human law. Even the inviolability of the oath is described by Hesiod as protected by the *Erinnyes*, who punished bad faith alike among gods and men.†

In the sphere of international law, heralds went between States as Divine officials (*κήρυκες Ἑρμοῦ*). A species of international custom, not formulated into law in the strict sense, was recognized as existing between Hellenic States, but not between Greeks and barbarians;‡ but it was considered to be Divine or unwritten law, it depended on the conscience and feeling of the individual State, and was regarded by some more than others. By the religious, however, it was considered more binding than the formal laws.§

Thus religion continued to be a sort of completion of public law. Where the latter was insufficient or inapplicable, or beyond the reach of the sufferer, the religious sanction was invoked in the form of a curse. Especially, international obligations were guarded by little more than the religious sanction. Any idea of Hellenic unity which existed had been the creation of religion; and the rights of even the Greek stranger or traveller, much more of the non-Greek, were almost wholly left to religion. Law was mostly confined to the relations between one citizen and another; and in the cases where (as in Athens) it touched the relation of a resident stranger to citizens, the stranger must be represented by a citizen, and could not himself have any standing before the law. Similarly, the traveller was under the protection of the gods of the road.

III. The Elements of Hellenic Religion.—Beyond other traceable but less important influences, three forces pre-eminently are to be distinguished in the history and formation of Hellenic religion. There was, first, that above-described pre-Hellenic cultus in the Greek lands, to which we may, like the Greeks themselves, apply the name Pelasgian: that cultus had certainly a very strong resemblance to the primitive Anatolian worship, and we have freely used certain obviously primitive ceremonies of the Greek lands as evidence of the character of the old Anatolian religion.

* *Odyssey*, xxiii. 296, *λέκτροιο παλαιοῦ θεσμόν*, is a faint echo of the religious idea.

† Hesychius, *s.v.* Πυλαιΐδες; Athenæus, xiii. 90, p. 609.

‡ Pausanias, VIII. xxxvi. 5.

* *Iliad*, ix. 454, 567, xv. 204; *Odyss.* xiv. 57 compared with xvii. 475. The names of the *Erinnyes* as personal beings are of later origin: the very plural is a development.

† *Op.* 802; *Theog.* 221.

‡ *κοινοὶ τῆς* Ἑλλάδος *νόμοι*: *νομιζόμενα* Ἕλλησι: *κοινὰ τῶν* Ἑλλήνων *νόμιμα* or *δίκαια*; cf. Thuc. iii. 59, iv. 97, etc.

§ *ἄγραφοι νόμοι, ἄγραπτα νόμιμα*, Soph. *Ant.* 454.

Into the question whether it spread from Anatolia into Greece, as so many later religious impulses did, we shall not enter, though it may be pointed out that the Greeks believed themselves to have derived some very characteristic early forms of Greek cult from Crete, which in its turn was certainly connected with and influenced by Asia Minor.

There was, in the second place, the influence exercised by surrounding nations on early Greek history and religion. Only one side of this influence can be considered here, viz. the Oriental. Under the name of Oriental may be included all influence which came from Asia Minor during the period commonly called historical, as well as all traces of Phœnician or other strictly Asiatic influence. There was certainly great importance attaching to this influence; yet its true character must be noted. It did not make Greek ideas, but was simply the raw material out of which the Greek mind drew part of its growth. The Greek mind, with its eager, ardent curiosity, learned from all its neighbours, and most of all from the most advanced neighbours.

In the third place, there was that special quality and tendency of the Hellenic mind, a unique and exquisitely delicate element, which selected and moulded, moderated and regulated, mixed and added life to, the food which it absorbed from the experience and the acquirements of various other nations. That spirit of Hellenism stood in such obvious relations to the peculiar geographical and other external conditions of Greece, that some writers regard it as absolutely produced by them.

But, in our view, there was a certain innate intellectual character in the formed Greek mind, which enabled them to see in nature what no other race could see, and to use opportunities as no other race could have used them. The spirit of Hellenism, it is true, was fostered by the geographical conditions, and could have acquired strength in no other land. It needed just those peculiar relations of sea and land to foster and strengthen it; it was, like the most delicate and exquisite of Hellenic goddesses, born on the sea, not on the land; but that sea must be the Ægean, the path and the roadway of the Greek peoples, which united the Greek lands instead of estranging and separating them (as other seas seemed to do).

One of the most noteworthy forms in which the strong Hellenic appreciation of individual personality and rights (without much feeling of individual duty) showed itself was the love of competition and prizes. The individual Hellene trained himself to the highest pitch attainable in competition with his fellows, and his eagerness was stimulated by the prize of victory. The prize, in the true Hellenic idea, was simply the victor's garland, the recognition by his peers that he had won the victory. In the early stages of Hellenism the mere honour of victory was hardly sufficient to tempt the competitive ardour without prizes of value; and when in later times the Hellenic games were introduced in the Asiatic cities, it was the custom there to give valuable prizes (*θέματα*); while even the Hellenic contests in that later time were made practically valuable by privileges and money rewards from the victor's own State. Only in the fullest bloom of the Hellenic spirit were the honour and crown sufficient to attract all Hellenes.

Many religious ceremonies were modified or developed by the introduction of such competitions. While the barbarism of primitive funeral rites was developed by the Romans into gladiatorial combats, it was developed among the Greeks into the system of funeral sports and prizes. The crown of wild olive, which originally was simply the garland of the foliage sacred to the god, worn by every worshipper at Olympia, was by the Hellenes given as a prize to the victor in a competition.

The view, then, which we take is that the character of Greek religion arose in the country, and sprang from the Greek genius, which took into itself, assimilated, and gave new life and character to elements gathered from its own past and from every race with which the Greeks came in contact, so far as those races offered anything worth learning; but in this process the Greek spirit, so long as its bloom and vigour lasted, only grew more and more intensely Hellenic. The more the Greeks learned from Phœnicians or Phrygians, the more unlike them they became. In many of the Hellenic deities there is a certain Oriental element, but how utterly different in character and spirit is the Hellenic Aphrodite from a Phœnician goddess. Although Aphrodite, as she was worshipped in the cultus of the Greeks, bore strong traces of the ugly, gross, material Orientalism, and though Phœnician elements in origin can be assigned to her more confidently than to any other Greek deity, yet the Hellenic genius is almost more conspicuous in the graceful, exquisite, smiling Aphrodite of the *Iliad* than in any other Greek deity. The Greek spirit could make her beautiful without making her moral in the modern sense.

IV. The Growth of Hellenic Religion.—(1) *Continuity of development.*—The Hellenic religion which was built on that older Greek foundation had in itself little of true religious character and depth. It was in many ways a beautiful development of artistic feeling, harmony, and grouping, instinct with the Hellenic sense of individual rights and liberty, and indissolubly intertwined with the political institutions of the free, self-governing, progressive Greek City-State. The city was the highest creation of the Hellenic genius, with its free institutions and its education of the individual man; and the Hellenic religion was the ideal counterpart of the Hellenic city.

But, when we try to sound the real religious depths of the Greek nature, we must go to the worship of the dead or of the sacred stones (the *Hermai*), or the mystic worship of the deities of the old Pelasgian type. Yet the difference between the old religion and the formed Hellenic worship does not amount to absolute opposition. The later grew out of the earlier by a simple process of easy development. No definite and unvarying line divides the older gods of Greece from the properly Hellenic gods. There is hardly one of the latter who has not also in some district, or on account of some aspects of his worship, a place among the former.

(2) *Growth of mythology.*—The old personages of myth and religion continued to acquire new meaning and character amid the historical vicissitudes of the people. Just as among the Germanic and Scandinavian tribes the old Aryan tales took on a Christian character in their later development, so the old pre-Hellenic Divine personalities bear the impress of later history, or (to vary the metaphor) formed centres round which the floating beliefs and facts of later times gathered. Thus the name of Zeus goes back to the primitive Aryan stock, but he came to be the bearer of new thoughts and ideals in the Hellenic mind. To admit that Cadmus represents a Phœnician element in Greek history does not necessarily imply that Cadmus must be a Phœnician name. To take a typical case of a markedly late development: As the Oriental seclusion of women began to spread among the Greeks in general, the familiar use of boys and male favourites in domestic service, with the vices that accompanied this custom, became general. As was invariably the case, a mythical or religious parallel and example was

found, and Ganymedes became the mythical representative of the new custom in all its worst features. But, while one recognizes this, one may carry back the history of the mythic figure Ganymedes much further, and see in him one of the numberless local impersonations of the freshness and bloom of nature, the Good Genius who came from heaven and returns again to it.

The old legends can be traced in Greece in never-ceasing transformations. They appear in the Lyric poets in a very different form from what they bear in Homer; and the Tragic poets take them and again remodel them, while in Pausanias we find occasional traces of local forms differing from all the literary embodiments. The Odysseus of Homer is not the Odysseus of Sophocles. But the inference, which has sometimes been drawn, that the Tragic poets did not know the Homeric poems in the form in which we possess them, has no validity. The Lyric and the Tragic poetry represent a deeper phase—certainly a very different phase—of thought and religion from the Epic; and those later poets treated the myths as their poetic or dramatic property, and read in them or into them the thoughts of their own time.

(3) *Polytheism and the Hellenic unity.*—The older Greek religion, as we have seen, was comparatively simple. There was not a large number of gods worshipped in any one district. But the conception and names of the Divine beings varied in different districts to some degree. Though fundamentally the same, the idea of 'the God' tended in each district to assume some of the special character of the people, and to run through a special kind of development according to the succession of immigrant tribes or the varying experience of the original tribe. New religious conceptions came in with new tribes. The special deity of each race reflected in his nature the whole history of his people. The power of each deity was confined to his own district and the circle of his own worshippers.

But the idea of Hellenic unity became a political force, founded on a religious basis and strengthened in the literary development of the country. This unity was merely ideal, and never became a political reality: it was a power which exerted a certain influence on events: it was an end which some persons saw dimly before them in the distance. The Delphic Oracle was to some extent guided by that ideal in the leading which it gave to the Greek States when they consulted it; but its influence was never directed to modify the character of local or tribal religion. It always supported the established customs of each State. But it favoured uniformity by introducing new gods (πυθόχρηστοι) into almost every city of Greece: *e.g.* Aphrodite, Dionysos, Demeter, and Kora were all introduced at Erythræ by oracles from Delphi. Thus the local religions tended towards a common type by adopting each other's gods.*

Political or social unity, to the ancient mind, could exist only through common religion. Those who worshipped different gods and practised hostile religious rites could have no unity. Therefore, as a Hellenic ideal unity grew, the varying religions of the various States composing that unity could not be felt as essentially different from or really hostile to one another. If there was an ideal unity in the political sphere, there must necessarily be an ideal unity in the religious sphere; and the gods of one Hellenic State were recognized as gods by the others. Those gods quarrelled with one another, as brothers and sisters quarrel, or as the Hellenic States warred with one another. But the States met in the common recognition of the Hellenic deities. Especially the four great Pan-Hellenic games—Olympian, Pythian, Nemean, and Isthmian—formed peaceful meeting-places for all Hellenes, where religion kept the peace and all celebrants felt the benign influence of the Hellenic gods.

(4) *Formation of the Hellenic Pantheon.*—But when all the various gods who obtained Pan-Hellenic recognition were thus set side by side, the religious consciousness demanded some theory of the relation between them. Various theories, in which a religious system was built up, came into existence. But out of these the great unifying forces, literature and the Delphic Oracle, formed a generally recognized Pantheon. No two expressions of that system are precisely the same. Different writers conceived it with slight variations, but the general type is clear. The conception of a household, as it were, consisting of twelve great deities is found in several parts of Greece; but it was far from being universal, and the twelve selected were not everywhere the same. Again, in no district did the Hellenic Pantheon correspond exactly to the actual popular religion.

Everywhere both literary and popular conceptions tended towards a common form, which had its root in the popular mind and the popular ideas. It was the great poets who most of all gave shape to it, and made it familiar over the whole country and in the Greek colonies. Hence the popular Greek idea that the Hellenic religion was the creation of Homer and Hesiod had a certain truth. They beyond all others gave expression to the popular tendencies, and were the chief instruments in moulding the recognized, or, as one might almost call it, the 'orthodox' Greek Pantheon.

(5) *The Hellenic Religion an ideal.*—This common religion, which we shall continue to term the Hellenic religion, must be carefully distinguished from the actual religion of any single Hellenic State. Like the political unity which originated along with it, the Hellenic religion was much more an ideal than an actual, realized fact. Its centre and crowning idea is the supremacy and almighty power of Zeus; but very seldom do we find that Zeus is in actual worship the most important god of any State. In Athens, *e.g.*, Athenaia was the great divinity and tutelary goddess of the State; and her festivals were celebrated with greater magnificence and public interest than any others. The honour and safety of the State were bound up with her worship, not with that of Zeus. Zeus, at least so far as actual ritual is concerned, occupied quite a secondary position.

But under this local diversity it is clear that a general likeness existed. We can hardly consider that men who merely performed stated ceremonies had a religion. That term we can use only with reference to men who thought about the ideas involved in these rites; and it was the approximation to a general Hellenic type in their local religion that engaged general attention. Though they spent most care and most money on the festival of Athenaia, of Hera, or of Poseidon, their thought was concerned most with Zeus as *the* god, and with Athenaia or the others only as his representatives. Especially is this common or Hellenic religion the religion of the literature to which the most thoughtful men gave shape. But a national literature, though it be in advance of the prevalent standard of thought, is not in opposition to it. Homer and Plato only gave clearer form to the thoughts that were present in all educated minds. This common character, this Hellenic religion, is the true line in which the actual religion of Greece tended to develop. All intercourse of Greek with Greek, all education,

* νόμος πόλεως, Xen. *Mem.* iv. 3. 16; Dem. *Mid.* § 51.

all feeling of pride in their common blood and nationality, tended to foster it throughout the country, but, of course, in unequal degree according to the unequal strength of these influences in different parts of the country. Hence the Hellenic type was not equally apparent everywhere, just as it was not equally realized by all men. Some tribes went more rapidly, others very slowly, but all were tending in one direction. Various lines of argument lead to the conclusion that this Hellenic religion assumed a definite form by the middle of the 8th cent. B.C. Changes continued to take place, new ideas were added, new gods and new rites were popularized after that date, and indeed down to the latest time when Greek gave place to a new religion, which was thoroughly non-Hellenic and even anti-Hellenic, though to some considerable extent it has been influenced by Greek ideas. But at that period the religion of Hellas seems to have assimilated all its essential elements and to have established itself as a power over all the Greek tribes, which acted chiefly from a religious centre recognized by all the Hellenes —viz. the Delphic Oracle.

In fact, from that time onwards it was not so much blood or locality that determined the right of different tribes to the common name of Hellenes, as recognition of this Hellenic religion and participation in the Hellenic rites.

The history of the Greeks in modern times presents a remarkable parallel. For centuries the Greek religion was the only bond that held together the Greeks in different regions. Every other bond was gone. No Greek government, education, or literature existed. The national name had perished, and the people were serfs to a barbarous race. The tie of language had in many cases disappeared, and even at the present day there are Greeks in Asia Minor who do not know a word of the Greek tongue. Community of blood was confined to a small part of the Greek world, so called. But the religion remained to unite the people, and it proved a stronger tie than any other. Cretans of the Greek Church are Greeks, Cretans whose fathers became Mohammedans are non-Greek. This common religion was enough to preserve all the old feeling; and when the country was awakened from the sleep of centuries, when education and literature came in to help, as strong a national feeling and as complete a severance in the national mind between Greek and the rest of the world have been made manifest as ever existed in olden times. In the western parts of Asia Minor the movement can still be watched in progress. The schools have not yet been universally established, but, wherever they have been planted, a single generation develops the religious feeling into a strongly national one.

(6) *Theory of the Hellenic Pantheon.*—Further, there was a polytheistic element in the primitive Greek religion; and there grew up very early an idea that around the chief deity there were other great deities, in whom the Divine power existed in more narrowly circumscribed fashion: thus a system of higher and lower divinities was formed in such an ancient cultus as that of Eleusis. In the growth of a unified Hellenic religion this idea was developed. According to this system Zeus is the supreme god, father of gods and men, protector of right and punisher of evil: as Ἑρκεῖος and Κτήσιος he is the patron of family and household, as Ξένιος and Ἱκέσιος he is the guardian of hospitality and of friendly intercourse between different countries; finally, he is the protector of cities and public life, and the fountain of law and of morality: from him originates all revelation of the will of heaven (Πανομφαῖος). His will is fate; and the course of events is the gradual consummation of his purposes. In the whole *Iliad* the will of Zeus was wrought out (Διὸς δ' ἐτελείετο βουλή). In the tale of Melampus and Iphiclus, as it is narrated in the *Odyssey*, xi. 290 ff., the fate from the god fettered the prophet, but, when the full time came, he was released and the purpose of Zeus was perfected. The other gods and goddesses are the ministers of the will of Zeus. Each has his special province: Apollo speaks to mankind in oracles what Zeus wishes to reveal; Hestia is the goddess of family life; Poseidon rules the sea; and so on.

The province or sphere of action assigned to each deity * in this Hellenic idea had not much influence on the local cultus. When we take the Hermes of Imbros we find, not the Hellenic idea of the messenger of Zeus, but the Imbrian idea of the Divine power. But the Hermes who was adopted in many Greek cities under the Hellenic impulse was the Hellenic idea; and the popular view approximated to the Hellenic view. The average Greek thought of Aphrodite as the deity of love and beauty, Hermes as the god of heralds, and so on, irrespective of the cultus; and their names passed often into proverbial popular usage in this connexion.

This religion as we find it in Homer was practically the general religion of Greece. While in each district the same gods as of old were worshipped with special care, and the regular *cultus* at their sanctuaries was traditionally fixed among the priests, the other Pan-Hellenic gods were recognized beside them, and occasionally a Pan-Hellenic cultus even eclipsed the native worship. Thus at Olympia, Hera (perhaps associated in the Holy Marriage, ἱερὸς γάμος, with Zeus Καταιβάτης, the naturalistic deity) was the native goddess; but the festival of Zeus Olympius, a later institution, far surpassed the older worship in magnificence. In general, however, the native worship remained the chief one, and the 'orthodox' Hellenic system was recognized either by altars and worship of other gods separately, or by an altar of all the gods or of the Twelve Gods. See (14).

(7) *Moralization of the Hellenic gods.* — The most important element in the progress of Greek religion lay in the tendency to make its gods more and more into moral conceptions. In the case of the greater gods, the physical character that had once belonged to them almost entirely disappeared from the Hellenic mind. In this respect the view of Homer may be taken as identical with that which prevailed generally during the 6th or 5th century. The gods are concerned with human life and human action; they influence the course of nature solely as a means of aiding or hindering the works of men. While the gods had thus become almost purely moral conceptions, the tendency to see Divine life in external nature remained as strong as ever.

(8) *The Daimones and the Divine in the physical world.* — When once the tendency to polytheism had been established, it increased rapidly. The physical world was filled with Divine beings. Every place, every natural object which impressed men with its beauty or solemnity, became to them the seat of a deity. The nymphs of the old Pelasgian religion formed a convenient expression for this pantheistic idea; and nymphs were seen in every tree and every stream, every glen and every mountain.

In moral conceptions a Divine nature was equally conspicuous; and altars to Pity, Shame, Friendship, etc.,† were erected in different places. Many

* τιμὰς καὶ τέχνας διελόντες, Herod. ii. 53.

† ἔλεος, αἰδώς, φιλία, ὁρμή, φήμη, φόβος, γέλως, εἰρήνη, ἐργάνη, πειθώ, εὐνομία, εὔκλεια, σωτηρία, ὁμόνοια, καιρός, νίκη, ἀρά, κ.τ.λ.

of these names are known as actual epithets of different deities; Athena *Ergane* and Athena *Nike* are well known; Artemis *Eukleia* was worshipped at Thebes. Ara or the Arai are sometimes an independent conception, sometimes a name of the Erinnyes or Eumenides. In such deities as Eros or the Charites we have forms which were in some instances worshipped as the great embodiment of the Divine conception and chief gods of the places (so Eros at Thespiæ, the Charites at Orchomenos); but generally they were only inferior figures attendant on the great gods. The Greeks themselves found it difficult to determine how far a god as worshipped under two epithets continued to be one being. Socrates (Xen. *Symp.* c. 8, 9) knows not whether there is one Aphrodite or two, Ourania and Pandemos; for Zeus himself, whom men count one, has many surnames. Xenophon was wont to sacrifice to Zeus Soter and Zeus Basileus; but a soothsayer of Lampsacos showed him that he had sinned in not sacrificing also to Zeus Meilichios. It cannot here be accidental that Xenophon's first sacrifices acknowledged only the Olympian religion, whereas Zeus Meilichios is a Chthonian deity. Solon's laws ordered that men should swear by three gods, Ἰκέσιος, Καθάρσιος, Ἐξακεστήριος; but these, though expressly called three gods, are obviously epithets of Zeus. It is therefore not surprising to find that epithets gradually tend to acquire distinct personality and a separate worship.

This tendency is seen already in Homer, who personifies the Λιταί. The sea-monster Scylla he calls a goddess, and Chimæra, Echidna, Sirens are godlike beings (θεῖον γένος). So pestilence and hunger are called gods by Sophocles (*Œdip. Tyr.* 28) and Simonides of Amorgos (vi. 102). These and all other striking instances of natural power, real or fabulous, were equally representative of the Divine nature. The term *daimon* (δαίμων) was often applied to such powers. In Homer the term δαίμων denotes a distinctly less personal conception than θεός: hardly anywhere except in *Il.* iii. 420 is a special god called δαίμων: the δαίμων is bearer of the Divine power which works in nature and in human life: the δαίμων has not been so formed, bounded and defined by mythology and cultus as θεός: δαίμων is sometimes even used impersonally (especially in the *Odyssey*) in the sense of *numen.* There is a certain tendency in Homer to attribute a bad influence to the δαίμων, and the preponderance of evil is distinctly marked in the *Odyssey.**

In the post-Homeric usage δαίμων acquired a more definite meaning, and was applied to certain godlike beings intermediate between the great gods and mankind. In Hesiod the spirits of men of the Golden Age are appointed by Zeus to watch and guard men, and are called *daimones,* and the name is also applied to Phaethon, appointed by Aphrodite as guardian of her shrine. Hence it is generally applied to the train of inferior beings attendant on the chief gods, as Satyrs, Corybantes, Erotes, etc. (Plato, *Legg.* 848 D). These *daimones* are often conceived as the executors of the will of Zeus in particular cases.† The analogy with some phases of the Hebrew doctrine of angels is interesting. In Arcadia men sacrificed to Bronte and Astrape, evidently *daimones* of Zeus. Wind-gods‡ are worshipped in a similar fashion, though they are not expressly so named. *Daimones* as companions and guardians of individual men are mentioned by Theognis (161 ff.), and frequently in later authors.* The words εὐδαίμων, δυσδαίμων probably imply such a view. They are not found in Homer; and ὀλβιοδαίμων (*Il.* iii. 182) is one of many suspicious expressions in the passage where it occurs. Εὐδαίμων is used by Hesiod (*Op.* 824). The Roman idea of a genius of city or people is not found till a late date. After the Christian era the *Tyche* of the city was worshipped; and the head of the city-goddess appears on coins. This, of course, must be distinguished from the genuine ancient cult of Tyche.† In Athens a cult of the *Demos,* alone or along with the *Charites,* is mentioned in inscriptions of the last cent. B.C.

Some order was introduced into this motley throng of Divine beings by the idea of a train of inferior deities attendant on each of the greater gods. Dionysos had a troop of followers from Sileni and Satyrs down through all grades of life to wild beasts. The train of attendants is a sort of epitome of the sphere of action belonging to the god, and that of Dionysos represents all phases of the life and energy of nature which are included in the special significance of that deity. So it is with many other gods. All the deities and *daimones* of the sea form a court round their sovereigns Poseidon and Amphitrite. To Aphrodite is attached every variety of love and grace, Eros, Himeros, Pothos, the Charites, etc. Art had much to do in determining the form of all these trains of beings; and they seldom attained such importance as to be recognized in public cult.

(9) *Restrictions on the nature of the gods.*—The originally restricted character of the Greek gods continued to cling to them. Their power was once confined to a narrow district, their worship to a small circle. As the gods changed from physical to moral conceptions, the range of their power widened, and the circle of their worshippers was increased; but still there was a universal feeling that a defined boundary did exist, and that new worshippers were admitted into a select and exclusive company. The cultus of a god was often transferred to a new place, where his worship was established in a form as closely as possible resembling the original (ἀφίδρυσις); but blood and race were usually the cause of such a transfer. The worship of the mother city thus spread to the colonies. When smaller communities were concentrated in a great State, as the Attic towns were in Athens, the worship of each was transferred to the central city; and the chief festival of the god was constituted a memorial of the original transfer by a procession to the ancient seat of the worship. Thus the old image of Dionysos was taken from Eleutherai to Athens, and an imitation left in its place. But the Eleusinian worship was left in its own home, with Athens as a secondary seat of the cultus.

This process was common in Greek history, and a well-known example in historical times is the foundation of Megalopolis by Epaminondas, in order to establish a centralized Arcadian State in counterpoise to the power of Sparta. When this was done the gods and worship of the minor States were incorporated in the greater, and the memory of their relation was kept up in the annual festival and procession between the cities. The importance of this custom for the development of inter-communication in Greece has been well shown by Curtius.‡ A system of roads to connect the chief city with the minor ones was a necessity of the growing cult. When the worship was left in the minor State as too holy to be dis-

* Kröcher, *Gebrauch des Wortes* δαίμων, reckons that the word occurs there eighteen times in action unfriendly to men, fourteen times indifferent or friendly. Fick derives δαίμων from the root *das,* 'to teach,' and identifies it with the Sanskrit *dasmant,* 'wise.'

† So in Plato (*Legg.* v. 730 A), ὁ ξένιος ἑκάστου δαίμων καὶ θεός, τῷ ξενίῳ συνεπόμενος Διί.

‡ Herod. vii. 178, 189.

* Cf. Plato, *Phædon,* 107 D.

† Paus. vi. 25. 4; ii. 7. 5; iv. 30. 2.

‡ *Geschichte des Wegebaus bei den Griechen.*

turbed, a road between the two cities was equally required. This conception of the roads is related to the utilitarian view described in A, § I (1), etc.: the use of the roads for the god's service was the guarantee and consecration of their usefulness for all his worshippers, and ensured that they were respected by all who reverenced his power.

Thus originated the sacred roads of the processions of Athens, of Megalopolis, of Sparta to Amyclæ, of Elis to Olympia. The road from Athens to Marathon, by which the god had been brought to Athens, was, as Curtius has emphasized, always traversed by the θεωρίαι sent by Athens to consult the Delphic Oracle. There they found the road that connected Marathon with Delphi, marking the way along which the worship of the god had once been borne; and they travelled by the Sacred Way in preference to the direct path from Athens to Delphi. Hence they watched the lightning over Harma before starting; in other words, they observed the signs of the weather in the direction of Marathon. The most famous Sacred Way in Greece was the path by which Apollo had come to Delphi with the Dorians from the north of Thessaly, and every fourth year the sacred procession to Tempe kept alive the old relation. These processions are among the most interesting features of Greek religion. War was often stopped to allow them to be carried out. But in the Peloponnesian war this was not the case: for years after the Spartans occupied Dekeleia the procession by land to Eleusis ceased, till Alcibiades, by guarding the way with soldiers, enabled it to be held in safety.

(10) *State gods and gods within the State.*—Even in the State itself only a few of the gods were worshipped by the whole people. These were the θεοὶ πατρῷοι, γενέθλιοι, ἀρχηγέται, with whose worship the safety, honour, and existence of the State were bound up. They have to be distinguished from θεοὶ πάτριοι, a term which includes all the gods legally recognized in the community.

Every set of persons within the city united in any relation had their own god. But voluntary associations for the worship of a god, and united by no other bond but this worship, belong to a later time, including those which were made in a city like Athens by a set of strangers for the purpose of their own national worship: see below, C, § III.

Besides the patron-gods of each city (θεοὶ πατρῷοι), all gods legally worshipped in the State required respect from the State. If any of them were injured, or if their full rights were not given them, their anger was shown not merely against the individual wrong-doer, but also against any one in his company, and against the whole community.* Hence it was only prudent for the State to extend its support to the worship of every god, to contribute to the expense of his sacrifices and festivals (δημοτελῆ ἱερά), and to give dedicatory offerings from time to time. At the same time, it was obviously necessary to guard against the introduction of new gods into the State (see (14) below).

(11) *Extension of the worship of a god.*—It depended entirely on the worshippers themselves to determine how far their circle should be widened. In some cases a rigid exclusiveness was maintained, and new members were admitted only as a special honour. In the family worship of Zeus Ktesios some did not allow even the domestic slaves to participate (Isaios, *Ciron.* § 16); but the general custom was to admit the household slaves to the household worship (cf. Æsch. *Agam.* 1026). To the public worship of some States no strangers were admitted, as was the case in the Panionion (Herod. i. 143). At Argos no stranger could sacrifice in the Heraion (Herod. vi. 81). Athens was in general far more hospitable (Dem. *Neær.* § 79). This exclusiveness is rather a relic of the past than a real characteristic of the Hellenic religion, and it disappeared sensibly as time elapsed. The worshippers were the chief source of revenue to the priests and the temple (Lucian, *Phalar.* ii. 8), and were generally encouraged to come from all quarters.

* Æsch. *Sept.* 581; Eur. *El.* 1353; Hor. *Od.* iii. 2. 26, etc.

Apart from the formal ritualistic service of the temples, viz. the public festivals, admission to which was a matter of public concern, what may be called occasional worship, depending on the wishes and needs of individual worshippers, was a considerable element in the Hellenic religion. The cost of the public ceremonies was defrayed by the State: private worshippers in the temple also existed. This element was an increasing one, and was encouraged by the Oracle and by the priesthood in general. Pindar's house in Thebes was close by the temple of Rhea, and he honoured the goddess greatly (Pyth. iii. 77): the term indicates not mere vague respect, but practical acts of worship and offering were implied in 'honouring a god.' Neighbourhood to a particular god had the same effect in other cases (Plaut. *Bacch.* ii. 1, 3): even travellers passing a shrine or a sacred tree ought to show some token of respect, were it only to kiss the hand to it.

It is doubtful how far such worship was admitted from all comers. Probably the strict rule, in older time, was that only the privileged circle of worshippers could be admitted; and Herodotus (v. 72, vi. 81) shows cases of exclusion of extraneous worshippers. But it is probable that these cases were exceptional, that worshippers were rejected only in some excitement of national feeling, that the principle of Hellenic religion, which gradually established itself in most of the temples of local cults, was that all Hellenes might worship in Hellenic temples, and that, in such cases as Herodotus mentions, the intending worshipper acted on this principle.

(12) *State recognition of the Pan-Hellenic Religion.*—The idea of a Hellenic religion of gods common to all Hellenes never gained complete ascendency, but is seen in many individual cases. Zeus *Hellenios* or *Panhellenios* was worshipped in Athens (Paus. i. 18. 9; Ar. *Eq.* 1253) and in Ægina (Pind. *Nem.* v. 10; Paus. i. 44. 9). The expression κοινοὶ θεοί and others similar (Herod. ix. 90, etc.) show the same feeling. Invocation of all the gods together is not infrequent (Dem. *de Cor.*, *init.*; *Mid.* § 52). An altar of all the gods (βωμὸς κοινὸς πάντων θεῶν) existed at Olympia; and at Ilium there was a priest of all the gods (τῶν πάντων θεῶν). Altars of the Twelve Gods, as a convenient summary of the chief Hellenic gods, were frequent. Later we find in Messene statues of all the gods ὁπόσους νομίζουσιν Ἕλληνες.

(13) *The Hellenic Religion a part of the City-State.*—In the fully formed Hellenic city the State religion was one part of the commonwealth, and the State gods had a recognized claim to certain perquisites. The relation of the gods to the State lost the religious and pious character, and came to be conceived as a purely legal matter (νόμῳ γὰρ τοὺς θεοὺς νομίζομεν, Eur. *Hec.* 800). Here the verb does not mean so much as 'believe in the existence of' nor so little as 'practise the rites of'; it may be paraphrased by the preceding sentence. Not that the law could abolish the gods and their worship. The original thought that the Divine nature was a necessary part of the world, and help from it a necessary element in human life, was indelible and beyond the legal power to alter. A State without religion was as little conceivable as a State without laws; the good citizen and the religious citizen were equivalent expressions.

(14) *The Hellenic conception of piety.*—Εὐσέβεια, 'piety,' consisted in giving the gods their due; righteousness is justice to the gods.* Mythologically, the idea is expressed by Hesiod (*Theog.* 535) as a regular compact of mutual duties and rights (κρίνεσθαι) made in Methone between Zeus and Prometheus as the representatives of gods and men. Law and public opinion required that the gods be given their due; but that personal honour be paid them there was no necessity. Their character and position might be ridiculed so long as no intention was shown to do away with their worship. The γραφὴ ἀσεβείας was directed only against him that sought to alter or infringe the established ceremonial. The atheist (ἄθεος) was obnoxious to the law because his principles made the cultus unnecessary.

The worship of new deities was forbidden in Athens, until the Ecclesia, or the Nomothetai acting under its direction, sanctioned the introduction of a new cult, and settled the ceremonial belonging to it. But the effective prohibition of foreign rites was hindered by various causes. It was no one's business to protest against a new worship or prosecute the worshippers; the duty, disagreeable and entailing ill-will from a considerable section of the people, was left to the patriotic piety of the nation to carry out, and seldom found any one to perform it. An openness to novelties, a receptivity for foreign thought, characterized the Athenians; and foreign citizens and foreign religions (ἐπίθετοι) found in general an equally free access to the city. See below, C, § III; above, A, § VII (2).

A higher conception of εὐσέβεια, however, was not wanting. Fear of the god was from the first no prominent part of the idea of piety. Throughout the literature, love is a much more important element. Zeus is the father of gods and men, not as being their creator, but as a father-like ruler (Aristot. *Pol.* i. 12). The good man is the man beloved of God. The gods were full of goodwill towards men. The passages where the fear of God is mentioned often show that a high idea is implied in the word 'fear' (ἵνα γὰρ δέος, ἔνθα καὶ αἰδώς, Plat. *Euth.* 12 C). The word δεισιδαίμων occurs in the sense of 'pious' in Xenophon and Aristotle (*Pol.* v. 11. 25).

But the other conception of God as hurtful to men, and of the Divine action as showing itself in calamity, is not absent (see C, § I). In later times δεισιδαιμονία, as the superstitious fear of God, is distinguished from εὐσέβεια. This sense is first found in Polybius, if we except the doubtful chapter of Theophrastus (*Char.* xvi.). Moreover, the expression 'justice towards God' is often used in a better sense than that of mere compliance with an external law. But such finer thoughts probably belonged only to the few; it is hardly possible to attribute any ideas of the kind to Nicias, who was to many the ideal of a pious man. The picture that Plato gives of the religion of his time is a very dark one. In one place (*Legg.* x. p. 885) he says that some disbelieve in the gods, and others think that they are moved unjustly by gifts and vows. Still worse is the account given by Adeimantos and Glaucon in *Rep.* ii., where the strolling soothsayers who sell pardons to the people, and teach them that a few ceremonies and a little money will gain forgiveness for all sins, are especially inveighed against.

It must, however, be remembered that these passages are purposely one-sided. The truth is that popular thought was unable to reconcile the love of the gods and the fear of the gods, which constituted the central antithesis of Hellenic religion. Their religion provided no help in the difficulty. Ideas of sin, of the wrath of Heaven, were present to all men; and those who could not themselves rise to higher thoughts sank to superstitious practices to avoid the consequences of the guilt which they felt themselves laden with. The mythological legends handed down from an older stage of religion, and frequently gross and revolting in character, still clung to the gods of the national religion. The gods seemed themselves to sanction hateful and immoral acts, and exposed themselves as much to the ridicule of men as to that of their peers (*Il.* i. 600; *Odyss.* viii. 343). The better thought of Greece rejected and abolished these fables; but the vulgar often justified their evil deeds by the example of the gods.*

As the Hellenic State grew, and as art separated itself from the service of religion, the secularization of all cultus proceeded with rapid strides. The productions of the fine period of art were not made to be worshipped, but to be admired in the temple. The spectacular side of religion became every year more prominent. If it could not satisfy the religious wants of the people, it aimed at least at satiating them with fine shows. In many temples the cultus, though never wholly wanting, was quite subordinate to the purposes of State offices and of occasional pageants, which had far more of a political than a religious character. See also C, § III (4).

Art no longer formed, as it once did, a part of religion; but it influenced the popular theory of religion very materially. The Artemis of cultus was developed mainly by the artistic element into the huntress maiden; and this conception of the goddess, though not ruling in cultus, was certainly the common Hellenic idea. In this and other ways the gulf between the ancient cult and the actual thought of the people was widened.

V. The Hellenic Classification of Deities as Olympian and Chthonian. — This distinction, so characteristic of and peculiar to Hellenic thought, has already been anticipated as if familiar. One can hardly speak about Hellenic religious thought without assuming it.

(1) *Hellenism and the thought of death.*—In the thought which belongs to and constitutes Hellenism, looked at in its relation to religion, the first moment was the revolt of man against the hard law of nature—a revolt springing from the energetic, joyous consciousness of individual power and freedom. This thought expressed itself in the gods whom it pictured to itself—gods of beauty and of enjoyment. There was a tendency to eliminate from the traditional conception of the Divine beings everything that conflicted with this sentiment, and leave only gods of life and brightness. The Athenaia of actual Attic cult died, and was mourned for every year according to the old religious idea of the annual death and rebirth of the life of nature; but the Athena of Hellenic thought was lifted far above death. The grave of Dionysos was a central fact in the actual ritual, but drops out of the literature almost entirely.

The older views as to the dead, which made them into and worshipped them as gods, were not in accordance with the Hellenic spirit, and are not conspicuous in Greek literature. But the continuance of the ritual and worship of the dead in practice among the Greeks is everywhere presupposed and sometimes alluded to. There was in this respect a deep gap between the educated spirit of Hellenism and the actual conduct of the ordinary Greek man or woman. The Hellenic spirit hated and avoided the thought of death. It was concerned with life and brightness and enjoyment, with show and festival and art. Homer

* Cf. Plat. *Protag.* 331, *Rep.* i. 331 B; Cic. *de Nat. Deorum,* I. 41, 116.

* Plat. *Euth.* 5 E; Ar. *Nub.* 905, 1080; Eur. *Hipp.* 451, *Ion.* 449; Ter. *Eun.* iii. 5. 36.

describes the *Eidola* of the dead as preserving in the realm of death a shadowy and wretched existence which is worse than the most miserable lot in life. Yet in the Homeric poems the old rites are seen in practice at the graves of Patroclus and Achilles (*Odyss.* xxiv. 65, etc.) That old ritual was systematized and formulated under the influence of the Delphic Oracle (whose rule always was to recognize and regulate the ancient religious usages); and this systematization was repeated in the Solonian legislation, and doubtless all over Greece.*

Hellenism could not maintain itself at this stage: the hard facts of the world and of life demand and force recognition. Thus comes in the second moment in the Hellenic religious idea — the inevitable awe before this irresistible power, the power of nature, stern, inexorable, irresistible, which may be regarded either impersonally as Fate or Necessity (Εἱμαρμένη, Ἀνάγκη), or personally as a god whose power or will constitutes and moves and orders the course of nature. Here the gods of the old régime returned into the Hellenic consciousness. They were more closely connected in the Greek mind with the power of nature and the one great fact in nature, Death. Life, the other side of that great fact, was not, as a rule, apprehended by the Greeks in its true relation to Death. The Greek mind had sought to make for itself gods of life alone; and the two antithetic sides of the religious conception were to a great extent developed separately from one another. In this way, probably, must be explained the remarkable fact that in the Hellenic religion life and death are apportioned, so far as that is possible, to two different moods of thought and two different sets of deities. Only in the highest development of Greek thought in some rare minds, and there only in a very imperfect way, was the antithesis reconciled in a higher conception of the Divine nature (see C, § I, below).

(2) *The Olympian and the Chthonian gods.*— The difference between the gods of the old religious ideas and of the newer or Hellenic thought tended to crystallize in the distinction between Chthonian and Olympian gods, though this distinction never became absolute and universal, and there is hardly any deity who belonged everywhere and at all times to the one class and never to the other. But the worship of the dead, *i.e.* of the heroes, and of the Chthonian gods, was marked off by broad lines from that of the Olympian gods; and most of what was really deep and heartfelt religion in Greece belongs to the former, while most of what is artistic and a permanent possession for the civilized world belongs to the latter.

The even numbers and the left hand belonged to the Chthonian deities, the odd numbers and the right hand to the gods of heaven (Plat. *Legg.* iv. 717 A). White was the appropriate colour of the Olympian gods, the East their abode, and the direction to which their temples looked and their worshippers turned when sacrificing to them. The forenoon was the time suitable for their worship. The Chthonian gods preferred blood-red or black; the West was the direction to which their worshippers faced, the afternoon their chosen time. Offerings to the Olympian gods were shared in by men; offerings to the Chthonian gods were burnt whole. Men had community in the sacrifice with the former, with the latter they had none. One who had partaken of the black sheep offered to the hero Pelops in his grove in the Altis might not enter the temple of Zeus (Paus. v. 13). The priestess Theano refused to curse Alcibiades and devote him to the infernal gods, on the ground that her duty was only to bless (Plut. *Alc.* 22).

* See U. Köhler's commentary on the famous Cean inscription, *Athen. Mittheil.* i. 139; Plutarch, *Solon*, 21.

The worship of the Chthonian deities was for the most part mystic; and a very brief description of the character of the ritual of the Mysteries has already been given in A, § VII. This mystic and secret character shielded the Chthonian gods against the Hellenizing tendency; and thus the awe that attached to them remained unimpaired. Awe was foreign to the spirit of Hellenism; but the human spirit demands an element of awe, and the Hellenes were human. Accordingly, Hellenism protected the Chthonian gods against itself by keeping them private, mysterious, and apart.

VI. The Religion of Apollo and the Delphic Oracle.—To attain a conception of the spirit and character and the infinite variety of Hellenic religion and its relation to Hellenic life, it is above all necessary to study the practical development of the individual gods out of their primitive form into the full Greek idea. We can here take only one example. We might select Athenaia, the champion and mother of Athens, originally a form of the Pelasgian Mother-Goddess, who became step by step an almost purely Olympian deity (at least in the popular idea, though never in the actual cultus*), patron of what the world holds in memory as most characteristic of Athens, protector of the democracy, of art and of letters, opposed to and yet closely connected with Poseidon, who was the champion of the oligarchic and aristocratic element in the city.† But Apollo is, on the whole, the most typical and representative Hellenic deity, and his oracle at Delphi was the most powerful influence in guiding and moulding the growth of Hellenism. And as, in the much debated subject of Greek religion, it is useful to see more than one view, Mr. L. R. Farnell, the author of *Cults of the Greek States*, will treat this part of it.—

[If the study of any single Hellenic divinity can suffice for the comparison of the pagan and Christian classical world in respect of religious thought and rite, one may be justified in selecting the Apolline worship for the purpose. It may not indeed present us with the highest achievement of the Hellenic spirit in religious speculation: for instance, to trace the gradual evolution of ideas that made for monotheism, we must turn rather to the worship of Zeus. Nor, again, did it attempt to satisfy, as did the Dionysiac and Eleusinian cults, the personal craving for immortality and happiness after death which was working strongly in the Hellenic world before the diffusion of Christianity. Currents of mystic speculation, coming partly from the East, and bringing new problems concerning the providence of the world and the destiny of the soul, scarcely touched and in no way transformed the personality of Apollo. Until the old Hellenic system was passing away, he remained a bright and clearly outlined figure of the early national religion, a Pan-Hellenic god, whose attributes reflected and whose worship assisted the various stages of material, social, and moral development through which the race had passed. The study of the cult is of the highest value for the student of Hellenism, and not without value for the wider study of European ethics and religion.

To understand this, we must distinguish more carefully than is often done between the figure of worship and the figure of myth. This is the more necessary in the case of a religion such as the Hellenic, that was not fortified by any strong and imperious dogma which might bring the mythic

* Her relation to the Eumenides, the Gorgon, and the serpent-footed Erichthonios, shows her Chthonian and antique character.

† See Neil's edition of Aristophanes' *Knights*, p. 83.

fancy under control. Hence Greek myth, though usually bright and attractive, and often illuminative of actual worship, is sometimes repulsive, and no adequate expression of the serious mood of the worshipper. If we confine our view, then, to the public cults—Greek devotion being mainly public—and to the myths that illustrate these, we soon discover that Apollo did not instantly reveal himself, as he emerged above the horizon of prehistoric Hellas, as the divinity of the higher life who brought a higher message to his worshippers. The Apollo of Æschylus and Pindar is not quite the same as the Apollo of the earliest Greek tribes. The records of the historic period still preserve the impress of a wilder and more savage age.

The meaning of the name Apollo, like that of most of the Divine names in Greece, escapes us. A modern etymology that connects it with ἀπέλλα, the Doric word for 'assembly,' would yield us, if we could accept it, the very interesting result, that the aboriginal deity was not a mere 'Nature-god,' a personification of some portion of the natural world, but already a political divinity full of promise for the future public life of the race. But for etymological reasons the word ἀπέλλα could not give rise to the derivative Ἀπόλλων, though they might both come from some common stem.

We must content ourselves with having the right to believe that he is at least an Aryan god, brought in by the Hellenic conquerors, and the common possession of several of the leading tribes. In countries where the autochthonous population claimed to have survived, such as Attica and Arcadia, he is clearly an immigrant, not an indigenous deity. And Greek ritual preserved and hallowed the memory of his original entrance into Hellas from the north. It seems that in Herodotus' time the Delians were still in the habit of receiving certain cereal offerings at the festival of Apollo that purported to come from the 'Hyperboreans.' The route which the offerings followed entered Greece from the north-west, and, passing southward as far as Dodona, then struck across eastward to the Malian Gulf, and so by the Eubœan Carystos to Delos. Wild fancies have been conceived and foolish theories devised about these Hyperboreans. Error arose from the illusory belief that any people, known however dimly to the Greeks, and known to be worshippers of Apollo, could have been styled 'the people who live beyond the north wind.' The key to the puzzle has been undoubtedly found by Ahrens, who as a philologist has made one of the very few philological contributions to the study of Greek religion that are of any value. He discovered that the word Ὑπερβόρειοι is a slight popular corruption for Ὑπερβόροι or Ὑπερβερεταῖοι, a well-attested Macedonian dialect form for the Delian word Περφερέες that Herodotus declares was applied to the sacred 'carriers' of Apollo's offerings. They are then northern Greeks, all bearing pure Greek names, which all have a religious origin proper to their ritualistic function. And it is of the greatest interest to note that the route by which the oblations of the North-Greek tribes are reported to have travelled is the natural route of invasion which the Aryan conquerors are now supposed by modern historians to have followed.

Can we discover the original character of this divinity in the earliest days of the worship in Greece? A belief that still appears to prevail in ordinary classical scholarship is that he began his career as a sun-god, displacing earlier and less personal solar powers, and became gradually humanized and withdrawn from this elemental sphere. But the belief is uncritically held, and breaks down before the evidence of the cult-facts. The epithets whereby a Greek divinity was addressed in prayer and official hymns give the best clue to the ideas of ancient worship. None of those that are attached to Apollo can be naturally interpreted as designating a god of the sun or of the lights of heaven. Λύκειος, one of his most common titles, can come from the stem of λύκο-ς, 'wolf,' and not phonetically from the stem of λύκη, an assumed old Greek word for 'light.' Λυκηγενής, an epithet only used twice in the *Iliad* in a conversation between Athena and the Lycian Pandaros, can mean, in accord with the laws of word-formation, either 'Lycian-born' or 'wolf-born': the latter significance being in harmony with a well-attested legend. Αἰγλήτης, 'the god of the gleam' at Anaphe, appears to have been a later transformation for an older form Ἀσγελάτας, a term of quite different import.

At a comparatively later period, Apollo comes into touch with Helios, especially in Asia Minor: the same may be said of other divinities, for whom no one would claim a solar origin. The first to identify him with Helios was Euripides; but this poet is often quite reckless of the popular religious view, and the statement belongs to a certain theory of his.

In pagan North Europe, and in pagan Greece, the leading practices of ritual that have been discovered and interpreted by modern research aimed at ensuring fertility and growth in the vegetable and animal kingdoms. This must be the chief interest of primitive society in the pastoral and agricultural age; and it is this that gives function and much of their character to most of the Hellenic divinities throughout all periods of their career, and especially to Apollo.

Doubtless, the earliest Hellenic invaders had already advanced beyond the social level of the hunter and the shepherd. Yet early cult and cult-ideas that survived the changes and progress of the ages preserve the traits of savage life. Here and there Apollo was still the cave-dweller: for instance, near Magnesia on the Mæander, where his image and spirit filled his priests with superhuman force, so that in wild frenzy they bounded down steep rocks and uprooted strong trees: even in cultured Athens he was still worshipped in a cave on the Acropolis. To this period belong such conceptions as that of Apollo Λύκειος, the wolf-god, the son of a wolf-mother, the god to whom wolves were offered in Argive ritual. In Cyprus we come upon the worship of Apollo Ὑλάτης, the deity of the woodland, to whom certain trees were sacred; and the bow, the weapon of early man, and always the chief badge of Apollo, belongs to him as the divinity of the chase, to whom the huntsman even in the days of Arrian offered a tithe of the spoil. Throughout all Hellas he was worshipped also as the deity of flocks and herds, who tended sheep and horned cattle in the pastures, and brought plentiful supply of milk, as Νόμιος and Γαλάξιος. The agricultural life, which is again a higher stage, is also under his care. He guards the crops from mildew and vermin, preserves the boundaries of the tenements, and to his shrines at Delphi and Delos the Greek States far and wide send their tribute of corn.

His festivals, which fell in spring, summer, and early autumn, but never in winter, attest very clearly his vegetative and agricultural character. At Amyclæ, in Laconia, he succeeded to and absorbed the cult of an old hero of vegetation, Hyacinthus, probably a pre-Hellenic personage, the beautiful youth who dies young and is bewailed as the incarnation of the bloom and the early fruits of the year. His grave was beneath the basement of Apollo's statue, and the first part of the *Hyacinthia* festival was consecrated to him; the note of sorrow in the ritual is an echo from the primitive life of the husbandman and harvester in Europe and Asia. The Laconian festival of the

Κάρνεια is one of peculiar interest, and it is impossible here to cope with the questions that arise concerning it. Our own view is that Apollo Κάρνειος, whose name means 'the cattle-god,' was worshipped by the Dorians in North Greece, and probably by the Dryopes before the Dorian conquest of the Peloponnese; that the Dorians established his worship in Megara, Sicyon, Argos, and Sparta, though a previous migration, possibly of the Dryopes, may have already planted the worship in certain parts of Southern Greece. The Spartan ritual has been well interpreted by Mannhardt: for nine days all the people lived in tents or huts, a reminiscence of primitive life, and the chief act of the festival was the pursuit of a man called 'the runner,' who was covered with garlands, by youths who carried grape clusters; if they caught him, it was a good omen for the crops and vintage. The ritual is vegetation-magic and old European. Upon this, as upon the ritual of the *Hyacinthia*, the higher worship of the god of song and music was engrafted.

To this early pastoral and agricultural period belongs the rite of human sacrifice which survived here and there in the worship of Apollo, and which was probably more frequent in the earlier period when it was common to all Aryan and to less progressive races. In Cyprus those who touched the altar of Apollo were thrown from a rock; from the famous Leucadian promontory in Acarnania a victim was hurled once a year 'as a piacular offering' to Apollo; and in the Attic Θαργήλια, an early harvest-festival consecrated to Apollo, where most of the ritual was harmless vegetation-magic, the cruel rite may have prevailed, even in the civilized age, of leading forth two human scapegoats and putting them to death by stoning or burning. The human oblation, which Greek civilization tended to abolish or modify, is a practice—whatever its true meaning—that is rooted in savagery. Yet it sometimes contains the germ of the idea of piacular and vicarious atonement that can bear fruit in a higher religion.

So far it has only been the primitive character of Apollo that we have attempted to outline. His real significance for the Greek πόλις touches higher issues. He becomes, or already at the dawn of Greek history he was, one of a special group of deities that presided over the communion of the family, the clan, the village, and finally of the πόλις, the last development of these. His cone-shaped pillar stood in the street before the door of the citizen; and Apollo Ἀγυιεύς becomes Apollo Προστατήριος, the god 'who stands before the door' and shields the household from terrors of the seen and unseen world. To the Ionic communities he stood in the special relation of ancestor, and the Dorian cities honoured him as the leader of their colonies, and sometimes as the founder and organizer of their social institutions.

Two instances may be selected from the many that might be quoted, to show the importance of his cult for social and political progress. At Athens the court called ἐπὶ Δελφινίῳ was founded to try cases of homicide where justifiable circumstances were pleaded. When criminal law becomes able to consider such pleas, it is advancing from the barbaric to the civilized stage. It is of importance, therefore, to note that this great advance was associated at Athens, in part at least, with the name and cult of Apollo. Again, at Delphi the worship of the Pythian Apollo played a very useful part in the emancipation of slaves. The slave who saved money could not, of course, be sure of buying his freedom from his master, for the latter might lay hands on the money and retain the slave; but he could, and from a vast number of Delphic inscriptions we have evidence that he very frequently did, deposit the money with the god, who then purchased him from his master, and let him go free with a religious guarantee, that was legally effective, against further violence or constraint. This excellent system prevailed in other worships elsewhere, but was specially in vogue at Delphi.



To the development of ethical thought the Apolline cult contributed one vital conception, that of purification from sin, an idea that belongs to other cults also, but is most prominent in this. We must not interpret this conception as having at the outset any essential relation to inward or moral purity, or as even enforcing any austere ideal of sexual abstinence. Purification in the Apolline and other Hellenic cults must be understood in a ritualistic sense: the process of purification aimed at washing away certain stains from a man's person that rendered him ritualistically unclean, that is, unable to approach the altars and temples of the gods, or to mix with his fellows without spreading a deadly miasma around him: such stains would be contracted by harmless physical acts, but specially by contact with blood. It is therefore the shedder of blood who stood in special need of the Delphic ritual of purification, in which the use of the laurel and the lustration with swine's blood are combined. Now, these kathartic practices are not proved to have been very ancient in Greece; the poet Arctinus of the 8th cent. B.C. is the first who records them, and he associates them with Apollo and Artemis. There is reason for believing that they were introduced into Delphi from Crete, the land whence the Athenians summoned Epimenides to purge the city from the stain of the Cylonian massacre, and whither Apollo himself repaired to be purified from the blood of Python. The Athenian Θαργήλια was partly a feast of purification; and the idea was still more prominent in the Delphic feast of the Στεπτήρια, held every eight years in the early summer, when, after a dramatic representation of the slaughter of Pytho, the Delphians selected a beautiful and high-born boy, who was temporarily an incarnation of the god, and who proceeded to Tempe, and, after purification, returned by the 'Sacred Way,' bearing the pure laurel through many an old seat of Apollo's worship in Thessaly, Oeta, and Malis. This ritualistic idea of cleanliness, so prominent in the Apolline cult, at first a non-ethical idea, is of the greatest importance for the history of ethics, for from it has grown the advanced conception of moral purity and the civilized horror of bloodshed.

Finally, Apollo was pre-eminently a god of the arts and the higher intellectual life, the leader of the Muses, the deity to whom the stateliest forms of music and song were consecrated. In pre-Homeric days the Pæan was already his special hymn of praise. In its earliest period the Pythian festival was a musical, not an athletic, contest; it came to include a competition of poets, and even of painters, thus fulfilling some of the functions of a Royal Academy of Arts. It is, in fact, the distinction of the Greek as compared with other high religions of the world that it conceived of the Divinity as revealed in the achievements of art and human science no less fully than in the moral life of the household and the State.

It remains to give a very brief outline of the Oracular worship of Delphi; for this presents the salient features of the god in the strongest light; and the Delphic tripod was the chief source of his power, and one of the few bonds of religious union in the Hellenic world. The god had seized upon Delphi or Pytho before the period of the Homeric poems, that is to say, before the Greek colonization of Asia Minor.

We may ask how Apollo became pre-eminently the prophetic god, while the power of divination was always inherent and often active in every deity and many a departed hero. His special distinction in this sphere was probably not due to any fundamental fact in his original character. The prestige of Delphi was probably the cause rather than the effect of the oracular prestige of Apollo; what it was that won for Delphi this unique position is a question that cannot now be raised.

We are certain, at any rate, that it was from the Delphic rock that the fame of the prophetic god spread far and wide over the Hellenic and non-Hellenic world; and affiliated shrines were planted in Greece consecrated to Apollo Pythæus.

The sanctity of the temple was safeguarded by the Amphictyonic Council, whose constitution reflects the pre-Homeric age of Greece, and whose members bound themselves by a solemn oath to defend the shrine, and never to destroy or allow the destruction of an Amphictyonic State. It was not the fault of the religion that the oath was shamefully broken, and that this ideal of a higher national union remained barren.

The manner of divination at Delphi is interesting, and in one respect peculiar. The 'mantic' art in Greece has been defined as twofold; one kind being ecstatic, enthusiastic, insane, the other sane and rational. The diviner of the former type is possessed by the spirit of the god who enters into him or her through the sacramental eating or drinking of a substance in which the spirit of the god was supposed to reside; so possessed, the human frame becomes an organ of the voice of God, and the human lips are moved in madness with utterances that the skilled can interpret. Of the latter type is soothsaying from birds and other animals, inspection of entrails, the drawing of lots, which may be corn-stalks or notched pieces of wood. The soothsayer in this case is sane enough, and may be said to practise rationally an art or science that is merely based on a false hypothesis. To these we may add a third: prophecy by means of dreams that were supposed to well up from the earth and the earth-spirit into the sleeper's brain. The second type is regarded as specially Apolline, ecstatic enthusiasm being considered to be alien to the character of the sane god. All three were once practised at Delphi—the third when the Oracle was under the dominion of the earth-goddess, the two former after Apollo's arrival. But the only divination that was in real vogue there in the historic period was of the ecstatic, enthusiastic, epileptic type. The Pythoness drinks the water of the holy stream, chews the sacred laurel-leaf, mounts the tripod above the chasm whence the mephitic vapours rose, and then speaks words of frenzy which the Ὅσιοι, the five priests of the noblest Delphic blood, holding office for life, who sit near her listening, interpret according to some system of their own. This oracular madness has been supposed to be un-Apolline, and due to the strong influence of the Bacchic cult at Delphi. The theory is plausible, but not convincing. The priestess of the Argive shrine of the Pythian Apollo, a very early offshoot of Delphi, was also 'possessed by the god,' though the possession was wrought by a draught of the blood of the sacred lamb that was offered to him in the night. What strikes us as really un-Apolline is inspiration by means of the subterranean vapour: this may be a heritage from the pre-Apolline and 'Chthonian' period of the Oracle, for the subterranean world and its agencies are wholly alien to him.

The Pythoness was merely a virtuous woman, often of humble origin, a mere tool in the hands of the 'Holy Ones.' The history of the Oracle is really the history of the generations of those Ὅσιοι, the record, if we could gather it, of their varying attitude towards the national ethics, politics, and religion; and a complete list of the oracles would give us a marvellous insight into the average mind of Hellas. For these priests must be taken as reflecting the better average character of the nation, not as inspired teachers with a definite mission and advanced dogma. But their power was really great, and their exercise of it and their claims remind us dimly of the Papal power in the Middle Ages. In one respect their work was evil, and through conservative instinct they lagged behind the growing morality of their age; many a legend and record attest that, so far from softening the harsher traits in Greek religion, they encouraged and insisted on the maintenance of human sacrifice. The savage rite gradually passed away in spite of Delphi.

The political career of the Oracle cannot be dealt with here. It may be enough to say that the oracles which have been preserved display no settled policy; usually, but not always, the Oracle is on the side of constitutional government as against the tyrant, and was nearly always the devoted friend of Sparta, owing much of its great prestige in the 7th and 6th cent. to the support of that State.

In a famous oracle concerning the Spartan plan of Arcadian conquest, Apollo's voice was on the side of righteousness, but the utterance suggests a quasi-Papal claim to dispose of territory. But with all her influence Delphi was too weak to menace the liberties of the Greek States. Her best political activity was in the sphere of colonization; the Ὅσιοι have every reason to be considered the best informed agency for emigration that any State has ever possessed. Of course, neither in this nor in any other matter could they dictate; they merely advised and pointed the route to adventurous spirits; and they advised very well, so that at last no body of colonists were likely to start without the sanction of Delphi. There is reason for thinking that this colonizing of Apollo began in prehistoric times. The Dorian migration was probably blessed by the Oracle; and, what is still more important, we have good evidence from the legends, of the custom of dedicating to Delphi a tithe of the captives taken by any conquest: these appear to have been sometimes sent forth as a colony of the god's.

A few last words may be added concerning the part played by the Oracle in Greek religion and morality. In spite of the dark exception mentioned above, its influence, which was certainly great, was often good, and generally innocent. The priests were propagandists of two departments of cult especially: the cult of Dionysos, who was Apollo's confrère at Delphi, and the cult of heroes. The latter is an interesting feature of Greek religion, for it explains the spread of later saint-worship in the Mediterranean; and as no departed holy person could be canonized without the sanction of the Pope, so no departed athlete, warrior, or benefactor could be, or was likely to be, the object of public worship without the authorization of Delphi. Usually, the Delphic rule in religion is to encourage each State to maintain the religion and ritual of their forefathers.

In the sphere of private morality, in the ethics of the conscience, the Oracle often did good service; and this short epitome of a large theme may close with a few illustrations of this. Herodotus has preserved for us the stern and significant words with which the Oracle denounced Glaukos for tempting the god to connive at fraud: the terrified sinner craved forgiveness for his evil thoughts;

but the Pythoness told him that God would punish evil intent as well as evil act. This was then almost a new phase in the world of Greek ethics. Again, at a later time the Oracle reveals how far the moral thought of Greece had advanced out of the old bondage to ritual: a brave and good man had slain his own friend by accident while defending him in a deadly encounter with robbers; horror-stricken, with his friend's blood upon him, he flees to Delphi to ask what atonement or ritual can wash off the sin; but a better voice greets him than might have greeted Œdipus: 'Thou didst slay thy friend, striving to save his life; go hence, thou art purer than thou wert before.' Akin to the ethical idea embodied here is a χρησμὸς τῆς Πυθίας preserved in the Anthology: 'Enter the shrine of the pure God, pure in soul, having touched thyself with holy water: lustration is easy for the good; but a sinner cannot be cleansed by all the streams of ocean.' The genuineness of these oracles is a matter of indifference; they prove a rising tide of ethical feeling, which originated in the philosophical schools of Greece, and was imputed to Delphi. The conservative Oracle itself came to be regarded as playing its part in freeing men from that ancient heavy burden of ritual that in an older period may have aided certain growths in the moral world, but had long been a clog upon moral advance.

This short exposition of a great chapter in Greek religion puts forth many unproved and undeveloped statements. The present writer hopes to be able to deal more fully and more satisfactorily with doubtful and important points in the fourth volume of his *Cults of the Greek States.*

LEWIS R. FARNELL.]

C. *LATER DEVELOPMENT OF RELIGION IN THE GREEK WORLD.*—I. RELIGION IN LITERATURE AND PHILOSOPHY. — The essential inconsistency and self-contradiction involved in the idea of the Hellenic Pantheon was apparent, in a dim way, even to the common mind. Zeus was himself an individual with a history full of faults and selfishness. While his rule was often a mere capricious despotism, the other gods were a court surrounding him, each with his own schemes clashing both with the will of Zeus and with the wish of his fellow-deities. Thus the power of the highest god was limited, and overruling fate then became an inexorable law, before which even he must bow. However unwilling, he must surrender his own son Sarpedon to the death that fate had allotted him.

The contradictions and inconsistencies which were inherent in the system were felt by the common people. Thus Euthyphron defends his action against his father by the analogy of Zeus's treatment of his own father Kronos. The worship of the different gods in the State was loosely coordinated into a religion. In Athens the enjoyment and splendour of the great festivals of Athena were supplemented by the solemn impressiveness of the Mysteries. The feeling of awe, the fear of God, and the dread of divinely-sent calamity, grew with the spread of education into a vague consciousness of sin, and of the need for reconciliation with an offended God. On this consciousness the Orphic Mysteries were based; and in them certain observances ensured Divine forgiveness and future happiness. Strolling prophets even professed to sell indulgences, and in return for money to ensure, by performing certain rites, safety from punishment. At the same time a vague idea was growing in the popular mind that a good and pious life was needed to please God, quite as much as compliance with a stated ritual.

There was only one possible cure—raising the conception of God and intensifying the tendency to monotheism inherent in human thought, and not entirely lost sight of in the Greek religion. No adequate provision existed in the religion for educating the people and purifying itself. The Delphic with other Oracles had carried on this work for centuries, and ἐξηγηταί, appointed with its sanction in many States, were judges in difficult points of religion, and had some influence in coordinating the several cults; but the influence of the Oracles began to grow weaker after the end of the 6th cent., and their character deteriorated. The established religion became purely conservative, and the effort of all its ministers was solely to keep up the traditional state of things. The only hope lay in the literature of the age and the spread of higher thought. As poets had formulated with the help of the prophets the prevailing system, they with the help of the philosophers had now to raise its character. This was the religious work that the Gnomic poets, Pindar, and the Tragic poets successively performed.

The first adequate recognition in modern times of this important side of Greek literature is probably to be found in the pages of Zeller and of Trendelenburg, to whom especially we owe much in the following paragraphs.

Although the religious thought expressed in Greek literature and philosophy tended constantly to separate itself from the common religion, yet it was only the development of the latent capacities of that common religion. In its earlier stages literature worked hand in hand with the Delphic Oracle. The great Lyric and even the Tragic poets were recognized as the servants and ministers of the god. They wrote hymns for the worship which the Oracle propagated over Greece; and there is every reason to think that their finest conceptions of religion were practically those of the Oracle. Those brief proverbial utterances in which the wisdom of the 7th and 6th cents. concentrated itself are in the records expressly brought into connexion with the Oracle, over whose entrance was inscribed the μηδὲν ἄγαν of the Wise Man.*

But the relation between the two did not always continue so peaceable. Apart from those who simply denied the truth of the prevailing religion, those who like Æschylus or Socrates continued in sympathy with, and tried to read a higher meaning in, the established religion, found themselves in frequent danger of being misunderstood. Æschylus was accused of revealing the Mysteries to the profane, and Socrates was condemned as seeking to introduce new deities into the State. The Delphic rule of maintaining the hereditary order of things (τὰ πάτρια) was generally on the side of the uneducated, though the Oracle seems on the whole to have appreciated the work and character of Socrates. The conflict of religion and science, which had begun in the 5th cent. or even earlier, was the prominent fact in the 4th.

Two questions rose naturally to the minds of all who thought about the common religion: first, what was the relation of Zeus to the other gods, and how could will and power in them be reconciled with his omnipotence? And, second, what was the relation of Zeus to that overpowering fate that seemed at times to control even his will? In truth, the two questions are but two aspects of the same difficulty, and the answer to one involves the answer to the other. As long as the conception of God contains any of the capricious human element, so long must the will of Zeus clash with the will of the other gods and be overruled by the unbending, unvarying order of nature. When the Divine nature is conceived as absolutely

* See especially a paper on Freedom and Necessity in Greek Philosophy in Trendelenburg's *Beiträge.*

regular and the Divine will as absolutely free from arbitrariness and caprice, opposition between the will of the different gods and disagreement with the course of fate tend to disappear.

As we have already seen, the religious view in Homer varies between the opposite and inconsistent views, and the same wavering is seen throughout Greek literature.

Herodotus represents more completely the lower view of Divine nature than any other of the great writers. In his view, success produces pride; man believes in his own power and sufficiency, and recognizes not the unseen power of God: the gods blind him and lead him into destruction through his own arrogance. This view, that the gods, acting as the instruments of an inscrutable fate, blind men, involves essentially the same idea of fate as the other view, that the gods are friends of men, but that fate is over the gods and too powerful for them. The latter view is summed up in the words of Pittacos, *ἀνάγκᾳ δ' οὐδὲ θεοὶ μάχονται*. To Herodotus mere success is in itself a defying of the Divine law: the Divine power is chiefly seen in the misfortune which it sends on men. The order and regularity of the world, recognition of which is the fundamental idea of his work, is quite above and apart from human reason; man cannot adapt himself to it, but only mourn when he has felt its power. Only when he dies is a man safe from the calamity that the god may at any moment send on him.

But in the literature Zeus became by degrees more completely the bearer of a moral rule, and the other gods the willing ministers of his providence and will. As this idea was more thoroughly grasped, the opposition between Fate and God was in some degree reconciled; the order of nature (Εἱμαρμένη) became a moral and knowable law, the will of God: man, by learning and living in accordance with that will, can avoid the calamity which must otherwise overtake him. So in Pindar, Zeus causes all that happens to man; he can turn night to day, and day to night: nothing that man does is hid from him; only where he shows the way is a blessing to be hoped for. The constant theme of Æschylus is the unerring, unfailing justice displayed in the course of nature. He uses Justice (Δίκη) and Zeus sometimes as convertible terms; and both denote that order in nature which through suffering teaches knowledge and conformity with itself, and the recognition of which is the only consolation in time of doubt. He recognizes a development in the history of religion; the triumph of Zeus over the older dynasty of the Titans is the triumph of a moral providence over a lower order of gods. He directly combated the ancient saying as it appears, *e.g.*, in Herodotus (*παλαίφατος λόγος*), and declares that it is the actual sin of man, not the mere fact of his prosperity, that brings on him the divinely-sent calamity (*Agam.* 750; *Eum.* 531); and in many other passages he shows in clear words that such calamity is simply the way in which wisdom is taught to men even against their will. The law of Zeus, or the course of justice, is to learn by suffering (*παθεῖν μαθεῖν, πάθει μάθος, Agam.* 170). The law is a kindly one, the gracious dispensation of one that has power to make his will into Necessity. The older dynasty had represented the rule of fear: Necessity was only a punishing power, which man must dread but cannot understand; and was exercised by the gods of that dynasty—

> *τίς οὖν ἀνάγκης ἐστὶν οἰακοστρόφος;*
> *Μοῖραι τρίμορφοι μνήμονες τ' Ἐριννύες·*

and Heraclitus declares that if the sun were to transgress his bounds the Erinnyes would punish him. But under the completed sway of Zeus the avenging power of the older gods is merged in the helping and benignant power of the younger deities, for Necessity is changed into order and reason, which man can learn and respect, and thereby avoid the punishment and gain the good. Socrates seems even to have substituted *Pronoia*, Providence, for Necessity; but his biographer did not understand him.

In Sophocles, polytheism perhaps appears in its most perfect form; the other gods are only representatives of the one God, or instruments used in turn by a moral providence. To Pindar, also, Zeus is not so much a god, as the one God.

Euripides was clearly conscious of the essential self-contradiction involved in polytheism; he perceived clearly and felt strongly that it results in degrading the several gods and making the world irrational: he gave as emphatic and open expression to this as he dared: for example, in the Apollo of the *Ion*, whose criminal conduct towards Creusa in the past is even surpassed by the dishonesty of his attitude towards her and towards Xuthus in the play. That Euripides was fully conscious of this aspect of the action seems undeniable: that the general Athenian public had only some vague, uneasy sense that the poet was maligning the gods seems equally certain. It is doubtful if Euripides had any solution to offer that satisfied himself; but at any rate the conditions under which he had to work precluded his formally offering any solution, for he dared not make his views about the gods too explicit, and could only suggest difficulties and put questions. But, although his plays are remarkably instructive as regards the attitude of a section of the thinking and educated Greeks towards polytheism, the subject is too large for our limits.

At the same time, the other side of religious thought grew correspondingly. The idea of a larger cycle of life in which the apparent injustice of earthly existence might be eliminated and all men receive their deserts—an idea of which the most scanty traces appear in Homer and Hesiod—grows more apparent in Pindar: future punishment is the climax of the Divine vengeance in Æschylus, it is often referred to in Sophocles, and Euripides says, 'Who knows if death is not really the life, and life the death?' This recognition of a single rule in life and after death reconciles the antithesis of Olympian and Chthonian deities.

The influence of literature penetrated gradually through the people. The more educated were, of course, more open to it, and thus tended to become estranged from the popular beliefs as superstitions. Hence in the 5th and 4th cents. there was a growing gap between the religion of the educated and the religion of the common people. Both, so far as we have yet gone, were equally polytheistic. Philosophy entered on a bolder path, and directly combated the polytheism and anthropomorphism of the popular religion. While the poets saw in the ancestral religion the germs of higher thoughts, they did not try to free these thoughts from the sensuous symbolism in which the prevailing religion enveloped them. Philosophy naturally tended more to rise above the traditional and accepted ideas. Hence it appears to Plato in the Tenth Book of the *Republic* that in the conflict between philosophy and the vulgar crowd the poets are among the latter.

The fundamental doctrine of Greek philosophy is always the unity of the world. Some conceive this unity under the form of God, others under the form of Nature. Heraclitus conceives this unity as the Divine *λόγος*, which constitutes the correlation and intelligibility of phenomena: and Anaxagoras as *νοῦς* or Reason. It is therefore the philosophic expression of that fate or order of nature which is recognized by the poets and by religion; but the philosophers from the first maintain it as a knowable law.

The attitude of the philosophers towards the established religion is various. Some do not trouble themselves about it, others use it where it suits them. Heraclitus approaches most closely the Æschylean point of view; he declares that, whereas men see contradiction and perplexity in the world, God sees only unity and consistency; and, like Æschylus, he calls the order of nature 'Justice' (Δίκη). Man learns what is this Justice, and in learning achieves his own character and works out his own fate: τὸ ἦθος ἑκάστῳ δαίμων (compare Æsch. *Eum.* 520 f.). On the other hand, the worship of images and the offerings of beasts seem to Heraclitus hateful.

Democritus and Empedocles bring in the gods of the established religion as part of the system of things evolved from their primordial principles.

A third class of philosophers simply oppose the common religion, and would fain sweep it away to make room for a higher belief. Xenophanes cannot find strong enough terms to express his hatred for such doctrines as the plurality of gods, with all their moral failings. The anthropomorphism of the current religion, where gods are born and die, revolts him. God is infinite, and finite characteristics are foreign to His nature. God does not change and move like the vulgar deities; He is motionless, for He is all that exists, and there is nothing outside of Him into which He could move or change.

To the Sophists (who may be broadly distinguished from the Greek philosophers by their utter lack of sense for the unity of nature, and the limitation of their view to the multiplicity of phenomena) religion was created by voluntary compact among men; the variety of religions proved that it could not exist by nature, for if it came by nature it would be one. That the variety of religious thought was the necessary consequence of the variety of character produced in men by variety of external circumstances, their analysis of the world was too superficial to show. But this very superficiality of theirs is more representative of popular thought than the philosophy of deeper men, and shows better what was the religion of the educated in their own time.

Nothing sets in so clear a light the degradation of the gods in popular thought as the comedies of Aristophanes. Much as he hates the Sophists, and bitterly as he attacks their irreligion, he himself shows the gods of the established religion in more ludicrous and degrading situations than any of the Sophists cared to do. The Sophists approved of these gods as a very useful device, and inculcated respect for them as the means of developing morality among the people.

Isolated outbreaks of popular fury, in times when calamity terrified the people into piety and roused in them a temporary and quickly evanescent reaction against the growing irreligion of the time, were of no avail 'to stem the torrent of descending time.' Purely conservative, without any provision for deepening its character and keeping pace with the rapid growth of thought and of political and commercial life, the established religion continued, as a trammelling and impeding institution, losing its hold year by year on all classes of the people. How intense was the religious feeling of Athens is shown by such outbreaks as took place in B.C. 415 and 410. A longing for something more is everywhere manifest in the literature, and history shows the dissatisfaction to have been as strong in the mass of the people. The feeling was vague, for the people knew not what they sought; and it showed itself at first only in blind outbursts of fury against more prominent violations of the established religion, though in reality these violations were merely stronger examples of the universal dissatisfaction.

Only a prophet with a deeper revelation could bring the strong religious feeling of the people and the decay of the national worship into harmony; and, after Socrates had sealed with his life his belief in freedom of religious thought, the succession of philosophy to the position once occupied by the Delphic Oracle as leader of Greek religion was accomplished. It was, however, the misfortune of Greek life, and a proof of its religious weakness in comparison with the Hebrew race, that the prophetic mantle found no new wearer. In the dangerous path of pointing out the true and divinely ordained course in actual public life,—that path in which Palestine produced a constant succession of great thinkers to walk,—Socrates found no follower. Plato, while fully acknowledging that the true philosopher should take part in public life, found the actual world too full of evil to allow philosophy to enter it. Greek thought therefore remained abstract from actual life; it found its work and its heavenly kingdom, not in the world, but apart from it. Thus, in Greece, there never took place that application of philosophy to practical work which makes for development in religion; and there was never exerted that influence of philosophy on public life and on the mass of the people which is the marvellous feature of Hebrew history.

Socrates only expresses more definitely and in simpler terms the theory of the older poets: one God rules all for the best. He expresses no disbelief in the other gods, and often uses the plural θεοί; but they are not an important element, and he never, so far as our accounts go, expressed any opinion about their relation to the great God. Plato regards the common religion as the exoteric form of a deeper truth; it is generally mythical, *i.e.* it expresses in sensuous language spiritual truths. This exoteric religion is proper for the education of children, and necessary for those who cannot rise to understand the reality pictured to them in the tales of the gods. But the popular mythology must be purified: it is full of hateful and false tales which have crept in through the influence of poets and corrupted the genuine myths.

Aristotle has the same view. Polytheism is a State-engine for education. On the other hand, he sometimes tries to connect it with his system, by placing the gods in the stars; but the subject gets little notice from him.

Aristotle was the last purely Hellenic philosopher; Greek thought had now run its course. With the victorious march of Alexander, Greek civilization went forth to conquer the East; and Greek thought was now brought directly in contact with Oriental religion, and particularly with the genuine monotheism of the Hebrews. The Greek contempt for barbarians gradually disappeared before the actual experience of a religion greater than their own; while the narrowness of the Jews recognized the high character of Greek philosophy. In the last centuries before Christ, constant attempts were made on both sides to unite Hebrew and Greek thought into one system. The doctrine of angels and devils, which was mixed up (in later times) with the Hebrew monotheistic belief, was assimilated with the Greek polytheism. The gods who surrounded Zeus became *daimones* who interposed between God and the world and bridged over the gulf between the infinite and the finite. The idea became common that all men are the children of God; that the true service of God lay, not in the cult-observances of any particular religion, but in a virtuous life; and that a priesthood to mediate between man and God was needless and wrong. The λόγος of Heraclitus and of Plato became in the Jewish school of Alexandria the Divine Word which is the bearer of all Divine power. Most of these attempts at a union of Hellenic and Jewish thought ended in an ascetic system; for all aimed at combining the two by dropping elements from each. In Christianity alone both find their completion and perfection, without loss of any of their true character.

Stoicism was the most remarkable Greek attempt to produce a synthesis of Hellenic and Oriental thought. It was to a great extent a religion, but it was an artificial religion with none of the vigour of natural unconscious life. As Zeller says, the whole Stoic view of the world was founded on the idea of one Divine being, father of all, containing and sustaining all, ruling all, manifest everywhere. God was to the Stoics the beginning and the end of the world's development. Virtuous action consists in fulfilling the Divine will and law. The true philosopher is sufficient for himself, master of his fate, above all surrounding circumstances, perfectly happy in his own knowledge, lord of all things, a true king—and a self-satisfied prig. As all men stand in the same relation to God, all men are brothers.

In its theoretic character Stoicism was wholly careless of and uninfluenced by the popular religion. But in practice the Stoic philosophers inculcated acquiescence in the religion which was accepted by common opinion and a restraint on the passions of the common people. They spoke with contempt of many points in the popular faith, the temples, the images, the fables; but they found real germs of truth in it, and thought these sufficient to justify its continuation.

Better almost than in any other writer we may see in Horace the effect of these religious philosophies on the world of Greece and Rome. To think and reason about conduct and good action and wisdom is his only religion. The gods to him are little more than names and fables. When he supported the attempt of Augustus to re-create the old religious cults, the poet and the emperor were alike urged on by the feeling that religion was a political and social machine so useful as to be indispensable to good government.

II. THE ATTITUDE OF ST. PAUL TO GREEK PHILOSOPHY.—In this brief, imperfect outline of the religious side of Greek literature—a subject which calls for a much more serious and systematic treatment than it has ever received—it has been shown how clearly the Greek thinkers conceived the problem, and how lofty was the plane on which they pitched their thoughts; but we have refrained from dwelling on their weaknesses and errors. But naturally St. Paul, who frequently alludes in very disparaging terms to the *Sophia* of the world, was most keenly sensible of its faults and imperfections. Three characteristics seem to have specially offended him.

In the first place, its method was shallow; it frequently offered irrational 'fables and endless genealogies' (1 Ti 1[4]) in place of real attempts to grapple with the problems, and was quite content with these pseudo-solutions: those genealogical explanations, not unknown even to the deepest Greek thinkers (as in Æschylus, *Agam.* 738 ff.), became more frequent in the later period, and were applied in all departments of pseudo-research, geographical, historical,* etc.

* See, *e.g.*, the account given of early Tarsian history and topography by Athenodorus, the greatest philosopher and politician whom the city produced, quoted by Stephanus Byz., *s.v.* 'Anchiale'; also pseudo-Plutarch, *de Fluviis*, etc. (*Expositor*, Dec. 1901, p. 412).

In the second place, the fibre in the popular philosophic speculation of the later Greek time (which alone was presented to the members of the Pauline Churches) was poor and its results disappointing. There came from the study no real advance in knowledge, but only frivolous argumentation and 'questionings' (1 Ti 1[4]).

In the third place, the Greek *Sophia* was entirely devoid of power over the will and heart of mankind. It remained purely theoretical and abstract: it could do nothing for men; it was the property of a few, and had no effect, or a miserably inadequate effect, on the life and character even of those few. Where it did to some degree touch the heart and affect the life of some rare individual, it produced a philosophic and affected prig rather than a true man; and in the case of some of its most eloquent exponents, such as Seneca, there was a woeful contrast in spirit between their words and their life. But the essential feature in St. Paul's teaching was that he propounded a doctrine of power, not of theory. That is what he lays special stress upon; and of that he found not a trace in the *Sophia* of the time. The Greek philosophers had sometimes observed that the unwritten laws which rested on religion had more influence on the will and conduct of men than the written laws of the State (see above, B, § II); but they had not carried out this observation to a practical result.

In this last observation lies the essence of the whole matter. The best and the most characteristic Hellenic thought was bound inevitably to regard the higher life, at which the good man must aim, not as the striving after an ideal above and beyond human nature, but as the proper and natural development of his human nature. There was in Hellenic thought no real conception of sin. There could not be such a conception, for it is of the essence of Hellenism to be perfectly content with the human nature, to rejoice in it, to find in it the Divine perfection. The counsel which Hellenic philosophy gave to man, which it must give so long as it continued true to the Hellenic spirit, was, 'Be yourself: do not fall short of your true and perfect development.' Such an idea as rising above oneself, trampling one's nature under foot as sinful, striving after the Divine nature, is essentially anti-Hellenic, and it is only rarely that any faint traces of it can be found even in those Hellenic philosophers who have been most affected by foreign thought. But it was in this revolt from the yoke of sin, in this intense eagerness after the Divine, that St. Paul found the motive power to drive men on.

But, though St. Paul saw so clearly and resented so strongly the faults of the Greek *Sophia*, it would be wrong to infer (as has been too often done) that he was either ignorant of or uninfluenced by it. It is a general fact that the great creative minds in philosophy have been more alive to the faults of their predecessors than to their excellences, and have given larger space and more emphasis in their writings to criticism of preceding philosophers than to expression of indebtedness to them. They were probably not fully conscious of their obligation, but it was very real. So it has been with St. Paul. He owed much to the Greek philosophy and thought, gained partly in formal education at Tarsus, partly by assimilation of the knowledge which floated on the surface of a more or less educated society and became insensibly the property of all its members. On this see the excellent papers by E. Curtius on 'Paulus in Athen,' and Canon E. Hicks, 'St. Paul and Hellenism,' in *Studia Biblica*, iv.; and on his probable debt (in common with Seneca) to the philosophy of Athenodorus, which must have been the staple of education and educated conversation at Tarsus in St. Paul's childhood, the present writer's remarks in *St. Paul the Traveller*, p. 300 ff., may be consulted.

Further, while St. Paul often harshly criticises the current *Sophia* in his letters to his young Churches, he was conscious that he was a debtor both to the educated Hellenes and to the uneducated non-Hellenes, both to the philosophically trained and to those who had no such training (Ro 1[14]). And he would not have his Churches lose anything of the excellences of the Greek spirit. His extreme fondness for the word *charis* can hardly be quite separated in his mind, and could not possibly be separated in the minds of his numerous Hellenic hearers, from the Greek *charis*, the grace and charm which is of the essence of Hellenism. And he sums up in three Greek words his counsel to the Colossians and the Asians generally, when he urged them to 'make their market to the full of the opportunity which their situation offered them' (Col 4[5], Eph 5[16]; cf. Ph 4[4. 8]).

III. Degradation of the Hellenic Religion. —(1) *Foreign influence.*—In Greece as in Anatolia (see A, § VII (4), above), the history of religion after a certain period of progress and elevation was a continuous process of deterioration. The changes in religion were for the most part forced on by external causes, viz. by the pressure of foreign worships; and their influence was almost wholly bad. This character resulted partly from the way in which the influence reached the Greek races and cities (see (3), below), and partly from deeper causes which cannot be described in this short sketch (though they have been briefly indicated in A, § VIII (9), above): those deeper causes combined to destroy that sensitiveness to the Divine nature, and that desire to hear and readiness to obey the Divine voice, which make for progress and elevation in religious thought.

(2) *Susceptibility to foreign religious influence.* —Some influence was exerted on the religion of the Greeks by almost every race with whom they came in contact. Even the despised and barbarous Thracians could make their Bendis and Kotys or Kotytto powerful and reverenced in cultured Athens. But it was mainly cults from the East that affected the Greek peoples during the period which is best known to us.

The foundation of this influence was always the same. The Hellenic religion, with its invariable tendency to concentrate attention on the bright side of nature and life, and to permit only reluctantly, under mystic and half-acknowledged forms, any ritual appealing to the sense of fear in the worshippers, could never completely satisfy human needs; and more was always sought after, and seemed to be found in the more impressive foreign religions. Especially the enthusiastic, emotional, and impressive Oriental forms of religion exercised on Greece an influence which acted continuously throughout ancient history. As we have seen in B, § III, the Oriental character and the primitive Pelasgian character in many deities were fused, during the vigorous growth of the Hellenic spirit, into a new form, becoming truly Hellenic conceptions; and although, in the cultus especially, the original characteristics can be traced in the Hellenic deity, yet the completed product is essentially and generically different from the Oriental type.

Thus far back in Athenian history we can observe the entrance of the Brauronian Artemis, a figure analogous to the Ephesian Artemis and the Phrygian Cybele, with her attendant animals and her Amazon priestesses; but myth tells how the invading Amazons were expelled by the hero of Athenian Hellenism; and the Artemis who established herself was the graceful huntress-maiden, a purely Hellenic conception, however much of the primitive forms could be traced in the actual cultus. But as the youth and creative energy of Hellenism passed away the Oriental influence asserted itself more effectively, and was less modified by the spirit of Greece. Asklepios never became so thoroughly Hellenized as Dionysos, but he was a distinctly later introduction into the Hellenic circle of deities.

In all of those deities the Hellenic character is evident; but in later times Hellenism touched only very slightly, if at all, the gods of Phrygia, of Syria, and of Egypt, who were naturalized in Greek lands and cities. In an age when half-Greek or wholly barbarian kings and Roman emperors were worshipped as gods in Hellenic cities, it was clear that the spirit of Hellenism had grown very weak.

Those Oriental deities appealed to the side of human nature which was alien to, and could not be satisfied with, Hellenism and the bright festival-loving gods of Hellenic political and municipal life. But in earlier times, as any Oriental deities penetrated into the Greek circle, Hellenism tended to lend them its peculiar grace and charm, to tone down the excesses and the abandon of their rites, but at the same time to detract from their power to satisfy that deep-seated craving for an awe-inspiring deity. Even as late as the 3rd cent. B.C. the Cybele, who was worshipped at Athens in the Mêtroön, was sometimes invoked under the name of Aphrodite;* and the first signs of the Hellenizing of a naturalized foreign deity was the substitution of a Hellenic for the barbarous name.

The Egyptian Isis, the Phrygian Cybele, and many others, can be traced as far back as knowledge reaches, pressing upon and forcing their way into the mind and the worship of Greece. The worship of Isis was known very early in the Greek colony of Cyrene (Herod. iv. 186); for the Greeks of Cyrene were necessarily in close relations with Egypt, and doubtless Egyptians visited or resided in Cyrene, and, moreover, there was invariably a tendency in the ancients to worship the gods of the land to which they had migrated, in the belief that those gods were powerful in the land which belonged to them.

Cybele was introduced from Phrygia into the Ionic Greek colonies on the west coast of Asia Minor at a very early time, and in much the same way as Isis was introduced at Cyrene. The Phrygian traders came in numbers to Miletus, as Hipponax mentions in the 6th cent. B.C., and they brought their religion with them. Moreover, in times of danger the Greeks turned to Cybele for help, and found her efficacious and powerful; in this respect the story of the introduction of her worship at Miletus is instructive, and may be taken as typical of what happened in many other cases.

The party of the old kingly dynasty in Miletus, having been expelled, took refuge in Assesos, and were there besieged by the tyrant of Miletus. Being hard pressed they consulted the Oracle, and were informed by the god that helpers would come to them from Phrygia, who would release them and Miletus from misfortunes. Thereafter two young men came from Phrygia, bringing the sacred things (τὰ ἱερά) of the Kabeiroi † in a basket, and approaching the wall of Assesos by night asked admittance, as they had come at the order of the god, bringing sacred things from Phrygia for the good of the people of Assesos and Miletus. In the issue the tyrant was defeated and slain, and the new rites introduced into Miletus.‡ Here the

* See Foucart, *Associations Religieuses*, p. 98, and Appendix, No. 16; cf. 10 and 11.

† This term must indicate the Phrygian rites with the sacred objects displayed to the worshippers in Phrygia.

‡ Nic. Damasc. 53.

reception of the native Anatolian ritual into Miletus is connected with the straits of a political party during a serious dissension in the city. Similarly, the introduction of the worship of the Dioscuri at Rome and the building of their temple in the forum was coincident with the struggle against the tyranny of the Tarquins, the Etruscan intruders, when the Twin Brethren aided the young republic.

(3) *Manner in which foreign religion entered Greece.*—As to the way in which these foreign gods came to be adopted by the Greeks, no clear information has come down to us about the very earliest times, though myth and legend on the subject can be interpreted by comparison with later historical facts. But the facts quoted as typical in the last few paragraphs are taken from a comparatively early period, and they agree in general with the fuller evidence that survives with regard to the later centuries (which will be stated in the following paragraphs). From all these sources of evidence, it results that nothing like intentional spread of religious belief by the adherents of any of those foreign cults occurred; that each body of worshippers rather desired to keep to itself its own gods, and was unwilling to extend the circle except for some distinct present advantage to themselves and their worship; that the spread of a cultus was connected with migration or colonization, both because the migrating people carried their gods with them and because settlers adopted also the gods of the land in which they settled; the adoption of a new god was frequently connected with and suggested by some calamity, which was attributed by popular superstition or by Oracular authority to neglect or contempt of the god in question.

The Oracle was often consulted in such cases of calamity, and often recommended that a novel worship should be introduced. Such was the way in which Rome adopted the Phrygian Cybele in B.C. 204, and Athens in 430. But the Oracle in these cases (as is always probable and in some cases certain) simply confirmed the popular impression, that the new deity if properly invoked would be able to help; and this popular impression was produced by seeing the worshippers of the deity in question, and by the superstitious fear that that deity was very powerful (which the worshippers attested) and was being outraged by neglect.

The religious history of Athens in later times is better known than that of any other Greek State, and may be taken as typical. Athens showed itself more hospitable to foreign cults than any other city, but it was also more hospitable to foreigners. There came into existence in Athens a bewildering multiplicity of gods; but the same process of multiplication went on in all Greek cities more or less, and the increase was greatest in those cities where the largest number of foreign visitors or residents was found.

There was, of course, in Athens (and doubtless in Greece everywhere) a formal law (in some less civilized places, perhaps, only a general principle and 'unwritten law'), confirmed at first by, and indeed originating from, a strong popular feeling, which forbade the introduction of strange or new gods. The penalty was death. The formal permission of the State was necessary before any new god could be introduced. But this law and this originally strong popular feeling were, in practice, far from effective. The following were the usual circumstances.

Commerce and intercourse brought to Athens, the Piræus, and other great trading centres large numbers of foreigners. As these foreigners conduced to the increase of trade, the city which desired to become a great trading centre was forced to encourage them; otherwise, in the keen competition of Greek trading cities, they would have been driven away to more hospitable places. Those strangers naturally desired to practise their own peculiar worship; and, obviously, a State which encouraged them must tolerate their practice of their rites. As early as the legislation of Solon this necessity was recognized by the law which is attributed to him. A body of foreigners who desired to conduct their native worship in Athens might form a religious society (θίασος); and the State granted to the society permission for the rules which it might lay down for its members, and toleration for its rites, so long as its aims and regulations did not conflict with the public law or tend to subvert peace and order in the city. The constitution of those religious societies was modelled on that of the State. The assembly (ἐκκλησία) of members (θιασῶται) framed rules, elected priests and other officials, who were responsible to it, and inflicted fines on disobedient members; the fines could be enforced by action before the legal tribunals of the State. New members were welcomed to these societies, not from the desire to affect the life or conduct or belief of the outside world, but because increase in numbers increased the wealth and influence of the body.

In strict legal effect the Athenian State merely tolerated, but did not encourage, the rites of the religious societies (θίασοι). Special leave was required from the Athenian Assembly (Ἐκκλησία) before any such society could build a sanctuary for itself. As regards the rites celebrated by the societies, if these seemed to the State to be unsuitable or disorderly, the primary law came into force prohibiting the introduction of new deities on pain of death. The ritual was permitted only to the foreigners who constituted the society; and when, as occasionally happened, an alarm was raised that Athenian citizens were going after those strange gods, the primary law was liable to be brought into operation, and the offending society with its gods expelled. Thus in B.C. 430 the strolling priest (μητραγύρτης) who had initiated Athenian women into the rites of the Phrygian goddess was executed. But when the plague immediately afterwards broke out, owing to the overcrowding of the city due to the invasion of Attica by the Peloponnesian armies, an alarm arose, and the Delphic Oracle (which was consulted) attributed the epidemic to the wrath of the goddess at the murder of her priest, and ordered the State to atone by building her a temple. In consequence, the temple of the Mother-Goddess (Mêtroön) was built at the Piræus.

The question arises, whether, and how far, the building of the Mêtroön implied the introduction of the ritual of the Phrygian Mother-Goddess as part of the State religion. It was, of course, necessary that in her temple there should be a cultus of, and offerings to, the goddess: it was also obviously necessary that the ritual of the temple should be such as she loved. But that does not imply that the complete ritual and mysteries of the Phrygian deity were adopted and practised at the expense and under the sanction of the Athenian State. On the contrary, Demosthenes* holds up Æschines to public contempt because he had assisted at the performance of the Phrygian Mysteries; and he could hardly have done so if they had been part of the State religion. Probably the public worship in the Mêtroön was selected and toned down by something of Hellenic restraint and order. But the Phrygian ritual was performed at the Mêtroön by a private society of

* Demosth. *de Cor.* p. 259; cf. Aristophanes, *fr.* 478, *Lys.* 388, *Pax*, 10; Cicero, *de Legg.* ii. 15, 37.

'Ὀργεῶνες, and elsewhere by strolling priests and *Metragyrtai*; and was still despised by the educated and the patriotic citizens, and discouraged by the State.*

The reason why the foreign rites spread was in Athens the same as elsewhere. The State religion, with its purely external show, did not satisfy the deep-lying religious or superstitious cravings of the people: the West turned to the more intense and enthusiastic religion of the East. While the educated classes in the later centuries were trying to unite Greek philosophy with Oriental ideas about the nature of God and his relation to man, the lower orders took refuge in the practice of the direct and undisguised Eastern rites. First naturalized in the Piræus among the lowest and most ignorant class of Athenians, who filled the harbour-town with the 'sailors' licence,'† those new rites, though scouted and despised by the more educated citizens, spread, and by degrees reduced the national worship to comparative neglect.

There was probably no period when Greece was not affected by such religious influence; but in Athens the movement assumed much greater strength through the influx of foreign merchants, attracted by the commercial supremacy and liberal policy of the city in the 5th cent. B.C.

Thus, *e.g.*, the rites of Adonis were introduced before the outbreak of the Peloponnesian war in B.C. 431.‡ The festival was being celebrated at the time when the great expedition was setting sail for Sicily in B.C. 416, as Plutarch mentions (*Alc.* 18). The rites had come from Cyprus (and ultimately from Syria); one of the female conspirators in the *Lysistrata* of Aristophanes (performed B.C. 412) swears by the Paphian Aphrodite; and the ritual is ridiculed in the same play (389, 557). The chief ceremony was entirely non-Hellenic, with its vehement mourning for the goddess's dead favourite Adonis, the search for the body and its discovery, the planting of quick-growing plants in pots as the Garden of Adonis, the revivification of the god in the garden, and the joyous conclusion of the festival.

The Thracian rites of Kotytto were satirized by Eupolis in the *Baptæ*, and the fragments of that comedy show how ugly was the character of the ritual; while the fact that Eupolis had Alcibiades in view in the play, suggests how far the rites had spread in Athens. Æschylus had previously described the Edonian worship of Kotys and Dionysos in a lost tragedy; but there the worship was foreign, though its place in the tragedy shows how great interest it had for the Athenians. The rites were of similar general character to the Phrygian ritual of Cybele and Attis or Sabazios.

Through the analogy of these cases the nature of the introduction of any foreign worship in the very early Hellenic period can be readily gathered from the associated myths and legends. The worship of Dionysos was essentially of the same kind and character as the Phrygian ritual. When it began to penetrate into Greece, through the influence of foreign settlers or a foreign tribe, it aroused the strongest opposition from the native and patriotic party, and from the government which represented the wisdom and long experience of the governing class. But it won its way through its hold on the masses; and supposed or real calamities occurring to those who had expressed contempt or made open resistance to the new god were taken as proofs of his power. The religion of Dionysos was gradually accepted over Greece, and the god himself was received as the associate of Apollo in Delphi; but in general it rested on the devotion of the lower orders and the democracy,* and was resisted by the aristocracy and the governing classes. And even that religion was strongly affected by the Hellenic spirit; and its Greek ritual lost much of its Asiatic character and some of its most repulsive features.

(4) *Itinerant priests.*—The strolling impostors who dealt in religious and purificatory rites, and practised on the superstitions of the common people, have been mentioned above, and are often alluded to by the ancient writers. They generally claimed to be representatives of the old Orphic Mysteries, and to possess prophecies of Orpheus, Musæus, and other ancient seers. They had formulæ by which they could bend the gods to their will, and make them favour or injure whom they pleased; and this power they were ready to exercise in favour of any one who paid them. At a trifling cost, and without any personal trouble, one could gain forgiveness of sins, revenge on one's enemies, and a happy life in the future world. At other times the rites of the Mother-Goddess, or some other foreign ceremonial, formed the engine of their power. Some of them cured madness by ecstatic dances, either round the patient sitting in a chair or in company with him. *Orpheotelestai*, *Metragyrtai*, etc., are common names for such impostors, and little distinction can be drawn between different kinds of them. They were generally of a very low class, and addressed themselves to the lower orders of the people. Their equipment was poor, and they often carried about the instruments of their ritual on an ass.†

Some of their customs are described by Apuleius, *Met.* viii. 25 ff. Among them was included a parody of the confession and expiation (see A, VII (6 f.), above): one of the strolling band (who are described as *Galli*) in a loud voice confessed publicly that he had been guilty of violating the law of the goddess in some way, and demanded from himself the just punishment of his crime (in the same way as the goddess is represented in the confessional steles as demanding expiation and penalty from the criminal). Thereupon the devotee took a whip and beat himself, till the blood flowed and the sympathy of the multitude showed itself in gifts.

(5) *Magic.*—The practices of such impostors as are described in the previous section are not always distinguishable from magic, into which they shade off by imperceptible gradation. Magic in the strict sense was always felt by the Greeks to be a foreign and specially an Oriental art, as is shown by the very name μάγος, a magician, literally a magian or Persian priest. The magical art was called γοητεία in reference to the loud howling utterance of magic formulæ.‡

In Homer, apart from the tale of the obviously Oriental Circe, little approach to magic appears except in the art of medicine, which was to a great extent learned from the older civilizations of the East, and which always assumes an uncanny character to a primitive people: charms (ἐπαοιδοί) are uttered over wounds: Helena has a care-soothing drink, *nepenthe*; Aphrodite, a love-producing girdle; and Athena changes the form of men. But the use of all such arts is confined to gods and half-Divine heroes, and is therefore clearly distinguished from magic.

Later, the power of transforming men into other shapes, of making love-philtres, of stilling the

* See Foucart, *Les Assoc. Relig.* pp. 80, 88, 134, 156.

† ναυτικὴ ἀναρχία, Eurip. *Hecuba*, 607.

‡ They are mentioned as common, Ar. *Pax*, 420.

* Compare, for example, the story of Cleisthenes, the democratic tyrant of Sicyon, who expelled the aristocratic hero Adrastus, and substituted *Dionysia* for Adrastus festivals (Herod. v. 67).

† Ar. *Ran.* 159; cf. Plat. *Rep.* ii. 364, *Euthyd.* 277 D; Theophr. *Char.* xvi.; Apul. *Metam.* viii. c. 27; Lucian, *As.* ch. 35.

‡ See W. Headlam in *Class. Review*, 1902, p. 52.

winds, causing rain, etc., was believed to be attainable by human beings through arts which were strictly magical, and quite distinct from the process whereby (according to a primitive form of religious belief) priests through their prayers and rites could induce the gods to do those things.* The magical art whereby men could attain such powers was so well known and widely practised in Thessaly that the word *Thessalis* was used in the sense of 'witch.' Witches could draw down the moon (as Aristophanes says, *Clouds* 748), turn men into wolves, still the winds, and so on. This magic power was gained by *compelling* the gods; in other words, by appealing to a higher and supreme power to which the gods must bow. Magical art, then, was associated with an older pre-Hellenic religion and the Divine power of a more ancient system, and was always related to the Chthonian religion and the gods of the world of death.

The foreign origin of magic as practised in Greece must not be pressed too far. There can hardly be any doubt that it embodied elements of the primitive pre-Hellenic religion, which persisted in the form of popular superstition and occult lore after the public and acknowledged religion had assumed a new form.

The power of magic was most frequently invoked to attract reluctant persons to a lover, or to bring disease and death upon an enemy. Numerous examples of curses of this latter kind have been found in recent years, and have considerably enlarged our knowledge of the subject. They were usually scratched rudely on plates of lead, the proper metal, and buried in the ground, often in a grave, or in the Temenos of Chthonian deities. They were, however, also turned to a utilitarian purpose, and employed, *e.g.*, almost like advertisements of lost or stolen property, the finder of which was subjected to a terrible curse if he failed to restore it to the owner. Such curses were intended to be seen by the thief, and must therefore have been publicly exposed; but even these seem to have been connected with Chthonian worship, and attached to the shrines of Chthonian deities. The penalty invoked most frequently in all curses was fever, the hidden fire of the gods of death, which burns up imperceptibly the strength and life of the sufferer.†

To this subject belong also the belief in the evil eye (which, while specially injurious to children and domestic animals, was dangerous to all) and other forms of baleful influence, and the use of charms and preservatives against them (ἀποτρόπαια). This belief was a debased form of the doctrine seen in Herodotus, that the gods are jealous of any surpassing success, or power, or beauty, or happiness in man, and interfere to destroy it; and that it is wise to propitiate them by voluntarily sacrificing part of one's good fortune or wealth: hence arose the common practice of guarding against evil by spitting, and by ugly or obscene gestures.

It would, however, serve no useful purpose at present to enumerate the various forms which magic and other superstitious practices assumed in the Greek world. For our purpose, the important point is, that they were alien to and in the long-run stronger than the true Hellenic religion, and helped to destroy it.

(6) *The worship of living men as deities.*—The deification of living men was not in itself alien to the spirit of Hellenism, but, on the contrary, was quite in harmony with the Hellenic satisfaction and delight in human beauty and nobility. The worship of the dead as heroes was developed by Hellenism in a way that tended in that direction, as when the dead freebooter Philip was worshipped as a hero by the people of the Greek colony of Segesta (whom he had wantonly attacked in piratic fashion), simply on account of his personal beauty.* It was an easy step to identify the man of surpassing excellence, physical or mental, with a god either after his death or during his lifetime, when the perfection of human nature was regarded as Divine. Thus Pythagoras after death was worshipped under the form of Apollo Hyperboreios, Lycurgus as a god, Sophocles as Asklepios-Dexion. Sacrifices were offered to Brasidas and Hippocrates, and the term θύειν, which properly denotes the offering to a god as distinguished from a hero,† is used about them. According to Plutarch, the first man to whom worship was paid as a god during his lifetime was Lysander (*Lys.* 18). It is significant that this first step was made among the Asiatic Greek cities. While there was nothing essentially non-Hellenic in such deification of human nature, yet the Hellenic sense of order and measure and grace long shrank instinctively from such a step as an excess; but, in Asia, Hellenism never was so pure as in Europe.

The Thasians honoured Agesilaos in a similar way. From the time of Alexander the deification of kings was customary, as a mere recognition of 'divine right.' Roman generals were often honoured by Greek cities with festivals and games, which implied deification.‡ Every Roman emperor in succession was worshipped; and it was inscribed on the coins and the engraved decrees of the greatest Greek cities as a special honour that they were temple-wardens (νεωκόροι) of the emperors.

IV. Religion of the Græco-Asiatic Cities.—In the Hellenized cities of Asia Minor, which had such importance in the early history of Christianity, all these forms of religious thought and act were busy simultaneously. The old Anatolian superstition retained no vestige of its early simplicity and its original adaptation to the needs of a primitive people, and had been brutalized and degraded by the exaggeration of its worst features and the importation of barbarian superstitions; but it was still strong, especially in the cities of the inner country. The Hellenic religion in its decaying forms was introduced and talked about by the Hellenes of the cities. Greek or Græco-Asiatic philosophy exercised a considerable influence on the thought of the educated classes in those cities, and many sayings and principles and scraps from it had passed into the popular language and conversation of society; but it had little influence on life, except in the way of producing disbelief in current religions and contempt for the most vulgar kinds of superstition. But on the great mass of the population all kinds of superstition and magic exercised a very strong influence, and were on the whole in harmony with the spirit of the Anatolian religion in its modern form.

As to the philosophic speculation current in those cities, in spite of its many faults and its obvious weakness as a practical force, the account given in § I makes it easy to understand how and why philosophy, though so depreciated and scouted by St. Paul, was, after all, his ally in a certain degree against the gross forms of vulgar superstition which were the only active religious force

* Compare, for example, Pausanias, ii. 34. 2 (at Methana in Argolis), viii. 38. 4 (at the spring Hagno on the Arcadian mountain Lycæus).

† See Wuensch in *Corpus Inscript. Att.*, Appendix.

* Herod. v. 47.

† The distinction, however, was not strictly maintained: θυσίαι were offered to Philip at Segesta.

‡ Cicero in *Verr.* ii. 21, 51, *ad Q. Fr.* i. 1. 26, *ad Att.* v. 21. 7; Plutarch, *Lucull.* 23, *Flam.* 16.

in the cities. One can also readily understand why, to the educated observer in contemporary Græco-Roman society, such as Sergius Paulus in Paphos, or the Stoic and Epicurean philosophers in Athens, he seemed to be a new teacher of philosophy, more or less impressive in himself, but not essentially different in type from scores of other lecturers who were striving to catch the ear of the educated world.

V. Decay and Death of the Hellenic Religion.—While the religion of the country ceased to satisfy the wants of the people, the outward show became greater and greater. The Scholiast on Aristophanes (*Vesp.* 661) says that the year consisted really of only ten months, as two were occupied by festivals; and Strabo (vi. p. 429) says that finally at Tarentum there were more feasts than days in the year. But the spirit in which the rites had once been performed was now lost; people tolerated the duties as traditional ceremonial, and enjoyed the festivals merely as fine shows. The word ἀφοσιοῦσθαι, 'to discharge oneself of what is due to the gods,' came to denote careless and perfunctory performance. The duty of performing the public sacrifices was hired out to the lowest bidder. Zeus had to mourn the neglect into which he had fallen compared with the more recent gods (Lucian, *Icarom.* 24).

In truth, the Hellenic religion in its most typical form could not permanently maintain its hold on human nature. It was the evanescent, rare, and delicate product of a peculiar period and of special conditions in human history. It was the belief of an aristocracy of talents and opportunities, filled for the moment with the delight of activity and expansion, and the mere joy of living. It required the Hellenic City-State for the theatre of its development, and the existence of a class, supported and set free from mere drudgery by a large enslaved population, but too numerous and too various in worldly circumstances to be only a narrow, privileged, and idle aristocracy of birth. But such conditions are rarely possible, and can never last long. Where an approximation to them occurs for a time in any considerable section of the population of any land, there results a tendency to a similar artistic development of religion. But there has never been elsewhere an experiment on such a scale as in Greece, where economic and social facts, natural surroundings, and relation to foreign nations, conspired to give a glory and an intoxicated consciousness of life to the small, energetic, busy, keenly competing cities of the Hellenes.

But even there the conditions soon ceased. Greece sank into its inevitable place as a third-rate province in some larger empire. It was essential to true Hellenism that it should be supported by the spirit of a self-governing people; its proud self-consciousness and joy in its own life and activity were inconsistent with servitude.

A mournful consciousness that the 'gods of Greece' were dead is often apparent in the later Greek literature, as, for example, in the well-known story preserved by Plutarch (*de Defectu Orac.* 17), that in the reign of Tiberius, when a ship sailing from Greece to Italy was among the Echinades Islands, off the Acarnanian coast, a voice was heard summoning by name a certain Egyptian pilot who chanced to be on board; and, when he answered the third summons rather reluctantly, the voice bade him announce when he reached Palodes that 'Pan the great is dead.'

It is a fitting conclusion to Hellenic religion that the Oracles became dumb; and especially that the Delphic Oracle, which had played so important and, for a time, so noble a part in guiding its development, lost first its influence and finally its voice. As a force in history it had long lost all power; in the 1st cent. after Christ, Delphi and Ammon had given place to Chaldæan astrologers, as Strabo and Juvenal agree in saying, and Plutarch wrote a treatise inquiring into the reason;* and in the 4th cent., when Julian sent to consult the Delphic Oracle, the last response was uttered for him: 'Tell the king, to earth has fallen the beautiful mansion; no longer has Phœbus a home, nor a prophetic laurel, nor a fount that speaks: gone dry is the talking water.' †

*εἴπατε τῷ βασιλῆι, χαμαὶ πέσε δαίδαλος αὐλά·*
*οὐκέτι Φοῖβος ἔχει καλύβαν, οὐ μάντιδα δάφνην,*
*οὐ παγὰν λαλέουσαν· ἀπέσβετο καὶ λάλον ὕδωρ.*

The religious forms of Greece had served their day; they were now antiquated, and the world passed on to other forms. The alternatives presented to the people were Christianity or vulgar superstition, while a steadily diminishing remnant of the educated class clung to a philosophical form of paganism.

Literature.—Besides the many general Dictionaries and works on Greek Antiquities, which usually include Religious Antiquities, such as Daremberg-Saglio's *Dict. des Antiquités gr. et rom.* (A-M published in 1902), Pauly-Wissowa, *Real-Encyclopædie* (A-Dem. in 1902), Smith (who includes Mythology under Biography, and Ritual under Antiquities), etc., the works devoted expressly to Greek Religion (under which some casual information is given about cults of Asia Minor), either generally or in some particular department or aspect, are extremely numerous, and complete enumerations unnecessary and hardly possible. The reader who looks at the discussion of any detail in a few of the following works will find in them sufficient indications to guide him to the vast literature (much of it not in itself valuable) that has accumulated round most of the chief topics. Owing to the capricious and subjective nature of the treatment (which can hardly be avoided), the information which is most important for an investigator from a novel point of view may, however, be passed unnoticed in several of the most elaborate works, and may be found only by looking into some of the older or the less important and honoured works. The old-fashioned and unpretending *Handwörterbuch der griechischen u. röm. Mythologie* of Jacobi (Coburg, 1835), with its bare and bald lists of references to ancient authorities, is still often most practically useful for the investigator, because there he gets facts unencumbered with opinions: in the voluminous and indispensable, and in many respects far more complete, work of Roscher, *Lexicon der griech. und röm. Mythologie* (still unfinished: A-Par. published in November 1902), facts are apt to be concealed by opinions: but the variety of writers in the *Lexikon* on cognate topics often supplies a useful diversity of opinion. Those who desire to study the history of modern opinion will find the following list, while inadequate, yet a sufficient introduction from which to make a beginning (only, as a rule, one work by any author is named: the most recent writers as a rule are given, and the older can be followed up from them).—

Maury, *Histoire des Religions de la Grèce ancienne*; Farnell, *Cults of the Greek States*, i. and ii. 1896 (sequel not ready in 1902); Foucart, *Recherches sur l'origine et la nature des Mystères d'Eleusis*, 1895, etc.; Preller-Robert, *Griechische Mythologie*[4], 1887; A. Mommsen, *Feste der Athener* (new edition of *Heortologie*); E. Curtius, *Gesammelte Abhandlungen*, etc.; Dieterich, *Nekyia*; Diels, *Sibyllinische Blätter*, 1890; Bouchè-Leclercq, *Histoire de la Divination*; Usener, *Religionsgeschichtliche Untersuchungen*, 1889, *Griechische Götternamen*, etc.; Gruppe, *Die griech. Kulte u. Mythen*; Ridgeway, *Early Age of Greece*, 1901; many articles and other works by these writers, and also by S. Reinach, Miss J. E. Harrison, Wernicke, Wilamowitz, Robert, Maass, Kuhnert, Körte, Bloch, Drexler, Vitry, Perdrizet, Berard, Cumont, Studniczka, Rohde, Tümpel, Marillier, Beurlier, Miss A. Walton, Krause, Keller, Stengel, Weinhold, Crusius, Hoffmann, Reichel, Thraemer, Toepffer, von Fritze, Ziebarth, Ziemann, Buresch, Dümmler, etc. Anrich, *Das Antike Mysterienwesen*, 1894; Wobbermin, *Religionsgesch. Studien*, 1896; Gardner, *Origin of the Lord's Supper*, 1894, etc., treat of the relation of the Mysteries to early Christianity: Anrich is the least imaginative; Gardner takes a more subjective view. Cf. also S. Cheatham, *The Mysteries* (Huls. Lect. 1896–97).

On the origin of rites and their relation to savage ritual, Bötticher, *Baumkultus*; A. B. Cook, *Animal-Worship in the Mycenæan Age*; Frazer, *Golden Bough*[2] (nominally on Italian, really more on Greek), 1900; Mannhardt, *Wald- und Feld-Kulte*, etc.; Jevons, *Introduction to the History of Religion*, 1896 (totemistic). In Bursian's *Jahresbericht* from time to time reviews of the entire literature can be found.

* Juv. *Sat.* vi. 553; Strab. xvii. p. 1168; Plutarch, *de Defectu Oraculorum.*

† Cedrenus, i. p. 532, has preserved the oracle, which is perhaps the work of a triumphant Christian or of one of the last pagan philosophers.

On the religious ideas in the Greek poets and philosophers: Zeller, 'Entwickelung des Monotheismus bei den Griechen' in his *Vorträge und Abhandlungen Geschichtl. Inhalts*, 1865, *Ueber das Wesen der Religion*, Tübingen, 1845; Trendelenburg, 'Nothwendigkeit und Freiheit in der griech. Philosophie' in the second volume of his *Historische Beiträge zur Philosophie*; and many scattered references and discussions in the commentaries on the leading authors, and in the Histories of Literature and Philosophy. Verrall, *Euripides the Rationalist*, states well some of the difficulties which are caused by a too superficial view of the thought of Euripides; but the solution suggested suffers from the want of any attempt to estimate the place of that poet in the development of Greek thought, and the failure to emphasize that Euripides must be studied in relation to the preceding and succeeding writers.

W. M. RAMSAY.

## STYLE OF SCRIPTURE.—

i. Historical introduction.
ii. Characteristics of Biblical style due to earliness of date or to the Semitic idiosyncrasy of the Hebrews.
iii. Peculiarities of style purposely adopted upon occasion by *all* classes of Scripture writers.
iv. Peculiarities of style for which a preference is shown by *particular* classes of Scripture writers.
v. Conclusion. Observations on the *critical* and *doctrinal* significance of differences of style on the part of Scripture writers.

Literature.

i. HISTORICAL INTRODUCTION.—The question of the style of Scripture has formed the subject of discussion from a very early period. The diversity of forms in which prophecy, *e.g.*, makes its appearance was a point of too much interest to escape the notice of the scribes. Hence we already encounter in the Talmud a saying which contains an excellent illustration of the formal differences that exist between prophecies. We refer to the words: 'Everything that Ezekiel saw, Isaiah also saw; but Ezekiel with the eyes of a rustic who has seen the king, Isaiah with the eyes of a citizen who has seen him' (*Ḥăgîga*, 13*b*). The meaning is, that the descriptions found in the Book of Ezekiel are elaborated in much greater detail and sometimes developed at greater length than is the case in the Book of Isaiah (cf., *e.g.*, Ezk $1^{3}$-$2^{3}$ with Is $6^{1-8}$). It may have been simply this diversity which marks the prophetical literature that gave rise to the judgment pronounced in *Sanhedrin*, 89*a*: 'No two prophets prophesy in the same style' (בסיגנון אחר), although this remark primarily concerned the differences disclosed by a comparison between Ob $^{3}$ and Jer $49^{16}$. In the former of these passages we read 'The pride of thine heart (זְדוֹן לִבְּךָ) hath deceived thee,' but in the parallel passage we find 'Thy terribleness (תִּפְלַצְתְּךָ) hath deceived thee.' Such differences between parallel passages of the OT as affect especially their linguistic colouring were not upon the whole unnoticed in antiquity. This may be seen from the *Massora magna* to Ex $20^{17}$ etc., or from the tractate *Ṣōphĕrîm*, 8, etc. (cf. Ed. König, *Einleitung ins AT*, § 16).

Among early *Christian* writers no one has treated the question of the style of Holy Scripture in more detail than Adrianos in his Εἰσαγωγὴ εἰς τὰς θείας γραφάς (*aus neuaufgefundenen Handschriften herausgegeben, übersetzt und erläutert*, von Friedr. Goessling, Berlin, 1887). His whole book is devoted to the subject of the present article. He points out stylistic peculiarities of particular parts of the OT, *e.g.* the Psalter (§§ 99, 105). He also drew already the distinction between prose and poetry in Scripture. Taking the word 'prophecy' in the wider sense which it assumed in later times (cf. Ed. König, *Einleit.* p. 457), he remarked in the final paragraph of his work: 'It ought also to be known to the initiated that one kind of prophecy is composed in prose, like the writings of Isaiah and Jeremiah and their contemporaries, but another kind in regular measure adapted for singing (ἡ δὲ μετ' ᾠδῆς ἐν μέτρῳ), like the Psalms of the blessed David, and the prophecy [Ex $15^{1-18}$ and Dt 32 f.] contained in the second and fifth books of Moses' (§ 134).

This question of the style of Holy Scripture is of great importance in its bearing upon the judgment we form regarding its perspicuity and its inspiration. From this point of view, the style of the Biblical writers has been discussed by the authors we now proceed to name. Flacius Illyricus, in his famous *Clavis Scripturæ Sacræ* (1567, etc.; ed. Basileensis, 1628 f.), vol. i. Præfatio, fol. 3*a*, writes: 'Objiciunt illi [*i.e.* pontificii] de sensu ac intelligentia litem esse. Eam illi volunt ex Patribus peti oportere. At contra Augustinus et Hilarius contendunt ex collatione Scripturæ loca aut dicta obscuriora esse illustranda.' The other passages of his work which treat of style are $2_{32}$ $420_{25}$ $433_{39}$ ('Lapsus styli ex alio in aliud') $489_{47}$ ('De plenitudine styli') $508_{49}$ ('Stylus Paulinus'). These points, however, are much more fully discussed by Glass in his important *Philologia Sacra*, which went through a number of editions from 1623 onwards. To these questions he devotes the whole of the third and fourth tractates of the first of the five books into which his work is divided (4th ed. 1668, pp. 186–246). He sets out with the following statement: 'Inter rationes, quibus Bellarminus Scripturæ Sacræ obscuritatem probatam dare vult, occurrit etiam illa quam a styli seu modi dicendi in Scripturis usitati ambiguitate desumit,' and he brings forward good arguments in refutation of this charge against Holy Scripture. The same point of view has been since then considered by many scholars, and is touched upon by Sanday in his admirable Bampton Lectures on *Inspiration* (1st ed. 1893, p. 403), and C. A. Briggs in his comprehensive *General Introduction to the Study of Holy Scripture* (1899, p. 328). This highest point of view from which the question of the style of Scripture has to be considered, is not, however, the only one. It is a question which is not only an eminently religious one, but of importance as regards the history of culture. For it is an extremely interesting inquiry how far the *art* of description by means of language was developed among the Hebrews and the writers of the NT. In what follows we shall endeavour to satisfy both interests, the religious and the secular.

ii. CHARACTERISTICS OF BIBLICAL STYLE DUE TO EARLINESS OF DATE OR TO THE SEMITIC IDIOSYNCRASY OF THE HEBREWS. — The most important of these phenomena, arranged according to their noteworthiness and frequency, are the following:—

1. We have only to proceed a short way in our reading of the first book of the Bible to be struck with the great frequency with which the word 'and' occurs. The opening sentence of Genesis is followed by the statement 'And the earth was without form and void' (*tōhû wā-bōhû*). In like manner, the third sentence 'And darkness was upon the face of the deep' is tacked on by 'and,' while the fourth runs 'And the spirit of God moved upon the face of the deep.' And so in this same chapter there is a direct succession of some sixty sentences, all beginning with 'and.' This *preference for the copulative conjunction* may be observed no less in the frequent **Polysyndeton** which characterizes the style of Scripture, as, for instance, in 'Shem and Ham and Japheth' (Gn $9^{18}$); or 'Elam and Asshur and Arpachshad and Lud' ($10^{22}$); or 'thou nor thy son nor thy daughter nor thy manservant nor thy maidservant nor,' etc. etc. (Dt $5^{14}$); or 'Thou shalt not kill, neither shalt thou commit adultery, neither shalt thou steal, neither,' etc. etc. ($5^{17-21}$ $6^{5}$). Nay, this preference for 'and' went so far that we even find new books of the OT commencing with 'and.' This is the case not only with the five books of the Pentateuch, but also

with Joshua, Judges, Ruth, etc. It cannot be inferred from this form of opening that these books once formed parts of a continuous work, for the Book of Esther begins with the same formula 'And it came to pass,' although its subject is an isolated episode. The correct view of this phenomenon is that the expression 'And it came to pass' was so much in use that one came to write it from force of custom and almost unconsciously. On this same account, the fact that the Book of Ezekiel opens with 'And it came to pass' is no indication that something has dropped out before this formula, as is contended by Budde and others (see the controversy on this point between Budde and the present writer in *Expos. Times*, xii. [1901] 39 ff., 375 ff., 525 ff., 566 f.; xiii. 41 ff., 95). The expression 'And it came to pass' had become as common as the phrase 'And it shall come to pass,' with which circumstantial statements of time, etc., were introduced (cf. Is $2^{2}$ 'And it shall come to pass in the last days that,' etc.).

When we compare even so simple a writer as 'the Father of History,' this Hebrew fashion of connecting sentences is striking. After giving his own name and dividing mankind into the two categories of Hellenes and barbarians, Herodotus begins his narrative with the following sentences: '*Now* the learned among the Persians say that the Phœnicians were the authors of the discord (namely, between the Greeks and other peoples). *For*, after they (the Phœnicians) came from the sea that is called the Red Sea to this (the Mediterranean) sea, and settled in the land which they still inhabit, they immediately devoted themselves to great enterprises by sea. *But* in the course of transporting Egyptian and Assyrian goods, they frequently visited Argos as well as the rest of the country.' There is no need for proceeding further with the translation of Herodotus' *History*, in order to show the striking contrast in structure and connexion presented by its opening sentences and those of the Bible. The numerous principal sentences which are *co-ordinated* in Gn $1^{1ff.}$, and the stereotyped 'and' by which they are connected, have ceased, as a rule, to strike us, because from our earliest days we have been used to this characteristic of the Biblical narratives, and this fashion of writing, which is peculiar to Biblical history in the widest sense, was also very well calculated to impress our minds. For this way of adding principal sentence to principal sentence, and of connecting them for the most part by 'and,' is the childish device which always meets us at the naïve stage in the history of culture. We encounter it in the childhood of the individual, we find it amongst the uneducated masses of the people, and it shows itself at the primitive stages in the development of the human race. For instance, 'The Homeric speech loves the *co-ordinating* of sentences' (G. Curtius, *Gr. Gram.* § $519_{5}$; Hentze, *Parataxe bei Homer*, 1889), and it is very interesting to note how the number of conjunctions in the later Hebrew and other Semitic languages underwent increase: for illustrations see Ed. König, *Historisch-Comparat. Syntax der heb. Sprache*, §§ 377–396*r*).

There are other four principal marks of the simple method followed by Hebrew writers in grouping their ideas and their sentences. —(*a*) There are such forms of expression as 'Let them be for signs and for seasons and for days and years' (Gn $1^{14}$), words which mean, in all probability, 'Let them serve as signs for seasons,' etc. This is the same simple method of *co-ordinating ideas* as is familiar to us from the 'pateris libamus et auro' of Vergil, *Georg.* ii. 192, and is commonly known as **Hendiadys.** Other instances of it in Scripture are: 'a city and a mother in Israel,' *i.e.* a mother-city, a metropolis (2 S $20^{19}$); 'feasting and gladness' = feasting of gladness (Est $9^{18}$); 'I heard whispering and a voice,' *i.e.* whispering of a voice (Job $4^{16b}$); 'changes and war' = changes of war (Job $10^{17c}$); 'glory and strength' = glory of strength (Ps. $29^{1}$ $96^{7}$); 'time and judgment' = time of judgment (Ec $8^{5}$); 'cloud and smoke' = cloud of smoke (Is $4^{5}$); 'trouble and darkness' = dark, *i.e.* irremediable, trouble (Is $8^{22}$). In like manner the Heb. 'consumption and determination' is rightly changed in EV to 'consumption, even determined' (Is $10^{23}$ $28^{22}$), and 'end and expectation' is correctly replaced by 'an expected end' (Jer $29^{11}$). The same co-ordination of ideas meets us in 'the roll and the words' for 'the roll of the words' (Jer $36^{27}$). An illustration of the same fondness for simple co-ordinating of ideas is found also in 'her hand . . . and her right hand' (Jg $5^{26}$); or 'my hand . . . and my right hand' (Is $48^{13}$); or 'the LORD . . . and his glory' (Is $60^{2}$); or 'the LORD . . . and his strength' (Ps $105^{4}$). This mode of expression is known as καθ' ὅλον καὶ μέρος, and a counterpart to it has been recently noted by the present writer in the words 'Who will bring me into the strong city? Who will lead me into Edom?' (Ps $60^{9}$ ‖ $108^{10}$; cf. Ed. König, *Fünf neue arabische Landschaftsnamen im AT*, 1902, p. 33 f.).—(*β*) There is the frequent throwing in of the interjection 'Behold!': *e.g.* 'And God saw . . . and, *behold*,' etc. (Gn $1^{31}$ $6^{12}$ $8^{13}$ $18^{2}$ $19^{28}$ etc.; cf. Ed. König, *Heb. Syntax*, § 361*g*).—(*γ*) We have the very frequent employment of *direct speech*. The list of examples of this begins with the words 'Let there be light' (Gn $1^{3}$); it is continued in 'Let there be a firmament,' etc. (v.$^{6}$), 'Behold, I have given you,' etc. (v.$^{29}$), and so on it goes (cf. *Syntax*, § 377). The NT also shares abundantly in this preference for the *oratio directa* (Mt $1^{20.\ 23}$ $2^{2.\ 5}$ etc.).—(*δ*) The fourth mark of the naïve simplicity of style which is wont to be employed by the Biblical writers may be observed from the following instance: 'Till thou return unto the ground . . . for dust thou art, and unto dust shalt thou return' (Gn $3^{19}$). Here we have first a destiny indicated for man, then the reason for this, and finally the destiny itself is once more repeated. Many of our readers must have noticed the same movement of thought in the conversation and letters of persons belonging to the lower classes. This process whereby one returns to the original starting-point is called **Palindromy,** and there are various species of it. Here are some other instances of the class represented by Gn $3^{19}$: 'And it repented the LORD that he had made man, etc., and the LORD said, I will destroy, etc., for it repenteth me that I have made them' (Gn $6^{6f.}$); 'The earth also was corrupt, etc., for all flesh had corrupted,' etc. (v.$^{11f.}$); 'The LORD scattered them abroad, etc. Therefore is the name of it called Babel, etc., and from thence did the LORD scatter them abroad,' etc. ($11^{8f.}$); 'Every beast of the forest is mine, etc., If I were hungry, I would not tell thee, for the world is mine' (Ps $50^{10-12}$); 'O that my ways were directed to keep thy statutes, then shall I not be ashamed when I have respect unto all thy commandments' ($119^{5f.}$); 'Surely he hath borne our griefs, etc., for the transgression of my people was he stricken' (Is $53^{4-8}$); 'The LORD said, etc., because I have spoken it' (Jer $4^{27f.}$); 'Because ye multiplied, etc., because of all thine abominations' (Ezk $5^{7-9}$). —Another species of *Palindromy* is represented by the words 'The land was not able to bear them, that they might dwell together; for their substance was great, so that they could not dwell together' (Gn $13^{6}$). There the course of ideas turns from the fact to its cause, and then returns to the fact or the consequence. The same mental movement may be observed in: 'Judah, thou art he whom thy brethren shall praise; thy hand shalt be in the neck of thine enemies; thy father's children shall bow down before thee' (Gn 49$^{8}$); 'The nakedness of thy mother shalt thou not uncover; she is thy mother, thou shalt not uncover her nakedness' (Lv 18$^{7}$); and the same is the case in v.$^{15}$ 'My strength is dried, etc., for dogs have compassed me, etc., I may tell all my bones' (Ps 22$^{15-17}$); and in Is 53$^{11f.}$ 'By his knowledge, etc., Therefore will I divide him a portion with the great, etc., because he hath poured out his soul unto death.' Essentially the same phenomenon recurs in 1 Ch 9$^{44}$ 'Azel had six sons, and these are their names: Azrikam, etc., these were the sons of Azel.'—A third species of *Palindromy* is made up of instances like 'God created man in his own image, in the image of God created he him' (Gn 1$^{27}$); 'Make thee an ark, etc. Thus did Noah, according to all that God commanded him, so did he' (6$^{14. 22ab}$); 'Thou shalt speak all that I command thee, etc., and Moses and Aaron did as the LORD commanded them, so did they' (Ex 7$^{2ff. 6ab}$). The same mode of expression meets us in Ex 12$^{2ab. 28. 50}$ 39$^{32. 43}$ 40$^{16}$, Lv. 4$^{20}$, Nu 1$^{54}$ 5$^{4}$ 8$^{20}$ etc., Ec 1$^{6}$, Dn 8$^{1ff. 20}$ etc. (see Ed. König, *Stilistik*, etc. p. 171 f.).

Another feature that strikes us in the structure of clauses in the OT presents itself in 'I am the LORD thy God which *have* brought,' etc. (Ex 20$^{2}$). Other examples of the same fashion are Dt 5$^{3b.}$ ('all of *us*')$^{6}$, Jg 13$^{11}$ ('the man that *speakest*'), 1 S 25$^{33}$ ('and thou which *hast*'), Ps 71$^{20}$ ('thou which *hast*'), Neh 9$^{7}$ ('thou art the God who *didst*'), 1 Ch 21$^{17}$ ('I it is that *have* sinned').

2. It requires no great acquaintance with the language of Scripture to enable one to recall such forms of expression as the following: 'Joseph was the *son* of his old age' (Gn 37$^{3}$), *i.e.* he was born when Jacob was advanced in years, forming thus a contrast to the 'children of youth,' *i.e.* children begotten by a man at the period of his full strength (Ps 127$^{4}$, cf. Gn 49$^{3}$). Where we now find in the EV the expressions 'son(s) of' or 'children of,' the Hebrew is בֶּן or בְּנֵי, and their use constitutes such a characteristic feature of the style of Scripture that it deserves somewhat fuller illustration. —(*a*) The בֶּן (*ben-*) is sometimes retained in the EV: *e.g.* Ben-ammi (Gn 19$^{38}$), *i.e.* 'belonging to my people'; Ben-oni (35$^{18}$), *i.e.* 'born in my sorrow'; Boanerges (Mk 3$^{17}$), *i.e.* 'sons of thunder.' Seven proper names show the Aramaic form of *ben-*, namely *bar-*: Bartholomew (Mt 10$^{3}$), Barjonah (16$^{17}$), Barabbas (27$^{16}$), Bartimæus (Mk 10$^{46}$), Barsabbas (Ac 1$^{23}$), Barnabas (4$^{36}$), Barjesus (13$^{6}$).—(*β*) בֶּן or בְּנֵי are reproduced by 'son(s) of' or 'children of' in the following expressions: 'son of his old age' (Gn 37$^{3}$); 'thy mother's sons,' or the like, *i.e.* brothers who have not only the same father but the same mother (Gn 27$^{29}$, Jg 8$^{19}$, Ps 50$^{20}$, Ca 1$^{6}$); 'children of his people' (Nu 22$^{5}$); 'children of Sheth' (24$^{17}$), *i.e.* friends of war tumult [according to Sayce, *Expos. Times*, xiii. 64$^{b}$, the 'Sutu], at least Jeremiah in the parallel passage (48$^{45}$) speaks of 'sons of tumult' (*bĕnê shā'ôn*); 'children (son, sons) of Belial' (Dt 13$^{13}$ [RV 'base fellows'], Jg 19$^{22}$ 20$^{13}$, 1 S 2$^{12}$ 10$^{27}$ 25$^{17}$, 1 K 21$^{10. 13}$, 2 Ch 13$^{7}$), *i.e.* worthless persons (cf. Ed. König, *Syntax*, p. 309, n. 1 [against Cheyne]), cf. 'children of wickedness' (2 S 3$^{34a}$ 7$^{10}$, 1 Ch 17$^{9}$); 'son of wickedness' (Ps 89$^{22b}$); 'children of iniquity' (Hos. 10$^{9}$); 'son of Hinnom' (?=wailing; Jos 15$^{8}$ 18$^{16}$, Jer 7$^{31}$ etc.); 'son of the morning' (Is 14$^{12}$); 'children of strangers' (2$^{6b}$); 'sons of strangers' (60$^{10}$)= 'strangers' (Ezk 44$^{7}$ etc., Ps 18$^{44f.}$ 144$^{7. 11}$, Neh 9$^{2}$); 'children of whoredom' (Hos 2$^{4}$); 'children of the needy' (Ps 72$^{4}$); 'children of youth' (Ps 127$^{4}$); 'children of the province' (Ezr 2$^{1a}$); 'children of the captivity' (4$^{1b}$ 6$^{19f.}$ 10$^{7. 16}$); 'son of man' (Nu 23$^{19}$, Job 16$^{21b}$ 25$^{6}$ 35$^{8}$, Ps 8$^{4}$ 80$^{17}$ 144$^{3}$ 146$^{3}$, Is 51$^{12}$ 56$^{2}$, Jer 49$^{18b. 33}$ 50$^{40}$ 51$^{43}$, Ezk 2$^{1}$ etc., Dn 7$^{13}$ 8$^{17}$, Mt 8$^{20}$ etc.);* 'sons (=disciples) of the prophets' (1 K 20$^{35}$, 2 K 2$^{3}$ etc., Am 7$^{14}$); 'children'='disciples' (Mt 12$^{27}$); 'sons' = 'disciples' (Lk 11$^{19}$); 'son(s)' or 'children' = 'citizen(s)' or 'adherent(s)' (Mt 8$^{12}$ 13$^{38}$, Ac 13$^{10}$); 'children of (*i.e.* those that prepare) the bride-chamber' (Mt 9$^{15}$, Mk 2$^{19}$, Lk 5$^{34}$); 'son(s)' or 'children'='belonging to' or 'sharing in' (Mt 23$^{15}$, Lk 10$^{6}$ 16$^{8}$ 20$^{34. 36}$, Jn 12$^{36}$ 17$^{12}$, Ac 3$^{25}$, 2 Co 6$^{18}$, 1 Th 5$^{5}$, 2 Th 2$^{3}$, Eph 2$^{2}$ 5$^{6}$, Col 3$^{6}$).—(*γ*) בֶּן or בְּנֵי are paraphrased in the following passages: Gn 5$^{32}$ 'Noah was five hundred years *old*,' lit. 'a son of five hundred years' (and so in many similar passages); 15$^{2b}$ 'the steward,' for the possessor or heir; 29$^{1}$ 'the people (lit. sons) of the East' (cf. Jg 7$^{12}$ 8$^{10}$, 1 K 5$^{10}$, Job 1$^{3}$, Is 11$^{14}$, Jer 49$^{28}$, Ezk 25$^{10}$); 'his ass's colt' (Gn 49$^{11}$); 'the bullock' lit. 'son of the cattle' (Lv 1$^{5}$); 'young' lit. 'son(s) of' (1$^{14}$ 4$^{3. 14}$ 5$^{7}$ etc.); 'their people' lit. 'children of their people' (Lv 20$^{17}$, cf. Nu 22$^{5}$); 'rebels' lit. 'sons of refractoriness' (Nu 17$^{10}$); 'meet for the war' lit. 'sons of might' (Dt 3$^{18b}$ AV; RV 'men of valour'); 'men of valour' or the like (Jg 18$^{2a}$, 1 S 14$^{52}$ 18$^{17}$ etc.); 'worthy' (Dt 25$^{2a}$); 'breed' (32$^{14a}$); 'surely die' lit. 'son of death' (1 S 20$^{31b}$ 26$^{16a}$, 2 S 12$^{5}$, cf. Ps 79$^{11b}$ 102$^{20b}$); 'wicked men' lit. 'sons of wickedness' (2 S 3$^{34a}$); 'hostages' lit. 'sons of pledges' (2 K 14$^{14}$ ∥ 2 Ch 25$^{24}$); 'young' lit. 'son of' (2 Ch 13$^{9}$); 'kids' lit. 'sons of' (35$^{7}$); 'those that had been carried away' lit. 'sons of the exile' (Ezr 8$^{35}$); 'sparks' lit. 'sons of flame' (Job 5$^{7}$); 'a man' lit. 'son of man' (16$^{21b}$); 'lions' whelps' lit. 'sons of pride *or* savagery' (28$^{8}$)= 'children of pride' (41$^{34}$); 'arrow' lit. 'son of the bow' (41$^{28}$); 'arrows' lit. 'sons of his quiver' (La 3$^{13}$); 'young' lit. 'son of' (Ps 29$^{6b}$ 147$^{9}$); 'any of the afflicted' lit. 'son of affliction' (Pr 31$^{5}$); 'appointed to' lit. 'sons of' (31$^{8}$).

This characteristic of Scripture style attains all the greater prominence because the same derived usage is frequently met with in the case of the term 'daughter.' For instance, 'daughters of Heth' stands for Hittite women (Gn 27$^{46}$). The same usage appears in 28$^{1. 8}$, Nu 25$^{1}$, Jg 11$^{40}$; 'the daughters of Shiloh' (Jg 21$^{21}$); 'daughters of Dan' (2 Ch 2$^{14}$); 'daughter of Tyre' (Ps 45$^{12}$)='princess of Tyre'; 'daughters of Judah,' etc. (Ps 97$^{8}$, Ca 1$^{5ff.}$); 'daughters of Zion,' etc. (Is 3$^{16}$ etc., Jer 49$^{3αβ}$, Ezk 16$^{27}$); 'daughter of Zion'='inhabitants of Zion' (2 K 19$^{21}$, Ps 9$^{15}$ 137$^{8}$, Is 1$^{8}$ 10$^{30. 32}$ 16$^{1}$ 22$^{4}$ 23$^{10. 12}$ 37$^{22}$ 47$^{1a. 5}$ 52$^{2}$ 62$^{11}$, Jer 4$^{11. 31}$ 6$^{2. 14. 23. 26}$ 8$^{11. 19. 21-23}$ 9$^{6}$ 14$^{17}$ 46$^{11. 19. 24}$ 48$^{18}$ 50$^{42}$ 51$^{33}$, La 1$^{6. 15}$ 2$^{1f. 4f. 8. 10f. 13. 15. 18}$ 3$^{48}$ 4$^{3. 6. 10. 21f.}$ [on 'company,' etc., Ezk 27$^{6b}$, see Ed. König, *Heb. Syntax*, § 306*m*], Mic 1$^{13b}$ 4$^{8. 10. 13}$, Zeph 3$^{10.}$ [against Hommel's art. in *Expos. Times*, 1899, p. 99 f., see the present writer's *Fünf neue arab. Landschaftsnamen im AT*, 1902, p. 58]$^{14}$, Zec 2$^{11. 14}$ 9$^{9}$ [on Is 1$^{8}$ etc., see esp. *Stilistik*, p. 32$_{1ff.}$]; 'daughter of Belial,' *i.e.* of worthlessness (1 S 1$^{16a}$); Hos 1$^{3}$; Mic 5$^{1}$; 'daughter of a strange god,' *i.e.* a female worshipper of him (Mal 2$^{11b}$); 'the daughters of music'=musical tones (Ec 12$^{4}$); θυγατέρες 'Ααρών (Lk 1$^{5}$)=remote descendants of Aaron; and a similar sense is conveyed by 'daughter of Abraham' (13$^{16}$), 'daughters of Jerusalem' (23$^{28}$), ἡ θυγατὴρ Σιών (Mt 21$^{5}$, Jn 12$^{15}$), θυγατὴρ θεοῦ (2 Co 6$^{18}$)=one belonging to the Kingdom of God.

A similar characteristic of the style of Scripture is its fondness for *employing substantives for adjectives*. There are numerous examples of this, even leaving out of account the instances in which the phenomenon disappears in the EV. Thus we find 'jewels of silver,' etc. (Gn 24$^{53}$, Ex 3$^{22}$ etc.); 'men, etc., of truth' (Ex 18$^{21}$, Pr 12$^{19}$ 22$^{21a}$). 'Few in number' is lit. 'men of number' (Gn 34$^{30}$, Dt 4$^{27}$,

* On this expression in all its senses, see art. SON OF MAN in vol. iv.

1 Ch 16[19], Job 16[22], Ps 105[12], Is 10[19], Jer 44[28a], Ezk 12[16a]). Cf. 'the king's court' (Am 7[13]); 'city of confusion' (Is 24[10]); 'an iron pen' (Job 19[24]); 'instruments of death' (='deadly,' Ps 7[13]); 'sorrows of death' (Ps 116[3], cf. Rev 13[3. 12] πληγὴ τοῦ θανάτου); 'sacrifices, etc., of righteousness'=just *or* right *or* righteous sacrifices, etc. (Dt 33[19], Job 8[6], Ps 4[1. 5] 23[3] 51[19] 118[19], cf. 119[7. 62. 106. 160. 164], Pr 8[20] 12[28] 16[31], Is 1[26] 61[3. 10], Jer 50[7], Am 6[12]); 'habitation of justice' (Jer 31[23]); 'Branch of justice' (33[15]); 'garments of salvation'=garments which diffuse healing (Is 61[10]); 'God, etc., of my salvation' (1 Ch 16[35], Ps 18[2b. 46] 24[5] 25[5] 27[9] 65[5] 68[20] 79[9] 85[4], Mic 7[7], Hab 3[18]); עֹז 'of strength' is at times replaced by 'strong' (Jg 9[51], Jer 48[17], Ezk 19[11. 14] 26[11], Ps 61[3] 71[7] 89[10]), or 'mighty' (Ps 68[34]), or 'loud' (2 Ch 30[21]); but we find, on the other hand, 'God of my strength' (Ps 43[2]), 'the rock of my strength' (62[7]), 'rod of thy strength' (110[2], cf. 132[8]), 'pride of your power' (Lv 26[19]), 'fury of his power' (Dn 8[6b]), 'gall of bitterness' (Ac 8[23]), πᾶσα ψυχὴ ζωῆς='every living soul' (Rev 16[3]).

Another of the peculiarities which belong to the *Semitic* idiosyncrasy of the Scripture narratives is the frequent introduction of *genealogies*. The interest was strong in the correct preservation of ancient tradition, and thus the genealogical connexions of families and tribes were noted. Hence we find many genealogical trees in the historical books of the Bible. A number of them form considerable lists, *e.g.* Gn 4[17ff.] 5[3ff.] 10[2ff.] 11[10ff.]; many others are shorter, *e.g.* Jos 7[18], Ru 4[18-22], 1 S 1[1] 9[1] 14[49-51] etc., 1 Ch 1[1ff.], Ezr 7[1-5] ('Ezra, the son of Seraiah, the son of Azariah, the son of Hilkiah, the son of Shallum, etc., this Ezra went up from Babylon'), Neh 11[-2], Est 2[5], Job 32[2], Mt 1[1-17] Lk 3[23ff.].

A similar interest accounts for the arrangement of the Book of Genesis. It is an extremely noteworthy feature of its structure that the narrative regarding the main line of the human race, *i.e.* the citizens of the Kingdom of God, stands, like the trunk of a tree, in the centre of the whole. The branches of the race, which diverged from the main stem, are regularly dealt with at the outset briefly, but a detailed enumeration of the successive representatives of the main stem follows. Thus the final compiler, *i.e.* the author proper of the first book of the Bible, advances from the outside inwards, or from the remote to the near in chapters 4 (the Cainites) and 5 (the Sethites, from whose line sprang Noah, who carried the human race over the period of the Flood and ensured its perpetuation thereafter); in 10[1-20] (Japhethites and Ḥamites) and vv.[21-32] (Semites); in 11[1-9] (the human race, which rises in revolt against God in building the Tower of Babel) and vv.[10-25] (the Semites, and, above all, the Hebrews); in 11[26-32] (the Terahites in general, cf. the supplementary list in 22[20-24]) and 12 ff. (Abraham). In like manner the collateral branches of the descendants of Abraham are treated of in 25[1-18], but the main stem in v.[19ff.]; and the descendants of Esau are given in ch. 36 before the commencement of the history of which Jacob is the central figure (37[1ff.]). The principal line is always set forth last, because it forms the starting-point for the earthly mediators and heirs of the future salvation.

An interesting light is thrown upon the *social* conditions under which the Biblical writers lived, by the phenomenon we now proceed to describe. There are two sets of passages in which 'thou' alternates with 'my lord,' or 'I' with 'thy servant' (or 'thy handmaid'). The first set finds its earliest illustration in 'Hear us, my lord' (Gn 23[6]), and recurs, *e.g.*, in 'The LORD said unto my *lord*, Sit *thou*,' etc. (Ps 110[1] etc., cf. *Stilistik*, p. 244). Thus persons in a subordinate position addressed their superiors as 'thou,' but frequently interjected 'my lord,' in order to express their subjection. In the same way they took care that the 'I' with which they introduced themselves should often alternate with 'thy servant.' *E.g.* 'If now I have found favour in thy sight, pass not away from thy servant' (instead of 'from me,' Gn 18[3]). Similarly, 'thy servant' and 'unto me' alternate (Gn 19[19]), or 'me' and 'thy servant' (Ps 19[12b. 13a]), or 'I' and 'thy servant' (Dn 9[16a. 17a]). Further, 'I' is resolved into 'your servant' in Gn 18[5] and 19[2], where we read 'Turn in, I pray you, into your servant's house.' Again, 'we' alternates with 'thy servants' in 'We are true men, thy servants are no spies' (Gn 42[11]); or 'thy servants' has its parallel in 'our' (v.[13]); cf. 'Prove thy servants . . . and let them give *us* pulse to eat,' etc. (Dn 1[12] etc.), and the Aram. sentence 'Tell thy servants the dream, and we will show the interpretation' (2[4] etc., cf. *Stilistik*, p. 252).

Another characteristic feature of Biblical style may be regarded at one and the same time from the *national* and the *religious* point of view. We refer to the frequent use of blessings and cursings. The series of blessings opens with Gn 1[22], and is continued in v.[28] 2[3] (blessing of the beasts, of man, and of the Sabbath) 5[2] 9[1. 26f.] 12[3] 14[19] 25[11] 28[1] 35[9] 47[7. 10] 48[15] 49[28], Ex 39[43], Nu 23[7ff.], Dt 33[1ff.], 1 K 8[14. 55], 2 Ch 6[3]. To the same class belongs also the frequent exclamation 'O the happiness of Israel!' or the like (Dt 33[29], 1 K 10[8], Ps 1[1], and so on to Ec 10[17]); Mt 5[44] 'Bless them that curse you'; Lk 24[50f.] 'bless'=bid farewell; Mt 21[9], Mk 11[9f.], Lk 19[38], Jn 12[13], cf. Ps 118[26]. The series of cursings begins with Gn 3[14] (the curse pronounced upon the serpent), and is continued in v.[17] 4[11] 9[25] 12[3] 27[29] 49[7], Nu 5[18ff.], Dt 27[15ff.] 28[16ff.], Jos 6[26] 9[23], Jg 5[23] 21[18], 1 S 14[24. 28] 26[19], Job 3[8] ('cursers of the day'), Ps 119[21], Pr 3[33] 28[27], Jer 11[3] 17[5] 20[14ff.] 48[10], Mal 1[14ff.]. To this list must be added the instances in which a 'Woe!' is addressed to any one: Nu 21[29] ('Woe to thee, Moab!') 24[14], 1 S 4[7f.], Ps 120[5], Pr 23[29], Ec 4[10] 10[16], Is 3[9. 11] 6[5] 24[16], Jer 4[13ff.], Ezk 16[23] etc., Hos 7[13] 9[12], Mt 11[21] 18[7] etc., Mk 13[17] 14[21], Lk 6[24] etc., Jude [11], Rev. 9[12ff.] 12[12] etc. This form of expression is connected partly with the ancient custom of blessing one's children or friends and cursing one's enemies (Nu 22[6] etc.), and partly with the habit of the religion of Israel of postulating happiness for the godly and punishment for transgressors.—By the way, these last two categories possess certain features of special interest. The series of blessings has its first representative as early as the narrative of the Creation, that of cursings does not open till after man's first sin. The Psalter, again, contains twenty-five examples of the phrase 'O the happiness!' (cf. *Syntax*, § 321*g*), but only once (120[5]) the exclamation 'Woe!' The list of blessings is longer than the other, and does not end till the last chapter of the last book of the Bible. Its last utterance is 'Blessed are they that wash their robes [*or* do his commandments],' Rev 22[14].

iii. PECULIARITIES OF STYLE PURPOSELY ADOPTED UPON OCCASION BY ALL CLASSES OF SCRIPTURE WRITERS.—These devices will be set forth in such a way as to have regard to the interests, successively, of the human intellect, the will, and the feelings.

1. The Biblical writers aim at clearness, and this quality is not prejudiced (*a*) by the use, which is common to man, of Metonymy and Synecdoche.

Noteworthy instances of **Metonymy** are the following: 'seed' stands for descendants in Gn 3[15] etc.; 'the earth,' as the source of its products, is put for the latter in 'In sorrow shalt thou eat it (*i.e.* the earth=its products),' 3[17b], cf. Is 1[7b]. *Nābî*, 'prophet,' is correctly rendered 'prophecy' by AV in Dn 9[24b]; but 'prophet' in Mt 5[17] and Lk 16[29. 31] has the same meaning; and 'Moses' stands for the Law in the expression 'Moses is read' (2 Co 3$^{15}$). 'Tongue' became naturally an expression for speech (Gn 10$^{5}$ etc.). 'Lips' stands in Hos 14$^{2b}$ for the confession of sin proceeding from the lips; the prophet means to say, 'We will offer as sacrifices of calves the confession of our sins.' Similarly, 'throat' means in Ps 5$^{10}$ conversation. 'Hand' is often equivalent to activity (Ex 3$^{19}$ etc. 'by a mighty hand'). 'Horn' represents power or rule (1 S 2$^{1}$ etc., 'My horn is exalted,' etc.). In parallelism to 'peace,' 'sword' stands for war (Mt 10$^{34}$). 'Yield unto thee her strength' (Gn 4$^{12}$) is= give the product of her strength, *i.e.* her fruits. 'Lest ye be consumed in all their *sins*' (Nu 16$^{26}$)= through the consequences of their sins, *i.e.* the punishment for them. In 'dust thou art' (Gn 3$^{19}$), dust=produced from dust (2$^{7}$). We encounter the same Metonymy in 'dust and ashes' (18$^{27}$ etc., Sir 10$^{9a}$). 'Wood' or 'tree' is a term for the cross in Ac 5$^{30}$, Gal 3$^{13}$ etc.—When we read 'Two nations are in thy womb' (Gn 25$^{23}$), we must plainly understand this to mean the ancestors of two nations. In the same way 'covenant' in Is 42$^{6}$ stands for the mediator of the covenant, and 'blessing' in Gn 12$^{2b}$ for the formula wherewith the blessing is invoked.—The *possessor* naturally often stands for the *possession*. Thus Lebanon is put for the cedars (Is 10$^{34b}$) which symbolize the host of the Assyrians; and the cup stands for its contents in 1 Co 11$^{25}$ etc. 'Heart and reins' (Ps 7$^{9}$ 26$^{2}$ etc.) refers to thoughts and volitions. In Mk 5$^{35}$ ἀπὸ τοῦ ἀρχισυναγώγου means 'from the house of the ruler of the synagogue.' So 'the hour' (Mk 14$^{35}$) might stand for the events of that period of time.—A *mark of distinction* points impressively to its *bearer* in 'A sceptre shall rise out of Israel' (Nu 24$^{17}$). So also in Is 23$^{3}$ the Shihor, *i.e.* the Nile, stands for Egypt.—The *contents* may stand for the *container*: for instance, in Ps 9$^{14}$ 'the gates of the daughter of Zion,' the daughter, *i.e.* the population, of Zion must be the equivalent of Zion itself. In like manner 'testament' (2 Co 3$^{14}$)= book of the covenant, and 'prayer' (Ac 16$^{16}$)= place of prayer.

Characteristic instances of **Synecdoche** are such as the following: 'the Jebusite,' etc. (Gn 10$^{16f.}$); 'and the Canaanite was then in the land' (12$^{6}$); 'the man' (Ps 1$^{1}$ 32$^{1}$ etc.). This employment of *a part for the whole* may be seen also in other expressions. 'Father' is equivalent to all kinds of ancestors (Gn 47$^{9}$, Ex 12$^{3}$, Nu 14$^{18}$, Ps 22$^{5}$ 39$^{13}$ 106$^{6}$ etc.). Again, in Abraham's words to Lot 'we are brothers' (Gn 13$^{8}$), 'brothers' stands for all degrees of relationship, and so also in Ex 2$^{11}$ and Nu 16$^{10}$. The principal members of a class could very readily be used to represent the whole class: *e.g.* 'a land flowing with milk and honey' (Ex 3$^{8.17}$ 13$^{5}$ 33$^{3}$, Nu 13$^{27}$ etc., Dt 6$^{3}$ etc., Jos 5$^{6}$, Jer 11$^{5}$ 32$^{22}$, Ezk 20$^{6.15}$). So also a principal part could stand for the whole in the following: 'the shadow of my *roof*' (Gn 19$^{8}$), *i.e.* of my house; 'The ark of God dwelleth within *curtains*' (2 S 7$^{2}$, cf. 1 Ch 17$^{1}$, Ca 1$^{5}$, Jer 4$^{20}$ 10$^{20}$ 49$^{29}$, Hab 3$^{7}$), *i.e.* in a mere tent; 'Thy seed shall possess the *gate* of his enemies' (Gn 22$^{17}$ 24$^{60}$, Dt 12$^{15}$ 15$^{7}$ etc., Ps 87$^{2}$, Is 3$^{26a}$ 14$^{31}$, Mic 1$^{9}$), *i.e.* their city. The 'soul' stands for the whole man in Gn 9$^{5a}$ 12$^{5}$ ('the souls that they had gotten in Haran')$^{13}$ 14$^{21}$ 17$^{14}$ 46$^{18}$, Ex 12$^{15}$, Lv 7$^{20f.}$ etc.; 'Let every soul,' etc. (Ro 13$^{1}$, Ac 2$^{43}$ 3$^{23}$, 1 Co 15$^{45}$, Rev 16$^{3}$); 'three thousand souls,' etc. (Ac 2$^{41}$ 7$^{14}$ 27$^{37}$, 1 P 3$^{20}$); cf. 'Thou art my bone and my flesh' (Gn 29$^{14}$, Jg 9$^{2}$, 2 S 5$^{1}$ 19$^{13f.}$, 1 Ch 11$^{1}$)=my blood relation; 'flesh and blood' (Sir 14$^{18}$ 17$^{31}$, Mt 16$^{17}$, 1 Co 15$^{50}$, Gal 1$^{16}$)=man; 'How beautiful upon the mountains are the *feet* of him that bringeth good tidings' (Is 52$^{7}$, Nah 2$^{1}$, Ac 5$^{2}$, Ro 10$^{15}$), the feet being the organs most necessary to a messenger.—In 'Blessed be the LORD God of Shem' (Gn 9$^{26}$), the designation of the whole ('Shemites') is put for that of the principal constituent of the race, namely Israel (cf. 10$^{21}$). The general expression 'the river' stands for the Euphrates, because for Western Asia this stream was 'the great river' (Gn 15$^{18}$), *i.e.* possessed most importance (31$^{21}$, Ex 23$^{31}$, Dt 1$^{7}$ 11$^{24}$, Jos 1$^{4}$ 24$^{2f.14f.}$, 2 S 10$^{16}$, 1 K 4$^{21.24}$ 14$^{15}$, 1 Ch 5$^{9}$ 19$^{16}$, 2 Ch 9$^{26}$, Ezr 8$^{36}$, Neh 2$^{7.9}$, Ps 72$^{8}$ 80$^{12}$, Is 7$^{20}$ 8$^{7}$ 11$^{15}$ 19$^{5}$ 27$^{12}$, Jer 2$^{18}$, Mic 7$^{12}$, Zec 9$^{10}$). 'The high' κατ' ἐξοχήν is the heavens (2 S 22$^{17}$, Job 16$^{19}$, Ps 7$^{7}$ 18$^{16}$ 71$^{19}$ 93$^{4}$ 144$^{7}$ 148$^{1}$, Is 24$^{18.21}$ 32$^{15}$ 33$^{5}$ 40$^{26}$ 57$^{15}$, Mic 6$^{6}$).—To this category belongs also the employment of *the abstract for the concrete*: as, for instance, 'a help' (Gn 2$^{20}$); 'captivity' (2 K 24$^{15}$ 25$^{27}$, 1 Ch 5$^{22}$, Ezr 1$^{11}$, Neh 7$^{6}$, Est 2$^{6}$, Is 20$^{4}$ 45$^{13}$, Jer 24$^{5}$ 28$^{4}$ 29$^{16.22}$ 40$^{1}$ 52$^{31}$, Ezk 1$^{1f.}$ 33$^{21}$ 40$^{1}$, Am 1$^{6.9.15}$, Ob $^{20b}$, Zec 6$^{10}$). In Ps 110$^{3b}$ 'youth' is employed in the same way as *iuventus*=*iuvenes*.

(*b*) Clearness of style can hardly be said to be prejudiced by the following devices.

It was natural that a single verb should express two cognate actions. Thus שׁוּף (Gn 3$^{15b}$) is used for the hostile action both of the seed of the woman and of that of the serpent, and is thus equivalent in the one instance to 'bruise' and in the other to 'sting.' This employment of only one verb is known as **Zeugma.** Other examples of its use are: Ps 76$^{3}$ 'There brake he the arrows, etc., and [finished] the battle'; Ezk 6$^{9}$ 'I am broken,' etc.; Hos 2$^{18}$ 'I will break the bow, the sword, and the battle.'—Elsewhere we meet with *a play upon the double meaning of words*. For instance, in Gn 48$^{22}$ שׁכם has the two meanings of 'mountain ridge' and 'portion.' Further, Isaiah announces to his people, 'Though thy multitude, O Israel, be as the sand of the sea, a remnant of them shall return' (10$^{22a}$), *i.e.* 'a remnant certainly, but only a remnant' (Cheyne, 1884, *ad loc.*). Again, when Isaiah says to his people, 'God will lift up his staff over thee' [*i.e.* for thy protection] בְּדֶרֶךְ מִצְרַיִם (10$^{24b.26b}$), he means by דֶּרֶךְ, in the first instance, 'manner' or 'way.' That is to say, God will help Israel in the *way* in which He helped them once before, when He brought them forth from Egypt. But, further, בְּדֶרֶךְ מִצְרַיִם has in view the notion that God will deliver Israel by destroying the Assyrian army on the *way* to Egypt, as actually happened in B.C. 701 (Is 37$^{36}$). 'A phrase of double meaning, such as Isaiah loves,' is Cheyne's comment on Is 10$^{22}$. He adduces no other example, but we find a similar 'Janus-word' in 22$^{23b.24}$, where כָּבוֹד is used in the two senses of 'honour' and 'weight.' Both originated from the radical notion of the word, namely 'heaviness.' Again, one and the same term שׁוּב means both 'turn away' and 'return' (Jer 8$^{4b}$). The other instances of this *ambiguity* will be found enumerated in *Stilistik*, p. 11 f.—The striving after a witty use of words in a double sense culminates in the **Riddle**; and, in accordance with the general custom of Orientals of diverting themselves by putting and solving riddles, we find that the writers of Scripture have interwoven a number of these with their histories and arguments. The earliest example is Jg 14$^{14}$ 'Out of the eater came forth meat, and out of the strong [eater] came forth sweetness.' Both the occurrences mentioned here are opposed to ordinary experience, and thus awaken reflexion. The answer to this riddle was in turn given (v.$^{18}$) as a riddle, namely, 'What is sweeter than honey, and what is stronger than a lion?' Once more, the words 'The horseleech hath *two* daughters, crying, Give, give. There are *three* things,' etc. (Pr 30$^{15}$), furnish a specimen of the enigmatic sayings which the Jews called מִדָּה 'measure,' because they lead to the measuring, *i.e.* exhausting of the scope of a notion.

The other instances are Pr $6^{16-19}$, Sir $23^{16}$ $25^{2.7f.}$ $26^{5ff.19}$ $50^{25}$. Also the name SHESHACH in Jer $25^{26}$ contains a species of riddle. The key to it is found in the custom of interchanging letters. In one of these systems the last letter of the alphabet was substituted for the first, the next to the last for the second, and so on. In this way *Sheshach* (ששך) would stand for *Babel* (בבל). The same phenomenon presents itself in Jer $51^{1}$, where the words 'in the midst of them that rise up against me' represent the Heb. *Leb-ḳamai* (לב קמי), which, on the same system of interchange of letters, would = *Kasdim* (כשדים), *i.e.* Chaldæans.

The following instances of *interchange of pronoun and substantive* may also be traced to natural motives, and are thus readily intelligible: 'God created man, etc., in the image of God created he him' (Gn $1^{27}$). The words 'of God' take the place of 'his,' because prominence is meant to be given to the concept 'God.' The same preferring of the name 'God' to the pronoun is to be noted in the following passages: 'And the LORD said unto Abraham, etc., Is anything too hard for the LORD' (Gn $18^{13f.}$) = 'for me'? 'The LORD rained fire from the LORD,' etc. ($19^{24}$); 'Thou (O LORD) shalt destroy them that speak leasing, the LORD will abhor,' etc. (Ps $5^{6ab}$), instead of 'thou wilt abhor,' etc.; 'He (the LORD) answered, etc., and the LORD,' etc. (Is $6^{11f.}$); 'concerning his Son, etc., which was made, etc., and declared to be the Son of God' (Ro $1^{3f.}$). In the same way 'thou' and 'the king' alternate in 2 S $14^{12ab}$, and the title 'king' on many other occasions takes the place of the pronoun: *e.g.* 'O king, the eyes of all Israel are upon thee, that thou shouldest tell them who shall sit on the throne of my lord the king,' etc. (1 K $1^{20}$ $8^{1ab}$ $22^{15b}$ etc.); or 'Thine arrows [O king] are sharp in the heart of the king's enemies' (Ps $45^{5}$ etc.; cf. *Stilistik*, 154).—It was no less natural that the bare pronoun should frequently be used to point to the personage who is the main subject of any particular discussion. For instance, the hero who was called from the rising of the sun to deliver the exiles (Is $41^{1-7}$) is indicated by the simple pronoun in $41^{25}$ $45^{13}$ $46^{11}$ $48^{14}$, and perhaps $55^{11b}$. Who, now, was a more important subject than God Himself, in religious texts such as are contained in the Bible? Hence the reference of the pronoun 'he' is not doubtful in the words 'if he destroy him from his place' (Job $8^{18a}$), or in $9^{3a}$ 'for he is not a man,' etc. In both passages God is self-evidently the other party. The same function is discharged by 'he' in $12^{13f.}$ $13^{16b}$ $19^{8}$, and 'God' is quite justifiably substituted by AV for the Heb. 'he' in $20^{23}$ and $21^{17b}$. The same use of the pronoun 'he' to refer to God is found in the following passages: 'In them (the heavens) he set a tabernacle for the sun' (Ps $19^{4}$); 'Judah was his sanctuary' ($114^{2}$); 'He will no more carry thee away into captivity' (La $4^{22}$ etc., cf. *Stilistik*, p. 115 f.). Thus 'God' came to be the *great logical subject* or *object of the Bible.* Almost more natural still was it that 'God' should be the *great logical vocative* of Scripture. Examples of the latter are: 'Salvation belongeth to the LORD, *thy* blessing is upon *thy* people' (Ps $3^{8}$), or 'Put your trust in the LORD,' and 'LORD, lift *thou* up the light of *thy* countenance upon us' ($4^{5f.}$), or 'the LORD shall judge the people, judge me, O LORD,' etc. ($7^{8}$). This involuntary turning of the religious man to his God is met with again in 'I have set the LORD always before me,' and 'for *thou* wilt not leave my soul in hell,' etc. (Ps $16^{8-10}$), or in 'He sent,' etc., and 'at *thy* rebuke,' etc. ($18^{14f.}$ etc. $69^{23b}$ $76^{4}$ etc.). The same natural apostrophizing of God is found in the well-known words 'therefore forgive them not' (Is $2^{9b}$), or in 'and the LORD hath given me knowledge of it . . . then thou shewedest me their doings' (Jer $11^{18}$). Many similar passages are collected in *Stilistik*, p. 243.

Besides these forms of transition from pronoun to substantive, there are other rapid transitions characteristic of the style of Scripture.—

(*a*) After Joseph has been extolled in the words 'Joseph is a fruitful bough,' etc., he is addressed directly: 'even by the God of *thy* father,' etc. (Gn $49^{21-24.25f.}$). A similar transition shows itself in such instances as the following: 'Let her cherish him, and let her lie in *thy* bosom' (1 K $1^{2}$); 'who eat up my people,' etc., and '*you* have shamed the counsel of the poor,' etc. (Ps $14^{4b.6a}$). The complaint '*they* are gone away backward' is continued by the question 'Why should *ye* be stricken any more?' (Is $1^{4f.}$); cf. Hab $2^{7f.}$ etc. The opposite transition, from apostrophe to the objective and calmer treatment of a person, may be observed in the words 'Reuben, *thou* art my firstborn . . . *he* went up to my couch' (Gn $49^{3f.}$). The same change occurs again in 'O Jacob . . . *he* shall pour the water out of his buckets,' etc. (Nu $24^{5-7}$); or in 'Worship *thou* him' and '*her* clothing is of wrought gold' (Ps $45^{11-13}$); or in '*Thou shalt* be called the city of righteousness' and '*Zion shall* be redeemed,' etc. (Is $1^{26f.}$); or in '*Thy* men shall fall by the sword,' etc., and '*her* gates shall lament,' etc. ($3^{25f.}$ etc. $22^{16b}$ etc.; cf. *Stilistik*, pp. 238–248). There are, further, many passages in which the employment of the *third* person passes over into a preference for the *first*. A large proportion of these cases is explained by the circumstance that the writer passes to the use of direct speech: *e.g.* 'He feared to say, she is *my* wife' (Gn $26^{7}$); 'The rulers take counsel together. . . . Let *us* break,' etc. (Ps $2^{3}$); 'He maketh . . . know that *I am* God' ($46^{9f.}$); 'The LORD of Hosts doth take . . . and *I* will give children to be their princes' (Is $3^{1a.4a}$); 'He fenced . . . and now judge between *me*,' etc. ($5^{2f.}$). Other instances are due to the author's including himself in the same group as the persons spoken of: *e.g.* 'They went through the flood on foot, there did *we* rejoice in him' (Ps $66^{6}$); 'The daughter of Zion is left as a cottage . . ., except the LORD of Hosts had left unto *us* a very small remnant' (Is $1^{8f.}$). It might also happen that a collective personality like the Servant of the Lord (Is $41^{8}$ etc.) found its herald in a prophet. In this way is explained the employment of 'I' in the expressions 'In the LORD have I righteousness,' etc. (Is $45^{24}$ $48^{16b}$ $49^{1}$ $50^{4}$ $53^{1}$ $61^{1}$).—Less frequent is the transition from the *first* person to the *third*, as in 'Lamech said, Adah and Zillah, Hear *my* voice, ye wives *of Lamech*, hearken unto my speech' (Gn $4^{23}$). It is obvious that this form of transition is a very natural one. The 'I' or 'my' is replaced by the name of the person concerned. The same phenomenon appears in 'Balaam lifted up his eyes and said, Balaam the son of Beor hath said,' etc. (Nu $24^{2f.}$). 'David' is used instead of 'I' in 2 S $7^{20a}$. In the words 'I shall not be greatly moved' and 'How long will ye imagine mischief against a man?' (Ps $62^{2b.3a}$) the poet passes over from himself to the general category to which he belongs. With special frequency does the 'I' of a Divine message pass over into the third person. In some passages the place of the Divine 'I' is taken by a Divine name, as in the words 'Will *I* eat flesh of bulls? . . . Offer unto *God* thanksgiving,' etc. (Ps $50^{13f.}$), or in 'The LORD said unto my lord, Sit thou at *my* right hand . . . the LORD shall send the rod,' etc. ($110^{1f.}$). In other passages where the first person alternates with the third, we observe the language of God passing into that of His interpreter. An indisputable example of this transition is found in the words 'I will command the clouds that they rain no rain upon it, for the vineyard of *the LORD* is,' etc. (Is $5^{6f.}$). So also in 'Mine anger in their destruction . . . *the LORD of Hosts* shall stir up,' etc. ($10^{25f.}$ etc., cf. *Stilistik*, pp. 249–256).

(β) Another phenomenon very frequently met with in the OT is the *transition from plural to singular*, and *vice versâ*. For instance, we read 'And ye shall observe this thing for an ordinance to thee and to thy sons for ever' (Ex $12^{24ab}$). There 'all the congregation of Israel' (v.[3]), which in vv.$^{5-24a}$ is addressed by the plural 'your,' is treated in v.$^{24b}$ as a singular, and this singular has probably at the same time an individualizing force, and a warm parenetic tone. But the reader of the OT is not misled thereby, for this transition meets him very frequently: *e.g.* Ex $13^{5-16}$ $20^{24}$ etc., Dt $6^{25}$ etc., Jg $12^{5}$, Ps $17^{12a}$ ('a lion'), Is $56^{5b}$ (where 'them' instead of 'him' has a levelling effect), Mal $2^{14}$ ('yet *ye* say . . . the LORD hath been witness between *thee* and the wife of *thy* youth') $^{15b}$ etc.; cf. *Stilistik*, pp. 232–238.

(γ) Still less surprising is the *sudden transition from one subject to another*. The first instance of this is met with in the words 'When the sons of God came in unto the daughters of men, and they bare children to them' (Gn $6^{4}$). This example is more difficult in the Hebrew text, where there is no equivalent for 'they,' and the verb *yālĕdû* might also mean 'beget' and be connected with the 'sons of God.' The next example is 'God shall enlarge Japheth, and he shall dwell in the tents of Shem' ($9^{27}$). Here 'God' cannot be the subject of 'shall dwell,' for He has been already extolled in v.$^{26a}$ as the ally of Shem. The same phenomenon appears in 'And he believed in the LORD, and he counted it to him for righteousness' ($15^{6}$). There are not a few instances of this rapid change of subjects (cf. *Stilistik*, p. 257 f.), seeing that it is favoured by the so-called **Chiasmus,** of which an excellent specimen is presented by the words 'And the LORD had respect to Abel and his offering, but unto Cain and his offering he had no respect' (Gn $4^{4b.\ 5a}$). Here the words that come first in v.$^{4b}$ correspond to those that form the conclusion of v.$^{5a}$. On the other hand, the words with which v.$^{4b}$ closes and the words that commence v.$^{5a}$ are closely akin. It is readily explicable psychologically that similar ideas should be treated at the end of one sentence and directly afterwards at the beginning of a second. Hence *Chiasmus* is an extremely frequent occurrence in the OT. Here are a few further instances: 'The LORD knoweth *the way* of the righteous, but *the way* of the ungodly shall perish' (Ps $1^{6ab}$); 'Why do the nations rage, and the peoples imagine a vain thing?' (Ps $2^{1ab}$); 'It was full of judgment, righteousness lodged in it' (Is $1^{21}$); 'The vineyard of the LORD of Hosts is the house of Israel, and the men of Judah his pleasant plant' ($5^{7}$). An exceedingly instructive example is furnished by the words: 'Make the *heart* of this people fat, and make their *ears* heavy, and shut their *eyes*; lest they see with their *eyes*, and hear with their *ears*, and understand with their *heart*' (Is $6^{10}$). Here a threefold correspondence may be observed. A number of other examples will be found in *Stilistik*, pp. 145–148.

None of the above phenomena, as they are psychologically explicable, diminish the perspicuity of the style of Scripture, and there are a number of devices whereby its clearness is *increased*.—

The first place amongst these is held by the **Simile.** What a bright light is thrown upon the number of Abraham's descendants by the declaration that they shall be 'like the dust of the earth' (Gn $13^{16}$ $28^{14}$), or 'as the sand which is upon the seashore' ($22^{17}$ $32^{12}$), or 'as the stars of the heaven' ($15^{5}$ $22^{17}$ $26^{4}$ etc.)! How clearly defined is the victory of the theocratic king by the words 'Thou shalt dash them in pieces like a potter's vessel' (Ps $2^{9}$)! With what terrible distinctness the persecutor stands before our eyes when it is said 'lest he tear my soul like a lion' ($7^{2}$ $10^{9}$ $17^{12}$)! The few words 'Zion is left as a cottage in a vineyard' (Is $1^{8}$) describe the situation of besieged Jerusalem more clearly than could have been done in a series of sentences. With what a shuddering feeling we hear the words 'In that day they shall roar against them like the roaring of the sea' ($5^{30}$)! We will only note, further, the characteristic words spoken of Ahaz, 'His heart was moved as the trees of the forest are moved with the wind' ($7^{2}$).—A special form of the Simile is the **Example.** For instance, when it is said 'We have sinned with our fathers . . . our fathers understood not thy wonders in Egypt,' etc. (Ps $106^{6f.}$), this is equivalent to 'We have sinned like our fathers,' etc. The παράδειγμα or *Exemplum* is merely a Simile introduced in a peculiar manner. The Example is rare in the OT, there being hardly any more instances of it than the following: Mal $2^{15}$ (Abraham), Ps $99^{6}$ (Moses, Aaron, and Samuel), $106^{30f.}$ (Phinehas), Neh $13^{26}$ (Solomon). Later generations had much more occasion to introduce characters from earlier history for the purpose of encouragement or of warning. The following are cited as examples for imitation: Abraham, Moses, and others in the 'Praise of Famous Men,' Sir 44 ff., in Jth $4^{22}$ $8^{19f.}$, or in 1 Mac $2^{52-60}$; David as a pattern of self-restraint (cf. 2 S $23^{16}$) in 4 Mac $3^{6-17}$; the queen of the south (*i.e.* Saba) in Mt $12^{42}$; the widow of Sarepta in Lk $4^{26}$ etc. We have, held up to warning: the Egyptians in Wis $17^{2ff.}$; the Sodomites in Mt $10^{15}$ $11^{23f.}$; Lot's wife, that μνημεῖον ἀπιστούσης ψυχῆς (Wis $10^{7}$) in Lk $17^{32}$; Theudas and others in Ac $5^{36f.}$ etc. The OT is somewhat richer in instances of the Example, if we include those that are drawn from the animal world. When, *e.g.*, we read 'The ox knoweth his owner,' etc. (Is $1^{3}$), what is this but an example which puts man to shame? Similar is the force of the saying 'The stork in the heaven knoweth his appointed times,' etc. (Jer $8^{7}$), and every one is familiar with the call 'Go to the ant, thou sluggard, consider her ways and be wise' (Pr $6^{6}$). For further instances see *Stilistik*, p. 78 f.—Closely akin to the Example is the **Proverb.** For the function of the latter is simply to describe the usual working of an Example. It must, however, suffice here to note the high value of the Proverb as a device for lending vividness to a description. For further details, see art. PROVERB in vol. iv.—While, on the one hand, shortened forms of the Simile may be seen in the Example and the Proverb, this figure of speech assumes, on the other hand, expanded forms in the **Parable** and the **Fable,** as well as in those passages of the OT which may be called **Paramyths.** These three species of picturesque description are explained in the art. PARABLE (in OT) in vol. iii.

The second principal stylistic device for illustrative ends is the **Metaphor** and its cognates. The source of the metaphor is a vivid simultaneous contemplation of the main elements in two notions. For instance, the notions of joy and of light are naturally combined, because both exercise a liberative and elevating influence upon the health of man. On the other hand, unhappiness and darkness both weigh man down, as it were. Thus we explain sayings like the following: 'Thou wilt light my candle, the LORD my God will enlighten my darkness' (Ps $18^{28}$). For the same reason, a sorrowful period in one's life is described as a passing 'through the valley of the shadow of death' ($23^{4}$). So we read 'The people that sat in darkness have seen a great light' (Is $9^{2}$), *i.e.* they shall attain to political freedom and deliverance from guilt and sin. In a similar way 'fire' could be an expression for 'anger,' as may be seen in the words 'therefore the inhabitants of the earth are burned' (Is 24$^{6}$). The 'dew' was quite naturally used as a symbol for a great many phenomena of a cheerful order, so that there is no difficulty in understanding the expression in Ps 110$^{3}$ 'Thou hast the dew of thy youth' (lit. 'Like the dew are thy young men'). On the other hand, the 'floods' and similar expressions stand for hosts of foes (Ps 18$^{4b.16b}$ etc.). The 'earthquake' may point an allusion to political disturbances, as in 'Thou hast made the earth to tremble,' etc. (Ps 60$^{2f.}$). The 'rock' is an equally natural figure for a place of refuge (Ps 27$^{5}$ 'He shall set me up upon a rock'), as 'depth' is for catastrophe or misfortune (Ps 69$^{2}$ 'I am come into deep waters'; cf. v.$^{14b}$, and 130$^{1}$ 'Out of the depths have I cried unto thee'). Regarded from another point of view, the 'deep' was naturally employed as a symbol of the inexhaustible and unfathomable. Hence we read, 'O the depth of the riches,' etc. (Ro 11$^{33}$, cf. 2 Co 8$^{2}$), and for the same reason 'deep' in the sense of 'mysterious' is used of the heart (Ps 64$^{6b}$, Jth 8$^{14}$) or of the lip, *i.e.* the speech (Is 33$^{19}$, Ezk 3$^{5f.}$). Thus 'to be deep' is equivalent to 'to be unfathomable' (Ps 92$^{5}$ 'and thy thoughts are very deep'), and a matter that is incomprehensible is compared to the great primeval flood (תְּהוֹם רַבָּה Ps 36$^{6}$ 'a great deep').—The number of combinations of phenomena from the different spheres is almost endless. We can note only a few of them. 'Shield' is an expression for 'protector' (Gn 15$^{1}$ etc.), and 'star' is a beautiful figure for a conquering hero (Nu 24$^{17}$ 'There shall come a star out of Jacob'; cf. Is 14$^{12}$, Dn 8$^{10}$, Rev 22$^{16}$, and Ovid, *Epist. ex Ponto*, III. iii. 2, 'O sidus Fabiæ, Maxime, gentis'). 'The waters,' again, stands for hostile troops (Ps 124$^{5}$, Is 8$^{7}$, Rev 17$^{1}$ etc.), and 'branch' for 'descendant' (Ps 80$^{11b}$, Is 11$^{1}$ 60$^{21}$ etc.).—From the sphere of animated nature we have 'lion' as a honorific title for a strong hero (Gn 49$^{9}$ 'Judah is a lion's whelp,' cf. 2 S 23$^{20}$ etc.); and 'goats' might be symbolic either of leaders of the people (Is 14$^{9}$, where the Heb. is כָּל־עַתּוּדֵי אָרֶץ 'all the goats of the earth'; cf. Zec 10$^{3}$), or of refractory elements in the community (Ezk 34$^{17}$); while 'sheep' was an honourable designation for gentle and pious men (Ps 79$^{13}$ 100$^{3}$, Is 53$^{7}$, Ezk 36$^{38}$, Mt 25$^{32f.}$, Jn 10$^{1}$ etc.). The expression 'on eagles' wings' (Ex 19$^{4}$) portrays the triumphant fashion of the Divine intervention in the course of history (cf. Dt 32$^{11}$, Ps 17$^{8b}$).—Lastly, certain objects in the inanimate sphere were often regarded as if they had life, and even as if they were human beings. Thus the blood has a voice attributed to it in the words 'The voice of thy brother's blood crieth unto me from the ground' (Gn 4$^{10}$); and when the prophet says, 'Hear, O heavens, and give ear, O earth' (Is 1$^{2}$), this only falls short of *personification*. The same figure may be observed in the call to ships to howl (Is 23$^{1}$); and in the passages where it is said that 'the stone shall cry out of the wall' (Hab 2$^{11}$), or that 'if these should hold their peace, the stones would immediately cry out' (Lk 19$^{40}$), how vividly the scene presents itself to our eyes! Since metaphorical expressions portray, as it were, to our eyes a spiritual process, they readily combine to form whole pictures. We have an instance of this in 'The whole head is sick, and the whole heart faint; from the sole of the foot even unto the head,' etc. (Is 1$^{5f.}$); and another in 'There shall come forth a rod out of the stem of Jesse, and a branch shall grow out of his roots' (11$^{1}$). A continued series of metaphorical expressions of this kind receives the name of **Allegory.** This figure meets us *in* the Song of Songs, as, for instance, in the words 'I sat down under his (*i.e.* my beloved's) shadow with great delight, and his fruit was sweet to my taste' (2$^{3}$), or in 'A garden enclosed is my sister,' etc. (4$^{12ff.}$, cf. 7$^{7f.}$), but it is not the case that the *whole* Song is an allegorical poem regarding the Messiah and His Church (cf. further, *Stilistik*, pp. 94–110, and art. SONG OF SONGS in vol. iv.).

2. The Biblical writers naturally desire to give their words the highest possible degree of *emphasis.* It is this aim that gives rise to not a few characteristic features of the style of Scripture. —(*a*) The employment of a *prospective pronoun*, as in 'This is that night of the LORD to be observed,' etc. (Ex 12$^{42}$); 'I shall see him, but not now,' etc. (Nu 24$^{17}$), the effect in this last instance being to awaken strongly the interest in the star which is then mentioned. So also 'Thou shalt not go thither unto the land which I give,' etc. (Dt 32$^{52}$); 'the Most High himself' (Ps 87$^{5}$); 'to this man will I look, even to him that is poor,' etc. (Is 66$^{2}$; cf. *Stilistik*, p. 153 f.).—(*b*) Emphasis is sought, again, by the repetition of one and the same expression, giving birth to the so-called **Epizeuxis.** The list of its occurrences begins with 'Abraham, Abraham' (Gn 22$^{11}$), and is continued in the following: 'the red, the red' (25$^{30}$ AV 'that same red pottage'); 'Jacob, Jacob' (46$^{2}$); 'Amen, Amen' (Nu 5$^{22}$, Ps 41$^{14}$ 72$^{19}$ 89$^{53}$, Neh 8$^{6}$); 'of justice, justice' (Dt 16$^{20}$ AV 'altogether just') 'Come out, come out' (2 S 16$^{7}$); 'My God, my God' (Ps 22$^{1}$); 'Return, return' (Ca 6$^{13}$); 'peace, peace' (Is 26$^{3}$, where AV has 'perfect peace,' although it retains 'peace, peace' in 57$^{19}$, Jer 6$^{14}$ 8$^{11}$); 'Comfort ye, comfort ye, my people' (Is 40$^{1}$); 'Ho, ho' (Zec 2$^{6}$ etc.; cf. *Stilistik*, p. 155 f.). A specially high degree of emphasis was naturally expressed by the thrice-repeated employment of a word. This is seen in 'Holy, holy, holy is the LORD of Hosts' (Is 6$^{3}$); or 'The temple of the LORD, the temple of the LORD, the temple of the LORD' (Jer 7$^{4}$); or 'O earth, earth, earth' (22$^{29}$); or 'I will overturn, overturn, overturn it' (Ezk 21$^{27}$); or 'The LORD revengeth,' etc. (Nah 1$^{2}$). The same *emphatic repetition* occurs also with the conjunctions, as when the words 'We will arise and go and live and not die' (Gn 43$^{8}$) furnish us with a speaking picture of anxious impatience. Again, the double use of the conditional particle in '*If* ye have done truly . . . and *if* ye have dealt well with Jerubbaal' (Jg 9$^{16}$) serves very well as a reminder that the point was open to question. Once more, to indicate how well deserved a punishment was, we have a repeated 'because, because' (Ps 116$^{1f.}$); or 'for, for' (Is 1$^{29f.}$); or 'therefore, therefore' (5$^{13a.14a}$); or 'for, for' (Jer 48$^{5ab}$ etc.; cf. *Stilistik*, p. 159).—Emphasis is also aimed at in such words as 'Get thee out of thy country, and from thy kindred, and from thy father's house' (Gn 12$^{1}$), where a series of words is so arranged as to designate an ever-narrowing circle of persons. Abraham must separate himself from even the most intimate circle of his relations (cf. Jos 24$^{2}$), in order to follow the Divine call. Such a form of expression is known as a **Climax,** and examples of it meet us frequently in the Bible. Here are a few: 'His bread shall be *fat*, and he shall yield *royal* dainties' (Gn 49$^{20}$); 'The children of Israel have not hearkened unto me, how then shall Pharaoh hear me?' (Ex 6$^{12}$); 'the day . . . and the night' (Job 3$^{3}$); 'ungodly . . . sinners . . . scornful' (Ps 1$^{1}$); 'my friend or brother' (35$^{14}$); 'Forget thy own people and (even) thy father's house' (45$^{10}$); 'in the twilight, in the evening, in the black night' (Pr 7$^{9}$); 'Are they Hebrews . . . Israelites . . . seed of Abraham . . . ministers of Christ?' (2 Co 11$^{22f.}$); 'which we have heard, which we have seen, which we have looked upon, and our hands have handled,' etc. (1 Jn 1$^{1}$). Speci-

ally common is the Climax in connexion with the use of numbers: *e.g.* 'He will deliver thee in *six* troubles, yea in *seven* there shall no evil touch thee' (Job $5^{19}$); 'God hath spoken once, twice have I heard this' (Ps $62^{11}$); 'Give a portion to seven, and also to eight' (Ec $11^{2}$); 'two or three . . . four or five' (Is $17^{6}$); 'for three transgressions and for four,' etc. (Am $1^{3.6.9.11.13}$ $2^{1.4.6}$); 'Of three things my heart is afraid, and before the fourth I fear greatly' (Sir $26^{5}$); 'Where two or three are gathered in my name,' etc. (Mt $18^{20}$; cf. *Stilistik*, p. 163 f.). Quite similar is the phenomenon which presents itself in such expressions as, 'They go *from strength to strength*' (Ps $84^{7}$); 'affording from species to species' (Ps $144^{13}$ AV 'all manner of store'); 'from wickedness to wickedness' (Sir $13^{21}$ $40^{13}$), *i.e.* to ever new forms of wickedness; 'Add iniquity to their iniquity' (Ps $69^{27}$); 'The sinner heaps sin upon sin' (Sir $3^{27}$ $5^{5}$); 'A chaste woman shows grace upon grace' ($26^{15}$; cf. Jn $1^{16}$ 'grace for grace,' *i.e.* ever self-renewing grace).

3. In conformity with the nature of their subjects, the Biblical writers seek to invest their language with a high degree of *seriousness* and *dignity*. Both these qualities appear to be prejudiced by certain peculiar forms of expression. The first of these is the **Hyperbole,** a figure which is undoubtedly employed in the Bible. What is it but Hyperbole when the posterity of Abraham is compared to the sand upon the seashore (Gn $22^{17}$ etc.)? Even a theologian like Flacius admits this (*Clavis Script. Sacr.* 1628, ii. p. 383 ff.). But we must also assign to the same category forms of expression like the following: 'under *every* green tree' (from Dt $12^{2}$ to 2 Ch $28^{4}$); 'The cities are great and walled *up to heaven*' (Dt $1^{28}$ etc.); 'though thou set thy nest *among the stars*' (Ob $^{4}$ etc.); 'Saul and Jonathan were swifter *than eagles*' (2 S $1^{23}$ etc.); 'I am a *worm*,' etc. (Ps $22^{6}$; cf. *Stilistik*, pp. 69–77). But the employment of such expressions does not detract from the seriousness, not to speak of the truthfulness, of the style of Scripture. The Biblical writers simply conformed in this matter to the usage of their people and their time, and every hearer or reader of such expressions knew in what sense he must understand them. Nor will it be questioned that the same is the case with the examples of **Litotes** that occur in the Bible. Such are the following: 'A broken and a contrite heart, O God, thou wilt *not despise*' (Ps $51^{17}$), *i.e.* wilt accept and praise; 'The smoking flax shall he *not quench*' (Is $42^{3}$), but supply with fresh oil; 'He setteth in a way that is *not good*' (Ps $36^{4}$); 'Thou, Bethlehem, art *not the least*,' etc. (Mt $2^{6}$); 'when we were *without strength*' (Ro $5^{6}$), *i.e.* laden with sin and guilt. It is true also of these and other expressions of a similar kind (cf. *Stilistik*, pp. 45–50), that they were not strange to readers of the Biblical writings, but were a well-understood equivalent for the positive statement in each case. The same principle holds good of the examples of **Irony** in the Bible. For instance, we have 'Go and prosper,' etc. (1 K $22^{15}$), an ironical imitation of the words of the false prophets; 'No doubt but ye are the people, and wisdom shall die with you' (Job $12^{2}$); 'It pleased God by the *foolishness* of preaching to save them that believe' (1 Co $1^{21}$); 'Now ye are full, now ye are rich,' etc. ($4^{8}$, cf. 2 Co $12^{10}$ $11^{19}$ $12^{13}$). The Biblical writers were not afraid of prejudicing the seriousness of their utterances by resorting to Irony, nor had they any occasion to be afraid, seeing that every one knew to convert these ironical expressions into their opposite. Hence we find this figure employed even in utterances attributed to God: 'Let them (the false gods) rise up and help you' (Dt $32^{38}$); 'Go and cry to the gods whom ye have chosen, let them deliver you' (Jg $10^{14}$); 'and give me to know' (Job $38^{3b}$ AV 'answer thou me'); 'Gather my saints together unto me' (Ps $50^{5}$). Nay, even sayings of Jesus are reported which exhibit the use of Irony. Amongst these we do not include καθεύδετε τὸ λοιπὸν καὶ ἀναπαύεσθε, AV and RV 'Sleep on now and take your rest' (Mt $26^{45}$ ‖ Mk $14^{41}$), for τὸ λοιπόν means 'later,' 'afterwards.'* But Irony is present (cf. *Stilistik*, p. 43) in the words 'Full well ye reject the commandment of God, that ye may keep your tradition' (Mk $7^{9}$). There are other undoubted occurrences of the same figure, as, for instance, in Jn $7^{28}$ 'Ye both know me, and ye know whence I am.' To the Biblical writers Irony was simply what it is to human speech in general—a means of heightening the effect of an utterance. A similar intention underlies the occurrence of **Sarcasm** in Scripture. There is a scoff in David's question to Abner, 'Art thou not a valiant man?' (1 S $26^{15}$), as well as in the exclamation 'How hast thou helped him that is without power!' (Job $26^{2}$), or the statement 'As a jewel of gold in a swine's snout, so is a fair woman which is without discretion' (Pr. $11^{22}$). Then there are the numerous familiar passages in which the gods of the heathen are the object of *satirical* persiflage: 'Elijah mocked them and said, Cry aloud, for he is a god, either he is talking,' etc. (1 K $18^{27}$; cf. Ps $115^{4ff.}$, Is $40^{19}$ etc.). We have similar instances of satire in the question 'Is this the city that men called the perfection of beauty, the joy of the whole earth?' (La $2^{15}$); in the affirmation 'They that be whole need not a physician' (Mt $9^{12}$); and in the indignant substitution of 'concision' (κατατομή) for 'circumcision' (περιτομή) in Ph $3^{2}$ (cf. *Stilistik*, pp. 42–45). The Biblical writers, in short, avail themselves of all natural means of reaching their end, to teach and to warn men. In this respect as in others their heart was filled with the wish expressed by the apostle in the words 'I desire to change my voice' (Gal. $4^{20}$).

4. The writers of Scripture sought to give to their words that ennobling effect which springs from regard to *purity* or chastity. Of this we find a considerable number of positive traces in the so-called **Euphemisms** such as the following: 'Adam *knew* Eve his wife' (Gn $4^{1.25}$; cf. v.$^{17}$ $19^{5.8}$ $24^{16}$ $38^{26b}$, Nu $31^{17f.35}$, Jg $11^{39}$ $19^{25}$ $21^{11f.}$, 1 S $1^{19}$, 1 K $1^{4}$, Mt $1^{25}$, Lk $1^{34}$); 'The sons of God *came in* unto the daughters of men' (Gn $6^{4}$; cf. $16^{2}$ $19^{31}$ $29^{23}$ $30^{6.16}$ $38^{2.8f.}$ etc., Ps $51^{2b}$ etc.); '*come near* her' (Gn $20^{4}$, Lv $18^{14}$, Dt $22^{14}$, Is $8^{3}$, Ezk $18^{6}$); 'to *touch* her' (Gn $20^{6}$, Pr $6^{29}$, 1 Co $7^{1}$); '*lie with*' (Gn $19^{32}$ $26^{10}$ $30^{15f.}$ $34^{2.7}$ $35^{22}$ etc.); 'Thou *wentest up to thy father's bed*' ($49^{4}$); '*discover his father's skirt*' (Dt $22^{30}$ $27^{20}$); 'she *eateth*,' said of the adulteress (Pr $30^{20}$; cf. *Stilistik*, p. 39); 'Let the husband render unto the wife *due benevolence*' (1 Co $7^{3}$). Another series is represented by euphemistic expressions like the following: 'the *nakedness*' (Gn $9^{22f.}$, Ex $20^{26}$ $28^{42}$, Lv $18^{6ff.}$ $20^{11ff.}$, 1 S $20^{30}$, Is $47^{3}$, La $1^{8}$, Ezk $16^{36f.}$ $22^{10}$ $23^{10}$); 'her young one that cometh out from between her *feet*' (Dt $28^{57}$); 'he *covereth his feet*' (Jg $3^{24}$, 1 S $24^{3}$, cf. Is $7^{20}$); '*flesh*' (Lv $15^{2f.19}$ $16^{4}$, Ezk $16^{26}$ $23^{20}$ $44^{7}$ etc.; cf. *Stilistik*, pp. 36–38).—There are only a few passages where it appears to us that the Biblical writers might have shown a little more reserve in dealing with 'the secrets' (Dt $25^{11}$). We have no exception to take to those instances in which 'shame' is employed (Is $20^{4}$ $47^{3}$), for this is still a veiled epithet. But the impression of a want of delicacy is given by modes of speech like the following: 'He lifteth up the beggar from the dunghill,' etc. (1 S $2^{8}$); 'I did cast them out as the dirt in the streets' (Ps $18^{42}$); 'Thou didst make us as the off-

* The present writer in his *Stilistik* (p. 43) anticipated Professor Potwin (see *Expos. Times*, Aug. 1901, p. 481), who rightly denies the presence of Irony in the above passage.

scouring,' etc. (La 3[45], 1 Co 4[13]); 'Dost thou pursue after a dead dog, after a flea?' (1 S 24[14]); 'Am I a dog's head?' (2 S 3[8]); 'a dead dog' (9[8] 17[9]); 'The carcass of Jezebel shall be as dung upon the face of the earth' (2 K 9[37]); 'They made it a draught-house' (10[27]); 'that they may eat their own dung,' etc. (18[27] ‖ Is 36[12]); 'They became as dung for the earth' (Ps 83[11]). Two facts, however, have to be taken into account with reference to such modes of expression. In the first place, they are in accordance with the fashion of earlier times, and were not so repugnant to men then as they are to us. But, further, the choice of such strong expressions served in some of the passages in question to increase the emphasis of the prophetic denunciation. This latter point of view helps us also to explain and to excuse certain passages in Ezekiel, notably 16[3ff.] and 23[3ff.]. We may assume that in these passages the idolatry of Israel is described in such detail as adultery, in order to deter subsequent generations from a repetition of this sin. At the same time, it must be admitted that the prophet could equally have achieved his purpose by a different method of treatment. In like manner, the description of the 'navel' and the 'belly' of the Shulammite (Ca 7[2ff.]) is somewhat too realistic.

5. The Biblical writers are by no means indifferent to *euphony* in their style.

(*a*) The very first words of the OT furnish evidence of this, the Heb. words *bĕrēshîth bārā* ('In the beginning created') being an instance of the first means of securing euphony, namely **Alliteration.** Other instances of it are found in *Nôaḥ yĕnaḥămēnû* 'Noah shall comfort us' (Gn 5[29]); *shemen shĕmekha* 'ointment thy name' (Ca 1[3]); *'āphār wā-'ēpher* 'dust and ashes' (Gn 18[27], Job 30[19] 42[6]); *yishshōm wĕ-shārak* 'shall be astonished and shall hiss' (1 K 9[8], Jer 19[8] 49[17] 50[13]); *simḥā wĕ-sāsôn* 'joy and gladness' (Est 8[16f.]); *hôd wĕ-hādār* 'honour and majesty' (Job 40[10], Ps 21[5] 96[6] ‖ 1 Ch 16[27], Ps 104[1] 111[3]); *shāmîr wā-shayith* 'briers and thorns' (Is 5[6] 7[23-25] 9[18] 10[17] 27[4]); *sāsôn wĕ-simḥā* 'gladness and joy' (Is 22[13] 35[10] 51[11]); *shôd wā-sheber* 'desolation and destruction' (Is 51[19] 59[7] 60[18]); *shommu shāmayim* 'Be astonished, O heavens' (Jer 2[12]); *ḳôẓîm ḳāẓĕrû* 'shall reap thorns' (12[13]); *sar(r)êhem ṣôrĕrîm* 'their princes are revolters' (Hos 9[15]), etc. etc.; σήμερον σωτήρ 'this day a Saviour' (Lk 2[11]).

(*b*) In other passages we meet with expressions like *tōhû wā-bōhû* 'waste and void' (Gn 1[2], Jer 4[23]). These words exhibit what is called **Assonance,** a phenomenon which recurs in *ṣôrēr u-môre* 'stubborn and rebellious' (Dt 21[18] etc.); *'ôyēb wĕ-'ôrēb* 'the enemy and the lier in wait' (Ezr 8[31]); *nĕsûy* ‖ *kĕsûy* 'forgiven' ‖ 'covered' (Ps 32[1]); *zādôn* ‖ *ḳālôn* 'pride' ‖ 'shame' (Pr 11[2]); *hôy gôy* 'Ah nation' (Is 1[4]); *kî* ‖ *yōphî* 'burning' ‖ 'beauty' (3[24]); *hôy hôdô* 'Ah his glory' (Jer 22[18]); σχῖνος 'mastic' and πρῖνος 'holm' (Sus [54. 58]); κτηνῶν 'beasts' and πτηνῶν 'birds' (1 Co 15[39]). In a good many instances Alliteration and Assonance are combined: *nā' wā-nād* 'a fugitive and a vagabond' (Gn 4[12. 14]); *Ḳayin* 'Cain' and *ḳānîthî* 'I have gotten' (Gn 4[1]); *Ḳênî* 'Kenites' and *ḳên* 'nest' (Nu 24[21]); 'Achan' and 'Achor' (Jos 7[24]); the frequently recurring 'Cherethites and Pelethites' (2 S 8[18] 15[18] 20[7], 1 K 1[38. 44], 1 Ch 18[17]); *'attā 'attā* 'thou, now' (1 K 21[7]); *'ănîyyā* ('poor') *'Anāthôth* (Is 10[30]); 'Jezreel' and 'Israel' (Hos 1[4]), etc.; πορνεία 'fornication' and πονηρία 'wickedness' (Ro 1[29]); φθόνου 'envy' and φόνου 'murder' (*ib.*), etc.; cf. *Stilistik*, pp. 287–295.

(*c*) The superlative degree of this harmony of elements in style is observable in such collocations as the following: *wayyakkirēm wayyithnakkēr* 'and he knew them, and made himself strange' (Gn 42[7ab]); *wa-hăshimmōthî . . . wĕ-shāmĕmû* 'and I will bring into desolation . . . and they shall be astonished' (Lv 26[32]); *shō'ā u-mĕshō'ā* 'desolate and waste' (Job 30[3] 38[27], Zeph 1[15], Sir 51[10c]); *'im lō ta'ămînû kî lō tē'āmēnû* 'if ye will not believe, surely ye shall not be established' (Is 7[9]); *mûsād mus(s)ād* 'of founded foundation' (28[16]). Many other instances might be cited of this species of Euphony, which is usually called **Paronomasia** or **Annominatio.** The number is particularly increased by the very frequent explanations of Proper Names, which form a noteworthy feature in the style of the Hebrew historical books. In Genesis we have the following combinations: *'ădāmā* 'tillable land' and *'ādām* 'man (Adam)' (Gn 2[7]); *'ishshā* 'woman' and *'îsh* 'man' (v.[23]); *shêth* 'Seth' and *shâth* 'hath appointed' (4[25]); *yapht* 'shall enlarge' and *Yāpheth* 'Japheth' (9[27]), etc.; cf. *Stilistik*, p. 296. Elsewhere in the OT we have the following examples of Paronomasia: *Môshe* 'Moses' and *māshîthî* 'I drew' (Ex 2[10]); *Lēwî* 'Levi' and *yillāwû* 'they may be joined' (Nu 18[2]); *Mārā* and *hēmar* 'hath dealt bitterly' (Ru 1[20]); *'Edom* and *'ādôm* 'red' (Is 63[1f.]); *Jerusalem* and *shĕlômîm* 'wholly' (Jer 13[19]); *Solomon* and *shālôm* 'peace' (1 Ch 22[9]); Πέτρος and πέτρα (Mt 16[18]), etc.; cf. *Stilistik*, pp. 295–298.

(*d*) Euphony is aimed at also by making the same words recur at certain intervals. The various *nuances* that thus arise may be illustrated from the following groups of examples: (α) *bārûkh* 'blessed' occurs at the *beginning* of a number of sentences in Dt 28[3-6]. This usage is called **Anaphora,** and we note it also, for instance, in the *'ārûr* 'cursed' with which vv.[16-19] commence; cf. also 'I will sing . . . I will sing' (Jg 5[3]); 'Many . . . many' (Ps 3[1b. 2a]); 'Lift up your heads, O ye gates . . . lift them up' (24[9ab]); 'and it was full . . . and it was full' (Is 2[7ab. 8a]); 'Woe . . . woe,' etc. (5[8. 11. 18. 20-22]); 'and I will cut off . . . and I will cut off,' etc. (Mic 5[11a. 12a. 13a]); 'All things are lawful for me, but, etc. . . . all things are lawful for me, but,' etc. (1 Co 6[12]); 'Have we not power . . . have we not power?' (9[4f.]); 'All our fathers . . . and all . . . and all . . . and all' (10[1b-4]), etc.—(β) In 'We perish, we all perish' (Nu 17[12]), we find the same expression repeated at the *end* of two successive sentences—a method of securing Euphony which is called **Epiphora.** We encounter it again in the eleven times recurring 'and all the people shall say Amen' of Dt 27[15-26]; cf. 'Take them alive . . . take them alive' (1 K 20[18ab]): and we find at the end of sentences repetitions like the following: 'the king of glory' (Ps 24[10ab]); 'shall be bowed down' (Is 2[11. 17]); 'when he raiseth up,' etc. (vv.[19b. 21b]); 'shall lament her' (Ezk 32[16ab]); 'as a child' (1 Co 13[11]); 'so am I' at the close of three sentences (2 Co 11[22]); 'in watchings often . . . in fastings often' (v.[27]), etc.—(γ) A superior degree of Euphony is sought by *beginning* one sentence and *closing* another with the same expression. This so-called **Ploke** is exemplified in 'Ceased . . . in Israel . . . they ceased' (Jg 5[7]); 'Blessed shall be . . . she shall be blessed' (v.[24ab]); 'He lieth . . . he lieth' (Ps 10[9]); 'Wait on the LORD . . . wait' (27[14ab]), etc.; 'Vanity . . . vanity' (Ec 1[2]); 'Hope that is seen is not hope' (Ro 8[24]); 'Rejoice in the LORD . . . rejoice' (Ph 4[4]), etc.—(δ) Specially frequent is the attempt to secure Euphony by making the same word *end* one sentence and *begin* the next—the so-called **Anadiplosis.** The earliest example of it in the Bible is *shôphēkh dam hā'ādām bā'ādām dāmô yishshāphēkh* 'Whoso sheddeth man's blood, by man shall his blood be shed' (Gn 9[6]); 'The kings came and fought, then fought,' etc. (Jg 5[19]); '. . . the way, but the way,' etc. (Ps 1[6ab]); 'and gathered themselves together, yea . . . gathered themselves together' (35[15ab]); *lābēsh* ('is clothed'), *lābash* (Ps 93[1]); *lākhēn yĕyêlîl Mô'āb lĕ-Mô'āb kulloh* *yĕyêlîl* 'therefore shall Moab howl, for Moab shall every one howl' (Is 16$^{7}$); *ha-ḳêẓ bâ, bâ ha-ḳêẓ* 'the end is come, it is come the end' (Ezk 7$^{6}$), etc.; 'That which the palmerworm hath left hath the locust eaten, and that which the locust hath left hath the cankerworm eaten,' etc. (Jl 1$^{4}$) etc.; 'In him was life, and the life,' etc. (Jn 1$^{4f.}$); 'Faith cometh by hearing, and hearing by the word of Christ' (Ro 10$^{17}$); 'He that soweth sparingly, sparingly shall he also reap' (2 Co 9$^{6}$); 'The trying of your faith worketh patience, but let patience,' etc. (Ja 1$^{3}$) etc.; cf. *Stilistik*, pp. 298–304.

iv. PECULIARITIES OF STYLE FOR WHICH A PREFERENCE IS SHOWN BY *PARTICULAR* CLASSES OF SCRIPTURE WRITERS.—1. In certain parts of the Bible the so-called 'lower' style is employed, while others are marked by the use of a 'higher' style. The difference may be observed even by readers of the Bible who have no acquaintance with Hebrew. They will note how in certain portions of the OT the employment of metaphorical expressions has a special vogue. Every one is familiar with the phrase 'daughter of Zion,' *i.e.* the inhabitants of Zion, and at times = Zion itself. But where do we meet with this phrase for the first time in the OT? From the beginning of Genesis we may read straight on to 2 K 19$^{21}$ before we encounter it, and the passage just named is the only one in the historical books of the OT where it occurs. How has it found its way here? Simply because in this passage we have a report of words spoken by Isaiah (cf. Is 37$^{22}$), in whose writings this and similar phrases are found repeatedly (1$^{8}$ 10$^{30.\ 32}$ 16$^{1}$ 22$^{4}$ 23$^{10.\ 12}$ 37$^{22}$; cf. [Deutero-] Is 47$^{1\ bis.\ 5}$ 52$^{2}$ 62$^{1}$). The reader of the English Bible may, further, remark how, for instance, in the Book of Isaiah, the beautiful metaphors of darkness and light are employed (5$^{30b}$ 8$^{22}$ 9$^{1f.}$ etc.), and how at one time the hosts of the enemy and at another time the Divine judgments figure in the oracles of this prophet as irresistible floods (8$^{7f.}$ 28$^{17}$ etc.). Any ordinary reader of the Bible will notice, again, how in Isaiah there are far more questions and exclamations than in the Book of Kings. For instance, 'How is the faithful city become an harlot!' (1$^{21}$); 'Woe unto the wicked!' (3$^{11}$); 'O my people!' (v.$^{12}$); 'Woe unto them!' etc. (5$^{8ff.}$); 'Woe is me!' etc. (6$^{5}$); 'Bind up the testimony!' (8$^{16}$); 'Shall the axe?' etc. (10$^{15}$); 'This people was not!' (23$^{13}$). Nor can the reader of this book help noticing the dialogues and monologues it contains. How lifelike, for instance, are the words 'The voice said, Cry, and he (the person formerly addressed) said, What shall I cry?' followed by the answer of the first speaker, 'All flesh is grass,' etc. (40$^{6}$). The same quality excites our admiration in 'Can a woman forget her sucking child?' etc.; 'Yea, they may forget . . . Behold, I have,' etc. (49$^{15f.}$); or in the question 'Wherefore have we fasted,' etc. (58$^{3}$), etc.; cf. *Stilistik*, pp. 229–231. But the reader of the original text of the OT will recognize much more clearly still that certain portions and even whole books are distinguished from others by a *higher style*. He will observe that many components of the Hebrew vocabulary are used only in certain passages. For instance, there is no occurrence in Gn 1–4$^{22}$ of *he'ĕzîn* 'give ear,' a synonym of *shāmă'* 'hear' which is used in 3$^{8.\ 10f.}$. On the other hand, *he'ĕzîn*, which is translated 'hearken' in 4$^{23}$, recurs in the following additional passages: Ex 15$^{16}$, Nu 23$^{18}$ (one of the Balaam oracles), Dt 1$^{45}$ 32$^{1}$, Jg 5$^{3}$, 2 Ch 24$^{10}$ (perhaps an imitation of Is 64$^{3}$), Neh 9$^{30}$ (in a prayer), Job 9$^{16}$ etc., Ps 5$^{2}$ etc., Pr 17$^{4}$, Is 1$^{2.\ 10}$ 8$^{9}$ 28$^{23}$ 32$^{9}$ 48$^{23}$ 51$^{4}$ 64$^{3}$, Jer 13$^{15}$, Hos 5$^{1}$, Jl 1$^{2}$. The same is the case with the word *'imrā* 'speech,' which likewise does not occur prior to Gn 4$^{23}$, and after that is preferred to its synonym *dābār* only in the following passages: Dt 32$^{2}$ 33$^{9}$, 2 S 22$^{31}$, Ps 12$^{7}$ etc., Pr 30$^{5}$, Is 5$^{24}$ 28$^{23}$ 29$^{4}$ 32$^{9}$, La 2$^{17}$. Consequently, the choice of these two words suffices to bring Gn 4$^{23}$ into connexion with other portions of the OT where the same comparatively rare terms occur (cf. *Stilistik*, pp. 277–283). To take other two illustrations of a similar kind, the dative 'to them' is expressed by the usual *lāhém* in Gn 3$^{21}$ etc., but by *lāmô* in the following passages: Gn 9$^{26b.\ 27b}$, Dt 32$^{32.\ 35}$ 33$^{2}$, Job 3$^{14}$ etc. (10 times), Ps 2$^{4}$ etc. (21 times), Pr 23$^{20}$, Is 16$^{4}$ 23$^{1}$ 26$^{14.\ 16}$ 30$^{5}$ 35$^{8}$ 43$^{8}$ 44$^{7.\ 15}$ 48$^{21}$ 53$^{8}$ (?), La 1$^{19.\ 22}$ 4$^{10.\ 15}$, Hab. 2$^{7}$. Again, 'man' is expressed by *'ādām* from Gn 1$^{26}$ onwards, but *'ĕnôsh* is the term selected in the Song of Moses (Dt 32$^{26}$) as well as in Job 4$^{17}$ etc. (18 times), Ps 8$^{5}$ etc. (12 times), Is 8$^{1}$ 13$^{7.\ 12}$ 24$^{6}$ 33$^{8}$ 51$^{7.\ 12}$ 56$^{2}$, Jer 20$^{10}$, 2 Ch 14$^{10}$; cf. the Aram. *'ĕnāsh* in Ezr 4$^{11}$ 6$^{11}$, Dn 2$^{10}$ etc.

2. The portions of the OT which are characterized by the 'higher' style embrace the two categories of *addresses* and *poems*. This may be noted clearly enough, we think, by comparing the Book of Isaiah and the Psalms with one another. For instance, Is 1$^{2f.}$ reads—

'I have nourished and brought up children,
  and they have rebelled against me.
The ox knoweth his owner,
  and the ass his master's crib:
  but Israel doth not know,
  my people doth not consider.'

Here we find that peculiar construction of clauses to which, so far as the present writer is aware, the name 'parallelismus membrorum' was first given by Robert Lowth in the Fourteenth of his famous *Prælectiones de poesi Hebræorum* (Oxonii, 1753). But this ideal rhythm (explained psychologically and comparatively in *Stilistik*, pp. 307–311) is not met with everywhere in Isaiah. For instance, when we read 'When ye come to appear before me, who hath required this at your hand to tread my courts?' etc. (1$^{12-14}$), it would be precarious here to attribute to the author an aim at *parallelismus membrorum*. As little can any such intention be detected in sentences like 'In that day a man shall cast his idols of silver and his idols of gold, which they made each one for himself to worship, to the moles and to the bats' (2$^{20}$). Such instances occur frequently in the prophetical books; and if these contain also sentences which exhibit the *parallelismus membrorum*, it must be remembered that the higher form of prose, as employed especially by good speakers, was not without a certain kind of rhythm. This is pointed out by no less an authority than Cicero in the words 'Isocrates primus intellexit etiam in soluta oratione, dum versum effugeres, modum tamen et numerum quendam oportere servari' (*Brutus*, viii. 32); and we find a confirmation of his statement when we examine the opening words of his own First Oration against Catiline: 'Quousque, tandem, abutere, Catilina, patientia nostra? Quamdiu etiam furor iste tuus nos eludet? Quem ad finem sese effrenata iactabit audacia?' The word *nābî'*, indeed, means literally 'speaker' (cf. the present writer's *Offenbarungsbegriff des AT*, i. 71–78), and prophecies as such could be co-ordinated with the productions of poets only if *all* prophetical utterances bore upon them the characteristic marks of poetical compositions. But no one would venture to assert this, for instance, of Zec 1–8 or of the Books of Haggai and Malachi. The last-named portions of the OT lack even those elements of the higher diction described above, (1). Further, the author of Ps 74$^{9}$ did not count himself a prophet, for he says expressly of the age in which he lived, 'There is no more any prophet' (see, further, *Stilistik*, p. 318 f.).

A characteristic feature of the OT prophecies is that they begin with a Divine utterance, which they then go on to develop. For instance, the Book of Isaiah contains at the outset God's declaration 'I have nourished and brought up children,' etc. (vv.$^{2b. 3}$), which the prophet as God's interpreter ($30^{2a}$) then illustrates in detail. Note the words '*They* have forsaken *the LORD*,' etc. ($1^{4b}$), and 'Unless the *LORD of Hosts* had left *us*,' etc. (v.$^{9}$). Many similar instances will be found in *Stilistik*, p. 255 f. Another peculiarity of the style of the Prophets is that many of them commence with censure, then speak of the punishment of the impenitent, and close with the announcement of deliverance for the godly. This order is found, for instance, in Am $7^{1}$–$9^{15}$ [on $9^{8-15}$ see Driver, *Joel and Amos*, pp. 119–123], Hos $1^{2}$–$2^{3}$, Is $1^{2}$–$2^{4}$ $2^{5}$–$4^{6}$, Mic $4^{9f. 11-13}$ $5^{1f.}$ etc.

The true relation of the Prophets of Israel to poetry consists, in the opinion of the present writer, in the circumstance that here and there they intersperse their addresses with poetical compositions. Thus in Is $5^{1-6}$ we have a 'song' about the vineyard of Jahweh, and specially frequent are passages which reproduce the rhythm of the lament for the dead (the *ķînā*). This rhythm, which resembles the elegiac measure of the Romans, is heard in such passages as Am $5^{2}$—

'The virgin of Israel is fallen,
she shall no more rise,
She is forsaken upon her land,
there is none to raise her.'

The same rhythm is found also in the Prayer of Hezekiah in Is $38^{10-20}$. Another 'elegy' occurs in Jer $9^{11}$—

'And I will make Jerusalem heaps,
and a den of dragons,
And I will make the cities of Judah desolate,
without an inhabitant.'

And such 'elegies' recur in v.$^{21}$, Ezk $19^{2. 14}$ $26^{17}$ ('How art thou destroyed,' etc.) $27^{3ff. 32}$ $28^{12ff.}$ $32^{2ff. 16. 19ff.}$. See, further, art. POETRY, vol. iv. p. 5.

3. The structure of the other poetical parts of the OT (cf. מַעֲשַׂי 'my works,' *κατ' ἐξ.* Ps $45^{1}$) is not easy to determine. But certain conclusions may be affirmed with confidence, and the first of these is that the rhythm of ancient Hebrew poetry does *not* consist in the alternation of short and long syllables. W. Jones held, indeed (*Poeseos Asiaticæ Commentarii*, London, 1774, cap. ii.), that the poems of the OT exhibit a regular succession of syllables of different quantity, such as we find in Arabic poems. But he was able to prove his point only by altering the punctuation and by allowing the Hebrew poets great freedom in the matter of prosody. The conclusion on this subject reached by the present writer in *Stilistik* (p. 341) is maintained also by Sievers (§ 58): 'Hebrew metre is not quantitative in the same sense as the classical.' Hence it is now admitted in all the more recent literature on Hebrew poetry, that the rhythm of the latter is based upon the alternation of unaccented and accented syllables. Still there are various *nuances* to be observed in the views held by those who have investigated this subject. G. Bickell (*Metrices Biblicæ Regulæ*, etc., 1879, etc.) holds that 'the metrical accent falls regularly upon every second syllable.' But, in order to make this law apply to the Psalms, he has either removed or added some 2600 vowel syllables and proposed some 3811 changes, as is pointed out by J. Ecker in his brochure, 'Professor G. Bickell's *Carmina Veteris Testamenti metrice* das neueste Denkmal auf dem Kirchhof der hebräischen Metrik' (1883). Nevertheless, Bickell has adhered to his principle, and gives us his transcription, for instance, of Job $32^{6}$ thus—

'Ẓa'ír 'aní leyámim
W'attém sabím yeshíshim
Al-kén zaḥált wa'ira'
Meḥávvoth dé'i 'éthkhem.

That is to say, he makes Elihu speak in Iambic Tetrameter Catalectic. But, in order to reach this result, he introduces in v.$^{aβ}$ the superfluous word *sābîm* 'grey-headed,' while in v.$^{bα}$ he robs *zaḥaltî* of its ending *-î*, which in Hebrew is the characteristic of the 1st person singular. In spite of such objections, Duhm in his Commentary on Job (*Kurzer Hdcom.* 1897, p. 17) accepted without reservation Bickell's theory of the rhythm of ancient Hebrew poetry. Afterwards, however, he rightly abandoned it (in his Commentary on the Psalms in the same series, 1899, Einleit. § 24). The falsity of Bickell's view is demonstrated by the present writer in *Stilistik* (p. 339 f.), and in like manner Sievers (§ 55) declares, 'I can take no further account of Bickell's system.'—A preferable view of the rhythmical character of OT poetry is that which is represented especially by J. Ley. According to this theory, the ancient Hebrew poets paid regard only to the accented syllables (cf., on this point, *Stilistik*, pp. 330–336). But even the advocates of this view are divided into two schools. The majority (*e.g.* Duhm, *Psalmen*, 1899, p. xxx) hold that the Hebrew poets aimed at an equal number of 'rises' in the corresponding lines. To this group belongs also Sievers (cf. §§ 52 and 88 of his *Metrische Studien*, 1901, Bd. i.). But Budde and still more the present writer have come to the conclusion that a Hebrew poet aimed at nothing more than the *essential symmetry* of the lines that answer to one another in his poem. This may be observed, for instance, in the following four passages: 'Be instructed, ye judges of the earth' (Ps $2^{10b}$), 'and rejoice with trembling' (v.$^{11b}$), 'and ye perish from the way' (v.$^{12b}$), and 'blessed are all they that put their trust in him' (v.$^{12d}$). Our conclusion is confirmed also by the poetical compositions which are sung by the inhabitants of Palestine at the present day (see *Stilistik*, pp. 337, 343). Cornill (*Die metrischen Stücke des Buches Jeremia*, 1901, p. viii) supports the same view, so far at least as the Book of Jeremiah is concerned: 'For Jeremiah an exact correspondence of the various *stichoi* was not a formal principle of his metrical system.' Duhm, it is true, in his Commentary on Jeremiah (*Kurzer Hdcom.* 1901) remarks on $2^{2b}$: 'In all Jeremiah's poetical compositions the *stichoi* contain three and two "rises" alternately.' But, to make good his theory, he has to deny to Jeremiah a passage like $2^{4-13}$ because 'the metre of Jeremiah is wanting' in it. Such a conclusion, however, would be valid only if he were able to adduce other, independent, reasons for the excision of this passage. He urges, indeed, that v.$^{4}$ contains a fresh notice of the Divine commission to Jeremiah. But this is nothing strange; such notes occur very frequently in Jeremiah and the later Prophets (see the passages in *Stilistik*, p. 174). Moreover, vv.$^{29-37}$ of the same chapter are allowed by Duhm himself to be Jeremiah's, and yet v.$^{29f.}$ is followed by a fresh call, 'O generation, see ye the word of the LORD,' quite in the manner in which v.$^{4}$ follows upon v.$^{2f.}$ Further, Duhm thinks himself entitled to deny $2^{4-13}$ to Jeremiah because the people of the LORD are addressed in v.$^{4}$ as 'house of Jacob,' a designation which Duhm believes to be unused except by later writers. But 'house of Jacob' occurs also in Is $2^{3}$ and $8^{17}$, both of which passages are regarded by Duhm himself (in Nowack's *Hdkom.*) as Isaianic; and the same expression is found in Am $3^{13}$ and Mic $2^{7}$ $3^{9}$, passages which cannot be attributed to 'later writers.' Finally, Duhm's view of Jer $2^{4-13}$ raises the difficulty that Israel is treated in v.$^{2f.}$ as a feminine, but in v.$^{14}$ as a masculine, subject. But, if v.$^{14}$ is the sequel of v.$^{13}$, Israel is naturally treated as masculine, because it has just been designated in v.$^{13}$ by the masculine word *'am* 'people.' In any case, it may be added, the supposed interpolator of vv.$^{4-13}$ knew nothing of the metrical system which Duhm attributes to Jeremiah, else he would have accommodated the form of these verses to their surroundings. Hence the present writer is unable to accept Duhm's view as to 'the metre of Jeremiah,' quite apart from the fact that, according to our foregoing contention (see above, (2)), Jeremiah was not a poet.

4. Some interesting features of style occur sporadically in various parts of the OT.—(*a*) There are **alphabetical acrostics.** The present writer cannot, indeed, admit that Nah $1^{2-10}$ belongs to this category [but see art. NAHUM in vol. iii. p. 475], which, however, probably includes Ps 9 f., and certainly Ps 25. 34. 37. 111 f. 119. 145, Pr $31^{10-31}$, La 1–4, and Sir $51^{13-29}$, as is shown by the recently discovered Heb. text (cf., further, *Stilistik*, pp. 357–359). There is another species of acrostic which we do not believe to be found in the OT. The letters, for instance, with which the lines of Ps $110^{1b-4}$ commence are not intended to point to שמען, as the name of Simon the Maccabee, who reigned B.C. 142–135. That such is the case is represented, indeed, by Duhm (*Kurzer Hdcom.* 1899, *ad loc.*) as unquestionable. But, in the first place, it is surely awkward that the alleged acrostic should include only part of the poem. Secondly, as has been shown by Gaster (*Academy*, 19th May 1892), the name *Shim'on* is written upon the coins (where the vowel letters are relatively rare) 40 times with and only once without the ו. Yet the latter is the way in which, upon Duhm's theory, it would be written in Ps 110. Once more, the clause 'until I make thine enemies thy footstool' (v.$^{1b}$) would be in glaring opposition to the statement of 1 Mac $14^{41}$ that Simon was to hold office 'until a trustworthy prophet should arise.' The former (Ps $110^{1b}$) promises the highest degree of triumph for the king who is there addressed, the latter (1 Mac $14^{41}$) reminds Simon that his choice to be prince was subject to recall.—(*b*) Other poetical compositions in the OT are marked by frequent use of the figure *Anadiplosis* described above (iii. (5)). Such is the case with the fifteen psalms (120–134). For instance, the 'dwell' of 'that I dwell in the tents of Kedar' (Ps $120^{5b}$) is taken up again in the 'dwell' of 'my soul hath long dwelt with him' (v.$^{6a}$). Again, the two lines 'that hateth peace' (v.$^{6b}$) and 'I am for peace' (v.$^{7a}$) have a connecting link in the word 'peace.' The same characteristic is still more marked in Ps 121, as may be seen from the clauses 'From whence shall my help come?' (v.$^{1b}$) and 'My help cometh from the LORD' (v.$^{2a}$). The familiar title of these fifteen psalms 'Songs of *Degrees*' (AV; RV 'Songs of *Ascents*') has reference, in the opinion of the present writer, to their rhythmical peculiarity as well as to their destination to be sung by the caravans of pilgrims journeying to Jerusalem (cf. *Stilistik*, pp. 302–304).—(*c*) **Rhyme** is found in the poetry of the OT only in the same sporadic fashion as in the plays of Shakespeare (where, *e.g.*, 'rise' rhymes with 'eyes' at the close of *Hamlet*, Act I., Scene ii., or 'me' with 'see' in Act III., at the end of Ophelia's speech). Rhyme of this kind may be observed in the very earliest poetical passage of the OT, namely Gn $4^{23f.}$, where *ḳôlî* 'my voice' rhymes with *'imrâthî* 'my speech.' But such rhymes, which could not readily be avoided in Hebrew, are not found at the end of *every* line of an OT poem. H. Grimme claims, indeed (in an article entitled 'Durchgereimte Gedichte im AT' in Bardenhewer's *Biblische Studien*, Bd. vi. 1901), to have discovered poems of this kind in Ps 45. 54 and Sir $44^{1-14}$. But our suspicions are awakened at the very outset by the circumstance that the poet does not exercise his rhyming skill at the opening of his composition (Ps $45^{2}$). Grimme offers, it is true, a scansion of the verse, marking it as he does with the sign of *arsis*, but he cannot point to the presence of rhyme in it. Further, with reference to the following lines, are we to hold that the poet considered an identity of final *consonants* (as in *'oznēkh* and *'ābîkh* of v.$^{11ab}$) to amount to rhyme, although the standing and correct conception of the latter demands an assonance of the preceding *vowel*, such as is heard even in the *rime suffisante* (*e.g.* in 'soupir' and 'désir') of the French? Again, Grimme, in order to establish a rhyme between the end of v.$^{3b}$ and v.$^{4b}$, drops in v.$^{3b}$ the closing word (*lĕ'ôlām*) of the MT, and alters the preceding words. In like manner he transposes the words in v.$^{4a}$, and again drops two words in v.$^{10b}$. Lastly, all the rhymes which Grimme discovers in Ps 45 consist simply of the assonance of the pronominal suffix *-kh*, and he increases the number by making the masculine form for 'thy,' namely *-khā*, the same as the feminine form, namely *-kh*. Thus instead of the MT *hădārékhā* (v.$^{3(4)b}$), 'thy majesty,' he would pronounce *hădārăekh*, a course of procedure which is shown to be wrong by R. Kittel in his treatise *Ueber die Notwendigkeit und Möglichkeit einer neuen Ausgabe der hebräischen Bibel* (1901), §§ 62–68. The weakest point in Grimme's contention is found in the circumstance that the rhymes he discovers depend upon an assonance of a series of pronouns, which could not be avoided in Hebrew. Why should not the composer of Ps 45 have placed at the end of v.$^{4b}$ a word to rhyme with the final *lĕ'ôlām* of v.$^{3b}$? At all events, the tradition which allowed *lĕ'ôlām* to stand at the end of v.$^{3}$, knew nothing of any intention on the part of the author of Ps 45 to provide all the lines of his poem with rhymes. Grimme's attempt to demonstrate the presence of rhyme in Ps 54 and Sir $44^{1-14}$ must equally be pronounced a failure (see the present writer's brochure, *Neueste Prinzipien der alttest. Kritik geprüft*, 1902, p. 24).

5. The last feature we wish to notice as discoverable in the stylistic structure of the OT is the construction of **strophes.** Those scholars who at present are disposed to co-ordinate the prophecies and the poems of the OT, speak of strophes also in the Book of Isaiah, discovering them, for instance, in $2^{6-11}$ vv.$^{12-17}$ and vv.$^{18-21}$. But even an orator may unfold his subject in sections of nearly equal length, and may conclude each of these with the same sentence, the so-called *Epiphora* (see above, iii. (5*dβ*)). Lately, the opening of the Book of Amos has been a favourite field for attempts to discover a strophic structure. The earlier attempts are examined in *Stilistik*, pp. 347–352, and Sievers (i. § 103) agrees with the judgment expressed there by the present writer. But a renewed effort of the same kind has been made by Löhr in his *Untersuchungen zum Buche Amos*, 1901. He proposes to regard the four prophecies against Damascus, Gaza, Ammon, and Moab ($1^{3-5}$ vv.$^{6-8}$ vv.$^{13-15}$ $2^{1-3}$) as four strophes, each consisting of 4+2+4 *stichoi*. But, in order to make out this uniformity, he is compelled in $1^{3}$ to reckon the object 'Gilead' as the fourth *stichos*. Similarly, in $2^{1}$ the fourth *stichos* has to be made up simply of *lassîd* ('into lime'). Short parts of sentences have thus to be counted as whole lines, although in the corresponding passage of the prophecy against Ammon ($1^{13-15}$) a whole clause ('that they might enlarge their border,' v.$^{13b\beta}$) is found, which Löhr himself takes as the fourth *stichos* of the 'strophe' $1^{13-15}$. The creating of *stichoi* in such a fashion, in order to form strophes, appears to the present writer to be an artificial procedure, the responsibility for which belongs, not to the

prophet Amos but to modern upholders of the theory that the Prophets of Israel meant to employ 'strophes.' Our view of the matter is that also of Cornill in the *Theol. Rundschau* (1901, p. 414 f.). Sievers (*Metrische Untersuchungen*, ii. p. 473) gives up the attempt to establish an exact equality between corresponding lines, for, according to him, $1^{3b}$ ('because they have threshed,' etc.) contains four feet, while v.$^{6b}$ has five, v.$^{13b}$ six, and $2^{1b}$ seven.—In the real poems of the OT there are not a few traces of an aim at a strophic structure. The latter cannot be denied, for instance, to the author of Ps 2, who evidently meant to exhaust his subject in four sets of three verses each. Such an aim was connected also with the construction of alphabetical acrostics (see above, (4)). What, for instance, are the twenty-two groups of eight verses each of which Ps 119 is made up, but strophes? Such divisions of a poem are at times indicated even externally. We have an instance of this in the occurrence of quite similar clauses, 'Surely every man at his best estate is wholly vanity' and 'Surely every man is vanity,' in Ps $39^{5b}$ and v.$^{11b}$. In $42^{5.11}$ $43^{5}$, again, we have the thrice repeated 'Why art thou cast down, O my soul, and why art thou disquieted within me?' and there are a good many similar 'refrains' in the Psalter (cf. $46^{7.11}$ $49^{12.20}$ $57^{5.11}$ $136^{1b.2b}$ etc., see *Stilistik*, p. 346 f.).

v. CONCLUSION.—1. In so far as the stylistic differences between Biblical writings depend upon the choice of words, the style is not without significance for the purposes of *literary criticism.* This is proved in the present writer's *Einleit. ins AT*, pp. 147–151, and its truth reaffirmed, in reply to recent doubts expressed by W. H. Cobb, and defended, with fresh materials, in the *Expository Times*, xiii. (1901) p. 134. For instance, the relative pronoun is expressed by אֲשֶׁר in Is $1^{1.29ab.30a}$ $2^{1.8b.20b}$ $5^{5a.28a}$, but זוּ is not met with till $40^{24}$ and $43^{21}$. Again, the negative לֹא may be counted at least sixteen times in Is 1–6. Yet how easily we might have had at least one occurrence of בַּל, the word used in $40^{24}$ $43^{27}$ $44^{8ff.}$. Now, these and other words selected in chs. 40 ff. belong to the vocabulary of the 'higher' style of the Hebrews, and it is a fact that in chs. 1 ff. Isaiah cultivates the most elegant mode of writing. Why should he, then, have avoided in these chapters all those elements of the higher style for which a preference is shown in chs. 40 ff.? Such conduct would be all the more incomprehensible, seeing that the most of the linguistic peculiarities which mark Is 40 ff. concern expressions which, on account of their frequency, are employed without deliberate choice and almost without consciousness.—But a number of the more recent expounders of the OT have thought to discover a critical touchstone also in features of Biblical style which do not depend upon the choice of words. Duhm, for instance, says in his Commentary on Isaiah in Nowack's *Hdkom.* p. 30: 'The fate of the unknown city is depicted in $3^{25f.}$ in too elegiac a strain to allow of our assigning these verses to Isaiah.' He has in view the words 'Thy men shall fall by the sword, and thy mighty in the war,' etc. But to say that this is 'in too elegiac a strain' is simply a subjective opinion, whose correctness is not proved by Duhm, and cannot be proved. For the strongest expressions of grief over the catastrophes that overhang Israel are given utterance to by Isaiah in other passages, such as $1^{5-9}$ and $6^{11-13}$, which are allowed by Duhm himself to be genuinely Isaianic. A number of similar critical judgments, which have been built in recent times upon the mannerisms of style in certain portions of the OT, are examined in the present writer's brochure, *Neueste Prinzipien der alttest. Kritik geprüft*, 1902, pp. 13–19.

2. The differences in style between various books of Scripture have a special significance from the point of view of the *history of religion.* It is a weighty circumstance that Nathan's prophecy, which is found in 2 S $7^{11b-16}$, is reproduced somewhat differently in 1 Ch $17^{10b-15}$, and that the oracle of Is $2^{2-4}$ has another form in Mic $4^{1-3}$. From this we gather that the Israelites of earlier times cared for nothing more than to preserve the contents of revelation in their essential identity. The form was of importance only in so far as it served for the preservation of the contents, and thus, even with the Prophets, the form was the human element. God permitted His interpreters to make use of the language of their own time. If this statement required proof, it would be found in such facts as the following. In the prophetical writings the two forms for the pronoun 'I,' namely *'ānōkhî* and *'ănî*, stand to one another in the following ratios: —in Amos as 10 : 1, in Hosea as 11 : 11, in Micah as 1 : 2, in Jeremiah as 35 : 51, in Ezekiel as 1 ($36^{28}$) : 138, in Daniel as 1 ($10^{11}$) : 23, in Haggai as 0 : 4, in Zec 1–8 as 0 : 9, in Malachi as 1 : 8. Then in the historical books, Samuel has 48 *'ānōkhî* to 50 *'ănî*, Kings 9 to 45, Ezra 0 to 2, Nehemiah 1 to 15, Chronicles 1 (1 Ch $17^{1}$ ∥ 2 S $7^{2}$) to 30, Esther 0 to 6. A number of other evidences will be found in the present writer's article 'Prophecy and History' in the *Expository Times*, xi. (1900) pp. 305–310. The above assertion that the form of the language is the human element in the Bible, is subject only to the reservation that the contents of a prophecy were naturally not without influence upon its form, and this was the case also with the spirit which animated the prophets (Mic $3^{8}$, Is $8^{11}$ etc.). But we are convinced that there is still another point to be observed. When, for instance, we read 'They pierced my hands and my feet' (Ps $22^{16}$), the present writer cannot believe this sentence to have been written without the co-operation of the Divine Spirit, who was the supreme director of Israel's history. Such expressions were meant to pre-establish a harmony between the Old and the New Covenant, so that believers who lived under the new dispensation might be strengthened in their faith by noticing the presence of such features in the earlier history of God's saving purpose.

LITERATURE.—In addition to the works mentioned in the introductory part of the above article, the present writer's *Stilistik, Rhetorik, Poetik, in Bezug auf die Biblische Litteratur komparativisch dargestellt* (1900) may be consulted throughout. For special points, reference may be made to Karl J. Grimm's *Euphemistic Liturgical Appendices in the OT* (1901), pp. 3–5, and Ed. Sievers' *Metrische Untersuchungen*, 2 vols. (1901).

ED. KÖNIG.

## SYMBOL, SYMBOLICAL ACTIONS.—

i. Distinction between Metaphor and Symbol.
ii. Symbols in Scripture.
iii. Symbolical actions: (A) in common life; (B) in the religious life: (*a*) constant or usual actions; (*b*) unusual actions. The symbolical actions in the prophetical literature.

i. DISTINCTION BETWEEN METAPHOR AND SYMBOL.—Both these terms stand for something which is not used in its barest literal sense or for its proper purpose. Both describe methods which are employed to give concrete expression to ideas belonging to the realm of spirit. But what the *Metaphor* is in the sphere of speech, that the *Symbol* is in the sphere of things. 'Metaphorical' applies to expressions, 'symbolical' is an attribute of objects and actions. How closely allied the two conceptions are is shown by the fact that in familiar speech the terms are occasionally interchanged. For instance, we recently met with this sentence: 'If the ordinary man is to fulfil the command to love God above everything, the word "love" must be understood merely as a symbolical [*sinnbildlich*] designation for two dispositions of mind for which there is no more fitting expression' (*Die Grenzboten*, 1900, p. 447). The correct term here would be 'metaphorical,' not 'symbolical.'

The varieties of Metaphor which occur in Biblical literature are enumerated and explained in the present writer's *Stilistik, Rhetorik, Poetik, in Bezug auf die Biblische Litteratur komparativisch dargestellt* (1900). But the notions of 'Symbol' or 'symbolical' could not be handled there, because they have not to do with a sphere in which language is the agency at work. Hence the explanation there given (pp. 93–109) of Metaphor and the present article will be found to supplement one another.

ii. SYMBOLS IN SCRIPTURE.—The extent to which symbolism pervades the Biblical literature is a doubtful question. The following may be regarded as the surest instances :—

(*a*) The word *'ăshēra*, which had all along, in the sense of 'gracious,' been an attribute of 'Astarte, and hence appears also as a personal name for her (1 K 15$^{13}$ [=2 Ch 15$^{16}$] 18$^{19}$, 2 K 21$^{7}$ 23$^{4.7}$), came in later times to be used mainly as the name for the symbol of this goddess, namely a tree, in allusion to the fruitfulness of the life of nature (Ex 34$^{13}$, Dt 7$^{5}$ etc., 2 Ch 34$^{7}$).—Further, the *hammānîm* (Lv 26$^{30}$, Is 17$^{8}$ 27$^{9}$, Ezk 6$^{4.6}$, 2 Ch 14$^{5}$ 34$^{4.7}$ *et al.*) were miniature obelisks, which represented the sun's rays. They were symbols of the sun-god who in Phœn. inscriptions is called בעל חמן or בעל חמנן, and the like (cf. Bloch, *Phön. Glossar*, p. 22).—The *maẓẓēbôth*, again ('pillars,' Gn 28$^{18}$ etc.), were not set up on their own account. They were not meant to be dwelling-places of the Deity, but were symbols, expressive of gratitude for a Divine revelation (Gn 28$^{22}$ 31$^{13}$ etc.); primitive altars (cf. Ex 20$^{25}$, Is 19$^{19}$); allusions to the rock (*Ẓûr*), which formed the surest ground of trust for Israel (Dt 32$^{4.15.18}$ etc.; *Stilistik*, p. 99$_{32-34}$); or they were symbols of the twelve tribes of Israel (Ex 24$^{4}$, cf. 1 K 18$^{31}$).

(*b*) It is equally unmistakable that the visible dwelling-place of God, *i.e.* the Tabernacle and the Temple, was a symbol of His invisible dwelling-place. In point of fact, the Holy Place and the Holy of Holies correspond respectively to the heavens and the highest heaven (שְׁמֵי הַשָּׁמַיִם 1 K 8$^{27}$ etc.), while the forecourt was the analogue of the earth, which, according to Is 66$^{1}$, is God's footstool. Josephus was quite right, then, when he said long ago that the subdivision of the sanctuary was an imitation of the constitution of the universe (*Ant.* III. vi. 4: πρὸς μίμησιν τῆς τῶν ὅλων φύσεως). The same notion is favoured by He 9$^{24}$ οὐ γὰρ εἰς . . . ἀντίτυπα . . . ἀλλ' εἰς αὐτὸν τὸν οὐρανόν. Hengstenberg contended that the OT sanctuary was to be viewed as symbolizing the pre-Christian stage of the Kingdom of God (*Authentie des Pent.* ii. 628 ff.). But in that case the arrangement of the sanctuary of the religion of Israel would have pointed to the imperfection of that religion; and the view that this arrangement was chosen in order to express the truth that the OT religion was imperfect, is unnatural. Still less conceivable is the notion (Schegg, *Bibl. Arch.* 1887, p. 418) that 'the sacred tent typified the Christian Church.'

(*c*) A symbolical meaning of *numbers* cannot be certainly demonstrated for the OT. This question has already been so exhaustively discussed in art. NUMBER in vol. iii., that only a very little needs to be added here.—The circumstance that the sanctuary was divided into three parts, has just been explained. It was not, then, on account of the number 'three' that this arrangement was adopted. That number was not a symbol of the Deity (Schegg, *l.c.* 420) at the OT stage of religion. As little is a symbolical meaning of the number 'four' evident in the construction of the Sanctuary. Nor was the number 'ten' meant to express the idea of 'perfection' (Schegg, *l.c.* 419), as one may see from the fact that the Holy of Holies in Solomon's temple formed a cube of 20 cubits (1 K 6$^{3}$).

(*d*) With somewhat more foundation it may be contended that the *colours* selected for the adornment of the OT sanctuary had a symbolical meaning. Why, for instance, does blue- or violet-purple (*tĕkheleth*) occupy the first place among the four colours of the curtains of the sanctuary (Ex 26$^{1}$)? Without doubt, because it was meant to allude to the unclouded sky and thus to God. But, to take another instance, it appears to the present writer doubtful whether the red-purple (*'argāmān*) 'recalls the God of judgment,' as was suggested by Franz Delitzsch in his interesting work, *Iris: Studies in Colour and Talks about Flowers*, 1888, p. 55. On the other hand, the white colour which we note in the high priest's dress (Ex 28$^{5b}$ etc., Rev 4$^{4}$), and in the horses, etc., of Zec 6$^{3a}$ and Rev 6$^{2}$ 19$^{11}$ (cf. 14$^{14}$), is as certainly a symbolical expression of purity, salvation, and victory as black (Zec 6$^{2a}$, Rev 6$^{5.12}$) is a symbol of death.

(*e*) It may be added that the forms of the CHERUBIM in the Tabernacle (Ex 25$^{18}$ etc., 26$^{1.31}$) and the Temple (1 K 6$^{23.32.35}$, Ezk 41$^{18}$) were symbols of the presence of God (cf. Ps 18$^{11}$). Again, what but God's dominion over nature can have been meant to be represented by the carved *palms and flowers* (1 K 6$^{32.35}$ 7$^{36}$, 2 Ch 3$^{7}$)? As to the *lions*, finally, which were to be seen on various pieces of the furniture of the Temple (1 K 7$^{29.36}$) and on the throne of Solomon (10$^{20}$), were these not symbols of the power exercised by the heavenly or the earthly king of Israel? This symbolical significance of the lion shows itself also in the description of the Cherubim (Ezk 1$^{10}$ 10$^{20}$) and the four apocalyptic creatures (Rev 4$^{7}$); and in the same passages we find the *ox*, the *eagle*, and the *man* as symbols of strength, swiftness, and reason.

iii. SYMBOLICAL ACTIONS.—While it is a debateable question how far the realm of Symbol extends in the Biblical literature, the sphere of *symbolical actions* is defined with almost complete precision. For it is easy, in the case of each particular action, to perceive whether it is performed for its own sake or *in order to express an idea.* But what is the best classification for the wide department of symbolical actions? Perhaps as suitable a course as any will be to distinguish symbolical actions (A) of common life and (B) of religious life. The latter class will then be subdivided again into ordinary and extraordinary actions.

A. *SYMBOLICAL ACTIONS IN COMMON LIFE.*—(*a*) The very *beginning* of life was connected with a symbolical transaction. The newborn child used to be placed on the knees of the father, not merely to be caressed by him (Is 66$^{12b}$), but also to be acknowledged as his offspring. This is the most probable meaning of Job's question, 'Why did the knees receive me?' (Job 3$^{12a}$). For in the two *stichoi* of v.$^{12}$ it is most natural to find a reference to the action respectively of the father and the mother, and the placing of the newborn child on the knees of the father is encountered also outside Israel as a recognition of the child by the father (cf. *Il.* ix. 455, etc., and Lat. *tollere*). It is essentially the same act that is referred to when in the MT of Gn 50$^{23b}$ it is said that great-grandsons of Joseph were 'born upon his knees.' The expression עַל־בִּרְכֵּי answers to the question Whither?, and the meaning is that great-grandsons of Joseph were brought after their birth to the supreme head of the family that they might be recognized by him as new members of it. It is quite natural that this statement should have come in later times to be regarded as incredible.

Hence in the Samaritan Pentateuch we find the reading בִּימֵי 'in the days of' substituted. But if this had been the original text, as is assumed in Kautzsch's translation of the OT, and by Holzinger in the *Kurzer Hdcom.* (*ad loc.*), it is unintelligible how such a strange reading as the other should have arisen. And how does the גַּם 'also' witness against the reading of the MT, as Holzinger contends? This conjunction really couples the two facts that Joseph lived to see grandsons not only in the line of Ephraim, but also in that of Manasseh. Holzinger further argues that, supposing the statement in Gn $50^{23b}$ refers to adoption, Joseph may have adopted Machir but cannot have adopted his sons. 'Machir certainly gained the same standing as Manasseh, but his sons did not.' But is it really established as a necessary conclusion that the narratives found in the patriarchal history simply reflect the later history of the tribes of Israel? Is it not rather possible that the story of Gn $50^{23b}$ contains an argument against the correctness of this recent theory?—Further, adoption on the part of the mother is clearly expressed in the words attributed to Rachel in Gn $30^{3b}$ 'And she (Bilhah) shall bear upon my knees, and so shall I come into possession of a family from her.'

(*b*) Not only the beginning of life but also *new steps* in life were marked by symbolical transactions. A woman captured in war, who is chosen by an Israelite to be his wife, 'is to shave her head and pare her nails' (Dt $21^{12}$). In this way she is to indicate that her former state of mourning has ceased, and 'that she is about to begin life again under new auspices' (Driver, *Deut. ad loc.*). It is not possible to discover in either of the two actions 'expressions of grief,' as is done by Bertholet (*Kurzer Hdcom. ad loc.*). On the one hand, this interpretation is not required on the ground of $14^{1}$. For in the last-named passage and in Jer $16^{6}$ and Ezk $7^{18}$ it is not the simple shaving off of the hair (Dt $21^{12}$) that is forbidden, but 'the making of a baldness between the eyes, *i.e.* on the forehead.' On the other hand, Bertholet's view of Dt $21^{12b}$ is reduced to an impossibility in view of v.$^{13a}$. For it is added there that the woman in question is also to put off 'the raiment of her captivity,' which is quite a different thing from 'to strip herself naked like a mourner' (Bertholet). Consequently the three actions described in Dt $21^{12b. 13a}$ are really meant to illustrate the fact that a happy change has taken place in the woman's life. It is true that she is still to be allowed a month's time to bewail her parents. But during this she is not to return to her previous absolute mourning. This is proved beyond question by the laying aside of her captive garb (v.$^{13a}$). The intention rather is merely that during the month specified she may have time to reconcile herself to the transition from the old to the new condition of things. Thus her situation during this month is a mingling of grief and joy.—A happy advance in life was very clearly expressed by the 'breaking of the yoke,' a symbolical action introduced in Jer $28^{10}$; cf. Is $58^{6}$, Ezk $30^{18}$, Nah $1^{13}$.

(*c*) Symbolical actions which denote a *disturbance* of one's life or its *end.*—The border of the garments, especially over the breast, is rent: *e.g.* Gn $37^{29. 34}$ $44^{13}$, Nu $14^{6}$, Jos $7^{6}$, 1 S $4^{12}$, 2 S $1^{2}$ $3^{31}$ $13^{31}$ $15^{32}$, 2 K $2^{12}$ (לִשְׁנַיִם קְרָעִים) $5^{8}$ $11^{14}$ $18^{37}$ $22^{19}$, Is $36^{22}$ $37^{1}$, Jer $36^{23f.}$ $41^{5}$, Jl $2^{13}$, Job $1^{20}$ $2^{12}$, Est $4^{1}$, Ezr $9^{3. 5}$, 2 Ch $23^{13}$ $34^{27}$, 1 Mac $2^{14}$ $3^{47}$ $4^{39}$ $5^{14}$ $11^{71}$ $13^{45}$, Mt $26^{65}$, Mk $14^{63}$, Ac $14^{14}$ (Barnabas and Paul), Jos. *BJ* II. xv. 4 (*γυμνοὺς τὰ* **στέρνα** *τῶν ἐσθήτων περιερρηγμένων*). Further, one puts on sackcloth, a primitive article of dress, in order to show that one is giving up every convenience and every ornament: *e.g.* Gn $37^{34}$, 2 S $3^{31}$ $14^{2}$ $19^{24}$ $21^{10}$, 1 K $21^{27}$, 2 K $6^{30}$, Is $3^{24}$ $15^{3}$ $20^{2}$ $22^{12}$ $50^{3}$ $58^{5}$, Jer $4^{8}$ $6^{26}$ $49^{3}$, Ezk $7^{18}$, Jl $1^{8}$, Am $8^{10}$, Jon $3^{5-8}$, Ps $30^{12}$ $35^{13}$ $69^{12}$, Job $16^{15}$, La $2^{10}$, Est $4^{1f. 3}$, Dn $9^{3}$, 1 Mac $2^{14}$ (*περιεβάλοντο σάκκους*), Mt $11^{21}$ (cf. $3^{4}$), Lk $10^{13}$, Rev $11^{3}$ (cf. $6^{12}$ *σάκκος τρίχινος*).* One goes barefooted (2 S $15^{30}$, cf. Is $20^{2}$) and without turban (Ezk $24^{17a}$), or neglects washing oneself (2 S $12^{20}$). Ashes are sprinkled upon the head: 2 S $13^{19}$, Is $58^{5}$, Est $4^{3}$, Jos. *BJ* II. xv. 4 (*τῆς κεφαλῆς κόνιν*); cf. G. Jacob (*Altarab. Parallelen*, p. 15, where it is shown how the pre-Islamite Arabs were also wont to sprinkle ashes upon the head in token of great grief); or one simply sits in the ashes: Jer $6^{26}$, Ezk $27^{30}$ $28^{18}$, Jon $3^{6}$, Job $2^{8}$ (cf. La $3^{16}$). In this way one clothed himself as it were with ashes (Est $4^{1}$, cf. Dn $9^{3}$, Is $61^{3}$), and thus proclaimed in a visible fashion that he was indifferent to the joy of life. Or, again, the hand might be laid upon the head (2 S $13^{19}$, Jer $2^{37}$), to express the fact that the soul was bowed down by a heavy sorrow. One covered the head (2 S $15^{30}$, Jer $14^{3b}$, Est $6^{12}$), or at least the beard (Lv $13^{45}$, Mic $3^{7a}$, Ezk $24^{17b. 22}$, cf. 2 S $19^{24}$ †) and thereby the mouth, in order to mark oneself as a person who could neither see nor speak for grief. Perhaps the smiting of the thigh or the breast (Jer $31^{19}$, Ezk $21^{17b}$, Lk $18^{13}$) were also meant to express mental suffering.

(*d*) A special group of symbolical actions expresses the *establishing of a relation* between persons. This is above all symbolized by the *giving of the hand*: 2 K $10^{15}$ ('give me thine hand then'), Ezr $10^{19a}$ ('and they gave their hand'), Jer $50^{15a}$, Ezk $17^{18b}$, La $5^{6a}$, 2 Ch $30^{8b}$, Pr $6^{1}$ $11^{15}$ $17^{18}$ $22^{26}$. In 1 Ch $29^{24}$ the giving of the hand by the vanquished is the sign of submission, and thus a pendant to the placing of the conqueror's feet upon his neck (Jos $10^{24b}$). An alliance is likewise cemented by the one party *laying hold of the right hand* of the other: Is $41^{13}$ $45^{1}$, Ps $73^{23}$ (cf. $80^{18}$).—The concluding of an agreement was also symbolized by *a common meal* (Gn $26^{30}$ $31^{54}$, Ex $24^{11b}$, 2 S $3^{20}$), and it is very natural to find that on such an occasion not only bread (Jos $9^{14a}$, cf. v.$^{5b}$) but, above all, salt was eaten. For salt serves to keep other articles from putrefaction and consequent destruction, and might thus fittingly point to the security of the agreement. The same is still the practice among the modern Arabs (d'Arvieux, *Merkwürdige Nachrichten von einer Reise*, etc., Bd. iii. p. 164 f.), and hence the OT speaks of the 'salt of the covenant' (Lv $2^{13}$) and of 'a covenant of salt' (Nu $18^{19}$, 2 Ch $13^{5b}$).—The establishing of a connexion with a property is indicated by a man casting one of his shoes upon it (Ps $60^{10a}$ ‖ $108^{10a}$. See art. SHOE in vol. iv.). This is based upon the fact that walking upon a piece of ground is a sign of proprietorship. We may recall the Roman custom of bringing before the prætor a clod of earth from the field which one claimed as his property.—A certain relation was established also when Elijah the prophet cast his mantle upon Elisha (1 K $19^{19b}$). A special meaning may be discovered in this act, namely, the investiture with the prophetic mantle (2 K $2^{13}$, cf. Is $20^{2}$). So the covering of a woman with one's mantle (Ezk $16^{8}$, Ru $3^{9}$) expresses the intention of becoming her protector *par excellence*, *i.e.* of marrying her. This is the interpretation already given to Ru $3^{9}$ in the Targum ('and let thy name be named [cf. Is $4^{1}$] over thy handmaid, to take me to be thy wife'), and by Rashi (*ad loc.*: 'this is an expression for marrying' [לשון נישואין]); and 'thy wing' here does not mean 'thy protecting arm,' as M. Peritz (*Zwei alte arab. Uebersetzungen des Buches Rûth*, 1900, p. 37) holds. The correct view of Ezk $16^{8}$ and Ru $3^{9}$ is confirmed by

* Perhaps the *rending of the garments* and the *putting on of sackcloth* should be regarded as the earlier and the later form, respectively, of the same announcement of mourning (so M. Jastrow; cf. *Expos. Times*, 1901, p. 337 f.).

Arab custom. 'The son who, in the heathen period of Arab history, took over the widow of his father, threw his garment over her. So, too, Mohammed cast his mantle over the Jewess Safîja, captured at Khaibar, as a token that he desired to have her in marriage' (G. Jacob, *l.c.* p. 23, where other instances of the same thing will be found). Other actions whereby the conclusion of the marriage bond was symbolized, are not mentioned in the OT, unless we are to reckon among these the loading of Rebekah as Isaac's bride with presents (Gn $24^{53a}$), and Isaac's conducting of her into the tent of his mother (v.$^{67a}$).

(*e*) The opposite condition of things, namely, the *dissolution of relations*, is indicated as follows. One person takes off another's shoe (Dt $25^{9a}$ 'וְחָלְצָה וגו), or the wearer removes it himself (Ru $4^{8b}$ 'וַיִּשְׁלֹף וגו). The idea at the basis of this act may be explained thus. Seeing that one enters upon the occupancy of a field by treading upon it with his shoes (see above, on Ps $60^{10}$ ‖ $108^{10}$), the pulling off of the shoe indicates the intention of *not* carrying out this occupancy. The drawing off of the shoe was also, among the Arabs, a special sign of the dissolution of a marriage. This is shown by the use of خُلْعٌ (*khul'un=extractio*) for 'divorce.' 'The drawing off of a shoe also meets us in still later times as the symbol of renunciation of allegiance. When a ruler was declared to have forfeited the throne, it was customary to cast off the shoe in a solemn assembly' (Ign. Goldziher, *Zur arab. Philologie*, Bd. i. p. 47). A parallel to the above-cited passage, Ru $4^{8b}$, will be found also in Burton, *The Land of Midian*, vol. ii. p. 197.—A very energetic expression for the complete dissolution of a connexion consists in the *shaking off the dust from one's feet* (Mt $10^{14}$ ἐκτινάξατε τὸν κονιορτόν, κ.τ.λ.; Mk $6^{11}$ ἐκτινάξατε τὸν χοῦν, κ.τ.λ.; Ac $13^{51}$).—The superlative degree of separation from a person may be seen in the *covering of his face* (Est $7^{8b}$ 'and they covered Haman's face'). By this act he was marked as if non-existing. A similar symbolical action was practised among the Macedonians (Curtius, IV. viii. 22) and the Romans (cf. Bertheau-Ryssel in *Kgf. exeg. Hdb. ad loc.*). Similar to a certain extent is the Turkish custom of sending a silken cord to one who is condemned to death.

(*f.*) *Symbolical actions affecting certain classes of society.*—(α) If a Hebrew slave declined to avail himself of the liberty that was open to him after seven years' service, *one of his ears*—probably the right one—*was bored through with an awl against the door and thus pinned to it* (Ex $21^{6b}$, Dt $15^{17}$). This was meant to indicate that the service of his ears—*i.e.* his obedience—must henceforth be indissolubly devoted to this house. The pierced ear is found also amongst other nations as the mark of the slave (Nowack, *Heb. Arch.* i. 177).

(β) The office of house steward was conveyed to one by *laying the key of the house upon his shoulder* (Is $22^{22}$, cf. Rev $3^{7}$). The investiture with the prophetic office is once, too, symbolized by the *giving of a book to eat* (Ezk $3^{1}$).

(γ) We find quite a number of symbolical actions intended to indicate a man's rank as ruler. First of all there is *anointing* (Jg $9^{8}$, 1 S $9^{16}$ $10^{1}$ $15^{1}$ $16^{3ff.}$, 2 S $2^{4}$ $3^{39}$ $5^{3}$, 1 K $1^{39}$ $19^{15}$, 2 K $11^{12}$ $23^{30}$, Ps $45^{8}$ $89^{21}$, 1 Ch $29^{22}$, 2 Ch $22^{7}$ $23^{11}$, but not Ps $2^{2}$). Although this practice of anointing princes is witnessed to even in the Tel el-Amarna letters (*KIB*, Bd. v., Brief $27^{50-53}$ $37^{6f.}$), it acquired a peculiar meaning in Israel. For the oil which fed the lamps of the sanctuary readily became a symbol of Divine illumination, and so a vehicle of the Holy Ghost. —In the second place, the elevation of a man to be ruler was expressed by putting on his head a *diadem* (2 S $1^{10}$, 2 K $11^{12}$, Ps $132^{18}$, 1 Mac $11^{13}$, Rev $19^{12}$) or a *crown* (2 S $12^{30}$, Ezk $16^{12}$ $21^{26}$ $23^{42}$, Zec $6^{11b}$, Ps $21^{4}$, Est $8^{15}$, 1 Ch $20^{2}$).—Thirdly, a ruler was acknowledged by the act of *kissing*. Thus Samuel kissed Saul after he had anointed him king over Israel (1 S $10^{1}$). The kiss, as an act of homage, is found, not indeed in Gn $41^{40a}$, but in Ps $2^{12}$, 1 K $19^{18}$, Hos $13^{2}$, Job $31^{27}$, and the same custom prevailed among the Assyrians (Schrader, *KAT*² 455) and other peoples.—Again, a person may be recognized as a sharer in rule by being *caused to sit at one's right hand* (1 K $2^{19}$, Ps $45^{10}$ $110^{1}$, Job $30^{12}$, 1 Mac $10^{62-65}$, Mt $19^{28}$ $20^{21}$, Ac $7^{55f.}$, Ro $8^{34}$, He $8^{1}$ $12^{2}$, Jos. *Ant.* VI. xi. 9: παρακαθεσθέντων αὐτῷ, τοῦ μὲν παιδὸς Ἰωνάθου [1 S $20^{25}$] ἐκ δεξιῶν). Thus Nero made Tiridates, king of Armenia, sit on his right (Sueton. *Nero*, c. xiii.: 'Juxta se latere dextro collocavit'), and Sallust (*de Bello Jugurth.* xi. 3) tells us: 'Hiempsal . . . dextra Adherbalem adsedit . . . quod apud Numidas honori ducitur.' Moreover, when a person is spoken of who stands in need of protection, the man who stands at his right hand is his patron (Ps $16^{8b}$ $121^{5a}$).—Finally, the act of *intercourse with the concubines* of a ruler was meant to indicate seizure of his sovereignty. This was a natural interpretation of the act in question, and is sufficiently authenticated by 2 S $3^{7}$ and 1 K $2^{22a}$. But it was not *necessarily* its meaning, as von Bohlen (Com. on *Genesis*, 1835) maintains with reference to Gn $35^{22}$ and $49^{4}$, and as has been held since by a number of scholars, as, *e.g.*, Guthe, *GVI* (1899) § 1. 4. In these two passages the act in question may denote merely a gross violation of filial duty, and the same interpretation is put upon it in 2 S $16^{21b}$, whereas the struggle for the kingly sway was indicated by other acts ($15^{1ff.}$). It is not to Judah, whose tribe actually strove for the hegemony in Israel, that intercourse with one of his father's concubines is attributed.

(*g*) Another group of symbolical actions expresses *thoughts, feelings, and aspirations.*—(α) The consciousness or the assertion of innocence was symbolized by *the washing of the hands* (Dt $21^{6}$, Mt $27^{24}$, Herod. i. 35: καθαρὸς χεῖρας ἐών, cf. Verg. *Aen.* ii. 719 f.).—(β) A feeling of aversion to a person is proclaimed by *spitting in his face* (Nu $12^{14a}$ יָרֹק יָרַק בְּפָנֶיהָ, Dt $25^{9a}$).—(γ) Bitterness and anger show themselves by *gnashing of the teeth* (Ps $35^{16}$ $37^{12}$ $112^{10}$, Job $16^{9}$, La $2^{16}$, Mt $8^{12}$ $13^{42}$ etc.). Hostile desires express themselves in a similar way: one *gapes with the mouth* as if he would swallow a person (Ps $35^{21}$, Job $16^{10}$, La $2^{16a}$).—(δ) *Clapping the hands* is a gesture expressive sometimes of ill-feeling (Ezk $6^{11}$ $21^{17.22}$ $22^{13}$), sometimes of joy (2 K $11^{12}$, Is $55^{12}$, Nah $3^{19}$, Ps $47^{2}$ $98^{8}$).—(ε) Scoffing wonder is expressed by *shaking of the head* or *the hands* (2 K $19^{21}$, Is $37^{22}$, Jer $18^{16}$ $48^{27}$, Zeph $2^{15}$, Ps $22^{8}$ $44^{15}$ $109^{25}$, Job $16^{4}$, La $2^{15}$, Sir $13^{7}$, Mt $27^{39}$), silent astonishment by *laying the hand upon the mouth* (Jg $18^{19}$, Mic $7^{16}$, Job $21^{5}$ $29^{9}$ $40^{4}$) or *pressing the lips closely together* (Is $52^{15a}$, Ps $107^{42}$, Job $5^{16}$). —(ζ) The fear of profaning a place consecrated to the Deity is expressed by *putting off the shoes*, these being not only a product of man's work, but also dirty (Ex $3^{5}$ 'שַׁל וגו, Jos $5^{15}$, Ex $29^{20}$, Lv $8^{23}$, cf. the covering of the feet in Is $6^{2}$).—(η) The dread of looking upon the holy God found expression in the *covering of the face* (Ex $3^{6b}$ 'וַיַּסְתֵּר וגו, 1 K $19^{13}$ 'וַיָּלֶט וגו, Is $6^{2}$ 'יְכַסֶּה וגו), and Verg. *Aen.* iii. 405 ff. describes the offering of a sacrifice thus—

> 'Purpureo velare comas adopertus amictu,
> Ne qua inter sanctos ignes in honore deorum
> Hostilis facies occurrat et omina turbet.'

(θ) The meaning of the interesting ceremony described in 1 S $7^{6}$, when the Israelites, moved to repentance by the words of Samuel, *drew water and poured it out* before Jahweh, is unfortunately not clear. But perhaps we shall not be wrong to find in it an expression of humility. Bowed down with grief for its sin, the soul melts like water before its God (Ps $6^{7}$), and prostrates itself before Him (Ps $22^{15}$ 'like water I am poured out,' La $2^{19}$).—($\iota$) Much clearer is the meaning of the action attributed in Zec $9^{9}$ to the future ideal king, namely, the *riding upon an ass.* This is a striking allusion to the eminently peaceful aims of his rule. For the ass was the riding animal not of poverty (cf. 1 K $1^{33}$) but of peace, whereas the horse along with the battle-bow is to be expelled from the future kingdom of God (Zec $9^{10}$, Is $2^{4}$ $30^{15}$, Mt $21^{7}$ $26^{52}$, Jn $18^{36}$).

(*h*) A connecting link between the symbolical actions of common life and those of the religious sphere is found in the *lifting up of the hand*, by which swearing is symbolized. The first instance of this meets us in Abraham's words, הֲרִמֹתִי יָדִי 'I have lifted up my hand' (Gn $14^{22}$), and we have noted the same gesture as mentioned in the following passages: Ex $6^{8}$ (נָשָׂאתִי), Nu $14^{30}$, Dt $32^{40}$, Ezk $20^{6.15.23.28}$ $36^{7}$ $44^{12}$ $47^{14}$, Ps $106^{26}$, Neh $9^{15b}$, Dn $12^{7}$ †. To the same category belongs the somewhat obscure expression יָד עַל־כֵּס יָהּ (Ex $17^{16}$), whether כֵּס be regarded as a by-form of כִּסֵּא 'throne,' which to the present writer appears impossible, or whether it is a corrupt form of נֵס 'standard.' The latter view seems to us the correct one, because the words manifestly point back to the rod of God (v.$^{9b}$), which had once more evinced its character as the standard of Jahweh by the defeat of the Amalekites (vv.$^{10-13}$). The most probable rendering would thus be: 'With my hand on the standard of Jahweh I declare [as interpreter of the Divine oracle in v.$^{14b}$], War continues for Jahweh against Amalek from generation to generation.' Swearing is symbolized, further, by *placing the hand under the thigh*: Gn $24^{2.9}$ $47^{29}$. See art. THIGH in vol. iv.

There are also two isolated actions mentioned in the OT, which are performed not on their own account, but in order to express an idea. We refer to the *cutting in pieces* of the concubine of the Levite (Jg $19^{29}$), and of Saul's two oxen (1 S $11^{7}$), both of which tokens bear the marks of symbol.

B. *SYMBOLICAL ACTIONS IN THE RELIGIOUS LIFE.* — (*a*) *Constant or usual actions.* ($\alpha$) In *prayer* we find, first of all, the spreading out of the palms of the hands (כַּפַּיִם, Ex $9^{29.33}$, 1 K $8^{22.38.54}$, Is $1^{15}$, Ps $44^{21}$ $63^{5}$, Job $11^{13b}$, Ezr $9^{5b}$, 2 Ch $6^{12b.13b.29}$; cf. Ps $141^{2b}$, La $2^{19}$ $3^{41}$). This gesture symbolizes the thought that one comes forward as a suppliant and desires to obtain gifts from God. Hence it is intelligible how also at times the hands simply (יָדַיִם) are spread out (Ps $143^{6}$, La $1^{17a}$), or lifted up (Ps $28^{2}$ $134^{2}$, Neh $8^{6}$, 1 Ti $2^{8}$), or stretched forth (2 Mac $3^{20}$ *προτείνειν τὰς χεῖρας*). It is not at all likely that the word כַּפַּיִם 'palms of the hands' was chosen because originally it was the custom to stroke the image of the god (Wellhausen, *Reste*$^{2}$, 105). Would *this* have been a reason for retaining כַּפַּיִם with the verb 'spread out'? It may be noted that the heathen Arabs also lifted up their hands to heaven in the act of prayer: *e.g.* we read, 'Then he lifted up his hand towards heaven, and said, O Allah, give me victory over Nahd!' This is a parallel to Ex $17^{11f.}$ (G. Jacob, *Altarab. Parallelen*, p. 8).—Further, in praying, one practised bowing down (Gn $24^{26}$ $47^{31}$, 1 K $1^{47}$, Job $1^{20}$, Neh $8^{6}$, Jg $9^{1}$) or kneeling (1 K $8^{54}$, Ps $95^{6}$, Dn $6^{11b}$, Ezr $9^{5b}$, 2 Ch $6^{13b}$, Ac $20^{36}$ *θεὶς τὰ γόνατα*), sinking of the head (1 S $1^{26}$, 1 K $18^{42}$, Ps $35^{13}$, Dn $9^{20}$). There can be no doubt as to the idea expressed by these actions. They amount to a confession that man humbles himself before his Lord and Judge.

($\beta$) In the act of *blessing*, the hand is laid upon the head of the recipient, or at least stretched out towards him (Gn $48^{14}$, Lv $9^{22}$, 2 K $13^{16}$, Mt $19^{13}$, Mk $10^{16}$, Lk $24^{50}$). This imposition or motion of the hand is meant to symbolize the passing over of the blessing from the one party to the other—an idea which is expressed by the imposition of hands in other cases as well. Cf. the following groups of passages: Nu $8^{10}$ $27^{18}$, Dt $34^{9}$, Ac $6^{6}$ $13^{3}$, 1 Ti $4^{14}$ $5^{22}$, 2 Ti $1^{6}$; Lv $16^{21}$ $24^{14}$, Sus $^{34}$; Ex $29^{10}$, Lv $1^{4}$ etc.; Mt $9^{18}$, Mk $5^{23}$ etc., Rev $1^{17}$.

($\gamma$) Other parts of the cultus also provided rich material for symbolical actions. To follow up what was said a moment ago, the *incense offering* is interpreted in Ps $141^{2}$ and Rev $5^{8}$ $8^{3f.}$ as expressing the idea of prayer ascending to heaven. And no less are the other *offerings* the medium whereby such feelings as gratitude or penitence or the longing for reconciliation with God are expressed in an unmistakable fashion. For a God who is spirit has no need of such offerings for Himself (Ps $50^{13}$; cf. Is $40^{16}$ and Ac $17^{25}$).

($\delta$) Symbolical actions with a *negative* purpose included, in the first place, the oft-mentioned *washings* (Ex $19^{10}$ etc.). Washing oneself is spoken of elsewhere as an act of self-consecration (Jos $3^{5}$ $7^{13}$, 1 S $16^{5}$; cf. *Odyss.* iv. 759), and least doubtful of all is this symbolical sense in the case of Jesus' washing of His disciples' feet (Jn $13^{7ff.}$).—Again, the *circumcision* of male children, when eight days old, as this rite was practised among the Israelites, had a symbolical meaning, being intended to indicate that the child in question belonged to the religious community of Abraham.—Within this community smaller circles receive a higher degree of consecration, and this, too, was effected by means of symbolical transactions. In the case of *priests* we read of washing, anointing (see above), etc., Ex $29^{1}$ $40^{13}$, Lv $8^{12.30}$. Again, the symbolical actions whereby the separation of NAZIRITES was proclaimed, are described in Nu $6^{1-21}$ (cf. Jg $13^{7.13f.}$, Am $2^{12}$, and Ed. Vilmar, 'Die symbolische Bedeutung des Nasiräatsgelübdes' in *SK*, 1864). Once more, there are symbolical actions, although their number is very small, connected with *prophets.* The one action of which we read in this case is anointing, and the mention even of this is doubtful. In 1 K $19^{16}$ it is merely in parallelism with 'Jehu shalt thou anoint to be king' that it is said 'and Elisha shalt thou anoint to be prophet'; and in Is $61^{1}$ it is from the possession of the spirit that the inference is drawn 'therefore hath Jahweh anointed me.' Consequently we hear much in the prophetical writings of symbolical actions, and these demand a more detailed examination.

(*b*) *Unusual actions in the sphere of religion.*—This category does not yet include the writing up in public of Divine oracles in the way we find the prophets sometimes enjoined to do (Is $8^{1}$ $30^{8}$, Hab $2^{2}$; cf. Jer $36^{2}$, Ezk $24^{2}$). For this was not intended to give publicity to an oracle itself so much as to emphasize one quality of it, namely, its importance. With more reason may this class be held to include those instances in which prophets *gave a symbolical name* to a person or a thing: *e.g.* 'A remnant shall return' (*Shĕ'âr-jâshûb*), etc., Is $7^{3}$ $8^{3}$; $7^{14b}$ $8^{8b.10b}$; $30^{7b}$; Zec $11^{7}$. For Isaiah, in bestowing upon one of his sons the name *Shĕ'âr-jâshûb* (Is $7^{3}$), gave an embodiment to the hope that at least a minority of Israel would return to their God; and as often as the bearer of this name walked the streets, *he performed a symbolical action by the bearing of this name.* Although silent, he preached a sermon whose text was Is $6^{13}$. But, in the most proper sense, the category with which we are dealing has to do with the following passages:—

The prophet Ahijah tore his garment into twelve pieces, to illustrate the Divine determination to divide the kingdom of Israel (1 K $11^{30-32}$).

A parallel to this passage was found by 'some,' as Abulwalîd (*Riqma*, ed. Goldberg, p. 215, lines 28–30) says, in 1 S $15^{27b}$. They presupposed the reading וַיִּקְרָעֵהוּ, and took Samuel to be the subject of the statement 'and he rent it' (namely, his upper garment). But the subject of the preceding clause וַיַּחֲזֵק וג׳ is Saul, as the second of two persons that have been mentioned is frequently in the OT taken for granted as the subject of an action (Gn $3^{10a.\ 11a}$ etc.; cf. König, *Stilistik, Rhetorik, Poetik*, p. 180, lines 29 ff.). But a symbolical action is really recorded in 1 K $20^{35ff.}$, where we read that one of the 'sons of the prophets' got one of his comrades to smite him, in order that he might exhibit by his wounds the punishment that king Ahab had deserved. A symbolical character belonged also to the iron horns which the false prophet Zedekiah put on, in order to express the notion that Ahab was to push the Syrians as with horns of iron (1 K $22^{11}$). Something analogous is seen in the conduct of Tarquinius, who struck off poppy heads (Livy, i. 54) to indicate that his son should deal in like manner with the nobles of the city. While the imperative הַךְ 'strike' in Am $9^1$ is not certainly addressed to the prophet, chs. 2 and 3 of the Book of Hosea belong to the present category. Again, according to Is $20^{2-4}$, the prophet Isaiah announced the defeat of Egypt and Ethiopia beforehand, by going about half-clothed (cf. $58^{7b}$) and barefooted, like a captive. We may notice, in passing, the contrast to this presented by the words of Rev $11^3$ *προφητεύσουσι περιβεβλημένοι σάκκους*. Jeremiah, too, speaks of similar actions in $13^{1-12}$ (the journey to the Euphrates), $18^{1-6}$ (the work of the potter), $19^{1-15}$ (the bottle cast out into the Vale of Hinnom), $25^{15-31}$ (the handing of the cup, which is full of Jahweh's fury), $27^{2ff.}$ (putting on of fetters), $28^{10-13}$ (wearing and breaking a yoke), $32^{7-15}$ (purchase of the field in Anathoth); cf. also the offering of wine to the Rechabites ($35^{2ff.}$), and the building in of great stones ($43^9$). In the Book of Ezekiel the following passages come into account: ch. 4 (the lying upon the left and upon the right side), ch. 5 (the cutting off, etc., of the hair), $12^{3ff.}$ (the procuring of baggage appropriate to a captive), v.$^{17ff.}$ (eating bread with trembling), $21^{11\,(6)}$ (sighing), v.$^{19\,(14)}$ (smiting the hands together), vv.$^{24-28\,(19-23)}$ (the appointing of two ways), $24^{3ff.}$ (the setting on of the seething caldron), $37^{16ff.}$ (the two sticks which represent the two separated portions of Israel). Finally, the prophet to whom we owe Zec 9–11 tells how he was appointed to be shepherd of the sheep for slaughter ($11^{4ff.}$), and received instructions to take to himself the instruments of a foolish shepherd (v.$^{15}$).

With reference to the above passages from the prophetical literature, the difficult question now arises, what we are to hold as to the literal performance of the actions mentioned by the prophets. We will examine the various possible solutions of the problem, in order to arrive at the correct solution.

(*a*) As in dealing with other questions, the proper course will be to consider the OT data themselves. It appears to the present writer that a starting-point from which a sure conclusion may be reached is to be found in Jer $25^{15ff.}$. There we read: 'For thus saith Jahweh, the God of Israel, unto me, Take the cup of the wine of this fury at my hand, and cause all the nations, to whom I send thee, to drink it (v.$^{15}$). Then took I the cup at the hand of Jahweh, and made all the nations to drink, unto whom Jahweh had sent me (v.$^{17}$), namely, Jerusalem and the cities of Judah,' etc. (vv.$^{18-26}$). Now, it is obvious that the causing of whole cities and peoples to drink *cannot* have been carried out literally. But when, in spite of this, the narrative of this transaction runs as if it had been so, we have at least *one* certain instance of a prophetical action which to all appearance was literally performed, although its performance is seen to have been an impossibility. Jeremiah thus means nothing more than that he was stirred up by his Divine director to a certain action, and that he carried this out in his inner life. The purpose meant to be served by the Divine commission and the record of it, is to set forth the determination of God with the greatest clearness. Incidents belonging to the spiritual sphere are to pass like an earthly drama before the eyes of the hearer and reader.

The position of matters disclosed in Jer $25^{15ff.}$ furnishes a ground for holding that some of the other symbolical actions of which we read in the prophetical books, could also have been performed only ideally. The prophets, like Jeremiah in the above passage, might so relate the symbolical transaction as to guide their hearers to the correct conclusion as to its actual or ideal occurrence. Let us examine this point in detail.

Jeremiah records in $13^{4-7}$ how he was commanded by God to bury a girdle by the 'Perath' (פְּרָת), and that he carried out this commission. If the contemporaries of Jeremiah must necessarily—and no other possibility can be plausibly made out—have understood by 'Perath' the well-known great river of Asia, the Euphrates, they must at the same time have been aware that the prophet had not actually gone to the Euphrates.—Again, the circumstance noted in Is $20^{2-4}$ that the prophet went about *for three years* half-clothed and barefooted, is far from natural. But it may be that the statement of time here is not original. The mention of a definite period seemed to be required, and so it was inserted in the form of a so-called round number. We venture to add another remark on this passage. The form of expression, 'At that time Jahweh spake *by* Isaiah' (v.$^2$) is extremely surprising, seeing that the following words are addressed *to* Isaiah. The form is not at all explained by such passages as Ex $9^{35}$, Lv $10^{11}$, 1 K $12^{15}$, Jer $37^2$, Hag $1^{1.\ 3}$, which are cited by Duhm (in *Kurzer Hdcom.* on Is $20^2$), for in none of these does any Divine message follow, addressed to the person who is introduced by 'by' (בְּיַד). Is it too much to assume that the man who wrote the words 'by Isaiah' meant to mark the contents of vv.$^{2-4}$ as containing nothing more than the report of an announcement by God? Have we not the same indication in the strange form of v.$^3$, where the words of God are reported in a definite form meant for the people? Was it not Isaiah's intention by this *narrative* to call attention to the overthrow of Egypt and Ethiopia?

But, be this as it may, the history which meets us in Hos 1 and 3 was certainly enacted only in the spiritual sphere. By means of the Divinely inspired narrative of the experiences of the prophet with an unfaithful wife, the ideal relations are meant to be portrayed, which had partly been realized in the case of the prophet's Master and the people of Israel, and were partly to follow by way of punishment. It is true that, even in recent times, there have not been wanting exegetes who have seen in these chapters the record of *actual* experiences (Nowack, *Die kleinen Propheten*, p. 29; Valeton, *Amos und Hosea*, 1898, p. 221 f.; O. Seesemann, *Israel und Juda bei Amos und Hosea*, 1898, p. 32 ff.). But the objections to this view appear to the present writer to be too weighty to be set aside. The marriage of the prophet with a harlot, if it had been an actual incident, would have been altogether too repulsive. And it may be remarked, in passing, that what the prophet was commanded to do was to take to himself a wife of whoredom and children of whoredom ($1^2$). The notion that 'the impure inclinations of this woman did not reveal themselves to Hosea till after marriage' (Wellhausen, *Skizzen und Vorarbeiten*, v. p. 104 f.; similarly W. R. Smith, *Prophets of Israel*, p. 181 f., and G. A. Smith, *Book of the Twelve Prophets*, i. 238 f.) cannot be reconciled with the text. Our first main argument may be reinforced by the following questions. Would Hosea, even supposing his wife to have been thus guilty, have inscribed her name on the page of history and thus pilloried her for ever? Or would the name of his wife have been so much as named, had it not been a significant one? No, the designations *Gomer bath-diblayim* (Hos 1$^{3}$) do not really form a proper name. We are constantly told, indeed, that these designations defy all attempts to explain them as appellatives (Nowack, Valeton, *et al.*). But why may not *Gomer* mean 'completion' (Frd. Delitzsch, *Prolegomena*, etc. p. 200), or, better, 'ripeness' (namely, for judgment), or 'end' (cf. גמר Ps 7$^{10}$ etc.)? Why may we not find in *diblayim* the sense of 'double compression' (cf. E. Meier, *Wurzelwörterbuch*, p. 163 f.; Wünsche, *Erklärung des Hosea*, p. 15; Arab. *dabala*='coegit')? May not, then, the epithet *bath-diblayim* characterize Gomer as one who had to do with two husbands? (We may recall the question: 'How long halt ye on both knees? If Jahweh is God, follow him; and if Baal, follow him,' 1 K 18$^{21}$). Finally, it would surely have been a strange circumstance if Hosea's real wife had had a name composed of two elements, capable of being explained as='ripeness *or* end,' and 'double copulation.'

Further, Zec 11$^{4ff.}$ records how the prophet was told to call one of the two staves, with which he was to shepherd the people of Israel, 'graciousness,' and the other 'union,' 'community of fate' (cf. Ed. König, *Syntax*, § 244*c*). Would not these very names be enough to show to the prophet's contemporaries that the actions recorded in vv.$^{4ff.}$ were not actually performed? This conclusion is favoured by the circumstance that there is no mention of the execution of the command given in v.$^{15}$.

Of greatest weight for the solution of the problem before us are the indications supplied by the prophet who speaks most of symbolical actions, namely Ezekiel. The data are as follows:—In the first place, in his narratives regarding symbolical actions, it is only rarely (12$^{7}$ 24$^{18}$) that he states that these when commanded were carried out. Secondly, in place of mention of the actual performance of these, we find rather an account of their symbolical meaning (4$^{16f.}$ 5$^{5}$ 12$^{19}$ 21$^{24-28}$). Thirdly, the external performance of the charge 'thou shalt eat thy bread with trembling, and drink thy water with trembling and despair' (12$^{18}$), would have been scarcely noticeable. The intention of presenting clearly the Divine decree as to the final chastisement of Israel was realized by the bare narrative about a Divine command as effectively as would have been the case if the command had been actually performed. Fourthly, God's command to carry out a symbolical transaction is expressly introduced in these terms: 'Give to the rebellious house a parable (*māshāl*) and *say* (!) to them, Thus saith the LORD God, set on the caldron, and pour water into it,' etc. (24$^{3}$, cf. also 21$^{5b}$). This, too, favours the conclusion that Ezekiel's statements about commands from God to perform symbolical actions, do not differ essentially from the parables spoken in 17$^{2ff.}$ and 18$^{3ff.}$. But, as a matter of fact, these narratives may be understood as parables, whose subject is the prophet as the representative now of God and now of his people. As the *representative of God* he is to smite one hand against the other (21$^{17}$), to depict the conflict which Jahweh, to His sorrow, has to wage against the unfaithful majority of Israel (21$^{24}$), just as the smiting together of the hands is attributed to Jahweh Himself in 22$^{13}$. In the same capacity Ezekiel is also called on to depict vividly the rejection of Israel, to which God has been compelled to resort by the excessive unfaithfulness of His people (3$^{24-27}$ 24$^{25-27}$). Hence, when the prophet has to picture forth the highest degree of the Divine displeasure, he does so by becoming dumb, *i.e.* by ceasing to act as a reprover (3$^{26}$), and by refraining from articulate expressions of grief at the destruction of Jerusalem, in order to impress upon the people about him the truth that this turn in their fortunes was a just punishment from God. This dumbness continued till, with the fall of Jerusalem, the Divine justice was satisfied, and then the Divine grace in the person of the prophet turned anew to the people (33$^{21f.}$), and sought to win their love.—Again, as *representative of his people*, Ezekiel is the subject of those narratives in which actions of Jahweh against Israel are vividly portrayed. This comes out with special clearness in the words, 'But thou, O son of man, behold, *they* shall put bands upon thee' (3$^{25}$), and 'Behold, I put bands upon thee' (4$^{8a}$). In this way the punishment impending from God upon Israel is described as inflicted upon the prophet, and the purpose of this is evident enough. The exiles who, living far from their native land, could not be onlookers at the act of judgment to be executed upon Judah and especially upon Jerusalem, were to have a clear reflexion of the fate of Jahweh's people placed before their eyes.

Such are the positive grounds for holding that Ezekiel's accounts of symbolical actions, whose actual performance is not specially mentioned (12$^{7}$ 24$^{18}$), make up a species of parables, whose subject was the prophet as representative either of Jahweh or of Israel (cf. the present writer's art. 'Zur Deutung der symbolischen Handlungen des Propheten Hesekiel' in the *Neue kirchliche Zeitschrift*, 1892, p. 650 f.). The same conclusion, however, is supported by weighty considerations of a negative kind. For instance, is it credible that Ezekiel should literally have lain upon his left side for 390 days (4$^{5}$), *i.e.* for more than a year? Did the neighbours count the days? Or is it likely that he actually baked his barley cakes, using human excrement for fuel (4$^{12}$)? These negative considerations have led even Smend (*Kgf. exeg. Hdb.* 'Hesechiel,' 1880, p. 27) to the conclusion that 'it is evident that such a transaction as that of 4$^{4-8}$ cannot have been literally carried out.' Practically, the same standpoint is occupied also by Kuenen (*Hist.-crit. Einleitung*, ii. p. 258 f.), Toy ('Ezekiel' in *SBOT*, 1899), and Hühn (*Die Messianischen Weissagungen*, 1899, p. 160); and a similar judgment is passed by Frankenberg (in Nowack's *Hdkom.*, 'Sprüche,' 1898, p. 18). It may further be noted that Hos 1 and 3 are called 'parabolæ' by Wenrich (*De poeseos hebraicæ atque arabicæ origine*, p. 152).

($\beta$) But in the most recent times there have been a number of exegetes who have held that all the symbolical actions mentioned in the Book of Ezekiel were externally performed. These scholars fall into two groups. The one group is made up of v. Orelli (in Strack-Zöckler's *Kgf. Kom.*, 'Hesekiel,' p. 3) and Giesebrecht (*Die Berufsbegabung der alttest. Propheten*, 1897, p. 171), who both found their interpretation upon the appearance of literalness in the language of the passages in question. In particular, Giesebrecht simply asserts that 'the symbolical actions of Ezekiel cannot be understood as mere figures.' But this is no argument.—The other group comprises the following scholars:—Klostermann, in his art. 'Ezechiel: Ein Beitrag zur besseren Würdigung seiner Person und seiner Schrift' in *SK*, 1877, p. 391 ff.; L. Gautier, *La mission du prophète Ézéchiel*, 1891, p. 85 ff.; Bertholet, in Marti's *Kurzer Hdcom.*,

'Hesekiel,' 1897, p. 24 f.; and Kraetzschmar, in Nowack's *Hdkom.*, 'Ezechiel,' 1900, p. v. They have come to this conclusion in consequence of accepting the hypothesis regarding the person of Ezekiel put forward by Klostermann in the above-named article. Hence it is necessary to examine this hypothesis, and to ask whether it can supply a ground on which to defend the view that the symbolical actions of which Ezekiel speaks were literally performed.

Klostermann's theory is based on the assumption that the dumbness of Ezekiel ($3^{24-27}$ and $24^{25-27}$) was due to a temporary *alalia* from which the prophet finally recovered ($33^{21f.}$); and that his long-continued lying posture ($4^{4ff.}$) was the result of *hemiplegia* (*l.c.* pp. 417 f., 422). But to this hypothesis there are the following objections:—(*a*) The Divine command to the prophet to shut himself up in his house and keep dumb ($3^{24.26}$), or to refrain from articulate lamentation ($24^{16.27}$), and to lie upon his left side ($4^{4-8}$), must be interpreted in the same manner as the command to shave his head and beard with a sharp sword ($5^{1ff}$). It is impossible to pick and choose amongst the various records of symbolical actions contained in the Book of Ezekiel. If, then, symptoms of disease on the part of the prophet are to be discovered in Ezk $3^{24ff.}$ $24^{16ff.}$ and $4^{4-8}$, all symbolical actions of which he speaks must be traced back to some disease of his, and we must be permitted to bring all the particular features of the narratives of $3^{24ff.}$ $24^{16ff.}$ and $4^{4-8}$ into a causal connexion with some pathological habit of Ezekiel. But it may be asked whether, among other disordered inclinations, he had a fancy for using human excrement for fuel ($4^{12}$). Did he at one and the same time suffer from temporary *alalia* and also have the peculiarity at one time of sighing ($21^{6}$), and at another time of crying aloud (v.$^{12}$)? If the Divine command to refrain from any articulate lament for the dead ($24^{16}$) is to be explained by a temporary speechlessness, then the non-shedding of tears, which is enjoined in the same verse, must be derived from a bodily idiosyncrasy of Ezekiel.—(*β*) It must be observed that in $3^{24-26}$ Ezekiel speaks not of dumbness in general, but of keeping silence with any prophetic message. This is obvious from the single circumstance that, in order to carry out the injunction of silence, the prophet had to shut himself up in his house—a course of action which would have been unnecessary if he had been suffering from temporary speechlessness. The same conclusion follows, on the positive side, from the circumstance that his silence is to evidence itself by his not coming forward as a reprover ($3^{26a}$), and that it is to come to an end when his God again makes disclosures to him (v.$^{27}$).—(*γ*) If Ezekiel had suffered from temporary *alalia*, this could not have been unknown to his neighbours, whose principal representatives used to assemble in his house ($8^{1}$ $14^{1}$ $20^{1}$). But, in that case, a new attack of this dumbness could have had no symbolical meaning to them.—(*δ*) It must truly have been a remarkable *hemiplegia* which compelled the prophet to lie for exactly 390+40, *i.e.* 430 days, and thus to furnish a parallel to the 430 years (Ex $12^{40}$) of Israel's bondage in Egypt.—(*ε*) If it was, as alleged, a bodily infirmity that prevented the prophet from articulate wailing ($24^{25-27}$), he could, and no doubt would, at least have expressed his grief at his bitter loss by practising all the other mourning usages. But, as he did not do so, it is unmistakably plain that his neglect of the lament for the dead was due, not to a bodily indisposition but to a higher impulse. What a novel kind of *alalia*, by the way, which had its cessation foretold ($3^{26}$ $24^{27}$)!

Consequently, the view that all the symbolical actions mentioned in the Book of Ezekiel were literally performed, fails again to find any support from Klostermann's hypothesis about the condition of the prophet's health. On the contrary, in $3^{24-26}$ $24^{25-27}$ and $4^{4-8}$ he is only represented as the subject of a symbolical action in the same way as in $5^{2f.}$ etc. It is also intelligible how he should be introduced as afflicted with dumbness. For God meant to symbolize the extreme of His displeasure against Israel by breaking off His revelations ($3^{27}$). Again, Ezekiel is described in $4^{4-8}$ as lying, because Israel's captive condition might suitably be regarded also as a lying, just as it is elsewhere (Hos $3^{3a}$) compared to a sitting in isolation.

A subdivision of symbolical actions may be formed of those which depict some feature of the future consummation of the Kingdom of God. They may be called προφητεῖαι δι' ἔργων (Adrianos, Εἰσαγωγὴ εἰς τὰς θείας γραφάς, ed. Goessling, § 130) or 'types.' But it is questionable whether the OT speaks of any actions which were meant to be performed with the intention of pointing beforehand to some incident in the life of Christ. This is doubtful even in the case of the passage in which Adrianos (*l.c.*) appears with a measure of certainty to have discovered a προφητεία δι' ἔργων. We refer to Gn $22^{2}$ 'Take now thy son Isaac, thine only son, whom thou lovest,' etc. This story is rather intended to express the notion that the God who has revealed Himself to Israel, holds human sacrifices in abhorrence. It could all the less have been meant to point to the time of Christ, seeing that God did not spare Himself the sorrow of offering His only Son as a sacrifice for the sin of mankind. Nor was the Flood sent to serve as an allusion to baptism, although it might afterwards be viewed as an analogue to the latter (1 P $3^{21}$). This has been noted also by J. D. Michaelis in his interesting work, *Entwurf der typischen Gottesgelartheit*², 1763, p. 37.

The most familiar symbolical actions of the NT (Jn $13^{4ff.}$, Ac $6^{6}$ ἐπέθηκαν αὐτοῖς τὰς χεῖρας, etc.) have been already referred to in speaking of symbolical *washing* and the *imposition of hands* (which see). To these may be added *the cursing of the fig-tree* (Mt $21^{19}$, Mk $11^{13f.}$), the texts relating to which are not meant to be a mere 'symbolical narrative,' as has been recently maintained in the *Theol. Ztschr. aus der Schweiz*, 1899, pp. 228–238. Further, the *casting of lots* (Ac $1^{26}$) is merely an external parallel to the previously (v.$^{24}$) mentioned prayer; and, finally, the *breaking of bread* (κλάσις τοῦ ἄρτου, Mt $26^{26}$, Lk $24^{35}$, Ac $2^{42}$) and *baptism* (Mt $28^{19}$) have a fundamentally symbolical character. See BAPTISM in vol. i. and LORD'S SUPPER in vol. iii.

LITERATURE.—This has been indicated in the body of the article.

ED. KÖNIG.

## RELIGION OF EGYPT.—

Introduction. Official religion and popular faith.

i. COSMOGONY.

(*A*) Creation of the world.

(1) Supposed reciprocal relation between deities and men.

(2) Creation myths attributing the formative effect to *acts*: (*a*) separation of heaven and earth, (*b*) origin of the sun, (*c*) origin of gods and men, animals and plants, (*d*) methods of creation.—(*α*) a series of births, (*β*) artificial construction, (*γ*) procreation.

(3) Creation myths attributing the formative effect to *words*. Supposed connexion between an object and its name. Creation by inarticulate sounds a late conception.

(*B*) Destruction of the world.

(1) Supposed allusions.

(2) A deluge checked by the Deity.

(3) Rā's partial destruction of the human race.

ii. THE GODS.

(*A*) Historical development of the power of particular gods.

*Introduction.*—In studying the religion of ancient Egypt we encounter a phenomenon which it has in common with almost all religions. Two forms of conception may be distinguished, which started from the same principles and exercised a permanent influence upon one another, but which at the same time exhibit a number of radical differences in the view they take of Divine things. These two are, respectively, the official religion of the upper classes, and the popular faith. It is true that the difference is not so pronounced in the Nile valley as elsewhere, since the Egyptian religion was never subjected to a systematizing process and a logical establishing of its various dogmas, but always remained in a fluid condition, so that even the official religion was thus permanently exposed to powerful influence from the side of the popular conceptions.

The sources of information of which modern investigation can avail itself in seeking to arrive at a knowledge of the official religion of ancient Egypt are very copious. It is the subject of the inscriptions on temples, and of almost all the texts found in tombs and on monuments (including the religious papyri) dedicated to the worship of the dead. Far fewer materials have to be taken account of in estimating the popular religion. Its adherents belonged in general to the poorer classes, who were not in a position to erect any fine monuments. Besides, in the texts they destined for publicity, such persons almost uniformly employed the terminology and the formulæ of the official monuments, even in cases where they understood the dogmas in view differently from the priestly colleges of the great sanctuaries. In order to recover this realm of ideas belonging to the popular faith, our main resources are a series of ill-executed sepulchral steles and rock-inscriptions, sporadic passages in the temple texts and those concerning the dead which show traces of popular influence, and in which, notably for instance in the so-called Book of the Dead, the popular doctrine could occasionally not be passed over. When referred to, this doctrine is, strangely enough, spoken of as a great secret. Lastly, we have to take account of the statements of the classical writers, who, like their countrymen that were settled in the Nile valley, were brought into contact less with the priests and the upper classes than with the great mass of the people proper, so that their accounts reproduce primarily the notions of the latter. What holds good of these Greeks applies also to the Israelites, who, if they



acquired information or received stimulus from Egypt, must have derived these from the middle classes or the lower orders, and not from study of the doctrines in the temples which were so difficult of access to a non-Egyptian, or of the inscriptions which must have been almost always unintelligible to a foreigner.

Under these circumstances, it will be necessary in the present article to lay more emphasis on these popular notions than it has been usual, in view of the above described meagreness of the sources, to do in descriptions of the Egyptian religion. But, on the other hand, owing to the want of materials and the constant interpenetration of the two forms of conception, it becomes impossible to treat the two apart; the difference between their points of view can only be indicated from time to time in the course of our exposition.

i. COSMOGONY.—(A) *Creation of the world.*—(1) From the earliest times from which we possess Egyptian religious texts down to the period when the ancient polytheism gave way to the Christian faith, the relation between Divinity and humanity was thought of by the inhabitants of the Nile valley as reciprocally conditioned. Man dedicates to the Deity food, drink, clothing, a dwelling-place—the things which the Deity, who shares in all earthly qualities and needs, requires for comfort. The Deity gives in return such benefits as he can dispense — long life, endurance, joy, victory over enemies, health, and the like. If either party neglects his duty, the other is at once set free from any counter obligation. Man offers only to *that* god who shows himself helpful to him; the god favours only *that* man who does him some service. Thus in the inscriptions the god says to the king, 'I give thee victory in proportion to thine offerings,' and the king threatens to discontinue his worship if the god will not bestow long life upon him.

As in every instance where similar notions are cherished, this way of thinking led in Egypt to the continuance of a polytheistic system. Upon the assumption that only one or only a few gods existed, or that their supremacy was universal, it was difficult to conceive how, in view of the conflicting interests of different individuals, any decisive pressure could be exerted on the Divine will by a particular suppliant. This was more practicable if a man could apply to special gods who had to be considered in relation to only *one* or only a few individuals. Then, when he had obtained the good graces of these, he could leave it to them to accomplish their will in the circle of their fellow-gods, or to bring it at the proper moment under the notice of a higher god. The kings of the gods were accessible, if necessary, to the Pharaohs and their court; the sphere of their activity was far too exalted to permit of their rendering continuous help to ordinary mortals.

In this way the notion that every family and every locality or province possesses and must retain for itself its special deities, persisted for thousands of years, and was never absolutely suppressed. At no time was there a religious system in which every Egyptian was bound to believe; the belief in the gods always exhibits a particular form and development in the different divisions of the country, the so-called nomes (see below, p. 182[b]).

It is quite recently that historical science has come to recognize the above characteristic of the Egyptian religion. Only some thirty years ago it began to be urged and demonstrated that, in order to obtain a correct view of the faith of the ancient Egyptians, we must examine individual conceptions and individual deities, instead of setting up *a priori* principles. Up till then it had been the fashion to attribute to this people now an obscure monotheism, now a professedly profound but in reality perfectly unintelligible pantheism, or some other religious system, and to support such pretensions by sentences of the inscriptions torn from their context. From the point of view of scientific inquiry, the ancient Egyptian religion is made up of a long series of particular religions and separate spheres of ideas, which one has to follow in their development, unconcerned at first with the question which of the various conceptions is the oldest and whence each originated. The time may come when it may be possible to bring a number of the deities into connexion with the various elements that gave birth to the Egyptian people of history; with the Libyan aborigines, the conquering Ḥamites, and the Semite peaceful immigrants. But at present the materials at our disposal are far too scanty to lead to any certain conclusions, and the hypotheses that have been started about the Egyptian religion are already so numerous that in the interests of the progress of science any multiplying of them is to be deprecated.

(2) The variety of ways in which myth-forming speculation could view one and the same event forces itself at once on our observation when we essay a survey of the most important of the Egyptian myths intended to explain the origin of the world and of gods and men. It will be best to commence our study of the religion of Egypt with an account of these myths, because we can here take account at the same time of a number of fundamental ideas of the ancient Egyptians about religious questions, which exhibit resemblances to, or differences from, certain classes of notions that prevailed among the Israelites.

In the opinion of the ancient Egyptians, as with other peoples, our world, the heavens and the earth, and the beings that inhabit them, did not exist from the beginning, but were created. Not, indeed, out of nothing, but out of a fluidity which the Egyptians called *Nu*, and which may be compared with the *Chaos* of the Greeks. While this filled the universe, there was, as a text expresses it, 'not yet the heaven; not yet was the earth, not yet were formed the good and the evil serpents.' Or, as it is put in an inscription in the pyramid of a king belonging to the 6th dynasty (Pepi I. l. 663 f.), *i.e.* *c.* 3000 B.C., 'not yet was the heaven, not yet the earth, men were not, not yet born were the gods, not yet was death.'

(*a*) In this primeval mass lay hidden the germs of the future world, but no text as yet discovered points to any attempt on the part of the Egyptians to form a clear and harmonious picture of the relation of these germs to one another. It is only as to particular points that we have indications. Thus, according to a widely diffused notion, in primeval times the heaven, Nut (thought of as female), reposed in the close embrace of the earth, Seb or Keb (thought of as male). Besides the primeval fluid, Nu, there existed, according to Egyptian ideas, prior to the creation, *one* deity, who appears sometimes alone as a male god, and at other times falls apart into a male and a female form. This deity calls into existence from Nu the world that is to be. The means employed are very variously described, but they may be conveniently divided into two great categories, namely, *acts* and *words*.—Amongst the myths belonging to the first class the most popular is that which describes how the creating deity forced his way between heaven and earth, tore them from their embrace, trod the earth under foot, and raised the heaven on high with his arms. For the most part, it is Shu that appears as the separating deity, but his place is taken at times by Bes (Petrie, *Hawara*, pl. 2). We possess numerous pictures (especially from the period *c.* 1500–1000 B.C.), showing, with slight variations of detail, the breaking up of the ancient union. For the most part, the act is represented as just completed. The goddess of heaven, Nut, supports herself on her hands and feet, and so arches herself over the earth-god Seb, who is still falling. A number of other deities are generally to be seen, notably the gods of the Osiris circle. These are regarded as the children sprung from the union of Seb and Nut; they were gradually generated, but first made their appearance at the moment when their parents were torn apart.

Other pictures show a somewhat later scene in the process of creation. We see the earth-god lying wearied on the ground, while the separating god stands over him, holding up the goddess of heaven with his hands. To save himself from fatigue, he has sometimes called assistants to his aid: these either hold up particular portions of the heaven, or even form points of support for the arms of the god himself.—A variant of this legend found it unworthy of the god that he should himself permanently play the part of an Atlas, and be thus hindered from exercising his power in other ways. Accordingly, we are told how the god erected four bifurcated supports—one each in the north, the south, the east, and the west—to bear the arch of heaven. And, in order to ensure the stability of these supports, upon whose existence the continuance of the earth depended, a deity was set over each to guard it. It is the notion of these supports that underlies the figures of the four pillars which, in some pictures of the separation scene, appear beside the god. The names of the supporting deities are variously given. At times they are the usual deities of the regions of heaven: Horus for the south, Set for the north, Thoth for the west, Septi for the east; at other times the place of these gods is taken by goddesses. But the four supports mark the end of the world; and, when the Pharaoh desires to emphasize the fact that he is the lord of all lands, he declares that he rules 'to the supports of the heaven.'

The goddess of heaven is for the most part thought of as a woman, but at times also as a cow—two forms which from the point of view of Egyptian mythology are really identical. For in the Nile valley in general the only purpose served by the goddess is to be the mother and nurse of the future god. The natural symbol for this among an essentially agricultural people was the domestic animal that was most common, the cow, which hence appears as the form of manifestation of practically all the goddesses in their maternal activity. If, for instance, the Egyptians desire to represent the king drinking from the goddess, in order to imbibe, along with her milk, the immortality inherent in her, they introduce him in contact sometimes with the breast of an anthropomorphic form, sometimes with the udder of a cow. Even when such a Divine nurse is portrayed in human form, she is not infrequently provided with a cow's head, in order to indicate with corresponding emphasis her most important function (cf. *e.g.* Naville, *Deir el baḥari*, ii. pl. 53).

On the body of the goddess of heaven the celestial bodies move to and fro, the sun by day, the stars by night; hence she is often depicted with her whole body studded over with stars.

While in the above instances the deity of heaven always appears as female, there is another series of cosmological conceptions where a partition into a female and a male form takes place. We meet with these from about B.C. 1500 downwards, and it is quite possible that they originated at the date just mentioned, for during this period the whole Egyptian mythology is ruled by the effort to divide as far as possible all divinities into a male and a female form of manifestation. This is bound up with a phenomenon that appears even in the language. When the Egyptians wish to express a totality with the utmost possible clearness, they write both the masculine and the feminine of the word, thus exhausting the genders of a language that has no neuter. Thus they say 'every male and every female death,' 'every male and every female disease,' when they mean all forms of death or of disease. In like manner they seek to exhaust the totality of the notion of any particular deity by emphasizing the male and the female form of manifestation. This partition of the divinity is in most instances the result, not of a logical development of religious processes of thought, but of an artificial formation, the female supplementary being obtained simply by adding the feminine suffix *-t* to the name of the male deity. Thus from Ḥer was derived a Ḥer-t, from Rā a Rā-t, etc. (see p. 184[b]).

In thus partitioning the deity of heaven, they usually thought of the female form as overarching the upper, inhabited, side of the earth, while the male form correspondingly arched the under side, both being thus placed at a distance, either above or below, the earth-god Seb. Starting from this conception, the rising of the sun is occasionally so depicted that the subterranean god of heaven holds up the sun at arm's length, while the *cynocephali* that have to greet the rising sun offer their praises to it.

Occasionally, although rarely, the sex of the deities of heaven is reversed, the upper heaven being male and its counterpart female. Thus in texts of the 13th cent. B.C. the rise of the sun in the under world is so depicted that the male god of the heaven of day hands the bark with the sun-god to the female deity of the nightly heavens, as she stands upon the spherically conceived under world.

(*b*) The above described cosmogonic conception is connected with another, intended to explain the origin of the sun, but to which we have as yet only brief allusions. One of these is found in the so-called Book of the Dead, a collection of magical formulæ, whose purpose is to procure, for the deceased, entrance into the world beyond and authority there. In pronouncing these the deceased is to identify himself with certain deities, and to endeavour to obtain advantages by pointing to this fictitious identity. One of the chapters (54), which we can trace back to about the year B.C. 2500, begins thus: 'I am the double lion of the egg of the great cackler, I guard the egg which the god Seb drops from the earth' (cf. *PSBA* vii. p. 152, xv. p. 288). This double lion is the horizon. Here sat, according to Egyptian notions, back to back two lions, which represented yesterday and to-day, the issue of the sun from the under world and his entrance into the upper world (cf. *Tombeau de Ramses IV.*, ed. Lefébure, pl. 40), and whose charge was to guard the sun as he rose between them. The sun himself is often called 'the egg of the great cackler,' while this cackler, again, is the earth-god, who was supposed to have let fall, *i.e.* laid, the egg. Hence he had assigned to him as his sacred animal the goose, which he frequently bears upon his head in those pictures in which he is introduced in human form as a man. How he conceived the egg is not expressly said in the texts, but a picture on a coffin of *c.* 1200 B.C. (Lanzone, *Diz. di mit.* pl. 159) points to the explanation. Here we see the earth-god strain himself under the male nightly heaven till his erected *phallus* points to his mouth. That is to say, he must have impregnated himself, and the sun portrayed behind him is the egg which he will detach from himself as the result of this act.

Alongside of the myth of the great cackler which in the form of a goose lays the sun-egg, runs another, according to which the sun- and also the moon-egg are fashioned by a deity upon the potter's wheel, a process in which it is especially the by-form of the god of Memphis, Ptaḥ-Tatunen (relief at Philæ, in Rosellini's *Mon. del culto*, pl. 21), that we find engaged. To Ptaḥ is attributed also the creation of the whole world, in which rôle he is called 'the great artificer,' so that in this instance we have to think not of a crude tearing apart of the primeval mass, but of an artificial construction of the universe. In this work the god had a number of coadjutors, the so-called *Chnumu* or 'formers.' These are little, dwarf-like, deformed, thick-headed forms, which, eight in number, were regarded as sons of Ptaḥ, or, at a later period, also of Rā. Images of them were frequently put in a grave along with the corpse. As they had once co-operated in the forming of the world, they would now in the world beyond devote themselves to the reconstruction of the deceased, and help him to attain to a new and everlasting life.

(*c*) But the creation of the world was a subject of far less interest to the Egyptians than the origin of the living beings and the objects it contains, gods and men, animals and plants. But in the myths connected with this subject we meet again with that want of systematizing which shows itself everywhere in the Egyptian world of ideas. We have statements as to the origin of particular beings and objects, but there is no finished story of creation such as we find, for instance, at the beginning of the Bk. of Genesis. It is this inability to combine individual notions into a whole that explains also how it was possible for the numerous particular statements to maintain their existence side by side in spite of their contradictions. Since it was not required to unite them into a harmonious system, there was no need to separate duplicate legends, or to exclude or harmonize irreconcilable elements.

For the most part, one was content to celebrate in general terms the praises of this or that god as creator. Thus, *c.* 1500 B.C., it is said of Osiris (stele in Paris, Bibl. Nat., published by Ledrain in *Mon. égypt. de la Bibl. Nat.* pll. 21–26; cf. Chabas, *Rev. arch.* XIV. i. 65ff., 193ff.): 'He formed with his hand the earth, its water, its air, its plants, all its cattle, all its birds, all its winged fowl, all its reptiles, all its four-footed creatures.' Again, we read of the ram-headed god Chnum: 'He created all that is, he formed all that exists, he is the father of fathers, the mother of mothers,' 'he fashioned men, he made the gods, he was father from the beginning,' 'he is the creator of the heaven, the earth, the under world, the water, the mountains,' 'he formed a male and a female of all birds, fishes, wild beasts, cattle, and of all worms.' In another passage the god of Thebes, Amon-Rā, is celebrated as 'the father of the gods, the fashioner of men, the creator of cattle, the lord of all being, the creator of the fruit trees, the former of the grass, the giver of life to the cattle.'

Similar functions are attributed also to other members of the Pantheon, and it even happens not infrequently that in the same tomb or temple different deities are hailed as creator in almost identical terms, without any sense of contradiction. It is seldom, however, that one gets beyond general language; and above all it is impossible to establish a fixed order in the succession of creative acts. Sometimes it is gods that first come into being, at other times men, or again animals or plants, etc.

(*d*) The choice of methods of creation, again, is left to the different deities—nay, one and the same god adopts one method according to one author, and another according to another. (α) Relatively most frequent is the conception of creation, after the analogy of earthly conditions, as a series of births. A god and a goddess are placed at the beginning of the development; these unite and have children born to them, who in their turn are gods. But gradually their posterity degenerates, becoming demi-gods and at last men. To avoid the difficulty of having to postulate the pre-existence of two deities, a myth, which recurs from the Pyramid era down to that of the Ptolemies, makes only one god pre-exist, namely Tum, who by means of Onani formed the first divine pair, Shu and Tefnut (Pyramid Pepi I., l. 465 f. = Mer-en-Rā, l. 528 f.; Papyr. Brit. Mus. 10188, ed. Budge, 'On the Hieratic Papyrus of Nesi-Amsu' in *Archæologia*, lii., 1891; cf. Pleyte, *Rec. de trav. rel. à l'Égypt.* iii. p. 57 ff.; Budge, *PSBA* ix. p. 11 ff.; Brugsch, *Religion der alten Aegypter*, 470 f.; and, for the creation myth, Wiedemann, *Urquell*, ii. p. 57 ff., where a collection will be found also of further ancient statements bearing upon the same circle of conceptions). Then were born to Shu and Tefnut the god Seb and the goddess Nut, who were the parents of Osiris and the gods of his group, whose children multiplied upon this earth. This genealogy shows that the Onanistic creation was placed before the heavens and earth were formed, the representatives of these first making their appearance as grandchildren of the pre-existing god.

It was not only gods that originated from a primeval deity by the instrumentality of Onani; men also were formed in the same way. In the tomb of Seti I., founded *c.* 1350 B.C., there are portrayed (Leps. *Denkm.* iii. 136[b]) the four races of men, which, according to the Egyptian view, peopled the earth, and which are characterized as the flocks of the sun-god Rā. They are the reddish-brown 'men,' *i.e.* the Egyptians: the dark-yellow Asiatic Semites; the black negroes; and the whitish-grey Libyans. According to the accompanying inscription, these beings were created by another form of the sun-god, namely the hawk-headed Horus; the negroes by Onani, the Egyptians by his tears, the Libyans by the shooting forth of his eye, *i.e.*, apparently, by his warming beams.

A great creative power is attributed also in other inscriptions to the tears of a deity. They play a part in the most diverse periods of Egyptian history. There are other texts besides the above which trace the origin of the Egyptians to them. But then the sun as well brought other things into being by *his* tears. 'When the sun weeps a second time,' we read in a papyrus of *c.* 800 B.C. (Papyr. Salt, No. 825 in London, tr. by Birch in *RP* vi. p. 115), 'and lets water fall from his eyes, this changes itself into working bees, which pursue their task in flowers of every kind, and honey and wax are produced instead of water.' Further products of the tears of the sun-god Horus are cloth-stuffs, wine, incense, oil, the most varied objects used for offerings, which, accordingly, are designated 'the eye of Horus.' The tear of the goddess Isis, which falls into the Nile, causes the inundation of the river, and thus brings to the land abundance, wealth, and the means of nourishment.

Not only the tears but other fluids from the body of a deity have creative power attributed to them. From the blood that issued from the *phallus* of the sun-god when he cut himself, sprang, according to the Book of the Dead (chs. 17. 23), two gods, Ḥu (Taste) and Sa (Perception), who henceforth remained in his train. After the slaughter of the bull, in which Batau, who in the fable of the Two Brothers (composed *c.* 1300 B.C.) is conceived of as almost a divine being, had incarnated himself (Papyr. d'Orbiney, pl. 16, l. 8 ff.), two drops of blood fell upon the earth, and from these sprang two great trees, which now served Batau as an embodiment.—Side by side with the blood is the saliva. When saliva flows from the mouth of the senile sun-god and falls upon clayey soil, Isis forms from these materials a serpent, which at once assumes life, and whose bite threatens to be fatal to the sun-god (Wiedemann, *Rel. of Anc. Egypt*, 54 ff.).

The root idea is the same in all these instances. In every part of the body of the god, in everything that proceeds from him, there is a portion of his Ego, something Divine and therefore capable of development and life-producing.

(β) A further way to the formation of living beings was found in the artificial methods attributed to the gods. We have already had occasion to mention how Ptaḥ, the god of Memphis, was supposed to fashion the sun-egg on the potter's wheel. In like manner, according to the view that prevailed in Upper Egypt, the ram-headed god Chnum fashioned the king and his *ka* upon a similar wheel (relief at Luxor, in Maspero, *Hist. anc.* i. p. 157). If no wheel was available, the god was capable also of forming human beings in a simpler way. When the sun-god, in the fable of the Two Brothers (Papyr. d' Orbiney, pl. 9, ll. 6–8), found his favourite Batau alone, and desired to furnish him with a wife, Chnum 'built' a woman for him. Since the latter owed her origin to a god, she was more beautiful in her limbs than any woman in the whole land, and all gods were in her. The word 'built' has here for its determinative the picture of a man erecting a wall, so that the Egyptian writer thought of an actual construction of a woman—a manner of origin for which the reconstruction of the dismembered body of the god Osiris supplied him with a fitting analogy, for after this reconstruction the god at once acquired new life (cf. p. 195[a]).

(γ) Procreation is another process which is not left out of account by the ancient Egyptians in connexion with the formation of man. It is employed above all by the sun-god when his earthly representative and son, the Pharaoh, has to be brought into being. In each successive case the god assumes the form of the present occupant of the throne, unites himself with the queen, and thus generates the future ruler (see the detailed representations in Naville, *Deir el baḥari*, ii. pll. 47–53). This belief in the Divine origin of the monarch was held fast down to the Greek period. When Alexander the Great gave himself out as the son of Jupiter Amon, he was thoroughly accommodating himself to the notions of his Egyptian subjects. The ram's horn, moreover, which, in conformity with this origin, shows itself in the pictures of Alexander and his successors, has its prototype in the ancient Pharaohs, who (so, above all, Seti I. at Abydos) likewise, as sons of Amon, bear this horn.

For the most part, the king is satisfied with one god as his father; but at times a step further is taken, and the Pharaoh claims a plurality of heavenly fathers. Thus Ramses II. makes the gods of Egypt declare that they had generated him as their son and heir, while the goddesses tell how they nursed and brought him up, so that in a sense at least they performed maternal functions for the monarch.

(3) In all the forms of creation hitherto discussed, some *act* of a deity is required in order to call something new into being; it may be an act of violence, or a procreative act, or a shedding of tears, etc. But, side by side with these, there was a considerable series of myths which did not regard any active exertion on the part of the creator as necessary, but attributed the result simply to *speech*, the uttering of words.

The Egyptian assumed—and this is a very important notion from the point of view of the history of religion—that an inward and indissoluble connexion subsists between an object and its name (cf. Wiedemann in *L'Égypte*, i. 573 ff., and in the *Muséon*, xv. 49 ff.). Every thing has a name; without name is no thing, and without thing no name is conceivable. Thus the name becomes an imperishable component of the Ego, on a footing of equality with soul, form, heart, etc., and its continued existence is indispensable if the whole man is to enter upon immortality. Any one who utters the name of a god correctly is sure of his favour. When the goddess Isis succeeded by her wiles in inducing the sun-god Rā to whisper to her his real name, she thereby obtained the power of this god and became the supreme goddess. Any one who in the under world was able to call a demon by name was safe from any further harm at his hands; a gate must open its leaves to any one who named it correctly.

As acquaintance with the name of a god gave power over the god, so did acquaintance with a man's name give power over him. Hence it was very dangerous to one to have his name known to an enemy, who could make use of it in connexion with magic, and only required to introduce it into a formula to bring disease and death upon its bearer. The anxiety to escape such a result was sometimes so keen that the Egyptian bore two names—one civilian, by which he was called in his ordinary life, and one sacred, which was introduced only into religious texts, in the hope that its holy environment would avail to save its bearer from destruction. We meet with analogous notions among various peoples, it being sometimes the case that even the man himself does not know his real name, for fear of his inadvertently betraying it. The ancient Egyptians did not go so far as this, but the true name was uttered only in the narrowest possible circles. In the above-mentioned myth of the sun-god Rā, the god himself is made to say, 'My name was uttered by my father and my mother, and then was it concealed in me by my parent that no spell might be formed to bewitch me.' For these reasons it is often said of the great gods that their name is hidden, and from the second millennium B.C. downwards the Divine name *Amon* was explained to mean 'the hidden one,' as if the word had been derived from the root *ȧmen*='to be hidden,' which indeed is not true to fact.

The theory of the connexion between name and thing gave rise to quite a number of creation myths, which all go back to the same fundamental idea, however they may differ in details. The moment the deity in the exhilaration of his creative activity utters a word, the object designated by that word springs into being, even if it should happen that the word in the particular instance has quite a different meaning. The word had sounded so or so, and thereupon the notion inherent in it made its appearance, the word had assumed the form corresponding to it, and co-existed now with its notion to all eternity. Some examples taken from the presently to be described legend of the destruction of the human race, will best show how the Egyptians record the process of creation in such instances as we have in view. There the god says, 'I give thee authority to send forth thy messenger (*hab*), then originated the ibis (*habi*),' or 'I let thee turn (*ānān*) to the peoples of the north, then originated the *cynocephalus* (*ānān*).' Sometimes the word uttered is not even the exact name of the object, in which case a resemblance of sound sufficed to bring the latter into being. Thus in one text it is said, 'I let thee comprehend (*ȧnh*) both heavens, then originated the moon (*ȧāh*).'

Especially in the later periods of Egyptian history, from the 17th cent. downwards, such theories of creation, which in the earlier literature occur only sporadically, find favour, until in the Ptolemaic era a perfect passion for them sets in. Long, fantastic, occasionally unconnected, ætiological myths bring the god into the most diverse situations, in order to cause him to utter the word that shall bring into being one or another portion of the *materia sacra* of a particular sanctuary. And in such myths as little concern is displayed for logical connexion as for grammatically correct derivations (cf. *e.g.* the legend of the winged solar disc at Edfu, tr. by Brugsch in *Abhandlungen der Göttinger Akad.* xiv.).

The god who, above all, created by means of words, was Thoth; who appears sometimes, as at Hermopolis, the principal seat of his worship in Upper Egypt, as exercising this function on his own initiative, at other times as acting as the instrument of the creator proper, for whom he speaks. This was a rôle to which he was specially called, as lord of the words of the gods, composer of the most powerful magical formulæ, god of wisdom. Since he knows what is correct and gives it correct expression, he comes to be also the god of wisdom, who, along with his two embodiments, the ibis and the *cynocephalus*, is revered above all the gods by scholars and devout students of magic.

In all the ancient Egyptian literature known to us, actual words require to be uttered by the god in the act of creation. The notion that *inarticulate sounds*, his laugh and the like, could produce the same results, meets us first in the later Greek papyrus-literature of the Hellenistic and post-Christian period, and then in the Gnostic writings (cf. Maspero, *Études de mythol.* ii. p. 376). How far this belief is older than Hellenism cannot be determined. At all events, there is a connexion between it and the strange statement of the Church Fathers that the inhabitants of Pelusium paid Divine honours to flatulence and to the onions that caused it (Jerome, xiii. *in* Is 46; cf. Clem. Alex. x. 76; Minucius Felix, *Oct.* 28; Theoph. Ant. *Oct.* i. 15; Orig. *c. Cels.* v. 36).

The Egyptians had at their disposal a wealth of materials bearing upon the above doctrines, when it was desired to record the causes and the course of creation, but—to emphasize this point again and once for all—they never succeeded in harmonizing the particular conceptions and constructing out of them a finished system of cosmogony.

(B) *Destruction of the world.*—(1) While the ancient Egyptians have much to tell of the creation of the world, they know far less about its destruction, or even about a partial destruction of the world or of man. Presumably, this world appeared to the ancient Egyptian in a light so fair that in general he was unable to conceive of a time when it should be no more, and when no Egyptian should dwell any more on the banks of the Nile. It is true that recent investigators, founding upon some statements of a Saitic priest reported by Plato (*Timæus*, 22), have frequently attributed to the Egyptians a belief in a great world-conflagration. But the truth is that in the passage in question what is said is that, if a conflagration of the world should set in in consequence of the stars leaving their courses, the Nile would protect Egypt by its inundation. Egyptian papyrus-passages which have been cited for the same purpose (Ebers, *Papyrus Ebers*, p. 15), contain equally little to bear out the contention built upon them. They tell of a fire which threatened to be fatal to Horus, the son of the goddess Isis, and which Isis extinguished. But there is no thought here of a conflagration of the world, but of a local fire, presumably in a hut in the Delta where Horus happened to be at the time. The means, again, employed by Isis are little suited to the extinguishing of a world-conflagration (see Schaefer, *Aegyp. Ztschr.* xxxvi. p. 129 ff.).

(2) The only allusion as yet discovered to a deluge that threatened to destroy the whole earth, or at least parts of it, is contained in a papyrus of *c.* 1200 B.C. (Leps. *Denkm.* vi. 118, ll. 34-39 [the tr. by Pierret in *Études égyp.* 1 ff., is not free from errors]), which contains a hymn of praise to the pantheistically conceived Deity. Here we read: 'Thine (*sc.* the god's) overflowing water [lit. 'Thy spreading-itself-out'] rises to the heavens, the roaring water of thy mouth is in the clouds, thy jackals are upon the mountains [*i.e.* the jackals which, according to an Egyptian doctrine, drew the bark of the sun-god, have been compelled to retire before the flood to the mountain-tops]. The water of the god Horus covers the tall trees of all lands, the overflowing water covers the circuit of all quarters of the heavens and of the sea. A scene of inundation would all lands (still) be, were they not under thine influence. The waters (now) move themselves in the way which thou assignest them, they pass not over the bounds which thou settest them, (the path) which thou openest for them.' The Deity, that is to say, saved the world from destruction by the deluge, and now by his providence prevents a recurrence of that event.

(3) Another text treats of the destruction of a portion of the human race by the Deity, against whom they had rebelled, and thus belongs to the category of so-called Deluge legends in the wider sense of the term. We have this legend in two copies in Theban kings' tombs belonging to the period B.C. 1400-1200 (Lefébure, *Tombeau de Seti I.*, part 4, pll. 15-18, *Tombeau de Ramses III.*, pll. 2-5: cf. Bergmann, *Hierogl. Inschriften*, pll. 75-82; Naville in *TSBA* iv. p. 1 ff., viii. p. 412 ff.; Brugsch, *Religion*, etc., 436 ff., and *Die neue Weltordnung*, Berlin, 1881; Maspero, *Les Origines*, 164 ff. [*Dawn of Civilization*, 164 ff.]; Wiedemann, *Religion*, etc. [Eng. ed.], 58 ff.). There is a further allusion to this myth in Papyrus Sallier IV., of the Ramesside period (cf. Chabas, *Le calendrier des jours fastes et néfastes*, Chalons, 1870), which contains a list of the days of the year, with an appended note as to whether they are to be considered lucky or unlucky, and a record of the mythological occurrence which gave them this character. This text remarks on the 13th Mechir: 'Unlucky, unlucky, unlucky! Go not out in any wise on this day. It is the day on which the eye of Sechet grew terrible and filled the fields with desolation. On this day go not out at sundown.' The same occurrence is in view also in the plates of glazed clay which exhibit the lion-headed goddess Sechet, with a huge eye introduced behind her. These were intended, in all probability, to protect their owners from a fate similar to what then befell guilty men. Their pretty frequent occurrence down to a late period proves that the legend in question not only found its way occasionally into Egypt, but had wide and long-continued vogue.

The myth itself relates how the sun-god Rā ruled over gods and men. But men observed that he had grown old, his bones had turned into silver, his joints into gold, and his hair into lapis-lazuli. When Rā noticed how men were thus inclined towards rebellion, he secretly summoned the rest of the gods to Heliopolis to take counsel as to counter measures. The gods advised him to send forth his eye, the goddess Sechet (the sun in its consuming strength), against men to destroy them, although the rebels, filled with fear, had already begun to seek refuge in flight. Rā followed their counsel, and Sechet slaughtered mankind, wading for several nights in the blood of her victims, from Heracleopolis Magna in Middle Egypt to Heliopolis. But Rā quickly repented of having instigated this massacre. Not venturing directly to forbid the goddess to complete the task assigned her, he had recourse to stratagem. He caused beer to be brewed and poured into the blood of the slain. When the goddess saw this next morning, and found the fields flooded with it, she rejoiced, drank the mixture till she was intoxicated and could not recognize men. Thus mankind was rescued; but Rā was dissatisfied with himself, because he had not left their destruction unchecked. He saw in this a token of his weakness, and determined to abdicate his sovereignty voluntarily before a new weakness should overtake him. At first he set out, on the back of the cow of heaven, for the Mediterranean coasts. At this spectacle men were seized with contrition. They besought Rā to remain with them and destroy his enemies. But the god went on his way, men followed him, and, when it was morning, they came forth with their bows and joined battle with the enemies of the god Rā. Then spake Rā: 'Your transgression is forgiven. The slaughter (which ye have wrought on my behalf) compensates the slaughter (which my enemies intended against me).' In spite, however, of his forgiveness of men, Rā did not continue to dwell with them. He betook himself to higher regions, created the Fields of Peace and the Fields of Aalu, and settled many men there. Then he handed over his sovereignty of the earth to his son Shu (who was likewise a sun-god), called into being a number of sacred animals such as the ibis and the *cynocephalus*, and charged the earth-god Seb to give heed to the serpents, which must be charmed by means of magical formulæ.—In these details, which are not explained by the legend itself, some part is played presumably by the recollection of other myths, in which the serpents appeared as opponents of the sun-god, and with which the author assumed an acquaintance on the part of his readers.

ii. THE GODS.—(A) *Historical development of the power of particular gods.*—(1) We have already remarked that the Egyptian religion was not a unity. Nor did it form a concentrated system any more than the Egyptian State. The latter had originated in early times from a number of small States, which either peaceably or as the result of conquest had become united under a single ruler, without thereby making a complete surrender of their former independence. To these ancient petty States corresponded the later so-called *nomes* (Egyp. *hesp*), of which there were generally reckoned 22 for Upper and 20 for Lower Egypt. The number underwent not infrequent variations, adjacent nomes being sometimes united for administrative purposes, while at other times particular nomes might be partitioned owing to rights of succession or other causes. Nevertheless, these nomes, especially in Upper Egypt, continued to be the same on the whole from the Pyramid era down to that of the Greeks and Romans.

The nomes were independent from not only a political but a religious point of view. In their principal city stood the temple of the chief god of the nome, and here the conception and the worship of this higher being developed themselves independently of the religious development in other parts of Egypt. The cultus, however, was not confined to this nome god; worship was offered in his temple to other gods as well. In this way groups were readily formed, a goddess and a son or a larger family being assigned to the god, or the latter was conceived as the supreme deity, with a circle of inferior gods surrounding him. Nor did his cult exclude the worship of other gods in other localities of the same nome or in other temples of the same metropolis. The nome god was simply regarded in general as the tutelary lord who had the first claim upon the inhabitants in all specially important matters, and, above all, when their common interests were concerned.

(2) The authority of the nome god was not so firmly established but that it might be overshadowed, even in his own nome, by other deities, although such an experience was relatively rare. Thus the god of the Thinite nome was originally Ȧnḥer. At a later period, Osiris, the god of the city of Abydos, in the same nome, gained such preponderance that he stepped into the place of Ȧnḥer in the nome cult as well. In the Thebaid the principal rôle appears to have been played at first by Mont (Ment), the god of the ancient metropolis Hermonthis. With the advance of Thebes and the growing importance of its temple of Amon, the latter became from the 12th dynasty onwards the principal deity. But as the power of Thebes waned more and more during the Saitic period, the prestige of its god also sank in the nome, and the significance of Mont once more revived.

In other instances nome gods were able to extend their worship beyond the limits of their own province. Thus shrines were occasionally built to their own gods by men who had migrated from one nome to another. If these shrines were richly endowed, other Egyptians might be led to attach themselves to the newly introduced cult. As far as we can trace the matter back, in such cases the gods who from of old had been in possession were always tolerant, and took no umbrage at the introduction of the new divinities so long as these made no claim to supremacy over themselves. But cults of this kind, whose introduction was due to private persons, had no importance outside a limited sphere. The authority of a nome god increased in far greater measure when the princes of his province raised themselves to the rank of Pharaohs. The god had procured for his prince the supreme power in Egypt, and thereby showed that he was mightier than the other nome gods. The maintenance of his cult was consequently the primary duty of the royal house and of all the courtiers and officials connected with it, not indeed in the sense that an officially prescribed State cult was introduced, but one that had the force of consuetudinary propriety in view of the religious notions which had been cherished from olden times by the now reigning Pharaonic house. But similar considerations would gain over other Egyptians also to the new cult, and move the various priestly colleges to grant it admittance into their temples. This advance in the honours paid to some particular god, followed by a decline when the power of the dynasty from that nome decayed, may still be traced, by aid of the inscriptions, in the case of Amon, Bast, and other Divine figures. With other gods the change of prestige has taken place prior to the commencement of the literary tradition accessible to us. In primitive times, for instance, great significance was possessed by the jackal-headed god Ȧp-uat, who was ultimately regarded as the nome god of Siut. His image was borne upon a standard before the king, and the jackal's tail, in allusion to his cult, was, down to the latest times, worn by the Pharaohs, attached to their girdle behind, as a symbol of rule. In the course of Egyptian history, however, Ȧp-uat receded quite into the background in the cult. In the Old Empire he still held the place of one of the chief gods of the dead, in the Middle Empire even this prestige begins to decay, and under the New Empire in almost every necropolis his place is taken by another jackal-god, Anubis, who, in the train of Osiris, the god of the dead, obtains growing significance in the conceptions of the under world.

(3) In all these instances a political development of Egypt, originally quite apart from religious considerations, had brought with it as a logical consequence a change of faith, without the co-operation of any external compulsion on the part of the State. Once only was it otherwise, namely, when Amenophis IV. sought at one bound forcibly to raise to the chief place the cult of Aten, the solar disc, worshipped as one of the natural bodies—a cult which under his predecessors had been slowly growing in importance. The rest of the gods were to take only a secondary place, if indeed the attempt was not made, as in the case of Amon, to prevent their worship altogether, and to damage the god by destroying his name in inscriptions, etc. This violent revolution had no success. After the death of the innovator, even his own family speedily lost interest in his god. The temples consecrated to Ȧten were deserted and destroyed, his worship survived in only a few places, and even there to only an insignificant extent.

(4) In order that the heavenly figures should enjoy Divine authority, it was not necessary for them to be the chief gods in one of the nomes of Egypt; the enormous number of Egyptian divinities is itself sufficient to exclude such a supposition. Some of them even enjoyed widespread regard throughout Egypt, without ever having possessed any such local authority. Some even of the chief deities of the whole country have no place among the nome gods, as for instance the goddess of Truth Maāt, the god Nefer-Tum, the Nile god Ḥāpi, and, above all, the principal god of historical Egypt, Rā. This sun-god was indeed specially worshipped at Heliopolis, a city which was called after him by the sacred name *Pa-Rā*, 'house of Rā,' but the nome god here was originally not Rā but Ȧtum (Tum). The latter is likewise a sun-god, who even in later times always enjoyed veneration side by side with Rā, an attempt being frequently made to represent him as a partial form of Rā, namely, the god of the evening sun. For his veneration over the whole of Egypt, Rā is indebted, accordingly, not to any local authority possessed by him,—as a city Heliopolis never had any very great importance,—but to the doctrine concerning him and to the development of religious conceptions in the Nile valley.

In the time of the early dynasties, whose power was concentrated in Upper Egypt, and which, it would appear, succeeded only gradually in conquering the Delta, Rā plays no considerable rôle. Even under the 4th dynasty, which had its residence at Memphis, not far from Heliopolis, he is still quite in the background. With the accession of the 5th dynasty these conditions are changed. A fabulous story, dating from *c.* 2000 B.C., makes the first three kings of this dynasty to have been the offspring of the god Rā by the wife of a priest of Rā in an otherwise unknown place of the name of Sachebu. How old this legend is we cannot tell, but it is certain that from the 5th dynasty onwards all the Pharaohs give themselves out to be sons of Rā. Nevertheless, the god does not at first appear very frequently in the inscriptions, although king Rā-en-user of the 5th dynasty already caused a great sanctuary to be erected to him at Abusir (cf. *Aegyp. Ztschr.* xxxvii. 1 ff., xxxviii. 94 ff., xxxix. 91 ff.). It is not till the time of the Middle Empire that Rā is mentioned with ever-increasing frequency, and that the conception of the specially close relation between deity and sun begins at the same time to influence the conception formed of other gods. This leads, for instance, in the case of the Theban Amon, to a complete amalgamation of the old god of Thebes with the sun-god—a result which finds outward expression in the usual name for this deity under the New Empire, namely Amon-Rā. But, even when this new name is not employed, the simple name Amon is always during this period to be understood of the deity who had become a solar one. The same happened with other Divine figures. Sometimes the amalgamation is indicated by the name (Sebek-Rā, and the like), at other times the old name is retained, and it is merely the conception of the god that is influenced by solar notions. In the first millennium B.C. practically the whole of the more important Egyptian gods became more or less clearly defined sun-gods, and processes of thought derived from the solar faith were allowed to influence even the conceptions of the gods of the under world who were connected with the Osirian doctrine of immortality (see below, p. 195[b]).

But, although the nature of the Egyptian deities was in later times prevailingly solar, we must be careful not to carry inferences from this back to earlier periods. We can trace the progress of the process by aid of the monuments, and are not at liberty offhand to place the result at the beginning of the development of Egyptian religion.

(5) In consequence of the independence of the various nome gods, the doublets already referred to were bound to arise in the circle of the higher powers. In his own district each nome god is at once creator, preserver, ruler of the world, quite untrammelled by similar pretensions on the part of his Divine neighbour. The Egyptians never attempted to remove the logical contradiction that thus arose. Quite the reverse! In taking over a foreign god to a new nome, they calmly took over also his titles and his myths, quite unconcerned that in this way a *Doppelgänger* to the old nome god found entrance into the nome. The only concession occasionally made in favour of more systematized thought was that deities of this kind were declared to be essentially identical or emanations of the same Divine notion, without, however, the further step being taken of abandoning the assumption of an independent individuality for each particular form. Especially in later texts it is often asserted that the nome or temple god bears in other places the names of the local deities, but one must not infer from this, as has frequently been done, *e.g.* even by Brugsch, that the forms in question are actually identical. Such statements are merely intended to characterize the particular god as the possessor of all Divine power—a position which in other places might quite well be attributed to any other who was the ruling deity there.

(6) In principle, then, the nome gods have equal importance, they may all of them, if the occasion demands it, have omnipotence attributed to them; but we have already noted that this relation might assume a different form in practice, according to the power of their particular nome. The material at our disposal does not indeed always give us a trustworthy picture of the actual conditions. We have an exact knowledge only of those deities whose places of worship and temples survive and have been already excavated. Our views are thus subject to constant shifting when new texts and monuments emerge from places that had not been previously examined. Chance plays so great a part in the matter that it is quite possible that gods at present scarcely known to us had great importance in antiquity, and, conversely, that the forms which are frequently named in our sources once possessed only slight significance. Here, as little as elsewhere in Egyptological questions, are we at liberty to forget that, in spite of the wealth of monuments that have survived, their number is relatively small considering the thousands of years of Egyptian history, and hence their data must be used with caution in drawing inferences as to ancient conditions in general. This must be kept in view in judging of the following list of the most important Egyptian deities. These are the forms of which the extant texts principally speak; and, above all, they are those which possessed the greatest interest for the nations of antiquity outside Egypt.

(B) *List of gods*:—1. *NATIVE EGYPTIAN DEITIES*.—**Rā** is the god of the sun, who, conceived of as a man, or as a man with a hawk's head, guides the heavenly bodies, creates new life by his rays, and thus blesses mankind, although at times he also shoots forth consuming fire (his eye is the goddess Sechet, cf. above, p. 182). The centre of his worship is Heliopolis (Egyp. *An* [Heb. אֹן] or *Pa-Rā*, Gr. Ἡλιούπολις [Heb. בֵּית שֶׁמֶשׁ]), where the kings of the 12th dynasty built him a great temple. For the most part he stands alone, but occasionally an artificially formed consort (see above, p. 179[a]), Rā-t (Rā-t-ta-ui), is placed by his side. The monuments of the cult of Rā resemble the conical stone in which among others he embodied himself at Heliopolis. In the time of the Old Empire huge buildings were erected to him in the form of a flat-topped pyramid surmounted by an obelisk. The best known of these was that erected by king Rā-en-user at Abusir (see above, p. 183[b]).

The god pursued his course in the heavens by ship. Two barks, bearing the names Mādet and Sekti, are generally attributed to him; in later times he is supposed to use a special vessel for every hour of the day. The name of Rā is associated with numerous legends which depict him as a king decaying with age, against whom gods and men rebel, but who always emerges victorious from the resulting conflicts. The texts name a number of other sun-gods along with and often confused with Rā. Of these we now proceed to notice the five most important—

(1) **Horus.**—Our treatment of this god is rendered difficult by the circumstance that under this name were understood two deities, who were originally quite distinct, although afterwards they passed into one another: Horus, the son of Isis (see below, p. 194[b]), and Horus the sun-god. The latter, again, is separated into a number of independent individual forms, which are distinguished by additions to the name Horus. Thus we have: *Ḥer-ur*, 'Horus the ancient,' of Letopolis; *Ḥer-men-ti*, 'Horus of the two eyes,' of Shedenu in the Delta; *Ḥer-chent-àn-ma*, 'Horus in the condition of not seeing,' of Letopolis; *Ḥer-em-chuti*, 'Horus on the horizon,' the Greek Harmachis, at Tanis, and in the environs of Memphis, where the great sphinx of Gizeh is his symbol; *Ḥer-nub*, 'the golden Horus,' who is regarded especially as the midday sun; *Ḥer-beḥudti*, 'Horus of Edfu,' whose symbol, the winged solar disc, used to be placed as an omen-averter on temples, steles, etc. Then, again, *Ḥer-ka*, 'Horus the bull'; *Ḥer-desher*, 'the red Horus'; *Ḥer-àp-shetu*, 'Horus the revealer of the secret,' answer to the planets Saturn, Mars, Jupiter, which were thus thought of as solar forms.—*Ḥer-t* is a later-formed female complementary form of the male Horus (see p. 179[a]).

(2) **Cheperá,** 'he that becomes' (Germ. 'der Werdende'), is primarily the morning sun. A Turin text declares: 'I am Cheperá in the morning, Rā at midday, Tum in the evening,' but the three deities just named are usually thought of in pretty much one and the same way as = the sun in general.

(3) **Tum** or **Atum** is the god of Heliopolis, and

is frequently regarded as the creator; he is portrayed mostly as a man with the crowns of Egypt. A great temple dedicated to him was situated at the modern Tell el-Maskhuta, and known as *Pa-Tum* ('house of Tum,' the biblical Pithom; cf. Naville, *The Store-city of Pithom*, London, 1885).

(4) **Shu** appears, above all, as creator, and at Thebes and Memphis is named as one of the Egyptian kings of the gods. His female consort and twin sister is the lion-headed **Tefnut.** The notions cherished regarding this goddess, and especially her genealogical place in the Egyptian religious system, underwent numerous variations. In the myths she does not come at all prominently forward.

(5) **Åten,** 'the sun's disc,' of whom we have spoken already (see p. 183[b]), is, in contrast to Rā, not an anthropomorphic form, but the celestial body itself. He is portrayed as the solar disc from which rays stream down towards the earth. These end in hands which reach down the signs for life, power, etc. Amenophis IV. (*c.* 1450 B.C.) desired to make Åten the ruling god in Egypt, called himself in honour of him *Chu(achu)-en-àten*, 'splendour of the solar disc,' and built him a great temple at Tel el-Amarna in Central Egypt, to whose neighbourhood he removed the royal residence, which had been at Thebes. Apart from the prominence it gave to the new god, the henotheistic (*not* monotheistic) reformation of this king made little change in Egypt. The organization of officials remained the same (cf. Baillet, *Rec. de trav. rel. à l'Egypt.* xxiii. 140 ff.), and so did the cultus and the religious formulæ, in which the ancient Divine names were simply replaced in many instances by that of Åten. In numerous hymns, touched with poetical feeling, which have been found in the tombs of el-Amarna, the god is hailed as beneficent star, bringer of light and heat, rejoicer of man and beast, creator and nourisher of all things and beings, the only deity that is worthy of veneration, etc. As a matter of course, no myth is attached to the nature god himself.

**Amon** of Thebes was presumably at first a god of the reproductive natural force which generates animals and plants, as were his neighbour gods, **Ment** of Hermonthis and **Min** of Koptos. The three names probably go back to the root *men* (='stand'), the allusion being to the erected *phallus.* At a later period Amon blends more and more with the sun-god (see above, p. 184[a]), and thus arises Amon-Rā, who is now hailed repeatedly in hymns as creator, dispenser of nourishment, etc. More and more he arrogates the functions of other gods, and is first invoked in a henotheistic sense, and then designated pantheistically as god of the All, the other gods being his members and parts. During this period the custom originated of deriving his name from *àmen* ('to be hidden'), the idea being that his true name, *i.e.* his real nature, is concealed (see above, p. 181[a]). He is portrayed as a man with a high feather crown.

At Thebes Amon does not usually appear alone, but in company with the goddess **Mut** and their son **Chunsu.** There is thus constituted a Divine family, a triad, the members of which, however, always remain independent, and never blend into a trinity. It was generally held in ancient Egypt that a god, like a man, grows old and dies. In order to secure, in spite of this, the perpetual life of the god, he is supposed to generate by his wife, who is usually also his sister, a son like himself, who, when the father dies, steps into his place. He in turn generates, by her who had been his own mother, a son like himself—he becomes, as the Egyptians say, *ka-mut-f*, 'husband of his mother,' —who succeeds him on his death. Strangely enough, there is no word of the goddess dying. But this is probably due, not to any real immortality being attributed to her, but to the meagre significance of goddesses in Egyptian mythology.

Besides the triad, we find in Egyptian temples groups of four or eight, and especially of nine deities. The composition of these groups rests upon a variety of principles: at times the forms have actually a close connexion, at other times one of the gods is regarded as king, the others as his court, etc. Pre-eminent in this class is the ennead of Heliopolis, in the formation of which a mythological system co-operated, and which then exercised an influence upon other temples as well (cf. Maspero, *Ét. de myth.* ii. 337 ff.). In place of a single ennead some temples have two, a great and a small, while others have a still larger number.

**Mut,** depicted as a woman with a human head or that of a lion, had a temple of her own to the south of Karnak in Thebes (Benson-Gourlay, *The Temple of Mut in Asher*, London, 1899), where she passed for queen of heaven and eye of Rā, and where numerous lion-headed statues were dedicated to her or to Sechet (see below, p. 186[a]), particularly by Amenophis III. and Sheshonk I. Instead of her we occasionally meet with the grammatically formed goddess **Åment** by the side of Amon. She has nothing to do with the almost homonymous goddess of the under world, *Åmenti*, 'she who belongs to the realm of the dead.'

**Chunsu** appears to have been primarily a moon-god [*chens*='pass through,' here with reference to the motion of the stars]. He bears upon his hawk's head a moon-crescent and sun's disc, and the mention of him runs parallel with that of the other moon-deities (Thoth, Åāh, etc.). In later times he becomes the god of healing, and falls apart into two forms, 'Chunsu, the beautifully resting one,' who always abides in the temple at Thebes, and 'Chunsu, the executor of plans,' who is sent out by the other as physician and magician. To the first of these a great temple was erected at Karnak by Ramses III. and his successors; the latter had a small sanctuary beside it, which is mentioned as late as the Ptolemaic era (cf. *Aegyp. Ztschr.* xxxviii. 126).

**Ment** was worshipped at various places in the Thebaid; he has a hawk's head, solar disc, and the Amon feathers, and in the Theban period of Egyptian history he is regarded especially as the god of war, to whom the Pharaoh, as he sets out for battle, is compared. His embodiment at Erment is the Bacis (see below, p. 190[a]).

**Min** [formerly read *Chem* or *Åmsi*] was the god of Panopolis, Koptos, and other places; he presents himself as an ithyphallic man, and is viewed as the god of procreation. Harvest and other joyous festivals are held in his honour, and he often coincides with Amon *ka-mut-f*, as the god who constantly reproduces himself and thus lives for ever.

**Chnum** or **Chnuphis,** the ram-headed god of the cataract region, is creator of the world, which he fashioned upon the potter's wheel, and of human beings, whom he 'constructed.' By his side appear the goddesses to be presently mentioned, Sati and Anukit. In addition, we find occasionally coupled with him the frog-headed goddess **Ḥekt,** who is frequently mentioned from the earliest times downwards, without our being able, however, to fix her exact significance. At all events, she played a part in the resurrection dogma, which was symbolized down to the Christian-Coptic era by her sacred animal, the frog.

**Ptaḥ** (Gr. Φθᾶ) was the god of Memphis, and,

as such, well known to the Greeks, who for unknown reasons call him *Hephæstos*. Herodotus visited and described his temple (Herod. ii. 99, 101, 121, 176). Ptaḥ appears in mummy form, swathed, with only the head free; the feet are placed upon the sign for truth. In Memphis he was regarded as the first king of the country and as creator, a rôle which at Philæ is assigned to *Ptaḥ-Tatunen*, a combination of Ptaḥ and Tanen or Tatunen, a deity who makes his appearance especially in Nubia, and who, as earth-god, recalls the Egyptian Seb (Keb). Ptaḥ is also combined with other deities so as to form new special gods. Thus we have *Ptaḥ-Âten-en-pet*, 'Ptaḥ solar disc of the heaven,' who illumines the earth with his rays; *Ptaḥ-Nu*, the father of the gods; *Ptaḥ-Ḥâpi*, Ptaḥ the Nile; and, above all, *Ptaḥ-Sokaris*, to whom *Ptaḥ-Sokaris-Osiris*, *Ptaḥ-Osiris*, and Sokaris alone (see below) correspond. The triad at Memphis is composed of Ptaḥ along with Sechet and their son Nefer-Tum or Imhetep (Imûthes).

**Sechet** (Sechmet) is a lion-headed sun-goddess, who, under the title of 'the eye of Rā,' slaughters Rā's enemies. In her essential significance she coincides pretty nearly with the lion-headed Mut of Thebes, Tefnut, Pacht of Speos Artemidos, and the cat-headed Bast of Bubastis.

**Nefer-Tum** appears, particularly in more recent texts, as a man whose head is surmounted by a budding lotus, from which we may infer that he was a god of the regeneration and reawakening of nature, although there are no specific details of this in the inscriptions. **Imḥetep,** 'he who comes in peace,' is depicted as a youth with a closely-fitting cap upon his head. He generally appears seated, with a rolled-up papyrus upon his knees. In earlier times his figure does not seem to occur, but in the later New Empire, and, above all, in the Saitic period, numerous bronzes of him are found, notwithstanding which he does not become any more prominent in the texts, where he is introduced as a learned god. — For the associates of Ptaḥ, see above, p. 179[b].

**Sokaris,** conceived of as hawk-headed, is primarily a sun-god. His principal festival fell at the winter solstice, and in the Ptolemaic period was celebrated on the morning [at an earlier period perhaps on the evening] of the 26th of Choiak (cf. Brugsch, *Rev. égyp.* i. 42 ff.). He was worshipped especially in the neighbourhood of the necropolis of Memphis (where there is still a reminiscence of him in the name *Saqqarah*), and thus became blended on the one side with the Memphitic Ptaḥ, and on the other with the god of the dead, Osiris, whose symbols were, in consequence, often assigned to him.

**Nechebit** of Eileithyiaspolis, the vulture-formed tutelary goddess of Upper Egypt, generally appears in company with the serpent-formed **Uat'-it** of Buto, the tutelary goddess of Lower Egypt. The combination of the two stands for the empire of the Pharaoh, who united both their spheres of authority under his sway.

**Hathor,** 'the house of Horus' according to the later etymology, is mentioned times without number, and had her principal temple at Denderah. She is the goddess of joy, the patroness of mirthful gatherings. Her sacred animal was the cow, in consequence of which she occasionally appears with a cow's head, and, even when she wears a human form, she has very frequently cow's ears. Another Hathor is regarded as the goddess of the under world, and yet other Hathors are the seven female beings who made their appearance at the birth of a child and, like our fairies, foretold its fortune.

**Sebak** (Suchos) appears with a crocodile's head or as a crocodile. Under this same name, however, we must distinguish at least three different deities. In the first place there was a sun-god, who is combined with Rā and makes his appearance pre-eminently at Ombos, side by side with the sun-god Aroëris. Another Sebak constitutes a kind of by-form of Osiris. Finally, there is a Sebak who is regarded as the god of evil. His sacred animals were the crocodiles, which were supposed to be the associates of Set in the under world, and which in most of the nomes of Egypt were hunted to the death. The centre of worship of a Sebak who was well disposed to men continued till a late period to be the Fayum.

(2) *FOREIGN DEITIES.* — The Egyptian gods during the flourishing period of the country's history were not exclusive. They admitted into their number such of the gods of neighbouring peoples as had been found to be powerful and capable of resistance. It is a sign of deterioration that such a course was not followed with the Greek and Roman deities, who had no place assigned to them in the temple cult, but had to be content with the worship of certain circles of the people who would regard them as special gods. In the first millennium B.C. the Egyptian religion was too ossified to permit of its assimilation of new ideas. And this all the more because at this very time an archaizing tendency made itself felt in religion, so that from the time of the 25th dynasty the oldest attainable religious formulæ are in the most unmistakable fashion sought out and employed once more. In earlier times it was different. Libyan, African, Semite deities were then worshipped in the Nile valley along with the native gods.

(*a*) From the *Libyans* the Egyptians, in invading their future settlements, presumably borrowed the goddesses Neith and Bast, who at the beginning of Egyptian history play a considerable part, then recede entirely, and come forward once more in the Saitic period (from B.C. 700 onwards).

**Bast** appears pre-eminently as the local goddess of Bubastis in the Delta, where she had a share in the cult of the principal temple (Naville, *Bubastis*, London, 1891; *Festival Hall of Osorkon II.*, London, 1892). She is portrayed with a cat's head, and, like all lion- and cat-headed goddesses, is regarded as an embodiment of the sun. She plays no considerable part in the mythology.

**Neith** was thought of as an armed woman, with bow and arrow in her hand. As local goddess of Sais she was well known to the Greeks. In mythology she is regarded as the mother of Rā, and then becomes blended with Isis, along with whom she plays a rôle in the Osirian festivals, which under the New Empire had one of their centres at Sais. The Libyans of the time of Seti I. tattooed the ideogram of Neith upon their arms and wove it into their clothes (cf. Mallet, *Le culte de Neith à Sais*, Paris, 1889; Petrie, *Naqada*, p. 64).

Amongst deities that were originally Libyan should perhaps be included also the two goddesses **Sati** and **Ânukit,** who at a later period make their appearance in the cataract district as companions of Chnum (see above). Sati is depicted with the crown of Upper Egypt and the cow's horns, and is regarded as queen of heaven and of Egypt, queen of all gods, and is compared by the Greeks with Hera, although she has fundamentally nothing in common with her. Anukit wears a feather crown, is regarded above all as mistress of the island of Sehel in the neighbourhood of Philæ, and is compared with Hestia, but never succeeded in gaining any firm footing in Egypt proper.

(*b*) Bes and Ta-urt and their companions appear to be of *African* origin, by which is not meant that we are to think of divinities of a pronounced negro type. We have to do rather with deities whose acquaintance the Egyptians made through the medium of the tribes on the southern border of their empire, and to whom they left their grotesque forms, although these stood in the most glaring opposition to the refined forms of the genuine Egyptian gods, and permanently retained the stamp of their barbarian origin.

**Bes** is portrayed as a bearded dwarf, with long ears, bandy legs, long and generally bent arms, with a feather crown on his head. Behind him hangs down to the ground a long tail, probably that of the *cynœlurus guttatus*, whose name (*bes*) the god himself bears. Apart from occasional ornaments, he is represented naked, and almost always as of the male sex. It is only rarely that a female form appears beside him. In later times a number of by-forms (Ḥait, Aḥti, Sepd, Åḥaui, etc.) take their place by his side. These are at one time identified with him, and at another remain independent. In the Old Empire he seems to have as yet played no part; in the Middle Empire there is still little mention of him; it is during the New Empire, especially in the Saitic period, that he attains his bloom (cf. Krall in *Jahrb. d. Wien. Kunsthist.* Samml. ix. p. 72 ff.; A. Grenfell, *PSBA* xxiv. 21 ff.). He is regarded as a deity who renders aid at the birth of gods and kings, who amuses the newborn babe with his dances and waits upon it, protecting it at the same time from all evil, and especially against witchcraft. He thus becomes one of the most important of the omen-averting deities. At times he is confused with the young sun, and at a later period is thought of also as a pantheistic divinity.

**Ta-urt's** embodiment is a female hippopotamus standing upon its hind legs, with thick belly and pendant breasts, and often with a long mane hanging down to the ground. She, too, is ready with her aid at the birth of gods and kings, and in certain localities she is regarded, in her by-form Åpet, as mother of Osiris. In representations of the under world she takes her place by the side of the cow-formed Hathor. She appears at the entrance to necropoleis and to the realm of the dead, presumably occupying this position that she may render aid at the new birth of the dead, the resurrection. Her symbol is one of the most frequently occurring amulets in tombs belonging to the more recent periods of Egyptian history.

(*c*) *Asiatic*, principally *Semitic*, deities (cf. Meyer, *ZDMG* xxi. 716 ff.; W. Max Müller, *Asien u. Europa*, 311 ff.) found their way into the Egyptian temples under the New Empire, a period during which the Egyptian people was much brought into contact, alike in peace and war, with the different tribes of Western Asia. The principal deities of this class are Baal, Reshpu, Åstarte, Anta, and the city goddess of Ḳadesh. The last named will be dealt with in the same category as the Egyptian city goddesses (see below, p. 191[a]).

**Baal** was worshipped notably in the Ramesside period, and indeed his cult appears to have had its starting-point at the city of Tanis in the eastern Delta, where Ramses II. gave to this god a place even in the chief temple. His name has frequently for its determinative the sacred animal of the god Set, with whom he thus appears to have been identified—a result which would be reached all the more readily because the by-form of Set, namely Sutech, was also regarded elsewhere as god of the Asiatics. No statues of Baal have been discovered in Egyptian temples up till now.

**Reshpu**, the Phœnician *Reseph*, carries a lance, exhibits Semitic features, and makes his appearance frequently upon steles belonging to the flourishing period of Egyptian history.

**Astarte** was worshipped in several Egyptian temples. The most frequently mentioned is her shrine at Memphis, which existed down to the Ptolemaic period, and must have stood not far from the Serapeum. In the treaty between Ramses II. and the Asiatic Kheta, she appears as goddess of the Kheta, but even Ramses II. himself esteemed her so highly that he named one of his sons after her—*Mer-Å-(s)trot* (Wiedemann, *Herodot's Zweites Buch*, 433; cf. Spiegelberg, *PSBA* xxiv. 41 ff.).

**Anta** likewise makes her appearance as goddess of the Kheta. She bears shield, lance, and battle-club, and is occasionally mounted on horseback. Ramses II. and III. worshipped her, and the first named of these monarchs called his favourite daughter and future wife after her—*Bent-Ånta*, 'daughter of Anta.' But neither her cult nor that of her Semitic associates appears to have laid hold upon the mass of the people. It remained an official cult, quite in contrast with that of the Libyan and African divinities, who appear to have found their principal worshippers in popular circles.

(3) *DEIFIED MEN.*—In treating of the Egyptian religion, great importance has frequently been attached to the worship of the king of the land, and a whole pantheon of kings has been attributed to the Egyptians. But this way of putting it is not correct. The Pharaoh was, as we have seen already (p. 180[b]), the direct offspring of a god, and hence bore the title 'beautiful god,' and felt himself to belong to the order of heavenly beings. Even during his lifetime hymns were composed which attributed to him all manner of divine attributes (for examples see Maspero, *Genre épist.* 76 ff.); he is portrayed with the insignia of the gods; his subjects approached him as a god, and no doubt offered adoration to him in the popular cult and elsewhere. But in the temple cult his worship had a very subordinate place. Amenophis III. indeed prays to his own *ka*, and obtains from the latter the promise of all kinds of heavenly gifts. Ramses II. admits himself into the number of his temple gods, etc. But, upon the whole, even these monarchs stand a long way behind the great gods. It may be noted also as a circumstance connected with this, that the cult ceases as a rule upon the death of the particular Pharaoh concerned. It is true indeed, that occasionally, even after their death, offerings continue for a considerable time to be presented to them in accordance with their own directions and from funds left by them for the purpose, until later generations apply these gifts to their own use, but it is seldom that the defunct Pharaohs continue to be invoked as actual heavenly powers. Only a few of them are mentioned after the lapse of centuries as deities (cf. *e.g.* for the kings of the first dynasties, Erman, *Aegyp. Ztschr.* xxxviii. 121 ff.), and even then only in company with others. The temples to the dead, which the Pharaohs erected to themselves, appear to have been nearly all very quickly alienated from their proper use.

Still less frequently than kings did ordinary mortals attain to Divine honours after death. One of these rare instances is found in the time of Amenophis III. in the person of Amenophis the son of Ḥapu, who is still regarded as a god as late as the Ptolemaic period (cf. Wiedemann in *PSBA* xiv. 334, *Urquell*, vii. 289 ff.; Sethe, *Ægyptiaca*, 107 ff.). Another is the prince of Cush, Pa-ser, who for a length of time bears the title of 'the god' (Wiedemann, *PSBA* xiv. 332 f.), and there are examples of the same in other two private persons under the 18th dynasty (Wiedemann, *Orient. Ltztg.* iii. 361 ff.). The Greeks assert, further (see the citations in Wiedemann,

*PSBA* xiv. 335), that in the otherwise unknown city of Anabis a man was venerated as a god, and had gifts presented for him to eat. But such notices are isolated; the veneration of such men being confined as a rule to the narrow circle of the clan to which they belonged, or the officials of the building erected by them.

Naturally, we must not confound Divine veneration of this kind with the proper cult of the dead, the object of which was to ensure a supply of food and drink to the deceased so as to prevent his wandering about as a ghost, but which did not necessarily imply the attributing to him of any Divine attributes in the stricter sense of the term.

(4) *THE POPULAR GODS.—Partition of the great gods.*—The older investigators of the history of Egyptian religion proceeded on the principle that the best way to arrive at a thorough knowledge of the character of the particular deities was to collect all the references to them in the monuments and to draw conclusions from these. But the progress of study showed that identity of name is in the Nile valley no necessary guarantee for identity of deity, that, for instance, Horus of Edfu is quite a different form from Horus of Letopolis or Horus the son of Isis. This circumstance it was sought in the first instance to explain by assuming that the original Egyptian gods were worshipped at different places, and that, under the influence of the varying local development of doctrine, the varying images, etc., there arose in course of time different conceptions of the gods, which found expression in the local by-names for the primeval divinities. This view is in general correct, but the phenomenon had a much fuller scope than was formerly supposed. It happened not infrequently that even in one and the same place the same god was worshipped under several forms, and that each of these forms was regarded as an independent personality.

When in invocations a god appears with different by-names, as for instance Amon-Rā the king of the gods, side by side with Amon-Rā the lord of the throne of the world, our first impulse is to find here two titles of one and the same god, and we shall thus do justice upon the whole to the notion of the worshipper. But when in pictorial representations we see a number of forms seated together who all represent the same god, but with the addition in each instance of a different by-name, and who are worshipped together, the Egyptians held in such cases that each of the pictures had also a special divine personality corresponding to it. Thus Thutmosis III. appears at Karnak (Leps. *Denkm.* iii. 36 *c*, *d*) in the act of worshipping ten gods who are seated side by side and who are all called Amon, but one is Amon the lord of the throne of the world, another Amon-Rā the lord of heaven, another Amon of western Thebes; and these are followed by Amon the bull of his mother, Amon-Rā the great in love, etc. Sometimes the texts in such instances indicate that one is to address the god by his names. But in Egypt to name any one must not be understood in our weakened sense; the name is an independent part of the Ego, the different names have different independent forms corresponding to them. This occurrence of different forms of one and the same primeval god, if one might use the expression, explains how it is that upon certain steles the same god is portrayed in a variety of embodiments. Thus a stele now at Berlin (No. 7295, publ. by Wiedemann in *Mélanges déd. à Harlez*, p. 372 ff.) represents one of the king's shoemakers, Amen-em-âpt (about the 20th dynasty), engaged in worshipping the following forms: (1) the human-formed Amon-Rā in the valley, the lord of heaven; (2) the goose-formed Amon-Rā, the lion of valour, the great god; (3) the ram-formed Amon-Rā of Surerii, *i.e.* probably the deity who lived in animal form in a shrine erected by Surerii.

It will scarcely be safe to assume that in such instances as the above there has been uniformly a partition, due to local conditions, of the god into a number of individualities. Rather may we find in not a few of these forms originally independent deities, whose old names afterwards became by-names of a greater divinity, without the memory of their original independence being thereby permanently lost. Many indications in the texts suggest that there was once a god known as 'lord of heaven,' another as 'lord of the All,' a third as 'great in love,' etc., and that these titles were gradually drawn into the sphere of Osiris, Amon, etc., just as happened, for instance, in Greece with deities like Hygieia, Eubuleus, Basileia, and others (cf. Usener, *Götternamen*, 216 ff.). But the old deities never became completely absorbed in the new form, but always detached themselves from it afresh, as may be seen from the variety of their embodiments. To each particular form of the deity a special form of embodiment must correspond, for the Egyptians recognized no gods but such as were conceived of personally, whether as man or beast or any other perceptible object. Thus there could be in the same place different embodiments of the same great god, the latter being only apparently a unity, but in reality composed of a long series of Divine individualities independent of one another.

(*a*) The Divine forms for *heaven* and *earth* are supplied, in the Egyptian mythology known to us, by personal forms that animate these concepts, namely, the goddess of heaven, Nut, and the earth-god, Seb, to whom we have referred already in dealing with the creation myths. So is it also with the *heavenly bodies.* Here, again, there is in general no mention of the worship of the natural body but of that of a deity animating it. For the most part, it is true, these remained special gods; it is only in a few instances that we have to do with great gods whose functions extended beyond giving its proper movement to the heavenly body. Occasionally, however, the attempt was made to combine the special god with a great god, in the same way as at Thebes the special gods were readily brought into relation to Amon-Rā (see above, p. 185[a]). We thus hear of Isis-Sothis instead of Sothis alone as goddess of the dog-star, or of Bennu-Osiris instead of Bennu (Phœnix). The combination of Horus with the planet-gods also belongs to this category. The old month-gods were almost wholly replaced by great gods, to whom the months were dedicated; the lists of later times have preserved of the old deities, properly speaking, only 'the great heat' and 'the little heat' for the two principal summer months (see, for lists of such divinities, Leps. *Denkm.* iii. 170 f.). The gods of the particular days of the week were also combined with great gods, whereas the goddesses of the hours of day and night were able to preserve their independence down to the latest times. It is only rarely then that we find an invocation of the stars themselves, or that a particular star is mentioned as a god except in star catalogues.

The proper moon-god Āāḥ gradually passed into the god Thoth, and, even when he is not exactly amalgamated with the latter, he is depicted similarly to him. In later times he is further attached also to Osiris. In the case of Thoth it is probable that, at least in some localities, we have in him an actual moon-god whose personality originally ran parallel with that of Āāḥ, and to whom the *cynocephalus* was sacred; whereas the later more important Ibis-Thoth, associated with writing and the healing art, is, to all appearance, of a different origin. Egyptology has not as yet succeeded in separating the various Divine primary elements combined in the same god, although the task is one that in the Nile valley is at once suggested and facilitated by the presence of the various sacred animals.

(*b*) *Stone* worship prevailed especially in Heliopolis, where the sun-god embodied himself, amongst other forms, in a stone. It is hard to say whether we should detect here the influence of the Semites, in whose native land Divine stones played a great part, or whether we have to do with genuine Egyptian notions. In any case, this species of worship exhibits itself as long established. The form of the deity appears to have varied; the texts speak now of a pyramid, now of an obelisk (whence the obelisks in the classical period of Egyptian history are always dedicated to Rā or to some deity amalgamated with him), and again of a kind of pillar; but the essential form is always that of a cone, the shape common to the Semites. It was probably owing simply to the influence of Heliopolis that the belief in this embodiment of Rā found entrance into other temples. The god Set, the opponent of Osiris, was occasionally thought of as embodied in a stone, as is shown by the determinative of his name, which is a stone in the shape of a brick-mould. Late texts mention also worship paid to the metals and to half-precious stones, but such notices are rare.

(*c*) The worship of *high places* could naturally attain to no great proportions in the Nile valley, as characteristic elevations are in general wanting in the flat plateaus that stretch along both banks of the river; but instances of it do occur. The circumstance that the temple of the Hathor of the copper mines of the Sinaitic peninsula was situated upon a mountain height, may, it is true, have been due to Semitic influence. But we find a similar state of things in other places as well. At Heliopolis there was a sandhill, on which sacrifices were offered to the sun-god at his rising (Piānchi stele, l. 102). At Gebel Barkal the mountain on which the temples were situated was called the holy mountain, probably because it was itself regarded as holy, and not merely because of the sanctuaries to which it afforded shelter. From the end of the second millennium B.C. come some notices pointing to the paying of Divine honours to the mountain peak over Sheḥ Abd el-Gurnah at Thebes. This peak has prayers addressed to it; a *ka*, a Divine personality, is attributed to it; transgressions may be committed against it, which it punishes severely, or forgives if entreaty to that effect is addressed to it. In other texts it is brought into connexion or even identified with the serpent Mer-seker ('she who loves silence'), one of the most popular deities of the Theban necropolis. But originally the mountain was an independent Divine form (cf. the texts in Maspero, *Ét. de myth.* ii. 402 ff.; Capart, *Revue de l'Université de Bruxelles*, vi. [April 1901]), which, amongst other functions, was supposed to discharge those of a healing deity. A more exact study of the rock-inscriptions of Egypt may be expected to bring to light more of these high-place deities; in temple-inscriptions, on the contrary, they appear to be practically wanting, showing that here they were not regarded as of sufficiently high rank to find mention by the side of the great gods.

(*d*) The cult of *springs* and *streams* was in the Nile valley naturally confined to a few instances, there being so slender a supply of independent watercourses. Of springs, the only one, properly speaking, that comes into consideration, is at Heliopolis. In it, according to a stele of the 8th cent. B.C. (Piānchi stele, l. 102), the sun-god Rā washed his face, and his example was followed by kings when they visited the sanctuary. It is not said whether the spring actually received Divine honours, but it certainly possessed a certain sacredness, which it retained even after the fall of the Egyptian State. The Arabs regarded it as the fountain of the sun; and, according to the Christian legend, the Virgin Mary, when fleeing from Herod, washed the swaddling-bands of the infant Jesus in it (*Evang. Inf. Arab.* c. 24; Abd Allatif, *Rel. de l'Égypte* [French tr. by de Sacy], p. 88 ff.).

Far more important was the place held by the Nile (Ḥāpi), on whose flow and inundation the prosperity and even the existence of Egypt depended, and which was conceived of as a fat man with nipple-formed breasts, flowers upon his head, and wearing a loin-cloth composed of sedge. He had temples in a number of places (Nilopolis near Memphis, Heliopolis, etc.); in other instances he was received into the important temples in company with other deities. The greatest of the popular festivals were held in his honour and to mark the phases of his increase; numerous hymns celebrating his beneficence have come down to us, being found even engraved upon rock-walls along with lists of offerings to be presented to him (cf. *e.g.* Stern, *Aegyp. Ztschr.* 1873, p. 129 ff.; Maspero, *Hymne au Nil*, Paris, 1868). In these texts he is hailed as giver of life to all men, bringer of joy, creator, nourisher of the whole land. In all this we have no myth in the proper sense of the term, and the Nile comes into no further relations with the great deities of the temples. Occasionally the Nile is not viewed as one divinity, but is divided into the Nile of Upper and of Lower Egypt. When these two bind together for Pharaoh the plants that characterize them, he is thereby constituted lord of the whole land. There are other instances where the process of partition is carried still further, and each nome has its own Nile.

In the train of the Nile appear a number of forms which embody the blessings dispensed by him. Thus we have the god of provisions, Ka (not to be confounded with the soul-form *ka*), who is also called the father of the gods; the gods Ḥu, T'efā, and Resef, which stand for abundance and nourishment; the goddess of corn, Neperȧ, and the serpent-headed goddess of the harvest, Rennut.

(*e*) The worship of *animals* (cf. Wiedemann, 'Culte des animaux' in the *Muséon*, viii. 211 ff., 309 ff.; *Mél. de Harlez*, 372 ff.; *Herodot's Zweites Buch*, 271 ff.) has been regarded from ancient times as one of the most remarkable features of Egyptian religion. In discussing this subject we must distinguish between the Divine honours paid to certain individual animals, and the high regard for whole classes of animals sacred to certain gods. In the latter instance it was supposed that certain animals were specially dear to certain gods, whether because they were fond of incorporating themselves in these, or for some other mythological reason. The animals in question must not be hurt or killed, in their lifetime they must be fed, after their death they were frequently embalmed and buried, but were not worshipped. The phenomenon with which we are dealing may be compared with the high regard for certain animals shown in other lands: for instance, at the present day, for the stork in N. Germany; it is not animal worship, properly so called. Almost every species of animal found in Egypt is included in this category of sacred animals (see list in Parthey's Plutarch, *de Is.* 261 ff.), but regard for a particular species is commonly confined to particular nomes or districts, and one nome had no scruple about killing and eating the sacred animals of another.

The case is quite different with individual animals that ranked as Divine. In them a particular god embodies himself when he descends to earth, and lives on in this incarnation in the temple. The cult is then occupied essentially with this god-animal, which is duly supplied with food, drink, adornments, etc. We learn this, above all, from the classical writers; the inscriptions in such cases always speak of the god himself. These animal deities were immortal in the sense that, whenever the animal incorporation died, a fresh embodiment of the god in an animal of the same species immediately took place. Moreover, the death of the first embodiment was not a complete one; its immortal soul passed, like that of man, as Osiris, into the world beyond. Hence the Osiris dirge was raised for the animal, and it was solemnly interred, sometimes in an isolated tomb, sometimes in a spot where there were numerous such graves of animals. Besides real animals, we encounter, amongst these embodiments of deity, certain fabulous creatures. Pre-eminent amongst these is the *phœnix*, an embodiment of Rā. The Egyptians came to look upon these fancied forms as actually existing creatures, like the sphinx, the griffin, etc., which were supposed to inhabit the desert (cf. *e.g.* Leps. *Denkm.* ii. 131).

The most important of the god-animals, or at least the most frequently mentioned in the classical authors, are the following:—

**Apis** (Egyp. *Ḥāpi*)—a bull in the form of which Ptaḥ of Memphis embodied himself, and whose worship is attested from the 4th dynasty down to the time of the emperor Julian. This animal was believed to be engendered by a moonbeam; the cow which gave birth to him shared in the veneration paid him. He was recognized by a number of marks, about whose appearance tradition varies as to details. Solemnly introduced into the temple, the animal gave oracles, partly directly, and partly through his attendants. His death occasioned general mourning; his place of burial, from the middle of the 18th dynasty, was a rock-cut catacomb, the so-called *Serapeum*, in the middle of the necropolis of Memphis. The soul of the animal passed as Osiris-Apis into the world beyond, and this double form became blended, in the minds of the Greeks who were settled in Egypt, with the notions of Pluto and Asclepios. Thus arose the hybrid god Sarapis or Serapis, whose cult at the beginning of the Christian era was diffused over the whole of the Roman Empire (cf. *e.g.* Lafaye, *Hist. du culte des divinités d'Alexandrie*, Paris, 1884).

**Mnevis**—an incorporation of Rā as a bull, at Heliopolis.

**Bacis**—a bull form of Rā (Mont), at Hermonthis.

**Suchos**—a crocodile embodiment of Sebak in a lake in the Fayum, which likewise gave oracles, and was interred in the catacombs of the labyrinth.

A *ram* form belonged, amongst others, to Osiris at Mendes, and Amon-Rā at Thebes. Thoth had the form of an *ibis* at Hermopolis Magna, and, it would appear, also in a temple at Memphis, where the ibis was regarded as a sacred animal, and buried accordingly.

The **Phœnix** (*bennu*), in earlier times conceived of as a heron, in later also as an eagle, was an embodiment of Rā, especially as the morning sun, in a temple at Heliopolis (cf. Wiedemann, *Aegyp. Ztschr.* 1878, p. 89 ff.), but worshipped also in other places in Egypt, and one of the forms of the blessed dead, whose resurrection was guaranteed by that of the Phœnix itself.

The **Sphinx**, a lion with human head, was an embodiment of Rā-Harmachis, who is represented in this manifestation-form by the great Sphinx of Gizeh. The Sphinx, further, represents more generally the form assumed by various deities when they descend to the earth as watchers. The figures representing sphinxes generally have the features of the dedicator of the particular sphinx, *i.e.*, for the most part, the features of a king. The majority of sphinxes are of the male sex. But if the deity portrayed should be female, and the dedicator of the monument a woman, the sphinx may also have a female form. The sphinx was originally unwinged; it was only under Asiatic influence that it came to assume wings.

The *cow* was an embodiment of Hathor and of other maternal deities.—The *serpent* was the form of embodiment of several deities of the tomb districts—above all, of Mer-seker (see above, p. 189[a]), as well as of harvest deities like Rennut and many others.

(*f*) In the Nile valley there is less frequent mention of the worship of *plants and trees* than one might expect in the case of an essentially agricultural people. This deficiency of statement is explicable on the ground that the cult of vegetable life was part of the popular religion, and only found occasional admittance into the temple cult. Even when the latter was the case, one can always see clearly how loose was the connexion of the cult of plants with that of the great gods, and how little, in consequence, this connexion was maintained.

Thus, a religiously important tree is the *sycomore* which stood in the West on the way to the world beyond, and from which a goddess, who is more or less identified with the tree, supplied the dead with food and drink for their wanderings. This notion took its rise from the actually existing isolated trees growing at the commencement of the desert, in small hollows where water is found. Under the shadow of these the shepherd or the huntsman would seek rest, and express his gratitude by paying veneration to them. A great deal of vacillation is shown as to the particular deity with whom this sycomore is to be brought into relation. The one usually selected was Hathor, the mistress of the West, but besides her we find Isis, Selkit, Neith, Nut (cf. Wiedemann, *Rec. de trav. rel. à l'Egypt.* xvii. 10 f.). Within the sacred domain of the temples there were groves, the trees of which were occasionally venerated in the same sense as everything else connected with the temple. In the Ptolemaic period an attempt was made systematically to establish this veneration in the case of all temples, and thus to include the various species of sacred trees in the lists of *materia sacra.* Thus in 24 nomes we find the Nile acacia, in 17 the *Cordia myxa* (?), in 16 the *Zizyphus Spina Christi*, in 1 or 2 the sycomore, the *Juniperus Phœnicea*, and the *Tamarix Nilotica.* In all, 10 species of trees appear as sacred. Of these as many as 3 are sometimes venerated in the same nome (Moldenke, *Ueber die in altägyp. Texten erwähnten Bäume*, 8 ff.). So far as we know, the only tree that played a considerable rôle in the temple cult was one that grew at Heliopolis near the spot where the sun-cat killed the Āpepi serpent. From this tree the Phœnix took flight, and on its leaves Thoth or Safecḥ inscribed the name of the king in order thus to endue him with everlasting life (cf. Lefébure, *Sphinx*, v. 1 ff., 65 ff.).

The most surprising circumstance in connexion with the whole subject of plant worship is that the tree which is most characteristic of the Nile valley, namely the palm, makes its appearance only very rarely in the cultus inscriptions. Thus, the palm is found instead of the sycomore of Nut upon a relief now at Berlin (No. 7322); and a stele at Dorpat (*PSBA* xvi. 152) mentions the goddess Ta-urt of the Dum palm; but such notices are only exceptional.

With greater frequency than sacred trees we encounter the special gods of corn, who, as noted above, are sometimes assigned to the train of the Nile god. Also the dogma of the resurrection of Osiris is brought into connexion with plant life, and Osiris awakening to new life is portrayed as a mummy lying upon its back, and with corn sprouting from it (Papyr. Louvre, v. 27, in Pierret, *Dogme de la resurrection*; relief at Philæ, in Rosellini, *Mon. del culto*, p. 23). Allusions to this doctrine are found as early as the Middle Empire (Birch, *Coffin of Amamu*, pl. 276), and then repeatedly in the Book of the Dead. Even in the Osiris festivals of late times the sprouting of grains of corn from the figure of Osiris still plays a part; and in a tomb of the time of Amenophis III. proof has been discovered by Loret (cf. *Sphinx*, iii. 106 f.) that it was occasionally the practice then, in connexion with burial, to make corn grow from an image of Osiris as a kind of pledge of human immortality.

(*g*) Of *city divinities* there must have been a considerable number, but only one of them is mentioned somewhat frequently, namely the goddess of Thebes, who was conceived of as an armed woman, and who appears in two forms, namely Uas-t 'Thebes,' and 'she who is there in sight of her lord' (originally the necropolis of Drah abu Neggah; cf. Maspero, *Ét. de myth.* ii. 403). As yet, we know nothing of temples erected in honour of such personifications. Even a foreign city deity found admittance into the Egyptian pantheon, namely the goddess **Kadesh,** who derived her name from a Syrian city on the Orontes, and who comes before us as queen of heaven, mistress of all gods, daughter of Rā. She is portrayed, with a front view, as a woman standing upon a lion. To what foreign deity she originally answered, whether a Semitic Astarte in her local form as worshipped at Ḳadesh, or a Hittite goddess, cannot be determined, but the fashion of her portraiture makes the latter supposition the more probable.

(*h*) There were also certain *buildings*, temples, pyramids, and the like, that were temporarily regarded as divinities to whom veneration was due.

(5) *DEIFIED ABSTRACT NOTIONS.*—These hold a special place in the list of Egyptian objects of veneration. It would be a mistake to look upon such deification as the result of profound philosophical speculation; it is simply a development of the fundamental idea which never ceased to make itself felt in Egypt, namely, that every word must have corresponding to it a perceptible form, a kind of personality, which could be portrayed and, if necessary, worshipped. The number of abstract notions known as yet from lists of gods or from other indications, is pretty large; the discovery of fuller lists will no doubt increase the number. The base of an altar (now at Turin, pub. in *TSBA* iii. p. 110 ff.) dating from the time of king Pepi I. (6th dynasty), supplies the following group: Day (*Hru*), Year (*Renpt*), Eternity (*Ḥeḥ*), Unendingness (*T'et-ta*); followed by Life (*Ānch*), Stability (*Ṭeṭ*), and Joy (*Fu-t-āb*). Further, we find here Seeing (*Ma*), and Hearing (*Sen*), and, finally, Right Speaking (*Maā-cher*). In other inscriptions appear Taste (*Hu*), Perception (*Sa*), Strength (*Us*), etc. When it is desired to portray these abstract notions, they are simply provided with a human form having the appropriate written sign on its head, or their ideographic hieroglyph sign is drawn with arms and legs appended to it. In the temple cult these forms in general scarcely received actual worship, although some of them are mentioned not infrequently under the New Empire. A number of abstract notions seem to make their appearance as a connected group at Hermopolis, where the so called eight elementary deities enjoyed Divine honours. These eight, divided into four pairs, each with a male and a female, were Eternity (*Ḥeḥ*), Darkness (*Kek*), Heavenly Water (*Nu*), Earthly Water of Inundation (of the Nile, *Nenú*); see the Literature in Wiedemann, *Orient. Ltztg.* iv. 381 ff. From this starting-point they found admittance into other temples as well.

There was only one abstract notion which by itself played a prominent part, namely the goddess Maāt, 'Truth,' who appears as a woman, with the ideogram for 'truth' upon her head. She is quite materialistically conceived of; one can eat and drink the truth, in order to become truthful. Maāt is mentioned from the earliest times onwards, but, in spite of the widely diffused veneration for her, she had seldom a sacrificial cult of her own. When prominent officials are called 'priests of the truth,' this is probably rather a title intended to characterize them as specially truthful, and not the name of an actual office. Occasionally we hear of two Truths, in which case there was probably in view the distinction between truth in action, *i.e.* justice, and inward sincerity. The goddess of Truth, when represented as human, appears at times blindfolded, because she judges without respect of persons. She conducts the dead into the judgment-hall of Osiris, where she attends to the weighing of the heart. In mythology she plays no part; and if at times she appears as the consort of Thoth, this has nothing to do with her proper significance, but rests upon later speculation, which desired to bring the god of wisdom into connexion with the truth. A similar judgment is to be passed on the statement that Maāt is a daughter of Rā. This is simply an expression of the thought that the light of the sun brings the truth to view. None of these notions has been further worked up (cf. for Maāt, Stern, *Aegyp. Ztschr.* 1877, pp. 86 ff., 113 ff.; Wiedemann, *Ann. du Musée Guimet*, x. 581 ff.).

iii. THE CULTUS.—The worship of the deity in the temple was concerned, above all, with the charge of the image of the god or the sacred animal that found a place in the holiest part of the building, the *naos*. The door leading to the *naos*, or the barred gate giving access to the god-animal, was fastened by a priest every evening with a strip of papyrus, the ends of which were smeared with clay and a stamp impressed upon them. The following morning it was one of the first sacred functions to break this seal, and thus to renew the possibility of communion between the deity and man. Regarding this ceremony and others which accompanied or followed the breaking of the seal, we are informed through the ritual books of various temples which have come down to us, and which describe the various sacred duties to be performed on the morning of each day. We have the ritual at Abydos, in the time of Seti I., for Osiris, Isis, Horus, Amon, Rā-Harmachis and Ptaḥ (publ. by Mariette in *Abydos*, i. 34–86); at Karnak (in the Hall of Pillars, back wall), from the time of Seti I., for Amon-Rā (not yet publ.). Then there are isolated pieces; mostly with reference to royal visits to the temple, containing also pictures of the various ceremonies, mostly in the correct order, but furnished with abbreviated legends. These are to be met with on most temple walls, on the outside of the *naos*, temple doors, obelisks, etc. Further texts may be found in Papyr. Berlin 55 [now 3055] for Amon, and 14 and 53 [now 3014 and 3053] for Mut, both dating from the time of the 20th dynasty (publ. in

*Hieratische Papyr. aus der Königl. Mus. zu Berlin*, i., Leipzig, 1896–1901); cf. Lemm, *Ritualbuch des Ammondienstes*, Leipzig, 1882; and Moret, *Le rituel du culte divin journalier en Égypte*, Paris, 1902. For the parallel texts of the ritual for the dead, cf. especially Schiaparelli, *Il Libro dei Funerali*, ii., where numerous examples are given; for the meaning and translation of the latter texts, cf. Maspero, *Ét. de myth.* i. 283 ff. A number of the statements that come under the present category are already found in the Pyramid texts of the 6th dynasty. These surviving accounts of the ritual show that the ceremonies were nearly the same in almost all Egyptian temples.

There is first a brief indication of the ritual act to be performed, with a picture of it also when the text happens to be engraved in relief on the temple wall, and then follow the terms of the prayer which the priest is to utter as he performs each of the acts named. These prayers consist almost exclusively of invocations of the deity, without any further point of interest, whereas the acts themselves have a higher significance, as they let us see what was the form of the ancient Egyptian divine service. They show at the same time that the latter was very much of one cast, for the same ceremonies as were performed before the god every morning were performed also by the king when he brought a great offering to the temple in the hope of obtaining from the god in return the promise of victory over his enemies, joy, strength, or everlasting life. Much the same usages were followed, moreover, when the object was to reanimate a dead man, that he might be able to enter the world beyond and eat and drink there. We cannot go more fully into these ceremonies here, but we must speak of their order:—(1) There was first the 'striking *or* rubbing of the fire,' *i.e.* a spark was generated by striking a flint or rubbing dry pieces of wood against each other, and this spark was regarded as Divine and as an effluence of the eye of the sun-god Horus. It furnished the means of lighting the temple and of kindling the fire for the burnt-offering. The latter was the main object, for now follow: (2) the taking hold of the censer, (3) the placing of the incense-container on the censer, (4) the casting of the incense into the flame. Thereupon (5, 6) the ministrant advanced to the elevated place, the *naos*, (7) loosed the band that fastened its door, (8) broke the seal, (9) opened the *naos*, and thus (10) made the face of the god himself visible, and (11) looked upon the god. Reverently (12–17) he cast himself upon the ground, raised himself, and repeated the prostration a number of times, keeping his face all the while turned towards the earth, and then (18, 19) commenced a hymn of praise to the god. When this was ended, a series of offerings were presented to the god: first of all (20) a mixture of oil and honey, with which it was customary to anoint the images of the gods, and then (21) incense. After this the priest stepped back from the *naos* into the adjoining room of the temple, where (22) he uttered a short prayer. Then (23, 24) he took his place once more in front of the *naos*, and (25) solemnly praying ascended the steps which led from the temple floor to the level of the interior of the *naos*. Whereas he had hitherto stood lower than the deity, he now felt himself, after performing the above-mentioned ceremonies, to be on an equal footing with him, and might thus stand on the same level. But scarcely had he taken this step when he was seized once more with awe of the god, whose countenance was now distinctly visible (26, 27), he looked upon him (28), and repeated the prostrations he had previously performed (29–34). Then he burned incense (35, 36), and uttered one or more prayers and hymns in honour of the god (37–41). A figure of the goddess of Truth was now presented to the god (42), who, in order to be truthful, must receive the truth into himself by eating or drinking. Then followed an incense-offering, meant not only for the god who was the special object of worship, but for all his companions who shared the veneration of the temple (43). Then began the purifying and clothing of the god. First of all the priest laid both his hands upon the god himself (44), then upon the upper side of the case in which the figure was placed, in order to effect its purifications as well (45). Then he purified the deity with four libation-pitchers full of water (46) and with four red pitchers full of water (47), fumigated him with incense (48), brought a white sash (49) and put it on the god (50). Then he put on him, successively, a green, a bright-red, and a dark-red sash (51–53), after which he brought to him two kinds of ointment (54, 55), then green and black eye-paint (56, 57), an act which was followed by scattering dust before the god (58), in order thereby to make even the spot, on which the god or the sacred animal stood, clean. The priest next walked four times round the god (59), and this ceremony explains why the temple *naos* occupied a detached position in the sanctuary, namely, in order that this walking round it might be possible. At the close of this performance the presentation of offerings again took place. First the god received natron with which he was purified (60), then he was fumigated with incense (61), and underwent a purification with four grains of a substance brought from the south, and then with four grains of the same from the north (62, 63), then a purification with water (64), followed by a fumigation with ordinary incense, and another with the Ānti incense from Arabia (65, 66). Here ended the regular Divine service.

The object of all these acts was to clothe and to purify the god. The latter point was considered important, because the Egyptians in all matters of religion laid special stress upon bodily cleanness. Washings of every kind were required before any sacred transaction; even the gods must wash themselves repeatedly if they desire to consult the sacred books. Fumigating and rubbing with ointment also come under the category of purification, it being the custom in the Nile valley to perfume oneself before important transactions of a civil as well as a religious character. The man who above all had to wash himself was the priest, who was accordingly designated 'the clean' (*āb*, *uāb*), the ideogram for which is a man over whom water is poured or who finds himself beside water, in allusion to these frequent washings.

In addition to the purifying, the supplying of food and drink to the god or to the sacred animal played a part in the cultus; but here we have no extensive books of ritual to tell us in detail, for instance, about the prayers to be uttered in connexion with the performance of the various acts. No doubt, all this was regulated by as exact a code of ceremonial as the actions and prayers connected with the clothing and the purifying of the god. In regard also to other religious ceremonies we are without the prescriptions as to the occasions and the ordering of processions, burnt-offerings, and various consecrations. There are merely allusions in the inscriptions, but these show that here too everything was fixed by a hard-and-fast rule instead of being left to the discretion of the individual worshipper or the temple college.

iv. CONCEPTIONS OF A FUTURE LIFE.—(1) The notions as to a world beyond (cf. Wiedemann, *The Realms of the Egyptian Dead*, London, 1901), where gods and the dead have their home, are primarily connected in the Nile valley with the sun and his 24-hours' course. The sun rises in the east in the morning, and sails in his bark to the west; for the motion of the sun, like that of all the heavenly bodies, is conceived of by the Egyptians as effected by a vessel, the waters on which it sails being sometimes viewed as a heavenly ocean, and sometimes as a Nile that flows through the brazen heaven. The sun-bark is generally supposed to be carried along by the stream, requiring merely to be steered; it is only exceptionally that it is represented as drawn by jackals which run on both banks of the heavenly stream. In the cabin of the bark sits the sun-god, while other gods man the vessel. The day voyage lasts 12 hours, that is to say, the Egyptians divided the time from sunrise to sunset into 12 equal parts, these being consequently, as a matter of course, longer in summer than in winter.

The sun sets in the west, and commences now upon a subterranean stream its night voyage, which also lasts 12 hours. The whole voyage of the sun is compared by the Egyptians to the life of man. The god is born in the morning, grows old during his course, sinks in the evening, as an old man, into the night, to rise again as a new god the following morning. Usually the whole process is accomplished, as indicated above, within four and twenty hours; more rarely, instead of this, it is spread over a whole year or over longer periods of 365 and more years. Wherever the sun comes, he finds gods and spirits, but the distribution of these beings over heaven, earth, and the under world is variously conceived of at different times.

(2) As to the dwelling-place of the gods themselves we have only meagre data. In the matter of the cultus, apart from the offerings which were daily offered to the sun upon open-air altars, the whole concern was with the embodiments of the gods that dwelt in the temples. If *Doppelgängers* who did not dwell on earth were postulated for these, they were spoken of without any precise localizing of them, or they were called by such general titles as 'lord of heaven *or* earth *or* Egypt,' etc. In later times, in addition to this, the various gods are frequently conceived of pantheistically as inhabiting the whole world. Thus it is said (Horrack, *Lamentations d' Isis*, pl. 5, l. 2) of Osiris: 'The heaven contains thy soul, the earth contains thy forms, the under world (*Duat*) contains thy secrets.' A dwelling-place of the gods in the sense of the Greek Olympus is unknown to the Egyptians.

(3) Far more numerous than the statements regarding the abodes of gods are those about the region which was believed to be the place of sojourn of dead men when they were awakened to new life. This region is variously placed—

(*a*) *Above the earth, in heaven.*—Different views prevailed as to how the soul succeeded in gaining admittance into the sun-bark among the stars or into the spreading Plain of the Blessed. According to some, the soul, immediately upon a man's death, hastened to the west to the spot where the sun sank through a narrow opening into the deep, and there clambered into the solar bark. On board of the latter it passed through the under world, and the following morning rose to heaven. Others believed in a ladder, by whose aid the soul could climb to heaven. Another set of notions attached themselves to the cremation of the dead; the soul was supposed to ascend with the smoke from the burning corpse. But the most widely diffused view was that the soul had the form of a bird, that of kings being in the form of a hawk, that of other men in that of a bird with a human head. In this shape it left the body as it grew cold in death, and flew upwards.

On reaching heaven, the soul dwelt in the company of the gods and of the souls that had arrived there before it. How a place was assigned it here is a question on which the Egyptians in general do not appear to have had settled convictions. Only the Pyramids of the 5th and 6th dynasties notice it, the dead Pharaoh being here represented as seizing the supremacy of the other world by force. With the aid of his servants he captures the gods on his arrival, causes them to be slaughtered and cooked, and devours them along with their souls and attributes, crowns and bracelets. In this way their magical power passes over to him, and he becomes the mightiest of the gods. The texts give no indication, it is true, of how he was able to maintain this position against a subsequently dying Pharaoh, or to avoid being himself captured and eaten in turn.

(*b*) *Under the earth.*—Here lay *Duat*, 'the deep,' which the sun passed through by night, and which was divided into 12 parts, corresponding to the 12 hours of night. These were separated from one another by doors, or, according to another view, by massive gates. This realm is described in words and illustrated by pictures in a number of texts, notably in the Book of *Am-Duat*, 'that which is in the deep,' and the Book of the Gates, the beginnings of which go back to the Middle Empire, but which were widely circulated above all in Thebes from the 18th to the 20th dynasty. In later times they were less frequently copied. While their accounts are similar in their fundamental ideas, there are far-reaching differences in details. Through the midst of *Duat* flows a Nile, upon which floats the bark containing the ram-headed night sun. On the banks to right and left were found innumerable demons of the most varied forms, men, animals, especially serpents, or hybrid forms, human and animal. Many of them attend upon the sun, aiding him in his course. Others, with the great Āpepi serpent at their head, labour to destroy the sun, but are always overcome, although this does not prevent their always commencing afresh the conflict of darkness with light—a conflict whose end the Egyptians never attempted to portray, and probably never expected.

The souls of men joined the sun in the west when he entered *Duat*. The god assigned them fields in the various divisions. Here they lived under conditions that were in general far from enjoyable, and had to render help to the god on subsequent nights. Each of them had the benefit of only a single hour's sunshine upon their land. As soon as the god had left any division, night reigned in it, illuminated at most by the seas of fire in which enemies of the sun-god were burned, or by fire-vomiting serpents. Originally it was held that all men, good and bad, kings and subjects, would experience much the same lot in these regions. Only those who were expert in magic might escape from *Duat* and pursue their journey in company with the sun till they reached a new day. In later times *Duat* became the scene of a process of judgment, in which sentence was pronounced concerning good and evil. The good were then allowed to till the fields, the bad were punished by being plunged in seas of water and fire.

Similar and as little reassuring is the account of the future world contained also in other Egyptian works; hence, above all, the numerous exhortations to enjoy life which were in vogue from ancient times down to the closing period of Egyptian history. Here the future world is presented as a land of sleep and darkness, whose inhabitants recognize neither father nor mother, in which they pine for water and fresh air, and where there is a reign of absolute death, which shows no tenderness to its worshippers, and regards not the offerer of sacrifice.

(c) *On the earth.*—On this theory the realm of the dead appears to have been for long sought in the north, in the Delta. This Plain of Peace or Plain of *Åalu* (*i.e.* 'of marsh plants'; later, by popular etymology, explained as Plain 'of worms'), as it was called, was thought of as a district traversed by a stream and divided by numerous canals and river-arms into islands, which were the abode of the gods and the dead. The latter were mainly occupied with agriculture, which provided them with the necessary food. When the Delta came to be better known, the realm of the dead was naturally banished from it. At first it moved further north, still continuing on earth, but was afterwards transferred to heaven, being located in the region of the Great Bear.

In that form of Egyptian conceptions of the future world which prevailed in later times, above all in the Osirian faith, a realm of the dead, similarly thought of and named, lies in another quarter of the heavens, in the west, where the sun sets. Whether this notion is as old as that of the dwelling of the dead in the north—which appears most likely—or was of later origin, cannot be made out from the texts. From the time of the Middle Empire the adherents of the Osirian system are likewise at one regarding the western situation of the Plain of Åalu. The dead man, before he could arrive there, must first traverse the desert. In his earthly form, with the traveller's staff in his hand, he set out on his journey, commencing, according to the commonest view, at Abydos, from which a number of caravan roads ran to the west. Hunger and thirst threatened him; with Divine help he procured refreshment from the presiding deities of isolated trees; by means of magical formulæ he overcame the serpents which beset him, and the crocodiles which filled the streams he had to pass through. He was aided by the same kind of formulæ also when he wished to pass terrible demons, or had to go through mysterious rooms, or was terrified by all kinds of dangers. These formulæ, consequently, appeared to be indispensably necessary for reaching the life beyond; and they were collected into a compilation called by modern scholars the Book of the Dead. From the time of the Middle Empire it was a favourite practice to commit these formulæ to the grave along with the body of the deceased, inscribing them at times on the walls of the tomb or on the coffin, at other times entrusting them to the corpse itself, written on papyrus or on the swathings of the mummy. In the various copies extant the terms of the formulæ are approximately the same, but their order varies very frequently. The Egyptians did not mark off the road to the world beyond with geographical precision; the notions on this subject changed again and again; the order of the demons to be encountered and of the various realms of the gods is not the same. Only the starting-point is given, the western mountain-chain of Egypt, and the goal, the Hall of Judgment, in which the verdict is pronounced on the dead (see below, p. 197[a]). If this was favourable, they entered the Plain of Åalu, to dwell there for ever, or at least to find a home, which they left only if it was their own wish to do so. In the latter event, they could assume any other form they pleased, visit the earth, or even change themselves into gods.

(4) *The Osirian doctrine of immortality.*—We have already noticed in the preceding pages a considerable number of Egyptian conceptions of the future life. In this matter there was no uniform system of belief in the Nile valley. It appears to have been a generally accepted dogma that man's life endures for ever; but this was represented and developed by each nome in conjunction with its own religious conceptions, without any regard to the possible prevalence of contradictory notions amongst their neighbours. They even went further than this in their want of system. The very same individuals occasionally regarded views of the future life which were logically self-contradictory as equally legitimate, and gave them a place side by side in their funeral texts. We must here pass over a long list of such doctrines, and rest content with giving a short account of the most important of them—a dogma which already played a part in the earliest period of Egyptian history, and became from *c.* 2000 B.C. the prevailing conception of the future life, till, finally, in the first millennium B.C. it was practically the only doctrine on the subject that was taken account of by the great mass of the Egyptian people.

(*a*) This doctrine connects itself with the fortunes of the god Osiris. The first biography of this god we possess comes from the post-Christian period, being found in Plutarch's *de Iside et Osiride*; but allusions in the monuments show that much the same story of his life was known as early as the Old Empire. It is true that, besides this main narrative, there were a number of others which showed deviations in details. Above all, the conceptions regarding the most important episode in the god's existence, namely his resurrection, differed very widely, especially in the later texts. This may be due to the fact that, now that the Osirian doctrine was the prevailing one, the attempt was made to assimilate to it other doctrines of immortality, which originally started from other divine conceptions, or, conversely, to assimilate the Osirian doctrine itself to these heterogeneous processes of thought. The most widely current version, however, continued, to all appearance, to be that handed down by Plutarch, which is essentially as follows:—

Rhea (Nut), the consort of Helios (Rā), had sexual relations with Kronos (Seb). Helios observed this, and laid a curse upon her to the effect that she should not give birth to a child in any month of the year. But Hermes (Thoth), who was also in love with the goddess, succeeded in evading the curse. He won from Selene (Åāh) at draughts the 70th part of each day, and formed from these 5 intercalary days, which he placed at the end of the year. Osiris was born on the first of these days, Aroëris (Ḥer-ur, the elder Horus) on the second, Set on the third, Isis on the fourth, Nephthys on the fifth. Osiris and Aroëris pass for children of Helios, Isis of Hermes, Set and Nephthys of Kronos. According to some accounts, Osiris and Isis had already intercourse in their mother's womb, the result being the birth of Aroëris. In general Osiris and Isis appear as one married couple, Set and Nephthys as another. After a time Osiris became king of Egypt, ruled mildly, gave laws, taught the doctrines concerning the gods, and then journeyed over the world as an introducer of civilization. On his return he was murdered, on the 17th of Athyr, in the 28th year of his life or his reign, by Set, who had associated with him as fellow-conspirators 72 men and a queen of Ethiopia named Aso. Isis' grief was profound, but she found a companion in Anubis, a son of Osiris and Nephthys. Besides, she had herself a son by Osiris, namely Horus, who later became a helper to her after having during his youth been often threatened with danger at the hands of Set. According to Plutarch, Isis discovered the coffin in which Set had deposited Osiris, at Byblos in Phœnicia, and brought it from there to Egypt. Set, however, found the coffin which had been concealed by Isis, tore the corpse of Osiris to pieces, and scattered them. When Isis discovered this outrage, she searched for the different parts of her husband's corpse, and, wherever she found one of them, erected an Osiris tomb. Then she and Horus commenced a campaign against Set, which ended in the victory of Horus. By way of appendix Plutarch states that Isis had intercourse even with the dead Osiris, the result of which was the birth of Harpocrates (*Her-pe-chrut*, 'Horus the child').

When we look more closely at the treatment of the corpse of Osiris, as described in Plutarch's narrative, we are struck with one feature which points to a mixing up of originally different accounts of the fate of the corpse. At first the latter rests as a whole in the coffin, then it is cut in pieces, and, finally, the pieces are again brought together. As a matter of fact, we have here a reflexion of the chief points in the Egyptian treatment of dead bodies; the only feature wanting is cremation, which in the earliest times was practised in the case of kings, and later occurs sporadically and in connexion with human sacrifice. This omission must be due to the circumstance that, at the time when the Osirian doctrine was attaining to full vigour, cremation was no longer sufficiently in vogue to demand consideration. During the Naqada period, a dismemberment of the corpse was customary at burial. In the Pyramid era this was generally replaced by the burial of the whole body, which it was sought at the same time to preserve from decay by a more or less complete process of embalming. During this same period we find also a transition form, by which the corpse was first allowed to decompose, and then the bones were collected and placed again in the proper order of a skeleton. At a later period the custom that had practically exclusive sway in the Nile valley was that of embalming, which then came in general to be regarded as that applied to Osiris. During the process of embalming the latter, Nephthys and Isis were said to have sung dirges over the god, in order to aid in his resurrection; and a similar practice for a like purpose was followed also in connexion with human interments (see the texts in Horrack, *Lamentations d'Isis et de Nephthys*, Paris, 1866; Budge, *Archæologia*, lii. 11 ff., 65 ff. The festivals in commemoration of the burial and the resurrection of Osiris at the end of the month Choiak are portrayed at Denderah; cf. Loret, *Rec. de trav. rel. à l'Égypt.* iii. 43 ff., iv. 21 ff., v. 85 ff.).

In addition to the embalming of the god, we hear of the reconstruction of his body. This connects itself with the erecting of his spinal column, and a festival in its honour was held on the 30th of Choiak especially at Busiris in Lower Egypt. Finally, side by side with this there lingers on till the latest times the conception of the dismemberment, in consequence of which various parts of Osiris' body remained at different places in the land, and continued to be venerated as relics in the particular temples, the so-called *Serapeums*. Upon this theory, then, there was no such collection of the parts of the body as is referred to by Plutarch. Thus the head of the god was said to be preserved at Memphis, the neck at Letopolis, the heart at Athribis. There is, however, no fixed system in the matter; occasionally the same parts rest at different places, according to the tradition of the temples concerned. Thus the head, for instance, is claimed not only for Memphis but for Abydos, and the legs are catalogued as Divine relics at a plurality of sanctuaries.

(*b*) Taken as a whole, Osiris stands in Egypt for the prototype of the man who after a virtuous life must die, but who afterwards rose again to life for ever. Even in early times, moreover, an influence on the conception of Osiris entered from the side of the sun-religion. This movement appears to have originated at Memphis, where Osiris was identified with Sokaris, the local god of the dead and of the sun, — in Abydos this amalgamation rarely meets us. Then, when the sun-worship was centralized in Rā, the latter assumed the character of a parallel to Osiris. The custom grew up of identifying the fate and the death of Osiris with the fate of the sun; and, as the old Osiris myth was also retained, duplicate dates were thus obtained for the period of the year that marked the occurrence of the different events in the life of Osiris. For instance, the murder of Osiris fell, according to Papyrus Sallier iv. (19th dynasty) and Plutarch, upon the 17th of Athyr. Numerous other texts (from the 18th dynasty onwards), on the other hand, transfer this event to the end of the month Choiak, the period of the shortest days of the year, within which the death and the regeneration of the sun are accomplished. It is this contamination between the Osiris and the sun-god myths that explains how Osiris, from being a human king of divine descent, becomes a complete god. Thus a text of the 18th dynasty describes him in detailed fashion as creator of the world (see above, p. 179[b]), although, remarkably enough, it contains also copious allusions to the usual Osiris myth, and remarks: 'Isis the glorious, the avenger of her brother (Osiris), sought him and rested not while she journeyed through this land full of grief; she ceased not until she had found him; a wind she stirred up with her feathers, a breeze she created with her wings; she performed the panegyrics usual at burial; she raised up the wearied parts of him whose heart is still (the dead Osiris); she took his seed and fashioned an heir for herself.' The extraordinary method by which Horus is here generated after the death of his father is mentioned also in Plutarch, and meets us already in the Pyramid texts. This was a matter of faith then during the whole period of Egyptian history, and is even frequently (in Abydos and Denderah) the subject of pictorial representation (cf. Wiedemann, *Rec. de trav. rel. à l'Égypt.* xx. 134 ff.).

(*c*) Osiris in his lifetime had been a king on earth, after his death he became ruler in the world beyond. He there passed judgment on the dead, to him were presented the prescribed offerings which were meant to procure food and drink for the dead. His sisters Isis and Nephthys play no rôle in the world beyond. In general, Set, the murderer of the god, is of course tabooed there, and hence his name is avoided in sepulchral texts. This is carried so far that king Seti I., in the inscriptions on his tomb, in writing his own name, everywhere replaces the *Set* by *Osiris*. It is true that alongside of the usual tradition a wholly different class of conceptions is found attached to the god Set. In Tanis, for instance, he is regarded as a good god and a favourite of the sun-god, on whose behalf he pierces with his lance the Āpepi serpent—in contrast, again, to the Theban conception, in which Set himself corresponds essentially to the Āpepi serpent. This difference is probably connected with the circumstance that at Thebes one started from the original form of the Osiris myth, where Set appears as the murderer of Osiris; whereas, at Tanis, Set or Sutech, as god of the desert and of foreign parts, was amalgamated with the foreign god Baal, who was thought of as the sun-god, the result of which was that in this roundabout way Set assumed a wholly altered character.

Of far more importance in the future world than Set is the jackal-god Anubis, who is generally presented as a son of Osiris and Nephthys, but occasionally also as a son of Rā. He had aided Isis and directed the embalming of Osiris. According to the usual view, he was one of the guides of the dead, whom he, alternating in this function with Thoth, conducted into the judgment-hall of Osiris. His cult had no great vogue, whereas in early times a prominent part was played by another jackal-god Ȧp-uat (see above, p. 183). The worship of the latter had its centres at Lycopolis in Upper Egypt and Lycopolis in the Delta. In consequence of this double local worship, we frequently hear of two gods of the same name, who are called, respectively, 'Ȧp-uat of the south' and 'Ȧp-uat of the north,' and, further, by a combination of Ȧp-uat with Anubis, two jackals are frequently portrayed upon steles of the dead as guardians of the under world.

(*d*) The doctrine of immortality attached to the name of Osiris is the best known to us of all the Egyptian conceptions of the future life. To it is devoted the so-called Book of the Dead, whose oldest texts date from the Middle Empire (cf. Lepsius, *Aelteste Texte des Todtenbuchs*, Berlin, 1867; Birch, *Egyptian Texts of the Coffin of Amamu*, London, 1886; Lepsius, *Denkm.* ii. 98 f., 145–148; Maspero, *Mém. de la Miss. du Caire*, i. 155 f. [These texts show a great resemblance to the Pyramid texts which Maspero published in *Les inscriptions des Pyramides de Saqqarah*, Paris, 1894, a reprint from *Rec. de trav. rel. à l'Égypt.*, vols. iii.–xiv.]). Its period of bloom, to which belong the copies that are relatively freest from verbal errors and best illustrated, falls within the period from the 18th to the 20th dynasty (for the texts see Naville, *Das aegyp. Todtenbuch der 18–20 Dynastie*, Berlin, 1886; le Page Renouf, *Facsimile of the Papyrus of Ani*, London, 1890 [2nd ed. by Budge, 1894–1895, with Introduction and Translation]; Budge, *Facsimiles of the Papyri of Hunefer*, etc., London, 1899 [among them notably the very important text of the Papyrus of Nu]. Translations have been published by le Page Renouf in *PSBA* xv. ff. [recently continued by Naville]; Budge, *The Book of the Dead*, 3 vols., London, 1898 [abridged ed. under same title, London, 1901]. Renouf's notes are mainly on the language; Budge discusses also the history of the Book of the Dead, with the later and the supplementary texts). In later times many passages were no longer intelligible to the scribes, who, accordingly, frequently produced very faulty copies. To this category belongs the Turin exemplar (emanating from the Ptolemaic period) published by Lepsius, which is now used as the basis for citations from the Book of the Dead (Lepsius, *Todtenbuch der Aegypter*, Berlin, 1842). A similar but less complete text is found in the Papyrus Cadet used by Champollion, and published in the *Description d'Égyp. Ant.* ii. 72–75. Translations, mainly based on the Turin exemplar, have been published by Birch (in Bunsen's *Egypt's Place in Universal History*, v. 123 ff.) and Pierret (*Le Livre des Morts*, Paris, 1881).

At a late period, from about B.C. 1000 onwards, there grew up, side by side with the Book of the Dead, numerous religious compilations, based upon the same doctrines, and utilizing the Book itself as a source. Thus we have the various Books of 'Breathing,' the Book of 'Journeying through Eternity,' the Book of 'May my name flourish,' and the like. (Texts of this class have been published and discussed by, amongst others, Maspero, *Les momies royales de Deir el-Bahari*, p. 594 f.; cf. Budge, *The Book of the Dead*, 1898, ii. pp. clxxxiii ff. [text of Nesi-Chunsu]; Horrack, *Livre des Respirations*, Paris, 1877 [another text in Budge, *l.c.* p. cxcv ff., publ. by Budge with the Book of the Dead of Hunefer]; von Bergmann, 'Das Buch vom Durchwandeln der Ewigkeit' in *Sitzungsber. der Wiener Akad.* 1886, p. 369 ff.; Lieblein, *Le Livre Égyptien 'Que mon nom fleurisse,'* Leipzig, 1895; Papyrus Louvre, No. 3283, ed. by Wiedemann in *Hieratische Texte*, Leipzig, 1879). These works help in some measure to fill up *lacunæ* in the conceptions of the Book of the Dead. Further supplements, emanating from the same circle of ideas, are furnished by the rituals for the process of embalming (Rhind Papyri, ed. by Birch, London, 1863, and Brugsch, Leipzig, 1865; a 'hieratic Papyrus from Vienna' in von Bergmann's *Hieratische Texte*, Vienna, 1887; texts from Gizeh and Paris in Maspero's *Mém. sur quelques papyrus du Louvre*, Paris, 1875) and for the ceremonies at the door of the tomb (Schiaparelli, *Libro dei Funerali*, Turin, 1831–1890; cf. Maspero, *Ét. de myth.* i. 283 ff.).

These texts yield an uncommonly large number of notices with reference to the notions of immortality that attached to Osiris, but they contain nothing like a systematic Osirian religion. This is due to the circumstance that from first to last the Book of the Dead was a collection of hymns to gods and of magical formulæ, which were based upon the most diverse fundamental doctrines, and were united in a single work without any attempt being made to remove the contradictions and establish a harmony. As time went on, this compilation always received fresh accessions in the shape of independent passages; and, in addition to this, the already existing texts were constantly being expanded at every turn, without any regard to the harmony of the various doctrines expressed.

(*e*) Thus the same confusion that reigns in Egyptian religion in general, prevails also in the Book of the Dead and its supplementary texts. It is impossible here to illustrate this in detail; we must be content to sketch briefly the principal features of the Osirian faith, passing over all incidental points and particular deviations.

Originally, the adherents of Osiris appear to have held, in accordance with the teaching of the Book of the Dead, that the dead man as a whole would enter upon the way to the world beyond. The name Osiris — and this custom persisted through the whole course of Egyptian history — was then given to him, in the hope that, like the god Osiris, he would attain to immortality. In earlier times, so far as we know, the deceased was always thought of as male. It was only at a later period, after *c.* 500 B.C., that women began to have their sex left to them, and to be sometimes called in the funeral texts by the name Hathor instead of Osiris.

As experience proved more and more that mummies did not leave the sepulchres, a distinction was drawn between the mummy (*cha*) and the Osiris; the former remained in the coffin, the latter passed to the Plain of Ȧalu. All the same, however, the two were thought of as essentially identical. The mummy was equipped for the journey to the world beyond, the necessary amulets and magical formulæ were given to it, the tomb was so arranged that it could serve as a dwelling-place of the Osiris, and offerings of food and drink were put in it.

While, on the above view, the immortal part of the deceased, his soul as we should say, was an Osiris, thought of as with an earthly human form, in other places the soul was quite differently conceived. But these divergent views were, even at an early, and still more fully at a later, period amalgamated with the Osiris conception just mentioned, without on that account being completely given up. Thus it came about that a man was credited with a number of souls that pursued their course side by side. It was then supposed that in the man's lifetime these souls were united, while at death they forsook the corpse and sought, each one independently, the way to the next world. If they succeeded in this, and if the deceased was found righteous when tried before Osiris, his souls once more united within him and lived with him in the Plain of Åalu, as they had once done on earth. The fact that these part-souls are borrowed from originally independent doctrines, explains how the views of their nature frequently clash and contradict one another, and, above all, how a number of attributes are ascribed to several of the part-souls. Here, again, there is a complete lack of any systematic harmonizing of the various doctrines, which must of necessity be logically contradictory. Besides, it is to be remarked that the texts in general do not introduce all the part-souls at once, and that now one and now another, according to place and time, came more to the front. The following is a list of the most important of them, along with some notes on the main significance attributed to each of them (cf. Wiedemann, *The Ancient Egyptian Doctrine of the Immortality of the Soul*, London, 1895, and 'Le Livre des Morts' in the *Muséon*, xv. 40 ff.):—

*Ka* had the same form as the man, and corresponded to the Osiris, standing in much the same relation to the man as that in which the word stands to the thing, the name to the person. The *ka* was born with the man, and could, even during his lifetime, separate itself from him to a certain extent: thus Amenophis III. honoured his own *ka* as a god. After a man's death, the *ka* could at any time return into the mummy, animate it, and assume the dignity of the '*ka* living in his coffin.' For the most part, the cult of the dead recognized in the *ka* the essential personality of the deceased, the sacrificial formulæ were addressed to it, the tomb is its house, its temple, etc.

*Ba* has the form of a bird, mostly with human head and arms. At death it takes flight from the body, but visits it occasionally, and brings it food and drink. The *ba* itself, like the *ka*, also requires nourishment, being thus as little as the rest of the part-souls thought of as an immaterial being.

*Ab* or *ḥāti* is the heart. At death it leaves the man and goes by itself into the next world. In the Hall of Judgment it encounters its former possessor, and gives evidence, if need be, against him. In the event of his being pronounced righteous, it was restored to him; in the opposite case, the heart was supposed to live on in the Dwelling-place of Hearts. The deceased being bereft of his heart was thereby consigned to annihilation, for without a heart no existence was possible. This notion led to a peculiar practice. In the process of embalming, the readily decomposing heart was removed from the body. But, as neither the latter nor the Osiris could live without this organ, an artificial heart was substituted for the natural one. For this purpose they selected an amulet in the form of a small vase or of a *scarabæus* beetle, the latter symbolizing the notions of Becoming, Being, and Resurrection in general.

*Sāḥu* is the form, the envelope of the man.

*Chaibit* is the shadow cast by the man, which has an existence of its own, and is depicted as a black human form, or figuratively as a fan.

*Chu* (*achu*) is a shining transfigured soul, which was frequently, it may be assumed, conceived of in bird form.

*Sechem* is the personally conceived strength and power of the man; occasionally it appears to stand also for the form of the dead.

*Ren* is the name of the man. As long as this survived, and monuments associated with it lasted, as long as sacrificial formulæ, which commemorated it, were uttered, the dead man also continued to live in the other world. In the Saitic period in particular, great importance was attached to the *ren*, the conception of which at times coincides with that of the *ka*.

LITERATURE.—Jablonski, *Pantheon Aegyptiorum*, Frankfort, 1750–1752 (the best collection of the passages from the classical writers, the most important of which are those found in Plutarch's *de Iside et Osiride* [good edition by Parthey, Berlin, 1850]). ‖ Champollion's *Panthéon Égyptien*, Paris, 1823–1831, and Wilkinson's *Manners and Customs of the Ancient Egyptians* (last vol.), London, 1841, have a mainly historical interest. ‖ Lanzone, *Dizionario di mitologia egizia*, Turin, 1881–1886 (alphabetical list of the gods, with citations of the sources, and illustrations. This work is very difficult to procure). ‖ E. de Rougé, *Revue archéologique*, Nouv. sér. i.; Pierret, *Essai sur la Mythologie Égyptienne*, Paris, 1879; le Page Renouf, *Lectures on the Origin and Growth of Religion*, London, 1880 (emphasize the monotheistic, or, more correctly, henotheistic element in Egyptian religion). ‖ Tiele, *Histoire comparative des anciennes religions*, Paris, 1882, and E. Meyer, *Geschichte Aegyptens*, 1887 (attempt to trace the historical development of Egyptian religion, but the materials used by them are not sufficient to justify any very far-reaching conclusions). ‖ H. Brugsch, *Religion und Mythologie der alten Aegypter*, Leipzig, 1885–1890 (an attempt, principally with the aid of texts belonging to the late period of Egyptian history, to elucidate a connected religious system, somewhat on the lines of Plutarch's ideas. Brugsch's views, however, lack the support, above all, of the older monuments. Nevertheless, the materials collected by him have an importance of their own). ‖ Strauss und Torney, *Der altägyptische Götterglaube*, 2 vols., Heidelberg, 1889–1891 (draws upon second-hand sources). ‖ Maspero, *Études de mythologie et d'archéologie*, 4 vols., Paris, 1893–1900 (a collection of the extremely important articles of Maspero on general questions of Egyptian religion, and on various religious compositions such as the Book of the Dead and of Åm-duat, together with reviews of modern works on questions of the same kind); cf. also the relevant passages in Maspero's *Histoire ancienne de l'Orient classique*, Paris, 1895–1899. ‖ Wiedemann, *Die Religion der alten Aegypter*, Münster, 1890 [Eng. ed., freshly revised, and with illustrations, under the title 'Religion of the Ancient Egyptians,' London, 1897].

A. WIEDEMANN.

## PHILO.—

- i. Life.
- ii. Works.
- iii. System of thought.
  1. The general character and basis of Philo's system.
  2. The origin and nature of philosophy.
  3. Philo's theory of the universe.
  4. Man as the microcosm.
  5. The doctrine of God as eternal Being: (*a*) His existence; (*b*) His nature, ἄποιος; (*c*) His attributes.
  6. The doctrine of the Divine powers: (*a*) existence and character; (*b*) relation to God; (*c*) function.
  7. The doctrine of the Logos: (*a*) meaning of the term; (*b*) the supreme idea; (*c*) the Divine Logos twofold; (*d*) God's son and image; (*e*) mediator between God and matter; (*f*) relation to Wisdom, Spirit, and *logoi*; (*g*) Was the Logos a person?
  8. The higher relations of man: (*a*) general relation to God; (*b*) ethics.
- iv. Influence on Christian writers.
  Literature.

i. LIFE.—Philo, called *Judæus*, to distinguish him from others of the same name, was a resident, probably a native, of Alexandria. Born about the year B.C. 20, or perhaps a little earlier, he was an older contemporary of Jesus Christ; and this fact lends a peculiar interest to his writings, as revealing the intellectual and religious position of a Hellenist who was at once enlightened and conservative. If these writings did not directly influence the earliest expressions of Christian faith, they certainly exhibit the line of philosophical thought, to some extent the phraseology, and the method of Scripture exegesis, to which that faith resorted when it first appealed to the Græco-Roman world as a system of theology.

Little is known of Philo's life. He belonged to a wealthy and distinguished family, his brother enjoying Imperial favour, and holding the high position of *alabarch*. Familiar with cultivated society and the luxuries of Alexandria, he did not regularly practise the asceticism which he sometimes admired in others. But he led a blameless and studious life, amply availing himself of those opportunities of learning which Alexandria at that time afforded, with its Museum and Library, its concourse of lecturers and students, and the commingling of ideas which resulted from its position as a meeting-place of East and West. He was well versed in Greek literature, especially in the works of the great philosophers, whom he regarded with admiration; but, instead of being led by this admiration to despise the simple records of the Pentateuch, he found whole and untarnished in the sacred books of Israel the wisdom which was partially contained in the writings of Greece, so that, with all his width of culture, he remained a devout and believing Jew. He was strongly attached to his own people. On some occasion he was sent to Jerusalem to offer prayer and sacrifices; and late in life, notwithstanding his aversion to the turbulence and anxieties of political life, he was so moved by the brutal riots in which the Jews were barbarously treated, that he went on an embassy to Caligula, in the winter of A.D. 39-40, to seek for redress and security against further outrage. From such an Emperor nothing was to be obtained but insult and even blows, so that the members of the embassy were glad to escape with their lives. Philo describes himself as old and grey-headed when writing an account of this transaction. The year of his death is unknown.

ii. WORKS.—Philo's collected works have appeared in several editions, of which that of Thomas Mangey is still the standard. This edition, however, published in 1742, is neither sufficiently complete nor sufficiently accurate, and will be superseded by that of Cohn and Wendland, of which four volumes have appeared (November 1902). A convenient edition is that of Richter, in eight volumes (1828–1830), containing in addition to Mangey's text the treatises *de Festo Cophini* and *de Parentibus Colendis*, and the books translated from Armenian into Latin by Aucher. From this the Tauchnitz edition (1851–1853) was taken, with some slight alterations.

The works fall into several groups. 1. There is a series of *philosophical works*, which are believed by Cohn to have been written in Philo's early life, because they contain little of his characteristic thought, and seem like exercises in philosophical style and dialectic. The difference of their character from that of the other writings of Philo has led to suspicions of their genuineness; but Cohn thinks their style so specifically Philonean that there ought not to be a doubt on this point. This series comprises:—**1.** *de Incorruptibilitate Mundi.* This has been commonly regarded as spurious, but its genuineness has been defended by F. Cumont in the Prolegomena to his edition of the treatise (Berlin, 1891), and is accepted by Cohn. At the close it promises a sequel, which, however, has not been preserved. **2.** *Quod omnis probus liber sit*, which, as we learn from its opening lines, was preceded by a discourse Περὶ τοῦ πάντα δοῦλον εἶναι φαῦλον. **3.** *de Providentia*, in two books, preserved in Armenian (with considerable fragments in Greek), of which the genuineness of the first, which has been somewhat injured in transmission, has been questioned. **4.** *Alexander, sive de eo quod rationem habeant bruta animalia*, preserved in Armenian. The mention, in § 54, of an embassy to Rome cannot refer to the embassy to Gaius, as it occurs not in a speech of Philo's, but in the treatise of Alexander which Philo begins to read in § 10. But, as Cohn points out, the consulship of Germanicus, in A.D. 12, is alluded to in § 27, so that the book must be later than this, but might still be a comparatively early work. Philo, however, in § 73, says 'ex juventute in hac nutritus sum disciplina,' so that he probably wrote this treatise in middle life.

2. There is the great collection of writings containing *explanations of the Pentateuch.* This embraces three extensive works. **1.** The large group of allegorical commentaries, designed for educated Jews. These begin with the treatises now known as *Sacrarum Legum Allegoriæ* (a title which once had a more extended application), and dealt with the text of Gn 2–20, certain parts being omitted for special reasons. There are several gaps, some of which were certainly, and others probably, filled by books which are lost. This group, following the order observed in the editions, ends with the two books (originally five) *de Somniis.* To this series must have belonged the two lost books 'On Covenants,' to which reference is made in *de Mutatione Nominum*, 6 [i. 586].* A second book 'On Drunkenness' also, with the exception of some fragments, is lost; and yet another treatise, 'On Rewards' (founded on Gn 15[1]), is referred to as having preceded *Quis rerum divinarum heres* (1 [i. 473]). The fragment *de Deo*, preserved in Armenian, may have belonged to this group, and formed part of a treatise between *de Mutatione Nominum* and *de Somniis*. A few pages which appear in Mangey (ii. 265 ff.) as part of a separate tract, *de Mercede Meretricis*, have been restored by Cohn and Wendland to their proper place in the *de Sacrificiis Abelis et Caini*, § 5. The first section belongs to the treatise *de Sacrificantibus*, where it should be inserted between sections 4 and 5. **2.** The explanation of portions of the Pentateuch in the form of question and answer. This was intended to cover the whole Pentateuch; but it is uncertain whether it was completed. Several books on Genesis and Exodus have been preserved in an Armenian translation, and some fragments in Latin and Greek. Though this work is shown by references to be later than the great group of allegorical commentaries, certain difficulties suggest that the two works may to some extent have proceeded simultaneously. **3.** An exposition of the Mosaic legislation, in which allegorical explanation is sparingly used. The plan of this series is clearly described by Philo himself in the opening of the treatise *de Præmiis et Pœnis.* It dealt first with the account of the Creation, then with history, and lastly with laws, the following treatises being a supplement. It is clear, therefore, that the tract *de Mundi Opificio*, which occupies the first place in the editions, formed the beginning of this group. This indeed foreshadows the general plan, and is expressly referred to as 'the former composition' in the opening of the treatise *de Abrahamo*, which introduces the second division. The object of this division was to illustrate the excellence of the laws through typical examples. The essays on Isaac and Jacob are lost; and the three books on the Life of Moses do not belong to the series. The tract on Joseph is succeeded by one 'On the Decalogue,' and this again by four books on 'Special Laws.' The first of these has been broken up into several distinct treatises, beginning with that 'On Circumcision,' and the second and fourth books also comprise treatises with distinct titles. The essays on Fortitude, Philanthropy, and Penitence form a kind of appendix, and the work is completed by a dissertation on Rewards and Punishments, and on Curses.

3. There are several *historical treatises*, which were complete in themselves. **1.** *de Vita Mosis*, originally in two, but now arranged in three books.

* The first number refers to the section in Richter and Tauchnitz; the subsequent figures to the volume and page of Mangey.

**2.** A work called Ὑποθετικά, of which only fragments have been preserved. This is perhaps the same as—**3.** The Apology for the Jews, from which Eusebius extracted an account of the Essenes (*Præp. Ev.* viii. 11), and to which perhaps belonged the *de Vita Contemplativa*, containing an account of the Therapeutæ. The genuineness of the latter has been sharply disputed by Lucius and others, and ably defended especially by Massebieau and Conybeare (the former in the *Revue de l'Histoire des Religions*, xvi. [1887] pp. 170 ff., 284 ff.; the latter in his edition of the treatise, 1895. There are some valuable remarks also in Edersheim's article on Philo in Smith and Wace's *Dictionary of Christian Biography*, iv. 368 ff., and some of the principal objections are considered in a review of Conybeare in the *Jewish Quarterly Review*, 1896, p. 155 ff.). **4.** *in Flaccum*. **5.** *Legatio ad Gaium*, which survives out of five books Περὶ ἀρετῶν, describing the persecutions of the Jews, and the sad fate of the persecutors.

The editions contain also certain works, the spuriousness of which is generally admitted: *de Mundo*; and, in Armenian, *de Sampsone* and *de Iona*.

For fuller information and references, see the excellent section on the writings of Philo in Schürer's *GJV*³ iii. 487 ff. The above classification is in the main that suggested by Ewald (*GVI*² vi. 294 ff.), who, however, regards the Life of Moses as an introduction to group 2 (**3**), and places the leading groups in a different order. We have followed the careful classification of Cohn ('Einteilung und Chronologie der Schriften Philos,' published in *Philologus, Zeitschr. für das classische Alterthum*: Supplementband vii. Heft 3, 1899). A similar classification, though somewhat differently arranged, is given, with other interesting matter, in an earlier article by Cohn, on 'The latest Researches on Philo of Alexandria' in the *Jewish Quarterly Review*, v. [Oct. 1892] pp. 24–50.

iii. System of Thought.—1. *The general character and basis of Philo's system.*—The peculiarities of Philo's thought are largely due to the influence of his time and place. In Alexandria, Greek philosophy and Oriental mysticism met and mingled; and while the former, in its decline into scepticism, sought for support in eclectic schemes or in positive revelation, the latter endeavoured to justify itself before the world of thought by clothing its ideas in the language of philosophy. Jews, living in the midst of intellectual culture, and deeply versed in the finest portions of Greek literature, could no longer be satisfied with the crude ideas of their forefathers, and it became necessary to show that their ancestral religion was in harmony with the highest philosophy. Of those who made this attempt Philo was by far the most eminent, and his writings possess a singular interest for the Christian student, not only as revealing an instructive phase of human thought, but on account of the influence which they exercised, directly and indirectly, on the theology of the Church. He combined in himself the two tendencies which were seeking for reconciliation; for he was at once a religious man, full of devout feeling and moral enthusiasm, and, although his philosophy was largely borrowed, distinguished by no small share of speculative faculty. Of the truth and Divine authority of the Jewish religion he was profoundly convinced. His system avowedly rested upon the Scriptures, which were inspired in the minutest details. The prophets speak nothing of their own, but only what the Divine Spirit suggests, while the voluntary powers are in suspense. This condition, transcending the ordinary operations of the will, is open to good and wise men, and Philo does not hesitate to speak of his own enjoyment of it (*de Migrat. Abr.* 7 [i. 441]). Moses, however, was the supreme prophet, as well as king, legislator, and high priest; and his law remained, among the vicissitudes of States, unchangeable and eternal. Nevertheless, Philo did not resort to the Hebrew Scriptures, but, accepting the current story of the miraculous origin of the LXX, he assumed that the Hebrew and Greek were one and the same both in the facts and in the words. But, though he was ready to attach the utmost importance to a letter or even to an accent, he is not remarkable for the correctness of his citations. This subject has been investigated by Siegfried, who arrives at the following results:—A large part of Philo's citations consists of paraphrases from memory; in many instances the citation and the interpretation are so blended that a complete separation is impossible; there are many examples of double citation, one agreeing with the LXX, the other deviating from it; many of his deviations are found in single manuscripts of the LXX; others are explicable from the Hebrew text; some instances occur which point to a Hebrew text different from the Massoretic; and others indicate an attempt to improve the Greek. Passages also occur in which Philo bases an interpretation on an expression which is not found in our text of the LXX. And, finally, some variations must be ascribed to errors of transcribers. (See Siegfried's *Philo von Alexandria als Ausleger des Alten Testaments*, 1875, p. 162, where he sums up the results of three articles in Hilgenfeld's *Zeitschr. f. wiss. Theol.* 1873. See also Dr. H. E. Ryle's *Philo and Holy Scripture: or the Quotations of Philo from the Books of the OT*, 1895, where the subject is carefully treated in the Introduction, § ii.; and two articles in the *JQR*, v. [Jan. 1893] pp. 246–280, and viii. [Oct. 1895] pp. 88–122, 'On the Philonean Text of the Septuagint,' so far as it may be gathered from the Armenian version of the *Quæstiones et Responsiones*, by F. C. Conybeare, who surmises that 'Philo, at different times, and in writing his different works, used different texts of the LXX'; which would not be surprising, as the text must by that time have swarmed with variants). His canon must have been substantially the same as that which is now recognized, though there is no direct proof that he accepted Ruth, Esther, Ecclesiastes, Song of Songs, Lamentations, Ezekiel, or Daniel. (See the subject fully treated in Dr. Ryle's work, Introduction, § i. This volume contains also the text of Philo's quotations from Scripture).

Notwithstanding his apparent narrowness of view and rigid scripturalism, Philo was far from limiting his sympathies to the Jewish nation. The man who conformed to the Law was, he conceived, a citizen of the world. He himself attended the theatre as well as lectures on philosophy, and was a shrewd observer of the habits and emotions of men. But philosophy could not satisfy him; for, owing to the difficulty of its problems, it was broken up into conflicting schools, and, while he found in all the great sects certain elements of Divine truth, he took the teaching of Moses with him as a clue to guide him amidst their contending thoughts. He was not, however, content with carrying the great monotheistic faith and noble moral principles of Judaism into the disputes of the lecture-room; he believed that Moses had anticipated the philosophers, and that the sublimest speculations of Greece lay embedded in the Pentateuch. But how was it possible to find the philosophy of Plato or of the Stoics in the simple tales of Genesis? By the method of allegorical interpretation, which had already been applied by some of the philosophers, and especially by the Stoics, to the ancient mythology, and which Philo seriously adopted in order to rescue the wisdom of Scripture. If anything in the venerated records appeared on the surface to be childish and absurd; if any statement was made which appeared derogatory to God; if there was something contradictory, or a representation which was contrary to known fact,—any of these cases was in itself an indication of some hidden meaning which was worthy of a Divine author; and so a method of exegesis which must seem to us false and arbi rary grew out of the exigencies of the time, and was reduced to a kind of rule among the interpreters of Scripture. The rules which are followed by Philo are carefully classified by Siegfried in the above-mentioned work (p. 168 ff.); and it is evident that allegorical interpretation, however absurd and fantastic it must appear to us, was not left wholly to individual caprice, but followed certain definite lines which were considered as established among the students of allegory. Several of these canons, though differently applied, are found in the Haggadic interpretation of Palestine; but this connexion may be due less to Philo's knowledge of Rabbinical methods than to the general tendencies of thought which characterized the age. While thus holding that almost everything in the Pentateuch was related allegorically, Philo did not reject the literal meaning of that which seemed intrinsically credible or reasonable; and he insists that the ceremonial laws, though possessing a spiritual significance, must be observed according to the letter. Many things, however, especially anthropomorphic expressions, could be understood only allegorically; and here we may observe that no distinction is drawn between allegorical and simply figurative language. Philo's mode of treatment, being that of a commentator rather than a thinker, leaves no room for a systematic exposition of the problems of philosophy, and his theory of the universe must be gathered and pieced together from an immense number of unconnected passages. His style, though flowing and ornate, is often tedious, and the modern reader grows weary of interpretations which destroy the living beauty of the original text, and make the patriarchs the puppets of Alexandrian speculation. Yet the patient student may find many a golden saying, and perceive that Philo's rambling disquisitions are bound to one another by a thread of coherent thought.

From what has been already said, it is evident that for a proper understanding of Philo some knowledge of Greek philosophy, especially of the Platonic doctrine of ideas and of the Stoical doctrine of the Logos, must be presupposed. This the reader must necessarily seek elsewhere. The Old Testament, too, prepared the way both for the main problem of philosophy and for the special mode of solving it. The problem may be thus stated: How was the transcendent and infinite Spirit to be brought into connexion with the material universe and with the souls of men? An answer was partly suggested by the doctrine of angels, and by the poetical personification of Wisdom, while 'the word of the Lord,' frequently translated λόγος, furnished the very expression which Heraclitus and the Stoics had selected to denote the all-pervasive reason of the cosmos, and so provided a scriptural basis for the speculations of the thinker.

2. *The origin and nature of philosophy.*—According to Philo, philosophy originated in the contemplation of the cosmos, especially of the orderly movements of the heavens; but, as this suggested problems which seemed to him insoluble, he turned to the study of human nature, which permitted a closer and more fruitful examination. Thus he was led to the universal Mind, to Him who alone is real Being. Philosophy, accordingly, concerned itself with the whole nature of things, visible and invisible, and with the regulation of conduct, its end being wisdom, which consisted in the knowledge of Divine and human things and their causes. The incentive to it was found in the hope of blessedness (εὐδαιμονία). Before entering on so serious a pursuit, it was necessary to have a good moral and intellectual education, and to master the preparatory or 'encyclical' studies—grammar, geometry, and rhetoric. Philosophy itself had been divided into physics, ethics, and logic. Of these Philo assigns the lowest place to logic, and entertains a very poor opinion of physics or cosmology, as presenting nothing higher than fruitless conjecture. To ethics, which includes theology, or the knowledge of God, is assigned the highest and only worthy position.

3. *Philo's theory of the universe.*—Notwithstanding his depreciation of physics, Philo believed that the invisible could be entered only through the door of the visible cosmos, and he was fairly familiar with the science of his day. In order to understand some of his speculations, it is necessary to know in what sort of universe he conceived himself to be living. The earth, apparently regarded as spherical, was its fixed centre, and around it extended the heavens in successive spheres. Enclosing all was the vast sphere of the fixed stars, with its daily revolution from east to west. Within this were the seven spheres of the planets, the Sun occupying the centre; above it Saturn, Jupiter, and Mars; below it Mercury, Venus, and the Moon. This arrangement was symbolized by the golden candlestick. Matter was divided into four elements—fire, air, earth, and water, the ἀρχάς τε καὶ δυνάμεις of the cosmos. The air extended from the earth to the lunar sphere, beyond which was the ether, the salutary form of fire, as distinguished from the useful but destructive form with which we are familiar on the earth. The various objects of nature which admit of classification were constituted by a process of rational differentiation. First, things were divided into animate and inanimate. The latter comprised things which remained unaltered, through the possession of 'habit' (ἕξις), and things which had the higher property of 'nature' (φύσις), involving nutrition, change, and growth. The animated kingdom, divided into rational and irrational, was distinguished by the presence of soul (ψυχή), which rose above φύσις by having the attributes of perception, mental representation, and impulse. To these, rational beings add reason and free preferential power. Air, or πνεῦμα, was the element which constituted habit, nature, and soul. The air, the life-giving element, must be full of living beings, and therefore was peopled by invisible and immortal souls. It seemed impious to suppose that the stars were only fiery masses of earth. They were unmixed and Divine souls, 'manifest and perceptible gods.'

This survey of the phenomenal world led to many important questions, the answers to which must be briefly given. The universe, notwithstanding the multiplicity of its phenomena, was proved both by monotheistic faith and by pantheistic philosophy to be one, all its parts being mutually related, and each object depending for its perfection upon its place and function in the entire system. The heavenly bodies, besides shedding down light upon the earth, gave indications of future events through eclipses and other celestial occurrences; but Philo rejected the Chaldæan astrology, as deifying fate and destroying human responsibility. This unity, which presented the universe to the eye of reason as a well-ordered city, showed that there were powers by which the several parts were united, and an everlasting law, stretching from centre to circumference, and forming a bond that could not be broken. It was assumed that this universe, being the work of the greatest Creator, must be itself perfect, that is to say, complete in itself, and not depending on anything extraneous for the supply of its wants. Its perfection proved that it was the only cosmos; for it could not be perfect unless the whole substance of the elements had been used up in its production, and the Creator, being one, made it resemble himself in solitude. To the question whether the cosmos was self-existent and eternal a Jew could give but one answer: there was a time when the universe was not. That which is eternal is immutable; and therefore the universe, which is constantly changing, must have come into existence. Its genesis, however, did not take place in time; for time began with the interval of days and nights, and the six days of creation denote not a chronological succession, but an order in thought. Nevertheless, as the cosmos came into existence, Philo is driven into the expression, 'there was once a time when it was not' (*Dec. Orac.* 12 [ii. 190]). The archetype of time is eternity, in which nothing is either past or future, but only present. The genesis of the world was, according to a philosophical maxim, the beginning of its corruption; but the natural process might be stayed by the providence of the Creator, and thus Philo was able to believe that the entire cosmos endures for ever. But, while he admitted the dependence of the universe on an eternal and transcendent Cause, he was not a monist. The four elements pointed to something prior to themselves, of which they were differentiated forms. This was matter (οὐσία or ὕλη). It was conceived as the necessary substratum of the forms impressed upon it by reason, and as therefore in itself wholly destitute of rational distinctions. It was accordingly described by negative predicates, ἄποιος, ἄτακτος, ἄψυχος, ἄμορφος, ἀνείδεος, ἀσχημάτιστος, ἀτύπωτος, ἄσημος, ἄπειρος, πλημμελής, ἀνώμαλος, ἄνισος, νεκρός. Matter was thus only the passive condition of the exercise of efficient causality. Its existence was postulated by a necessity of thought; for causality involved four things—the agent, the material, the instrument, and the end in view. Matter being thus the condition of the efficient causality of God, was itself uncaused and eternal. Nevertheless, Philo does not seem quite at home with dualism, for he nowhere explicitly asserts the eternity of matter, and he occasionally uses expressions which, on a cursory perusal, seem inconsistent with it, but on more careful consideration appear not to be so. Again, he was not a dualist in the sense of accepting an eternal principle of evil. Dead matter could not be an efficient cause of imperfection, or limit the agency of God. Passages are, however, cited which establish Philo's belief that the created universe limited in some way the flow of Divine power. This limitation was due, not to the opposition of matter but to the very fact of creation, for the phenomenal is necessarily contrasted with that which is not phenomenal, and therefore could not be a full expression of Eternal Being. And, again, the parts of the universe were, in the original design of God, arranged in an ascending scale, and so could experience Divine benefits only in proportion to the capacity of their being. These considerations sufficiently explain Philo's language, without attributing to matter a causality which is expressly denied.

4. *Man as the microcosm.*—From the macrocosm we pass to the microcosm, man, considering him at present simply as a natural object. He combines in himself the powers which we have already encountered, ἑκτική, φυτική, ψυχική, and adds to these λογική and διανοητική. It is accordingly from the study of man that we derive our knowledge of God; for the higher principle in man corresponds with the supreme Mind in the cosmos. Man, then, is a duad, composed of body and soul. The body is made out of the same four elements as the rest of the material world. Soul is distinguished by the possession of αἴσθησις, which, being an εἴσθεσις, introduces things to the mind through the five channels of sensation, which are signified by the creation of animals on the fifth day; of φαντασία, which is an impression (τύπωσις) left in the soul by what the senses have communicated; and impulse (ὁρμή), which has the two forms of desire and aversion. The human soul, however, is twofold, and, in addition to the lower part which it shares with the animals, has the higher principle of reason. The lower part of the soul, the vital principle, consists of blood, or, more properly, of air which is mixed with blood, and carried by it to every part of the body. Like the sphere of the planets, it has seven parts or natures. These are the five senses, speech, and the faculty of reproduction. Being material, it is mortal. The higher principle is regularly spoken of as νοῦς. The possession of νοῦς in a qualified sense is indeed sometimes extended to the lower animals; but this vacillation in the use of language does not necessarily indicate any contradiction in Philo's thought. The rational principle, in its highest sense, was distinctive of man, and in him it was the sovereign part (τὸ ἡγεμονικόν). Several able interpreters believe that Philo derived the substance of the rational soul from the ether, and to that extent was a materialist, although he sometimes wavers. A remarkable passage seems decisive. He alleges that we cannot know the substance (οὐσία) of mind, and nevertheless asserts parenthetically, as though this one point were certain, ἀλλ' οὐ σῶμα, ἀσώματον δὲ λεκτέον (*de Somn.* i. 6 [i. 625]). To resolve his doubts he appeals to the statement of Moses, 'God breathed into his face a spirit of life,' meaning by spirit 'not air in motion, but a certain stamp and character of Divine power' (*Quod det. pot. ins.* 22, 23 [i. 207]). Accordingly, the substance of the higher soul is 'Divine spirit' (*de Concup.* 11 [ii. 356]), 'derived from nothing at all that is originated, but from the Father and Sovereign of the universe' (*de Mundi Op.* 46 [i. 32]). It is accordingly τῆς μακαρίας φύσεως ἐκμαγεῖον ἢ ἀπόσπασμα ἢ ἀπαύγασμα (*ib.* 51 [i. 35]). In one of the passages which are thought to contradict this view he is simply stating the opinions of others; one or two more admit of an interpretation which is consistent with his more clearly expressed view; and in the remainder the word 'ethereal' may readily be understood figuratively of a pure and heavenly origin. Philo is a rhetorical writer; and his highly wrought language must frequently be interpreted by reference to his more careful and exact statements. The immaterial soul was by its nature incapable of division, and accordingly corresponded with the unbroken sphere of the fixed stars, and so completed the analogy between the microcosmos and the macrocosmos. It belonged to the tribe of souls who peopled the air. These fell into two divisions: some, endowed with a more Divine constitution, living close to the ether; others descending into mortal bodies. The former were called by Moses angels, as bearing messages between God and man. The desire of the latter to descend into bodies is not clearly explained, and seems to imply an original moral distinction among souls. The souls of the wise, indeed, may have come to increase their experience and wisdom; but others abandoned wisdom, and were swept away by the earthly torrent. In either case, however, the soul was intrinsically immortal.

We must now view the soul in its temporary connexion with the body. Its seat is the heart or brain, more probably the brain, which is so closely connected with the senses. There it acts as a 'god' of the irrational part (*Leg. All.* i. 13 [i. 51]), through which, though itself incapable of severance, it is wholly diffused. This diffusion is effected by means of the ductile powers, which, without rupture, not only pervade the body but extend far beyond it, reaching even to God Himself. The analogy for this extension of an inseparable monad confined to one small portion of space is found in the sun, which, without leaving its place, sends its rays into every part of the cosmos (*de Somn.* i. 14 [i. 632]). These powers, however, are not dependent on the soul that has them, but are in their nature imperishable, so that the individual mind only has its share of those spiritual essences which belong equally to countless others. Beyond the division into rational and irrational, Philo does not venture on any systematic classification, though numerous powers are casually alluded to. We must confine our attention to the most important. Man alone, upon earth, has been endowed with freedom and the power of voluntary choice between good and evil, and is therefore justly subject to praise and blame (the most important passage is *Quod Deus immut.* 10 [i. 279 f.]). He alone is capable of sin, for higher beings are above the reach of temptations, and the animals, being subject to necessity, are below it. It is not inconsistent with the power of choice between alternatives that God is represented as the sole originating Cause; but one fragment pushes this so far as to be inconsistent with the general doctrine, the writer's mind being for the time overwhelmed by his sense of the nothingness of the creature (see J. Rendel Harris, *Fragments of Philo Judæus*, p. 8). The logos is another faculty which raises man above the brute. Here Philo, except in his scriptural allegories, simply follows the Greek philosophers. The logos is twofold: ὁ ἐνδιάθετος, ὁ κατὰ διάνοιαν λόγος, by virtue of which we are rational; and ὁ προφορικός, or ὁ κατὰ προφοράν, or ὁ γεγωνὼς λόγος, whereby we are able to converse. The latter is the interpreter (ἑρμηνεύς) of the mind, and therefore ought to be cultivated, so as to do justice to the thought. The virtues of the double logos were symbolized by the Urim and Thummim (δήλωσις and ἀλήθεια) on the breastplate of the high priest. The sources of knowledge are sensible perception and reason. The former brings the mind into connexion with the material world, and is the starting-point of all our knowledge; for the intuitive apprehension of the intelligible cosmos arises only on occasion of some sensible experience, as space is apprehended from the perception of bodies at rest, and time from perceiving bodies in motion. Nevertheless noümena shine by their own light, and in their higher forms reveal themselves only to the pure. Knowledge, however, which depended simply on the natural faculties, was insecure. As a rule, things were known only by comparison with their opposites, and that which required something else to support it could not be depended on. The formula of scepticism, that it is safest to suspend one's judgment (ἐπέχειν), is advocated in a long passage, in which the errors of the senses and the conflicting views of men are dwelt upon (*de Ebriet.* 41–49 [i. 383–388]). Through the varying opinions of the philosophers, therefore, Philo took for his unerring guide the laws and customs divinely communicated to the Jews.

5. *The doctrine of God as eternal Being.*—(*a*) The belief in the *existence* of one supreme God was fundamental in the Jewish religion. In the world of speculation, however, this was opposed by atheistic and pantheistic hypotheses, and it was therefore necessary to support the belief by philosophical arguments. The microcosm, man, suggested the true solution of the problems presented by the macrocosm. As the visible body was presided over by the invisible mind, so the universe which engages our vision must be held together and governed by an unseen sovereign. This conclusion is confirmed by the evidence of design and harmony in the objects around us. The cosmos has all the appearance of being a work of art, and consequently cannot be itself ὁ πρῶτος θεός, but must have proceeded from an intelligent and providential artificer. Again, the universe, as we have seen, bore the marks of transience and dependence, and so pointed to a πρῶτον or πρεσβύτατον αἴτιον, which could be none other than supreme Reason or Mind (ὁ τῶν ὅλων νοῦς), which alone could produce a world that bore everywhere the impress of rational thought. But the highest mode of approaching God was by religious intuition. The world was only a shadow, which left men subject to conjecture; but God shone by His own light, revealing Himself to the eyes of the soul, and imprinting immortal thoughts upon the mind. This intuition is not universal. It requires solitude, detachment from earthly cares, and freedom from the sway of the senses. Self-knowledge, leading to self-despair, opened the way for this diviner knowledge; and he who had despaired of himself knew the Self-existent. Accordingly, the apprehension of God not only varied in different persons, but in the same person changed with changing moods.

(*b*) In forming an opinion about the Divine *nature* we are necessarily hampered by the limitations of our own consciousness. The human analogy evidently fails in a fundamental point. Man is a derived being, placed in a world which he has not created, while God is the underived Creator of the universe. He is not only without the human form, but without human passions. The highest truth is expressed by the statement that 'God is not as man' (Nu 23[19]), and it is only for purposes of admonition that He is said to be 'as man' (Dt 1[31]), and to have bodily organs, and such passions as enmity and wrath. This thought is frequently insisted on. The two most instructive passages are *de Sacr. Ab. et Caini*, 28–30 [i. 181–183], and *Quod Deus immut.* 11–14 [i. 280–283]. The former, explaining the necessary use of anthropomorphic language on account of our weakness, sums up in these words: ἀφελεῖς οὖν, ὦ ψυχή, πᾶν γενητὸν θνητὸν μεταβλητὸν βέβηλον ἀπὸ ἐννοίας τῆς περὶ θεοῦ τοῦ ἀγενήτου καὶ ἀφθάρτου καὶ ἀτρέπτου καὶ ἁγίου καὶ μόνου μακαρίου. The higher faculties in men, however, reason and the preferential freedom of the will, were peculiar to them among created beings, and must be regarded as essentially Divine; so that we may regard God as free, self-determining, ever active Mind (ὁ τοῦ παντὸς νοῦς), possessed of τὸ αὐτεξούσιον κράτος, even His beneficence being ascribed, not to His inability to do evil, but to His preference for the good (*de Plantat. Noe*, 20 [i. 342]).

When we seek to pass beyond this description, and inquire into the essence of God, we are met with blank mystery. The essence of the human mind is impenetrable, much more that of God, so that we can know only that He is, not what He is: ὁ δ' ἄρα οὐδὲ τῷ νῷ καταληπτὸς ὅτι μὴ κατὰ τὸ εἶναι μόνον· ὕπαρξις γὰρ ἔσθ' ἣν καταλαμβάνομεν αὐτοῦ, τῶν δέ γε χωρὶς ὑπάρξεως οὐδέν (*Quod Deus sit immut.* 13 [i. 282]). Accordingly, He is in the strictest sense without a name. There are, indeed, numerous appellations which serve to denote Him, and He is called in Scripture κυρίῳ ὀνόματι ὁ ὤν (*de Abr.* 24 [ii. 19]); but these do not reveal His essence, so as to communicate a perfect knowledge of what

He is. In spite of this opinion, Philo constantly assumes that we have a very extensive knowledge of God, and it is generally supposed that his whole doctrine is involved in hopeless contradiction. This, however, may be resolved by a strict attention to the meaning of words. According to Philo, God is a simple uncompounded unity. But, when we speak of Him as rational, good, powerful, we violate His unity, and represent Him as manifold. This is due to the imperfection of our thought, which cannot comprehend the essence in which these things are one, but can notice only the different effects of the Divine causality in the manifoldness of nature. As a simple essence, God is without qualities (ἄποιος, a word which expresses not, as is often said, the absence of attributes, but the impossibility of classification). God is not a sort of God, or a sort of anything, but is alone in His incomprehensible perfection. How, then, are we to regard His attributes? A man is good by partaking of goodness, which, as it may be shared by others, makes the man a particular sort of man. God, however, is not good by partaking of goodness, as though it were something extraneous to Himself. Goodness and all such attributes are among the ἰδιότητες of God; and if other beings may be classified as good, it is only because they participate in the Divine essence, in the eternal and archetypal ideas which the fulness of God exhausts and transcends. Οὐδὲν γάρ ἐστι τῶν καλῶν, ὃ μὴ θεοῦ τε καὶ θεῖον (*de Sacr. Ab. et Caini*, 17 [i. 174]); πλήρης δὲ ἀγαθῶν τελείων, μᾶλλον δὲ, εἰ χρὴ τὸ ἀληθὲς εἰπεῖν, αὐτὸς ὢν τὸ ἀγαθόν, ὃς οὐρανῷ καὶ γῇ τὰ κατὰ μέρος ὤμβρισεν ἀγαθά (*de Septen.* 5 [ii. 280]); ὁ τῶν ὅλων νοῦς ἐστιν εἰλικρινέστατος καὶ ἀκραιφνέστατος, κρείττων ἢ ἀρετὴ καὶ κρείττων ἢ ἐπιστήμη καὶ κρείττων ἢ αὐτὸ τὸ ἀγαθὸν καὶ αὐτὸ τὸ καλόν (*de Mundi Op.* 2 [i. 2]).

(*c*) There is, then, no contradiction in ascribing *attributes* to Him whose uncompounded essence is so inscrutable. He is eternal, incorruptible, and immutable, and thus differentiated in the most absolute way from every thing created. Hence He is not only the one only God, but He is the indivisible, archetypal unity, without parts or members. He is invisible, except as spiritual light revealing itself to the soul. He is omnipresent, and 'has filled the cosmos with Himself' (*de Post. Cain.* 5 [i. 229]), having stretched his powers through the earth and sky, so as to leave no part empty. Being independent of place, He is at once everywhere and nowhere, and all terms of motion, like up and down, are inapplicable, except figuratively, to God in His essence (τῷ κατὰ τὸ εἶναι θεῷ; see especially *Conf. Ling.* 27 [i. 425]). He is equally independent of time, which belongs only to the phenomenal world. Every thing being thus present to His view, He is omniscient, and no man can hide himself from Him. As sole efficient Cause, He is omnipotent. He is also perfect, that is, complete in Himself, so that nothing could add to the fulness from which all things come; and, regarded as pure Being, He is out of all relation (τὸ γὰρ ὄν, ᾗ ὄν ἐστιν, οὐχὶ τῶν πρός τι), but some of His powers are, as it were, relative (ὡσανεὶ πρός τι); a phrase which implies that, though they are described by relative terms, their character is not altered by the relation, but they impart all and receive nothing (see *de Mut. Nom.* 4 [i. 582]). Philo habitually teaches that God has no participation in evil, and is the source only of good. With him are οἱ θησαυροὶ μόνων ἀγαθῶν (*de Fuga et Invent.* 15 [i. 557]). In one passage, however, this is verbally contradicted, εἰσὶ γὰρ ὥσπερ ἀγαθῶν οὕτω καὶ κακῶν παρὰ τῷ θεῷ θησαυροί (*Leg. All.* iii. 34 [i. 108]). This may illustrate the kind of inconsistency into which Philo is betrayed by his allegorical interpretation of different passages; but here the contradiction is relieved by the consideration that in one passage he is dealing with moral evil, and in the other with Divine punishments. When we add that God enjoys perfect blessedness and uninterrupted peace, we have completed this preliminary survey of His attributes.

And now a profound question arises which philosophy was bold enough to answer. Why did a Being so perfect, and in need of nothing, create the universe? Because He was good and munificent, and did not grudge to matter a share of His own best nature; and in thus bestowing His favours He acted from His own sole initiative, οὐδενὶ δὲ παρακλήτῳ—τίς γὰρ ἦν ἕτερος;—μόνῳ δὲ αὑτῷ χρησάμενος (*de Mundi Op.* 5, 6 [i. 5]). From the same source springs His providential care, with which He pours forth the abundant riches of His favours, blessing the imperfect, and pitying the unworthy. But His mercies are measured out in due proportion, for not even the whole world could contain them in their purity. Every doctrine of Providence, however, is required to account for the existence of pain and of moral evil. The questions thus suggested are discussed by Philo in his treatise on Providence, where he gives the usual philosophical answers, on which it is unnecessary to linger. We must pass to the more characteristic problem, How are we to reconcile the absolute simplicity and unity of God with His manifold activity in the world of phenomena?

6. *The doctrine of the Divine powers.*—(*a*) *Their existence and character.*—When we survey this world and observe the mutual relation of its several parts, we are driven to the conviction that it is one system, and therefore that it is held together by a pervasive and enduring power. But this power is manifested in a vast variety of objects, which embody distinct ideas or rational forms; and nothing but the presence of a compelling force can prevent them from sinking back into amorphous matter. We are therefore constrained in thought to recognize a multitude of powers, such as habitual, vital, rational. God being the only efficient Cause, these powers must be Divine, and so constitute the link between God and matter. They belong therefore to the Divine essence, and, as that essence is unknown, the powers too hide their essence, and reveal only their effects. They are uncircumscribed, timeless, and unbegotten, holy and unerring as God Himself, and consequently they are only partially exercised in creation. From this brief description it is apparent that they correspond with the Platonic *ideas*, and accordingly Philo adopts this part of Platonic philosophy. The principal passage bearing on this subject may be quoted. God is represented as replying thus to Moses: 'As, among you, seals, whenever wax or any similar material is applied to them, make innumerable impressions, not suffering the loss of any part, but remaining as they were, such you must suppose the powers around Me to be, applying qualities to things without quality, and forms to the formless, while they experience no change or diminution in their eternal nature. But some among you call them very appropriately *ideas*, since they give ideal form to each thing, arranging the unarranged, and communicating determinate limits and definition and shape to the indeterminate and indefinite and shapeless, and, in a word, altering the worse into the better' (*de Monarch.* i. 6 [ii. 218 f.]). The function of these powers or ideas in the work of creation is described in the following passage: 'For God, as being God, anticipating that there could never be a beautiful imitation without a beautiful pattern, or any perceptible thing faultless which was not modelled in conformity with an archetypal and intelligible idea,

when He wished to fabricate this visible cosmos, first shaped forth the intelligible, in order that, using an immaterial and most Godlike pattern, He might work out the material cosmos, a more recent copy of an older one, destined to contain as many perceptible genera as there were intelligible in the other. But it is not to be said or supposed that the cosmos which consists of the ideas is in any place; but in what way it subsists we shall know by following up an example of what takes place among ourselves. Whenever a city is founded to gratify the high ambition of some king or emperor, claiming autocratic authority, and at the same time brilliant in thought, adding splendour to his good fortune, sometimes a trained architect having offered his services, and inspected the good temperature and suitability of the place, describes first within himself almost all the parts of the city that is to be erected—temples, gymnasia, town-halls, market-places, harbours, docks, lanes, equipment of walls, foundations of houses and other public edifices. Then, having received the forms of each in his own soul, as in wax, he bears the figure of an intelligible city, and having stirred up the images of this in his memory, and, still more, having sealed there its characters, looking, like a good workman, to the pattern, he begins to prepare that made of stones and timber, making the material substances like each of the immaterial ideas. Similarly, then, we must think about God, who, when He purposed founding the great city, first devised its forms, out of which, having composed an intelligible cosmos, He completed the perceptible, using the former as a pattern. As, then, the city which was first formed within the architect had no exterior place, but had been sealed in the artist's soul, in the same way not even the cosmos that consists of the ideas could have any other place than the Divine Logos which disposed these things into a cosmos. For what other place could there be for his powers which would be adequate to receive and contain, I do not say all, but any one unmixed?' (*de Mundi Op.* 4 f. [i. 4]). The ideas are not mere names, which could have no efficiency, but are real essences, to which the qualities of things are due (see especially *Sacrificant.* 13 [ii. 261 f.]), and which maintain in material objects the permanence of ideal types. They are eternal, and do not perish with the things on which their seal has been set; for wisdom and goodness do not die with the wise and good man. In their combination they form the *κόσμος νοητός*, which is the archetype of the *κόσμος αἰσθητός*. They have no locality but the Divine thought, or God Himself, who is the 'immaterial place of immaterial ideas' (*Cherub.* 14 [i. 148]), the primal archetype, or rather older and higher than the archetype, the Idea being only one mode of the eternal Thought. From this point of view the *κόσμος νοητός* is the son of God, and its counterpart, the *κόσμος αἰσθητός*, is his younger son. Philo attempts no careful classification of the powers; but there are a few on which he frequently dwells. The highest of all is the Logos. Next to this comes the creative power, *ἡ ποιητική*, and then, in succession, *ἡ βασιλική*, *ἡ ἵλεως*, and the two divisions of *ἡ νομοθετική*, the preceptive and the prohibitive. The lowest on the scale, which are virtually only two, are subordinate varieties of the two powers above them, affecting the life of men, and not the entire cosmos. The two great powers, the creative and the regal, have their unity in the Logos. They are otherwise called *ἀγαθότης* and *ἐξουσία*, for by goodness God generated the universe, and by authority He rules it. Scripture represents this distinction by the two titles, *θεός* and *κύριος*. Under the latter power is ranked the punitive, for it is the business of a ruler to punish the guilty; but this is not inconsistent with goodness, 'the oldest [*i.e.* the highest and best] of the graces,' for punishment is intended as a prevention or correction of sin.

(*b*) We must now notice a very difficult question, What was *the relation of the Divine powers to God*? It is generally said that Philo is here involved in hopeless contradiction, sometimes treating the powers merely as attributes, sometimes regarding them as distinct persons. Philo himself felt that the subject was obscure, and not to be rashly spoken of before those who were incapable of philosophical reflexion (see, especially, *de Sacr. Ab. et Caini*, 15 and 39 [i. 173 f. and 189]). The most definite statement is found in an allegorical interpretation of the visit of the three men to Abraham. These symbolized the Father of the universe, and His two oldest and nearest powers, the creative and the regal. These present to the seeing intelligence a mental image, now of one, and now of three,—of one, whenever the soul, being perfectly purified, presses on to the idea which is unmingled and complete in itself; but of three when it is unable to apprehend the self-existent Being from itself alone, but apprehends it through the effects. That the triple image is virtually that of one subject is apparent not only from allegorical speculation, but from the word of Scripture, which represents Abraham as addressing his visitors, not as three but as one, and as receiving the promise from one only (*de Abr.* 24 f. [ii. 18 ff.]). It is clear from this passage that the creative and regal powers are not conceived as beings distinct from God, but only as answering to our imperfect modes of apprehension, while to a true perception both are lost in the supreme and unbroken unity of God. In other words, our highest thought, when it penetrates to the Divine unity, can apprehend God only as pure Being; but, when we view Him through the variety of His operations, we are obliged to think and speak of certain aspects of that Being. An instructive analogy is furnished by a description of the 'power' in the wise man. It receives various names, piety, natural philosophy, ethical, political; and the wise man contains these and numberless other powers; but in all he has one and the same *εἶδος* (*de Ebriet.* 22 [i. 370 f.]). Agreeably to this view, the powers are spoken of collectively as equivalent to the 'invisible' or 'eternal nature' of God. It is not surprising, therefore, that God and His power or powers are used interchangeably. Again, there are several passages in which the powers are regarded as predicates of God, and God is referred to as Himself being or doing what is implied by their several names.

(*c*) What, then, is *the function of the powers*? They are not intended, as is so often said, to act as personal agents who can take the place of God in all mundane affairs, but to present to our thought the mode in which we may conceive of the Eternal Mind as acting in time and space; or, in other words, they are not meant to separate God from the material world, but to bring Him into contact with it. It is through them that the self-existent Being (*ὁ ὤν* or *τὸ ὄν*) is omnipresent, having filled the universe with *Himself*. He 'stretches' them into every part, as we may stretch our mind to a speaker, or the energies of our souls to God. It is through the powers that God 'touches' the soul; for we can receive only a broken and partial revelation. The passage which is thought to prove decisively the separate personality of the powers is the following: *ἐξ ἐκείνης* [*οὐσίας*] *γὰρ πάντα ἐγέννησεν ὁ θεός, οὐκ ἐφαπτόμενος αὐτός· οὐ γὰρ ἦν θέμις ἀπείρου καὶ πεφυρμένης ὕλης ψαύειν τὸν ἴδμονα καὶ μακάριον, ἀλλὰ ταῖς ἀσωμάτοις δυνάμεσιν, ὧν ἔτυμον ὄνομα αἱ ἰδέαι, κατεχρήσατο πρὸς τὸ γένος ἕκαστον τὴν ἁρμόττουσαν λαβεῖν μορφήν* (*Sacrificant.* 13 [ii. 261]). Yet even here it is God, evidently used in the highest sense, who generated the universe, and the powers are really 'ideas,' which impart form to every genus. God did not touch matter Himself, for that would imply that He communicated to it the totality of the Divine idea, and that the universe, instead of affording fragmentary glimpses of the Divine thoughts, was a complete revelation of His nature. Again, it is quite in conformity with Philo's abundant use of figurative language when God and His powers are compared to a sovereign and his attendant bodyguard. Similarly, the human mind, as a king, has its bodyguard of attendant powers (*de Migrat. Abr.* 31 [i. 462], and several other passages); and the passages where the Divine powers figure most clearly as separate persons may all be explained as instances of this rhetorical style. It is impossible for us to survey these in detail. Some confusion arises also because expositors are not careful to separate Philo's literal interpretations from his allegorical. Thus the three visitors to Abraham might literally be angels, and yet allegorically might be designed to represent God under three aspects of His being. A different order of reflexion arises in connexion with the creation of man. The words 'Let us make man' point to a plurality of persons. These words would have been quite intelligible if Philo had looked upon all the Divine powers as distinct persons; but in fact he feels their difficulty, and declares that the truest reason for them is known to God only. He treats of them in four passages of considerable length (*de Mundi Op.* 24 [i. 16 f.]; *Conf. Ling.* 33–36 [i. 430–433]; *de Fuga et Inv.* 13 f. [i. 556]; and *de Mut. Nom.* 4 [i. 582 f.]); and in these he professes to give only a plausible conjecture. One distinction is made perfectly clear. Man, unlike the rest of the creation, has been partly formed by inferior agents, whereas the whole cosmos, heaven and earth and sea, was made by the architect Himself, without the co-operation of others. This proves conclusively that the subordinate agents, to whom is assigned the partial creation of man, were not regarded as identical with the Divine powers which were exercised in every part of creation. Man occupies a unique place in that he is liable to sin; and therefore God delegated the creation of man in part to others, in order that, if evil arose, it might not be ascribed to the Supreme Goodness. These others are angels, and angels are souls flying in the air, and 'under-servants of God's powers' (τοὺς ὑποδιακόνους αὐτοῦ τῶν δυνάμεων ἀγγέλους, *de Monarch.* ii. 1 [ii. 222]). Nevertheless, they are themselves spoken of as God's powers. This apparent inconsistency is easily explained. All objects which embodied a rational idea might be spoken of as powers; but these created and finite manifestations of Divine thought in the elements, in all the lovely sights of nature, and in pure angelic souls inhabiting the air, are not to be identified with the infinite and unbegotten powers which, in our modern language, must be described as attributes of God. While, however, they are distinct to our thought and perception, they participate in the same nature; for it is only through sharing in a Divine idea that matter can receive the impress of rational form, or souls concentrate in themselves the characters of personality.

7. *The doctrine of the Logos.*—(*a*) At the head of the hierarchy of Divine powers was the Logos. This word occasions a good deal of difficulty to interpreters of Philo, owing to the want of any precise English equivalent. It denotes, in its highest sense, the mind itself, but more especially the rational faculty. Then it is applied to any rational thought or idea residing within the mind, and is extended to any relation which may be rationally conceived, to an underlying principle or law, for instance, of numbers or harmony, and to the meaning of anything. From this it passes to any kind of outward expression of some thought or idea, particularly in spoken or written language. Probably its best representative in English is 'Thought,' a word which has some approach to the same variable application.

(*b*) We have already seen that the cosmos presented a picture of rational forms or ideas; and, as these were combined in one harmonious whole, they constituted one cosmic thought. This thought was the highest genus, under which the multitudinous ideas took rank as species; or, more strictly, God, as pure Being, was the most generic, and His reason or thought was second. The Logos, therefore, regarded as a Divine power, was the unitary principle of all beneath it. It was by virtue of His reason that God was both ruler and good; or, in other words, creation and providence were both expressions of reason. If so, a νοητὸς κόσμος must have existed in the mind of God prior to the visible world; and, as it was the sum of the Divine thoughts, it was the Logos of God. 'The intelligible cosmos,' says Philo, 'is nothing else than God's Logos, when he is already engaged in making a cosmos; for neither is the intelligible city anything else than the reflexion (λογισμὸς) of the architect when he is already intending to create the city' (*de Mundi Op.* 6 [i. 5]). From this point of view the Logos is the supreme archetypal idea (ἰδέα τῶν ἰδεῶν), which by its impress, as of a seal, on matter constitutes the visible universe. Matter, however, was inherently incapable of retaining what was once impressed upon it; and hence its ideal forms were forces or powers constantly present and active, and might be regarded as a law, the eternal and pervasive law of 'right reason,' which, stretching from centre to circumference, was a bond of the universe that could not be broken. The same supreme Logos appeared in man as the moral law, enjoining what was right and forbidding what was wrong. Thus the Logos, the intelligible cosmos, became manifest in the universe, where it dwelt as an 'intelligent and rational nature,' ministering as a high priest in the cosmic temple of God.

(*c*) It is well known that the human logos was divided into ἐνδιάθετος and προφορικός, and that these terms were, in the later theology, extended to the Logos of God. Now Philo, while familiar with this distinction in the case of man, never applies to God the technical language by which it was described. Hence it is sometimes maintained that the distinction in the Divine Logos was absent from his thought. But the conception of a twofold Logos is involved in the account which we have already given, and it is quite explicitly recognized by Philo. The principal passage is in the *Vita Mosis*, iii. 13 [ii. 154], where it is said that the 'Logos is double both in the universe and in the nature of man,' and the former is divided into that which relates to immaterial ideas, and that which relates to the visible objects of the perceptible cosmos. Nevertheless, the analogy between man and God was incomplete; for God had no organs of speech, and His word was seen in His works, and not heard by the ears (see, especially, *de Migrat. Abr.* 9 [i. 443 f.]). Philo may therefore have shrunk from adopting the usual terms, as one of them suggested anthropomorphic ideas.

(*d*) The Logos, as the sum and unity of the world of ideas, was identical with the Divine reason; and this reason was not an essence extraneous to God, by sharing in which God became rational, but was a mode of the Divine essence, and in no way broke the solitude of God which existed prior to creation. God, however, was more than reason (κρείσσων ἢ πᾶσα λογικὴ φύσις, *Fragments*, ii. 625); and therefore it was possible to apprehend the Divine reason, though none could reach God in His essence. Since thought may be regarded as a product of the mind, the Logos, as the cosmic thought, might be conceived as produced by God, and in this aspect is spoken of under the figure of a *son*, πρεσβύτατος or πρωτόγονος υἱός. The epithet implies that there were other and younger sons; and this is agreeable to Philo's view of God as ὁ πατὴρ τῶν ὅλων or τῶν ὄντων. As the son of God, the firstborn archetypal idea, which by its impress has converted formless matter into a cosmos, it is God's *image*, in accordance with which the rational soul in man was created. Or, in another figure, it is the shadow of God, disclosing by its incidence upon matter the rational form of which the substance is invisible.

(*e*) It is now apparent in what sense the Logos was conceived as *mediator* between God and matter. It was not a personal demiurgus, creating, under orders, a universe which God Himself would not touch, but rather the effectual Divine Thought, through which God made His own work (τὸ ἴδιον ἔργον, *Quis rer. div. her.* 42 [i. 502]), impressing it, like a seal, upon matter. As the hidden Reason of God, it is eternal; as the objective Thought of God, impressed upon matter, it has come into existence. As essentially Divine, it might be spoken of, but only imperfectly (ἐν καταχρήσει), as God (*de Somn.* i. 39 [i. 655]); and once it is described as ὁ δεύτερος θεός (*Fragments*, ii. 625). This we can understand, if we bear in mind that matter was not regarded as simply put into shape, and then left to itself, but its cosmic form was the living presence of Divine thought, the sum of all that man could truly apprehend of God, though he could rise to the knowledge that Reason was not exhaustive of Being, but transcendent beyond it was the eternal Cause, whose essence was unknowable.

(*f*) Philo, following the Old Testament, frequently refers to *Wisdom*. In many passages this is identified with the Logos. In others the two terms are distinguished; and it is a little perplexing to find that their mutual relations are inverted, Wisdom being the fountain of the Logos, and the Logos being the fountain of Wisdom. Probably the difficulty may be resolved by the difference between the universal and the particular. Human reason or wisdom, distributed among many souls, flows from the supreme Wisdom or Reason, which are identical with one another in either the higher or the lower sphere. The term Wisdom is almost always used in relation to man, and is more applicable than Logos to some forms of character and attainment; but the latter term is generally preferred, both on account of its philosophical associations, and perhaps owing to Philo's preference for a masculine substantive.

Another word which is sometimes used instead of Logos is πνεῦμα. This occasionally denotes 'air in motion'; but in its higher sense it is identical with Logos. In the latter sense it is used only in connexion with men, and under the suggestion of some passage of Scripture.

The cosmical Thought necessarily contained a multitude of subordinate thoughts or *logoi*. This Stoical doctrine was fully adopted by Philo, who used the word *logoi* as synonymous with the Platonic ideas, the powers which constituted the essence of things. In relation to man they are 'the right words of wisdom,' seen with the eyes of the soul, ethical ideas or laws, the heavenly manna by which the soul is fed.

(*g*) The question of the *personality* of the Logos is one beset with difficulty, and consequently receives conflicting answers. It may be maintained that Philo regarded it as a person, that he did not so regard it, or that he vacillated illogically between the two conceptions. The doctrine hitherto laid down does not involve the attribute of personality. Large allowance must be made for Philo's excessive love of poetical personification. Laughter is the ideal son of God, and the graces are his virgin daughters. Similar figures are abundantly applied to the Logos. It is a 'charioteer and umpire,' a 'physician,' a 'military officer,' a 'spear-bearer,' and a 'champion.' This use of personification is largely suggested by the allegorical interpretation of the persons in Genesis, who represent ideas, including the Logos. Passages where such figures are employed could hardly induce any one to ascribe personality to the Logos; but they may warn us to be very careful in other passages where the figurative meaning is not so obvious. We must briefly survey the arguments which have most weight. The Logos is the image of God and the archetype of man: could this be true of anything but a person? The answer must depend on the writer's style of thought and language; and this is clearly revealed in his treatment of the number seven. This number is the 'image' of God, and is referred to as if it were the very essence of the Logos. It is everywhere impressed upon creation. There are seven stars in the Pleiades and in the Bear. There are seven planets. There are seven zones marking the divisions of the sky. There are seven days in the week, determined by the changes of the moon. The same law extends to man. The head has seven essential parts—two eyes, two ears, two nostrils, and the mouth. We need not give further details. In brief, the number seven is a mirror in which the Maker and Father of the universe is manifested (see especially *de Mundi Op.* 30 ff. [i. 21 ff.]; *Leg. All.* i. 4, 5 [i. 45 f.]; *de Decal.* 21 [ii. 198]). This presents to us in a very striking way the mode in which Philo conceived that the Divine Thought was impressed upon matter, and became there an image of its originator. Regarded as the archetype of human reason, the Logos is simply the rational power of God, by participation in which man becomes rational. 'The suppliant Logos' (ὁ ἱκέτης λόγος) is sometimes the suppliant cry of men; and once, where it is represented as standing between God and creation, the ambassador of the one and the suppliant of the other, it seems clearly to mean, in a figure, the cry 'of the mortal pining always for the incorruptible,' seeking for the complete realization of the Divine idea (*Quis rer. div. her.* 42 [i. 501 f.]). Whether the title παράκλητος is ever applied to the Logos is at least doubtful; if it is so at all, it is only to the Logos as identified with the cosmos. The passages which are most relied on as proving the personality of the Logos are those in which the term 'angel' is applied either to it or to the *logoi*. Of these there are no fewer than seventeen, and it is impossible for us to consider them here one by one. The key to the true interpretation of all of them is to be found in Philo's system of allegorical interpretation. The angels of the Old Testament become in this system Divine thoughts, just as the patriarchs, Moses and Aaron, and other persons, have fixed symbolical meanings attached to them. As we might expect in dealing with such a visionary world, Philo's language is not always quite consistent and clear; but, with a little care, every passage will yield its allegorical sense, and will save us from the necessity of forcing on Philo the absurd supposition that the great cosmic Thought of God was a soul flying in the air, that Jacob literally wrestled with this uncircumscribed and incorporeal power, and that ordinary men eat showers of angels. The Scripture is accustomed to describe heavenly visitations under the name of angels; but these, when applied to the various characters represented by the persons whom they visited, symbolize the Divine thoughts, precepts, or laws which come with their heavenly messages to the soul. We may be permitted to sum up in words which have been used elsewhere: 'The Logos is the Thought of God, dwelling subjectively in the infinite Mind, planted out and made objective in the universe. The cosmos is a tissue of rational forces, which images the beauty, the power, the goodness of its primeval fountain. The reason of man is this same rational force entering into consciousness, and held by each in proportion to the truth and variety of his thoughts; and to follow it is the law of righteous living. Each form which we can differentiate as a distinct species, each rule of conduct which we can treat as an injunction of reason, is itself a Logos, one of those innumerable thoughts or laws into which the universal Thought may, through self-reflexion, be resolved. Thus, wherever we turn, these Words, which are really Works of God, confront us, and lift our minds to that uniting and cosmic Thought which, though comprehending them, is itself dependent, and tells us of that impenetrable BEING from whose inexhaustible fulness it comes, of whose perfections it is the shadow, and whose splendours, too dazzling for all but the purified intuitions of the highest souls, it at once suggests and veils' (Drummond, *Philo Judæus*, ii. p. 273).

8. *The higher relations of man, and the ethical principles which rested upon them.*—(*a*) The Logos was the archetype of human reason; and this reason was the true generic man, made according to the image of God, and not yet divided into species, which arose with the 'moulded' man, who participated in quality, consisted of body and soul, was man or woman, and naturally mortal. We have seen that Philo believed in the pre-existence of the soul; but how he reconciled this doctrine with the biblical account of the creation of man is not apparent. The first man, having proceeded more directly from God, was the most perfect, while his descendants, who sprung from men, underwent continual degeneration. Adam himself made a wrong choice, being led astray by woman, sensation, which acted under the seduction of the serpent, pleasure. But participation in the original type of humanity was never lost. Man was the true temple of God, and none was so base as never to be visited with noble thoughts. The highest form of this visitation was prophecy, which came only to the wise and good, who in moments of ecstasy were possessed by God, and spoke nothing of their own. The knowledge of grand ideals, combined with the power of wrong choice, made man a moral and responsible being; and Philo deals so abundantly with ethical questions that it is possible to gather his unsystematic utterances into some sort of orderly arrangement.

(*b*) The supreme end of human life is εὐδαιμονία, and this consists of 'the practice of perfect virtue in a perfect life' (*Quod det. pot. ins.* 17 [i. 203]). But, while virtue should be followed for its own sake, it is something higher to follow it for the sake of honouring and pleasing God. He is the perfect good; and to follow Him, and find refuge with Him, is eternal life (ζωὴ αἰώνιος), while departure from Him is death (*de Fuga et Invent.* 15 [i. 557]). The supreme evil, then, is φιλαυτία, otherwise described as μεγαλαυχία, ἀσέβεια, or ἀμαθία. This ignorance is a forgetfulness of our indebtedness to God, to whom alone it is congruous to say 'mine'; and 'whoever dares to say that anything is his own shall be written down a slave for all eternity' (*Leg. All.* iii. 70 [i. 126]). The conditions of responsibility are, first, the possession of a twofold nature, inclining respectively to the eternal and the transient; consequently the power of choice between alternatives; and, thirdly, a knowledge of the better and the worse, which is given by the conscience. It is man's bodily constitution that renders him liable to sin; for the body, being phenomenal, is opposed to the eternal, and sin consists of a preference for the transient and partial instead of the eternal and universal. The body, accordingly, is a prison, a tomb, or a foreign land, which impedes the reason in the pursuit of its true end. Pleasure (ἡδονή), one of the irrational passions, is the principle which brings mind and sensation together; and it is the desire for pleasure that leads us into moral evil. Ἐπιθυμία is generally used in a bad sense, as the desire 'for absent things which are looked upon as good, but are not truly so,' such as food and drink, wealth, glory, power. From this source all public and private wrongs have sprung. Nevertheless, Philo distinctly disapproves of asceticism. 'If,' he says, 'you see any one not taking food and drink at the proper time, or declining the use of baths and ointments, or neglecting covering for his body, or sleeping on the ground and keeping an uncomfortable house, and then from these things counterfeiting temperance, take compassion on his error, and show him the true way of temperance' (*Quod det. pot. ins.* 7 [i. 195]). If the perfect man reaches a state of ἀπάθεια, this is only a deliverance from the sway of the irrational passions through the joyous energy of love and trust. As the end of man's probation, Philo expected the triumph of good over evil. The Israelites would be gathered together into their own land; but there is no clear recognition of a Messiah, still less of any identification of him with the Logos. The punishment of sin is a living death, and the final reward of virtue is to have the Divine Spirit of wisdom within, and to hold communion with the Unbegotten and Eternal.

iv. PHILO'S INFLUENCE ON CHRISTIAN WRITERS.—The interest which is felt by Christian theologians in the writings of Philo is due not only to the light which they throw on Hellenistic thought in the time of Christ, but still more to the wide influence which they exerted on the development of Christian theology. The beginning of this influence is sometimes traced in the doctrine and language of the Fourth Gospel. The doctrine of the Logos set forth in the Prologue has several points of contact with Philo's, and through the remainder of the Gospel many other parallels have been pointed out. Nevertheless there is no obvious quotation, and the style of the author is entirely different from that of Philo. His vocabulary too is strikingly different, as any one may see by looking through Siegfried's 'Glossarium Philoneum,' which fills more than 83 pages of his *Philo von Alexandria* (pp. 47-131). A few examples of classes of words, taken at random, may be given. Philo is fond of compounds with δυς-, having 28 words of this kind; the Gospel has none. Philo has 40 compounds with εὐ-; the Gospel has only 2 quite common words. Philo has 73 compounds with ἐκ-, not one of which is in the Gospel, though the latter has 14 such compounds, nearly all very common words. Philo has 67 compounds with ἐπι- which are not in the Gospel, the Gospel having 11 ordinary words. If the writer was versed in the writings of Philo, it is strange that he has not even inadvertently borrowed an appreciable quantity of his characteristic vocabulary. Even in the doctrine of the Logos the characteristic phraseology is wanting in the Gospel: πολυώνυμος, ὁ ἑρμηνεὺς τοῦ θεοῦ λόγος, ὁ τομεύς, πρεσβύτατος υἱός, ὁ ἀγγέλων πρεσβύτατος, ἀρχάγγελος, εἰκών, ὁ κατ' εἰκόνα ἄνθρωπος, ἀπεικόνισμα, παράδειγμα, ἰδέα τῶν ἰδεῶν, ἀρχέτυπος ἰδέα, ὁ νοητὸς κόσμος, τύπος τοῦ ἐκ τῶν ἰδεῶν κόσμου, σφραγίς, χαρακτήρ, σκιὰ θεοῦ, δεύτερος θεός. We may further observe that the multitude of philosophical terms descriptive of God is entirely absent from the Gospel. In reading the valuable collection of parallels made by Professor Julius Grill (*Untersuchungen über die Entstehung des vierten Evangeliums*, Erster Teil, 1902, pp. 106–138), where the Greek text of Philo is fully presented, one cannot fail to be impressed by the marked difference in the style and phraseology of the two writers. Amid many interesting resemblances of thought, which indicate the presence of a similar religious and philosophical atmosphere, there are some striking contrasts; and, in the few cases where the same words are used, the identity may be explained without the hypothesis of direct literary dependence. These facts show that it is not unreasonable to suppose that the resemblances may be due to the common stock of ideas which belonged to thoughtful men at that time. There are two lines of evidence which strengthen the probability that this may be the case. First, Philo himself had an extensive acquaintance with Palestinian interpretation. For particulars see Siegfried, *Philo von Alexandria*, p. 145 ff., and Bernhard Ritter, *Philo und die Halacha: Eine vergleichende Studie unter steter Berücksichtigung des Josephus*, 1879. Secondly, other books of the New Testament also contain a number of parallels to Philo's exposition; and, although we cannot prove that the writers of these books had not read Philo, it seems more probable that the coincidences are due to the general drift of thought. Even the Synoptic Gospels furnish some striking resemblances in phraseology and sentiment. The Epistles of St. Paul approach Philo more nearly, and even contain examples of allegorical interpretation. It is perhaps more surprising to find that the Epistle of James has many words and figures, allusions and precepts, in common with Philo, and that the two writers agree in some of their doctrines, both in substance and in the mode of presenting them. The author of the Epistle to the Hebrews betrays an obvious affinity with the Alexandrian school; and yet, even in his case, we cannot prove a direct dependence upon Philo. See particulars, and other works referred to, in Siegfried, and in Anathon Aall, *Geschichte der Logosidee in der christlichen Litteratur*, 1899, who assumes a more direct dependence upon Philo than seems securely established by the evidence. On the wide prevalence of a Logos-doctrine in the 1st cent., and its connexion, through the mediation of Stoicism, with the old Egyptian theology, see many interesting particulars in R. Reitzenstein's *Zwei religionsgeschichtliche Fragen nach ungedruckten griechischen Texten der Strassburger Bibliothek*, 1901.

When we pass from the New Testament, the connexion with Philo gradually becomes more and more obvious, especially through the predominance of that vicious mode of interpretation of which he made such extensive use. This is seen in the Epistle of Barnabas, which follows some of the principal rules of allegory. It is still further exemplified in the writings of Justin Martyr, where the whole false system is fully established. The Apologist, moreover, in his doctrine of the Logos, has many points of agreement with Philo, which are wholly wanting in St. John; and it is certainly not improbable that a philosopher had studied the works of the Alexandrian sage. Similar appearances are presented by the works of other apologists, Tatian, Athenagoras, Theophilus. When we come to the great Alexandrian writers, Clement and Origen, there is no longer any room for doubt; for they expressly refer to him. They inherit from him the rules of allegorical interpretation, and are dependent on him in some of their important doctrinal statements. Eusebius frequently quotes him, and borrows his doctrines and interpretations; and he was read even in the West, for Ambrose makes ample use of him, and sometimes transfers his very words, in a Latin translation, to his own pages. Jerome, too, is familiar with his writings, and avails himself especially of his interpretations of scriptural names, though sometimes correcting him. It was probably, for the most part, through Jerome that these explanations passed on to other Latin Fathers. See the whole subject treated by Siegfried, p. 303 ff., where other works are referred to. This widely spread knowledge of his writings shows the high estimation in which Philo was held; but, nevertheless, we cannot place him among the world's great original thinkers. To class him, as ancient writers did, with Plato, must seem to us an absurd exaggeration of his powers. His system of interpretation, borrowed indeed but extended and popularized by him, may have helped for a time to save the reverence due to the Scriptures, but was in its ultimate effect purely mischievous, hiding the real beauties of the ancient records, and reducing Revelation to a fantastic puzzle. But he gave eloquent expression to a great movement of thought, and prepared a sort of philosophical mould in which the fluid doctrines of Christianity could acquire consistency and shape; and amid his tedious interpretations there are splendid flashes of spiritual thought, while his ethical teaching reaches an exalted purity, without transgressing the bounds of sober sense, and is always flushed with the hues of religious faith, and reverence for the Will and Spirit of God.

LITERATURE.—In the foregoing article only the most important references have been given; for the opinions of Philo are collected from such a number of passages that the complete references would occupy an undue amount of space. They will be found in the present author's work, *Philo Judæus: or the Jewish-Alexandrian Philosophy in its Development and Completion*, 2 vols., London, 1888, where also there is a much fuller discussion of controverted points. In addition to works already referred to, it may be sufficient to mention the following: August Gfrörer, *Philo und die alexandrinische Theosophie*, 1831; August Ferdinand Dähne, *Geschichtliche Darstellung der jüdisch-alexandrinischen Religions-Philosophie*, 1834; Friedrich Keferstein, *Philo's Lehre von den göttlichen Mittelwesen*, 1846; Zeller, *Die Philosophie der Griechen in ihrer geschichtlichen Entwicklung*, iii. Thl. 2 Abth. 1881; Henry Soulier, *La Doctrine du Logos chez Philon d'Alexandrie*, 1876; Anathon Aall, *Geschichte der Logosidee in der griechischen Philosophie*, 1896. A fuller bibliography may be consulted in Schürer, *GJV*³ iii. 542 ff. An interesting *Florilegium Philonis* has been collected and published by Mr. C. G. Montefiore in the *JQR* [April 1895 vii. pp. 481–545.

JAMES DRUMMOND.

## TEXTUAL CRITICISM (OF NT).—

i. §§ 1, 2. The Object of Textual Criticism.
ii. §§ 3, 4. Materials for Textual Criticism, and Critical Editions.
iii. §§ 5–84. Methods and Principles.

§§
5. Two rival schools, 'Traditional' and 'Critical.'
6–8. The 'Traditional' School as represented by Mr. Miller.
9. Their claim to take account of the whole evidence. [Note on the difference between 'the date of a document' and 'the date of the text contained in it'].
10. Suggested causes for the corruptions of the text. [Note on the attitude of Westcott and Hort to the 'Synoptic Problem'].
11. The rise of the 'Critical' School.
12–15. Mr. Miller's account of the triumph of the 'Traditional' Text tested by reference to the period 381–450 A.D.
16 f. Dr. Hort's challenge with regard to the ante-Nicene evidence for 'distinctively Syrian' readings.
18. *Prima facie* evidence for the existence of the readings in 1 Timothy.
19–22. Examination of these readings in the light of 'Intrinsic' evidence and of the evidence of Versions and ante-Nicene Fathers.
23. The Traditional Text of Mk $1^{1-28}$ printed so as to indicate its relation to other types of text current in early times, with a detailed examina-

tion of all the variants in the light of the 'Internal Evidence of Readings.'

§§
24. The groups of Authorities brought to light by this examination.
25–28. Are the names 'Syrian,' 'Western,' 'Alexandrian,' 'Neutral,' applied by Dr. Hort to these groups, 'question-begging'?
29. The fundamental importance of the 'subjective' element in Textual Criticism illustrated by the examination of Mk $1^{1-28}$, leading to a description of the checks on personal idiosyncrasy provided by 'Intrinsic' and 'Transcriptional' Probability, and by the 'Internal Evidence of Documents.'
30. The principle of Genealogy.
31–34. The consequences of this principle.
35–59. Grounds for the 'Critical' rejection of the Traditional Text illustrated by reference to 'distinctively Syrian' readings in Mk $1^{1-28}$.
36 f. The argument from 'Conflation.'
38–41. Ante-Nicene evidence.
42–48. Detailed examination of the evidence for τοῖς προφήταις in Mk $1^{2}$.
49. And for ἔμπροσθέν σου.
50–51. Conclusion with regard to ante-Nicene evidence.
52. Summary of the evidence against 'Syrian' readings.
53–55. Evidence of editorial activity in the production of the Traditional Text.
56–58. The argument *a priori*.
59. The argument from ecclesiastical use.
60–62. The characteristics of the 'Western' readings in Mk $1^{1-28}$.
63. The acceptance of these readings not precluded by 'Genealogy.'
64–66. 'Alexandrian' readings in Mk $1^{1-28}$.
67 f. 'Neutral' readings in Mk $1^{1-28}$.
69. The value of B as determined by the 'Internal Evidence of Readings.'
70. The relation of B to other primary authorities.
71–76. The relation of ℵ to B.
77–81. ℵ and B in relation to the oldest forms of the Latin and Syriac Versions, especially k and Syr-*sin*.
82. The value of ℵB in opposition to Syriac and Latin evidence combined.
83 f. Conclusion.

i. OBJECT.—1. The object of Textual Criticism is to recover the *ipsissima verba* of the documents of which the NT is composed, and to present them to modern readers as nearly as possible in the form in which they left their authors' hands. This definition is based on the assumption that all the copies of the different books we possess, whether in Greek or in a translation, are capable of being traced back in the last resort to one and the same original. The assumption is a natural one, and not to be surrendered without very cogent reason. Still we cannot exclude the possibility that any particular book may have been current from Apostolic times in two closely related but distinct forms. St. Paul may, as Lightfoot suggested,* have issued a second edition of his Epistle to the Romans. St. Luke may, as Blass maintains, have issued two editions, both of his Gospel and of the Acts. The phenomena presented by the text of St. Mark, not only in regard to the last twelve verses but throughout the Gospel, may need the same hypothesis for their adequate solution.† In such cases the task of the critic becomes still more delicate. He has to disentangle and present distinctly not one original but two, which were once current side by side, but which have in the course of time been blended together, in almost inextricable confusion, in all our extant authorities.

2. From this definition of the object which all textual critics alike have before them two consequences follow, to which it will not be superfluous, judging from the past history of the science, to call attention before we pass on.

The first is this. There is at present, and there must remain, room for legitimate difference of opinion. We must be careful not to arrogate to the form of text which we ourselves prefer an exclusive right to represent the true 'word of God.'

* See the papers by him and by Hort, reprinted from the *Journal of Philology* in *Biblical Essays*, pp. 287–374.

† See Blass, *Textkritische Bemerkungen zu Markus.*



The necessity for this caution is perhaps not so great as it was in the days of Griesbach.* The appeal made in a recent pamphlet by the leading supporter of one of the two rival schools of Textual Criticism to a standard which has yet to be fixed is a most hopeful sign.†

The second consequence which follows from our definition of the object of Textual Criticism is this. As all textual critics are engaged on one and the same sacred study, and are fellow-workers to a common end, they will do well to take special pains to cultivate mutual respect. It is strange, but it is none the less true, that the study of Textual Criticism seems to have a peculiarly disastrous effect upon the temper. The virulence with which Walton, Mill, Griesbach, and Lachmann were assailed, not to speak of more recent examples, is a deep stain on the annals of the study.‡

ii. MATERIALS.—3. It does not fall within the scope of this article to describe at length the materials available for the Textual Criticism of NT. In part they are dealt with under separate heads (see A, ℵ, B, C, D, Arabic Version, etc.). For a complete list (and for purposes of reference anything short of a complete list is unsatisfactory) the student must be referred to the recognized storehouses of information, *e.g.* Tregelles, vol. i. of Horne's *Introduction to the New Testament*, revised 1856, by no means to be neglected; *Prolegomena to Tischendorf*, ed. C. R. Gregory, 1884–94; Scrivener's *Introduction to the Criticism of the New Testament*[4], 1894, revised by E. Miller and others; Gregory, *Textkritik des Neuen Testamentes*, Leipzig, 1900. The evidence, so far as it had been ascertained at the time of publication, was collected in two great critical editions.

4. The edition by Tischendorf, ed. viii. 1869–72, is at present indispensable for students, but it needs throughout to be carefully checked and supplemented. The edition of Tregelles (1857–79) is no less a marvel of patient accuracy. Unfortunately, the first two Gospels were issued before the discovery of ℵ, and, though the evidence is supplied in an Appendix issued by Hort and Streane after the author's death, it is awkward to use. The statement of the evidence is, however, given with great clearness. And the method adopted—a deliberate limitation of the authorities, whose evidence was to be represented, to the uncial

* See the Prolegomena to his second edition, Sect. I. § 3, p. xlv f. [ed. London, 1809], esp. 'Deinde non ideo *verbum Dei* mutatur, quia in textu vulgari unum alterumve vocabulum deletur aut additur aut cum alio permutatur. Quod hebraico magis quam latino nomine verbum Dei appellare solent, continetur *sensu* Scripturæ sacræ; non autem ita in ipsis syllabis atque literis consistit, ut mutato (ob gravissimas rationes et auctoritates, ac salvo sensu) vocabulo quodam, ipsum Dei verbum, hoc est doctrina Christi ac Apostolorum, pereat. Nulla emendatio a recentioribus editoribus tentata ullam Scripturæ sacræ doctrinam immutat aut evertit; paucæ sensum sententiarum afficiunt. Ad has posteriores quod attinet, tenendum porro est, principium, ut aiunt, peti ab iis, qui verbum Dei ab editore mutari existiment. Nempe hoc est id ipsum, de quo disputatur, utrum scilicet lectio vulgarium editionum, an vero lectio aliorum ac meliorum codicum, genuina sit verbi divini pars. Nemo itaque *verbum Dei* se defendere ideo jactet, quia textum Elsevirianum tuetur. Nam *æquo* jure ii, qui manuscriptorum codicum textum defendunt, dicere possent, verbi divini integritatem a se propugnari contra corruptorum interpolationes.'

† See *The Textual Controversy and the Twentieth Century*, by Edward Miller, M.A., p. 24: 'Thus I submit my case to all the learned in Christendom. When I speak of the Traditional Text, I mean that recension of the Received Text which shall ultimately be settled by the voice of Christendom upon an exhaustive examination of all the evidence in existence. My own Commentary, so far as it goes, is meant to be a contribution towards such a settlement.

'Accordingly, neither does my theory consciously override facts, nor must my expressions be taken to be dogmatic, when convenience in writing leads me to drop hypothetical language.'

‡ See Tregelles, *Account of the Printed Text*, pp. 115–117, 254–256.

MSS, a few select cursives, all the Versions, and the Fathers up to Eusebius—has a real advantage, as it concentrates attention on that period in the history of the text about which there is room for serious difference of opinion.*

Editions which aim at giving only a selection of readings such as Baljon's (1898) are radically unsatisfactory. It is impossible to estimate the value of any authority in any single book without studying the whole of its readings through that book.

Editions such as that published by E. Nestle at Stuttgart in 1899 are convenient as indicating concisely the differences between the most important among recent critical editors, but do not profess to give the grounds on which their judgments are based. *A Textual Commentary upon the Holy Gospels*, edited by E. Miller largely from materials collected by the late Dean Burgon, of which part i. (Mt 1-14) appeared in 1899, will afford a useful index to the Gospel references to be found in the Fathers down to the latest period. This list is based directly on the indexes compiled with enormous labour by Dean Burgon, now in the British Museum. It has not apparently been supplemented by reference to other sources, *e.g.* Tregelles, or Hort in the Notes on Select Readings in his Appendix. It needs, besides, and will no doubt in due course receive, careful sifting. Scholars, however, cannot but be grateful for the labour that has been bestowed on its preparation.

It is only right to add that Mr. Miller's judgment on the drawback to the use of Patristic evidence from the uncritical character of the current editions of their works † must be checked in the light of Barnard's edition of the *Quis dives salvetur*, and his account of 'The Biblical Text of Clement of Alexandria' in *Cambridge Texts and Studies*, v. 2 and 5. Nestle also has some pertinent remarks, with illustrations, in his *Textual Criticism of NT*, p. 144 ff., Eng. tr.

Mr. Miller's edition embodies, besides, the results of recent collations, chiefly of cursives. A certain number of misprints are inevitable in a work of this scope. Students, however, should be warned that Mr. Miller has not incorporated all the various readings for which there is MS evidence. Nor does he always quote completely the subsidiary authorities, *e.g.* the MSS of the Latin Versions, in the passages which he selects for comment. Again, the authority of the Revisers is quoted constantly for readings on which it is clear that they were never called upon to pronounce an opinion.

iii. METHODS AND PRINCIPLES.—5. The main purpose of this article is to discuss the methods and principles by the help of which we may hope to secure the best result from our use of the materials available for Textual Criticism. This, it is well to remember, is the true province of the textual critic. It is, no doubt, of first-rate importance for any one who wishes to bring out a critical edition, that he should have a certain amount of experience in the direct handling of MSS. But to imagine, as Dean Burgon seems to do, that the value of a man's opinion on a matter of Textual Criticism depends directly on the extent of his first-hand acquaintance with original documents, is very like measuring the skill of a jeweller by the amount of his experience in the work of a diamond field or of a gold mine, or refusing to accept a historian's estimate of a document unless he has himself inspected the MS from which it was printed. In fact, the qualities that go to make an ideal collator, such as Scrivener for instance, are very rarely combined with the capacity and the opportunity for taking such a comprehensive and intelligent survey of the whole evidence as can qualify a man to pronounce a sound judgment on the relative importance of any particular element in it. The constant growth of available material makes it increasingly important to lay stress on the radical distinction between the two functions—the function of collecting and the function of interpreting the materials of criticism.

It is strange, and not a little sad, that after nearly two centuries of discussion there should as yet be no general agreement among textual critics on the fundamental principles or even the methods of their science. Yet so it is. Critics have from the first been divided into two main schools—the 'Traditional' and the 'Critical.' They approach the problem from diametrically opposite points of view, and are at present almost as far from coming to an agreement as they have ever been. The 'Oxford Debate,' however, at least indicates a desire for mutual understanding, and is so far a sign of better days in store.

6. The Traditional School is represented by a small but vigorous band of English scholars, at the head of whom stands Mr. Miller,* to whom reference has already been made more than once.† This school has, so far as known to the present writer, no support on the Continent, though readings of the Traditional Text constantly commended themselves to the veteran French commentator, Godet.

7. Traditionalists are strong in the prescriptive right due to fifteen centuries of almost unchallenged supremacy. They have, or had,—for the 19th cent. has not left matters as they were in this respect,—what Mr. Gwilliam in writing of the Peshitta (Scrivener[4], vol. ii. p. 17) fairly calls 'the advantage of *possession*.' They are, however, fully alive to the necessity of establishing their position on the ground of a reasoned and not an unreasoning faith. They are busy, therefore, in justifying their position by argument in the court of truth and fact, which, as they cannot but feel, must cast prescription to the winds if there is a flaw in their title. Their fundamental canon, as formulated by Mr. Miller (*Oxford Debate*, p. xii), runs as follows:—

'It (the true text) must be grounded upon an exhaustive view of the evidence of Greek copies in manuscript in the first place, and, in all cases where they differ so as to afford doubt, of Versions or Translations into other languages, and of Quotations from the NT made by Fathers and other early writers.'

On p. xiv we read further: 'In the ascertainment of this text, or these readings, guidance is to be sought under Seven Notes of Truth, viz.—(1) Antiquity, (2) Number, (3) Variety, (4) Weight, (5) Continuity of Witnesses, (6) The Context of Passages, (7) Internal Evidence. These Seven Notes of Truth, which are essential to the Traditional Text, sufficiently exhibit the agreement of it with the Canons laid down. In fact, coincidence with the first Canon implies coincidence with all the rest.'

* Von Soden's *Die Schriften des NT*, etc. (Bd. i. Abt. 1, 1902) is a worthy fruit of the recent revival of German interest in NT Textual Criticism. He has already revolutionized the catalogue of NT Greek MSS. When completed, the work cannot fail to mark an immense advance in the scientific presentment of the materials for Criticism.

† *l.c.* p. xiii: 'I am persuaded that more is made of this drawback than would be if it were generally known how little modern editing of the best kind, perhaps not in Eusebius, but in most authors, alters the quotations.'

A somewhat lurid light is thrown on this remark by a sentence in Nestle, *l.c.* p. 145, Eng. tr. 'As late as 1872 an Oxford editor, in bringing out Cyril of Alexandria's Commentary on the Gospel according to St. John, wrote down only the initial and final words of the quotations in his manuscript, and allowed the compositor to set up the rest from a printed edition of the Textus Receptus.'

* Mr. Miller died while the present art. was passing through the press.

† Mr. Miller is the author of—(1) *A Guide to the Textual Criticism of the NT*, 1886; (2) *The Oxford Debate*, 1897; (3) *The Present State of the Textual Controversy*, 1899; (4) *The Textual Controversy and the Twentieth Century*, 1901. He is joint author with Dean Burgon of *The Traditional Text of the Holy Gospels*, 1896; and *The Causes of the Corruption of the Traditional Text*, 1896. He also edited the 4th ed. of Scrivener's *Introduction*.

8. There is no indication of the kind of differences between MSS which 'afford doubt,' and render it necessary to call in the evidence of Versions or Quotations; nor is there any hint of the method of determining the 'weight' of a witness. Judging from his *Textual Commentary*, Mr. Miller's own habit is to weigh uncials against uncials and cursives against cursives, and he feels no doubt so long as there is a clear numerical preponderance in each class in favour of the same reading. In 7 cases an adverse group is characterized as 'Western.' In 5 of these it includes ℵ and B. In one case (Mt $9^{13}$) a reading attested by ℵBD + $6^{unc}$ $30^{cu}$ all latt. exc. c $g^{1.2}$ Syr-*vg* (against *cur* and *sin*) and Clem. Rom. (ii. 2), is described as 'Syrio-Low-Latin with Alexandrian support.' These are the only cases in which he gives any guidance in the classification of MSS.

In 4 cases, viz. Mt $6^{28}$ (pl. verb after τὰ κρίνα), $13^{25}$ (ἐπέσπειρεν for ἔσπειρεν), $13^{36}$ (διασάφησον for φράσον, 'prob. a Latin gloss adopted by Origen'), $13^{57}$ (ἰδίᾳ for αὐτοῦ, disregarding Jn $4^{44}$), he suspects 'Latinization.' In $14^{24}$ (σταδίους πολλοὺς ἀπὸ τῆς γῆς ἀπεῖχεν for μέσον τῆς θαλάσσης ἦν) he hints at retranslation from Syriac. Here, again, we might wish that the suggestions were more illuminating. In 5 cases he discusses the possibility of the influence of Lection systems; in 2 of assimilation to St. Mark; in one case ($14^{30}$) he appeals to 'internal testimony' (construction of βλέπω). For the rest, he is content to let his lists speak for themselves. The mere recital of a long list of authorities ought, he has no doubt, to bear down opposition by sheer weight of numbers. It is true that in the 'Seven Notes of Truth' antiquity stands before number. But his power to estimate the antiquity of witnesses is limited by his failure to grasp clearly the distinction between *the date of a document* and *the date of the text contained in it*, or at least by his failure to apply this distinction consistently.* In practice, his convenient assumption, that the almost universal prevalence of the Traditional Text in the Greek Church after the end of cent. iv proves that text to be Apostolic, frees him from any qualms arising from the demonstrable antiquity of those witnesses which he is content to disregard.

9. At this point it will be well to examine a little more minutely the claim of the Traditionalists to be the only school that takes account of the whole available evidence. It would, no doubt, be a strong point in their favour if they could substantiate it. Unfortunately for them, the assertion is utterly baseless. Their most formidable antagonist, Dr. Hort, framed his text, as any one who has read his *Introduction* must know, at least as directly as any Traditionalist, on a patient examination of all the evidence. And he lays at least as much stress on the importance of bringing the knowledge gained by the examination of all the facts to bear on the interpretation of the evidence in each case that comes up for decision. When at last a choice has to be made between two rival groups of authorities, the one or the other must be rejected. But it does not follow that its claims have not been fully considered. Otherwise, the Traditionalists themselves would be open to the charge of 'taking no account' of what seems to others the most significant part of the evidence. This charge would, of course, be untrue. And it is an encouraging sign of a *rapprochement* between the two schools, that the Traditionalists are beginning to admit the necessity for accounting for the existence of the various readings which they reject, on some more satisfactory theory than that of the blind or malignant perversity of the individual scribe of ℵ, B, or D. A great step towards ultimate agreement will have been made when it is admitted on both sides that no solution of a textual problem can be final which does not leave room for a rational account of the origin of all the extant variants.

10. The cause of corruption on which Mr. Miller is at present inclined (*Oxford Debate*, p. xv) to lay most stress, is a striking admission of the antiquity of the texts affected by it. He traces it back to forms of the oral Gospel which may have been in existence 'even before the Gospels were written.' A similar source was suggested long ago by Dr. Hort as a possible explanation of certain remarkable insertions in the text of D and its allies. It remains to be seen whether the characteristic differences between the text of ℵB and the text of the later Gospel MSS are best explained on the same hypothesis. The suggestion does not at first sight commend itself. In the text of ℵB the separate Gospels stand before us, each with a marked individuality of its own. In the Traditional Text the specific differences in the several reports of the same utterance or the same incident which help to define this individuality, are constantly obliterated. Now, of course, it is *a priori* possible that this uniformity was original, and that the variations came from a corrupting force, which may well have been very potent while it lasted, but which can, *ex hypothesi*, only have been in operation during a very limited period. Only in that case it is difficult to see why it should not have affected all the Gospels equally.

On the other hand, we are bound to make allowance for an undeniable tendency towards the assimilation of parallel passages—a tendency which must have acted with growing intensity as the comparative study of the Gospels developed (as it did very early), and especially in a country which possessed a popular 'Harmony' (cf. Chase, *Syro-Latin Text of the Gospels*, p. 76 ff.). It is unlikely, therefore, that Mr. Miller's suggestion will

* As this distinction is of primary importance in estimating the weight to be attached to a document, and as beginners in Textual Criticism sometimes find a difficulty in understanding it, it may be worth while to explain that the 'date of a document' is, strictly speaking, the date at which it was written, and, when the MS is not expressly dated by the scribe, is settled by palæographical considerations. 'The date of the text contained in the document' is, of course, primarily the date of the autograph. But in the case of a text like that of NT, which has a continuous history, the 'date of the text' refers naturally to the time when the particular form of text contained in the document was current, either generally or in some particular district. *E.g.* D (Codex Bezæ) is a document of cent. vi, but its text represents a type which was widely prevalent in cent. ii. 'k' (Bobiensis) is usually assigned to cent. v. Mr. Burkitt has recently given strong grounds for dating it early in cent. iv, but the text of 'k' is the text current in Africa in the days of Cyprian, A.D. 250 (see *Old-Latin Biblical Texts*, ii.).

It is interesting to notice that Mr. Miller is alive to this distinction in regard to Syr-cur and Syr-sin (p. xviii of *Text. Com.*). But he habitually ignores it in the case of ℵ and B. The confusion in this case goes back to Scrivener, who writes in a note (p. vi, *Advers. Crit. Sacr.*), describing the work of Dean Burgon, which underlies Miller's *Text. Com.*: 'He had been engaged day and night for years in making a complete index or view of the MSS used by the Nicene (and ante-Nicene) Fathers, by way of showing that they were not identical with those copied in Codd. ℵ and B, and, *inasmuch as they were older, they must needs be purer and more authentic* than those overvalued uncials' [italics are the present writer's]. He also quotes, 'as helping to annul much of Dr. Hort's erroneous theories' (p. xxviii), an extract from Mr. Rendel Harris, which exactly expresses Dr. Hort's fundamental contention on the matter. 'It is not a little curious to the person who commences the critical study of the documents of the NT to find that he can discover no settled proportion between the age of a MS and the critical weight attached to it. . . . A little study soon convinces the tyro of the impossibility of determining any law by which the value of a codex can be determined in terms of its age only without reference to its history.'

This quotation can have no point in Scrivener's note, except on the assumption, which Mr. Miller adopts without hesitation, that Westcott and Hort attached fundamental importance to the dates at which ℵ and B were written in arriving at their estimate of the weight to be ascribed to them.

obtain any wide acceptance as an explanation of the characteristic readings of ℵB.*

11. In treating of the problems raised by the felt necessity of offering an explanation of the origin of variant readings, we have reached what is really the starting-point of the labours of the 'Critical' school. Ever since the collection of the evidence for the text of NT began in earnest, in the great edition published by Mill in 1707, the attention of critics was attracted by the nature of the variants from the 'Traditional' text contained in the writings of the earliest Fathers, in the Versions, and in a few of the oldest MSS.†

* This seems the most convenient place to notice Dr. Salmon's criticism of Westcott and Hort for their lack of interest 'in the question of the origin of the Synoptic Gospels; that is to say, in inquiries whether the narratives of the three have any common basis, oral or written' (*Some Criticism of the Text of NT*, ch. v.). It is strange that in making this criticism Dr. Salmon should have forgotten Dr. Westcott's *Introduction to the Study of the Gospels*, the most powerful statement in any language of the case on behalf of the old 'oral' hypothesis, and the share Dr. Hort took in the formation of the plan of (Abbott and) Rushbrooke's *Synopticon*, which was designed as an instrument for testing any 'Documentary Theory' that might be started. Otherwise, he might have looked for some other reason than 'lack of interest' to account for the silence of their *Introduction to the NT* in regard to the Synoptic Problem. The fact is, that to have called in one out of many possible solutions of the Synoptic Problem to fix the weight to be attached to MSS of the Gospels, would have been to explain *obscurum per obscurius*.

It is strange also that so close a reasoner should have failed to notice that his application to the Synoptic Problem of Dr. Hort's method for 'the recovery of the text of a single lost original, assuming the fact of exclusive descent from it to have been sufficiently established,' must fail from the neglect of two vital considerations. He has failed to allow (see Hort, p. 55, l. 6) for the possibility of 'mixture' between the representatives of his different groups. But, what is even more serious, he has overlooked the primary condition of 'exclusive descent.' For, while we may well believe that the three Synoptics take us back to a common original, whether that original be our St. Mark or an Ur-Marcus, no one, least of all Dr. Salmon, has ventured to suggest that St. Matthew and St. Luke had no independent information. In fact, if St. Matthew had anything to do with the Gospel that bears his name, it may well preserve genuine elements in certain incidents that had failed to attract St. Peter's attention. From this point of view, the story of the 'Canaanitish woman' (Mt $15^{21f.}$, Mk $7^{24f.}$), where there is no serious question of reading, affords an instructive parallel to 'the rich young man' (Mt $19^{16}$, Mk $10^{17}$, Lk $18^{18}$). In each case Matthew follows a distinct but by no means necessarily inconsistent tradition. (On 'the rich young man' see G. Macdonald, *Unspoken Sermons*, 2nd series).

It is clear that in settling the text of the Gospels we have to allow for the operation of forces acting in opposite directions: (1) a constant tendency to assimilation, affecting all the Gospels alike, complicated by (2) a tendency to dissimilation, produced by various accidents in the special history of the transmission of each Gospel.

No mechanical rule can therefore be laid down, and we may be thankful that in this, as in other cases, the editors were content to follow consistently the evidence of the MSS which, taking everything into account, they found most reason to trust, whether it made for likeness (*e.g.* Mt $8^{9}$ $15^{26}$) or for difference (as in Mt $19^{16}$) between the Evangelists, instead of revising their decision in each case with an eye to the Synoptic Problem. No doubt, the questions cannot be ultimately dissociated. But, after all, we must provisionally settle our text of the Gospels before we can solve the problem of their inter-relation.

† A few dates may with advantage be noted here. In the time of Mill (1707) the only 'primary uncials' of the Gospels of which full collations were available were A and D. Bengel (1734) had access as well to 'select readings' of C. Griesbach, in his first edition, used full collations of ACDL. No collation of B was published till 1788. ℵ was discovered in 1859.

In the light of these facts, Mr. Miller's method of accounting for the preference shown by the 'Critical' school for the small over the large group of authorities needs correction. 'The explanation,' he says (*Oxford Debate*, p. 6), 'is what has frequently been called by other men the extreme adulation paid to B, especially by Dr. Hort and men of that side. I think some of it is very natural, and that history quite accounts for it. They [ℵ and B] are the two oldest MSS; and in early times, when people had in their view only a small amount of evidence, it was very natural that they should say that these two MSS, which come to us as the earliest, and were therefore nearest to the original autographs, should be right.'

In the interests of 'true history' and 'sound logic' we must remember that the foundations of the Critical position were laid, not only long before ℵ was discovered, but even while the readings of B were almost entirely unknown.

It must, no doubt, have given B a peculiar interest in the eyes of Griesbach when he found how exactly it verified results which he had arrived at independently (see Tregelles, *Intr.* p.

Not only was the authority for these variants demonstrably early, but it was again and again so much easier to account for the origin of the variants on the supposition that the Traditional Text was wrong. In fact it soon became clear that the substantial uniformity of the bulk of the later copies of the Greek Text was due to a gradual process, by which the variety of texts current in cent. iv were in the course of three or four centuries transformed after a common type. This common 'Traditional' type Bengel called 'Byzantine.' It is the same as that which Dr. Hort calls 'Syrian' and some modern scholars 'Antiochian.'

It is interesting to notice that there is now no controversy as to the fact of this transformation.* The only question at issue is the significance to be attached to it. Mr. Miller contends that the triumph of the Traditional Text was due to the fact that it was already widely diffused at the beginning of the period in documents of such excellence, and so highly accredited, that it simply crushed all rivals out of existence.

12. This contention clearly demands careful examination. In order that the investigation may be as precise as possible, it will be well to define the field which it is proposed to explore. As Mr. Miller's language (*e.g.* Preface to *Oxford Debate*, p. xiv) is quite general, all periods may be assumed to come alike to him. Let us take, then, the period between the Council of Constantinople in 381 and the Council of Chalcedon in 450. It is the latest that we can choose that will give us evidence which can in any real sense be said to speak with the voice of the whole Eastern Church. During this period the development of Christian thought was determined by influences emanating from three main centres: from Alexandria, fresh from the triumph over Arianism, which Athanasius had done so much single-handed to secure; from Antioch; and from the Church which ecclesiastically was the daughter of Antioch, from Constantinople. Of these three centres it is not, the present writer thinks, too much to say that Alexandria never accepted the Traditional Text. The date of the Bohairic Version must, we suppose, still be regarded as uncertain. If, as seems to be at present the verdict of the most competent Coptic scholars, it is to be assigned to cent. iv or v, it would give us exactly the evidence that we need as to the state of the text officially recognized in Egypt either at the beginning or at some point in the course of our period. The Bohairic constantly sides with ℵ and B against the Traditional Text.

Nor does this evidence stand alone. The same type of text † is found in the two great Alexandrian writers of this period, Didymus (†394) and Cyril (†444). Further evidence on this point will, no doubt, come to light with the progress of Egyptian exploration. It is too soon as yet to summarize the evidence of the papyri.‡ Here, then, at the outset, the boasted 'universality' breaks down. On textual matters, as the earliest nomenclature for describing the 'families' of readings might have warned us to expect, there was a permanent distinction between Constantinople and Alexandria.

13. Nor is this all. Jerome's revision of the Old Latin Versions was made at Rome *c.* 382 by the aid of the Greek MSS which he judged most trustworthy. It is true, as Nestle says (*Textual Criticism*, p. 124), that it is not yet clearly made out

131), a forecast only less brilliant than that which was verified by the discovery of the Curetonian and Sinaitic Syriac.

* See Miller's *Text. Cont.* p. 29: 'Thenceforward [from the end of the 4th cent.] till the 19th [? 18th] cent. was far advanced it [the Traditional Text] reigned without a rival, though perhaps the thorough establishment of it did not take effect till the beginning of the 8th century.'

† See Hort, p. 550 of WH Text, smaller ed.

‡ Yet see Burkitt's Introduction to Barnard's *Biblical Text of Clement*, p. viii ff.

what these MSS were. But it is remarkable that the latest editors of the Vulgate have seen reasons to infer for them a close kinship with ℵ and B.* At any rate, Jerome had not been taught by his stay in the East to believe in the exclusive validity of the Traditional Text.

14. The other two centres, Antioch and Constantinople, resolve themselves into one, at least in the person of Chrysostom, the most prominent representative of the Imperial city. Here, no doubt, we do find clear evidence of the coming supremacy of the Traditional Text. But even here the agreement is by no means as complete as it might appear to a casual observer. Each writer, even of those connected with these centres, has his own degree of approximation to the Traditional Text, and can be identified by his readings.

The fact to which we allude is in itself so striking an evidence both of the phenomenon to which we wish to call attention, and of the insight of the scholar who alone in our generation seems to have mastered the textual problems presented by Patristic citations, that we venture to transcribe in full the account which Dr. Hort gave of the steps by which he was led to the discovery of the lost commentaries of Theodore of Mopsuestia. He is referring to commentaries in Latin on ten of St. Paul's Epistles contained in a Corbey MS to which Pitra had recently called attention, claiming their authorship for Hilary of Poitiers. He writes (*Journal of Classical and Sacred Philology*, No. xii., Feb. 1860, p. 303 f.) as follows:—

'What led me to the true authorship was, first, the character of the text used in the quotations; and, secondly, two passages on Gal 4[24. 29], referred to by Pitra among the "splendidiora, quibus sibi haud impar identidem Hilarius emicat." St. Hilary employs, as is well known, a tolerably pure form of the Old Latin version of the NT: the text of the commentary is distinctively Greek of a late and bad type. No Father using any known Latin text could have so written; it contains many corruptions not found in the very worst copies of the Vulgate, much less in earlier versions. It is too corrupt in its character for any considerable Greek Father even of cent. iv, except those connected with the Syrian school, and, among them, a shade too bad for St. Chrysostom or Theodoret. These facts considerably narrowed the question of authorship. And when, in commenting on the passages of Galatians, the author showed himself a vehement opponent of allegorical interpretation, it was easy to see that he must have been a literalist of too decided a character to be unknown,—in fact could not well be any other than Theodore himself, the chief of the literalists, or his brother Polychronius. Reference to a catena at once put an end to all speculation; the Greek fragments of Theodore appeared in the Latin along with their lost context.'

15. Now, if Alexandria persistently rejected the Traditional Text, if Jerome came back from the East convinced of the excellence of the MSS that least resembled it, if there are marked differences during this period even between individual members of the Antiochene-Constantinopolitan school, it is difficult to know where to look for evidence of the universal, not to say exclusive, predominance of the Traditional Text in cent. v. Even the Peshiṭta, which Mr. Gwilliam† believes, and no doubt rightly (*Oxford Debate*, p. 32), that he can trace back with minute accuracy to the shape which it possessed in this same cent. v, is very far from affording that undivided support which Mr. Miller desiderates; a fact which perhaps accounts for the coldness with which he receives a statement that used to be regarded almost as a commonplace—to wit, that 'the Syriac Version is the sheet-anchor of the Traditionalist position.' We are not sure that he would have been pleased with the suggestion, for which nevertheless there is something to be said, that Theodore of Mopsuestia should be promoted to the place left vacant by the Peshiṭta.

16. These, however, are matters of minor importance. It has all along been admitted that the Traditional Text was in existence in substantially its present form by the middle of the fourth century. The really vital point is to determine whether there is any evidence of its existence in the preceding period. On this point Dr. Hort 20 years ago made a statement, which was precise and definite enough, one might have thought, to ensure patient and attentive consideration on the part of those whose whole system must fall to the ground if the position laid down in it should prove to be well founded. His words are these (*Introduction*, p. 114, § 162): 'Before the middle of the third century, at the very earliest, we have no historical signs of the existence of readings, conflate or other, that are marked as distinctively Syrian by the want of attestation from groups of documents which have preserved the other ancient forms of text.' For the identification of the readings referred to, full directions are given in §§ 225 f., 343. And any one who chose to take the trouble could make out lists of them for himself and test the accuracy of the contention. Mr. Miller refuses to take this method of attempting to understand the position of his opponent. He prefers a method which is not a little surprising in a writer who lays such stress on the importance of sound logic. His words (p. xv, Preface to *Oxford Debate*) are as follows:—

'We entirely traverse the assertion, that "no distinctly (*sic*) Syrian (*i.e.* Traditional) readings" are found amongst the earliest Fathers. Very many of the readings in the Traditional Text which are rejected by the other school are supported by those Fathers: and there is no evidence, as we maintain, to show that they pertain to the other side or to any other Text rather than to us, or that readings confessedly old and found in the Traditional Text did not belong to that Text.'

In other words, 'we entirely traverse' a statement, which has express reference to one element in the Traditional Text, by asserting propositions which have never been denied with regard to the other elements which on any hypothesis are recognizable in its composition. It would have been simpler to deny altogether the existence of 'distinctively Syrian readings' as defined by Dr. Hort. That at least is a question which can be brought to a definite issue. On that point the *Apparatus Criticus* will be recognized as an impartial arbiter.

17. Let us, then, examine the facts for ourselves. It is clear that in this article we shall have to limit ourselves to illustrative specimens, as an example of a method which any one can learn to apply for himself to any part of the NT that he chooses. At the same time it is important for the right understanding of the method, that it should be seen in application to continuous portions of the text—and not in isolated examples chosen because they possess special features of interest or importance. The weight of authorities in cases of primary importance can be learnt only by patient attention to details which in themselves may seem absurdly trivial and insignificant.

We propose therefore to set forth and to examine first a list of all the readings which have a claim to be regarded as distinctively Syrian in 1 Timothy, and then to attempt a more comprehensive analysis of all the variants in Mk 1[1-28]. It is true that the ultimate decision of the true text in the Pastoral Epistles is less secure than it is in the case of most of the books of the NT, owing to the absence not only of B, but also of any demonstrably early Latin or Syriac evidence—apart from the isolated quotations in Cyprian; but these considerations will not seriously affect the identification of 'distinctively Syrian readings,' and the specimen chosen has the advantage of enabling us to study the influence of similar but not identical contexts on one another in a way that may throw light on a class of readings that meet us constantly in the Synoptic Gospels.

* Wordsworth and White, *N.T. Latine Epilogus*, cap. vi. 'De regulis a nobis in Textu constituendo adhibitis.'

† Mr. Burkitt's essay (*Texts and Studies*, vii. 2) goes far to prove that the Peshiṭta is in fact a revision made in this century.

18. The first step is to collect all the readings supported by the mass of later documents without the support of any of the five leading uncials ℵACD$_2$G$_3$.

(1) 1 Ti 1$^2$—ἡμῶν (after πατρός) ℵ*AD$_2$*G$_3$ cu$^6$ Lat-vg Boh Go Arm : Orig$^{int}$.
+ ϛ c. rell. Syrr Sah Æth : Chr, etc.
See v.$^1$, and note similar addition in 2 Ti 1$^2$, Tit 1$^4$, 1 Th 1$^1$.
It forms part of the true text in all the other Pauline salutations except Galatians.

(2) 1 Ti 1$^4$ (*a*) οἰκονομίαν, ℵAG$_3$K$_2$L$_2$P$_2$ most cursives Arm Boh : Chr, etc.
(*b*) οἰκοδομήν, D$_2$* Iren Lat-vg Go Syr.
(*c*) οἰκοδομίαν, ϛ$^e$ D$_2^c$ and a few cursives.
Note characteristic Pauline use of οἰκονομίαν ; cf. Eph 3$^2$.
οἰκοδομίαν (not found elsewhere in Gr. Bible) combines the sound of (*a*) with the sense of (*b*).

(3) 1 Ti 1$^9$ πατρο- μητρολῴαις, ℵAD$_2$G$_3$ (P$_2$) (K$_2$) 17 37 137.
πατρα- μητραλῴαις, ϛ c. rell.
The spelling πατρο- is due to a false analogy ; but the question we have to settle is not which spelling is right in itself, but which St. Paul is most likely to have used.

(4) 1 Ti 1$^{13}$ τὸ πρότερον ὄντα, ℵAD$_2$*G$_3$P$_2$ cu$^7$ : Chr $^{mosc\ 1}$ Cyr.
τὸν πρότερον ὄντα, ϛ c. rell. Lat-vg : Chr, etc.
Here the neuter is clearly the more idiomatic.

(5) 1 Ti 1$^{17}$ μόνῳ θεῷ, ℵ*AD$_2$*G$_3$ cu$^3$ Lat-vg Syr-hr Boh Sah Arm Æth : Eus Cyr Chr $^{com}$ Tert.
μόνῳ σοφῷ θεῷ, ϛ c. rell. Go Syr-hcl : Chr $^{txt\ not\ com}$, etc.
Cf. Ro 16$^{27}$ where σοφῷ has point, cf. 11$^{33}$ ; and note similar insertion in Jude $^{25}$.

(6) 1 Ti 2$^9$ ὡσαύτως γυναῖκας, ℵ*AP$_2$(D$_2$*G$_3$ add καί) : (Clem) (Orig).
ὡσαύτως καὶ τὰς γυν., ϛ c. D$_2^{b.c}$ rel : Chr.
Cf. *v.l.* in 1 P 3$^1$, and note neighbourhood of τοὺς ἄνδρας.

(7) 1 Ti 2$^9$ ἐν πλέγμασιν καὶ χρυσῷ ἢ μαρ., ℵAD$_2$*G$_3$ Syr-vg Boh : Orig ½.
ἐν πλέγμασιν ἢ χρυσῷ ἢ μαρ., ϛ c. rell. (exc. P$_2$al$^3$) f m Lat-vg Syr-hcl Go Sah : Clem Orig ½ Cypr Chr.
The combined evidence of Versions and Fathers, if the details may be trusted, proves that this variant is pre-Syrian. It is possibly Alexandrian.
Cf. *v.l.* in 1 P 3$^3$. There seems to be a point in the distinction between the treatment of the hair and of the jewels.

(8) 1 Ti 2$^{12}$ διδάσκειν δὲ γυναικί, ℵAD$_2$G$_3$P cu$^{11}$ Lat-vg Arm : Orig Cypr.
γυναικὶ δὲ διδάσκειν, ϛ c. rell. Syrr (Boh) Sah : Chr.
The emphasis clearly lies on διδάσκειν.

(9) 1 Ti 2$^{14}$ ἐξαπατηθεῖσα, ℵ*AD$_2$*G$_3$P$_2$ cu$^{11}$: Chr ¼.
ἀπατηθεῖσα, ϛ c. rell : Chr ¾.
ἐξαπ. Pauline, cf. 2 Co 11$^3$. ἀπατ. has come in from context.

(10*) 1 Ti 3$^3$ — μὴ αἰσχροκερδῆ, ℵAD$_2$G$_3$KLP cu$^{37}$ verss : Orig$^{int}$ Tert Chr.
+ ϛ c. rell. Syr-hcl-mg.
Insertion from v.$^8$, Ti 1$^7$ ; cf. Ti 1$^{11}$, 1 P 5$^2$. Here superfluous, see ἀφιλάργυρον.

(11) 1 Ti 3$^{16}$ ὃς ἐφανερώθη, ℵ*A*C*F$_2$G$_3$ cu$^3$ Boh Sah Syr-hcl-mg : Orig$^{int}$.
ὃ ἐφανερώθη, D$_2$* Lat-vg Syr-vg-hcl Arm.
θ̅ς ἐφανερώθη, ϛ c. ℵ$^c$C$^c$D$_2^c$KLP rell.
F$_2$ is quoted here, though the present writer does not believe that it has any authority independent of G$_3$, because it is sometimes quoted wrongly in support of θεός. The line above ο is not horizontal, and corresponds exactly to the line which elsewhere indicates a rough breathing in this MS. There is no trace of a sagitta in the ο.
On this reading see Hort, Appendix, p. 132 ff.
Note especially the evidence of the Versions.

(12) 1 Ti 4$^{12}$ ἐν ἀγάπῃ ∧ ἐν πίστει, ℵACD$_2$G$_3$ cu$^9$ verss : Clem Chr.
ἐν ἀγ. ἐν πνεύματι ἐν π., ϛ c. rell.
Insertion awkward ; 1 Co 4$^{21}$, 2 Co 6$^6$ no parallels. Prob. from Col 1$^8$.

(13) 1 Ti 4$^{15}$ φανερὰ ᾖ πᾶσιν, ℵACD$_2$*G$_3$ cu$^2$ verss.
φαν. ᾖ ἐν π., ϛ c. rell : Chr.
Cf. Ac 4$^{16}$.

(14*) 1 Ti 5$^4$ ἀποδεκτόν, ℵACD$_2$G$_3$KLP cu$^{pl}$ Lat-vg Syrr Æth : Chr.
καλὸν καὶ ἀ., ϛ c. rell. incl. Boh Go Arm.
Insertion from 2$^3$. The only other instance of ἀποδ. in NT.

(15) 1 Ti 5$^{21}$ Χριστοῦ Ἰησοῦ, ℵAD$_2$*G$_3$ cu$^3$ Lat-vg Boh Sah Arm Æth : Clem Ath.
κυρίου Ἰ. Χ., ϛ c. rell. Syrr Go : Chr.
Cf. 2 Ti 4$^1$. Fuller titles characteristic of later MSS.

(16) 1 Ti 5$^{25}$ τὰ ἔργα τὰ καλά, ℵAD$_2$G$_3$P$_2$ cu$^3$.
τὰ καλὰ ἔργα, ϛ c. rell : Chr.
Perhaps from Mt 5$^{16}$, note οὐ δύναται κρυβῆναι v.$^{14}$.

(17) 1 Ti 5$^{25}$ (*a*) πρόδηλα, ℵA 67**.
(*b*) πρ. εἰσι, D$_2$G$_3$P$_2$ cu$^7$.
(*c*) πρ. ἐστι., ϛ c. rell : Chr.
Here (*b*) and (*c*) are insertions of a common type. (*c*) apparently a correction of (*b*) to bring it into agreement with classical rules ; cf. 2 Ti 4$^{17}$.
The plural is by no means uncommon in later Greek.

(18*) 1 Ti 6$^5$ διαπαρατριβαί, ℵAD$_2$G$_3$L$_2$P$_2$, etc. : Clem Chr.
παραδιατριβαί, ϛ 'not many cursives.'
διαπαρα — in itself a rarer form of compound—is much more vigorous, connoting an intensified form of παρατριβή, 'friction' or 'collision.'

[19] 1 Ti 6$^5$ – ἀφίστασο ἀπὸ τῶν τοιούτων, ℵAD$_2$G$_3$ cu$^3$ Lat-vg Boh Sah Go Æth.
+ ϛ c. rell. incl. Syrr Arm : Chr ; cf. Cypr.
An insertion, of an unusually bold type for this form of text, to complete a misunderstood construction. The evidence of Cyprian shows that it is not purely 'Syrian.' It is of a Western type.

(20) 1 Ti 6$^7$ (*a*) ὅτι οὐδὲ ἐξ., ℵ*AG$_3$17 (Lat-vg-codd) r Sah Boh Arm : Ath.
(*b*) ἀληθὲς ὅτι ο. ἐ., D$_2$* m Go : Cypr al. aliter.
(*c*) δῆλον ὅτι ο. ἐ., ϛ c. ℵ$^c$D$_2^{bc}$K$_2$L$_2$P$_2$ : Chr.
(*b*) and (*c*) are independent attempts to mend (*a*).
See Hort, Appendix, p. 134. He conjectures that the true reading is simply οὐδὲ ἐξ. This is found in Arm Cyr. Cyprian also seems to omit ὅτι.

(21*) 1 Ti 6$^{12}$ εἰς ἣν ἐκλήθης. All uncials, many cursives, all versions (exc. Syr-hcl) : Chr.
εἰς ἣν καὶ ἐ., ϛ c. rell.
An echo of Col 3$^{15}$.

(22) 1 Ti 6$^{17}$ ἀλλ' ἐπὶ θεῷ (or τῳ θεῷ), ℵAD$_2$*G$_3$P$_2$ cu$^{13}$ : Orig Chr.

ἀλλ' ἐν τῷ θ., ϛ c. rell.

It seems difficult to find a clear case of ἐλπ. ἐν in NT. Certainly not Ph $2^{19}$, and 1 Co $15^{19}$ is more than doubtful.

ἐπί is found regularly, *e.g.* 1 Jn $3^{3}$, 1 Ti $4^{10}$, and in this verse.

(23*) 1 Ti $6^{17}$ *πάντα πλουσίως*, all uncials exc. G, most cursives, all versions (exc. Æth): Orig Chr.

*πλουσίως πάντα*, ϛ Æth, not many cursives.

$G_3$ omits *πάντα*.

(24) 1 Ti $6^{19}$ *ὄντως*, ℵ$AD_2$*$G_3$ cu[10] verss.

*αἰωνίου*, ϛ c. rell. (37 'conflates' *αἰωνίου ὄντως*): Chr.

*αἰωνίου* is habitual with *ζωῆς*; cf. v.[12].

*ὄντως* is striking, and characteristic of this Ep.; cf. $5^{3.\,5.\,16}$.

(25*) 1 Ti $6^{20}$ *παραθήκην*, all uncials, most cursives: Clem Ign.

*παρακαταθήκην*, ϛ with many cursives: Hipp Chr.

*παρακαταθ.* is said to be the Attic form.

19. Here, then, are 25 readings which have a *prima facie* claim to be regarded as 'Syrian' or 'post-Syrian.' The criterion, as Dr. Hort warns us (§§ 324 f., 343), is not an infallible one. We need not be surprised, therefore, to find among them 2 readings (7 and 19) which are proved by Old Latin evidence to be pre-Syrian; we may therefore strike them out of our list. The whole 25 belong to the Received Text. How many of them Mr. Miller would assign to the Traditional Text it is impossible to say. No. 2, the support for which is infinitesimal, may be assumed to disappear. We shall therefore exclude it also from consideration. Nos. 10, 14, 18, 21, 23, 25 (which are distinguished above by an asterisk), when there is serious division among the cursives, must be regarded as at best uncertain. Dr. Hort would call them post-Syrian; it would be interesting to know how many of them Mr. Miller would class as 'post-Traditional.' In any case, they witness to a progressive deterioration in the text of the Epistle. We shall not, however, strike them out of the list, as their internal characteristics show a striking 'family likeness' to their predecessors. They may well be regarded as later results of the working of one and the same tendency. We shall, however, where possible, mark a distinction between them and the other readings. We have no wish to take an unfair advantage of the Traditional Text.

20. The first point that strikes us on a survey of the list as a whole is the triviality of by far the greater number of the examples. One (3) is a mere matter of spelling, (4, 6, 16) affect only an article, 3 (8, 16, 23*) relate to the order of words, 2 (13, 22) to prepositions, 3 (9, 18*, 25*) to different compounds of the same root, 4 (1, 17, 20, 21*) are quite trivial insertions; there are only 7—2 changes of words (11, 24) and 5 insertions (5, 10*, 12, 14*, 15)—which can be regarded as at all important. Of these, only 1 (11) can be supposed to affect any point of doctrine, and, as the Nicene Fathers managed to make shift without the reading of the Traditional Text, we need not be afraid to keep the demonstrably older reading.

21. The next point of interest is the distribution of support on the different sides on the part of Fathers and Versions.*

In the Patristic evidence the result is remarkable. Taking the whole number of passages (25), ante-Nicene evidence is quoted against the 'Syrian' Text 18 times, and only once (25*—a reading in Hippolytus incapable of verification) in support of it. If we leave out the 6 doubtful examples, the numbers are 12 against, 0 for. Chrysostom's text shows a marked contrast. He is quoted in all on 20 of the passages. In the 6 doubtful cases he supports the ante-Nicene in 5. In the remaining 14 his authority is quoted on both sides in 3 cases (4, 5, 9). He supports the Traditional Text in 12 (or 9) cases, he opposes it in 2 (or 5).

* We have taken the evidence from Tischendorf and Tregelles. We have not thought it worth while to subject the whole to an independent verification. The Patristic evidence includes, it will be noticed, all the ante-Nicene quotations, together with the quotations in Chrysostom.

Among Versions the results are as follows :—

| | | | | | | |
|---|---|---|---|---|---|---|
| Latin Vulg. | supports the | Trad. Text | 1, | opposes it | 13 (9) | times. |
| Bohairic . | ,, | ,, | 2 (1) | ,, | 10 (7) | ,, |
| Sahidic . | ,, | ,, | 1 | ,, | 10 (7) | ,, |
| Syriac Vulg. | ,, | ,, | 3 | ,, | 9 (5) | ,, |
| Harclean Syriac | ,, | ,, | 4 | ,, | 8 (4) | ,, |
| Æthiopic . | ,, | ,, | 1 | ,, | 10 (6) | ,, |
| Armenian . | ,, | ,, | 1 (0) | ,, | 12 (9) | ,, |
| Gothic . | ,, | ,, | 4 (2) | ,, | 6 (5) | ,, |

All the extant Versions are combined in 10*, 11, 12, 13, 23*, 24, in each case against the Received Text.

22. It remains to indicate briefly the character of the readings of the Traditional Text. Clearly, its most noteworthy feature is its fulness. In one case (16) it errs by defect, it drops one article out of two, while it contains 9 (6) additions. The most potent factor in this expansion of the text is, without doubt, the tendency to assimilate cognate passages. A second feature we may fairly describe as general weakness. In no single case has any of the editors collated by Nestle in his Stuttgart edition accepted any of those distinctively Traditional readings.

The net result of our examination may, we think, be fairly stated as follows: There is a demonstrably late element in the Traditional Text of 1 Tim.; the readings, which may fairly be regarded as distinctive of it, in which it is unsupported by any member of the numerically insignificant group ℵ$ACD_2G_3$, are both weak in themselves and can very rarely be traced back historically into ante-Nicene times, and then they seem to belong also to other types of text.

23. We pass* now to our second specimen passage, Mk $1^{1\text{-}28}$.

This time—as we wish to study the whole structure of the Traditional Text, and not merely to sift out 'distinctively Syrian' readings—we must begin by printing the verses at length, marking as clearly as the typographical means at our disposal will allow, the relation in which this text stands to the other types of text out of which, on the Critical hypothesis, it was constructed. In one case (v.[16]) where 'the verdict of the MSS' seemed decisive, we have ventured to print as 'traditional' a reading which is not found in the Received Text. Otherwise, the text printed here agrees with that which Scrivener edited for the Cambridge University Press as representing the Greek Text that may be presumed to underlie the AV.

[In the form of the extract the following points should be noticed: Words in ordinary type, and undistinguished by any signs above or below them, are common to all forms of text alike; words in heavy type belong to readings which, either in particular words or in arrangement or combination of words, may be regarded as 'distinctively Syrian,' because *as they stand* they agree exactly with no other form of text.

The relation in which the text as a whole stands to the 'Western' Text is indicated by continuous lines. These lines are drawn under the word

* A careful collation of the readings of 1 and the MSS related to it in Mk 1 has just been published by Mr. Lake in *Cambridge Texts and Studies*. It contains a few variants which have not been noticed above, notably λίνα for δίκτυα in v.[18].

when the Traditional Text has accepted, above the word when it has rejected, a 'Western' reading. Its relation to the 'Alexandrian' Text is similarly indicated by spaced lines.

In a few cases, where it is desired to call attention to some evidence for or against a reading of the Traditional Text, though the authorities cannot be assigned with certainty to any of these types, the words affected are indicated on the same principle by a row of dots.

The 'Neutral' Text may be assumed to be at variance with the Traditional Text in all cases where words are underscored; all the other words in ordinary type are supported by it. Slight differences in form and spelling have in this case been neglected].

1 Ἀρχὴ τοῦ εὐαγγελίου Ἰησοῦ Χριστοῦ υἱοῦ **τοῦ** θεοῦ· 2 ὡς γέγραπται ἐν **τοῖς προφήταις**· Ἰδοὺ ἐγὼ ἀποστέλλω τὸν ἄγγελόν μου πρὸ προσώπου σου, ὃς κατασκευάσει τὴν ὁδόν σου **ἔμπροσθέν σου**· 3 φωνὴ βοῶντος ἐν τῇ ἐρήμῳ, Ἑτοιμάσατε τὴν ὁδὸν Κυρίου, εὐθείας ποιεῖτε τὰς τρίβους αὐτοῦ. 4 Ἐγένετο Ἰωάννης ^ **βαπτίζων ἐν τῇ ἐρήμῳ καὶ** κηρύσσων βάπτισμα μετανοίας εἰς ἄφεσιν ἁμαρτιῶν. 5 καὶ ἐξεπορεύετο πρὸς αὐτὸν πᾶσα ἡ Ἰουδαία χώρα καὶ οἱ Ἱεροσολυμεῖται ^· καὶ ἐβαπτίζοντο **πάντες** ἐν τῷ Ἰορδάνῃ ποτάμῳ ὑπ' αὐτοῦ, ἐξομολογούμενοι τὰς ἁμαρτίας αὐτῶν. 6 ἦν δὲ ^ Ἰωάννης ἐνδεδυμένος τρίχας καμήλου, καὶ ζώνην δερματίνην περὶ τὴν ὀσφὺν αὐτοῦ καὶ ἐσθίων ἀκρίδας καὶ μέλι ἄγριον. 7 Καὶ ἐκήρυσσεν λέγων Ἔρχεται ὁ ἰσχυρότερός μου ὀπίσω μου, οὗ οὐκ εἰμὶ ἱκανος κύψας λῦσαι τὸν ἱμάντα τῶν ὑποδημάτων αὐτοῦ. 8 ἐγὼ μὲν ἐβάπτισα ὑμᾶς ἐν ὕδατι· αὐτὸς δὲ βαπτίσει ἐν Πνεύματι Ἁγίῳ.

9 Καὶ ἐγένετο ἐν ἐκείναις ταῖς ἡμέραις ἦλθεν ^ Ἰησοῦς ἀπὸ Ναζαρὲτ τῆς Γαλιλαίας, καὶ ἐβαπτίσθη **ὑπὸ Ἰωάννου εἰς τὸν Ἰορδάνην.** 10 καὶ εὐθέως ἀναβαίνων **ἀπὸ** τοῦ ὕδατος εἶδε σχιζομένους τοὺς οὐρανούς, καὶ τὸ Πνεῦμα ὡς περιστερὰν καταβαῖνον ἐπ' αὐτόν. 11 καὶ φωνὴ ἐγένετο ἐκ τῶν οὐρανῶν· Σὺ εἶ ὁ υἱός μου ὁ ἀγαπητός, ἐν **ᾧ** εὐδόκησα.

12 Καὶ εὐθὺς τὸ Πνεῦμα ^ αὐτὸν ἐκβάλλει εἰς τὴν ἔρημον. 13 καὶ ἦν **ἐκεῖ ἐν τῇ ἐρήμῳ** ἡμέρας τεσσαράκοντα πειραζόμενος ὑπὸ τοῦ Σατανᾶ, καὶ ἦν μετὰ τῶν θηρίων· καὶ οἱ ἄγγελοι διηκόνουν αὐτῷ.

14 Μετὰ δὲ τὸ παραδοθῆναι τὸν Ἰωάννην ἦλθεν ὁ Ἰησοῦς εἰς τὴν Γαλιλαίαν κηρύσσων τὸ εὐαγγέλιον τῆς βασιλείας τοῦ θεοῦ, 15 καὶ λέγων, Ὅτι πεπλήρωται ὁ καιρὸς καὶ ἤγγικεν ἡ βασιλεία τοῦ θεοῦ· μετανοεῖτε καὶ πιστεύετε ἐν τῷ εὐαγγελίῳ. 16 **περιπατῶν δὲ** παρὰ τὴν θαλάσσαν τῆς Γαλιλαίας εἶδεν ^ Σίμωνα καὶ Ἀνδρέαν τὸν ἀδελφὸν **αὐτοῦ τοῦ Σίμωνος βάλλοντας ἀμφίβληστρον** ἐν τῇ θαλάσσῃ· ἦσαν γὰρ ἁλιεῖς· 17 καὶ εἶπεν αὐτοῖς ὁ Ἰησοῦς, Δεῦτε ὀπίσω μου, καὶ ποιήσω ὑμᾶς γενέσθαι ἁλιεῖς ἀνθρώπων. 18 καὶ εὐθέως ἀφέντες τὰ δίκτυα **αὐτῶν** ἠκολούθησαν αὐτῷ. 19 Καὶ πρόβας **ἐκεῖθεν ὀλίγον** εἶδεν Ἰάκωβον τὸν τοῦ Ζεβεδαίου καὶ Ἰωάννην τὸν ἀδελφὸν αὐτοῦ καὶ αὐτοὺς ἐν τῷ πλοίῳ καταρτίζοντας τὰ δίκτυα. 20 καὶ εὐθέως ἐκάλεσεν αὐτούς· καὶ ἀφέντες τὸν πατέρα αὐτῶν Ζεβεδαῖον ἐν τῷ πλοίῳ μετὰ τῶν μισθωτῶν ἀπῆλθον ὀπίσω αὐτοῦ.

21 Καὶ εἰσπορεύονται εἰς Καπερναούμ· καὶ εὐθέως τοῖς σάββασιν εἰσελθὼν εἰς τὴν συναγωγὴν ἐδίδασκεν ^. 22 καὶ ἐξεπλήσσοντο ἐπὶ τῇ διδαχῇ αὐτοῦ· ἦν γὰρ διδάσκων αὐτοὺς ὡς ἐξουσίαν ἔχων, καὶ οὐχ ὡς οἱ γραμματεῖς. 23 καὶ ^ ἦν ἐν τῇ συναγωγῇ αὐτῶν ἄνθρωπος ἐν πνεύματι ἀκαθάρτῳ, 24 καὶ ἀνέκραξε λέγων, Ἔα· τί ἡμῖν καὶ σοί, Ἰησοῦ Ναζαρηνέ; ἦλθες ἀπολέσαι ἡμᾶς; Οἶδά σε τίς εἶ, ὁ ἅγιος τοῦ Θεοῦ. 25 καὶ ἐπετίμησεν αὐτῷ ὁ Ἰησοῦς λέγων, Φιμώθητι καὶ ἔξελθε ἐξ αὐτοῦ ^. 26 καὶ σπαράξαν αὐτὸν τὸ πνεῦμα τὸ ἀκάθαρτον ^ καὶ κράξαν φωνῇ μεγάλῃ ἐξῆλθεν ἐξ αὐτοῦ. 27 καὶ ἐθαμβήθησαν πάντες ὥστε συζητεῖν πρὸς αὐτοὺς λέγοντας, **Τί ἐστιν τοῦτο; τίς ἡ δίδαχὴ ^ ἡ καινὴ αὕτη, ὅτι κατ' ἐξουσίαν** καὶ τοῖς πνεύμασιν τοῖς ἀκαθάρτοις ἐπιτάσσει καὶ ὑπακούουσιν αὐτῷ; 28 ἐξῆλθε **δὲ** ἡ ἀκοὴ αὐτοῦ εὐθὺς ^ εἰς ὅλην τὴν περίχωρον τῆς Γαλιλαίας.

V. 1 Om. τοῦ ℵ$^{a}$BDL.

om. υἱ. τ. θ., ℵ* 28 255 Lat-vg-cod Syr-hr: Iren$\frac{1}{3}$ Orig *Jo*$^{3}$; *Cels*; *Rom.* Lat. Ruf Bas Hier$^{2}$ al$^{4}$. See Hort, *Select Readings*, p. 23, *Suppl.* (Burkitt) p. 144.

V. 2 (1) καθώς, ℵBLΔ unc$^{2}$ cu$^{8}$: Orig$\frac{3}{4}$ al$^{4}$; cf. 9$^{13}$ 14$^{21}$.

ὡς, ADP rell: Orig$\frac{1}{4}$ Iren al; cf. 7$^{6}$.

καθώς an unclassical form, usual in NT with γέγρ.

ὡς γ. is rare, but is found in par. Lk 3$^{4}$.

(2) τῷ Ἡσαΐᾳ τῷ προφήτῃ, ℵBDLΔ cu$^{26}$ Latt Syrr-vg-hcl-mg-h Boh Go (Arm$^{mss}$): Orig Iren$^{gr}$ Porph al$^{8}$.

(-τῷ 1°, D cu$^{17}$: Orig Iren) (tol* omits altogether).

τοῖς προφήταις, AP rell Syr-hcl-txt Arm$^{ed}$ Æth: Iren$^{int}$.

Notice here the strength of the early Patristic evidence, and of Versions, coupled with the obvious reason for change. On the tendency to insert 'Isaiah,' see Hort, *Select Read.* p. 13; cf. Burkitt, *ib.* p. 143.

(3) ἐγώ, om. BD 28 (Latt) Syr-vg Boh: Iren$^{int}$ Orig$\frac{1}{5}$ (Orig$^{int}$) Tert; so Lk 7$^{27}$ (ℵBDL).

Ins. ℵAPLΔ rell Syr-hcl Go Arm Æth: Orig$\frac{4}{5}$ Eus; so Mt 11$^{10}$.

LXX (not ℵ or B) ins. in Mal 3$^{1}$ with Heb.

(4) ἀποστελῶ, ℵ al pauc Boh, assimilating to neighbouring tenses.

So in Mt. in a few MSS, not in Lk.

(5) ἔμπροσθέν σου, om. ℵBDLKP a b c l q Lat-vg-codd Boh Syr-vg-hr: Iren Orig *diserti*.

Ins. AΔ rell f ff$^{1.2}$ g$^{1.2}$ Syr-hcl; cf. Mt. and Lk. (D a l Tert$^{marc}$ om.). In Heb. and LXX of Mal. the phrase is found here, but not after ἄγγ. μου.

V. 3 αὐτοῦ, ℵABLΔ rell ff$^{1}$ g$^{1}$ l q Syr-vg-hcl-txt Boh Arm Æth: Orig.

τοῦ θεοῦ ἡμῶν, (D) (34$^{mg}$) a b c f ff$^{2}$ g$^{2}$ Syr-hcl-mg Go: Iren$^{int}$ (D 34$^{mg}$ υμων). Assimilation to Isaiah, LXX and Heb.; found also in Latin and Syriac texts, Mt., Lk.

V.$^{4}$ (*a*) ὁ βαπτίζων ἐν τῇ ἐρήμῳ κηρύσσων, B 33.

(*b*) ὁ βαπτίζων ἐν τῇ ἐρήμῳ καὶ κηρύσσων, ℵLΔ Boh.

(*c*) ἐν τῇ ἐρήμῳ βαπτίζων καὶ κηρύσσων, D 28 Latt (exc. f) Syr-vg.

(*d*) βαπτίζων ἐν τῇ ἐρήμῳ καὶ κηρύσσων, A rell f Syr-hcl.

The clue to the readings here, as the present writer finds hinted in a MS note of Dr. Hort's, lies in Mark's use of Ἰω. ὁ βαπτίζων (6$^{14. 24}$, not 8$^{28}$; yet see 28 2$^{pe}$) as a title for the Baptist. The original reading is: (*a*)='John the Baptizer appeared in the wilderness preaching.' (*b*) is an Alexandrian emendation, the Marcan idiom not being recognized, and the article causing difficulty in consequence ='There appeared John who used to baptize in the wilderness and preach.' (*c*) shows the Western handling of the difficulty, dropping the troublesome article, inserting καί, and, because the wilderness was a strange place to be specially connected with the baptisms, transposing the words. (*d*) is 'distinctively Syrian,' and conflates (*b*) and (*c*), keeping the order of (*b*) and dropping the article with (*c*). This is a first-rate example of the excellence of B in Ternary Variations. The connecting particle with ἐγένετο in ℵ* and Boh should be noticed. It could preclude the conn. of vv.$^{1}$ and $^{4}$ which Orig *Joh* favours.

V.$^{5}$ (*a*) πάντες after Ἱερ., ℵBDLΔ 28 33 versions: Orig Eus.

after ἐβαπτ., AP rell (69 cu$^{4}$ om. πάντες= Mt.).

(*b*) ποτάμῳ, om. D a b c ff$^{2}$ Eus; cf. the 'Western' and 'Syrian' reading in Mt.

(*c*) ὑπ' αὐτοῦ after ἐβαπτ., ℵBL 33 Latt (exc. a) Arm: Orig Eus.

after ποτάμῳ, ADP rell a Syr-hcl Go.

Note, further (*d*), that ℵ 69 a om. καί before ἐβαπτ.

In (*d*) the omission was probably due to the idea that the subj. of ἐξεπορεύετο was complete at χώρα (cf. the post-Syrian ἐξεπορεύοντο). The result is a strange statement that the city folk took the lead in accepting baptism, which can hardly be historical.

The Syrian change of the position of πάντες may be a modified echo of this. It is more likely due to a misunderstanding of the characteristically Marcan indefiniteness of ἐβαπτίζοντο='men' were being baptized. πάντες with ἐβαπτ. is hyperbolical after a fashion to which Luke supplies parallels, not Mark.

In (*b*) and (*c*) notice once more how the Syrian Text combines the language of the 'Neutral' with the order of the 'Western' Text. The result is a close assimilation to Mt.

V.$^{6}$ (1) καὶ ἦν, ℵBL 33.

ἦν δὲ, AD$^{gr}$P rel.

Mark's resolute adherence to καί causes constant difficulty to scribes. At least 40 times δέ has been wrongly introduced into the Syrian Text; cf. vv.$^{14. 16. 28}$ in this extract.

(2) ὁ Ἰω., ℵBL unc$^{9}$ cu$^{62}$.

-ὁ, ADΔ rell? assim. to v.$^{4}$. Otherwise the tendency in these authorities, esp. D, is to insert articles before proper names. See vv.$^{9. 14. 16. 29. 36}$.

(3) For τρίχας καμήλου D$^{gr}$ reads δέρρην (=δέρριν) καμ., 'a' *pellem* and 'd' *pilos*. δέρριν in LXX (of raiment) Jg 4$^{18. 21}$, Zec 13$^{4}$ only.

In Zec 13$^{4}$ δέρριν=אַדֶּרֶת, found also (Heb. not LXX) for Elijah's mantle in 1 K 19$^{13. 19}$, 2 K 2$^{8. 13f.}$.

This is remarkable, because the clause καὶ ζώνην δερμ. π.τ. ὀσφ. αὐτοῦ, omitted by D, is found exactly in 2 K 1$^{8}$ in another description of Elijah. δέρριν (=the prophetic mantle) was probably regarded as a concise and picturesque equivalent for the whole phrase. But the man who introduced it must have known his Hebrew Bible and his LXX. Note that 'a,' which also omits καὶ ζώνην, κ.τ.λ., places v.$^{6}$ after v.$^{8}$.

V.$^{7}$ ἔλεγεν αὐτοῖς for ἐκήρυσσεν λέγων, D (a). In 'a's' arrangement of the verses, αὐτοῖς has a point which is lost in D. In view of the rest of vv.$^{7. 8}$ in D, it is safe to say that ἔλεγεν comes from Lk 3$^{7}$ or Mt 3$^{7}$. ἐκήρυσσεν is characteristic of Mk. (cf. *e.g.* 1$^{38}$ and Lk 4$^{43}$, 1$^{45}$ and Lk 5$^{15}$, 6$^{12}$ and Lk 9$^{6}$. It is curious that in these passages there should be no par. in Mt.). It has also point as resuming v.$^{4}$.

Vv.$^{7. 8}$ (1) D a (ff$^{1}$) read: Ἐγὼ μὲν ὑμᾶς βαπτίζω ἐν ὕδατι, ἔρχεται δὲ ὀπίσω μου ὁ ἰσχυρότερός μου οὗ οὐκ εἰμὶ ἱκανὸς λῦσαι τὸν ἱμάντα τῶν ὑποδημάτων αὐτοῦ· καὶ αὐτὸς ὑμᾶς βαπτίζει ἐν πνεύματι ἁγίῳ. Notice first the order of the clauses, natural in Lk 3$^{16}$, which this reading reproduces almost *verbatim*, but weak in Mk., where there is no ref. in the context to popular surmises about John. Notice also the omission of the characteristic Marcan κύψας.

A clear case of assimilation in the 'Western' text.

(2) The Syrian text adopts μέν from this text, or from Mt. and Lk. ℵBL 33 69 124 Orig om.; cf. Jn 1$^{26}$. μέν rare, in Mk 4$^{4}$ 9$^{12}$ 12$^{5}$ 14$^{21. 38}$ only; cf. 10$^{39}$.

(3) Also ἐν 1° against ℵBΔH cu$^{8}$. ἐν 2° against BL b Lat-vg.

In Mt 3$^{11}$ Jn 1$^{26. 33}$ ἐν is found with both words without variant. In Ac 1$^{5}$ ὕδ. and ἐν πν. without variant. In Lk 3$^{16}$ ὑδ. (exc. D 1 13 69 al ἐν ὑδ.) and ἐν πν. without variant. There seems, therefore, no tendency to omit ἐν where it is clearly genuine, even to balance phrases, *e.g.* Ac 1$^{5}$. The tendency to insert from par. must have been very strong.

V.$^{9}$ (1) ταῖς ἡμέραις ἐκείναις, DΔ Latt (exc. a c).

ἐκεῖνος never comes after ἡμέρα in Mk. without special emphasis.

Only in 13$^{19. 32}$ 14$^{25}$, all three eschatological passages.

(2) ὁ Ἰησ., DMΓΔ 13 28 69 al. See on v.$^{6}$.

(3) εἰς τὸν Ἰορδ. ὑπὸ Ἰωάν., ℵBDL cu$^{15}$ (ἐν τῷ, 1-28, etc.) Latt (c f) Syr-vg Boh.

ὑπὸ Ἰωάν. εἰς τὸν Ἰορδ., AP rell c f Syr-hcl Arm Æth Go.

Notice the converse change in v.$^{5}$. Here clearly the important fact is that the baptism was administered by John, not that it took place in the Jordan. ὑπὸ Ἰω. is therefore rightly kept to the last.

V.$^{10}$ (1) εὐθέως or εὐθύς, om. D a b.

A peculiarly difficult word for the textual critic in Mk., clearly characteristic, offending some scribes and some translators by its recurrence, at the same time always to hand when an adventurous scribe wished to 'improve' the story. We find ourselves therefore driven by sheer perplexity to take refuge in obedience to the one golden rule of sound criticism and to 'trust our MSS.' The result will show if our confidence is misplaced.

One point we can lay down at the outset. A close examination of the facts shows that the effect of Synoptic parallels on the text of Mk. must, so far as this word is concerned, have been uniformly towards omission: Mk 14$^{45}$ om. D 251 2$^{pe}$ a c ff$^{2}$ k q (Mt 26$^{49}$ 'non fluctuat') is the only possible exception.

The facts are interesting, and we may allow ourselves this one excursion into the field of Synoptic criticism. Assuming the WH text as our standard, εὐθύς occurs 40 times in Mark. In 29 of these there are parallel contexts in both Mt. and Lk., in 8 there is a parallel in Mt. only, in 2 in Lk. only, in 1 there is no parallel in either. In one case, 1[42] = Mt 8[3] = Lk 5[13], εὐθ. is found in all three Gospels. In none of the other 30 cases where Lk. has a parallel context is εὐθ. found: in 7 the whole phrase to which εὐθ. belongs in Mk. is transformed; in 17 εὐθ. is simply omitted; in 5 he substitutes παραχρῆμα, in 1 εἶτα. Of the 37 places where Mt. presents a parallel, εὐθ. is retained in 12; in 8 the whole phrase, in 15 the word, disappears; in 2 ἀπὸ τῆς ὥρας ἐκείνης does duty as an equivalent. In one case Lk. (21[9] = Mt 24[6] = Mk 13[7]) substitutes οὐκ εὐθέως for οὔπω.

Assuming, as it is probably worth while to do at present, that our Mk. was in the hands of both Mt. and Lk., the figures given above supply a good illustration of the delicate literary criticism to which Mark was subjected, esp. by Luke. This general result is not seriously affected by questions of text. In 6 places TR *ins.* where WH *om.*, in 4 TR *om.* where WH *ins.* But it is worth notice that the 'Western' Text, esp. in D and in the various MSS of Lat-vet, shows a clear tendency to omit εὐθ. The chief passages are 1[10. 28. 29] 2[8] 3[6] 4[16] 5[2. 42] 6[25. 50] 9[20] 14[43. 45]. The same tendency is found in the same authorities in Mt., *e.g.* 4[22] 21[2].

In the case before us (1[10]) the genuineness of εὐθύς in Mk. is, we think, supported by its presence in Mt 3[16]. There are only 2 cases (24[29] 27[48]) where Mt. in a parallel context shows a εὐθ. which is not represented in the true text of Mark. And in neither of these does any authority for the text of Mk. attempt to assimilate.

(2) ἐκ τοῦ ὕδ., ℵBDL 13 28 33 69 124.
ἀπό, AP rell; cf. Mt 3[16].

Here, again, ἐκ is characteristic of Mark. In 4 other cases it corresponds to ἀπό in a parallel context in Mt., and in 10 cases in Luke. A similar reaction on the MSS of Mk. also in 1[5. 26] 7[15] 9[9] 16[3].

(3) σχιζομένους, ℵAB rell.
ἠνυγμένους, D Latt ('apertos') = Mt. and Luke.

Here there is nothing to account for the change of ἀνεῳγμένους if it were genuine, while σχιζομένους is at once vivid and difficult.

(4) καταβαῖνον εἰς αὐτόν, BD 13 69 124 a.
καταβαῖνον ἐπ' αὐτόν, ℵAP rell, but note that ℵ 33 insert καὶ μένον before ἐπ' from Jn 1[32].

Fondness for εἰς is another characteristic feature of Mark's style. It occurs in all about 157 times. Of these, 42 are found in both Mt. and Lk., 39 in Mt. alone, 19 in Lk. alone, 57 belong to sections or phrases peculiar to Mark. In 3 places Lk. substitutes ἐν, in 2 ἐπί, in 1 ἐν μέσῳ. Mt. substitutes ἐν in 5 places and ἐπί in 4. Here (1[10]) Mt. and Lk. agree in substituting ἐπί as they agree in substituting ἐν in 11[8]. In 4 cases Mt. or Lk. supports εἰς when the other has changed it.

On the other hand, ἐπί *with acc.* occurs only 32 times in Mark. There is only very slight evidence of a tendency to change it into εἰς. See 6[53] 15[22. 46], and perhaps d (not D) in 9[13]. In no case is there a real parallel to the phrase here, which must have suffered from 'assimilation.'

V.[11] (*a*) Om. ἐγένετο, ℵ* D ff[2] mt (a f 'venit'; 28 2[pe] g[1] ἠκούσθη).

Here, again, light is thrown on the reading by a careful study of Mark's usage. He is fond of γίνεσθαι, and uses it to cover a great variety of different meanings. It occurs 52 times in the WH Text; of these, 6 are found both in Mt. and Luke. Besides these, Mt. retains only 16, Lk. only 9; and even in some of these instances slight modifications are introduced. (Mt. has a parallel context in 49, Lk. in 36 cases). The text of Mk. shows similar traces of the attempt to obliterate this individualism. See 1[17] 2[27] 4[4. 11] 5[16] 6[2] (9[6]) 9[7] 10[43] 12[11] 14[4]. 9[6] seems to be Syrian. In all the other cases, except 1[17] 2[27] 5[16], D appears in the group which either omits or provides a substitute for γίν. D is generally supported by some Old Latin MSS and various members of the group 1-28, etc. The most instructive case is the closely par. 9[7] ἐγένετο φωνὴ ἐκ τῆς νεφέλης (ℵBCLΔ), where AD rell inc. Syr-sin read ἦλθεν (exc. k 1 Syr-vg-codd *om.*), while ἰδού from Mt. and λέγουσα from Lk. also find support. In Lk 9[35] ἐγένετο . . . λέγουσα is found without variant, except that D reads ἦλθεν, Syr-cu-sin ἠκούσθη. In 10[44] the Syrian Text has γενέσθαι, ℵBC(D)LΔ εἶναι. The omission of ἐγένετο may therefore safely be regarded as 'Western.'

(*b*) ἐν σοί, ℵBD[gr]LPΔ 1 13 22 33 69 cu[25] Lat-vg a c ff[1. 2] g[2] l Boh ? Syr-vg-hcl-txt Arm Æth Go.
ἐν ᾧ, AΓΠ unc[8] rell b d g[1] f Syr-hcl-mg.
In Lk. there is virtually no doubt (apart from the very early 'Western' variant υἱός μου εἶ σύ) about the reading σὺ . . . ἐν σοί.
In Mt. the reading is οὗτος . . . ἐν ᾧ, exc. that D a Syr-cu read σὺ—ἐν ᾧ; Syr-sin σὺ . . . ἐν σοί.
ἐν σοί was peculiarly liable to change from the association with Is 42[1] = Mt 12[18]; cf. 2 P 1[17].

V.[12] (1) τὸ πν. add τὸ ἅγιον, D.

The tendency to add ἅγιον is much less than might have been expected (see 2[8], Jn 7[39]). Its presence here, perhaps due to Lk 4[1], is more likely meant to mark the contrast with the Tempter.

(2) (*a*) ἐκβάλλει αὐτόν, DΔ 33–69.
(*b*) αὐτὸν ἐκβάλλει, ℵABL rell.

The order in (*b*) is somewhat unusual, though relatively commoner in Mk. than in Mt. or Luke. See 3[6. 11. 12] 5[4] 11[3. 18] 12[13. 34] 14[65] 16[7].

V.[13] (1) (*a*) ἐν τῇ ἐρήμῳ, ℵABDL 13 33 346 Boh: Orig Eus.
(*b*) ἐκεῖ KΠ 1 69 124 131 209 al[15] Syr-sin Arm.
(*c*) ἐκεῖ ἐν τῇ ἐρήμῳ, Δ unc[9] rel Syr-vg.

Here (*a*) is apparently the original reading. The repetition εἰς τὴν ἐρ., ἐν τῇ ἐρ. is thoroughly Marcan; cf. v.[16]. It is interesting to notice that Mt. keeps εἰς τὴν ἐρ. and Lk. ἐν τῇ ἐρ.

(*b*) is a substitute for (*a*) to avoid the repetition.

(*c*) is a simple conflation of (*a*) and (*b*).

The only alternative is to regard (*c*) as a reduplication of the regular Marcan type (*e.g.* ὀψίας δὲ γενομένης ὅτε ἔδυ ὁ ἥλιος), of which (*a*) and (*b*) are alternative redactions. But Mark's pleonasms are never, we think, weakly tautological, as this would be; *e.g.* in 5[11] ἐκεῖ πρὸς τῷ ὄρει, the second clause brings out a fresh and important feature in the scene; cf. v.[28].

(2) τεσσ- ἡμ., ℵBL 33: Orig Eus.
ἡμ. τεσσ., ADΔ rell = Mt. Lk. without variant.

V.[14] (1) καὶ μετά, BD[gr] a (c) Boh ?
μετὰ δέ, ℵAL rell.
See on v.[6].

(2) τὸ εὐαγγέλιον, om. τῆς βασιλείας, ℵBL 1 28 33 69 209 b c ff[2] Syr-sin Boh Arm.
Add AD rell Lat-vg a f ff[1] g[1. 2] Syr-vg Æth.

τὸ εὐαγγέλιον is used without further definition 5 times in Mk. (cf. Ac 15[7]). In 1[1] Ἰησ. Χρ. is added. In Mt. εὐαγ. occurs 4 times, 3 times defined by τῆς βασιλείας. εὐαγ. is not found in Lk. or John. The full phrase τὸ εὐ. τ. βασ. τ. θεοῦ is not found anywhere else. It is most likely that τ. βασ. came in from Mt. assisted by its recurrence in v.[15]. No good reason can be given to explain its omission, if it were genuine. The phrase ἡ βασ. τ. θεοῦ is constant (14 times) in Mk., and never seems to have provoked alteration.

(3) (*a*) καὶ λέγων, BLΔ unc[3] 1 33 69 rel a b ff[1] g[2] Lat-vg Boh Syr-vg-hcl.
(*b*) λέγων, ℵ[a]AD unc[8] cu[30] f ff[2] g[1] Go.
(*c*) Om. ℵ* c mt Syr-sin : Orig.

This is a difficult case. It is surprising how many of the various readings in Mk. involve the insertion or omission or change of λέγων. In some cases the insertion is clearly due to assimilation, 9[7] 11[9] 14[4] 15[34]. In others the word is omitted or changed because it seemed bald or pleonastic, 1[7] 6[25] 8[28] 10[49] 11[31] 12[14]. The aberrant text is almost uniformly supported by D, some MSS of Lat-vet, and some members of the 'Ferrar Group.'

In 3 cases besides this, 1[25] 2[12] 15[4], no certain decision is possible. In 2 of these, 1[25] 15[4], ℵ is the chief authority for omission. It is difficult to account for the change of (*a*) either into (*b*) or (*c*) if it be genuine. (*a*) is also open to suspicion from Mt 4[17].

The asyndeton in (*b*) might have led to (*a*) and (*c*) as independent simplifications (cf. 1[40]). But it is harsh even for Mark.

(*c*) might have caused difficulty, because v.[15] can hardly be regarded as merely epexegetic of τὸ εὐαγγέλιον τῆς βασιλείας.

V.[15] πεπλήρωνται οἱ καιροί, D a b c ff[2] g[1] mt, probably due to the association in thought of passages like Lk 21[24] and esp. Eph 1[10], the singular seeming too tame.

V.[16] (1) καὶ παράγων, ℵBDL 13 33 69 124 346 Latt Boh Arm Syr-hcl-mg.
περιπατῶν δέ, AΔ rell Syrr = Mt.
For δέ see note on v.[6].
παράγων recurs in 2[14] (= Mt 9[9]) and 15[21]; cf. Mt 9[27] 20[30], Jn 9[1].

It is never found in Luke. He has no strict par. here. In both the other cases he avoids it. There seems no reason why περιπατῶν should have been changed, if it were original.

(2) Σίμωνα, D 28 69 124 346 add τόν.
See note v.[6].

(3) (*a*) Σίμωνος, ℵBLM al a Boh Arm.
(*b*) τοῦ Σίμωνος, AE[2]Δ 1 69 al[20]. See on v.[6].
(*c*) αὐτοῦ, ς DGΓ 33 al vix mu Latt (exc. a) Syr-sin-vg Æth.
(*d*) αὐτοῦ τοῦ Σίμωνος, EFH unc[5] al plus[120] Syr-hcl Go.

(*a*) is here clearly the original reading. The repetition of the subst. is a trick of the Marcan style (see 3[17]). (*c*) is an inevitable 'Western' correction agreeing with Matthew. (*d*) is a simple conflation.

(4) (*a*) ἀμφιβάλλοντας, ℵBL 33.
(*b*) ἀμφιβάλλοντας τὰ δίκτυα, D 13 28 69 124 346 Latt.
(*c*) ἀμφιβάλλοντας ἀμφίβληστρον, AΔ unc[11] Boh Syr-hcl Go.
(*d*) βάλλοντας ἀμφίβληστρον, E[2]MΓΠ[2] al pl Arm = Mt.

Here, again, (*a*) is clearly original. Its full force not being understood (or requiring in translation the express mention of the object), the 'Western' reading (*b*) supplied τὰ δίκτυα from v.[18]. On the other hand, the influence of Mt. suggested (*c*) ἀμφίβληστρον. Finally, by substituting βάλλοντας (*d*), the resemblance to Mt. was made complete.

V.[17] γενέσθαι, om. 1 13 28 69 118 209 al[10] b Syr-sin-vg Æth.
See on v.[11]. Here the omission is helped by text of Mt.

V.[18] (*a*) τὰ δίκτυα, ℵBCL al[10] ff[1] g[2] Lat-vg Boh Arm = Mt.
(*b*) πάντα, D a b c ff[2] = Lk.; cf. 10[28].
Note that D a c have already used δίκτυα in v.[16].
(*c*) τὰ δίκτυα αὐτῶν, A unc[12] al pl f g[1] Syrr Æth Go.
Notice a similar addition in vv.[19. 22] etc.

V.[19] (*a*) ὀλίγον, BDL 1 28 118 124 131 209 2[pe] a b ff[2] g[1] Boh Syr-vg (sin).
(*b*) ἐκεῖθεν, ℵ* = Mt.
(*c*) ὀλίγον ἐκεῖθεν, ℵ[c] 33.
(*d*) ἐκεῖθεν ὀλίγον, AC unc[12] al pl c f ff[1] g[1.2] Syr-hcl Arm Go.

Here there is no doubt of the genuineness of ὀλίγον. ἐκεῖθεν seems to have come in from Matthew. The tendency to omit ἐκεῖθεν is very slight in the Gospels, and confined to quite insignificant MSS, exc. in Jn 11[54].

(*c*) and (*d*) represent independent conflations of (*a*) and (*b*).

V.[20] ἀπῆλθον ὀπίσω αὐτοῦ, ℵABC rell Syrr.
ἠκολούθησαν αὐτῷ, D Latt Boh = Mt. ; cf. v.[18].

ἀπερχ. ὀπίσω is a remarkable, apparently unique phrase (Jn 12[19] is no true parallel), which has suffered assimilation. Perh. a Syriasm; but ἀκολ. is a common word, not wont to provoke alterations.

V.[21] (1) (*a*) εἰσπορεύονται, ℵABC rel d.
(*b*) εἰσπορεύεται, 1 6 22 71 121 al pauc.
(*c*) εἰσπορευόμενος, Orig (c) (e).
(*d*) εἰσεπορεύοντο, D[gr] 33 (61) (a b f).

A reading worth looking at. At first sight (*a*) seems entirely natural, and we wonder why it should have caused any trouble. Then we notice the sequence of verbs, ἀπῆλθον, εἰσπορεύονται, ἐδίδασκεν. The subject of no two of them is the same, though they are linked by καί, but in genuine Marcan fashion the reader is trusted to infer the subject of each himself.

Again the sequence of tenses, an historic present, characteristic of Mk., between an Aor. and an Imperfect. (*b*) and (*c*) are independent attempts to smooth over the change of subject, (*d*) assimilates the tenses.

(2) (*a*) τοῖς σάββασιν εἰσελθὼν εἰς τὴν συναγωγὴν ἐδίδασκεν, ABD rell Latt (exc. c) Syr-hcl.
(*b*) εἰσελθὼν τοῖς σαβ. ἐδίδασκεν εἰς τὴν συναγ., 33 124.
(*c*) τοῖς σάββασιν ἐδίδασκεν εἰς τὴν συναγ., ℵL 28 346 2[pe] : Orig.
(*d*) ἐδίδασκεν ἐν τοῖς σάββασιν εἰς τὴν συναγ., C Boh Syr-sin-vg.
(*e*) τοῖς σάββασιν εἰς τὴν συναγ. ἐδίδασκεν, Δ 69.
(*f*) et ingrediens cum eis sabb. in synag. Capharnaum docebat populum c.
Note that Syr-sin omits καὶ εἰσ. εἰς Καφ.

This is a strange case of confusion affecting the simplest of sentences. The omission of εἰσελθών, which is common to (*c*) (*d*) and (*e*), produces a reading which at first sight seems attractive. It is short and vigorous. And the pregnant use of εἰς might easily have led to the insertion of εἰσελθών. On the other hand, the group ℵCLΔ, which supports the omission, is, the present writer believes, in Mark typically 'Alexandrian,' in Dr. Hort's sense of the term. They exhibit constantly a type of readings quite their own, which, though always interesting, rarely succeed in establishing their claim to preserve the original text. The most favourable examples are 3[6. 7] 4[22. 28] 11[11] 15[1. 44]. Here it is worth noticing that in (*f*) *ingrediens* may stand either for εἰσπορευόμενος or εἰσελθών. And it is possible that the repetition may have given offence to the linguistic sense of the Alexandrians, and have led to the dropping of εἰσελθών. Both words are well established in Mark's vocabulary. For though πορεύεσθαι never occurs (outside 16[9-21]) exc. perhaps in 9[30], εἰσπορ. is found 8 times.

Nor is Mk. fond of the pregnant use of εἰς. 1⁹ 1³⁹ (2¹ *v.l.*) 13⁹·¹⁶ 14⁹ are the only examples; and even κηρύσσειν εἰς (1³⁹ 14⁹) hardly justifies διδάσκειν εἰς.

The larger omission in Syr-sin may well be due to the difficulty of supposing that the work from which Simon had been called (v.¹⁶) lay at any distance from his home (v.²⁹).

(3) αὐτοὺς *post* ἐδίδ., D (Latt) Syr-hcl Arm Æth Go. Probably from v.²².

There is no difficulty in the absolute use of διδάσκειν, which occurs fairly often in all the Gospels, and generally causes no trouble. Mt 4²³ is the only parallel. Curiously enough, in Mt 21²³ 26⁵⁵ Lk 23⁵ some auth. omit διδάσκειν altogether. Mark is never tired of emphasizing this aspect of our Lord's activity. In 9 cases (out of 17) the word is not paralleled either in Matthew or Luke.

V.²² καὶ *ante* οὐχ, om. D*b c d e.
Cf. v.¹⁴ (3) (*b*).

V.²³ (1) εὐθὺς *post* καί, ℵBL 1 33 131 209 Boh: Orig. Om. ACDΔ rell.
Cf. on v.¹⁰ (1). It is not found in Lk 4³³.

Here the word would be specially liable to alteration, as it expresses simply the suddenness of the interruption, without reference to any definite point of time.

(2) αὐτῶν *post* συναγωγῇ, om. DL 72 b c e ff² g¹ Boh.

The presence of the word is remarkable. It has no antecedent. συναγ. is regularly defined in Mt., but very rarely in Mark or Luke. Only Mk 1²³·³⁹, Lk 4¹⁵ (where as here D a b l om.). But there is no trace of any tendency to supply αὐτῶν mechanically with συναγ. in either Mark or Luke. Lat-vg in Lk 13¹⁰ is an instructive exception. So it is unlikely that it has come in here from Matthew. On the other hand, Mark has no quite similar case (exc. 9⁴⁸, where αὐτῶν has come in from LXX) of an indefinite αὐτῶν. It is possible that it may represent Mark's transformation of what on St. Peter's lips was 'our' synagogue.

V.²⁴ (1) Ἔα om. ℵBD 157 2ᵖᵉ Latt Boh Syr-sin-vg Æth.
Ins. (A) CLΔ rell. Syr-hcl Arm Go: Orig Eus=Lk 4³⁴ (where as here D cu⁴ Lat-vet Boh Syr-sin-hier Æth om.).

Another 'Alexandrian' reading, this time adopted by the 'Syrian' Text, against the 'Neutral' and the 'Western.' Granted that the 'Western' authority here must be discounted because of its behaviour in Lk 4³⁴, still the 'Neutral' reading is preferable because it alone explains the phenomena in the two passages taken together. There seems no reason why Ἔα (however it is to be understood) should have caused trouble. All is simple, if we suppose that the 'Alexandrian' and 'Syrian' texts here assimilated Mark to Luke, while conversely the 'Western' assimilated Luke to Mark.

(2) οἴδαμεν, ℵLΔ Boh Arm Æth: Tert Irenⁱⁿᵗ Orig Eus.
οἶδα, ABCD rell Latt Syrr=Lk 4³⁴ (where only Arm has pl.).

Neither reading has any intrinsic difficulty. It is simply a question whether the Alexandrian Text introduced the pl. in consequence of ἡμῖν (cf. ᾔδεισαν, v.³⁴), or whether the rest assimilated Mark to Luke. The fact that the Alexandrians omitted to insert the corresponding change in Luke is not a fatal objection to the first hypothesis.

V.²⁵ (1) ἀπ' for ἐξ, HL 33 cu¹⁶ c f g¹=Lk.

See on v.¹⁰. ἐκ is habitual in cases of possession in Mark. In these cases it is never retained either by Matthew or Luke.

(2) (*a*) τοῦ ἀνθρώπου for αὐτοῦ and + πνεῦμα ἀκάθαρτον, D (8ᵖᵉ) Latt (exc. f) (Go Æth).
Go Æth add πν. ἀκ. but read αὐτοῦ. 8ᵖᵉ τὸ πν. τὸ ἀκ.
(*b*) ℵABCLΔ rell: Orig Syr-sin read αὐτοῦ without πν. ἀκ.=Lk.

Here we have to balance the chance that (*b*) has arisen out of (*a*) by assimilation to Luke, against the chance that (*a*) has arisen out of (*b*) by assimilation to 5⁸. (*a*), as 5⁸ shows, is thoroughly Marcan; but the evidence for it, as our experience even in these few verses is enough to suggest, is far from trustworthy. Again, if we may allow any weight to our provisional hypothesis as to the relation between Luke and Mark, there is no reason to suppose that Luke would have modified (*a*) if his text of Mark had contained it. In 8²⁹ (=Mk 5⁸) he retains the words, though putting them into the *oratio obliqua*. His agreement with Mark in these verses, 4³³⁻³⁵ = Mk 1²³⁻²⁶, is exceptionally close. There is no par. in Matthew.

V.²⁶ (1) The whole verse reads as follows in D:—
καὶ ἐξῆλθεν τὸ πνεῦμα τὸ ἀκάθαρτον σπαράξας αὐτὸν καὶ κράξας φωνῇ μεγάλῃ ἐξῆλθεν ἀπ' αὐτοῦ.

With this e agrees (only omitting τὸ ἀκάθαρτον), and ff² (only transposing σπαρ. αὐτ. with τὸ πν. τὸ ἀκ.).

It is difficult not to believe that this exhibits a conflation of two readings: (*a*) καὶ ἐξῆλθεν τὸ πν. τὸ ἀκ. σπαράξας αὐτὸν καὶ κράξας φωνῇ μεγάλῃ, with (*b*) the reading in the text. Some such conflation must also underlie the reading of D in v.³⁴. (*a*) might have arisen out of (*b*) by free assimilation to Mk 9²⁶, where also we find the masc. καὶ κράξας καὶ πολλὰ σπαράξας ἐξῆλθεν.

(2) κράξαν is read by AC(D) rell.
φωνῆσαν, ℵBL 33: Orig.

Neither phrase is objectionable in itself. φων. φ. μεγ. is found in Lk 23⁴⁶, Ac 16²⁸, but not in contexts likely to have suggested themselves here. κράζω, on the other hand, is constantly used of the cries of the possessed, and κράξας φ. μ. occurs in Mk 5⁷.

(3) ἀπ' is read for ἐξ by C(D)ΔM 33 Latt.
See on v.²⁵.

V.²⁷ (1) (*a*) αὐτούς, ℵB (b e ff² q).
(*b*) πρὸς ἑαυτούς, ACDΔ unc⁹ al⁹⁰.
(*c*) πρὸς αὐτούς, GLS rell verss.

It is difficult to find any test to enable us to judge between these readings. The reciprocal use of πρὸς ἑαυτ. is characteristic of Mk 9¹⁰ 11³¹ 12⁷ 14⁴ 16³, besides *v.l.* 9¹⁴·¹⁶·³³ 10²⁶. It is not found in Matthew. It occurs in Lk 20⁵ (=Mk) 22²³ (*v.l.* 20¹⁴=Mk), and in Jn 12¹⁹. On the other hand, ℵB exhibit no special animus against it. They seem clearly right on the three other occasions (9³³ 10²⁶, Lk 20¹⁴), where they combine to attest an alternative reading. συνζητεῖν is used absolutely in 12²⁸ and Lk 24¹⁵. The construction of Mk 9¹⁰ is ambiguous. In 9¹⁴·¹⁶ the true reading is clearly πρὸς αὐτούς, though here ℵ in each case reads ἑαυτ. These facts, so far as they go, are in favour of (*a*), as is the fact that some of the authorities for πρός (ACE* MΔ² al²⁰) give what is perhaps a further sign of the influence of Lk 4³⁶ by reading λέγοντες for λέγοντας. αὐτούς has a real point (cf. on αὐτῶν in v.²³) if it indicates a distinction between the circle immediately round our Lord, and that part of the congregation whose astonishment found vent in the words that follow.

(2) (*a*) τί ἐστιν τοῦτο; διδαχὴ καινὴ κατ' ἐξουσίαν, ℵBL 33 (1 118 131 2ᵖᵉ al³ +αὕτη) Boh.
(*b*) τίς ἡ διδαχὴ ἐκείνη ἡ καινὴ αὕτη ἡ ἐξουσία ὅτι, D (evv³ Latt).
(*c*) τί ἐστιν τοῦτο; τίς ἡ διδαχὴ ἡ καινὴ αὕτη ὅτι κατ' ἐξουσίαν, (A)CΔ rel (A τίς ἡ κ. αὐ. διδ.) (69 τίς ἡ κ. διδ. αὐ.).

Note that the Latin renderings are very various.

They agree with D in leaving out *τί ἐστιν τοῦτο*; Some omit *καινή*. Most, if not all, may represent *κατ' ἐξουσίαν*, none exc. 'd,' *ἐξουσία*.

The simplest solution is to regard (*a*) as the original reading; it is vigorous and vivid, and its abruptness might easily offend. (*b*) would then be a 'Western' paraphrase, (*c*) a 'Syrian' conflation of (*a*), with one or other of the various forms of (*b*).

V.[28] (1) *καὶ ἐξῆλθεν*, ℵBCDLΔM 33 al[11].
*ἐξῆλθεν δέ*, A rel.
See on v.[6].

(2) *εὐθύς*, om. ℵ* 1 28 33 131 al[2] b c e ff[2] (g) q Boh Syr-sin Arm Æth.
See on v.[11].

(3) *πανταχοῦ*, ante *εἰς ὁλ.*, ℵ[c]BCL 69 124 b e q Boh.
Om. ℵ* ADΔ rell c f ff[1. 2] g[1. 2] Lat-vg Syr-sin-vg-hcl.

A characteristic pleonasm, part of which is represented in Mt 4[24] *εἰς ὅλην*, part in Lk 4[37] *εἰς πάντα τόπον*. See on v.[13].

(4) (*a*) *τῆς Γαλιλαίας*, ℵ[c]ABCD rell.
(*b*) *τῆς Ἰουδαίας*, ℵ*, cf. Lk 4[44]; but there is no indication in Mk., as there is in Lk., of a use of *Ἰουδαία* to include the whole of Palestine.
(*c*) *τοῦ Ἰορδάνου*, 28; cf. Mt 3[5], Lk 3[3].
(*d*) *ἐκείνην*, s[scr*]; cf. Mt 14[35], *v.l.* Mk 6[55].

24. The facts are now before us. We can judge for ourselves the kind of variations that are to be met with on every page of the Gospels, and the kind of considerations by which we can attempt to discriminate between alternative readings, before we are in a position to assign a special value to any particular authority, or group of authorities, over the rest. It is true that we have in one or two particulars anticipated results that must be verified by further examination. We have treated certain groups of authorities, which even within the limits of this passage can be seen to mark themselves off from time to time from all the rest, as approximately constant units, and we have given distinctive names to the particular sets of readings which they attest. The fact that the authorities do exhibit this tendency to fall into groups is now generally admitted, and even the Traditionalists are beginning to see that a careful study of these groups is the first step towards the understanding of the history of the changes through which the text, taken as a whole, has passed. They point out, however, quite rightly, that the term 'text' as applied to these groups must be used with caution. It does not necessarily imply, *e.g.*, that there ever existed an edition of the 'Western Text,' including all the variants that we should be prepared to class as 'Western,' and excluding all their rivals, in the sense in which Westcott and Hort include, with a few exceptions, all the 'Neutral' readings; or, again, in which Mr. Miller prints the Traditional Text. No critic is likely to take serious exception to the definition which Mr. Miller puts forward of the sense in which he is himself prepared to use the word. 'What is properly meant,' he writes,* 'is that of the variant readings of the words of the Gospels which, from whatever cause, grew up more or less all over the Christian Church, so far as we know some have family likenesses of one kind or another, and may be traced to a kindred source.'

25. More serious exception has been taken by Dr. Salmon to the names which Dr. Hort gave to the different groups. He calls them 'question-begging.' But it is by no means easy to see the exact point of his criticism. The names are as free as possible from any invidious connotation, differing in this respect *toto cœlo* from the name 'Neologian,' which Mr. Miller regards as a fair description of the text of any editor who rejects a 'Traditional' reading. They are all descriptive of certain clearly marked and carefully defined characteristics of the groups to which they are applied. The 'Syrian' Text is so called because its most constant support is found, as we have seen, in the writings of Fathers connected directly with the Church of Antioch. An objection may no doubt lie against it, because it must suggest to an uninstructed reader that the chief support for these readings is to be found in the Syriac versions; but in itself it is purely descriptive, and implies no judgment on the genuineness of the readings connoted by it.

26. 'Western' again, as Dr. Hort himself pointed out, is an inadequate title for readings which have early Greek, Syriac, and Egyptian support, as well as Latin. But he retained it because it was established by long usage, and there seemed no sufficient reason for obscuring the continuity of the development of the science of Textual Criticism by any unnecessary change in the accepted terminology. The name as he defined it connoted nothing more than the fact that this group of readings had first attracted the attention of scholars by the support that it receives in the great Græco-Latin MSS and in the Latin versions. There was nothing in the name to imply that no readings in this group could be regarded as genuine.

27. The name 'Alexandrian' was chosen simply because the authorities supporting it are, so far as we can judge, exclusively confined to Alexandria. It had, no doubt, already been applied to all non-Western pre-Syrian readings by Griesbach. Neither ℵ nor B was, however, accessible to Griesbach when he made his classification. And, now that in the light of the new evidence a further subdivision of Griesbach's Alexandrian family has become possible, no serious difficulty is likely to arise from appropriating to one division the name which belonged to the whole class before its elements were fully differentiated.

28. It would be difficult to devise a more scrupulously colourless name than the last on our list—the name 'Neutral.' It was chosen to express the fact that the authorities supporting it were habitually found in opposition to the 'distinctive' readings of both the 'Western' and the 'Alexandrian' groups. It is true that these 'distinctive' readings are, from the nature of the case, in the great majority of instances corruptions that have affected one particular line of transmission; so a group that has escaped them must be, so far as these corruptions are concerned, a relatively pure text. But there is nothing in the name to imply that all the readings attested by it must necessarily be genuine, or to exclude the possibility that the rival authorities may in any individual case have preserved the genuine text. To adopt the name 'Early Alexandrian' for this group, as Dr. Salmon suggests, on the strength of the number of names connected with Alexandria which appear among its most prominent constituents, would obscure the fact, to which attention must be called later, that the attestation to it is by no means confined to Alexandria, besides obscuring the clearly marked distinction between this group and the one last described. It is difficult, therefore, to see what question any one of these names as defined by Dr. Hort can be supposed to beg.

29. It will be noticed that the points suggested for consideration in the notes, as likely to afford a presumption either for or against the genuineness of the different variants, are exclusively of an internal

* *Trad. Text*, p. 118. The light thrown on the extent to which Mr. Miller is prepared to believe in the existence of 'editions' in very early times by his note (*l.c.* p. 22) should not be overlooked.

character. This limitation is deliberate, because at this stage of the investigation our purpose must be simply to determine which reading in each case has the best claim to be regarded as original, apart from any preconceived theory as to the weight to be attached to the authorities by which it is attested. Some minds are, no doubt, constitutionally impatient of this class of considerations, and profoundly sceptical of any conclusions which are based on them. And, no doubt, there would be far less room for difference of opinion, and far less need of patient study and careful and exact scholarship in Textual Criticism, if we could start with some external standard, and so dispense with internal considerations altogether. Nothing, for instance, can be easier, if one may assume that the mass of authorities must always be right, than to prove that a numerically insignificant group of dissentients must be worthless, just because the evidence of 'the many' can always, *ex hypothesi*, be described as 'overwhelming.' But when the precise question at issue is the relative weight to be attached to the rival groups, no amount of erudition can conceal the fact that a demonstration constructed on these lines has no logical value; it does 'beg the question.' It is well, therefore, to realize from the outset that the element of personal judgment can never be eliminated from the processes of Textual Criticism. A clear realization of this fact is necessary if we are to understand the importance of a careful study of the laws which must regulate the use of the critical faculty, and of the different methods which other workers in the same field have found useful as safeguards to minimize the dangers arising from unconscious caprice or personal idiosyncrasy. The criteria for testing *the internal evidence of Readings* are of two kinds: *Intrinsic Probability*, or 'the consideration of what an author is likely to have written,' and *Transcriptional Probability*, or 'the consideration of what a copyist is likely to have made him seem to have written.' No doubt, taken separately, they are, as Mr. Miller calls them,* 'weak pillars.' But, when they combine in favour of any variant, their testimony is overwhelming. Such cases are indeed comparatively rare. They are numerous enough, however, to enable us to form, first a provisional, and then a more carefully balanced estimate of the characteristic excellences and defects of each authority with which we have to deal. They enable us—that is, in cases where the internal evidence of the readings is ambiguous—to appeal to *the internal evidence of the Documents* by which the different variants are attested. But even this is not enough. The same document may be of very different value in different parts.

30. We have therefore still to inquire what methods are available when, as in the case of most of the MSS of the NT, whether uncial or cursive, the documents are of a very mixed character, and considerations derived from internal evidence alone are in consequence unusually precarious.†

It is at this point that the real importance of *the principle of Genealogy* comes full into view. It is based on the obvious fact that our documents, to quote the words of Dr. Hort to which Mr. Miller has called special attention, 'are all fragments, usually casual and scattered fragments, of a genealogical tree of transmission, sometimes of vast extent and intricacy.' It is true, as Mr. Miller points out, that the analogy with human relationship which the word suggests is not complete. There is a variability in the transmission of acquired characteristics in human heredity which is lacking under normal conditions in derivation by a process of copying. But this difference is all in favour of the textual critic, and enables him to tread securely even in cases where the normal conditions of transmission are disturbed by the presence of 'mixture,' *i.e.* when the scribe at work on a particular MS embodies either constantly or occasionally readings derived from more than one exemplar. For the process depends on the principle, which it is encouraging to notice that Mr. Miller accepts without reserve, that 'identity of reading implies identity of origin.'

31. The consequences that follow from the acceptance of this principle and the careful application of this method are far-reaching. Its chief importance lies in this, that it opens a field for strictly historical investigation into facts which can be brought to definite tests. These tests no doubt require the greatest delicacy and skill in their application, but the facts are in themselves concrete and quite independent of subjective considerations.

It has, however, one or two subsidiary consequences to which we may call attention before we pass on. We may notice, first, that it justifies at once the treatment of groups of documents, which are found constantly associated in the support of the same variants, as approximately constant units: to this point attention has already been called. It also suggests the explanation of one of the paradoxes of Textual Criticism which has puzzled Dr. Salmon (p. 55). It is certainly strange that the evidence of two witnesses should be lowered in value by being associated with, rather than opposed by, a third; that, for instance, more weight should be assigned by Dr. Hort in the Pauline Epistles to $B+D_2-G_3$, than to $B+D_2+G_3$. As long as each document is regarded as an independent witness, it is clearly impossible to assign a negative value to its evidence. But when we realize that each document has a composite character determined by its ancestry, and that in consequence we have to determine in each case which strain is represented in any particular reading before we can estimate the value to be assigned to its evidence, the paradox disappears. The value of any group is simply the value of the element common to all the members composing it. Thus B in the Pauline Epistles is largely 'Neutral' with a decided 'Western' element: $D_2$ is Western with a decided 'Neutral' element: $G_3$ is almost purely 'Western' with a Syrian admixture. The combination $B+D_2$ may therefore be either Neutral or Western, both elements being present, though in different proportions, in each document. And the reading attested by $G_3$ can be either Western or Syrian. But a reading supported by $B+D_2+G_3$ in opposition to all other authorities must be distinctively 'Western.'

32. One further remark may be allowed before we leave this paradox. It is, no doubt, tempting to illustrate different stages in the critical process by comparison with the everyday procedure of the Law Courts, especially when one's object is to interest Englishmen in the minutiæ of a dry and technical study. But the habit is a dangerous one. The legal and the scientific methods are fundamentally distinct, and, in consequence, serious fallacies, as this paradox shows, may lurk even in the most specious analogy. But the worst effect of yielding to it is that it tends insensibly to merge the critic himself in the advocate, and to make him 'the champion of an opinion,' for whom

* *Trad. Text*, p. 238; cf. Hort's *Summary*, ed. minor, p. 543.

† The mixed character of the text in the uncials will be obvious from the study of any *App. Crit.* If any one wishes to realize the mixed character of the text even in the cursives, he cannot do better than study Mr. Hoskier's admirably thorough examination of the codex 604. The only surprising thing is that he should imagine that the facts he has observed disturb any of the results at which Dr. Hort arrived. Compare also the introduction to Scrivener's c llation of 20 MSS with Tregelles' remarks upon it (Horne, *Intr.* p. 145).

the value of an argument is measured by its immediate effectiveness rather than 'the single-hearted lover of truth,' who knows that there is no influence against which he must guard more resolutely than the influence of the popular prejudices which tend to warp his own judgment, and which respond most readily to a rhetorical appeal.

33. Dr. Salmon suggests in another place (p. 43) that the dogmatic tone of WH's *Introduction* is due to the influence of the established Cambridge method of mathematical teaching. A closer parallel would seem to be provided by ordinary text-books in any department of Natural Science. We expect to find in them a description of the methods, and a classified record of the results, of an investigation into a series of phenomena which the student is no doubt expected to take on trust, but only until he has repeated the experiment and verified the result by his own observation. The extraordinary insight and skill in classification which the *Introduction* reveals, reflect the expert botanist more than the mathematician.

34. The last consequence of the acceptance of the principle of 'Genealogy' to which we wish to call attention, is the light that it throws on the radical unsoundness of any system of Textual Criticism which bases itself directly on a numerical calculation of the attesting documents, before the significance of the numbers has been checked and interpreted by descent. It is, no doubt, a remarkable fact that one of the types of text which were current side by side in the fourth century is represented to-day in extant MSS by a progeny 'like the stars of heaven in multitude';* while the representatives of the others are few and for the most part fragmentary. But the principle of Genealogy reminds us that, however numerous the progeny of any MS may be, their united value can never be higher than that of their common original. And it has yet to be seen whether that common original can, in the case of distinctively Syrian readings, be traced back beyond the 4th century. The facts which we have already noticed in the history of the text of one of the Pauline Epistles prove that the answer to that question cannot be taken for granted. We must not forget that, if 'identity of reading' implies 'identity of origin,' identity in a demonstrably wrong reading, except in the case of a primitive error, implies a common original later than the autograph. And in such cases it becomes of primary importance to determine as precisely as possible the date of the common original.

35. We can now pass on to consider what light is thrown by our examination of the variants in Mk $1^{1-28}$ on the character of the witnesses by which they are supported. We must begin with those variants that are the exclusive property of the Traditional Text, and by which in consequence the value of the authorities supporting it can be most effectively tested. We have included provisionally as belonging to it all the readings which are attested by none of the five MSS, ℵBCD or L. Further examination will show which, if any, of these readings have a claim to be regarded as belonging also to one or other of the alternative texts. Sixteen examples occur. The points affected are in almost every case extremely trivial, but they are none the less significant as indications of documentary relationship.

(1) V.[1] om. *τοῦ* before *θεοῦ*.
(2) V.[2] *τοῖς προφήταις* for *'Ησ. τ. προφ.*
(3) V.[2] add *ἔμπροσθέν σου*.
(4) V.[4] *βαπτίζων ἐν τῇ ἐρήμῳ καὶ κηρύσσων*. Conflate.
(5) V.[5] transpose *πάντες*.

* See *Trad. Text*, p. 233.

(6) V.[9] transpose *ὑπὸ 'Ιωάννου*.
(7) V.[10] *ἀπό* for *ἐκ*.
(8) V.[11] *ᾧ* for *σοί*.
(9) V.[13] *ἐκεῖ ἐν τῇ ἐρήμῳ*. Conflate.
(10) V.[16] *περιπατῶν δέ* for *καὶ παράγων*.
(11) V.[16] *αὐτοῦ τοῦ Σίμωνος*. Conflate.
(12) V.[16] *βάλλοντας ἀμφίβληστρον* for *ἀμφιβάλλοντας*.
(13) V.[18] add *αὐτῶν*.
(14) V.[19] *ἐκεῖθεν ὀλίγον*. Conflate.
(15) V.[27] *τί ἐστιν τοῦτο; τίς ἡ διδαχὴ ἡ καινὴ αὕτη ὅτι κατ' ἐξουσίαν*. Conflate.
(16) V.[28] *δέ* for *καί*.

36. Now, it is surely remarkable that in no single one of these cases does the internal evidence, taken as a whole, point unequivocally in favour of the Traditional reading. In many cases it seems to be definitely adverse. Again, it is surely remarkable that even in this short passage five of the readings, vv.[4. 13. 16. 19. 27], admit of a ready explanation on the supposition that they were produced by combining, with more or less modification, two alternative readings which were at one time current independently. In other words, they suggest the presence of Conflation as a factor in the production of the Traditional Text. This hypothesis is rendered distinctly more probable by the observation which rests on a wide induction of undisputed facts, that the normal tendency of scribes in all ages is towards addition and not subtraction.* The exceptions to this rule, which spring from purely accidental causes, *e.g.* 'Homoeoteleuton,' are clearly not in point here. Nor, again, can we logically give any weight here to the charge of a deep-seated tendency to omission brought against the scribes of all our oldest authorities: because again and again the only evidence adduced in support of it is that the text they attest is habitually shorter than the Traditional, and we are looking for an assurance that the Traditional Text itself is free from addition.

It is true that there is evidence that some scribes, the originators of the 'Western' readings, did in the course of their extraordinarily rash recasting of the text omit a word here and there without introducing an equivalent. But there is no evidence to show that a tendency to omit affected a large proportion of their work. And the common ancestor of ℵ and B was, so far as we can judge, entirely unaffected by 'Western' influence.

37. The suspicion of Conflation is deepened when we indicate to the eye, as has been done in the passage as printed above, the relation in which the Traditional Text stands to the earlier texts out of which on this hypothesis it must have been constructed. The passage certainly illustrates with remarkable vividness the phenomena which Dr. Hort's description would have led us to expect. His words run as follows:—

'To state in a few words the results of examination of the whole body of Syrian readings, distinctive and non-distinctive, the authors of the Syrian Text had before them documents representing at least three earlier forms of text, Western, Alexandrian, and a third. Where they found variation, they followed different procedures in different places. Sometimes they transcribed unchanged the reading of one of the earlier texts, now of this, now of that. Sometimes they in like manner adopted exclusively one of the readings, but modified its form. Sometimes they combined the readings of more than one text in various ways, pruning or modifying them if necessary. Lastly, they introduced many changes of their own where, so far as appears, there was no previous variation. When the circumstances are

* See Tregelles, *The Printed Text of the NT*, p. 184.

fully considered, all these processes must be recognized as natural' (§ 165).

When the whole text has the appearance of being conflate, individual readings combining elements which can be proved to have existed independently are more naturally accounted for on the hypothesis of Conflation than on any other. It would seem impossible to determine *a priori* what proportion of such readings we should expect to find in a passage of any given length. Mr. Miller is probably right when he says, 'I venture to think that, supposing for a moment the theory to be sound, it would not account for any large number of variations, but would at the best only be a sign or symptom found every now and then of the derivation attributed to the Received Text.'* This is exactly the impression that an attentive reader would receive from Dr. Hort's carefully measured language in reference to them.†

38. The last point to be examined in regard to these readings is the presence or absence of ante-Nicene Patristic support. What has already been said on the principle of Genealogy will put us at the right point of view for appreciating the significance of this part of our investigation. For it is clear that, unless we can discover some evidence external to the MSS for locating and dating the readings contained in them, we shall find it difficult, if not impossible, to make sure of the direction actually taken by the different streams of textual change. The primary source of such evidence is provided by fully verified and tested Patristic quotations.

39. We must not, however, hide from ourselves the difficulty of the task. Even at the risk of some repetition, we must remind ourselves that it is always necessary, in cases where the text of a Father appears to agree with the Traditional Text, to make allowance for the possibility that that agreement would disappear if we had access to his autograph, even though there is no variation in the printed editions or in any of the extant MSS of his work. No conclusions can be based on such evidence unless the correctness of the reading is guaranteed by the context.

40. Again, in a passage like the one before us (Mk $1^{1-28}$), which has parallels throughout either in one or in both of the other Synoptics, and in which a considerable proportion of the variants suggest the influence of assimilation, it is clearly unwise to build any conclusions on a Patristic reference to the text in its assimilated form, unless the writer gives us independent means of determining the particular Gospel from which he is quoting.

41. Again, in applying the knowledge derived from such evidence, after it has passed all our tests, to the interpretation of the facts of textual history as indicated by the groups into which the MSS are observed to fall, we have to bear in mind that it is impossible on MS evidence alone to determine precisely what readings, other than 'conflate,' are to be classed as distinctively Traditional—*i.e.* are to be regarded on the Critical hypothesis as having originated with the 'Syrian' revisers, and not merely been adopted by them from some pre-existent text. For, as the evidence of the Latin, Syriac, and Egyptian versions shows, the preservation of at least the 'Western' types of text in Greek MSS is incomplete and fragmentary. So that it is practically certain that some of the readings which are at present attested only by MSS of a markedly Traditional type are not really the exclusive property of the Traditional Text. They must have belonged also, at one time, to one or other of its rivals. We must be ready, therefore, to make allowance for the possibility that some of the readings in our provisional list, and in any other list drawn up on the same rough-and-ready principle, may be 'Western,' 'Alexandrian,' or even 'Neutral,' as well as 'Syrian.'

42. Ante-Nicene evidence is quoted by Tischendorf or Tregelles on one side or the other in 7 out of the 15 readings in our list. In the first case (v.[1]), the insertion of τοῦ before θεοῦ, the ante-Nicene evidence disappears on close examination. The passages in Irenæus which contain the clause are extant only in Latin, and are therefore indecisive. The clause is wanting in the one passage where we have access to the Greek of Irenæus, and in Origen. We may note, however, that Severianus (fl. 400) and Victor of Antioch (d. 430) both omit the article. Cyril Alex. (d. 444) is the earliest authority quoted in support of it. The second reading τοῖς προφήταις for 'Ησ. τῷ προφ. finds a place as No. 14 in Mr. Miller's select 30 (*Trad. Text*, p. 108), and is also discussed at length by Dean Burgon (*Causes of Corruption*, p. 111 ff., cf. *Trad. Text*, App. iv.). So in this case we have the advantage of a full statement of the evidence that can be put forward on behalf of the Traditional reading. It will be instructive to examine this statement in detail.

43. Only a summary of the evidence is given in *Trad. Text*, detailed references being promised in *Causes of Corruption*. In the summary, 6 names appear as supporting τοῖς προφ.: Titus of Bostra, Origen, Porphyry, Irenæus (p. 205), Eusebius, Ambrose. 7 names appear on the other side: Irenæus (p. 191), Origen (*Cels.* ii. 4; *in Joan.* i. 14), Titus of Bostra (*adv. Manich.* iii. 4), Basil (*adv. Eunom.* ii. 15), Serapion, Victorinus of Pettau (*in Apoc. Joh.*), Epiphanius (twice over—the second time with a ref. *adv. Hær.* II. i. 51). When we come to *Causes of Corruption* we are met by a statement that Tischendorf quotes 13 Fathers against the Traditional reading: Irenæus, Origen, Porphyry, Titus, Basil, Serapion, Epiphanius, Severianus, Victor, Eusebius, Victorinus, Jerome, Augustine. We are then told that 'from this list serious deductions must be made. Irenæus and Victor of Antioch are clearly with the Textus Receptus. Serapion, Titus, and Basil do but borrow from Origen, and with his argument reproduce his corrupt text of Mk $1^{2}$. . . . Victorinus and Augustine, being Latin writers, merely quote the Latin version, which is without variety of reading. There remain Origen (the faulty character of whose codices has been remarked upon already), Porphyry the heretic (who wrote a book to convict the Evangelists of mis-statements, and who is therefore scarcely a trustworthy witness), Eusebius, Jerome, and Severianus. Of these, Eusebius and Jerome deliver it as their opinion that the name of "Isaiah" had obtained admission into the text through the inadvertency of copyists. Is it reasonable, on the slender residuum of evidence, to insist that St. Mark has ascribed to Isaiah words

* *Causes of Corruption*, p. 270.

† As curious misapprehensions are current on this point, it may be well to quote the sentences in full, italicizing the significant phrases. The reff. are to paragraphs in the *Introduction.* § 133, 'The clearest evidence . . . is furnished by conflate readings, where they exist; and in the case of some of the primary groupings of the textual documents of the New Testament *they are fortunately not wanting.*' In § 165, already quoted, notice the words, '*Sometimes* they combined the readings of more than one Text in various ways, pruning or modifying them, if necessary.' In § 185, '*Occasionally* also the readings of two of the antecedent Texts were combined by simple or complex adaptations.' We may also compare the language used in the short statement of the principles of Textual Criticism printed at the end of the volume containing the text (p. 548, ed. minor). 'The priority of two at least of the three Texts just noticed to the Syrian Text is further brought to light by the existence of *a certain number* of distinctively Syrian readings, which prove on close examination to be due to a combination of the Western with the Neutral readings.' The number of readings in Mk $1^{1-28}$ that have a claim to be considered as 'conflate' is distinctly larger than this language would have led us to anticipate. But we must not forget that the genealogical antecedents of the component elements are in some cases obscure.

confessedly written by Malachi?' The passage concludes with a lecture on the duty of 'carefulness' and 'honesty.'

44. If, in the light of this statement, we come back to the summary in *Trad. Text*, the result is startling. Of the 6 names quoted on behalf of the TR, the evidence of the first 3 in favour of the rival reading is discussed and discounted. But no hint is given of any justification for the appearance of their names on the opposite side. Of the other 3, Ambrose is left unnoticed; Irenæus, whose name appeared in the summary, like the names of Origen and Titus, on both sides, is boldly claimed exclusively for the TR. Of Eusebius we gather that he is usually quoted in favour of the opposite side, but that he felt the difficulty of that reading so much that he regarded the text as corrupt. (It is difficult to see how he could have failed to refer to a difference of reading among MSS on the point had he been conscious that any such difference existed). A reference to the Latin version of Irenæus is rather a 'slender residuum' from the original 6, even when supplemented by a claim to Victor of Antioch, whose date no doubt excluded his name from the summary. This result, we may notice in passing, does not inspire confidence in the accuracy of the summary, or in the conclusions built on it. But that is not the point immediately before us.* We must turn to a closer examination of the details of the evidence in the light of Dean Burgon's comments upon them.

45. The earliest witness is Irenæus. Three passages in his writings (pp. 187, 191, 205) come up for consideration. Two (pp. 187, 205) are extant only in Latin; but, as Grabe showed (see note in Stieren), there is no reason to question the accuracy of the translation. The reading '*in prophetis*,' for which they vouch, cannot have come in through the Latin version, and it is, besides, strongly, though not quite conclusively, confirmed by the context (p. 205). The passage on p. 191 is, fortunately, extant both in Greek and Latin. The Latin reads '*in Esaia propheta*' with no recorded variant. The Greek is attested in various ways. It is found in an extract from Irenæus preserved by Anastasius

* Mr. Miller's 30 passages are meant to supply materials for comparison between the Patristic evidence to be derived from writers who died before A.D. 400 to the Traditional and the 'Neologian' texts respectively. It is impossible to discover the principle which underlies this selection. He professes to choose passages in which 'evidence is borne on both sides.' But in 8 out of the 30 he can find no Patristic evidence on the 'Neologian' side.

The selection is certainly not regulated by any consideration of the distribution of MS authority. 24 out of the 30 are supported by one or more members of the group ℵBCDL. Nor, again, is any care taken to choose passages where the Patristic evidence is free from the uncertainty caused by the presence of Synoptic parallels. The only element common to all the 30 is that they are printed in thick type by Scrivener in the Cambridge Greek Testament, *i.e.* each of them has, at one time, been adopted by one or more of the critical editions collated at the foot of Scrivener's pages.

It is equally difficult to see the bearing of this evidence on the point at issue. It is true that at the beginning of the chapter a vague reference is made (p. 95) to a statement of Dr. Hort's, and it is assumed at the end that his contentions have been shown to be baseless. But we are left to divine, as best we may, how the collection of reff., reaching to the end of the 4th cent., relating to readings four-fifths of which are obviously not distinctively Syrian, affects Dr. Hort's position that there are no historical signs of the existence of distinctively Syrian readings before the middle of the 3rd cent. There is no excuse for this flagrant *ignoratio elenchi*. Dr. Hort's position was precisely formulated in words which called special attention to the fundamental importance of the fact which he claimed to have observed. The passage reads as follows (*Int.* § 162): 'Before the middle of the third century, at the very earliest, we have no historical signs of the existence of readings, conflate or other, that are marked as distinctively Syrian by the want of attestation from groups of documents which have preserved the other ancient forms of text. This is a fact of great significance, ascertained as it is exclusively by external evidence, and therefore supplying an absolutely independent verification and extension of the results already obtained by comparison of the internal character of readings as classified by conflation.'

of Sinai. Here the reading is certainly ἐν Ἠσ. τῳ προφ. The only recorded variant is ἐν βίβλῳ λόγων Ἠσ. τοῦ προφ. in a Florentine MS containing an extract from Anastasius. This independent confirmation of the reading of the Latin version makes the fact that Irenæus in this passage wrote ἐν Ἠσ. τῷ προφ. practically certain. Nor does it stand alone. The same passage of Irenæus is quoted in an anonymous scholion preserved in Evv. 237, 238, 259 (Matthäi's *d*, *e*, *a*). And in each case, according to Matthäi, the reading is ἐν Ἠσ. τῷ προφ. It is therefore not a little difficult to understand how Dean Burgon, in a note expressly based on a reference to the scholion in Ev. 238, should print '*in the prophets*.' If his translation is based on an independent examination of the MS, it was unkind of him not to give a hint that Matthäi's transcript was in error. If not, we have another illustration of the danger of trusting to printed texts when they agree with TR.

Mk $1^2$ is quoted also in a short introduction to St. Mark, attributed in some MSS to Cyril Alex. and in others to Victor of Antioch, in the same form ἐν Ἠσ. τῷ προφ. printed in Combefis, i. p. 436. It is true that Germanus (Patriarch of Constantinople, A.D. 715), who has drawn on this same passage of Irenæus, writes ἐν τοῖς προφ. But the natural suspicion that he has in this case assimilated the text of his author to the text with which he was himself familiar, is confirmed by the observation that this same Germanus, a few lines earlier, in his extract, writes τοῦ δὲ Ἰησοῦ Χριστοῦ ἡ γέννησις in a quotation by Irenæus of Mt $1^{18}$ in accordance with TR, though, in view of the special stress laid by Irenæus on the point in a well-known passage (p. 204), there can be no doubt that the Latin version '*Christi* autem generatio' preserves the text as Irenæus wrote it.

We may fairly, therefore, claim Irenæus as a witness to both readings in Mk $1^2$. It is, no doubt, strange that he should have gone from one codex to another and back again in less than 20 pages, but a similar phenomenon with regard to the reading in v.[1] shows that something of the kind must have happened. The difficulty, such as it is, would disappear if we might accept Dr. Hort's suggestion (App. *in loc.*) that the whole of the peculiar passage (p. 191) was derived by Irenæus from an earlier writer. As the passage contains the well-known argument proving from 'the nature of things' that the number of Gospels cannot be more or less than four, the conclusion has consequences of wider interest than can attach to the solution of any merely textual problem. If this strange argument was already traditional in the time of Irenæus, it throws back the evidence as to the closing of the Gospel Canon, which is rightly felt to be involved in its very strangeness, into the generation that preceded him.

46. The next authority in point of date is Origen. Tischendorf gives 4 references. Mr. Miller's summary is content with 2. In one passage Origen deals expressly with the problem of the composite quotation. He does not regard the difficulty as serious. He writes ($4^{126}$): δύο προφητείας ἐν διαφόροις εἰρημένας τόποις ὑπὸ δύο προφητῶν εἰς ἓν συνάγων πεποίηκε· καθὼς γέγρ. ἐν Ἠσ. His evidence is discounted by Dean Burgon on the ground that his codices were bad. As this condemnation is based mainly on the fact that his quotations constantly support 'the few' against 'the many,' it need not delay us at this stage. The significant fact for us is that the MSS used by Origen at different periods during the long course of his literary activity (d. 248) in different centres of Church life read uniformly Ἠσ. τῷ προφ.

47. The next witness is Porphyry, the Neo-Platonist philosopher, a leading opponent of Chris-

tianity from the standpoint of philosophic paganism, who endeavoured, among other things, to confute Christians out of their own Gospels. These facts must, of course, be taken into consideration in estimating his evidence, and no doubt they would make him 'scarcely a trustworthy witness' on a question of Christian doctrine. But it is difficult to see that they invalidate his testimony on a simple question of fact. Indeed the character of the work in which the quotation occurs offers the strongest possible guarantee that he found *ἐν Ἠσ. τῷ προφ.* in his copy of the Gospels. It is impossible to suppose that he invented it in order to create a difficulty. The retort to which he would have exposed himself would have been too obvious and too crushing. As it is, it is not easy to see how, if his opponents were familiar with the existence of the alternative reading, they should not have mentioned it in reply. Controversialists find it difficult to resist the temptation to accuse an opponent of corrupting the text, when he follows a reading to which they are unaccustomed. However easy, therefore, it may be, after the approved style of forensic oratory, to discredit the character of this witness, if one find his evidence inconvenient, we have in this instance a strong guarantee that he gives a true report of what he has seen, and the most venerated names in Church history can do no more. Dean Burgon himself has no scruples about appealing to this same extract from Porphyry for evidence in support of a Traditional reading (*Trad. Text*, p. 286). It would not be easy to find a better illustration of the fact that the help to be derived from Patristic quotations in elucidating the course of Textual History has nothing whatever to do with the personal 'respectability' of the writer from whom it is taken. It is determined entirely by the more tangible considerations of his locality and his date.

48. The other authorities quoted on this text are not included in the chronological limits within which our examination is at present confined. So we must not delay upon them, except to notice that, when a later writer embodies in his own work thoughts derived from one of his predecessors, his evidence is not necessarily worthless. If he repeats an argument which deals directly with the difficulty inherent in a particular reading, the adoption of the argument will be evidence of the continued prevalence of the reading. In any case, we shall have a fresh assurance that the text of his predecessor has been accurately preserved. For instance, Victor of Antioch, as preserved in the catena edited by Possinus, adopts Origen's explanation of the difficulty caused by the reading *ἐν Ἠσ. τῷ προφ.* '*ἐπιτεμόμενος οὖν ὁ εὐαγγελιστὴς ὡς ὑπὸ Ἠσαίου εἰρημένας τὰς δύο χρήσεις παρέθηκεν.*' The fact that in the same catena the text of Victor's quotation from St. Mark contains the reading *ἐν τοῖς προφήταις* (*Trad. Text*, p. 285), is therefore only a fresh instance of the necessity for caution in accepting any reading which reproduces the Traditional Text. Again, Basil's words seem to Dean Burgon to reflect Origen. They present also remarkable affinities with Irenæus. In either case, and especially in the latter, the confirmation of his predecessor's text should not be overlooked.*

49. The next point of reading that we have to consider is the presence or absence of *ἔμπροσθέν σου*. The omission is supported by Irenæus. The passage (p. 187) is known only in Latin. But there is evidence in the context to show that the translator is at any rate not mechanically substituting the Latin version, with which he must have been familiar, for the Greek text in front of him. For this is the first of the two passages in which he gives '*in prophetis*,' when the uniform reading of the Latin versions is '*in Esaia propheta*.' We may fairly therefore assume that *ἔμπροσθέν σου* was wanting also in the Greek of Irenæus. Origen in one place ($4^{126}$) calls special attention to the absence of the words from the quotation as given by St. Mark. We are quite justified, therefore, in refusing to accept the reference to St. Mark as printed on the preceding page ($4^{125}$) in support of the inclusion of the words. Of the 2 other passages in Origen quoted in favour of the words, one ($3^{769}$) is really a direct quotation from the prophet, in the other ($1^{389}$) there is nothing in the context to decide whether the words did or did not stand as part of the quotation as Origen made it. The passage in Eus. $^{dem\ 430}$, which is also quoted on the same side, is really indecisive. He gives the quotation at length from the prophet, and then tells us that Mk. makes use of it. He does not write out Mk.'s text at length.

50. In no other case is any ante-Nicene evidence alleged in favour of the Traditional side of any of our 16 readings. In v.$^4$ the 'Western' Text is supported by Eus$^{dem}$. In v.$^5$ Origen $4^{130.\ 126}$ Eus$^{dem}$ are quoted against the TR, and in v.$^9$ Origen and in v.$^{12}$ Origen and Eus$^{dem}$ reappear against it. In 8 out of the 16 no ante-Nicene evidence is alleged on either side.

To sum up our results. The comparative weakness of the *Trad. Text* in ante-Nicene support is obvious at the first glance. The only support it can muster that will stand examination is Irenæus in 2 places out of 3 on v.$^2$, and possibly one passage in Origen on v.$^3$.

51. Before we can decide whether this support is wholly lacking to the 'distinctively Syrian' readings, we shall have to consider more closely the attestation and the internal characteristics of the readings in v.$^2$ and v.$^3$. In regard to v.$^2$, it is certainly remarkable that the reading *ἐν τοῖς προφ.*, if not genuine, must be a deliberate emendation of the text, of a bolder type than the other readings of the group, and quite in the 'Western' spirit. When we add to this that Irenæus is one of the most constant supporters of the 'Western' Text, it will not seem unreasonable to class this reading provisionally as an early 'Western' reading of exceptionally limited circulation, which was afterwards taken up into the 'Syrian' Text. We shall thus cease to regard it as 'distinctively Syrian.' In v.$^3$, if the reading in Orig. $1^{389}$ be accepted, there would be nothing unnatural in classing it as Alexandrian. It is attested by Δ, one of the small group which, as we shall see, have a large Alexandrian element in this Gospel. It also may disappear from the 'distinctively Syrian' list.

So much then for the ante-Nicene evidence. The passages clearly do not afford sufficient ground for any wide generalization. But enough has been said to illlustrate the method of investigation which has to be followed, and the results as far as they go are in general agreement with what Dr. Hort's words would lead us to expect.

52. We have now completed our examination of

* The passage in Basil runs as follows: *ὁ μὲν Ματθαῖος τῆς κατὰ σάρκα γεννήσεως ἐξηγητὴς γέγονεν ὥς αὐτός φησιν· Βίβλος γενέσεως Ἰησοῦ Χριστοῦ υἱοῦ Δαβίδ, υἱοῦ Ἀβραάμ. Ὁ δὲ Μᾶρκος ἀρχὴν τοῦ εὐαγγελίου τὸ Ἰωαννοῦ πεποίηκε κήρυγμα εἰπών· Ἀρχὴ τοῦ εὐαγγελίου Ἰησοῦ Χριστοῦ καθὼς γέγραπται ἐν Ἠσ. τῷ προφ. Φωνὴ βοῶντος, κ.τ.λ.* In Irenæus we read: *Ματθαῖος δὲ τὴν κατὰ ἄνθρωπον αὐτοῦ γέννησιν κηρύττει λέγων· Βίβλος γενέσεως Ἰησοῦ Χριστοῦ υἱοῦ Δαβείδ, υἱοῦ Ἀβραάμ. καὶ Τοῦ δὲ [Ἰησοῦ] Χριστοῦ ἡ γέννησις οὕτως ἦν· ἀνθρωπόμορφον οὖν τὸ εὐαγγέλιον τοῦτο . . . Μᾶρκος δὲ ἀπὸ τοῦ προφητικοῦ πνεύματος τοῦ ἐξ ὕψους ἐπιόντος τοῖς ἀνθρώποις τὴν ἀρχὴν ἐποιήσατο λέγων· Ἀρχὴ τοῦ εὐαγγελίου Ἰησοῦ Χριστοῦ ὡς γέγραπται ἐν Ἠσ. τῷ προφ.*

It should be noticed that Basil here passes straight from the mention of the prophet's name to the quotation which is taken from him—omitting the intervening quotation from Malachi. In this he is supported by Epiphanius and Victorinus. It seems not unlikely that this represents another attempt to escape the difficulty.

the distinctively Syrian readings under the different heads suggested by Dr. Hort's analysis, §§ 132–168. And we have before us examples which will help to give 'actuality' to most of the different classes of phenomena to which he calls attention. We are therefore in a position to estimate to some extent the strength of the case against the Traditional Text. If this passage be, as there is no reason to doubt, a fair specimen of the general character of that text, as indicated by the internal evidence of its 'distinctive readings,' if some of those readings are 'conflate,' if they prove on careful examination to be destitute of ante-Nicene support, we can understand why critics should be driven to the conclusion that, in spite of the vast number of witnesses that support Traditional readings, the true text must be sought elsewhere. We can see also in its true proportions the nature of the issues at stake between the rival schools. In the vast majority of cases the differences relate to points in themselves exceedingly minute and trivial—the loss or the preservation of delicate distinctions in style and phraseology between different Evangelists, the question whether a particular saying of our Lord is recorded by one witness or by two; at the highest, whether narratives of incidents or recorded words which admittedly embody traditions of the Apostolic period, and have the sanction of centuries of ecclesiastical use, were or were not actually incorporated by the Evangelists themselves in the Gospels that they wrote.*

53. Again, a careful comparison of these readings with their rivals will help us to understand why it has now come to be admitted on both sides that the differences between the Traditional Text and the 'Neutral' or the 'Western' cannot be explained as due merely to the normal accidents of transmission. The changes bear too clearly stamped upon them the marks of method and deliberation, and have been carried out too consistently, not to be the result of design. Dr. Hort expressed his opinion on this point with remarkable boldness and precision, asserting that a thorough examination of the facts pointed not to one only, but to two careful revisions under editorial supervision—the first after the death of Origen, and the second about the middle of the 4th century. This second revision he saw reason, as has been already pointed out, to connect with the Church of Antioch. None of his conclusions has roused so much scorn and indignation among his opponents, or has been so unsparingly denounced as groundless and visionary. But time and further study under the stimulus of controversy have brought a more intelligent appreciation of the phenomena. Dean Burgon (*Trad. Text*, p. 234), though 'not so simple as to pretend to fix the precise date and assign a definite locality to the fontal source, or sources, of our perplexity and distress,' yet suspects 'that in the little handful of authorities which have acquired such a notoriety in the annals of recent Textual Criticism, at the head of which stand Codices B and א, are to be recognized the characteristic features of a lost family of (once well-known) 2nd or 3rd cent. documents, which owed their existence to the misguided zeal of some well-intentioned but utterly incompetent persons who devoted themselves to the task of correcting the Text of Scripture, but were entirely unfit for the undertaking.' Mr. Miller sees reason to place this editorial activity at an even earlier period (*Causes of Corr.* p. 22, note); 'I am inclined to believe that, in the age immediately succeeding the apostles, some person or persons of great influence and authority executed a Revision of the NT, and gave the world the result of such labours in a "corrected Text." The guiding principle seems to have been to seek to *abridge* the Text, to lop off whatever seemed redundant, or which might in any way be spared, and to eliminate from one Gospel whatever expressions occurred elsewhere in another Gospel. Clauses which slightly obscured the speaker's meaning, or which seemed to hang loose at the end of a sentence, or which introduced a consideration of difficulty,—words which interfered with the easy flow of a sentence,—everything of this kind, such a person seems to have felt at liberty to discard. But, what is more serious, passages which occasioned some difficulty, as the *pericope de adultera*; physical perplexity, as the troubling of the water; spiritual revulsion, as the agony in the garden,—all these the reviser or revisers seem to have judged it safest simply to eliminate. It is difficult to understand how any persons in their senses could have so acted by the sacred deposit; but it does not seem improbable that at some very remote period there were found some who did act in some such way. Let it be observed, however, that, unlike some critics, I do not base my real argument upon what appears to me to be a not unlikely supposition.'

54. When we add to this that the result of the revision was to produce 'a Thucydidean compactness, condensed and well pruned according to the fastidious taste of the study,' 'exactly that which does not in the long-run take with people who are versed in the habits of ordinary life' (*Trad. Text*, p. 291), we have a picture of the characteristic differences between the rival texts, the main outlines of which it would be difficult to improve, blurred though they are in parts by a failure to discriminate between features peculiar to the Western and features belonging to both the Western and the Neutral types. Students may safely be left to decide for themselves between the rival methods of explaining the character and accounting for the origin of these differences.

It is true that in neither case has any record of this work of revision survived in historical tradition. Mr. Burkitt,* however, has shown, by reference to a far more complete transformation in a biblical text—the exchange of the LXX version of Daniel for Theodotion's by the Church of Africa during the 3rd cent.—that no conclusion unfavourable to Dr. Hort's hypothesis can be based on this silence.

55. For the sub-Apostolic period, to which Mr. Miller would relegate us, historical evidence is at its scantiest, so that the absence of any allusion to the revision which he postulates has virtually no weight at all. Such writings, however, as have survived to show what manner of men the Church produced during that period do not indicate any very high degree of literary power or intellectual distinction. What a delightful surprise it would be, if among the Egyptian papyri even a fragment could come to light representing original work by some leading member of this early-second-century school of critics, who, unlike any other Greek writers of their time, loved Thucydidean

* Dr. Salmon seems hardly to do justice to the attitude of WH on this last point. It is true, in a sense, that, as he says (p. 155), they investigated the subject merely as a 'literary problem.' It is difficult to see how, if their work was to have any scientific value, and to provide materials on which a student of the Apostolic age can work with confidence, they could have done otherwise. All considerations of immediate edification had to be rigorously excluded. At the same time they would be the last people in the world to dispute Dr. Salmon's doctrine of 'the well-illuminated penumbra.' A highly developed literary conscience does not necessarily imply a rigidly mechanical theory of Inspiration.

The text adopted by the Revisers really represents that kind of compromise which Dr. Salmon's argument would desiderate. In it distinct recognition is given to 'prescriptive rights.' Passages like the *pericope de adultera* and Mk 16[9-20] are retained in their familiar places for public use. At the same time, the student receives due warning of the difference in authentication between these passages and their surroundings.

* *The Old Latin and the Itala*, pp. 7, 8.

compactness of style, not wisely, indeed, if it betrayed them into tampering with the text of Scripture, but with a masterful power of reproducing it, and who anticipated by seventeen centuries modern scientific perplexities. It might do far more to shake the foundations of Dr. Hort's position than the discovery of the early history of the cursive script, which seems to Mr. Miller so clear a proof that the world is drifting away from his opponents (*Trad. Text*, p. 238 f.).

56. The points that remain under this head demand reverent handling. They belong to that side of the subject where the textual critic is bound to give an account of the position that he occupies on fundamental articles of Christian faith. Dean Burgon claims that faith in the Inspiration of Scripture carries with it, as a corollary, faith in a special Providence watching over the transmission of the text, and that the same ecclesiastical tradition which guarantees the list of books which are to be accepted as Canonical must be held also to guarantee the type of text which all believers in the authority of the Church are bound to uphold (*Trad. Text*, ch. i.).

57. Let us take these points in order. If there is one doctrine more than another that has in the Providence of God been forced on the attention of Christian students during the course of the last century, it is the doctrine of Inspiration. And if any result with regard to it may claim to be established by the trial through which God has seen fit to test and discipline the faith of those that believe in Him, it is surely this: that there is no subject on which *a priori* arguments are so liable to be upset when they are brought to the test of facts. Here as elsewhere we are forced to acknowledge that God's ways are not as our ways. The course of events has followed again and again a very different line from that which we should naturally have anticipated. And while we may, I think, confidently affirm that the result of this last century of freest discussion has been to deepen and strengthen the faith of men in the reality of the inspiration of the Prophets of the Old Covenant, and of the Apostles and Evangelists of the New, it has shown that there is no royal road to the discovery of the laws by which Inspiration works, except through the most patient and attentive study of the books which owe their form and their contents to its influence.

58. The Church in the 2nd cent. was led by processes, which we have no reason to distrust because they were to a large extent 'instinctive,' to make a provisional selection of the books that had a claim to be regarded as Canonical. The list of books "of whose authority was never any doubt in the Church,' is amply sufficient as a standard by which we can estimate the claims of those whose credentials are less complete. Centuries of pious use and devout meditation, even if sometimes 'not according to knowledge,' have shown the rich stores of spiritual fruit which can be drawn from them. But the Church, as a whole, has never attempted to put forward an authoritative definition of Inspiration. This being so, we are clearly not in a position to formulate any theory with regard to the course which the Providence of God may be assumed to have followed in regard to the preservation, in literal exactness through the ages, of the text as it left the hands of the inspired writers. Even the languages in which the books are written are living languages no more. Not one Christian in 10,000 can read either Testament in the original. We have therefore no grounds *a priori* to expect that kind of accuracy in the Traditional Text which Dean Burgon would postulate for it.

59. 'But,' it will be said, 'you must at least admit that the claims of the Traditional Text on our acceptance rest on the same Church authority that guarantees the Canon.' Supposing the contention to be true, the patent differences which exist to-day in point of actual content between the Greek, Latin, Syriac, and English Bibles would show that we must expect to find in Textual Criticism, as we find in regard to the contents of the Canon, many questions which cannot be foreclosed by an appeal to 'authority.' The text recognized by the most explicit conciliar decision as alone authoritative for the Latin part of Western Christendom is fundamentally distinct from that for which Dean Burgon claims the prescriptive sanction of undisputed and universal possession. But the contention itself will not bear examination. The differences of use between the different centres of Christendom in regard to the contents of the Canon at the beginning of the 4th cent. were perfectly definite, and the problems arising out of the differences claimed immediate and special attention. The *Ecclesiastical History* of Eusebius is a permanent memorial of the interest taken in them, and of the general principles that were applied, at least in some quarters, to their solution. But there is nothing even remotely parallel to this in regard to the development of thought on the problems of Textual Criticism. If it is true, as Dean Burgon asserts (*Trad. Text*, p. 11), 'that in the time of Origen the first principles of the science were not understood,' it would hardly be rash to hazard the assertion that Origen at least shows more interest in the subject, and takes more pains to compare the readings of different MSS, and to mention any variants that he found existing, than all the Greek Fathers from Athanasius to Chrysostom put together.*

It would indeed be strange if, in the stress of the battles which they had to fight for the defence and elucidation of the fundamental verities of the Christian faith, the great protagonists of the Nicene period and of that which immediately succeeded it, had had time to spare for such comparative minutiæ. And, unless it can be proved that they ever took more than an occasional and passing interest in the question, what is it but a gross abuse of a great principle to appeal to their authority in a matter like this, as if it stood on the same level as their authority on the great problems which we may well believe they were raised up by God to solve for the guidance, not of their own generation only but of all the generations that were to come after them?

60. We must pass on now to examine such specimens as the same passage (Mk $1^{1-28}$) provides of characteristic readings belonging to the other, and, if the conclusion we have reached with regard to the Traditional Text be right, presumably earlier types of text.

The first of these to attract attention is the 'Western.' It will be worth while to print the list *in extenso*, marking the readings which it shares with other types.

(1) V.[2] ὡς for καθώς, also Syrian.

(2) om. ἐγώ, also Neutral. Ins. Syr. and Alex.

(3) V.[3] τοῦ θεοῦ ἡμῶν or ὑμῶν for αὐτοῦ, with further addition from the prophet in c.

(4) V.[4] ἐν τῇ ἐρήμῳ βαπτίζων καὶ κηρύσσων for ὁ β. ἐν τῇ ἐρ. κηρ.

* The *prima facie* grounds for this assertion are strong enough to justify its being put forward for examination. Unfortunately, no systematic collection has yet been made of the materials by which it could be tested. The list of reff. to passages in the Fathers in which express reference is made to ἀντίγραφα, which Nestle has compiled (*Intr.*, Appendix ii.) from Tischendorf's *Apparatus Criticus*, is a preliminary step of great importance. It is much to be hoped that the matter will not be allowed to rest there.

(5) V.[5] ἐν Ἰορδάνῃ for ἐν τῷ Ἰ. ποτάμῳ with transp. of ὑπ' αὐτοῦ.
(6) V.[6] δέ for καί, also Syrian.
(7) Vv.[6-8] completely recast (see above). Chiefly assimilation to parallels in other Gospels. Note, however, δέρρην (= δέρριν) for τρίχας.
(8) V.[9] ταῖς ἡμέραις ἐκείναις for ἐκ. τ. ἡμ.
(9) V.[10] om. εὐθύς.
(10) V.[10] ἠνυγμένους for σχιζομένους.
(11) V.[10] εἰς for ἐπ', also Neutral. Against Syr. and Alex.
(12) V.[11] om. ἐγένετο.
(13) V.[12] add τὸ ἅγιον.
(14) V.[12] ἐκβάλλει αὐτόν for αὐτ. ἐκβ.
(15) V.[13] ἡμέρας τεσσαράκοντα for τεσσ. ἡμ. Assimilation.
(16) V.[14] καί for δέ, also Neutral. Against Syr. and Alex.
(17) V.[14] add τῆς βασιλείας, also Syr. Assimilation.
(18) V.[15] λέγων perhaps for καὶ λέγων.
(19) V.[15] πεπλήρωνται οἱ καιροὶ for πεπ. ὁ καιρός.
(20) V.[16] αὐτοῦ for Σίμωνος.
(21) V.[18] πάντα for τὰ δίκτυα. Assimilation.
(22) V.[20] ἠκολούθησαν αὐτῷ for ἀπῆλθον ὀπίσω αὐτοῦ.
(23) V.[21] εἰσεπορεύοντο for εἰσπορεύονται.
(24) V.[21] add αὐτούς after ἐδίδασκεν.
(25) V.[22] om. καί.
(26) V.[23] om. εὐθύς.
(27) V.[23] om. αὐτῶν.
(28) V.[25] om. ὁ Ἰησοῦς.
(29) V.[25] τοῦ ἀνθρώπου for αὐτοῦ.
V.[25] add πνεῦμα ἀκάθαρτον.
(30) V.[26] Recast (see above). Note κράξας (cf. Syrian) for φωνῆσαν, and ἀπό for ἐξ.
(31) V.[27] πρὸς αὐτούς, with Syrian and perhaps Alex.
(32) V.[27] τίς ἡ διδαχὴ ἐκείνη ἣ καινὴ αὕτη ἡ ἐξουσία for τί ἐστιν τοῦτο; διδαχὴ καινὴ κατ' ἐξουσίαν.
(33) V.[28] om. πανταχοῦ, with Syrian.

To these we should probably add, as we have seen—

($1^b$) V.[2] ἐν τοῖς προφήταις for ἐν Ἡσ. τῷ προφ.

61. The difference in general character between these readings and the 'distinctively Syrian' series is obvious. Without for the most part seriously affecting the sense, they yet show, if we take the Neutral text as our standard, a remarkable freedom in altering the form of expression, 'the love of paraphrase,' which Dr. Hort's description (§ 173 f.) would have led us to anticipate. And in most cases, as we have seen, there is little doubt that the change was made by the 'Western' scribe. This fact will help us to realize the true character of a reading such as δέρριν in (7), which, if it stood alone, or was supported only by one or two carefully chosen examples, might quite easily appear unquestionably original, or, at least, a correction due to the author himself. It is in itself remarkably vigorous and appropriate. And, if we were dealing with the work of scribes of a normal type, we should say at once that they could not have had either the inclination or the capacity to invent it. But the matter presents a different aspect where we find in the same company readings like (29) τοῦ ἀνθρώπου for αὐτοῦ, (20) αὐτοῦ for Σίμωνος, (21) πάντα for τὰ δίκτυα, (22) ἠκολούθησαν for ἀπῆλθον ὀπίσω, (30) κράξας for φωνῆσαν, (10) ἠνυγμένους for σχιζομένους. There is no such ground for attributing these to the hand of the author. And a scribe capable of introducing them may well have been capable of changing τρίχας to δέρριν if the word occurred to him. This assumption is strengthened when we note that this spirit of licence has affected not single words only but whole sentences, *e.g.* (7) (30) (32); where, in like manner, it would seem impossible to attribute the readings to a revision by the author himself.

This case, we may notice in passing, is a good example of the importance of attending to what Dr. Hort called the 'Internal Evidence of Documents,' before deciding finally on particular readings. No conclusion can safely be built on a mere selection of readings, however striking in themselves.*

62. The general character of these readings, then, is not such as to inspire confidence. It is not likely that any editor will be found to accept them as a whole, and construct his text throughout from the documents that contain them. Editions, indeed, like Professor Blass's edition of the Acts and St. Luke, which enable the two recensions to be studied side by side, supply a real need. At the same time, the character of these readings, and the very early date at which they must all have originated, will ensure for them a large share of attention. Certainly, the most fruitful work that has been done in this department of Textual Criticism in recent years, if we except the closely kindred work done by Professor Sanday and Mr. Burkitt on the early history of the Latin Version, is work that has been devoted to the investigation of their origin. The first step was taken by Mr. Rendel Harris in the 'Study of the Codex Bezæ,' printed in the series of Cambridge *Texts and Studies* in 1891. The thesis of this stimulating but inconclusive essay was that the origin of the peculiar readings in the Greek text of Codex Bezæ, the primary authority for the Western Text in its Greek dress, can be traced to the influence of the Latin version that accompanied it in various stages of its history. At the same time, he claimed to trace the Latin version, in the form in which it has accompanied D, back to Carthage early in the 2nd century. One direct result of his work was the publication of two vols. by Dr. Chase on 'The Old Syriac element in Codex Bezæ' and 'The Syro-Latin Text of the Gospels,' in which he collects the evidence in support of the thesis that the true source of the peculiar elements in the Bezan text is to be found, not in Latin but in Syriac. And he emphasized, following a suggestion thrown out by Dr. Sanday in a review of Rendel Harris, the claims of Antioch as the centre from which this influence had spread. It is difficult to doubt that the swing of the pendulum will ultimately bring us back to a simpler, if more commonplace, solution, and we shall be content to believe that the bulk of the Western readings originated in Greek, excepting those which may fairly be regarded as individualisms of D. The influence of Syriac can hardly have been more than occasional and spasmodic. If the suggestion with regard to Antioch can be established, important consequences will flow from it. It would be rash, perhaps, to say more at present.† In any case, it is in striking agreement with the opinion expressed by WH (§ 153): 'On the whole, we are disposed to suspect that the "Western" Text took its rise in North-Western Syria or Asia Minor, and that it was soon carried to Rome, and thence spread in different directions to North Africa and most of the countries of Europe. From North-Western Syria it would easily pass through Palestine and Egypt to Ethiopia. But this is at present hardly more than a speculation; nor do any critical results depend upon it.' It is interesting, however, to notice that, as Mr. Lake has pointed out in his little book on the *Text of NT* (p. 89), this view

* This caution is specially necessary in judging of any list of readings which from the nature of the case can consist only of specimens: *e.g.* in Blass's article on 'The Western Text of St. Mark,' and in Nestle's 'Critical Notes on various Passages.'

† See esp. Chase, *Syro-Latin Text*, p. 141.

would at the same time satisfactorily account for most of the phenomena in the remarkable series of interpolations in Acts which Prof. Ramsay has sought to elucidate.

63. A further question, of some importance with regard to this class of readings, still remains. Even if it be granted that, as a whole, the 'Western' represents an aberrant type of text, 'it does not follow,' as WH themselves point out, (§ 237), 'that none of its distinctive readings are original.' The special class of 'Western non-Interpolations' to which they called attention may or may not be regarded as favourable specimens.* At any rate they show that WH did not start, as Dr. Salmon's humorous illustration might lead the unwary to conclude, with an invincible prejudice against any reading that might be called 'Western.' The fact is that their uniform habit, in their preliminary examination of the text of each book of NT, was to make a list of all the Western readings that were not obvious corruptions. In Mk. more than 200 such readings were tabulated. The list so made was then subjected to repeated revisions, and no reading of any interest was passed over without full consideration. In Mk. more than 60 of these readings were recorded in their first edition under one form of notation or other on the same page as the text. In the smaller edition 12 rank as strictly alternative readings, 51 are printed as Noteworthy Rejected Readings in a list at the end of the volume. Whether this list would have received large additions had they had access to Syr-*sin* is an interesting question on which something must be said presently. The only point which it is worth while to emphasize at this stage is this. They state expressly that they were not prevented by any genealogical considerations from accepting any 'Western' reading. Only, they found very few that seemed to them commended by internal evidence (§§ 269–273).

We must postpone for the present the question, raised by Mr. Burkitt,† whether we are bound to attach such weight to the demonstrable antiquity of the readings supported by a combination of the earliest Syriac and the earliest Latin authorities as to enable us to dispense with the necessity of applying the test of 'the Internal Evidence of Documents' to the readings of this as of any other group, before taking it as the foundation for a reconstruction of the text.

64. The Alexandrian readings in our passage are few, but thoroughly representative of the class. They include—

(1) The insertion of *καί* before *κηρύσσων* in v.$^{4}$.

(2) The omission of *εἰσελθών*, with various rearrangements of the words in v.$^{21}$.

(3) The insertion of Ἔα in v.$^{24}$.

(4) *οἴδαμεν* for *οἶδα* in the same verse.

To these we should add—

(5) V.$^{2}$ ins. *ἐγώ*, also Syrian.

(6) V.$^{14}$ *δέ* for *καί*, also Syrian.

(7) V.$^{27}$ *πρὸς αὐτούς*, perhaps Alex. as well as Western and Syrian.

These readings are relatively far less numerous and less startling than the 'Western,' and in consequence their identification by WH as a distinct class was a triumph of delicate and patient analysis,‡ and writers who are not alive to the necessity for finding a clue through the maze of the *concordia discors* of the small group of demonstrably early authorities, still find it possible and convenient to despise the evidence on which this part of WH's classification rests. No one, however, who will be at the pains to study the readings of the group ℵCLΔ through the rest of the Gospel will doubt either the soundness or the importance of the conclusion. WH tabulate upwards of 70 examples, printing 11 either in text or margin; see $1^{21.24.45}$ $3^{6.7}$ $4^{8}$ $8^{21.25}$ $10^{43}$ $11^{11}$ $15^{1}$. The readings similarly treated, $3^{17}$ $4^{22}$ $5^{23}$ $6^{14.23.33}$ $9^{9.30}$ $12^{30}$ $15^{44}$, seem to differ from these only by the fact that they were adopted by the Syrian revisers. We must not, however, forget that these are all picked specimens, and cannot be fairly judged apart from their companions.

65. The results of our examination were not favourable to the genuineness of any of the 6 (or 7) examples that are immediately before us. Our study will, however, help us to appreciate the accuracy of WH's sketch of the general characteristics of the class (§ 183). 'The changes made have usually more to do with language than matter, and are marked by an effort after correctness of phrase. They are evidently the work of careful leisurely hands, and not seldom display a delicate philological tact which unavoidably lends them at first sight a deceptive appearance of originality.' 'Some of the modes of change described above as belonging to incipient paraphrase occur as distinctly here as in the Western texts, though as a rule much more sparingly; and the various forms of assimilation, especially harmonistic alteration and interpolation in the Gospels, recur likewise, and at times are carried out in a very skilful manner.'

The example in v.$^{4}$ is an excellent specimen of the class referred to in the closing sentence of § 184: 'The most instructive distributions, as exhibiting distinctly the residual pre-Syrian text, which is neither Western nor Alexandrian, are those produced by the simultaneous aberration of the Western and Alexandrian texts, especially when they severally exhibit independent modes of easing an apparent difficulty in the text antecedent to both.'

66. The subsidiary attestation that they receive both from versions and from ante-Nicene Patristic quotations is remarkable.

In (1) they have the support of the Bohairic.

In (2) (in one form or another) of Boh Syr-sin and some old Latin MSS, besides Origen in 4 places.

In (3) they are supported by Origen and Eusebius.

In (4) by Boh Orig$^{2}$ Eus$^{4}$, besides Orig$^{\text{int } 1}$ Iren$^{\text{int } 1}$ Tert.

In (5) by Orig $\frac{3}{5}$ Eus.

In (6) by Orig Eus.

67. We come now to the last and in many respects the most difficult part of our task—the examination of the evidence for 'the residual pre-Syrian Text, which is neither Western nor Alexandrian,' and to which in consequence WH gave, as we have seen, the name 'Neutral.' The specimens before us, with the authorities attesting them, are these—

(1) V.$^{2}$ *τῷ Ἠσ. τῷ προφ.*, ℵB(D)LΔ 1 33 Latt Syr-vg Boh: Orig Iren$^{\text{gr}}$ Porph.

(2) V.$^{2}$ om. *ἐγώ*, BD am fu Syr-vg Boh: Iren Orig $\frac{1}{5}$ Tert.

(3) V.$^{4}$ Ἰ. *ὁ βαπτίζων ἐν τῇ ἐρ. κηρύσσων*, B 33.

(4) V.$^{5}$ *ὑπ' αὐτοῦ* after *ἐβαπτ.*, BL 33 (ℵ 69).

(5) V.$^{6}$ *καί* for *δέ*, ℵBL 33 Lat-vg b d ff$^{1}$ g$^{1}$ Boh.

(6) V.$^{6}$ *ὁ* Ἰω. for Ἰω., ℵBPL al$^{8}$ 1 69.

(7) V.$^{8}$ om. *μέν*, ℵBL 33 69: Orig.

(8) V.$^{8}$ om. *ἐν*, 1° ℵBΔH 33 al$^{8}$ Lat-vg: Orig.

(9) V.$^{8}$ om. *ἐν*, 2° BL b Lat-vg.

(10) V.$^{10}$ *εἰς* for *ἐπ'*, BD 69 a 8.

* See esp. Dr. Chase's note, *ibid.* p. 130.

† Introd. to Barnard's *Biblical Text of Clement*, p. xvii ff.

‡ It is important to bear in mind the fact, to which attention has already been called, that the discovery was only rendered possible by the help in different ways of both ℵ and B. Griesbach, therefore, whom we might naturally have expected to lead the way in this as in other directions, had not the materials on which to show his skill as a pioneer.

(11) V.[13] *τεσσαρ. ἡμ.* for *ἡμ. τεσσ.*, ℵBL 33: Orig Eus.
(12) V.[14] *καί* for *δέ*, BD[gr] a (c) Boh ?.
(13) V.[14] om. *τῆς βασιλείας*, ℵBL 1 33 69 b c ff[1] Boh Syr-sin: Orig.
(14) V.[16] *Σίμωνος*, ℵBLM (a Boh AE[2] Δ 1 69).
(15) V.[16] *ἀμφιβάλλοντας* without add., ℵBL 33.
(16) V.[18] om. *αὐτῶν*, ℵBCL ff[1] g[2] Lat-vg Boh (D).
(17) V.[19] *προβὰς ὀλίγον*, BDL 1 a b ff[2] Syr-vg Boh.
(18) V.[19] om. *αὐτῶν*, ℵABC*DL Latt Boh.
(19) V.[23] add *εὐθύς*, ℵBL 1 33 Boh: Orig.
(20) V.[23] om. *Ἔα*, ℵBD Latt Syr-sin-vg Boh.
(21) V.[26] *φωνῆσαν* for *κράξαν*, ℵBL 33: Orig.
(22) V.[27] *αὐτούς* for *πρὸς αὐτούς*, ℵB (b e ff[2] q).
(23) V.[27] *τί ἐστιν τοῦτο; διδαχὴ καινὴ κατ' ἐξουσίαν*, ℵBL (1) 33 Boh.
(24) V.[28] *καί* for *δέ*, ℵBCDLΔM 33.
(25) V.[28] add *πανταχοῦ*, BC(ℵ[c]L) 69 b e 9 Boh.

68. The internal evidence, as we have seen, is strongly in favour of the 'Neutral' Text in many of these cases. In none is it clearly unfavourable. What are we to say of the documents by which it is supported?

The first point that will strike us as we go through the list is the variation in size in the attesting groups. At times, *e.g.*, (1) we have an array as strong and varied in its contents as we could desire, including 7 good MSS, all the early Versions, and abundant ante-Nicene Patristic evidence. Side by side with this we find in (3) only one uncial and one cursive. In fact the only constant supporter of the whole series of readings is the single uncial MS, B. Clearly we must test our ground most carefully if we are to rest securely on evidence that is liable from time to time to be reduced to such slender proportions.

69. What, then, is the real foundation for the authority which WH claim for B?

First and foremost it rests, they tell us, on 'Internal Evidence of Readings.'* They claim that the great majority of readings, even when but slenderly supported, approve themselves as genuine after repeated examination. The 25 examples before us certainly tend to confirm this judgment. The case does not, however, rest purely on internal considerations. It is confirmed, so far as the evidence at our disposal will enable us to speak, by 'genealogy.' In this connexion the reading in v.[4] is once more most instructive. It supplies us with a clear proof of the existence of a third type of text distinct alike from the Western and Alexandrian, and presenting a reading which may well explain the origin of both, and it helps us to appreciate the significance of the fact that in other cases the same MS, which in cases like this is seen to preserve a text independent of both the other early groups, supports now one and now the other of these groups against its rival. In other words, except in the comparatively rare cases in which both the Western and Alexandrian text have gone astray in the same place, B has uniformly the support of one set of authorities or the other, *i.e.* it would naturally rank both as an early Western authority as compared with the Alexandrian group, and as an early Alexandrian authority against the Westerns. Or, to put the same thing from the other side, both the Western and the Alexandrian texts are fundamentally 'neutral' in a large proportion of their readings. And the further back we can trace either of them, and more especially the Western, where the evidence, though still far from complete, is yet relatively abundant, the more closely do its readings as a whole approximate to the 'Neutral' Text.

70. In the light of this fact we may estimate more truly the extent of the confirmation which the text of B receives from other primary authorities. *E.g.* in the passage before us it is supported by ℵ in 19, by L in 18, by 33 in 12, by D in 9 out of the 25 cases. C is extant in 10, and supports B in 3. Latin evidence of one kind or another supports B in 16, the Bohairic in 13, Syr-*sin* in 2 out of 8 passages where it definitely supports one or other of the variants (in 3 passages Syr-*sin* presents us with a new variant). Origen, who in some cases supports the rival reading as well, is quoted in support of B in 8 cases, and Irenæus in 2. These results correspond closely with the anticipations which Dr. Hort's words in § 235 would have led us to form.

71. In the case of ℵ and the oldest form both of the Latin and of the Syriac Versions, it is important to examine the extent and the limitations of their support more closely.

Let us take first the relation of these two MSS of the Greek text to one another. The amount of agreement between ℵ and B in readings in which they stand almost or altogether alone is so great that there can be no doubt, on 'genealogical' grounds, that for a considerable part of their contents they preserve unchanged the text of a common original. What, then, we are forced to ask, is the length of the interval which separates each of them from this common ancestor? Or, in other words, to what extent are we justified in regarding their testimonies as 'independent'?

72. To Mr. Miller the case seems very simple. The MSS were certainly written in the same generation; in part, as it would seem, by the same scribe. What more is wanted, in view of their admitted agreement in a peculiar type of text, to prove that they are 'twin products of a lost exemplar,' and to justify us in quoting them as 'ℵ-B,' linked by a hyphen, as certain groups of cursives are linked, and as Mr. Cronin (*JTS* vol. ii. p. 590) has proved that the Codices Purpureæ (N-Σ-Sinop) should be linked, because they are all derived directly from one and the same MSS?

Dean Burgon was more cautious. His minute comparison of the two MSS had impressed him very strongly with the extent not only of the agreement, but of the differences between them. He writes of them (*Trad. Text*, p. 33) as 'closely resembling one another, yet standing apart in every page so seriously that it is easier to find two consecutive verses in which they differ than two consecutive verses in which they entirely agree.' And, though he would have it that the 'idea of fixing the date of the common ancestor of B and ℵ is based upon pure speculation' (groups of attested variations being for some unexplained reason excluded from the category of facts), yet he was perfectly well aware that the differences between the two MSS required 'several generations' of transcription to account for them. Only he was able to persuade himself that, at a time when the demand for fresh copies must have been very great, these generations could 'have been given off in two or three years' (*ib.* p. 73).

73. The treatment of the problem in WH (*Intr.* §§ 287–304) is very different in character. Few better examples could be found of Hort's inexhaustible fertility in conceiving hypotheses which might fit the

* Dr. Bernhard Weiss has published in various numbers of *Texte und Untersuchungen* a careful examination of the text of the leading uncials as determined exclusively by a study of 'the Internal Evidence of Readings.' His results are summarized conveniently in Kenyon's *Handbook to the Textual Criticism of the NT*, p. 264 f. They supply a striking and entirely independent corroboration of WH's estimate of the relative purity of the text of B.

The present writer is glad of this opportunity of calling attention to Dr. Kenyon's *Handbook*. It contains, besides other matter which none but so expert a palæographer could supply, a statement of the questions at issue in the present state of Textual Criticism which is eminently clear and fair.

facts by which he was confronted, and the patient consideration which he was prepared to give to each before he pronounced judgment on it. The passage is too long to extract, and too condensed already to admit of further condensation. It cannot, however, be too earnestly commended to the consideration of all students.

Far too many of the theories that have been recently put forward have been framed without reference to the facts to which these paragraphs call attention. Meanwhile we must content ourselves with the summary of his conclusions, given by Hort himself (*ed. min.* p. 559): 'If B and ℵ were for a great part of their text derived from a proximate common original, that common original, whatever might have been its own date, must have had a very ancient and a very pure text. There is, however, no tangible evidence for this supposition; while various considerations, drawn from careful comparison of the accessory attestation of readings supported by ℵB together, by B against ℵ, and by ℵ against B respectively, render it morally certain that the ancestries of B and of ℵ diverged from a point near the autographs, and never came into contact subsequently; so that the coincidence of ℵB marks those portions of text in which two primitive and entirely separate lines of transmission had not come to differ from each other through independent corruption in the one or the other.'

74. The passage of Mark already before us will supply material by which we can at once illustrate and test the force of the argument on which this conclusion rests. We have already examined the most remarkable of the readings in which ℵ and B agree in the course of our study of the 'Syrian,' 'Western,' and 'Neutral' texts in these verses; and certainly the standard of excellence which the two MSS reach in combination is very high. Whatever the date of their common original, 'it must,' judging by internal considerations in those parts of it which we can at once restore with confidence, 'have had a very pure text.' The accessory evidence for a large proportion of these readings makes it clear at the same time that it is also 'a very ancient' text.

75. The following list of readings in which the two authorities disagree will give us examples of the 'various considerations' to which Dr. Hort alludes, and so enable us to appreciate the rest of the passage:—

(1) V.[1] +*υἱοῦ θεοῦ*, ℵ$^{a}$BDL etc.: Iren $\frac{2}{3}$ Orig$^{int}$.
–ℵ*: Iren $\frac{1}{3}$ Orig Syr-hr.
(2) V.[2] –*ἐγώ*, BD am fu Syr-vg Boh: Iren Orig $\frac{1}{5}$ Tert.
+ℵAPLΔ etc. Syr-hcl: Orig $\frac{4}{5}$ Eus.
(3) V.[2] *ἀποστέλλω*, B etc. *ἀποστελῶ*, ℵ Boh.
(4) V.[4] *ἐγένετο*, B etc. *καὶ ἐγένετο*, ℵ* (Boh).
(5) V.[4] *κηρύσσων*, B 33. *καὶ κηρύσσων*, ℵLΔ Boh.
(6) V.[5] *καὶ ἐβαπτίζοντο*, B etc. *ἐβαπτ.*, ℵ* 69 a.
(7) V.[7] *ὀπίσω*, B: Orig $\frac{1}{2}$. *ὀπίσω μου*, ℵ etc.
(8) V.[8] *πνεύματι ἁγίῳ*, BL b Lat-vg. *ἐν πν. ἁγ.*, ℵ etc.
(9) V.[9] *ἐγένετο*, B (a). *καὶ ἐγένετο*, ℵ (ff$^{2}$ mt Boh) etc.
(10) V.[10] *εἰς*, BD 69 a (g$^{1}$). *καὶ μένον ἐπ'*, ℵ 33 Latt Boh.
(11) V.[11] *φωνὴ ἐγένετο*, B etc. *φωνή*, ℵ*D ff$^{2}$ mt.
(12) V.[14] *καὶ μετά*, BD$^{gr}$ a (c) Boh ?.
*μετὰ δέ*, ℵALΔ etc. Latt Syrr: Orig Eus.
(13) V.[15] *καὶ λέγων*, BKLΔ unc$^{2}$ a b ff$^{1}$ g$^{2}$ Lat-vg Boh Syr-vg.
–ℵ* c mt Syr-sin: Orig.
(14) V.[18] *ἠκολούθουν*, B. *ἠκολούθησαν*, ℵ etc.
(15) V.[19] *ὀλίγον*, BDL 1 a b ff$^{2}$ Syr-vg (sin) Boh.
*ἐκεῖθεν*, ℵ* (33).
(16) V.[21] *εἰσελθών*, ABD etc.
–ℵ (C) L (Δ) (33 69) (c) (Syr-sin-vg) (Boh).
(17) V.[24] *σύ*, ABΔΓ (a curious instance of accidental coincidence in an *itacism*).
*σοί*, ℵ etc.
(18) V.[24] *οἶδα*, ABCD etc. *οἴδαμεν*, ℵLΔ: Iren$^{int}$ Orig Eus Tert.
(19) V.[25] +*λέγων*, B etc. *om.* ℵ* (A*?): Dam.
(20) V.[26] –*πνα τό*, B by homœoteleuton. +ℵ etc.
(21) V.[28] +*εὐθύς*, B etc.
–ℵ* 1 33 b c e ff$^{1.2}$ (g$^{1}$) Boh Syr-sin.
(22) V.[28] *Γαλιλαίας*, ABCD etc. *'Ιουδαίας*, ℵ* (cf. 28 s$^{scr*}$).

76. From this list we may at once eliminate (17) and (20), which are clearly only slips of the pen; and (4), (14), (22), as possibly individualisms. In a certain number of the cases that remain—(2), (5), (12), (16), (18), where, as we have seen, the readings may be classed as either Alexandrian, or Alexandrian and Syrian—it is possible that the variants might have come in together, if the archetype of ℵ had been collated with a MS containing a strongly-marked Alexandrian text. There remain, however, 12 variants, even in these 28 verses, supported on both sides by early evidence, and by no means the same evidence in the different cases, which can only have come into the aberrant text, whichever it is, at different times in the course of an eventful history. We can see, then, what kind of evidence is available in support of Dr. Hort's 'various considerations.' Further evidence will be forthcoming from the investigation which we have yet to make, into the relation in which these two primary MSS of the Greek text stand to the two earliest Versions—the Latin and the Syrian.

77. A complete examination of this, the most important problem that still awaits solution in Textual Criticism, is not as yet possible. Mr. Turner has recently reminded us (*JTS* vol. ii. p. 602) that the 'African Latin' had a history before Cyprian. The evidence of k, priceless as it is, is only part of the evidence that will become available in due course as the result of the work at present being carried on at Oxford under the direction of Prof. Sanday on the text of Irenæus and kindred subjects. Similarly, we must not forget that the history of the 'Old Syriac' did not begin with Syr-*sin*. The total amount of evidence for enucleating this history is still lamentably small, and inaccessible to those who are not themselves good Syriac scholars. Students, however, have long been cheered by the announcement that Mr. Burkitt has in hand an edition of the Syriac Gospels which, they have good reason to know, will leave nothing to be desired that wide reading, accurate scholarship, and brilliant genius can supply.

78. Meanwhile something can be done with the evidence already accessible. Dr. Sanday contributed a valuable essay on the Greek text underlying k to the Oxford edition of that MS.* The various lists are, unfortunately for our present purpose, admittedly incomplete. Still they afford a sufficiently wide basis for the experimental investigation, which is all that can be attempted here. A collation of Syr-*sin* with the readings tabulated by Dr. Sanday supplies a list of upwards of 200 cases in which the evidence of the 4 authorities is simultaneously available for comparison. These may well be taken as samples of the ore which this mine will supply.

It is worth while to tabulate and print these

* *Old Latin Biblical Texts*, No. II. pp. 95-122.

examples in full, as the tables will need to be carefully checked and supplemented by better equipped scholars; and no merely numerical summary of results can give even an approximately true impression of the facts.

79. List I. ℵB k Syr-*sin* in combination against later 'Western' or 'Syrian' readings.

Mt $4^{12}$ – ὁ Ἰς.
$5^{11}$ – ῥῆμα.
$5^{27}$ – τοῖς ἀρχαίοις.
$5^{44}$ 3 omissions.
$6^{4}$ – αὐτός.
$8^{7}$ – ὁ Ἰς.
$8^{12}$ – αὐτῆς.
$8^{13}$ – καί.
– ἐν τῇ ὥρᾳ ἐκείνῃ.
$8^{29}$ – Ἰου.
$8^{31}$ ἀπόστειλον ἡμᾶς.
$8^{32}$ εἰς τοὺς χοίρους.
$9^{5}$ ἀφίενται.
$9^{12}$ – αὐτοῖς.
$9^{15}$ πενθεῖν.
$10^{8}$ + νεκροὺς ἐγείρετε.
$11^{10}$ – γάρ.
$12^{10}$ – ἦν.
$12^{15}$ – ὄχλοι (Syr-*sin ut vid.*).
$12^{25}$ – ὁ Ἰς.
$13^{9}$ – ἀκούειν.
$13^{36}$ – ὁ Ἰς.
$13^{40}$ – τούτου.
$13^{44}$ – πάλιν.
$13^{46}$ εὑρὼν δέ.
$13^{51}$ – λέγει αὐτοῖς ὁ Ἰς.
$14^{12}$ πτῶμα (Syr-*sin ut vid.*).
$15^{30}$ αὐτοῦ for τοῦ Ἰου.
Mk $8^{20}$ λέγουσι for οἱ δὲ εἶπον.
$8^{25}$ διέβλεψεν (Syr-*sin e lacuna*) for ἐποίησεν αὐτὸν ἀναβλέψαι.
$8^{28}$ εἶπαν for ἀπεκρίθησαν.
$9^{7}$ – λέγουσα.
$9^{14}$ ἐλθόντες . . . εἶδον for ἐλθὼν . . . εἶδεν.
$9^{16}$ αὐτούς for τοὺς γραμματεῖς.
$9^{24}$ – μετὰ δακρύων.
$9^{44}$ om. verse.
$9^{45f.}$ – εἰς τὸ πῦρ, κ.τ.λ.
$10^{29}$ – ἢ γυναῖκα.
$11^{26}$ om. verse.
$13^{22}$ δώσουσι (σημεῖα) for ποιήσουσιν.
$14^{36}$ – θέλεις (Syr-*sin ut vid.*).
$14^{70}$ – καὶ ἡ λαλιά σου ὁμοιάζει.
$15^{46}$ – καὶ ἀπῆλθεν.
$16^{9-20}$ omit.

List II. B *v.* ℵ k Syr-*sin*.

Mt $9^{22}$ + Ἰς.
$13^{16}$ – ὑμῶν.
$14^{16}$ + Ἰς.
Mk $8^{21}$ πῶς οὐ for οὔπω.
$15^{44}$ ἐθαύμασεν for ἐθαύμαζεν.

List III. ℵ *v.* B k Syr-*sin*.

Mt $5^{9}$ – αὐτοί.
$8^{10}$ { οὐδὲ ἐν τῷ Ἰσρ. τοσ. πίστιν. / παρ' οὐδένι τοσ. πίστιν, κ.τ.λ. (Syr-*sin aliter*).
$9^{28}$ + δύο.
$9^{35}$ + ἐν τῷ λαῷ.
$11^{15}$ – ἀκούειν.
$13^{17}$ – γάρ.
$13^{35}$ + Ἡσαίου.
{ + κόσμου. / – B k (Syr-*sin* paraphrases).
Mk $8^{16}$ { ἔχομεν. / ἔχουσιν, B k (Syr-*sin* paraphrases).
$11^{3}$ + ὅτι.
$12^{15}$ ἰδών for εἰδώς.
$14^{22}$ + ὁ Ἰς. { – B k. / – λαβὼν ὁ Ἰς., Syr-*sin*.
$14^{46}$ αὐτῶν for αὐτῷ.
$15^{24}$ σταυρώσαντες for σταυροῦσιν . . . καί.

List IV. Syr-*sin v.* ℵB k.

Mt $1^{22}$ + Ἡσαίου.
$1^{25}$ τὸν υἱὸν αὐτῆς for υἱόν.
$4^{10}$ + ὀπίσω μου.
$4^{16}$ – μέγα.
$4^{20}$ + αὐτῶν.
$5^{25}$ – ὁ κριτής.
$5^{45}$ ὅς for ὅτι.
ἀγ. καὶ πον. for πον. καὶ ἀγ.
$8^{3}$ + ὁ κύριος ἡμῶν.
$8^{9}$ ἔχων ἐξουσίαν for ὑπὸ ἐξου. τασσ.
+ λέγω.
$8^{13}$ + αὐτοῦ.
$8^{15}$ αὐτοῖς for αὐτῷ.
$8^{25}$ + οἱ μαθηταὶ αὐτοῦ.
$9^{5}$ + σοι αἱ ἁμ. σου for σοῦ αἱ ἁμ.
$11^{17}$ + ὑμῖν.
$11^{23}$ ἡ . . . ὑψωθεῖσα for μὴ . . . ὑψ.
$12^{22}$ + ἀκούειν.
$12^{25}$ ἰδών for εἰδώς.
$12^{31}$ + αὐτῷ (sentence recast).
$12^{35}$ + τῆς καρδίας αὐτοῦ.
$12^{50}$ ποιεῖ *ut vid.* for ἂν ποιήσῃ.
$13^{10}$ + αὐτοῦ.
$13^{22}$ + τούτου.
$13^{37}$ + αὐτοῖς.
$13^{43}$ + ἀκούειν.
$15^{25}$ προσεκύνησεν for προσεκύνει.
$15^{33}$ + αὐτοῦ.
Mk $9^{3}$ + ὡς χιών for οἷα γναφ. κ.τ.λ.
$9^{23}$ εἰ πιστεύεις πάντα δυνατά σοι γενέσθαι.
$9^{24}$ + κύριε.
$9^{29}$ + νηστείᾳ καί.
$9^{38}$ + λέγων.
$9^{42}$ – τῶν πιστευόντων [εἰς ἐμέ, B].
$10^{13}$ τοῖς προσφέρουσιν for αὐτοῖς.
$10^{24}$ + τοὺς πεπ. ἐπὶ χρήμ.
$10^{49}$ αὐτὸν φωνηθῆναι for φωνήσατε αὐτόν.
$12^{27}$ + ὑμεῖς δέ.
$13^{8}$ + καὶ ταραχαί.
$13^{15}$ + εἰς τὴν οἰκίαν.
$14^{24}$ + καινῆς.
$14^{52}$ + ἀπ' αὐτῶν.
$14^{54}$ καθήμενον for συγκαθ.
$14^{72}$ – εὐθύς.

List V. k *v.* ℵB Syr-*sin*.

Mt $1^{3}$ – καὶ τὸν Ζαρὰ ἐκ τῆς Θάμαρ.
$4^{4}$ – ἀλλ' ἐπὶ παντὶ . . . Θεοῦ.
$4^{16}$ εἶδεν φῶς μέγα (Syr-*sin* – μέγα).
φῶς εἶδεν μέγα, ℵB.
$4^{23}$ ὅλην for ἐν ὅλῃ.
$4^{24}$ – καὶ ἐθεράπευσεν αὐτούς.
5 v.[5] before v.[4].
$5^{11}$ δικαιοσύνης for ἐμοῦ, ℵB. 'My own name's sake,' Syr-*sin*.
διώξ. καὶ ὀνειδ. { ℵB ὀνειδ. καὶ διώξ. / Syr-*sin* only διώξ.
$5^{25}$ ἐν τῇ ὁδῷ μετ' αὐτοῦ for μετ' αὐτοῦ ἐν τ. ὁ.
$5^{32}$ – ὅτι.
– καὶ ὃς ἐάν. . . μοιχᾶται, + ℵ Syr-*sin* (B).
$5^{36}$ { ποιῆσαι τρίχα μίαν λευκὴν ἢ μέλαιναν. / μίαν τρ. λ. ἢ μέλ. ποι., ℵB (Syr-*sin* paraphrases).
$5^{46}$ ἕξετε for ἔχετε.
$6^{1}$ ἐλεημοσύνην for δικαιοσύνην.
$6^{8}$ – ὁ θεός { + ℵB. / + 'Hou' Syr-*sin*.

Mt $8^{8}$ – ὁ παῖς μου.
$9^{11}$ εἶπον for ἔλεγον, ℵB. λέγουσι, Syr-*sin*.
$9^{12}$ + Ἰς.
$9^{17}$ ῥήσσει ὁ οἶνος, κ.τ.λ. { ℵB ῥήγνυνται οἱ ἀσκ. / Syr-*sin* conflates. }
$9^{32}$ + ἄνθρωπον { – ℵB. / + τινα, Syr-*sin*. }
$10^{2}$ – καί bef. Ἰάκ.
$10^{3}$ Λεββαῖος for Θαδδαῖος, ℵB.
Ἰούδ. Ἰάκ. Syr-*sin*.
$10^{10}$ ῥάβδους for ῥάβδον.
$11^{10}$ καί for ὅς.
$13^{24}$ σπείροντι for σπείραντι.
$13^{30}$ – αὐτὰ εἰς, + ℵB (Syr-*sin ut vid.*).
$13^{55}$ Ἰωσῆς, B Syr-*sin* Ἰωσήφ. ℵ Ἰωάννης.
$14^{3}$ – Φιλίππου.
Mk $8^{35}$ (besides om. ὃς δ' . . . ψυχήν) τοῦ εὐαγγελίου, ℵB ἐμοῦ καὶ τοῦ εὐαγγ. Syr-*sin* τοῦ ἐμοῦ εὐαγ.
$9^{15}$ gaudentes for προστρέχοντες.
$9^{35}$ – καὶ λέγει . . . διάκονος.
$9^{38}$ + ὃς οὐκ ἀκολουθεῖ ἡμῖν after δαιμόνια.
– ὅτι οὐκ ἀκολούθει ἡμῖν after αὐτόν.
$9^{43}$ ὁπου ἐστι for εἰς.
$10^{10}$ + secreto.
$10^{19}$ μὴ μοιχ. μὴ πορν. { B Syr-*sin* μὴ φον. μὴ μοιχ. / ℵ only μὴ φον. }
$10^{22}$ + et agros.
$11^{1}$ – Βηθφαγὴ καί. + ℵB (Syr-*sin*).
$11^{8}$ ἔκοπτον for κόψαντες, ℵB.
+ καὶ ἐστρώννυον. – ℵB (Syr-*sin* omits the whole sentence, ἄλλοι δὲ . . . ὁδόν, app. by homœoteleuton).
$11^{9}$ + τῷ ὑψίστῳ.
$12^{14}$ interrogabant eum farisæi dicentes for ἐλθόντες λέγουσιν αὐτῷ. Syr-*sin aliter*.
+ εἰπὲ οὖν ἡμῖν τί σοι δοκεῖ.
$12^{42}$ – πτωχή.
$12^{43}$ – ἡ πτωχή.
$13^{2}$ + καὶ διὰ τριῶν ἡμερῶν ἄλλος ἀναστήσεται ἀνεὺ χειρῶν.
$13^{14}$ + τὸ ῥηθὲν . . . προφήτου.
$13^{18}$ + ἡ φυγὴ ὑμῶν . . . μηδὲ σαββάτου.
$13^{22}$ – ψευδόχ. καί.
$13^{27}$ – αὐτοῦ after ἐκλεκτούς.
$14^{4}$ + καὶ λέγοντες { – ℵB. / + λέγοντες, Syr-*sin*. }
$14^{8}$ + αὕτη { – ℵB. / – ἔσχεν αὕτη, Syr-*sin*. }
$14^{19}$ + καὶ ἄλλος μήτι ἐγώ.
$14^{20}$ + ἀποκριθείς.
$14^{37}$ + ἰσχύσατε for ἴσχυσας.
$14^{45}$ – ἐλθὼν εὐθύς.
$15^{23}$ + πιεῖν.

List VI. B Syr-*sin* *v.* ℵ k.

Mt $12^{49}$ + αὐτοῦ after τὴν χεῖρα.
$13^{11}$ + αὐτοῖς.
Mk $8^{20}$ + αὐτῷ.
$10^{19}$ μὴ φον. μὴ μοιχ. { k μὴ μοιχ. μὴ πορν. / ℵ only μὴ φον. }
$10^{30}$ + οἰκίας . . . ἀγρούς.
$14^{71}$ + ὃν λέγετε.
$15^{20}$ + αὐτόν after σταυρώσουσιν.
14 { $^{30}$ + δίς. – ℵ k.
$^{68}$ – καὶ ἀλέκτωρ ἐφώνησεν. + k *not* ℵ.
$^{72}$ + ἐκ δευτέρου. – ℵ *not* k.
+ δίς. – ℵ. }

List VII. B k *v.* ℵ Syr-*sin*.

Mt $12^{44}$ – καὶ before σεσαρ.
$13^{35}$ – κόσμου. + ℵ (Syr-*sin* paraphrases).
$15^{22}$ ἔκραζεν for ἔκραξεν.
Mk $8^{22}$ ἔρχονται for ἔρχεται.
Mk $13^{27}$ – αὐτοῦ after ἀγγέλους.
$13^{33}$ – καὶ προσεύχεσθε.

List VIII. ℵB *v.* k Syr-*sin*.

Mt $5^{11}$ + ψευδόμενοι.
$5^{22}$ – εἰκῆ.
$5^{41}$ – ἔτι ἄλλα.
$5^{46}$ τὸ αὐτό for οὕτω.
$8^{21}$ – αὐτοῦ after τῶν μαθητῶν.
$9^{11}$ ἔλεγον. k εἶπον. Syr-*sin* λέγουσιν.
$9^{27}$ + καὶ λέγοντες.
$9^{32}$ – ἄνθρωπον. + k. Syr-*sin* τινα.
$10^{23}$ – κἂν ἐν τῇ . . . ἄλλην.
$11^{16}$ ἐν ταῖς ἀγοραῖς for ἐν τῇ ἀγ.
$11^{19}$ ἔργων for τέκνων.
$12^{6}$ μεῖζον for μείζων.
$13^{48}$ ἦν ὅτε for ὅτε δέ (? Syr-*sin*).
Mk $8^{9}$ – οἱ φαγόντες.
$8^{10}$ εὐθὺς ἐμβάς for ἀνέβη.
$8^{36}$ ὠφελεῖ for ὠφελήσει.
$10^{2}$ + προσελθόντες [οἱ] φαρισαῖοι.
$10^{5}$ ὁ δὲ Ἰς for καὶ ἀποκ. ὁ Ἰς.
$10^{6}$ – ὁ θεός.
$10^{29}$ ἔφη for ἀποκ. . . . εἶπεν.
$11^{8}$ κόψαντες for ἔκοπτον, k.
– καὶ ἐστρώννυον. + k. Syr-*sin* omits app. by homœoteleuton.
$11^{31}$ + οὖν.
$12^{30}$ – αὕτη πρώτη ἐντολή.
$12^{31}$ αὕτη for ὁμοία αὐτῇ.
$14^{4}$ – καὶ λέγοντες.
$14^{8}$ ὃ ἔσχεν ἐποίησεν προέλαβεν μυρίσαι τὸ σῶμά μου εἰς τὸν ἐνταφ.
k : quod habuit hæc, præsumpsit et unguentavit, etc.
Syr-*sin*, 'For that which she hath done, behold as if for my burying she hath done it, and hath anointed my body beforehand.'
$14^{9}$ + δέ.
$14^{14}$ μου after τὸ κατάλυμα.
$14^{16}$ – αὐτοῦ after οἱ μαθηταί.
$14^{19}$ – οἱ δέ.
$14^{27}$ – ἐν ἐμοί.
$14^{43}$ + εὐθύς.
– πολύς.
$14^{51}$ + ἐπὶ γυμνοῦ.

80. List I. contains 44 passages in which all four authorities are agreed. Generally (not always) they form the nucleus of a small group of authorities in opposition to the bulk of later evidence. In no case do they stand quite alone. Of course this list represents only a small part of the total amount of agreement between the four texts. The most noteworthy reading in the list is the omission of Mk $16^{9-20}$—verses which must on internal grounds, as even their most strenuous supporters are now prepared to admit, have had an origin in some respects different from that of the rest of the Gospel. See, *e.g.*, *Trad. Text*, p. 305.

Lists II.–V. contain passages in which each of the four stands in turn unsupported by any of the rest. Lists VI.–VIII. represent the various combinations of the authorities taken two together.

B stands alone in 5 places.

ℵ stands alone in 14. In 4 of these Syr-*sin* has a reading of its own differing both from ℵ and B k.

Syr-*sin* stands alone in 44 places.

k stands alone in 56. In 15 of these Syr-*sin* presents a third alternative, ℵ in 2.

B and Syr-*sin* range against ℵ k in 7 places (besides the 4 closely connected readings referring to the cock-crowings in Mk.).

B and k oppose ℵ Syr-*sin* in 6 places.

ℵB oppose k Syr-*sin* combined in 31 cases, besides 4 cases in which k and Syr-*sin* offer divergent alternatives.

210 passages in all come before us. In five-sixths B is supported by ℵ, in three-fourths it has the support either of k or Syr-*sin*. And, what is even more remarkable, B (and in a less degree ℵ) is decidedly more nearly allied to both k and Syr-*sin* than k and Syr-*sin* are to one another.

81. What, then, shall we say of the significance of these facts?

First, surely, that they amply vindicate Hort's contention that the 'Neutral' text was by no means confined to Alexandria.

Next, that they demonstrate the absurdity of supposing that the text of ℵB was in any sense the result of a 'recension' by Origen.* At least five-sixths of their characteristic readings are demonstrably at least a century older than his time. Even if, as must no doubt have been the case, his judgment on a reading, as expressed in his commentaries, affected the opinions of some of the scholars and scribes—notably, *e.g.*, Pamphilus—who came after him, his influence in the case of the readings where ℵB are opposed by k Syr-*sin* would as often have led away from as towards ℵB.

Thirdly, since both B and ℵ, as we have already seen, are more nearly allied to k than Syr-*sin* is, judging by the standard of k, B and ℵ are better than Syr-*sin*. Similarly, judging by the standard of Syr-*sin*, B and ℵ are both better than k. So it would seem that, on the evidence of the Versions themselves, the value either of ℵ or of B, and *a fortiori* the value of the two combined, is distinctly higher than that of either version separately.

82. It only remains to consider the problem which arises when the two versions combine against the two MSS. Their very divergences would seem to reinforce Mr. Burkitt's argument from geography, and to lend a peculiar weight to their evidence in the readings in which they are found to agree. As we have already seen, even if these readings are to be regarded as distinctively 'Western,' genealogical considerations offer no insuperable objection in the way of their acceptance (WH, *Intr.* § 237). It is true that Hort had had to examine a closely kindred group, k Syr-*cu* in Mt., and had not found reason to reject outright any of the readings of ℵB in their favour. Still he would have been the first to insist on a careful re-examination of the whole evidence in the light of any new discovery, not to speak of a discovery of such primary importance as Syr-*sin*. He would, however, have approached the question from a point of view different in many important respects from Mr. Burkitt's. It would clearly have been no surprise to him to learn that fuller knowledge brought into clearer light the fundamentally 'Western' character of Clement's biblical text (*Intr.* § 159). He would have needed no special exhortation to come out of 'the land of Egypt,' because he had said from the first that the 'Neutral' text in remote times was not confined to Alexandria (§ 178); and the fresh evidence that has come to light since he wrote, esp. the discovery of Syr-*sin*, has brought abundant fresh confirmation in support of his original contention. On the other hand, he would no doubt have been inclined to question very seriously the assumed independence of 'East' and 'West,' of 'Carthage' and 'Edessa,' on which so much of the force of Mr. Burkitt's appeal depends.† Mr. Turner may no doubt be quite justified in contending (*Journal of Theol. Studies*, vol. ii. p. 602) that 'the agreement—when they do agree—of the two great pillars of the "Western" text, the African Latin and the Sinai Syriac, can hardly be explained away as due to any identity of their immediate source. Both may have first seen the light, it is true, in some part of Northern Syria, and both may have been produced within the limits of the same generation; but that is the only extent to which a common origin can be ascribed to them, and it is not enough to qualify seriously the weight of their consentient testimony.' It is, however, more than enough, if any part of Northern Syria is really to be regarded as the birthplace of the Latin Version, to weaken considerably the force of Mr. Burkitt's argument. For the agreement of two parts, even allowing them to be different parts, of Northern Syria, is a very poor substitute for the agreement 'of East and West, of Carthage and Edessa.' We shall require at least some clear internal evidence to induce us to go to 'some part of Northern Syria' for a surer foundation than ℵB for the text of the Gospels. In fact the ultimate appeal must lie, as Dr. Hort's words (§ 373) indicate, and Dr. Westcott's words* (*Intr.*[2] p. 328) state expressly, to the Internal Evidence of the Readings of the opposing groups. Judged by this standard, if the readings of List VIII. prove, as the present writer thinks they will, to be a fair sample of the whole, it is extremely unlikely that more than a very few of the readings of k Syr-*sin* will ultimately make good their claim to a place in the text. *E.g.* Mk 10[2] the omission of φαρισαῖοι may with considerable probability be regarded as genuine, but hardly any other in the whole list, least of all the insertion of εἰκῇ, Mt 5[22].

83. On the whole, then, there seems no reason to anticipate that the present revival of interest in the early history of the 'Western' text will in the end be found to upset the estimates formed by WH of the relative importance of the different groups of textual authorities, or to modify in more than a mere handful of passages the judgments which they formed on individual readings.

84. As this article is drawing to its conclusion the news comes in rapid succession of the deaths of the two last surviving protagonists in the textual controversies of the nineteenth century. Fundamentally as the present writer differs from the position taken up by Prebendary Miller in his published works on Textual Criticism, and strangely as he seems to him to have overlooked or failed to understand the plainest statements put forward on the other side, he must not close this article without a warm tribute of admiration for his unwearied industry, his enthusiasm for his subject, and his profound conviction of the sacredness of the cause which he felt called to defend.

The loss of Dr. Westcott will naturally be felt most keenly in spheres of Christian thought and activity that are of deeper, broader, and more universal interest than Textual Criticism. But it may be permitted to call attention here to the witness borne to the intrinsic importance of the

* It is interesting to notice that Koetschau ('Bibelcitate bei Origenes,' *Z. f. w. Theol.* p. 321 ff.) has recently expressed his agreement with the opinion of Griesbach and Hort (*Intr.* § 249; cf. Nestle, *Intr.* p. 185 ff.) that Origen 'never made anything like a recension of the New Testament.'

† Intr. to Barnard's *Clement*, etc. p. xviii: 'Let us come out of the land of Egypt, which speaks (as Clement's quotations show) with such doubtful authority, and let us see whether the agreement of East and West, of Edessa and Carthage, will not give us a surer basis upon which to establish our text of the Gospels.'

* His words are: 'The discovery of the Sinaitic MS of the Old Syriac raises the question whether the combination of the oldest types of the Syriac and Latin texts can outweigh the combination of the primary Greek texts. A careful examination of the passages in which Syr-*sin* and k are arrayed against ℵB would point to this conclusion.' The best comment on the last sentence is supplied by the specimens of Dr. Westcott's habitual method of working, as shown in the introductions to his commentaries on the Gospel and Epistles of St. John, and on the Epistle to the Hebrews. It does not, as Nestle seems to think (*Intr.* p. 923), involve a surrender at discretion to the authority of Syr-*sin* and k. It simply calls for a systematic comparison of the distinctive readings of the rival groups before a final judgment is passed on their respective merits.

study by the fact that it occupied so large a share of the time and attention of such a man. The fact that the writing of the *Introduction* fell to Dr. Hort has prevented scholars generally from realizing the nature and the extent of Dr. Westcott's share in that wonderful monument of the labour of 28 years. The minds and methods of the two fellow-workers were remarkably distinct, and well fitted to check and complement each other. And their work is in the strictest sense the resultant of their combined forces, and not, as in weaker hands work on the same principle might tend to become, a mere compromise appreciably feebler and weaker than either scholar would have produced independently.

All the time the present writer was engaged on this article he was looking forward to the day when he could present it to Dr. Westcott as some acknowledgment, however unworthy, of a debt of gratitude that has been accumulating for 24 years, and gather from his kind but searching criticism what measure of success had attended this attempt to expound and illustrate the principles on which he and his great collaborator had worked. Now he can only inscribe it with reverence and affection to their memory. Christian scholarship will for all time be the richer for the example of their 'implicit confidence in all truth' and their 'guileless workmanship' (*Intr.* § 425).

J. O. F. MURRAY.

**VERSIONS (ENGLISH).**—Owing to the length of the subject, it may be found convenient to divide it into the following sections: (i.) Anglo-Saxon; (ii.) Anglo-Norman; (iii.) Wyclifite; (iv.) Reformation period; (v.) Puritan; (vi.) Elizabethan; (vii.) Roman Catholic; (viii.) The 'Authorized' and its successors; (ix.) The 'Revised'; (x.) The 'American Revised.'

i. ANGLO-SAXON.—At the head of this period it is usual to place **Cædmon** († *c.* 680), although he did not, properly speaking, translate any part of the Bible. The work ascribed to him is an alliterative poem, in which he paraphrases the Scripture account of the chief events in Genesis, Exodus, and Daniel. A continuation of the poem, now imperfect, treats of portions of the life of Christ. His story is picturesquely told by Bede (*HE* IV. xxiv.),—how, from a servant, he became a monk in the mixed monastery under St. Hilda; and how, when bidden to exercise his newly found gift of song, he burst forth into a hymn of praise of the great Creator. Bede gives in Latin the substance of this hymn. On the margin of some MSS of Bede a short West-Saxon poem of nine lines is found, purporting to be the original. At the end of the Moore MS (Camb. Univ. Lib. Kk. v. 16) the verses are found in the Northumbrian dialect; and, as this would be Cædmon's own tongue, it has been considered to be the older form. But whether any of these is the original vernacular of Cædmon, or only a retranslation from Bede's Latin, cannot be pronounced with certainty. The hymn bears only a general resemblance to the beginning of the poems, and hence doubts have been thrown on the Cædmonian authorship of the latter.* The poems exist, so far as is known, in one manuscript only (Bodleian, Junius xi.). It was given by Archbishop Ussher to Francis Dujon, or Junius, librarian of the Earl of Arundel, and by him bequeathed to the Bodleian. It was printed at Amsterdam in 1655, and was edited with an English translation by Benjamin Thorpe in 1832, and again published by Grein in his *Bibliothek* in 1857. A short passage from Thorpe's literal rendering, on the subject of Nebuchadnezzar's chastisement, will give some notion of Cædmon's style—

'To thee shall not be meal-meat,
save the mountain's grass,
nor rest assigned:
but thee the rain's shower
shall waken and chastise.'

**Bede** († 735) himself is known to have translated portions of Scripture into his native tongue. Purvey, indeed, in his General Prologue,* asserts that 'if worldli clerkis loken wel here croniclis and bokis, thei shulden fynde, that Bede translatide the bible.' No authority, so far as is known to the present writer, can now be found for this statement. But Bede expressly says, in a letter to Bishop Ecgbert (c. v.), that he had often translated the Creed and Lord's Prayer for uneducated priests.† And the touching passage is familiar to all, in which his biographer Cuthbert describes the end of his life approaching, before he had finished his version of St. John.‡ It is a matter for regret, that not even this version should have escaped the ravages of time.

**King Alfred** († 900) added to his other titles to the name of Great an expressed conviction that his code of civil laws must be based upon the revealed law of God. Acting on this conviction, he prefaced his code of Saxon laws with a free translation of the enactments in Ex 20–23, and of the letter sent by the apostles in Jerusalem, contained in Ac 15. His reason for the addition, at first sight apparently singular, of this passage from the NT, was to show how the harshness of the Hebrew *lex talionis* was modified by the teaching of Christianity. In king Alfred's translation there are some noticeable peculiarities. In Ex 20[11] 'for in six days the Lord made heaven and earth,' for 'Lord' (*Dominus*) he puts, not *Dryhten*, the usual word, but *Crist*:—'forðam on .VI. daȝum *crist* ȝewohrte heofonas ⁊ eorðan.' The explanation is that, in a contemporary Anglo-Saxon poem, Christ is made to describe how He created the earth; and *Dominus*, in the Vulgate of the NT, is of course frequently used of Christ. Another singular change is his transposition of a clause in the Fifth Commandment. He places 'which the Lord thy God giveth thee' directly after 'thy father and thy mother,' apparently wishing to take 'land' in the general sense of earth, and so removing the limitation. A third alteration is made at the end of Ac 15[29]. In the Latin text followed by him there is an interpolated clause: 'et quod vobis non vultis fieri, non faciatis aliis.' This is duly rendered: '⁊ þæt ȝe willen þæt oðre men êow ne don, ne doð ȝe ðæt oþrum monnum'; 'and what ye would that other men should not do to you, that do ye not to other men.'§

Besides these, there are extant various MSS by unknown authors, containing Anglo-Saxon versions of the Psalms and of the Gospels. One such version of the Psalter, contained in a MS found in the National Library of Paris about the be-

* See the edition of Bede's works by Plummer, 1896, vol. ii. p. 252, where the question is ably discussed, and F. Graz's *Beiträge zur Textkritik der sogenannten Caedmonschen Genesis*, Königsberg, 1896. An interesting study of this 'Milton of our forefathers' will be found in R. S. Watson's *Cædmon, the first English Poet*, 1875.

* Forshall and Madden's *Introduction*, p. 59.

† 'Propter quod et ipse multis sæpe sacerdotibus idiotis hæc utraque, et symbolum uidelicet et dominicam orationem, in linguam Anglorum translatam optuli.'

‡ See Appendix ii. to vol. i. of Plummer's edition. A difficulty is caused, as the editor points out, by the reading of the St. Gallen MS, which appears to make Bede's translation extend only to Jn 6[19]. Such a limitation spoils the sequel of the story; unless we understand it to mean that the translator had got no further, when the premonitory symptoms of his illness came upon him.

§ See *The Legal Code of Ælfred the Great*, ed. by Professor Milton Haight Turk, Boston (U.S.A.), 1893, pp. 33–37. The explanations given in the text are from Professor Turk, who in turn acknowledges his indebtedness to the late Dr. F. J. A. Hort.

ginning of this century, has been thought to be, in part at least, the work of Aldhelm († 709), bishop of Sherborne. If so, it would be as early as the 7th century. There seems, however, no evidence that it is his work, or as early as his time. In this version the first fifty Psalms are rendered into prose, the remainder into verse. It was published by Benjamin Thorpe in 1835.* Two other versions were published—one edited by Spelman in 1640, and the other by Stevenson in 1843.†

Of the Gospels, in like manner, three Anglo-Saxon versions were published, from MSS—one by Archbishop Parker, in 1571 ; another by Marshall, rector of Lincoln College, in 1665 ; and the third by Thorpe, in 1842.‡ It had been a complaint of scholars that no proper estimate could be formed, from these detached publications, of the relative value of the original MSS, or their relation to one another.§ This cause of complaint has now been removed. In the edition of the Gospels just referred to, put forth by Skeat,‖ not only is a larger number of MSS brought into requisition, but their comparative date and value are ascertained. Two well-known 'glosses' are also included in this collection—the Lindisfarne, or Durham Book, and the Rushworth. In these the Latin is interlined with a *verbatim* rendering in Anglo-Saxon. The date of the Latin text of the Lindisfarne is, roughly speaking, about A.D. 700 ; that of its 'gloss,' the work of a priest named Aldred, some two and a half centuries later. The gloss in the Rushworth MS (so called from its donor) is derived from the Lindisfarne. In a note at the end of St. John's Gospel the names of the two makers of the gloss (in this case little more than transcribers) are given : Færmen, or Farman, a priest of Harewood in Yorkshire, and Owun.¶ It is obvious that, from the nature of its construction, a word for word gloss can scarcely be called a translation.

Before leaving the Anglo-Saxon period, a brief mention should be made of the metrical version, with many abridgments and omissions, of the Pentateuch, and the books of Joshua, Judges, Kings, Esther, Job, Judith, and Maccabees, the work of **Ælfric,** Abbot of Peterborough in 1004, and Archbishop of York in 1023. What remains of this version was published in 1698 by Edward Thwaites, at Oxford, under the title *Heptateuchus, Liber Iob, et Evangelium Nicodemi*, etc. It was reprinted by Thorpe in 1834, in his *Analecta Anglo-Saxonica*, and still more recently by Grein in his *Bibliothek*. This version, like all those previously mentioned, is from the Latin.**

* See the Preface to Forshall and Madden's Wycliflte Bible, p. i, and Mombert's *English Versions*, p. 9, where a specimen of the translation is given.

† See Moulton's *History of the English Bible*², p. 8. In 1885 the Vespasian Psalter (an interlinear Anglo-Saxon gloss, so called from its being contained in the Cotton MS Vespasian A. 1) was edited by Henry Sweet for the Early English Text Society. Its date is the first half of the 9th century. The text of a later one, the Eadwine Canterbury Psalter, was also edited for the same Society by F. Harsley in 1888.

‡ Forshall and Madden, as before.

§ Westcott, *History of the English Bible*, 1872, p. 6, n. 2.

‖ *The Holy Gospels in Anglo-Saxon, Northumbrian, and Old Mercian versions*, ed. by the Rev. Walter W. Skeat . . . 1871–1877, 4to.

¶ These particulars are taken from Skeat's edition. See also the Preface of Forshall and Madden. With regard to the MS versions, Skeat considers the C.C.C. Cambridge MS (No. 140), the Bodleian (441), and the Cottonian (Otho C. 1), to be practically duplicate copies of an unknown original. The MS in the Camb. Univ. Libr. (Ii. 2. 11) is closely akin, perhaps a little later. This evidence is of value as pointing to the existence of a common Anglo-Saxon version.

** A specimen of Ælfric's translation will be found at p. 16 of Mombert's *English Versions*. See also Eadie's *English Bible*, vol. i. pp. 15, 16. In the Handbook for the Wyclif Exhibition, arranged by Sir E. M. Thompson, 1884, p. 4, there is a description of an early 11th cent. MS of Ælfric (Cotton, Claudius B. iv.) ; and also, at p. 1, a full account of the precious 'Durham Book,' mentioned above.

It is a characteristic of the Anglo-Saxon idiom, in the versions described, that it prefers rendering foreign words, even though clumsily, to retaining and assimilating them. Thus 'centurion' becomes 'hundred-man,' 'disciple' 'leorning-cniht,' 'parable' 'bigspel,' 'sabbath' 'reste-dæg,' 'treasury' 'gold-hórd,' and so on.* It will be borne in mind, also, that the Latin text from which these versions have been made is not the Vulgate as we have it, but in some cases the earliest of Jerome's revisions, in others the *Vetus Itala*.†

ii. ANGLO-NORMAN.—During the three centuries that elapsed after the Conquest, the changes going on in the national life and character were not favourable, at any rate for a time, to the spread of vernacular translations. Apart from the sudden disruption in government, and the diversion of men's thoughts to war rather than religion or literature, the infusion of Norman-French, with its swifter current, into the slower English speech, like the influx of the Rhone into the Saône, would tend to check the formation of a common literary tongue. The native strength of the invaded language prevailed in the long run ; but for a while, as all know, the Norman-French remained the language of the court, the school, the bar, while its rival held possession of the farmhouse and the cottage. A collateral result of this state of things was, that the educated classes were the more readily satisfied with Latin, as the language for religious use ; while the need, or the possibility, of devotional books in one common native tongue was less and less thought of.‡

Yet even in this period, as Forshall and Madden have pointed out, the Anglo-Normans had translated into their own dialect, before the year 1200, the Psalter and Canticles of the Church in prose.§ More remarkable still, they are said to have executed in this country a prose translation into their own tongue of the entire Bible.‖ Metrical paraphrases of Scripture stories, such as are found in the *Ormulum*,¶ would help to keep alive a knowledge of Holy Writ.

It will suffice, however, here to give a short account of two works, both belonging to the first half of the 14th cent. ; of one of which it is said that it is 'the earliest version in English prose of any entire book of Scripture.' Both are prose versions of the Psalms. The author of the first is commonly believed to be the **William of Shoreham** (de Schorham), of whom we have a number of English poems remaining. William himself was probably a monk of the priory of Leeds in Kent. Shoreham, presumably his native place, is between four and five miles from Sevenoaks. When the rectory of Chart Sutton, in Kent, was impropriated by Walter Raynolds, Archbishop of Canterbury from 1313 to 1327, to Leeds priory, William of Shoreham became its first vicar.** In this capacity, like an earlier George Herbert, he poured forth his

* See Bosworth and Waring's *Gothic and Anglo-Saxon Gospels*, 1865, p. xvii.

† Moulton, *The English Bible*, p. 9. See also Bosworth and Waring, as before, Pref. p. x, where examples are given.

‡ See Traill's *Social England*, vol. ii. (1894) p. 538, and Freeman's *Norman Conquest*, v. p. 508.

§ *Preface*, p. iii. They refer, in evidence, to Cotton MS Nero C. iv., Trinity Coll. Camb. MS R. 17. 1, and others.

‖ *Ib.* The editors refer to the *Catalogue des MSS françois de la Bibliothèque du Roi*, by M. Alexis Paulin Paris ; in vol. i. pp. 1–3 of which is a description of a MS (No. 6701) entitled *Traduction littérale de la Sainte Bible*. M. Paris thinks that the writing and dialect of the MS, which is assigned to the 14th cent., prove it to have been 'exécuté en Angleterre.' The other two MSS referred to by Forshall and Madden contain, according to M. Paris (*Catalogue*, t. vii. pp. 183, 200), only 'traductions en vers' from the Bible.

¶ The *Ormulum*, so called from its author Ormin, or Orm, an Augustinian canon of the 12th cent., was edited by R. M. White (2nd ed. 1878). Notes on its spelling will be found in an edition of the *History of the Holy Rood*, by A. S. Napier (Early English Text Society), 1894.

** These particulars are taken from the Preface to *The Religious Poems of William de Shoreham*, edited for the Percy Society by Thomas Wright, 1849. Wright's text is criticised in many passages by Konrath in his *Beiträge zur Erklärung und Textkritik des W. von Schorham*, Berlin, 1878.

soul in verse. So far as is known, his poems are contained in one solitary manuscript,* which also contains a prose version of the Psalter in English of this period. Whether the two productions are to be referred to the same author, has been made a matter of question. That the poems are the work of William of Shoreham, is not doubted. His name is found in the colophon to some of them. And it might be thought sufficient evidence of unity of authorship, under the circumstances, that the handwriting is the same throughout. But Konrath argues, on the other side, that the dialect in which the version of the Psalter is written is not Kentish, as 'Schorham's' would naturally be, but Midland.†

The subjoined extract, containing the opening verses of Ps 56 (in the Latin Bible 55), will enable the reader to judge of the style of the version:—

*Miserere mei, deus, quoniam conculcauit me homo: tota die impugnans diabolus tribulauit me.* Haue mercy on me, god, for man haþ defouled me. Þe fende trubled me, feȝtand alday oȝayns me. *Conculcauerunt me inimici mei tota die, quoniam multi bellantes erant aduersum me.* Myn enemys defouled m[e] alday, for many were feȝtand oȝains me. *Ab ascendine diei timebo te: ego uero in te sperabo.* Y shal drede þe fram þe heȝt of þe daye: Y for soþe shal hope in þe. *In deo laudabo sermones meos in deo speraui: non timebo quid faciat michi humana caro.* Hii shal hery my wordes, what manes flesshe doþ to me. *Tota die mala uerba mea execrabantur: aduersum me omnes cogitaciones eorum in malum.* Alday þe wicked acurseden myn wordes oȝains me: alle her þoutes ben in iuel. *Inhabitabunt in inferno & abscondent se ibi. ipsi calcaneum meum obseruabunt.* Hii shul wonen in helle, and þer hii shul hiden hem, and hii shul kepen mid fouleinges. *Sicut sustinuerunt* .i. temptauerunt *animam meam, pro illo saluos faceres eos & in ira tua populos istos constringes* .i. aduersabis. As hii tempteden my soule for nouȝt, þou shalt make hem sauf and ȝou shalt bringe to nouȝt þes folkes in þyn ire. *Deus, uitam meam annuntiaui tibi: posuisti lacrimas meas in conspectu tuo.* Ha, god, ich telde my lyf to þe: þou laidest min teres in þy syȝt.‡

Whatever doubt there may be as to the authorship of the version of the Psalter known as Shoreham's, there is none regarding that assigned to **Richard Rolle** of Hampole († 1349). Richard was a native of Thornton, near Pickering, in Yorkshire, and was sent to Oxford by Thomas de Nevile, archdeacon of Durham. At the age of nineteen, obeying an inward impulse, he left the university, and became a hermit at Hampole, near Doncaster.§ His commentary is devotional and mystical, and, as such, is often quoted by Adam Clarke in his notes on the Bible. The following specimens will show his method, which is to set down, after each verse of the Latin in order, a literal rendering of it, and then to add his own comments:—

Ps 135¹ *Confitemini Domino quoniam bonus: quoniam in eternum misericordia eius.* ¶ Shrifis til lorde for he is gode: for withouten end the mercy of him. ¶ Grete louyng of this psalme is shewyd in paralypomenon,‖ where it is red. that when the sunnys of israel began to loue god and sey *confitemini domino.* the ioy of god fulfilde goddis hous. also nere is the presens of goddis grace, if hit be purly seyd. loue we god here that we may loue him with aungels: his louying is our fode. for no delite is like it.

Ps 136¹ *Super flumina babilonis illic sedimus & fleuimus: dum recordaremur syon.* ¶ Abouen the flodes of babilon thar we sat and gret: whils we vmthouȝt* of syon. ¶ fflodis of babilon are all thinges that are lufid here. and passis, that holy men beholdis and forsakes, sittand abouen thaim. & gretis thair oun pilgrymage & thair synne. that are rauysht in til the flodis. whils thei thynk of syon. that is, of heuen, where nothing rennys, bot all that ioy is to gedur. worldis men gretis. bot nouȝt bot for tynsil of thair godes or thair frendis. as thei ioy nouȝt bot in thair welth. ilk man shal grete. bot thinkand of syon.

iii. Wyclifite.—To understand aright the Biblical labours of Wyclif and those who worked with him, we must take a brief survey of the events amidst which he grew up, and try to discern their general drift.

The reign of Edward III. is often described as one of outward glory and prosperity. It was so in part, but it was much more (the latter part of it, at least) a period of upheaval and slow-working revolutionary movements. It was a period in which the sentiment of national independence became more strong and definite, both in civil and religious matters. In 1338 the German electors asserted their right to choose a king, whose title should not need confirmation by the pope.† The 'captivity' of the papacy itself, when from 1378 to 1409 an anti-Rome was fixed at Avignon, tended materially to strengthen this sentiment. The claims of a spiritual sovereignty, the visible seat of which was at a spot just outside the French frontier, became perceptibly weakened, as regards England at least, in a country which regarded France as its natural enemy. Evidence of the growth of this anti-papal feeling was shown in the passing of the Statute of Provisors in 1351, of the Ordinance of Præmunire in 1353, and of the formidable statute bearing that name in 1393. The great battles of the reign, and its great calamity of the Black Death, both, rightly interpreted, taught the same lesson. At Creçy and Poitiers it was the national militia of England that overthrew the feudal chivalry of France; the yeoman's cloth-yard shaft that unhorsed the mail-clad noble. After the Black Death of 1348–49, which ceased only after it had swept away half the entire population, those of the working classes who were left, whether as labourers in the fields or handicraftsmen in the towns, were masters of the situation. No statutes of labourers could prevent them from demanding and obtaining higher wages. For the next thirty years the struggle went on between the forces of upheaval, on the one hand, and repression on the other, till it culminated in the Peasant Revolt, and in the scenes of riot at Bury and St. Albans.

This spirit of the age is seen reflected in the two poets who, with Wyclif, are the greatest names in its literature. William Langland, born about 1332, took for the hero of his discursive poem, no noble, but a peasant, Piers the Plowman, who 'rises, in the poet's conception, from being only a representative English labourer, to the type of Christ himself.'‡ And of the many characters who grew into life under the creative hand of Chaucer, the one drawn with the finest and most loving touch, the 'poure persoun of a toune,' was a ploughman's brother.

Of **John Wyclif** himself, at least for the earlier part of his life, but few facts are known with certainty. He was a Yorkshireman, and, according to Leland,§ came from the village of Wyclif-on-Tees. That he entered Oxford is certain; and, as he was afterwards Master of Balliol College, a college founded not long before by a neighbouring

* No. 17,376 of the Additional MSS in the British Museum. It is on vellum, 7¾ by 5¼ in. in size. A memorandum by the late Sir F. Madden, on the fly-leaf, relates the curious adventures through which the MS passed before it finally came into the possession of the Museum in 1849. The writer notes also the resemblance of the version of the Psalter to that in a MS in the Library of Trinity College, Dublin, ascribed to John Hyde.

† *Beiträge*, as before, p. 1. It was, however, a tendency of the Mercian, or Midland, to absorb collateral dialects into itself; and possibly some who spoke Kentish might write Mercian. See a passage quoted from John de Trevisa in Traill's *Social England*, ii. p. 538.

‡ The English of this passage was given as a specimen in the Guide-book to the Wyclif Exhibition, before mentioned, p. 10. We have inserted the Latin text from the MS itself, fol. 50. It is noticeable how much it differs from the Vulgate.

§ See the edition of *The Psalter or Psalms of David and certain Canticles* . . . by Richard Rolle, of Hampole, ed. by H. R. Bramley, 1884, p. v. The MSS used by the editor are Univ. Coll. MS lxiv.; Sidney Sussex Coll. MS Δ 5. 3; and the Laudian MS 286.

‖ Chronicles. The reference is to 2 Ch 7¹.

* Thought about. So *umgang*, with the prefix used as in German.

† Traill, *Social England*, ii. p. 159.

‡ *Ib.* p. 226.

§ *Collectanea*, ii. 329. For the claims of a supposed 'Spresswell' to be his birthplace, see the Introduction to Wyclif's *English Works*, by F. D. Matthew, 1880, p. i.

family, the Balliols of Barnard Castle, it may be reasonably concluded that this was the place of his education. In 1360 he became, as has just been said, Master of Balliol; and in 1361 he was presented to the rectory of Fillingham in Lincolnshire, resigning his Mastership soon after. This living he exchanged, in 1368, for that of Ludgers hall in Buckinghamshire, probably as being nearer Oxford. Whether he was the John Wyclif appointed by Archbishop Islip, in 1365, warden of his secularized foundation of Canterbury Hall, is doubtful.* In 1366 his pen was employed in the service of Parliament, which had rejected the claim of pope Urban V. for payment of arrears of the annual tribute first imposed on king John. On this occasion he terms himself 'peculiaris regis clericus.'† In 1371 he advocated the proposal that the revenues of the Church should be subject to the general taxation. In 1374, being by this time a Doctor of Divinity, he was nominated on a commission appointed to confer with the pope's representatives at Bruges about the exercise of papal Provisions.‡ In his protracted stay on the Continent his mind may well have been stirred by what he saw, to speculate 'de optimo statu ecclesiæ,' as More's was, when on a similar mission on secular business, in the same region, to speculate 'de optimo statu reipublicæ.' The embassy was a fruitless one. Possibly as a reward for his services, Wyclif was presented, in 1374, to the Crown living of Lutterworth; where, having resigned Ludgershall, he remained till his death.

In 1377 came the first open attack made upon him by the authorities of the Church. He was cited to appear before Convocation, assembled at St. Paul's on Feb. 19th. But the prosecution was really a political one, aimed at John of Gaunt, through Wyclif, and the proceedings came to nothing. Papal bulls then arrived, requiring his prosecution on nineteen specified articles. For a time these were suspended owing to the death of Edward III. in June of the same year. But in the spring of 1378 he appeared at Lambeth to stand his trial. Once more, however, the prosecution was arrested, this time by the influence of the Princess of Wales, widow of the Black Prince.§ In 1382 he had a stroke of paralysis, from which he partially recovered. But on Innocents' Day, 1384, he was again struck down, while engaged in Divine service, and died on the last day of that year.

Such are the bare outlines of Wyclif's life. It would seem that one of the subjects most in his thoughts, suggested in part, no doubt, by the events through which he lived, was that of lordship or dominion. By what title did the pope, the abbot, the secular governor, claim the power he exercised? Was that 'lordship' dependent, in any way, on his own personal character? Did it involve a reciprocity of service? The theories he formed appear to have been suggested by the *de Pauperie Salvatoris* of Richard Fitz Ralph, archbishop of Armagh, who died in 1360.‖ But in the mind of Wyclif they did not remain mere speculative theories, but became actively aggressive principles. One of his propositions was: 'Quod ad verum dominium seculare requiritur iustitia dominantis, sic quod nullus in peccato mortali est dominus alicuius rei.'* From this great principle, which Wyclif intentionally made a prelude to his *Summa in Theologia*, the line of action he subsequently followed may in large measure be deduced. His life was a rebellion against what he believed to be unjust dominion—a rebellion analogous to the national one going on in more than one country of Europe at the time.

As a justification of this course of conduct, since ecclesiastical authority was adverse to him, he fell back upon the teaching of Holy Scripture. The Word of God, he believed, would support him in his position, though the religious orders might assail him, and archbishops condemn. Hence he began to lay stress on the importance of a study of the Bible, and the necessity that people should be able to read it in their own tongue. In his tract on the Pastoral Office, probably written not later than 1378,† he pleads for an English translation. After instancing the gift of tongues at Pentecost, and the fact of St. Jerome's making a translation of the Bible, he continues: 'Also the wurthy reume of fraunse, not-with-stondinge alle lettingis, hath translatid the bible and the gospels with othere trewe sentensis of doctours out of lateyn in-to freynsch, why shulden not engliysche men do so? as lordis of englond han the bible in freynsch, so it were not ayenus (against) resoun that they hadden the same sentense in engliysch; for thus goddis lawe wolde be betere knowun & more trowid for onehed of wit (believed for unity of meaning), & more acord be be-twixe reumes.'‡

At what precise date Wyclif began himself to supply this want, we have not the means of knowing. No doubt, his thoughts had long been turned to it. But the genuineness of what is commonly cited as his first work in this field, a Commentary on the Apocalypse, with translation, has been called in question. At any rate, by the year 1380 he was busily occupied with the task of translating the NT, while a fellow-worker, **Nicholas of Hereford**,§ was engaged upon the OT. Hereford's work, of which the original MS is extant, breaks off abruptly in the middle of a verse, Bar $3^{20}$. The cause of this sudden interruption has been conjectured to be a summons to appear before a synod of preaching friars, served upon Hereford in 1382, followed by an adjourned trial held at Canterbury, which ended in his being excom-

* F D. Matthew inclines to the view that he was. See the *Introduction* as before, p. iv, n. Sir E. M. Thompson, in the account of Wyclif prefixed to the Guide-book before referred to, thinks the evidence for it conclusive.

† Compare the title 'clericus specialissimus domini regis,' borne by Philip Repyngdon. It appears to mean king's chaplain, and not, as some think, a special clerk or commissioner.

‡ Stubbs, *Constitutional History*, 1880, ii. p. 463.

§ *Ib.* p. 484.

‖ See the Preface to R. L. Poole's edition of the *de Dominio*, 1890, pp. xxxiv-xxxvi.

* *Ib.* p. xlvii. For the evidence that the *de Dominio* is Wyclif's, see p. xxii.

† *English Works*, ed. by F. D. Matthew, pp. 405, 429. The editor makes no doubt that this is Wyclif's own composition. In another tract, on the Office of Curates, probably not by Wyclif himself, but by one of his school (*ib.* p. 141), the language used is very decisive. Speaking of the opposite party, the writer says: 'thei crien opynly that seculer men schullen not entirmeten (meddle) hem of the gospel to rede it in heir modir tonge, but heere her gostly fadris preche & do after hem in alle thingis; but this is expresly ayenst goddis techynge.'

‡ Mr. Matthew suggests (p. 530) that the French translation referred to in this passage may be that described by M. Paris. See above, p. $237^b$ note ‖. Bender, in his *Der Reformator Johann Wicklif*, 1884, pp. 11-20, collects the passages, from Foxe and others, which seem to indicate the existence of vernacular Bibles in England before Wyclif's time. But if any such had been known to Wyclif, his argument in the text would have lost its force.

§ Nicholas of Hereford was an Oxford man, and Fellow of Queen's, with which college Wyclif also is said to have been connected. He was implicated in the confession of John Ball in 1381. Throughout the Lent of 1382 he was preaching zealously at the University Church in support of Wyclif's doctrines; but on June 15th was suspended from all public functions. On July 1st, failing to appear at his trial, he was excommunicated. From this sentence he appealed to the pope, and set out for Rome. Hence probably the sudden termination of his manuscript work, before referred to. More than once he narrowly escaped being handed over to the secular power. At length, after being, according to Foxe, grievously tormented in Saltwood Castle, he recanted, probably in 1391. He afterwards himself sat in judgment on heretics, was treasurer of Hereford Cathedral in 1397, and died in the Carthusian monastery of St. Anne, Coventry, somewhere about 1420.—See R. L. Poole's article in the *Dict. of Nat. Biography*.

municated on July 1st. Who continued and finished the OT * we do not know. It would no doubt be under Wyclif's superintendence; but it was in this year that he had his first seizure of illness, and it is difficult to believe that he could, single-handed, have finished his own NT work, and also what was wanting of Hereford's. It is usual, however, to assign to him the whole of the NT translation and the remainder of the OT.

The want of uniformity perceptible in the work, added to the defects naturally attending a first attempt, rendered a complete revision necessary. This was at once taken in hand; but, before it could be finished, death removed the master mind. A faithful disciple of Wyclif, **John Purvey**,† carried on the work, and, somewhere about 1388, the whole task of revision was accomplished.

In a lengthy 'Prolog' to the OT thus revised, Purvey states the principles by which he had been guided. Out of a charitable desire, he says, 'to saue alle men in our rewme (realm), whiche God wole haue sauid, a symple creature hadde myche trauaile, with diuerse felawis and helperis,‡ to gedere manie elde biblis, and othere doctouris, and comune glosis,§ and to make oo Latyn bibel sumdel (somewhat) trewe.' He then describes the process of revision, as the workers compared the version made with 'the glose,' and other doctors, 'and speciali Lire ‖ on the elde testament, that helpide ful myche in this werke.' A third time their performance was tested, by a reference to grammarians and early writers, in order to settle

* It should be remembered that, according to the arrangement of the books of the OT in the Vulgate, the portion remaining after Baruch is not large—Ezekiel, Daniel (with its continuations), the Minor Prophets, and 1 and 2 Maccabees.

† The important part taken by Purvey in Wyclif's great work makes some particulars of his life desirable. He is said to have been a native of Lathbury in Buckinghamshire, born about 1354. Wyclif, it will be remembered, was at one time rector of Ludgershall in that county. During Wyclif's residence at Lutterworth, Purvey was closely associated with him, and, after his master's death, went, as one of the itinerant preachers, to Bristol, a city in sympathy with the new movement. Proceedings were taken against him by the Bishop of Worcester, and in 1390 he was imprisoned. In 1400–1 he was brought before Convocation, and recanted. In August 1401 he was presented to the vicarage of West Hythe in Kent; but, his mind being ill at ease, he resigned it in Oct. 1403. In 1421 we find him again imprisoned by Archbishop Chicheley. He was alive in 1427, after which nothing seems known of him.—See the article by J. W. Hales in the *Dict. of Nat. Biography*, vol. xlvii. p. 52.

‡ Who these helpers were we can only conjecture. The three following were noted adherents of Wyclif at the time, and it is not improbable that one or more of them had a hand in the work:—John Aston, or Ashton, is said to have been of Merton College, Oxford. If Wyclif was seneschal of Merton, this might account for their friendship. In 1382 he was conspicuous as one of Wyclif's itinerant preachers. In that year, along with Lawrence Bedeman, Nicholas Hereford, and Philip Repyngdon, he was summoned to appear at Blackfriars, in London, before Archbishop Courtney. By a royal patent, July 13th, he was expelled from his university. On Nov. 27th he recanted, but we find him again denounced as a Lollard, and prohibited from preaching.

Lawrence Bedeman, otherwise Stevine, was an Oxford man, like his companions, being of Stapeldon Hall, afterwards Exeter College. It fared with him, in 1382, as with Aston. Brantingham, Bishop of Exeter, took proceedings against him for his conduct as an itinerant preacher in Cornwall. After making his submission, he became rector of Lifton, Devonshire, and was there as late as 1410.

Philip of Repyngdon was probably a native of Repton. He was educated at Broadgates Hall, Oxford, and before 1382 was an Augustinian canon of St. Mary de Pré, Leicester. Like Hereford, he was a vigorous upholder of Wyclif's tenets in sermons at Oxford. When exposed to the same trial, he appears to have succumbed at once, becoming afterwards a great favourite with Henry IV., with the style of 'clericus specialissimus domini regis Henrici,' and in 1404–5 being made Bishop of Lincoln. On Sept. 18th, 1408, he was created a cardinal by Gregory XII., and died in 1424.—See the articles by C. L. Kingsford and R. L. Poole in the *Dict. of Nat. Biography*.

§ The *glossa ordinaria*, or 'comune glose,' was the work of Walafrid Strabo, about A.D. 840. The interlinear gloss was later.

‖ Nicolaus de Lyra, so called from the place of his birth in Normandy, was a converted Jew. Hence the special value attached to his commentary on the Old Testament. He died at Paris in 1340.

the precise use and meaning of words and phrases. And yet once again there was a final scrutiny, by a committee, as we should say, when there were present 'manie gode felawis and kynnynge at the correcting of the translacioun.' *

That the work, after so much preliminary care, was well and thoroughly done, need not surprise us. Purvey's revision appears to have aimed chiefly at making the rendering more idiomatic, both in respect of the vocabulary and the construction of sentences. In particular, too close an imitation of the participial construction of the Latin had often led the earlier translators into difficulties. 'Wyclif's own part,' says a competent judge,† 'offends less in this respect than Hereford's; but the work of each needed anglicizing or englishing; and this was the improvement Purvey set himself to carry out.' A few examples will make this clearer. It should be premised that not only was the Vulgate the sole authority for the translation, but that, as Purvey himself says, the text of the Vulgate was then in a bad state. 'The comune Latin biblis,' he declares, 'han more nede to be correctid, as manie as I haue seen in my lif, than hath the English bible late translatid.' This was particularly the case with the Psalms, St. Jerome's version of which was not used in the services of the Church, 'but another translacioun of othere men, that hadden myche lasse kunnyng and holynesse than Jerom hadde.'

In Ex $7^{22}$ the *malefici* of the Vulgate is rendered 'the clepers of deuels to doon yuel' by Hereford; 'witchis' by Purvey.

Jos $10^{17}$ 'lurking in the spelunk of the cite' (H.); 'hid in the denne of the citee' (P.).

Jg $5^{23}$ *Maledicite terræ*, 'curse ye *to* the loond' (H.); 'curse ye the lond' (P.).

Ps 77 (78) $^{70}$ *De post fetantes accepit eum*, 'fro the after berende blet he toc hym' (H.); 'he took hym fro bihynde scheep with lambren' (P.).

Ps $113^{4}$ 'The maumetis of Jentilis syluer and gold' (H.), 'The symulacris of hethene men *ben* siluer and gold' (P.).

Lk $14^{15}$ 'Whan sum man of sittinge at the mete had herd' (H.); 'And whanne som of hem that saten togider at the mete had herd' (P.).

Ro $13^{11}$ 'And we witinge this tyme, for hour is now, vs for to ryse of slepe' (H.); 'And we knowen this tyme, that the our is now, that we rise fro sleep' (P.).‡

Besides the general 'Prolog' already spoken of, there are separate prologues, some of them very short, to most of the books of the OT and NT. These are usually translated from St. Jerome. The order of books in the main follows the Vulgate, but 'Deeds' (Acts) stands between Hebrews and James. The Epistle to the Laodiceans, inserted after Colossians in the first version, was left out by Purvey.§ The later version has also a number of marginal glosses or notes in place of the short textual insertions common in the earlier. These glosses, it may be remarked, whether textual or marginal, are not of a controversial nature. They are simply explanatory. There does not appear to be any desire to use them for party purposes. Thus, on the passage relating the institution of the Lord's Supper, a subject on which Wyclif's views were elsewhere so strongly pronounced, there is no note at all. Neither is there on Mt $16^{17}$, with the exception of a textual

* Forshall and Madden, vol. i. p. 57. The General Prologue fills 60 pages in this edition. It is strictly a prologue to the OT, hardly mentioning the NT, to which Purvey may have intended to prefix a similar prologue.

† J. W. Hales, in the article before quoted. By the publication in a convenient form of *The Book of Job, Psalms*, . . . etc., from Hereford's version as revised by Purvey (Oxford, 1881, 8vo), Skeat has made it easy for the ordinary reader to form an opinion of Hereford's style, though not as he originally wrote.

‡ The list of such passages may be easily extended from Eadie or Mombert.

§ As none of the volumes in Forshall and Madden's great edition has a table of contents, Skeat was at the trouble to compile one for a paper read by him at a meeting of the Philological Society, June 5th, 1896. He distinguishes the different MSS used by the editors in each part of their work. See the *Transactions of the Philological Society*, 1896, p. 212 ff.

gloss, explaining *Bariona* as 'the sone of culuer' (a dove).

This being the case, one is perplexed to know on what ground Sir Thomas More should inveigh so bitterly against Wyclif's translation:—'In which translacyoun he purposely corrupted the holy text, malycyously placyng therin suche wordys as myght in the reders erys serue to the profe of such heresyes as he went about to sow; which he not only set forth with his own translacyon of the byble, but also with certayne prologes and glosys which he made ther vpon.'* Such prologues and glosses as we have do not answer this description. 'The ecclesiastical authorities in England' at the time, writes an unexceptionable witness,† 'most certainly approved of various copies of the actual versions now known as Wyclifite.' Some of these extant copies are shown, by the autographs and inscriptions they bear, to have belonged to high personages in Church and State. What is the explanation? A very daring one has been started by Father Gasquet.‡ He endeavours to prove that the versions of which we have been speaking, those we call the Wyclifite, are not Wyclifite at all; that we have been under a delusion all these years; that the heretical translation of the Bible due to Wyclif and his followers, if it ever existed, has completely disappeared; and that what we possess under that name is neither more nor less than an authorized Catholic translation of the Bible. The existence of such orthodox versions is attested by the evidence of Sir Thomas More, who declares that 'the whole byble was longe before his (Wyclif's) dayes by vertuous & well-lerned men translated into the englysh tonge, & by good and godly people with deuocyon & sobernes well & reuerently red.'§ In another well-known passage he speaks of having seen 'Bibles fair and old.' It is to be observed that More speaks of such orthodox versions as were made *long* before Wyclif's days. The Bibles he has seen are *old*. That no authorized version was made at, or after, Wyclif's time, follows plainly, it would seem, from another passage a little later on in this same *Dyaloge*. 'And surely howe it hathe happed that in all this whyle god hath eyther not suffered or not prouyded that any good vertuous man hath had the mynde in faythfull wyse to translate it, and ther vpon eyther the clergy or at the lest wyse some one bysshop to approue it, this can I nothynge tell.'‖

If, then, the orthodox English versions seen by More were old ones; if, as he implies, no fresh ones were made by authority from Wyclif's day to his own, how is the fact to be explained that the Bible, now suddenly claimed as Catholic, while found, wholly or in part, in nearly 200 MSS, should be found nowhere but in MSS written in or soon after Wyclif's time? Why should the style, in every instance, fix the composition to the last quarter of the 14th century? What can have caused this sudden and prolific growth of orthodox Bibles just then, when no link is visible to connect them with an earlier stage?

Father Gasquet's paradox is a bold one, and, it need not be said, ingeniously and forcibly defended. But, if it is proved untenable, the resorting to it will be one more testimony to the candour and good faith of the Wyclifite translation.¶

iv. Reformation Period.—The century that intervened between the death of Wyclif and the birth of Tindale has been rightly called a century of preparation. For a time the spread of Lollard opinions was checked. The passing of the Act *de hæretico comburendo* in the reign of Henry iv., and the condemnation of unauthorized versions of the Bible in the Synod at Oxford in 1408, threatened to be a deathblow to the hopes of Wyclif's followers. But the wave which had retreated for a while was soon to return with redoubled force. The fall of Constantinople in 1453 threw open to the Western world the treasures of Greek literature. The invention of printing, about the same period, furnished the means of spreading abroad the results of the new learning. In 1466** was born one destined to be perhaps the greatest exponent of that new learning, Desiderius Erasmus. Hitherto authority had triumphed against conviction: it was now to be seen whether it would triumph against conviction allied with knowledge.

* *A Dyaloge of syr Thomas More Knyghte* . . . 1530, f. cviii.

† The Rev. F. A. Gasquet, O.S.B., in an article which originally appeared in the *Dublin Review*, July 1895, reprinted and enlarged in *The Old English Bible, and other Essays*, 1897, p. 176.

‡ In the work just cited, pp. 102–178.

§ *Dyaloge*, as before, f. cviii.

‖ *Ib.* f. cxiv. vers., letter G.

¶ See, further, an article by F. D. Matthew in the *English Historical Review* for January 1895, and Kenyon's *Our Bible and the Ancient Manuscripts*, 1895, p. 204 ff.

** That 1466 and not, as commonly said, 1467 was the date of Erasmus' birth, has been shown by Kan, the learned headmaster of the Erasmiaansch Gymnasium at Rotterdam.



Between the years 1480 and 1490, possibly in the same year that Luther was born at Eisleben, **William Tindale** first saw the light, it is believed, in the little village of Slymbridge, Gloucestershire.* Foxe says that 'from a child' he was brought up in the University of Oxford. If so, as he did not take his Bachelor's degree till 1512, nor his Master's till 1515,† it would seem that his first years there were spent, not in college but in school. And with this agrees the statement that he entered Magdalen Hall, then known as Grammar Hall, the school preparatory to the great foundation of William of Waynflete. As a boy there, he may have seen Colet, who was probably of Magdalen; but Colet left Oxford on being appointed Dean of St. Paul's in 1505, and it is not likely that Tindale could have come, in any direct manner, under his influence. 'Spying his time,' says Foxe, Tindale presently left Oxford for Cambridge. The exact year of this migration we do not know, nor the immediate cause of it. It is natural to connect it with the presence of Erasmus in the sister university, where he was Lady Margaret professor from 1511 to 1515. But here, again, the date of Tindale's M.A. degree is a difficulty.

After leaving the university, about 1521, as we may suppose, he became tutor in the family of Sir Thomas Walsh, a knight of good position and well connected, at the manor house of Little Sodbury, not far from the place of his birth. Here he remained till the latter part of 1523. The need of reform in matters ecclesiastical in Gloucestershire may be inferred from the fact that from 1512, when Sylvester de Giglis returned to Rome, to 1535, when Hugh Latimer was consecrated, there was no resident bishop of Worcester. The see was held by Italians; one of them being afterwards Clement vii. As men's thoughts were turned to such abuses, we can hardly wonder that a blunt, free-spoken man like Tindale occasionally got into heated arguments with the local clergy and others who frequented the manor house. These he silenced by a translation of the *Enchiridion* of Erasmus; but, beginning to preach in an irregular manner to the neighbouring villagers, he was summoned to appear before a clerical tribunal, presided over by Parker, chancellor of the diocese.

Though no proof of heretical teaching was established against him, Tindale began to turn his thoughts to another scene. The idea of an English Bible had been long present to his mind. In London the idea might become a fact. He would address himself to the Bishop of London, Tunstall, the friend of More, a man of repute as a statesman and a scholar. Armed with a translation of Isocrates to be his introduction to the bishop, and a letter from his patron to Sir Harry Guildford, he came to London. The reception he met with from Tunstall, though not surprising to us, and the disappointments he experienced in other quarters, convinced Tindale, as he sorrowfully owns, 'not only that there was no rowme in my lorde of londons palace to translate the new testament, but also that there was no place to do it in all englonde.'‡

During his short stay in London he met with one faithful friend. This was Humphrey Monmouth, afterwards an alderman and sheriff, and knighted, who chanced to hear him preach in the

* We follow in this account the *Life of Tyndale* by R. Demaus, revised edition 1886. The Reformer, it may be noted, spelt his own name Tindale (*ib.* p. 9), the spelling adopted throughout this Dictionary.

† See Boase, *Register of the University of Oxford*, 1885, i. pp. ix, 80. He supplicated for his degree in the name of Huchens, or Hychyns, a name by which some previous generations of his family appear to have been known. The dates furnished by the *Register* make the earlier year suggested for Tindale's birth improbable.

‡ *Preface to the Pentateuch.*

church of St. Dunstan in the West. Monmouth took him into his house as chaplain, at a stipend of £10 a year.* For this he afterwards got into trouble; and his petition to Cardinal Wolsey, between four and five years later, is valuable for the picture it gives us of Tindale's manner of life while in his house. After relating his first acquaintance with him, Monmouth continues: 'So I took him into my house half-a-year; and there he lived as a good priest as methought. He studied most part of the day and of the night at his book; and he would eat but sodden meat by his good will, and drink but small single beer.'†

At the table of Monmouth, a merchant who had travelled, and visited Rome and Jerusalem, Tindale would be sure to meet with men who could tell him of the doings abroad, and especially of Wittenberg and Luther. Determined at length, as the safest course, to entrust his contemplated work to a foreign printer, he made choice of Hamburg, and in or about the month of May 1524 set sail for that busy city. As Hamburg is said to have possessed no printing-press at this time, it is a matter of dispute whether or not Tindale stayed there till his translation was ready for printing. He may have gone to visit Luther at Wittenberg, as is implied in statements of More and others. If so, he returned to Hamburg, to receive his remittance from Monmouth, and then went on to Cologne, to arrange for the printing of his English Testament at the press of Peter Quentel. Three thousand copies of the work, in small quarto size, were to be struck off. The printing had advanced as far as signature K, when the authorities of the city unexpectedly gave orders for the work to be stopped, and the printed sheets confiscated. An enemy, Cochlæus,‡ had been dogging the footsteps of the English scholar, and from him came the information given to the senate. Tindale and his companion Roye§ hastily caught up what they could of their materials, and took passage up the Rhine to Worms, where they would be in less fear of interruption. From the difficulty of matching Peter Quentel's type at the press of Peter Schoeffer (son of the partner of Faust), Tindale seems to have given up the thought of completing the 4to edition; and instead to have had his work printed in small 8vo, without notes or glosses. But, not to waste the copies of the sheets printed in 4to at Cologne, he sent them on to England. In this way, about March 1525-26, there appeared the first English New Testament ever printed, the one in 8vo, complete, and the portion of the one in 4to. Of this latter, the first printed in point of time, only one solitary fragment is known to remain; and of the former, only two copies, neither of them complete.‖

Before pausing to consider these translations in detail, we must briefly conclude the story of the author's life.

The summer of 1526 was probably spent by Tindale at Worms, in making arrangements for the transmission of his books to England.* Obstacles in the way of their reception soon began to appear. Besides the warning given by Cochlæus, Edward Lee, the king's almoner, afterwards Archbishop of York, wrote from Bordeaux on Dec. 2nd, 1525, to report what he had heard of the suspected work in his journey through France. One active agent in the distribution of the books was Simon Fish, author of *The Supplicacyon for the Beggars*, then living near the White Friars. Standish, bishop of St. Asaph,† was the first to bring the matter under the cognizance of Wolsey. The great cardinal was disposed to make light of it, but Tunstall was urgent for the condemnation of the anonymous version, and it was ordered that the books should be burnt, wherever found. To make the condemnation more impressive, a public burning was appointed, to follow a sermon by the Bishop of London at Paul's Cross.‡ A mandate to the like effect was issued by Warham, Archbishop of Canterbury, on Nov. 3rd; and by the end of the year the part taken by Tindale and Roye came to be publicly known, and an active search was made for them. West, a priest of the community to which Roye belonged, was sent abroad to track them, and letters from him and Hermann Rinck, during 1528, give an account of their efforts. Tindale and Roye, however, had separated, and their machinations were thus baffled. In 1527, or thereabouts, Tindale went to Marburg in Hesse, the seat of a university, and there, towards the end of 1528, was joined by Frith. At Marburg (anglicized in his colophons as 'Marlborow') he printed several of his controversial works, and, what more concerns us, the first instalment of his long-meditated version of the OT. The Pentateuch was here printed by Hans Luft, and published Jan. 17th, 1530.§ Several copies of this exist, but only one (now in the Grenville Library) in a perfect condition. It is remarkable for the 'piebald' appearance of the printing; Genesis and Numbers being in Gothic letter; Exodus, Leviticus, and Deuteronomy, in Roman. The explanation probably is that the books were prepared for separate issue, the five having no collective title-page. The following year Tindale printed, at

* Equal to about £120 now.

† Monmouth's petition is in the Harleian MSS. See Demaus, p. 88 n.

‡ John Dobenek, who latinized himself as *Cochlæus*, was born about 1503 in a village near Nürnberg. He was a violent opponent of Luther. As he was himself passing a book through Quentel's press at the time, he had peculiar opportunities for learning the business of the two Englishmen. See the letters from him in Arber's *First Printed English New Testament*, 1871, pp. 18-24.

§ William Roye, who had been an Observant Friar at Greenwich, was acting as Tindale's amanuensis. As would be guessed from his poem, he was an uncongenial spirit, and Tindale was glad to get rid of him as soon as he could.

‖ The fragment in 4to is now in the Grenville Library of the British Museum, No. 12,179. It consists of 31 leaves, and goes to the end of sheet H, ending abruptly with the words 'Friend, how camest thou in hither, and' (Mt 22[12]). It has been photo-lithographed, with an Introduction, by Mr. Arber. Of the 8vo edition there is an imperfect copy in the Library of St. Paul's Cathedral, and a perfect one (all but the title-page) in the Library of the Baptist College, Bristol. The singular vicissitudes through which this last book has passed are told by Demaus, p. 126.

* It is a mystery whence the money was obtained for defraying the first cost of these editions. 3000 copies of the 8vo edition are said to have been struck off at Worms. Whether the 4to edition was completed there, is disputed. No trace of such a complete edition is left, beyond the fragment printed at Cologne. Still, even the existence of *this* was not known till 1834.

† For this person, see Erasmus' Letter to Justus Jonas (Eng. tr. 1883, p. 42).

‡ As need hardly be said, this buying up and burning the copies of Tindale's first edition proved the readiest means of providing money for a second. But it is not fair to call Tindale, as Dore does, a 'participator in the crime' because he let the books be sold, knowing to what purpose they would be put. The motives of the two parties were different. The bishops wished to destroy this translation; Tindale wished to replace it by a better. See Dore, *Old Bibles*, 1888, p. 26.

§ Genesis alone has the colophon: 'Emprented at Marlborow in the lande of Hesse, by me Hans Luft, the yere of oure Lorde M.CCCCC.XXX. the xvij dayes of Januarij.' From the peculiarity of 'Marlborow' as an equivalent for Marburg, and from an impression that Hans Luft never had a printing-press there, Mombert endeavoured to prove that the Pentateuch was really printed at Wittenberg, and that 'Marlborow' was a pseudonym. 'It is painful,' says one writer, accepting this as proved, 'to think that an intentional misstatement should be on the imprint of the first part of the English bible ever issued' (Dore, *Old Bibles*, 1888, p. 67). The pain may fortunately be relieved, and the fair fame of Tindale cleared, by observing the evidence furnished by an able reviewer of Mombert in the *Athenæum*, Apr. 18th, 1885, to show that Hans Luft really had an itinerant press at Marburg at this time, and that in fact one publication of this very year, the *Compendious olde Treatise* used by Foxe, bears the colophon: 'Emprented at Marlborow in the lāde of Hessen by me Hans Luft.'

Antwerp most probably, his translation of the Book of Jonah.* Antwerp was a dangerous retreat, but it was conveniently situated for communicating with England. Here accordingly he resided from 1533, if not earlier, to his arrest in 1535. The last two years of his life were years of great literary activity. In 1534 appeared at Antwerp his revision of the Pentateuch, Genesis being the only book in which any changes were made; † and in November of that year his revised NT. ‡ This is commonly called the second edition, and it is strange that nine years should have elapsed before Tindale himself published one.§ But if there had been any delay, there was none now. Two editions appeared in 1535. These must be carefully discriminated. The first is entitled: *The newe Testament dylygently corrected and compared with the Grcke by Willyam Tindale, and fynesshed in the yere of oure Lorde God A.M.D. and XXXV.*‖ No place or printer's name is given, but it is considered to be from the press of Hans van Ruremonde at Antwerp. It is in 8vo. A striking peculiarity of this edition is the curious misspelling of English words, such as 'faether' for father, 'stoede' for stood, and the like. This gave rise to the fancy that Tindale had adapted his version to the pronunciation of the Gloucestershire farmers. But the more rational explanation is that Dutch or Flemish compositors were employed upon this edition; and that in fact it was not superintended by Tindale at all, but a private enterprise of Dutch printers, who had observed the censure passed on Joye's unauthorized production of the previous August, and wished to anticipate the final revision which Tindale was understood to be preparing.¶

This last revision, in which 'yet once again' Willyam Tindale addressed the reader, has two titles, the first bearing date 1535, the second 1534; denoting, we may suppose, the times of publication and printing. It is in 8vo size, with black letter type, and has a calendar prefixed. While bearing no printer's name, or place, it has a printer's mark with the initials G. H. These were conjectured by Stevens to denote Guillaume Hychyns, a form of the translator's name; ** but the late Henry Bradshaw has shown convincingly that they are the initials of the Antwerp publisher, Godfried van der Hagen, who latinized himself as *Dumæus*. The printer he employed was frequently Martin Emperour, who was probably the printer of this last revision.††

We must hasten to the close. On the 23rd or 24th of May 1535 Tindale was entrapped and carried off from Antwerp to the fortress of Vilvorde, where he was strangled and burnt on Oct. 6th, 1536. Even in his imprisonment he was not idle. In the touching letter ‡‡ to the governor of the fortress, the Marquis of Bergen-op-Zoom, in which he petitions for warmer clothing, he asks also for a Hebrew Bible, grammar, and dictionary. And it is said that he finished in prison a translation of the books Joshua to 2 Chronicles inclusive.* His last words at the stake were: 'Lord, open the king of England's eyes!'

The influence exercised by Tindale's version on subsequent ones will be best considered later on. But it seems proper to notice here a question that has been raised as to his competence for the work of translating. Was he able to form an independent judgment on his Greek and Hebrew originals, or did he take his Pentateuch from Luther, and his New Testament from Luther and Erasmus? † It may be admitted at once that Tindale availed himself freely of the labours of both these scholars. His object being what it was, he would probably have thought it mere perverseness not to do so. But he did not borrow as one who could not pay back. Even in the prologues, he sometimes not only differs from, but argues against, the German translator, as in the case of the prologue to James. Tindale's great aptitude for languages is shown by various testimonies. That of Herman von dem Busche ‡ would be thought high-flown if we did not know that it came from one not likely to be imposed upon. As regards Hebrew, in particular, one of the seven languages that von dem Busche declared Tindale to be at home in, it is not likely that he would have found it difficult to obtain instruction in it at Cologne, or Worms, or other cities where he stayed.

The question is one that, after all, can be settled only by an induction of passages on a sufficiently large scale. For that there is no room here. We give a few, taken almost at haphazard from the NT; some of which will show Tindale's obvious indebtedness to previous versions. But the general impression conveyed by them will be, we think, that he used these helps as a master, and not as a servant.§

Lk $2^{49}$ An nesciebatis, quod in his quæ patris mei sunt, oportet me esse?
Wissent ir nit, das ich seyn muss in dem das meins vatters ist?
Wist ye not that I must goo aboute my fathers busines? (Compare, as showing Tindale's freedom, the Rhemish of 1582, closely following the Latin, 'I must be about those things which are my father's').

Ac $9^{15}$ Vade, quoniam organum electum est mihi iste.
Gang hyn, deñ diser ist mir ein ausserwelet rüstzeüg.
Goo thy wayes: for he is a chosen vessell vnto me ('vessell' representing the Greek σκεῦος more closely than the Latin or German).

Ac $27^{30.31}$ Nautis uero quærentibus fugere e naui . . . sub prætextu uelut e prora ancoras extensuri, dixit Paulus centurioni . . .
Da aber die schiffleutt die flucht suchten . . . vnd gaben fur, sy wolten ancker auss dem hinder schiff auss strecken, sprach Paulus zu dem vnderhauptman . . .
As the shipmen were about to fle out of the ship . . . vnder a coloure as though they wolde have cast ancres out of the forshippe: Paul sayd vnto the vnder captayne . . . (Compare 'hinder schiff' with 'forshippe.' The term 'vnder captayne,' for centurion, seems clearly due to the German).

Ro $2^{18}$ . . . institutus ex lege; vnd weyl du auss dem gesetz vnderricht bist; in that thou arte informed by the lawe (κατηχούμενος ἐκ τοῦ νόμου. Note 'by' instead of 'out of').

1 Co $9^{19}$ . . . quo plures lucrifaciam; auff das ich ir vil (=ihrer viel) gewinne; that I myght wynne the moo (more). (The comparative is rightly kept, with the Greek and Latin, against the German).

---

* Copies of this had so completely disappeared, that some began to doubt its ever having existed. But in 1861 Lord Arthur Hervey discovered a copy, bound up in an old volume with other pieces, in his library at Ickworth.

† Dore, *Old Bibles*, 1888, p. 69, where the book is described.

‡ *The newe Testament, dylygently corrected . . . by Willyam Tindale.* It was printed in Gothic letter by Martin Emperour, in 8vo. This is the edition used in Bagster's *Hexapla*. In Fry's *Bibliographical Description* it is No. 3. The copy in the British Museum is marked C. 23. a. 5.

§ This is not taking count of surreptitious editions, such as Dore gives instances of (*op. cit.* p. 27), nor of Joye's unauthorized edition in August 1534. For this last, see Westcott, *General View*, 1872, pp. 46–49.

‖ The titles of this and of the next are taken from the Catalogue of the British Museum Library. The press-marks of the two copies are C. 36. a. 2 and C. 36. b. 5.

¶ See the Introduction to Bagster's *Hexapla*, p. 19, col. 1. This edition is the one numbered 5 by Fry.

** See above, p. 241b, note †.

†† See Bradshaw's paper, 'Godfried van der Hagen,' reprinted from the *Bibliographer*, 1886.

‡‡ Reproduced in facsimile by Fry, with a translation.

* The English version of these nine books in 'Matthew's' Bible is not Coverdale's, and reasons are given to show that it was by Tindale. See Moulton, p. 127.

† The reviewer in the *Athenæum* before referred to (May 2nd, 1885) holds very strongly that he did both. Admitting that Tindale possessed a fair knowledge of Greek, he yet insists that the wholesale borrowing of Luther's prologues and marginal notes, in the first Cologne fragment, justifies the charge that the work was adapted from Luther. If this was done with a Greek original, and with Erasmus' Latin rendering as an assistance, what would be done with a Hebrew original? Where could Tindale, travelling about from place to place, and busy with the publication of his treatises, find opportunities of acquiring a sound knowledge of so difficult a language? The reader will find in Eadie, i. pp. 143, 209, a collection of passages from various writers, conveying this imputation more or less directly.

‡ For this writer, sometimes latinized as Dumæus, see the 'Index Biographicus' to Böcking's edition of the *Epistolæ Obscurorum Virorum*, to which he was one of the contributors. His biographer, Hermann Hamelmann, speaks of him as the friend of Colet, More, and Fisher. Erasmus was one of his correspondents.

§ The editions used for this comparison are the third of Erasmus' *Novum Testamentum*, Basle, 1522; Luther's *Das neue Testament*, 'zu Basel, durch Adam Petri,' 1522 (the first edition of all came out, we believe, in September 1522, at Wittenberg); and Tindale's New Testament of 1534, as reprinted in Bagster's *Hexapla*.

 VERSIONS (ENGLISH)

2 Co 4$^{7}$ Habemus autem thesaurum hunc in testaceis uasculis; in irdischen gefessen; in erthen vessels. (Probably Tindale took 'erthen,' that is, of earthenware, from the German. Wyclif's 'britil' preserves one side of the Latin *testaceis*, *ὀστρακίνοις*, as referring to Gideon's pitchers).

Ph 1$^{20}$ secundum expectationem; wie ich endlich wartte; as I hertely loke for. (Tindale seems to catch the force of *ἀποκαραδοκίαν*, the 'earnest expectation' of one looking out eagerly for news).

Ph 1$^{27}$ . . . adiuuantes decertantem fidem euangelij; vnnd sampt (sammt) vns kempfft (kämpfet) über dem glauben des Euangeli; labouringe as we do, to mayntayne the fayth of the gospell.

Ph 2$^{7}$ . . . semetipsum inaniuit; hat sich selbs geeüssert; made him silfe of no reputacion (literally 'emptied himself.' Note the freedom of the rendering).

Ph 4$^{3}$ . . . compar germana; mein artiger geferte (mein trewer geselle, 1534); faythfull yockfelowe. (Wyclif has: 'Also I preie & the german felowe').

Ph 4$^{5}$ . . . modestia uestra; euwere lindigkeit; youre softenes. (Here probably the term used is suggested by the German).

Ph 4$^{10}$ . . . quod iam tandem reuiguit uestra pro me solicitudo; das ir der mals eyns wider ergrunet seyt von mir zu halten (das ir widder wacker worden seid, fur mich zu sorgen, 1534); that now at the last ye are revived agayne to care for me.

Ja 1$^{23}$ . . . faciem natiuitatis suæ; sein leiplich angesicht; his bodyly face.

Ja 3$^{5}$ Ecce, exiguus ignis quantam materiam incendit; Sihe, ein klein feür, welch einen walt zündet es an; Beholde how gret a thinge a lyttell fyre kyndleth.

When we turn to the Old Testament there is, so far as the present writer can pretend to judge, less evidence of originality in Tindale's translation; but instances are not wanting to show that he did not follow blindly either Luther or the Vulgate. Sometimes he differs from both. In many cases he sides with one as against the other; sometimes mistakenly, but quite as often, we think, taking the right side. A few examples will suffice:*—

Gn 3$^{14}$ *inter* omnia animantia; *vor* allem viech; *of* all catell. (Tindale's *of* is nearer to the original 'out of,' 'from among'—see RVm—than the others).

Gn 4$^{21}$ pater canentium cithara et organo; die mit harpffen vnd pfeyffen vmbgiengen; all that excercyse them selves on the harpe and on the organs. (Here it would have been better to render 'pipe' instead of 'organ,' with the German).

Gn 21$^{23}$ et posteris meis stirpique meæ; meine kinder . . . meyne näffen; my childern nor my childern's childern. (Tindale, alone of the three, appears to aim at keeping the alliterative cast of the Hebrew).

Gn 30$^{11}$ Dixit: Feliciter, et idcirco vocavit nomen ejus Gad; da sprach Lea, Rustig, vñ hiess in (ihn) Gad; Then sayde Lea: good lucke; and called his name Gad. (Compare the rendering in AV).

Gn 35$^{19}$ hæc est Bethlehem; die nũ heist BethLehem; which now is called Bethlehem. (The words are now held to be a gloss. Tindale plainly followed Luther).

Gn 37$^{3}$ fecitque ei tunicam polymitam; vnd machet im einen bundten rock; and he made him a coote of many coloures.

(The rendering 'of many colours' is retained even in the RV, though in the margin 'a long garment with sleeves' is given. The LXX supports the former, having *ποικίλον*; and probably the same meaning was meant to be conveyed by 'polymitam' (*πολύμιτον*), 'of many threads,' in the sense of damasked).

Ex 3$^{14}$ Ego sum qui sum; Ich werde seyn der ich seyn werde; I wilbe what I wilbe. (See RVm).

Ex 12$^{6}$ ad vesperam; zwischen abents; aboute euene. (The German is the most literal).

Ex 15$^{14.\,15}$ (Tindale has the past tense, along with the Vulgate and Luther; the AV has the future).

Ex 16$^{15}$ Dixerunt ad invicem, Manhu? quod significat, Quid est hoc? Das ist Man, denn sie wysten nicht . . . They said one to another: What is this? for they wist not . . .

Ex 39$^{1}$ Fecit vestes, quibus indueretur Aaron; amptkleider zu dienen in Heyligthum; the vestimentes of ministracion to do seruyce in. ('Vestments of ministration' is as literal as the AV 'cloths of service,' and more dignified).

Lv 19$^{20}$ . . . vapulabunt ambo; das sol gestrafft werden; there shalbe a payne vpon it (RV 'they shall be punished'; lit. 'there shall be an inquisition.' Tindale gives the sense, though not pointedly. AV 'she shall be scourged' conveys a wrong impression).

Tindale's last words were a prayer that the Lord would open the king of England's eyes. It is remarkable that the English version of the Bible made by the next translator we have to treat of, bore, in one of its forms, that king's imprimatur.

**Miles Coverdale** was born in 1488, probably in Richmondshire, in the North Riding of Yorkshire.

* The texts used are, besides a modern Vulgate, the Basel edition of Luther's Pentateuch, 1523, and the 1530 edition of Tindale's, printed by Hans Luft.

He studied at Cambridge, where he entered the convent of Augustinian Friars. In 1514 he took priest's orders. Though senior to George Stafford and Bilney, he probably fell under the same influences as they. When Barnes, who became prior of the Augustinians in 1523, was arrested and conveyed to London, Coverdale attended him, and helped him to prepare his defence. About this time he laid aside his conventual habit. In 1529 he is said by Foxe to have assisted Tindale in his work at Hamburg. In 1551 he was consecrated bishop of Exeter, but deprived in 1553, on the accession of Mary, and imprisoned. His deliverance is said to have been due to the intercession of the king of Denmark, whose chaplain, Dr. John Macbee, was his wife's brother-in-law. After living abroad in Denmark and Geneva, he returned to England in 1558, and died in Feb. 1569, at the age of 81.*

What first turned Coverdale's thoughts to the translation of the Bible is uncertain. It seems to have been, at least in part, the encouragement to undertake the task given by Thomas Cromwell, with the knowledge, if not the express approval, of Sir Thomas More.† The earliest document of Coverdale's we possess is a letter addressed by him to Cromwell, undated, but probably written in 1527, in which he reminds him of the 'godly communication' that Cromwell had held with him in the house of Master More.‡ As he goes on to speak of now beginning to 'taste of holy scriptures,' of being 'set to the most sweet smell of holy letters,' and of needing books for his work, the natural inference is that he was then engaged in the task of Bible translation. At any rate there appeared, as the result of his labours, two issues in 1535, followed by later ones, of the first complete translation of the Bible into English. The titles present an interesting, but perplexing, variety—

'Biblia | The Bible, that | is, the holy Scripture of the | Olde and New Testament, faith|fully and truly translated out | of Douche and Latyn | in to Englishe. | M.D.XXXV.' (followed by texts).

'Biblia | The Byble: that | is, the holy Scrypture of the | Olde and New Testament, | faythfully translated in | to Englyshe. | M.D.XXXV.' (texts). The title of an edition of 1536 varies from this last only in the spelling of one word. That of an edition of 1537 is: 'Biblia | The Byble, that | is the holy Scrypture of the | Olde and New Testament, fayth|fully translated in Englysh, and | newly ouerseene & corrected. | M.D.XXXVII.' (texts). 'Imprynted in Sowthwarke for James Nycolson.' The word 'Biblia' in all is in Roman capitals, the rest in black letter, occupying the central compartment of a page within a border of figures.§

On comparing these titles, two important differences will be noticed. Before 1537 no place of publication is given; and in the first alone is it specified that the translation is made 'out of Douche and Latyn.' With regard to the place, while there can be no doubt that the editions of 1535 and 1536 were printed abroad, opinions differ as to the claims of Antwerp and Zürich. In favour

* Art. by H. R. Tedder in the *Dict. of Nat. Biography*.

† Dore, *Old Bibles*, p. 90.

‡ *Remains* (ed. Parker Soc.), p. 490; Moulton, p. 96.

§ See Plates i.–iv. of Fry's *The Bible by Coverdale*, 1867. No perfect copy of Coverdale's Bible is known. In the British Museum (C. 18. c. 9) is a fine copy, with titles in facsimile by J. Harris. The size of leaf is $11\frac{3}{4}$ in. $\times 7\frac{1}{2}$. The dedication, 'Unto the most victorious,' etc., begins near the top of leaf ♣ 2, and ends on the obverse of leaf ♣ iiij. In line 13 it speaks of 'your dearest iust wyfe and most vertuous Pryncesse, Quene Anne.' On the reverse of ♣ iiij. begins the 'Prologe,' 'Myles Couerdale vnto the Christen reader,' ending on obv. of ♣ 7. On the reverse of this last begins a list of 'The Bokes of the hole Byble,' ending on obv. of leaf viii., and on rev. of this begins 'The first Boke of Moses, called Genesis.'

of the former is a statement of Symeon Ruytinck, in his Life of Emanuel van Meteren, 1618, that Jacob van Meteren of Antwerp, the printer, employed 'un certain docte escolier, nommé Miles Coverdal,' on the work of an English translation of the Bible.*

On the other hand, certain peculiarities of type point to Zürich; and Westcott, supported by Ginsburg, is convinced that Froschover of Zürich was the printer. As to the description of the sources from which the version was made, it is most natural to suppose that the words 'out of Douche and Latyn' were omitted after the first issue, as likely to offend some English supporters of the undertaking. The mention of 'Douche' (German), in particular, might suggest a Lutheran bias. But the description was an accurate one, and in his Dedication and Prologue Coverdale openly acknowledges it. He had 'purely and faithfully translated,' he says, 'out of five sundry interpreters.' And again: 'To help me herin, I have had sondrye translacions not only in latyn, but also of the Douche interpreters, whom (because of theyr synguler gyftes and speciall diligence in the Bible) I have been . . . glad to folowe.' What the 'five sundry interpreters' were is a question of much interest. Coverdale's indebtedness to the Vulgate, the Latin version of Sanctes Pagninus (first published at Lyons in 1528), Luther, the Zürich Bible (the work of Zwingli, Leo Judæ, Pellicanus, and others, 1524–29), and Tindale, are unmistakable.† But, as he specifies only 'Douche and Latyn' on his title-page, he may not have meant to include Tindale as one of the five; and if so, the fifth source may have to be sought for in some other Latin or German interpreter. In any case, the perfect candour of Coverdale's declaration in his Prologue is apparent. He had not sought the work; but when it was put upon him he had executed it with the best helps he could obtain. One or two short specimens will show the style of his translation—

Gn $49^{22-25}$ The frutefull sonne Joseph, that florishinge sonne to loke vpon, the doughters go vpon the wall. And though the shoters angered him, stroue with him, and hated him, yet his bowe bode fast, and the armes of his handes were made stronge by the handes of ye Mightie in Jacob. Of him are come herdmen & stones in Israel. Of ye fathers God art thou helped, of the Almightie art thou blessed, with blessynges of heauen from aboue, with blessynges of the depe that lyeth vnder, with blessynges of brestes and wombes.

2 K (*i.e.* 2 S) $5^{6-8}$ And the kynge wente with his men to Jerusalem, agaynst the Jebusites, which dwelt in the londe. Neuertheles they sayde vnto Dauid: Thou shalt not come hither but the blynde and lame shal dryue ye awaie. (They thoughte planely, that Dauid shulde not come in). Howbeit Dauid wanne the castell of Sion, which is the cite of Dauid. Then sayde Dauid the same daye: Who so euer smyteth the Jebusites, and optayneth the perquellies, the lame & the blynde, which (Jebusites) Dauids soule hateth. Herof commeth the prouerbe: Let no blynde ner lame come in to the house.

Jer $38^{7-11}$ Now when Abdemelech the Morian beynge a chamberlayne in the Kynges Courte, vnderstode, that they had cast Jeremy into the dongeon: he went out of the Kynges house, and spake to the kynge (which then sat under the porte off Ben Jamin) these wordes: My lorde the kynge, where as these men medle with Jeremy the prophet, they do him wronge: Namely, in that they haue put him in preson, there to dye of honger, for there is no more bred in the cite. Then the kynge commaunded Abdemelech the Morian. . . . So Abdemelech toke the men with him, & went to ye house of Amalech, & there vnder an almery he gat olde ragges & worne cloutes, and let them downe by a corde, in to the dongeon to Jeremy.

The tender beauty of Coverdale's translation has never been surpassed. In the Psalms especially this characteristic is noticeable. In 1662, at the last revision of the Book of Common Prayer, while the Gospels, Epistles, and other portions of Scripture made use of, were directed to be taken from the newer version, the Psalter was left unchanged, the older version being regarded as more rhythmical for singing. Hence it is that, if the majesty or the pathos of the Psalms has sunk deep into myriads of English hearts, to Coverdale above others their debt of gratitude is due.

Coverdale's Bible had not been more than two years in circulation when there appeared what purported to be a new version, printed in 1537. To this version, commonly known as **Matthew's Bible,** some mystery attaches. The title runs:* '¶ The Byble | which is all the holy Scrip- ture: in whych are contayned the | Olde and Newe Testament truly | and purely translated into En|glysh by Thomas | Matthew. | Esaye i. | ☞ Hearcken to ye heauens and | thou earth geaue eare: for the | Lorde speaketh. | M·D·XXXVII.' Across the page at the bottom is, 'Set forth with the Kinges most gracyous lycẽce.' This may accordingly be termed the first Authorized Version. On the reverse of the title is a notice of various additions made, including 'many playne exposycyons,' in the margin, 'of svch places as vnto the symple and vnlearned seame harde to vnderstande.' A calendar and similar matter fills the next two leaves. The fourth leaf begins with 'An exhortacyon to the studye of the holye scrypture gathered out of the Byble,' and has at the bottom I. R. in large floriated capitals. The rev. of this leaf and obv. of next have, 'The summe & content of all the Holy Scrypture . . . ,' and on the rev. of the fifth leaf is the dedication 'To the moost noble and gracyous Prynce Kyng Henry the eyght, kyng of England and of Fraunce . . . Defender of the faythe: and vnder God the chefe and supreme head of the church of Engeland . . .' This ends on rev. of sixth leaf with, 'So be it. Youre graces faythfull & true subject Thomas Matthew,' followed by H. R. in capitals. The seventh leaf, signed * *, has an address 'To the Chrysten Readers,' followed by an alphabetical 'Table of the pryncypall matters,' ending on rev. of eighth leaf. This 'Table' shows a strong controversial bias—*e.g.* 'Abhomynacyon. Abhomynacyon before God are Idoles & Images, before whom the people do bowe thẽ selues, Deut. vii. d.' 'Confessyon. Judas, which confessed hym selfe to the prestes of ye lawe, and not to God, is damned, Mat. xxvii. a.' 'Cursynge. God doth curse the blessynges of the preastes, and blesseth their curssyng, Mal. ii. a.' The ninth leaf has 'The names of all the Bokes of the Byble,' with a full-page woodcut of the Garden of Eden. With the tenth leaf a regular system of numbering the leaves begins. The first of the four sections into which the Bible is here divided closes on fol. cxlvij with 'The Ende of the Ballet of Ballettes of Salomon, called in Latyne Canticum Canticorum.' Following this is a leaf, unsigned, forming the title of the second section, or prophetical books. This title has on the obv. a centre-piece, surrounded by a woodcut border in sixteen compartments; and on the rev. a centre-piece (the seraph touching Isaiah's lips), with four large floriated capital letters at the four corners—R. G. along the top, and E. W. along the bottom. With Isaiah the numbering by folios begins afresh, and ends with Malachi on rev. of leaf xciv. Underneath are two capital letters, W. T. The Apocrypha follows, with similar title (but only fifteen compartments in border), and extends to lxxvi leaves. The New Testament in like manner is numbered to cxi leaves; and a leaf not numbered completes the work, with the colophon: '¶ To the honour and prayse of God | was this Byble prynted and fy|nesshed in the yere of oure |

* Quoted by Henry Stevens in his *Catalogue of the Caxton Celebration*, p. 88.

† See Westcott, Append. iv., for the sources of Coverdale's notes (sixty-six in all), and Eadie, i. p. 285 ff.

* The copy described is in the Library of the Brit. and For. Bible Society, marked Ss. 9. 2. It is in folio; size of leaf, $11\frac{3}{8} \times 8\frac{5}{8}$ inches.

Lorde God a. | M·D·XXXVII.' There is nothing to show where the book was printed, though the woodcut on the title, and that of Adam and Eve before mentioned, have been traced to the blocks used for a Dutch Bible printed at Lübeck in 1533. The most probable place is Antwerp; 'the larger types being apparently identical with those of Martin Emperour in the edition of Tyndale's N.T., 1534.'* While passing through the press, the sheets appear to have been bought by the London printers, Richard Grafton and Edward Whitchurch, whose names are not obscurely indicated by the capital letters R. G. and E. W. Grafton, in a letter to Archbishop Cranmer (Strype's *Cranmer*, App. 20), speaks of having invested £500—a large sum for those days—in the production of the work, and mentions that the impression would consist of 1500 copies. To prevent infringement of his rights as publisher, Grafton prays the archbishop to use his influence with Cromwell to the end that the king's licence might be obtained for the publication. Cranmer, who was probably already interested in the project, exerted himself so effectually that the king's licence was soon granted for the new translation 'to be bought and read within this realm.'† To this English version, then, as has been said, the term 'Authorized' may first be properly applied.‡

Three other points require elucidation: the meaning of the capital letters I. R. subscribed to the 'Exhortacyon,' of W. T. at the end of the Old Testament, and of the name Thomas Matthew on the title-page. The initials may be taken, with all but absolute certainty, to denote John Rogers and William Tindale. Rogers, a native of Deritend, near Birmingham, where he was born about 1500, after graduating from Pembroke Hall, Cambridge, the college of Whitgift, Bradford, and Ridley, had gone out, at the end of 1534, to be chaplain to the English factory at Antwerp. There, according to Foxe (*Acts and Mon.* vi. 591), he came under the influence of Tindale and Coverdale to such an extent as to join them 'in that painful and most profitable labour of translating the Bible into the English tongue, which is entitled "The Translation of Thomas Matthew."' As Rogers moved on to Wittenberg soon after 1536, it is doubtful whether he could have had much personal intercourse at Antwerp with Coverdale; but it is highly probable that Tindale, who suffered October 6th, 1536, may have given his manuscript versions and the like into the hands of Rogers at his first arrest. John Rogers, it may be added, was the first to suffer in the Marian persecution, being burnt at Smithfield, February 1555.

Why, assuming that the Bible before us was edited by John Rogers, it should have been put forth under the name of Thomas Matthew, is not easy to explain. Some have supposed it to be a disguise for William Tindale, whose name, if openly given as the author of the greater part of the version, would have roused opposition in high quarters. Others, that it was the real name of a sharer in the work. Both suppositions seem negatived by the fact that, in the register recording the arrest of John Rogers later on, he is described as John Rogers *alias* Matthew. The same motive that made him veil the name of Tindale under initials, might lead him to suppress his own.

An examination of the contents of the book shows that the Pentateuch and NT are certainly Tindale's, with slight variations, the latter having been taken, as Westcott has shown (pp. 183, 184), from the revised ed. of 1535. With equal certainty the books from Ezra to Malachi inclusive, and the Apocrypha (excepting the Prayer of Manasses), may be assigned to Coverdale. The books from Joshua to 2 Chronicles inclusive present a difficulty. It might have been expected that they would be taken from Coverdale's version, that being the only English version as yet extant in print. As a matter of fact, however, they are evidently not so taken. And it has been shown, by a comparison of renderings of identical words found in Tindale's Pentateuch and 'Epistles,' as well as in these historical books, that the version must almost certainly be Tindale's. It has already been mentioned as probable that Tindale, at or before his arrest, would consign his unfinished translations, and the like, to the care of John Rogers.

As to the Prayer of Manasses, which was omitted by Coverdale, the translation may very well be set down to Rogers himself. It owes much to Olivetan's rendering in the French Bible of 1535. Rogers executed his task of general supervision as editor well and carefully.* But the controversial character of his annotations, and his inclusion, almost unaltered, of Tindale's Prologue to Romans, were probably among the causes which led to the production of the 'Great' Bible.

**Taverner's Bible.**—In the same year as the Great Bible, 1539, appeared a new edition, which, from its close relation to Matthew's, it will be convenient to examine first. Its title runs:† 'The most | sacred Bible, | whiche is the holy scripture, con|teyning the old and new testament, | translated in to English and newly | recognised with great diligence | after most faythful exemplars by Rychard Taverner. | Harken thou heuen . . . Esaie i. | Prynted at London in Fletestrete at | the sygne of the sonne by John Byd|dell for Thomas Barthlet. | Cum privilegio . . . M·D·XXXIX.'

The title is followed by 15 leaves, not numbered, of which the first has on the recto an Address to Henry VIII., on the verso 'an Exhortacion'; the next 'the Contentes of the Scripture,' and the remainder 'The names of the Bokes,' etc., followed by 'A Table of the principall maters conteyned in the Byble.' From Gn 1 the numeration of leaves begins, ending with 'Salomons Ballet' at ccxxx. The prophets are numbered afresh, to the end of Malachi, at lxxxxi. The Apocrypha and NT have each a separate title-page, and number lxxv and ci leaves respectively; three unnumbered leaves of 'Table' completing the work.

In the Address to Henry VIII. the king is described as 'in erth supreme heed immediately vnder Chryst of the churche of England'; and among all his services to religion it is declared that none is greater than his sanction of the English Bible. Being essentially a 'new recognition' of Matthew's Bible, we do not look for much originality in Taverner's work. But he gives himself a much freer hand than some suppose. The more violent controversial remarks in his predecessor's notes are softened down, or omitted. Thus, in the 'Table of the principall maters,' Matthew began his section on Altars with the words, 'An aulter was neuer commaunded to be made, but only to God,' and ended with, 'So we have no aulter but Christ.' Taverner begins, 'An aulter was commaunded to be made to God,' and leaves out the concluding sentence. Under 'Purgatorye' Matthew wrote, 'He then that wyl pourge hys synnes through fyer or by any other meanes then by the passyon of Christ, denyeth hys sayd passyon . . . and shal be greuously punyshed, because he hath despysed so greate a grace.' Taverner omits the section altogether. The last chapter of Acts ends on leaf liiii; Romans begins on lxi. The inference naturally is that an intermediate sheet of six leaves had been meant to contain Tindale's Prologue to Romans, but had been cancelled.

A few examples will indicate the nature of the changes made in rendering. It will be seen that they are chiefly due to (*a*) the seeking after a plainer, more idiomatic rendering, (*b*) the influence of the Vulgate, (*c*) a better knowledge of Greek.

* Note in the Brit. Mus. Catalogue. Mr. Sidney Lee (art. 'John Rogers' in *Dict. of Nat. Biogr.*) assigns the work to the press of Jacob van Meteren.

† Jenkyns, *Remains*, vol. i. p. 197.

‡ An edition of Coverdale's Bible in 4to (the first printed in that size), by James Nycolson, of Southwark, which appeared in this same year, 1537, had also the notification: 'Set forth with the Kynges most gracious licence.'

* Examples will be found in Westcott, pp. 182, 183; Moulton, pp. 129, 130.

† We quote from the copy numbered 4. c. 5 in the Brit. Mus. Library. It is in small folio; size of leaf, 11½×7¼ inches.

(*a*) Gn $2^{1}$ with all theyr furniture (Matthew 'apparell,' AV 'host'); Nu $24^{22}$ neuertheless (M. 'neuerthelater'): Is $2^{2}$ in the last dayes (M. 'in processe of tyme'); Mt $2^{16}$ was very wrothe (M. 'exceding wrothe'); Mt $5^{11}$ (and elsewhere) pursue for 'persecute'; Mt $8^{9}$ vnder authority (M. 'subject to the authorytye of another'); Lk $2^{4}$ wente up for 'ascended'; Ac $3^{7}$ anone (M. 'immediately').

(*b*) Gn $43^{11}$ a quantitie of bawlme (M. 'a curtesye bawlme,' Vulg. *modicum resinæ*); Gn $49^{6}$ they threw down the walls of the city (M. 'they houghed an ox,' Vulg. *suffoderunt murum*); 1 K $21^{21}$ incluse and furthest (M. 'prisoned and forsaken,' Vulg. *inclusum et vltimum*).

(*c*) Lk $13^{8.9}$ and it it beare frute, *well and good*, if not, &c. (M. 'to se whether it will beare frute, and yf it beare not,' &c.); Ro $8^{20}$ creature (M. 'creatures'); Mk $14^{7}$ for ye *have* poore with you alwayes (Tind. 'shall have').

His acquaintance with the Greek article does not, however, save him from such oversights as *a* pinnacle (Mt $4^{5}$), *a* candlestick ($5^{15}$), *a* prophet (Jn $7^{40}$), can faith saue him? (Ja $2^{14}$). In Jn $7^{40}$ 'vndoubtedly' is not an improvement on the earlier 'of a truth.' Dore (*Old Bibles*, p. 148) asserts that the translation of 3 Esdras, at least in part, is original. But, so far as the present writer has examined it, it agrees with the one in Matthew.

Richard Taverner was a client and pensioner of Cromwell, who in 1536 appointed him clerk of the Privy Seal. The fall of his patron in 1540 put a stop to his literary work, and made his position unsafe. For a time he was committed to the Tower. He succeeded, however, in regaining the royal favour, and under Edward VI., in 1552, received a general licence to preach, though a layman. He died in 1575.*

**The Great Bible.**—Before the execution of Cromwell, on July 28th, 1540, that statesman had just time to see brought to a successful issue one great scheme on which he had set his heart. This was the production of an amended version of the Bible in English. Circumstances seemed to favour Cromwell's project. Coverdale, on whom he chiefly relied for an improved translation, was in Paris, where, in 1538, he had brought out an edition of the New Testament in Latin and English, printed by Regnault. Paper and printing were both better at that time in Paris than in London. Francis I., so long as his relations with Henry kept good, was willing, upon certain conditions, to sanction the work of Coverdale and Grafton and the French printer Regnault.† No private opinions were to be introduced. The work was to be 'citra ullas privatas aut illigittimas opiniones.' Bonner, shortly to be made Bishop of Hereford, was transferred from the court of the emperor to that of Francis, and charged 'to aid and assist the doers thereof in all their reasonable suits.' So far, at least, he seems to have regarded the translating of the Bible without disfavour. For a time, therefore, matters went smoothly. But in December 1538 the French king inclining more and more to the side of the emperor, the Inquisition was allowed to interpose, and the printers and others engaged in the enterprise had to flee for their lives. According to Grafton's own statement (*Abridgement of the Chronicles*, etc., 1564, sub anno 29 Hen. VIII.), eighty finished copies were 'seased and made confiscat.' If this was so, no copy of the eighty, which would have Paris as the place of publication, appears to have escaped destruction. Foxe is the authority for a story that 'four great dry vats full' of the printed sheets were rescued from a haberdasher, who had purchased them 'to lay caps in.' But Kingdon (p. 63) discredits the statement, on the ground that the materials seized, for the restitution of which Cromwell and Bonner were making constant efforts, would be in the custody of the university. However this may be, Cromwell succeeded in getting most of the plant transferred to London, and there, from the press of Richard Grafton and Edward Whitchurch, newly housed in the vacated precinct of the Gray Friars, appeared, in April 1539, the first edition of the Great Bible.

The name 'Great Bible,' as being 'of the greatest volume' (both terms being used by Grafton himself), is a convenient one by which to denote the seven editions of this work issued during the years 1539–41. Of these the second and subsequent ones had a preface by Cranmer, and the name 'Cranmer's Bible' may be properly applied to them. But it is not correct to use it, as is often done, of the first edition as well, in the preparation of which the archbishop had no direct share. The dates of the seven are as follows:—(i.) April 1539; (ii.) April 1540; (iii.) July 1540; (iv.) ready in November 1540, but kept back till the following year, on account of the fall of Cromwell in July 1540; (v.) May 1541; (vi.) November 1541; (vii.) December 1541. Though no two issues are identical, the family likeness is so strong that it will suffice to describe the first, and to indicate briefly the features by which later ones may be identified. The title of (i.) is:* 'The Bible in | Englyshe, that is to saye, the con | tent of all the holy scrypture, bothe | of y^e^ olde and newe testament, truly | translated after the veryte of the | Hebrue and Greke textes, by y^e^ dy|lygent studye of dyuerse excellent | learned men, expert in the forsayde | tonges. ¶ Prynted by Richard Grafton & | Edward Whitchurch. | Cum priuilegio ad imprimen|dum solum | 1539.' This title, in black and red letters, is surrounded by a singularly spirited woodcut, bearing no artist's name or mark, but commonly believed to be by Holbein. In the centre at the top, a king, his crown laid aside, is prostrate on the ground before a figure of the Saviour appearing in the clouds. Lower down the central line, the same king, seated on his throne, and now easily recognizable as Henry VIII., is giving a clasped volume lettered *verbum Dei* to a group of ecclesiastics on his right, headed by Cranmer, and to a corresponding group of lay nobles and others on his left, headed by Cromwell. Beneath, on the dexter side, a preacher, not unlike Colet (who, however, had been dead twenty years), is addressing a mixed multitude on the words of 1 Ti $2^{1}$. Labels, with suitable inscriptions in Latin, issue from the mouths of the chief characters. Some little boys, too young to have learned Latin, cry 'God save the king' in English.† Five more leaves of preliminary matter follow, containing (1) 'The Kalender,' ending with 'an Almanach for xix years'; (2) 'An exhortacyon to the studye' . . . ; (3) 'The summe and content of all the holy scripture' . . . ; (4) 'A prologue' . . . ; (5) 'A descripcyon and successe of the kynges of Juda' . . . ; (6) 'With what iudgement the bokes of the Olde Testament are to be red.' Genesis begins on the seventh leaf, marked 'fo. 1.' It is worth while to give some extracts from the Prologue, 'expressynge what is meant by certayn signes and tokens that we have set in the Byble. First, where as often tymes ye shall fynde a small letter in the texte, it sygnifyeth that so moche as is in the small lettre doth abounde and is more in the common translacyon in Latin, then is founde ether in the Hebrue or in the Greke. . . . Moreouer, where as ye fynde this figure ☩ it betokeneth a dyuersyte and difference of readynge betwene the Hebrues and the Chaldees in the same place. . . . We haue also (as ye maye se) added many handes both in the mergent of thys volume and also in the

* See art. by A. F. Pollard in *Dict. of Nat. Biography*.

† The royal permission, along with many interesting letters from Coverdale and Grafton, is given in facsimile in J. A. Kingdon's *Incidents in the Lives of Thomas Poyntz and Richard Grafton*, privately printed, 1895. See also the correspondence in Pettigrew's *Bibliotheca Sussexiana*, 1839, p. 281 ff.

* The copy used is that marked C. 18. d. 1 in the Library of the British Museum. It is a singularly fine copy, the leaves measuring 15 × 10 inches. A sumptuous copy on vellum, meant for Cromwell himself, is in the Library of St. John's College, Cambridge. In this the title is somewhat abridged.

† A full description of the woodcut is given in Moulton, pp. 138, 139, and in Mombert, pp. 204, 205.

text, vpon the which w^e purposed to haue made in the ende of the Byble (in a table by themselues) certen godly annotacions: but for so moch as yet there hath not bene soffycient tyme minystred to the Kynges moost honorable councell for the ouersyght and correccyon of the sayde annotacyons, we wyll therfore omyt them, tyll their more conuenient leysour. . . . God saue the Kynge.' The colophon is: 'The ende of the new Testamēt: | and of the whole Byble, ffynisshed in Aprγll, | Anno M.CCCCC.XXXIX.* | A Dño factū est istud.'

Peculiarities by which the various issues of the 'Great Bible' may be distinguished one from another have been minutely tabulated by Fry (*Description of the Great Bible*, fol. 1865). The first three editions alone have the ☞ as a reference for Coverdale's intended 'annotacyons,' the 'conuenient leysour' for which never came. The same three editions also are the only ones which present Cromwell's coat of arms, in Holbein's woodcut, unerased. After his attainder and execution, July 28th, 1540, the circle containing his arms is left blank. Cranmer's Prologue, as was said, is prefixed to the second and following editions. In it he distinguishes two classes of people: some being too slow, and needing the spur; others too quick, and needing the bridle. 'In the former sorte be all they that refuse to read the scripture in the vulgar tongue. . . . In the latter sorte be they which by their inordinate reading, vndiscrete speaking, contentious disputing, or otherwyse by their licentious living, slaunder and hynder the worde of God. . . .' The Introduction to the Apocryphal Books, for which, however, Cranmer is not in the first instance responsible, has a curiously confused account of the term 'Hagiographa,' by which for some reason they are described:—'because they were wont to be reade, not openly and in comen, but as it were in secret and aparte.' The mistake was repeated in the editions of April and July 1540, and of May and December 1541. In the fourth of the seven, the first which shows Cromwell's arms erased, the title presents, by way of compensation, the names of Cuthbert [Tunstall], Bishop of Durham, and Nicholas [Heath], Bishop of Rochester, as those by whom the work was 'oversene.' In the title to this edition, also, the king is styled 'supreme heade of this his churche and Realme of Englande.'

Who were the 'dyuerse excellent learned men,' expert in Hebrew and Greek, who helped Coverdale, we are not informed. But traces of their work may perhaps be seen in the translation of musical terms in the Psalms, and in the retention of the Hebrew titles of some of the books of the OT. Thus the first book is described as 'called in the hebrue Bereschith, and in the latyn Genesis.'

If we take it for granted that Coverdale was the working editor of the Great Bible, we shall be prepared to find that he reproduces in it very much of his own earlier version of 1535, as well as of what had been incorporated with Tindale's work in 'Matthew's' Bible of 1537. But in the OT there is evidence that this reproduction was carefully revised by the help of an edition of the Hebrew text, published at Basle in 1534-35, with a new Latin rendering by Sebastian Münster. 'Thus,' Westcott goes so far as to say (*Hist.* p. 187), 'Coverdale found an obvious method to follow. He revised the text of Matthew, which was laid down as the basis, by the help of Münster. The result was the Great Bible.' This is too unqualified a statement. For instance, in the opening chapters of Genesis, a book the version of which in Matthew's Bible was by Tindale, we find not a few examples of Coverdale's own rendering in 1535 being preferred, or of a fresh rendering being made. A very few specimens must suffice—

'Then of the euening and the morning was made *one day*' (C.); 'And the euening . . . *one day*' (G. B.); 'And so of the . . . was made *the fyrst daye*' (T.); 'Et *fuit* uespera . . . dies unus' (Münster); 'Factumque est . . . dies unus' (Vulg.).

'And God *set* them in the fyrmament' (C. and G. B.); '*put* them' (T.).

'And all the *hoost* of them' (C. and G. B.); 'apparell' (T.). The Vulg. here has *ornatus*, Münster *exercitus*.

'The Lorde God shope man, euen of the *moulde of the erth*' (C. and T.); . . . 'of the dust from of the grounde' (G. B.).

'In Eden *towarde ye east*' (C.); 'from the begynnynge' (T.); 'eastward from Eden' (G. B.). The Vulgate, followed by T., has *a principio*; Münster *ab oriente*.

The version of Isaiah in Matthew is by Coverdale. But that this was diligently revised for the Great Bible, a few examples from the first two chapters will show—

'An oxe knoweth his LORDE' (M.); 'The oxe hath knowne his owner' (G. B.).

'Like a watchouse in tyme of warre' (M.); 'lyke a beseged cytie' (G. B.).

'Ye tyrauntes of Sodoma' (M.); 'ye Lordes of Sodoma' (G. B.).

'Cease from doinge of evell & violence' (M.); '& violence' omitted (G. B.).

'Leade' (M.); 'tynne' (G. B.).

'Al heithen shal prease vnto him' (M.); 'all nacyons' (G. B.).

'So that they shal breake . . . to make . . . & sawes therof' (M.); 'They shall breake theyr swerdes also in to mattockes . . . to make sythes' (G. B.).

In the NT the relation of the version found in the Great Bible of 1539 to those of Tindale (1534) and Coverdale (1535) may be conveniently traced by the parallel passages from St. Matthew, 52 in number, set down by Westcott (pp. 174-176), for the purpose of comparing the two latter. If the Great Bible be compared with these it will be found to agree with Tindale in 5 places, with Coverdale in 33, and to differ from both (though on the whole nearer to Coverdale) in the remaining 14.

As regards the relation of the text found in the Great Bible of April 1539 to that of the succeeding editions, Westcott has shown, by a full induction of passages, that while in the OT there is little change in the versions of the Pentateuch and the earlier historical books, a careful revision of the Hagiographa and the prophetical books is apparent in the issue of April 1540. The authority most relied on for the changes thus made is Münster. A curious circumstance pointed out by Westcott is the fact that, instead of the alterations being progressive, the text of Nov. 1540 shows a tendency to recur to that of April 1539; so that practically two groups or recensions may be recognized:—(1) April 1539, Nov. 1540, May 1541, Nov. 1541; (2) April 1540, July 1540. In the NT Erasmus occupies the position which Münster has done in the OT. A single example will show the deference paid to Erasmus—

**Ja 1[13]** 'Deus enim intentator malorum est: ipse autem neminem temptat' (Vulg.).
'For Gode cannot temte vnto euyll, because he tempteth no man' (G. B., Apr. 1539).
'Nam Deus ut malis tentari non potest, ita nec ipse quemquam tentat' (Eras.).
'For as God cannot be tempted with euyll, so neither he himself tempteth any man' (G. B., May, Nov. 1540).

In the Preface to the Book of Common Prayer it is noted that 'the Psalter followeth . . . the translation of the great English Bible, set forth and used in the time of King Henry the Eighth and Edward the Sixth.' This arrangement, which was unavoidable in 1549, was left unaltered in 1662, the rhythm of Coverdale's version, and its greater fitness for singing, having in the meantime endeared it to the people. The present text of the Pr. Bk. Psalter does not, however, represent the text of any edition of the Great Bible exactly, and it contains some misprints (*e.g.* 'sight' for 'light' in Ps 38[10]). See Preface to Driver's *Par. Psalter*, and esp. the elaborate collation in M'Garvey's *Liturgiæ Americanæ* (1895), pp. 1*-51*.

Though Bishops Tunstall and Heath had allowed their names to stand on the title-pages of several editions of the Great Bible, and Bonner, after the royal proclamation of 1540, had duly caused six copies of the Bible to be set up for public reading in St. Paul's, it is plain that the Episcopal bench generally were only half-hearted as yet in the work of translating the Scriptures into English. A motion was brought forward in Convocation, in 1542, for undertaking a fresh version, but was

* Kingdon (*Grafton*, p. 63), following in this Strype's *Cranmer*, i. p. 120, endeavours to show that the impression of 2000 copies, seized in Paris, was *intended* to appear in April 1539, and dated accordingly; but that, when the embargo was removed, and the copies got over to London, they were not actually published there till 1540.

shelved by Gardiner, who stipulated for the transliteration, not translation, of many words of the original, such as *ecclesia*, *pœnitentia*, *pascha*, *zizania*, *didrachma*; including even some of which the meaning was obvious, as *simplex*, *dignus*, *oriens*. To have constructed a version on these principles would have been to anticipate the worst faults of the Rheims and Douai translations.

v. PURITAN.—Meantime, however, while the bishops at home were hesitating, the work of a new version, or rather of a vigilant revision of existing ones, was being actively carried on abroad. The result was the **Genevan Bible**.*

When, on the accession of Mary Tudor, in 1553, the leaders of the Reforming party sought safety on the Continent, Frankfort became for a time a centre for the refugees. But when dissensions on the subject of the English Liturgy broke out between the moderate section, headed by Cox, afterwards dean of Durham, and the more violent spirits, who followed John Knox, the latter withdrew to Geneva. Among them was William Whittingham, a native of Chester, who in 1545 had been made Fellow of All Souls', Oxford, and Senior Student of Christ Church in 1547.† In 1557 he published anonymously at Geneva a new version in English of the NT in small 8vo, bearing date 'This x of June.' This was a prelude to a greater work, an English version of the whole Bible, on which some of the exiles were engaged. The news of queen Mary's death, in 1558, drew most of these back to England; but Whittingham remained at his post, to finish the work, and with him, as Anthony a Wood tells us, there remained 'one or two more.' These 'one or two' were probably Anthony Gilby, of Christ's Coll., Cambridge, who afterwards became rector of Ashby-de-la-Zouche; 'a fast and furious stickler against Church discipline,' as he is called by Fuller, but a good scholar; and Thomas Sampson. Sampson had entered Pembroke Hall, Cambridge, but apparently had not taken any degree. After refusing the bishopric of Norwich in 1560, he was made dean of Christ Church, Oxford, in 1561. Beza gives him the character of being of 'an exceedingly restless disposition.'

By the labours of these men, and of others whose names have not come down to us, there was issued from the press of 'Rovland' Hall, at Geneva, in 1560, an English Bible, commonly called, from its place of publication, the Genevan, which was destined to attain lasting popularity. Its title was: 'The Bible | and | Holy Scriptvres | conteyned in | the Olde and Newe | Testaments. | Translated accor| ding to the Ebrue and Greke, and conferred With | the best translations in diuers langages. | With moste profitable annota|tions vpon all the hard places, and other things of great | importance as may appeare in the Epistle to the Reader.' Below is a woodcut of the Israelites crossing the Red Sea, bordered by texts in small italic character. On the reverse of the title is a list of the books of the Bible, including the Apocrypha (ending with 2 Mac.). Leaves ii and iii are occupied by a Dedication to 'the moste vertvous and noble Qvene Elizabeth,' from her 'humble subjects of the English Churche at Geneva.' Leaf iiii is filled on both sides with an Address 'to ovr Beloved in the Lord, the Brethren of England, Scotland, Ireland, &c.,' dated 'from Geneua, 10 April, 1560.' The regular foliation begins on the fifth leaf, and ends with the close of the Apocrypha on f. 474. The NT begins with fresh foliation, and ends on f. 122, being followed by 12 unnumbered leaves, containing proper names, with interpretation, and chronological tables. A map, folded into two leaves, is placed next after the title of the NT.

If we inquire into the causes which made the Genevan Bible so long a favourite one (Hoare estimates that 160 editions of it appeared between 1560 and the outbreak of the Civil War in England), they are not far to seek. The mere shape and size of the volume as it first appeared, a handy 4to,* was a recommendation as compared with the ponderous folios of the Great, or the Bishops', Bible. It was printed throughout in Roman and italic, not Gothic, letter. It adopted the division into verses, first introduced by Stephen in 1551, and followed by Whittingham in his NT of 1557. It retained the marginal notes, Calvinist in tone, but generally free from offensive asperity, of the NT of 1557, with the addition of similar notes for the OT,—the Apocrypha being but slenderly furnished with them. It indicated by marks of accent the pronunciation of proper names. It had woodcuts,† and convenient maps and tables.

The version of the OT is substantially Tindale's; that of the NT Whittingham's; but both are vigilantly revised. A comparison of the Genevan version of a passage from Ac $27^{13}$–$28^{4}$ with that of Whittingham,‡ and with that of the Bishops' Bible in 1568, will suffice to show this—

| | | |
|---|---|---|
| Ac $27^{13}$ | W. | lowsed *nearer* (ἄραντες ἆσσον). |
| | G. | losed *nearer*. |
| | B. | loosed unto *Asson*. |
| v.$^{14}$ | W. | there arose *agaynst Candie*, a stormye wynd out of the northeast (κατ' αὐτῆς). |
| | G. | there arose *by it* a stormie winde called Euroclydon. |
| | B. | there arose *against their purpose* a flawe of winde out of the northeast. |
| v.$^{15}$ | W. | and *draue* wyth the wether (ἐφερόμεθα). |
| | G. | and *were caryed away*. |
| | B. | and *were dryuen* with the weather. |
| v.$^{16}$ | W. | and we were caryed *beneth* a litle yle . . . to come by *the* boat (τῆς σκάφης). |
| | G. | and we rã *vnder* a litle yle . . . to get *the* boat. |
| | B. | but we were caryed *into* an Ile . . . to come by *a* boat. |
| v.$^{17}$ | W. | *vndergirding* the shyp . . . they let slip *the* vessel (τὸ σκεῦος). |
| | G. | *vndergirding* the ship . . . *the* vessel. |
| | B. | and *made fast* the shippe . . . *a* vessel. |
| v.$^{21}$ | W. | and to haue *gayned* this iniurie and losse (κερδῆσαι). |
| | G. | so shulde ye haue *gained* this hurt and losse (=haue saued the losse by auoiding the danger—marg. note). |
| | B. | neither to haue *brought* vnto vs this harme and losse. |
| v.$^{27}$ | W. | were *caried to and fro* in the Adriatical sea (διαφερομένων). |
| | G. | were *caryed to & fro* in the Adriatical sea. |
| | B. | were *saylyng* in Adria. |
| v.$^{40}$ | W. | they committed *the ship* (italics) (εἴων). |
| | G. | they committed *the ship* (italics). |
| | B. | they committed *themselues* (smaller type). |
| v.$^{42}$ | W. | should *flie* away. |
| | G. | shulde *flee* away. |
| | B. | should *runne* away. |
| v.$^{44}$ | W. | on *broken peces* (both words in italics) (ἐπί τινων τῶν ἀπό, κ.τ.λ.) . . . that they *came* all *safe*. |
| | G. | on *certeine pieces* (*pieces* in italics) . . . yᵗ thei *came* all *safe*. |
| | B. | on *broken* peeces . . . that they *escaped* all. |
| $28^{2}$ | W. | the Barbarians . . . the *showre which appeared* (τὸν ὑετὸν τὸν ἐφεστῶτα). |
| | G. | the Barbarians . . . the *present showre*. |
| | B. | yᵉ straungers . . . the *present rayne*. |
| v.$^{3}$ | W. | a *fewe* stickes. |
| | G. | a *nomber* of stickes (φρυγάνων τι πλῆθος). |
| | B. | a *bondell* of stickes. |
| v.$^{4}$ | W. | the *worme* (τὸ θηρίον). |
| | G. | the *worme*. |
| | B. | the *beast*. |

* A series of useful articles on this subject, by N. Pocock, will be found in vols. ii. and iii. of the *Bibliographer*, 1882–83. See also an essay on 'The English Bible from Henry VIII. to James I.,' by H. W. Hoare, in *The Nineteenth Century* for April 1899.

† He is said to have been Calvin's brother-in-law; but this is disputed by A. F. Pollard in his art. on W. Whittingham in the *Dict. of Nat. Biography*.

* The size of page in the copy before the present writer (Brit. Mus. C. 17. b. 8) is 9¾ by 6⅝ inches.

† Some of these are said to be from the French Bible of A. Davodeau, published at Geneva earlier in the same year.

‡ Whittingham's translation is included in Bagster's *English Hexapla*, from which we quote it.

A few peculiarities of spelling may be noticed. The desire to economize space, as shown in the frequent contractions, even of short words like 'mā' (man), 'rā' (ran), has led to the reduction of double consonants and diphthongs—in many instances, to single letters. Thus we find 'delt,' 'hel,' 'wildernes,' 'confunded,' 'thoght,' and many more of a like kind.

A 4to edition of the Genevan Bible, printed at Geneva in 1570, by John Crispin, professes to be the second edition; but Pocock has shown that this title really belongs to one issued at Geneva in folio without any printer's name, the OT being dated 1562 and the NT 1561. The first edition published in England was one in small folio, with Roman type, issued in 1576 by Richard Barkar (*sic*). An edition of the metrical version of the Psalms by Sternhold and Hopkins was prepared for binding up along with this. Later on, in 1578, we find the Book of Common Prayer, somewhat garbled, printed in the same volume with the Genevan Bible.

No other change need be noticed, except the partial displacement of the Genevan NT by a fresh version, made in 1576, by Laurence Tomson, a private secretary of Sir Francis Walsingham. Tomson closely followed Beza, putting 'that' for the *ille* by which Beza had rendered the Greek article. Thus, in Jn 1[1], we have 'that Word' for 'the Word.' Tomson's notes were more pronouncedly Calvinistic than before. His NT was often bound up with the Genevan OT, and, as a separate book, is said to have been preferred to the other.

vi. ELIZABETHAN.—**The Bishops' Bible.**—It was not to be expected that the Elizabethan bishops should acquiesce in the popularity of the Genevan version. Its Calvinism, if we may judge from Whitgift's example later on, might have been tolerated by them, but not its hostility to their office. Accordingly, a move was made by Archbishop Parker for a new translation, or rather for a fresh revision of that contained in the Great Bible. The steps taken can be followed, with fair certainty, in the *Parker Correspondence*. There is extant a letter, dated Nov. 26, addressed by the archbishop to Sir William Cecil. This is referred, in the Calendar of State Papers, to the year 1566. But if, as Pocock suggests, it should be placed a year earlier, it would present to us one of the first acts in the proceedings. For in this letter the archbishop not only acquaints Cecil with his plans, but asks the busy statesman (out of compliment, we may well suppose) to undertake some portion of the translation. The general principle on which the work was to be carried out, was for certain books to be assigned to individual bishops, or other biblical scholars, who should work on the text of the Great Bible as their basis, and transmit their portions, when finished, to the primate, for his final revision.

The defects of such a scheme were obvious. There was no meeting together for the discussion of various renderings. No provision was made to secure uniformity of style. The final revision to be expected from one with so much business on hand as Archbishop Parker, one not specially distinguished as a scholar, and one who had, moreover, reserved certain books as his own particular share, was not likely to be thorough, even if deputed in part to other learned men. Accordingly, we are not surprised to find traces of haste, if not of negligence, in the work. Thus the revision of Kings and Chronicles was despatched by Bishop Sandys in about seven weeks. As an incentive to diligence, the initials of each contributor were to be printed at the end of the books undertaken by him. Comparing these with a list sent by Parker to Cecil, Oct. 5th, 1568,* we can identify nearly all the workers with fair certainty.

According to this list, the archbishop himself undertook, besides Prefaces and other introductory matter, Genesis, Exodus, Matthew, Mark, and 2 Cor.–Hebrews inclusive. Andrew Pierson, prebendary of Canterbury (a conjectural expansion, supported by the initials A. P. C., of the single word 'Cantuariæ'), had Leviticus, Numbers, Job, and Proverbs. The Bishop of Exeter (Wm. Alley) had Deuteronomy. The Bishop of St. Davids (Rd. Davies) had Joshua–2 Kings.† The Bishop of Worcester (Edwyn Sandys) had 3 and 4 Kings and Chronicles. Andrew Perne, Master of Peterhouse and Dean of Ely (a conjectural inference, like the former, by help of the initials A. P. E., from 'Cantabrigiæ'), had Ecclesiastes and Canticles. The Bishop of Norwich (John Parkhurst) shared the Apocryphal books with the Bishop of Chichester (Wm. Barlow). The Bishop of Winchester (Rt. Horne) had Isaiah–Lamentations; the Bishop of Lichfield and Coventry (I. Bentham) taking the rest of the Greater Prophets. The Minor Prophets fell to the Bishop of London (Edmund Grindal). The Bishop of Peterborough (Ed. Scambler) took Luke and John; the Bishop of Ely (R. Cox) Acts and Romans; the Dean of Westminster (Gabriel Goodman) 1 Corinthians; and the Bishop of Lincoln (N. Bullingham) the General Epistles and the Revelation.

It will be noticed that Parker's list omits the Book of Psalms. The initials appended to this book in the Bible itself are T. B., supposed by Strype to designate Thomas Becon, formerly one of Cranmer's chaplains, afterwards a prebendary of Canterbury. The Psalms had in fact been originally assigned to Edmund Geste, Bishop of Rochester; and if the revised rendering had been made by him on the principles he does not scruple to avow,‡ the work might well need to be sent on to some other scholar for correction. A difficulty is also caused by the fact that the initials at the end of Daniel, T. C. L., do not appear to correspond with the 'I. Lich. and Covent.' of the list. But the explanation of Burnet is a plausible one, that Thomas Bentham, Bishop of Lichfield and Coventry (1560–1580), is meant in both cases, the confusion of I. and T. being easy; and that he was accustomed to sign himself 'Covent. and Lich.,' reversing the usual order.

By these united efforts there was produced, in 1568, from the press of Richard Jugge, dwelling in St. Paul's Churchyard, what well deserved the designation by which it was often known, 'the Bible of largest volume.'§ The title-page is chiefly occupied by an ornamental border, having within it, on an oblong label at the top, 'The holie Bible,'‖ and in the centre, within an oval, a portrait of queen Elizabeth: above it, the royal arms; beneath, in three lines, the text *Non me pudet . . . credenti* from Ro 1[16]. The next three leaves have 'A Preface into the Bible folowynge,' by Archbishop Parker. The fifth, sixth, and part of the seventh leaves are taken up with Cranmer's 'prologue or preface.' Other preliminary matter follows, extending to the twenty-sixth leaf, Genesis beginning on the twenty-seventh. One interesting point among the subjects treated of in the Introduction, peculiar, we believe, to this Bible, is the caution to ministers against heedlessly reading aloud words or phrases which might sound objectionable. Certain 'semy circles' are used as marks to denote what 'may be left vnread in the publique reading to the people.'¶ This scrupulousness, which would have satisfied Selden, might well have been extended to the designs used for initial letters; some of which (notably that at the beginning of Hebrews in the ed. of 1572) would be more appropriate for an edition of Ovid's *Metamorphoses* than for an English Bible. Besides the copperplate engraving of Elizabeth already mentioned, there is one of the Earl of Leicester at the beginning of Joshua, and another of Sir Wm. Cecil (to represent king David?) at the beginning of the Bk. of Psalms.

* Printed in the *Correspondence of Archbishop Parker* (Parker Society), pp. 335, 336.

† That is, 2 Samuel.

‡ 'Where in the New Testament,' he writes to the archbishop, 'one piece of a Psalm is reported, I translate it in the Psalm according to the translation thereof in the New Testament, for the avoiding of the offence that may arise to the people upon diverse translations.'—*Parker Corresp.* p. 250.

§ In the copy before the present writer (Brit. Mus. 1. e. 2) the size of page is 15½ by 10¼ inches.

‖ Some copies have the additional words: 'conteyning the olde Testament and the newe.'

¶ The note is on the fifteenth leaf, signed * 1, next after the list of 'faultes escaped.'

The 'other perusal,' of which Parker had assured Cecil that the travail of the Revisers would have the benefit, showed itself in an amended edition, published by Jugge, in 4to, the following year, with the brief title, 'The holi Bible.' But only negligent use had been made of the criticisms called forth. Some interesting specimens of these, by a schoolmaster named Laurence, have been fortunately preserved by Strype,* and the way in which they were incorporated in the edition of 1569 shows strikingly the want of care exercised. Two examples must suffice. In Mt $28^{14}$ the traditional rendering of ἀμερίμνους, namely 'harmless,' had been retained. Laurence pointed out that 'careless' (in the sense of *securus*) was rather the word. But he must have been surprised to find himself taken so literally that in 1569 the rendering appeared, 'We will make you careless.' Again, in Mt $21^{38}$ the Revisers, following the Great Bible in preference to the Genevan, had rendered κατάσχωμεν 'let us enjoy' instead of 'let us take' (RV). Laurence found fault with this, on the ground that the original signified 'let us take possession or seysyn (seizin) upon.' In the edition of 1569, and in every subsequent one, this appeared as 'let us *season upon* his inheritance' ('sease on' in AV of 1611).†

The most singular part of the matter is that, while corrections (of whatever value) were freely admitted into the second edition of 1569, the third of 1572 went back in many particulars to the first. A few examples will make this clear. For brevity, the editions may be denoted by A, B, C.

In Gn $36^{24}$ in A Anah is a woman : 'she fedde'; in B, correctly, a man : 'he fedde ;' C goes back to 'she.'—In Jg $5^{10}$ A reads, 'ye that dwell by Middin' (RV 'that sit on rich carpets'); B 'ye that syt vppermoste in iudgment'; C goes back to A.—In Mt $15^5$ A has 'by the gyft that [is offered] of me, thou shalt be helped'; B 'what gift soeuer shold haue come of me'; C agrees with A.—In Lk $2^2$ A has 'and this first taxing was made'; B 'this taxing was the first and executed when,' etc.; C goes back to A.—In Ac $1^1$ A and C have 'O Theophilus'; B 'deare Theophilus.'—In Ac $7^{34}$ A and C have 'I haue seene, I haue seene'; B 'I haue perfectly sene.'—In 1 Ti $1^2$ A has 'a natural sonne'; B 'his naturall sonne'; C goes back to A.

The edition of 1572, moreover, exhibited two versions of the Psalms in parallel columns : that of the Revisers themselves, and that from the Great Bible. Many subsequent editions appeared. Dore (*Old Bibles*, p. 239) enumerates nineteen in all, from 1568 to 1606 inclusive; Pocock seventeen, speaking doubtfully also of one of these, as never seen by him, an alleged folio of 1606. The British Museum Catalogue does not show this last, nor yet an 8vo (included by Dore) of 1577.

The Bishops' Bible appears never to have received the royal sanction. Parker, indeed, in his letter of Oct. 5th, 1568, before quoted, tried to procure, through Sir Wm. Cecil, such a mark of recognition. 'The printer,' he writes, 'hath honestly done his diligence. If your honour would obtain of the Queen's Highness that this edition might be licensed and only commended in public reading in churches, to draw to one uniformity, it were no great cost to the most parishes, and a relief to him for his great charges sustained.' But, so far as is known, the application was unsuccessful. Accordingly, the claim to be 'set foorth by auethoritee,' made by the editions of 1574 and 1575, must be referred to the sanction of Convocation, given in 1571. The *Constitutions and Canons Ecclesiastical* of that year expressly ordain that 'every archbishop and bishop should have at his house a copy of the holy Bible of the largest volume as lately printed at London.' A like injunction was laid upon cathedrals; and, 'as far as it could be conveniently done,' upon all churches.*

vii. ROMAN CATHOLIC.—It was not likely that English Roman Catholics should continue unmoved by this untiring work in translating the Bible. Every fresh version made by scholars of the Reformed Church was a tacit reflexion on them for making none. Accordingly, it was resolved by the leading members of the newly founded English College at Douai, that this reproach—so far as they admitted it to be a reproach—should be wiped away. The moving spirit in this undertaking, as in the foundation of the college itself, was Dr. William Allen,† made cardinal afterwards in 1587. But the actual work of making the new translation devolved almost entirely on Dr. Gregory Martin, a native of Maxfield in Sussex, who had been one of Sir Thomas White's first batch of students at St. John's College, Oxford, in 1557. Having chosen to forsake Oxford for Douai, he was made by Allen the teacher of Hebrew and Biblical literature there.‡ Dr. William Reynolds, formerly of New College, Oxford, Richard Bristow, a Worcester man, and others, took a share in the work of revision.

Amid such circumstances, recalling in some measure the origin of the Genevan version, the translation known as the **Rhemes and Doway** took its rise. The entire Bible appears to have been ready for issue together. But, owing to want of funds, a portion only could be published at a time. The NT was properly given the preference, and appeared in 1582 with the following title :—

'The | Nevv Testament | of Iesvs Christ, trans|lated faithfvlly into English | ovt of the authentical Latin, according to the best cor|rected copies of the same, diligently conferred vvith | the Greeke and other editions in diuers languages: vvith | Arguments of bookes and chapters, annota|tions, and other necessarie helpes, for the better vnder|standing of the text, and specially for the discouerie of the Corrvptions of diuers late translations, and for | cleering the Controversies in religion, of these daies.—In the English College of Rhemes. . . . Printed at Rhemes | by John Fogny | 1582 | *cum privilegio*.'

The volume is in a convenient 4to size,§ printed in clear-cut Roman type, no black letter being used. In some respects the arrangement of the RV is anticipated. The text is broken up into paragraphs, not verses. But the verse numeration is given in the inner margin, an obelus being prefixed to the beginning of each verse. Quotations from the OT are printed in italics. At the head of each chapter is an 'Argument,' and 'Annotations' at the end.

Of the preliminary matter, the long Preface to the Reader, occupying leaves a ij–c iv, well merits attention. The writers address themselves to three special points: (1) the translation of the Holy Scriptures into the vernacular, and, in particular, into English; (2) the reasons why the present version is made from the Vulgate; (3) the principles on which the translators have proceeded. They do not publish their translation 'vpon erroneous opinions of necessitie that the holy scriptures should alwaies be in our mother tongue, or that they ought or were ordained of God to be read

* *Life of Parker*, ed. 1821, vol. iii. p. 258. It has been conjectured, with much probability, that the Laurence in question, 'a man in those times of great fame for his knowledge in the Greek,' was Thomas Lawrence, appointed head-master of Shrewsbury in 1568.

† See Pocock's art. in the *Bibliographer*, vol. i. p. 113, where more examples are given.

* Cardwell, *Synodalia*, i. 115.

† Allen was born in 1532 at Rossall in Lancashire; entered Queen's College, Oxford, in 1547. He founded the seminary at Douai in 1568, and removed with it to Rheims in 1578, when disturbances in Flanders made Douai unsafe. He died at Rome in 1594.

‡ See the art. by Thompson Cooper in the *Dict. of Nat. Biography*. Martin and Bristow both died of consumption at a comparatively early age.

§ In the copy before the present writer (Brit. Mus. 1008. c. 9) the page measures $8\frac{1}{2}$ by $6\frac{1}{8}$ inches.

indifferently of all . . . . but vpon special consideration of the present time, state and condition of our country.' Holy Church, while not encouraging, had not absolutely forbidden such versions. Using the freedom thus left, divers learned Catholics, since Luther's revolt, had already translated the Scriptures into the mother tongues of various nations of Europe; yet still repudiating the notion that all people alike might indifferently read, expound, and talk of them.

That the Latin Vulgate should have been taken as the basis of their work, in preference to any Greek text, is defended on the ground of its antiquity, of its freedom from the discrepancies visible in MSS of the Greek, and of its having been defined as exclusively authentic by the Council of Trent. Usually it would be found that the Vulgate agreed with the received text of the Greek; and where that was not so it would probably be found in accord with readings relegated to the margin, but not necessarily of less authority on that account. The issue, we think, within ten years of the date of this Preface, of the Sixtine edition of the Vulgate in 1590, and the Clementine in 1592, with the momentous corrections of 'preli vitia,' as Bellarmin called them,* must have been a shock difficult for these apologists to withstand.

As regards the style of their translation, the Rhemists profess to have had one sole object in view. This was, without partiality and without licence, to express the sense of the Vulgate with the least possible change of form; 'continually keeping ourselves as near as is possible to our text, and to the very words and phrases which by long use are made venerable . . . [not doubting] that all sorts of Catholic readers will in short time think that familiar which at the first may seem strange.' In carrying out this principle it is inevitable that some felicitous phrases and turns of expression should be hit upon in the course of a long work. 'A *palpable* mount' (He $12^{18}$) is better than 'the mount that might be touched' of the AV. In the first chapter of James alone it is to the Rhemish version that we owe 'upbraideth not' (v.$^{5}$), 'nothing doubting' (v.$^{6}$), 'the engrafted word' (v.$^{21}$), 'bridleth not' (v.$^{26}$).† As Plumptre has pointed out, so great an authority as Bacon (*Of the Pacification of the Church*) goes out of his way to praise the Rhemists for having restored 'charity' to the place from which Tindale had ousted it in favour of 'love.' In particular, the closeness with which the translators kept to the Vulgate helped to save them from that needless variation in the rendering of the same or cognate words, which is an undoubted blemish in the AV. Thus, while *δικαιοῦν* is correctly rendered in our version 'to justify,' *δίκαιος* and *δικαιοσύνη* are more often than not represented by 'righteous' and 'righteousness.'‡ Once more, the antiquity of the MSS from which the Vulgate translation was made causes its readings at times to accord with the results of the highest critical scholarship. It will follow that the Rhemish version occasionally comes nearer our RV than does that of king James. Thus in Mt $5^{44}$ the clauses, interpolated from the parallel passage in St. Luke, which find no place in the RV, are partially omitted in the Rhemish. So, too, this latter agrees with the RV in reading 'Christ' for 'God' in 1 P $3^{15}$.

But, when every allowance of the kind is made, the fact remains that, to ordinary English readers, the translation in question must often have seemed one into an unknown tongue. What else could have been thought of such specimens as these: 'I wil not drinke of the generation of the vine' (Lk $22^{18}$); 'the passions of this time are not condigne to the glorie to come' (Ro $8^{18}$); 'For our wrestling is . . . against Princes and Potestats, against the rectors of the world of this darkenes, against the spirituals of wickedness in the celestials' (Eph $6^{12}$); 'But he exinanited himself' (Ph $2^{7}$); 'Yet are they turned about with a little sterne, whither the violence of the director wil' (Ja $3^{4}$)?*

In 1593 the English College returned from Rheims to their old quarters at Douai, and completed their biblical labours by the issue, in 1609 and 1610, of two volumes, containing the OT and Apocrypha. In size, type, and general execution, they closely resemble the volume of the NT published nearly thirty years before. The title is: 'The | Holie Bible | Faithfvlly trans-|lated into English, | ovt of the avthentical | Latin | Diligently conferred with the Hebrew, Greeke, | and other Editions in diuers languages. | With Argvments of the Bookes, and Chapters: | Annotations: Tables: and other helpes, | for better vnderstanding of the text: for discouerie of | corrvptions in some late translations: and | for clearing controversies in Religion.| . . . . Printed at Doway by Lavrence Kellam, | at the signe of the holie Lambe. | M.DC.IX.' The first volume extends to the end of Job. The second volume, bearing a similar title, and the date M.DC.X., comprises from Psalms to 4 Esdras. A preface to 'the right welbeloved English Reader' goes over much the same ground as that prefixed to the Rhemes NT, but more cursorily, being only about half the length of the other. The hindrances, which had delayed the appearance of the work, had all proceeded from 'one general cause, our poore estate in banishment.' The arguments for translating from the Vulgate are re-stated. The retention of Latinisms, or original forms of words, is defended. If English Protestants keep 'Sabbath,' 'Ephod,' 'Pentecost,' 'Proselyte,' and the like, why not 'Prepuce,' 'Pasch,' 'Azimes,' 'Breades of Proposition,' 'Holocaust,' and others of the same kind?

This uncompromising principle gradually gave way. In 1749–50, and again in 1763–4, editions of the Doway OT and the Rhemes NT, each edition in five vols. 12mo, were published by Richard Challoner, Bishop of Debra, *in partibus*, with the assistance of William Green, afterwards President of the College at Douai, and Walton, afterwards Vicar Apostolic of the northern district of England.† As thus revised, it is substantially the version used at the present day by English-speaking Roman Catholics. In Cardinal Wiseman's opinion, 'though Challoner did well in altering many too decided Latinisms, he weakened the language considerably by destroying inversion . . . and by the insertion of particles where not needed.'‡

The nature and extent of these changes may be judged of by a comparison of a few passages from the older and newer versions, side by side with the RV of 1885:—

| 1609–10. | 1763–4. | 1885. |
|---|---|---|
| 2 K [2 S] $21^{19}$ Adeodatus the sonne of the Forest a broderer . . . | Adeodatus the son of Forrest an embroiderer . . . | Elhanan the son of Jaare-oregim§. . . |

* See the passages quoted by Westcott in his article on 'The Vulgate' in Smith's *DB*, vol. iii. pp. 1706, 1707.

† See Moulton, p. 187, where more examples are given.

‡ See an article in *The Month*, June 1897, pp. 578, 579. The writer appears to think that *χειροτονήσαντες*, in Ac $14^{23}$, should be translated 'by imposition of hands.'

* See now especially J. G. Carleton, *The Part of Rheims in the Making of the English Bible*. Oxf. 1902.

† See the art. on 'Challoner' by Thompson Cooper in the *Dict. of Nat. Biography*. Challoner was born at Lewes in 1691, and died in 1781. His parents were Protestant dissenters. But, losing his father in infancy, he was brought up in Roman Catholic families, and sent to Douai in 1704.

‡ Cotton, *Rhemes and Doway*, p. 49 n., specifies, as an additional fault, Challoner's excessive fondness for 'that' as equivalent to 'who,' 'whom,' 'which.'

§ *Oregim*, 'weavers' (thought by Kennicott to be a transcriber's insertion from the latter end of the verse), evidently suggested the *polymitarius*, 'broderer,' of the Vulgate. Want of space forbids any attempt at a commentary on these passages.

| 1609-10. | 1763-4. | 1885. |
|---|---|---|
| 2 Es [Neh] 9[17] and gaue the head to returne to their seruitude. | and set the head to return to their bondage. | and appointed a captain to return to their bondage (marg.). |
| Job 26[13] and his hand being the midwife, the winding serpent is brought forth. | and his artful hand hath brought forth the winding serpent. | His hand hath pierced the swift serpent. |
| Ps 67 [68][15. 16] The mountane of God a fat mountane. A mountane crudded as cheese, a fatte mountane. Why suppose you crudded mountanes? | The mountain of God is a fat mountain. A curdled mountain, a fat mountain. Why suspect ye curdled mountains? | A mountain of God is the mountain of Bashan; An high mountain is the mountain of Bashan. Why look ye askance, ye high mountains? |
| Jer 50[39] Therefore shall the dragons dwel with the foolish murderers. | Therefore shall dragons dwell there with the fig-fauns. | Therefore the wild beasts of the desert with the wolves (Heb. 'howling creatures') shall dwell there. |

The free manner in which Challoner borrowed from the AV (itself enriched by earlier borrowings from the Rhemes and Doway version) has been often remarked. A few verses will suffice in illustration.

Ro 8[18] For I reckon that the sufferings of this present time are not worthy to be compared with the glory to come, that shall be revealed in us.
Eph 6[12] For our wrestling is not against flesh and blood, but against principalities and powers; against the rulers of the world of this darkness; against the spirits of wickedness in the high places.
Ph 2[6. 7] Who being in the form of God thought it not robbery to be equal with God: But debased himself . . .
He 13[16] And do not forget to do good and to impart; for by such sacrifices God's favour is obtained.

viii. THE 'AUTHORIZED.'—The so-called Authorized Version of 1611 had its origin in the Hampton Court Conference, held on Jan. 14th, 16th, and 18th, 1604. On the second of these days, one of the four representatives of the Puritan party, Dr. John Reynolds, President of Corpus Christi College, Oxford, a learned and temperate divine, 'moved His Majesty that there might be a new translation of the Bible,'* alleging in support of his request the presence of many faults in the existing ones. It is not likely that much would have come of the motion, but for its happening to chime in with the mood of the king. The caustic remark of Bancroft, Bishop of London, that 'if every man's humour should be followed, there would be no end of translating,' probably indicates the spirit in which the proposal would have been received by his party generally. But, while they were content to let the matter drop, James was thinking out his plans for carrying Dr. Reynolds' suggestion into effect. By July of that year we find him writing to the Bishop of London, informing him that he had made out a list of fifty-four learned divines, to whom the work he had at heart might be suitably entrusted. He also drew up, for the guidance of the workers, a paper of instructions, too long to be given here in full,† but containing some sensible rules. In this he requires the bishops to see that provision be made, where necessary, for those engaged on the task of translation. The king's letter, dated July 22nd, 1604, was communicated by Bishop Bancroft ‡ to his brother prelates on the 31st. In this letter king James speaks of having already appointed 'certain learned men, to the number of four and fifty, for the translating of the Bible.' But, for some unexplained reason, the scheme did not come into operation till 1607. Possibly the death of some of those selected, or the difficulty of providing for the maintenance of others, may have caused the delay. However, by 1607 all was in working order. A list of the companies of revisers was issued, together with a paper of rules to be observed in the conduct of the work. Bancroft, no doubt, had a hand in drawing up both these documents. The most important of the rules were the following:*—

I. The ordinary Bible read in the church, commonly called 'the Bishops' Bible,' to be followed, and as little altered as the truth of the original will permit.
III. The old ecclesiastical words to be kept, videlicet, the word 'church' not to be translated 'congregation,' etc.
VI. No marginal notes at all to be affixed, but only for the explanation of the Hebrew or Greek words . . .
VIII. Every particular man of each company to take the same chapter or chapters, and having translated or amended them severally by himself, where he thinketh good, all to meet together, confer what they have done, and agree for their parts what shall stand.

As each company finished one book, they were to send it to the other companies for their careful consideration. Where doubts prevailed as to any passage of special obscurity, letters were to be sent to 'any learned man in the land' for his judgment. Finally, 'three or four of the most ancient and grave divines in either of the universities, not employed in translating,' were to be 'overseers of the translations as well Hebrew as Greek.'

It will be seen at once how much more effectual were the provisions made for securing accuracy and thoroughness in the work than those devised by Parker and his coadjutors for the Bishops' Bible.

The lists of translators which have been preserved offer some difficulties. The king, in his letter before referred to, speaks of the workers appointed as numbering fifty-four. Burnet's list, which he obtained from the papers of one of the company engaged in the work, gives only forty-seven names. The discrepancy may be accounted for by the death of members (as in the case of Mr. Lively, who died in May 1605), or some of the other changes to be looked for in a period of three years. Wood supplies two additional names—those of Dr. John Aglionby, Principal of St. Edmund's Hall, and Dr. Leonard Hutton, Canon of Christ Church. Others may still remain to be discovered.†

The entire body was divided into six groups or companies, of which two held their meetings at Westminster, two at Cambridge, and two at Oxford. Some uncertainty being allowed for, the lists are as follows:—

FIRST WESTMINSTER COMPANY.

(*Genesis*—2 *Kings*).

(1) Dr. Lancelot Andrewes, Dean of Westminster; Master of Pembroke Hall, Camb., 1589-1605; Bishop of Winchester, 1619-26. (2) Dr. John Overall, Dean of St. Paul's; Master of St. Catherine's Hall, Camb., 1598-1607; Regius Professor of Divinity, 1596-1607; Bishop of Norwich, 1618-9. (3) Dr. Hadrian à Saravia, best known as the friend of Hooker; b. at Hesdin in Artois, 1531; made Professor of Divinity at Leyden, 1582; in-

* *Sum and Substance of the Conference* . . . by William Barlow, dean of Chester, reprinted in Cardwell's *History of Conferences*, ii. 187, 188.

† It may be seen in Cardwell's *Documentary Annals*, ed. 1844, pp. 145, 146.

‡ Bancroft was appointed to the see of Canterbury at the latter end of 1604. Whitgift having died in February of that year, Bancroft discharged in the interval some of the archiepiscopal duties.

* They will be found in Cardwell's *Synodalia*, ed. 1844, ii. pp. 145, 146. Cardwell took them from Burnet, who 'himself took his list from a copy belonging originally to Bishop Ravis.'

† Mr. J. S. Cotton has kindly referred the present writer to Clark's *Register of the Univ. of Oxford* (Oxf. Hist. Soc. 1897, ii. 141), where a dispensation from the statutable exercises for the degree of D.D. is granted to Arthur Lakes, 14th May 1605, 'because engaged on the translation of the NT in London.' Arthur Lake, or Lakes, was at this time Master of St. Cross, afterwards Bishop of Bath and Wells. A similar dispensation, for a like reason, dated 6th May 1605, is granted to John Harmar. In the Calendar of State Papers, Domestic Series, under 11th Apr. 1605, mention is made by Bishop Bilson, writing to Sir Thomas Lake, Sec. of State, of Dr. George Ryves, Warden of New College, as a translator. This ref. also we owe to Mr. Cotton. The names of Lakes and Ryves are new. The three dates given are interesting as furnishing evidence that some of the translators, at least, had got to work as early as the spring of 1605.

corporated D.D. at Oxford, 1590; Prebendary of Canterbury, 1595; d. 1613. (4) Dr. Richard Clerke, Fellow of Christ's Coll., Cambridge; one of the six preachers at Canterbury, 1602; d. 1634. (5) Dr. John Leifield, or Layfield, Fellow of Trin. Coll., Camb., 1585–1603; 'Lector linguæ Græcæ,' 1593; Rector of St. Clement Danes, 1601–17; d. 1617. Noted for his skill in architecture (Collier, *Eccl. Hist.* ed. 1852, vii. 337). (6) Dr. Robert Teigh, or Tighe, Archdeacon of Middlesex, 1601; incorporated at Oxford from Trin. Coll., Cambridge, where he graduated in 1582; d. 1616. (7) 'Mr. Burleigh,' probably Dr. Francis Burley, one of the earliest Fellows of King James's College at Chelsea. (8) 'Mr. King,' probably Geoffrey King, Fellow of King's Coll., Cambridge; succeeded Dr. Robert Spalding as Regius Professor of Hebrew, 1607. (9) 'Mr. Thompson,' taken to be Richard Thompson, of Clare Hall, Cambridge; called, from the land of his birth, Dutch Thompson; the friend of Casaubon and Scaliger. (10) 'Mr. Beadwell,' taken in like manner to be William Bedwell, scholar of Trin. Coll., Oxford, 1541; Rector of St. Ethelburga's, Bishopsgate Street, 1601; tutor of Pocock.

FIRST CAMBRIDGE COMPANY.

(*1 Chron.—Ecclesiastes*).

(11) Edward Lively, Fellow of Trin. Coll., 1572–8; Regius Professor of Hebrew, 1575;* d. 1605. (12) Dr. John Richardson, successively Master of Peterhouse, 1609, and Trinity, 1615; Regius Professor of Divinity, 1607–17; previously Fellow of Emmanuel. (13) Dr. Laurence Chaderton, first Master of Emmanuel Coll., 1584–1622; previously Fellow of Christ's Coll. One of the four Puritan representatives at the Hampton Court Conference. (14) Francis Dillingham, Fellow of Christ's Coll., 1581. Praised for his knowledge of Greek. (15) Thomas Harrison, Vice-Master of Trin. Coll., 1611–31. (16) Dr. Roger Andrewes, brother of the bishop, Master of Jesus Coll., 1618–32. (17) Dr. Robert Spalding, Fellow of St. John's Coll., 1593; succeeded Lively as Regius Professor of Hebrew, 1605; d. 1607?. (18) Dr. Andrew Byng, Fellow (?) of Peterhouse; Regius Professor of Hebrew, 1608. About 1605 a stall in the cathedral church of York to be kept for him; d. 1651.

FIRST OXFORD COMPANY.

(*Isaiah—Malachi*).

(19) Dr. John Harding, Regius Professor of Hebrew, 1591–8 and 1604–10; Canon of Lincoln, 1604; President of Magdalen Coll., 1607; d. 1610. (20) Dr. John Rainolds, or Reynolds, Dean of Lincoln, 1593; President of Corpus Christi Coll., 1598; d. 1607. His share in the Hampton Court Conference has been already mentioned. (21) Dr. Thomas Holland, Fellow of Balliol, 1573; Regius Professor of Divinity, 1589; Rector of Exeter Coll., 1592; d. 1612. (22) Dr. Richard Kilbye, Rector of Lincoln Coll., 1590; Prebendary of Lincoln Cathedral, 1601; Regius Professor of Hebrew, 1610; d. 1620. (23) Dr. Miles Smith, student of Corpus Christi Coll., about 1568, afterwards of Brasenose; Canon of Exeter, 1595–9; Bishop of Gloucester, 1612–24; d. 1624. To him, along with Bishop Bilson, the final revision of the work was entrusted, and he wrote the Preface. (24) Dr. Richard Brett, Fellow of Lincoln Coll., 1586; Rector of Quainton, Bucks, 1595; d. 1637. Praised as an Orientalist. (25) Mr. Richard Fairclough, scholar of New Coll., 1570; incorporated at Cambridge, 1581; Rector of Bucknell, Oxon, 1592.

SECOND CAMBRIDGE COMPANY.

(*The Apocrypha*).

(26) Dr. John Duport, Fellow of Jesus Coll., 1580; Master, 1590; Prebendary of Ely, 1609; d. 1617. (27) Dr. William Branthwait, Fellow of Emmanuel, 1584; deputy Lady Margaret Professor of Divinity; Master of Caius Coll., 1607; d. 1620. (28) Dr. Jeremiah Radcliffe, Fellow of Trin. Coll. (29) Dr. Samuel Ward, Lady Margaret Professor of Divinity, 1623; Master of Sidney Sussex Coll., 1610. Had previously been scholar of Christ's and Fellow of Emmanuel. One of the English representatives at the Synod of Dort; d. 1643. (30) Mr. Andrew Downes, Fellow of St. John's Coll., 1571; Regius Professor of Greek, 1585–1628; d. 1628. He corresponded in Greek with Casaubon. (31) Mr. John Bois, Fellow of St. John's Coll., 1580; Greek Lecturer, 1584–95; Prebendary of Ely, 1615. When the Apocrypha was finished, he joined the first Cambridge company at their urgent request. (32) Robert Ward, of King's Coll., Prebendary of Chichester; Rector of Bishop's Waltham, Hampshire.

SECOND OXFORD COMPANY.

(*Gospels, Acts, Revelation*).

(33) Dr. Thomas Ravis, Dean of Christ Church, 1596–1605; Bishop of Gloucester, 1605; of London, 1607; d. 1609. (34) Dr. George Abbot, Master of University Coll., 1597; Dean of Winchester, 1600; Archbishop of Canterbury, 1611–33; d. 1633. (35) Dr. Richard Edes, student of Christ Church, 1571; Dean of Worcester, 1597; d. 1604. As he died thus early, some have thought that Dr. James Montague, who succeeded him in the Deanery, was the 'Mr. Dean of Worcester' in Burnet's list. Wood gives, in place of Edes, Dr. John Aglionby, who was Principal of St. Edmund Hall, 1601; d. 1610. (36) Dr. Giles Thompson, matric. from University Coll., 1575; Fellow of All Souls', 1580; Dean of Windsor, 1602; Bishop of Gloucester, 1611; d. 1612. (37) Sir Henry Savile, Warden of Merton Coll., 1585; Provost of Eton, 1596; editor of St. Chrysostom, 1610–13; founder of the Savilian Chairs of Geometry and Astronomy; d. 1622. (38) Dr. John Perrinne, or Perne, Fellow of St. John's College, 1575; Regius Professor of Greek, 1597–1615; Canon of Christ Church, 1604–15; d. 1615. (39) 'Dr. Ravens,' assumed to be Dr. Ralph Ravens, Fellow of St. John's Coll.; Rector of Great Easton, Essex, 1605; d. 1616. In his stead Wood gives the name of Dr. Leonard Hutton, Canon of Christ Church. (40) Dr. John Harmar, Fellow of New College; Regius Professor of Greek, 1585–90; Head-Master of Winchester, 1588–95; Warden of Winchester, 1596–1613; d. 1613.

SECOND WESTMINSTER COMPANY.

(*Romans—Jude*).

(41) Dr. William Barlow, Fellow of Trinity Hall, Cambridge, 1590; Dean of Chester, 1602–5; Bishop of Lincoln, 1608–13; d. 1613. (42) 'Dr. Hutchinson,' taken to be Mr. William Hutchinson, of St. John's Coll., Oxford; Archdeacon of St. Albans, 1581; Prebendary of St. Paul's, 1589; d. 1616. (43) Dr. John Spenser, President of Corpus Christi Coll., Oxford, 1607–14; Chaplain to James I., and Fellow of Chelsea College; d. 1614. (44) Dr. Roger Fenton, Fellow of Pembroke Hall, Cambridge; Preacher of Gray's Inn, 1599; Prebendary of St. Paul's, 1609; d. 1616. (45) 'Mr. Rabbet,' identified with Michael Rabbet, B.A., of Trinity Coll., Cambridge, 1576; incorporated at Oxford, 1584; Rector of St. Vedast's, 1604–17; d. 1630. (46) 'Mr. Sanderson,' identified in like manner with Thomas Sanderson, Fellow of Balliol, 1585; Archdeacon of Rochester, 1606–14; Canon of St. Paul's, 1611; d. 1614?. (47) Mr. William Dakins, Fellow of Trinity Coll., Cambridge, 1594; Professor of Divinity in Gresham Coll., 1604; d. 1607.

With such machinery prepared, the work went on apace. From an expression in the Translators' Preface we may infer that their task took something less than three years in completion. Contrasting their own labours with those bestowed on the Septuagint version, finished, according to tradition, in seventy-two days, they say, 'The work hath not been huddled up in seventy-two days, but hath cost the workmen, as light as it seemeth, the pains of twice seven times seventy-two days and more.' Of the method of procedure we have an interesting glimpse left us by Selden.* 'The Translation in King James' time,' he writes, 'took an excellent way. That part of the Bible was given to him who was most excellent in such a tongue (as the Apocrypha to Andrew Downes), and then they met together, and one read the Translation, the rest holding in their hands some Bible, either of the learned Tongues, or French, Spanish, Italian, &c.: if they found any fault they spoke; if not, he read on.' The final preparation for the press seems to have been entrusted to six delegates, two from each centre.† Dr. Downes and Bois are mentioned by name as of the party, and the time thus occupied is said to have been nine months.

At length, in 1611, the volume appeared from the press of Robert Barker, with this title: 'The | Holy | Bible, | Conteyning the Old Testament, | and the New: | Newly Translated out of the Originall | tongues, & with the former Translations | diligently compared and reuised, by his | Maiesties speciall cõmandement. | Appointed to be read in Churches. | Imprinted at London by Robert | Barker, Printer to the Kings | most Excellent Maiestie. | Anno Dom. 1611.' The title occupies the centre of a copperplate engraving, being flanked, right and left, by figures of Moses and Aaron, and having the four Evangelists at the corners. Above is the Paschal Lamb, surrounded by Apostles; and below is a pelican, symbol of piety. At the summit, in Hebrew characters, is the sacred name of God; on either hand the sun and moon; the Holy Dove beneath; and at the bottom of the plate the artist's signature, 'C Boel fecit in Richmont.'

The NT has a separate title, within a woodcut

* The Cambridge Calendar (unofficial) gives 1580. A touching picture of the close of this great scholar's life—inferior as a Hebraist to Pocock alone—is reproduced, from a contemporary funeral sermon, in Cooper's *Athenæ Cantab.*

* *Table Talk*, ed. 1868, p. 20. We owe the ref. to Dr. Westcott.

† *Life of John Bois*, by Dr. A. Walker; printed in Peck's *Desiderata curiosa.*

border, representing, down one side, the tents and badges of the twelve tribes of Israel, and down the other the twelve Apostles. At the corner are the four evangelists with their emblems.

The second title runs: 'The | Newe | Testament of | our Lord and Sauior | Jesvs Christ | ¶Newly translated out of | the Originall Greeke: and with | the former Translations diligently | compared and reuised, by his | Maiesties speciall Com | mandement. | Imprinted | at London by Robert | Barker, | Printer to the | Kings most Excellent | Maiestie. | Anno Dom. 1611. | cum Priuilegio.'

The first, or general, title is followed by the 'Epistle Dedicatorie' (A 2–3), and this by 'The Translators to the Reader' (A 3 *verso* to B 4 *verso*). Calendars, Tables to find Easter, and the like, occupy the remaining preliminary leaves. The text of this *editio princeps* is in black letter. Headlines and summaries of the contents of chapters (the latter by Dr. Miles Smith) are in Roman letter. Words supplied, which would now be in italics, are in small Roman.* Various head-pieces, initial letters, and other embellishments, from the Bishops' Bible, the further reprinting of which was discontinued after 1606, were used again in this edition. The figure of Neptune is now found at the beginning of St. Matthew, and the crest and arms of Walsingham and Cecil are left on in the Psalms.† By what warranty the clause 'Appointed to be read in Churches' was inserted in the title is not easy to determine, seeing that there can be found for it, so far as is known, 'no edict of Convocation, no Act of Parliament, no decision of the Privy Council, no royal proclamation.'‡ The true explanation probably is that, as the new revision was meant to supersede the old Bishops' Bible, it naturally took the place, and succeeded to the privileges, of that work. But, as has been before mentioned, the Bishops' Bible was ordered, by the *Constitutions and Canons Ecclesiastical* of 1571, to be placed in all cathedrals, and, so far as it was practicable, in all churches. Thus the new version was simply the heir of the old. It may be remarked, in passing, that the clause is not found in the NT title of the *editio princeps*, nor at all in the first 8vo and some other early editions.§ It will be observed also that the OT and NT are spoken of in the general title as 'newly *translated* out of the original tongues'; and the Preface is headed 'the *Translators* to the Reader.' This might be thought a disregard of the very first of the king's instructions. But we must bear in mind how the alternative word *revised* was then used, as for instance in this very title. And the 'Translators' themselves, while content to use this designation in their Preface, make it quite clear what their conception of their duty was in this respect. 'But it is high time to leave them,' they say, referring to Romanist objectors, 'and to shew in brief what we proposed to our selves, and what course we held in this our perusall and survey of the Bible. Truely (good Christian Reader) we never thought from the beginning, that we should need to make a new Translation, nor yet to make of a bad one a good one . . . but to make a good one better, or out of many good ones, one principall good one, not justly to be excepted against; that hath been our indeavour, that our mark.'

Whether or not the translators reached their mark, is now no matter of opinion: history has spoken. Especially as a well of English undefiled, drawing its waters in part from yet older springs, it has solaced the heart, and satisfied the taste, of peasant and scholar alike. One well entitled to be heard (the late Bishop Lightfoot), writing on a subject which made him rather a severe critic than a willing eulogist,* speaks of the 'grand simplicity' in which the language of our English Bible 'stands out in contrast to the ornate and often affected diction of the literature of that time.' Another, than whom few, if any, have studied the text of Holy Writ with minuter care, marvels at 'the perfect and easy command over the English language exhibited by its authors on every page.'† And yet another, whose testimony may be of the greater value from the fact that, when he gave it, he had ceased to be in the communion of the English Church, pays a generous tribute to the benefits derived from listening, in the course of public service, to the 'grave majestic English,' in which are enshrined 'the words of inspired teachers under both Covenants,' and from associating religion with 'compositions which, even humanly considered, are among the most sublime and beautiful ever written.'‡

But it is of more importance, especially as bearing on the question of subsequent revision, to form a just estimate of the defects of the AV than to record the language of panegyric. Some specimens of these defects, taken almost at haphazard, are accordingly given. But it must be borne in mind that their cumulative force loses its effect when a short list only can find place.

Gn $15^{2}$ 'And the steward (*r.* possessor, *or* inheritor) of my house'; $20^{16}$ 'Thus was she reproved' (*r.* And so thou art cleared); $25^{18}$ 'And he died' (*r.* settled); $49^{5}$ 'Instruments of cruelty,' etc. (variously emended); $49^{6}$ 'digged down a wall' (*r.* houghed oxen); $49^{14}$ 'between two burdens' (*r.* between the cattle-pens); Ex $13^{4}$ 'This day came ye out' (*r.* go ye forth); $15^{2}$ 'prepare him an habitation' (*r.* praise, *or* glorify him); $32^{25}$ 'had made them naked' (*r.* had let them loose); $33^{7}$ 'tabernacle of the congregation' (*r.* tent of meeting—distinct in use from the tabernacle); Nu $11^{25}$ 'and they did not cease' (*r.* but they did so no more); $21^{18}$ 'by the direction of the lawgiver' (*r.* with the sceptre; but variously rendered); Jg $5^{16}$ 'for the divisions' (*r.* by the brooks, *or* watercourses—see also vv.$^{10. 13-15. 17}$); $8^{13}$ 'before the sun was up' (*r.* from the ascent of Heres); 1 S $13^{1}$ 'Saul reigned one year' (*r.* Saul was [thirty] years old when he began to reign—see margin of RV); 1 K $20^{38}$ 'with ashes upon his face' (*r.* with his headband over his eyes); $22^{38}$ 'and they washed his armour' (*r.* now the harlots washed themselves); 2 K $11^{15}$ 'without the ranges' (*r.* between the ranks); $11^{16}$ 'they laid hands on her' (*r.* made way for her); $21^{6}$ 'observed times' (*r.* practised augury); 2 Ch $22^{6}$ 'because of' (*r.* of); Job $36^{33}$ 'the cattle also concerning the vapour' (*r.* concerning the storm, *or* concerning him that cometh up); Is $29^{16}$ 'Surely your turning of things upside down shall be esteemed as the potter's clay' (*r.* Ye turn things upside down! Shall the potter be counted as clay?); Ezk $13^{18}$ 'kerchiefs upon the head of every stature' (*r.* kerchiefs for the head of persons of every stature); Mal $2^{3}$ 'I will corrupt your seed' (*r.* I will rebuke the seed for your sake).

Mt $25^{8}$ 'are gone out' (*r.* are going out); $26^{55}$ and elsewhere 'a thief' (*r.* a robber); Mk $6^{27}$ 'an executioner' (*r.* a soldier of the guard); Lk $1^{59}$ 'called' (*r.* were calling, *or* would have called); $19^{13}$ 'occupy' (*r.* trade, *or* do business); $22^{56}$ 'by the fire' (*r.* in the light of the fire); Jn $4^{27}$ 'with the woman' (*r.* with a woman); $10^{16}$ 'one fold' (*r.* one flock); Ac $19^{38}$ 'the law is open, and there are deputies' (*r.* court days are held, and there are proconsuls; *or* the courts are sitting, and there are magistrates); 1 Co $14^{23}$ 'one place' (*r.* the same place); 2 Co $9^{13}$ 'experiment' (*r.* proof); Eph $4^{12}$ 'for the work of the ministry' (*r.* to a work of ministration,—removing the comma after 'saints'); Ph $3^{21}$ 'our vile body' (*r.* the body of our humiliation); $4^{2}$ 'Euodias' (*r.* Euodia); 2 Ti $4^{6}$ 'I am now ready to be offered' (*r.* I am already being offered); He $2^{16}$ 'He took not on him the nature of angels' (*r.* it is not of angels that he taketh hold, *i.e.* to succour *or* support); $4^{8}$ 'Jesus' (*r.* Joshua—so also in Ac $7^{45}$); Ja $1^{17}$ 'gift . . . gift' (*r.* giving . . . gift); Rev $4^{4}$ 'seats' (*r.* thrones).

If we knew with certainty what were the original texts chiefly relied on by the translators, we should be better able to account for some of the flaws in their work. So far, indeed, as the OT is concerned,

* The copy used for this description is the one marked 466 i. 6 (1) in the Library of the British Museum. Size of page, 16×10½ inches.

† See Loftie, *A Century of Bibles*, 1872, p. 6.

‡ Eadie, ii. 204.

§ A list of those in which it is wanting is given by Dore, *l.c.* p. 326.

* *On a Fresh Revision of the English NT*, 1871, p. 191.

† Scrivener, *The Authorized Edition of the English Bible*, 1884, p. 141. This is a reprint, with additions and corrections, of the same author's Introduction to the Cambridge Paragraph Bible, 1873.

‡ J. H. Newman, *Grammar of Assent*, 1874, p. 56.

the variations found among different editions of the Hebrew Bible then printed are less material than might have been supposed. And for this part of their work the translators had good helps. Besides the Latin version of the Hebrew Bible made (1575–9) by Immanuel Tremellius (a converted Jew, who became Professor of Divinity at Heidelberg), revised by his son-in-law Francis Junius, who added a similar version of the Apocrypha, 'an interlinear Latin translation of the Hebrew text, based on that of Pagninus,'* had been appended in 1572 to the Antwerp Polyglott by the Spanish scholar, Arias Montanus. The Complutensian Polyglott had been available since 1517. Moreover, in the interval, versions into several modern languages had appeared:—a revised edition of the French Bible, in 1587–8, at Geneva; an Italian translation by Diodati, in 1607, also at Geneva; and two Spanish versions, one by C. Reyna, Basle, 1569, and the other, based on it, by C. de Valera, Amsterdam, 1602.† But, as regards the NT, the translators fared worse. The great MSS of the Greek Testament, with which scholars are now familiar, were then unknown. The science of biblical criticism was not yet competent to deal with them, had they been available. The third edition of Robert Stephen, 1550, furnished a *textus receptus*, representing what was best in the Complutensian and Erasmus. To supplement this, the translators had the several editions of Beza's Greek Testament with his Latin version, preferably the fourth, of 1589. It may be going too far to assert, with Hartwell Horne,‡ that 'Beza's edition of 1598 was adopted as the basis' of the Authorized Version. But even Scrivener, who combats the assertion, admits that, out of 252 passages examined, the translators agree with Beza against Stephen in 113 places, and with Stephen against Beza in only 59; the remaining 80 being cases in which the Complutensian, Erasmus, or the Vulgate were followed in preference to either.

Poor, however, as was the *apparatus criticus* at the command of the translators, they had an advantage, which it would not be easy to overestimate, in the existence of previous English versions. Some of these the king's letter of instructions had specially directed them to consult. Two others, not named in those instructions, they consulted frequently, and with the greatest benefit to themselves. These were the Geneva Bible and the Rhemish NT. The Douai OT appeared just too late to be of use, not being issued till 1610. It would be exceeding our limits to enter into the statistical calculations, by which it has been sought to apportion aright the indebtedness of the AV to each of its two rivals. It must suffice to say that its obligation to both was great;—to the one for principles of interpretation, to the other for an enriched vocabulary. At the same time its independence was never sacrificed. 'It differs from the Rhemish Version in seeking to fix an intelligible sense on the words rendered: it differs from the Genevan Version in leaving the literal rendering uncoloured by any expository notes.'§

The gradual efforts that have been made from time to time to emend and perfect this noble translation will be most fittingly noticed when we come to speak of the Revised Version of 1881. A few words remain to be said on the relation in which the first edition of 1611 stands to its immediate successors; and mention must be made briefly of some of the most conspicuous among the almost countless descendants of king James's Bible.

* Westcott, *General View*, p. 268. † *Ib.* p. 269.

‡ See Scrivener's *Supplement to the AV*, 1845, p. 8; and the same writer's *Authorized Edition*, 1884, p. 60. The edition of 1598 was Beza's fifth and last, judged less correct than that of 89.

§ Westcott, *l.c.* p. 269.

That the edition described above as the first was really the *editio princeps* of the AV, few scholars will be found to deny.* But, when we come to inquire which of the others is to be placed next to it, we are met by a difficulty. A number of Bibles are in existence, the first, or general, title of which agrees in wording with that of the assumed first edition, but differs slightly in the division of lines, and also in not having for border Boel's copperplate engraving, but a woodcut, similar to the NT border of A.† For date, the first title of B has 1613 (sometimes 1611); while the second, or NT title, has regularly 1611, and has also, what that of A has not, the words (in italics) 'Appointed to be read in Churches.'‡ In what relation, now, do A and B stand to each other? It has been held that they represent 'two contemporary issues . . . separately composed and printed, for the sake of speedy production, in 1611.'§ But this supposition is negatived by the fact that in both these Bibles—and indeed in all the black-letter folios of the AV, save only one of 1613, in smaller type—the printing is so arranged that every leaf ends with the same word. The sheets, notwithstanding many internal differences, could thus be interchanged, and in point of fact are often found so interchanged in copies of the editions dated 1611, 1613, 1617, 1634, 1640. It follows that no two could have been set up simultaneously from two corrected Bishops' Bibles used as 'copy' by separate compositors. They could not by accident have brought their leaves to end uniformly at the same word. The alternative remains of supposing B derived from A, or A from B. Of these Dr. Scrivener chooses the latter. He considers B 'to have been printed first, and rejected by the translators on account of its inaccuracy in favour of the more carefully revised A edition; but to have been ultimately published, by a kind of fraud on the part of the printers, after the translators were dispersed.' ‖ Notwithstanding the learning and ability with which this opinion is defended by its author, it will hardly gain the credit of being more than a brilliant paradox, with those who weigh impartially the evidence furnished by the errors and corrections observable in the two volumes.

In endeavouring to single out the more noticeable in the almost endless list of editions of the AV that have appeared since 1611, our attention is first arrested by those which are conspicuous for the number of errors admitted, or for the efforts made to eliminate previous errors. A few preliminary words thus become necessary on the responsibility of printers in the 17th century.

It is a mistake to suppose that the appointment of King's or Queen's Printer, then or formerly, implied any obligation to greater vigilance in ensuring accuracy of printing. It was simply a matter of purchase. In this way Robert Barker's father, Christopher, had bought, in 1577, a patent granted by Elizabeth a few years before to Sir Thomas Wilkes, and thus became Queen's Printer. In this capacity he opposed the claim of Cambridge, in 1583, to maintain a university press. In 1627 the Barkers assigned their rights to Bonham Norton and John Bill. But in 1635 Robert Barker's second son, of the same name, bought back the reversion of the patent; and it continued in their family till

* The adverse opinion of Dr. Scrivener will be mentioned presently.

† For brevity, we will so denote the assumed first edition; and the one we are describing, by B.

‡ The actual copy described is that marked 3051 g 10 (1) in the Library of the British Museum.

§ Art. 'English Bible,' by the late Rev. J. H. Blunt, in *Encyclop. Brit.*[9] vol. viii. p. 389.

‖ We adopt the convenient summary of Scrivener's views (for which see his *Authorized Edition*, p. 5 ff.) given by the Rev. Walter E. Smith in his valuable monograph, *A Study of the great 'She' Lible*, 1890, p. 5.

1709, having had a run of 132 years. The subsequent stages, through Thomas Baskett, need not be particularized. In 1799 a fresh patent was granted to George Eyre, Andrew Strahan, and John Reeves; and so we come to the present distinguished firm of Eyre & Spottiswoode.*

It is obvious that purely business transactions, such as these, would not of necessity give rise to any lofty ideal of responsibility in a King's Printer. He would feel it his first duty to recoup himself for the sums laid out. Any higher standard of work must be prompted by his own sense of *noblesse oblige*. Accordingly, we are not surprised to find traces of bad workmanship multiplying in editions of the AV, as the years roll on. A flagrant example of such negligence is to be seen in the 8vo edition of 1631,† printed by Robert Barker and the assignees of J. Bill. In this, besides many other mistakes, the 'not' is left out in the Seventh Commandment (Ex 20[14]). For this, it is fair to say, the printers were fined in the then substantial sum of £300 by the Court of High Commission, with Laud at its head. With the proceeds of the fine, Laud, it is said, designed to purchase a fount of Greek type for the university press of Oxford; but it does not appear that payment of the money was ever enforced.

The universities, to which we are now accustomed to look for accuracy and beauty of typography, were late in the race. Cambridge, as we have seen, had pleaded the privilege of its press as far back as 1583. But in point of fact no English Bible issued from it till 1629; nor from that of Oxford till 1673–5. The Cambridge folio of 1629, printed by Thomas and John Buck, is a creditable piece of work, and shows traces of careful revision. But it is the first to exhibit a misprint, which held its ground, it is said, till 1803—'thy doctrine' for 'the doctrine,' in 1 Ti 4[16].

In 1638 a still more serious attempt at revision was made by a little band of Cambridge scholars, at the command, we are told, of Charles I. Their names are preserved in a manuscript note, made in a copy of the Bible in question, by a contemporary Master of Jesus College. They were Dr. Goad, Rector of Hadleigh in Suffolk, an old Eton and King's man; Dr. Ward and Mr. Boyse (Bois), both already spoken of in the lists of translators; and Mr. Mead, more familiar to us as Joseph Mede. Dr. Scrivener, while speaking favourably of their work as a whole, points out some fresh *errata* due to them: among these the substitution of 'ye' for 'we' in Ac 6[3], foolishly believed by some to be not an accidental misprint, but a deliberate change, made under Nonconformist influences.

Of other editions of the AV, an 8vo, printed at Edinburgh in 1633, may be noticed as the first printed in Scotland; the earliest in Ireland not appearing till 1714, and in America not till 1752.‡ A 12mo of 1682, professing to be printed in London, but in all probability from a press in Amsterdam, may be taken as a specimen of a number of editions, produced in Holland, but counterfeiting the imprints of London publishers, with the object of imposing upon English readers. They are mostly full of errors. Conspicuous for the magnificence of their typography are the noble folios of John

* See the articles on Chr. and Rob. Barker, and on Thomas Baskett, by Mr. H. R. Tedder in the *Dict. of National Biography*.

† Scrivener, *Authorized Edition*, p. 25 n., gives 1632 as the date, and speaks of one copy only as known to be in existence, namely at Wolfenbüttel. Mr. Henry Stevens (*Cat. of the Caxton Celebration*, 1877, p. 114) shows both these statements to be incorrect. The name 'Wicked Bible' originated with Mr. Stevens in 1852.

‡ This last was issued surreptitiously, bearing the false imprint of 'Mark Baskett, London.' A 12mo, produced at Philadelphia in 1782, is believed by Cotton to be the earliest English Bible avowedly published in America.



Baskett (Oxford, 1717) and John Baskerville (Cambridge, 1763). In the former of these, however, a misprint of 'vinegar' for 'vineyard' (or 'vinegarth'?) in the headline over Lk 22, has caused it to be commonly known as 'The Vinegar Bible.'

Passing over the folio of 1701, revised by Bishop Lloyd, in which for the first time dates, taken in the main from Ussher, were added in the margin, we come to two editions which, from their proximity of date and similarity of aim, may be conveniently studied together. These are (1) an edition in folio and one in quarto (2 vols.), printed by J. Bentham at the Cambridge University Press in 1762, revised by Dr. Thomas Paris, Fellow of Trinity College; and (2) an edition, also in folio and quarto, issued from the Clarendon Press at Oxford in 1769, revised by Dr. Benjamin Blayney. The fame of Dr. Paris has to some degree suffered eclipse; partly from the later editor having his predecessor's work to improve upon, and partly from the accident of a fire at Dod the bookseller's having destroyed the greater part of the impression of 1762.* Yet competent judges have pronounced the work of Dr. Paris to be at the least not inferior to that of his successor. There is extant a report, dated Oct. 25th, 1769,† addressed by Dr. Blayney to his employers, the delegates of the Clarendon Press, in which he states the principles by which he, and by implication Dr. Paris, had been guided. The restoration of the exact text of 1611, where not itself corrupt; the modernizing of the spelling; the weeding-out of references to passages in no way parallel, and the replacing of them by fresh ones; the making clear the allusions contained in Hebrew proper names by adding their English equivalents in the margin; the rectification of the use of italics; the reform of the punctuation,—such were some of the objects aimed at. Oxford has done honour to Dr. Blayney, by making his two revisions of 1769 the standard text for its university press. Dr. Scrivener associates the work of Dr. Paris with his as deserving of equal praise, pronouncing their labours to be 'the last two considerable efforts to improve and correct our ordinary editions of Holy Scripture.' With these, accordingly, the present section may fitly close. But a parting word of tribute must not, in justice, be withheld from the work of Dr. Scrivener himself, whose *Cambridge Paragraph Bible* (in 3 parts, 1870–3) is a model of care and laborious exactness.‡

* Somewhat singularly, the copies of Dr. Blayney's edition suffered, though apparently not to the same extent, from a fire at the Bible Warehouse, Paternoster Row.

† Reprinted from the *Gentleman's Magazine* (xxxix. 517) as App. D in Scrivener's *Authorized Edition*.

‡ We have not considered it within our province to notice versions of detached portions of Holy Scripture. But an exception seems properly made in favour of Sir John Cheke's translation of St. Matthew and part of the first chapter of St. Mark. This singular work is in a fragmentary state, and there is nothing to show how far the author meant to carry it. The MS, in Cheke's beautiful handwriting, is preserved in the Library of Corpus Christi Coll., Cambridge. It is unfortunately defective, having lost a leaf containing Mt 16[25]–18[7] inclusive, wanting also the last ten verses of ch. 28. It ends abruptly with the words 'Capernaum, and' in Mk 1. Marginal notes are added, dealing chiefly, as befitted the scholar who 'taught Cambridge and king Edward Greek,' with the wording of the original. Cheke's translation, though probably made about 1550, lay unpublished till 1843, when it found a competent editor in the Rev. James Goodwin, B.D. Its chief peculiarity lies in the attempt deliberately made to exclude words of foreign origin, and like Barnes, the Dorset poet, to use solely, or as nearly so as possible, words of native growth. Thus for 'captivity' he writes 'outpeopling'; for 'lunatic,' 'mooned'; for 'publicans,' 'tollers'; for 'apostle,' 'frosent'; for 'proselyte,' 'freschman'; for 'crucified,' 'crossed.' His principles in this respect were the opposite of those held by Gardiner and his school. Sometimes he is not consistent. Thus in Mt 3 (he adopts the division into chapters, but not into verses) he uses 'acrids' for locusts; but in Mk 1 he retains 'locustes,' putting ἀκρίδας in the margin. Sometimes his system reduces him to hard shifts, as when for 'tetrarch' he gives 'debitee of y[e] fourth part of y[e] contree.' His method of spelling is interesting, from the light it throws on the pronunciation of the time. To indicate that a vowel is

IX. THE 'REVISED' VERSION.—It must be constantly borne in mind that the work of 1611 was not a new translation, but a revision of an old one. In any such case the thought is readily suggested that the revision may itself need revising. If in nothing else, the revisers may have erred in excess or defect: they may have changed too much or too little. Nor can men who have undertaken to correct the faults of others reasonably complain if their own performance is subjected to unsparing criticism. So it fared with the AV and its authors. Even before the work had seen the light, it became evident that, in certain quarters, it would meet with a hostile reception. And the origin of this hostility is instructive to notice, as disclosing the mixed motives by which men may be influenced under such circumstances.

The leader of the attack was the learned Hebraist, Hugh Broughton; a scholar whose erudition would have fully justified his inclusion in king James's company, but whose lack of judgment and impracticable temper would have made it impossible for him to work with the rest. Rainolds and Lively were old antagonists of his. Moreover, he had himself projected a fresh translation of the Bible. In a letter to Lord Burleigh, dated 21st June 1593, he explained what his plan was. He proposed to have the assistance of five other scholars; to make none but necessary changes; and to add short notes. His views on the subject he further set out in 'An Epistle to the learned Nobility of England, touching translating the Bible from the Original,' published in 1597.* And when the AV was in preparation he showed his determination even yet to have a say in the matter, by writing an 'Advertisement how to execute the translation now in hand, that the first edition be onely for a triall, that all learned may have their censure.'† We can understand that, when at length the revised translation appeared without his co-operation being asked or his advice attended to, his indignation knew no bounds. A copy of the finished work was sent him for his opinion, and he gave it. Writing to a 'Right Worshipfull Knight attending upon the King,' he passionately exclaims: 'Tell his Majesty that I had rather be rent in pieces with wild horses, than any such translation by my consent should be urged upon poor churches.' It 'bred in me,' he had just said, 'a sadnesse that will grieve me while I breath. It is so ill done.'‡ The reader will judge how far this was prompted by personal feeling; and how far, as Broughton's learned editor contends, the words were spoken 'in zeal and vindication of the truth.'§

As time went on, the faults which Broughton had detected, or thought he could detect, in the AV, were supplemented by an ever-lengthening list of errors due to the carelessness of printers. After the breaking out of the Civil War more especially, learning, and its handmaid, the art of printing, became held in less esteem; and the presses of Holland found their account in doing what the king's printer, or an English university, should have done. But the editions of the Bible thus imported were, it need hardly be said, in most cases extremely incorrect. So serious was the mischief judged to be, that, as early as 1643, the Assembly of Divines made a report to Parliament on the subject. In it they complained of the faultiness of these Dutch editions. To substantiate their charge, they were content with three instances only; but these, it must be admitted, were enough:—Gn $36^{24}$ 'found the *rulers*' for 'found the mules'; Ru $4^{13}$ 'gave her *corruption*' for 'gave her conception'; Lk $21^{28}$ 'your *condemnation*' for 'your redemption.' The Assembly's report was followed up by an appeal from the learned Dr. John Lightfoot. In a sermon preached before the Long Parliament, Aug. 26th, 1645, he urged upon the members the necessity for a 'review and survey of the translation of the Bible,' that by this means people 'might come to understand the proper and genuine reading of the Scriptures by an exact, vigorous, and lively translation.'*

long, he doubles it. Thus we have 'taak' (take), 'swijn' (swine), 'ameen,' 'propheet,' 'Herocd,' and the like. 'Church' (p. 67) is said to be sounded 'moor corruptly and frenchlike' than the north-country 'Kurk.' Speaking generally, the value of the work is philological rather than biblical.

* Printed in H. B.'s collected *Works*, Lond. 1662, p. 557 ff. For several particulars in this account the present writer is indebted to the Rev. Alex. Gordon's art. in the *Dict. of National Biography*.

† Sloane MSS, No. 3088, leaf 120 *verso*.

‡ *Works*, p. 661.

§ *Works*; Dr. John Lightfoot's Pref., sig. C.

It does not appear that either report or sermon produced any immediate effect. There exists, indeed, the draft of a bill, proposed to be brought before Parliament in 1653, authorizing the appointment of a committee 'to search and observe wherein that last translation appears to be wronged by Prelates or printers or others.'† But the spirit which prompted the motion for such an inquiry was too obvious, and nothing came of it. There were, in truth, vested interests at stake, and abuses connected with them, not easy to reform, even under a Protectorate.

Henry Hills and John Field (who had obtained his patent from Cromwell) were the licensed printers to the University of Cambridge. But the fact that they had to pay for their privilege a yearly bribe of £500 to certain persons in power,‡ prepares us to expect from them little conscientious work. Accordingly, when, in 1659, William Kilburne, Gent., printed at Finsbury his *Dangerous Errors in Severall Late printed Bibles: to the great scandal and corruption of sound and true Religion*, it was chiefly against these two printers that his attack is directed. The longer title, or Advertisement, of the tract§ describes it as 'discovering (amongst many thousands of others) some pernicious erroneous & corrupt Erratas Escapes & Faults in several Impressions of the Holy Bible and Testament within these late years commonly vended & dispersed, to the great scandal of Religion, but more particularly in the Impressions of Henry Hills and John Field, printers . . .' Kilburne brings heavy charges; but he fully justifies them. Two specimens must suffice. Both are from pocket Bibles printed by Field, in 1656 and 1653 respectively:—Jn $7^{39}$ 'this spake he of the *spirits*' for 'this spake he of the Spirit'; 1 Co $6^{9}$ 'the unrighteous *shall inherit*' for 'the unrighteous shall not inherit.'

The improvement which authority, regal and republican alike, had seemed powerless to effect, was brought about by private effort and the slow but unvarying growth of public opinion. If any one will take the trouble to go through a list of editions of English Bibles, and parts thereof, which have appeared from about the middle of the 17th to the middle of the 19th cent., he can hardly fail to be struck with the steady increase, first, of paraphrases, and then of new or emended versions of separate books of Holy Scripture. The names of Edward Wells and Zachary Pearce, of Chandler, Harwood and Gilbert Wakefield, of Archbishop Newcome and Bishop Lowth, not to mention many others, will meet him at every turn in this field of inquiry. Or let him apply a simple numerical test to the first fifty years of the 19th cent., taking Cotton's *List of Editions* as a con-

* Newth, *Lectures on Bible Revision*, p. 92.

† *Ib.* p. 93.

‡ Scrivener, *Authorized Edition*, p. 26; Loftie, *Century of Bibles*, pp. 12, 13.

§ Reprinted by Loftie, *ib.* pp. 31–49.

venient basis for his calculation. He will find that there are only nine years out of the fifty in which there has not appeared some fresh translation, or new edition of such translation, of some or all the books of the Bible. And Cotton's *List* is not exhaustive.*

Whatever might be the merits or defects of these versions—and some of them are very defective, especially in point of style†—they had the effect of keeping alive an interest in the subject. Men were constantly reminded that the revision of 1611, with all its high qualities, could not be accepted as final. Moreover, by the labours of Brian Walton, Kennicott, Mill, Bentley, and others, the only sure foundation for the reviser's work had been laid, or had at least begun to be laid, in fixing, on sound principles, the original texts.

Forces were thus slowly gathering, which culminated during the middle third, or nearly so, of the last century. Many causes contributed to bring about this result. The after-swell of the Reform Bill agitation and of the Oxford movement was still felt, making men less satisfied with things as they were, simply because they were. It was the period of the biblical labours of Tischendorf and Tregelles, of Wordsworth and Alford, of Trench and Scrivener, of Lightfoot, Westcott and Hort. Public attention had been called afresh to the subject of revision by a series of pamphlets and reviews. In 1849 appeared the third and enlarged edition of Professor Scholefield's learned *Hints for an improved Translation of the New Testament.* In October 1855 an Edinburgh reviewer, discussing the merits of an *Annotated Paragraph Bible*, published by the Religious Tract Society two years before, in which corrections of the AV had been freely introduced, expressed the conviction, not only that 'our Common Version requires a diligent revision, but that the great body of the people are aware of it; and that their trust in its perfection, which has been so long opposed against any suggestion of improvement, can no longer be alleged as a pretext for delaying the attempt.'* On March 1st, 1856, Canon Selwyn brought the matter before the notice of the Lower House of Convocation, and followed this up, in the autumn of the same year, by the pamphlet just cited. In July 1856 Mr. James Heywood, M.P. for North Lancashire, moved in the House of Commons an address to the Crown, 'praying that Her Majesty would appoint a Royal Commission of learned men, to consider of such amendments of the authorized version of the Bible as had been already proposed, and to receive suggestions from all persons who might be willing to offer them, and to report the amendments which they might be prepared to recommend.'† After a short discussion the motion was withdrawn. But its author did not let the subject drop; publishing *The Bible and its Revisers* in 1857, and the *State of the Authorized Bible Revision* in 1860. In 1857 a good pattern of what such a revision should be was set in the publication of *The Gospel according to St. John . . . revised by five clergymen.* In 1863 a remark by the Speaker of the House of Commons (J. Evelyn Denison, afterwards Lord Ossington), suggested the undertaking of the 'Speaker's' Commentary, one express object of which was 'a revision of the translation.'

Not to dwell longer on preliminary matters, by the spring of 1870 things were ripe for action. On February 10th of that year, the Bishop of Winchester (Dr. S. Wilberforce), anticipating a motion which Canon Selwyn had prepared to introduce into the Lower House, moved in the Upper House of Convocation of the Southern Province, 'that a Committee of both Houses be appointed, with power to confer with any Committee that may be appointed by the Convocation of the Northern Province, to report upon the desirableness of a revision of the AV of the NT, whether by marginal notes or otherwise, in all those passages where plain and clear errors, whether in the Hebrew or Greek text originally adopted by the translators, or in the translation made from the same, shall, on due investigation, be found to exist.'‡ The Bishop of Llandaff (Dr. A. Ollivant) carried an amendment, to include the OT in the terms of the motion. When the motion, thus amended, had been agreed to, it was sent down to the Lower House (Feb. 11), where it was accepted without a division. In pursuance of it, a joint Committee, consisting of eight members of the Upper House and sixteen of the Lower, was formed. The Convocation of the Northern Province had in the meantime declined to co-operate. They admitted the existence of blemishes in the AV. They were 'favourable to the errors being corrected.' But they 'would deplore any recasting of the text.' Notwithstanding, the work went on; and on May 3rd a Report of the joint Committee, embodied in five Resolutions, was laid before both Houses of the Southern Convocation. The Resolutions affirmed—

'1. That it is desirable that a revision of the AV of the Holy Scriptures be undertaken.
2. That the revision be so conducted as to comprise both marginal renderings and such emendations as it may be found necessary to insert in the text of the AV.
3. That in the above Resolutions we do not contemplate any new translation of the Bible, or any alteration of the language, except when in the judgment of the most competent scholars such change is necessary.
4. That in such necessary changes the style of the language employed in the existing version be closely followed.

* A good summary of the steps finally leading to the revision of 1881, so far at least as the year 1863, is given in Professor Plumptre's article on the Authorized Version in vol. iii. of Smith's *Dictionary of the Bible.* A list of works, bearing more or less directly on the revision of the AV, beginning with Robert Gell's *Essay*, fol., 1659, will be found in the App. (pp. 216–9) to Trench's *On the A V of the NT*, 1859.

† It is almost a slaying of the slain to quote Dr. Edward Harwood (*A Liberal Translation of the NT*, 2 vols. 8vo, 1768), who thus begins the parable of the Prodigal Son: 'A gentleman of a splendid family and opulent fortune had two sons. One day the younger approached his father, and begged him in the most importunate and soothing terms to make a partition of his effects betwixt himself and his elder brother. The indulgent father, overcome by his blandishments, immediately divided all his fortunes betwixt them.' Ja $2^{2.3}$ appears thus: 'For should there enter into your assembly a person arrayed in a magnificent and splendid dress, with a brilliant diamond sparkling on his hand, and should there enter at the same time a man in a mean and sordid habit; Your eyes being instantly attracted by the lustre of this superb vest, should you immediately introduce the person thus sumptuously habited into the best seat,' etc. A revised version of the Bible by J. T. Conquest, M.D. (2nd ed. 1846), purports to contain 'nearly twenty thousand emendations.' The following are a few brief specimens:—

Is $9^{1\text{-}3}$ 'Nevertheless the darkness shall not be such as was in her anguish
When at first he rendered contemptible
The land of Zebulun and the land of Naphtali,
So shall he confer honour upon them
By the way of the sea, beyond the Jordan, in Galilee of the nations.
The people who walked in darkness, have seen a great light:
Those who dwell in the land of the shadow of death, upon them the light shineth.
Thou hast multiplied the nation,
Whose joy thou didst not increase. . . .'

1 Co $15^{12}$ 'How say some among you, that there is no resurrection and future existence of the dead?'

He $7^{3}$ 'Without recorded father or mother, without descent, having neither predecessor or successor in office. . . .'

* *Notes on the proposed Amendment of the Authorized Version* . . ., by William Selwyn, Canon of Ely, 1856, p. 11.

† Newth, as before, p. 103; Ellicott, *Considerations on Revision*, 1870, p. 5.

‡ Westcott, *Eng. Bible*, p. 338, quoting *Chronicles of Convocation.* The words 'Hebrew or' will be noticed as indicating a motion originally wider in its scope. Three members of the NT Revision Company (Drs. Westcott, Newth, and Moulton) have left accounts of these proceedings.

5. That it is desirable that Convocation should nominate a body of its own members to undertake the work of revision, who shall be at liberty to invite the co-operation of any eminent for scholarship, to whatever nation or religious body they may belong.'

This Report was unanimously adopted by the Upper House, and eight bishops were at once nominated, in accordance with the terms of the last Resolution, to be its quota towards the new joint Committee. On May 5th the report was discussed in the Lower House. Some opposition was there shown to the principle embodied in the last clause of the fifth Resolution; but, on a division, the adoption of the Report was carried, with but two dissentients. On May 6th eight of their own body were chosen, to co-operate with the others in forming the new Committee. This new, or second, joint Committee held its first meeting on May 25th, 1870. It then passed a series of Resolutions, indicating the lines on which the work should be carried out. In substance these were as follows, the more important ones being quoted in full:—

I. Committee to separate into two Companies—one for OT, the other for NT.
II. Names of the members of Convocation, nine in all, forming the OT Company.
III. Names as before, seven in all, for the NT Company.
IV. OT Company to begin with Pentateuch.
V. NT " " " Synoptical Gospels.
VI. Names of 'Scholars and Divines' (18) to be invited to join the OT Company.
VII. Names of 'Scholars and Divines' (19) to be invited to join the NT Company.*
VIII. That the general principles to be followed by both Companies be as follows:—
'1. To introduce as few alterations as possible into the text of the Authorized Version, consistently with faithfulness.
2. To limit, as far as possible, the expressions of such alterations to the language of the Authorized and earlier English versions.
3. Each Company to go twice over the portion to be revised, once provisionally, the second time finally, and on principles of voting as hereinafter is provided.
4. That the Text to be adopted be that for which the evidence is decidedly preponderating; and that when the Text so adopted differs from that from which the Authorized Version was made, the alteration be indicated in the margin.
5. To make or retain no change in the Text on the second final revision by each Company, except *two-thirds* of those present approve of the same, but on the first revision to decide by simple majorities.
6. Cases in which voting may be deferred.
7. Headings of chapters, etc., to be revised.
8. Permission to consult learned men, 'whether at home or abroad.'
IX. The work of each Company, on completion, to be communicated to the other, to secure, as far as possible, uniformity in language.
X. 1. 2. 3. 'Bye-rules' as to the mode of making corrections.

The invitation given in accordance with Resolutions VI. and VII. was declined by Canon F. C. Cook, Dr. J. H. Newman, Dr. Pusey, and Dr. W. Wright of the British Museum. The last-mentioned, however, subsequently joined the OT Company. Of those who accepted it, Dr. S. P. Tregelles was prevented by ill-health from joining in the work, while Professor M'Gill was removed by death in 1871. Dean Alford, one of the original members appointed by Convocation, died in the same year. Two other members of like standing, Dr. Chr. Wordsworth, Bishop of Lincoln, and Dr. Jebb, Dean of Hereford, resigned their seats at an early stage of the proceedings. Seven new members were chosen in their stead, of whom one, Dean Merivale, resigned in 1871. Others were added subsequently. The lists of members were accordingly as follows:—

MEMBERS OF THE OT REVISION COMPANY.†

The Rt. Rev. Connop Thirlwall, Bishop of St. Davids (Chairman till 1871).
The Rt. Rev. E. H. Browne, Bishop of Ely, afterwards of Winchester (Chairman from 1871).
The Rt. Rev. Chr. Wordsworth, Bishop of Lincoln.
The Rt. Rev. Lord Arthur C. Hervey, Bishop of Bath and Wells.
The Rt. Rev. Alfred Ollivant, Bishop of Llandaff.
The Very Rev. R. Payne Smith, Regius Professor of Divinity, Oxford; afterwards Dean of Canterbury.
The Ven. Benjamin Harrison, Archdeacon of Maidstone.
The Ven. H. J. Rose, Archdeacon of Bedford.
Dr. W. L. Alexander, Professor of Theology, Congregational Church Hall, Edinburgh.
Mr. R. L. Bensly, Fellow and Hebrew Lecturer of Gonville and Caius College, Cambridge.
The Rev. John Birrell, Professor of Oriental Languages, St. Andrews.
Dr. Frank Chance, Sydenham.
Mr. T. Chenery, Lord Almoner's Professor of Arabic, Oxford.
The Rev. T. K. Cheyne, Fellow and Hebrew Lecturer of Balliol College, Oxford; afterwards Oriel Professor of the Interpretation of Holy Scripture, Oxford.
Dr. A. B. Davidson, Professor of Hebrew, Free Church College, Edinburgh.
Dr. B. Davies, Professor of Hebrew, Baptist College, Regent's Park, London.
Dr. George Douglas, Professor of Hebrew, and afterwards Principal of Free Church College, Glasgow.
Dr. S. R. Driver, Fellow and Tutor of New College, Oxford; afterwards Regius Professor of Hebrew, Oxford.
The Rev. C. J. Elliott, Vicar of Winkfield, Windsor.
Dr. P. Fairbairn, Principal of the Free Church College, Glasgow.
The Rev. F. Field, author of *Otium Norvicense*; editor of Origen's *Hexapla*.
The Rev. J. D. Geden, Professor of Hebrew, Wesleyan College, Didsbury.
Dr. C. D. Ginsburg, editor of *Ecclesiastes*, etc.
Dr. F. W. Gotch, Principal of the Baptist College, Bristol.
Dr. John Jebb, Dean of Hereford.
Dr. W. Kay, late Principal of Bishop's College, Calcutta.
The Rev. Stanley Leathes, Professor of Hebrew, King's College, London.
The Rev. J. R. Lumby, Fellow of St. Cath. Coll., afterwards Norrisian Professor of Divinity, Cambridge.
Dr. J. M'Gill, Professor of Oriental Languages, St. Andrews.
Dr. J. J. S. Perowne, Professor of Hebrew, St. David's College, Lampeter; afterwards Bishop of Worcester.
Dr. E. H. Plumptre, Professor of NT Exegesis, King's College, London.
The Rev. A. H. Sayce, Fellow and Tutor of Queen's College; afterwards Professor of Assyriology, Oxford.
Dr. W. Selwyn, Canon of Ely; Lady Margaret's Professor of Divinity, Cambridge.
The Rev. W. Robertson Smith, Professor of Hebrew, Free Church College, Aberdeen; afterwards Lord Almoner's Professor of Arabic, and Fellow of Christ's College, Cambridge.
Dr. D. H. Weir, Professor of Oriental Languages, Glasgow.
Dr. W. Wright, Professor of Arabic, Cambridge.
Mr. W. Aldis Wright, Librarian, afterwards Bursar, of Trinity College, Cambridge.

MEMBERS OF THE NT REVISION COMPANY.*

The Rt. Rev. C. J. Ellicott, Bishop of Gloucester and Bristol (Chairman).
The Rt. Rev. S. Wilberforce, Bishop of Winchester.
The Rt. Rev. G. Moberly, Bishop of Salisbury.
The Most Rev. R. C. Trench, Archbishop of Dublin.
The Rt. Rev. Charles Wordsworth, Bishop of St. Andrews.
The Very Rev. E. H. Bickersteth, Dean of Lichfield (Prolocutor of Lower House of Convocation).
The Very Rev. Henry Alford, Dean of Canterbury.
The Very Rev. A. P. Stanley, Dean of Westminster.
The Very Rev. Robert Scott, Dean of Rochester.
The Very Rev. J. W. Blakesley, Dean of Lincoln.
The Very Rev. Charles Merivale, Dean of Ely.
The Ven. William Lee, Archdeacon of Dublin.
The Ven. Edwin Palmer, Archdeacon of Oxford.
Dr. Joseph Angus, President of the Baptist College, Regent's Park, London.
Dr. David Brown, Principal of Free Church College, Aberdeen.
Dr. John Eadie, Professor of Biblical Literature in the United Presbyterian Church, Glasgow.
Dr. F. J. A. Hort, afterwards Hulsean Professor of Divinity, Cambridge.

---

* The names in Resolutions II., III., VI., VII. are included in the final lists given below.

† This and the following list are drawn up, in the main, from those prepared by Dr. Philip Schaff for his *Companion to the Gr. Test.* 1883. It will be noticed that the present list contains 37 names, Dr. Schaff's only 27. There is no real discrepancy. The difference of 10 is made up by including those who were removed by death or resignation during the progress of the work. If they had sat as members, for however short a time, it seemed fair to include them. The losses by death in the OT Company up to 1875, after which year no new names were added to the list, were 7, and by resignation 3. Under the former head come Bishop Thirlwall, Archdeacon Rose, Canon Selwyn, Principal Fairbairn, and Professors M'Gill, Weir, and Davies. Under the latter, Bp. Wordsworth, Canon Jebb, and Professor Plumptre.

* Dr. Schaff's list (exclusive of the Secretary, the Rev. John Troutbeck) contains 24 names; the present one, 28. The difference is accounted for by the presence or absence of the names of Bishop Wilberforce, Dean Alford, and Professor Eadie (removed by death), and of Dean Merivale (resigned).

The Rev. W. G. Humphry, Prebendary of St. Paul's.
Dr. B. H. Kennedy, Canon of Ely; Regius Professor of Greek, Cambridge.
Dr. J. B. Lightfoot, Hulsean Professor of Divinity, Cambridge; afterwards Bishop of Durham.
Dr. W. Milligan, Professor of Divinity, Aberdeen.
Dr. W. F. Moulton, afterwards Master of The Leys School, Cambridge.
Dr. S. Newth, Principal of New College, Hampstead.
Dr. Alexander Roberts, Professor of Humanity, St. Andrews.
Dr. F. H. A. Scrivener, afterwards Vicar of Hendon.
Dr. G. Vance Smith, afterwards Principal of the Presbyterian Coll., Carmarthen.
Dr. C. J. Vaughan, Master of the Temple; Dean of Llandaff.
Dr. B. F. Westcott, Canon of Peterborough; Regius Professor of Divinity, Cambridge; afterwards Bishop of Durham.

The two Companies, thus constituted, began their labours in June 1870. On the morning of June 22nd the members of the NT Revision Company met together in Henry VII.'s Chapel, to join in Holy Communion, as the best preparation for the work then to be begun. The OT Company first assembled for business on June 30th. One of the NT Revisers, Dr. Newth, has left us a minute and interesting description* of the mode of procedure observed in the Company to which he belonged. Much of what he says will apply equally to both Companies; but want of space forbids all but the briefest extracts. The place of meeting was the historic Jerusalem Chamber, placed at their disposal by Dean Stanley. Here, on four consecutive days of every month in the year, except August and September, the NT Revisers met. The session lasted from eleven to six, with half an hour's interval for lunch. The ordinary routine is thus described:—Preliminary matters over, 'the Chairman invites the Company to proceed with the revision, and reads a short passage as given in the AV. The question is then asked whether any *textual* changes are proposed; that is, any readings that differ from the Greek text as presented in the edition published by Robert Stephen in 1550. If any change is proposed, the evidence for and against is briefly stated, and the proposal considered. The duty of stating this evidence is, by tacit consent, devolved upon two members of the Company, who, from their previous studies, are specially entitled to speak with authority upon such questions—Dr. Scrivener and Dr. Hort. . . . After discussion, the vote of the Company is taken, and the proposed reading accepted or rejected.' The reading being thus settled, questions of rendering followed, and were dealt with in a similar way.

It is evident that, with such methods, progress would necessarily be slow. In fact, at the close of their ninth sitting the NT Company had finished the first revision of not more than 153 verses, or an average of 17 a day.† It was even proposed, for more expedition, to divide the Company into two sections; one beginning the Epistles, while the other proceeded with the Gospels. Fortunately, the proposal was negatived.

Meantime an event occurred which, while promising to make the work more thorough, seemed likely to render it still more protracted. This was the association with the English‡ Revisers of two Companies of American biblical scholars. The arrangements were not completed till Dec. 7th, 1871, and work was not actually begun by the American contingent till Oct. 4th, 1872, after they had received from England the first revision of the Synoptic Gospels.§ But there is evidence that such co-operation had been thought of, almost from the very first. 'On July 7th, 1870, it was moved in the Lower House of Convocation by the present Prolocutor (Lord Alwyne Compton) that the Upper House should be requested to instruct the Committee of Convocation to invite the co-operation of some American divines.' This was at once assented to by the Upper House.* Difficulties naturally arose, but were overcome by patience and tact, and by the good feeling displayed on both sides. A visit of Dr. Angus to New York in August 1870, and of Dr. Schaff to this country in the following year (when he was present, unofficially, at one of the meetings of the English NT Revision Company and observed their methods), helped to smooth the way. A representative Committee of American scholars and theologians was formed, with Dr. Schaff for President, and this resolved itself into two Companies, as follows:—

Old Testament Revision Company (American).

Dr. W. H. Green (Chairman), Theological Seminary, Princeton, N.J.
Dr. G. E. Day (Secretary), Divinity School of Yale College, New Haven, Conn.
Dr. C. A. Aiken, Theological Seminary, Princeton, N.J.
Dr. T. W. Chambers, Collegiate Reformed Dutch Church, N.Y.
Dr. T. J. Conant, Brooklyn, N.Y.
Dr. J. de Witt, Theological Seminary, New Brunswick, N.J.
Dr. G. E. Hare, Divinity School, Phila.
Dr. C. P. Krauth, Vice-Provost of the University of Pennsylvania, Phila.
Dr. T. Lewis, Professor Emeritus of Greek and Hebrew, Union College, Schenectady, N.Y. (d. 1877).
Dr. C. M. Mead, Theological Seminary, Andover, Mass.
Dr. H. Osgood, Theological Seminary, Rochester, N.Y.
Dr. J. Packard, Theological Seminary, Alexandria, Va.
Dr. C. E. Stowe, Hartford, Conn.
Dr. J. Strong, Theological Seminary, Madison, N.J.
Dr. C. V. A. Van Dyck, Beirût, Syria (consulting member on questions of Arabic).

New Testament Revision Company (American).

Dr. T. D. Woolsey, New Haven, Conn. (Chairman).
Dr. J. H. Thayer, Theological Seminary, Andover, Mass. (Secretary).
Dr. Ezra Abbot, Divinity School, Harvard University, Cambridge, Mass
Dr. J. K. Burr, Trenton, New Jersey.
Dr. Thomas Chase, President of Haverford College, Pa.
Dr. Howard Crosby, Chancellor of New York University, N.Y.
Dr. Timothy Dwight, Divinity School, Yale College, New Haven, Conn.
Dr. H. B. Hackett, Theological Seminary, Rochester, N.Y. (d. 1876).
Dr. James Hadley, Professor of Greek, Yale College, New Haven (d. 1872).
Dr. Charles Hodge, Theological Seminary, Princeton, N.J. (d. 1878).
Dr. A. C. Kendrick, University of Rochester, N.Y.
The Rt. Rev. Alfred Lee, Bishop of the Diocese of Delaware.
Dr. M. B. Riddle, Theological Seminary, Hartford, Conn.
Dr. Philip Schaff, Union Theological Seminary, N.Y.
Dr. Charles Short, Columbia College, N.Y.
Dr. E. A. Washburn, Calvary Church, N.Y. (d. Feb. 1881).

It will be noticed that four members of the above Company died before seeing the fruit of their labours, but not before they had each taken part, for a longer or shorter time, in the work. Two names are not included—those of Dr. G. R. Crooks of New York, and Dr. W. F. Warren of Boston—both of whom accepted the invitation to join the Company, but found themselves unable to attend. The place of meeting was the Bible House, New York. Owing to the start they had gained, the English Companies had finished the first revision of the Synoptic Gospels, and been twice over the Pentateuch, respectively, by the time their American brethren were ready to begin. The manner in which their fellow-work was then carried on is described in the Preface to the Revised NT.

'We transmitted to them from time to time,' say the English Revisers, 'each several portion of our First Revision, and received from them in return their criticisms and corrections. These we considered with much care and attention during the time we were engaged on our Second Revision. We then sent over to them the various portions of the Second Revision as they were completed, and received further suggestions, which, like the former, were closely and carefully considered. Last of

* *Lectures*, as before, p. 117 ff.
† *Ib.* p. 121.
‡ The word 'English' is used in its widest sense.
§ Schaff, as before, p. 391 ff. Dr. Schaff was himself the President of the American Committee.

* *Times*, May 20th, 1881, quoted by Schaff.

all, we forwarded to them the RV in its final form; and a list of those passages in which they desire to place on record their preference of other readings and renderings will be found at the end of the volume.'

The first revision of the entire NT occupied six years of labour; the second, about two years and a half. What was to some extent a third revision, together with various necessary details, prolonged the task of the English Company till Nov. 11th, 1880, 'on which day, at five o'clock in the afternoon, after ten years and five months of labour, the revision of the NT was brought to a close.' * The Preface bears that date. But further causes of delay intervened; and it was not till Tuesday, May 17th, 1881, for London, and Friday, May 20th, for New York, that the actual publication took place. The scene in each city on both those days—the congestion of streets in the booksellers' quarter, the stoppage of all other traffic, the night-and-day labours of the work-people employed—will not soon be forgotten by those who witnessed them. Dr. Schaff computes that at least three million copies of the Revised NT were sold, in this country and the United States together, within the first year of its publication.

Meantime the revision of the OT was advancing, on similar lines, but more slowly, from the greater extent of ground to be covered. The Revisers in this case were more conservative than their fellow-workers on the NT, and their version differs less in proportion from the Authorized than does the other. The Preface, dated July 10th, 1884, speaks of the revision of the OT as completed in eighty-five sessions, ending on June 20th, 1884, having occupied 792 days, usually of six hours each. The day of actual publication, May 19th, 1885, was marked by little of the excitement which attended the publication of the NT four years before. The Revised Bible, in its complete form, bore the title:—'The | Holy Bible | containing the | Old and New Testaments | Translated out of the Original Tongues | Being the Version set forth A.D. 1611 | Compared with the most ancient Authorities and Revised. | Printed for the Universities of | Oxford and Cambridge | Oxford [*or* Cambridge] | At the University Press | 1885.'

No mention has thus far been made of any revision of the Apocrypha. Such an extension of the work does not appear to have been contemplated by Convocation. That it was finally included in the scheme was a result of the negotiations about copyright. In the course of 1872 an agreement was entered into between the Committee of Convocation and the representatives of the University Presses of Oxford and Cambridge, by which the latter, on condition of acquiring the copyright of the RV, when completed, agreed to provide a sum sufficient to cover the bare cost of production, including the travelling expenses of members of the Companies; whose labour, in other respects, was a labour of love.† It was then for the first time stipulated by the University printers, that the Apocrypha should be included in the scheme of revision. This was assented to.

In pursuance of the compact thus made, it was arranged between the two English Companies of Revisers (the Americans not joining in this part of the work), that, as soon as the NT Company should have finished its task, it should resolve itself into three committees for the purpose of beginning the revision of the Apocrypha.‡ These were to be called, in imitation of their predecessors of 1611, the London, Westminster, and Cambridge Committees. The first of the three had assigned to it the Book of Sirach; the second had 1 Mac., to which were afterwards added Tobit and Judith; the third was to take Wisdom and 2 Maccabees. The London Committee began work on May 11th, 1881, and finished the second and final revision of Sirach on May 25th, 1883. The Westminster Committee completed their second revision of 1 Mac. on Nov. 3rd, 1881, and the remainder of their task on Oct. 11th, 1882. The work of the Cambridge Committee lasted from the spring of 1881 to the summer of 1892. During this comparatively long interval space was found for giving the difficult Book of Wisdom a third revision.

The OT Revision Company having in the meantime (July 1884) come to the end of their own proper labours, passed a resolution, appointing six of their number a committee for revising the remaining books of the Apocrypha. Of these six, two were unable to take any part in the work; and Dr. Field, one of the OT Company, whose co-operation had been invited for the settlement of the text, died in April 1885. A small committee of four members—Professor Lumby, Professor Robertson Smith, Mr. Bensly, and Mr. W. Aldis Wright—had thus the task of revising what remained of the Apocrypha, comprising 1 and 2 Esdras, Ad. Esther, Baruch, Song of the Three Children, the History of Susanna, Bel and the Dragon, and the Prayer of Manasses. For one of these books (2 Esdras) they had the benefit of Bensly's careful reconstruction of the text, and were thus able to give a translation of the 'missing fragment' ($7^{36-105}$). In the other instances no critical settlement of the existing text was attempted. The revised Apocrypha was published early in 1895. It bore the title: 'The | Apocrypha | Translated out of the | Greek and Latin tongues | Being the Version set forth A.D. 1611 | Compared with the most ancient Authorities and | Revised A.D. 1894 | Printed for the Universities of | Oxford and Cambridge | Oxford [*or* Cambridge] | At the University Press | 1895.'

In endeavouring to form a just estimate of the merits of the RV, it will be convenient to take the component parts of it in the order in which they appeared. The NT, moreover, challenges our attention first, because of its surpassing importance, because the changes made in revising it were relatively much more numerous than in the case of the OT, and because the attack and defence were here the most strenuous. As was not unnatural, the strife grew fiercest about the form in which the Lord's Prayer was now set forth. In both its forms (Mt $6^{9-13}$, Lk $11^{2-4}$) alike it was now without the doxology. The form in Luke was much curtailed. For 'Our Father which art in heaven' it had simply 'Father.' It lacked altogether two petitions—'Thy will,' etc., and 'Deliver us from evil.' These changes were made on MS authority, believed to be the highest; and the clauses omitted were duly noted in the margin. So far, the Revisers were within their rights. But a further alteration of 'from evil' to 'from the evil one' could not be so easily defended. It was understood to have been accepted mainly through the influence of Bishop Lightfoot. A chief argument for the change, the alleged fact that ῥύσασθαι ἀπό, as distinguished from ῥύσασθαι ἐκ, denotes deliverance from a *person*, not a *state*, was controverted by other scholars; and we cannot but wish that, in this instance, the renderings in the text and margin could have changed places.*

* Newth, as before, p. 125.

† Westcott, *English Bible*, pp. 346, 347.

‡ Preface to the *Apocrypha* in the RV, from which most of the particulars immediately following are taken.

* See, for an outline of the controversy, the Bishop of Durham's three letters in the *Guardian* of Sept. 7th, 14th, and 21st, 1881, reprinted in *A Fresh Revision of the NT*, 3rd ed. 1891, and Canon F. C. Cook's *A Second Letter to the Lord Bishop of London*, 1882.

Fault was also found with the change—the uncalled-for change, as it seemed to many—in the order of the words in the familiar Song of Simeon. What was gained, men would ask, by thus re-grouping the well-remembered lines—

> 'Now lettest thou thy servant depart, O Lord,
> According to thy word, in peace'?

A more perfect parallelism, it might be replied, and a closer adherence to the order of the original. But the further question might be pressed: How far is this latter quality essential to a good idiomatic translation?

More irritating, however, than such changes in important passages as we have noticed, were the incessant alterations in small particulars, which tripped up the reader at every turn.* One accustomed to 'Jesus stood on the shore,' in Jn $21^{4}$, could not take kindly to 'Jesus stood on the *beach*,' even though assured that the rendering of *αἰγιαλός* was thus kept uniform. Nor would one who knew how deeply the phrase 'vials of wrath' was embedded in our language, fail to demur, if he read Rev 15, at having '*bowls* of the wrath of God' substituted for the familiar expression. The Revisers of 1611 and those of 1881 both equally admitted that no two words in different languages cover precisely the same ground. But from this common axiom they proceeded to opposite conclusions. The older translators felt justified by it in varying the rendering of the same word in the original. They even made a merit of doing so. 'We have not tied ourselves,' they say in their Preface, 'to an uniformity of phrasing or to an identity of words, as some peradventure would wish that we had done. . . . That we should express the same notion in the same particular word; as, for example, if we translate the Hebrew or Greek word once by *purpose*, never to call it *intent* . . . thus to mince the matter, we thought to savour more of curiosity than wisdom.'

The liberty thus claimed is freely used in the AV, and, it must be admitted, deserves at times rather to be called licence. The translation may gain in spirit and buoyancy, but at the cost of losing other qualities yet more precious. How much is lost, for instance, by the capricious alteration of 'destroy' to 'defile,' in 1 Co $3^{17}$?—'If any man destroyeth the temple of God, him shall God destroy.' Nothing but the love of variety for its own sake could have prompted the double rendering of *διαιρέσεις* in 1 Co $12^{4-6}$ by 'differences' and 'diversities,' and of *ἐνεργημάτων* and its cognate verb by 'operations' and 'worketh.' Hardly less injurious to the sense, in many passages, is the converse fault of using the same English word to translate different words in the original. Thus 'light' serves as the equivalent of *φῶς*, *φωστήρ* (Ph $2^{15}$), *φωτισμός* (2 Co $4^{4}$), *φέγγος* (Lk $11^{33}$), *λύχνος* (Mt $6^{22}$); 'know' of *οἶδα*, *γινώσκω*, *ἐπιγινώσκω*, and *ἐπίσταμαι*. The Revisers of 1881 were fully alive to the difficulties placed in their way by this peculiarity of their predecessors' labour, and speak in their Preface of the principles on which they endeavoured to solve the problem thus presented to them. They discriminated, as far as possible, between 'varieties of rendering which were compatible with fidelity to the true meaning of the text' and 'varieties which involved inconsistency, and were suggestive of differences that had no existence in the Greek.' To the former class they professed themselves lenient. Some have thought that they would have acted more wisely if they had made this class more comprehensive, instead of sacrificing so much for a uniformity of rendering, not always attainable even by themselves.*

It may be well, as helping the reader to form a judgment for himself, to set down a short list of passages from the NT in which the rendering of the RV is generally admitted to be an improvement, followed by another of passages in which the changes made are considered by many to be for the worse.

(A) *Changes admitted to be for the better.*

| AV 1611. | RV 1881. |
|---|---|
| Mt $12^{15}$ But when Jesus knew it [as if for a time he had not known it]. | Mt $12^{15}$ And Jesus perceiving it. |
| Mk $4^{21}$ Is a candle brought to be put under a bushel . . . and not to be set on a candlestick? | Mk $4^{21}$ Is the lamp brought to be put under the bushel, . . . and not to be put on the stand? |
| Mk $4^{38}$ And he was in the hinder part of the ship, asleep on a pillow. | Mk $4^{38}$ And he himself was in the stern, asleep on the cushion. |
| Mk $7^{19}$ . . . purging all meats. | Mk $7^{19}$ *This he said*, making all meats clean [καθαρίζων, masc. in ℵ, A, B]. |
| Mk $10^{42}$ exercise lordship over them. | Mk $10^{42}$ lord it over them. |
| Lk $23^{42}$ when thou comest into thy kingdom. | Lk $23^{42}$ when thou comest in thy kingdom. |
| Lk $24^{17}$ . . . as ye walk, and are sad? | Lk $24^{17}$ . . . as ye walk? And they stood still, looking sad. |
| Jn $4^{1}$ . . . made and baptized. | Jn $4^{1}$ . . . was making and baptizing. |
| Jn $21^{16}$ Feed my sheep. | Jn $21^{16}$ Tend my sheep. |
| Ac $23^{27}$ This man was taken of the Jews, and should have been killed of them: then came I with an army, and rescued him. | Ac $23^{27}$ This man was seized by the Jews, and was about to be slain of them, when I came upon them with the soldiers, and rescued him. |
| Ac $26^{28}$ Almost thou persuadest me to be a Christian. | Ac $26^{28}$ With but little persuasion thou wouldest fain make me a Christian. |
| Ac $27^{40}$ And when they had taken up the anchors, they committed *themselves* unto the sea. | Ac $27^{40}$ And casting off the anchors, they left them in the sea. |
| 1 Co $7^{28}$ . . . but I spare you. | 1 Co $7^{28}$ . . . and I would spare you. |
| 1 Co $9^{5}$ Have we not power to lead about a sister, a wife . . .? | 1 Co $9^{5}$ Have we no right to lead about a wife that is a believer . . .? |
| Ph $4^{6}$ Be careful for nothing. | Ph $4^{6}$ In nothing be anxious. |
| 2 Th $2^{1}$ . . . by the coming. | 2 Th $2^{1}$ . . . touching the coming. |
| 1 Ti $3^{13}$ . . . purchase to themselves a good degree. | 1 Ti $3^{13}$ . . . gain to themselves a good standing. |
| 1 Ti $6^{5}$ . . . supposing that gain is godliness. | 1 Ti $6^{5}$ . . . supposing that godliness is a way of gain. |
| 2 Ti $2^{26}$ . . . who are taken captive by him at his will [pronouns ambiguous]. | 2 Ti $2^{26}$ . . . having been taken captive by the Lord's servant unto the will of God [see also m.]. |
| Tit $1^{12}$ The Cretians are alway liars, evil beasts, slow bellies. | Tit $1^{12}$ Cretans are alway liars, evil beasts, idle gluttons. |
| Ja $1^{25}$ . . . he being not a forgetful hearer, but a doer of the work. | Ja $1^{25}$ . . . being not a hearer that forgetteth, but a doer that worketh. |

(B) *Changes not so admitted.*

| AV 1611. | RV 1881. |
|---|---|
| Mt $5^{26}$ . . . till thou hast paid the uttermost farthing. | Mt $5^{26}$ till thou have paid the last † farthing. |

* Professor Plumptre computes the number of variations in rendering from the AV of the NT to be more than 35,000. Others make them 36,000. See Canon Cook's *Second Letter*, p. 6 and n. Cook further estimates that the deviations from the Greek text of 1611 in that adopted by the Revisers exceed 5000. Edgar (*The Bibles of England*, 1889, p. 342) agrees, making the exact number 5002. The Greek text used by king James's translators, so far as it could be ascertained, was published at Cambridge by Scrivener, and had, as footnotes, the readings preferred by the Revisers. A similar work, but with converse arrangement of text and notes, was published at Oxford by Archdeacon Palmer. The calculation was thus made easy.

* See the examples of inconsistency in rendering in the RV collected by Edgar, p. 362. *διδάσκαλος* is 'teacher,' 'doctor,' 'master'; *κύριος* has four equivalents; *παράκλησις* and *σπλάγχνα* each five. Of course, some of these are AV renderings allowed to remain.

† Gr. *ἔσχατον*. A high authority, Dr. F. Field, himself one of the Revisers, characterizes this change as one 'than which no single verbal alteration has met with more general reprobation' (*Notes on the Translation of the NT*, 1899, Pref. p. xiv n.).

| AV 1611. | RV 1881. |
| --- | --- |
| Mt $13^{32}$ . . . it is the greatest among herbs. | Mt $13^{32}$ . . . it is greater* than the herbs. |
| Mk $16^{2}$ . . . they came unto the sepulchre . . . | Mk $16^{2}$ . . . they come to the tomb . . . |
| Lk $5^{5}$ . . . we have toiled all the night, and have taken nothing. | Lk $5^{5}$ . . . we toiled all night, and took nothing.† |
| Jn $17^{2}$ . . . that he should give eternal life to as many as thou hast given him. | Jn $17^{2}$ . . . that whatsoever thou hast given him, to them he should give eternal life. |
| Ac $21^{37}$ Canst thou speak Greek? | Ac $21^{37}$ Dost thou know ‡ Greek? |
| Ac $27^{16}$ . . . we had much work to come by the boat. | Ac $27^{16}$ . . . we were able, with difficulty, to secure § the boat. |
| Ro $5^{7}$ Yet peradventure for a good man some would even dare to die. | Ro $5^{7}$ for ‖ peradventure for the good man some one would even dare to die. |
| Ro $5^{15}$ For if through the offence of one many be dead, much more the grace of God, and the gift by grace, which is by one man, Jesus Christ, hath abounded unto many. | Ro $5^{15}$ For if by the trespass of the one the many died, much more did the grace of God, and the gift by the grace of the one man, Jesus Christ, abound unto the many. |
| 1 Co $5^{1}$ It is reported commonly . . . | 1 Co $5^{1}$ It is actually ¶ reported . . . |
| 2 Co $10^{2}$ . . . that I may not be bold when I am present with that confidence, wherewith I think to be bold against some, which think of us as if we walked according to the flesh. | 2 Co $10^{2}$ . . . that I may not when present show courage with the confidence wherewith I count to be bold against some, which count of us as if we walked according to the flesh. |
| Gal $2^{16}$ Knowing that a man is not justified by the works of the law, but by the faith of Jesus Christ. | Gal $2^{16}$ . . . knowing that a man is not justified by the works of the law, save [m. but only] through faith in Jesus Christ.** |
| Gal $3^{16}$ Now to Abraham . . . were the promises made. | Gal $3^{16}$ Now to Abraham were the promises spoken. |
| 1 Ti $3^{2}$ A bishop . . . | 1 Ti $3^{2}$ The bishop . . . |
| 1 Ti $6^{10}$ For the love of money is the root of all evil. | 1 Ti $6^{10}$ For the love of money is a root of all kinds of evil.†† |
| He $11^{5}$ . . . for before his translation he had this testimony, that he pleased God. | He $11^{5}$ . . . for before his translation he hath had witness borne to him that he had been well-pleasing unto God. |
| He $12^{7}$ If ye endure chastening, God dealeth with you as with sons. | He $12^{7}$ It is for ‡‡ chastening that ye endure; God dealeth with you as with sons. |
| He $13^{5}$ Let your conversation §§ be without covetousness. | He $13^{5}$ Be ye free from the love of money. |
| Rev $19^{5}$ Praise our God, all ye his servants. | Rev $19^{5}$ Give praise to our God, all ye his servants. |

The Revisers of the OT had a task before them in some respects more difficult, in others easier, than that which the NT Revisers had had to face. On the one hand, their subject was a much longer one; more varied in its contents, and hence requiring more diversified knowledge in those who dealt with it; beset, moreover, with greater obscurities, and not illustrated by the light shed from many quarters upon the NT. On the other hand, the confessed obscurity of many passages formed a justification of the Revisers' work; fewer persons were competent to criticise their work; and they had the advantage of an interval of four years after the appearance of the revised NT, in 1881, in which to profit by the verdict passed by public opinion upon the performance of their colleagues. Above all, they were not hampered by the constant necessity of deciding between rival texts of the original. Very wisely, we think, they came to the conclusion, as stated in their Preface, that 'as the state of knowledge on the subject is not at present such as to justify any attempt at an entire reconstruction of the text on the authority of the Versions, the Revisers have thought it most prudent to adopt the Massoretic Text as the basis of their work, and to depart from it, as the Authorized Translators had done, only in exceptional cases.'

Being carried out on the same lines as the revised NT, we find in the present work the same improvements in the arrangement of the English text: the grouping by paragraphs, the indication by spaces of a change of subject, the clearer marking of quotations, the system of parallelism adopted for poetical books and passages, and the like. As in the NT, the direction of Convocation is obeyed, that no change of reading be admitted into the English text if not approved, at the final revision, by a majority of at least two-thirds of the Revisers present. Hence it may often be the case that a particular reading in the margin is one which a majority—though not the requisite majority—of the Revisers would have wished to see inserted in the text. It is permissible to conjecture that an example may be found at the outset in Gn $1^{2}$, where 'the spirit of God moved upon' is left undisturbed, but the margin offers the alternative rendering 'was brooding upon' (cf. Dt $32^{11}$). As in the case of the NT also, another rule of Convocation is not observed—that, namely, which directed that the revision should extend to 'the headings of pages and chapters.' Both classes of headings have been omitted altogether; with the twofold advantage that space is gained, and the province of the commentator is not encroached upon.

In passing to the more important subject of the merits of the revised translation itself, the first question that will occur to many minds is, whether the changes made are proportionately as numerous as in the NT. Is there, in particular, so frequent an infringement of the rule laid down by the Committee of Convocation 'to introduce as few alterations as possible into the text of the AV, consistently with faithfulness'? The prevalent opinion is that there is not. But to give a decisive answer is less easy than might be supposed; partly from the extent of the ground to be covered, and partly from the fact that the language of the OT is in general less familiar to most persons than that of the NT.* Thus in Jon $4^{6}$ we had 'to deliver him from his grief'—a vigorous and appropriate expression at the time, although it may well be asked how many modern readers are acquainted with the old meaning of 'grief.' Instead of this, we now have 'to deliver him from his evil case'—a rendering which, while closer to the

* Query, used here as a superlative? μείζων is so used in Mt $18^{1}$ and elsewhere. The tendency of the superlative *form* of adjs. to disappear in NT Greek (noticed by Rutherford in the Pref. to his new translation of *Romans*, 1900) is illustrated by the fact that μέγιστος is only found once in the NT (2 P $1^{4}$).

† Justified by RV on ground of aorist tenses.

‡ For the ellipse of λαλεῖν with Ελληνιστί, see Field, *in loc.*

§ 'Difficulty' not found in AV. 'Secure,' as a verb, only in Mt $28^{14}$ (ὑμᾶς ἀμερίμνους ποιήσομεν), where the Revisers have substituted 'rid you of care.' As a rendering of περικρατεῖς γενέσθαι in the present passage, 'secure' is inappropriate, unless (as is probable enough) the RV uses it as simply equivalent to 'get hold of.'

‖ The 'for' refers to a thought suppressed, by a common Gr. idiom. Rutherford thus supplies the ellipse: 'I say barely conceivable, not wholly inconceivable; for,' etc. As left in the text the words are scarcely intelligible.

¶ 'Actually' in this sense is a modernism.

** Burgon (*The Revision Revised*, p. 147) quotes Bp. Wordsworth of Lincoln as saying that the statement thus put forth, with 'save' instead of 'but,' or 'but only,' 'is illogical and erroneous, and contradicts the whole drift of St. Paul's argument in that Ep. and in the Ep. to the Romans.'

†† πάντων τῶν, not παντοίων, is 'all,' not 'all kinds of.' With ῥίζα, anarthrous as predicate, Field (*in loc.*) aptly compares (after Wetstein) Athen. vii. p. 280 A, ἀρχὴ καὶ ῥίζα παντος ἀγαθοῦ ἡ τῆς γαστρὸς ἡδονή.

‡‡ εἰς has undoubtedly better authority than εἰ. But, with this allowance, let the two versions be compared simply as English.

§§ Gr. ὁ τρόπος. 'Let your manners be without auarice' (Rhemish). It must be admitted, however, that the AV is very unintelligible here, or, if intelligible, gives a totally false sense to a modern reader.

* A writer in the *Church Quarterly Review* (Oct. 1885, pp. 190, 191) reckons that there are about 830 changes in Judges, 684 in Pss 1–41, 335 in Hosea, and 1389 in Job, 'the most difficult book in the OT.' In the *Edinburgh Review* of the same date, p. 483, similar results are obtained. The reviewer notes 2094 changes in the entire Book of Psalms, 1278 in Jer., 1550 in Ezekiel. On an average of nine books, the changes marked 'important' number about one-sixth of the whole. But it is obvious that opinions might differ widely as to what changes were important.

Hebrew,* lacks the spirit and force of the other. Objection has been taken, again, to the substitution of 'my provocation' for 'grief' in 1 S 1$^{16}$, where Hannah pleads: 'Out of the abundance of my complaint and grief [but is this the meaning of the Heb. כַּעַס ?] have I spoken hitherto.'

The OT Revisers made it a principle not to depart from the Massoretic Text save in 'exceptional cases.' One such case occurs in Jg 18$^{30}$, where are described the idolatries of the tribe of Dan, and the participation in them of Jonathan, the son of Gershom, the son—as we now read—of Moses. The AV in place of Moses has Manasseh. The explanation is simple. To save the great lawgiver from the reproach of having an idolatrous descendant, the Massoretes suggested a corruption of the text in the passage in question, by writing a 'suspended N' over and between the M and S in Moses, thus converting it, so far as the consonants are concerned, into Manasses.† The Revisers have rightly restored Moses, which is also the reading of the Vulgate.

To take another example. In Ps 24$^{6}$ the AV reads: 'This is the generation of them that seek him, that seek thy face, O Jacob'; with the marginal variant, 'O God of Jacob.' All attempts to make sense of the former reading being, to say the least, far-fetched, the Revisers have wisely placed in their text that supplied by the margin; in which they have the support of the LXX, the Vulgate, and the Syriac.

The advantage gained by forsaking the received text for the ancient versions being in these and some other instances‡ indisputable, it is perhaps to be regretted that the Revisers did not use the term 'exceptional' with a greater latitude of meaning. To have done so might have saved them at times from the necessity of encumbering their margin with variants (as in the case of Pss 2$^{12}$ and 22$^{16}$), only perplexing the reader, and leaving him to reconcile conflicting renderings as best he can.

A word must be said in passing on the treatment of archaisms by the OT Revisers. The principle they lay down in their Preface appears at first sight to be a sound and consistent one. 'Where an archaic word or expression was liable to be misunderstood, or at least was not perfectly intelligible,' they have changed it for another. Where, 'although obsolete,' it 'was not unintelligible,' they have suffered it to stand. Thus, to take their own illustration, 'to ear' (1 S 8$^{12}$) and 'earing' (Gn 45$^{6}$) are replaced by 'to plow' and 'plowing,' as being now not only obsolete, but misleading. On the other hand, 'bolled' is retained in Ex 9$^{31}$ ('the flax was bolled'), as the word is still occasionally met with in country parts, and has no English equivalent to express its meaning—that of 'podded for seed.' But, as often happens, a principle, good in itself, is here found to work imperfectly in practice; the reason in this case being, that words and phrases intelligible to one class of readers are unintelligible to another, and hence it is difficult to know where to draw the line. The result is at best a compromise. 'Artillery' is gone from 1 S 20$^{40}$; but 'bravery,' in the sense of adornments or beauty,§ is retained in Is 3$^{18}$. Cain is now a 'wanderer,' not a 'vagabond'; the inlets of the shore, where Asher abode, are 'creeks,' not 'breaches'; the question of Achish (1 S 27$^{10}$) is made clear by the simple change of 'road' to 'raid.' But we still meet with 'occurrent' for 'occurrence' (1 K 5$^{4}$), 'chapmen' for 'traders' (2 Ch 9$^{14}$), 'sith' for 'since.' In 1 S 17$^{22}$ 'carriage' is properly changed to 'baggage,' as in Is 10$^{28}$ and elsewhere; and in 2 K 23$^{17}$ 'title' (from the Vulgate) is in like manner replaced by 'monument.'* Yet the house in which the leper king Azariah dies is still called a 'several,' instead of a 'separate,' house (2 K 15$^{5}$); and, yet more strangely, the Latinism 'desired' for 'regretted' is still found in the description of the death of Jehoram (2 Ch 21$^{20}$).

In spite, however, of defects and inconsistencies, of which only a very few specimens have been given, it is but just to the OT Revisers to admit that they have corrected many a faulty rendering, and by so doing have thrown light on a multitude of obscure passages. In 2 S 1$^{18}$, for instance, David's bidding '*the use of* the bow' to be taught to the children of Judah has always been felt to be out of place at the beginning of the dirge. By the simple change of *use* to *song*, as the word to be supplied, it is seen that the dirge itself, 'the song of the bow,' was the thing enjoined to be taught. The inconsequent statement in Is 10$^{22}$, 'though thy people Israel be as the sand of the sea, *yet* a remnant of them shall return,' is made logical by reading '*only*' for '*yet*'; both words being alike in italics. Much improved also is the rendering of the next verse. In the AV it stands: 'For the Lord God of hosts shall make a consumption, even determined. . . .' In the RV it is: 'For a consummation, and that determined, shall the Lord. . . .' 'The ships of Tarshish,' in the older rendering of Ezk 27$^{25}$, by a poetical but not very intelligible metaphor, 'did sing of thee in thy market.' Now, in simple prose it is: 'were thy caravans for thy merchandise.' In a very obscure passage, Hos 5$^{2}$ 'the revolters are gone deep in making slaughter' can at least be understood, which is more than can be truly said of the earlier version: 'are profound to make slaughter.' Hab 1$^{11}$ gains much in terseness, not to say fidelity, by the rendering 'whose might is his god,' in place of 'imputing this his power unto his god.' Other examples crowd upon the memory, but these will suffice.

As we try to view the work of the Revisers upon the two Testaments as a finished whole, the question inevitably arises: Is their work a failure or a success? Will the Bible, in the form in which they leave it to us, become the Bible of the English-speaking people, or will it be quietly laid aside, to be referred to occasionally as a useful commentary on the older version? Fortunately, we are spared the necessity of replying, as time alone can give the answer. We do not forget how slowly, for a long while, the AV itself won its way to general acceptance; and how the Psalter it contains has not even yet displaced the older version in the Book of Common Prayer.† Knowing as we do the long and unselfish labour bestowed by the Revisers upon their task, we cannot but sympathize with the aspirations with which their Prefaces close. But as it is a hazardous undertaking to attempt to restore—not renovate—an ancient building, so is it perilous to apply the touch of any but the most loving and cautious, as well as skilful, hands to the venerable structure of the Version of 1611. For its 'marvellous English,' to recall a familiar

* מֵרָעָתוֹ, literally rendered in the LXX by ἀπὸ τῶν κακῶν αὐτοῦ.

† See Lord Arthur Hervey's note, *ad loc.*, in *The Speaker's Commentary*.

‡ As Ps 16$^{2}$, Ps 22$^{16}$, 1 Ch 6$^{28}$. See the article in the *Church Quarterly Review*, before referred to, pp. 186, 187, where these passages are discussed.

§ See the marginal reading of Is 4$^{2}$.

* The Hebrew word צִיּוּן, here so rendered, is translated 'sign' in Ezk 39$^{15}$ (AV and RV), while in Jer 31$^{21}$ its plural is 'waymarks.' See Edgar, as before, p. 319 n.

† See some remarks on this by Scrivener, *Authorized Edition*, p. 139. Professor Cheyne, who quotes the passage (*Expositor*, 3rd ser. vol. v. p. 304), justly urges in reply the claims of sense as against sound. But in a translation of poetical books both must be studied. As a passing illustration, let the reader call to mind two sentences from the older version of Ps 147$^{9. 18}$ 'Who giveth fodder unto the cattle,' and 'He bloweth with his wind and the waters flow'; and ask himself what has been gained by the alteration of these in the RV.

passage of F. W. Faber, 'lives on in the ear like a music that never can be forgotten. . . . Its felicities seem often to be almost things rather than mere words.' The makers of that version erred, no doubt, in many places. Small credit is ours, if, with the added knowledge of nearly three centuries, we can discern their faults. But great will be the praise of that scholar, or that band of scholars, who shall be judged to have removed the blemishes of their handiwork, without marring its beauties.*

The revision of the *Apocrypha* was, as before said, an afterthought. It was simply a matter of agreement between the Revisers and the representatives of the University Presses of Oxford and Cambridge. Moreover, whilst, in the *Speaker's Commentary*, the Apocr., issued in 1888, was included under the general title of 'The Holy Bible,' the title-page of the revised edition of 1895 makes no such claim. The Preface ends simply with the unassuming hope 'that it will be found helpful to the student, and acceptable to the general reader of the Apocrypha.' This seems to make a few words desirable on the position held by the Apocrypha in our English Bibles.†

The first printed English Bible containing the Apocrypha was that of Miles Coverdale, 1535. In a short prologue, Coverdale describes these writings as 'The bokes and treatises which amonge the fathers of olde are not rekened to be of like authorite with the other bokes of the byble, nether are they founde in the Canon of the Hebrue.' After giving a list of them, which agrees in order with our own as far as the end of Sirach, the translator adds: 'Unto these also belongeth Baruc, whom we haue set amonge the prophetes next vnto Jeremy, because he was his scrybe and in his tyme.' He then explains that these books 'are not iudged amonge the doctours to be of like reputacion with the other scripture, as thou [good reader] mayest perceaue by S. Jerome *in epistola ad Paulinum.* And the chefe cause therof is this: there be many places in them, that seme to be repugnaunt vnto the open and manyfest trueth in the other bokes of the byble. Neuertheles, I haue not gathered them together to the intent that I wolde haue them despysed, or little sett by, or that I shulde think them false, for I am not able to proue it.

The above 'gathering together' of the Apocryphal books into one place, while it might seem an appropriate bridging over of the interval between the Old and New Testaments, undoubtedly tended to make deeper and more sharply cut the line dividing the canonical from the uncanonical books, and to diminish the esteem in which the latter were held. So long as these were interspersed among the canonical, as in the Greek and Latin Bibles, it was natural that, in the popular mind, the two classes should be indiscriminately regarded as Scripture. Even Colet, in his *Ryght fruitfull Monicion*, cites or refers to Sirach more frequently than any other book; and later still, in the two Books of Homilies (1547 and 1563), we find passages from the Apocr. quoted as 'Scripture written by the Holy Ghost,' or as 'the Word of God.'* But, when the Apocryphal writings were grouped together by themselves, the thought easily suggested itself, to the Puritan at any rate, that they might be dispensed with altogether. It is said that some copies of the Genevan Bible of 1576 were issued without the Apocrypha.† In any case, the practice of printing Bibles not containing the Apocr. must have continued, for in 1615 it was judged of sufficient importance by Archbishop Abbot to be prohibited, under pain of one year's imprisonment. This prohibition was of little avail in arresting the course of public opinion. In 1643 Dr. John Lightfoot, when preaching before the House of Commons, complained of the privilege, curtailed as it was, still enjoyed by the Apocryphal writings. He speaks of them not as connecting, but as separating, the Old and New Testaments. 'Thus sweetly and nearly,' he exclaims, 'should the two Testaments join together, and thus divinely would they kiss each other, but that the wretched Apocrypha doth thrust in between.' 'Like the two cherubins in the temple oracle,' he continues, the Law and the Gospel would touch each other, 'did not this patchery of human invention divorce them asunder.'‡

But in fact the concessions made to the Puritan party at the Hampton Court Conference itself, with regard to the use of the Apocr. in the Lectionary of the Church, and the large excisions then agreed to,§ furnish evidence enough, if any were still needed, of the diminished esteem into which the Apocryphal books were falling, and help to explain the comparative carelessness with which these books were revised in 1611. That the revision of the Apocr. then made shows signs of less care and deliberation than was bestowed upon the canonical books, is certain. The task was assigned to the second Cambridge Company, a body which comprised perhaps fewer scholars of eminence than any of the others. They were the first to finish their allotted share of the work. 'For the rest,' says Scrivener,‖ 'they are contented to leave many a rendering of the Bishops' Bible as they found it, when nearly any change must have been for the better; even where their predecessor sets them a better example they resort to undignified, mean, almost vulgar words and phrases; and on the whole they convey to the reader's mind the painful impression of having disparaged the importance of their own work, or of having imperfectly realized the truth that what is worth doing at all is worth doing well.'

One peculiarity of the AV of the Apocr. could

* It will be instructive to note the progress made in a parallel revision movement—that concerned with the German Luther Bible. We are enabled to do this by a paper of Dr. Philip Schaff's in the *Expositor*, 3rd ser. vol. v. p. 468 ff. The work was begun, in 1863, by the Eisenach German Evangelical Church Conference, and the result of their labours appeared at Halle, in 1883, under the title: *Die Bibel, oder die ganze Heilige Schrift des Alten und Neuen Testaments nach der deutschen Uebersetzung D. Martin Luthers.* The revised NT had been already published separately. The Halle publication was regarded as a *Probe-bibel*, or specimen of what was proposed. The revision was carried out with extreme care, but in too conservative a spirit; as may be judged from the fact that, while the English revised NT contained some 36,000 changes, the German contained only 200. Failing to please either party—those who desired and those who deprecated change—'it was recommitted by the Eisenach Conference of 1886 for final action.' After being subjected to a second and more thoroughgoing revision, and kept back for the proverbial nine years, the Luther Bible was issued again at Halle in 1892. A Preface by Dr. O. Frick, Director of the v. Canstein Bible Society, gives an interesting account of the progress of the work, and the lines on which it had been carried out. Still more than in the English revision, the difficulty was how to steer judiciously between opposite extremes: to correct errors and remove archaisms, without needlessly disturbing the venerable 'rust' on Luther's handiwork; to keep in view the wants of school and congregation, while not forgetful of the more fastidious taste of scholars;—in short, to pacify alike those who would summarily recast the whole version, and those who would leave it altogether untouched—the large class of those whom Dr. Frick might have described as holding to the opinion of Magr. Petrus Lapp, in the *Epp. obscur. Virorum*: 'Sacra scriptura sufficienter est translata, et non indigemus aliis translationibus.'

Dr. Frick refers, for fuller information on the subject, to *Das Werk der Bibelrevision*, Halle, 1892. See also two articles by Dr. H. L. Strack in the *Expositor*, 3rd ser. ii. pp. 178–187; v. pp. 193–201; and Funck's *Beurteilung der rev. Ausgabe d. N.T. 1892*, . . . Cannstadt, 1896.

† For a fuller treatment of the subject, see the art. Apocrypha in vol. i., that by Bishop Ryle in Smith's *DB*, and Dr. Salmon's General Introduction to the Apocr. in the *Speaker's Commentary*.

* This was noticed by Pusey in his *Eirenicon*. See the *Church Quarterly Rev.*, Oct. 1888, p. 140. In the first part of the *Sermon of Swearing*, a quotation from Wisdom is introduced by the words: 'Almighty God by the wise man saith.'

† Churton, *Uncanonical and Apocr. Scripture*, Introd. p. 21.

‡ Salmon, Gen. Introd. (*l.c.*) p. xxxvii.

§ A full list of these is given in Perry, *Hist. of the Eng. Church*, i. pp. 105, 106.

‖ *Authorized Edition*, p. 140. Scrivener notes that Dr. Robert Gell in his *Essay*, 1659, formed a like unfavourable opinion of the revision of the Apocr. in the AV.

hardly fail to strike the reader, though it might not occur to him to ascribe it to its true cause—simple negligence. This is the scarcity of words in italics, or, in case of the early black-letter editions, in small Roman type. As first published, there were only fifty-four examples to be found in the whole Apocrypha. 'In fact only three instances occur at all later than Sir 45[4], after which [ ], or sometimes ( ), are substituted in their room.' *

It may be of service for forming a just estimate of the merits of the AV and RV respectively, so far as the Apocr. is concerned, to set down two or three short extracts, taken almost at random from the Bishops' Bible, and notice some of the changes made in the revisions of 1611 and 1895. The copy of the Bishops' Bible used is one of the 2nd ed. of 1572. The first passage taken shall be from the description of a friend in Sir 6. And here we are struck at the outset by the advantage the later Revisers have gained in recognizing, by a system of parallelisms, the poetical character of the book. The same remark applies to Wisdom. This in turn suggests the question: why, if the principle of stichometry was admitted in the case of the Sapiential books, it should have been ignored in other parts of the Apocrypha. Why should it not have been applied to portions, at least, of Baruch, to the psalmic Prayer of Manasses, and to the Song of the Three Children? The result, as we have it, seems to point to a want of uniformity of plan.

SIRACH 6 (*Bishops' Bible*, 1572).

6 Holde frendship with many, neuerthelesse haue but one counseller of a thousande.

7 If thou gettest a freende, prooue him first, and be not hasty to geue hym credence.

8 For somme man is a freende but for his owne turne, and wyl not abide in the day of trouble.

9 And there is somme freende that turneth to enmitie, and taketh part agaynst thee: and yf he knoweth any hurt by thee, he telleth it out.

10 Agayne, somme freende is but a companion at the table, and in the day of neede he continueth not.

11 But in thy prosperitie he wyl be as thou thee selfe, and deale plainely with thy householde folke.

12 If thou be brought lowe, he will be agaynst thee, and wyl be hydden from thy face.

Here, in v.[6], for 'Holde frendship,' etc., the AV has, more literally, 'Be in peace with many'; the RV, still more exactly, 'Let those that are at peace with thee be many'—*οἱ εἰρηνεύοντές σοι ἔστωσαν πολλοί*. In v.[7], for 'If thou gettest' (Coverdale and Bish.) the AV and RV needlessly, 'If thou wouldest get.' It is exactly 'If thou art getting' (or 'acquiring'), *εἰ κτᾶσαι*. For 'to geue hym credence' (so, too, Cov.), the AV, not so well, 'to credit him.' The RV, more simply, 'to trust him.' In v.[8], for the cumbrous 'somme man is,' etc., retained by the AV, the RV has, more neatly, 'there is a friend that is so for,' etc. Not to delay over lesser matters, a more important question is, What is the friend referred to in vv.[11. 12]? Is it a faithful friend (so the Lat. 'Amicus si permanserit fixus,' followed by Coverdale, 'But a sure frende,' etc.), or is it the time-server of v.[10]? The Bish. and AV are undoubtedly right in taking the latter view, but obscure the sense by beginning v.[11] with 'But' instead of 'And.' The RV makes the meaning clear—

'And in thy prosperity he will be as thyself,
And will be bold over thy servants:
If thou shalt be brought low, he will be against thee,
And will hide himself from thy face.'

'Be bold over' is not a happy rendering of *παρρησιάσεται ἐπί*, 'will be plain-spoken with.'

SUS 52 (*Bishops' Bible, agreeing with Coverdale*).

'When they were put asunder one from another, he called one of them, and sayd vnto hym, O thou olde cankarde carle, that haste vsed thy wickednesse so long, thyne vngratious deedes whiche thou haste donne afore, are now comme to lyght.'

In this passage the interest centres on the vigorous paraphrase ('O thou . . . long') of *πεπαλαιωμένε ἡμερῶν κακῶν*. The AV has the less forcible but terser rendering, 'O thou that art waxen old in wickedness,' and this is retained in the RV. At the same time it should be observed that *παλαιοῦσθαι* is not a mere synonym of *γηράσκειν* (cf. He 8[13]), but involves the notion of becoming stale, decrepit, worn out (Lk 12[33]). Nor is 'wickedness' quite adequate as a translation of *ἡμερῶν κακῶν*. On the other hand, the rendering in the RV of *ἥκασι* by 'are come home to thee' is excellent.

WIS 7[22-25] (*Bishops' Bible, here differing much from Cov.*).

22 For Wisdome, whiche is the woorker of al thinges, hath taught me: for in her is the spirite of vnderstandyng, whiche is holy, one only, manifolde, subtile, quicke, moouing (marg. *or* liuely), vndefiled, plaine, sweete, louyng the thing that is good, sharpe, whiche can not be letted, dooing good.

23 Kinde to man, stedfast, sure, free from care, hauyng al vertues (marg. *or* power), circumspect in (marg. *or* hauyng regard of) al thynges, and passing through al vnderstandyng, cleane and subtile spirits.

24 For wisedome is nimbler than al nimble thinges, she goeth through and atteyneth to al thinges, because of her cleannesse.

25 For she is the breath of the power of God, and a pure influence flowyng from the glory of the almyghty [God]; therefore can no defiled thing comme vnto her.

The spirit of Divine Wisdom is here described by a string of epithets, numbering in the Greek text twenty-one (7×3). The rendering of the AV is a great improvement on that of the earlier versions. In the RV, where further changes are made there is a slight tendency to diffuseness. Thus *νοερόν*, 'intelligent' ('understanding,' AV), becomes 'quick of understanding'; *εὐκίνητον*, 'mobile' ('lively,' AV, with which compare the double sense of 'quick'), becomes 'freely moving'; *τρανόν*, 'penetrating,' 'distinct' ('clear,' AV), becomes 'clear in utterance,' as if to harmonize with the Lat. 'disertus.' The rendering of *μονογενές* by 'alone in kind' also seems doubtful. On the other hand, 'unhindered' is a terser rendering of *ἀκώλυτον* than 'which cannot be letted' (AV): and there are several others of this type.

One of the minor defects pointed out in the RV of the Apocr. is a want of consistency in the spelling of proper names. The Revisers, in their Preface, show themselves aware of this, and plead in mitigation the difficulty of securing 'uniformity of plan in the work of the four committees.' But the fault lies deeper. Inconsistencies are met with in the same verse. Thus in 2 Es 2[18], where the AV had consistently 'Esay and Jeremy,' the former is altered to 'Esaias' in the RV, while the latter is left untouched. In 1[40] of the same book, one solitary change is made in a string of proper names—that of 'Aggeus' to 'Aggæus'; and this is left betwixt such incongruous forms as 'Nahum and Abacuc, Sophonias, . . . Zachary and Malachy.' In Jth 8[1] 'Elcia,' as it is in the AV, is altered to 'Elkiah,' which represents neither the Hebrew form of the word (חִלְקִיָּה Ḥilkiah), nor the Greek (Ἐλκειά), nor the Latin (Elai).

More serious is the charge brought against the Revisers of neglecting the help which the Oriental Versions were capable of affording them.* For example, in Sir 25[15] they are content to reproduce the meaningless rendering of the AV, 'There is no head above the head of a serpent,' without any hint of a better sense being procurable. Yet help is not far to seek. The Syriac version, as Edersheim points out, is literally 'there is not a head *more bitter* than the head of a serpent.' And this at once suggests—what Bissell and others had already perceived—that the Hebrew word, here rendered κεφαλή, 'head,' in the Greek, was probably רֹאשׁ, which in Dt 32[33] and elsewhere denotes 'venom.' The meaning then becomes simple and natural, 'There is no poison above (more virulent than) the poison of a serpent.'

Or, again, take Sir 51[10] 'I called upon the Lord, the Father of my Lord.' If the words had been written from a Christian point of view, they would have been unexceptionable. But such was not the point of view of Jesus Ben Sirach. 'The Syriac shows us,' writes Edersheim, 'that the original text signified, 'unto the Lord, my father, O Lord.'

It is but fair to add that, in two at least of the books, Wisdom and 2 Esdras, the Versions have been freely resorted to, and with happy effect. In 2 Esdras, more particularly, the Greek original of

* Scrivener, *ib.* p. 72. Some have thought that in the RV the use of italics is overdone. See the point raised in the *JQR*, vol. viii. (1895–96), pp. 322, 323, where 'a *Greek* place of exercise' is censured as the rendering of *γυμνάσιον* in 2 Mac 4[9. 12]. In Sir 22[3] (wrongly cited as 12[3]) 'a *foolish* daughter is born to his loss,' the reviewer shows good cause for omitting *foolish*. But it is justified by the parallelism of the passage.

* In an able review of the revised Apocr., which appeared in the *Times* of Nov. 19, 1895, this charge is pressed home.

which is not extant, many passages have been corrected through this means. A single chapter will furnish sufficient instances. In 2 Es $3^{18}$ the AV has 'thou didst set fast the earth,' which does not suit the context. The verb in the Arabic version is rendered by Gildemeister *concussisti*, which justifies the translation of the RV, 'Thou . . . didst shake the earth' (as if ἔσεισας had been corrupted to ἔστησας). In v.[34] is a singular diversity of rendering: 'and so shall thy name nowhere be found but in Israel' (AV); 'and so shall it be found which way the scale inclineth' (RV). The Arabic again bears out the RV. In the Latin, as Hilgenfeld suggested, *momentum* may have got perverted to *nomen tuum*. Other examples will be found in vv.[21. 28. 30] of this same chapter. But, on the whole, the Oriental Versions might have been consulted with profit to a much greater extent than they appear to have been.

There are a few instances of conjectural emendation of the text, one or two of which deserve mention. One of the most felicitous is noted in the margin of 2 Mac $7^{36}$. By the slight change of πεπτώκασι to πεπώκασι the construction is simplified, and the sense altered from 'having endured a short pain that bringeth everlasting life, have now died under God's covenant,' to 'having endured a short pain, have now drunk of everflowing life under God's covenant.' Another, the merit of which is assigned to Dr. Hort,* is admitted to the text of 2 Mac $4^4$. It consists in reading Μενεσθέως, '*son* of Menestheus' (as in v.[21]) for the inappropriate μαίνεσθαι ἕως (or rather, ὡς), 'did rage as,' etc. In 2 Es $1^{38}$ the Revisers give 'O father' (*pater*, Cod. S) in place of 'brother' (AV). But neither is suitable, the speaker being God. Bensly suggested that the true reading in the Greek might have been περίβλεψον, *circumspice*, and that the contracted form of περί had got mistaken for one of πάτερ. But this conjecture, though ingenious, was not acted upon.†

Subjoined are some examples of changes of rendering made by the Revisers, which have met with approval, or the reverse :—

(A) *Changes generally approved.*

| AV 1611. | RV 1895. |
|---|---|
| 1 Es $1^{38}$ And he bound Joacim and the nobles. | 1 Es $1^{38}$ And Joakim bound the nobles. |
| 1 Es $4^{21}$ He sticketh not to spend his life with his wife. | 1 Es $4^{21}$ And with his wife he endeth his days. |
| 2 Es $14^{42}$ and they wrote the wonderful visions of the night that were told, which they knew not. | 2 Es $14^{42}$ and they wrote by course the things that were told them, in characters which they knew not.‡ |
| Jth $3^9$ near unto Judea (m. or *Dotea*). | Jth $3^9$ nigh unto Dotæa [*i.e.* Dothan]. |
| Ad. Est $13^5$ differing in the strange manner of their laws. | Ad. Est $13^5$ following perversely a life which is strange to our laws.§ |
| Wis $1^4$ the body that is subject unto sin. | Wis $1^4$ a body that is held in pledge‖ by sin. |
| Wis $7^3$ and fell upon the earth, which is of like nature. | Wis $7^3$ and fell upon the kindred earth (ὁμοιοπαθῆ . . . γῆν). |
| Wis $17^{18}$ a pleasing fall of water running violently. | Wis $17^{18}$ a measured fall, etc.¶ |
| Sir $15^{15}$ If thou wilt, to keep the commandments, and to perform acceptable faithfulness. | Sir $15^{15}$ If thou wilt, thou shalt keep the commandments; And to perform faithfulness is of *thine own* good pleasure.** |

* *London Quarterly Rev.*, April 1896, p. 6.

† On the value of Mr. R. L. Bensly's assistance in this section of the work, and the facts connected with his discovery of the 'missing fragment' of 2 Esdras, see a full and discriminating review of the revised Apocr. in the *Guardian* of 24th Dec. 1895.

‡ The RV translates the text adopted by Bensly (*Fourth Book of Ezra*, 1896), in which, *ex successione*, the reading of Cod. C. displaces the meaningless *excessiones* of the Latin. The correction of *noctis* to *notis* is borne out by the Eastern versions.

§ Gr. διαγωγὴν νόμων ξενίζουσαν παραλλάσσον.

‖ κατάχρεω, *oppignerato*.

¶ ῥυθμὸς ὕδατος πορευομένου βίᾳ. But is 'fall' a necessary part of the idea? The context seems to point to ῥυθμός being 'the measured *sound*' or cadence.

** The construction of the second clause in the Greek—καὶ πίστιν ποιῆσαι εὐδοκίας—is disputed.

| AV 1611. | RV 1895. |
|---|---|
| Sir $22^{11}$ make little weeping for the dead, for he is at rest. | Sir $22^{11}$ weep more sweetly for the dead, because he hath found rest.* |
| Bar $5^6$ God bringeth them unto thee exalted with glory, as children of the kingdom. | Bar $5^6$ God bringeth them in unto thee borne on high with glory, as *on* a royal throne.† |
| Pr. Man $^1$ O Lord, Almighty God of . . . etc. | Pr. Man $^1$ O Lord Almighty . . . thou God of, etc. |
| 1 Mac $2^{21}$ God forbid . . . | 1 Mac $2^{21}$ Heaven forbid . . .‡ |
| 1 Mac $11^{63}$ purposing to remove him out of the country. | 1 Mac $11^{63}$ purposing to remove him from his office.§ |
| 2 Mac $4^9$ to write them of Jerusalem *by the name of* Antiochians. | 2 Mac $4^9$ to register the inhabitants of Jerusalem as *citizens* of Antioch.‖ |
| 2 Mac $8^{20}$ the battle that they had in Babylon with the Galatians. | 2 Mac $8^{20}$ the *help given* in the land of Babylon, even the battle that was fought against the Gauls.¶ |

(B) *Changes not so approved, or not made where needed.*

| AV 1611. | RV 1895. |
|---|---|
| 1 Es $4^{39}$ With her there is no accepting of persons or rewards. | 1 Es $4^{39}$ (the same).** |
| Jth $16^{11}$ Then my afflicted shouted for joy, and my weak ones cried aloud; but they (m. *the Assyrians*) were astonished: these lifted up their voices, but they were overthrown. | Jth $16^{11}$ Then my lowly ones shouted aloud,<br>And my weak ones were terrified and crouched for fear:<br>They lifted up their voice, and they were turned to flight.†† |
| Wis $8^7$ she teacheth temperance and prudence, justice and fortitude. | Wis $8^7$ she teacheth soberness and understanding, righteousness and courage.‡‡ |
| Wis $11^{15}$ being deceived they worshipped serpents void of reason, and vile beasts. | Wis $11^{15}$ they were led astray to worship irrational reptiles and wretched vermin.§§ |
| Sir $6^2$ that thy soul be not torn in pieces as a bull [straying alone]. | Sir $6^2$ that thy soul be not torn in pieces as a bull.‖‖ |
| Sir $24^{14}$ I was exalted like a palm tree in En-gaddi. | Sir $24^{14}$ I was exalted like a palm tree on the sea shore.¶¶ |

* ἥδιον κλαῦσον κ.τ.λ., *Modicum plora* (Lat.).

† ὡς θρόνον βασιλείας. For θρόνον some MSS read υἱούς (*filios*, Lat.), followed by the AV.

‡ As the Revisers note in their Preface, the words 'God' and 'the Lord' never occur in the best Greek text of 1 Maccabees. See the point fully discussed in Fairweather and Black's ed. of 1 Mac. (*Camb. Bible*), 1897, Introd. p. 46.

§ χρείας, 'office,' is a better supported reading than χώρας, 'country,' which has very little authority.

‖ Ἀντιοχεῖς ἀναγράψαι. The rendering of the AV throughout this passage needs emending in several points. Thus δι' ἐντεύξεως (v.[8]) is translated 'by intercession,'—a meaning which the word bears in 1 Ti $2^1$, but inappropriate here. *Data per congressum occasione* is Wahl's explanation.

¶ It is with some hesitation that this passage is placed among the improved renderings. As to the construction, the words τὴν ἐν τῇ B. should probably be connected, not with ἀντίληψιν, but with the following παράταξιν. The reading of several MSS, τὴν ἐν τῇ B. πρὸς τοὺς Γαλάτας γενομένην παράταξιν, supports this view. The marg. note, 'Gr. *Galatians*,' appended to 'Gauls,' is confusing. Γαλάται may mean Galatians; but, like Κέλται, it may also mean Gauls. The question is, which does it mean here? See Bissell's note on 1 Mac $8^2$.

** The Gr. says nothing about rewards: οὐκ ἔστι παρ' αὐτῇ . . . διαφορά. Truth '*indifferently* ministers justice.'—Other passages in this book, where the rendering of the AV needs correction, are $2^{20}$ 'are now in hand' (ἐνεργεῖται, 'are being pushed on'), and $8^{91}$ 'children' (νεάνιαι, 'youths').

†† The sense is obscured by this rendering. The fault is due (as was pointed out by a reviewer in the *Times*, before quoted) to the true parallelism not being observed. When properly arranged, the first two clauses refer to the Israelites, the last two to their enemies—

Then my lowly ones raised their battle-cry (ἠλάλαξαν),
And my weak ones gave a shout (ἐβόησαν, not ἐφοβήθησαν);
And they (the Assyrians) were affrighted,
They lifted up their voice (in fear) and were overthrown

‡‡ The names of the four cardinal virtues, needlessly altered.

§§ ἄλογα ἑρπετὰ καὶ κνώδαλα εὐτελῆ.—If 'creeping things' be substituted for 'serpents,' the rendering of this clause in the AV may perhaps be judged preferable.

‖‖ The simile has no meaning. The Lat. couples *velut taurus* with *Non te extollas*, etc., preceding, and thus makes sense; but the reading differs widely from the Greek. Mr. Ball (*Variorum Apocrypha*, in loc.) suggests 'as by a bull'; comparing, for the construction, the LXX of Is $5^{17}$ and Jer $50^{11}$.

¶¶ The Vatican MS has ἐν αἰγιαλοῖς 'on beaches,' which the Revisers follow. But, as Edersheim pertinently remarks, 'palms are not supposed to attain any special height by the sea shore'; whereas En-gedi of the Amorites, as its other name Hazazon-tamar shows, was noted for its palm trees. The Cod. Sinait., by second-hand, has εν ενγαδδοισ; the Lat. *in Cades*; the Arabic 'at the fountain of Gad.' Hence the AV is most probably right. Kautzsch (*Apok. u. Pseud.*, 1900) accepts *Engeddi*.

| AV 1611. | RV 1895. |
|---|---|
| Sir 24[27] He maketh the doctrine of knowledge appear as the light. | Sir 24[27] That maketh instruction to shine forth as the light.* |
| Sus 45 a young youth. | Sus 45 (the same).† |
| 1 Mac 3[48] And laid open the book of the law, wherein the heathen had sought to paint the likeness of their images. | 1 Mac 3[48] and laid . . . concerning which the Gentiles were wont to inquire, seeking the likenesses of their idols.‡ |
| 1 Mac 6[43] and supposing that the king was upon him. | 1 Mac 6[43] and the king seemed § to be upon him. |
| 1 Mac 6[62] Then the king entered . . . but when he saw . . . he brake, etc. | 1 Mac 6[62] And the king entered . . . and he saw . . . and set at nought . . . and gave . . . ‖ |

On the whole, a study of the RV of the Apocr. cannot fail to make us aware of the great amount of work still to be done before such a translation as we desire to see can be produced: work in settling the text, in harmonizing proper names, in elucidating obscure passages.¶ But it cannot fail to make us conscious also of the vast amount of work done. That there are inequalities in the workmanship none will deny. Wisdom is better done than Sirach, 2 Mac. than 1 Maccabees. But let the fair-minded reader take any of these books, and compare carefully the rendering of a few consecutive chapters in them with that in the AV. He will meet, no doubt, with changes that he demurs to as uncalled for or even wrong. He will be perplexed, on the other hand, by the seeming neglect of alterations, where he had thought them necessary. But for one such case he will find a score, in which the new version is an improvement upon the old, in point of exactness, or finish, or consistency of diction. The Revisers have at any rate thrown down the gage, and may now say to their critics: *Si non placebit, reperitote rectius.*

x. THE 'AMERICAN REVISED' VERSION,** 1900 and 1901.—With the completion of their work in 1885, the English members of the joint Revision Company regarded their corporate existence as at an end. The American members retained their organization. In assigning the copyright to the two University Presses, it had been stipulated that for fourteen years every copy issued from those presses should contain in an appendix the readings preferred by the Americans; and that the latter, for their part, should give their sanction to no other version for the same number of years. It became evident, however, as time went on, that the American Revisers would not be content with a version in which the renderings they preferred were permanently consigned to an appendix. Accordingly they continued their labours, it might almost be said without interruption from 1885; and the result has been a fresh recension of the RV of the NT in 1900, and of the whole Bible in 1901.

The book is well printed by Thomas Nelson & Sons, of New York. Each page has two columns. The space running down the middle of each is occupied by marginal references. Various readings printed in italics are grouped at the foot of each column, or in the side margins, according to the size of the book. Along the top of each page runs a headline summarizing the contents of that page. The Apocryphal books are not included. The titles present several noticeable variations from the customary form. The NT title-page begins: 'The New Covenant, commonly called The New Testament of our Lord and Saviour,' but the title of the whole Bible (there being no separate title of the OT) does not exhibit the word 'covenant.' 'S.' for Saint is not prefixed to the names of the writers of the NT. 'The Acts' is the sole title of the historical book; The Epistle to the Hebrews bears no author's name; the term 'general' is discontinued before the Catholic Epistles; and the last book is simply 'The Revelation of John.'

In their Preface the translators indicate with clearness the ends they chiefly desire to attain. The principal of these are: that the name 'Jehovah' be inserted, wherever it occurs in the Hebrew, instead of 'LORD' or 'God,' which had hitherto taken its place. That 'Sheol' in the OT and 'Hades' in the NT be used to express that unseen world which had been imperfectly or inconsistently denoted by 'the grave,' 'the pit,' 'Gehenna.' Throughout the NT they would replace 'Holy Ghost' by 'Holy Spirit.' The translators desire to bring the diction as much as possible into harmony with that in use at the present time. To this end they would always write 'who' for 'which,' when referring to persons; 'are' for 'be,' in using the indicative; and so on in many other instances.

It is obvious that in this last respect consistency cannot be ensured at once; and fault will no doubt be found with the new revision on the ground of want of uniformity.

To advert for a moment to the special objects first spoken of as desirable, there can be little doubt that the restoration of the name 'Jehovah' will be a gain, wherever special stress is laid on it as that of the God of the Hebrews, as in Ex 3[14. 15]. But in many other passages, notably in the Psalms, the frequent repetition of the name cannot but be felt a burden—a result which was avoided under the old system by the use of two short but impressive words, 'Lord' and 'God.'*

Whether the words 'Sheol' and 'Hades,' one or both, will ever become naturalized in the English Bible is not easy to forecast. We have assimilated 'Sabbath' and 'Pentecost,' and many more such terms. Why, it may be asked, not these also? Experience alone can decide.

So in the case of 'Holy Spirit' and 'Holy Ghost.' There can be no question about the intrinsic merit of the former. The one great objection to making the change is that 'Holy Ghost' has become so deeply embedded in the creeds and formularies of the Church that it would be difficult

* A comparison of vv.[25-27] shows that the similes are taken from rivers:—Pishon and Tigris, Euphrates and Jordan, *x* and Gihon. Hence, from considerations of symmetry, *x* should represent, not 'light,' or anything of the kind, but the name of a river. Edersheim thinks that the Greek translator had כָּאֹר before him, which in Am 8[8] and elsewhere means not 'as the light,' but 'as the river' (*i.e.* the Nile), as if כַּיְאֹר; and that he wrongly took the former rendering.—See the review in the *London Quarterly*, before cited, p. 7.

† Gr. παιδαρίου νεωτέρου, 'a young lad' (Bissell). Cf. Jn 6[9].

‡ The RV follows the best-supported reading of the Greek. But Fritzsche, on the authority of some cursives, with the Complut. and the Aldine of 1518, inserts τοῦ ἐπιγράφειν ἐπ' αὐτῶν before τὰ ὁμοιώματα. Such a mode of desecrating the sacred books would be intelligible. Other explanations may be seen in Bissell. All that is here contended for is, that the RV takes no account of the plural in περὶ ὧν, makes ἐξηρεύνων do double duty for 'were wont to inquire, seeking,' and gives a very obscure sense.

§ The AV appears to have followed the reading of some cursives, ᾠήθη, 'he (Eleazar) supposed.' The RV adopts the common reading ὤφθη, better taken impersonally (see Grimm), 'it seemed that,' just as in the Lat., 'et visum est ei quod . . .'

‖ This is cited as an instance of the principle, very closely observed throughout this book, of *parataxis*, or co-ordination, as distinguished from subordination, of clauses. By retaining this peculiarity, the Revisers have reproduced more exactly the form of the original, but at the cost of sacrificing English idiom.

¶ A help towards this has been gained by the introduction, in 1898, of marginal references throughout the RV.

** 'The | Holy Bible containing the | Old and New Testaments | translated out of the original tongues | being the version set forth A.D. 1611 | compared with the most ancient authorities and revised | A.D. 1881-1885 | newly Edited by the American Revision Committee | A.D. 1901 | Standard Edition | New York | Thomas Nelson & Sons.' |

* In Pss 1-41 the name 'Jehovah' occurs 272 times, and in Pss 90-150 it occurs 339 times (see Kirkpatrick, *Psalms*, Introduction, p. 55).

to displace it. This holds good of the American Church as well as of our own.

It will perhaps be most serviceable to the reader to set down a few passages in which the new recension may be instructively compared with its immediate predecessor. It will be noticed in how many instances the American Version reverts to that of 1611.

Ec 12[5] 'desire shall fail' (Am. RV); 'the caper-berry shall fail' (RV). This would not be intelligible without the help of a commentator. It is explained that caper-berries were eaten before meals to give a whet to the appetite. If they failed to do so, it might be a sign of the coming on of old age.

Dt 32[14] 'with the finest of the wheat' (Am. RV); 'with the fat of kidneys of wheat' (RV, retaining the Hebrew figure of speech, by which the choicest parts of an animal for sacrifice were taken to express what was finest in other objects. See Ex 29[13]).*

Zec 4[14] 'these are the two anointed ones' (Am. RV); 'the two sons of oil' (RV, retaining the Hebraism in its unmodified form).

Jer 17[9] 'The heart is . . . exceedingly corrupt' (Am. RV); 'the heart is . . . desperately sick' (RV).

Jg 5[12] 'lead away thy captives' (Am. RV); 'lead thy captivity captive' (RV).

Pr 13[15] 'the way of the transgressor is hard' (Am. RV); 'the way of the treacherous is rugged' (RV).

Ac 17[22] 'Ye men of Athens, in all things I perceive that ye are very religious' (Am. RV); 'somewhat superstitious' (RV). It is noticeable how the influence of the Vulgate has drawn all the English Versions, down to the AV inclusive, into rendering δεισιδαιμονεστέρους by some form of 'superstitious.' But it is certain that St. Paul would not have raised a prejudice against himself by using an offensive term at the very outset of his address. Hence 'religious' (a sense in which the word is used by Josephus) is wisely taken as its equivalent. But in prefixing 'very' the American translators obscure the delicate shade of meaning in the comparative.

Ph 2[6] 'who, existing in the form of God, counted not the being on an equality with God a thing to be grasped' (Am. RV); 'who, being . . . counted it not a prize . . .' (RV). This rendering of ὑπάρχων by 'existing' is a distinct improvement on the 'being' of the RV. 'Prize' (RV) renders more neatly than the later equivalent the ἁρπαγμόν of the Greek, but not so literally (see Moule's note on the passage). 'Grasped' should rather be 'grasped at.'

1 Th 2[6] 'might have claimed authority' (Am. RV); 'might have been burdensome' (RV, with 'claimed honour' in the margin). The Greek is ambiguous, δυνάμενοι ἐν βάρει εἶναι. The use of ἐπιβαρῆσαι in v.[9] in the sense of 'prove a burden to,' seems to carry ἐν βάρει εἶναι with it. But, as Ellicott points out, this is counterbalanced by the close connexion of the clause with δόξαν, so that the American Revisers may be right.

2 Ti 2[26] 'having been taken captive by him unto his will' (Am. RV); 'having been taken captive by the Lord's servant unto the will of God' (RV). In aiming at perspicuity the RV has given a comment rather than a translation. The Am. RV leaves an ambiguity in the pronouns 'him' and 'his.' A point would be gained if 'His' were written with a capital letter.

He 11[5] 'for he hath had witness borne to him that before his translation he had been well-pleasing unto God' (Am. RV); 'before his translation he hath had witness borne to him that he had been well-pleasing unto God' (RV). The tenses speak for themselves.

He 11[1] 'now faith is assurance of things hoped for, a conviction of things not seen' (Am. RV); 'now faith is the assurance of things hoped for, the proving of things not seen' (RV). The former of these renderings has been praised as much the better of the two. But, as Westcott points out, 'it is difficult to suppose that ἔλεγχος can express a state'; and he himself gives 'substance' and 'test' for ὑπόστασις and ἔλεγχος.

If, in the above examples, the advantage may be claimed for the American RV, the same can hardly be said in the case of those which follow :—

Ex 20[13] 'thou shalt not kill' (Am. RV); 'thou shalt do no murder' (Prayer-Book Version and RV). It is interesting to observe that each of these newest renderings has gone back to an earlier pattern,—the RV to that in the Prayer-Book, and the Am. RV to that of 1611. There is this merit in the last, that it harmonizes with the word used in our Lord's summary of the Commandments (Mt 19[18]). But the word 'kill' does not necessarily imply a criminal act, and in so far the rendering of the Am. RV is inadequate.

Ps 24[6] 'This is the generation of them that seek after him, that seek thy face, even Jacob' (Am. RV); '. . . that seek thy face, O God of Jacob' (RV). The difficulty lies in supplying the ellipse 'O God of.' It is admitted that, if the Massoretic text be followed, the first of these renderings is the right one; but in that case, as Kirkpatrick points out, 'the construction is harsh; a vocative is needed after *thy face*; and *Jacob* does not by itself convey this sense.' His conclusion is that 'the AVm and RV rightly follow the LXX, Vulg., and Syr. in reading "O God of Jacob."'

Ps 148[12] 'young men and virgins' (Am. RV); 'young men and maidens' (RV). What is gained by the change?

Lk 24[26] 'Behooved it not the Christ to suffer these things, and to enter into his glory?' (Am. RV). Except in the spelling of the first word this rendering repeats that of the RV, and is therefore open to the same objection. By retaining the coordinate construction with 'and' instead of the subordinate, the sense is missed. It should have been 'by suffering these things to enter into his glory,' or 'to suffer these things and so enter,' etc. This will be seen more clearly by comparing such a sentence as Mt 23[23] 'these things ought ye to have done, and not to leave the others undone'; which would appear to charge the Pharisees with neglecting the ceremonial observances of the law. The sense requires: 'without therefore leaving the others undone.'

Ac 8[32] 'The passage of Scripture' (Am. RV); 'The place of the Scripture' (RV). The change of 'place' to 'passage' has not been made by the Am. RV in Lk 4[17].

Gal 1[10] 'am I now seeking the favor of men, or of God?' (Am. RV); 'am I now persuading men, or God?' (RV). While it is admitted that a verb of kindred meaning with πείθω should be supplied by zeugma to govern θεόν, it does not seem necessary that the meaning of πείθω with ἀνθρώπους should also be thus modified.

Tit 1[8] 'given to hospitality' (Am. RV and RV) for the simple 'hospitable' (φιλόξενον).

He 9[16.17] In this passage διαθήκη is rendered 'testament,' not 'covenant,' both by the Am. RV and the RV. But, as Westcott has shown, 'there is not the least trace of the meaning "testament" in the Greek Old Scriptures, and the idea of a

* For this and one or two other examples the writer is indebted to an appreciative article by Professor H. M. Whitney, in the April number of the *Bibliotheca Sacra* (Ohio), 1902.

"testament" was indeed foreign to the Jews till the time of the Herods.'

Ja $1^{17}$ 'every good gift and every perfect gift' (Am. RV, in this agreeing with the AV); 'every good gift and every perfect boon' (RV). This latter rendering fails because 'boon' is not a cognate word to 'gift,' as δώρημα in the original is to δόσις. The American Revisers, in making 'gift' serve for both these terms, confess themselves unable to surmount the difficulty.

Rev $2^{24}$ 'as they are wont to say' (Am. RV); 'as they say' (RV). The latter is preferable, the Greek being simply ὡς λέγουσιν.

The inference to be drawn from this brief comparison of renderings, as well as from a more general survey of the work, is that it is premature as yet to call it, as is done on the title-page, a 'standard' edition. It seems evident that, even if the principles of the latest Revisers be admitted, a considerable time must elapse before they can be thoroughly carried out in practice. An illustration taken from one single department of the subject will suffice. In the case of archaic or obsolete words much progress has been made. Many a 'howbeit' has given place to 'yet'; 'or ever' to 'before'; 'evil entreated' to 'ill-treated'; 'meat' to 'food'; and the like. But how many still remain! 'Gendereth' is altered to 'bringeth forth' in Gal $4^{24}$, but left unaltered in Job $38^{29}$. 'High-minded,' which is now an epithet of praise, is left in 1 Ti $6^{17}$ in the sense which it bore in the days of the Gunpowder Plot. 'Took knowledge of' for 'recognized' still remains in Ac $4^{13}$. 'Nephews' is rightly changed to 'grandchildren' in 1 Ti $5^{4}$; but 'piety,' in the Latin sense of the word, still remains in the same passage.

We may see from these few instances that it is vain to hope that a standard edition of the English Bible will be soon forthcoming; and still more vain to dream that the desired object has been attained already. That many improvements have been made upon the Revision of 1885, none would wish to deny. It is reasonable to anticipate that, when the next Revision is accomplished on this side the Atlantic, it may in its turn show a superiority in some respects over that of 1901. But the end to be kept in view is not that the scholars of the two countries should pass and repass each other 'adversi spatiis,' but that they should advance 'facta pariter nunc pace.' The aspiration to which utterance was given in the Preface to the Joint-Revision of the NT in 1881, is not yet, we trust, out of season—that the labours of the fellow-workers, 'thus happily united, may be permitted to bear a blessing to both countries, and to all English-speaking people throughout the world.'

*** In concluding this article, the writer desires to acknowledge his indebtedness to his sons (especially the Rev. J. M. Lupton, assistant master in Marlborough College) for much valuable help in the course of it.

LITERATURE.—I. Abrahams, art. on the RV of the Apocr. in *JQR*, vol. viii. [1895–1896] pp. 321–329; Chr. Anderson, *Annals of the English Bible*, 1845; E. Arber, *The First Printed English NT*, 1871; *The Athenæum*, 1885, pp. 500–502, 562–565 (review of Mombert), *ib.* 1888, p. 243 (art. on the Bishops' Bible), 1889, ii. p. 246 (review of Edgar); Bagster's *English Hexapla* (Introduction), n.d.; the Ven. Bede, *Works*, ed. Plummer, 1896; J. A. Beet, 'RV of NT' in *Expos.* 2nd ser. ii., iii.; W. Bender, *Der Reformator J. Wiclif als Bibelübersetzer*, 1884; *Bibliotheca Sacra* (Andover), April 1858 and 1859, pp. 56–81 (early edd. of AV), *ib.* (Ohio), April 1899 (Cædmon); E. C. Bissell, *The Apocrypha with a Revised Translation*, n. d.; J. H. Blunt, art. on Eng. Bib. in *Encyc. Brit.*[9]; Bosworth-Waring, Pref. to *The Gothic and A. S. Gospels*, 1865; H. Bradshaw, *Godfried v. d. Haghen*, 1886; British Museum, *Cat. of . . . Bibles*, pt. i. 1892; Hugh Broughton, *Works*, ed. by John Lightfoot, 1662; J. W. Burgon, *The Revision Revised*, 1883; Cædmon's *Metrical Paraphrase*, ed. B. Thorpe, 1832; E. Cardwell, *Documentary Annals*, 1844, *Synodalia*, 1844, *Hist. of Conferences*[3], 1849; J. G. Carleton, *The Part of Rheims in the Making of the Eng. Bible*, 1902; *The Catholic World* (New York), 1871, pp. 149–170; *The Christian Examiner and General Review* (Boston), 1833, vol. xiv. pp. 327–371 (Eng. VSS); *Church Quarterly*, July 1885 (on RV of OT); T. K. Cheyne on RV Psalms and Isaiah, in *Expos.*, 3rd ser. v., vi., vii.; A. S. Cook, *Biblical Quotations in Old Eng. Prose Writers* (Introd. on Old Eng. Bibl. Versions), 1898; F. C. Cook, '*Deliver us from Evil,' a Letter to the Bishop of London*, 1881, *The Rev. Version of the First Three Gospels*, 1882, *A Second Letter to the . . . Bp. of London*, 1882; H. Cotton, *List of Editions of the Bible*, 1852, *Rhemes and Doway*, 1855; M. Coverdale, *Memorials of* (anon.), 1838; A. B. Davidson, 'Job in RV,' *Expos.*, 3rd ser. iv.; R. Demaus, *Wm. Tyndale: A Biography*, 1886; J. R. Dore, *Old Bibles*, 1888; S. R. Driver 'Gen. to Josh. in RV,' *Expos.*, 3rd ser. ii.; John Eadie, *The Eng. Bible*, 1876; Eadwine's *Canterbury Psalter*, ed. by F. Harsley, pt. i. 1889; *Edinburgh Review*, Oct. 1885 (RV of OT); A. Edgar, *The Bibles of England*, 1889; C. J. Ellicott, *Considerations on Revision*, 1870; T. S. Evans, 'Crit. Remarks on RV,' in *Expos.*, 2nd ser. iii., v.; articles by various writers on the Failure of the RV, in *Expos. Times*, iii., iv.; F. Field, *Notes on the Translation . . .*, 1899; Forshall-Madden, *The Holy Bible* (Wyclifite Versions), 1850; F. Fry, *Description of the Great Bible*, 1539 . . ., 1865, *The Bible by Coverdale*, 1867, *Bibliogr. descr. of the edd. of NT*, 1878; E. Gasner, *Beitr. z. Entwickelungsgang d. neuengl. Schriftsprache . . . wie sie auf Wyclif u. Purvey zurückgehen soll*, 1891; F. A. Gasquet, *Old English Bible*, 1897; R. Gell, *Essay toward the Amendment* (of the AV), 1659; F. Graz, *Beitr. z. Textkritik Cædmons*, 1896; *The Guardian*, 16th Feb. 1870 (Action of Convocation), 27th Nov. 1895 (letters on use of RV), 24th Dec. 1895 (review of RV of Apocr.); E. Harwood, *A Liberal Tr. of the NT*, 1768; J. Heywood, *State of the Authorized Bible Revision*, 1860, *The Bible and its Revisers*, 1857; H. W. Hoare, artt. on the Eng. Bible in the *Nineteenth Cent.*, May 1898, April 1899, *Evolution of the Eng. Bible*, 1901, 2nd ed. 1902; T. W. Hunt, *Cædmon's Exodus and Daniel*; J. Jacobs, 'Rev. OT' in *Bibl. Archæology*, 1894; A. C. Jennings and W. H. Lowe, 'A Crit. Estimate of RV of OT,' *Expos.*, 3rd ser. ii.; B. H. Kennedy, *Ely Lectures*, 1882; F. G. Kenyon, *Our Bible and the Anc. MSS*, 1895; W. Kilburne, *Dangerous Errors in . . . Bibles*, 1659; J. A. Kingdon, *Incidents in the Lives of Tho. Poyntz and Ric. Grafton* (priv. printed), 1895; A. F. Kirkpatrick, 'Judges to Neh. in RV,' *Expos.*, 3rd ser. i., ii., iii., v.; M. Konrath, *Beitr. z. Erkl. u. Textkr. des William v. Schorham*, 1878; G. V. Lechler, *John Wyclif*, tr. by P. Lorimer, 1884; J. Lewis, *Life of Pocock*, Pref. p. 13 ff., *Complete Account of Translations . . .*, 2nd ed. 1739; J. B. Lightfoot, *On a Fresh Revn. of the English NT*, 1871 (3rd ed. 1891, reprinting Letters in the *Guardian*, 7th, 14th, 21st Sept. 1881); W. J. Loftie, *A Century of Bibles*, 1872; *London Quarterly Review*, 1896 (art. on the 'RV of the Apocr.'); R. Lovett, *The Printed Eng. Bible, 1525–1885*, 1895; M'Clellan, *Four Gospels* (Introd.), 1875; M'Clintock-Strong, *Cycl.* (art. on Eng. VSS), 1873; G. P. Marsh, *Lectures on the Eng. Language*; E. Miller, *The Oxford Debate on the Textual Crit. of the NT*, 1897; G. Milligan, *The Eng. Bible, a Sketch of its History*, 1895, and art. on VERSIONS (ENG.) in vol. iv.; J. I. Mombert, *Eng. VSS of the Bible*, 1883; *The Month*, June 1897, pp. 573–586, July 1897, pp. 43–62 (Rheims and Douay); Sir T. More, *A Dyaloge*, 1530; W. F. Moulton, *The Hist. of the Eng. Bible*, 2nd ed. 1884; S. Newth, *Lectures on Bib. Revision*, 1881; *Notes and Queries*, 5th ser. x. pp. 261, 262 (Trevisa); G. Offor, MS Collections (Brit. Mus., Addl. and Eg. MSS 26,670–26,673); *The Ormulum*, ed. R. M. White, 1878; A. G. Paspati, *Remarks on the RV of the NT*, 1883; T. H. Pattison, *Hist. of the Eng. Bible*, 1894; Percy Society's Publications, *Religious Poems of Wm. de Shoreham*, 1849; T. J. Pettigrew, *Bibliotheca Sussexiana*, vol. ii. 1839; C. Plummer, Pref. to *Ven. Bædæ Hist. Eccl.* 1896; E. H. Plumptre, art. on the AV in Smith's *DB*; N. Pocock, artt. in *The Bibliographer*, vols. i.–iv. on the Bishops' and Genevan Bibles; R. L. Poole, *Wyclif and Movements for Reform*, 1886; Prime Wendell, *Fifteenth Cent. Bibles*, 1888; *The Quarterly Review*, April 1870, p. 129 ff., Oct. 1885, pp. 281-329 (RV of OT); R. Rolle, of Hampole, *The Psalter . . .*, ed. H. R. Bramley, 1884; W. G. Rutherford, *St. Paul's Ep. to the Romans* (Introd.), 1900; W. Sanday, 'RV of NT' in *Expos.*, 2nd ser. ii.; P. Schaff, *Companion to Gr. Test.* 1883; J. Scholefield, *Hints for an Improved Transl. . . .*, 3rd ed. 1849; F. H. A. Scrivener, *Supplement to the AV*, 1845, *The Authorized Ed. of the Eng. Bib.* 1884; W. Selwyn, *Notes on the Proposed Amendment of the AV*, 1856; W. S. Simpson, *Catalogue of St. Paul's Cathedral Library*, 1893; W. W. Skeat, *The Holy Gospels in Anglo-Saxon . . .*, ed. by W. W. S. 1871–1877, Pref. to *The NT in English* (Purvey's rev.), 1879, *Dialect of Wyclif's Bible* (in Trans. of Philolog. Soc., pt. i. for 1895–1896); W. E. Smith, *A Study of the Great 'She' Bible*, 1890; H. Stevens, *Cat. of Bibles in the Caxton Celebr.* 1877; Stevenson-Waring, *The Lindisfarne and Rushworth Glosses* (Surtees Society's Publns., Nos. 28, 39, 43, 48); E. Thwaites, *Heptateuchus . . .*, 1698; B. Thorpe [see above, 'Cædmon']; *The Times*, 19th Nov. 1895 (review of RV of Apocr.); W. Tindale, see Lansdowne MSS (Brit. Mus.), 979, f. 150; R. C. Trench, *On the AV of the NT, in connexion with some Rec. Proposals for its Revn.*, 2nd ed. 1859; M. H. Turk, *The Legal Code of King Ælfred the Great*, 1893; C. J. Vaughan, *Auth. or Rev.* 1882; R. S. Watson, *Cædmon . . .*, 1875; B. F. Westcott, *A Gen. View of the Hist. of the Eng. Bible*[2], 1872, *Bible in the Church*, 1875, *Some Lessons of the RV of the NT*, 1897; S. W. Whitney, *Revisers' Gr. Text*; Lea Wilson, *Bibles . . . in the Collection of*, 1845; John Wright, *Early Bibles of America*, 1893; J. Wyclif, *English Works* of (ed. by F. D. Matthew, 1880), *de Eccl. Notione* (ed. F. Wiegand, 1891), *Opus Evangelicum*, 1895.

J. H. LUPTON.

## DEVELOPMENT OF DOCTRINE IN THE APOCRYPHAL PERIOD.—

SOURCES.—

B.C. 200–100: Sirach; Daniel; Ethiopic Enoch 1–36, 83–90, 91–104; Baruch 1–3[8]; Tobit; Sibylline Oracles (part of Book iii.); Testaments of the Twelve Patriarchs (B.C. 140–A.D. 30); Book of Jubilees; Judith.

B.C. 100–1: Ethiopic Enoch 37–70; 1 Maccabees; Psalms of Solomon; 2 Maccabees.

A.D. 1–100: Assumption of Moses; Book of Wisdom; Philo; Slavonic Enoch; 4 Maccabees; Josephus; Apocalypse of Baruch; Book of Baruch (from 3[9] onwards); 2 (4) Esdras; Ascension of Isaiah; Shemoneh Esreh.

[In the above list of authorities the Targums are not included. They undoubtedly contain fragments as old as the time of John Hyrcanus; but as they were not published until, perhaps, the 3rd or 4th cent. A.D., they must obviously be used with caution as sources for estimating the development of Jewish doctrine during our period].

Introduction.
1. The question stated.
2. Relation of later Judaism to foreign systems of thought.
   (1) Persian influence.
   (2) Greek influence.
3. Decay of the older Hebraism.
4. Classification of the Apocrypha according to the national influences under which they were composed.

i. THE DOCTRINE OF GOD.
1. The OT position.
2. The position of this doctrine in Jewish writings of the Apocryphal period.
3. The extent to which foreign influences affected the doctrine of God as reflected in these writings.
4. Popular superstitions regarding the name Jahweh.
5. The Christian doctrine of God.

ii. THE DOCTRINE OF THE WISDOM.
1. In OT presented not only as human, but also as Divine.
2. Hellenizing of the Heb. *Ḥokhma* in the Alexandrian Wisdom of Solomon.
3. The Logos of Philo.
4. The Memra of the Targums.
5. NT conception of the Logos.

iii. ANGELOLOGY AND DEMONOLOGY.
A. Angelology.
1. OT doctrine of angels.
2. Post-exilic development of angelology on Persian lines seen in (1) Daniel, (2) Tobit, 2 Mac., 2 (4) Esdras.
3. Conception of elemental angels in post-canonical Jewish literature.
4. Doctrine of angels as held by the Essenes and by Philo.
5. Denial of angels by the Sadducees.

B. Demonology.
1. The position as reflected in the earlier OT literature.
2. The Satan of Job, Zechariah, the Chronicler, and the Similitudes of Enoch.
3. The doctrine of evil spirits in the Apocrypha and in Josephus.
4. Demonology of the Alexandrian Jews.
5. Development of demonology in the Jewish pseudepigrapha.

C. Relation of the religious consciousness of our Lord to current beliefs about angels and demons.

iv. ANTHROPOLOGY. Teaching of the Apocrypha and Pseudepigrapha as to—
1. Psychological nature of man.
2. Original moral condition of man.
3. Immortality of the soul.
4. The first sin and its consequences.
5. Free will and foreordination.
6. Ethics: (1) Palestinian; (2) Alexandrian.
7. Final shape given by Christian doctrine to Jewish anthropology

v. THE MESSIANIC HOPE.
1. Meaning of the expression.
2. The OT position.
3. The Messianic idea in the Apocrypha.
4. Transformation into Apocalyptic ideas.
5. The Messianic idea in later Palestinian books.
6. The Messianic expectation in Hellenistic Judaism.
7. Peculiarities of the later Messianic hope.
8. Question as to retrogression of Messianic idea during the post-Prophetic period.

vi. ESCHATOLOGY.
1. Position of eschatological doctrine in OT.
2. Post-canonical development, with special reference to—
   (1) Future judgment.
   (2) Realms of the departed: (*a*) Sheol; (*b*) Paradise; (*c*) Heaven; (*d*) Gehenna.
   (3) The Resurrection.
3. Question as to the influence of Zoroastrianism upon Jewish eschatology.

Literature.

*Introduction.*—1. *The question stated.*—Our first concern in discussing the subject of doctrinal development in the Apocryphal period is to get a clear conception of the true bearings of the question. The field over which our investigation is to extend consists practically of the intervening space between the Old and New Testaments. We have to deal with a transition period, to be considered with due reference both to what precedes and what follows; we are to look back on the OT, and forward to the NT. In short, we must have the OT basis from which to start, and the NT position to which we are to be led up, both in full vision. The question might be broadly stated, then, as the relation of Jewish views of theology at this time to the Old and New Testaments—the special point to be elucidated being whether and how far the Apocrypha and other non-canonical pre-Christian Jewish writings bridge the distance between them. They do so historically; do they do so doctrinally? Is there evidence of real doctrinal development?

The student of theology will hardly say there is no felt want of such a bridge. While the NT stands most intimately related to the OT, and would be a real enigma without it, it is yet true that the difference between them is of the most marked description. And many, instead of following the somewhat doubtful course of leaping from the one to the other, naturally prefer to tread the path, indistinct and curiously winding though it be, that undoubtedly leads through the gloom of these 400 years into the full-orbed light of the Christian era. They claim that amid much that is admittedly of questionable value, and amid much to which distinct objection can be taken in these Apocryphal writings, the latter nevertheless furnish stepping-stones by means of which it is possible gradually to climb the long ascent from Malachi to Matthew. Nor is there anything *a priori* extravagant in this claim. In virtue of its own inherent living power of growth, and in accordance with the divinely chosen method of its gradual delivery to man, revealed truth must have gained something, if not in actual content, at least in clearness of expression, during such a period. As a matter of fact we find that, in the two centuries immediately preceding the Christian era, Jewish literature, though obviously past its prime, has still a measure of vigorous life. It throbs with patriotic feeling, of which indeed (in the Books of Maccabees) it reflects perhaps the most signal instances on record. It shows also that during these 'Middle Ages of sacred history' the lamp of true piety continued to burn, and, so long as that was the case, scriptural doctrine could not altogether have stood still, but must of necessity have undergone some development in its application to the circumstances of the age. And this theological development must have made itself felt in the Jewish religious books of the period. As will be seen from the list of authorities given above, these numbered many more than those included in the OT Apocrypha. Among other extant works falling within the limits of our period are the remarkable and mysterious Palestinian *Book of Enoch* (preserved in Ethiopic), parts of which date from the 2nd cent. B.C.; the Græco-Jewish-Christian *Sibylline Oracles*, which, from a large Jewish nucleus issued from Alexandria towards the middle of the same century, grew first under Jewish and subsequently under Christian hands, into a 'chaotic wilderness' of fourteen books; the *Book of Jubilees*, assigned by the most recent scholarship to *c.* 130 B.C.; the *Psalms of Solomon*, dating from B.C. 70–40; and the *Assumption of Moses*, which appears to have been written practically at the dawn of the Christian era (A.D. 7–30). These and other pseudepigrapha dating from the early centuries of our era (*e.g.* the *Apocalypse of Baruch* and the *Ascension of Isaiah*) are mostly apocalyptic, and, while throwing a valuable supplementary light on the religious views of the Jewish people in the time of our Lord, do not take rank with the 'deutero-canonical' books. Although they are sometimes termed apocryphal (Iren. *Hær.* i. 20), they form no part of the OT Apocrypha properly so called, and perhaps we may take the latter as representing on the whole the continuity both of literature and dogma. At the same time, for the sake of completeness, it will be necessary to include in our historical survey material supplied by the pre-Christian Jewish literature generally, as well as by the writings of Philo and Josephus, which date from the 1st cent. of the Christian era.

The history of the Church, moreover, no less than the expansive power of Divine truth, leads us to expect that there should be such a bridge between OT and NT doctrine. Almost any 400 years of Church history have witnessed important new developments of doctrine; and every age has found occasion to sift and discuss many points that never suggested themselves to those of an earlier time. Our own religious perspective has distinctly changed within a relatively shorter period. And, *mutatis mutandis*, is it at all likely that the Jewish theology of the post-Prophetic period took no colour of its own from the special circumstances, struggles, and aspirations of the age? No doubt it is true, as Langen * points out, that the OT could never have developed itself into the NT, as the seed does into the plant, seeing that a new and miraculous fact which could not develop, but was accomplished by Divine statute at a definite moment (viz. the Incarnation), came in and sharply defined the boundary line between the old and new economies, and expressed their essential difference of character. But, though the term *development* be inapplicable here, it is otherwise as regards doctrine, which must always of necessity develop itself. This is a natural law in the spiritual world which will not be denied. Are we, then, to suppose that this organic development within the sphere of Jewish theology met with a sudden check after the issue of the books composing the Heb. Canon,—ceased, in fact, in order to the subsequent sudden appearance of quite new truths? Such a thing, to say the least, would be a great anomaly, and to many the Apocryphal books have furnished some tangible and valuable links in the chain of biblical truth.

Certainly, none can with reason refuse to believe that in the eventful period of Jewish history to which they owe their origin there was produced, and in these works preserved, something of significance for the universal Church of God. Yet they have been denounced as worse than worthless. Few will now accept the bitterly hostile verdict of the Edinburgh Bible Society in 1825, that 'the whole work (*sic*) is replete with instances of vanity, flattery, idle curiosity, affectation of learning, and other blemishes; with frivolous, absurd, false, superstitious, and contradictory statements.'† For while the Apocrypha admittedly do contain inaccuracies, offences against good taste, and even serious deviations from 'sound doctrine,' it is ridiculous to speak of the whole collection as 'bad in itself, bad in its effects, bad in every point of view,'* or as a 'miserable heap of fables and romances, of pitiful fooleries and base falsehoods, of vile impostures and gross immoralities.'† Such an estimate of the main portion of the religious literature of the centuries preceding the advent of Christ amounts to the negation of the great law of spiritual evolution, according to which utter stagnation in the matter of doctrinal development is a virtual impossibility. The developments of such a period may have been strange, retrograde, and misguided, as well as normal, progressive, and healthy; but development of some sort there must have been. And we must look for the reflexion of this, such as it was, in the Apocryphal literature as the written repository of the religious thought of the age. Reasonable as this view of the case appears to be, it has been too often either quite overlooked or vehemently rejected. By those who concede to these books no right save that of being anathematized, it will of course be considered monstrous to take account of them at all in connexion with biblical doctrine. And this class has had, and probably still has, its representatives in various quarters. For rooted aversion to the Apocrypha has not been confined to Scotland. A German writer ‡ rather wildly says, 'They tear asunder the code of Divine revelation'; but the real question, which we must not allow to be obscured by a statement of this sort, is, How does NT doctrine stand related to that of the Hebrew Canon? Is there any middle ground? And do these post-canonical books furnish us with that middle ground? Do they show us any doctrines in a transition stage of development between the OT and NT positions? 'Science,' says Reuss, 'can never ignore or neglect with impunity the regular succession and natural connexion of facts, and it acts under a singular illusion when it attempts to bring together the two ends, after cutting away the thread which unites them' (*Apostolic Age*, i. p. 70, Eng. tr.). May not the Apocrypha in this case be the uniting thread which some have been too eager to cut away?

2. Another interesting and important factor here enters into the discussion, viz. *the relation in which the later Judaism stood to foreign systems of thought*, for it was undoubtedly owing to the influence of these, combined with a certain decay of the older Hebraism itself, that it assumed its distinctive character.

The choice of Israel did not absolutely exclude the rest of the human race from being the objects of Divine regard (Jn 1[9]). On the contrary, it was distinctly contemplated that they should ultimately be received into the larger Israel of the Christian Church (Mt 8[11], Jn 10[16]). While the Jews were selected for the discharge of the missionary function of transmitting the Divine revelation to the world, God was also by His providence gradually and surely preparing the world for Christianity. Consequently, the idea of other nations making some contribution towards the sum-total of the religious knowledge attained in pre-Christian times is not one to be summarily rejected as unworthy of consideration. When in Jn 1[9] Christ is designated 'the true Light, which lighteth every man that cometh into the world,' may we not warrantably trace to this source the reasonings and yearnings of a Socrates for a future and endless life, and the profound thoughts of a Plato concerning the immortality of the soul? After a struggle with his native Jewish prejudices, the Apostle Peter perceived that 'God is no respecter of persons: but in every nation he that feareth God and worketh righteousness is accepted with him' (Ac 10[34f.]). That other nations besides the Jews had at least some measure of light is therefore a fact which should be thoughtfully acknowledged rather than grudgingly admitted. It can in no way derogate from the supreme honour due to the religion of Jesus Christ to recognize that Confucius taught obedience to parents; that Buddha based his system of morality on the notion of the equality of all, and enjoined the widest toleration; that Zoroaster, so far from being accurately described as a 'famous impostor' and 'very crafty knave,' was a teacher of monotheism and of many valuable ethical principles; or that in

* *Judenthum in Palästina zur Zeit Christi*, p. 64.
† *Statement relative to the circulation of the Apocrypha* (1825), Appendix, p. 8.

* *Second Statement*, etc. (1826), p. 60.
† *Rev. Andrew Lothian*, at annual meeting of E.B.S., 1827.
‡ Keerl, *Das Wort Gottes und die Apokryphen des AT*, p. 17.

ancient Egypt men were familiar with the conceptions of immortality and eternity. These were only so many 'past stars getting light from the everlasting sun.' All that was true or good in these ancient faiths was derived from Jesus Christ. The providential shaking together of the nations which took place during the centuries immediately preceding the Christian era enabled each to pour what contribution it could into the great treasury of religious thought and sentiment. The fusion of the diverse tendencies and thoughts of East and West was not without its effect in developing in a forward direction (though not uniformly so) the truth that God had communicated to His people; and the constant intermingling of ideas that took place was, under God, destined to result in nothing less than the inbringing of a cosmopolitan religion, equally suitable for all climates and peoples, and capable of assimilating all that was noblest and purest in human aspiration and culture. Whatever of real advance in doctrinal development is anywhere traceable during this important and formative period is therefore still to be attributed to the revealing Spirit and guiding hand of Jehovah, and is not to be regarded as simply the product of human reason or philosophical speculation.

With the exception of certain modes of thought and expression, including perhaps the ponderous visionary style so much employed by Ezekiel, the patriotic Jew apparently brought back with him from Babylon no new literary possession. His religious borrowing was upon a still smaller scale: he had viewed the idolatrous practices of his captors with lofty scorn (Is $44^{9\text{-}20}$). But his debt to Persian and Greek religious thought proved to be much more considerable.

(1) *Persian influence.*—The worship of the One Supreme God which was common to both Persians and Jews (Ormazd and Jahweh being to this extent practically identified) sufficiently accounts for the bond of religious sympathy which undoubtedly united the two peoples. They were at one in their repudiation of idolatry; both looked for the absolute reign of the good. That the final destruction of evil is well within the horizon of Zoroaster appears from the *Gāthās*, or hymns, the only part of the *Avesta* claiming to be from the prophet's own hand. (For further details, see art. ZOROASTRIANISM in vol. iv., and Cheyne in *Expos. Times*, ii. (1891) 202, 224, 248). Apart from the influence inevitably exerted on one another by men of diverse creeds who are brought by circumstances into close mutual relationship, these fundamental resemblances between their respective faiths naturally led to a certain interaction of belief in other directions also. For example, the Zoroastrians, like the Jews, expected a Saviour (*Saoshyant*, of the stem of Zoroaster) at whose advent the powers of evil were to be overthrown. Again, it need not be doubted that the Zoroastrian expectation of a glorious and happy future, in which the faithful, freed from all contact with evil, should enjoy eternal fellowship with Ormazd and his angels, led the Jews towards a clearer apprehension at least of the hitherto but dimly entertained and scarcely formulated doctrine of a personal immortality. Persian ideas have been traced in the OT itself (Dn $10^{13.\,20}$ $12^{1}$); they are certainly present in the Apocr. (To $12^{15}$); and seem to have passed through the earlier Jewish apocalyptic (En $90^{21f.}$) into the NT Apocalypse of St. John ($1^{4}$ $8^{2}$). A noticeable feature of Zoroastrianism is its artistic and lavish use of numbers and images. This tendency was specially developed in connexion with the doctrine of good and evil spirits, and is already reflected in the later canonical books of the OT (1 Ch $21^{1}$, Zec $3^{9}$ $4^{10}$), and still more, as we shall see, in the post-canonical literature. These foreign elements began to produce a freer play of the imagination within the sphere of things sacred than had been possible under the former limitations; they supplied the old faith with a new stock of names and images. That Jewish ritual as well as doctrine was affected by Persian influence appears not only from the institution of the Feast of Purim, but in connexion with such a matter as the saying of the first prayer (*Shĕma'*) in the temple at daybreak.

(2) *Greek influence.*—The tide of Hellenism, which began to flow over the whole civilized world after the brilliant conquests of Alexander the Great, affected Palestine as well as other countries. During the period of the Ptolemies and the Seleucidæ the Greek spirit took possession of the land; native customs and traditional ways of thinking everywhere yielded to this subtle overmastering force. In the purely Judæan district, however, the Hellenistic spirit was so far kept at bay. No new Greek cities sprang up within that essentially Jewish area, and when the rising wave of Hellenism dashed up against the rock of Judaism the latter was strong enough to withstand the shock. Only its sharper corners were worn off in the process, and this was necessary in order to the fulfilment of the function assigned in providence to the Heb. faith as the historic preparation for the world-wide religion of Christ. The influx of Greek culture was met by a fresh and resolute devotion to the legalistic ideal developed by the scribes. Such was the result of the conflict epigrammatically referred to by Zechariah in the words: 'Thy sons, O Zion, against thy sons, O Greece' ($9^{13}$). Proudly conscious of their privileged position as the chosen people, and punctilious to the last degree with regard to their observance of the temple worship, the Jews gained rather than lost in national sentiment. But if the Hellenistic spirit was denied an entrance into the *religious* citadel of Judaism, it crept insidiously into every other department of life (1 Mac $1^{15}$, 2 Mac $4^{9\text{-}14}$).

Alexandria, and not Athens, was now the proud 'mother of arts and eloquence,' and it was in this Egyptian city that non-Palestinian Judaism came into closest contact with Hellenistic thought and culture. The spiritual atmosphere of the place was altogether peculiar, and charged with elements derived alike from the East and the West. Two such powerful and opposite streams of tendency could not meet without mutually influencing each other, and the world has profited by their fusion. The translation of the Heb. Scriptures into Greek made them the property of all nations, while the Greek language and philosophy provided the Jewish religion with splendid weapons for apologetic and missionary purposes. Judaism and Hellenism were thus complementary factors in creating a type of thought and life wider and fuller than either of them could have produced of itself. A distinctly religious conception of the universe had hitherto been as foreign to the Greek as the rules and abstractions of metaphysics had been to the Hebrew. But the Greeks were now provided with a direct Divine revelation, capable of filling with life every groove of their languishing philosophical systems; and the Jews, besides appropriating certain Greek conceptions, found the means of giving scientific expression to the contents of their religious consciousness. The result of this union of two great forces was seen in the rise and development of the Jewish-Alexandrian philosophy of religion. In this system, unfortunately, the literal meaning of Scripture was discarded in favour of allegorical interpretations. From the time of Aristobulus (2nd cent. B.C.), who maintained that the Greek philosophy had been borrowed from Moses, to that of Philo Judæus (*c.* 20 B.C.–50 A.D.), who still further developed the allegorical method, philosophers used the Bible largely as a prop for their own speculations. To Judaism the results were sufficiently serious, but it emerged at last from the keen battle which had to be waged as the price of its partnership with 'the wisdom of men,' if not without wounds, yet also enriched with spoil.

There were thus two great streams of influence flowing in upon the Jewish theology of this period, an Eastern and a Western, a Persian and a Greek. Of these by far the stronger was the Greek, though the Persian is as distinctly traceable. The one may be likened to an ordinary under-current, and the other to the Gulf Stream. The Persian current was that of Zoroastrianism; the Greek cannot be associated with a single name. Out of these two forces, which were new, or newly felt, acting upon the native Judaism of Palestine, which was old, was formed that *third* which we meet within the home Jewish theology of the period. But there was also, as we have seen, a Jewish theology outside of Palestine altogether. Not only did foreign influences flow in upon Judaism, but Judaism, now no longer confined to Palestine, went out to meet them. Thus the hitherto unbroken river of OT ideas and doctrines divided itself at this point into three separate streams. One, the main current, continued to flow on in Palestine; while on the east and west of it ran two other streams—the one through Persian territory, and the other through Greek. The tributaries of Persian and Greek ideas by which these streams respectively were fed necessarily caused their waters to be of a composite character, exceedingly difficult to analyze so as to say definitely, 'This is Jewish, that is Persian,' or 'This is Jewish, that is Greek.' These currents, however, into which Judaism was divided, and through which it was widened, were destined in some degree to find a meeting-point again in the religion of Christ, which assimilated what was good not only in Judaism, but also in the splendid creations of foreign philosophical and theological thought.

We find, then, that human speculation had a great function to perform in so acting upon OT dogma as to soften and widen it in the direction of the larger truths of the perfect revelation in Christ. This revelation was certainly the more easily received and apprehended that the Greeks had lived and thought. The contribution of the thinkers of the West to the universal religion was their philosophical culture and spirit. That, joined to the sacred depository of truth that composed the faith of the Hebrews, went to form a religion wide enough for every section of humanity. It wanted only the material force of Rome to fuse the nations into the outward and political union that was to consolidate the deeper union which the interchange of spiritual thought and feeling had already in great measure brought about.

3. *Decay of the older Hebraism.*—If, moreover, in the later canonical books we already find traces of the influx of foreign influences on the one hand, we also discover signs of the decay of pure Hebraism on the other. In particular, we can discern in Ezekiel and Zechariah distinct traces of the process by which the old supremacy of the prophet passed first into the hands of the priest, and subsequently into those of the scribe, the spiritual ancestor of the NT Pharisee. For instance, it is very significant that in the fifth vision of Zechariah the two 'anointed ones' who jointly sustain the spiritual life of Israel are the civil and priestly heads of the nation, and that the prophet is accorded no place by their side. Quite foreign, too, to the older prophecy is the way in which Zechariah introduces mediators to bridge the distance between men and Jahweh, who is conceived as reigning in the remote heaven and maintaining intercourse with the world through the medium of invisible messengers. In Malachi we detect not only a certain scholasticism of style that is new, but also, as contrasted with Isaiah and the other great prophets, a tincture of the legalistic spirit ($4^4$) which was destined to become so strong in the near future. 'Joel starts, like any older prophet, from the facts of his own day, but these hurry him at once into apocalypse; he calls, as thoroughly as any of his predecessors, to repentance, but under the imminence of the day of the Lord, with its supernatural terrors, he mentions no special sin and enforces no single virtue. The civic and personal ethics of the earlier prophets are absent. In the Greek period, the oracles, now numbered from the ninth to the fourteenth chapters of the Book of Zechariah, repeat to aggravation the exulting revenge of Nahum and Obadiah, without the strong style or the hold upon history which the former exhibits, and show us prophecy still further enwrapped in apocalypse.' * That the ceremonial had now taken precedence of the moral and the spiritual is also clear from a comparison of the historical books of this period with those of earlier times. The Chronicler is concerned chiefly about the outward holiness of Israel, and knows nothing of the ethical earnestness of the older prophets. In the Apocryphal literature of the Gr. period we see the spirit of Pharisaic Judaism altogether in the ascendant.

4. The foregoing considerations supply us with a convenient basis for *the classification of the Apocrypha.* They range themselves into three classes according to the national influences under which they were composed, and it will be important for our present inquiry to view them in that connexion, bearing in mind, of course, that no classification of this sort can be absolutely exhaustive, and that traces of Pers. influence, *e.g.*, may be met with in books prevailingly Gr. or Pal. in their origin, and *vice versâ.* †

(1) The Persian-Palestinian books. These are characterized chiefly by their deep-seated horror of idolatry; by the extraordinary value they attach to alms-giving and other works of benevolence; by a very elaborate doctrine of angels, and especially of demons; by the prominence they give to the miraculous; by a distinct doctrine of immortality, and indications of belief in a future judgment; by the doctrines of the mediation of the saints and the efficacy of prayers for the dead; and by the sure hope of the resurrection of the just. To this class belong Tobit, Baruch, 2 Mac., and the Additions to Daniel. Here it will be observed, on the one hand, what a curious deviation there is in some particulars from OT doctrine, and, on the other, how marked an approximation there is on some other points towards the NT position.

(2) The pure Palestinian books, viz. Sirach, 1 Maccabees, and possibly Judith. These are distinguished by their keen attachment to Judaism, as seen in the way in which they magnify the Law, and celebrate the praises of Zion and the temple services; by the much smaller place given to the miraculous; by their defective ideas about a future life, the only immortality known to them being apparently that of being remembered; by their silence concerning the resurrection; and by their crude notions with respect to a Divine retributive judgment. Here we are in contact with the central stream of Judaism, and hence find no such decided deviations from OT doctrine as in those books written under Persian influence. There is, however, as might be expected, also less of real development towards NT positions. The Pharisaic party, we know, were dominant in Palestine, and did what they could to prevent foreign influences from being introduced. There was thus less violent collision between opposing elements, and hence less pronounced results were produced both in the

* G. A. Smith, *The Twelve Prophets*, vol. ii. p. xi.

† This is the principle of classification adopted by Bretschneider in his important work, *Die Dogmatik der Apokr. Schriften des AT*, Leipzig, 1805 (4th ed. 1841).

normal and in the abnormal directions. Yet even here there was a gradual widening as generations passed, and as new influences forced themselves even into the citadel of Judaism.

(3) The Jewish-Alexandrian books. These include 1 Esdras, the Wisdom of Solomon, and the Prayer of Manasses. While also showing an attachment to Judaism, they lay more stress upon a holy life than upon the outward *cultus* of the Mosaic Law. But the chief peculiarity of this third class is that they bear distinctly the colouring of the Greek philosophy. Especially is this true of the Book of Wisdom. This important work is far from being an ordinary sample of Alexandrian theosophy, but neither is it conceived precisely in the spirit of the older Heb. literature. In passing from those OT books to which it bears the closest resemblance, viz. Proverbs and Ecclesiastes, we are conscious of a certain change of atmosphere, and of the presence of a new element which gives a distinct tone to the whole. This new factor is none other than the subtle spirit of Hellenism. The work deals in an abstract and philosophical manner with such subjects as the creation, wisdom, man, history, etc. It also contains the Platonic doctrine as to the four cardinal virtues. In this division of the Apocr. we naturally again meet with more variation from OT doctrine. With regard to sundry points, it would be vain to attempt to reconcile the Canonical and Apocryphal statements. *E.g.*, the position taken up in Wisdom as to creation and the soul of man is not that of the OT. These discrepancies arise apparently from an effort on the writer's part to harmonize the scriptural and philosophical positions. The general strain of the book, however, is thoroughly biblical, only the truths of revelation are viewed through the medium of Gr. learning. While the prevailing standpoint is essentially that of the OT, we not infrequently meet with passages conceived in the larger and freer spirit of the NT. For over against the variations mentioned we must place the fact that there is a clear advance upon some OT doctrines, notably with regard to that of immortality. Ewald says we have in this book 'a premonition of John' and 'a preparation for Paul' (*HI* v. p. 484). And, in fact, altogether apart from the claim that St. John's doctrine of the Logos is found in germ here, St. Paul's argument in Romans that men are inexcusable who do not find out to some extent from nature even the knowledge of God, his description of the Christian's armour in Ephesians, and the expressions used with reference to the Person of Christ in the anonymous Epistle to the Hebrews, are all embodied already in this Apocryphal work ($13^{1ff.}$ $5^{17ff.}$ $7^{26}$).

While it is important to recognize the facts just mentioned, we must not put forward an extravagant claim on behalf of the post-canonical Jewish writings. 'These books belong to the decaying period of the nation's life. The earliest of them were written only at the close of the Persian dominion, and belong to a time when prophecy had ceased, and when men were looking not for what might be revealed, but to what had been revealed.'* The statement in 1 Mac $9^{27}$ that 'there was great tribulation in Israel, such as was not since the time that no prophet appeared unto them,' illustrates the prevailing feeling on this point. There was no longer any proper scope for prophecy as the medium of further revelation. A period when attention to legalistic details became the paramount tendency in religion was not one to call forth men filled with great ideas, and eager in the name of God to unfold them to the people. And, in fact, religious activity was practically confined to the expository handling by the scribes of the revelation already given in the Law and the Prophets. 'Fresh principles and truths were no longer developed, though of course this did not exclude development in the case of what had already found expression.'* The only further revelation now possible was that which was to burst through the limitations of Judaism and bring in a religion for man. The Maccabæan revolt, however, regenerated in a wonderful degree the religious life of the period, and gave rise to a literature of its own which really amounted to a renaissance of a very fruitful kind. Our claim, then, in regard to the Apocr. and other non-canonical Jewish writings of the period is, that, while forming no essential part of OT revelation, they yet supply a very welcome link between the OT and the NT, and contain not a little that is of value in their illustrations and applications and further developments of the principles already revealed. It has been too readily assumed that these books are wholly without 'evidences of the Divine Spirit leading on to Christ.'

* *Camb. Bible for Schools*, 1 Mac., Introd. p. 14.

i. The Doctrine of God.—The first thing that naturally demands attention when we come to look at the dogmatic of the Apocr. is the doctrine of God. Now here, perhaps, it was not possible as regards the general doctrine that there should be any advance, and we are rather concerned to ask, Is the lofty presentation of the OT, as given especially in Ex $34^{6f.}$, sustained? On the whole, there need be no hesitation in saying that it is, although in some of the Apocryphal books the conception of God is much higher than in others. It is at its lowest in Judith, and at its highest in Sirach and Wisdom. But in general, throughout the Apocr., one finds essentially the OT view of God, as that had been evolved during centuries of theocratic guidance.

1. *The OT position.*—While the general idea of God is everywhere expressed in the OT by the name El (also Elōăh, Elōhīm), the earliest conception of the Divine nature within the sphere of revelation is that conveyed in the name El Shaddai=(?) 'God Almighty.' Although probably of pre-Mosaic origin, it was only at a later stage of revelation (Ex $3^{14}$ $6^{2f.}$) that the name Jahweh came to be apprehended in its essential significance as the absolutely independent, faithful, and immutable covenant God of Israel. God was next conceived as the Holy One (Ex $15^{11}$),—just (Dt $32^4$, Ps $36^{6f.}$), and jealous (Ex $34^{14}$), but also merciful and gracious (Ex $34^6$). In the prophetic writings He is further designated as the Lord of Hosts (Is $1^{24}$ $2^{12}$, Jer $10^{16}$, Hab $2^{13}$ etc.), and in the *Ḥokhma* literature as the all-wise (Job $35^5$, Ps $147^5$, Pr $2^6$, Sir $2^{26}$). See, further, art. God (in OT) in vol. ii.

Precisely the same conception of the Divine Being predominates in the Apocrypha. The only point about which there could be any difficulty in maintaining this identity is the spirituality of God; and with regard to this we hope to show that in the Apocr. there is something that may not unfairly be described as intermediate between the perfect revelation of the NT and the more materialistic view of the OT. While the fundamental conception of God remains unchanged from that of the OT Canon, there is at the same time a decided movement towards a more spiritual conception of the Supreme Being.

2. *The position of this doctrine in Jewish writings of the Apocryphal period.*—(1) Of the Pal. books the most important here, and the oldest, is Sirach. This book (written in Heb. *c.* 180 B.C., translated into Greek B.C. 132) has much to say about God, especially about His relation to the world physical and moral. The fullest statement of God's relation to the material universe is found

* *Camb. Bible for Schools*, 1 Mac., Introd. p. 14.

in $42^{15}$–$43^{33}$; and what is distinctive of the writer's view as here expressed is his assertion that the mighty works of God's wisdom are beyond the power of His saints to declare ($42^{17}$). He is above all human praise ($43^{30}$). 'Who hath seen him, that he may declare him? And who shall magnify him as he is?' ($43^{31}$). There is no doubt that this represents a distinct step in the development of the doctrine of God. 'From the point of view of Ecclesiasticus,' says Nicolas, 'it is not only anthropomorphic representations which give false ideas of deity; not even the most elevated conceptions of the human spirit can declare it as it is. No feat of imagination, no effort of intelligence can reach it. Jesus, son of Sirach, has pronounced the word: the Eternal is incomprehensible in His essence by the limited faculties of man.'* The book also contains many statements regarding God's relationship to the moral world. There is a beneficent design in creation, 'for all things are created for their uses' ($39^{21}$). 'In the hand of the Lord is the authority of the earth,' and also 'the prosperity of a man' ($10^{4f.}$). 'Poverty and riches are from the Lord' ($11^{14}$), and 'he hath not given any man licence to sin' ($15^{20}$). God is represented as 'visiting' men; but 'as his majesty is, so also is his mercy' ($2^{18}$). Sometimes the contrast is drawn from the opposite side, as in $16^{12}$ 'As his mercy is great, so is his correction also; he judgeth a man according to his works.' As judge, there is with Him no respect of persons ($35^{12}$). In the assertion that 'the Most High also hateth sinners' ($12^{6}$) we have a deviation from the true biblical position that while hating sin God loves the sinner. The writer addresses God as 'Father and Master of my life' ($23^{1}$), and recognizes Him as the hearer of prayer ($21^{5}$ $35^{16}$ $38^{9}$ etc.). A gracious Providence watches over the godly ($34^{16}$), but the sacrifices of the wicked are vain ($34^{19}$). God is regarded as specially the God of the Jews, but yet as the God of all, and loving all ($36^{1-5, 17}$ $18^{13}$). The relation of God to evil is thus laid down: 'Say not thou, It is through the Lord that I fell away; for thou shalt not do the things that he hateth. Say not thou, It is he that caused me to err; for he hath no need of a sinful man' ($15^{11f.}$). This passage is one of several in this book, the tenor of which is practically repeated in the Epistle of St. James ($1^{13f.}$). Except in the two particulars noted above, there is nothing in all this either in advance of, or at variance with, what is met with in the Canonical books of the OT upon the subject of the nature and character of the Supreme Being. The conservative instincts of the writer have even brought upon him the charge of adhering to 'a not so much untrue as antiquated form of religious belief.'†

In the various sections of Enoch the conception of God is practically that of the OT, although occasional divergences occur. *E.g.* the idea of God rejoicing over the destruction of the wicked ($94^{10}$) is quite foreign to the OT (cf. Ezk $18^{23, 32}$ $33^{11}$). This book employs a great multiplicity of titles for God. Of these, which are collected in the Index to Charles's edition, some of the most striking are, 'eternal Lord of glory' ($75^{3}$), 'God of the whole world' ($84^{2}$), 'Head of Days' ($46^{2}$), 'Honoured and Glorious One' ($14^{21}$), 'Lord of the sheep' ($89^{16}$), 'Lord of spirits' ($37^{2}$), 'Lord of the whole creation of the heaven' ($84^{2}$).

In the remaining Pal. books the conception of God undergoes little modification. According to the author of Jubilees, Israelites are God's children because physically descended from Jacob ($1^{28}$); but He is also the God of all ($22^{10, 27}$ $30^{19}$ etc.). The idea of God presented in Judith is of the narrowest Jewish type. God is the God of Jews only. He ranks as the greatest of national deities, who will wreak vengeance on the foes of His people. Their misfortunes are due to their having departed from the law of Moses. God hears their prayers when they 'cast ashes upon their heads and spread out their sackcloth before the Lord' ($4^{11}$). $16^{16}$ is conceived in a higher strain; but apparently it is borrowed, like a similar passage in Sirach, from Ps 51. The general scope of the book, as regards the relation of the story to the character of God, detracts from the value of its separate statements. God is represented as countenancing the deceit practised by Judith in order to the deliverance of her nation, and by consequence the assassination of Holofernes. This book ranks fairly high as a literary work, but we cannot justify its morality without subscribing to the maxim that the end justifies the means. It contributes nothing to the doctrine of God beyond the general impression arising from the history, and that certainly is such as to convey a conception of Him far inferior to the lofty position maintained in Sirach. The First Book of Maccabees, being wholly historical, contains nothing to the point. Indeed, according to the true text, the name of God does not once occur in the book. Although inserted in several passages of the AV ($2^{21}$ $3^{53, 60}$ $4^{55}$ etc.), it is absent from the Greek text. In $3^{18}$ a few MSS do contain the word 'God,' but there is a preponderance of authority against the reading. While it breathes throughout a spirit of unfeigned faith in God as the defender and helper of His people ($4^{8ff.}$ $12^{15}$ $16^{3}$), exhibits the deepest reverence for the Law and the temple worship ($12^{9}$ $2^{21}$), and recognizes the overruling providence of God ($1^{64}$ $3^{18}$) and His unfailing support of those who put their trust in Him ($2^{61}$), yet the general conception of the Divine Being, so far as presented in this book, is not that of Jahweh dwelling among His people, but that of God enthroned in the distant heaven ($3^{50}$ $4^{10}$). In Test. Levi 3, God is designated 'the Great Glory,' as in Enoch $14^{20}$ $102^{3}$. 2 (4) Esdras, while presenting no distinctive doctrinal feature on this head, contains, besides an enumeration of the Divine attributes ($7^{62ff.}$) and a summary of much OT teaching about God, the striking invocation of $8^{20-23}$.

(2) Of the Pers.-Pal. books Bar $1$–$3^{8}$ is perhaps the oldest. Baruch's idea of God is simply that He is the guardian of Israel ($2^{11}$ $3^{1, 4}$). In spite of disciplinary trials, they enjoy peculiar privileges ($2^{15}$). To them alone has the Divine wisdom been revealed; and had they not abandoned it, they would not have been in subjection to the heathen ($2^{1, 4}$ $3^{8}$). The Book of Tobit has a wider conception of God. The writer hopefully contemplates the time when 'all the nations shall turn to fear the Lord God truly, and shall bury their idols. And all the nations shall bless the Lord' ($14^{6f.}$). The Jews will be raised above all other nations, not, however, because they are Jews, as Baruch holds, but because they do the will of God. In this book we have an illustration of the post-exilic tendency to accumulate names for God. He is spoken of as 'the Most High' ($1^{4}$), 'the Lord of heaven and earth' ($7^{18}$), 'God of our fathers' ($8^{5}$), 'the Holy One' ($12^{12}$), 'our Lord,' 'our Father' ($13^{4}$), 'the Lord of righteousness,' 'the everlasting King' ($13^{6}$), 'the Lord God' ($13^{11}$), 'the King of heaven' ($13^{7, 11}$), 'the Lord of the righteous' ($13^{13}$), 'the great King' ($13^{15}$). Those who fear God shall be recompensed ($4^{14}$); indeed the fear of God is the true standard of wealth ($4^{21}$). The burden of the book is to prove that God's favour is reached through good works, such as fastings, the giving of alms, and the burial of the dead ($12^{8ff.}$). In this distinctly unbiblical position (cf. Sir $3^{3, 30}$, which, though pure Palestinian, comes under the excep-

* *Des Doc. Rel. des Juifs*, p. 160 f.

† Cheyne in *The Expositor* (1st series), xi. p. 351.

tion noted above, p. 275) we may perhaps trace the influence of Zoroastrianism. According to that system, man's future destiny is determined by his life on earth, apart altogether from any idea of a Saviour. In the books of heaven every man is credited with his good deeds, while he is debited with his evil works. 'After death the soul arrives at the accountant's bridge over which lies the way to heaven'; a balance is struck, and according as the good or evil predominates so will his future be. In the case of equality between the good and the evil, the soul is relegated to an intermediate state until the last judgment, when his fate is finally fixed. The biblical doctrine of forgiveness is foreign to the system of Zoroaster, although it teaches that in view of man's ignorance, and his liability to be led astray by the powers of evil, Ormazd graciously resolved to send a prophet (Zoroaster himself) to point out to men the right way, and so rescue them from everlasting perdition. Still, in the last resort, this is essentially salvation by works—a doctrine propounded in Tobit, but utterly alien to Holy Scripture, the teaching of which on this head has been well voiced in two lines by Tennyson—

> 'For merit lives from man to man,
> And not from man, O Lord, to Thee.'
> (*In Memoriam*).

In the Assumption of Moses, a pure Pal. composition, the OT conception of merit is still adhered to ($12^7$), although in the Apoc. of Baruch, a composite book belonging to the first century of our era, justification by works is taught ($51^7$ $67^6$) just as in the Talmud.

(3) If some of the Jewish-Alexandrian writings contain little that is noteworthy, from our present standpoint, regarding the doctrine of God, there are others which furnish us with much that is germane to our purpose. In the second section of Bar. ($3^9$ onwards) there occurs the following passage: 'This is our God, and there shall none other be accounted of in comparison of him. He hath found out all the way of knowledge, and hath given it unto Jacob his servant, and to Israel that is beloved of him. Afterward did she appear upon earth, and was conversant with men. This is the book of the commandments of God, and the law that endureth for ever: all they that hold it fast are appointed to life; but such as leave it shall die' ($3^{35}$–$4^1$). Owing to a misinterpretation, this was treated as a *locus classicus* in the Arian controversy; the reference in $3^{37}$ is not to the incarnation of the Logos, but to Wisdom personified, as in Sir $24^{10}$. The really special feature of the passage is 'the view which it expresses of the sacred law. This wears the appearance of full creative originality. The Law is the final manifestation on earth of the wisdom of God Himself, which has taken a sort of bodily form, bestowing life and salvation on all who keep it. This constitutes a totally new combination of the older representation of wisdom as the revelation of God in the world with the deep veneration for the law which had recently arisen.'* In Baruch there is therefore no real development of the doctrine of God.

The Wisdom of Solomon, on the other hand, is here of first-rate importance. In this book we have the very highest conception of God, and are lifted entirely above the limitations of the Jewish idea. God 'is manifested to them that do not distrust him' ($1^2$); 'he visiteth his holy ones' ($4^{15}$). Men please him, not by their Judaism but by the purity of their life. God is described both in His relation to the physical and moral worlds, and also in regard to His nature and essence. His all-powerful hand created the world out of formless matter ($11^{17}$); by His word He made all things, and by His wisdom He formed man ($9^2$). But while 'He created all things that they might have being' ($1^{14}$), 'God made not death' ($1^{13}$). As 'sovereign Lord of all' ($6^7$), He exercises moral supervision over mankind in general: 'being righteous thou rulest all things righteously' ($12^{15}$). God's infinite resources are used in behalf of the righteous and against the ungodly ($5^{15.17}$ $11^{17ff.}$). Stern, however, as are the writer's delineations of the Divine judgments against sin, he is not oblivious to the correlative truth of the Divine mercy ($11^{23}$ $12^{16}$ etc.). The sovereign Lord is also the lover of men's lives=souls ($11^{26}$), and 'the saviour of all' ($16^7$). Full recognition is accorded to the truth of God's gracious and sleepless providence ($4^{17}$ $12^{13}$ $14^{5.3}$; $17^2$). The philosophy of Israelitish history is explained by the fact that 'by measure and number and weight thou didst order all things' ($11^{20}$).

While the view of the Divine nature presented in Wisdom has manifestly much in common with that of the OT generally, it is also decidedly tinged with Hellenism. God is spoken of as 'the first author of beauty' ($13^3$), a designation which would never have occurred to a Heb. mind uninfluenced by Gr. thought. All wisdom is in His hand ($7^{16}$), and is the reflexion of His essential glory and goodness. In a noble *locus classicus* the author says: 'She is a breath of the power of God, and a clear effluence of the glory of the Almighty; therefore can nothing defiled find entrance into her. For she is an effulgence from everlasting light, and an unspotted mirror of the working of God, and an image of His goodness. And she, being one, hath power to do all things; and remaining in herself, reneweth all things: and from generation to generation passing into holy souls she maketh men friends of God and prophets' ($7^{25ff.}$). This is the language of the educated Greek as well as of the pious Jew. Such metaphysical abstractions and recondite conceptions are altogether alien to the genius of the unsophisticated Hebrew. What is distinctive in the idea of God presented here is that He is regarded not from the point of view of power and majesty, but from that of wisdom. The author's philosophy led him to value wisdom more than power. With him wisdom is the most excellent of all things, the noblest ideal that can be pursued, and the highest Being is necessarily the wisest Being. There is also something non-Hebraic about the following statements bearing on the spirituality and omnipresence of God:—'The spirit of the Lord hath filled the world' ($1^7$); 'thine incorruptible spirit is in all things' ($12^1$); 'verily all men by nature were but vain who had no perception of God, and from the good things that are seen they gained not power to know him that is' ($13^1$). On account of Ex $3^{14}$ we should perhaps exempt the last from this category, but the other passages look very like Jewish modifications of Gr. thought. The idea of the all-pervasiveness of the Divine spirit occurs also in Ps $139^8$, but there is a difference in the mode of its presentation. In Wisdom the personality of God is kept more in the background, and is conceived in a vein of idealistic pantheism. With Plato, God is not a person but the all-comprehending idea of the Good, and our author's language seems to indicate a certain bias in this direction. But at the same time he emphasizes the spirituality of God; in the passages referred to we certainly have this apprehended in a very remarkable degree. If they lack the directness and finality of that great revealing word, 'God is spirit' (Jn $4^{24}$), they nevertheless furnish an intermediate link between it and the more materialistic standpoint of the OT.

It will be necessary for us here, and at subsequent stages in our investigation, to take account

* Ewald, *HI* v. p. 208.

of the theological position of the Jewish-Alexandrian philosopher Philo, whose views, as marking a notable development of Judaism intermediate between the Apocrypha and the NT, cannot reasonably be passed over. Although not the first, 'he is quite the most important representative of Hellenistic Judaism, and his writings give us the clearest view of what this development was and aimed at.'* One of its most cherished aims was the substitution of more abstract teaching for the numerous anthropomorphisms of the OT. And in this field Philo did extensive service. He held that grief, envy, wrath, revenge, etc., cannot be attributed to God, and that when He is represented as showing such emotions and affections the motives of the Divine activity are only being expressed in a way that specially appeals to the human mind. But, strongly influenced as he was by Gr. philosophy, Philo did not abandon Judaism. On the contrary, he did his best to propagate it. In opposition to the Stoic doctrine that God is the (impersonal) soul of the world, Philo declares Him to be essentially different from the world, of which He is the Creator and Preserver. And thus, in spite of such approximations to pantheistic thought as we meet with in his writings, and his free use of Gr. philosophical language and method, Philo stands firmly on theistic ground. Frequently, no doubt, he conveys the impression of sinking the concrete God in a conception of almost purely ideal content. According to this philosopher, God is pure Being, of whom no quality can be predicated, and it is only through the medium of an infinite multiplicity of Divine Ideas or Forces, distinct from his own proper being, that any active relation between God and the world is rendered possible. Regarding the nature of these mediating ἰδέαι or δυνάμεις, however, he has no very definite conception. He follows Plato in calling them *Ideas*, and the Stoics in also designating them *Forces* and *Logoi*, *i.e.* parts of the Reason which operates in the world; while at the same time he further identifies them with the Jewish *Angels* and the Gr. *Dæmons*, *i.e.* intermediaries between God and the world. It is not surprising that this vagueness of conception with regard to a fundamental theological distinction should involve him in a serious contradiction. Philo is unable to avoid the inconsistency of declaring on the one hand that the sum-total of Ideas, the κόσμος νοητός, is nothing more than the Reason of God as Creator, while yet on the other hand he represents these Ideas as so many distinct and independent entities. If God works in the world through the medium of His Ideas or Forces, then the latter cannot be separated from Him; but if He does not come into direct relationship with the world, then they must have an independent existence. See, further, art. PHILO in the present volume.

3. *The extent to which foreign influences affected the doctrine of God as reflected in these writings.*—How far, speaking generally, did external views modify the OT conception of this fundamental doctrine? As regards the influence of Persian thought, it must be said that, although traceable, it was yet in this connexion comparatively inoperative. The references in the visions of Zechariah to 'the seven eyes of Jehovah' (3$^{9}$ 4$^{10}$) are probably derived from Zoroastrian imagery; but, if we except the idea that the favour of God is obtained through good works (To 12$^{8ff.}$), there is hardly anything in the Apocrypha touching the doctrine of God which can be attributed to Persian influence. Allusion has already been made to the general identification of Jehovah with Ormazd. But, if there were points of union between the religion of the Persians and that of the Hebrews in their conception of the Supreme Being, there were also points of cleavage. *E.g.*, unlike Judaism, Zoroastrianism starts from a dualistic scheme of the universe. In the persons of their representatives Ahura-mazda (Ormazd) and Angrô-mainyush (Ahriman) good and evil have existed from all eternity. These two spirits divide the world between them; and its history is the record of their contest for the possession of the human soul. Man has been created by, and is accountable to, Ormazd, but he is a free agent, and may, if he choose, become the abettor of evil. To do evil is to serve the interests of Ahriman; to live righteously is to advance the kingdom of Ormazd. The two original spirits wage war by means of their respective creatures. Thus Ormazd is practically an idealized Oriental monarch surrounded by his ministers or *Amesha-Spentas* (mod. Pers. *Amshaspands*) who execute his will. But for the pious Jew, after the Exile as before it, there is no such dual proprietorship of the world; on the contrary, there is one 'Creator of all' (Sir 24$^{8}$), 'the God of all' (Sir 50$^{22}$), and 'sovereign Lord of all' (Wis 6$^{7}$ 8$^{3}$).

But, if the Pers. influence was slight, the Gr. influence on the OT conception of God was considerable. The necessary consequence of Judaism meeting Gr. thought appears in nothing more clearly than in the way in which the LXX translators habitually tone down anthropomorphic expressions about God. A few examples taken from only two OT books will suffice to illustrate this tendency. In Is 42$^{13}$, where the Heb. text reads, 'Jehovah shall go forth as a mighty man,' the LXX has 'The Lord God of powers (κύριος ὁ θεὸς τῶν δυνάμεων) shall go forth,' while in the same passage, as also in Ex 15$^{3}$, for His designation as 'a man of war' is substituted the general idea of 'stirring up war' (συντρίβων πολέμους). The statement of Ex 19$^{3}$ that 'Moses went up unto God, and J″ called unto him out of the mountain' is modified as follows: 'Moses went up unto the mount of God, and God called unto him from heaven, saying,' etc. In Ex 21$^{6}$ it is said of the slave who prefers his master's service to freedom, 'his master shall bring him unto God' (RV), but the Gr. tr. runs, 'unto the judgment of God.' An obvious avoidance of the idea of seeing God occurs in Ex 24$^{10}$, where the Heb. text—'They saw the God of Israel'—is expanded into 'they saw the place where stood the God of Israel'; and in Is 38$^{11}$, where Hezekiah's lament, 'I shall not see the Lord in the land of the living,' becomes 'I shall not see the salvation of God,' etc. But, while in the case of the bolder anthropomorphisms used by the Heb. writers the LXX translators were thus careful to put more abstract language in their place, they did not of course go the full length of pantheism. That would indeed be a strange travesty of the OT which should attempt to represent J″ as an impersonal Deity, devoid of self-conscious reason and will. All that can be affirmed is a distinct tendency to guard the idea of God from misconception, by making use of language studiously abstract and sober. The same tendency is observable in the Apocrypha. As the majority of these books were written originally in Greek, we cannot trace the process so visibly as in the case of OT books rendered into Greek, but it shows itself none the less in the much rarer employment of names of members of the human body (anthropomorphisms), and in the much rarer ascription of affections of the human mind (anthropopathies), to set forth the personal activity, moral freedom, and spirituality of the living God. Even Wisdom, however, is not wholly free from anthropomorphisms; it speaks of God's ear (1$^{10}$), and of His hand (5$^{16}$ 7$^{16}$ 10$^{20}$ etc.); it contains the expression, 'them the Lord shall laugh to scorn' (4$^{18}$), and it 'retains a picture

* Schürer, art. 'Philo' in *Encyc. Brit.*

which was removed by the Targumist Jonathan as too anthropomorphic.' *

Philosophy has often wavered between pantheism and the recognition of a personal Deity. The human mind has difficulty in uniting the two conceptions of the Absolute and concrete personality. Revelation, however, has done this, and has done it without detracting from the significance of either, or setting the one above the other. The personality of God is not, as in the more popular view, emphasized to the virtual exclusion of the conception of the Absolute, for it is expressly declared that the heaven of heavens cannot contain Him (1 K $8^{27}$); nor, on the other hand, is the idea of the Absolute pressed, as in the strictly scientific view, to the exclusion of the individual personality, for God is represented as saying, 'I am the Lord, and there is none else, there is no God beside me' (Is $45^{5}$ etc.). In the Apocrypha likewise each of these conceptions gets its true position. This appears from such a passage as Wis $1^{7}$ 'The spirit of the Lord hath filled the world, and that which holdeth all things together hath knowledge of every voice.' Here the author pronounces against Greek pantheism by representing God as a living, personal Being; yet in the second half of the verse the attributes of omnipotence and omnipresence are predicated of the Divine spirit in the most abstract way. In short, God is presented as knowing and willing and actively working, just as in the OT, but He is spoken of in a more philosophical way. In another passage the writer excuses to some extent those who have been led to hold pantheistic views from the mistaken notion that personality is not compatible with absolute Godhead. At the same time, while giving them credit for diligent search after God, he laments that they should 'yield themselves up to sight, because the things that they look upon are beautiful,' and not 'sooner find the Sovereign Lord of these his works' ($13^{6ff.}$).

4. *Popular superstitions regarding the name Jahweh.*—Owing, perhaps, to their more figurative language, the Pal. Jews had not the same aversion as their Hellenistic brethren to representations of God which ascribed to Him visible features or human passions. But even they felt it necessary to harmonize the corporeal conceptions of the theophanies with the many biblical assertions of the spirituality of God. This they sought to do by the theory that God Himself did not appear to the patriarchs and to Moses; they saw only a manifestation of God—His word, His glory, His Shekinah. Persian ideas had as little to do with this attitude of the Pal. Jews as Greek, for Zoroastrianism did not concern itself with religious metaphysics. It was not due to any external influence. They had simply come to build their doctrine of God more upon the spiritual basis of such teaching as that of Ex $3^{14}$ $10^{28}$ etc. Unfortunately, they 'did not know how to retain it within the limits of spiritualism. It fell gradually into the excess of a gross theosophy of reveries and superstitions.' † Like the philosophers of Alexandria, the illiterate Jews of Palestine had arrived at the conclusion that God cannot be known to human intelligence. Unlike the former, however, they could not give philosophical expression to this idea, and held it only in the form of a superstitious belief that it is unlawful to utter the sacred name. The Kabbalists refer to it as 'the name of the four letters.' According to Jewish tradition, it was pronounced only once a year by the high priest when he entered into the Holy of Holies, and Simon the Just was the last who did this. He who knew how to pronounce this mysterious name was believed to have a magical power over the forces of nature, and was designated among the Rabbis בַּעַל שֵׁם = 'master of the name.' Mystic speculations upon the name of J″ naturally led up to wild surmises regarding the essence of God and the origin of things, referred to possibly in Sir $31^{21f.}$, practised among the Essenes (Jos. *BJ* II. viii. 9), and embodied later in the Kabbala. The tendency of the period was towards an abstract conception of Deity. Starting from the principle that God was too pure to have immediate relations with created things, men were forced to have recourse to the theory that He governs the world through intermediary beings. And here the Jews of Palestine virtually joined hands with Philo.

* Langen, *Judenthum*, etc. p. 205, n. 8.
† Nicolas, *Des Doc. Rel. des Juifs*, p. 159.

5. *The Christian doctrine of God.*—In Palestine the strongest influence opposing the growth of the Hellenistic spirit was the partisan life which the people had come to lead. Samaritan separatism and Pharisaic pride gave the most determined resistance in their power to everything foreign. According to Dillmann ('Enoch' in Schenkel), the Book of Enoch was the first known attempt to defend the biblical conception of the world against the inroads of Hellenism. The work of the scribes in expounding and elaborating the Law helped still further to erect and strengthen the 'middle wall of partition' between Jew and Gentile. Yet it is plain that, when Christ appeared, the doctrine of God was very variously conceived. It was reserved for Him to clear away the heathen elements that, in spite of all efforts to the contrary, had clustered round it, and to reveal God as the loving Father of His creatures, by whom the hairs of our head are numbered, and the sparrows protected and fed (Mt $10^{29f.}$). Christ thus made God known to men as He had never been known before, and gave full expansion to OT glimpses of truth. And we know how in doing this He united the most popular expressions and modes of thought with the most abstract conceptions. His teaching 'joins, in the highest degree possible,' says Wendt (*Teaching of Jesus*, § ii. ch. 1), 'popular intelligibility and rich significance.' The truth is, both elements are necessary. The exclusive use of either the popular language of the imagination or the philosophical terminology of the schools must lead to a defective and one-sided conception of God. In the former case the concrete personality comes to clear expression, but the elaborate use of popular images may seriously interfere with the thought of essential spiritual Godhead. When, as in the OT, He is represented as writing, laughing, bearing the sword, etc., we are brought within measurable distance of such a humanistic conception. That the Israelites were constantly in danger of obscuring the conception of God as the Absolute is shown by their repeated lapses into idolatry, which really meant the putting of many separate deities in the place of the One. On the other hand, a conception of God that is limited to the philosophical language of the schools must always be deficient on the religious side. The free, personal life of Deity can become intelligible to us only when expressed in terms taken over from human life. Such language is of course figurative, but it sets forth the Divine activity in a way singularly fitted to impress us. Our minds cannot lay hold of God in His invisible Being; we need some tangible object on which to fix our thoughts. We see God's glory in the heavens, but we cannot live on abstract ideas of Being and Omniscience. We long for a Person whom we can love, to whom we can tell our sorrows, whom we can approach with confidence. Instinctively we cry, 'Show us the Father.' This great need of the human soul is fully supplied in the Person of Christ. He is the Word of life, whom men's eyes have seen, and men's hands have handled.

Our conclusion, then, is that in at least one of the most important Apocryphal books, The Wisdom of Solomon, there is an appreciable development towards a more spiritual idea of God, and that what of grossness yet remained in the conception of Him was purged away by Christ. In the Christian doctrine of God we have also the true corrective to the exaggerated idealism of Philo, according to which God has no direct connexion with the world which He has made.

ii. THE DOCTRINE OF THE WISDOM.—Among Oriental nations in general, and among the Hebrews in particular (1 K $4^{30f.}$, Jer $49^7$), there was a strongly marked tendency of mind known distinctively as 'wisdom,' and comparable to, though not identical with, the speculative philosophy of Greece. Whether indeed the Hebrews can be said to have possessed a philosophy at all, depends on the meaning ascribed to the term. Of metaphysical speculation about God and the world they had none, believing as they did that 'in the beginning God created the heavens and the earth,' but they had a 'sacred' philosophy of their own, which was, above all, religious and practical in its aims. Between secular philosophy and the human wisdom of Israel there was thus an essential difference. They differed in standpoint, in method, and in spirit. The Greek philosopher exercised reason upon the phenomena of the universe (τὸ πᾶν) as he found it, with the view of making it yield up its secret; the Hebrew philosopher had his ethical and religious principles to start with, and merely verified them in the actual occurrences of life.

1. *Wisdom presented in OT not only as human but as Divine.*—In its *human* aspect Wisdom is the ability to recognize, the capacity to understand, and the disposition to co-operate with the Divine purpose as it affects the physical world and the life of men. Theoretically and practically, 'the fear of the LORD is the beginning of wisdom.' Moral and intellectual wisdom are seldom dissociated: the righteous man is the 'wise' man, and the ungodly is the fool (Ps $5^5$, Wis $4^{17}$ $12^{23}$). Among the people of Israel the human wisdom assumed different phases from time to time. From being a doctrine of Providence in the widest sense, according to which 'the LORD hath made all things answering to their end' (Pr $16^4$), it came to be so in a narrower sense when the events of history appeared irreconcilable with the *a priori* principles contained in the Law (cf. Ps 37. 73, and the Bk. of Job). There came, too, 'a period of comparative quiescence in the presence of difficulties, which are themselves drawn into the general scheme, and shown, as parts of it, to have their own utility.' *

In the OT, however, Wisdom is presented not only as human, but also as *Divine*. By Divine Wisdom is meant the world in its totality as inhabited by God and expressing in its varied phenomena His mind and character and mode of working. As the unity of thought and force underlying the manifold forms of creation, it may be ideally differentiated from God. It is so, *e.g.*, in the passage of most significance—the remarkable generalization of Pr 8. Wisdom is spoken of in such a way as to make it impossible to believe that only the Divine attribute of wisdom is meant. Nor perhaps can we regard this description of wisdom as 'certainly nothing more than a poetical personification of the Divine Intelligence.' † Rather is it here the active, organized, and conscious embodiment of the Divine principles empirically manifested in creation and providence. It is something outside of, yet standing alongside of, God, created by Him so as together with Him to fashion the world. God is the actual worker, but Wisdom is with Him as His workman and fellow. Realizing itself thus in the work of creation, Wisdom is further represented as 'playing' like a child before Jehovah in His habitable earth, in all the glow of conscious power, and as taking special delight in the sons of men. Such qualities are ascribed to it as to make it almost identical now with the Spirit, now with the NT Logos.

In different parts of the Heb. Scriptures God's revelation of Himself is attributed to His word. Gn 1 at once suggests itself in connexion with the idea of the Word as creative; God *speaks*, and the world starts into being. Later on, it appears as the regular medium of the prophetic oracles. In certain psalms ($33^6$ $107^{20}$ $147^{15}$) and in Isaiah ($55^{11}$) we find the Word personified and set forth as the agent and messenger of the Divine will. It came thus to be conceived as distinct from God Himself, force being perhaps lent to the distinction by the fact that nearly all Heb. words for speech include the notion of *standing forth*. The Word is essentially connected with the idea of mediation, and indeed the whole Jewish revelation is pervaded by the thought that God never manifests Himself except through a medium. He sends His angel, His word, His prophet, His only-begotten Son; but, as for Himself in His essential Being, 'no man hath seen God at any time.'

It is thus possible to find the germ of the doctrine of the Logos already in the opening verses of Scripture, which represent God as having called things into being by speech. But, doubtless, it was only in connexion with the later development of the Wisdom that the origin of the Logos doctrine was referred back to this source. The whole subject is beset with much difficulty. This is partly due to the variable meaning attached to the Wisdom by biblical writers. Sometimes it is conceived as a pure abstraction, sometimes as a simple personification of the Divine Intelligence, and sometimes as virtually a distinct person objective to God Himself. From Pr 8 it is clear, on the one hand, that to the writer Wisdom exists alongside of God in a special sense applicable to none of His attributes; and, on the other, that his picture of the perfectly harmonious coexistence of God and Wisdom excludes the hypothesis of a duality in the Godhead. The Logos is more than a simple personification of Wisdom, and yet is not altogether conceived as a distinct person. The conception is more than poetical, without, however, clearly passing beyond the poetical category. A very near approach is made to the idea of the hypostasis of the Logos, but there is no definite expression given to it. No other passage of the OT affords a deeper glance into the inner Divine life, and yet it is not easy to say what precisely we gain from it in this, to us, necessarily mysterious department of knowledge. Possibly Langen is right—although it may be difficult to reconcile such an opinion with a strict view of inspiration—when he says with regard to the statements of the sacred writer: 'It would really seem that in those expressions he has presented his own dark surmisings about the essence of his "Wisdom of God" rather than clear-cut thoughts' (*l.c.* p. 252).

2. *Hellenizing of the Heb. Hokhma in the Alexandrian Wisdom of Solomon.*—In Sirach the conception of Wisdom is often of the vaguest kind. Wisdom may be reason, or foresight, or knowledge, or virtue. He does use it, however, in a more definite sense. Objectively, it is that everlasting

* A. B. Davidson in *The Expositor* (First Series), xi. p. 340.

† Godet (*Prologue to St. John's Gospel*), who adds: 'When combined, however, with the notion of the Angel of the LORD, this idea of Wisdom assumes the character of a real personality.' It is difficult to see what good purpose is served by thus mixing up the two ideas. A great deal is predicated of Wisdom that is not in the OT applied to the Angel of the LORD; they have, in fact, nothing in common beyond the notion of representing God to the chosen people.

power by which God created and governs the world. Immanent from all eternity ($1^4$ $24^9$), it became active at the creation. It must therefore be conceived at once as an emanation from God and as standing alongside of God. Subjectively, it is the possession of the man who discovers the Divine Wisdom through the investigation of God's works in nature, and the knowledge of His will as revealed in the Law. The personification in Sir 24, although sharper and bolder than that of Pr 8, does not go beyond the latter in the direction of asserting a distinct personality. Wisdom is represented as a premundane creation of God (v.[9]), which 'came forth from the mouth of the Most High, and covered the earth as a mist' (v.[3]). All-embracing (v.[5]), and with a footing in every nation (v.[6]), it makes its home in Israel (vv.[8. 10f.]), takes root, grows, blossoms, and brings forth fruit (vv.[12-17]), and is enshrined in the Mosaic law (v.[23]). To Wisdom is thus given the special aspect of the revelation of God in the Law and in 'the assemblies of Jacob.' But, although in this way it corresponds somewhat to the NT λόγος, there is no clear ascription to it of personality: 'the conception of it still floats, so to speak, "as a mist."'* Thus we find nothing in Sirach, or in Baruch who agrees with him (cf. $3^{12ff.}$), beyond a highly coloured personification after the manner of the OT writings. They stand, in spite of Greek influences, where the author of Pr 8 stood. But these influences told very strongly in 'that highly original synthesis of Jewish, Platonic, and Stoic elements,' the later Alexandrian Book of Wisdom.

Heraclitus, who was a pantheist, appears to have been the originator of the Greek doctrine of the νοῦς or λόγος. Matter, he said, is God, but the animating νοῦς gave it shape. Anaxagoras improved on this by his threefold system of Godhead, λόγος, and matter, holding that God as the highest Being made use of the λόγος or νοῦς = Divine Intelligence, as the regulative principle of the universe. To Anaxagoras belongs the merit of having asserted the ascendency of Mind, although his theory was much obscured by the attempt to adduce explanations from material causes. In opposition to the physical philosophers, and in continuation of the work of Socrates, Plato put forth his theory of Ideas, in accordance with which he maintained that the phenomena of the universe could be accounted for only by 'The good,' *i.e.* the Final Cause. This philosopher gave a further development to the views of Anaxagoras by holding that the λόγος or νοῦς which gave form and order to the world designed it after the pattern of its own perfections. A supreme Mind, he contended, must as Intelligence work with some end in view; but, as the perfect Intelligence can fittingly have for its object only that which is best, it must have reflected its own attributes in the shaping of the world. Thus 'God is the measure of all things' (*de Leg.* iv.). The νοῦς holds together the κόσμος νοητός, but, as regards its relation to God Himself, Plato is clear only in saying that it is not identical with Him. For, according to this greatest of Gr. philosophers, the Divine essence is to be sought, not in Intelligence but in the idea of the Chief Good; and, when he speaks of God as νοῦς, it is only as Creator of the world that He is so designated. Still, Plato does not go the length of representing the νοῦς as a distinct personality.

It is not difficult to see how the Alexandrian Jews found their Heb. חָכְמָה (*Ḥokhma*) in this Greek doctrine of the νοῦς. Not to take account of differences, Plato and Solomon—or the writer of Pr 8 it should perhaps rather be said—were agreed that Wisdom must be distinguished from God, that it nevertheless belongs to Him, and that through it as a medium He actively works. Here, then, was a distinct point of union; and it is only natural that in passing from Sirach to Wisdom, written in another country and at a later time, we should meet with a considerable development of the OT doctrine, which was still substantially repeated there. This development is in the direction of Hellenizing the Heb. doctrine of Wisdom.

The writer introduces his discussion of Wisdom with the remark that he will explain what it is, and how it arose ($6^{22}$). Further, the doctrine is set forth in the abstract terms of Platonism, and not in language current among the ancient Hebrews. There is in Wisdom 'a spirit quick of understanding, holy, alone in kind, manifold, subtil, freely moving, clear in utterance, unpolluted, distinct, unharmed, loving what is good, keen, unhindered, beneficent, loving towards man, stedfast, sure, free from care, all-powerful, all-surveying, and penetrating through all spirits that are quick of understanding, pure, most subtil' ($7^{22f.}$). This summation of the attributes of Wisdom in no fewer than 21 particulars is quite after the Hellenistic style. The computation is indeed moderate when compared with the 150 epithets applied by Philo to vicious men.* The whole description of Wisdom recalls the manner in which the Gr. philosophers were accustomed to speak of their νοῦς. In point of subtlety of thought and expression the passage is manifestly framed after the Gr. rather than the Heb. models. It is also worthy of note that this does not profess to be a description of Wisdom itself, but only of *a spirit that is in her*. In this connexion Langen says: 'There was a disinclination to transfer directly to Wisdom itself what the Greeks said of the νοῦς, because σοφία in the abstract is only a bare conception, and therefore in the case of such a transference the qualities mentioned ran the risk of being handed over from their more substantial bearer (νοῦς) to a purely ideal one. On this account the writer elevated σοφία into a substance, while investing it with a spirit (πνεῦμα). And hereby there was therefore also implied an actual doctrinal advance, inasmuch as the essential character (*Wesenseigenthümlichkeit*) of Wisdom came to clearer expression than was possible through the figurative language of Solomon (*i.e.* Pr. 8). Yet this advance can be treated only as formal and not material, since Solomon also, through his anthropomorphic presentation of Wisdom playing before God, had already plainly enough raised it above the purely ideal.'† As regards the description itself, it would seem that, when the writer speaks of Wisdom as 'a clear effluence of the glory of the Almighty,' 'an effulgence from everlasting light,' 'an unspotted mirror of the working of God,' and 'an image of his goodness,' he means to represent it as standing in a relation to God that is not shared by the Divine creations —a relation so close and peculiar as to constitute Wisdom the very image or reflexion of His own essential Being, in a sense in which man cannot be said to be so. Here at all events Wisdom is no mere personification, but a real essence of purest light, the image of the Godhead, streaming forth as a substance from God before the creation of the world. At the same time there is no sharp distinction of personality drawn between God and His Wisdom. While, in conjunction with the Gr. doctrine of the νοῦς, the Heb. doctrine of the Wisdom came to be more clearly conceived and expressed, it was not as yet, either in the mind of our author or of his contemporaries, hypostatized into a second and subordinate God, as it afterwards was by Philo. There is in more than the usual sense a personification of Wisdom, yet we

* De Wette, *Ev. Joh.* p. 12 (Leipzig, 1837).

* *De Mercede Meretricis*, ed. Mang. ii. 268.
† *Judenthum*, etc. p. 259 f.

are led only half-way to personality. As Schürer says, 'The author applies the term *Wisdom* of God to represent the notion of an intermediary hypostasis, so far as he entertains it' (*HJP* II. iii. p. 376 n.). It is, however, important to note that, as the result of the combination and interaction of the Greek and the Jewish mind, the Book of Wisdom marks a distinct step towards greater definiteness of conception and expression in reference to this doctrine.

In the Bk. of Wisdom the Heb. *Ḥokhma* is practically identified, however, not only with the Gr. *νοῦς*, but also with the Holy Spirit and with the Logos. In the OT, God's Holy Spirit is the giver of all good; so to the Alexandrian was Wisdom. It is not wonderful therefore that the author of our book virtually identifies the two, and attributes to Wisdom just what the OT (*e.g.* in Is 11[2]) does to the Spirit of J″. At all events, the idea of the Spirit of God is intermixed with that of Wisdom, for it is Wisdom that inspires the prophets (7[27]). In one passage in particular (9[17]) Wisdom and the Holy Spirit are spoken of in quite parallel terms as the sole avenues to knowledge of the Divine counsel. Although not known to most of the Apocryphal writers, the Holy Spirit is, beyond doubt, expressly mentioned here. See art. HOLY SPIRIT in vol. ii. In at least one passage there also seems to be an identification of the Wisdom with the Gr. *λόγος*. Regarding the destruction of the firstborn in Egypt it is said, 'Thine all-powerful word leaped from heaven out of the royal throne, a stern warrior into the midst of the doomed land, bearing as a sharp sword thine unfeigned commandment; and standing it filled all things with death; and while it touched the heaven it trode upon the earth' (18[15f.]). The description here given of the *λόγος* inevitably suggests what the writer has already said of Wisdom as sharing God's royal throne (9[4]); and besides, as Langen has pointed out, there is merely a transference to the *λόγος* of what was before said of Wisdom, viz. that it 'pervadeth and penetrateth all things' (7[24]), and 'reacheth from one end of the world to the other' (8[1]). In support of the view that God's Word is here only another name for His Wisdom, we have the general doctrine, otherwise clearly expressed in our book, that God executes His will through His Word (16[12]). It can make no difference that in this case His will was to punish Egypt, and was not associated with any creative or healing purpose. A comparison of this passage with 10[19] shows that what is here ascribed to the *λόγος* might equally well have been attributed to the agency of the Wisdom. Bretschneider, on the other hand, maintains (*l.c.* p. 254 f.) that *λόγος* here denotes the destroying angel, and that nowhere either in the Apocrypha or in the LXX is it the equivalent of חָכְמָה, which is always translated by *σοφία*. But can the epithet *παντοδύναμος* be fittingly applied to an angel? However this may be, it seems quite plain that the doctrine of Wisdom in the Apocrypha is intermediate between that of the OT and the Logos of Philo, just as in Philo again we have the transition from the Apocryphal to the Johannine doctrine. In the Book of Wisdom there is assuredly development of some sort, however we may be disposed to characterize it. If our author says no more than the OT, he certainly says it more clearly. If there be no material advance on the OT doctrine, we have that doctrine presented in a much fuller and more developed form, and this we may regard as the legitimate service of Greek thought. Hagenbach recognizes 'the more definite and concrete form which, at the time when the Apocryphal writings were composed, was given to the personifications of the Divine word and the Divine Wisdom found in the OT.'* And so good an authority as A. B. Davidson says, 'If in the Alexandrian Wisdom of Solomon a progress directly in *advance* of what is found in Proverbs viii. on the doctrine of Wisdom may be justly contested, there is certainly what may be called a progress *round about*,—the ideas about Wisdom are expanded and placed in new lights, and made to enter into new relations in such a way that a general approximation to the NT doctrine of the Logos is the result.'† See, further, the articles WISDOM and WISDOM OF SOLOMON in vol. iv.

3. *The Logos of Philo.*—Already in the OT (Pr 8) there had been drawn the distinction between God Himself and the Wisdom of God, and in connexion with the Platonic doctrine of the *νοῦς* a further development is traceable in the Apocrypha, particularly in the Book of Wisdom. The designation of the Wisdom as *λόγος* furnishes the transition to another notable development—that which we find in the teaching of Philo. According to this philosopher, the relation of the Wisdom to the Logos is that of the source to the stream; the Logos is just Wisdom come to expression. Sometimes, however, he identifies the two (*de Profug.* i. 56). The whole world of ideas is embraced in the single conception and supreme Idea of the Logos or Reason of God. All empirical knowledge of God is referred to the Logos, who ranks indeed as a second, but also secondary, God. It is he who created and who reveals himself in the world, while the true God is inconceivable, and 'hides Himself behind the impenetrable veil of heaven.' The Logos is not in himself God; he is, however, an emanation from God, His firstborn son, and formed in His image. He is the manifested reflexion of the Eternal—the shadow, as it were, cast by the light of God. He is at once the medium and the mediator between God and the world; as 'the many-named archangel' he is the bearer of all revelation; and in him as high priest God and the world are eternally reconciled. With striking vigour and originality of thought Philo built up a religious philosophy, in which the Logos is endowed with personality and represented as a hypostasis standing between God and the world. In thus raising the Logos from an impersonal power to the level of a mediatorial hypostasis he passes beyond the OT and the Apocrypha, and makes his Logos correspond exactly neither to the Jewish Wisdom nor to the Platonic *νοῦς*. His teaching under this head is, however, characterized by the same ambiguity that attaches to his doctrine of God. By no possible ingenuity can the Logos be consistently represented as at once the immanent Reason of God, and yet also as a distinct hypostasis mediating between the spiritual and the material, the Divine and the finite. And in general it may be said that, 'owing to the manifold relations in which Philo places the Logos,—to Divine powers, ideas, and angels, to the supersensual and to the visible world, to the thought, speech, and creation of God, and again to the human spirit, whose heavenly prototype he is,—a perfectly clear and consistent conception of this mythical figure is rendered a virtual impossibility.'‡ Moreover, the service done by Philo in giving clear expression to the personality of the Logos is seriously curtailed by his theory of subordination, which, although no doubt in his view necessitated by the pronounced monotheism of the OT, detracted from the position previously assigned to the Logos, and even anticipated in some measure the fashion of Gnostic polytheism.

* *Hist. of Doctrines*, i. p. 106, Eng. tr.

† Art. 'Apocrypha' in *Encyc. Brit.*

‡ Lipsius, art. 'Alexandrinische Religionsphilosophie' in Schenkel's *Bibellexicon*.

4. *The Memra of the Targums.*—Before we come to consider the teaching of the NT regarding the Logos, reference may be made to a kindred expression which occurs very frequently in the Targums. The name given to the Logos in these writings (but never in the Talmud) is *Memra* = 'Word.'

*Memra* is not, however, always the equivalent, nor is it, strictly speaking, ever the precise equivalent, of Logos, which has the additional meaning of *reason*; and one result of the adoption of this narrower term was to give fresh significance to the statement that the world was created by the word of God (Gn 1[3], Ps 33[6]). Still, the mediation of the Memra or Word is not, as in the OT and in Philo's theosophy, represented as specially connected with the creative activity of God; rather is it applied to the whole scope of His activity in the world. With the Targumists it stands in much the same relationship to God as the *Ḥokhma* or σοφία of the earlier Jews, only it is allowed a wider range. By His Word God enters into covenant with men and exercises guardianship over them; to His Word they pray, and by His Word they swear. There is, however, considerable vagueness in the use of the term. Sometimes anthropomorphisms are avoided by the introduction of *word* or *glory*. Thus in Gn 28 the glory of J″ appears to Jacob, who declares that the Word of J″ shall then be his God. But in some passages, when there can be no such motive, Memra or Word is used for the Spirit of J″, apparently to avoid referring directly to the Divine Being the processes of the inner life of Godhead. A distinction is made between the Word as spoken (*Pithgama*) and the Word as speaking or revealing Himself (*Memra*). *E.g.* in Gn 15[1] 'After these things came the *Pithgama* of J″ to Abram in a vision (? in prophecy), saying, Fear not, Abram, my *Memra* shall be thy strength and thy exceeding great reward.' 'A critical analysis shows that in 82 instances in Onkelos, in 71 instances in the Jerus. Targum, and in 213 instances in the Targum pseudo-Jonathan, the designation *Memra* is not only distinguished from God, but evidently refers to God as revealing Himself.' *

From what has been said, it will be apparent that, while the Memra plays a rôle somewhat similar to it, it is not to be altogether identified with the Logos of Philo. In one respect, however, the Targumists are at one with the Alexandrian theosophy of which he became the leading exponent; the Deity Himself remained in the background, and everything that can be known by us about God's essential Being is transferred to the Word. This is shown, *e.g.*, by their treatment of 1 S 26[20], where, instead of 'Let not my blood fall to the earth before the face of the Lord,' we have 'Let not . . . before the *Word* of the Lord.' Even affections are attributed to God only mediately through the Word (Gn 6[6], 1 S 15[10], Is 42[1]). With the Alexandrians God is without qualities (ἄποιος); with the Targumists He is virtually unknowable. While, then, the Memra of the Targumists is not to be identified with the Logos doctrine of the Alexandrian school, the former being at bottom religious and the latter philosophical, the two conceptions are yet in some measure related. Indeed the difference between the position reflected in the Targums and the standpoint of the Book of Wisdom is most satisfactorily explained on the assumption that the Alexandrian doctrine of the Logos, as representing the knowable in Deity, was not unfamiliar to Pal. circles, at any rate so far as its general features and results were concerned. In all probability it was to a large extent welcomed and adopted as a ready-made and serviceable conception. This may be inferred from the fact that the expression Memra is used almost to excess, and in the most varied connexions. While really connoting much less than the Jewish σοφία = Gr. λόγος, it was given a far more extended application than is warranted by the doctrine of the σοφία as presented in the Book of Wisdom.

It was in keeping with the spirit of the age that the Targumists should hail a doctrine which made for the purification of the conception of God by excluding the ascription to God in His essential Being of all direct activity in the world or contact with man, and of all such affections of the soul as seemed to savour of the finite and human, and so to import a certain limitation and degradation of the Deity. They did not, however, like Philo, speculate about the position of the Word relatively to God. They were content to connect their generalizations with the OT representation of the creation of the world mediately through Wisdom. And as in the sacred writings the conception of Wisdom is not a fixed one, but appears now as merely a personified Divine attribute, now as virtually a distinct entity or hypostasis, they secured their object by the simple method of giving to it a wider scope. In the hands of the Targumists, however, the Logos doctrine underwent no essential development; they did nothing to give precision or clearness to the obscure and indeterminate position in which it is found in Proverbs and Wisdom, and also in the earlier writings of the Alexandrian school.

For generations thinking men had been grappling with the problems suggested by the OT doctrine of the Logos in conjunction with philosophical speculation, and it would appear as if at length by the first century of our era the hope of a satisfactory conclusion ever being reached had been to a large extent abandoned. Men were weary of wandering in what seemed an interminable maze. For while on the one hand there was a disposition to surmise that the unity of the Godhead was not in all respects absolute, on the other hand it was recognized that the phenomena of the inner life of Deity were secrets undecipherable by man's intellect, and only darkly hinted at even in revelation. Through the dense maze of subtleties and theorizings which had overrun the path of investigation Philo had boldly cut his way to clearer ground by ascribing to the Logos a distinct personality, albeit with the rank of an inferior God. Others went to the opposite extreme, and took no cognizance whatever of the subject. The writer of 2 (4) Esdras, *e.g.*, ignores the whole development of the Logos doctrine. Although that doctrine was specially associated with the creation of the world, and had obtained in Palestine a new significance as Memra, the term 'Word' is used by the writer simply as denoting the spoken word, even where he speaks of God as having created heaven and earth by His Word. All mystery is eliminated from the doctrine, and no consciousness betrayed of the existence of the many enigmas which had gathered round it.

5. *NT conception of the Logos.*—But the whole position with reference to this doctrine was about to undergo a development of the utmost consequence through the promulgation of the Christian idea of the Logos. This is set forth in the Prologue to the Fourth Gospel. Here we are taught that the Logos is a Divine personal Subsistence, and, as such, exists in a twofold manner: first, as coexistent with God from eternity, as resting in Him before all time; second, as outwardly existing, *i.e.* as manifested, first of all in order to the act of creation, and finally in His Incarnation in order to the redemption of the world. 'In the beginning was the Word, and the Word was with God, and the Word was God. The same was in the beginning with God. All things were made by him. . . . And the Word was made flesh, and dwelt among us, full of grace and truth.' In these bold, concise, and unmistakable utterances, St. John, moved and enlightened by the Holy Ghost, at once completely solves the long-standing riddle of centuries, and communicates a new revelation. Joining on his representation to that of the Mosaic account of the creation as containing the first revelation of the activity of the Logos, he proceeds to erect upon this foundation his great doctrinal superstructure. The opening verses of the OT had already declared that in the beginning God created the heaven and the earth, and through His Word gave shape and order to formless chaos. St. John supplements this statement by further declaring that 'in the beginning' the Word already existed alongside of God and partook of the Divine nature. He thereby also confirms the language of Pr 8, which speaks of Wisdom as 'set up from everlasting,' and as occupying the very closest relation to God. True, he does not make use of the term Wisdom, but of the term Logos. The latter, however, is employed, not in its older meaning of *Nous* but in its then current sense of *Word*. The connexion with Pr 8 is obvious enough, and the Evangelist's representation makes it impossible to put any other interpretation upon the passage than that which it must bear when read in the light of his words.

The question is often asked, How far was the writer in his view of the Logos influenced by current philosophical speculations, and more especially by those of Philo? In seeking an answer we must keep in mind the fact that when the Gospel was written the name Logos was a familiar one, alike in Jewish and in non-Jewish circles. The air was

* Edersheim, *Life and Times of Jesus the Messiah*, i. p. 47.

full of such doctrines as Philo's, and that of the Logos in its essential features not only existed in Alexandria before his day, but must also have gained currency in Palestine, seeing there was constant communication between Egypt and that country. Consequently, it is not surprising that the author of the Gospel uses the name without explanation as one which his readers would be prepared to understand. Two extreme views have been propounded, and, as frequently happens, the truth would seem to lie somewhere between them. The first is, that the philosophy of the time had no influence whatever on the Prologue to this Gospel, and was not kept in view by the writer. In this case the name Logos is not regarded as derived from the Schools, but as having sprung up solely within the Church, in the sense of *oratio*='word,' 'revelation.' But, if we thus exclude the meaning *ratio* and confine it to *oratio*, we cannot put a satisfactory construction on the words ἐν ἀρχῇ ἦν ὁ λόγος. For though we may regard creation as a self-revelation of God, wrought through the Logos, who was as Logos at the beginning *of the world*, yet if, as we believe, ἦν denotes the pre-temporal existence of Christ, we cannot accept the narrowed meaning. It is only as λόγος ἐνδιάθετος that the term can denote His eternal existence *before* time; and this we find to be an outstanding truth in the record of the Logos made flesh. The other and opposite view, that the writer merely expands and embodies the teaching of Philo, is likewise untenable. Even those who deny the Johannine authorship must reject it, for the two conceptions, if in some respects similar, are yet essentially at variance. While the idea of an Incarnation is utterly destructive of Philo's doctrine of the Logos, it is the central truth of the Christian faith that God's revelation is not completed until it is embodied in a human life. On the assumption that the Gospel is St. John's, this view is incredible. Can we suppose that the disciple whom Jesus loved, who drew from the Saviour the principles that gave character to his life, who pondered deeply and long what he had seen and heard, would have founded his conception of his Master on the crude notions of an expiring philosophy? The matter, then, would seem to stand thus: The author derived his view of Christ's Person from Christ's life and teaching, and his own reflexion upon them, guided by the illumination of the Holy Spirit. Like St. Paul, he might have expressed these views independently of any philosophical system. At the same time he recognized in the name and conception of the Logos a suitable vehicle for his own thought, and adopted it accordingly. In other words, he recognizes and declares that there is a great Truth after which men had been thus groping, that there *is* a Divinity working in the world, as the Greek had faintly perceived, and that there is need for a revealer of the invisible God, as the Jew had come to feel.

Very noticeable in connexion with St. John's solution of an enigma which had become more and more complicated as time went on, is the contrast between the firm tread of Scripture and the hesitating vagaries of the unaided human intellect. In the Prologue to this Gospel there is a note of certainty, of finality, of quiet confidence, and of powerful persuasiveness, which is foreign to Alexandrian theosophist and Jewish Targumist alike. The Logos became flesh: in this simple yet momentous declaration he conveyed to the world the secret of the inner life of the Godhead as he had learned it from the Holy Spirit working in the soul of one who had been so intimately associated with Jesus, and who, more than any other of the Apostles, was capable of being animated by the mind of the Master. That which he had seen and heard, and which had never faded from his adoring consciousness, he announced to men not only as an answer to their problems, but also as the redemption of their souls. The two loftiest ideas in OT revelation are those of Wisdom and the Messiah, and, although the Jews had no proper conception of this, and latterly even lost the consciousness of it, the two ideas were essentially one. It was his knowledge of this that enabled St. John to unlock the mystery which would yield to no other key. To as many as received Him on the footing of His being at once the Word and the Anointed of God, the Eternal Word gave power to become the sons of God. The jarring note in the Evangelist's account of this glorious gospel is the record that 'he came unto his own, and his own received him not.' It needed the lurid light of the cross to show the harmony and inseparableness of these two ideas, and to prove that Christ, as combining in His own Person everything ascribed to the Logos and the Messiah, is made unto us 'wisdom from God, and righteousness, and sanctification, and redemption' (1 Co $1^{30}$).

iii. ANGELOLOGY AND DEMONOLOGY. — A. *ANGELOLOGY*.—1. *The OT doctrine of angels.*—There was throughout the East a general belief in angels as inhabitants of the spirit-world. In the OT these are recognized as spirits intermediate between God and man, and acting as the messengers and servants of Providence. Their nature, while superior to that of man, is not purely spiritual; their main function is that of executing the Divine behests. They are poetically conceived as forming the host of heaven (1 K $22^{19}$), who praise God in the sanctuary above (Ps $148^{2}$ $150^{1}$), act as the ministers of His will (Ps $103^{20f.}$), attend Him when He manifests Himself in His kingly glory (Dt $33^{2}$?; see Driver, *ad loc.*), and form His retinue when He appears for judgment (Jl $3^{11}$, Zec $14^{5}$). The mention of the captain of the Lord's host in Jos $5^{13ff.}$ is too slender a basis for the conclusion that the ancient Hebrew regarded the angels as an organized celestial hierarchy in which the cherubim and seraphim hold their respective ranks. Nowhere are the cherubim endowed with independent personality; they are only ideal representations, varying according to the conception of the writers who make mention of them. In like manner the seraphim of Is 6 seem to be only symbolic appearances. There is, however, a very perceptible development of angelology in the OT itself. At first the LORD God speaks directly to man (Gn $3^{9}$); then He appears to men through His messengers, who are called 'sons of God' (Job $1^{6}$, Ps $29^{1}$ $89^{6}$). We have further the conception of the Angel of the LORD, who is in some passages identified with J″ (Gn $18^{20}$, cf. with $19^{13}$), and in others hypostatically distinguished from Him (Gn $24^{7}$, Zec $1^{12}$). Whether this name is to be applied specifically to one angel who represents God's presence, or is to be extended to any angel with a special commission, remains therefore a moot point. The doctrine that Israel was led by the angel of J″ paved the way for the belief in angelic guardianship of individuals, which some would find in Ps $34^{7}$ $91^{11}$, although it is doubtful whether these passages contain more than a poetical expression of trust in a beneficent Providence. On the other hand, angels were regarded as the instruments of judgment (2 S $24^{16}$, 2 K $19^{35}$, Ps $78^{49}$), and even the forces of nature came to be personified as God's messengers (Ps $104^{4}$).

Prior to the Exile, with rare exceptions such as Is $6^{2-6}$, the prophets do not introduce angels, but already in the visions of Ezekiel and Zechariah they play a prominent part, and the mystic number of seven (Ezk $9^{2}$, Zec $4^{2.10}$) possibly points to the hierarchical idea which certainly afterwards gained ground (To $12^{15}$, Rev $8^{2}$). Ezekiel calls them men; Zechariah calls them both men and messengers. By these prophets special prominence is also given to one angel who acts as Instructor or Interpreter. This is the fruitful germ from which has sprung the widespread invocation of angels and spirits in the worship of the Christian Church. Then, as in modern monastic piety, it appears to have arisen from a false conception of God as reigning in the remote heaven; angels were employed to bridge the gulf that separated Him from men. Zechariah is the first prophet to recognize different orders and ranks among the angels ($2^{3.4}$ $3^{1.4}$).

2. *Post-exilic development of angelology on Persian lines.*—In the post-exilic period, chiefly under the Parsi influences brought to bear upon the Jews of the Dispersion, the OT doctrine of angels underwent a curious and interesting development. Not that the Jews adopted wholesale the doctrine of Zoroaster either on this or on other points; but the inevitable social and religious influences amid which many of them lived in contentment and peace, could not but tell on their theology. All the more was this the case that Zoroastrianism was in the zenith of its prosperity as a religious system, and in many respects indeed, as we have seen, was allied to Judaism. In no direction did it influence Jewish thought more than in the department of angelology. Men's minds were strongly attracted to the superhuman, and angels were multiplied until God was conceived as governing the world by hosts of these 'intermediary beings who concerned themselves with the affairs of men with very various ends.' The belief in a regularly graded hierarchy of good and evil spirits, which characterized the religion of Zoroaster, began to be distinctly reflected, at least as to its main features, in the Jewish theology of the period. The position reached with regard to this whole doctrine in the later Judaism was apparently the result of the Persian conception of pure beings who surrounded Ormazd as his servants, acting upon the ancient Jewish belief that the angels were the messengers of Jehovah's will. Development of the doctrine on Iranian lines was facilitated by the general and undefined nature of the Heb. angelology. The latter offered no bar to the acceptance of an ideal structure based upon a common principle; and the religious character of the Mazdean doctrine of pure spirits gave it the appearance of being the complete form of their own more rudimentary belief. In the later Jewish literature, accordingly, the angels are viewed as a well-organized host, whose recognized chiefs (Dn $10^{13}$) are admitted into God's immediate presence, and form His secret council (Enoch $14^{22}$). They are seven in number (To $12^{15}$). Three are named in Daniel and Tobit, viz. GABRIEL, *i.e.* 'man of God,' whose special function seems to have been to communicate Divine revelations (Dn $8^{16}$ $9^{21}$, Lk $1^{19}$); MICHAEL, *i.e.* 'who is like God?' the guardian of Israel (Dn $10^{13.21}$ $12^{1}$, Bar $6^{7}$, cf. 1 Th $4^{16}$, Jude $^{9}$, Rev $12^{7}$); and RAPHAEL, *i.e.* 'God heals,' whose mission it was to cure disease (To $3^{17}$), and to present the prayers of the saints before God's throne (To $12^{15}$, cf. Zec $1^{12}$). Three more are mentioned in 2 (4) Esdras: URIEL, *i.e.* 'God is light' ($4^{1}$); JEREMIEL, *i.e.* 'God hurls' ($4^{36}$); and PHALTIEL (the Syriac has *Psaltiel*, $5^{16}$).* Who was the seventh? Is the silence of the pre-Christian Jewish literature on this point merely accidental, or was J″ Himself reckoned the first of the seven archangels, as Ormazd was the chief of the seven *amshaspands*?† On the latter supposition the analogy would be complete, but it would have been alien to all Jewish tradition to compare Ormazd or any of the archangels with J″. To them He was far above, and of another nature than, angels or archangels, who were only His servants. They borrowed the idea of the seven *amshaspands*, and made them the chiefs of the heavenly host; but they regarded them, their chief included, as beings entirely subordinate to J″.

The Persian influence is seen so far in the pronounced angelology of the Book of Daniel. What is new here is that angels, who are designated 'watchers' (עִירִין. In LXX עִיר is Grecized into εἴρ, but Aq. and Symm. render ἐγρήγορος), have recognized princes with particular names, whereas in ancient Israel none of the angels were known by proper names. The angel in Jg $13^{18f.}$ refuses to tell his name. That the names of the angels *ascenderunt in manu Israelis ex Babylone** is expressly acknowledged by the Rabbins themselves. It is also taught in Daniel that the nations have their own special tutelary spirits, who fight actively in their behalf ($10^{13.20}$). This identification of particular angels with different nations carries us a step further than the intercession of the angels in Zechariah's first vision. There is also in Daniel a further development of the former prophet's vision of a hierarchy among the angels; they are classified in categories, of which each has particular functions.

But it is in the Apocryphal writings that we discern the full strength of the Persian influence. The great Books of Sirach and Wisdom have little or nothing to say about angels. Judith speaks of none, and 1 Mac. refers only once to the destroying angel ($7^{41}$). In Baruch also there is but a single reference to the subject ($6^{7}$). The other books, and mainly 2 (4) Esdras, Tobit, and 2 Mac., are our sources. The most important passage, and one which formed the groundwork, so to speak, of many subsequent delineations of man's relation to the spirit-world, is To $12^{12-15}$ (cf. Rev $8^{4}$): 'When thou didst pray, and Sarah thy daughter-in-law, I did bring the memorial of your prayer before the Holy One: and when thou didst bury the dead, I was with thee likewise. . . . And now God did send me to heal thee and Sarah thy daughter-in-law. I am Raphael, one of the seven holy angels, which present the prayers of the saints, and go in before the glory of the Holy One.' This passage teaches still more clearly than the Books of Zechariah and Daniel that there is a distinction of rank among the angels. Raphael is one of seven who stand in the immediate presence of God; from Lk $1^{19}$ and Rev $8^{2}$ we learn that Gabriel was also a member of Tobit's heptarchy. This idea, which was probably taken from the customs of Oriental palaces, where dignitaries were wont to gather round the throne, and which at all events had been embodied in the religion of Zoroaster, attains great prominence in the Jewish Apocalyptic literature. In spite of the weighty authority of A. B. Davidson, who observes, 'The number seven already appears in Ezk $9^{2}$, and there is no need to refer it to Persian influence' (art. ANGELS in vol. i.), it is difficult to resist the conviction that the seven *amshaspands* or princes of light suggested the seven Jewish archangels. So Winer, *RWB*, art. 'Engel'; Ewald, *HI* v. p. 185; Nicolas, *Des Doctrines Religieuses des Juifs*; Cheyne, *OP* p. 335. At the same time there is no reason to suppose that the entire scheme of the supersensible world elaborated in the Avesta became part of the creed of Judaism. While the Persian influence is traceable, and while there are general points of resemblance in the angelology of

* Cf. Enoch $20^{7}$ (Uriel, Raphael, Raguel, Michael, Sariel, Gabriel).

† These are called (1) Vohu-Manô = 'the good mind'; (2) Asha-vahista = 'the highest holiness'; (3) Khshathra-vairya = 'good government'; (4) Spenta-armaiti = 'meek piety'; (5) Haurvatât = 'perfection'; (6) Ameretât = 'immortality'; (7) Ahura-mazda = 'the supreme god himself.'

* Jerus. Talmud, *Rôsh-hashânâ*, p. 56.

the two systems, there is nothing like absolute identity. It is further implied in the passage under review, that according to their position in this hierarchy particular functions are performed by particular angels. The great business of 'the seven' is to 'present the prayers of the saints.' It seems to follow from this that the prayers of the pious are directed to the angels for this purpose; compare, on the other hand, Rev 22[8f.]. Another belief, clearly reflected in Tobit, is that some angels are charged with the protection of individual men: 'A good angel shall go with him, and his journey shall be prospered, and he shall return safe and sound' (5[21]). 'Good' is here evidently not descriptive of the angel's character as opposed to evil angels, but to his office of guardianship, in keeping with the statement of v.[16] 'God . . . shall prosper your journey; and may his angel go with you.' The Israelites thought of the superhuman powers, not as good and evil but as benevolent or antagonistic. If the idea of angelic guardianship of individual men appears at all in the OT (Ps 34[7] 91[11]), it does so in a far less definite shape than here. In NT times, on the other hand, this belief seems to have been quite current (Ac 12[15]). An interesting example of its recurrence in modern literature is found in Lessing's *Nathan der Weise*, where Recha, Nathan's adopted daughter, is made to say—

> 'Ich also, ich hab' einen Engel
> Von Angesicht zu Angesicht gesehn ;
> Und *meinen* Engel.'

The same idea was extended to nations and armies (Dn 12[1], 2 Mac 11[6] 15[23]). Indeed we find in 2 Mac. almost a repetition of the old Roman legend of Castor and Pollux mounted on white steeds and appearing at the head of the Jewish armies (3[25ff.]). A somewhat similar tale is told in 10[29f.], where five such 'men' appear, 'two of them leading on the Jews.' In 15[23] Judas Maccabæus is represented as praying for 'a good angel' to terrify the enemy, and in v.[27] the Jews are described as having been 'made exceeding glad by the manifestation of God.' This idea as applied to nations seems to underlie the Heb. text followed by the LXX translator of Dt 32[8] 'The Most High set the bounds of the people according to the number of the *angels of God*' (בְּנֵי אֵל) instead of 'sons of Israel' (בְּנֵי יִשְׂרָאֵל). Perhaps also Ben Sira may have had the angels in view when he wrote: 'For every nation he appointed a ruler' (Sir 17[17]).

3. *Conception of elemental angels in post-canonical Jewish literature.*—Allusion has already been made to the personification of the forces of nature in the OT. The same tendency showed itself later in the conception of the elemental angels. Sir 39[28ff.] speaks of 'fire and hail, and famine and death; teeth of wild beasts, and scorpions and adders' as 'spirits (πνεύματα) that are created for vengeance.' Although these are not angels, they are said to rejoice in executing God's commandment, and the language used by the writer certainly prepared the way for the introduction into Palestine of the Gr. idea of attributing to every separate thing its δαίμων or angel. In the Book of Enoch, the sea, the hoar frost, the snow, the mist, the dew, and the rain,—each has its special spirit (60[16ff.]). This idea is still further developed in the Book of Jubilees (B.C. 135–105); the different elements are represented as each containing a spirit, and this again its angel, so that it becomes possible to speak of the angels of the fire-spirit, the wind-spirit, etc. The fullest development, however, of the tendency in question is found in the Targums. Thus in that of Jonathan the pestilence of Hab 3[5] becomes the angel of death. That even abstract conceptions had their angels bound up with them appears, *e.g.*, from the statement of the *Testament of Benjamin* that the souls of the virtuous are led by the angel of peace (ἄγγελος τῆς εἰρήνης).

To sum up. The Jewish people, under the influence of what they saw in the religion of Zoroaster, formulated their doctrine of angels with more precision than they had done previously. Especially was this the case with regard to these points: (1) the angels as a whole were conceived as forming a celestial hierarchy with seven princes; (2) those angels who acted as intermediaries between heaven and earth were designated by proper names; (3) the Jews began to follow the custom (which, however, was no less Greek than Persian) of peopling the whole world with angels, and of giving to every man his own protecting spirit or δαίμων; (4) they formed the conception of the elemental angels.

4. *Doctrine of angels as held by the Essenes and by Philo.*—That the Jewish angelology had not reached its full development even at the beginning of the Christian era is evident from the fact that a cardinal point in it, viz. the doctrine propounded in the Talmud and the Targums regarding the creation of angels on the second day of the creation of the world, is entirely absent from the NT as well as from the later pre-Christian Jewish writings. The same conclusion is pointed to by the vagueness in several respects (*e.g.* in the exact division of angelic tasks, and in the varying names given to the last three archangels) of the angelology of the two centuries before Christ, which seems to have been a product of popular imagination rather than the deliberate teaching of the Rabbis. The Palestinian and Babylonian Jew was, however, quite satisfied with an angelology which not only supplied some tangible link between him and the Deity, but also afforded the comfortable assurance that in heaven his destinies were watched over by the accredited commissioners of J″. It was otherwise with the Jews of Alexandria and the Essenes, who were concerned with the speculative rather than the practical, and with whom the doctrine of angels took the form of a theory of cosmic powers. By the latter sect the popular belief in angels was spiritualized into an esoteric system, in which the angels were only metaphorically the servants and messengers of God; in reality they were descending grades of being, differing in purity and in power in proportion to their distance from the First Cause, of which they were all emanations. It was the privilege of the initiated to be informed as to the distinctive names of this graduated series of spirits, and of the relations in which they stood to the whole and to one another. Any one admitted to their sect had to take an oath that he would 'equally preserve' their peculiar books and the names of the angels (Jos. *BJ* II. viii. 7). In all this we see the allegorizing and Gnostic tendency already at work.

Philo's doctrine of angels, although much akin to that of the Essenes, bore the peculiar stamp of its birthplace. It was a Platonized version of the ancient Hebrew beliefs. The latter formed, indeed, the common basis of both the Palestinian and the Alexandrian angelology; the differences in the developed products were due to the fact that in the one case Zoroastrian, and in the other Platonic, influences were at work. According to Philo, the angels are incorporeal beings who inhabit the air, and are in number equal to the stars. They are comprehended in two main divisions—the inferior angels, who dwell nearest to the earth and are capable of descending into human bodies; and the higher and purer intelligences (λόγοι = Ideas), whose habitat is the upper regions of the air. It is through the latter that God, who as the perfect Being cannot enter into relations with corruptible matter, communicates with the universe. These intermediaries, whose action is purely spiritual, Philo identifies not only with the Platonic Ideas and Stoic Forces, but with the Dæmons of the Greeks and the Angels of the Jews. Their function is to execute the commands of the Most High, and to protect and direct the souls of good men. Among the infinite variety of the powers two are supreme—goodness and might. It must be said, however, that Philo has no clear-cut conception of these mediating forces. At times he speaks as if they were mere abstractions, at other times as if they were persons. But this is the necessary result of the premises from which he starts. As the media by which He works in the world His Ideas must be inseparable from God; while at the same time, on the assumption of His aloofness from the world, they must rank as independent entities.

5. *Denial of angels by the Sadducees.*—In certain quarters, however, during the post-exilic period the doctrine of angels seems to have met with entire rejection. The position of the Samaritans is not quite clear, but at all events they had a doctrine of angels, and in this respect differed from the Sadducees, who maintained that 'there is no resurrection, neither angel, nor spirit' (Ac 23[8]). This is so far supported by Josephus, who says that according to the teaching of the Sadducees the soul dies with the body (*Ant.* XVIII. i. 4). How much does this denial of angels by the Sadducees imply? It is possible that they only rejected the oral Pharisaic tradition and the developed angelology of their day, while accepting the written Scriptures and a rationalistic interpretation of the old angelophanies. Yet they were evidently pure materialists, and repudiated the idea of a future life. It does seem strange that they should nevertheless have believed in God; but their God was, like the deities of Epicureanism, entirely separated from the world. In their view the present life was complete in itself, and man had no future judgment to face. As adherents of the Epicurean philosophy, they could not accept either the doctrine of a future life, or the Jewish angelology which postulated a spirit-world created by God, and judged by Him.

B. DEMONOLOGY.—1. *The position as reflected in the earlier OT literature.*—The development in demonology is still more marked than that of angelology. Among the ancient Hebrews the belief in evil spirits seems to have been of the most rudimentary description, hardly amounting to more than a vague popular superstition. The data furnished by the earlier OT literature is extremely meagre. Ruins and waste places were peopled with weird spectres (*sĕ'îrîm*), including a night-monster, Lilith, who was specially dangerous to infants (Is 13[21] 34[14]).* Mental disease was attributed to the malign influence of evil spirits, but in such cases the evil spirit is said to have proceeded from the LORD (1 S 16[14]). As His Providence comprehended alike the evil and the good (1 S 2[6], Ps 78[49]), there was really no place for demons viewed as the source of evil. The *shêdîm* of Dt 32[17] and Ps 106[37], though illegitimate objects of worship, are not in OT the noxious spirits which they became in the later Judaism, and the story of the serpent in Gn 3[1-7] is not elsewhere alluded to in any pre-exilic writing. If the belief in evil spirits can be said to have existed in Israel before the Exile, it certainly was not in the widespread

* Although these passages are probably exilic, and coloured by Babylonian influence, the mention of jackals and other animals in connexion with the *sĕ'îrîm* warrants the conclusion that demons were supposed to dwell in all those animals which haunt the solitary waste.

form which it afterwards assumed. Although those interpreters who have detected a personal being in Azâzel (=(?) 'God strengthens,' Lv 16[8]) are probably right, in view of the fact that Jehovah receives the one goat and Azâzel the other, it does not follow that the conception of the latter arose at an early date in Heb. history. It is probable that the Priestly Code is not of Mosaic origin, and that this allusion to the ritual of the scapegoat belongs to post-exilic times. There is no subsequent mention of Azâzel in OT, although he reappears in the Book of Enoch as a leader of the (fallen) angels. Cheyne ('Azâzel' in *Encyc. Bibl.*) thinks he was 'a personal angel substituted for the crowd of *sĕ'îrîm* (or earth-demons) to whom the people sacrificed; just as the scapegoat was the substitute for the sacrificial victims.' However this may be, it is clear that he was regarded as in some sense antagonistic to J″; and that the conception of him, if not identical with that of Satan, as Origen (*c. Cels.* vi. 305) and others have supposed, was at least a step in the direction of that of the devil.

2. *The Satan of Job, Zechariah, the Chronicler, and the Similitudes of Enoch.*—In the Prologue to Job we have the first trace of the Satan or Adversary, *i.e.* the angel whose function it is to act as Accuser and to execute God's purposes of judgment. As a member of God's council (1[8]) he stands in contrast to those angels whose ministry is concerned with errands of mercy, but while an angel of evil he is not in his own nature an evil angel. Although showing a strong disinclination to believe in human virtue, he does not in Job, as in Jude, contend with God; he is content to act by His permission. But while he is not here represented as an evil spirit, he is yet on the way which led later to his being so conceived. He performs his task with a too evident relish, and instigates God against Job (2[3]). It is still a question among critics whether the Book of Job is pre-exilic, but the other OT writings in which the word Satan is used to denote this minister of God undoubtedly belong to the Jewish period. In Zec 3[1.2] he appears as the pitiless accuser whom J″ repels. The cruel and malicious way in which he exercises his office against the broken-down Church of the Restoration calls forth the rebuke of Divine grace. Here there is an approach to the conception of him as an evil spirit, without his being regarded, however, as an embodiment of all evil; he is still God's servant. In 1 Ch 21[1] Satan is used without the article as the distinctive designation of the spirit who stands up against Israel as their enemy. It is at his instigation that David numbers the people, an act ascribed in earlier times to J″ (2 S 24[1]). The possibility of such an interchange is owing to the fact that in either case the angel who tempts David is the minister of J″. Angels are but the ministers of His will. Even to the 'lying spirit' mentioned in 2 Ch 18[21] we are not to ascribe an evil character. That passage does not prove that at this stage evil spirits were not only believed in, but viewed as having power to 'possess' individual men. The spirit who misled the infatuated Ahab is Jehovah's messenger, and goes forth from His immediate presence. In the Satan of Zechariah and the Chronicler, then, even more than in that of Job, there seems to be some approach to the conception of an evil spirit. At the same time he has not yet become an actual demon. The period was one of transition: foreign influences were at work among the Pal. and Bab. Jews, and primitive Semitic beliefs were undergoing a process of transformation. Thus in the earlier post-exilic age Satan was neither a Heb. angel pure and simple, nor a Jewish demon of the developed type familiar to us in NT. Later, in the *Similitudes* of the Book of

Enoch, written, according to Charles, B.C. 95–80, he appears as ruler of the angels whom he has made subject to him (54[6], cf. Mt 12[24ff.]). These, who are designated Satans, have access to heaven, but are subject to the Lord of spirits (40[7]). Like those of Satan in NT, their functions are tempting (69[4. 6], cf. Mt 4[1ff.], Lk 22[3]), accusing (40[7], cf. Rev 12[10]), and punishing (53[3] 56[1], cf. 1 Co 5[5]). It was long before Satan came to be conceived in Palestine as Beelzebub, or prince of devils. There is, in fact, a strange reticence regarding the existence and nature of Satan in the literature of the period between the Testaments. He is not mentioned in the Apocrypha (Satan being most probably used in Sir 21[27] merely in the general sense of adversary) or by Josephus. There is not, however, the same silence with regard to demons. Under the influence of Mazdeism a more concrete form was given to floating Semitic superstitions about evil spirits. Not that this influence went very deep, for Persian dualism could not seriously affect Hebrew monotheism.

It is a moot point whether the conception of Satan may not have been taken over from the Persians. This is denied by many scholars, *e.g.* Oehler, who maintains that 'the Satan of the OT is devoid of essential characteristics which must be present to justify a comparison with Ahriman' (*OT Theol.* ii. p. 291, Eng. tr.). So also Renan. Cheyne thinks it 'a matter for argument. But who can fail to see that the Satan of the Book of Revelation is the fellow of Ahriman?' (*OP*, p. 282). G. A. Smith, while admitting the difficulty of the question, ranges himself on the negative side (*The Twelve Prophets*, ii. p. 319). According to Wellhausen, however,—who thinks that 'the influence of Parsism upon Judaism was not so great as is usually assumed,'—'Satan has some relation to old Hebrew conceptions (1 K xxii.), but nevertheless is essentially the product of Zoroastrian dualism' (art. 'Israel' in *Encyc. Brit.*). Bruce suggests that the divergence of 1 Ch 21[1] from 2 S 24[1], referred to above, may have been due to a feeling on the part of the Chronicler, begotten of Iranian influence, that temptation was no fit work of God (*The Moral Order of the World*, p. 63). The influence of the Persian dualism, which represents Ahriman as the antagonist of Ormazd, may also possibly be reflected in Zec 3. Here Satan appears as accuser of Joshua the high priest, standing, as was customary upon such occasions, at his right hand (Ps 109[6]). The rebuke administered to him exactly coincides with that of Jude[9], where Michael the archangel is said to have disputed with him about the burial of Moses. It is, however, doubtful whether in Zec. Satan is not used merely in the general sense of the Adversary; the occurrence of the article seems to preclude the view that we have here a regular proper name as in 1 Ch 21[1]. In the art. ZOROASTRIANISM in vol. iv., J. H. Moulton, while characterizing as 'absurd' the idea that Satan was borrowed from Angra Mainyu, is ready to concede that 'the ranking of demons and the elevation of one spirit to their head may have been stimulated by Parsism.' This writer also allows that 'the abandonment of earlier ideas, like Azâzel and the serpent' 'in favour of the Satan,' is to be ascribed to Persian influence. See, further, art. SATAN in vol. iv.

3. *The doctrine of evil spirits in the Apocrypha and in the writings of Josephus.*—Although the Apocrypha say nothing of Satan (unless Wis 2[24], on which see below, refers to him), they clearly teach the doctrine of δαιμόνια or evil spirits. These are not angels, nor, apparently, fallen angels. They have power to plague and even slay men, but can be driven away by fumigation, and bound by the angels. Asmodæus is represented in To 6[14] as being in love with Sarah, daughter of Raguel, and as having killed in succession seven unfortunate men to whom she had been married (3[8]). The angel Raphael advises Tobias the son of Tobit to marry her, and provides him with a charm, in the shape of the heart and liver of a fish thrown upon the ashes of incense, to drive away the demon. The smell causes the evil spirit to flee into Egypt, where he is bound by Raphael (8[1-3]). If all the other spirits were like this one, they must have had bodies, and must have been inferior in power to the angels. The writer of the Book of Tobit was evidently acquainted with Mesopotamia, and therefore with the Persian demonology, which is reflected in his work, although not to the extent of representing the demon as a rival power to that of God. He stops short of actual dualism. The author of 1 Mac., speaking of the Akra or citadel which was the headquarters of the Syrian garrison, describes it as 'an evil adversary (διάβολος) to Israel,' *i.e.* 'an adversary or devil in stone'; but this simply reflects the popular conception of the devil as hostile to God's true worshippers.

Josephus, though silent as to Satan, has a good deal to say about evil spirits, and we may fairly take his views as those current in his time. His theory is that demons are the spirits of wicked men departed, who enter into the living and kill them unless they can obtain deliverance (*BJ* VII. vi. 3). The art of exorcizing evil spirits is also known to him. By the use of certain incantations, and especially by the application to the nostrils of the demoniac of a fire-coloured root called *barras*, which grew near the fortress of Machærus, the demon can be expelled. Josephus speaks of this as the discovery of Solomon, and says he saw one Eleazar releasing demoniacs in this fashion (*Ant.* VIII. ii. 5). He gravely affirms that great care must be exercised in the handling of this root, otherwise fatal consequences will follow. On the soil being removed, it may, however, be safely taken by tying a dog to it; as soon as the dog moves, it dies, but the plant has been rendered innocuous (*BJ* VII. vi. 3).

4. *Demonology of the Alexandrian Jews.*—If the Pal. demonology of the two centuries preceding the fall of Jerusalem be characterized by an element of triviality, that of the Alexandrian Jews is marked by one of vague generality. In the LXX heathen gods are uniformly demons, and not merely nonentities as in the Heb. text. The same view is taken by the Alexandrian author of Bar 3[8]–5[9], who in his hatred of idolatry charges the Israelites with having sacrificed to devils and not to God (4[7]). In the Book of Wisdom the subject is dealt with on a higher plane of thought. 'God created man for incorruption, and made him an image of his own proper being; but by the envy of the devil death entered into the world, and they that are of his portion make trial thereof' (2[23f.]). This is interesting as being the first clear allusion in Jewish literature to the narrative of the Fall as told in Genesis. It is also a philosophy of the history, for it 'substitutes a personal devil for the serpent,' and is, moreover, a tolerably precise statement of the doctrine of original sin. But it is only a passing allusion that the writer makes to the subject; he does not return to it, and his views do not reappear in other writings of the Alexandrian Jews. Philo, who makes only a single reference to evil spirits as exciting impure desires in man, adopts another explanation of the Fall (*de Gig.* 4). Yet the recurrence of this view in Rev 12[7], and its acceptance by Christian theologians, show that it must have had its advocates.

5. *Pronounced development of demonology in the Jewish pseudepigrapha.*—In the Jewish pseudepigrapha, highly composite works containing many Christian elements, and ranging over one or two centuries before and after the Christian era, much light is thrown upon the development of demonology. These writings embody a mass of heterogeneous material which had considerable influence in shaping NT doctrines, and in no direction is this influence more marked than in that of demonology. The only demon named in the Apocrypha is Asmodæus (To 3[8. 17]), but in the pseudepigrapha we meet with many others. Beliar, probably the Belial of 2 Co 6[15], appears in the Testaments of the Twelve Patriarchs, in the Sibylline Oracles (2[167]), and in the Ascension of Isaiah (4[2]) as the Antichrist. The latter work further describes him as the ruler of the world (1[8] 2[4]), which will be the scene of his manifestation (4[2]). In the Book of

Enoch, which seems to embrace all the superstitions of the period, a list is given of the chief of the demons to the number of eighteen ($6^7$), and another of (evil) 'angels' to the number of twenty (so the Greek text of $69^2$), followed by a further enumeration of their chiefs, with an account of the particular direction in which each showed himself active. In both instances the leader of the demons is Semjâzâ. No place is given in either of the lists (which belong to different sections of the work, and differ considerably from each other) to Asmodæus, or to Sammael, who figures in the Ascension of Isaiah as ruling in the firmament along with Beliar ($4^2$ $7^8$), and in the Targum of Jonathan as the angel of death (Gn $3^6$). It was he who tempted Eve (*Jalkut Shim.* 'Beresh.' 25). As the special foe of Israel he was the counterpart of Michael (*Shem rabba* 18).

In Enoch $16^1$ the demons are spoken of as the disembodied spirits of the giants, who were the progeny of the fallen angels and the daughters of men, and who will carry on their work of moral ruin upon the earth unpunished till the final judgment (cf. Mt $12^{43ff.}$ and $8^{29}$ 'Art thou come hither to torment us *before the time*?'). This is clearly a legendary expansion of Gn $6^{2.4}$, which, however, says nothing about a fall of angels, and nothing condemnatory of the love shown by the sons of the Elohim for the daughters of men. The Heb. tradition, which was not without its analogies in pagan mythologies, arose naturally enough in an age in which no surprise was felt at the fact of familiar relations between God and men. It is not easy to trace the process by which the narrative of Genesis was gradually metamorphosed into the legend of the Book of Enoch; but by the time when the LXX translation was made there was apparently a disposition to look askance upon the union of the sons of God with the daughters of men. This seems the most natural explanation of the curious divergence by which in that translation the simple fact of the existence of giants gives way to the representation of the giants as the offspring of that union. This theory once accepted, it would then be an easy enough deduction from it that such a relationship was a blot upon angelic sanctity. M. Nicolas (*Des Doctrines Religieuses des Juifs*, p. 264 f.) thinks that the legend of the fall of angels and of their transformation into demons, as well as the Book of Enoch itself, originated among the Pharisaic and ascetic Jews who gathered round the temple of Leontopolis in Egypt during the high-priesthood of Onias IV. But this view, of course, involves the assumption that the Book of Enoch was originally written in Greek, whereas according to Ewald and more recent authorities (*e.g.* Charles, *The Book of Enoch*, p. 21 f.) it is a Pal. composition with a Heb. original.

C. *THE RELATION OF THE RELIGIOUS CONSCIOUSNESS OF OUR LORD TO THE CURRENT BELIEFS ABOUT ANGELS AND DEMONS.*—We can only briefly touch upon this question, as the discussion properly belongs to NT theology.

It is remarkable that Jesus added nothing to the doctrine of angels. He certainly used it as it existed for the advancement of His own purposes, but He nowhere demands faith in angels as necessary to discipleship. In this respect both Judaism and Christianity are distinguished from the religion of Islam. Can we conclude, then, that Jesus made use of angels merely in the way of symbolism? Or does not such a saying as this compel us to the opposite conclusion: 'Take heed that ye despise not one of these little ones; for I say unto you, That in heaven their angels do always behold the face of my Father which is in heaven'? (Mt $18^{10}$). Although it is used with a certain poetic freedom, an angelology is clearly implied in the NT.

The popular belief in Satan and demons is nowhere assailed by our Lord. It may be that this did not lie to His hand as the herald of the heavenly kingdom. But did He accept it? If He had meant to lay stress upon the reality of the idea, would He have used it so exclusively in figure or parable as He has done? Owing to the number of factors (anthropological, physiological, psychological, and theological) involved, the subject is admittedly full of difficulty, and it seems equally perilous either to try to explain it away or to dogmatize upon it. It comes out strongly in NT writings, yet not in such a way, perhaps, as to make it possible to formulate any very definite doctrine. Schenkel and theologians of his school maintain that the belief in Satan and demons in NT literature is only the reflex of the popular Jewish belief produced through foreign influences, but already more or less given up by the educated classes of the period, and that it is therefore no peculiar product of the Christian idea. The difficulty presses most in connexion with the frequent cases of casting out demons recorded in the Synoptic Gospels. How are they to be explained? The theologians referred to do so on the Accommodation Theory, which men like Pressensé again have always consistently rejected; others would explain them psychologically, and diagnose them as cases of delirium or insanity; Schleiermacher and Matthew Arnold speak of the power of a dominant will over a crushed spirit; stricter pietists have clung to the literal doctrine of external evil spirits; Keim has put forward the theory that Christ freed an enslaved self-consciousness from the morbid dispositions engendered by superstition; Bruce attributes the confession of the Messiah by the demoniacs to the prevalence of the Messianic hope, and its special sway over shattered minds. According to a recent writer, the demonic possession recorded in NT is genuine, and has as its distinctive features (1) insanity or mental disease of some sort, forming the natural element; (2) the confession of Jesus as Messiah, forming the supernatural element (Alexander, *Demonic Possession in NT*, pp. 121, 150). The presence of the latter element is the criterion of real demonic possession, which was a counter-movement on the part of the powers of evil to the Incarnation. In this way only three typical cases occur—those of the demoniacs of Capernaum (Mt $9^{3f.}$, Lk $11^{14}$) and Gerasa (Mt $8^{28ff.}$, Mk $5^{1ff.}$) and the youth at the Transfiguration-hill, and the sufferers are regarded as having been the victims of epileptic insanity, acute mania, and epileptic idiocy respectively. Interesting and able as is this writer's treatment of the subject, he has not proved his case, and the last word upon the problem has not yet been spoken. There is perhaps no satisfactory middle ground between 'the view that what Christ accepted must be true, and that which sees in His attitude to demonic possession a particular example of Kenosis.' Three things seem clear—(1) Jesus recognizes a Satanic activity and a Satanic mastery over the possessed; (2) He usually reduces the legions of devils commonly believed in to a single Satanic being, though in one passage (Mt $12^{45}$ ‖ Lk $11^{26}$) He speaks about the unclean spirit taking with him seven other spirits more wicked than himself (the question arises here, If we accept the personality of the devil, must we also believe in his angels?); (3) He conceives the relation of Satan to man as a *moral* one, and so gives to the whole doctrine an ethical basis. From this standpoint there is a good deal to be said for the ancient view that there is a possession bound up with moral obliquity.

iv. ANTHROPOLOGY.—The development in regard to the doctrine of man is not so remarkable. In general we find just the OT anthropology in the Apocrypha, though it is in some respects stated with greater precision and clearness. On one or two important points, however, there is a distinct deviation from the OT position.

1. *Psychological nature of man.*—As to his nature and origin, man is a creature of God, consisting of soul and body. There seems to be no distinction made between πνεῦμα and ψυχή; at all events there is no trichotomy. The fullest conception of man's personality is found in the Book of Wisdom; but, although on some other points the phraseology of that book is distinctly of a Platonic cast, it nowhere adopts Plato's doctrine of a tripartite nature in man, 15[11] being only an apparent exception. This is the more remarkable in that it was the accepted theory of the Alexandrian school, and became one of the tenets of Philo (*de Somn.* i. 22) and of Josephus (*Ant.* I. i. 12). But we have here only one instance out of several in which the writer shows his independence of the Hellenistic philosophy; he can apply it on occasion to the kernel of OT dogma with very fruitful results, but he is not its slave. His position as to the derivation of the human soul is that of creationism, not traducianism. The spiritual ego, which is distinct from the body, comes directly from God, and attaches itself to the body at birth. But at this point we meet with a real variation from OT doctrine. Our author teaches the pre-existence of the human soul. When good, it enters an undefiled body (8[19f.]). Some dispute this interpretation of the passage, but the influence of Gr. philosophy is undoubtedly traceable here, as also in the further statement that the body is only an 'earthly frame' for the mind (νοῦς, 9[15]). The soul is temporarily lent to the body, which must after a brief space restore it and then return to dust (15[8]). Here the Jewish doctrine of the resurrection of the body is abandoned in favour of the Gr. conception of the immortality of the soul. The writer's ideas of pre-existence and dualism are borrowed from the Pythagorean and Platonic doctrines respectively. With regard to pre-existence, we may compare the disciples' question in Jn 9[2] 'Who did sin, this man or his parents, that he was born blind?' This remained for long the main prop of the pre-existence doctrine, and it shows how readily uneducated people must have picked up many philosophical doctrines which did not seem directly to clash with sacred religious customs. One of the alternatives here is, of course, that possibly the man had sinned before his birth. Viewed in the light of the subsequent remark to the man himself, 'Thou wast altogether born in sins,' this seems incapable of explanation except on the theory that there had become visible in this way the punishment of sin committed in a pre-existent state. The saying is probably to be traced to the influence of the Essenes, who in spite of their exclusiveness commanded the reverence of the populace as strict moralists, and as a secret order representing the occult and mysterious. At all events, it shows how deeply foreign views had imprinted themselves on the Jewish theology of the time, and that with regard to anthropology as well as other doctrines. In the attempt to solve the perennial riddle, What is man? the dualistic theory lies midway between the two extremes of materialism and pantheism. But, while dualism is right as to the combination in man's nature of the animal and the spiritual, it settles nothing as to the union of those two elements. On this point, indeed, the Gr. philosophers, and after them the Gnostics, indulge in the wildest speculations. Sense is made to take the place of sin, and the body is viewed as in itself evil, seeing it originates from a principle opposed to the Divine element in the human spirit. In contrast to this the Jewish anthropology as embodied in the OT taught the creation of man, of his body, and his soul, by an act of the Divine will (Gn 1[27] [P] 2[7] [J]). Pre-existence is nowhere taught in the OT, Ps 139[15], which is perhaps the nearest approach to it, being simply a poetic description of growth in the womb. That in the centuries immediately preceding the Christian era the scriptural doctrine was seriously endangered from the side of speculative philosophy, is clear from the Book of Wisdom itself. According to Langen, the writer does no more than clothe genuine Jewish doctrine in a Gr. dress, thereby establishing it with a precision corresponding to the danger it had to meet; but, in view of his position with regard to pre-existence and dualism, the statement requires modification. In connexion with the latter point it should be noted that if in 9[15], influenced by the Platonic idea that the body is the soul's prison, the author means that the body led man into sin, he ascribes this in another passage to the envy of the devil (2[24]). The most probable explanation of this divergence appears to be that he was trying to find a *via media* between philosophy and Scripture.

Although the work is considerably under the influence of Hellenism, the doctrine of creationism is traceable in 4 Mac. (13), where God is spoken of as giving their souls to men. The reverse is the case with Enoch, and yet trichotomy is taught in at least one passage (67[8]). The expressions of Josephus on this subject are vague and even contradictory (*Ant.* I. i. 2, *BJ* VII. viii. 7). His description of the soul as a part of godhead (μοῖρα θεοῦ) is only his way of affirming its likeness to God, and is not to be interpreted pantheistically; it is evidently used to emphasize the contrast between the perishable material body and the immortal soul. He is at one with Platonic dualism in maintaining the unsuitability of the union of spirit and matter in one body, and, although he nowhere expressly adopts the view of the Essenes, it is doubtful whether he contemplates a bodily resurrection. The one point upon which he is clear is that there is a continued personal existence of the soul after death.

2. *Original moral condition of man.*—According to Gn 1[26f.], man was made in the image of God. This is the positive foundation on which the later Jewish theology bases its view about the moral dignity of the human race. But, although the phrase is uniformly referred not to physical form but to mental and moral characteristics, it is not always understood in precisely the same sense. According to Sirach, man's likeness to God consists in his sovereignty over the rest of creation, and in his intellectual endowments, particularly in the power to discern good and evil (17[2. 8]). In Wisdom this resemblance is seen not only in man's dominion over the creatures and in his moral direction of the world (9[2f.]), but also in the fact that he was created for immortality (2[23]). By Philo the Divine image in man is conceived as mediated through the Logos. The reasonable soul is a transcript of the eternal Word (*de Plant. Noe*, 5), and it is in the rational element or νοῦς that we are to look for the Divine image (*de Mund. Opif.* 23), in virtue of which man is a product, not of earth but of heaven (*de Plant. Noe*, 4). Strangely enough, Josephus makes no allusion to the subject.

3. *The immortality of the soul.*—In Wisdom the idea of a future life is much more prominent than in the earlier OT canonical books. The old vague delineations of Sheol, and intermediate references to the realm of the shadow of death, no longer suffice for the cultured Alexandrian. Materialism is met by a clear and pointed statement of the view that the soul is immortal (2[23] 3[1]). The writer

of 2 Mac. adopts the same standpoint (6[26] 12[43f.]). And if in both books stress is mainly laid upon the fact of the future life of the righteous who were apparently destroyed by persecution, this does not warrant the inference that the writers deny the future existence of the wicked. 2 Mac 7[14] (cf. Jn 5[29]) lends no support to this view, and the reference to punishment after death implies the continued existence of the sinner (12[43f.]).

Apparently, the future existence of the wicked was also accepted by orthodox Pal. Jews. The common phrase 'destruction of the ungodly' must be interpreted in the light of those passages in OT and Apocryphal books which have in view the eternal punishment of the wicked. By the 'removal' of the godless in Enoch 1[1] is meant their being handed over to the place of punishment, and not their annihilation; cf. 22[13], which speaks of sinners whose 'souls will not be slain on the day of judgment.' 'There are degrees of suffering in Sheol. The worst penalty appears to be "the slaying of the soul," but even this did not imply annihilation' (Charles; see this writer's further notes on Enoch 99[11] 108[3]). Even in the Ascension of Isaiah, which says that the destruction by fire of the ungodly will cause them to be *as if* they had not been created (4[18]), absolute annihilation is not intended.

In the doctrinal position of the Sadducees as summed up in Ac 23[8] (cf. 4[2], Mt 22[23ff.]) the anthropological element is the most important. Their denial of angels was of little consequence compared with their denial of the resurrection. A love for Hellenistic worldliness had rendered attractive to them the idea that this life is complete in itself, that death is no mere shadow but a reality, and that a resurrection is not to be thought of. Along with the resurrection of the body, the Sadducees naturally denied the immortality of the soul. They were pure materialists, who made no earnest attempt to reach a philosophy of the nature and life of the human spirit, and took no account of the Scripture fact that the separation of soul and body is the punishment of sin. At the opposite pole from the Sadducean doctrine was the extreme spiritualism of the Essenes, who denied the possibility of a resurrection, but believed in the immortality of the soul. They accepted the Pythagorean doctrine that the human soul is derived from the purest ether, and that its connexion with the body is accidental and necessarily temporal. Its preexistence they regarded as a necessary consequence of immortality and the dualistic opposition between spirit and matter. The practical effect of these views was seen in a rigid bodily asceticism and in an earnest pursuit of moral ideals. Immortality and the resurrection both formed part of the creed of the Pharisees. Josephus, indeed, says they taught the transmigration of the souls of the good, and the eternal punishment of the wicked. But, so far as the former idea is concerned, this deviation is really more one of form than of substance, the only difference being that in the one case it is asserted that the material frame does not remain the same, while in the other it is held that every soul has its own particular body. It is quite after the manner of Josephus to make a Jewish doctrine as little objectionable as possible to men of other races, and this may account for his curious confusion of the Jewish doctrine of the resurrection with the widely prevalent pagan doctrine of the transmigration of souls. The idea of the punishment of the wicked was certainly not excluded from the doctrine of transmigration, although the resurrection was frequently spoken of as confined to the good. It was conceived only as a resurrection to life, in which, of course, the lost had no part. What was really but a qualification of the resurrection was thus transferred to the resurrection itself, and Josephus was at once right and wrong in limiting the resurrection to the good, while representing the wicked as delivered up to punishment. But in general it is true of this writer that he has no decided anthropological views of his own, and that his pages reflect the most diverse opinions upon this subject current in the Palestinian Judaism of his time.

4. *The first sin and its consequences.*—In Sirach we have exactly the biblical account of the Fall: 'Of the woman came the beginning of sin, and through her we all die' (25[24]); and this may be taken as representing the general opinion among the Jews of Palestine two centuries prior to the Christian era. As practical reformers, the prophets did not concern themselves with religious metaphysics; but during an epoch when the Law was the one subject of study it was inevitable that attention should be concentrated upon the problem which agitated the whole ancient world—that of the origin of evil. And, naturally, the narrative in Gn 3 formed the starting-point in this discussion. Only gradually was the doctrine of original sin clearly formulated. In Sir 8[5] all are indeed said to be worthy of punishment; but if there be transgressors who are 'a deceivable seed,' those who love and fear the Lord are 'an honourable plant' (10[19]). The writer of Wisdom says, 'By the envy of the devil death entered into the world, and they that are of his portion make trial thereof' (2[24]). This speculative treatment of the narrative of the Fall in Genesis in no way alters its content. The language clearly implies the doctrine of original sin, which, however, is not conceived as inconsistent with a certain predisposition towards good (8[19]). That this goodness, on the other hand, is in any case not absolute, is shown by the writer's statement that apart from Divine aid he could not possess wisdom (8[21]).

In Enoch the eating of the tree of knowledge is treated as the source of a radical moral and spiritual transformation in man, which showed itself in his instant recognition of the impropriety of being naked. It carried death with it also, not as a punishment but as a natural consequence (69[11]). Although Dillmann would read this into 108[11], it is doubtful whether the book knows anything of a natural bias of all men towards evil. The question of original sin is scarcely in the view of the writer, whose concern is rather to explain the great moral difference in men. This he attributes to an initial difference of natural disposition. Philo treats the narrative of the Fall allegorically. Man represents the spiritual, woman the physical, side of our being. By teaching man to exchange the celestial for the terrestrial life, woman was the cause of the first sin (*de Mund. Opif.* 53 ff.). Through his descent into a sensible body, the first man caused the most evil consequences to his whole posterity. Sense as such being evil, sin is inborn with human nature (*de Vita Mosis*, ii. 157). Josephus (*Ant.* I. i. 2–4) gives a sort of allegorizing version of the biblical account of the Fall. By eating the forbidden fruit our first parents attained the height of knowledge, but it proved their destruction. Their punishment is made to consist in labour and adversity, in the swift advance of old age and the near prospect of death. Of an original immortality nothing is said. In a somewhat embellished account of the Creation the Book of Jubilees takes cognizance of Adam's sin, and represents it as involving his expulsion from Paradise, with other attendant penalties. But it goes no further. It declares neither that death is the consequence of sin, nor that Adam's transgression resulted in the depravity of the race.

It would appear, then, that in Jewish post-exilic tradition no clear views had been formulated on the subject of anthropology. A certain degree of latitude prevailed alike as regards the philosophical conception of the constitution of man and the theological position as to the original condition of our race. In particular, no doctrine of original sin had, for the most part, been arrived at. With some exceptions, however,—notably that of Josephus,—the recognized necessity of death was connected with the fall of our first parents. Yet, curiously enough, this was usually considered a distinct gain, inasmuch as through the first sin man had audaciously possessed himself of knowledge divinely prohibited. In other words, he had sinned to his own advantage. So that in this particular, as Langen points out, 'pre-Christian tradition agrees rather with the Prometheus-myth than with the biblical account' (*l.c.* p. 365).

In 2 (4) Esdras we meet with the doctrine of original sin in a highly developed form. Already in the angel Uriel's promise to teach him 'wherefore the heart is wicked' ($4^{4}$), the writer assumes that the question will interest his readers, and in several passages he gives to it a distinct and definite answer. The sins of Israel are fruits of the first fall ($3^{21ff.}$). So also in $4^{30}$ it is said, 'A grain of evil seed was sown in the heart of Adam from the beginning, and how much wickedness hath it brought forth unto this time! and how much shall it yet bring forth until the time of threshing come!' As in our nature the evil far outweighs the good, so the perishing outnumber the saved ($7^{44}$ $8^{3}$ $9^{15}$). In view of the pessimistic tone of the writer, it would not be safe to infer that his outlook was that of the Judaism of the period, although in days of troublous events it was doubtless shared by many. The element of truth underlying his morbid presentation is that emphasized by our Lord, viz. that relatively few enter in at the strait gate. This is quite in keeping with the strict demands of OT morality, in which the writer finds a point of contact for his doctrine of original sin. He gives clear expression, however, to what was only obscurely wrapped up in Jewish tradition. But in his handling of this doctrine he does not confine himself to abstract theory; he approaches the problem also from the practical side. With the deep feeling of a soul crushed by the curse of sin he cries out, 'O thou Adam, what hast thou done? for though it was thou that sinned, the evil is not fallen on thee alone, but upon all of us that come of thee' ($7^{48}$). Although the writer's views are coloured by Christian influence, that influence is only a reflex one. He was himself no Christian, and no propagator of Christianity. His work is essentially Jewish, and its aim is to revive the Jewish hope. Nothing is further from his intention than the appropriation of foreign matter, yet it was inevitable that expressions forged in the heat of the conflict attending the early development of Christian doctrine should have appealed to his susceptible spirit. On its austerer side Christianity ministered to his gloomy spiritual tendency. In its milder aspects it seems to have awakened no answering echo within him. What, consciously or unconsciously, impressed him was its delineation of the race as sunk in universal sinfulness and exposed to the wrath and curse of God, of the human heart as naturally wicked, and of the comparatively small number of the saved. Yet he is so far from denying the possibility of salvation that he even specifies what is necessary in order to find it, viz. works and faith ($9^{7}$ $13^{23}$). As the thought already appears in Gn $15^{6}$, there is no need to ascribe the expression to the influence of St. James.

5. *Free will and foreordination.*—The OT clearly affirms, on the one hand, the doctrine of Divine providence and foreordination, and, on the other, the freedom of the human will. All the later Jewish writings take the same position with regard to man's moral liberty. According to Wisdom, God is found of such as seek Him in singleness of heart ($1^{1ff.}$). Wisdom is attainable by him who loves her and will diligently pursue her ($6^{12.\ 14}$). 'For her true beginning is desire of discipline; and the care for discipline is love of her; and love of her is observance of her laws; and to give heed to her laws confirmeth incorruption; and incorruption bringeth near unto God; so then desire of wisdom promoteth to a kingdom' ($6^{17ff.}$). Thus along the entire line of the soul's moral development the way lies open to man. Owing to innate wickedness ($5^{13}$), he cannot tread this path without Divine help ($8^{21}$); but for this he can pray ($7^{7}$), and it will be given him if he shows himself worthy of it ($1^{2ff.}$), and does not court death by unrighteous words and deeds ($1^{12.\ 16}$). To the same effect is the teaching of Sirach. The Lord 'showed men good and evil' ($17^{7}$), and 'left him in the hand of his own counsel' ($15^{14}$). 'Before man is life and death; and whichsoever he liketh, it shall be given him' ($15^{17}$). It is noteworthy that, in thus affirming man's power to distinguish between good and evil, the writer stoutly assails the contrary opinion ($15^{11ff.}$). As he would never have controverted an unknown theory, the doctrine of predestination must have had its exponents in Jewish circles. Free will in man, it was held, could not consist with God's government of the world. Providence meant predestination, and man is but a passive agent in the hand of God. This is the point of view against which Ben Sira directs his polemic; and, although we cannot tell with what Pal. school he was specially identified, it is evident that during this period theological questions were keenly debated. In view of the full recognition of human freedom, and in opposition to Sadducean rationalism, special stress was laid in some quarters upon the heavenly ordering of earthly things. This thought gradually came to be expressed under the figure of a heavenly book or heavenly tables, in which was set down the whole course of events as these would unfold themselves in actual history. The idea of a book of life is not foreign to the OT (Ex $32^{32}$, Ps $69^{28}$), but it was more freely employed in the later literature; cf. *e.g.* Enoch $104^{1}$ $108^{2}$ $47^{3}$. In the Book of Jubilees sins are said to be written in the eternal books which are before the Lord ($39^{6}$); while Abraham and Levi are written down as just in the tables of heaven ($19^{9}$ $30^{20}$). The same idea occurs in Dn $10^{21}$. It corresponds to the Platonic world of Ideas or Divine world-plan, and seems to have been the Jewish expedient for retaining the old doctrine of Divine providence in the face of Hellenism. Philo finds the distinctive nature of man and the most direct consequence of his likeness to God in the faculty of self-determination. The moral liberty belonging to the rational element in man is the very condition of virtue. By a spontaneous act of will man can choose to practise good or evil, and so arrive at honour or condemnation. His destiny is thus in his own hands. According to Josephus, the chief difference between the three leading Jewish sects was connected with the question of human freedom; but, except as adherents of one or other of these, men seem to have troubled themselves little about the relation to each other of the two factors of human liberty and Divine prearrangement. The peculiar use of εἱμαρμένη for θεός affords an example of Josephus' liking for Hellenistic terms as a medium for the expression

of Jewish ideas (*Ant.* XIII. v. 9, XVIII. i. 3; *BJ* II. iii. 1).

6. *Ethics.*—In the sphere of morals the vital question must ever be, What is sin, and what is virtue? According to OT ideas, sin consists in deviation from the law of God, and virtue in the observance of that law. But for the most part the OT is content with laying down general principles, leaving men to apply these to their own special circumstances in accordance with their individual judgment. In post-exilic Judaism we meet with two marked developments differing on opposite sides from the OT position. The one is that of Pharisaism, according to which the main element in morality is the literal observance of positive precepts; the other is that identified with the Alexandrian school, according to which the principal importance is attached, not to the outward act itself but to the sentiment inspiring it.

(1) Palestinian Jews based their ethical system on the Mosaic law, which is not a philosophy but a revelation. It does not deal with the general conditions of moral existence as such, but with the particular conditions that obtained in Israel. Naturally, therefore, the scribes were not philosophers; they were interpreters of the sacred Law. For Ezra and his coadjutors this formed the unique standard, not only of religion and morals but also of economics and politics. Every department of life was regulated by it. No distinction was made between the ceremonial and the moral; Sabbath observance and rules about food were enjoined by the same law that commanded the love of God and just dealing towards men. National law and not conscience was the recognized norm of morality, which thus became synonymous with jurisprudence. In point of fact, the practice of well-doing was often dictated by the love of good for its own sake (To $4^{7ff.}$, Sir $4^{28}$ etc.), but in theory morality was simply a matter of mechanical obedience to legalistic prescriptions. This conception of ethics led to the Law being developed in quite a wrong direction. Every biblical commandment was surrounded by a network of petty regulations. No allowance was made for changing circumstances; full obedience to the Law in all its particulars was inexorably demanded of every Jew. To the precepts of the Written Law were added those of the *Halakha* or Traditional Law, which was handed down as a sacred trust from generation to generation, and ultimately embodied in the Talmud. It took centuries for the Oral Law to reach its completed form, but its birth dates from the restoration of Israel under Ezra and Nehemiah. An attempt was thus made to bring every conceivable case within the scope of the Law, and with merciless logic to regulate the whole of human conduct by strict rule of thumb. Legal details were multiplied until religion became a trade, and life an intolerable burden. Men were reduced to moral automatons. The voice of conscience was stifled; the living power of the Divine word was neutralized and smothered beneath a mass of external rules. Hence our Lord's accusation against the Pharisees, that by their traditions they made void the Law. Not that in Palestinian ethics the inner motive was absolutely disregarded. The literature of the period recommends the practice of the Law out of respect to God who gave it (To $1^{12}$ $4^{5ff.}$ etc.); and, from the efforts made in the 2nd century A.D. to crush out the modified spiritualism represented by Sirach and the school of Gamaliel and Hillel, we may reasonably infer that the Pharisaic affirmation of the merit of works met with considerable opposition at an earlier date. Liberalism disappeared only when the observance of the Ceremonial Law became the one safeguard of Israel's nationality. Yet there is no doubt that externalism held the field, and that more and more, as the one thing needful.

A conspicuous example of legalistic Judaism is furnished in connexion with the observance of the Sabbath (see vol. iv. p. $320^{b}$). No fewer than 39 species of servile work are forbidden on that day, and each of these includes numerous particulars. To observe scrupulously the prescribed rules about food is viewed as morally meritorious (Dn $2^{8ff.}$, Jth $8^{6}$ etc.). From the days of Noah downwards, the eating of blood seems to have been considered criminal. In Enoch $4^{5}$ the giants are depicted as dreadful cannibals because guilty of this enormity. The Book of Jubilees also attaches much importance to this prohibition. 'Eat no blood whatever . . . that thou mayest be preserved from all evil' ($21^{6.\ 18ff.}$). This appears to be a superstitious gloss upon the biblical statement, 'the blood is the life' (Lv $17^{14}$). At all events, it shows us that an ethical significance was given to mere externalities having none. Almsgiving is represented as purging away all sin (To $12^{9}$ $14^{11}$). This error as to the value of good works passed over into Christianity with Jewish Christians, and formed the subject of St. Paul's great controversy. In the special religious conditions of the Jews this mechanical and minute system of ethics was perhaps inevitable. It seems to be a law of religious history that all written tradition gives rise to an oral tradition, and that the latter always claims to dominate conscience; especially is this the case where, as in Mosaism, written tradition is at once a religion and a revelation (Nicolas, *Des Doctrines Religieuses des Juifs*, p. 381). Church history shows that even (official) Christianity has not always refrained from lording it over the conscience in matters of detail not included within the scope of the Divine commandments. Closely connected with the value attached to good works was the exclusiveness which distinguished the Pal. Jews of this period. It was no longer their birth only that marked them off from other nations; in virtue of their observance of the Law they occupied a position of superiority over 'sinners of the Gentiles' (Gal $2^{15}$). The strength of this feeling is reflected in the jealousy afterwards shown by Jewish Christians towards their brethren of pagan extraction, and in the demand that all such should at least perform the obligations of proselytes. The misapprehension as to the nature of sin on the part of orthodox Judaism led naturally to a wrong view regarding absolution from sin. In this connexion there was apparently no thought of a moral renewal of the heart. To judge from the attitude of later Rabbinism, it was all a question of calculation. Sin could be atoned for by counterbalancing good works; and if a man's good deeds exceeded his evil deeds, then he was both morally good, and would stand in the judgment. But evidence is not wanting that in the Judaism of the period room was found for the conception that a soul may reach a point in sin which constitutes a state of moral banishment from God. According to Jubilees ($26^{3.\ 31}$), Esau committed 'a sin unto death' in renouncing the yoke of his brother, while 2 (4) Es $7^{49}$ speaks of 'works that bring death,' *i.e.* for which, on earth at least, there is no forgiveness.

With regard to retribution, the Pal. Apocrypha strongly maintain that a holy life will bring happiness, and that the wicked will meet with misfortune and punishment (Sir $35^{11}$ $28^{1}$). The writers mostly confine their view to the present life. Tobit joins with Sirach in laying great stress on almsgiving as a means of securing the Divine favour, but only, it would seem, with reference to this life; though in one passage he speaks of death as more profitable for him than life, and desires to be released from distress that he may 'go to the everlasting place' ($3^6$). Future retribution, however, is also taught (Jth $16^{17}$, 2 Mac $7^{14}$, 2 (4) Es $7^{36. 79f.}$).

(2) The moral ideas of the Alexandrian Jews reflect a different and, in one respect at least, more scriptural atmosphere. Moral worth is determined, not by the measure of obedience to positive prescription but by the inner purpose of the heart. The spirit of the Law is not subordinated to the letter. Morality is a quality of soul (Wis $1^4$ $6^{10}$), and has its roots in fellowship with God ($15^3$). Wisdom, which has its source in the four cardinal (Platonic) virtues—soberness, understanding, righteousness, and courage ($8^7$)—corresponds somewhat strikingly to what St. Paul designates faith. 'To be acquainted with thee is perfect righteousness, and to know thy dominion is the root of immortality' ($15^3$). According to Philo, religious reverence is the source of virtue, and the perfect law is the disinterested love of the good for its own sake.

But, if the Alexandrian ethics coincides with OT teaching in the place which it assigns to the heart's intention, it deviates from the scriptural position in virtually setting aside the practice of the Mosaic law. In Wisdom sacrifice is mentioned only incidentally, while stress is laid upon the importance of prayer ($16^{28}$), and upon the word of God as the true nourishment of the soul ($16^{26}$). Philo expressly teaches that God takes no pleasure in sacrifices, but is pleased only with purity of heart (*de Victim. Offer.* 3). The virtuous soul is His temple, and its homage the true offering. So far he may be said to anticipate the spirit of Christianity. But in opposing the mechanical morality of the Pal. schools the Alexandrians fell into an unhealthy spiritualism. The writer of Wisdom shows a distinct leaning towards asceticism. In his view the body is the enemy of the soul, upon which it acts as a heavy drag ($9^{15}$), and celibacy is better than the anxious lot of him whose children are only too likely to be given to wickedness ($3^{12ff.}$ $4^1$). Philo goes still further, and allegorically reduces all the positive precepts of the OT to the one idea of overcoming sense by the life of the spirit. It is the duty of the wise man to loosen the bonds that bind the spirit to the material frame in which it is imprisoned (*de Migrat. Abr.* 1). Although the application of this general principle frequently coincides with OT precepts, it amounts to a rejection of the positive teaching of revelation. That there is no fundamental agreement is shown by the difference between the Philonic and OT conceptions of sin. According to OT revelation, the sinner's restoration may be effected by his penitent return to God; in Philo's system there is no healing for the soul that has deliberately sinned. Neither does the Alexandrian theosophist acknowledge any degrees of heinousness in sin, seeing that he attaches no importance to the outward act, but takes account only of the freedom and decision with which the sin is committed. This writer's ascetic bias is so far corrected by his declaration that the care of the soul and devotion to God should not render us oblivious to our duties towards our fellow-men (*de Decal.* 22).

In contrast to the Palestinians, the Alexandrian Jews applied the idea of retribution to the future as well as to the present life. Wisdom clearly teaches the doctrine of future rewards and punishments ($3^{1ff.}$). The Day of Judgment is expressly mentioned ($3^{7. 18}$). The terrors of an evil conscience and the thought of future condemnation are jointly set forth in $17^{21}$. In $19^4$ the hardening of Pharaoh's heart is represented as a necessary doom, quite after the analogy of the Greek *Nemesis*.

Another distinctive note of the Alexandrian ethics is its universalistic tendency. According to Wisdom the peculiar advantage of the Jew consists, not in his birth but in his possession of the knowledge of God. Pagans are sinners, not because they are not of Abraham's race but because they are without the knowledge of the true God ($13^{3ff.}$). It is from this standpoint that idolatry is regarded as the source of evil and the corruption of life ($14^{12}$). Philo departs even more emphatically than Wisdom from the Jewish particularism taught in Palestine. All men are brethren, similarly organized and endowed; before all is set the same task of emancipating the soul from the bondage of the body. Slavery is the greatest of all evils, and virtue consists in obeying the voice of conscience. It is the mission of the Israelites to be the priests and prophets of the whole human race, and herein lies their privilege. But in order to accomplish this momentous task they must have a true spiritual understanding of their Law, *i.e.* they must become philosophers. This extreme spiritualism was due partly to the influence of Greek philosophy, and partly to the distance of the Alexandrian Jews from Palestine. Equally shut off from contact with the schools of the home land, and from the observance of the Ceremonial Law, they soon idealized their religion.

7. *Christian doctrine gave final shape and precision to the Jewish anthropology*, and threw a flood of light upon the obscurities of a period unrivalled for religious wavering and confusion. To many things in the current theological teaching Christ gave His assent; with regard to others He set men upon the right track; others still He rejected or supplanted by positive doctrine of a contrary character. To a large extent this was done through the use of well-known ideas and expressions. The words of Jesus with reference to unpardonable sin (Mt $12^{31f.}$ ||; cf. 1 Jn $5^{16}$, He $6^{4ff.}$) probably reflect a phraseology familiar to the Judaism of the age. *A propos* of this example, Langen suggestively remarks that the key to many theological difficulties of NT passages lies in approaching them from the standpoint of their historical connexion (*Judenthum*, p. 381). Without essentially altering its content, Christian doctrine introduces light and definiteness into the well-nigh chaotic mass of religious thought and theory which represented the accumulation of centuries. As to the nature of man, it distinguishes between soul and spirit without embracing Plato's doctrine of trichotomy, and rejects the Pythagorean view of the connexion between soul and body. It teaches, further, that there is a personal future life for man, a resurrection to life, but also to judgment. In St. Paul's Epistles we have the facts of redemption joined on to the teaching of the opening chapters of Genesis, and raised to a definite system. Sin, death, and grace appear in their true significance and connexion. On the one hand, we have the loftiest ideal towards which to strive in our moral and spiritual growth and development, and on the other the Almighty will working from eternity towards the fulfilment of His purposes (Ro 8). While not showing how the two doctrines can be held in combination without neutralizing each other, it teaches both free will and an overruling Providence. Finally, Christian ethics neither ignores the motive inspiring conduct, nor minimizes the importance of the external act. It teaches that, while the moral quality of an action is determined by the inner motive, its outward manifestation is also worthy of praise or blame (Mk $14^6$).

v. THE MESSIANIC HOPE.—1. *Meaning of the expression.*—The word Messiah (Heb. מָשִׁיחַ, Gr. Χριστός) means 'anointed,' and is used most frequently in OT of the theocratic king of Israel (1 S $12^3$ etc.), but with a special significance when applied to David and his descendants (Ps $18^{50}$

$89^{19ff.}$). In Dn $9^{25}$ the reference is apparently to Cyrus (cf. Is $45^{1}$). The title does not occur either in the Apocrypha or in the Apocalyptic literature written during the last century and a half B.C. In the latter especially there are undoubtedly Messianic passages, but the style of composition lent itself most naturally to the use of the symbolical. The earliest extant instance of its distinctive use as a technical form is found in the anti-Sadducean Psalms of Solomon ($17^{36}$ $18^{6.8}$), composed *c.* 140 B.C. It may be noted here also that the expression 'Messianic hope' is not free from a certain ambiguity, seeing that under this title are frequently comprehended two things which should be carefully distinguished, viz. the expectation of the Messianic *era*, and the expectation of the Messianic *king*. In tracing the development of the Messianic idea in Israel it is necessary to keep in view the fact that many Prophetic and Apocalyptic writers who look forward confidently to a glorious future for the nation entertain no expectation of a personal Messiah. The Jews cherished a strong belief in the restoration of their national prestige as Jehovah's chosen people. After purifying the nation by discipline, He would bestow upon them all that heart could wish. This faith, already preached by the prophets of the 8th cent. B.C., they firmly held apart from and prior to the notion of a unique personal deliverer in the form of the Messiah. In certain sections of Judaism also, and at certain periods, when the latter expectation grew dim, the wider hope was never relinquished.

2. *The OT position.*—The prophets Amos, Hosea, and Joel give clear expression to Messianic hopes for Israel and Judah, but say nothing of a personal Messiah. What they predict is the revived glory of the Davidic house (Am $9^{11f.}$) and the return of the children of Israel (Hos $3^{5}$). Nor does Zephaniah, in depicting the happy future that shall follow the Divine judgment on Israel and the nations ($3^{9-20}$), introduce at all the figure of Messiah. Jeremiah announces the coming of a king of David's line, but seems to think of a succession of them ($17^{25}$ $22^{4}$ $33^{15.17}$); and Obadiah (v.$^{2}$) speaks of a plurality of saviours on Mount Zion. The same thought appears to be implied in Ezk $43^{7}$ $45^{8f.}$, and elsewhere this prophet idealizes the reign of David, referring to him as the 'shepherd' of Israel and 'their prince for ever.' In Isaiah, Micah, and Zechariah we meet with a great advance in the development of Messianic expectation. These prophets do not confine the blessing to their own nation, and clearly bring forward the person of a particular descendant of David (Is $7^{13-16}$ $9^{6f.}$, Mic $5^{2ff.}$, Zec $9^{9}$ $14^{9}$). The terms in which this king is described perfectly fit the character of the Messiah as that came to be recognized in Jewish theology.

3. *The Messianic idea in the Apocrypha.*—While confidently predicting better times for Israel, the Apocrypha afford but few materials for the construction of the doctrine of the Messiah. Baruch, Tobit, and Sirach may be noticed first as falling within the period between the cessation of prophecy and the commencement of the Maccabee revival. Baruch comforts Jerusalem and the Jewish nation by the assurance of the destruction of their enemies, and of the return of their prosperity as a united people 'gathered together by the word of the Holy One' ($4^{21ff.}$). There is no Mediator known to Baruch as accomplishing all this. Many of the Fathers pointed to another passage ($3^{35ff.}$) as a prophecy of the Incarnation; but the words 'afterward did she (AV 'he') appear upon earth, and was conversant with men' are more properly regarded as a personification of Wisdom. Tobit's point of view is somewhat different. He predicts the same happiness for Israel, and a return to Jerusalem, there to re-establish with great pomp the worship of the Lord God. But he speaks of no vengeance to be wreaked on their enemies, over whom they are rather to obtain a glorious triumph in the shape of their conversion to Judaism ($13^{5.11.16ff.}$). Ben Sira knows no more of a personal Messiah than either Baruch or Tobit. The idea of a glorious future is present to his mind, although he expresses himself on the subject with great sobriety. He recalls the promises made by God to Abraham and to David ($44^{21}$ $45^{25}$ $47^{11}$), and looks for the return of the scattered Jews, for the punishment of their oppressors ($36^{10ff.}$), and for the breaking of 'the sceptres of the unrighteous' ($35^{18}$). In spite of a dim Messianic expectation in 44–50 that is in no special way connected with an individual Messiah, his real interest is in the perpetuity of the Israelitish people. 'The days of Israel,' he says, 'are innumerable' ($37^{25}$), and 'their glory shall not be blotted out' ($44^{13}$). The only other passage we need refer to is one which is generally thought to be of later origin on account of the great contrast it bears to the prevailing doctrine of the book, viz. $48^{10f.}$. This passage, which recalls the closing lines of the prophecy of Malachi, speaks of Elijah returning at the inauguration of the Messianic kingdom, and that in such a way as to seem to imply that the author had hopes of living to see it all. But the Gr. text is obscure, and it is certainly not safe to conclude that he speaks of a future life.

'From the little and in part doubtful evidence that remains to us, it would seem that in the period between the Captivity and the rise of the Maccabees the Messianic hope resolved itself into vague anticipations of a glorious and happy future, in which the presence of God would be more manifest, but of which a Messiah would form no essential feature' (Drummond, *Jewish Messiah*, p. 199). This is exactly the position of those modern Jews who say the Messiah is not a person, but an epoch.

In 1 Mac. three passages have been singled out for discussion in this connexion:—(1) 'David for being merciful inherited the throne of a kingdom for ever and ever' ($2^{57}$). These words are put into the lips of Mattathias, and it is possible that the writer, without ascribing this expectation to the priest of Modin, contemplated the restoration of the Davidic kingdom through the appearance of the Messiah. (2) 'They pulled down the (desecrated) altar, and laid up the stones in the mountain of the house in a convenient place, until there should come a prophet to give an answer concerning them' ($4^{46}$). There is here certainly no specific reference to the Messiah. (3) 'The Jews and priests were well pleased that Simon should be their leader and high priest for ever, until there should arise a faithful prophet' ($14^{41}$). Although the absence of the article makes it difficult to identify the 'prophet' in question with the Messiah, 'the allusion may still fairly be regarded as Messianic in the general sense that the expected "faithful prophet" first appeared in Christ' (Camb. Bible, *ad loc.*). In 2 Mac. there is only one passage of Messianic import—'In God have we hope, that he will quickly have mercy upon us, and gather us together out of all the earth into the holy place' ($2^{18}$). The use of 'quickly' seems to imply the expectation of the near approach of the Messianic kingdom. There is nothing in Judith beyond the mention of 'the Day of Judgment,' when the Lord Almighty will take vengeance on the enemies of Israel ($16^{17}$).

In the Alexandrian Wisdom of Solomon likewise we meet with little that can claim to be directly Messianic. We have the same belief expressed as to the punishment of the enemies of God's people, and the elevation of the latter to a position of supremacy, but all in very general terms ($3^7$ 5). There is just one passage—$2^{12-20}$—which has been often reckoned to be Messianic. It describes the suffering of the righteous at the hands of the ungodly, here and there in such language as makes it very natural to interpret it of the Messiah. Most probably, however, it is Israel as a nation that is spoken of here; and many of the expressions are to be applied rather to the present than to the future. In $16^{17}$ and other passages Israel is called ὁ δίκαιος. Besides, some of the things said scarcely admit of Messianic application, *e.g.* 'Let us lie in wait for the righteous man,' 'He is grievous unto us even to behold,' 'We were accounted of him as base metal.' These expressions all point to national enmities. Moreover, the next chapter proceeds to speak of the righteous in the aggregate. It is inconceivable that, had the hope of a Messiah been clear to his own mind, this writer would not have brought it forward in an unmistakable way in his references to the glorious kingdom awaiting the godly ($5^{16}$). At the same time it may be conceded to Ewald that 'this work should, . . . in consideration of its central idea and ultimate purpose, be reckoned among the Messianic productions' (*Hist.* v. p. 484).

With the exception of the material supplied by 2 (4) Esdras, which is dealt with below, this sums up what the Apocrypha contain with regard to the doctrine of the Messiah; and certainly it is impossible to claim anything in the way of development here. Indeed, 'in the post-Exilian time the limitation of Messianic apprehension to OT forms becomes again much greater than with Jeremiah and Deutero-Isaiah' (Riehm, *Messianic Prophecy*, p. 231).

4. *Transformation of Messianic hopes into Apocalyptic ideas.*—In the post-exilic period the ancient Messianic promises gradually assumed a new aspect. The *Apocalyptic* presentation of the Messiah-hope appears for the first time in the Book of Daniel, which seems to have formed the model of most of the subsequent literature bearing this name. The work dates from the Maccabæan struggle against the tyrannical attempt of Antiochus Epiphanes (the 'little horn' of ch. 7) to suppress Judaism by force. Its aim is to revive the courage of the Jewish people. This it seeks to do by pointing them to the splendid example of religious constancy set by the heroes of a former age (1–6), and to the glorious destiny awaiting them in the future (7–12). It deals with the restoration of Israel, and the victorious establishment of the worship of J" under a Davidic prince, but with a wealth of detail that is new, and with a reference of the facts to the history of the four great nations which in succession ruled the world. The kingdom of God is represented as the fifth and last monarchy ($2^{44f.}$), the final consummation of the Divine purposes to which the whole series of revolutions, political and religious, consecutively lead up. It will be preceded by the Abomination of Desolation ($9^{27}$ $12^{11}$), the culminating point in the career of the transgressors ($8^{23}$). This will continue for a fixed period, and then the last and vilest of the heathen powers will be crushed by the special interposition of the Most High, who will transfer the dominion to His saints ($7^{18}$). The glorious deliverance will be signalized by a partial resurrection of the dead, of whom some shall rise to everlasting life, and some to shame and everlasting contempt ($12^2$). So shall be inaugurated the Messiah's kingdom, which shall extend to all nations and never be destroyed ($7^{14}$). Some think there is here no trace of the Messiah, and that the person in human form who appears in the vision of Dn 7 is merely the personification of Israel, as the four animals are the personification of the four empires; but the majority of scholars ascribe to him a supernatural character (cf. article SON OF MAN in vol. iv. p. 583 f.). In any case, the Messianic idea appears here in a more precise form than in Sirach. Instead of vague predictions of a prosperous future, there is a definite date assigned to the downfall of Israel's enemies, and to the assumption by the chosen people of universal dominion. Those who have fallen victims to persecution will not be without their reward; they will be raised up to share in the glories of the Messianic era.

Subsequent Apocalyptic writers follow the Book of Daniel in connecting the advent of the Messiah with the general development of human history, although they differ from it and from one another in their mode of mapping it out. Sometimes it is divided simply into the period preceding and that following the Messiah's coming; sometimes into three periods of 1000 years. The Testaments of the Twelve Patriarchs (Levi 17 f.) speak of seven weeks, Enoch of ten weeks, and the Sibylline Or. ($2^{15}$) of ten generations. Other books, however, represent the time of the Messiah's advent as known only to God (2 Es $6^{7ff.}$). Already in Daniel the enemies of God's chosen people are supported by the rebel angels ($10^{18f.}$ $12^1$), and in the later literature their last and greatest enemy is represented, not only as a pagan king but as the prince of demons, leading all the hosts of evil against the Messiah. Some other notable developments occur, such as the preparation of the way of the Lord by the reappearance not only of Elijah as in Malachi, but also of Moses, Isaiah, and Jeremiah; the dating in mystical numbers of the main events that usher in the Messianic era; a resurrection *of the just* (qualifying Dn $12^2$; cf. Jos. *Ant.* XVIII. iv. 3, *BJ* VIII. i. 4); the giving of a new law for the whole world (Sib. Or. $3^{755ff.}$); and the millennium, or reign of the Messiah on earth for 1000 years. These elements sufficiently distinguish the apocalypses from the ancient Heb. prophecies. To speak more generally, the former are differentiated from the latter by their almost purely transcendental character, and by the wider sweep of their horizon. If the essential features of the picture are the same as in the prophetic writings, the main interest is shifted from the present to the future, and the canvas is enlarged. There is greater precision, more fulness of detail, and bolder colouring. This gradual transformation of Messianic hopes into apocalyptic beliefs was the necessary consequence of the political situation in Israel. As each new crisis overtook them, a way had to be found of reconciling the prophetic promises with present misfortunes.

But there is an element in Jewish Apocalyptic literature which forbids us to regard it as a mere extension of OT Messianic teaching. Foreign influence is clearly traceable in such ideas as those of a partial resurrection, a millennial reign, etc. And in this instance the external impulse was not Greek, but Persian. Between Hellenism and Jewish Apocalyptic there is no affinity: the one conceived the golden age as past, the other as future. In the atmosphere of Alexandrian Judaism the Messianic hope lost its vitality, and resolved itself into little else than a philosophy of human betterment from the point of view of religion and morals. On the other hand, apocalyptic beliefs are closely associated with Babylonia under the Persian rule. The scene of the Book of Daniel, in which they were first propounded, is laid in Babylon, and the Pal. Apocrypha show that it was among the Jews who either as returned exiles or as citizens had intimate relations with Babylon that these views found acceptance. Moreover, the sacred writings of the Persians (*Vendîdâd*, etc.) speak of the coming of a deliverer in the last days, of the overthrow of the enemies of Ormazd, and the consequent establishment of an era of happiness analogous to that contemplated in the Messianic expectation of the Jews. The resemblance extends even to such details as the idea of a fifth monarchy, the resurrection of the dead, the millennial reign of the saviour, etc. Not that these elements were simply adopted by the Jews as an addition to their own Messianic hopes by way of supplementing and completing them. In no case does the resemblance amount to identity, and on certain points, as, *e.g.*, that of the final restoration of the wicked, the Persian doctrine was distinctly rejected by the Jews. This again influenced their views of the resurrection, which they conceived as partial and not universal. The Persian elements traceable in the Jewish beliefs of the period merely show that, in the fresh interpretation of ancient documents induced by their changing circumstances, the Jews were influenced by the recollection of something analogous in Mazdeism.

We have a typical specimen of Jewish Apocalyptic in the Book of Enoch. Difficult critical questions arise with reference to this strange and interesting book,—questions of date, authorship, and constituent elements,—but it is unnecessary for our purpose to discuss them. (See the general and special Introductions in Charles' ed.). Two well-marked sections of the book treat of the Messianic expectation, viz. the *Similitudes* (37–71) and the *Dream Visions* (83–90). The date assigned by Charles to the latter section is B.C. 166–161, or a little later than Daniel. The work of a Hasidæan in full sympathy with the Maccabæan insurrection, it contains two visions, of which the first deals with the judgment of the Deluge, and the second gives a bird's-eye view of the entire course of human history from the Creation down to the establishment of the Messiah's kingdom. In the first vision no attempt is made to explain the origin of human sin. According to the representation of the writer, the judgment that first fell upon the world was caused by the sin of the rebel angels, and not by that of man. In the second vision, which employs a symbolism akin to that of the Book of Daniel, special stress is laid upon the distressful condition of Israel after the Exile. This is ascribed to the faithlessness of the seventy shepherds, who wickedly destroyed those whom God entrusted to their care ($89^{19ff.}$). But in the midst of this oppression, from the party of the Hasidæans and in the person of Judas Maccabæus (the 'great horn' of $90^{9}$), there will arise a deliverer whose sword shall destroy their enemies. God Himself shall appear, and the earth shall swallow them up ($90^{6-19}$). Then will ensue the judgment of the fallen watchers, the shepherds, and the apostate Jews, who will be cast into a fiery abyss ($90^{24ff.}$). This will be followed by the setting up of the new Jerusalem, the conversion of the remanent Gentiles, and their submission to Israel ($90^{28ff.}$), the resurrection of those who have succumbed to persecution, and the gathering of the dispersed of Israel ($90^{33}$). Finally, the Messiah ('a white bullock') will appear ($90^{37}$); all the saints will be changed into his likeness, and God will rejoice over them ($90^{38}$). We have here 'the Messiah coming forth from the bosom of the community. He is a man only, but yet a glorified man, and superior to the community from which he springs. So far as he is a man only, he may be regarded as the prophetic Messiah as opposed to the Apocalyptic Messiah of the Similitudes, and yet he is not truly the prophetic Messiah; for he has absolutely no function to perform, and he does not appear till the world's history is finally closed. Accordingly, his presence here must be accounted for purely through literary reminiscence, and the hope of the Messiah must be regarded as practically dead at this period. The writer felt no need of such a personality so long as the nation had such a chief as Judas Maccabæus' (Charles, *Introd.* p. 30 f.).

5. *The Messianic idea in later Palestinian books.*—The Book of Jubilees (written, according to Charles, B.C. 135–105). This work is distinguished by the spirituality of its description of the Messianic kingdom, although the person of the Messiah, whom the writer expects to arise from Judah, is alluded to only once ($31^{18}$). It is neither strictly apocalyptic in form, nor chiefly concerned with the subject of the Messianic hope. Only two or three passages are of importance for our purpose. Ch. 1 speaks of the day when the sanctuary of God will be established in the midst of Israel for ever and ever. Corrected by reproof, the people will abandon their idolatry. After having been dispersed among the heathen, the penitent Israelites will be gathered into one, and God will come and dwell among them. On the setting up of the Messianic kingdom, 'the heavens and the earth' . . . 'and all the luminaries shall be renewed' ($1^{29}$). This idea of the gradual transformation of nature as well as man appears to have been taken from Mazdeism (Söderblom, *La Vie Future d'après le Mazdéisme*, p. 254). In ch. 23 the death of Abraham at the age of 175 years gives occasion for some reference to the duration of human life, and this again leads the writer to portray in glowing colours the future vicissitudes of Israel. By reason of sin the infant of three weeks will look like a centenarian. But they will begin to renounce the sins of their fathers, and then their days will gradually lengthen to a thousand years, and the servants of the Lord 'will again pursue their enemies.' In another passage universal empire is promised to kings of Jacob's line ($31^{18}$). The statement that life will be short until the day of the Great Judgment ($23^{11}$) seems to indicate that the writer conceives the Judgment as intervening at the point when after protracted trial a new generation penitently kisses the rod. This marks the rise of the Messianic era. 'Jubilees will pass away,' however, before a perfectly pure Israel shall dwell in quiet throughout the land.*

We must next take account of the *Similitudes* of Enoch (chs. 37–71), which Charles refers to B.C. 95–80. This work exhibits the genuine religious spirit of Judaism. The Messianic doctrine in particular finds here unique expression. Dealing with the old problem, How can the temporary triumph of wickedness consist with the justice of God? the writer finds the answer in a comprehensive review of the world's history from the first beginnings of evil down to the final extrication wrought by the establishment of the Messianic kingdom. His method is strictly apocalyptic. Men were led astray by the watchers, who became subject to Satan ($54^{6}$). After this sinners deny the Lord of spirits ($38^{2}$), and the mighty oppress God's elect children ($62^{9ff.}$). But the Son of Man along with the Head of Days will appear for judgment. Punishment will be meted out to the fallen angels ($54^{6}$), the kings and the mighty ($38^{5}$), and the godless ($38^{3}$ etc.), and 'unrighteousness will disappear as a shadow' from the earth ($49^{2}$). Heaven and earth will be transformed ($45^{4f.}$), and the elect will live in the light of eternal life ($58^{3}$). The Elect One will dwell among them, and 'with that Son of Man will they eat and lie down and rise up for ever and ever' ($62^{14}$). Most frequently the Messiah is desig-

* While Charles admits that this is a correct statement of the case 'if v.11 is correctly handed down and to be taken literally,' he argues that the view that the Final Judgment precedes the Messianic kingdom is precluded by the writer's conception of this kingdom as 'a gradual and progressive transformation. Cf. the same writer's note on $23^{30}$.

nated 'the Elect One' ($40^5$ $45^3$ etc.), but also 'the Righteous One' ($37^3$), 'the Anointed' ($48^{10}$ $52^4$), and 'the Son of Man' ($46^{2ff.}$ $48^2$ etc.). His pre-existence seems to be affirmed in $48^{2-6}$. This is a solitary instance of religious speculation on the part of this Apocalyptic writer; and certainly it is rare to find in a Pal. work of pre-Christian date such a union of the Messianic idea with the Logos doctrine of Alexandrian and the Wisdom doctrine of Pal. Judaism. It probably appealed to him, however, as 'the fittest means of preserving intact the religious content of the Messianic idea' (Langen, *Judenthum*, p. 414). In the *Similitudes* the Messiah appears as (1) Prophet and teacher. Wisdom is poured out like water before him ($49^1$); its secrets stream forth from his mouth ($51^3$). He is the last and highest embodiment of the spirit of prophecy ($49^3$), and the revealer of all that is hidden ($46^3$). (2) Vindicator and ruler of the righteous. He has been revealed to the elect ($62^7$), and will be a staff to the righteous ($48^4$). He preserves their lot, and is the avenger of their life ($48^7$). They shall have the earth for their dwelling-place ($51^5$); He will abide over them ($62^{14}$); and their faces will be lighted up with joy ($51^5$). (3) Judge. The writer's spiritual conception of the Messianic idea comes out specially in connexion with the judicial function assigned to him. The Lord of spirits has chosen the Messiah as judge ($49^4$). For this work he is fitted by reason of his perfect righteousness ($46^3$). No matter by what death they have perished, all the righteous will be raised by him to life again ($51^1$ $61^5$), and no evil shall stand in his presence ($49^2$). He possesses the spirit of might ($49^3$), and rules over all ($62^6$). All judgment is committed unto him, and he will sit on the throne of his glory ($45^3$ $69^{17}$). The consequences of judgment are presented in $45^{3ff.}$. In the transformed heaven and earth no place will be left for sinners. Azâzel and all his associates he will judge ($55^4$). On all men and angels, good as well as bad, he will pronounce sentence ($61^8$), and in his presence falsehood will be impossible ($49^4$ $6^{23}$). While the writer thus boldly represents the Messiah as the supernatural Son of Man, clothed with the attributes of Deity and separating the righteous from the wicked, it is noteworthy that, like other pre-Christian Jewish authors, he knows nothing of a Second Advent. The Messiah is spoken of simply as the deliverer of the righteous, the light of the Gentiles ($48^4$), and the judge of the world, and his whole activity is connected with a single appearance. This may help to explain the fact that to the later Judaism, and even to the first Christian disciples, a suffering Messiah seemed a contradiction in terms. Rather, it was thought, must the Messiah on his coming 'abide for ever' (Jn $12^{32ff.}$), in keeping with the view already presented in Enoch of his single and continual presence upon earth.

That the Messianic expectation grew stronger as the end of the Jewish State drew near is evidenced by the Psalms of Solomon, a collection of 18 psalms breathing the spirit of OT poetry, and dating from the early years of the Roman supremacy in Palestine (B.C. 70–40). Of these poems, which are of Pharisaic authorship, only two (17 and 18) give expression to such hopes. The writer strikingly combines the thought of God Himself being the King of Israel ($17^1$) with that of an endless Davidic monarchy ($17^5$). After recalling the beginnings of royalty in Israel, and bewailing the havoc wrought by the stranger (?=Pompey), he pleads with God for their restoration under 'a son of David' ($17^{23}$). He then goes on to describe the person of the future Messianic king, on which he lays greater stress than his predecessors (Daniel, Sirach, etc.). This ruler will gather again the holy people, over whom he will reign in righteousness ($17^{28}$). The heathen ($17^{25. 27. 31}$) and the 'proud sinners,' *i.e.* the Hasmonæans (vv.$^{26f. 41}$), will be driven from the inheritance usurped by them. The subject nations will come to a purified Jerusalem to bring her wearied children as gifts, and to see the glory of the Lord ($17^{32ff.}$). Himself without sin ($17^{41}$), there is no unrighteousness in his days, for all are saints, and their king is the Lord's Anointed ($17^{35}$). Ordinary methods of warfare he will not resort to ($17^{37}$), but will smite the earth with the word of his mouth ($17^{39}$). The period of his dominion is limited: 'he shall not faint all his days.' Such is the beauty of the king of Israel, and happy are they who are born in his days ($17^{47}$ $18^7$). This bright expectation of a Messiah in face of the triumph of the Roman arms shows that the downfall of the national dynasty was marked by a distinct revival of Messianic hopes. The writer contrasts the evils of the present with the glorious future awaiting Israel when they shall have returned to God. The Messianic idea is treated, however, more with reference to its bearing on the earthly prospects of the Israelitish people than is the case in Enoch, and it is very doubtful whether the supernatural at all enters into the poet's conception of his hero. While there is no secularization of the Messianic idea, the future king is represented as David's successor upon the earthly throne (11. $18^{6-10}$).

At the commencement of the Christian era the Messianic idea in its spiritual significance had faded largely from the popular mind. It was in truth the secularization of this idea that led to the crucifixion of Jesus. A Messiah of another sort was wanted. This feeling found its strongest manifestation in the fanaticism of the Zealots, who, on the principle that God had already (under the Maccabees) delivered Israel from the yoke of a great heathen empire, continually fomented rebellion against the power of Rome. At the opposite pole from this was the exclusively spiritual conception of Messianic prophecy which had become the specialty of apocalyptic authors. Both of these elements originally entered into the Messianic idea, but gradually they came to be sharply distinguished.

In the Assumption of Moses, written according to Charles A.D. 7–30, but doubtless embodying views current *before* its composition, the Jewish lawgiver recounts to Joshua the future history of the nation down to Messianic times. The work is apocalyptic, and gives expression to the Messianic idea on its purely religious side. There is no mention of any victory over the heathen. The writer abandons the hope of an earthly Messiah,* and some would even detect hostility to this hope in the statement that 'the Eternal God alone . . . will appear to punish the Gentiles' ($10^7$). In the beautiful passage forming ch. 10 there is nothing beyond an ardent expectation that J″ will manifest Himself for the punishment of their enemies and the salvation of the chosen people. The theocratic kingdom, which will be preceded by a day of repentance ($1^{18}$), will extend to 'the whole creation' ($10^1$). The dominion of the devil shall have an end, and Israel's enemies shall be punished by the hands of the angel (Michael), $10^{2. 8}$. God will also exalt Israel to heaven ($10^8$), whence they shall joyfully behold their enemies in Ge(henna).†

The trend of Jewish Messianic expectation just before and after the destruction of Jerusalem by the Romans is exhibited in the Apocalypses of Baruch and 2 (4) Esdras. These two writings

* Hilgenfeld's identification of 'Taxo' ($9^1$) with the Messiah is purely arbitrary. Cf. vol. iii. p. 449b.

† According to the conjecture of Charles, who for ἐν γῇ (=*in terram*) reads *in Gehenna*, and thus certainly gets a better sense.

have so many affinities that some have regarded them as from the same hand; but, according to the most recent scholarship as represented by Kabisch and Charles, they are composite works derived from several authors. Baruch reflects the Judaism of the latter half of the 1st cent. A.D. The Messianic portions, which present an optimistic view of the earthly prospects of Israel, seem to have been written prior to A.D. 70. They are three in number—(1) 27–30[1]. The coming tribulation, which will fall into twelve periods, will extend to the whole earth, and the enemies of Israel will be destroyed. After that the Messiah will appear, and the surviving 'remnant' will feed not only on the flesh of animals and the fruits of the earth, but on manna from the skies. It will be a time of plenty, of marvels, and of joy. At the end of his reign the Messiah 'will return in glory' to heaven. (2) 36–40. Four successive world-empires antagonistic to Zion will rise and perish. When the last and most terrible of these (Rome) is ripe for destruction, then will be revealed 'the principate of my Messiah, which is like the fountains and the vine, and when it is revealed it will root out the multitude of his host.' The last surviving leader (?=Pompey) will be put to death by 'my Messiah,' whose reign will endure for ever, until the world of corruption is at an end. Here the Messiah plays a more active part than in the former section, the protection of Israel and the overthrow of their enemies being represented as his sole work. (3) 53–74. In this section, which magnifies the Law while expressing the popular Messianic expectation, the writer divides the history of the world into twelve periods of evil (black waters) and good (bright waters) alternately, followed by a period of woes (the last and blackest waters). To these succeeds the Messiah's kingdom (the bright lightning). He will judge the nations, sparing those who have not trodden down the seed of Jacob, but slaying the enemies of Israel. He will then continue to sit on the throne of his kingdom, and all tribulation will vanish before the universal joy.

The representation of 2 (4) Esdras (written, according to Schürer, in the reign of Domitian, A.D. 81–96), while of the same spiritual type, is marked by some striking peculiarities of its own. Among the Jews hitherto the thought of a glorified Messiah had been universally prevalent, but pseudo-Ezra speaks of him as dying after an activity of 400 years, and says nothing of his resurrection. After the death of Christ, the world, he says, shall relapse into primeval silence for seven days, 'so that no man shall remain.' Then the new world shall be ushered in, the earth shall restore its dead, and the Most High shall be revealed upon the seat of judgment (7[28ff.]). In contrast to the view presented in the Assumption of Moses, this writer not only sharply distinguishes the Messiah from J" Himself, but also gives a figurative delineation of his person. He is described as a lion rising up out of the wood and rebuking the eagle (*i.e.* imperial Rome) for her unrighteousness. While he has been kept by the Most High unto the end in order to condemn the Romans, the rest of the Jewish people shall live happily under his sway until the Day of Judgment (12[31ff.]). Again he is pictured as a man coming up from the midst of the sea, and flying with the clouds of heaven (13[3]). Planting himself upon a great mountain (the emblem of Zion), he encounters a mighty host who have gathered themselves against him from the four winds of heaven, and destroys them by the flaming breath of his lips. Coming down from the mountain, he then calls to him another and 'peaceable' multitude (the ten tribes). These figures, it is explained, are used of 'this my son' (13[37]); and, although it is not easy to deduce from them a very concrete doctrine of the Messiah's person, one or two points are sufficiently clear. The writer dissociates himself from the view current in the Judaism of his time: according to him, the Messiah is in no sense an earthly king. At the same time it is plain, from the representation he gives of him as dying, that he does not conceive him as possessing essential Deity. Neither is he depicted as an ordinary man: he comes up out of the sea, 'as it were the likeness of a man,' and flies with the clouds of heaven. As fire melts wax, so his voice burns those that hear it (13[3f.]). It would therefore seem that in this apocalypse the Messiah is conceived as a created being of a quite peculiar kind, who appears as a man among men for the destruction of Jehovah's enemies and the restoration of His people, although not as an earthly potentate. The Most High has reserved him for long (13[26]), until the moment appointed for his coming. 'No man upon earth can see my son, or those that be with him, but in the time of his day' (13[52]). Then he shall be revealed (7[28]), and his appearance will herald that revolution which shall destroy the power of Rome and bring together the scattered tribes of Israel.

It is clear from the Shemoneh 'Esreh—the chief prayer which it was the duty of every Israelite to repeat thrice daily, and which, although it attained its final form only after A.D. 70, must be considered much more ancient as to its groundwork—that the hopes expressed in these apocalypses were cherished by the nation as a whole. Prayer is offered for the gathering of the dispersed, the rebuilding of Jerusalem, the revival of the Davidic kingdom, and the restoration of the sacrificial service.

6. *The Messianic expectation in Hellenistic Judaism.*—If in Palestine the hope associated with the advent of the ideal Davidic king had not altogether waned in presence of the political and religious liberty enjoyed under the Hasmonæan dynasty, the people were at least content to wait for the rise of a new prophet (1 Mac 14[41]). But in Egypt, where they were still under Gentile dominion, the Jews seem to have cherished more warmly the hope of a Messianic deliverance. Thus about B.C. 140 the oldest Jewish portions of the Sibylline Oracles predict the approach from the East of a God-sent king, who will take vengeance on his adversaries, and make war to cease throughout the earth. Heathen opposition to the temple will collapse under the stroke of the Immortal, whose children will live in peace and quietness under the protection of His hand. At sight of this the Gentiles shall accept God's law, and bring gifts to the temple. So shall be inaugurated the reign of peace. God will set up an eternal kingdom over all mankind, with Jerusalem as its central seat, and under the just sway and judicial control of the prophets (3[652-794]). Although the Messiah is not named, and although the main stress of the prophecy is laid on the triumph of the Law, the introduction of the figure of the Messianic king into the writer's delineation of the future is nevertheless very significant in view of the abstract spiritualism affected by Alexandrian Judaism generally, and already traceable in the LXX. No less remarkable is it that even a speculative moralist like Philo, in his delineation of the happiness in store for the righteous, should avail himself of the image of the Messianic king. According to this writer, all adherents of the Law will be liberated 'at a given sign on one day.' Led by a Divine appearance, visible only to the delivered, they will rebuild the ruined cities, and the desert will be fertilized (*de Exsecr.* 8–9). On their deliverance the dispersed Israelites will stream together to a certain place: the indefiniteness here is probably

due to a spiritualizing in Philo's mind of the Zion of the prophets. The coming era will be signalized by the tameness of wild beasts (*de Præmiis et Pœnis*, 15 ff.); by the saints' bloodless victory in battle ['Then, says the prophecy (Nu $24^7$, LXX), a man who goes to battle and makes war shall go forth and subdue great and populous nations, God Himself sending help to His saints' (*ib.* 16)]; by the blessing of physical health and strength (17–18); and by that of wealth and prosperity (20). Athough there is here no express mention of a personal Messiah, the latter is nevertheless clearly indicated in the warrior who subdues great nations. The use of such language, alien as it is to Philo's general point of view, is a proof of the prevalence of the Messianic idea in his time. It is more after his manner to lay stress upon the liberating power of virtue, and this he contrives to do, without, however, altogether excluding the activity of the Logos as a fundamental factor in the future salvation.

The Hellenistic sympathies of Josephus are apparent in his treatment of the Messianic idea. He studiously ignores it. Only in two passages of his writings does it find the faintest expression. In recording Daniel's interpretation of Nebuchadnezzar's dream he declines to explain the meaning of the stone which was cut out of the mountain and destroyed the image (Dn $2^{45}$), on the ground that as a historian he is not concerned with the future (*Ant.* X. x. 4). Again, in remarking upon the fulfilment of several of Balaam's predictions, he takes no account of the Messianic prophecy in Nu $24^{12ff.}$, but merely adds: 'One may easily guess that the rest will have their completion in due time' (*Ant.* IV. vi. 5). No further evidence is required to show that in his presentation of Jewish history the Messianic prophecies of the OT are deliberately ignored. When he says of Jesus, 'This is the Christ' (*Ant.* XVIII. iii. 3), all he means to convey is that He was popularly regarded as the Jewish Messiah. Certainly, the words do not contain the confession of his own faith. That he had personally abandoned (if indeed he ever understood) the Messianic hope is clear from his declaration to his fellow-countrymen at the siege of Jerusalem that Rome was invincible, and that God had now given the dominion to Italy (*BJ* V. ix. 3), as well as from his impudent transference of it to the rule of Vespasian (*BJ* VI. v. 4).

After the Exile the doctrine of the Messianic expectation appears to have assumed two very different forms—one in Palestine, and the other in Egypt. The increased clearness of the prophetic doctrine had been accompanied in Palestine by an increased departure from the true understanding of the scriptural position. In the prevailing popular conception the religious character of the Messiah was overlooked. Men either thought of him as a temporal prince, or lost sight of the personal element altogether in their anticipation of a temporal kingdom. 'The theocratic views of the people made it impossible for them to separate the thought of the Messiah from that of a victorious earthly king, and caused them to cling to the political idea till it was finally extinguished in the ashes of the Holy City.'* In Egypt the doctrine had a different history. If the notion of a Messianic ruler did not cease to be popularly contemplated, no place at all was given to a visible Messiah in the Jewish-Alexandrian philosophy. Where Philo does introduce the figure of the Messianic king, this is done purely as a concession to the popular sentiment, and not because it falls in with his ethical view. The conception of the Alexandrian philosophers was wholly ideal, and exclusive of personal Messianic activity. The Law and wisdom were all the Messiah they wished. No other view would square with their philosophical system, which did not favour the concrete and visible side of things. This was the opposite extreme of the development in Palestine, and it is not improbable that what yet remained of true Messianic hope in the latter country was due to the tenacity with which their brethren in Egypt clung to the mystical conception of the Messianic deliverance.

7. *Peculiarities of the later Messianic hope.*—From the situation as broadly reflected in Palestine and in Egypt it is clear that the hope of a bright future, which formed an integral part of the religious consciousness of Israel, assumed various aspects in different minds and at different periods of the national development. Particularly noteworthy are some well-marked points of contrast between the older and the later Messianic hope. These have been well stated by Schürer (*HJP* II. ii. p. 129 ff.), whom we here follow. (1) Upon the whole, the former contemplated nothing more than the advent of better times, when a purified nation under a wise and just Davidic king should occupy a place of power and influence, and enjoy all the blessings of peace and prosperity. (2) While the former was almost entirely national, the latter growingly assumed an individual character. Every pious Jew would share in the glory of the future kingdom, and for this end the righteous dead would be raised to life again. (3) The former did not go beyond the circle of earthly circumstances, whereas the latter conceives the future salvation as transcending the sphere of the present. (4) In later times, and in the hands of the scribes, the Messianic hope assumed a more scholastic form than in the earlier prophetic days. 'The poetic image was stiffened into dogma' in a way not possible so long as the Messianic expectation was a living reality. While this characterization is broadly true, it is to be remembered that 'even in later times the old hope of a glorious future for the nation maintained the supremacy. This forms, even in the later view of the future, the determining ground-plan of the picture. And just as upon this foundation the characteristic peculiarities of the later view have stronger or weaker influence, and produce this or that alteration, is the old image now more now less, now in one way now in another, specially modified and supplemented' (*HJP* II. ii. p. 135).

8. *Question as to the retrogression of the Messianic idea during the post-Prophetic period.*—Was there a break in the development of this doctrine? Did the distinctively Messianic hope disappear with the cessation of prophecy, to be revived only with the advent of Christianity? It would be wrong to suppose that it ever became absolutely extinct. In order to this the Prophetic books of the OT must have perished, and the synagogues must have been closed. Neither of these things had happened. Even in the darkest days there yet remained some earnest souls who clung to the old faith and tried to revive it. It is, however, undeniable that the expectation of a personal Messiah went greatly down after the Prophets were silent. The hope of a bright future for Israel never wavered, yet there was a very strong disposition no longer to associate it with the raising of an ideal Davidic king to the throne. For many, the Prophetic picture of such a king had lost its first attractiveness. They had waited for him long enough, and he had not appeared. Thus among the great mass of the Jewish people there was no living faith in a personal Messiah at the time when the Apocrypha were composed. What was the reason of this retrogression? So far as we can judge, it was due to two considerations—(1) The hope of the Jews was a distant

* See the author's *From the Exile to the Advent* (Clark's Handbook Series), p. 175.

hope. It was in books—that was all. They took for granted that there would be no great realization of it in their time, and looked upon the living realities of Divine grace as confined to the past and the future. Such want of heart manifested in regard to this great central doctrine was necessarily a crushing blow to the national development. (2) Their hope was a political hope. The transient glory of the Maccabæan period gave a measure of religious life, but any further deliverance that was longed for was rather along the same lines. 'The speedy triumph of the Maccabees satisfied for a time the aspirations of the people; and a longer period of suffering and disappointment was needed to develop the hope of a Messiah into a passion among the masses of the nation, and into a doctrine in the schools of the learned' (Drummond, *Jewish Messiah*, p. 269). The hopes centred on the Hasmonæan princes were gradually seen to be delusive, and in the struggle for supremacy between a secularized hierarchy and the Pharisees or party of the Law the people took the side of the latter. Turning from all human kingship, they looked for deliverance to the king whom J″ Himself would raise up from David's line. That in the time of Christ this hope was generally prevalent is manifest from the Gospels. It had been abundantly proved that the kingdom of God could not perfect itself under the restrictions of an earthly State. But that stone which the builders rejected was soon to become the head of the corner in the prophetic building; and in the person and work of Jesus as Messiah the true spiritual idea of the Divine kingdom was to arise and prevail.

vi. ESCHATOLOGY.—In the OT, eschatological doctrine appears in a very undeveloped form, and, though it cannot be said to occupy a large place in the Apocrypha either, there is yet enough in these post-canonical books to show that in the period after the Exile there was a much clearer apprehension of a future life than there had been in the earlier stages of the nation's history. It is, however, in the Apocalyptic literature of the two centuries preceding the Christian era that the most marked development in eschatology is met with. In these works the inherent importance of the subject, connected as it was with the Messianic hope, combined with the Jewish fondness for elaborate and fantastic presentation of truth to give it a foremost place.

1. *The OT position.*—By many scholars (Stade, Schwally, Charles) the eschatological ideas of the early Hebrews are traced to the ancestor worship of Semitic heathenism. However this may be, it is certain that in the Mosaic legislation the outlook is confined to the present sphere of existence: virtue is rewarded, and vice punished, during this life. Both in pre-Mosaic and in Mosaic times, however, the view that death does not end the conscious life of all had taken possession of the popular mind. It comes out in connexion with the translations of Enoch (Gn $5^{22ff.}$) and Elijah (2 K $2^{11}$), although immortality is here conceived as a possibility only for soul and body together, previous to death, and not after it. The thought of Jehovah's power restoring the dead through human instrumentality (1 K $17^{22}$, 2 K $4^{35}$), which is of later occurrence, also implies the thought of a future life. According to the Heb. conception, death does not mean absolute extinction. Although the dead person does not in any real sense live, he still subsists. He descends into Sheol, a dreary region of darkness (Job $10^{21}$), a land of silence and forgetfulness (Ps $94^{17}$ $115^{17}$), the house appointed for all living (Job $30^{23}$). In this shadowy existence, the dreamy counterpart of his past life, he has no fellowship with the living, whether men or God (Ps $6^5$, Is $38^{18}$). He has nothing to fear, and nothing to hope for. Into this conception of Sheol no moral element enters; there is no distinction made between good and bad. Personal identity, however, is not lost, and the kingdom of the dead reflects the family and other distinctions of the upper world. Thus men are gathered into tribes (Gn $25^{8f.}$ etc.), and kings sit upon thrones (Is $14^{9f.}$).

Although they did not actually formulate either the doctrine of immortality or that of the resurrection, the Prophets by their ethical tendency prepared the way for a more spiritual development. Their insistence upon the fact that Israel's relation to J″ is morally conditioned, was fitted to awaken the consciousness of a new life through fellowship with God. The conception of a life of blessedness beyond the grave was the necessary corollary of the law of individual retribution as proclaimed by Jeremiah ($31^{29f.}$) and developed by Ezekiel ($18^4$). That this law as thus stated caused much perplexity to the afflicted righteous is evident from Job and Ecclesiastes as well as from several of the Psalms. And, although the doctrine of a blessed future life in which the wrongs of the present will be righted is nowhere definitely taught in these books, they contain passages in which it certainly seems to be implied (Job $14^{13ff.}$ $19^{25ff.}$, Ps 49. 73). If in Job the immortality of the individual is no more than a deep aspiration, in Ps 49 and 73 it becomes a settled spiritual conviction. Early in the 3rd cent., and even perhaps late in the 4th, it was merged in the larger doctrine of the resurrection, which embraced not only the idea of an individual immortality, but also that of the Messianic kingdom. Thus for a time the former idea completely fell into the background, since to the Jew the future blessedness of his nation was more than the well-being of the individual.

This eschatology of the nation is reflected in the Prophetical books of the OT, especially in the conception of the day of J″, when judgment will be meted out to Israel's enemies, and unmingled happiness to the chosen people, the judgment on the former being the inaugural prelude to the national blessedness of the latter. We have here the oldest expression of a conception which subsequently assumed various forms. In the 7th cent., when the Jews chafed under the cruelty of their Assyrian oppressors, Nahum and Habakkuk reasserted it with only slight modification. According to Amos, however (and also Hosea, who, while not using the expression 'day of Jehovah,' predicts the judgment which it denotes, $13^{12ff.}$), it is upon Israel itself that the judgment will most severely fall ($3^{2f.}$), for in His 'day' J″ will manifest Himself, not in order to the triumph of Israel, but for the vindication of His own righteousness. In Isaiah and Micah the judgment is represented as falling chiefly upon Judah and Jerusalem (Is $1^{24ff.}$ $29^6$, Mic $3^{12}$), while in Zephaniah it is set forth for the first time as embracing the whole world ($1^{18}$), and leaving only a righteous remnant in Israel ($3^{12f.}$). In Jeremiah the day of J″ is mainly, although not exclusively, directed against Judah ($37^{6ff.}$); but at the same time there is held out the hope that the national life will be regenerated and restored ($23^{7f.}$ $24^{5f.}$), and that the Gentiles shall be converted, and only the impenitent destroyed ($12^{16f.}$).

The epoch of the Exile witnessed a revival of individualism in religion. According to Ezekiel and his followers, judgment means the destruction of the Gentiles and the purification of Israel man by man in order to the establishment of the Messianic kingdom, which will be introduced by the day of J″. In the post-exilic age the idea of judgment recedes before that of a universal Messianic kingdom. Through Israel as the Servant of J″ all nations shall embrace the true religion (42[3f.] 49[6] 52[13]-53[12]), and yield themselves to Him of their own accord (Is 2[2ff.] = Mic 4[1ff.]). In Is 19[16-25] Egypt and Assyria are placed alongside of Israel as sharing in her spiritual blessedness, while in Mal 1[11] we have the language of unqualified universalism, and the acceptance by J″ as a pure offering even of the unconscious sacrifices of the heathen. In contrast to this standpoint, however, the particularism of Ezekiel continued to have its advocates, and the Messianic kingdom was viewed as the close preserve of a reunited Israel (Hos 3[5], Mic 5[3], Is 9[1ff.]), the Gentiles being either excluded or represented as in subjection to Israel. In Hag. (2[20ff.]) and Zec. (1[18ff.]) the day of J″ is depicted as involving the destruction of the heathen powers, and the establishment of the Messianic kingdom as consequent on the rebuilding of the temple. Joel's point of view is already apocalyptic; the nations generally will be destroyed, and Israel justified; there is no moral sifting of Israel as in older prophets. In the apocalypse of Daniel it is taught that when evil has reached its height the end of the world will ensue.

It needed a combination of both the individual and the national aspects of the thought of a blessed future for the righteous to form the fuller doctrine of the resurrection as apparently conceived by the end of the 4th or beginning of the 3rd cent. B.C. If we accept Cheyne's view as to the date (*c.* 334 B.C.) of the remarkable passage Is 26[19], and Charles' interpretation of its meaning, it was then held that immortality would indeed be secured to the righteous individual, but would consist in his resurrection to share in the blessedness of the Messianic kingdom.

2. *Post-canonical development.*—But, although the doctrines of immortality and the resurrection were thus steadily establishing themselves in Jewish thought, it was only very gradually that they won their way to general recognition among the people. In several of the OT Apocrypha there is no mention of them. Sirach limits to this life both the punishment of wickedness and the reward of righteousness. Even after the doctrine of the resurrection was being regularly taught in the schools of the Pharisees, many of the Jews evidently had no clear ideas upon the subject (Mk 9[10]). At the same time, in the post-canonical literature there is undeniably a further development of the eschatological conceptions of the later prophets. The new views regarding the future destiny of man assumed two distinct forms—one in Palestine, the other in Egypt. To the Pal. Jew the future life was made real only through a bodily resurrection; to the Alexandrian, it was the necessary consequence of the immortality of the soul.

The 2nd cent. B.C. witnessed a great advance in eschatology. Instead of the old indefiniteness of the day of J″, we have the formulation of distinct ideas. The Book of Enoch especially describes the last things and the other world in minute detail.

(1) *Future judgment.*—A prominent feature in the eschatological development of the period is the strongly expressed certainty with regard to future retribution, in contrast to the admitted uncertainty that men will in this life be rewarded according to their works. In the view of the apocalyptic writers of this century the establishment on earth of the Messianic kingdom will be preceded by judgment and just recompense for all men living, and for some or all of the Israelitish dead, as well as for the fallen angels. To a certain extent punishment has already been administered through the first world-judgment on the angels who formed unions with the daughters of men, on their children, and on all men living at the time of the Deluge (Enoch 10[1-12]). These angels are bound fast in gloomy caverns under the hills (10[4f. 12]), while the souls of men are relegated to Sheol (22), until the final judgment that shall usher in the reign of the Messiah. Then will judgment be pronounced upon the impure angels, the demons who have hitherto escaped punishment (16[1]), and, with the exception of one special class of sinners (22[13]), upon all Israel. The fact of an individual judgment after death is thus already taught in the oldest section of the Book of Enoch. It is also found in Jubilees (4[23] 5[9ff.] etc.) in special connexion with the idea of 'heavenly tables,' on which 'judgment is written down for every creature and for every kind.' We have it embodied likewise in the Apocalypse of Baruch (4[4ff.]), according to which those who have rejected God's law will first behold the righteous invested with the splendour of angels, and 'afterwards depart to be tormented.' There is here no limitation of the idea to faithless Israelites. In the contemporary Book of Daniel (B.C. 168), which presents a contrast to the Book of Enoch in respect that it has in view the future of the nation rather than that of the individual, judgment is executed by the saints (7[22]) as a prelude to the final judgment at the hands of the Almighty (9[12ff.]). Although nothing is said as to the judgment of angels, that of the angel princes of Persia (10[13. 20]) and Greece (10[20]) is implied. In Enoch 83-90 (written B.C. 166-161), the last judgment is likewise placed at the inauguration of the Messianic kingdom. Special reference is made to the judgment wrought by the 'great sword' of Judas Maccabæus (90[19]), whose victorious campaigns against the Syrians were being carried on when this part of Enoch was written. In this section of the book the thought of a general individual judgment is set forth in great judicial detail. A throne is erected for the Lord of the sheep; the sealed books are opened; the seven archangels are commanded to bring before Him the evil angels (the fallen Watchers), who are cast into an abyss of fire; the seventy faithless 'shepherds' of Israel and the 'blinded sheep' (*i.e.* apostate Jews) share the same fate. After this the Messianic kingdom is set up *on earth*; a new Jerusalem takes the place of the old, and the righteous who have suffered oppression are brought into it (90[20ff.]).

During the last century B.C. there occurred a radical change in Jewish eschatology. What lay at the root of this was the conviction that an eternal Messianic kingdom cannot be suitably manifested on the present earth. Such a view had obviously an important bearing upon the whole field of eschatological thought. It led the writers of this century to take new ground with respect to the kingdom, and the place of the Final Judgment relatively to it. Some cut the knot by denying the eternity of the earthly Messianic kingdom (Enoch 91-104); others by postulating the idea of a new heaven and a new earth (Enoch 37-70). The latter section of the Book of Enoch is the only work of this century which still places the Final Judgment at the inauguration of the Messianic kingdom. All others dating from this period (Enoch 91-104, Ps.-Sol., etc.), appear to relegate it to its close. As to the scope of the Judgment, the view of the former period remains unaltered; it extends to all men and angels, righteous and wicked. Enoch 91-104 follows Daniel in speaking of a preliminary judgment wrought through the instrumentality of the saints. In Ps-Sol 17. 18 the Messiah himself is judge, although the act of judgment here is probably confined to the destruction of the hostile powers.

The Pal. Judaism of the 1st cent. A.D. continued virtually to reflect the eschatological position arrived at in the preceding century. In the Assumption of Moses, as well as in the Apocalypse of Baruch and 2 (4) Esdras (certain sections excepted), there is conserved the idea of a preliminary judgment. The Final Judgment on men and angels is placed at the close of the Messianic kingdom, or, failing the expectation of such a kingdom, at the close of the age (Apoc. of Baruch), or on the completion of the number of the righteous (2 (4) Esdras).

So far as the doctrine of a Future Judgment is concerned, it would therefore appear from the above that the Apocryphal period witnessed very decided developments. Although the OT idea of judgment through the overthrow of existing hostile powers was to some extent retained (Enoch $90^{18f.}$, Assumption of Moses 3, Apoc. of Baruch $72^6$, 2 Es $13^{14}$), this gradually gave way to that of a forensic act. The Judgment was placed for the most part at the end of the Messiah's reign instead of at its commencement. It tended to assume a growingly personal and individual character. The scope of the Judgment was also extended so as to include all, men and angels alike. Obviously, we have here a distinct approximation to the doctrine of the Judgment as given by Christ Himself. 'He employs many of the terms which were current, while He relieves the popular beliefs of all that was gross, fantastic, or trivial. He brings to the OT conception the extension and the certainty which it needed. The spiritual principles of His teaching, and the things which it adds to the Heb. faith on the subject, make the old doctrine a new one.' * That He is Himself the Judge, that every man will be judged by Him 'according to his works,' and that His judgment is final,—these are the transforming elements by which all the deficiencies of the pre-Christian conception are removed, and the doctrine of a Future Judgment is raised to a clear and definite position in the doctrinal structure of revealed religion.

(2) *Realms of the departed.*—(*a*) *Sheol.*—In Dn $12^2$, according to the most probable reading, this is designated 'the ground (land) of dust,' and seems to be used in its OT sense as denoting a region devoid of moral distinctions. It is represented as the final abode of all mankind save the best and the worst in Israel, of whom the former shall rise to 'æonian life,' and the latter be cast into Gehenna. For these two classes Sheol is only a temporary and intermediate abode. The writer appears to have in his mind the faithful and the apostates in the struggle with Antiochus Epiphanes.

From the detailed description in Enoch 22 it is manifest that during the 2nd cent. B.C. the conception of Sheol underwent a radical change. From being a place free from moral distinctions it has become a place of retribution, where men are dealt with according to their deserts. Here all souls assemble ($22^3$), and await the Judgment in their respective habitations. Of these there are four—two for the spirits of the righteous, (1) for those who have died an unmerited death, (2) for the rest of the righteous; and two for the spirits of the wicked, (1) for those who have already been punished in this life for their wickedness, (2) for those who escaped punishment in the upper world. From three of these divisions there is a resurrection to final judgment; but from the fourth, the abode of sinners to whom death came as the punishment of their crimes, there is no resurrection. In their case Sheol is equivalent to hell. Ethically, this represents a great advance upon the old Heb. conception, although it is of too cast-iron a description to be truly ethical. The soul can neither become better nor worse, and 'Sheol thus conceived is only a place of petrified moralities and suspended graces' (Charles, *Eschatology*, 187).

Soon, however, this fault was to be remedied, for in 2 Mac $12^{42ff.}$ moral transformation in Sheol is considered possible. Judas is said to have offered sacrifice for the fallen warriors, 'for if he were not expecting that they that had fallen would rise again, it were superfluous and idle to pray for the dead.' During the last century B.C. Sheol is regarded (1) as the intermediate abode of the dead, whence all Israelites (2 Mac $6^{23}$), and possibly all without distinction (Enoch $51^1$), rise to judgment; (2) as the final abode of the wicked, *i.e.* as hell (Enoch $56^8$, Ps-Sol $14^6$ etc.), where souls are slain (Enoch $99^{11}$). In Enoch 91-104 Sheol is almost synonymous with Gehenna, and in Ps.-Sol. entirely so. The *Similitudes* conceive Sheol as the preliminary abode of those dying previous to the establishment of the Messianic kingdom. Subsequent to this, however, it becomes the final abode of the wicked ($63^{10}$). This view of Sheol was almost a necessary consequence of the belief that only the righteous would be raised from the dead.

In the 1st cent. A.D. Sheol is represented as the intermediate abode of all the dead prior to the last judgment (Apoc. Bar $23^5$ $48^{16}$, 2 (4) Es $4^{41}$). According to Josephus, the Pharisees taught that the righteous are rewarded and the wicked punished under the earth (ὑπὸ χθονὸς, *Ant.* XVIII. i. 3), or in Hades (καθ' ᾄδου, *BJ* II. viii. 14), *i.e.* in Sheol. The righteous rise again, and possess other bodies; but for the wicked there is no resurrection. Between the righteous and the wicked in Sheol there was, according to the prevailing conception of the period, a great gulf fixed. The former inhabited 'the treasuries' (Apoc. Bar $21^3$ etc., 2 (4) Es $7^{95}$) of restful bliss; the latter dwelt in a place of torment (Apoc. Bar $30^5$).

It appears, then, that during the Apocryphal period the conception of Sheol was by no means a fixed quantity. Rather was it in a somewhat fluid condition, and underwent considerable variation. It had, however, 'come to be regarded as a definite *stadium* between death and judgment, with preliminary penalties, and, in some forms of thought, with moral processes. The idea of an intermediate state took a larger and larger place in Judaism, and in this matter Christian theology to a great extent served itself heir to Jewish theology. But all this is in the strongest possible contrast to Christ's own teaching. His words fix our thoughts on the present life and the final issues. . . . They give little or no place to the thought of an intermediate state.' *

(*b*) *Paradise.*—According to Schrader,† the word 'paradise' is of Perso-Indogermanic origin (*pairidaēza*, from *pairi*, 'around,' and *daēza*, 'a rampart'), and signifies an enclosure or 'park.' From this it came to denote a pleasure-garden generally, as in Neh $2^8$, Ec $2^5$, and was ultimately adopted as the distinctive designation of the seat of the blessed, whether conceived as earthly or heavenly. According to the conception that prevailed in the 2nd cent. B.C., Paradise was reserved for those who had been directly translated in the flesh. In other words, its gates had been opened only for Enoch and Elijah. From the way in which it conceives Sheol as 'the place of condemnation' ($7^{22}$ $22^{22}$), the Book of Jubilees, however, seems to imply that Paradise is the intermediate abode of the righteous dead until the Final Judgment. But this work also shares the point of view of the later 2 (4) Esdras, according to which

* Salmond, *Christian Doct. of Immortality* 3, p. 318.

* Salmond, *Christian Doct. of Immortality* 3, p. 345 f.

† *COT* ii. p. 71.

Paradise is conceived as the final abode of the righteous ($7^{36.\ 123}$ $8^{52}$). Already in the 1st cent. B.C. it is viewed as 'the garden of the righteous' (Enoch $60^{23}$), and the dwelling-place of 'the elect' (Enoch $60^{8}$ $61^{12}$). In the *Similitudes*, however, it is not the eternal abode of the holy, who pass from it to the Messianic kingdom.

It would appear, therefore, that no very definite position had been reached either with regard to the geographical situation of Paradise or with regard to its inhabitants. This is clear from the varying representations of the Book of Enoch under both of these heads. 'In $32^{2f.}$ it lies in the East: in $70^{2ff.}$ between the West and North: in $77^{3}$ in the North. . . . It is apparently empty in Enoch's time in $32^{3ff.}$, and the righteous dead are in the West, 22: it is the abode of the righteous and the elect in Enoch's and Noah's times in $61^{12}$ $60^{8.\ 23}$: the abode of the earliest fathers in Enoch's time, $89^{52}$.' *

In spite of the uncertainty thus attaching to the term 'Paradise' in Jewish thought, the later Rabbis constructed an elaborate topography of it, with 'Abraham's bosom' as the place of highest honour. The general popular conception in the time of Christ is perhaps fairly well reflected in that of the Essenes, who, according to Jos. (*BJ* II. viii. 11), regarded Paradise as a region situated beyond the ocean, where there was no uncongenial rain or cold or heat, and where righteous souls were perpetually refreshed by gentle zephyrs blowing from the sea. The word is very sparingly used in NT. In the recorded sayings of our Lord it occurs but once (Lk $23^{43}$), and not in such a way as to throw much light upon His own conception of the term. He employs it in a very general sense, and possibly as the word which would convey most meaning and comfort to the listener.

(*c*) *Heaven.*—It is not until the last century B.C. that we find heaven represented in Apocalyptic writings as the abode of the righteous subsequent to 'the day of the great judgment.' This view is first met with in Enoch 91-104, where the righteous are described as the objects of angelic intercession ($104^{1}$). To them will the portals of heaven be opened ($104^{2}$); their joy will be like that of the angels of heaven ($104^{4}$); and they will yet become companions of the heavenly host ($104^{6}$). According to the later Apoc. of Baruch, they will be made like unto the angels ($51^{10}$), while in the *Similitudes* of Enoch it is claimed that they will themselves become angels in heaven. The Book of Jubilees ($23^{31}$) and the Assumption of Moses ($10^{9}$) also regard heaven as the eternal home of the righteous.

(*d*) *Gehenna.*—From denoting the scene of idolatrous sacrifices 'Gehenna' (from the Hebrew גֵּי הִנֹּם = 'valley of Hinnom,' Gr. Γέεννα) came to signify the place where apostate Jews are punished in the sight of the righteous (cf. Is $50^{11}$). In Dn $12^{2}$ it becomes the final abode of all such apostates. But in the last century B.C. this idea took on quite a new complexion. Gehenna is now no longer exclusively reserved for apostate Jews, and is the place of punishment for the nations generally (Jth $16^{17}$). More particularly is it intended for kings and the mighty (Enoch $48^{8f.}$ $53^{5}$ $54^{2}$). Again, whereas according to the older view the torments of the wicked were to afford a constant spectacle to the righteous (Enoch $27^{2f.}$ $90^{26f.}$), in the *Similitudes* this spectacle, although still to be witnessed ($62^{12}$), is only of temporary duration. This fresh development is necessitated by the writer's view with respect to the transformation of heaven and earth at the advent of the Messiah. In the new heavens and the new earth there was no place for Gehenna, which accordingly disappears from the sight of the righteous from henceforth ($62^{13}$). Still another modification of the older view of Gehenna occurs in Enoch 91-104, where the wicked are cast into the furnace of fire as incorporeal spirits ($98^{3}$). Hitherto the punishment of Gehenna had been thought of as both bodily and spiritual, but here the former element is eliminated. In this book no distinction is made between Sheol and Gehenna ($99^{11}$ etc.). 2 (4) Esdras contains the following statements: 'The Most High shall be revealed upon the seat of judgment' ($7^{33}$), and 'the pit of torment shall appear, and over against it shall be the place of rest: and the furnace of hell (Gehenna) shall be showed, and over against it the paradise of delight' ($7^{36}$). The nations that are raised from the dead will then be called upon to behold the contrast between the delight and rest on one side, and fire and torments on the other ($7^{37f.}$). It was only in the later Rabbinism that the word was used to denote a temporary purgatory as well as the abode of the wicked after death. As employed by Christ in the Synoptic Gospels, 'Gehenna' retains its older meaning as 'the final retributive scene or condition, not any intermediate place, whether of penalty or of purification, between death and the resurrection.' * On the momentous and difficult question as to the *eternity* of the penal condition in Gehenna, the student is referred to the discussion in bk. iii. ch. vi. of the work just quoted.

(3) *The Resurrection.*—The first occurrence in the OT of the idea of a resurrection is in Hos $6^{2}$, where the hope expressed is clearly not individual but national. It appears again in a national sense in Ezekiel's vision of the valley of dry bones ($37^{1-14}$). Chronologically, the next reference to this idea is found in the post-exilic prophecy of Is 24-27. Here there is a distinct advance upon former conceptions. Although the thought of a resurrection is still, as in Hosea and Ezekiel, limited to Israel ($26^{14}$), its application to individuals ($26^{19}$), even if the prophets' words do breathe a pious hope rather than contain a clear-cut doctrine, is new. One other OT passage is of importance in this connexion, viz. Dn $12^{2}$ 'And many of them that sleep in the dusty ground (lit. *the ground of dust* ? = Sheol) shall awake, some to everlasting life, and some to reproaches and everlasting abhorrence.' There is here taught for the first time a resurrection of the *wicked*, as also the doctrine of a diversity of lot reserved for the righteous and the wicked in the future. In both cases the writer thinks of Israelites only, and does not even include all of these. Only those are in his view who have distinguished themselves either by their promotion of, or antagonism to, the Divine kingdom.

In the subsequent development of the doctrine the extent of the resurrection was variously conceived. In Dn $12^{2f.}$ the writer thinks of a partial resurrection of both righteous and wicked; Enoch 1-36 speaks of a resurrection of all the righteous and some of the wicked; the *Similitudes* represent at one time that all will be raised up, good and bad alike ($51^{1f.}$), and at another contemplate the resurrection of the righteous only ($61^{5}$); while Enoch 91-104, and the later Jewish literature generally, limit the idea of the resurrection to the righteous (Enoch $91^{10}$ $92^{3}$, 2 Mac $9^{14.\ 36}$, Ps-Sol $3^{16}$ $13^{9}$ etc.). It is in all these cases the resurrection of Israel that is spoken of; there is as yet no thought of a general resurrection.

Different views were held also as to the nature of the resurrection itself. From 2 Maccabees (which as a professed epitome of the work of Jason of Cyrene must be taken to reflect the eschatological views of the century preceding that in which it appeared) it is evident that in the 2nd cent. B.C. the doctrine of the resurrection of the

* Charles' ed., note on $60^{8}$.

* Salmond, *op. cit.* p. 360.

body was very distinctly held. In the account of the cruel death of the seven brothers and their mother, the resurrection is represented at once as a resurrection to eternal life ($7^{9.36}$) in fellowship with the risen righteous ($7^{29}$), and as a resurrection of the body ($7^{11}$). By thus uniting the doctrine of a resurrection with that of immortality, 2 Mac. takes up a more advanced position than any other Apocryphal work.

During the last century B.C. the mode of conceiving the resurrection underwent a change in keeping with the altered view as to the scene of the Messianic kingdom. So long as the latter was regarded as an eternal kingdom on this earth, the idea of a bodily resurrection seemed quite in place. But, after it became usual to think of that kingdom as having its only fitting manifestation in a new heaven and a new earth, the resurrection was conceived either as purely spiritual (Enoch 91–104, Ps.-Sol.), or as one in which the risen righteous shall be invested with garments of glory and of life (Enoch $62^{15f.}$). The *Similitudes*, however, reflect the older view of a bodily resurrection.

Although at the beginning of the Christian era the limitation of the resurrection to the righteous was the accepted view of Judaism, there were still different ideas held with reference to the resurrection itself. According to Jos. (*BJ* II. viii. 14), the Pharisees taught that 'the souls of good men only are removed into other bodies,' *i.e.* bodies of another nature than the present, while the Essenes believed in the soul's immortality, but not in a bodily resurrection. In the Jewish-Alexandrian writings the resurrection is regarded as wholly spiritual, and as taking place immediately after death.' * Matter being essentially evil, there can be no resurrection of the body. As the true self, the soul only is immortal, and can be redeemed only through Wisdom (Wis $8^{13}$). The knowledge of God's dominion is the root of immortality ($15^{3}$). The author starts from the position that 'righteousness is immortal' ($1^{15}$) as God is immortal. Then follows the statement that 'God created man for incorruption' ($2^{23}$); in consequence of his Divine origin he bears the stamp of immortality. Death would have been unknown but for the envy of the devil ($2^{24}$). Eternal life in fellowship with God is therefore the portion of the righteous. To them death is but an apparent calamity ($3^{3f.}$). The ungodly, on the other hand, are doomed to death ($2^{24}$), and are punished for their crimes both here and hereafter ($3^{17f.}$). In this book only the larger thought of immortality is emphasized; it leaves it to be implied that there must be a previous (spiritual) resurrection to life. The righteous dead, moreover, are not merely as in OT said to dwell in Sheol, but in immediate nearness to God ($6^{19}$).

The same view is set forth still more explicitly in the writings of Philo. According to this author, the body is only the temporary and polluted prison-house of the rational soul, which, as an emanation of Deity, is immaterial and imperishable. This is essentially the Platonic doctrine; although Philo, for whom Genesis is only an allegorical history of the soul's development, found it already taught in the statements that God made man in His own image ($1^{26f.}$) and breathed into him His spirit ($2^{7}$). Philo's view as to the essentially evil nature of matter precludes the possibility of a bodily resurrection. He quotes approvingly the word-play of Heraclitus, who calls the body (σῶμα) the tomb (σῆμα) of the soul (*Leg. Alleg.* i. 33).

The doctrine of an incorporeal immortality is also taught in 4 Maccabees in connexion with the famous story of the martyrdom of the seven brothers and their mother. It describes the brothers as 'running in the way of immortality' ($14^{5}$); the mother as 'again giving birth to the entire number of her sons for immortality' ($16^{13}$); and both them and her as 'assembled together to the company of their fathers, having received again from God pure and immortal souls' ($18^{23}$).

* According to the Book of Jubilees and the Assumption of Moses, which were of Pal. origin, the resurrection of the spirit takes place only after the Final Judgment.

Another point, in regard to which no agreement had been arrived at when Christ came, was the *time* of the resurrection. According to Enoch $51^{1}$, it was to take place immediately before the Messianic era; according to the Apoc. of Baruch and 2 (4) Esdras, it was to synchronize with its close.

The only Jewish works of the 1st cent. A.D. which teach the doctrine of a general resurrection of the entire human race are the Apoc. of Baruch ($30^{2-5}$) and 2 (4) Esdras ($7^{32-37}$). Even on this view, something was done to conserve the idea that the resurrection is a privilege pertaining to the righteous. In connexion with the appearance of the Messiah, reference is made to 'those that be with him' (2 Es $13^{52}$) in such terms as to suggest a retinue of saints whose special prerogative it is to 'rise first' (cf. 1 Th $4^{16}$) and accompany Him when He assumes His earthly dominion. The nature of the resurrection body appears to have been the subject of frequent discussion. In Apoc. Bar $49^{2}$–51 it is taught that the bodies of the dead will be raised in precisely the same form as that in which they were committed to the ground, so that they may be recognized. After their identity has been established, they will undergo a transformation in order to endless spiritual existence in glory or in torment. This supplies a link with St. Paul's teaching on the resurrection in 1 Co $15^{35ff.}$.

That the belief in a personal resurrection was not, however, universal during the Apocryphal period is shown by the fact that certain books belonging to it retain the old view of Sheol (Sir $17^{27f.}$ $41^{4}$, Bar $2^{17}$). Indeed, from the evidence adduced it will be seen that during this period 'the belief had a varied and interesting history. It underwent certain enlargements, and became more established. But it developed at the same time some doubtful elements, and remained subject to some uncertainty.' * If immortality cannot be said to have been a dogma of the later Judaism, certainly the idea, along with that of the resurrection which stands or falls with it, was one generally current among the Jews. Yet we know that it met with a vigorous opposition from the Sadducees, who made use of the Greek materialism to combat a doctrine that occupied so rudimentary a place in the OT. This party, however, could not succeed in Israel; and the hopes which had long animated those known by that name gradually tended to fix themselves in a clear and definite doctrine, which found its completion in the teaching of Him who declared God to be the God not of the dead but of the living, and Himself to be the resurrection and the life. In these words Christ indicates that man's relationship to God is such as to secure not only his continued existence, but his existence in his whole being, bodily and spiritual. His language, even as reported in the Fourth Gospel, points, moreover, not to a bare immortality in the Hellenic sense, but to a bodily resurrection (Jn $5^{25f.}$). It is further set forth in His teaching that the resurrection will be universal. The expression 'the resurrection of the just' (Lk $14^{14}$), so far from limiting the scope of the resurrection, actually suggests the very different lot of the wicked when they shall be raised up. There is a 'resurrection unto life' and a 'resurrection unto condemnation.' Beyond what may

* Salmond, *op. cit.* p. 331.

be gathered from the comparison between the condition of the risen and that of 'the angels in heaven' (Mt 22[30], Mk 12[25], Lk 20[36]), Christ's doctrine furnishes no information with reference to the nature of the resurrection body.

3. *Question as to the influence of Zoroastrianism upon Jewish eschatology.*—The development in eschatology during the Apocryphal period was undoubtedly of the most pronounced character. How are we to explain it? How is it that with the Messianic hope sunk so low there should have been not only an advance in eschatology, but an arrival at such fixed forms as we meet with in the Jewish literature of the age? A living faith in a personal Messiah was not always essential to Messianic expectation and the belief in a Future Judgment; and what we find in Amos and other OT prophets we may be prepared to see repeated. But the position of the apocryphal and pseudepigraphic books is here so much clearer and fuller than anything in the OT that we are constrained to ask, How was it reached? It can hardly have been the result of metaphysical speculation. Was it, then, simply a legitimate development upon doctrines potentially existing in the OT? Those who take this view point to the fact that the restoration of the chosen nation is set forth under the figure of a rising again to authority and influence (Ezk 37). The later Jews, it is said, put their own construction upon such passages, and thence formulated to some extent a doctrine as to the way in which the righteous would come to the enjoyment of the Messianic kingdom. When it should be inaugurated, they would be raised up and have part in it.

Many scholars, however, explain the eschatological development of the period on the theory of the contact of Judaism with foreign systems of thought, and in particular maintain that the doctrine of the resurrection was arrived at through the medium of Zoroastrianism, or at all events assumed the form it did under the stimulus of Persian influence. It can no longer be reasonably doubted that the resurrection formed part of the creed of the ancient Persians; and at any rate we have the express testimony of Theopompus (preserved in Plutarch, etc.) that this doctrine was held by the Zoroastrians at the time of Alexander the Great, *i.e.* previous to its appearance in Daniel, and at least as early as Is 26[19]. This theory is therefore historically possible. But can it be substantiated? Apart from the general presumption that the Jews would be disposed to regard favourably the religion of Cyrus, their deliverer, stress is laid upon the fact that the doctrine of an individual resurrection appears in the OT only in writings dating from, or subsequent to, the Pers. period, and is (?) first put forward in a book, the writer of which had special connexion with Babylonia. These considerations, however, do not prove that the Jewish doctrine of the resurrection was derived from the religion of Zoroaster. As Nicolas has said, 'Ideas do not pass ready-made and complete from one nation to another like the fruits of industry which are transported in caravans.' And, in fact, the Jewish and Persian beliefs with regard to the resurrection of the body are not identical. Zoroastrianism knew nothing of a partial resurrection, whether of the righteous and wicked as in Daniel, or of the righteous only as in 2 Mac. etc., and, unlike Judaism, looked for the final restoration of the wicked after the resurrection. The idea of simple borrowing is further precluded by the gradual formation of the Jewish doctrine, the development of which, in its principal stages, is distinctly traceable. This doctrine was of no sudden growth in Israel. It had long been nascent, when the persecution under Antiochus Epiphanes gave it life and vigour as the grand sustaining hope of those who did battle for God's law. This was a great turning-point in Judaism, and gave to it, as regards religious beliefs, modes of thought, and ethical practice, a character which has been stamped on all its subsequent history. Scribes and people were united by a common patriotism. The religious conscience was awakened; men looked eagerly for the promised Deliverer, and in the assurance of His coming found a new life. Those who shed their blood to prepare the advent of His kingdom would be raised up to share in its bliss. The resurrection of the dead was thus the necessary complement of the Messianic hope, and in its earlier form was set forth as the first act of the victorious Messiah, and as the privilege of Jews only. This is the genuinely Jewish form of the doctrine of the resurrection of the body, and had a distinct place in an order of ideas called forth by the crisis which overtook the Jewish nation in the second quarter of the 2nd cent. B.C. It did not owe its existence to foreign influence, but was the result of internal development.

But there may be stimulus without transference, and this appears to be what really happened in the case before us. The foreign influence was not such as to supply or even fundamentally to affect the doctrine itself; at most it helped to determine the form of its development. Naturally, therefore, it does not seem to count for much in any single passage in which it can be traced; yet the cumulative effect of its presence in frequent instances is not to be denied. For an interesting enumeration of passages from the OT and post-canonical literature giving evidence of Parsi influence on Jewish eschatology, see par. 7 of the article ZOROASTRIANISM in vol. iv. Among other (and more doubtful) examples the following perhaps may be safely allowed. Is 24[21f.] speaks of an intermediate place of punishment for evil powers, where they are imprisoned prior to their final judgment. Even Charles, who thinks that the influence of Zoroastrianism on Jewish eschatology was but slight, admits that the ideas here expressed 'appear as a foreign element in the OT, and may be derived from the Mazdean religion.'* Cf. in this connexion Jude[6], Enoch 18[14. 16] 21[6]. The new heaven and new earth of Is 65[17] 66[22], to be ushered in after the Last Judgment and overthrow of evil, corresponds to the Pers. doctrine of 'renewal' after the world's purification by 'the ordeal of molten metal.' The latter may also have suggested the figure used in Mal 3[2] 4[1]. In Ps 17[15] 49[14] there is probably a reflexion of the Pers. conception of the dawn as a daily emblem of the resurrection. In the later Apocalyptic literature also traces of Parsism occur. In Enoch (45[4f.]) reference is made to the transformed heaven and earth; and its location of the mountain of God's throne in the *south* (18[6]), taken along with the placing of a hell in the *north* (Secrets of Enoch, 10), recalls another characteristic of Parsi literature. Through the medium of earlier Jewish apocalyptic, many Persian ideas found their way also into the Apocalypse, *e.g.* the binding of the old serpent, Satan's futile attack upon heaven, the millennium, etc. In the peculiar and epoch-making circumstances of their nation the Jews assimilated certain foreign elements, and grafted them upon the data supplied by their own sacred books—so modifying them, however, as to make them fit into and complete their own doctrinal system, with a view to the fuller expression of their own spiritual needs.

LITERATURE.—Besides the OT Theologies of Oehler, Schultz, and Dillmann, and various articles in the best Bible Dictionaries, see Bretschneider, *Die Dogmatik der Apokr. Schriften des AT*[4]

* *Eschatology*, p. 159.

(1841); Nicolas, *Des Doctrines Religieuses des Juifs* (1860); Langen, *Judenthum in Palästina zur Zeit Christi* (1866); Kohut, *Jüdische Angelologie* (1866); Vernes, *Histoire des idées Messianiques depuis Alexandre jusqu' à l'empereur Hadrien* (1874); Wellhausen, *Die Pharisäer und Sadducäer* (1874); Ewald, *HI*; Drummond, *Jewish Messiah* (1877); Stanton, *The Jewish and the Christian Messiah* (1886); Stade, *GJV* (1888); Schürer, *HJP* (Index); Cheyne, *OP* (1891); Schwally, *Das Leben nach dem Tode* (1892); Hühn, *Die Messian. Weissagungen des Israel.-Jüdischen Volkes bis zu den Targumim* (1899); G. A. Smith. *The Twelve Prophets* (1896–98); Charles, *Eschatology* (1900), and the same writer's editions of *Enoch*, *Assumption of Moses*, *Baruch*, *Jubilees*; Salmond, *The Christian Doctrine of Immortality* (1901); Alexander, *Demonic Possession in the NT* (1901); Bousset, *Die Religion des Judentums im neutest. Zeitalter* (1903).

W. FAIRWEATHER.

**TRINITY.**—

*A.* In the Jewish Apocrypha and pre-Christian Jewish writings: (*a*) In Palestine; (*b*) in Alexandria.
*B.* In the NT.
  i. In the Advent and Incarnation.
    (1) Testimony of the Holy Spirit and the return of Prophecy.
    (2) Birth of Jesus Christ.
    (3) Baptism of Jesus.
    (4) The Holy Spirit given to Jesus for ministry.
    (5) Temptation and Transfiguration of Jesus.
    (6) Outline of NT doctrine of the Trinity.
  ii. Teaching of Jesus.
    (1) In Synoptics.
    (2) In the Fourth Gospel.
    (3) The Apostolic Commission and Baptism.
  iii. Apostolic Teaching.
    (1) Among Jewish Christians—Acts, Hebrews, and Catholic Epistles.
    (2) Teaching of St. Paul.
    (3) Teaching of St. John.
  iv. Trinity involved in the Life of the Apostolic Church.
    (1) Equipment of the Apostles.
    (2) Establishment of the Church.
    (3) Work of Missions.
    (4) Test of Doctrine.
    (5) Christian Worship.
      Literature.

*A.* IN JEWISH APOCRYPHA AND PSEUDEPIGRAPHA.—Jewish theology in the period between the OT and Christ made some progress towards a Trinitarian view of God. It was marked (1) by a monistic and transcendent conception of God, which put Him far away from man, and avoided all anthropomorphisms about Him (cf. Weber, *Altsynag. Theologie*, 144 f.). On the other hand, the Law was largely put in place of the immanent J″, and God made a student of the Law; that is, a *Judaizing* of J″ took place, which ended in the dualism of a transcendent God and a Rabbi schoolmaster God. (2) This remoteness of God led men to seek after mediators between the far-off One, whose very name was a mystery (Enoch $69^{14f.}$; Weber, 144), and the earth. Angels and other beings were made prominent; but especially the Messiah was felt after. In Palestine the mediating 'Word' of the prophets, the מֵימְרָא, was taught (cf. Weber, p. 174); while in Alexandria Philo elaborated his doctrine of the Divine λόγος, whom he identified with 'the Angel' and all Divine manifestations in OT (cf. Siegfried, *Philo*, p. 219 f.; Drummond, *Philo*, ii. 239 f.). This 'Word' was regarded sometimes as Divine thought or revelation or action. Again, it was presented as a Divine hypostasis, personal if not a person (4 Ezr $6^{43}$, Apoc. Bar $56^4$, Wis $8^1$). Biesenthal goes so far as to hold (*Trostschreiben d. Ap. Paul an d. Hebr.* 69) that 'the Generatio æterna filii vel Messiæ was in no wise a later doctrine of Christianity, but belonged to the very oldest teachings of the synagogue.'

The transcendent view of God arose in the schools of the scribes in opposition to surrounding polytheism; and, while it called for a Mediator, it also tended to make him transcendent as was God. This may be the reason for the practical disappearance of the thought of king Messiah in the period just before Christ, and the appearance, through study of the OT, of a heavenly Mediator (cf. Baldensperger, *Selbstbewusstsein Jesu*, 1892, p. 69). This Mediator, the 'Word,' was Divine, in heaven (Dn $7^{9.13}$, Enoch 46. 48. $6^2$), pre-existent, a supernatural 'Son' of God (En $105^2$), who would come in due season to reign on earth (En $45^4$, Ps-Sol $17^{23f.}$). He sits upon the same throne with J″, shares His knowledge (En 46) and glory (En 62, 4 Ezr $2^{43}$), and will be final judge (En $47^3$). All that is involved in the 'Word' Enoch ascribes to 'the Messiah' ($52^4$); though Philo does not identify the λόγος with the Messiah. As soon as Jewish theologians systematically studied the OT, they found a God-like Being set forth somewhat after the manner of NT writers and early Christians. He was the 'Wisdom' of Pr 8 (cf. Midrash *in loco*), 'the Angel' (Targ. Ex $23^{16}$); He spoke to Moses at the bush; He was the Heavenly Man of Dn $7^{13}$ (cf. 4 Ezr $13^3$), and the Eternal One of Mic $5^1$. All other middle beings are set aside by this supreme Mediator, who is the 'firstborn' of God (Targ. Ps $2^7$; Baldensperger, p. 88), and 'Christ the Lord' (Ps-Sol $17^{28.35.36}$; cf. La $4^{20}$, Lk $2^{11}$). The writings which describe His coming are called 'apocalypses,' for He would unveil the very face of God (4 Ezr $6^{72}$ $7^{28}$, Assump. Mos $10^7$). With him 'Deus palam veniet' (*l.c.*). Here Judaism reaches a half-metaphysical, an Arian conception of the Son of God, beyond which it could not go. Only the incarnation in Jesus Christ could lead men further.

(3) With the Messiah would come also the Holy Spirit, which had left prophetic men since Malachi (Weber, p. 78). But how it was related to God and His Christ was not evident. It is identified with Divine wisdom (Wis $7^9$ $9^{17}$), with the Angel (Ps-Sol 10), and with the Memra (Wis $7^{22f.}$). The Spirit is felt to be distinct from J″; the Targums (on Mic $2^7$, Zec $4^6$ etc.; cf. Schlottmann, p. 82) often distinguish the Spirit from God, and that with the same formula מִלִּפְנֵי ׳׳=מִן קֳדָם (*e.g.* Gn $1^2$, Jg $3^{10}$, 1 S $10^6$ $16^{13}$) where no such distinction is in the Heb. text. Philo gave to the λόγος the designations ὁ δεύτερος θεός and ὁ πρεσβύτατος υἱός, also 'an image of God' (*de Somn.* ii. 6); and the Spirit he calls an 'impress' of this λόγος image of God. This Spirit of the λόγος of God is the principle of all life. Both 'Word' and Spirit inhere in God: the Spirit is personal (Weber, p. 185), Divine, God's voice in man, the Eternal Wisdom. Again, we hear it called a creature, and made on the first day. Further than this Judaism could not go. We have here, perhaps for the first time, the absolute designation 'the Holy Spirit' (Ps-Sol $17^{14}$, 4 Ezr $14^{23}$, Wis $9^{17}$); and He comes with 'Christ the Lord' (Ps-Sol $18^8$), who appears 'in wisdom of the Spirit and righteousness and power' (cf. Lk $24^{49}$, Ac $1^5$).

(4) This Jewish teaching was comprehensive but confused. It had elements of the Trinity in it, but did not know what to do with them. It believed in God transcendent and 'God with us,' but could not correlate them. Its Christology found three things in OT—(1) the Son of God, heavenly, Divine, eternal, and the Son of Man, also in heaven (Dn $7^{13}$, Enoch $62^9$); (2) the human Messiah, who would be a glorious king of all the earth; and (3) the suffering Servant of J″. How to combine these was beyond the power of Judaism (cf. Enoch 5. 10. 25. 90. 98). The heavenly and the earthly elements would not meet. Two Messiahs were sometimes taught; and most Jews looked for a Messianic kingdom such as actually appeared in Mohammedanism. The Holy Spirit was also beyond Rabbinical grasp. Perhaps the 'still in the land,' from whom NT Christians chiefly came, 'full of the Holy Ghost,' knew more than did the theologians. Philo speaks of 'the Divine Spirit' (*de Gig.* 5); others preached a created spirit, a ministering spirit, like the angels (Weber, 184). The Spirit was needful for holy living; but it was

now withdrawn and hidden, to come again with the Messiah. The *Bath Ḳôl* took the place of the Spirit, the scribe took the place of the prophet. The fulness of OT teachings lies here, but confused, waiting for the NT doctrine of Father, Son, and Holy Ghost.

*B.* In the New Testament.—i. *Advent and Incarnation.*—(1) With the close of the OT the spirit of Prophecy left Israel. Judaism, in spite of particular workings of the Spirit, did not have the Holy Ghost (Jn $7^{39}$). It was said to have left the nation with Malachi, and was little looked for by Rabbis and scribes (cf. Gunkel, *Wirkungen d. heil. Geistes*, 55). But as the Advent of Christ drew nigh, His great forerunner, the Spirit of God, suddenly reappeared, and a group of saints in Israel, filled with the Holy Ghost, prepared His way. The last OT prophet foretold the first NT prophet; and both, led by the Spirit, proclaimed Messiah the Lord (Mal $4^5$ $3^{1f.}$, Mk $1^7$). Jesus and the Evangelists regard gospel history as beginning especially with John the Baptist (Lk $16^{16}$) and his inspired testimony to the Son of God. He announced the coming of Jesus as the coming of J″ (Is $40^3$, Mk $1^3$, Lk $1^{76}$). He showed the return of the prophetic Spirit as the Spirit of Christ (Mk $1^8$, Lk $1^{67}$), which alone knew the deep things of the Law and the Prophets, and led to Christ as the fulfilment of both. Now for the first time we hear a prophet clearly preaching salvation as repentance towards God the Father (Mt $3^2$), faith in a coming King, the Son of God (Mk $1^1$, Jn $1^{29}$), who takes away the sin of the world, and a baptism of the Holy Ghost, given by the Son of God (Mt $3^{11}$, Mk $1^8$, Lk $3^{16}$, Jn $1^{33}$).

(2) The work of Jesus was inseparable from His Person. What He did rested on what He was, for His preaching included Himself. None born of woman was greater than John the Baptist; but he was less than the least in Christ's kingdom, and beyond measure less than the King Himself (Mt $3^{11}$, Mk $1^7$, Jn $1^{34}$). John was filled with the Holy Spirit from the womb (Lk $1^{15}$), through the Holy Spirit Christ became man. To the one He imparted character, to the other He gave being. The *Gospel to the Hebrews* (ed. Hilgenfeld, $17^1$) calls the Holy Ghost the spiritual Mother of Jesus, as Mary was His bodily mother. Angels now appear again as messengers of God, and their chief mission (Lk $1^{15.\,35}$) is to proclaim the entrance of the Spirit into humanity, and to set forth the mystery of the Incarnation by the Holy Ghost. To the inquiry of Mary how she could become mother of the Son of the Highest (Lk $1^{34}$), Gabriel replied that it would take place through the co-operation of the Holy Ghost and the power of the Most High (v.[35]) upon her. The Most High means here God the Father (Lk $6^{35.\,36}$): both Father and Spirit caused the Incarnation (cf. Is $48^{16}$). The Father, by His power, appeared as an overshadowing cloud above the Virgin, as later over Jesus when He called Him 'my beloved Son' (Mt $17^5$). The Spirit is said to 'come upon' (ἐπελεύσεται) Mary, as the power of the Father 'shadowed upon' her (ἐπισκιάσει); so that the conception is more specifically described as of the Holy Ghost (Mt $1^{18.\,20}$): yet Jesus is called the Son of the Father. It is evident that the Holy Spirit is here more than a Divine influence; otherwise, the addition 'the power of the Highest' would be meaningless. It seems also clear that, while the Spirit acts as a Person, the parentage is ascribed to the Father. The God with whom Mary found favour appears in personal distinctions of Father and Spirit in the conception of Jesus, as was perhaps foreshadowed in the creation of Adam (Gn $2^7$). The result of this supernatural conception was twofold: first, Jesus was holy, corresponding with His relation to the Spirit; and, second, He was the Son of God (Lk $1^{3.\,5}$), corresponding with His r lation to the Father. He was as sinless as the Holy Ghost. His sinlessness and His supernatural birth are put together. The RV of Lk $1^{35}$ shows the one was rooted in the other; because of this Divine origin 'wherefore, also, that which is to be born shall be called holy, the Son of God.' It was to bring out the truth that 'it was not the *Sonship* but His *holiness* from His very birth, which was secured by the miraculous conception,' that the Revisers were so careful to correct the translation here (Dr. D. Brown in *Presb. and Ref. Rev.* 1896, p. 232; cf. Hofmann, *NT Theol.* 25). His sinlessness was not incidental, but was of His very being. The *non potuit peccare* lay in His nature; otherwise, through childhood and youth He could not have developed without some falls into sin. He was one with the Holy Ghost. He is also so one with the Father that His name is 'God with us' (Mt $1^{23}$); and His kingdom, like that of J″, is everlasting (Lk $1^{33}$). The angel of the Lord calls Him Christ the Lord (Lk $2^{11}$); for the identification of the Messiah with Jehovah, long foretold, was now a historic reality.

(3) The birth of Jesus was of God and of the Spirit of God; in like manner He was baptized for service in the name of the Father, Son, and Holy Ghost. The Baptist says that Jehovah sent him to watch for the coming of the Son of God; and the sign of His coming, as all Israel knew (Is $11^{2}$), would be the descent and abiding upon Him of the Holy Ghost. His great mission, in contrast to that of John, would be to baptize men with the Holy Ghost. In the *Gospel to the Hebrews* ($3^{14-17}$) the Holy Spirit says, '*Fili mi, in omnibus prophetis expectabam te, ut venires et requiescerem in te. Tu es enim requies mea, tu es filius meus primogenitus, qui regnas in sempiternum.*' The most Jewish Christians had definite views of the Divine Christ and the personal Spirit. We are not sure (Jn $1^{15-18}$) where the testimony of John passes over into that of the Evangelist; in any case, the witness is remarkable. He knows that the Son came from heaven (Jn $3^{31}$), was pre-existent, and because of His heavenly origin was above all human forerunners ($1^{27.\,30}$). What Christ taught He learned by seeing and hearing it from God ($3^{32}$). He bore the sins of the world (Jn $1^{29.\,36}$), because He was the Lamb of God and a heavenly offering (v.[30]). He was the final Judge of the sinners of the world (Mt $3^{12}$), because He was Jehovah and His way was the way of J″ (Jn $1^{23}$). Such was the Son of God whom John recognized at baptism, through the statement of the Father that the Spirit would rest as a dove upon the Son. John adds, 'I saw and bare record that this is the Son of God' (Jn $1^{34}$). The Synoptists add that the Father spake from heaven when the Spirit descended, saying, 'Thou art my beloved Son' (Mt $3^{17}$, Mk $1^{11}$ $3^{22}$). The objective dove symbol was an indication that the Spirit was distinct from the Father who spake, and from the Son who heard the Father's voice and beheld the dove descend (Mk $1^{10}$).

(4) The double witness of Father and Spirit to the Son was regarded as His commission to enter upon His ministry of redemption. And, what is of special importance, Jesus now received authority to baptize men with the Holy Ghost. The Baptist and all four Evangelists regard this as the great truth set forth in Christ's baptism (Mt $3^{11}$, Mk $1^8$, Lk $3^{16}$, Jn $1^{23.\,26}$); and the risen Lord confirms their view (Jn $3^5$, Ac $1^5$). His work was as far above John's as the Spirit of God is above water. The OT taught that the Holy Spirit would come *with* the Messiah (cf. Jl $2^{28}$, Is $11^{2-4}$); the Baptist takes a long step beyond this in proclaiming that the

Holy Spirit comes directly from the Messiah as Son of God. The truth here developed is that the Holy Ghost stands in the same relation to the Son that He does to the Father (cf. Is 44$^{3}$). He is the Spirit of God; He is also the Spirit of Christ. At the birth of Jesus the Son appeared as conceived by the Spirit; now the Spirit appears as proceeding from the Son. In the one case Jesus received of the Spirit; in the other the Spirit received of Christ. The Spirit in relation to Jesus Christ cannot be cause in the same sense in which He is effect. We touch here the mystery of the God-man, in which apparently contradictory statements respecting Him find their simplest solution by reference to His human and Divine natures (cf. Novatian, *de Trin.* xi.; Augustine, *de Trin.* i. 8). As man the Messiah needed the Spirit as means of perfect human development; as God He imparted the Spirit to believers for regeneration and full redemption.

(5) The Temptation of Jesus was closely connected with His baptism as introduction to service. The conflict with Satan had to do with the true relation of the Son to the Father; and it was the Spirit that drove Him to this conflict (Mk 1$^{12}$). 'If thou be the Son of God' was the repeated taunt. The second Adam stood where the first Adam fell. The threefold temptation was the same—lust of the flesh, lust of the eye, and pride of life; bread good for food, to know as much as God, to have the kingdoms of the world, so pleasant to the eyes, at once in Messianic possession. It was a battle of the evil spirit and the Holy Spirit with ministering angels (Mt 4$^{11}$). It was a struggle of the Son of God and the god of this world, in which the aim of the tempter was to tear Christ out of His oneness with the Father. The same truth appears in the Transfiguration (Mt 17$^{2-8}$). In face of Satan (16$^{23}$), doubting disciples, and the cross (17$^{9}$), the Son stood to reveal what is called the Trinity. The bright cloud of the presence of Jehovah (1 K 8$^{10.11}$) is here: the Father addressed Jesus as 'my beloved Son,' telling the Church to 'hear him' as the great Prophet (Dt 18$^{15.18}$); and He was transfigured by the Holy Ghost (μετεμορφώθη; cf. ἐν μορφῇ θεοῦ, Ph 2$^{6}$, 1 Ti 3$^{16}$) in anticipation of His return to the glory of the Father. Christ was now ready for His public ministry. Born of the Spirit, baptized of the Spirit, victorious over the devil by the Spirit, He returned in the power of the Spirit into Galilee (Lk 4$^{14}$). His first public utterance in Nazareth was, 'The Spirit of the Lord is upon me'; and 'the eyes of all . . . were fastened upon him; for he said, This day is this scripture fulfilled in your ears' (Lk 4$^{18}$). He knew that both Himself and His gospel came from God the Father and the Spirit of God.

(6) The NT doctrine of the Trinity, presented as it is chiefly from the point of view of the Son, contains the following elements:—

First, There is one God, Jehovah, the Father everlasting.

Second, Ever with Him was His Divine Spirit.

Third, With Him also, from before the foundation of the world, was His only-begotten Son, enjoying perfect knowledge of the Father, and sharing His glory.

Fourth, In the fulness of time the Son came into this world (*a*) by incarnation (Jn 1$^{1.14}$) through the co-operation of the Father and Spirit (Mt 1$^{18.20}$, Lk 1$^{35}$), and (*b*) by humiliation, ἑαυτὸν ἐκένωσεν (Ph 2$^{7}$).

Fifth, This coming was for the salvation of men; it was preceded by the love of the Father and followed by the work of the Spirit.

Sixth, In His incarnate mission to save men, the Son was endued with the Holy Ghost without measure.

Seventh, Following the work of humiliation, which ended in death and burial, came the resurrection and exaltation of the Son through the co-operation of the Spirit (1 P 3$^{18}$) and His ascension to the Father where He was before.

Eighth, This ascension was a triumph over Satan and his kingdom, a reward for the Son, in which He received all Divine gifts for men, these gifts being summed up in the Holy Ghost, whose coming to earth was inseparable from the Son's glorification in heaven. The two foci of NT Christianity are: (*a*) God sending the Son from heaven to earth to redeem men, and (*b*) the risen and glorified Christ sending the Holy Spirit to make men partakers of that redemption.

Ninth, The Church is under the constant providence and mediatorship of the exalted Son and the immanent Spirit: this is sometimes presented as what Christ has done for us, and, again, as what He does in us, by the Spirit.

Tenth, When the end comes, the Son will return and judge mankind; He will then terminate all that is temporal in His kingdom; and Father, Son, and Holy Spirit will continue for ever in those Divine relations which took on the colour of time and space in the history of redemption. Of these inner relations of the Trinity neither Jesus nor the Apostles speak. The Scriptures reveal only the side of the Divine being which has to do with God's relation to the world and man; yet the doctrine of the Godhead in these respects is so set forth as Father, Son, and Holy Spirit, that, if such representations rest upon reality, we seem constrained to believe that there are personal distinctions within the Divine Essence.

When we pass to Christ's entrance upon His ministry, we touch the whole sequence of thought here outlined as involved in the Trinity. In the Synoptic accounts Jesus presents the gospel as the kingdom of God the Father, to enter which men must not only accept the words of Christ, but have faith in Him as Saviour; in the Fourth Gospel Jesus offers salvation as eternal life. This life is in the Son, and is imparted by the Spirit.

ii. *Teaching of Jesus*.—(1) In the Synoptic Gospels Jesus appears (*a*) as proclaimer and bringer of God's kingdom. He came from the Father (Mt 20$^{28}$; cf. Jn 16$^{1}$), had all the Father had (11$^{27}$ 28$^{18}$), and entered this world able to seek and to save the lost (Mt 15$^{24}$ 18$^{11}$, Lk 19$^{10}$). In this implied pre-existence Jesus claimed more than ethical oneness with God. Ethical pre-existence is no true pre-existence. It was Jewish theologians whom He challenged to tell whose son the Messiah is (Mt 22$^{45}$); and when they answered 'the son of David,' He replied that David, speaking by the Holy Ghost — whom Jesus presupposed as well known from the OT — called his son his Lord. Isaiah knew (11$^{1}$) that the Messianic 'rod' and 'branch' sprang from the stem of Jesse, and pointed to a Lord and kingdom above that of David; so Jesus teaches that His sonship was not simply from David, but from a source which made Him David's Lord. He was David's Lord in heaven before He appeared as Jesus on earth (cf. Mt 10$^{40}$, Mk 9$^{37}$, Lk 9$^{48}$). Such seems to be the argument. This heavenly origin made Him well-pleasing in the sight of God (Mt 3$^{17}$ 12$^{18}$ 17$^{5}$), set Him above the angels in heaven, put Him next the Father (Mk 13$^{32}$), and gave Him authority from the Father to forgive sins (Mk 2$^{10}$). As Son of God He cast out devils and empowered others to cast them out (3$^{15}$). Jehovah said, 'Look unto me, and be ye saved, all the ends of the earth; for I am God, and there is none else' (Is 45$^{22}$); Jesus does not hesitate to put Himself in place of J" in the same invitation: 'Come unto me all ye that labour' (Mt 11$^{28}$). Salvation depends upon Him (11$^{27}$), and He is always present to save (Mt $18^{20}$). Because He was ever with God (Mt $24^{3}$; cf. Dn $7^{13}$), He can judge men from the beginning of time to the end. As Son of Man He will welcome the saints to glory (Mt $25^{34}$, Lk $23^{69}$) and sentence the wicked to outer darkness. Jesus knows God as well as God knows Him (Mt $11^{27}$). Only the omniscient Father can know the being of the Divine Son ($16^{17}$, Lk $10^{22}$). The sole confession of faith which He approved was that of His own Divinity (Mt $16^{17}$); and upon that He built His Church (v.$^{18}$, cf. Jn $17^{8}$). He did not declare sins forgiven: He imparted forgiveness (Mk $2^{5}$). The consciousness of Jesus speaks as of one who was with God before all time, through all time, and who continues in eternity with God. His words were thus understood by the Jews (Mk $2^{7}$, Jn $5^{18}$) and by the Apostles (Mt $10^{40}$, Jn $4^{34}$ $5^{23}$ $6^{38-40}$, 1 Co $15^{47}$, 1 Th $1^{10}$ $4^{16}$). The words imply such a relation as theologians call the Trinity.

(*b*) The fellowship of Father, Son, and Holy Spirit appears still more personal and essential in the actual work of man's redemption. The religious value of Father, Son, and Spirit appears to be the same. The Spirit is not prominent in the teachings of Jesus, first, because its work, internal, subjective, tender, must be felt rather than described; and, second, because the outpouring of the Holy Spirit was not to come till after His ascension. Yet the Spirit is there (Mt $10^{20}$), for faith in God involves also faith in Christ and the Holy Spirit; since each has part in man's salvation. This truth appears whether considered from God downwards, from man upwards, or from Christ the centre outwards. This last is specially important in NT teachings, for Jesus ever looks back to the Father and forward to the Spirit. He is the only, the living bond between them. No man can come to the Father but by Him (Mt $11^{28}$, Jn $6^{44}$); no man can come to Him unless the Father draw him (Mt $11^{25}$, Lk $10^{21}$); neither can any man come to Father and Son unless born of the Holy Ghost (Mk $13^{11}$, Mt $5^{45}$, Lk $11^{13}$). Salvation, Jesus teaches, depends upon right relations to Father, Son, and Holy Spirit. Unless men enter the kingdom of the Father through faith in God they will be lost (Mk $1^{15}$ $11^{22}$). Unless they believe in the Son as Saviour they will be left under sin (Mt $11^{28}$ $24^{30.44}$ $25^{34}$). And unless they accept the Holy Spirit they will incur eternal death (Mk $3^{29}$). The kingdom of heaven comes from the Father (Mt $6^{10}$), is brought by the Son (Mk $1^{15}$ $12^{34}$), and put in the hearts of men by the Holy Spirit. When Jesus showed the Holy Ghost casting out devils He said, 'Then is the kingdom of God come unto you' (Mt $12^{28}$). Both Father and Son hear the prayer prompted by the Spirit (Mt $6^{6}$, Jn $14^{14}$); and all the blessings of the kingdom of God flow from the Father in heaven through Christ, who bids us ask what we will; and the Holy Spirit, who brings all the gifts of the heavenly Father to His children on earth (Mt $7^{11}$, Lk $11^{13}$), will impart it unto us. Jesus taught that the full establishment of the kingdom would be the work of the Holy Ghost (Lk $24^{49}$, Ac $1^{8}$).

(*c*) The Trinity underlies the kingdom of God; it is also the revelation of God which overthrows the rival kingdom of the devil (Mt $12^{26}$). God the Father is at the head of the one, the devil the father is at the head of the other (Mt $13^{38}$, Jn $8^{44}$). Jesus came to destroy the works of the devil (Gn $3^{15}$, Mk $1^{24}$, 1 Jn $3^{8}$), and the Holy Spirit was the power of God in His hands to cast out Satan. The world of demons was much more prominent in NT thought than we sometimes suppose (cf. Weinel, *Wirkungen des Geistes*, pp. 1–26). Jesus summed up the Lord's Prayer in 'Thy kingdom come' and 'Deliver us from the evil one.' His commission to the Twelve consisted essentially in 'Preach the gospel' and 'Cast out the devil' (Mk $1^{22.23.39}$ $3^{11}$ $16^{15.17}$, Lk $4^{32-34}$ $9^{1.2}$); His own work might be similarly summed up. The destroyer and the Saviour were thought of together: *Nullus diabolus, nullus Redemptor*, seems to be the NT nexus of thought. It was a conscious conflict of personalities. The demons assailed Christ, or appealed to Him as the Son of God, doubtless understanding more by that title than did the Jews (Mk $3^{11}$); and He replied that He carried on a war of destruction by means of the Holy Spirit (Lk $9^{43}$ $11^{20}$, Mt $12^{28}$), who was given by the Father (Lk $11^{13.14}$). The evil spirit was cast out by the Holy Spirit; and the Holy Spirit came from the Father through the Son (Mt $12^{28}$). That Son and Spirit are both Divine and personal, Jesus shows in the terrible passage Mt $12^{22-32}$; cf. Mk $3^{22-30}$, Lk $12^{10}$. Men saw the Son through the Spirit casting out devils, and were so blind as to call it the work of Beelzebub. Looking at the sun they called it midnight. Such confounding of spiritual values meant moral chaos. All other impulsive blasphemies against Father or Son would be forgiven; but to see the personal Holy Ghost at work and call Him the personal devil meant death to spiritual distinctions. It was blasphemy against the Holy Ghost (perhaps, as the derivation of the word, βλάπτειν τὴν φήμην, suggests, attack on personal character), and involved 'guilt of eternal sin' (Mk $3^{29}$). It was also, so one are Son and Spirit, in some sense an unforgivable sin against the Son (cf. Lk $12^{10}$ 'a word against the Son'), 'because they said he hath an unclean spirit.' So pointed is the personal antagonism that Jesus seems also to teach: *Nullus diabolus, nullus Spiritus Sanctus.* The blasphemy which Jesus declared fatal was against the Holy Spirit; the blasphemy which the Apostles first feared was against the Son of God (Ac $13^{45}$, Ja $2^{7}$, 1 Ti $1^{13}$). The two sins which have no forgiveness are lying to or about the Holy Ghost, and putting the Son of God to the shame of open denial (Mk $3^{29}$ $8^{38}$, Lk $9^{26}$; cf. Ac $5^{3}$, He $6^{6}$). The destiny of man's soul depends upon his attitude towards the Son of God and the Holy Spirit; we can hardly think of higher claims for the Divinity and Personality of both.

(2) The record of Christ's teaching in the Fourth Gospel presupposes the Synoptics, and in Apostolic perspective, under illumination of the promised Spirit, unfolds their final meaning. Were this Gospel not from John, it still would show how the most spiritual Christians in Apostolic days recalled the words of Jesus respecting the Son and Spirit, and how their experience witnessed to them. In the Apocalypse, Jesus appears, after the manner of the Synoptists, as Son of Man exalted as Son of God; in the Fourth Gospel, Christ is revealed as the Divine Son incarnate, not humbled, but with His eternal glory veiled by temporary abode among men, only to burst forth again in full splendour at His ascension. Jesus here presents Himself as central in salvation; He is the eternal life ($6^{33.35}$), of which men must partake or perish. From this central position Jesus ever looks up to the Father and forward to the Spirit. He speaks much more here of the Holy Spirit than He does in the Synoptics. He enlarges and unfolds here what He indicated there. He identifies Himself more closely with the Gospel. The kingdom appears here as eternal life, and that life is in Christ ($1^{4}$ $3^{36}$ $5^{40}$ $6^{53}$). He is not a guide to the way, or a preacher of truth: He *is* the way, the truth, and the life ($14^{6}$). When John's disciples wondered at His knowledge of men, He told them that He was Jacob's ladder, reaching all the way to God ($1^{50.51}$). To see Him was to see the Father ($14^{9}$). His solemn words, Ἀμὴν ἀμὴν . . . ἐγώ εἰμι ($8^{58}$), seem to reflect the 'I AM' of Ex $3^{14}$. In His typical interview with Nicode-

mus, the Jewish theologian, He presented salvation as flowing from Father, Son, and Holy Spirit. Baur says Jn $3^{16}$ sums up all Christian truths, and from it the Trinity appears as 'the most definite expression of the peculiar relation between God and man which has been realized through the revelation of Christianity' (*Lehre von d. Dreieinigkeit*, i. 80 f.). Nicodemus addressed Jesus as 'teacher' ($3^{2}$); but Jesus replied that He was 'eternal life' (vv.$^{15.\ 16}$), and pointed out as the three steps in man's redemption, (1) regeneration by the Holy Ghost (vv.$^{5.\ 6}$); (2) faith in the Son of God, who came from heaven to save men by His death (vv.$^{13-15}$); and (3) the love of God the Father, who gave His only-begotten Son to redeem the world (v.$^{16f.}$). The elaborate teachings of Jn 14–17 are but an unfolding of what is here taught as the way of salvation. Moving from heaven to earth, as the thought of Jesus does in the Fourth Gospel, we find His theology consists of (1) God the Father in glory and the glorification of the Father in the redemptive work of the Son; (2) the salvation of men through the incarnation, death, and exaltation of the Son; and (3) the establishment of a kingdom (so in the Synoptics) of eternal life (so in Fourth Gospel) through the Church, in which by the special revelation of the Holy Spirit men will be born again and equipped with spiritual gifts for service, and all to the glory of the Father and the Son (Jn $5^{17.\ 21.\ 24.\ 43}$). Even when speaking to a Samaritan woman and early in His ministry, Jesus related acceptable worship to Father, Son, and Holy Spirit. He taught that God is His Father ($4^{21-26}$), and, through Him, Father of believers only ($1^{12}$ $8^{44}$); and that the Father is to be worshipped in spirit and in truth, that is, in the Spirit of truth ($4^{24}$, cf. $14^{17}$). To the Jewish theologian as an inquirer, to the Samaritan woman as indifferent, and to the eager disciples ($14^{6.\ 13.\ 16f.}$) the Lord's theology is the same—to the Father, through the Son, by the Holy Spirit. In the farewell discourses (14–17) the Father, Son, and Spirit are so repeatedly spoken of as if persons, as acting together and apart, as going forth one from another, and returning one to another, that the question of difficulty is not: How can one God subsist as Father, Son, and Spirit, but rather: How can the Father, Son, and Spirit, here respectively set forth by Jesus, constitute one God?

In these discourses Jesus sheds some light upon the inner Trinitarian relations of the Godhead. He shows first that the work of redemption involves His triumphant return to the glory which He had with the Father before the world was ($6^{62}$ $13^{31.\ 32}$ $17^{5}$). It was Divine, eternal glory to which the Son returned: such glory only a Divine Being could lay aside and take again. It remained ever with Him as Son of God, but was veiled in the incarnation ($1^{14}$ $2^{11}$ $11^{40}$). Jesus says the Son is so one with the Father that He has glory of His own, has eternal life in Himself ($5^{26}$ $11^{25}$); in fact, that all that the Father has the Son has ($5^{21}$ $16^{15}$ $17^{2.\ 5}$). Men may believe in Him as in the Father ($14^{1}$), seek life from Him as from the Father ($6^{47}$), pray to Him as to the Father ($14^{4}$), and are as safe in His hands as in the Father's hands ($10^{28.\ 29}$). And for this equality with God He gives a remarkable reason: 'My Father is greater than I.' He describes His relation to the Father in the paradoxical words: 'I and my Father are one' ($14^{28}$ $10^{30}$), and again, 'My Father is greater than I' ($14^{28}$ $10^{29}$). Jesus never calls Himself God; but ever claims to be Son of God, and does this through a perfect human consciousness ($14^{16}$ $17^{3}$ $20^{17}$). He knows that both as Son of Man and Son of God He came from heaven ($13^{6}$ $8^{38}$); and He calls Himself the Son of Man who is in heaven ($3^{13}$). He claims to be 'the Son' in an absolute sense, as God is to Him 'the Father' in an absolute sense ($6^{40}$ $3^{35}$ $5^{20.\ 19.\ 21.\ 22.\ 23.\ 26}$ $8^{35.\ 36}$ $14^{13}$). It is from this relation of God incarnate that He says, 'My Father is greater than I.' For Moses or Paul or Luther to say, 'God is greater than I am,' would be absurd. Equally absurd would it be for Christ unless He were conscious of superhuman being, as the Jews saw at once ($5^{23}$). In the two places where He thus speaks ($10^{29}$ $14^{28}$) He addressed His disciples. He might thus speak from the point of view of His humiliation by the incarnation or in reference to the precedence ever given the Father before the Son and Spirit; but, plainly, His purpose here is to cheer believers. He does not say, 'I am less than the Father'; His mind dwells upon the absolute oneness with the Father, so that all the greatness and fulness of the Father are for His people. Hence He says to His disciples ($10^{29}$), 'My Father is greater than all' opponents, and (v.$^{30}$) 'I and my Father are one.' Again ($14^{28}$) He says, 'If ye loved me ye would rejoice, because I go unto the Father; for my Father is greater than I.' The greatness of the Father is not apart from the Son, but belongs to the Son, and through the Son becomes His people's. The Father was not greater than the Son by way of contrast or separation, but in the way of likeness and perfect oneness. No mere ethical union of Jesus with God fully explains this 'one.' Only one Divine Being seems able to include such relations and make the infinite fulness of the Father the possession of the Son. Only God could receive all of God. Of such Divine being Christ seems plainly conscious ($3^{13}$ $6^{46}$ $8^{28.\ 38}$ $10^{35}$). When charged with making Himself God ($10^{33}$) He answered that He was Son of God, and gave, as proof, that He was sinless (cf. Lk $1^{35}$, Jn $10^{36}$), sanctified and sent of God—a thing no mere man could claim. The salvation of all the redeemed hangs upon Jesus Christ; only a oneness of being with God can bear such a load of weal and woe. It is into this transcendent and real relation of Father and Son that Jesus roots the gospel of redemption. It begins and ends in heaven. Because the Son came from God and went to God ($13^{13}$) He could wash the disciples' feet, and as Di ine Providence be ever with His people. From this transcendence He speaks as Jehovah to His people (Ac $9^{5.\ 10f.}$), and from it He sends forth the Holy Spirit. The Spirit is spoken of as in heaven with the Father and Son, and coming to earth at the intercession of the Son.

If there is anything cardinal in NT teachings ($14^{16-19.\ 26}$ $15^{26}$ $16^{7}$ $17^{1}$ $20^{22}$, Lk $24^{49}$, Ac $1^{5.\ 8}$ $2^{4.\ 17.\ 33}$, Ro $1^{4}$ $8^{1.\ 9}$, Gal $3^{1.\ 2}$), it is that the gift of the Holy Ghost comes through the glorification of the Son. This is the theme of Jn 14–17, especially of $16^{5-15}$. Here Jesus sends another Paraclete to continue His personal work ($14^{16}$). Jesus never spoke of the Spirit as created; there is a power from on high (Lk $24^{49}$), but its source is the personal Spirit (Ac $1^{8}$). Nor does He ever speak of the gift or outpouring of the Spirit, as John himself does (1 Jn $4^{13}$). Jesus speaks of the Holy Spirit as a Personal Being, coming from the Father, sent by the Son, to testify before men to Father and Son ($15^{26.\ 27}$). Hence the disciples would not be 'orphans' when Jesus left them ($14^{18}$). When He said, 'I will come unto you' ($14^{18}$), He meant by the Spirit: the one is as personal as the other. The incarnate Son was more of manifestation of God then than the Father; so Jesus says that the Spirit can do greater things for men than the Son, because the Son returned to the glory of the Father and the Son ($14^{16}$ $15^{26}$ $16^{7f.}$). Each takes precedence in His peculiar work. The Father can no more complete the work of redemption without the Son than the Son could begin it without the Father. They are so one that Jesus could say that the Father sanctified Him ($10^{36}$) or that He sanctified Himself ($17^{19}$). The Father sends the Son; and the Son comes Himself. Jesus excludes in all His teachings separate action of Father and Son (14$^{9.10f.}$ 17$^{10.21}$). And the mission of the Spirit is to witness to Father and Son. This indicates the equal Divinity of all. Unless the Son were God, He could not send the Spirit of God; and the Holy Ghost would not testify to and glorify a man. Jesus teaches that Father, Son, and Spirit are all equally present in the souls of believers (7$^{38.39}$); yet none loses His personality or is confounded with another. The witness of the Spirit, Jesus says, is twofold—first to the Church, and second to the world. To Christians He would so recall the teachings of Jesus and add to them that believers would know the Son as never before. Jesus taught 'these things' (14$^{25}$); the Spirit would teach 'all things' (v.$^{26}$), that is, the things of the Father and Son (16$^{13}$), as the Spirit ever hears (16$^{13}$, note the present sense in ἀκούσῃ) them in Divine omniscience. To the world also, through the Church, the Spirit would testify for Christ (16$^{8-15}$). As in the Synoptics, so in the Fourth Gospel, Jesus reveals the Father, Son, and Holy Spirit as building up God's kingdom and destroying that of the devil. The Spirit was to convince the world that it had not glorified the Son. To hate the Son was to hate the Father (15$^{23}$), and to hate the Son called forth the protest of the Spirit (15$^{23.26}$). Only the Spirit, coming from the glorified Christ, could overcome this hatred (16$^{7}$). And this co-operation of Son and Spirit rested on essential relations to one another and to the world (11$^{to}$ 16$^{7}$). Almost dramatically it is said of the personal Spirit that ἐκεῖνος ἐλθών (15$^{26}$) would convict the world of a threefold sin. The triple attack of Satan upon the Son (Lk 4$^{3f.}$) is met by a triple defence of the Spirit. The first world sin was disbelief in Christ; the second was sin against the righteousness of Christ (cf. 'eternal sin,' Mk 3$^{29}$). Conviction of this sin the Spirit wrought through the triumphant resurrection of Jesus (cf. 1 P 3$^{18}$ 4$^{6}$, 1 Ti 3$^{16}$, He 9$^{14}$), and His return to the Father, with whom only the righteous can dwell. The third sin, like the third temptation (Mt 4$^{9}$), was putting Satan in the place of the Son of God. The Spirit would show that the death of Jesus meant the destruction of the devil: 'the prince of this world is judged' (Jn 16$^{11}$). As intimated in the Synoptics, Jesus here teaches that God is to destroy the kingdom of evil by His Son and Spirit. The prince of this world is judged and doomed. The Son testifies (14$^{17}$) that the world is lost because it cannot know and receive the Spirit; the Spirit testifies that the world is lost because it does not accept and honour the Son. The only hope of man, Jesus teaches, lies in coming to God through the Son and the Holy Spirit. The Divinity of both and their place in the Trinity appear to be inextricably involved in Christ's own gospel. In most solemn manner He asks the once blind man (9$^{35}$), 'Dost thou believe on the Son of God?' He accepts his confession of faith in Him as such, 'Lord, I believe.' He also accepts, as He had done before (Mt 14$^{33}$ 16$^{16}$), worship as Son of God. Here His testimony to His own Divinity and equality with God culminates. But with it He ever associates the Holy Ghost as coming from God (14$^{13-17}$) and continuing the work of the Son in leading men to God (3$^{5-8}$ 14$^{16}$).

(3) The Synoptic Gospels present, by way of just historic accommodation, the teaching of Jesus to the Jews, though showing incidentally, especially after the resurrection, the higher self-consciousness of Christ as found in the Fourth Gospel (cf. especially Mt 11$^{27}$ and Lk 10$^{22}$). This last, given intentionally for disciples (Jn 21$^{23-25}$), for the Church, and for man as man, unfolds the deeper character and words of Christ. There are two symbolical acts, which show how the doctrine of the Trinity appears with equal naturalness in all the Gospels. Jesus breathed upon His disciples and imparted the Holy Ghost (Jn 20$^{22}$). He also bade them baptize their converts in the name of the Father, Son, and Holy Ghost (Mt 28$^{18.19}$). Here in brief symbol and formula He sets forth the Trinity conception of Jn 14–17. He breathed upon the disciples from His own glorified body and said, 'Receive ye the Holy Ghost.' He speaks as Lord, 'Take'; it is a word of command with which He sends forth the Spirit. He begins to do what He said He would do (16$^{7}$). Speaking as God (cf. Gn 2$^{7}$, Ezk 37$^{5}$), He exercised the authority to impart the Spirit of God. Through His word of command and His vital breath the Holy Ghost proceeded from God the Father to the hearts of men. The Apostles received the baptism of the Holy Spirit for service, as had Jesus Himself for His great Apostleship (Mk 1$^{8.10}$, Jn 1$^{32}$, He 3$^{1}$). The authority to bind and loose given by Jesus (Mt 18$^{18}$) is now ascribed to the Holy Ghost (Jn 20$^{23}$). Both Son and Spirit forgive sins through the Apostles. The gift of the Spirit (Jn 20$^{22}$) corresponds with the baptismal command (Mt 28$^{19}$). Both set forth the Apostolic commission; and both do so in the name of Father, Son, and Holy Ghost. In the Fourth Gospel, Jesus sends forth the Twelve in His own name, with the authority of the Father and inspired by Him with the Spirit (20$^{21}$). In Mt 28$^{20}$ He claims all power in heaven and on earth, and bids them disciple and baptize men in the name of the Father, Son, and Holy Ghost. Jesus began His own work with baptism, which He said was from God (Mt 21$^{25}$), and referred to communion with Himself as baptism (Mk 10$^{38}$); hence His command to baptize is not strange. He would send His disciples to the Gentile world with the same ordinance with which John came to Israel. It is the Trinitarian formula that challenges criticism (cf. Wendt, *Teaching of Jesus*, ii. 349, 374). True, there is no text evidence against it (Resch, *Paralleltexte*, 3 Ev. ii. 393 f.); and it occurs in the most Jewish Gospel, where such teachings are improbable unless from Jesus. Later references to baptism in the name of Jesus (Ac 2$^{38}$ 19$^{5}$, 1 Co 1$^{13}$) seem either to describe the acceptance of Christianity, without reference to the mode of baptism, or to prove that the Trinitarian form was not the only one in use. Where the form of baptism is expressly referred to, it is always in the name of Father, Son, and Holy Ghost (*Didache*, vii. 3; Justin M., *Ap.* i. 61; cf. Resch, *l.c.*). If the teachings in Jn 20$^{21-23}$ are from Jesus, Mt 28$^{19}$ is quite natural. If the Apostles were sent by the Father and the Son, and inspired by the Spirit to declare converts' sins remitted, what more natural than to add 'baptize them in the name of the Father, of the Son, and of the Holy Ghost'? We can hardly think of Paul, some 25 years after Christ's ascension, writing 'the grace of the Lord Jesus Christ, and the love of God, and the communion of the Holy Ghost, be with you all,' or John reporting Jesus (16$^{7-15}$) as building His gospel upon Father, Son, and Holy Ghost, unless the Lord had taught essentially what is in Mt 28$^{19}$. The teachings of Jesus seem fairly to include the following: (1) He approved of the baptism of John, and His disciples continued it (Jn 3$^{32}$ 4$^{1}$); (2) after the death of John, He let this preparatory baptism drop (*a*) because the kingdom foretold had actually come, (*b*) because Messianic baptism led to false views of the kingdom and provoked opposition, (*c*) because Jesus gradually turned to the special instruction of the Twelve; (3) His teaching on baptism identified it with the Holy Ghost, as all the evangelists tell us (Mt 3$^{11}$, Mk 1$^{8}$, Lk 3$^{16}$, Jn 1$^{33}$, Ac 1$^{5}$), hence, as soon as the Holy Spirit was given at Pentecost, the Apostles felt that the time

had come for the renewal of external baptism also; (4) baptism 'in the name of Jesus' would then mean, as Jesus taught, baptism of the Holy Ghost and into the service of Christ, in contrast with Johannine baptism; (5) Luke shows that Jesus had the same view of baptism and the Trinity as appears in Mt $28^{19}$. He taught (*a*) the coming of the Holy Ghost, (*b*) this coming was a baptism of the Holy Ghost, and (*c*) the Father and Son participated in this baptism of the Holy Ghost ($24^{49}$, Ac $1^{5}$). Here are the same elements of doctrine as are contained in Mt $28^{19}$. If we suppose with Haupt (*Apostolat im NT*, 38 f.), that this is not a formula of baptism, but a summary by the Evangelist of Christ's teachings on baptism and what it meant, we reach the same result: the only confession of faith and baptism that Jesus taught meant sharing the redemption of Father, Son, and Holy Ghost. The Apostolic form 'in the name of Jesus' would then mean just what is taught in Mt $28^{19}$. It was baptism in the Spirit unto Christ: hence, when St. Paul found disciples (Ac $19^{3}$) who had not received the Holy Ghost, he asked unto what they had been baptized: baptism had special reference to the Holy Ghost. It also referred to all the redemptive work of the Son (Gal $3^{26f.}$, Ro $6^{3}$), as well as to the full activity of the Spirit (1 Co $12^{13}$, Tit $3^{5.6}$).

St. Paul also puts baptism and the Holy Spirit together (1 Co $10^{2.3}$) in a way to make it seem certain that he traced both to Christ ($11^{23}$, cf. Mt $20^{22}$). St. Peter, too, describing conversion (Ac $2^{38}$), united baptism in the name of Jesus, and reception of the Holy Ghost, just as we should expect on our view. Baptism 'into the name' meant baptism unto God (Jer $14^{9}$), who is revealed, not through but in the Father, Son, and Holy Ghost. Jehovah was the name of God for the OT covenant; the new name of God for the new covenant in Christ is Father, Son, and Spirit. Their equal Divinity, personality, and participation in man's redemption so form the doctrine of God and His work in the teachings of Jesus, that Mt $28^{19}$ may well be regarded as a culmination and synopsis of the gospel of the risen Lord. This baptismal formula was the centre of a solemn act of worship in which Father, Son, and Holy Ghost were equally adored. It was a solemn profession of faith in which each was regarded as indispensable ground of man's salvation. It was a solemn confession of covenant relation in which each was equally looked to as source of consecration and blessing. Jesus speaks of these distinctions as of spiritual realities. It seems impossible to paraphrase His words into, 'Baptizing them into the name of the Father, and of the Messiah, and of God as Spirit,' as some modern critics say Jesus meant (cf. Kaftan, *Wesen der Chr. Rel.* ii. 345 f.; see H. M. Scott, *Nicene Theol.* 255 f.). 'The Trinity of revelation, according to Jesus' own teachings, leads up to a Trinity of Being' (Schlottman, *Compendium d. Bib. Theol.* 134). The historicity of Mt $28^{19}$ is not weakened by later opposition to Gentiles entering the Church (Ac $11^{10}$ $15^{16}$, Gal $2^{16}$); for that controversy turned not on the fact but on the mode of their admission: must they enter the Church through the synagogue or not? (cf. Schmid, *Theol. of NT*, 163). On the other hand, this Trinitarian confession has an argumentative relation to all nations; the spread of the gospel would be a proof of the truth of the doctrine. Upon such teaching Christ promised His blessing; with it He would be in His Church unto the end of the world (v.$^{20}$, cf. Mt $24^{14}$ $30^{31}$). Out of this confession of faith in baptism, taught by Jesus, has grown the first and only creed of all the ages: 'I believe in God the Father . . . and in Jesus Christ our Lord . . . and in the Holy Ghost.' 'The baptismal symbol in its whole *contents* goes back beyond all question to the Apostolic age' (Caspari, *Quellen z. Gesch. d. Tauf-symb.* i. 5); and no other than a Trinitarian formula has ever appeared in the history of the Church (cf. Resch, 424 f.); 'Trinitarian baptism was universal in the earliest churches and among the earliest heretics.' No Judaizer or Gnostic administered Christian baptism without the τρισμακαρία ἐπονομασία, the 'trina invocatio, nomen trinæ beatitudinis,' that sprang from Father, Son, and Holy Ghost (Clem. *Hom.* ix. 23).

iii. *Apostolic Teaching.*—(1) The outpouring of the Holy Ghost upon the Apostolic Church brought first the personality of the Spirit into greater prominence, and, secondly, shed new light from the Spirit upon the Son. (*a*) This new light showed (α) the great importance of the *Person* as well as the words of the incarnate Christ—He was much more than a prophetic Messiah; (β) the unique value of His atoning death; and (γ) the vital relation for believers between this shameful death and His glorious resurrection and ascension to the right hand of the Father, where He represents and rules His people. The first martyr, full of the Holy Ghost, saw the heavens opened and Jesus standing on the right hand of God (Ac $7^{55.56}$; cf. 1 P $1^{19-21}$ $3^{18f.}$, Ph $2^{6f.}$, He $1^{3}$). He who ascended to Divine glory, it was felt, must ever have dwelt in Divine glory; and His incarnation, instead of being His life, was but an incident in His eternal existence. These Jewish Christians all start from Ps $110^{1f.}$, and declare by the Holy Ghost that the Psalmist knew by the Holy Ghost that Christ was Lord of David and Lord of all (Ac $2^{34.36}$ $10^{36}$ $11^{23}$, Ja $2^{1}$, Jude $^{4}$; the *Didache* calls him 'the God of David,' $10^{6}$). 'Our God and Saviour Jesus Christ' and 'our Lord and Saviour Jesus Christ' meant the same thing (2 P $1^{1.11}$ $2^{20}$). Jesus was equal with Jehovah (cf. Weiss, *NT Theol.*$^{6}$ 132); His throne was God's throne (He $1^{5.8}$ $3^{13}$); because He was God (He $1^{8}$). Language failed these Jewish Christians to say more of the glory of the Son of God. The whole OT, as revelation of the Holy Spirit, testified to the Divine Christ (He $3^{7}$ $1^{5.8f.}$ $2^{2f.}$ $5^{6}$ $10^{5}$). The ruling idea in Hebrews is that the old covenant of Jehovah with Israel was supplanted by the new, in which Jesus takes the place of Jehovah, Christians take the place of Jews (cf. Ep. of Barnabas 4), and the Holy Spirit, which led Israel towards Canaan, leads Christians through the Son to the rest in heaven ($1^{2}$ $2^{3.4f.}$ $4^{1f.}$). This eternal Son is as the Jehovah of the OT (He $1^{3.13}$ $8^{1}$ $12^{2}$), and is described there as such (Ps 110, He $1^{13}$, Ps $102^{26-28}$, He $1^{10}$). He became incarnate to save men; and, in co-operation with the Holy Ghost the eternal Spirit ($9^{14}$), the eternal Son ($1^{8}$) became author of eternal salvation ($5^{9}$), and eternal redemption ($9^{12}$) unto an eternal inheritance ($9^{15}$). The relations of Father, Son, and Holy Spirit are eternal. An attempt is made to set forth the connexion of the Son with the Father by comparing it with a brightness streaming from the Divine glory. Christ is one with God as a ray of light is one with the sun: out of such relation He takes form as a Personal Being distinct from the Father, yet so one with Him that to see the Son was to see the very glory which constitutes the Father (He $1^{3}$), the very 'character of His being' (cf. Weiss, 493). 'He was everything lofty that could be imagined. Everything that can be said of Him was already said in the first two generations after His appearance' (Harnack, *Dogmengesch.* i. 66).

(*b*) Equally marked is the Apostolic conception of the Holy Ghost and His relation to Father and Son. In the Gospels Jesus speaks 25 times of the Spirit, and the Evangelists make a like number of references; but in the Acts and Epistles over 160 statements are made about the Holy Ghost (Scofield, *The Holy Spirit in NT Scripture*, 11). In the Gospels the Spirit 'was not yet' (Jn $7^{39}$), that is, not in the fulness and abiding power of post-Ascension days. But, after Christ's return to the Father, Apostolic men were 'full of the Holy Ghost' (Ac $4^{8}$). At Pentecost the Spirit came as Jesus predicted (Jn $3^{8}$ $16^{5-15}$), to inspire and equip the Church. He came also in judgment, as Jesus had said (Mk $3^{28}$, Lk $12^{10}$). The first mention of the 'Church' (Ac $5^{3}$) shows Ananias and Sapphira dead upon its threshold for lying to the Holy Ghost. To lie to the Spirit was to lie to God (v.$^{4}$); for it is the Spirit of both God (1 P $4^{14}$) and His Christ (1 P $1^{11}$). Regeneration is the work of the Spirit, who uses the word (1 P $1^{23}$, Jude $^{19.\ 20}$); it is also the work of God (1 P $5^{10}$). The writer of Hebrews speaks little of the Spirit in believers; but when he comes to set forth the eternal high priesthood of the Son ($6^{20}$), which was 'after the power of an endless life' ($7^{16}$), he emphasizes the doctrine that Christ's eternal intercession takes place through the eternal Spirit ($9^{14}$). If Spirit means here (cf. Delitzsch, *ad loc.*) 'the Divine inward being of the God-man,' we meet once more the view that Father, Son, and Holy Ghost are eternally one with God who is a Spirit.

(*c*) St. Peter as leader of the Jewish Christians preaches the gospel as from Father, Son, and Holy Ghost. He sums it up doctrinally (1 P $1^{2}$) as ($\alpha$) election by God the Father, ($\beta$) through the Holy Spirit, ($\gamma$) unto salvation by Jesus Christ. This is the order from the side of God: from the side of man he describes it to inquirers and twice over to a court of Jewish theologians (Ac $2^{38}$ $4^{12}$ $5^{32}$) as ($\alpha$) repentance towards God, ($\beta$) faith in the Lord Jesus Christ, and ($\gamma$) receiving the Holy Ghost. He says the conversion of Cornelius was acceptance of the Holy Ghost as a gift of God, and faith in the Lord Jesus Christ (Ac $11^{16}$, cf. 1 P $1^{17f.}$). He describes Christians as those who have 'faith in the righteousness of our God and Saviour Jesus Christ' (2 P $1^{1-11}$), where Jesus is both God and Saviour. He adds that both the preacher and the Word must be witnessed to by the Holy Spirit, to have any effect (1 P $1^{11}$ $4^{11}$). This Trinitarian gospel of St. Peter is that of St. Stephen (Ac $7^{48f.}$), St. James ($1^{5}$ $2^{1}$ $4^{5}$), and St. Jude (vv.$^{19-21}$). The beginning of the Christian life takes place through presentation of the Son in the Word; for such applying the things of Christ by the Spirit (1 P $2^{3}$) regenerates the heart. All Christian growth depends upon being in Christ ($3^{16}$ $4^{1}$ $5^{14}$). The three Apostolic conditions of entering the kingdom of God were repentance (Ac $5^{31}$ $11^{18}$, Ro $2^{4}$, 2 Co $7^{9.\ 10}$; cf. Mt $9^{13}$, Lk $24^{47}$), faith (Ac $3^{16}$ $14^{27}$ $20^{21}$, Ro $9^{10}$, 1 Co $13^{13}$), and holiness (Ac $26^{20}$, He $6^{1}$, Ja $2^{17}$, Ro $16^{3}$); and these rested upon Father, Son, and Holy Spirit. Faith in Christ works by love (Gal $5^{6}$) towards the Father, the Son, and the brethren, and purifies the heart by the indwelling of the Holy Spirit (Ac $15^{9}$). These constant allusions to the Trinity, with no further explanations, show that this doctrine was taken for granted among the Apostolic Churches. From the adoration of Jesus Christ, the centre of the Trinity, as God by Jewish Christians, light must have fallen in all directions upon the conception of God as Father, Son, and Holy Ghost.

(2) St. Paul sets out from fundamental belief in one God (Gal $3^{20}$, 1 Co $8^{6}$, 1 Ti $2^{5}$), but at once proceeds to teach that in the gospel God is the Father of the Lord Jesus Christ. (*a*) Upon this essential relation of Father and Son he built all his hopes (Ro $1^{3.\ 8}$, 1 Co $1^{2-4}$, 2 Co $4^{6}$). In the eternal Son believers were chosen before the foundation of the world (Eph $1^{4}$). He is called κύριος and even θεός, side by side with the Father (Ro $9^{5}$, cf. $7^{25}$, Tit $2^{13}$). He shares Divine attributes, and, together with the Father, is worshipped and glorified (1 Co $1^{2}$, Ro $13^{10}$, Eph $5^{19}$, 1 Ti $1^{12}$). Yet He is never identified with the Father, but is carefully distinguished from Him (1 Co $8^{6}$, Ro $1^{4}$ $8^{32}$). He is the image of the invisible God (Col $1^{15}$), and shares the invisible glory of God; He is also 'a man' Christ Jesus (1 Ti $2^{5}$). As sharing the glory of the Father, He is called the 'firstborn' of all creation (Col $1^{15}$). As Jesus spoke of the Father as greater than He, when claiming all the Father has as His, so St. Paul describes the glorified Christ as Head of Creation, in reference both to God and the universe. In Him all things subsist, because He is the Son and receives all from the Father (2 Co $4^{6}$). He is described as 'existing before the world in the eternal Godhead, yet He did not cling with avidity to the prerogatives of His Divine majesty, did not arbitrarily display His equality with God; but . . . took upon Him the form of a servant' (Lightfoot's paraphrase of Ph $2^{6f.}$). St. Paul does not use metaphysical terms, but teaches here that the μορφὴ θεοῦ involved participation in the οὐσία θεοῦ. Similarly, Bengel remarks (in Nösgen, *Gesch. NT Off.* i. 19) that the term θεότης as distinguished from θειότης expresses 'non modo divinas virtutes sed ipsam divinam naturam.' St. Paul regards the Incarnation as serving the double purpose of showing God's love as Father (Gal $4^{4}$, Ro $8^{3}$; cf. Jn $3^{16}$), and of revealing the inner relations of Christ's premundane and Divine being (2 Co $8^{9}$, Ph $2^{6f.}$). A God of love seemed to involve personal subjects and objects of love within the Godhead, from which God who loved the world sent forth the Son of His love to save men. The Father gave the Son (Ro $8^{32}$), the Son gave Himself (Gal $1^{4}$), surrendered His glory and died on the cross; the Holy Spirit witnesseth to the Son and wins sinners to accept Him (Ro $1^{1.\ 4.\ 5}$). That is St. Paul's gospel (Ro $1^{16.\ 17}$), which has proved itself the power of God unto salvation. He often sums up his gospel, and it is always Trinitarian (Ro $5^{1-5}$ $8^{2f.}$ $15^{16.\ 17}$, 1 Co $2^{1-4}$ $12^{3f.}$, 2 Co $3^{3}$, Gal $4^{4-6}$, Eph $1^{3-5.\ 13}$ $2^{18}$ $4^{4-6}$, Col $1^{3.\ 4.\ 8}$; cf. He $1^{1.\ 9}$ $2^{3.\ 4}$ $10^{26.\ 29.\ 31}$ $11^{22.\ 24.\ 29}$). Over every sermon he can pronounce the benediction of Father, Son, and Holy Spirit (2 Co $13^{14}$).

(*b*) St. Paul, like all the Apostles, supports his theology by the Old Testament. His central theme, the Divine Christ, he sets at once in inseparable relations to Jehovah. The Jewish teachings of his day confounded אלהים and יהוה (so Jehovah is rendered θεός in LXX of Nu $22^{13}$ $28^{8}$, while אל and אלהים appear as κύριος in Nu $28^{8}$, Gn $21^{2.\ 6}$); but St. Paul, with a few possible exceptions (1 Co $3^{5}$, Ro $14^{4f.}$), agrees with St. James ($1^{1}$ $2^{1.\ 5}$) and St. Peter (Ac $2^{36}$) in distinguishing them as two Divine Persons. The Father is θεός, though the name is also given to the Son (Ro $9^{5}$), and the Son is κύριος. This personal distinction of Father and Son is traced by St. Paul to the OT distinctions of אלהים and יהוה, and to the different relations of God to man expressed by those names (cf. Seeberg, *Die Anbetung d. 'Herrn' bei Paulus*, p. 8 f.). The distinction of God in Himself and the revealing Jehovah in the OT, St. Paul sees fully unfolded in the personal distinction of Father and Son. Christ did not *become* Lord; His κυριότης was but a form of His activity as a personal Divine Being. He was God before He was manifested as Lord; and He will be God after He ceases to rule as Lord (1 Co $15^{25}$; cf. August. *l.c.* i. 8). He is Lord, not in relation to God but in relation to man (Ro $5^{1.\ 11.\ 21}$ $6^{11}$ $14^{8}$, 1 Co $1^{2.\ 10}$). St. Paul, too, goes back to Ps 110, which he quotes oftener than any other OT passage (Ro $8^{34}$, Eph $1^{20}$, Col $3^{1}$, 1 Co $15^{23}$). He found there the Lord Christ reigning with the Lord God until all enemies to God's kingdom were subdued, and sharing the Divine majesty and power inseparable from God. This prophecy was fulfilled in the incarnate Lord conquering death and Satan, and through the Resurrection sitting down at the right hand of God, with all enemies at His footstool (Ro 8[34], Eph 1[20]). The glorified Christ is the Lord of glory (Ph 2[9], Ja 2[1]). Not till after the Resurrection was Jesus Lord, though He was ever Divine (1 Co 2[8]; cf. Mt 22[41f.]). Christ saves us as triumphant Lord (Eph 4[3], 1 Co 7[32]). He is also the Providence of the Church (Gal 2[2], 1 Co 4[19] 16[7]). When all believers are saved His lordship ceases; He gives the kingdom which He undertook to the Father and resumes the eternal relations of the Son (1 Co 15[25]). From the Resurrection to the Last Judgment is the rule of Christ. He rules with the Father (1 Co 15[10], Ro 8[30]), as He saves with the Father (Col 1[3], Ro 8[8]). God's work for man, St. Paul teaches, is never apart from Christ's work. They are as rays of heat and light in the same sunbeam. Hence St. Paul was called to be an Apostle by both Father and Son (Gal 1[1]), who formed one Divine power (as omission of διά before θεοῦ and singular predicates show; cf. 1 Ti 1[1], 1 Th 3[11], 2 Th 2[17], 1 Co 15[8. 10]; Seeberg); and he sees the final judgment as by both God and Christ (2 Th 1[6f.], 1 Co 4[5]). All between these in St. Paul's survey of life is done equally by the Father and Son. 'The active rule of the exalted Lord is, according to Paul, such that in every act of it contemporaneously an act of God the Father is completed' (Seeberg, p. 35). The grace of the Son is as much a Divine element in salvation as is the love of the Father (Tit 3[6. 7]); hence, with the possible exception of Ro 8[34], St. Paul never speaks of intercession of the Son with the Father, so one are they considered in working. His God, in opposition to polytheism, is 'one God the Father, of whom are all things, and one Lord Jesus Christ, by whom are all things' (1 Co 8[6]). He says (v.[4]), 'there is none other God but one,' and that one God is the Father and Son. These were equally God for St. Paul from Ps 110 to his own last experience. The subordination of the Son was but a stepping-stone to lift the saints to the glory of the Father, which was shared by the Son. The words 'Christ is God's' (1 Co 3[23]) support the assurance 'ye are Christ's,' as the statement 'the head of Christ is God' upholds the teaching that 'the head of every man is Christ' (1 Co 11[3]). St. Paul follows Jesus' teachings that the Father was greater than the Son, not by way of contrast, but in a unity, which communicates all the greatness of the Father through the service of the Son (cf. Col 1[19] 2[9] 3[11]).

(*c*) St. Paul's theology is Christo-centric. He proceeds from Christ outwards to Father and Spirit, yet everywhere recognizing the Divine relation of the Spirit to the Father and Son. The living bond between the Son, exalted as Lord, and man is the Holy Ghost. St. Paul echoes Jesus' doctrine (Jn 16[14]) that the Spirit teaches Christ and is an earnest of all good things to come (2 Co 1[22] 5[5], Eph 1[19]). So one in working are they that he calls Christ a life-giving Spirit (1 Co 15[45]), and says, 'the Lord is the Spirit' (2 Co 3[17]). They are one as in the Godhead, yet distinct, both in their subjective and objective relations to man; for he adds: 'where the Spirit of the Lord is, there is liberty,' and elsewhere (Gal 5[1]) says, 'stand fast in the liberty wherewith Christ hath made us free.' St. Paul's theology grew out of his experience. He knew the personal Divine work of Son and Spirit in his own soul (Ph 3[3], Ro 8[9] 9[1]). He had extraordinary gifts of the Spirit (1 Co 14[18]). He knew that all religious life comes from the Spirit (Ro 15[19], Gal 3[2. 3]). He knew, also, that Christ in him was his life, his hope of glory (Col 1[27]). But he sharply distinguished the revelation of the Lord in him (Ac 22[7]), and the sending of the Son that we may become sons of God, from the sending of the Spirit to awaken us to the life of sons (Gal 4[4-6]). He did not regard the Spirit as merely the spiritual disposition produced in us by Christ. Christian life is equally related to both Son and Spirit; they are equally Divine, but not identical. The Spirit proceeds from the Son as the Spirit of Christ (Ro 8[9], Gal 4[6], 1 Co 2[16], Eph 4[8]), as well as from the Father; and in his experience St. Paul found the Son to be the fundamental type of the form of life into which believers are brought by the Spirit (so Nösgen, ii. 262). The Spirit is the impelling power, the Son is the abiding life element, in the Christian (Ro 8[14], Gal 1[18]). The same fruits spring from both (Gal 5[5. 16. 22. 24], Eph 5[9], Ph 1[11]). Both make us free from the Law (Gal 5[1. 18]). We are to have the mind of both (1 Co 7[40], Ro 8[27]); both intercede with the Father for us (Ro 8[34. 27]), and with us for the Father (Ro 8[9], 2 Co 13[5]). We cannot trace the limits of the working of Father, Son, and Holy Spirit; but St. Paul plainly teaches that there are such limits. The Spirit begins the life of the soul in man, but all NT writers ascribe the resurrection life of the body to the risen Christ (2 Co 4[10]). The Spirit makes man a new personality, the Son makes man a member of His body, the Church (Nösgen, *l.c.*) The Son may become angry and condemn in wrath (1 Co 15[22]), the Spirit is only grieved (Eph 4[30]). The constant use of the names shows a corresponding distinction of functions within the Godhead.

(*d*) St. Paul's worship also is of Father, Son, and Holy Spirit. The Spirit is for him personal, searching the deep things of God, with a will of His own for man's good, and showing Divine treasures to man (1 Co 2[11]; cf. Lk 24[49], Jn 15[26]). The Spirit does the work of the Father and Son (Ph 4[13], Gal 3[5] 4[6]). Father, Son, and Spirit must have been for St. Paul Divine realities. He could not pray to mere names or personifications. He never suggests that one is more or less Divine or personal than the other. That most solemn claim of Jehovah—'I have sworn by myself . . . that unto me every knee shall bow' (Is 45[23])—St. Paul applies to Christ as God (Ro 14[11], Ph 2[10]). For a Jew with the First Commandment as the creed of his life, prayer to Jesus Christ meant full equality with God; for neither OT (Is 42[8] 48[11f.], Jer 10[11f.], Ps 18[22]) nor NT (Ro 1[24f.], 1 Th 1[9]) allows worship of anything but God. The blasphemy of Antichrist was claiming Divine honours (2 Th 2[4]). St. Paul warned against worshipping φύσει μὴ οὖσι θεοῖς (Gal 4[8]), hence he must have worshipped Christ as φύσει ὄντι θεῷ. A Christian was a man calling on the name of the Lord Jesus Christ for salvation (Ac 9[14. 21]); and St. Paul, like St. Stephen (Ac 7[59]) and all saints (Rev 22[20]), prayed to Christ Himself (Ac 22[16]) and taught others to do so (1 Co 2[1]). To call on Christ was the same thing as prayer to God (Ps 88[10], Is 45[23]). St. Paul's test of a Christian was 'calling on' the Son (2 Ti 2[22]). False teachers knew this test, and did not dare to omit it (2 Ti 2[22]), because praying to Jesus was the recognized way of salvation (Ro 10[12. 13]). A Christian meant a worshipper of Christ (1 Co 1[2]). St. Paul prays to the Son to send the Spirit (Eph 3[14]). The Spirit prays in him to the Father, echoing the familiar 'Abba' of the Lord's Prayer (Ro 8[15], Gal 4[6]). He unites Father, Son, and Holy Ghost in doxologies of adoration and praise (2 Co 13[14]). He prays for the same things—men's salvation—to Father and Son, and in the same Spirit to both. He thanks the Father through the Son (Ro 1[8] 7[25]). He does not pray to them alternately, or in succession, but at the same time (2 Th 1[2], Gal 1[3], 1 Co 1[3]). He cannot separate them in his worship. In certain thanksgivings St. Paul prays to God as the Father of Jesus Christ (Ro $15^{6}$, 2 Co $1^{3}$, Eph $1^{3}$), showing that he knew the Lord was within the Godhead as Son. He thanks the Father through the Son, because Christ's work was the ground of all thanksgiving to God. The Son is the completer of the Father's work for man. The love of God and the grace of Christ and the fellowship of the Spirit of love meet, therefore, in the spirit of gratitude. St. Paul's three cardinal virtues are, faith in Jesus Christ, love to God the Father, and hope in the spirit of promise (Eph $1^{13}$, Gal $3^{14}$, 1 Co $13^{13}$). They are all fruits of the Spirit (Gal $5^{22.23}$), and come from the Father through the Son. St. Paul certainly taught all the data of a doctrine of the Trinity, however theologians may differ as to its formulation. He could not have learned his fixed, confident doctrine of Father, Son, and Holy Spirit from Jewish theology; neither did pagan thought suggest such teachings: he evidently received it as part of the gospel given him by Christ (cf. Gal $1^{3-8}$).

(3) St. John's teachings take their perspective (*a*) from his doctrine of the λόγος, which he sees prefigured in the OT. This is central in his Gospel, as it is in the doctrine of the Trinity. The Divine λόγος became incarnate in Jesus. This may be why Christ's conception of the Holy Ghost is not referred to, and why the Spirit is spoken of as a gift, and not made so clearly personal as in the words of Jesus Himself (1 Jn $3^{24}$ $4^{13}$). The Fourth Gospel presents Christianity as a double revelation of God through the Spirit and through the Son; the Evangelist bears witness chiefly to the Son, and lets the Son testify to the Spirit. Because St. John beholds the eternal Son prominent in the OT (Gn $1^{1}$, Ps $33^{4.6}$, Is $40^{8}$ $55^{11}$, Jn $1^{1.14}$), he does not describe the Incarnation as a humiliation, as St. Paul does (Ph $2^{6}$), or rise to it through the thought of His ascension to glory involving pre-existent glory, as in He $1^{3}$ $2^{9}$ $10^{12}$. He sees the Divine Son, the Creator of the universe ($1^{3}$), carry the glory of God veiled with Him into the world ($1^{10-14}$), and, when His work of redemption was complete, move calmly again into the glory which He had with the Father before the world was. His emphatic statements that the λόγος *was* in the beginning with God, and that the beginning of the being of all things was through Him, set forth the eternal Being of the Son. And because of His Divine Sonship He was a Divine revelation: 'No man hath seen God at any time, God only-begotten (μονογενὴς θεός, as in ℵ B C L), who is in the bosom of the Father, he hath declared him.' What can transcend 'God only-begotten'? St. John exhausts all Jewish descriptions of Divine manifestations to set forth the glory of the Son. He embodied them all. He was one with the יקר, the evident 'glory' of God ($1^{14}$ $2^{11}$ $12^{41}$, Targ. to Is 6; cf. Schlottmann, 130, Mt $16^{27}$, Mk $8^{38}$). His coming is the coming of the Divine glory, which Ezekiel said ($43^{1-7}$ in Targ.) should dwell for ever with God's people. Jesus had identified Himself with the Shekinah (Mt $18^{20}$; cf. *Pirke Aboth*, iii. 3): He even said that His presence was greater than the Shekinah in the temple (Mt $12^{6}$): St. John proceeds to identify the Son with the *Memra* or 'Word' ($1^{14}$). In one statement he combines the *Memra* (λόγος), the *Yekar* (δόξα), and the Shekinah (in σκήνοω), and applies all to the incarnation of the Son of God ($1^{14.18}$). Jesus Christ reveals the personal glory of God, not temporarily, but incarnate, tabernacling among His people as Jehovah tented among Israel (Ex $25^{8}$ $29^{45}$, He $1^{3}$). Philo called the λόγος figuratively δεύτερος θεός; St. John calls Him simply θεός; for He is on one side the λόγος of God, and, on the other, God. Philo's λόγος is πρωτόγονος υἱός, or, as an angel, ἀρχάγγελος (cf. Riehm, *Heb.* 146 f.): but St. John puts the Son-Logos far above all angels; He is one with God, truly personal and incarnate as the Messiah, all of which is foreign to Philo's allegorical exegesis. St. John's theology shows no connexion with that of Philo. Like St. Paul, he comes to Jesus from the OT, and finds that it is the revealed God, the Jehovah, the Lord of David, the 'Memra' that took flesh in Jesus ($1^{2}$ $14^{9}$). The relation of the Son to the Father is expressed by St. John as in He $1^{3}$, by the terms 'light,' as 'God is light' (1 Jn $1^{7}$), 'life,' as 'God is life' ($1^{2}$)—only the Son is called 'the life' or 'eternal life' (1 Jn $5^{20}$), because the Son is the manifestation of Divine life and its source for man—and especially by the word μονογενής ($1^{14.18}$ $3^{16.18}$, 1 Jn $4^{9}$; cf. $1^{1}$). Christ was the only-begotten Son of God, as the widow's son was her only child (Lk $7^{12}$), as the ruler's daughter was his only daughter (Lk $8^{42}$), and as the possessed boy was his father's only son (Lk $9^{38}$). He was the 'only-begotten' in such a sense that He might be called the only-begotten Son or the only-begotten God. He was the Son absolutely, and in a sense shared by no other being. He was so one with God that St. John says He was God ($1^{1.14}$); or, as put elsewhere (1 Jn $5^{5.20}$), He was the 'true God' revealing the true God. He was also 'with God' ($1^{1.2}$), *i.e.* not God without a property peculiar to Him as Son of God. From this Divine Sonship flows St. John's Gospel. In it he finds the source of all blessing and eternal life ($20^{31}$, 1 Jn $5^{12.13}$). From it come (1) the power to become sons of God ($1^{12}$), (2) sonship through faith in the Son ($9^{35}$), (3) sonship through the will of the Father ($1^{13}$), (4) participation in the truth, grace, glory, and indwelling of the Father ($1^{14}$, 1 Jn $4^{15}$); (5) an experience of the fulness of the Godhead in the Son ($1^{16.17}$), through union with whom (6) believers share the victory of the Son of God over the devil (1 Jn $3^{8}$), and (7) have the witness of sonship in themselves (1 Jn $5^{10}$). No Divine Son of God, no other sons of God. If God be not the Divine Father of the Divine Son, He is the religious Father of no man: that is the theology of St. John's Gospel.

In the Apocalypse, which has a strong Jewish colouring, we find the same high conception of the Father and the Son. As conqueror over Satan and Saviour of the saints, Jesus sits in Divine glory, adored and praised as omniscient ($2^{23}$), omnipresent, and eternal ($1^{18}$ $2^{8}$ $3^{21}$ $5^{8.14}$ $7^{12}$ $11^{15}$ $20^{6}$ $22^{1.3}$). He is the Son of Man, in heaven with the Ancient of days (Dn $7^{13}$, Rev $14^{14}$), while judge of all men on earth ($2^{27}$ $12^{5}$ $19^{15}$). His face shines as the face of God ($1^{16}$); and before Him the prophet falls down as before Jehovah ($1^{17}$). He is King of kings and Lord of lords ($17^{14}$ $19^{16}$), nay, He is Lord God Almighty ($15^{3}$). Weiss concludes (p. 560): 'It is certain that the Messiah appears here as an original Divine Being,' side by side with the Father.

(*b*) Of the Holy Spirit and His relation to the Father and Son, St. John says little; but his constant presentation of Christianity as life, birth from God and a birth to holiness, presuppose the Comforter. He makes the full teachings of Jesus on the Holy Spirit (14–17, cf. $7^{39}$) his own; and says the Apostolic experience and testimony through the Holy Ghost, after the glorification of Christ, were as rivers to drops, compared with what they were before ($7^{39}$). The water of life is from the Spirit as from the Son ($7^{37}$). Jesus taught the Spirit as Paraclete on earth representing the Father and Son (cf. παράκλησις of Holy Ghost, Ac $9^{31}$); St. John adds the doctrine that the Son is a corresponding Paraclete in heaven with the Father, representing men (1 Jn $2^{1}$). The 'new birth' is mentioned five times in the NT. It is a παλινγενεσία of the whole creation through Christ (Mt $19^{28}$), and of a single soul in conversion through the Spirit (Tit $3^{5}$); St.

James ($1^{18}$) sees Christians 'come into the world' (ἀποκυεῖσθαι) begotten of the Father; and St. Peter twice speaks of God begetting us again (1 P $1^{3.23}$). St. John has the further conception that the birth from God takes place through the Holy Ghost ($1^{13}$, 1 Jn $2^{29}$ $3^{9}$ $4^{7}$ $5^{1.4}$), for there is no doubt that by born *of God* he means *by the Holy Spirit* ($3^{6}$). In two passages he shows that the indwelling of the Father and the Son depends upon the Spirit (1 Jn $4^{13}$ $3^{24}$). He presents religion also as a command of the Father to believe on the Son (1 Jn $3^{23.24}$), and then says that this obedience of faith is possible only through the indwelling of the Father and Son by the Spirit. The only way to keep out evil spirits is to be possessed of the Holy Spirit; and we know, he says, which is the Holy Spirit, by its testifying to the incarnation of the Son of God (1 Jn $4^{2.3}$ $5^{5.6}$) and to nothing else ($16^{13}$). In the passage on the Three Witnesses (1 Jn $5^{6.8}$) the Holy Spirit testifies to the Son as Divine Redeemer, (*a*) because from Him flows the double stream of life-giving, cleansing water (Jn $7^{38}$ $19^{34}$) and atoning blood; (*b*) because the witnessing Spirit is 'the truth'; and (*c*) because the Father testifies also to the Son (1 Jn $5^{9}$).

(*c*) St. John touches here a thought which runs through the whole NT. God, who is transcendent, incarnate, and immanent as Father, Son, and Holy Ghost, establishes His kingdom in opposition to the god of this world, who is the devil and Satan (Rev $12^{9}$ $20^{2}$). The kingdoms of light and darkness run in growing opposition through the Fourth Gospel ($6^{70}$ $7^{20}$ $8^{44.48}$ $10^{20}$ $13^{2}$). St. John knows of demoniacs (cf. 'signs,' etc., $4^{48}$ $20^{30}$), but the only man he describes as possessed of the devil ($13^{2.27}$) is Judas, the son of perdition, who betrayed the Son of God. To deny the incarnate Son is to join the ranks of Antichrist, to deny the Father also (1 Jn $2^{22}$), and to show that the new birth from God has not taken place (1 Jn $3^{9}$). That is, the only way to oppose the devil is to be born of God by the Spirit (1 Jn $5^{18}$). Christians are sons of God through the Son of God (1 Jn $3^{1f.}$), who came to destroy the works of the devil (v.$^{8}$); and they prove both their sonship and their opposition to the devil by obeying the Spirit in them, testifying to the incarnate Son. Thus both the begotten beginning and the triumphant end of the Christian life are inseparable from Father, Son, and Holy Ghost (1 Jn $5^{1.5.6}$). Amid the OT imagery of the Apocalypse we move upon the same high plane. It opens with a benediction ($1^{4.5}$), like that of St. Paul (1 Co $13^{13}$), in which salvation is set forth as coming from God, the seven spirits before His throne,—evidently the sevenfold, perfect revelation of the Spirit promised the Son (Is $11^{2}$),—and from Jesus Christ. Salvation is ever ascribed to God and the Lamb ($7^{10}$ $4^{11}$), and is mediated by the Spirit to the Churches ($2^{7.11.17.29}$ $3^{6.13.22}$ $14^{13}$ $22^{17}$). The rapt Christian 'in the Spirit' hears the voice of Jesus saying, 'Hear what the Spirit saith unto the Churches.' As in the Gospel, so here, the Spirit appears both as between Jesus and the Father ($1^{4}$), and as possessed by Christ ($3^{1}$). The Son and the Spirit are so identified that what one says is from the other ($2^{7.8.12.17}$ $3^{5.6}$). The glorified Christ and the prophetic Spirit are here actually at work as foreshadowed in the OT view of the Word and the Spirit of God. The Paracletes in heaven and on earth are also here. The glorified Christ says, 'Blessed are the dead which die in the Lord,' and the responsive Spirit replies, 'Yea, that they may rest from their labours' ($14^{13}$). The Spirit and the Bride say, 'Come'; that is, 'Come to Jesus' ($22^{17.20}$); and Jesus is the only way to the Father.

iv. *Teachings in the Life of the Apostolic Church.*—The Trinity was not a theory from without, but part of the gospel, life, work, and worship of the Apostolic Church. It lived in devotion long before it appeared in theology. The Father, Son, and Holy Ghost were as much part of Church life as body, soul, and spirit were elements of every believer's life. They are not introduced or explained, but everywhere taken for granted and present. No man can share NT worship without using Trinitarian forms. This natural and incidental yet constant reference to Father, Son, and Holy Spirit in Apostolic Churches presupposes just such a development as our study has indicated. The later and clearer statements are always in full agreement with what had been already taught. What the first disciples received from Jesus went far beyond what is recorded in the Gospels; it went far beyond all that He said or did; for after His ascension they became conscious that Jesus was not only a teacher, but Saviour and Lord, and imparter of the Holy Ghost. The teachings and work of Christ in Apostolic experience expanded much more rapidly than they could have done in any process of merely natural development. The order, too, of growth is just what we should expect: new teachings of Jesus about God as Father, then the teachings of Apostles about the Son, and, last of all, the full reference to the Holy Spirit. This order repeats itself in the history of doctrine which took form in the Nicene Creed. Through the words of Jesus, the Synoptic Gospels, St. Paul, Hebrews, St. John, and the Acts, there runs a harmonious and growing representation of God as Father, Son, and Holy Spirit. Jesus sets Himself as Son above all the servants of God (Mt $21^{33}$, Mk $12^{1-9}$, Lk $3^{22f.}$); He $1^{1.2}$ gives the same doctrine in theological form, declaring the Son above all created beings 'God for ever and ever.' St. Paul presents an intermediate view, in which God and His Christ are central (1 Co $1^{3}$, 2 Co $1^{2.3}$, Gal $1^{3}$, Eph $1^{2}$); but puts it at once in vital union with the Trinitarian conception of God as Father, Son, and Holy Ghost (2 Co $13^{14}$, Eph $3^{14-16}$). The Acts shows historically that Father, Son, and Holy Ghost were inseparable from the life and thought of believers; while the Fourth Gospel presents the same teaching as the culmination of NT theology ($16^{7-10}$). (For further indications of doctrinal growth, cf. the articles GOD IN NT and HOLY SPIRIT in vol. ii.). These early disciples knew that there is an infinite eternal God (2 Co $4^{17.18}$, 1 Ti $1^{7}$); they knew also that He is personal, and personal only as Father, Son, and Spirit. How the Infinite can be personal is ever a mystery; to Apostolic men the threefold personality of the infinite God was no greater mystery than any personality of the Infinite. They also knew that there is a God of Absolute Right, the Supreme Lawgiver, the Holy Father in heaven (Jn $17^{11}$, Ro $7^{7.12}$, Rev $4^{8}$); on the other hand, they knew that God had broken through His own law, and, by His revelation in the Son and Spirit, opened heaven and poured supernatural grace and blessing upon men (Ro $3^{26}$ $4^{5}$, 1 P $1^{2-5}$). Their practical experience found that this personality of the Father, and the mediating personalities of the Son and the Spirit, were indispensable to fellowship with God through grace and faith, and in the struggles against sin. Illustrations of this practical Trinity may be seen (1) in the equipment of the Apostles, (2) the establishment of the Church, (3) the work of Missions, (4) the test of sound Doctrine, and (5) the nature of Christian Worship.

(1) The risen Lord gave His commands no more directly to the Apostles, but through the Holy Ghost (Ac $1^{2}$). As inseparable as the Father and the Son appear before the Crucifixion, just as inseparable appear the Son and the Spirit after the Resurrection. To the Son as mediator of the Father, and to the Spirit as mediator of Father and Son, the Apostles turn as to the source of all power and authority.

St. Peter says he opened the Church to the Gentiles because the Lord Jesus Christ from heaven told him to do so (Ac 11$^{8}$), and because the Holy Spirit told him to do so (Ac 10$^{19}$ 11$^{12}$). St. John says the Spirit of truth in the Apostles made them men of God (1 Jn 4$^{2. 6}$), and witnessed through them that the Father sent the Son to give life to believers (vv.$^{13. 14}$). The Spirit in the Apostles made them preach the incarnate Son, and denounce all contrary preaching as of the devil (1 Jn 3$^{8-10}$). The Lord Jesus sent Ananias to St. Paul that he might be filled with the Holy Ghost (Ac 9$^{17}$); then St. Paul preached Christ, that He is the Son of God (v.$^{20}$). St. Paul supported his claim to be an Apostle by appealing to the call of God the Father and His Son Jesus Christ (Ro 1$^{1}$, Gal 1$^{1. 15. 16}$, 1 Co 1$^{1}$), who filled him with the Holy Ghost at his conversion for apostleship (Ac 9$^{17}$ 1$^{2}$). He traces the grace of apostleship and of all work in the Church to the Holy Spirit (1 Co 12$^{13}$) and the Son (v.$^{27}$, 1 Ti 1$^{12}$, 1 Co 7$^{2-5}$, 2 Ti 2$^{2. 11}$); and he spoke from experience. These Apostles tested all Christ's Trinitarian promises. In His name, as the name of God, they cast out devils (Mk 16$^{17}$, Ac 16$^{18}$), healed the sick (*ib.* Ac 3$^{6}$ 9$^{34}$), and raised the dead (Ac 9$^{40}$ 20$^{10}$). The Holy Ghost in their work honoured the Son as He honoured the Father (Jn 5$^{23}$ Ac 3$^{6}$ 16$^{18}$, Ja 2$^{19}$). St. Peter found that the Spirit inspired him to speak as Jesus promised (Mt 10$^{19. 20}$, Lk 12$^{12}$), and, thus inspired, he preached repentance towards the Father and faith in the Son as the way of life (Ac 4$^{8. 10. 31. 33}$). He saw also in the OT covenant of God with parents and their children a point of connexion for the doctrine of approach to the Father through the Son (Ac 2$^{38. 39}$ 3$^{13. 17}$). Sins were remitted or retained by the Apostles on the authority of the Son and as inspired by the Spirit (Mt 18$^{18}$, Jn 20$^{22. 23}$, Ac 8$^{20f.}$). They imparted the Holy Spirit for service (Ac 8$^{17}$), and, full of the Holy Ghost, acted in the name of Christ as ministers of discipline (Ac 15$^{29}$), in conscious opposition to the kingdom of Satan (1 Co 5$^{4. 5}$ 6$^{11}$). They could pronounce Anathema in view of the coming Lord. Christ in the midst, and the Spirit in the midst with the Apostles as ministers, formed the Supreme Court of the Church. St. Paul sums up his apostleship (Ac 20–24) in (*a*) the constant witness of the Holy Spirit, guiding him through bonds and persecutions of Satan and bad men; (*b*) a ministry received from the Lord Jesus Christ; and (*c*) a gospel of the grace of God revealed in His Son. That was his practical work, and not a theological elaboration (Ro 15$^{16. 19}$). The Apostles claimed and exercised doctrinal authority over the Church (1 Jn 4$^{6f.}$, 1 Co 4$^{21}$ 5$^{4}$ 9$^{1f.}$ 11$^{23}$), resting their claims on the command of the Son through the Spirit (Ac 1$^{2}$). They alone perfectly knew the meaning of Jesus (1 Co 2$^{16}$), as Jesus alone perfectly knew the meaning of the OT. They also had the Spirit of prophecy, so that they could declare the future glories of Christ's kingdom, and the overthrow of the kingdom of the devil (1 Co 5$^{5}$ 16$^{22}$, 1 Ti 1$^{20}$, 1 Jn 2$^{22}$ 4$^{3}$, Rev 2$^{9}$ 3$^{9}$).

(2) The Apostolic Church was built upon faith in Father, Son, and Holy Ghost. Pentecost was in an important sense the birthday of the Church; and St. Peter explained it by saying that the Son at the right hand of the Father, having received the promise of the Spirit, 'shed forth this which ye now see and hear.' The Holy Ghost sent by the glorified Son made the Church. If anything is certain, it is that the Apostolic Church saw its foundation laid in the ascension of Christ and the descent of the Spirit. This Spirit of Christ was the regenerating, sanctifying, working power in the Church. If any man had not the Spirit of Christ, he was none of His (Ro 8$^{9}$). Surrounded by pagans whose gods were devils (1 Co 10$^{20}$), and by Jews who were led by Satan to crucify the Lord (Jn 6$^{70}$ 8$^{44}$ 13$^{2}$), Christians were kept by the power of the Holy Ghost (Ro 5$^{5}$). They met heresy in the same power (1 Jn 4$^{2f.}$), and were given by the Spirit a twofold defence: (1) the Old Testament, inspired at first by the Spirit, and now made practical by the Spirit; and (2) growing faith in the Son of God. The Spirit revealed Him in the hearts of believers as the personal, glorified, triumphant Lord (1 Co 2$^{14}$). The OT and Christ were shown to be essentially the same Word of God, once spoken by the prophets, now incarnate and glorified in Christ. But, as in the OT, so in the NT, the Spirit is never confounded with the Word or with Christ. Whether speaking through Apostles or Prophets, the Spirit ever declares Jesus Christ to be the true cornerstone of the Church (Eph 2$^{20}$, 1 P 2$^{6}$). Through the Spirit believers already share the glory of Christ, and through Him receive all the gifts of the Spirit (1 P 3$^{7}$, Eph 1$^{3}$ 6$^{14}$, 2 Co 1$^{22}$, Ro 8$^{16}$).

(3) From the Trinity also started the Mission of the Church (Mt 28$^{19f.}$). The Holy Spirit appeared at once as the great propagating power. He repeated the 'Come' and 'Go' of Jesus (Mt 11$^{28}$ 28$^{19}$, Ac 1$^{8}$) and continued His work. Jesus declared that the work of foreign missions was the aim of His death (Jn 12$^{20. 23-36}$). It was furthered by the Father (v.$^{28f.}$), and carried out by the Spirit, who inspired the first missionaries, Peter (Ac 4$^{8}$), Stephen (6$^{5}$), Barnabas (11$^{24}$), Philip (8$^{29}$), and Paul (13$^{4}$), to preach the gospel and cast out devils (Jn 2$^{31}$; cf. Ac 8$^{7}$). 'Separate me Barnabas and Saul for the work whereunto I have called them,' said the Spirit (Ac 13$^{2}$); 'Go ye into all the world and preach the gospel to every creature,' said Jesus. 'Baptize them in the name of the Father, Son, and Holy Ghost,'—that is the Trinitarian foundation of missions. St. Paul is intelligible only as a man who regarded himself as an organ of the Holy Ghost, fighting the powers of darkness (Ro 8$^{38}$, Eph 6$^{12}$) to save men by the Son of God (1 Co 2$^{4}$ 1$^{4-7}$). He had more gifts of the Spirit than other Apostles, and was the greatest missionary of Christ (1 Co 14$^{18}$). The Holy Spirit directed him to his field of labour (Ac 16$^{7}$), and the Son told him what to expect in those fields (9$^{15}$). The same is true of St. Peter (Ac 1$^{15f.}$ 2$^{4. 17-38}$) and the rest.

(4) The NT Church also regarded the Trinity as the doctrinal assurance that any man was preaching the gospel. Unless he preached the Son of God in personal witness of the Spirit, he was not true to Christ. St. Paul urged Timothy (2 Ti 1$^{13. 14}$) to hold fast the Apostles' form of sound words, which consisted in faith and love towards Christ, who is God our Saviour (1 Ti 2$^{3}$), and was committed unto Him by the Holy Ghost. False teachers left the Church because they denied the Father and the Son, and had no unction of the Holy Ghost (1 Jn 2$^{19. 20. 22}$). Only those preaching the Divine Son had the witness of the Spirit: to such there came the demonstration of the Spirit and of power (1 Co 2$^{4}$, 1 Th 1$^{5}$, Ro 9$^{1}$). Supernatural signs of the Holy Ghost encouraged such missionaries to preach, and roused the careless to hear of the Son of God as Saviour (He 2$^{3}$, 1 P 1$^{12}$, Eph 1$^{13f.}$). As Christ knew what was in man, in like manner did the Spirit in Apostolic preachers so reveal the hearts of heathen in Christian meetings that they fell down crying, 'God is in you of a truth' (1 Co 14$^{25}$). The two heresies against which the Apostles warned were an incipient Gnosticism, which rejected Christ as Lord and Head (Col 2$^{6. 8. 19}$, 1 Ti 1$^{2. 3}$), and an allied Antinomianism, which set at naught the Holy Ghost (Eph 5$^{6. 9. 18}$, Rev 2$^{13. 17. 20f.}$, 1 Co 3$^{17}$). The Holy Ghost warned (1 Ti 4$^{1}$) against 'doctrines of devils' which opposed the Son, and 'seducing spirits' which fought against the Spirit of God. By the laying on of hands the Holy Spirit was

given to NT workers that they might preach the Son of God as Saviour (1 Ti 4[14. 16. 6]). Only such preaching of Father, Son, and Holy Ghost would actually reform and save men (Eph 1[17] 2[4-6. 18] 3[1. 2. 5. 14-16] 4[3-6. 13. 14] 5[1. 2. 9. 18-20]). St. Paul's test description of the gospel against Judaizers is, 'God sent forth His Son . . . to redeem them . . . under the law,' and make them 'sons'; also, 'God hath sent forth the Spirit of His Son' into men's hearts, 'crying, Abba, Father' (Gal 4[4-6]). All men sent of God would preach this sending of Son and Spirit as the true gospel of Christ (1 Co 12[3f.]), and not 'another Jesus,' and 'another Spirit,' constituting 'another gospel' (2 Co 11[4]).

(5) The NT Church meant two or three gathered together with the Son in their midst (Mt 18[17. 20]). The meetings for worship were of two kinds—first, that of the Lord's Supper, in which Christ was central; and, second, the public service of οἰκοδομή, in which the Holy Ghost was central; but each carried with it the Trinity. The general worship was charismatic. Its aim and purpose was edification of the saints through the χαρίσματα granted the various participants by the Holy Ghost (1 Co 14[26]). The worshipping people were the body of Christ (1 Co 10[16] 12[27], Eph 4[12]), in which each member edified the others as an organ of the Holy Spirit (Jn 6[45] 7[38], 1 Co 3[16]). Each brother who took part was moved by the Spirit of the glorified Head of the Church, the Lord Christ (Eph 1[22] 4[15], Col 1[18]). St. Paul traces all the elements of worship—tongues, prophecy, teaching, interpretation, prayer, singing—to the Holy Ghost (1 Co 14[1f.]; cf. Jude [20]); but not apart from the Father and the Son; for in this worship were diversities of gifts by the same Spirit, differences of administration by the same Lord Jesus, and diversities of operations by the same God and Father (1 Co 12[4-6]). The order of St. Paul's thoughts in worship appears as he prays for the Ephesians (3[14-17]) to the Father that He would strengthen them by the Spirit, so that Christ might dwell in them. He asks the Romans (15[30]) to pray in like manner on his behalf. The doxology to Father, Son, and Holy Ghost, spoken of God rather than to God, with which St. Paul opens and closes Epistles (Ro 1[7] 16[27], 1 Co 1[3] 16[23], 2 Co 1[2] 13[14]), doubtless appeared also at the opening and close of Christian worship (2 Co 1[2. 3. 9] 13[14]). The synagogue worship began with 'Blessed be Jehovah' (cf. Schürer, *GJV*[3] ii. 377); the Christian service began with such an invocation as 'Blessed be the God and Father of our Lord Jesus Christ . . . the God of all comfort' (2 Co 1[3]). The Jewish worship closed with the threefold benediction: 'The Lord bless thee . . . the Lord keep thee . . . the Lord give thee peace'; the Christian service ended also, probably, with a threefold benediction of Father, Son, and Holy Spirit (cf. Ro 15[12. 13. 16], 2 Co 13[14], Rev 1[4-6] 11[13] 14[7] 16[9] 19[7]). St. Paul uses the word κύριος nearly 150 times, and always of the Son of God, uniting the Lord Jesus and the Lord God in his worship (cf. Seeberg, p. 3). Both Jewish and Gentile Christians, filled with the Holy Ghost, worshipped equally the Father and the Son—a thing impossible to men whose Bible was the Old Testament, unless they accepted what we understand religiously by the Trinity (Eph 5[19], Ph 1[19]).

A similar recognition of the Trinity underlies the worship of the Lord's Supper. Only those baptized in the name of Father, Son, and Holy Ghost were to partake of this Holy Supper (1 Co 10[1-4] 14[16-19], Gal 3[27f.], Ac 2[38] 8[12] 19[3]; *Didache*, x.). It called to mind the Father, in whose kingdom the new wine would be drunk (Mt 26[29], Lk 22[16]). It was celebrated in remembrance of the Son, who sealed the new covenant with His blood (Mt 26[28], Mk 14[24], Lk 22[19]); while the solemn reference to Christ's return to the Father and the coming thereby of His kingdom implies the work of the Holy Ghost (Lk 22[18]). The wonderful discourses (Jn 14–17) on the mission of the Comforter were spoken in connexion with the Supper. The washing of the disciples' feet while at the table (Jn 13[5. 13]) symbolized the work of the Spirit. The worship of all who were here fed by the Son was charismatic (Ac 20[7]), and conducted by men full of the Holy Ghost. Jesus said, 'this do in remembrance of me'; St. Paul said, 'till he come' (1 Co 11[26]); the Spirit-filled disciple at the feast prayed especially to the Lord Jesus, saying, 'Come, Lord.' This appears as part of the ritual (*Didache*, x.), and St. Paul's use of it in the original 'Maran Atha' (1 Co 16[22]) shows that it was already liturgical in NT days (cf. Rev 22[20]). The object of adoration here, as in all worship, was the Lord Jesus Christ, who, according to promise (Mt 28[20]), was invisibly present, feeding the Church, and guiding all her activities (Ac 1[24] 2[47] 4[31]). The hymns of the Church must have started from this Christian Passover (Mt 26[30], Mk 14[26]); they are all 'spiritual songs' (Eph 5[19]), arising in men filled with the Holy Ghost (5[18], cf. Col 3[16]), and without exception glorifying the Son of God (Eph 5[20], Col 3[17], 1 Ti 3[16], Rev 19[1-3. 6f.] 11[17f.] 4[11] 5[9-13]). For St. Paul the Lord's Supper consisted in (1) a celebration of the Lord's death, and (2) communion with the glorified Christ (1 Co 11[24f.] 10[16f.]). This κοινωνία of the body and blood of Christ, which united all to worship the Son, was the creative work of the Spirit, which made a group of individuals a Church of God. After Pentecost, believers continued in this κοινωνία (Ac 2[42]), which was a gift of the Spirit (v.[38]). The Holy Ghost led believers at the Communion Supper to break bread in memory of the Son and offer prayer to Him as Lord of all. From NT days onwards, the Spirit led Christians at the Lord's Supper to pray to Christ as both Creator and Redeemer (1 Co 10[21. 26], *Didache*, ix.); and in both offices He was inseparable from the Father. The communion of the Lord's Supper was 'unto the κοινωνία of His Son Jesus Christ,' to which we are called by the Father (1 Co 1[9]); and in it as the family gathering of the Holy Brotherhood 'the communion of the Holy Ghost' was indispensable (2 Co 13[14]). The community of goods (Ac 2[42f.]), which was an enlargement of the Lord's Table to provide for the poor of the Church, arose through men 'all filled with the Holy Ghost' (Ac 4[31. 32]), speaking the word of God and witnessing to the glorified Christ (v.[33]). And the sin of Ananias and Sapphira against this communion —St. Paul calls the contribution for the saints a κοινωνία (Ro 15[26])—was lying to the Holy Ghost (Ac 5[3. 9]). The men chosen to serve these tables of the Lord and His poor were 'full of the Holy Ghost and wisdom' (6[3]); and when the first of them, Stephen, began to preach, his gospel was the Most High God and the Glorified Christ, whom he adored as Lord. In urging the Jews to be saved, he declared that opposition to God and His Christ was resisting the Holy Ghost (7[48. 59. 51]). The NT connects also the sacrament of Baptism and that of the Supper. The one was God's Israel marching in covenant with the Lord through the sea; the other was the spiritual meat and drink given to feed them by the way (1 Co 10[1-4] 12[13]). And, what is very important, both sacraments profess faith in Father, Son, and Holy Ghost. St. Paul sees in Baptism a profession of fellowship with the Son (Ro 6[3], 1 Co 1[13]), into whom believers are baptized by the Spirit (1 Co 12[13]), showing that he agrees with Mt 28[19]; and in the Supper, which commemorates the Son, he says we 'drink of the Spirit' (1 Co 12[13]; cf. Nösgen, ii. 333). The sent Son and the sent Spirit appear in both sacraments as the only way to communion with God. The Lord's Supper embodies the thought of covenant with the Father through confession of the Son. Jesus called it a new covenant in His blood (Mk $14^{24}$). To eat and drink of this Supper was a test of loyalty to Father, Son, and Holy Ghost (1 Co $10^{20.16}$ $11^{22.20.29}$ $12^{13}$; cf. Mk $14^{18}$, Lk $13^{26}$ $24^{30}$, Jn $13^{18}$). At the foot of the cross the sacrificial meal of loyalty to Christ was eaten. It was a place of spiritual life or death; hence St. Paul, following Jesus (1 Co $11^{23}$, Jn $8^{44}$), sees the alternative here to be the kingdom of God or the kingdom of Satan; table of the Lord Jesus or table of the devil; Spirit of God or spirit of evil,—that is the crucial confession-test at the Holy Supper (1 Co $10^{16-21}$ $12^{3}$). The charismatic communicant, speaking excitedly with tongues, might seem unworthy to sit down at the Lord's Table; St. Paul's supreme and only criterion is, 'No man can say that Jesus is the Lord but by the Holy Ghost' ($12^{3}$). The test of every Christian in all worship, including the most sacred service of the Lord's Supper, was belief in the Holy Ghost, who testified to the Divine Son, who came forth from the Father. The real presence of the Son of God, set forth in the bodily symbol of the broken bread, experienced in the communing Church, which is the body of Christ, ever one with her Divine Head, and witnessed to by the Holy Ghost, without whose presence there can be no Christian worship, is a doctrine of the NT to which the Church in all ages has borne testimony. In the believer's experience, as in the Bible history of redemption, this doctrine grows upon him. Not till the OT revelation ended was it evident that God was Father; only the Son could perfectly reveal the Father. Not till Jesus had finished His work and returned to the Father was it fully evident that He was the Divine Christ; only the Holy Ghost could perfectly reveal the Son of God. And not till the Church has ended her work on earth and become glorified with her Lord, and the historically revealed economic Spirit has completed her sanctification, will the Divinity and Personality of the Holy Ghost be perfectly manifest. Only in the heavenly life, where the Spirit may cease to be subjective and inseparable from our spirit in religious consciousness, will His distinctive character appear as manifest as that of the Father and the Son.

LITERATURE.—There is no recent literature on this subject. See art. GOD IN NT in vol. i. Besides the works quoted in the text and the sections in *Bibl. Theology of the OT*, by Oehler, Riehm, Schultz, Smend, and *Bibl. Theol. of NT*, by Holtzmann, Beyschlag, Gould, see the Literature under artt. JESUS CHRIST, CHRISTOLOGY, MESSIAH, HOLY SPIRIT, in this Dictionary; and in Herzog-Hauck, *PRE*³. In our day the Trinity is treated chiefly from the point of view of Christology: cf. Kähler's art. 'Christologie' in *PRE*³; Cremer, *Bibl. Theol. Wörterb.* 8, *s.vv.* λόγος, υἱός, πνεῦμα ἅγιον; Gore, *The Incarnation*; Caspari's essay, 'Der Glaube an die Tr. Gottes in d. Kirche des 1 Chr. Jahrh.' (1894), is valuable. The discussion on the Apost. Creed started by Harnack in his *Das Apost. Glaubensbekentniss* (1893), 27 ed., and shared by Zöckler, *Zum Apostolikum*, and Swete, *The Apost. Creed* (1894), sheds side light upon the subject.

HUGH M. SCOTT.

## REVELATION.—

i. THE PHILOSOPHY OF REVELATION.
   1. The present position regarding the Bible.
   2. Man and Religion.
   3. Religion and Revelation.
   4. Revelation and Inspiration.

ii. THE HISTORY OF REVELATION.
   1. Characteristics of OT revelation.
   2. Limitation of God's action.
   3. Fulfilment of the OT revelation in Jesus Christ.
   4. Christ's connexion with the OT.
   5. Relation of Christ to the NT.
   6. Limits of the NT revelation.
   7. Relation of Criticism to the History of Revelation.
   8. Assumptions regarding the Supernatural.
   9. History and Literature of Revelation.

iii. THE DOCTRINE OF REVELATION.
   1. The OT doctrine of Revelation.
   2. The doctrine in the NT regarding the revelation in the OT.
      (*a*) The use of the OT by Christ.
      (*b*) The use of the OT in the Gospels and Acts.
      (*c*) The use of the OT in St. Paul's Epistles.
   3. The NT doctrine of Revelation.

iv. THE EVIDENCE OF REVELATION.
   1. Evidence of the Bearers of Revelation.
   2. Evidence of the Literature of Revelation.
   3. Evidence of Experience.
   4. Reception of Divine Revelation.

SUMMARY.

Literature.

This article is intended not simply to state what the teaching of the Bible on the subject of Revelation is, but also to show what is the nature of the revelation preserved in the Bible, and what are the wider relations to human thought and life held by it. It will deal accordingly with the *philosophy*, the *history*, the *doctrine*, and the *evidence* of Revelation. Topics already discussed in previous volumes will again be referred to, but the new point of view from which they will be regarded should prevent repetition, and, wherever possible, reference to previous articles will take the place of detailed treatment. The subject will be handled with this intention and under these limitations.

i. THE PHILOSOPHY OF REVELATION.—1. *The present position regarding the Bible.*—It is generally admitted that a great change in theological thought has taken place during the last century, especially in regard to the Bible. We cannot now think of it as our fathers did. We cannot believe that its science must determine our view of nature; that its historic records can never be convicted of mistake; that its every part alike gives us the whole counsel of God; that the imperfect morality which is found in some whom it commends as holy, or commissions as teachers, must be explained by the discovery of mystic meanings; that every word it utters regarding man's duty, devotion, and destiny must be accepted as authoritative. This change of attitude regarding the Scriptures is due to several causes. *Firstly* must be mentioned the ethical spirit of the age. In the records of the Bible, deeds are reported and approved in the name of God as done by men recognized as servants of God which our conscience must condemn. There are views of God's relation to men presented which contradict man's consciousness of freedom, on which his moral duty and worth alike depend. Can God approve injustice and cruelty? Can man be the creature of a Divine omnipotence? Such questions are being asked, and cannot be answered without considerable modification of the traditional views of the Scriptures. *Secondly*, science has been making many discoveries, if also manufacturing a few theories. Everywhere it finds unbroken order, unchanging law, continuous development. In claiming that miracle and inspiration are possible the Bible seems to come into conflict with science, and harmony can be restored only by a reconsideration of current conceptions regarding the Bible. *Thirdly*, the philosophical conception of evolution, which has so transformed every mode of man's mental activity, has been brought to bear on the Scriptures with results in many ways opposed to the thoughts which have hitherto ruled in the Christian Church. *Lastly*, the literary and historical criticism of the writings themselves has led to conclusions about date, authorship, mode of composition, literary character, and historical value, which are very far removed from the opinions on these matters which have been handed down in the Church. On these grounds, the common views about the Bible hitherto held are being very widely and boldly challenged.

But, on the other hand, we seem to be furnished now with a more secure foundation on which we may build our apology for the worth of the Scriptures. For, *firstly*, within the last century philosophy in the person of the idealist thinkers of Germany has become more favourable to religion, recognizing its use and worth in making man rational, and accepting the conception of God as the necessary, ultimate principle of thought. In more recent sociological theory the value of religion in moralizing man has been recognized. Without expecting very much help from philosophy and science in vindicating the claims of the Bible, we must yet acknowledge that the much more respectful attitude towards religion which now generally prevails among thinkers does offer the promise of more careful and sympathetic consideration of any defence of the Scripture which may be advanced. And, *secondly*, what calls itself the science of Comparative Religion has shown that man is everywhere religious, even as he is rational and moral, although the forms in which these higher activities are expressed are often imperfect and inadequate. Although the discoveries made in this inquiry regarding man's religion have sometimes been used to discredit the unique value of the Bible, yet in an impartial comparison with other religions Christianity need not fear that it will lose its pre-eminence, nor will the Holy Writings of our faith fail to assert their superiority. Keeping these general considerations in view, we may now apply ourselves more closely to the subject of Revelation with special reference to the Scriptures. In dealing with this, it will not be enough to inquire what claim the Bible makes for itself, and what worth the Christian consciousness assigns to it; it will be necessary to verify this claim, and vindicate this worth in relation to man's thought and life. It is the purpose of this preliminary philosophical discussion, therefore, to show that man's nature implies religion, and religion revelation, and revelation inspiration; but that while all these belong to man as man, yet the perfect religion, the ultimate revelation, and the authoritative inspiration are found in only one Person, who is, however, so related to a historical development going before and to a historical development following after Him, that He cannot be viewed apart from their record, or they be seen apart from Him.

2. *Man and Religion.*—It must be here assumed that the attempt to explain man *empirically*—that is, as a product of nature—has failed, and that he must be interpreted *ideally*, as a person in and yet above the process of nature. If *Materialism*, or *Naturalism*, or *Agnosticism* be true, then human religion is a delusion, and Divine revelation an impossibility. But none of these theories can offer a guarantee for the truth of science, or a reason for the claims of conscience; and each of them fails to explain all that man feels to have the highest worth for him. Idealism alone can so interpret man as not to lower the value of his spiritual interests and pursuits. What, then, is the idealist interpretation of man? As *rational*, he seeks truth, the harmony of thought and being; as *moral*, he seeks what from different points of view may be described as holiness or freedom, or the harmony of law and will; as *emotional*, he seeks what from different points of view may be described as blessedness or love, the harmony of his whole self with his whole environment. Now, although these ideals are not always consciously present to his mind, even although they may disguise themselves in the forms of lower desires and expectations, yet they are ever determining his actions both as motive for and as end of his development. These ideals as realized in one Being afford man his conception of God. Of course it is not affirmed that man's religious consciousness reaches this conception by any such analysis or argument; all that is here indicated is that man's ideal nature adequately interpreted implies the conception of God, and that his belief in his ideal involves his faith in a reality corresponding thereto, for such a reality alone can afford him the assurance that his ideal can be realized. Unless the intelligence and the intelligible world have their ground in one reason, the harmony of thought and being can never be reached; unless the activity of man can be derived from the same character as is expressed in moral standards, the harmony of will and law seems unattainable; unless the same purpose is expressed in the desires of men and the process of the world, there will be no escape from the struggle of the self and the environment. Man has ever sought to form relations with, by rendering services to, or seeking benefits from the Being on whom he is proved by his very nature dependent, and with whom, as rational, moral, emotional, he claims affinity. The communion of God and man finds expression in *Religion*, which from a speculative standpoint may be defined as *necessary*, and from a historical as *universal*. It is true that attempts have been made to prove that there are peoples without religion; but in the instances produced it has subsequently been found that closer investigation modified first impressions; and, even should there be any doubt left in a few cases, it can be confidently asserted that peoples without religion have not yet reached the full development of their humanity. Without attempting now to disprove the contentions of the thinkers who do not interpret man's morality and religion as true, but account for them as fictitious, we may assert that the origin of religion cannot be inconsistent with its functions. If man's ideal implies religion, its origin lies not in what is lowest but in what is highest in him. Imperfect as were the forms in which the instincts, impulses, and intuitions of religion at first were manifested, yet we have warrant in the history of religions for concluding that man's consciousness of God developed along with his consciousness of self and the world. The communion he sought with God had necessarily the inadequacy of his purposes for himself, or the uses he made of the world. If religion be thus implied in man as mind and heart and will, the inquiry as to the organ of religion in him is evidently due to a misconception of its nature. Religion is not one of a number of spiritual functions; it is the relation between man's whole personality and the Being who is its ground, law, type, ideal, in whom all his varied functions have their source and reason. Hence religion has his whole nature as its organ, and finds expression in all his spiritual functions. Religion is not primarily or exclusively intellectual (Hegel), or moral (Kant), or emotional (Schleiermacher), but embraces mind and will and heart alike. Just as man responds to his natural environment in knowledge, feeling, deed, so does he respond to his spiritual environment in reason, conscience, reverence. His consciousness of God is at least as varied as his consciousness of the world, or of his own self. But in the history of religions the proportion and harmony of these three elements has not been maintained. Religion as truth and as righteousness has often been subordinated to religion as the satisfaction of emotions. This is sought in worship, from which all intellectual and all moral elements cannot be altogether excluded. In Greece, for instance, we find the popular idolatry completely divorced from the ethical inquiry of a Socrates and the speculative effort of a Plato. The intellectual and moral content of religion has again and again been allowed to fall

behind the stage reached by science and morality, while the ritual elements were made unduly prominent. Yet it is quite evident that the consciousness of God ought to have a content adequate to the demands of reason and the dictates of conscience. The religious development of mankind has not been normal; it has been disturbed and perverted by sin. Renewal as well as progress is needed. Hence God's activity in religion must be redemptive as well as perfecting.

3. *Religion and Revelation.*—It follows from the very nature of religion that God is active as well as man. If man raises himself above his natural to his spiritual environment, from self and world to God, God responds to that approach; nay, it is to the attraction of this spiritual environment that man yields. Unless religion is a delusion, man is not holding intercourse merely with a transfigured self or an idealized world. Religion is not an imagination, which robs the world of its finitude, or lifts the self above its limitations. It is because neither the world nor the self is adequate to his ideal conceptions, or can satisfy his ideal necessities as a spiritual being, that man in religion elevates himself to a region not of his own abstractions, but where Divine reality meets him, and enters into reciprocal relations with him. The truth, pureness, and power of religion depend on the completeness of this elevation. When the consciousness of self or the world dominates, we have conceptions of God false and unworthy. Paganism never so delivered itself from the consciousness of the world as to rise to a true and pure conception of God. Its deities remain natural beings, and therefore not ideally rational or moral. When it did rise above the consciousness of the world, and even strove to rise above the consciousness of self, it reached a pantheism in which God was merely τὸ ἓν or τὸ ὄν. Neither by observation of the world nor by contemplation of the self can the consciousness of God be reached, for neither is adequate to give content to the conception. The world may suggest a final purpose and an ultimate cause, the relation of the self to the world a common ground for both, the self reason and righteousness transcending man's, so much truth there is in speculative theism. But, nevertheless, no effort of man, unaided of God, has reached His reality. Not through nature nor in self does man know God, but only as God makes Himself known. Just as for his natural existence man and nature must be in reciprocal relations, so for his spiritual experience must man and God be alike active. To deny God's action on man in his religion is to destroy its truth, worth, and claim. His religious knowledge is not self-projection, his religious life is not self-subjection, his religious feeling is not self-satisfaction. So to treat religion is not to interpret it as true, but to account for it as fictitious, however necessary and universal the fiction may be allowed to be. Or to explain religion as the action of nature on man is equally to contradict its essential character. It is further to deny that God can have reciprocal relations with the spirit who has affinity with Himself. It is to affirm that God who is absolutely, and man who is relatively, above nature can have no personal relations except through nature; that God who is communicative, cannot communicate unless under such conditions as make the communication inadequate for His bounty and man's need; that God is unable to constitute such direct relations with man as a complete human development demands. This is to subject both God and man to nature. If man in religion is conscious of elevating himself above nature that he may more completely ally himself with God, shall we say that God is unable so to detach Himself from nature that He may respond to man's effort? May we not believe rather that God stands in such personal relations to man that He can out of His own fulness meet the need of Himself which He has implanted; that the spirit that seeks for knowledge of Him, because it has been made for it, will gain it, and not be mocked by a transfigured self or an idealized world? Yet mystic thinkers have been mistaken when they thought that God could be known only in abstraction from the consciousness of self and the world. It is not by losing the finite consciousness that the Infinite reality is known. Nay, it is in such an elevation and purification of the consciousness of self and the world as carry us beyond their finitude and reveal to us their absolute source and purpose. This is a real distinction, the verbal expression of which is not easy. We do not know God apart from the world and self, and yet we know Him as different, though not separated, from both. We do not leave the world and the self behind when we rise to God, but we see the self and the world in God. Although God is manifested, yet He is not exhausted in world and self. God has a revelation of Himself in nature and history on the one hand, and man's own spiritual being on the other; but that revelation cannot be identified with human discovery in the realm of nature, human reflexion on the course of history, human insight into character. All these human activities imply Divine action, as in God we live, and move, and have our being; yet, to be in the full sense a revelation to man, nature and history, reason and conscience must become the organs of a Divine activity, not of creation, or preservation, or government only, but distinctly of self-communication. Nature as a succession of phenomena, history as a series of events, and personality as an organism of varied functions, are not revelations, but become so when man knows that in them God is speaking to him, and making Himself known.

This revelation, it is to be understood, is permanent and universal. It is not to be supposed that the spiritual activity of man, which seeks God in nature, history, self, summons into activity the spiritual self-revealing function of God; but all these media of Revelation are to be conceived as permanently and universally so related to God that they constitute His manifestations, and man is so made that he interprets them as such when in religion he seeks God. But man's receptivity does not always and everywhere respond to this activity of God. While he is made for intercourse with God, he does not maintain it unbroken; nay, he may even suffer it altogether to cease. God is still active, but man is not responsive. The consciousness of self and of the world are raised into a false independence of the consciousness of God; and, it may be, ultimately exclude it, or so pervert it as to make it but the expression of spiritual deformity. Man's responsiveness to this permanent and universal Divine activity must not only be stimulated and sustained, but the consciousness of self and the world must be put in their true and right relation to the consciousness of God. But since, as the history of heathenism has shown, this consciousness of God has not been mediated, but perverted by the consciousness of self and the world, God must in thought be first detached from self and the world, that the right and true relation may at last be apprehended and appreciated. In other words, God's *transcendence* must be asserted, in order that His *immanence* may be understood. The spiritual vision, so to behold God as above and beyond nature and history, is lacking to man, as neither his inner nor outer experience can stimulate or sustain it, and therefore God, who is Himself the *light*, must bestow on men the *sight* to behold Him. These *objective* and *subjective* requirements have been met in that special revelation of God, the literature of which lies before us in the Holy Scriptures.

4. *Revelation and Inspiration.*—In passing from general to special revelation, we must take note of a certain ambiguity which attaches to the common use of the term 'revelation.' The sense in which the term has been used in the previous discussion is this. Nature, history, conscience, reason, are so constituted that they show what God is; but man has not received this knowledge in its purity and completeness, for he does not know God as He makes Himself known. His receptivity to the Divine revelation must be restored, so that his consciousness of God, obscured and perverted, may be purified and perfected. God must, on the one hand, so act on him as to make him capable of this purified and perfected consciousness; and, on the other hand, that there may be continuity in his spiritual development, this consciousness of God must be mediated by a progressive purifying and perfecting of his consciousness of self and the world. This *action of God on the nature of man* we call 'inspiration'; its *result*, the perfected and purified consciousness of self and the world and God, is 'revelation.' The latter term is sometimes loosely used for the subjective process as well as the objective product, but it is desirable that the method and the purpose of God's action be thus distinguished, and the term Inspiration be reserved for the one and the term Revelation for the other. While the essential content of this revelation is the character and purpose of God, the contingent form is the consciousness of the self and the world of the inspired agent. It is quite possible to imagine that this Divine action might have been universal; and yet, if we consider what is God's method in the progress of the race, we shall recognize that this restriction of inspiration to individuals is not contrary to but in accord with it. Although the form of St. Paul's argument raises great difficulties for our thought, yet the fact must be admitted that there is a Divine election of individuals and nations. God deals with mankind as one body, of which the several members have not one function, but are mutually dependent. Science, art, philosophy, culture of many kinds, is the Greek's contribution to the treasures of mankind. From the Roman the nations have learned law, order, government. The speciality of the Hebrew was religion. Each function was assigned to each people, not for self-enrichment only but also for mankind's greater good. As limitation of effort and concentration of energy are the necessary conditions of the greatest efficiency and fullest service, it would seem that in no one people could all the functions of a complete humanity be developed: to each must be assigned the development of one function, the results of this development in each being in course of time made the property of all. If we compare the historic peoples with the savage races, we may ask, Why has God made them so to differ? Surely the answer is, that to the historical peoples may be given the generous task of imparting the treasures of thought and life, which they have won by ages of toil and struggle, to the savage races, who may have been incapable of gaining them for themselves. The Parable of the Labourers has an application to the history of the world. The labourers hired at the eleventh hour also received a penny. It is to be remembered that God's election is to service through sacrifice, as the world's saviours are also its sufferers. As the Hebrew people was chosen to be the school of the knowledge of God for the world, the lessons were taught in national pain, loss, ruin. This revelation was not only limited in space, but also conditioned by time. A perfect revelation would be wasted on an imperfect nation. Religion, or man's receptivity for God's communication, can make progress only as conscience and reason, morals and institutions are developed. That a revelation may be effective for the ends for which it is intended, it must be adapted to the stage of growth of the persons to whom it is given. Accordingly, the idea of evolution, the application of which has been so fruitful in other branches of knowledge, not only may but must be utilized in the interpretation of this revelation. Viewed from this standpoint, it shows a steady if slow progress, not without relapses followed by recoveries, yet with the dominant tendency to truer thought, purer worship, and better life, until in Jesus Christ the promise of the Hebrew religion found its fulfilment, and from Him went forth the power which has made, and is still making, the Christian religion the final and perfect satisfaction of man's need of God. The theoretic proof of the superiority of the Christian to all other religions is being confirmed by the practical proof that, wherever it is known and understood, the imperfections of the religion hitherto cherished are recognized, and its higher claim and greater worth are acknowledged. In its idea of God as Father it offers the truest object for faith; in its law of love it affords both the highest principle and the strongest motive for morality; in its promise of eternal life it inspires the brightest hope; and in the salvation from sin it offers it delivers mankind from its greatest danger and meets its deepest need.

Before passing to consider more closely the history of this revelation, two remarks, for which the preceding discussion affords the warrant, may be added. *Firstly*, there is no religion without revelation. In so far as men have sincerely sought God, however inadequate their conceptions or imperfect their methods, He has been really found of them. The truth and worth of any religion depends on the measure of man's responsiveness to God's revelation. *Secondly*, we cannot altogether deny the inspiration of the great religious personalities who have in any degree reformed or revived religion, such as Confucius, Buddha, Zoroaster, and Mohammed. In so far as they saw any clearer light than their contemporaries, God gave them sight; but, as any revelation which came through them has done immeasurably less for man's progress than the revelation in Christ, they cannot be regarded as His rivals, but at best as tutors to lead to Him.

ii. THE HISTORY OF REVELATION.—1. *Characteristics of OT revelation.*—In dealing with this history it will not be necessary to enter into any minute details, as these have already been presented in such articles as ISRAEL in vol. ii. and OLD TESTAMENT in vol. iii., but the characteristic features and decisive factors may be briefly shown. The revelation was to and by individuals, lawgivers, judges, priests, and prophets—men who were chosen, called, and fitted by God to be the teachers and leaders of their fellow-countrymen, rebuking their sins, withstanding their unbelief, correcting their mistakes as to God's relation to men, communicating His will and His purpose, and announcing His judgments and His promises. Otherwise it could not have been; for just as peoples are chosen for special functions, so in these peoples persons are chosen, by whose enlightenment and stimulus they are fitted for the discharge of their respective functions. To the minds and hearts and wills of a few men God commits His message and mission to the many. But these few are not isolated from or independent of the society for which their work is done. Not only do the words and works of the individual not suffice for the full expression of the content of Divine revelation, but he in isolation would be incapable of being the organ of Divine communication. As the individual lives not to himself but for society, God's will for him cannot be expressed apart from His purpose for society. God's moral commands, involving as these do the relations of men to one another, can find adequate expression only in the customs, laws, and manners of a society. So communion with God for its variety and vigour needs community with men. If an individual message is not to be wasted, it must be delivered to a society with a measure of responsiveness. But this involves that each teacher or leader does not stand quite alone, but that he has entered into other men's labours, and that he is sowing seed of which others will reap the fruit. Each is continuing a work already begun, and is transferring to others a task waiting to be completed. There must be this inheritance from the past, and this bequest to the future at each stage; for the whole counsel and purpose of God cannot be communicated at once. As God's communication must at each stage be conditioned by man's receptivity, and the development of that receptivity was very gradual, the revelation was progressive. Men were led from lower to higher thoughts of God, from poorer to richer life in God, from narrower to wider hope from God. We must, to complete our conception of the process of revelation, not only consider God's action through the inspiration of men, but must also take into due account God's guidance of the whole course of the history of the people for whom this revelation was intended, and His control of all the events which affected its fortunes and development; for what God had done or was doing in judgment or mercy to punish or to save, was the content of the message and mission of the leaders or teachers. It was not through nature that God discovered Himself; it was not by brooding over their own inner life that God's spokesmen found the word of the Lord. They read the signs of the times in the rise and fall of empires; in famine, pestilence, and invasion; in the wrongs and miseries of the poor, and the tyranny and luxury of the rich; in moral and social conditions as well as in political circumstances: and the signs of the times were to them a Divine language. Accordingly, the history must be included in the revelation, in the measure in which God was seen to be acting, or was heard to be speaking by the inspired persons in all events and experiences. The external history afforded the occasion for the internal revelation, but did not limit its range, as inspired men learned and taught more about God than was immediately suggested by facts. It would be to ignore the most prominent feature of this history not to lay special stress on the redemptive character of it. God again and yet again showed Himself to be a Saviour in delivering His people from the evils which they had brought upon themselves by their transgression. The Exodus from Egypt and the Return from Babylon, to mention only the most momentous instances, were both decisive factors in the process of God's revelation.

2. *Limitation of God's action.*—It is by so viewing the history of Revelation in a nation that we escape some difficulties to which we expose ourselves, if we consider only the inspiration of individuals. It has often been asked, why should we restrict inspiration to Hebrew lawgiver, or judge, priest, or prophet, and refuse it to Greek sage or Roman statesman? Without entangling ourselves in any abstract psychological discussion about the subjective process of inspiration, we can answer the question by pointing out first of all, that, whatever true or holy utterance regarding God or the spiritual order may have fallen from the lips of Greek sage or Roman statesman, it was not addressed to a society, conscious of itself as discharging a Divine function in the world, as constituted by a Divine covenant and regulated by a Divine law; did not connect itself immediately with prior Divine utterances, which were alike the condition of its intelligibility and the basis of its authority; did not mark a stage in the progressive development of the knowledge of God, and of a moral and religious life corresponding thereto. We may most gladly admit that every good and perfect gift is from above, from the Father of lights, and that all truth concerning God is of God; yet we must maintain that such isolated, and for the most part impotent, utterances cannot have for us the same significance as utterances which find their due place and play their needful part in the expression of an ever more adequate and influential knowledge of God in a progressive national history. The distinctively religious character of this history is usually recognized, but is variously explained. The Hebrew people has been credited with *a genius for religion*, an innate tendency towards monotheism, a passion for righteousness. It has accordingly been maintained that we do not need to recognize in this progress any but the ordinary historical factors. Just as the Greeks had the genius of arts and letters, and the Romans the genius of law, so the Hebrews had the genius of religion. But the very phrase in which the function of this people in the world-economy is expressed, forces us to recognize what is claimed for itself by the literature which this genius has produced. If the argument developed in the previous section is valid, religion implies a reciprocal relation of God and man. The consciousness of the world and the self cannot constitute, although they may mediate, the consciousness of God. Nay, those tend to pervert or even exclude this, unless restrained and corrected by an intensified religious life, which is an increased responsiveness to the presence and action of God. Hence a genius for religion implies an activity of God which a genius for art and letters, or for law, does not. The character and the result of religious genius implies a revelation of God by Himself as no other genius does. But besides this consideration, two other evidences of the Divine action in Hebrew history may be indicated. On the one hand, we do not find any of the peoples who had the closest racial affinity to the Hebrews display any innate tendency towards monotheism, or any passion for righteousness; and, on the other, the history of the nation itself shows with what difficulty and delay it learned the lessons of faith and duty, which God was giving to it both by His dealings with it in events, and by His teaching of it by His messengers.

3. *Fulfilment of the OT revelation in Jesus Christ.*—This revelation has its issue and consummation in Jesus Christ. As religion seeks to bring man into such reciprocal relations with God that there may be a community of thought, feeling, and life, in His God-manhood religion had its ideal realized. As the purpose of revelation is to communicate to man such a knowledge of God as shall be adequate to answer the questions of his mind regarding God, to satisfy the longings of his heart for God, to determine his actions by the will of God, in the consciousness of Jesus, who knew the Father as He was known of the Father, in the testimony of Jesus, who being in the bosom of the Father has declared Him, revelation reached its goal. But we must add, inasmuch as man's relation to

God in religion had been disturbed, and his capacity to respond to God's revelation had been destroyed by sin, in Him also was accomplished that redemption from the guilt, power, lust, and curse of sin, and that restoration to the knowledge, love, and life of God, which made it possible for man to receive Christ's revelation of God and to enter on the realization of His ideal of religion. In completing, Christ transcended the Hebrew religion and revelation. He came in the fulness of the time, but He was sent into the world by the Father. Accordingly, we have to recognize in Him two aspects—a historical and a metaphysical, a natural and a supernatural. It is not within the scope of this article to discuss the evidence for His Divinity (see article JESUS CHRIST in vol. ii.). Let it suffice to assert that it seems to the writer impossible otherwise to account, without violation of all historical probability, for the records of His teaching, work, character, and influence which have come down to us; for the growth, the spread, and the worth of the society He founded; for the moral and spiritual forces which proceed from Him to transform the life of individuals, nations, races; and that it appears to him both true and right to regard the universe as the gradual fulfilment of a purpose of self-revelation in a series of existences of ever higher worth, greater truth, and nobler grace, which is not closed by man, capable under limitations of understanding and welcoming this revelation, but finds its most fitting and worthy close in the union of the Creator and the creature, the Word who became flesh. But be it noted that the truth, worth, and claim of the Christian religion and revelation depend on the reality of the Divine incarnation. There may be a better religion and a truer revelation, although our intelligence cannot conceive their character and content, if Christ be only one of the prophets. Only if He is the Son, can we be quite sure that we have found at last, and can never again lose, the infinite and eternal Father.

There cannot be an adequate discussion here of the doctrine of the Person of Christ. But to determine accurately the range and limits of the revelation in Him, the limitations necessarily involved in a Divine incarnation (see article INCARNATION in vol. ii.) must be recognized. We must inquire how far the mode, the form, and even the content, of His teaching was dependent on His relation to His age and His people. Without entering into the very complex problems which His knowledge raises, it seems necessary for the purpose of this article to state two general principles. *Firstly*, He knew all that it was necessary for Him to know, that, as Son, He might reveal the Father, and that, as Saviour, He might redeem mankind from sin and death, and restore it to truth, love, holiness, God. His was unerring moral insight and spiritual discernment. *Secondly*, as regards the facts about nature and history, which men can discover for themselves by the exercise of their faculties of perception and reasoning, He probably knew what and as His age and people knew. All questions about God's character and purpose, and man's duty and destiny, He can answer with infallible authority. But questions about the authorship of a writing, or the date of an event, or the cause of a disease, it was not His mission to answer; and, therefore, regarding all such matters we are warranted in believing that He emptied Himself of all Divine omniscience. Although we cannot account for Him by birth, training, surroundings, yet He must be interpreted through the thought and life of His age and race. As born of Mary and of the seed of David, as brought up in the home, and doubtless taught in the school at Nazareth, as seeking His knowledge of God in the beliefs, fulfilling the will of God in the laws, and observing the worship of God in the rites of Judaism, as linking His precepts with the commands, His words with the teaching, and His claims with the authority of the Hebrew Scriptures, He stands in close and constant relation to the Divine revelation to the Hebrew people. He so attached Himself to it, that we may trace along three lines its progress towards Him.

4. *Christ's connexion with the OT.*—The truth entrusted to the Hebrew people was the conception of the character and purpose of God (see article GOD in vol. ii.). As the Divine discipline of Israel advanced, this conception became richer, wider, purer. At first thought of as might, then as wisdom and righteousness, He is at last conceived as longsuffering, mercy, pity, even love. At first viewed as so bound up with the fortunes of His people that their disasters are His dishonour, He is at last seen to fulfil His larger ends in their loss and ruin. At first regarded as pleased with offerings and won by worship, He is at last recognized as served by pure hearts, clean hands, and true lips. To this spiritual and ethical prophetism, and not to the legal and ceremonial Judaism of His own time, did Jesus ally Himself, and gave to this teaching a wider range and a deeper reach. The conception of God has a very intimate connexion with the organization of life. In the Hebrew people the idea of God was in a pre-eminent degree the regulative principle of life, the national law, and the social morality. All the teaching of the prophets and all the efforts of the reformers were directed to bring the life of the people into accord with its faith. It was this morality which Jesus accepted, unfolding its full meaning, and applying its principles to the inward motives as well as the outward actions, making wider the circle of those to whom the duties were due, correcting imperfections which had been allowed for the hardness of men's hearts, but, above all, supplying stronger and sweeter motives in the recognition of man's filial relationship to God, by the inspiration of His own moral enthusiasm and example, and by the constraining love of gratitude to Him for His sacrifice and salvation. As God came to be more clearly known, and the claims of righteousness to be more fully recognized, a need was more and more felt. The loftier the view of God and His will became, the greater did men's shortcomings appear to be. Of this sense of need was born the hope (see article MESSIAH in vol. iii.) of God's help; and just as God was known to be merciful as well as just, did this hope gain assurance; and just as men learned their helplessness and the failure of all their efforts at reform, did the hope gain urgency; and just as they learned in national disaster God's method of dealing with sin, did the hope gain distinctness. The true Messianic hope was born of a moral need, and grew for a religious end. The false Messianic hope was the offspring of an unethical patriotism and an unspiritual bigotry. Christ fulfilled the true Messianic hope, and was rejected by the Jewish people because He would not accept the false; yet even this true Messianic hope He transcended. Whatever was merely national, legal, ceremonial, had no fulfilment; only what was universal, ethical, spiritual, was realized in Him. He did not leave what He took from the Old Testament as He found it, but transformed it, and it is only as fulfilled by Christ that the older revelation has authority for the Christian Church.

5. *Relation of Christ to the NT.*—Between the two Testaments there is not only an interval of time, there is also a change of religious thought

and life. A trinitarian conception of God takes the place of a unitarian; instead of a national there is an individual and thus universal relation of man to God: a ceremonial is superseded by a spiritual worship of God; an outward is changed to an inward morality; the hope of a deliverance promised yields to the assurance of a salvation possessed. Of course these contrasts are subject to some qualification, as there are parts of the OT which anticipate some of the higher elements of the NT, and there are features in the Apostolic Church as presented in the NT which are survivals of the lower elements of the OT. But that a new creation had been accomplished, no one comparing the two literatures can doubt. How can the NT be accounted for? Not by a mythical process (Strauss), nor by polemical tendencies (Baur), but by the historical person and work, life and death of Jesus Christ. The writers of the Gospels and Epistles give us what is an adequate explanation of their character and contents. In Jesus they had learned to recognize and confess not only the Messiah, but the Son of the living God, in more than the Messianic sense, even the Lord from heaven, and the Word who became flesh. As Healer and Teacher He stood alone above other men. He could not be ensnared by sin, or holden of death. As Crucified, He was to them the power and the wisdom of God unto salvation. In Him, as Risen and Ascended, God was reconciling the world unto Himself. This conception of Him which they give us as not only His own claim for Himself, but as the witness of their own experience of what He had been to them in the flesh or was still in the Spirit, is in perfect harmony with the words which they report as falling from His lips, and the deeds which they record as done by His hands. The Evangelical history and the Apostolic interpretation are in perfect unison. Whatever common sources the Evangelists used, each writes from his own standpoint, and their representations agree. It is unintelligible and incredible that this portrait of sinless perfection and gracious beauty can be a work of the imagination, and not a copy of reality. Four imperfect men could not have succeeded in producing this harmonious picture. Surely the impression and influence of the Original so inspired the writers that they were able to preserve for all time and all lands the grace and glory of the life of which only for a short time a few men were the witnesses.

But the NT offers not only this record, but also an interpretation; and there is at present a tendency to distinguish these two very sharply from one another. Some scholars and thinkers strive to free Christianity as Jesus taught it from the Hellenistic metaphysics of St. John and the Rabbinic exegesis of St. Paul. We must, therefore, inquire whether the Apostolic interpretation does not belong to the revelation in Christ, whether in disowning St. John's philosophy and St. Paul's theology we are not refusing Christ's own testimony to Himself by His Spirit in St. John and St. Paul. It seems necessary to insist that not only Christ's consciousness of Himself, but also the Christian consciousness of Him, belongs to His revelation. If the Person and work of Christ are the objective cause in the revelation, the spiritual contemplation of St. John and the moral conflict of St. Paul are the subjective effect; and the one should not be separated from the other. To know Christ fully, we must not only know what He said and did Himself, but also what He made of the men who fully surrendered themselves to His grace and truth. To grasp His truth in its entirety, we must know it not only as expressed in Him, but also as it finds expression in men of varied capacity and different character. He must present Himself not only as the perfect ideal, but also as the sufficient power for realizing that ideal in imperfect men. When we see Him taking men so different from Himself in nature, habit, character, and making them like Himself, the crooked straight and the rough plain, then only do we learn the fulness of power and the surety of promise which dwell in Him. Because in St. John's conception of the Person of Christ we can discern his mental habits, and in St. Paul's doctrine of Christ's work we can discover his character and experiences, it by no means follows that either of them is false. Nay, rather it follows that Christ evoked what was truest in St. John and best in St. Paul, and that the mind of the one and the soul of the other enable us better to understand Christ, who made them both what they were. He was the centre of numberless relations, the source of countless developments, the cause of manifold influences. Through many varied personalities He needed to exhibit the content of His Person. With regard to St. Paul especially there is an inclination among those whose spiritual experience has not afforded them the ability to understand his, to maintain that his views about sin and grace are morbid, exaggerated, unnatural, too much coloured by the Judaism which he claimed to have laid aside, too much involved in the legalism which he professed to be contending against. The lack of such an experience as St. Paul's gives no man the right or reason to deny its worth, which has been proved to many in the history of the Christian Church because they have shared it. To the present writer, at least, it seems beyond all doubt that without St. Paul's interpretation of the relation of Christ to sin, law, death, grace, and life, the revelation of God in Christ would not have been complete. Is not St. Paul's view of the Cross one of those truths which Christ could not fully disclose to His disciples, because they could not bear it, but into which the Spirit of truth led them? Is it altogether vain to suggest that St. Paul never knew Christ according to the flesh that he might gain his knowledge of Christ in the Spirit through inward struggle and anguish, and might thus in his writings give expression to an experience through which many after him would be called to pass? St. Paul's interpretation of Christ's work has not lacked the confirmation of some of the most notable Christian experiences. The criticism which imagines that when it has traced the exegetical methods of St. Paul to the Rabbinic schools, or the philosophical terminology of St. John to Alexandrian speculation, it has adequately accounted for what is distinctive in them, deludes itself. Behind their words there is their personal experience. These but afford the form, that gives the content. Had St. John not seen all in Christ and Christ in all, the doctrine of the *Logos* had never been. Had St. Paul not passed from sorrow and struggle to peace and power in Christ, he would never have construed the work of Christ as he does. The personalities have to be accounted for, and not merely their forms of speech traced. We may freely and frankly recognize much that was temporary and local in the modes of expressing the truth, and yet be warranted in asserting that the truth expressed is permanent and universal.

6. *Limits of the NT revelation.*—It may be objected, that if the Christian consciousness of Christ has authority even as the testimony of Christ to Himself, why should we limit this authority to the consciousness of St. Peter, St. John, St. Paul, and the other persons whose writings have found a place in the NT? Why should such works as the *Imitation of Christ* or the *Pilgrim's Progress* not be as authoritative as the Gospel of St. John or

the Epistles of St. Paul? From the standpoint of this article the traditional answer, that the latter works are inspired and the former not, cannot be given, because the general principle assumed in this discussion is, that the inspiration of any writing in the distinctive sense in which we apply the term to the Holy Scriptures can be inferred only from its position and function in the history of revelation. The answer from this standpoint cannot be given in so few words, but it will be indicated as briefly as possible. *Firstly*, the men whose writings form the NT stood in an immediate historical relation to Christ, such as no men since have done. They were either eye-witnesses, or had received from eye-witnesses what they had declared. St. John had enjoyed intimate fellowship with Christ. St. Paul, though one 'born out of due time,' lived in such constant and intense realization of the Risen One that he could declare, 'to me to live is Christ.' St. James, although he was not the companion of Jesus during His earthly ministry, yet had known Him according to the flesh, and shared in that vivid and potent consciousness of the exalted Lord which was bestowed on the Church at Jerusalem after Pentecost. The author of the Epistle to the Hebrews, whoever he was, had connexion with the Church at a time when the Lord's presence, though withdrawn from sight, yet wrought signs and wonders among believers. As the history of the Canon (see articles CANON in vol. i., and OT CANON, NT CANON in vol. iii.) shows, the Christian consciousness hesitated about the admission of some writings, because they had not such warrant, or at least it was doubtful if they had. The value of the writings varies with the closeness of the contact of the writers with Jesus Christ. *Secondly*, a comparison of the writings which have been admitted with those which, though seeking admission, have been rejected, justifies the conclusion that the Christian consciousness, not as expressed in decrees of councils or the authority of bishops, but in a growing unanimity of use and esteem in the Churches, was guided by the Spirit of God in what it accepted as kindred with, and what it rejected as alien to, the deposit of truth and grace committed to it by Christ. That judgment has been confirmed by growing Christian experience. While some, because they lack the sympathetic insight, may reject this book or that, yet individual peculiarities are corrected by the general Christian consciousness. The critical questions which some of the books raise, such as *2 Peter* and *Jude*, are as open as ever to discussion, and may result in the conclusion that these writings should have been excluded, and not included; but that does not affect the conviction that there is a limit to the books which the Christian consciousness will recognize as authoritative, because recording the revelation of God in Christ. *Thirdly*, this conviction is not without grounds in reason. It is altogether reasonable to conclude that those who were brought into contact with Christ Himself or with the Christian Church, in which He manifested His presence and power in an intensified spiritual life and in varied spiritual gifts, should be qualified by His Spirit authoritatively to interpret His mind and will. It is equally rational to conclude that this unique relation was destined to be, not permanent but temporary, continued only until the whole content of the unique personality of Christ, so far as was necessary for the practical ends of revelation, should find a place in the minds and win a hold on the wills of men. The introduction of so unique a Personality into the course of historical development must necessarily have established unique relations between Himself and those immediately connected with Him, and commissioned to proclaim and diffuse the truth historically exhibited in His Person. The varied relations in which men might stand to Him were then displayed; the limits to and the lines of the normal development of the Christian life were then indicated. Just as the seed, when it falls into fit soil, begins to grow, and has in it already, though undeveloped, the promise and the pattern of the full-grown plant, so the seed of the Divine life, finding its fit soil in the souls of disciples and apostles, displayed what is the type to which Christian life must conform. Not that the content was then fully developed, but that the form of that content and the laws of its development were then given. *Fourthly*, a note of revelation is originality. Religious life, however varied and intense, which is dependent on a past development and is not originative of a future development, cannot be accepted as a revelation. Hence, while Christianity is progressive, it is also permanent. It develops, but does not augment, 'the truth as it is in Jesus.' To suggest that religious works of later times may be equally inspired with the writings of the NT, is to ignore this characteristic of the revelation in the Son of God—a revelation which, as it has been shown, must include not only His own words and works, but also the interpretation of His person, which is given in the relations which He formed with, and the transformation which He wrought in, those who came into direct historic contact with Him in that manifestation of His presence and power which immediately accompanied His incarnation. We do not need to deny the high spiritual value of subsequent Christian literature, or doubt that it is the Spirit of God which is still guiding His people into truth. Nay, we should believe that God reveals Himself in the experience of every man whom in Christ He saves and blesses, and that his life in the Spirit is an inspired life; yet the revelation and the inspiration alike are mediated by faith in God's grace in Christ, and are therefore dependent on the original revelation and inspiration. We do not need to affirm that all the writings of the NT are equally inspired, and that no other books are inspired; but nevertheless we may acquiesce in the judgment of the Christian Church, that the Christian Revelation is presented adequately and effectively in the NT Scriptures.

7. *Relation of Criticism to the history of Revelation.*—In this sketch of the Christian revelation and its herald, the Hebrew, critical problems have not been discussed, not because the writer has ignored or been indifferent to their existence in forming his conclusions, but because the scope of the article seemed to him to exclude their treatment, and because in many other articles they have been fully dealt with. But a reference to the bearing of these questions on the conception of revelation cannot be altogether avoided. Whether myths, legends, and traditions were employed by the writers of the Hebrew records or not, whether the patriarchs were historical persons or personifications of tribal characteristics and relations, how much or how little was involved in the relation between Jehovah and Israel mediated by Moses, how far the prophets were innovators teaching new truths or conservators recalling old beliefs, what were the stages of the development of the Law before it assumed its final form in the Pentateuch, — these all are questions on which scholarship must be left to pronounce judgment. Questions of literary ethics, such as the use of older sources without acknowledgment, the composition of speeches for historical persons, the ascription of later developments of the ritual system or the moral code to Moses, the treatment of history from the religious standpoint of a later

age, must be dealt with, not by applying modern standards but by recognizing the customs of each writer's age. That the critical reconstruction of the OT exhibits far more clearly than did the traditional views of date and authorship the progress of revelation, must be frankly admitted. That this progress is to be regarded as a merely natural evolution is a conclusion which no results of a legitimate and sober literary and historical criticism warrant, which involves philosophical and theological presuppositions, the acceptance of which must lead to the denial of the reality of a Divine revelation altogether, and which is contradicted, as will be shown in the next section of this article, by the testimony which the OT Scriptures bear to themselves. So long as criticism recognizes the presence and operation of God in the history of the Hebrew people, it may change our opinion of the mode, but it does not affect our conviction of the fact of a Divine revelation. The essential content of that revelation, the idea of God, the law of life, and the hope of salvation, as just described, will not be contradicted by any of these results. The idea of evolution seemed to many Christian thinkers a denial of the fact of creation; but now Christian theism has recovered from its panic, and confidently affirms that evolution is a creative mode and not a creating cause. So will it be with the results of criticism: it will be seen that it affects only the conception of the mode of revelation, and not the certainty of the fact. When we turn to the NT, it must be frankly conceded that Christian faith must be much more concerned about the results of criticism. If the portrait of Jesus is not substantially historical; if the witness of the Apostles to His resurrection, and the reception of the Spirit by them, is not to be believed; if St. Paul's interpretation of the Cross is nothing else or more than an individual, and in no way a typical experience; if St. John's doctrine of the *Logos* is a theological speculation, for which the historical Person of Jesus affords no justification,—then assuredly the character and content of Christian faith would be thoroughly changed, as the revelation of God in Christ would be essentially altered. Some indications have already been given how this criticism is to be met; but the fuller answer must be reserved until the last section of this article on the *Evidences of Revelation* has been reached.

8. *Assumptions regarding the Supernatural.*—Criticism may have much to tell us about the local and temporary forms of the revelation, about the personal characteristics and historical circumstances of the writers, about the literary methods of the writings,—in short, about the earthen vessel which holds the heavenly treasure; but the serious, even decisive, issue for faith lies not in any of these questions, however interesting, but in the affirmation or denial of the fact that God has spoken to mankind in the revelation, of which the Bible is the literature. In asserting this fact, care must be taken not to assume an untenable position. Even the most cautious criticism has made impossible the assumption of *ultra-supernaturalism*, which asserts the absolute infallibility and authority of all the writings in the Bible, which maintains that all human conditions are transcended by Divine revelation, so that its agents must have been raised quite above their individuality, environment, and stage of development into such a relation to God that the Divine content and the human form can be identified; that they may be regarded as altogether undetermined by their own capacity, character, or circumstances, and that accordingly the literature need not be interpreted by the history, as it may have no relation to the needs of the time when it was written, but may anticipate the needs of another age. The vehement defence which is sometimes met with of the Mosaic authorship of the Pentateuch, of the unity of Isaiah, of the accuracy of all the historical narratives, of the literal fulfilment of prophecy and apocalyptic, involves this assumption. This may for a long time yet remain the popular attitude, and here and there will be found a theologian in panic, who will seek to save the ark of God by appealing against the findings of scholarship to the prejudices and the passions of the multitude in the Churches; but in an article such as this it is not necessary to waste any effort in refuting it. What, on the contrary, is much more relevant to the present purpose, is to examine closely the opposite assumption of *anti-supernaturalism*, with which it would be unjustifiable to charge the Higher Criticism as a whole, but which does evidently account for some of the views advanced by some of its representatives.

Without at present entering on any detailed discussion of the subject of *miracles* (see article MIRACLE in vol. iii.) and *inspiration*, the denial of the supernatural operation of God in revelation must be dealt with. The denial may be due to either a supposed scientific interest or an assumed philosophical necessity; *the uniformity of nature* or *the continuity of thought* may be alleged as objections to the supernatural. So long as life, mind, and will cannot be explained by the simple application of the principle of causality, that is, so long as more complex forms of existence call for more adequate categories of thought, the uniformity of nature cannot be asserted so as to exclude the possibility of the supernatural, which is the highest conceivable category. The idea of evolution, with its recognition of a progress in which each successive stage transcends each preceding, is not a hindrance but a help to the belief in the supernatural; as it presents nature to us, not as a rigidly fixed system but as an ever-developing organism, full of surprises in its fresh manifestations, with a possible future inexplicable by its actual past. That personality in this progress appears as the highest stage, forbids the limitation of our conception of the whole process by the application of any of the lower categories, which are inadequate for the interpretation of this highest stage. And personality, which in its religious function reaches out beyond the natural to the supernatural, and recognizes not only its dependence on the order of nature beneath it, but also its affinity with the Maker of nature above it, itself holds the promise of unexhausted possibilities of existence. The categories of science do not explain all forms of being, and therefore cannot determine what may or may not be beyond the range of their application.

Without venturing on the unwarranted course of denying the possibility of the supernatural in the name of science, some writers try to get rid of it by denying the sufficiency of the evidence. But, in the estimate of the value of evidence, mental prejudice, if unconsciously, often affects the decision. Often when the trustworthiness of the witnesses is denied, they have been prejudged false witnesses on the assumption that miracles do not happen. How is it that many are prepared to accept as trustworthy the report of the sayings of Christ in the Gospels, and yet refuse to receive their record of His works? Is there not as much and as good evidence for the fact of the Resurrection as for any of the ordinary events of ancient history about which no doubt is felt? In this so-called scientific examination of the witnesses a philosophical presupposition is involved. Nature is conceived as a self-enclosed and self-sufficient system; but so to think of it is to allow the consciousness of the world to exclude the consciousness of God. When the attention is fixed on the world solely, then order, system, law become the guiding categories of thought. But when attention is turned to God also, then it is recognized that reason, character, will ought to be the predominant conceptions. In accordance with these the consciousness of the world must be transformed. The consciousness of the world suggests necessity, the consciousness of God freedom in the relation of God to the world; the former makes nature appear as a complete unity, the latter leads us to think of it as part of a larger whole; the former constrains us to look at nature as a sphere in which unvarying physical law maintains itself, the latter warrants us in regarding it as a scene in which a moral and spiritual purpose is being realized, to the accomplishment of which the physical order must be regarded as subordinate. The question of the probability of the supernatural is really identical with the question, whether the religious consciousness of God shall transform the scientific consciousness of the world, or the latter be allowed to determine the former. If we follow our religious consciousness, we shall be able to deal without prejudice with all the evidence for the supernatural submitted to us; if the scientific consciousness is allowed to rule over us, however much we protest our impartiality, the improbability of the supernatural will be an influential factor in our treatment of the evidence. The consciousness of God will also afford us the regulative principle in dealing with the narratives. We shall recognize that there is an assertion of the supernatural, due to ignorance of the laws which regulate unusual natural phenomena; that expectation of the supernatural has sometimes led to an assumption of it; that only such evidence to the supernatural can be accepted as valid as justifies it in relation to our consciousness of God, that is, in the supernatural there must be manifested Divine reason, righteousness, or grace. It is only if we view the world teleologically as the expression of Divine purpose that we can admit the supernatural, when it can be shown to be necessary to, and explicable by, the fulfilment of this end. In other words, we must be able to show an intelligible and credible reason why the supernatural order has been manifested in the natural.

A few words will suffice to meet the objection that the supernatural breaks the continuity of thought. If the world is viewed as the manifestation of the Idea or Reason, it is argued by some that no new factor can be admitted, but that each stage of the development must be explicable by that which precedes. But it may with reason be asked whether the limitation of the evolution of the Idea to the natural order is justified; whether we should not rather conceive that the rational system of the universe has the supernatural as the complement of the natural; whether man's thought has warrant to set limits to possible reality. This objection seems to be due to an exaggeration of the achievement and authority of man's self-consciousness. Let us recognize that there may be factors in the historic progress of revelation, inexplicable by our consciousness of ourselves or of the world, but of which the consciousness of God may afford the explanation. The world is something more than the evolution of categories, and its rationality vaster than any logical system. Reason is often set in opposition to revelation, but reason can give no adequate or satisfying interpretation of the world or of self without the regulative conception of God; and reason cannot develop for itself the full content of this conception without religion, or conscious relation to God, which, as has already been shown, presupposes revelation, or God's conscious relation to man. Man's reason is his capacity so to order and relate all his knowledge that the universe will appear to him an intelligible unity; but this unity cannot be constituted without the idea of God; and if man is to affirm a reality corresponding to this idea so that he may be able to base this mental structure on the solid foundation of real existence, it is only by religion, responsive to revelation, that he can bridge the gulf between thought and being. Hence reason must recognize as regulative of the consciousness of self and of the world the consciousness of God, and is therefore dependent on revelation; and that not an abstract revelation discoverable in individual minds, but, as man's reason has developed in human history, the concrete revelation in Christ in which man's conception of God has found its most adequate and satisfying content. If we confine our regard to the intelligence within or the intelligible without, the supernatural may seem unintelligible; but if we develop our sense of God, especially of our need of God to save and bless us, we shall gain the moral insight and spiritual discernment to apprehend and appreciate the supernatural.

9. *History and Literature of Revelation.*—Hitherto revelation has been discussed as a history and not a literature, as a life and not a book. This seems to the writer the proper standpoint. The inspiration of the writings contained in the Bible has in the traditional view too long been allowed to hold the foremost place; and the Higher Criticism has undoubtedly rendered us a service in compelling us to relate the literature to the history. To say that the Bible is the record of the revelation is inadequate, unless we give an extended sense to the word 'record.' While the narrative parts of the OT and NT do record the history of the Divine guidance and rule of the Hebrew people and the Christian Church, which is an essential element in revelation, yet in the Prophetic and Apostolic writings we have more distinctly and directly the literature of revelation, the expression of the inspired consciousness of the bearers of God's message to men. In the Psalms and the Wisdom literature we find the utterance of the devotional mood and the practical or speculative wisdom which a more or less close contact with Divine revelation produced. As in Christ the Spirit dwelt without measure, all His words and works are revelation; and the witnesses of them for us, in so far as they were influenced and impressed by this revelation, were inspired. The inspiration of all the writings is not of the same intensity, but varies with the stage of God's revelation reached, and with the degree in which the writer submitted himself to the presence and power of God's Spirit in it. The primary matter is God's action in events and persons to make Himself known, not in abstract truths about His nature but in concrete deeds in fulfilment of His purpose; altogether secondary is the literature resulting from that action. Although we must approach this revelation through its literature, the value of which is that it perpetuates and universalizes the revelation made temporally and locally, yet we must never allow ourselves to forget that the revelation was before the literature; and that even for us the literature is not an end in itself, but only a means to bring us here and now into vital contact and personal communion with the God who thus revealed Himself that He may continue to reveal Himself to us in a deeper knowledge, and warmer love, and better use of the Bible.

iii. THE DOCTRINE OF REVELATION.—1. *The OT doctrine of Revelation.*—Whatever stages Hebrew faith may have passed through before it reached absolute monotheism, yet in its doctrine of Revelation it is assumed that there is only one God, and that idols are nothing (Ps $18^{31}$, 1 S $2^{2}$, 2 S $7^{22}$, Jg

$6^{31}$, Ex $19^{5}$). Not only the history of the chosen people is ordered by Him (Ps 78. 105–107), but His judgments are also seen in the destinies of other nations (Am 1. 2. $9^{7}$). He makes Himself known to persons who do not belong to the elect nation, as Melchizedek, Laban, Hagar, Pharaoh, Abimelech, Balaam, Cyrus, Job. His worship goes back to the beginnings of human history (Gn $4^{26}$), and even the heathen may offer Him an acceptable worship (Mal $1^{11}$). Nature reveals His glory (Job 38–41, Ps 8. 19. 29. 93, Is $40^{12-26}$). Man's conscience, reason, spirit, as coming from Him, reveal Him (Gn $1^{26}$, Nu $16^{22}$, Dt $30^{14}$, Lk $3^{12}$, Job $32^{8}$, Ps $8^{5}$ $36^{9}$, Pr $2^{6}$ $9^{10}$ $20^{27}$, Ec $2^{26}$). But limiting our attention to the revelation to the chosen people, which, however, is conceived as having a relation to all mankind (Gn $12^{3}$, Is $49^{6}$), God's intercourse with the patriarchs is often represented in language which is startling in its frank and free anthropomorphism. He appears to and talks with them. The references in Genesis to theophanies are so numerous that they need not be specially mentioned. (If with the aid of a concordance the word 'appeared' is tracked through the book, the relevant passages will be easily found). Sometimes the Lord appears or speaks in dreams, as to Jacob, Joseph, Pharaoh, Samuel, and Solomon. Sometimes He makes Himself known in a vision, as to Moses, Isaiah, and Ezekiel. A sign of His presence in the camp of Israel was the pillar of fire and cloud; afterwards His presence was found in the ark of the covenant (1 S 4–5). A sound in the tops of the mulberry trees was to David the proof of God's action (2 S $5^{24}$). To Elijah, God came not in the whirlwind, earthquake, or fire, but in the 'still, small voice' (1 K $19^{11-13}$). Through the priesthood, inquiry was made of Jehovah for guidance in perplexity by *Urim and Thummim* (see article in vol. iv.), or otherwise (Jg $20^{27.28}$, 1 S $14^{36.37}$ $22^{10}$), and through it He communicated His blessing and instruction (Nu $6^{22-27}$, Dt $33^{10}$). The seer also is consulted (1 S 9). God's leading is sought and found by various signs (Gn $24^{13.14}$, 1 S $10^{3}$, Jg $7^{13.14}$).

When the conception of God's transcendence tended more and more to supersede that of His immanence, greater prominence was given to supernatural organs of revelation, as His *Spirit*, *Word*, *Wisdom*, and *Angel*. (Consult the articles on all these subjects). The Angel is sometimes identified with, sometimes distinguished from, Jehovah, but may on the whole be regarded as a manifestation rather than as a messenger. The name of God (see articles on NAME in vol. iii. and GOD in vol. ii.) is the epitome of the revelation of God. It is sometimes so personified as to be virtually equivalent to God Himself, and to be the subject or object of actions (Ps $20^{1}$ $5^{11}$ $7^{17}$, Is $29^{23}$ $52^{5}$ $18^{7}$ $30^{27}$, Dt $28^{58}$ $12^{11}$, 1 Ch $29^{16}$, Ex $9^{16}$ $20^{24}$, Ezk $20^{9}$, 2 S $7^{13}$, 1 K $8^{17-20}$). In Ex $23^{21}$ the name of God is represented as dwelling in the Angel. A new name marks a fresh stage of revelation (Ex $3^{13.15}$ $6^{3}$). But, while God reveals Himself, it is recognized on the one hand that He cannot be fully known by man (Job $26^{14}$ $28^{12}$ $36^{26}$ $37^{15}$ $42^{3}$, Pr $25^{2}$ $30^{3}$, Is $45^{15}$), and on the other that there is peril for the man who sees Him or His angel, or even looks on or touches the outward sign of His presence (Gn $32^{30}$, Ex $3^{6}$ $19^{12}$ $20^{19}$ $24^{11}$ $28^{35}$ $30^{21}$, Lv $16^{2}$, Jg $6^{22}$, 1 S $6^{19}$, 2 S $6^{7}$). Piety and morality, however, are the conditions of gaining such a knowledge of Him as avails for the needs of the soul, and of enjoying close communion with Him (Job $28^{28}$, Ps $17^{15}$ $25^{12}$ $27^{8}$ $42^{2}$, Dt $29^{29}$).

The most prominent and authoritative organs of revelation are the *prophets* (see article PROPHECY AND PROPHETS in vol. iv.). All new beginnings in the life of the nation are made by the authority of prophets. Both Abraham and Moses are regarded as prophets (Gn $20^{7}$, Dt $18^{18}$). Quite in the spirit of the OT, St. Peter describes David as a prophet (Ac $2^{30}$). Samuel sanctions the introduction of the monarchy, and even Saul after his anointing is mightily seized by the prophetic spirit (1 S 8–10). Nathan first approves David's intention to build the temple, but afterwards conveys God's prohibition (2 S 7). The division of the two kingdoms is first announced by Ahijah, who also intimates the fall of Jeroboam's house (1 K $11^{29}$ $14^{7}$). Rehoboam's attempt to subdue the rebellion by force is forbidden by Shemaiah (1 K $12^{22}$). Elijah not only announces to Ahab God's judgment on his family, but also anoints Hazael to be king over Syria, and Jehu over Israel (1 K $21^{22}$ $19^{16}$). The part played in the national history by the later prophets, especially Isaiah and Jeremiah, is so familiar that it needs no detailed discussion here. The prophetic consciousness is of special significance for the doctrine of Inspiration; but it would be beyond the scope of this article to discuss this subject fully, nor is it at all necessary, for in the article on PROPHECY AND PROPHETS in vol. iv. it has already been dealt with by a masterhand. Suffice it here to call attention to the important and decisive fact, that while, unless in a few exceptional cases, the prophet continues in the normal exercise of all his faculties, yet he does with confidence distinguish between his own subjective meditations and the objective message of God. It is from this fact we must start in dealing with the question whether the OT does contain a revelation from God, or only the reflexions of men. That in this revelation God may have employed abnormal inward states, as dreams or visions (see articles DREAMS in vol. i. and TRANCE and VISION in vol. iv.), or extraordinary outward signs, is by no means incredible, as these may have been a necessary adaptation to the condition of those whom He used as the organs of His communication. The language about God's coming to and talking with the patriarchs we cannot accept literally, but must recognize the necessarily imaginative character of these narratives, although they probably have some historic basis in tradition, as the revelation of Jehovah through Moses seems to presuppose some antecedent revelation to the fathers of the people. Such conceptions as the *Spirit*, the *Word*, the *Wisdom*, or the *Angel* of God must be regarded as efforts of the human mind to explain God's presence and communion with men in revelation, while maintaining the idea of His transcendence and absoluteness; but in them we may recognize anticipations, however imperfect and inadequate, of the Christian revelation of God as Father, Son, and Holy Spirit.

2. *The doctrine of the NT regarding the revelation in the OT.*—The recognition of the OT in the NT may be traced along three lines—historical, theological, literary. The Hebrew is recognized as an elect and privileged nation, as the bearer of God's special revelation (Ro $3^{1.2}$ $9^{4.5}$ $11^{16}$). Although the Jews by their unbelief have forfeited their claim, yet God has not forsaken His people, and their partial and temporary rejection is the divinely appointed means of a universal and final salvation (Ro 9–11). The promise had been given to this people in Abraham that it should be a blessing to other nations (Gal $3^{8}$); God had delivered it from Egyptian bondage, and entered into covenant with it, so that it was pledged to obedience to His law. While St. Paul insists that the promise came before the Law (Ro $4^{1-16}$), the old covenant is regarded as distinctively a covenant of law, and, as such, is contrasted with the new covenant which has been established by Christ (2 Co 3; cf. also He 8, and see article COVENANT in vol. i.).

Admitting the Divine origin and consequent spiritual character of the Law, its insufficiency to secure righteousness is acknowledged by St. Paul (Ro $7^{7-25}$). The author of the Epistle to the *Hebrews* equally acknowledges the inefficiency of the ritual sacrifices to cleanse the conscience and to restore communion with God (He 7). Thus the NT recognizes the imperfection and limitation of the former revelation; and Jesus, in contrasting what was of old (Mt $5^{21. 27. 33. 38. 43}$), because of the hardness of men's hearts, with His own teaching, seals with His own authority this Apostolic doctrine. The greatest persons of the old revelation are transcended by the supreme Person of the new, and fall far short of the privileges of the humblest and simplest believers. Abraham rejoiced to see the day of Christ (Jn $8^{56}$). Moses and Elijah met Him in the Mount (Mt $17^{3}$). While law came by Moses, grace and truth came by Jesus Christ (Jn $1^{17}$). Greater is He than Solomon (Mt $12^{42}$). Greatest of prophets, the Baptist is inferior to the least in the kingdom (Mt $11^{11}$). The saints of old longed in vain to see what the disciples see (Mt $13^{16}$). Nevertheless, what is best and truest in the old is carried on and completed in the new revelation. Jesus came not to destroy but to fulfil the Law and the Prophets (Mt $5^{17}$). He fulfils the Law by disclosing its essential principles, and by giving to these wider and more inward applications, by securing by His sacrifice the salvation from sin's guilt and power, which by obedience to the Law could not be attained, and by imparting a spiritual energy the Law could not offer. He fulfilled Prophecy generally by carrying on to its last and highest stage the Prophetic ideal of morality and religion, but especially by realizing in His own person the aspirations and expectations of saints and seers regarding the Day of the Lord, the Messiah in the narrower sense of the term, the Servant of the Lord, and the Priest after the order of Melchizedek (see articles on MESSIAH in vol. iii. and PROPHECY in vol. iv.).

The extent to which the writers of the NT regard this fulfilment as being carried will be shown in considering next the use of the OT in the NT, which yields us the following conclusions regarding their views:—(1) The OT Scriptures are cited as an organic unity, ἡ γραφή, αἱ γραφαί, τὰ γράμματα. (2) They are cited as authoritative, as appears from the formulæ of citation, γέγραπται, καθὼς εἶπεν ὁ θεός, from the purpose of the quotations to establish a proof, and from the frequency of the references in exact or approximate quotations or historical allusions. (3) Christ expressly assigns authority to the OT in the words 'the Scripture cannot be broken' (Jn $10^{35}$); 'How then doth David in the Spirit call him Lord'? (Mt $22^{43}$). (4) The inspiration (see article INSPIRE, INSPIRATION in vol. ii.) of the Scriptures is expressly asserted in two passages (2 Ti $3^{16. 17}$, 2 P $1^{21}$) which, however, are not definite enough to yield a doctrine. (5) The quotations are often inexact, and are drawn from the LXX as well as the Hebrew (see article QUOTATIONS in vol. iv.). To suggest a provisional conclusion at this stage of the discussion, it is evident that, while the writers of the NT treat the whole of the OT as authoritative because inspired, yet the inaccuracy of many of the quotations as well as the use of the LXX show that, even if they would have formally accepted a theory of verbal inspiration, yet they were not limited and controlled by it practically; but this general impression must seek confirmation in a more detailed discussion.

(*a*) Not only does *Jesus Himself* quote from the OT frequently, but in His own language the modes of speech of the OT are recalled. It ministered counsel and comfort to His own personal experience (Mt $4^{4. 7. 10}$, Lk $4^{18}$, Mt $27^{46}$, Lk $23^{46}$). It was appealed to in His teaching (Mt $5^{21. 27. 31}$ $15^{4}$ $19^{19}$ $22^{32. 37}$). It was His weapon in controversy (Mt $9^{13}$ $15^{8}$ $21^{13. 33. 38. 43}$ $22^{44}$). OT history served to illustrate His work, as the serpent in the Wilderness, the preaching of Jonah, and the doom of the cities of the Plain. His use of the OT leads us to recognize it as a Divine revelation akin in spirit and purpose to His own. A few quotations there are which raise points of difficulty, as His use of the words of God to Moses in proof of the Resurrection (Mk $12^{26}$), His appeal to the taunt to the unjust judges as a justification of His claim to be the Son of God (Jn $10^{34}$), His assumption of the Davidic authorship of the 110th Psalm (Mk $12^{36}$), His allusion to Jonah's story as an illustration of His own resurrection (Mt $12^{40}$). There is good reason for regarding this last allusion as a gloss which has crept into the text; and the other quotations, it may be pointed out, are used in controversy as *ad hominem* arguments, on which it would be perilous to base any conclusions about Jesus' exegetical methods; yet in each case we can discern the connecting link of thought between the quotation and its use, which justifies it as neither arbitrary nor artificial. The allusion to Jonah and the reference of the 110th Psalm to David have been used to drag the authority of Christ into modern controversies of literary and historical criticism. Without comment on the reverence or the prudence of this procedure, this argument can be met from the critical standpoint without recourse to the objectionable explanation that He accommodated Himself to His hearers. For, *firstly*, no wise teacher raises avoidable disputes on questions which lie beyond the range of His purpose of teaching, but uses the popular language in all matters indifferent. It shows a strange lack of moral insight and spiritual discernment to assume that it was so important that the Jews should have correct views about historical and literary questions, that Jesus was bound to spend time and take pains to put them right on these before He could impart to them the gospel of His grace. He came to preach the gospel, and nothing else; and, even if He had held other views than His contemporaries, there was no need of His discussing them with His ignorant and prejudiced hearers. This whole argument is due to a confusion of the accidentals and the essentials of Divine revelation. *Secondly*, the present writer is prepared to go further, not for the sake of getting altogether rid of this argument, but in the interests of a true Christology. One cannot read the Gospels with an open mind without coming to the conclusion that no claim for the omniscience of Jesus is made, nay, even, facts are recorded which disprove such a claim; that His consciousness of the Father whom He came to reveal did not include a knowledge of all the facts of nature and history which can be ascertained by the exercise of ordinary human powers of observation and inference; that His perfect wisdom and absolute truth, His moral insight and spiritual discernment, had no relation whatever to the treatment of literary and historical problems; that, as not embraced in His message and mission, His views on all such questions were the opinions of His age, which He had learned in the same way as all His contemporaries. If the purpose of revelation is practical—the salvation of men by the self-sacrifice of God—then the more complete the reality of the Incarnation, the subjection of the Son to the limitations of humanity, the more thorough is the fulfilment of this purpose. It is as much in the interests of Christian faith as for the sake of intellectual liberty that the limitation of the knowledge of Jesus must be confidently affirmed. But, to return from this necessary digression to the main course of the discussion, the investigation of Jesus' use of the OT shows that He recognized the kinship of His own religious life to that of the saints of old; that in His teaching He assumed as the condition of the understanding of His words the knowledge of the Law and the Prophets; that in the moral standards He imposed the principles of the Jewish theocracy were applied and developed, and that His own historic mission was conceived in relation to a continuous and progressive historical activity of God in and by the chosen people; but, on the other hand, the manner of His use of the OT does not discharge us from the duty, far less forbid the attempt, to free by sound exegetical and critical methods the universal and permanent content of truth in the OT revelation from its local and temporary forms of expression.

(*b*) The distinctive use of the OT in the *Gospels* and the *Acts* is this, that the whole life of Christ is viewed as the fulfilment of prophecy. We observe differences of emphasis, according to the speaker or writer, the hearer or reader. Without entering into details, it may be said that when the writer or speaker is himself imbued with the spirit of Judaism, or addresses himself to Jews, then the argument from prophecy is more prominent than when Gentiles are being spoken or written to by one of broader sympathies. Generally, the OT is appealed to as authoritative by or for those whose religious life had already been developed by it. How large a place this conception fills in the minds of the historical writers of the NT will be best shown by a brief summary of the facts of Jesus' life, in which they find predictions realized. He is *born of a virgin* in *Bethlehem*, and as an infant returns from *Egypt* to *Nazareth.* His public ministry is *heralded* by John the Baptist. He begins His work in *Galilee* by claiming *the endowment of the Spirit*, and in Judæa by showing *His zeal for God's house.* His ministry in Northern Galilee brings *light to dark places.* In His acts of healing He *takes upon Himself the burden of men's infirmities.* As befits the *Servant of God*, He is *humble, silent, patient.* He is compelled by the stupidity of the people *to speak in parables.* He *enters Jerusalem in lowliness, seated on an ass.* He is greeted *as coming in the name of the Lord.* His message is *not believed*; He is *rejected by the leaders of the people*; He is *betrayed for money*; He is *forsaken by His followers*; He is *reckoned among transgressors*, and *hated without cause. His garments are divided; His bones are not broken*, although His *side is pierced*; He is not *suffered to be holden of death*; He is *exalted to God's right hand.* By His gift the Spirit is *poured forth upon all flesh.* Although in Him all *the nations of the earth are blessed*, yet against Him *the heathen rage, and the rulers are gathered together.* In His exaltation as *Son of the Highest* all *who scorn Him are put to shame.* He proves Himself a *light to the Gentiles*, and in *Him alone can the ruin of Jerusalem be repaired.*

There can be no doubt whatever that the OT revelation reaches its highest point in the hopes which Christ fulfils, for there is a vital, organic connexion between it and Him. The Messianic hope did in many of its most striking features anticipate the characteristics of His life and work. On the other hand, these writers treat the whole OT as prophetical, even when it is purely historical or didactical, and thus use some passages for quite another purpose than their original intention. Yet even in these cases the interpretation cannot be pronounced altogether arbitrary and artificial. For if Christ may be regarded as the end and reason for all God's historical activity in the Hebrew people, then its whole development may be conceived as a movement towards Him in whom the promises which had never found fulfilment, the hopes which had again and again been blighted with disappointment, the aspirations which neither moral performances nor ritual observances could satisfy, all found their consummation,—then the spiritual experiences of God's saints of old may be viewed as an anticipation of the life hid with Christ in God, and the sufferings for righteousness' sake of God's witnesses to an unbelieving people as a participation in the Cross of the Just and Holy One. These writers, therefore, were entitled to assume the unity of the life of God's Anointed with the history of His chosen people, the prophetical character of its great personalities and the typical significance of its main institutions, although it must be acknowledged that they laid stress on minor details which may be adequately accounted for as coincidences, and need not be regarded, as they regarded them, as immediate prophecies. It has sometimes been assumed that these coincidences are not to be explained by similar conditions and experiences, due to the unity of the principle underlying the whole development of religion and revelation, which not only ends but is summed up in Christ, but must be accepted as Divine harmonies. To the mind of the present writer at least such a view gives an artificiality to, and hides the reality of, the connexion of Christ and the OT. There are cases, however (Mt $27^{9.10}$, Ac $2^{30}$), where this connexion is imposed rather than discovered. Again, to note briefly the conclusion to which this part of the investigation leads, we are constrained to recognize the continuity of the revelation of the OT and the NT; and, on the other hand, that the writers of the NT tend to regard the parallelism as more exact than it actually is, owing to their peculiar method of exegesis in treating passages apart from, even in spite of, their historical setting. It need not surprise us to find that the men who were fitted by the Spirit to be both receptive and communicative of the truth as it is in Jesus were lacking in scientific method and historical insight. Their inspiration did not raise them above their times in these respects, and consequently we must, on the one hand, form such a conception of revelation as admits such limitations, and, on the other, maintain that the OT must be interpreted by the grammatical and historical methods of a scientific criticism, unhindered and undisturbed by appeals to the usages of NT writers.

(*c*) In *St. Paul's Epistles* the doctrinal aspects of the OT are more prominent. The frequency of his quotations depends on the subject he is dealing with, and the destination of the letter. Generally speaking, he appeals to the OT most frequently when he is asserting the independence of Christianity against Judaistic objections, and not when he is developing its unique contents. His so-called *Rabbinisms* (1 Co $10^{1-4}$, 2 Co $3^{13}$, Gal $3^{16}$ $4^{21-31}$) need not excite any surprise and cause any difficulty: that they are so few in number is a testimony to his mental vigour and spiritual discernment. Sometimes he does give to a quotation an application which the context does not justify (Ro $9^{25.26}$ $11^{9.10}$ $12^{19}$, 1 Co $9^{9}$ $14^{21}$ $15^{27}$, Gal $3^{13}$). Even in his normal use the OT language sometimes, on the one hand, obscures the Christian conception, and, on the other hand, his Christian conception transforms the meaning of the OT words. Sometimes his use gives a harder, at other times a more gracious, tone to the passages quoted than they have in their own context. The language of the OT is not adequate for his gospel, the essential inspiration of which we may assert and maintain without committing ourselves to an acceptance of his exegetical methods. The occasion and the purpose of the *Epistle to the Hebrews* explain the characteristically Jewish use of the OT. Sentences are taken without any regard to context; stress is laid on single words; allegorical explanations are given of historical references. This reading of the New Faith into the Old does violence to the historical significance of the one and the Divine originality of the other. The *Apocalypse* is steeped in the OT imagery, and applies the Messianic prophecies to the Second Advent. Without any closer examination of the other NT writings, enough evidence has already been produced to justify the conclusion that in every part the NT treats the OT as a Divine revelation, but that the exegetical methods of the NT writers are such as to forbid our basing on their use of the OT any dogmatic theory of verbal inspiration.

3. *The NT doctrine of Revelation.*—Although the NT recognizes the Divine revelation in the OT, it does not limit God's manifestation of Himself to the Hebrew history and literature. The Prologue to St. John's Gospel takes up the OT conception of the Divine *Word*, *Wisdom*, or *Spirit* in its doctrine of the *Logos*, and teaches a permanent and universal revelation in nature and in man as well as in the history culminating in Christ. As significant is St. Paul's teaching regarding the witness of nature to God, in his speech at Lystra (Ac $14^{15-17}$); regarding man's affinity to God, in his speech at Athens (Ac $17^{22-31}$); regarding the wilful ignorance of God, to which he traces the religious degradation and the moral depravity of the Gentiles, and the testimony borne to God by conscience, in his Epistle to the Romans ($1^{18-32}$ $2^{14-16}$); and regarding the Divine purpose in the pre-Christian stage in human history, in that to the Galatians ($4^{1-9}$). A study of the science of Comparative Religion does not contradict, but confirms, this doctrine of a permanent and universal revelation in which OT and NT agree. In many religions we find the higher elements suppressed by the lower, and in only a few the higher elements asserting themselves over the lower. Even in the corrupt and superstitious paganism with which Christianity in its earliest days came in contact, there was in its philosophical schools an approach to an ethical monotheism which, imperfect as it was, proved to some men a tutor to lead them to Christ.

As regards the NT doctrine of the OT revelation, enough has been said in the preceding paragraph; we must now consider what it teaches about the origin and the method of the Christian revelation. Jesus Christ is pre-eminently the revealer of the Father; this function He claims for Himself (Mt $11^{27}$, Jn $17^{26}$), and it is accorded to Him by St. Paul, St. John, the writer to the Hebrews (Jn $1^{18}$, Col $1^{15}$, He $1^{1-3}$). Yet it is only by the Spirit of God that men are enabled to recognize in Him the Son of God (Mt $16^{17}$, Gal $1^{15}$). To know God in Christ is to receive a revelation which transforms all things, so that self and world alike appear as a new creation (2 Co $5^{17}$). An interesting evidence of St. Paul's consciousness that the Christian revelation was both in continuity with and in contrast to the older revelation, is his use of the word 'mystery.' The Divine purpose which has hitherto been concealed is now revealed (Ro $11^{25}$ $16^{25}$, 1 Co $2^{7}$, Eph $1^{9}$ $3^{3.\,4}$ $5^{32}$ $6^{19}$, Col $1^{26}$ $2^{2}$ $4^{3}$). A completion of the old revelation (Mt $5^{17}$, Gal $3^{24}$ $4^{4}$, Jn $5^{38}$), the new revelation can claim permanent validity, as it will not be superseded by any other (Mt $24^{35}$). On the other hand, the comprehension of the perfect revelation by man is imperfect relatively to the full and clear vision of Christ, which is the Christian's hope for the hereafter (1 Co $13^{12}$, 1 Jn $3^{2}$): Christ's consciousness of perfect knowledge of, love for, and obedience to the Father is explained only by the confession of His essential unity with the Father. The promise of Jesus to His disciples, that the Spirit should be given to them, was fulfilled at Pentecost; and in the outpouring of the Spirit on that day St. Peter was bold enough to see the fulfilment of Joel's prophecy of a universal prophetic inspiration (Ac $2^{17.\,18}$). Both in the *Acts* and in *St. Paul's Epistles* it is assumed that all believers are inspired; in the exercise of their charisms, spiritual gifts, the presence and power of the Spirit in them is revealed. But for the instruction and government of the Church (see art. CHURCH in vol. i.) it was believed that Apostles and Prophets possessed an authoritative inspiration. The Apostles had seen the Lord, and were witnesses to the Resurrection (Lk $24^{48}$, Ac $1^{8.\,22}$ $2^{32}$, 1 Co $9^{1}$). They showed the signs of an Apostle (1 Co $9^{2}$, 2 Co $12^{12}$), and they had received a call from God (1 Co $12^{28}$, Eph $4^{11}$). They were endowed as well as the Prophets with that higher energy of the Spirit which qualified them for special revelations (see articles APOSTLE in vol. i. and PROPHET IN NT in vol. iv.). Most instructive in this respect are the writings of St. Paul, as to defend the truth of his gospel it was needful for him to establish his claims as an Apostle. He asserts his independence of human instruction and his reception of his gospel by Divine revelation (Gal $1^{11-24}$). In his own instructions to the Churches which he had founded he distinguishes between the commandments of the Lord and his own judgment (1 Co $7^{25.\,40}$), but expresses the confidence that even in the exercise of this he has the Spirit of God. He testifies that, in a state of ecstasy, he was transported to the third heaven and heard unspeakable words, unlawful to utter (2 Co $12^{2.\,3}$). Not only did Jesus appear to him on the way to Damascus (Ac $9^{17}$, 1 Co $15^{8}$), but on other occasions also did He come and speak to him in trance or vision (Ac $18^{9}$ $22^{17}$ $26^{16}$). At Troas he was guided to cross to Macedonia by a vision in the night (Ac $16^{9}$). The angel of God conveyed an assurance of safety to him (Ac $27^{23}$). St. Peter, too, was taught his duty towards the Gentiles in a vision during a trance (Ac $10^{10}$). An angel appeared to Mary in a vision (Lk $1^{26-38}$), and to Joseph in a dream (Mt $1^{20-23}$). The visions in the Book of Revelation may be, as is common in Apocalyptic literature, a literary device, but there may have been some basis for them in unusual psychic conditions. Of such mental states as trance, vision, dream as organs of revelation, we must beware of judging by our modern standards. For us such means of Divine communication may seem less credible than inward intuition, but even to a St. Paul these methods of revelation seemed significant and valuable. (The articles on DREAM in vol. i. and TRANCE and VISION in vol. iv. may with advantage be consulted). In closing this section of the article a few general considerations may be offered. The Prophet, or Apostle, or even Christ Himself, is confident that God is revealing His mind and will to him, but distinguishes God's words from his own. With the Prophet, it would seem, the inspiration was not constant; his whole personality did not become the permanent organ of the Spirit. In the Apostle the spiritual possession is more constant and complete. He may still distinguish his own opinions from his Lord's commands, but his inspiration is derived from an intimate personal union and communion with the living Christ Himself. As the natural life has been more completely transformed by the supernatural, their contrast is less evident than in the prophetic consciousness. In Christ the union of

God and man is so complete, that, so to speak, the absolute quantity of the inspiration guarantees the perfect quality of the revelation. There is, therefore, no uniformity in the intensity of the inspiration or the sufficiency of the revelation in the Holy Scriptures; but we must distinguish degrees of the one as we recognize varieties of the other. In the OT the prophetic consciousness exhibits revelation at its highest; the spirit of devotion as expressed in the Psalms may be reckoned nearest to this; then we may perhaps place the meditations in the Wisdom literature on the problems of life and duty; and, lastly, come the historical records, inspired in so far as they regard the history as the development of God's purpose and the fulfilment of His promises. The Apostolic interpretation varies in the fulness of the understanding of the mind of Christ, dependent on the closeness of the fellowship with the life of Christ, in whom revelation and inspiration alike culminate. The OT increases as a revelation as it approaches Him, and the NT varies as a revelation as it receives more or less of His Spirit.

iv. THE EVIDENCE OF REVELATION.—1. *Evidence of the Bearers of Revelation.*—The first line of evidence is to be found in what has just been mentioned at the close of the previous section—the consciousness of the bearers of the revelation. They bear witness that they are not speaking of themselves, but that God is communicating to them what they are declaring to others. The truth of the reality of the revelation, and the sincerity of its organs,—these two are not the same, for a man professing to communicate a revelation might be a deceiver or self-deceived,—cannot be proved by any outward attestation, but only by the moral and spiritual quality of the revelation, and by the personal character it forms in the bearer. The fulfilment of prophecy is not, unless in exceptional circumstances, a test that can be immediately applied, and the performance of miracles does not afford a decisive criterion, as the natural may be made to appear as supernatural. But these two evidences are quite out of court for us. For, where the character of the bearer and the content of the revelation do not inspire confidence, denial that any real prediction has been made, or any actual miracle has taken place, cannot be disproved. If at one time prophecy and miracle were relied on as attesting a revelation, such an argument is worthless at the present day. For, on the one hand, the more critical attitude towards the records of revelation which is becoming more general forbids that unquestioning belief that predictions were made and that miracles did happen which was once common; and it is being more clearly recognized, on the other hand, that a Divine revelation must be able to commend itself morally and spiritually to the conscience and reason of mankind, and that a revelation which could not so commend itself could never be accepted on any external evidence without such an abdication of reason and conscience as would involve a far more serious injury and wrong to the moral and spiritual nature of man than could be compensated for by any such revelation.

2. *Evidence of the Literature of Revelation.*—But, when we get to this position that the evidence of revelation is in the quality of its contents and the character of its bearers, we, to whom this revelation has not come at first hand, but has been transmitted by a literature, have to ask this further question: Is the literature trustworthy in its testimony to the consciousness and character of these bearers and to the contents of this revelation? This is the point at which the history of the formation of the *Canon* of the OT and NT forces itself on our attention. This story has already been told in previous articles, and need not be told again; but one fact deserves special notice, that it was not by formal decree of any ecclesiastical authority that certain writings were selected as sacred, recognized as inspired, and accepted as authoritative for faith and life; but this was brought about by their use in worship and for edification. We need not claim an infallible judgment for either the Jewish or the Christian Church, but what must be insisted on is that it was the religious consciousness which was the court of appeal with regard to the writings to be treated as the literature of revelation. The importance of such a literature cannot be overestimated. Only if God had revealed Himself uniformly to all mankind, would there be no need for such a literature. Reason has already been shown why along with a general revelation we may believe in a special. To perpetuate and to diffuse this special revelation, limited both spatially and temporally, the written record was necessary. Jesus Christ would be incomprehensible without the record of the revelation which led up to Him, and His grace and truth would be inaccessible to the mind and heart of mankind without the report of the revelation realized in and proceeding from Him. Yet a difference between the importance of the two Testaments must, in view of the modern critical position, be clearly recognized and frankly explained. What were the stages and phases, the features and factors, of revelation in the OT is an interesting and important question for our understanding of the OT; but it does not in the slightest degree affect the historical reality of Jesus Christ. Not the view of the OT which most unquestioningly accepts as historical all its narratives and all the traditional opinions about authorship and date of the writings makes Christ most credible, but that which makes to us most intelligible the progress of revelation towards Him, and the fulfilment of its promise in Him. Accordingly, we can, without troubling or bewildering our faith with a task for which it is not competent, leave to a reverent scholarship, which makes neither ultra-supernatural nor anti-supernatural assumptions, all historical and literary questions regarding the OT. The NT, however, holds a much more immediate and vital relation to the revelation in Christ, and from Him through His witnesses. If the substantial historicity of the Gospels and the Acts cannot be maintained, if the image of the Person of Christ presented there is mainly a work of fiction and not a copy of fact, if Jesus did not really so impress and influence men as He is represented to have done, if the Apostles who have undertaken to interpret to us their experience of His grace ascribed to His Spirit what was due to their heredity, individuality, or environment, then the Christian revelation must lose so much of its contents as to affect its character. If, for instance, a filial consciousness towards God and a fraternal consciousness towards mankind was all that Jesus revealed, if He put Himself in no way into relation to the sin of mankind to save men from its guilt and curse, then undoubtedly Christianity becomes a religion of illumination, and not of redemption. But if the historical character of the NT as the record and report of the life and work of Christ, and the interpretation of the experience wrought by His spirit, is more necessary to Christian faith, it can be maintained as that of many parts of the OT cannot. We have more nearly contemporary evidence of the existence and the acceptance as authoritative of the NT writings than for any of the OT. The contents of many portions of the NT are self-evidencing to reason and conscience as revelation, as many portions of the OT cannot be

said to be. The character of Christ, the existence of the Church, the experience of St. Paul,—all these are proofs of the reality of the Christian revelation as presented in the NT such as can meet doubt and help faith. That the NT can be accepted as a true record and a faithful interpretation of the revelation in Christ, is a conclusion which the best scholarship allows and Christian faith claims.

3. *Evidence of Experience.*—No conclusion of scholarship on so difficult and delicate a problem as the date, authorship, historical accuracy, and theological authority of these writings can compel faith. Scholarship, as honest and as competent as that which is found in the Christian Churches, has not felt this compulsion, and has been able to maintain an opposite conclusion. For this conclusion depends not only on the outward data, but on the inward attitude with which the data are approached. If, through the Person and Teaching and Work of Christ, God does not here and now draw near to a man, make Himself known to him, meet his greatest need, and bring him his highest good, neither the OT nor the NT can be proved to him the record and the interpretation of a Divine revelation. He might assent intellectually to the whole process of argument, but a mere assent to the claims of the Holy Scriptures has no religious value or significance. The evidence of revelation is a present experience, the impression the Holy Scriptures make, and the influence they wield, in reproducing in men the same relation to God as was perfectly realized by Christ, and is being progressively realized in men by the presence and power of the Holy Spirit. The intellectual process cannot be ignored, and the spiritual experience alone recognized. If it were proved to a man's reason that the NT is not a true book, he might find an æsthetic gratification, but he could not get a spiritual satisfaction in the life and work of Christ. It will enlarge and strengthen a man's faith, if he not only yields himself to the impression Christ makes on him, and the influence He gains over him, when the NT is read and studied on the assumption that it is true, but if he also sees what evidence there is to justify that assumption. The evidence may at first not go beyond the more probable, or the less improbable, but that is itself enough to justify a man, under the pressure of his practical necessities, in putting Christ to the proof, with all honesty and sincerity, whether He is indeed able to save to the uttermost all who come unto God through Him. The results in personal experience and character will in most cases raise the probability to a certainty, and the man will be able to say that he knows whom he has believed, and is persuaded that He is able to be to all who trust Him all that the NT represents Him as being.

4. *Reception of the Divine Revelation.*—It is with this proving of Christ's grace that the present evidence of Divine Revelation must begin. But the acceptance of Christ as from God will so change the mental attitude, the moral disposition, the spiritual capacity, that a personal apprehension, appreciation, and appropriation of the entire revelation of God in the Holy Scriptures will become increasingly possible. There may remain incidents incredible and doctrines unintelligible, and no Christian man is required to do violence either to conscience or to reason by forcing himself to believe anything which does not evidence itself to him as from God. On the one hand, a large liberty of reserve should be claimed, and, on the other, a wide tolerance of difference should be shown. But no man who has found God in Christ can treat with indifference any element in the Christian revelation. He must feel that his insensibility to impression from or influence by any part of the Holy Scriptures is his own spiritual loss, the narrowing and the impoverishing of his experience; and he should so strive to widen his intelligence and deepen his sympathy by fuller submission to the Spirit of truth and love in Christ, that he will be able at last to secure and rejoice in the whole counsel of God, all the truth as it is in Jesus. Only by this receptive and responsive attitude can a man become the possessor of the Divine revelation as his personal treasure. As in olden times God revealed Himself in outward signs and sounds, so in the Holy Scriptures, read with intelligence, reverence, aspiration, does He still reveal Himself. Not a distant but a present, not an indifferent but an interested, not an indolent but an active Father meets us in Christ by the Spirit, and deals with us here and now. The significance and value of the old revelation is that it is the medium of an ever new revelation. God Himself proves that He spake and wrought of old by speaking and working in us now His own good will and pleasure, even our salvation. Every Christian man should be an inspired man, because the Spirit is in Christ given to all men according to their faith; and, in this experience of the Spirit, God is really revealing Himself. But inasmuch as this revelation comes from this inspiration, and this inspiration is conditioned by faith in Christ's grace, and that faith is not found apart from a knowledge of the Gospel as contained in the Holy Scriptures, this continuous revelation and universal inspiration in Christ is not a rival to or substitute for the revelation and inspiration of the Holy Scriptures, as the former is dependent on and controlled by the latter. We know that God reveals Himself in us only as we know the revelation of the Father in the Son; but to the testimony of the writers of the Scriptures to their own authority and the witness of the Church to the worth of these Scriptures for its faith and life there must be added, to produce that perfect confidence in God's revelation which it demands and deserves, the experience in the individual soul of God's presence and power in His Son and by His Spirit.

*Summary.*—Let us sum up in a few words the arguments of this article. Man is by necessity of his nature religious. Religion implies revelation; man's approach to God is in response to God's approach to man. As religion is, so is revelation universal; but its quality varies with human capacity and development. It is in accord with God's method that He should through one nation bless all mankind. In the history of the Hebrew people there can be traced a progressive revelation, the record of which is in the OT. This culminates in Christ, in whom the ideal of religion is realized, and the perfect revelation is given. To secure full historic reality to this revelation, the image of His person and the influence of His work must be perpetuated and diffused, as is done by means of the NT. The Holy Scriptures as the literature of revelation offer us a doctrine of its range, method, and purpose. The bearers of the revelation bear a witness to their own qualifications and authority, which is confirmed both by their characters and the contents of their message. This evidence is further strengthened by the recognition of the worth of the OT in the Jewish Church and of the NT in the Christian Church. But the full evidence of revelation is not possessed until its purpose has been fulfilled and its effect realized in the experience of the Christian, saved from sin and death and doom by the love of the Father in the grace of the Son through the fellowship of the Holy Spirit.

Literature.—The special articles referred to may be consulted for the Literature relating to their respective subjects. For the more general literature, the note at the end of the article Bible in vol. i. may be referred to. To the books there mentioned may be added Caird's, Pfleiderer's, and Sabatier's *Philosophy of Religion*; Fairbairn's *The Philosophy of the Christian Religion*; and Illingworth's *Reason and Revelation*. Bruce's *Apologetics* deals with many of the topics touched on, and his *Chief End of Revelation* is still worth consulting. Herrmann's *Communion of the Christian with God* offers an original and suggestive treatment of the subject of Revelation.

Alfred E. Garvie.

**THEOCRACY.**—The terms 'theocracy' and 'theocratic' have been used somewhat freely in connexion with the history of Israel, but it is not altogether easy to determine with precision what ideas should be attached to them. It may seem that, if these words are to denote an actual constitution of human society, they must imply the absorption of the State in the Church, or at least the supremacy of the Church over the State. When applied, as they are, to the form and aims of the mediæval Papacy, they have this meaning; and so taken they would be true only of the period, or periods, of Jewish history when the people were under a hierarchy, with the high priest at its head. Wellhausen and other critics of his school do, in fact, restrict the notion of the Theocracy thus, and consequently hold, in accordance with their view of the documents, that it was realized only after the Exile. The question of the best use of the term must not, however, be identified with that of the date of the Priestly Code. Readers of the Bible, generally, taking the Pentateuch as it stands, and believing the constitution therein described to have been given and actually established by Moses, have regarded those early days as ideal ones for the Theocracy. But it may be doubted whether they have derived the impression that its essence lay in priestly rule, or whether this is in reality suggested in the Bible; while a more elastic conception must certainly be formed if justice is to be done to the teaching of the OT as a whole.

i. *The use of the term by Josephus.*—The term 'theocracy' was coined by Josephus on the model of others expressive of various kinds of political constitution, in order to explain to Gentile readers the distinctive characteristics of the national life of Israel. He uses it but once, and then with an apology. In *c. Ap.* ii. 16, after referring to differences between States in respect to the seat of power—a single sovereign, a few, the multitude—he proceeds: *ὁ δ' ἡμέτερος νομοθέτης εἰς μὲν τούτων οὐδοτιοῦν ἀπεῖδεν, ὡς δ' ἄν τις εἴποι βιασάμενος τὸν λόγον, θεοκρατίαν ἀπέδειξε τὸ πολίτευμα, θεῷ τὴν ἀρχὴν καὶ τὸ κράτος ἀναθείς.* 'Our lawgiver had an eye to none of these; but, as one might say, using a strained expression, he set forth the national polity as a theocracy, referring the rule and might to God.' As Josephus introduced the term, it may be worth while to consider a little more fully what he intended to convey by it; and this may help us to clear our own minds. There is the more reason for doing so, because statements in regard to his meaning, which the present writer believes to be in different ways misleading, have been made by such writers as Stanley, *Jewish Church*, Lecture 18 *init.*, and Wellhausen, *Proleg. to Hist. of Israel*, Eng. tr. p. 411, 3rd German ed. i. p. 436.

In the sequel to the words just quoted, Josephus says, by way of explanation or expansion of them, that Moses led the Israelites to recognize God as the source both of the good things bestowed on all mankind, and of deliverances granted to themselves in their distresses in answer to their prayers; that to the whole people he imparted a knowledge of God such as at most a philosopher here and there among other nations had attained to; and that he gave them Divine laws and customs to mould and train their national character.—A broader or more unexceptionable statement as to the special relation of the true God to Israel as their ruler, and of their relation to Him as His subjects, it would be difficult to imagine.



In other places, however, Josephus describes the Mosaic constitution as an 'aristocracy,' connecting this with the view that it is also a theocracy, which he indicates without using the term. Thus in his version of Moses' address to the people at the close of his life,—in which he gives more prominence, so far as provision for government was concerned, to the judges who were to be appointed in all their gates, of whom Moses had spoken (Dt $16^{18}$ $1^{15f.}$; cf. *Ant.* IV. viii. 14), than to the priests,—he makes Moses say, 'An aristocracy is best, and the life in harmony therewith; let not desire for another polity take hold of you, but cherish this one, and having the laws as your masters, do all things according to them; for it suffices to have God for your ruler' (*Ant.* IV. viii. 17). Later on he explains Samuel's grief at the people's demand for a king by his hatred of kings and conviction that an aristocracy is Divine, and that it makes those happy who have it for their form of polity (*Ant.* VI. iii. 3). Once more, of the Return from Exile he writes that those who then settled in Jerusalem adopted 'an aristocratic constitution with an oligarchy, for,' he adds, 'the chief priests were at the head of affairs till the descendants of the Hasmonæan became kings' (*Ant.* XI. iv. 8). See, further, art. Religion of Israel, II. iii. 1.

It is to be observed that Josephus lays no stress on the 'holiness,' either official or personal, of the ruling class, as he would have done if he had held the view attributed to him by Wellhausen; and in the last passage cited he even distinguishes the 'oligarchy' of priests from that 'aristocracy' which he regards as so desirable. It appears that for him the *theocratic* character of the system lay, not in its formal institutions but in the fact that they were of a kind to throw much on the people themselves. There was no excessively eminent human personage to intercept the regards that should be turned on God alone. Men were to submit to the laws because they had received them from God, and to depend on His guidance and protection—which included, no doubt, the raising up of leaders for times of special need.

ii. We pass to the actual history of the belief in Jehovah's kingship over Israel. (*a*) *The connexion of the belief with Semitic religious ideas.*—This was one of those conceptions derived from the general stock of Semitic religious ideas, which in Israel came to be immeasurably refined and exalted. In the OT itself we have evidence that in other instances also the tribal or national god was regarded as the king of the tribe or nation. In early times it was the specific duty of the chieftain or king to lead in war, so that the notion of chieftainship or kingship is itself involved in the belief implied in the language of Jephthah (Jg $11^{24}$) that the god fought for his people, and won and held the territories in which they dwelt (cf. 1 S $26^{19}$, Ru $1^{14f.}$, and the phrase in Is $10^{10}$ 'the kingdoms of the idols'). For evidence from other sources, see W. R. Smith, *RS*$^1$ 66 f.

(*b*) *The view attributed to Gideon and to Samuel that the establishment of an earthly kingship implied disloyalty to Jehovah.*—In two passages in OT the proposal to establish an earthly monarchy is treated as an infringement of Jehovah's rights, Jg $8^{23}$ and 1 S 8 with $12^{12}$. It will be necessary that we should discuss briefly the historical value of these notices. And, first, a few words as to the documents.

There is a large amount of agreement among critics to the effect that in the Book of Judges the work may be traced of a compiler of the age of Deuteronomy, *i.e.* the latter period of the Jewish kingdom, who has provided a framework into which he has fitted narratives, and perhaps a collection of narratives, of an earlier age. Some touches, also, are assigned to a post-exilic editor. The question whether Gideon's refusal of the kingship is a trait introduced by one of the later hands will have to be considered in connexion with the similar view of human monarchy appearing in 1 Samuel. In the portion of that book which relates to the choice of Saul, two accounts are combined which give distinct, and in some respects differing, views of the transaction. That one in which the desire for a king is represented as an act of disloyalty to Jehovah is generally regarded as the later of the two. Wellhausen refers it, chiefly because of its attitude on this point, to the exilic or post-exilic time, when the monarchy had been overthrown and the government was in the hands of the chief priests (*Prolegomena*, Eng. tr. pp. 249, 253–6, and 3rd German ed. i. pp. 260, 265–8). The statement in regard to Gideon in Jg $8^{23}$ he necessarily supposes to have been introduced at the same period (*ib.* Eng. tr. p. 239, and 3rd Germ. ed. p. 249). Other competent critics, however, point out marked affinities between the document embodied in 1 Samuel, which is now in question, and E of the Pentateuch (Budde, *ZATW* p. 230 f.; Driver, *LOT*$^{6}$ p. 177 f.); and in the connexion of this document with the Northern Kingdom is to be found, according to Budde, the true explanation of its low estimate of the monarchy (*ib.* pp. 235, 236). He accounts for the words of Gideon in like manner ('Richter' in *Kurzer Handcom. in loc.*, and *Einleit.* lix f.). If we must choose between these views, the latter is certainly the more reasonable. It is a pure figment of the imagination, and opposed to all the evidence which we possess, to suppose that, under the constitution established after the Exile, men learned to depreciate the monarchy. On the contrary, we know that the hope of its restoration was still cherished; and, although there was a period in which this hope died down, there is no sign that any other ideal was formed of a nature to exclude it. Indeed, if such had been the case, its revival, without leaving any trace of a struggle between it and other aspirations, would have been well-nigh impossible. There were, on the other hand, no sacred associations with any one of the successive dynasties in the Northern Kingdom, and prophets had been brought into far more frequent and sterner conflict with individual kings. It would be more conceivable that here religious men should have become convinced of an inherent incompatibility between human and Divine sovereignty. But evidence is wanting that such was the case. [In Hos $13^{10}$ no opposition to kingship on principle is implied. With regard to Hos $10^{9}$, see G. A. Smith in *Expositor's Bible*, p. 288, n. 1.]

The admission that the narrative of Gideon's judgeship may not have been committed to writing till long after the events, and that the document used in 1 Samuel with which we are concerned may probably have been composed in the latter part of the 9th or even in the 8th cent. B.C. (on date of E, see Driver, *LOT*$^{6}$ p. 123), does not make it unsuitable for us to ask whether the view respecting the institution of monarchy which is found in them may not be due to a sound tradition. That view does not seem to be out of harmony with the character of the early age to which the narratives refer, and with natural tendencies of the human mind. And its appearance merely in two isolated instances, which cannot be shown to have anything in common with the experience and feeling of better known periods of Israelite history, is sufficient to suggest that it is a survival. We do not indeed know of the existence outside of Israel of the same view. But it would surely be quite in accordance with the relations supposed to exist between the god and his worshippers (see W. R. Smith, *RS*, Lect. 2) that a tribe or group of tribes which adhered to its primitive organization, or want of organization, should insist that its god was its king, contrasting itself in this respect with neighbouring nations that had adopted monarchy; or even that the notion of the permanent chiefship or kingship of the god should have been evolved before that of permanent human kingship. And, when a movement arose to substitute a monarchy for the older and looser constitution of society, it would be natural that in some quarters it should meet with opposition from a spirit of conservatism, which would call religious beliefs to its aid. We shall, moreover, be justified in regarding the fact that we have an example of this in Israel, though not elsewhere, as due to a peculiar intensity of religious feeling and faithfulness to the God whom they acknowledged, by which not the whole people but individuals amongst them were already distinguished.

(c) *The Theocracy subsequent to the establishment of the Monarchy.*—But while there is reason to think that belief in Jehovah's kingship over Israel existed before the regular establishment of an earthly monarchy, and that it afforded a ground with some for objecting to this institution, the sense of the Divine sovereignty over Israel was not in the event impaired by this change of national polity. It is a mistake to speak of the transition to this new period as 'the close of the Theocracy' (so Stanley does, *Jewish Church*, Lect. 18 *init.*). The same work in which the document that describes resistance to the introduction of monarchy is embedded, has in its second book set forth Jehovah's covenant with David and his descendants in terms which virtually make the reigning prince of this house the earthly vicegerent and representative of the heavenly King, under whose control he still remains (2 S $7^{1-17}$). Some other passages, which show how the relation of the king to God was regarded, are 2 K $11^{17}$ $23^{3.4}$, Ps $89^{27}$, Neh $13^{26}$, and even as to the Northern Kingdom 1 K $14^{14}$. In Dt $17^{14-20}$ we have 'the law of the kingdom' set forth in subjection to the principle of the Theocracy (cf. Driver, *LOT*$^{6}$ p. 92). The remarkable expression in 2 Ch $13^{8}$ should also be particularly noticed:—'the kingdom of Jehovah in the hand of the sons of David'; the lateness of the work in which it occurs makes it the more important. The use of the title King for God belongs especially to the Prophets and Psalms. Some instances in which God is called King of Israel, or in which His being so is most directly implied, are of the times of the Monarchy or the first part of the Exile, and occur in writers to whom, beyond question, the Divine sanctions of the earthly kingdom were no unfamiliar thought (Zeph $3^{15}$, Ps $48^{2}$ $89^{18}$ [AV and RVm], Is $33^{22}$, Jer $8^{19}$). Passages of a later date are Is $43^{15}$ $44^{6}$. It is to be added that, where God is spoken of simply as King, or as King over all the earth, the special relation of Israel to God may be, and in some cases certainly is, present to the writer's mind, the thought being that Jehovah, who has made Zion His favoured seat, from His capital exercises a world-wide dominion (Zec $14^{9.16.17}$, Jer $10^{10}$ $48^{15}$ $51^{57}$, Ps $95^{3}$ $98^{6}$ $145^{1}$). Where individuals with special devotion address God as their King, it is impossible to say always whether they held that the privilege and the power to do so were consequences of their membership in the chosen people; but sometimes they seem to have recognized this (Ps $5^{2}$ $44^{4}$ $68^{24}$ $74^{12}$).

In conclusion, we may say that if we are to be guided by OT thought and language, as assuredly we ought to be, in determining the meaning to be given to the term *theocracy*, it must be employed to designate, not any one of the forms of government under which the Israelites lived, but a great conviction. It will describe the faith that God exercised a special and effective rule over Israel by blessings, punishments, deliverances, by prophets, whom He sent to instruct them, and the visitations of His providence, throughout all the stages of their chequered history. And in that Kingdom of Heaven, of which our Lord spake so much, the Theocracy found its enlargement and fulfilment.

V. H. STANTON.

## HEBREWS, GOSPEL ACCORDING TO THE.—

Introduction.
- i. Patristic and other evidence of existence.
  1. Jerome.
  2. Epiphanius.
  3. Eusebius (including Hegesippus).
  4. Clement of Alexandria, and Origen.
  5. Muratorian Canon (silent), Irenæus, Papias, Ignatius.
  6. Nicephorus, and a minuscule codex of 9th or 10th cent.
- ii. Extant fragments.
- iii. Theories of origin and character.

Literature.

*Introduction.*—Under the designation 'according to the Hebrews' several Church Fathers, from the 2nd to the 5th cent., speak of a Gospel which existed in their day, though to Greek-speaking Christians known but vaguely, if at all. Many of the statements made with regard to it are of ambiguous meaning, as if the writers themselves were but imperfectly acquainted with the subject; and hence it is little wonder if the most divergent theories have been held about it. Was the Gospel according to the Hebrews a particular book, or was it a type of tradition which was embodied in several different books? Did it exist in Greek as well as in a Semitic tongue? and was the Hebrew a translation from Greek, or the original? Was it a source of the canonical Gospels or derived from them, or quite independent of, and parallel to, them? In the absence of any certain answer to these questions, some of which may never be finally disposed of, the Gospel according to the Hebrews has been made to fill a place in connexion with each successive theory of the origin of the Gospels; some, as Lessing, and more recently Hilgenfeld, regarding it as the primary root of the whole of the Gospel literature; the Tübingen school seeing in it the earliest written expression of the Jewish-Christian position; while others hold that it was never important, and that, while it may have contained some true reminiscences, its tradition on the whole was secondary and derived. Recent discussions, however, by Hilgenfeld,* Zahn,† Handmann,‡ Harnack,§ and Nicholson,‖ have rendered the subject less shadowy. While there is still much difference of opinion on special points, the Gospel according to the Hebrews is coming into view as it actually existed in the early centuries.

i. Patristic and other evidence of existence.—1. More facts are to be learned on the subject from *Jerome* than from any other Father; and it is best to begin with what he tells us, referring afterwards to the statements before him and after him. What is here said about Jerome is based on the admirable discussion by Zahn, in which the passages are collected.

Jerome went twice to the East. He lived 374–379 a hermit life at Chalcis in Northern Syria, and in 385 he was at Antioch on his way to Palestine, to spend the rest of his life in the monastery he founded at Bethlehem. He was much in contact with Syrian Christians, who helped him to learn Hebrew, and told him many interesting things. In particular, he gathered from them much information as to the Gospel they used. This he describes by various phrases which at first sight seem somewhat inconsistent with each other. At one time he calls it 'the Hebrew Gospel'; at others, and most frequently, 'the Gospel according to the Hebrews' (*juxta* or *secundum Hebræos*). These words may be a description, not a title, and do not of themselves require us to think of a written work; they might refer to the Evangelical tradition current in the East, which might exist in more than one form. Jerome frequently says that the Nazarenes use this Gospel, or are in the habit of reading it. If the 'Nazarenes' of Jerome were a particular sect, their Gospel would be a particular book. But the name is more probably, in most of the passages where he uses it, a general one for the Jewish Christians of the East; so that the Gospel they used might have various forms. In one passage (*ad* Mt 12[13]; No. 8¶) Jerome says the Nazarenes and the Ebionites used this Gospel. Here he must be held to be speaking very loosely. There were Ebionites who were, to the eye of the Churchman, heretics, and they had a Gospel of heretical tendency of which fragments are preserved, though not by Jerome. But the term 'Ebionite' was also used as a general designation of the Christians of Palestine who kept up a Jewish form of belief in Christ. It is not therefore to be inferred from this expression of Jerome that he identified the heretical Gospel of the Ebionites with that according to the Hebrews, which he does not elsewhere regard as heretical. More probably he is guilty of a confusion, and adds the Ebionites to the Nazarenes, though the two were identical: if this is so, his expression need not point to more than one book. But all doubts as to what he means by his 'Gospel according to the Hebrews' are set at rest by his other statements. In his *de Viris Illustribus* (ii. 3) of the year 392 he speaks of a book which existed at that day in the library at Cæsarea, which the martyr Pamphilus took such pains to form; and he says that the Nazarenes at Berœa (Aleppo) showed him the same work, and allowed him to copy it (No. 2). Here we come to another puzzle. In this passage he calls the book, of which he knew two copies, *ipsum Hebraicum*, 'the original Hebrew.' Now, he is speaking in this passage of the Gospel according to Matthew, so that he appears to think, like Cureton in later days, that what he had copied out was the original Hebrew of Matthew, of which the canonical First Gospel in Greek was a translation. In his commentary on Mt 12[13] (the passage cited above) he says that the Gospel used by the Nazarenes and Ebionites was called by many 'the original of Matthew' (*Matthæi authenticum*). And in his work against the Pelagians he speaks of 'the Gospel according to the Hebrews, which is written in the Chaldæan and Syrian tongue [*i.e.* Aramaic, cf. Zahn, p. 659. It is Chaldaic as appearing in the OT, Syriac as a living language], but in Hebrew letters, which the Nazarenes use to this day; according to the Apostles, or, as many are of opinion, according to Matthew, which has a place in the library at Cæsarea (No. 3).' And this book, he tells us, he had translated into Greek and Latin. To these translations of his own he frequently refers. There can be no doubt that he made them; there is evidence, indeed, that they occasioned some little scandal in the Church, and were regarded as an indiscretion on his part, as if he had sought to add a fifth Gospel to the sacred four acknowledged by the Church.

There are many difficulties and confusions in Jerome's statements on this subject, but the following facts clearly appear from them:—1. The Christians of Syria used in the 4th cent. a Gospel in Aramaic, written in the square Hebrew character, and not identical with any of those in the Canon. 2. There was great uncertainty as to the origin of this work. Many held it to be the original work of the Apostle Matthew. Some identified it with the Gospel of the Twelve Apostles, the surviving fragments of which, not preserved by Jerome but by others, show it to have been a different work (see Harnack, *Chronologie*, ii. 627). Those who knew little about it could say that it was used by the heretical Ebionites as well as by the ordinary Oriental Christians. 3. It was unknown at this period in the West; Jerome knew of no Greek or Latin version of it; his designation of it 'according to the Hebrews' indicates its circle of readers; it was used by Hebrew-speaking Christians, not by others. 4. The identification with the Apostle Matthew shows that it resembled our First Gospel more than the others; yet Jerome knew that it was in many respects different from the canonical Matthew, else he need not have translated it.

2. From *Epiphanius*, Jerome's contemporary, who also spent part of his life in the East, we have various statements as to the Gospel used in Palestine, and on the whole a confirmation of the facts obtained from Jerome. It is from Epiphanius that we derive our fragments of the Gospel according to the Ebionites. He tells us that that Gospel began with John the Baptist, without any genealogy or story of the Infancy, and that the early Docetics,

* *NT extra Can. Rec.*, Fasc. 1. *Evangeliorum sec. Hebræos*, etc., 1884.

† *Geschichte des NT Kanons*, ii. 642–723.

‡ *Texte und Untersuchungen*, v. 3.

§ *Chronologie*, ii. 1, pp. 625–651.

‖ *The Gospel according to the Hebrews*, 1879.

¶ The numbering of the Fragments in this article is that of Preuschen's *Antilegomena*.

Cerinthus and Carpocrates, had used it. The fragments show an ascetic tendency, and in one of them there is an account of the baptism of the Lord quite different from that in the Gospel 'sec. Hebr.' Nicholson, however, prints them as part of the same book; for which he can allege the passage of Jerome given above, and also a statement of Epiphanius, who says that the Ebionites called this Gospel 'according to the Hebrews,' and that it was the Hebrew Matthew. The latter statement the extracts plainly disprove; and if we add to it the statement made by the same Father, that Tatian's *Diatessaron* was called by many 'according to Matthew,' we have some measure of the confusion which, in this Father's mind at least, rested on the whole subject. As to the Nazarenes, whom he treats as another set of heretics, but in his description of whom we may recognize the features of the ordinary Jewish Christian of the East who cherished the Law as well as the Gospel, Epiphanius says they have a 'very full Matthew in Hebrew.' This book, however, he has never seen; he cannot even tell whether or not it opened with a genealogy.

3. The work with which Jerome made such close acquaintance was known to Fathers of the two centuries before him; some of the extant fragments are found in their writings, and we find them considering how much authority is to be allowed to a Gospel which, though not recognized by the Church, was not suppressed, but in some quarters warmly cherished. *Eusebius*, who lived half a century before Jerome, and was much interested in the question of the books to be adopted by the Church, quotes several times 'the Gospel which has reached us in Hebrew characters,' or 'the Gospel which is with the Jews in the Hebrew language.' He does not speak of any translation of it into Greek, and we do not know how he got the Greek versions he gives us. In his famous list of the New Testament Scriptures (*HE* iii. 25) he gives 'sec. Hebr.' a place, not among the acknowledged books of the Church, but among the Antilegomena, the books which are accepted in some quarters of the Church but not generally, such as the Shepherd of Hermas, the Teaching of the Apostles, and, in the view of some, the Johannine Apocalypse. 'In this class,' he says, 'some count the Gospel according to the Hebrews, which is most used by those of the Hebrews who have accepted Christ' (*ᾧ μάλιστα* 'Εβραίων *οἱ τὸν Χριστὸν παραδεξάμενοι χαίρουσιν*). Harnack sees in these words an implied statement that there were Greek-speaking as well as Hebrew-speaking Christians who used this Gospel, and holds them to prove the existence in Eusebius' day of a Greek translation, which had disappeared when Jerome wrote. But the *μάλιστα* may be taken with *ᾧ* rather than with 'Εβραίων, and may indicate that the Christians of Syria clung to this Gospel more than to the *Diatessaron* or any other Syriac translation. Similarly, Eusebius says (iii. 27) that 'sec. Hebr.' was used by the better set of Ebionites, *i.e.* by the Christians of Syria who kept up their attachment to the Law, as their only Gospel: 'by the others they set small store.' Eusebius, then, respects the practice of the Jewish Christians in using a Gospel which had come down to them in their own tongue; but a work of such limited circulation could not be taken to belong to the accepted collection of the Church. He nowhere identifies it with the Hebrew of Matthew, though he does speak of that work, in which early tradition firmly believed, when he says (v.[10]) that Pantænus found in India the Gospel of Matthew in Hebrew, which had been carried there by the Apostle Bartholomew. What he knew of 'sec. Hebr.' is all in the direction of the difference of that work from Matthew, not of their similarity. In a statement about *Hegesippus*, who travelled from the East to Rome in the latter half of the 2nd cent., he tells us that that Father wrote a book of Memoirs, in which he gave extracts from the Gospel according to the Hebrews and the Syriac, translating them himself. Whatever may be the precise meaning of this, whether it credits Hegesippus with using two Gospels of Semitic language or only one, it shows Eusebius to have considered 'sec. Hebr.' to have been in the possession of the Christians of the East from a very early period.

4. Going back more than a century to *Clement* and *Origen*, with whom, as is well known, the Canon of Christian Scriptures was only emerging into definite form, we find 'sec. Hebr.' in the position of a well-known book, which, while it may not rank as Scripture,—yet in one passage of Clement (see below) it almost seems to do so,—is treated with respect, and regarded as a possible source of genuine information as to the Gospel narrative and teaching. Of Origen, Jerome tells us that he frequently used this Gospel; and there are three passages in the works of the great commentator in which he is seen to do so. He furnishes two of the extant fragments, introducing one of them (Jn 2[12]) with the words: 'If any one gives credence to the Gospel according to the Hebrews, where the Saviour Himself says' (No. 5*a*), and saying of another (Mt 19[16]), 'It is written in a certain Gospel which is called "according to the Hebrews," if at least any one choose to accept it *not in the way of authority, yet* (this phrase is thought by Zahn to be a gloss) for the bringing out of the question before us' (No. 11). Origen, then, who firmly believes that the Church had only four Gospels (*Hom. in Luc.* 1), knows of another to which some attach value, and he does not condemn that work as either heretical or absurd, but leaves it open to those who are so inclined to accept its statements, and regards them himself with great interest.

With regard to Origen's predecessor, Clement, we have the one fact that he twice quotes a saying from 'sec. Hebr.,' on one occasion (*Strom.* ii. 9. 45) introducing it with 'So also in the Gospel according to the Hebrews it is written' (No. 24); where the phrase 'it is written,' the ordinary formula for quotation from Scripture, is held by some to indicate that he regarded 'sec. Hebr.' in that light. But with Clement the Canon is not a very definite quantity; he names as Scripture a number of books which, according to Eusebius (vi. 14, 1), he does not seem to have held to belong to the NT. That Origen and Clement had 'sec. Hebr.' in a Greek translation is asserted by Harnack; but he does not succeed in accounting for the disappearance of such a version, if there was one, before the time of Jerome; and both Fathers were in a position to quote from a work in Aramaic.

5. It is not necessary to go further back. The *Muratorian Canon*, drawn up at Rome in the last quarter of the 2nd cent., does not name our Gospel. *Irenæus*, writing in the West some time after, knows that there are Christians, whom he calls Ebionites, who use only the Gospel of Matthew, and repudiate the Apostle Paul as an apostate from the Law. He shows no knowledge of the Gospel 'sec. Hebr.,' and his statement may be understood as a vague reflexion in the West of the fact that there were believers in Christ in the East who used only one Gospel and connected it, in the way we have seen, with the name of the Apostle Matthew. Of *Papias*, first author, so far as we can discern, of the statement that Matthew had written a Gospel-work in Hebrew, Eusebius tells us that he had the story of the woman accused to the Lord of many sins—a story which Eusebius says 'sec. Hebr.' also contained (No. 23). He does not say that Papias derived it from that source. Finally, it is a very

curious circumstance that *Ignatius*, in the early part of the 2nd cent., quotes the narrative in which the risen Christ summons His disciples to satisfy themselves that He is 'not a bodiless spirit' (No. 19). Eusebius, who knew our Gospel, declares that he does not know from what source Ignatius derived this; and to conclude, as Harnack does, that Ignatius knew 'sec. Hebr.,' seems scarcely necessary.

6. The history of our Gospel after Jerome translated it is soon told. In a Stichometry, or list of the books of Scripture with the number of lines in each, appended to a copy of the chronography of *Nicephorus*, Patriarch of Constantinople 806–813, the Gospel according to the Hebrews is named among the Antilegomena of the NT. It is in company here with the Apocalypse of John, the Apocalypse of Peter, and the Epistle of Barnabas. Good reasons have been given for thinking that the copy containing this list originated, not at Constantinople but at Jerusalem, and that the list was drawn up in Palestine. It may have been a century or two old when the MS was written; and thus we are given to know that though the Canon of the Church prevailed in Jerusalem as well as elsewhere, yet the work which had once been the only Gospel of the Christians of the East was still held in affection there, and read, if not in Church, yet privately. Its appearance on this list shows that it was in Greek when the list was made. And we may suppose that it was Jerome's translation which was thus half canonized. The Stichometry informs us how large a book our Gospel was, and how it compares in this respect with those of the Canon. 'Sec. Hebr.' had 2200 lines; it was longer than Mark, which had 2000, but shorter than Matthew, which had 2500.

The last fact of the external history of our Gospel is derived from *a minuscule codex of the First and Second canonical Gospels*, which dates from the 9th or 10th cent., and was brought by Tischendorf from the East to St. Petersburg. The Gospel according to Matthew is said in it to have been taken from old copies at Jerusalem. There are four marginal notes on Matthew, giving readings from τὸ Ἰουδαικόν; and one of these agrees with matter quoted by Jerome from the Gospel according to the Hebrews. We thus learn that that work was extant in Greek, and was a matter of interest in the East up to the time when this copy was made, and probably some time after. It is open to us to believe, with Zahn, that here also we are on the track of Jerome's Greek translation. From this point the Gospel according to the Hebrews is lost, and, till the book itself turns up in some corner in the East, we are left for our knowledge of it to the shadowy history which has been traced, and to what may be learned from the scanty fragments which are preserved.

ii. Extant fragments. — The fragments are 24 in number. They are collected in a very convenient form in Preuschen's *Antilegomena* (Giessen, 1901), the passages in which they occur being also given; and also in Nestle's *Novi Testamenti Græci Supplementum* (Leipzig, 1896); also in Nicholson, Zahn, and Handmann. They are various in their nature—some being linguistic, stating a different word, phrase, or name which stood in our Gospel; while some give a piece of narrative of a different tenor from that in the canonical Gospels, or additional to what they supply. A few give isolated utterances of the Lord not found in our New Testament. The fragments show that the Gospel contained the baptism of Jesus by John, a piece which may be connected with either the Transfiguration or the Temptation, the Lord's Prayer, the story of the man with the withered hand, the confession of Peter, the piece about forgiving seven times, the interview with the rich young man, the triumphal entry, the impeachment of the Pharisees, the parable of the Talents, Peter's denial, Barabbas, a catastrophe in the temple at the crucifixion, two appearances of the risen Lord; to which is to be added the story of the woman accused of many sins. That the narrative proceeded after the same scheme as our Matthew cannot be proved or even shown to be probable; some narratives are fuller than in that Gospel, and some additional to it; yet the work was considerably shorter than Matthew. A Gospel for the use of Hebrews would probably contain a genealogy, though on this point Epiphanius confesses ignorance; it might also have a narrative of the Infancy, though the evidence on this point is not conclusive.

The linguistic variations have been thought by many scholars to show that 'sec. Hebr.' was a translation from Greek; but recent writers take a different view, and hold our Gospel to give valuable corrections of the Greek Gospels of the Church, and to show an earlier tradition. Thus its reading *Bethlehem Juda* is better than *Bethlehem of Judæa* in Matthew, pointing to the district, not the country; and when *Barabbas* is explained to mean 'the son of their Master' (Jerome; No. 16), we remember Origen's statement, that the name of this person was Jesus, and see that our Gospel may have been right in taking Barabbas, not as a name but as a title. Origen also says that the word is to be translated 'son of the teacher.' In the Lord's Prayer the fifth petition ran, 'Give us this day to-morrow's bread' (No. 7). Here it has been held that the Aramaic *mahar* was a translation of ἐπιούσιος, taken as derived from ἡ ἐπιοῦσα, 'the coming day.' But the converse is possible; ἐπιούσιος may be a translation of *mahar* (see Lightfoot, *Fresh Revision*, App. I. 195): in this prayer as originally given only very simple terms would be employed, which can scarcely be said of ἐπιούσιος if derived from οὐσία, and denoting 'necessary,' or (as Jerome) 'supersubstantial.' To-day's work is done among simple people for the bread of to-morrow, and the prayer in this form might accompany the work without implying the anxiety forbidden in Mt $6^{31}$.

The narrative pieces are of extreme interest.

No. 3: '*Behold, the Lord's mother and brothers said to him, John the Baptist is baptizing for remission of sins; let us go and be baptized by him. But he said to them, What sin have I done that I should go and be baptized by him; unless perhaps what I have now said is ignorance?*' Here the title 'Lord' applied to Christ, and that of 'the Baptist,' belong to a time when the tradition was already formed; but the revelation of Christ's family circumstances at an early time, and the words He utters, appear such as could not have been invented. The absence of any consciousness of sin, and at the same time the attitude of humility, agree with all we know of His early life; but, as we see from Mk $10^{18}$ with its parallels, the tradition tended to discard His self-depreciation. Mt $3^{14}$ shows that reflexion early took place on the meaning of Jesus' baptism by John.

No. 4. The Baptism: '*It came to pass when the Lord had ascended out of the water, the whole fountain of the Holy Spirit came down and rested upon him, and said to him, My son, in all the prophets I was looking for thee, that thou shouldest come, and that I should rest in thee. For thou art my rest; thou art my firstborn son, who reignest to eternity.*' Here more distinctly than in any of the canonical Gospels the baptism is the act by which Jesus is made acquainted with His destiny to bring about the highest revelation of God. The dove is not mentioned; the Holy Spirit itself descends on

Him. The heavenly voice is that not of the Father but of the Spirit, afterwards spoken of as feminine, and is addressed as in Mark, not to the bystanders or to John but to Jesus Himself. The Spirit is to dwell with Him, not as in the prophets occasionally and provisionally, but in full and ultimate manner; He is firstborn of the Spirit, and is to have an endless reign. This passage also can scarcely be thought to be invented. It has the appearance, like the next extract, of a communication made by Jesus Himself to His intimate friends, and setting forth His experience, as does also that of the Temptation, in a symbolic narrative.

No. 5. The Flight to Mount Tabor: '*The Holy Spirit, my mother, took me just now by one of my hairs, and carried me away to the great Mount Tabor.*' This extract occurs 5 times in Origen and Jerome; it must have made a great impression. Jesus appears to be telling of an experience He has just had; it seems scarcely possible to connect it with either the Temptation or the Transfiguration, though early tradition held Tabor to be the scene of the latter: Jesus has been carried off, not as in the former by the devil, or as in the latter with any companions. The Holy Spirit, the Heb. word for which (רוּחַ) is usually feminine, has taken Him (cf. Ezk $8^{3}$, Bel and the Dragon v.$^{36}$) for some communication which He alone is to hear.

No. 7. The man with the withered hand (Mt $12^{9-13}$) is in this Gospel said to be a builder, and to entreat help in such words as these: '*I was a builder, seeking my living with my hands; I pray thee, Jesus, restore to me my health, that I may not basely beg my bread.*' The R.C. commentator Stapula states, when dealing with this story in Matthew, that the man with the withered hand made a strong appeal to Jesus' compassion; accepting this as a fact from Jerome citing this Gospel. The story reads awkwardly without this feature; in its absence the energy of Jesus appears to be called forth by His indignation against the Pharisees, or by the desire to establish the view that cures may be wrought on the Sabbath: neither alternative is very satisfactory.

The simple freedom which is apparent in these narratives meets us also in the Christophanies recorded in the Gospel. In one of them (No. 18) we are told how '*the Lord after handing over the linen cloth to the servant of the high priest* (the guard at the tomb is accordingly not Roman but Jewish), *went to James and appeared to him* (cf. 1 Co $15^{7}$); *for James had sworn that he would eat no bread from the hour at which the Lord had drunk the cup* (of death), *till he should see him rising again from those who are asleep. . . . Bring, the Lord says, a table and bread.*' . . . And then it goes on: '*He took bread, and blessed, and broke it, and gave it to James the Just, and said to him: My brother, eat thy bread, for the Son of Man is risen from those who are asleep.*' Here, as in the former pieces, the embellishing touches of a later time are unmistakable, while the tradition itself has a look of originality, and is independent of our NT.

The narratives from the ministry also present surprising variations from those of our NT, as when we hear the Lord (No. 11) addressing the *second* rich man with the exhortation to part with his possessions, and showing him that he has not kept the Law, since there are people dying of hunger about his gates and no supplies are sent them out of his well-furnished house. The parable of the Talents (No. 14) had three types of service, not only two as in our NT, and the hard sentence was directed not to him who hid his lord's talent in the earth, but to the servant who had devoured his lord's substance with harlots and flute-players. It was not the veil of the temple that was rent at the Crucifixion, but the lintel (No. 17), a stone of immense size, that was broken in two; in which, however we may compare the two physical facts, we see at least a different symbolism.

We find, lastly, a number of sayings of the Lord not recorded in the canonical Gospels, but which are accepted by scholars as not unfit to stand with those formerly known to us. It is reckoned among the greatest crimes '*that one should have saddened the spirit of his brother*' (No. 20). '*Never be glad but when you have looked upon your brother in charity*' (No. 21). The following is more difficult: '*I will choose for myself the well-pleasing; the well-pleasing are those whom my Father in heaven gave me*' (No. 22; from a work of Eusebius in Syriac; the translation is disputed; cf. below, p. 346[a]). Could this come from the same mouth which said, 'I came not to call the righteous, but sinners'? It speaks at least of a more Jewish colouring in this tradition. Yet the same Gospel contained the story of the woman accused to the Lord of many sins, which, whether parallel to Jn $8^{1-11}$ or to Lk $7^{36-50}$, or a different story, must have had a lesson of compassion for human infirmity.

iii. THEORIES OF ORIGIN AND CHARACTER.—From these extracts, reminding him now of one of the Gospels of the NT and now of another, and in some cases appearing to add to what these Gospels give, the reader will readily see what questions are here suggested to scholarship. That 'sec. Hebr.' was a translation from Greek into Aramaic, drawing its information from the canonical Gospels, mostly, no doubt, from Matthew, but also from Luke, has now ceased to be believed. If, however, Matthew wrote a Gospel-work in Hebrew, as Papias declares and as early Christendom believed, our Gospel may be related to that Apostolic work. This is held by Hilgenfeld, Nicholson, and Zahn, in different ways. Hilgenfeld, as the principal opponent of the now prevailing view of the priority of Mark to Matthew, is naturally led to claim for 'sec. Hebr.,' which agreed on the whole with Matthew, but was more Jewish and less universalistic, a very early and independent position. He considers 'sec. Hebr.' to be the work of Matthew of which Papias speaks, and to be the earliest Gospel, from which the study of the Gospels must set out as its point of Archimedes. Nicholson, in a book full of learning and of interest, concludes that 'Matthew,' not necessarily the Apostle, wrote both 'sec. Hebr.' and canonical Matthew, the latter of which may have been translated from Aramaic, and was probably first produced. This would be another instance in the NT of an author who wrote two versions of his book, both of which got into circulation. Zahn considers that Matthew wrote, as Papias says, in Hebrew, and that 'sec. Hebr.' followed him, but was written in a broader and more popular style (as some of the fragments show), which caused the original Matthew to disappear before it. It follows that on points of language the non-canonical Gospel, being nearer Matthew's original than the canonical, is more correct, but that its tradition is derived from Matthew, and is to be regarded as secondary.

The present state of opinion as to the origin of the Synoptic Gospels is opposed to the views of these scholars, and none of them has found followers on this subject. If, as is now generally believed, the sources of Matthew, Mark, and Luke alike were Greek; and if Matthew, as appears to many to be capable of demonstration, composed his Gospel with Mark before him, and another work, also Greek, before him from which Luke also drew, then any Aramaic work Matthew used must have been subsidiary to his main sources. That canonical Matthew was originally composed in Greek, not translated, is not now questioned.

The position, accordingly, is that we know the Gospel tradition to have been put into Greek by A.D. 70, when attempts were made to construct out of it continuous Gospels for the use of Christians. These underwent various modifications, the textual critics assure us, after they were written, and tended to become always more dignified, more intelligible to men of all lands, and to part with any features they might have at first of too great naïveté and simplicity. But the tradition, though translated into Greek, continued to exist in its original Aramaic; and it is no matter of wonder if it was seen in course of time to be different in some respects from that of the Church, if it remained more Jewish, more particular, and in many instances more realistic and quaint. Zahn explains these features of 'sec. Hebr.' as due to the exuberance of a popular preacher, and therefore quite secondary; but they may also be explained as signs of an earlier stage of the tradition which, while the Church outgrew it, survived among 'the Hebrews.'

The date of the work Jerome translated cannot be fixed with any precision. Papias may not have known it, as Hilgenfeld thinks, nor Ignatius, as Harnack. Its anonymity, its primitive character, and the authority it afterwards enjoyed, point to a very early origin. It may have come into existence about the same time as the Synoptic Gospels, and in obedience to some at least of the same motives as led to their appearance.*

LITERATURE.—In addition to the works mentioned in the body of the above article, which are the most recent and important, the student may consult, for the history of the subject, Lessing's *Theol. Nachlass*, p. 45; the NT Introductions of Eichhorn, Hug, de Wette, Reuss, and Hilgenfeld; Weizsäcker's *Untersuchungen über die evangelische Geschichte*; Baur's and Holtzmann's works on the Gospels; Lipsius' art. 'Apocryphal Gospels' in Smith's *Dict. of Christian Biography*. The subject is discussed by Strauss and Keim in their works on the Life of Christ, while the most recent publication of this kind, Oscar Holtzmann's *Leben Jesu* (1901), treats 'sec. Hebr.' as a coordinate source with the Synoptic Gospels and weaves its statements into the narrative.

ALLAN MENZIES.

## AGRAPHA.—



i. NAME.—The name *Agrapha* was first used in 1776 (J. G. Körner, *De sermonibus Christi ἀγράφοις*, Leipzig) for the Sayings purporting to come from Jesus Christ but transmitted to us outside of the canonical Gospels. The term was suggested by the idea that these Sayings are stray survivals from an unwritten tradition, orally preserved and running parallel with the written Gospels. It is now recognized that this description does not strictly apply to many Sayings which must be included in any collection of such material; but the name has proved convenient, and since the publication of Resch's elaborate monograph ('Agrapha: Aussercanonische Evangelienfragmente in möglichster Vollständigkeit zusammengestellt und untersucht,' in *Texte und Untersuchungen*, v. 4, 1889), has passed into general use.

* Cf., further, on various points dealt with in this article, the following art. AGRAPHA.

ii. CERTAIN SAYINGS NOT TO BE INCLUDED.—In a collection of Agrapha it is, however, neither customary nor advisable to include all that falls under the definition just given. The long discourses ascribed to Jesus in such works as the *Didascalia*, or to the Risen Christ, as in the *Pistis Sophia*,* have no claim to authenticity, and are profitably studied only in their original context. The same is to be said of most of the comparatively few Sayings of Jesus found in the religious romances known as Apocryphal Gospels, whether Gnostic or Catholic, and in the Apocryphal Acts, as well as of the Letter of Christ to Abgar (Euseb. *HE* i. 13). And of some of the Sayings now usually and rightly included in the lists it must be said that if their full context were known it would probably at once appear that they were of this same sort, and were better omitted. Of a different character are the Sayings preserved from those uncanonical Gospels which were designed, like the canonical Gospels, to embody Evangelical tradition for serious public or private use. To this class of writings belong the *Gospel according to the Hebrews*, together with the (far less valuable) *Gospel according to the Egyptians*, and the *Ebionite Gospel* (mainly based upon the canonical Gospels) known to Epiphanius. With these would be placed also the *Gospel according to Peter*; but the only fragment of it extant contains no Saying of Jesus excepting a peculiar form of the word from the cross of Mk 15[34], Mt 27[46].

It is also to be remarked that in nearly all the published collections of Agrapha a considerable number of Sayings will be actually found which for various reasons have no right to be included as independent Agrapha. (*a*) Some of these are obviously mere parallel forms or expansions or combinations of Sayings found in the canonical Gospels.

For instance—

Ephr. Syr. *Testamentum* (*Opp. Græce*, ed. Assemani, vol. ii. p. 232), τοῦ γὰρ ἀγαθοῦ διδασκάλου ἤκουσα ἐν τοῖς θείοις εὐαγγελίοις φήσαντος τοῖς ἑαυτοῦ μαθηταῖς· μηδὲν ἐπὶ γῆς κτήσησθε: 'For I heard the Good Teacher in the divine Gospels saying to his disciples, Get you nothing on earth.' Cf. Mt 6[19] 10[9], Lk 12[33].

With regard to such cases, the process of alteration of some of the Sayings of Jesus to be seen within the Synoptic Gospels themselves, whether as shown by the parallel forms in the several Gospels, or by the variant readings of Greek MSS and the renderings of early Versions, should be a warning against assuming too easily the presence of an independent Saying. There is a strong presumption in favour of accounting for half-strange Sayings of Jesus from the universally current canonical Gospel tradition. But, in determining whether or not a Saying is to be regarded as an independent Agraphon, individual judgments will necessarily vary. For other Sayings which might be classed here, see below, 'List of Agrapha,' Nos. 38, 49.

(*b*) In other cases, by a mere slip a passage from Scripture has been wrongly ascribed to Jesus by an ancient writer. For instance—

*Didascalia Apostolorum Syriace* (ed. Lagarde, p. 11, l. 12), 'For the Lord saith, Wrath destroyeth even wise men.' From Pr 15[1].—*De aleatoribus*, iii., 'Monet Dominus et dicit: Nolite contristare Spiritum Sanctum qui in vobis est, et nolite exstinguere lumen quod in vobis effulsit': 'The Lord also warneth

* For certain Sayings found in the *Pistis Sophia*, which have a somewhat different character from the mass of that work, but are not included in the List of Agrapha given below, see Harnack, 'Uber das gnostische Buch Pistis-Sophia' (*TU* vii. 2), 1891, p. 30 f.; Ropes, *Sprüche Jesu*, pp. 63 f., 117-119, 135 f., cf. p. 141.

and saith, Grieve not the Holy Spirit which is in you, and quench not the light which has shone in you.' From Eph $4^{30}$, 1 Th $5^{19}$.

(*c*) In another class of cases the ancient writer never intended to give the impression that he was quoting a Saying of Jesus, but has merely paraphrased in homiletical fashion Jesus' thought. Thus—

Hippolytus, *Demonstratio adv. Judæos*, vii., ὅθεν λέγει· γενηθήτω, ὦ πάτερ, ὁ ναὸς αὐτῶν ἠρημωμένος: 'Whence he says, Let their temple, Father, be desolate.' Here the context shows that the apparent quotation is meant simply as an explanatory paraphrase of Ps $69^{25}$, of which the writer is giving a connected exposition.

Petrus Siculus, *Historia Manichæorum*, 34 (ed. Mai, *Nova Patr. Bibl.* iv. 2), ἑταῖρε, οὐκ ἀδικῶ σε, ἀπέλαβες τὰ σὰ ἐν τῇ ζωῇ σου· νῦν ἆρον τὸ σὸν καὶ ὕπαγε: 'Friend, I do thee no wrong, thou receivedst thy reward in thy lifetime; take up that which is thine and go thy way.' The context shows that this is an address to certain specific errorists, made up by combining Mt $20^{13f.}$ with Lk $16^{25}$, and put by the author into the mouth of the Judge at the Last Assize.

(*d*) Other Sayings have occasionally been included through sheer mistake of some kind, as—

*Epist. Barnabæ*, iv. 9, 'Sicut dicit filius Dei, Resistamus omni iniquitati et odio habeamus eam': 'As the Son of God says, Let us resist all iniquity and hold it in hatred.' Here the Greek text (first published from Cod. ℵ in 1862) ὡς πρέπει υἱοῖς θεοῦ ἀντιστῶμεν, κ.τ.λ., makes it apparent that *sicut dicit filius Dei* is a textual corruption of *sicut decet filios Dei*.

(*e*) Still another class of Sayings to be found in the lists owe their places only to the guess of some modern scholar trying to discover the source of an ancient quotation. Resch, especially, has in a number of cases been led by his theory about the origin of the whole body of Agrapha to assume without sufficient ground that a quotation of unknown origin is from the words of Jesus.

Examples of this will be found in his treatment of 1 Co $2^{9}$, Eph $5^{14}$, Ja $4^{5}$, or such a case as the following:—

Clemens Alex. *Strom.* i. 8. 41 (Potter, 340), οὗτοι οἱ τὰ κατάρτια καταστῶντες καὶ μηθὲν ὑφαίνοντες, φησὶν ἡ γραφή: 'These are they who ply their looms and weave nothing, saith the Scripture' (cf. Resch, *Agrapha*, p. 226 f.).

A more plausible suggestion is that Rev $16^{15}$ (Resch, *Agrapha*, p. 310; Ropes, *Spr. Jesu*, No. 145) is an Agraphon.

iii. METHOD AND RESULTS OF CRITICISM OF THE AGRAPHA.—The criticism of the Agrapha has first to determine the source or sources by which, independently of other sources known to us, the Saying in question has been preserved. The Agrapha were much copied by ancient writers from one another, and even an imposing array of attesting authorities is in most cases reducible to one. This genealogical criticism of the sources accomplished, the next question is whether the earliest authority for the Saying is of such date and character that he might reasonably have had access to trustworthy extra-canonical tradition. For Papias or Justin Martyr this will be admitted; for a writer of the 4th cent. it will not. Finally, a third question must be considered, viz. whether the Saying is conceivable in the mouth of Jesus, in view of what the canonical Gospels make known to us of His thought and spirit. On the answer to this question will depend the ultimate decision as to the probable genuineness of the Agraphon. But, even if a negative conclusion is here reached, the proof is not complete until a fair explanation of the actual rise of the Agraphon has been furnished.

The criticism of the Agrapha is in most cases more difficult and less satisfactory than that of the Sayings of Jesus contained in the Gospels, because the history of their preservation and early transmission is, as a rule, utterly obscure, and because of their isolated character, lacking, as they often do, all context. The setting of the canonical Sayings in a great body of material all of the same general character, touching on the same topics, and transmitted to us by the same process, is a factor of unspeakable significance and value in Gospel criticism.

For detailed criticism of the Agrapha the reader must be referred to the literature of the subject. Here only a general summary can be furnished.

(*a*) Of the following list of Agrapha, Nos. 1, 17, 19, 21, 34, 35, 38, 39, 42, 43, 44, 46, 48, 59, 60 are, for various reasons, certainly not genuine Sayings of Jesus.

(*b*) Of most of the others so positive a statement cannot be made, but to the present writer Nos. 2, 3, 5, 6, 9, 22, 28, 40, 41, 45, 50, 54, 56, 63, 64, 65, 66 seem decidedly to lack the marks of genuineness; while in favour of Nos. 7, 8, 10, 12, 14, 16, 18, 20, 23, 26, 27, 29, 30, 31, 32, 33, 36, 37, 49, 51, 52, 53, 61, 62 a better, though not a conclusive, case can be made out. Some of them may have concealed within them a genuine kernel.

(*c*) Nos. 4, 11, 13, 15, 24, 25, 47, 55, 57, 58 (distinguished by an asterisk) all seem with considerable probability to possess historical value. At the head in trustworthiness stands No. 13 (Ac $20^{35}$), which possesses the same right to be accepted as any Saying in the Gospel of Luke. The others vary in the strength of their claim.

The fact that after all Christian literature has been thoroughly searched there can be found outside of the New Testament only a bare handful of Sayings of Jesus which can possibly be thought to convey trustworthy tradition of His words, is striking and important. Its significance is increased by the comparatively trifling intrinsic interest which attaches even to these few Agrapha. The cause of this state of things seems to be that the authors of the First and Third Gospels gathered up practically all that the Church in general possessed of traditions of the life and teaching of Jesus Christ. Any tradition embodied in the Fourth Gospel seems to have belonged to a comparatively small circle, if to more than one person. Living tradition may have persisted for a time in Palestine (possibly leaving a trace in the Gospel according to the Hebrews), but it was cut off by the destruction of Jerusalem and the withering of Jewish Christianity. The treasures that the earliest tradition had brought to the Gentile Churches were collected and arranged in our Synoptic Gospels; and the Evangelists did their work so well that only stray bits here and there, and these of but slight value, were left for the gleaners.

The Agrapha from Mohammedan sources are chiefly of merely curious interest.

iv. LIST OF AGRAPHA.—

[*Note.*—In the following list, numbers preceded by R. refer to the numbered Sayings in Ropes, *Sprüche Jesu*; numbers with Ag. to the 'Logia' enumerated in Resch, *Agrapha*; and with Ap. to the 'Apokrypha' given by Resch.]

(*a*) 1–15. *Agrapha from the NT or from some NT manuscripts.*—

1. (R. 113) Mt $6^{13}$ (TR), ὅτι σοῦ ἐστιν ἡ βασιλεία καὶ ἡ δύναμις καὶ ἡ δόξα εἰς τοὺς αἰῶνας. ἀμήν.

2. Mt $17^{21}$ (TR), τοῦτο δὲ τὸ γένος οὐκ ἐκπορεύεται εἰ μὴ ἐν προσευχῇ καὶ νηστείᾳ.

3. (R. 114) Mt $17^{26f.}$ (*Arabic Diatessaron*; cf. Cod. $713^{evv}$), 'Simon said unto him, From strangers. Jesus said unto him, Therefore the sons are free.

Simon saith unto him, Yea. Jesus said unto him, Give thou also unto them as if a stranger. And lest it should distress them, go thou to the sea, and cast a hook.'

*4. (R. 153) Mt 20[28] (DΦ verss), *ὑμεῖς δὲ ζητεῖτε ἐκ μικροῦ αὐξῆσαι καὶ ἐκ μείζονος ἔλαττον εἶναι. εἰσερχόμενοι δὲ καὶ παρακληθέντες δειπνῆσαι μὴ ἀνακλίνεσθε εἰς τοὺς ἐξέχοντας τόπους, μήποτε ἐνδοξότερός σου ἐπέλθῃ, καὶ προσελθὼν ὁ δειπνοκλήτωρ εἴπῃ σοι· ἔτι κάτω χώρει, καὶ καταισχυνθήσῃ. ἐὰν δὲ ἀναπέσῃς εἰς τὸν ἥττονα τόπον καὶ ἐπέλθῃ σου ἥττων, ἐρεῖ σοι ὁ δειπνοκλήτωρ· σύναγε ἔτι ἄνω, καὶ ἔσται σοι τοῦτο χρήσιμον* : 'But ye seek from the small to increase, and from the greater to be less. But when ye come in, even by invitation, to a feast, sit not down in the distinguished places, lest one grander than thou arrive, and the giver of the feast come and say to thee, Go further down, and thou be ashamed. But if thou sit down in the meaner place, and one meaner than thou arrive, the giver of the feast will say to thee, Join [us] further up, and that shall be to thine advantage.'

5. (R. 115) Mk 9[49] (TR), *καὶ πᾶσα θυσία ἁλὶ ἁλισθήσεται.*

6. (R. 116) Mk 16[15-18] (TR), *καὶ εἶπεν αὐτοῖς· πορευθέντες εἰς τὸν κόσμον ἅπαντα κηρύξατε τὸ εὐαγγέλιον πάσῃ τῇ κτίσει· ὁ πιστεύσας καὶ βαπτισθεὶς σωθήσεται, ὁ δὲ ἀπιστήσας κατακριθήσεται. σημεῖα δὲ τοῖς πιστεύσασιν ἀκολουθήσει ταῦτα, ἐν τῷ ὀνόματί μου δαιμόνια ἐκβαλοῦσιν, γλώσσαις λαλήσουσιν, καὶ ἐν ταῖς χερσὶν ὄφεις ἀροῦσιν, κἂν θανάσιμόν τι πίωσιν οὐ μὴ αὐτοὺς βλάψῃ, ἐπὶ ἀρρώστους χεῖρας ἐπιθήσουσιν καὶ καλῶς ἕξουσιν.*

7. (R. 132; Ag. 27) Lk 6[4] (Cod. D), *τῇ αὐτῇ ἡμέρᾳ θεασάμενός τινα ἐργαζόμενον τῷ σαββάτῳ εἶπεν αὐτῷ· ἄνθρωπε, εἰ μὲν οἶδας τί ποιεῖς, μακάριος εἶ· εἰ δὲ μὴ οἶδας, ἐπικατάρατος καὶ παραβάτης εἶ τοῦ νόμου* : 'On the same day, seeing one working on the Sabbath, he said to him, Man, if thou knowest what thou doest, blessed art thou; but if thou knowest not, thou art accursed and a transgressor of the Law.'

8. (R. 136) Lk 9[55f.] (TR), *καὶ εἶπεν· οὐκ οἴδατε οἵου πνεύματός ἐστε ὑμεῖς· ὁ γὰρ υἱὸς τοῦ ἀνθρώπου οὐκ ἦλθε ψυχὰς ἀνθρώπων ἀπολέσαι ἀλλὰ σῶσαι.*

9. Lk 11[2] (Greg. Nyss. *de Orat. Dom.* iii. p. 738), *ἐλθέτω τὸ ἅγιον πνεῦμά σου ἐφ' ἡμᾶς καὶ καθαρισάτω ἡμᾶς* : 'Let thy Holy Spirit come upon us and cleanse us.'

10. (R. 137) Lk 23[34] (TR), *ὁ δὲ Ἰησοῦς ἔλεγε· πάτερ, ἄφες αὐτοῖς· οὐ γὰρ οἴδασι τί ποιοῦσι.*

*11. (R. 146; Resch, p. 341) Jn 7[53]–8[11] (TR), *Pericope Adulteræ.*

12. (R. 138) Ac 1[5] 11[16], *Ἰωάνης μὲν ἐβάπτισεν ὕδατι, ὑμεῖς δὲ ἐν πνεύματι βαπτισθήσεσθε ἁγίῳ οὐ μετὰ πολλὰς ταύτας ἡμέρας.*

*13. (R. 141; Ag. 12) Ac 20[35], *μνημονεύειν τε τῶν λόγων τοῦ κυρίου Ἰησοῦ ὅτι αὐτὸς εἶπεν· μακάριόν ἐστιν μᾶλλον διδόναι ἢ λαμβάνειν.*

14. (R. 139) 1 Co 11[24f.], *τοῦτο ποιεῖτε εἰς τὴν ἐμὴν ἀνάμνησιν. τοῦτο ποιεῖτε ὁσάκις ἐὰν πίνητε εἰς τὴν ἐμὴν ἀνάμνησιν.*

*15. (R. 154) 1 Th 4[15-17], *τοῦτο γὰρ ὑμῖν λέγομεν ἐν λόγῳ κυρίου, ὅτι ἡμεῖς οἱ ζῶντες οἱ περιλειπόμενοι εἰς τὴν παρουσίαν τοῦ κυρίου οὐ μὴ φθάσωμεν τοὺς κοιμηθέντας· ὅτι αὐτὸς ὁ κύριος ἐν κελεύσματι, ἐν φωνῇ ἀρχαγγέλου καὶ ἐν σάλπιγγι θεοῦ, καταβήσεται ἀπ' οὐρανοῦ, καὶ οἱ νεκροὶ ἐν Χριστῷ ἀναστήσονται πρῶτον, ἔπειτα ἡμεῖς οἱ ζῶντες οἱ περιλειπόμενοι ἅμα σὺν αὐτοῖς ἁρπαγησόμεθα ἐν νεφέλαις εἰς ἀπάντησιν τοῦ κυρίου εἰς ἀέρα. καὶ οὕτως πάντοτε σὺν κυρίῳ ἐσόμεθα.*

(*b*) 16–25. *From Gospel according to the Hebrews.*—26. *From Gospel according to the Egyptians.*

16. (R. 134; Ap. 11) Clemens Alex. *Strom.* ii. 9. 45 (Potter, 453), *ἢ κἂν τῷ καθ' Ἑβραίους εὐαγγελίῳ, ὁ θαυμάσας βασιλεύσει, γέγραπται, καὶ ὁ βασιλεύσας ἀναπαύσεται*; v. 14. 96 (Potter, 704), *ἴσον γὰρ τούτοις ἐκεῖνα δύναται· οὐ παύσεται ὁ ζητῶν ἕως ἂν εὕρῃ, εὑρὼν δὲ θαμβηθήσεται, θαμβηθεὶς δὲ βασιλεύσει, βασιλεύσας δὲ ἐπαναπαύσεται* : 'For those words have the same meaning with these others, He that seeketh shall not stop until he find, and when he hath found he shall wonder, and when he hath wondered he shall reign, and when he hath reigned he shall rest.'

17. (R. 93; Ap. 14) Origen, *in Joann.* tom. ii. 6 (cf. *in Jerem. hom.* xv. 4), *ἐὰν δὲ προσίεταί τις τὸ καθ' Ἑβραίους εὐαγγέλιον, ἔνθα αὐτὸς ὁ σωτήρ φησιν· ἄρτι ἔλαβέ με ἡ μήτηρ μου τὸ ἅγιον πνεῦμα ἐν μιᾷ τῶν τριχῶν μου καὶ ἀπήνεγκέ με εἰς τὸ ὄρος τὸ μέγα Θαβώρ* : 'And if any one goes to the Gospel according to the Hebrews, there the Saviour himself saith: Just now my mother the Holy Spirit took me by one of my hairs and carried me off to the great mountain Tabor.'

18. (R. 150; Ap. 17) Origen, *in Matt.* tom. xv. 14 (*vetus interpretatio*), 'Scriptum est in evangelio quodam, quod dicitur secundum Hebræos, si tamen placet alicui suscipere illud non ad auctoritatem sed ad manifestationem propositæ quæstionis: Dixit, inquit, ad eum alter divitum: Magister, quid bonum faciens vivam? Dixit ei: Homo, leges et prophetas fac. Respondit ad eum: Feci. Dixit ei: Vade, vende omnia quæ possides et divide pauperibus et veni, sequere me. Cœpit autem dives scalpere caput suum et non placuit ei. Et dixit ad eum Dominus: Quomodo dicis, legem feci et prophetas, quoniam scriptum est in lege, Diliges proximum tuum sicut te ipsum; et ecce multi fratres tui, filii Abrahæ, amicti sunt stercore morientes præ fame, et domus tua plena est multis bonis, et non egreditur omnino aliquid ex ea ad eos. Et conversus dixit Simoni discipulo suo sedenti apud se: Simon, fili Joannæ, facilius est camelum intrare per foramen acus quam divitem in regnum cœlorum': 'It is written in a certain Gospel, the so-called Gospel according to the Hebrews, if any one likes to take it up not as having any authority but to shed light on the matter in hand: The other, it says, of the rich men said unto him, Master, by doing what good thing shall I have life? He said to him, Man, do the law and the prophets. He answered unto him, I have. He said to him, Go, sell all that thou hast, and distribute to the poor, and come, follow me. But the rich man began to scratch his head, and it pleased him not. And the Lord said unto him, How sayest thou, I have done the law and the prophets, since it is written in the law, Thou shalt love thy neighbour as thyself; and behold, many brethren of thine, sons of Abraham, are clad in filth, dying of hunger, and thy house is full of good things, and nothing at all goes out from it to them. And he turned and said to Simon his disciple, who was sitting by him: Simon, son of John, it is easier for a camel to enter through the eye of a needle than for a rich man to enter into the kingdom of heaven.'

19. (R. 95; Ap. 18) Eusebius, *Theophania*, xxii., *τὸ εἰς ἡμᾶς ἧκον Ἑβραϊκοῖς χαρακτῆρσιν εὐαγγέλιον τὴν ἀπειλὴν οὐ κατὰ τοῦ ἀποκρύψαντος ἐπῆγεν, ἀλλὰ κατὰ τοῦ ἀσώτως ἐζηκότος· τρεῖς γὰρ δούλους περιεῖχε, τὸν μὲν καταφαγόντα τὴν ὕπαρξιν τοῦ δεσπότου μετὰ πορνῶν καὶ αὐλητρίδων, τὸν δὲ πολλαπλασιάσαντα τὴν ἐργασίαν, τὸν δὲ κατακρύψαντα τὸ τάλαντον· εἶτα τὸν μὲν ἀποδεχθῆναι, τὸν δὲ μεμφθῆναι μόνον, τὸν δὲ συγκλεισθῆναι δεσμωτηρίῳ* : 'The Gospel which has come down to us in Hebrew characters gave the threat as made not against him who hid [his talent], but against him who lived riotously; for [the parable] told of three servants, one who devoured his lord's substance with harlots and flute-girls, one who gained profit many fold, and one who hid his talent; and how in the issue one was accepted, one merely blamed, and one shut up in prison.'

20. (R. 151; Ap. 21*b*) Eusebius, *Theophania Syr.*

(ed. S. Lee), iv. 12, pp. 233–34, 235, ܐܓܒܐ ܠܝ [ܗܠܝܢ] ܫܦܝܪܐ. ܫܦܝܪܐ ܗܢܘܢ ܕܝܗܒ ܠܝ ܐܒܝ ܕܒܫܡܝܐ: '[The cause, therefore, of the divisions of the soul, that comes to pass in houses, he himself taught, as we have found in a place in the Gospel existing among the Hebrews in the Hebrew language, in which it is said], I will select to myself the good, those good ones whom my Father in heaven has given me.'

21. (R. 98*a*; Ap. 30) Jerome, *adv. Pelag.* iii. 2, 'Et in eodem volumine (*sc.* evangelio iuxta Hebræos): Si peccaverit, inquit, frater tuus in verbo et satis tibi fecerit, septies in die suscipe eum. Dixit illi Simon discipulus eius: Septies in die? Respondit Dominus et dixit ei: Etiam ego dico tibi, usque septuagies septies; etenim in prophetis quoque, postquam uncti sunt spiritu sancto, inventus est sermo peccati': 'And in the same volume it says, If thy brother sin in word and give thee satisfaction, receive him seven times in the day. Simon, his disciple, said to him, Seven times in the day? The Lord answered and said to him, Yea, I say unto thee, until seventy times seven; for with the prophets also, after they were anointed with the Holy Spirit, there was found sinful speech.'

See also Scholion in Cod. 566[evv], Mt 18[22] τὸ Ἰουδαϊκὸν ἑξῆς ἔχει μετὰ τὸ ἑβδομηκοντάκις ἑπτά· καὶ γὰρ ἐν τοῖς προφήταις μετὰ τὸ χρισθῆναι αὐτοὺς ἐν πνεύματι ἁγίῳ εὑρίσκετο ἐν αὐτοῖς λόγος ἁμαρτίας.

22. (R. 105; Ap. 50) Jerome, *de Viris Illustribus*, ii., 'Evangelium quoque quod appellatur secundum Hebræos et a me nuper in Græcum Latinumque sermonem translatum est, quo et Origenes sæpe utitur, post resurrectionem Salvatoris refert: Dominus autem cum dedisset sindonem servo sacerdotis ivit ad Iacobum et apparuit ei. Iuraverat enim Iacobus se non comesturum panem ab illa hora qua biberat calicem Domini, donec videret eum resurgentem a dormientibus.

'Rursusque post paululum: Afferte, ait Dominus, mensam et panem. Statimque additur: Tulit panem et benedixit ac fregit et dedit Iacobo Iusto et dixit ei: Frater mi, comede panem tuum, quia resurrexit filius hominis a dormientibus.'

'Also the so-called Gospel according to the Hebrews, which was recently translated by me into Greek and Latin, which Origen, too, often uses, relates after the resurrection of the Saviour: But when the Lord had given the linen cloth to the priest's servant, he went to James and appeared to him. For James had taken an oath that he would not eat bread from that hour in which he had drunk the cup of the Lord, until he should see him rising from them that sleep.

'And again, a little further on: Bring me, saith the Lord, a table and bread. And there follows immediately: He took the bread, and blessed, and brake, and gave to James the Just, and said to him, My brother, eat thy bread, inasmuch as the Son of Man hath risen from them that sleep.'

23. (R. 133; Ap. 2) Jerome, *adv. Pelag.* iii. 2, 'In evangelio iuxta Hebræos . . . narrat historia: Ecce mater Domini et fratres eius dicebant ei: Ioannes Baptista baptizat in remissionem peccatorum; eamus et baptizemur ab eo. Dixit autem eis: Quid peccavi, ut vadam et baptizer ab eo? nisi forte hoc ipsum, quod dixi, ignorantia est': 'In the Gospel according to the Hebrews . . . is the following story: Behold, the Lord's mother and his brethren were saying to him: John the Baptist baptizes unto the remission of sins; let us go and be baptized by him. But he said unto them: What sin have I done, that I should go and be baptized by him? unless perchance this very thing which I have said is an ignorance [*i.e.* sin].'

*24. (R. 147; Ap. 7) Jerome, *in Ezech.* 18[7], 'In evangelio quod iuxta Hebræos Nazaræi legere consueverunt inter maxima ponitur crimina, qui fratris sui spiritum contristaverit': 'In the Gospel which the Nazarenes are accustomed to read, that according to the Hebrews, there is put among the greatest crimes, he who shall have grieved the spirit of his brother.'

*25. (R. 148; Ap. 8) Jerome, *in Ephes.* 5[3f.], 'In Hebraico quoque evangelio legimus Dominum ad discipulos loquentem: Et numquam, inquit, læti sitis, nisi quum fratrem vestrum videritis in caritate': 'In the Hebrew Gospel, too, we read of the Lord saying to the disciples, And never, said he, rejoice, except when you have looked upon your brother in love.'

26. (R. 135; Ag. 30, Ap. 16) 2 Clem. Rom. xii. 2, ἐπερωτηθεὶς γὰρ αὐτὸς ὁ κύριος ὑπό τινος, πότε ἥξει αὐτοῦ ἡ βασιλεία, εἶπεν· ὅταν ἔσται τὰ δύο ἕν, καὶ τὸ ἔξω ὡς τὸ ἔσω, καὶ τὸ ἄρσεν μετὰ τῆς θηλείας, οὔτε ἄρσεν οὔτε θῆλυ: 'For the Lord himself, having been asked by some one when his kingdom should come, said, When the two shall be one, and the outer as the inner, and the male with the female, neither male nor female.'

Clemens Alexandrinus: (1) *Strom.* iii. 6. 45 (Potter, 532); cf. iii. 9. 64 (Potter, 540), and *Exc. ex Theodoto*, § 67, τῇ Σαλώμῃ ὁ κύριος πυνθανομένῃ, μέχρι πότε θάνατος ἰσχύσει, οὐχ ὡς κακοῦ τοῦ βίου ὄντος καὶ τῆς κτίσεως πονηρᾶς, μέχρις ἄν, εἶπεν, ὑμεῖς αἱ γυναῖκες τίκτετε: 'When Salome asked how long death should have power, the Lord (not meaning that life is evil and the creation bad) said, As long as you women bear.'

(2) *Strom.* iii. 9. 63 (Potter, 539 f.), οἱ δὲ ἀντιτασσόμενοι τῇ κτίσει τοῦ θεοῦ διὰ τῆς εὐφήμου ἐγκρατείας κἀκεῖνα λέγουσι τὰ πρὸς Σαλώμην εἰρημένα, ὧν πρότερον ἐμνήσθημεν· φέρεται δέ, οἶμαι, ἐν τῷ κατ' Αἰγυπτίους εὐαγγελίῳ. φασὶ γὰρ ὅτι αὐτὸς εἶπεν ὁ σωτήρ· ἦλθον καταλῦσαι τὰ ἔργα τῆς θηλείας, θηλείας μὲν τῆς ἐπιθυμίας, ἔργα δὲ γέννησιν καὶ φθοράν: 'And those who oppose the creation of God through shameful abstinence allege also those words spoken to Salome whereof we made mention above. And they are contained, I think, in the Gospel according to the Egyptians. For they say that the Saviour himself said, I came to destroy the works of the female,—the female being lust, and the works birth and corruption.'

(3) *Strom.* iii. 9. 66 (Potter, 541), τί δὲ οὐχὶ καὶ τὰ ἑξῆς τῶν πρὸς Σαλώμην εἰρημένων ἐπιφέρουσιν οἱ πάντα μᾶλλον ἢ τῷ κατὰ τὴν ἀλήθειαν εὐαγγελικῷ στοιχήσαντες κανόνι; φαμένης γὰρ αὐτῆς· καλῶς οὖν ἐποίησα μὴ τεκοῦσα, ὡς οὐ δεόντως τῆς γενέσεως παραλαμβανομένης, ἀμείβεται λέγων ὁ κύριος· πᾶσαν φάγε βοτάνην, τὴν δὲ πικρίαν ἔχουσαν μὴ φάγῃς: 'And why do not they who walk any way rather than by the gospel rule of truth adduce the rest also of the words spoken to Salome? For when she said, Therefore have I done well in that I have not brought forth, as if it were not fitting to accept motherhood, the Lord replies, saying, Eat every herb, but that which hath bitterness eat not.'

(4) *Strom.* iii. 13. 92 (Potter, 553), διὰ τοῦτό τοι ὁ Κασσιανός φησι· πυνθανομένης τῆς Σαλώμης, πότε γνωσθήσεται (*lege* γενήσεται) τὰ περὶ ὧν ἤρετο, ἔφη ὁ κύριος· ὅταν τὸ τῆς αἰσχύνης ἔνδυμα πατήσητε καὶ ὅταν γένηται τὰ δύο ἕν, καὶ τὸ ἄρρεν μετὰ τῆς θηλείας, οὔτε ἄρρεν οὔτε θῆλυ: 'Therefore Cassian says: When Salome inquired when those things should be concerning which she asked, the Lord said, When ye trample on the garment of shame, and when the two shall be one, and the male with the female, neither male nor female.'

(c) 27–33. *The Oxyrhynchus 'Logia.'*—

[*Logion* 1, καὶ τότε διαβλέψεις ἐκβαλεῖν τὸ κάρφος τὸ ἐν τῷ ὀφθαλμῷ τοῦ ἀδελφοῦ σου, is part of Lk 6[42]].

27. *Logion* 2, λέγει Ἰησοῦς· ἐὰν μὴ νηστεύσητε τὸν κόσμον οὐ μὴ εὕρητε τὴν βασιλείαν τοῦ θεοῦ· καὶ ἐὰν μὴ σαββατίσητε τὸ σάββατον οὐκ ὄψεσθε τὸν πατέρα: 'Jesus saith, Except ye fast to the world, ye shall in no wise find the kingdom of God; and except ye make the sabbath a real sabbath, ye shall not see the Father.'

28. *Logion* 3, λέγει Ἰησοῦς· ἔ[σ]την ἐν μέσῳ τοῦ κόσμου, καὶ ἐν σαρκὶ ὤφθην αὐτοῖς, καὶ εὗρον πάντας μεθύοντας καὶ οὐδένα εὗρον διψῶντα ἐν αὐτοῖς, καὶ πονεῖ ἡ ψυχή μου ἐπὶ τοῖς υἱοῖς τῶν ἀνθρώπων, ὅτι τυφλοί εἰσιν τῇ καρδίᾳ αὐτῶ[ν] καὶ οὐ βλέ[πουσιν]: 'Jesus saith, I stood in the midst of the world, and in the flesh was I seen of them, and I found all men drunken, and none found I athirst among them, and my soul grieveth over the sons of men, because they are blind in their heart, and see not.'

29. *Logion* 4 . . . [τ]ὴν πτωχείαν: '. . . poverty.'

30. *Logion* 5, [λέγ]ει [Ἰησοῦς· ὅπ]ου ἐὰν ὦσιν [β, οὐκ] ε[ἰσὶν ἄ]θεοι, καὶ [ὅ]που ε[ἷς] ἐστιν μόνος, [λέ]γω ἐγώ εἰμι μετ' αὐτ[οῦ]· ἔγει[ρ]ον τὸν λίθον κἀκεῖ εὑρήσεις με, σχίσον τὸ ξύλον κἀγὼ ἐκεῖ εἰμί: 'Jesus saith, Wherever there are two, they are not without God; and wherever there is one alone, I say, I am with him. Raise the stone and there shalt thou find me; cleave the wood and there am I.'

31. *Logion* 6, λέγει Ἰησοῦς· οὐκ ἔστιν δεκτὸς προφήτης ἐν τῇ πατρίδι αὐτ[ο]ῦ οὐδὲ ἰατρὸς ποιεῖ θεραπείας εἰς τοὺς γινώσκοντας αὐτόν: 'Jesus saith, A prophet is not acceptable in his own country, neither doth a physician work cures upon them that know him.'

32. *Logion* 7, λέγει Ἰησοῦς· πόλις οἰκοδομημένη ἐπ' ἄκρον [ὄ]ρους ὑψηλοῦ καὶ ἐστηριγμένη οὔτε πε[σ]εῖν δύναται οὔτε κρυ[β]ῆναι: 'Jesus saith, A city built upon the top of a high hill and stablished, can neither fall nor be hid.'

33. *Logion* 8, λέγει Ἰησοῦς· ἀκούεις [ε]ἰς τὸ ἓν ὠτίον σου, τὸ . . .: 'Jesus saith, Thou hearest with one ear . . .'

(d) 34–46. *From various ancient documents, Catholic and heretical.*—

34 (R. 96; Ap. 21c) Clem. Alex. *Strom.* vi. 6. 48 (Potter, 764), αὐτίκα ἐν τῷ Πέτρου Κηρύγματι ὁ κύριός φησι πρὸς τοὺς μαθητὰς μετὰ τὴν ἀνάστασιν· ἐξελεξάμην ὑμᾶς δώδεκα μαθητὰς κρίνας ἀξίους ἐμοῦ—οὓς ὁ κύριος ἠθέλησεν—καὶ ἀποστόλους πιστοὺς ἡγησάμενος εἶναι, πέμπων ἐπὶ τὸν κόσμον εὐαγγελίσασθαι τοὺς κατὰ τὴν οἰκουμένην ἀνθρώπους γινώσκειν ὅτι εἷς θεός ἐστιν, διὰ τῆς [τοῦ χριστοῦ] πίστεως ἐμῆς δηλοῦντας τὰ μέλλοντα, ὅπως οἱ ἀκούσαντες καὶ πιστεύσαντες σωθῶσιν, οἱ δὲ μὴ πιστεύσαντες ἀκούσαντες μαρτυρήσωσιν, οὐκ ἔχοντες ἀπολογίαν εἰπεῖν· οὐκ ἠκούσαμεν: 'Straightway, in the Preaching of Peter, after the resurrection the Lord says to the disciples, I chose you twelve disciples, having judged you worthy of me (those whom the Lord wished), and having accounted you to be faithful apostles, sending you into the world to preach, that the men on the earth should know that God is one; and through faith in me to show what is to be, in order that they who hear and believe may be saved; but those who believe not, having heard, may bear witness, having no excuse for saying, We did not hear.'

35. (R. 106; Ap. 51) Clem. Alex. *Strom.* vi. 5. 43 (Potter, 762), διὰ τοῦτό φησιν ὁ Πέτρος εἰρηκέναι τὸν κύριον τοῖς ἀποστόλοις· ἐὰν μὲν οὖν τις θελήσῃ τοῦ Ἰσραὴλ μετανοήσας διὰ τοῦ ὀνόματός μου πιστεύειν ἐπὶ τὸν θεόν, ἀφεθήσονται αὐτῷ αἱ ἁμαρτίαι. μετὰ δώδεκα ἔτη ἐξέλθετε εἰς τὸν κόσμον μή τις εἴπῃ· οὐκ ἠκούσαμεν: 'Therefore Peter says that the Lord said to the apostles, If then any one of Israel wishes to repent and believe through my name on God, his sins shall be forgiven him. After twelve years go forth into the world, lest any one say, We did not hear.'

36. (R. 130; Ag. 15) *Apostolic Church-Order*, xxvi. (Hilgenfeld, *NT extra Canonem*[2], iv. p. 118), προέλεγε γὰρ ἡμῖν, ὅτε ἐδίδασκεν, ὅτι τὸ ἀσθενὲς διὰ τοῦ ἰσχυροῦ σωθήσεται: 'For he said to us before, when he was teaching, That which is weak shall be saved through that which is strong.'

37. (R. 131; Ag. 26) *Didascalia Syr.* ii. 8 (ed. Lagarde, p. 14), λέγει γὰρ ἡ γραφή· ἀνὴρ ἀδόκιμος ἀπείραστος: 'For the Scripture saith, A man is unapproved if he be untempted.'

Tertullian, *de Bapt.* xx., 'Vigilate et orate, inquit, ne incidatis in tentationem. Et ideo credo tentati sunt, quoniam obdormierunt, ut apprehensum Dominum destituerint, et qui cum eo persititerit et gladio sit usus, ter etiam negaverit. Nam et præcesserat dictum: Neminem intentatum regna cœlestia consecuturum': 'Watch and pray, he saith, that ye enter not into temptation. And so I think they were tempted, because they fell asleep, so that they failed the Lord after his arrest; and he who continued with him and used the sword even denied him three times. For the saying had also preceded, that no one untempted should attain to the heavenly realms.'

38. (R. 101; Ap. 45) *Hom. Clem.* iii. 53, ἔτι μὴν ἔλεγεν· ἐγώ εἰμι περὶ οὗ Μωϋσῆς προεφήτευσεν εἰπών· προφήτην ἐγερεῖ ὑμῖν κύριος ὁ θεὸς ἡμῶν ἐκ τῶν ἀδελφῶν ὑμῶν ὥσπερ καὶ ἐμέ· αὐτοῦ ἀκούετε κατὰ πάντα. ὃς ἂν δὲ μὴ ἀκούσῃ τοῦ προφήτου ἐκείνου, ἀποθανεῖται: 'Moreover, he said: I am he concerning whom Moses prophesied, saying, A prophet shall the Lord our God raise up for you from your brethren like unto me; hear him in all things; and whoever shall not hear that prophet, shall die.'

39. (R. 86; Ag. 11) *Hom. Clem.* x. 3, θεοῦ τοῦ τὸν οὐρανὸν κτίσαντος καὶ τὴν γῆν καὶ πάντα ἐν αὐτοῖς πεποιηκότος, ὡς ἀληθὴς εἴρηκεν ἡμῖν προφήτης: 'God having created the heaven and the earth, and made all things therein, as the true Prophet hath told us.'

40. (R. 7; Ag. 13) *Hom. Clem.* xii. 29, ὁ τῆς ἀληθείας προφήτης ἔφη· τὰ ἀγαθὰ ἐλθεῖν δεῖ, μακάριος δέ, φησί, δι' οὗ ἔρχεται· ὁμοίως καὶ τὰ κακὰ ἀνάγκη ἐλθεῖν, οὐαὶ δὲ δι' οὗ ἔρχεται: 'The Prophet of truth said, Good things must come, but blessed, saith he, is he through whom they come; in like manner, It must needs be also that evils come, but woe to him through whom they come.'

41. (R. 89; Ag. 22) *Const. Apost.* viii. 12, ὁσάκις γὰρ ἂν ἐσθίητε τὸν ἄρτον τοῦτον καὶ τὸ ποτήριον τοῦτο πίνητε, τὸν θάνατον τὸν ἐμὸν καταγγέλλετε ἄχρις ἂν ἔλθω: 'For as often as ye eat this bread and drink this cup, ye do show my death until I come.'

42. (R. 52; Ap. 21a) Epiphan. *Hær.* xxx. 13, ἐν τῷ γοῦν παρ' αὐτοῖς εὐαγγελίῳ κατὰ Ματθαῖον ὀνομαζομένῳ, οὐχ ὅλῳ δὲ πληρεστάτῳ, ἀλλὰ νενοθευμένῳ καὶ ἠκρωτηριασμένῳ (Ἑβραϊκὸν δὲ τοῦτο καλοῦσιν) ἐμφέρεται ὅτι ἐγένετό τις ἀνὴρ ὀνόματι Ἰησοῦς, καὶ αὐτὸς ὡς ἐτῶν τριάκοντα, ὃς ἐξελέξατο ἡμᾶς. καὶ ἐλθὼν εἰς Καφαρναοὺμ εἰσῆλθεν εἰς τὴν οἰκίαν Σίμωνος τοῦ ἐπικληθέντος Πέτρου, καὶ ἀνοίξας τὸ στόμα αὐτοῦ εἶπε· παρερχόμενος παρὰ τὴν λίμνην Τιβεριάδος ἐξελεξάμην Ἰωάννην καὶ Ἰάκωβον, υἱοὺς Ζεβεδαίου, καὶ Σίμωνα καὶ Ἀνδρέαν καὶ <Φίλιππον καὶ Βαρθολομαῖον καὶ Θωμᾶν καὶ Ἰάκωβον τὸν τοῦ Ἀλφαίου καὶ> Θαδδαῖον καὶ Σίμωνα τὸν Ζηλωτὴν καὶ Ἰούδαν τὸν Ἰσκαριώτην καὶ σὲ τὸν Ματθαῖον καθεζόμενον ἐπὶ τοῦ τελωνίου ἐκάλεσα, καὶ ἠκολούθησάς μοι. ὑμᾶς οὖν βούλομαι εἶναι δεκαδύο ἀποστόλους εἰς μαρτύριον τοῦ Ἰσραήλ: 'In their Gospel, called "according to Matthew," though not fully complete, but falsified and mutilated (and they call it "the Hebrew"), is contained the following: There came a certain man, by name Jesus, and he was about thirty years old, who chose us. And when he had come to Capernaum he came into the house of Simon, surnamed Peter, and he opened his mouth and said, As I passed by the lake of Tiberias I chose John and James, sons of Zebedee, and Simon and Andrew and

<Philip and Bartholomew and Thomas and James the son of Alphæus and> Thaddæus and Simon the Zealot, and Judas Iscariot, and I called thee Matthew, sitting at the receipt of custom, and thou didst follow me. You therefore I wish to be twelve apostles for a witness to Israel.'

43. (R. 92; Ap. 6) Epiphan. *Hær.* xxx. 16, *ὡς τὸ παρ' αὐτοῖς (sc. τοῖς 'Εβιωναίοις) εὐαγγέλιον καλούμενον περιέχει, ὅτι ἦλθον καταλῦσαι τὰς θυσίας, καὶ ἐὰν μὴ παύσησθε τοῦ θύειν, οὐ παύσεται ἀφ' ὑμῶν ἡ ὀργή*: 'As their [the Ebionites'] so-called Gospel runs: I came to destroy the sacrifices, and except ye cease from sacrificing, wrath shall not cease from you.'

44. (R. 94; Ap. 15) Hippolytus, *Philosoph.* v. 7, *περὶ ἧς διαρρήδην ἐν τῷ κατὰ Θωμᾶν ἐπιγραφομένῳ εὐαγγελίῳ παραδιδόασι [sc. οἱ Ναασσηνοί] λέγοντες οὕτως· ἐμὲ ὁ ζητῶν εὑρήσει ἐν παιδίοις ἀπὸ ἐτῶν ἑπτά· ἐκεῖ γὰρ ἐν τῳ τεσσαρεσκαιδεκάτῳ αἰῶνι κρυβόμενος φανεροῦμαι*: 'Concerning which in the Gospel inscribed "according to Thomas" they [the Naassenes] have expressly a tradition as follows: He that seeketh me shall find me in children from seven years old onwards, for there I am manifested, though hidden in the fourteenth age.'

45. *Acta Thomæ*, vi. (M. R. James, *Apocrypha Anecdota*, Second Series), *οὕτως γὰρ ἐδιδάχθημεν παρὰ τοῦ σωτῆρος λέγοντος· ὁ λυτρούμενος ψυχὰς ἀπὸ τῶν εἰδώλων, οὗτος ἔσται μέγας ἐν τῇ βασιλείᾳ μου*: 'For thus were we taught by the Saviour, who said, Whoso redeemeth souls from idols, he shall be great in my kingdom.'

46. (R. 100; Ap. 44) *Acta Philippi*, xxxiv. (Tisch. *Acta apost. apocr.*), *εἶπεν γάρ μοι ὁ κύριος· ἐὰν μὴ ποιήσητε ὑμῶν τὰ κάτω εἰς τὰ ἄνω καὶ τὰ ἀριστερὰ εἰς τὰ δεξιά, οὐ μὴ εἰσέλθητε εἰς τὴν βασιλείαν μου*: 'For the Lord said to me, Except ye make the lower into the upper and the left into the right, ye shall not enter into my kingdom.'

(*e*) 47–48. *Agrapha from the Mishna.*—

*47. (R. 152) *Aboda Zara* 16*b*, 17*a*, 'The Rabbis have the following tradition: When Rabbi Eliezer was once imprisoned for heresy (*minuth*, *i.e.* inclination to the forbidden Christian religion), he was brought before the (Roman) court to be judged. The judge said to him, Does such a mature man as thou occupy himself with such vain things? Eliezer replied, The Judge is just to me. The judge thought that Eliezer was speaking of him; in fact he referred to his Father in heaven. Then the judge said, Because I am held by thee to be just, thou art acquitted. When Eliezer came home, his disciples came to comfort him, but he would accept no comfort. Then R. 'Akiba said to him, Permit me to say to thee something of that which thou hast taught me. He answered, Say on. Then R. 'Akiba said, Perhaps thou hast at some time heard a heresy which pleased thee, because of which thou wast now about to be imprisoned for heresy. Eliezer replied, 'Akiba, thou remindest me. I was once walking in the upper street of Sepphoris; there I met one of the disciples of Jesus of Nazareth, named Jacob of Kephar Sekhanya, who said to me, In your law it reads: Thou shalt not bring the hire of an harlot into the house of thy God (Dt 23[18]); is it lawful that from such gifts one should have a draught-house built for the high priest? I knew not what to answer him to this. Then he said to me, Thus taught me Jesus of Nazareth: Of the hire of an harlot hath she gathered them, and to the hire of an harlot shall they return (Mic 1[7]); from filth it came, to the place of filth shall it go. This explanation pleased me, and therefore have I been arrested for heresy, because I have transgressed the word of Scripture: Remove thy way far from her (Pr 5[8]), *i.e.* from heresy.'

48. (R. 117) *Shabbath* 116*a*. *b*, 'Imma Shalom, the wife of R. Eliezer and sister of Rabban Gamaliel (II.), had a philosopher as a neighbour, who had the reputation of never accepting a bribe. They wished to make him ridiculous. So Imma brought him a golden lampstand, came before him, and said, I wish to be given my share of the family estate. The philosopher answered them, Then have thy share. But Gamaliel said to him, We have the law: Where there is a son, the daughter shall not inherit. The philosopher said, Since the day when you were driven from your country, the law of Moses has been done away, and the Gospel has been given, in which it reads: Son and daughter shall inherit together. The next day Gamaliel brought to the philosopher a Libyan ass. Then the philosopher said to them, I have looked at the end of the Gospel; for it says: I, the Gospel, am not come to do away with the law of Moses, but I am come to add to the law of Moses. It stands written in the law of Moses: Where there is a son, the daughter shall not inherit. Then Imma said to him, May your light shine like the lampstand! But Rabban Gamaliel said, The ass is come, and has overturned the lampstand.'

(*f*) 49–66. *Agrapha from early Christian Writers.*—

49. (R. 2; Ag. 2) Clem. Rom. xiii. 1 f., *μάλιστα μεμνημένοι τῶν λόγων τοῦ κυρίου 'Ιησοῦ, οὓς ἐλάλησεν διδάσκων ἐπιείκειαν καὶ μακροθυμίαν· οὕτως γὰρ εἶπεν·*

*ἐλεᾶτε, ἵνα ἐλεηθῆτε·*
*ἀφίετε, ἵνα ἀφεθῇ ὑμῖν·*
*ὡς ποιεῖτε, οὕτω ποιηθήσεται ὑμῖν·*
*ὡς δίδοτε, οὕτως δοθήσεται ὑμῖν·*
*ὡς κρίνετε, οὕτως κριθήσεσθε·*
*ὡς χρηστεύεσθε, οὕτως χρηστευθήσεται ὑμῖν·*
*ᾧ μέτρῳ μετρεῖτε, ἐν αὐτῷ μετρηθήσεται ὑμῖν.*

'Most of all remembering the words of the Lord Jesus which he spake, teaching forbearance and long-suffering; for thus he spake: Have mercy, that ye may receive mercy; forgive, that it may be forgiven to you. As ye do, so shall it be done to you. As ye give, so shall it be given unto you. As ye judge, so shall ye be judged. As ye show kindness, so shall kindness be showed unto you. With what measure ye mete, it shall be measured withal to you.'

50. (R. 57; Ap. 28) 2 Clem. Rom. iv. 5, *διὰ τοῦτο, ταῦτα ὑμῶν πρασσόντων, εἶπεν ὁ κύριος· ἐὰν ἦτε μετ' ἐμοῦ συνηγμένοι ἐν τῷ κόλπῳ μου καὶ μὴ ποιῆτε τὰς ἐντολάς μου, ἀποβαλῶ ὑμᾶς καὶ ἐρῶ ὑμῖν· ὑπάγετε ἀπ' ἐμοῦ, οὐκ οἶδα ὑμᾶς πόθεν ἐστέ, ἐργάται ἀνομίας*: 'For this cause, if ye do these things, the Lord said, Though ye be gathered together with me in my bosom, and do not my commandments, I will cast you away, and will say unto you, Depart from me, I know you not whence ye are, ye workers of iniquity.'

51. (R. 149; Ap. 10) 2 Clem. Rom. v. 2–4, *λέγει γὰρ ὁ κύριος· ἔσεσθε ὡς ἀρνία ἐν μέσῳ λύκων. ἀποκριθεὶς δὲ ὁ Πέτρος αὐτῷ λέγει· ἐὰν οὖν διασπαράξωσιν οἱ λύκοι τὰ ἀρνία; εἶπεν ὁ 'Ιησοῦς τῷ Πέτρῳ· μὴ φοβείσθωσαν τὰ ἀρνία τοὺς λύκους μετὰ τὸ ἀποθανεῖν αὐτά· καὶ ὑμεῖς μὴ φοβεῖσθε τοὺς ἀποκτέννοντας ὑμᾶς καὶ μηδὲν ὑμῖν δυναμένους ποιεῖν, ἀλλὰ φοβεῖσθε τὸν μετὰ τὸ ἀποθανεῖν ὑμᾶς ἔχοντα ἐξουσίαν ψυχῆς καὶ σώματος, τοῦ βαλεῖν εἰς γέενναν πυρός*: 'For the Lord saith, Ye shall be as lambs in the midst of wolves. But Peter answering said unto him, What, then, if the wolves should tear the lambs? Jesus said unto Peter, Let not the lambs fear the wolves after they are dead; and ye also, fear ye not them that kill you and are not able to do anything to you; but fear him that, after ye are dead, hath power over soul and body, to cast them into the Gehenna of fire.'

52. (R. 5; Ag. 7) 2 Clem. Rom. viii. 5, *λέγει γὰρ ὁ κύριος ἐν τῷ εὐαγγελίῳ· εἰ τὸ μικρὸν οὐκ ἐτηρήσατε,*

*τὸ μέγα τίς ὑμῖν δώσει; λέγω γὰρ ὑμῖν ὅτι ὁ πιστὸς ἐν ἐλαχίστῳ καὶ ἐν πολλῷ πιστός ἐστιν*: 'For the Lord saith in the Gospel, If ye kept not that which is little, who shall give unto you that which is great? For I say unto you that he who is faithful in the least, is faithful also in much.'

53. (R. 110; Ap. 95) Irenæus, v. 33. 3 f., 'Quemadmodum presbyteri meminerunt, qui Ioannem discipulum Domini viderunt, audisse se ab eo, quemadmodum de temporibus illis docebat Dominus et dicebat: Venient dies in quibus vineæ nascentur singulæ decem millia palmitum habentes, et in uno palmite dena millia brachiorum, et in uno vero palmite (*lege* brachio) dena millia flagellorum, et in unoquoque flagello dena millia botruum, et in unoquoque botro dena millia acinorum, et unumquodque acinum expressum dabit vigintiquinque metretas vini. Et cum eorum apprehenderit aliquis sanctorum botrum, alius clamabit: Botrus ego melior sum, me sume, per me Dominum benedic. Similiter et granum tritici decem millia spicarum generaturum, et unamquamque spicam habituram decem millia granorum, et unumquodque granum quinque bilibres similæ claræ mundæ: et reliqua autem poma et semina et herbam secundum congruentiam iis consequentem: et omnia animalia iis cibis utentia, quæ a terra accipiuntur, pacifica et consentanea invicem fieri, subiecta hominibus cum omni subiectione. Hæc autem et Papias, Ioannis auditor, Polycarpi autem contubernalis, vetus homo, per scripturam testimonium perhibet in quarto librorum suorum: sunt enim illi quinque libri conscripti.

'Et adiecit dicens: Hæc autem credibilia sunt credentibus. Et Iuda, inquit, proditore non credente et interrogante: Quomodo ergo tales genituræ a Domino perficientur? dixisse Dominum: Videbunt qui venient in illa.'

'As the elders, who saw John the disciple of the Lord, relate that they had heard from him how the Lord used to teach concerning those times, and to say: The days will come, in which vines shall grow, each having ten thousand shoots, and on one shoot ten thousand branches, and on one branch again ten thousand twigs, and on each twig ten thousand clusters, and in each cluster ten thousand grapes, and each grape when pressed shall yield five-and-twenty measures of wine. And when any of the saints shall have taken hold of one of their clusters, another shall cry, I am a better cluster; take me, bless the Lord through me. Likewise, also, that a grain of wheat shall produce ten thousand heads, and every head shall have ten thousand grains, and every grain ten pounds of fine flour, bright and clean; and the other fruits, seeds, and the grass shall produce in similar proportions; and all the animals, using these fruits which are products of the soil, shall become in their turn peaceable and harmonious, obedient to man in all subjection. These things Papias, who was a hearer of John and a companion of Polycarp, an ancient worthy, witnesseth in writing in the fourth of his books, for there are five books composed by him.

'And he added, saying, But these things are credible to them that believe. And when Judas the traitor did not believe, and asked, How shall such growths be accomplished by the Lord? he relates that the Lord said, They shall see, who shall come to these (times).'

Hippolytus, *Comm. in Danielem*, lib. iv. (ed. Braike, p. 44), *τοῦ οὖν κυρίου διηγουμένου τοῖς μαθηταῖς περὶ τῆς μελλούσης τῶν ἁγίων βασιλείας ὡς εἴη ἔνδοξος καὶ θαυμαστή, καταπλαγεὶς ὁ Ἰούδας ἐπὶ τοῖς λεγομένοις ἔφη· καὶ τίς ἄρα ὄψεται ταῦτα; ὁ δὲ κύριος ἔφη· ταῦτα ὄψονται οἱ ἄξιοι γινόμενοι*: 'So when the Lord told the disciples about the coming kingdom of the saints, how it was glorious and marvellous, Judas, amazed at what was spoken, said, And who then shall see these things? And the Lord replied, These things shall they see who become worthy.'

54. (R. 88; Ag. 21) Justin Martyr, *Dial.* xxxv., *εἶπε γάρ· πολλοὶ ἐλεύσονται ἐπὶ τῷ ὀνόματί μου, ἔξωθεν ἐνδεδυμένοι δέρματα προβάτων, ἔσωθεν δέ εἰσι λύκοι ἅρπαγες· καί· ἔσονται σχίσματα καὶ αἱρέσεις*: 'For he said, Many shall come in my name, clad without in sheepskins, but within they are ravening wolves; and, There shall be schisms and heresies.' Cf. *Didascalia Syr.* vi. 5 (ed. Lagarde, p. 99, l. 9).

*55. (R. 142; Ag. 39) Justin Martyr, *Dial.* xlvii., *διὸ καὶ ὁ ἡμέτερος κύριος Ἰησοῦς Χριστὸς εἶπεν· ἐν οἷς ἂν ὑμᾶς καταλάβω, ἐν τούτοις καὶ κρινῶ*: 'Wherefore also our Lord Jesus Christ said, In whatsoever things I apprehend you, in those I shall judge you.'

56. (R. 91; Ag. 51) Justin Martyr, *Apol.* i. 15, *εἶπε δὲ οὕτως· οὐκ ἦλθον καλέσαι δικαίους, ἀλλ' ἁμαρτωλοὺς εἰς μετάνοιαν· θέλει γὰρ ὁ πατὴρ ὁ οὐράνιος τὴν μετάνοιαν τοῦ ἁμαρτωλοῦ ἢ τὴν κόλασιν αὐτοῦ*: 'And he said this, I came not to call righteous but sinners to repentance; for the heavenly Father desireth the sinner's repentance rather than his punishment.'

*57. (R. 143; Ag. 41) Clem. Alex. *Strom.* i. 24. 158 (Potter, 416), *αἰτεῖσθε γάρ, φησί, τὰ μεγάλα, καὶ τὰ μικρὰ ὑμῖν προστεθήσεται.*

Origen, *de Orat.* ii., *τὸ μὲν ὃ δεῖ· αἰτεῖτε τὰ μεγάλα, καὶ τὰ μικρὰ ὑμῖν προστεθήσεται, καί· αἰτεῖτε τὰ ἐπουράνια, καὶ τὰ ἐπίγεια ὑμῖν προστεθήσεται*: 'That which is needful: Ask for the great things, and the small shall be added to you; and, Ask for the heavenly things, and the earthly shall be added to you.'

*58. (R. 144; Ag. 43) Clem. Alex. *Strom.* i. 28. 177 (Potter, 425), *εἰκότως ἄρα καὶ ἡ γραφή, τοιούτους τινὰς ἡμᾶς διαλεκτικοὺς οὕτως ἐθέλουσα γενέσθαι, παραινεῖ· γίνεσθε δὲ δόκιμοι τραπεζῖται, τὰ μὲν ἀποδοκιμάζοντες, τὸ δὲ καλὸν κατέχοντες*: 'Rightly, therefore, the Scripture also, in its desire to make us such dialecticians, exhorts us, Be approved money-changers, disapproving some things, but holding fast that which is good.'

Cf. Orig. *in Joh.* tom. xix. (*τηρούντων τὴν ἐντολὴν Ἰησοῦ λέγουσαν· δόκιμοι τραπεζῖται γίνεσθε*); Apelles *ap.* Epiphan. *Hær.* xliv. 2; *Didascalia Syr.* ii. 36 (ed. Lagarde, p. 42); *Pistis Sophia*, p. 353 [Lat. p. 220]; *Hom. Clem.* ii. 51.

59. (R. 87; Ag. 17) Clem. Alex. *Strom.* v. 10. 64 (Potter, 684), *λέγει γὰρ ὁ προφήτης· παραβολὴν κυρίου τίς νοήσει εἰ μὴ σοφὸς καὶ ἐπιστήμων καὶ ἀγαπῶν τὸν κύριον αὐτοῦ; ἐπ' ὀλίγων ἐστὶ ταῦτα χωρῆσαι. οὐ γὰρ φθονῶν, φησί, παρήγγειλεν ὁ κύριος ἔν τινι εὐαγγελίῳ· μυστήριον ἐμὸν ἐμοὶ καὶ τοῖς υἱοῖς τοῦ οἴκου μου*: 'For the Prophet saith, Who shall know the parable of the Lord except the wise and understanding and that loveth his Lord? It belongeth to a few only to receive these things. For not grudgingly, he saith, did the Lord declare in a certain Gospel, My mystery is for me and for the sons of my house.'

60. (R. 107; Ap. 53) Clem. Alex. *Strom.* iii. 15. 97 (Potter, 555), *πάλιν ὁ κύριός φησιν· ὁ γήμας μὴ ἐκβαλλέτω καὶ ὁ μὴ γήμας μὴ γαμείτω· ὁ κατὰ πρόθεσιν εὐνουχίας ὁμολογήσας μὴ γῆμαι ἄγαμος διαμενέτω*: 'Again the Lord saith, Let him that is married not put away, and let him that is unmarried marry not: let him that with purpose of celibacy hath promised not to marry remain unmarried.'

61. (R. 129; Ag. 8) Clem. Alex. *Excerpta ex Theodoto*, ii. (Potter, 957), *διὰ τοῦτο λέγει ὁ σωτήρ· σώζου σὺ καὶ ἡ ψυχή σου*: 'Therefore the Saviour saith, Be saved, thou and thy soul.'

62. (R. 128; Ag. 5) Origen, *Hom. in Ieremiam*, xx. 3, 'Legi alicubi quasi Salvatore dicente, et quæro sive quis personam figuravit Salvatoris, sive in memoriam adduxit, an verum sit hoc quod dictum est. Ait autem ipse Salvator: Qui iuxta me est, iuxta ignem est; qui longe est a me, longe est a regno': 'I have read somewhere what pur

ports to be an utterance of the Saviour, and I query (equally if some one put it into the mouth of the Saviour, or if some one remembered it) whether that is true which is said. But the Saviour himself saith, He who is near me is near the fire; he who is far from me is far from the kingdom.'

63. (R. 90; Ag. 36*b*) *de montibus Sina et Sion*, xiii., 'Ipso (*sc.* Domino) nos instruente et monente in epistula Johannis discipuli sui ad populum: Ita me in vobis videte, quomodo quis vestrum se videt in aquam aut in speculum': 'He himself instructing and warning us in the Epistle of John his disciple to the people: Ye see me in yourselves, as one of you sees himself in water or mirror.'

64. (R. 85; Ag. 3) Epiphan. *Hær.* lxxx. 5, *ἄξιος γὰρ ὁ ἐργάτης τοῦ μισθοῦ αὐτοῦ· καὶ· ἀρκετὸν τῳ ἐργαζομένῳ ἡ τροφὴ αὐτοῦ*: 'For the labourer is worthy of his hire; and, Sufficient for the labourer is his maintenance.'

65. (R. 125) Augustine, *Contra adversarium legis et prophetarum*, ii. 4. 14, 'Sed apostolis, inquit, Dominus noster interrogantibus de Iudæorum prophetis quid sentiri deberet, qui de adventu eius aliquid cecinisse in præteritum putabantur, commotus talia eos etiam nunc sentire, respondit: Dimisistis vivum qui ante vos est et de mortuis fabulamini. Quid mirum (quandoquidem hoc testimonium de scripturis nescio quibus apocryphis protulit) si de prophetis Dei talia confinxerunt hæretici, qui easdem litteras non accipiunt?' 'But (he says) when the apostles asked our Lord what ought to be thought about the prophets of the Jews, who were believed formerly to have prophesied his coming, he, angry that they even now had such thoughts, answered, You have sent away the living who is before you, and prate about dead men. What wonder, seeing he has brought out this quotation from some apocryphal scriptures, if heretics who do not accept the same writings, have invented such things about the prophets of God?'

66. (R. 97; Ap. 24) Ephr. Syr. *Evang. conc. expos.* (ed. Mösinger, p. 203), 'Quod autem turbatus est consonat cum eo, quod dixit: Quamdiu vobiscum ero et vobiscum loquar? et alio loco: Tædet me de generatione ista. Probaverunt me, ait, decies, hi autem vicies et decies decies': 'Now that he was distressed agrees with what he said, How long shall I be with you and speak with you? and in another place, I am weary of this generation. They proved me, he said, ten times, but these twenty times and ten times ten times.'

(*g*) For examples of unauthentic Agrapha from very late sources, see Ropes, *Sprüche Jesu*, pp. 111, 116, 120, 121.

(*h*) *Agrapha from Mohammedan sources.*—The following 48 Agrapha from Mohammedan sources were published by Prof. D. S. Margoliouth in the *Expository Times*, Nov., Dec. 1893, Jan. 1894, pp. 59, 107, 177 f.

1. Castalani, *Commentary on Bukhari*, i. 163, 'Jesus asked Gabriel when the hour (*i.e.* the day of judgment) was to come? Gabriel answered, He whom thou askest knows no better than he who asks.'

2. Jaḳut's *Geographical Lexicon*, i. 1, 'Jesus said, The world is a place of transition, full of examples; be pilgrims therein, and take warning by the traces of those that have gone before.'

3. Baidawi, *Commentary on the Ḳoran*, p. 71, ed. Constantinop., 'Jesus said, Be in the midst, yet walk on one side.'

4. Zamakhshari, *Commentary on the Ḳoran*, p. 986, 'In the sermons of Jesus, son of Mary, it is written, Beware how ye sit with sinners.'

5. *El-Mustatraf*, etc., i. p. 20, 'Jesus said, I have treated the leprous and the blind, and have cured them; but when I have treated the fool, I have failed to cure him.'

6. *El-Hadaik El-Wardiyyah*, i. p. 27, 'God revealed unto Jesus, Command the children of Israel that they enter not my house save with pure hearts, and humble eyes, and clean hands; for I will not answer any one of them against whom any has a complaint.'

The following are from El-Ghazzali, *Revival of the Religious Sciences*:—

7. i. 8, 'Jesus said, Whoso knows and does and teaches, shall be called great in the kingdom of heaven.'

8. i. 26, 'Jesus said, Trees are many, yet not all of them bear fruit; and fruits are many, yet not all of them are fit for food; and sciences are many, but not all of them are profitable.'

9. i. 30, 'Jesus said, Commit not wisdom to those who are not meet for it, lest ye harm it; and withhold it not from them that are meet for it, lest ye harm them. Be like a gentle physician, who puts the remedy on the diseased spot.' According to another version: 'Whoso commits wisdom to them that are not meet for it, is a fool; and whoso withholds it from them that are meet for it, is an evildoer. Wisdom has rights, and rightful owners; and give each his due.'

10. i. 49, 'Jesus said, Evil disciples are like a rock that has fallen at the mouth of a brook; it does not drink the water, neither does it let the water flow to the fields. And they are like the conduit of a *latrina* which is plastered outside, and foul inside; or like graves, the outside of which is decorated, while within are dead men's bones.'

11. i. 50, 'Jesus said, How can he be a disciple who, when his journey is unto the next world, makes for the things of this world? How can he be a disciple who seeks for words in order to communicate by them, not to act according to them?'

12. i. 52, 'God said unto Jesus, Exhort thyself, and if thou hast profited by the exhortation, then exhort others; otherwise be ashamed before me.'

13. i. 177, 'Jesus said, If a man send away a beggar empty from his house, the angels will not visit that house for seven nights.'

14. i. 247, *Prayer of Jesus*—'O God, I am this morning unable to ward off what I would not, or to obtain what I would. The power is in another's hands. I am bound by my works, and there is none so poor that is poorer than I. O God, make not mine enemy to rejoice over me, nor my friend to grieve over me; make not my trouble to be in the matter of my faith; make not the world my chief care; and give not the power over me to him who will not pity me.'

15. ii. 119, 'God revealed to Jesus, Though thou shouldst worship with the devotion of the inhabitants of the heaven and the earth, but hadst not love in God and hate in God, it would avail thee nothing.'

16. ii. 119, 'Jesus said, Make yourselves beloved of God by hating the evil-doers. Bring yourselves nearer to God by removing far from them; and seek God's favour by their displeasure. They said, O Spirit of God, then with whom shall we converse? Then He said, Converse with those whose presence will remind you of God, whose words will increase your works, and whose works will make you desire the next world.'

17. ii. 134, 'Jesus said to the apostles, How would you do if you saw your brother sleeping, and the wind had lifted up his garment? They said, We should cover him up. He said, Nay, ye would uncover him. They said, God forbid! Who would do this? He said, One of you who hears a word concerning his brother, and adds to it, and relates it with additions.'

18. ii. 154, 'They say that there was no form of address Jesus loved better to hear than "Poor man."'

19. ii. 168, 'When Jesus was asked, How art thou this morning? he would answer, Unable to forestall what I hope, or to put off what I fear, bound by my works, with all my good in another's hand. There is no poor man poorer than I.'

20. iii. 25, 'Satan, the accursed, appeared to Jesus, and said unto him, Say, there is no God but God. He said, It is a true saying, but I will not say it at thy invitation.'

21. iii. 28, 'When Jesus was born, the demons came to Satan, and said, The idols have been overturned. He said, This is a mere accident that has occurred; keep still. Then he flew till he had gone over both hemispheres, and found nothing. After that he found Jesus the son of Mary already born, with the angels surrounding him. He returned to the demons, and said, A prophet was born yesterday; no woman ever conceived or bare a child without my presence save this one. Hope not, therefore, that the idols will be worshipped after this night, so attack mankind through haste and thoughtlessness.'

22. iii. 28, 'Jesus lay down one day with his head upon a stone. Satan, passing by, said, O Jesus, thou art fond of this world. So he took the stone and cast it from under his head, saying, This be thine together with the world.'

23. iii. 52, 'Jesus was asked, Who taught thee? He answered, No one taught me. I saw that the ignorance of the fool was a shame, and I avoided it.'

24. iii. 52, 'Jesus said, Blessed is he who abandons a present pleasure for the sake of a promised (reward) which is absent and unseen.'

25. iii. 65, 'Jesus said, O company of apostles, make hungry your livers, and bare your bodies; perhaps then your hearts may see God.'

26. iii. 67, 'It is related how Jesus remained sixty days addressing his Lord, without eating. Then the thought of bread came into his mind, and his communion was interrupted, and he saw a loaf set before him. Then he sat down and wept over the loss of his communion, when he beheld an old man close to him. Jesus said unto him, God bless thee, thou saint of God! Pray to God for me, for I was in an ecstasy when the thought of bread entered my mind, and the ecstasy was interrupted. The old man said, O God, if thou knowest that the thought of bread came into my mind since I knew thee, then forgive me not. Nay, when it was before me, I would eat it without thought or reflexion.'

27. iii. 81, 'Jesus said, Beware of glances; for they plant passion in the heart, and that is a sufficient temptation.'

28. iii. 87, 'Jesus was asked by some men to guide them to some course whereby they might enter Paradise. He said, Speak not at all. They said, We cannot do this. He said, Then only say what is good.'

29. iii. 87, 'Jesus said, Devotion is of ten parts. Nine of them consist in silence, and one in solitude.'

30. iii. 92, 'Jesus said, Whosoever lies much, loses his beauty; and whosoever wrangles with others, loses his honour; and whosoever is much troubled, sickens in his body; and whosoever is evilly disposed, tortures himself.'

31. iii. 94, 'Jesus, passing by a swine, said to it, Go in peace. They said, O Spirit of God, sayest thou so to a swine? He answered, I would not accustom my tongue to evil.'

32. iii. 107, 'Jesus said, One of the greatest of sins in God's eyes is that a man should say God knows what he knows not.'

33. iii. 108, 'Malik, son of Dinar, said, Jesus one day walked with his apostles, and they passed by the carcass of a dog. The apostles said, How foul is the smell of this dog! But Jesus said, How white are its teeth!'

34. iii. 134, 'Christ passed by certain of the Jews, who spake evil to him; but he spake good to them in return. It was said to him, Verily these speak ill unto thee, and dost thou speak good? He said, Each gives out of his store.'

35. iii. 151, 'Jesus said, Take not the world for your lord, lest it take you for its slaves. Lay up your treasure with Him who will not waste it,' etc.

36. iii. 151, 'Jesus said, Ye company of apostles, verily I have overthrown the world upon her face for you; raise her not up after me. It is a mark of the foulness of this world that God is disobeyed therein, and that the future world cannot be attained save by abandonment of this; pass then through this world, and linger not there; and know that the root of every sin is love of the world. Often does the pleasure of an hour bestow on him that enjoys it long pain.'

37. iii. 151, 'He said again, I have laid the world low for you, and ye are seated upon its back. Let not kings and women dispute with you the possession of it. Dispute not the world with kings, for they will not offer you what you have abandoned and their world; but guard against women by fasting and prayer.'

38. iii. 151, 'He said again, The world seeks and is sought. If a man seeks the next world, this world seeks him till he obtain therein his full sustenance; but if a man seeks this world, the next world seeks him till death comes and takes him by the throat.'

39. iii. 152, 'Jesus said, The love of this world and of the next cannot agree in a believer's heart, even as fire and water cannot agree in a single vessel.'

40. iii. 153, 'Jesus being asked, Why dost thou not take a house to shelter thee? said, The rags of those that were before us are good enough for us.'

41. iii. 153, 'It is recorded that one day Jesus was sore troubled by the rain and thunder and lightning, and began to seek a shelter. His eye fell upon a tent hard by; but when he came there, finding a woman inside, he turned away from it. Then he noticed a cave in a mountain; but when he came thither, there was a lion there. Laying his hand upon the lion, he said, My God, Thou hast given each thing a resting-place, but to me thou has given none! Then God revealed to him, Thy resting-place is in the abode of my mercy: that I may wed thee on the day of judgment . . . and make thy bridal feast four thousand years, of which each day is like a lifetime in this present world; and that I may command a herald to proclaim, Where are they that fast in this world? Come to the bridal feast of Jesus, who fasted in this world!'

42. iii. 153, 'Jesus said, Woe unto him who hath this world, seeing that he must die and leave it, and all that is in it! It deceives him, yet he trusts in it; he relies upon it, and it betrays him. Woe unto them that are deceived! When they shall be shown what they loathe, and shall be abandoned by what they love; and shall be overtaken by that wherewith they are threatened! Woe unto him whose care is the world, and whose work is sin; seeing that one day he shall be disgraced by his sin.'

43. iii. 153, 'Jesus said, Who is it that builds upon the waves of the sea? Such is the world; take it not for your resting-place.'

44. iii. 153, 'Some said to Jesus, Teach us some doctrine for which God will love us. Jesus said, Hate the world, and God will love you.'

45. iii. 154, 'Jesus said, Ye company of apostles, be satisfied with a humble portion in this world, so your faith be whole; even as the people of this world are satisfied with a humble portion in faith, so this world be secured to them.'

46. iii. 154, 'Jesus said, O thou that seekest this world to do charity, to abandon it were more charitable.'

47. iii. 159, 'Jesus used to say, My condiment is hunger, my inner garment fear, and my outer garment wool. I warm myself in winter in the sun; my candle is the moon; my mounts are my feet; my food and dainties are the fruits of the earth; neither at eventide nor in the morning have I aught in my possession, yet no one on earth is richer than I.'

48. iii. 161, 'The world was revealed unto Jesus in the form of an old woman with broken teeth, with all sorts of ornaments upon her. He said to her, How many husbands hast thou had? She said, I cannot count them. He said, Hast thou survived them all, or did they all divorce thee? She said, Nay, I have slain them all. Jesus said, Woe unto thy remaining husbands! Why do they not take warning by thy former husbands? Thou hast destroyed them one after another, and yet they are not on their guard against thee.'

The following two Sayings are quoted by Levinus Warnerus, in notes to his *Centuria proverbiorum Persicorum*, Lugd. Batav. 1644, p. 30 f. (see Fabricius, *Cod. apocr. NT*, iii. p. 394 f.):—

49. 'Jesus, son of Mary (to whom be peace), said, Whoso craves wealth is like a man who drinks sea-water; the more he drinks, the more he increases his thirst, and he ceases not to drink until he perishes.'

50. 'Jesus, son of Mary, said to John, son of Zacharias, If any one in speaking of thee says the truth, praise God; if he utters a lie, praise God still more, for thereby shall thy treasure be increased in the list of thy works, and that without any labour of thine, that is, his good works are carried to thy list.'

Finally, we have the following Saying:—

51. Ḳoran, Sur. 5 *fin.*, 'Remember, when the apostles said, O Jesus, Son of Mary, is thy Lord able to cause a table to descend unto us from heaven? he answered, Fear God, if ye be true believers. They said, We desire to eat thereof, and that our hearts may rest at ease; and that we may know that thou hast told us the truth; and that we may be witnesses thereof. Jesus, the son of Mary, said, O God our Lord, cause a table to descend unto us from heaven, that the day of its descent may become a festival-day unto us, unto the first of us, and unto the last of us; and a sign from thee; and do thou provide food for us, for thou art the best provider. God said, Verily I will cause it to descend unto you; but whoever among you shall disbelieve hereafter, I will surely punish him with a punishment wherewith I will not punish any other creature.'

LITERATURE.—Much of the material relating to the Agrapha was collected by the older editors of Patristic texts. Especially the notes of Cotelier (*Patres apostolici* 2, Antwerp, 1698; *Ecclesiæ Græcæ monumenta*, Paris, 1677–86) have been quarries of erudition for later workers. In recent years important contributions have been made by Anger (*Synopsis Evangeliorum*, Leipzig, 1852); Hilgenfeld (*NT extra Canonem Receptum* 2, Leipzig, 1884); and Zahn (*Gesch. d. neutest. Kanons*, 1888–92), as well as by the writers who have discussed the fragments of the Gospel according to the Hebrews (notably Nicholson, Handmann, Zahn). Collections of Agrapha have been frequently made since those of Grabe (in his *Spicilegium*, Oxford, 1698) and Fabricius (in his *Codex apocr. NT*, Hamburg, 1703). See, among others, R. Hofmann, *Leben Jesu nach den Apokryphen*, 1851; Westcott, *Introduction to the Study of the Gospels*, Appendix C, 1860, 81894; J. T. Dodd, *Sayings Ascribed to Our Lord*, Oxford, 1874; Schaff, *History of the Christian Church*, vol. i., 1882, pp. 162–7; Nestle, *NT supplementum*, Leipzig, 1896, pp. 89–92; Preuschen, *Antilegomena*, 1901, pp. 43–47, 138 f.; J. de Q. Donehoe, *Apocryphal and Legendary Life of Christ*, 1903. Resch brings together a vast amount of material relating to the whole subject, and uses the Agrapha as a leading argument for his theory (founded on that of B. Weiss) of the origin of the Synoptic Gospels. He holds to an original Gospel, called in ancient times τὰ λόγια, and composed in Hebrew by Matthew shortly after the death of Christ. This document is supposed to have been the main source of the three Synoptic Gospels (its matter constituting four-fifths of Matthew, three-fourths of Luke, and two-thirds of Mark), to have been used by St. Paul and St. John, and to have been known for many centuries to the writers of the Church. From it are derived the Agrapha, and to varying translations of it are due not only the variations of the Synoptic Evangelists, but also many of the countless textual variants in the Gospels, especially those of the 'Western Text,' as preserved both in MSS and in Patristic quotations. A reconstruction of the 'Logia' is attempted in Resch, *Die Logia Jesu nach dem griechischen und hebräischen Text wiederhergestellt*, 1898; see also his 'Aussercanonische Paralleltexte zu den Evangelien' (*TU* x. 1–5), 1893–96.

Resch's contention that 75 Agrapha are probably genuine Sayings of Jesus would, if accepted, furnish some reason for supposing a single common source of such material. In fact, however, most of Resch's Agrapha do not commend themselves to other scholars as probably genuine; and his solution of the Synoptic Problem has been generally rejected. See J. H. Ropes, 'Die Sprüche Jesu die in den kanonischen Evangelien nicht überliefert sind: eine kritische Bearbeitung des von D. Alfred Resch gesammelten Materials' (*TU* xiv. 2), 1896. For criticism of Resch's views, see also Jülicher in *ThLZ*, 1890, col. 321–330; *Church Quarterly Review*, Oct. 1890, pp. 1–21; Knowling, *Witness of the Epistles*, 1892; Rahlfs in *ThLZ*, 1893, col. 377 f.; C. C. Torrey in *AJTh*, Oct. 1899, pp. 698–703.

Blomfield Jackson (*Twenty-five Agrapha, annotated*, London, S.P.C.K., 1900) offers sensible and interesting discussions, with some fresh illustrative material. More complete notices of literature in Resch, *Agrapha*, and Ropes, *Sprüche Jesu*.

On the Oxyrhynchus 'Sayings of Our Lord,' see the *editio princeps*, Grenfell and Hunt, ΛΟΓΙΑ ΙΗΣΟΥ, *Sayings of Our Lord*, London, 1897; Lock and Sanday, *Two Lectures on the 'Sayings of Jesus,'* Oxford, 1897 (with full bibliography); Grenfell and Hunt, *The Oxyrhynchus Papyri*, pt. i., 1898, pp. 1–3.

On the Sayings from the Talmud, see Laible, *Jesus Christus im Thalmud*, 1891 [Eng. tr. by Streane, 1893]; and Literature given in Ropes, *Sprüche Jesu*, pp. 115, 151.

On the Sayings of Jesus in Mohammedan writers, see J. A. Fabricius, *Codex apocr. NT*, iii., Hamburg, 1719, pp. 394–7; Jeremiah Jones, *New and Full Method of Settling the Canonical Authority of the NT*, i., Oxford, 1798, pp. 451–71; R. Hofmann, *Leben Jesu nach d. Apokryphen*, 1851, pp. 327–9; D. S. Margoliouth in *Expository Times*, vol. v. pp. 59, 107, 177 f., Nov., Dec. 1893, Jan. 1894; W. Lock in *Expositor*, 4th ser. vol. ix. pp. 97–99, 1894.

J. H. ROPES.

**PAPYRI.**—The manner in which papyrus was used as writing-material in the ancient world, the dates of its adoption and abandonment, and the countries in which it was employed, have been described in vol. iv. of this Dictionary (art. WRITING). The object of the present article is to show what actual writings on papyrus, bearing upon the study of the Bible, have come down to us, and what kind of information is to be derived from them.

i. THE DISCOVERIES OF PAPYRI. — The first papyrus rolls to be brought to light were the product of the excavations on the site of Herculaneum in the middle of the 18th century. In 1752 a small room was discovered, which proved to be a library; and on the shelves round its walls were found several hundreds of rolls, calcined to the semblance of cinders by the eruption of Vesuvius, which buried the town in A.D. 79. These, however, when patiently unrolled and deciphered, were found to contain philosophical treatises of the Epicurean school, and do not concern us here. All other papyri that have hitherto come to light are derived from Egypt, where alone the conditions of soil and climate are such as to admit of the preservation of so perishable a material. The date of the first discovery of papyri in Egypt is 1778, when a collection of rolls was discovered by fellaheen, probably in the Fayum; but, since no purchaser was immediately forthcoming, all were destroyed but one, now in the Museum at Naples, containing a list of labourers in the reign of Commodus. For a century after this date discoveries were merely sporadic, though some important literary papyri were among the fruits of them.

The first find upon a large scale was made in 1877, on the site of the city of Arsinoë, in the Fayum, from which several thousand papyri (nearly all fragmentary) were derived, most of which are now at Vienna. With this event the modern period of papyrus discovery begins, and the quarter of a century that has elapsed since that date has witnessed an ever-increasing flood of papyri, partly due to the systematic searches of European explorers, and partly to the irregular zeal of the natives. The principal localities from which papyri have been drawn are the Fayum, a detached province lying to the west of the Nile in Central Egypt, and the neighbourhoods of the towns of Oxyrhynchus, Hermopolis, Heracleopolis, and Thebes. They are found in the rubbish-heaps of buried towns or villages, in the cartonnage of mummy-cases of the Ptolemaic period (in which layers of papyrus, covered with plaster, took the place of wood), and in cemeteries; one remarkable discovery (by Messrs. Grenfell and Hunt, on the site of the ancient Tebtunis) being that of a cemetery of crocodiles, in which the animals were found wrapped in rolls of papyrus, while other rolls had been stuffed inside them. There are now tens, or even hundreds, of thousands of papyri (the majority, no doubt, being mere fragments) in the possession of the museums and learned societies of Europe, many of which have not yet been unrolled or deciphered. Some of these are literary works, relics of the books which once circulated among the educated classes, native or foreign, of Egypt; but the vast majority consists of non-literary documents, including official and commercial papers of all descriptions (census-rolls, tax-registers, receipts, petitions, sales, leases, loans, etc.), as well as private letters and accounts. It is from these that some of the most instructive materials for our present purpose are obtained.

ii. Egyptian Papyri.—The papyri of which we have chiefly to speak are Greek, belonging to the period after the conquest of Egypt by Alexander and the establishment of the Ptolemaic dynasty. But in addition to these some mention must be made of papyri in the ancient Egyptian language, which precede the Greek period or coincide with the earlier part of it; and in the later Egyptian language, commonly known as Coptic, which coincide with the latter part of the Greek period and continue after the practical disappearance of Greek. Ancient Egyptian papyri have only an indirect bearing upon the study of the Bible. Concurrently with the monuments of stone, they give us records of the history of Egypt, with which that of the Hebrews is in contact in so many places; while many of them contain copies of the Book of the Dead, the principal document of the Egyptian religion, with which the Israelites may possibly have become acquainted to some extent through their intercourse with their neighbours. These are written in *hieroglyphics*, the earliest form of writing practised in Egypt. Two other forms were successively developed from it—the *hieratic* and the *demotic*. Hieratic papyri are relatively scarce, and contain nothing to our purpose; demotic are very difficult to translate, and are mostly of the nature of business documents or stories. One document of the latter class, written about the end of the 1st cent., has been held to show certain resemblances to the narrative of the Nativity of our Lord; but the resemblance is, in truth, very slight and unessential (Griffith, *Stories of the High Priests of Memphis*, 1900, pp. 43, 44). On the whole, therefore, the later Egyptian papyri contain little that concerns the biblical student as such.

iii. Hebrew Papyri.—If papyrus was used in Palestine at all as writing material (see art. Writing, *l.c.* § ii.), no specimens of it could be expected to survive in that country; and even in Alexandria, where the colony of learned Jews no doubt possessed copies of the Hebrew Scriptures on papyrus, the soil is too damp to admit of their preservation. Consequently it is not surprising that, up to a very recent date, no Hebrew papyrus was known to exist. The first publication (containing fragments of prayers and business documents, from papyri in the Berlin Museum) was made by Steinschneider in 1879; but these are not earlier than the 7th century. Portions of a liturgical papyrus-codex, assigned to the 9th cent., are in the Cambridge University Library, and there are a few fragments at Oxford and Vienna. Far earlier and more valuable than these is a fragment acquired in 1902 by Mr. W. L. Nash, and by him presented to the Cambridge University Library. It is assigned on palæographical grounds to the 2nd cent. after Christ, though the materials for comparison (consisting mainly of inscriptions) are very scanty. It contains the Ten Commandments and the commencement of the *Shema'* (Dt $6^{4ff.}$), in a text differing markedly from the Massoretic. The Decalogue is in a form nearer to Dt $5^{6-21}$ than to Ex $20^{1-17}$. The Sixth and Seventh Commandments are transposed, as in Cod. B and in Lk $18^{20}$. The *Shema'* immediately follows the Decalogue, but has the introductory words, 'These are the statutes and the judgments which Moses commanded the children of Israel, when they came out of the land of Egypt,' which appear in the LXX (and OL). So far as it goes, therefore, this interesting fragment tends to support the theory that the LXX not infrequently represents a genuine pre-Massoretic Hebrew text. (S. A. Cook, *PSBA* xxv. 34, 1903).

iv. Greek Papyri.—Up to the present time, out of all the great mass of Greek papyri which have been brought to light, not many have any direct bearing on the Bible text or history. Nevertheless, all lists speedily become antiquated by the publication of fresh discoveries. The following list is believed to be complete up to June 1903:—

A. *Biblical texts**—

1. Gn $1^{1-5}$, in versions of LXX and Aquila. 4th cent. Amherst Pap. 3*c* (Grenfell and Hunt, *Amherst Papyri*, pt. i.).
2. Gn $14^{7}$; probably a quotation in a theological treatise, since the text on the *verso*, in the same hand, is not biblical. 3rd cent. Brit. Mus. Pap. 212.
3. Ex $19^{1. 2. 5. 6}$, Dt $32^{3-10}$. 6th cent. Amherst Papp. 191, 192 (*op. cit.* pt. ii.).

3*a*. 2 S $15^{36}$–$16^{1}$. 4th cent. Strassburg Pap. 911. *Archiv. f. Papyrusforschung*, ii. 227.

4. Job $1^{21. 22}$ $2^{3}$. 7th cent. Amherst Pap. 4 (*ib.* pt. i.).
5. Ps $5^{6-12}$. 5th or 6th cent. Amherst Pap. 5.
6. Ps 10 $(11)^{2}$–18 $(19)^{6}$ 20 $(21)^{14}$–34 $(35)^{6}$. 7th cent. Brit. Mus. Pap. 37 (Tischendorf, *Mon. Sac. Ined.*, Nov. Coll. i. 217).
7. Ps 11 $(12)^{7}$–14 $(15)^{4}$. Late 3rd cent. Brit. Mus. Pap. 230 (Kenyon, *Facsimiles of Biblical MSS.*, pl. 1).
8. Ps 39 $(40)^{16}$–40 $(41)^{4}$. Berlin Museum (Blass, *Zeitschr. f. äg. Sprache*, 1881).
9. Ps 107 $(108)^{13}$ 108 $(109)^{1. 2. 12. 13}$ 118 $(119)^{115-122. 127-135}$ 135 $(136)^{19-28}$ 136 $(137)^{1. 6-8}$ 137 $(138)^{1-3}$ 138 $(139)^{20-26}$ 139 $(140)^{1-6. 10-14}$ 140 $(141)^{1-4}$, with several additional small fragments. 7th cent. or later. Amherst Papp. 6, 200 (Grenfell and Hunt, *op. cit* pts. i. and ii.).

* In addition to the papyri here enumerated, there are several biblical fragments in the Rainer collection at Vienna and the Bibliothèque Nationale at Paris, as to which no precise details have yet been published.

10. Ca $1^{6-9}$. 7th or 8th cent. Bodl. MS. Gr. Bibl. g. 1 (P) (Grenfell, *Greek Papyri*, i. 7).
11. Is $38^{3-5. 13-16}$. 3rd cent. Rainer Pap. 8024 (*Führer durch die Ausstellung*, 1894, No. 536).
12. Ezk $5^{12}$–$6^{3}$, with Hexaplaric symbols. 3rd cent. Bodl. MS. Gr. Bibl. d. 4 (P) (Grenfell, *Greek Papyri*, i. 5).
13. Zec 4–Mal 4. 7th cent. (?) Heidelberg University Library (Specimen facs. in *Times*, Sept. 7, 1892; to be edited by Deissmann).
14. Mt $1^{1-9. 12. 14-20}$. 3rd cent. Pennsylvania Univ. Library (Grenfell and Hunt, *Oxyrhynchus Papyri*, i. 2).
15. Lk $1^{74-80}$ $5^{3-8}$ $5^{30}$–$6^{4}$. 4th cent. Paris, Bibl. Nat. (Scheil, *Mém. de la Miss. arch. française au Caire*, ix.).
16. Lk $7^{36-43}$ $10^{38-42}$. 6th cent. Rainer Pap. 8021 (*Führer*, No. 539).
17. Jn $1^{23-31. 33-41}$ $20^{11-17. 19-25}$. 3rd cent. Brit. Mus. Pap. 782 (Grenfell and Hunt, *Oxy. Pap.* ii. 208).
18. Ro $1^{1-7}$. 4th cent. Harvard University Library (*ib.* ii. 209).
19. 1 Co $1^{17-20}$ $6^{13-18}$ $7^{3. 4. 10-14}$. 5th cent. Uspensky Collection at Kiew.
20. 1 Co $1^{25-27}$ $2^{6-8}$ $3^{8-10. 20}$. 5th cent. St. Catherine's, Sinai (Harris, *Biblical Fragments from Mt. Sinai*, No. 14).
21. 2 Th $1^{1}$–$2^{2}$. 4th or 5th cent. Berlin Museum P. 5013.
22. He $1^{1}$. 3rd or 4th cent. Amherst Pap. 3*b* (Grenfell and Hunt, *Amherst Papyri*, pt. i.).

B. *Extra-canonical writings*—

23. Fragment from narrative of St. Peter's denial, consisting of parts of seven lines. 3rd cent. (?) Rainer Pap. (Bickell, *Mitth. Erzh. Rainer*, i. 52).
24. Logia Jesu; one leaf, containing seven sayings of our Lord, with remains of an eighth. The first (imperfect) agrees, so far as it goes, with Lk $6^{42}$; part of the sixth is nearly identical with Lk $4^{24}$; the seventh is an expansion of Mt $5^{14}$; the rest are new. Found at Oxyrhynchus. 3rd cent. Bodl. MS. Gr. th. e. 7 (P) (Grenfell and Hunt, *Sayings of our Lord*).
25. The Ascension of Isaiah, ch. 2. § 4–4. § 4; the only extant MS of any part of the work in the original Greek. 5th or 6th cent. Amherst Pap. 1 (Grenfell and Hunt, *Amherst Papyri*, pt. i.).

C. *Theological works*—

26. Philo, τίς ὁ τῶν θείων κληρονόμος and περὶ γενέσεως Ἀβέλ. 3rd cent. Formerly at Gizeh, now in the Louvre (Scheil, *Mém. de la Miss. arch. française au Caire*, tom. ix.).
27. Hermas, *Pastor*, *Sim.* ii. 7–10, iv. 2–5. 3rd cent. Berl. Mus. Pap. 5513 (Diels and Harnack, *Sitzungsb. d. Berl. Akad.* 1891).
28. Hermas, *Pastor*, *Vis.* i. 2–3, 12–13; *Mand.* xii. 1; *Sim.* ix. 2, 12, 17, 30; the last fragment contains a portion of the text hitherto known only in translations. 6th cent. Amherst Pap. 190 (Grenfell and Hunt).
29. Tract on prophecy, including quotation from Hermas, *Mand.* xi. 9. Harnack suggests that it may be part of the work of Melito περὶ προφητείας. 3rd–4th cent. Oxyrhynchus Pap. 5 (Grenfell and Hunt).
30. Fragment on the higher and lower soul; according to Harnack, from a Gnostic work of the Valentinian school. 3rd–4th cent. Oxyrhynchus Pap. 4 (*ib.*).
31. Theological fragment of uncertain character. 3rd cent. Oxy. Pap. 210 (*ib.*).
32. Early Christian hymn, in irregular metre. 4th cent. Amherst Pap. 2 (Grenfell and Hunt).

32*a*. Admonitions, perhaps *logia*, very fragmentary. 4th cent. Strassburg Pap. 1017. *Archiv. f. Papyrusforschung*, ii. 217.

33. Basil, *Epp.* v. 77 E, vi. 79 B, ccxciii. 432 B, cl. 239 C, ii. 72 A. 5th cent. (?) Berlin Museum (*Philologus*, 1884).
34. Gregory of Nyssa, *Life of Moses*; extracts. 5th cent. Berlin Museum (Blass, *Zeitschr. f. äg. Sprache*, 1880).
35. Cyril of Alexandria, *de Adoratione*, p. 242 E–250 D, 286 B. 6th or 7th cent. In private hands (Bernard, *Royal Irish Acad.* xxix. pt. 18).
36. Prayer to our Lord for deliverance from sickness and evil spirits, including elements of a creed; regarded by its first editor as drawn from the Gospel of the Egyptians, but without adequate grounds. 4th–5th cent. Gizeh Pap. 10263 (Jacoby, *Ein neues Evangelienfragment*, Strassburg, 1900).
37. Fragments of lives of SS. Abraham and Theodora. Louvre Papp. 1704–8 *bis* (Wessely, *Wiener Studien*, 1889).

38–44. Unidentified fragments of theological works. 5th–7th cent. Amherst Papp. 194–199, 201 (Grenfell and Hunt).

45–48. Ditto. 6th–7th cent. Brit. Mus. Papp. cxiii. 12*a–c*, 13 (Kenyon, *Catal. of Greek Papyri*, vol. i.).

49–51. Ditto. 6th–7th cent. Brit. Mus. Papp. 455, 462, 464 (*ib.* vol. ii.).

52. Ditto. 6th cent. (?) Brit. Mus. Pap. 873 (*Catal. of Additions to Dept. of MSS in British Museum*, 1894–99).
53. Hymn or incantation in Christian terms. 7th cent. (?) Brit. Mus. Pap. 1029 *verso* (unpubl.).
54. Prayer. 7th cent. Brit. Mus. Pap. 1176 (unpubl.).
55. Unidentified theological fragment. Berlin Museum. (Blass, *Zeitschr. f. äg. Sprache*, 1881).
56. Liturgical fragments, apparently choir slips. 7th–8th cent. Amherst Pap. 9 (Grenfell and Hunt).
57. Fragments of a Hebrew-Greek *Onomasticon Sacrum*. Heidelberg University Library (Deissmann, *Encycl. Biblica*, iii. 3560).

D. *Documents illustrative of Church history*—

58–60. Reports of appeals by Jews heard by the Roman emperors (Claudius and Trajan). Berl. Pap. 7118 (*Gr. Urk.* 511), Paris Pap. 68 + Brit. Mus. Pap. 1, Berl. Pap. 8111 (*Gr. Urk.* 341). See Wilcken, *Hermes*, xxx. 485 ff.; Bauer, *Archiv für Papyrusforschung*, i. 29, who compares these documents to the early Christian *Acta martyrum*.

61, 62. *Libelli*, or certificates of conformity to the State religion, issued by magistrates during the Decian persecution, A.D. 250. Berl. Pap. 7297 (*Gr. Urk.* 287) and Rainer Pap. (Krebs, *Sitzungsb. d. k. Akad. zu Berlin*, 1803, No. 48; Wessely, *Anzeiger d. k. k. Akad. in Wien*, 3rd Jan. 1894).

63. Letter from a Church dignitary in Rome to a Christian community in the Fayum, containing references to Maximus (bishop

of Alexandria, A.D. 264–282) and his successor Theonas. Amherst Pap. 3*a* (Grenfell and Hunt, *Amherst Papyri*, pt. i.; Harnack, *Sitzungsb. d. Berl. Akad.*, Nov. 1, 1900).

64. Letter from the presbyter Psenosiris to the presbyter Apollo with regard to a woman sent to the Great Oasis by the prefect of Egypt (perhaps a Christian banished during the persecution of Diocletian). Brit. Mus. Pap. 713 (Grenfell and Hunt, *Greek Papyri*, ii. p. 115; Deissmann, *The Epistle of Psenosiris*).

65. Inventory of furniture of a Christian church in the village of Ibion (in the Fayum). 5th–6th cent. Bodl. MS. Gr. th. d. 2 (P) (Grenfell and Hunt, *op. cit.* p. 160).

66. Festal letter from a Patriarch of Alexandria to his clergy. Probably A.D. 577. Brit. Mus. Pap. 729 (*ib.* p. 163).

67. Rescript from the emperors Theodosius II. and Valentinian III. to Apion, bishop of Syene and Elephantine, in reply to his petition for protection. Reference is made to churches on the island of Philæ. A.D. 425–450. Leyden Pap. Z (Wilcken, *Archiv für Papyrusforschung*, i. 396 ff.).

68. Christian amulet, including the Lord's Prayer. 6th cent. Papyrus found at Heracleopolis in 1899, but since burnt (*ib.* p. 429 ff., where references are given to other amulets).

v. VALUE OF THE PAPYRI.—The direct value to biblical science of the papyri above enumerated can be briefly estimated. The earlier biblical fragments (those of the 4th cent. or earlier) are too few and too small to be of much textual importance; but so far as they go their evidence in the NT supports the now dominant textual theory associated with the names of Westcott and Hort. They range themselves with the Codices ℵB and their allies, thus supporting not merely the type of text which WH have shown to be earlier than the Textus Receptus, but that particular form of it (WH's 'Neutral') which there is good reason to associate with Egypt. In the OT nearly all the papyrus fragments yet discovered are later than the great vellum uncials, and throw no new light on the textual problems of the LXX; but No. 12 is noticeable as containing a Hexaplaric text, with the earliest extant specimens of the symbols used by Origen. Outside the range of the canonical books, the Vienna fragment (No. 23) is too small to admit of any secure deductions; but the 'Logia' papyrus is exceptionally interesting, though there is no evidence to establish either the immediate source of its contents or the amount of authenticity which can be allowed to them. The 'Ascension of Isaiah' MS is also of considerable value as the only extant witness to the Greek text of the work; and the same may be said, to a less degree, of the Hermas fragments (No. 28). The other theological papyri do not amount to very much.

The greater part, however, of the value of the papyri lies in another direction, and arises from the light which they throw on the circumstances under which the LXX and the NT were written and circulated in the earlier ages. Occasionally they provide us with direct evidences of early Christianity, as in the case of Nos. 61–63 in the foregoing list; but the indirect evidence is greater, both in bulk and in importance. In the Greek papyri of the Ptolemaic period we have a mass of documents, literary and non-literary, written in the very country in which the LXX was produced and at the very same time, and showing us both how books were written at that time and what manner of Greek was spoken by the foreign residents in Egypt. Similarly, in the papyri of the early Roman period, from the 1st to the 4th cent., we have examples of books, letters, and business documents contemporary with the writers of the NT books, and illustrating the methods of book production and book circulation before the adoption of vellum and the date of the great vellum uncials which are the foundation of our textual knowledge. The results can be indicated only in outline within the limits of this article.

(*a*) *Linguistic.*—Previous to the great discoveries of papyri, it was usual to treat biblical Greek as a thing apart, due to a combination of Hebrew influences with the common Greek dialect, which operated only in Hellenistic (Jewish-Greek) circles. There is, no doubt, a considerable amount of truth in this view. Hebrew idioms naturally influenced the translators of the LXX, and acquaintance with the LXX naturally affected the style of the writers of the NT; but it is a view which requires modification. The papyri show us the dialect of Greek Egypt in many forms,—the language of the Government official, of the educated private person, of the dwellers in the temples, of the peasantry in the villages; and in many of them, which cannot be suspected of being subject to Jewish influences, we find words and phrases previously known only in the LXX or the NT. Thus the 'instrumental' use of the preposition ἐν by St. Paul in 1 Co 4[21] (ἐν ῥάβδῳ ἔλθω πρὸς ὑμᾶς) has habitually been regarded as a Hebraism; yet an exact parallel to it occurs in a group of petitions from a village in the Fayum (Tebtunis Papp. 16[14] 41[5] 45[17] 46[15] 47[11. 12] 48[19] Μαρρείους σὺν ἄλλοις πλείοσι ἐν μαχαίραις παραγινομένου, ἐπελθὼν Λύκος σὺν ἄλλοις ἐν ὅπλοις, κ.τ.λ.). Another papyrus from the same neighbourhood (50[12]) contains the expression ἐπιβαλὼν συνέχωσεν, in the sense 'he *turned to** and blocked up' (a canal), which may be compared with the obscure use of the same participle in Mk 14[72] καὶ ἐπιβαλὼν ἔκλαιεν. Prof. A. Deissmann, who, if not the first to notice this topic of interest in the papyri, was the first to develop it at length, has given the following list of words occurring in the LXX or NT, the use of which is elucidated or confirmed by the papyri:—

ἀγγαρεύω, ἀδελφός (of members of religious communities), ἄδολος, ἀθέτησις, ἀκατάγνωστος, ἀμετανόητος, ἀναφάλαντος, ἀντιλήμπτωρ, ἀντίλημψις, ἀπέχω, ἄρκετος, ἀρχισωματοφύλαξ, ἀσπάζομαι, ἄφεσις (ὑδάτων), γῆ ἐν ἀφέσει (but here D.'s explanation cannot be accepted, the phrase meaning land not held directly of the king), βαστάζω, βεβαίωσις, γένημα, γογγύζω, γραμματεύς, γράφω (γέγραπται), διάδοχος, διακούω, διῶρυξ, δοκίμιος, ἐάν (=ἄν), εἰ μήν, ἐλαιών, εἰς (=dat. commodi), ἐνταφιαστής, ἔντευξις, ἐνώπιον, ἐργοδιωκτής, ἐρωτᾶν (=request), ἔσθησις, εὐίλατος, θεμέλιον, καθαρὸς ἀπό, κατάκριμα, κυριακός, λειτουργία, λικμάω, λίψ (=west, which is normal in the papyri), λογεία, μετὰ καί (or σὺν καὶ), μικρός (=iunior), νεόφυτος, νόμος (=nome, the territorial division of Egypt), ὄνομα (in such phrases as ἔντευξις εἰς τὸ τοῦ βασιλέως ὄνομα), ὀφειλή, ὀψώνιον, παράδεισος, παρεπίδημος, πάρεσις, παστοφόριον, περιδέξιον, περίστασις, περιτέμνεσθαι (but D.'s interpretation of ἄσημος as=ἀπεριτέμνητος is untenable), ἀπὸ πέρυσι, πῆχυς (genitive πηχῶν), ποτισμός, πρᾶγμα ἔχειν, πράκτωρ, πρεσβύτερος (designating an official), πρόθεσις (ἄρτων), προφήτης, πυρράκης, σιτομέτριον, σκευοφύλαξ, σμαράγδινος, σουδάριον, συγγενής (as court-title), συμβούλιον, συνέχω, σφραγίζω, σφυρίς, σῶμα (=slave), τήρησις, υἱὸς θεοῦ (used as title of Augustus), ὑποζύγιον (=ass), ὑποπόδιον, φίλος (as court-title), χάραγμα, χειρόγραφον, χωρίζομαι.

In addition to the light thus thrown on the

* ἐπιβαλών might also be taken to mean 'heaping up (earth)'; but the construction without an object would be strange, and the expression somewhat tautological, since συνέχωσεν alone would give the same sense.

vocabulary of the Greek Bible, the papyri furnish evidence with regard to the orthography and the grammatical forms in use in Ptolemaic and Roman Egypt; but on these topics it is impossible to say much until the work of classifying the materials provided by the papyri has proceeded further than is at present the case. A beginning of the application of the material to biblical study has been made by A. Thumb (*Die sprachgeschichtliche Stellung des biblischen Griechisch*).

(*b*) *Historical.*—On the historical side, the papyri provide a mass of information with regard to the usages, official and private, of Egypt under Ptolemaic and Roman rule, which from time to time throws light on the biblical narrative. We have letters with which to compare those which St. Paul wrote to his fellow-Christians; some of them recalling, by the number of salutations with which they conclude, the terminations of the Epistles to the Romans or Colossians (*e.g.* Brit. Mus. Pap. 404); others, in which a large autograph signature closes a letter written by a scribe, illustrating St. Paul's expressions in Gal 6[11] (*e.g.* Brit. Mus. Papp. 311, 413). We have official, legal, and business formulæ in large numbers, including, for example, reports from one magistrate to another, similar to that sent by Claudius Lysias to Felix (Ac 23[26-30], where it may be observed that the doubtful word of salutation, ἔρρωσο, in v.[30], which is omitted by the best MSS, is decisively condemned by Egyptian usage, which admitted the use of this phrase only in letters addressed to an inferior). We have records of trials before magistrates, including brief summaries of the speeches of counsel, which recall the report of the speech of Tertullus in Ac 24[2ff.]. The double name of St. Paul (Σαῦλος ὁ καὶ Παῦλος) ceases to be remarkable or to cause any difficulty, when we find in the Egyptian census-lists scores of such double names, showing that it was customary for the natives of Oriental provinces to assume a Greek or Roman name in addition to that which they had among their own people (*e.g.* Ἡρώδης ὁ καὶ Πετενεφρῆς, Ἰσίδωρος ὁ καὶ Πανᾶς, κ.τ.λ.). The same census-records throw an interesting light on the census of Quirinius recorded in Lk 2[2]. They prove that a census was held every 14 years in Egypt under Roman rule, at least as far back as A.D. 20; while at the same time all the extant indications tend to show that this system did not exist under the Ptolemies. It is natural, therefore, to regard these facts as having some bearing on the statement in Luke; but the only attempt to work out the problem in detail is that of Prof. W. M. Ramsay (*Was Christ born at Bethlehem?* 1898, p. 131 ff.). A.D. 5–6 (the Egyptian year beginning on Aug. 29), the date of the unquestioned governorship of Quirinius, is one of the census-years: B.C. 10–9, the natural date for the immediately preceding census, is too early for the Nativity; but Ramsay argues that the special circumstances of Judæa under Herod's rule would account for the census having been held a few years later in that province—probably in B.C. 6. Complete evidence on the subject is not yet forthcoming; but the instance is suggestive of the way in which the papyri may elucidate the chronology of the NT.*

(*c*) *Textual.*—Yet another branch of biblical study which is illustrated by the papyri is that of the history of the text. They furnish us with numberless examples of Greek writing of the period in which the LXX and NT were produced, and enable us to realize the conditions under which books circulated in the early ages of the Christian Church; and thereby they suggest a natural explanation of the genesis, at a very early date, of the divergent types of text which we find already established by the time that our most ancient vellum codices were written. This topic has, however, been already dealt with (see art. WRITING in vol. iv. pp. 951, 952), and need not be reconsidered here.

* They may also assist Patristic chronology; *e.g.* Justin's *Apology* is fixed to a point shortly after A.D. 150 by the mention of the prefect Munatius Felix in Brit. Mus. Pap. 358.

vi. COPTIC PAPYRI.*—The importance of the Coptic versions of the Bible for the purposes of textual criticism is well known (see vol. i. p. 672); but, as in the case of Greek MSS, the majority of the Coptic biblical MSS are on vellum. Only one Bohairic papyrus (a number of small fragments of a Psalter of the 10th cent., divided between the British Museum and the Rylands Library) is in existence; all the rest are in the Sahidic or Middle Egyptian dialects. With one or two notable exceptions, to be named below, the biblical papyri hitherto discovered are small and unimportant fragments. On the other hand, Coptic papyri have proved unexpectedly valuable in respect of apocryphal writings (some orthodox and others heretical) which were hitherto unknown, or known only by name and in a few quotations; while they also include a considerable number of Patristic texts and a very large quantity of documents bearing upon monastic and ecclesiastical life in Upper Egypt. Catalogues of these papyri are, however, still almost wholly wanting, so that no complete lists can be given: the following are the most notable individual MSS of which the existence has yet been notified:—

1. Brit. Mus. MS. Or. 5000; a large and complete codex, containing the entire Psalter in the Sahidic dialect. Prob. 7th cent. Edited by E. A. W. Budge (*The earliest known Coptic Psalter*, London, 1898). Its text agrees markedly with that of the largest Greek papyrus Psalter (No. 6, above).

2. Brit. Mus. MS. Or. 5984; part of a very large codex, containing considerable portions of the Sapiential books (Prov., Eccles., Song, Wisdom, Sirach), with one small fragment of Job, in Sahidic. Portions of the Song, Wisdom, and Sirach are wholly new, and in the other books the text sometimes differs from that published. Prob. 7th cent. Described in the forthcoming catalogue of Coptic MSS in the British Museum, by Mr. W. E. Crum.

3. Sixteen leaves (apparently out of an original 32) of a papyrus book at Cairo, containing a narrative of the Resurrection and conversations between our Lord and the disciples. It appears to purport to be a document issued by the Apostles to the Church in general, for its information. It is orthodox in teaching, and directed against the early Gnostics, Cerinthus (MS Κόρινθος) and Simon being mentioned by name. The MS may be assigned to the 4th or 5th cent., the work itself to the first half of the 2nd cent. Described by C. Schmidt (*Sitzungsb. d. Berl. Akad.* 1895, p. 705 ff.), but not yet published.

4. Papyrus at Heidelberg, containing the *Acta Pauli* in Sahidic, and showing that (1) the Acts of Paul and Thecla, (2) the apocryphal correspondence between Paul and the Corinthians, (3) the *Martyrium Pauli*, all hitherto generally regarded as independent works (but cf. opinions quoted by Harnack, *Altchrist. Litteratur*, i. 128 ff.), are really parts of this early and popular romance, which for a time circulated with the canonical books. Prob. 7th cent. Described by C. Schmidt (*Neue Heidelberger Jahrbücher*, vii. 217 ff., 1897), but not yet published.

5. Twenty-two leaves of a book, partly at Berlin and partly at Paris, in Akhmimic dialect, containing (*a*) an anonymous vision of Heaven and Hell, imperfect at the beginning and perhaps at

* For information with regard to this section the present writer is much indebted to Mr. W. E. Crum.

the end ; (*b*) prophecies of the history of the world and the coming of Antichrist and Messiah, entitled 'Apocalypse of Elias.' A Sahidic papyrus at Paris contains six leaves of the latter work, coinciding with and supplementing the Akhmimic MS, together with one leaf of the Apocalypse of Zephaniah. The Akh. MS is assigned to the 4th–5th cent., the Sah. to the 5th (the published facsimiles would perhaps rather suggest the 4th cent. for the former and the end of the 5th for the latter). Published by Steindorff (*Texte u. Unters.*, N. F. ii. 3*a*, 1899).

6. Papyrus at Strassburg, containing two mutilated leaves of an apocryphal Gospel in Sahidic, which, however, there is no reason to identify (with the editor) with the Gospel according to the Egyptians. The narrative appears to relate to the period between the Resurrection and the Ascension. The papyrus is of the 5th–6th cent., but there seems no reason to place the composition of the Gospel earlier than the 3rd cent. Published by A. Jacoby (*Ein neues Evangelienfragment*, Strassburg, 1900).

7. Papyrus at Turin, containing the *Gesta Pilati* or Gospel of Nicodemus in Sahidic, of which Greek and Latin texts are already extant. Published by F. Rossi (*I Papiri Copti del Muséo Egizio di Torino*, 1887).

8. Papyrus at Berlin, containing (*a*) the *Evangelium Mariæ* (also called the *Apokryphon Johannis*), (*b*) Σοφία Ἰησοῦ Χριστοῦ, (*c*) Πρᾶξις Πέτρου, in Sahidic. Prob. 5th cent. The *Evangelium Mariæ* is quoted (without title) by Irenæus (i. 29) as a Gnostic work, and is consequently earlier than *circ.* 185. This discovery is especially interesting as enabling us to test the accuracy with which Irenæus represents his opponents' views. Described by C. Schmidt (*Sitzungsb. d. Berl. Akad.* 1896, p. 839 ff.); the Πρᾶξις Πέτρου has recently been published by him (*Texte u. Unters.*, N. F. ix. 1, 1902), but the other treatises have not yet appeared.

9. Bruce Gnostic Papyrus, at Oxford, containing (*a*) the two 'books of Jeu,' a work akin to the *Pistis Sophia*, but earlier in date, belonging probably to the first half of the 3rd cent. ; (*b*) an unnamed work, somewhat earlier still, being assigned by Schmidt to the end of the 2nd cent. Both are in Sahidic dialect. According to Schmidt, the first belongs to the Severian type of Gnosticism ; the second to the kindred, but not identical, Sethite-Archontican type. Edited by C. Schmidt (*TU*, Bd. viii. 1892).

10. Papyrus at St. Petersburg, containing fragments of apocryphal Acts of the Apostles, viz. the Acts of Bartholomew, Philip, and Andrew and Matthew, in Akhmimic. Edited by O. von Lemm (*Bull. de l'Acad. Imp. des Sciences de St. Petersburg*, nouv. sér. 1, No. 4, 1890).

11. Papyrus at Leyden, containing (*a*) a magical prayer and exorcism attributed to St. Gregory ; (*b*) the correspondence of Christ and Abgar, in Sahidic. Edited by Pleyte and Boeser (*Manuscrits Coptes du Musée d'Antiquités à Leide*, 1897, p. 441 ff.).

12. Brit. Mus. MS. Or. 5001, a large and complete codex of 174 leaves, containing ten Patristic homilies, in Sahidic. Described in Crum's catalogue of Coptic MSS in the British Museum.

13. Brit. Mus. Pap. 36, containing the Canons of Athanasius, in Sahidic. Described by Crum, *op. cit.*, and to be edited by him shortly in the publications of the Text and Translation Society.

14. Papyrus at Turin, containing the Life of Athanasius and records of the Council of Nicæa. Edited by F. Rossi (*I Papiri Copti*, 1884).

15. Legends of saints, homilies, etc., in papyri, at Turin, edited by Rossi, *op. cit.* (1885–1892).

The numerous papyri (mostly small) containing letters and other documents which illustrate ecclesiastical life in Egypt, fall outside the scope of this article.

LITERATURE.—Kenyon, *Palæography of Greek Papyri*, 1899, ch. i.; the annual *Archæological Reports* of the Egypt Exploration Fund, including sections on ancient, Græco-Roman, and Christian Egypt (from 1893); P. Viereck, 'Bericht über die ältere Papyruslitteratur' [before 1877] and 'Die Papyruslitteratur von den 70er Jahren bis 1898' (in *Jahresb. ü. d. Fortschritte d. class. Altertumswissenschaft*, vols. 98 and 102); Seymour de Ricci, 'Bulletin Papyrologique' in the *Revue des Études Grecques* (intermittently from 1901); *Archiv für Papyrusforschung*, edited by Wilcken (from 1900); Deissmann, *Bibelstudien* (1895) and *Neue Bibelstudien* (1897), with Eng. tr. of both series by A. Grieve (*Bible Studies* 1901); Moulton, 'Grammatical Notes from the Papyri,' in *Classical Review*, xv. 31, 434, *Expositor*, Apr. 1901 and Feb. 1903; the principal publications of papyri (Egypt Exploration Fund, British Museum, Berlin Museum, Rainer collection at Vienna, Lord Amherst's collection, etc.); and works cited in the course of this article.

F. G. KENYON.

**WAGES.**—The usual OT term for 'wages' is שָׂכָר *sākhār*; less frequently the cognate מַשְׂכֹּרֶת *maskōreth*, and פְּעֻלָּה *pĕ'ullah*. אֶתְנַן *'ethnan* is the reward paid to a prostitute. As wages are the price paid or the reward given for labour, מְחִיר *mĕḥîr*, 'price,' may sometimes* be translated 'wages' or 'hire'; and conversely the terms for 'wages' are sometimes translated 'reward.'† The usual NT term is μισθός, *misthos*. The term ὀψώνιον, *opsōnion*, is translated 'wages' in Lk $3^{14}$ (of soldiers), Ro $6^{23}$ ('the wages of sin is death'), and 2 Co $11^{8}$. According to Sanday-Headlam on Ro $6^{23}$, ὀψώνιον '=(1) "provision-money, ration-money, or the rations in kind given to troops"; (2) in a more general sense, "wages."' It is used in the Apocrypha of wages paid to soldiers.‡

(*A*) OLD TESTAMENT.—There are only a few references to wages in the Old Testament, because in Israel, as in the ancient world generally, most work was done either by members of the family or by slaves. We may, however, take 'wages' in a broad sense as the price of labour without regard to the status of the labourer. From this point of view we may consider wages as paid to five classes: (i.) the farmer and his family living chiefly on the actual produce of their work; (ii.) relations outside the family in its narrow modern sense; (iii.) slaves; (iv.) priests, soldiers, hired labourers, etc., giving all their time to a master; (v.) craftsmen, smiths, carpenters, etc., working for different customers. It may be as well to say at once that the available data are extremely meagre, so that only general statements are possible.

i. *A farming family* living chiefly by its own labour on its own land depended for the return for its labour on its industry, the fertility of the land, and the stage of development of agriculture. These, of course, varied: for the general condition of things, see AGRICULTURE (in vol. i.), PALESTINE (in vol. iii.), etc. But the accounts which we have of the families of Saul and of Jesse of Bethlehem suggest that in earlier times the yeomen-farmers, as we should call them, obtained a good return for their labour. The prophets of the 8th cent. (Is $3^{14}$ $5^{8}$ $10^{32}$, Am $2^{6-8}$ $3^{9.10}$ $5^{11.12}$) and the Book of Nehemiah (ch. 5) show that towards the close of the monarchy, and after the Return, the small farmers were burdened with various charges,§ taxes, usury, etc., and hardly made a livelihood.

ii. *Remuneration of dependents.*—There were often associated with the actual family, more distant relations and other dependents. These shared the work and the life of the family, probably, as a rule, on no fixed terms, but receiving, as we should say, board and lodging; living 'as

* *e.g.* Mic $3^{11}$. † *e.g.* Ru $2^{12}$.
‡ 1 Mac $3^{28}$ $14^{32}$, and (apparently) 1 Es $4^{56}$.
§ This is rather an inference for the period of the close of the monarchy.

one of the family,' but often with inferior comfort and less consideration. Thus the 'poor relation' would be provided for; and 'the poor within thy gates and the Levite,' who are so often commended to the charity of the pious Israelite (Ex $23^{11}$, Dt $12^{18.19}$ $14^{26-29}$ $15^{7.8}$), would no doubt be expected to render some service to their benefactors. Thus Moses kept the flocks of his father-in-law Jethro (Ex $3^{1}$); and Jacob, at the beginning of his sojourn with Laban, rendered similar service for board and lodging (Gn $29^{15}$). The sequel (cf. § iv.) shows that dependents might also become hired servants at fixed wages.

iii. *Remuneration of slaves.*—Their remuneration, like that of the previous class, consisted of 'all found,' and varied according to the circumstances, character, and goodwill of the master. We should gather that the slaves were well treated, as is commonly the case in the East. See also art. SERVANT in vol. iv.

iv. *Wages of hirelings in continual employment.*—The class of whom we read most are the priests; their wages in earlier times consisted of a share of the sacrifices, and of freewill offerings. Probably, as a rule, either a priest had land as a family inheritance, or the sanctuary held land. Some priests received a stipend from the owners of a private or tribal sanctuary. Moses' grandson was hired by Micah of Ephraim to be priest of his sanctuary for a yearly salary of 10 pieces of silver (shekels), a suit of clothes, and his board and lodging (Jg $17^{10.12}$). No doubt this was fairly liberal; yet when the Danites invited him to go with them 'he was pleased' (*Polychrome Bible*), probably expecting a larger income. Thus he became priest of the sanctuary of the northern Danites at Dan. The Priestly Code has very large ideas as to the proper revenues of priests and Levites, but these were never fully realized; see art. PRIESTS AND LEVITES (in vol. iv.), § 8 **f**, § 10 **b**.

In early times there were no professional soldiers; probably the leader or the king may have made some contribution of provisions or arms to the levy engaged in actual warfare. The chief wage of the soldier was plunder. The bodyguard, the foreign mercenaries, and the forces of horsemen and chariots must have received some regular pay and have been provided with fodder and stabling, board and lodging (1 K $4^{26-28}$). In 2 Ch $25^{6}$ Amaziah hires 100,000 mercenaries for 100 talents of silver; the hiring would be for a single campaign, which might perhaps last a month. The wages of a successful soldier would be augmented by royal gifts, as in the case of David (1 S $17^{25}$), and grants of land. Thus we read in 1 S $8^{14f.}$ 'The king will take your fields, and vineyards, and oliveyards, even the best of them, and will give them to his servants. And he will take the tenth of your grain, and of your vineyards, and give to his officers, and to his servants.'

Little is said about the pay of other classes of hirelings. Jacob purchased a wife by seven years' service (Gn $29^{18}$), and of course had 'all found' during the period; afterwards he was paid by a portion of the increase of the flock ($30^{31ff.}$); but we do not know the normal price of wives; it probably depended on the eagerness of the would-be son-in-law.

The hireling is not referred to in the JE legislation (Ten Commandments, Book of the Covenant, etc.), so that, apparently, work for wages was rare in early times. It increased with the growth of civilization. The hirelings were sufficiently numerous to be the subject of ordinances in the later codes, Dt $24^{14}$, Lv $22^{10}$ (H), Ex $12^{45}$ (P). The payment of wages would be increased by the attempt of the Priestly Code (Lv $25^{39-55}$) to minimize slavery amongst the Jews. The hireling seems to have been at the mercy of his employers as to the amount of his wages, and even as to getting them paid at all. Laban changed Jacob's wages ten times (Gn $31^{7}$). Both the Prophets and the Law intervene on behalf of the wage-earner (Dt $24^{14}$, Jer $22^{13}$, Mal $3^{5}$); he was to be paid promptly, usually, as it seems, at the end of each day (Dt $24^{15}$, Lv $19^{13}$, Job $7^{2}$), but Lv $25^{53}$ refers to a 'servant hired year by year.' The hireling was considered inferior in industry to a slave, of whom it is said in Dt $15^{18}$ 'to the double of the hire of a hireling hath he served thee.' In the earlier periods of Israelite history, when almost every family had its own land, it would be the exceptionally poor 'ne'er-do-well' who was on bad terms with his kin, or the foreigner, that hired himself into service. Dt $24^{14}$ speaks of the hireling as 'poor and needy . . . of thy brethren or of thy strangers.' Naturally the connexion of the hireling with the family was less close than that of the slave; he has no share in the family *sacra*; he may not eat the passover (Ex $12^{45}$ [P]); nor may the hired servant of a priest eat the holy food (Lv $22^{10}$). When we consider these facts, together with the control of the labour market by the employer, and the full advantage which the latter took of the situation, we may be sure that the usual rate of wages afforded only a bare subsistence to the free labourer. The description of the miserable condition of the working classes in Job $24^{1-12}$ will refer to hired servants. In the case of the *corvée*, or compulsory service for public works, no wages were paid beyond food and lodging. The *corvée* was used by Solomon to build the temple (1 K $5^{13}$ $12^{4}$), and doubtless by other kings and nobles (Jer $22^{13}$).

v. *Wages for occasional pieces of work.*—Prophets, priests, judges, etc., received payment under different names for the occasional services rendered by them to their clients (Mic $3^{11}$). These payments or fees were variously known as gifts, shares of victims (cf. above), or even bribes. The gifts or bribes varied with the importance of the occasion, the wealth of the giver, and the standing of the recipient. Saul considered that Samuel would accept a quarter of a shekel as a sufficient fee for information about his lost asses (1 S $9^{8}$). Jeroboam's wife going to Ahijah, disguised as an ordinary woman, took him 'ten loaves, and cracknels, and a cruse of honey' (1 K $14^{3}$). But the princes who consulted Joseph (Gn $41^{41f.}$), Balaam (Nu $22^{17}$), and Daniel (Dn $2^{6}$ $5^{16}$), made them munificent offers of wealth, power, and honour.

There are references to various kinds of craftsmen who must have worked 'by the job' so to speak, especially to smiths and carpenters, but we are not told how they were paid. Judah's payment of a kid to Tamar (Gn $38^{17}$) may be mentioned here.

*Code of Hammurabi.*—This code, which is dated about B.C. 2285–2242 (Johns), includes provisions as to the fees to be paid to doctors and builders; and as to the wages of boatmen, reapers, threshers, shepherds, labourers, brickmakers, tailors, stonecutters, and carpenters; and as to the hire of oxen, cows, waggons, and boats. If a doctor performs for a noble a successful operation for a wound or an abscess in the eye, he receives ten shekels of silver; if for a poor man, five; if for a slave, two. But if the noble dies or loses his eye, the doctor's hands are cut off; in the case of a slave, the doctor replaces him if he dies; pays half his price if he loses his eye. For minor operations, the doctor receives five, three, or two shekels, according to the rank of his patient. A cow- or sheep-doctor receives one-sixth of a shekel of silver for a cure, and pays the owner a quarter of the animal's value if it dies. A builder is to be paid in proportion to the size of the house; and if it collapses through faulty construction and the owner is killed, the builder is to be put to death; if other damage is caused, suitable compensation is to be paid.

Oxen, boatmen, reapers, threshers, and shepherds were hired for the year; the hire for the ox being 4 *gur** of corn, of a boatman or thresher 6, of a reaper or shepherd 8.

There were also hirings by the *day*, as follows: (*a*) reckoned

* Worth, according to Johns, a shekel of silver *per gur*.

in *ka* * of corn; for threshing, ox 20, ass 10, calf 1; oxen, waggon, and driver, 180; or waggon, 40; (*b*) reckoned in *še* † of silver; boat, 3; carpenter, 4; tailor, brickmaker, or stonecutter, 5; labourer, for first five months of the year, 6; for the last seven months, 5. A freight boat to carry 60 *gur* of corn could be hired for one-sixth of a shekel a day.

In this code many regulations are laid down as to slaves; little is said as to their treatment or the provision made for their maintenance, but we may conclude that they were treated with the comparative humanity and consideration usually accorded to them in the ancient East. For instance, the code implies that a master would be willing to pay two shekels, or the equivalent of three months' wages to a shepherd, for the cure of a slave. Moreover, if a slave married a free woman, the children were free.

It will be noticed that wages, as in mediæval codes, are fixed by law. We may surmise, from the analogy of the Middle Ages, that these regulations were made in the interests of the employers; and that, practically, the rates fixed were a minimum, and that higher wages were often paid.

(*B*) The Apocrypha and the New Testament.—The references to wages in the Apocrypha and the New Testament are still comparatively few, and do not suggest that any very important changes had taken place.

i. The *farmers*, etc., profited by the order maintained by the Roman government and the Herods, but probably this advantage was more than counterbalanced by the weight of taxation and the fraudulent extortions of the publicans.

ii. *Dependents*, poor relations, etc., probably were very much in the same position as of old.

iii. *Slaves* were still well treated in the East, and fairly well when serving in the households of Greeks or even Romans, but the provision made for slaves working in factories or on large farms, or manning ships, was often scanty and sordid. Cf. art. Servant in vol. iv.

iv. *Wages paid for continuous service.*—In To $5^{14}$ the angel Raphael, professing himself to be a member of a distinguished Jewish family akin to Tobit, is hired by the latter as travelling companion to his son, and subsequently sent to collect a large debt; so that hired servants were sometimes placed in positions of trust. Raphael's wages were to be a drachma a day and 'all found,' with the promise of a bonus at the end of the engagement if he gave satisfaction. Similarly, the labourers in the vineyard (Mt 20) received a *denarion* or denarius, whose value 'was the same as that of' the drachma 'in ordinary transactions' (art. Money in vol. iii. p. $428^b$). The shekel contained rather more silver than a half-crown, and the denarius about $\frac{4}{5}$ as much silver as a shilling; probably, too, the labourers received food. The mere statement of the weight of silver, however, tells us nothing as to real wages; and to a large extent our data rather serve to fix the value of silver than the real wages of labour. If we may reckon the price of wheat in NT times at from 16s. to £1 a quarter, a denarius or drachma, about $9\frac{1}{2}$d. a day, with food, would be very roughly equivalent to the present wages of a London charwoman, about 2s. a day with food, wheat being about 29s. a quarter.

We are told ‡ that before the time of Julius Cæsar a foot-soldier was paid $\frac{1}{3}$ of a denarius a day, a centurion $\frac{2}{3}$, a horse-soldier a denarius; that these wages were doubled by Julius Cæsar, and further increased by Augustus, and again by Domitian. The Prætorian guards received double pay.

There are various references to the payment of wages and the services of wage-earners. Sir $7^{20}$ speaks of the 'hireling who giveth thee his life' (marg. 'soul'). On the other hand, we are bidden (Sir $37^{11}$) not 'to take counsel . . . with a hireling in thy house about finishing his work.' It was still necessary (Sir $34^{22}$, and later still Ja $5^4$) to denounce those who kept back the wages of their hired servants. Mercenary soldiers appear in 1 Mac $6^{29}$.

In Mk $1^{20}$ Zebedee has a paid crew (μισθωτοί) for his fishing-boat; and hired servants (μίσθιοι) appear in the parables of the Prodigal Son (Lk $15^{17.19}$) and of the Labourers in the Vineyard (Mt $20^{1.2}$). The former implies that the household of a wealthy man included several hired servants; and the latter, that there was a class of free labourers who were, as in the Old Testament, hired and paid by the day. So, too, the reaper receives wages (Jn $4^{36}$, Ja $5^4$). The service of the 'hireling' or free labourer is still lightly esteemed: 'the hireling . . . fleeth because he is an hireling, and careth not for the sheep' (Jn $10^{13}$); and the Apostles style themselves and their fellow-Christians the 'slaves' (δοῦλοι), never the 'hired servants,' of Christ. The preachers of the gospel receive wages, 'hire' (μισθός), from men whom they serve (Lk $10^7$, 2 Co $11^8$, 1 Ti $5^{18}$). God is said to give 'hire' or wages (Mt $5^{12}$ $20^8$, He $11^6$ etc.); on the other hand, there are 'the wages (ὀψώνια) of sin' (Ro $6^{23}$) and 'the wages (μισθοί) of unrighteousness' (2 P $2^{15}$ etc.).

Mt $5^{41}$ 'whosoever shall impress thee to go one mile' implies the existence of the *corvée* or exaction of forced labour.

v. *The wages of occasional service.*—The Apocrypha and the New Testament give us no definite information as to the payment for pieces of work done by smiths, carpenters, etc.

Literature.—Ewald, *Antiquities of Israel*, pp. 185, 217 f.; Nowack, *Lehrbuch der Heb. Arch.* i. pp. 221–250; Benzinger, *Heb. Arch.* pp. 204–223; W. H. Bennett, 'Economic Conditions of the Hebrew Monarchy (Labour),' in *Thinker*, April 1893; C. H. W. Johns, *The Oldest Code of Laws in the World* (*Code of Hammurabi*), 1903.

W. H. Bennett.

**SHIPS AND BOATS.**—Under the designation 'ships' are included in the Bible vessels of all sizes, from the sea-going ships whose Phœnician crews 'did their business in great waters' (Ps $107^{23}$), and traded for kings Solomon and Hiram (1 K $9^{26.27.28}$) from the head of the Gulf of 'Aḳabah in the Red Sea to Ophir in the Indian or Arabian Sea, down to the mere fishing-boats of the Sea of Tiberias (Jn $6^1$ $21^1$; called Sea of Galilee in Mt $4^{18}$, Mk $7^{31}$, Jn $6^1$; and Lake of Gennesaret in Lk $5^1$), such as that in which our Lord was awakened from sleep during a storm and rebuked the wind and sea and reproached His timid disciples for their want of faith (Lk $8^{22-25}$). 'Boats' are mentioned in the AV only twice. The term is applied once to what were, apparently, lake fishing-craft (Jn $6^{22.23}$ πλοιάριον). It is used again, in the story of St. Paul's voyage and shipwreck, of the boat (σκάφη) of a sea-going ship which was hoisted up on account of bad weather after being towed astern during the first part of the voyage (Ac $27^{16}$). This boat was afterwards lowered again by the crew of the ship, but cut adrift by the soldiers on St. Paul's advice (vv.$^{30.32}$).*

*A*. Ships of the Old Testament.—It seems proper to make mention here, as belonging to the category of 'ships,' although denominated an 'ark' (תֵּבָה), of the huge three-decked vessel said to have been built by Noah under Divine direction (Gn $6^{14.15.16}$), and apparently without mast, sail, or any means of steering or propulsion. It was to be of gopher wood (an unknown timber), and was intended as a means of saving Noah and his family, and such animals as were necessary for the per-

* 300 *ka* = 1 *gur* (Johns). † 180 *še* = 1 shekel (Johns).

‡ Ramsay's *Roman Antiquities*, p. 391.

* A 'ferry-boat' is perhaps mentioned in 2 S $19^{18}$, if the MT וְעָבְרָה הָעֲבָרָה is correct, although such a meaning of עֲבָרָה is not found elsewhere. But prob. Wellhausen (followed by Driver, *et al.*) is right in reading וַיַּעַבְרוּ ה׳, 'and they crossed over the ford.' This is implicitly supported by the LXX καὶ ἐλειτούργησαν τὴν λειτουργίαν (*i.e.*, by confusion of ד and ר, וַיַּעַבְדוּ הָעֲבֹדָה, the reading adopted by Budde in *SBOT*).

petuation of the species, from destruction by water. If we assume the form of the ark to be conceived as that of an ordinary ship, we have no historical mention of its dimensions as given in Gn 6[15] being exceeded until the construction of the *Great Eastern* steamship, built at Millwall by Brunel in 1858, with accommodation for 4000 passengers, and with a capacity of 24,000 tons, which is slightly in excess of the apparent size of the ark. See, further, art. FLOOD in vol. ii. p. 16. The earliest Scripture mention of ships properly so called (אֳנִיּוֹת) is in Gn 49[13], where Zebulun is spoken of in the Blessing of Jacob as a haven for them. The next is in Nu 24[24], where the Balaam oracles speak of ships from the coast of KITTIM as taking part in the destruction of Assyria. These latter would be ships of war as distinguished from commercial ones. Merchant ships are mentioned in 1 K 9[26] (cf. 10[22] 'a navy of TARSHISH'); and in Ps 107[23-30] is given the heart-stirring description of a sailor's life in a sea-going ship. In Pr 31[14] the foresight of the thrifty housewife forms the point of comparison between her and the merchant ships which bring goods from afar. In Pr 30[19] 'the way of a ship in the midst of the sea' is mentioned as one of the four things which were too wonderful for the writer. The absence of chart and compass, with the sun and stars only for a guide to the Phœnician mariner, and these often, as in St. Paul's voyage (Ac 27[20]), invisible, made the art of navigation a mystery known only to those who, like these experts, were gifted with the hereditary instinct of their profession. Moreover, the pressure of the wind on the sails from a direction opposed to the ship's course, nevertheless urging her through the water on the way she would go, seems almost as wonderful as that the disposition of the muscles and feathers of an eagle should enable it to soar to invisible heights, or swoop to the earth in a moment without apparent motion of its wings, or that the slippery serpent should glide rapidly over a smooth rock without any external means of locomotion. In 1 K 9[26] (‖ 2 Ch 8[17f.]) and 10[22] (‖ 2 Ch 9[21]) we have the account of the building of Solomon's merchant ships at 'Ezion-geber at the head of the Gulf of 'Aḳabah, and the furnishing of them with experienced Phœnician pilots by Hiram king of Tyre, the friend of Solomon's father, David; and of their voyage to Ophir and back with 420 talents of gold (equal to £2,583,000). The last of the above passages has a notice of the triennial visit of Solomon's and Hiram's ships 'to Tarshish,'* bringing back gold and silver (the latter being considered so plentiful as to be regarded of no account), ivory, apes, and peacocks. These were genuine sea-going ships, and the whole of the above references, except those from Genesis and Numbers, relate to the same century and to the 40 years of Solomon's reign (*c.* 970–930 B.C.), when Tyre was at the height of its prosperity, and Shashank (Shishak) I., of the 22nd dynasty, or his immediate predecessor, was the ruling Pharaoh of Egypt. Unfortunately, the Phœnicians have not left us either literature or sculptures from which we can form an idea of the kind of ships used on these voyages; nor have we any Assyrian representations of them until two centuries later in the time of Hezekiah and Sennacherib, when all the sea trade of the Assyrians was in the hands of the Phœnicians, who had also absorbed that of the Egyptians (Herodot. i. 1). A century later still

* The Chronicler here confuses a 'ship of Tarshish' (*i.e.* a large vessel fitted to go long voyages) with a ship going *to Tarshish*. Wherever the latter port was, whether (as most believe) identical with Tartessus in Spain, or Tarsus, or some district in Greece or Italy, it could not have been reached by a vessel sailing from 'Ezion-geber unless by circumnavigating [on every ground a most unlikely supposition] the continent of Africa.

Ezekiel (27[5-8]) speaks of the royal merchant ships of Tyre, which traded with Syria and various Mediterranean ports and to the far East, as having planks of fir and masts of cedar, whilst the oars were of oak of Bashan, and the benches of the rowers of ivory inlaid in wood from the isles of Kittim, the sails of fine embroidered linen, their crews from Ẓidon and Arvad, and their pilots from Tyre. But this description, although no doubt applicable to the royal yachts, may be considered to some extent poetical as applied to commercial ships.

The question of the much disputed situation of the port of Ophir to which Solomon's ships traded from 'Eẓion-geber in the Gulf of 'Aḳabah, bringing back gold, ivory, almug trees, and peacocks (1 K 9[28] 10[22]), belongs to another section of this Dictionary (see art. OPHIR in vol. iii.); but the length of time occupied in the voyage, inferred from the interval of three years (1 K 10[22]) between the arrivals of the ships at 'Eẓion-geber, indicates a great distance, such as Central or Southern Africa, or the island of Ceylon, where peacocks still abound. Such voyages would necessitate the ships being laid up in some safe port between the months of May and October, during the bad weather and heavy sea which accompany the S.W. monsoon, as is the case at the present day with the Indian and Arab trading vessels which annually frequent the port of Berbereh opposite to Aden.*

Although we have no contemporary representations of Phœnician sea-going ships of Solomon's time, we have drawings of Egyptian ones to refer to of a much more ancient date, and of a type after which we may suppose the ships of the early Phœnicians and those of Hiram and Solomon to have been constructed. These drawings, no doubt, give us a faithful picture of the ships, their crews, and their merchandise from a general point of view; but they are more or less conventional, and the technical errors in our own marine historical pictures point to the necessity of not relying too much upon accuracy of nautical detail, as the drawings may have been made by artists who did not take part in the expeditions and were not seamen. Unfortunately, also, many important details are missing from the models of ancient ships in the museums. The Egyptian ships were for the most part unloaded at a port in the Red Sea, and their cargoes transferred overland to Koptos on the Nile.

The first Red Sea voyage of which we have any knowledge is mentioned in an inscription at Wady Gassûs, near Kosseir, in the Valley of Hammamât, on the road from Koptos to the Red Sea. This commemorates the expedition sent by Pharaoh Sankh-Ka-Ra of the 11th (a Theban) dynasty to the 'Land of Puânit' (or Punt), the site of which is as much disputed as that of Ophir or Tarshish, and is considered by M. Edouard Naville to be but a 'vague geographical designation.' See, further, art. PUT in vol. iv. p. 176 f. The destination of the expedition was evidently, however, somewhere in Tropical Africa, and was in all probability in the vicinity of the present Somaliland on the east coast, where there existed an *entrepôt* for the ivory, frankincense, myrrh, gold dust, and ostrich feathers, and for the ostrich eggs so much prized by the Egyptians of those days. This first expedition to Punt must have taken place, according to Brugsch, 250 years after the founding of Tyre, if Herodotus (ii. 44) was correctly informed by the Tyrians, *i.e.* about 1500 years before the time of Solomon, and 500 years before the birth of Abraham; but, according to Mariette, even earlier than this. We have no account of this expedition, nor

* Findlay's *Directory for the Navigation of the Indian Ocean*, 1870, p. 559.

any sculptures showing the kind of ships employed on it.

The next important Red Sea expedition mentioned on the monuments was sent during the 18th dynasty, also to the Land of Punt, in the reign of queen Hatsepsu I., sister of Thothmes II. (during the sojourn of the Israelites in Egypt); the sculptures on the walls of Deir el-Bahri, near the Tombs of the Kings at Thebes, fully illustrate this important event, including the ships used (see Flinders Petrie, *History of Egypt*, ii. 82 ff.). The place of departure by the overland route from the Nile to the Red Sea, on the outward voyage, as well as the port of reshipment of the goods brought by the expedition on its return by the same route, was doubtless the ancient Koptos (now Qoft), as in the earlier expedition before mentioned; the Red Sea port of embarkation and disembarkation being Tua or Œnmun, known later as Philoteras (after it had been so renamed by the Ptolemies), and now as Old Kosseir, not far from the modern port of that name in lat. 26° 7′ N., and distant from Koptos about 100 miles. As regards the African port depicted in the sculptures as the object of the expedition, and called the Land of Punt, there is some doubt. But for the African ebony (*Dalbergia melanoxylon*, G.P.R., so much in request for temple furniture in Egypt) and other trees which are represented as growing near the place of landing,* the land-locked port of Berbereh already spoken of, which has always been a great mart for the products of the interior, might be intended; and even these trees may have been artistically introduced to indicate a part of these products.

Although the Children of Israel must, at the time of queen Hatsepsu's expedition, have been at the height of their prosperity in the land of Goshen (Gn 47^{14. 27}, Ex 1[7]), which they had inhabited for more than a century, it is probable that, as their occupation was that of shepherds and cattle-dealers located in the midst of the Delta, they would see and know but little of what was going on so far south of them as Koptos and Thebes, and absolutely nothing of the sea-going ships of which the expedition was composed. Consequently, no knowledge of the building or handling of ships or boats was carried away with them from Egypt at the time of the Exodus; and the forty years of subsequent wandering in the wilderness would have sufficed to ensure the obliteration from their memories of any such knowledge had it been acquired.

It was not until the reign of Solomon that the Israelites commenced to build ships (1 K 9[26]), an art which, through the friendship of Hiram king of Tyre for David and his son (2 S 5[11] ‖ 1 Ch 14[1] and 1 K 5[1]), they learned from the Phœnicians, who supplied the pilots and mariners for these ships (1 K 9[27]). Whether the Phœnicians brought their knowledge of shipbuilding with them from Western Arabia at the time of their early migration (Herod. i. 1, vii. 89) or learnt it from the Egyptians, is a mystery. Boatbuilding was certainly a very ancient art in Egypt, as in the tomb of Ti at Sakâra (5th dynasty, *c.* 3680-1500—3660 B.C. [Petrie]) it is represented in the wall sculptures in all its details.

The merchant ships of queen Hatsepsu's expedition to the Land of Punt, as delineated on the walls of the temple of Deir el-Bahri,* are long vessels curved upwards at each extreme, as we see the Phœnician triremes of the 7th cent. B.C. depicted

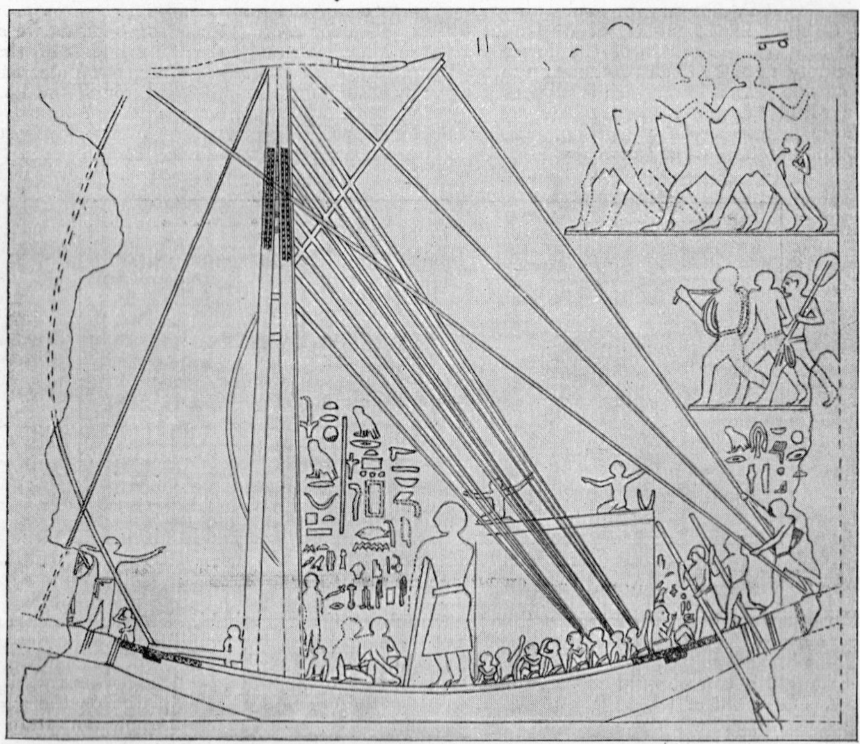

1. DESHÂSHEH (MIDDLE EGYPT). W. WALL, N. HALF. TOMB OF ANTA, B.C. 3600. SAILING SHIP WITH ANTA STANDING BY THE CABIN.

* These trees are not now found near the seashore.

* *Egyp. Expl. Fund*, pt. iii. vol. 15, pl. lxxii., lxviii., lxxiv., lxxv.; Petrie, *l.c.* p. 84. Cf. figs. 3 and 4 on p. 364.

on the Assyrian monuments, but without their figureheads; the stern is recurved towards the bow like the uplifted trunk of an elephant, and ends in a trumpet mouth—the conventional representation of the papyrus plant—a form adopted also by the Phœnicians and Assyrians; there is also a raised forecastle and poop. The mast, instead of being of the more ancient 'sheerlegs' form (as we see it in fig. 1 on the walls of the tomb of Anta at Deshâsheh, 5th dynasty, *c.* B.C. 3600), consists of a single spar, placed a little forward of the centre of the ship, and is kept in its place by 'shrouds' and a 'stay'; whilst additional support, when the sail is set, is given by a pair of very stout 'jeers,' or halliards, attached to each side of the 'bunt,' or middle of the 'yard,' and secured to the gunwale of the vessel. The sail is of the square form and secured to two yards, the lower of which is as long as the ship herself, but the upper one is a good deal shorter. Each yard is in two pieces, 'fished' together in the middle of its length by means of cordage, the centre of the lower yard being securely lashed to the mast near the level of the gunwale. This lower yard is supported by numerous 'lifts' * at uniform intervals (apparently about seven in number on each side), which are 'rove' through 'sheaves' or 'snatches' placed one above the other at the head of the mast, so that one rope answers for a lift on both sides of the yard. These lifts are so tightened as to give to the yard the form of a bow curving upwards at each extremity. The head of the sail is attached, in accordance with modern usage, to the upper yard, which can be hoisted to the masthead when the sail is set, or lowered so as to lie on the lower yard or remain aloft with the sail 'brailed up' at pleasure. This upper yard has a single lift on each side, attached half-way between the mast and the yardarm. The 'foot' of the sail is attached to the lower yard at intervals when the sail is set, but quite detached from it when the sail is furled. The 'braces' of the upper yard (not always represented in the drawings) are single ropes attached to the upper yard at the same spot as the lifts, and lead thence to the deck or gunwale; they were usually under the control of the helmsman, as we see them on the walls of the tomb of Anta at Deshâsheh. There are 15 oarsmen, seated on either side of the ships, all engaged in rowing (not pushing the oars), although the sails are set (pl. lxxiii.), and only one man plies each of the 30 oars—a universal rule in ancient ships. The distance between the rowers in a fore and aft direction is, apparently, about 4 ft., but possibly only 2 cubits, as we see in Greek and Roman ships of later date. A noticeable arrangement for strengthening these sea-going ships is a tightly stretched and very stout cable secured to the bow and stern in the centre of the ship, inside, passing high over the heads of the rowers, and supported on strong wooden props with forked heads. This is doubtless to afford support to the weakest or curved portion of the ship at her two ends, neither of which is water-borne—a very necessary precaution under such conditions when a vessel is straining in a heavy sea. Assuming the distance between the rowers to be 4 ft., the space between the foremost oar and the extremity of the bow is about 18 ft. in length, so that the total length of the ships appears to have been 102 ft., of which a length of about 58 ft. only is water-borne, the remainder being the curves of the bow and stern. A row of port-holes, corresponding in number to the oars, is indicated on the side of the ships below the gunwale. These were probably intended for a second tier of oars, as we see in the Phœnician and Assyrian triremes of the 7th and 8th cents. B.C. The ships are steered, not 'by a single rudder passing through the keel,' as in the more modern arrangement described by Herodotus (ii. 96), but by two very stout paddles, one on each quarter, having simple broad blades without the remarkable letter D form of the Phœnician ones represented on the Assyrian monuments in the time of Sennacherib, but having long 'looms' or handles, which first pass through 'strops,' or loops of rope, placed on the gunwale midway between the upper end of the stern-curve and the point where the stern first touches the water; immediately above these strops, at a vertical height of about 4 ft., the upper portion of the looms rests on the summit of a post fixed to the gunwale close to the strop; here is placed a crutch or notch in which the loom revolves by means of a tiller fixed to its upper portion and curving downwards to the hand of the helmsman below. The ordinary mode of steering was precisely as by the modern rudder, the normal position of the blades of the paddles being nearly vertical and 'fore and aft.' We see the same arrangement of tiller in the papyrus sail-boats painted on the tomb of the priestess of Mera at Deshâsheh,* a few miles south of the Fayum (not to be confounded with the tomb of Mera at Sakârah, belonging also to the 5th dynasty), nearly 2000 years before queen Hatsepsu's time. A stout stirrup of rope is attached to the upper part of the post on which the loom rests, and hangs over the outside of the ship, apparently for the helmsman to put one of his feet in whilst he placed the other against the outside of

2. DESHÂSHEH (MIDDLE EGYPT). COFFIN OF MERA, B.C. 3500. BOAT CONVEYING OFFERINGS TO THE TOMB.

* Precisely as shown in the model of an Indian ship in the Indian Institute Museum at Oxford.

* *Egyp. Expl. Fund*, vol. 15, pl. xxvii. See above, fig. 2.

the ship in order to obtain leverage in working the paddle on special occasions when the loom must have been previously lifted out of the crutch; but the stirrup may also have been used to support the rudder-paddle when not in use, or when it was 'triced up.' Occasionally ships had only one rudder-paddle, as shown in tomb paintings and in the model of the Scandinavian ship lately found at Christiania, to be seen in the Pitt-Rivers Collection at Oxford, which rudder-paddle being on the starboard side explains the derivation of this word from 'steer-board.' Other tomb paintings show as many as three rudder-paddles on one side. Four-oared boats, without masts or sails, are also represented in the Deir el-Bahri paintings of queen Hatsepsu's expedition as bringing off goods to the ships, and these have only one paddle-rudder, which is shipped in a crutch in the centre of the stern, but with the same stirrup as shown in the ships.

There is no visible *anchor* of any kind on board the ships, nor any arrangement for using one; but the pilot on the forecastle has a long pole in his hand with which he is sounding the depth of the water. The only anchor used in those early days was a heavy weight, generally a large stone or a basket full of smaller ones. No anchor, properly so called, is represented in any Egyptian sculpture or painting. The hooked anchor (ἄγκυρα) is first mentioned by the poet Pindar (I. v. 18) in the 5th cent. B.C.; it was without flukes. Homer always uses the word *εὐναί*, meaning a stone anchor; and Ephorus, the historian of the 4th cent. B.C. (Strabo, vii. 3), attributed the invention of the two-armed anchor to Anacharsis, a Scythian prince of the 6th cent. B.C. In the time of Herodotus (ii. 96) the merchant ships of the Egyptians on the Nile, when sailing down stream, used a heavy stone attached to a rope from the stern as a drag to keep their heads straight, in conjunction with a raft of tamarisk floating on the water, attached to the bow, so as to be acted on by the current which pulled the ship down stream, whilst the stone held her back, as is still the practice on the river Euphrates;* but there is no mention of the use of a bow anchor, whether of stone or any other material.

The form of the Egyptian ships admitted of their lying at anchor as easily by the stern as by the head, and, paddles which could be lifted out of the water being used instead of rudders, there was no fear of the latter being broken by the sea, as was the case when the modern rudder, hung on 'gudgeons' by means of 'pintles,' was substituted in later times. The advantage of anchoring by the stern in narrow waters or when suddenly shoaling water at night, as in the case of St. Paul's ship off the island of Melita (Ac $27^{28.\ 29}$), where the rudder-paddles were triced up clear of the water, is obvious. But this vessel had means of anchoring by the bows if desired (v.$^{30}$), and no doubt the Egyptian ships also; large stones, wooden tubes, or sacks filled with lead or other heavy weights being used as anchors.

The *masts* of queen Hatsepsu's ships were probably derived, like the Egyptian ships in the time of Herodotus (ii. 96), and even at the present day, from the gum-arabic tree of Nubia (*Acacia nilotica*, Delile), known to modern Arabs as the *sont*, a corruption of the ancient Egypt name *shant*, which is as old as the 4th dynasty, or of one of the many varieties of this tree in that region. The equally common *seyâl*, or 'ash' of the ancient Egyptians (*Acacia seyâl*, Delile), which Canon Tristram supposes to be the 'shittim' wood of the Bible (Ex 25. 26. 37. 38), is scarcely more than a variety of the *sont*, and, like it, is frequently

* Chesney, vol. ii. p. 640.

mentioned in the hieroglyphs, and is of the same antiquity.

The ships of Solomon built at 'Eẓion-geber (1 K $9^{26}$) were probably of the fir and cedar supplied by Hiram (1 K $5^{8.\ 9.\ 10}$), which do not grow in Egypt or Nubia, although much imported for use in Egyptian temples from the 5th dynasty downwards. No mention, however, is made in the Bible of the material used in shipbuilding. According to Onesecritus, chief pilot to Alexander the Great (Pliny, vi. 24), the ships which traded in the 5th cent. B.C. between Taprobane (Ceylon) and the country of the Prasians (Calcutta) during four months of the year, the voyage lasting 20 days, were rigged like the Nile boats, and were built of papyrus stems as we see them in process of construction depicted 3000 years earlier on the walls of the tomb of Anta at Deshâsheh; but these were only coasting vessels. The Egyptian merchant vessels in the time of Herodotus are described by him (ii. 96) as being built without ribs, the planks, 2 cubits in length, being arranged 'like bricks' (*i.e.* probably the planking was double, the middle of the outer plank overlaying the two ends of the inner one), and joined together by long 'tree-nails'; the planks were caulked with stems of 'byblus' (*Papyrus antiquorum*, L.), the sails being made of the same material, which seems incredible; but whether of flax or byblus, the 'cloths' of the sails were placed horizontally instead of vertically as now. The ropes of Egyptian ships continued to be made of byblus (Herod. vii. 25, 34) or of palm fibre as late as the 27th or Persian dynasty (B.C. 480), and, according to the same authority (Herod. ii. 96), the sails also,—whilst those of the Phœnicians were made of flax. But it is doubtful if the Nile boats, described by Herodotus, were really sea-going vessels like those of queen Hatsepsu and Solomon, though they carried many thousand talents (more than 100 tons) of cargo; and, as the making of linen cloth was an Egyptian speciality, it was probably used for the sails of sea-going ships by them as well as by Solomon and Hiram, who imported it from Egypt (Ezk 27).

At Deir el-Bahri* we see the queen's ships being laden in a port of the Land of Punt after the same fashion as we may suppose those of Solomon to have taken in their cargoes at Ophir, by means of porters and 'gang-boards' connecting the ships with the shore. The cargo, which is being carried and stowed on the deck by the crew, consists of sacks of frankincense of various kinds (especially that called 'anti'), gold dust, ebony, elephants' tusks, gum, ostrich eggs and feathers. Live apes are climbing about the rigging as we see them in the boat depicted on the tomb of Mera at Deshâsheh 2000 years earlier—an indication probably of the fauna of the Land of Punt, which includes the giraffe, peculiar to tropical Africa.

We may safely assume that Solomon's Mediterranean ships were similar to those built by him at 'Eẓion-geber, on the Phœnician model, and that the latter, again, resembled those of queen Hatsepsu, although with possibly some modifications of no great importance. There seems, also, no reason to suppose that the ships built at 'Eẓion-geber by Jehoshaphat king of Judah a century later (1 K $22^{48}$), or the passenger ship in which Jonah embarked at Joppa some thirty years later for Tarshish (Jon $1^{3}$), and in which the vain use of the oars in the ships to endeavour to make the land is so graphically described, belonged to a different type.

*Ships of war.*—The Egyptian sailors or boatmen formed, according to Herodotus (ii. 164), one of the seven classes into which the population of the

* *Egyp. Expl. Fund*, pt. iii. vol. 15, pl. lxxiv. See figs. on p. 364.

country was divided, the office of pilot or steersman ranking above all other grades. Probably those belonging to merchant ships formed a superior subdivision of these. We may take it for granted that the Phœnicians and Tyrians followed the same practice in the time of Solomon as with certain modifications the Greeks did in later times. The crews of war ships seem to have been placed in a separate category with the soldiers, who, from constant practice at the oar on the Nile, were themselves expert galleymen. Whether any of these latter were on board queen Hatsepsu's or Solomon's ships we are not told; but, although these were both commercial expeditions, it is probable that the ships were prepared are stationed in a 'top' or cage at the masthead. During the engagement the sail was 'brailed' up, and there was apparently no lower yard to the square sail as we see in the ships of queen Hatsepsu of a later date. According to Wilkinson (iii. 204), ramming was used in the attack; but the ships had no beak for this purpose as in Roman days, a lion's, ram's, or other animal's head covered with metal taking its place.

There seems to be little doubt that the Egyptian men-of-war also took part in the Mediterranean in the transport of troops and in sea fights during the reign of the Ramses Pharaohs against the ships of various nations inhabiting the littoral, as they did in the time of Pharaoh-

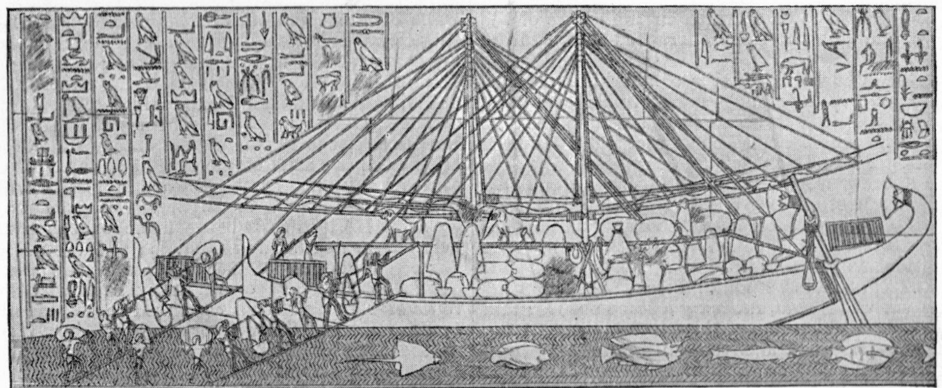

3. TEMPLE OF DEIR EL-BAHRI. MIDDLE COLONNADE. SOUTH WALL. QUEEN HATSEPSU'S EXPEDITION TO PUNT, B.C. 1500. LOADING EGYPTIAN SHIPS AT PUNT.

4. MIDDLE COLONNADE. SOUTH WALL. LADEN EGYPTIAN SHIPS LEAVING PUNT.

to fight if need be. That men-of-war were specially fitted out by the Egyptians for fighting purposes in the Arabian Gulf we know from Herodotus (ii. 102) and Diodorus (i. 55), who both mention the fleet of 'long vessels' built expressly for war (called by them *ua*) to the number of 400, whilst the transports were called *usch* (broad), and the galleys *mensch*;* and the employment of such vessels on the expeditions of the Pharaohs to Ethiopia was frequent, the officers who commanded them being mentioned on the monuments, and the title of 'chief *or* captain of the king's ships' being not uncommon. A sea fight is represented at Thebes, in which the Egyptian soldiers in military dress are seen rowing. In the men-of-war of the 4th and 5th dynasties slingers

* Wilkinson, *Anc. Egypt.*, vol. i. p. 274.

necho (Herod. ii. 159); their victories over combined forces of Dardanians, Teucrians, Mysians, and, apparently, over Pelasgians, Daunians, Oscans, and Sicilians, being recorded on the monuments.

Of the *Phœnician* war vessels which were contemporaneous we have no knowledge; and it is to the Assyrian monuments of a later date that we are indebted for pictorial representations of them in a very crude way. During the three invasions of Syria and Phœnicia by Shalmaneser IV. in the reigns of Hezekiah king of Judah and Hoshea king of Israel (B.C. 726–721, 2 K 18[9, 10]), Josephus tells us, on the authority of Menander (342–291 B.C.), that the Assyrian monarch, in order to quell a revolt in the island of Tyre, made use of 60 Phœnician galleys with 800 men to row them, but was utterly defeated by the Tyrians with 12 ships, which took 500 prisoners.*

Sennacherib, who had sent the Rabshakeh to Hezekiah to reproach the living God (2 K 19[20. 34]), and demand the surrender of Jerusalem the second time within three years, took, a few years later, his Phœnician shipwrights across Mesopotamia to the Tigris and built a fleet of his own, with which he made a successful raid on the Chaldæan settlement in Susiana at the north end of the Gulf of Persia. It is these Phœnician *cataphract* triremes, with two tiers of oars, and having beaks, masts, and sails, that we see represented in the sculptures of Kouyunjik.† In Sargon's sculptures the Phœnician vessels of this time have 4 or 5 oarsmen on each side, but in Sennacherib's they have 8, 9, or 11, and also two steersmen. It was not until Sennacherib's time that the Assyrians began to build war vessels, which even then were only imitations of Phœnician ones. These trireme war galleys were what is called *aphract, i.e.* the upper tier of rowers were unprotected and exposed to view. The apertures for the oars are like those

5. WAR GALLEY IN THE SERVICE OF SENNACHERIB, KING OF ASSYRIA.

in queen Hatsepsu's ships, no oars being shown in them in the drawings in either case. The beak is somewhat like the snout of a fish; the shields of the soldiers are seen suspended inside the bulwarks, they themselves being partly visible; the pilot is in the bow, and the steersman aft, with part of the crew standing near the mast, the two steering-paddles having blades in the form of the letter D, which is perhaps only conventional.

The war ships of Kittim (Dn 11[30]), which were to conquer Antiochus Epiphanes, are Roman vessels. In 2 Mac 4[20] we have the first mention of galleys (τριήραι).

*B.* New Testament Ships and Boats.—An account of Greek and Roman ships of war (νῆες μακραί, *naves longæ*), of which ample details are given by Boeckh,‡ Graser,§ Guhl and Koner,‖ and Torr,¶ seems to be out of place here, as, apart from the fishing and passenger vessels on the Sea of Galilee, in which our Lord embarked (described in the AV as 'ships' [except in Jn 6[22. 23], where it has 'boats'], and in the RV as 'boats' [Mt 4[22] 14[22. 24. 32. 33], Mk 6[32. 45. 47. 51. 54], Lk 5[2. 3. 7. 11] 8[22. 37], Jn 6[17. 19. 22. 23. 24]]), the interest in ships mentioned in the NT centres in the voyage of St. Paul from Cæsarea to Puteoli, about 60 A.D. During this voyage he and his fellow-traveller, St. Luke the physician, experienced what seems to have been his fourth shipwreck (2 Co 11[25]). The account of this voyage is remarkable for accuracy and conciseness in the use of nautical terms, though wanting in the descriptive details which a professional seaman would have added. In the *Onomasticon* of Julius Pollux of Naucratis in the Egyptian Delta, written about a century and a half later, we have a collection of Greek nautical terms, containing most of those used in St. Luke's description of the voyage. Of the ship of Adramyttium, a seaport of Mysia (which had then been for half a century part of the Roman province of Asia Minor), in which they embarked at Cæsarea, no details are given; but the two Alexandrian corn-ships in which the voyage was completed from Myra (Ac 27[6. 7. 8]), a port of Lycia, to Fair Havens in Crete, and to the island of Melita (28[1]), and thence to Syracuse, Rhegium, and Puteoli (28[11. 12. 13]), were evidently of large size, if the reading in both AV and RV of 276 as the number of persons on board, including the crew, besides a cargo of wheat, is correct.* This number was not extraordinary, as Josephus tells us that only a few years later he himself was wrecked on a voyage from Palestine to Puteoli in a ship having about 600 persons on board.

For the type of these ships we can refer to contemporary paintings found at Herculaneum and Pompeii which 'afford valuable details, and have the advantage of synchronizing perfectly with the voyage of St. Paul, the catastrophe to which they owe their preservation having happened less than twenty years after his shipwreck.'† The term πλοῖον used by St. Luke throughout his account of this voyage, except in Ac 27[41], when

* Rawlinson, *Anc. Monarch.* vol. ii. pp. 405, 449.
† Layard's *Nineveh*, 1st series, p. 71, etc.; and pl. in Rawlinson, *Anc. Monarch.* vol. ii. p. 176.
‡ *Urkunden über das Seewesen des Attischen Staates*, etc., 1840.
§ *De veterum re navali.*
‖ *The Life of the Greeks and Romans*, 3rd ed. pp. 253-264.
¶ *Ancient Ships*, 1894.

* WH and others read 'about (ὡς) 76.'
† J. Smith, *Voyage and Shipwreck of St. Paul*, 4th ed. 1880, p. 182.

ναῦς is used, was a common one for a merchant ship in general, but does not point to any one in particular of the many kinds of sea-going ships (*phaseli, corbitæ, cybææ*, etc.), of the 'round' or merchant class (στρογγύλη ναῦς, *navis oneraria*) in use at that time; but the fact of the wrecked vessel being a corn-ship of Alexandria suffices. Lucian (2nd cent. A.D.) in one of his dialogues* gives an account of one of the great merchant ships employed in carrying corn from Egypt to Italy about 150 A.D. Her length was 180 ft., and breadth 45 ft., the depth from upper deck to keel being 43½ ft. Such a ship would carry a burthen of 10,000 talents or *amphoræ*, equal to 250 tons. But ships of much larger capacity were built for special purposes, such as the one described by Pliny as having, about twenty years before St. Paul's voyage, taken the Vatican obelisk, by order of the emperor Caligula, from Egypt to Rome, together with four blocks of stone to form its pedestal, the whole weighing nearly 500 tons, in addition to 1000 tons of lentils in the hold as a bed for the obelisk to rest on. The mast of this ship, which Pliny describes as the most wonderful vessel ever seen afloat, was a single fir spar, and required four men with extended arms to encircle it. This event occurred within Pliny's own knowledge as a youth of seventeen; but if he is correct as to the size of the ship, that of the mast is almost incredible, unless he was in error as to its not being a built one.† Julius Cæsar tells us that these ships carried movable three-storeyed turrets on the upper deck for defensive purposes.‡

According to Lucian's description, the ship had both bow and stern curved upwards like those of the ancient Egyptian and earliest Greek ships, the ends terminating in a gilded *cheniscus*, one of which was in the form of the head and neck of a swan, and the other either similar or a 'figure-head.' Somewhere between the stem and stern was a statue of the presiding deity of the State or port of origin of the ship. On each bow was painted a large eye, or a figure illustrative of her name.

From a painting still to be seen in a tomb at Pompeii, and another found at Herculaneum,§ we know that such ships had projecting galleries at bow and stern, with bulwarks of open rails, and that the upper ends of the two paddle-rudders (πηδάλια, *gubernacula*) passed through holes in the ship, as described by Herodotus, instead of being externally attached to rope straps on the gunwale as in the Egyptian vessels and in the Scandinavian one already spoken of, and were often connected together by a rope attached to the tillers stretched across the ship, called χαλινός, which kept the two paddle-blades parallel to one another; ‖ but this, from St. Luke's account of the shipwreck, must have been done in such a way as not to prevent the rudders from being triced up clear of the water in case of anchoring by the stern. We also see in the Herculaneum painting a portion of one of the ship's cabins described by Lucian. There are also depicted what are, apparently, cable arrangements for anchoring by the stern, though no anchor is visible. She has two masts with 'square' yards and sails, as we see represented on the coins of the 2nd and 3rd centuries A.D.; and this seems to have been the normal number, though occasionally there were three at this period; but only one mast is shown in the Pompeii ship. The masts were supported by 'shrouds' placed abreast of and abaft the mast, with 'stays' to support it from the bow as now. These as well as the 'running rigging' were made of hide, flax, or hemp, or, probably in many cases, a combination of them and papyrus.

The ships of this—the merchant—class were built almost exclusively of fir or pine, as also the masts and yards, the latter (κεραίαι or *antennæ*) being in two pieces 'fished' together like those of both ancient and modern Egyptian vessels. The sails at this period were almost universally made of flax as now; the 'bolt rope' surrounding them being of hide. One of the sails is called ἀρτέμων by St. Luke (Ac 27[40]), and, although this word is not found in Julius Pollux or in any other ancient or mediæval Greek author, a mast and sail, each termed *artemon*, are mentioned by the Romans, Lucilius, Labeo, and Seneca, almost contemporaneously with St. Paul's shipwreck, as being, apparently, inferior in importance or magnitude to the principal mast and sail of a ship; they are represented on an Alexandrian coin of A.D. 67* as a sort of bowsprit and spritsail, and again on a Roman coin of A.D. 186 in the Museum at Avignon as a foremast and square foresail.† The word *artemon* is translated in the AV 'mainsail,' but in the RV 'foresail'; and there can be little doubt but that the latter is the more correct term as applied to the sail hoisted when the ship was purposely run aground. The word is still in use in the French marine as the name of the mizen or sternmost mast, and the sails on it; whilst the term *misaine* is applied to the foremast and its sails. The word *artemon* is now obsolete in the Italian language, but in the 16th cent. it was applied at Venice to the largest sail of a ship, which appears then to have been the foresail; and, possibly, the ignorance of this fact, as suggested by Smith, may have led the AV translators into error.‡

The sails were triced up to the yards by numerous 'brails' (καλώδια) when it was desired to reduce or take them in, and these were worked by the crew from the deck below; the yards were also furnished with 'lifts' and 'braces' for trimming the sails. The anchors (ἄγκυρα), which were suspended as now, one on each bow from 'catheads' (ἐπωτίδες), were made of lead, iron, or wood coated with lead, and of the modern form, as on the coins of Pæstum we see the stock and flukes or palms and ring duly represented; besides the 'bower' anchors there were others, four of which were let go at the stern of St. Paul's ship when shoaling water (Ac 27[29. 30]), whilst a pretence was made by the crew of also laying out the bower anchors by boat.

Oars (κώπη, *remus*) are not mentioned as being used on board; and as these were often absent from large merchant vessels, or only sufficient in number to be used as 'sweeps' during a calm, this was probably the case here. Such vessels had movable 'topmasts,' to the summit of which was hoisted the upper corner of the triangular sail, called in Latin *supparum*. It is to the lowering down to the deck of these topmasts that the expression (Ac 27[17]) 'strake sail' in the AV and 'lowered the gear' in the RV probably refers; to 'strike' a topmast is the proper nautical term in use at the present day. Seneca tells us that Alexandrian wheat-ships,§ on arrival at Puteoli, alone had the privilege of keeping their topsails up, all others being obliged to lower them down on entering the bay. The phrase ἀντοφθαλμεῖν τῷ ἀνέμῳ (Ac 27[15]), translated in the AV 'bear up into the wind,' and in the RV 'face the wind,' would be, in nautical language, 'beat up against the wind.' To 'bear up' is the sea phrase for doing exactly the reverse of what is

* πλοῖον ἢ Εὐχαί.
† Pliny, *HN* xvi. 76 and xxxiv. 14.
‡ *de Bello Gallico*, iii. 14; *de Bello Civili*, i. 26.
§ *Antichità di Ercolano*, tom. ii. pl. xiv. cit. J. Smith, *V. and S. of St. Paul*, p. 206.
‖ Guhl and Koner, *Life of the Greeks and Romans*, fig. 291, p. 257.

* Torr, *Ancient Ships*, pl. vi. 27. † *Ib.* pl. vi. 28.
‡ Smith, *V. and S. of St. Paul*, pp. 192-200.
§ *Epist.* 77, cit. Smith, *V. and S. of St. Paul*, p. 157.

expressed in the AV, and means to put a ship before the wind. Captain Sturmy* in describing a naval sea fight says, 'Bear up before the wind that we may give him our starboard broadside,' and again, 'He bears up before the wind to stop his leaks'; ἀντοφθαλμεῖν, as a nautical expression, may have reference to the eyes painted on each bow of ships in general; the term 'eyes of the ship' is still in general use as a sea term for the inside part of her which lies nearest to the stem. The rope cables (σχοινία, ἀγκύρια, *ancoralia* or *funes ancorales*) which passed, as now, through holes on each side of the bow, were of from 6 in. to 4½ in. in diameter, equal to from 13½ in. to 18 in. modern hemp cables, and were 'hove in' by a capstan (στροφεῖον) to weigh the anchor. Chain cables were then used only by ships of war, and, in so far as the English Navy is concerned, were not introduced till the beginning of the 19th century.

The terms 'helps' and 'undergirding' (Ac 27[17] βοήθειαι, ὑποζωννύντες) refer to the modes in use of strengthening an old or weak ship in bad weather by bracing the two curved ends of the ship, which were not water-borne, together by means of a stout rope or cable passing along the outside of the ship longitudinally, and generally below the water-line, several times; or by passing it under the keel and round the hull in a direction transverse to its length, and probably sometimes by a combination of both these methods. 'Undergirding' is a literal translation of the Greek nautical term for the operation of passing the above ropes or cables (ὑποζώματα) around or under a ship; but it has never been an English sea term, although the process of transverse undergirding has occasionally been resorted to by our sailing ships when dangerously overstrained, and was then termed 'frapping' the ship.† The internal longitudinal rope support of the ancient Egyptian ships seems to have been still in use in Roman ships to some extent under the name of *tormentum*,‡ probably from the two or four parts of rope of which it consisted being tightened, as required, by means of a piece of wood inserted between them and twisted round; the transverse external support was termed *mitra*. The longitudinal support became unnecessary when the length of the ends of the ship not water-borne became greatly diminished and the amount of deck increased; with improved shipbuilding the long curves disappeared. All Greek and Roman ships of war of the rank of triremes and upwards seem to have had the *hypozomata* permanently fixed in their places on board to enable them to better withstand the shock of ramming, and were also supplied with extra ones as part of their stores; but, in the case of merchant vessels (φορταγωγαί) such as St. Paul's ship, these 'helps' were probably improvised out of their ordinary gear. The term σκευή, translated 'tackling' (AV and RV Ac 27[19]), which the crew (and passengers [AV]) threw overboard with their own hands on the third day of the gale, probably refers to the spare stores of various kinds which followed some heavier undescribed weights (v.[18]), and it was only as a last resort that the cargo of wheat (v.[38]) (on which the commercial success of the voyage depended, and which was in charge of the 'supercargo' (ναύκληρος, v.[11]), to whose ill advice and that of the sailing-master (κυβερνήτης) St. Paul attributed their mishap) was 'jettisoned' in order to so lighten the ship, that, when the cables were slipped (v.[40]) and the foresail hoisted, she might run high up on the beach they had selected (v.[39]).

From the depth of water in which soundings were taken (Ac 27[28]), viz. in 20 and 15 fathoms, it is evident

* *The Compleat Mariner*, bk. i. p. 20, A.D. 1669.
† Isidore Hisp. *Op.* Fol. Par. 1601.
‡ Hor. *Carm.* i.-xiv. 6, 7.

that a sounding-lead attached to a line (καταπειρατηρία, *catapirates*) was used, as we see it on a bas-relief in the British Museum, suspended from the volute of the bow,* and probably 'armed' with grease at its lower end to determine the nature of the bottom, as in the time of Herodotus (ii. 5) and Lucilius.† The anchoring by the stern when rapidly shoaling water at night (Ac 27[29]) was good seamanship, and, in a vessel shaped alike at both ends, offered no practical difficulties, the rudder-paddles being afterwards triced up clear of the water. The ship carried at least one boat (σκάφη), like all others of her class, for general purposes, such as laying out anchors (v.[30]), communicating with the shore or with other ships; and this boat was towed astern in charge of one of the crew,‡ in accordance with usual practice in fine weather, being either hoisted up to 'davits' outside the ship, or hoisted on board altogether, for greater security (v.[16]), when bad weather came on.

The ship in which St. Paul embarked from the island of Melita seems to have been of the same type as the wrecked one, but we have the additional detail given of her 'sign' (παράσημον, *insigne*) (28[11]), indicating her name Διόσκουροι, translated 'Castor and Pollux' in the AV and 'The Twin Brothers' in the RV. Whether the *parasemon* was, in this case, a painting on either side of the stem denoting the *fratres Helenæ*, sons of Jupiter, who were then specially venerated as the patrons of sailors,§ like St. George and St. Nicholas in modern days, or whether they formed her 'figurehead,' we do not know; but both modes of indicating a ship's name, and, occasionally, a combination of the two, were in vogue at that time in Roman ships. That these ships were capable of 'working to windward' like modern sailing ships there can be no manner of doubt, although, possibly, not lying so close to the wind as within 5 or 6 points of the compass; but the quotation from Pliny (*HN* ii. 48) does not refer to 'beating,' and merely states that ships with the same wind sail in opposite directions according to the 'tack' they are on, and often meet one another, which can obviously be done with the wind fair or abeam.‖ The modern nautical term corresponding to the Greek περιελθόντες κατηντήσαμεν εἰς Ῥήγιον (Ac 28[13]), translated in the AV 'we fetched a compass and came to Rhegium' (RV 'made a circuit'),¶ would be 'we beat up to Rhegium,' the only course open to her in making for that port from Syracuse with a northerly wind, which is clearly indicated by her waiting there a day for a change of wind to the south. That these ships were fast sailers we know from contemporary statements of ancient authors, and especially from Pliny, who, in speaking of the marvellous utility of the flax plant, of which sails were made, in reducing the time occupied in a voyage from Egypt to Italy, instances a voyage recently made from the Straits of Messina to Alexandria, by two Roman prefects, E. Galerius and Balbillus, in 7 and 6 days respectively; and another voyage from Puteoli to Alexandria by Valerius Marianus, a Roman senator, 'lenissimo flatu,' in 9 days.** St. Paul's voyage from Rhegium to Puteoli (180 miles) was effected in 2 days (but see art. ROADS AND TRAVEL (IN NT), p. 379).

Of the fishing and passenger boats on the Sea of Galilee (Lake of Tiberias), which were evidently very numerous in our Lord's time, we have no description.

* Guhl and Koner, *Life of the Greeks and Romans*, fig. 294, p. 259.
† Torr, *Ancient Ships*, p. 101. ‡ *Ib.* p. 103.
§ Hor. *Carm.* i. 3.
‖ Smith, *DB*², art. 'Ships and Boats.'
¶ WH (following BN¹) read περιελόντες, 'cast loose.
** *HN* xix. 1.

LITERATURE.—Champollion and Rosellini, *Monuments de l'Égypte*; August Boeckh, *Urkunden über das Seewesen des Attischen Staates*; B. Glaser, *Über das Seewesen des alten Ægypten*; M. Jal, *Archéologie Navale*; F. Steinitz, *The Ship, its Origin and Progress*; Carl R. Lepsius, *Denkmäler aus Ægypten und Ethiopien*; Dümichen, *Die Flotte einer Egyptischen Königin*; A. H. Layard, *Monuments of Nineveh*, and *Nineveh and its Remains*; Cecil Torr, *Ancient Ships*; James Smith, *Voyage and Shipwreck of St. Paul*; Wilkinson, *The Ancient Egyptians*; Canon G. Rawlinson, *The Seven Ancient Monarchies*; *Egypt. Exploration Fund*, Tomb of Pateri at el-Kab, Deshâsheh (tomb of Anta and Mera), Deir el-Bahri (Punt Expedition); G. Maspero, *The Dawn of Civilization*; E. Guhl and W. Koner, *The Life of the Greeks and Romans*; Canney, art. 'Ship' in *Encycl. Biblica*.

R. M. BLOMFIELD.

## ROADS AND TRAVEL (IN OT).—

I. ROADS.
- i. Position and conformation of Palestine.
- ii. Hebrew terms for 'road.' Metaphorical usages.
- iii. Various kinds of roads.
- iv. The roads of the OT.
  1. Roads connecting Palestine with other countries: (*a*) Arabia, (*b*) Egypt, (*c*) Syria, Assyria and Babylonia.
  2. Roads in Palestine: in (*a*) Judæa, (*b*) Samaria, (*c*) Galilee, (*d*) the Jordan Valley (including the fords), (*e*) on the east of the Jordan.

II. TRAVEL.
- i. Motives for travelling: (*a*) attendance at religious festivals, etc., (*b*) commerce, (*c*) political relations, (*d*) ill-health, (*e*) war. Travelling hampered for Jews by the Sabbath law.
- ii. Modes of travel: on foot, riding (asses, mules, camels, horses), chariots, ox-waggons, caravans.
- iii. Provision for the wants of travellers. Inns a late institution. *Khans*. Oriental hospitality.

Literature.

I. *ROADS*.—i. POSITION AND CONFORMATION OF PALESTINE.—The land inhabited by the Israelites seemed from its position to have been predestined to form a meeting-point in the world's lines of communication. On the western side its situation brought it into connexion with the Mediterranean coasts; on the south-west the country was closely bound to Egypt, that land of ancient civilization; on the south to Arabia, which was traversed by richly laden caravans; while on the north there were approaches from the coast by the *Merj 'Ayyûn* ('the entering in of Hamath,' Nu $34^8$, Jos $13^5$, and often), and by the S.E. side of Antilibanus, to the cultured lands beyond, and further to the great empires of the Euphrates. It was only on the east that an insurmountable barrier to communication was presented by the cheerless desert.

For the Israelites themselves, however, these advantages of situation had not the significance that might have been expected. The seacoast with its harbours, some of which were poor enough, was (apart from the period referred to in Gn $49^{13}$) in the hands of the Phœnicians and the Philistines, to whom thus belonged the important points at which the caravans coming from Damascus or Arabia unloaded their goods for further transport by sea. Consequently the Israelites, when they sought to take a share in international commerce, found themselves compelled to make the distant port of 'Ezion-geber the starting-point of their shipping trade. It was not till the latest period of Jewish history that they got Joppa into their hands, a possession afterwards supplemented by the harbour of Cæsarea, which had been repaired by Herod.

The ancient caravan road connecting Damascus with Arabia, the modern Pilgrim Road, ran along the eastern side of the territory of the Israelites, and thus was of no service to them. In like manner the important caravan road from Gaza to Arabia touched only a small and thinly peopled tract of their country. On the other hand, the great caravan road connecting Damascus with the middle part of the Mediterranean coast and with Egypt ran right through the territory of Israel, and offered its people a variety of advantages, which they did not fail to utilize when the State reached under Solomon the culminating point of its culture.

In the interior of the country the extensive stretch of mountains, interrupted by steep descents, presented a serious obstacle to communication. Any one who has made journeys in Palestine knows from experience how travelling is a course of up hill and down, and how at every turn declivities have to be passed which it is a severe task for one's horse to mount or to descend. For the most part, one has to ride at a walking pace; it is but rarely that valleys are encountered with a level surface where horses can gallop for any long stretch. Besides, the tract on the western side of the Jordan is separated from that on the eastern side by the deep depression of that river. In the dry season, it is true, communication between the two parts of the country is kept up by numerous fords, but during the rainy season these are for the most part impassable; while, on the other hand, the winding and impetuous course of the stream makes it impossible to use it as a waterway between north and south. The only exception in this respect is the broad expanse of the Lake of Gennesareth, offering great advantages to the dwellers upon its shores.

Nevertheless, the gradually developed high civilization of the Israelites led to the difficulties of communication being overcome as far as was practicable, and there arose, as the Old Testament shows, a network of roads covering all the inhabited parts of the country. From this point of view, the monarchical period, from the reign of Solomon onwards, must have been of special significance; but, on the other hand, the difference between the earlier and later periods must not be exaggerated. The country to which the Israelites came as settlers already possessed a certain measure of civilization. The Tel el-Amarna letters, which in so many respects have enlarged our knowledge of the pre-Israelite history of Canaan, mention, amongst other things, caravans which the Egyptian vassal-princes in Canaan were in the way of sending under escort to Egypt.* This points to the existence of routes of communication. We gather also from the Song of Deborah that in the period of the Judges there were roads with a brisk traffic in the Northern kingdom, for the condition of things that had supervened owing to the weakness of the Israelites is described in these terms: 'The highways were unoccupied, and the travellers walked through byways' (Jg $5^6$).†

ii. HEBREW TERMS FOR 'ROAD.'—The usual Hebrew word for 'road' is דֶּרֶךְ (*derekh*), which, from its etymology, probably means 'ground trodden upon.' Side by side with it we have the word מְסִלָּה (*mĕsillāh*), which occurs also in the Inscription of Mesha, and whose radical meaning is undoubtedly that of a road which has been constructed by the filling up of hollows, and which is kept up by artificial methods. More poetical is the employment in Hebrew of the word אֹרַח (*'ōraḥ*), which, on the other hand, is the usual term in Aramaic. Likewise more poetical are נָתִיב (*nāthîbh*) or נְתִיבָה (*nĕthîbhāh*) and (common in Aramaic and Arabic) שְׁבִיל (*shĕbhîl*). A narrow road shut in on both sides was called מִשְׁעוֹל (*mish'ōl*, Nu $22^{24}$ only); the road that ran right through a valley or led over a stream was מַעֲבָר (*ma'ăbhār*) or מַעְבָּרָה (*ma'bārāh*); the steep road up a declivity, מַעֲלֶה (*ma'ăleh*), or, down it, מוֹרָד (*môrād*).

In the *figurative* language of the OT the notion

* Cf. Nos. 180, 189, 242, 256 in Winckler's edition [Petrie, Nos. 254, 231, 42, 41].

† That there were much frequented roads also in the southern portion of the land is evident from the narrative of Gn 38, where the *ḳĕdēshah* takes her seat by the wayside to be seen by passers-by.

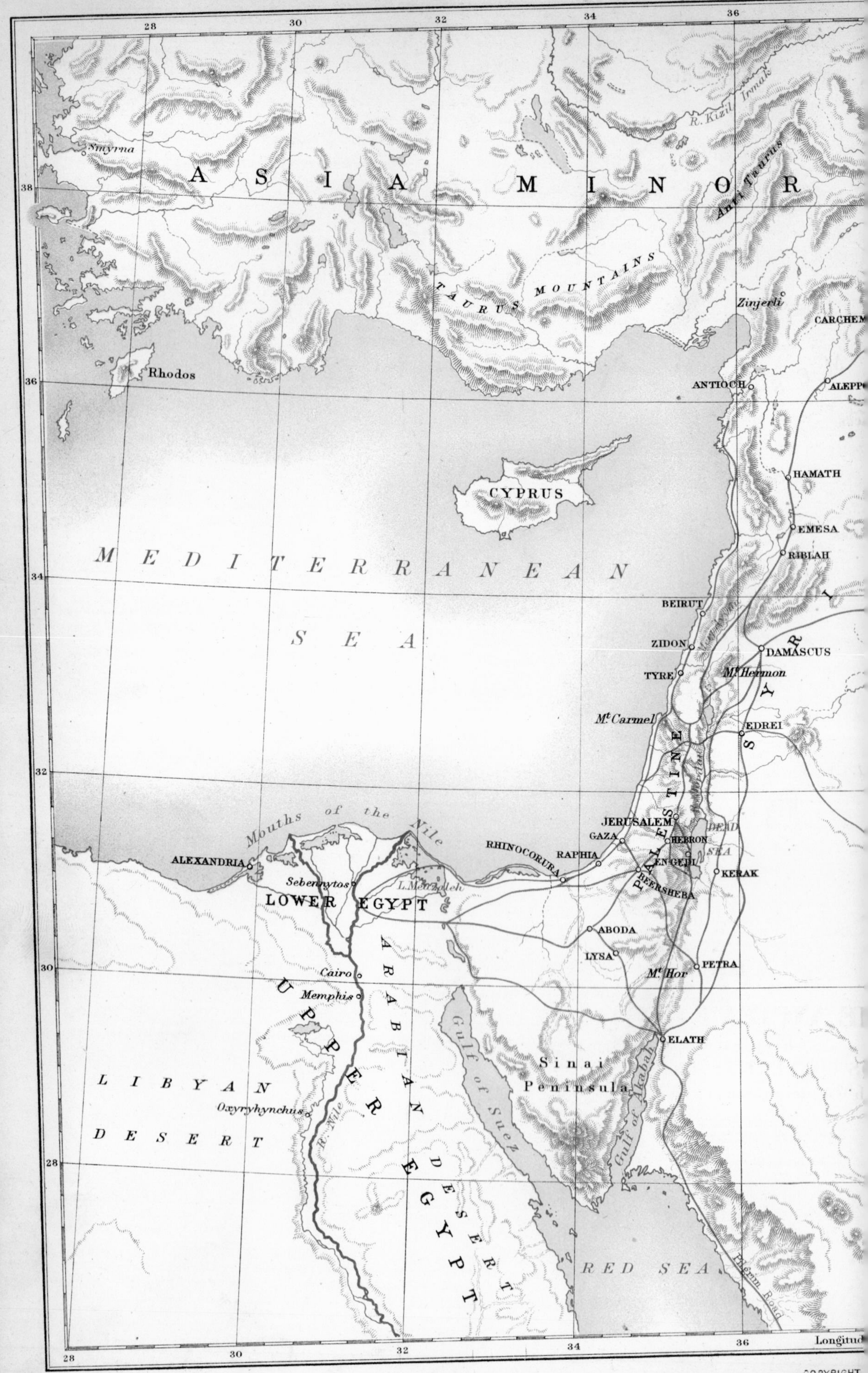

28
30
32
34
36
38
36
34
32
30
28
Smyrna
A S I A M I N O R
R. Kizil Irmak
Anti Taurus
TAURUS MOUNTAINS
Zinjerli
CARCHEM
Rhodos
ANTIOCH
ALEPP
CYPRUS
HAMATH
EMESA
RIBLAH
M E D I T E R R A N E A N
S E A
BEIRUT
ZIDON
DAMASCUS
TYRE
Mt. Hermon
Mt. Carmel
EDREI
S Y R I
PALESTINE
JERUSALEM
GAZA
HEBRON
DEAD SEA
RHINOCORURA
RAPHIA
ENGEDI
KERAK
BEERSHEBA
Mouths of the Nile
ALEXANDRIA
Sebennytos
L. Menzaleh
LOWER EGYPT
ABODA
LYSA
PETRA
Mt. Hor
Cairo
Memphis
UPPER EGYPT
ARABIAN DESERT
Gulf of Suez
ELATH
Sinai Peninsula
Gulf of Akabah
LIBYAN DESERT
Oxyryhynchus
R. Nile
RED SEA
Pilgrim Road
Longitud
Engraved & Printed by
COPYRIGHT.

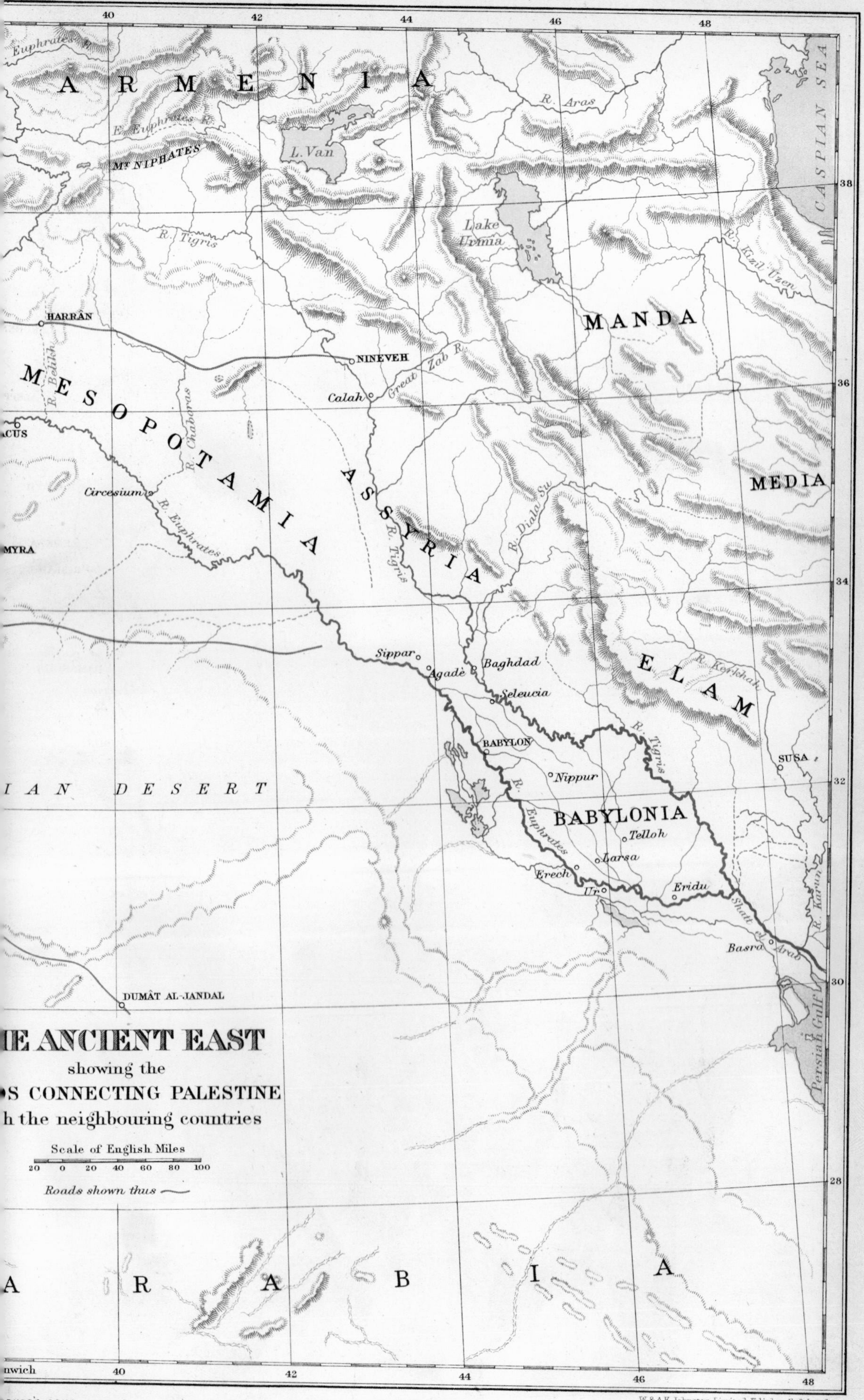


IE ANCIENT EAST
showing the
S CONNECTING PALESTINE
h the neighbouring countries

Scale of English Miles
20 0 20 40 60 80 100

Roads shown thus

BNER'S SONS

W. & A.K. Johnston, Limited, Edinburgh & London.

of 'road' or 'way' plays a prominent part, a circumstance probably connected not with the increase of communication but with recollections of the nomadic pre-historic period of Israel's history. In the desert the discovery of the right path is often a question of life, for the wanderer who fails to find a well of water or who stumbles upon an enemy's quarters speedily falls a prey to death. In this way the language of the OT is to be understood when it speaks of a way to life and one to death (Pr 6$^{23}$ 10$^{17}$ 12$^{28}$ 14$^{12}$ 21$^{16}$, Jer 21$^{8}$), or of a way that perishes (Ps 1$^{6}$), or that is shut up (Job 19$^{8}$). When God means to destroy a nation He closes up its way with a wall * or with thorns (Hos 2$^{6\,(8)}$). His law teaches Israel the right way, from which, however, the people constantly wander (Jer 3$^{13}$, cf. Is 2$^{3}$). He who follows the example of another walks in his ways (1 K 15$^{26}$ and often). Illustrations of similar usages might be multiplied indefinitely. The same figurative mode of expression prevails also in the Ḳoran, whose first hearers must have been familiar with the importance of path-finding to the Bedawîn.

iii. Various kinds of Roads.—In many passages of the OT the word 'way' or 'road' undoubtedly stands for a simple bridle-path. It is the latter that is the initial stage in the process whereby men and beasts tread the same ground year after year. Thus the very old Pilgrim Road from Damascus to Arabia consists merely of a number of parallel tracks without any artificial construction, and recalls the passages in the ancient Arab poets where such roads are compared to striped cloths from S. Arabia. On the hills of Palestine the hard limestone soil forms a firm foundation for the roads, which for long stretches require nothing more in the way of construction, and present no inconvenience to the traveller except at spots where the winter rains have washed down accumulations of stones. The existence of artificially formed roads is not necessarily implied in the passages where chariots or waggons are spoken of. According to the OT, the great plain between the hills of Samaria and Galilee was the proper home of chariots of war, which could move here with ease (Jg 4$^{2}$, cf. 2 K 9$^{20}$). But besides this we hear also of vehicles traversing the hill-country proper—*e.g.* Gn 45$^{27}$ (from Ḥebron to Egypt), 1 S 6 (from Ekron by way of Beth-shemesh to Kiriath-jearim), 2 S 6 (from Kiriath-jearim to Jerusalem), 2 S 15$^{1}$, 1 K 1$^{5}$, Is 22$^{18}$, Jer 17$^{25}$ (from and to Jerusalem), 1 K 12$^{18}$ (from Shechem to Jerusalem), 1 K 22$^{22\text{ff.}}$ (from Ramoth-gilead to Samaria), 2 K 7$^{14\text{f.}}$ (from Samaria to the Jordan), 2 K 5$^{9.\,20\text{ff.}}$ (from Damascus to Samaria), 2 K 10$^{15\text{f.}}$ (from Jezreel to Samaria, cf. 9$^{27\text{ff.}}$). With reference to Gn 45$^{27}$ Robinson (*BRP*$^{2}$ i. 214 f.) declares that the road from Ḥebron to the south cannot possibly have been traversed by waggons, and hence he assumes that they must have made a circuit by the *Wādy el-Khalîl*. In like manner he asserts that the road between Ḥebron and Jerusalem must have been impracticable for anything on wheels. But in that case the OT could not have spoken at all of vehicles travelling from and to Jerusalem, for none of the roads leading to the capital are a whit better than the Ḥebron road. Nor can it well be doubted that the chariots which Absalom collected in connexion with his projected rebellion (2 S 15$^{1}$) were procured at Ḥebron. As a matter of fact, there is no ground for Robinson's remark if one keeps in mind that the light two-wheeled chariots of war and the clumsy ox-waggons (1 S 6) could travel not only on perfectly primitive roads, but even along unbeaten ground.* Of course the progress under such conditions was often very slow, and the journey was attended with inconveniences and dangers such as are expressly alluded to in 2 S 6$^{6}$.

But, although a number of the roads mentioned in the Bible are nothing more than primitive natural tracks, it is a well established fact, on the other hand, that the Israelites had also artificially constructed roads. It is a circumstance of special importance from this point of view that the Moabite king Mesha records in his Inscription (l. 26) how he caused the road along the Arnon to be constructed (עשתי מסלה). For it may be inferred that what was done by this prince would also be done by the Israelite monarchs of the same period. A testimony in favour of this may be found in the very word מְסִלָּה (*mĕsillāh*) noticed above. It is also expressly said in Dt 19$^{3}$ that the roads leading to the three Cities of Refuge are to be kept in good repair (הכין). In Sir 21$^{10}$ the writer says figuratively, 'The way of sinners is made smooth with stones.' Contrariwise, Job (30$^{13}$) speaks of a tearing up or destroying (נתס) of the road, which likewise presupposes one that has been artificially formed. The expression 'the king's highway' (דֶּרֶךְ הַמֶּלֶךְ) used for the great trunk-road of the country (Nu 20$^{17}$, cf. v.$^{19}$ מְסִלָּה) appears to point to the fact that it was especially the kings who saw to the repairing of the roads, a procedure which was natural even on military grounds.† We are not, of course, to think of such roads as possessing any special excellence; they were probably similar in character to the 'Sultan's roads' as these existed in Palestine down to recent years. Accordingly, when kings went upon a journey, people were sent out to prepare the roads, for instance by removing loose stones from the surface (cf. Is 40$^{3}$ 57$^{14}$ 62$^{10}$, and Diod. Sic. ii. 13). It is also related by Josephus that Vespasian took workmen along with his army, whose duty it was to remove inequalities in the roads, and to cut down any bushes that might be in the way.‡ On the other hand, it is improbable that the Israelites built any *bridges*, as there is no word in the OT (nor even 2 Mac 12$^{13}$) which can be proved to mean 'bridge,' and none of the existing remains of ancient bridges over the Jordan are earlier than the Roman period. Any one who wanted to cross the Jordan had to avail himself of the *fords*, unless he followed the example of Jonathan the Maccabee (1 Mac 9$^{48}$) and swam over.§ In desert regions a '*waymark*' (צִיּוּן *ẓîyyûn*, or תַּמְרוּר *tamrûr*) was set up for the guidance of travellers (Jer 31$^{21}$), a practice which is also mentioned frequently by the ancient Arab poets. But *milestones* were first introduced by the Romans; the Israelites reckoned distances by the number of days' journey (Gn 30$^{36}$ 31$^{23}$, 1 K 19$^{4}$, 2 K 3$^{9}$), and appear in general to have had no measure for long stretches of road.‖

iv. The Roads of the OT.—The mention in the OT of the then existing roads is naturally of a

* The method of blocking a road by means of a wall (גָּדֵר) formed of loose stones is described by Guthe in *Mitteil. u. Nachrichten des deutschen Pal. Vereins*, 1896, p. 9.

* Cf. *e.g.* the illustrations in W. Max Müller, *Asien u. Europa*, 301, 366.

† But when Josephus (*Ant.* VIII. vii. 4) records that Solomon caused the roads leading to Jerusalem to be paved with black stone, it is certain that he attributes to this monarch the work of a later age. A stone pavement is mentioned in the OT in 2 K 16$^{17}$, Ezk 40$^{17}$, Neh 3$^{8}$ (?), 2 Ch 7$^{3}$, cf. Aristeas, 38.

‡ *BJ* III. vi. 2. Cf. vii. 3, where it is recorded how Vespasian, when he had determined to besiege Jotapata, first despatched workmen in the direction of the city to level the mountain road, which was difficult for foot-passengers to traverse and wholly impracticable for horsemen. Josephus adds that in four days they succeeded in making a wide military road.

§ On the other hand, it may be assumed that the Phœnicians understood how to build some kind of bridge, for the deep Liṭāny gorge which is crossed by the undeniably ancient road between Ẓidon and the *Merj 'Ayyûn* cannot be passed in any other way (cf. Robinson, *BRP* iii. 50).

‖ Whether the word כִּבְרָה (*kibhrah*, Gn 35$^{16}$ 48$^{7}$, 2 K 5$^{19}$) really stands for a larger measure of length, is very uncertain.

somewhat incidental character, and is influenced exclusively by regard to the scenes of the history that is being narrated. Nevertheless, it is worth while to enumerate the most important of these roads, since we thus obtain at all events a view of the condition of things at the time. They were supplemented by the later Roman roads, which as a rule followed the old lines of communication (cf. the following article).*

1. We shall first examine *the roads that connected Palestine with the surrounding countries.*—(*a*) From *Arabia* it was possible to reach Palestine by a variety of roads. One led in a straight line from Elath, by way of Lysa (*Wādy Lussan*), to Gaza.† At Aboda (*'Abde*) it met the road coming from Ḥebron by Beersheba and Elusa. The portion of this road lying between Lysa and Elath is probably to be identified with 'the way to the *Yam Ṣuph*' mentioned in Nu $14^{25}$ $21^{4}$, Dt $1^{40}$ $2^{1}$. Another road ran up from Elath to the north through the 'Arabah depression. The traveller who made choice of it in order to reach Judah, might either make his way to Ḥebron by the ancient Ascent of 'Aḳrabbim; or he might journey through the 'Arabah as far as the south end of the Dead Sea and thence gain the hills and reach Ḥebron by way of *Zuwêre et-Taḥta* and *el-Fôḳâ*; or he might pursue his way along the west side of the Dead Sea and make use of the ascent at En-gedi (see below). These roads must have been under the control of the Israelites at the time when Solomon opened the sea trade from 'Eziongeber. Close by the watershed a road parts from the 'Arabah route and goes down to the metropolis, Petra. This city, however, may be reached also by a direct road over the high land. From Petra a main road leads by *eṭ-Ṭafila* to Kerak in Moab. This may perhaps be identified with 'the king's highway' of Nu $20^{17}$. But it is extremely doubtful whether it is the same that is referred to in the parallel narrative, Dt $2^{8}$, for here the road from Elath to Ma'ân and thence (coinciding with the great Pilgrim Road) to the east side of Moab suits much better. The Pilgrim Road itself, which leads on further by Edre'i and Muzêrîb (probably the ancient Ashtaroth-ḳarnaim) to Damascus, marks an old established and very important connexion between Syria and Arabia, and also opens up, by means of various branches running westwards, a further connexion between Arabia and Palestine. At Edre'i it takes up a road coming from Dumah (*Dumât al-Jandal*). The oasis of Tema mentioned in the OT (Job $6^{19}$, Is $21^{14}$) may be reached both from Dumah and from the southern continuation of the Pilgrim Road. Along these roads travelled not only peaceful caravans, but also the Bedawîn tribes upon the occasion of their forays upon the civilized districts east of the Jordan, or their plundering campaigns to the west of that river.

(*b*) Palestine was connected with *Egypt* by two roads. One of these ('the way of the land of the Philistines,' Ex $13^{17}$) ran along the shore of the Mediterranean, and is probably identical with the present caravan road which leads past *Ḳanṭarat el-Khazne.*‡ By this road Sargon advanced against the Egyptians, and defeated them at Raphia; and Necho doubtless availed himself of it when he set out to march through Palestine (2 K $23^{29}$). At a later period Titus made his way from Egypt to Judæa along this road, his halting-places being Ostrakine, Rhinocorura, Raphia, Gaza, Ascalon, Jamnia, Joppa, and Cæsarea.* The other road is called in the OT 'the way to Shur' (Gn $16^{7}$, 1 S $15^{7}$). The researches of F. W. Holland have shown that it deviated from the caravan road from Beersheba, and ran north from *Jebel Yeleḳ*, then by *Jebel Mughara*, and finally over undulating ground to *Isma'îlîya.*† See, further, art. SHUR in vol. iv.

(*c*) On the northern frontier of Palestine there were three entrances to the country. These marked the connexion not only with *Syria* but also with the Euphrates lands, *Assyria and Babylonia*, for any direct communication with the latter through the waterless Syrian desert was difficult. We shall look first at the points of entrance, and then at the routes which converged upon them.

The first entrance is the road along the Mediterranean coast, leading from Beirut by Ẓidon to Tyre and on to the south. Somewhat to the north of Beirut it was blocked by a rocky projection at the *Nahr el-Kalb*, but even in pre-Israelite times this obstacle had been overcome, for among the figures cut on the rocky wall, at the spot where the course of the road is hewn past the rock, is that of Ramses II.—a circumstance which throws an interesting light upon the conditions of communication in these early times.—The second entrance was the *Merj 'Ayyûn*, into which debouched the road leading from Riblah (2 K $23^{33}$ $25^{6.\ 20f.}$) through the valley between Lebanon and Antilibanus.—The third starting-point was Damascus, from which several roads led to the west and the south. One ran along the foot of Hermon to Dan, whence the traveller could reach Ẓidon, Tyre, and Galilee (see below). Another ran in a S.W. direction past *el-Ḳunêtra* in Golan, and struck the Jordan at the spot where afterwards the Bridge of Jacob's Daughters was built. We shall presently describe more fully how from this point it traversed Western Galilee and led by one branch to Acco and by another to the Plain of Jezreel. By means of its further continuation along the Mediterranean coast it formed the principal connexion between Damascus, with its hinterland, and Egypt. In the Middle Ages it was called *Via Maris*, and there is a strong probability that it is to be identified with the road that bears the corresponding name דֶּרֶךְ הַיָּם (*derekh hayyām*, 'way of the sea') in Is $9^{1}$.‡ Besides this there was still another road from Damascus through the trans-Jordanic territory, which crossed the Jordan at Bethshean, and thence led to the Plain of Jezreel or into the hill-country of Samaria.

Having now learned what were the points of entrance to North Palestine, we must notice briefly the roads leading thence to Syria and the Euphrates lands, for the Israelites had not infrequently the misfortune to see armies advancing against them along these roads, or had themselves to tread them as deported captives. The oldest principal line of communication between North Palestine and the Euphrates lands contrived to avoid the desert by a long circuitous route through Syria, passing Riblah (2 K $23^{33}$ $25^{6.\ 20f.}$), Ḥamath, Emesa, and Aleppo, and along the Upper Euphrates till in the fertile Belikh Valley it reached the city of Ḥarrân, where the roads from Armenia and Babylonia met. This was probably the route chosen, for instance, by Pharaoh-necho (2 K $23^{29}$), who was met by Nebuchadrezzar at Carchemish. It was doubtless along the same road that the Assyrian kings advanced

* Of maps to be consulted on what follows, we should recommend, in addition to the two accompanying ones and large English ones of the *PEF*, the special maps of the *ZDPV*, vols. iii. and xix. Cf. also Bartholomew-Smith's *Map of Palestine* (Edin., T. & T. Clark, 1901).

† Regarding the stations of the Peutinger Table, cf. Buhl, *Gesch. der Edomiter*, p. 18.

‡ Cf. Brugsch, *Deutsche Revue*, ix. 350 ff.

* Jos. *BJ* IV. xi. 5. Regarding the ancient Egyptian fortresses on this road, see W. Max Müller, *Asien u. Europa*, 134.

† *Proceedings of Royal Geog. Soc.* xxii. 455 f.; Trumbull, *Kadesh Barnea*, 349 f.; Guthe, *ZDPV* viii. 217.

‡ Schumacher, *PEFSt*, 1889, p. 78 f.; G. A. Smith, *HGHL* 426 f.

on their expeditions of conquest.* From Ḥarrân a road led direct to Nineveh, while Babylonia could be reached through the Mesopotamian Plain. At a later period Thapsacus was a favourite crossing-place. It was here, for example, that the younger Cyrus and Alexander the Great crossed the Euphrates. This brought one nearer to the desert on the west of the river, but it was still possible to keep on the edge of the cultured land. In the Roman period, on the other hand, a much frequented route was the shorter road from Damascus by way of Palmyra and a number of water stations in the desert to the spot where the Chaboras joins the Euphrates.† It is possible, however, that in much earlier times this desert road had a predecessor. H. Winckler ‡ seeks to show that as early as the 14th cent. B.C. the Babylonian king Kadašman-ḫarba, finding the old road through N. Mesopotamia closed against him by the extension of the sway of Assyria, caused water stations to be established in the desert, in order that he might have a direct road from Babylon to Damascus after his conquest of the Suti who lived in this desert. The circumstance that Palmyra is first mentioned towards the close of the pre-Christian period is of course no argument against this view, for a water station may very well have existed there prior to the building of the famous city. Which of these roads was followed by the exiles on their way back from Babylon cannot be determined with certainty. The descriptions in Is 40[1ff.] 43[14f.] 49[9ff.] presuppose that a desert has to be traversed by the returning company. We may also recall the circumstance that those who accompanied Zerubbabel took with them, according to Ezr 2[66], not only horses and mules and asses, but 435 camels, and that those who returned with Ezra were exposed to danger from 'liers in wait' (Ezr 8[31]). But this will suit equally well a journey through the mostly unpeopled N. Mesopotamia, and does not point of necessity to a course through the desert proper. According to Berosus (*ap.* Jos. *c. Apion.* i. 19), Nebuchadrezzar, after he had cleared Syria of the Egyptian troops, being informed of his father's death set off for Babylon by forced marches through the desert. At the same time he left instructions with his generals to conduct the Jewish, Phœnician, and other prisoners of war, along with the baggage of the army, thither. In this latter instance, evidently, the way round about the desert was to be followed.

2. *Roads in Palestine.*—(*a*) When we turn to *Judæa*, we are best informed as to the roads leading from Jerusalem. The ancient main road from the capital to the Maritime Plain led past Gibeon and Beth-ḥoron, from which there was a steep ascent to the plain (cf. *e.g.* Jos 10[10], 2 S 2[24] 13[34] [LXX] 20[12], Ac 23[23. 31]; Jos. *BJ* II. xii. 2, xix. 8). The present road from Jerusalem to Jaffa or Lydda is first mentioned a few times by Eusebius.§ From the Philistine Plain various passes led into the mountains and to the capital.* From Ashdod the main road led through the *Wādy es-Sunṭ*, called in earlier times the Vale of Elah (cf. the narrative of 1 S 17[1ff.]). From 'Eḳron a road ran to Beth-shemesh in the *Wādy es-Surâr* further to the north. Hither the kine brought the ark of Jahweh, and thence it was afterwards conveyed to Ḳiriath-jearim and finally to Jerusalem (1 S 6, 2 S 6).—Towards the south Jerusalem was connected by an ancient road with Ḥebron and beyond it with Beersheba (cf. *e.g.* 2 S 15[9] 16[15], 1 K 19[3]). By this road Lysias, according to 1 Mac 4[29ff.], attempted to reach the capital, but was completely routed by Judas at Beth-ẓur. It was presumably this road also that was chosen when a journey was undertaken from Judæa to Edom. The ancient highroad, before it was modernized a few years ago, bore every trace of having been always the main route between Jerusalem and the south; it was carried in a straight line, and was in many places artificially constructed, and that apparently from early times. Like the generality of such roads, it presented not a few difficulties, leading as it did over steep hills, and being covered at not a few spots with large stones.† An hour's journey south of Jerusalem a road strikes off from it, which brings one in 13 minutes to Bethlehem (cf. Jg 19[1ff.]). — From Jerusalem to En-gedi there was also a much frequented road. It is mentioned in 2 Ch 20. As the הַצִּיץ (*Haẓẓiẓ*) of v.[16] is no doubt to be identified with the modern *Wādy Ḥaṣâṣâ*, the ancient road followed exactly the same course as the later Roman road. A part of this road is probably in view also in 1 S 24[2f.], whereas the road named in the parallel narrative (26[3]) should more likely be found in that between En-gedi and Ḥebron, if, that is to say, the hill Ḥachîlah is rightly identified with *Ḍahr el-Kôlâ*. From En-gedi one can proceed further to the southern shore of the Dead Sea and to Edom.—The ancient main road between Jerusalem and Jericho (Lk 10[30]) probably coincided with the Roman road.‡ It ran, according to 2 S 15[23] [LXX] 16[5], over the Mount of Olives and then by the city of Baḥurim. Its further course, which may be presumed to have been the same as that of the later road (before it was modernized), led through the waterless and sun-scorched desert to *Tal'at ed-Dâm*, a name which probably points back to the old 'Ascent of *Adummim*' by which the low ground is reached (Jos 15[7] 18[17]). This was the usual road taken by pilgrims coming from the east of the Jordan. The latter, as a rule, included also Galilæans who desired to avoid the road through Samaria. There was another, but a longer, road from the capital to the N.W. shore of the Dead Sea and Jericho. It first follows the lower Ḳidron Valley by Mar-saba; then passes the *Munṭar* hill, and crossing the small plain of *Buḳa'* finally arrives through beautiful scenery at the low ground. It was probably by this road that king Ẓedekiah fled from Jerusalem to the Jordan (2 K 25[4f.], Jer 39[4]).—The present main road from Jerusalem to the north, which at some spots is very bad and uncomfortable, meets us in the narrative of Jg 19[13], where the Levite, turning aside from Jerusalem, proposed to pass the night at Gibeah or Ramah.§ Its northern continuation, which ran past Gophna, is mentioned in *Onom.*[2] 300. 94. It is the same road which is called in Jg 20[31] the way from Bethel to Gibeah. By this road Titus moved on

* Shalmaneser II. describes (H. Winckler, *Keilinschr. Textbuch*, 2) how, when the Euphrates was in high flood, he crossed the river on vessels constructed from sheeps' skins, and defeated the king of Carchemish and others.

† M. v. Oppenheim, *Vom Mittelmeer zum persischen Golf*, i. 331.

‡ *Altorient. Forschungen*, i. 146; *Die politische Entwickelung Babyloniens und Assyriens*, 14. The active intercourse between Babylon and Palestine-Egypt by means alike of royal messengers and traders is witnessed to by the Tel el-Amarna letters, *e.g.* Winckler, Nos. 10, 11 [Petrie, Nos. 22, 124].

§ *Onom.*[2] 109. 27, 271. 40, 233. 83. If the NT Emmaus should be identical with *Ḳolôniye*, the way to it would coincide with the beginning of the Jaffa road; but if Emmaus is *el-Kubêbe*, the reference in Lk 24[13] will be to the road to this village by way of *Nabi Samwîl*. If Ḳiriath-jearim be rightly identified with *Ḳaryet el-'Ineb*, it was by the eastern portion of the present Jaffa road that the ark travelled from this city to Jerusalem (1 S 6).

* Josephus (*BJ* III. ii. 3) says that these passes were occupied by the Romans when the Jews projected an attack on Ascalon. On the ancient roads from Jerusalem to *'Artûf*, see *ZDPV* x. 134 f.

† Robinson, *BRP*[2] i. 214 f.

‡ Cf. v. Kasteren, *ZDPV* xiii. 95 ff.

§ Ramah is the modern *er-Râm*; Gibeah in all probability is *Tulêl el-Fûl*, somewhat to the south of it.

Jerusalem, for he passed the night at Gophna, then at *Gabath-Saul, i.e.* Gibeah, and came finally to Scopus, from which he descried Jerusalem with its magnificent temple.* On the other hand, Isaiah ($10^{28ff.}$) makes the Assyrian conqueror advance against Jerusalem by another road further to the north-east—a circumstance which at least suggests that in olden times armies coming from the north approached Jerusalem by this road, and not by the one first named. As a matter of fact, the two roads unite further to the north, but it is strange all the same that considerable armies should have preferred the very difficult passage by the *Suweiniṭ* gorge (cf. 1 S $14^{4}$). The road named by the prophet, which can be reached either by way of 'Anathoth or by the present road to the south of *Tulêl el-Fûl*, runs past *Ḥizma* and *Geba'* to the *Suweiniṭ* gorge, north of which Michmash is reached. At all events Michmash was, as 1 S $13^{18}$ shows, an important meeting-point, from which roads ran in all directions. Towards the south one could go to 'Ai and 'Ophrah. A road running west connected Michmash with Beth-ḥoron and the Maritime Plain. And, lastly, there was a fourth road going in a south-eastern direction to the Valley of Ẓeboim, by which we should no doubt understand the great *Wādy el-Ḳelt*, from the northern edge of which an ancient road leads down to Jericho.† It is very probable that it was this route that the Israelites followed when they moved into the country to the west of the Jordan; so that here again we have to do with a road of extreme historical interest.‡ Since there is a direct course from Michmash to 'Ai, everything is in favour of the latter city having been the first to be attacked by the Israelites; and by the same road they could always retire upon their fixed camp in the Jordan Valley (cf. Jos $9^{6}$).

(*b*) The continuation of the road leaving Jerusalem for the north leads to *Samaria*, namely by way of Bethel to Shechem (cf. Jg. $21^{19}$, a passage which shows that the ancient road, like the modern one, ran to the west of Shiloh).§ The scene of Jos $4^{5ff.}$ is the spot where this road bends to the west and leads into the Vale of Shechem. The different roads leading from Shechem are referred to generally in Jg $9^{25}$, and in v.$^{37}$ there is special mention of the way that came from 'the Soothsayers' Oak.' But several of these roads were of special importance, and the scanty allusions to them in the OT must be explained on the ground that detailed narratives are so seldom connected with this district. As the well-watered and fertile *Wādy Sha'îr*, running west from Shechem, opens a connexion with the Maritime Plain, so does the *Wādy el-Fâri'a*, which runs east, provide an approach from the Jordan Valley. Neither of these roads is mentioned in the OT, except in the narrative of Jacob's immigration (Gn $33^{17f.}$); but in later times we read of Vespasian coming from Emmaus and descending by way of Shechem to Koreæ, *i.e.* the beautiful oasis *Ḳurâwa* at the mouth of the *Wādy el-Fâri'a*.‖ The story of Abimelech's march from Shechem to Thebeẓ (Jg $9^{50}$) introduces us to another main road leading out from Shechem, namely that which runs in a north-eastern direction by way of *Tûbâṣ* to Bethshean, and thus connects Shechem with the trans-Jordanic region and Damascus.—Lastly, there is a road to the north, running from Shechem to *Jenîn*, where opens one of the approaches that lead from the Plain of Jezreel into the hills of Samaria. Here we are at the starting-point of the great road which led from the Plain and from Galilee past Shechem to Jerusalem and to the south of the country.* Hence we find king Ahaziah of Judah at this spot when he sought to flee to his home before Jehu — an attempt, however, which failed because his wounds compelled him to hasten to *Megiddo*, westward from Jenîn (2 K $9^{27f.}$). At Jenîn we encounter also those Galilæans who in their pilgrimage to the temple passed through Samaria (cf. the story of the murder of Galilæans perpetrated here by the Samaritans, Jos. *Ant.* XX. vi. 1; *BJ* II. xii. 3). Special importance attached to this Jenîn road for the further reason that it formed the approach from the north to the capital, Samaria, the great *Jenîn-Shechem* road throwing off two side-roads to *Sebastiyeh*. One of these branches off at the beautifully situated village of *Jebna*, the other at the more southerly *Beit Imrîm*.† Here then we have the route followed, for instance, by Jehu when he drove from Jezreel to Samaria (2 K $10^{12ff.}$), and probably also by an enemy advancing from the Jordan against the capital ($7^{14f.}$).

In addition to the two roads already mentioned which gave access from the north to the hill-country of Samaria by way of *Bethshean* and *Jenîn*, there were a number of other passes at the choice of travellers coming from the Plain of Jezreel. The most important of these is the road leading by *Lejjûn* (probably the ancient Megiddo) over the hills in a S.W. direction to the Judæan and Philistine Maritime Plain; for this is the continuation of the above-mentioned great caravan road (the *Via Maris*) connecting Damascus with Egypt. This road was traversed not only by patient caravan camels, but by many great armies —*e.g.* by the Assyrians when marching against Egypt; by Necho's troops on his march to the Euphrates, which king Josiah made a vain attempt to stop at Megiddo (2 K $23^{29}$); by Cambyses in his Egyptian campaign, etc. It was presumably followed also by the Aramæan kings of Damascus, when they extended their military expeditions to the Philistine Maritime Plain (2 K $12^{18}$ $13^{22}$ [LXX]).‡—But besides this main route there was another caravan road to the southern Maritime Plain, which was preferred by those who crossed the Jordan at Bethshean. It is described by Robinson (*BRP* iii. 158 f.) as running west from *Jenîn* into the hill-country and touching the Plain of Dothan between *Kefr Ḳud* and *Ja'bud*. Its great antiquity is shown by Gn $37^{25}$, where a caravan travelling from Gilead to Egypt passes Dothan.—Finally, it was possible for one coming from the northern part of the country to reach the Judæan Maritime Plain by keeping right along the seashore, for an artificially widened passage led by the foot of Carmel; but this route was chosen only by those who from their start in the north had followed the way by the coast.

(*c*) Among the roads in *Galilee* we have first to deal with that part of the *Via Maris* which touched

* Jos. *BJ* v. ii. 1 ff. From Gibeah a road led to Gibeon, if Budde's very attractive emendation in Jg $20^{31}$ is correct. In any case such a road exists, and in all probability it was followed by the legion which came from Emmaus to join Titus at Gibeah.

† The name *Wādy Abu Ḍabá'*, recalling the name *Ẓĕbō'îm*, is still attached to a branch of the *Wādy el-Ḳelt*.

‡ Cf. G. A. Smith, *HGHL* 264.

§ In Dt $11^{30}$ it is usual to discover a reference to the main road which passes to the east of Shechem, but perhaps Steuernagel is right in questioning the correctness of the text in this passage.

‖ Jos. *BJ* IV. viii. 1.

* In Jth $4^{7}$ the high priest writes to the inhabitants of Bethulia, directing them to seize the mountain passes because by them was the way to Judæa, and it was easy to hinder an approach, as the pass was narrow, with space for two men at most. It is plain that the author has in view here the narrow valley of *Jibleam*, behind Jenîn.

† Robinson, *BRP*[2] ii. 311. Samaria is connected with Shechem by a road which turns off to the right from the *Wādy Sha'îr*.

‡ On the ground of these passages, Wellhausen (*Comp. d. Hex.* 254) identifies the Aphek mentioned in 1 K $20^{26.30}$, 2 K $13^{17}$, with the Aphek of the Maritime Plain, on the situation of which cf. especially G. A. Smith, *HGHL*[4] 675.

this district. After passing the Bridge of Jacob's Daughters, the road ascends to *Khan Jubb Yusuf*, from which it runs to the N.W. shore of the Lake of Gennesareth at *Khan Minyeh.** Thence it runs up through the Vale of el-Ḥammâm to *Khan et-Tujjâr*, and reaches the Plain of Jezreel in the neighbourhood of Tabor. At *Ḳarn Ḥaṭṭîn* it throws off a branch in a westerly direction to Acco.—Of the remaining roads in Galilee, which, owing to the dense population of this part of the country, must have been very numerous, we may notice the following. The cities which Tiglath-pileser conquered in succession (2 K $15^{29}$) lay on the road from *Ḳedesh* to the *Merj 'Ayyûn.*† But the main road from the *Merj 'Ayyûn* to the south probably kept closer by the Jordan, till it finally united with the *Via Maris.* From *Âbil* (the ancient Abel beth-Maacah) a road ran westwards to Tyre; it connected the latter city with Damascus. On the western side of the Galilæan hills the protuberance known as the Ladder of Tyre (*Scala Tyriorum*) presented an awkward obstacle to communication. Nevertheless, the Phœnicians succeeded in making this difficult point passable even for chariots, as is proved by the ancient marks of wheels; and so we hear of various armies moving from Syria along the seacoast.‡ What roads are referred to in the narrative of 1 K $17^{9}$ and Mt $15^{21}$ cannot be determined with certainty owing to the brevity of the descriptions.

(*d*) In the *Jordan Valley* an ancient road on the western side of the river supplies the connexion between north and south. On the west shore of the Lake of Gennesareth, where the bordering hills leave only a somewhat narrow strand clear, this road connected the numerous villages that were found here in ancient times. From the crossing-place at Bethshean it was followed by Pompey in his campaign against Aristobulus.§ Along its northern portion, between the Lakes of Gennesareth and Ḥûleh, Jonathan marched (1 Mac $11^{67}$).‖

The Jordan, as already remarked, possesses a considerable number of *fords*. The most southern of these is called *el-Ḥenu*; next comes the ford at the pilgrims' bathing-place; and, further up the river, that at the road from Jericho to *es-Salṭ*, where the crossing is now made by a bridge. At one or other of these points we must seek the ford of *Pěsîlîm* (Jg $3^{26}$ [see art. QUARRY in vol. iv.], cf. 2 S $19^{16}$). At the next principal entrance to the hill-country, namely the *Wâdy el-Fâri'a* coming from Shechem, we encounter the ford *ed-Dâmiye*, likewise with a bridge, which by the way stands at present on dry ground, the river having hollowed a new bed for itself.¶ This much frequented crossing to the central part of the trans-Jordanic district meets us in the OT under the name *Adam* (Jos $3^{16}$, and probably also 1 K $7^{46}$, where Moore happily suggests reading 'the ford (*ma'abhrath*) Adam'). Further north is the most important crossing-place, the ford *'Abâra* at Bethshean, which was that chosen, for example, by Judas on his return march from the east of the Jordan (1 Mac $5^{52}$), and by Pompey in his above-mentioned campaign. The importance of this spot is readily intelligible in view of the fact above noted, that a whole series of great caravan roads from east and west converge upon it.—There are yet other two crossing-places further up the river—one by the bridge *el-Mujâmi*, ½ hour south of the mouth of the Jarmuk; the other immediately south of the exit of the Jordan from the Lake of Gennesareth, a point (*Bâb el-Tumm*) where some traces of an ancient bridge remain. The ford last named had special importance for such of the dwellers on the shore of the Lake as did not avail themselves of boats. Between the Lake of Gennesareth and that of Ḥûleh is the Bridge of Jacob's Daughters, at the spot where the old caravan road, already referred to more than once, crosses the Jordan.*—Lastly, in the northern Jordan Valley there is a road from Galilee to *Dân*, where the different sources of the Jordan have to be crossed, a task now accomplished for the most part by bridges. In the OT this road is alluded to in such passages as Jg $18^{7}$.

(*e*) About the roads on *the east side of the Jordan* the Bible gives us little information. On the other hand, the Roman roads give a good picture of the later routes of communication, and from these we may draw backward inferences as to the earlier roads. The way from *Maḥanaim* to the Jordan Valley (2 S $2^{29}$ $4^{7}$) probably ran through the *Wâdy 'Ajlûn.* Nothing can be said about the road mentioned in 2 K $10^{16}$ until the site of Ramoth-gilead has been determined. Coming down to a later time, the route followed by Judas Maccabæus after his conquests in the districts to the west of the Ḥauran range can be fixed with tolerable certainty. *Ephron* (1 Mac $5^{46}$) is in all probability identical with *Gephrun* (Polyb. V. lxx. 12), a name which is recalled by that of the deep *Wâdy Ghafr*, in which the city will thus have lain which Judas had to pass through.† Josephus speaks incidentally of the roads which led from the city of *Julias* to *Gamala* (the modern *Jamli* (?)) and *Seleucia* (now *Selûḳiye*).‡ We have already spoken of the road from Damascus to the Bridge of Jacob's Daughters.

II. *TRAVEL.*—i. MOTIVES FOR TRAVELLING.—Journeys were undertaken only on a very small scale by the Israelites after they had exchanged the shifting nomadic stage of existence for a settled life; for the inconveniences and dangers attached to travelling were many and the advantages few. Any one who left his home and family gave up, according to the ancient Oriental conception, the best part of his human rights, and became a *gêr* (see art. GER in vol. ii.), whose welfare and whose life were entirely at the mercy of those with whom he sojourned. This was, above all, the case if he lived in a foreign land, where, as David expresses it (1 S $26^{19}$), he had to serve other gods. The traveller was frequently exposed to the risk of being plundered and maltreated on the way.§ In the desert he was threatened with all the perils characteristic of such places (Is $30^{6}$, Jer $2^{6}$ etc.). On the sea his life was in constant danger (Jon $1^{4}$, Ps $107^{23ff.}$, Enoch $101^{4}$).‖ Journeys for pleasure in our sense of the term were thus quite unknown to the Israelites. Nor do we find any who undertook travels for purposes of research, moved by a scientific interest, like Herodotus or Ibn Batûta; although they enjoyed listening to the tales of those who had visited foreign parts (cf. Job $21^{29}$). The Israelite who travelled had a definite and practical aim in view. Such aims might of course be purely accidental and individual, as, for instance, when one did not dare or wish to remain at home, like Jacob, or the Levite

* In this neighbourhood, in the time of Christ, was the customs boundary (Mt $9^{9}$).
† Janôaḥ may be sought most fittingly in *Hunîn*.
‡ Jos. *Ant.* XIV. xv. 11; *BJ* I. xiii. 1, III. ii. 4; *Vita*, 74.
§ Jos. *Ant.* XIV. iii. 4.
‖ It continues its course to the north as the great road leading over the Liṭâny river to Ẓidon.
¶ A photograph of this bridge will be found in the *Mitteilungen und Nachrichten des deutschen Pal. Vereins*, 1899, p. 34.

* Cf. the picture of the bridge in *ZDPV* xiii. 74.
† Cf. Schumacher, *Northern Ajlûn*, 179, 181; Buhl, *Studien zur Topogr. d. nördl. Ostjordanlandes*, 17 f.
‡ Jos. *Vita*, 71.
§ Cf., for different periods, Jg $9^{25}$, Hos $6^{9}$, Jer $3^{2}$, Ezr $8^{22}$, Pr $23^{28}$, Lk $10^{30}$; Jos. *Ant.* XIV. xv. 5, XX. vi. 1.
‖ Cf. the diverting poem in Nöldeke's *Delectus carminum arab.*, Carmen 62, in which a Bedawî describes the terrors that had beset him on his passage by sea.

who was dissatisfied with his abode at Bethlehem-judah (Jg 17[7ff.]); or when one had to go in pursuit of runaway slaves or a fugitive wife (1 K 2[39f.], Jg 19[1ff.]); or when a prophet was commanded to betake himself for concealment to another country (1 K 17), etc. But, in addition to such casual instances, there were regularly recurring occasions which necessitated the facing of the hardships of a journey.

(*a*) In part these occasions were connected with *religious observances*. Even in earlier times the Israelites were accustomed to assemble for the great festivals at certain of the more important sanctuaries (1 S 1[3], Ex 34[23f.]); and when, after the Deuteronomic reformation, the temple at Jerusalem was recognized as the only legitimate sanctuary, these festival pilgrimages received a strong impulse, and became a main element in the life of an Israelite. From all parts of Palestine, and afterwards from all quarters of the then world (see art. DIASPORA in the present volume), Jews poured into Jerusalem, which, on the occasion of these festivals, was a seething mass of humanity. Those who had most acquaintance with the dangers of such a journey were the Galilæan Jews, who had to pass through the hostile territory of the Samaritans (Jos. *Ant.* XX. vi. 1). On this account many of them preferred to take the roundabout way by the east of the Jordan, where they were liable to no such misadventures.*—It must be remembered, moreover, that in early days men often visited a sanctuary for the purpose of obtaining oracles or receiving instruction on a point of ritual (Gn 25[22], 2 K 1[2], 1 S 3[20] 9[6], Zec 7[3]).

(*b*) Further, the increasing Jewish *commerce* supplied many with a motive for travelling. In the earlier period it was mostly foreigners that travelled through the land and carried on trade with its inhabitants (cf. the story of Joseph, Gn 37[28ff.], Ex 21[8], Dt 14[21], and the term *ṣōḥēr* used for the trader by whose standard money was weighed, Gn 23[16], 2 K 1[2. 5]). But as early as the monarchical period and still more in the later post-exilic times the Israelites began to take an active part in both home and international trade, and this involved frequent journeys in their own land as well as to foreign parts. The trade in horses carried on by Solomon led his buyers to the neighbouring States (1 K 10[28f.]), while the shipping trade from 'Ezion-geber inaugurated by him gave the Israelites an acquaintance with travelling by sea. Israelitish merchants established factories in foreign cities, as at Damascus, where Ahab was able to obtain State permission for his subjects to erect dwellings in a certain quarter of the city (1 K 20[34]). In the later post-exilic period Jewish commerce made a great advance, particularly after the Jews came into possession of some seaports on the Mediterranean; and it was all the easier for them to undertake trading journeys, because they could count with certainty on meeting with countrymen of their own in all foreign trading towns. The wife of an Israelite now knew that it meant a distant journey when her husband on setting out took the money-bag with him (Pr 31[14]).

(*c*) A third motive for travelling was supplied by the *political and diplomatic relations* into which the Israelites entered with other peoples. A nation that was in vassalage to another required to send men to hand over the tribute (Jg 3[15ff.]). The later kings of Israel had often to go in person to a foreign court to pay homage to their powerful suzerain (2 K 16[10], Jer 51[59]). But more especially attempts to arrange political alliances led to a constant coming and going of ambassadors (Is 30[2ff.] 31[1]; and on the other side 14[32] 18. 39, Jer 27[3]).—Journeys of an involuntary character are seen in the deportation of conquered peoples, a fate which befell the Israelites more than once. But there were also occasions when one voluntarily left his home to find safety in a foreign land (Jer 43). A happier condition was that of the travelling companies which by the grace of their sovereign were permitted to return to their homes (Ezr 1. 8). Moreover, the sojourn of a portion of the people of Israel in the Diaspora gave occasion for frequent journeys between the foreign land and the home country, as we see from Jer 29[3], Zec 6[10], Neh 2[5ff.] 13[6ff.].

(*d*) A special motive for undertaking a journey was *ill-health*, which led to the visiting of foreign places in the hope of a cure (cf. 2 K 5). This habit finds illustration particularly in later times, when the various hot springs in the Jordan Valley were much frequented.*

(*e*) Lastly, *wars* of conquest and plunder may in a certain sense be reckoned among the motives to travel, which brought great multitudes of men to foreign lands.

Travelling on the part of Jews was beset by a peculiar difficulty in the shape of the Sabbath law, after so strict an observance of it had been introduced that on the Sabbath day and on those festival days on which sabbatical rest was enjoined it was unlawful to walk more than a fixed number of paces. Thus Josephus (*Ant.* XIII. viii. 4) mentions incidentally that the Syrian king, Antiochus Sidetes, out of consideration for Hyrcanus who accompanied him, remained for two days by the river Lycus, on account of a Jewish festival being then in progress. On the other hand, the Law accommodated itself to the needs of travellers in so far as it permitted those who were on a journey in the month of Nisan to celebrate the Passover in the following month (Nu 9[10f.]).

ii. MODES OF TRAVEL.—Those who were not particularly well-to-do, especially if they were young, strong men, went for the most part *on foot* (Gn 28, Jos 9[13], 1 K 19[4ff.], Is 52[7], and the Gospel narratives). Hence the first attention shown to an arriving guest was to wash his feet (Gn 18[4], Jg 19[21]). Women and elderly well-to-do men *rode upon asses*, which also carried the baggage (Jg 19[3], 1 S 25[20], 2 S 17[23], 1 K 2[40], 2 K 4[24], Lk 10[34]); people of high rank also used *mules* (2 S 13[29], 1 K 1[38]). *Camels* were less frequently employed, and only when the journey led through the desert (Gn 24). *Horses*, on the other hand, were used only in war, being either ridden or harnessed to the chariots. The *chariots* mentioned in the OT are, as a rule, chariots of war, but they were used by kings also in journeying from one part of the country to another (1 K 12[18], 2 K 10[16]; and the story of Naaman in 2 K 5, where, however, we have to do with a foreigner). In 1 S 6[7] we meet with an *ox-waggon* as a vehicle of transport; and in the case of the waggons sent from Egypt to convey the old men, the women, and the children, we should probably think also of similarly simple vehicles (Gn 45[19]). From a later period we have the story of the Ethiopian chamberlain (here again a foreigner) driving in a chariot (Ac 8[27ff.]). Josephus (*Ant.* XIX. viii. 1) speaks of a larger kind of chariot (ἀπήνη), in which Agrippa, accompanied by other kings, drove out to meet the Roman prætor.† In Ca 3[9] we read of a sedan chair

* Special risks naturally attended those travelling companies that carried with them large sums of money, as, for instance, in connexion with the transmission of the poll-tax of the Babylonian Jews. Hence these companies included many thousand persons (Jos. *Ant.* XVIII. ix. 1).

* Cf. Dechent, 'Heilbäder u. Badeleben in Palästina' in *ZDPV* vii. 173 ff.

† When Josephus (*Ant.* VIII. vii. 3 4) relates how Solomon often drove out to his gardens at Etham, he is simply adding a picturesque touch of his own.

or palanquin (אַפִּרְיוֹן, φορεῖον) being used by people of high rank.

On account of the attendant risks, one did not care to go on a long journey alone,* but had at least one companion, who received a daily wage and, if the journey terminated happily, a present besides (To $5^{15f.}$). When Nehemiah travelled from the Persian court to Jerusalem, he carried with him letters from the king to the governors of the various provinces commanding them to grant him free passage and an armed escort (Neh $2^{7ff.}$). The favourite method was to combine into large companies (*caravans*, originally a Persian word), which were accompanied by armed men (cf. Ezr $8^{22}$). Such caravans, travelling under military protection, are referred to in the Tel el-Amarna letters (see above, p. 368b). In the wilderness they were conducted by the Bedawin tribes, *e.g.* the Dedanites (Is $21^{13}$). When unknown regions had to be traversed, a guide acquainted with the roads had to be procured (Nu $10^{31}$), or parties were sent in advance to make inquiry about the way and about the cities that had to be passed (Dt $1^{22}$). The deadly danger of a caravan when the water of which it has come in search is found dried up, is portrayed with poetic beauty in Job $6^{18}$.

iii. PROVISION FOR THE WANTS OF TRAVELLERS.—For the *comfort* and the *refreshment* of travellers very little provision was made. In the wilderness the inhabitants of the oases might, as described in Is $21^{14}$, meet the exhausted caravans with water and bread; but, in the main and as a matter of course, a traveller through the desert had to provide for himself by bringing the necessaries of life with him (Gn $21^{14}$). But the same was the case even in travelling through inhabited regions. The Levite of Jg 19 takes with him fodder and straw for the asses as well as bread and wine (v.[19]); and a similar course is followed by the Gibeonites when they seek to give themselves the appearance of having come from far (Jos 9). In Nu $20^{17ff.}$ we read of a great company binding itself, as it passed through a country, to keep to the highway, to touch nothing in the vineyards or the fields, and to pay for the water drunk by man and beast.

Of *inns* in the proper sense of the term we do not hear till NT times (Lk $10^{34f.}$); and the very circumstance that the Greek word πανδοχεῖον there employed was adopted by the Jews as פּנדוק, proves that the whole institution was a new and foreign appearance.† In earlier times there may have been establishments at least somewhat akin to the modern *khans*—large empty buildings surrounding a courtyard, in which travellers can pass the night, but where the necessaries of life are not sold.‡ Some have thought to find the corresponding word in Hebrew in the גֵּרוּת (*gērûth*) of Jer $41^{17}$; but the real meaning of this word is very uncertain, and even the text is doubtful, for Josephus (*Ant.* X. ix. 5) read the word גדרות ('hurdles,' 'sheep-pens'). Likewise the word מָלוֹן (*mālôn*) has to be considered; for, even if in some passages it appears to mean simply the place where one takes up his quarters at night, the sense of *khan* fits very well passages like Gn $42^{27}$ $43^{21}$, Jer $9^2$. The king was attended on his journeys by a שַׂר מְנוּחָה (*sar mĕnûhah*, lit. 'captain of the resting-place,' RV 'chief chamberlain,' RVm 'quarter-master'), whose duty was to look after night quarters for the royal party (Jer $51^{59}$).

* R. Meir, in an epigram, called the solitary traveller a 'son of death' (W. Bacher, *Die Agada der Tannaiten*, ii. 17).

† Cf., on the further travels of this word, S. Krauss, *Griech. u. Latein. Lehnwörter im Talmud, Midrasch, u. Targum*, ii. 428. In the form *Funduḳ* it still occurs as the name of a village in southern Samaria, the *Fondeḳa* of the Talmud (Neubauer, *Géog. du Talmud*, 172).

‡ According to Herodotus (v. 52), there were such caravanserais (καταλύσεις) on the roads in the Persian empire.

In general, then, in early times the traveller, unless he carried his victuals with him and preferred, like Jacob, to sleep in the open air, had to fall back on the hospitality of the inhabitants of the place; but this he could do with confidence, for in all ages *hospitality* has been one of the most beautiful virtues of the Oriental. Although it is not expressly enjoined in the Law,* narratives like Gn $18^{1ff.}$ $24^{31}$, Ex $2^{20}$ show how highly it was esteemed; and Job, in the passage where he casts a backward glance on his former life in order to prove his integrity, says, amongst other things, 'The stranger did not lodge in the street, but I opened my doors to the traveller' ($31^{32}$). Passages like Jg $19^{15}$ indicate how severe was the judgment passed on those who suffered the traveller to pass the night outside; while the story related in Gn 19 and that in Jg 19 are meant to show the enormity of the offence of offering violence to the defenceless guest. The deed of Jael alone is praised (Jg $5^{25ff.}$), although, according to ancient Semitic notions, her guest ought to have been specially sacred to her, because he had drunk from her milk-bowl. But in this instance duty to a guest is regarded as overshadowed by duty to one's country.

When one reached a city at nightfall he took up his position on the open space before the gate, and waited to see if any one would invite him in (Jg $19^{15ff.}$). In like manner a traveller in the country took his stand before the tent or the house into which he desired to be invited (Gn $18^2$). When the guest entered, his feet were washed, and a meal was prepared for him. In the latter instance, a wish to honour him was marked, as still happens regularly in the East at the present day, by the killing of an animal from the herd (Gn $18^7$, 2 S $12^4$). At his departure he was expected to eat heartily to strengthen him for his further journey (Jg $19^5$, cf. 1 S $28^{22}$). To take payment from a guest was contrary to good manners, and hence it is a perfectly genuine touch that Josephus adds to the narrative of Gn 24, when he makes Rebekah decline Eliezer's offer to pay for his entertainment by telling him not to think they were parsimonious people (*Ant.* I. xvi. 2). In later times hospitality specially flourished among the Essenes, who, according to Josephus (*BJ* II. viii. 4), took nothing with them on a journey, as everything belonging to their co-religionists was at their command. There was even an official appointed in every city, whose duty it was to provide travelling Essenes with clothing and all other necessaries. An instance of a permanent guest-friendship is supplied by the story of Elisha and the wealthy lady of Shunem (2 K $4^{8ff.}$). In later times, under Roman and Greek influence, this practice was greatly extended. Thus we hear for instance of guest-friends in Jotapata, whose death was bewailed at Jerusalem, after the little fortress was taken by the Romans; † cf. also Ac $10^6$ $21^{16}$. That a guest's lot, however, was not always a happy one, and that he was exposed to many disagreeable experiences, is noted by that always acute and dispassionate observer, Ben Sira (Sir $29^{21ff.}$).

LITERATURE.—Riehm, *HWB*[2], artt. 'Reisen' and 'Wege'; G. A. Smith, *Historical Geography of the Holy Land*, *passim*; F. Buhl, *Geographie des alten Palästina*, 125–131; H. Guthe, *Kurzes Bibelwörterbuch*, art. 'Wege.'

FRANTS BUHL.

****ROADS AND TRAVEL** (IN NT).‡—I. *ROUTES BY LAND AND BY SEA.*—i. ROME THE CENTRE OF THE EMPIRE.—The system of communication

* The Deuteronomic law regarding duties to the *gêr* (Dt $11^6$ $24^{14.\,17}$ etc.) belongs to a different category.

† Jos. *BJ* III. ix. 5. Several of the stories in the *midrāshim* have to do with Jewish guest-friends in different lands.

‡ See Table of Contents, p. 402.

in the world of the first century after Christ was dominated and determined by one single motive, viz. to seek direct connexion with Rome, the capital and centre of the Empire and of the world. Within the bounds of the Empire, the principle of Roman Republican government had originally been to connect every subject, country, and district as closely as possible with Rome, and to keep them as much as possible disconnected from one another, so that each should look to Rome as the centre of all its interests, its trade, its finance, and its aspirations, and regard all other subjects as rivals and competitors for the favour of the governing city. Though the ideal and the ultimate aim of the Imperial government was different, and did not tend to make Rome the governor of subjects, but rather to educate and elevate the subjects to equality with Rome by a slow but steady process, yet in the first century the older idea still was practically effective to a large extent, and governed the system of communication. Hence the first point is to examine how each province of the Empire communicated with Rome.

Along the great arteries that led to Rome all new ideas and movements of thought and religious impulses naturally moved, without any definite purpose on the part of the originators, even perhaps in spite of their intentions in some cases. It was, as a rule, an easier and more rapid process for a new idea to spread from a distant province to Rome than to spread from that province to its neighbour, if the neighbour did not lie on the road to Rome, or was not connected with the first province by some old bond of intimacy. Hence the fact, for example, that Christianity spread very early to Rome constitutes no proof, and does not even afford a presumption, that there was any purpose or intention of carrying it thither. Such conscious, deliberate purpose can be proved only by some clear evidence of its existence, and especially by deliberate statement on the part of those who entertained the purpose.

For example, we know that the purpose of visiting Rome was distinctly expressed by St. Paul (Ac 19[21]) several years before he was able to carry it into effect; and we can infer from the general character of his action that the purpose was in his mind, latent or perhaps expressed orally, long before the date at which he first mentions it in his extant letters. But even at that time Rome contained already a body of Christians, and St. Paul's aim was twofold—partly to extend the limits and affect the character of the Church in Rome, 'to impart unto you some spiritual gift,' and 'that I might have some fruit in you also, even as in the rest of the Gentiles' (Ro 1[11. 13]); but still more to use Rome as a basis from which to affect the West, especially Spain, 'to be brought on my way thitherward by you' (Ro 15[24]). Just because Rome was the centre and meeting-place of all roads, it lay on the way for any traveller or missionary going from Syria to the West: he could not go direct, but must tranship in Rome.

When one keeps this principle clearly in mind, the interpretation of Clem. Rom. i. 5 becomes evident and certain. Clement says of St. Paul that 'after he had preached in the East and in the West, he won the noble renown which was the reward of his faith, having taught righteousness unto the whole world, and having reached the furthest bounds of the West.' If Clement had caught the least spark of the Pauline and the Roman spirit and thought, he could not have called Rome (as some modern scholars maintain that he did) * 'the goal of the West' or 'his limit towards the West,' τὸ τέρμα τῆς δύσεως; and Lightfoot has rightly expressed the general Roman point of view in that age, which looked on Rome as the centre of empire, not as its limit, nor as belonging to the Western part of the Empire.

ii. Seasons and Routes open for Travelling.—The route of communication was not always the same throughout the whole year. When the crossing of any considerable stretch of sea formed an essential part of a line of communication, the route in question was closed almost completely during a considerable part of the year. The times were stated by the ancients themselves as follows:—The sea was closed from 10 November to 10 March; but perfectly safe navigation was only between 26 May and 14 September,* while there were two doubtful periods 11 Mar.–26 May, and 15 Sept.–10 Nov., when merchants might risk sailing, but fleets of war vessels were loath to do so.

It is not the case that the closure was absolute. In case of necessity or urgency a voyage was at times attempted in the season when navigation was closed. Julius Cæsar's army crossed from Brundisium to Epirus during Nov. 49,† and Pompey's army had crossed similarly in Jan. 49.‡

Again, Claudius proposed great inducements to traders who carried corn to Italy during the winter, guaranteeing a certain rate of profit, and insuring them against loss of their vessels by storm. His proposal probably applied chiefly to the short voyages from Sardinia and Africa, in which it was possible to watch an opportunity for a less dangerous voyage even in the stormy season; but, in the long voyage from Alexandria, such waiting upon opportunities would be a much more serious matter. See Suet. *Claud.* 18.

When Flaccus was recalled from the government of Egypt, early in October A.D. 38, he sailed immediately, and had much stormy weather at sea; but Philo (*in Flac.* 13–15) gives no information as to the route. Shortly afterwards Philo and four other envoys sailed from Alexandria, in urgent need, to present a petition to Caligula: their route also is not recorded, and the length of their voyage is uncertain; but they were in Rome in the spring of A.D. 39, and had an audience there of the Emperor; and Philo refers in feeling terms to their troubles on the sea.§ In both cases we need not doubt that the ships sailed along the coast, according to the opportunities of getting on from point to point.

But only the exigencies of government service, or of urgent religious and national duty (and to the ancients national duty was necessarily a matter of religion, for patriotism was a religious idea), would cause such winter voyages. Doubtless, Philo and the other four envoys had to pay largely to induce any ship to sail after 11 November. In ordinary circumstances the regular course was to lay up at the beginning of winter and wait for

* It is, of course, necessary for those who believe that St. Paul was put to death at the conclusion of the two years' imprisonment in which he wrote Colossians and Philemon, to force this unnatural meaning on the plain words of Clement—words which no person at that time could have misunderstood. Only aloofness from the spirit of the first century makes it possible to doubt as to the meaning.

* *Secura navigatio*, Vegetius, iv. 39, v. 9; *statos æstivis flatibus dies et certa maris*, Tacitus, *Hist.* iv. 81.

† Nominally, Jan. 48 in the unreformed old calendar (which was 67 days wrong in B.C. 47).

‡ Nominally, March A.D. 49. When the old calendar differed by two months from the true calendar, obviously the rules could not be calculated by the days of the existing calendar, but by the stars.

§ They sailed μέσου χειμῶνος; but this phrase cannot be pressed to mean about the winter solstice: it might mean only 'in full winter,' as distinguished from Flaccus' departure ἀρχομένου χειμῶνος in October. The Jewish envoys had every reason to hurry after him in order to present their case to Caligula. Moreover, they sailed at no great interval after Agrippa had visited Alexandria in July or early August 38 (Philo, *in Flac.* 16, *de Leg.* 28). Their voyage probably began not later than November, perhaps already in October.

spring. Thus Horace speaks (*Od.* iii. 7. 5) of Gyges as returning from Bithynia, but detained at Oricum in Epirus until spring returned and the Adriatic was open; and of another Roman sailor waiting (probably in Syria, *Od.* iv. 5. 9)* till spring returned and he could cross the Carpathian Sea (the sea near Rhodes).

This dread of storms and dislike to travel in winter was not confined to voyages by sea. Even on land there are many proofs that, where mountain ranges or high plateaus had to be crossed, as in going across Asia Minor, ordinary persons avoided winter travelling and waited till spring. Basil of Cæsarea, who speaks in *Epist.* 20 of a 'continuous stream of travellers' on a great route, such as that which led from Cæsarea to Athens, says that in a severe winter 'all the roads were blocked till Easter' (*Epist.* 198), and that 'the road to Rome is wholly impracticable in winter' (*Epist.* 215). His meeting with the Bishop of Iconium must be fixed 'at a season suitable for travelling' (*Epist.* 191); yet the road between Cæsarea and Iconium is wholly on the level, and crosses no pass or elevated ground. Even a mild winter 'was quite sufficient to keep him from travelling while it lasted' (*Epist.* 27). A modern traveller or missionary would traverse the roads of the plateau at any time;† but for ancient travellers there was a close time, during which travelling was almost entirely suspended, and no journeys were planned or thought of, except by professional travellers (Basil, *Ep.* 198). Vegetius (iv. 39) mentions that land travel was stopped as completely as sea travel between 10 Nov. and 10 March.

The reason lay, not simply in the snow,—although Basil speaks in *Epist.* 48 of 'such a heavy fall of snow that we have been buried, houses and all, beneath it,'—but quite as much in the spring rains and the extremely cold winds of early winter, which are very trying, though not likely to keep an active traveller indoors. The Taurus is in some places, however, impassable in winter except with considerable personal danger: see, *e.g.*, the account given by Prof. Sterrett in the *Wolfe Expedition to Asia Minor*, p. 80. In time of heavy rain the surface of the plateau becomes, in most places, a sea of mud, though perhaps the principal Roman roads may have been well enough built in the time of St. Paul to rise above that sea.

This is a factor of considerable importance in determining the chronology of St. Paul's journeys. The broad and lofty ridge of Mount Taurus is for the most part really dangerous to cross in winter, owing to the deep snow obliterating the roads. The roads leading from Perga direct towards Ephesus, and from Tarsus through the Cilician Gates towards Lycaonia and the north and west generally, cross a lower summit height, and are actually traversable by well equipped or determined travellers through most part of the winter, except during any temporary block caused by snowstorms. But we must estimate the time of year when St. Paul would be likely to cross Taurus (Ac 13[14] 14[24] 16[1] 18[23]) according to the customs of the period.

To estimate this factor rightly, we should know the precise limits of the close season in popular usage. This is difficult. For example, towards the end of May 1882 snow was lying in all these uplands. In the crossing of the Cilician Gates during the early part of June 1902 there was a thunderstorm, accompanied by severe cold and heavy rain, almost every day. During the season when such weather was fairly probable, we can hardly believe that it was customary or usual for

* Lycia or Cilicia are also possible.

† Ramsay, *Impressions of Turkey*, p. 222, and *Quarterly Review*, vol. clxxxvi. No. 372, p. 430 f.

ordinary persons among the ancients to arrange their journeys. Basil, as quoted above, may be taken as a fair specimen of ancient views.

It is true that even in ancient times Cicero crossed Taurus by the Cilician Gates in November 51 and April 50 B.C.* Antigonus vainly tried to cross Taurus from Cilicia in B.C. 314, but lost many soldiers owing to the snow. His second attempt at a more favourable opportunity succeeded (Diodor. xix. 69. 2).

To take another example from later history, in the autumn of A.D. 803 the Emperor Nicephorus broke the peace, thinking that he could do so safely at that late season with the winter at hand. Nicephorus relied on the customary closed time, when the march of an army was impossible. But he was taken unawares† by the Caliph Harun er-Rashid, who crossed Taurus in the winter season before the end of the year (the Mohammedan year ended about 20 December in A.D. 803). Harun did not consider himself bound by the ordinary custom, and he must have passed the Cilician Gates about November or early December.‡

The question, however, in such a matter is not what is possible, but what is customary. Just as it was possible to cross the sea during the closed season, so it was possible to traverse the Cilician Gates in the winter by taking a favourable opportunity, and yet the winter was a closed season, when ordinary people would not attempt to cross. The ordinary traveller had not the equipment of a Roman governor, like Cicero, nor was he like such a general as Antigonus, anxious to surprise an enemy, and willing to risk the lives of his soldiers in the attempt. Yet even Antigonus must wait a favourable opportunity.

Although the exact limits of the travelling season must remain uncertain, yet probably the ordinary custom of the sea ruled also on land. If there was any difference, it would naturally be that on land the closed season began and ended a little later than on sea. All travel across the mountains was avoided between the latter part of November and the latter part of March; and ordinary travellers, not forced by official duties, but free to choose their own time, would avoid the crossing between October (an extremely wet month on the plateau) and May.

iii. Variations in the Routes at different Seasons.—Where a long sea passage was involved, it does not follow that the route from the province to Rome was the same as the return from Rome to the province. The winds which favoured the voyage from Rome might prohibit the return voyage, or *vice versâ*. We shall see one such case below: in summer the winds favoured a quick voyage from Italy to Alexandria, but seriously hindered the return voyage. In general, the path from Rome to the East followed a different line from the path which led from the East to Rome; and an envoy from the East would go to Rome by one path and return by another.

Both these causes contributed to complicate the communications between the province of Syria (including Palestine) and Rome. There were four lines of communication: (1) by sea to or from Puteoli on the Gulf of Naples, and by land between Puteoli and Rome; (2) by sea to Corinth, and thence to Brundisium, and by land between Brundisium and Rome; (3) by land to Ephesus, thence

* In the incorrect calendar current at that time (which varied sixty-seven days from the true calendar in B.C. 47) he started north from Tarsus on 5 January, and reached Tarsus on his return journey on 5 June. But, according to the true calendar, he evidently avoided the most snowy season in Taurus.

† Weil, *Gesch. der Khalifen*, ii. p. 159.

‡ The other road, by Germanicia, which the Arabs often employed, seems never to have been used by Harun, and would be more unsuitable for a winter expedition.

by sea to Corinth, etc., as in the preceding route; (4) the land route across Asia Minor, and, after crossing to Europe, along the Egnatian Way to Dyrrachium, and thence across the Adriatic Sea to Brundisium.

The first-named was the great route, preferred by trade and by travellers who desired to make a rapid journey eastward from Italy. It was closely connected with the Egyptian communication with Rome; and in fact it was the splendid and regular service of ships between Alexandria and Puteoli that made this route so important and so rapid. We shall therefore describe the Alexandrian service at this point. The Syrian service connected itself with the Alexandrian as it best could, and used the latter as much as possible. The excellence of the Alexandrian service was due to the fact that Egypt was the mainstay of the Imperial corn supply for feeding the gigantic city of Rome. When one considers the vast population of Rome (probably not very much under a million), the smallness of the Italian harvest (for Italy was naturally far more productive of wine, oil, and fruits than of grain; and Italian wheat could no longer be grown at a profit in competition with sea-borne grain), and the fact that scarcity in Rome meant discontent, mutiny, and probably revolution after the murder of the Emperor who had let the corn supply fail, it becomes obvious that the maintenance of a steady and trustworthy service between Rome and the principal corn-producing countries was an Imperial concern of the very first importance. With the defective means of commerce and transport then available, private enterprise was quite incapable of feeding the great population of Rome; the corn supply was a most important department of the Imperial administration; and, in particular, the long transport from Egypt was mainly performed by a fleet in the Imperial service. Transport from the other chief producing countries—Sicily, Sardinia, and Africa—was easier, and private enterprise had probably greater scope there; but the Egyptian corn was the greatest source of supply for Rome.

Of course it is not to be supposed that there was no private trade between Puteoli and Egypt; on the contrary, there was doubtless a good deal. But the corn trade seems to have been an Imperial business, carried in Imperial ships (III. § ix.). Egypt was kept far more closely under the immediate Imperial administration than any other part of the Empire, and practically the whole supply available for exportation was marked for the Roman service and managed by the Emperor's own private representatives. No great Roman nobles were allowed even to set foot in Egypt, except on rare occasions by special permission. The land of Egypt was managed as a sort of great private appanage of the reigning Emperor. In a few cases we read of corn from Alexandria being brought to other cities of the Empire; but this was in case of famine, and must have required the special grace of the Emperor, to relieve the distressed population of one of his towns.

iv. VOYAGE FROM ROME TO EGYPT DIRECT AND THENCE TO PALESTINE.—Communication from Puteoli to Alexandria was maintained direct across sea. The prevalent summer wind in the east Mediterranean waters was westerly; and the ships ran in a direct course from the south of Italy to the Egyptian coast, keeping at the outset well out south from the Italian coast, in order to avoid the land winds and to get into the steady Mediterranean currents of air.

The pilots or sailing-masters had acquired great skill in these long voyages, and could make their harbour with almost unerring accuracy: they are compared by Philo to skilful charioteers driving their teams of horses. Such a service required also careful study of the seasons and the winds. Experience showed that there were seasons when the winds could be reckoned upon with confidence, and others when the long voyage was unsafe or impossible. The important period to notice is that of the Etesian winds; and it is doubtful whether the direct voyage was hazarded (as a rule) except when they were blowing. In the year A.D. 38, when Agrippa was eager to go quickly from Rome to occupy his kingdom in northern Palestine, he was advised to wait for the Etesian winds, and then sail direct to Alexandria and thence cross to Palestine. He reached Alexandria in a few days,* arriving apparently early in August. This passage of Philo (*in Flac.* 5) is extremely important for the system of communication with Syria and Egypt.

In the open Mediterranean Sea and the Levant the Etesian winds are said to have blown from the north-west steadily for forty days after 20 July (or thirty days from 1 August); and at this season it was difficult for news from the East to reach Rome (Tac. *Hist.* ii. 98); and the Etesian winds prevented a voyage from Alexandria to Italy (Cæsar, *de Bell. Civ.* iii. 107),† or from Rhodes to Athens (Cicero, *ad Att.* vi. 7). They began to blow each day towards noon, but never earlier in the morning. There is much difference among the ancients as to the direction and duration of the Etesian winds; but the diversity is due doubtless to the facts that (1) they vary in different seas, (2) any regularly recurring time of fairly steady wind was Etesian (*i.e.* annual).

The statements as to the Etesian winds drawn from the ancient writers (see the quotations in Facciolati and Forcellini's *Lexicon*) are entirely confirmed by modern meteorological experience, except that 'the north-west winds prevail in the summer months' generally, and not exclusively during the forty days from July 20. These winds prevail in that season 'throughout the whole of the Mediterranean, but mostly in the eastern half.' In fact it is probable that, to the sailors of the Alexandrian Roman fleets, the Etesian winds meant simply the summer winds, and roughly corresponded to the period of open sea from the end of May to the middle of September. The statements restricting the number of days during which the winds blow are probably taken from Greek writers who were speaking more of the Ægean Sea.‡

But Agrippa had to wait some little time for a ship. The delay is explained by Philo as due to waiting on the winds; but in all probability this is not quite a complete account. It was necessary also to wait until a fleet of ships was ready. Single vessels did not venture on the long sea course.

The reason why the long voyage was made by a whole fleet in company was, doubtless, safety. One ship could aid another. There is, of course, a good deal of exaggeration in Philo's account of the certainty with which the ships reached their goal. A single ship could not be certain of making directly the harbour of Alexandria after being six or eight days out of sight of land; and might easily miss Egypt altogether and sight Cyrene on the one hand or Syria on the other. But with a large fleet sailing with a widely extended front, the ships keeping within signalling distance of one

* The expression ὀλίγαις ἡμέραις must not be pressed too closely; it is opposed to the long coasting passage (see p. 379b), and probably indicates a period of 15 to 20 days: see below.

† Here the Etesian winds are spoken of as blowing in early October; but this is due to the disorder of the Roman calendar. Cæsar reached Alexandria on 3 Oct.; but this date was really equivalent to late July or early August.

‡ See the excellent discussion, with quotations from modern experience at sea, in James Smith, *Voyage and Shipwreck of St. Paul*, pp. 64, 76 ff.

another, the experience of one would guide the others; when the ship on the extreme right came in sight of the Cyrenaic or Egyptian coast, it would signal accordingly, and the news would spread to the extreme left immediately; or if, on the other hand, after having run far enough, the ship on the right had not sighted any land, or that on the left of the fleet had sighted Crete,* this would show that all had taken too northerly a course; and sailing directions would be signalled over the whole fleet.

Similarly, the westward-going vessels tried to sail in a body, as we see from Seneca, *Epist. Mor.* 77, 1. But exceptions occurred on this route, if vessels were belated and obliged to make the voyage alone (as in Ac 27[6] 28[11]).

It is not to be supposed that all the corn vessels sailed in one single fleet at the same time. There could not possibly be facilities for loading nearly all the vessels simultaneously; and it would have been an absurdly wasteful method for the first to wait until the last were loaded. Beyond a doubt, there must have been several successive companies, which sailed together: when a certain number were ready they would start. Moreover, it is known that even single corn ships were occasionally engaged on a voyage, as we have seen in the preceding paragraph. A dedicatory inscription, erected by the master of a corn ship which was evidently wintering in the harbour of Phœnix, is quoted by James Smith (*Voyage and Shipwreck of St. Paul*, p. 261; also in *CIL* iii. 3).

It cannot be supposed that a passage on government vessels was allowed to every one, any more than that the Imperial postal service by land was open to every one. In the latter case it is known that no one could use the Imperial service without a *diploma* signed by the Emperor (who made a rule of entrusting a certain number of *diplomata* to governors of provinces, which the governors gave to persons travelling on public service, and to some others in exceptional circumstances).† But, naturally, officers on government service, like the centurion in Ac 27[9-11], took advantage of an Imperial corn ship with full authority; and it is evident from the language of Ac 27[11] that in such a case the centurion was in supreme command of the vessel as the highest officer of the Imperial service on board, and, after consulting with the sailing-master and the captain and with any other persons whom he chose, settled how far the ship was to go and when it was to be laid up for the winter (*St. Paul the Traveller*, p. 324).

As regards the time which news from Rome took to reach Egypt, a much exaggerated idea of the speed of communication has been propagated by Friedländer (*Sittengeschichte Roms*, ii. p. 31), and has been incautiously quoted from him as the foundation of their argument by many modern scholars.‡ This distinguished scholar infers from Pliny and Diodorus that ships frequently sailed from the Sea of Azoff to Alexandria in fourteen days, and from Rhodes to Alexandria in four; and that on a fortunate voyage a ship could reach Marseilles in twenty days from Alexandria, and Alexandria in seven days from Utica or in nine days from Puteoli (Pliny, *Nat. Hist.* xix. 1; Diodor. iii. 34: see also below, § vi.).

These, if correctly recorded, must have been quite exceptional voyages, and cannot be used as examples of ordinary life.

But when Agrippa sailed from Puteoli, as above described, in A.D. 38 (probably in July, possibly as early as June),* he reached Alexandria in a few days (ὀλίγαις ὕστερον ἡμέραις, Philo, *in Flac.* 5), before any news of his elevation had reached the East. This seems to imply a very short voyage; but Philo is of course speaking comparatively, and we need not suppose that he means less than ten days, but rather even a little more than ten. Still this seems to be a case in which the time from Rome to Alexandria can hardly have exceeded twenty days. With this as a standard, it must be inferred that in the open season it would be a tedious and unfortunate voyage which failed to bring passengers and news from Rome to Alexandria under twenty-five days.

The speed with which the news of a grave Imperial event like the death or accession of an Emperor reached the provinces would be the test of extremest ordinary speed. There can be no doubt both that such news would be carried by quick special messengers faster than ordinary travellers would go, and that the State messengers would travel at a fairly uniform speed (except so far as winds or storms favoured or prevented them). Yet the statistics collected by Wilcken (*Griech. Ostraka*, i. p. 799 ff.) vary in a very perplexing way. But this variation is more in appearance than in reality. Setting aside mere examples of the ignorance in small villages or remote towns of events at Rome,† we find that probably sixty to sixty-five days was an ordinary period for news of such great events to penetrate from Rome to Egypt. A good example is afforded at the accession of Pertinax (1 Jan. A.D. 193): the prefect of Egypt issued at Alexandria instructions with regard to the celebration of that important event (ἐπὶ τῇ εὐτυχεστάτῃ βασιλ(ε)ίᾳ).‡ It cannot be supposed that any time was lost in such a case. The instructions are dated 6 March, and the news is not likely to have been then more than a day old. At that season, therefore, in the slowest and most difficult time for travelling, the news travelled from Rome to Alexandria in sixty-four days. The route by which messages of this kind were transmitted will be considered hereafter: see below, §§ ix. xii.

But, on the other hand, there are cases of much more rapid transmission; as, for example, the accession of Galba was known officially in Alexandria within twenty-seven days.§ This speed, however, was due to the fact that Galba was proclaimed on 9 June, and at that season news would come by the direct sea route from Puteoli to Egypt, whereas the clearest examples of news of such events taking about sixty days to arrive in Egypt belong to the winter or spring. We have seen that the direct sea route to Alexandria was hardly ventured upon except between 27 May and 15 September.

v. Voyage from Alexandria to Rome.—The voyage from Alexandria to Rome was a much more difficult and tedious matter than the voyage from Rome to Alexandria, owing to the prevalence during summer of westerly winds in the

* This must have been common, for the lofty Cretan mountains are visible far out at sea; probably it may have been the usual intention to get bearings by sighting Crete.

† Pliny apologized to Trajan for permitting his own wife to use the public service with a *diploma* in a case of pressing haste.

‡ So, for example, von Rohden in Pauly-Wissowa (*Realencycl.* i. 2, p. 2621), and against him Wilcken (*Griech. Ostraka*, i. p. 799).

* Ships ready to sail from Puteoli in June must doubtless have started from Alexandria in the previous year (like St. Paul's ships); those which started from Alexandria at the very beginning of the open season would not be able to sail from Puteoli till the end of July. See below, § vi.

† Mere carelessness must also be allowed for in remote places: thus Nero's death was matter of current knowledge in Elephantine within fifty-seven days; and yet on the fifty-eighth day a document was dated in Thebes by his reign (though Thebes must have received the news before Elephantine). Again, in (villages of the city) Arsinoë the accession of Pertinax (1 January) was currently known on 19 May, but ignored on 2 June: it was known in the Fayum before 1 April. Wilcken (*loc. cit.*) also gives examples of an Emperor ignored in common documents five or even eight months after his accession.

‡ *Berl. Gr. Urkunden*, No. 646, Wilcken, *l.c.* p. 802.

§ There is no evidence as to the exact time occupied in transmission, except that it was less than twenty-seven days (Wilcken, *loc. cit.*; *CIG* 4957).

Mediterranean. The ships had to help themselves by the uncertain and fitful breezes on the coasts. Now it was unsafe to keep too southerly a course owing to the great quicksands, Syrtes, on the African coast: even if the winds permitted, ships could not venture from Alexandria on a course which would keep them near the Cyrenaic shore lest the wind might shift round towards the north and drive them too far south (Ac 27[17]). They were compelled to take a northerly course, keeping as much to the west of north as the wind would allow. Thus they might fetch the Lycian coast, or, in very favourable circumstances, possibly ships might even make the Rhodian or Cretan coast; but it may be regarded as absolutely certain that they could never attempt a course across sea from the Egyptian coast direct to Italy or Sicily. Rather they would make for the south-east end of Crete—at the best—though with the prevailing west or north-west winds such a course could rarely have been sailed. In ordinary circumstances, the usual aim of ships from Alexandria undoubtedly was to reach the Lycian coast, keeping west of Cape Akamas in Cyprus; but sometimes they made too much leeway, and failed to clear the western point of Cyprus. In the former case the harbour of Myra was, apparently, the usual point to which ships ran (Ac 21[2]). In the latter case ships seem to have run for the Syrian coast, perhaps because the south coast of Cyprus was dangerous from its shallow and harbourless character. Examples of voyages northwards from Alexandria are given below: on the voyage south from Rhodes to Alexandria, see p. 382b.

After reaching some point on the south coast of Asia Minor the westward-bound ship was obliged to work along the coast from point to point, taking advantage of the land breezes. Dion Chrysostom in his second Oration at Tarsus speaks of the fitful and uncertain character of those breezes, comparing to them the policy of a city governed for brief periods by a succession of magistrates.* Not a moment could safely be lost in taking advantage of such a breeze, lest it should fall again, or change its direction, before the ship got past the promontory ahead. The progress along the coast in this part of the voyage was necessarily slow, and sometimes exceedingly tedious. St. Paul's ship took fifteen days from Cæsarea to Myra (Ac 27[5] [Western text]).

This part of the voyage frequently ended with the harbour of Rhodes. Vespasian touched at Rhodes on his voyage from Alexandria to Rome in A.D. 70.† So did Philotimus on his way from Cæsar in the East to Cicero at Brundisium in July, B.C. 47 (see footnote on p. 387a). Herod the Great sailed in winter from Alexandria by the Pamphylian coast and Rhodes to Rome by way of Brundisium in B.C. 40, and in B.C. 14 touched at Rhodes on his voyage from Cæsarea to the Black Sea,‡ as did St. Paul when making the reverse voyage (Ac 21[1]).

Gregory of Nazianzus in the 4th cent. sailed from Alexandria to Greece, keeping under (*i.e.* south and west of) Cyprus, and reached Rhodes apparently on the twentieth day (*Carm. de vita sua*, 128 ff.; *de rebus suis*, 312; *Or.* xviii. 31).

The ship on which St. Paul sailed for Rome is not stated to have touched at Rhodes, and the expression that it came over against Cnidus (Ac 27[7]) suggests that it kept north of Rhodes as if intending to cross among the Cyclades to Malea. Lucian's *Ship*, also, sailed north of Rhodes.

After reaching the south-western extremity of Asia Minor the ships ran down to the eastern promontory of Crete, Salmone, and proceeded to work along its south coast in the same way as before (Ac 27[7. 13]). This was the safe course, in preference to the north side of Crete, because there, if a north wind came sweeping down the Ægean, the ship would be in danger of being driven on the coast, which has few harbours.* On the south coast there was not the same danger of running ashore, partly because the harbours were more numerous, and still more because the south winds in this sea are much more gentle, as a rule, than the north winds.†

Only one piece of evidence (see below) known to the present writer describes the voyage between Crete and the Italian coast. But the course of such a voyage is indubitable: the ships would take an opportunity of running for the south point of Cythera, and thence off Zakynthos and across the mouth of the Adriatic to the south coast of Italy, usually to Hydruntum (*Itin. Mar.* p. 489). They would not shrink from running direct to Italy if the wind at any moment were from the north. An ancient fleet could safely run from Cythera or Zakynthos for the wide angle between Italy and Sicily; the ships on the wings would guide the whole fleet by signal.

The evidence of Lucian in the beginning of his dialogue, *Navigium*, is clear: the corn ships in ordinary course sailed across from the south-west of Crete to sight Cythera; ‡ but they sometimes missed their course under the influence of southerly winds and got into the Ægean Sea.

There is not in the Ægean or the Adriatic the same prevalence of westerly winds in summer as in the Levant and the open stretch of the Mediterranean. Northerly and southerly winds are more characteristic of those seas; and therefore this part of the voyage would in general be much more easily accomplished than the preceding part. Hence in a favourable voyage the runs from Alexandria to Myra, and from Crete to Rhegium and thence to Puteoli, would not be slow; but, even at the best, a considerable time would necessarily be spent on the coasting voyage from Myra to the west end of Crete.

It is noteworthy that this wide stretch of sea between Crete and Italy, being affected by the prevalent winds of the Adriatic, was called by the sailors Adria (Ac 27[27]). We note also that westward-bound ships kept well to the north in this part of the sea to catch the Adriatic winds, while eastward-bound ships must have kept more to the south in order to profit by the general Mediterranean current of air setting for the Syrian coasts and the hot deserts behind them (see § iv.).

On the other hand, in unfavourable times, if the ship failed to clear Akamas, or did not get suitable winds west of Crete, all three parts of the voyage might be tedious. The scene in which Lucian's dialogue, *Navigium*, is laid is most probably taken from a real event. The ship failed to clear the point of Akamas on the seventh day from Alexandria, and, after being driven to Zidon, and on the tenth day from Zidon § reaching the Cheli-

* *ὥσπερ οἱ τοῖς ἀπογείοις, μᾶλλον δὲ τοῖς ἀπὸ τῶν γνόφων πνεύμασι πλέοντες*, xxxiv. 36, p. 424. He had probably experienced these winds on the voyage back from Alexandria.

† Josephus, *BJ* VII. ii. 1; Suet. *Vesp.* 7; Dion Cass. lxvi. 9; Zonaras, xi. 17. He landed at Brundisium.

‡ Josephus, *Ant.* XIV. xiv. 2 f.; *BJ* I. xiv. 3; *Ant.* XVI. ii. 2.

* *δυσλίμενος* (Eust.), which does not mean (as some scholars have understood) that there was no harbour on the north coast, but only that they were too few.

† It is different in the Adriatic, where, as Horace (*Od.* i. 3. 15) says, the south wind is the *arbiter*.

‡ *ἔδει τὴν Κρήτην δεξιὰν λαβόντας, ὑπὲρ τὸν Μαλέα πλεύσαντας, ἤδη* (*i.e.* before the seventieth day from Alexandria) *εἶναι ἐν Ἰταλίᾳ*. A glance at the map shows with perfect certainty how this must be interpreted.

§ The exact course is mentioned: the ship sailed through the Aulon or channel between Cyprus and the Cilician-Pamphylian coast, the same course as St. Paul's ship took. That course was necessarily and invariably followed by westward-bound ships from the Syrian harbours.

donian Islands (east of Myra), it met a storm, narrowly escaped sinking, and thereafter had a run of bad luck south of Crete, and was finally driven by southerly winds into the Ægean, and had to put into the Piræus after a voyage of 70 days.

vi. TIME BETWEEN ALEXANDRIA AND ROME.—From this voyage, as described by Lucian, combined with the statement in Ac 27[5], that St. Paul's ship reached Myra on the fifteenth day from Cæsarea, we can state with very considerable accuracy the fair time to Myra from Alexandria as nine days, and from Zidon as twelve to thirteen. Now two days was ample time from the Straits of Messina to Puteoli (Ac 28[13]), when the wind favoured; and ten to twelve days must be allowed from Crete to the Straits. This leaves thirteen to eighteen days for the coasting voyage from Myra to the west extremity of Crete, in the passage described in the next paragraph as a favourable one. Gregory of Nazianzus took twenty days to Rhodes (say ten to Myra, and ten from Myra to Rhodes); this is a little slower.

Examples of the average length of passage from Alexandria to Rome are difficult to get, as most of those which are mentioned are exceptional and tedious voyages. But the following may be taken as probably a fair average voyage in the best season. No. 27 of the Berlin Greek Papyri is a letter written from Rome on 2 August, towards the end of the 2nd cent., by a sailor or officer on an Alexandrian ship. He mentions that he 'came to land' on 30 June, finished unloading on 12 July (perhaps in Puteoli),* and reached Rome on 19 July. Now the ship cannot be supposed to have left Alexandria long before 26 May, for the statement of Vegetius about the period when the sea was fully open was almost certainly inspired by the rules for the Alexandrian corn ships. If the ship in question sailed in the first fleet it would probably be ready to start on the first day of open sea, and the voyage would have occupied thirty-six days. But, further, the ships would probably be ready to take advantage of a favourable opportunity some days before the 26th, for it cannot be supposed that the day was fixed with absolute precision (Ac 28[11]). The voyage in this case, therefore, may be taken as lasting probably about forty days; and we must understand that it was a favourable passage. In this argument we have assumed that the ship arrived as one of a fleet and not as a single stray ship; but it may fairly be assumed that stray ships came in at unusual times, very early or late, and that a ship reaching Puteoli on 30 June was sailing in the ordinary course. Probably this was near the ordinary time for the first fleet of the year to arrive, as described by Seneca (*Epist. Mor.* 77, 1), in a year when the voyage was very good. As a rule, vessels with a heavy cargo like corn did not unload at Puteoli, but went on thence to Ostia, whereas valuable cargo was discharged at Puteoli and carried to Rome by land.

On the other hand, Lucian, in the passage quoted above, says that the ship which he describes, at the time when it was forced to put into the Piræus by stress of weather on the seventieth day from Alexandria, ought in ordinary course to have been already in its harbour in Italy if it had not been driven astray into the Ægean Sea.† This seems to imply that the voyage to Italy just mentioned was an unusually quick one. Had forty days been about the usual length, Lucian would naturally have said that his *Ship* should have been already *for a long time* in an Italian harbour on the seventieth day.

Accordingly, we conclude that, when not detained unduly, fifty days was a more common length of passage from Alexandria to Rome. It would be roughly divided thus—

6 days to Akamas in Cyprus.
3 ,, ,, Myra.
10 ,, ,, Rhodes (Gregory's time).
15 ,, ,, west end of Crete.
13 ,, ,, the Straits.
1 day in the Straits.
2 days to Puteoli.

When a ship was delayed beyond sixty or seventy days the passage would begin to be considered an unfortunate one; but no anxiety would be felt, for it must often have been the case that ships were carried far from their course,* and detained even till the following year. Phœnix, in the south-west of Crete, was evidently a common harbour for laggard ships to spend the winter in (Ac 27[12]; also p. 379[a]): it was convenient as being near to the west end of the island, so that ships could there be on the outlook for promise of a fair passage across the wide sea to Cythera and Italy.

There can hardly be any doubt (though no proof formally exists or could be expected) that the remarkably early Christianization of Crete was due to the ships from Alexandria and Syria having occasionally to winter there. Such a result was natural when crew and passengers were doomed to remain for some months in harbour. On the other hand, the many voyages along the coasts of Pamphylia and Lycia appear to have produced little or no effect, for those provinces seem to have been less affected by Christianity in the early centuries than any other part of Asia Minor. The reason, doubtless, was that passengers in ships on the coasting voyage could never count on an hour's delay. The fitful land winds might change or begin or end at any time, and the passenger was bound to the ship.† Only those who have had the experience can realize how absolutely prohibitive this uncertainty is as regards any intercourse with the country along which the coasting voyage leads. Pamphylia or Lycia could not be Christianized in the same way as Crete, but only by deliberate and intentional missionary effort such as that of Ac 12[13].

vii. VOYAGES TO ASIA, THE ÆGEAN AND EUXINE SEAS, PALESTINE AND EGYPT.—During the rest of the year, except the open season, the voyage to Egypt was made by way of the coasts of Asia Minor and Syria—the same route that war vessels would take even in the very height of summer. Caligula intended to sail by that course, *viâ* Brundisium, when he thought of going to Egypt. This was the more luxurious though the slower route, as he could rest quietly on land every night (Philo, *de Leg.* 33, cf. *in Flac.* 5).

Smaller vessels or ships of war never ventured on such long sea courses as were needed in the voyages hitherto described, but kept closer to the shore. Only the large, heavily-built merchant vessels were suited for such a voyage (Philo, *de Leg.* 33); they alone had sufficient spread of canvas, or strength of build, or storage room, to go a long voyage and remain out of sight of land for a number of days. The war ships were slighter in construction, moved in a more agile way, and were not dependent on the wind or able to make such use of the wind, for they trusted chiefly to oars.

* If we assume that he started as soon as unloading was finished, Puteoli would be certain. The Berlin editor gives μηδὲν ἀναπολελύσθαι: read μηδέναν ἀπολ., 'that none of the corn-traders has got leave to depart.'

† It would appear probable that this ship, which sighted Akamas on the seventh day from Alexandria, was on the extreme right of the fleet. It would signal the others, but was itself too far east to be able to clear the promontory.

* Lucian's *Ship* carried to the Piræus; two to Malta, Ac 28[1.11].

† Cf. Dion Chrysostom as quoted on p. 380[a], note *.

The voyages made by the south coast of Asia Minor are naturally similar in many respects to voyages between Rome and the ports of the Ægean Sea or the Euxine. These also may therefore be suitably noticed at this point. Puteoli was the chief harbour of this trade in the Roman Republican times and the first century after Christ. When Delos was the great centre and market of the Ægean, before the massacre of Roman traders by Mithridates in B.C. 88, Puteoli was called Lesser Delos.* When Delos was destroyed, no other harbour of the Ægean was heir to its greatness, and Puteoli became more important than ever. It was crowded with traders and settlers from all the Eastern lands and harbours. These brought their religion with them; and Puteolanian inscriptions reveal a mingled, strange picture of foreign deities, cults, and societies and traders (see the interesting article by M. Dubois on 'Cultes et Dieux à Pouzzoles' in *Mélanges d'Histoire et d'Archéologie*, 1902, p. 23).

From Puteoli thus started, and to it came in, a vast body of trade. After the completion of the great works by which Trajan improved the harbour, Portus Augusti, at the mouth of the Tiber, which Claudius had planned and in part made, that port supplanted Puteoli to a considerable extent as the emporium of the Eastern trade. But in New Testament times it claimed most of that trade, though some part (especially the heaviest goods) always went direct to Ostia without breaking bulk at Puteoli.

All ships trading between one or other of these harbours and any part of the East passed through the Straits of Messina. Beyond that, there were the three lines—one keeping well south to seek Alexandria, one keeping as near the line to Cythera as was possible, but often tending northwards towards Zacynthos. The ships from and to the Ægean kept north of Cythera, rounding Cape Malea. Trading vessels coming from Egypt and Syria kept south of Cythera: as to those which were going to Egypt or Syria, it is probable that they kept north of Cythera and through among the Cyclades: such at least was Jerome's course—see the end of this section. Doubtless, war vessels and small trading ships always kept north of Cythera, and crept on from harbour to harbour and island to island. Thus a very large number of vessels must constantly have been passing and repassing through the southern Greek waters.

There can be no doubt that all, or almost all, heavy merchandise travelled by this route between Rome and the Ægean or Black Sea harbours. The alternative route by Corinth required transshipment and transportation across the Isthmus of Corinth, which would have seriously added to the cost of freight. In earlier times, when Cape Malea was an object of dread to sailors in small ships, the trouble of the Isthmus crossing might be incurred in carrying goods, but the Roman merchant ships seem to have lost the old dread: on a gravestone at Hierapolis in Phrygia we read that a certain Zeuxis had rounded Cape Malea seventy-two times. Though Nero revived the old scheme of a ship canal through the Isthmus, he was probably impelled more by the tradition than by any real apprehension felt in his own time; and the canal would not produce any great saving in hours of voyage except to ships from (and to) the Adriatic, or Epirus, or Acarnania. These facts, or the disturbed state of the Empire soon after, caused the scheme to be abandoned; and there was no good reason to bring about its resumption by a later Emperor, though Herodes Atticus talked about it.

* Paulus ex Festo, xi. p. 91, *s.v.* 'Minorem Delum,' quoting the phrase from Lucilius, *Sat.* iii. 94 (Lachmann).

Ephesus was the great harbour of the Asian produce, though Smyrna vied with it; and other harbours also were used, such as Miletus, Caunos, etc. But most ships seem to have put in at Ephesus, even though bound to other ports; and it became a custom for the Roman governors of Asia to land first there. This custom was finally recognized and made compulsory by a formal enactment of the Emperor Antoninus Pius. The enactment probably sprang from some complaint on the part of the great rival cities, Smyrna and Pergamus; and the Imperial rescript marked and confirmed the recognition (perhaps originating from Hadrian) of Ephesus as the capital of Asia. Ephesus was *de facto* the capital of the province long before it was formally recognized as such by the Imperial law.*

Passengers, also, as well as goods went sometimes by this route to the Asian coast. Pliny the younger went in this way in August A.D. 111 to Ephesus, and experienced contrary winds. There he changed ship, and went on northwards in small coasting vessels to his Bithynian province.

Trade with the Black Sea harbours followed the same route as far as Ephesus, and then went on through the Hellespont and the Thracian Bosporus. At Ephesus it met the line of ships trading between the north Ægean or Euxine harbours and Syria or Egypt. This latter line of ships was now far less important than it had been under the Greek kings in the last centuries B.C., when Canon Hicks thinks it safe to assert that daily ships ran on the line.† The causes stated above prevented such trade on any great scale between the provinces of the Empire. Still there was an appreciable trade, and Diodorus (iii. 34) gives a statement of the length of voyage from the Sea of Azoff to Crete and Egypt (which, as we saw reason to think, conveys a very exaggerated idea of the swiftness of the voyage).‡

From this passage of Diodorus it is clear that the long over-sea voyage to Alexandria was made direct from Rhodes: with a westerly or north-westerly wind that was the natural line, and not any longer than the run from the Lycian coast. With a west wind the ancient ships could hardly have reached Alexandria from Lycia on a direct course; now the object was to make Alexandria on a straight run. Thus we see that there were three long lines common in the Levant voyages: (1) from Rhodes to Alexandria; (2) from Alexandria past Akamas towards Myra, though the latter part of this voyage could not have been made on a straight course; (3) from Myra or Patara to one of the Syrian harbours, as in Ac 21.

It is impossible that ancient ships ordinarily sailed from the Sea of Azoff to Crete in ten days. A voyage from Crete to Alexandria in four days is more credible, because ships could often have a continuous run with a steady breeze, and a lucky voyage might reach Alexandria in four days. But there is a great variety inevitable in the former part of the voyage—changes of direction, changes of wind, passing from sea to sea, and through the long narrow passages of the Bosporus and Dardanelles. Finally, the statement that ten days was the time from Alexandria up the Nile to Ethiopia is entirely inconsistent with the tendency of all the evidence that Wilcken has collected as to the length of time needed for even great Imperial events to become known in Upper Egypt (even though in many cases the indifference and carelessness of the peasants may account for their ignorance).

In an admirable excursus to his posthumously

* See vol. iii. art. PERGAMUS, p. 751[a].

† See Paton and Hicks, *Inscriptions of Cos*, p. xxxiii.

‡ Diodorus is more probably speaking of ships in his own time than quoting from some Greek account of older voyages.

published Commentary on First Peter, Dr. Hort traces the course of the messenger who carried that letter from Rome to a harbour on the south coast of the Black Sea: he considers that Sinope was the harbour, but Amastris seems more probable. Sinope was no longer so important a harbour under the Romans as it had been in older times: Amastris surpassed it, and bore the title Metropolis Ponti. Moreover, if the messenger had landed at Sinope, he would naturally have visited Cappadocia before Galatia, whereas Dr. Hort has rightly argued that the strange order of enumeration of the provinces is due to the order of the messenger's journey. He landed at Amastris, visited Pontus first, then passed through North Galatia to Cæsarea and perhaps Tyana, and thence through South Galatia to Asia, and finally reached Bithynia.

It may be added to Dr. Hort's examination of the facts, that the journey in its eastern part probably corresponds to the actual order in which Christianity spread; that is to say, the new religion was carried by ship to the Bithynian and Pontic harbours, and thence spread south into the northern and north-eastern regions of the province Galatia, including inner Pontus* and the north of Cappadocia. Thus we find that this new thought and teaching, 'floating free on the currents of communication across the Empire,' spread first directly along the great tracks that led to Rome, as every free and natural movement of thought necessarily did owing to the circumstances of that period, and from that centre was redirected to the outlying parts of the Empire. As Christianity spread from Syria and Cilicia through the Cilician Gates, it did not radiate out west and north and north-east, but passed along the great route that led by Ephesus, Corinth, and the sea-way, or by Troas and Philippi and the overland way, to Italy.

It is extremely difficult to get even an approximate idea of the time required on these courses between Rome and the various eastern provinces. There was no rule possible in this case, such as we could determine roughly in the direct Alexandrian passages, and as we shall be able to determine more accurately in the overland postal route (see § ix.). The ships generally were merchant vessels, liable to minor variations in their course according to the conditions of the carrying trade, and sometimes waiting in harbours for some time to unload or take in fresh cargo, as in Ac 20. Thus their voyages were evidently slow, as a rule. Probably they were generally much smaller than the Alexandrian ships, and some would not venture to do more than make short runs from harbour to harbour or point to point, in the ancient Greek fashion: the last class of vessels had more reason to dread Malea than the better built traders. Even war vessels, which were comparatively independent of winds, evidently required much longer time for the eastern voyage than the large Alexandrian trading vessels.

Statistics as to the time which despatches during the Republican period, or private letters under the Empire, required to reach a distant destination on this course, are of little value as indications of the rate of travel: there was no regular postal service, and the letter-carriers were liable to many delays and interruptions. Hence the recorded facts vary widely. Friedländer (p. 31) quotes two cases of letters from Syria addressed to Cicero in Rome: one, dated 31 Dec., took over a hundred days in delivery; the other, dated 7 May, hardly over fifty:* presumably the latter was carried straight through, while the other was carried by a messenger who was detained on the way. The slow letter was sent during the worst season of the year, the quick letter during the best; but in the case of land travelling (if either went in that way), the season ought not to make any serious difference. Both were sent by men of high standing, who could command all the resources of the State for quick transmission; but the period was disturbed, and the machinery of government was dislocated and liable to stoppages. The quick letter travelled at much the same rate as the Imperial postal service organized by Augustus (see below, § ix.), taking only a few days more than Imperial despatches probably required. The slow letter perhaps went by ship.

A business letter written in Puteoli on 23 July, A.D. 174, was delivered in Tyre a hundred and seven days later,† though it was sent in the most favourable season for sailing. This letter would not be transmitted by the Imperial service, but by private agents, travelling doubtless by ship. It could hardly have been sent by one of the large ships running direct to Alexandria, but was more probably sent on a trading vessel which went by Cape Malea and the Asian coast, and probably spent time in various harbours. St. Jerome sailed in August from Portus Augusti, by Malea, through the Cyclades, by the Asian coasts and Cyprus to Syrian Antioch, whence he went on to Jerusalem, which he reached in winter;‡ this voyage was made along the same route by which the letter to Tyre travelled, but seems to have been quicker.

With similar variation in speed, letters from Rome in Cicero's time reached Athens—in one case arriving on 14 October in twenty-one days, in another case in forty-six days during July and August:§ the former is mentioned as showing great activity on the part of the messenger; the latter, though so slow, came in the most settled season of the year.

viii. Overland Route and Imperial Post-road from Rome to the East.—While passengers to and from Egypt or Syria seem frequently to have travelled along the coasts of Asia Minor and Crete, it is not probable that the Imperial despatches and news went regularly by that route, which was uncertain and (at least during a considerable part of the year) liable to great variation in time. The fast sea passage (see § iii.) was of course preferred during the open season; but it may be regarded as probable that during the rest of the year the Imperial service to the eastern provinces was conducted by the overland route through Macedonia and Thrace. Only in this way could that regularity of communication which was important for administrative purposes be attained. For those purposes reasonable certainty as to when instructions would be received was in many cases even more important than the chance of the messages being delivered more quickly; and, where speed was important, it was always possible to send a special messenger in addition by the route which offered the chance of more rapid delivery. Hence even Syria and Egypt probably communicated regularly with Rome by the overland route during the stormy and the doubtful seasons of the year.

Hudemann (*Geschichte des röm. Postwesens*, p. 163 f.) and other writers have rightly maintained that ships were used only as a subsidiary and occasional method of communication for Imperial

* See the article Pontus in vol. iv., where emphasis is laid on the important, but often neglected, distinction between Provincia Pontus on the coast (which was united with Bithynia) and *mediterraneus* Pontus (a kingdom at first, in Prov. Galatia till about 106, thereafter in Prov. Cappadocia).

* Cicero, *ad Fam.* xii. 10. 2 (false number in Friedländer, p. 31, note), *ad Att.* xiv. 9.

† The case is quoted by Friedländer from Mommsen in *Ber. d. Sächs. Gesellsch.* 1850, ii. p. 61, to which the present writer has not had access.

‡ Hieron. *c. Rufin.* iii. 22, ed. Vallars. ii. 51.

§ Cicero, *ad Fam.* xvi. 21. 1; xiv. 5. 1. See also § xii. 5.

purposes, and not as a regular and permanent part of the postal system, at least under the early Empire; but under Hadrian a procurator (*procurator pugillationis et ad naves vagas*) was stationed at Ostia (or Portus Augusti), possibly to regulate the transmission of despatches by occasional or special ships (*CIL* xiv. 2045).*

Moreover, the overland route was the shorter for many provinces, even in the open season, and had therefore to be maintained in full efficiency throughout the year. Hence it must have been the main route for administrative purposes; and every other route, even the short sea route in summer, was merely subsidiary and additional to the great way for the Imperial couriers.

An incidental proof of the preference of land to sea travel for Imperial communication is furnished by two of Pliny's despatches to Trajan. He mentions (*Ep.* 63) that a courier came to him at Nicæa from the king of Bosporus (Pantikapæum on the European side of the entrance to the Sea of Azoff); but it is also implied there and in *Ep.* 67 that the embassy from Bosporus on its way to Rome would pass through Bithynia, and be obliged in courtesy to pay a call on him as governor in passing. The official way, then, was not to sail from the Crimea to the Hellespont or to Byzantium, but to take ship to Amastris or Sinope, the shortest sea passage, and then travel by land. The purely land route from the Crimea through South Russia round the north-western coasts of the Black Sea was not open to the Roman service, because it led through foreign territory.

The regular course for the couriers carrying despatches from Rome was along the Appian Way to Brundisium. Then they crossed from Brundisium to Dyrrachium or Aulona, and thence went by the Via Egnatia to Thessalonica and Philippi and its harbour Neapolis. The direct and apparently easy route along the coast to Neapolis was avoided by the Roman road (as the Itineraries are agreed): the road turned away from the crossing of the Hebrus at Amphipolis (Ac 16) inland to Philippi, the great Roman *colonia*, before seeking the harbour; but there was, doubtless, always a path in local use from Amphipolis direct to Neapolis.

Very little evidence exists as to the exact route beyond Neapolis. The way to Syria under the later Empire was by Byzantium, Nicomedia, and Ancyra; but it is certain that that route was not in use so early as New Testament times, for the roads of the provinces Galatia and Cappadocia seem not to have been constructed until the end of Vespasian's reign; and Cappadocia was not even properly organized as a province until about A.D. 74. Previously, viz. from A.D. 17 to 74, it had been a procuratorial province, which implied that it was governed not after the fully developed Roman system (which permitted a considerable degree of autonomy or home rule in internal matters), but after the native fashion and on monarchical lines by a procurator who represented the Emperor. The procurator represented the native king, whose rule had been deliberately chosen by the people, when the Romans had offered them their liberty and autonomy in B.C. 95 (Strab. p. 540): when the last king proved incapable, and the province was still unfit for real Roman provincial organization, a procurator was sent in place of the king, who gradually raised the country to the Roman level. After A.D. 74 Roman roads began to spread over the combined provinces of Galatia—Cappadocia (united under one governor, but as a double, not a single uniform homogeneous province). Thus there gradually grew up a great through route from the Bosporus opposite Byzantium by Juliopolis to Ancyra, Archelais-Colonia and Tyana, and the Cilician Gates, joining the older line of the Overland Route and also that of the Central Route* to the Gates at Colonia Faustiniana or Faustinopolis, which was founded by Marcus Aurelius beside the old native village of Halala (the Byzantine Loulon), 23 miles S.S.W. from Tyana, and named after his wife, who died there. That new through route, the 'Pilgrims' Route,' is described by the present writer in *Hist. Geogr. of Asia Minor*, p. 240 ff., and more fully in sections in the *Geograph. Journal*, 1903, and by Anderson in *Journ. of Hell. Stud.* 1899, p. 53 ff.

* Mommsen, *Staatsrecht*, ii. 3 p.1030 (approved by O. Hirschfeld), denies this, and understands that the procurator's duty was to register the ships as they singly entered the harbour. Accepting this, however, we must observe that such registration was necessary for the postal service, and might naturally be combined with it.

It is therefore highly probable that messengers for Syria and Egypt during the first and early second centuries went by the same route as messengers to Asia.† They sailed from Neapolis, the port of Philippi, to Alexandria Troas (Ac $16^{10}$ $20^{6}$). Galen, it is true, sailed (from Troas) to Thessalonica; but he implies that this was an unusual course, taken for the special purpose of visiting Lemnos (*Op.* ed. Kühn, xii. 171).‡ Those who preferred to avoid even this short voyage seem to have crossed the Hellespont at Lampsacus and thence followed the route given in the Antonine Itinerary, p. 334, by Ilium to Troas.

In general, travellers from the East would prefer the less fatiguing route by Corinth (§ x.); but there would always be many travellers from the northern provinces on the overland road, and in winter it was the only route that was always open. Hence Aristides, when he travelled to Rome in the winter (probably of A.D. 143–144), went by that road. He describes the hardships of the journey—the rain, the frozen Hebrus, the snow, the wretched inns, the sullenness and ill-will of the barbarous natives; he lay long sick in Edessa; and thus, although for a time he went as fast as the Imperial post, he finally reached Rome on the hundredth day from his own home (which probably is to be understood as Hadrianoutheræ in Mysia, though Pergamus or Smyrna are also possible).§

From Lampsacus or Troas the way for Syrian couriers doubtless went by Pergamus (still the capital of Asia in the 1st cent.), Philadelphia, and on through the Cilician Gates to Tarsus, Antioch, Palestine, and Egypt. The way from Philadelphia to the Gates is described more fully below, § xi.

An important and typical route deserves fuller discussion. In the reign of Trajan, Ignatius was conducted to Rome from Syrian Antioch by land through many cities (the only one mentioned by name being Philadelphia) to Smyrna,‖ thence he went (probably on shipboard) to Troas and Neapolis for Philippi, and then went along the Egnatian Way, and so on to Rome. There is one unusual feature in this journey, viz. the detour to Smyrna. Presumably, some special duty required the escort to go to Smyrna; possibly prisoners under sentence were to be taken from thence; but the exact reason must remain uncertain. The ordinary course for such a party would have been

* See below, § x.

† A new route came into use before A.D. 193: see § xii.

‡ Returning from Rome to Asia, he again wished to visit Lemnos; but this time he took ship from Neapolis for Thasos, and thence to Lemnos.

§ *Or.* 24, p. 305 (i. 481 f., ed. Dindorf).

‖ Friedländer, *Darstellungen aus der Sittengeschichte Roms*, p. 30, mentions only the absurd account of the *Acta* (Antiochian), that Ignatius went by sea from Seleucia to Smyrna, and says that this ignorant statement, whether true or invented, is at least the work of one thoroughly acquainted with the way. On the contrary, it proceeds from one who mixes up and confuses quite inconsistent routes and methods of travel, as is shown in the sequel.

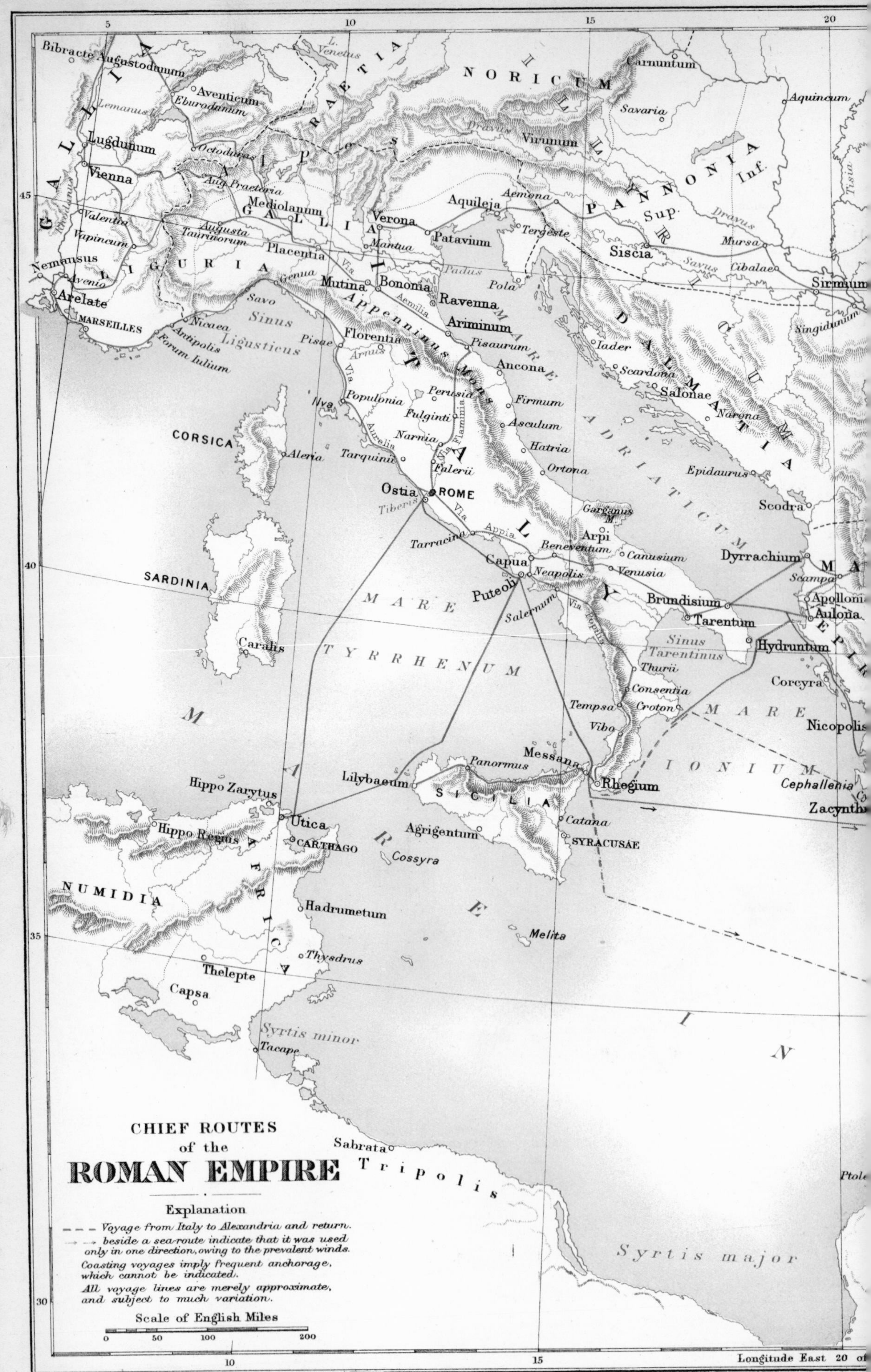
CHIEF ROUTES
of the
ROMAN EMPIRE
Explanation
Voyage from Italy to Alexandria and return.
→ → beside a sea-route indicate that it was used only in one direction, owing to the prevalent winds.
Coasting voyages imply frequent anchorage, which cannot be indicated.
All voyage lines are merely approximate, and subject to much variation.
Scale of English Miles
0 50 100 200
Longitude East 20 of
Engraved & Printed by
COPYRIGHT, 19
GALLIA
RAETIA
NORICUM
PANNONIA Inf.
PANNONIA Sup.
ALPES
GALLIA
LIGURIA
ITALIA
ILLYRICUM
DALMATIA
CORSICA
SARDINIA
SICILIA
AFRICA
NUMIDIA
Tripolis
MARE ADRIATICUM
MARE TYRRHENUM
MARE IONIUM
MARE INTERNUM
Sinus Ligusticus
Sinus Tarentinus
Syrtis minor
Syrtis major
Appenninus Mons
Bibracte
Augustodunum
Aventicum
Eburodunum
Lemanus
Lugdunum
Vienna
Octodurus
Aug. Praetoria
Mediolanum
Valentia
Vapincum
Augusta Tauriuorum
Nemausus
Avenio
Arelate
MARSEILLES
Nicaea
Antipolis
Forum Iulium
Genua
Savo
Placentia
Verona
Mantua
Patavium
Aquileja
Aemona
Tergeste
Pola
Padus
Mutina
Bononia
Ravenna
Ariminum
Pisaurum
Ancona
Firmum
Asculum
Hatria
Ortona
Pisae
Florentia
Arnus
Populonia
Ilva
Perusia
Fulginti
Narnia
Tarquinii
Falerii
Aleria
Ostia
ROME
Tiberis
Via Aemilia
Via Aurelia
Via Flaminia
Via Appia
Tarracina
Capua
Neapolis
Puteoli
Salernum
Beneventum
Garganus M.
Arpi
Canusium
Venusia
Brundisium
Tarentum
Hydruntum
Thurii
Consentia
Croton
Tempsa
Vibo
Messana
Rhegium
Panormus
Lilybaeum
Agrigentum
Catana
SYRACUSAE
Cossyra
Melita
Caralis
Carnuntum
Aquincum
Savaria
Virunum
Dravus
Siscia
Savus
Mursa
Cibalae
Sirmium
Singidunum
Iader
Scardona
Salonae
Narona
Epidaurus
Scodra
Dyrrachium
Scampa
Apollonia
Aulona
Corcyra
Nicopolis
Cephallenia
Zacynthus
Hippo Zarytus
Hippo Regius
Utica
CARTHAGO
Hadrumetum
Thysdrus
Thelepte
Capsa
Tacape
Sabrata
Tisia

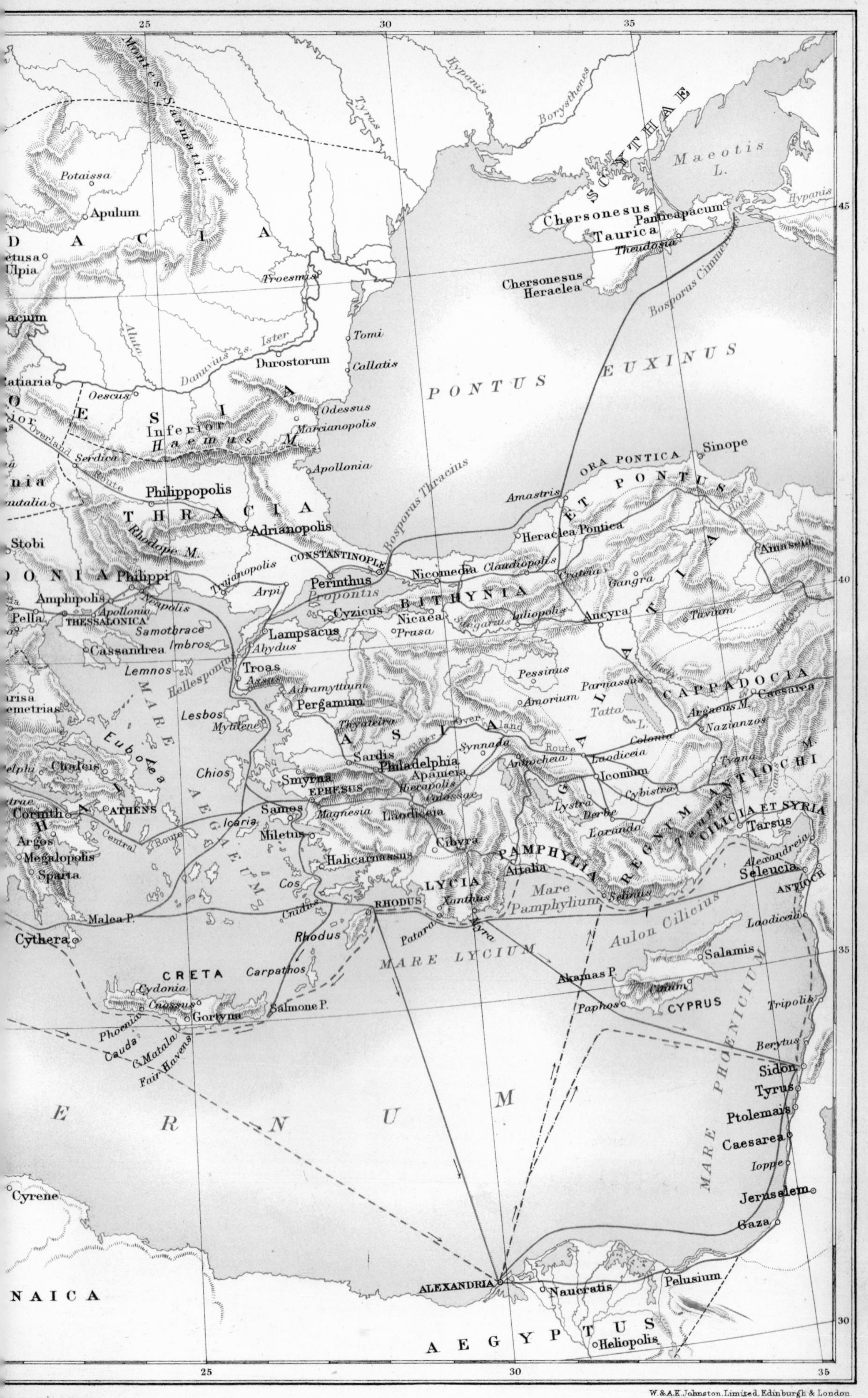

W.&A.K. Johnston Limited, Edinburgh & London
CRIBNER'S SONS

to report to the governor at Pergamus; but special orders must have been sent to alter the usual course. From Smyrna the natural course would be to sail to Troas and Philippi; and it is certain that Ignatius passed through both of those towns, and that he sailed from Troas to Philippi.

If we could assume that the convoy travelled by the Great Highway, through Philomelium, Julia, Apamea, and Laodicea, it would be necessary to suppose that the call to Smyrna was received at Philadelphia. Had the orders to visit Smyrna been known at Laodicea, the natural course would have taken the party through Tralles and Ephesus. But it may be regarded as most probable that the Roman officer followed the direct path west from Julia straight through Prymnessus and near Acmonia to Philadelphia and Pergamus, and that the convoy, travelling by this ordinary route, was called away to Smyrna from Philadelphia. This establishes a probability that the path Julia-Prymnessus-Philadelphia was the usual one for Imperial business under the early Empire. That path was an important Roman road in the early Empire, and less important later (see *Cities and Bish. of Phrygia*, ii. p. 588 f.).

The reason why the officer who conducted Ignatius (with other prisoners) preferred the land road to the direct voyage from the Syrian coast, did not lie in the season of the year. Friedländer says the voyage from Seleucia to Smyrna was made in late autumn or winter; but, as we saw, there was no such voyage, and indeed that voyage could hardly have been made in winter: he is wrong also as to the period, for Ignatius was at Smyrna on 23 August, and is therefore likely to have started from Antioch in early July.* According to the *Acta*, he entered Rome and was martyred on the feast of the *Sigillaria*, 20 Dec., which would point to a later start; but no statement in the *Acta* as to the journey carries the smallest weight; and that authority must be disregarded except when confirmed by other evidence, especially that of the letters themselves. Better authorities † give 17 October as the day of his martyrdom and presumably of his entry into Rome, for those two days were wrongly identified by the hagiographers: see p. 386.

We must therefore suppose that the land road was followed because it was the ordinary official route for government messages and parties; and that for Imperial administration and communication ships were used only occasionally as opportunity offered: that conclusion was stated on general grounds at the beginning of this section, and is confirmed by the circumstances of this special case. A similar conclusion is distinctly suggested by Ac 27[2. 6] 28[11]: it is evident that, but for the accidental meeting with a convenient Alexandrian corn ship at Myra, the centurion would have conducted St. Paul and the rest of his convoy to Smyrna, Troas, Neapolis, and so on by the same route as Ignatius travelled from Smyrna.

When Ephesus became the regular seat of government of the province Asia, the ordinary course for such a party would perhaps have been by Julia, Apamea, Laodicea, Tralles, and Magnesia to Ephesus, to report themselves there to the governor; but, as we have seen, it was probably not before the time of Hadrian that Ephesus became the official capital, as it had long been the practical and commercial capital of the province. Now by that time the road-system across Asia Minor was greatly developed: the roads of Galatia and Cappadocia were built on a great scale under the Flavian dynasty, when the administration of central and eastern Asia Minor was remodelled in A.D. 74. It is possible that under that dynasty the government couriers from Rome to Syria began to travel by Byzantium, Nicomedia, Juliopolis, Ancyra, Tyana, and the Cilician Gates, though the route followed by Ignatius's guards would suggest that the older and longer route through the province Asia was retained in ordinary use as late as Trajan's time. But during the 2nd cent. (before A.D. 192, see below, § xii.) the Bithynian route or 'Pilgrims' Road' was made official and ordinary. Already in A.D. 112 Juliopolis was an important point on a Roman route (Pliny, *Epist.* 77).

According to the *Acta*, Ignatius took ship at Dyrrachium and sailed through the Adriatic and Tyrrhenian Seas to Portus Augusti, the new harbour completed by Trajan at the mouth of the Tiber: he desired to land at Puteoli, but strong wind would not permit. There can be little doubt that this voyage, like that from Seleucia to Smyrna, is a pure invention: the short passage to Brundisium would be preferred as the natural and ordinary conclusion of the march along the Egnatian Way.

The truth is, as Hilgenfeld has seen (though Lightfoot* argues against him), that the writer of the *Acta*, who possessed no authority except the letters (of which he made very little use), and who had extremely little knowledge of roads and geography, tried to model the journey on St. Paul's so far as the few facts known to him permitted. He took the journey to Seleucia from Ac 13[4]: there he made the martyr embark for Smyrna, *i.e.* on board a ship 'to sail by the coasts of Asia' (Ac 27[2]), and afterwards on another which sailed close to Puteoli (Ac 28[13]), but was blown past it to the great harbour (which the writer had heard of in his own time, but which had probably not been completed when Ignatius died). He speaks as if Ignatius exercised as much authority on this ship as St. Paul did on his (Ac 27[9]), which is evidently absurd. The brethren come forth from Rome to greet the martyr, as they did to welcome St. Paul (Ac 28[15]). Everything is fanciful and invented; and all is the invention of a person who had only rather vague ideas of the journey.

The distances by land on this route may be roughly estimated as follows, according to the Itineraries:—

| | |
|---|---|
| Rome to Brundisium . . . | 360 miles |
| Brundisium to Dyrrachium or Aulona . . . . . . | 2 days |
| Dyrrachium or Aulona to Neapolis | 381 miles |
| Neapolis to Troas . . . | about 3 days |
| Troas to Antioch by Philadelphia and Julia . . . . . . | 880 miles |
| Troas to Antioch by Laodicea . | 930 ,, |
| Antioch to Cæsarea . . . | 365 ,, |
| Cæsarea to Alexandria . . . | 435 ,, |
| Total: Rome to Alexandria by Neapolis, Troas, and Julia, 5 days and | 2420 ,, |
| Rome to Alexandria by Neapolis, Troas, and Laodicea . 5 days and | 2470 ,, |
| Dyrrachium or Aulona to Callipolis | 630 miles |
| Callipolis to Lampsacus . . . | 2 hours |
| Lampsacus to Troas . . . | 60 miles |
| Total: Rome to Alexandria by Lampsacus . . 2 days and | 2730 or 2780 ,, |
| Dyrrachium or Aulona to Constantinople . . . . . . . | 750 ,, |
| Constantinople by Ancyra to Antioch . . . . . . . | 750 ,, |
| Total: Rome to Alexandria by Ancyra . . . 2 days and | 2660 ,, |

ix. DURATION OF JOURNEYS ON THE POST-ROAD BETWEEN ROME AND THE EAST.—The time re-

* See the calculation of time for the journey as given in the following section.

† The earliest are Chrysostom and the early Syrian Martyrology. See Lightfoot, *Ignatius and Polycarp*, ii. p. 416 f.

* *Ignatius and Polycarp*, ii. p. 389.

quired to travel by the overland route requires a much more complicated investigation than is the case with the sea routes; the time would vary within very wide limits, according to the taste and character and equipment and physical powers of the individual traveller; as a rule, the government couriers went most rapidly; ordinary travellers in carriages came next to them, and sometimes equalled them; travellers on foot were of course much slower, and travelled shorter daily stages. But on the whole we shall find reason to think that current views, which are all founded on Friedländer, exaggerate the speed of travelling, and neglect the practical facts which restrict the rate over a long journey; the eminent authority just named takes exceptional cases (which are mentioned because they were exceptional, whereas the ordinary cases are not recorded, just because they were ordinary and familiar) as examples of the regular practice.

(*a*) Travellers on foot seem to have accomplished about 16 or 20 Roman miles per day. This estimate of 20, as stated in the present writer's *Church in the Roman Empire*, p. 65, was founded on experience and observation in the country. It is confirmed by a fragmentary itinerary of a journey through the Cilician Gates, dating from the 1st cent., in which the daily stages vary from 18 to 22 Roman miles,* and by the principle of Roman law (mentioned by Friedländer, p. 25) that the number of days' grace allowed by the prætor to parties at a distance was reckoned at the rate of one day for each 20 miles. The estimate may seem short, but a consideration of the distances, *mutationes* and *mansiones*, on the Bordeaux Pilgrim's Itinerary would suggest that the average daily stage was even shorter, viz. 16 to 18 Roman miles;† and this shorter estimate is in accordance with the following unbiassed testimony. Sir H. Johnston, in the *Nineteenth Century*, 1902, pp. 728, 729, speaking of the rate of travel on foot, suited for the presumably hardy and strong African workmen going to the Transvaal mines, says: 'It should be laid down as an absolute rule that not more than 15 miles [*i.e.* 16 or 17 Roman miles] are to be accomplished in one day.'

It may therefore be confidently assumed that the ordinary rate for a long journey on foot was about 17 Roman miles per day. At this rate the distance from Antioch to Rome would be completed by the party in which Ignatius travelled in about ninety-five days continuously: eighty-six being spent in walking, seven on shipboard between Smyrna and Neapolis,‡ and two between Dyrrachium and Brundisium. To this some days must be added for detention in Smyrna and Troas, where evidently some halt was made, and there may possibly have been some other such stops by the way, especially in Tarsus, for the officer in command to report to the Roman governor of Cilicia,—say, about 104 days from start to finish.

Now of this total the journey to Smyrna would require forty-four, to which we may add two for delay in Tarsus and elsewhere, and four for the interval spent in Smyrna before the letter to the Romans was written (evidently on the eve of departure); and, as that letter was written on 24 August, the party must have started from Antioch about 6 July, and arrived in Rome about 17 October, on which day he reached Rome according to the oldest authorities (properly interpreted): see p. 385[a]. By this rough yet not inaccurate reckoning we are forced to the conclusion that Ignatius is likely to have reached Rome about the day mentioned in the oldest tradition; and it seems not improbable that this day was correctly remembered in tradition, with the probably incorrect addition that he was put to death on the same day that he arrived.

But it is more natural and probable that the execution was postponed until some great festival, when, amid the sports of the amphitheatre, Ignatius formed one of the crowd of criminals collected from all parts of the Empire, who were made to struggle with, or die unresistingly before, the starved wild beasts. The later hagiography delighted to represent the Roman government as intent on and wholly absorbed in the punishment of the martyr, and as hurrying him to death the moment he reached Rome; whereas, in reality, no official in Rome thought or cared about the one individual amidst a crowd of criminals reserved to make the next Roman holiday.

The journey of Ignatius may serve as a fair example of numberless similar journeys made by martyrs to Rome to meet the same kind of death for the amusement of a populace, which was in this way kept in good humour by the Imperial policy. There seems to be nothing exceptional or unusual about this journey. Ignatius was treated somewhat harshly by the soldiers who guarded him and the other prisoners; but naturally the guards were severe with the criminals, whom they were bound to watch, and for whose safe custody they were responsible (Ac 27[42]).

(*b*) Travellers driving along the road may probably be taken as going ordinarily at the rate of 4 Roman miles an hour. That is the rate which the writer calculated for the journey of Aristides from Smyrna to Pergamus,* and the minute details which Aristides gives make it possible to attain approximate certainty as to the rate. Ordinary travellers were weighted by luggage, and would not go faster than the heavy waggon on which it was carried. But where they wished, they were able to travel at the faster rate of the Imperial post: see below.

The regular day's journey for this class of travellers was perhaps only 25 Roman miles—half as long again as the foot traveller's ordinary journey (faster travellers went double distance, a few quadruple: see below). Twenty-five miles was the average distance between the *mansiones* on the roads; and, as Friedländer points out (p. 19), the distance between Bethlehem and Alexandria (which is about 400 Roman miles) was reckoned to be sixteen days' journey (*mansiones*).† Between each two *mansiones* the rule seems to have been that there should be two *mutationes*, though we have not a complete list for any road, for even the Bordeaux Itinerary omits some.

The roads, therefore, appear to have been divided into stages of about $8\frac{1}{3}$ Roman miles in length. The length of the stages was, undoubtedly, closely related to the average daily distances in ordinary travelling.

(*c*) The rate at which the Imperial couriers travelled is difficult to estimate with any exactness. Chambalu (*de magistratibus Flaviorum*, p. 8) supposes that they travelled at the rate of 160 Roman miles per day; and Friedländer (p. 23) quotes this estimate with apparent approval. But such a rate is entirely inconsistent with the long interval which (as we have seen) elapsed before

* The passage is discussed in the Appendix to a paper on 'Tarsus, Cilicia, and the Cilician Gates' in the *Geographical Journal*, 1903.

† Double the unit of distance, $8\frac{1}{3}$ Roman miles, while the traveller in carriage or waggon went three units, as is shown below. No Itinerary gives a complete list of the stages or units.

‡ Allowance for waiting on winds must be made (see Pliny, *Epist.* 15, 17, who travelled at nearly the same season, Aug. or Sept. A.D. 111); otherwise five days would be an ample allowance.

* *Journal of Hellenic Studies*, 1881, p. 49.

† Sulpicius Severus, *Dial.* i. 4. So twenty-five *mansiones* from Edessa to Jerusalem (*S. Silviæ Aq. Peregrin.* 47); the distance by Antioch is not much under 625 miles.

events at Rome of great importance in the Imperial family became known in Egypt. If the couriers travelled at that rate, important events in Rome, like the proclamation of an Emperor, ought to have been known at Alexandria within twenty days at all seasons of the year; but news seems to have taken three or four times as long, except when it could be carried by ship direct from Italy. We have seen in § iv. a clear case: the accession of Pertinax on 1 January had just become known (probably on the preceding day) to the prefect of Egypt in Alexandria on 6 March A.D. 193, implying a period of sixty-four days spent on the journey.

This may seem to imply a very slow rate of travel for government couriers; and even if we suppose that the prefect in early March A.D. 193 was absent from Alexandria, and had to be summoned, the delay cannot have been more than a day or two. Had the governor been far from Alexandria, he would not have waited till he returned there before issuing his edict. Neglect or delay in celebrating the accession would have been disloyal, and, in the Roman sense, impious. Moreover, another well-attested interval confirms this case. News of the death of Gaius Cæsar at Limyra on the coast of Lycia on 21 February A.D. 4 reached Pisa on 2 April.* If we allow that it reached Rome four days earlier, this would give thirty-six days from Limyra to Rome. News of this tragic event of Imperial importance would not linger on the way; and there seems no reason to think that it would be concealed on arriving in Rome. Doubtless, public mourning was ordered instantly by Augustus.

Moreover, for a long journey such a rate of travelling was sufficiently fatiguing. The couriers, undoubtedly, were soldiers; † only to them could such an important service be entrusted; and doubtless picked men alone were employed. The service must have been planned with a view to be consistent with what can judiciously be expected from good soldiers as a permanent duty. It would appear that a courier carried through to its destination the despatches with which he was entrusted, and that these were not passed from hand to hand. The latter method would have given greater possibility of speed, but the former was more safe and useful. Hence, for example, Tacitus (*Hist.* ii. 73) mentions that the couriers (*speculatores*) from Syria and Palestine gladdened Vitellius by describing how the Eastern legions had taken the oath to him. See Suet. *Aug.* 42.

Chambalu and Friedländer have been misled by some exceptional cases of rapid travelling. A great effort can be made for a few days; but the steady all-the-year-round rate of travelling for the couriers must be estimated on a very different scale. We are not told how many horses were killed in those exceptional rides. We have laid down as the ruling principle of the government courier-service that regularity and certainty were more prized than mere speed; the government desired to know confidently at what date it could be reckoned that instructions would be received and put in effect. The headlong speed of modern government messages had no analogy in ordinary Roman practice, though exceptional characters, like Julius Cæsar and some others, knew the value of speed in critical circumstances, and risked everything to attain it.

The postal service across Asia Minor before the railways were opened may be taken as a fair example of the probable rate per hour: horses were changed frequently; no halts were made except at government offices in the great cities; and the rate of riding was about 5 Roman miles per hour.* Friedländer (p. 22) rightly estimates that the Imperial post travelled at this rate, though he considers that military couriers travelled at exactly double the rate—10 miles per hour (*loc. cit.* p. 24).†

Aristides, on the journey to Rome by the Egnatian Way in A.D. 144, as above described, says he travelled as fast as the Imperial couriers; and this we may confidently take as 5 Roman miles per hour. Similarly, before the railways were opened in Asia Minor, private travellers often rode with the post when they desired to make a rapid journey.

The rate per day of the couriers depends on the number of hours they rode. As to this no certain estimate is possible; but it seems probable that double the ordinary traveller's journey was the distance required daily of the couriers. A faster rate seems inconsistent with the length of time which Imperial news took to reach distant places.

We conclude, then, that 50 Roman miles per day was the post rate for the Imperial couriers. At this rate about fifty-four days would be needed for despatches from Rome to Alexandria, forty-six to Cæsarea (the capital of Palestine), thirty-nine to Syrian Antioch, twenty-four to Byzantium, and seven to Brundisium. But, further, no allowance need be made for halts at the great administrative centres—Cæsarea, Antioch, Ancyra, and Nicomedia (or the Asian capital when that route was followed). The Turkish post used to halt to allow provincial governors to send on despatches to the more distant provinces, and some time must be allowed for preliminary consideration of the despatches which the courier had brought; Imperial couriers, however, carried their despatches, as a rule, from Rome to their destination, waiting for nothing by the way.

But, even if the Imperial couriers may sometimes have made such halts by the way, it is entirely improbable that the news of the death of an Emperor and the accession of his successor would be allowed to linger in such a fashion. Couriers would in such a case surely go straight on to their own destination. They would carry official intimations to the governor of each province, and it was the duty of the governor to circulate the news by special edict. Doubtless, a special courier started from Rome for each different province, and the Alexandrian message was carried direct without any serious halt by the way. Hence it can hardly be supposed that the news of the accession of Pertinax, which took sixty-three or sixty-four days to reach Alexandria, travelled by this route, unless we allowed for a long detention by stress of weather at Brundisium. But in § xii. we shall see that the news in that case probably travelled by a different route.

As we have seen, hurried travellers went as rapidly as the government couriers. Aristides mentions that he did so; and Friedländer (p. 24) quotes the following cases, which all evidently imply journeys of 50 miles per day:—

| | | |
|---|---|---|
| Tarraco to Bilbilis . | 224 miles | —fifth day. |
| Mutina to Rome . | 310 ,, | —sixth day. |
| Rome to Puteoli . | 141 ,, | —third day.‡ |

* Orelli, *Del. Inscr. Latin*, No. 643. Philotimus took 36 days (July 9–Aug. 14) from Rhodes to Brundisium (Cic. *ad Att.* xi. 23; *ad Fam.* xiv. 24; *pro Ligar.* 7).

† They were called *speculatores*: a certain number were attached to each legion. The *speculatores* of the Prætorian guard were closely attached to the Emperor's person, and formed a sort of bodyguard, ready for confidential service at any time. They were, of course, selected men.

* The rate for ordinary travellers on horseback on a long journey is 3¾ or 4 Roman miles per hour; but one finds it quite easy to keep up with the post for a short time, as the writer knows from experience.

† It is not clear why he distinguishes the post rate from that of military couriers. The post was carried by military couriers.

‡ Martial (x. 104) says that the fifth carriage will perhaps bring his correspondent from Tarraco to Bilbilis: he evidently

Still more rapid journeys are mentioned. Julius Cæsar is said to have travelled for eight days from the Rhone to Rome at the rate of 100 miles per day. Couriers carrying urgent news sometimes rode for several days in succession at the rate of 150 miles per day. Friedländer gives 160, but the facts seem to point rather to 150, or six *mansiones.* Icelus carried the news of Nero's death to Galba in seven days or a little less (Plut. *Galb.* 7), presumably going to Tarraco by ship in four days, and thence over 300 miles by land. But such journeys were only performed in stress and need, and afford no standard for ordinary life.

The relation of all these varying rates to the fundamental 25 miles is manifest.

We have made a much more modest estimate of Roman rates of travel than Friedländer. He estimates the foot-traveller's daily journey at 26 or 27 Roman miles, that of the ordinary traveller by carriage at 40 to 50 miles, and that of the courier anywhere from 130 to 160 miles. We regard all these rates as exceptional, and as true even then only for short distances.

The rates which we have found reason to accept as customary may seem slow, but they are probably quite as great as is consistent with the climate and the character of the people. Travel was performed chiefly in the summer season, and there is no doubt that the day's journey began early in the morning, and that a stop was made by noon, after six hours (25 miles); while, in the case of ordinary travellers who were not in a hurry, it is probable that no second journey was begun after the heat of the day was passed.* Couriers and rapid travellers did one stage before noon and a second in the evening, each of five hours, 25 miles. As has been pointed out in art. TYRANNUS in vol. iv. p. 822[b], ordinary people regarded the day's work in summer as finished by the fifth hour, one hour before noon, though active, energetic persons still kept up the older Roman strenuous custom of a distinctly longer day.

Practical experience will show that walking 16 miles or driving 25 miles day after day without intermission, in the hot season, is quite sufficient for the strength of the ordinary man, and that only men of more than average strength and endurance can stand a long course of riding 50 miles per day. We have quoted the testimony of experience as to the rate of walking journeys; and as to carriage travelling, the following may be quoted from a *Times* telegram from the Transvaal about a journey performed in a carriage, with all the careful equipment that can now be commanded, in January 1903: 'Mr. Chamberlain's journey to-day amply testified to his physical strength and powers of endurance. The thirty miles constitute a formidable trek . . . and the sun proved very trying.' On the other hand, in the wet season or the winter a long course of travelling is even more fatiguing, from other reasons. During that period very few travellers except government couriers and carriers of goods would be on the road.

The question might be raised whether during the most temperate months of the year a quicker rate of travelling was required of the post couriers. The evidence at our disposal does not permit a certain reply; but it is most probable that the rate was uniform for the whole year. Every season offers, or may offer, its own special hindrances to rapid travel; and it would be necessary either to have one uniform rate, or to estimate the proper rate for each journey separately according to the weather and circumstances, which would be absurd.

x. THE CENTRAL ROUTE BETWEEN ROME AND THE EAST.—The routes which we have described were those by which goods were sent, and which were, as a rule, employed by travellers contemplating a steady, continuous journey, without halts. Travellers along the land route were indeed able to stop when they pleased, or when it was necessary to do so; but as a rule they undertook the journey for the sake of reaching Italy, and not with any thought of staying in the little civilized and rather inhospitable regions through which the Egnatian Way led. Thessalonica, Philippi, and a few other towns on that part of the road were doubtless much like the ordinary second or third rate cities of the Grecized countries east of the Ægean Sea; but west of Thessalonica the traveller passed into half-barbarous lands, where there was no temptation to stop, though occasionally (as was the case with Aristides through sickness, see p. 384) a halt was unavoidable. On the sea route there was, as we have seen, rarely any opportunity of stopping (except in Crete during a winter detention).

But the route most favoured by those travellers who intended to make halts by the way, whether for business or for pleasure, passed across the Isthmus of Corinth and through Ephesus, the two great business and commercial centres of the Ægean world. This was in many respects the greatest and most typical road to the East, most patronized by tourists and travellers, and by far the most important in the history of early Christianity; for along that road, incomparably more than by any other, travelled and intermingled the thoughts, the inventions, the intercommunication, of the busiest parts of the ancient world. Thus, as we have seen, the sea routes carried Christianity direct to Rome, and did not affect the lands and cities by the way except Crete. The overland route, also, was not very important in the diffusion of Christianity. Philippi and Thessalonica, two early centres of the new religion, were Christianized almost, as it might seem, accidentally, and hardly anything is known with regard to any important development along the road, nor did those two cities play any leading part in early Christian history. But Ephesus and Corinth are critical points in that history, and continued to be centres of activity and development for many centuries.

The great stages on this road were Cæsarea, Syrian Antioch, Tarsus, Cybistra,* Derbe, Iconium, Pisidian Antioch, Apamea, Laodicea, Ephesus, and Corinth or Athens. Each of these was a knot where the roads of a whole district met, and where its trade and intercommunication and education found a centre.

Thus this great artery was the channel in which the life-blood of the Empire mainly flowed. It was not the route along which goods mostly moved, but it was the route of those who directed trade, as well as of thoughts and inventions. Along this road it was St. Paul's early idea to move towards Rome. In his second journey, Ephesus attracted him as the city 'in which the East looked out on the West,' *i.e.* on Rome; † but he was diverted by Divine impulse to Philippi. Again, the last missionary idea which he had in mind before his final imprisonment and condemnation was to winter in Nicopolis (Tit 3[12]), a point on

thinks of five days as the post-distance. The distance is 214 miles in the Antonine Itinerary; but Friedländer gives 224. From Mutina to Rome he gives 317: the Antonine has 313, but even this seems too great (Cic. *ad Fam.* xi. 6. 1; Philost. *Apoll. Tyan.* vii. 41).

* Even in the Republican period it was not thought idle to be ready for the principal meal (after work and exercise and bath were all finished) full four hours before sunset.

* There was a more direct road from Cybistra by Hyde, Savatra, Laodicea Katakekaumene, Philomelium, and Julia, to Apamea (p. 390); but it did not lead through the great cities, and the list of names shows that it did not play such an important part in early Christian life as the longer road.

† See Hort, *Lectures on Ephesians*, p. 813.

the coasting voyage between Corinth and Brundisium.

The route involved a good deal of variety, change of transport and method in travelling. It was partly a sea route, partly a land road. From Syria to Ephesus it was usually a land road (though it was free to the traveller to vary it by using the sea for this part of the journey). Between Ephesus and Corinth the communication was by sea; and again between Corinth and the coast of Italy. Though a land road was possible for a great part of the way in this latter stretch, it was rarely or never employed except for purely local communication, since it traversed barren, mountainous, and sparsely populated, almost barbarous lands, and there were on it no great cities or centres of thought and trade. But the sea way touched several important centres before it reached Italy.

Either of two sea ways to Italy was open from Corinth. Probably the more common was along the coast of Acarnania and Epirus, by Nicopolis, to Brundisium, as described in part in the *Itinerarium Maritimum*, p. 488, and thence by the Appian Way, the 'Queen of Roads,' through Tarentum, Venusia, Beneventum, and Capua to Rome.

But Ostia or Puteoli was sometimes substituted for Brundisium as the Italian harbour in this route. Ælius Aristides travelled by this way from Rome to Miletus and Smyrna, starting in September A.D. 145. Friedländer (p. 28 f.) thinks he reached Miletus in fourteen days from Rome; but this is certainly erroneous, and the interpretation of Aristides's words must be incorrect. Masson reckons the fourteen days from Corinth to Miletus, which is much more probable. This would be a very slow and tedious passage, but not improbable, if winds were unfavourable. Friedländer supposes that Aristides sailed in thirty-six hours from Sicily to Cephallenia, which is incredible;* the steamers of the Messageries Maritimes would take nearly that time for the crossing. The distinguished German scholar has made the mistake of ignoring the halt which (as we have already pointed out) probably took place at Corinth, and perhaps at islands in the Ægean Sea as well as at Miletus. Finally, Aristides says that he did not reach Smyrna until winter had begun, which implies a journey of nearly two months, if not more; for he seems to mean that the bad weather of winter had begun, and it is rare for such weather to begin before the middle of December or even later.

In truth, it is vain to think of reckoning the average time required on this journey. It was not made continuously. Its importance and character arise from the fact that travellers frequented it with the intention of staying at various points on its course, seeing and talking and learning and teaching and transacting private or public business.

These statements should not be taken as involving an assertion that no one ever travelled without halts by this route: there are no universal rules in human conduct. But continuous unhalting travel was not the intention of this route; and even when halts are not actually mentioned, it cannot be assumed in any case without careful consideration that no halts were made. The two great breaks and changes, at Corinth and at Ephesus, required new arrangements at those places, thus caused at least some short delay, and easily led to considerable halts. The traveller from Rome landed at Lechæum, on the Corinthian Gulf, and had to find a new vessel at Cenchreæ for his eastern passage. He naturally waited for some time at so famous a city as Corinth while making the new arrangements. The *diolkos*, or portage of vessels across the Isthmus, could be used only for very small vessels, and cannot be reckoned as a factor in the ordinary travelling system.

This tendency, at a break between voyages, as at Corinth, or at a change from land to sea travel or *vice versâ*, to make a halt which might last for days, is illustrated in St. Paul's journey from Philippi to Jerusalem (Ac 20. 21). Philippi was so near Neapolis that no detention at the harbour need be expected. But at Troas there seems to have been a change of ship with detention of seven days; and at Cæsarea the change to land travelling was accompanied by a detention of some days and the preparation for a journey by road (see below, p. 398[b]). On the other hand, the transhipments at Patara and at Myra (Ac 21[1] 27[5]) seem to have entailed no delay, as in each case the change of ship appears to have been unpremeditated, and due to the opportunity that presented itself of a larger and more convenient sea-going ship. The change at Troas from land to seafaring made it a good centre and starting-point for mission-work, 'a door opened' (2 Co 2[12]).

This discontinuous character of travel on the Central Route to the East shows very clearly—what has been already stated, p. 382, on other grounds—that there was no serious need for a ship canal at Corinth under the Roman Empire, and little prospect of such a canal being any more remunerative than the modern canal is. It would have been disadvantageous to Corinth under the conditions of the Roman Empire that there should be continuous unbroken navigation past its gates. The scheme of Nero and of Herodes Atticus was an archaistic fancy, and not a sound practical scheme resting on a solid commercial basis.

Again, owing to the character of this route, the cities on it grew steadily in importance. Travellers did not pass through them as mere hostelries and stations for a night: they were visitors who stayed for a time, taught and learned, transacted business or performed political and social duties. Corinth, in particular, is mentioned as profiting by these opportunities. It was the half-way house between Italy and Asia. Hence Gaius of Corinth was 'the host of the whole Church' (Ro 16[23]), and Corinthian hospitality is mentioned several times by Clement of Rome in his letter.*

We have described this route only as an Imperial highway, neglecting its local character and noticing only the great stages. It will be described more fully among the inter-provincial routes in the following section.

xi. INTER-PROVINCIAL ROUTES IN THE EAST.—These were, as has been said in § i., only of subordinate consequence in the Imperial time. But, of all inter-provincial routes in the Roman Empire, those in the East were the most frequented and important. The older Greek trade between the Levant and Ægean harbours had not been entirely destroyed; and many hundreds, doubtless, of small vessels were constantly plying along all those coasts from Egypt or even Cyrene round to Corinth. Travellers were always able to find readily a ship to carry them in either direction along the coast. They might not always find one to do exactly what they desired: the first ship

* Aristides, *Or.* 24, p. 305 (ed. Dindorf, vol. i. p. 481). Eastward-bound ships made for Cyllene in Elis, six days from Sicily (Philost. *Apoll. Tyan.* viii. 15. 1; Paus. vi. 26. 3). Friedländer quotes Apollonius's voyage (vii. 10. 1), five days, Corinth to Puteoli; but common men needed longer time.

* Under CORINTH, vol. i. p. 480[b], the *Corinthiaca* of Dion Chrysostom, *Or.* 37, is erroneously referred to: the passage intended is in his *Isthmiaca*, *Or.* 8, pp. 138–139, which speaks of the Greek period, but is true also of the Roman.

might not be going as far as the harbour which they aimed at, and they might have to tranship (Ac 21²) : their ship might omit to visit a harbour where they would have liked to stop, or it might stay several days in a harbour where they had no wish to remain (Ac 20¹⁶).* They would have to accommodate themselves to the course of the ship, and remain close to it even when it was lying at anchor, except when it went into harbour to load or unload, or when it was laid up for the winter (§ vi.).

There were also ships plying between the Euxine harbours and those of the Ægean and the Levant. Diodorus gives the time for vessels between the Sea of Azoff and Alexandria (see § iv.) : such a vessel would run down to Amastris or Sinope, then coast to Rhodes, and thence run direct to Alexandria, if Egypt were its destination ; or to Myra, and thence west of Akamas to the Syrian coast, if such were its aim.†

The land roads connecting the provinces of Asia Minor were fairly developed, because in many cases the same roads that led to Rome also connected the different provinces with one another : Asia Minor is a bridge stretching from east to west, from Asia to Europe ; and the roads that passed across it westward, besides leading to Rome, traversed several provinces and connected their most important cities.

1. The great Trade Route by which the products of Cappadocia were carried to Ephesus was also the direct path from Cappadocia to Rome, and those products were carried to Ephesus as the harbour for the trade with the West: the Trade Route had been developed under the Greek kings, and became even more important under the Roman Empire. It is not to be supposed that all Cappadocian trade with Rome passed through Ephesus. All heavy merchandise would inevitably follow the natural law of seeking the nearest harbour, viz. Tarsus for southern Cappadocia and Amisus for northern Cappadocia. It is noteworthy that the single Cappadocian product which is expressly mentioned as carried to Ephesus by land—red earth used for colouring—would be in small bulk and of light weight (Strabo, p. 623). The Trade Route, which went from Ephesus by Laodicea, Apamea, Julia, Laodicea Katakekaumene to Cæsarea, is fully described in the *Historical Geography of Asia Minor*, chs. iii. iv.

In the east of Cappadocia the old Trade Route was in the time of Trajan, or perhaps already under Vespasian, merged in the military road system for the defence of the Euphrates frontier.‡

2. The Syrian Route coincided with the Trade Route from Ephesus through Tralles, Laodicea, Colossæ, Apamea, etc., as far as Laodicea Katakekaumene. From that city the most direct path kept away along the north edge of the low range of hills called now Boz-Dagh, by Savatra to Hiera Hyde and Kybistra. But general intercourse avoided this path and turned south to Iconium, Derbe, Laranda, and Kybistra.

We may call this route the Syrian, as the Gates through which it issued from Laodicea on the Lycus were called the Syrian Gates.§ It was identical with the Eastern section of the Central Route of the Empire, § x., and coincided in part with the Overland Route, § viii.

An alternative for part of the way kept eastward from Apamea through Apollonia and Pisidian Antioch, Neapolis, and Pappa to Iconium, where it rejoined the other. This is the line that plays most part in the NT. More important cities lay along it ; in practice it seems to have been the most important way.

A modification of this alternative route, made under the Emperor Augustus, was of some importance for a time. That Emperor founded a series of six military *coloniæ*, with Pisidian Antioch as the centre, to control the barely conquered tribes of the northern Taurus (*i.e.* Isauria and Pisidia). These six *coloniæ* were connected by a series of military roads, each of which was called *Via Sebaste*, the Augustan Way.* The road coming from Apamea coincided between Apollonia and Antioch with the Augustan Way coming from the western *coloniæ* ; and again south of Antioch it coincided for a long distance with the Augustan Way that leads to Lystra.

This Augustan Way is mentioned in the *Acts of Paul and Thekla* as τὴν βασιλικὴν ὁδὸν τὴν εἰς Λύστραν φέρουσαν: starting from Antioch it coincided with the other road to a point about 24 miles from Iconium (west of the village Kizil-Euren), where it probably turned south to Lystra : in the story of Thekla, Onesiphorus went out to this point on the Basilike or Augustan Way and waited till Paul should pass.† This line had more importance in a military and official point of view than in practical life.

Another alternative to part of the Syrian Route ran between Ephesus and Pisidian Antioch ; it traversed the higher Phrygian lands,‡ and was useful only for travellers on foot or on horseback. It kept nearly in an easterly line from the one city to the other, ascending the Cayster valley, crossing the high and hilly region where the Cogamis rises, and through which the Mæander breaks in a deep cañon, going through Seiblia and Metropolis, and again crossing a ridge of mountains to reach Antioch. It is mentioned Ac 19¹.

3. An important route led from the harbours of the Propontis and Bosporus, and from Nicomedia and Nicæa, almost due east through Bithynia, Paphlagonia, and Pontus, keeping nearly parallel to the Black Sea coast. It traversed the long valley of the Amnias in Paphlagonia—a valley which is divided both from the sea and from the Central Plateau by two parallel mountain ridges. Many of the campaigns in the history of the Pontic and Bithynian kings were fought along this valley. The road must have played a considerable part in the development of society and religion in those northern provinces under the Roman Empire ; but hardly anything is known on the subject owing to the almost entire loss of evidence.

4. Another very important road from the Propontis and Bosporus harbours and from Nicomedia, ran south through Nicæa to Dorylaion. There was a road-knot at Dorylaion : here met many ways : from Smyrna and Philadelphia on the south-west : from Synnada and the south : from Iconium and Lycaonia : from the Cilician Gates and Cilicia : from Ancyra and the East. The last mentioned way was afterwards the great Byzantine military road, which is very fully described in the *Historical Geography of Asia Minor*, ch. G. The other roads that radiated from Dorylaion also became far more important in later times, when

* The view taken by many scholars, that St. Paul and the delegates chartered a vessel for their own voyage, is probably incorrect. See *St. Paul the Traveller*, p. 295.

† Diodorus, iii. 34.

‡ On these eastern roads, see Anderson in *Journal of Hellenic Studies*, 1897, p. 22 ff.

§ *Cities and Bish. of Phrygia*, i. p. 35.

* In *St. Paul the Traveller*, p. 64, the name is given not quite correctly as the 'Royal Way' : the Greek term was βασιλικὴ ὁδός, which might be rendered rightly so in English : but the Latin name, recently discovered on three milestones, proves that βασιλική here is to be understood as 'belonging to the Emperor,' who was called Βασιλεύς in purer Greek, Σεβαστός in technical and common Greek.

† The line of the Basilike, as given in the map attached to *St. Paul the Traveller*, requires to be corrected near Lystra by recent discoveries : the difference does not affect the argument or any other opinions in the book.

‡ *i.e.* High or Central Phrygia, see vol. iii. pp. 865ª, 867ª.

Nicomedia first, and Constantinople afterwards, were successively capitals of the Roman world, and when the roads that connected the various districts of Asia Minor with the capitals acquired immensely greater consequence. But of them all only the road from Smyrna to Dorylaion was of considerable importance in Roman times, as it connected Bithynia with the two leading cities of Asia—Smyrna and Ephesus. It passed through Philadelphia, and coincided for a long distance with the road Philadelphia–Julia (see above, § viii.).

The road from the south to Dorylaion was evidently the one along which St. Paul travelled when he had been forbidden to preach in Asia (Ac 16[6]). He turned away north towards Bithynia, intending to preach in the great Greek cities of that province, Nicæa and Nicomedia. But when he came nearer the frontier, probably at Dorylaion, he was forbidden to enter that province; and he then turned towards the west, keeping near the frontier, perhaps in the hope that he might be permitted to enter at another point. He was, however, impelled onwards towards the sea, until at last he came out on the Ægean coast at Troas. A possible memory of this journey is preserved in local tradition near the spot where he must have crossed the river.*

5. A road of considerable importance in Roman times connected Perga, the capital of Pamphylia, with Ephesus and the Asian cities. It crosses the Taurus at a low elevation, and comes down on the Lycus valley: there is no difficulty in the path, which is marked out by nature. According to some recent theories, St. Paul was thinking of making his way to Ephesus already on his first journey from Perga (Ac 13[14]); but if Ephesus had been his aim, he would have taken the easy, natural, and frequented road which trade and intercourse ordinarily followed. Instead of doing so, he crossed Taurus by a very difficult path, which can never at any time have been of any importance, and which had no object except to permit occasional communication between the districts of Perga and of Pisidian Antioch: it seems beyond doubt that a person who went by this way as far as Antioch had as his aim simply to reach that city.

xii. Other Routes.—Of the many other important roads of the Empire, few played any part in the early history of Christianity, at least so far as the New Testament is concerned.

1. The road round the north of the Adriatic Sea, from Rome by the Flaminian Way, about 210 miles, to Ariminum, and thence through Ravenna, Altinum (by ship), and Aquileia, led to Mœsia, Dacia, and the regions of the Middle and Lower Danube generally, and on to Thrace and Constantinople.

This road was of growing importance in later times, as the countries through which it passed increased in civilization. It was of little importance in NT times, and was valueless as a through route for communication with the East because it traversed the still purely barbarian country of Thrace, which was formed into a procuratorial province† by Claudius in B.C. 46. Only under Trajan was Thrace constituted as a fully organized province of the Empire. From that time onwards the route which we are describing possessed some considerable importance, not merely as a connexion with many great and improving provinces, but also as an alternative, purely overland road, ultimately the Imperial post-road, to the East.

This route crossed the delta of the Padus by ship from Ravenna to Altinum; but the purely land road went round by Bononia (Bologna) along the Æmilian Way, then north to Verona, and east to Aquileia. By the latter way the distances were (according to the Itineraries)—

| | | |
|---|---|---|
| Rome to Verona 370, and to Aquileia | 520 | miles |
| Thence to Sirmium (Lower Pannonia) | 400 | ,, |
| ,, ,, Sardica (Thrace) . . | 311 | ,, |
| ,, ,, Constantinople . . | 349 | ,, |
| Total: Rome to Constantinople . | 1580 | ,, |
| Rome to Alexandria . . . | 3130 | ,, |
| Courier's time, Rome to Alexandria . . . . . . | 63 | days |
| Rome to Cæsarea in Palestine . | 2680 | miles |
| Courier's time, Rome to Cæsarea . | 54 | days |

But if we suppose that a courier went direct from Ariminum by Ravenna, thence by ship to Altinum, and thence riding to Aquileia,* and that he took even one or two days on ship and other two days for the land journey to Aquileia, 95 miles, he would save two or three days.

These results seem to show clearly that this was the road by which the news of the accession of Pertinax travelled from Rome to Alexandria: the messenger, starting on 1 Jan. A.D. 193, arrived only about the sixty-third or sixty-fourth day in Alexandria. If so, it would follow that this route was established as the regular official path to the East before the end of the 2nd cent., and after the time of Trajan.

The reason for the change of route was doubtless twofold. The northerly route was far the most important: it passed through many great military centres and the capitals of several provinces, while it communicated with the capitals of several others which lay off the line of the road. Moreover, the long and sometimes stormy crossing of the Adriatic Sea was avoided by the northern route, which necessitated no voyage except the short and always easy passage of the Bosporus. Thus we can imagine that the northern road developed more and more at the expense of the road through Brundisium. It may be asked whether the latter road would not be kept in use during the more temperate seasons of the year, even if the sea-crossing was avoided in the most stormy months. That may have been so: for the accession of Pertinax, the most conclusive case known to us, falls in January, the stormiest month of the year. But it is perhaps more probable that when the northern route was established it superseded the other: it was for many reasons convenient to have permanent and unvarying conditions of travel: moreover, at least during the decay that characterized the administration of the 3rd cent., it is unlikely that more than one route was maintained permanently with a full working postal establishment.

2. The country of the Upper Danube, Rhætia, etc., was approached by the Augustan Way over the Brenner Pass (*viâ* Claudia Augusta).

3. Gaul and its adjuncts and tyrants, the two provinces of the Rhine frontier, Lower and Upper Germany, were approached by several roads: (*a*) The Flaminian Way to Ariminum, and the Æmilian Way to Placentia, continued to Milan and the Alps, and across the Cottian Alps (Mont Genevre) to Arles (Arelate), or the Graian Alps (Little St. Bernard) to Vienna, Lugdunum, and Augusta Remorum (Rheims). The distance from Rome to the Rhone was not much short of 800 Roman miles, and was said to have been traversed by Julius Cæsar in eight days. The distance to Rheims is given as 1170 miles in the Antonine Itinerary, by a very circuitous route.

(*b*) The Aurelian Way led along the coast of Italy, Liguria, and Gaul to Massilia (Marseilles) and Arelate.

(*c*) The Cassian or the Clodian Way led to Florence, and thence it joined the Aurelian Way

* See Mysia, vol. iii. † See above, p. 384[a].

* *Anton. Itiner.* p. 126.

or else went across the Apennines to join the Æmilian Way at Bononia. This route had only local importance, and was then merged in the preceding.

4. Spain, which St. Paul hoped to visit from Rome (Ro 15[24]), might be reached either by sea to Tarraco, or by the roads to South Gaul, which were continued across the Rhone through Narbo and over the eastern end of the Pyrenees to Tarraco, and thence by the Via Claudia Augusta to Valentia, Cordova, and Cadiz. News of the battle of Munda (not far from Cordova) is said to have been brought to Rome in thirty-five days, which is at the rate of about 50 miles a day; while Julius Cæsar reached Rome from Obulco (35 miles from Cordova) within twenty-seven days. The distance from Cordova to Rome was about 1700 miles.

5. The route to Britain went on from Lugdunum by the valley of the Saone (Arar), by Soissons and Rheims to Amiens and Boulogne, where the channel was crossed to Rutupiæ (Richborough). The distance from Rome to Bononia was about 1250 miles by the shortest route through Helvetia. Letters from Britain reached Cicero in twenty-three, or twenty-seven, or twenty-nine days:* there can be little doubt that all were carried by special military couriers, who came bearing Cæsar's despatches.

6. Africa was reached either by sea from Ostia or Portus, or by land and sea combined. The direct voyage in very favourable circumstances was made in three days; but this can only have been a rare and exceptional passage. Pliny's statement, that Africa could be reached on the second day, must be set aside as very doubtful. The land route followed the Appian Way to Capua, and thence the Popilian Way, keeping near the coast, to Rhegium, about 450 miles from Rome; thereafter it traversed Sicily from Messana to Lilybæum, and crossed the narrow seas to Africa. The total land journey was about 650 miles. A letter from Africa reached Rome in one case in twenty-two days:† doubtless it travelled either by the land route or by a coasting voyage.

II. *THE GENERAL EQUIPMENT OF THE ROMAN ROAD SYSTEM.*—i. MAINTENANCE, REPAIRS, AND SAFETY.—While the maintenance of the great roads in Italy was entrusted to special officials of prætorian or even of consular rank,‡ the care of the roads in the provinces was part of the duty of the provincial governors. At important points, and especially at knots in the road system, permanent military guards in special guard-houses were stationed. These *stationes* were charged not merely with the care of the roads, but still more with the keeping of them safe from robbers or brigands, and in general with the safety of the public in the region around. In the more important *stationes*, at least, the commander was a centurion *regionarius*. A soldier in such a *statio* was called *stationarius*.§ On the subject, see O. Hirschfeld in *Berl. Sitzungsber.* 1891, p. 864 f.; Mommsen, *Strafrecht*, p. 307 ff., esp. p. 312; Domaszewski, *Röm. Mittheil. Instit.* 1902, p. 330 ff.

Thus the charge of the roads was closely connected with the maintenance of peace and order in the districts served by the roads; and there grew up in the later time a tendency to name some districts of Italy according to the great road which connected them with Rome.

* Cicero, *ad Q. frat.* iii. 1. 13; 17. 25; *ad Att.* iv. 17. 3.
† Cicero, *ad Fam.* xii. 25. 1.
‡ Curators of the greatest roads, sometimes *consulares*.
§ The name *statio* was used widely in military service; but *stationarius* was practically restricted to *stationes* for police duty and public safety, and the use of the word belongs to a later period than the NT.

But, in spite of these attempts to keep the peace along the roads, there was a considerable amount of insecurity. The inscriptions often mention guards or travellers slain by robbers.* Juvenal speaks of the brigands of the Campanian roads, who when actively pursued in their usual haunts find it the safest course to take refuge in Rome itself (*Sat.* iii. 305 f.). The case described in Lk 10[30] was no uncommon one. St. Paul's 'perils of robbers' (2 Co 11[26]) were very real: it was especially in journeys through mountainous districts, where roads were not carefully guarded, that he had experienced those dangers, as Ac 13[14. 51] 14[24] 16[8]; but there was sometimes danger on the most frequented roads. Poorer travellers were those who suffered most, as was natural; the rich had large trains: important persons were granted an escort in some cases, *e.g.* Lucian was escorted by two soldiers through Cappadocia (*Alex.* 55).

The Roman roads were probably at their best during the 1st cent., after Augustus had put an end to war and disorder. In the troublous period at the close of Nero's reign, disorder crept in again; and it is doubtful if the Flavian rule ever succeeded in repressing it so completely as Augustus had done. Thus St. Paul travelled in the best and safest period, and yet the roads even then were in some places far from safe (though probably this was only in exceptional parts). In the decay of the Empire and the general relaxation of order during civil wars and during the growing weakness of administration in the 3rd cent., travelling was much less secure. On the whole subject see Friedländer, p. 46 ff.; O. Hirschfeld, 'die Sicherheitspolizei im röm. Reich' (*Berl. Sitzungsber.* 1891, p. 845 ff.), 'die aegypt. Polizei der röm. Kaiserzeit' (*ib.* 1892, p. 815 ff.).

The Roman roads only traversed properly organized provinces, and not either foreign countries or territory not yet administered on thorough Roman principles, such as Cappadocia. That province occupied a peculiar position in the Roman Empire, as we have described it above, § viii. In the Pauline time, therefore, there was no Roman road leading across it from Ancyra to the Cilician Gates. That road could not have been made before A.D. 74, when Vespasian made Cappadocia into a fully organized province.

There was one remarkable exception to this general rule. The road from Derbe to Tarsus led almost entirely through non-Roman territory (governed in St. Paul's time by Antiochus IV.). Yet that road had been necessary for Roman communication with the province Cilicia ever since that province was organized in B.C. 104. The precise authority which Rome exercised along the road, and the relation between Roman and regal power over it, are wholly obscure. It was impossible to leave a road, along which Roman officials and couriers were frequently obliged to travel in the exercise of their duties, entirely under non-Roman authority; and yet it seems practically certain that Rome did not exercise authority over the cities on the course of the road before the time of Vespasian. It is in accordance with this anomalous position of affairs that no reference is made in Acts to that part of the road: it is wholly dropped out of sight, and the author speaks as if St. Paul passed directly from Cilicia into the Roman territory of Galatia at Derbe. St. Paul and his historian were thoroughly penetrated by the Roman spirit, and simply ignored non-Roman, *i.e.* non-provincial, territory.

ii. CONSTRUCTION, MEASUREMENTS, MILESTONES.—As to the construction of the Roman

* *CIL* ii. 2968, 3479, iii. 2399, 2544; *Cities and Bish. of Phr.* i. p. 328, No. 133; Sterrett, *Epigr. Journey*, No. 156; Boissier, *Inscr. de Lyon*, 478, iv. etc.

roads, it is unnecessary to speak here. The manner and measure varied greatly; and in the East it is not probable that the roads were built on the same massive scale as the Appian Way. Ten feet seems to have been a common breadth. The road through the long pass over Taurus, which leads from Tarsus to Tyana and to Kybistra, and which was built in a very costly and grand style, was 10 feet broad; but this breadth was required to be entirely serviceable; and where the road was cut through solid rock, the distance left between the rock walls seems to have been always fully 13 or 14 feet. The road across Taurus from Laranda to Olba and Korykos seems to have been narrower: it remains in a fairly complete condition about one to five miles from Korykos. But, again, some miles south of Ancyra, near Gorbeous, the Pilgrims' Route seems to have been very much broader.

Milestones are frequently found in groups of three or four, new stones having been erected when repairs were made. But the later Emperors, especially those of the 4th cent., were usually satisfied with the substitution of their names for those of some earlier Emperors on an old milestone: this may be classed along with many other examples of slovenliness and carelessness during the degradation of the Empire. After the 4th century hardly any milestones are known—one of many proofs that the Byzantine government had greatly degenerated from the thoroughness of method that characterized the Roman Empire.

iii. INNS AND ENTERTAINMENT.—Inns, taverns, and places of refreshment certainly existed in numbers along the great roads. Little is known about them, and the little that is known gives no favourable picture of them. Aristides complains of their half-ruinous condition, with leaky ceilings and general discomfort and disagreeable conduct on the part of the owners, on the road from Neapolis to Dyrrachium. His account suggests that he found the inns on this road poorer than those to which he was accustomed in Asia. To judge from all that is mentioned,—though one must not press too closely the complaint of travellers,—in the less civilized countries they were, as a rule, dirty, ill kept, and badly managed by churlish and ignorant hosts.* Hence wealthier travellers carried their own equipment, and the hospitality of private houses was much sought after.

On the other hand, in the Eastern provinces inns seem to have been much superior and far more numerous: competition raised the standard of equipment (as Plutarch says, *de vit. Pud.* 8, p. 532), and the art of innkeeping was very ancient in the province of Asia.† Epictetus, who originated from Hierapolis in the Lycus valley, speaks of the traveller being tempted to linger long in a splendid hotel.‡ The *Panhormus* which is mentioned near the summit of the road above the narrow pass of the Cilician Gates, must have been at least a large establishment, though probably more of the nature of a khan (in which only room, but no furniture,§ was supplied) than of a hotel; but at least there can be no doubt that food was supplied, whereas in modern khans nothing but coffee can be procured by the traveller. The present reason for this defect, viz. want of capital or of trading instinct, did not exist in Roman times; but it is mentioned in earlier Greek times, when the land was poorer (Plutarch, *Apophth. Lacon. var.* 44).

The fact that Aristides, travelling in Asia between Smyrna and Pergamus,* went to an inn before going to a friend's house, which Friedländer rightly notes, may serve as an indication of the superior character of inns in that province, though it must be remembered that he was travelling by night (*Or.* 27, p. 347 ff.). His discontent with the inns in Macedonia on the Egnatian Way shows probably that he was used to better accommodation in Asia (see above, § viii.).

Imperial officials, judges, soldiers on the march, and even municipal magistrates,† had the right to free quarters in the towns through which they passed. They were billeted on residents (though physicians and teachers of grammar, philosophy, and rhetoric were exempted by Vespasian). The behaviour of many of those who enjoyed the right of free quarters was rude and oppressive; and Plutarch (*Cat.* 12), in describing the modest and courteous behaviour of the younger Cato in this respect, shows by contrast what was done by others. Towns might avoid the burden by erecting a public house of entertainment,‡ as is stated in the inscription published by Waddington, *Inscr. de la Syrie*, No. 2524, on which see the remarks of Domaszewski in *Mittheil. des Instit. Röm.* 1902, p. 333. Such oppressive conduct was frequent, in spite of all attempts to repress it.§ Trajan wrote about it to Pliny (*Epist.* 77). Provincial governors were charged by the general *mandata* of the Emperor to prevent it.‖

Inns, taverns, or houses of better class for the entertainment of high officials (*prætoria*) were often erected by municipalities: see *CIL* iii. 6123. Friedländer, p. 41, quotes Man in *Bull. d. Instit.* 1882, p. 116 (but it may be a private *hospitium* or inn).

In one respect, however, the ancient inns were almost universally bad. They were little removed in character from houses of ill-fame; and such are sure (like their owners) to degenerate in general character. The profession of innkeepers was dishonourable, and their infamous character is often noted in Roman laws.¶

The story of the birth of St. Theodore of Sykea bears witness to an equally depraved condition of things in the 6th cent. after Christ; and in the Middle Ages the pilgrims to Jerusalem saw no improvement, and found that a decent stranger, if his ship were lying in harbour, would be wise to return to it at night rather than stay in an inn. In ancient writers allusion is often made to the way in which hosts and hostesses tried to induce travellers to enter their inns, also to their cheating and shamelessness. Finally, hostesses were often said to practise witchcraft.

The bad character of the inns imparts new meaning and stronger emphasis to the repeated and emphatic references made in early Christian literature to the duty of hospitality.** It was not necessary to recommend this virtue because it was neglected in the society of that period, as, *e.g.*, purity and various other virtues are urgently pressed on the attention of the early Christians,

* Sidonius Apoll. *Epist.* viii. 11. 3; Pliny, *Hist. Nat.* ix. 154, xvi. 158; Script. Hist. Aug. *Hadr.* 16; Plutarch, *de San. Præc.* 16, p. 130; Dioscor. *de Ven.* ii. præf., ed. Sprengel, ii. p. 5. All are quoted by Friedländer. See above, p. 384.

† On its antiquity, the writer's *Cities and Bish. of Phrygia*, ii. p. 416 n., may be consulted.

‡ *Diss.* ii. 23. 36.

§ Not much furnishing, of course, is needed, or would be comfortable, in warm countries.

* This journey is very fully discussed in *Journ. of Hell. Stud.* 1881, p. 48 ff.

† Pliny, *Nat. Hist.* ix. 26, *Epist.* ix. 33. 10.

‡ Pliny, *Epist.* viii. 8. 6.

§ It was called διασεισμός, διασείειν, Lk. 3[14] (addressed to the soldiers on duty at an Imperial estate, probably near Jericho, who in later times would have been called *stationarii*, see Domaszewski, *loc. cit.*); *CIL* iii. 12336, 14191; *Pap. Oxyrynch.* ii. 240, 284, 285.

‖ *CIL* iii. 14191 (Appia in Phrygia), 12336 (Skaptopara in Thrace).

¶ Ulpian, *Dig.* iii. 2. 4. 2; xxiii. 2. 43. 1 and 9; *Cod.* iv. 56. 3; Tertullian, *de Fuga in Persecut.* 13; see also Marquardt, *Privatl.* p. 471, n. 5.

** See, *e.g.*, Ro 12[13], 1 Ti 3[2], Tit 1[8], 1 P 4[9], He 13[2]; Clem. Rom. *ad Cor.* i. 10–12. 35.

because ordinary society lacked them and cared not for them. On the contrary, hospitality was in all probability generally and regularly practised in pagan society. Nor was hospitality recommended merely on the general ground that it is a good thing: the advice and exhortations in early Christian literature are always given with a clear reference to the actual position and failings and interests of the people concerned. The reason for recommending it lies in the needs of the Christian travellers: they ought not to be left to the corrupt and nauseous surroundings of the inns kept by persons of the worst class in existing society. Gaius of Corinth, that meeting-place of nations, was remembered by Paul as the host of himself and of the whole Church (Ro $16^{23}$).

The reference in Lk $10^{35}$ opens up the question of the expense of inns. The Samaritan there pays two denarii, about two francs, for the expense incurred at an inn for two persons for one night; he can hardly have intended this to cover part of any future expense, as the wounded person needed further care; for he promised to pay any expenditure beyond that amount, and it is not clear that there was any surplus after paying the night's expenses. The pay of a private in the Roman legions during the 1st cent. was a little over half a denarius per day, of a prætorian apparently two denarii; but the soldiers were discontented and mutinied, claiming a full denarius of daily pay (Tacitus, *Annals*, i. 17 and 26). Perhaps the action of the Samaritan was only a liberal payment of the bill already incurred, with a promise to pay any further expenses.

iv. CUSTOMS, ROAD-TAXES OR TOLLS, AND FRONTIER DUTIES.—Among the incidents of travel, custom-house examinations did not fail. Personal effects were free from duty; but merchandise of every kind was liable to a duty, sometimes by tariff, generally *ad valorem*, at the frontier of each of the provinces. Duties collected from travellers to pay for the maintenance of roads may be summed up along with the customs duties: there is not enough of evidence about them, but their existence seems certain.

Attempts to defraud the customs officers were numerous and varied: *mille artibus circumscribimur*, says the advocate of the customs officials in Quintilian, *Declam.* 341. The result necessarily was greater strictness on the part of the officers: the law gave them the right of searching the luggage and the person of all travellers (except that personal search of matrons was forbidden):* they sometimes disturbed and turned over personal luggage in the search for contraband articles.†

Officials, soldiers, and certain distinguished persons, by special favour of the Emperor, travelled duty-free, and safe from such troublesome examination (ἀτέλεια).

The customs duties (*portoria*) formed a most important item in the revenues of the Roman State, and their regular and complete exaction was a matter of the utmost moment.‡ They were levied at the frontier stations in the nearest cities, which all bore the title *portus*, λιμήν, whether they were maritime towns or frontier towns on the great land roads. Hence, *e.g.*, Derbe, which was a frontier town of the province Galatia, is called λιμήν by Stephanus Byzantinus.§

Only in the case of the province Achaia was there an exception perhaps made. Dessau (*Hermes*, xix. p. 532) expresses the opinion that the Romans exacted no customs duties in that province during the Imperial period, and thinks that Athens collected customs in the harbour of Piræus for its own benefit at that time, according to an inscription of Piræus (published in *Philologus*, 1870, vol. xxix. p. 694). If he is right, there were no customs duties in the great harbour of Corinth (except in so far as that city was permitted to charge for its own advantage); and this freedom would greatly encourage the passage of intercourse through the city.

The duties payable at the frontier varied widely in amount. In Sicily, in all the provinces of Illyricum,* perhaps in Africa, the charge was five per cent. all round, in Gaul and in Asia two and a half per cent. In Syria it was levied by tariff (*πινάκιον*), varying for different wares and products, and reckoned according to a formal statement or invoice (*professio*, ἀπογραφή): the tariff system is known to have existed at the great Euphrates-bridge, Zeugma, and at Palmyra,† and may therefore be supposed general for the whole of Syria.

v. THE TELONAI IN THE GOSPELS.—With regard to the tax-gatherers, or 'publicans,' *τελῶναι*, mentioned in the Gospels, there are some incorrect views which have obtained practically universal acceptance in books relating to the NT. (1) The *telonai* are usually described by modern authorities as if they were identical with, or agents of, the *publicani*—those great financial corporations which in the Republican period had farmed the revenues of entire provinces: in fact, the current translation, 'publicans,' bears witness to the almost universal acceptance of this mistake. (2) The *telonai* are also described by modern writers generally as being collectors of customs duties, and it is regularly pointed out that Capernaum and Jericho were near the frontier‡ (Lk $5^{27}$ $19^{1,2}$, Mk $2^{14}$ etc.). But it is impossible to suppose that mere custom-house officers on the frontiers could be either so numerous or the object of such bitter and fanatical hatred as were those *telonai*. To see the falseness of the current view, and the true nature of the *telonai*, it is necessary to recapitulate briefly the history of the recent Roman practice in Palestine, and we accept the views stated by Rostowzew.§

In B.C. 57 Gabinius reorganized Judæa. He did not (as many authorities have supposed) make it a part of Syria or treat it as a province: this is proved with great probability by Unger.‖ Gabinius introduced a partial autonomy, dividing Palestine into five parts, each with a capital city and an

* See the case of the lady who hid 400 pearls in her bosom, Quintilian, *Declam.* 359.

† References in Freidländer, p. 46, n. 1.

‡ 'The frontier duties (*portoria*) formed the principal part of the State Revenue' (Rostowzew, 'Gesch. der Staatspacht in der röm. Kaiserzeit,' *Philol. Suppl.* ix. p. 409).

§ See DERBE, vol. i. p. 595; GALATIA, ii. p. 87a; LYCAONIA, iii. p. 175b. This important fact about Derbe remains entirely disregarded by writers on the subject; and λιμην is commonly altered to λίμνη.

* The character of the Illyrian system during the first century is unknown. From the time of Hadrian onwards the eight provinces Rhætia, Noricum, two of Pannonia, two of Mœsia, Dacia, Dalmatia, were organized for this purpose as a single governmental district, though dues were levied at the frontier of each district, as in Africa dues were levied probably at the frontiers of the four districts into which the province was divided (Rostowzew, pp. 393, 402): *quattuor publica prov. Africæ* was the full title of the African customs.

† Fronto, *Princ. Hist.* 209 (Naber); Philostr. *Vit. Apoll. Tyan.* i. 18: on Palmyra, see the important inscr. of A.D. 137, Dessau, *Hermes*, xix. 486 ff., 526 ff.: Rostowzew, p. 405 (Reckendorf, *Zft. d. d. morgenl. Gesellsch.* 1888, p. 370 ff., gives both Greek and Aramaic texts). Schürer, *Gesch. d. jüd. Volkes*3, i. p. 475, wrongly supposes that Palmyra collected the tax for its own benefit, following Dessau, *loc. cit.*; Rostowzew shows that it acted on behalf of the fiscus, and was assisted or watched by Imperial officials.

‡ It is, however, by no means clear that Capernaum was the frontier city on the road, though it was not far from the frontier. Jericho was at the frontier between procuratorial Judæa and Herod Antipas's Peræa. Rostowzew (p. 481) makes some not quite accurate geographical statements on this point.

§ 'Gesch. der Staatspacht,' u.s.w., p. 475 ff.

‖ See his paper on Josephus IV. in *Sitzungsber. Bayer. Akad.* 1897, i. 189 ff.; Rostowzew, p. 476.

aristocratic *synhedrion* to administer the government. But a direct tax, *stipendium*, instituted by Pompey in B.C. 63, was paid by each part.* For taxation Palestine was treated along with Syria, the collection of the taxes in both being contracted for by one society of *publicani*. The *publicani* made their arrangements with the five *synhedria*, and the five capitals formed so many centres of administration and collection of the *stipendium* for and by the *publicani*.

Julius Cæsar restored the single government with the capital and centre at Jerusalem (Mommsen, *Provinces*, ii. p. 175). With this was united a remodelling of the regulations regarding the *stipendium*. The tax, at first, had to be paid in Zidon (as the central office of the company of *publicani*, doubtless); † but, after a year or two had elapsed, the control of the *publicani* was abolished, so far as concerned Palestine, and the ethnarch was made solely responsible for the levying of the tax and the payment of it to the Roman government. ‡ The autonomy of Judæa was thus restored very completely, except for the payment of a *stipendium*, but the tax was collected by the ruler of the nation in native fashion. Hence the census of Syria (according to Lk 2[1]), which began in B.C. 8, was probably conducted by Herod over Palestine according to the Jewish tribal divisions (Ramsay, *Was Christ Born in Bethlehem?* ch. viii.).

This financial system lasted till A.D. 6, when Quirinius, in his second governorship of Syria, made Judæa a province, and subordinated it to Syria. It is quite obvious that the system of *publicani* was not then reintroduced. The census which Quirinius made shows that the Roman State retained the tax under its own control; whereas the previous *census* between 8 and 6 B.C. had evidently been made in Palestine according to native methods, because the taxation was levied by such methods.

Perhaps collection of taxes by the Roman State was now introduced, and the division of Judæa into eleven *toparchiai* must have probably been intended to facilitate this: these had their *metropoleis* and *komai*, and were probably not divided into *poleis* on the Greek system.

Many taxes were paid in the province Judæa—a heavy poll-tax, customs duties payable at the frontiers, road-tax on those who used the roads, land-tax, and many others. § The system was probably much the same as in the Seleucid times.

The so-called 'publicans,' τελῶναι in NT, were the agents in collecting these taxes. It is obvious that these 'publicans' have no connexion with or relation to the old *publicani* of the Roman Republic. Those old *publicani* had been financiers on a vast scale, who farmed the taxes of an entire province, paid a lump sum to the Roman State, collected the taxes by their own staff of agents, and made large profits out of the revenue which they collected. Their staff was a highly trained band of clerks and agents, consisting chiefly of their slaves and freedmen, who were familiar with the work of tax-collecting, ready to be employed in any province farmed by the financial company, almost always foreigners and not natives of the province where they were stationed. But the *telonai* of the NT were Jews, who prayed in the temple, and with whom Jesus and His disciples sat at meat. They were contractors or farmers on a small scale: they arranged for the collecting of one tax in one town or small district. Their precise relation to the Roman government and their method of remuneration is not attested, but Rostowzew regards it as practically certain that they did not pay down a lump sum by contract and retain all that they could collect over that amount, and he suggests that they perhaps may have been paid through a percentage on the amount collected.

Hence the *telonai* in a town were very numerous (Lk 5[27-30], Mk 2[16. 17], Lk 19[1ff.], Mt 9[9ff.]). Each had his own office, where he sat, where he collected his own special tax alone or with others, for associations or companies of *telonai* sometimes united to make the contract. Those *telonai* were persons of some property, as is quite distinctly implied in the Gospels (cf. also Josephus, *BJ* II. 14. 4 [Niese, § 287]). They were permitted by law to collect only a certain fixed duty according to law or tariff, though there were many instances in which they illegally collected more than the proper amount; see Lk 3[12. 13]. They had no right of exacting arrears, but could merely denounce and accuse defaulters before the officers of the State (συκοφαντεῖν, Lk 19[8]; Rostowzew, p. 343 f.): their powers, therefore, fell far short of those exercised by the old Republican *publicani* and their agents. These *telonai* were evidently all natives of the country; and the fiscal system was practically the same as in Roman Egypt, a slightly modified continuation by Augustus of the Hellenistic system, which utilized the native population as collectors.

The change which Julius Cæsar in B.C. 47–44 introduced, and which Augustus in A.D. 6 confirmed, in abolishing the sway of the *publicani* in Judæa,* was only part of the general change introduced gradually in the Empire. The exactions and tyranny of the *publicani* had been the greatest evil of Republican Roman government in the provinces. The Emperors gradually increased the activity of the government, narrowly watched the conduct of the *publicani*, reduced their gains, collected the new Imperial taxes (such as that on inheritances) without their aid, and finally abolished them entirely, as Rostowzew has shown with admirable skill in the dissertation from which we have so frequently quoted. The collection of customs duties (*portoria*) was the sphere in which the *publicani* had persisted longest, because in that department, through their immense staffs of trained agents, they had a great advantage; but even there they were superseded, at latest in the 2nd cent., in Judæa already by the arrangements of Julius Cæsar. The Imperial government rarely substituted direct collection by its own officials and staff; sometimes it employed the cities, *e.g.* Palmyra, as above pointed out, but generally it used a large staff of small farmers of revenue, who collected each one tax in a small district, and who were carefully superintended by Imperial officials, to whom they had to refer all doubtful cases.

In the Republican period the *publicani* had been, of course, subject to the jurisdiction of the proconsul or other governor of the province. But their situation, subject to the governor of a year,—who had no knowledge from his previous training of the facts and methods of tax-collecting, and was therefore quite unable to understand the real character of many of the complicated questions

* This *stipendium*, an unusual kind of tax in the Roman State, was probably imitated from the Seleucid custom in Syria.

† This, of course, implies that the tax in Palestine was collected, not by agents of the *publicani* but by the government of the land of Judæa, which in turn paid it to the *publicani*. This avoided the worst evils.

‡ Mommsen and others suppose that Judæa was freed from the tax by Cæsar, and that the edicts on the subject (Josephus, *Ant. Jud.* XIV. v. 6) refer only to Joppa. Niese in *Hermes*, xi. 435, and Viereck, *Sermo Græcus*, p. 100, show that the text of Josephus must not be tampered with (as Mommsen has to do). Appian mentions Herod among the kings who paid tribute.

§ Goldschmid, 'Les Impôts et Droits de Douane en Judée sous les Rom.' (*Rev. d. Ét. Juives*, 1897, p. 192 ff.); also Ruggiero, *Diz. Epigraph.* iii. p. 126; Wilcken, *Griech. Ostraka*, i. 247.

* Schürer does not admit this, *Gesch. d. jüd. Volkes*[3], i. p. 478; and sets aside Wieseler, *Beitr. z. richt. Würdigung d. Evangelien*, 1869, p. 78 f., who had seen rightly.

connected with the vast business-organization, whose correct working he was supposed to keep an eye upon,—was very different from the situation of the contractors under the Empire, who were watched over by an Imperial procurator, trained to the duty, selected by the Emperor, as a rule, on account of his familiarity with the duty, remaining for years in the same office, and commanding all the collected information that was stored up in the Imperial bureau. It was necessary under the Empire for the contractors to be very much more careful, when the regular methods of overseeing had gradually established fixed and minute rules of procedure, than under the Republican régime when there were only vague and general principles laid down as to tne conduct of the collectors, and it was rarely difficult, and usually extremely easy, to hoodwink even a just and strict governor. The *publicani* of the Republic had been the masters, tyrants, and scourges of the provinces, able to seize, torture, and ill-treat as they pleased any provincial whom they declared to be in arrears—permitted by the governors of provinces (who were almost all ignorant and either feeble or corrupt) to exact what they wanted in any way they pleased—gaining great wealth with little or no responsibility in practice. The tax-contractors (*telonai*) of the Imperial time, or even the *publicani* where they continued in that period to exist, were far more closely and efficiently superseded: the amount which they could collect legally was much better known through the tariff: the *telonai* had not such a direct interest (though they had some interest) in collecting too much, and had no power to collect arrears at all, but could merely denounce the defaulter to the proper Imperial officials. It is probably the case that, if a *telones* failed to prove his case against a defaulter, he had to forfeit a penalty (possibly fourfold the sum claimed, for Zacchæus's obscure and unexplained statement in Lk 19[8] was perhaps founded on legal usage).*

The *telonai* collected taxes paid in money, not tithes or other dues paid in kind. The Jews regarded it as a fundamental principle of their religion that they should pay no money except to the temple and the priests. But the *telonai*, exacting the many various kinds of taxes, intruded unpleasantly into the life of the people at every turn, and were a constant reminder of their subjection. Moreover, the fact that they were Jews, who made themselves the agents of the oppressor, and acquired money by exacting it from their own brethren, made them even more despised than if they had been Romans or slaves of Romans, like the agents of the old *publicani*.

So far as we can judge from the Gospels, the method of tax-collecting was, generally speaking, the same in the procuratorial province of Palestine and in Herod Antipas's kingdom of Galilee and Peræa. Small contractors for a single tax in a district performed the work of collecting both in the province and in the kingdom. The superintendence of these contractors lay with the supreme taxing authority. In the province the authority was, of course, the Imperial government. In the kingdom the authority is not quite certain. While it is possible that Antipas was permitted to collect the taxes for the Romans in his kingdom, as his father Herod had done, it seems more probable that he was not so honourably treated as Herod the Great had been, and that Roman officials supervised the *telonai* in his kingdom as in the province.

III. *MEANS AND POPULARITY OF TRAVEL.*—i. TRAVEL AS PICTURED IN THE CLASSICAL LITERATURE.—To judge from many expressions used by the leading men of letters and philosophic moralists in classical times, travelling might seem not to have been popular. Those writers often speak as if travelling, especially by sea, were confined to traders who risked their life to make money, and as if the dangers were so great that none but the reckless and greedy would incur them; and the opinion is often expressed, especially by poets, that to adventure oneself on the sea is an impious and unnatural act. The well-known words of Horace (*Od.* i. 3) are typical of that point of view.

But that point of view was traditional among the poets; it had been handed down from the time when travelling was much more dangerous and difficult, when ships were small in size and fewer in number, when seamanship and method were inferior, when few roads had been built, and travel even by land was uncertain. Moreover, seafaring and land travel were hostile to the contentment, discipline, and quiet orderly spirit which Greek poetry and thought loved to dwell on and to recommend: they tended to encourage the spirit of disorder, rebellion against authority, self-confidence and self-assertiveness, the ναυτικὴ ἀναρχία, stigmatized by Euripides in the *Hecuba*. In Roman literature the Greek models and the old Greek sentiments were looked up to and imitated as sacred and final; and those expressions of the Roman writers, like the Corinthian Canal and the dread of Cape Malea,* were a proof of their bondage to their Greek masters in thought.

When we look deeper, we find underneath and behind those superficial sentiments very different views expressed by the writers who wrote in closer contact with the real facts of the Imperial world. Writers like Philo and Pliny in the 1st cent., Appian, Plutarch, Epictetus, Aristides in the 2nd cent., are full of admiration of the Imperial peace and its fruits: the sea was covered with ships interchanging the products of different regions of the earth, wealth was vastly increased, comfort and well-being improved, hill and valley covered with the dwellings of an increasing population: wars and pirates and robbers had been put an end to, travel was free and safe, all men could journey where they wished, the most remote and lonely countries were opened up by roads and bridges: such is the picture of the Roman world which those writers place before us.†

It is the simple truth that travelling, whether for business or for pleasure, was contemplated and performed under the Empire with an indifference, confidence, and, above all, certainty, which were unknown in after centuries until the introduction of steamers and the consequent increase in ease and sureness of communication.

ii. TRAVEL IN THE CHRISTIAN LITERATURE.—The impression given by the early Christian writings is in perfect agreement with the language of those writers who spoke from actual contact with the life of the time, and did not merely imitate older models and utter afresh old sentiments. Probably the feature in those Christian writings, which causes most surprise at first

* ἐσυκοφάντησα in that passage is commonly misunderstood and mistranslated: it does not mean 'exacted': the passage means 'if I have accused any defaulter before the government and had him condemned to pay up arrears.' It is possible that, in mentioning this detail, Zacchæus was replying to the unspoken accusation of unfair conduct levelled at all his class, and that he meant 'as to this accusation, my reply is that when I have made an unfair claim for arrears, I forfeit as a penalty four times the sum claimed: this makes it practically impossible for us to act so unfairly and extortionately as we are accused of doing.' But the first part of his statement would still remain as obscure as it is on the ordinary interpretations.

* See above, pp. 382, 389.

† Friedländer quotes Philo, *Leg. ad Gaium*, 7 and 21, pp. 552, 566; Plut. *de fort Rom.* 2; Appian, *Præf.* 6; Epict. *Diss.* iii. 13. 9; Plin. *Nat. Hist.* xiv. 2, xxvii. 2 f.; Aristides, *Or.* ix. εἰς βασιλέα, p. 66 (Dind. i. p. 111).

to the traveller familiar with those countries in modern times, is the easy confidence with which extensive plans of travel were formed and announced and executed by the early Christians. In Ac 16[1ff.] a journey by land and sea through parts of Syria, Cilicia, a corner of Cappadocia, Lycaonia, Phrygia, Mysia, the Troad, Thrace, Macedonia, and Greece is described, and no suggestion is made that this long journey was unusual or strange, except that the somewhat heightened tone of the narrative in 16[7-9] corresponds to the rather perplexingly rapid changes of scene and successive frustrations of St. Paul's intentions. But those who are most intimately acquainted with those countries know best how serious an undertaking it would be at the present time to repeat that journey, how many accidents might occur in it, and how much care and thought would be advisable before one entered on so extensive a programme.

Again, in 18[21] St. Paul touched at Ephesus in the ordinary course of the pilgrim-ship which was conveying him and many other Jews to Jerusalem for the Passover. When he was asked to remain, he excused himself, but promised to return as he came back from Jerusalem by a long land journey through Syria, Cilicia, Lycaonia, and Phrygia: that extensive journey seems to be regarded by speaker and hearers as quite an ordinary excursion. In Ro 15[24], when writing from Corinth, St. Paul sketches out a comprehensive plan. He is eager to visit Rome: first he must go to Jerusalem, but thereafter he is bent on visiting Spain, and his course will naturally lead him through Rome, so that he will, without intruding himself on them, have the opportunity of seeing and affecting the Romans and their Church on his way. Throughout mediæval times nothing like this off-hand way of sketching out extensive plans was natural or intelligible: there were then, indeed, some great travellers, but those travellers knew how uncertain their journeys were, and they would hardly have expressed such rapid plans as a matter of serious business, because they were aware that any plans would be frequently liable to interruption, and that nothing could be calculated on as reasonably certain: they entered on long journeys, but regarded them as open to modification or even frustration: in indicating their plans they knew that they would be regarded by others as attempting something great and strange. But St. Paul's methods and language seem to show clearly that such journeys as he contemplated were looked on as quite natural and usual by those to whom he spoke or wrote. He could go off from Greece or Macedonia to Palestine and reckon with practical certainty on being in Jerusalem in time for a feast day not far distant: 'I must by all means keep this feast that cometh in Jerusalem; but I will return again unto you, if God will' (Ac 18[21] AV). The last condition is added, not as indicating uncertainty, but in the usual spirit of Eastern religion, which forbids a resolve about the future, however simple and sure, to be declared without the express recognition of Divine authority—like the Mohammedan 'inshallah,' which never fails when the most ordinary resolution about the morrow is stated.

iii. TRAVEL CONFINED TO THE ROMAN EMPIRE.—One of the main causes for that certainty and confidence in travel lay in the unification of the Empire and the profound peace and security established by the Emperors over all the Mediterranean world. Travellers were everywhere in their own country. Travel in foreign countries was never common among the ancients. Although many considerable journeys in foreign and barbarous lands had been made, they were adventurous and exceptional, and stand on quite a different platform from the easy, sure journeys which we are describing as characteristic of the early Imperial period. The Roman traveller travelled in the Roman world; but that world was now so extensive that his journeys could be made on a much greater scale. Moreover, war was no longer to be dreaded; only civil war was now possible, since a foreign army could not be thought of within the Roman bounds; and when St. Paul was travelling, civil war had long ceased to be considered as a possible contingency (though it broke out shortly after his death). Again, Augustus had exterminated piracy by sea and brigandage by land, as Epictetus said; and though, as we have seen, the statement can only be accepted with certain limitations, it was fairly correct during a vigorous period of provincial government (such as that between A.D. 47 and 61, during which most of St. Paul's travelling was performed), and in the thoroughly organized parts of the Empire.

When St. Paul confined his work and his immediate plans so entirely to the Roman world, he was not merely acting in the spirit of his time, which he had unconsciously assimilated during his childhood as a Roman Tarsian, but he was guided by the practical possibilities of communication and travel at the time. The 'door' was open wide in the one direction, in the other it was closed. That the Scythian was ultimately to be included in the universal Church, was of course part of his ideal; but that lay further away and beyond the sphere of immediate work, and, moreover, the prevalent idea in the Roman world doubtless was that the Roman rule and Empire was steadily growing wider and taking in more and more of the alien world. New provinces were continually being added during St. Paul's lifetime. A little more than twenty years after his death, Dion Chrysostom was wandering among Scythians and Getæ through South Russia and Hungary from the mouth of the Borysthenes to the Upper Danube, and soon afterwards a new province of Dacia was formed on the north of the Danube.

iv. CLASSES OF TRAVELLERS, AND MOTIVES FOR TRAVELLING.—In the NT we find a large number and a great variety of travellers: Lydia, the 'Lydian woman' from Thyatira, dealing in turkey-red stuffs at Philippi:* Luke, the doctor, at Troas: Aquila, the Pontic tent-maker, with his wife at Rome and Corinth and Ephesus, and back at Rome again: Bar-Jesus, the Jewish magician at Paphos: Paul, taken in many cities for a lecturer on ethics and philosophy wandering in search of fame and a situation: Apollos coming to Ephesus probably in the same way: the agents of Chloe travelling between Ephesus and Corinth, probably for business purposes (*Expositor*, February 1900, p. 104): the centurion conducting a body of prisoners to Rome: besides these, many travellers for Church purposes, like the deputation in Ac 20 and 21, Titus at Corinth, Timothy and Silas sent to Macedonia, and so on.

There was a similar variety of travellers in the ordinary society of the Roman world. Then, as now, there was a tendency in the people to crowd into the cities: farming and country life were found to be hard and not very profitable. Officials and messengers were continually travelling backwards and forwards between Rome and the various provinces, or from province to province, as they were transferred from one to another: centurions and soldiers in charge of prisoners, a few occasionally for trial who were Romans, most mere criminals intended for the *venationes* (like Paul the Roman citizen and the criminals who were conducted along with him, Ac 27): many recruits, of whom at least

* See LYDIA (country) in vol. iii. and THYATIRA in vol. iv.

20,000 annually were needed for the armies, those of the west being filled up from the western provinces in general, those of the east from the eastern (though Hadrian changed that Augustan system, and arranged a series of territorial armies with local recruiting, which would diminish the number of travelling recruits). Embassies from the cities to Rome, or to provincial governors, are known from inscriptions to have been very common, *e.g.* Byzantium sent every year two complimentary embassies, one to the Emperor in Rome and one to the governor of Mœsia, until Trajan ordered the city to content itself with letters. Travelling for purposes of education, pleasure, or health kept thousands on the roads. Vast crowds flocked to the great festivals of Greece and Italy: Dion Chrysostom's account of the Isthmian festival is doubtless founded on what he had seen, though it is placed in the time of Diogenes.* Students flocked to the great universities, Athens, Alexandria, Rome, etc. Strabo mentions it as a peculiarity of Tarsus that no students came to it from abroad, but its lecture-rooms were crowded with native students, though some of the young Tarsians went abroad to study. Curative springs and the famous medical schools which were often attached to great religious centres (such as the temple of Men Carou, near Laodicea, of Asklepios at Pergamus, etc.) attracted large numbers of patients, often from great distances: thus we saw above that Spanish invalids visited Vicarello in Tuscany for centuries. Voyages were made for the sake of health: Gallio did so twice at least—once when he was governor of Achaia, another time long after from Rome to Alexandria (see *St. Paul the Traveller*, p. 261: these two voyages are often confused): we believe that St. Paul made a similar journey to the high country of Pisidian Antioch (Ac 13[14]). Tourists for the mere pleasure of sightseeing were numerous, and Pliny expresses his wonder that Italian people went away in numbers to see foreign scenery and remained ignorant of the wonders and beauties of their own country (*Epist.* viii. 20).

Again, there was a great deal of emigration in search of employment. This led chiefly to the great cities, and, above all, to Rome. In the great city men of all nations were found; and the Syrian Orontes, as Juvenal (*Sat.* iii. 62) says, emptied itself into the Tiber. But in every city visitors or strangers resident for business purposes were common: they came as traders, actors, and artists, physicians, magicians, and quacks, teachers of grammar, philosophy, and rhetoric, and so on. The inscriptions of every province offer numerous examples.

Formal geographical accounts of the products, resources, cities, and monuments of various countries in the Roman world were in existence. Strabo's *Geography*, written about A.D. 19, and Pausanias's elaborate account of all that was worth seeing in Greece (written in the 2nd cent.), were the outcome of a great many previous works of similar kind.

v. Road Maps, Guide-books, and Statistics.—Maps of the roads, lists of halting-places and distances both by land and by sea journeys, and other means whereby intending travellers could plan out and reckon their route, were evidently common. A fragment of an account, indicated day by day, of a journey through the Cilician Gates, has been found in Rome;† and it is quite probable that such an itinerary on papyrus could be purchased in Tarsus in the time of St. Paul. Many such itineraries in more or less complete form have been preserved, belonging mostly to a later time. But similar ones were at the disposal of the geographers such as Strabo (B.C. 64–A.D. 19), whose account even of countries which he had not seen is accurate to a degree otherwise impossible of attainment. Four silver vases have been found at Vicarello in Etruria, shaped like milestones, and inscribed with the full itinerary from Cadiz to Rome. They belong to different periods, and represent therefore a long-continued custom: they can hardly be explained otherwise than as dedications made at the famous baths of Vicarello by Spaniards, who in gratitude left a memorial of themselves and their journey as a votive offering to the Divine healing power at the baths.

* *Isthmiaca*, Or. 8. By a slip his *Corinthiaca* is quoted in its stead in the art. on 'Corinth' in vol. i. p. 479.

† *CIL* vi. 5076; *Hist. Geogr. of Asia Minor*, p. 68; see art. on 'Tarsus and the great Taurus Pass' in *Geogr. Journal*, 1903.

vi. Means of Locomotion in Journeys by Land.—The land journeys mentioned in the NT seem to have been for the most part performed on foot. There is one evident exception. In Ac 21[15. 16] a journey of 68 Roman miles is described from Cæsarea to Jerusalem. That long distance was traversed in two days: that this was the duration of the journey is shown clearly in the Western text, which mentions that the travellers rested for the night in a village at the house of Mnason and went on to Jerusalem the next day, while the Cæsarean disciples returned home. Though this meaning is not so clearly evident in the accepted text of Ac 21[16], it appears on closer consideration to lie in it also: v. [15], they set about the journey to Jerusalem (*imperfect* tense): v. [16], they lodged with Mnason, to whose house the Cæsarean disciples conducted them: v. [17] they reached Jerusalem and were welcomed (see *Expositor*, March 1895, p. 214 ff.).* It is clearly irreconcilable with the results which we have attained, that a miscellaneous body of travellers from various cities of Greece and Asia Minor, who must have had some personal luggage with them, could perform a journey of 68 miles in two days on foot without horse or carriage.

Now, in 21[15] the preparation for this journey is described: the writer at the beginning of the land stage of the long journey felt it necessary to explain that some preparations were made. The word used is ἐπισκευασάμενοι,† which Chrysostom renders 'we took what was needed for the land journey' (τὰ πρὸς τὴν ὁδοιπορίαν λαβόντες). There must lie in this some allusion to the horses or vehicles for the journey; and it is not impossible that ὑποζύγια or ζῷα is to be understood with τά in Chrysostom's explanation. But, however that may be, equipment and preparation obviously imply means of conveyance. In the case of persons who simply rose up and walked to Jerusalem, there would have been no room or need, in this extremely concise narrative, for describing their preparations. The narrative, therefore, makes it clear that there was some amount of luggage to be carried to Jerusalem, and that horses or carriages had to be employed. Now ἐπισκευάσαι ἵππον means 'to saddle or to load a horse,'‡ and it seems quite possible in Greek to take the middle voice as meaning 'we got ready or saddled horses for our use.'§ Both horses and carriages could undoubtedly be hired for journeys in such a city as Cæsarea (see Friedländer, p. 20 ff.).

vii. Ships and Shipping Arrangements.—Little that could be said on this point has any bearing on the NT.

The art of shipbuilding had been so greatly improved that vessels of very considerable size were

* We regard the Western text here as a skilful and correct commentary on the briefer reading, but not as the original Lukan language.

† ἀποσκευασάμενοι in a few MSS. can hardly be correct.

‡ Aristot. *Oecon.* ii. 24; Xen. *Hell.* v. 3. 1; Pollux, x. 14.

§ Grotius (as Professor Knowling mentions) understood it as *sarcinas iumentis imponere*. See also *Expositor*, March 1895, p. 216 f.

constructed. Lucian's *Navigium* describes an Alexandrian corn vessel towards the end of the 2nd cent. as 120 cubits, or 180 feet, in length; from which James Smith (*Voyage and Shipwreck of St. Paul*[3], p. 182 ff.) calculates the tonnage as between 1100 and 1200, a much more sober estimate than some scholars reach. Josephus (*Vit.* 3) sailed for Rome in a ship which carried 600 passengers, St. Paul in one carrying 276.*

In shape and in rigging, however, there had not been much improvement on the more ancient and primitive vessels. There was still a great deal of unnecessary and useless length in the high bow and stern, which stood far out above the water; so that there was a great difference between the length of that part of the keel which was immersed and the total length of the ship. The ship was sailed mainly by one large sail on the single mast: hence it was always difficult to shorten sail and to adapt the ship to a wind as it grew stronger. Moreover, the leverage of the single huge sail on a single mast exercised a tremendous disruptive power on the hull of the vessel: hence ancient vessels encountered much greater danger in the open sea than modern sailing vessels have to face, and were often sunk owing to the timbers being wrenched asunder by the straining of the mast, and the ship being thus made leaky and unfit to keep out the water; whereas modern sailing vessels are usually safe in the open sea and more in danger near shore.

In addition to the great sail † other sails were also used, though apparently only as subsidiary; and they were not employed in every ship. There was sometimes a topsail (*supparum*) above the great sail. Moreover, there were one or more small storm-sails, which could be substituted for the great sail when the wind was too strong: some such subsidiary sails were an absolute necessity in a ship which had to go on a voyage far from home.

There were also small sails—one or more on the bow, and one behind the great sail towards the stern. These seem all to have been only occasionally used as supplementary. In Ac 27[40] the *artemon* was set to work the disabled ship. A single sail, set to work a large ship, must have been either rigged on the great mast, or set further forward. If the mast was still fit to be used, the former would be more probable; but some analogous cases point to the *artemon* being rather a foresail, set on the bow, where a small mast was often placed (as is shown in several works of ancient art). The case mentioned by Juvenal (*Sat.* xii. 69), where a ship disabled by a storm manages to make its way into harbour by the sail on the prow, the only remaining one, which the scholiast explains as the *artemon*, must in this obscure subject be regarded as the strongest piece of evidence available.‡

Ships of war were more lightly built, for the sake of rapid manœuvring, and were as a general rule impelled partly at least by oars. Hence they were independent of the winds to a great degree. But, owing to the slightness of their build, they could not venture on long over-sea voyages: moreover, they had not storage room for the equipment needed for such voyages. See above, I. § vii. p. 381.

viii. Passenger Ships.—The ships of which travellers availed themselves were doubtless as a rule trading ships, whose movements were determined mainly by considerations of freight and lading, not of passengers; in other words, the ships made money mainly from the freight, and not from the passengers' fares. Hence regular services at stated intervals for the convenience mainly of passengers probably did not exist. Travellers embarked in a vessel that happened to be going in their direction, and were dependent on the chances of the trade; and, as we have seen above, this often affected the arrangement of their journey.

There must, however, have been certain exceptions. The large numbers of persons who visited the great religious festivals and games must have required special vessels where a sea had to be crossed; and just as special steamers now run from Smyrna and Athens for the festival of the Panagia of Tino, so in ancient times the people of the Ionian race were conveyed to the great national reunion in the festival of Apollo of Delos, whose place the Panagia has taken. In some cases, where presence at the festival was a national duty, the city probably sent the people at State expense. But in many cases, and especially in later times, when national ties were weakened, and the festivals were visited chiefly from motives of curiosity, artistic and athletic interest, or enjoyment, the ships were run from commercial motives, and the owners profited by the fares of passengers.

One case of this class is of great importance as affecting the NT. Thousands of Jews of the Diaspora were able to go up to the Passover at Jerusalem only by ship: the land journey from distant cities would have been too tedious and slow. It may, *e.g.*, be regarded as certain that all Jews who went up to the Passover from the western, the northern, and even the eastern coasts of the Ægean, travelled on board ship; and that ships were run for their special benefit in order to make money from the passengers. Such pilgrim-ships would run for the special purpose of the festival, and would lose no time by the way from stopping for other purposes. Thus it would be safe to start from such a port as Corinth or Ephesus much later than would be prudent on an ordinary trading vessel, liable to stop for days in harbours on the way to load or unload. The time of absence from home and business required for the journey was thus much shortened.

The position of Jews in the Diaspora was affected in various ways by the pilgrim-ships. On the one hand, those ships immensely facilitated communication, and made it possible for far larger numbers of Jews to go up to the Feast: thus they strengthened the national feeling and sense of unity, which so marvellously resisted the dissociating influence of distance and of difference between the Diaspora and the Palestinian Jews in language, customs, and education On the other hand, they offered opportunities for oppressing and annoying the Jews in every harbour that the ship had to enter: mere strictness in enforcing harbour regulations might cause delay, and this could be best avoided by bribery: greed or positive ill-will might prolong the detention so as to endanger the purpose of the voyage or compel the payment of large sums: the mere fact of a great number or Jews being collected in one ship gave opportunity for many acts of injustice and malevolence. Hence it is easy to see why numerous edicts of kings and Roman officials and Emperors in favour of the Jews reiterate the provision for unimpeded liberty to journey to Jerusalem.

* Some scholars say that the ship Dioscuri, which wintered at Malta, took on board the whole 276 (Ac 28[11]); but this is not stated in the text, though it may possibly be true: if the Dioscuri could take on board 276 passengers beyond its own complement—even crowded in for a short voyage of a few days—it must have been a very large vessel.

† It is advisable to avoid the name 'mainsail,' which is a technical term with a different connotation in modern ships.

‡ *Quod superaverat unum, velo prora suo.* The scholiast says *artemone solo velificaverunt.* It is possible that he was only making an inference from Acts or some other similar passage; but such a mere possibility cannot be considered to counterbalance the probability in his favour or to invalidate his evidence.

The right understanding of Ac 20[1ff.] is influenced by this fact. St. Paul was on the point of sailing from Corinth to Palestine: he was going to be for ten days or more in the company and the power of a body of Jews, including the most zealous and, in some cases, fanatical among them. The situation was at the best a dangerous one. It became known that some of the Jews were openly stating their intention of using this favourable opportunity to get rid of their enemy: murder on shore was too dangerous, but murder at sea on a ship where all except a few sailors were Jews* might be easily carried out in such a way as to defy investigation and probably even to escape notice: the loss of one pilgrim in a crowd might probably never even be observed. It was therefore resolved that St. Paul must avoid this obvious and serious danger. He was quite ready and resolute to adventure himself in Jerusalem, where the danger was equally great. But there in the great city at the Feast his death, if it came, would be a public protest in favour of truth and freedom: on shipboard it would be unknown and useless, so far as these high ends were concerned. Moreover, he was in charge of a considerable sum of money contributed at Corinth (see next paragraph), and was responsible for its safe delivery at Jerusalem. It was, however, impossible by that time to reach Jerusalem for the Feast by any ordinary vessel; and therefore St. Paul sailed for Philippi and spent the Passover there.

Presumably, the delegates who were to accompany him to Jerusalem carrying the voluntary contributions of the Pauline Churches (just as among the Jews then 'men of noble birth are entrusted with the conveyance to Jerusalem' of the accumulated annual dues paid by the Jews in the Diaspora) † had arranged to meet him at Ephesus. On the new arrangement the Asian delegates came on to Troas to meet him and the Macedonian delegates (Ac 20[4]). The party was dependent now on the chances of trading vessels, and therefore the start was made from Philippi as soon as the Passover and the Days of Unleavened Bread were ended. There was no detention at Neapolis, which is not even mentioned. Owing to the great importance of the passage between Neapolis and Troas, as we have seen, vessels of one kind or another must have been constantly, probably daily, available there. At Troas, however, there was a detention of seven days; and then there seems to have been a choice of vessels—one going round the west and south coast of Asia Minor, making a short stay of three or four days at Miletus, but otherwise only the ordinary nightly halts of coasting vessels; the other intending to put in at Ephesus and make a considerable stay there for some purpose connected with her freight. In these circumstances Paul, though desirous of seeing the Church of Ephesus, chose the ship that sailed past that city, because he was desirous of reaching Jerusalem in time for the Feast of Pentecost, and did not wish to run any risk of being too late (Ac 20[16]). Some commentators suggest that he was also unwilling to go to Ephesus, from fear lest trouble might arise there, as on his previous residence; but when a perfectly sufficient reason is stated in our authority, it seems unjustifiable to add another reason.‡ This case is a very instructive example of what might happen in voyages made by common travellers.

* Such ships may probably have been owned and perhaps in part manned by Jews; though the existence of Jewish sailors is not much attested at that time.

† As Philo, *de Mon.* ii. 3 (ii. 24, Mangey), says. The passage is quoted by Prof. Schürer in the art. DIASPORA, above, § v.

‡ Moreover, it is quite unnatural to suppose that in the great city of Ephesus the return of a single Jew for a week or so must necessarily be observed.

ix. IMPERIAL TRANSPORT SHIPS.—We have, above, spoken about the Alexandrian corn ships as belonging to the Imperial service. In the strictest point of view that is not quite accurate. Those ships were not government vessels, like men-of-war. They belonged to private owners, or rather great trading companies, who contracted in open market with the Imperial government* for the conveyance of the corn. As in the collection of taxes, the government found it easier to give out the work to contract than to organize for itself the enormous machinery in men and equipment needed for that great service. But, on the other hand, those ships were exclusively used for the Alexandrian service (as other companies contracted for other special services and purposes);† the companies received certain subventions from the State (including a free gift of all the wood needed for building), and immunities for all members from various public burdens; and thus they were bound in a great degree to the State service, and became almost part of the State equipment. Gradually it was found advisable in the public interest to bind them more closely, until at last they became hereditary servants of the State for that duty, and unable to free themselves from the service, which descended from father to son, and which was remunerated by percentage ‡ at a rate fixed by law, and no longer given out at contract. See Marquardt, *Röm. Privatalt.* ii. 405 ff.

x. CORRESPONDENCE.—Communication by letter had been common from remote antiquity. The familiar use of writing leads to correspondence between absent friends as inevitably as the possession of articulate speech produces conversation and discussion. Now it is becoming more certain and evident through the progress of discovery that writing was widely and familiarly used from an extremely early period. There was, of course, a very marked line of distinction, in ancient society, between the educated section of the population, which could read and write, and the uneducated, which could not; and the distinction did not at all correspond to the distinction between free and slave; on the contrary, many of the slaves in households of the educated class were specially highly and carefully educated, when their abilities were such that education would make them more useful to their masters.

With the great development of travel and communication in the Roman Imperial period, it might have been expected that communication by letter should have been greatly developed and increased. It is, however, extremely doubtful if that was the case.

The weakest side of the Imperial system always was its comparative carelessness of the intellectual and spiritual well-being of the population. To feed and to amuse ('panem et Circenses') nearly summed up its ideal of treatment for the masses. Real education, which the Greek cities admired and aimed at, grew weaker and poorer as the Empire grew older. The fact that in the purely barbarian provinces, such as Pannonia, Mœsia, etc., the introduction of the Roman civilization and government caused an educated class to grow up, should not be allowed to conceal the real fact that the educated class was not enlarged proportionately over the whole Empire.

And, similarly, epistolary correspondence was probably not much, if at all, increased in those

* *Ad hastam locamus ut nobis ex transmarinis provinciis advehatur frumentum* (Columella, *de Re Rust.* 1, *pr.* 20).

† Special ships were built for the transport of the immense blocks and monolithic columns of coloured marble: the nature of the transport required that, and Pliny mentions that *naves marmorum causa fiunt* (*Nat. Hist.* xxxvi. 2).

‡ In the 4th cent. the rate was 4 per cent. of the cargo, and an *aureus* for every thousand bushels.

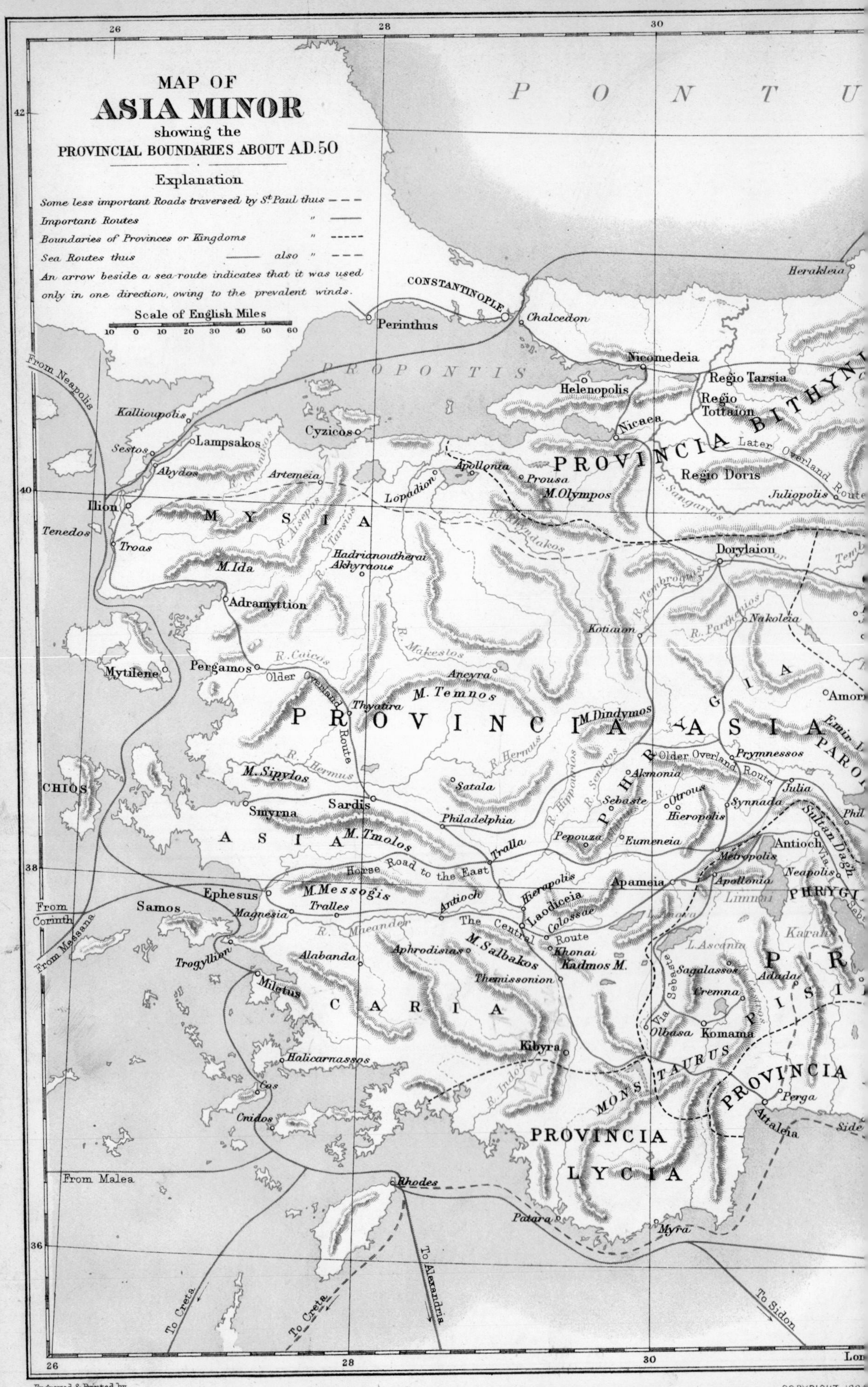

MAP OF
ASIA MINOR
showing the
PROVINCIAL BOUNDARIES ABOUT A.D.50
Explanation
Some less important Roads traversed by St. Paul thus
Important Routes "
Boundaries of Provinces or Kingdoms "
Sea Routes thus also "
An arrow beside a sea-route indicates that it was used only in one direction, owing to the prevalent winds.
Scale of English Miles
10 0 10 20 30 40 50 60
PONTUS
PROPONTIS
CONSTANTINOPLE
Perinthus
Chalcedon
Herakleia
Nicomedeia
Helenopolis
Nicaea
Regio Tarsia
Regio Tottaion
PROVINCIA BITHYNIA
Later Overland Route
Regio Doris
Juliopolis
Kallioupolis
Lampsakos
Sestos
Abydos
Cyzicos
Artemeia
Apollonia
Prousa
M.Olympos
Lopadion
Ilion
Tenedos
Troas
MYSIA
M.Ida
Hadrianoutherai
Akhyraous
Dorylaion
Adramyttion
Kotiaion
Nakoleia
Mytilene
Pergamos
Older Overland Route
Thyatira
Ancyra
M.Temnos
PROVINCIA ASIA
M.Dindymos
PHRYGIA
Prymnessos
Julia
Synnada
CHIOS
M.Sipylos
Satala
Akmonia
Sebaste
Otrous
Hieropolis
Smyrna
Sardis
Philadelphia
ASIA
M.Tmolos
Tralla
Pepouza
Eumeneia
Metropolis
Antioch
Sultan Dagh
Horse Road to the East
Apameia
Apollonia
Neapolis
Ephesus
M.Messogis
Hierapolis
Laodiceia
Colossae
Samos
Magnesia
Tralles
Antioch
The Central Route
Khonai
Kadmos M.
From Corinth
From Messana
From Neapolis
Trogyllion
Alabanda
Aphrodisias
M.Salbakos
Themissonion
Sagalassos
Cremna
Adada
Miletus
CARIA
Via Sebaste
Olbasa
Komama
PISIDIA
Kibyra
MONS TAURUS
PROVINCIA
Perga
Attaleia
Halicarnassos
Cos
Cnidos
PROVINCIA LYCIA
From Malea
Rhodes
Patara
Myra
To Creta
To Creta
To Alexandria
To Sidon
26
28
30
42
40
38
36
Engraved & Printed by
COPYRIGHT, 1904

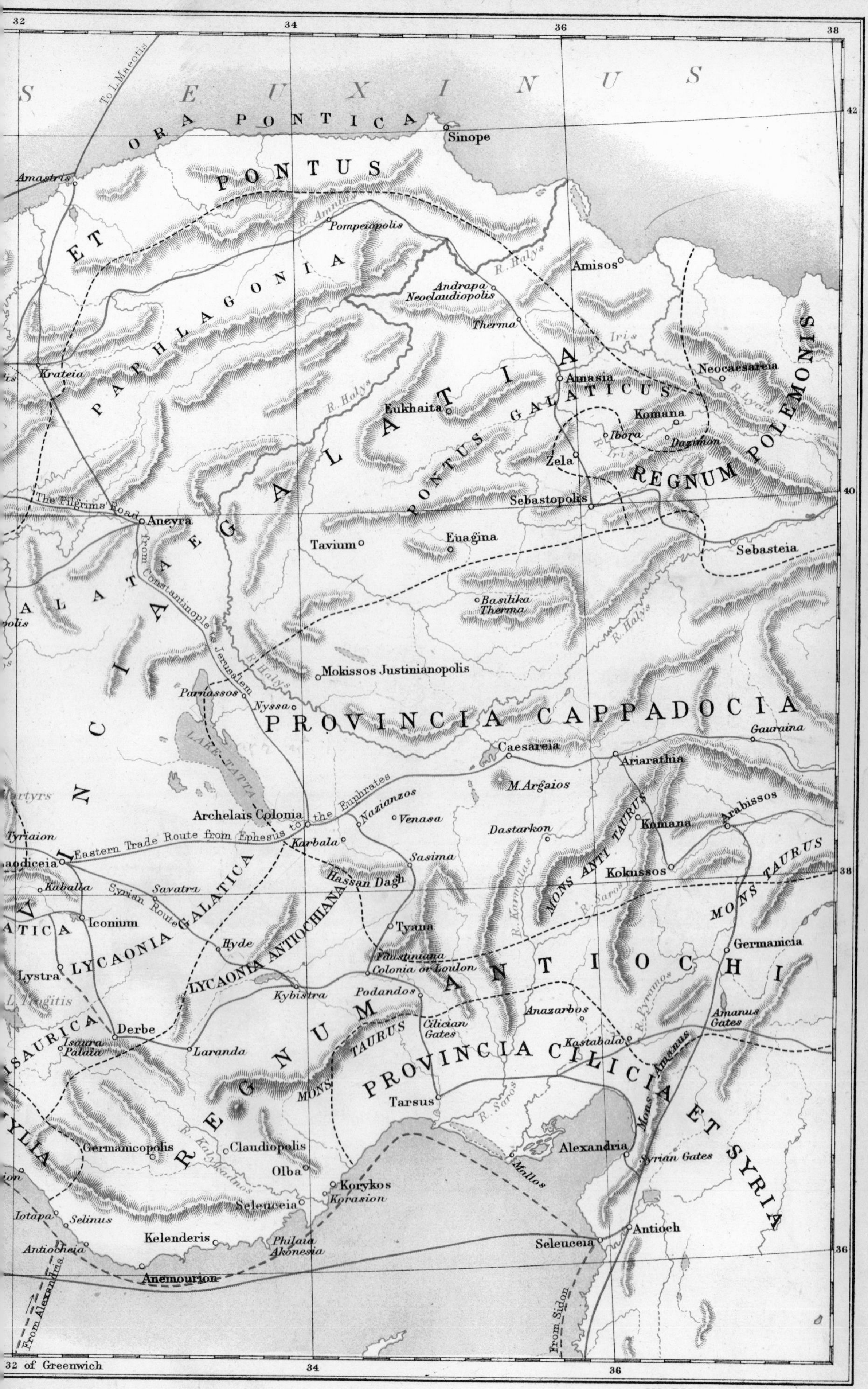

RIBNER'S SONS

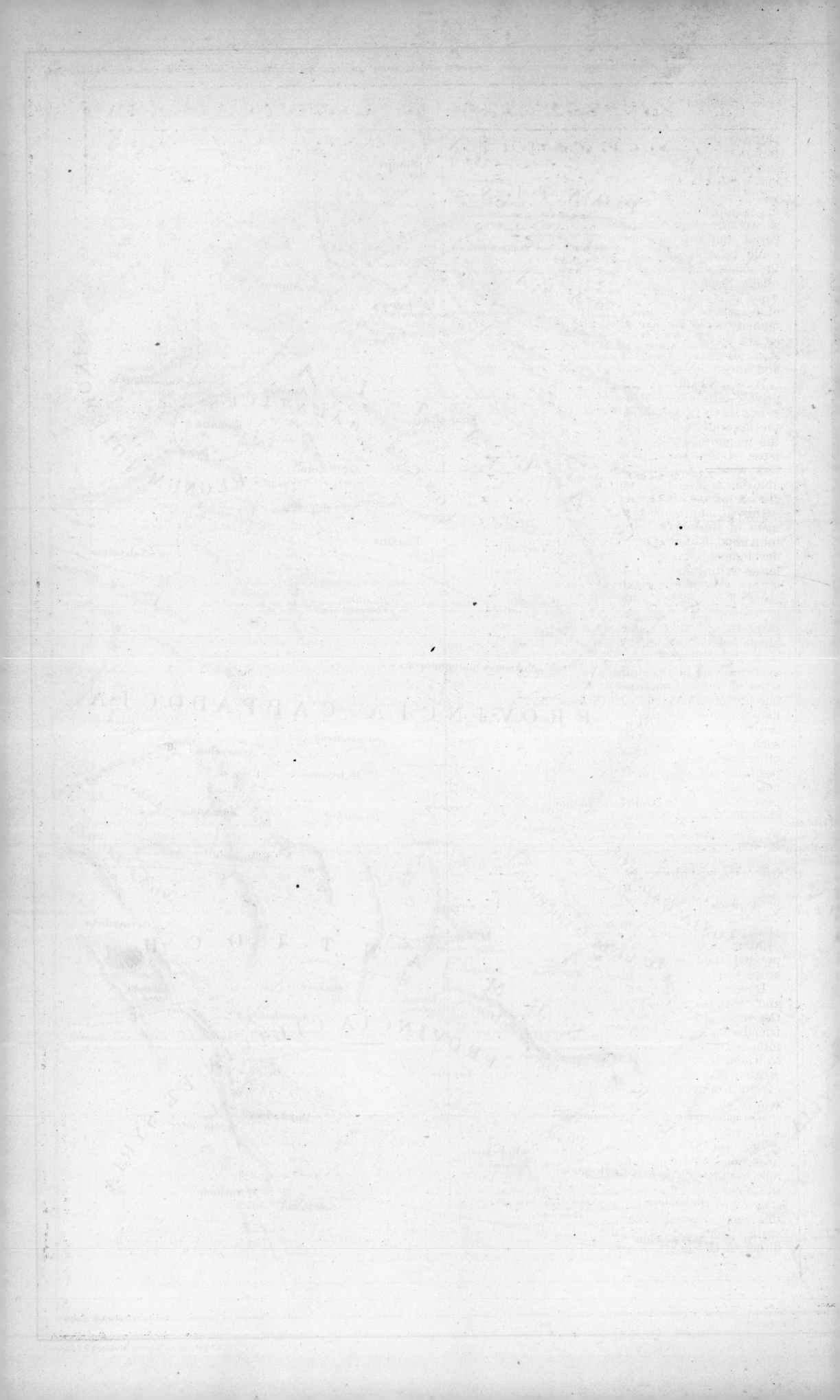

parts of the Empire where civilization and education had existed before the Roman conquest. The Imperial government made no attempt at, and never even seems to have thought about, carrying the correspondence of private persons, or facilitating such communication between them. The post, as we have seen, was absolutely confined to Imperial and strictly official needs. Private letters could be sent only by special messengers, or by the hands of friends or acquaintances, or by some other chance opportunity. Such opportunities were, it is true, more numerous when the number of travellers was greater; but this led to no permanent development of the idea. Such statistics as are preserved seem to show that the transmission of private letters continued slow, irregular, and uncertain: see p. 383.

It is probably true that a larger number of private letters has been preserved of the Imperial period than of an earlier time; but this is due to the naturally more nearly complete destruction of the memorials of the older period in the longer lapse of time, especially inasmuch as private letters were written for the most part on perishable materials, which survive nowhere and in no climate except in Egypt.

Only in one respect was there any real development of epistolary communication between private individuals under the Roman Empire; and this development was not so much in the frequency of letter-writing as in the purpose and character of letters written by private individuals. The Christians developed the letter into new forms, applied it to new uses, and placed it on a much higher plane than it had ever before stood upon. In their hands communication by letter became one of the most important, if not the most important, of all agencies for consolidating and maintaining the sense of unity among the scattered members of the one universal Church. The scattered congregations had for centuries no real unifying and directing centre of life: Jerusalem had been in some degree such a centre at first; but whether or not it could otherwise have maintained that authoritative position, all chance of its continuing to be the head and centre of the universal Church disappeared with its siege and capture by Titus and the changes that were forced on by that event; and no other city took, or could take, its place for several centuries. The unity of the separate and equal congregations was kept alive by travel and by correspondence. By such means the congregations expressed their mutual affection and sympathy and sense of brotherhood, asked counsel of one another, gave advice with loving freedom and plain speaking to one another, imparted mutual comfort and encouragement, and generally expressed their sense of their common life. Thus arose a new category of Epistles.

Deissmann, following older scholars, has rightly and clearly distinguished the two older categories, the true letter—written by friend to friend or to friends, springing from the momentary occasion, intended only for the eye of the person or persons to whom it is addressed—and the literary epistle—written with an eye to the public, and studied with careful literary art. But he has erred in trying to reduce all the letters of the NT to one or other of these categories. Though he shows some vague sense of the insufficiency of the two older categories, yet he has not seen with sufficient clearness, nor stated with sufficient precision, that in the new conditions a new category had been developed—the general letter addressed to a whole class of persons or to the entire Church of Christ. Letters of this class are true letters, in the sense that they spring from the heart of the writer and speak direct to the heart of the readers; that they rise out of the actual situation in which the writer conceives the readers to be placed; that they express the writer's keen and living sympathy with and participation in the fortunes of the whole class of persons addressed; that they are not affected by any thought of publication for a wider public than the persons immediately addressed. On the other hand, the letters of this class express general principles of life and conduct, religion and ethics, applicable to a wider range of circumstances than those which have called forth the special letter; and the letters appeal as emphatically and intimately to all Christians in all time as they did to those addressed in the first instance. Such letters have a certain analogy to the edicts and rescripts by which Roman law grew, documents arising out of special circumstances but treating them on general principles. As expressing general truths and universal principles, those letters must have been the result of long and careful thought, though the final expression was often hasty and called forth by some special occasion. This more studied character differentiates them from the mere hasty unstudied expression of personal affection and interest.*

Those general letters of the Christians express and embody the growth in the law of the Church and in its common life and constitution. They originated in the circumstances of the Church. The letter of the Council at Jerusalem (Ac $15^{23-29}$) arose out of a special occasion, and was the reply to a question addressed from Syria to the central Church and its leaders; the reply was addressed to the Churches of the province of Syria and Cilicia, headed by the Church of the capital of that province; but it was forthwith treated as applicable equally to other Christians, and was communicated as authoritative by Paul and Silas to the Churches of the province Galatia (Ac $16^{4}$).

The peculiar relation of headship and fatherhood in which St. Paul stood to the Churches which he had founded, developed still further this category of letters, as is well shown in the article on EPISTLES, vol. i. p. 730. A still further development towards general philosophico-legal statement of religious dogma is apparent on the one hand in Romans, addressed to a Church which he had not founded, and on the other hand in the Pastoral Epistles, addressed to friends and pupils of his own, partly in their capacity of personal friends,—such portions of the letters being of the most intimate, incidental, and unstudied character,—but far more in their official capacity as heads and overseers of a group of Churches—such parts of the letters being really intended more for the guidance of the congregations than of the nominal addressees, and being, undoubtedly, to a considerable extent merely confirmatory of the directions and instructions already given to the congregations by Timothy and Titus. The double character of these Epistles is a strong proof of their authenticity. Such a mixture of character could only spring from the intimate friend and leader, whose interest in the work which his two subordinates are doing is at times lost in the personal relation.

The Catholic Epistles represent a further stage of this development. First Peter is addressed to a very wide yet carefully defined body of Churches in view of a serious trial to which they are about to be exposed. Second Peter, James, and First John are quite indefinite in their address to all Christians. But all of them are separated by a broad and deep division from the literary epistle written for the public eye: they are informed and inspired with the intense personal affection which the writers felt for every individual of the thou-

*See EPISTLE, vol. i. p. 730; Deissmann, *Biblical Studies* (an improved edition of his *Bibelstudien* and *Neue Bibelstudien*), also his article on 'Epistolary Literature' in *Encycl. Bibl.* ii. p. 1323.

sands whom they addressed. A serious study of all the NT and early Christian Epistles from this point of view is much needed, and would bring out in strong relief their real, human, individual and authentic character. The seven letters to the seven Churches contained in Rev 1–3 are full of touches special to the individual Churches, many of which have hardly been observed in modern times, but which show close personal knowledge of the cities on the part of the writer; and yet they are written on a uniform plan, which gives them a certain literary type to a degree and of a kind differing from any of the other letters. They stand by themselves, written in the inspiration of one single occasion, which expressed itself suitably to the individual circumstances of each of the seven Churches, yet conformed to certain general lines.

This remarkable development, in which law, statesmanship, ethics, and religion meet in and transform the simple letter, was the work of St. Paul more than of any other. But it was not due to him alone, nor initiated by him. It began before him and continued after him. It sprang from the nature of the Church and the circumstances of the time. The Church was Imperial, the Kingdom of God, and its leaders felt that their letters expressed the will of God. They issued their truly Imperial rescripts: 'it seemed good to the Holy Spirit and to us' is a bold and regal expression in the first Christian letter.

Christian letters in the next two or three centuries were often inspired by something of the same spirit. Congregation spoke boldly and authoritatively to congregation, as each was moved by the Spirit to write: the letter partook of the nature of an Imperial rescript, yet it was merely the expression of the intense interest taken by equal in equal, and brother in brother. The whole series of such letters is indicative of the strong interest of all individuals in the government of the entire body; and they form one of the loftiest and noblest embodiments of a high tone of feeling common to a very large number of ordinary, commonplace, undistinguished human beings.

Such a development of the letter in that widely scattered body of the Church was possible only through the greatly increased facilities for travel and intercourse. The Church showed its marvellous intuition and governing capacity by seizing this opportunity. In this, as in many other ways, it made itself really a rival to the Imperial administration. It did, and did better, what the Imperial policy was trying to do.

The bishop, as the representative of the congregation in its relations to other congregations, was charged with the maintenance of correspondence, just as he was charged above other members with the exercise of hospitality to Christian visitors. The letter which he wrote might be regarded either as emanating from the congregation or as his personal letter. The letter of Clement to the Corinthians is expressed as really the letter of the Roman Church to the Corinthian Church. It is the present writer's belief that the Epistle to the Hebrews was the letter of the Church in Cæsarea, and mainly of Philip as leader of that Church.

In the absence of a proper postal system, special messengers had to be found to carry these letters. These messengers may be assumed to have been, from the beginning, always Christians: such were Epaphroditus, Tychicus, Titus, Phœbe, and many others.

Dr. Hort, in the Appendix to his posthumous Commentary on First Peter, has shown that such a messenger carried that Epistle from Rome to the Churches of Asia Minor, sailing to Amastris, where he landed and went across Pontus into North Galatia, Cappadocia, South Galatia, Asia, and finally Bithynia.

LITERATURE.—Friedländer, *Darstellungen aus der Sittengeschichte der röm. Kaiserzeit*, ii.[5] ch. i., is excellent, though we have found ourselves obliged often to differ from his views. Miss Caroline Skeel has published a useful little work, *Travel in the First Century*. Most useful and fundamental is Parthey and Pinder's edition of the *Itineraria*. Compare Bergier, *Histoire des grands Chemins de l'Empire rom.*; Berger, *Die Heerstrassen des röm. Reichs*. On the Imperial Post, see Hudemann, *Geschichte des röm. Postwesens*; Rittershain, *Die Reichspost der röm. Kaiser*, Berlin, 1880; de Rothschild, *Histoire de la Poste aux Lettres*, Paris, 1873; Hirschfeld, *Röm. Verwaltungsgeschichte*, p. 98 ff.; Marquardt, *Röm. Staatsverwaltung*, i. p. 558 ff.; Mommsen, *Röm. Staatsrecht*, ii.[2] p. 987 ff., ii.[3] p. 1029 ff.; Stephan, *Das Verkehrswesen im Alterthum*, is quoted by Friedländer from Raumer's *Histor. Taschenb.* 1868, p. 120. Cf. Breusing, *Die Nautik der Alten*, 1886; Vars, *L'Art Nautique*, 1887. Many other books are incidentally referred to in the preceding pages.

TABLE OF CONTENTS OF ABOVE ARTICLE.



W. M. RAMSAY.

## CONTINENTAL VERSIONS.—

- i. French.
- ii. Italian.
- iii. Spanish.
- iv. Portuguese.
- v. German.
- vi. Dutch.
- vii. Danish (and Norwegian).
- viii. Swedish.
- ix. Hungarian.
- x. Bohemian.
- xi. Polish.
- xii. Russian.
- xiii. Modern Greek.

i. FRENCH VERSIONS.—The earliest reference to the *lingua Romana rustica*, in connexion with France, comes to us in the 7th cent., when Mummolinus was elected bishop of Noyon because he could speak both German and Romance; but the oldest written French is found in detached words written in the 8th cent. as glosses on a Latin Bible, inserted to explain the meaning of the Latin words. These are the well-known Reichenau and Cassel glosses. The 9th cent. gives us, in the Strassburg oaths of 842, the first continuous French. Earlier in the same century, in 813, it had been ordered at the Synod of Tours that the Latin homilies were to be translated *in linguam Romanam rusticam aut Theotiscam*. This does not, however, imply more than an oral translation; but it is significant of the widening breach between the language of the common people and the Latin of the clergy—a breach which had no doubt been widened unnaturally by Charlemagne's efforts to prevent the deterioration of written Latin. By the next century, the 10th, we find the great broad division appearing, into the *langue d'oil* of the centre and north of France, and the *langue d'oc* of the south. By the end of the 11th cent. the first of these was marked off into at least four dialects: Norman in the N.W. (and in England), Picard in the N.E., Burgundian in the east, and French in the Île de France. This last gradually became supreme as the literary dialect, owing to the widening political supremacy of the lords of France, with Paris as their capital, and by the 14th cent. its supremacy was complete. In the south, the *langue d'oc* attained its chief literary importance in the 12th and 13th cents., and after the defeat of the south in the Albigensian war in 1272 it was supplanted for literary purposes by the northern French, on which, however, it exercised a considerable influence.

1. The earliest MSS of a French version of any part of the Bible which have come down to us belong to the 12th century. These contain the Psalter, the Books of Kings, the Apocalypse, and five chapters of St. John's Gospel. All but the last are, in the earliest MSS, in the Norman dialect; the last is in Provençal, and was probably copied at Limoges.

(*a*) Two MSS of the Psalter, the so-called Eadwin Psalter in the library of Trinity College, Cambridge, and a Paris MS of the 12th or 13th cent. (*Fonds lat.* 8846), translate Jerome's *Psalterium Hebraicum*, *i.e.* his rendering of the Psalter from the Hebrew. In the Cambridge MS, which was written by Eadwin at or near Canterbury about 1120, the French is an interlinear gloss written over the Hebrew in a triple Psalter. The Paris MS, which contains only Ps 1–98[6], has a Latin text which probably represents a revision made in Normandy at Bec under Lanfranc's influence. These Psalters were edited by Michel at Paris in 1876. Besides the *Psalterium Hebraicum* of Jerome, his *Psalterium Gallicum*, or Latin translation based on the Hexaplar text, was used as the version which underlies another group of early French Psalters. The most important MS of this group is that written at Montebourg in Normandy before the year 1200. This is now in the Bodleian Library (MS Bodl. Douce 320), and was edited by Michel at Oxford in 1860. It is written in the Norman dialect. Several other MSS belonging to this family are known, three of which are connected with England, viz. a Cotton MS (Brit. Mus. Nero C. iv.) of the end of the 12th cent. written at Shaftesbury; an Arundel MS 230 of the same date with an English calendar; and a 14th cent. MS also in the British Museum (MS Harl. 1770) from Kirkham in Yorkshire. In the Arundel MS the interlinear French gloss is put word for word over the corresponding Latin. Two other MSS of this family are Bibl. Nat. *Fonds lat.* 768, of the early 13th cent., and a Munich MS 16 of the 14th century. This version of the Psalter, of which the Arundel MS is perhaps the most ancient representative, and of which Berger mentions nearly a hundred MSS, was the basis of all the French translations of the Psalter down to the edition of Olivetan. Between this and the version based on Jerome's Hebrew Psalter there is 'no difference of glossary or of grammar.' The underlying Latin is of course different, but the French in both is the Norman dialect, resembling that of the Oxford MS of the *Chanson de Roland* of the latter half of the 12th century.

(*b*) The version of the Books of Kings is found in several MSS, the most important and the oldest of which is a Mazarin MS 70 of about the year 1170. Another MS mentioned by Berger is in the Arsenal Library at Paris, No. 5211, and to these P. Meyer (*Romania*, xvii. 126) adds Bibl. Nat. 6447, and in the same library *Nouv. acq. fr.* 1404. The version is not literal, but has many glosses, and is in parts versified. It is a translation of a text of the Vulgate not unlike the revision of Alcuin, written in Anglo-Norman, and not, as Leroux de Lincy thought, in the dialect of the Île de France.

(*c*) The Apocalypse is preserved in 'pure Norman of the 12th cent.' in an early 13th cent. MS (Bibl. Nat. *fr.* 403); in a slightly different version in Bibl. Nat. MS *fr.* 13096 (A.D. 1313); and in the dialect of the Île de France in Bibl. Nat. MS 1036. The version, originally one and the same, has been reproduced in more than eighty MSS and in various dialects. There is also an early 13th cent. version of 1 and 2 Mac., of which there have been several editions, in a dialect which has been the subject of much controversy.

(*d*) The five chapters of St. John are found in a MS dating from the end of the 12th cent. in the British Museum (MS Harl. 2928), and are the earliest representative of the Bible in the dialect of southern France.

2. About the same date we meet with several references to the existence of partial translations of the Bible in the south and east of France in connexion with the Waldenses, or followers of Peter Waldus of Lyons, and the natives of the Vaud. Thus Walter Mapes, who was himself present at the Lateran Council of 1179, tells how certain Waldenses *librum domino papæ præsentaverunt lingua conscriptum Gallica in quo textus et glossa psalterii plurimorumque legis utriusque librorum continebatur*. Again, Stephen of Bourbon, writing soon after 1225, says that a man named Waldus, a native of Lyons, arranged with two priests to translate the Gospels for him, and that besides this they also translated 'several books of the Bible.' Again, a Bull of Innocent III., dated 12th July 1199, refers to the translation into French of the Gospels, St. Paul, the Psalter, the *moralia* on Job, and other books, and bids the bishop and Chapter of Metz make inquiries about them. The *moralia* Leroux de Lincy edited with the Books of Kings from a late 12th cent. MS (Bibl. Nat. *fr.* 24764) in a dialect which he thought to be Burgundian, but which P. Meyer says belongs to the neighbourhood of Liège. The MSS connected with Provence and Vaud have been made the subject of two monographs by Berger in *Romania*, xviii. 353 ff. and xix. 506 ff. The MSS themselves belong to a later date than the references just mentioned, but probably the version goes back to the religious movements in the 12th and early 13th centuries—movements of which an important feature was a study of the Bible; and the text they contain has close affinities with one which circulated in the districts mentioned, in the 13th century. Amongst the Latin MSS of the Bible we find a group with a peculiar mixed text, quite local in its distribution, containing only the NT, and

marked by curious divisions of the text. They 'present a recension quite peculiar, which cannot be confounded with any other family of text, and which can confidently be called Languedoc.' It is important to remember that these Latin MSS belong to the beginning of the 13th century. Now, the earliest of the Provençal MSS is in the library at Lyons, and is dated by P. Meyer in the third quarter of the 13th century. This translation is based on the local Latin text just mentioned (as in the long interpolation found in a few Latin MSS at Mt $20^{28}$), and that a glossed text in which the Latin was written above the Provençal. Another Provençal MS (Bibl. Nat. MS *fr.* 2425) is not earlier than the beginning of the 14th cent., and Meyer regards the version as not much older, while its linguistic peculiarities indicate an origin in the south or south-east of Provence. The translation is more free than that found in the Lyons MS, but is not independent of that MS, with which it agrees in some misreadings or misrenderings of the Latin. The two MSS exhibit 'the greatest differences, and striking resemblances.' Thus, in St. Mark the texts differ widely, in St. John the resemblances and differences are both great; on the other hand, in the Epistle of St. James and those of St. Paul the text seems to be the same. A third MS (Bibl. Nat. MS *fr.* 6261) of the Provençal belongs to the 15th century. The version is 'free, often abridged, sometimes paraphrased or accompanied by glosses.' The Latin text on which the translation rests is 'that which was in use throughout France from the 9th to the middle of the 13th cent.,' and there is hardly any trace of the local Languedoc readings already mentioned. There are other indications that the translation is earlier than the end, and perhaps than the middle, of the 13th century. In *Romania*, xviii. 430, Meyer mentions another fragment of the 14th cent. containing the same translation, on the whole, as that found in the MS just mentioned — a translation independent of that in the first two MSS, and bearing marks of having its origin among the sect of the Cathari. Another Provençal MS of the 15th cent. (Bibl. Nat. MS *fr.* 2426) contains the historical books of the OT. This translation was made not from the Latin, but from the French. Berger thus sums up (*Romania*, xix. 559–561) the history of the Provençal Bible: 'The first Provençal translation comes to us from Limoges. It consists of five chapters of St. John. The MS which contains it was copied in the 12th cent., perhaps in the Abbey of St. Martial. There is no reason to think that it is a fragment of a more complete translation, for it is a liturgical section. About one hundred years after, in the south of Languedoc, and very probably in the department of Aude, an interlinear version of the NT was made over the text then used in that district. This version, preserved for us in the Lyons MS, was the official translation of the Cathari, and undoubtedly exercised a great influence in the south. It is difficult to believe that the Vaud version and the second Provençal version (MS *fr.* 2425) have not been, to some extent, influenced by it. . . . Finally, in the 15th cent., beyond a doubt, the Provençal Bible was completed by a translation of the historical books of the OT. . . . This new sacred history was not derived from the Latin, but from a French compilation, a composite work due to several translators.'

3. Another group of MSS contains a text certainly used by the inhabitants of the Vaud, but there is nothing at all to prove that the translation was their work. Five of these MSS have been carefully examined by Berger. The oldest is the Carpentras MS, No. 22, in the Municipal Library, which dates from the 14th cent., and contains, besides the NT, the Sapiential books. Another MS closely allied to the preceding is a Dublin MS, dated 1522, which 'would seem to be a reproduction of the MS of Carpentras,' only that it contains eight chapters of Ecclesiasticus not found in the latter. Two other MSS, one at Grenoble and another at Cambridge, are closely related. The first is particularly interesting because of a liturgical point, implying a connexion with Bohemia; and both have a curious translation of the latter part of the Acts derived from an Italian version. The last MS of this family, at Zürich, belongs to the 16th cent., and has been influenced by the text of Erasmus.

Of the relation of this group to the Provençal, Berger writes (*Romania*, xviii. 405) that 'it is not possible to give a decided answer. There are innumerable differences of all kinds between the two families, and the most important perhaps is that their Latin text is not absolutely the same. . . . It is not impossible that the relation of the Vaud and Provençal texts may be thus explained. After the first edition [*i.e.* of the Provençal text], represented by the Lyons MS, a redaction of the interlinear Provençal text might have been made into more modern language, and one which the translator believed to be more in accord with the Latin. Into this work variants of every kind, even of the Latin text, might have found their way.'

Of the OT, the only part which has found a place in these MSS is that which includes the Sapiential books, and that probably has a different origin from the NT. The version is based on the Latin, corresponding exactly with the revision made at Paris at the beginning of the 13th cent., and 'contains none of the peculiarities of the southern texts of the end of the 13th cent., of which the Vaud NT seems to be the translation.'

4. All these translations with which we have so far been engaged were local and partial; but the same century which gave birth to the translations of Provence and Vaud also saw the origin of the first complete French Bible. This dates from some time after the year 1226, the time to which Roger Bacon assigns the Paris revision of the Vulgate, the chapter divisions of which (as found in MSS Bibl. Nat. *lat.* 15185, 15467) are adopted by the French Bible. An inferior date is fixed by the second Dominican revision of the Vulgate made by Hugh of St. Cher about 1250. The limits of time within which this complete French Bible was made are therefore fixed pretty narrowly. The translation was made at Paris 'by several translators working under the same guidance and using several Latin MSS, of which the chief was a copy of the Bible, corrected by the University.' The character of the translations varies widely in the different parts of the Bible. Some books, for example Genesis, are glossed throughout; in the rest of the Pentateuch there are no glosses, in other books there are few. The translation also varies very much in merit in respect of style and accuracy. There are many resemblances between the Gospels and the Prophets. The translation of the Acts and Catholic Epistles is poor; on the other hand, that of St. Paul's Epistles, especially the Epistle to the Romans, is very good. Some MSS give two versions of the Epistle to Titus. All these things indicate that the work was not that of one translator, but of many.

Of the entire Bible we have only one perfect MS (Bibl. Nat. *fr.* 6 and 7), which dates from the end of the 14th century. Another MS in the same library (*fr.* 899) is a good deal older, dating from about 1250; but several books are not found in it, and it is mutilated at the beginning and end, for it begins with Gn $2^{14}$ and ends with 1 P $2^{21}$. Of the first part of the Bible we have three MSS of the 13th and 14th cents., viz. Arsenal MS 5056.

Brit. Mus. Harleian 616, and Cambridge MS Ee. 3. 52. Of the second part of the Bible we have very many MSS. Amongst the oldest and most important of these, all of them belonging to the 13th cent., are Mazarin 684, Bibl. Nat. *fr.* 398, Brussels MS A. 211, Bibl. Nat. *fr.* 12581. It is not, however, easy to distinguish between MSS of the second part of the French Bible and MSS of the second volume, the so-called *Bible Historiale* (which incorporated bodily the Bible text), unless the MSS are older than the date of the *Bible Historiale.* This work was a translation into French of the *Historia Scholastica*, composed by Peter Comestor about 1179. It was a *résumé* of Bible history, incorporating many legends and a good deal of secular history. The French translation, or edition, was made by Guiars des Moulins, of Aire, in the N.E. of France, at the end of the 13th cent. He dealt very freely with the original, sometimes abridging, sometimes inserting, extracts of Bible text. The *Bible Historiale Complétée*—of which the oldest MS (A.D. 1312) is Brit. Mus. i. A. xx.—is the name given to Guiars' work when accompanied by a translation of the actual text of the Bible. The smallest copies do not contain the text of Chron., Ezra, Neh., Job. Some add Job, while the so-called *Grandes Bibles Historiales* give the complete text of Chron., Ezra, and Nehemiah. The popularity rapidly attained by the work of Guiars des Moulins secured a wide circulation for the French translation of the Bible of which it incorporated so much.

5. In the 14th cent. there are only three translations which require to be noticed—

(*a*) The first is an Anglo-Norman version made in England, which never had any influence in France. The earliest MS (Bibl. Nat. *fr.* 1) ends with He 13, and belongs to the first half of the 14th century. A second MS (Brit. Mus. i. C. iii.) dates from the 15th cent., and contains from Genesis to Tobit. The translation is not a good one.

(*b*) The second translation belonging to this period is the so-called Bible of king John, at whose command the work was begun by John of Sy in the diocese of Rheims. It is found in a MS (Bibl. Nat. *fr.* 15397) of the year 1355. Berger describes it as an 'excellent revision of the Anglo-Norman Bible,' giving a text independent of the 13th cent. translation.

(*c*) Thirdly, we have to notice the incomplete version made by Raoul de Presles. This is the 'Bible of Charles V.,' a revised text of which, containing the whole OT, is found in MS Bibl. Nat. *fr.* 158, a 14th cent. MS.

6. The 15th cent. is 'the age of MSS retouched, and of the beginning of printed texts.' The earliest printed text is that which appeared in Lyons in 1477 or 1478 with the names of Jullien Macho and Peter Farget as editors. It reproduces the text of the 13th cent. Bible, but is an edition of no importance. Much more important is the edition printed by Verard (with no date on the title-page), at dates variously given as 1487 and 1496. This contains a text very much like that in MS *fr.* 159, and embodies a revision made by John de Rely, confessor of Charles VIII.

7. With the beginning of the 16th cent. we come to the important work of le Fèvre d'Étaples, which appeared between 1523 and 1530. The NT was published by Simon de Colines at Paris in 1523, and often reprinted later. The completed Bible appeared at Antwerp in 1530. The OT is largely a new translation from the Vulgate, and the glosses of the *Bible Historiale* for the most part disappear from the French Bible for the first time. But, save where J. de Rely had given the paraphrase of the *Bible Historiale,* and not the Bible text, le Fèvre only 'revised' his predecessor's work, comparing it with the Latin. The translation is described as 'painfully literal,' but the marginal notes with which it was accompanied were thought to savour of Protestantism, and in 1546 the book was put on the Index, and many copies were destroyed. A few years later a revision of the Antwerp Bible was undertaken by two Louvain divines in the interests of Roman Catholicism, and appeared in 1550. Very few changes from le Fèvre's version were made, but the translation was authorized and frequently revised (in 1608, 1621, 1647) and reprinted.

8. The translation of Olivetan of Noyon in Picardy marks an epoch in the history of the French Bible. This, the first French Protestant version, was published in 1535 at Serrières near to Neufchatel, and is sometimes called the Bible of Serrières. It was frequently republished with numerous revisions in the successive editions. The work of Olivetan has been the subject of several articles by Reuss in the *Revue de Théologie* (series iii. vols. 3 and 4), in which his relation to preceding workers is carefully examined in detail. His chief contribution was in the translation of the OT. This is, according to the estimate of Reuss, not only a work of erudition and merit, but a real *chef d'œuvre.* He had the Antwerp Bible before him, but generally the changes are so numerous that it would be hard to prove his use of it. There is no doubt that we have in the OT a new translation in which he sought faithfully to reproduce the original. Simon asserts that Olivetan had little or no Greek or Hebrew knowledge, and Pétavel that he was really dependent on Pagninus' Latin version of the Hebrew; but Graf says his marginal notes show that he does not follow Pagninus slavishly, but himself consulted and studied the Hebrew. In the Psalter, Olivetan translated from the Hebrew, whereas le Fèvre's version, in the Antwerp Bible, was based, like nearly all the mediæval French Psalters, on the Gallican Psalter of Jerome, which, as we have seen, represented a Hexaplar text. In the Apocrypha (*Revue de Théologie*, iii. 4. 14) he did not himself make a new translation, but 'confined himself to reproducing, with very slight and superficial corrections, the translation printed at Antwerp.' The marginal notes show the amount of work he himself did, sometimes explaining the Hebrew, in other places substituting one French word for another. These notes show that the Greek has been used in some cases, while elsewhere it has been quite neglected. The NT is substantially the same as that printed in the 1523 edition of le Fèvre, but there are changes probably due to the use of the fourth edition of Erasmus (1527), in which the Greek text, a Latin translation of it, and the Vulgate are placed side by side. That he has carefully used the Greek is seen by the care with which he marks the words in le Fèvre's version which are not in the Greek. These he prints in small type. Reuss regards his work, judged by the standard of that time, as indicating an 'erudition really prodigious.' It has been often asserted that Calvin collaborated with Olivetan in this work, but there is no proof of any association with Olivetan in the original translation, or in any revision before 1545. Before this latter date many editions had appeared,—including an anonymous one under the name of Belisem de Belimakom (*i.e.* 'no name from nowhere'),—and many changes had been made.

The first really important revision was that published at Geneva in 1588, which checked for a while the changes which had been introduced from time to time into Olivetan's version, and it is important not because of the changes made by the Geneva revisers, but because the edition became official.

Of the Geneva translation there were very many editions in the 17th and 18th cents. which had a wide circulation. The work of Martin (NT in 1696, Bible in 1707) and Roques' revision of it (1736) are comparatively unimportant.

A more complete and important revision of Olivetan's work was carried out by Osterwald, who published a Bible at Amsterdam in 1724. This was followed in 1744 by a much more thorough revision, which regarded mainly the French idiom and the exegetical views of the time. It is clearer than Martin, and bears the marks of careful work, but as a translation is heavy in style. Another Geneva edition of some importance appeared in 1802–1805, and in 1822 a revised edition of Osterwald was published by the Bible Societies of Lausanne and Neufchatel, which in turn was revised more than once later. In 1834 a committee was formed at Paris to make a good translation, and they proposed 'to combine Martin and Osterwald, keeping the exactness of the one and the clearness of the other.' As a result, a NT was published in 1842 at the expense of the S.P.C.K., and this was followed by the OT in 1849. But the Bible of Osterwald was still the most popular, and feeling was so strong that in 1863 a disruption of the Bible Societies in France was the result, the majority wishing to circulate other texts, while a minority was anxious to adhere to Osterwald.

9. Leaving, at this point, the history of Olivetan's version, we must go back chronologically to mention the French translation made by Castalion of Geneva, on which he had been at work since 1544, and which he published in 1555. This translation was made, not from his Latin version published in 1551, but from the Hebrew and Greek. His chief aim was to produce a work intelligible to the common people; and to effect his object he did not hesitate, if necessary, to coin a word. The style is brief, nervous, and often effective, but the expressions chosen are sometimes undignified. While its language was strongly censured by some when it appeared, as by Henry Stephen and the Genevan professors, it has been more highly valued by later Protestants as 'the first translation truly French and truly modern.'

10. It is not necessary to delay over the many Catholic versions of the 17th cent., connected with the names of Corbin (1643), Marolles (1649, etc.), Amelote (1666), Bouhours (1697), which were all based, more or less, on the Vulgate, and are chiefly interesting as showing the existence of a need among the French Catholics.

The only one of lasting importance is the work of the Port Royalists, which is associated with the names of Antony and Louis Isaac le Maistre. The last named is better known as de Sacy. The translation of the NT from the Vulgate was begun by Antony le Maistre before 1657, and revised and completed by Louis le Maistre, who used the original Greek. The whole was revised by Arnauld and others, with the help of the ancient Versions and Patristic commentaries. The translation was finally authorized, and the NT appeared at Mons in 1667. The OT translation was the work of de Sacy himself during his imprisonment in the Bastille; but the publication was authorized only if notes were added to the translation. This was done, and the result was that the publication begun in 1672 was only completed in 30 volumes, the last of which appeared in 1695. 'The translation made from the Vulgate is not always literal enough: it pays more attention to clearness and elegance than to faithfulness. Of all the French versions, it is the purest from the point of view of the language, and the best written.' It has been often reprinted with and without notes, and during the last century it was circulated even by the Bible Societies.

11. Numberless translations of the whole or part of the Bible have been published both by Roman Catholics and Protestants during the last century, which need not detain us. It is only necessary in conclusion to notice the translation of the NT published by Oltramare in 1872 and that of the OT by Segond in 1874. These were combined in an edition published by the French Bible Society in 1882. Segond completed his translation of the whole Bible by publishing a NT in 1880, which, though not so good as Oltramare's version of the NT, has been circulated widely by the English and French Bible Societies. In 1900 the French Bible Society again published the OT of Segond, and the NT version of Oltramare.

LITERATURE.—S. Berger, *La Bible Française au moyen age*, Paris, 1884, 'Les Bibles Provençals,' etc., in *Romania*, vols. xviii. and xix.; E. Mangenot, art. 'Françaises Versions de la Bible' in Vigouroux's *Dictionnaire de la Bible*; le Long, *Bibliotheca Sacra*; E. Reuss, numerous articles in the Strassburg *Revue de Théologie*; Douen, *Histoire de la Société Biblique Protestante*; Herzog, *RE*[3] iii. 127 ff.

ii. ITALIAN VERSIONS.—1. None of the MSS of the Italian Bible which have survived probably belong to an earlier date than the 14th cent.; but the evidence they afford as to the text from which they are derived enables us to refer the origin of the translation to the middle or second half of the preceding century. It is not likely that the whole Bible was translated as early as this. That part is earlier than the 14th cent. is clear from the differences between the text of the Italian version and the Latin texts of the 14th and 15th cents., and its frequent agreement (*e.g.* at Ex $34^{28}$, Nu $3^{45}$) with the peculiar local readings of earlier Latin MSS circulating in Northern Italy. An early date is also indicated by other evidence furnished by some of the MSS. Thus the order of the books, and the divisions of the text found in two Paris MSS, and another at Siena, agree with those of Latin MSS prior to the 13th century. Other facts preclude the obvious suggestion that the resemblance is due to the use of the early Latin MSS by a 14th cent. translator. The beginnings of the version are to be traced to the 'religious and literary influence of France,' and it has many points in common with the early French MSS, more particularly those connected with Provence and the valleys of the Vaud. These resemblances occur throughout the whole Bible. Thus the Italian Psalter is in close agreement with one of the earliest French Psalters. Of the Gospels, again, M. Berger writes: 'The Italian Gospels stand in so close a relationship to the different Provençal texts that we have to look to each of them in turn for parallels to the peculiarities of our version.'* The Provençal text to which the Italian is related is an early form of that text. The same is true of the rest of the Italian version of the NT, but there are indications that it belongs to a somewhat later date. One of the most striking illustrations of the relationship between the Italian and Provençal texts is to be found in Jn $1^1$, where 'In the beginning was the Word' is rendered by the Italian version 'In the beginning was the Son of God.' This is found also in Provençal MSS, and other versions connected with them. Another parallel between the Italian and Provençal is found in the famous passage 1 Jn $5^{7.8}$.

Probably in Italy, as elsewhere, only single books or sections of the Bible were first translated; and those the books most in use for devo-

* *Romania*, xxiii. 386. In this article the late M. Berger gives a very careful account of the early Italian Bible, and many facts have been taken from it.

tional purposes, or for edification, such as the Gospels, the Psalms, and the Sapiential books of the OT, and more particularly the Book of Proverbs. Thus the earliest MS of the version which is assigned doubtfully to the 13th cent., a MS in the library of St. Mark at Venice (Cl. i. *ital.* 80), is a translation only of the Gospels and Epistles of the Sundays according to the Roman year. Other MSS of the Gospels consist of extracts, making a harmony of the Four Gospels, beginning sometimes with one, sometimes with another, this harmony being often paraphrastic. Others give a complete text of the Gospels; and of these complete MSS Berger enumerates six of the 14th and 15th centuries.

2. To those parts of the Bible which have been mentioned, translations of the rest were subsequently added, the OT being for the most part the latest to be dealt with. The completion of the translation was probably the work of the Dominicans of the 14th cent.; but complete Bibles, owing to their expense, were rare. As elsewhere, the historical books of the OT were at first paraphrased rather than translated, on the plan of the *Historia Scholastica* or the French *Bible Historiale*, modelled on it. In this form we find a good deal of the OT in a Siena MS (I. v. 5) of the 14th century. Another Siena MS (F. iii. 4) is 'our best MS' of the OT, the whole of which it contains. This last MS dates from the 14th or 15th cent., and is interesting for the old order in which the books of the Bible are found, and the old system of divisions of the text. Other noteworthy MSS are two belonging to the Riccardi Library in Florence, one of which (MS 1250) is a 15th cent. MS of the whole NT; the other (MS 1252) is a 14th cent. MS of the second half of the Bible from Ecclesiasticus to Revelation. The first half of the Bible, Genesis to Ps 14, is found in a Laurentian MS (Ashb. 1102) of the year 1466; while a Paris MS (*ital.* 3 and 4) of the year 1472 contains the second and third volumes of a Bible, beginning with Ezra. The only complete MS of the whole Bible which has come down to us is also in the Bibliothèque Nationale at Paris (MS, *ital.* 1 and 2). This dates from the end of the 15th cent., and with the other Paris MS came from the library of the kings of Naples, and no doubt represents a version made there.

3. The MSS, in which the version is contained either wholly or in part, have many of them been carefully examined with a view to the evidence which they afford in regard to its general character and history. This may be summarized as follows. The language is, as a rule, the Tuscan dialect as spoken at Florence in the 14th cent.; but in some cases, *e.g.* in the Psalter contained in the St. Mark MS, *ital.* 57, the influence of the Venetian dialect is evident, and the MS of the Gospels (MS, *ital.* i. 3) in the same library is in pure Venetian. The text found in both these MSS, as might be expected, represents a different underlying text from that found in the majority of MSS.

In the Pentateuch the MSS as a rule present one and the same version; but one MS (Riccard. 1655), containing Genesis only, preserves a text quite different from that of the other MSS, such as Siena MS, F. iii. 4. In the historical books we have two versions—one more incorrect, abounding in glosses and paraphrase, and therefore probably the earlier, found in the Siena MS (I. v. 5); the other more literal and exact (Siena MS, F. iii. 4, Paris, Bibl. Nat. *ital.* 3). In the Psalter we find many variants in the comparatively large number of MSS, but these really represent only one original version. In the Book of Proverbs, one of the earliest books to be translated, there are almost as many versions as there are MSS. Of the Book of Judith there are two versions—the one free, the other literal. For the rest of the OT, though there are many variants, yet these do not indicate more than one translation.

Passing to the NT, we find that most of the MSS of the Gospels go back to one and the same version. An exception must be made in respect of the Venetian text (Marc. MS, *ital.* i. 3) already mentioned, which stands alone. The MSS of the Acts vary in the glosses which they insert; and Minocchi traces three redactions of the version, but these are not independent. The translator's name is given in a prologue found in some MSS as Domenico Cavalca, a Dominican of Pisa, who died in 1342. A curious fact mentioned by Berger (*l.c.* pp. 391, 392) is that this version has been used in two MSS connected with the Vaud, and is the source of an otherwise untraced rendering of Ac 16 onwards, found in those MSS. The process of Italian indebtedness to France has here been reversed. In St. Paul's Epistles there is only one version, though it has passed through more than one redaction. The version found in Riccard. 1252 seems at first sight to be independent; but there are expressions, which it has in common with other MSS, which point the other way. In the Catholic Epistles we find, as elsewhere, two translations—the one incorrect and glossed, the other literal. Most MSS of the Apocalypse contain the same text, but one (Riccard. 1349) is quite independent, and is related to the Provençal texts. The most striking and sufficient proof of this is the rendering of the words 'one like unto the son of Man' by 'one like the son of the Virgin,' a rendering found in several versions connected with the south of France.

In regard to the text of the version, Berger (*l.c.* p. 417) sums up as follows: 'We cannot affirm that it was translated entire by one single person, or by the same group of translators. . . . As for the NT, it appears to have come entirely from one pen, and that the pen of a man who knew the Provençal language perfectly, and who had the Provençal Testament under his eye or in his memory. Many readings of the Latin which the translator adopts are those which were current at the beginning of the 13th cent. in Languedoc. Sometimes the Italian text is not a translation of the Latin text, but of the Provençal or Vaud version.'

4. The name of one translator, Cavalca, has been already mentioned, but probably all he did was to revise an older text resembling those of southern France. Another name connected with the old Italian version as a translator is that of John of Tavelli, born in 1386, and afterwards bishop of Ferrara, who is said to have translated the version printed at Venice. An old Life of him ascribes a translation to him, but is indefinite as to the extent of the supposed translation; and the statement as to the Venice edition is disproved by the fact that the printed version is contained in 14th cent. MSS, while John of Tavelli was then too young to have done the work ascribed to him. The early versions have also been assigned to James of Voragine, Passavanti, and others. Passavanti is himself excluded by the way in which he speaks of the versions which existed in his time, and the mention of his and other names is probably due to the wish to assign the version to persons well known in connexion with the formation of early Italian prose.

5. Of course, in connexion with the Reformation movement, several translations came into existence. The earliest is associated with the name of A. Brucioli, one of those who championed Florentine liberty, and suffered for so doing. His translation was begun in 1528, and the NT was first

published by Giunti at Venice in 1530. This was followed by the Psalms in 1531, and the whole Bible in 1532. This complete translation (and also translations of the separate books) was frequently reprinted. On his title-page Brucioli claims that the version was made from the Hebrew and the Greek. He probably knew Hebrew; but Simon has proved that no great knowledge of Hebrew is shown, and the author very probably relied on Pagninus' Latin version for the OT, and that of Erasmus for the NT. His commentaries betray Protestant ideas, and his work was condemned and put on Paul IV.'s Index of 1559, and after this it practically ceased to be reprinted. In 1538 a Dominican of some repute, named Marmochino, issued a translation which was in reality only a redaction of Brucioli's work, bringing it more into conformity with the Vulgate. The 16th cent. produced many other translations of separate books, with and without commentaries, but none are of any special interest.

6. The most important translation, which is still the official Bible of Italian Protestants, circulated by the British and Foreign Bible Society, is that of J. Diodati, who was born at Lucca in 1576, and died in 1649. Diodati was a very good scholar, and when only twenty-one was appointed by Beza professor of Hebrew at Geneva. His work is described as remarkable from the point of view of literature and of scientific accuracy. As a rule he keeps close to the Vulgate, except in the Psalter, where the Vulgate follows the LXX. An edition of the whole Bible was published at Geneva in 1607. The NT was published separately at Geneva in 1608 and at Amsterdam in 1665. An edition with commentaries appeared in 1641. A carefully revised edition was published by the London *Society for Promoting Christian Knowledge* in 1854.

7. Of Catholic translations there were fewer in this country than elsewhere. The prohibition, by Pope Pius IV. in 1564, of the reading of the Bible in the vulgar tongue was not removed till 1757, when Benedict XIV. gave a qualified permission, and so for two centuries the Catholics had no need of a translation. The only one which need be mentioned is that of Martini, archbishop of Florence, published in 1776 at Turin, and circulated by the British and Foreign Bible Society in editions of the NT (1813) and of the OT (1821).

8. In conclusion, it is necessary to speak briefly of the earliest editions of the Italian Bible. One of these was printed by Wendelin at Venice in August 1471, and bears on its title-page as the name of the translator Nicolo di Malherbi. Berger says of it that 'the text in general differs much from that of the MSS'; but it is really not a new translation, but the old version with a few changes, chiefly dialectical, from the Tuscan of the MSS to Venetian. Of the frequent later editions of Malherbi's translation, one—that of 1490—is noteworthy if, as Carini says, the designs for its ornamentation were the work of Bellini and Botticelli. Another edition, which followed immediately in October of the same year, is that published by Jenson, the text of which was based partly on that of the MSS, partly, as in the NT and Psalter, on that of Malherbi's edition. The explanation of this is that the printing was begun simultaneously at different points. Berger says of it (*l.c.* p. 364) that it is 'faithful to the MSS, and those as a rule the best'; but the value of the edition is enormously depreciated by the fact of its being in large measure a reproduction of Malherbi's work. It had become a bibliographical rarity, for it was not in great demand, and was reprinted with a valuable introduction by Negroni in 1882–1887 in ten volumes.

LITERATURE.—S. Berger, 'La Bible Italienne au moyen age' in *Romania*, 1894, p. 358 ff. (with bibliography, and list of MSS appended); S. Minocchi, art. 'Italiennes Versions de la Bible' in Vigouroux's *Dict. de la Bible*; Negroni, *La Bibbia volgare*; Carini, *Le Versioni della Bibbia in volgare italiano*; le Long, *Bibliotheca Sacra*.

iii. SPANISH VERSIONS.—1. The history of the Bible in Spain begins with Priscillian and Lucinius of Bætica, the correspondent of Jerome (*Epp.* lxxi. and lxxv.); and four centuries later the school of sacred palæography at Seville and afterwards at Toledo, from which came the *Codex Toletanus* and *Codex Cavensis*, might well detain us. The importance of the Visigothic text of the Vulgate, and the influence of Theodulf and the Latin Bible of Spain beyond the border of that country, are other interesting subjects closely connected with the Spanish Bible.

2. But our immediate object is to trace the history of the Bible in the Spanish language. To this there is no allusion before the 13th cent., when John I., king of Arragon, passed a royal decree in 1233 at Tarragona, that no one, clergy or laity, was to keep in his house any translation into the vulgar tongue of the OT or NT. This prohibition implies the existence of such a translation. A few years later, however, the reign of Alphonse X., surnamed 'the Wise' (1252–1284), marks a period of literary activity, especially in regard to the translation of ancient writings into Spanish. Among other works he is said to have ordered a translation of Jerome's text of the Bible. One of the most important productions of this reign was the commencement, at any rate, of a *Historia General* very similar in character to the *Bible Historiale* (see above, p. 405[a]), but in its original form probably more general, and containing less of the Bible text than the French work. The *Historia* was divided into five parts, the first of which corresponded roughly to the Pentateuch; the second covered from the death of Moses to the death of David; the third the Psalter, Sapiential books, and some of the Prophets; of the fourth we do not know the contents; the fifth contained some of the Prophets, the Apocryphal books, and a large part of the NT. It is probable that the first two parts alone go back to the time of Alphonse X., and that in Spain, as elsewhere, the earliest form of the composition had comparatively little of the actual text of the Bible, though a good deal of it was paraphrased. Of this work we have many MSS of the 14th and 15th cents., some with, some without, the text of the Bible. It is impossible, however, to define precisely the date and origin of the Bible text contained in the work, the later MSS of which in Spain as in France no doubt gradually incorporated more and more of the *ipsissima verba* of the Bible. Comparatively little, if any, can be assigned to the date of Alphonse X.

3. One almost unique feature in the history of the Spanish version of the Bible, as compared with those made in other countries, is the large proportion of early translations made from the Hebrew text, the work of Jewish Rabbis. The history of these, and of the translations made from the Latin, has to be recovered from an examination of the text of MSS contained in the Escurial and elsewhere, and from such other information as these MSS give in the way of prefaces, notes, etc. Much has been done in this direction by Éguren in the work mentioned at the end of this section, and by Berger in a detailed comparison of the text of the MSS in two articles in *Romania* for 1899, where a full description of a number of MSS and a bibliography will be found.

Among the important MSS which contain translations from the Hebrew may be mentioned two in the Escurial, I. j. 8 and I. j. 6. The first of these is a 15th cent. MS, which contains a large part of the first half of the Bible, including the Psalter. This version of the Psalter is said, in a note prefixed to it, to be the work of Herman, a German, and to be made from the Hebrew. Now a man of this name, known as a translator of Aristotle, is connected with Toledo about the year 1240. There is no reason, then, to doubt that the Psalter was translated about that time by Herman. He probably used the *Psalt. Heb.* of Jerome, and so we find *ṣelah* (in Ps 51 [Eng. and Heb. 52]$^5$) rendered by 'always'; but the translation shows an independent knowledge of Hebrew, as at Ps $41^2$ and $41^7$. The second MS mentioned above is assigned to the 14th cent., and contains the second half of the Bible. The Spanish used is that of the early 14th cent., and there are many points of resemblance, in respect of the text divisions, summaries, etc., between this MS and the Codex Toletanus, the Bible of Theodulf, and the Visigothic text—a resemblance which points to an early date for the translation. There are various other MSS containing versions from the Hebrew, *e.g.* Escur. Bibl. MS 4, and a bilingual (Lat. and Spanish) MS belonging to the Royal Hist. Library at Madrid, which begins with the Major Prophets and ends with 2 Maccabees. The best known of these translations is the so-called Bible of the Duke of Alba, the MS of which is now in the Liria Palace at Madrid. This is described by Berger as an 'unrivalled monument of Spanish art and science,' 'an enterprise unrivalled in the Middle Ages.' The work was ordered in 1422 by Louis de Guzman, master of the order of Calatrava, who paid more than £3000 for it. The translation was carried out between 1422 and 1430 by Rabbi Moses Arragel (*i.e.* 'the Expert') of Maqueda, near Toledo. It was not a new translation, but a revision of older texts.

Of versions made from the Latin Vulgate may be mentioned—(1) the Bible of Quiroga (Escur. MS 4), given by Cardinal Quiroga to Philip II. In this the order of the books is that of the Vulgate; and the Apocryphal books, not in the Hebrew, are translated; (2) a translation made for Alphonse V., king of Arragon (1416–1458). This MS contains the books from Proverbs to the Apocalypse; (3) a translation made by Martin de Lucena (about 1450) of the Gospels and St. Paul's Epistles contained in Escur. MS 11, a MS now lost; (4) a translation (in Escur. MS 7) of the books from Lv 7–2 Kings.

4. The earliest printed edition of any part of the Spanish Bible is that of the Pentateuch printed at Venice in 1497, which was the work of Spanish Jews exiled from their native country. By far the most important and the best known of the early Spanish Bibles is the so-called *Bible of Ferrara*, which contains the whole OT except Lamentations, and was the work of two Portuguese Jews, Duarte Pinel and Jerome de Vargas. It is not really a new translation, but only an editing of the old revision made with reference to the Hebrew. The translation, we are told, leaves much to be desired in respect of elegance and correctness, and is often inexact and full of Hebraisms. Some corrections were made in later editions, of which there have been very many between 1611 and the present day, published in many cases at Amsterdam. Besides the Bible of Ferrara, there have been many Jewish versions of the whole or parts of the OT: thus Plaine mentions three editions of the Pentateuch at Amsterdam, six versions of the Psalter (between 1625 and 1720), a translation of the Song of Songs, of the 'First Prophets,' of the Hagiographa, and of Isaiah and Jeremiah.

5. Translations made by Catholics in the 16th, 17th, and early 18th centuries are comparatively unimportant. The Council of Trent prohibited the reading of the Bible in the vulgar tongue, and one of the rules of the Inquisition was stringent in the same direction. It was not till 1757 that Benedict XIV. permitted the reading of the Bible in the language of the country under certain conditions; and fifteen years later, in 1782, the Spanish Inquisition gave similar permission. Moreover, in the 16th cent. at any rate the bulk of the Catholic theology of Spain was written not in Spanish but in Latin. For the most part, therefore, the efforts of Catholics in regard to Bible translation were confined to those parts of it which had a place in the liturgy, and several of these attempts were never printed. Of the Gospels, four complete or partial translations are recorded. The first is a translation of the liturgical Gospels and Epistles by Montesiro, which was printed at Madrid in 1512; the second is an anonymous translation of the four Gospels, contained in MS Escur. I. j. 9, but never printed, which is not dated, but is later than the Complutensian Bible of 1514–1517 which it uses; the third is a translation by a Benedictine, John de Robles, made in 1550 which is found in MS Escur. H. i. 4, but was never printed; the last is a translation of St. Matthew and St. Luke by Siguenza. Of the Psalms there were several translations, including one by Villa, a Benedictine of Montserrat, which was afterwards put on the Index; another by Cornelius Snoi, published at Amsterdam in 1553. The Sapiential books also found many translators, including the famous Louis of Léon, an Augustinian who translated the Book of Job. There was also a version of the Apocalypse by Gregory Lopez, which was published after his death.

6. More important were the Protestant translations. The earliest of these was the version of the Psalter by Juan de Valdes, a Lutheran, the MS of which is at Vienna. This was not published till 1880. To the same translator belongs the version of Romans and 1 Corinthians, printed at Venice in 1536 and 1557. The first published Spanish NT was the work of Francis of Enzinas, printed at Antwerp in 1543, and reprinted many times later. Another version, regarded by some as a model of Castilian style, was the translation of the NT from the Greek, and the Psalter from the Hebrew, the work of Juan Perez of Pineda, who fled to Geneva to escape the Inquisition. The first published edition of the whole Bible is the *Biblia del Oso*, so called from the bear which appeared as the frontispiece. This was the work of Cassiodore de Reina, a distinguished Hellenist, and occupied twelve years. The OT portion was probably little more than a translation of the Latin version of Pagninus. It is regarded as a satisfactory translation, and was published at Basle in 1567–1569. The edition by Cyprian de Valera (Amsterdam, 1602) was practically only a revision of the work of Cassiodore.

7. In the period after 1782, when the Inquisition revoked the prohibition against reading the Bible in the vulgar tongue, a number of Catholic translations appeared of the Psalms, Sapiential books, and Gospels. Only two of these Catholic versions are important. The first is the work of Philip Scio, afterwards bishop of Segovia, and was published at Valencia in 1791–1793. A second edition was published at Madrid in 1795–1797. This translation is based on the Vulgate, and is on the whole 'correct and elegant, though sometimes lacking in clearness and exactness, and more often in warmth and life.' As the first complete version by a Spanish Catholic it was received with enthusiasm, and went through many editions. But the

need of a translation based on the Hebrew and Greek began to be felt, and in 1807 Charles IV. ordered such a one. This was the work of Felix Torres y Amat, afterwards bishop of Astorga, and was published 1823–1825. Though very successful and often reprinted, it did not supplant the translation of Scio, of which numerous editions still appear. There are no recent Protestant translations. The copies circulated in large numbers by the British and Foreign Bible Society are practically only reprints of the early Protestant translations of Enzinas, Cassiodore de Reina, and Cyprian de Valera already mentioned, and of the later Catholic versions of Scio and Torres Amat.

8. Besides the Castilian versions of the Bible of which we have hitherto spoken, the translation into Catalan, the language of Catalonia, also demands attention in connexion with the history of the Bible in Spain. Both by language and by political ties the district of Catalonia was in the early Middle Ages closely connected with southern France, and we are not surprised therefore to find a close resemblance between the Catalan version and those of France. According to Berger (*Romania*, xix. 523), the version 'is not older than the 14th cent., and was made in all probability by a native of Catalonia, educated at the University of Paris.' Its dependence on the French version is shown by the way in which it reproduces the most characteristic glosses of the French Bible.

The oldest MS of the version is a Marmoutier MS of the NT now at Paris (Bibl. Nat. *Fonds esp.* 486) of the 14th century. We have also later MSS —(1) Bibl. Nat. *Fonds esp.* 2–4; (2) Bibl. Nat. *Fonds esp.* 5; (3) Brit. Mus. Egerton 1526, all of the 15th cent., and all containing the same portions of the Bible,—which enable us to trace the history of the text to some extent. These later MSS preserve the same general text as that contained in the 14th cent. MS, but the glosses of the French Bible have been removed. 'The foundation of the version is the same: the phrases of the 15th cent. MSS from end to end are modelled on those of the 14th, and a number of characteristic expressions attest the original identity of the translation.' Of MSS of the Psalter in this language Berger mentions ten, and in them he distinguishes three independent versions. One is found in Bibl. Nat. *Fonds esp.* 5, another is contained in Bibl. Nat. *Fonds esp.* 2, and Egerton 1526, and a third in Bibl. Nat. *Fonds fr.* 2434. The first, like the other Catalan Psalters, is based on the Gallican Psalter; the second seems to rest on the Hebrew Psalter, but this is really not the case; the third represents the most ancient form of the text, and this last is based on a French version, for 'all the peculiarities of the Catalan text are explained by the French, and several are only explained by it.' The Sapiential books show evidence of the use of French and Latin as bases for translation. In the Book of Proverbs both French and Latin influences are clear, in Wisdom there is no evidence of French, in Sirach the two alternate. There is a similar want of uniformity in regard to the Prophets. The translation of Isaiah is made from the Vulgate, but shows French influence. In Jeremiah, Ezekiel, and Daniel there is no trace of such influence. Nor is the underlying Latin text the same; for, while Isaiah and Daniel rest on the ordinary Paris text of the 13th cent., there is no sign in Jeremiah and Ezekiel of the characteristic readings of that text. Of the Gospels we have three Catalan versions—one very inexact and paraphrased, the others literal. Two of these have many points of resemblance to the Provençal, by the help of which they were made, viz. those contained in the Marmoutier MS and Bibl. Nat. *Fonds esp.* 2; the third contained in a Barcelona MS does not appear to have anything in common with the Provençal text. In regard to St. Paul's Epistles, there is 'no doubt but that the Catalan Bible of the 15th cent. is dependent on that of the 14th, and the latter on the Bible in the language of France' (*langue d'oil*). The Apocalypse was based not on the French, but on the Vulgate; but in the middle of this translation made from the Latin we find reminiscences of the French. Berger sums up as follows in regard to the NT: 'I conclude by saying that the Catalan version of the NT was made at the latest in the 14th cent. in some places from a French text, in others from a Latin text very similar to those in use at Paris. The writer probably incorporated into his work an earlier translation of the Gospels.'

The names of two translators are met with in writings on this version. The one is Boniface Ferrer, to whom is ascribed the translation printed near Valencia in 1477–1478; but, while the version belongs to the 14th cent., Ferrer lived in the 15th. A more important name is that of Sabruguera, a Dominican of the beginning of the 14th century. He studied at Paris about the year 1307, and this would agree with the character of the version, as indicated by the MSS. Further than this, one MS attributes to him a version of the Psalter.

The only early edition is that just referred to; but nothing of it remains except four pages of one copy now in the monastery of Porta Cæli, near Valencia. A note on one of these pages preserves the name of Ferrer as the translator, and tells us the translation was made by him, with the assistance of other scholars, from the Latin. During last century, by the efforts of the British and Foreign Bible Society, a version of the NT in Catalan was made and circulated. The first edition was printed in London in 1832, and later it was reprinted in London and Barcelona.

LITERATURE.—S. Berger, 'Nouvelles recherches sur les Bibles Provençales et Catalanes' in *Romania*, xix. 505 ff., 'Les Bibles Castillanes,' etc., *ib.* xxviij. 360 ff., 508 ff. (with a bibliography and list of MSS, etc.); Eguren, *Memoria descriptiva de los Codices notables*, etc., Madrid, 1859; Plaine, art. 'Espagnoles Versions de la Bible' in Vigouroux's *Dictionnaire de la Bible*; Borrow, *The Bible in Spain*; Mayor, *Spain, Portugal, and the Bible.*

iv. PORTUGUESE VERSIONS.—1. A 14th cent. MS in the Escurial (O. j. 1) contains a Portuguese translation of the first part of the *Historia General* of Alphonse (see p. 408[b]), which of course had a Scripture basis. This translation may have been made by order of king Denis (1279–1325), the grandson of Alphonse, but it does not give the literal text of the Bible. In the same century we are told that king John I. (1385–1433) had a translation made by distinguished scholars of the Gospels, Acts, and St. Paul, but nothing more is known of it. His granddaughter Philippa, who died in 1497, is said to have had a translation made from French into Portuguese of the Gospels and Epistles of the Church year, and the MS of such a translation now exists at Lisbon.

2. A 15th cent. catalogue of the library of king D. Duarte (1433–1438) mentions among the books a translation of Genesis, another of the Gospels and Acts, another of the Books of Solomon. From this we may infer that before the date of his death a Portuguese version of these books existed.

3. In the same century we hear of the compilation of a Life of Christ preserved in a MS of the monastery of Alcobaça; and a paraphrase of the Acts, mixed with a good deal of legend, is found in another MS of the same monastery. We also know from the writings of D. Manuel of Cenaculo, bishop of Beia from 1770–1802, that twenty years

before he wrote there was in existence a paraphrastic translation made in the 15th cent. by a Portuguese acquainted with Hebrew. Of this he gives a specimen from the beginning of the Book of Genesis, which shows that the translation kept fairly close to the text of the Bible. There was also in a MS of Alcobaça, which has since been lost, a less literal translation, or rather summary, of OT history. Some extracts of this which have been preserved are said to be written in language of the 14th cent., more archaic than the passage quoted by Cenaculo.

Most of the statements mentioned here are incapable of being tested by the evidence of MSS containing the version, but there is nothing improbable about them, and they imply that the Portuguese translation dates from the 14th cent., that at first only some parts of the Bible were translated, and those the parts most likely to be in use, and that the translation was made from the Spanish and the French, and no doubt also from the Latin.

4. It is not till the end of the 17th cent. that we meet with the first printed Portuguese Bible. This was a translation made by a native of Lisbon, John Ferreira d'Almeida, who went out to the East as a Roman Catholic missionary, and afterwards became a Protestant. He began with the NT, which, after being revised, was printed at Amsterdam in 1681; and a second edition appeared in 1712. Almeida's work, completed only as far as Ezekiel, was continued by others, and gradually the whole Bible was published, the last part to appear being the Major Prophets, which was printed in 1751. Almeida's version was not very popular, partly because it was antiquated in style, and partly, perhaps, from prejudice on account of his change of religion.

5. In 1784 a Catholic translation by Anton Pereira de Figueiredo was published at Lisbon. This work, with notes, in twenty-three volumes, was based on the Vulgate, but does not follow it slavishly, and sometimes departs from it in favour of the Greek. A revised edition was begun some years later, but not completed till 1819.

Both of these translations have been circulated in Portugal by the British and Foreign Bible Society, but not in very large numbers.

LITERATURE.—S. Berger in *Romania*, xxviii. p. 543, where a full bibliography will be found.

v. GERMAN VERSIONS.—1. The oldest fragment of the Bible in German is to be found in a MS, twenty-three leaves of which are at Vienna (MS N. ccxxxiii.) and two at Hannover. These leaves, recovered from the bindings of other MSS, come from a MS of the 8th cent. which belonged to the Bavarian monastery of Monsee, and they preserve fragments of a Latin and German translation of St. Matthew, the first of which begins at $8^{33}$ and the last ends with $28^{20}$. The ending of the Gospel is followed by a Latin subscription, from which it is clear that only this Gospel was translated. The translation is unexpectedly good. The Latin is closely but not slavishly followed, and there are few mistakes due to misunderstanding the Latin. The German is clear, and 'it was the aim of the translator to give not only correct but good German,' in a dialect which is 'a Bavarian redaction of a Frankish or Alsatian original.' There is an edition of this very early and interesting MS by Massmann (Vienna, 1841), and more recently by Hench (Strassburg, 1890).

2. The next documentary evidence bearing on the Old German Bible is a translation of Tatian's Harmony of the Gospels, contained in a St. Gall MS (No. 56) of the second half of the 9th cent., in which the Latin and German are given in parallel columns. The Latin version rests on that of the Fulda MS of the 6th cent., and this is closely followed by the German, in an East Frankish dialect. The translation is not, as Sievers supposed, the work of a number of men, but of one, who perhaps received assistance from others, and may perhaps have used already existing translations of the separate Gospels made by different translators. The style of translation is not so vigorous as that of the Monsee St. Matthew, but it is clear, and runs easily. In one section there are peculiarities, best explained by supposing that there was a defect in the MS copied, which was supplied from another source.

3. We must leave on one side, as not properly belonging to our subject, such sacred poems, embodying a good deal of the Bible narrative, as the *Krist* of Otfrid and the *Heliand* by an unknown author. Both these belong to the middle or second half of the 9th century.

4. To the 10th or early 11th cent. belongs the work of Notker Labeo (d. 1022), a monk of St. Gall, who translated and commented on Job and the Psalter. His work on Job has been lost. That on the Psalter is contained in its entirety only in one MS (No. 21) at St. Gall, but fragments of different MSS of it are to be found at Munich, Basle, Maihingen, and elsewhere. The method adopted is to give each verse of the Psalms in the shortest possible sentences, first in Latin and then in German. This is followed by commentary or paraphrase. Above the Latin words an interlinear German rendering is given in the St. Gall MS; but this is later than Notker, and is not contained in the fragments in other libraries. Probably Notker's work was intended not for reading in the services, but for students in the monastery.

5. A little later than Notker is to be placed the work of Williram, abbot of Ebersberg in Bavaria (d. 1085), who translated and commented on the Song of Songs. Of this work many MSS survive, showing its popularity. The Latin text of the Vulgate is written in the middle of the page; on the left of this comes a Latin paraphrase in leonine hexameters, and on the right an explanation in German appended to little sections of the text in German, which are of varying length. The German translation is generally very free, often too free, but the style is good and almost ideal. 'Such a true translation was only possible because Williram loses himself in his text, and has sought to reproduce it even to the smallest details. Williram has absorbed the Song of Songs into his very being, and from his being it has welled out in purest German.'

6. The next fragments of Bible text are some portions of the four Gospels recovered from the bindings of volumes at Vienna (now Suppl. 2559) and Munich (now c.g.m. 5250) attributed by Walther (p. 456) to the 12th century. These are clearly copied from a MS belonging to an older, perhaps a much older, date. The sections are marked for liturgical use, both in the Latin and the German, and the 'use' points to the diocese of Constance, perhaps to St. Gall. The aim of the translator has been to give a 'flowing and popular' German version; and in this, in spite of an imperfect knowledge of Latin, he has succeeded. It is possible, but cannot be certainly proved, that the version was made for reading at church services.

7. To the 12th cent. belongs a MS of the Psalter now at Munich (*Cod. Germ.* 17), which came from the monastery at Windberg, and is dated 1187. With this may be discussed another MS of the Psalter belonging to the same century, now at Vienna (MS 2682). Both these are Latin Psalters with interlinear German versions. In the Wind-

berg Psalter the Latin is represented sometimes by more than one synonym, and a fuller explanation given in the margin; the German is often omitted, or given only in part, possibly, as Walther suggests, because the scribe could not read the German he was copying. The synonyms were probably added later, possibly from a MS like the Vienna Psalter. The translation in this last Psalter is less exact than that in the Windberg Psalter.

8. To the next century Walther ascribes a Zürich MS (Stadtbibl. C. 55. 713) of the Gospels, which, like a later MS of the same family at Basle (A. iv. 44), shows signs of being copied from an earlier MS, in which corrections had been made, for two German words are often given for one Latin. Walther notices the effective and impressive character of the translation.

9. The beginning of the 14th cent. marks, according to Walther, an epoch in the history of the German Bible, and MSS begin to multiply. We need not therefore pursue beyond that date the history of separate MSS of the whole or part of the Bible. The multiplication of MSS is explained by the desire of the Christians in Germany to have translations of the Bible to which they might appeal in regard to matters of doctrine and practice, as the authority of the Pope was weakened by the events of the early 14th century. The result was that a number of independent translations were made, often very inexact and inadequate.

Walther enumerates altogether 203 MSS, beginning with those which have been mentioned, and going down to the 16th century. Of these, 10 contain the whole German Bible; 6 others were originally, but are no longer, complete Bibles; 5 contain the OT and 8 the NT. Of the whole number no fewer than 128 belong to the 15th century.

In connexion with all these MSS it is only possible to summarize the results as given in Walther's exhaustive work on the German Bible of the Middle Ages, and to mention one or two MSS of special interest or importance. The most important of the MSS, to which no reference has yet been made, if importance is to be measured by the amount of controversy of which it has been the occasion, is the so-called *Codex Teplensis.* It is so called because it is to be found in the library of the Præmonstratensians at Tepl in Bohemia. The controversy, of which it is the centre, is the relation, if any, between the German translation and the work of the Waldenses. On the one hand, Haupt maintained that the pre-Lutheran German Bible, with which this MS generally agrees, had a Waldensian origin; and, on the other hand, Jostes denied that there was any sufficient evidence of this. In this discussion many other scholars besides the two already named took part. The *Codex Teplensis* contains, among other things, a longish treatise on the '7 stücke dez heiligen christlichen Gelauben' (seven articles of the holy Christian faith) appended to a short discussion on the '7 heilikheit der kirchen' (*i.e.* the sacraments), and it is their inclusion which suggests to Haupt the Waldensian origin of the MS; and, as the text of this MS agrees with that of the first printed German Bibles, he goes on to infer the connexion of the German Bible with the Waldenses. Walther (*l.c.* pp. 193, 194) says: 'As a result of the controversy between Haupt and Jostes we may recognize that only the treatise at the end of the MS, and that very probably, originated among the Waldenses, while the other additions may have come as well from a Waldensian as from a Catholic. At the same time, it is by no means certain that the man who inserted the last piece was aware of its heretical origin, or was himself a Waldensian.' Other evidence is afforded by marks in the margin drawing attention to certain passages of doctrinal importance. But these marks do not all imply the same doctrinal views on the part of the person who added them. Some are Catholic, others Waldensian, and all in the same hand. These marks therefore only prove, according to Walther, that the MS was used and marked by one of the Waldenses.

Another MS which deserves attention is the splendid Bible in six volumes at Vienna (MS N. 2759–64) called the 'Wenzel Bible' after king Wenzel. It contains the greater part of the OT, and was the work of Martin Rotlev between 1389 and 1400. The importance of the MS lies not so much in the text as in the elaborate illustrations. Some of these are found in other MSS, and their origin and purpose are not always clear.

A third MS to be noticed is the so-called Florian Psalter, a trilingual version, in Latin, Polish, and German, chiefly interesting in connexion with the early history of the Polish Bible. This is also a sumptuous volume so far as illustrations are concerned, but for some reason or other they were never completed.

Among early groups of MSS one of the most interesting is that which contains a translation of the Psalter made by Henry of Mügeln about 1350. The oldest representative of this family is a MS of the Cistercian monastery of Rein near Gradwein, but the version is found in 18 other MSS. The MSS give a continuous translation with a Latin text on the margin and a gloss derived largely from Nicholas of Lyra. Of the translation represented by this group Walther writes (p. 718): 'His work on the Psalter cannot be brought into line with the other German Psalters, for his chief purpose is to provide a popular work, and he has succeeded in his object.'

Another group of MSS of the Psalter is one which goes back either to the original Hebrew text or to Jerome's *Psalterium Hebraicum.* As preserved in the MSS the text has been corrected by the help of the Vulgate.

10. From the MSS we pass to the early printed editions of the German Bible. Of these Walther enumerates as belonging to the period from 1466, the date of the earliest, to 1521, eighteen editions of the complete German Bible—fourteen in High German and four in Low German—besides thirty-four of Psalters or other separate books of the Bible. The four earliest bear no indication of the date or place of publication, and their order of precedence has been very carefully examined by Walther. The result of his investigation is to vary the order as previously given by Hain. Walther has proved that the earliest Bible is that printed by Mentel at Strassburg. In a note at the end of the copy in the Munich Library it is stated that 'this book was bought on the 27th of June 1466 for 12 gulden'; and a note at the end of a copy at Stuttgart says that it was printed in 1466. The second edition of the Bible is that of Eggestein, also printed at Strassburg. On the strength of a note in the Stuttgart copy, which says that it was printed in 1462, Eggestein's used to be regarded as the earliest German printed Bible. Walther shows that it is later than Mentel's edition, on which it is based, and that it dates from about 1470, as a note in the Gotha copy implies. The third, dependent on Eggestein, is Pflanzmann's Augsburg edition of about 1473. The fourth, also an Augsburg edition by Zainer, is a revision of Eggestein, for 'they have many most striking misprints in common.' This is assigned to about 1473, and is to be regarded as earlier than the Swiss edition, printed probably at Basle, which used to be put fourth. Of this Swiss

edition one copy only, at Göttingen, out of the thirty-two known to us, bears a date, 1474. On Zainer's edition of 1473 the Swiss edition and three other Augsburg editions, printed by Zainer (1477) and Sorg (1477 and 1480), depend. The next edition, published by Koburger at Nuremberg in 1483, professes to be and is 'a revision made with great diligence,' his corrections being possibly derived from those in the Cologne Low German Bible, with which Koburger's edition has many illustrations and other points in common. The last five editions of the complete High German Bible which preceded Luther are dependent on that of Koburger. They were published, one at Strassburg (1485) by Grüninger, and four at Augsburg—two by Schönsperger in 1487 and 1490, and two by Otmar in 1507 and 1518. Walther thus sums up the result of his exhaustive investigation of the early printed Bibles: 'Our conclusion from the comparison of these Bibles is that they all belong to the same family of translations, but that the Bible first published by John Mentel at Strassburg in 1466 was revised about 1473 by G. Zainer at Augsburg, and that this new and revised edition received at the hands of A. Koburger at Nuremberg, and afterwards in the two last Bibles of the Middle Ages, a further slight correction.'

The text represented by this succession of printed Bibles is found also in various Psalters printed at various dates and in various places between 1473 and 1498, and also in an edition of the Apocalypse (1498) and of Job (1488). Besides printed editions of this recension of text, Walther enumerates fourteen MSS in which it is found, nine of which, however, are copies of a printed Bible, as is evident from the misprints which they reproduce, while a tenth also depends on a printed text. Two of the other MSS (at Wolfenbüttel and Nuremberg) are MSS of the early part or middle of the 15th century. That at Nuremberg contains only Joshua, Judges, and Ruth, but is interesting on account of the reasons given by the translator—John Rellach of Resom, in the diocese of Constance—for undertaking the work of translation. The other two are MSS of the NT—the one at Freiburg in Saxony; the other, already mentioned, at Tepl in Bohemia. These are 14th cent. MSS, having many points of resemblance, but neither is a copy of the other. From a careful examination Walther concludes that Mentel's Bible represents the text of this family in a purer and more original form than these, the oldest MSS which contain it. This text, based of course on the Latin, shows many points of agreement with old MSS of the *Itala*, and in the NT many points of agreement with the Greek against the Latin, but only in cases where the Greek has a reading not contained in the Vulgate; for if the Vulgate has a fuller reading than the Greek, the Vulgate is followed. The question to be decided is whether the German translator himself enriched his text by using several MSS of the Vulgate, or used a MS of the Vulgate which itself contained the additions which he has translated. Walther decides in favour of the second alternative, and finds such a MS in a Latin MS at Wernigerode, which has 37 of the 45 additions common to the first Bible and the Freiburg and Tepl MSS; and many, but by no means all, of these are found also in the Provençal version connected with the Waldenses. But the resemblances are not, as we have seen above (see p. 412[a]), sufficient in number or distinctive enough to prove a Waldensian origin of the earliest German printed Bibles.

11. The work of Luther marks an epoch in the history of the German Bible. His labours in translation began with some of the Psalms, the Lord's Prayer, the Ten Commandments, sections of the Gospels and the Epistles, all clearly intended for the edification of the unlearned.

The idea of making a complete translation of the Bible dates from 1521, but it was thirteen years later before the work was carried out in its entirety. The first part to appear was the NT, the translation of which was done at the Wartburg. This was the so-called *Septemberbibel*, so called because it appeared in September 1522, at Wittenberg, but without any date or the name of the publisher on its title-page. Of this a photographic facsimile appeared in 1883 on the four hundredth anniversary of Luther's birthday. The first edition was followed by a second in the same year 1522, and by 1580 more than seventy editions of the NT had appeared.

The translation of the OT was a more difficult task, to which Luther then turned. He tells us that in the translation of Job days were sometimes spent over a few verses, and the erasures in the MS of his work, now in the Royal Library at Berlin, are sufficient evidence of the trouble which he took. The OT translation was published in parts, beginning with the Pentateuch, which appeared in 1523. The historical Books and Hagiographa were followed in 1532 by a complete translation of the Prophets, and in 1534 by the Apocrypha, and so 'in a relatively short time the most epoch-making work of modern times came to light.' For the translation Luther was himself responsible, though he consulted numerous friends. Though he is not wholly independent of the work done by his predecessors, some of whose mistakes he reproduces, he was not by any means dependent on them. Both in the OT and NT he translates from the original text, using in the OT the Brescia edition of 1494, and in the NT Erasmus' edition of 1519, which he follows, for instance, in the curious reading ἐν ταῖς ἡμέραις ἐμαῖς at Rev 2[13]. He had also the assistance of the LXX, Vulgate, and the *Glossa ordinaria*. The object Luther set before himself was not to produce a literal translation, but one which should be clear and intelligible to the people; and in this he was successful, largely because he was a thorough German, fully conscious of the needs of the people, and in sympathy with them. The result was that this translation had an incalculable effect on the development of the German language and literature, leading to the predominance of one dialect throughout the country. Outside the limits of Germany it was the basis of the versions used in Denmark, Sweden, Norway, and Holland.

His work had no sooner appeared than it was the subject of much criticism, which came chiefly from the Roman Catholics. The earliest critic was Emser, who in 1523 published a volume, in which he called attention to the many mistakes and doctrinal errors contained in the work of Luther. Emser's work was the precursor of many others, and it is no doubt possible to point to mistakes due to a defective knowledge of Hebrew or Greek. But the best testimony to Luther's work is the permanent hold it has had on the German nation, as shown by the innumerable editions through which it has passed. Some of these are interesting because of the changes of different kinds which they introduced in many cases with the object of supporting special doctrinal views. Others had a linguistic purpose. More modern and familiar words and constructions were introduced in place of those which had become obsolete. One of these revised editions, which obtained a very large circulation, is that of 1703, of which the Canstein Bible Institute at Halle has since 1717 circulated, according to Nestle, more than five million copies.

12. Such was the position which Luther's translation occupied in Germany, that while it was generally admitted that revisions and corrections were necessary, many of the attempts in this direction roused great opposition; and while some would have been content with merely removing words which were obsolete or of uncertain meaning, others were in favour of a more thorough revision. Finally, a commission, representative of various theological views, was appointed, charged to make the minimum of necessary corrections, and the first result of their labours was the NT, published at Halle in 1867; and finally in 1883 appeared at Halle, 'The Bible, or the complete Scriptures of the Old and New Testament according to the German translation of D. Martin Luther. First impression of the Bible revised by order of the Eisenach German Protestant Church Congress.' This is the so-called *Probe-Bibel* or Proof-Bible. Two years were allowed for criticism, and then the final revision of the Proof-Bible began, during which numerous opinions and reports were sent in. In January 1890 the great final conference of all who had taken part in the theological and linguistic revision was begun at Halle, and at last in the beginning of 1892 the revised edition was issued by the Canstein Bible Press at Halle. This completed the work begun as long ago as 1855, when Pastor Mönckeburg of Hamburg made an appeal to the Bible Societies to unite in preparing a uniform text. It was inevitable that the result should be freely and variously criticised, and the amount of literature produced has been large. The defects are due not so much to the revisers as to the limitations set in regard to the amount of change they were to make, which were fixed before the work was begun.

13. The rapid and widespread popularity obtained by Luther's translation, when it first appeared, made other attempts in the same field rare, and the only important edition in the 16th cent. is the Zürich Bible of 1530, which followed the publication of the Prophets and Apocrypha in the preceding year. The translation was for the most part that of Luther, only unimportant linguistic changes being introduced. The only portion of the Bible of which a new translation was made was the Hagiographa, including Job, Psalms, Proverbs, Ecclesiastes, and Song of Songs; and this was not satisfactory, especially on the linguistic side. A later edition of 1548 is said to be based on a comparison with the Hebrew, but the changes are not important. This edition of 1548 became itself in turn the basis of later revisions. Of such later revisions the most important is that of Breitinger, who published a NT in 1629, which introduced many changes, and aimed at extreme literalness. An attempt to secure a thorough revision aroused such opposition that it led to no result. It was not till the 19th century that any satisfactory or effective revision took place, and, as a consequence of these revisions, Nestle says that 'its dialectical character has now disappeared, and in respect of accuracy it may be compared with the best: it certainly has not come from one mould, and the effort after exactness has frequently led to bombastic language and lack of clearness.' In 1858 a commission was appointed in Switzerland to revise the work again, and in 1893 a NT and Psalter appeared, in which account has been taken of the results of scientific criticism of the Greek text.

14. Another Protestant translation of importance is that of J. Piscator, first published at Herborn in 1602, and afterwards in use at Bern and elsewhere. Nestle describes it as a weak translation, abounding in Latinisms, which indicate a use of the Latin versions of Junius and Tremellius. Mention should also be made of the Socinian version of Crell and Stegman (Rackau, 1630) and another by the Socinian Felbinger which was published at Amsterdam in 1660. Another translation, which had leanings to mysticism, was the Berlenburg Bible (1726–1742), based partly on Luther's version, partly on the Zürich Bible. Other versions, such as the Wertheim Bible of 1735, were rationalistic in tendency, and explained away the supernatural. The same object was kept in view in Bahrdt's translation of *The latest revelations of God* (Riga, 1773). Of 19th cent. translations those of de Wette (1809–1814) and Bunsen (1858–1869) are the most important. The first mentioned combined scholarly exactness with happiness in expression, the second aimed at being popular and easily understood by the masses.

15. The German translations made in the interests of Roman Catholics have not been very numerous or very important. The earliest is a translation of the NT by Beringer, published at Spires in 1526. This was almost a reprint of Luther's version. In the next year Emser, who has been mentioned as one of Luther's first critics, published a NT at Dresden, which also differs very little from Luther's save that glosses have been added in places, and the text of the Vulgate in some instances preferred. Emser's version has been many times reprinted. A few years later, in 1534, Dietenburger, a Dominican, printed a Bible at Mainz. In his translation he followed Luther in the OT, though he sometimes adopted the Vulgate rendering. The Apocrypha is a reproduction of the translation of Leo the Jew made for the Zürich Bible. The NT closely follows Emser's version. The version of J. Eck, Luther's famous antagonist (Ingolstadt, 1537), was in the NT only a reproduction of Emser, but in the OT the pre-Lutheran translation was followed as a rule. It does not seem to have been successful, and Nestle says of it that the 'German is beneath criticism.' In the 17th cent. the only Catholic version of importance is that of Ulenberg, based on the Sixtine edition of the Vulgate. This was published at Cologne (1630), and afterwards, as revised by the theologians of Mainz (Cologne, 1662), was known as the Catholic Bible. In the 18th cent. several translations appeared, that of Erhard (Augsburg, 1722) being perhaps the most often reprinted. At the end of the century appeared the work of Braun (Augsburg, 1788–1805) in thirteen volumes. This was afterwards revised by Allioli (1830). These and other Roman Catholic versions kept the Vulgate mostly in view, but a free rendering of the Greek of the NT was made by Brentano (1790). His translation of the OT from the Hebrew he did not complete himself, but his work was continued by others. The 19th cent. Roman Catholic versions are, like the earlier ones, based on the Vulgate, though the Hebrew and Greek texts are not neglected. The version of Kistemaker (1825) was the Roman Catholic version which was adopted by the British and Foreign Bible Society.

LITERATURE.—W. Walther, *Die deutsche Bibelübersetzung des Mittelalters*, Brunswick, 1889; Nestle in Herzog's *RE*³ iii. 61 ff., where a full bibliography is given; Vigouroux, art. 'Allemandes Versions' in *Dictionnaire de la Bible*.

vi. DUTCH VERSIONS.—1. The earliest translation of the substance of any part of the Bible into Dutch is to be found in metrical versions of the Biblical narrative; but these do not represent *literal* translations of the text of Scripture.

2. Of literal translations of the whole or of parts of the Bible, Isaac le Long in his *Boekzaal der nederduitsche Bybels* enumerates twenty-four MSS; and to these Walther, in his work on the German translation (see p. 721 ff.), has added others. The

oldest MS, according to Walther, is a Vienna MS in two volumes (MSS 2771–2), which he assigns to the second half of the 14th century. Among other early MSS are a MS at Paris of the historical books of the OT, two MSS in the Bodleian Library, one (dated 1472) of the Gospels, and another of the Acts, St. Paul, and the Apocalypse. All these contain a version made from the Latin, probably about 1300, by a Fleming, for the benefit of those unlearned in that language. Such a translation, according to the unnamed translator, was desirable in spite of 'the opinion of many clergy that the mysteries of the Bible should be kept from the ordinary man.' To the translation are added explanations based mainly on the *Historia Scholastica* of Peter Comestor; but these are distinguished from the text by being written in a different character. Moreover, some parts which it was thought undesirable to popularize (*e.g.* Dt 22[13ff.]) are left out, and for these the reader is referred to the original Latin. The first edition of this translation, but without the Psalms and New Testament, was printed at Delft in 1477.

3. It was inevitable that Luther's version should be translated very soon into Dutch, in spite of the opposition of the Inquisition and the edicts of Charles V., and an edition appeared at Antwerp in 1522, for which so much of this version as was available was used. In 1525 and 1526 other editions appeared of the New Testament at Basle, and in 1525 the whole Old Testament was published at Antwerp in four small volumes, the Pentateuch and Psalms being based on Luther, the rest on the Delft Bible. The first complete Bible was printed at Antwerp by Jacob van Liesveldt, and in the second edition of 1532 Luther's version of the Prophets was adopted as a basis. Several editions followed before 1546, when the printer was condemned and put to death for unorthodox statements in the notes. Liesveldt's Bible was revised by Vorsterman with the help of the Complutensian Polyglott.

4. It was only to be expected that efforts should be made by the Roman Catholics to secure a translation for their own needs. Editions of the New Testament appeared in 1527 and in later years, a Latin-Dutch version in 1539, and finally in 1548 editions of the whole Bible were published at Cologne and at Louvain. The first was the work of a Carmelite, the second of a Canon of Louvain, Nicholas von Wingh. This last, which contained a vigorous preface dealing with the mistakes of Protestant Bibles, was approved by the Theological Faculty at Louvain, and published with the sanction of Charles V. It has passed through many editions, was revised in 1599 after the Vulgate of 1592, and issued by the Plantin press at Antwerp, and has been many times reprinted. A later revision of this version dates from 1717, and is the work of Ægidius Wit, a Ghent divine. This is in the idiom of Flanders and Brabant, and follows the Vulgate, though in certain parts the original texts have been used. In 1820 permission was given to circulate a translation without note or comment for the benefit of Roman Catholics, and the edition of 1599—the so-called Moerentorf Bible—was reprinted at Brussels in 1821, and to its circulation the British and Foreign Bible Society contributed.

5. Amongst the various sects various translations circulated, each after a time preferring its own. Thus the *Lutherans*, who had used Liesveldt's Bible, in 1558 adopted one based on a Magdeburg edition, and the 1558 edition was many times revised and reprinted. The *Memnonites* used an edition of the Bible published by Viestkens in 1560, and of the New Testament published in 1562. A few years earlier the *Reformed Churches* acquired a translation printed at Emden in 1556. This was the work of Jan Gheylliart. In the earlier half of the Bible, down to and including Job, he used the text of Liesveldt, revised by the help of the Zürich edition of 1548–9; the rest of the Bible was a translation of this Zürich text. A separate edition of the New Testament was published in 1556, and this was many times revised. A few years later, in 1562, a translation based on Luther's version was adopted, the so-called *Deux Æs* or *Eulenspiegel* Bible. The *Remonstrants* for a long time used the version made by order of the States General, and first published in 1637. This sect was opposed to the views of those who took part in the translation just mentioned, but after careful examination they were so satisfied as to its accuracy that they adopted it, and have used the Old Testament ever since. A version of the New Testament was made for their use by Christian Hartsoeker, an Arminian minister; but, although it professes to be a new translation, it follows in the main the version hitherto used.

6. The first attempt to revise the existing Dutch version by use of the original texts seems to have been made by W. Baudartius of Zütphen, who in 1614 produced such a revised text, with the help of various scholars and earlier editions. Any such individual or private attempts were dwarfed by the combined effort in the same direction made by the States General, which resulted in the edition of 1637, to which reference has been already made. The necessity of procuring an improved version based on the original texts was generally recognized some time before any steps were taken to deal with the need. In 1594 the States General determined on undertaking such a work, and entrusted it in the first instance to Philip Marnix. The matter was discussed at several sittings of the Synod of Dort in 1618–9, but it was not till ten years later that the work was begun by six translators and eight revisers for the Old Testament and the same number for the New, the scholars being selected by the Synod, and paid by the States General. The translation was finished in 1632, and the revision in 1635. The first edition was printed in 1636, and published at Leyden in the following year. In the next thirty years many editions appeared at different places, and with slight revisions and changes in orthography (such as the unsuccessful revision contained in the edition of Henry Cats of 1834) it has been adopted up to the present day.

7. About the middle of last century (1848) an attempt was made to combine the various Protestant sects in the work of revision, and members of various theological faculties were entrusted with the task; but jealousy and distrust prevented a successful completion of the plan, and when the New Testament was ready in 1866 it was not welcomed. The work on the Old Testament, after an abrupt cessation, was resumed in 1884, and its publication at Leyden began in 1897.

8. The only modern translation not based on the edition of 1637 which need be mentioned is that of Professor Van der Palm of Leyden, published in 1825. This enjoyed great popularity during the thirty years after its publication, but was never adopted in churches.

LITERATURE.—Isaac le Long, *Boekzaal der nederduitsche Bybels*, 1732; Bagster, *Bible of Every Land*; Nestle, *Urtext und Uebersetzungen*, p. 179 ff., and literature there mentioned.

vii. DANISH (AND NORWEGIAN) VERSIONS.—1. The earliest translation of the Bible into Danish is found in a 15th cent. MS now at Copenhagen. This contains the OT as far as 2 Kings, and is based on the Vulgate, which it follows very closely. The MS has been edited by Molbech at Copenhagen in 1828. The version belongs to the 15th or possibly the 14th century. This appears to be the only MS containing any large section of the Bible which has survived of the many which, according to the statement of Hvitfeldt (died 1609) in his Danish Chronicle, were to be found in the monastic libraries in his time. Of the Psalter there are several MSS of about the same date, and fragments of Biblical translations are also to be met with.

2. At the time of the Reformation, Denmark was the earliest of the Scandinavian kingdoms to possess a complete version of its own in the vernacular. The king, Christian II., entrusted the work of translation to his secretary, John Michaelis,—or Hans Mikkelsen,—who had heard Luther at Wittenberg. The NT appeared at Leipzig in 1524, and was reprinted at Antwerp in 1529. The translation of the Gospels was based on the Latin version of Erasmus, and the rest of the NT follows very closely Luther's German translation. The language into which Mikkelsen translated was not pure Danish, but a mixture of Danish and Swedish, and the work was not very well received.

3. In 1528 two Danish versions of the Psalter appeared. The one, based on the Hebrew, in which the Latin and German were also used, was the work of Wormord, a Dutchman, and was published at Rostock, but had no great success. The other was the work of C. Pedersen (1480–1554), a man 'who had the same importance for Danish literature that Luther had for German.' This version was based on the Hebrew text and Jerome, and was printed at Antwerp, and afterwards reprinted at Copenhagen. In 1529 he published an edition of the NT which he based on Michaelis' translation, but used also 'the help of the best available theologians,' *i.e.* Luther and Erasmus. Two years later another edition appeared at Antwerp, and also a version of the Psalter. In 1535 Tausen published at Magdeburg a translation of the Pentateuch, in which Luther's version, the Hebrew, and Vulgate were used. In 1539 a translation of the Book of Judges by Tidemann, based on the Vulgate and Luther, appeared at Copenhagen, and two years later the same translator issued a version of Wisdom and Sirach.

4. The year 1550 marks an epoch as the date of the appearance of the first complete Bible. This was the work of the Theological Faculty at Copenhagen, and among the collaborators Pedersen took a prominent place. The work was done by command of Christian III., who ordered Luther's version to be followed as closely as the Danish would allow. An edition of 3000 copies was published, and in 1589 a second edition followed, in which the archaisms of the first were removed.

5. The first translation based on the original languages was the work of Resen, bishop of Zealand, who, not finding the editions of 1550 and 1589 literal enough, undertook a revision, which was completed in 1607, the NT appearing two years earlier. This work of Resen was not very successful owing to its indifference to Danish idiom, and another edition of the older version appeared at Copenhagen in 1633, with slight changes. This is known as the Bible of Christian IV.

6. Resen's translation was revised by Swaning, bishop of Zealand, and others in 1647, and of this revision very many copies were circulated by the College of Missions, founded in 1714. Later it was adopted by the British and Foreign Bible Society, and with only slight changes it is the version which circulates generally at the present day. During last century revised editions of the NT (1819) and OT (1824) were published under the superintendence of Bishop Munter. Another revision of the whole Bible appeared in 1872, under the superintendence of Bishops Martensen and Hermansen.

7. The Bible used in Denmark was current also in Norway till the separation of the two countries in 1814. An important revision of the 1647 Bible was begun in 1842, and the work was carried on over many years. The translation of the OT as finally approved did not appear till 1890. Of the NT a new translation was made by Bishop Bugge, and revised by other scholars.

LITERATURE.—Bruun, *Biblioteca Danica*; le Long, *Bibliotheca Sacra*; Herzog, *RE*³ iii. 146 ff.

viii. SWEDISH VERSIONS.—1. The earliest reference to the Bible in Sweden is connected with the name of St. Bridget at the beginning of the 14th century. She is said to have had a translation of the Bible made for her. About the same time a great Bible in Swedish is mentioned in the will of king Magnus Smek, which may have been the same as that mentioned as made for St. Bridget, and probably was not a complete Bible, but an exposition of the Pentateuch made by Bridget's confessor Matthias, which was no doubt to have been continued in the other books. Towards the end of the next century the Books of Joshua and Judges were translated by Nils Ragnvaldson, and a little later Budde translated Judith, Esther, Ruth, and the Books of Maccabees. A version of the Apocalypse of about the same date also survives. No other parts of the Bible are known to have been translated. All those which have been mentioned are based on the Vulgate.

2. In 1523 Sweden separated from Denmark, and, in order to secure linguistic as well as political independence, Gustav Vasa commanded a translation to be undertaken. Two translations were ordered—one in the interests of the Church of Rome, for which Vasa had recourse to the archbishop of Upsala; the other, based on Luther's version, which was the work of Laurence Andreas, afterwards chancellor. Of the first, no part was ever printed. Of the second, the NT was published at Stockholm in 1526, and many times reprinted since. A few years later (in 1536) the Psalter and Sapiential books were translated, and in 1541 the first Swedish version of the whole Bible appeared at Upsala, the OT being translated from Luther's Bible of 1534 by Laurence Petri and others, and the NT being the translation of Andreas already mentioned. This is substantially the Bible in use at the present day. At the beginning of the 17th cent. a committee was appointed to collate various editions of Luther with the object of producing an improved Swedish version. The results were known as the *Observationes Strengnenses*—so called from Petri, bishop of Strengnäs; but the edition for which the notes were made did not appear till 1617, when it was printed at Stockholm. It was practically a reprint of the 1541 Bible with certain additions, and corrections of typographical errors. Several subsequent editions were issued, some of them with deviations from the text of the original. At the beginning of the 18th century a revision was ordered by Charles XII., and entrusted to Benzel, bishop of Strengnäs. Very few alterations from the 1617 text were admitted, and the work was published at Stockholm in 1703. During the 18th century many editions appeared; but, owing to their cost, the circulation was not large till the Swedish and British and Foreign Bible Societies took up the work. They worked together for some time, but the connexion between them was severed by a difference of opinion as to the inclusion or exclusion of the Apocrypha. The current translation of the NT appeared in 1882, and was slightly revised next year, and approved.

LITERATURE.—Herzog, *RE*³ iii. 146 ff.; Bagster, *The Bible of Every Land*, 185 ff.

ix. Hungarian Versions.—1. The introduction of Christianity into Hungary towards the end of the 10th cent. was soon followed by sermons in the vernacular, but Latin still remained the language of the Court. The earliest specimens of Hungarian which have survived are a funeral oration in a 13th cent. MS, and another fragment of the 14th cent. on the virginity of Mary. The Hussite movement had some effect on Hungary, and some parts of the Bible were translated into Hungarian; but the inroads of the Turks checked any development in this direction. The earliest translation of which we have any remains dates from the beginning of the 15th cent., and was the work of two Franciscan monks, Thomas and Valentine, who, under stress of persecution, fled from Bohemia into Hungary. Fragments of their work survive in a Vienna MS (No. 47), which contains part of the OT; in a Munich MS, dated 1466, which contains the Gospels; and in a MS, belonging to the bishop of Stuhlweissenburg, containing the Psalms, Canticles, and Gospels. The Vienna and Munich MSS were published by Dobrentei in 1838–1842. The translation, which is based on the Vulgate, is described as terse and exact.

2. To the beginning of the 15th cent. is to be assigned a translation by Ladislaus Batori (d. *circa* 1456). Many fragments of this version, including Pentateuch, Joshua, Judges, and NT, are said by Schwicker to survive in the library at Gran. A MS of the year 1519 contains a Hungarian version, perhaps the one by Ladislaus, complete. An almost complete translation of the Psalms is also to be found in a MS of 1522.

3. The beginning of the 16th cent. was a time of great literary activity in Hungary. The earliest printing-press in Hungary was established at Ofen in 1473, and many others followed in the 16th century. The earliest Hungarian book to be printed was Komjati's translation of St. Paul's Epistles. This was followed by a translation of the Acts, the work of the same scholar, which was based on the Vulgate. This was printed at Cracow in 1533. The next translation to appear was one of the Gospels by G. Pesti, also based on the Vulgate, but a successful rendering, more free and independent than that of Komjati. More important was the translation of the NT by John Sylvester (Erdösi), who had been a pupil of Melanchthon at Wittenberg, and was commended by him as a man rich in knowledge and wisdom. This scholarly but rather high-flown translation was printed at Uj-Sziget, the first Hungarian Protestant printing-press, in 1541, and afterwards at Vienna in 1574. A few years later (1551–1562) appeared a careful translation of the OT and NT, based on the Hebrew, by Kaspar Heltai, also, like Sylvester, a pupil of Melanchthon. Other translations followed; but none is of any importance till we come to that of Kaspar Karolyi, the most important Protestant translation. This was based on the Hebrew and Greek, the Vulgate and other translations being also used. It was first printed in 1589–1590 at Visoly near to Gönz, and is known as the Visoly Bible. It was revised in 1608 by Albert Molnar of Szencz, and has passed through many editions, and is still in use.

4. In the beginning of the 17th cent. we have a Roman Catholic translation, based on the Vulgate. This was the work of a Jesuit, George Kaldi, and is a vigorous and faithful version. It was published at Vienna in 1625; a second edition followed in 1732, and it is still in use among the Roman Catholics. About the middle of the century a revision was undertaken by Count Stephen Bethlen D'Iktar, who established a printing-press for the purpose at Waradin. The work of printing was but half finished when the town was taken and burnt by the Turks in 1660, and nearly half of the whole edition was destroyed.



5. During this century the use of the Hungarian language spread, though Latin was also used, and there was a great increase in the number of printed books. At the same time, even as late as 1682, we meet with complaints as to the scarcity of books, for the supply had apparently not kept pace with the demand. Towards the end of the century a complete Protestant translation of the Bible was undertaken by Georg Csipkes of Komorn, who had been a student of Hebrew under Leusden at Utrecht. This was based on the original languages, and finished in 1675. Owing to various political and religious obstacles the publication was delayed, and it was not till 1715 that arrangements were made with Vitringa at Leyden for the production of an edition of 4000 copies. A large number of these were burnt before delivery, by the intervention of the Jesuits.

6. The 18th cent. saw a great decline in the interest taken in the Hungarian language and literature; but copies of the Bible were difficult to procure, and costly. Steps were therefore taken to collect funds for reprinting Karolyi's translation, and this was done five times at Utrecht. Three editions also appeared at Basle.

7. At the beginning of the 19th cent. the British and Foreign Bible Society interested itself in the circulation of Bibles in Hungary as elsewhere, and for a time printed Bibles in Hungary itself, because the introduction of Bibles was forbidden. From 1852 till 1867 no agents of the Society were allowed in the country; but with the accession of the emperor Francis Joseph, in 1867, permission to circulate copies of the Bible was again given. In 1886, on the initiative of a Hungarian scholar, and with the help of the British and Foreign Bible Society, a revision of the old text was undertaken, and the archaisms of Karolyi were removed without interfering with the general vigour of his translation. After many delays the first part, the Hexateuch, appeared in 1896. A revision of Karolyi's NT had previously been published in 1878 at Budapest. In the interests of Roman Catholics, a revision of Kaldi's translation was entrusted by the archbishop of Erlau to his secretary Béla Tárkányi, who, after nine years' work, completed a translation with notes, the first edition of which was published at Erlau in 1862–1865, and a second edition appeared in 1892. Balogh in his account of the version in Herzog's *RE*[3] (iii. p. 118) sums up by saying that, between 1541 and 1871, 78 editions of the Hungarian Protestant Bible, and only 8 of the Roman Catholic Bible, appeared.

Literature.—Herzog, *RE*[3] iii. 115 ff.; Schwicker, *Geschichte der Ungarischen Litteratur*; art. 'Hongroises Versions' in Vigouroux's *Dictionnaire de la Bible*.

x. Bohemian Versions.—1. The oldest MSS of a Bohemian version of Scripture belong to the 14th century. There can be little doubt that the translation of some parts of the Bible was made considerably earlier, possibly as early as the 10th or 11th century, for the Eastern Slavs had many versions by that time (see vol. iv. p. 863 f. 'Slavonic Version'), and the Western Slavs, to whom the Bohemians belong, would be sure to follow the Eastern branch before long, and certainly had a Slavonic liturgy very early. No MSS, however, have reached us, for the fragments of a Bohemian version of St. John's Gospel, assigned to the 10th cent., are probably a forgery of Hanka.

2. Here, as elsewhere, the Psalter was one of the first books to be translated, and we have several early MSS of it, two of which are assigned to the 14th century. These are the Wittenberg Psalter, edited by Gebauer, which contains a Latin Psalter and an interlinear Bohemian version, and the rather later Clementine Psalter in the University Library

at Prague. In all, four different early translations of the Psalter have been distinguished by Gebauer. Besides the Psalter, other books of the OT were translated in or before the 14th cent., including Isaiah, Jeremiah, and Daniel. The earliest parts of the NT to be translated were the parts used in Church services, and so it is not surprising that traces of Slavonic influence should have been found in the Bohemian version due to the use of a Slavonic liturgy. The translation was no doubt made from the Vulgate; but Vondrak, who has carefully examined the text with reference to any evidence of Slavonic influences, writes: 'It is true they took a Latin text for basis, but the translator, or rather "glosser," had also a Church Slavonic text before him.' Traces of similar influence Vondrak also finds in the Psalter. On the other hand, Dobrofsky maintains that there is not the slightest trace of Slavonic influence.

3. Besides translations of the parts of the Gospels used in Church services, complete Gospels in Bohemian were also extant in the 14th century. Wyclif mentions that Anne of Luxemburg, wife of Richard II., had a Gospel *in lingua triplici exaratum scilicet in lingua Bohemica, Teutonica, et Latina*, about the year 1380. To a slightly later date belong the MSS at Dresden (*c.* 1400), Leitmeritz (*c.* 1411), and Olmutz (1417). The text of these MSS is, according to Leskien, a 'conglomeration of the already extant older translations of single books of the Bible made by different persons at different times in different recensions.'

The important point is that the text of all these MSS is older than the time of Hus. He 'did almost as much for his native tongue as Luther for German. He corrected the translation of the Bible, rearranged the Bohemian alphabet, and fixed the orthography.' This revision had some reference to the Vulgate as the underlying text, but was directed mainly to removing obsolete words and expressions. During the interval which separated the death of Hus in 1415 from the first printed Bohemian Bible in 1488, many revisions of the text took place, and many MSS of this period, both of the whole Bible and of the NT, are mentioned by Dobrofsky, all dependent on the Vulgate. Some of these are only copies of other MSS, while others contain independent translations.

4. In 1487 the first printing-press was established at Prague, and next year appeared the first edition of the Bohemian Bible, interesting as 'the first instance on record of the application of the newly invented art of printing to the multiplication of the Scriptures in a living tongue.' On this first edition, with only slight alterations and corrections, many later editions are based. The edition of the NT which appeared in 1518 is interesting as the first work of the 'United Brethren' carried out by order of Lucas of Prague. But this and subsequent revisions were relatively unimportant when compared with the so-called 'Kralitz *or* Brothers' Bible,' published in six volumes at Kralitz in Moravia (1579–1593). This work is described as 'an eternal monument of the beauty of the Bohemian language,' for which the United Brethren did so much. The work was superintended by John Blahoslav, 'the first profound student of the Bohemian language,' who himself translated the NT from the Greek (1564). In the translation of the OT thirteen scholars besides Blahoslav took part. The Hebrew text of the Antwerp Polyglott was used as a basis, but previous Bohemian versions are also quoted.

5. The disastrous battle of the White Mountain in 1620 was followed by the crushing out of the Bohemian nationality. 'Books in the Chekh language were hunted up in all quarters and burned. The Jesuits were very active in these labours: one especially, Andrew Konias, probably the greatest book-burner whom the world has ever seen, boasted that he had been instrumental in destroying 60,000 volumes.' Owing to the proscription of the national language in 1621, and the activity of the Jesuits just mentioned, the circulation of the Bohemian version languished. But a demand on the part of Roman Catholics led to the publication of the so-called 'Wenzel Bible,' edited by Jesuits (1677–1715). The text of the Venice edition of 1506 was used as a basis, but the Brothers' Bible was also used. Another Catholic edition, which is a revision of the Wenzel Bible, was the work of Durich and Prochaska (1778–1780), and this in turn was again revised by Prochaska, the NT appearing in 1786 and the whole Bible in 1804. In 1808 Palkovitch published a reprint of the text of the Kralitz Bible, with a list of words which had become obsolete, and this was circulated later by means of the British and Foreign Bible Society.

LITERATURE.—Dobrofsky, *Geschichte der Böhm. Sprache*; Vondrak, *Die Spuren der altkirchenslavischen Evangelienübersetzung in der altböhmischen Literatur*; Morfill, *Slavonic Literature*; numerous articles in the *Archiv für Slavische Philologie* [see especially Supplementband, pp. 145, 146] and in the *Centralblatt für Bibliothekswesen*, 1897; Leskien in Herzog, *RE*[3] iii. 161 ff.

xi. POLISH VERSIONS.—1. The earliest specimen of the Polish language which has survived is the well-known Florian Psalter, so called because it was discovered at the monastery of St. Florian near to Linz in Austria. This MS (St. Florian iii. 206) is trilingual, richly illuminated, in two columns. The versions represented are Latin, Polish, and German, a verse in Latin being followed first by a Polish and then by a German rendering of the same verse. It is uncertain whether the letter M and the arms of Anjou found in the MS signify that it belonged to Margaret the first wife of Louis king of Hungary and Poland, and daughter of Charles IV., or refer to Mary the sister of the Polish queen Hedwig of Anjou, and daughter of king Louis. In either case the date would be about the same, viz. the middle of the 14th century. It is asserted by Leciejewski that it is a copy of a much older text, and the version may well be referred to the 13th cent., to the end of which Macieowski assigns a version of Ps 50. The St. Florian Psalter shows a very close adherence to the Latin, and also a use of the Bohemian version. It is sometimes called the Psalter of queen Margaret, and has been carefully edited by Nehring.

2. Another important MS is the so-called Bible of queen Sophia, now in the library at Saros Patak in Hungary. According to a 16th cent. statement it was written for Sophia, the fourth wife of Jagello, about the year 1455. Other authorities date it a century earlier. This MS was edited by Malecki in 1872. It is perhaps copied from a complete Polish Bible, but is itself very incomplete, containing only the earlier books of the OT (according to Morfill, the whole Pentateuch; according to Leskien, Genesis only), Joshua, Ruth, Kings (and, according to Leskien, also Chronicles), and fragments of other books of the OT. The writing of five different scribes is traceable in the MS. The translation it contains is based on the Bohemian version, with occasional reference to the Vulgate.

3. Various other Polish translations were made after the beginning of the 16th cent., 'the classical age of Polish literature,' as it has been called. The first was a translation of the NT, the work of a Lutheran, Seklucyan, a competent Greek scholar, whose translation was 'made from the Greek, with the use of the Latin and other versions.' This was printed at Königsberg in 1551. The first

version of the whole Bible was published at Cracow ten years later. This, the 'Old Cracow' Bible, was intended for Roman Catholic use; but the Pope refused to sanction it, because of the use made in it of the Bohemian Bible. The next important edition is the so-called Radzivil or Brest Bible, published at Brest for the Calvinists in 1563, at the expense of Prince Nicholas Radzivil. The son of this prince, who was a Roman Catholic, on his father's death bought up and burnt all copies of this translation. This version claimed to be based on the original texts, Hebrew and Greek, but was regarded as Socinian in places. It did not, however, satisfy this sect, for whom a version was made by Budny in 1570 'from Hebrew, Greek, and Latin,' and this was reprinted, with certain changes, in 1572. Another Socinian translation appeared in 1577.

4. Another important translation made from the original language was that published at Dantzig in 1632, and afterwards reprinted. A large number of copies of this edition were bought up and burnt by the Jesuits. At the beginning of the 19th cent. the text of the Dantzig Bible was adopted by the Berlin Bible Society for the edition circulated by that Society.

5. Of Catholic translations the first to be noticed is the Leopolita Bible, the translation of John of Lemberg, based on the Vulgate, and published in 1561. But the most important of the Catholic versions is that made by Jacob Wuyck, and published at Cracow in 1599. This was based on the Vulgate; but use was made by the translator of the original text, and also of previously existing Polish translations. It was sanctioned by Pope Clement VIII., and has been often reprinted. At the beginning of the 19th cent. the text of this edition was used by the St. Petersburg Bible Society in 1813, and it has since been reprinted and widely circulated.

LITERATURE.—Herzog, *RE*[3] iii. 165 ff.; numerous articles in the *Archiv für Slavische Philologie*; Morfill, *Slavonic Literature*.

xii. RUSSIAN VERSIONS.—The early history of the Bible in Russia is dealt with, in regard to its origin, and the MSS in which the version is preserved, in vol. iv. p. 863 f. In the present article the history may be taken up with the first edition of the Bible, and continued to the present day.

1. The first Russian book was an *Apostol* (the name given to the MS or volume which contained the Acts, Cath. Epp., and St. Paul's Epistles), printed at Moscow in 1564. The innovation of printing was not well received, and the printers, Theodorof and Mstislavetz, had to flee from Moscow into Lithuania. Here editions of the Gospels (1569), the Apostol (1574), and, finally (1581), of the whole Bible appeared.

This last is the famous Ostrog Bible, so called from the place at which it was printed, the first complete printed Bible in Slavonic. For this work, brought out under the auspices of Constantine, prince of Ostrog, various MSS of the Slavonic were used; the Slavonic text was compared with the Greek, and sometimes with the Latin; modern expressions were substituted for those which were obsolete, and therefore often unintelligible; and errors were corrected. Another work—the Bible of Skorina, (Prague, 1517–1525)—emphasized the growing need of a translation into the ordinary language of the time, and a few years later Gregory's version of the Gospels (1556–1561) marks the first definite beginning of a translation into Russian, as distinguished from Old Slavonic. The printing-press was re-established at Moscow by Ivan the Terrible (1533–1584), but the prejudice against introducing corrections caused the perpetuation of the mistakes found in the Slavonic MSS. At last the agitation for, at any rate, necessary reforms became powerful enough to be effectual. In this agitation the famous Nicon, who became patriarch of Russia in 1652, took a prominent part. Scholars were summoned to Moscow, and in 1653 Greek MSS were brought from Mt. Athos. This revision was the beginning of dissent in Russia, for many adhered to the use of the unrevised books. In face of the opposition, progress was slow, and it was not till 1674 that a revision of the Slavonic Bible according to the Greek text was ordered, and begun under the superintendence of Epiphanius Slavenetzki. In 1683 a translation of the Psalter into Russian by Pheersof appeared.

2. The age of Peter the Great marked an epoch in the history of the Bible, as in other things. He revised the alphabet, removing some letters and introducing the character with which the reader of modern Russian is familiar, but the Old Slavonic remained in use for ecclesiastical purposes. In 1712 a revision of the text was ordered by Peter the Great, but the printing of this revised edition was delayed by his death. His successor, Catherine, continued the support given by her predecessor; but it was not till Elizabeth's reign that anything effective was done, owing to the persistent opposition to the work of revision. In 1744 Elizabeth ordered the Synod to proceed with the work, and finally in 1751 appeared the so-called Bible of Elizabeth. With very few changes this is the Bible in ordinary use in Russia at the present time, the text of the second edition of Elizabeth's Bible (1756) being the one adopted.

3. The reign of Alexander I. (1801–1825) marks the next event of importance in connexion with the Bible, viz. the establishment of the Russian Bible Society. This was in the first instance due to the energy of John Paterson, an agent of the British and Foreign Bible Society, and with the warm support of the emperor the first depôt of the Russian Bible Society was opened at St. Petersburg in 1813. In 1818 the first edition of the Gospels in Slavonic and Russian was printed, in 1822 an edition of the NT followed, and a beginning was made on the OT, a Psalter appearing in the same year. But the work of the Society was to be shortlived. It met with opposition from rationalists on the one hand and conservative Bible students on the other, and fell into disfavour also with the emperor on the suggestion that there was about it somewhat of the nature of a secret political society. It 1824 the work of translation was discontinued, and the existing copies burnt; and two years later the Society was finally dissolved by the emperor Nicholas, after having during its short existence translated parts of the Bible into fourteen new languages, and circulated nearly a million copies of the Bible or some parts of it in twenty-six different languages or dialects.

4. But the demand for Russian Bibles continued to be keenly felt; and Philaret, the famous bishop of Moscow, made attempts, but without much success, to prosecute the work of translation. The first attempt to translate the OT from the Hebrew original into Russian was made by Pavski, professor of Hebrew at the Academy of St. Petersburg; but this work was not for general use. Similar work was being done by Macarius, and his translation was submitted to the Holy Synod, with a representation as to the urgent need of completing the Russian translation. At last the Synod was moved to action, and in 1860 the translation of the Gospels appeared, followed, in 1862, by the Acts, Epistles, and Apocalypse. The first part of the OT to be published was the Pentateuch in 1868, but the whole work was only com-

pleted in 1875, nearly twenty years after the passing of the original resolution of the Synod in 1857. This was the first translation approved by the Czar and the Synod, and is in ordinary use. A translation of the OT made from the Hebrew into Russian by the British and Foreign Bible Society (London, 1875) was not allowed to circulate, but the same Society was allowed to print the translation made by the Synod, and to circulate it without the Apocrypha of the Greek and Latin Bibles translated by the Synod.

LITERATURE.—This is for the most part in Russian. See Scrivener's *Introduction*, ii. 157 ff.; art. by the present writer in the *Church Quarterly Review*, October 1895 [from which the above facts are summarized], and the Literature there referred to; Nestle, *Urtext*, etc., 211 ff.; Kean, *The Bible in Russia*.

xiii. MODERN GREEK VERSIONS.—1. The earliest translation into modern Greek dates from 1547, when the Pentateuch, the five 'Rolls,' and the other parts of the OT read in the Jewish services were translated from the Hebrew, and printed at Constantinople, in three columns which contained the Spanish, modern Greek, and the Targum of Onkelos. All three columns were printed in Hebrew characters; but the edition had no widespread circulation, and had a literary rather than a religious value.

2. The first really important translation was that of the New Testament made by Maximus Callipoli. This was printed at Geneva in 1638 at the expense of the Government of the United Provinces, and contains an introductory preface by Cyril Lucar, patriarch of Constantinople, who had studied at Geneva. This translation, in the Greek of the 17th cent., follows closely the original text; and of the edition of 1500 copies many were by permission distributed in the East.

3. The translation of Maximus was reprinted in 1703 in London at the expense of the Society for the Propagation of the Gospel, after having been revised by Seraphim; and after further correction by Anastasius and Kollettis an edition was published at Halle in 1710 at the queen of Prussia's expense.

In Greece the favourable reception originally given to Maximus' work was modified later, on the ground that it was made in a dialect, and therefore not generally intelligible. The real underlying ground of opposition was distrust of Protestant influence. Whatever the cause, the circulation of Seraphim's work was forbidden by the patriarch Gabriel, as that of Maximus had been earlier.

The influence of the British and Foreign Bible Society at the beginning of the 19th cent. made the matter of a modern Greek version again prominent. In 1810 Maximus' translation of the New Testament was reprinted, and several editions were circulated before 1830, the necessary permission having been obtained from the patriarch Cyril in 1814.

4. But the need of revision was recognized, and accordingly in 1819 the archimandrite Hilarion was entrusted with the work, the ultimate responsibility for the revision being undertaken by the learned archbishop Constantius of Sinai. Certain difficulties arose as to the inclusion of the OT Apocrypha, for Hilarion's version of the Old Testament was made from the Septuagint. Ultimately it was decided by the British and Foreign Bible Society that the translation of the Old Testament should be made from the Hebrew, and the headquarters of the work were established at Corfu. Here two English scholars, with a knowledge of Hebrew, and with the help of other scholars, including two learned Greeks, Bambas and Tipaldo, began the work, using not only the Hebrew, but the French translation of Martin, the Italian of Diodati, the Septuagint, Vulgate, and other versions. Parts of the Old Testament (*e.g.* the Psalms) were printed and circulated as they were finished, and by 1836 the whole Old Testament was completed. The New Testament translation of Hilarion was also revised by Bambas, and an edition appeared in 1848. This 'revision is considered so correct and idiomatic that it has now completely superseded that of Hilarion.'

As once before, so again, a reaction set in against Western influences, and Biblical translations were forbidden in the Orthodox Church. But, in spite of this, the British and Foreign Bible Society continued to print translations into modern Greek.*

LITERATURE.—Legrand, *Bibliographie Hellénique*, 1885–1895; Bagster, *Bible of Every Land*; Nestle, *Urtext*, etc. p. 178 ff.; *Bible Society Reporter* for Jan. and May 1902.

LL. J. M. BEBB.

## APOCRYPHAL GOSPELS.—

i. Definition.
ii. Origin.
iii. Value.
iv. Reception and influence.
v. Classification.
Literature.

i. DEFINITION.—The history of the word 'Apocrypha' accounts for its various uses, and its etymology explains its diverse meanings (see art. APOCRYPHA in vol. i. p. 112). 'Apocryphal' was a title of honour when it was applied to writings which were *hidden* on account of the unique value of their contents; their secret doctrines imparted to them a special authority (*auctoritas secreta*). But 'apocryphal' was a term of reproach when it was applied to writings which were *hidden* on account of the heterodoxy of their contents; their heretical teaching rendered them specially harmful. An approximation of the two opposite senses of 'apocryphal' may, however, be traced; for the secrecy which was originally a claim to peculiar regard soon became a mark of inferiority, owing to the suspicion which rests on books of hidden origin. From these differences in the application of the word it is not difficult to understand how it came to pass that Gospels which were held in high esteem, as, *e.g.*, by Gnostic sects, were condemned by the Christian Church and declared to be unworthy of a place in the Canon, notwithstanding that for some of them Apostolic authorship was claimed; it is also not difficult to understand how Gospels, which were not condemned for their false teaching, were excluded from the Canon because of their inferiority to the writings of the four Evangelists. Hence 'apocryphal,' which in the early Fathers means *heretical*, acquired the sense of *uncanonical*, which it now most frequently bears.

Under the heading of 'Apocryphal Gospels' it is customary to include all extra-canonical writings which claim to be Gospels, whether they are rivals of or supplements to the canonical Gospels, whether they are dependent on or independent of the writings of the four Evangelists, whether the tradition they embody has the appearance of being authentic or is manifestly fictitious. But when the term 'apocryphal' has this wider denotation, it has a narrower connotation. To Jerome this extension of the meaning of the word is generally ascribed, for he applies it to those Jewish writings which had a place in the LXX Greek version of the OT but were not included in the twenty-two books of the Hebrew Canon (*Prologus Galeatus*: '*Quidquid extra hos est, inter* ἀπόκρυφα *esse ponendum*'). Nevertheless, Jerome held that some of the OT apocryphal books might be read 'for the edifica-

* These were sanctioned on condition that the ancient Greek text was printed in parallel columns with the modern Greek version. But in 1901 ecclesiastical and patriotic prejudices were roused by a modern version or 'paraphrase,' circulated at the expense of queen Olga, and, in consequence, the circulation of any Greek version except the ancient Greek text has been denounced by the Synod and prohibited by the Government.

tion of the people, not for confirming the authority of Church dogmas' (*Prol. to Books of Solomon*); his description of these non-canonical books as apocryphal does not therefore imply that he condemned them as false and worthless. This must be borne in mind when 'apocryphal' is defined as *uncanonical* in its application to Gospels. Apocryphal Gospels are uncanonical Gospels; but all uncanonical Gospels are not necessarily apocryphal in the bad meaning which adheres to the word. A Gospel may be neither spurious nor heretical, though it is apocryphal; it may be based upon a genuine tradition, though it is uncanonical.

ii. ORIGIN.—The resemblances and the variations in the Synoptic Gospels furnish a problem which requires for its solution either an oral tradition which gradually became as stereotyped as though it had been written, or documentary sources modified by oral traditions. Most critics recognize elements of truth in the oral as well as in the documentary theory of the origin of the Gospels. Those who adopt the documentary hypothesis allow for the influence of traditions current in the Church, though not committed to writing. The problem presented by the apocryphal Gospels is to determine how far their additions to the narratives of the four Evangelists are derived from authentic sources, also to decide how far the fictitious accretions are due to fraudulent intentions or the heretical tendencies of the respective writers. The external evidence for the existence of an apocryphal Gospel must be weighed together with the evidence derived from a careful study of its contents before any judgment can be pronounced as to its origin. But no pre-judgment of the issue in any particular case is involved in the statement of some general considerations which must guide every such inquiry. The author of *Supernatural Religion* thinks that 'apologetic critics' are prejudiced by 'canonical glamour'; but there may be an unreasonable bias against as well as a reasonable presumption in favour of the canonical Gospels. The reverence they enjoyed for centuries is a significant fact, and is not satisfactorily accounted for by the statement that they were 'more fortunate' than the Gospels which were never included in the Canon of Scripture (*The Gospel according to Peter*, p. 132). The claim of an uncanonical Gospel to represent an early form of the Christian tradition cannot be dismissed on *a priori* grounds, nor can it be admitted without the most thorough investigation. The author may have derived the narratives of unrecorded incidents in the life of Jesus, or the reports of His unwritten sayings, from sources unknown to the four Evangelists. Jesus did 'many other things' (Jn 21[25]) than those which the canonical Gospels relate; before St. Luke wrote the Third Gospel many had 'taken in hand to draw up' similar, if less complete, narratives (Lk 1[1]). Moreover, the manufacture of fanciful traditions is not always to be ascribed to the zeal of heretics, but sometimes to an eager desire to satisfy—without critical discrimination between the nucleus of fact and the embellishments of fiction—curiosity in regard to those periods in our Lord's life about which the four Evangelists tell us nothing. Pseudo-Matthew had persuaded himself that the motive which impelled him to write was love for Christ (*Liber de infantia Mariæ: 'amor ergo Christi est, cui satisfecimus'*). But before any apocryphal Gospel is assumed to contain an earlier and purer form of the Evangelic tradition it must be examined in the light of indisputable evidence that writers of Gnostic tendencies (cf. Epiph. *Hær.* xxvi. 8, 12) published fictitious and pseudepigraphic works to support their peculiar tenets, claiming that their works imparted knowledge, secretly handed down to them, of the things hidden by Jesus from the multitude to whom He spoke in riddles which none but His most favoured disciples understood. Origen (*c.* 240) says: 'There are some believers exactly like drunken people who treat with violence their own body, for they falsify and alter the text of the Gospels three or four times, in order that they may evade its remonstrances' (*contra Celsum*, ii. 27. See Harnack, *Chron.* i. 590).

The variations in the texts of such apocryphal Gospels as are extant in different recensions cannot, in the judgment of Tischendorf, be explained as unintentional alterations; often the sense of a passage is completely altered, these Gospels being treated with a freedom which is inconceivable on the supposition that they were held in as high esteem as the canonical Gospels (*de Evv. Apocr. origine et usu*, p. 121: '*Fraudis apocrypha* (*evangelia*) *convincuntur ex mira qua laborant textus ambiguitate, a qua immensum canonica differunt, quamquam et ipsa haud exigua lectionum varietate premuntur*'). The authors of the apocryphal Gospels, whether they were influenced by dogmatic motives or by a desire to satisfy curiosity, adopted, as Hofmann points out, similar methods of composition. In both classes of writings there are some stories which are pure inventions, but there are others in which a *causa media* may be discovered. Sometimes elaborate narratives are developed out of a mere allusion in the canonical Gospels, sometimes words of Jesus are transformed into deeds, sometimes a slavishly literal fulfilment of an OT prophecy is recorded, and sometimes Jesus is represented as working marvels closely resembling and frequently surpassing OT miracles (Herzog, *PRE*[3] i. 655).

iii. VALUE.—The revival of interest in the apocryphal writings of the NT is due partly to the discovery of new documents, and partly to the attraction exerted upon the minds of many scholars by the fascinating and complex problem of the literary origin of the Gospels. Amongst the questions upon which light is sought are the following: Do these uncanonical Gospels impart any additional knowledge of the words and works of the Lord Jesus? In this respect it is generally agreed that their value is slight. Do they help to establish any theory of the origin of the Gospels? In this respect their value differs greatly: until more complete and more accurate texts of some of these Gospels are accessible it is impossible to express any positive judgment in regard to their relation to the canonical Gospels. It may, however, be said that the theory of a common oral tradition deserves more careful consideration than it has received from some modern critics, whose arguments are valid only on the assumption that priority to the canonical Gospels and direct dependence on them are the only possible alternatives.

The apocryphal Gospels contain information which is of considerable value to the student of the manners and customs of the Jews in early Christian times. It is true that their statements are sometimes in flagrant contradiction to history; but it is, as a rule, not difficult to discover the dogmatic bias which led to a perversion of the facts. When no such motive is discernible, and the details given violate neither psychological nor historical probability, the writer's source may be an authentic tradition. For example, the setting of some of the fabulous stories of our Lord's childhood has an interest for the antiquarian who regards the fantastic miracles as quite incredible. It is also probable that, in the near future, these Gospels will prove of even greater value to historians as they strive to disperse the gloom which still hangs over the first two centuries of the Christian era,—the period when heretical tendencies appeared within the Church, and heretical sects were formed outside it. In the controversy which has arisen on this question there has been on the one side a tendency to forget that in the 4th cent. opinions might be regarded as heterodox which were not so regarded in the 2nd cent.; but on the other side there has been a tendency to claim the sanction of the early Church for later forms of asceticism and Gnosticism, on the insufficient ground that some of these Gospels which originated in heretical circles found some favour amongst Christians. Von Dobschütz, who has studied these writings from this point of view, has called attention to facts which have an important bearing on the discussion, as, *e.g.*, that the adherents of Gnosticism who claimed to belong to the Christian Church, and sought to propagate their peculiar views within its borders, did not of their own accord leave the Church,—it was the Church that excluded them; also that the Docetic type of Christianity current in Egypt at the end of the 1st and at the beginning of the 2nd cent. was at a very early date discredited as heretical, though it long continued to dominate Christian thought as expressed in Christian art (*Theol. Lit.-Zeitung*, 1903, No. 12).

In this article the contents of the various apocryphal Gospels are given, sometimes in full, but always in sufficient detail to enable the reader to judge of their worth. This course has been taken in the belief that first-hand acquaintance with these writings establishes, by contrast, the unique value of the canonical Gospels, and furnishes the most conclusive refutation of the theories which seek to lift these extravagant stories to the same level as the narratives of the four Evangelists. To pass from the NT to these apocryphal Gospels, in so far as they embody independent traditions, involves a complete change of psychological climate. The wisdom of Westcott's words is confirmed by recent research: 'The completeness of the antithesis which these spurious stories offer to the Divine record appears at once—if we may be allowed for a moment to compare light with darkness—in relation to the treatment of the three great elements of the Gospel history—Miracles, Parables, and Prophecy, the lessons of power, of nature, and of providence. In the apocryphal miracles we find no worthy conception of the laws of providential interference; they are wrought to supply personal wants, or to gratify private feelings, and often are positively immoral. Nor, again, is there any spiritual element in their working . . . The apocryphal Gospels are also entirely without parables; they exhibit no sense of those deeper relations between nature and man—between corruption and sin—which are so frequently declared in the Synoptic Gospels. . . . Yet more, they do not recognize the office of Prophecy. History in them becomes a mere collection of traditions, and is regarded neither as the fulfilment of the past nor as the type of the future' (*Introd. to Study of the Gospels*, Appendix D).

iv. Reception and influence.—In tracing the influence of these writings no question arises, as in regard to the OT Apocrypha, of their reception by any section of the Church as canonical or deutero-canonical books. In the 2nd cent. four Gospels, and only four, were recognized. There is also ample evidence, as will hereafter be manifest, that most of the apocryphal Gospels have always been condemned by orthodox Christians. A few, however, had an extensive and early circulation amongst Christians in the East: for example, the Protevangelium of James was read in churches in the 4th cent., and was translated into the Syriac, Arabic, and Coptic languages. Details of such usage will be given in the notes on the several Gospels; but in general it may be said that these writings were condemned by the Western Church until the Middle Ages, when a sufficient period of time had elapsed for their origin to be forgotten. Pseudo-Chrysostom (*c.* 600) is said to have made use of the apocryphal Gospels of the Childhood of Jesus, and from the 10th cent. onwards they formed the material for legendary poems and miracle-plays, whilst some of their traditions were embodied in paintings and other works of art. The first of a series of Latin poems by Hroswitha (d. 968), a Saxon nun, is based on the fictitious accounts given in these Gospels of the perpetual virginity of Mary. Vincent of Beauvais, a Dominican, did much to popularize these apocryphal stories by including many of them in his *Speculum Majus* (*c.* 1250); the third part of this work, the *Speculum Historiale*, contains twelve chapters from the Gospel of pseudo-Matthew, and several from the Gospel of the Nativity of Mary. In the 14th cent. the *Speculum Historiale* was translated into French and other European languages. In his *Speculum Sanctorum* de Voragine (d. 1298) made use of almost the whole of the Gospel of the Nativity of Mary, and of a few chapters from the Gospel of pseudo-Matthew. This work, better known as the *Legenda Aurea*, and the *Speculum Historiale* of Vincent were amongst the earliest printed books in the 15th cent.; they are the chief sources from which many popular Roman Catholic compilations of these stories are derived. Yet Vincent put the Gospels he made use of into the category of 'doubtful' writings; and amongst Roman Catholic divines who have denounced them as unauthoritative, Tappenhorn mentions Alcuin (d. 804), St. Bernard of Clairvaux (d. 1153), and Thomas Aquinas (d. 1274). As recently as 1884, Pope Leo XIII. reaffirmed the judgment of the learned Pope Benedict XIV., which declares the Protevangelium of James and other works on the Nativity of Mary to be 'impure sources of tradition' (*de Festis B.M.V.* lib. ii. cap. 9: '*Cum plures scribere voluerint, ex turbidis fontibus, quæ tradiderunt, hausisse videntur*'). Tappenhorn, whose work is published with episcopal authority, laments that these fictions are often accepted as embodying 'ancient and pious traditions.' 'The veil which the Holy Spirit in the Gospels has drawn over the birth and early life of the Mother of God, we ought not to try to remove by means of untrustworthy, apocryphal narratives' (*Ausserbiblische Nachrichten*, p. 18 f.).

Some of the fables of these Gospels are found in the Ḳoran, as, *e.g.*, the vow of Mary's mother to consecrate her virgin daughter to the temple-service, the feeding of Mary by an angel, the use of rods to discover by lot a guardian for Mary, the making by the boy Jesus of twelve sparrows out of clay, etc. Kessäus, the famous commentator on the Ḳoran, refers in his notes to more of these stories (cf. Forbes Robinson, *Coptic Apocr. Gospels* in 'Texts and Studies,' IV. ii.; 1896).

v. Classification.—There is an article on the Gospel of Nicodemus in vol. iii. p. 544 ff., and an account of the Gospel of Marcion in art. Luke (Gospel of), *ib.* p. 168 f. Separate articles on the Gospel according to the Hebrews (see above, p. 338 ff.), and on the Gospel of Tatian (see art. Diatessaron, below, p. 451 ff.), appear in the present volume. In the present article the most important of the apocryphal Gospels, other than those above mentioned, will be treated in the following order:—

*A*. Gospels (or fragments of Gospels) which, in the opinion of some critics, embody an early tradition, and rival the canonical Gospels. In regard to the date, character, and tendencies of these

Gospels there has, however, been much controversy; they are known as—

1. Gospel according to the Egyptians.
2. Gospel according to Peter.
3. Fayûm Gospel Fragment.

*B.* Gospels which claim to fill up the gaps in our knowledge of the parents of Jesus, or of His infancy and childhood, viz.—

1. Protevangelium of James, including the Latin recensions known as—
   (*a*) Gospel of pseudo-Matthew,
   (*b*) Gospel of the Nativity of Mary.
2. Gospel according to Thomas.
3. Arabic Gospel of the Childhood.
4. Arabic History of Joseph the Carpenter.
5. The Departure of Mary (*Transitus Mariæ*).

*C.* Gospels whose heretical origin is universally acknowledged, viz.—

1. Gospel of the Twelve Apostles.
2. Gospel according to Philip.
3. Gospel according to Matthias.
4. Gospel according to Basilides.

*D.* Gospels of which almost nothing is known except their name. These will be mentioned in alphabetical order, and, as far as possible, described.

LITERATURE.—In 1552 Bibliander's edition of the 'Protevangelium Jacobi' appeared; this work is also the only Gospel in the earliest collection of NT Apocrypha: *Apocrypha, h.e. narrationes de Christo, Maria, Joseph, cognatione et familia Christi, extra Biblia*, etc., 1564, added by M. Neander Soraviensis to his *Catechesis Mart. Lutheri parva.* Fabricius published the first critical edition in 1703: *Codex apocryphus NT*; this work is the basis of Jones' *A New and Full Method of settling the Canonical Authority of the NT*, and of Birch's *Auctarium cod. apocr. NT Fabriciani.* In 1832 Thilo's *Codex Apocryphus NT* appeared with valuable Prolegomena; this work is the basis of Borberg's *Bibliothek der NT Apokryphen*, and of Brunet's *Les évangiles apocryphes.* A new impetus to the study of these writings was imparted by the publication of the results of Tischendorf's learned researches: *Evangelia Apocrypha*, 1853, 2nd ed. 1876; this standard edition was preceded by Tischendorf's prize essay: *de Evang. Apocr. origine et usu*, 1851; in the same author's *Wann wurden unsere Evangelien verfasst?* there is a chapter on 'Apocr. Literatur.' Hilgenfeld's *NT extra canonem receptum*, 4th ed. 1884, contains, in the section entitled 'Librorum Deperditorum Fragmenta,' learned notes on some of these Gospels.

In recent years elaborate investigations of the apocryphal Gospels have been published. Invaluable to all students are those found in Harnack's *Altchristliche Litteraturgeschichte* and Zahn's *Geschichte des NT Kanons.* Holtzmann's *Einleitung in das NT*, 3rd ed. 1892, contains an appendix on the 'NT Apocrypha.' Admirable introductions to these Gospels, with complete translations of their contents, are given in *Die Apokryphen des Neuen Testaments*—a comprehensive work shortly to be published under the editorship of Dr. Hennecke, who, with Prof. A. Meyer, has contributed the greater part of the section on the apocryphal Gospels.

Preuschen's *Antilegomena: Die Reste der ausserkanonischen Evangelien und urchristlichen Ueberlieferungen*, presents a critically edited text of the extant fragments of these writings. The Syriac Versions are brought within the student's reach by Wright's *Contributions to the Apocryphal Literature of the NT*, and his articles in the *Journal of Sacred Literature*, 1865; the Coptic Versions by Forbes Robinson's *Coptic Apocryphal Gospels.*

Other works are: Hofmann, *Leben Jesu nach den Apokryphen*, 1851; Kleuker, *Ueber die Apokryphen des NTs*; Tappehorn, *Ausserbiblische Nachrichten* (a Roman Catholic work); Pons, *Recherches sur les apocryphes du nouveau Test.*; Nicholas, *Études sur les Évangiles Apocryphes*; Variot, *Les évangiles apocryphes* (a Roman Catholic work); Barnes, *Canonical and Uncanonical Gospels*; Baring-Gould, *Lost and Hostile Gospels*; Ellicott, 'On the Apocr. Gospels' in *Cambridge Essays*, 1856; Krüger, 'The Apocr. Gospels' in Gillett's translation of *Early Christian Literature*; Cruttwell, 'Early Apocr. Literature' in *A Literary History of Early Christianity*; Westcott, 'On some of the Apocryphal Gospels' in *Introduction to the Study of the Gospels*, Appendix D; Salmon, 'Apocryphal and Heretical Gospels' in *Introduction to the NT*, lect. xi.; Orr, *NT Apocryphal Writings*, with brief and scholarly notes—a volume of the 'Temple Bible'; Hone's 'catchpenny' *Apocr. New Testament* is sufficiently described by Orr as 'critically worthless.' Excellent English translations are given in Walker's *Apocryphal Gospels, Acts and Revelations* (Ante-Nicene Christian Library); vol. ix., an extra volume of the series, contains 'the Gospel of Peter.'

Important and lengthy articles on these Gospels are contributed by Hofmann to vol. i. of *PRE*[3]; by Lipsius to vol. ii. of the *Dict. of Christ. Biography*; shorter articles by James to vol. i. of the *Encycl. Biblica*, and by Charles to vol. xxv. of the *Encycl. Britannica.* Hofmann's article has the most complete Bibliography.

A. 1. *EGYPTIANS, GOSPEL ACCORDING TO THE.*—

i. Meaning of the title.
ii. Evidence of existence.
   1. Clement of Alexandria.
   2. Origen (Jerome, Ambrose).
   3. Hippolytus and Epiphanius.
   4. The so-called Second Epistle of Clement of Rome.
   5. Hypothetical sources.
iii. Contents.
iv. Origin and character. Place and date.
   Literature.

i. MEANING OF THE TITLE.—In the title which Clement of Alexandria first applies to this Gospel—τὸ κατ' Αἰγυπτίους εὐαγγέλιον—the preposition κατά cannot have the same meaning as in the titles of the canonical and other Gospels, where it is used with a proper name in the singular. The reference is not to authorship, but to the region in which the Gospel found acceptance, or to the circle from which it sprang. It is improbable that the Gospel was written in the Egyptian, *i.e.* the Coptic language; Clement of Alexandria quotes from it, but there is no evidence either that he made use of a translation or that he had learnt Coptic during his residence in Egypt. On account of the resemblance of the title to that of the Gospel according to the Hebrews, Harnack (*Chronologie*, i. 612 f.) suggests that one Gospel circulated amongst the Jewish Christians residing in Egypt, and the other Gospel amongst the Christians who were natives of Egypt; it is also a possible inference that the Gospel was not called καθ' Ἕλληνας, because Christianity had more adherents amongst the native Egyptians than amongst the Greek residents in Egypt. But there is insufficient foundation for Harnack's argument, when he maintains that the title—the Gospel of the Egyptians, or the Egyptian Gospel—signifies that this was the only Gospel known to these Egyptian Christians. 'If, in the same circles, the Gospels according to Matthew, Mark, etc., had been read with equal or even higher authority, it would have been impossible in those circles to describe this Gospel as *the* Gospel of the Egyptians.' Harnack's conclusion rests upon his statement that the name was given to the Gospel by Egyptian writers, *i.e.* by Clement of Alexandria and Origen; he acknowledges that if non-Egyptian Fathers had thus described this Gospel, 'we might, nay we must, have believed that because the Gospel came from Egypt it was called the Egyptian Gospel, just as the Palestinian Gospel was called τὸ εὐαγγέλιον καθ' Ἑβραίους, or Ἑβραϊκόν, or Ἰουδαϊκόν.' But although Origen was a native of Alexandria, Clement was an Athenian. Zahn (*Geschichte*, ii. 630) can find no intimation in the writings of Clement and Origen that they regarded themselves as Αἰγύπτιοι; his explanation of the title, therefore, is that whilst the Church at Alexandria kept to the canonical Gospels, this non-canonical Gospel had considerable popularity in the provinces of Egypt during the 2nd century. This conclusion is a probable inference from the scanty facts; moreover, it is in accord with the history of the Church in Egypt during the 3rd and 4th cents., when the provincial Churches diverged in their theology from the teaching of the Alexandrian Fathers.

ii. EVIDENCE OF EXISTENCE.—1. The Gospel according to the Egyptians is first mentioned (175–200) by *Clement of Alexandria.* After quoting a passage which Julius Cassianus (*c.* 170) ascribes to 'the Lord,' Clement adds: 'We have not this saying in the four Gospels that have been handed down to us, but in the Gospel κατ' Αἰγυπτίους (*Strom.* iii. 13, 92). The Gospel is not described as a heretical writing, but it is regarded as outside the class to which the four Gospels belong (τοῖς παραδεδομένοις ἡμιν :έτταρσιν εὐαγγελίοις).

2. *Origen* in his Commentary on Lk $1^1$ (*c.* 220)

gives the unknown authors of τὸ κατ' Αἰγυπτίους εὐαγγέλιον the first place in his list of those who 'took in hand to draw up a narrative of Gospel occurrences.' With these writers who took the matter in hand he contrasts the four Evangelists who wrote as they were moved by the Holy Spirit (ἐξ ἁγίου κινούμενος πνεύματος). Latin translations of Origen's notes on this passage are given by *Jerome* and by *Ambrose*; both place the Gospel in the class of heretical writings. Jerome's words are: '*Ecclesia quatuor habet evangelia, hæreses plurima, e quibus quoddam scribitur "secundum Ægyptios."*' (Cf. Zahn, *Geschichte*, ii. 625). After naming other apocryphal Gospels, Jerome says '*et alia plura legimus*': these words are not in the extant Greek text; but as it bears elsewhere signs of abbreviation, and as Ambrose in his independent version essentially agrees with Jerome, the Latin is probably a correct rendering of Origen's words. Harnack and Zahn conclude that Origen had this Gospel in his hands; hence we may, with some degree of confidence, accept his judgment as to the character of a work which he had himself read.

3. This Gospel was known by name to two other authors. *Hippolytus* (155–235) quotes from a Naassene work a passage which treats of the constitution of the human soul, and says (*Philos.* v. 7) that this Gnostic sect found support for their fantastic theories ἐν τῷ ἐπιγραφομένῳ κατ' Αἰγυπτίους εὐαγγελίῳ. Of the Naassenes little is known. Lightfoot (*Biblical Essays*, 1893, pp. 408, 411–418) sought to prove that the ἑτεροδιδασκαλοῦντες of the Pastoral Epistles closely resembled them; but Hofmann, B. Weiss, and Hort (*Judaistic Christianity*, 1894, pp. 130–146) have shown that this view does not meet the requirements of strict exegesis. The Naassenes were not Jewish legalists, but Gnostics 'in whose syncretistic system there were Jewish elements' (cf. Zahn, *Einleitung*, i. 476).—*Epiphanius* (377) states that the Sabellians appealed to this Gospel in support of their doctrine; he does not give a quotation from it, but says that it represents 'the Saviour' as teaching His disciples that the Father, the Son, and the Holy Spirit are the same (τὸν αὐτὸν εἶναι πατέρα, τὸν αὐτὸν εἶναι υἱόν, τὸν αὐτὸν εἶναι ἅγιον πνεῦμα); he also asserts that the heresy was derived from apocryphal sources, especially from 'the Egyptian Gospel' (ἐξ ἀποκρύφων τινῶν, μάλιστα ἀπὸ τοῦ καλουμένου Αἰγυπτίου εὐαγγελίου). The slight change in the title (Αἰγύπτιον εὐαγγέλιον) renders still more probable the view taken above of its meaning; Epiphanius (*Hær.* xxx. 13) also speaks of a Hebrew Gospel (Ἑβραϊκόν), and the natural explanation yields good sense in both cases: the Gospels would fitly be so described which were used respectively by the Egyptians and by the Hebrews.

4. *The so-called Second Epistle of Clement of Rome.*—Of writings which are supposed to contain quotations from this Gospel, although it is not named, the most important is the 'Ancient Homily,' which from the 5th cent. was known as the Second Epistle of Clement of Rome to the Corinthians (130–140). Pseudo-Clement—unlike the genuine Clement, whose Scripture references are almost exclusively to the OT—makes many allusions to the Evangelic history, using both the canonical Gospels and apocryphal narratives. In one passage there are verbal agreements with the Gospel according to the Egyptians: 'For the Lord Himself, being asked by a certain person when His kingdom would come, said, *When the two shall be one, and the outside as the inside, and the male with the female neither male nor female*' (2 Clem. xii.). Lightfoot concludes (*Apost. Fathers*, pt. i. vol. ii. p. 238) that 'our pseudo-Clement would seem to have employed this apocryphal Gospel as a principal authority for the sayings of our Lord.' Harnack is quite certain that he did, but the evidence does not warrant a positive statement; there are differences as well as agreements in the two forms in which the saying is quoted (cf. iii. below). The two versions may therefore be derived from a common source, either oral or written, the purer form of the saying being found in pseudo-Clement. Zahn and Resch oppose the identification of the source as strongly as Hilgenfeld and Harnack assert it; Harnack assigns three other quotations in the Homily to this Gospel (*Chron.* i. 618). Ropes says that it is impossible to express a confident opinion (*Die Sprüche Jesu*, pp. 132, 146).

5. In recent criticism there has been manifested a tendency to refer back to this Gospel sayings of our Lord and narratives of events found in other fragmentary sources. Harnack favours the theory that the *Logia* in the Oxyrhynchus Fragment were taken from this Gospel (cf. *Expositor*, 5th series, vi. 411); Sanday does not adopt this view, but is of opinion that 'they may well have had their birth in proximity to it' (*Crit. Rev.* viii. 140); Armitage Robinson says: 'I am not at present prepared to say that the newly discovered sayings are excerpts from the Gospel according to the Egyptians. I must content myself with the statement that such a view is not improbable' (*Expositor*, 5th series, vi. 421). It is a mere conjecture that the *Fayûm Fragment* (Mk $14^{26-30}$ abbreviated, with v.[28] omitted) is an extract from this Gospel. Harnack (*Chron.* i. 590) suggests the Gospel according to the Hebrews as an alternative source, whilst Zahn regards the verses as the fragment of a homily (*Geschichte*, ii. 789 f.). Völter (*Petrusevangelium oder Ægypterevangelium?*) holds that the Gospel of Peter is identical with this Gospel, in which, however, he is compelled to acknowledge the presence of interpolations. The reasoning has failed to convince scholars who have made a special study of the Gospel of Peter (cf. *Crit. Rev.* v. 299). Other conjectures, as, *e.g.*, that this Gospel is related to the *Didache* and to Tatian's *Diatessaron*, are mentioned by Harnack, but he does not deem it needful to discuss them. On the general question, it may be said that it is hazardous to treat one Gospel, whether canonical or apocryphal, as dependent on another, because similar reports of our Lord's words or deeds are found in both; they may be independent of each other, but dependent on a common source, oral or written.

iii. CONTENTS.—The passages from this Gospel quoted by Clement of Alexandria are taken from the discourse of Jesus with Salome. (For the Greek text, see Harnack, *Geschichte*, i. 13; Preuschen, *Antilegomena*, p. 2 f.). To Salome's question, 'How long shall Death reign?' Jesus replies, 'So long as ye women give birth; for I came to destroy the works of the female.' Salome says, 'Then should I have done well, if I had borne no children?' and the Lord makes answer, 'Eat every herb, but the bitter one eat not.' [Salome's words are καλῶς οὖν ἐποίησα μὴ τεκοῦσα; Lightfoot proposes 'an easy change of reading' (ἂν ἐποίησα) to avoid the contradiction to the canonical narratives implied in the rendering 'then I did well that I bare not.' But, as Zahn points out, this rendering would require οὐ in place of μή; all difficulty is removed by adopting Harnack's note of interrogation]. To a further question of Salome, 'When shall these things be known?' the Lord replies, 'When ye tread underfoot the garment of shame, and when the two become one, and the male with the female neither male nor female.' (Cf. ii. 4 above for pseudo-Clement's version of this saying).

Another extract from this Gospel is given by

Hippolytus in his refutation of the Naassene heresy (*Philos.* v. 7): 'They affirm that the soul is very difficult to discover, and hard to understand; for it does not remain in the same figure or the same form invariably, or in one passive condition, that either one could express it by a sign or comprehend it substantially. But they have these varied changes [of the soul] set down in the Gospel inscribed "according to the Egyptians."'

Epiphanius (*Hær.* lxii. 2) states that this Gospel was a chief source of Sabellian heterodoxy; but, although he asserts that in it many such things are ascribed to the Saviour 'with a mystical significance' (μυστηριωδῶς), he mentions only one: 'the same [person] is Father, the same is Son, the same is Holy Spirit.'

In Harnack's judgment, three more passages found in the homily of pseudo-Clement (*Ep.* c. 4, c. 5, c. 8) are quotations from this Gospel, viz.: 'The Lord said, Though ye be gathered together with me in my bosom and do not my commandments, I will cast you away, and will say unto you, Depart from me, I know you not whence ye are, ye workers of iniquity.' (Cf. Lk $13^{27}$, Mt $7^{23}$). 'For the Lord saith, Ye shall be as lambs in the midst of wolves. But Peter answered and said unto him, What then, if the wolves should tear the lambs? Jesus said unto Peter, Let not the lambs fear the wolves after they are dead; and ye also, fear ye not them that kill you and are not able to do anything to you; but fear him that after ye are dead hath power over soul and body, to cast them into the gehenna of fire.' (Cf. Lk $10^{3}$, Mt $10^{28}$, and Lk $12^{4.5}$). 'For the Lord saith in the Gospel, If ye kept not that which is little, who shall give unto you that which is great? For I say unto you that he which is faithful in the least, is faithful also in much.' (Cf. Lk $16^{10}$, Mt $25^{21.23}$).

iv. ORIGIN AND CHARACTER.—There is great divergence of opinion in regard to the character of this Gospel. All are agreed that it circulated amongst various heretical sects or schools; but was it, therefore, a heretical Gospel as regards its origin? or was it, as Harnack believes, 'part of the *original* Evangelic literature in the strict sense of the word?'

The facts of which any satisfactory solution of the problem must take account are these: 1. Clement of Alexandria's statements (*Strom.* iii. 9, 13, 91) that the Gospel was used (*a*) by Cassian, the Gnostic leader (ὁ τῆς δοκήσεως ἀρχηγός) of the Encratites who were ascetics and condemned marriage, and (*b*) by Theodotus, the Egyptian pupil of the Gnostic Valentinus. 2. Hippolytus asserts that the Naassenes, who were also Gnostics, quoted it in support of their speculations about the soul of man. 3. Epiphanius says that the Sabellians found passages in it which taught a modalistic doctrine of the Trinity. 4. Clement of Alexandria classes it apart from 'the four Gospels.' 5. Origen puts it at the head of the list of heretical Gospels.—Is Origen's judgment confirmed by the extant fragments of this Gospel? To this question Lipsius (*Dict. Christ. Biog.* ii. 712) replies: 'The Gospel was a product of pantheistic gnosis'; unquestionably, it contains traces of the teaching that the true gnosis imparts 'insight into the unsubstantial character of all the distinctions which prevail among, and separate one from another, the things of this visible world'; it reflects also the practical as well as the mystical aspect of Gnosticism, for the Encratite prohibition of marriage was the natural consequence of insight into the vanity of the distinctions of sex. Some amount of Encratism is recognized by Harnack, but he contends that it is not present to such an extent as to justify those who describe the Gospel as heretical and Gnostic. He is right in maintaining that the ascetic tendency of some of the sayings has been exaggerated, and in urging that the entire Gospel may have contained material derived from purer sources than the fragments known to us. But to establish the non-heretical character of this Gospel more conclusive evidence is required than its use by pseudo-Clement, which, as we have seen, cannot be regarded as a certainty. The least convincing part of Harnack's investigation is that in which the inference that this Gospel bears the Synoptic stamp, and is closely akin to Matthew and Luke, is made to rest upon the insufficiently attested assertion that it was used by pseudo-Clement. 'It contained nothing heretical,—if it had, the Church at Rome in 170 would certainly not have read it' (*Chron.* i. 619). But if pseudo-Clement drew from the same source as this Gospel, the phenomena of the text would be satisfactorily explained, especially the expanded and less credible form given in this Gospel to the words of Jesus. Moreover, this solution of the problem is quite consistent with Harnack's view that this Gospel is not dependent on the Synoptics, but 'derives from the sources of the Synoptics.' The strongest argument adduced to prove that this Gospel must have contained much orthodox teaching, is based upon the fact that Clement of Alexandria held it in good esteem and gave a different, if mystical, interpretation to those passages which the Encratites quoted in support of their ascetic practices. The most probable conclusion which the evidence now available warrants is that the Gospel according to the Egyptians is a Gnostic writing derived, it may be, from a good source; but if its unknown author had access to material as valuable as that of which the Evangelists made use, he treated it more freely, and both added to and modified the Evangelic tradition.

In regard to the *place* where this Gospel was written, Zahn suggests Antioch; Harnack prefers Egypt. Its *date* cannot be later than the middle of the 2nd cent., probably about 140. Harnack, however, holds that the *terminus ad quem* is 130.

LITERATURE.—Emmerich, *de Evang. sec. Ebrœos, Ægypt.* etc., 1807; Schneckenburger, *Ueber das Evang. der Ægypt.* 1834; Hennecke in *Die Apokryphen des NT.* See also Hilgenfeld, Harnack, Zahn, in *opp. citt.*, and cf. Resch, *Ausserkanonische Paralleltexte zu den Evangelien*, 1894, p. 28.

## A. 2. *PETER, GOSPEL ACCORDING TO.*—

i. Evidence of existence prior to its discovery.
  1. Serapion.
  2. Origen.
  3. Eusebius, etc.
  4. Some doubtful testimony.
ii. Contents of recently discovered Fragment.
iii. Relation to the canonical Gospels.
iv. Alleged use by early writers.
v. Character and tendencies.
vi. Date and place of origin.
  Literature.

i. EVIDENCE OF EXISTENCE PRIOR TO ITS DISCOVERY.—1. The earliest evidence of the existence of this Gospel is found in a letter of *Serapion*, who became bishop of Antioch *c.* 190. Eusebius mentions amongst the memorials of his 'literary industry' a work composed 'on the so-called Gospel of Peter,' and gives the following extract from it (*HE* vi. 12 [McGiffert's translation, p. 258]): 'For we, brethren, receive both Peter and the other apostles as Christ; but we reject intelligently the writings falsely ascribed to them, knowing that such were not handed down to us. When I visited you, I supposed that all of you held the true faith, and as I had not read the Gospel which they put forward under the name of Peter, I said, "If this is the only thing which occasions dispute among you, let it be read." But now, having learned from what has been told me that their mind was involved in some heresy, I will hasten to come to you again. . . . For having obtained this Gospel from others who had studied it diligently, namely, from the successors of those who first used it, whom we call Docetæ (for most of their opinions are connected with the teaching of that school), we have been able to read it through, and we find many things in accordance with the true doctrine of the Saviour, but some things added to that doctrine, which we have pointed out for you further on.'

2. *Origen*, writing *c.* 246, not only mentions this Gospel, but also shows some knowledge of its contents. 'Some say, basing it on a tradition in the Gospel according to Peter, as it is entitled, or the Book of James, that the brethren of Jesus were sons of Joseph by a former wife, whom he married before Mary' (*Com. on Mt.* bk. x. 17 [Ante-Nicene Christian Library, p. 424]). Eusebius tells us (*HE* vi. 21) that Origen was summoned to Antioch by Mammæa, the mother of the emperor Alexander Severus, and 'a most pious woman,' though it is not said that she was a Christian. From Serapion's statements about this Gospel it is evident that it was not widely circulated; but if Origen saw it during his visit to Antioch (probably 218), his uncertainty in regard to a particular passage is only what might be expected, and does not detract from the value of his testimony to its general character.*

3. Besides quoting Serapion's estimate of this Gospel, *Eusebius* (*c.* 324) refers to it twice (*HE* iii. 3, 25). 'The so-called Acts of Peter, however, and the Gospel which bears his name, and the Preaching, and the Apocalypse, as they are called, we know have not been universally accepted, because no ecclesiastical writer, ancient or modern, has made use of testimonies drawn from them.' In his chapter on the Canon of Holy Scripture, Eusebius classifies the books into *Homologoumena* or 'accepted,' *Antilegomena* or 'disputed,' *νόθοι* or 'spurious,' *i.e.* orthodox but not canonical. After enumerating the writings which are placed under these several heads, he adds: 'We have felt compelled to give this catalogue in order that we might be able to know both these works and those that are cited by the heretics under the name of the apostles, including, for instance, such books as the Gospels of Peter, of Thomas, of Matthias, or of any others besides them, and the Acts of Andrew and John and the other apostles, which no one belonging to the succession of ecclesiastical writers has deemed worthy of mention in his writings.'

The statement of Jerome (*de Vir. Illust.* 1) that this Gospel is a heretical work, also the condemnation pronounced upon it in the so-called 'Gelasian decretal' ('*evangelium nomine Petri apostoli apocryphum*'), are in agreement with, and possibly are based on, the judgment of Eusebius.†

4. Historical critics of different schools regard the testimony of *Theodoret* (*c.* 450) as untrustworthy. He says that this Gospel was used by the Nazarenes, of whom, however, he knows nothing except that they 'honour Christ as a righteous man' (*Hær. fab.* ii. 2). Zahn points out in detail the marks of confusion in Theodoret's references to the Jewish Christian sects (*Geschichte*, ii. 743); Harnack inserts a note of interrogation, and attaches no more value to this than to most of 'this historian's remarkable statements' (*Chron.* i. 623); Hofmann thinks that Theodoret meant the Gospel according to the Hebrews (*PRE*³ i. 663).

* For other traces of the use of this Gospel by Origen, see J. O. F. Murray's article in the *Expositor* (4th series, vii. 55 f.).

† Other writers who were probably acquainted with the Petrine Gospel are the author of the *Didascalia* and *Apostolical Constitutions* (cf. Harnack, *Bruchstücke*, p. 41 f.), and *Cyril of Jerusalem* (cf. Swete, 'The Akhmim Fragment,' in his edition of the Gospel of Peter, xxx ff.).

There has been much discussion in regard to the meaning of a phrase in *Justin Martyr's* (*c.* 150) *Dialogue with Trypho.* Some have thought that this Gospel is referred to as the 'Memoirs of Peter' in the passage: 'And when it is said that he changed the name of one of the apostles to Peter; and when it is written in the Memoirs of him (*ἀπομνημονεύματα αὐτοῦ*) that this so happened, etc.' The difficult problem of the relation to this Gospel of Justin Martyr's quotations cannot be discussed until its contents have been given; but it is important that the discussion should not be biassed by the assumption that 'the name "Memoirs" cannot with any degree of propriety be applied to our canonical Gospels,' as the author of *Supernatural Religion* asserts (*The Gospel according to Peter*, p. 22). It may be granted that the *αὐτοῦ* is more naturally interpreted as referring to Peter and not to Jesus; but the judgment of such an expert as Lipsius (*Dict. Christ. Biography*, ii. 712) must not be forgotten: 'In the passage in question the right reading is most probably not *ἀπομνημονεύματα αὐτοῦ* (*i.e.* of Peter mentioned just before), but *ἀπομν. αὐτῶν* (*i.e. τῶν ἀποστόλων* as elsewhere).' But if, contrary to his invariable practice, Justin here attaches a name to the Evangelistic writings, it is by no means certain that he speaks of this apocryphal Gospel as the 'Memoirs of Peter.' He may refer to the Second Gospel, for many ancient authorities support the testimony of Origen: 'The Gospel published by Mark may be called Peter's, whose interpreter Mark was' (*adv. Marcion.* iv. 5), and in Mk 3¹⁷ there is a record of the fact mentioned by Justin: 'Simon he surnamed Peter.'

ii. CONTENTS OF RECENTLY DISCOVERED FRAGMENT.—In 1892 M. Bouriant published the manuscript known as 'the Akhmim Fragment'; it contains portions of the Gospel of Peter, of the Apocalypse of Peter, of the Book of Enoch, and of the Acts of St. Julian. This parchment manuscript and a papyrus collection of mathematical problems were discovered by the French Archæological Mission during the winter of 1886–87 in the tomb of a monk at Akhmim, the ancient Panopolis, in Upper Egypt. A heliographic reproduction of the manuscript greatly assisted palæographists to determine the true text, in regard to which scholars are now generally agreed. The parchment codex is assigned to a date between the 8th and the 12th century. The following translation by Dr. J. Armitage Robinson was carefully revised by him in accordance with the photographic facsimile (Ante-Nicene Christian Library, vol. ix. p. 7 f.):—

1. But of the Jews none washed his hands, neither Herod nor any one of his judges. And when they had refused to wash them, Pilate rose up. And then Herod the king commandeth that the Lord be taken, saying to them, What things soever I commanded you to do unto him, do.

2. And there was standing there Joseph the friend of Pilate and of the Lord; and, knowing that they were about to crucify him, he came to Pilate and asked the body of the Lord for burial. And Pilate sent to Herod and asked his body. And Herod said, Brother Pilate, even if no one had asked for him, we purposed to bury him, especially as the Sabbath draweth on; for it is written in the Law that the sun set not upon one that hath been put to death.

3. And he delivered him to the people on the day before the unleavened bread, their feast. And they took the Lord and pushed him as they ran, and said, Let us drag away the Son of God, having obtained power over him. And they clothed him with purple, and set him on the seat of judgment, saying, Judge righteously, O king of Israel. And one of them brought a crown of thorns and put it on the head of the Lord. And others stood and spat in his eyes, and others smote his cheeks; others pricked him with a reed; and some scourged him, saying, With this honour let us honour the Son of God.

4. And they brought two malefactors, and they crucified the Lord between them. But he held his peace, as though having no pain. And when they had raised the cross, they wrote the title, This is the king of Israel. And having set his garments before him they parted them among them, and cast lots for them. And one of those malefactors reproached them, saying, We for the evils that we have done have suffered thus, but this

man, who hath become the Saviour of men, what wrong hath he done to you? And they, being angered at him, commanded that his legs should not be broken, that he might die in torment.

5. And it was noon, and darkness came over all Judæa: and they were troubled and distressed lest the sun had set whilst he was yet alive: [for] it is written for them, that the sun set not on him that hath been put to death. And one of them said, Give him to drink gall with vinegar. And they mixed and gave him to drink, and fulfilled all things, and accomplished their sins against their own head. And many went about with lamps, supposing that it was night, and fell down. And the Lord cried out, saying, My power, my power, thou hast forsaken me. And when he had said it, he was taken up. And in that hour the vail of the temple of Jerusalem was rent in twain.

6. And then they drew out the nails from the hands of the Lord, and laid him upon the earth, and the whole earth quaked, and great fear arose. Then the sun shone, and it was found the ninth hour; and the Jews rejoiced, and gave his body to Joseph that he might bury it, since he had seen what good things he had done. And he took the Lord, and washed him, and rolled him in a linen cloth, and brought him into his own tomb, which was called the garden of Joseph.

7. Then the Jews and the elders and the priests, perceiving what evil they had done to themselves, began to lament and to say, Woe for our sins; the judgment hath drawn nigh, and the end of Jerusalem. And I with my companions was grieved; and being wounded in mind we hid ourselves: for we were being sought for by them as malefactors, and as wishing to set fire to the temple. And upon all these things we fasted and sat mourning and weeping night and day until the Sabbath.

8. But the scribes and Pharisees and elders being gathered together one with another, when they heard that all the people murmured and beat their breasts, saying, If by his death these most mighty signs have come to pass, see how righteous he is—the elders were afraid, and came to Pilate, beseeching him and saying, Give us soldiers that we may guard his sepulchre for three days, lest his disciples come and steal him away, and the people suppose that he has risen from the dead and do us evil. And Pilate gave them Petronius the centurion with soldiers to guard the tomb. And with them came elders and scribes to the sepulchre, and having rolled a great stone together with the centurion and the soldiers, they altogether who were there set it at the door of the sepulchre; and they affixed seven seals, and they pitched a tent there and guarded it. And early in the morning as the Sabbath was drawing on, there came a multitude from Jerusalem and the region round about that they might see the sepulchre that was sealed.

9. And in the night in which the Lord's day was drawing on, as the soldiers kept guard two by two in a watch, there was a great voice in the heaven, and they saw the heavens opened, and two men descend from thence with great light and approach the tomb. And that stone which was put at the door rolled of itself and made way in part; and the tomb was opened, and both the young men entered in.

10. When therefore those soldiers saw it, they awakened the centurion and the elders; for they too were hard by, keeping guard. And, as they declared what things they had seen, again they see three men come forth from the tomb, and two of them supporting one, and a cross following them: and of the two the head reached unto the heavens, but the head of him that was led by them overpassed the heavens. And they heard a voice from the heavens saying, Thou hast preached to them that sleep. And a response was heard from the cross, Yea.

11. They therefore considered one with another whether to go away and show these things to Pilate. And while they yet thought thereon, the heavens again are seen to open, and a certain man to descend and enter into the sepulchre. When the centurion and they that were with him saw these things, they hastened in the night to Pilate, leaving the tomb which they were watching, and declared all things which they had seen, being greatly distressed, and saying, Truly he was the Son of God. Pilate answered and said, I am pure from the blood of the Son of God: but it was ye who determined this. Then they all drew near and besought him and entreated him to command the centurion and the soldiers to say nothing of the things which they had seen: For it is better, say they, for us to be guilty of the greatest sin before God, and not to fall into the hands of the people of the Jews and to be stoned. Pilate therefore commanded the centurion and the soldiers to say nothing.

12. And at dawn upon the Lord's day Mary Magdalen, a disciple of the Lord, fearing because of the Jews, since they were burning with wrath, had not done at the Lord's sepulchre the things which women are wont to do for those that die, and for those that are beloved by them—she took her friends with her, and came to the sepulchre where he was laid. And they feared lest the Jews should see them, and they said, Although on that day on which he was crucified we could not weep and lament, yet now let us do these things at his sepulchre. But who shall roll away for us the stone that was laid at the door of the sepulchre, that we may enter in and sit by him and do the things that are due? For the stone was great, and we fear lest some one see us. And if we cannot, yet if we but set at the door the things which we bring for a memorial of him, we will weep and lament, until we come unto our home.

13. And they went and found the tomb opened, and coming near they looked in there; and they see there a certain young man sitting in the midst of the tomb, beautiful and clothed in a robe exceeding bright; who said to them, Wherefore are ye come? Whom seek ye? Him that was crucified? He is risen and gone. But if ye believe not, look in and see the place where he lay, that he is not [here]; for he is risen and gone thither, whence he was sent. Then the women feared and fled.

14. Now it was the last day of the unleavened bread, and many were going forth, returning to their homes, as the feast was ended. But we, the twelve disciples of the Lord, wept and were grieved; and each one, being grieved for that which was come to pass, departed to his home. But I Simon Peter and Andrew my brother took our nets and went to the sea; and there was with us Levi the son of Alphæus, whom the Lord . . .

iii. Relation to the canonical Gospels.—A careful study of the contents of this Gospel reveals many close resemblances to, and some striking divergences from, the canonical Gospels. The author of *Supernatural Religion* endeavours to prove that it is not dependent on them, and describes those who differ from him on this question as 'apologetic critics' (*op. cit.* 107 f.). But Harnack's judgment is that acquaintance with Mark is 'proved or almost proved,' on the other hand acquaintance with John is 'not proved'; in regard to Matthew and Luke he is uncertain whether their points of agreement with this Gospel show that its author made use of their narratives, or of the same sources as the Evangelists (*Bruchstücke*, p. 32 f.). Zahn holds that 'the only sources from which the Gospel of Peter has drawn its materials are our four Gospels,' and shows that there is close agreement with each Gospel as well in forms of expression as in subject-matter. He accounts for the divergences by allowing time for the development of variations in the text of the canonical Gospels (*Das Evangelium des Petrus*, p. 47). But, whilst the evidence available may suffice to establish the probability of dependence upon the four Gospels as a source, it is not sufficient to prove that they were the only source. The subject is exhaustively treated in the introduction to Swete's edition of this Gospel ('The Akhmim Fragment,' xiii ff.). The Petrine Passion-history 'exceeds by about one-fourth the average length of the four canonical narratives,' and this notwithstanding many significant omissions; the result of a verbal comparison reveals coincidences which, in Swete's judgment, prove that the use of the First and Second Gospels by the author of the Petrine Fragment is 'scarcely doubtful'; that there is a 'strong presumption' in favour of his use of the Third Gospel; and that traces of verbal indebtedness to the Fourth Gospel are fainter, though it is 'at least probable that he had access' to it. From the nature of the case absolute proof is not attainable, but the solution of this complex problem, to which the investigations of many scholars point, is that the Petrine Gospel is later than the canonical Gospels; that its author was acquainted with them; that his sources are treated with great freedom, many of the changes being due to his recasting of the Gospel history in the form of a personal narrative; and that possibly he had access to other sources, which may have included, as Harnack rightly says, some good traditions (*Chron.* i. 624).

iv. Alleged use by early writers.—Traces of the Petrine Gospel have been diligently sought in the works of authors who wrote before the date at which it is known to have been in circulation. The author of *Supernatural Religion* argues for the probability that *Tatian* possessed this Gospel, but reveals an apologetic interest in the establishment of a conclusion which might 'lead to the opinion that Tatian's *Harmony* was not composed out of four Gospels, but out of five' (*op. cit.* p. 41). It is, however, an indisputable fact that there are signs of harmonizing in this Fragment: to refute the argument that Tatian used it by proving that its author used Tatian is impossible, but in all probability a Harmony, such as the *Diatessaron*, was known to him. This is Swete's view, though he does not think that the Petrine writer was 'limited to the use of the Diatessaron' (*op. cit.* xxiv.). Dr. Rendel Harris, in his 'Popular Account' of the Gospel, clearly states the facts, but reserves his final judgment.

There is much more to be said in favour of the view that *Justin Martyr* (*c.* 150) was acquainted with the Petrine Gospel, as a comparison of the following passages with the Fragment will show. 'The Spirit of prophecy foretold . . . *the conspiracy* which was formed against Christ by Herod, the king of the Jews, and *the Jews* themselves, and Pilate who was your governor among them, with his *soldiers*' (*Apol.* i. 40). 'And as the prophet spoke, they tormented Him, and *set Him on the judgment-seat, and said, Judge us*' (*Apol.* i. 35). 'Those who crucified Him parted His garments among themselves, *each casting lots for what he chose to have*, and receiving according to the decision of the lot' (*Dialogue with Trypho*, 97). The words and sentences in *italics* are the most important parallels to the Petrine Gospel in Justin's writings, and the most striking of these is the statement that Jesus, not Pilate (cf. Jn 19[13]), sat on the judgment-seat. But Justin's account bears a closer resemblance to John's than to the longer narrative in the Petrine Fragment; if there be dependence, Justin's seems to be primary. This conclusion is confirmed by a fact to which Dr. Salmon calls attention, viz., that Justin—who, *ex hypothesi*, believed this Gospel to be Peter's, and therefore a document of paramount authority—'in every case where the account in this Gospel differs from that in the canonical, and where we have the means of judging which Justin prefers, follows the latter without hesitation' (*Introd. to NT*, Appendix, p. 587).

*The Epistle of Barnabas* (vii. 3–5) resembles this Gospel in representing Jesus as drinking gall mingled with vinegar, and in its description of the fasting and mourning that followed the Crucifixion. Dr. Swete thinks that it may 'not improbably have come into the hands of the party from which the Petrine Gospel emanated.' He is also of opinion that the resemblances between the *Sibylline Oracles* (bk. 8) and the Petrine Fragment are 'for the most part superficial.'

v. CHARACTER AND TENDENCIES.—Serapion, who first mentions 'the so-called Gospel of Peter,' states that it was used by the Docetæ; after reading it through, he pronounced it orthodox in general, but condemned it on account of its heterodox additions. Is this judgment as to the character and tendencies of the Petrine Gospel sustained by the knowledge gained of its contents from the discovery of the Akhmim Fragment?

Docetism in the 2nd cent. had various forms. Ignatius combated a Docetic heresy which Lightfoot describes as 'Judaic,' for it combined a denial of the reality of Christ's passion with a tendency towards Judaizing. But the author of the Petrine Fragment does not doubt that Christ had a true body, and he manifests an anti-Judaic spirit in his endeavour to fasten on the Jews the responsibility for the crucifixion of Jesus. Irenæus describes an Ophite system, which more nearly resembles the teaching of this Gospel; but Swete points out that, according to that system, the Christ withdrew from Jesus before the Crucifixion, whereas the Petrine Gospel 'regards the higher nature of the Lord as remaining with Him on the Cross up to the moment of His death' (*op. cit.* xxxix. f.). Hippolytus (*Philos.* viii. 8, x. 12) refers to a Gnostic sect, which bore the name of *Docetæ*, although they taught that Christ was born of the Virgin Mary, and had a true body. On the ground that Serapion could not have spoken so favourably of a work which denied the reality of Christ's body, McGiffert identifies the *Docetæ*, who used the Petrine Gospel, with this Gnostic sect, whose speculations added to true doctrine (Eusebius, *Church History* [McGiffert's tr.], p. 258, n. 8). There are, however, points of contact between the Petrine Fragment and the comments of Valentinian writers who accepted the facts of the Gospel history, but made it the vehicle of Gnostic teaching. Dr. Swete inclines to the belief that the Petrine writer, though not himself a Valentinian, 'felt the influence of the Valentinian school.' It is not necessary to decide between the claims of these different types of Gnostic Docetism to see that a writer of either of these schools would be likely to produce just such a Gospel as Serapion describes. Moreover, his judgment as to its character and tendency is fully sustained by the contents of the Akhmim Fragment, which has many features in common with the canonical Gospels, and yet has many additions to the Evangelic tradition, some being obviously unorthodox. The amplifications of the Gospel history, which clearly reveal a Docetic purpose, are: the statement that the Lord was silent on the Cross 'as though having no pain' (sec. 4); the cry, 'My power, my power, thou hast forsaken me,' followed by the description of His death as an ἀνάληψις: 'and when he had said it, he was taken up' (sec. 5). The conclusion arrived at implies that Eusebius too severely condemns this Gospel; it compares favourably with the other Gospels assigned by him to the 'heretical' category, though it is not free from Docetic tendencies which characterized some forms of early Gnosticism.

vi. DATE AND PLACE OF ORIGIN.—From Serapion's evidence the *terminus ad quem* for the date of this Gospel cannot be placed later than A.D. 170. The fixing of the *terminus a quo* depends upon the decision arrived at in the foregoing discussions. Critics who, like Harnack, hold that Justin used the Gospel, assign its composition to the beginning of the 2nd century. The opposite conclusion implies A.D. 130–150 as the probable date; in Swete's opinion, it cannot be placed earlier than A.D. 150. There is no evidence of the circulation of this Gospel in the West; a probable inference from the places of residence of the writers who were familiar with it is that it was a Syrian Gospel.

LITERATURE.—Bouriant, *Mémoires publiés par les membres de la mission archéol. française au Caire*, ix. 1 (1892); Stülcken in *Die Apocryphen des NT*; Harnack, *Texte u. Unters.* ix. 2; Zahn, *Das Petrusevangelium*; Völter, *Petrusevangelium oder Ægypterevangelium?*; also editions by von Gebhardt, Kunze, Lods, A. Sabatier, von Schubert. English editions by Rutherford in extra vol. of Ante-Nicene Christian Library, Robinson and James, Swete, Rendel Harris, and the author of *Supernatural Religion*; also Macpherson's translation of von Schubert's work—a useful edition with synoptical tables and critical apparatus. There are important articles by Baljon in *Theol. Studien*, 1894, 1 ff.; Funk in *Theol. Quartalschr.* 1893, 278 ff.; Hilgenfeld in *Zeitschr. f. wiss. Theol.* 1893, 220 ff.; von Soden in *Zeitschr. f. Theol. u. Kirche*, 1893, 52 ff.; Stanton in *Journal of Theol. Studies*, Oct. 1900; Murray in *Expositor*, 4th series, vol. vii.; Macpherson in *Crit. Rev.* v. 296.

## A. 3. *FAYÛM GOSPEL FRAGMENT.*—

i. Discovery.
ii. Contents.
iii. Theories of origin. Date.
Literature.

i. DISCOVERY.—Fayûm is a province of Egypt about 50 miles south of Cairo. It has become famous within the last 25 years owing to the discovery at Medinet, its capital, and elsewhere, of a large quantity of papyri in Latin, Greek, Coptic, and other languages. In 1882 the Austrian Archduke Rainer bought a mass of documents which are now in the Imperial Museum at Vienna. In this valuable collection a small and mutilated fragment of a Gospel was found. The honour of deciphering and restoring the true text belongs to Dr. Bickell, Roman Catholic Professor of Christian Archæology in the University of Innsbruck. In the *Zeitschrift für katholische Theologie* (1885, iii. 498 ff.), Bickell published the Fragment, and his judgment in regard to its antiquity and value. Since then his conclusions have been subjected to keen criticism by many scholars. The principal contributions to the discussion have been made by Harnack and Zahn; the result of their critical investigations is given below. An instructive account of the Fayûm papyri in general, and of this Fragment in particular, was published by Professor Stokes of Dublin in the *Expositor* (3rd series, i. 334, ii. 132, vii. 449).

ii. CONTENTS.—The Greek text of the Fragment, as finally restored by Bickell, is as follows: Μετὰ δὲ τὸ φαγεῖν ὡς ἐξ ἔθους, πάντες ἐν ταύτῃ τῇ νυκτὶ σκανδαλισθήσεσθε κατὰ τὸ γραφέν· πατάξω τὸν ποιμένα καὶ τὰ πρόβατα διασκορπισθήσονται. Εἰπόντος τοῦ Πέτρου· καὶ εἰ πάντες οὐκ ἐγώ. ἔφη αὐτῷ· ὁ ἀλεκτρυὼν δὶς κοκκύξει καὶ σὺ πρῶτον τρὶς ἀπαρνήσῃ με.

Certainty in regard to some details of the reconstruction cannot be attained. At first Bickell read ὡς ἐξῆγον, the letters being here obscure. Zahn (*Geschichte des NT Canons*, ii. 785) prints what he regards as the most probable text in a way which shows at a glance the mutilations at the end of the lines—

> . . . ὑμνησάντων δὲ αὐτῶν
> μετὰ τὸ φ]αγεῖν ὡς ἐξ ἔθους, πά[λιν εἶπε·
> ταύτῃ] τῇ νυκτὶ σκανδαλισ[θήσεσθε
> κατὰ] τὸ γραφέν· "πατάξω τὸν [ποιμένα, καὶ
> τὰ] πρόβατα διασκορπισθήσ[εται." εἰπόν-
> τος δὲ το]ῦ Πετ. "καὶ εἰ πάντες, οὐκ ἐγώ,"
> ἔφη· "πρὶν] ὁ ἀλεκτρυὼν δὶς κοκ[κύξει σή-
> μερον, σὺ τρὶς με ἀ]παρν[ήσῃ" . . .

According to Zahn's reconstructed text, the contents of the Fragment are: 'Now when they had sung a hymn, after eating according to custom, He said again: This night ye shall be offended according to the Scripture, "I will smite the shepherd, and the sheep shall be scattered." When Peter said: Even though all, yet not I, He said: Before the cock shall crow twice this day, thou shalt deny me thrice.'

iii. THEORIES OF ORIGIN.—The passages in the canonical Gospels which correspond to the contents of the Fayûm Fragment are Mt $26^{30-34}$, Mk $14^{26-30}$, the resemblances to Mark being more close. The words used for 'cock' and 'crow' (lit. 'cry cuckoo') are not found in the NT. In Bickell's judgment these few verses are a genuine relic of early Evangelic tradition, and the Fragment is part of such a document as Luke mentions in the preface to his Gospel. Harnack inclines to Bickell's view, though he admits that the words may be a free quotation from Mark rather than a part of the original material used by the Synoptic writers ('Das Evangelienfragment von Fajjum' in *Texte und Untersuchungen*, v. 4). The use of different words for 'cock' and 'crow' does not disprove the latter theory, but tends rather to confirm it. The Fragment has ἀλεκτρυών for ἀλέκτωρ, and κοκκύζειν for φωνεῖν. ἀλεκτρυών is the more usual word in classic prose; κοκκύζειν is more expressive than the colourless φωνεῖν. 'It is most probable that the words used in the canonical Gospels are more original, and that a preacher substituted in one case a more elegant, and in the other case a more significant expression' (Zahn, *op. cit.* ii. 787). Hort favoured the view that the passage is an extract from the Synoptic Gospels, and uttered a timely warning against hasty deductions from one scanty fragment (*Times*, 25th June 1885). Other conjectural explanations of its origin are that it is a quotation from the Gospel according to the Hebrews, or the Gospel according to the Egyptians (Harnack), and that it is a Gnostic recension of the canonical Gospels (Stokes).

The style of writing and the methods of contraction employed in this Fragment furnish, in the judgment of eminent palæographists, a strong argument for fixing the *date* of its composition in the 3rd century.

LITERATURE.—This has been sufficiently indicated in the body of the above section of the article.

### B. 1. *JAMES, PROTEVANGELIUM OF.*—

i. Title.
ii. Evidence of existence.
  1. Fourth century writers.
  2. Origen.
  3. Possible traces of anonymous use.
iii. Summary of contents. Variations in *pseudo-Matthew* and *Nativity of Mary*.
iv. Character and tendencies.
v. Relation to Latin recensions—
  1. Gospel of *pseudo-Matthew*.
  2. Gospel of the *Nativity of Mary*.
vi. Date.
Literature.

i. TITLE.—This work claims to have been written by James the Just, in Jerusalem, but its author does not describe it as a Gospel. Its title in the manuscripts is 'The History of James concerning the Birth of Mary.' Early writers do not refer to it as εὐαγγέλιον, but describe it as διήγησις, λόγος ἱστορικός, ἱστορία or γέννησις Μαρίας. The name of *Protevangelium* was probably given to it by Oriental Christians; it is not known to have existed before the 16th cent., when the Latin version of Postellus and the Greek version (πρωτευαγγέλιον) of Michael Neander appeared.

ii. EVIDENCE OF EXISTENCE.—1. The Protevangelium, in its present form, was known to 4th cent. Fathers. *Epiphanius* (*c.* 376) made use of it (*Hær.* lxxix. 5, lxxviii. 7); Harnack (*Chron.* i. 601) finds reference to it in *Gregory of Nyssa* (*Orat. in diem Natal. Christi*, iii. 346), *Eustathius*, and the *Excerpta Barbari*.

2. If this work had been known in early times as 'the Gospel of James' the evidence of *Origen* (*c.* 246 A.D.) would have been less trustworthy. There is, however, little doubt that he refers to it as 'the Book of James' (ἡ βίβλος Ἰακώβου) in a passage where he distinguishes its title from that of 'the Gospel according to Peter,' and yet refers to both writings as common sources of the tradition that our Lord's brethren were 'sons of Joseph by a former wife, whom he married before Mary.' Origen adds: 'Now those who say so wish to preserve the honour of Mary in virginity to the end' (*in Matt.* tom. x. 17); this comment is an accurate description of the purpose of the Protevangelium.

3. *Possible traces of anonymous use.*—Points of contact between this work and other writings have been found. *Peter of Alexandria* (d. 311) in all probability derived from it his account of the death of Zacharias (Routh, *Rell. Sac.* iv. 44). *Clement of Alexandria* (*c.* 200 A.D.) may have learnt from it the story of the attestation of Mary's virginity after the birth of her son, but the indefinite words 'some say' may refer to oral tradition (*Strom.* vii. 16). *Justin Martyr* (*c.* 140 A.D.) has several remarkable 'concordances' with the Protevangelium. Both combine (*Apol.* 33) the angel's message to Mary (Lk $1^{32}$) with his words to Joseph (Mt $1^{21}$); both state (*Dial.* 78) that our Lord was born in a cave; both speak (*Apol.* 33) of Mary's overshadowing by 'the power of God'; both attach importance (*Dial.* 100) to the Davidic descent of Mary; both assert that 'Mary received joy,' though Justin (*Dial.* 100) connects the words καὶ χαρὰν λαβοῦσα Μαρία with the angelic salutation, whilst in the Protevangelium the same words are associated with the priest's benediction. Zahn regards the dependence of Justin on this Gospel as proved. But the more exact resemblances would

be satisfactorily explained if both writers made use of a common tradition; and the variation in the context of the statement about Mary's joy points, in the judgment of many scholars, to the use by Justin of an older text of the Protevangelium. On the whole, the evidence cannot be said to prove that he used this Gospel in its present form.

iii. SUMMARY OF CONTENTS.—[Two Latin Gospels of the Childhood—*pseudo-Matthew* and the *Nativity of Mary*—either depend on the Protevangelium, or on the sources used by its author. In so far as the contents of these Latin Gospels are parallel to its narrative, the chief variations will be noted; they furnish important data for the solution of the problem of the mutual relations of these Gospels].

1. On a great festival, Joachim, an exceedingly rich man, brings double offerings to the temple; they are rejected because he is childless. In his grief he retires to the desert and fasts forty days, prayer being his food and drink. 2. Anna, the wife of Joachim, being reproached by Judith her maid-servant, prays to God under a laurel, and asks that to her, as to Sarah, a child may be given. 3. Beholding a sparrow's nest in the laurel, Anna laments that she is not like the fowls of the heaven, which are 'productive before Thee, O Lord.' 4. An angel of the Lord announces to Anna that her prayer is heard; she vows that her child shall be a gift to God. Another angel bids Joachim return home; he obeys, and takes with him flocks for an offering. Anna and Joachim meet at the gate.

In *pseudo-Mat.* 3 the angel bids Anna meet her husband at the Golden Gate; in *Nat. Mary* 4 the angel bids Joachim meet his wife at the Golden Gate. Cf. Ac 3[2].

5. On the following day Joachim brings his offering to the temple and goes down to his house 'justified.' In course of time a daughter is born to Anna and Joachim; Anna calls the child Mary.

In *Nat. Mary* 5 the name Mary is given at the command of the angel.

6. When the child is six months old, Anna sets her on the ground 'to try whether she can stand, and she walks seven steps'; Anna vows that Mary shall not walk on this earth until she has been taken to the temple of the Lord. When Mary is a year old, Joachim makes a great feast; the chief priests bless the child, and Anna sings a song to the Lord. 7. When Mary is three years old, her parents take her to the temple in fulfilment of their vow. After the high priest has blessed her, he 'sets her down upon the third step of the altar'; she 'dances with her feet, and all the house of Israel love her.'

In *pseudo-Mat.* 4 the child is put down before the doors of the temple, and 'goes up the fifteen steps so swiftly, that she does not look back at all.' In *Nat. Mary* 6 the virgin of the Lord goes up all the steps without help 'in such a manner that you would think she had already attained full age.' The Lord 'by the indication of this miracle' foreshowed the greatness of 'His virgin.'

8. Mary dwells in the temple 'as if she were a dove,' and is fed by the hand of an angel. When she is twelve years old, Zacharias the high priest summons the widowers in order that the Lord may signify whose wife Mary is to be.

*Pseudo-Mat.* 6 adds many marvels, as, *e.g.*, the angels often speak to Mary and most diligently obey her; sick people who touch her go home cured. Both in *pseudo-Mat.* and *Nat. Mary* the age of Mary is fourteen when she refuses to be given in marriage, and announces her resolve to be a virgin to God.

9. Joseph, throwing away his axe, obeys the summons; the widowers present their rods to the high priest in the temple. A dove comes out of Joseph's rod and rests upon his head—the sign that he is chosen to keep the virgin of the Lord. 10. When Joseph refuses, saying, 'I have children, and I am an old man,' the priest warns him of the guilt of disobedience. Joseph therefore takes Mary from the temple to his home.

In *pseudo-Mat.* 8 the tribe of Judah is chosen by lot; then every man of that tribe, 'who has no wife,' takes his rod to the temple. The high priest does not at first bring Joseph's rod out of the Holy of Holies 'because he was an old man.' Joseph asks: 'Why do you hand over to me this infant, who is younger than my grandsons?' In *Nat. Mary* 8 Joseph withholds his rod; God is consulted a second time, and Joseph is found out; also Joseph's rod produces a flower on which the Spirit descends in the form of a dove (cf. Is 11[1.2]).

11. The angel of the Lord announces to Mary at the well the coming upon her of the power of the Lord.

In *pseudo-Mat.* 9 the angel appears to Mary in her chamber, while she is working at the purple for the veil of the temple.

12. Mary visits Elisabeth, who greets her as 'the mother of my Lord.' 13. Mary returns home after her three months' visit to Elisabeth; Joseph reproaches her, and with weeping she maintains her innocence. 14. The angel of the Lord appears to Joseph. 15. Annas the scribe accuses Joseph of stealthily marrying Mary; the officers bring her with Joseph to the tribunal. 16. Joseph and Mary drink the water of the ordeal and remain unhurt.

*Pseudo-Mat.* 10–12 describes with even less restraint the incidents recorded in chs. 13–16. In *Nat. Mary* 9 the words of the angel to Mary are much expanded; from one addition it would seem that when this apocryphal book was written the doctrine of the Immaculate Conception was unknown: 'that which shall be born of thee shall alone be holy, because it alone, being conceived and born without sin, shall be called the Son of God.'

17. Joseph takes Mary and his sons to be enrolled in Bethlehem. In Mary's face sometimes there is laughter and sometimes sorrow; she explains to Joseph, 'I see two peoples with my eyes; the one lamenting, and the other rejoicing.'

*Pseudo-Mat.* 13 adds 'she saw the people of the Jews weeping, because they have departed from their God; and the people of the Gentiles rejoicing, because they have been made near to the Lord.' But cf. Gn 25[23] or Lk 2[34].

18. Joseph leaves Mary in a cave in charge of his two sons, whilst he seeks a woman to minister to her needs. The sky is astonished and the birds keep still. 19. When the woman enters the cave a great light shines, but it gradually decreases until the infant's birth. 20. The woman tells Salome of the strange event; Salome demands proof. Her hand is made to burn with fire as a punishment for her unbelief, but is restored when she touches the infant. 21. The Magi are led by the star to the cave, and present their gifts. 22. Herod sends murderers to kill the children from two years old and under. Mary puts her child into an ox-stall. A mountain is cleft to receive Elisabeth and John.

*Pseudo-Mat.* adds many details. The star is 'larger than any that had been seen since the beginning of the world.' The ox and the ass 'incessantly adore Him,' fulfilling the word of Habakkuk the prophet: 'Between two animals thou art made manifest.' (Hab 3[2] LXX *ἐν μέσῳ δύο ζῴων γνωσθήσῃ*, by slight change in Hebrew text: שְׁנַיִם חַיִּים for שָׁנִים חַיֵּיהוּ).

23. Zacharias is murdered, because he cannot tell the officers of Herod where his son is. 24. A priest hears a voice saying, 'Zacharias is murdered'; the body of Zacharias is not found, but his blood is turned into stone. Simeon is chosen in his place. 25. The author says that he withdrew into the wilderness, because of the commotion that arose about the death of Herod. Doxology.

iv. CHARACTER AND TENDENCIES.—From the summary of contents given above, it will be seen that chs. 1–17 of the Protevangelium are occupied with the story of Mary—her birth and childhood, her life in the temple, and her betrothal to Joseph. In chs. 18–20 the style of the narrative is changed, the direct form is assumed: 'I, Joseph, was walking,' etc. The writer, laying aside all reserve, enlarges upon the marvel of the birth of Jesus, and upon the perpetual virginity of Mary. The remaining portion of this work (chs. 21–25) consists of (*a*) the account of the visit of the Magi, which closely follows the narrative of the canonical Matthew; and (*b*) the story of the marvellous escape of John from Herod's massacre, and of the murder of his father Zacharias.

The extravagances of chs. 18–20, the Gnostic tendencies of the narrative, and the abrupt introduction of Joseph as the speaker, are sufficient reasons for regarding this section of the Gospel as derived from an independent source. Harnack calls this section *Apocryphum Josephi.* Some light has been cast upon chs. 22–24, which Harnack calls *Apocryphum Zachariæ*, by the researches of Berendts (*Studien über Zacharias-Apokryphen*, 1895); he holds that the Protevangelium does not contain these legends in their oldest form. Confirmation of this theory is found in the fact that Origen (*in Matt.* tract. 25), who was acquainted with the Book of James, gives a very different account of the martyrdom of Zacharias; his account may have come from an independent source, but the recognition of this possibility renders no less probable the suggestion of Harnack (*Chron.* i. 601) that the βίβλος Ἰακώβου to which Origen refers is essentially identical with chs. 1–17 of the Protevangelium. The evidence of Origen, therefore, like the evidence of Justin, yields no proof of the existence of this Gospel in its present form; he becomes, however, the oldest witness for the γέννησις Μαρίας, the story of the Nativity of Mary.

The result of the foregoing analysis is to show that in all probability the Protevangelium is a composite work. The facts do not warrant the inference that its author had three separate documents before him of which he made free use, adding his own embellishments; they point rather in the direction of the conclusion at which Lipsius (*Dict. Christ. Biog.* ii. 703) arrives by a different course of reasoning. The author's acquaintance with Jewish customs is manifest to every reader; but, as Lipsius points out, such incidents as the refusal of Joachim and his sacrifice, the bringing up of Mary in the temple, and the drinking by Joseph of the water of the ordeal, are quite contrary to Jewish ideas and usages; moreover, there are traces of Gnostic speculation, especially in the *Apocryphum Josephi* and the *Apocryphum Zachariæ.* 'This curious admixture of intimate knowledge and gross ignorance of Jewish thought and custom compels us to assume and distinguish between an original Jewish-Christian writing and a Gnostic recast of it.'*

v. Relation to Latin Recensions.—1. *The Gospel of pseudo-Matthew.* This Gospel claims to be Jerome's translation into Latin of what the holy Evangelist Matthew wrote in Hebrew and 'set at the head of his Gospel.' It gives, with variations such as are noted above, the same narrative as the Protevangelium; but, instead of ending with the martyrdom of Zacharias, it describes (chs. 18–24) the flight into Egypt, and enlarges upon the marvels of the journey—*e.g.* the adoration of the infant Jesus by dragons, lions, and panthers; the bending of a palm-tree at His word, in order that His mother may gather its fruit; the shortening of the way, so that in one day they accomplish what would otherwise have taken thirty days; the prostration of the idols when Mary with her child enters the Egyptian temple. The rest of this Gospel, in what Tischendorf regards as its complete form (*Evang. apocr.* 51–112), gives the story of the boyhood of Jesus in a form even more extravagant than the Gospel according to Thomas, an account of which is given below. There is little doubt that, in so far as this Gospel is parallel with the narrative of the Protevangelium, it is independently derived from the same sources. It alone records the special series of miracles wrought in Egypt and on the way thither; in the narratives which it has in common with the Protevangelium there is a marked development of the marvellous nature of the incidents; the growing exaltation of Mary is also very apparent.

2. *The Gospel of the Nativity of Mary.*—This short Latin Gospel, entitled the *Evangelium de Nativitate Mariæ*, covers the same ground as the early part of the Gospel of *pseudo-Matthew*; its last words describe the birth of Jesus at Bethlehem. It is found amongst the works of Jerome, and has every appearance of being an orthodox revision of the Latin Gospel of *pseudo-Matthew.*

vi. Date.—According to the view taken above of the composite character of this Gospel, the original Jewish-Christian work dates from the middle of the 2nd century. The Protevangelium in its present form embodies the result of a Gnostic recast, and cannot be earlier than the latter part of the 3rd century. To the 4th cent. or perhaps the 5th must be assigned the Gospel of *pseudo-Matthew*, of which the Gospel of the *Nativity of Mary* is a later redaction.

Literature.—In 1552 Bibliander's Latin edition was published, Postellus having prepared the text from a Greek MS. In 1840 Suckow issued a separate edition, *ex. cod. MS Venetiano.* See A. Meyer in *Die Apokr. des NT*, p. 47; also Neander Sor., Thilo, Tischendorf, Harnack, Zahn, Borberg, Wright, Orr, in *opp. citt.* Translation by A. Walker in Ante-Nicene Christian Library, also by Conybeare from an Armenian MS in *Amer. Journ. of Theol.* i. 1897, p. 424 ff. Articles by Hilgenfeld in *Zeitschr. f. wiss. Theol.* xii. p. 339 f., xiv. p. 87 note; Conrady, *Die Quellen der kanonischen Kindheitsgeschichten*, and in *SK* lxii. p. 728 ff.

### B. 2. *THOMAS, GOSPEL ACCORDING TO.*—

i. Evidence of early writers.
   1. Hippolytus.
   2. Origen, Eusebius, etc.
ii. Present form.
iii. Summary of contents.
iv. Character and tendencies.
v. Date.
Literature.

i. Evidence of early writers.—1. A Gospel κατὰ Θωμᾶν was, according to *Hippolytus* (155–235), in use among the Naassenes. A passage, in which they found support for their teaching in regard to the 'nature of the inward man' (φύσιν . . . τὴν ἐντὸς ἀνθρώπου), is quoted from the Gospel: 'He who seeks me shall find me in children from seven years old; for there will I, who am hidden in the fourteenth æon, be manifest' (Ἐμὲ ὁ ζητῶν εὑρήσει ἐν παιδίοις ἀπὸ ἐτῶν ἑπτά· ἐκεῖ γὰρ ἐν τῷ ιδ' αἰῶνι κρυβόμενος φανεροῦμαι).

2. *Origen* (*c.* 246) mentions this Gospel (*Hom. i. in Luc.*), and *Eusebius* (*c.* 324) places it with the Petrine Gospel amongst the 'heretical' writings (*HE* iii. 25). *Cyril of Jerusalem* (d. 386) states that the Manichæans wrote it (*Catech.* iv. 36), and in a later passage of the same work traces its origin to 'one of the three base disciples of Moses' (vi. 31). Later writers refer to the high esteem in which it was held by the Manichæans.

ii. Present form.—A Gospel, entitled 'Thomas the Israelite philosopher's Account of the Infancy of the Lord' (Θωμᾶ Ἰσραηλίτου φιλοσόφου ῥητὰ εἰς τὰ παιδικὰ τοῦ Κυρίου), is extant in two Greek recensions, also in a Latin and in a Syriac version. Tischendorf gives the longer Greek recension

* The secondary character of this Gospel, in so far as it can be compared with the narratives of Matthew and Luke, is recognized by critics of various schools, notwithstanding the attempt of Conrady to show that the Evangelists borrowed from it (*Die Quellen der kanonischen Kindheitsgeschichte Jesus*). 'It would have been a literary miracle if the opening chapters of St. Matthew and St. Luke, with their lifelike touches and tender humanities, had been derived from a work teeming with superstitious trivialities' (Dr. T. Nicol in *Critical Review*, xii. 35).

(*Evang. apocr.* pp. 140-157), the shorter Greek recension (pp. 158-163), and the Latin version, which Harnack describes as a compilation, with striking resemblances to the apocryphal Gospel of Matthew (pp. 164-180). The Syriac version (Wright, *Apoc. Lit. NT*, p. 6 f.) is a somewhat abbreviated form of the longer Greek recension. (For English translations of the two Greek and the Latin versions, see Walker's *Apocr. Gospels*, p. 78 ff.; and for a detailed account of the variations in the several texts, see Lipsius' article in *Dict. Christ. Biog.* ii. 704). None of these four recensions contains the Naassene quotation from this Gospel which is given by Hippolytus. Does he refer to a different Gospel, or to an original Gospel of which the longest extant version contains only fragments? The attempt to answer these questions must be deferred until the outline of the contents of these four recensions has been given. But one important piece of evidence is here in place. *Nicephorus* (d. 599) mentions this Gospel in his *Stichometry*, and states that it contained 1300 *stichoi*. Therefore, inasmuch as the longest extant recension does not contain half of that number of *stichoi*, it is possible, though not certain, that the copy known to Nicephorus contained the passage quoted by Hippolytus.

iii. Summary of contents.—The narratives contained in this Gospel of the Childhood of Jesus consist of (*a*) stories of His superhuman knowledge, (*b*) stories of His superhuman power. The different versions frequently disagree, as well in their statements in regard to the scenes of the miracles and the names of the chief actors, as in the form of the narratives and in the arrangement of the various incidents. The following summary is based on the longer Greek recension:—

(*a*) To his teacher, Zacchæus, the child Jesus repeats the letters of the alphabet, 'from the Alpha even to the Omega, clearly and with great exactness'; He questions His teacher about the first letter, and convicts him of ignorance of the nature of Alpha, and therefore of inability to teach others the Beta. 'Thou hypocrite! first, if thou knowest, teach the A, and then we shall believe thee about the B. . . . And in the hearing of many the child says to Zacchæus: 'Hear, O teacher, the order of the first letter' [the old Phœnician A was written ≮ or ∀], 'and notice here how it has lines, and a middle stroke crossing those which thou seest common; (lines) brought together; the highest part supporting them, and again bringing them under one head; with three points [of intersection]; of the same kind; principal and subordinate; of equal length. Thou hast the lines of the A.' The amazement of Zacchæus, as he listens to this allegorizing, is thus expressed: 'That child does not belong to this earth. . . . What great thing he is, either god or angel, or what I am to say, I know not.' The shorter Greek recension represents Jesus as saying: 'I know more than you, for I am before the ages. . . . When you see my cross, then will ye believe that I speak the truth.' When Joseph takes the child to another master, who tries 'to flatter him into learning his letters,' Jesus immediately reads a book that lies on the desk, and by the Holy Spirit teaches the Law to those that are standing round. The account of the child's visit to the temple with His parents follows closely the narrative of Luke ($2^{41-52}$). It describes Him as 'sitting in the midst of the teachers, both hearing the law and asking them questions,' but adds: 'And they were all attending to him, and wondering that he, being a child, was shutting the mouths of the elders and teachers of the people, explaining the main points of the law, and the parables of the prophets.'

(*b*) Some of the miracles ascribed to the child Jesus are works of beneficence, but others are deeds of vengeance. When five years old He makes twelve sparrows out of clay, and as soon as He claps His hands they fly away. At the same age He raises to life a child killed by a fall; and also a young man who, whilst splitting wood, cut the sole of his foot in two, and died from loss of blood. 'And he said to the young man, Rise up now, split the wood, and remember me.' When six years old He breaks a pitcher, but fills His cloak with water and carries it to His mother; He stretches a short piece of wood, and makes it equal to the longer piece. At the same age He cures His brother James, who was dying from the effects of the bite of a viper; He also performs two more miracles of raising from the dead. But His miracles of vengeance make such an impression that the parents of a boy whom Jesus has killed say to Joseph: 'Since thou hast such a child, it is impossible for thee to live with us in the village; or else teach him to bless, and not to curse, for he is killing our children.' The son of Annas the scribe is 'dried up' at His word; a boy who runs up against Him is struck dead; one of His teachers incurs His wrath, and at His curse swoons and falls to the ground; His accusers are smitten with blindness, and dare not provoke Him to anger lest His rebuke should maim them.

iv. Character and tendencies.—To the evidence of Hippolytus that this Gospel was known to the Naassenes, and of Cyril of Jerusalem, who regards it as a Manichæan work, should probably be added the witness of Irenæus (*c.* 190) to its use amongst the Marcosians, a Gnostic sect, whose leader boasted that he had improved upon his master, Valentinus. It is true that Irenæus does not name the 'spurious writing'; but he accuses the Marcosians of pulling to pieces 'the dispensations of God, in themselves so striking, by means of Alpha and Beta,' and of bringing forward 'that false and wicked story' that the Lord said to His teacher: 'Do thou first tell me what Alpha is, and then I will tell thee what Beta is.' 'This they expound as meaning that he alone knew the Unknown, which he revealed under its type, Alpha' (*Hær.* I. xx. 1; cf. xvi. 3). The value of this passage consists in its testimony to a second-century Gnostic interpretation of an incident which is recorded in the extant Gospel according to Thomas. Harnack (*Chron.* i. 594) assigns to this apocryphal Gospel, in its original form, a saying of Jesus, which Irenæus charges the Marcosians with misinterpreting: 'I have often desired to have one of these words, and I had no one who could utter it' (*Hær.* I. xx. 2). The saying may, however, be a loose quotation from the canonical Gospels (Lk $10^{24}$; cf. Lk $19^{42}$).

The question asked above may now be answered. If one sect of Gnostics found in the contents of this Gospel—not to assume that the Gospel itself was in their hands—support for their speculations, the Syrian Gnostics (Naassenes) may have used the same Gospel, though the passage quoted in Hippolytus is not found in the extant fragments. The saying (see § i.), whatever be its true meaning, is clearly a Gnostic interpretation of some of our Lord's sayings about childhood, with Gnostic accretions (cf. Mt $7^8$ $18^5$). Ropes (*Die Sprüche Jesu*, p. 100) expounds it as signifying that only when a child attains to full intelligence can the image of Christ be manifested in it. The saying is not so entirely out of harmony with this Gospel of the Childhood as to compel the ascription of it to an unknown Gospel of Thomas. The undoubted difference between this saying and the fabulous contents of the Gospel that has been preserved would be explained if the Gospel quoted in Hippolytus was revised by an anti-Gnostic editor and abbreviated in accordance with his views. Such an anti-Gnostic would be a heretic in the judgment of writers like Origen, for in the canonical Gospels the child Jesus works no miracles. It is probable, as Lipsius suggests, that this Gospel originated in an attempt 'to enlist the miraculous stories of the Childhood on the Catholic side. . . . The child Jesus [it might be argued] must certainly have worked some miracles in order to rebuke the Gnostic error, which made the Christ to descend upon Him for the first time at His baptism' (*Dict. Christ. Biog.* ii. 704).

v. DATE.—Zahn holds that this Gospel was one of the sources used by Justin Martyr (*c.* 140), who says (*Dial.* 88) that Jesus 'was in the habit of working as a carpenter when among men, making ploughs and yokes' (ἄροτρα καὶ ζυγά); there is a verbal coincidence with this Gospel which describes Joseph as a carpenter who 'made ploughs and yokes.' But Justin, who was a native of Palestine, would scarcely require a written source for this tradition, nor is he likely to have used a heretical Gospel as an authority. Justin cannot, therefore, be quoted to prove the existence of this Gospel in the first half of the second century; a legitimate inference from the evidence already given is that in its original form it was written *c.* 160–180. But Harnack does well to add that it is impossible to say certainly how much of the Gospel in its present form was derived from the longer work. There may, of course, be interpolations in the abbreviated versions of this Gospel.

LITERATURE.—Cotelerius published a fragment from a Paris MS of the 15th cent. in his notes to the *Const. Apost.* vi. 17; also Mingarelli a larger portion: *Nuova raccolta d'opuscoli scientifici*, tom. xii., Venet. 764, pp. 73–155. See A. Meyer in *Die Apokr. des NT*, p. 63; Conrady in *SK*, 1903, Heft 3; also Thilo, Tischendorf, Wright, Borberg, Harnack, Zahn, Orr, in *opp. citt.*

B. 3. *CHILDHOOD, ARABIC GOSPEL OF THE.*—

i. Sources.
ii. Contents.
iii. Characteristics. Date.
Literature.

i. SOURCES.—This Gospel is entitled in Tischendorf's corrected Latin version (*Evang. Apocr.* pp. 181-209), *Evangelium Infantiæ Salvatoris Arabicum.* The Arabic text is a translation from the Syriac. The work is a compilation. The author refers to 'the book of Joseph, the high priest' (c. 1), to 'the Gospel of the Infancy,' and to 'the perfect Gospel' (c. 25), and concludes: 'Here endeth the whole Gospel of the Infancy, with the aid of God Most High, according to what we have found in the original.' For the first part of this Gospel (1-25) the compiler claims the authority of Joseph Caiaphas, whose book Lipsius (*Dict. Christ. Biog.* ii. 705) identifies with 'the Gnostic work made use of in the Protevangelium, and which bore the name of Joseph (not Caiaphas, of course, but the husband of Mary)'; the earlier portions of his narrative are to a large extent parallel to the Protevangelium and to the Gospel of *pseudo-Matthew*; but he also draws largely on 'the perfect Gospel.' though he records 'very many miracles' of the Lord Jesus which are not found either in it or in less 'complete' Gospels of the Infancy. In the second part (26-55) his chief source is the Gospel according to Thomas.

ii. CONTENTS.—This Gospel begins by quoting a word of Jesus spoken, when He was lying in His cradle, to Mary His mother: 'I am Jesus, the Son of God, the Logos, whom thou hast brought forth.' Miracles are narrated for which no parallel can be found either in the canonical Gospels or in the apocryphal writings, as, *e.g.*, the Lady Mary gives to the kings from the East one of her child's swaddling-bands, which 'the fire was not able to burn or destroy' (8); a demoniac boy, the son of an Egyptian priest, is healed by putting upon his head a newly washed garment of the Lord Christ (11); the water in which Mary washes Jesus cleanses from leprosy (17); by witchcraft a youth has been transformed into a mule; Mary puts Jesus on the mule's back and asks Him to exert His mighty power, whereupon the animal 'became a young man, free from every defect' (21); the Holy Family fall into the hands of two robbers, Titus and Dumachus; Titus bribes Dumachus to let them go free, and Jesus tells His mother that in thirty years 'these two robbers will be raised upon the cross along with me, Titus on my right hand and Dumachus on my left; and after that day Titus shall go before me into Paradise' (23); at the age of twelve, Jesus discourses in the temple to astronomers on the heavenly bodies, 'their course, direct and retrograde, the twenty-fourths and sixtieths of twenty-fourths, and other things beyond the reach of reason' (51); also to a philosopher 'skilled in treating of natural science' He explains 'physics and metaphysics, hyperphysics and hypophysics . . . and other things beyond the reach of any created intellect' (52); 'from this day' (*i.e.* from His twelfth year) 'he began to hide his miracles and mysteries and secrets, and to give attention to the law, until he completed his thirtieth year' (54).

iii. CHARACTERISTICS.—The extracts given from this Gospel prove that its author not only drew largely from his sources, canonical and apocryphal, but also allowed his imagination free play, with the result that his work is a strange conglomerate of authentic Evangelic tradition and the most fantastic legends. In one respect alone does it compare favourably with the apocryphal Gospels it most closely resembles; from its fabulous stories there is an absence of miracles of vengeance such as are found in the Gospel according to Thomas and the Gospel of *pseudo-Matthew.* There are many traces of the influence of Gnosticism in this Gospel, but it also contains a clear recognition of the humanity of Jesus: the mother of a dying boy who is healed by 'the smell of the clothes of the Lord Jesus Christ' says to Mary: 'Now I know that the power of God dwelleth in thee, so that thy Son heals those that partake of the same nature with himself' (30). The central section of this work has been aptly described as 'thoroughly Oriental in its character, reminding one of the tales of the *Arabian Nights*, or of the episodes in the *Golden Ass* of Apuleius' (Walker, *Apocr. Gospels*, x.).

No definite *date* for the composition of this Gospel can be fixed. Lipsius is content to say that it was compiled 'comparatively late, but probably earlier than the Mahometan times.'

LITERATURE.—In 1697 Henricus Sike published an Arabic text with Latin translation: *Ev. Inf. vel Liber apocryphus de Infantia Salvatoris.* See Fabricius, Jones, Schmid, Thilo, Tischendorf, in *opp. citt.*

B. 4. *JOSEPH THE CARPENTER, ARABIC HISTORY OF.*—

i. Sources.
ii. Contents.
iii. Characteristics. Date.
Literature.

i. SOURCES.—This Gospel is entitled in Tischendorf's Latin version (*Evang. Apocr.* pp. 122–139), *Historia Josephi Fabri Lignarii*; his edition takes note of variations in the Sahidic and Memphitic dialects of the Coptic, from which language the Arabic text was a recension. The author relates briefly the life of Joseph, and at greater length his death and burial; he also represents Jesus as uttering lengthy and rhapsodical lamentations. For the greater part of his narrative there is no parallel in other writings, but in the sections which describe the choice of Joseph to be the guardian of Mary, his betrothal to her, Herod's search for the children, and the flight into Egypt, the author is in close agreement with the Protevangelium. If he used it as a source, he omitted the portents which it describes as accompanying these events; it is more probable, however, that his source was the earlier Jewish-Christian tradition, for the rest of his work does not suggest that Gnostic embellishments would have been distasteful to him. There are more distinct traces of his dependence upon the Gospel according to Thomas in the account given of Joseph's perplexity and the words of the angel (17); Lipsius (*Dict. Christ. Biog.* ii. 706) adds that in the Coptic recension 'the use made of the Gospel of Thomas is still more evident.'

ii. CONTENTS.—In the introduction to this history the author states that it was related by our Lord to His disciples on the Mount of Olives. The speaker throughout is Jesus, who says of His mother: 'I chose her of my own will, with the concurrence of my Father, and the counsel of the Holy Spirit. And I was made flesh of her, by a mystery which transcends the grasp of created reason' (5), a mystery which 'no creature can penetrate or understand, except myself, and my Father, and the Holy Spirit, *constituting one essence with myself*' (14).* Joseph before his death asks Jesus for pardon (17); Jesus sees Death and Gehenna approaching: 'accordingly I drove back Death and all the host of servants which accompanied him' (21); when Joseph died, 'he had fulfilled a hundred and eleven years; never did a tooth in his mouth hurt him, nor was his eyesight rendered less sharp' (29); of Joseph's body Jesus says: 'Not a single limb of it shall be broken, nor shall any hair of thy head be changed. Nothing of thy body shall perish, O my father Joseph, but it will remain entire and uncorrupted even until the banquet of the thousand years' (26).

iii. CHARACTERISTICS.—The motive of this history is revealed in words spoken by the Apostles to Jesus: 'Thou hast ordered us to go into all the world and preach the holy gospel; and thou hast said: Relate to them the death of my father Joseph, and celebrate to him with annual solemnity a festival and sacred day. And whosoever shall take anything away from this narrative, or add anything to it, commits sin' (30). There is another reference to the day of Joseph's commemoration (26); the work is doubtless, as Lipsius suggests, 'a festal lection for St. Joseph's day.'

The words of Jesus to Mary, 'Thou, O my virgin mother, must look for the same end of life as other mortals,' point to a *date* of composition earlier than the 5th cent., when the Assumption of Mary was taught. Tischendorf decides for the 4th century.

LITERATURE.—In 1722 Wallin published an Arabic text with Latin translation. See Tischendorf, Hofmann, in *opp. citt.*

B. 5. *MARY, THE DEPARTURE OF.*—

i. Versions.
ii. Summary of contents.
iii. Characteristics. Date.
Literature.

i. VERSIONS.—Tischendorf published in his *Apocalypses Apocryphæ* the Greek text of a work sometimes described as the *Evangelium Joannis*; its full title is, *The Account of St. John the Theologian of the Falling Asleep of the Holy Mother of God.* Two Latin versions are printed by Tischendorf, and the writing is generally known as the *Transitus Mariæ* or *The Departure of Mary.* Wright has edited three recensions of a Syriac text. Arabic, Sahidic, and Ethiopic versions are also extant. Lipsius finds the nearest approximation to the original text in the Greek and in the Syriac versions known as B and C. Syriac B was edited by Wright (*Journal of Sacred Literature*, 1865), and Syriac C is published in his *Contributions to the Apocr. Lit. of the NT*, pp. 24–41. Walker's translation of the Greek text is used in the following section ('Ante-Nicene Christian Library,' *Apocryphal Gospels*, etc. p. 504 ff.).

ii. SUMMARY OF CONTENTS.—'The all-holy glorious mother of God and ever-virgin Mary' goes to 'the holy tomb of our Lord' to burn incense and to pray. She is invisible to the guards. Gabriel informs her that her request is granted: 'thou having left the world, shalt go to the heavenly places to thy Son, into the true and everlasting life.'

Mary and her three virgins return to holy Bethlehem; in answer to her prayers the Apostles are summoned to her deathbed. John is 'snatched up by a cloud from Ephesus' and assures Mary that her 'holy and precious body will by no means see corruption.' By a whirlwind the Holy Spirit brings 'Peter from Rome, Paul from Tiberias, Thomas from Hither India, James from Jerusalem.' The Apostles who have fallen asleep are raised from their tombs, but the Holy Spirit says: 'Do not think that it is now the resurrection; but on this account you have risen out of your tombs, that you may go to give greeting to the honour and wonder-working of the mother of our Lord and Saviour Jesus Christ, because the day of her departure is at hand, of her going up into the heavens.'

Mary, sitting up in bed, asks the Apostles to tell her how they had been summoned. John says, 'I was going in to the holy altar in Ephesus to perform Divine service'; Mark says, 'I was finishing the canon of the third [day] in the city of Alexandria'; Matthew says, 'I was in a boat and overtaken by a storm, the sea raging with its waves; on a sudden a cloud of light overshadowing a stormy billow, changed it to a calm, and having snatched me up, set me down beside you.' Similar experiences are narrated by the other Apostles.

Marvels accompany Mary's departure: the sun and the moon suddenly appear about the house; all who are 'under disease and sickness' are cured, if they touch 'the outside of the wall of the house' where Mary was lying. The Jews, 'boiling with rage,' say to the Procurator, 'The nation of the Jews has been ruined by this woman; chase her from Bethlehem and the province of Jerusalem.' The Procurator refuses, but yields to importunity and 'sends a tribune of soldiers against the Apostles to Bethlehem.' The Apostles leave the house 'carrying the bed of the Lady, the mother of God'; they are 'lifted up by a cloud' and transported to 'the house of the Lady' in Jerusalem. The priests and the people 'being the more moved with hatred' take the wood and fire, 'wishing to burn the house where the Lord's mother was living with the Apostles'; but many Jews are burnt up by 'a power of fire suddenly coming forth from within by means of an angel.'

The Holy Spirit reminds the Apostles that 'on the Lord's day' Gabriel made the Annunciation to the Virgin; 'on the Lord's day' the Saviour was born; 'on the Lord's day' the children of Jerusalem welcomed Him with palm-branches and Hosannas; 'on the Lord's day' He rose from the dead; and 'on the Lord's day' He will come to judgment. 'On the Lord's day' Christ comes with a host of angels and says to His mother, 'Thy precious body will be transferred to Paradise.' Mary kisses and adores the right hand of the Lord; she beseeches Him as 'God, the King of the

* The words in italics are omitted in the Coptic version.

Ages, the only-begotten of the Father,' to bestow His aid 'upon every man calling upon, or praying to, or naming the name of, thine handmaid.' The Lord replies, 'Every soul that calls upon thy name shall not be ashamed, but shall find mercy, and comfort, and support, and confidence, both in the world that now is, and in that which is to come, in the presence of my Father in the heavens.'

Whilst the Apostles sing a hymn, and the powers of the heavens respond with Alleluia, the blameless soul of Mary departs. When Jephonias puts his hands upon the couch on which her holy body lies, 'an angel of the Lord by invisible power, with a sword of fire, cut off his two hands from his shoulders, and made them hang about the couch, lifted up in the air.' At the word of Peter the hands are 'fixed on again.'

Different accounts are given of the transference of Mary's 'spotless and precious body' to Paradise. One describes the translation as taking place after the body had lain for three days in Gethsemane in a new tomb; another represents 'twelve clouds of light' as snatching up the Apostles with the couch and 'the body of our Lady' into Paradise; and another narrates the miraculous resuscitation of the Virgin's body. 'Anna, the mother of the Lady,' is one of the heavenly choir that sing the Alleluia and adore 'the holy relics of the mother of the Lord.'

iii. CHARACTERISTICS AND DATE. — Although, as Lipsius points out (*Dict. Christ. Biog.* ii. 707), 'a comparison of the various texts proves that the original narrative was now abbreviated and now enlarged in manifold ways with all manner of foreign additions and strange ornaments,' yet, in all the various forms in which this work is extant, the *Departure of Mary* (κοίμησις τῆς Μαρίας, *Transitus Mariæ*) contains many evidences of a desire to furnish Apostolic sanction for Mary-worship of an advanced type. Traces of the *Protevangelium Jacobi* and of Gnostic apocryphal writings are found in some texts, but the narrative common to all versions is undoubtedly 'a Catholicizing recast of an heretical work.' Such phrases as 'the holy altar,' 'the canon of the third day,' *i.e.* a part of the Church service consisting of nine odes, 'cast incense and pray,' are internal evidence of a Catholic development of ecclesiastical ritual. Lipsius says: 'The Catholic recast plainly belongs to a time when the worship of the Virgin is already flourishing, *i.e.* at the earliest, the close of the 4th, and most probably the beginning of the 5th century.' Proof of the wide circulation of this work is afforded by the number of extant versions of it; in Catholic circles it has had great influence. Orr and Wright quote with well-merited approval the judgment of Ewald: 'This book has become from the first the firm foundation for all the unhappy adoration of Mary, and for a hundred superstitious things, which have intruded with less and less resistance into the Churches, and have contributed so much to the degeneration and to the crippling of all better Christianity.'

LITERATURE.—Cureton's *Ancient Syriac Documents*, p. 110; Enger published the Arabic text in 1854 (*Joannis apostoli de Transitu Beatæ Mariæ Virginis liber*); Zoega gives some particulars of the Sahidic version in the *Catal. Codd. Copt. Borjianorum*. See Tischendorf, Wright, in *opp. citt.*; also Orr's Introduction and Notes (*NT Apocr. Writings*).

### C. 1. *TWELVE APOSTLES, GOSPEL OF THE.*—

i. Evidence of existence :—
  1. Not identical with the Gospel according to the Hebrews.
  2. Identical with the heretical Gospel of the Ebionites.
ii. Contents of fragments preserved by Epiphanius.
iii. Character and tendencies. Date.
  Literature.

i. EVIDENCE OF EXISTENCE.—1. A Gospel entitled τὸ ἐπιγεγραμμένον τῶν δώδεκα εὐαγγέλιον (Jerome: 'juxta XII apostolos' and 'Evang. XII apostolorum') is placed by *Origen* (*c.* 230) amongst the heretical Gospels (*Hom. 1 in Lucam*). But Origen esteemed highly 'the Gospel according to the Hebrews,' which Jerome (417) confuses with 'the Gospel according to the Apostles' (*adv. Pelag.* iii. 2). Of modern scholars who accept Jerome's identification of the two Gospels, the most distinguished are Resch (*Agrapha*, p. 327) and Lipsius (*Dict. Christ. Biog.* ii. 710 f.). Zahn (*Geschichte des NT Kanons*, ii. 662, 724) and Harnack (*Chronologie*, i. 629) discuss the question in detail, and agree in the conclusion that Jerome misunderstood Origen, from whom all his information about this Gospel was derived (see art. HEBREWS [GOSPEL ACCORDING TO THE] above, p. 338 ff.). Lipsius considerably modifies his acceptance of Jerome's statement by his confession: 'One thing is certain, that at various times and in different circles it took very different shapes'; he frankly recognizes the existence of 'contradictory phenomena,' and suggests that the Gospel known to these Fathers was 'a recast of an older original' (*op. cit.* ii. 711).

2. By those who regard this Gospel as an independent work it is often called 'The Gospel of the Ebionites.' In their view the Ebionites who composed and used it were not Jewish Christians who observed the Mosaic law, though to them the name was first given (Orig. *adv. Cels.* ii. 1); they were the heretical sect of Ebionites, more correctly described as Elkesaites, and characterized by 'an abhorrence of sacrifice and by an objection to the use of flesh meat' (cf. Salmon, *Introd. to NT*, p. 159 f.). Owing to the ambiguity in the meaning of 'Ebionites,' conflicting interpretations are given to the statement of Jerome (398) that the Gospel, of which he speaks indifferently as 'according to the Hebrews' or 'according to the Apostles,' was used 'by the Nazarenes and by the Ebionites' (*Comm. in Matt.* $12^{13}$). If he means orthodox Jewish Christians, he is 'guilty of a confusion, and adds the Ebionites to the Nazarenes, though the two were identical' (Menzies, above, p. $339^{b}$); if, however, he means Elkesaites, his original mistake in identifying two different Gospels may account for his mentioning together the two parties by whom the two Gospels were respectively used.

Epiphanius (377) was acquainted with a Gospel which the Ebionites called 'the Gospel according to Matthew, not entire and perfectly complete, but falsified and mutilated (οὐχ ὅλῳ δὲ πληρεστάτῳ, ἀλλὰ νενοθευμένῳ καὶ ἠκρωτηριασμένῳ), which they call the Hebrew Gospel' (*Hær.* xxx. 13). The last sentence has no weight, for Epiphanius also says that Tatian's *Diatessaron* was called the Hebrew Gospel (*op. cit.* xlvi. 2); the value of his statement consists in its correct description of the Gospel of the Twelve Apostles, of which he alone has preserved fragments, neither lengthy nor numerous, but sufficiently extensive to prove that the author of this Gospel used Matthew's narratives or his source, mutilating it, and falsifying it by additions which have an Elkesaite tinge.

ii. CONTENTS.—The extant fragments of this Gospel are found in one of the writings of Epiphanius (*Hær.* xxx. 13–16, 22). Zahn gives the Greek text (*Geschichte des NT Kanons*, ii. 725) of all the passages that in his judgment are quotations. (Cf. Preuschen, *Antilegomena*, 9 ff.; also Westcott, *Introd. to Study of Gospels*, 465 ff.).—

1. 'The beginning of their Gospel is this: It came to pass in the days of Herod, king of Judæa (in the high priesthood of Caiaphas), that a man called John came baptizing with a baptism of repentance in the river Jordan, who was said to be

APOCRYPHAL GOSPELS

of the race of Aaron the priest, a son of Zacharias and Elisabeth; and all went out to him' (cf. Mt $3^{1}$, Lk $1^{13}$).

2. 'There arose a man called Jesus, and he was about thirty years old, who chose us. And when he came to Capernaum he entered the house of Simon who was surnamed Peter, and opened his mouth and said: As I passed along the Lake of Tiberias I chose John and James, sons of Zebedee, and Simon and Andrew and Thaddæus and Simon Zelotes and Judas Iscariot; and thee Matthew I called as thou wast sitting at the receipt of custom, and thou followedst me. Therefore, I wish you to be twelve Apostles, for a testimony unto Israel' (cf. Mt $4^{12f. 18ff.}$ $9^{9f.}$, Lk $3^{23}$).

3. 'And John arose baptizing; and Pharisees went out to him and were baptized, and all Jerusalem. And John had raiment of camels' hair, and a girdle of skin about his loins; and his food (the Gospel says) was wild honey, the taste of which was the taste of manna, like a honey cake steeped in oil' (cf. Mt $3^{7ff.}$).

4. 'When the people were baptized, Jesus also came and was baptized by John. And as he came up from the water, the heavens were opened, and he saw the Holy Spirit in the form of a dove, which came down and came upon him. And a voice came from heaven, saying: Thou art my beloved Son, in thee I am well pleased. And again: To-day have I begotten thee. And immediately a great light shone round about the place; and John, when he saw it (the Gospel narrates), says to him: Who art thou, Lord? And again a voice came from heaven to him [John]: This is my beloved Son, in whom I am well pleased. And then (the Gospel says) John fell down before him and said: I beseech thee, Lord, do thou baptize me. But he forbade him, saying, Suffer it, for thus it is becoming that all be fulfilled' (cf. Mt $3^{13ff.}$).

5. 'I came to put an end to sacrifices, and unless ye cease from sacrificing, [God's] anger will not cease from you.'

6. = Mt $12^{47-50}$; the last verse reads: 'They who do the will of my Father are my brethren and mother and sisters.'

7. 'Have I earnestly desired to eat this flesh, the Passover, with you?' (cf. Lk $22^{15}$).

Westcott adds—

8. 'They say, according to their absurd argument: It is sufficient for the disciple to be as his Master' (cf. Mt $10^{25}$).

iii. CHARACTER AND TENDENCIES.—The foregoing extracts furnish the material upon which any judgment as to the characteristics of this Gospel must be based. Its verbal agreements with the canonical Gospels are evident; references to parallel passages in the Synoptics might have been multiplied. Zahn inclines to the view that its author made use of all four Gospels (*Geschichte des NT Kanons*, ii. 732 f.), though he grants that dependence on the Fourth is doubtful. The use of the Johannine designation 'Lake of Tiberias' is noted, and the unique position of John at the head of the list of the Apostles. The most striking parallels with Luke occur in extracts 1 and 7. It is certain that the writer had access either to the Synoptic Gospels or to their sources; but it is also evident that he has altered the meaning of some passages and made additions to others. His heretical tendencies appear in 5, which gives expression to the Elkesaite abhorrence of sacrifices; in 7, which disparages the Passover by adding the word 'flesh' and by turning our Lord's statement into a question to which a negative answer is implied. The vegetarian practices of the sect account for the omission in 3 of 'locusts' from the Baptist's food; the comment of Epiphanius on this passage is instructive, and his play on words shows that he was using a Greek and not a Hebrew text of Matthew: 'that they may convert the word of truth into a lie, and put *honey-cakes* (ἐγκρίδας) for *locusts*' (ἀκρίδας). It is plain from 1 that this Gospel had no narrative of the birth of Jesus and no genealogy; but these omissions may not have any significance, for the story of the virgin-birth was accepted by some Gnostic Ebionites, and the resemblance to Mk $1^{1}$ is obvious. The account of the baptism of Jesus should be compared with the corresponding narrative in the Gospel according to the Hebrews (Nos. 3 and 4. See HEBREWS [GOSPEL ACCORDING TO], above, p. 341b); the different traditions embodied in the two Gospels supply a strong argument for their distinctness. This section also shows that the author did not always make skilful use of his sources; the statement that Jesus forbade John is irrelevant, and inconsistent with the context. Only eight Apostles are mentioned in 2, but the emphatic reference to 'the Twelve' in the immediate context imparts probability to the suggestion that the omission of four names is due rather to a scribe's error than to the author's carelessness.

The examination of the contents of the extant fragments of this Gospel yields slight evidence for its dependence upon the Gospel according to the Hebrews, and brings to light differences in the parallel narratives which point to the use of different sources. The facts have a satisfactory explanation, if the Gospel is a distinct work compiled to some extent from good material by an author who did not scruple to modify the Evangelic tradition, and to introduce spurious details in order to adapt his work to the principles and practices of a heretical Ebionite sect. The inconsistencies presented by the extant passages of this Gospel are so marked as to lead Westcott to contemplate the possibility that the information of Epiphanius may have been 'derived from different sources'; but he does not exclude the alternative and, on the whole, more probable view that the incongruous elements 'had been incorporated in the Gospel in the time of Epiphanius' (*Introd. to Study of Gospels*, p. 466).*

Zahn assigns an early *date* to this Gospel (170), but his argument is not convincing. He supposes Clement of Alexandria (*c.* 190) to refer to it when he says that 'the Lord announced in some Gospel or other: My mystery is for me and for the sons of my house' (*Strom.* v. 10, 64). The ultimate source of this saying is the LXX rendering of Is $24^{16}$; but in what apocryphal Gospel Clement found his version of the passage it is hazardous to affirm. This Gospel was known to Origen, and it reflects a Gnostic form of Ebionite teaching; the latter part of the 2nd or the early part of the 3rd cent. is the probable date of its composition.

LITERATURE.—A. Meyer in *Die Apokryphen des NT*, p. 24. See Hilgenfeld, Harnack, Zahn, Westcott, in *opp. citt.*

### C. 2. *PHILIP, GOSPEL ACCORDING TO.*—

i. Evidence of existence.
ii. Contents of extant Fragment.
iii. Characteristics. Date.

i. EVIDENCE OF EXISTENCE.—The Coptic-Gnostic work known as *Pistis Sophia* testifies to the existence, in the second half of the 3rd cent., of a Gospel ascribed to Philip. This Apostle is represented as having written in a book the mysteries which the risen Lord revealed to His disciples: '*Et quum Jesus finisset dicere hæc verba, exsiliens Philippus stetit, deposuit librum, qui in sua manu, iste γὰρ est, qui scribit res omnes, quas Jesus dixit et quas fecit omnes*' (see Harnack, *Christliche Urlitteratur*, i. 14, where the whole passage is quoted). *Epiphanius* (377) knew that the Gnostic heretics, against whom he wrote, used a Gospel which bore Philip's name (εἰς ὄνομα Φιλίππου τοῦ ἁγίου μαθητοῦ εὐαγγέλιον πεπλασμένον). He quotes from it the passage given below. *Leontius of Byzantium* (d. 543) states that the Manichæans had composed a Gospel of Philip; but that he is referring to the work known to Epiphanius cannot be affirmed (*de Sectis*, iii. 1).

ii. CONTENTS OF EXTANT FRAGMENT.—The passage quoted by Epiphanius (*Hær.* xxvi. 13) from this Gospel is thus translated by Lipsius (*Dict. Christ. Biog.* ii. 716): 'The Lord revealed to me what the soul ought to say when she mounts to heaven, and what answer she should give to

* The quotations given by Epiphanius from this Gospel have been compared by J. Rendel Harris with the contents of a Syriac MS edited by him. In his judgment the Syriac work is an extract from an adaptation of an earlier lost Gospel, and not a version of the Gnostic Gospel of the Twelve Apostles (*The Gospel of the Twelve Apostles*, etc., edited from the Syriac MS, Camb. 1900).

the higher powers: "I have known myself and gathered myself together, and begotten no children for the Archon of this world, but have torn up his roots, and gathered the scattered members; and I know thee and who thou art! for I also am descended from the upper world."'

iii. CHARACTERISTICS.—The Fragment has a few points of contact with the Fourth Gospel, but the resemblances are too slight to prove dependence (cf. Jn $11^{52}$ $8^{23}$). The ascetic and Gnostic tendencies of the work are both manifested in the single sentence, 'I have begotten no children for the Archon of this world.' Lipsius notes that this brief extract also dwells on a favourite theme of Gnostic writings, viz. 'The prayers of the departing soul as she passes through the various heavens' (*op. cit.* 716).

Zahn (*Geschichte des NT Kanons*, ii. 767) thinks it probable that Clement of Alexandria (*c.* 190) had the authority of this Gospel for his assertion that it was Philip to whom our Lord said, 'Leave the dead to bury their own dead,' etc. (Lk $9^{60}$). Whence Clement derived this tradition cannot now be determined, but the conjecture cannot be accepted as evidence for an early *date.* Harnack decides for the end of the 2nd or the first half of the 3rd cent., and bases his argument on the nature of the Gnosticism which the extant Fragments of this Gospel reflect.

### C. 3. *MATTHIAS, GOSPEL ACCORDING TO.*—

i. Evidence of existence.
ii. Conjectural identifications.
iii. Supposed contents.
iv. Origin and date.

i. EVIDENCE OF EXISTENCE. — *Origen* (*c.* 246) mentions a Gospel κατὰ Ματθίαν (*Hom.* 1 *in Luc.*), and *Eusebius* (*c.* 324) places it, together with the Gospels according to Peter and to Thomas, in his list of 'heretical' writings (*HE* iii. 25). The name of this Gospel is also found in later lists of apocryphal works, but no writer who uses this title gives any quotation from the Gospel.

ii. CONJECTURAL IDENTIFICATIONS. — *Hippolytus* (155–235) states that the Basilidians appealed to 'secret discourses' which had been communicated to them by Matthias, who had been privileged to receive private instructions from our Lord: 'φασὶν εἰρηκέναι Ματθίαν αὐτοῖς λόγους ἀποκρύφους, οὓς ἤκουσε παρὰ τοῦ σωτῆρος κατ' ἰδίαν διδαχθείς' (*Philos.* vii. 20). If from other sources the contents of this Gospel were known, it might be possible to identify it with these ἀπόκρυφοι λόγοι, but the reference is not of necessity to a 'writing' (Lipsius, *Dict. Christ. Biog.* ii. 716); and it would be satisfactorily explained if the Gospel of Basilides, mentioned by Origen (*tract.* 26 *in Matt.* 33, 34), claimed for the teaching of his school the authority of Matthias. The name of one who was not chosen to be an Apostle during the life of Jesus would naturally suggest itself to a Gnostic writer who knew that the only way to trace his doctrine to our Lord was to invent the fiction of secret teaching given to an Apostle in the interval between the resurrection and the ascension.

*Clement of Alexandria* (175–200) quotes three passages from the 'Traditions of Matthias' (Παραδόσεις Ματθίου). The three quotations given below are respectively introduced by the following formulæ: 'Matthias exhorting in the "Traditions" says'; 'They say that Matthias also taught thus'; 'They say in the "Traditions" that Matthias, the Apostle, constantly said.' Clement refers to the work known as the 'Traditions of Matthias' with respect. In the first passage he mentions it between Plato's *Theætetus* and the Gospel to the Hebrews; in the second passage he quotes its teaching immediately after a reference to our Lord's saying about the impossibility of serving 'two masters,' these being, in his view, 'pleasure and God.' Lipsius and Zahn identify this work with the Gospel according to Matthias mentioned by Origen. Lipsius allows that the identification is a conjecture; Zahn enters into a detailed argument in support of the suggestion (*Geschichte des NT Kanons*, ii. 751 ff.). But Harnack's refutation of this theory is powerful and convincing. In the earlier part of his work (*Christliche Urlitteratur*, i. 18) he speaks with qualified approval of Zahn's arguments in favour of identification, and assigns to them a measure of probability; but his more mature judgment is that they are inconclusive (*Chron.* ii. 597). In the work known to Clement the speaker is not our Lord, but Matthias. Neither this fact nor the title 'Traditions' is favourable to the hypothesis that it was in reality a Gospel. Some of Zahn's reasoning is based upon conjectural emendations of the text; but, unless these subjective alterations are accepted, the authorities he quotes refer not to Matthias but to Matthew.

iii. SUPPOSED CONTENTS.—The passages quoted by Clement of Alexandria from the 'Traditions of Matthias' are given here because they have an interest of their own apart from their relation to the Gospel according to Matthias, of which it is probable that we know nothing but the name.

'Wonder at the things present, for that is the first step towards a knowledge of the things beyond' (*Strom.* ii. 9).

'The flesh must be fought and evil entreated, and its unbridled lust must in no wise be yielded to; but the soul must grow through faith and knowledge' (*Strom.* iii. 4).

'If the neighbour of an elect person sin, the elect one sinned. For if he had conducted himself as the word enjoins, his neighbour would have so reverenced his manner of life as not to sin' (*Strom.* vii. 13).

iv. ORIGIN AND DATE.—In accordance with the views already expressed, nothing can be said of the 'Gospel according to Matthias,' except that it was known to Origen in the early part of the 3rd century. The 'Traditions of Matthias' was quoted with respect by a Christian Father towards the close of the 2nd cent., and it appears to have been highly esteemed by Gnostics on account of its ascetic teaching, though in the extant fragments there is nothing extravagant. Harnack finds in the phrase 'as the word enjoins' (ὡς ὁ λόγος ὑπαγορεύει) the stamp of Greek philosophy; but this is by no means certain.

### C. 4. *BASILIDES, GOSPEL ACCORDING TO.*—

i. Evidence of existence.
ii. Character and contents. Date.

i. EVIDENCE OF EXISTENCE.—*Origen* (*c.* 246) is the oldest and probably the sole authority for the statement that Basilides (*c.* 133), the founder of a Gnostic school in Egypt, 'had even the audacity (ἐτόλμησε) to write a Gospel κατὰ Βασιλίδην' (*Hom. in Luc.* 1). Later writers who express a similar judgment, but can scarcely be quoted as independent witnesses, are *Ambrose* (*Exp. in Luc.* 1) and *Jerome*, who includes a 'Gospel of Basilides' in his list of Apocryphal Gospels (*Præf. in Matt.*).

ii. CHARACTER AND CONTENTS.—More is known of Basilides' *Exegetica*, a commentary on 'the Gospel,' than of the Gospel which he is said to have written. Agrippa Castor, to whom Eusebius (*HE* iv. 7) refers as a 'most renowned writer,' who 'exposed the error' of Basilides, says that he 'wrote twenty-four books upon the Gospel' (εἰς τὸ εὐαγγέλιον βιβλία). A more specific title ('Εξηγητικὰ εἰς τὸ εὐαγγέλιον) is given to this work by Clement of Alexandria (175–200), who quotes from the twenty-third book (*Strom.* iv. 12) a passage which treats of the relation of sin to suffering and martyrdom. Lipsius thinks that Basilides is endeavouring to base his Gnostic teaching on an exposition of Lk 21[12ff.]; but Zahn suggests Jn 9[1-3], to which the resemblances are closer (*Geschichte des NT Kanons*, i. 767; cf. McGiffert, *Eusebius*, p. 179, n. 12).

Another fragment from 'the thirteenth book of the treatises (*tractatuum*) of Basilides' is preserved in the *Acta disputationis Archelai et Manetis*, c. 55 (see Galland, *Bibl. Patr.* iii. 608). This passage contains an exposition of the parable of Dives and Lazarus (Lk 16). Zahn traces to the *Exegetica* the Basilidian teaching about marriage in Clement (*Strom.* iii. 1), where the reference is clearly to Mt 19[11. 12]. It is reasonable to assume that the 'Treatises' and 'Expositions' of Basilides are different titles for the same work. In regard to the number of the canonical Gospels upon which the *Exegetica* were based nothing can be positively asserted; but it is known that the schools of Valentinus and Basilides used the Gospels on which the extracts from this work are based. The *Exegetica* almost certainly includes John as well as Luke, probably Matthew also.

In regard to the relation of 'the Gospel' to the *Exegetica* different opinions are held. McGiffert (*op. cit.*) suggests that 'Origen mistook the *Exegetica* for a Gospel'; but it is necessary neither to ascribe this confusion to him, nor to suppose that he inferred the existence of an apocryphal Gospel from the variations from the text of the canonical Gospels in the passages upon which he comments. There is evidence that the followers of Basilides made use of the 'Traditions of Matthias' (Hippol. *Philos.* vii. 20), and that he claimed to have received instruction from 'Glaucias, the interpreter of Peter.' Herein may be found the explanation of his departures from the Evangelic tradition. There is nothing inherently improbable in the hypothesis, which seems best to account for all the facts, that in the interests of Gnostic doctrine Basilides wrote a Gospel and afterwards a commentary on it. His Gospel may be described, with Zahn, as 'a kind of Harmony'; but the sources from which his narrative was derived appear to have been used with considerable freedom.

The *date* of this Gospel and of the *Exegetica* is probably 130–140, the period when Basilides appeared as the founder of a sect.

D. Of the following Apocryphal Gospels little is known but their name. Use has been made of Hofmann's list, derived from Fabricius (in *PRE*[3] i. 661)—

**1.** *ANDREW, GOSPEL OF.*—Possibly identical with the Gnostic 'Acts of Andrew' (περίοδοι Ἀνδρέου). Augustine refers to apocryphal writings of Andrew (*c. Adversar. Leg. et Prophet.* 20). See Lipsius, *Die apokr. Apostelgeschichte*, i. 543 f.

**2.** *APELLES, GOSPEL OF.*—Probably a mutilated version of a canonical Gospel by a disciple of Marcion. According to Epiphanius (*Hær.* xliv. 2) this work is the source of the familiar unwritten saying of our Lord: 'Become approved money-changers' (γίνεσθε δόκιμοι τραπεζῖται); see AGRAPHA, above, p. 349[b]. Cf. Harnack, *De Apellis gnosi monarchia*, 1874, p. 75.

**3.** *BARNABAS, GOSPEL OF.*—Mentioned in the Gelasian Decree, but nothing is known of its contents unless fragments of it have been preserved in the Mohammedan Gospel of Barnabas. See White's *Bampton Lectures*, 1784, and Axon's article in *Journal of Theol. Studies*, April 1902, p. 441.

**4.** *BARTHOLOMEW, GOSPEL OF.*—Mentioned in the Gelasian Decree, and by Jerome (*Præf. in Matt.*), in surroundings which suggest that it was a Gnostic work. There is no sufficient reason for identifying this Gospel with the Hebrew Gospel according to Matthew, which Bartholomew is said to have taken to India (Eusebius, *HE* v. 10).

**5.** *CERINTHUS, GOSPEL OF.*—Mentioned by Epiphanius (*Hær.* li. 7). Hofmann thinks that this work was a mutilated version of the Gospel according to Matthew, similar to that which the Carpocratians used.

**6.** *EVE, GOSPEL OF.*—Mentioned by Epiphanius as in use among the Borborites, an Ophite sect of Gnostics (*Hær.* xxvi. 2 ff.). Harnack is doubtful if it can properly be called a Gospel. Lipsius describes it as a 'Gnostic doctrinal treatise, though presented, it may be, in an historical form' (*Dict. Christ. Biog.* ii. 717). Preuschen prints the extracts quoted by Epiphanius as a fragment of an Ophite Gospel (*Antilegomena*, p. 80). Jesus is represented as saying in a voice of thunder: 'I am thou, and thou art I, and wherever thou art there am I, and in all things I am sown. And from whencesoever thou gatherest me, in gathering me thou gatherest thyself' (cf. Ropes, *Die Sprüche Jesu*, p. 56).

**7.** *JUDAS ISCARIOT, GOSPEL OF.*—According to the testimony of Irenæus (*adv. Hær.* i. 31), Epiphanius (*Hær.* xxxviii. 1), and Theodoret (*Hæret. Fab.* i. 15), this work was in use among the Cainites, a Gnostic sect. Lipsius says that it represents Judas's betrayal as 'a meritorious action, and the traitor himself as the perfect Gnostic who destroyed the dominion of the Demiurge by bringing about the crucifixion of our Lord.'

**8.** *THADDÆUS, GOSPEL OF.*—Mentioned in some MSS of the Gelasian Decree, but nothing is certainly known of its contents. The name of the author may be intended for the Apostle, or for one of the Seventy who, according to tradition, was sent to king Abgar (see art. THADDÆUS in vol. iv. p. 741 f.).

**9.** *VALENTINUS, GOSPEL OF.*—Mentioned by Tertullian (*de Præscript. Hæret.* c. 49), and usually identified with the 'Gospel of Truth' (*Evangelium Veritatis*) on the authority of Irenæus (*adv. Hær.* iii. 11), who says (1) that the 'Gospel of Truth' was used by the Valentinians, and (2) that it departed entirely from the canonical Gospels. Zahn holds that the two Gospels were probably separate works (*Geschichte des NT Kanons*, i. 748).

J. G. TASKER.

## DIDACHE.—



*Discovery in modern times.*—The publication in 1883 of the early Christian manual popularly known as the *Didache* marks an epoch in the study of primitive Christianity. One might compare it to the rediscovery of the genuine Ignatian Epistles in the 17th century. But the comparison would do scant justice to its real significance, which lies in the way in which the *Didache* bears on a wide range of early writings, and on phenomena in them which it causes to stand out in new and clearer light. It is needful, then, to do more than consider the actual contents of our MS, written in 1056 by 'Leo, notary and sinner,' and discovered about 1875 in the library of the Jerusalem monastery in Phanar, the Greek quarter of Constantinople, by Philotheus Bryennios, a scholarly Greek ecclesiastic. One must also try to estimate the various literary and historical relations of the original work which the MS brings to our knowledge, and of which it remains the prime representative. In this MS, doubtless Palestinian in origin, it occupies 203 lines, of 53 letters on an average; so that it is about the size of St. Paul's letter to the Galatians. But in all probability the original work, with which we are mainly concerned, was slightly shorter. Accordingly, our inquiries will fall under three main heads, viz., (A) The primal Didache: its contents, genesis, date; (B) the transformations which it underwent in various circles; (C) its significance in the history of Christianity.

A. *The Primal Didache.*—i. The Didache of our MS.—(*a*) *Title.*—Of the two titles in the MS, 'Teaching of the XII Apostles' and 'Teaching of the Lord through the XII Apostles to the Gentiles,' it seems natural to regard the latter as the more original. One can hardly imagine the fuller and more individual title being added between the commoner one and the text proper. It is unlikely, however, that either of them belonged to the earliest form of the 'Teaching,' corresponding roughly to chaps. i.-vi. of our MS. This body of precepts touching the *Two Ways* may perhaps, in its oral stage, have had some descriptive title, such as 'the Way of the Teaching'* (see ταύτης τῆς ὁδοῦ τῆς διδαχῆς in vi. 1), or 'the Way'; or it may have been known simply as 'the Teaching' (see ἄλλην διδαχὴν in xi. 2, cf. vi. 1; cf. Barn. xvi. 9 αἱ ἐντολαὶ τῆς διδαχῆς, also xviii. 1), or 'Teaching of the Lord' (perhaps preserved in our second title, Διδαχὴ Κυρίου, κ.τ.λ., cf. ἐντολαὶ Κυρίου, iv. 12 f.), the God of Israel (see παρεκτὸς θεοῦ, vi. 1). This would accord both with the contents of the original *Two Ways* and with the phrasing in Ac $13^{12}$ ἐκπλησσόμενος ἐπὶ τῇ διδαχῇ τοῦ Κυρίου, where reference has just been made to τὰς ὁδοὺς τοῦ Κυρίου τὰς εὐθείας (Hos $14^{10}$). Here 'Teaching' has the objective sense of 'Doctrine.'

As Dr. C. Taylor† says, 'the primitive Church had, instead of a New Testament, a body of teaching, which was at first, from the nature of the case, wholly unwritten. To this St. Paul alludes when he lays down that a bishop must be blameless, "holding to the faithful word which is according to *The Teaching*" (Tit $1^{9}$). Justin Martyr again expressly refers to it, speaking of Christ as attested "by the words of *The Teaching*, and the prophecies to Him ward" (*Dial.* 35). This teaching would sometimes be spoken of as the Lord's, and after a while as the Apostles' (2 Jn $^{9}$, Ac $2^{42}$), just as the Jews spoke of a Torah absolutely, and of a Torah of Moses, and of the Lord.' Certainly the way in which St. Paul refers to the 'type of teaching' (in relation to 'sin, unto death,' and 'obedience, unto righteousness') unto which the Roman Christians were 'committed' (Ro $6^{16f.}$), and which forbade the causing of division (διχοστασία, $16^{17}$, cf. Did. iv. 3 οὐ ποιήσεις σχίσμα), is very suggestive of a recognized form of 'Teaching' to converts, on lines similar to those of our *Two Ways*. Still full proof is lacking that it was so styled.

Nor can we be sure of the title under which the Teaching was first written down. 'Teaching of the Apostles' (cf. Ac $2^{42}$) is likely enough, especially if this was, as it appears, the earliest form in which it was known in Egypt. But, even were this more certain than it is, it would not necessarily be the original Palestinian form, which might be simply 'The Teaching' (like *Didascalia*, the title of a later Palestinian work suggested by our Didache). Still, the varied character of the witness to 'Teaching of the Apostles' rather supports this as the primitive title of the written *Two Ways*. Thus the Lat. version, the purest form of the *Two Ways* apart from our MS, has as its rubric *de doctrina Apostolorum*; so also Eusebius (*HE* iii. 25 τῶν ἀποστόλων αἱ λεγομέναι διδαχαί, which Rufinus renders *Doctrina quæ dicitur Apostolorum*), Athanasius (*Festal Epistles*, 39, διδαχὴ καλουμένη τῶν ἀπ.), and Nicephorus (διδαχὴ ἀποστόλων).

It looks, then, as if there were two distinct lines of transmission in the history of the *Two Ways*, of which the Latin and our MS are the types—a result borne out by textual criticism. The question of their mutual relations will be dealt with later on. Only, we may here observe that the phrase 'XII Apostles' is no less primitive than 'the Apostles' pure and simple. Thus in that part of the *Ascension of Isaiah* which represents a time prior to A.D. 100, it is 'the Twelve Apostles of the Beloved' who plant the Church (iv. 3); and it is 'the preaching (προφητεία) of his Twelve Apostles' that is forsaken by the mass of 'disciples' 'on the eve of His approach' (iii. 21). Hence the idea of 'the Lord's teaching through the Twelve Apostles to the Gentiles' is quite in keeping with an early date for the recension so described, especially if it belong to Palestine. And as it does not claim for its contents that they are the very words of the Apostles (cf. 'my child' in iii. 1–iv. 1), there is nothing pseudonymous about the work. It represents current teaching and usage at a time when it was natural to assume that these did but express the mind of 'the Lord'—which to the compiler of our Didache doubtless means, as in several other places (viii. 2, ix. 5, εἰς ὄνομα Κυρίου, xi. 2, 4, 8, xv. 4, xvi. 1, 7 f.), the glorified Christ.

(*b*) *Contents and structure.*—As it stands in our MS, the Didache has real organic unity. A natural development of thought is traceable throughout (save perhaps in one section near the beginning), as will appear from the following summary.

There are Two Ways in this world, one of Life and one of Death—so radically different are they. The Way of Life consists of love, (1) to God our Maker, (2) to one's neighbour as to oneself: this involves refraining from doing to another what one would not have done to oneself.

'Now of these words the Teaching is as follows':—

The Evangelical precepts which follow in our MS exemplify the thought of positive love to man, flowing from love to God. But the latter idea, the first element in the Great Commandment, is not formally developed. It is regarded as fulfilled in relation to man as God's image, whether in the fuller way represented by our MS, or up to the level of the negative form of the Golden Rule, which practically replaces the positive in the exposition or 'teaching' of the Way of Life in its original form (see below).

Then comes a section dealing with practical love to one's fellow in the spirit of the Sermon on the Mount, in which forgiveness of wrong and the relief of physical need by one's own goods are emphasized. In the latter case a warning to

* Cf. 2 P $2^{2}$ ἡ ὁδὸς τῆς ἀληθείας (τῆς δικαιοσύνης, $2^{21}$); and Ac $9^{2}$ $19^{9.23}$ 'the Way,' $18^{25}$ 'the Way of the Lord,' $22^{4}$ 'this Way,' $24^{14}$ 'the Way which they call heresy,' $24^{22}$ εἰδὼς τὰ περὶ τῆς ὁδοῦ.

† *The Teaching of the Twelve Apostles: Two Lectures*, p. 112.

the recipient is appended, as to his final accountability to God, if he take save when in want; likewise he who has whereof to give is bidden to make sure that he finds a fit recipient.

The exposition of the negative form of the Golden Rule opens (ch. ii.) with the words, 'Now the second precept of the Teaching (is).' It consists of an expansion of the second table of the Decalogue, beginning, after Jewish usage, with 'Thou shalt not kill'; but it also inserts the Third Commandment against perjury, in close connexion with false witness. The expansion in question is in terms of vices to which paganism was specially addicted.

The incidence of pagan failings explains the reversal of the order as to homicide and adultery found in the Latin version. This change confirms the view that its text represents Alexandria rather than Palestine; Dt $5^{17f.}$ LXX, cf. *JQR* xv. 309 ff.

No mention is made of the Sabbath or of honour to parents. The former seems to be omitted intentionally; the latter may be taken for granted, or may be omitted because pagan parents *must* be disobeyed. Abstinence from idolatry is naturally assumed: thus in iii. 4, vi. 3, things are forbidden as leading to or implying idolatry. This section ends with what is its keynote—prohibition of all evil purpose or feeling against another. Indeed it goes further: 'Thou shalt not hate any man; but some thou shalt rebuke, and for some thou shalt pray, and some thou shalt love above thine own life.'

The next section (ch. iii.), which has a unity of its own as regards its first five or six precepts at any rate (indicated by the recurrence of 'my child'), passes to the subtler sort of sins, which lead on to the grosser kind already dealt with. It makes the moral ideal more searching and exhaustive. In Jewish phrase, 'it fences the Law': 'My child, flee from every evil, and from everything like unto it.' Its Jewish colour is very evident; and the cardinal sins to which others lead are homicide, adultery, idolatry, theft, blasphemy. In contrast to the haughty and self-assertive temper, to which the last of these is traced, there follows a series of exhortations to humility of spirit and conduct which have a more specifically Christian ring; and the section ends with an exhortation meekly to accept the dispensations of Providence as good (which may once have followed the last of the more Jewish precepts, in an oral body of *catechesis* for proselytes to Judaism).

An easy transition to the last class of duties (ch. iv.), those of life in the religious community and family in particular, is presented by the inculcation of reverential docility towards 'him who speaks the word of God'; 'for where the lordship is spoken, there is the Lord' (a truly Jewish maxim). And here follow precepts on consorting with 'the saints'; on the avoidance of disunion, partiality in judgment, a doubtful mind; on selfishness and beneficence—the latter marked by a cheerful spirit, in view of Divine recompense and of the brethren's fellowship in the greater goods of immortality; on parental discipline and the mutual relations of master and bond-servant (2–11). The whole ends with the summary precepts:* 'Thou shalt hate all hypocrisy and whatsoever is not pleasing to the Lord. Thou shalt not abandon the Lord's precepts, but shalt keep what thou didst receive, neither adding nor taking away. In meeting thou shalt openly confess thy transgressions (cf. Ja $5^{16}$), and shalt not come to thy prayer with a bad conscience. This is the Way of Life.'

The Way of Death (ch. v.) is simply the opposite of all this, and takes the form of a List of Vices (§ 1 follows the order of chs. ii.–iii.), a common topic both in classical and Jewish literature.

In Judaism, indeed, there seems to have existed something like a standing list, to judge from the many points of contact between this list and those in the NT (*e.g.* Mk $7^{21f.}$, Ro $1^{29ff.}$, 1 Co $5^{10ff.}$, 2 Co $12^{20}$, Gal $5^{19\text{-}21}$, Col $3^5$, 1 Ti $1^{9f.}$, 2 Ti $3^{2ff.}$), on the one hand, and the traditional Confession of Sins in the Synagogue (*Vidui*), taken along with Wis $14^{22ff.}$, the Slavonic Enoch $10^{4f.}$, and Test. XII Patriarchs (Reuben 3, Levi 17), on the other: cf. *Clem. Hom.* i. 18, xi. 27, *Recogn.* iv. 36. Note the Jewish alphabetic number 22 in § 1: see Rendel Harris, *Teaching*, 82 ff.

Instruction in the 'Two Ways' ends (ch. vi.) in our MS with warning against deviation from 'this way of (the) Teaching' as deviation from God's truth. To which are added two postscripts: 'If, then, thou art able to bear the whole yoke of the Lord, thou shalt be perfect: but if thou art not able, what thou canst, that do. But touching food (βρῶσις), bear what thou art able; yet of that (food) which hath been offered to idols beware exceedingly; for it is a service of dead gods.'* The significance of these will be dealt with in the sequel.

Such was the Teaching† which should ring in the ears of the Gentile convert as he took upon himself the vows of Christian baptism. Of this, in a simple‡ form, the manual now goes on to speak (ch. vii.). And as it refers to fasting as an accompaniment of baptism, it passes naturally to the stated Christian Fasts and Prayers (ch. viii.),—in each case as contrasted with those of 'the hypocrites' (*i.e.* unbelieving Jews). Next comes a description of the special Eucharistic prayers preceding and following the actual eating of the Church's sacred meal (lit. 'being filled'). A striking feature of both groups of prayers is their reference to the fulfilment of the feast, and of its imagery, in the consummated state of the Church in the kingdom of God. It is added, however, that the liturgical forms here given (chs. ix.–x.) are not to bind 'prophets' in Eucharistic prayer.

At this point the manual pauses once more, to call attention to all that has gone before (ταῦτα πάντα τὰ προειρημένα) as the norm of true teaching on the matters in question, and the test of such as are to be received as teachers. 'If the teacher himself turn and teach another teaching to the undoing (of this), hear him not; but if to the increase of righteousness and knowledge of the Lord, receive him as the Lord' (xi. 2). And so we are led naturally to a description of the ministry of the Word, which is of the 'prophetic' or heaven-sent type. 'Apostles,' or divinely prompted missionaries,§ are described quite briefly, as being rather exceptional visitants. They are first named in conjunction with the prophets,‖ as persons provided for by 'the rule of the gospel' (κατὰ τὸ δόγμα τοῦ εὐαγγελίου); and then follow one or two rough and ready rules for their treatment, as they pass through existing churches on the way to their mission-fields (cf. 3 Jn $^{5\text{-}8}$). 'Prophets' occupy more space, probably as being a subject of more practical interest for those addressed. The need of tests, as between genuine and spurious claimants to the high authority and functions conceded to him who had the spirit of prophecy (a prime mark of the Messianic age, Ac $2^{17f.}$), was becoming acutely felt. But the simplicity of the tests here supplied—those of character merely, where the

* Probably part of the original framework of Jewish oral *catechesis*; cf. the re-emergence of 'my son' in the Latin version, which may here preserve an original touch.

* Wis $13^{10}$ 'But wretched they, and in dead (things) their hopes: for that they called "gods" the works of men's hands.'

† Compare the 'foundation of repentance from dead works and of faith towards God' in He $6^1$, with its own further διδαχή attached.

‡ Simpler originally than what now stands in Did. vii. 2–4; see below, iii. (*d*) *ad fin.*

§ By this time called 'evangelists' in most regions outside Palestine; cf. Eph $4^{11}$, 2 Ti $4^5$, Ac $21^8$ (written for non-Palestinian readers), Euseb. *HE* iii. 37; yet see Rev $2^2$.

‖ An unworthy 'apostle' is called a 'pseudo-prophet' (xi. 6)

recognized phenomena of 'speaking in Spirit' were present—shows that the age of 'enthusiasm' is still far from over (cf. Jude [12. 19], 2 P [2ff. 13]). As these two types of itinerant ministry are to be received according to certain rules, so the ordinary Christian stranger needs handling with prudence, including cases in which he wishes to settle among his new friends (ch. xii.). This in turn suggests the case in which even a prophet desires to settle in one community. His support is provided for by the principle that 'the labourer is worthy of his meat'; and this applies also to 'teachers,' a less spontaneous and more local type of the inspired ministry.* But it is the prophets, above all, who answer to the highest ministry under the OT; 'they are your chief priests' (esp. as offering the sacrifice of prayer at the Eucharist, x. 7, xiv. 1-3); and accordingly, to them, in the first instance, fall the first-fruits of various kinds (those specified are mainly country produce). Failing a prophet, first-fruits go to the poor (ch. xiii.).

After this excursus on matters of Discipline in relation to brethren coming to the community from outside,—suggested, it seems, by the mention of prophets in connexion with the Eucharistic Meal,—the compiler turns again to the chief features of internal church order, and so to the Eucharist, the stated Breaking of Bread on the Lord's day,† to lay down the conditions of its 'pure' observance (ch. xiv.). This depends on prior confession of trespasses (cf. iv. 14) between those uniting in the sacred 'sacrifice' of praise in prayer. None may partake while out of harmony with his fellow;‡ so shall their sacrifice of prayer§ be that pointed to by Mal [1^11. 14]. The thought of the Church's gathering on the Lord's day leads to mention of the local ministry, 'bishops' and 'deacons,' as those who, in a sense, share the sacred ministry (λειτουργία) primarily belonging to the ministers of the Word, prophets and teachers. Hence they are not to be looked down upon because their own special functions are of a humbler order, but are to rank as associates of their more gifted colleagues in the honour of the ministry (xv. 1, 2). With this apology for the administrative ministry, elected by the local community itself (and now assuming greater importance than in the past), the compiler returns to the thought of fraternal discipline, already alluded to in connexion with the Eucharist. He uses terms which imply that it was a matter of the Church itself, and not only of its bishops and deacons, and enjoins that it be dealt with 'as ye have it in the Gospel' (cf. Mt [18^15ff.]). This same Gospel standard‖ is to regulate their supplications (εὐχάς) and alms and all their actions (xv. 3, 4).

Finally, let them 'watch' in the interests of their 'life,' to be ready when the Lord comes. The last days may be very near, marked by abundance of pseudo-prophets and corrupters (already on the horizon, xi. 2) and by degeneration of the sheep. Then, as lawlessness increases, hatred shall go the length of persecution and treachery among the brethren, until there shall appear the world-deceiver as God's Son, with signs and wonders, and run a course of temporary triumph. Thus mankind shall be tested, and even many believers shall fail: 'but those who shall endure in their faith shall be saved by the curse* itself.' And then shall appear the signs of the truth: first, the sign of outspreading (the Crucified with outspread arms) in heaven;† next, the sign of a trumpet's voice; and third, resurrection of the dead—not of all, however, but, as it was said, 'the Lord shall come and all the saints with Him.' 'Then shall the world see the Lord coming upon the clouds of heaven.'

ii. Materials for comparative criticism.—In view of this summary most will agree with Harnack (Herzog's *PRE*[3] i. 713) when he says: 'Even if we knew nothing of the document from separate tradition, were aware of no later recensions of it, and were not in a position to supply its sources, we should—apart from some passages in the first chapter, which, in any case, raise the suspicion of being later additions—have to acquiesce in the assumption of the integrity of the writing.' Perhaps this is to overlook one or two secondary features in chs. vii.-xvi., particularly ch. vii.; but, broadly speaking, it is true. When, however, we turn to the traces of the work in the ancient Church, and to certain related documents that have reached us, perplexities and complications arise on every hand. These we must now examine, yet without ignoring the unity in style and language, as well as in feeling, which marks our Didache as a whole.

(*a*) *Textual witnesses:* (1) Primary—

(α) A = *Apostolical Constitutions*, vii. 1-32. This embodies the whole of the Didache, almost as found in our MS—the *Two Ways* largely *verbatim* (1-21), the rest with more reserve; but throughout occur large additions meant to suit the taste of certain circles of Syrian Christians in the latter half of the 4th century. Its special value lies at once in the relative completeness of its use of our Didache, and in the fact that it belongs, broadly speaking, to the same region.

It opens with the reference made by 'the lawgiver Moses' to choice between the Ways of Life and Death (Dt [30^19]), and having cited the words of 'the Lord Jesus,' 'No man can serve two masters,' continues: 'As in duty bound (ἀναγκαίως), we also, following the Teacher (διδασκάλῳ), Christ, . . . say that "Two Ways there are,"' etc. This rather points to knowledge of Διδαχὴ Κυρίου in the title, just as the opening of the *Apost. Const.* as a whole, πᾶσι τοῖς ἐξ ἐθνῶν πιστεύσασιν, points to τοῖς ἔθνεσιν. As to the *Twelve* Apostles, this is found in the title of the *Didascalia* (see below), the basis of *Apost. Const.* i.-vi., which runs: 'The Didascalia, or the Catholic Teaching of the Twelve Apostles and holy disciples of our Saviour.'

(β) B = *Epistle of Barnabas.* In chs. xviii.-xx. it quotes the bulk of the *Two Ways* as found in Did. i.-v., but in a very different order and with some textual variation (partly due to freedom of citation, partly, perhaps, also to original textual differences). There are slight echoes of the *Two Ways* in other parts of the Epistle, as also a rather close parallel in iv. 9, 10 to Did. xvi. 2. The great value of the Epistle of Barnabas is that it supplies an early date (see below, iii. (*b*)) in the literary history of the Didache.

(γ) CO = *Apostolic Church Ordinances*, 1-14. This compilation of about A.D. 300‡ does for the Egyptian Church what *Apost. Const.* vii. does for the Syrian; it works up the local recension of the Didache into a form more accordant with current sentiment. This work (which exists in Greek, Coptic, and Syriac) is our chief witness for the textual transmission of the *Two Ways* in Egypt; for there is

* Ja [3^1] 'Become not many of you teachers, my brethren'; cf. Ac [13^1], 1 Co [12^28], Eph [4^11], 1 Ti [5^17f.], 2 P [2^1], Barn. i. 8, iv. 9.

† Κυριακὴ κυρίου, perhaps as replacing the σάββατον κυρίου of the OT; cf. ch. viii., where new fast-days are prescribed.

‡ 'Transgression between man and his fellow the Day of Atonement does not expiate, until his fellow be reconciled' (Mishna, *Yômā*, viii. 9; cf. Mt [5^23f.], Ja [5^16]).

§ So the citation of this passage in *de Aleatoribus*, iv., has 'ne inquinetur et impediatur *oratio* vestra'; cf. Tert. *Apol.* 30, *adv. Marc.* iv. 1.

‖ Cf. Mt [5^23f.] [6^5ff.], Mk [11^25], for the conditions of true supplications (with an implied vow, εὐχάς), and Mt [6^1-4] for alms.

* For the idea of salvation through suffering, for Messiah's people as well as for Messiah, see Barn. viii. 6: 'In his kingdom there shall be evil and foul days, in the which we shall be saved: for he who suffers pain in the flesh is healed through the foulness of the hyssop'; cf. vii. 11 and Rev [1^9].

† Mt [24^30] 'the sign of the Son of Man in heaven' (so *Apost. Const.* vii. 32).

‡ The shorter recension found in Cod. Ottob. and two other MSS (see T. Schermann, *Eine Elfapostelmoral*, München, 1903) may be rather earlier.

no proof that the Epistle of Barnabas was written in Alexandria, rather than to it. Thus it is by the aid of CO that we are able to recognize the next document as a witness to the Egyptian type of text. But CO has one or two features due to the Epistle of Barnabas also.

(δ) L=The Latin version. Until recently this was known only in a fragment (Cod. Mellicensis), ending with Did. ii. $6^{a}$. But in 1900 it was published by J. Schlecht from a complete 11th cent. MS, now at Munich, and extending to vi. 1, after which come two or three concluding paragraphs peculiar to itself (see below). This version probably belongs to the 4th cent. (cf. Schlecht, *Die Apostellehre in der Liturgie der Kathol. Kirche*, 67 f.), and its value is great in two directions. It tends to confirm the idea that the original *Didache* consisted of the *Two Ways* and nothing more; and it is a most important textual witness in conjunction with CO and Barnabas. As to L and what of CO answers to it, we may say in general that they represent the same type of text at different stages of deviation from its primal form. On the whole L is further from our MS, and this not only because of such liberties as are natural to a translator. Sometimes it or its Greek original omitted and transposed,* and sometimes adopted additional touches from Barnabas and Hermas, at least in the opening paragraph.

'Viæ duæ sunt in sæculo, vitæ et mortis, *lucis et tenebrarum. In his constituti sunt angeli* duo, unus æquitatis, alter iniquitatis.' Here the words in italics echo Barn. xviii., ἥ τε τοῦ φωτὸς καὶ ἡ τοῦ σκότους . . . ἐφ' ἧς μὲν γάρ εἰσι τεταγμένοι φωταγωγοὶ ἄγγελοι τοῦ θεοῦ, ἐφ' ἧς δὲ ἄγγελοι τοῦ Σατανᾶ. L's deviation from B in describing the angels is due to Hermas, *Mandates*, vi. 2. 1, δύο εἰσὶν ἄγγελοι μετὰ τοῦ ἀνθρώπου, εἷς τῆς δικαιοσύνης καὶ εἷς τῆς πονηρίας. In view of this, one must assign to Hermas, *Mand.* ii. 4, the addition to iv. 8 (rather mangled at the end) of '*Omnibus enim dominus dare vult de donis suis.*'

As to its ending, L has special features which deserve attention. It runs as follows:—

(1) '*Abstine te, fili, ab istis omnibus, et vide ne quis te ab hac doctrina avocet, et si minus extra disciplinam doceberis.* (2) *Hæc in consulendo si cotidie feceris, prope eris vivo deo; quod si non feceris, longe eris a veritate.* (3) *Hæc omnia tibi in animo pone et non deciperis de spe tua* [*sed per hæc sancta certamina pervenies ad coronam per Dominum Jesum Christum regnantem et dominantem cum Deo Patre et Spiritu Sancto in sæcula sæculorum.* Amen].'

Here we may safely set aside the words in brackets as late, and probably due to the translator. But it is otherwise with the rest. As to 1, the fact that the injunction to avoid the things of the Way of Death is separated from immediate connexion with that section, is probably a mistake; while '*doctrina*' is secondary as compared with ὁδοῦ τῆς διδαχῆς, and '*extra disciplinam*' as compared with παρεκτὸς θεοῦ. On the other hand, L seems to preserve the more original form in '*abstine te, fili,*' the plural of our Didache being an adaptation to its fresh setting in the larger work. In 2 we may at present set aside '*in consulendo*' as ambiguous (yet see below, iii. (*b*)). But the simple religious phrase '*prope eris vivo deo*' looks at once primitive and Jewish in type; and the thought occurs that it is equivalent to 'thou shalt be a true proselyte.'† So Philo speaks of the proselyte as 'deserting to God' or 'to the Truth' (cf. Did. v. $2^{a}$), which corresponds exactly to the terms of L's antithesis. If this view be correct, L probably preserves the original form of Jewish-Christian 'Teaching' to converts, while Did. vi. 2, 3 represents the fresh form given to this clause by the author of the fuller Didache, in terms of current Palestinian conditions at the time when he wrote. In this light, $3^{a}$, with its reference to the believer's Hope, may also be original,* corresponding in function to the eschatological reference in Did. xvi.

(ε) Sch=The *Life of Schnudi*, an Egyptian monk of the Thebaid, who died about A.D. 451. Here we have in an Arabic version (ed. Iselin, *Texte und Unters.* XIII. i.) the bulk of the *Two Ways, i.e.* i.–iv. 8 (so CO) and traces of v., vi. 1.

(2) Secondary witnesses: containing textual evidence of a fragmentary or uncertain nature, like that of the *Sibylline Oracles*. The parallels in these, as in most of the writings here named, will be found in J. Rendel Harris' *Teaching of the Twelve Apostles.*—

Ignatius, *Smyr.* xiii. 1, *Magn.* iv.—Did. xvi. 2. *Preaching* and *Apoc. of Peter* (ed. M. R. James, 82). Hermas (*Mand.* ii. etc.)—our Didache. 2 Clement—apparently our Didache (xiii. 4, xvi. 4, Did. i. 3, 5; xvii. 3 f., Did. xvi. 1 f.). *Apol. of Aristides*, ch. xv. Justin—our Didache (Taylor, *Expositor*, III. vi. 359 ff.). Theophilus, *ad Autol.* ii. 34 *fin.* Irenæus—Did. i. 1, 5, xiv. 3; see below. Tertullian, *adv. Marc.* iv. 1—Did. xiv. 3, iv. 14. Clement of Alexandria—explicitly iii. 5 (calling it 'Scripture'), implicitly i. 5, iii. 2, ix. 2. Hippolytus, *Philosoph.* ix. 23—implicitly ii. 7; cf. i. 3. Origen†—implicitly ix. 2. Pseudo-Cyprian, *de Aleatoribus* (ch. iv.; Did. xiv. 2, xv. 3)—explicitly. Clementine Homilies. Pseudo-Clement, *de Virginibus. Didascalia* (Syriac and Latin). Lactantius and Commodian—echoes of *Two Ways* only. Athanasius, *Syntagma Doctrinæ*—clear traces of i.–vi., less clear of xii., xiii.; *de Virginitate*—quotes or paraphrases, ix., x.; *Fragment* περὶ ψευδοπροφητῶν, cf. xi., xii. Pseudo-Athanasius, *Fides Nicæna* and *Didascalia cccxviii. patrum*, two recensions of the *Syntagma*, in which the Did. is freely used. Serapion (of Thmuis, in the Delta), in his Prayer-Book, *c.* 350 A.D., quotes from ix. 4. Optatus, *de Schismate Donatist.* i. 21, quotes iv. $3^{a}$. Augustine cites Did. i. 5 *fin.* (see below, iii. (*d*)). *Canons of Basil* (Egyptian, 5th cent.) uses the *Two Ways.* Severinus, *Doctrina de Sapientia*—explicitly (*Two Ways*, and perhaps more). *Benedicti Regula*, iv. (*Two Ways*). John Climacus (*c.* 580)—implicitly i. 4, 5. Dorotheus of Palestine (*c.* 590)—implicitly iii. 1, 10. Boniface of Mainz, *Admonitio* (*S. Petri*) *sive prædicatio S. Bonifatii*, appears to know more than the *Two Ways.*

(*b*) *Historical testimonia*—

[Irenæus. The authenticity of the Pfaffian Fragment is too dubious to warrant citation of its δευτέραι τῶν ἀποστόλων διατάξεις].

Pseudo-Cyprian, *de Aleatoribus*, iv., 'Et in *Doctrinis apostolorum*: Si quis frater delinquit in ecclesia et non paret legi, hic nec colligatur donec pœnitentiam agat, et non recipiatur ne inquinetur et impediatur oratio vestra' (Did. xiv. 2, xv. 3).

Eusebius, *Hist. Eccl.* iii. 25, Ἐν τοῖς νόθοις (here =non-canonical books) κατατετάχθω καὶ τῶν Παύλου πράξεων ἡ γραφὴ ὅ τε λεγόμενος Ποιμὴν καὶ ἡ Ἀποκάλυψις Πέτρου καὶ πρὸς τούτοις ἡ φερομένη Βαρνάβα ἐπιστολὴ **καὶ τῶν ἀποστόλων αἱ λεγόμεναι Διδαχαί**—where Rufinus has *Doctrina quæ dicitur apostolorum* (so the Syriac).

Athanasius, *Festal Epistles*, 39, ἐστὶ καὶ ἕτερα βιβλία τούτων ἔξωθεν, οὐ κανονιζόμενα μὲν τετυπωμένα δὲ παρὰ τῶν πατέρων ἀναγινώσκεσθαι τοῖς ἄρτι προσερχο-

* Cases of omission or compression occur in iii. 3, $4^{a}$, $8^{a}$, iv. $13^{a}$, $14^{a}$, v. *fin.* (πανθαμάρτητοι); of transposition, in ii. 2, 3, where a different ethical emphasis is in view (CO is nearer our MS); of slight insertion, as i. 1, 'in sæculo'; ii. 2, 'deum *æternum*'; iii. 7, '*sanctam* terram'; iii. 9, 'nec honorabis te apud homines'; iv. 3, 'sciens quod tu judicaberis' (after 'judica juste').

† See art. PROSELYTE in present work, vol. iv. p. $134^{a}$; cf. *Apoc. Bar.* $41^{3}$ 'who have forsaken vanity and fled for refuge beneath thy wings.'

* The 'Teaching' as known to Barn. xxi. 1 seems to have had some such closing exhortations.

† Origen's quotation of what occurs in Did. iii. 10 is probably from Barnabas, which he has just cited. So the echo of the same passage in Dionysius of Alexandria may also be indirect.

*μένοις καὶ βουλομένοις κατηχεῖσθαι τὸν τῆς εὐσεβείας λόγον· Σοφία Σολομῶντος καὶ Σοφία Σιρὰχ καὶ Ἐσθὴρ καὶ Ἰουδὶθ καὶ Τωβίας* **καὶ Διδαχὴ καλουμένη τῶν ἀποστόλων** *καὶ ὁ Ποιμήν.*

Optatus, *l.c.*, ‘Et in capitibus mandatorum, *Non facies scisma*’ (Did. iv. 3[a]).

Rufinus, *Comm. in Symb. Apost.* 38, ‘In Novo vero Testamento libellus qui dicitur Pastoris sive Hermæ, [et is] qui appellatur *Duæ Viæ vel Judicium secundum Petrum.* Quæ omnia legi quidem in ecclesiis voluerunt, non tamen proferri ad auctoritatem ex his fidei confirmandam.’ These are ‘Ecclesiastical,’ not ‘Canonical’ books. But they are not ‘Apocryphal,’ or such as were not to be read in church. This distinction should be borne in mind in considering the following, and especially the silence of Western lists of canonical and other books, like that of Codex Claromontanus and the *Decretum Gelasii.**

Nicephorus, *Stichometry* (using list of sæc. v.–vi.).

*καὶ ὅσαι τῆς νέας ἀντιλέγονται·*
*Ἀποκάλυψις Ἰωάννου στιχ.* 1400
,, *Πέτρου* ,, 300
*Βαρνάβα ἐπιστολή* ,, 1360
. . . . .
*ὅσα τῆς νέας διαθήκης ἀπόκρυφα·*
*Περίοδος Παύλου*
,, *Πέτρου*
,, *Ἰωάννου*
,, *Θωμᾶ*
*Εὐαγγέλιον κατὰ Θωμᾶν*
**Διδαχὴ ἀποστόλων** *στίχ.* 200
. . . . . .

*Catalogue of the Sixty Books.*

*καὶ ὅσα ἀπόκρυφα·*
(OT apocryphal books, mostly not in LXX)
*Ἰακώβου ἱστορία*
*Πέτρου ἀποκάλυψις*
**Περίοδοι καὶ Διδαχαὶ τῶν ἀποστόλων**
*Βαρνάβα ἐπιστολή*
*Παύλου πρᾶξις*
. . . . .

The importance of this entry, which recurs in a list in Cod. Barocc. 206, is that the analogy of the *περίοδοι* of Apostles (seen from Nicephorus' list to include separate works) points to more than one work known as *Διδαχὴ τῶν ἀποστόλων*; and this in turn casts back light on Eusebius' phrase. On the other hand, the Syriac and Latin versions of Eusebius suggest that only one work of the name was generally known in Syria and Italy respectively, towards the end of the 4th century.

(*c*) *Conclusions.*—The impressions conveyed by this body of evidence may now be stated. (1) Knowledge of the *Two Ways* (=Did. i.–vi.) is far more general than that of the full Didache. (2) But in this matter a broad distinction long existed between Palestine, or Syria, and other centres of Christianity. In the former, the two seem to stand on much the same level down to Eusebius, though after his day one of them tended to fall out of use. This was probably the fuller form, now superseded by the *Didascalia* and *Apost. Const.* (3) Elsewhere the bulk of the rules in the full Didache seem never to have suited existing usage, or at least speedily fell out of touch therewith. Hence it is mainly the Eucharistic parts† which have left traces on the literature of the 2nd and 3rd cents., both in Egypt and in the West. Yet several Egyptian witnesses of the 4th and 5th cents. show various adaptations of phrases occurring in Did. xi.–xiii. Similar phenomena also crop up later in the West, possibly through use of such secondary sources. (4) In any case the *Διδαχὴ τῶν ἀποστόλων* meant to Athanasius, if not already to Clement, the shorter work, which was adapted to the instruction of catechumens. It was a book for general Christian edification, like *Wisdom* or the *Shepherd*; whereas the fuller work was known only to scholars, and by them used in an historical sense and as largely out of date. In the West, at least in Italy, to judge from Rufinus' words (compared with his Athanasian model), we gather that even the *Two Ways* had been given a local or Petrine setting. (5) All this tells against the view (*e.g.* of Funk) that the *Two Ways* as a distinct work was secondary, having been separated from the larger Didache for catechetical purposes. But it favours the theory that the full Didache reached Alexandria, from Palestine, only after the primitive Didache had become firmly established there. (6) Finally, there is no proof that the full Didache ever existed in Latin.

* As the Didache is not among ‘Apocrypha,’ it may have been one of the *Opuscula atque tractatus orthodoxorum patrum* not specified, to which perhaps the Epistle of Barnabas also belonged.

† Possibly the early prevalence of the use of Wednesday and Friday as fast-days, and of the three Jewish stated hours of prayer, also implies the influence of Did. viii. Again, Justin's *ὅση δύναμις αὐτῷ*, touching the president's Eucharistic prayer, may echo Did. x. *fin.* *ὅσα θέλουσιν.*

iii. Genesis of the Didache.—(*a*) *Genesis of the ‘Two Ways.’*—Setting aside the theory that the full Didache (with or without i. 3[b]–ii. 1) was prior to the *Two Ways* as a separate work,—which seems as little supported by internal* as by external evidence,—we must start from a closer consideration of the *Two Ways* as the nucleus of the whole. In substance it is clearly of Jewish origin. This is proved both by its structure and by its constant parallels with purely Jewish literature, and particularly with Rabbinic sources. This was first demonstrated by Dr. C. Taylor, and is reaffirmed, even to excess, by a Jewish scholar like Dr. Kohler.

Kohler's collection of Jewish parallels (*The Jewish Encyclopædia*, vol. iv., art. ‘Didache’) to the idea of ‘two ways,’ etc., is full and valuable. But he outruns the evidence when he assumes that the ‘Jewish manual’ (which he hastily infers to have existed) had matter bearing on love to God which the Christian redactor omitted. His *obiter dicta*, that ‘the whole book has fallen into disorder,’ and that ‘the whole first part of the “Didache,” dealing with monotheism, was tampered with by the Christian editor,’ are baseless conjectures.

Specially Jewish is the section in which the path to the graver sins is fenced by warnings against the lighter ones (iii. 1 ff.), each such warning being prefaced with ‘My son.’ Probably this section was borrowed from a self-contained unit of Jewish teaching for Gentile proselytes (including iv. 1). Of such instruction, which was sure to take more or less fixed shape on the lines of the Decalogue,† we have a good deal of indirect evidence (cf. Ro 2[19ff.]). And it is obvious that the first efforts of Jewish Christians, like the Hellenist missionaries of Acts, to instruct their Gentile converts, would naturally proceed on the existing lines. Hence we can well conceive the genesis of the Jewish-Christian *Two Ways* out of the oral *catechesis* of missionary Judaism. But there is no evidence that there was ever a purely Jewish *Two Ways* in writing, or even that all the elements in our *Two Ways* ever before existed as a unity. Indeed, some of its precepts were probably the creation of the new and gentler Christian spirit—a spirit well represented by the positive form of the ‘Golden

* Unless the *Two Ways* had lain before the compiler of the Didache, he would hardly have written ‘my child’ in iii. 1–iv. 1, his own tendency being shown in the ‘children’ at the end of the Way of Death, and the plurals throughout chs. vii.–xvi. Nor can we imagine i. 3[b]–ii. 1, vi. 2–3, being *omitted* by any one compiling a manual for catechumens subsequent to the date of the full Didache.

† Kohler (*l.c.*) points out that such emphasis on the Decalogue, especially in the Diaspora, was probably greater before Christian disparagement of the other Mosaic laws, as temporary usages, made Judaism more guarded in the matter.

Rule,' in contrast to the negative. In the original framework of the *Two Ways*, this negative form, 'according to the traditional Jewish * interpretation' (Kohler), practically cancels the larger spirit of the words of Lv $19^{18}$; so that on it the exegesis or 'teaching' proceeds. This defect was soon felt by the Christian consciousness, and was rectified in the fuller Didache.

Of course it is impossible to assign an upper limit to the date in the history of Christianity, when something like the *Two Ways* began to be used in the preparation of raw Gentile converts for baptism. But, in the endeavour to trace its earliest written form and to assign a rough date to it, the *Epistle of Barnabas* is our primary authority.

(*b*) *The witness of 'Barnabas.'*—Its witness, indeed, is ambiguous, and has been read in opposite ways by different scholars. One thing is certain, namely, that Barnabas did not know Did. i. $3^b$–ii. 2; else it would not have failed to echo these more Evangelical precepts. But the evidence, as we shall see, is rather against the fuller Didache ever having existed without them, and to this extent against Barnabas' use of it in any form. The affinity of thought between iv. 9 f. and Did. xvi. 2 does not prove the opposite; † both may be independent expressions of sentiments current in the same region and period (cf. He $10^{23-25}$). But, confining the issue at present to the most primitive Didache, does Barnabas presuppose a written or only an oral *Two Ways*? Probably the former.

The striking verbal agreement with the very phrasing of the *Two Ways* (as found in Didache, CO, and L), conjoined with great freedom of treatment,—involving changes in thought, as well as insertions and omissions,—all this points to use of a document rather than to quotation from a familiar stereotyped tradition. For an author would be less inclined to upset the order and wrest the sense of a body of teaching which he had learned by long use.

In the case of Barnabas, moreover, the use of such a fixed tradition is the less likely in view of the writer's sense of superiority to the religious ideal embodied in the 'Teaching,' which he aims at adapting to a higher level of spirituality. He finds it a form of instruction for would-be Christians in the rudimentary principles of the new Way of Life: he turns it into a vehicle for imparting ethical 'insight' (*gnosis*) even to mature Christians, to whom he is ever saying, 'Let us become spiritual' (iv. 11). That is not the way a man treats the catechism of his own church,‡ a formulary engraven *verbatim* on his memory by constant use. It is rather the way of one who, finding a terse and time-honoured body of precepts current in a community of somewhat different traditions from his own, seizes on it from the outside, as it were, and adapts it with sovereign freedom to the edification of his own spiritual kith and kin. This, of course, involves a special view as to the genesis of Barnabas—a theory which takes its personal references seriously, and sees in its author a more or less itinerant teacher (cf. Did. xiii. 2). Yet it is a theory which also emerges naturally out of due analysis of that author's handling of the *Two Ways*.

Provisionally, then, we assume that Barnabas presupposes a written *Two Ways*, perhaps known simply as 'The Teaching' (cf. αἱ ἐντολαὶ τῆς διδαχῆς, xvi. 9) or 'Doctrine of the Lord'; but that this was only in the hands of certain church teachers, or was written down for the first time at his request and for his benefit. Thus the question of a written form at this stage is of very slight moment in the place where our author wrote his Epistle. In any case, it is probable that it was about the date of Barnabas that the *Two Ways*, after an oral career of some duration, passed into written form. It may be that in this form it speedily followed the Epistle itself to Alexandria, possibly to satisfy a demand for fuller knowledge of it created by the latter. Thus would begin the Egyptian line of tradition, which is best represented by the Latin version, and in which it seems always to have been known as 'Teaching of the Apostles.'

As to the contents of the 'Teaching' as known to Barnabas, there is good evidence that it embraced the bulk of Did. i.–v. (*i.e.* except i. $3^b$–ii. 1, missing also from L, CO, Sch, etc.). The highly Jewish 'fencing of the Law' in iii. 1-6 would not commend itself to Barnabas, any more than the related iv. 1, which he modifies in a bold way (ὡς κόρην τοῦ ὀφθαλμοῦ for ὡς κύριον). But did he know ch. vi.? If so, in what form?

Immediately after the Way of Death in Barnabas we read: 'It is good, therefore, having learnt the ordinances (δικαιώματα) of the Lord, as many as have been written, to walk in them. For he that doeth them shall be glorified in the kingdom of God: he that chooseth those others (ἐκεῖνα) shall perish together with his works. For this cause is resurrection, for this cause recompense. . . . Near (is) the day wherein all things shall perish along with the Evil One. Near (is) the Lord and his reward. Again and again I entreat you: to each other (ἑαυτῶν) be good lawgivers; to each other (ἑαυτῶν) continue faithful counsellors (σύμβουλοι); take away from among you all unreality (ὑπόκρισιν).' This is certainly nearer to the line of thought in the Lat. than to our Did. vi. 2, 3. Nor should one overlook the parallelism between the ἑαυτῶν μένετε σύμβουλοι and L's '*in consulendo.*' But if Barnabas implies L's ending, what mean the points of contact which exist between Did. vi. 2 and Barnabas? Probably a common atmosphere (see below (*d*)).

*But what date must we assign to Barnabas?* As this is a crucial matter for our Didache, which was probably rather later, reason must be shown for fixing on the reign of Vespasian, in spite of much critical opinion to the contrary.

It is a mistake in method to rely mainly on the apparent reference in ch. xvi. to a rebuilding of the Jewish temple by the Romans as imminent. For such an expectation is quite as likely to have arisen in certain circles under Vespasian, soon after the staggering catastrophe of A.D. 70, as later under Hadrian. This being so, the dating in terms of Roman emperors, apocalyptically indicated in ch. iv., is really far more secure, when due note is taken of the very peculiar situation presupposed.

'And I saw the fourth beast to be wicked and strong, and more intractable than all the beasts of the earth; and how there arose from him ten horns, and from these a little horn, an excrescence (παραφυάδιον); and how that it abased at one stroke (ὑφ' ἕν) three of the great horns.' Now when it is noted that the text of Dn $7^{7ff.}$, which is here explicitly cited, does not furnish the most distinctive phrases in this description (for which Barnabas' Greek is here given), we are sure that they contain at once its emphasis and the key to its author's meaning. Keeping this in mind, we perceive that the reign of Vespasian alone suits the conditions. He and his two sons were, for a student of apocalyptic on the look-out for striking phenomena rather than for strict Roman theory, 'three' conjoint heads of the empire, which might be smitten down 'at one stroke.' The stroke was to be delivered by Nero, reappearing as Antichrist, himself an 'offshoot' of the series of emperors, to which he had once belonged. In this solution Lightfoot and

* In view, however, of the fact that the maxim ὃ σὺ μισεῖς ἑτέρῳ μὴ ποιήσῃς is attributed to Cleobulus (one of the Seven Sages of Greece), and that this form is close to that found in To $4^{15}$ (ὃ μισεῖς μηδενὶ ποιήσῃς) and in Philo (ἅ τις παθεῖν ἐχθαίρει μὴ ποιεῖν αὐτόν), one is led to suspect that this form was first adopted by the Diaspora as a maxim already current among those they wished to convert (cf. Hillel's use of it). This assumption would account for its interpolation in the 'Western' text of Ac $15^{20-29}$, and in a somewhat different form.

† The evidence of literary dependence, on the one side or the other, is weakened when we restore the text of Barnabas to its original form, by allowing for the reflex influence of the Didache on the Sinaitic MS (cf. Harris, 55 f.).

‡ This goes against the *Two Ways* being already in use in Egypt. Indeed, if Barnabas is addressed to Alexandria, the way in which the author cites and quotes *verbatim* this 'Teaching' excludes such an hypothesis.

Ramsay agree;* and it is hard to see why any should hesitate to accept it in some form, *e.g.* in Ramsay's, which includes Julius among the 'ten kings,' and excludes Otho and Vitellius as unlikely to count as emperors in Vespasian's day.† It is strange that any one should think that Nerva satisfies the unique situation hinted at by Barnabas, touching which he might well say to his contemporary readers, 'Understand, then, ye ought.' Further, it is natural to suppose that the coincidence between the political situation and Daniel would be noticed while the new conditions were still fresh in men's thoughts, that is, early in Vespasian's reign. Hence a date as early even as A.D. 71 is more likely than one towards the end of Vespasian's reign, especially as it would be before the Flavian rule was felt to be firmly established that the idea of Nero's return to overthrow the Flavians (like the shortlived emperors of 68–69) would most readily occur.

(*c*) *Origin of the fuller Didache.* — Assuming, then, that about A.D. 70, or soon after, the 'Teaching' of the *Two Ways* was already current in definite form in one or more of the Greek-speaking regions of Palestine (*e.g.* the Maritime Plain), how are we to imagine it growing into our Didache by the addition of the ecclesiastical sections (vii.–xv.) and the eschatological conclusion (xvi.), as well as the parts of ch. i. absent from other witnesses to the *Two Ways*? In the period following immediately on A.D. 70 there still existed in Palestine a strong sense that all sacred usages of the local Ecclesia rested upon the teaching of its Apostolic founders, particularly the Twelve. But it was also felt, with some dismay, that the personal influence of these authoritative exponents of the Gospel was yearly becoming less and less. Infirmity or death was rapidly removing those of them who had not already gone to other fields of work. How, then, was their influence to be preserved unimpaired, especially among Gentile believers, over whom it must from the first have been least assured, and who were most liable to change under outside influences, which would be at their maximum on the sea-board? Sooner or later the plan would suggest itself of putting into written circulation those usages which were held to be Apostolic, for the sake both of fixity and wider diffusion. Such a method was quite in keeping with Hellenistic habits, especially when influence on non-Jews was sought. Hence it was in every way natural that the first public catechism of the Christian life and of ordered Church fellowship should be addressed 'to the Gentiles.' It was equally natural that it should be issued by its Hellenistic author or authors as 'Teaching of the Twelve Apostles,' who were to all Palestinian Christians essentially *the* authorities as to their Lord's mind and will.‡ Finally, what more natural than to adopt an existing body of precepts like the *Two Ways*, already held to embody Apostolic teaching on the duty of the Gentile turned Christian, and to enlarge the scope of the title 'Teaching'—even at the risk of making it cover rather more than it would suggest § to a Greek at any rate?

* Lightfoot, *Clement*, ii. 503 ff.; Ramsay, *Church in the Roman Empire*, 307–309.

† This is clearly true of Vitellius, but not equally so of Otho, who was dead before Vespasian became a candidate for the purple. Accordingly, the present writer prefers to reckon from Augustus and to exclude Vitellius only (so Eusebius, *HE* iii. 5. 1, who may here reflect the view of contemporary writings). It is probable that St. John's Apocalypse also reckoned from Augustus, in its similar passage, $17^{9\text{-}11}$: see edition in the 'Century Bible,' 53 ff.

‡ Here one may observe that vi. 3 represents the spirit of the *concordat* of Ac $15^{20.\,28\text{f.}}$, now seemingly applied with larger liberty for the individual conscience.

§ Note the tendency to modify it as time goes on, whether into *Doctrinæ* (*de Aleatoribus*, iv.) or Διδασκαλία, the title of a work which was meant to supersede our Didache, at least as regards its ecclesiastical parts.

As the enlargement of contents consisted mainly in the addition of matter distinctively Christian in character, the Teaching or Doctrine was now referred, no longer to 'the Lord' God, but to 'the Lord' Christ, the special source of His Apostles' teaching. Thus would arise the title 'Teaching of the Lord, through the Twelve Apostles, to the Gentiles.'

(*d*) *Its exact contents.* — But while, no doubt, this enlarged Didache from the first contained the bulk of chs. vii.–xvi., did it contain all or any of the precepts now found in Did. i. $3^{b}$–ii. 1?

(1) Did. i. $3^{b}$–ii. 1 reads as follows:—

i. 3: 'Bless them that curse you, and pray for your enemies, but fast for them that persecute you. For what thank is there, if ye love them that love you? Do not even the Gentiles the same? But love ye them that hate you, and ye shall not have an enemy.

4: 'Abstain (thou) from fleshly and bodily lusts. If any one give thee a blow on the right cheek, turn to him the other also, and thou shalt be perfect. If any one compel thee to go with him one mile, go with him twain. If any one take away thy cloak, give him thy coat also. If any one take from thee what is thine, ask it not back, for neither canst thou.

5: 'Give to every one that asketh of thee, and ask not back; for to all the Father wills that gifts be given from his own bounties. Blessed is he that giveth according to the commandment; for he is guiltless. Woe to him that taketh; for if, indeed, any one having need taketh, he shall be guiltless; but he that hath not need shall give account wherefore he took anything and for what purpose; and being put in restraint, shall be examined concerning his conduct, and shall not come out thence till he have paid the last farthing. Yea, too, concerning this very matter it hath been said, Let thine alms sweat into thine hands, till thou have learnt to whom to give.

ii. 1: 'And the second commandment of the teaching is'—

The problem is a delicate one, and the evidence is earlier and fuller for i. 5 than for i. 3, 4. Thus we have nothing in Hermas parallel to i. $3^{b}$–4, as *Mand.* ii. 4–6 is parallel to i. 5; and the same holds also for Clement of Alexandria, if not for Irenæus.* Moreover, the phrase κατὰ τὴν ἐντολήν (i. 5) occurs twice in xiv. 5, 7; so that it seems characteristic of the original compiler of the full work. Again, it is only what we should have expected if the mind which added vii.–xvi. should find something wanting in an exposition of love to God and one's fellow which began with illustration of the negative form of the latter, without a word on its positive aspect. And when we look at the contents of the precepts for which we suppose him responsible, we find the one in which κατὰ τὴν ἐντολήν occurs to accord excellently with what we read in ix. 3. For there God's gifts of food and drink to mankind at large are referred to, and a verb (ἐχαρίσω) is used which contains the special notion expressed by the word for 'gifts' (χαρίσματα) in our passage.

The closing paragraph of ch. i. is of such importance, both for the date of our Didache and for its use in later times, as to merit special notice. 'But yet touching this topic, too, it hath been said, Let thy alms go on sweating into thine hands until thou perceive to whom to give' (ἀλλὰ καὶ περὶ τούτου δὲ [δὴ] εἴρηται, Ἱδρωτάτω ἡ ἐλεημοσύνη σου εἰς τὰς χεῖράς σου, μέχρις ἂν γνῷς τίνι δῷς). The sense of this is doubtful. On the whole, it seems best to regard it as qualifying the idea of indiscriminate giving suggested in the foregoing paragraph, which simply puts the *onus* on the person who asks and receives under false pretences. Here it is to be observed, as Dr. C. Taylor has shown,† that the limitation is not so much of what has been actually said (viz. that every one *who asks* is to receive, without question), as of what might hastily be inferred from it, viz. that there is no place for restraint and discrimination in giving. There is, in fact, the case where a man is ready to volunteer alms; and then he is right to hold his hand, and let the means of giving (gained by one's sweat) go on gathering it in, until a fit recipient be found. But, whatever its meaning may be, this saying touched a very living question in ancient and mediæval

* The relations of Hermas and Clement to our Didache are discussed below (p. $446^{a}$). As to Irenæus, the fragment (No. 10, ed. Harvey, ii. 477), ἐν ῳ ἂν τις δύναιτο (*var. lec.* δύναται) εὖ ποιεῖν τοῖς (*var. lec.* τοὺς) πλησίον καὶ οὐ (*var. lec.* μὴ) ποιεῖ, ἀλλότριος τῆς ἀγάπης (τοῦ) κυρίου νομισθήσεται, may well be an echo of Did. i. 5, read in its context as the fulfilment of the twofold law of love in i. 2.

† In an exhaustive discussion in *The Journal of Philology*, xix. 184 ff. See also the passage from John Climacus, below.

Christian ethics,* and so attracted a good deal of subsequent attention and comment. If, then, we may infer that the passage in the Did. is the fountainhead of this maxim in the Fathers and schoolmen, it proves that to some of them at least our Did. was known, down to the 5th cent. and later, and that in the West † as well as the East. It is true that at first sight the maxim, as introduced with *εἴρηται*, might seem to come rather from some OT Scripture, especially as Augustine cites it with '*et alio loco Scriptura dicit: Sudet,*' etc. But the nearest known OT passage is the *ἐὰν εὖ ποιῇς, γνῶθι τίνι ποιεῖς* of Sir 12[1]; while, had a nearer been known to Augustine and others, they would somewhere have given us more than the former's *alio loco*. Hence we may conclude that Sir 12[1] is in fact the ultimate basis of the *εἴρηται* in the Didache, but that its phrasing of the maxim is in terms of some current (? Rabbinic) paraphrase of it (cf. *ἐρρέθη* in Mt 5[33. 43]).

This is so far confirmed by a passage in Nicetas' catena on Mt 5[42]: 'We should do alms, yet with judgment and to the worthy, that we may *find a recompense from the Most High*.' ‡ In the words in italics there is a clear echo of Sir 12[2], so that what precedes is probably based on 12[1]. Thus this passage in Sirach seems to have been the *locus classicus* for the idea of giving *μετὰ κρίσεως καὶ τοῖς ἀξίοις*,—to use Nicetas' words; and the more concrete saying under discussion was perhaps a current form of it.§ Whether this maxim was already in the Didache as known to Clement of Alex. is an open question. But if we find him expressing the sentiment in immediate conjunction with the thought with which it is connected in the Didache, there is a presumption that he knew that work to contain it. Now this happens in his *Quis dives salvus*.‖ May it not be, too, that the 'libellus ab apostolis' known by Origen to contain 'Beatus est qui etiam jejunat pro eo ut alat pauperes,' was our Didache expanded in i. 5?

We have yet to consider the relations of Hermas and the *Didascalia* to our Didache i. 5 as a whole. The *Didascalia* (as reconstructed from the Syriac and the Verona Latin fragment) has the following in bk. iv. 2, 3: 'Truly blessed is he who is able to help himself, and so avoid pressing on the place of (relief belonging to) the orphan, the stranger, and the widow. This grace, moreover, is of God. *But woe to those who have and hypocritically take, or who take when able to help themselves.* But every one who takes shall give account to the Lord God in the judgment-day, wherefore he took. . . . *He who has and takes hypocritically, or through laziness*, instead of working and so helping himself and others, *shall incur judgment* with God. . . . He, then, who gives simply (*ἁπλῶς*) to all, gives well, as far as he is concerned ('sicut est illi'), and is guiltless ('innocens' = *ἀθῷος*). He, too, who takes because of affliction (*θλιβόμενος*) . . . takes well, and shall be glorified by God in life eternal.' Here the words in italics seem simply to make more explicit the middle clauses of Did. i. 5, viz. 'Woe to him that takes; for if indeed any one having need takes, he shall be guiltless (*ἀθῷος*); but he that hath not need, shall give satisfaction (*δώσει δίκην*) why and wherefore he took.' As to the rest of the quotation, it seems to echo our Didache ¶ in its antithesis *ἀληθῶς μακάριος, οὐαὶ . . . λαμβάνουσιν*, which is parallel to Did. alone.** On the other hand, Hermas is the probable source of the other matter. For its form follows closely the phrasing of Hermas, *Mand*. ii. 5 f., *e.g. οἱ μὲν γὰρ λαμβάνοντες θλιβόμενοι . . . ὁ οὖν διδοὺς* (*ἁπλῶς* thrice in the immediate context, besides *πᾶσιν ὑστερουμένοις δίδου ἁπλῶς* above) *ἀθῷός ἐστιν . . . ἔνδοξος παρὰ τῷ θεῷ . . . ὁ οὖν οὕτως ἁπλῶς διακονῶν, τῷ θεῷ ζήσεται.* Further, the idea of the pious labour and merit of the recipient, in praying for the donor, may well come from *Sim*. ii. 6, 7, just as the idea of the needy as God's altar, here and elsewhere (ii. 26, iii. 6, 7, 14) in the *Didascalia*, goes back to Polycarp, *ad Phil*. iv. 3.

As to the relative priority of our Didache and Hermas, the case seems here as clearly in favour of the former as elsewhere.* But if so, it is probable that Hermas' repeated *μὴ διστάζων* (*διακρίνων*) *τίνι δῷς ἢ τίνι μὴ δῷς* is a protest against the *μέχρις ἂν γνῷς τίνι δῷς* of Did., and that consequently *Ἱδρωτάτω*, etc., stood in the Didache as known to Hermas, and is, in fact, perhaps echoed in *ἐκ τῶν κόπων σου . . . δίδου*. It seems, indeed, that Hermas' protest is twofold. He protests, first, against trying to distinguish the good and bad; it is enough that they be needy; that, he says, is God's own principle (cf. Mt 5[45]). Then he goes further, and protests against trying to distinguish between real and apparent need; that, he says, is the receiver's look-out. But whatever Hermas may or may not have in mind, Did. i. 5 *fin*., in writing *ἀλλὰ καὶ περὶ τούτου δὴ εἴρηται*, probably means to apply what follows only to the need of distinguishing real from feigned need: so *Apost. Const*. iii. 4, *χρὴ γὰρ εὖ ποιεῖν πάντας ἀνθρώπους, μὴ φιλοκρινοῦντας τοῦτον ὅστις ἢ ἢ ἐκεῖνον· ὁ γὰρ κύριός φησι, Παντὶ τῷ αἰτοῦντί σε δίδου· δῆλον δὲ ὡς τῷ χρῄζοντι κατ' ἀλήθειαν.*

But we can hardly imagine the 'Teaching' proper, at any stage, to have opened abruptly with a section on giving; and, in fact, we observe in what immediately precedes in our MS that the phrase *καὶ ἔσῃ τέλειος* has its parallel in vi. 2. Nor is the parallel merely verbal. The idea of the phrase is probably the same in both cases, and belongs to the same mode of thought as meets us in Ja 1[25] 2[12] 3[2], touching a *νόμος ἐλευθερίας* and a *τέλειος ἀνήρ* in relation to it (cf. Mt 5[48] 19[21]).

The feeling that though a certain perfection of self-mastery was the Christian ideal, it could not be insisted upon for all in practice, seems to have been rather general among the second generation of Christians, when as yet even the most exacting Gospel precepts were taken seriously by all as the law of their new life. It meets us not only in Did. i. 4, vi. 2, 3, but also in Barnabas, and that in a way which does not point to dependence of the one on the other. In Did. vi. 2, 3 it takes this form: 'If, indeed, thou canst bear the whole yoke of the Lord, thou shalt be perfect; but if thou canst not, what thou canst, that do. But touching food, bear what thou canst; but of that offered to idols greatly beware, for it is worship of dead gods.' In Barnabas we read of 'the new law of our Lord Jesus Christ—without yoke of constraint as it is' (ii. 6); and of the spiritual, not ritual, obedience which belongs to it. On the other hand, we have in his *Two Ways* the exhortation, 'as much as thou canst thou shalt be pure (*ἁγνεύσεις*) in the interests of thy soul,' following on a specially exacting precept as to control of the tongue (xix. 8, cf. Ja 3[2] for the tongue as test of the 'perfect man'). This breathes the same spirit as speaks in Barn. iv. 11, 'Let us be spiritual, let us be a temple perfect to the Lord; as much as is in us, let us practise the fear of God; let us strive to guard his precepts.' Thus Barnabas has the same idea as Did. vi. 2, the meaning of which he helps to fix; but he puts it in his own way, without showing trace of Did. vi. 2 any more than of Did. i. 4.

Thus the author of our Didache intends his qualifying paragraph in vi. 2 to refer to the 'teaching' already given in i.–v.; and his recognition that 'the yoke of the Lord' includes what might overtax the moral power of some, becomes more natural if we suppose that he had in mind high counsels like those in i. 4, 5,† which he had himself introduced.

So far there seems good reason for holding that the full Didache originally embraced the precepts in Did. i. 4, 5. But was that all, and did it open, fitly enough, with the general precept, 'Abstain thou from bodily lusts'?

*Ἀπέχου τῶν σαρκικῶν καὶ σωματικῶν ἐπιθυμιῶν.* Here there may be dependence on 1 P 2[11]; but more probably *σαρκικῶν* is an interpolation from 1 P 2[11], to explain the less biblical *σωματικῶν*, which the *Apost. Const*. changes into *κοσμικῶν*. Cf. 4 Mac 1[32] *τῶν δὲ ἐπιθυμιῶν αἱ μέν εἰσιν ψυχικαί, αἱ δὲ σωματικαί.* The present writer cannot think (with Ropes, *Die Sprüche Jesu*, 40) that this maxim is to be viewed 'as an abstract reproduction of such passages as Mt 5[27 ff.]'. It goes too closely with what follows. The best parallel is Hermas, *Mand*. xii., where all virtues are referred to *ἡ ἐπιθυμία ἡ ἀγαθή* (*ὁ γὰρ φόβος τοῦ θεοῦ κατοικεῖ ἐν τῇ ἐπιθυμίᾳ τῇ ἀγαθῇ*, 2, 4), and all vices to *ἡ ἐπιθυμία ἡ πονηρά* (*Ἀπέχεσθαι οὖν δεῖ ἀπὸ τῶν ἐπιθυμιῶν τῶν πονηρῶν, ἵνα ἀποσχόμενοι ζήσητε τῷ θεῷ*, 2, 2). Cf. *Mand*. viii., with its maxim, *ἡ*

---

* Dr. Taylor is too ready to take the sense put upon the maxim by Augustine and later writers, specially in the West, as fixing its meaning in the Didache. Its original context in the Didache requires that the stress fall on the *μέχρις ἂν γνῷς τίνι δῷς*, *i.e.* the arrest of the impulse to give; while in Augustine, Cassiodorus, and Bernard, at any rate, the emphasis is on the *justum* which they insert ('*donec invenias justum cui eam tradas*').

† Here the divergences in text are against all being dependent on Augustine.

‡ The exact parallel to *Apost. Const*. iv. 3 which follows in Nicetas, with Κλεμ. in the margin, is, in fact, derived from that work, Clement of Rome being its supposititious author. Its attribution to Clem. Alex. is due to a mere guess of Corderius, the first editor of Nicetas' catena, as is shown by F. X. Funk, *Kirchengesch. Abhandlungen*, ii. 126 f.

§ Compare the Rabbinic saying, 'He that receiveth alms without needing the same, shall come to want before he dies' (*Kĕthûbôth*, 68*a*).

‖ Ch. xxxi. *ad fin*., where he says that the principle in Mt 10[41 f.], as to making friends by the worldly Mammon, is even more divine than *παντὶ τῷ αἰτοῦντί σε δίδου*, since it teaches one not to wait to be asked, *ἀλλ' αὐτὸς ἀναζητεῖν ὅστις ἄξιος εὖ παθεῖν*. That he has Did. i. 5 in mind, is suggested by his adding *θεοῦ γὰρ ὄντως ἡ τοιαύτη φιλοδωρία* to *παντί, κ.τ.λ.*, as Did. adds, *πᾶσι γὰρ θέλει δίδοσθαι ὁ πατὴρ ἐκ τῶν ἰδίων χαρισμάτων.*

¶ The *Didascalia* is certainly dependent on our Didache elsewhere (cf. Holzhey, *Die Abhängigkeit des syr. Didaskalia von der Didache*, München, 1898).

** The nearest known parallel is the sentiment in Ac 20[35], which the interpolated *Apost. Const*. iv. 3, actually substitutes here, in the form *ἐπεὶ καὶ ὁ κύριος μακάριον εἶπεν εἶναι τὸν διδόντα ἤπερ τὸν λαμβάνοντα.*

* Dr. Taylor's paper in the *Journal of Philology*, xviii. 297 ff., almost amounts to demonstration on both issues.

† Cf. John Climacus (sæc. vi.) *εὐσεβῶν μὲν τὸ αἰτοῦντι διδόναι, εὐσεβέστερον δὲ καὶ τῷ μὴ αἰτοῦντι· τὸ δὲ ἀπὸ τοῦ αἴροντος μὴ ἀπαιτεῖν, δυναμένους μάλιστα, τάχα τῶν ἀπαθῶν καὶ μόνων ἴδιον καθέστηκεν.* This passage suggests that *εἰ* has fallen out from the phrase *οὐδὲ γὰρ δύνασαι* at the end of i. 4. 'Nay, not even if thou art able' would make good sense after 'Ask not back' thine own.

'γκράτεια διπλῆ ἐστίν· ἐπί τινων γὰρ δεῖ ἐγκρατεύεσθαι, ἐπί τινων δὲ οὐ δεῖ . . . ἐγκράτευσαι οὖν ἀπὸ πονηρίας πάσης, ἐργαζόμενος τὸ ἀγαθόν: so *2 Clem.* xvi. 3, μὴ ἀντιπαρελκώμεθα ἀπὸ τῶν κοσμικῶν ἐπιθυμιῶν.

No doubt this has reference to what follows,—repression of the instincts to 'hit back' and to hold fast one's possessions. For such instincts spring largely from bodily impulse, while unresentfulness (ἀνεξικακία, cf. Justin, *Apol.* i. 16) is a victory of spirit over body, a supreme form of self-control (σωφροσύνη or ἐγκράτεια). Yet, admitting this connexion, would the 'Teaching' or exposition of the fundamental commands in Did. i. 2 be likely to begin with unresentfulness, rather than with what we find in i. 3, as also in Lk $6^{27f.}$? It is hard to decide. The very fact that i. 2 does precede might make the compiler pass at once to the most concrete and practical examples of the spirit of love, viz. unresentfulness and active charity, rather than dwell further on the feeling of love* and its secret acts of prayer and fasting. Again, it is rather strange that in i. 3 (and there alone) the plural 'Bless ye,' etc., appears at the head of precepts purporting to be addressed to the individual catechumen. For it is not as though at this time the *ipsissima verba* of the Lord's precepts were felt to be too sacred to be adapted to the context in which they were cited. Yet such arguments seem weaker than those pointing to i. 3 as originally part of our Didache. For, first, our Didache really has in mind not the single convert, but Christians in general, as comes out in its 'May ye, children, be delivered from all these' (at the end of the Evil Way). Next, the clauses, '*fast* for those who persecute you,' 'and ye shall not have an enemy,' are not found in our Gospels; and the latter at least seems to have influenced Justin Martyr both in his *Dialogue* and *Apology*. Indeed, Justin practically follows i. 3 as a whole, where it deviates from our Gospels.

*Apol.* i. 15, εὔχεσθε ὑπὲρ τῶν ἐχθρῶν ὑμῶν καὶ ἀγαπᾶτε τοὺς μισοῦντας ὑμᾶς καὶ εὐλογεῖτε τοὺς καταρωμένους ὑμῖν καὶ εὔχεσθε ὑπὲρ τῶν ἐπηρεαζόντων ὑμᾶς. The sentiment καὶ οὐχ ἕξετε ἐχθρόν is traced in *Apol.* i. 14, *Dial.* 254 B, as also in *Clem. Hom.* xii. 32, by Dr. C. Taylor (*Expositor*, 3rd series, vi. 364 f., where Justin's relation to the Did. is examined). To which may be added *Apol. of Aristides*, 15, τοὺς ἀδικοῦντας αὐτοὺς παρακαλοῦσι καὶ προσφιλεῖς αὐτοὺς ἑαυτοῖς ποιοῦσιν. Nor does it seem mere accident that *Mand.* ii., which begins Hermas' exposition of the faith and fear of God, in enjoining childlike ἁπλότης and ἀκακία first specifies abstinence from καταλαλία (καὶ εὐθηνίαν πάντοτε ἕξεις μετὰ πάντων), and then deals with the duty of giving (ἁπλῶς).

To sum up. The fuller Didache seems, from the first, to have contained all, or very nearly all,† of ch. i. as it stands in our MS. Its title was the second and longer one of our MS, under which it was perhaps known to Hermas, whose Twelve Mandates (ἐντολαί), artificially drawn out to that number, seem suggested by those of the Twelve Apostles. Again, they and their teaching 'to the Gentiles' may be alluded to in the Twelve nations‡ who inhabit the world, and to whom 'the Son of God was heralded by the Apostles.' Justin Martyr also shows himself familiar with the exact idea of this title, when he writes of τοὺς ἀπὸ παντὸς ἔθνους ἀνθρώπων διὰ τῆς παρὰ τῶν ἀποστόλων αὐτοῦ διδαχῆς πεισθέντας καὶ παραιτησαμένους τὰ παλαιὰ ἐν οἷς πλανώμενοι ἀνεστράφησαν ἔθη (*Apol.* i. 53, cf. ii. 2, τὰ καλὰ ἑαυτῷ συνεπιστάμενος διὰ τὴν ἀπὸ τοῦ Χριστοῦ διδαχήν, τὸ διδασκάλιον τῆς θείας ἀρετῆς ὡμολόγησεν). And, indeed, it may well be that the very form in which Justin, in common with the *Kerygma Petri*, Hermas, 2 Clement, and the *Apology of Aristides*, conceives Christianity, viz. as revealed 'teaching' on virtue and vice, owes much to the influence on the first half of the second century of the Christianity set forth in the Διδαχὴ κυρίου διὰ τῶν δώδεκα ἀποστόλων τοῖς ἔθνεσιν. This would help to explain the degree to which 'moralism,' with its notions of the Divine ἐντολαί and μισθὸς δικαιοσύνης, colours that literature. Certainly the title of our book suits the attitude of orthodox circles in the closing years of the first century, when Papias was on the look-out for those who related τὰς παρὰ τοῦ κυρίου τῇ πίστει δεδομένας (ἐντολάς), as witnessed by personal 'disciples of the Lord' (Euseb. *HE* iii. 39).

(2) As to chs. vii.–xvi., it is usually assumed that they are homogeneous, and contain nothing alien to the original Didache in its enlarged form. But this is hardly accurate; and though the accretions are wonderfully few and slight, when we remember the nature of the Didache and the drastic handling to which in other forms it has been subjected (see below, B. 'Transformations,' etc.), it is the more worth while referring to them, that they furnish the sole excuse for a paradoxical theory that our Didache 'did not exist as a book before the 4th century.'* Besides a number of mistaken or inconclusive criteria of lateness,† the treatment of Baptism in ch. vii. is rightly appealed to as unprimitive. It is true that Affusion has here nothing to do with '*clinic* baptism' (as Dr. Bigg supposes), and therefore is not in itself a mark of late date. But the change of address, from the plural of the community to the singular of the officiating minister, suggests a later hand; and the suspicion is borne out by the *Apost. Const.* (in what it has and has not), as well as by the unusual concern for detail—the casuistry of baptism, so to speak—which marks these clauses. They find their fullest parallel in the *Clementine Homilies* (ix. 19, xi. 26, iii. 73, xiii. 9, 11), and may belong to about the same period. This applies to vii. 2, 3, and to the end of vii. 4. But the injunction to the baptizer and baptized to fast beforehand, and to any others who can to join them in this, is probably original (cf. Justin, *Apol.* i. 61, ἡμῶν συνευχομένων καὶ συννηστευόντων αὐτοῖς). Other minor secondary features are the form of the Doxology in ix. 4, which the quotation in Athan. *de Virg.* (with the parallel passage in the *Apost. Const.*) shows once to have been, as elsewhere in the Didache, σοῦ ἐστιν ἡ δύναμις καὶ ἡ δόξα; and the possible insertion of ix. $5^b$ καὶ γὰρ περὶ τούτου εἴρηκεν ὁ κύριος, Μὴ δῶτε τὸ ἅγιον τοῖς κυσί. In this latter case the formula of citation εἴρηκεν ὁ κύριος is certainly not unprimitive; but the idea (the ἅγια ἁγίοις of later liturgies) is not found connected with Mt $7^6$ before Clement (*Strom.* II. ii. 7) and Tertullian (*de Præsc.* xli.). Further, it duplicates what appears in more primitive form in x. $6^b$, εἴ τις ἅγιος, ἐρχέσθω· εἴ τις οὐκ ἔστι, μετανοείτω; and the more elaborate parallel in *Apost. Const.*, which has the like

* Like *Test. Issachar*, 5, ἀγαπᾶτε κύριον καὶ τὸν πλησίον, πένητα καὶ ἀσθενῆ ἐλεᾶτε (the practical result of ἁπλότης to God and man).

† Observe the similar Evangelical matter in ch. xvi., which is generally admitted to have been part of the fuller Didache from the first. Yet while we find early traces of 'Ιδρωτάτω, etc., *e.g.* in Hermas (see above, p. $446^b$), it is otherwise with the penalty of the deceitful receiver; moreover, the connexion between 'Ιδρωτάτω, etc. and what precedes would gain by its omission. But if an interpolation, it must be early, as it is not assimilated to our Gospels.

‡ *Sim.* ix. 17. 1: so Dr. Taylor, *Journ. of Phil.* xviii. 298. Yet Hermas may rather have the spiritual analogue of the Twelve tribes of Israel in view (cf. Mt $19^{28}$). It is noteworthy that in *Mand.* xii. 3. 2 we read συνετέλεσεν οὖν τὰς ἐντολὰς τὰς δώδεκα, and then follows a rebuke of the suggestion that these ἐντολαί are too hard for man to keep. It looks as if Did. vi. 2 were being abused in the practice of some. On the other hand, the νηστεία τελεία of *Sim.* v. 3. 6 transforms the τελειότης of Did. i. 4, vi. 2, into 'merit.'

* Dr. C. Bigg, *Doctrine of the Twelve Apostles* (S.P.C.K. 1898).

† Some simply turn into proofs of *very* early date, *e.g.* the following: 'At what date would it be thought lawful to publish the Lord's Prayer and a collection of Eucharistic prayers in a book of this description?' This seems to the present writer to tell rather heavily against the relatively late dates of Harnack and others, and in favour of a first century date.

thought without citing the words of Mt $7^{6}$, shows how apt such an idea was to creep into the text. Finally, in xii. 5, the striking word 'Christmonger' (Χριστέμπορος, in contrast to Χριστιανός at the end of xii. 4) may be suspected of being late in origin. Certainly its use elsewhere is late, beginning perhaps with pseudo-Clement (*Epist. de Virg.* I. x. 4, xi. 4, xiii. 5) and Athanasius (*de Pseudo-proph.*, echoing Did.); nor does *Apost. Const.* make use of it, or indeed of xii. 2–5 as a whole. This, however, cannot do more than render the early date of xii. 5 or even xii. 2–5 rather less certain than that of the work as a whole. With such reservations, then, the original contents of the fuller Didache (probably as Hermas knew it) were practically those of our MS.

iv. CHURCH CONDITIONS IMPLIED IN THE DIDACHE.—This subject will be discussed more fully under C. Enough here to indicate certain features bearing on origin and date. Thus the degree to which its Christianity is still expressed in forms determined by Judaism, while yet its attitude to unbelieving Judaism ('the hypocrites') is one of bitter hostility, seems a highly primitive trait. It has more in common with the Epistle of James than with any other Christian document; only, the judgment which James felt near at hand has fallen, and has left Judaism as a whole still impenitent—apostate in the eyes of our author. Yet even he is swayed by Jewish sentiment in matters such as dietary restrictions (vi. 3), where inherited instinct would naturally leave a preference, even when Gentiles were concerned. And so vi. 3 shows a qualified survival of the compromise laid down in Ac $15^{20}$, with a clear distinction between different elements in it: 'Now touching food, bear what thou canst; but of food offered to idols greatly beware, for it is worship of dead gods.' Observe, too, the natural, allusive way in which it is said: 'All first-fruits . . . thou shalt take and give as the first-fruits to the prophets; for they are your chief priests. . . . Take the first-fruits and give according to the commandment' (xiii. 3, 5, 7). It is the age of transition, when the old forms of Palestinian Judaism are being adapted to the new religion of the Spirit, of which the prophet is the type.

But it is in the Eucharistic forms that this primitive continuity of thought and feeling is most apparent. We are still in the atmosphere of 'the breaking of bread' as it appears in Acts. The ideal implied in the Didache might (with the substitution of second-hand for first-hand Apostolic teaching) be summed up in the words of Ac $2^{42}$ 'They were keeping steadfastly to the teaching of the Apostles and to the communion—the breaking of bread and the prayers.' 'The breaking of bread' in Thanksgiving (Eucharist) is still viewed as 'the expressive act by which the unity of the many, as partakers of the one Divine sustenance, is signified' (Hort, *Christian Ecclesia*, 44): and here we have samples of 'the prayers' in which the thanksgiving was expressed. When we examine these prayers, they are seen to be transformed Jewish *Bĕrākhôth* over food; only, the parallel between the bodily and spiritual food reappears in a yet more impressive form, and the looking forward to the restitution of the Davidic Kingdom (here alluded to in 'the Holy Vine of David Thy servant'), with the festal joy of a united and blessed Israel, receives a nobler Messianic meaning. Indeed, the more the parallel with Ac $2^{42-47}$ is studied, the more the identity of spirit comes out; and a conviction arises that the writings belong to nearly the same epoch * (cf. the προφῆται καὶ διδάσκαλοι of Ac $13^{1}$ with Did. xiii. 1, 2, xv. 2). Particularly is this so, when we observe the agreement of Didache and Luke's Gospel (on either text) with respect to the order of the Cup and the Bread. For, however we may explain the liturgical usage here revealed, it is hard to believe that it would be thus enjoined, without a sign of embarrassment, once the Gospel of Matthew, with its opposite order in the story of the Last Supper, had become generally known in Palestine. Such a consideration tends to exclude the notion that the Didache means our Matthew in those cases where it cites 'the Gospel' (viii. 2, xi. 3, xv. 3, 4)—a view otherwise unlikely, owing to the fact that it also quotes Evangelical phrases found only in Luke. Add to this the nature of the ministry, especially the central significance of the prophet and the absence of any one presiding administrative official; the absence of any trace of public persecution, of any fixed creed, any conscious theological tendency, or any special heresy to be guarded against; and, finally, the type of its eschatology—and the general effect is that of a stage in primitive Christianity not later than the close of the 1st century.

* The present writer assigns the Lukan writings, like Barn., to Vespasian's reign.

J. Réville, *Les Origines de l'Épiscopat*, 260 f., well says: 'Certainly the compiler of the *Didache*, like all genuine Christians from the beginning, has a very lively sense of the unity of the Christian Society. But this unity is all spiritual and mystical: it does not yet manifest itself in any ecclesiastical organism. . . . The veritable organs of the essential unity of the Church are still the apostles and, above all, the itinerant prophets, all those who go from city to city, from village to village, to be the witnesses of one and the same evangelic tradition and the interpreters of one and the same Christian inspiration. Precautions have already to be taken concerning them, lest they abuse their position; but there is as yet no thought of subordinating them to any ecclesiastical authorities. The sovereignty of the Spirit is still undisputed, and knows no other control than that of the conscience of the faithful.'

v. DATE.—In trying to reach a yet more exact date, we are hampered by ignorance of the relative rate of development in different countries, especially as it happens that primitive features were likely to linger longest in Palestine, to which internal evidence points directly. Accordingly it is rash to say of Palestine, that after a given decade such a manual would no longer be in correspondence with its environment. Still it does seem possible to show that certain decades are more probable than others, even in Palestine. Nor is documentary evidence here quite so wanting as is often supposed, if we may take Dr. R. H. Charles' views on the *Ascension of Isaiah* as substantially correct. He shows that the striking Christian section (iii. $13^{b}$–iv. 18)—which he gives reasons for believing to have belonged originally to a larger 'Testament of Hezekiah' (known to Cedrenus)—reflects conditions as they existed within the lifetime of the last of those who had seen their Lord in the flesh (iv. 13), *i.e.* not later than A.D. 100. Further, the Hebraic cast of the style and the circle of ideas in this section point strongly to Palestine, or at least Syria, as the region to which its descriptions apply most directly. Here, then, are data for testing the state of things implied in the Didache by criteria belonging to a similar local type of Christianity. The following quotations exhibit the main points of contact. After an account of the first advent of 'the Beloved' (*i.e.* Messiah as God's παῖς, as in Did. ix. x.; see Mt $12^{18}$, citing Is $42^{1ff.}$) and 'the discipling of the Twelve' (ἡ τῶν δώδεκα μαθητεία), we read—

'He will send forth his disciples, and they shall disciple all the nations and every tongue unto the resurrection of the Beloved . . . and his ascension into the seventh heaven, whence he came: and many who believe in him will speak in the Holy Spirit. . . . And on the eve of his approach, his disciples will let go the preaching (προφητείαν) of his Twelve Apostles, and their faith and love and their purity (ἁγνείαν):

and there will be many factions on the eve of his approach. And there will be in those days many desiring to rule, though void of wisdom: and there will be many lawless elders and shepherds unjust towards their sheep, which shall be ravaged for want of pure shepherds. . . . And there will be much slander and vainglory . . . and the Holy Spirit will depart from the many: and there will not be in those days many prophets speaking sure things, but only one here and there in divers places, by reason of the Spirit of error and of fornication and vainglory and love of money, which shall be in those who will be called servants of that One and in those who will receive him. And there will be great hatred in the shepherds and elders towards each other.* For there will be much jealousy in the last days, for each will speak what is pleasing in his own eyes: and they will let go utterly the prophecies of the prophets who were before me (Isaiah): and these very visions they will treat as void, in order that they may utter the impulses of their own heart' (iii. 13-31).

Next follows a description of the descent of Beliar 'in the likeness of a man, a king, lawless, a matricide, one who himself—the king—will persecute the plant which the Twelve Apostles of the Beloved shall plant; and of the Twelve, one shall be delivered into his hands.' This Nero-Antichrist is then pictured as emulating the superhuman powers of the Messiah—

'He will act and speak like the Beloved, and will say, "I am God, and before me there has been none." . . . And the greater part of those who shall have been associated together in order to receive (=wait for) the Beloved, he will turn aside after him. . . . And he will set up his image before him in every city. . . . And many believers and saints, having seen him for whom they were hoping,' namely, Jesus the Christ, 'and those also who became believers in him—of these few in those days will be left as his servants, while they flee from solitude to solitude, awaiting the coming of the Beloved' (iv. 2-13).

It is true that one must not forget that in all this we are listening to an apocalyptist—one who as such is apt to dwell on the darker hues of days which he regards as the 'darkest hour before the dawn,' familiar to all apocalyptic. Yet allowing for this, as also for some phrases and clauses which may be due to the final redactor of the *Ascension*, the impression remains that the degree to which deterioration has invaded the communities specially in the writer's mind, particularly the degree to which 'the prophet' is already discredited,—not to speak of the greater relative prominence of the local 'pastors' and 'elders,'—that all this implies a state of things at least as late in the development of the Syrian or Palestinian† Churches as what meets us in the Didache. Surely such a picture of defection from the 'love and purity' of Messiah's 'Twelve Apostles' presents a wide contrast to the life among Christians as contemplated by the compiler of the Didache, and tells somewhat against a later date. In particular, the absence of explicit warning against possible faults in the local leaders, like those of the 'elders' and 'shepherds' cited above, deserves notice. Instead of this, the only hint of actual faults within the brotherhood is the injunction to 'reprove one another, not in wrath, but in peace,' and to visit with temporary spiritual ostracism the brother who offends against his fellow (xv. 3). In any case the attitude and mode of thought evidenced in the *Ascension*, in its reference to 'the preaching of his Twelve Apostles' as the norm of faith and conduct, to which Christians in the last days were like to prove unfaithful, furnishes a close parallel to the idea of the 'Teaching of the Lord, through the Twelve Apostles, to the Gentiles.' Thus it is natural to regard these two writings as almost contemporary attempts to extend the influence of the traditions going back to 'the Twelve Apostles.' Only, the author of the Didache did not see such difficulties in the way as were patent to the eye of the apocalyptist, writing further, perhaps, from the original centres of Apostolic activity, yet seemingly before A.D. 100. Accordingly, as to date, it seems best to say with confidence,* 'before rather than after A.D. 100,' and with diffidence, 'A.D. 80–90 is the most likely decade known to us.'

* So the Ethiopic, the Greek here being lost.

† There was probably enough common consciousness throughout the regions in question to warrant the argument as stated in the text.



The following weighty passage from Dr. C. Taylor's *Teaching of the Twelve Apostles*, p. 118, deserves quotation on several grounds:—

'Everything which goes to confirm its Jewish character has a bearing on the question of its date. If it is derived immediately from Jewish sources, it must either have emanated from a mere sect, which long preserved its Hebraic peculiarities, or it must have come down to us from the primitive age in which Christianity had but just separated itself from the parent stock of Judaism. The former alternative must be rejected, if at an early date we find it quoted with profound respect beyond the pale of Judaism; and we are thus finally led to regard it, in whatever may be its original form, as a genuine fragment of the earliest tradition of the Church.'

B. *TRANSFORMATIONS UNDERGONE BY THE DIDACHE.*—These have already been indicated in the section on 'Materials for comparative criticism.' But a few illustrations may here be given of the spirit prompting such efforts to adjust a primitive church-manual to developing 'Catholic' ideals. For they show at once the reluctance of the revisers to break altogether with this venerable monument of the first age of the Church, and the radical change in Christian ideals represented by the Catholicism of the 4th century. The only section in the Egyptian 'Apostolic Church Order' at all parallel to the ecclesiastical element in the Didache runs as follows (§ 12), the significant changes† being in italics—

Thomas said: 'Child, him that speaketh to thee the Word of God *and becometh to thee part-cause* (παραίτιον) *of life, and giveth thee the seal in the Lord*, thou shalt love as the apple of thine eye (=Barn. xix. 9); and thou shalt remember him night and day, thou shalt honour him as the Lord. . . . And thou shalt seek out *his* face daily and *the rest of* the saints. . . . *Thou shalt honour him as much as thou art able, from thy sweat and from the toil of thy hands.* For if the Lord deigned to give thee at his hands "spiritual food and drink and life eternal," thou oughtest much more to offer the corruptible and temporal food' (cf. Did. iv. 1, 2, xiii., xv. 2, x. 3, iv. 8b).

Here regard for the minister of Sacraments is added to that for those who minister the Word in any form.

Similar tendencies are seen in *Apost. Const.* vii.

Thus Did. vii. 1 appears as: 'But touching baptism, *O bishop or presbyter, . . . so shalt thou* baptize *as the Lord enjoined on us, saying*' (then follows Mt 28[19. 20a]). '*And thou shalt anoint, in the first place, with holy oil; next, thou shalt baptize with water; and, last of all, thou shalt seal with ointment*' (μύρῳ).

So with the Eucharistic prayers in Did. ix. x.; while Did. xv. 1, 2 is transformed so as to read—

'But ordain (προχειρίσασθε) bishops worthy of the Lord, *and presbyters* and deacons, men *prudent, just*, meek, etc. . . . , *dutiful* (ὁσίους), *impartial, able to teach the word of piety, orthodox in the doctrines of the Lord* (ὀρθοτομοῦντας ἐν τοῖς τοῦ κυρίου δόγμασιν). But do ye honour these *as fathers, as lords, as benefactors, as causes of well-being.*'

Besides these extant recensions of the Didache, in which the idea of 'Teaching of the Apostles' is turned into a pious fiction,—notably in the Egyptian 'Church Order,' which makes the several Apostles speak *seriatim*,—we hear from Rufinus of the *Duæ Viæ* or *Judicium Petri*, possibly the *Two Ways* in a setting adjusted to the taste of the Roman Church. Finally, there is some ground for supposing that an abbreviated edition of the full Didache, omitting archaic parts such as those touching Apostles and Prophets, was current in certain circles in the East. This would be antecedently probable, as an alternative method of

* With the widest and most varied *consensus* of scholars, cf. A. Ehrhard, *Altchrist. Litteratur und ihre Erforschung von 1884–1900*, p. 63. A weighty addition is the name of J. Réville, *Origines de l'Episcopat*, 234–261.

† In the shorter form of Cod. Ottob. (see p. 441b note) such changes are fewer.

preserving an ancient book in current use; and is the most natural explanation of the size of the Didache as known to Nicephorus or his (? Palestinian) source of *c.* 500 A.D., viz. about two-thirds of our MS. Another possibility is that this Didache was the fuller form of the *Two Ways* in *Apost. Const.* vii. (used in the ascetic maxims printed in *Oriens Christ.*, 1901, 49 ff.).

C. *The Significance of the Didache for Early Christianity.*—The historical value of the Didache is (*a*) direct, as it casts light on the first century of Christianity; (*b*) indirect, as it shows, by its wide and long-continued circulation, how such primitive ideas and usages continued to find a certain recognition after they had, on the whole, been forced into the background, or totally suppressed by the characteristic forms of Catholicism.

Under (*a*) the gain lies not so much in the way of new facts, as in the fresh light cast upon things already witnessed to by our existing documents, though in a manner too implicit to attract attention or win general assent as to their meaning. This is notably the case with the primary ministry of the Apostolic and sub-Apostolic ages—an unordained and largely an unlocalized ministry of the Word, including functions closely connected therewith, such as Eucharistic prayer—the ministry of Apostles, Prophets, and Teachers in the Spirit. Lightfoot, for instance, had already anticipated much of the truth as regards these; yet only for the few who could 'read between the lines' of our existing texts in the face of misleading traditions. With the aid of the Didache the blindest can, if they will, perceive the distinction in kind between the higher ministries of the Spirit and the ministries resting on gifts of a humbler but most necessary order, such as Bishops (Pastors) and Deacons. But there are other points almost equally important, even where less obvious. Such are (1) the congregational character of primitive Discipline, resting on the collective responsibility of all for each (xiv. xv. 3), side by side * with the existence of executive officers for this and other purposes (xv. 1, 2), whose appointment is attributed solely to the local community; (2) the Eucharist as still of the nature of a sacred meal of religious communion, in which, in some regions at least, the blessing of the Cup preceded that of the Broken Bread (ix. x., so Lk 22[17ff.], cf. 1 Co 10[16]); (3) the semi-Jewish nature of the two fixed Fast-days and three hours of Prayer, which passed into Christian use as suggested by, and in rivalry with, the practices of unbelieving Judaism (viii.); and (4) the idea of Christian Baptism as involving vows of renunciation of the Way of Death and self-surrender to the Way of Life.

In the last respect, as also touching the nature of the primitive Eucharist, the Didache illumines and is illumined by Pliny's report to Trajan about Christians in Pontus-Bithynia. Their early morning worship on the 'stated day' included a binding of themselves by solemn vow (*sacramento* is Pliny's word) 'not to any crime, but against the commission of thefts, robberies, adulteries, the breach of faith, the repudiation of a deposit when called upon.' This surely means that the moral vows taken at baptism were then renewed, and that such vows were more explicit than we had realized prior to the discovery of the Didache. Of course the usages in this matter may not have been exactly the same in Palestine and Bithynia. But the idea of an explicit moral covenant, as part of the new allegiance,† is common not only to these two, but also to many early Christian witnesses, such as Ignatius, Hermas, Justin, Tertullian, Origen;* to the *abrenuntiatio diaboli*, as found in the 'Canons of Hippolytus' onwards; and to the whole series of addresses to candidates for baptism or to the newly baptized, which extends well into the Middle Ages. Thus the very *Homiliarium* in which our Latin 'Doctrina Apostolorum' is preserved, comes next to an 'Admonitio S. Petri sive prædicatio sancti Bonifatii ep. de abrenuntiatione in baptismate.' Then, again, the Bithynian habit of meeting later on in the day 'to take food, but ordinary and harmless food,' confirms the Didache's picture of the Eucharist as one aspect of a religious meal, which could also be termed a 'love-feast,' as seemingly by Ignatius.†

There exists, indeed, a tendency in certain circles to discount the significance of our document in these and other respects—especially its 'dogmatic poverty'—on the plea that it is not representative of primitive Christianity, but only of some isolated and exceptional type of community, remote from the main stream of the Church's life. This is both unproved and improbable as regards Palestinian Christianity, which is the one type really in question. On the contrary, the Didache is in full accord with the piety of the Epistle of James and of those who furnished the author of Acts with the materials for his picture of Judæan Christianity; while it helps us to conceive the form of faith in which the readers of the Epistle to the Hebrews had been reared, and from which they tended to fall back into mere Judaism. The question, then, arises: Are we to regard ordinary Palestinian Christianity, during the Apostolic and sub-Apostolic ages, as 'representative' or normal as far as it went? Or are we to discount it as Ebionite, Judaic, or non-Apostolic, because it does not show certain features familiar to us from the Epistles of Paul (which form the bulk of our evidence) and those which, whether influenced by him or not, are hardly typical of the Palestinian Church (the Petrine Epistles, the Epistle to the Hebrews, where it represents its author rather than its readers, and the Johannine Epistles)? This issue is seldom faced. Yet on its answer largely depends our estimate of the Didache.

(*b*) But the case against the 'hole and corner' theory of the Didache goes much further. One can appeal to the history of its reception by the Church at large. To use Dr. C. Taylor's words once more, 'If at an early date we find it quoted with profound respect beyond the pale of Judaism,' we must regard it 'as a genuine fragment of the earliest tradition of the Church.' If it be rejoined that this applies more to the *Two Ways* than to the full Didache, the lesson is the same, namely, that the estimate of the ante-Nicene Church, particularly in the second century, was surprisingly appreciative of what some to-day find hardly Christian at all.‡ But when we consider the record

* Compare the picture of conjoint discipline of this sort, as late as the 3rd and 4th cents., reflected in *Apost. Const.* ii. 47, and its basis in the *Didascalia*.

† Justin, *Apol.* i. 61, describes candidates for baptism as those 'who are convinced . . . that these things which are taught by us . . . are true, and who promise that they are able thus to conduct their life.'

* Ignatius, *ad Eph.* xiv. 2 οἱ ἐπαγγελλόμενοι Χριστοῦ εἶναι, δι' ὧν πράσσουσιν ὀφθήσονται; Hermas, *Mand.* vi. 2, καλόν ἐστι τῷ ἀγγέλῳ τῆς δικαιοσύνης ἀκολουθεῖν, τῷ δὲ ἀγγέλῳ τῆς πονηρίας ἀποτάξασθαι; Justin, *Apol.* i. 65, τὸν πεπεισμένον καὶ συγκατατεθειμένον; Tertullian, *de Corona*, 3, 'contestamur nos renuntiare diabolo et pompæ et angelis ejus'; 11, 'Credimusne humanum sacramentum divino superduci licere et in alium Dominum respondere post Christum'? See also Origen, *contra Celsum*, iii. 51, 53; cf. the Elkesaite protestation of future holiness, in Hippolytus, *Philosoph.* ix. 15, which may well reflect something of normal baptismal usage.

† *Ad Smyrn.* viii., οὐκ ἐξόν ἐστιν χωρὶς τοῦ ἐπισκόπου οὔτε βαπτίζειν οὔτε ἀγάπην ποιεῖν; on which see Lightfoot's remarks.

‡ The justice of this complaint may well be doubted by those who recall the working faith of Francis of Assisi, and how much there is in common between its emphasis and that of the Didache. Of course the Passion of Christ forms a great point of contrast; but in the early Palestinian Church as a whole

set out above in A. ii., we are struck by the high prestige of the full Didache for more than two centuries. Only this can explain the way in which it is used, and even cited, as in *de Aleatoribus.* So with the influence it exerts on far later works, whether as their basis in one degree or another (*Didascalia* and *Apost. Const.*, Athanasius and pseudo-Athan.), or as an archaic writing of such repute as to call for an equivalent * more in keeping with current ecclesiastical usages (*Apostolic Church Order*). Its very rivals witness to its lasting acceptance. If it be not representative of sub-Apostolic Christianity, it is hard to see by what objective criteria any of the 'Apostolic Fathers' is to gain that credit.

LITERATURE.—Of the enormous literature connected with the Didache, full accounts will be found in the following: Schaff, *The Oldest Church Manual*, New York (3rd ed. 1889), containing a *catalogue raisonné* of books and articles down to March 1889; A. Ehrhard, *Die Altchristliche Litteratur und ihre Erforschung von 1884-1900*, Erste Abteilung, Freiburg im. Br. 1900, where, besides a full list of publications, an estimate of their general outcome is given by this liberal R. C. scholar.

*Typical editions.*—Bryennios, Διδαχὴ τῶν δώδεκα ἀποστόλων, Constantinople, 1883; Harnack, in *Texte u. Untersuch.* II. i. ii. (including O. von Gebhardt's 'Anhang' on a Latin fragment); Hilgenfeld, *NT extra canonem*, etc. (Leipzig); Wünsche (Leipzig); Hitchcock and Brown (New York); S. Orris and others (New York); de Romestin (Oxford: the most handy edition, with the related texts and a good list of minor literature during 1884); I. Prins, Leiden—all in 1884. P. Sabatier (Paris, 1885) lays just emphasis on the eschatological attitude of the piety reflected in the Didache, but draws a hasty inference from this and other early features in assigning it to 'the middle of the first century'; Schaff (as above), 1885, 1886, 1889; R. Majocchi (Milan, 1885, Modena, 1887, 1893); Spence (London, 1885); C. Taylor (Cambridge, see below), 1886; Harnack, *Die Apostellehre u. die jüdischen beiden Wege*, Leipzig, 1886 (inspired by Taylor's work) and 1896; Funk, *Doctrina duodecim apost.*, Tübingen, 1887 (with full Prolegomena and the related documents); Rendel Harris, London and Baltimore (with photographic facsimile of the MS; the most beautiful of all editions, and also among the most valuable, giving parallel texts and *testimonia* at length, and a number of suggestive elucidations, esp. from Jewish sources), 1887; J. Heron, *The Church of the Sub-Apostolic Age*, etc., London, 1888; E. Jacquier, Paris (with full bibliography), and J. M. Minasi, Rome, 1891; E. von Renesse, Giessen, 1897; C. Bigg in 'Early Church Classics,' 1898 (S.P.C.K., London); Funk, *Patres Apostolici*, i., 1901.

*Latin Version.*—At the close of 1900 appeared the full Latin text of the *Two Ways*, ed. Joseph Schlecht, Friburgi Brisgoviæ, sumptibus Herder, MCM (a handy edition of 24 pp., the Greek and Latin standing side by side); and more fully, with photographic reproduction of the Freisingen MS (now in Munich), in *Die Apostellehre in der Liturgie der Kathol. Kirche*, Freiburg, 1901. Of the Latin version, Harnack has a preliminary estimate in *Theol. Litztg.* 1900, 638–640, and Ladeuze in the *Revue d'Histoire ecclésiastique*, ii. 97–103; while E. Hennecke rests much on it in his article in the *ZNTW* ii. 58 ff., on the *Grundschrift* of the Didache and its recensions. [The text of *Two Ways* exists in two lines of transmission, viz. Δ (known to Hermas) = Lat. Did. and late Egyptian witnesses; and Δ′ = Barn. and *Apost. Church Order.* But this classification of texts is less likely than that into 'Syrian' and 'Egyptian' respectively].

*Typical discussions.*—Harnack, *Theol. Litztg.* 1884; Funk and Krawutzcky in *Theol. Quart.* (Tübingen), 1884; Duchesne, *Bulletin Critique*, 1884; G. Bonet-Maury, *La Doctrine des douze apôtres* (Paris; dates it after 160); Caspari, *Luthersk Ugeskrift*, Nos. 24, 25; Lightfoot at Church Congress, 1884 = *Expositor*, 1885, pp. 6–10, cf. *S. Ignatius*, i. 739, *Philippians* (1890), p. 349; Massebieau, *Revue de l'Hist. des Religions*, Sept.-Oct. 1884; Zahn, *Forschungen zur Gesch. des NT Kanons*, iii. 278-319; Holtzmann, 'Die Did. u. ihre Nebenformen' in *Jahrb. f. prot. Theol.* 1885, pp. 154–166 (regards Did. and Barn. as co-ordinate recensions of an earlier *Two Ways* or *Judicium Petri*); Langen in Sybel's *Hist. Zeitsch.* 1885, 193–214; Lechler, *Das Apost. u. Nachapost. Zeitalter*, Leipzig, 1885, pp. 553–593. Warfield and McGiffert in *Andover Review* and *Bibliotheca Sacra*, 1885, 1886; C. F. Arnold in *Z. f. Kirchenrecht*, 1885; and Bratke in *Jahrb. f. prot. Theol.* 1886,—all contribute to a genealogical theory of the related documents and types of text. C. Taylor, *The Teaching of the Twelve Apostles, with Illustrations from the Talmud*, Cambridge, 1886 (epoch-making as regards the Jewish character of the *Two Ways*), also in *Expositor* and *Journal of Philology*, as cited in the text; A. Chiappelli, *Studii di antica letteratura cristiana*, Turin, 1887, pp. 21-148; Wohlenberg, *Die Lehre . . . in ihrem Verhältniss zum NT Schrifttum*, Erlangen, 1888; Harnack, *Gesch. der altchr. Lit.* i. 86-92 (1893), ii. (*Chronologie*, 1897) 428 ff., in Herzog's *PRE*³ (1896), i. 711-730; N. Biesenthal, *Die urchristl. Kirche . . . nach der Did.* (Progr.), Insterburg, 1893; P. Savi, *La dottrina degli apostoli*, 1893; J. Réville, *Origines de l'Episcopat*, pp. 234–261, Paris, 1894; L. Iselin, 'Eine bisher unbekannte Version des ersten Teiles der "Apostellehre"' (*Texte u. Unters.* XIII. i.), 1895; O. Moe, *Die Apostellehre u. der Dekalog im Unterricht der alten Kirche*, Gütersloh, 1896; C. Holzhey, *Die Abhängigkeit der Syrischen Didaskalia von der Didache*, München, 1898; Funk, *Kirchengesch. Abhandlungen*, ii. 108–141, Paderborn, 1899 (on basis of earlier articles in *Theol. Quartalschrift*; valuable); A. Ehrhard, *op. cit.* 1900, 37–68 (an admirable summary); E. Hennecke, *l.c.* 1901; J. Schlecht, *op. cit.* 1901 (good summary of results, esp. as bearing on the Lat.); O. Bardenhewer, *Gesch. der Altkirch. Lit.* i. (1902) 76–86; K. Kohler in *Jewish Encyclopædia*, iv. 585 ff., London, 1903; P. Drews in *NT Apokryphen*, Tübingen, 1904, p. 182 ff.

J. VERNON BARTLET.

this was lost sight of in the rays of 'the glory' about to be revealed.

* In the Syriac version this is actually called 'Third Book of Clement: *Teaching of the Twelve Apostles*,' which may be its original title. Possibly, too, the idea of the Syrian 'Testament (Διαθήκη) of the Lord' owes its name and some of its contents to the Didache.

## DIATESSARON.—

i. Author and Date.
ii. Title, Language, and later History.
  (*a*) Testimony of Greek writers.
  (*b*) Testimony of Syriac writers.
iii. Non-Syriac versions of the Diatessaron.
  (*a*) The Armenian version of St. Ephraem's commentary on the Diatessaron.
  (*b*) Codex Fuldensis.
  (*c*) The Arabic version.
iv. Relation of the Diatessaron to the Old Syriac Literature.

i. AUTHOR AND DATE.—The Diatessaron, or Harmony of the four Gospels, was most probably compiled by Tatian, the disciple of Justin Martyr, towards the end of the 2nd cent. A.D., not long after the year 172 or 173, when Tatian returned from Rome to his native land of Mesopotamia. The scanty information that we possess regarding the early history of the author of this famous work is mainly derived from his no less celebrated *Oratio ad Græcos* (Λόγος πρὸς Ἕλληνας), a work which was probably composed soon after his conversion to Christianity. He is described by Clement of Alexandria (*Strom.* iii. 81), Epiphanius (*Hær.* 46. 1), and Theodoret (*Hær. Fab.* i. 20) as a Syrian; and this statement as to his nationality agrees with his own mention of the fact that he was born 'in the land of the Assyrians' (*Oratio*, 42, γεννηθεὶς μὲν ἐν τῇ τῶν Ἀσσυρίων γῇ). We may infer from his own writings that he was a man of good birth and position, and, as such, not without the temptation to embark on a military or political career; but his mind was early attracted to that pursuit of learning to which he devoted the greater part of his life. He spent many years in visiting the various schools, and in studying the different tenets, of heathen philosophy, and finally settled down in Rome, where, presumably through the influence of Justin, he embraced Christianity. Like the latter, he suffered persecution at the hands of Crescens; but it seems probable that he remained in Rome as a teacher some years after the martyrdom of Justin, in A.D. 165, among his pupils being Rhodon of Asia Minor. It was, no doubt, during this latter portion of his residence in Rome that Tatian developed that curious mixture of heterodox views with which his name is associated by later writers, and which, while causing him to be branded as a heretic, also necessitated his departure from Rome. Thus he undoubtedly advocated, like the Encratites, a rigid asceticism, condemning marriage and the use of wine and animal food; he also followed Marcion in distinguishing the Demiurge from the God of the New Testament, while he held a Gnostic theory of æons similar to that of Valentinus: his denial of the salvability of Adam alone marks a more original departure from the orthodox teaching of the Church. In view of the statements as to Tatian's heretical opinions made by Irenæus, Clement of Alexandria, Origen, Eusebius, etc., his heterodoxy can hardly be disputed; yet it is noticeable that Eusebius is the first to definitely associate him with any heretical party (see below, § ii. *a*). The date of Tatian's departure from Rome for the

East may be placed with tolerable certainty about A.D. 172–173.* How long he survived after his return to Mesopotamia is unknown; but it was there, probably at Edessa, that he composed for the Syrian Church that Harmony of the four Gospels which has rendered his name so famous.

Before leaving the personal history of Tatian we may note that no suspicion of heresy seems to have attached to his name in the Syrian Church — a fact which is most easily explicable on the supposition that, amid the primitive conditions of his native Church, Tatian had neither the occasion nor the inclination to air those views which had procured him so much disfavour at Rome. After his bitter experiences in the latter city, it was only natural that he should turn his attention towards a new field of activity such as that afforded by the compilation of his Harmony, rather than to the dissemination of his peculiar views. The plan of reproducing the fourfold history of the Gospels in the form of one simple connected narrative was no doubt a bold one, but the underlying motive was probably the desire to present his less cultivated countrymen with the story of the Gospel in a form which should at once preserve all that was essential in the narratives of the four Evangelists, while omitting all that might seem calculated to perplex and confuse.

ii. Title, Language, and later History.—The full title given by Tatian to his Harmony of the Gospels appears to have been 'The Gospel of Jesus Christ by means of the four [Gospels or Evangelists]' (ܐܘܢܓܠܝܘܢ ܕܝܫܘܥ ܡܫܝܚܐ ܕܕܝܛܣܪܘܢ = Εὐαγγέλιον Ἰησοῦ Χριστοῦ τὸ διὰ τεσσάρων), but the work was generally known and cited by the shorter title *Diatessaron* (ܕܝܛܣܪܘܢ; the forms ܕܝܐܛܣܪܘܢ and ܕܝܐܛܐܣܪܘܢ also occur). In addition to this Greek title, however, the Harmony also received the genuine Syriac name *Evangelion da-Mĕḥallĕṭē* (ܐܘܢܓܠܝܘܢ ܕܡܚܠܛܐ), or 'Gospel of the Mixed,' to distinguish it from the fourfold form of the Gospels, the *Evangelion da-Mĕpharrĕshē* (ܐܘܢܓܠܝܘܢ ܕܡܦܪܫܐ), or 'Gospel of the Separated (ones).'

The Greek title has been used, among others, as an argument in favour of the view that the Harmony was originally composed in that language; but no stress can be laid on this fact, since Greek titles, and especially Greek technical terms,† were largely employed by Syriac writers. Moreover, the balance of evidence seems to support the view that the Diatessaron was an original Syriac work, though no final opinion on the subject can be expressed until we have determined the question of its relation to the Old Syriac version (see below, § iv.). There can, however, be no doubt that, whether originally composed in Greek or Syriac, the work was intended for use in the Syriac Church, and was widely circulated in a Syriac form at an early date. Further, there is no direct evidence of the existence of a Greek original, and the scanty and indefinite nature of the information supplied by the Greek writers seems to show that the (Syriac) work was known to the Greek Church by name only.

(*a*) *Greek writers.*—The first notice of the Diatessaron occurs in Eusebius (*HE* iv. 36), who states that Tatian, whom he wrongly describes as the former leader of the Encratites, 'composed a sort of connexion and compilation, I know not how, of the Gospels, and called it the Diatessaron. This work is current in some quarters (with some persons) even to the present day.'* The work is also briefly mentioned by Epiphanius (*Hær.* 46. 1), who says: 'The Diatessaron Gospel is said to have been composed by him (Tatian). It is called by some the Gospel according to the Hebrews.'† Apart from these two writers no mention ‡ is made of the Diatessaron by either Greek or Latin writers until the 6th cent. (see below, § iii. *b*); and the silence of such writers as Irenæus, Clement of Alexandria, Jerome, or Augustine is explicable only on the supposition that the work was exclusively a Syriac one, and, as such, unknown to the Greek Church.

Before passing on to the evidence afforded by Syriac writers, we may note two points arising out of the above notices which tend to confirm the impression made by the silence of the Greek Fathers. The first is the omission of the clause 'I know not how' (οὐκ οἶδ' ὅπως) in the Syriac translation (4th cent.) of Eusebius' *History*.§ The explanation of this fact given by Hjelt ‖ is no doubt correct, viz. that the translator purposely suppressed the clause as irrelevant, since Tatian's work was well known both to himself and to his Syriac readers. Equally interesting is the translator's insertion of the words 'now this is the (*Evangelion*) *da-Mĕḥallĕṭē*' (Gospel of the Mixed) after the word 'Diatessaron,' which shows that the Syriac title of the Harmony was already current in the 4th century. The second point is connected with the confusion that existed, according to Epiphanius, in the minds of some with regard to the Diatessaron and the Gospel according to the Hebrews. As Zahn (*Forsch.* i. 25) has pointed out, the confusion admits of a tolerably easy solution on the supposition that the Diatessaron was a Syriac work. When the existence of another Gospel, written in the same or a nearly allied dialect, among the half-heretical Nazareans, *i.e.* in almost the same district, became known, it was not unnatural to suppose that the two were either closely allied or even identical. Such a mistake, however, could have arisen only amongst people who were either ignorant of Aramaic, or who possessed no knowledge of the works in question save at second hand.

(*b*) *Syriac writers.*—In contrast to the comparative ignorance displayed on this subject by Greek authorities, the statements made by Syriac writers concerning the Diatessaron, and the evidence of its use in the Syrian Church, are both clear and decisive. The earliest testimony is contained in the *Doctrine of Addai*, a work which, in its present form, is variously dated by critics from the middle of the 3rd cent. (Zahn) to the beginning of the 5th cent. (von Dobschütz, *Christusbilder*, p. 158 f.). But, though the form in which we now possess this text may not be earlier than A.D. 400, its contents are clearly based on very early tradition, and we may therefore safely follow Zahn (*Forsch.* i. 90 f.) in regarding it as a trustworthy witness to the practice of the Edessene Church during the 3rd century. The crucial passage states that 'much people gathered together day by day, and came to the prayer of the (Divine) service and to (the reading of) the Old Testament and the

* Zahn, *Forschungen*, i. p. 282 f.

† Cf. Χρονικόν, Ἐκκλησιαστική, Τετραευαγγέλιον, etc. Baethgen objects that these were used also as titles in Greek, and, as such, were taken over into Syriac, while *Diatessaron* is a Greek musical *terminus technicus*, and does not occur elsewhere in Syriac (*Evangelienfragmente*, p. 89; cf. Zahn, *Forsch.* i. pp. 104 f., 239 f.).

* ὁ μέντοι γε πρότερος αὐτῶν ἀρχηγὸς ὁ Τατιανὸς συνάφειάν τινα καὶ συναγωγὴν οὐκ οἶδ' ὅπως τῶν εὐαγγελίων συνθεὶς τὸ διατεσσάρων τοῦτο προσωνόμασεν, ὃ καὶ παρά τισιν εἰσέτι νῦν φέρεται.

† λέγεται δὲ τὸ διὰ τεσσάρων εὐαγγέλιον ὑπ' αὐτοῦ γεγενῆσθαι ὅπερ κατὰ Ἑβραίους τινὲς καλοῦσι.

‡ On the obscure scholion to Mt $27^{48}$ contained in Cod. 72, see Zahn, *Forschungen*, i. 26 f.

§ ed. Wright and M'Lean, Cambridge, 1898, p. 243.

‖ *Die altsyrische Evangelienübersetzung und Tatians Diatessaron*, p. 24 note.

New, (namely) the Diatessaron, and believed in the resurrection of the dead.'* Of a similar nature is the command given to his presbyters in Addai's parting speech: † 'The Law and the Prophets and the Gospel, wherein ye read every day before the people; and the Epistles of Paul which Simon Kephas sent us from the city of Rome; and the Acts of the Twelve Apostles, which John the son of Zebedee sent us from Ephesus: these writings (or Scriptures) shall ye read in the churches of Christ, and besides them nothing else shall ye read.' These two passages clearly show that the terms 'Diatessaron' and 'Gospel' were interchangeable, and also that the version of the Syriac Gospels adopted by the Edessene Church for use in Divine service was that which had been composed by Tatian. Internal evidence, again, shows that Aphraates, the bishop of the convent of St. Matthew near Mosul, made use of the same version, though the Gospel quotations in his *Homilies* (written between 336 and 345 A.D.) are not taken exclusively from Tatian's work. The most striking proof, however, of the widespread use of the Diatessaron in the Syrian Church during the 4th cent., and of the high repute in which it stood, is the fact that it forms the basis of the commentary on the Gospels written by the famous Ephraem Syrus (d. 373 A.D.; see below, § iii. *a*). It is noteworthy also that the Gospel quotations which are to be found in his genuine works appear to be also taken from the Harmony.‡

The beginning of the 5th cent. forms a decisive point in the history of the Syriac versions of the New Testament, inasmuch as it marks the introduction of a new version, which was destined to supersede all its predecessors. It was during the episcopate of Rabbūla, bishop of Edessa (A.D. 411–435), and under his direction that a revision of the existing Syriac translation of the NT was set on foot, with a view to bringing it more into conformity with the current Greek text. According to his biography § (written soon after his death) Rabbūla 'translated by the wisdom of God which was in him the New Testament from Greek into Syriac, because of its variations, exactly as it was.' To quote Mr. Burkitt,‖ 'It is only the belief, the erroneous belief, that the Peshiṭta NT was proved to be older than Rabbūla through the attestation given to it by St. Ephraem, which has hitherto prevented scholars from recognizing in these words a description of the making and publication of the Syriac Vulgate' or the Peshiṭta. But in order to establish the new revised version on a firm basis it was necessary to suppress all earlier translations. With a view, therefore, to securing this end, Rabbūla commanded his priests and deacons 'to take care that in all the churches there should be an *Evangelion da-Měpharrěshē*, and that it should be read.' The object of this canon was clearly to establish the new version at the expense of the Diatessaron.¶ How successful it was is shown by the fact that henceforth the Peshiṭta reigned alone as the accepted ecclesiastical text, while the Diatessaron almost entirely disappeared. An interesting notice of the thoroughness with which the crusade against Tatian's Harmony was carried out has been preserved in the writings of Theodoret, bishop of Cyrrhus (A.D. 423–457). In his treatise on heresies (*Hær. Fab.* i. 20) he states that Tatian 'composed the Gospel, which is called Diatessaron, cutting out all the genealogies and all such passages as show the Lord to have been born of the seed of David after the flesh. Now this work was used not only by those who belonged to his own sect, but also by those who follow the Apostolic doctrine, since they did not perceive the mischief of the composition, but used it in all simplicity on account of its brevity. And I myself found more than 200 such copies held in honour in the churches in our parts, and, having collected them all, I put them away, substituting the Gospels of the four Evangelists.'

Nevertheless, the vigorous measures adopted by Rabbūla and Theodoret failed to bring about the complete rejection of the Diatessaron. For, though Tatian's Harmony appears to have been effectually excluded from public worship in the Syrian Church, the evidence of later writers shows that the work was still in existence as late as the Middle Ages. Hjelt * suggests very plausibly that either the growing antagonism between the Monophysites (or Jacobites) and the Nestorians reacted on Church praxis, and caused the latter to retain the Gospels in the form to which they had been accustomed, or else that, for the same cause, the ecclesiastical reforms of Rabbūla met with no acceptance among the Syrians of the East. This theory is certainly an attractive one, and explains many of the phenomena connected with the later history of the Diatessaron; but the evidence at our disposal, while amply proving that Tatian's work was well known to and held in high esteem by the Nestorians down to the 14th cent., is scarcely sufficient to justify his further contention that it was retained by them in the services of the Church till that period. A more probable explanation of its continued existence is to be found in its connexion with the name of Ephraem. Ephraem's commentary on the Diatessaron was not only, as we shall see later, translated into Armenian, but also exercised a marked influence on the works of later (Syriac) NT commentators—an eloquent proof of the esteem in which that writer's work was held; and it can hardly be doubted that its association with the name of the great Syriac Father contributed very largely to the preservation of Tatian's work among the Syrians themselves. Some confirmation of this view is afforded by the way in which the later references to Tatian and his work, which are not confined to Nestorian writers but include several Jacobite authors, are closely connected with St. Ephraem's commentary.

Of the later Syriac writers who either refer to or quote from the Diatessaron (or Ephraem's commentary upon it), the first and most important is Ishoʻdad of Merv, the Nestorian bishop of Ḥadītha (or Ḥedhatta), who flourished about A.D. 850.† In his commentary on the NT we find the following statement in the Prologue to St. Mark: 'Matthew and John belonged to the Twelve, but Mark and Luke to the Seventy; but Tatianus the disciple of Justin, the philosopher and martyr, made a selection from the four Evangelists and combined (or mixed ܚܠܛ) and put together a Gospel and called it (the) Diatessaron, that is "of the Mixed" (*da-Měḥallěṭē*); and concerning the divinity of Christ he did not write. And on this (Gospel)

* ed. Phillips, p. 36, l. 15 f.
† Phillips, p. 46, l. 8 f.
‡ Burkitt, *Texts and Studies*, vol. vii. p. 56.
§ Overbeck, *S. Ephraemi Syri, Rabulæ, etc., opera selecta*, p. 172.
‖ *Op. cit.* p. 57.
¶ Overbeck, *op. cit.* p. 220. The term *Evangelion da-Měpharrěshē* must here denote, not the Old Syriac version (which was also so called), but rather any MS of the four Gospels, as opposed to the *Evangelion da-Měḥallěṭē* or Diatessaron.

* *Op. cit.* p. 29.
† For a full discussion of his commentary on the NT as contained in the Cambridge MS, Add. 1973, and of the passages bearing on Ephraem's commentary and the Diatessaron, see R. Harris, *Fragments of the Commentary of Ephraem Syrus upon the Diatessaron*, London, 1895, p. 10 f. Attention was first called to the importance of Ishoʻdad's work in this connexion by the American scholars, Dr. Hall and Professor Gottheil, *Journal of Biblical Literature*, vols. xi. and xii.

Mar Ephraem commented.' Hjelt (*op. cit.* p. 30 f.) argues with some force that the position of Tatian immediately after the four Evangelists, and the manner in which he is mentioned, seem to show that Isho'dad regarded his testimony as of equal value with that of the Evangelists; and this impression is confirmed by an examination of those passages in his commentary in which the Diatessaron is definitely cited, viz. Mt 1[20b] 3[4. 13f.] 21[1], Ac 1[13]. It is noteworthy that Isho'dad avoids the error into which so many of his successors have fallen, and draws a clear distinction between the Diatessaron of Tatian and that of Ammonius. Thus, in discussing the words 'as it is written in the prophet Isaiah' (Mk 1[2]), he says,* 'others (say): in the book of the Diatessaron which was composed in Alexandria, he (Mark) says "in the prophets" instead of "as it is written in Isaiah."'

The Jacobite bishop Moses bar-Kepha (d. A.D. 903), who was almost a contemporary of Isho'dad, also wrote a commentary on the NT in which there are clear traces of acquaintance with Ephraem's commentary, and apparently with an even earlier work (Harris, pp. 10, 18, 24, 85). He further makes direct mention of the Diatessaron in two passages in which he is discussing the canons of Eusebius. The whole passage runs as follows: 'Which shows who collected the four books of the Evangelists and set them in order in one book. And some people, indeed, say that Eusebius of Cæsarea, when he saw that Julianus (*sic*! for Ammonius) of Alexandria made the Gospel of the Diatessaron, *i.e.* "by means of Four," and changed the sequence of things [Hjelt: of the verses] in the Gospels, and that Tatian also the Greek, the heretic leader, made a Gospel which is called Tasaron (*sic*!), and he too changed the sequence of things; he, Eusebius, took care and collected the four books of the four Evangelists and set them in order and placed them in one book, and preserved the body of their compositions [Hjelt: the integrity of the text of the narratives of the Evangelists] as it was without taking anything from them or adding anything to them, and made certain Canons on account of their harmony one with another.'† Here we see that Bar-Kepha distinguishes the two Diatessarons, though apparently he only knew Tatian's work through the medium of Ephraem's commentary. The absence of any direct quotations from the Diatessaron as well as the epithets which he applies to Tatian may be due, as Hjelt suggests, to strong anti-Nestorian feeling.

The two lexicographers Isho' bar-'Ali (d. 873) and Bar-Bahlul (who flourished about the middle of the 10th cent.) both refer to the Diatessaron. The former defines the word 'Diatessaron' (for which he gives a variant *Diaqutrun*) as 'the Gospel of the Diatessaron, which Tatian made, the Mixed,' and adds that the author omitted both the human and the Divine genealogies of our Lord, and is on this account accursed, namely, Tatian: the latter statement is, however, not found in all MSS, and may be regarded as a later gloss. In Bar-Bahlul's lexicon the Diatessaron is defined (Hjelt, p. 48) as 'the collective Gospel which (was composed) from the four Evangelists': to this is added, 'This was composed in Alexandria, which the bishop Tatianus has written.' The latter sentence is, however, wanting in other MSS, and by its very form betrays its secondary character. It is interesting to find that Bar-Bahlul quotes the Diatessaron by its Syriac name *Evangelion da-Mĕḥallĕṭē*, while he cites the reading '*Jesus* Barabbas' (Mt 27[17]), which is found in the Sinaitic palimpsest, as occurring in the *Evangelion da-Mĕpharrĕshē*.

The evidence of our next witness, Jacob bar-Ṣalibi, the Jacobite bishop of Amida (d. 1171 A.D.) is largely based upon that of his predecessors. Thus in his NT Commentary he reproduces with but slight variations the statement of Isho'dad in connexion with the opening verses of St. Mark. He omits, however, the sentence 'and concerning the divinity of Christ he has not written,' but adds the remark 'now the commencement of the same was: In the beginning was the Word.' In like manner he follows Bar-Kepha in his statement concerning Eusebius and his canons (see above), though in another passage in his prologue to the Gospels (Harris, p. 28) he makes the extraordinary statement that Tatian and Ammonius were unable to bring the Gospel accounts of the Resurrection into harmony, and therefore desisted from the attempt.* Probably Zahn† is right in supposing that Bar-Ṣalibi has here confused Ammonius with Eusebius, and has assigned to the latter the rôle of Elias of Salamia (of whom he speaks elsewhere): for the fact that the canons of Eusebius stopped at Mk 16[8] was apparently treated by him as excluding the narrative of the Resurrection, while he ascribes the correction of this supposed error to Eusebius instead of to Elias. In any case it seems tolerably certain that Bar-Ṣalibi can hardly be treated as an independent witness to the existence of the Diatessaron, even though we reject the statement with regard to the Diatessaron which occurs in his commentary at Mk 1[2].‡

The statements of Bar-Hebræus (d. 1286 A.D.) in like manner appear to be mainly borrowed from the works of earlier writers, especially Bar-Ṣalibi. He follows the latter in reproducing Isho'dad's notice concerning Tatian with the same omission and insertion, but by a strange misunderstanding of his author applies the language of Eusebius with regard to the Diatessaron of Ammonius to Tatian's work.

Even at the end of the 13th cent. we still find striking evidence of the continued existence of the Diatessaron. The NT commentary of the celebrated 'Abd-isho' (Ebedjesu) bar-Berika (d. 1318), metropolitan of Nisibis and Armenia, has not been preserved, but in the preface to his *Nomocanon* § he describes Tatian's Harmony as the example of completeness and trustworthiness which he has endeavoured to imitate. The description is as follows: 'Tatian the philosopher having comprehended the meaning of the words of the Evangelists and grasped the plan of their Divine narrative, composed one admirable Gospel out of the Four. This is what he called the Diatessaron, in which he preserved with all care the accurate order of the sayings and deeds of the Saviour without having added a single word of his own.' From this notice it seems clear that 'Abd-isho' was well acquainted with the Diatessaron and its contents, even though he elsewhere ‖ confuses its author with Ammonius. The evidence of these later Syriac

* We have here followed the text of the Berlin MS as given by Hjelt (p. 35 note). For the text of the Cambridge MS, which seems less original, see Harris (p. 15); the latter refers the quotation '(as) it is written in Isaiah' to Tatian's reading at Mt 3[3].

† Harris, *op. cit.* p. 21.

* The passage runs as follows: 'Eusebius of Cæsarea took pains to compose the canons of the Gospel—and this, indeed, is known from his letter to Carpianus—and pointed out by their means the agreement of the Evangelists. Ammonius and Tatian had written a Gospel, the Diatessaron, *i.e.* of the Four, as we have said above, and when they came to the history of the resurrection, and saw that it varied, they gave up their works. But Eusebius took pains to make these canons and to point out in the same the agreement of the Evangelists' (Hjelt, p. 43).

† *Theol. Littbl.* 1896.

‡ 'Others (say): in the book of the Diatessaron, which was composed in Alexandria, which the bishop Tatianus has written,' *i.e.* the same gloss that appears in the lexicon of Bar-Bahlul.

§ Mai, *Script. Vet. Nova Coll.* x. 191.

‖ Assemani, *Bibl. Or.* iii. 12.

writers, at least from the 12th cent. onwards, is no doubt somewhat discounted by the fact that they appear to have mainly derived their information from the works of their predecessors; but the secondary nature of their evidence is more than outweighed by the additional testimony furnished by the following translations of the Diatessaron.

iii. NON-SYRIAC VERSIONS OF THE DIATESSARON.—The above sketch of the history of the Diatessaron proves beyond question: (1) That this form of the Gospels was very widely, if not exclusively, used in the Syrian Church during the 3rd and 4th cents.; and (2) that the work continued to be known and read by Syriac writers down to the beginning of the 14th century. But the evidence of the existence and influence of Tatian's Harmony is, as we have pointed out, not confined to the quotations and references of Syriac commentators; for though the Syriac Diatessaron has unfortunately not been preserved to us, yet we possess both Latin and Arabic translations of Tatian's work, together with an Armenian version of St. Ephraem's commentary upon it. These versions in themselves furnish incontrovertible proof of the great esteem in which the Harmony was held, and in that respect form a most important addition to the evidence set forth above; but their chief value lies in the fact that by their means we are enabled to obtain some conception, not only of the order and arrangement of Tatian's work but also of its actual text.

(*a*) *The Armenian version of St. Ephraem's commentary on the Diatessaron.*—It has been already suggested that St. Ephraem's commentary on the Diatessaron contributed in no slight measure to the preservation of the latter work. For the honour and esteem in which that writer and his works were held by the Syrian Church naturally extended to his Gospel commentary, and ensured the survival of Tatian's work at least in that form. We may even go further, and assume that the example set by so prominent a writer as Ephraem exercised a considerable influence on his successors, who were thus led to study—and so to preserve—a work which otherwise seemed destined to disappear. But, whatever its influence in the past, it is undoubtedly true that in modern times the publication of a Latin translation of the Armenian version of this commentary has been the means of once more arousing the interest of scholars in the Diatessaron, and of rescuing it from that oblivion to which it had been so long assigned. The Armenian version of the commentary first appeared in the edition of St. Ephraem's works issued in four volumes by the Mechitarist Fathers of St. Lazzaro in 1836. A Latin translation of the commentary was prepared by J. B. Aucher, one of the editors, as early as 1841, but was not published. The work was finally made accessible to scholars by Prof. Moesinger, who in 1876 published Aucher's translation, which he had revised and corrected by the aid of another MS, under the title: *Evangelii Concordantis Expositio facta a Sancto Ephraemo Doctore Syro.* Both the MSS on which this translation is based date from the year 1195, but the version itself is assigned to the 5th cent. (Moesinger, p. xi). That the Armenian version was made from the Syriac commentary of St. Ephraem seems to be fully established,* and we are therefore justified in treating the work as genuine.

Among the first to recognize the great importance of Moesinger's translation was Professor Zahn, to whom, indeed, all NT scholars are largely indebted for a knowledge, not only of a considerable part of the Diatessaron itself but also of a large number of facts bearing on its history and character. Those portions of the text which the author was able to restore with the aid of the new translation (and also of the *Homilies* of Aphraates) were incorporated in the first volume of his *Forschungen zur Geschichte des neutestamentlichen Kanons und der altkirchlichen Literatur* (Erlangen, 1881). In this work Zahn further gave a full and complete account of all that was then known of the Diatessaron and its author, and, to a large extent, solved the many complicated and difficult questions which are connected with its origin and history. The main interest of the volume, however, centres in his brilliant restoration of the text, and in the evidence which he has adduced in support of his reconstruction. We therefore append a brief description of the methods employed by Zahn in recovering the lost text.

The task of reproducing the order and arrangement of the Diatessaron, as Zahn discovered, was materially lightened by the character and form of Ephraem's commentary. For the latter consists of a series of lectures or discourses, which are largely homiletic both in form and substance, and appear to have been delivered orally. Moreover, each discourse was apparently preceded by the reading of the Gospel section which formed the subject of discussion; and though, unfortunately, the text of the section was not included in the commentary, the discourse itself affords sufficient evidence for identifying the passage of Scripture thus commented on. In reconstructing the text itself Zahn had to fall back upon the Gospel quotations contained in the commentary as translated by Moesinger,* and in the *Homilies* of Aphraates.†

The Gospel quotations that occur in the Latin translation of Ephraem's commentary naturally form the basis of the text. Those quotations,‡ however, which occur—chiefly by way of illustration—out of their context, *i.e.* in other discourses than the one to which they belong, are inserted in square brackets, as also the quotations from Aphraates, the latter being given, for the sake of clearness, in German instead of Latin. Further, all quotations, whether in Ephraem's commentary or in the *Homilies* of Aphraates, which are not given literally, but freely reproduced, are printed in italic type; and, lastly, all Zahn's own additions, *e.g.* references, etc., are enclosed in round brackets. In the voluminous notes appended to each section Zahn has compared the Curetonian and Peshiṭta versions, and, in many cases, also the Harklean; while in the more important passages reference is made to the Greek MSS (א, B and D) and to the Itala MSS.

It is no slight tribute to the skill and ingenuity of Zahn to say that he has by these means succeeded in restoring not only the broad general features of the Diatessaron, but also, to a relatively large extent, its actual text. The former we are able to control by means of the Latin (Codex Fuldensis) and Arabic translations of the Diatessaron, which confirm in the most striking manner the accuracy of Zahn's deductions; but these versions, unfortunately (see below) afford but little assistance in restoring the actual text.

Enough, however, of the original Diatessaron

* Zahn, *Forsch.* i. 46 f.; J. Hamlyn Hill, *A Dissertation on the Gospel Commentary of S. Ephraem the Syrian*, Edinburgh, 1896.

* A more accurate English translation from the Armenian MSS by Canon Armitage Robinson is given in Appendix x. to Dr. Hamlyn Hill's *The Earliest Life of Christ ever compiled from the Four Gospels, being the Diatessaron of Tatian*, etc.; and in the same writer's *Dissertation*, p. 75 f.

† Cf. Baethgen, *Evangelienfragmente*, p. 62 f., who points out that, though Aphraates knew and used the Diatessaron, his Gospel quotations are not taken exclusively from that work.

‡ The doubt expressed by Zahn as to whether these quotations were taken from the Diatessaron or from the Peshitta has now been dispelled once and for all. Since the publication of Mr. Burkitt's work on *S. Ephraem's Quotations from the Gospel*, it may be regarded as certain that Ephraem did not use the Peshiṭta.

has in this way been restored to enable us to make out both the object of the author and the methods which he followed. It is clear that the object of the Harmony was not to detract from, or impair, the authority of the four canonical Gospels, which undoubtedly form the basis of Tatian's work, but rather to put together a single connected account of the life of our Lord, which should contain all that was essential in the narratives of the Gospels. It was thus a popular rather than a learned work, and was designed to obviate those difficulties to which the fourfold form of the Gospels was only too apt to give rise. But, though the author was fully convinced of the genuineness of his sources, he did not adopt, as Zahn puts it, a 'superstitious attitude' towards them. He rightly perceived that divergent accounts did not necessarily imply more than a single occurrence of the same incident, and acted accordingly; while in cases of actual discrepancy or contradiction he boldly followed one authority to the exclusion of the others. Thus he followed St. Mark's ($10^{46}$) narrative of the healing of *one* blind man *after* leaving Jericho, in preference to that of St. Matthew ($20^{29.30}$), who speaks of *two* blind men, and to that of St. Luke ($18^{35}$), who places the miracle *before* the entry into Jericho. In this respect he appears to treat all four Evangelists as of equal authority; but, in the main, his scheme of our Lord's public ministry, which extends over three Passovers,* is based on the Fourth Gospel. In detail, however, the latter is treated with the same freedom as the Synoptists. Thus the purification of the temple (Jn $2^{14-22}$) and the discourse with Nicodemus ($3^{1-21}$) are transferred to the Feast of the Dedication at Jerusalem in the last winter of our Lord's life. The following example will perhaps give a better illustration, not only of the boldness with which Tatian treated his sources, but also of the keen insight and judgment displayed by Zahn in tracing out and determining the principles which appear to have guided him:—We find in the Harmony that Jn $6^{1-21}$ (§ 34. Feeding of the 5000 just before the second Passover) precedes Jn $4^{4-42}$ (§ 38. Discourse with the woman of Samaria) and Jn 5 (§ 40. Visit to Jerusalem and cure at the Pool of Bethesda), the two latter being separated by § 39 (the healing of the leper, Mt $8^{2-4}$, Mk $1^{40-45}$, Lk $5^{12-14}$). But § 38 (Jn $4^{4f.}$), which forms part of a journey from Judæa to Samaria, seems to be inconsistent with the preceding sections (14–37), which (with the exception of § 25) describe the Galilæan ministry. A further difficulty is presented by the isolated position of § 39, which is the only incident belonging to the Galilæan ministry which, presumably, stands in its proper position between the journey to Galilee (Jn $4^{1-43}$) and the visit to Jerusalem ($5^1$). The correct explanation is, no doubt, that offered by Zahn, who points out that Tatian has reversed the order of St. John, and assigned the two days' sojourn at Samaria (Jn $4^{4-42}$, § 38) to a journey *from* Galilee to Jerusalem. Tatian's procedure is bold, but it involves no alteration of Jn $4^{4-42}$, since these verses include nothing which requires that the sojourn in Samaria should form part of a journey from Judæa to Galilee. The remaining verses of ch. 4, it is true, clearly point to such a journey, but they form no part of § 38. For vv.$^{1-3}$ had already been given in § 13; of vv.$^{43-46}$ Tatian had only utilized v.$^{44}$ in § 32, while it is doubtful if v.$^{43}$ ever formed part of the Harmony: according to Zahn, vv.$^{46b-54}$ also were omitted by Tatian, their place being taken by § 39.† It naturally follows from this alteration of Tatian that the scene of § 39 is transferred from Galilee to Judæa. This second change, however, is certainly an improvement from the point of view of the history, for Mt $8^4$, Mk $1^{44}$, Lk $5^{14}$ appear to presuppose easy access to the temple and its priestly ritual. The complete chronological scheme underlying the Diatessaron, which has thus been restored, is as follows:—

| | | Sections |
|---|---|---|
| 1. | The Logos, Incarnation and Childhood of our Lord | 1–7 |
| 2. | The first Manifestation | 8–12 |
| 3. | The beginning of His public ministry. First Passover (Jn $2^{13}$) | 13 |
| 4. | Jesus in Galilee | 14–37 |
| 5. | Journey through Samaria. Second Passover (Jn 5) | 38–40 |
| 6. | Sojourn in Galilee | 41–51 |
| 7. | Visit to Jerusalem. Feast of Tabernacles (Jn $7^{2f.}$) | 52 |
| 8. | Journey to (Peræa or) Galilee and back | 53–58 |
| 9. | Feast of the Dedication in Jerusalem | 59–71 |
| 10. | Raising of Lazarus. Sojourn in Ephraim and return to Bethany | 72, 73 |
| 11. | From the Triumphal Entry to the Institution of the Lord's Supper | 74–89 |
| 12. | Passion, Resurrection, and Ascension | 90–100 |

(*b*) *Codex Fuldensis*.—That the Latin Harmony of the Gospels discovered by Victor, bishop of Capua, about the year A.D. 545, and ascribed by him, on the authority of the statements contained in Eusebius (*HE* iv. 36), to Tatian* does actually represent the Diatessaron, may now be regarded as proved.† A comparison of the two documents clearly demonstrates that they are closely allied, and that, at least as regards the *order*, they are, with few exceptions, in remarkable agreement. This agreement, unfortunately, does not extend to the text, for the copy of the Latin Harmony which Victor inserted (in place of the four Gospels) at the head of his edition of the New Testament is not so much a translation, whether of the original Syriac or of an intermediate Greek version, as a transference of the language of the original text into the language of the Latin Gospels as revised by Jerome. In other words, the form exhibited by the Latin Harmony of the Codex Fuldensis is that of the Diatessaron, the text is that of the Vulgate. We cannot, however, follow Hemphill‡ in attributing the form of the Latin text to Victor or to the scribe working under his direction. Such a supposition is inconsistent with Victor's own introductory remarks,§ which convey no hint of such a laborious task, and is directly excluded by an examination of the descriptive capitulation prefixed to the Harmony. For though the latter frequently disagrees with the enumeration of the chapters as given in the text, and was clearly, therefore, composed before the Harmony had assumed its present form, it has been preserved unchanged by the copyist. The following instances of this disagreement, taken from the commencement of the Harmony, are the more interesting as they serve in a large measure to ex-

* Cf. § iii. *c*. According to the Arabic version, no account of the first Passover is given by Tatian; this, however, does not affect the length of our Lord's ministry.

† These verses, however, occur both in the Latin and the Arabic translations, though in different contexts.

* 'Ex historia quoque ejus comperi, quod Tatianus, vir eruditissimus et orator illius temporis clarus, unum ex quatuor compaginaverit evangelium cui titulum diapente composuit' (*Codex Fuldensis*, ed. E. Ranke, 1868, p. 1 f.). The origin of the curious title 'Diapente' (διὰ πέντε) for 'Diatessaron' has long perplexed the minds of scholars. It is not found either in the original Greek of Eusebius or in the Latin (of Rufinus) and Syriac translations of that work. Further, it is expressly excluded by Victor's statement that the Harmony was compiled from the *four* Gospels (the numeral is also inserted in the translation of Rufinus). Zahn (*Forsch*. i. 2 f.) is probably right in regarding it as a *lapsus calami* either of Victor or of his scribe.

† H. Wace, *Expositor*, 1881, 2, p. 128 f.; Zahn, *Forsch*. i. pp. 1–5, 298 f.

‡ *The Diatessaron of Tatian*, p. xxiv.

§ Cf. Zahn, *Forsch*. i. p. 3 f.

plain the opposition with which Victor's identification of the Harmony was for so long received. The table of chapters commences: Præfatio I. *In principio verbum, deus apud deum, per quem facta sunt omnia.* From this heading we see that the Harmony commenced with Jn $1^{1-5}$, and that Lk $1^{1-4}$, which now precedes it in the Harmony, formed no part of the original work. In the same way we can explain the presence of the genealogies of the Lord, which, as we know, were omitted in Tatian's Diatessaron. The capitulation runs: V. *de generationem* (sic!) *vel nativitate Christi.* Here the word *generatio* is clearly identical with *nativitas*, and does not refer to the genealogies (Mt $1^{1-16}$, Lk $3^{34-38}$, Mt $1^{17}$) but to Mt $1^{18f.}$ (*Christi autem generatio sic erat*), which is given in the Codex at the beginning of ch. 5. Thus we see that the Latin Harmony originally commenced with Jn $1^{1}$, and did not contain the genealogies, the omission of which is so characteristic of Tatian's work.

The elimination of these later additions to the Latin Harmony undoubtedly removes two of the strongest objections that were urged against the identification of Victor's discovery with the Diatessaron. There still remains, however, the question of the language, since, in the opinion of many scholars, the Latin translation can have been made only through the medium of a Greek version, whether that of the original Diatessaron or of a translation made from the Syriac. But the evidence which we have examined affords no support, or rather is entirely opposed, to the theory of an original Greek Diatessaron, while the researches of Zahn (*Forsch.* i. 311 f.) have shown conclusively that the supposed need of a Greek intermediary translation lacks historical support. Thus a contemporary of Victor, the African Junilius, who was *Quæstor sacri palatii* at Constantinople about A.D. 545-552, made a Latin translation (*Instituta regularia divinæ legis*) of an introduction to the Scriptures, composed by the Syrian Nestorian Paul, a pupil and teacher of the school of Nisibis, and sent it to Primasius, bishop of Adrumetum.* Even at an earlier date Cassiodorus and the Roman bishop Agapetus (d. 536 A.D.) conceived the idea of founding a theological school at Rome on the model of those at Nisibis and Alexandria. Still more important is the testimony of Gennadius of Massilia, who wrote a continuation of Jerome's *de Viris Illustribus.* In the first chapter of this work (written about A.D. 495) he discusses at some length the *Homilies* of Aphraates, whom he identified with Jacob of Nisibis, and explains Jerome's silence with regard to this writer on the ground that his works had not been translated; for the works of the few Syriac writers which are included in Jerome's category were, by his own testimony, known to him only through Greek translations. Gennadius mentions further a Syriac chronicle of Jacob of Nisibis, the writings of two of Ephraem's pupils, and also those of Isaac of Antioch. It would seem, therefore, that the ignorance of Syriac, which prevailed among Western writers at the time of Jerome, had largely disappeared during the interval between the date of the latter and that of Victor of Capua. Probably, as Zahn suggests, this change was chiefly brought about by the Syriac monks who settled in Sinai, Palestine, Egypt, and Constantinople, and there came into contact with Western scholars. Hence it is by no means improbable that some Latin scholar in the 5th or at the beginning of the 6th cent. should have compiled that Latin form of the Syriac Diatessaron which has been preserved to us in the Codex Fuldensis.

It is obvious from what has been said above that the Codex Fuldensis can add nothing to our knowledge of the text of the Diatessaron. It is, however, an important witness to the general structure and arrangement of its Syriac original, though even in that respect it seems to have suffered from revision. Its chief value for our purpose consists, as we shall see, in the fact that it supplies us with the means of controlling the far more trustworthy evidence of the Arabic version.

(*c*) *The Arabic Version.*—This version was first published by A. Ciasca, one of the guild of scriptors at the Vatican Library, under the title: '*The Diatessaron which Tatian compiled from the Four Gospels* (in Arabic), *seu Tatiani Evangeliorum Harmoniæ Arabice. Nunc primum ex duplici codice edidit et translatione Latina, donavit P. Augustinus Ciasca*, etc., Romæ, 1888.' Of the two MSS which form the basis of this edition, one (Cod. Vat. Arab. xiv.) had been brought from the East by Joseph Assemani as early as A.D. 1719, and had been definitely described by its discoverer as 'Tatiani Diatessaron seu quatuor Evangelia in unum redacta' (*Bibl. Or.* i. 619). A statement to the same effect contained in the colophon* was also quoted by Stephen Assemani; nevertheless the MS was left unnoticed, except by Zahn, until the publication of Ciasca's *De Tatiani Diatessaron Arabica Versione*† in 1883. In this essay Ciasca gave a full description of the MS which, like Assemani, he assigned to the 12th century. He further defended the statement of the colophon, despite the fact that the Arabic Harmony commenced with Mk $1^{1}$ (instead of Jn $1^{1}$), and contained the genealogies according to Matthew and Luke. His conjecture that these additions were a later interpolation was substantially confirmed by a comparison with the second MS, which shortly afterwards came into his hands. This MS was presented to the Museo Borgiano in 1886 by the Copt, Galim dos Galî. It is probably to be assigned to the 14th century. It displays a less correct orthography than the Vatican MS, but presents the text in a more original form. Both the introductory notice and the colophon describe the work as the Diatessaron. It clearly begins with Jn $1^{1}$, Mk $1^{1}$ forming a sort of title, while the genealogies are not included in the text, but have been inserted before the colophon. For his Arabic text Ciasca has mostly followed the Vatican MS, but there are a number of passages in which he has adopted the readings of the later MS; the variants are in every case added in the footnotes. The usefulness of the Latin translation is a good deal impaired by Ciasca's attempt to adapt it to the style and character of the Clementine Vulgate; apart from this fact, it also contains too many inaccuracies to be of much critical value. This translation has been followed by Dr. Hemphill in his English edition of the Diatessaron (1888), and forms the basis of another English translation, which has been compared throughout with the original Arabic, published by Dr. Hamlyn Hill in *The Earliest Life of Christ.* A more literal and entirely independent English rendering of the Arabic has also been published by the Rev. Hope W. Hogg.‡

An interesting statement as to the origin of the Arabic translation has been preserved both in the introductory notice and in the colophon§ of the

* Kihn, *Theodor von Mopsuestia und Junilius Africanus.*

* 'In fine fol. 123 hæc a librariis adnotata reperies: Explicit auxilio Dei Sacrosanctum Evangelium quod ex quatuor Evangeliis collegit Tatianus, quodque Diatessaron vulgo dicitur. Et laus Deo' (Mai, *Script. Vet. Nova Coll.* iv. 2. 14).

† Pitra, *Analecta Sacra*, iv. 465-487.

‡ *Ante-Nicene Christian Library:* Additional Volume. 1897.

§ These are given in full by Hjelt, *op. cit.* p. 63 n., together with a discussion of the difficulties presented at the commencement of the Harmony by the various readings of the two MSS. Hjelt adopts the view (cf. Zahn, *Gesch.* ii. 538) that the material common to both MSS is probably the remains of an original title which perhaps ran as follows: 'The Gospel of Jesus Christ,

Borgian MS, according to which it was made by the 'excellent and learned priest' Abu'l Faraj 'Abdullah ibn aṭ-Ṭayyib. The colophon adds further that the Syriac exemplar was written by 'Isa (MS wrongly Gubasi) ibn 'Ali al-Mutaṭabbib, the pupil of Ḥonain ibn-Isḥaḳ. By means of these notices, the correctness of which we have no reason to doubt, we are able to fix the date both of the Arabic translation and of its Syriac original. Ibn aṭ-Ṭayyib was a well-known writer of the 11th cent. (d. 1043), who commented on the writings of Aristotle, Galen, and Hippocrates, translated the Gospels of SS. Matthew and John from Syriac into Arabic, and also wrote an Arabic commentary on the Gospels. The scribe who was responsible for the Syriac exemplar is most probably none other than the famous lexicographer Jesus bar-'Ali (see above, § ii. *b*), who flourished in the latter half of the 9th cent. (his teacher Ḥonain died in A.D. 873). Thus the date of the Syriac MS used by the translator of the Borgian MS is the latter half of the 9th cent., and that of the Arabic translation itself the first half of the 11th century.

It is disappointing to find that, though the Arabic translation has preserved the outward form and characteristics of Tatian's Harmony, and in that respect is a most important witness to the order and arrangement of the Diatessaron, the text which it exhibits has throughout been accommodated to that of the Peshiṭta, and is therefore of no value for restoring the original Syriac version. The data at our command are perhaps insufficient for determining whether this accommodation had already been effected in the Syriac exemplar which was used by the Arabic translator, or is to be assigned to the latter himself. Zahn * maintains that the translator entirely recast the Syriac in accordance with the existing Arabic versions of the Gospels, and that the history of the Arabic Harmony thus presents a close analogy to that of the Latin (Codex Fuldensis). In support of this view he urges that, when once the Diatessaron had been banished from the public worship of the Church, it would soon cease to have an interest for any but the learned, and the latter would have no motive in introducing any alterations. As evidence of such learned interest in the Diatessaron he points to the marginal references, attached to both the Arabic MSS and presupposed by the introductory notice in the Borgian MS, by which the source of each passage was indicated: these, presumably, already existed in the Syriac copy of the 9th cent., since the writer of the notice is silent on the subject; and they naturally formed no part of the original Diatessaron. It seems, however, more probable that the later type of text preserved in the Arabic version reflects the result of a process of revision by which the *Syriac* Diatessaron had been gradually brought nearer and nearer to the authoritative text of the Peshiṭta. For the Arabic, unlike the Latin Harmony, shows evident signs of its Syriac origin; and this fact alone makes it difficult to imagine that its text was entirely recast in a similar manner to that of the Codex Fuldensis. Moreover, it is not only, as Zahn admits, a faithful witness to the order and arrangement of the Diatessaron as a whole, but also reproduces in many cases the finer details which determine the internal composition of the individual sections. These arguments would naturally receive strong confirmation if we could follow Hjelt in his theory—which is undoubtedly supported by the fact of this 11th cent. Arabic translation—that the Diatessaron was retained in church use by the Nestorians down to the Middle Ages. For, had such been the case, the accepted text of the Peshiṭta could not have failed in course of time to exercise a marked influence on the older text. Hjelt's further suggestion, that the reference in the colophon of the Borgian MS to the work of 'Isa ibn 'Ali al-Mutaṭabbib, *i.e.* Jesus bar-'Ali, possibly contains a hint as to the authorship of that final revision of the Syriac Diatessaron, which is embodied in the Arabic version, can only be described as an ingenious conjecture. But, whatever its genesis, it is clear that the Arabic translation possesses far greater value for restoring the original work of Tatian, more especially in relation to its internal structure, than the Latin Harmony of Victor. Moreover, since a comparison with the quotations of Ephraem and Aphraates attests its trustworthiness in those parts for which the Syriac writers are available, we should be justified in admitting its evidence, even where the latter are silent. In such cases, however, some doubt would naturally exist, and it is therefore in this connexion that the importance of the sister Latin version is most apparent. For if, as can be shown, the Codex Fuldensis is in entire agreement with the Arabic version in passages which are otherwise attested by Syriac evidence, we may infer that their agreement elsewhere is also due to the fact that both have preserved the original form of the Diatessaron. This is the more certain, as the Arabic translation of the 11th cent. cannot be dependent on the Latin version of Victor in the 6th cent., while the theory of a common source for both is excluded by a comparison of their variations from the original.*

The testimony of the Arabic Harmony has naturally enabled Zahn to supplement his former work to a very considerable extent, while at the same time confirming in the most striking manner his reconstruction of the Diatessaron. In one respect only is a correction necessary in the chronological scheme (see above), viz. the omission of the first Passover (Jn $2^{13}$) †: otherwise the changes involved are confined to a few cases in which the order of the individual sections varies in the Arabic version.‡ Of these the majority are accepted by Zahn when the order of the Arabic Harmony is confirmed by that of the Codex Fuldensis.§

iv. Relation of the Diatessaron to the Old Syriac.—The term 'Old Syriac' is here used to denote that early form of the Syriac Gospels which existed alongside of the Diatessaron down to the beginning of the 5th cent., but which was then revised in conformity with the Greek by Rabbûla, with the result that the new version, the Peshiṭta, speedily became the accepted ecclesiastical text.‖ We have already seen (§ ii. *b*) that this version, with its separate Gospels, was frequently described as *Evangelion da-Mĕpharrĕshē* (Gospel of the Separated [ones]), to distinguish it from the Diatessaron or *Ev. da-Mĕḥallĕṭē* (Gospel of the Mixed). Of this version we now possess two codices, viz. that called the Curetonian Syriac (Sc), a Nitrian MS of about the middle of the 5th cent., which was published by Cureton in 1858, and the Sinai palimpsest (Ss), dating from the beginning of the 5th cent., which was edited by the late Prof. Bensly, J. Rendel Harris, and F. C. Burkitt in

viz. the Diatessaron.' In the Syriac exemplar, used by the Arabic translator, the original title was probably obscured by the substitution of 'the Son of God' (Mk $1^1$) for 'viz. the Diatessaron,' while later still the insertion of another marginal gloss from Mk $1^1$ (*ex Marco dic: Initium*) caused even further confusion.

* *Gesch.* ii. p. 530 f.

* Zahn, *Gesch.* ii. 535 f.

† *Forsch.* i. 250.

‡ Hamlyn Hill, *Earliest Life of Christ*, App. ix.

§ In two cases at least it would seem that Zahn has insisted too rigidly on the absolute agreement of the Arabic and Latin versions; see Hjelt, *op. cit.* p. 70 f.

‖ For a fuller account, see an article by the present writer in *The Church Quarterly Review*, April 1903, pp. 143-171.

1893. The two codices agree so closely—though they also display some important textual variations—that they may be suitably described as two recensions of one and the same translation. Of the two texts Ss is decidedly the purer, and may be regarded as a faithful witness to the text of the 2nd cent.; Sc, on the other hand, probably represents a later recension of the 3rd century. The question that naturally arises from a consideration of these two MSS of the Old Syriac is that of their relation to the Harmony of Tatian, which also involves the further question of the relation of the Old Syriac to the Diatessaron.

As the result of his exhaustive investigations in connexion with the Diatessaron, Zahn concluded that Tatian had based his Harmony on the text of the Old Syriac, which must have been made about the middle of the 2nd cent.; but had also made use of a Greek text of a similar type to that of the Codex Bezæ and of the oldest Itala MSS. This conclusion was, in reality, based on two misconceptions. For from a comparison of the text of Sc with that of the Diatessaron (T), Zahn argued that the former had influenced, and was therefore prior to, the latter; but, since he also identified Sc with the Old Syriac, the two errors did not affect the correctness of his main contention, that the Old Syriac was prior to T. The real relation of T to Sc was first established by F. Baethgen,* who, as Zahn admits, has shown conclusively that T clearly influenced, and was therefore prior to, Sc. The arguments adduced by Baethgen are, briefly: (1) the presence of an extraordinarily large number of harmonistic readings in Sc, which must be derived from the Harmony; (2) the numerous cases of abridgment which are to be explained in a similar way; (3) the specifically 'Alexandrine' readings, which point to a later date than the 2nd cent.; (4) the great freedom of rendering, which frequently lapses into paraphrase, and may be recognized as due to Tatian; (5) the dogmatic character of Sc.

(1) Even if we exclude those cases in which a harmonistic reading is attested by either a single Greek MS or one of the old translations, or a Patristic quotation, Baethgen has shown that there still remain some 150 cases in which Sc stands alone, except for the frequent agreement of T. This is the more remarkable, since such mixed texts are necessarily confined to passages for which there is a parallel account; while Zahn's restoration of the text of T, of which Baethgen makes use, is of a very fragmentary nature.

(2) It is of the very essence of a Harmony such as that compiled by Tatian that it should omit not only those incidents and sayings which are repeated by one or more of the Evangelists, but also many of the small clauses and words which, without affecting the sense, serve to characterize the narrative. But, though these omissions might naturally be expected to be restored in a translation of the four separate Gospels, nearly a half of the (roughly) 270 readings which are peculiar to Sc (excluding the harmonistic readings) belong to this category of abridgment or omission: hence we may infer that Sc has made use of the shorter text of T wherever such a course does not affect either the meaning or the context.

(3) As the result of an exhaustive examination, Baethgen pronounces the text of Sc to be of a decidedly 'Western' type, as is shown by its affinity with D, in part also with א and some minuscules (especially 69), and, lastly, with the 'African' text of the Old Latin. But Sc also displays traces of 'Alexandrine' influence, which seems, in fact, to be due to Origen. Hence the translation must certainly be assigned to a later date than that of the Diatessaron, and cannot be earlier than the 3rd century.

(4) In his discussion on the method of the translator of Sc, Baethgen (pp. 13–23) classifies the various expedients adopted in order to reproduce the sense of the Greek text. But similar examples occur with even greater frequency in T; and though naturally some of the latter's more striking translations are no longer to be found in Sc, yet the two so often agree that the dependence of the one on the other can hardly be denied (cf. Baethgen, p. 87). In view, therefore, of the priority of T which has been already established, it is highly probable that in this respect also Sc is dependent on the Diatessaron.

(5) It is, however, especially with regard to its 'dogmatic' character that Sc betrays the influence of Tatian. Clear traces of the latter's anti-Jewish or universalistic views appear to be preserved in Mt $1^{21}$ (*mundum* for τὸν λαὸν αὐτοῦ), Jn $6^{70}$ (πάντας for τοὺς δώδεκα), $7^{51}$ (the omission of ἡμῶν after ὁ νόμος).* The omission of the possessive pronoun with 'Father' in Mt $6^{15}$ $10^{32}$, Lk $2^{49}$, Jn $6^{32}$ $14^{21}$ is also, according to Baethgen, to be ascribed to a similar point of view. Further, Tatian's Encratite views seem to be reflected in those renderings of Sc which are clearly due to a desire to establish the perpetual virginity of the mother of our Lord. This is especially noticeable in Mt $1^{18-25}$.

The above arguments do not all possess the same evidential value, but the cumulative evidence which they supply is more than sufficient to justify Baethgen's conclusion as to the relative dates of Sc and T. It by no means follows, however, that the evidence which was conclusive in the case of Sc necessarily applies to its archetype, viz. the Old Syriac: hence Baethgen's further conclusion, that the Diatessaron was the earliest form of the Syriac Gospels, cannot be accepted without additional proof. In this connexion the discovery of the Sinai palimpsest is of the greatest importance. For if it can be shown that this codex agrees with Sc in exhibiting the same traces of T's influence, we can only infer that this agreement goes back to their common source, *i.e.* the Old Syriac, and that the latter is therefore posterior to Tatian's Harmony. That such is actually the case is maintained, among others, by Zahn and Nestle; but, in view of the arguments brought forward by Burkitt † and Hjelt, ‡ the contrary opinion seems to be the more probable. For a comparison of the text of Ss with that of Sc shows that those peculiar features of the text which clearly pointed, in the case of the latter, to the influence of T, are by no means so strongly marked, if not entirely wanting, in the former. This divergence of text is especially noticeable in respect to the harmonistic and 'dogmatic' readings which undoubtedly form the main support of Baethgen's arguments as to the relation of Sc to T. With regard to the former, Burkitt notes that sixteen, § or more than one-third, of the forty-three examples (quoted by Baethgen), where Sc stands alone (or with the Diatessaron), are not shared in Ss. Hence it is clear that, though Ss undoubtedly contains a large number of mixed readings, these by no means form such a distinctive feature of its text as they do in the case of Sc, and need not therefore be ascribed to the same cause. Their presence is more than sufficiently accounted for, whether we assign it to the well-known tendency of scribes to harmonize parallel passages unconsciously, or to the actual influence of the Diatessaron, which, as

* *Evangelienfragmente*, Leipzig, 1885.

* To these we may add Mt $10^{23}$ (the omission of τοῦ Ἰσραήλ).

† *Guardian*, Oct. 31, 1894.

‡ *Op. cit.* p. 107 f.

§ Hjelt, *op. cit.* p. 108 n., corrects this to fifteen, and points out that in four of these passages Ss is defective.

we have seen, was the accepted text of the Syriac Church during the 3rd and 4th centuries. In respect of their 'dogmatic' character, the difference between the two codices is even more strongly marked, since Ss exhibits no traces of Tatian's influence. A striking illustration of this fact is furnished by an examination of the two texts in the crucial passage, Mt 1[18-25]: v.[19] Ss *her husband*—Sc omits; v.[20] Ss *thy wife*—Sc *thy betrothed*; v.[21] Ss *and thou shalt call*—Sc (*his name*) *shall be called*; v.[24] Ss *his wife*—Sc *Mary*; v.[25] Ss *and she bore him a son, and* HE *called his name Jesus*—Sc *and he lived with her purely, until she brought forth the son, and* SHE *called his name Jesus.* (In this rendering of οὐκ ἐγίνωσκεν αὐτήν [omitted by Ss] Sc follows Tatian). But it is obvious that the lack of agreement between Ss and Sc on these points, which formed the basis of Baethgen's argument for the priority of T to Sc, materially weakens the case for the similar relation between T and Ss, since the other points of contact are not decisive in themselves and may have arisen equally well from the dependence of T on Ss.

Moreover, we are not without positive proofs of the priority of the Old Syriac (as represented by Ss). The most important of these is the omission in Ss of the last twelve verses of St. Mark, which, as Burkitt has pointed out, can only be a Greek variant, and must represent, therefore, the original form of the Old Syriac. But we know that Tatian included Mk 16[9-20] in his Harmony: hence its omission by Ss clearly points to the priority of the latter. Other omissions which point to the same conclusion are those of Mk 15[98], Lk 22[43. 44] (the Bloody Sweat) and 23[34] (the Prayer on the Cross), all of which are given in the Diatessaron.

Similar evidence is also afforded by the curious mistranslations of Ss which occur in Mt 22[16], Mk 7[26] 10[50], Lk 4[29]. In Mt 22[16] τοὺς μαθητὰς αὐτοῦ (Sc τοῦ Ἰησοῦ) for αὐτῶν (Sc τῶν Φαρισαίων); in Mk 7[26] Ss renders *from the border of Tyre in Phœnicia*, clearly identifying the Συρο in Συροφοινίκισσα with Tyre (צור); in Mk 10[50] ἀποβαλών is misread as ἀπολαβών; in Lk 4[29] its rendering presupposes ὥστε κατακρεμάσαι αὐτόν instead of ὥστε κατακρημνίσαι αὐτόν.* To these we should probably add Mt 5[4], Lk 2[25], where Aphraates renders παρακληθήσονται and παράκλησις according to the ordinary meaning of the verb, viz. *to pray*. Aphraates, as we know, made use of the separated Gospels, and has probably done so in the present case; for Tatian, who was well acquainted with Greek, would hardly have fallen into such an error. Ss, it is true, translates παράκλησις correctly in Lk 6[24], but makes a similar misrendering in Lk 2[25]; possibly, as Hjelt suggests, Ss does not represent the original text of the Old Syriac either in Lk 6[24] or in Mt 5[4].

But, apart from these omissions and mistranslations, which clearly attest the independence, and therefore the priority, of Ss, a comparison of the two texts shows no less clearly that 'in those cases in which they differ from one another, the former, as a rule, presents a form of text which appears to be the older and more original' (Hjelt, p. 155), while in many cases the rendering of T seems to be directly based on that of Ss, or of one similar to it. Space forbids a complete discussion of all the divergences of the two texts, but the following instance will afford sufficient illustration of this statement.

We have already seen from a comparison of the texts of Ss and Sc in Mt 1[18-25] that the former gives a plain unbiassed rendering of the passage, which is in marked contrast to that of Sc. But the variants of Sc in this passage reflect, to a large extent, that desire to emphasize the virginity of our Lord's mother, which is even more apparent in the Diatessaron—*e.g.* in the rendering (v.[18]) *antequam data est viro* for πρὶν ἢ συνελθεῖν, the omission of αὐτῆς, v.[19]; the rendering *in sanctitate habitabat cum ea* for οὐκ ἐγίνωσκεν, v.[25], and the transposition of v.[25] and [24b]. Possibly the clearest indication of the priority of Ss to T is given by v.[19], in which the rendering of T and (Sc) obviously presupposes that of Ss. Other passages which point to T's immediate dependence on Ss, or on a text similar to it, are Mt 10[23] 14[32], Lk 1[13], Jn 3[34b 35a]. In Mt 10[23] Ss renders *civitatem* by ܟܪܟܐ; while in Lk 10[10], which is here combined with the Matthew passage, the more usual ܡܕܝܢܬܐ is found. This difference of rendering, however, is preserved by T, who uses the latter word for *civitatem* in the introductory sentence which he has incorporated from Lk 10, but renders the πόλεις of Mat. by ܟܪܟܐ. In Mt 14[32] he translates ἐκόπασεν by two synonyms, the one (ܫܬܩ) being taken from Matthew, and the other (ܫܠܝ) from the parallel Mk 6[51]. The dependence of T is no less clear in Lk 1[13], where Ss renders διότι εἰσηκούσθη ἡ δέησίς σου quite freely by 'For, behold, God has hearkened to the voice of thy prayer'; for, though he has restored the passive construction of the Greek, he has also retained the addition of Ss in the form 'exaudita est deprecatio tua ante *Deum*.' Jn 3[34f.] offers a number of interesting Syriac variants;* but of these the rendering of T (οὐ γὰρ ἐκ μέτρου δίδωσι [τὸ πνεῦμα ὁ πατὴρ]† τῷ υἱῷ αὐτοῦ ἀγαπᾷ δὲ αὐτόν) seems to be based on that of Ss (οὐ γὰρ ἐκ μέτρου δίδωσιν ὁ θεὸς ὁ πατήρ, ἀγαπᾷ δὲ τὸν υἱὸν αὐτοῦ), the order of which he has slightly varied. Other passages in which Ss has preserved the more original reading are: Mt 4[6] (for βάλε σεαυτὸν κάτω), 5[4f.] (the order of the second and third Beatitudes), 10[6] (for πρὸς τὰ πρόβατα τὰ ἀπολωλότα τοῦ οἰκοῦ Ἰσραήλ), 16[13] 17[20] (for διὰ τὴν ἀπιστίαν ὑμῶν), 18[20] 21[28-31] (Ss here presents a 'Western' text), Mk 7[11] 9[23], Lk 2[14] (the rendering of εὐδοκία), 6[40] 17[21] (ἐντὸς ὑμῶν), Jn 2[19] (omission of τοῦτον after τὸν ναόν), 4[19] (omission of ἡ γυνή), 6[38. 39] 11[1. 25] (omission of καὶ ἡ ζωή).

In consideration of these facts we are justified in ignoring a large number of those passages which were formerly brought forward by Zahn‡ in support of his theory of the priority of T to Ss. For, though the majority of these attest the close affinity of the two texts, they do not of themselves furnish any evidence as to the origin of this affinity, *i.e.* as to the priority of T or Ss. Zahn's view, however, finds its main support in those traces of harmonistic readings which he discovered in Ss, which he naturally ascribed to the influence of T. Briefly, Zahn's theory was as follows: Ss and Sc are undoubtedly closely related, and may be described as two recensions of a single version. Their variations, in which Sc, as a rule, agrees with the Peshitta, are for the most part of a grammatical, lexical, and stylistic character; in others the agreement of Sc and P against Ss can be explained only by the supposition that the free, or less accurate, translation of Ss was altered in Sc and P, and brought into closer conformity with the Greek text. But Sc has also been shown to have much in common with T: hence it was natural to expect that Ss and T should be closely allied. The conclusion arrived at by Zahn, after an examina-

* Tatian apparently inferred that our Lord was actually cast over the cliff, but was miraculously preserved from harm [Moesinger, pp. 130 f., 212; Hamlyn Hill, *Dissertation*, p. 93).

* See Burkitt, *S. Ephraem's Quotations from the Gospel*, p. 50 f.; Zahn, *Forsch.* i. p. 129.

† So Aphraates, 123; Moesinger, 105, omits these words.

‡ *Theol. Littbl.* 1895, Nos. 1, 2, 3.

tion of the text of Ss, was that the latter was even more closely allied to T than Sc. The instances cited by Zahn in proof of his contention for the priority of T have been carefully examined by Hjelt,* who has shown that in the majority of cases the alleged dependence of Ss on T rests on insufficient evidence. A few traces of harmonization, it is true, are to be found in Ss, but these are probably to be ascribed to later interpolation.

Our examination, therefore, of the relation of the Diatessaron to the two codices of the Old Syriac version leads to the following conclusions as to the history of Tatian's Harmony. The two texts are closely related to each other, but a comparison of the two shows clearly that the Old Syriac is the earlier version: hence the latter must have been in existence before A.D. 172. At this date Tatian compiled his Diatessaron, or Harmony of the four Gospels, in Syriac from the older version, which it quickly superseded, revising it with the help of a 'Western' copy of the Greek text, and introducing a number of arbitrary changes in accordance with his theological views. Down to the end of the 4th cent. the Diatessaron was universally accepted by the Syriac Church, the extent of its influence being reflected in the later recension of the Old Syriac version represented by Sc. In A.D. 411 the Old Syriac version was revised, in conformity with the current Greek text, under the auspices of Rabbûla, who forcibly removed the Diatessaron from church use in order to make room for his new version, viz. the Peshiṭta. As the result of Rabbûla's action, the Diatessaron practically disappeared from the knowledge of the Syrian Church, the references to it in later writers being mainly connected with the better known commentary of St. Ephraem. All interest, however, in Tatian's work did not cease with its banishment as a service-book, for about the beginning of the 6th cent. it was translated, or rather transferred, into Latin by an unknown author. This translation, as preserved by Victor of Capua in the Codex Fuldensis, probably formed the basis of the German version made *c.* 820–830 A.D., and this again was utilized by the author of the Old Saxon poem known as *Heliand*. The last stage of the history of the Diatessaron was not reached until the 11th cent., when it was once more rescued from obscurity, this time in the form of an Arabic translation.

LITERATURE.—(1) General:—C. A. Credner, *Beiträge zur Einleitung in die bibl. Schriften*, 1832, p. 437 ff., *Gesch. der neutest. Kanons* (herausg. von G. Volkmar), 1860, p. 17 ff.; H. A. Daniel, *Tatianus der Apologet*, 1837; C. A. Semisch, *Tatiani Diatessaron*, 1856; Th. Zahn, *Forschungen zur Geschichte des neutest. Kanons*, i. (1881, 'Tatian's Diatessaron'), ii. 286 ff. (1883), iv. 225–246 (1891, 'Der Text des von A. Ciasca herausgegebenen arabischen Diatessarons von Dr. Ernst Sellin'), *Geschichte des Kanons* (1888), i. 369 ff. (cf. Harnack, *Das Neue Testament um das Jahr 200*, p. 90 ff.), ii. 530–556, art. 'Zur Geschichte von Tatian's Diatessaron im Abendland' in *Neue Kirchliche Zeitschrift*, 1894, pp. 85–120, art. 'Evangelienharmonie' in *PRE*³ v. 653 ff. (1898); A. Hjelt, *Die altsyrische Evangelienübersetzung und Tatian's Diatessaron*, Leipzig, 1901 (=Zahn, *Forschungen*, vii. 1, 1903); Fr. Baethgen, *Evangelienfragmente*, Leipzig, 1885; J. Rendel Harris, *The Diatessaron of Tatian*, Cambridge, 1890, *Contemporary Review*, Aug. 1895, pp. 271–278 (a reply to W. R. Cassels' article in *Nineteenth Century*, April 1895, p. 665 ff.), *Fragments of the Commentary of Ephraem Syrus upon the Diatessaron*, London, 1895; Isaac H. Hall and Professor Gottheil, *Journal of Biblical Literature*, xi. 11, pp. 153–155 (1891), xii. 1, pp. 68–71 (1892); Goussen, *Studia Theologica*, Fasc. 1 (1895); J. B. Lightfoot, *Essays on Supernatural Religion*, pp. 272–288; H. Wace, *Expositor*, 1881, 1882; Westcott, *History of the Canon*⁷, pp. 325–333; Fuller, art. in *Dictionary of Christian Biography*, ii. p. 140 ff.; Holzhey, *Der neuentdeckte Codex Sinaiticus untersucht*, München, 1896; Bewer, *The History of the NT Canon in the Syrian Church*, Chicago, 1900; F. C. Burkitt, *S. Ephraem's Quotations from the Gospel* (= *Texts and Studies*, vii. 2), Cambridge, 1901; art. in *Church Quarterly Review*, April 1903, pp. 143–171.

(2) Texts.—A. Ciasca, 'De Tatiani Diatessaron arabica versione' (in S. P. Pitra's *Analecta sacra spicilegio Solesmensi parata*, Paris, iv. pp. xxviii ff., 466 ff., 1883), *Tatiani evangeliorum harmoniæ arabice*, Romæ, 1888; Hemphill, *The Diatessaron of Tatian*, Dublin and London, 1888; J. Hamlyn Hill, *The Earliest Life of Christ, being the Diatessaron of Tatian*, Edinburgh, 1894, *A Dissertation on the Gospel Commentary of S. Ephraem the Syrian*, Edinburgh, 1896; Hope W. Hogg, 'The Diatessaron of Tatian' in *Ante-Nicene Christian Library*, Add. vol., Edinburgh, 1897; G. Moesinger, *Evangelii Concordantis Expositio; in Latinum translata*, etc., Venice, 1876 (Professor A. Robinson's more accurate English translation of the Gospel quotations occurring in the Commentary is given in Appendix x. of Hill's *Earliest Life*, and in his *Dissertation*, pp. 75–119); E. Ranke, *Codex Fuldensis: Novum Testamentum latine interprete Hieronymo ex manuscripto Victoris Capuani*, Marburg and Leipzig, 1868.

JOHN F. STENNING.

* *Op. cit.* pp. 113–130; see also *Ch. Quarterly*, April 1903, pp. 167–170.

## JOSEPHUS.—



i. LIFE.—Josephus, son of Matthias the priest, as he would be described by his countrymen,—or Flavius Josephus, to give him the name which he adopted out of gratitude for the benefits conferred on him by the Flavian emperors,—was born in the first year of the emperor Caligula, A.D. 37 or 38 (*Vita*, 5;* cf. *Ant.* XX. 267, where he identifies the thirteenth year of Domitian's reign with the fifty-sixth of his own life). He was of priestly descent, his father's line having been one of the noblest families, as he tells us, in the first of the twenty-four priestly courses; while on his mother's side he was connected with the royal Hasmonæan house (*Vita*, 2). So precocious was he in his studies, that at the age of fourteen, if we may believe him, his advice on questions concerning the Law was sought by the chief priests and principal citizens of Jerusalem. At the age of sixteen he determined to make trial of the three sects of his nation,—Pharisees, Sadducees, and Essenes,—and finally spent three years in the desert with one Banus, a hermit, who appears to have carried the ascetic practices of the last-named sect to an extreme. He returned to Jerusalem in his nineteenth year, and from that time adhered to the Pharisaic party, whose doctrines have left their mark on many of his pages. At the age of twenty-six, about the year A.D. 63, he went to Rome to plead the cause of certain priests who had been imprisoned by Felix and sent to Italy to be tried by the emperor. On this voyage, Josephus, like St. Paul a few years earlier, suffered shipwreck, but was picked up with some of his companions by a ship of Cyrene and brought safely to Puteoli. There he fell in with Aliturus, a Jewish actor in favour at court. Through the influence of this man with Poppæa, the shameless mistress and afterwards wife of Nero, who coquetted with Judaism [Josephus' remark, θεοσεβὴς γὰρ ἦν, *Ant.* XX. 195, implies that she was a proselyte], he obtained the release of the priests, and returned to Palestine laden with presents. The

* For the sake of brevity we have used the sections into which Niese has divided the text. These are also given in brackets in the other principal critical edition—that of Naber.

visit of Josephus to Rome nearly synchronizes with the period of St. Paul's imprisonment in that city; but the earlier dates now generally assigned to the latter portion of the Apostle's life * force us to the conclusion that he had already been liberated, and that his liberation cannot have been in any way connected, as Edersheim conjectured, with the mission of Josephus. Whether or no the Jewish priest became acquainted at this time with the life and work of the Apostle it is impossible to say: he has at all events maintained the same silence with regard to him with which he passes over all that concerns the history of the early Christian Church.

His brief visit to Italy seems to have impressed Josephus with a sense of the invincible power of Rome; and on his return to Judæa, where he found his countrymen ready for revolt, and everything pointing towards the immediate outbreak of war, he at first tried to pacify the war party, but in vain (*Vita*, 17). After the defeat of Cestius Gallus, the governor of Syria, in the defiles near Beth-horon, towards the end of A.D. 66, he realized that the irrevocable step had been taken. Josephus, then barely thirty years old, was appointed to the important post of the command of Galilee (*BJ* II. 568; *Vita*, 28). Apparently, his connexion with the priestly party obtained for him this office, as, in spite of his frequent assertions of his skill and strategy, he does not seem to have possessed many of the qualities necessary to a successful general. He found Galilee in a divided state: Sepphoris and Gamala were disposed to favour the Romans, Tiberias and Gischala were unwilling to submit to the commands of the newly-sent general. His first steps were to fortify the principal places, to reform the army after the Roman model by appointing a number of subordinate officers (*BJ* II. 577), and to appoint a council consisting of seventy of the principal Galilæans, who were to try cases, and would at the same time be hostages for the fidelity of the district (*Vita*, 79). But his efforts to enforce discipline and to secure the allegiance of the Galilæans were unavailing. He found many opponents, the most formidable being John of Gischala, who afterwards played so important a part in the siege of Jerusalem; and the spring of A.D. 67 was chiefly spent in civil war and in avoiding plots against his life. He was suspected, perhaps not without justice, of harbouring designs of betraying the country to Rome. At length John sent to the capital, accusing Josephus of setting himself up as a tyrant, and prevailed on the high priest Ananus and the principal men of the city to recall him from the command (*BJ* II. 627; *Vita*, 189). An embassy under the command of four leading men was accordingly sent to supersede Josephus. He, however, refused to accept the order, and succeeded in obtaining letters from Jerusalem by which he was reinstated (*Vita*, 309). Meanwhile Vespasian, who had been commissioned by Nero to conduct the war, was advancing from Antioch upon Galilee. Gadara was quickly taken, and Josephus, who at the first onset was half inclined to surrender, and wrote to Jerusalem for instructions on the subject (*BJ* III. 137), at length threw himself into Jotapata, and resolved to stand a siege.

Of this siege Josephus has given us a detailed account in the third book of the *Jewish War*, with much encomium upon his own skill, although he does not conceal the fact that at one period he meditated quitting his post and saving himself by flight. At length a deserter betrayed the fact to the Romans that the sentinels could no longer keep awake through the night, and advised them to make an attack in the early morning. This advice was acted on, and the place was taken after a siege of forty-seven days, on the 1st of the month Panemos (July A.D. 67). Josephus with forty others concealed himself in an underground cavern, where he was discovered by the Romans. He was ready to surrender himself, but was prevented by his comrades, who insisted on his sharing their fate, and dying either by their hands or his own. Josephus, by some stratagem, prevailed on them to draw lots as to the order in which they should put each other to death, and managed ['whether we must attribute it to chance or to Divine Providence' are his words] to be reserved till the last with another, whom without difficulty he persuaded to seek liberty along with himself. Being brought before Vespasian, he posed as a prophet, and foretold the elevation of the general and his son Titus to the empire, and was kept a prisoner, although treated with consideration. The prophecy of Josephus has been repeated by Roman historians—Suetonius (*Vesp.* 5) and Dio Cassius (lxvi. 1). Rabbinical tradition ascribes a similar prophecy with reference to Titus to Rabbi Jochanan ben Saccai, and both emperors are said to have been informed of the destiny awaiting them by heathen oracles (Tac. *Hist.* ii. 78, the priest Basilides at Mount Carmel to Vespasian; Suetonius, *Vesp.* 5, *Titus*, 5). Both Tacitus and Suetonius tell us that there was a widespread belief that at that time men coming from the East would become masters of the world (Tac. *Hist.* v. 13; Suet. *Vesp.* 4). Josephus could not but be aware of this belief, and might with no great shrewdness be able to read the signs of the times in the growing dissatisfaction with Nero's rule, which came to a climax in the following year.

By the end of A.D. 67 the whole of Northern Palestine was in the hands of the Romans. Only Jerusalem, where a bloody civil war was raging, remained to be taken. But its capture was delayed by the events of A.D. 68, which drew the attention of the generals to the West. News came first of the death of Nero, which took place in June, and then, in rapid succession, of the accession of Galba, Otho, and Vitellius. In July A.D. 69 Vespasian's legions took the law into their own hands, and proclaimed him emperor. One of his first acts as emperor was to liberate Josephus, whose prophecy had now come true; his chains, so the historian tells us, were, at Titus' suggestion, not merely loosed, but struck off, to indicate that he had been unjustly kept in bonds (*BJ* IV. 622). He now accompanied the emperor to Alexandria, and from there was sent back with Titus to take part in the siege of Jerusalem (*Vita*, 416). It is not the place here to describe the course of that memorable siege, which the historian has narrated in the fifth and sixth books of the *Jewish War*. The services of Josephus as interpreter and intercessor were more than once requisitioned by Titus (*BJ* V. 361, VI. 96); on one occasion he was hit by a stone, and barely escaped capture and death at the hands of his countrymen (*BJ* V. 541). He was, he tells us, at this time between two fires; for, while bitterly hated by the Jews, he was suspected by the Romans of treachery whenever they met with a reverse (*Vita*, 416). After the capture of the city and the destruction of the temple he was offered by Titus the choice of what he would from the ruins, but was content with requesting a copy of the Scriptures and the life of his brother and fifty friends. Subsequently he obtained the release of about a hundred and ninety of his friends, and was granted an estate outside Jerusalem (*Vita*, 422). He sailed with Titus to Rome, and witnessed

* The close of the Acts is placed early in A.D. 59 by Harnack, in 61 by Turner, 62 by Ramsay, and 63 by Lightfoot (see art. CHRONOLOGY OF NT in vol. i. p. 424).

the gorgeous triumphal procession of the two emperors, of which he has left us a description (*BJ* VII. 123 ff.). And now the erstwhile Jewish priest and patriot settled down to a life of ease as a *littérateur*. He was given apartments by Vespasian in the house which the latter had occupied before he became emperor, and honoured with the Roman citizenship and a pension (*Vita*, 423): he was thus among the first to be placed on the 'civil list' which was instituted by that emperor (Suet. *Vesp.* 18: 'Primus e fisco Latinis Græcisque rhetoribus annua centena constituit'). He was also awarded a further grant of land in Judæa. But the hatred of his countrymen still pursued him, and his security was from time to time endangered by their accusations. He mentions one Jonathan in particular, the leader of a Jewish revolt in Cyrene, who accused him of complicity in his designs; Vespasian, however, befriended Josephus, and had Jonathan put to death (*BJ* VII. 437; *Vita*, 424). Under Titus and Domitian he continued to receive the same honourable treatment; the latter emperor exempted his estate in Judæa from taxation. We know nothing as to the date of his death, except that he must have lived into the 2nd cent., since he wrote the *Life* after the death of Agrippa II. (*Vita*, 359), who died in the third year of Trajan's reign, A.D. 100 (Photius, *Bibliotheca*, Cod. 33).

The accuracy of the statement of Photius has, however, been called in question, and Niese (*Hist. Zeitschrift*, Bd. lxxvi. 193 ff.), identifying Epaphroditus, the patron of the historian, with the freedman of Nero, has conjectured that Josephus was involved in the ruin of his patron (Suet. *Dom.* 14), falling a victim to the suspicions of Domitian about A.D. 95.

Eusebius tells us that Josephus was honoured with a statue at Rome, and that his works were placed in the public library (*HE* iii. 9). He was married at least four times (*BJ* V. 419; *Vita*, 414, 415, 427): for his family connexions, see Schürer, *GJV*³ i. 77 [*HJP* I. i. 81].

ii. WORKS.—In the leisure which he enjoyed at Rome, Josephus composed the four works which, owing, no doubt, to the high esteem in which they were held by early Christian writers, have come down to us entire, namely, the *Jewish War*, the *Antiquities*, the *Life*, and the treatise *Against Apion*; nor is there sufficient ground for believing that he wrote any others.

1. *The Jewish War.*—This is the oldest of Josephus' works, having been written during the latter half of the reign of Vespasian (A.D. 69–79). That it was written late in this reign is shown by the fact that it had been preceded by other accounts of the war (*BJ*, *ad init.*), and also by the mention of the completion of the building of the temple of Pax (*BJ* VII. 158), which, according to Dio Cassius (lxvi. 15), was dedicated in A.D. 75. It was composed, in the first place, in the writer's native tongue, that is to say Aramaic, for the benefit of the Semitic peoples of inland Syria (τοῖς ἄνω βαρβάροις, *BJ* I. 3), and was afterwards rendered into Greek for the use of readers throughout the Roman empire. The original writing has not been preserved; probably it was a much shorter work than the Greek, and did not contain the two introductory books and the closing book of the *BJ*. For the translation, which shows no traces of its Aramaic parentage, and must have been practically a new work, Josephus employed certain *collaborateurs* (χρησάμενός τισι πρὸς τὴν Ἑλληνίδα φωνὴν συνεργοῖς, *c. Ap.* i. 50). Copies were presented to Vespasian and Titus, and to many Romans who had taken part in the war, and *sold* to Herod Agrippa II. and other learned men among his countrymen, all of whom, Josephus asserts, attested the accuracy of his work (*c. Ap.* i. 51 f.). Titus himself affixed his *imprimatur*, and Agrippa wrote as many as sixty-two letters in its support (*Vita*, 363 ff.). From two of these, which are quoted, it appears that the work was issued in parts, for Agrippa asks for the rest to be sent to him, while he offers to supplement the information of the writer at their next meeting (*ib.*).

This is undoubtedly a careful piece of work. The writer held the important post of commander of the forces in Galilee at the opening of the war, and throughout the siege of Jerusalem was in attendance in the Roman army. A great part of his account of the war must have been written from notes made during the events which he describes; though he must also, especially in the opening books, have had access to literary materials. He realized the magnitude and importance of the crisis [his exordium appears to be in imitation of the opening sentences of Thucydides with regard to the Peloponnesian War], and shows a high degree of literary skill in his dramatic presentation of the narrative. His chief defects may be said to be a tendency to exaggeration, especially in the matter of numbers,* and the bias which he shows, writing as he does under Imperial supervision, in extolling the achievements and the clemency of the Roman generals. Thus his account of the desire of Titus to spare the temple (*BJ* VI. 124, 236 ff.) runs counter to that of Sulpicius Severus, probably derived from Tacitus, according to which the general gave his sanction to its destruction ['At contra alii et Titus ipse evertendum in primis templum censebant,' *Chron.* ii. 30]. His representation of the Zealots as the only persons to blame for the obstinacy with which the siege was prolonged and the miseries endured, is probably an exaggeration, due to his personal antagonism to his old enemy in Galilee, John of Gischala. The rhetorical speeches which are put into the mouths of the principal actors, here and in the *Antiquities*, are a device which he shares in common with most ancient historians.

*Contents.*—Book I. gives a rapid sketch of Jewish history from the capture of Jerusalem by Antiochus Epiphanes to the death of Herod. Book II. carries on the history from the accession of Archelaus to the defeat of Cestius Gallus near Beth-horon, and the Jewish preparations for the war. Book III. describes the coming of Vespasian and Titus, the siege of Jotapata, and the war in Galilee. Book IV. contains the final scenes of the Galilæan campaign, the factions in Jerusalem, and the advance of Vespasian upon the city, from which he is called away to Rome on being elected emperor by his army. Book V. contains a description of the city and the temple, the investment by Titus, and the capture of the first and second walls. Book VI. describes the horrors of the famine and the taking of the castle of Antonia, which is rapidly followed by the burning of the temple and the capture and destruction of the city. Book VII. narrates the return of Titus to Rome, the triumph of the generals, and the capture of Machærus and Masada, the last strongholds of the most obstinate Jewish belligerents.

*Sources.*—The summary in Books I. and II. of the events from Judas Maccabæus to the outbreak of the war seems to be extracted from some Universal History, which contained occasional reference to Jewish history. It is most probable that this source was the great work of Nicolaus of Damascus. A comparison of this part of the work with the corresponding portion of the *Antiquities*, where the description is far more detailed, although there is occasionally *verbatim* agreement

* Tacitus (*Hist.* v. 13) gives the total number of the besieged as 600,000. According to Jos. (*BJ* v. 569) that was the number of the dead among the poorer classes alone, whose bodies were thrown out at the gates.

between the two works, forms an interesting study.

2. *The Antiquities.*—In this comprehensive work Josephus undertook to give a history of his nation from the creation of the world to the outbreak of the Jewish War. He tells us that he had such a work in mind when engaged on his earlier history, of the labour which it cost him, and how, after many misgivings and interruptions, it was only through the encouragement of his patron Epaphroditus that he was instigated to complete it (*Ant.* I. 6 ff.). This Epaphroditus, to whom he dedicated not only the *Antiquities* but also the *Life* and the *contra Apionem*, has often been identified with the freedman and secretary of Nero; but as the latter was put to death by Domitian (Suet. *Dom.* 14), and the *Life* at all events was written after the death of that emperor, this view is untenable. Schürer considers that the patron of Josephus should rather be identified with the grammarian of the name who, according to Suidas, lived in Rome under the emperors from Nero to Nerva, and collected a large library; the name, however, was not an uncommon one. The *opus magnum* was at length completed in the thirteenth year of Domitian and in the fifty-sixth of the life of the historian (A.D. 93–94, *Ant.* XX. 267). The division into twenty books was the writer's own (*ib.*), and in that arrangement as well as in the title (Ἰουδαϊκὴ Ἀρχαιολογία) he seems to have taken for his model the great historical work of Dionysius of Halicarnassus, entitled Ῥωμαϊκὴ Ἀρχαιολογία.

*Contents.*—In Books I.–X. the narrative closely follows the Biblical account down to the Babylonian captivity. Book XI. embraces the period from the return under Cyrus to Alexander the Great: XII. continues the narrative from the time of Ptolemy Philadelphus (B.C. 280) to the death of Judas Maccabæus (B.C. 161): XIII. gives the history of the Hasmonæan house to the death of Alexandra (B.C. 67): XIV. the history of the brothers Aristobulus II. and Hyrcanus, the coming of Pompey, and the accession of Herod to the throne of Judæa (B.C. 37): XV., XVI., and the first half of XVII. describe Herod's reign (B.C. 37–4): the rest of XVII. the reign of Archelaus (B.C. 4 to 6 A.D.): XVIII. contains a collection of notices with regard to Quirinius, Pilate, Tiberius, Herod Agrippa I., and the disturbances caused by the order of Gaius to erect his statue in the temple: the greater part of XIX. is occupied with the events leading up to the assassination of Gaius and the accession of Claudius (A.D. 41): the remainder of XIX. and XX. give a summary history of events to the outbreak of the Jewish War in A.D. 66.

*Sources.*—For the first ten books the principal source was the LXX text of the Bible, with occasional recourse to the Hebrew. This was supplemented by various legends, derived in part from Rabbinic tradition: for these and for the general treatment of the Biblical narrative the reader is referred to the next section of this article. But the Biblical narrative was further supported by quotations from secular historians and documents other than Biblical. Allusion is made to Berosus (I. 93, 107, 158, X. 20, 34, 219), Nicolaus of Damascus (I. 94 with other writers, 108 with others, 159 with others, VII. 101), the *Sibylline Oracles* (I. 118), Alexander Polyhistor (I. 240), for the annals of Tyre to Menander (VIII. 144, 324, IX. 283) and Dius (VIII. 147) and the original Tyrian archives (VIII. 55), also to Herodotus (VIII. 157, 253, 260, X. 20), Megasthenes, Diocles, and Philostratus (X. 227 f.). In the case of the lists of authorities cited in I. 94, 107 f., 158 f. (cf. the list in *c. Ap.* ii. 84) it should be noted that Nicolaus is quoted last, and it is probable that the other names are simply taken over from that author, of whom Josephus made considerable use in writing his *Antiquities.* It is thus not necessary to assume a first-hand acquaintance with all the authors mentioned: a parade of Greek authorities tended to impress the Greek readers for whom the history was written. Freudenthal (*Hellenistiche Studien*, 'Alexander Polyhistor,' 1875) has shown that Josephus was also acquainted with the Hellenistic versions of the Biblical narrative made in the 2nd cent. B.C. by Demetrius and Artapanus; but his knowledge of these was probably indirect, being derived from the extracts made by Alexander Polyhistor or others.

The account of the return from the Captivity is taken from the Greek 1 Esdras, a slight use being made of the canonical Books of Ezra and Nehemiah. This is followed by the story of Esther, also taken from the LXX, with the additions peculiar to that version.

The determination of the sources used for the post-Biblical period is a more difficult matter, and in recent times has given rise to considerable discussion. For the next two and a half centuries of Jewish history Josephus has little or no information; the interval from Nehemiah to Antiochus Epiphanes (B.C. 175) is bridged over by some legends with regard to Alexander (end of Book XI.), a long extract from the Letter of Aristeas, and a story of the mission of Joseph, the nephew of Onias the high priest, to Ptolemy Euergetes (Book XII.). The account of the persecution of the Jews by Antiochus Epiphanes and the history of the Maccabees to the death of Jonathan (B.C. 175–143), is taken from the First Book of Maccabees. There can be no doubt that Josephus used the Greek version of that book, and not, as has been maintained, the lost Hebrew original; but the almost complete neglect of the last chapters of that book raises a doubt whether they were contained in Josephus' copy. Some use has been made of Polybius, who is quoted in XII. 135 and 358. For the later history of the Hasmonæan houses after the point where the narrative of Polybius ended (B.C. 146), Josephus appears to have been without any special Jewish authorities, and to have derived his information from the sections dealing with the Jews in Universal Histories by Greek writers. His principal sources at this point were the lost history of Străbo and the voluminous work (extending to 144 books) of Nicolaus of Damascus, the friend of Herod the Great. From Books XIII. to XVI. of the *Antiquities* references to these two writers are frequent. Nicolaus is quoted in XII. 127, XIII. 250, 347, XIV. 9, 68, 104, XVI. 183 ff.; Strabo in XIII. 286, 319 (344 Timagenes, probably from Strabo, cf. 319), 347, XIV. 35, 68, 104, 111, 114 ff., 138, XV. 10.* It has, however, been maintained by some recent critics that these two authors have not been used except in the above-named passages, and that the narrative is mainly based on some authority who remains nameless. Niese (*Hermes*, xi. [1876] pp. 466–488) has pointed out that some of the quotations from Strabo are inserted out of place in the history (XIV. 35, 138 f.): emphasis is also laid on the καί with which the quotations from historians are introduced, as though they were merely intended to corroborate an account derived from other sources. These arguments have, however, been sufficiently answered by Schürer. He has traced the use of Strabo even where he is not named. The misplacing of some of the Strabo extracts is explained by the fact that Nicolaus was at those points the main authority. Traces of the style of Nicolaus, as seen in the extant fragments of his work, may

* Livy is once named (xiv. 68), but it is not likely that Josephus made any use of his history.

also be found, in the opinion of this writer, in this portion of the *Antiquities.*

There remains one argument to be considered which has been adduced in favour of this theory of an anonymous source. Destinon (*Die Quellen des F. Josephus*, 1882) was the first to call special attention to the use of the phrase *καθὼς δεδηλώκαμεν* (*καθὼς δεδήλωται*) in several instances where the references cannot be verified in the extant works of Josephus. The phrase is employed at the end of sections dealing with the history of the Seleucid dynasty, or, more generally, with the affairs of Syria and Parthia, where the writer reverts to Jewish history proper. Since there is no trace of any separate work on Syrian history by Josephus, Destinon maintained that these references were taken over bodily by him from his source. Further, as the phrase forms a link between the non-Jewish and the Jewish portions, the anonymous writer, from whom Josephus copied it, must, it is urged, have already combined Jewish and heathen materials. Josephus, according to Destinon, in this part of his work, found his history already made for him, and his only task was to insert occasional references to other historians such as Strabo and Nicolaus. The Syrian sections with the phrase in question are interspersed throughout the part which is based on 1 Maccabees; and Josephus, it is alleged, did not use that book at first hand, but found it incorporated in the anonymous work. This theory, which at first sight appears highly improbable, cannot be lightly dismissed. Such careless copying of authorities is not without parallels in ancient history; and the explanation of these references forms an interesting problem on which the last word has not yet been said. The facts are as follows:—(1) The first instance of the phrase occurs in *Ant.* VII. 393, *καθὼς καὶ ἐν ἄλλοις δεδηλώκαμεν* [Hyrcanus opens David's tomb and bribes Antiochus Eusebes with the treasures concealed there]. This might be a reference to the parallel account in *BJ* I. 61; but references in *Ant.* to *BJ* are usually more precise (*Ant.* XIII. 73, 173, XVIII. 11), and the allusion to one of the Seleucids is to be noted. (2) In *Ant.* XI. 305, *καθὼς ἐν ἄλλοις δεδήλωται* [Philip and Alexander], the reference may be, as elsewhere where the passive is used, to Greek historians generally. (3) In Books XII. and XIII. the personal *δεδηλώκαμεν* and the impersonal *δεδήλωται* are used interchangeably with some variation of readings in the MSS, and the reference is usually to the Seleucids (XII. 244, 390, XIII. 36, 61, 108, 119, 186, 253, 271, 347, 371, 372). (4) In Book XIV. the impersonal *δεδήλωται* is always used, and in two instances the phrase becomes 'as has been shown *by* others' (XIV. 122 *ὑπ' ἄλλων*, 301 *παρ' ἄλλοις*). The last instance, also with *δεδήλωται*, is XVIII. 54 [the death of Germanicus in A.D. 19]. The reference in these cases is nearly always to Parthian affairs, and, but for the use of the personal *δεδηλώκαμεν* in Book XIII., there would be no question that Josephus is here directing his readers for fuller information to Greek historians at large. (5) A comparison between *BJ* and *Ant.* in the following cases is specially interesting:—

*BJ* I. 179 [death of Crassus] *περὶ ὧν οὐ νῦν καιρὸς λέγειν.* — *Ant.* XIV. 119 [the same] *ὡς καὶ ἐν ἄλλοις δεδήλωται.*

*BJ* I. 182 [Parthian war of Cassius] *περὶ ὧν ἐν ἑτέροις ἐροῦμεν.* — *Ant.* XIV. 122 [the same] *ὡς καὶ ὑπ' αλλων δεδήλωται.*

In the earlier work a promise is made of a further description 'elsewhere': in the latter work the reader is referred to other writers. There can be no doubt that Josephus used the same authority or authorities when writing the parallel portions in *BJ* and *Ant.*, and it looks as if the common source at this point had some such phrase as *καθὼς ἐν ἄλλοις δεδηλώκαμεν*, which Josephus has retained with various slight modifications. On the other hand, it might be said that he did contemplate a work on Eastern history which still remained unwritten in A.D. 93 (the date of *Ant.*); that he had his own earlier work before him as well as the common source when writing *Ant.*; and that he has simply repeated himself, altering the phrase in view of his failure to carry out the projected Syrian history. But the former explanation appears to be the simpler of the two.

The following general observations may be made with regard to the phenomena. (*a*) The explanation that naturally suggests itself is that Josephus wrote a work on the Seleucids and Syrian history. The only external evidence in favour of this is a rather vague statement in Jerome (Com. on Is 11, *ad init.*: 'intelligant me non omnium probare fidem . . . sed ad distinctionem Josephi Porphyriique dixisse, qui de hac quæstione plurima disputarunt'), which implies that Josephus had written on the seventy weeks of Daniel. Such a work would of course have dealt with the Seleucid dynasty. But there is no allusion to it elsewhere; and Jerome, who quotes the interpretations of numerous writers on the seventy weeks in his Com. on Daniel, does not mention it again. Josephus himself in *Ant.* X., where he treats of Daniel, is quite silent on the subject, although his vanity must have led him to mention such a literary undertaking.

(*b*) The objections to Destinon's theory are that Josephus is elsewhere generally accurate in the matter of references: the formulas of reference used in the verifiable references are not unlike that used in the unverifiable cases: the first person, undoubtedly meaning Josephus, is used in close proximity to *καθὼς δεδηλώκαμεν* (*Ant.* XIII. 347): Josephus does not give the impression of being such a careless compiler as this theory would require us to assume. (*c*) If the phrase has been borrowed from a source, it is simpler, with Schürer, to identify this source with Nicolaus, in whose Universal History one or more books would probably be devoted to the history of the Seleucids, rather than, with Destinon, to invent an anonymous writer. (*d*) If we reject altogether the theory that the phrase is taken over from an earlier source, we may, with Drüner (*Untersuchungen über Josephus*, Marburg, 1896), suppose that Josephus refers to a preliminary work (*Vorarbeit*) to the *Antiquities*, which was never given to the world, in which he briefly sketched the history of the Seleucids. Niese (*Hist. Zeitschrift*, Bd. lxxvi.) regards the phrase merely as 'a convenient and euphonious formula for breaking off the narrative'; but this leaves unexplained its almost complete limitation to Syrian history.

For the history of Herod the Great, which occupies the greater part of four books (XIV. 158–XVII. 192), there can be little doubt that the principal source was Nicolaus of Damascus, from whom also, apparently, was derived the much briefer account in the *BJ.* Josephus, however, does not accept all his statements without question, and more than once censures him for the partiality which he shows to that monarch (XIV. 9, XVI. 183 ff.). He appears to have had access also to some document in which an unfavourable view was taken of the king. Mention is once made of the 'Memoirs of king Herod' (*τὰ ὑπομνήματα τὰ τοῦ βασιλέως Ἡρώδου*, XV. 174); but it is doubtful whether Josephus used these at first hand. A difference in the arrangement of subject-matter is to be noted in the two accounts of Herod. In *BJ* the external history of the reign is first given, ending with an account of Herod's buildings (to I. 430); and then, as a pendant to the picture of the patent prosperity (αἱ ὕπαιθροι εὐπραγίαι), is added the tragic story of the domestic dissensions. In *Ant.* this division is abandoned, and the events follow one another in chronological order.

After the death of Herod, when we should especially value any details which might throw light on the Gospel narrative, the history becomes meagre, expanding again into greater fulness when the reign of Agrippa I. is reached. With regard to him, Josephus would be able to obtain full information from his son Agrippa II., who had already offered his assistance in the composition of the *BJ* (*Vita*, 366); and for the events leading up to the war he could draw on his own recollections. The most striking feature in the latter part of the *Ant.* is the disproportionate length at which the somewhat irrelevant story of the assassination of Gaius and the accession of Claudius is given: it occupies the greater part of Book XIX. This must be derived from some contemporary source, and is of primary importance for the Roman historian. Mommsen (who is followed by Schemann) has suggested that this source was the history of Cluvius Rufus, who was present in the theatre at the time when Gaius came to his end, and of whom a remark is quoted by Josephus (*Ant.* XIX. 91 f.); but we do not know that Cluvius' work embraced more than the reign of Nero and the events of A.D. 69.

Throughout his history Josephus is careful to note the succession of the high priests; and at the close (XX. 224–251) he gives an enumeration of them, from Aaron to the destruction of Jerusalem, with some divergences from the earlier notices. (Destinon has laid stress on these divergences as pointing to the use of different sources). For this part of his work he must have had access to the priestly records, which, as he tells us, were kept with such strict exactitude (*c. Ap.* i. 36).

Of great value for the historian are the decrees, mainly concerning exemptions granted to Jews, which Josephus has grouped together at various points in the narrative (XIII. 260 ff., XIV. 149 ff., 185–267, 306 ff., XVI. 162–173). Of their genuineness there can be no doubt; whence Josephus obtained them is doubtful. He refers in two passages to the archives in the Capitol at Rome (XIV. 188, 266); but it is improbable that the decrees concerning the Jews of Asia Minor were preserved there. Niese (*Hermes*, xi. [1876] 466 ff.) has conjectured from *Ant.* XVI. 48, where Nicolaus, defending the Jews of Asia, appeals to similar decrees, that a collection of them had already been made in his Universal History, from which Josephus has borrowed them; Schürer (*GJV*[3] i. 86, note) has shown, however, that this will not account for all the documents quoted by Josephus.

As to the *character* of Josephus *as a historian*, very various estimates have been held, from that of Jerome, who extolled him as a 'Græcus Livius' (*Ep.* 22), to that of some modern critics, who have accused him of subjectivity and gross misrepresentation. The *apologetic* nature of the history is evident on the face of it. Its object is to represent the maligned Jewish nation in the best light to Greek readers. This has occasioned the suppression of some of the darker incidents in the Biblical story. But, granted this, there remains no very serious charge to be laid against the historian. His work is, on the whole, a skilful compilation, its value naturally varying with that of the authorities consulted, while the criticisms passed upon Nicolaus (XIV. 9, 183) show that these were used with discrimination. Attractiveness is one main object. To this end the narrative is diversified by legendary additions culled from all sources. Nor, it must be admitted, does the historian, with a view to greater picturesqueness, refrain from adding minor details of his own invention with regard to the strength of contending armies, names of localities, and the like (see Drüner, *Untersuch. über Josephus*, Marburg, 1896, p. 39 ff.). He, however, professes in several passages to have a high ideal of a historian's duty (*e.g. Ant.* XIV. 1 ff., XX. 154 ff.; *c. Ap.* i. 24 ff.); and, speaking generally, one must grant that, so far as it is possible to test him, he reaches a level of accuracy that gives him a high place among the historians of antiquity, setting aside those of the very foremost rank, while in extent and comprehensiveness he is far in advance of any of his predecessors in the same field.

[For the sources of the *Antiquities*, see especially Bloch, *Die Quellen des Flav. Josephus*, Leipzig, 1879; Destinon, *Die Quellen des F. Josephus*, Kiel, 1882; with the reviews of Schürer in *Theolog. Literaturzeit.* 1879, col. 567 ff.; 1882, col. 388 ff.].

3. The so-called *Life* (Ἰωσήπου βίος) is appended in the MSS to the *Antiquities*, and was certainly composed by Josephus as a sequel to that work, although it appears to be separated in time from the larger work by an interval of at least six or seven years. That it was planned as a sequel is shown by the promise at the end of the *Ant.* (XX. 266) of a brief account as to the author's family and life; by the fact that the *Life* begins without any prefatory remarks, being linked on to the *Ant.* by the particle δέ, and closes with a dedication of the whole work of the *Antiquities* (τὴν πᾶσαν τῆς ἀρχαιολογίας ἀναγραφήν) to Epaphroditus, who had been named in the exordium of *Ant.* (*Vita*, 430; *Ant.* I. 8); and by the fact that a passage from the *Life* is cited as from the *Ant.* by Eusebius (*HE* iii. 10). On the other hand, the *Antiquities* contains a formal conclusion of its own (XX. 267 f.), and was completed in the thirteenth year of Domitian (A.D. 93–94, *ib.*), while the *Life* implies that Agrippa II. was already dead (359 f.); and we learn from Photius (*Bibl.*, Cod. 33) that his death took place in the third year of Trajan (A.D. 100). The probability is that the autobiography was an afterthought, which was appended to later copies of the *Antiquities*, in which the sentence containing the promise of the Life (*Ant.* XX. 266) was then inserted for the first time. The immediate occasion for the production of the *Life* was the appearance of a rival history of the Jewish War by Justus of Tiberias, in which the writer accused Josephus of being the real cause of the outbreak of the war with Rome (*Vita*, 340). Justus had written his history twenty years before, but, according to Josephus, had kept it back until the chief actors in the war were dead, when there was nobody to convict him of inaccuracy (360). The appearance of Justus' work, with its damaging criticisms, was likely to endanger the secure position which Josephus had won for himself at Rome, and the earlier historian of the war felt bound to defend himself. The *Life*, then, by no means answers to its name. It is not a complete autobiography, but simply an apologetic statement as to the actions of Josephus as commander in Galilee before the outbreak of the war, to which have been added a few details as to the earlier and later events of his life, by way of prologue and epilogue. The defence which Josephus makes against Justus is an extremely lame one. He has to admit the part which he took in organizing the forces of the country against Rome, while endeavouring to show that he was not in favour of the war. It is an obviously one-sided statement, marked by excessive self-laudation, and the brochure must be pronounced to be the least satisfactory of the historian's works.

4. *Against Apion*, a work in two books.—The title, by which it is ordinarily known, is neither a

suitable one, since Apion is not mentioned until the second book is reached, nor original. It occurs first in Jerome. The older designations, both of which may be original, are Περὶ τῆς τῶν Ἰουδαίων ἀρχαιότητος (Eus. *HE* iii. 9) and Πρὸς τοὺς Ἕλληνας (Porphyry, *de Abstin.* iv. 11). It was undertaken as a reply to criticisms on the *Antiquities*, and a refutation of current attacks upon, and groundless prejudices against, the Jewish nation. It gives an interesting glimpse of the anti-Semitism of the first century. The writer begins by disproving the extreme antiquity claimed for the Greeks, and contrasts the discrepancies found in their writings with the carefully preserved and unanimous records of the Jews. He accounts for the silence of Greek writers with regard to Jewish history. He then proceeds to quote evidence for the antiquity of his nation from Egyptian, Phœnician, Chaldæan, and Greek sources. He passes next to a refutation of the malignant and often absurd accusations brought against his country by Manetho, Chæremon, Lysimachus, Apollonius Molo, and, the greatest offender of all, Apion. The object of Josephus' most biting satire enjoyed a considerable reputation as a grammarian and interpreter of Homer, but, from all accounts, he must have been a man of inordinate vanity, and a loquacious charlatan; the nickname of 'cymbalum mundi,' given him by Tiberius, corroborates the impression which we derive from Josephus; he is best known as the leader of the Alexandrian embassy to Caligula in A.D. 38, which brought accusations against the Jewish residents in that city, and was opposed by the counter-embassy of the Alexandrian Jews, headed by Philo. Josephus concludes his work with an able and eloquent defence of the Jewish lawgiver and his code, and contrasts his conception of God with the immoral ideas about the gods current among the Greeks. The book is, in short, an apology for Judaism, carefully planned and well worked out. The satire directed against Apion and the rest is pointed and lively, though sometimes, as in the allusion to Apion's death (ii. 143), it exceeds the bounds of good taste. The treatise gives us a higher idea than that we should form from his other works of the writer's literary skill, and of his genuine patriotism and zeal for his country's religion. A special value attaches to it from the numerous quotations from authors whose works are lost. It must have been written after A.D. 93 (the date of the *Antiquities*), but whether before or after the *Life* is uncertain.

*PROJECTED WORKS.*—At the close of the *Antiquities*, Josephus, after promising a brief autobiography, the *Life* which we possess, announces his intention, God willing, of writing two future works: (1) A summary of the Jewish War and the subsequent history of his nation down to the thirteenth year of Domitian; and (2) a work in four books 'on the opinions held by us Jews concerning God and His Being, and concerning the Laws, why some actions are permitted to us by them and others are forbidden.'* Neither of these works has come down to us, and there is no reason to suppose that either was carried out. But the work 'On Customs and Causes,' Περὶ ἐθῶν καὶ αἰτιῶν [Περὶ ἐθῶν καὶ νόμων or ἡ αἰτιολογία are other names which he suggests for it], appears, from the mention of the four books, to have been already mapped out in his mind, and was possibly begun. The project had been formed perhaps even at the time when the *Jewish War* was written (*BJ* v. 237), and there are frequent allusions to it in the earlier books of the *Antiquities*. The treatise was to contain, *e.g.*, an explanation why the first day is spoken of as 'day one' (*Ant.* I. 29; cf. Philo, *de Opif. Mundi*, 9, διὰ τὴν τοῦ νοητοῦ κόσμου μόνωσιν μοναδικὴν ἔχοντος φύσιν); the reasons for the dress worn by the high priest (*BJ* v. 237), for the practice of circumcision (*Ant.* I. 192, 214), for the changing of the shewbread every sabbath (*Ant.* III. 143), for the various sacrifices (*Ant.* III. 257), for the distinction between clean and unclean meats (*Ant.* III. 259); and a general rationale of Jewish laws and customs (*Ant.* IV. 198). It is to be regretted that this project remained, apparently, unfulfilled. Such a work would probably have preserved a considerable amount of valuable traditional lore, and put beyond a doubt the question whether Josephus was acquainted with the writings of Philo. At any rate, a comparison between the allegorical treatment of Scripture by the two writers would have been interesting.

*WORKS ATTRIBUTED TO JOSEPHUS.*—The so-called *Fourth Book of Maccabees*, or Περὶ αὐτοκράτορος Λογισμοῦ, was attributed to Josephus by Eusebius (*HE* iii. 10) and other Patristic writers. This rhetorical exercise has some points in common with Josephus; but that he was the author of it is disproved by the fact that it appears as an anonymous work in many MSS, by differences of style, and by the fact that it is based on 2 Maccabees, a book of which Josephus shows no knowledge in the *Antiquities*. The work, Περὶ τοῦ παντός [Περὶ τῆς τοῦ παντὸς αἰτίας, or Περὶ τῆς τοῦ παντὸς οὐσίας], ascribed by Photius (*Bibl.*, Cod. 48) to Josephus, is of Christian origin, and its author is almost certainly Hippolytus. On the alleged work of Josephus on the Seleucid dynasty, see above, p. 465[b].

iii. THE BIBLE OF JOSEPHUS AND HIS TREATMENT OF THE BIBLICAL NARRATIVE.—1. *Text.*—In the Preface to the *Antiquities*, Josephus professes that his account is based directly on the Hebrew writings, implying that he has translated them himself for his Greek readers (*Ant.* I. 5, ἐκ τῶν Ἑβραϊκῶν μεθηρμηνευμένην γραμμάτων; cf. X. 218, where his task is declared to be not to explain the difficulties of Scripture, but merely μεταφράζειν τὰς Ἑβραίων βίβλους εἰς τὴν Ἑλλάδα γλῶτταν). In reality this is not the case. The Bible of which he has made use throughout his work is, beyond a doubt, the collection of Greek translations commonly known as the Septuagint. The language of that version is constantly to be traced beneath the historian's paraphrase: passages occur which are peculiar to the Greek version, and probably never found a place in the Hebrew (*e.g.* the vapid answer of David to Goliath's question, 'Am I a dog?' Οὐχί, ἀλλ' ἢ χείρω κυνός, 1 S 17[43] [*Ant.* VI. 186]; cf. also *Ant.* VII. 173 with 2 S 13[21], *Ant.* VII. 190 with 2 S 14[27], *Ant.* VIII. 17 with 1 K 2[37] καὶ ὤρκισεν κ.τ.λ.). The writer's dependence on the Septuagint is most clearly seen in the use which he makes of 1 Esdras (including the story of the three pages, for which there is no Hebrew equivalent) and of the LXX additions to Esther. There can be no doubt that he has also used the Greek version of the First Book of Maccabees, not the lost Hebrew original.

As to the type of Greek text which he has followed, Mez (*Die Bibel des Josephus*, 1895) has made a special study of the subject for the historical books from Joshua to the end of the Books of Kings. He has examined the proper names of Josephus and the positive statements which deviate either from the MT or from the LXX. The conclusions to which he comes are as follows: (1) The text of Cod. B is never followed by Josephus where there is a diversity of reading. This statement is essentially, but not absolutely, correct: for instance, the answer of David to Goliath, mentioned above (1 S 17[43]), occurs in B but is absent from A, the Lucianic text, and the Hebrew.

* It is unnecessary to suppose that Josephus contemplated two distinct works—one on the Being of God, and one on the Laws.

(2) In Joshua, Josephus follows the Hebrew closely. (3) In the Books of Samuel he diverges from the MT and Codd. A and B, and agrees with the Lucianic text, whose errors he follows and whose language he sometimes misunderstands. (4) In Judges, Mez does not arrive at any definite decision.* Speaking generally, we may say that the LXX text of Josephus agrees most closely with the Lucianic text or that contained in Cod. A. The present writer tested the text of the Greek Bible of Josephus for 1 Esdras, and found that it almost invariably sides with the A text as against the B text (see vol. i. p. 762 f.) In 1 Maccabees, where B is wanting, Josephus sides with א as against A.†

Whether, and how far, Josephus used the Hebrew along with the Greek text has not yet, it seems, been ascertained with sufficient accuracy. There can hardly be a doubt that a man of his antecedents and education would be almost as well acquainted with Hebrew as with the Aramaic spoken in his day; but the indications that he made any use of the copy of the Hebrew Scriptures which he rescued from the ruins of Jerusalem (*Vita*, 418) are very slight. Practically, the only hint which he gives of a knowledge of Hebrew, and the only criterion which he offers us for testing the extent of his knowledge, is to be found in the etymological explanations which he appends to the Hebrew proper names throughout the narrative; many of these explanations, however, where they are not easily deducible from Scripture, are probably taken from contemporary *Midrashim*; while occasionally, as in the explanation of the names Μωυσῆς (*Ant.* II. 228) and Ἱεροσόλυμα (*BJ* VI. 438), he accommodates himself to his Greek readers, and accepts incorrect, or at best extremely doubtful, etymologies. See, on the whole subject, Siegfried, 'Die Hebräischen Worterklärungen des Josephus' (*ZATW*, 1883, pp. 32-52).

2. *Canon of OT.*—Josephus, as we have seen, in writing his *Antiquities*, draws freely upon Greek books, such as 1 Esdras and 1 Maccabees, which were never regarded as canonical; and no hint is given that the information derived from them is less trustworthy than that contained in the canonical books. In the opening of his work, using rhetorical language, he declares that 'the holy writings contain the history of five thousand years' (I. 13; cf. XX. 259 ff.). But that he was aware of the distinction between canonical and uncanonical books is made plain by a well-known passage in the *contra Apionem*, which is of primary importance for the history of the OT Canon, and must be quoted in full. Contrasting the reliability of Greek and Hebrew records, he says (*c. Ap.* i. 37 ff.): 'The writing [of the Scriptural records] was not within the power of all alike: nor is there any inherent discrepancy in what is written. It fell to the prophets alone to learn the events of the highest and most remote antiquity in virtue of the direct inspiration of God, and to record clearly the events of their own time just as they happened. It therefore naturally, or rather necessarily, follows that *we* do not possess ten thousand discordant and conflicting books. No; we have but two-and-twenty books, which contain the record of all time, and are justly credited.‡ And of these, five are those of Moses, containing the laws and the tradition from the origin of man up to the death of Moses: this period is little short of three thousand years. And from the death of Moses until that of Artaxerxes,* the successor of Xerxes on the throne of Persia, the prophets who succeeded Moses recorded the events of their time in thirteen books. The remaining four contain hymns to God and counsels for the life of men. But from Artaxerxes until our own time records of all things have been kept, but they have not been considered worthy of equal credit with the records of previous times, because there has not been the (same) uninterrupted succession of the prophets.' He goes on to say that, although so long a time has elapsed since the Scriptures were written, no one has ventured to add to them, or to remove or alter anything; and that all Jews from their birth instinctively regard them as the teaching of God, and are ready, if need be, to die on their behalf.

In this statement the following points are noticeable. (*a*) In the time of Josephus there was a canon of Scripture which had long been recognized. The test of the canonicity of a book was its antiquity. The mention of Artaxerxes, who in Josephus (*Ant.* XI. 184) and the LXX represents the Ahasuerus of the Book of Esther, must have special reference to that book. Nothing later than its reputed date was regarded as canonical. The 22 books of Josephus are generally taken to be: (1) the 5 books of the Pentateuch; (2) Joshua, Judges + Ruth, 1 and 2 Sam., 1 and 2 Kings, 1 and 2 Chron., Ezra and Neh., Esther, Job, Daniel, Isaiah, Jeremiah + Lamentations, Ezekiel, the 12 Minor Prophets (13 in all); (3) Psalms and Song of Songs ('the hymns'), Proverbs and Ecclesiastes ('the practical precepts').—(*b*) There is a tripartite division of Scripture, but not the ordinary Jewish division of Law, Prophets, Hagiographa. The second group of historical-prophetical books has in Josephus been increased by a number of books which the Rabbis placed among the Hagiographa. The Rabbinical arrangement is not chronological, nor based on the subject-matter, but is the result of the gradual growth of the Canon, and an indication of three stages in its development. In Josephus, on the other hand, the arrangement is one of subject-matter. Such an arrangement had already been attempted in the Greek Bible of which Josephus made use; but the exact division into groups of 5, 13, and 4 books is not met with elsewhere. It was natural that Josephus, writing for Greeks on the historical records of his nation, should place together all the historical or quasi-historical books.—(*c*) The number of books is given as 22, not, according to the commoner Jewish enumeration, as 24. Josephus is the only *Jewish* writer who gives the former number, but it recurs in the Christian Fathers such as Origen (on the authority of Hebrew tradition, *ap.* Eus. *HE* vi. 25) and Jerome (Preface to Books of Sam. and Kings); the latter writer gives 5 books of Moses, 8 of Prophets, 9 of Hagiographa, and alludes to the other enumeration of 24 books (see Ryle, *Canon of OT*, 221). The number 22 was arrived at by joining Ruth to Judges, and Lam. to Jeremiah; and a fanciful explanation was found for it in the number of letters in the Hebrew alphabet (Origen, Jerome, etc.). It is curious that this explanation is confined to Christian writers; it seems to be of Alexandrian origin. The number 24 appears to be the older, but the relation between the two numbers is still obscure. The idea of equalizing the number of books with the number of Hebrew letters need not have produced the division into 22 books; it may have been a later play of the imagination (Buhl), possibly the invention of Origen, who is the first to note it. In view of the parallels in

* It is to be noted that in this book Josephus transposes chapters 19-21 (the events leading up to the almost complete extermination of the tribe of Benjamin), placing them at the beginning of his account of the Judges.

† The Hellenized forms of Hebrew proper names employed by Josephus are given in Dr. Redpath's Supplement to the *Septuagint Concordance* (Fasc. i., Oxford, 1900).

‡ The word θεῖα ('which are with justice believed to be divine') is an addition of Eusebius, *HE* iii. 10.

* Or, according to another reading, 'until Artaxerxes.'

Origen and Jerome there can be no doubt that the number 22 in Josephus was arrived at by treating Ruth and Lam. as parts of Judges and Jeremiah. There is no ground for Grätz's inference, that Ecclesiastes and the Song of Songs had not been received into the Canon when Josephus wrote. See, further, Ryle, *Canon of OT*, 158–166, and the works of Buhl and Wildeboer on the OT Canon; also art. OT CANON in vol. iii. p. 607 f.

In a passage where allusion is made to the writings of Jeremiah and Ezekiel (*Ant.* x. 79) there is an enigmatical statement that Ezekiel was the first to write *two books* concerning the destruction of Jerusalem and the Captivity. Two explanations have been suggested for the *two* books: (1) The prophecy of Ezekiel may have been divided into two parts, chs. 1–39 and 40–48. But the latter portion contains no reference to the Exile. (2) The second book has been supposed to be an apocryphal work, from which are taken certain quotations made by Clem. Alex. and others which are not to be traced in the canonical Ezekiel (Fabricius, *Codex Pseudepig.* i. 1117). Both explanations leave unexplained the statement that Ezekiel wrote first, *i.e.* before Jeremiah. Eichhorn and Bertholdt have taken the words to refer to Jeremiah, and a division of his prophecy into two parts. See *Journ. Theol. Stud.* iv. p. 258 f.

3. *Additions to the Biblical narrative, mainly derived from Rabbinic tradition.*—Josephus has, with a view to rendering the Biblical narrative more attractive to his Greek readers, diversified and amplified it by a large number of additions. These additions may be divided into: (1) those derived from Rabbinic tradition, (2) those derived from Alexandrian and Hellenistic writers on Jewish history, (3) those which are the invention of the historian himself. It is not, however, always easy to distinguish between these three classes, and the attempt to do so has not been made in the present article. Additions for which Rabbinic parallels have been traced are indicated by an asterisk. For a fuller treatment of the relation of Josephus to Rabbinism, the reader is referred to the article of Edersheim in the *Dict. of Christian Biography*, and to the works of Bloch (*Die Quellen*) and others.† Edersheim, whose profound study of Rabbinic literature gives his opinion great weight, concludes that Josephus' knowledge of tradition was, like his acquaintance with Hebrew, not more than superficial.

We may begin by grouping together those additions and explanations which consist in the identification of places or persons, or in inferences deduced from bringing different passages of the OT into connexion. Among these may be named *the identification of the rivers of Paradise, Pishon = Ganges, Ḥiddeḳel = Tigris (so LXX) = Διγλάθ (*Ant.* I. 38 f.); *it was Nimrod, the builder of cities (Gn $10^{11}$), who counselled the building of the Tower of Babel, to revenge himself upon God for the Flood (*Ant.* I. 113 ff.); Dan was the name of one of the springs of Jor-dan (*Ant.* I. 177); Abraham's descendants by Ḳeṭurah occupied Troglodytis (*Ant.* I. 239, II. 213, where Gn $25^6$ merely names 'the east country'); *the daughter of Pharaoh who adopted Moses was named Thermuthis (*Ant.* II. 224; *Book of Jubilees* 'Tharmuth'); the injunctions in Nu 19 about the red heifer and the cleansing of one who touched a dead body are brought into connexion with the death of Miriam in Nu 20 (*Ant.* IV. 78 ff.); Mount Hor is identified with Petra (*Ant.* IV. 82); the mother of Abimelech was named Drumah (*Ant.* V. 233; unnamed in Jg $8^{31}$; the name is probably taken from that of her residence, Arumah, Jg $9^{41}$); the name of Jephthah's burying-place was Sebee in Gilead (*Ant.* V. 270; Jg $12^7$ 'one of the cities of Gilead'; Josephus may have had another reading, see Mez, *Die Bibel des Jos.* 16); Saul's uncle (1 S $10^{14}$) was Abner (*Ant.* VI. 58; cf. 1 S $14^{51}$);† the mention of Joab cutting off the water-supply of the Ammonites (*Ant.* VII. 159) has apparently arisen out of the name, 'the city of waters,' by which Rabbah is called in 2 S $12^{27}$; the queen of Sheba appears as the queen of Egypt and Ethiopia (*Ant.* VIII. 165); the prophet who prophesied against the altar of Jeroboam (1 K $13^1$) is named Ἰάδων (*Ant.* VIII. 231: has this arisen from ἰδού in the LXX, καὶ ἰδοὺ ἄνθρωπος τοῦ θεοῦ?); an anonymous prophet in 1 K 20 $(21)^{35}$ who foretold the death of Aḥab is identified with Micaiah (*Ant.* VIII. 389; cf. 403 and 1 K $22^8$); and the 'certain man who drew his bow at a venture' and gave Aḥab his death-wound is called Ἄμανος (*Ant.* VIII. 414; ? = Naaman); *the 'certain woman of the wives of the sons of the prophets,' who was persecuted by her creditors (2 K $4^1$), was the widow of Obadiah, who had borrowed money to support the prophets at the time of the famine (*Ant.* IX. 47); Tarshish, to which Jonah was sailing, is identified with Tarsus in Cilicia, and the prophet is said to have been cast up by the whale in the Euxine Sea (*Ant.* IX. 208, 213).

Some of the most striking among other legendary additions are the following: *Before the Fall all living creatures spoke a common language (*Ant.* I. 41), and the serpent for his malignity was punished by the loss of speech and feet (*Ant.* I. 50; so *Jubilees*, iii. 28, 'and on that day was closed the mouth of all beasts . . . for they had all spoken one with another with one lip and with one tongue'; see Charles' note; also the Targum of pseudo-Jonathan, 'upon thy belly shalt thou go, and thy feet shall be cut off'). Adam had daughters as well as sons (*Ant.* I. 52; *Jub.* iv. 1). Cain averted the punishment of death by a propitiatory sacrifice, and was banished with his wife and lived a life of luxury (*Ant.* I. 58 ff.). *The descendants of Seth invented astronomy, and left a record of their discoveries on two pillars of brick and stone, that they might not be lost to mankind in the flood or the fire which Adam had predicted (*Ant.* I. 69 ff.; cf. *Jub.* viii. 3, Cainan after the Flood finds an inscription which had been carved on the rock by the Watchers concerning the heavenly bodies). In *Ant.* I. 118 the Sibyl is quoted for the statement that the winds were employed by the gods to overthrow the Tower of Babel (cf. *Orac. Sibyll.* iii. 101 ff.). Abraham's knowledge of astronomy leads him to believe in one God (*Ant.* I. 155 ff.); in Egypt, God by an insurrection punishes Pharaoh for taking Sarah; while Abraham consorts with the most learned of the Egyptians, and teaches them mathematics and astronomy (*Ant.* I. 164 ff.). Potiphar's wife selects for her temptation of Joseph the occasion of a public festival, from which she begs to be excused on the plea of illness (*Ant.* II. 45). The interpretation of Pharaoh's dreams was shown him in his sleep, but forgotten by him (*Ant.* II. 75). *The birth of Moses was foretold to Pharaoh by a ἱερογραμματεύς, and to his father Amram by God (*Ant.* II. 205, 217); his mother was granted an easy deliverance, and so the birth escaped detection (*Ant.* II. 218). Moses' height and beauty (*Ant.* II. 224) were a common topic in tradition (cf. Ac $7^{20}$). *Josephus tells a story of how the child was brought to Pharaoh, and how, when the king playfully placed his diadem on his head, the child cast it away and trampled on it; and how the ἱερογραμματεύς detected that this was he whose birth he had predicted (*Ant.* II. 232 ff.; cf. the tragedian Ezekiel, *ap.* Euseb. *Præp. Ev.* ix. 440). But the most noticeable addition to the history of Moses

† The present writer has not had access to the works of Duschak (*Josephus und die Tradition*, Vienna, 1864), Tachauer (*Das Verhältniss des F. Jos. zur Bibel und zur Tradition*, Erlangen, 1871), and others named by Schürer.

† The scene of a battle between the Philistines and Israelites, unnamed in the OT (1 S $28^1$), is given as Ῥεγάν (*Ant.* VI. 325). This, however, as Mez has suggested, may be a corruption of φάραγγα.

is the account of his * Ethiopian campaign (*Ant.* II. 238–253). The Egyptians, whose country had long been ravaged by the Ethiopians, at God's advice appoint Moses as their general. He, after ridding the country of the serpents which infested the line of march, gained a complete victory over the enemy, with the help of Tharbis, the daughter of the Ethiopian king, whom he marries. This account should be compared with that of Artapanus (in Euseb. *Præp. Ev.* ix. 432c), who is probably the ultimate source from whom many of the Moses legends are derived by Josephus. In Artapanus, king Chenephres envies Moses, and sends him against the Ethiopians, hoping that he will be killed. The war lasts ten years; Moses ultimately gains the affection of the Ethiopians, and teaches them to practise circumcision. The Rabbinical accounts (see Edersheim, *Dict. Christ. Biog.* iii. 456) are rather different, representing Moses as fighting on the side of the Ethiopians. The story in its various forms has, no doubt, grown out of the reference to 'the Cushite woman' whom Moses married (Nu 12$^{1}$). Murmurs against Moses are magnified into attempts to stone him (*Ant.* II. 327, III. 12; with III. 307 cf. Nu 14$^{10}$). The prohibition to priests to marry innkeepers (*Ant.* III. 276, cf. Lv 21$^{7}$) is to be explained, as Edersheim suggests, by the fact that, in the story of Rahab, Josephus, in common with the Targum, translates זוֹנָה (harlot) by 'innkeeper.' * Balaam is said to have counselled Balaḳ to entice the Israelites by the beauty of the women of Midian, and so to draw them away from their religion (this does not occur in the narrative in Nu 24–25, but a hint of it is given later in Nu 31$^{16}$). He foretells slight disasters to Israel to be followed by renewed prosperity (*Ant.* IV. 128 ff.). As to Moses' end, we are told that he was accompanied to Mount Abarim by 'the senate,' Eleazar, and Joshua; the senate was then dismissed, and, while the prophet was still conversing with Eleazar and Joshua, a cloud covered him and he disappeared in a ravine. He described his own death in Scripture, for fear that it should be said that he had been translated to God (*Ant.* IV. 324 ff.).

For additional *legal ordinances*, we may note the injunction that the evidence of women and slaves is not to be accepted (*Ant.* IV. 219); the forty stripes allowed by Dt 25$^{3}$ become, in accordance with the later Rabbinical practice, 'forty stripes save one' (*Ant.* IV. 238, 248; cf. Targ. Jerus. i.; 2 Co 11$^{24}$); mention is made of the *seven* judges (*Ant.* IV. 214, 287); * the sexes are not to exchange dress, *especially in battle* (*Ant.* IV. 301; cf. Dt 22$^{5}$; Bloch refers to *Nāẓîr* 59*a*); the extraordinary statement that the Jews were not allowed to blaspheme the gods of other nations, or to rob their temples (*Ant.* IV. 207; *c. Ap.* ii. 237), seems to rest on the LXX of Ex 22$^{28}$ θεοὺς οὐ κακολογήσεις (where the Targums render אֱלֹהִים by 'the judges').

Among additions to and comments upon the Scripture narrative in books outside the Pentateuch, may be mentioned details with regard to Manoaḥ and his wife—how they used constantly to visit the suburb (τὸ προάστειον) to pray for children, and of Manoaḥ's jealousy of the angel who had visited his wife (*Ant.* V. 276 ff.). Solomon's judgment is that both children should be divided, which excites the mockery of the people (*Ant.* VIII. 31 f.); the exorcisms which Solomon invented were still in use and efficacious in Josephus' time (*Ant.* VIII. 45 ff.); his road-making is described (*Ant.* VIII. 187); his first deviation from virtue was in making images of oxen and lions (*Ant.* VIII. 195; cf. 1 K 7$^{25}$ 10$^{19}$). In the siege of Samaria doves' dung was bought *in place of salt* (*Ant.* IX. 62). Zedeḳiah disbelieved the prophecies of Jeremiah and Ezekiel because of their apparent discrepancy with regard to himself (*Ant.* X. 106). A description is given of a wonderful palace which Daniel built at Ecbatana, which was used as a mausoleum for the kings of Media, Persia, and Parthia (*Ant.* X. 246).

4. *Omissions from apologetic motives.*—Josephus, wishing to present the history of his nation in the best light, passes over in silence some of the less creditable incidents. We may note the omission of the selling of Esau's birthright, the story of Judah and Tamar (Gn 38), the killing of the Egyptian by Moses, the worship of the golden calf, the breaking of the first tables of the Law by Moses, the story of Micah (Jg 17. 18). The suppression of such incidents as these appears certainly to be due to apologetic motives, although other omissions may be the result of necessary compression; it must be admitted that some of the darker incidents in the picture are faithfully portrayed, though excuses are sometimes offered, as in the account of the slaughter of the Amaleḳites (*Ant.* VI. 136). It is rarely that Josephus condemns an action outright, as he does in the case of the sacrifice of Jephthaḥ's daughter (*Ant.* V. 266). The most striking omission of all is that of any reference to a Messiah. The words of the LORD God to the serpent, 'It shall bruise thy head, and thou shalt bruise his heel,' occasion no allusion to a future deliverer. Jacob's blessing is entirely omitted, nor do Balaam's prophecies call forth any hint of a Messiah. If Josephus held any such belief, he at all events felt that the doctrine would have no interest for his readers, or perhaps we should rather say that he studiously avoided a topic to which, in the circumstances of his time, it would have been dangerous to allude.

5. *Rationalistic explanations of the miraculous.*—Out of regard to the incredulity of his heathen readers, Josephus frequently suggests that miracles recorded in the history may have been due to natural causes, or he apologizes for mentioning them with the plea that he is only faithfully following the Biblical account. The readiness with which he has recourse to such explanations must, however, raise a doubt as to his own belief in miracles. Thus he appeals in support of his account of the crossing of the Red Sea, which, he says, happened εἴτε κατὰ βούλησιν θεοῦ εἴτε κατὰ ταὐτόματον, to the similar incident of the retreat of the Pamphylian Sea before Alexander the Great, adding, 'let every one think as he pleases as to these things' (*Ant.* II. 347 f.). The Biblical account of the healing of the bitter waters of Marah readily lent itself to a rationalistic explanation (*Ant.* III. 7 f.); cf. the account of the healing of the fountain by Elisha in *BJ* IV. 462 ff. (πολλὰ προσχειρουργήσας ἐξ ἐπιστήμης). The historian notes that quails are abundant in the Arabian Gulf, and that manna is still found in the region (*Ant.* III. 25, 31). As to the wonders of Sinai, every one is entitled to his own opinion, but the story must be told as it is given in the Sacred Books (*Ant.* III. 381). When Elisha procured water for the three kings in the wilderness, he was enabled to do so by rain having fallen some distance away in Edom (*Ant.* IX. 37, cf. 2 K 3$^{17}$ 'neither shall ye *see* rain'). The story of Jonah and the whale is given 'as I found it recorded' (*Ant.* IX. 213 f.). The same detachment from the narrative appears in the accounts of the deliverance of Daniel and his comrades from the fiery furnace (*Ant.* X. 214, φασί), and of Nebuchadnezzar's madness (*Ant.* X. 218: Josephus only undertook to translate the Hebrew books). A famine in the time of Herod was due either to God's wrath or to natural causes (*Ant.* XV. 299). Sometimes a rationalistic explanation of the miraculous is put into the mouth of a participant in the actions described. Thus the Philistines attribute the

sufferings brought upon them by the presence of the ark to natural causes (*Ant.* VI. 9); the old prophet gives Jeroboam a rationalistic explanation of the rending of the altar and the withering of the king's hand (*Ant.* VIII. 244); Elijah on Carmel bids the people approach to see that he did not conceal fire among the wood (*Ant.* VIII. 340); Daniel's enemies asserted that the lions left him unharmed because they had had their fill of food (*Ant.* X. 260).

6. *Prophecies in the OT.*—Josephus is careful to note the fulfilment of prophecy, and especially to reconcile apparent discrepancies in the predictions of different prophets. From the fulfilment of many of the prophecies of Balaam, even within the memory of the historian, one may conjecture that the remainder also will come true (*Ant.* IV. 125). Zedeḳiah, son of Chenaanah, is made to quote the prophecy of Elijah, that Ahab's blood was to be spilt in the field of Naboth, as contradicting the prediction of Micaiah that the king was to fall in battle against Ramoth-gilead, at a distance of three days' journey from Samaria. The historian notes the accomplishment of both predictions (*Ant.* VIII. 407 f., 418). Zedeḳiah, king of Judah, disbelieved the prophecies of Jeremiah and Ezekiel, because the former declared that he would be carried a prisoner to Babylon, while the latter said that he would not see Babylon. The statements were reconciled, as Josephus notes, in the putting out of the king's eyes (*Ant.* X. 106 f., 141). The fulfilment of the prophecies of Daniel affords a refutation of the opinions of the Epicureans (*Ant.* X. 277 ff.); he differed from other prophets in fixing a definite time, and in being a prophet of good things, and therefore enjoying popularity (*Ant.* X. 267). The spoliation of the temple by Antiochus Epiphanes was in accordance with a prophecy of Daniel (*Ant.* XII. 232), the building of the temple of Onias with a prophecy of Isaiah (*Ant.* XIII. 64; *BJ* VII. 432). In one instance Josephus refuses to reveal the meaning of a passage in Daniel, which he probably took to refer to the destruction of the Roman empire (*Ant.* X. 210). He holds that the gift of prophecy did not entirely fail in post-Biblical times. It was possessed by John Hyrcanus (*Ant.* XIII. 299), Judas an Essene (XIII. 311), Pollio (XV. 4), by Josephus himself (*BJ* III. 399), and others.

iv. RELATION OF JOSEPHUS TO PHILO AND ALEXANDRIAN JUDAISM.—Josephus only once mentions Philo, in a brief notice of the embassy to Caligula, which was led by the philosopher to oppose the counter-embassy of Apion (*Ant.* XVIII. 257 ff.). He there speaks of him in the highest terms as *ἀνὴρ τὰ πάντα ἔνδοξος . . . καὶ φιλοσοφίας οὐκ ἄπειρος*. It is impossible to say whether Josephus was acquainted with the detailed account of that embassy which Philo has left us in his *Legatio ad Gaium*, or how far he was acquainted with the other writings of the Alexandrian philosopher. Had he accomplished his projected work on the *Being of God* and the *Meaning of the Laws*, we should be in a better position to estimate the extent of the influence which Philo exercised upon him. Indications, however, are not wanting in the early books of the *Antiquities* of an apparently direct dependence upon Philo's writings. The following are the principal parallels which have been noted:—(1) The Preface to the *Antiquities* and the opening of the *de Opificio Mundi* show a striking agreement in the sequence of ideas. Both works raise the question why the Mosaic code is preceded by an account of the Creation. Josephus expects that his readers will wonder how it comes to pass that his work, of which the main purpose is to record laws and historical events, has so large an element of 'physiology' (*ἐπὶ τοσοῦτον φυσιολογίας κεκοινώνηκεν*). He explains that Moses, differing in this respect from other legislators, whose codes begin with contracts and the rights of man, considered it necessary, before laying down his code, first to elevate men's minds by setting the highest of all examples before them and inducing them to contemplate the nature and actions of God, especially as exhibited in the creation of the world (*Ant.* I. 18 ff.). Philo begins his work with a similar contrast between the procedure of Moses and that of other legislators. Moses did not commence by laying down commands and prohibitions, but gave as his exordium a most marvellous account of the Creation, in order to show the harmony existing between the world and the Law, and that the law-abiding man is a true citizen of the world. The unanimity of the Law and the universe is also expressed by Josephus (*Ant.* I. 24, *πάντα γὰρ τῇ τῶν ὅλων φύσει σύμφωνον ἔχει τὴν διάθεσιν*). Josephus (I. 15, 22) and Philo both refer to the mythical stories which disfigure the codes of other legislators. (2) In the same context, Josephus, quite in accordance with Philo's doctrine, admits that there is an *allegorical meaning in Scripture* as well as a literal (I. 24, *τὰ μὲν αἰνιττομένου τοῦ νομοθέτου δεξιῶς, τὰ δ' ἀλληγοροῦντος μετὰ σεμνότητος, ὅσα δ' ἐξ εὐθείας λέγεσθαι συνέφερε, ταῦτα ῥητῶς ἐμφανίζοντος*). It is not often that Josephus in the *Antiquities* resorts to such allegorical explanation [that was reserved for the projected *αἰτιολογία*]; but there is one striking instance, where the tabernacle and its furniture and the various articles in the dress of the high priest are explained as symbolical of the universe and its parts (*Ant.* III. 179–187). This is quite in the style of Philo, who gives a similar interpretation of the materials used for the woven hangings for the tabernacle and the high priest's apparel, in the *de Vita Mosis*, iii. 6, 12. The details of the explanation are not absolutely identical in the two writers, but for the general idea Josephus is not improbably directly dependent upon Philo. (3) In *Ant.* I. 29 an explanation of the use of *μία* for *πρώτη* in Gn $1^5$ is promised in the *αἰτιολογία*. For Philo's explanation, see *de Opific. Mundi*, 9. (4) Some of the explanations of Hebrew proper names are identical in the two writers: these, however, may go back to an earlier tradition. (5) Some expressions with regard to the nature of God have the ring of Philo, or at least of Alexandria. See *c. Ap.* ii. 167 (*ἀγένητον καὶ πρὸς τὸν ἀίδιον χρόνον ἀναλλοίωτον . . . δυνάμει μὲν ἡμῖν γνώριμον, ὁποῖος δὲ κατ' οὐσίαν ἐστὶν ἄγνωστον*); *Ant.* VI. 230 (*τὸν θεὸν τοῦτον ὃν πολὺν ὁρᾷς καὶ πανταχοῦ κεχυμένον*), X. 142, 278; *c. Ap.* ii. 284 (*ὁ θεὸς διὰ παντὸς τοῦ κόσμου πεφοίτηκεν*). The four cardinal virtues of Greek philosophy are traced by Josephus, as by Philo, in the Mosaic code (*c. Ap.* ii. 170; cf. Wis $8^7$, with Deane's note). But the indications which Gfrörer (*Philo*, 1831, ii. 356–367) has found in Josephus of the Logos doctrine of Philo—in the account of the three angels who visited Abraham, the burning bush, and the pillar of fire—are fanciful and far from convincing. See Siegfried, *Philo von Alexandria*, 1875, pp. 278–281.

v. THE ALLEGED WITNESS OF JOSEPHUS TO CHRIST.—The passage on which so much has been written occurs in *Ant.* XVIII. 63 f. [iii. 3], and runs as follows: 'Now about this time lived Jesus, a wise man, if indeed one should call him a man. For he was a doer of marvellous works, a teacher of such men as receive the truth with pleasure; and many of the Jews and many also of the Greeks did he win over to himself: this was the Christ. And when, on the indictment of the principal men among us, Pilate had sentenced him to the cross, those who loved him at the first ceased not [to do so]; for he appeared to them on the third day again alive, as the Divine prophets had declared these and ten thousand other wonderful things concerning him. And even now the race (τὸ φῦλον) of Christians, which takes its name from him, is not extinct.' The passage stood in the text of Josephus in the 4th cent., as Eusebius quotes it (*HE* i. 11; *Dem. Ev.* iii. 3. 105 f., ed. Gaisford), and from that time down to the 16th cent. its genuineness was undoubted. Its existence contributed largely to the high esteem in which Josephus was held by the Fathers. During the last 300 years a vast amount of literature has been written on the question of its authenticity. Very few critics at the present day accept the passage as it stands as from the pen of Josephus; but there is a division of opinion as to whether the whole is an interpolation, or whether Josephus did make a brief statement about Jesus Christ, which was afterwards augmented by a Christian hand.

(1) As to the *external* evidence, it is true that the passage occurs in all the MSS. But this is of comparatively little weight, as none of the Greek MSS containing Book XVIII. of the *Antiquities* is older than the 11th century. The old Latin version carries us much further back, to the time of Cassiodorus (beginning of the 6th cent.), and the quotation in Eusebius attests the existence of the passage still earlier, in the 4th century. On the other hand, it is practically certain that Origen in the preceding century did not find it in his text of Josephus. For, while he is aware of the passage in Josephus concerning James, the Lord's brother, he says: 'The wonder is that though he did not admit our Jesus to be Christ, he none the less gave his witness to so much righteousness in James' (*Comm. in Matt.* x. 17); elsewhere Origen, collecting all the indirect evidence for Christianity which he can find in Josephus, is silent on the above passage, and again states that Josephus 'disbelieved in Jesus as Christ' (*c. Celsum*, i. 47). This is a case where the negative evidence practically amounts to a positive proof that the passage was unknown.

(2) The *internal* evidence is decisive against the genuineness of the passage as it stands. The *style* affords no certain clue: it is not markedly different from that of Josephus in this part of his work: it may be granted that the interpolator has done his work with some skill. But the *contents* are not such as Josephus could have written. He is elsewhere, as was seen, silent on the subject of a Messiah. The sentence 'this *was* the Christ' (ἦν, not ἐνομίζετο) can have come only from a Christian pen, and it is certain that Josephus was not a Christian. The same may be said of the phrases 'if one should call him a man,' 'the truth,' and the statement about the appearance on the third day. Zahn has adduced an interesting parallel to the first of these phrases and the following words 'for he was a doer,' etc., from a Christian work, the *Acta Pilati* (quoted in Schürer). The passage is *out of place*, and breaks the sequence of the narrative. It is interposed between an account of the disturbances in Judæa caused by Pilate's disregard of Jewish scruples (55–62), and an account of scandals connected with the worshippers of Isis and the banishment of Jews from Rome (65–84). The opening of XVIII. 65, 'And about the same time another calamity disturbed the Jews,' connects that section directly with the section about Pilate. The mention of Pilate has of course led to the insertion of the passage at this point. The fact that the passage interrupts the sequence of the narrative is an argument for its spuriousness as a whole. Moreover, as Schürer has pointed out, a careful analysis of the section, eliminating all that must be of Christian origin, leaves practically nothing behind. The theory of *partial* interpolation is unsatisfactory.

Two other passages have to be taken into account in the discussion: (*a*) that concerning the death of 'John surnamed the Baptist' (*Ant.* XVIII. 116–119), who is described as a good man who bade the Jews practise virtue and be baptized, and who was put to death by Herod because he feared that John's influence over the people might lead to a rebellion; (*b*) that concerning the death of James, 'the brother of Jesus who was called Christ,' whom Ananus the high priest caused to be stoned (*Ant.* XX. 200 f.). Origen refers to both these passages. There is no reason why the former should not be accepted as genuine. The style is distinctly that of Josephus [*N.B.* the form ἁμαρτάς in xviii. 117]. The historian could refer to the preaching and baptism of John without giving offence to his Roman readers; he could not without personal risk allude to Messianic expectations at a time when the spirit of the Jewish revolt against Rome, the strength of which lay in those expectations, had not been completely quelled. The language of the second passage is not inconsistent with its authenticity. There is a marked difference between the words 'who was called Christ' and 'he was the Christ.' But since Origen, in referring to the passage (*c. Celsum*, i. 47), says that Josephus attributed the outbreak of the war to the putting to death of James (a statement which does not occur in our text), there is good reason to believe that here, too, there has been interpolation. This has taken various forms, one of which is that given by Origen.

We conclude, then, that the passage about Christ was introduced into the text by a Christian reader towards the end of the 3rd cent., between the time of Origen and that of Eusebius. For the literature and an admirable discussion of the question, see Schürer, *GJV*[3] i. 544–549 (to which the present writer is largely indebted). For the passage about James, see i. 581 ff. of the same work.

vi. STYLE.—A few remarks may not be out of place with regard to the style of the historian, upon which there can be no doubt that he spent considerable pains. He tells us as much in *Ant.* XX. 263; and, while he justly claims to have acquired a certain skill in the grammar, he confesses that long usage of his national language had prevented his mastering the Greek pronunciation (τὴν προφοράν). Elsewhere, he tells us that his chief aims are accuracy and beauty of style (τὸ τῆς ἑπαγγελίας κάλλος), so far as this is attainable by the choice of words and their arrangement, and the use of other ornaments of speech (*Ant.* XIV. 2). His fastidiousness in this direction may be illustrated by the way in which, while using the LXX, he regularly replaces certain words used by the translators by others of a more literary character. Thus he uses ἐσθής for LXX ἱμάτιον (-ισμός), ἐμπιμπράναι for ἐμπυρίζειν, κατόπιν for κατόπισθεν, νεανίσκος for παιδάριον, πέμπειν for ἀποστέλλειν, ὑπαντᾶν for συναντᾶν, ὑποστρέφειν for ἐπιστρέφειν. Similarly, he has taken the trouble to re-shape most of the sentences in the Letter of Aristeas, while retaining a good deal of the language. His Greek is almost entirely free from Hebraisms; the use of προστίθεσθαι (like Heb. יסף) is the only certain instance which Schmidt discovers (*de Flav. Jos. Elocutione*, p. 516). He tells us that, in writing the *Jewish War*, he employed *collaborateurs* to assist him with the Greek (*c. Ap.* i. 50, χρησάμενός τισι πρὸς τὴν Ἑλληνίδα φωνὴν συνεργοῖς), and no doubt he had similar assistance in writing the *Antiquities*. It would be interesting to know how far their work extended. Naturally, variations in the style and vocabulary occur, partly due to the different sources on which he draws, partly perhaps to the advice of different συνεργοί.

The most marked instance of change of style occurs in three of the later books of the *Antiquities* (XVII. XVIII. XIX.). Among the most striking of the phrases and uses peculiar to or characteristic of these three books, the following may be noted: a large use of the neuter participle (pres. aor. pf. fut.) with article as an abstract noun [*e.g.* XVII. 1, τὸ μὴ ἐπικοινωνῆσον; 171, ἐν ἐλπίδι τοῦ ἀνασφαλοῦντος 'of recovery': a list is given in Schmidt, *op. cit.* 361–368: the use is Thucydidean]; a more frequent use of the optative [Schmidt notes that the conjunctive is absent from Book XVII.]; the use of εἰ with inf. in *oratio obliqua*, of the Attic termination -ατο for -ντο (Thucydidean), of ὁπόσος where ὅσος is used in the earlier books, of ὁστισοῦν (παρ' ὁντινοῦν, οὕστινας = πάντας), and the phrases ἐκ τοῦ ὀξέος, μηδὲν εἰς ἀναβολάς (cf. Thucydides), and, combined, μηδὲν εἰς ἀν. ἀλλ' ἐκ τοῦ ὀξέος. The departure in these books from the ordinary practice of the writer extends to the orthography. Whereas elsewhere Josephus, according to the MSS, almost invariably writes the Attic ττ, in these books σσ is the rule, and ττ is almost unrepresented; it begins to recur towards the end of Book XIX., and in XX. the two spellings occur in almost equal proportions. It must be added that in these books the imitation of Thucydidean words and phrases is more marked; the writer has tried to reproduce the difficult style and involved periods of his model, with the result that he has often made his meaning very obscure, and the text has suffered much corruption. The subject-matter in this portion of the work is less carefully arranged, and there is not a single reference to authorities. Schmidt (*op. cit.* p. 368) has suggested that the peculiarities of this section are due to the use of Nicolaus of Damascus. But the remaining fragments of Nicolaus do not contain the usages in question; traces of his style may rather be found in the books preceding XVII. The use of a single authority for this long section is out of the question, and the difference of style is probably to be accounted for by the employment of another συνεργός and amanuensis. It is not unlikely that the work was laid by for some time when the end of Book XVI. was reached.

An interesting study has been made by Drüner (*Untersuchungen über Josephus*, Marburg, 1896, pp. 1–34) of the use made by Josephus of Thucydides as a model. The imitation is considerable in the earlier books of the *Antiquities*: from Book VI. to XII., and in XX., it is non-existent or very slight: in XIII.–XVI. it gradually increases, and reaches its climax in XVII.–XIX. It is not confined to the diction. The narrative of incidents in the history of the Israelites has been heightened by touches from the account of the siege of Platæa and the Sicilian expedition (cf. *Ant.* IV. 55 with Thuc. ii. 77, and *Ant.* IV. 91 f. with Thuc. vii. 83 f.). The Sicilian expedition especially has roused the Jewish historian to imitation. (See also Kennedy, *Sources of NT Greek*, 56 f.; J. A. Ernesti, *Observationes Philologico-criticæ*, etc., Leipzig, 1795). The style of Josephus has also been influenced, though in a less degree, by a study of Herodotus (Schmidt, *op. cit.* 509 f.).

Niese (*Hist. Zeitschrift*, Bd. lxxvi. 207) remarks on the language of the *Jewish War* that it is 'precious' (*gewählt*), and rich in poetical and rare words. 'It is not the simple speech of the Atticists, but approximates to the overladen fulness of the Asiatic oratory.' He finds the style of the *Antiquities* simpler and the poetical colouring almost wanting. The same care, according to Niese, is not spent in the *Antiquities* on the avoidance of hiatus; in both works, however, the crasis of article and noun (*e.g.* τἀδελφοῦ, τἀσφαλοῦς, θοιμάτιον, *BJ* ii. 148) appears to be the rule.

vii. EDITIONS AND TRANSLATIONS.—All previous editions of Josephus have been supplanted by the great critical edition of B. Niese in 7 volumes, containing a full critical apparatus and introductions on the relations of the MSS (Berlin, 1887–1895). Niese's only fault seems to have been a too great reliance on a single class of MSS, with the result that the true text is often to be looked for in the apparatus rather than in the text. In the manual edition of Niese, without critical apparatus (1888–1895), some corrections of the errors of the MSS have been introduced. On the basis of Niese's work, Naber has constructed a recension of his own (6 vols., Teubner, 1888–1896). Niese's edition is indispensable to the student, but that of Naber will also be found useful as supplementing and, to some extent, improving on the work of Niese.

Each of the works of Josephus has its own separate MS tradition: the MSS of the two halves of the *Antiquities* (I.–X., XI.–XX.) also have their own separate histories. For this history, and for the early versions of Josephus, it will be sufficient to refer the reader to the introductions to Niese's volumes and to Schürer, $GJV^3$ i. 95–99. With regard to the old Latin versions it need only be stated here that we have: (1) a version of the *Antiquities* and the *contra Apionem* undertaken at the instance of Cassiodorus (*de Institutione Div. Lit.* 17) in the 6th cent.; (2) a version of the *Jewish War* commonly attributed to Rufinus; (3) a very free Latin version of the *Jewish War*, which goes by the name of Hegesippus, a corruption of the name Josephus. The seven books are here compressed into five. The original is abbreviated, freely altered, and sometimes expanded: it has the appearance of being rather a new work than a translation. It goes back to the time of Ambrose of Milan, to whose pen it has sometimes, although probably incorrectly, been attributed. — Of the *Life* alone no Latin version exists.—There is a Syriac version of Book VI. of the *War*.

Of English translations the most serviceable, as containing the complete works, is that of Whiston, revised by Shilleto (London, 1889–1890), but the revision has been somewhat carelessly executed, and the translation is not always to be relied on. An English version of the *War* and the *Life* by Traill (London, 1862) is reported to be more reliable.

LITERATURE.—The literature on Josephus is immense. For a conspectus of the more recent works, the reader must be referred to the very full bibliography given by Schürer, *op. cit.* i. 100–106, to whose work the present writer is very greatly indebted. References will there be found to treatises on many interesting points, such as the chronology and geography of Josephus, which have not been touched on in the present article.

H. ST. J. THACKERAY.

## NUMBERS, HOURS, YEARS, AND DATES.*—



* Cf. artt. CHRONOLOGY OF THE OT and CHRONOLOGY OF THE NT in vol. i. Most of the points dealt with in the present article concern the NT alone, although some of the principles laid down, particularly in the first part of § iii., will be found to apply equally to the OT.

2. Dating by periodically elected magistrates.
3. Dating by priests or other officials.
4. Devices of historians for indicating important dates.
5. Character of the dating in the NT.
6. Dating by counting from a fixed era (Seleucid, Actian, etc.).
7. The Beginning of the Year in current use.
   (*a*) According to Roman custom, year began 1 January.
   (*b*) In Asia Minor and N. Syria, year began about autumn equinox.
   (*c*) In Southern Syria, year began about spring equinox.

Literature.

i. Numbers and Counting.—Important results sometimes turn on the precise meaning of such expressions as 'six days afterwards,' or 'on the sixth day afterwards,' and 'he was ten years old,' or 'when he was in his tenth year.' There is a tendency in English to differentiate between expressions containing the cardinal and the ordinal numbers, so that 'the tenth year of his age' refers to the interval between nine and ten, while 'ten years old' means that the person in question has lived ten years and something more. Sometimes, again, we find that, when the expression 'six days later' is used, the intention is not to reckon the day from which the period is counted as one of the six, whereas, when the expression 'on the sixth day after' is employed, the intention is to reckon the starting-point as one of the six (as, *e.g.*, 'the sixth year after' 1901 is 1906, but the phrase 'six years after' 1901 means 1907). Generally speaking, in Greek, Roman, and Græco-Roman usage there was no such difference between the expressions with cardinal and with ordinal numbers; but both classes of expression were used and understood as we in English tend to interpret the ordinal form. The older and popular expression in English also did not, as a rule, recognize such a difference: *e.g.* the idiomatic expression 'this day eight days' means the same day in the following week (the interval, *e.g.*, from Tuesday to the following Tuesday), and 'fifteen days' is still sometimes used to denote an interval of a clear fortnight. The following examples of ancient usage may be cited:—

Cicero (*ad Fam.* iv. 6. 1) says that Æmilius Paullus, the conqueror of Macedonia, lost two sons within seven days. Livy (xlv. 40) tells the story in more detail, that the younger son died five days before, and the elder three days after, his triumph over Macedonia was celebrated. Some scholars have remarked on the discrepancy between these statements. But there is no discrepancy when the numbers are counted according to the ancient fashion. If the triumph was celebrated, say, on the 14th day of the month, then, as Livy says, the younger son died on the 10th and the elder on the 16th; and, as Cicero says, the 16th is the seventh day after that on which the first son died.

Galba adopted Piso on 10 January A.D. 69. Then followed four complete days of sovereignty; and on 15 January Piso, in a speech to the soldiers, spoke of the day as the sixth since his adoption (Tacitus, *Hist.* i. 18 and 28).

There are some exceptions to this usage; but probably all could be explained as arising out of the special circumstances. Thus Tacitus elsewhere speaks of Piso's reign as lasting four days (*Hist.* i. 19 and 48). According to our reckoning, it lasted five clear days, from 10 to 15 January; but there were only four unbroken days of sovereignty.

The general rule that has just been stated must be applied in interpreting the numerical statements in the NT.—

1. The three days between the Saviour's death and resurrection are part of Friday (viz. the few hours that remained before sunset), the whole twenty-four hours from sunset on Friday to sunset on Saturday, and the few hours between sunset on Saturday and the early hour of the resurrection before sunrise on Sunday.

2. The three years and the fourteen years in Gal 1[18] 2[1] must be counted in the same way, the first and the last year in each period being only fractions of a year. Here the reckoning is complicated by the uncertainty as to how St. Paul counted the years. Was he thinking of years of his own age; or years reckoned from the day of his conversion as prominent in his mind at the moment; or years according to the common Asia Minor and N. Syrian reckoning, with New Year in the autumn; or years according to the S. Syrian style, with New Year in the spring (like the Jewish sacred year); or years according to the Roman style, with New Year on 1 January? (see § iii. 7).

The first two of these suppositions may be at once set aside as inconsistent with the ancient custom of thought and expression: years were counted by St. Paul as beginning and ending according to the current usage, and any part of the current year, however small, was counted as one year. It would be as unreasonable to consider that he counted the years as beginning and ending according to his birthday or his conversion day as it would be to consider that he counted days as beginning and ending according to the hour of either of those events. But the real difficulty lies in determining what system of years was ordinarily used by St. Paul in thinking and counting: in other words, what day was New Year's day in his estimation.

The present writer is not aware of any argument justifying an absolute and confident answer to this question. But the general impression made by the facts stated in § iii. 7 is that St. Paul counted according to the N. Syrian system, with the year beginning about the autumn equinox. This gives the general rule (stated only as probable, not as certain), that, in reckoning the number of years that had elapsed since any event, St. Paul counted the second year as beginning to run about the next autumn equinox: thus the interval between the event and the ensuing autumn equinox, however short, was reckoned as a year, and so with the interval separating the point down to which he counts from the last preceding autumn equinox.

According to this rule, the conversion of St. Paul (assuming, for the moment, the traditional day, 19 January, to be correct) and his first visit to Jerusalem (which he says took place three years after his conversion) might have occurred in two successive years of the Christian era. In his way of counting, the first year would be at an end about 23 Sept. or 1 Oct., after the conversion, the second year would end in the autumn of the following year, and any event in Oct. or later of that year would be in the third year. Thus, if the conversion were in January A.D. 31, the first visit to Jerusalem might have occurred in Oct.-Dec. A.D. 32, or in the first nine months of A.D. 33. On the other hand, if St. Paul was thinking of Roman years, the first visit could not be earlier than Jan. of 33, and might be as late as Dec. of 33. Thus a difference of nearly a whole year might be caused by the slight difference between those two methods of reckoning.

3. The statement in 2 Co 12[2] is also interesting. Fourteen years before writing, St. Paul had enjoyed the greatest vision, and the closest communion with the Divine nature, that had ever been granted him. There is probably little doubt in the mind of almost all scholars that these words were written during late summer or early autumn, about six months before the last journey to Jerusalem began. On the scheme of chronology which is followed in this article, this would be about Aug.

or Sept. A.D. 56; and the year in which the vision took place would be, on the Asia Minor and N. Syrian system, the year ending in autumn A.D. 43, on the S. Syrian system the year ending in spring A.D. 44, on the Roman system A.D. 43 (see § iii. 7).

4. In Ac 20[6] it is said that the deputation going to Jerusalem tarried seven days at Troas. As they sailed away from Troas on Monday morning, they must have arrived there on the preceding Tuesday before sunset. The journey from Philippi to Troas occupied five days, and therefore began on the Friday preceding. The five days' journey, doubtless, included one day's travel on Friday to Neapolis,* on Saturday they sailed for Troas, and, after a slow voyage (Ac 16[11]), they arrived probably early on Tuesday. These dates may be regarded as practically certain. Now it seems also practically certain that St. Paul started as soon as the days of Unleavened Bread were ended, for he was eager to be in Jerusalem in time for the Feast of Pentecost. In order to reach Jerusalem he was dependent on the uncertain chance of ships;† he had already been in Philippi for some time, and there was no special need for him to prolong his stay for a single day after the Feast was ended. Every consideration shows that he was bound to delay only for the festival season in Philippi, and to start immediately after. That is certainly the plain intention of the writer of Acts.

The long detention in Troas, waiting for a passage towards Syria, and the second shorter detention in Miletus, show how uncertain was the course of a ship, and prove that St. Paul could not afford to spend any time in Philippi after the feast was ended. On the other hand, when he had reached Cæsarea, and had only a land journey along a good road, on which the rate and time could be reckoned with confidence, he was able to wait several days, and go up to Jerusalem just before Pentecost.

Thus we reach the conclusion that, in the year in which St. Paul went up to Jerusalem, Passover began on a Thursday at sunset, and the days of Unleavened Bread came to an end on the following Thursday at sunset. From this it has been inferred (Ramsay, *St. Paul the Traveller*, p. 289) that the journey was made in the year A.D. 57; and the discussions which have taken place on the point seem to the present writer only to have established this result more clearly.‡

5. There is much difficulty in St. Paul's words, Ac 24[11] 'It is not more than twelve days since I went up to worship at Jerusalem.' The reckoning seems to show that it was a little more than twelve days. St. Paul reached Jerusalem after a journey, presumably after sunset, so that, though it was only next morning that he called on St. James, yet in the reckoning both events fall in the first day. Then we seem, at first sight, to have the following list of days and events:—

1st day. Arrival after sunset; visit to St. James next morning.
2nd ,, First day of Purification, Ac 21[26].
3rd ,, Second ,, ,,
4th ,, Third ,, ,,
5th ,, Fourth ,, ,,
6th day. Fifth day of Purification.
7th ,, Sixth ,, ,,
8th ,, Seventh ,, ,,* , Ac 21[27]; riot; St. Paul's speech.
9th ,, Council, Ac 22[30].
10th ,, { Dream by night, 23[11]. Conspiracy, 23[12]. Journey to Antipatris begins before sunset, 23[31].
11th ,, { Journey to Antipatris continues by night. Arrival in Cæsarea before sunset, 23[32f.].
12th ,, Detention in Cæsarea, 2nd day, 24[1].
13th ,, ,, ,, ,, 3rd ,,
14th ,, ,, ,, ,, 4th ,,
15th ,, ,, ,, ,, 5th ,, : trial.

This list seems to show that fifteen days at the least had elapsed between St. Paul's arrival in Jerusalem and the day when he declared that not more than twelve days had passed since he went up to Jerusalem.

The explanation probably lies in Ac 21[27] 'when the seven days (of purification) were about to be completed.'† In the above list this is understood as implying that the seventh day had arrived; but it may, perhaps, be taken as merely implying 'the seven days of purification were more than half finished, and the men were now coming near the end of the period.'‡ This seems quite consistent with the fifth day, and in that case St. Paul would be speaking on the thirteenth day since his entry into Jerusalem; and we may understand the peculiar expression 'not more than twelve days' as meaning 'the thirteenth day is not yet completed and past': this form of expression shows distinct analogy with the case quoted above from Tacitus (*Hist.* i. 19 and 48).

ii. Hours of the Day.—1. 'Hour' (*ὥρα*, *hora*) is a word used in a considerable variety of senses in the NT. The Latin *hora* was borrowed from the Greek (*ὥρα*), and was to a great extent determined in usage by the origin. The Greek word *ὥρα* meant, in a very wide and general sense, a distinguishable period of time, a division of time marked off by a beginning and an end, however vaguely the bounds might be indicated. Thus *ὥρα* meant, in the most general way, a measurable or estimable lapse of time; and this sense of the word never entirely disappeared, and is found in the NT, *e.g.* Mk 6[35] (twice), where it is rendered 'day' in both AV and RV; Mk 11[11], 2 Co 7[8], where it is rendered 'season' in AV and RV. The *ὧραι τῆς νυκτός* and *τῆς ἡμέρας* in Xenophon, *Mem.* iv. 3. 4, are not the 'hours' of night and of day, but the great 'periods,' the watches of night and the forenoon and afternoon of day.

The most characteristic division of time indicated by *ὥρα* in early time was the season of the year; and the mythological *Horai* were personifications of the Seasons. The use of the word in the sense of a division of the day, something approximating to an hour in the modern usage, hardly begins much before the end of the 4th cent. B.C. in the extant literature; but this quickly became the most common and widespread meaning of the word; and from some time, probably early in the 3rd cent. B.C. onwards, the Greek word in that sense was adopted in Latin. The division, which was probably of Babylonian origin

* No long detention is to be expected at Neapolis, where, doubtless, ships were to be found sailing for Troas every day (see above, p. 400, also pp. 384, 389); but still a certain amount of time must have been lost there.

† There were no pilgrim-ships (such as might have been got before Passover) sailing direct; and, even after a ship was found, its voyage might be broken at harbours on the way; see above, p. 400.

‡ Divergent views are stated by Mr. Turner, above, vol. i. p. 420, by Prof. Bacon in *Expositor* (1898, i. 123; 1899, ii. 351, 412; 1900, ii. 1). The latter argues on the false assumption that the strict and narrow Judaic practice of the later reaction against Roman and Christian science obtained also in the early years of the Imperial period.

* Assuming for the moment that the riot broke out on the last day of Purification; but we shall see below that it probably occurred on the fifth day.

† The rendering 'almost completed' in AV and RV is too strong for the Greek *ἔμελλον συντελεῖσθαι*.

‡ The Bezan text *συντελουμένης δὲ τῆς ἑβδόμης ἡμέρας*, which is inconsistent with our rendering, is evidently a later alteration to secure a more precise and definite sense than the true Lukan text.

(Herod. ii. 109), was according to the duodecimal system; and from an early time in the history of this usage traces occur both of a popular division of the period of light from sunrise to sunset (the natural day) into twelve parts or ὧραι, and of a scientific division of the double period of light and darkness from sunrise to sunrise, or from sunset to sunset (the civil or legal day), into twenty-four (twice twelve) parts.

Hours of the latter class, one twenty-fourth part of the fixed and unvarying period, a revolution of the earth round its axis, were of absolutely fixed and unvarying length; but the words *hora*, ὥρα, were rarely employed by the ancients in that sense: it was only astronomers that sometimes spoke of these ὧραι ἰσημεριναί, *horæ æquinoctiales*, as they were called. In ordinary usage among the ancients, these words *hora*, ὥρα, had a different meaning, which arose out of the only means of measuring hours known and used in ordinary life by the ancients, the sun-dial. The dial, originally a very simple instrument among the Greeks, was improved, until it afforded a means of dividing the time between sunrise and sunset into twelve equal parts or hours. These hours were equal in length to each other during the same day, but varied in length from day to day. The earliest systematic use of this division into twelve hours among the Greeks is said to have been made during the 4th century before Christ.

While hours of this new kind were in common and popular use, the astronomers found it necessary for their purposes to use the equinoctial or sidereal hours of unvarying length, which they calculated by means of *clepsydræ* or water-clocks.

There often occur in the NT examples of a system of numbering the hours of the day. The third, the sixth, and the ninth hour, as the main divisions between the four quarters of the day, occur very often. 'From the fifth to the tenth hour' Ac 19[9] (according to the Bezan text) is a note of the hours of lecturing in a public hall of quite unusual and even unique character in the NT; 'the eleventh hour' (Mt 20[9]) is proverbial of the approaching end of an allotted time. St. John uses the numbers with exceptional accuracy: 'the tenth hour,' 1[40]; 'the seventh hour' (in a medical observation), 4[52].

The precise meaning of these expressions in certain cases has been the subject of some doubt among NT commentators; but there is absolutely no uncertainty as to the meaning in ancient pagan usage, and the doubts expressed as regards the interpretation in a few passages of Christian writings are unnecessary. A certain amount of obscurity is introduced into the subject by the use of the word 'day' in two different senses: the period of light from about sunrise to sunset is called the natural day as distinguished from the period of darkness or night; a day and a night together constitute the period of the legal or civil Day. In the following remarks we distinguish these two senses by the convention that 'day' means the period of light as distinguished from the night (*Lichttag* in German), and that 'Day' means the legal period of a day and a night.

According to our own ordinary modern system of counting time, the legal Day is divided into 24 hours, and the hour is an unvarying and absolute duration of time; while the length of the day and the night are continually changing within certain limits (according to latitude), the day containing more hours and the night fewer at midsummer, and conversely at midwinter, while at the spring and the autumn equinox day and night are equal, and contain each 12 hours.

There are only the scantiest traces of such a meaning for the word 'hour' in ancient times, and it never occurs in popular usage, though it seems to have been known to astronomers from a very early time. The length of the ordinary ancient 'hour' varied continually from day to day throughout the year. The day, the period between sunrise and sunset, was divided into twelve equal parts called 'hours' (Jn 11[9]). The division was marked by the progress of the shadow from line to line on the sun-dial; and the progress was more widely published in houses of a more pretentious character by some such device as the blowing of a trumpet. In Trimalchio's house (Petronius, p. 26)* the trumpeter was an established institution; and in the old German Imperial city of Goslar the same ancient custom was maintained by the public authorities down almost to the present time: not many years ago, and perhaps still, the trumpeter in Goslar sounded every quarter of an hour, for the division of time is carried out more minutely in modern than in ancient times.

There is hardly any trace in popular Græco-Roman usage of any definite division of time shorter than the hour: *horæ momento*, 'in the motion of an hour,' *i.e.* the time that the shadow on the dial takes to creep from one line to the next, was a customary phrase for a brief interval (Horace, *Sat.* i. 1. 16). Hence the word 'hour' is often used in the NT to indicate a point of time, where the more emphatic expression of modern language would require some such term as 'instant' or 'moment,' *e.g.* Mt 8[13] 9[22], Mk 14[41], Lk 12[39. 40], Jn 17[1]. But this usage may really be much more emphatic than it appears at first sight. The Latin word *hora* certainly, and perhaps also the Greek ὥρα, are often used in the sense, not of the period that the shadow takes to creep from line to line on the dial, but of the brief moment in which the shadow crosses the line. Bilfinger has conclusively proved, contrary to the opinion of almost all other scholars, that the latter was the more frequent sense of the terms in Latin, *hora prima*, *hora secunda*: these generally indicated, not the whole time which the shadow required to move from the starting-point at sunrise to the first line, and from the first to the second line, but the moment † when the shadow reached the first or the second line. Hence *hora sexta* is frequently found, and almost always has the precise and exact sense 'at the point of noon.'

But Bilfinger tries to push too far the view which he champions. There are certainly some cases in which *hora prima* means the whole period from sunrise to the moment when the shadow on the dial reaches the first division. In truth, the ancients were far from being so accurate as modern people are; and probably many of them were hardly conscious of any difference between these two meanings, and used the term *hora prima* so loosely that they could hardly have specified which of the two meanings they had in mind. We ought not to try to make them out more accurate than they really were. Their vagueness in estimating the divisions of time must be allowed for. They had never been used to measure time so accurately or so minutely as we do. They had no division shorter than the hour; and they talked of the hours very loosely, making use chiefly of the prominent divisions—first, third, sixth, ninth, and twelfth hours. The third hour meant little more than 'during the forenoon'; and if an ordinary person, speaking of the third hour, were criticised and told that he should have said the sixth hour, he would probably have regarded the correction as too slight to be worth making, just as a Turkish peasant would at the present day. Modern peoples are so habituated to minute and

* Cf. also Martial, viii. 67, x. 48; Juvenal, *Sat.* x. 215 f.

† Bilfinger, *Der bürgerliche Tag.*

accurate divisions of time, and to precise punctuality, that their thought and language have acquired a precision which is wanting in the ancient writers,* and which we must not try to force on them by strained interpretation.

An example of the double meaning of the term 'hour' is seen if Mt $20^{9}$ be compared with Plutarch, *Crass.* 17. In the former passage 'the eleventh hour' is used metaphorically to indicate the last point of time, the last line and hour of the dial, before the allotted time, viz. the day, comes to an end, and the opportunity is lost for ever. In the latter passage 'the twelfth hour' is used to convey the same proverbial sense, as being the last period, which ends when the sun sets. St. Matthew thinks of the moment when the shadow crosses the last dividing line; Plutarch thinks of the interval that elapses between that moment and the sunset. The influence of Roman usage is here seen: dials and divisions of time seem to have been more familiar in the Roman time, and with greater familiarity came the use of *hora* to indicate the point of time when the shadow crosses the line.

When *hora prima* or *secunda* indicates a point of time, it means the moment when the shadow reaches the line at the end of the first or of the second hour after sunrise; and so on. Hence, in this usage, *hora prima* corresponds in logical sense, though not in time, to our expression 'one o'clock.'

The length of the hour varied, therefore, according to the length of the day: it was about 75 minutes long at midsummer, and hardly more than 45 at midwinter, while at the equinox it was exactly 60 minutes, like the hour in our modern custom. This sense of the word 'hour' as a period of time is found in such passages as Ac $19^{34}$ $5^{7}$,† Lk $22^{59}$, Mt $20^{12}$ $26^{40}$, Mk $14^{37}$. In popular language the varying length of the hour is alluded to in such expressions as *hora æstiva*. In both Greek and Roman times the conception of an hour as an unvarying period of time, the twenty-fourth part of the civil or legal Day, occasionally appears in books of a more scientific character, but never in popular literature or common life.

The division of the hour into 60 minutes is said to be of Babylonian origin, and may have had an existence in scientific thought and astronomical calculations; but such a minute division played no part in popular life, never affected popular thought, and was not expressed by any word in popular language. The hour was the shortest division of time known to ordinary people, as has been stated above.

In ordinary usage the night was divided, not into hours but into four watches, the second of which ended at midnight. The dial gave no means of dividing the night into hours; and the length of hours of the day could not, except with much trouble and careful adjustment (such as only men of science would be able to give), be applied to the night by such methods of measuring as the *clepsydra* or water-clock, because the night hours grew shorter as the day hours grew longer, and coincided with them in length only at the equinox. But, by analogy from the expression *hora sexta* for 'noon,' midnight was often called *hora sexta noctis* (Ulpian in *Digest.* xli. 3. 7; compare xl. 1. 1, xxviii. 1. 5; Aulus Gellius, iii. 2. 11). The Greek corresponding expression is not found in the NT (probably not anywhere in strictly Greek literature), but the similar expression 'at the third hour of night,' implying the end of the first watch, occurs in Ac $23^{23}$.* In Ac $16^{33}$ 'the same hour of the night,' the meaning is 'instant' or 'point of time,' as in the expressions described above.

It is accordingly involved in the very idea and origin of the hours in common usage that they begin from sunrise, and that the first hour ended when the shadow reached the first dividing line on the dial; and so on. These hours are parts of the natural day, the *Lichttag*, and cannot be counted except as beginning with the day. The hours, as parts of the civil Day, were a totally different conception, which, as we have seen, never affected or entered into popular usage and popular thought. Is it possible that those equinoctial hours might have been counted as beginning from the point when the Day was considered to begin (though only in scientific work)? We ask, then, when the Day was considered as beginning.

The legal or civil Day, comprising a complete period of day and night, was regarded as beginning from various points in the East and in the West. The Roman usage was the same as our modern usage: the Day was reckoned as the period from one midnight, *hora sexta noctis*, to the next. In the Jewish and the Greek usage the Day was reckoned from sunset to sunset; and it is in accordance with its Eastern origin and its early development amid Greek surroundings that the Church always reckoned the ecclesiastical Day as beginning at sunset. Bilfinger, indeed, maintains that both Greeks and Romans (except in matters of Roman law) counted the Day as beginning at daylight, either sunrise or roughly at dawn; but Unger has conclusively refuted his arguments on this point (see his article on 'Tagesanfang' in *Philologus*, 1892, pp. 14 ff., 212 ff.), allowing only that there was a Macedonian usage (traceable at Pergamos and other places where the Macedonian calendar was used), according to which the Day was counted to begin from sunrise. It may, however, be doubted whether those seeming cases of counting the Day from sunrise may not have been simply caused by the ordinary popular custom of counting the hours of the day as beginning with the light. But however that may be, it is certain that no example has ever been quoted from the ancient writers in which the hours were counted as beginning from midnight. Though the Roman legal Day began at midnight, yet the hours of the day were counted only as beginning from sunrise; and the hours of the night (in the rare cases in which hours of the night were spoken of) only from sunset. In popular usage probably no night-hours were spoken of except the third, sixth, and perhaps the ninth, as the beginnings of the second, third, and fourth watches; and those expressions were used, not because there was any device in ordinary use for dividing the night into twelve hours, but simply by analogy from the three main customary divisions of the day.

2. There has been among some NT scholars a certain degree of hesitation about accepting as absolutely and invariably true the principle that hours were counted only as beginning from sunrise; and some attempt has been made to show that the hours of the day were sometimes counted after a different fashion. This hesitation has been caused by the apparent discrepancy between Jn $19^{14}$ and Mk $15^{25}$. In the former passage it is said that the trial of Jesus was concluded and the judgment on the point of being pronounced '*about* the sixth hour,' and some more time was needed (but prob-

* The looseness shown by St. Luke in regard to time is noted in *St. Paul the Traveller*, p. 18, etc.

† In Ac $5^{7}$ ὡρῶν τριῶν διάστημα must mean 'the period of three hours'; it can hardly be, according to the usage described in the following paragraph, the interval that separates a line on the dial from the third following line, because that would give a space of only two hours, according to the ancient way of counting the starting-point as the first. Lk $22^{59}$ must be interpreted on the same analogy.

* It is sometimes said that the Greeks had only three watches, the Romans four. This is an error arising from misinterpretation of Pollux, i. 70. See Mr. Macan's note on Herodotus, ix. 5, in his forthcoming edition.

ably not long) to conduct Jesus to the place of execution and raise Him on the cross, so that the Crucifixion could hardly have been consummated before 12 noon. No other estimate is given by St. John of the lapse of time on that day, but towards sunset it was found that Jesus was dead already, though the other two sufferers were still living; thereafter the body was taken away by Joseph and Nicodemus for burial, apparently just before the day was ended, perhaps about 5.30 or 5.45 p.m.

In the latter passage, Mk $15^{25}$, it is stated that the Crucifixion was consummated 'at the third hour,' *i.e.* 9 a.m. (modern time), and that at the sixth hour darkness began and lasted till the ninth hour, when Jesus died: about the beginning of evening, very soon after 6 p.m. (modern time, *i.e.* sunset), Joseph took away the body for burial.

It has been suggested (and the view is advocated by some high authorities) that St. John counted the hours as beginning from midnight, so that according to him judgment was pronounced on Jesus about 6 a.m. (modern time); then after an interval of three hours followed the Crucifixion, and afterwards darkness began (according to the Synoptics) at noon. By this device all is shown to be in perfect harmony. It is urged that the difference in the way of counting the hours was due to the fact that St. John wrote in Ephesus, and counted in this one case according to the fashion of Asia Minor as being familiar to the public for which he wrote. An example of this supposed Asia Minor custom is sought in the martyrdom of Polycarp at the eighth hour. It is maintained that exhibitions of wild beasts, and executions by exposure to the beasts, ordinarily took place before noon (which is true),* and that therefore the eighth hour can only have been 8 a.m. (modern time).

It is needless to discuss fully the case of Polycarp; † the facts show beyond doubt that his case was exceptional, and that he did not suffer until after noon. He was arrested near sunset at a villa at some distance from Smyrna (to which he had retired after leaving his first refuge in a villa near the city) on a Friday, officers having been sent to arrest him in compliance with the shouts of the crowded audience at the conclusion of the *venatio* in the stadium at Smyrna on that day. He was permitted to pray for two hours after arrest; 'when the hour for departure arrived' (that is, evidently, early on Saturday morning) he was conducted to Smyrna; he was introduced for trial before the proconsul after the games in the stadium were concluded, because he could hardly have reached the city before the games began, and they would not be interrupted to allow the trial to proceed. It is clear that the games were over for the day when the trial was held, for Philip the Asiarch (who favoured Polycarp) declared that he could not reopen them in order to comply with the demand of the crowd that Polycarp should be exposed to the beasts. The games, of course, lasted more than one day; but it may be regarded as practically certain that they would not be continued after the fifth hour.‡ The interval between that hour and the eighth was occupied with the trial (for the forms of Roman law, even in a hurried trial, required some time) and the preparation for the execution; and the Jews, who could hardly have been present at the games on a Sabbath of especial sanctity, but who came in numbers to the trial, showed themselves active in procuring materials to burn Polycarp. Other examples of martyrdoms which took place in the afternoon are those of Zenobius and Zenobia at Aigeai in Cilicia on a Friday at the ninth hour (*Acta Sanct.* 31 Oct. p. 263), and of Pionius at Smyrna at the tenth hour (*Acta Pionii*).

In those exceptional cases the hour was remembered; but in ordinary cases the execution took place early in the day, commonly forming a part of the exhibitions or *venationes*.

Thus the one example that has been most confidently quoted to prove the existence of a peculiar way of numbering the hours in Asia Minor turns out to be an example of the ordinary custom. In truth, the idea that in Asia Minor people counted the hours from midnight is even more improbable than it would be in other countries; for, as has been shown above, there are many instances of even the civil Day, as well as the natural day, being reckoned there to begin with sunrise. Moreover, why should St. John in that one case count his hours from midnight? It is certain and admitted that elsewhere he counts them from sunrise.

The more closely the subject is examined, the more clear does it become that the numbering of the hours in popular usage always started from the beginning of the natural day. While the other kind of hours, the equinoctial, were sometimes used in scientific calculations, there is no appearance that they were numbered. The very idea of numbering the hours is a matter of practical convenience in everyday life, and has no scientific character.

It must be recognized that there is an absolute—and perhaps intentional and deliberate—difference between St. John and the Synoptists: the latter declare that the Crucifixion took place about three hours earlier in the day than the former admits. With regard to this difference there arise several questions bearing on the subject of this article: Which Evangelist shows himself most attentive and observant of details of time? what is the cause of the error which must exist on one side or on the other? what is its importance? with whom does it lie?

There can be no doubt that St. John is more careful about recording points and details of time. The two disciples of the Baptist went to the place where Jesus was, 'about the tenth hour' ($1^{39}$). Why does the historian record such a minute and in itself valueless detail? Obviously, he was naturally attentive to details of time, and that one remained in his memory because he had seen and known. 'About the sixth hour' Jesus sat down on the well of Jacob to rest ($4^{6}$). The official's son became free from the fever 'at the seventh hour' ($4^{52}$). In these cases there is no intrinsic importance (as there is in the case of the Crucifixion) to make the time of day memorable. The time when they occurred is stated, because the narrator remembered the details from personal knowledge; and only a person attentive to time-notes would have remembered what was the hour at which each event occurred.

While the question which authority is right cannot be discussed without a far wider estimate of facts and characteristics than belongs to the present article, yet the inference from the above-stated facts is in favour of St. John's superior trustworthiness in any statement of time; and the long interval of three hours which the Synoptists place between the consummation of the Crucifixion and the beginning of the darkness seems improbable.

The cause of the difference in this matter lies probably or certainly in the want of attention to the lapse of time on one side or the other. St. John shows himself distinctly more attentive, through a certain personal character, whereas most of the

* See the full discussion in Friedländer's *Röm. Sittengesch.* iii. p. 391 (349); also Martial viii. 67. 4, v. 65. 8.

† It is discussed at length in the *Expositor*, 4th Ser. [1893], vol. vii. p. 220 ff.

‡ See *Expositor*, *loc. cit.*, and the article TYRANNUS, vol. iv. p. 822b. Martial says *ad quintam varios extendit Roma labores.*

simple country people to whom the Synoptic tradition must go back are very unlikely to have paid any attention to an exact estimate of the passage of time, and may quite probably have erred in their recollection of the time. The reason for the difference lies simply in that inaccuracy in estimating and measuring the lapse of time which is observable in the thought and language of the ancients. The difference in opinion is not due to correct memory being obscured in the lapse of time; it dates from the event, and would be found in accounts written at the time, if witnesses of various character had been then ordered to state their impressions in writing.

As to the degree of importance to be attached to the contradiction between the witnesses, it is evident from the general considerations already stated that there is no importance in such a difference of recollection. Three events occurred successively during the day: the memory of most of the witnesses marked the sequence by recording that they occurred respectively at the third, the sixth, and the ninth hour, the only three divisions which the popular mind was used to note. But those three divisions were by most people used vaguely and roughly, without any accurate estimate of the precise hour indicated on the dial; and so it was in this case. The people who assigned the time of the Crucifixion as the third hour would have probably been much surprised if any one had in their presence used their testimony to pin down the event to an exact hour. Their thought and mind were not trained to such accuracy, they saw no importance in being accurate, and they were from habit not capable of even attempting to be accurate in respect of the lapse of time. The sixth hour, as being midday, was better marked than any other; but even in regard to it we must allow considerable latitude when ordinary persons speak of it. St. John alone in the NT stands out as habitually careful and accurate in this respect. The distinction between him and the other NT writers on this point is like the difference between Romans and Greeks. The Greeks made little use of the hours, and spoke little about them. The Romans used the hours in all departments of life, regulated their business and private life by them, and spoke frequently about them. St. John stood on the Roman plane.

iii. Years and Dates.—A convenient and practically useful system of chronology was developed only very slowly in the ancient world.

1. *Dating by the years of kings and emperors.*—In countries governed by monarchs, the custom of dating by the years of the current reign was natural and widespread. Such a system was of course confined almost absolutely to the limits of the monarchy. Beyond those limits it could hardly be used, or understood, or verified. Even within those limits it had many practical disadvantages for historical purposes. For instance, a considerable amount of trouble was often needed to discover the meaning and value of dates in past time; as amongst ourselves it would not be obvious, without some trouble, what interval elapsed between the fifteenth year of George III. and the third year of Victoria. The difficulties of this method are of course not so serious in contemporary dating: while a sovereign is reigning, the years of his reign, from whatever day it began, would be familiar to all the people, but after his death hardly any one remembers the exact limits of his reign.

The difficulty is increased by the fact that a king reigns not for an exact number of years, but for a period that must be reckoned by years, months, and days. If his first year is counted as running from the day of his accession, his last year is a broken one; and his successor's reign has to be counted as beginning from a different date. Thus a literal reckoning by the exact years of each king's reign becomes chronologically so complicated as to be extremely unwieldy and practically impossible.

Some modification was therefore commonly introduced for chronological purposes in this method of reckoning. The years of each king's reign were counted according to the current and recognized system of years, and not according to the day when the reign began: either the first year of the monarch was reckoned as ending with the last day of the current year (so that this nominal first year of his reign might last in reality only a few days or months), or the last year of the former monarch was counted as running up to the end of the year in which he died, and the first year of the new monarch was counted as beginning only with the first day of the local year next after he ascended the throne, or some other device of that kind was adopted in order to facilitate chronological reckoning.

Thus either the first year of Queen Victoria would have to be reckoned as ending on 31 Dec. 1837, and her sixty-fifth year would be running at the time of her death in the beginning of 1901: but in that case the rest of the year 1901 would be reckoned by subsequent chronologists as the first year of Edward VII., and in historical chronology 1837 would be called as a whole the first of Victoria and 1901 the first of Edward VII.: or else the whole of 1837 would have to be reckoned to William IV., 1838 would be the first year of Victoria, and 1901 would be her sixty-fourth, and would, as a whole, be reckoned as the last year of her reign. Whenever possible, it is desirable to investigate each writer's practice from his own writings. But, of the two alternative methods which have just been stated, the former was, on the whole, the more frequent and ordinary rule, and the one which must, in cases of doubt, be supposed to have been followed, as most likely to have been the practice of the writer in question.

On the other hand, in dating by years of the emperors, it is obvious that in Egypt the latter method was often practised, and many persons continued to date documents by the emperor who had been in office at the beginning of the year, even though his successor had already been in power for many months; see above, p. 379[b] (where many of the cases alluded to are probably due, not entirely to ignorance, but to the idea that the whole current local year should be reckoned to the emperor in whose name it had begun).

Practical convenience dictated the rule, and it may be regarded as universally observed that when ordinary persons spoke of a series of years they meant, and were understood by every one to mean, the current years of the country or State to which they belonged, and not years reckoned from some arbitrary epoch, such as the birth of an individual or the accession of a sovereign. Thus, in Egypt, the universal way of counting the years of the Roman emperors is known to have been according to the Egyptian year beginning on 1 Thoth (30 August). Similarly, we may be sure that in Syria people counted in ordinary usage according to the current local year (on which see § iii. 7).

There was no fixed and universal rule among chronologists regulating their practice in this respect; and the custom of each ancient writer should as far as possible be determined separately from a special study of his method. Many errors have been made by modern writers owing to misinterpretation of chronological statements according to Imperial years. For example, in the reign of Claudius, the dates (so important for NT chronology) of the great famine (Ac 12[1]) and of the edict expelling the Jews from Rome (Ac 18[2]) have been assigned to the fourth and ninth years of his reign. Now Claudius began to reign on 25 Jan. A.D. 41, and many writers have forthwith assumed that his fourth year ran from 25 Jan. 44 to 24 Jan. 45, and his ninth from 25 Jan. 49 to 24 Jan. 50. But that assumption is certainly wrong. We must first ask who is the authority responsible for the date, and what was his way of counting Claudius' years. Did he follow the Roman official reckoning of years of the reign, or did he follow any of the chronologists' methods? The authority is Orosius; and it is clear that he followed the method which reckoned A.D. 41 as the last year of Caligula and 42 as the first year of Claudius.* Hence his authority (such as it is) places the great famine in A.D. 45, and the edict expelling the Jews from Rome in A.D. 50. Ultimately, the value of his evidence depends entirely on the older authority or authorities on whom he was dependent: that is a topic that has to be treated by a careful comparative study of his account of the period as a whole. What concerns us here is that it is wrong to quote his evidence in favour of placing those events in A.D. 44 and 49.

It lies outside of the limits of this article to investigate the practice of the more scientific chronologists, which was not absolutely uniform. But so much is certain: the modern fashion of counting a sovereign's years from the day of his predecessor's death and his own accession was not followed by chronologists or historians in ancient times; and the reason lies in the hopeless cumbrousness of that method of reckoning. Such 'dynastic' years, as they may be termed, were hardly thought of or reckoned by the ancients. Current years, according to local usage, alone were taken into account.

The official Roman practice in reckoning the years of an emperor's reign varied. It was certainly not determined by scientific considerations of chronological convenience, and probably depended greatly on the choice or caprice of individual emperors. In general, the only part of the official description or titles of the reigning emperor that gave a clue to the length of his reign was the number of times that he had held the tribunician authority,† which was apparently chosen by Augustus as the characteristic feature and the fundamental element in his tenure of authority. The real foundation of his power, of course, lay in his command of the legions. That, however, was too harsh and repellent a feature; and in B.C. 23, after years of hesitation, during which he governed as triumvir by extraordinary appointment (for periods of five years, beginning from B.C. 42), or as consul by annual election (B.C. 31–23), he finally preferred to have the tribunician authority as Champion of the Commons conferred on him; and henceforth in his formal list of titles the number of years during which he had held that office was stated as being equivalent to the years of his reign. The custom was continued by subsequent emperors.

* This is pointed out by the present writer in *St. Paul the Traveller* (pp. 68, 254), where it is explained as due to a faulty reckoning of the years of Claudius; but in *Was Christ Born at Bethlehem?* p. 223, the right explanation is given that Orosius (or the older writer from whom he borrowed) reckoned intentionally after that fashion. We need not ask what was the New Year's Day in Orosius' reckoning: it was certainly late in our year, *St. Paul the Traveller*, p. 68.

† This number is always stated in the title (except in the abbreviated titles on coins): *trib. pot.* alone means the first year of the authority of the emperor in question. The consulships and the imperatorial salutations were also expressed numerically in his title; but the number gave no clue to the length of his reign. For example, the eleventh consulship of Augustus was in B.C. 23, but he continued to be called 'Consul XI.' till B.C. 5, when his twelfth consulship began.

Most of the emperors of the 1st cent. reckoned their years of tribunician authority from the day on which it had first been conferred on them, and disregarded the day on which their predecessor died, and on which their reign practically began. The theory was that their legal authority began when the people conferred on them tribunician and other powers, and thus made them Champion of the Commons, with the powers to make their championship effective. The later view, which makes dynastic succession the criterion, did not rule in the Roman practice of the 1st cent. and even later; and there is absolutely no justification for the common modern view, that the years of an emperor were counted in that century from the day of his predecessor's death.

According to this official Roman view—

The years of Augustus began 27 June.
" " Tiberius " "
" " Caligula " 18 March.
" " Claudius " 25 January.
" " Nero " 13 October (till A.D. 60).
" " Vespasian " 1 July.
" " Titus " "
" " Domitian " 13 September.

Nero's and Domitian's days coincided with those of their predecessor's death. Claudius' day was one day later than Caligula's death, Caligula's was two days later than Tiberius' death, and the other four had no connexion whatsoever with their predecessor's death.

Nero, in A.D. 60, introduced a new way of counting his own reign, and made the change retrospective. His seventh year had begun on 13 October in that year, but he ordered that his eighth year should begin on 10 December A.D. 60 (for the old Republican rule was that the Tribunes of the Commons entered office always on 10 December). Hence he was officially in the fifteenth year of his reign when he died on 9 June A.D. 68 (though according to our modern way of counting, by which many scholars interpret the chronological statements of the ancients, his fourteenth year was then still unfinished). But this way of counting the years of the reign from 10 December was not imitated by any of the 1st cent. emperors except Nerva and Trajan from the year 97 onwards, and could not have had any possible influence on NT usage.

2. From this follows a conclusion extremely important for NT chronology. There is no justification in Roman official usage for the view that when St. Luke (3[1]) mentioned the fifteenth year of Tiberius he was counting from the death of Augustus on 19 August A.D. 14, and meant the 12 months that began on 19 Aug. A.D. 28. We have previously seen that neither ordinary contemporary usage, nor the more scientific usage of chronologists, permits such an interpretation.* We must therefore conclude that, whatever St. Luke may have meant, he certainly did not mean the year 19 August A.D. 28 to 18 August A.D. 29. Yet the majority of modern writers assume as self-evident that that interpretation (which is founded only on modern custom and prejudice) must be what St. Luke had in mind. The question now is what bearing the special subject of this article has on the interpretation of that important date.

It may be regarded as practically certain that the custom of dating by the years of the reigning Roman emperor originated, not in Rome but in the Eastern provinces; and hence such dates are to be interpreted by Eastern, not by Roman, usage.

* They would consider that his reign began on 19 August, but that his first year ended at the conclusion of the current local year (which in many places would be on 22 or 30 September).

The Roman fashion of dating by consuls persisted in Rome far through the Imperial time; and so, *e.g.*, the *Annals* of Tacitus are arranged in strictly annalistic order, year by year, according to consuls, and not by years of the emperors. The prevalent method of counting in the Eastern provinces was a mixture of the dynastic method with the reckoning according to local years: as a general rule, the years of each emperor were counted according to the current local years, but his reign was considered to begin at the death of his predecessor. According to that method the fifteenth year of Tiberius would be the year beginning in spring A.D. 28, or in autumn A.D. 27, according as the local year began in spring or in autumn.* There were, however, some exceptions to this rule about the beginning of the reign, caused chiefly by collegiate government. Thus, in Egypt, the reign of Commodus, who had been colleague of his father, M. Aurelius, for some years, was counted continuously with his father's, as if there had been an unbroken rule from A.D. 161 to 192. Now, there were in the 1st cent. two emperors—Tiberius and Titus—who reigned for a time as colleagues of their predecessors. In their strictly official style, both counted their years of tribunician authority from a point long anterior to their predecessors' death. But Tiberius' tribunician authority was interrupted and remained in abeyance for a good many years, hence it was impossible to count the years of his reign from the first of his tribunician authority. There was, however, a second occasion when he was assumed as colleague of his predecessor with power over all the armies in all the provinces. This was a few days or weeks before 16 January A.D. 12, when, on his return from Pannonia, he celebrated his triumph. Before his arrival, probably at the meeting held in ordinary course on 1 January, the Senate had conferred on him those great powers; and it has been suggested with much plausibility that St. Luke (3[1]) considered his reign as beginning from that day, when he became colleague of Augustus, so far as the provinces and all provincial administration were concerned. If, as many hold on other grounds to be probable, St. Luke was writing under Titus, who counted his years from his collegiate appointment, there would be an Imperial contemporary analogy prompting the historian to this way of counting Tiberius' years.

One must take into account that, in the case both of Tiberius and of Augustus, it was extremely difficult to tell from what date their power ought to be counted as beginning. In both cases there were several different dates which might, with almost equal plausibility, be taken as the commencement of their reigns, while Roman custom (as we have seen) forbade that either reign should be counted as beginning from the death of the preceding ruler, the day which modern custom prefers.

It is therefore impossible to arrive, on the ground of custom or etiquette, at any sure conclusion about the sense that should be attached to the date in Lk 3[1]; and the meaning can be determined only by the general chronology of the life of Christ, which is not within the scope of this article. In this place there is only one further remark to make. St. Luke counted according to current years: but what, in his case, are to be understood as current years? He was certainly influenced in various ways by Roman feeling, but it seems highly improbable that he would count according to the Roman year; and there are absolutely no other facts mentioned in his writings to show with certainty what was his custom in respect of chronological reckoning. He was, however, Greek, and it seems improbable that he used any kind of year other than the Macedonian, Anatolian, and North Syrian, beginning at or near the autumn equinox. If we may start from this strong presumption, the fifteenth year of Tiberius began in autumn A.D. 25 or A.D. 27 (in the latter case year 1 of Tiberius would last only from 19 Aug. to 22 or 30 Sept. A.D. 14).

The passage is encumbered by another difficulty. The call of John the Baptist took place in that fifteenth year; but what relation does the call bear to the baptizing of Jesus, or, in other words, how long had John's preaching lasted before Jesus came to be baptized? It seems probable that the call of John and the coming of Jesus are to be placed within that fifteenth year, for otherwise the dating, which is here stated in such careful detail, would be valueless. But when an ancient historian specifies a date so elaborately as St. Luke does in this case, his object (as we shall see*) is to fix chronologically a critical event according to which the rest of the history is to be grouped.

Moreover, the narrative distinctly gives the impression that Jesus was one of John's early hearers. The baptism of Jesus in the Jordan belongs probably to the late winter season, as Lewin has shown;† and the call of John then must have taken place in the late autumn immediately preceding. The ancient customs of reckoning seem to leave only two possibilities: Jesus was baptized by John either in the beginning of A.D. 26 or in the beginning of A.D. 28, according as Tiberius' reign is counted as beginning from his collegiate power or dynastically from the death of Augustus.

2. *Dating by periodically elected magistrates.*—Far more difficult than the date according to the years of monarchs was the custom of dating by eponymous magistrates, which was introduced by the proud self-consciousness of Greek city life. No means existed of determining the interval between two events, for example, dated respectively in the archonship of Euclid and the archonship of Pythodorus, except to consult a list of archons and find out the number of names between them. Except in Athens, it would be extremely difficult to find a list of Athenian archons; even in Athens it would not always be easy to find such a list.

Almost every city in Greece made it a point of honour to date by its own magistrates. Thus the difficulty of this system was so much increased that in the majority of cases such dates are useless, and convey no chronological information. When we remember that in many towns those magistrates held office for only part of a year, the cumbrousness and absurdity of this pompous method of dating can be understood.

Only in the case of the *Roman* eponymous magistrates, the consuls, is a nearly complete list preserved; and the power of Rome spread the custom of dating by consuls far beyond the limits of the city. Consular dating was practised frequently even under the empire. It was complicated by the fact that the consuls who began their office on 1 January did not always remain in office throughout the year, and especially it became common under the empire that several pairs of consuls, the original and the later *suffecti*, held office in succession during each year. The old Roman rule, that the date should be given according to the existing consuls, whether or no they had come into office

* It will be argued in the sequel that the local year probably began at or soon after the autumn equinox.

* See below, 4.

† *Fasti Sacri*, p. 177: a slight change is needed to accommodate the reasoning to the difference of year in that admirable book. Though we disagree with its conclusions, it is by far the most useful work on the subject, on account of the care, fairness, completeness, and ingenuity with which it collects the evidence bearing on every single separate point.

on 1 January, was in force until the latter part of the 1st cent.; but at that time it began to be allowed that the whole year should be specified by the names of the pair of consuls who entered on office on 1 January; and gradually the superior convenience of this practice established it as the rule.

No dates in the NT are expressed by the consuls, but in early Christian times such dates were sometimes used. Thus they found their way into Eusebius and other important later authorities for the early history of Christianity; and often very important questions relating to early Christian chronology turn on this system of dating. The list of consuls entering office on 1 January is almost complete; but nothing like a complete list of consuls *suffecti* can as yet be recovered.

3. *Dating by priests or other officials.*—This was originally a mere variety of the system of dating by monarchs; for in many of the great religious centres the priest at an early period was a dynast or priest-king, who ruled over the people of the god as his representative and the interpreter of his will. In later times, when in general the priest had sunk to a much humbler level, the old custom still continued. Under the Roman Empire the governor of a province was often mentioned to specify a date: the Roman governor exercised the supreme power, and was in a sense a monarch for the time of his office, and, in fact, where a monarchy was formed into a province (for example, Asia, Bithynia, Cappadocia, etc.), the first governor succeeded the last king. In the Imperatorial provinces, such as Syria or Palestine, in which the governor regularly remained in office for several successive years, this way of dating was of small use without specification of the number of years of office (which was very rarely made, as it attributed too much of the monarchic character to the governor, and would be likely to offend the emperor); in the Senatorial provinces, where the governor by an almost invariable rule remained only one year, it was more useful.

4. *Devices of historians for indicating important dates.*—To lessen in some degree the difficulties entailed by such complicated and narrowly restricted systems of chronology, it was an occasional practice for historians to indicate the time of an event by several different ways of reckoning, when they wished to mark a date carefully, and to make their chronology readily intelligible to different classes of persons. Thus Thucydides (ii. 2) indicates an important date by the Athenian archon, the Lacedæmonian ephor, and the forty-eighth year of the priestess Chrysis in Argos, and by the fifteenth year of the Thirty Years' Peace. As a rule this was done, even by the most careful, only for some one or two critical events in their narrative. For the rest of the narrative they generally contented themselves with indicating the beginning and end of the single years more or less carefully, making the critical event a means of connecting the narrative as a whole with other departments and periods of history.

According to that traditional practice among historians, St. Luke dates the call of John the Baptist very elaborately, not merely by the fifteenth year of Tiberius, but also by the Roman procurator of Palestine, by the high priests (whom he seems to consider joint-priests), and by the tetrarchs of Galilee, of the Ituræo-Trachonitic land, and of Abilene. It is remarkable that he does not name the Roman governor of Syria, when he mentions the unimportant tetrarch of the small Syrian territory of Abilene; the governor of Syria was not brought into any relation with the subject of his narrative, but neither was the tetrarch of Abilene. It is also remarkable that he numbers the year only of Tiberius and not of any of the tetrarchs.

We must understand that this elaborate dating is intended to connect the whole book with general history, as was the usage of other ancient writers. There is no other purpose served by the carefully stated synchronisms. Now, the call of John the Baptist is of importance in the book only as leading up to the baptism of Jesus by John; and we therefore must understand that the dating is related to the baptism as well as to the call of John. If some vague, indefinite interval elapsed between the call and the baptism, the careful dating would be absolutely valueless for the book, whereas we have been forced to the view that such careful dating was used only for a critical point in the chronological sequence of the narrative.

5. *Character of the dating in the NT.*—Of the small number of dates which are given in the NT, most are specified according to the reigns of sovereigns; but a very few are expressed by officials or priests. Generally they are stated in the vague Greek fashion, 'when Quirinius was governor of Syria,' or 'in the high priesthood of Annas and Caiaphas'; and on this analogy, even when monarchs are concerned, 'in the days of Herod the king,' or 'Herod being tetrarch of Galilee' (Mt $2^1$, Lk $1^5$ $2^2$ $3^{1.2}$). The solitary exact date in the NT is the year of Tiberius, already discussed. This looseness as regards time seems more marked, when it is observed that almost all those scanty indications of dating are found in St. Luke: only one allusion that aids in providing a historical setting for the narrative is given by any other writer (Mt $2^1$). The few allusions to contemporary history that occur in the other writers are forced on them by their story; St. Luke alone makes intentionally chronological statements.

This chronological weakness is not a peculiarity special to the NT, but is characteristic of many ancient writers, even those whose purpose was more specially historical than was the case with the early Christians, among whom St. Luke alone seems to have had any thought of historical surroundings to his narrative. The chronological relations of ancient narratives are often so insufficiently marked that modern students are perplexed to arrange the events described in them according to the strict chronological order which present-day requirements demand. In Tacitus' biography of Agricola, the author obviously avoided chronological statements as out of keeping with fine literary quality. Only in the conclusion (ch. 44) he gives the exact years of the birth and death of Agricola according to the Roman consular method of dating. In the body of the work no date is given; but, by the allusions to contemporaries with or under whom Agricola served, and by our knowledge of the principles applicable to the Roman official career and of the legal intervals between the several offices, it is possible to arrange the chronology of Agricola very precisely: but much of the chronology is fixed by external evidence, and the biography alone would not be enough. If the history of the Eastern provinces in the NT period were well known, many of the chronological difficulties of the NT would disappear, and the references to the two kings, Herod Agrippa, to Sergius Paulus, Festus, Philip the tetrarch, etc., would be points chronologically fixed by external evidence, assuring the NT history that lies around them. If, on the other hand, the history of Rome and the rules of Roman official life in the time of Agricola were as obscure as the state of Palestine in NT times, if the dates of Suetonius Paulinus and M. Silanus were as uncertain as those of Pilate and Festus, of Aretas and Sergius Paulus, if the date of Galba and the consulship of Collega and

Priscus were the subject of as much controversy as the chief events in the reigns of the Herods, then the life of Agricola would offer many chronological problems; but with all its advantages and all modern research it has given rise to a good deal of chronological discussion, and a few of the dates are still uncertain.

6. *Dating by counting from a fixed era* (*Seleucid, Actian, etc.*).—The more rational and practically useful system of chronology, by counting the years from a conventionally fixed and generally accepted era, has not affected the NT; but dates according to such an era are found in the Books of Maccabees, where it is called 'the year of the kingdom of the Greeks' (1 Mac $1^{10}$). This name was applied to the era widely used in the central or Syrian part, rarely in the western or Asia Minor part, of the Seleucid Empire. It was fixed according to some uncertain event in the end of B.C. 312 or the early part of B.C. 311.

The rule in regard to all eras of this kind was not that the critical event on which the chronology depended was made the starting-point of the years of the era, but that the current local year in which that critical event occurred was counted the first year. Hence the year 1 of the era might last only a few days or weeks; and that was the case, for example, with the Actian era. In almost all lands where we know of that era being used, the current local years began at or about the autumn equinox (either on 23 September or on 1 October). Now, the battle of Actium was fought on 2 September in B.C. 31; and therefore the year 2 of the Actian era began at the following New Year, which was either on 23 September or on 1 October, according to the way of counting in different localities.

This rule, which is accepted by almost all recent writers on chronology, is disregarded once or twice in the excellent article on CHRONOLOGY OF THE NT in vol. i. p. 403, and therefore ought to be stated more emphatically here. It is proved definitely for the Actian era in the present writer's *Historical Geography of Asia Minor*, p. 441,* and has been illustrated and proved in other eras by various writers: see, *e.g.*, Th. Reinach, *Numismatic Chronicle*, 1902, p. 1 f. (who quotes the rule from the place just cited).

The rule has to be applied to the Seleucid era. M. Clermont-Ganneau has pointed out that, whereas in Syria generally that era was counted according to the Macedonian years, beginning from 1 October, in Damascus it was counted according to the local years, which began at the spring equinox.† He considers that the first year of the Seleucid era lasted in Syria generally from 1 October 312 to 30 September 311 B.C., and in Damascus from 23 March 312 to 22 March 311 B.C. But it is highly probable, though not as yet definitely proved, that wherever in the Syrian regions a different kind of year was in use (*e.g.* in Tyre, where the year began on 18 April, as Niese‡ has shown), the Seleucid era was counted accordingly.

A careful study, according to modern principles, of this era in its various forms (*e.g.* in Babylon, where it is said that the year 1 ran from 1 Oct. 311 to 30 Sept. 310 B.C.) is much needed, and would prove extremely useful; but that lies beyond the proper limits of the present article.§

There is an extraordinary variety of eras of this class. The idea seems to have been struck out in the effort which Greek civilization made, after Alexander the Great's time, to suit itself to the Asiatic dominions which it had conquered. The practical needs of governing greatly modified the character and outward expression of the Greek spirit; and the use of this kind of chronology was nearly confined to Macedonia and the subject lands of Western Asia. But the proud self-consciousness characteristic of the Greek cities reacted on this custom, and it was made a point of honour for each district and State and city to adopt an era of its own and count therefrom, instead of agreeing in the use of some common era. No ancient era, however, was used so widely or so long as the Seleucid, which continued to be employed for more than a thousand years, until the Arab conquest of Syria destroyed the Græco-Asiatic civilization in that country.

To those who regard St. Luke as a Syrian of Antioch, it must seem strange that he did not employ this familiar Syrian era in his careful datings in $3^1$. But to those who regard him as connected with Macedonia as well as with Antioch, his Greek character and feeling will sufficiently account for his employing a method of dating which is more akin to the style of Greek reckoning.

7. *The Beginning of the Year in current use.*—Local variation as to the day on which the year began was a most fruitful cause of chronological difficulties. The varieties were extremely numerous and perplexing; but of them all only a few have any bearing on NT questions.

(*a*) Roman custom made the consular year and the official year generally begin on 1 January. On careful examination, no probability can be found that those writers in the NT who speak about the lapse of any number of years counted them according to the Roman system. Still less chance is there that the Roman tribunician year, beginning on 10 December, had any influence on the NT. It is true that a few emperors* counted their reigns according to tribunician years, so that their first year ended on 9 December, and the second year began on 10 December, following their accession. But that could have no effect on NT usage.

(*b*) In Asia Minor and North Syria a year beginning about the autumn equinox was very widely used. It might, with great probability, be argued that men like St. Luke and St. Paul, brought up in lands where a year of that kind was certainly or probably in ordinary use, would naturally count according to it. That must be admitted as reasonable; and there seems to be no weighty consideration against it.

(*c*) In various regions of Southern Syria a year beginning at or near the spring equinox was in use: the years of Damascus (from 23 March) and of Tyre (from 18 April) have been referred to above (6). The Jewish sacred year began also about the spring equinox; but it was a lunar year, and therefore was not likely to be used for chronological purposes, for which the irregularity of lunar years made it unsuitable.

With that one exception, all the years which have been alluded to in this article are to be understood as solar years. They had all been transformed from an original lunar character to suit the Julian year, though keeping their New Year's Day at various different seasons.

LITERATURE.—On hours: besides the special articles in the treatises and Dictionaries of Antiquities (esp. M. Ardaillon, 'Horologium' in Daremberg-Saglio), see Bilfinger, *Die Zeitmessung der antiken Völker*, *Der bürgerliche Tag*, and *Die antiken Stundenangaben*; Unger, *Zeitrechnung der Griechen und Römer*, 1892; and Kaestner, *de Aeris*, 1890.

On chronology: the elaborate article 'Aera' by Kubitschek

* The reckoning was stated independently by M. Imhoof Blumer in *Griechische Münzen*, p. 33 (357), *Zft. f. Numism.* xx. p. 257: cf. Kaestner, *de Aeris*, p. 41 f.

† *Recueil d'Archéologie Orientale*, i. pp. 9 f., 72 f.

‡ Niese in *Hermes*, 1893, p. 208 ff.: cf. *Was Christ Born at Bethlehem?* p. 222.

§ The need is clearly shown by the meagre and uncertain account given of this era in Pauly-Wissowa, *Realencyclopädie*, *s.v.* 'Aera.'

* Nero (after 60), Nerva (in 97), and Trajan (as mentioned above, p. $480^b$).

in Pauly-Wissowa should be consulted; and Lewin, *Fasti Sacri*, should always be at hand. The discussion of numerous eras by the recent numismatists, especially M. Imhoof Blumer and M. Theod. Reinach, are highly instructive. The present writer has treated some of the principles in *Cities and Bishoprics of Phrygia*, i. p. 201 ff.; *Was Christ Born at Bethlehem?* chs. v.-x.

W. M. RAMSAY.

## GREEK PATRISTIC COMMENTARIES ON THE PAULINE EPISTLES.—

The subject will be dealt with in this article under the following heads:—



i. THE ORIGINAL BULK OF THE LITERATURE.—There is a sense in which nearly the whole of the writings of the early Christian Fathers may be said, and truly said, to be expositions of Holy Scripture. The controversy with the Jews turned on the interpretation of the Old Testament, the controversy with Valentinus and Marcion on the interpretation of the New: the theologians who dealt with these topics, which filled so large a space of the horizon of the Church in the 2nd and 3rd cents., like the theologians who dealt with the equally pressing danger of Arianism in the 4th, were all contributing their share to the explanation of the Prophetic and Apostolic writings. A book like the *adversus Hæreses* of Irenæus contains a mass of exegetical material; and few tasks in the domain of early Christian literature would be better worth doing than the collection and co-ordination of the fragmentary comments on passages of the NT which are scattered up and down the writings of the period anterior to the development of formal exegesis.

All this, and much more, would form part of a complete history of Patristic exegesis; but, since such a history cannot be written in these pages, it has seemed wisest to attempt only a limited and experimental treatment of one corner of the vast field, and to confine the scope of the present article to such Patristic writings as stand in direct connexion with the Pauline epistles.* Books which range over the whole of Scripture are therefore in the main excluded; and this affects two important departments of ancient Biblical literature: collections of Scripture proofs, of which the most famous instance is the *Testimonia* of St. Cyprian; and discussions of Scripture difficulties, such as the 'Mixed Questions' of Acacius (the successor of Eusebius at Cæsarea), or the *Quæstiones Veteris et Novi Testamenti* of Ambrosiaster. It is not, indeed, easy to draw a quite consistent line of demarcation: it has seemed worth while to note the occasional use of the great dogmatic theologians of the 4th cent. in the Catenæ (p. 498[b], below), and a place has been found in the list for one or two writings—such as the letters of Isidore of Pelusium, and the Euthalian 'edition' of the epistles (pp. 512[b], 524[b])—which perhaps cannot strictly be ranked as exegesis of St. Paul.

More serious objection might be taken to the absence of any notice of Latin commentaries (except in so far as they are translated from the Greek); and no doubt Ambrosiaster, Jerome, and Pelagius would have formed a natural pendant to Origen, Chrysostom, and Theodore. Yet, after all, it remains true that the lines of exegetical development were laid down in the East; the rival systems of allegorical and literal interpretation had been elaborated, the one at Alexandria, the other at Antioch, and both schools had produced expositions of the Epistles in imposing bulk, before a single Pauline commentary had seen the light in the Latin West. It may be hoped, therefore, that even in this inchoate form the following conspectus may prove of service to those who would know, with more detail than has hitherto been easily accessible, what was the measure of the devotion of the early Christian centuries to the special study of St. Paul.

No general or systematic list of the early Greek commentators on 'the Apostle'* as a whole, comparable to the Latin list of Cassiodorus, *Inst. Div. Litt.* 8, has survived. But in partial explanation of this fact it must be borne in mind that the continuous and uniform exposition of the whole series of the 13 or 14 epistles was unknown, or at any rate infrequent, in primitive times. The first extant commentary on the Epistles as a whole is that of the Latin Ambrosiaster (*c.* 375 A.D.); and though some of those commentators whose work is lost—such, *e.g.*, as Theodore of Heraclea—may have anticipated him, they can neither have been many in number nor much anterior in time. The work of the earliest interpreters of St. Paul was done, as a rule, on single epistles, or if on more than one, as in the case of Origen, yet still independently on the different epistles and unsystematically. Our estimate of the total mass of early exposition must be formed on such generalizations as can be drawn from the chance enumeration, by St. Jerome, of the books that were accessible about the end of the 4th cent. on three or four particular epistles.

(1) 1 Corinthians.—Jerome, *Ep.* xlix. 3 *ad Pammachium* [A.D. 393; Vallarsi, i. 233]: 'Origenes, Dionysius, Pierius, Eusebius Cæsariensis, Didymus, Apollinaris, latissime hanc epistolam interpretati sunt . . . revolve omnium quos supra memoravi commentarios et ecclesiarum bibliothecis fruere.' In *Ep.* cxix. 2–6 *ad Minervium et Alexandrum* [A.D. 406; i. 794] he quotes on 1 Co 15[51] the views of four commentators, Theodore of Heraclea, Diodore of Tarsus, Apollinaris, and Didymus, besides the 'Mixed Questions' of Acacius of Cæsarea.

(2) Galatians.—Jerome, *Præf. ad Comm. in Gal.* [between A.D. 386 and 392; Vallarsi, vii. 369: repeated in *Ep.* cxii., i. 733]: 'Aggrediar opus intentatum ante me linguæ nostræ scriptoribus, et a græcis quoque ipsis vix paucis ut rei poscebat dignitas usurpatum: non quod ignorem G. Marium Victorinum, qui Romæ me puero rhetoricam docuit, edidisse commentarios in apostolum . . . Origenis commentarios sum secutus: scripsit enim ille vir in epistolam Pauli ad Galatas quinque proprie volumina, et decimum Stromatum suorum librum commatico super explanatione eius sermone complevit; tractatus quoque varios et excerpta, quæ vel sola possint sufficere, composuit. prætermitto Didymum videntem meum, et Laodicenum

* In order further to limit the ground, the Epistle to the Hebrews has been excluded from detailed or special treatment; though, as nearly all the writers who will be enumerated accepted it without difficulty as a genuine work of St. Paul, some summary reference to it has occasionally been made.

* Ὁ ἀπόστολος is the regular phrase for the *corpus* of Pauline epistles, and dates back to the end of the 2nd century. If Eusebius (*HE* v. 27) tells us that Heraclitus (about A.D. 200) wrote εἰς τὸν Ἀπόστολον, the form of the title may perhaps be the historian's and not the commentator's; but in two other places (*HE* v. 17, 18), the phrase occurs in actual quotations from anti-Montanist writers of the same period: δεῖν γὰρ εἶναι τὸ προφητικὸν χάρισμα ἐν πάσῃ τῇ ἐκκλησίᾳ μέχρι τῆς τελείας παρουσίας ὁ Ἀπόστολος ἀξιοῖ (Anonymus), and Θεμίσων . . . μιμούμενος τὸν ἀπόστολον καθολικήν τινα συνταξάμενος ἐπιστολήν (Apollonius). So Clement of Alexandria, *Strom.* vii. 14: τό τε Εὐαγγέλιον καὶ ὁ Ἀπόστολος. So, too, the Latin Irenæus, *Hær.* IV. xxvii. 4: 'Domino quidem dicente [Lk 18[7]] . . . et Apostolo in ea quæ est ad Thessalonicenses epistola ista prædicante,' and often elsewhere, especially in Book V.: in two cases the Greek also is extant—V. ix. 3, where it, too, has Ἀπόστολος; and V. ii. 3, where the *Sacra Parallela* give ὁ μακάριος Παῦλος for 'beatus Apostolus'; but there can be no question that in such cases the Latin is our best guide. Doubtless, the use of the phrase goes back further still into the 2nd century.

de ecclesia nuper egressum,* et Alexandrum veterem hæreticum, Eusebium quoque Emisenum, et Theodorum Heracleoten, qui et ipsi nonnullos super hac re commentariolos [*v.l.* commentarios] reliquerunt . . . legi hæc omnia.' Again, in *Ep.* cxii. *ad Augustinum* [A.D. 404; i. 734], § 6: 'Primus Origenes in decimo Stromateon libro, ubi epistolam Pauli ad Galatas interpretatur, et ceteri deinceps interpretes . . . quid dicam de Ioanne, qui dudum in pontificali gradu Constantinopolitanam rexit ecclesiam, et proprie super hoc capitulo latissimum exaravit librum, in quo Origenis et veterum sententiam est secutus?'

(3) Ephesians.—Jerome, *Præf. ad Comm. in Eph.* [same date as *Comm. in Gal.*; Vallarsi, vii. 543]: 'Sciatis Origenem tria volumina in hanc epistolam conscripsisse, quem et nos ex parte secuti sumus, Apollinarium etiam et Didymum quosdam commentariolos edidisse, e quibus . . . pauca decerpsimus.'

(4) 1 Thessalonians.—Jerome, *Ep.* cxix. (*ut sup.*) 8-10, discussing 1 Th $4^{15-17}$, gives quotations from two commentators, Origen and Diodore, and alludes to two others, Theodore [of Heraclea] and Apollinaris.

The simple fact that of twenty or more Greek treatises on one or other of these four epistles which Jerome had (or had had) in his hands only one has survived to our day other than in Catena fragments, shows more eloquently than any argument could do the wealth and variety of the lost exegetical literature of the 3rd and 4th centuries. And if we further reflect that some of these twenty treatises would not, but for their casual mention by Jerome, have even been known by us to have existed at all, we shall realize what an imperfect picture the catalogue which we now proceed to draw up must give us of the labour which the 'age of the Fathers' devoted to the study of Holy Scripture.

ii. CATENÆ AND COMPILERS OF THE LATER PERIOD. — Before proceeding to speak of the Patristic commentaries separately, it will be convenient to say something of those more general and miscellaneous collections of later date which are often the only source from which we can now recover any fragments of the older writers. The subject of Catenæ was till quite lately an almost unexplored one; and no great advance can be made in the study of them until more of the material that exists abundantly in MSS has made its way into print. With regard to the Pauline epistles in particular, we need to know with more precision than is now attainable what material exists anterior to the two great compilers of the end of the 11th cent., Theophylact of Bulgaria and Euthymius Zigabenus. The scope of the brief sketch which now follows is limited to an enumeration of the matter in this department that has been either published or at least described in print: but something more will be said later on (see pp. 521-524) about the manuscript material.

**1.** The first Catena printed on the epistles is that known by the name of **Oecumenius,** published at Verona in 1532 under the following title: *'Εξηγήσεις παλαιαὶ καὶ λίαν ὠφέλιμοι βραχυλογίαν τε καὶ σαφήνε.αν τοῦ λόγου ἔχουσαι θαυμαστὴν ἐκ διαφόρων τῶν ἁγίων πατέρων ὑπομνημάτων ὑπ' Οἰκουμενίου καὶ 'Αρέθα συλλεχθεῖσαι εἰς τὰς τῆς νέας διαθήκης πραγματείας τάσδε· τοῦ μὲν Οἰκουμενίου εἰς τὰς Πράξεις τῶν 'Αποστόλων, εἰς τὰς ἑπτὰ Καθολικὰς λεγομένας ἐπιστολάς, εἰς τὰς Παύλου πάσας· τοῦ δὲ 'Αρέθα εἰς τὴν 'Ιωάννου 'Αποκάλυψιν.* The edition appeared under the same auspices as the slightly earlier (1529) edition of Chrysostom on the Epistles (see below, p. 505[a]); the patron, who bore the expenses of both editor and printers, was the illustrious Gian Matteo Giberti, bishop of Verona; the scholar entrusted with the work was Bernardino Donato; the type (and finer Greek type has never been produced) was set up 'apud Stephanum et fratres Sabios.' The whole contents of the volume were drawn from a single MS, presented to the bishop by John Lascaris, 'miro librarii artificio sumptuque descriptum apprimeque vetustum';* for the Epistles this MS gave in the text a continuous exposition as though by a single author, in the margin the names of the authors from whom the text was drawn: but use was also made of other MSS of a different class, which gave the quotations separately in the text, each under the name of its author. The work was attributed (quite rightly) to Oecumenius, on the ground that his name appears in the margin attached to the final comment on the Colossian epistle: *ἐκ τοῦ ἀντιγράφου μὴ εὑρὼν καλῶς τὰς παραγραφὰς τοῦ μακαρίου 'Ιωάννου τῆς πρὸς Κολοσσαεῖς ἐπιστολῆς, συνέγραψα αὐτὰς ὅπως ἠδυνάμην· ἐὰν οὖν εὑρεθῇ τι ἐν αὐταῖς ἢ κοῦφον ἢ ἐπιλήψιμον, ἴστω ὁ ἀναγινώσκων ἐμὸν εἶναι τὸ τοιοῦτον πταῖσμα.*† The editor concluded, on the strength of the one MS which was known to him, that the main and anonymous portion of the work is taken from Chrysostom, not indeed word for word,—for when that is done the name 'John' or 'Chrysostom' appears like any other in the margin,—but with much abbreviation and omission; that where Oecumenius takes an individual line he puts his own name in the margin, so that the reader may not be deceived as to the authority claimed for it; that the rest depends on various ancient authors, whose names are likewise given in the margin, and of whom Photius is far and away the most frequently cited. Theodoret—for the sign *Θεοδωρ.* refers to him and not to Theodore of Mopsuestia—comes next, and after him Severian, Cyril of Alexandria, and Gennadius. But the important point to bear in mind is that the sum-total of the rest of the quotations bears only an infinitesimal proportion to the bulk of the matter supplied by Chrysostom, Photius, and Oecumenius himself; in the nine epistles from Ephesians to Philemon there are only thirteen marginal references outside these three writers. This disproportion would, no doubt, be modified, though it is impossible to say how seriously, if we could estimate to what extent either Oecumenius in his original compilation, or the scribes who copied him down to the exemplar of John Lascaris, fell short of exactitude in inserting or reproducing the marginal ascriptions of authorship; for all such information as has accrued to us about Oecumenian MSS (see below, p. 488) points to the conclusion that the 'anonymous' portion of the printed text ought to suffer at least some reduction in favour of the rest.

It should also be noted that the printed text of Oecumenius prefixes to the exegesis a good deal of 'Euthalian' matter: (i.) *Διήγησις περὶ τοῦ ἁγίου ἀποστόλου Παύλου, Εὐθαλίου διακόνου πρόλογος*: (ii.) *ἀποδημίαι Παύλου τοῦ ἀποστόλου*: (iii.) *μαρτύριον Παύλου τοῦ ἀποστόλου*: (iv.) *ὑπόθεσις τῆς πρὸς 'Ρωμαίους ἐπιστολῆς*, [*inc.* *ταύτην ἐπιστέλλει*]: (v.) *κεφάλαια τῆς πρὸς 'Ρωμαίους ἐπιστολῆς*, [*inc.* *α' εὐαγγελικὴ διδασκαλία*]: (vi.) *σχόλιον πρὶν ἐπιδημῆσαι Παῦλον* . . .; similar matter to Nos. iv.-vi. is given with the other Pauline epistles. See below, on Euthalius, pp. 526, 527.

The edition of Donatus was repeated—without alteration of the Greek, so far as appears, but with the addition of the preface and Latin version

* He means, of course, Apollinaris of Laodicea.

* Perhaps identical with Paris gr. 219 (=Medic. Reg. 1886), sæc. xi., a copy of Oecumenius-Arethas which certainly at one time belonged to John Lascaris.

† So, too, on Eph $4^{16}$ the name Oecumenius is attached in the margin to the sentence *ὅρα τί κἀγὼ ἐνόμισα· οὔτε γὰρ ἐχώρησα τὰ τοῦ μακαρίου* [*sc.* Chrysostom] *νοῆσαι* of the text.

of Joannes Hentenius, A.D. 1545*—in the edition of F. Morel, Paris 'sumptibus Cl. Sonnii,' 1631; and the edition of Morel is incorporated in Migne's *Patrologia Græca*, vols. 118, 119. Thus we are still using Oecumenius on the authority of the MS of John Lascaris, modified, as Donatus' preface tells us, by other (apparently non-Oecumenian) MSS.

Who Oecumenius was—beyond the fact that he is said to have been bishop of Tricca in Thessaly—we do not know; as to his date, if the editions were right in making him use Photius (on which, however, see below, p. 488), he must be later than the middle of the 9th: but, if once the name Photius is removed, no obstacle remains to a much earlier period. See, further, p. 523.

**2.** Next of the great compilers to Oecumenius, both in order of history and in order of publication, comes **Theophylact,** archbishop of Bulgaria *c.* 1075 A.D. His commentary on the Pauline epistles was first published at London in 1636 as a posthumous work of Dr. Augustine Lindsell, bishop of Hereford, who died at the end of 1634. From the preface, addressed by T. Baily to archbishop Laud, it appears that the commentaries were copied out from a 'codex vetustus' of the earl of Arundel, and that the copy was compared with two Oxford MSS;† at Lindsell's death the edition was almost complete. The Greek text is accompanied by a Latin translation, based on that of Philippus Montanus, Antwerp, 1564.

As vol. ii. of a complete issue of the writings of Theophylact, the commentary on the Epistles was reprinted at Venice in 1755; the Greek was simply repeated from the edition—'satis nitidam et accuratam,' as the new preface calls it—of Lindsell, some 'manifest errors' only of the Latin being removed. The Venetian editor's contribution to the criticism of the text is, in fact, confined to the list on pp. 771–776 of readings from a Venice MS—presumably codex 32 of Zanetti's catalogue, sæc. xiv.—from which list, as he informs us with obvious satisfaction, he excluded everything (i.) that was manifestly wrong, (ii.) that injured either the style or the sense, (iii.) that the London edition had already noted as read in the Oxford MSS. No wonder that, though the variants were 'satis multæ,' he succeeded in reducing them 'ad mediocrem numerum'! Yet he tells us enough to show that the differences even among the MSS hitherto known are very considerable; the comments in one are now longer, now shorter, than in the rest; while at other times, though the general sense is the same, the language varies so much that the result is practically 'expositiones diversæ.' The most considerable merit of the Venice edition lies in its two indexes, Greek and Latin. The whole is reprinted in Migne, *Patrol. Gr.* vol. 124.

According to Ehrhard (in Krumbacher, *Geschichte der byzantinischen Litteratur*[2], 1897, p. 134), Theophylact shows a certain independence in the commentary on the Pauline epistles, and in particular cites many more names of earlier Fathers than in his commentaries on other books of the Bible—Clement of Alexandria, Methodius, Basil and the two Gregorys, Cyril of Alexandria, pseudo-Dionysius; but even here the majority of the explanations are quoted anonymously. Chrysostom is of course still the chief stand-by of the commentary: in his case, Theophylact even takes into consideration the *variæ lectiones* of the Scripture text (*bei dem er sogar die abweichenden Lesarten des Schrifttextes berücksichtigt*). Ehrhard is an authority from whom, speaking ordinarily, there is no appeal; but the present writer has been unable to find in either of the editions the references to the Fathers by name of which Ehrhard speaks.

**3.** The third of the great compilers, **Euthymius Zigabenus,** author of the *Panoplia Dogmatica*, was a younger contemporary of Theophylact, and flourished under the emperor Alexius Comnenus, *c.* 1100 A.D. C. F. Matthæi, the first editor of the original Greek of Euthymius' commentary on the Gospels, had found at Munich a MS of Euthymius on Romans and 1 Corinthians. But it is a Greek scholar, Nicolas Kalogeras, late archbishop of Patras, to whom the publication of the commentary on the Pauline epistles is due (Athens, 1887, 2 vols.). Kalogeras' preface, pp. 61–64, gives an interesting account of his search after a complete MS, which he found at last in MS gr. 6 (sæc. xiv.) of the Casatensian Library at Rome. The title of the commentary runs, according to the MS: Ἑρμηνεία τῶν ἐπιστολῶν τοῦ μεγάλου ἀποστόλου Παύλου φιλοπόνως ἐρανισθεῖσα, μάλιστα μὲν ἀπὸ τῆς ἐξηγήσεως τοῦ ἐν ἁγίοις πατρὸς ἡμῶν Ἰωάννου τοῦ Χρυσοστόμου, ἔτι δὲ καὶ ἀπὸ διαφόρων ἄλλων πατέρων, συνεισενεγκόντος τινὰ καὶ τοῦ ταύτην ἐρανισαμένου τοῦ Ζιγαβηνοῦ Εὐθυμίου μοναχοῦ. Besides Chrysostom, the chief sources used are said to be Basil and Gregory Nazianzen; but the citations are all made anonymously.* The agreement with Theophylact is often exact and verbal (Ehrhard in Krumbacher, pp. 84, 134). The order of the Pauline epistles in the MS is Romans, 1 and 2 Cor., Gal., Eph., Col., Philem., 1 and 2 Thess., Phil., Heb., 1 and 2 Tim., Titus.

**4. Nicetas of Serrae,** deacon of St. Sophia and afterwards archbishop of Heraclea, was another younger contemporary of Theophylact, and author of well-known Catenæ upon some of the Gospels and on the Epistle to the Hebrews. His claim to be regarded as author also of a Catena on the Pauline epistles rests on the evidence of the title of a single Florence MS, Laur. ix. 10, sæc. xii.: Ἐξήγησις τοῦ μακαριωτάτου μητροπολίτου [Νικήτα] Ἡρακλείας εἰς τὰς ἐπιστολὰς τοῦ ἁγίου Παύλου τοῦ ἀποστόλου: the name Νικήτα is not even by the original scribe, though he was presumably the person meant. A specimen of this MS, extending over chapters 1–8 of 1 Corinthians, was published in vol. v. of Jo. Lamius' *Deliciæ eruditorum* (Florence, A.D. 1738). It contains passages labelled with the name of Oecumenius, and on comparison with the printed text of the latter it is plain that the relation between the two Catenæ of 'Oecumenius' and 'Nicetas' is exceedingly close—so close that it is obvious to conjecture that the title of the Florence MS is a mere scribe's figment, and that the MS itself simply represents one of the numerous subdivisions of the 'Oecumenian' tradition. Still, the texts do not run quite on all fours with one another: as a rule, Lamius' text is only an abbreviated and corrupted form of the printed Oecumenius, but every now and then comes a section which is peculiar to the 'Nicetas' text; and, until more has been done for a critical edition of Oecumenius, it is hardly possible to be certain that the Florence MS may not, after all, embody a recension by Nicetas of the Oecumenian Catena.†

* Hentenius also rendered into Latin the commentary of Euthymius Zigabenus on the Gospels, 1544.

† The Arundel MS was the present British Museum Arundelianus 534, sæc. xiv., and the two Oxford MSS were Barocci 146, sæc. xv. (the Barocci MSS came in 1629), and Miscell. 20, sæc. xiv. (this MS is in the 1620 catalogue, and probably was given in 1604 by Winwood). Lindsell's *apparatus criticus* is confined to (i.) a considerable number of brief variants in the margin, to which the symbol γρ(άψον) is prefixed: (ii.) notice of a few more substantial divergences in which the two Oxford MSS agree against the Arundel, pp. 1033–1041.

* Except in the commentary on the Catholic epistles, vol. ii. pp. 473–664, which, however, is probably not by Euthymius.

† Dr. J. Sickenberger, 'Die Lukaskatene des Niketas von Heraklea' (*Texte und Untersuchungen*, N.F. vii. 4, A.D. 1902), p. 21, complicates the question still further by calling attention to the somewhat parallel title of a Paris Catena (MS. gr. 228, sæc. xiii. fol. 12): Ἑρμηνεία ἐκ τῶν ἑρμηνειῶν τοῦ Βουλγαρίας [sc. Theophylact] ὡς ἐν συνόψει εἰς τὰς ιδ´ ἐπιστολὰς τοῦ ἁγίου ἀποστόλου Παύλου ἐρανισθεῖσα παρὰ Νικήτα τοῦ Σαπωνοπούλου. But at pres-

**5.** Besides the three compilers, Oecumenius, Theophylact, and Euthymius, we have also in print the Catena on the Pauline epistles which Dr. **J. A. Cramer,** principal of New Inn Hall, published at Oxford between 1841 and 1844; it must, however, be remembered that Cramer's Catena, unlike the books hitherto mentioned, is not homogeneous, but is drawn from different MS sources for the different epistles. The volume on Romans, published last of all the epistles in 1844, is sufficiently described below in connexion with the list of Karo and Lietzmann (*d* and *e*, p. 488[b]), with Origen (p. 492), and with Dionysius of Alexandria (p. 497[a]). The volume on 1 and 2 Corinthians (A.D. 1841) is itself not uniform; the Catena on the First Epistle, drawn from MS Paris gr. 227, sæc. xvi., is of high value, and contains, for instance, over 80 references to Origen (see again, for this MS, Karo and Lietzmann, *e*, p. 488[b]); while that on the Second, of which Paris gr. 223, sæc. xi., was the source, does not differ widely from Oecumenius; two Bodleian MSS, Auct. T. i. 7, sæc. xi., and Roe 16, sæc. x., supplied some material (collected at the end of the volume) for the correction of the Oecumenian printed text.* The third volume (A.D. 1842) and the greater part of the fourth (A.D. 1843) consist of a Catena on the epistles from Galatians to Hebrews inclusive, taken from Paris coislin gr. 204, sæc. x.; while the remainder of vol. iv. is made up of a second Catena (Nicetas') on Hebrews, from Paris gr. 238, sæc. xiii. Portions of these Catenæ are, at least in their present and printed form, anonymous; some of the shorter epistles have only a colophon appended to them, indicating in a general way their sources—Chrysostom, Severian, Theodore of Mopsuestia (see below on Severian, p. 507[b]); but, on the whole, Cramer's volumes present a marked contrast to the other printed texts above enumerated in the vastly larger number of cases where the Patristic authorities are expressly cited, and his convenient indexes to each volume make it fairly easy to derive such a general conclusion as is embodied in the following table. The names are arranged in the order in which they are dealt with in this article, that is to say, in rough chronological order. Chrysostom occurs everywhere (except, strange to say, in the first of the two Catenæ on Romans), and is therefore not named. Authors named only once or twice are omitted. The Epistle to the Hebrews is left out of account:—

Origen: quoted frequently on Rom., 1 Cor., Ephesians.
Eusebius of Emesa: occasionally on Galatians.
Apollinaris: occasionally on Romans.
Diodore: occasionally on Romans.
Severian: occasionally on all the Epistles (most frequently, perhaps, on 1 Cor.) except 2 Corinthians.
Theodore of Mopsuestia: on all the Epistles except 2 Cor., most frequently on Rom. and 1 Corinthians.
Isidore: occasionally on Romans.
Cyril of Alexandria: frequently on Rom. and 1 Corinthians.
Theodoret: very frequently on Rom., frequently on 1 Cor., occasionally on 2 Corinthians.
Gennadius: frequently on Romans.
Theodore the Monk: occasionally on Romans.
Oecumenius: occasionally in the 2nd Catena on Rom., also on 1 Cor., 2 Cor., and Galatians.
Photius: occasionally on Rom., frequently on 1 Corinthians.

ent there seems nothing to show that the Florence Catena and the Paris Catena are the same thing: dependence on Theophylact is not suggested by Lamius' text of the Florence MS.

* Similar notes from the same MSS are appended also to vol. iii. (Gal.–2 Thess.).

**6.** About the same period that Cramer was working at the Catenæ in the libraries of Oxford and Paris, cardinal **Angelo Mai** was making the study of Catenæ at the Vatican one of the most productive forms of his marvellous literary fecundity; but, whereas Cramer published his Catenæ as they stood, Mai selected from his sources and separated whatever belonged to now one, now another, of the ancient writers whose remains he was rescuing from oblivion. The *Scriptorum Veterum Nova Collectio* (10 vols. 1825–1838) contains nothing, beyond minute fragments, of any Greek exegesis on St. Paul, though of the Latin it contains the commentaries of Victorinus Afer (vol. iii.) and the prologue to those of Claudius of Turin (vol. vii.). The *Spicilegium Romanum* (10 vols., 1829–1844) contains, of Latin material, the same Claudius on Philemon, and the 'canons' of Priscillian on St. Paul, both in vol. ix.; and in vol. iv. pp. 499–573 the Catena remains of Theodore of Mopsuestia on the Romans, from MS Vat. gr. 762.* Lastly, the *Nova Patrum Bibliotheca* (7 vols., 1844–1854; the 8th volume is Mai's, but was published after his death by Cozza-Luzi, 1871; the 9th volume is Cozza-Luzi's own) contains, besides fragments—(*a*) in vol. iii. part 1, pp. 1–127, extracts from Cyril of Alexandria on Romans, 1 and 2 Corinthians, from a Vatican MS,† and on Hebrews from a Milan MS, Amb. E. 63 inf.; (*b*) in vol. iv. part 3, pp. 114–146, extracts from Didymus on 2 Corinthians from the same Vatican MS; (*c*) in vol. vii. part 1, pp. 407, 408, a few quotations from Theodore of Mopsuestia on 2 Corinthians, again from the same MS, Vat. gr. 762. Mai's material for 2 Corinthians was a welcome addition to our knowledge, that being the one epistle on which Cramer had found no Catena that was not nearly related to the printed Oecumenius; on the other hand, most of his work on Rom. and 1 Cor. is anticipated (though probably with a less pure form of text) in the Catenæ which Cramer had published just before him.

It will not need pointing out to the reader who has followed the above account of the printed Catenæ, that many questions suggest themselves to which only a fuller examination of the still unpublished MS material can supply the answer. We have at the end of the 11th cent. two compilers, Theophylact and Euthymius Zigabenus, whose works on the Epistles are in print; but these works are, unless reinforced by other sources, useless for our purpose, since they systematically avoid naming the writers whose comments they incorporate. We have at an earlier date—but how much earlier is one of the questions that demand solution—one other compiler whose person is known, Oecumenius; and he adopts an intermediate method between the Catenæ and the compilers, since he sometimes gives his authorities, and leaves it apparently to be understood that the vastly preponderant portion of his work, which is anonymous, is abstracted and abbreviated from Chrysostom. But behind the compilers, as Cramer and Mai sufficiently show us, lies an older and more valuable group of writings, to which the name *Catena* properly belongs: these consist properly of named quotations, and the catenist's work is confined to the choice of his authorities and the selection of passages from them. The limited range of names in some of these Catenæ suggests a very early date, and the beginnings of the system may be sought at Antioch even as far back as the middle of the 5th century. In particular,

* The number of the MS is not given *ad loc.*, but in *Nova Patrum Bibliotheca*, vii. 407.

† The description of Mai (p. vii) is 'codex Vaticanus valde pretiosus, sæculi ferme xii.': it is, in fact, the same MS from which he drew his Theodore on Romans and his Didymus on 2 Corinthians, Vatic. gr. 762, which is now attributed to sæc. x.

the inclusion in the Catenæ of material from authors such as Origen and Apollinaris, Diodore and the two Theodores (of Heraclea and of Mopsuestia), remarkable as it is under any circumstances, would be tenfold more difficult to account for if it had originated after the middle of the 6th century. In days when Greek Churchmen, though they fought stoutly enough for dogmatic truth, had not yet enclosed themselves within the narrow ramparts of Byzantine orthodoxy, St. Cyril of Alexandria could lay down the rule (*Epistola ad Eulogium presbyterum*) that not all the writings of heretics are heretical: *οὐ πάντα ὅσα λέγουσιν οἱ αἱρετικοὶ φεύγειν καὶ παραιτεῖσθαι χρή, πολλὰ γὰρ ὁμολογοῦσιν ὧν καὶ ἡμεῖς ὁμολογοῦμεν.* Whether or no they definitely sheltered themselves under the authority of St. Cyril's *dictum*, it was in this spirit that the first catenists went to work; the precedent must have been set in the relatively untrammelled freedom of the days before Justinian; and all through the Byzantine middle age an occasional scribe found himself (doubtless much to his surprise) reproducing on equal terms, in this one form of literature, the words of those ancient writers whom he most approved and of those whom he most reprobated.

The Catenæ, then, have a special and unique value as preserving, however imperfectly, no small mass of the work of authors on whose writings, as a whole, a ban was set by later generations; and the study of Catenæ is therefore an indispensable preliminary to intelligent acquaintance with the development of Patristic exegesis. Unfortunately, even the few texts that are printed, such as Oecumenius and Cramer, fall far below the standard required in a modern edition. It would have seemed, therefore, in any case, essential to supplement this introductory section by attempting to give some idea of the Catenæ MSS contained in the libraries of Europe, especially of such as are earlier than the end of the 11th cent.; and this task is greatly facilitated since the appearance in 1902 of a work now to be described, which constitutes a very important addition to our knowledge of the subject.

**7.** In the *Nachrichten von der königl. Gesellschaft der Wissenschaften zu Göttingen* for 1902 (*philologisch-historische Klasse*, Heft i. pp. 1–66, iii. pp. 299–350, v. pp. 559–620), **G. Karo** and **J. Lietzmann** * published a classified list of Greek Catena MSS on both Old and New Testaments. Although in the total mass the Pauline epistles hold but a subordinate position, occupying only 13 pages (pp. 597–610) against 46, for instance, for the Psalms and 33 for the Gospels, yet eight different forms of Catenæ on them—besides that of Nicetas on the Hebrews—are distinguished and separately described; a summary account of all matter hitherto printed is prefixed, of which occasional use has already been made in the preceding portion of this article. Under each of the eight Catenæ some one passage is selected,—for the six which contain Romans the passage is Ro $7^{8ff.}$,—and the *incipit* and *explicit* are given of every comment on the passage or on any part of it: in this way additional MSS could without difficulty be assigned their proper place in the classification. The reasons for the order in which Karo and Lietzmann arrange their eight Catenæ are not easy to see, and a different order will here be adopted, a reference to the corresponding place in their account being given at the end of each section.

(*a*) A very large majority of the MSS described, 37 out of 49, give the Catena of Oecumenius; but a new test is supplied for grouping Oecumenian MSS, according as they do or do not contain citations from Photius. Thus for Ro $7^{8ff.}$ the extreme in one direction is represented by three MSS which give four passages from Photius by name; two or three others give the Photius passages, but without name and with minor transpositions; and one gives them in the margin only. All the rest, though they differ among themselves by omissions and transpositions, agree in containing no Photius; and ten of them agree further in giving the same 12 scholia on these verses in the same order. It would seem, therefore, to be certain that the Photius element is alien to the original Oecumenius, and that MSS in which the Photius element is present, whether with or without name, can be set aside as representing a later recension—a recension, however, already current in the 10th cent., to which two of its MSS belong. Among the 'Photius' MSS that group is, no doubt, the more ancient which gives the Photius passages under their author's name, since names are much more likely to have been omitted by the progressive carelessness of scribes than inserted by the accurate research of scholars. Tried by these tests, the printed Oecumenius comes out but badly; the four Photius passages are all present, but only one of them by name, and none of them in quite the same place as in the other MSS. On the other hand, the amount of agreement in detail between several of the earliest of the non-Photian MSS appears to be so considerable that a revised edition of Oecumenius, based on these alone, ought not to involve excessive labour in comparison with the advantage to be expected from it. [Karo-Lietzmann, vi. pp. 604–609: see below, p. 523].

(*b*) Of non-Oecumenian Catenæ only one covers the whole of St. Paul, and that one is represented only by a single MS, Paris gr. 216, sæc. x.; the scholia appear to be very brief, and to represent the same relatively late stage of the Catena tradition as Oecumenius, in not attaching to every citation the author's name. Nothing of this Catena is as yet published. [K. L. ix. pp. 610, 595].

The remaining Catenæ are all partial; and it may be convenient to mention first those which are in print. Two of them, with portions of a third, are contained in Cramer; Mai published from a completer MS further extracts of the third; the other three are still unprinted.

(*c*) Cramer's Catena for Galatians–Hebrews is drawn from a unique MS, Paris coislin 204, sæc. x. It is noteworthy on the one hand for the number of epistles which it covers, and on the other for its entire immunity from later accretions; it is almost, if not quite, the only Catena in which the name of Oecumenius does not occur. [K. L. iv. p. 602: see further below, p. 521[b]].

(*d*) Cramer's second Catena on Romans ($7^{7}$–end) is drawn from Munich gr. 412, sæc. xiii.; and as this MS (apart from two late copies of itself) is again the only known representative of its Catena, we have no means as yet of supplementing Cramer's edition. [K. L. ii. p. 601].

(*e*) Cramer's other Catena on Romans (chapters 1–8) is derived from a late Bodleian MS, Auct. E. ii. 20. Inexact statements have been made about this MS (see further in the fourth section of this article, p. 522[a]), but it is at any rate now clear that both this MS and the Paris MS gr. 227, which supplied Cramer's Catena on 1 Corinthians, are descendants * of the Vatican MS gr. 762, sæc. x., from which Mai extracted citations of Didymus, Theodore, and Cyril; and whereas the copies only contain Ro 1–8 and 1 Cor. respectively, the original

* Lietzmann had already, in 1897, published a pamphlet, *Catenen: Mitteilungen über ihre Geschichte und handschriftliche Ueberlieferung* (Freiburg i. B.: 85 pp.), which, however, contains no special material for the Epistles.

* The Paris Corinthians MS appears to be simply a transcript, the Bodleian Romans MS to be to some extent an abbreviation, of the corresponding parts of the Vatican MS.

covers the whole of the three epistles, Romans, 1 Corinthians, and 2 Corinthians. No known Catena has so wide a range of early sources; but side by side with primitive elements occurs the name of Photius. [K. L. i. pp. 598–601].

(*f*) How far the unpublished Catena on 1 and 2 Corinthians, Galatians, and Ephesians, contained in Vatic. gr. 692, sæc. xii., is independent of those already described, it is not easy to say: among the names frequently quoted is that of Oecumenius, but we find also Origen, Theodore, Cyril, Severus (*i.e.* Severian?), and on 2 Cor. Di(dymus?). [K. L. iii. p. 601: see below, p. 522a].

(*g*) The apparently imperfect Catena of a Vienna MS (gr. 166 [46], sæc. xiii.) on Ro $1^1$–1 Co $1^{12}$ cites no fewer than 24 authors; but a considerable proportion of these are comparatively late—Anastasius, John Climax, John of Damascus, Maximus, Oecumenius, Photius, Symeon Logothetes. A distinguishing feature of this collection is that it discriminates to some extent between the sources of its information. Chrysostom, Theodoret, and Gennadius are cited ἐκ τοῦ ὕφους, 'from the text,' *i.e.* direct from their respective commentaries; while among those cited as σχο' or ἐκ τοῦ σχο', *i.e.* from Catenæ, are Origen, Acacius, Severian, Theodore, Oecumenius, Euthalius, Photius. One source was presumably the Photian recension of Oecumenius; but it would seem that another and much more ancient Catena must also have been employed. [K. L. vii. p. 609].

(*h*) The last Catena is one on Romans and 1 Corinthians in Vatic. gr. 1270, sæc. xii. It appears to bear some relation to Oecumenius, but to contain less matter, and, apparently, to name its authorities—John (Chrysostom), Severian, Theodoret—more frequently. Perhaps it will be found valuable for identifying new matter from Severian on these two epistles. [K. L. viii. p. 610].

Lest attention should be unduly distracted from the main purpose of this article, further details about some of the more important MSS of Karo and Lietzmann's lists, as well as some notice of one or two which do not appear there at all, are relegated to a later point (p. 521). These preliminary pages are meant only to serve for introduction to the catalogue of commentators which follows, and for the better understanding of the process by which their works, or what remains of them, have to be rescued and reconstructed.

iii. PATRISTIC COMMENTATORS ON ST. PAUL.—

**1. Marcion.**—Whether the *Antitheses* of Marcion, which certainly contained what amounted to some sort of theological commentary on his Gospel, contained also similar expositions of his 'Apostolicon,'* is uncertain, though perhaps probable. We have no such definite statement for the Epistles as Tertullian has given in regard to the Gospel:† the evidence in the affirmative consists primarily of references in Jerome's commentaries on the Galatians and Ephesians—taken, no doubt, from Origen's books on the same epistles—which seem to point in this direction. Thus (*a*) on Gal $3^{13}$ (Vallarsi, vii. 434): '*Christus nos redemit de maledicto legis, factus pro nobis maledictum*; subrepit in hoc loco Marcion, de potestate creatoris, quem sanguinarium crudelem infamat et vindicem [*v.l.* iudicem], asserens nos redemptos esse per Christum, qui alterius boni dei filius sit.'—(*b*) On Gal $6^6$ (p. 523): '*Communicet autem is qui catechizatur verbum ei qui se catechizat in omnibus bonis;* Marcion hunc locum ita interpretatus est ut putaret fideles et catechumenos simul orare debere, et magistrum communicare in oratione discipulis, illo vel maxime elatus quod sequatur *in omnibus bonis*. cetera quæ sequuntur cum eius expositione non congruunt.'—(*c*) On Eph $5^{31ff.}$ (p. 659): '*Propter hoc relinquet homo patrem et matrem, et erunt duo in carne una: sacramentum hoc magnum est, ego autem dico in Christo et in Ecclesia* . . . interrogemus Marcionem qua consequentia locum istum, qui de Veteri usurpatus est Instrumento, in Christum et in Ecclesiam interpretari queat, cum iuxta illum scriptura vetus omnino non pertineat ad Christum.' Of Marcion's exegesis we can at any rate say that, unlike the interpretations of the Valentinian school, it was not allegorist, or rather that it was diametrically opposed to allegory; but the main interest with which he wrote was, no doubt, theological rather than directly exegetical.

**2.** A commentator on St. Paul is perhaps referred to by Origen on Eph $1^{13}$ (Cramer's *Catena in Eph.* p. 119; *Journal of Theological Studies*, iii. 242), where, commenting on the grammatically superfluous repetition of ἐν ᾧ (ἐν τῷ Χριστῷ ἐν ᾧ . . . ἐν ᾧ), he explains its presence by the 'saying of one of those who were before us, that, from his great love to Jesus, Paul continually, and as it might seem redundantly, makes mention of Him': ἔλεγε δή τις τῶν πρὸ ἡμῶν ἀπὸ τῆς πολλῆς περὶ τὸν Ἰησοῦν ἀγάπης τὸν Παῦλον συνεχέστατα αὐτοῦ μεμνῆσθαι καὶ ὡσπερεὶ παρελκόντως. The reference is, no doubt, not necessarily to technical exposition; yet the words most naturally suggest a homilist or commentator who was examining the details of the Apostle's style, and attention is therefore called to them in this place. It is tempting to identify this 'predecessor' with **Pantænus.** The testimony, indeed, of Jerome (*de Viris Illustribus*, 36), that many commentaries by Pantænus were extant when he wrote, is possibly nothing but an amplification of the vaguer words of Eusebius, *HE* v. 10, διὰ συγγραμμάτων τοὺς τῶν θείων δογμάτων θησαυροὺς ὑπομνηματιζόμενος. Still, Eusebius himself seems to imply that Pantænus did write commentaries (though he says nothing about their surviving to his time), and these would naturally have been accessible to Origen; but whether they included expositions of St. Paul, there is nothing to show.*

**3. Heraclitus.**—Eusebius in his *Hist. Eccl.* (v. 27), just after he has brought matters down to the death of the emperor Commodus and the succession of Pertinax (A.D. 192–193), mentions at the head of a number of books belonging to about that time, which he had himself read, the writings of Heraclitus on 'the Apostle' (τὰ Ἡρακλείτου εἰς τὸν Ἀπόστολον). Nothing is known of these commentaries or of their author; possibly he may be identical with the expositor alluded to by Origen. Nor have we any means of knowing whether Eusebius' dating was based on adequate grounds.

**4. Alexander 'the ancient heretic.'**—Among the works on the Epistle to the Galatians which Jerome had consulted before he wrote his own commentary (see p. 484b, above) was one by Alexander, 'veterem hæreticum.' Apparently, the only known Alexander with whom we could identify the commentator is the Valentinian whom Tertullian combats in his *de carne Christi* (after A.D. 200), 16, 17. But there is nothing in Tertullian's words that suggests any connexion of his Alexander with St. Paul, and the name was one of the commonest. At the same time, just as the Valentinian Heracleon was the earliest commentator on St. John, the Valentinian Alexander may have been one of the first commentators on St. Paul.

* *i.e.* his revised text of ten epistles of St. Paul, excluding the Pastoral epistles.

† Tert. *adv. Marcionem*, iv. 1.

* A still more probable source is perhaps the *Hypotyposes* of Clement of Alexandria, which ought to have been mentioned in the text at this place; the missing section will be found below, p. 520.

**5. Origen.**—The most important and most prolific of early exegetes of St. Paul was Origen, although even he did not write any uniform exposition of the Pauline epistles as a whole; it was not, as has been said (p. 484[b]), till a century later that any complete commentary on 'the Apostle' was published. The list of his works preserved to us in Jerome's *Ep.* xxxiii. *ad Paulam* (see Harnack-Preuschen,* *Geschichte der altchristlichen Litteratur*, i. 334; E. Klostermann gave an improved text in *Sitzungsberichte der k. preuss. Akademie der Wissenschaften*, 1897, p. 855) shows that the bulk of his exegetical writings on St. Paul must have exceeded that of any subsequent expositor in the Patristic period: the following commentaries and homilies are there enumerated:—

Romans: commentary in 15 books.
2 Corinthians: 11 homilies.
Galatians: commentary in 15 books; 7 homilies.
Ephesians: commentary in 3 books.
Philippians: commentary in 1 book.
Colossians: commentary in 2 books.
1 Thessalonians: commentary in 3 books; 2 homilies.†
2 Thessalonians: commentary in 1 book [not in Preuschen's text].
Titus: commentary in 1 book; 1 homily.
Philemon: commentary in 1 book.
Hebrews: 18 homilies.

The only epistles left unrepresented in this catalogue are 1 Corinthians and 1 and 2 Timothy; yet, strangely enough, Jerome himself with regard to 1 Corinthians bears witness, as we have seen, to the fact that Origen was among those who 'latissime hanc epistolam interpretati sunt.' And the list is altogether silent as to the third department of Origen's exegetical labours on the Bible, that of *scholia* or 'notes,' though reference will be found below to these in connexion with Rom., 1 Cor., and Galatians. The explanation of the discrepancy appears to be that the list in Jerome, *Ep.* xxxiii., is simply transcribed from the list given by Eusebius in his Life of Pamphilus, and therefore represents the collection as known to Eusebius. Jerome himself, while he knew books of Origen's that were not in the list, may very probably not have known many books that were in it. But the range of knowledge of either Eusebius or Jerome, partial and mutually exclusive though it be, contrasts painfully with the scattered débris which are all that time and theological animosity have spared to us of the vast labours which the father of Christian exegesis devoted to St. Paul. Much of his matter, indeed, remains accessible to us in the pages of later expositors, particularly of St. Jerome; but the direct tradition of his work, apart from fragments, is practically limited to a Latin version of the commentary on Romans, and to Catenæ notes on Romans, 1 Corinthians, and Ephesians.

Of the chronology of Origen's writings on St. Paul there is not much to be said. The *Stromateis*, of which the third book appears to have contained notes on Romans, the fourth on 1 Corinthians, and the tenth on Galatians (see below, pp. 492–493), were written at Alexandria, *i.e.* before 231, under the emperor Alexander Severus, *i.e.* after 222 (Eus. *HE* vi. 24). The commentary on Romans is mentioned in that on St. Matthew, and the commentary on 1 Thessalonians in the *contra Celsum* (see below, pp. 490[b], 496[a]): the commentary on St. Matthew and the *contra Celsum* were, however, almost Origen's latest works, so that in neither case does the information carry us very far. On the other hand, the homilies on 1 Corinthians had been written before the homilies on St. Luke (p. 492[b], below), and these latter are placed immediately after the departure of Origen from Alexandria. But it may be taken as probable that nearly all of his formal exegesis of the Epistles by way of commentaries and homilies belongs to the later or Cæsarean period of his life, A.D. 231–250.

The best account of the various editions of Origen's works is that given in bishop Westcott's article in the *Dictionary of Christian Biography*, iv. 140–142. No single Greek treatise was printed before the 17th cent.; of the Latin works of Origen collected editions appeared in 1512 (Jacques Merlin, Paris, 4 vols.; reprinted at Venice in 1516, at Paris in 1519, 1522, 1530) and 1536 (Erasmus, Basle, 2 vols.; reprinted with some additions in 1571). The first collected edition of Greek works was that of Peter Daniel Huet, afterwards bishop of Avranches, *Origenis in sacras scripturas commentaria quæcumque græce reperiri potuerunt*, 2 vols., Rouen, 1668 (reprinted at Paris 1679, at Cologne 1685): neither Latin works nor Catena fragments were included. Latin and Greek were first brought together in the great Benedictine edition of de la Rue, *Origenis opera omnia quæ græce vel latine tantum extant et eius nomine circumferuntur*, 4 vols., Paris, 1733–1759; the last volume, edited by Charles Vincent de la Rue after the death of his uncle, Charles de la Rue, is that which specially concerns us: from this edition all quotations in this article are taken. Migne, *Patrol. Gr.*, vols. 11–17 (Pauline epistles in vol. 14, cc. 837–1310), is a reprint, with a few additions, of de la Rue. Lommatzsch, 25 vols. (epistles in vols. 5–7), Berlin, 1831–1848, has the merit of handy size. The new Berlin edition of Origen has as yet only published St. John of all the NT commentaries. Editions of separate portions will be noticed under the epistle to which they belong.

(i.) *Romans.*

The commentary* in 15 books (Cassiodorus, *Inst. Div. Litt.* 8, has 'viginti'; but xx easily grows out of xv) is mainly known to us through the Latin version which Rufinus of Aquileia towards the end of his life made at the request of his 'brother,' the deacon Heraclius—after his translation of Origen *in Gen.*, *in Exod.*, *in Levit.*, *in Jos.*, *in Jud.*, *in Ps.* xxxvi., xxxvii., xxxviii., but before his translation of the Clementine *Recognitions* and of Origen *in Num.* (see his 'peroratio in explanationem Origenis super ep. Pauli ad Rom.,' de la Rue, iv. 688); probably, therefore, about A.D. 405. The 'preface' and the 'peroration' to this version raise important questions both about the state of the text of Origen's writings at the end of the 4th cent., and about the methods adopted by Rufinus in editing his exemplar for Latin readers.

(*a*) The incompleteness of the Greek text: 'Super omnes autem difficultates est quod interpolati sunt ipsi libri; desunt enim fere apud omnium bibliothecas (incertum sane quo casu) aliquanta ex ipso corpore volumina, et hæc adimplere atque in latino opere integram consequentiam dare non est mei ingenii sed . . . muneris fortasse divini' (*Præf. in explanationem*, etc., iv. 458). Preuschen in Harnack, *Altchr. Litteratur* i. 373, makes this into a double statement of incompleteness and interpolation; and if that were so, we should have to compare Rufinus' earlier treatise, *de adulteratione librorum Origenis* (A.D. 397: de la Rue, iv., Appendix, p. 48), where, on the strength of parallel

* It may be stated here once for all that the section on Origen is due to Dr. Preuschen.

† The 2 homilies may possibly belong to the Second Epistle: the list only says 'in epistolam ad Thessalonicenses.'

* The commentary on Romans was written before that on St. Matthew; cf. tom. xvii. *in Matt.* § 32 (de la Rue, iii. 821), referring to Ro 7[1]: *εἴρηται δὲ πλείονα ἡμῖν . . . ὁ ἡγουμένοις τὸ χωρίον τὸ τῆς πρὸς Ῥωμαίους ἐπιστολῆς ἐν τοῖς εἰς αὐτὴν ἐξηγητικοῖς.*

cases in the writings of other Fathers, and of a complaint by Origen himself in a particular instance, he maintained the theory of a wholesale falsification of the Origen literature by heretics. Jerome had no difficulty in proving (*adv. Ruf.* ii. 19) that the generalization was quite unreasonable. As a matter of fact, the Apollinarians are the only heretics against whom the charge of deliberate and systematic falsification of documents can be sustained, and they would certainly not have selected Origen for their authority; moreover, even if Origen's dogmatic writings had been manipulated, there is not the least reason to think that his exegesis would have been exposed to similar treatment. But, in truth, Rufinus, as the connecting particle *enim* shows, is not making two statements, but one: *interpolare* is 'to alter,' 'to corrupt,' not necessarily by interpolation: in this case the 'interpolation' consists simply in the imperfection of the booksellers' copies, and Rufinus himself appears to realize that that may have been merely accidental. The fact itself is interesting enough, and agrees curiously well with the evidence of the Athos MS (Laura, 184, B. 64) of the Epistles, which von der Goltz * has shown to contain not only a genuine Origen text of St. Paul, but some important Origen *marginalia*, among them the starting-points of the separate *τόμοι* of the commentary on Romans: for it is noted that tomes 11 and 14 were not extant (*οὐ φέρεται*). But as the Latin version gives a continuous commentary extending over the whole epistle—although arranged in 10 books in place of the original 15 †—we are bound to suppose that Rufinus had succeeded in securing a completer copy, so that the 'interpolation' has hardly affected the form in which the commentary has reached us.

(*b*) But, even if Rufinus possessed a complete Greek text, his own words reveal that he did not produce, or aim at producing, a complete Latin translation. Heraclius had begged him, he says, 'ut omne hoc xv voluminum corpus, quod græcus sermo ad quadraginta fere aut eo amplius millia versuum produxit, abbreviem et ad media, si fieri potest, spatia coarctem.' And if the figures are correct, it would seem to follow that this process of abbreviation was faithfully carried through; for whereas a translation ordinarily covers somewhat more space than its original, the translation of Rufinus occupies only 230 pages or about 25,000 half-lines (there being two columns to the page), while the 40,000 'verses' of Origen, at the normal rate of 16 syllables to the verse, would come to fully half as much again. The few passages preserved in the original Greek (see below) offer, of course, an obvious means of testing in individual instances the relation of the version to its exemplar.

Rufinus' translation of the commentary on the Romans was (as the list of extant MSS in Preuschen-Harnack, p. 400, amply demonstrates) by far the best known specimen in the West of Origen's work on the New Testament. While the East was piling up its anathemas, and Justinian was aspersing the name and memory of Origen in the vain hope of reconciling the Nestorians, the West, as represented in the Gelasian decree *de libris recipiendis*, approved of all such works of his as 'the blessed Jerome does not repudiate,' contenting itself with the rejection of 'the rest and their author.' Thus, to render unassailable Rufinus' translation of Origen on the Romans, nothing more was necessary than to make the substitution of the name 'Jerome' for the name 'Rufinus' in title, preface, and peroration; and this is what actually happened in the later MSS, and in the earlier editions before Erasmus.* The earliest extant MS of any part of the translation is a Lyons MS, cod. 483 (413); it contains, roughly speaking, the first five books (but without the beginning of Book I., and therefore without the translator's prologue and name), and is one of the oldest known specimens of the so-called semi-uncial writing—Delisle calls it 6th cent., but, in view of its habitual use of 'dom̄' for every case of *dominus*, and of the declension 'is̄,' 'iu̅,' 'im̄,' for *Iesus*, the present writer would prefer to call it 5th, so that it is perhaps the most ancient monument of Patristic exegesis that has come down to our times. Next in age would come a fragment (ascribed to about 700 A.D.) in a Monte Cassino MS, cod. 150, of which the first 64 pages contain our commentary, as far as $2^{16}$, including the prologue and name of Rufinus.†

Of the two fragments from Origen's commentary on the Romans, preserved in Rufinus' version of Pamphilus' *Apologia pro Origene* (de la Rue, iv., Appendix, pp. 25, 33), the second does not appear at all in Rufinus' version of the commentary itself (cf. de la Rue, iv. 466); the first appears only in an abbreviated and independent form (iv. 465).

The following authorities have preserved passages from, or references to, the original Greek of the commentary on Romans.

α. The *Philocalia* of Basil and Gregory (ed. Robinson, Cambridge, 1893) contains two passages: ch. xxv. *ὅτι ὁ ἐκ προγνώσεως ἀφορισμὸς οὐκ ἀναιρεῖ τὸ αὐτεξούσιον. ἐκ τοῦ α' τόμου τῶν εἰς τὴν πρὸς Ῥωμαίους ἐξηγητικῶν, εἰς τὸ Ἀφωρισμένος εἰς εὐαγγέλιον θεοῦ* (Ro $1^{1}$; Robinson, pp. 226–231): and ch. ix. *τίς ὁ λόγος τοῦ τὴν θείαν γραφὴν κατὰ διάφορα σημαινόμενα τῷ αὐτῷ. ὀνόματι κεχρῆσθαι πολλάκις καὶ ἐν τῷ αὐτῷ τόπῳ. ἐκ τῆς πρὸς Ῥωμαίους· τόμος ἔννατος, εἰς τὸ Τί οὖν; ὁ νόμος ἁμαρτία;* (Ro $7^{7}$; Robinson, pp. 54–58).

β. St. Basil, *de Spiritu sancto*, 73 (ed. C. F. H. Johnston, Oxford, 1892, p. 144): [Origen] *ἐν τοῖς εἰς τὴν πρὸς Ῥωμαίους ἐπιστολὴν ἐξηγητικοῖς, Αἱ ἱεραί, φησί, δυνάμεις χωρητικαὶ τοῦ Μονογενοῦς καὶ τῆς τοῦ ἁγίου Πνεύματος θεότητος.*

γ. St. Jerome, *Ep.* xxxvi. *ad Damasum* (A.D. 384; Vallarsi, i. 159), quotes no actual words: 'Origenes in quarto Pauli ad Romanos *ἐξηγήσεων* [*v.l.* *ἐξηγητικῶν*] tomo de circumcisione magnifice disputavit.'

δ. Socrates, *Hist. Eccl.* vii. 32 (ed. Bright, p. 316): *καὶ Ὠριγένης δὲ ἐν τῷ πρώτῳ τόμῳ τῶν εἰς τὴν πρὸς Ῥωμαίους τοῦ ἀποστόλου ἐπιστολὴν ἑρμηνεύων πῶς Θεοτόκος λέγεται πλατέως ἐξήτασε.*

ε. The Athos MS, whose discovery by von der Goltz has already been mentioned just above, embodies, as far as the Pauline epistles are concerned, an attempt at a critical edition according to the text used by Origen. The 10th cent. scholar to whom we owe the existing MS derived his text for the most part from an *ἀντίγραφον παλαιότατον*, 'a very ancient copy,' representing a similar attempt on the part of an earlier (probably much earlier) scholar, the accuracy of which the later scholar tells us he verified by the help of such commentaries or homilies of Origen on 'the Apostle' as were accessible to him. With regard,

* 'Eine textkritische Arbeit des zehnten bezw. sechsten Jahrhunderts, herausgegeben nach einem Kodex des Athosklosters Lawra, von E. von der Goltz' (*Texte und Untersuchungen*, Neue Folge; ii. 4, Leipzig, 1899). See further below, p. 491b.

† The contents of the separate books of the Latin are as follows:—Book I. = Ro $1^{1}$–$2^{1}$; II. = $2^{2}$–$3^{4}$; III. = $3^{5-31}$; IV. = $4^{1}$–$5^{11}$; V. = $5^{12}$–$6^{11}$; VI. = $6^{12}$–$8^{13}$; VII. = $8^{14}$–$9^{33}$; VIII. = $10^{1}$–$11^{36}$; IX. = $12^{1}$–$14^{15}$; X. = $14^{16}$–$16^{27}$. The tomes of the original Greek, as recovered by von der Goltz from the Athos MS, began as follows: tom. α' $1^{1}$; tom. β' $1^{8}$; tom. γ' $1^{26}$; tom. δ' $2^{12}$; tom. ε' $3^{5}$; tom. ϛ' $4^{1}$; tom. ζ' $5^{8}$; tom. η' $5^{17}$; tom. θ' $6^{13}$; tom. ι' $8^{9}$; tom. ια' (ὃς οὐ φέρεται) $9^{1}$; tom. ιβ' is not marked; tom. ιγ' $11^{13}$; tom. ιδ' (ὃς οὐ φέρεται) $12^{16}$; tom. ιε' $14^{10}$.

* The *editio princeps* of the Latin commentary, under the title 'Hieronymo interprete,' was printed at Venice in 1506.

† The rest of this MS consists of an earlier (6th cent.) copy of the commentary of Ambrosiaster.

however, to the Roman epistle—possibly because this epistle, standing at the head of the older MS, had suffered more than the rest in legibility—he copied his text not from the 'ancient copy,' but directly from the *lemmata* (*i.e.* the sections of text prefixed to corresponding sections of exposition) in his own MS of Origen's commentary on that epistle; but as the 11th and 14th tomes of the commentary—roughly speaking, chapters 9 and 13, 14—were wanting in that MS, he was there thrown back on the 'ancient copy,' helped out, where it was specially difficult to read, by the further testimony to Origen's text of the Romans contained in the notes on difficult passages in the third book of his *Stromateis*.* So far, we are dealing with the text only of the Origen commentary; but the Athos MS preserves also a few marginal citations from the commentary itself, and would have preserved more had not some Greek monk later on, after the fashion of his kind, set himself to erase with care anything that follows the name of the arch-heretic. It may be hoped that chemical reagents will yet prove victorious over the monastic scalpel: meanwhile von der Goltz has printed such matter as has escaped. The notes do not come to much; but they are valuable as showing how late some of the writings of Origen survived in the original Greek, and with what devoted care they were still studied—perhaps in the circle of archbishop Arethas of Cæsarea. Origen is cited in two cases (Ro $3^{16}$ $11^{8}$) as being unable to identify the sources of quotations in St. Paul, but for the most part (as doubtless also in the notes that have perished) to establish some question of reading. In $1^{7}$ both *lemma* and exposition omitted the words ἐν Ῥώμῃ; in $5^{17}$ the *lemma* had λαβόντες, but the exposition λαμβάνοντες; in $8^{24}$ the 'ancient copy' had ὃ γὰρ βλέπει τίς ἐλπίζει, the text of the Athos MS has ὃ γὰρ βλέπει τίς καὶ ἐλπίζει with ὑπομένει in the margin, so that it would seem that the reading of the 'ancient copy' was (exceptionally) given a place in the text, and that taken from the commentary relegated on this occasion to the margin; in $15^{14}$ both *lemma* and exposition apparently read καὶ αὐτοὶ μεστοί. On 1 Jn $4^{3}$ it is noted that that verse is quoted by Origen in tom. η′ on the Romans with the reading ὃ λύει τὸν Ἰησοῦν; similarly, 2 Co $12^{19}$ is said *ad loc.* to be adduced in tom. ϛ′ on the Romans in the form ἐνώπιον τοῦ κυρίου καὶ ἐναντίον τοῦ θεοῦ ἐν Χριστῷ λαλοῦμεν.

ζ. Cramer's Catena on the Romans (Oxford, 1844) consists of two Catenæ, both imperfect. Of these, the first, taken from a Bodleian MS, Auct. E. ii. 20, covers Ro $1^{1}$–$9^{1}$, and makes considerable use of Origen in more than 50 quotations,† belonging to the following verses: Ro $1^{1.\ 10.\ 11}$ $2^{8\text{-}9.\ 16.\ 27}$ $3^{2.\ 4.\ 10\text{-}12.\ 13\text{-}18.\ 19\text{-}20.\ 21.\ 25.\ 27.\ 28.\ 30.\ 31}$ $4^{3.\ 4.\ 7\text{-}8.\ 11.\ 12\ (?).\ 15.\ 16a.\ 16b.\ 17.\ 16.\ 18.\ 23\text{-}24}$ $5^{6}$ $6^{5.\ 9b.\ 12.\ 11\text{-}14.\ 19\text{-}20.\ 21.\ 22.\ 23}$ $7^{1.\ 6.\ 7.\ 8.\ 9.\ 13.\ 14.\ 15.\ 23.\ 24}$ $8^{3.\ 5\text{-}7.\ 24\text{-}25.\ 26a.\ 26b.\ 33.\ 37.\ 35\text{-}39}$. It will be seen that for considerable sections of these chapters—$3^{10}$–$4^{25}$ $6^{12}$–$8^{7}$ $8^{24\text{-}39}$—an almost continuous exposition could be restored from this Catena. Unfortunately, we do not yet know how far Vatic. gr. 762, which appears to be a direct ancestor of the Bodleian MS (see above, *e*, p. 488[b]), would supply additional Origen matter for the later chapters of the epistle, or a corrected Origen text for the earlier ones.

η. Cramer's second Catena, Munich cod. gr. 23 (now 412), sæc. xiii., extends from Ro $7^{7}$ to the end of the epistle (thus overlapping the Bodleian Catena for Ro $7^{7}$–$9^{1}$), but contains very few passages from Origen: Ro $7^{9.\ 11\text{-}12.\ 14.\ 23}$ $8^{5\text{-}7.\ 33.\ 38\text{-}39}$ $12^{20}$ seem to exhaust the list. Besides these, it quotes on $8^{30}$ a long passage ἐκ τῆς Φιλοκαλίας τοῦ Ὠριγένους (ed. Robinson, 226. 12–15; 227. 15–229. 29), which is really part of Origen's comment on $1^{1}$; on $9^{21}$ the still longer extract ἐκ τῆς Ἐκλογῆς τοῦ Ὠριγένους (Cramer, p. 340) is not from the commentary on the Romans, but from the *de Principiis*, and the brief paragraph Ὠριγένους ἐκ τῶν Ἐκλογῶν (Cramer, p. 349) has the same source (Robinson, p. xxx). Since all these references came not directly from Origen, but from the *Philocalia*,* we should be prepared to expect that the eight other quotations are similarly derived from some mediate source; and if we compare them with the Oxford Catena—seven out of the eight belong to the portion of the epistle, $7^{7}$–$9^{1}$, common to the two Catenæ—we shall find that, with the exception of the short passage on $7^{11\text{-}12}$ (Cr. 179. 13–18), all are already contained in the Oxford Catena. If we further consider that the last eight chapters are only represented by a single Origen quotation in the Munich Catena, it will scarcely seem over-bold to conjecture that the latter Catena drew its Origen, not of course from our actual Oxford MS, but from some similar MS, which was equally limited, whether by the original design or by accidental loss, to the first half of the epistle. The practical point of this conclusion, if correct, would be to reassure us that the loss of the earlier part of the Munich Catena has not seriously diminished our store of new matter from Origen.

It only remains to test by the evidence of the Greek texts, fragmentary though they are, the relation of Rufinus to his original. It has already been calculated that more than a third of the Greek must have been omitted to bring the Latin within its present compass; and Dr. Robinson says of the passages preserved in the *Philocalia* (p. xxxix) that in the translation they 'are so abbreviated that without the explanation of Rufinus we could scarcely have believed that they were intended to represent the corresponding sections in the *Philocalia* at all.' With regard also to the Latin text of St. Paul as given in Rufinus, bishop Westcott points out (*Dict. Chr. Biogr.* iv. 116*a*) that it makes no attempt to represent the Greek of Origen, but is rather an Old Latin text pure and simple—presumably, one may suppose, that of Aquileia.

*Scholia on Romans.*—The third book of Origen's *Stromateis*, or *Stromata*,† appears to have contained brief notes or 'scholia' on the Roman epistle, as the fourth book did on 1 Corinthians and the tenth book certainly on Galatians: see below, p. 493[a]. It is quoted in the Athos MS (von der Goltz, pp. 58, 59) for the readings of Ro $9^{20.\ 23}$.

(ii.) *1 Corinthians.*

The list of Eusebius-Jerome makes no mention of any work of Origen on 1 Corinthians; but Jerome mentions him as one of those who had commented on the epistle 'at great length,' and Cramer's Catena (Oxford, 1841; taken from MS Paris gr. 227, sæc. xvi.) gives an even larger mass of quotations from Origen than the same editor's first Catena on Romans does for that epistle. The number, in fact, is over 80, and they are in this case—with the exception of a single allusion by Origen himself, *Hom.* xvii. *in Luc.* (de la Rue, iii. 953), 'Memini cum interpretarer illud quod ad Corinthios scribitur *Ecclesiæ Dei*

* On Origen's *Stromateis* see also pp. 490[a], 492[b], 493[a].

† The list in Cramer's index should be supplemented by the following references: 22. 23; 73. 18; 74. 1; 105. 9.

* For which, however, they give a text independent of, and in some points better than, the extant *Philocalia* MSS; see Robinson, p. xxxi.

† The proper Greek name was no doubt Στρωματεῖς, 'bags for bedclothes,' 'carpet bags,' and so 'receptacles for miscellaneous odds and ends': Στρώματα would be the bedclothes themselves, and the form *Stromata*, whether in connexion with Clement or with Origen, seems to be found only in Jerome, and to be due probably to the difficulty of declining the word *stromateus* in Latin. See Hort and Mayor, *Clement of Alexandria*, pp. xi, xii.

*quæ est Corinthi cum omnibus qui invocant eum* [1 Co $1^{2}$] dixisse me diversitatem *ecclesiæ* et *eorum qui invocant nomen Domini*'*—the only authority of any sort for the book from which they are extracted. That this was not in the form of commentary but of homilies is shown (as Westcott points out) by the phrases used on $3^{1}$ περὶ ὧν καὶ πρώην ἐλέγομεν (Cramer, 51. 6), and on $6^{9}$ παρακαλοῦμεν οὖν καὶ ὑμᾶς, ὦ παῖδες (Cramer, 107. 19).† The following is a list of the passages commented on: 1 Co $1^{2a.\ 2b.\ 4.\ 7.\ 4\text{-}8.\ 9.\ 10.\ 11\text{-}12.\ 17a.\ 17b\ (bis).\ 18.\ 20a.\ 20b.\ 19\text{-}21.\ 22\text{-}25.\ 26.\ 27.\ 19\text{-}21,\ 26\text{-}31.\ 30}$–$2^{2}$ $2^{3.\ 6.\ 7\text{-}8.\ 9\text{-}10a.\ 9b\text{-}10.\ 11\text{-}15.\ 13\text{-}15}$ $3^{1\text{-}3a.\ 3b\text{-}4.\ 6.\ 9\text{-}12.\ 16\text{-}20.\ 21\text{-}23}$ $4^{1\text{-}5a.\ 5.\ 6\text{-}7.\ 7\text{-}8.\ 9\text{-}10.\ 15\text{-}18.\ 19b\text{-}20.\ 21}$–$5^{2}$ $5^{3\text{-}5.\ 7\text{-}8.\ 9\text{-}13}$ $6^{[2\text{-}3.]\ 4\text{-}9a.\ 9b\text{-}10.\ 12.\ 13a.\ 13b\text{-}14.\ 15a.\ 18.\ 19\text{-}20a}$ $7^{1\text{-}4.\ 5b.\ 5a\text{-}7.\ 8\text{-}12a.\ 12b\text{-}14a.\ 18\text{-}24.\ 25\text{-}28a}$ $9^{7\text{-}9a.\ 9b\text{-}11.\ 16\text{-}18.\ 19\text{-}22.\ 23.\ 24a}$ $10^{1\text{-}5.\ 6}$ $12^{[2.]\ 3a.\ 10.\ 28.\ 31.\ 34}$ $13^{1\text{-}2.\ 3.\ 4\text{-}5.\ 8b\text{-}11.\ 12}$ $14^{31.\ 34\text{-}35.\ 36.\ 37.\ 38}$ $15^{2.\ 12.\ 20\text{-}22.\ 36\text{-}37.\ 42\text{-}44}$ $16^{10\text{-}12.\ 13\text{-}14}$. The Vatican MS gr. 762, from which Cramer's Paris MS was copied, will probably not yield any fresh matter, but perhaps an improved text.

The Athos MS contains traces of erasure opposite 1 Co $2^{6}$ $3^{10}$ $4^{16}$ $6^{1}$ $7^{1}$ $10^{1}$ $11^{1}$ $12^{1}$ $13^{1}$ $14^{1}$ $15^{1.\ 58}$, which may possibly have marked the beginning of homilies. But however this may be, it preserves also clear indications that the fourth book of the *Stromateis* contained notes on this epistle; ἐν τῷ δ' τῶν Στρωματέων is appealed to for the readings of $7^{31.\ 34}$ $9^{20.\ 21}$ and $10^{9}$, and in each case several lines of the 'exposition' are quoted in support of the appeal. There can be little doubt that in the similar quotation on $6^{14}$ (ἐξήγειρεν for ἐξεγερεῖ) we ought also to read not, with von der Goltz, ἐν τῷ α' τῶν Στρωματέων, but ἐν τῷ δ' (Δ for Α).

(iii.) *2 Corinthians.*

The list mentions 11 homilies; but nothing is otherwise known of them, and published Catenæ on this epistle contain nothing from Origen: even Vatic. gr. 762, which is unpublished, can hardly contain any Origen, or cardinal Mai might have been expected to have put it before the world. Preuschen ingeniously proposes to read 'in ep. ad Cor. i.' (instead of ii.) in the list, and to identify these homilies with those from which the Catena on 1 Cor. is drawn. Yet the Origen quotations in that Catena are so full that it may be questioned whether so small a number of homilies as 11 could have provided so much matter. And though the *marginalia* in the Athos MS are scanty for this epistle, there is a long gloss on $1^{17\text{-}19}$ of which the first words have escaped erasure, οὕτως καὶ αὐτὸς ἐξηγεῖται λέγων . . . : and this is enough to make highly probable the employment of a definite exposition, whether commentary, homilies, or notes.

(iv.) *Galatians.*

The list mentions a commentary in 15 books and 7 homilies: Jerome, in the preface to his commentary on the epistle (see above, p. 484b), enumerates 5 'volumes' (of commentary), several 'tractatus' ( = homilies), and 'excerpts' (*i.e. scholia* or notes); and tells us also that the tenth book of Origen's *Stromateis* was devoted to a brief explanation of this epistle.

With regard to the *Stromateis*, one passage on the Galatians is extant: Jerome *in Gal.* lib. iii. (Vallarsi, vii. 494–496) gives us a literal version of the explanation of Gal $5^{13\text{-}23}$: 'hunc locum, quia valde obscurus est, de decimo Stromatum libro transferri placuit ad verbum'; and further on (vii. 505): 'in eo loco ubi supra de decimo Origenis Stromate verbum transtulimus ad verbum.' As eleven verses are covered in two columns and a half of Jerome's Latin, the exposition may justly be called, in comparison with the ordinary standard of Origen's work, 'brief.'

For the commentary the Athos MS has happily preserved the starting-point of each tome—tom. α' = $1^{1}$; tom. β' = $2^{3}$; tom. γ' = $3^{5}$; tom. δ' = $4^{6}$; tom. ϵ' = $5^{6}$—thus establishing the number given in Jerome's commentary against that of the list: beyond these numbers it has preserved nothing to our purpose. But two quotations, perhaps three, are embedded in Rufinus' version of Pamphilus' *Apologia pro Origene* (de la Rue, iv., Appendix, p. 35): (i.) 'Responsio ad tertiam criminationem: Quod non purus homo sed divinæ naturæ sit Christus. De primo libro epistolæ ad Galatas [on Gal $1^{1}$] . . . (ii.) Hæc in initio epistolæ dicens, in sequentibus libri ipsius similia adiecit [on Gal $1^{11.\ 12}$] . . . (iii.) Responsio ad quartam criminationem: Adversum eos qui dicunt eum per allegorias adimere omnia quæ a Salvatore scripta sunt corporaliter facta. Ex eodem lib. in epist. ad Galatas': but these last words are only in the margin, and if they do not rest on MS authority, no conclusive ground remains for connecting this lengthy and important passage with the Galatian commentary in particular among all the works of Origen. Conversely, the comment on Gal $3^{19}$ in the 'Responsio ad quintam criminationem,' which in the editions is entitled 'in tertio libro epistolæ ad Colossenses,' ought perhaps to read, 'in tertio libro epistolæ ad Galatas.'

Cramer's Catena on the Galatian epistle, taken from Paris coislin 204, contains no quotations ascribed by name to Origen; but as the quotations are nearly all anonymous, it is at least possible that Origen is among the writers of whom use is made, and it might be worth while to compare the Catena with the commentary of Jerome, in order to see if there is matter common to the two. For it is certain, both from Jerome's own words in the preface to his commentary and from the parallel case of the Epistle to the Ephesians—where the recovery of a good deal of Origen's Greek has made comparison possible between the two writers—that a very large proportion of the exhaustive commentary of Jerome is drawn directly from Origen.

(v.) *Ephesians.*

Both the list and Jerome (*Præf. ad Comm. in Eph.*) mention a commentary in 3 books (and nothing else) on this epistle. Although it has not come down to us in any continuous form, either in the original or in a translation,* yet enough survives in the Greek of Cramer's Catena and the Latin of Jerome's commentary to render feasible at least a partial reconstruction.

*a*. Cramer's Catena (Oxford, 1842), taken from Paris coislin 204, sæc. x., contains some 40 quotations from Origen, many of them of considerable length, but disfigured by the appalling blunders which, here as elsewhere, have to be set in the balance against the gratitude due to the only scholar who, during the whole 19th cent., effected any substantial addition to the printed texts of New Testament Catenæ. In this instance, however, a beginning has at last been made of a revision of the Cramer texts. In the *Journal of Theological Studies* for the year 1902 (iii. 233–244, 398–420, 554–576), the Rev. J. A. F. Gregg, of Christ's College, Cambridge, published from a fresh collation of the MS a continuous text of all the Origen fragments, equipped with full apparatus both of the Scripture references and of the parallels

* The interpretation alluded to is preserved, though in a corrupt and perhaps incomplete form, in the Catena, Cr. 7. 9–17: *e.g.* σπεύσωμεν οὖν ἀπὸ τοῦ 'ἐπικαλεῖσθαι' . . . ἀναβῆναι ἐπὶ τὴν 'ἐκκλησίαν' τὴν ἄσπιλον καὶ ἄμωμον.

† Yet it is just possible that the catenist was drawing on more than one work of Origen on the epistle, for on several occasions he seems to quote two different comments of Origen on the same passage.

* Preuschen in Harnack, *Altchr. Litteratur*, i. 375, goes beyond the facts in stating that Jerome actually translated the book. All the passages he adduces refer to the use Jerome made of Origen in his own commentary.

in Jerome. With the text re-collated, the punctuation revised, and the more obvious corruptions removed by the help of emendations from various English scholars, we can now for the first time read a substantial portion of a work by Origen on St. Paul in its original language and in an intelligible form. No doubt, the catenist has at many points contented himself with selections, and has abbreviated the superabundant material of the commentary; but the only considerable passages which are wholly unrepresented are Eph $2^{7-11}$ $3^{4-11.\,19b}$–$4^{2}$ $4^{8-10}$ $5^{25-33}$ (with the exception of two short notes on vv.$^{27}$ and $^{31}$) $6^{4-8}$.

*β*. The Athos MS contains at the end of the text of Ephesians a note to the effect that *ἀπὸ τῶν εἰς τὴν πρὸς Ἐφεσίους φερομένων ἐξηγητικῶν τόμων ἀντανεγνωσον ἡ ἐπιστολή*. The *vox nihili* *ἀντανεγνωσον* is, as von der Goltz points out, clearly a misreading of an uncial *ἀντανεγνώσθη* (ON for ΘH). The 'very ancient copy' (see above, p. 491[b]) had itself, therefore, been verified with the *lemmata* in Origen's commentary. The commencement of *τόμος α′* at $1^{1}$ is marked; unfortunately, no corresponding marks seem to have been preserved for tom. *β′* and tom. *γ′*.* In what remains of the marginal notes the 'exposition' is only mentioned twice: on $3^{18}$ as reading *βάθος καὶ ὕψος* (cf. *Journal of Theol. Studies*, iii. 411), where the *lemma* gave *ὕψος καὶ βάθος*: and on $2^{21}$ as *μίαν λέγουσα τὴν οἰκοδομήν* with the article, where the *lemma* gave *πᾶσα οἰκοδομή* without the article (*JThSt*, iii. 407; Robinson, *Ep. to the Ephesians*, p. 297).

*γ*. That Jerome's commentary in 3 books on the Ephesian epistle (published between 386 and 392) follows Origen with extreme fidelity is established by several convergent lines of testimony. We have his own preface, where, out of the three predecessors whose work he used, he distinguishes Origen, as the one whom he in some degree followed, from Apollinaris and Didymus, of whom he had only made occasional use: 'ex parte secuti sumus . . . pauca decerpsimus.' We have the Catena quotations; for—if the fragments extant for Eph 1 may be taken as a specimen of the whole—nearly three-fourths of the Catena Greek is represented by translation or paraphrase in Jerome's Latin. We have, lastly, the documents of the controversy between Jerome and Rufinus. Their mutual polemics centred round the allegation of Jerome's change of attitude towards Origen; and this in turn was argued out over the Ephesian commentary. In fact, in Jerome, *Ep.* lxxxiv. *ad Pammachium* [A.D. 400], § 2; Rufinus, *Apologia*, i. 22–43, ii. 2, 42; Jerome, *adv. Rufinum*, i. 16, 21–29, iii. 11, 13, we have a series of statements and replies which throw an interesting sidelight both on the writings of Origen and on the methods of Jerome. We must be careful to remember that it was Rufinus' cue to show that Jerome expressed or implied approval of all the matter he took over from Origen; just as it was Jerome's cue to show that he borrowed from other writers than Origen, that he often placed two divergent interpretations in simple juxtaposition, that in these cases he could not be supposed to be expressing agreement with both, and that therefore the same negative attitude on his part ought to be assumed even in cases where he gives the view of Origen only.

Jerome had claimed that his commentaries on Ecclesiastes and on the Epistle to the Ephesians would prove that he had always gone counter to the doctrines of Origen. Rufinus tests his allegation with reference to the Ephesian commentary, and adduces seventeen passages one after another as proving that Jerome, on several of the very points which he now charged against Origen and his followers as heresies, had used the words of Origen without in any way dissociating himself from them; indeed, while Origen had put forward his speculations cautiously and warily and with hesitation, his imitator had repeated them with curtness and decision 'as though the angel were speaking by Daniel, or Christ by St. Paul' (*Apol.* i. 43, ii. 42).

(*a*) *Unum esse corpus totius creaturæ rationabilis, id est angelorum et animarum.* Rufinus, *Apol.* i. 36–38, quotes from Jerome's comments on Eph $1^{22}$ $2^{15.\,17}$ (Vallarsi, vii. 568 C, 'potest ita responderi . . . purgasse perhibetur'; 569 D, 'non solum hominum . . . ecclesia intelligi potest'; 582 B, 'et hæc quidem iuxta vulgatam interpretationem . . . drachmis quæ salvæ fuerant copulaverit'; 582 D, 'quod autem ait, Ut duo conderet in semetipso . . . habitaturus est in novo mundo'): the Church includes angels and heavenly powers, and the Saviour's cross has cleansed them, and joined together things in earth and things in heaven, the near and the far, so that man will receive in the end the form of the angels.

(*b*) *De diabolo atque angelis refugis.* Rufinus, i. 34, quotes Jerome on Eph $2^{7}$ (vii. 576 A, 'quod nos qui quondam lege tenebamur . . . iuxta sedentium voluntatem incipient gubernari'): the rebellious principalities and powers will begin to be ruled according to the will of Christ and the saints who shall sit above them.

(*c*) *De animæ statu.* Rufinus, i. 25–30, 36, quotes Jerome on Eph $1^{4.\,5.\,11-12.\,17}$ (vii. 548 C, 'alius vero qui Deum iustum conatur ostendere . . . antequam humiliarer ego peccavi, et his similia'; 551 C, 'invadunt itaque in hoc loco occasionem . . . nisi causæ præcesserint quæ iustitiam Dei probent'; 558 C, 'si *speravimus* tantum dixisset *in Christo* et non præmisisset *ante* . . . benedicti sumus in cælestibus'; 563 C, 'quod vero ait *In agnitione eius* . . . et cetera his similia'): God's predestination of some to holiness—not to say also the inequality of human conditions—would conflict with God's justice, if we did not think of antecedent causes, known to God alone, which would supply the justification; and Scripture hints at a previous abode of the soul, which is contrasted with its present place of pilgrimage.

(*d*) *Quod animæ in corpore hoc vinctæ velut in carcere teneantur.* Rufinus, i. 37, 38, 40, quotes Jerome on Eph $2^{3.\,10}$ $3^{1}$ $6^{20}$ (vii. 573 B, 'nos vero dicimus . . . apposita sit ad malitiam'; 577 D, 'et diligenter observa quia . . . factura primum locum tenet, deinde plasmatio'; 587 B, 'quia in pluribus locis lectum est vinculum animæ corpus . . . per eum prædicatio compleatur'; 682 B, 'alius vero propter corpus humilitatis . . . spiritus Dei habitat in vobis'): the body of our humiliation, the body of death, fashioned later than the soul, is a 'chain' and 'prison' to the soul, and true knowledge is possible only to him who has put off his chain and been delivered from his prison.

With these passages may be combined the quotation in Rufinus, i. 22, from Jerome on Eph $5^{28.\,29}$ (vii. 659 A, 'foveamus igitur . . . quod nobis in cælestibus repromissum est'): women will become men, bodies will become souls, for we shall be like the angels.

(*e*) *De restitutione omnium.* Rufinus, i. 35, 39, 41, 42, quotes Jerome on Eph $1^{21}$ $2^{15-18}$ $4^{4.\,16}$ (vii. 566 C, 'si autem sunt principatus et potestates . . . et dominatione fiat'; 583 B, 'instaurationem novi hominis tunc plene perfecteque complendam . . . fiat voluntas tua sicut in cælo et in terra'; 608 E, 'quæritur quomodo una spes . . . et isti in nobis unum sint'; 618 C–620 A, 'in fine rerum cum Deum facie videre . . . in cælesti Jerusalem, quam in

* Both Jerome's commentary and Cramer's Catena are divided into 3 books; the former at Eph $3^{1}$ $4^{31}$, the latter at $2^{11}$ $4^{31}$. One or other of them is probably following Origen, whose Book iii. may therefore be fixed at $4^{31}$.

alio loco apostolus matrem sanctorum vocat'): not only in the present but in the future life there will be rising and falling, but in the end there will be a renewal of humanity, a restitution of all things, a perfect unity of all rational creation in common faith and common recognition of the Son of God, in the one hope of our calling, in the one body, in the perfect man.

(*f*) *Veritatem et perfectiorem doctrinam non esse omnibus publicandam.* Rufinus, ii. 2, quotes Jerome on Eph $4^{25}$ (vii. 627 E, 'propter quod Paulus ipse perfectus . . . in thalamum sponsi et penum regis inducat'): every man is to speak truth, but only to his neighbour—that is, to his neighbour in faith and virtue; to others he must shroud himself, as God does, in darkness and mystery.

It is not necessary to enter into the details of Jerome's answer to the individual charges. The controversy was so far simply *ad hominem* that Rufinus has to blame Jerome for Origenist statements which Rufinus, as an Origenizer, can hardly have considered seriously heretical; while Jerome has from time to time to make what defence he can for the Origenist colouring of a commentary written some ten years earlier, and certainly not reconcilable with the rigidity of his later views. What is valuable for the present purpose is simply Jerome's statement and defence of his methods as a translator and commentator.

'I,' writes Jerome,* 'in my commentaries, whether on the Ephesian epistle or elsewhere, have unfolded both my own opinion and that of others, making clear what is heretical and what is catholic. For this is the practice of commentators and of any one who has to explain things: they pursue their exposition through diverse theories, and set down the opinion of others as well as their own. And this is done not only by the interpreters of Holy Scripture, but by the commentators on secular literature, both Latin and Greek.' In the particular book under examination he had in the preface acknowledged obligations to three earlier commentators; but of these Origen differed from Apollinaris, Apollinaris from Didymus: if, then, he set down more than one opinion on the same passage, was he to be supposed to accept them both or all?† In two of the instances urged by Rufinus he had given three views anonymously, in simple juxtaposition: the first was in either case his own, the next that of Origen, the third that of Apollinaris.‡ Even if he had erred through modesty in not more definitely distinguishing his own from his predecessors' explanations, he could hardly be held responsible for all three at a time. In others of the inculpated passages he had not obscurely hinted at his own disagreement by such introductory phrases as 'alius qui conatur ostendere' and 'iuxta hæresim aliam,' or such summaries as 'quod ita intellectum et adversum eum facit.'§ But the one thing which, amid all the difficulties of translation, he had studiously set himself to avoid, was the habit, so dear to Rufinus, of doctoring Origen for Western readers. He himself either rendered the actual words,—*e.g.* 'ponamus tamen ipsa verba quæ in Origenis libro tertio continentur,'‖—or, where the exposition was a very lengthy one, reduced it to reasonable compass, yet without omitting anything either of the argument or of the illustrations.¶

To sum up: both the Paris Catena and the commentary of Jerome contain an amount of Origenian matter which must form no inconsiderable proportion of the whole of Origen's commentary on this epistle. Both, however, habitually abbreviate, so that, except in such rare cases as Jerome's *obiter dictum* in *c. Ruf.* i. 28, where, as was noted just above, he repeats from his commentary a passage of twenty-five lines (on Eph $5^{28.29}$) as a literal rendering from Origen, we can only then be sure of possessing the whole fulness of the original when our two authorities exactly agree. With regard to Jerome, there is of course the further question, how much of his matter to which parallels in the Catena are wanting can be ascribed to Origen. All the evidence we have tends to the conclusion that his own contributions and his requisitions on others of his predecessors put together do not equal his debt to Origen. The data of the controversy with Rufinus enable us happily to identify as taken from Origen a group of passages which, as they express with more than usual distinctness speculations afterwards accounted heretical, were of all the least likely to be preserved in a Catena.* Yet great as are Jerome's services in this matter of faithful representation, no one can compare the Greek and Latin where they run parallel without realizing how the very virtues of Jerome's writings—the limpid flow of words, the easy sequence, the direct straightforwardness of meaning—cause him to be, as perhaps every Latin translator must be, an inadequate interpreter of the more technical language of the great Greek theologian, of his more subtle thought, of his tentative and hesitating style, of his half-seen glimpses into mysteries that lie behind and beyond the letter.

(vi.) *Philippians.*

The list mentions a commentary in one book. Cramer's Catena on this epistle, as on the Galatians, is for the most part anonymous; but any extended use of Origen appears to be excluded by the colophon which names John (Chrysostom), Severian, and Theodore as its sources. The Athos MS contains two interesting *marginalia*: at the end of ch. 3 it notes *ἕως ὧδε ἡ ἐξήγησις*—*i.e.* Origen's commentary did not extend to the 4th chapter, which is personal rather than doctrinal; at $3^{14}$ *εἰς τὸ βραβεῖον τῆς ἄνω κλήσεως τοῦ θεοῦ* it records that 'in expounding these words he adds that some copies read *ἀνεγκλησίας τοῦ θεοῦ*'; and, as in another part of the same note it mis-writes this variant as *ἀνενέγκαι θυσίας τοῦ θεοῦ*, it would appear that here (as in the Ephesians) a note has been taken over from the 'ancient copy,' whose faded uncial writing has again given rise to error.

(vii.) *Colossians.*

The list mentions a commentary in 2 books; but we ought to read 'iii' for 'ii,' since the Athos MS marks not only *τόμος β′* at $2^{17}$, but *τόμος γ′* at $3^{16}$. The same MS notes at $4^{12}$ that the third tome ended there, the last words expounded being *ἵνα σταθῆτε τέλειοι*: so that in this, as in the previous epistle, the purely personal matter was left without comment by Origen. Of the contents of the exposition we only learn from the MS, that, in dealing with the words in $4^{11}$ *οἱ ὄντες ἐκ περιτομῆς*, 'he' (*αὐτός*, 'the master') 'developed wondrously the theme of the different senses of circumcision in the Scripture.' The only other extant

* *contra Rufinum*, iii. 11.

† *Ib.* iii. 13.

‡ *Ib.* i. 24, 25.

§ *Ib.* i. 22, 26.

‖ *Ib.* i. 28 = Vallarsi, vii. 658 D–659 A: 'dicamus illam carnem . . . in cælestibus repromissum est.' It is interesting to note that this commentary on Eph $5^{28.29}$ is absent from Cramer's Catena; the catenist avoids just what Jerome found interesting.

¶ *Ib.* i. 22: 'latissimam Origenis disputationem brevi sermone comprehenderim . . . nihil ab eo dictum prætermiserim . . . posui ergo omnia, licet brevius, quæ in græco reperi'; i. 26, 'latissimam Origenis expositionem, et eosdem sensus per diversa verba volventem, brevi sermone constrinximus, nihil exemplis et assertionibus illius auferentes.'

* Of all the passages alleged by Rufinus and catalogued above, only one, and that perhaps the shortest and least important, is preserved in full in the Catena (Jerome, 573 B = Cramer, p. 137). In one other case, the note on *ἐπίγνωσις* (563 C = Cramer, p. 130), part of the passage occurs in the Catena, but without the definite allusion to the pre-existence of souls. (The pages of Cramer are marked in Mr. Gregg's edition in *JThSt*).

reference to this commentary is in Rufinus' translation of Pamphilus' *Apologia pro Origene* (de la Rue, iv., App. p. 37), under the head 'Responsio ad quintam criminationem. Quod unus est Christus filius Dei:- In tertio libro epistolæ ad Colossenses.' But the passage which follows under this title is an explanation of Gal $3^{19}$ *διαταγεὶς δι' ἀγγέλων ἐν χειρὶ μεσίτου*; and it is impossible not to suspect that we should rather read 'in the third book of the epistle to the Galatians.' Cramer's Catena offers no help; its sources are again Chrysostom, Severian, and Theodore of Mopsuestia.

(viii.) *1 Thessalonians.*

The list gives a commentary in 3 books and 2 homilies. Both Origen himself and Jerome refer to the commentary. Origen, *contra Celsum* [A.D. 249], ii. 65, after quoting 1 Th $4^{13-15}$, adds: *τὴν δὲ φανεῖσαν ἡμῖν εἰς τοὺς τόπους διήγησιν ἐξεθέμεθα ἐν οἷς ὑπηγορεύσαμεν ἐξηγητικοῖς τῆς πρὸς Θεσσαλονικεῖς προτέρας ἐπιστολῆς* (de la Rue, i. 437); Jerome, *Ep.* cxix. *ad Minervium et Alexandrum*, 9 [A.D. 406: Vallarsi, i. 803], introduces a long comment of Origen's on 1 Th $4^{15-17}$, extending over nearly two columns, with the words 'Origenes in tertio volumine *ἐξηγητικῶν* epistolæ Pauli ad Thessalonicenses primæ, post multa quæ vario prudentique sermone disseruit, hæc intulit.' This is the only known quotation; the Athos MS has preserved no Origen *marginalia* on the epistle; but Cramer's Catena, as on the Galatians, is mostly anonymous, and may conceal Origen matter.

(ix.) *2 Thessalonians.*

The list—not in the older form, repeated by Preuschen-Harnack, but as printed from further MSS by E. Klostermann in the Berlin *Sitzungsberichte der k. preussischen Akad. der Wissenschaften*, 1897, p. 855—names a commentary in one book. The Athos MS several times refers to the 'exposition'—in three cases, $2^{14.17}$ $3^{10}$, for the readings it implies, on $2^{16}$ as establishing Origen's orthodoxy, *ἐξηγούμενος τοῦτο τὸ ῥητὸν σαφῶς μίαν τῆς Τριάδος λέγει ἐνέργειαν*. Nothing is otherwise known of it.

(x.) *Philemon.*

The list mentions a commentary in one book: but Greek authority almost wholly fails us. The Athos MS only notes on v.$^{12}$ that 'he too does not mention the word *προσλαβοῦ*'—presumably in his commentary. Cramer's Catena is again drawn from Chrysostom, Severian, and Theodore of Mopsuestia. Latin writers, however, again to some extent supply the defect. ($\alpha$) Rufinus-Pamphilus, *Apologia pro Origene* (de la Rue, iv., App. p. 38), 'Responsio ad sextam criminationem. Quod ea quæ in scripturis referuntur etiam secundum litteram gesta sint,' cites under the heading 'de epistola Pauli apostoli ad Philemonem' a passage taken from the comment on v.$^{5}$, concerning faith in the Lord Jesus and 'in all the saints,' which Origen interprets as meaning belief in the Old Testament histories. ($\beta$) Rufinus, *Apologia*, i. 40 (Vallarsi, ii. 625), quotes as Origen's an allegorical interpretation of v.$^{23}$ 'Epaphras my fellow-captive,' 'quod capti pariter et vincti in vallem hanc deducti sunt lacrimarum.' The passage quoted comes from Jerome's commentary on Philemon (Vallarsi, vii. 763), and strengthens the conclusion that Jerome in this, as in his other expository labours on St. Paul, wrote with the commentaries of Origen before him. It is true that in the preface to this particular commentary, unlike those to the Galatian and Ephesian epistles, he makes no mention of the debt due to his predecessors. But this may have been either because it seemed unnecessary to repeat information he was giving in the more or less contemporary commentaries on the two longer epistles, or perhaps because in the case of the Epistle to Philemon, which had so often been either rejected or passed over, he had had fewer predecessors, and so there was not the same need as elsewhere to distinguish the different writers to whom he lay under obligation. But that at least he made extensive use of Origen all the indications converge to show. The comment on v.$^{5}$, translated in Rufinus-Pamphilus, occurs in an independent and abbreviated version also in Jerome (vii. 752).

(xi.) *Titus.*

There is no evidence to show that Origen wrote anything on either of the epistles to Timothy, but for the epistle to Titus the list names a commentary in one book, and also a single homily. Of the latter nothing is known. For the former we have one reference in a Greek writer, several quotations in Rufinus-Pamphilus, and St. Jerome's commentary. ($\alpha$) In an interesting little 6th cent. tract of questions put to a Palestinian abbot, Barsanuphius (Gallandi, xi. 592; Migne, *Patr. Gr.* 86, c. 891), the questioner — the whole interest lies rather in the questions than in the answers—mentions having found the doctrine of the pre-existence of souls in Origen, Didymus, and Evagrius; and yet Origen himself asserts *ἐν τῷ αὐτοῦ ἐξηγητικῷ τῆς πρὸς Τίτον ἐπιστολῆς μὴ εἶναι τῶν ἀποστόλων μηδὲ τῆς ἐκκλησίας παράδοσιν τὸ πρεσβυτέραν εἶναι τὴν ψυχὴν τῆς τοῦ σώματος κατασκευῆς, ὡς αἱρετικὸν χαρακτηρίζων τὸν ταῦτα λέγοντα.* The assertion would be a strange one in the mouth of Origen. The explanation, as will appear in a moment, lies in the form of the passage alluded to, which is happily preserved in Rufinus. ($\beta$) Rufinus-Pamphilus, *Apologia pro Origene*, c. i. (de la Rue, iv., App. 21–23), quotes three passages (which are connected together by the phrases, 'post hæc paucis quibusdam per medium insertis adiecit' and 'post pauca addidit hæc') 'ex eo libro quem in epistolam Pauli apostoli ad Titum scripsit,' on the passage 'a man that is an heretic' (Tit $3^{10}$). The whole contains a valuable catalogue of the opinions which to Origen seemed to deserve the name of heresy. Again in c. ix. (*ib.* 43), 'Responsio ad octavam criminationem. De anima,' two further brief quotations are given from the same context, where Origen raises the question whether those who treat on matters not contained in the Rule of the Church —such as the origin of souls—ought to be treated as heretics, even if their opinion seems new and strange. It is clear that this is the passage referred to by the monastic questioner of Barsanuphius, and clear, too, that Origen, though his indirect manner of approaching the point may have deceived the monk, is really urging that, between what is of faith and what is heresy, there is a middle ground of debatable matter on such subjects as the pre-existence of souls. ($\gamma$) With regard to the relation of Jerome's commentary on this epistle to Origen's, what was said of the Epistle to Philemon holds here. Here, too, the long comment on Tit $3^{10}$, quoted by Rufinus from Origen, has been reproduced by Jerome; but on this occasion in a form so abbreviated as to deprive it of all its interest (Vallarsi, vii. 736).

In accordance with the plan of this article, the Epistle to the Hebrews is not separately dealt with: but those who wish for further details may refer to Preuschen-Harnack, p. 376.

**[Dionysius of Alexandria].**—The impulse to Biblical studies given by the teaching and example of Origen showed itself long after his death in the schools of Alexandria and Cæsarea. The next three writers to be mentioned were all noted Origenists. St. Dionysius the Great of Alexandria—head of the catechetical school, perhaps from A.D. 233, and afterwards, A.D. 247–265, bishop—is hardly represented at all in extant documents except by fragments of his numerous letters. But if, like his contemporary St. Cyprian, his primary importance lay in the influence which by means of his correspondence he exercised in the current ecclesiastical affairs both of his own province and of the Church at large, yet, like Cyprian, his literary activity was in no sense confined to this single channel. As a commentator he is known to have written on the Book of Ecclesiastes: but the case for regarding him as an expositor of particular books of the New Testament rests in several instances on single quotations, which (even if correctly ascribed to him rather than to some other Dionysius) may have come from other sources than a formal commentary or series of homilies. For the Pauline epistles the evidence seems somewhat stronger at first sight, seeing that Jerome, *Ep.* xlix. 3, includes him in the list of those who had interpreted 'very fully' the First Epistle to the Corinthians. Yet 'latissime' is certainly meant to apply to the half-dozen authors enumerated taken together, rather than to each individual; and even though there is no suggestion in Jerome's language of any limitation to the particular portion of the epistle (the 7th chapter) in reference to which their names are cited, it must not be overlooked that, of the six commentators named here, only two recur in the parallel list for 1 Co $15^{51}$ given in *Ep.* cxix. Is there, then, any trace elsewhere of Dionysius' work as a commentator on St. Paul? For if this allusion in Jerome stands quite alone, it will easily admit of a less stringent interpretation: a discussion on marriage, with express treatment of St. Paul's language on the subject, might easily have had a place in one of the lost letters. If, on the other hand, there are independent grounds for including Dionysius among the early commentators on any other epistle, the case for taking Jerome's statement literally will be immensely strengthened. And such evidence appears to be offered in the statement—quoted by Harnack, *Altchr. Litt.* i. 423, from Christopher Wolf, *Anecdota Græca*, iv. (Hamburg, 1724) p. 62—that Dionysius of Alexandria was largely used in a Catena on the Romans: 'illius mentio frequens est in Catena MS in epist. ad Romanos, quam B. Reiserus memorat in Catalogo MSS, p. 9.' The reference is to Antonius Reiser, *Index manuscriptorum bibliothecæ Augustanæ* (A.D. 1675), 'Cod. 23: Catena in epistolam D. Pauli ad Romanos viginti et quinque patrum græcorum, videlicet Acacii, Athanasii, Basilii Magni, Cæsarii, Chrysostomi, Clementis, Cyrilli, Damasceni, Didymi, Diodori, Carterii,* Dionysii Alexandrini, Dionysii Areopagitæ, Euthalii, Gennadii, Gregorii Theologi, Isidori, Maximi, Methodii, Nysseni, Oecumenii, Origenis, Photii, Severiani, Theodoreti, Theophili.' The Augsburg MSS passed during the course of the 18th cent. into the library of Munich, and the same MS is catalogued as græc. 412 in Ignatius Hardt, *Catalogus codicum manuscriptorum bibliothecæ regiæ Bavaricæ*, iv. (Munich, 1810) p. 269. Hardt notes that Reiser was in error in including the names of Athanasius and Carterius, and in omitting those of Theodore of Mopsuestia and of Apollinaris. It will be noted that neither catalogue says anything of a 'frequent' mention of Dionysius, or for that matter of any other writer; and in fact the Catena is nothing more nor less than the second of those printed by Cramer. Dionysius of Alexandria is there mentioned once only, and the quotation is one of exactly nine words: τὸ δὲ Πᾶς Ἰσραὴλ ἀντὶ τοῦ Οἱ πλειόνες κεῖται (p. 418; Ro $11^{26}$). The positive evidence is therefore reduced again to Jerome, and Jerome's words do not justify us in regarding Dionysius as a formal commentator on St. Paul.

**[Pierius].**—Another head of the catechetical school of Alexandria, towards the end of the 3rd cent., was Pierius. The evidence for connecting him with the study of St. Paul is again Jerome's list of commentators on 1 Co 7,—with this distinction, that Pierius' words are actually cited (*Ep.* xlix. 3; Vallarsi, i. 233): 'Pierius, cum sensum Apostoli ventilaret atque edisseret, et proposuisset illud exponere *Volo autem omnes esse sicut meipsum* [1 Co $7^{7}$], adiecit ταῦτα λέγων ὁ Παῦλος ἀντικρὺς ἀγαμίαν κηρύσσει.' As in the case of Dionysius, so in that of Pierius, there is no other evidence for a Pauline commentary than this reference in Jerome; Jerome's second list on 1 Co $15^{51}$ omits his name also; and since we have independent grounds for knowing (1) that Pierius commented at length on the opening of the Book of Hosea; (2) that the comment in question took the form of a homily or homilies at Easter, *i.e.* during the Easter eve vigil; (3) that in the first of his 'Paschal treatises' (ἐν τῷ πρώτῳ τῶν εἰς τὸ πάσχα) he strongly asserted that St. Paul had had a wife, but separated from her and dedicated her to God in the Church (Jerome, *de Vir. Ill.* 76; Philip of Side, fragments; Photius, cod. 119),—Harnack concludes, not without reason, that St. Jerome's citation is taken from this same treatise on the opening of Hosea, a passage which would offer an obvious opportunity for reference to 1 Co 7.

**[Eusebius of Cæsarea].**—From Alexandria we pass to the second centre of the influence of Origen—the school and church of Palestinian Cæsarea. Among the extraordinarily diverse writings of its bishop Eusebius (*c.* 270–340 A.D.) were certainly included commentaries, and those not exclusively on the Old Testament. But once more the evidence for ranking him with the expositors of St. Paul rests on the first of Jerome's two lists for the 1st Corinthian epistle, supported this time by a single quotation in Cramer's Catena (pp. 75, 477; 1 Co $4^{4.5}$). That, somewhere in the vast array of the works of Eusebius, Jerome should have found a discussion of 1 Co 7, and the catenist an explanation of a single passage in another chapter, seems much more probable than that a commentary by so well-known a writer should have left no other trace behind. If conjecture may be allowed, it would seem not unlikely that, as Pierius appears to have treated of 1 Co 7 in connexion with the Book of Hosea, and as Jerome in the preface to his commentary on Hosea places in immediate juxtaposition with the homily of Pierius a discussion by Eusebius in the (lost) 18th book of the *Demonstratio Evangelica*, the latter was also the occasion of Eusebius' exposition of the marriage teaching of St. Paul.

**6. Theodore of Heraclea** (commentaries on all the Epistles?)—

The results in the case of Dionysius, Pierius, and Eusebius have been almost wholly negative. Nothing more has been established than that somewhere or other in their writings they found occasion to expound one or two passages from 'the Apostle.' Of continuous commentaries or homilies, even on a single epistle, there is no real trace. But for Theodore, bishop of Heraclea-Perinthus in Thrace (from before 341 till between 355 and 358), the evidence is conclusive that, however little can be recovered of his work, he did publish commentaries on several, probably on all, of St. Paul's epistles. In Theodore we first come in contact with the great school of Antiochene interpreters. He is said to have been a pupil of the

* Carterius was the colleague of Diodore in the school of theology which Chrysostom and Theodore of Mopsuestia attended: as he is not known to have written any exegetical works, and as, further, his name occurs in Reiser's list out of its alphabetical order, it is tempting to take Carterii as a genitive depending on 'Diodori,' so that Diodorus Carterii would be parallel to Eusebius Pamphili.

first founder of that school, Lucian the martyr; and all that we know of his method shows that he worked on Antiochene rather than on Alexandrine lines. No interpreter of St. Paul in the first half of the 4th cent. could in his matter be wholly independent of Origen; but in his clear and literalist style of comment Theodore was not the follower of Origen so much as the predecessor of Chrysostom and Theodoret.

Theodore was perhaps the first commentator whose work was devoted mainly to the New Testament. Jerome (*de Vir. Ill.* 90) tells us that under the emperor Constantius he published commentaries on St. Matthew and St. John and on 'the Apostle,' distinguished by historical feeling and by clearness and elegance of style. Theodoret (*HE* ii. 3) speaks of his 'remarkable learning' and of his 'interpretation of the Divine Gospels' in immediate connexion with, and apparently as accounting for, his influence over the emperor. Yet, in spite of these testimonies to his importance, no single fragment of his work on St. Paul appears to have come down to us in the original. His merits as an expositor were unable to weigh down the balance against his faults as a theologian. Though he belonged to the more moderate section of the party, he was undoubtedly an Arian; and the whole of the Arian literature of the 4th cent. has perished, with such minute exceptions, that it requires some effort both of will and of imagination to reconstruct the vast stores of learning in chronicle, history, and commentary, which shared the fate of more strictly dogmatic writings.

The epistles on which we know for certain from St. Jerome's references that Theodore commented are 1 Thessalonians (*Ep.* cxix. § 8: Vallarsi, i. 802), 1 Corinthians (*ib.* § 2: i. 794), and Galatians (*Præf. ad Comm.*: vii. 369). For the latter epistle the reference is general; with regard to 1 Th $4^{15-17}$ we are told that Theodore's view agreed with that of Diodore, which is given at length (see below under No. **12**); only in the third case—on 1 Co $15^{51-53}$—are we given an actual version of an exposition contained in Theodore's 'commentarioli.' The diminutive form implies (what the Catena fragments on the Gospels amply bear out) that Theodore's comments were brief and succinct. The passage translated is for the most part a paraphrase, in clear and straightforward language, of the text, helped out by the parallel verses in 1 Th 4. It is to be noted that Theodore gives the Syrian reading, 'omnes quidem non dormiemus, omnes autem immutabimur,' without notice of any variant; from which it may perhaps be concluded that he was not interested in textual questions.

**7. Eusebius of Emesa** (on the Galatians).—Born at Edessa, Eusebius studied in succession at the chief centres of Christian learning in the East—at Edessa, at Cæsarea, at Alexandria, and at Antioch. But it was with Antioch, and with its successive Arian bishops, that his connexion was specially close. It was from Antioch that he was sent to the bishopric of Emesa or Hemesa in Syria, which he occupied till his death; and it was at Antioch that he was buried. The years of his episcopate roughly coincided with Theodore's: he did not become bishop till after 339, and he died under Constantius, *i.e.* not later than 360. Like Theodore, he was a leader of the Arian party, and like him a trusted adviser of the Arian emperor. Like Theodore, again, whom he immediately follows in Jerome's list of 'illustrious men' (*de Vir. Ill.* 91), he wrote largely on the New Testament—'ad Galatas libri decem, et in Evangelia homiliæ breves sed plurimæ'—with the same historical method, and with similar elegance of style.*

* Jerome speaks of his 'eloquence' again in contrasting him with Diodore of Tarsus (*de Vir. Ill.* 119).

Eusebius, however, was the more popular and rhetorical, and, if we may judge from the 'ten books' which he devoted to one of St. Paul's shorter epistles, the more diffuse writer of the two.

Jerome names Eusebius again in the preface to his commentary on Galatians (vii. 369), but nowhere quotes from him by name. Cramer's Catena on the Galatians—in other words, MS Paris coislin 204—includes a few, for the most part very brief, citations: on Gal $1^{1.2.4.11}$ $2^{9.18.20}$ $3^{23}$ $4^{4-7.12.14.20}$ $6^{13}$. Two points are noticeable about these fragments. In the first place, the predicate 'of Emesa' is found only on two occasions out of thirteen, though there does not seem any real reason to doubt that Cramer is right in attributing all Eusebius references to Eusebius of Emesa. In the second place, nine quotations out of the thirteen are introduced anonymously in the text with the phrase ἄλλος (ἕτερος) φησίν, the name Eusebius being supplied in the margin: but again there is no ground for doubting the correctness of the information. The annotator shows first-hand knowledge of particular interpretations of Eusebius on pp. 31, 90; and the only question is whether some of the anonymous quotations which have no marginal ascription of authorship may not likewise belong to our Eusebius.

That the catenist should have so far relaxed the rigidity of Greek orthodoxy as to make even this tentative and semi-anonymous use of an Arian commentator, is perhaps another indication of his early date: see above, p. 488[a].

**8. Asterius the Arian** (on the Romans).—The literary activity of this celebrated Arian philosopher, theologian, and exegete—of whom the *Dictionary of Christian Biography* contains no mention—is placed by Jerome (*de Vir. Ill.* 94) within the limits of the reign of Constantius;* but his history goes back to the great persecution, and he was a personal disciple of Lucian's. A Cappadocian by birth, an Antiochene by training, he was one of those to whom the Arian movement in its earliest stages owed most. No one did more than Asterius the layman to give it its philosophical basis, its theological terminology, and its literary expression. In the field of exegesis Jerome records that his labours included commentaries on the Epistle to the Romans and on the Gospels: but he tells us nothing about these books which would involve a first-hand acquaintance with them; and what he does say, namely, that they were assiduously studied in Arian circles, when taken in connexion with the complete absence of citations from them in the Catenæ, perhaps suggests that the Arian animus was more marked in his exegesis than in that of Theodore of Heraclea and Eusebius of Emesa.

**[Athanasius, Basil of Cæsarea, Gregory of Nazianzus, Gregory of Nyssa].**—That citations from the great Fathers of the 4th cent., whose writings served as the authoritative standard of Greek dogmatic theology, should be found scattered here and there throughout the Catenæ, is only what we should expect. The references to Athanasius, indeed, in Cramer's four volumes on the Pauline epistles amount—excluding, here as elsewhere, the Epistle to the Hebrews—to no more than two. Those to Basil, outside the Roman epistle, are also only two: for the Roman epistle they are fairly numerous. The few quotations

* If Asterius of Scythopolis, philosopher and commentator on the Psalms (Jerome, *Epp.* lxx. 4, cxii. 20: Vallarsi, i. 427, 747), were identical with our Asterius the Arian, also a philosopher and also a commentator on the Psalms (Jerome, *de Vir. Ill.* 94), we should have a further proof that Jerome placed him after Eusebius of Cæsarea and Theodore of Heraclea. But, even if the identification were more probable than it is, Jerome's chronology is not infallible.

from Gregory Nazianzen occur also mainly, those from Gregory of Nyssa exclusively, in the Catena on the same epistle. It will be remembered that Cramer's sources are for the Roman epistle a Bodleian Catena and a Munich Catena (see above, p. 487[a]): for each of the Corinthian epistles a separate Paris MS: for the other ten epistles a continuous Catena in a single Paris MS, coislin 204. Of these, the second or Munich Catena on the Romans ($7^{7}$-end) is responsible for all but nine of the whole number of quotations from these four Fathers on the Pauline epistles: and this fact alone is enough to create some presumption that none of them had written on any of the other epistles, since commentaries of such distinguished authorship could hardly have escaped the notice of a catenist; and even a commentary on the Romans, had there been such a one, must have played its part in the Bodleian as well as in the Munich Catena. Further, many of the citations from these particular Fathers are introduced not only with the name of their author, but of the book from which they are taken. Thus for Athanasius: 1 Co 7 (Cramer, *in Epp. ad Cor.* 478 * = Benedictine edition, ii. 1272 = Migne, *Patr. Gr.* 27 c. 1403), *τοῦ ἁγίου Ἀθανασίου ἐν τῷ Περὶ τοῦ σεμνοῦ γάμου*. For Basil: in the Munich Catena on Romans, *ἐκ τῶν Ἀσκητικῶν* (eight passages), *ἐκ τῶν Ἀντιρρητικῶν* (three), *ἐκ τοῦ Ὅτι οὐκ ἔστιν αἴτιος τῶν κακῶν ὁ Θεός* (two), *ἐκ τοῦ Εἰς τὸν λβ′, εἰς τὸν λγ′, εἰς τὸν μδ′, ψαλμόν* (one each), *ἐκ τοῦ Περὶ εὐχαριστίας λόγου* (one): on Col $1^{15}$ *ἐν τοῖς κατ' Εὐνομίου λόγοις* (two). For Gregory Naz.: Munich Catena on Romans, *ἐκ τοῦ Ἡττημένου* (one), *ἐκ τοῦ Περὶ υἱοῦ β′ λόγου* (one), *ἐκ τῶν Περὶ φιλοπτωχίας* (two): on Col $1^{15}$ *ἐν τῷ Περὶ υἱοῦ δευτέρῳ λόγῳ*: on Eph $1^{17}$ *ἐν τῷ Περὶ υἱοῦ λόγῳ*. For Gregory Nyssen: Munich Catena on Romans, *ἐκ τοῦ κατὰ Εὐνομίου β′ λόγου, ἐν τῷ τέλει τοῦ κατὰ Εὐνομίου ἑβδόμου λόγου*. Such passages as still remain unaccounted for show themselves on examination to be derived from sources still extant: thus the rest of the Basil quotations in the Munich Catena on Romans can mostly be traced to the *adversus Eunomium* and the apparently spurious *Homilia de Spiritu sancto*. Of Catenæ other than Cramer's, Karo and Lietzmann's lists (see pp. 488–489, above, *a* and *g*) show an occasional use, but no more, of the great dogmatic writers. Thus Oecumenius gives one quotation from Athanasius, three from Basil (one of them *ἐκ τῆς Πρὸς Σωζοπολίτας ἐπιστολῆς*), one from Gregory Nazianzen *εἰς τὸν β′ Περὶ υἱοῦ λόγον*, two from Gregory Nyssen. The Vienna Catena on Romans has none from Athanasius, but four from each of the Gregorys, and nearly 20 from Basil, the sources being generally given in the case of Basil and Gregory Nyssen. Thus for Basil: *Ἀσκητικῶν* (five passages), *Ἑξαημέρου, Εἰς τὸν λγ′ ψαλμόν, Εἰς τὸ Πάτερ ἡμῶν, Περὶ φθόνου, Ὅτι οὐκ ἔστιν αἴτιος κακῶν ὁ Θεός, ἐν τῷ Πρὸς Ἀμφιλόχιον κε′, Εἰς τὸ μαρτύριον Ἰουλίττας, ἐν λακιζ* (?) *ὁμιλ.* (all one each); for Greg. Nyss. *Εἰς τὸ Πάτερ ἡμῶν β′ ὁμιλίας* and *πρὸς Εὐνόμιον λο*. Some of these references are probably identical with references noted above from Cramer: in any case the general result is the same. There is no reason whatever to suppose that any of these Fathers wrote a commentary on any part of St. Paul.†

**9. Didymus of Alexandria** (commentaries on 1 and 2 Corinthians, Galatians, Ephesians).—

By far the most striking figure among the heads of the catechetical school of Alexandria in the 4th cent. is the blind presbyter Didymus. Born about the end of the first decade of the century, he became head of the school under Athanasius, was still living when Jerome wrote his catalogue of 'illustrious men' in 392, and only died, according to the *Lausiac History* of Palladius, about the year 399. In spite of total loss of sight in early childhood, he mastered all the secular and sacred science of the time, and poured out the wealth of his knowledge, 'night and day,' for the benefit of visitors and correspondents, among whom were numbered Antony, Jerome and Rufinus, Palladius and Isidore. His special strength lay in the exegesis of Holy Scripture. It was with the object of learning his views on points of doubt ranging over the whole Bible that Jerome visited him in 386. Palladius tells us that he dictated explanations of the whole of Scripture. Jerome, *de Vir. Ill.* 109, after enumerating some ten works, nearly all of them exegetical, adds that there were countless others, 'quæ digerere proprii indicis est'; and, in fact, besides the commentaries there mentioned on St. Matthew and St. John, we know from Cassiodorus that he wrote on the Catholic epistles, and from Jerome himself that he commented on the 1st Corinthian, Galatian, and Ephesian epistles (*Epp.* xlix. 3, cxix. 2 [Vallarsi, i. 233, 794], *Præf. ad Comm. in Gal.* [*ib.* vii. 369], *Præf. ad Comm. in Eph.* [*ib.* vii. 543]). The volumes of Cramer's Catena on the Pauline epistles contain only a single citation from Didymus, on Ro $7^{20}$. But Mai in his *Nova Patrum Bibliotheca*, iv. (1847) part 3, 115–146, published from a Vatican Catena * more than fifty excerpts upon 2 Corinthians: many of these are of considerable length, and at several places they form so continuous an exposition that there can be no doubt whatever they were taken from a commentary.† Thus the question naturally arises whether the commentaries on these four epistles were independent of one another, like Origen's, or were parts of a complete and homogeneous Pauline commentary. It is not in itself decisive that Jerome speaks of the *commentarioli* of Didymus on the Ephesian epistle,‡ while he includes him among those who had interpreted 'latissime' the First Epistle to Corinth. Yet neither the long explanation which Jerome translates from Didymus on 1 Co $15^{51-53}$ (*Ep.* cxix. 5: i. 795 D–798 A), nor yet the Mai fragments on 2 Corinthians, seem quite to suit the diminutive applied to the commentary on Ephesians. And since Didymus was in almost all respects a close follower of Origen,—with regard to his exegesis Jerome mentions this expressly in introducing the fragment on 1 Cor., 'non pedibus sed verbis in Origenis transiens sententiam,'—the evidence as a whole appears to be best satisfied if we suppose that he also imitated Origen in treating the different epistles separately and not always on a uniform scale. In that case there will be no reason left for postulating lost commentaries by this author on the remaining nine epistles. He may easily have written on more than the four of which we have definite information, but it is not necessary to suppose that he wrote on all; and which of the others, if any, he expounded besides 1 and 2 Cor., Gal., and Eph., we shall be able to

* Cramer gives only the introductory words; the Benedictines give a passage of some ten lines.

† A tract by Gregory of Nyssa on 1 Co $15^{28}$ 'Then shall the Son also himself . . .,' is printed in vol. i. pp. 838–853 of the Paris 1615 edition. Its genuineness has been contested, perhaps without reason.

* Cardinal Mai gave no sort of indication of the number of the MS: but (*a*) he noted the folio on which each Didymus citation is found—the first is on fol. 340, the last on fol. 411; (*b*) he mentioned that he had already printed some Cyril of Alexandria from the same MS. It is, in fact, the already often cited MS, Vat. gr. 762.

† The verses at which the different excerpts begin are as follows: 2 Co $1^{1. 2. 3. 6. 7. 11. 12. 13. 15. 23}$ $2^{3. 10. 12. 15. 17}$ $3^{1. 4. 7. 17}$ $4^{4. 5. 7. 8. 11. 13}$ $5^{1. 2. 13. 14. 16. 17. 21}$ $6^{3. 7. 10. 11. 14}$ $7^{2. 6. 12. 13}$ $8^{13. 20. 22}$ $10^{1. 3. 17}$ $11^{1. 7. 12. 13. 21}$ $12^{2. 7. 19}$ $13^{11}$.

‡ In the case of the Galatian epistle the MSS of Jerome (*Præf. ad Comm. in Gal.*: Vallarsi, vii. 369) appear to vary between 'commentarii' and 'commentarioli.'

say only if further and fuller knowledge comes to our assistance.*

**10. Apollinaris (or Apollinarius) † the younger of Laodicea** (commentaries on all the Epistles?).—

The problem in the case of Apollinaris is not unlike that for Didymus, but the balance of evidence inclines perhaps the other way. It is certain that he commented on five of the Pauline epistles, and it seems likely that he commented on all. St. Jerome mentions him among those who interpreted 'latissime' the 1st Epistle to the Corinthians, and among the authors of 'commentarii' or 'commentarioli' on the Galatian and Ephesian epistles. On 1 Co $15^{51}$ he notes that Apollinaris' exposition agreed in substance though not in language with that of Theodore of Heraclea, and on 1 Th $4^{15}$ that Theodore, Apollinaris, and Diodore all adopted the same interpretation (Vallarsi, i. 233, 795, 802; vii. 369, 543). Thus on every epistle where Jerome has occasion to refer to older commentators, he includes Apollinaris among them; while in the *de Viris Illustribus*, 104, he speaks of him as 'in sanctas scripturas innumerabilia scribens volumina.' The Catenæ enable us to add yet another epistle; for Cramer's Bodleian Catena on the Romans contains 36 citations from Apollinaris, of which 21 belong to the first two chapters, and are therefore sufficiently numerous to imply a continuous exposition. It would not then appear to be rash to suppose that Apollinaris, like the writers of the school of Antioch with which he stood geographically in such close contact, commented on the whole of St. Paul. That the Catenæ for most of the Epistles do not quote from him is sufficiently accounted for by his equivocal reputation as a theologian. Apollinarianism was the special *bête noire* of the 5th cent. Antiochenes, and Apollinaris was so far in a worse position than either Origen or Theodore of Mopsuestia, as he may be said to have died out of communion with the Church, though apparently still in possession of his bishopric. That Jerome on the other hand, in spite of his heresy, used him extensively and spoke of him with respect,—he calls him nothing worse than 'the Laodicene who lately left the Church,'—is due partly to his admiration for a man who had been a powerful champion of Catholic Christianity against Arianism and paganism, partly also to the loyalty he always retained (and it is one of the most pleasing features of Jerome's character) for his old teachers.‡ Of the residuum of Jerome's commentary on the Ephesians, after the Origen matter has been subtracted, much certainly came from Apollinaris. In the cases which he discusses in detail (cf. p. $495^{a}$, above), wherever he had given three interpretations, the first was his own, the second that of Origen, the third that of Apollinaris. And though the amount which can at the present stage of our knowledge be definitely recovered out of St. Jerome's writings for Apollinaris is small,§ yet Jerome's evidence is singularly clear in respect to his general character and relationships as an exegete. On the Ephesians Apollinaris habitually differed, according to Jerome's express statement (p. $495^{a}$, above), from Origen on the one side, as on the other from Didymus; while in his exposition of the two passages from the Corinthian and Thessalonian epistles, discussed by Jerome in *Ep.* cxix., he agreed with Theodore of Heraclea against Origen and Didymus in the one case, in the other with Diodore and with Theodore again against Origen. His exegetical position was therefore influenced more by his geographical connexion with the city of Antioch than by his opposition to the teaching of its school in the sphere of theology. Among Antiochene expositors there is no one whose loss, if we may judge by the fragments that remain, we have more reason to deplore. The Catena quotations on St. Matthew's Gospel are often very striking, and betray a singularly original and independent mind. Of the few on St. Paul, that on Ro $1^{1}$ in Cramer may serve as an example: *κεχωρισμένος καὶ* ἀφωρισμένος εἰς *τὸν εὐαγγελισμόν, ὡς ὁ νόμος ἀφόρισμα καὶ ἀφαίρεμα λέγει τὸ χωριζόμενον τῶν θυμάτων θεῷ καὶ ἱερεῦσιν.*

**11. Eunomius the Anomœan** (commentary on Romans).—

Eunomius, disciple of Aetius, and his successor in the leadership of the Anomœan or extreme Arian party, was believed by Jerome, when he was writing his 'Catalogue of Illustrious Men' in 392, to be still alive (ch. 120), but is last heard of in history some years before that date. A prolific writer on theological questions, he drew forth answers from the principal theologians of his day—Apollinaris, Didymus, Basil of Cæsarea, Gregory of Nazianzus, and Gregory of Nyssa. His contribution to exegesis was a commentary in seven tomes on the Epistle to the Romans, known to us only through the criticism of Socrates (*HE* iv. 7), who speaks of him as 'ignorant of the Holy Scriptures, and unable to understand them, but copious in language and given to tautology': his commentary on the Romans was an illustration of his defects as a writer and thinker, for, verbose as it was, it never really grasped the meaning (*σκόπος*) of the epistle: many words and few ideas would be found in all his writings alike. No fragments of the commentary are extant, and it is possible to conjecture its method of exegesis only from the geographical and historical conditions of the writer's career. Eunomius was by birth a Cappadocian; was educated at Constantinople and, under Aetius, at Alexandria; accompanied his master to Antioch in 358; and was intruded bishop of Cyzicus in 360. Although he did not long retain the bishopric, he appears to have lived, with intervals of exile, in or near Constantinople for some twenty years, till he was finally banished to his native Cappadocia about 383. All the probabilities point to his exegesis being rather Antiochene than Alexandrine; but a more direct influence than that of the Antiochene school in general will, no doubt, have been the commentary of his Arian predecessor Asterius on the same epistle [No. **8**, above, p. $498^{b}$].

**12. Diodore of Tarsus** (commentaries on all the Epistles?).—

If Eunomius can be spoken of only loosely as an Antiochene exegete, there is no doubt that in Diodore we have a representative of the Antiochene school in its strictest sense; and indeed, both for his own writings, and as the teacher of its two most illustrious members, Chrysostom and Theodore of Mopsuestia, he may rightly be called its second and greater founder. Diodore was born at Antioch, perhaps *circa* 325–330, and, with the exception of a time spent in study at the university of Athens, lived wholly at Antioch until his elevation to the bishopric of Tarsus in A.D. 379. For twenty-five or thirty years before that date, as layman, as monk, and finally as priest and head of the theo-

* It is worth noting that Didymus is not included among the commentators on 1 Thessalonians whom Jerome enumerates in *Ep.* cxix. 8–10.

† According to Zahn, *Forschungen*, v. 99 ff., the correct form is Apollinaris in Latin, Ἀπολινάριος in Greek. But Jerome seems most often to write Apollinarius.

‡ Jerome, *Ep.* lxxxiv. 3 (A.D. 400): 'Apollinarium Laodicenum Antiochiæ frequenter audivi et colui; et cum me in sanctis scripturis erudiret, numquam illius contentiosum [super sensu] dogma suscepi.'

§ Two passages, however, can be identified by the help of Jerome, *c. Rufinum*, i. 24, 25: (*a*) 'in tertia [expositione] quid Apollinarius simpliciter explanaret' = *Comm. in Eph.* ii. 7 (Vallarsi, vii. 576 D–577 A), 'alius vero . . . dici potest': (*b*) 'in tertia quid Apollinarius contra illius [*sc.* Origenis] vadens dogmata sentiret' = *Comm. in Eph.* iii. 1 (vii. 587 B), 'licet quidam . . . carnis acceperit.'

logical school, Diodore was standard-bearer of the Catholic cause in the capital of the East; and, important as was the see of Tarsus, Jerome (*de Vir. Illust.* 119) is no doubt right in saying that his greatest fame was as a mere presbyter of Antioch. When Jerome wrote, he was apparently still living; but he must have died soon after, for a new bishop signs for Tarsus at a Council in 394. If Jerome tells us that Diodore was an imitator of Eusebius of Emesa, and that, though he followed his ideas, he could not rival his eloquence owing to his ignorance of secular literature, we must remember that Jerome would be bitterly, if naturally, prejudiced against him as the real author of the consecration of Flavian to the Antiochene episcopate after the death of Meletius in 381. The West refused communion to the party of Flavian; and Jerome, for all his profound interest in Greek Christian learning, was a thoroughgoing Western in matters of party controversy. Of the 'many' books of Diodore, not enough has perhaps survived to test the soundness of the criticism;* but whatever amount of truth it may have had, we cannot but regret the almost total loss of the exegetical writings of one who holds so important a place in the history and development of Christian exegesis. Photius (cod. 223) appears to have known him only through his book 'on Fate'; and though he praises the clearness of Diodore's language, he seems to imply that the book did not show any corresponding clearness of thought. From Socrates (*HE* vi. 3, followed by Sozomen, *HE* viii. 2) we learn that Diodore's fame was that of an exegete, and an exegete of the literalist school: 'he wrote many books, attending to the letter only of the Divine Scriptures, declining to find recondite senses in them' (*τὰς θεωρίας αὐτῶν ἐκτρεπόμενος*).

According to Leontius of Byzantium, Diodore commented on the whole of Scripture. In the list given by Suidas, and derived by him apparently from the Ἐκκλησιαστικὴ Ἱστορία of Theodorus Lector, commentaries on many books of the Old Testament are mentioned by name, and, of the New, 'On the Four Gospels,' 'On the Acts of the Apostles,' 'On the Epistle of John the Evangelist'; besides a treatise on the principles of exegesis, 'What is the difference between *θεωρία* and *ἀλληγορία*?' It is curious that, while there is no notice of any commentary on the Pauline epistles in this list of Suidas, Jerome mentions such commentaries specifically, 'extant eius in Apostolum commentarii'; indeed, as he mentions no other work of Diodore's by name, but dismisses the rest under the general description 'et multa alia,' it may fairly be inferred that he attached particular importance to them. Whether these 'commentaries on the Apostle' extended to all the Pauline epistles is not certain, though Jerome's language and the analogy of other Antiochene commentaries perhaps suggest it. Jerome himself (*Ep.* cxix., A.D. 406: see pp. 484, 485 above) includes Diodore among the commentators on 1 Corinthians, and quotes in full his exposition of 1 Th $4^{15-17}$: that he omits to name him in the prefaces to his commentaries on Galatians and Ephesians (before 392 A.D.) may only mean that Diodore's commentaries had not at that time come into his hands. Of Cramer's Catenæ only those on the Roman epistle cite him—the Bodleian Catena on the earlier half of the epistle 32 times, the Munich Catena on the later half only thrice ($10^{5}$ $11^{12. 32}$). Even in the Bodleian Catena the comments are not scattered evenly over the eight chapters, but begin only at $5^{15}$, being fairly constant from that point as far as $8^{21}$; the references are $5^{15. 16. 18. 20}$ $6^{1. 5. 12. 19. 23}$ $7^{1. 5. 7. 9. 13. 14. 15. 18. 21. 23. 24}$ $8^{1. 2. 3. 9. 15. 16. 19. 21}$.* A reference to previous expositors should be noted (Cramer, 48. 22), *ἔνιοι μὲν οὖν . . . ᾠήθησαν*.

The exegesis of Diodore is concise, clear, intelligent; but an Antiochene expositor — and Diodore's theology in respect of the doctrine of grace does not appear to be substantially different from his pupil Theodore's†—was perhaps hardly qualified to sound in these particular chapters the full depth of the Apostle's thought. With one exception the catenist's citations from Diodore are short, but a passage of six pages (108. 4–114. 12), which ranges over the whole of Ro $7^{5}$–$8^{2}$, follows on the name of Diodore; and there seems no valid reason for denying it to him. It would, therefore, form the natural starting-point for further investigation into the exegetical principles and methods in which Chrysostom and Theodore were trained, and from which, in opposite directions, they developed.

**13. Chrysostom** (commentary on the Galatians; homilies on the rest of the Epistles).—

John, surnamed *Chrysostom*,—born at Antioch about 347, ordained priest there in 386, consecrated bishop of Constantinople early in 398, driven into final exile in 404,—is the earliest of the Greek Fathers whose exposition of all the Pauline epistles has come down to us. With the single exception of the Galatians, which is represented by a continuous commentary (and even this was perhaps prepared for oral delivery, see below on that epistle, p. 503ᵃ), the method of treatment is, in every case, by a series of homilies actually preached in church. The benefit of his hearers, says the patriarch Photius at the close of an interesting criticism of the most illustrious of his predecessors (codd. 172-174), was the one great object of Chrysostom, in comparison with which all else was neglected; and he accounts in this way for the absence in the *Homilies* of any attempt to penetrate into the 'deeper' sense (*τὰ βαθύτερα, ἡ βαθυτέρα θεωρία*). And while it is certainly true that Chrysostom was in full agreement (fuller than Photius would perhaps have liked to admit) with the exegetical principles of Diodore, his master, and Theodore, his friend,—witness, for instance, his general introduction on the chronology of the Epistles, which he defends on the ground that *συντελεῖ ἡμῖν πρὸς τὰ ζητούμενα οὐ μικρὸν ὁ τῶν ἐπιστολῶν χρόνος* (*Hom. in ep. Rom.*, ed. Field, p. 4),—it is also true that the warm moral interest and direct purpose of edification animating the *Homilies* raises him above the arid intellectualism which was the danger of the literalist school of Antioch. To each homily is appended, at the end of the exposition proper, an 'ethical' application of the lessons to be learnt from the passage expounded; and this is sometimes given the separate heading *ἠθικόν* in the MSS. Of the homiletic expositors of 'the Apostle,' St. Chrysostom ranks as indubitably the greatest, and subsequent commentators and compilers bear testimony to his popularity as an exegete by the extensive use they make of his work; indeed his *Homilies*, shorn of the 'ethical' or directly hortatory passages, form the groundwork of most of the extant Catenæ on the Epistles.

In what manner and by what methods the *Homilies* of Chrysostom were preserved for posterity there is little direct evidence to show. Writing at Constantinople a generation after his death, the historian Socrates excuses himself from

* Harnack's attribution to Diodore of a group of four treatises that pass under the name of Justin Martyr ('Diodor von Tarsus' in *Texte und Untersuchungen*, N. F. vi. 4, 1901) has not yet secured general assent.

* The comments on $8^{24}$ $9^{3}$ ascribed to Diodore in Cramer, pp. 142, 162, are said to belong to Theodore (see Swete, *Theodore of Mopsuestia*, p. lxxiii n.).

† *e.g.* on Ro $5^{16}$: 'the sin of Adam was one, but . . . condemned *τοὺς πολλούς*, because they imitated Adam,' reading *μιμήσασθαι* for *μισήσασθαι* (Cramer, 49. 33).

entering into detail on the characteristics of the *Homilies*, or from attempting to explain their popularity, by the remark that any one who wished to gain an idea of their brilliance and attractiveness had only to turn to their published form. He appears to distinguish between two classes of homilies—those that were published by Chrysostom himself, and those that were simply taken down, as he preached, by shorthand writers (οἵ τε ἐκδοθέντες παρ' αὐτοῦ λόγοι καὶ οἱ λέγοντος αὐτοῦ ὑπὸ τῶν ὀξυγράφων ἐκληφθέντες, *HE* vi. 4). The distinction thus made is borne out by such evidence, both external and internal, as we possess. On the one hand, the finished character of the homilies, for instance, on Romans seems certainly to imply that the preacher had himself prepared them for publication; and with this corresponds the fact that references (intended to excuse the preacher from dwelling on topics which he had already elaborated elsewhere) are more than once made to previous discourses as still accessible in book shape, *e.g.* to the homilies on St. John and to the homilies on the change of name from Saul to Paul (*Hom.* vii. *in 1 Cor.*, *Comm. in Gal.*: both passages are quoted in full below, pp. 502[b], 503). On the other hand, the less polished style of some other series of Chrysostom's homilies, such as those on Philemon, has suggested that in them we have only the report at second hand of unprepared addresses; while those on Hebrews are known to have been first published after his death from notes taken by the presbyter Constantine.

The manuscripts (and Socrates, as cited in the previous paragraph) give to the *Homilies* the title λόγοι; and this must be taken as their correct name, at least in the form in which they were prepared for publication. Photius, however, while admitting that he found them—he is speaking particularly of the homilies on Genesis—circulating under that title, urges that, as they consist throughout of direct addresses to an audience, they are really not λόγοι but ὁμιλίαι (cod. 172: ὡς παρόντας ὁρῶν τοὺς ἀκροατάς, οὕτω πρὸς αὐτοὺς ἀποτείνεται καὶ ἐρωτᾷ καὶ ἀποκρίνεται καὶ ὑπισχνεῖται).

Photius also bears witness to the high place among all the writings of St. Chrysostom which is due to the homilies on the Pauline epistles, taken as a whole, and at the same time draws a distinction, which develops rather than contradicts that suggested by Socrates, between different series among them: πανταχοῦ γὰρ τοῖς λόγοις αὐτοῦ τὸ καθαρὸν καὶ λαμπρὸν καὶ εὐκρινὲς μετὰ τοῦ ἡδέος τεχνουργῶν, τούτοις τε ἐνταῦθα [*sc.* in his interpretations of 'the Apostle' and of 'the Psalter'] μάλιστα διαπρέπει καὶ τῇ τῶν παραδειγμάτων εὐπορίᾳ καὶ τῇ τῶν ἐνθυμημάτων ἀφθονίᾳ καὶ (εἴ που δέοι) καὶ δεινότητι· καὶ ἁπλῶς ἔν τε λέξει καὶ συνθήκῃ καὶ μεθόδῳ καὶ νοήμασι καὶ τῇ ἄλλῃ [*v.l.* ὅλῃ] κατασκευῇ ἄριστα τάσδε τὰς συγγραφὰς ὑπεστήσατο. ἀλλὰ τὰς μὲν εἰς τὸν Ἀπόστολον ἔστιν ἐξ αὐτῶν ἐκείνων ἐπιγνῶναι, ποῖαι τε αὐτῶν ἐν Ἀντιοχείᾳ διατρίβοντι ἐξεπονήθησαν, αἳ καὶ μᾶλλον διηκρίβωνται, καὶ ποῖαι ἀρχιερατεύοντι ἐποιήθησαν . . . εἴ τις τὴν δύναμιν καὶ τὴν ἄλλην ἀρετὴν τοῦ λόγου θαυμάζων, σχολάζοντα αὐτὸν μᾶλλον ἀλλ' οὐ πράγμασι κοινοῖς ἐνστρεφόμενον ταύτας φαίη ἐξεργάσασθαι.

In proceeding, therefore, to say something separately with regard to each set of homilies on the Pauline epistles, we shall rely not only on indications of place and time, but, where such precise data fail us, on the more general characteristics of careful preparation and literary finish.* But if evidence of this sort on the whole suggests Antioch, we shall, on the other hand, not too hastily conclude that an authoritative and apparently episcopal tone necessarily points to Constantinople; for Tillemont has collected references to such language in homilies indubitably Antiochene, and supposes that Flavian, on ordaining Chrysostom priest, entrusted him with a large share of his own episcopal authority (*Mémoires*, vol. xi. 'Saint Jean Chrysostome,' article xiii.).

(i.) *Romans.*—33 homilies; in the earlier editions arranged as 32, the first homily being treated separately as the 'argument' (so similarly for the Philippians). In this series Chrysostom perhaps reaches the zenith of his achievements as an expositor: in them more than anywhere else throughout his writings—such is the judgment of Isidore of Pelusium, himself no mean critic—'did John, the wisest of men, pour out the full treasures of his wisdom'; and he pays him the highest compliment in the power of any critic when he goes on to assert that 'if the divine Paul had received the gift of Attic language so as to be his own expositor, his exposition would have coincided with that of Chrysostom, οὕτω καὶ ἐνθυμήμασι καὶ κάλλει καὶ κυριολεξίᾳ κεκόσμηται ἡ ἑρμηνεία (*ad Isidorum diaconum, Epp.* lib. v. 32). If, then, the rule of Photius holds good, these homilies must belong to the Antiochene period; and in favour of this view may be quoted a passage in *Hom.* ix. [viii.] p. 508 B,* οἶδα ὅτι ὑπὸ τὸν σηκὸν ἐσμεν τὸν αὐτὸν καὶ τὸν ποιμένα, and possibly another in *Hom.* xxxi. [xxx.] p. 743 C, μετὰ τοσοῦτον χρόνον εἰσιόντες ἔνθα ἔμεινε Παῦλος, ἔνθα ἐδέθη, ἔνθα συνεκάθισε καὶ διελέχθη, πτερούμεθα καὶ πρὸς τὴν μνήμην ἐκείνην ἀπὸ τῶν τόπων παραπεμπόμεθα. Tillemont, indeed, reserves judgment on the ground that in the phrases used at the end of *Hom.* xxx. [xxix.] the preacher ranks himself among ποιμένες and ἄρχοντες; but these words hardly appear to go beyond others which Tillemont himself, as above mentioned, had noted as belonging to Antioch. A series of comments on Ro $5^{12}$–$6^{3}$ taken from *Hom.* xi. [x.] are cited, together with other passages from St. Chrysostom, by Augustine (*contra Julianum*, I. vi. 27), in order to rebut the force of Julian's appeal to Chrysostom's authority in the Pelagian controversy. Yet how far Chrysostom was in reality removed from the standpoint of Augustine may be illustrated by his explanation of Ro $8^{28}$ (τοῖς κατὰ πρόθεσιν κλητοῖς οὖσιν), where, in order to emphasize man's contributory share in his own salvation, he erroneously interprets the πρόθεσις as man's and not God's (οὐχ ἡ κλῆσις μόνον ἀλλὰ ἡ πρόθεσις τῶν καλουμένων τὴν σωτηρίαν εἰργάσατο, p. 595 B; quoted by R. Simon, *Hist. Crit. des Commentateurs du NT*, p. 174).

(ii.) *1 Corinthians.*—44 homilies; also ranked among Chrysostom's best work. The evidence of place is here unusually important, since it covers not only these homilies but others as well. In *Hom.* xxi. p. 188 E, Chrysostom urges that niggardliness in almsgiving was especially inexcusable at Antioch (καὶ ταῦτα ἐν Ἀντιοχείᾳ, ἐν ᾗ πρῶτον ἐχρημάτισαν Χριστιανοί . . . ἐν ᾗ πολὺς ὁ τῆς ἐλεημοσύνης τὸ παλαιὸν ἐκόμα καρπός); in *Hom.* xxvii. p. 242 C he cites Mt $18^{7}$ and says he has already explained the passage at length, when dealing with the Gospel (ταῦτα μὲν εὐρύτερον ἐν αὐτῷ γενόμενοι τῷ χωρίῳ διελέχθημεν); and similarly in *Hom.* vii. p. 53 A he refers to his exposition of the Gospels for fuller treatment of Jn $7^{28}$ $8^{19}$ (ἀλλὰ τίς ὁ τρόπος τῆς ἀναγνώσεως ταύτης καὶ τίς ἐκείνης, ἐν τοῖς εὐαγγελίοις ἤδη εἴρηται· καὶ ὥστε μὴ συνεχῶς τὸ αὐτὸ στρέφειν, ἐκεῖ παραπέμπομεν τοὺς ἐντυγχάνοντας). The homilies on

* Savile, Tillemont, Montfaucon, have all dealt with this subject; but the most complete and convenient discussion will be found in Field's Preface to his edition of St. Chrysostom on the Hebrews, pp. xi–xvi. For an account of the editions of St. Chrysostom's *Homilies*, see below, pp. 505[a]–507[a].

* References to the *Homilies* are given in the paging of the Benedictine edition, because this numeration is also to be found in the outer margins of Field's pages.

1 Corinthians were therefore delivered at Antioch, but probably towards the end of St. Chrysostom's residence there.

(iii.) *2 Corinthians.*—26 homilies. A reference to Constantinople appears in *Hom.* xxvi. p. 625 C: before the tombs of the tentmaker and the fisherman at Rome the very emperor humbles himself to ask their intercession; and so, too, at Constantinople, Constantius conceived he could pay his father no higher honour than to bury him 'in the antechamber of the fisherman'—that is, at the porch of the church which contained relics of the Apostles. Savile, although he rated the style of these homilies above the average, yet thought himself forced by this passage to place them at Constantinople; but Tillemont, Montfaucon, and Field rightly deduce from it just the opposite conclusion. Two citations from these homilies were made in the Second Council of Nicæa (A.D. 787), the sixth session of which consisted of the reading of an elaborate refutation of the 'decree' of the Iconoclastic Council of 754. The latter had appealed to St. Paul's words in 2 Co $5^{7}$ 'by faith, not by sight,' and $5^{16}$ 'even though we have known Christ after the flesh, yet know we him so no more'; and in answer to that appeal expositions of these texts are given from Cyril of Alexandria (see below, p. $515^{a}$) and from Chrysostom. Ἰωάννης ὁ ὑπὲρ χρυσίον καὶ λίθον τίμιον διδασκαλίαν κεκτημένος is quoted for both verses,—Mansi, xiii. 288, 289 [Labbe-Coleti, viii. 1122, 1123]=*Hom.* xi. p. 514 C, *Hom.* x. p. 508 C,—and the quotations are of sufficient length (twenty-five and six lines respectively in Field's text) to be of some value for testing the character of the MS tradition.*

(iv.) *Galatians.*—A continuous commentary without break of any sort, for the chapters into which it is divided by the earlier editors are in no way represented in the MSS. This continuity necessarily carries with it the absence of the 'ethical' sections which in the other epistles form the close of each homily; but, curiously enough, the use of the second person, which would seem to be as alien to a commentary as it is characteristic of a homily, occasionally recurs, *e.g.* in the passage 673 E quoted just below, or in the comment on Gal $2^{14}$, p. 688 D: μηδὲ αὔτη ὑμᾶς θορυβείτω ἡ λέξις. Either, then, the commentary was composed for ultimately homiletic purposes, or it may be that the direct speech of Chrysostom the preacher flowed naturally from the pen of Chrysostom the writer. Perhaps because of this uniqueness as a commentary among so many homilies, critics have differed much in their estimate of the literary value of this work; Savile and Tillemont rank it high enough to be allotted to Antioch, and the latter adds that the 'book' on the change of name from Saul to Paul, referred to in this commentary (p. 673 D E), consists of homilies that were certainly preached at Antioch (ed. Bened. iii. 98–140), and was therefore more likely to be accessible to Antiochenes than to Constantinopolitans: ἵνα μὴ τοῦ κατεπείγοντος ἀποστὰς μακρότερον ποιήσω τὸν λόγον . . . καὶ ἡμῖν δὲ εἴρηταί τις ὑπὲρ τούτων λόγος ὅτε περὶ τῆς μεταθέσεως αὐτοῦ τῆς προσηγορίας πρὸς ὑμᾶς διελεγόμεθα . . . εἰ δὲ ἐπιλέλησθε, ἐντυχόντες ἐκείνῳ τῷ βιβλίῳ πάντα εἴσεσθε ταῦτα. A brief citation from 'John Chrysostom,' ἐκ τοῦ ὑπομνήματος τῆς πρὸς Γαλάτας ἐπιστολῆς, is preserved in Photius' account (cod. 229, part 3) of a work by Ephraem, patriarch of Antioch A.D. 527–545, in defence of the Council of Chalcedon; but the words themselves—ὅτι, φησί, τὸ λέγειν σαρκὶ παθεῖν τὸν θεὸν λόγον φρόνημα τῆς ἐκκλησίας ἐστίν, ὥσπερ καὶ βλάσφημον καὶ ἀποβλητὸν τὸ κηρύττειν αὐτὸν παθεῖν τῇ φύσει τῆς θεότητος—appear to be neither akin to Chrysostom's normal theological style nor identified in his Galatian commentary.

(v.) *Ephesians.*—24 homilies. Allotted by Savile, on account of their unfinished style, to Constantinople, but by Tillemont and Montfaucon, on the ground of historical indications, to Antioch. Tillemont points to the impassioned appeal against schisms in the Church at the end of *Hom.* xi. (after the exposition of Eph $4^{4-16}$) p. 86 ff., which naturally connects itself with the Eustathian separatists at Antioch; Montfaucon to various laudatory references to the monastic inhabitants of the neighbouring hills,—*Hom.* vi. p. 44 A, *Hom.* xiii. p. 44 E; cf. *Hom.* xxi. p. 162 D,—whereas at Constantinople the monks were not dwellers in hills, and are mentioned rather with blame than praise. If further argument is needed, it may be found in the mention without definition, as of a saint well known to the audience, of Babylas, martyr-bishop of Antioch under Decius (ὁ μακάριος μάρτυς Βαβύλας, *Hom.* ix. p. 70 C).

Citations from or references to these homilies are made (1) by Theodoret, *Dialogus II.* '*Inconfusus*,' ed. Schultze, IV. i. p. 158, ἐκ τῆς ἑρμηνείας τῆς πρὸς Ἐφεσίους ἐπιστολῆς: (*a*) *Hom.* i. p. 7 D, κατὰ τὴν εὐδοκίαν . . . γέγονεν: (*b*) *Hom.* iii. p. 20 D, περὶ τούτου φησὶν Ὁ θεὸς τοῦ κυρίου ἡμῶν Ἰησοῦ Χριστοῦ, οὐ περὶ τοῦ θεοῦ λόγου: (*c*) *Hom.* iv. p. 26 F, καὶ ὄντας ἡμᾶς . . . περὶ τοῦ κατὰ σάρκα πάντα εἴρηται*—(2) by Ephraem of Antioch (see just above) in Photius cod. 229 for the use of ὁ ἄνθρωπος with the article of the human nature of Christ (ὁ Χρυσόστομος ἐν τῇ ἑρμηνείᾳ τῆς πρὸς Ἐφεσίους ἐπιστολῆς τρίτης ὁμιλίας): the whole passage 18 E–19 C is more or less in point, but the specific reference is perhaps to 20 D, τὸν ἄνθρωπον εἰς μέγα ὑψηλότητος ἀνήγαγε—(3) by Facundus of Hermiana in the middle of the 6th cent., *pro Defensione Trium Capitulorum*, xi. 5 (ed. Sirmond, p. 486; Gallandi, *Bibl. Vet. Patrum*, xi. 788), 'beatus Ioannes . . . in commento epistolæ ad Ephesios libro tertio,' translating into Latin (*a*) *Hom.* iii. pp. 18 F–19 A, ἐννόησον ὅσον . . . τοῦ θεοῦ λόγου οὐδαμῶς, and (*b*) *Hom.* iii. p. 20 C D, δύο γὰρ τὰ μέγιστα . . . οὐ περὶ τοῦ θεοῦ λόγου.†

(vi.) *Philippians.*—16 homilies; in the earlier editions 15, because the first homily was separately treated as the 'argument' (so also in Romans). This is the first set of homilies which the majority of critics place at Constantinople, on the ground partly of general negligence of style, partly of language that is supposed to be definitely episcopal in the 'ethical' part of *Hom.* x. [ix.], p. 268 F onwards, where the preacher rebukes his congre-

* Comparison of the two texts reveals the following variants:—(1) Field, p. 128, l. 7, καὶ πάλιν τούτου αὐτοῦ (*sc.* of being no longer κατὰ σάρκα) ἀρχηγὸν τὸν Χριστὸν ὄντα δείκνυσι: Conc. Nic. καὶ πάλιν τοῦ αὐτοῦ· Ἀρχηγὸν τὸν Χριστὸν ὄντα δείκνυσι, as if a second quotation from Chrysostom began at Ἀρχηγόν. (2) Field, l. 15, ἀλλὰ νῦν οὐκέτι: Conc. Nic. ἀλλὰ νῦν οὐκέτι γινώσκομεν. ὅτι εἰ καὶ παθητὸν ἐγνώκαμεν τὸν Χριστόν, ἀλλὰ νῦν οὐκέτι. Here the Council is clearly right, and the MSS have omitted a line through *homœoteleuton*. (3) Field, ll. 15, 17, ἡμῶν μὲν . . . Χριστοῦ δέ: Conc. Nic. ἐπὶ ἡμῶν μὲν . . . ἐπὶ δὲ Χριστοῦ, probably wrongly. (4) Field, l. 22 [Jn $14^{30}$], οὐκ ἔχει οὐδέν: Conc. Nic. εὑρήσει οὐδέν. Both readings have good support; but the latter is less likely to be the posterior insertion into Chrysostom's text, and is therefore probably genuine. (5) Field, l. 24, τὸ ἐκτὸς σαρκὸς εἶναι: Conc. Nic. omits σαρκός, perhaps accidentally. (6) Field, p. 120, l. 29, ἵνα μήδεις: Conc. Nic. ἵνα μήτις. (7) Field, l. 29, εἴπῃ, ἀκούων ὅτι ἐκδημοῦμεν; Conc. Nic. εἴπῃ, τί οὖν; λέγοντός σου ἐνδημοῦντες ἐν τῷ σώματι ἐκδημοῦμεν. It is difficult here to decide. (8) Field, l. 31, τοῦτο: Conc. Nic. omits. (9) Field, l. 33, ἐν ἐσόπτρῳ καὶ ἐν αἰνίγματι: Conc. Nic., less pointedly, completes the quotation by prefixing ἄρτι βλέπομεν and subjoining τοτε δὲ πρόσωπον πρὸς πρόσωπον.

* Theodoret's polemical quotations, at least from early writers, are not to be relied on; it is therefore all the more important to note that his differences from Field's text are relatively slight. In one case (p. 7 D, ὡς ἄν τις εἴποι for ὡς ἄν [τις] ἔχοι) he supports Cramer's Catena against all the direct MS tradition. Did he use the Catena?

† Facundus entirely supports Field in his return to the text of the Verona edition against Savile and the Benedictines; *e.g.* 20 D he reads 'in sanguine eius salvavit'=τῷ αἵματι αὐτοῦ ἔσωσεν (Field, Veron., and 3 MSS, against omission by the rest) and 'præter hoc'=χωρὶς τούτου, with the same authorities, where the rest omit χωρίς.

gation for their grudging support of the clergy.* Yet even for this epistle grave doubt must be felt in presence of a passage indicated by Tillemont, *Hom.* xvi. [xv.] p. 318 C D, where Chrysostom, enumerating the drawbacks to earthly royalty, ends his dark catalogue of misfortunes with the catastrophe in which Valens perished, while "he that now rules, ever since he put on the diadem, has lived among labours, dangers, despondencies, calamities, conspiracies.' Chrysostom was a bold preacher; but even in Chrysostom's mouth such language is more natural at a distance from the court. And it is not easy to see why the argument should leap from Valens to Arcadius without any hint at the critical fortunes of the intermediate reign of Theodosius (A.D. 379–395); yet if Theodosius is meant by ὁ νῦν κρατῶν, the homilies again belong to the Antiochene period. In a Catena from the Fathers contained in Book i. of Leontius of Byzantium, *contra Nestorianos et Eutychianos*,† are included passages from Chrysostom's *Hom. in 1 Tim.* (see just below) and *in Phil.*—the latter passage is from *Hom.* vii. [vi.] p. 235 B, μορφὴν δούλου ἔλαβε . . . ἡ μορφὴ τοῦ θεοῦ.

(vii.) *Colossians.* — 12 homilies. For the first time the indications are decisive in favour of Constantinople. Not only is the style considered to be below the average of the other epistles, but the preacher is quite certainly a bishop; in *Hom.* iii. p. 349 D–F he sits ἐπὶ τοῦ θρόνου τούτου, to him belongs τὸ τῆς ἐπισκοπῆς ἀξίωμα. *Hom.* vii. contains two illustrations drawn from current or recent events: p. 374 F, 'the man who but yesterday was exalted in the tribunal, who had heralds to proclaim aloud his dignity and crowds of attendants hustling a way for him in the forum,' who to-day is living deprived of all this pomp and station, can only be the minister Eutropius between his fall at the beginning, and his death at the close, of A.D. 399; p. 375 E, 'my own city (ἡ πόλις ἡ ἡμετέρα) gave offence to a previous monarch, and he ordered it to be destroyed to the uttermost, inhabitants and buildings alike . . . but when our neighbours of the city on the coast interceded on our behalf, our citizens went about saying that that intervention was a worse humiliation than the destruction of the city would have been'—St. Chrysostom, in fact, is giving his audience at Constantinople the story of the experiences of 'his own' city of Antioch after the 'statues' riot of A.D. 387. It may be noted that the 2nd and 3rd homilies were preached on successive days: p. 338 A, σήμερον ἀναβαλλομένους αὔριον τοῦτο προθεῖναι δεῖ: 343 B, τήμερον ἀποδοῦναι ἀναγκαῖον τὸ ὄφλημα ὅπερ χθὲς ἀνεβαλόμην. Perhaps the days were Saturday and Sunday.

(viii.) (ix.) *1 Thessalonians.* — 11 homilies; *2 Thessalonians.*—5 homilies. Both sets of homilies appear to be episcopal utterances, and were therefore preached at Constantinople: cf. 1 Thess. *Hom.* x. p. 495 C, κἂν . . . τῆς ἐκκλησίας ἀπαγάγω ἢ τῆς κοινῆς εὐχῆς ἀπείρξω: *Hom.* xi. p. 504 E, ὑπεύθυνος ἐγενόμην τῆς ἁπάντων ὑμῶν προστασίας: 2 Thess. *Hom.* iv. p. 533 E, ἀλλά, φησίν . . . σὺ ἀξιοῖς τὸν λαὸν ὑπὲρ τοῦ ἡγουμένου παρακαλεῖν, p. 535 E, ἡμεῖς δήμου τοσούτου προεστῶτες, cf. p. 533 B C.

(x.) (xi.) *1 Timothy.*—18 homilies; *2 Timothy.*—10 homilies. The supposed inferiority of the style of these homilies led Savile to attribute them, according to Photius' canon, to the Constantinopolitan period. Montfaucon, however, while admitting that on none of the Epistles is it so difficult to decide as on these, considers that the unstinted eulogy of monks in *Hom. in 1 Tim.* xiv., and the absence of any indication of episcopal position in dealing with the qualifications for the ministry laid down by St. Paul (contrast the passages quoted above on 1 and 2 Thess.), point on the whole to Antioch. The homilies on 1 Timot y are named by Ephraem of Antioch and Leontius of Byzantium; Ephraem (*ap.* Photius, cod. 229), appealing this time to the teaching of the Fathers on the Unity of Christ's Person, includes ὁ Χρυσόστομος τὴν πρὸς Τιμόθεον πρώτην ἑρμηνεύων ἐπιστολήν: Leontius (see just above on Philippians) cites from *Hom. in 1 Tim.* vii. p. 586 B, ἐπειδὴ γὰρ δύο φύσεων . . . οὕτω καὶ θεὸς ἦν.

(xii.) *Titus.* — 6 homilies. The principle laid down above, that caution must be exercised in interpreting passages which at first sight seem to imply episcopal oversight on the part of the preacher, receives abundant justification in these homilies. For whereas on the one hand *Hom.* i. p. 735 B speaks of the πατρικὴ διάνοια which forbids treating any one τῶν ἀρχομένων other than gently 'however much trouble he give us,' on the other hand *Hom.* iii. p. 746 C contains an indisputable reference to Christian attendance at non-Christian sanctuaries at Antioch. 'What must we say of those who keep the same fasts as they do, who observe sabbaths, who go off to places dedicated to their worship, such as the spot at Daphne, the so-called cave of Matrona?'*

(xiii.) *Philemon.*—3 homilies. These homilies appear to present no features suggestive of either Antioch or Constantinople. The majority of critics suppose that the relatively unfinished style is decisive, according to Photius' canon, for Constantinople; Venables (*Dict. Chr. Biogr.* i. 533*b*) even speaks of them as perhaps 'extemporaneous addresses taken down by others.' Yet such is the uncertainty of this sort of criterion that Montfaucon can assert that 'parem diligentiam et accurationem alibi in scriptis eius vix reperias.'

No Latin translation of any part of Chrysostom on St. Paul was known to Cassiodorus when he wrote his summary account of extant commentaries, *de Institutione Divinarum Litterarum*, ch. 8; but he possessed a complete set of them in the original Greek, which, as he says, could be translated if wanted—if, that is to say, the Latin commentaries which his library could manage to procure should turn out insufficient. 'Commemoratas tamen epistolas a Ioanne Chrysostomo expositas Attico sermone, in suprascripto octavo armario dereliqui, ubi sunt græci codices congregati: ut si latina non potuerint latiora commenta procurari, de istis subinde transferatur quod plenissimam poterit præstare notitiam.' Two things are here worth notice. In the first place, Chrysostom was, for the Latins, *the* Greek commentator *par excellence*: if Cassiodorus knew of the existence of any others, they were at any rate not in his hands. In the second place, the quality which distinguished Chrysostom in Cassiodorus' eyes from all the Latins was his fulness: there he was in the library, ready to be

* The most definite words of all, πατήρ εἰμί (p. 272 D), do not, however, appear in Field's text.

† According to F. Loofs' masterly discussion of this important but obscure writer (*Texte und Untersuchungen*, iii. 1, A.D. 1887), the treatise *contra Nest. et Eutych.* was published between 529 and 544. Leontius is not mentioned in the *Dictionary of Christian Biography*. These passages from Chrysostom are in the Latin version of H. Canisius, *Lectiones Antiquæ* (re-edited by J. Basnage, *Thesaurus Monumentorum*, i., Antwerp, A.D. 1725, p. 554), and in the Greek of the important Bodleian MS of Leontius, cod. Laudianus gr. 92 B, foll. 55*b*, 56*a*: but they are omitted (with many others) in Migne's edition, vol. 86, c. 1309, 'minuendi voluminis gratia.'

* One would naturally suppose that allusions to the well-known name of the Antiochene Daphne implied heathen worship: but the fasts and sabbaths are, of course, Jewish, and from *Hom. adv. Iudæos* i. (ed. Bened. i. 595 D) it appears that there was a Jewish synagogue at Daphne, besides that in Antioch: καὶ τοῦτο οὐ περὶ τῆς ἐνταῦθα λέγω συναγωγῆς μόνον ἀλλὰ καὶ τῆς ἐν Δάφνῃ, πονηρότερον γὰρ ἐκεῖ τὸ βάραθρον ὃ δὴ καλοῦσι Ματρώνης . . . ἐμοὶ καὶ τὸ Ματρώνης καὶ τὸ τοῦ Ἀπόλλωνος ἱερὸν ὁμοίως ἐστὶ βέβηλον.

translated if no Latin commentary of equal 'latitude' should come into the hands of the monks of Vivarium.

That the *Homilies* should have been early translated into Syriac is only what we should expect; and the evidence of the catalogue of Syriac MSS in the British Museum fully confirms such expectations. The material falls naturally into the three classes of (*a*) translations at full length; (*b*) abridgments extending over several or all of the Epistles; (*c*) fragmentary quotations.

(*a*) Translations. *Romans:* MS dccxlv.* (Brit. Mus. Add. 17164) is for the most part a palimpsest of a 6th or 7th century MS of the homilies on Romans. *1 Corinthians:* MS dlxxxix. (Add. 14563), sæc. vii.–viii., *Hom.* xx.–xxxiii.; MS dxc. (Add. 12160), A.D. 584, *Hom.* xxxiv.–xliv. *2 Corinthians:* MS dxci. (Add. 14564), sæc. vi.–vii., complete save for a few *lacunæ*; MS dxcii. (Add. 12180), sæc. vi.–vii., complete. *Ephesians:* MS dxciii. (Add. 14565), sæc. vi.–vii., complete. *Philippians, Philemon:* MS dxciv. (Add. 14566), sæc. vi., fragments. *Colossians, Titus:* MS dxcv. (Add. 14566, part 2), sæc. vi.–vii., considerable portions. *1 and 2 Thessalonians:* MS dxcvi. (Add. 17152), A.D. 594, complete.†—In this group of MSS all the Epistles are represented except Galatians and 1 and 2 Timothy.

(*b*) Whereas the MSS of translations in full of the *Homilies* range from 550 to 750 A.D., those of abridgments and extracts—in which all or most of the Epistles are treated in a single MS—belong to the later centuries; and this is probably not an accidental distinction, but is a parallel phenomenon to the supersession of commentaries by Catenæ in general.—MS dccxiv. (Add. 14683), foll. 1–141, sæc. x.: parts 3 and 4 (with two great *lacunæ*) of a commentary on the Pauline epistles abridged from Chrysostom, containing Galatians [Gal $6^{12}$–end, Eph., Ph $1^{1-11}$ lost], Philippians, Colossians, 1 and 2 Thessalonians [1 and 2 Tim., Philem., He $1–10^{7}$ lost], He $10^{8}$–end; on fol. 140*b* is a complete list of the number of Chrysostom's homilies on each epistle.—MS dccclii. (Add. 12168), foll. 166–233, sæc. viii.–ix.: Pauline epistles, with extracts throughout from Chrysostom; Colossians comes at the end between Titus and Hebrews.—MS dcccliii. (Add. 12144), foll. 123–176, A.D. 1081: Catena on all the Epistles, principally, but in this case not exclusively, from Chrysostom.

(*c*) The fragmentary quotations are far too many to enumerate here, and must be sought for in the catalogue itself, and in Wright's invaluable index to it. Often, of course, the motive for the choice of the passages is the dogmatic interest: thus MS dccclvii. (Add. 12155), sæc. viii., consists largely of *testimonia* collected from the Fathers with a view to the refutation of various heretics; and citations, or groups of citations, from Chrysostom on the Epistles occur on no fewer than twelve occasions, representing on one or other occasion each set of his *Homilies*.

It remains to give an account of the principal editions of the Greek text, and of the manuscript authority on which they are based.

The *editio princeps* of the original Greek text of Chrysostom on St. Paul is the Veronensis, a superb piece of typography in four folio parts,‡ published at Verona 'per Stephanum et fratres a Sabio' in 1529; the patron, according to the preface addressed to pope Clement VII. by Donatus of Verona, was Gibertus, bishop of the see.* Part i. contains the homilies on the Romans (foll. 1–132) and Ephesians (133–204); part ii. the two Thessalonian epistles (foll. 1–33, 34–47), Colossians (48–86), 1 Corinthians (87–255); part iii. the Second Epistle to the Corinthians (1–93), Titus (93–108), Hebrews (109–205), Philippians (205–249); part iv. the two Epistles to Timothy (1–42, 42–70), Philemon (71–78), and Galatians (78–107). The Greek is given without any Latin translation. The homilies on all epistles except 1 and 2 Thess., Col., and 1 Cor. are divided each into two parts, the more strictly homiletic portion at the end being separated off with the title ἠθικόν. The general title of the homily and its running headline is λόγος α', λόγος β', and so on. Even the commentary on Galatians has the running title λόγος α' throughout; but, being a commentary and not homilies, it has of course no 'ethical' section. The text of the whole edition is taken apparently from a single manuscript, identified by Heyse (see below on the Oxford edition) with the Venice MS, Marcianus 103, sæc. xi. The unusual order in which the Epistles occur in the edition is no doubt faithfully reproduced from the order of the MS: as each series of homilies circulated from the first independently, and were rarely brought together into a single MS, there was no fixed rule to follow, and the sequence in the Venice MS may be assumed to be accidental. The Verona edition is, apart from the matter of punctuation, warmly praised by Savile; its faults were due to the imperfect condition of the 'half-eaten' MS on which it was based. Indeed it is now clear that, as regards the *type* of text used, succeeding editors (until we come to Field) progressively deteriorated from the standard of the *editio princeps* rather than improved upon it.

In 1603 an unimportant edition appeared at Heidelberg 'in bibliopolio Commeliniano,' which claimed to restore to its integrity the mutilated Greek of the Verona edition by the help of MSS at Heidelberg and Augsburg; but the character of the edition is far from corresponding to the promise of the title-page.

A very different work soon followed. In Sir Henry Savile's great edition of the complete works of Chrysostom (Eton, 1612) the Pauline epistles are to be found in vols. iii. and iv.—in vol. iii. Romans to Ephesians, in vol. iv. Philippians to Philemon. Information about the MSS used must, however, be sought in vol. viii. (the concluding volume) col. 225 ff. The groundwork of Savile's text throughout was the Verona edition, but he modified it by the help, on each epistle, of some one MS from the libraries of France and Germany. For the Romans he used a codex 'Regius' of Paris—apparently Paris gr. 731, sæc. xi.; for 1 Cor. a MS of New College, Oxford—no doubt cod. lxxvii. sæc. xii. ineunt.; for 2 Cor. a Paris 'Medicean' MS; for Gal. a Paris 'Regius' MS; for Eph. an Augsburg MS—presumably Munich gr. 353, sæc. x.; for Phil. a Vienna MS and the copy of a Vatican MS—perhaps Vatic. gr. 551, sæc. x.; for the remaining seven epistles also an Augsburg MS—perhaps Munich gr. 377, sæc. x. For the Roman epistle he further gives in an Appendix, vol. viii. cc. 981–988, a collation again of an Augsburg MS—apparently Munich gr. 457, sæc. xi. A large number of suggestions and emendations are also printed in the margin of the texts. By using more than one manuscript, and still more by drawing on his own critical ingenuity and that of other scholars, Savile was able to make in many ways a very substantial contribution to the improvement of the text of St. Chrysostom; but the *type* of text re-

* The roman numerals are those of Wright's catalogue.

† The homilies on 2 Thessalonians are reckoned not as five homilies, but as an introduction and four homilies; compare the arrangement for Romans and Philippians in the earlier editions of the Greek (above, pp. 502b, 503b).

‡ That is, it is *paged* with four separate paginations, but there is only one colophon, and no copy that the present writer has seen is *bound* in four volumes. Possibly it was issued in sheets only, and bound in volumes at each purchaser's discretion.

* Compare the account of the Verona Oecumenius, p. 485, above.

presented by his new MSS was inferior for the most part to the type represented by the Venice MS employed for the Verona edition.

A new edition was published at Paris in 1636 by the king's printer, C. Morel, of which volumes iv.–vi. contain the homilies on the Epistles. Morel's edition does not pretend to do more than follow Savile's Greek text, incorporating at the same time Latin translations revised by the Jesuit Fronton du Duc.

The Benedictine edition of St. Chrysostom was the latest of the vast labours carried through by dom Bernard Montfaucon. Vol. ix. (A.D. 1731) contains the homilies on Romans; vol. x. (A.D. 1732) contains 1 and 2 Cor., Gal.; vol. xi. (A.D. 1734) the remaining epistles. According to the convenient custom of Benedictine editors, a Latin translation faces on each page the Greek text; but the latter is generally judged to be inferior to the text of Savile. The manuscripts used were exclusively Parisian: on Romans [the numbers of the modern catalogue of M. Omont are substituted, where identification is possible, for those of Montfaucon] MSS Paris gr. 732, sæc. xi., and 734, sæc. xiii.; on 1 Cor. MS gr. 738, sæc. x.; on 2 Cor. MS coislin 74, sæc. x.; on Galatians none; on Eph. MSS coislin 74 (as on 2 Cor.), coislin 75, sæc. xi., gr. 1017, sæc. x.; on Phil. apparently MSS coislin 75 and gr. 1017 (as on Eph.); on Col. MSS gr. 1017 (as on Eph.), gr. 731, sæc. xi., gr. 743, sæc. xi.; on 1 Thess. apparently gr. 743 (as on Col.), gr. 1017 (as on Eph.), and one other; on 2 Thess. gr. 743 (as on Col.), and a second 'Colb. 616,' which may perhaps be gr. 744, sæc. ix.; on 1 Tim. 'Colb. 616' (as on 2 Thess.) and gr. 743 (as on Col.); on 2 Tim. nothing is said; on Titus gr. 745 (imperfect), sæc. xii., and 744 (fragmentary), sæc. ix.; on Philemon gr. 745 (as on Tit.) Montfaucon does not appear to have made exhaustive use even of the early MSS of the Paris Library; the reissue of the Benedictine edition, Paris, 1834–1840, takes account of several additional MSS: *e.g.* for Romans gr. 731, sæc. xi.; for 1 Cor. gr. 739, sæc. xi., and 740, sæc. xi.; for 2 Cor. gr. 741, sæc. xv.; for Gal. gr. 675, sæc. xi., and 1017 (imperfect), sæc. x.

Meanwhile, before the appearance of the second Benedictine edition, attention had been called to the importance of Chrysostom's *Homilies* for the history of the text of St. Paul, by C. F. Matthæi, whose critical edition of the New Testament appeared at Riga towards the close of the 18th cent.: part vi. (Romans, Titus, Philemon) in 1782, part vii. (1 and 2 Corinthians) in 1783, part viii. (Galatians, Ephesians, Philippians) in 1784, part x. (Hebrews, Colossians) also in 1784, part ix. (1 and 2 Thessalonians, 1 and 2 Timothy, together with a 'Præfatio in omnes D. Pauli epistolas') in 1785. Matthæi was professor at Moscow, and his MSS of the *Homilies* were exclusively drawn from the library of the Holy Synod in that city—many or most of them had come originally from Mount Athos: a list of them may be inserted here.

Mosq. xcvii. = Matthæi (vi. 262) 3, A.D. 917: Romans.
„ c. = (vi. 264) 8, sæc. x.–xi.: Romans.
„ ci. = (vii. 277) 1, A.D. 993: Hebrews, Colossians.
„ cii. = (vii. 275) 9, sæc. x.–xi.: 2 Cor., 1 Timothy.
„ ciii. = (vi. 275) σ or 6, sæc. x.–xi.: 2 Cor., Titus.
„ civ. = (vii. 274) 7, sæc. ix.: 1 Corinthians.
„ cv. = (vii. 274) 2, A.D. 990: 1 Corinthians.
„ cvi. = (vii. 276) 4, sæc. xi.: Philippians, Hebrews.
„ cvii. = (vii. 279) 5, sæc. x.: Hebrews.
Mosq. cviii. = (vi. 275) β, sæc. x.–xi.: Eph., Philippians, Philemon.
„ cix. = (vi. 276) α, sæc. ix.–x.: 1 Tim., 2 Tim., Philemon, 1 Thess., 2 Thessalonians.

In the 'Præfatio' above referred to—a singularly perverse piece of writing—Matthæi explains his reasons for devoting such special attention to the MSS of Chrysostom's *Homilies*. To Chrysostom, he maintains, are largely due the difficulties which beset the attempt to reconstruct the original text of St. Paul. Partly through his copying Origen—the loss of whose commentaries Matthæi professes to regret only because he would like to apportion the amount which Chrysostom borrowed from him,—partly through his own carelessness and inexactness of quotation, the text of the Epistles as used in his *Homilies* was seriously depraved; while, owing to the popularity he enjoyed, the text thus depraved, copied by John of Damascus, Theophylact, and others, reacted upon the current manuscripts of the New Testament. Thus, in order to grasp the whole extent of the corrupting influence of the Greek Fathers upon our existing MSS, it is necessary to identify the Chrysostom reading of each disputed passage in turn; for whatever else is right, that is sure to be wrong. But this identification must rest not on the editions of Savile or Montfaucon,—since neither used enough codices, nor followed those they used,—but on a fresh and thorough examination of a larger number of MSS.

Matthæi's own work on the Chrysostom MSS was naturally limited to collation of the text of the Epistles as embedded in the *Homilies*: but a complete edition on a wider basis of MS authority, as demanded by him, was in fact produced for the Oxford Library of the Fathers by the Rev. F. Field, better known perhaps as the editor of the *Hexapla*. Collations were supplied—in Italy by Theodor Heyse, at Munich by J. G. Krabinger, at Paris and Vienna by other scholars. Among the MSS employed for the first time—and many of those that older editors had used were re-collated for the new edition—were (1) for *Romans*: Paris gr. 1016 A, sæc. xi.; Vatic. gr. 550, sæc. x.; Venice Marcianus 98, sæc. xi., and 564, sæc. xi.; Vienna Lambec. cxli. (*Hom.* i.–xxix.) 'antiquus.'* (2) For *1 Corinthians*: Paris gr. 683 (imperfect), sæc. xii., and suppl. 226 (*Hom.* xxi.–xxxiii.), sæc. ix.; Munich gr. 373 (beginning in *Hom.* iv.: 'omnium præstantissimus'), sæc. x.; Venice Marcianus 99, sæc. x., and Append. 77, sæc. xii.—the two latter only partially collated. (3) For *2 Corinthians*: Paris gr. 742 (contains only the 'ethical' or homiletic portions), sæc. xiii.; Vienna Lambec. cxxxv. 'antiquus,' cxxxvi. 'pervetustus,' and cxxxvii. 'pervetustus.' (4) For *Galatians*: Paris gr. 725, sæc. xii.; Munich gr. 373 (as for 1 Cor.); Vienna Lambec. cxxxv. (as for 2 Cor.), and cxl. 'antiquus'; and an unidentified Venice MS. (5) For *Ephesians*: Munich gr. 353, sæc. x.; Vienna Lambec. cxxxvii. (as for 2 Cor.: only used in part), and cxxxviii., sæc. xi.; Florence Laurent. plut. viii. 2, sæc. xi.; Vatic. 551, sæc. x. (6) For *Philippians*: Mus. Brit. Burney 48, sæc. xiv., and Vienna Lambec. cxl. (as for Gal.). (7) For *Colossians*: Mus. Brit. Burney 48 (as for Phil.); Vienna Lambec. cxxxix. 'pervetustus,' and cxl. (as for Gal. Phil.). (8, 9) For *1 and 2 Thessalonians*: Mus. Brit. Burney 48 (as for Phil. Col.); Florence Laurent. plut. viii. 2 (as for Eph.). (10, 11) For *1 and 2 Timothy*: Mus. Brit. Burney 48 (as for Phil. Col. Thess.). For *1 Tim. only*: Florence Laurent. plut. viii. 2 (as for Eph. Thess.). (12) For *Titus*: Burney 48 again, and Munich gr. 353 (as for Eph.). (13) For

* These adjectives of Lambecius' catalogue must be taken for what they are worth.

*Philemon:* again Burney 48.—Besides these, the Catenæ published by Cramer are mentioned for every epistle except 2 Cor.; the first of the two Catenæ on Romans contained practically no Chrysostom, but in every other case the Catena texts are stated to be of great value, and sometimes to preserve the true text against all the MSS of the *Homilies* themselves. These latter MSS are divided by Field into two classes—the first containing a purer and more original text, the second the recension of some later scholar. Since the first is represented more or less by the Verona edition, the second by Savile,—Montfaucon's is set aside as being critically of less importance than either,—Field's text represents to a large extent a return to the *editio princeps*. How well justified he was in doing this may be seen from the note to the quotations by Facundus of Hermiana from *Hom. in Eph.* iii. (p. 503[b], above); just as his dependence on Cramer's Catena against the direct MS tradition is in another case supported similarly by Theodoret (*ib.*). In fact, Field's is the only edition which can be called in any real sense critical; and although the number of MSS used might perhaps with advantage be increased and more use might be made of the Syriac, it is not likely that the work of this eminent scholar will for a long time to come be superseded.

Field's volumes appeared in the following order: 2 Corinthians, 1845; 1 Corinthians, 1847; Romans, 1849; Galatians, Ephesians, 1852; Philippians, Colossians, 1 and 2 Thessalonians, 1855; 1 and 2 Timothy, Titus, Philemon, 1861; Hebrews (with indexes to the whole), 1862.

About the same time with the Greek edition, and under the same auspices, an English translation of the *Homilies* was undertaken at Oxford as part of the large series of translations in the 'Library of Fathers of the Holy Catholic Church.' In 1839 appeared in two parts the homilies on 1 Corinthians, translated by H. K. Cornish and J. Medley (from the Benedictine text, but modified from Savile); in 1840 those on Galatians, translated anonymously, and on Ephesians, translated by W. J. Copeland; in 1841 the homilies on Romans by J. B. Morris (from Savile's text, modified by the new collations of MSS); in 1843 a volume containing Philippians by W. C. Cotton (from Savile), Colossians by J. Ashworth, and 1 and 2 Thessalonians by J. Tweed (all these from the reissue of the Benedictine text, compared with Savile); in the same year another volume containing 1 and 2 Timothy, Titus, Philemon, also by J. Tweed (from the new Benedictine text, with Savile, and occasionally with material from collations); and in 1848 the homilies on 2 Corinthians by J. Ashworth and J. F. Christie (from Field's text, which, as above mentioned, had been published as early as 1845).

**14. Severianus of Gabala** (commentaries or homilies on all the Epistles?).—

Severianus, bishop of Gabala, on the Syrian coast south of Antioch, is principally known to us as one of the main instruments of St. Chrysostom's misfortunes. It was common knowledge that Chrysostom's fame as a preacher was the cause of his selection to the episcopate of Constantinople, and therefore other Syrian bishops who had acquired a local reputation in the pulpit were moved to follow in his footsteps, and, neglecting their flocks, to transfer their oratorical gifts to a more comprehensive sphere. Antiochus of Ptolemais and Severian of Gabala came in this way to reside in the capital; and whether or no they were moved by jealousy of the bishop's preaching powers, they soon showed themselves two of the most persistent and unscrupulous of his enemies. History has not cared to tell us more of them: they are visible on the stage for a moment in the light which radiates round the personality of St. Chrysostom, and when that light is withdrawn they pass on into darkness again. Nor in the case of Antiochus do any literary remains survive to enable us to judge how far his friends were justified in bestowing on him the rival appellation of the 'Golden Mouth'; even Gennadius, *de Viris Illustribus*, 20,* knew only a single one of his homilies. Severian was perhaps the more eminent preacher of the two, and certainly the more considerable exegete: Gennadius (*op. cit.* 21) describes him as 'in divinis scripturis eruditus et in homiliis declamator admirabilis,' and had read his exposition on the Galatians. The evidence of the Catenæ points to his having written on at least several others of St. Paul's epistles: Oecumenius quotes him on Romans, 1 Corinthians, 2 Thessalonians;† Cramer gives several quotations from him in each of his two Catenæ on Romans, many in that on 1 Corinthians, several again on Galatians, Thessalonians, and the Pastoral epistles, while for the four epistles of the Roman captivity the colophons at the end of the Catenæ summarize their sources, and in each case Severian is named among them. Ephesians: *Τῶν εἰς τὴν πρὸς Ἐφεσίους ἐπιστολὴν Παύλου τοῦ ἀποστόλου ἐξηγητικῶν ἐκλογῶν τόμος ἀπὸ φωνῆς Ὠριγένους, τοῦ μακαρίου Ἰωάννου, Σευηριανοῦ, Θεοδώρου.* Philippians: *Τῶν εἰς τὴν πρὸς Φιλιππησίους ἐπιστολὴν ἐξηγητικῶν ἐκλογῶν τόμος α' τοῦ μακαρίου Ἰωάννου ΙΩ. Σευηριανοῦ Σ. Θεοδώρου Θ.* Colossians: *Αἱ ἐκλογαὶ τῆς ἑρμηνείας τῆς παρούσης ἐπιστολῆς ἐκ τοῦ κατὰ πλάτος ὑπομνήματος τοῦ σοφοῦ καὶ οἰκουμενικοῦ διδασκάλου Ἰωάννου τοῦ ἐπισκόπου τῆς βασιλίδος πόλεως καὶ Σευηριανοῦ τοῦ Γαβάλης καὶ Θεοδώρου τοῦ Μοψουεστίας· ἔχει καὶ μίαν χρῆσιν τοῦ μακαρίου Κυρίλλου.* Philemon: *Τῶν εἰς τὴν πρὸς Φιλήμονα ἐπιστολὴν ἐξηγητικῶν ἐκλογῶν τόμος α'. ἡ ἑρμηνεία τῆς ἐπιστολῆς τοῦ μακαρίου Ἰωάννου τοῦ Χρυσοστόμου, Σευηριανοῦ, Θεοδώρου Μοψουεστίας.* It is clear that the statements of these colophons imply something more than the occasional use which could be made of miscellaneous homilies and the like: they are satisfied only by supposing that Severian had formally written on these epistles.‡ The same thing follows for 1 Corinthians from the extensive quotations from him, 90 in number, in Cramer's Catena. Add to this the express testimony of Gennadius for the Galatians, and we have six epistles which Severian can be proved to have expounded—whether in commentaries, or like Chrysostom in homilies, has not so far been established. As Severian is further represented on each of the remaining epistles (to a greater or less degree) in Cramer's Catena, the deduction is a probable one, that, like his other contemporaries of the Antiochene school, his exposition covered the whole range of the Pauline epistles.§

Severian is, as we should expect, a commentator

* Gennadius, a presbyter of Marseilles, published about A.D. 495 a supplement to the *de Viris Illustribus* of St. Jerome, enumerating exactly one hundred writers for the century that had elapsed between the original work and the continuation.

† One of the Catenæ in Karo and Lietzmann's list, Vat. gr. 1270, sæc. xii., Romans and 1 Corinthians (p. 489[a], above, *h*), appears to be related to Oecumenius but to name its authorities more frequently; and may possibly prove useful for identifying further quotations from Severian for these two epistles.

‡ As the contributions of both Chrysostom and Theodore for these four epistles can be identified,—in the case of Chrysostom from his *Homilies*, in the case of Theodore from the Latin version (see below, p. 510[b]),—it ought to prove possible, by a process of exclusion, to put together the residue that belongs to Severian; but the attempt has not yet been made.

§ Venables, in *Dict. Christ. Biogr.* iv. 626*b*, speaks of the possibility that quotations given as from Severian may really belong to Severus, the great Monophysite patriarch of Antioch in the early 6th century. But he was not apparently acquainted with the decisive testimony of Cramer's Catena; nor is Severus, active writer as he was, known to have commented formally on any of the Pauline epistles. See further below, p. 522[a].

of the literalist or historical type. An interesting testimony to his reputation as a preacher outside the limits of the influence of either Constantinople or Antioch, is the fact that in the Coptic Church his *Homilies* are prescribed as lessons in Holy Week, together with those of Athanasius, Chrysostom, Shenoute the Copt, and Severus of Antioch the Monophysite.

**15. Theodore of Mopsuestia** (commentaries on all the Epistles).—

1. *THE POSITION OF THEODORE IN HISTORY AMONG SYRIANS, GREEKS, LATINS.*—Theodore—called sometimes of Antioch, where he was born about 350, but more often of Mopsuestia, of which he became bishop in 392—was pupil of Diodore, friend of Chrysostom, and after the latter's death the most influential teacher, whether as theologian or as exegete, within the Eastern Church. Intellectually the greatest of the Antiochene writers, Theodore's greatness was seriously qualified by the defect of one-sidedness: in exegesis he represented the extreme of the reaction against the allegorizers, minimizing or explaining away the Messianic element in the Old Testament; in Christology he dwelt on the ethical value of the human example of Christ so exclusively as almost to make 'the Master' (ὁ δεσπότης Χριστός) a different Person from the indwelling Word. In both aspects Theodore's thought may not unfairly be called rationalizing; and yet there is both in his theology and in his exegesis an important element of truth, such as specially needed emphasis in his day and perhaps also in ours. He died at the end of 428, 'taken away from the evil to come,' just as the theological tendency which he represented and fostered was coming to a head in the Nestorian controversy.

Naturally, Theodore became one of the great saints and doctors of the Nestorian communion. Throughout the long centuries of its prosperity he was to it, *par excellence*, 'the Interpreter': most, if not all, of his commentaries on Holy Scripture were translated into Syriac, and were read in that language for at least 1000 years. Yet, so far, only the commentary on St. John has been in this way recovered: we owe the greater part of our extant Syriac literature to the Monophysite monastery of Nitria in Egypt, and consequently writers of the school of Theodore are but scantily represented in it.

Naturally, again, in proportion as Theodore became an authority among the Nestorians, he became an object of suspicion within the Church. In the first generation, indeed, after the Council of Ephesus in 431, the 'Churches of Syria and Cilicia' remained faithful to the memory of their great teacher: 'we believe as Theodore believed, long live the faith of Theodore.' The Council itself, though in one of its later sessions it had condemned the use of a creed which appears in fact to have been Theodore's, neither on that occasion mentioned his name nor took any other opportunity of aspersing his memory. Cyril of Alexandria did not conceal his own conviction that Theodore and Diodore 'had borne down full sail upon the glory of Christ,' and were the true parents of Nestorianism; he collected and answered a series of propositions taken from their writings; but happily for the peace of the re-united Churches, and in spite of pressure from his more extreme adherents, he declined to commit himself to the fatal policy of *post mortem* anathemas. For a century, therefore, after Theodore's death it remained possible for orthodox Christians of the 'East' to study the Biblical writings of 'the Interpreter' without being calumniated as fautors of heresy: and it is at least not improbable that it was within this period that the Catenæ in which most use is made of him were originally compiled. But the stubborn and protracted resistance which the Chalcedonian definition encountered in so many quarters, caused the centre of gravity in matters theological to shift further and further from the standpoint of the older Antiochene school; while the sensitive orthodoxy which was engendered by the struggle made it easier for each party to procure the condemnation of the extreme wing on the opposite side than to protect the extreme wing on its own. When Justinian anathematized Theodore to please the Monophysites (as he had already anathematized Origen to please the Nestorians), he failed, indeed, to reconcile the separatists, but he might at least claim that his policy had incurred no serious resentment among Greek churchmen. The accusation of Nestorianizing tendencies, repeated under a series of Monophysite emperors, had already driven the orthodox section of the school of Antioch to sacrifice Theodore; and if we may believe the evidence produced in 550 at a council at Mopsuestia,—held, it is true, under pressure from Justinian,—the name of Theodore had been erased from the diptychs of that Church, and the name of Cyril substituted, as far back at any rate as the end of the 5th century.

For the Eastern empire the action of Justinian and his councils was final: the Chalcedonian party in the Greek Church had enough to do to maintain their own orthodoxy and that of the Fourth Council without taking under their protection the favourite teacher of the Nestorians; Theodore's writings, Biblical as well as theological, were placed under a tacit ban, and circulated only, so far as they circulated at all, in fragmentary and emasculated form in the Catenæ. But the Latins were less trammelled by fear of emperors or Monophysites; the resistance, indeed, of pope Vigilius was after a time overcome, but the Churches of Africa and North-eastern Italy broke off communion (and the latter body maintained their separation for over a century) from men who had dared to anathematize not only the opinions, but the name, of one who had 'departed this life in the peace of the Church and the praise of the Fathers.' Justinian employed force; the opposition resorted to the pen. Rusticus, the pope's nephew and deacon, published an improved Latin version of the Acts of Chalcedon. The *Breviarium* of Liberatus, archdeacon of Carthage, and the *pro Defensione Trium Capitulorum* of another African, Facundus, bishop of Hermiana, state the contemporary case against the condemnation, Facundus especially giving us valuable particulars in regard to Theodore's life and writings. Junilius, an African official at Constantinople, introduced Theodore's principles of exegesis to the West under the title *Instituta regularia Divinæ Legis*; while it was probably about the same time, and perhaps also in Africa, that the commentaries of Theodore on the lesser Pauline epistles were translated into Latin and so preserved for the use of future generations. But the controversy of the Three Chapters died out at last, and the same silence about the person and history of Theodore as already prevailed among the Greeks overspread the Western Church also.

2. *GENERAL ESTIMATE OF THEODORE'S STYLE (AS GIVEN BY PHOTIUS).*—Before all first-hand knowledge of Theodore's works had quite disappeared, the patriarch Photius, in the 9th cent., placed on record the only criticism we possess of 'the Interpreter's' literary style. The three books which came into Photius' hands were (α) the 25 or 28 books ὑπὲρ Βασιλείου κατὰ Εὐνομίου, cod. 4, with which in cod. 6 Photius compares and contrasts the treatise, bearing the same title, by Gregory of Nyssa; (β) the commentary in 7 tomes

on Genesis, cod. 38; (γ) the 5 books Πρὸς τοὺς λέγοντας φύσει καὶ οὐ γνώμῃ πταίειν τοὺς ἀνθρώπους, cod. 177. According to his custom, Photius supplements his account of each work with a summary judgment of the merits or defects both of its style and of its subject-matter; and, by combining the three notices, we may form a fair general idea of the impression made by Theodore's writings on a competent and not wholly unsympathetic reader. Strong in power of thought and in his handling of Scripture, Theodore's weak points, according to Photius, are obscurity and prolixity. His style (φράσις) cannot be called lucid (σαφής)—although his vocabulary is simple enough—still less brilliant (λαμπρός); it is, in fact, ungraceful and unpleasing (ἄχαρις καὶ ἀηδής). Its obscurity is due to long-winded periods (σχοινοτενέσι περιόδοις); to the accumulation of parentheses (παρεμβολαῖς ἀλλεπαλλήλοις), which distract the mind from the subject; to fondness for oblique cases and participial constructions (ταῖς τῶν ὀνομάτων πλαγίαις καὶ ταῖς μετοχικαῖς λέξεσι); to continual and inartistic tautology, in which the repetitions are more circumstantial than the original statements (τὰς ἐπαναλήψεις πλέον τῶν διηγήσεων ταῖς περιστάσεσι μεμεστῶσθαι). On the other hand, Theodore's writings are packed close with thought and argument (ταῖς διανοίαις καὶ τοῖς ἐπιχειρήμασι λίαν πυκνός); in fertility and in massiveness of proof (τὸ πλῆθος τῶν ἐπιχειρημάτων καὶ τὸ γόνιμον) he is as much superior to Gregory of Nyssa as he is his inferior in beauty, brilliancy, and charm (κάλλει τε καὶ λαμπρότητι καὶ τῷ ἡδυντάτῳ). Whatever his other faults, the continuous labour he spent on Holy Scripture (φιλοπονώτερον διατεθῆναι), and his wealth of apposite citations from it (ταῖς γραφικαῖς ἄριστα πλουτῶν μαρτυρίαις), deserve full recognition. As an exegete, he avoided allegory as far as possible, and interpreted historically.

The criticisms passed by Photius upon Theodore's style and method would perhaps apply less seriously to exegesis than to some other departments of literature. A wide acquaintance with Scripture, an unwearied devotion to its study, when combined with unusual powers of thought, albeit not of expression, are no contemptible equipment for 'the Interpreter' of St. Paul.

3. *HISTORY OF THEODORE'S COMMENTARY ON THE EPISTLES.*—(i.) *The first complete list.*—The fullest information about Theodore's commentaries, and the first quite definite statement that he expounded the whole series of Pauline epistles, come to us from the great catalogue of Syriac writers drawn up for the Nestorians by their metropolitan Ebed-jesu (died A.D. 1318), and printed in vol. iii. pp. 1-362 of J. S. Assemani's *Bibliotheca Orientalis Clementino-Vaticana* (Rome, A.D. 1725: for Theodore, see pp. 30-35, ch. xix.). The bulk of Theodore's works, Ebed-jesu begins by telling us, amounted to 150 times that of the Prophets: as they were arranged in 41 [it is possible that we ought to read 51] 'divisions' or 'parts,' each part must have been thrice the size of the sixteen Prophets put together. Of these parts, the commentaries on the Old Testament appear to have occupied 18; St. Matthew, St. Luke, St. John, and the Acts, one each; and the Pauline epistles 5. The latter are enumerated as follows (Assemani gives, in parallel columns, the Syriac text and a literal translation into Latin):—

'epistolam quoque ad Romanos ad Eusebium exposuit.
binas ad Corinthios epistolas tomis duobus dilucidavit et illustravit rogatu Theodori.
Eustratius postulavit expositionem quattuor epistolarum quas sum commemoraturus: epistolæ ad Galatas et ad Ephesios et ad Philippenses et ad Colossenses.
binas autem ad Thessalonicenses Iacobo efflagitante exposuit.
epistolam ad Timotheum utramque explicavit ad Petrum.
Cyrino etiam deprecante exposuit epistolam ad Titum et ad Philemonem.
item epistolam ad Hebræos ad eundem Cyrinum dilucidavit.
quinque autem tomis finem imposuit commentariis suis in totum Apostolum.'

If we may assume, as appears probable, that the words *pelga* ('division') and *penqiata* (πίναξ, 'volume') are, for the purpose of the catalogue, identical,—Assemani translates both by 'tomus'—then, of the five parts into which the commentary on St. Paul was distributed, the 1st, 2nd, and 3rd must have contained respectively Romans, 1 Corinthians, and 2 Corinthians; the 4th, Galatians—Colossians, with perhaps 1 and 2 Thessalonians; the 5th, the Pastoral Epistles, Philemon, and Hebrews. This, however, was probably no more than a mere library arrangement of the Syriac volumes: what takes us back nearer to the original composition of the commentaries is the grouping according to their various addressees—Eusebius, Theodore, Eustratius, James, Peter, Cyrinus. Theodore's exposition of St. Paul was therefore not a book carried through continuously and published as a single whole, but a series of at least six parts, which, so far, may or may not have belonged to the same period of his long literary activity, and may or may not have been written after the same method and on the same scale. Like Chrysostom's homilies on the Epistles, Theodore's commentaries must have been too bulky to be compressed within a single binding; and they must therefore have circulated separately or in groups, with the result that one writer would naturally have acquaintance only with some of them, another only with others; exactly as the evidence now to be described shows to have been the case.

(ii.) *Earliest isolated references.*—Ebed-jesu bears witness to the knowledge of Theodore's commentaries on the epistles, and the position held by them, among the Nestorians of the Middle Ages: we have now to turn back to the earlier but more fragmentary references which can be picked out from the controversial writings of the reign of Justinian.

*a.* The first specific mention of any of Theodore's commentaries on the Epistles is in Leontius of Byzantium, *contra Nestorianos et Eutychianos*, between 529 and 544 (see above, p. 504[a]). To each of the three books into which that work is divided a Catena is appended of χρήσεις or *pièces justificatives*, those of Book iii. being taken from Theodore, Diodore, and Paul of Samosata. Mai (*Script. Vet. Nov. Coll.* vi. 299-312) has printed the Theodore passages, with the prologue to them: Leontius there complains bitterly that Theodore's followers were so carefully on their guard against committing any of his writings to the uninitiated, that his own selections had been perforce restricted to the single work περὶ (he intentionally miscalls it κατὰ) τῆς ἐνανθρωπήσεως. From the exegetical books he consequently quotes nothing beyond a single passage on the Psalms; but he gives a list of those which were known to him by name, and compounds for ignorance of their contents by ingeniously vituperative mis-statements of their titles. In this list he includes (besides the books on Genesis, Job, Psalms, St. Matthew, St. John, St. Luke) 'the false interpretation' (τὴν παρεξήγησιν) of the Epistles to the Hebrews, Corinthians, and Galatians.

*β.* The Acts of the Council of Constantinople in 553, which anathematized Theodore, are extant in

Latin. The 32nd of the series of quotations from his works, which were read at the fourth 'collatio' or session, is taken 'ex commento epistolæ ad Hebræos' (Labbe-Coleti, *Concilia*, vi. 55; Mansi, *Concilia*, ix. 216); Theodore there deduces from Ac 10[38a] and Ps 44 (45)[8] that the unction or Messiahship of Jesus was a 'reward.' The *Constitutum ad Imperatorem* of pope Vigilius in the same year examines the Council's quotations one by one, and condemns, under the same heading 'ex commento epistolæ ad Hebræos,' the passage just mentioned (Labbe-Coleti, v. 1336; Mansi, ix. 82): the Latin of the quotation is identical (save for transcriptional errors) in the Acts and in the *Constitutum*, so that probably an official Latin version was ordered by the Council and supplied to the pope. A later pope, Pelagius II., writing to the bishops of Istria in 585,* quotes (from one or other of the above sources) the same passage under the same title (Labbe-Coleti, vi. 269; Mansi, ix. 443).

γ. Facundus of Hermiana (iii. 6; ed. Sirmond, p. 127) quotes in defence of Theodore a passage on Ro 1[8] 'in commento epistolæ ad Romanos,' as showing that he admitted both Messianic prophecy and the unity of Person in the two natures: 'et prophetas de domino Christo locutos et ipsum dominum Christum hominem confitetur et Deum.'

(iii.) *Printed collections of fragments on the epistles from Catenæ.*—α. The first considerable contribution was that of Mai's *Spicilegium Romanum*, iv. (1840) pp. 499–573, consisting of passages from a Vatican Catena on Romans: the number of the MS is not there given, but it is supplied in *Nov. Patr. Bibl.* vii. 407 as Vat. gr. 762 (on which see Karo and Lietzmann's list of Catenæ above, p. 488, *e*). In his *Nova Patrum Bibliotheca*, vii. (1854) 1, pp. 407–408, Mai adds (i.) one more fragment from the same MS on Ro 1[8]; (ii.) 14 or 15 fragments from the same MS on 2 Cor.; (iii.) two small fragments from Vat. gr. 765 (sæc. x.) on Gal 3[3. 22]—which, however, as Lightfoot (*Galatians*[5], p. 229 n.) points out, really belong to Theodoret.

β. Between the earlier and the later publication of Mai, Cramer was issuing the successive volumes of his Catenæ on the Epistles, and thereby adding largely to our stock of fragments from Theodore. The first or Bodleian Catena on Romans (chs. 1–8) contains 54 quotations from Theodore; but since this Catena is beyond doubt descended, directly or indirectly, from the Vatican Catena on which Mai had already drawn (see above, p. 488[b]), no real addition to our knowledge was thereby made. The second or Munich Catena on Romans contains no more than 10 pieces from Theodore, and those quite brief, so that it, too, hardly comes into account. But for 1 Corinthians [the Catena is taken from Paris gr. 227] there are 58 passages from Theodore; and in the same way the Catena on the lesser epistles from Galatians to Philemon [taken from Paris coislin 204] supplied Cramer with no inconsiderable number (see just below, in connexion with the Latin version of the commentary on those epistles).

γ. Of A. F. V. von Wegnern's *Theodori Antiocheni Mopsuestiæ episcopi quæ supersunt omnia*, only the first part, embracing the commentary on the Minor Prophets (Berlin, 1834), ever appeared. But in 1847 the scattered fragments of Theodore's work on the New Testament, as they had appeared in Mai's *Spicilegium* and Cramer's Catena, were put together and arranged in order by O. F. Fritzsche, *Theodori episcopi Mopsuesteni in Novum Testamentum commentariorum quæ reperiri potuerunt* (Zürich). Of this useful volume, pp. 45–107 belong to Romans (Facundus' fragment, and the Catena fragments of Mai and Cramer combined); pp. 108–119 to 1 Cor. (Cramer, with corrections); p. 120 to 2 Cor. (one fragment on 6[6] from Cramer; Mai's *Nova Patrum Bibliotheca*, vii., had not then been published); pp. 121–172 to Galatians–Hebrews (Cramer, with corrections). Fritzsche detected some cases of incorrect attribution to Theodore made by either Cramer's copyist or his MS; but he did not examine the MSS himself, and he worked without the help of the criterion now put into our hands by the discovery of the Latin version. Of his preface, the most interesting part is the disquisition on the unknown writer 'Theodorus monachus.' Cramer's Munich Catena on Romans assigns to this author 39 pieces, but Theodore of Mopsuestia (on the authority of Mai's Vatican Catena) claims 16 out of the 39, and Diodore (on the authority of Cramer's Bodleian Catena) 4, while 2 are Theodoret's. Among historical personages known as 'Theodore the Monk,' the easiest to identify with the exegete of the Catenæ would be, Fritzsche thinks, the Severianist monk Theodore of Alexandria at the beginning of the 6th cent.; but the result of Fritzsche's analysis of the 39 fragments on Romans points rather in the direction of some unknown compiler of the Antiochene school (see below, p. 519[a]).

δ. The edition of Theodore in Migne's *Patrologia Græca*, tom. 66, is, so far as concerns the Pauline epistles (cc. 787-968), reprinted direct from Fritzsche, with the addition of a Latin translation and of the fragments from Mai's *Nov. Patr. Bibl.* vii.*

(iv.) *The Latin version of the commentaries on Galatians–Philemon.*—More important for our knowledge of Theodore than even the discoveries of Mai and Cramer was the identification of a Latin version of the commentary on the ten shorter epistles. The Benedictine editors of St. Ambrose noticed that, of two sister MSS of an exposition of St. Paul belonging to the great library of the abbey of Corbie, near Amiens, the first contained on Romans and on 1 and 2 Corinthians the well-known commentary of Ambrosiaster, the second contained on the remaining epistles (Hebrews not being included) a commentary wholly unknown to them save that Rabanus Maurus had obviously made large use of it (*Ambrosii Opera*, ii., Paris, 1690, App. p. 21).† The next scholar to concern himself with the Corbie commentary (which meanwhile, since the time of the Revolution, had become Nos. 87 and 88 in the public library at Amiens) was another Benedictine, dom, afterwards cardinal, J. B. Pitra. Pitra saw that the unknown commentary was a genuine and unadulterated survival from the Patristic period, far older than the 9th cent.—the date both of Rabanus and of the Corbie MS; and believing that he had found the true author in the person of St. Hilary of Poitiers, he published in 1852, under that Father's name, the full commentary on Galatians, Ephesians, and Philemon, with brief notes on the rest (*Spicilegium Solesmense*, Paris, i. pp. xxvi–xxxv, 49–159). But a comparison of Pitra's text with Cramer's lately published Catena on the same epistles revealed the fact that in the Greek fragments which bore the name of Theodore was to be found the equivalent, so far as they went, of the

* The letter was really written by Pelagius' deacon, Gregory, afterwards pope Gregory the Great.

* E. Sachau's *Theodori Mopsuesteni fragmenta Syriaca e codicibus Musei Britannici Nitriacis* (Leipzig, 1869) appears to contain nothing from any of the commentaries on the Epistles.

† Besides Rabanus (who, however, for Gal. and Eph. used the real Ambrosiaster, and only began his use of the unknown authority with Philippians), we can now add Amalarius, *de Ecclesiasticis Officiis* (Philippians and 1 Timothy), and archbishop Lanfranc's commentary on St. Paul (Galatians to Philemon), as well as an isolated reference on Galatians in the *Collectanea* of Sedulius Scotus; see Swete's *Theodore*, pp. xlvi–li, and vol. ii. p. 346.

Latin of the Corbie MS; and the only possible conclusion was that in the latter we possessed a complete version of Theodore's commentary on these epistles. The comparison was made, and the conclusion drawn, by J. L. Jacobi in 1854 (*Deutsche Zeitschrift für christliche Wissenschaft und christliches Leben*), and, independently, by Dr. Hort in 1859 (*Journal of Classical and Sacred Philology*, iv. 302-308). Dr. Hort afterwards discovered a second and slightly earlier MS in Brit. Mus. Harley 3063, from Cusa on the Moselle; and an edition of the Latin version, with a re-collation of Cramer's Greek fragments for the ten epistles covered by it, was published in 1880 by Dr. H. B. Swete (*Theodore of Mopsuestia on the minor Epistles of St. Paul: Theodori Mopsuesteni in epistolas B. Pauli commentarii*, 2 vols., Cambridge)—a book of the rare kind for which praise is superfluous.

The Latin supplies us on the one hand with some sort of representation of Theodore's meaning over long pages where the Greek entirely fails us, and on the other with a test for the verification of what really in the Catena belongs to Theodore. It is satisfactory to find that the net result has been to add to the number of fragments admitted as genuine by Fritzsche; for whereas only seven of his passages have to be struck out, there are nearly 40 others in the Catena of which Theodore had wrongly been deprived (Swete, p. xvii, n. 3 and 4). That the catenist can now be shown to have often abridged and occasionally paraphrased his author (Swete, p. xxxv), is no more than the parallel experience of other writers in the Catenæ might have led us to expect.

The translator may be credited on the whole with faithfulness and conscientiousness; but neither his knowledge of Greek (at any rate of Theodore's Greek) nor his command of his own tongue was sufficient to produce what could be called, from a literary point of view, a successful version. As to his date, it is natural to bring the attempt to introduce Theodore to Western readers into connexion with the circle of Facundus and Junilius, and to place him conjecturally at or soon after the middle of the 6th cent.; and the conjecture is in harmony with the evidence of his Biblical text, which (when it is not simply a literal rendering of Theodore's) displays sometimes reminiscences of the Vulgate, but more often reminiscences of the Old Latin (see, for fuller details on all these points, Swete, pp. xxxv–lviii). It is a less easy question to answer, whether his translation included also the longer epistles. The evidence of Rabanus Maurus suggests that there were MSS which gave Ambrosiaster for Rom.-Ephesians, Theodore for the rest; the existing MSS with Lanfranc (and, presumably, Sedulius) make the change from Ambrosiaster to Theodore between 2 Cor. and Gal.; possibly, therefore, it may be argued, other MSS may have existed which supplanted Ambrosiaster by Theodore at a still earlier point or even from the beginning. Yet we have seen (p. 509ᵇ) that Theodore's Greek commentaries on the epistles did not circulate in a single volume; and in the absence of definite indications to the contrary it is safest to suppose that the translator had access to only a portion of them, and that the whole of his work has now been recovered. As an imperfect commentary, there was an obvious reason for completing it by borrowing the missing epistles from some other commentary, such as Ambrosiaster's; and the accident that the missing epistles happened to be the first in the series explains also how it was that the name already attached to them came to be attached to the rest of the series as well, so that Carolingian scribes and scholars read Theodore of Mopsuestia under the pseudonym of Ambrose of Milan.

(v.) *Order and date of Theodore's commentaries on the Epistles.*—Of the order in which Theodore commented on the different epistles of St. Paul he gives several indications by cross-references from one commentary to another (Swete, p. lxiii).—(α) *Galatians after Romans:* on Gal $3^{23}$ (Swete, i. p. 51, l. 6) he refers to Ro $11^{32}$: 'si nostram decurrere voluerit interpretationem in qua latius id explicasse videmur.'—(β) *Galatians after Hebrews:* on Gal $4^{24}$ (i. 76, l. 10) he says, 'in epistola illa quæ ad Hebræos est interpretantes ostendimus evidentius.'*—(γ) *Galatians after several (?) other epistles:* on Gal $2^4$ (i. 16, l. 20) he alludes to previous notes on many passages, 'multis enim in locis coniunctiones a beato Paulo non cum debita sequentia positas esse ostendimus.'—(δ) *Ephesians after Galatians:* on Eph $1^4$ (i. 123, l. 4) he refers to his comment on Gal $3^{23}$: 'dixi ['dixit' MSS, wrongly] namque et in epistola Galatarum.'—(ε) *Colossians after Philippians:* on Col $1^{17}$ (i. 272, l. 12) he refers to Ph $2^{6-8}$: 'hoc enim ostendimus ['ostendemus' MSS, but the confusion of i and e is very common] fecisse apostolum et Philippensibus scribentem.'—(ζ) *1 Timothy after Philippians:* on 1 Ti $3^8$ (ii. 118, l. 13) he refers to Ph $1^1$: καὶ τοῦτο ἐπεσημηνάμεθα καὶ ἐν τῇ πρὸς Φιλιππησίους.—(η) *1 Timothy after most of the other Epistles:* on 1 Ti $1^{3,4}$ (ii. 71, l. 12) he mentions 'interpretationem nostram quam propemodum per omnes epistolas explicasse videmur.'—(θ) *Titus after 1 Timothy:* on Tit $1^6$ (ii. 237, l. 20) he refers to 1 Ti $3^2$: 'dictum est nobis hoc idem latius in illa epistola quam ad Timotheum inprimis dudum scripseramus.'

Thus, with the exception that Hebrews came somewhere near the beginning of the list, Theodore appears, so far as we can judge, to have written on the Epistles in the order of our New Testament Canon. But both the separate dedications of the different groups recorded by Ebed-jesu (p. 509, above), and the interval between the commentary on Titus and that on 1 Timothy 'quam dudum scripseramus,'† suggest that the whole exposition may have been spread over some considerable number of years. The work on at least the later Epistles was posterior to the work on the Gospels: on Col $1^{17}$ (i. 273, l. 5) he refers to the explanation of Jn 5, 'si interpretationem nostram decurrere voluerit in illam partem evangelii Iohannis'; on 1 Ti $1^4$ (ii. 74, ll. 2–6) to the explanation of the genealogies, 'interpretationem nostram . . . quam de evangeliis expressisse visi sumus'; and on 1 Ti $3^{16}$ (ii. 137, l. 14) to his exegesis of the Epistles and Gospels as a whole, 'sicut non solum in apostolica interpretatione id ostendimus, sed et in evangeliorum interpretatione identidem id demonstravimus.'

Seeing that Theodore's prolonged span of exegetical activity extended over the whole of the last quarter of the 4th cent. and of the first quarter of the 5th, the conclusion so far reached with regard to the date or dates of his commentaries on the Epistles is not very precise. One line of argument, however, still remains to be examined which may bear upon the chronology, namely, the relation of his commentaries to those of other more or less contemporary exegetes.‡

* Note that the Epistle to the Hebrews comes next *before* Galatians in the Sahidic version (Scrivener, *Introd. to the Criticism of the NT*⁴, i. 57, ii. 138): next *after* Galatians in the system of chapters running through the Pauline epistles in the margin of B (*op. cit.* i. 56, 57).

† Yet 'dudum' may only represent ἤδη, as perhaps in Swete, i. 112, l. 2.

‡ Dr. Swete (p. lxi) emphasizes in this connexion the use apparently made by Theodore of the Euthalian 'chapters' as indicating a date after A.D. 396. Some attempt will be made later on in this article (see p. 524) to deal in outline with the intricate questions that centre round the name of Euthalius.

Ancient commentators were accustomed to study and copy earlier models, and were studied and copied by later imitators in their turn. Theodore, though he was of too independent a mind to copy his predecessors as much as others did, probably studied them quite as much, to judge from the frequency with which he records the views of 'certain people' and expresses disagreement with them. To Origen's system of exegesis he, of course, stood in fundamental opposition. The material is hardly sufficient to enable us to estimate the extent of his undoubted debt to Diodore; and even if it should be proved that he used also Chrysostom and Severian—both of them more nearly his contemporaries than was Diodore—yet even their expositions might have been in his hands before the year 400 A.D. Of his successors, Theodoret can be shown to have exploited him freely (below, p. 517[a]); but Theodoret probably wrote after Theodore's death, and furnishes us therefore with no new *terminus ad quem*. But between Diodore and Chrysostom on the one hand, and Theodoret on the other, there is yet one other commentator whose evidence is crucial for the chronology of Theodore. The date of Pelagius' Latin exposition of St. Paul falls within the years 401–409, and since his points of contact with Theodore appear to be unambiguous (Swete, pp. lxxiv–lxxvi), we get a new *terminus ad quem* or *a quo* for the latter, according as we make his share in the common matter original or derivative. The question can be fully answered only when the true text of Pelagius has been restored from a comparison of the various recensions in which he has come down to us.* Dr. Swete inclines to the view that Theodore borrowed from Pelagius; but it would be unusual to find a Greek writer using a Latin authority, and in two at least of the parallels (Gal 3[20], 2 Ti 2[20]), while Theodore states his own view and no other, Pelagius prefixes to the view that coincides with Theodore the formula 'ut quidam putant.'† If then Pelagius drew on Theodore, and that for the later as well as the earlier Epistles, it would follow that Theodore's exposition of St. Paul was completed very early in the 5th century: nor does there seem to be anything which seriously conflicts with such a conclusion.

4. *THEODORE AS A COMMENTATOR ON ST. PAUL.*‡—Theodore is the typical Antiochene exegete, not in the sense that he serves as a standard for judging other commentators of the school, or as a mean from which in one direction or another they diverge, but in the sense that the literal and historical method of interpretation, which (with whatever qualifications) is distinctive of them all, is in him carried out to its most rigorous extreme. The present age is impatient of any form of allegorizing, and so is inclined to sympathize with Theodore; and yet it might be well to recollect that it was Origen's allegorical interpretation of the early chapters of Genesis which, as much as anything else, aroused the opposition of the Antiochenes, and that Theodore's literalist principles committed him to the acceptance of the story of Jonah as a record of actual historical fact. No doubt, Messianic applications of the Old Testament had often led to exegesis that was arbitrary in the extreme, and Theodore voices the reaction of common-sense; no doubt also it can be urged, with show of truth, that at least in the New Testament there is no place for allegory, and that Theodore's position is here inexpugnable. And he would be a singularly unfair critic who failed to recognize and appreciate the services of Theodore's severely logical mind in expounding the often difficult connexion and concatenation of the Apostle's thought; in this direction probably no ancient expositor either attempted or achieved as much; and for that alone, if all other merits were refused them, these commentaries of his would possess a real and permanent value. But it is also just this relentless sense of logic which from another side sets a fatal limitation on Theodore's powers of exegesis; for he approaches the study of the Epistles, unconsciously no doubt to himself, with the expectation of finding in them, not merely a theological system as complete as his own, but the particular system at which he had himself arrived. St. Paul's thoughts do not always consent to be labelled and put in their proper place as parts of an organized and coherent body of doctrine; and so far as they do admit of it, it is not quite on Theodore's lines. The contrast between ἡ πάρουσα and ἡ μέλλουσα κατάστασις, which dominates Theodore's whole scheme of the universe, is a fruitful one, but it does not exhaust, and in part it does not even correspond to, the theology of St. Paul. To Theodore the 'present condition' and 'future condition' are indeed those of sin and sinlessness, but they are also those of death and immortality, of change and changelessness; and it is on this aspect of the contrast that Theodore's optimistic thought habitually dwells. Redemption tends to be predominantly the restoration of the gift of immortality, moral lapse a weakness of our mortal condition, Christ our human example in the successful struggle with it. It would be rash to say that there is no room for Theodore's conceptions in the wide cycle of Christian theology; but they are not the characteristic conceptions of St. Paul, and so far Theodore could not be his ideal 'Interpreter.'

**16. Isidore of Pelusium** (letters on detailed points of exegesis).—

With Isidore a new chapter opens: we are on the threshold of the era when Greek exegesis ceases to be strictly original, and begins to reproduce what seemed most worthy of preservation in the great writers of the past; and however great the loss in vigour and freshness which this change entailed, it carried with it at least the compensating advantage of expanded sympathies. Allegorical and literalist systems could each claim the sanction of illustrious names: neither could be wholly rejected by those who wished to walk in the footsteps of the 'Fathers.' St. Isidore is the earliest expositor in whose case geographical position is not the decisive factor in determining exegetical affinities. His nationality and all the external circumstances of his life connected him exclusively with Alexandria, while his literary studies and his ecclesiastical hero-worship tended rather to make him a follower of the great homilist of Antioch. The interest which attaches to him in these respects is sufficient excuse for finding a place in this article for a writer whose exegetical remains consist only of answers to correspondents about difficulties in the explanation of detached passages of the Sacred Text.

Isidore, as his name suggests, was an Egyptian; and his whole career, so far as we know, was spent

* With the appearance of H. Zimmer's book *Pelagius in Irland* (Berlin, 1901), all previous discussions of the subject of Pelagius' commentary, and of the related commentaries of pseudo-Jerome and pseudo-Primasius (cf. Swete, p. xlv), were at once superseded; see a review of Zimmer by the present writer in *Journal of Theological Studies* (October 1902), iv. 132–141.

† Of course a common source for Theodore and Pelagius—in that case probably Diodore—is conceivable; but Theodore's work is the more likely to have reached the West.

‡ See Swete, pp. lxv–lxxi, lxxix–lxxxvii, and Kihn, *Theodor von Mopsuestia und Junilius Africanus als Exegeten* (Freiburg im Breisgau, 1880). The first 200 pages of Dr. Kihn's admirable monograph are devoted to Theodore and his Biblical exegesis: unfortunately, he wrote before the publication of Dr. Swete's edition, and pays little or no attention to the commentaries on St. Paul.

in Egypt. Of Alexandrine family (according to Ephraem of Antioch, in Photius cod. 228), and, to judge from his extensive learning, of Alexandrine training, he early embraced the monastic life and commenced the prolonged residence at Pelusium, the frontier-city between Egypt and Palestine, which has given him the title that distinguishes him from his namesake of Seville. From Pelusium he carried on, during a period of which different critics extend the limits as far back as 395 and as far on as 450, the vast correspondence on which his fame mainly rests. It is enough for the present purpose to say that Isidore, when writing to Cyril of Alexandria during and after the Council of Ephesus in 431, employs towards the archbishop a familiarity and even authority of tone which imply either advanced age or long-established reputation.

The dogmatic interest was a much stronger one than the exegetical in the generations which succeeded Isidore; and it appears probable that his letters owe their survival as a collection to the use made of them in the Monophysite controversy. Whether or no he survived till the outbreak under Dioscorus of the secular struggle, Isidore was sufficiently Antiochene, in theology as well as exegesis, to have spoken with no uncertain sound about the truth of Christ's manhood: *Θεοῦ πάθος οὐ λέγεται, Χριστοῦ γὰρ τὸ πάθος γέγονε, σαρκωθέντος δηλονότι Θεοῦ καὶ τῇ προσλήψει τῆς σαρκὸς τὸ πάθος ὑπομείναντος* (*Ep.* i. 124); *ἐκ φύσεων δυοῖν ὁ εἷς ὑπάρχων υἱός* (*Ep.* i. 323, to Cyril); *ἐν ἑκατέραις ταῖς φύσεσιν εἷς ὑπάρχει υἱὸς Θεοῦ* (*Ep.* i. 405). Consequently we find the writers on the Chalcedonian side, Ephraem of Antioch, Leontius of Byzantium, Facundus of Hermiana, appealing to his authority; while the great Monophysite writer Severus attempts (according to Stephen Gobar, in Photius cod. 232) to turn the edge of the appeal by accusing Isidore of Origenism. The principal stronghold at Constantinople of the Chalcedonians was the monastery of the *Acœmetæ* or 'Sleepless ones'; and it was the Acœmetæ who, somewhere in the century 450–550 A.D., collected and published an edition of 2000 of Isidore's letters. Facundus apparently quotes from this collection; and nearly fifty letters were excerpted from it and translated into Latin (together with a very numerous series of documents bearing on the Nestorian controversy) by a scholar of the time of Justinian, whose work is preserved to us in two MSS of the 12th cent., Casinensis 2 and Vaticanus 1319.

From the same collection of 2000 letters, and from no other source, all our Greek MSS are derived. The oldest of them (Grotta Ferrata B α I), written in 985, and never yet employed for the printed texts, contains 1600 letters, numbered from 1 to 600, and from 1001 to 2000; another at Paris (gr. 832, of the 13th cent.) contains the first 1213 letters; while two 16th cent. MSS at the Vatican (Vat. gr. 649-650 and Vat. Ottob. gr. 341-383) contain the whole 2000, numbered through continuously from the first to the last. One or two more give some portion of the collection in its proper order; but a much larger number give groups of letters selected out of the rest because of their connexion with some particular topic. Thus Bodl. Laud. gr. 42, sæc. xii., contains thirty-eight letters on the Psalter, arranged in the order of the Psalms with which they deal, though to each letter is still prefixed its proper number in the continuous series. Within this class one MS distinguishes itself from the rest, both for the large bulk of letters which it contains and for the influence which it has exercised upon the printed texts,—Venice Marcianus 126, sæc. xiv.: of its 1148 letters, the first division, 484 in number, are concerned exclusively with the exegesis of different parts of Scripture.*

Unfortunately, the history of the printed texts became entangled at an early point with this other or indirect line of the manuscript tradition. The *editio princeps*, prepared by the abbé Jacques Billi, and published posthumously at Paris in 1585, was taken, indeed, from the Paris MS above mentioned, and consisted therefore of the first 1213 letters of the original collection. These were divided by the editor, it is not clear on what grounds, into three books, the first comprising 500, the second 300, and the third the remaining 413; but, apart from this division into books, the letters then printed were printed in the exact order in which the Acœmetæ had arranged them. To the next editor, Rittershusius, or rather to the MS on which he relied, is due the confusion which still prevails in the printed texts of Isidore. He used a Munich copy of the Venice MS, and found in it as many as 230 letters which had not appeared in Billi's edition; his own edition, published at Heidelberg in 1605, repeated Billi's three books, and added to them a fourth, consisting of the 230 new letters, thus raising the total number to 1443. As we have seen that the interest of the scholar (whoever he was) who put together the collection of the Venice MS was in the first place exegetical, it is not surprising that the fourth book should contain a specially large proportion of strictly exegetical letters, or that the editor who finally completed the printed collection, the Jesuit A. Schott, though he was able to add 569 new letters from the Vatican Library, added few of the more strictly exegetical sort. Schott published his 569 letters as a fifth book† (without reprinting the earlier books), first in Greek alone, Antwerp 1623; next in a Latin version only, Rome 1624; and finally in both Greek and Latin, Frankfort 1629. The four books of Billi-Rittershusius and the fifth book of Schott were combined in the Paris edition of Morel, 1638; and this edition (which has Greek text and Latin translation throughout) has never been superseded, though the imperfections of its text are only less glaring than its faults of typography and defective indexes. Something was done for the improvement of the text in the publication by P. Possinus, Rome 1670, of collations made from Roman MSS, under the direction of cardinal Barberini, some thirty years earlier; and these notes of Possinus are incorporated at the foot of the page in Migne's reprint of Morel's text (*Patr. Gr.* 78). Four dissertations by German, French, Swedish, and Italian scholars respectively — Niemayer, (Halle, 1825; reprinted in Migne), E. L. A. Bouvy (Nîmes, 1884), V. Lundström (in *Eranos*, vol. ii. [Upsala, 1897] p. 68), and N. Capo in *Studi di filologia classica*, ix. (Florence, 1901)—have each contributed something to our knowledge of the MSS of Isidore; but a new edition remains one of the *desiderata* of Patristic literature.‡

Among the letters of Isidore which deal with the study of Holy Scripture in general may be mentioned *Epp.* i. 369; iv. 91, 140, 208, 221; v. 281, 293, 318. More nearly approaching the subject of exegesis are the letters on linguistic topics, such as that on the use of *μήποτε* in Scripture (ii. 270), or those on Scripture synonyms [Trench, *Synonyms of*

* There is some reason to think that Isidore's letters may have been translated into Syriac: two British Museum MSS (cod. dcccxxvii. = Add. 14731, sæc. xi., and cod. xlix. of Rose and Forshall's catalogue, sæc. xiii.) contain selections from his correspondence.

† The total number of letters thus became 2012; but Rittershusius had printed in his fourth book several that were really already in Billi, and in the same way Schott's fifth book contained several that had appeared in Rittershusius.

‡ Fuller details about the history, MSS, and editions of the collection of Isidore's letters will be found in a paper by the present writer, *Journal of Theological Studies*, 1904.

*the New Testament*, pp. xiv–xvi, does not seem to know of them] (iii. 92 ; iv. 130 ; v. 128, 203, 286, 337, 338, 411). Far more numerous are the letters which are exegetical in the strictest sense, as explaining passages in which Isidore's correspondents had appealed to him for help.

The prominent place which belongs here to the Pauline epistles may be explained naturally enough on the ground of their inherent difficulties ; but it also corresponds to the special veneration which Isidore displays towards the Apostle. He never tires of drawing on the resources of his vocabulary for fresh phrases with which to do him honour : St. Paul is *ὁ θεσπέσιος Παῦλος, τὸ σκεῦος τῆς ἐκλογῆς, ὁ τῶν τοῦ Χριστοῦ νοημάτων ταμίας, ὁ γῆν καὶ θάλασσαν ῥυθμίσας, ὁ βαρβάροις φιλοσοφεῖν ἀναπείσας* (ii. 124) ; *ὁ κορυφαῖος [τῶν νομίμως τὸν παρόντα βίον διαθλησάντων]* (iii. 207) ; *ὁ τῶν ἀνθρωπίνων πραγμάτων ἀκριβῶς βασανίσας τὴν φύσιν* (iii. 351; cf. v. 74) ; *ὁ ἐξ Ἰουδαικῆς ἐπάλξεως εὐαγγελικὸν μηχάνημα γεγονώς* (v. 197) ; and see especially iv. 80 (on St. Paul as the *σκεῦος ἐκλογῆς*, and on miracles) and v. 299 (on the reasons for our veneration of St. Paul, and on the contrast between him and those who claim to be his successors).

The following is a list of the letters, some eighty in number, which are directed exclusively or primarily to the interpretation of passages in the Pauline Epistles :—

| | *Epp.* | | *Epp.* |
|---|---|---|---|
| Ro $1^{22}$ | ii. 213; iii. 350; iv. 194. | 1 Co $9^{27}$ | iii. 265 ; v. 144. |
| $1^{28}$ | iv. 59. | $10^{12}$ | iv. 14. |
| $1^{32}$ | iv. 60 (cf. v. 74). | $10^{27}$ | iv. 68. |
| $2^{10}$ | iv. 61. | $12^{27}$ | iv. 103. |
| $3^{25}$ | iv. 100. | $13^{11}$ | i. 443, 444. |
| $6^{12.\,23}$ | iv. 52. | $13^{12}$ | ii. 56. |
| $7^{8}$ | iv. 62. | $14^{20}$ | i. 442. |
| $8^{8}$ | i. 477. | $15^{29}$ | i. 221. |
| $8^{18}$ | iv. 63. | $15^{31}$ | iii. 399. |
| $8^{28}$ | iv. 13, 51. | $15^{56}$ | iv. 52. |
| $9^{1-3}$ | ii. 58. | 2 Co $4^{7}$ | ii. 4, 5. |
| $11^{8}$ | iv. 101. | $5^{13}$ | iii. 266. |
| $12^{1}$ | iii. 75. | $5^{16}$ | iv. 46. |
| $12^{18}$ | iii. 284, 285 ; iv. 36, 37, 120, 220. | $12^{9}$ | i. 423 ; iii. 182. |
| $12^{20}$ | iv. 11. | $13^{7}$ | iv. 7. |
| $13^{1}$ | ii. 216. | Gal $1^{8}$ | iii. 165. |
| $13^{3.\,7}$ | iv. 12, 102. | $3^{15}$ | ii. 196. |
| $13^{7}$ | iv. 16. | Eph $2^{15}$ | iii. 53. |
| $13^{13}$ | i. 456. | $4^{26}$ | ii. 189, 239. |
| 1 Co $1^{20}$ | i. 429. | $4^{31}$ | i. 328. |
| $2^{2}$ | iv. 150. | Ph $1^{29}$ | iv. 104. |
| $2^{14}$ | iv. 81, 127. | $2^{3}$ | iv. 22. |
| $3^{1.\,2}$ | i. 445. | $2^{6}$ | i. 139. |
| $3^{8}$ | v. 82. | $3^{19}$ | iii. 186, 187, 188. |
| $3^{18}$ | iv. 6. | Col $1^{15}$ | iii. 31. |
| $4^{5}$ | iv. 94. | $2^{9}$ | iv. 166. |
| $6^{7}$ | iv. 95. | $2^{15}$ | iv. 108. |
| $6^{10}$ | iv. 42. | 1 Ti $3^{1}$ | iii. 216 ; iv. 219. |
| $6^{18}$ | iv. 129. | $3^{16}$ | ii. 192. |
| $7^{29}$ | i. 413. | $4^{3}$ | iv. 112. |
| $9^{5}$ | iii. 176. | $5^{8}$ | ii. 124. |
| $9^{20.\,21}$ | ii. 138. | Tit $1^{16}$ | ii. 64 ; iv. 85.* |

None of the printed Catenæ on the Epistles have made any extended use of this large body of letters. Isidore is quoted once in Cramer's Bodleian Catena on Romans : $7^{8}$=*Ep.* iv. 62 ; eleven times in his Munich Catena on Romans : $7^{8}$ as before ; $8^{8}$=i. 477 ; $8^{28}$=iv. 51 ; $9^{1-3}$=ii. 58 ; $11^{8}$=iv. 101 ; $12^{1}$=iii. 75 ; $12^{18}$=iv. 220 ; $12^{20}$=iv. 11 ; $13^{1}$=ii. 216 ; $13^{7}$=iv. 16 ; $13^{13}$=i. 456 ; and twice in his Catena on 1 Corinthians : $6^{18}$=iv. 129, and $9^{20.\,21}$=ii. 138. Among Karo and Lietzmann's Catenæ, No. vii. (on Romans) quotes, we are told, *Epp.* 1245, 1244, 1323, 1337 ; but these letters belong exactly to that part of the collection where it is not at present possible to bring the old numeration into comparison with the printed text—no doubt they are all to be found in Book iv.

Isidore as an independent interpreter has a terseness and directness of his own : but perhaps the reason why he is not more often quoted in the Catenæ is that his explanations are sometimes only echoes of those of Chrysostom ; compare, for instance, the comment on Ro $12^{18}$ in *Ep.* iii. 284 with the parallel passage in the latter's *Homilies.* Isidore's panegyric on Chrysostom's whole exposition of the Romans has been mentioned above (p. 502[b]) ; and elsewhere he cites the letter of Libanius to Chrysostom as illustrating *τὴν τοῦ ἀοιδίμου Ἰωάννου* [*sc.* Chrysostom] *γλῶτταν καὶ τὸ κάλλος τῶν νοημάτων καὶ τὴν πυκνότητα τῶν ἐνθυμημάτων* (ii. 42). Nor was admiration for his writings divorced in Isidore's mind from admiration for his life and character : Chrysostom is called by him (in reference to his *de Sacerdotio*) *ὁ τῶν τοῦ θεοῦ ἀπορρήτων ὑποφήτης, ὁ τῆς ἐν Βυζαντίῳ ἐκκλησίας καὶ πάσης ὀφθαλμός* (i. 156) : in the cause of Chrysostom he can speak plainly about one patriarch of Alexandria, or plead boldly with another ; Egypt, he says, by making use of Theophilus *τὸν λιθομανῆ καὶ χρυσολάτρην, τὸν θεοφιλῆ καὶ θεολόγον κατεπολέμησεν ἄνθρωπον* (i. 152), and he writes to Cyril, in the interests of peace and reconciliation, a letter that is universally understood to allude to the restoration of St. Chrysostom's name to the diptychs (i. 370).

Thus, just as in doctrine he represents a reaction in Egypt from the extremer type of Egyptian theology, so too in exegesis Isidore, Egyptian and Alexandrine though he was, modified the allegorical traditions of Alexandrine exegesis under the influences of Chrysostom's writings. He takes up a middle position between those who interpreted the whole of the Old Testament directly of Christ, and those who refused so to interpret any of it : *ἐγὼ δὲ ἀναγκαίως φημὶ ἀμφότερα γεγενῆσθαι, τό τε μὴ πάντα λελέχθαι περὶ αὐτοῦ καὶ τὸ μὴ παντελῶς τὰ κατ᾽ αὐτὸν σεσιγῆσθαι* (ii. 195). He will not refuse to allow some place to allegorical interpretations, and he gently rebukes a correspondent who had asked for a purely literalist explanation of some provisions of the Mosaic legislation : *τοὺς τὰς θεωρίας ὑποφαίνοντας καὶ τὸ γράμμα εἰς τὸ πνεῦμα μεταρυθμίζοντας οὐκ οἶδ᾽ ὅπως αἰτιασάμενος, καίτοι πολλάκις ὠφέλιμά τινα τοῖς ἀκροωμένοις λέγοντας, αὐτὰ τὰ πράγματα ἑρμηνευθῆναί σοι λιπαρῶς παρεκάλεσας* (ii. 81). Even in matters belonging to the New Testament, allegorical interpretations can be found in Isidore ; but to what a subordinate position, at least in dealing with the Pauline epistles, he relegates the allegorical sense, may be illustrated from *Ep.* iv. 129, where, in enumerating many possible explanations of the precise meaning of 1 Co $6^{18}$ *εἰς τὸ ἴδιον σῶμα ἁμαρτάνει*, he has recourse to allegorizing as a ninth alternative only : *εἰ δὲ καὶ τραπῆναι ἡμᾶς βούλει εἰς τὴν τῆς ἀλληγορίας ὁδόν, ἐνάτη ἔστω ἡ λεχθησομένη.*

**17. Cyril of Alexandria** (commentaries on Romans, 1 Corinthians, 2 Corinthians).—

Cyril, the great opponent of Nestorianism, was archbishop of Alexandria from 412 till his death in 444. Nothing is known as to the date of his birth. His relations to Isidore of Pelusium seem to have been those of a younger to an older man, but he was of sufficiently mature years in 403 to be present, in the train of his uncle and predecessor Theophilus, at the Council of the Oak which condemned Chrysostom. The overpowering dogmatic

* For completeness' sake, references to the Hebrews may here be added : He $1^{3}$=*Epp.* iii. 58 ; $2^{15}$=iv. 146 ; $4^{8}$=iv. 147, v. 91 ; $4^{13}$=i. 94 ; $9^{17}$=iv. 113 ; $10^{28}$=iv. 168 ; $12^{7}$=iii. 184 ; $12^{16}$=i. 320 ; $12^{17}$=iv. 26 ; $13^{4}$=iv. 192.

interest of Cyril's career and writings has naturally tended to obscure the interest of his exegetical work; yet the bulk even of what is preserved of the latter class is far more considerable than that of the former, and the original discrepancy must have been greater still. Too much stress need not be laid on the statement of Cassiodorus, in the preface to his *Inst. Div. Litt.*, that Cyril was one of those who had expounded in the Greek language the Divine Scriptures of the Old and New Testament 'ab ipso principio usque ad finem'; for not only Clement of Alexandria (of whose *Hypotyposes* it was more or less true, see below, p. $520^b$), but Chrysostom, Gregory, and Basil, are included under the same heading, and there is every reason to suppose it inexact in the case of the latter writers. But out of the seven volumes which make up the only complete edition of Cyril's works—that of Aubert (Paris, 1638)—four consist wholly of exegetical matter; and yet this edition contained nothing on the New Testament except the portions which have survived of the commentary on St. John. For two centuries after Aubert little more was done; but the last seventy years have witnessed the recovery of a Syriac version of the commentary on St. Luke, and of considerable fragments in the original Greek of commentaries on St. Matthew and on some of the Pauline epistles.

That Cyril had commented on the Epistle to the Hebrews there was a good deal of ancient evidence, in Theodoret, Leontius, Facundus, and others, to show; but for the epistles of St. Paul, properly speaking, the only direct witness that was in print until within the last sixty or seventy years appears to have been a solitary quotation (itself perhaps taken from a Catena) in the Acts of the Second Council of Nicæa in 787 (Mansi, xiii. 289). The 'definition' of the Iconoclastic Council of 754 had appealed to 2 Co $5^{16.\,17}$, and the answer of the orthodox appeals, among other interpreters, to Cyril: *καὶ Κύριλλος δὲ ὁ Ἀλεξανδρεὺς ὁ ὑπέρμαχος τῆς εἰλικρινοῦς ἡμῶν πίστεως σαφηνίζων ἡμῖν τὸ αὐτὸ ῥητὸν οὕτως διερμηνεύει· Ἐπειδὴ γὰρ γέγονεν ἄνθρωπος ὁ μονογενὴς τοῦ Θεοῦ Λόγος* (there follows a passage of some 18 lines).*

Cramer's Catenæ on the Epistles to the Corinthians (A.D. 1841) and Romans (A.D. 1844) first supplied sufficient material to prove the existence of continuous commentaries; for his Catena on 1 Corinthians contained sixty quotations from Cyril, his Bodleian Catena forty-four quotations for Ro 1–8, and his Munich Catena about seventy for Ro 7–16. Similar proof for 2 Corinthians (the epistle cited in the Second Nicene Council) was not long delayed, for the 3rd volume of Mai's *Nova Patrum Bibliotheca*—the title-page of which bears the date 1845, though the year 1849 is mentioned in the preface—published from the Vatican Catena, MS gr. 762, a whole series of Cyrilline excerpts on Romans (pp. 1–47), 1 Corinthians (pp. 48–82), and 2 Corinthians (pp. 83–103), together with one fragment apiece from other sources for Galatians and Colossians; a Latin translation follows in part 2 of the same volume, pp. 1–67. For the first two epistles Mai had been largely anticipated by Cramer, since two of the latter's MSS (that on 1 Cor. and the Bodleian Catena on Romans) were descendants, collateral or direct, of Mai's Vatican MS; but for the latter chapters of Romans Mai's matter was partly, and for 2 Corinthians it was wholly, new.

A commencement of a comprehensive reissue of Cyril's works was made by the late P. E. Pusey, and the following portions had appeared when the work was prematurely cut short by his death in 1880: the commentary on the Minor Prophets (2 vols., Oxford, 1868), the commentary on St. John (3 vols., 1872), and two volumes of dogmatic treatises (1875, 1877). Happily for our present purpose, the third volume of the commentary on St. John was extended to include the remains of the commentaries on St. Paul: Romans (pp. 173–248), 1 Corinthians (pp. 249–319), 2 Corinthians (pp. 320–361, as well as Hebrews, pp. 362–440). This edition entirely supersedes those of Cramer (whose two MSS on the Romans were re-collated) and Mai; for it combines their material with additional fragments on the two Corinthian epistles from an early Catena in the monastery of Pantocrator on Mount Athos (see below, p. $522^b$),* and with a few new fragments on Ro 1 (Pusey, pp. 173–175) drawn from a Vienna Catena (Karo and Lietzmann's No. vii.: see above, p. $489^a$). Several important changes are also made in this edition in the matter of passages incorrectly ascribed to St. Cyril.†

From the Athos Catena the division of Cyril's commentaries on the two Corinthian epistles into *τόμοι* and *λόγοι* can to some extent be reconstructed, though it must of course be remembered that these 'tomes' and 'chapters' do not necessarily begin at the verses where they happen to be quoted. The following indications are supplied: 1 Co $6^{18}$ *ἐκ τοῦ γ' τόμου*, $7^{21}$ *ἐκ τοῦ δ'* [MS ᾳ for Δ] *τόμου*, $10^{1}$ *τόμος δ' λόγος γ'*, $11^{3}$ *τόμος δ' λόγος δ'*, $12^{3}$ *τόμος ϵ' λόγος α'*, $14^{2}$ *τόμος ϵ' λόγος β'*, $14^{10}$ *τόμος ϵ' λόγος γ'* [MS inverts the two numbers], $15^{1}$ *τόμος ϵ'* [MS omits *ϵ'*] *λόγος δ'*, $15^{35}$ *ἐκ τοῦ ζ' τόμου*. And for 2 Corinthians: $1^{1}$ *τόμος α' λόγος α'*, $1^{18}$ *τόμος α' λόγος β'*, $3^{4}$ *τόμος β' λόγος α'*, $4^{7}$ *τόμος γ' λόγος α'*, $4^{16}$ *τόμος γ' λόγος β'*, $5^{5}$ *τόμος δ' λόγος α'*. The Syriac fragments catalogued in the next paragraph testify, wherever they give details, to a similar arrangement: on 1 Co $15^{20}$ the 'fifth tome' is quoted, and on $15^{42}$ the 'seventh tome'; on 2 Co $5^{3}$ the 'third tome,' and on $13^{3}$ the 'fourth tome.'

The Greek evidence of which an account has so far been given would by itself create a strong presumption that Cyril had not commented on any but the longer epistles of St. Paul; for the diligence of Cramer, Mai, and Pusey, between them, has found nothing on the shorter epistles save two or three citations on Galatians and Colossians. But isolated citations from Fathers of great theological repute are presumably taken, as was shown on p. 498 above, from their dogmatic writings. Thus the Vienna Catena just referred to cites Cyril for the Epistle to the Romans, not only *ἐκ τοῦ ὕφους*,—'from the text of the commentary,' or perhaps we should best represent the words by translating them '*ad loc.*,'—but also from the *κατὰ Λουκᾶν*, from the *Θησαυρός*, from the *πρὸς Ἑρμίαν*, from the *Περὶ τῆς ἐν Πνεύματι λατρείας*, Book vi., and from the *κατὰ Ἰουλιανοῦ*. The *μία χρῆσις* in Cramer's Catena on Colossians (pp. 305, 340: see above, p. $507^b$) is from the *Θησαυρός*,‡ and the two cited from a MS of Oecumenius on the same epistle (*op. cit.* p. 411) are from the *Περὶ τῆς ἐν Πνεύματι λατρείας*. And this conclusion is reinforced by the testimony of the Syriac manuscripts, where there is no trace of any commentary (apart from Hebrews) save those on the Roman and Corinthian epistles, though Cyril

* The printed Oecumenius contained six quotations by name from Cyril on Romans, three on 1 Corinthians, one on 2 Corinthians, two on Galatians; but these might conceivably have been all culled out of his dogmatic writings.

* Unfortunately, a fresh element of confusion is introduced by the fact that the quotations from Vat. 762 and the Athos MS, though they tally in sense, rarely tally in words: the former appears to contain more Scripture citations, the latter more technical theology.

† Thus about a dozen of the passages quoted in the Munich Catena on Romans are identified as belonging to other writings of St. Cyril (the *ad Herniam* and the *Thesaurus*), and three or four to other writers altogether—Chrysostom, Theodoret, Photius.

‡ The citation on p. 320 of Cramer headed *Κυρίλλου* belongs really to the *Homilies* of Chrysostom, *ad loc.*

was of course an author much used in the Monophysite circles from which this Syriac literature comes to us. Even the commentary on Romans was but sparsely known: from the two Corinthian epistles the quotations are more numerous, as the following list of British Museum MSS will show:—

*Severus of Antioch against Julian:* MS dcxc. (Add. 12158), A.D. 588, quotes Cyril on 1 Cor., foll. 11*a*, 26*b*; on 2 Cor., fol. 119*b*.

*Monophysite treatise:* MS dccxcviii. (Add. 14535), sæc. ix. ineunt.: on 1 Cor., fol. 3*a*.

*Catenæ patrum* (the last of the six exegetical, the rest doctrinal)—

MS dccclvi. (Add. 14529), sæc. vii.–viii.: on (1?) Cor., fol. 20*a*.

MS dccclvii. (Add. 12155), sæc. viii.: on 1 Cor., fol. 125*a*; on 'the epistles to the Corinthians,' foll. 63*a*, 68*b*.

MS dccclviii. (Add. 14532), sæc. viii.: on 2 Cor., foll. 37*b*, 48*b*.

MS. dccclix. (Add. 14533), sæc. viii.–ix.: on 1 Cor., fol. 103*b*; on 2 Cor., foll. 53*a*, 59*b*.

MS dccclxiii. (Add. 14538), sæc. x.: on 1 Cor., fol. 23*a*.

MS dcccliii. (Add. 12144), A.D. 1081; on Rom., 1 Cor., 2 Cor.

No external data appear to exist which would enable us to date the commentaries on the three epistles. According to Bardenhewer (*Patrologie*², p. 321), the commentary on St. John is later than the outbreak of the Nestorian struggle, but earlier than the other NT commentaries. His ground for the latter statement appears to be that these commentaries represent a progressive advance in the direction of emphasis on the literal sense, which contrasts strongly with the book, for instance, on Worship in Spirit and Truth, where the Pentateuch is allegorically explained. It is, no doubt, true that we do find a mixture and combination of elements in the exegesis of the Epistles: for instance, in explaining Ro 8[28] τοῖς κατὰ πρόθεσιν κλητοῖς, Cyril explains that one would not err in saying that some are called κατὰ πρόθεσιν τήν τε τοῦ κεκληκότος καὶ τὴν ἑαυτῶν. But it would seem premature to draw from these features any definite conclusion as to date; and there are not wanting, in the history of the Catenæ (see below, p. 522[b]), indications which suggest that the commentaries of Cyril passed into circulation at no inconsiderable interval before those of Theodoret.

**18. Theodoret of Cyrrhus** (commentaries on all the Epistles).—

Theodoret, the younger contemporary of Cyril and typical representative of the orthodox Antiochene theology as Cyril of the orthodox Alexandrine, was born at Antioch in the latter part of the 4th cent., and became bishop of Cyrrhus in eastern Syria about A.D. 423: he died not many years after the Council of Chalcedon in 451. Like Cyril too, although his fame rests primarily on the share he took in the dogmatic controversies of his day, his own literary activity (to judge at least by those works of his which have been preserved) was more largely exegetical than either doctrinal or ecclesiastical or historical or apologetic, though his *Dialogues*, his *Letters*, his *Church History*, and his *Cure for Pagan Affections*, survive to show us what a many-sided theologian he was. Of the four volumes of Sirmond's edition (Paris, 1642), vols. i. and ii. are taken up with OT exegesis, and the first half of vol. iii. with the commentary on the Pauline epistles:* of the ten volumes (5 tomes, each in two parts) of J. L. Schulze's edition (Halle, 1769–1774), the first four are OT, the fifth (tom. iii. part 1) is our Pauline commentary (the editing of which was in fact done for Schulze by J. A. Noesselt), while the last two contain little more than dissertations and indexes.

The editions of Sirmond, to which Garnier added a supplementary volume in 1684, and of Schulze-Noesselt, which incorporates the material of both Sirmond and Garnier, have remained—with the exception of Migne, *Patr. Gr.*, vols. 80–84 (Pauline epistles in vol. 82, cc. 35–878)—the only collected editions of the works of Theodoret. But for his commentary on St. Paul the Oxford Library of the Fathers made a real advance towards a critical edition, though the standard reached may not have been so high as in Field's sister edition of Chrysostom (p. 506[b], above). Mr. Charles Marriott of Oriel College, to whom the task was entrusted, was, of all the Oxford Tractarians, perhaps the most deeply versed in Patristic scholarship. At the moment of the too early breakdown of his health, the first volume, containing Romans, 1 and 2 Corinthians, and Galatians, had already been issued (1852)*; the second and concluding volume was nearly complete, but the usual delays that attend posthumous publication prevented its appearing till 1870. A brief account of the editions of the text, and of the MSS used in them, is prefixed to the first volume. Sirmond appears to have used only one MS, but gives no details by which it can be identified. Noesselt used two: an 'Augustanus' which he called A—this is no other than the familiar Munich Catena on Ro 7[7]–16—and a 'Bavaricus,' B, no doubt identical with Munich gr. 18, sæc. xvi.† Marriott took over Noesselt's material and his symbols A and B, but his main reliance was on two Paris MSS, coislin 82, sæc. xi. (C), and gr. 217, sæc. x. (D). By the help of the latter MS, brought from Constantinople to the Royal Library after Sirmond's day, a *lacuna* in the commentary on Galatians (2[6-14], pp. 336. 14–339. 20) was for the first time filled up. Marriott made use also of the printed Oecumenius, and of such of Cramer's Catenæ as contained material from Theodoret. Unfortunately, he restricted within very narrow limits the improvements he allowed himself to make upon Noesselt's text; nor was it easy to build up definitive results out of MSS so few in number as those he employed.

Unlike Chrysostom, and apparently unlike Theodore, Theodoret expounded the whole of the fourteen epistles on one scale and in a single work, to which is prefixed a common preface (προθεωρία) and a common title ([τοῦ μακαρίου] Θεοδωρήτου ἐπισκόπου Κύρου ἑρμηνεία τῶν ιδʹ ἐπιστολῶν τοῦ ἁγίου ἀποστόλου Παύλου). To this difference in method and system between Theodoret and his predecessors corresponds a difference in the bulk of their respective expositions; for whereas Chrysostom's *Homilies* on St. Paul fill seven fairly thick octavo volumes, Theodoret's are all comprised within two quite thin ones. When Theodoret wrote, the reaction was probably already in full swing against what must have seemed the long-windedness of the older commentators—Origen, Chrysostom, even Theodore. There was a real gap to fill with an exposition of the literal sense, that should be less discursive and homiletic than Chrysostom's, less ambitiously conceived than Theodore's; and it could hardly have been filled better than by the commentary of Theodoret. In two succinct phrases he has sketched his plan and its limits: τὰς ἀφορμὰς ἐκ τῶν μακαρίων συλλέξω πατέρων· συντομίας δὲ ὅτι μάλιστα φροντιῶ.

An earlier passage in the preface indicates that the 'blessed Fathers' whom Theodoret especially

* Though this was the *editio princeps* of the original Greek of Theodoret on St. Paul, a Latin version by Gentianus Hervetus had been published as far back as 1552.

* Although Migne's edition was not published till 1864, it does not seem to have taken any account of this volume.

† This MS is not improbably a direct copy of a Venice MS of Theodoret on St. Paul, Marcianus 36, sæc. x.

followed were two in number: he might well, he says, be indicted for shameless audacity in setting his own hand to the 'interpretation of the Apostle,' μετὰ τὸν δεῖνα καὶ τὸν δεῖνα τοὺς τῆς οἰκουμένης φωστῆρας. That he is there referring to Chrysostom and Theodore is beyond question. It has been long recognized of his commentary 'que ce ne soit qu'un abrégé de Saint Chrysostome' (Simon, *Hist. Crit. des Commentateurs du NT*, p. 314): and, now that part of Theodore's work has been recovered, Simon's further divination, 'Je ne doute point qu'il n'ait aussi consulté les commentaires de Théodore de Mopsueste,' is abundantly verified; though at the same time it is to be remembered that Theodoret avoids carefully the less orthodox speculations of his predecessor, and indeed seldom, if ever, verbally reproduces him (Swete, *Theodore*, p. lxxvi). When, then, it is admitted that Theodoret's commentary, 'for appreciation, terseness of expression, and good sense, is perhaps unsurpassed,' and that 'if the absence of faults were a just standard of merit, it would deserve the first place' (Lightfoot, *Galatians*[5], p. 230), all and more than all is conceded which Theodoret would have wished to claim.

To what period of Theodoret's life the commentary on St. Paul belongs, is a question which four cross-references to it in his own writings enable us to answer within comparatively narrow limits.

*a*. *Ep*. 1 is addressed to an (unfortunately) unnamed correspondent, to whom Theodoret had sent τὴν εἰς τὸν θεῖον Ἀπόστολον συγγραφεῖσαν βίβλον, and who had read it through and returned it without any expression of opinion about it. It would seem that the letter, if it did not even precede, must have immediately followed the publication of the commentary; but there is nothing whatever to fix its date.

*β*. In *Quæst*. 1 *in Leviticum* Theodoret gives a brief summary of some of his writings, mentioning those 'against the Greeks,' 'against Heresies,' 'against the Magi,' the 'interpretation of the Prophets,' and the 'notes on the Apostolic epistles,' τῶν ἀποστολικῶν ἐπιστολῶν ὑπομνήματα. Of these *Quæstiones* on the Octateuch we know that they were earlier than the *Quæstiones* on the Books of Kings; but as they are not mentioned in the next two lists, it is probable that they are themselves posterior to A.D. 440.

*γ*, *δ*. In two parallel and not far from contemporary letters (*Epp*. 82 *ad Eusebium Ancyranum* and 113 *ad Leonem ep. Romæ*, A.D. 448–449), Theodoret, under the stress of the early years of the Monophysite controversy, is appealing for assistance alike to East and West; and in both letters he reviews a number of his earlier works—books written 'either before the Synod of Ephesus, or at any rate not less than twelve years ago,' 'twenty years or eighteen years or fifteen years or twelve years ago'—as guarantees that the orthodox doctrine he now professed was no new thing with him. To Eusebius he says: 'I expounded all the Prophets, and the Psalter, and the Apostle; and I wrote long ago against Arians and Macedonians and Apollinaris and Marcion; and I composed a μυστικὴ βίβλος, and another on Providence, and yet another against the questions of the Magi, and the Life of the Saints, and many other books as well.' The list given to Leo is the same in substance, though different in order and in detail: 'I wrote against Arians and Eunomians; against Jews and Greeks; against the Magi in Persia; on Universal Providence; on Theology and the Divine ἐνανθρώπησις: I interpreted, by the grace of God, both the Apostolic writings (τὰ ἀποστολικὰ συγγράμματα) and the Prophetic oracles.'

In both these bare estimates of the writings of a single decade the commentary on St. Paul finds a place, and it would be unreasonable to reject the evidence that thus fixes it between A.D. 429 and 438. But the internal characteristics of the commentary enable us to go a step further and reduce this interval by some years. For Theodoret closes his comment on Col $2^{9}$ (ἐν αὐτῷ κατοικεῖ πᾶν τὸ πλήρωμα τῆς θεότητος σωματικῶς) with the words θεὸς γάρ ἐστι καὶ ἄνθρωπος, καὶ τὸ ὁρώμενον τοῦτο πᾶσαν ἔχει ἡνωμένην τοῦ μονογενοῦς τὴν θεότητα, and he would hardly have thus expressed himself, until the progress of the Nestorian controversy had led the more moderate Antiochenes about A.D. 432 to adopt the terminology of the ἕνωσις as a definite guarantee of their orthodoxy.

**19. Gennadius of Constantinople** (commentaries on all the Epistles).—

Gennadius, patriarch of Constantinople from 458 till 471 A.D., was not only a supporter of the Council of Chalcedon and an opponent of the Monophysites, but had even in earlier life—during the interval between the Council of Ephesus in 431 and the Reunion in 433—written against the Twelve Articles of St. Cyril. Facundus, to whom we owe this information (*pro Defens. Trium. Capit.* ii. 4, ed. Sirmond, pp. 76–81), renders into Latin some specimens of Gennadius' controversial style (such as 'quales Cyrilli Aegyptii et quantas blasphemias incurri . . . anathematizaturus est te Deus, paries dealbate'), in order to contrast the censures meted out, for no stronger language about Cyril, to Theodoret and Ibas with the immunity enjoyed by 'sanctus Gennadius,' 'beatæ memoriæ Gennadius.' The theological tendencies of Gennadius being thus obviously Antiochene, it is natural to conclude that his affinities as an exegete would be of the same type; and it was in the domain of exegesis rather than of dogmatic theology that his special interests lay. Such at least is the impression left on us by the account of him in Gennadius of Marseilles, *de Viris Ill.* 90: 'Gennadius Constantinopolitanæ ecclesiæ episcopus, vir lingua nitidus et ingenio acer, tam dives ex lectione antiquorum fuit ut Danielem prophetam ex integro ad verbum commentatus exponeret; homilias etiam multas composuit.' The expression 'ex integro ad verbum' seems to imply that Gennadius found something to say on every word of his text; in any case, what was regarded as his most marked characteristic was his 'reading of the ancients,' that is, apparently, his knowledge of the works of earlier commentators. Gennadius in fact, like Isidore and Theodoret, belongs to the generation of exegetes intermediate between the more original writers on the one hand and mere catenists on the other, —to those who, either out of the whole bulk of existing commentaries, or from the one or two predecessors to whom they specially attached themselves, selected and abbreviated material which they combined in varying degrees with what was properly their own.

The published remains of Gennadius have been collected in Migne, *Patr. Gr.* 85, cc. 1611–1734; the department of exegesis is represented chiefly by Catena fragments on Genesis and on St. Paul. For the latter, Migne's only Greek sources were: (i.) the Catena of Oecumenius, which, in the printed text, ascribes to Gennadius five passages on Romans, four on 1 Corinthians, one on 2 Corinthians, two on Galatians, one on 2 Thessalonians; (ii.) the Catenæ of Cramer, of which the Bodleian Catena on Romans has 57 Gennadius citations, the Munich Catena on Romans 64 citations,* the Catena on 1 Corinthians two citations. Another

* Since the two Catenæ overlap for Ro $7^{7}$–$9^{1}$, some of these citations occur twice over, and the total is therefore considerably less than the sum of 57+64. It is curious that no citations from Gennadius occur before Ro $5^{12}$.

Catena can now be added to the list of those which use Gennadius, Karo and Lietzmann's No. vii. (*g* on p. 489[a], above), which appears to draw on him both directly and indirectly, *i.e.* both from the text of his commentary (ἐκ τοῦ ὕφους) and from earlier Catenæ. Since this Catena is also on the Romans (it breaks off at 1 Co 1[12]), the mass of Gennadius material on that one epistle is so large compared with the mere fragments that have come down to us on the other twelve, that the question may arise whether, after all, Gennadius commented formally on any other epistle than the Romans. But there is more than one reason which makes any such suspicion untenable.

In the first place, the longer epistles are very much better represented in the known Catenæ than the shorter ones; and, so far as printed material enables us to judge, the range of authors employed is decidedly larger on the Roman even than on the Corinthian epistles. No doubt, the explanation of this may lie partly in the fact that more commentaries were actually accessible on the Romans than on the rest; we have seen, for instance, that the two Arian writers, Asterius and Eunomius, commented on that epistle only (pp. 498[b], 500[b]): but it may also well be that among the original compilers, of whose labours our existing Catena MSS are the ultimate result, were some who started working at the first of the Epistles on a scale and with a thoroughness which were never equalled by the scholars who dealt, then or later, with the rest. For the seven epistles, Philippians–Philemon, no Catena material (besides Oecumenius) has yet been described other than the unique MS, Paris coislin gr. 204, printed by Cramer; and that Catena, since no name is cited in it later than Theodore of Mopsuestia, may actually have been put together in the first half of the 5th cent., before the commentaries of Gennadius, or even of Theodoret, had passed into circulation. In face, then, of the quotations in Oecumenius, few and scattered though they be, the absence of Gennadius material on these epistles in other sources might probably be discounted.

In the second place, we have definite external evidence which would outweigh the argument from silence, even if that were stronger than it is. The *Chronicle* of Marcellinus (a 6th century continuation, with special interest in Constantinople, of the *Chronicle* of Jerome), as printed in the earlier editions, concludes a notice of Gennadius, under the year 470, with the words 'et Pauli epistolas omnes exposuit.' It is true that these words are rejected by Mommsen (*Mon. Germ. Hist.*, *Chronica Minora*, ii. 56) as not part of the original Marcellinus; but they are found in the Bodleian MS of Marcellinus, written about A.D. 600, and they belong, therefore, at least to a very early recension. The correctness of the information is of course quite independent of the authorship of Marcellinus, and there is no reason at all for doubting it.

Gennadius, then, commented on all the Epistles. But it still remains true that our knowledge of his commentaries is practically confined to what Cramer's two Catenæ on the Romans have preserved for us; and to Cramer's volume we must turn if we are to get to closer quarters with the exegesis of Gennadius. The two characteristics which we have learnt so far to associate with him are Antiochene sympathies and wide reading in the literature of exegesis; and the Catena fragments bear ample testimony to both of them.

(*a*) The commentator's erudition is apparent. The quotation of Aquila's rendering of Is 8[14] κατὰ τὴν ἔκδοσιν τοῦ Ἀκύλου . . . Αὐτὸς φόβημα ὑμῶν καὶ αὐτὸς θρόησις ὑμῶν καὶ ἔσται εἰς ἁγίασμα καὶ εἰς λίθον προσκόμματος καὶ εἰς πέτραν σκανδάλου, in illustration of Ro 9[32] (Cramer, 367. 9–21), must be one of the latest instances of the use of the unauthorized Greek versions of the OT. And the references to previous expositors are quite unusually numerous, though unfortunately all anonymous; Ro 8[34] (Cramer, 152. 2) οὐ γάρ, ὥς τινες ᾠήθησαν . . . : Ro 8[37] (289. 31) τὸ ὙΠΕΡΝΙΚΩΜΕΝ οὕτως ἀπέδωκέ τις : Ro 9[2. 3] (161. 24) αὕτη μὲν οὖν ἡ τῆς προεκτεθείσης πίστεως* ἀκριβὴς ἑρμηνεία· κωλύει δὲ οὐδὲν καὶ τὴν δόξασαν ἑτέροις εἰπεῖν (where there can be no doubt that the 'others' are right and Gennadius wrong). In the middle of one long exposition of an earlier commentator's view (on Ro 9[19ff.])—extending from 349. 30, ἕτερος δὲ τοῦτο οὕτως ἑρμήνευσεν, as far as 351. 1, ταῦτα πρὸς τοῦτο . . . ἀντειπών, ἑρμηνεύει λοιπὸν καὶ τῶν προτεθεισῶν ῥήσεων τὸν σκοπόν—occur the words ἀλλὰ γὰρ ὃ τινῶν ἐπὶ τοῦ παρόντος τεθαύμακα, τοῦτο καὶ πρός σε, φίλτατέ μοι Πέτρε, βούλομαι διελθεῖν : and this address to 'dear Peter' is therefore not Gennadius' own, but is taken over with the rest of the passage from his source. What the source was, it would be interesting to know; the turn of the phrase suggests perhaps rather a letter than a formal commentary.

(*b*) In several directions the fragments betray the Antiochene temper of Gennadius' commentaries. He uses, if not so frequently as Theodore and Theodoret, the title ὁ δεσπότης Χριστός (Cramer, 63. 35; 410. 21; 478. 34). He speaks of the καινὴ κατάστασις (43. 15), and dwells with special emphasis on ζωή, ἀθανασία, ἀπάθεια (*e.g.* 50. 33; 56. 29; 60. 2; 117. 11; 118. 32; 146. 25). In commenting on Ro 8[3] his Christology expresses itself in language which contrasts strongly with the more guarded and accurate phraseology of Diodore (Cramer, 124. 3–11) on the same passage: 123. 13, τὸν γὰρ υἱὸν πέμψας τὸν ἑαυτοῦ, σάρκα τὴν αὐτὴν ἡμῖν ἔχοντα παθητήν τε καὶ ἁμαρτεῖν ἐπιδεχομένην· ὉΜΟΙΩΜΑ γὰρ ΣΑΡΚῸΣ ἉΜΑΡΤΊΑΣ τὴν ἐνδεχομένην ἁμαρτῆσαι σάρκα φησίν, ὡς καὶ τὸ ἘΝ ὉΜΟΙΏΜΑΤΙ ἈΝΘΡΏΠΟΥ ΓΕΝΌΜΕΝΟΣ ἀντὶ τοῦ Γενόμενος ἄνθρωπος. So in the treatment of the problems raised in the Pelagian controversy: on Ro 5[12] ἐφ' ᾧ πάντες ἥμαρτον, πάντες is equivalent, he writes (43. 1–11), to οἱ πολλοί, since, though it is true that all have died, it is not true that all have sinned; infants, for instance, οἱ οὔτε πράξεως οὔτε διακριτικῆς προαιρέσεως ὄντες ἐντός, πῶς ἂν εἶεν ὑπεύθυνοι πλημμελήματι;

As we should therefore expect, Gennadius shows himself to be no allegorizer, and devotes himself to the literal meaning. Special mention may be made of his notes on the 'idioms' of Scripture: Ro 7[11] (93. 23 = 176. 7), on personifications κατὰ τὸ τῆς θείας ἔθος γραφῆς of abstractions such as Sin or Righteousness: Ro 7[14] πεπραμένος (100. 13 = 186. 1), on the use of metaphors, according to the ἰδίωμα γραφικόν, without the introductory ὡς: Ro 8[20] ἡ κτίσις (139. 8–19), on personifications of inanimate creatures: Ro 15[5. 6] ὁ δὲ θεός . . . τὸν θεόν (499. 18–25), on repetition of the name of the subject (τὸν θεόν instead of αὐτόν) as an ἰδίωμα τῆς γραφῆς. Interesting specimens of an exegesis which is rather clear than deep may be found on the following passages: Ro 9[1] (159. 4–162. 16), a summary of the Jewish position and of St. Paul's attitude towards it: Ro 13[1] (458. 3–22), how the overflow of new life and power in the spiritual charismata of the primitive Church created a danger which called out the Apostle's exhortation to civil obedience and orderliness: Ro 14[15-17] (482. 12–25), on the simplicity and effectiveness of every detail in the style of these verses.

With Isidore and Cyril, Theodoret and Gennadius, we have reached the close of the golden age of Greek exegesis. Of the three names that still remain for cursory notice, the first two, Theodore the Monk and John of Damascus, appear to have

* So Cramer: Dr. Sanday suggests ῥήσεως.

confined themselves exclusively to the task of compilation from previous commentators, while the third, the patriarch Photius, stands at the very limit of the Patristic period; and all three might perhaps have found a more appropriate place at an earlier point in this article (p. 485).

**20. Theodore the Monk** (commentary on Romans?).—

In Cramer's Munich Catena on Ro $7^7$–16 nearly forty citations are given under the name of an otherwise unknown exegete, Θεοδώρου Μοναχοῦ: and mention was made above (p. 510[b]) of Fritzsche's analysis of these passages, from which it appeared that many of them are found elsewhere ascribed to Diodore, Theodore, or Theodoret. So large a proportion, indeed, recur as Theodore's (16 out of 39), that the doubt inevitably rises whether the Θεοδώρου Μοναχοῦ of the Munich catenist may not, after all, have been a misunderstanding of Θεοδώρου Μο(ψουεστίας); but, tempting at first sight as this explanation is, it breaks down when confronted with the facts. It does not account for the Diodore passages;* of the fourteen citations from Theodore the Monk in that part of the epistle (Ro $7^7$–$9^1$) which is covered also by the Bodleian Catena, four, indeed, reappear in the latter under the authorship of Theodore of Mopsuestia, but two, and parts of two more, under the authorship of Diodore.† And it is inconsistent with the introductory phrases under which Theodore the Monk ushers in his borrowed matter, for these betray at once the compiler's hand: thus Cramer, 175. 7, τινὲς δέ φασι (what follows is from Theod. Mops.): 248. 4 ἕτερος δὲ ἀπεφήνατο (from the same writer): 328. 25 and 379. 6, ἔφη τις: 417. 25, ἔφη δέ τις περὶ τούτων καὶ οὕτως. Less stress can be laid on the use of ἤ, ἢ τάχα, ἢ καὶ οὕτως, since nearly all commentators from time to time give alternative interpretations; but their relative frequency in Theodore the Monk serves to bear out the conclusion that the Munich catenist has stumbled somehow upon an unknown compiler, the staple of whose material was derived from writers of the Antiochene school, and principally, it would seem, from Diodore and Theodore. The anonymous form of his quotations, τις, τινές, ἕτερος, may be accidental, or it may conceal the desire to recommend the subject-matter of the two great expositors, who had fallen under the odium of Nestorian heresy, in quarters where suspicion might be awakened by the express mention of their names. There is nothing to show when the Monk lived; but the data on the whole point to the 6th century.

**21. John of Damascus** (commentary on all the Epistles).—

St. John Damascene belongs to the time—he was born about 685 and died about 760 A.D.—when Greek theology, though it had still to produce Theodore of Studium, was approaching the close of its creative era; and it was his unique work to sum up the results of previous thinkers in that domain and to combine them in a great constructive system. But theology cannot be divorced from New Testament exegesis, and systematic theology moved therefore on parallel lines with Catena compilations: in the West the author of the *Summa* was the author also of the *Catena Aurea*; and in the case of John of Damascus, side by side with the systematic treatise *On the Faith* may be set the commentary on the Pauline epistles which will be found in le Quien's edition of his works (Paris, 1712, vol. ii., pp. 1–274) or in Migne's reprint (*Patr. Gr.* 95, cc. 439–1034).

The very title of this work, as le Quien prints it, shows at once that John aims at nothing further than the selection of what is best and most authoritative in the exegesis of the past: ἐκ τῆς καθόλου ἑρμηνείας Ἰωάννου τοῦ Χρυσοστόμου ἐκλογαὶ ἐν ἐπιτομῇ ἐκλεγεῖσαι παρὰ Ἰωάννου τοῦ Δαμασκηνοῦ. But the sources of the commentary are not, le Quien points out, confined in fact exclusively to Chrysostom. Although on the longer epistles John follows him closely, the case, it is said, is different with the shorter ones; attention is called to the note on Col $2^9$, where, in the technical language of the Nestorian controversy, a merely 'relative' (σχετικός or συναπτικός) indwelling of the Word in Christ is expressly rejected: in the commentary on the epistles to the Ephesians, Colossians, Philippians, and Thessalonians, le Quien could find no trace at all of the use of Chrysostom, and according to the same authority the commentaries both of Cyril (to judge by the parallels in the Oecumenian Catena) and of Theodoret are exploited by John. An obvious objection to le Quien's view as thus stated is that we have seen reason to conclude (p. 515) that it was on the longer epistles only that Cyril wrote;* and a further analysis of John's commentary is all the more desirable, because it may probably be found to have exercised a dominant influence on later compilations such as those of Photius and Theophylact.

For this purpose, however, a new edition of the commentary would appear to be essential; le Quien based his text on an ancient but imperfect MS (Paris gr. 702 [=Reg. 2331], foll. 252–434, sæc. x.), and warns us in his preface 'codicem multis passim mendis scatere mutilumque esse, ut sensus sæpe impervius sit et obscurus.' But he had heard also of a MS at Patmos; and No. 61 (ξα') of Sakkellion's new catalogue of the Patmos library (Athens, 1890) contains, in fact, the commentary of John. In its present condition this MS, which is attributed to the beginning of the 10th cent., has lost most of the commentary on Romans, and Sakkellion was therefore unable to fix the authorship; but the portions of the text which he prints, such as the argument for 1 Corinthians and the opening words of the commentary on the same epistle, are amply sufficient for the identification. In the Patmos MS, then, together with a re-collation of the Paris MS, material for the revision of the text is ready to hand.

It is interesting to note that, according to le Quien, the *lemmata* prefixed to the exposition give a text of the epistles which is not that used by St. Chrysostom—another reason for a new and completer edition.

**22. Photius of Constantinople** (commentaries on all the Epistles?).—

In the person of Photius (A.D. 820–891), statesman, ecclesiastic, scholar, exegete, the illustrious line of Greek writers on St. Paul that began with Origen finds a fitting close; and indeed his many-sided qualities and multifarious learning bring him, intellectually if not morally, into comparison rather with Origen than with any intermediate commentator. Considering the position of authority which Photius has enjoyed in the Byzantine Church, it is a little strange that his exposition of the Pauline epistles has neither been discovered in any direct MS tradition, nor yet extracted from the Catenæ and separately collected either in the volumes of Migne (*Patr. Gr.* 101–104) or in

* Theodoret appears to come into the question only through the mistake of Cramer's index; the last three passages there ascribed to Theodorus Monachus are given in the text as Θεοδωρήτου.

† *Diodore:* Cramer, 188. 19=105. 4; 199. 19=114. 16; 212. 30=120. 17; 226. 29=128. 21. *Theodore:* Cramer, 175. 7=94. 6; 202. 22=116. 10; 239. 32=131. 6; 248. 6=135. 30 and 137. 19.

* If John could be shown to have used Cyril through the medium of the Oecumenian Catena, this would constitute a further proof of the early date which recent discoveries (see p. 523, below) have vindicated for Oecumenius.

the Greek edition of Photius' works at present in process of issue. Yet the material is abundant, and could easily be worked, as the following conspectus will show.

(*a*) A later recension of the Oecumenian Catena (see p. 488[b], above) distinguishes itself from the original work exactly by a large use of Photius; in Karo and Lietzmann's specimen (Ro 7[8ff.]) four passages are taken from Photius as against twelve from all other writers. The principal MSS known to give this recension are: at Milan, Ambros. D 541 inf., sæc. x.; at Rome, Vat. Palat. gr. 204, sæc. x.; at Venice, Marcianus 33, sæc. xi. In these MSS the Photius passages are incorporated in the text: other methods of grafting the new matter on to the Oecumenian stock are illustrated (i.) by Paris coislin 27, sæc. x., where the Photius passages are inserted in the margin by the second hand; and (ii.) by Oxford Magd. Coll. gr. 7, sæc. xi. ineunt. (containing, however, only Romans and 1 and 2 Corinthians),* which adds at the end of each epistle *τὰ λείποντα*, that is to say, a large number of quotations from Photius and a small number from Gennadius.

(*b*) Though these Oecumenian MSS would be the principal means of the reconstruction of the commentaries of Photius, yet for the longer epistles considerable assistance would be given by other Catenæ. The Catena of Vat. gr. 762, so far as we can restore it from Cramer's texts, should contain something from Photius on Romans, and a good deal on 1 Corinthians. Cramer's Munich Catena on Ro 7[7]–16 has about 25 quotations from him. Karo and Lietzmann's Vienna Catena (*g* on p. 489, above) cites him 'sæpius,' but apparently from an earlier Catena rather than direct from the text of his commentary, and perhaps only through the Photian recension of Oecumenius.

Since Photius' literary activity falls in the second half of the 9th cent., and five out of the Catena MSS just enumerated belong to the 10th or 11th cent., there is a fair presumption that his text could be restored from them with tolerable correctness; and the attempt would be worth the making. But it is not possible to say, without further analysis of the quotations from him than has yet been undertaken, whether the result would contribute—in the measure in which an edition of John of Damascus, for instance, ought to contribute—to our knowledge of that exegetical tradition of the earlier centuries which it is the purpose of this article to illustrate.

**23.** *ADDENDUM* (to p. 489[b], above). **Clement of Alexandria** (notes on all the Epistles?).—

The series of commentators on the Pauline epistles should have included the name of Clement; for the express evidence of Photius makes certain, what is indeed already implied by Eusebius, that the lost Ὑποτυπώσεις or *Outlines* included notes on the Epistles.† Eusebius tells us (*HE* vi. 14, § 1) that 'in the *Hypotyposes* Clement gave concise accounts (*ἐπιτετμημένας πεποίηται διηγήσεις*) of the whole of canonical Scripture, including such doubtful books as Jude and the other Catholic epistles and Barnabas and the so-called Apocalypse of Peter'; and he adds some few details about Clement's treatment of the Epistle to the Hebrews and of the Gospels. Photius testifies more clearly (cod. 109) to the exegetical side of the work: of the three writings of Clement, presbyter of Alexandria, *Hypotyposes*, *Stromateus* (*sic*), and *Pædagogus*, the *Hypotyposes* 'contain discussions on selected verses (*διαλαμβάνουσι περὶ ῥητῶν τινῶν*) up and down both Testaments, in the form of a summary exposition and interpretation' (*ὧν καὶ κεφαλαιωδῶς ὡς δῆθεν ἐξήγησίν τε καὶ ἑρμηνείαν ποιεῖται*). Photius proceeds to criticise the theology of the *Hypotyposes* from the standpoint of Byzantine orthodoxy, and concludes thus: 'All these things he attempts to establish from phrases found here and there in Scripture; and there are countless other follies and blasphemies committed either by Clement himself or by some one who has usurped his name. This blasphemous nonsense occupies eight volumes: the author continually repeats himself, and distorts his texts (*παράγει τὰ ῥητά*) promiscuously and indiscriminately like a lunatic. Speaking roughly, the general scheme of the work consists of explanations (*ὁ δὲ ὅλος σκοπὸς ὡσανεὶ ἑρμηνεῖαι τυγχάνουσι*) of Genesis, Exodus, the Psalms, the epistles of Saint Paul, the Catholic epistles, and Ecclesiastes.'*

Though both Eusebius and Photius have something to say about the *Hypotyposes*, neither of them has preserved much of its actual words: it is to a Western scholar that we owe the only considerable portion which survives. We have already seen (in connexion with Cyril of Alexandria, p. 515[a]) that Cassiodorus named Clement—no doubt with reference to the *Hypotyposes*—at the head of those Greek commentators who had explained the whole of both Testaments: and when he comes to deal with the Catholic epistles (*Inst. Div. Litt.* 8) he tells us that Clement 'quædam Attico sermone declaravit' about 1 Peter, 1 and 2 John, and James; that in expounding them he said many things that were acute, but a few that were over-hasty; and that therefore he himself had arranged for the commentary to be rendered into Latin in such a way that Clement's teaching, strained free of some small causes of offence, might be fearlessly absorbed. About the identity of this translation with the extant *Adumbrationes Clementis Alexandrini in epistolas canonicas*—although the four epistles actually expounded there are 1 Peter, 1 and 2 John, and (not James but) Jude—there can be as little real doubt as about the intended equivalence of *Adumbrationes* to Ὑποτυπώσεις.

Zahn's text of these *Adumbrationes* covers only fourteen pages in all; and though it must be borne in mind that Cassiodorus ordered the omission of certain passages of the original, it would seem that Photius was abundantly justified in speaking of the exegesis as 'summary' and 'select' (*κεφαλαιωδῶς, ῥητά τινα*). A commentary which ranged over the whole Bible in eight 'books' must needs have been of the nature of an epitome. In fact it becomes clear that, side by side with the tradition of lengthy and detailed exposition, which had its rise among the Gnostics (Basilides, as we know, devoted twenty-four books of *Exegetica* to 'the Gospel') and was taken up and developed in the commentaries of Origen, another and very different method, modelled possibly on Papias' 'Exposition of the Sayings of the Lord,' can claim an equal or almost equal antiquity. Origen himself was no stranger to the system of interpretation by 'scholia' or notes: see above, in connexion with the Roman, Corinthian, and Galatian epistles, pp. 492, 493. Among early commentaries on the canonical Gospels, that of Victorinus on St. Matthew is described by Cassiodorus in the phrase 'de quo [*sc* Matthæo] et Victorinus . . . nonnulla disseruit' (*Inst. Div. Litt.* 7): nor does the work of Hippolytus on the same Gospel appear to have contained anything like a continuous exposition.†

* The second half of the Magdalen College MS is in the Cambridge University Library, Ff i. 30; and the arrangement of it is the same.

† On this subject the indispensable monograph is Th. Zahn's *Forschungen zur Geschichte des NTlichen Kanons und der altkirchlichen Literatur*, iii.: 'Supplementum Clementinum,' pp. 64–103, 130–156.

* Not Ecclesiasticus: see Zahn, p. 66, n. 1.

† See a paper by the present writer, 'An Exegetical Fragment of the Third Century,' in *JThS* v. 218-241 (especially pp. 225–227), Jan. 1904.

Twelve comments on passages in the Pauline epistles are directly cited from the *Hypotyposes* (Zahn, *op. cit.* pp. 66–77; Preuschen in Harnack, *Altchr. Litteratur* 303–305): eleven of these occur in the Catena of Oecumenius, and one in the *Pratum Spirituale* of John Moschus (died A.D. 620). The formula of quotation in the latter case is Κλήμης ὁ Στρωματεὺς ἐν τῷ πέμπτῳ τόμῳ τῶν Ὑποτυπώσεων. . . τὸ ἀποστολικὸν ῥητὸν ἐξηγούμενος τὸ λέγον εὐχαριστῶ κ.τ.λ. (1 Co 1[14]). The references in Oecumenius are not merely marginal ascriptions of authorship, such as are given to other authors in this Catena, but are part of the text itself, and in every case but one are appended and not prefixed to the quotation: οὕτως ὁ Κλήμης ἐν τετάρτῳ* [once ἐν δ'], ἐν πέμπτῳ, ἐν ἑβδόμῳ [once ἐν ζ'] Ὑποτυπώσεων. It is natural to conclude from this that Oecumenius drew direct from Clement himself rather than through the agency of a Catena.

Five different epistles are represented in Oecumenius' quotations: 1 Corinthians (11[10] διὰ τοὺς ἀγγέλους), 2 Corinthians (5[16] 6[11, 12]), Galatians (5[24]), 1 Timothy (2[6] καιροῖς ἰδίοις, 3[16] ὤφθη ἀγγέλοις, 5[8] τῶν ἰδίων καὶ μάλιστα οἰκείων, 5[10] εἰ ἁγίων πόδας ἔνιψε, 5[21] χωρὶς προκρίματος, 6[13] τοῦ μαρτυρήσαντος ἐπὶ Ποντίου Πιλάτου), and 2 Timothy (2[2] διὰ πολλῶν μαρτύρων). The comments on both Corinthian epistles are quoted from the 4th book; that on Galatians from the 5th book; those on 1 and 2 Timothy from the 7th book. Zahn points out (pp. 150, 156) that Clement, like the Muratorian Canon, appears to have drawn a marked line between the epistles to Churches, which he expounded in the 4th and 5th books of the *Hypotyposes*, and the personal epistles, which are dealt with in the 7th, the Pauline series being interrupted in the intermediate book by notes on the Acts and perhaps also on the Gospels.

To these twelve passages from Oecumenius and Moschus it is possible that several more should be added from other Catenæ. Neither Zahn nor Preuschen seems to mention the fact that Cramer's Munich Catena on Romans contains three citations (on Ro 8[39] 10[2, 3] 10[5]), and his Catena on 1 Corinthians two citations (on 1 Co 1[20] 1[21]), under the heading Κλήμεντος; while the Catena of Vat. gr. 692, so Dr. Mercati informs the present writer, contains at least five. It is probable that some of these came from the *Hypotyposes*.

As the example of the Latin *Adumbrationes* would lead us to expect, these comments of Clement on St. Paul are brief—for the most part very brief. The exegesis is of course predominantly allegorical. The ἄγγελοι of 1 Co 11[10] are 'righteous and virtuous men': according to one interpretation (not, however, finally accepted) of Gal 5[24], Christians are the σάρξ Χριστοῦ, and the whole verse means 'there is no law against such as have crucified the flesh of Christ,' *i.e.* their own body: in 2 Ti 2[2] the πολλοὶ μάρτυρες are the Law and the Prophets, cited regularly by the Apostle as 'witnesses' to the contents of his preaching. But the *Hypotyposes* also—in this again resembling the work of Papias—adduce traditions of Apostolic history in explanation of the sacred text: such matter was hardly to the purpose of catenists, but Eusebius has preserved a few bearing on other NT books, and the solitary quotation in John Moschus is of this character. Clement, he tells us, in expounding 1 Co 1[14], 'relates that Christ is said to have baptized Peter only, Peter to have baptized Andrew, Andrew to have baptized John and James, and they the rest.'

* The comment on 1 Co 11[10] is in the printed text of Oecumenius given as ἐν τρίτῳ; but Zahn points out that the Bodleian MS, Auct. T. i. 7, cited on p. 465 of Cramer's Catena on the Corinthian epistles, reads ἐν τετάρτῳ, and this is doubtless right.

iv. Summary of unpublished or inadequately published MS Material.—The aim of the present section is to point out the lines along which it is likely that the labours of the next generation of scholars could be most profitably directed, with a view to our further knowledge of the Patristic writings enumerated in this article. The material groups itself naturally under four headings: A. Anonymous Catenæ; B. Catenæ of known authorship; C. Original commentators as preserved in the Catenæ; D. Commentators whose text is preserved independently of Catenæ. Thus three of the four headings of the section are concerned, directly or indirectly, with Catenæ; and that fact is enough of itself to foreshadow the predominant part which will belong in the immediate future to this branch of research. To a large extent the following paragraphs will do no more than focus the results of preceding sections, and bring into one comprehensive scheme the isolated points that have already been indicated at various stages of the inquiry: but fuller details will be given here than was possible above about the more important Catena MSS; and, in a few cases where for one reason or another there had been no previous opportunity for introducing it, the matter is entirely new (see A 4 and 5, p. 522[b], and B 1, p. 523[a]).

A. *Anonymous Catenæ.*—

1. The most ancient of the Pauline Catenæ, to judge by the limitation of its sources, is the Paris MS, coislin 204, sæc. x. (311 folios), from which Cramer published his Catena on the eleven epistles, Galatians–Hebrews (Karo and Lietzmann's No. iv.). The Fathers regularly cited are Origen (on the Ephesians), Eusebius of Emesa (on the Galatians), and, throughout, John Chrysostom, Severian, and Theodore of Mopsuestia: while Basil, Gregory Nazianzen, and Cyril are quoted once each on the Colossians. Putting aside the Epistle to the Hebrews—the Catena on which may perhaps have had a separate origin and history—there is nothing later than the first half of the 5th century, and, if we except the one passage from Cyril, nothing later than the first years of that century. Cramer employed a 'scriba Parisiensis' to copy out the MS for him, and expresses in his preface the fear that the copyist 'non semper codicis lectionem vere repræsentaverit.' How well justified his fears were, the re-collation of the Origen comments on Ephesians for Mr. Gregg's edition in *JThS* iii. (1902) abundantly demonstrated. The Theodore, too, was re-collated for Dr. Swete's edition; but for the remaining Fathers, and especially for Severian, Cramer's edition is still our only authority, and for critical purposes it is quite valueless. See, for previous references to this Catena, pp. 487[a] (Cramer); 488[b] (Karo-Lietzmann); 493[b], 494[a], 495[b], 496[a] (Origen); 498[b] (Eusebius of Emesa); 499[a] (Basil and Greg. Naz. on Col 1[15]); 507[b] (Severian); 510[ab], 511[a] (Theodore of Mopsuestia); 515[b] (Cyril); 518[a] (absence of Theodoret and Gennadius).

2. Next perhaps in antiquity of origin, and not inferior in the importance of its contents, comes the Vatican Catena, gr. 762, sæc. x., an enormous MS of 411 folios; the Catena for Romans commencing on fol. 1*a*, that for 1 Corinthians on fol. 218*a*, and for 2 Corinthians on fol. 340*a*.* The handwriting is very fine: the blank spaces left, *e.g.*, on foll. 343, 350, show that the exemplar of that part at any rate of the MS could no longer be deciphered, and was probably, therefore, already an old MS when it was being copied in the 10th century.

* For many new details about the Vatican Catenæ, and for an important reference in the case of Oecumenius, the writer is indebted to the unwearied kindness of his friend Dr. Mercati, of the Vatican Library.

In Karo-Lietzmann it is No. i.; their list of the authors cited is divided, according to their custom, into two classes: the first (at least 10 citations apiece) includes Apollinaris, Cyril, Didymus, Diodore, Gennadius, John Chrysostom, Oecumenius, Origen, Photius, Severus of Antioch,* Severian, Theodore, Theodoret; the second consists of Acacius of Cæsarea (4 times on Romans), Basil (3 times on Romans), Clement (twice on 1 Corinthians), Dionysius the Areopagite (once on 1 Corinthians), Gregory Nyssen (once each on Romans and 1 Corinthians), Isidore (5 times), Methodius (once on 1 Corinthians), Theodulus chorepiscopus (once on Romans). This account is, however, not quite exhaustive, and omits, for instance, a *scholion* on fol. 403*b*, written in smaller characters but by the original scribe, under the heading Ἀλεξάνδρου ἐπισκόπου Νικαίας. Alexander of Nicæa lived in the first half of the 10th cent., and may conceivably have been the editor of the Catena in its present form. Both Oecumenius and Photius are laid under contribution: the passages taken from the latter are considerable both in number and length. Where both of them are cited together, Oecumenius always comes first.

Of the two late MSS of parts of this Catena which alone were at Cramer's disposal—Paris gr. 227 and Bodl. Auct. E. ii. 20 (=Miscell. gr. 48)—the latter, on the ground of its rather curious history, may claim a few words here.

MS Bodl. Auct. E. ii. 20, containing in a 16th century hand a Catena on Ro $1^1$–$9^1$, was presented to the Library in 1659 by S. Cromleholme, master of St. Paul's School in London; at an earlier date, in 1601, it had been given to Dr. G. Ryves, warden of New College, by John Lloyd (Johannes Luidus), rector of Writtle in Essex. Lloyd's inscription on the fly-leaf is headed 'Ex manubiis Gaditanis,' indicating that the MS was part of the spoils of the Earl of Essex's Spanish expedition in 1596; but whether it was taken in the sack of Cadiz itself, or formed part of the library of bishop Osorio of Algarve, which is known to have fallen into Essex's hands on the homeward journey,† cannot be said for certain. At the end of the text on the last leaf is the word λείπει; and on the following guard-leaf, in different ink but perhaps in the same handwriting as the body of the MS, are epitaphs by John Lascaris (see above, p. 485[b]) on himself and on his wife Catherine. These two epitaphs were actually inscribed on Lascaris' tomb in the church of S. Agata dei Goti at Rome; and since, in the MS, they are separated by a floriated cross, such as one might expect on a tombstone, it looks as if they had been actually copied *in situ*. If so, the presumption is strong that the MS itself was written in Rome, and that Vat. gr. 762 was its direct exemplar.

See above, for these MSS, pp. 487 (Cramer and Mai); 488[b] (Karo-Lietzmann); 492, 493[a] (Origen); 499[b] (Didymus); 501[a] (Diodore); 510 (Theodore of Mopsuestia); 514[a.b] (Isidore); 515[a] (Cyril); 517[b] (Gennadius); 520[a] (Photius); 521[a] (Clement).

3. More importance than the brief account in Karo-Lietzmann (No. iii., *op. cit.* p. 601) would suggest seems to attach to the Catena on the Corinthian, Galatian, and Ephesian epistles contained in Vat. gr. 692, foll. 1–93. These scholars attribute the MS to the 12th cent., and name Cyril, John Chrysostom, Oecumenius, Origen, Severus, Theodoret, Theodore, and (on 2 Corinthians) 'Δι,' as the writers more frequently cited; Clement, Gennadius, Isidore, and Gregory Nyssen as cited respectively three times, twice, twice, and once. But the date should be moved back to sæc. x.–xi.; the names of Nicolas, Methodius, Basil, Eusebius, Photius should be added to the list of Fathers cited; from Clement of Alexandria not three only, but at least five quotations are made; Di(dymus) is very common on 2 Corinthians; Severian is once named in full (fol. 59*a*), and the substitution of this Father's name for Karo and Lietzmann's Sev(erus), proposed on p. 489[a] above, is thus amply justified. On many occasions the catenist compares expressly the views of different authors—*e.g.* Clement, Eusebius of Cæsarea, Gregory Nazianzen, Chrysostom, Severian, Theodoret, Cyril—and sometimes adds to his authors' names precise references to their books. On comparing this Catena with the last, Vat. gr. 762, for the Corinthian epistles, it results that the quotations common to both are briefer in 692 than in 762: and this is what the relative bulk of the two MSS would lead us to expect.

See above, pp. 489[a] (Karo-Lietzmann); 507[b] (Severian); 521[a] (Clement); too little was known of this Catena for full use to be made of it in the foregoing pages.

4. The most important addition that has to be made to Karo-Lietzmann's list of Pauline Catenæ is a MS that has once been mentioned above (p. 515[b]), in connexion with Pusey's edition of Cyril of Alexandria — Athos Pantocrator cod. 28. According to the catalogue of Sp. Lambros (i. 95), the MS is of the 9th cent., and contains the (Acts and) Pauline epistles, the names most frequently cited being Isidore of Pelusium, John Chrysostom, Severian, Diodore of Tarsus, Theodore of Mopsuestia, and Apollinaris. Photographs of eleven pages of this MS, covering 1 Co $7^{34}$–$11^{11}$, were taken by Prof. Kirsopp Lake, and are now in the Bodleian (MS gr. th. f. 8): the principal authors in these pages are Chrysostom, Severian, Cyril, and Theodore of Mopsuestia. The absence of Theodoret is noticeable; and as all the eight writers known to be used in the Catena are earlier than Theodoret, it is possible that its origin goes back to the period anterior to the publication of his commentary. If that is so, it ranks with our earliest Catenæ; but a serious drawback to its value is that the evidence of its Cyril texts (see above, note on p. 515[b]) seems to suggest that the catenist may have not only abbreviated but otherwise re-cast the passages he extracted from his sources.

5. Patmos σξγʹ (=No. 263, p. 127 of Sakkellion's catalogue), sæc. x., is described as containing, on foll. 1–119, not a continuous commentary, but a series of notes on the Acts and some of the Catholic and Pauline epistles (2 Cor., Eph., Phil., Col., 1 and 2 Thess., 1 and 2 Tim., Titus), with an unusually extensive range of authorities: Athanasius, Ambrose, Anastasius of Antioch, Apollinaris, Archelaus the bishop, Basil, Cæsarius, Cyril of Alexandria and of Jerusalem, Eusebius, Gennadius, Gregory Nazianzen and Nyssen, Hyp(atius?), Irenæus, [Isidore] the Pelusiote, John Chrysostom, John [Damascene], Josephus, Leontius the Monk, Maximus the Monk, Methodius of Patara, Origen, Severian, Theodore, Theodoret. From the specimens given in the catalogue it would seem that the quotations are, for the most part, so brief as to promise little in the way of profitable result.

Of other anonymous Catenæ, the editing of Cramer's Munich Catena on Romans appears to be a much better piece of work than that of his Paris Catena on the shorter epistles: to Karo-Lietzmann's account of their No. vii. Catena, from Vienna, the present writer has nothing to add: of their No. viii. something will be said below, at the end of the account of Oecumenius, p. 524[a].

* If this is correct, and not really a confusion with Severian, the last note on p. 507[b] above should be modified. But, in the case of the Catena next to be mentioned, Karo and Lietzmann have wrongly expanded Σευ into Severus instead of Severian.

† Of the many books which came by gift from Essex to the Bodleian in A.D. 1600 a considerable number were printed in Spain and Portugal.

B. *Catenæ of known authorship.*—

1. Those who have followed down to this point the argument of the present article will have gathered that the origin of the Catenæ in general is to be looked for in a more remote age than it has been customary to ascribe to them. In particular, the Catena of Oecumenius (see pp. 485, 486[a], 488[b]) is to be placed not, as hitherto, after the time of Photius, but before it. Recent investigations tend still further to accelerate this backward movement, and make it probable that the true date of Oecumenius is about 600 A.D.

In a 12th cent. MS at Messina, cod. S. Salvatoris 99, a complete commentary on the Apocalypse under the name of Oecumenius has been lately found by a German scholar, Fr. Diekamp of Münster (see a paper by him in *Sitzungsberichte der k. preuss. Akademie der Wissenschaften*, Berlin, 1901, pp. 1046–1056); and the internal evidence of the commentary is sufficient to establish roughly both the date and the theological standpoint of the writer. The comment on 1[1] ἐν τάχει states that 'a period of more than 500 years had elapsed' since the date of St. John's vision. The Christology is Cyrilline or even Severianist rather than Chalcedonian: ἐν πρόσωπον καὶ μίαν ὑπόστασιν καὶ μίαν ἐνέργειαν is the nearest approach to a formulated doctrine of the Incarnation. The writer was therefore, if not actually a Monophysite, at any rate one of those who still sought for a common ground with Monophysitism.

Diekamp somewhat hastily concludes that his discovery is fatal to the genuineness of the Oecumenian Catena on St. Paul, in which he would see only the work of a later compiler excerpting Oecumenius in precisely the same way as he excerpted other ancient authorities. But neither of his reasons will stand examination.

*a.* 'Photius is used in the Oecumenian Catena; but Photius lived in the 9th cent., and the real Oecumenius cannot therefore have quoted him.' But it has been shown above (p. 488[b]), following Karo-Lietzmann, that it is not the original Oecumenius, but a later recension only, which makes use of Photius.

*β.* 'Oecumenius' work on the Apocalypse is a commentary, not a Catena; but the so-called Oecumenius on St. Paul is a Catena, not a commentary.' The argument is specious rather than sound. For, in the first place, Oecumenius on St. Paul is not quite a Catena on the ordinary model: see p. 485[b] above. In the second place, Diekamp sufficiently answers himself when he shows that Oecumenius is the earliest of the Greek commentators on the Apocalypse: if there were no commentators before him, it is difficult to see how he could have compiled a Catena. Of the two other ancient Greek commentators known to us, Arethas of Cappadocian Cæsarea wrote about A.D. 900, Andrew considerably earlier. That Arethas is found by Diekamp to make use of both Oecumenius and Andrew, is only what we should expect of a scholar as profoundly versed as Arethas in Patristic learning (cf. p. 492[a], above); but Diekamp also makes it clear, first that Andrew and Oecumenius are not independent of one another, and secondly that it was Andrew who used Oecumenius, and not *vice versâ*. In his comments on 4[5] 6[1] 9[5. 15] Andrew introduces the explanations of τινὲς or τις τῶν πρὸ ἡμῶν; and in every case the explanation so introduced is found in Oecumenius. Especially cogent is the case of μῆνας πέντε in 9[5], because there Oecumenius, after balancing the 'apocatastasis' doctrine of the Origenist Evagrius with the more rigid eschatology of other writers, compromises on a doctrine of punishment which should be eternal indeed in duration, but after the 'five months' modified in intensity (ὑφειμένως). When, then, we find Andrew quoting with the formula τινὲς ἔφησαν the very conclusion at which Oecumenius had painfully arrived by way of compromise, it would be unreasonable to doubt that Oecumenius is the source on which Andrew draws.

But if Oecumenius on the Apocalypse quotes no predecessors for the simple reason that he had no predecessors to quote, he does as a matter of fact approach the method of Oecumenius on St. Paul by not infrequent references to the Fathers generally. Cyril is quoted four times; Gregory Nazianzen and Eusebius, twice each; Aquila, Josephus, Clement (the *Stromateis*), Gregory Nyssen, and Evagrius, once each. The commentator on the Apocalypse and the commentator on St. Paul are equally versed in Patristic literature, and employ it equally in the measure appropriate to the two works. It may be added that, while the former is, as has been seen, rather Cyrilline than Chalcedonian in the expression of his Christology, the latter too appears to have worked on anti-Nestorian lines; for the Catena on St. Paul never once cites Theodore of Mopsuestia, and, considering the number of names adduced in it, this omission can hardly be accidental. On internal evidence, therefore, there is no reason at all to question their identity.

The external evidence to the commentary of Oecumenius on the Apocalypse is confined to a single quotation in a Syriac *Catena Patrum* of the 7th cent. (Brit. Mus. Add. 17214 = Wright cod. dccclv., fol. 72 *b*). In this MS, which is a collection of explanations of Bible passages, the principal authority employed is Severus of Antioch, and Theodore of Mopsuestia is cited as 'Theodore the heretic': its Monophysite leanings are therefore clear, and we are not surprised to find that Oecumenius, in the phrase with which the quotation from him is introduced, is brought into close connexion with Severus: 'Of Oecumenius, a diligent man, and one who is very orthodox, as the letters of the patriarch Mar Severus which are written to him show: From the sixth book of those composed by him about the Revelation of John the Evangelist.' If the Syriac writer is correct, Oecumenius the commentator on the Apocalypse was a favoured correspondent of the great Monophysite, and must therefore have been of mature age before the death of Severus, *circa* A.D. 540: so that the internal evidence of the commentary, both as to date and as to the theological affinities of its author, would be carried somewhat further by the Syriac catenist. But among all the extant correspondence of Severus the only person bearing the name of Oecumenius is a Count to whom Severus addressed two dogmatic letters before A.D. 512: and it is probable, therefore, that the Syriac writer has blundered in identifying the commentator with the correspondent, for the interval of 'more than 500 years' since the vision of the Apocalypse is inconsistent with anything earlier than the second half of the 6th century. At the same time, the fact that the mistake could be made suggests that the commentary was not quite a new thing when the Syriac MS was written. We shall hardly err in placing the commentary on the Apocalypse about 600, and the Catena on St. Paul within the limits 560–640.

Of the original non-Photian form of the Oecumenian Catena on St. Paul the following MSS in Karo-Lietzmann's list (*op. cit.* p. 605) are attributed to the 10th century:

i. Paris coislin 95, foll. 348.
ii. Vatic. gr. 766, foll. 249.
iii. Oxford Bodl. Roe 16, foll. 255.
iv. Venice Marcianus 546, foll. 59–205 (but foll. 134–173, Gal 3[21]–1 Ti 4[10], are a later insertion).

v. Milan Ambros. C 295 inf., foll. 190.
vi. Florence Laurent. plut. x. 6, foll. 286.
vii. Paris gr. 224, foll. 1–222 (contains also the Apocalypse).
viii. Paris coislin 224, foll. 151–328 (contains also Acts, Cath. Epp., Apoc.).
ix. Vatic. gr. 1430, foll. 267.
x. Vatic. Palat. gr. 10, foll. 268.
xi. Athens 100, foll. 377 (1 Co 15[29]–He 11[37]).

Of these eleven MSS the first five are, so far as can be gathered, homogeneous in the matter which they contain. No data are given about the last two; the remaining four, Nos. vi.–ix. (save that No. viii. perhaps contains only excerpts), while agreeing with the first five for all the anonymous citations in Oecumenius, differ from them with regard to the (in number much fewer) named citations, which they either transpose or, more rarely, omit. Both classes of MSS give the anonymous citations in one and the same continuous series marked by Greek numerals; and the choice appears to lie between the hypothesis that the named citations, though they entered into the Catena long before the Photian matter, are yet no part of the original Oecumenius, and the more probable hypothesis that in the original form of the Catena the named citations were separated in some way from the continuous series of the anonymous citations,—perhaps by being written in the margin,—and so were exposed, in the course of the propagation of the text, to special danger of either transposition or omission.

Another Catena, Vatic. gr. 1270, which is treated as an independent Catena in Karo-Lietzmann's scheme (*op. cit.* No. viii. p. 610), should perhaps, as was suggested on p. 489[a], above, be treated as belonging to the Oecumenian group. This MS, which was written in southern Italy about A.D. 1100, contains the Acts and Catholic epistles, and on foll. 79–164 a Catena on Romans and 1 Corinthians. From Karo-Lietzmann it would not be possible to deduce more than that the names of Chrysostom, Severian, and Theodoret were found in it; but Acacius, Cyril, Gennadius, and Oecumenius also occur, and once at least Basil ἐκ τοῦ πρὸς Σωζόπολιν ἐπιστολῆς (*sic*). It is significant that a similar reference to this last appears in Oecumenius; see above, p. 499[a].

2. On the need for a new edition of the commentary on the Pauline epistles by John of Damascus, and on some of the MS material for it, enough has already been said on p. 519[b].

3. Cod. Vatic. gr. 1650, A.D. 1037, is a commentary on the Pauline epistles written by Nicolas, archbishop of Reggio in Calabria. Ehrhard (in Krumbacher's *Geschichte der byzantinische Litteratur*[2], p. 133), who mentions the MS, gives no details of its contents, so that it is impossible to say whether it contains ancient elements.

C. *Original authorities as preserved in the Catenæ.*—

It is obvious that not much can be done under this head until the Catenæ themselves are made accessible in trustworthy texts; and how far that is from being the case at the present date it has been the business of the preceding paragraphs to demonstrate. But, as soon as this preliminary work has sufficiently advanced, it would be the turn of definitive collected editions of the more important writers. Since the Catenæ are mainly on the longer epistles (see especially p. 518[a] above), the results to be anticipated from this line of research will be, in the case of the majority of writers, most marked on the Roman, or on the Roman and Corinthian, epistles.

*Origen.*—The work has already been done tentatively for the Ephesians (pp. 493–495, above); but it still remains to be done for the Romans, and for the First at any rate of the Corinthian epistles (pp. 492, 493[a]).

*Didymus:* p. 499.—It does not seem likely that much can be restored for any other epistle than 2 Corinthians; but Mai's text (from Vat. gr. 762) will need re-editing, and the Didymus material of Vat. gr. 692 (see pp. 489[a], 522) will need to be tested, though it may turn out to be not independent of the other MS.

*Diodore:* p. 501.—The evidence here rests wholly on Vat. 762, and a separate edition might probably wait for Harnack's promised undertaking of a 'Corpus operum Diodori' (see his 'Diodor von Tarsus,' *Texte und Untersuchungen*, N. F. vi. 4, 1901, p. 68).

*Severian:* p. 507.—Severian is perhaps the author for whom most is to be expected from a careful cross-examination of the Catenæ: on the Romans (unless Oecumenius should here come to the rescue) less has been preserved from him than from several other writers; but for 1 Corinthians, Ephesians, Philippians, Colossians, Philemon, and probably for the other shorter epistles as well, a rich harvest should be yielded.

*Theodore of Mopsuestia.*—For the shorter epistles the work has been done by Dr. Swete (p. 511[a]): for the longer epistles the texts of Mai and Cramer (p. 510[a]) would need revision, and for Theodore, as for Didymus, the Catena of Vat. 692 may or may not add new matter.

*Cyril:* p. 515.—The only source from which any additions to Pusey's collection could be hoped for would be a re-edited Oecumenius.

*Gennadius:* p. 518[a].—Oecumenius and the various Catenæ on Romans ought between them to add something, though perhaps it may not be much, to the fragments put together by Migne.

*Photius:* p. 520[a].—Here again a separate edition, for which the Photian recension of Oecumenius would supply the main material, is an imperative and probably a not really difficult task.

D. *Authors preserved independently of Catenæ.*—

In this department, as was to be expected, more work has already been done; but something still remains to do. The commentaries of Chrysostom (p. 506[b]) and Theodoret (p. 516[b]), and the Latin version of Theodore (p. 511[a]), have been adequately edited by English scholars: Rufinus' version of Origen on the Romans is to be expected in the Berlin series of the Ante-Nicene Fathers: with regard to the letters of Isidore of Pelusium, the need for a new and better edition, and the material which would make such an edition feasible, were pointed out with sufficient emphasis on p. 513. And besides the many Fathers who expounded the Epistles there were some also who edited them. It will be seen in the course of the next (and concluding) section that patient investigation may hope ultimately to restore, with approximate correctness, the text and apparatus of these early editions of St. Paul.

V. PATRISTIC EDITORS OF THE PAULINE EPISTLES.—**Evagrius** and **Euthalius.**—The name Euthalius conjures up more questions than with the information at our disposal it is possible to answer. Of late a revolution in Euthalian criticism has been made every few years; and though material is accumulating rapidly, the time has not yet come for the last word to be said. But no estimate of Patristic labours on St. Paul would be adequate which did not try to give some account of the earliest attempts to produce what would now be called an edition, with Introduction and Prolegomena, of the sacred text.

(*a*) 'Euthalian matter' is a convenient term, of which use has already been made (p. 485[b]) in this article, denoting a whole literature of documents, 'prologues, *argumenta*, *programmata*, lists of OT citations, lists of chapters, colophons, and scraps of all kinds,' found in part or in full in many Greek MSS of the Acts and Epistles, and first published with any approach to completeness by L. A. Zacagni, *Collectanea monumentorum veterum ecclesiæ Græcæ ac Latinæ quæ hactenus in Vaticana bibliotheca delituerunt* (Rome, 1698), pp. liv-lxxvii, 401-708. It falls into two parts—an edition of the Pauline epistles, and a subsequent edition of the Acts and Catholic epistles with which we are here concerned only in so far as it may throw light on its author's previous work on St. Paul. To each of the two editions is prefixed a prologue; and these prologues in some MSS are anonymous, and in others bear the name of Εὐθαλίου διακόνου or Εὐθαλίου ἐπισκόπου Σούλκης. According to Zacagni, the proper title of the Pauline prologue is 'Euthalius the deacon,' and of the other prologue 'Euthalius bishop of Sulca,' the author having been raised to the episcopate in the interval between the composition of his two works. Zacagni printed the fullest collection of texts accessible to him; and though he was not prepared to claim the authorship of Euthalius for all his documents, he certainly attributed the great mass of them to him. On the strength of a note of time attached in some MSS to one of his Euthalian documents, the *Martyrium Pauli*, he fixed the date of the edition of the Pauline epistles at A.D. 458.

(*b*) For nearly two centuries no serious advance was made upon Zacagni's statement of the problem. The credit of the first contribution of new material belongs to a paper by Dr. A. Ehrhard in the *Centralblatt für Bibliothekswesen*, 1891, vol. viii. pp. 385-411. Ehrhard called attention to the occurrence of the name Evagrius in two MSS which contain Euthalian material: (i.) codex H of the Pauline epistles, a fragmentary MS of the 6th cent., written in στίχοι or sense lines,—'per cola et commata,' to use the more technical term,—the colophon of which is written in the first person, and in clearly 'Euthalian' language, by a certain Evagrius;* (ii.) codex Neapolitanus II. a 7 of the Acts and Epistles (in Gregory's notation =Ac. 83=Paul. 93), a later but completer MS, comprising much Euthalian matter without the name of Euthalius, together with the Evagrius colophon as in cod. H. No one had ever been able to identify Euthalius the deacon or Euthalius the bishop of Sulca with any known historical personage; and Ehrhard proposed to eject him altogether, and to substitute instead the name Evagrius. By moving back the date of the Pauline apparatus from Zacagni's 458 (a secondary date found in only a few MSS of the *Martyrium Pauli*) to 396 (a date found in all of them without exception), he brought the work of his Evagrius within the limits of the lifetime of the well-known Origenist writer, Evagrius Ponticus, who died in Egypt about 399.

(*c*) Dr. J. Armitage Robinson's *Euthaliana* ('Cambridge Texts and Studies,' iii. 3, A.D. 1895) was principally directed to the analysis of Zacagni's Euthalian collection, with a view of discriminating the original matter from that which had accrued at later stages. Accepting Dr. Ehrhard's connexion of the *Martyrium Pauli* with the year 396 and with the name Evagrius, Dr. Robinson maintained that the *Martyrium* is itself a secondary document, dependent on the Euthalian prologue to the Pauline epistles; and he argued back to an original Euthalius, to whom is due the prologue and whatever in the Euthalian collection is covered by the sketch which the prologue gives of its author's proposed edition. The table of Old Testament quotations, the table of chapter-divisions, and the arrangement of the text by sense lines, constitute the sum, according to Dr. Robinson, of all that we can safely attribute (in addition to the prologue) to the pen of Euthalius himself. The date of Euthalius would then fall somewhere between the date of the *Chronicle* of Eusebius (which is cited in the prologue) and the date of the *Martyrium Pauli*. Dr. Robinson's tentative results have been superseded by the discovery next to be mentioned; but the value of his method is independent of it and unaffected by it.

(*d*) The first part (1902), which alone has yet appeared, of H. v. Soden's elaborate but far from lucid textual Introduction to the NT, *Die Schriften des NT in ihrer ältesten erreichbaren Textgestalt hergestellt auf Grund ihrer Textgeschichte*, has settled once for all, not indeed the whole problem of Euthalian criticism (as the author seems to suppose), but the vexed questions of Euthalius' place and date. In his discussion on Euthalius (pp. 637-682), von Soden prints from an Athos codex (Laura 149, sæc. xi. foll. 1-4) a 'confession of Euthalius, bishop of Sulca, concerning the orthodox faith.' The document belongs to the days of the Monothelite controversy, after pope Martin's Lateran Council (A.D. 649), and after the death of Maximus Confessor 'of blessed memory' (A.D. 662), but presumably, since no mention is made of it, before the Sixth Council (A.D. 680). Latin theologians—Ambrose, Augustine, Leo—are cited in this Greek confession of faith on equal terms with Athanasius and Cyril; the mention of the 'Holy Catholic and Apostolic great church of Rome' is given precedence over the mention of the 'four Holy and Œcumenical Synods'; and Western origin is made quite certain, if further proof were needed, when the writer attributes his attack on Maximus, of which he is now making public retractation, to the instigation of John the 'exceptor' or official of the 'duchy,' ὁ ἐκσκέπτωρ τῆς δουκιανῆς ἀρχῆς, for the term 'ducatus' or duchy points to the Western provinces of the Byzantine empire. Thus there can be no doubt that the see of Euthalius is, after all, the only known city bearing a name anything like Sulca—that is to say, Sulci in Sardinia. The difficulty which was naturally felt in making a Greek writer bishop in Sardinia in the 4th or 5th cent. vanishes when we transfer him to the 7th, a period when even Rome, through the closeness of its renewed relations with Constantinople, became for the time half-Greek again.*

What is the effect of von Soden's discovery upon the Euthalian question? Its main result is naturally to enhance the importance of Ehrhard's Evagrian discoveries, since Evagrius, even if he was not the person who in 396 put together the *Martyrium Pauli*, is mentioned in the 6th cent. codex H, and is consequently earlier than Euthalius. Dr. Armitage Robinson aimed at rescuing out of the Euthalian congeries such documents as he thought could be attributed to Euthalius himself rather than to his successors, Evagrius or others: our present aim must be the exact converse of this, namely, to discriminate what can be attributed to Evagrius or other predecessors before Euthalius set his hand to the collection. With this view we proceed, firstly, to draw up a list of the Pauline documents contained in Zacagni's edition, and, secondly, to enumerate the sources earlier than the 7th cent. which include any of

* The name has been erased, but there appears to be now no doubt at all as to the original reading.

* It is perhaps worth while in this connexion to call attention to the Laudian MS of the Acts, which we know to have been in Sardinia at some date before 735. The third correcting hand, which is attributed to the 7th cent., added in the margin a series of chapter-divisions which appear to be either those of Euthalius' edition or at least closely related to them.

this Euthalian matter, since so much at least must be earlier than Euthalius himself.

1. *COMPLETE LIST OF EUTHALIAN DOCUMENTS* (with reference to the pages of Zacagni's edition).

(i.) p. 515: *πρόλογος προτασσόμενος τῶν ιδ' ἐπιστολῶν Παύλου.* A sketch of firstly the life, secondly the writings, thirdly the chronology of St. Paul: the latter is summarized, says the writer, from the Χρονικοὶ Κανόνες of Eusebius Pamphili, though in fact the *History* of the same author appears to be as largely employed. At the end of the second section of this prologue, the analysis of the Epistles, some indication is given of what the reader may expect to find in the sequel: *τὰ μὲν κατ' ἐπιτομὴν παρ' ἡμῶν εἰρήσθω περὶ αὐτῶν ἐπὶ τοσοῦτον· καθ ἑκάστην δὲ συντόμως ἐπιστολὴν ἐν τοῖς ἑξῆς προτάξομεν τὴν τῶν κεφαλαίων ἔκθεσιν ἑνὶ τῶν σοφωτάτων τινὶ καὶ φιλοχρίστων πατέρων ἡμῶν πεπονημένην· οὐ μὴν ἀλλὰ καὶ τὴν τῶν ἀναγνώσεων ἀκριβεστάτην τομήν, τήν τε* [*v.l.* δὲ] *τῶν θείων μαρτυριῶν εὐαπόδεκτον εὕρεσιν ἡμεῖς τεχνολογήσαντες ἀνεκεφαλαιωσάμεθα ἐπιπορευόμενοι τῇ τῆς ὑφῆς ἀναγνώσει· ἐκθησόμεθα δ' οὖν ταύτην εὐθὺς μετὰ τόνδε τὸν πρόλογον.* That is to say, immediately after the prologue should come a convenient and summary conspectus of the quotations in the Epistles; while to each several epistle would be prefixed a list of its chapters, taken over from an earlier Father. What the 'exact division of the *ἀναγνώσεις*' means, whether it was taken over from the earlier Father or, like the list of quotations, was an original work, and in the latter case whether it too came immediately after the prologue, are more difficult questions, the consideration of which must for the moment be postponed.

(ii.) p. 535: *μαρτύριον Παύλου.* A brief statement of the Apostle's martyrdom at Rome, important as containing a note that the interval since the martyrdom was 330 years 'down to the present consulship, Arcadius IV. Honorius III.,' *i.e.* A.D. 396. One particular class of the MSS contains also the further note that 63 years had elapsed between the last mentioned consulship and 'this present consulship, Leo Augustus I.,' *i.e.* A.D. 458. In view both of the statements in the prologue (see just above) and of the order of the documents, *e.g.*, in the Naples MS (see p. 528[b], below), it is doubtful whether the *Martyrium* is in its proper place here —unless, indeed, it is to be treated (as perhaps it should be) as a mere appendix to the prologue.

(iii.) p. 537: *ἀνακεφαλαίωσις τῶν ἀναγνώσεων καὶ ὧν ἔχουσι κεφαλαίων καὶ μαρτυριῶν καθ' ἑκάστην ἐπιστολὴν τοῦ ἀποστόλου καὶ ὅσων ἑκάστη τούτων στίχων τυγχάνει.* A summary of the 'lections' for each epistle of the Apostle; and how many chapters, how many quotations, how many verses each 'lection' contains. In this case there is no doubt that the *ἀνάγνωσις* or lection is a division of an epistle, containing several *κεφάλαια* or chapters. The *στίχος* is presumably the measured line of 16 syllables, equivalent to a hexameter verse.* Thus the Epistle to the Romans contained 5 lections, 19 chapters, 48 quotations, 820 verses. It may be added that the number of *στίχοι* is noted not only for the actual text of the Epistles, but for several of the accompanying documents,—for instance, the prologue is reckoned at 300 *στίχοι*, the *Martyrium* (not including the second date) at 16 *στίχοι*,† the summary with which we are now concerned at 60 *στίχοι*,—and it may be conjectured that their presence or absence is a criterion which distinguishes one stratum from another in the 'Euthalian' collection.

(iv.) p. 542: *πρόγραμμα.* Introduction (of 7 *στίχοι*) to No. v. (summary table of Scripture quotations), explaining the use of black and red numerals in the following table [this will be best understood from a concrete case; see the next paragraph]: every red numeral would be found repeated in the margin of the text itself; the series of both red and black numerals would begin afresh for each epistle.

(v.) p. 542: *ἀνακεφαλαίωσις θείων μαρτυριῶν* (78 *στίχοι*). Carrying out the rules just given, the table begins as follows: 'In the Epistle to the Romans xlviii. [quotations]; Genesis vi., namely, 6, 8, 9, 11, 12, 13; Exodus iii., namely, 15, 16, 40,' and so on, meaning that the six quotations from Genesis are the 6th, 8th, 9th, 11th, 12th, and 13th in order among the 48 OT quotations in Romans. The numbers here represented in *roman* numerals would be black letters in the Greek, those in *arabic* numerals would be red, and the same red letters would be found opposite to the quotations in the body of the text: thus in the margin of Ro 4[3] *ἐπίστευσεν δὲ Ἀβραὰμ τῷ θεῷ, κ.τ.λ.*, we should expect *ϛ' Γενέσεως*, and of Ro 4[17] *πατέρα πολλῶν ἐθνῶν τέθεικά σε*, we should expect *η' Γενέσεως* (the numeral in each case in red), meaning that the quotations came from Genesis, and were respectively the sixth and eighth OT quotations made in the epistle.

(vi.) p. 546. List of the places from which the Epistles were written (12 *στίχοι*).

(vii.) p. 547. List of the names associated with St. Paul's in the headings to the Epistles (12 *στίχοι*).

(viii.) p. 548: *πρόγραμμα* (not reckoned by *στίχοι*). Introduction to No. ix. (second or fuller table of Scripture quotations), explaining that all St. Paul's quotations would be found written in full, with the name of the book from which each was taken, and with two numbers, red and black respectively: the red signified the place in the series of quotations contained *in* that particular epistle,—a fresh reckoning in red beginning with each epistle,— while the numeration in black was continuous throughout the Epistles, and signified the number in the series of quotations taken *from* that particular book of the OT. The same red number (but not the black) recurred in the margin of the text at the point where the quotation was made.

(ix.) p. 549: *ἀνακεφαλαίωσις θείων μαρτυριῶν* (not reckoned by *στίχοι*). To illustrate the above rule, let us turn to the table for 1 Corinthians, and we should find it begin somewhat thus: *Α' Ἡσαίου προφήτου ΙΕ' ἀπολῶ τὴν σοφίαν τῶν σοφῶν καὶ τὴν σύνεσιν τῶν συνετῶν ἀθετήσω*, where the Α' would be in red, signifying the first quotation in 1 Corinthians, and the ΙΕ' in black, signifying the fifteenth quotation from Isaiah, fourteen having been marked already in Romans.* Now it seems obvious that (viii.) (ix.) are not additional to, but a substitution for, the other table of Scripture quotations described above (iv.) (v.): the title is the same, *πρόγραμμα· ἀνακεφαλαίωσις θείων μαρτυριῶν*: the use of the red numbers in the summaries and in the margin of the text is the same, but the use of the black numbers is different and inconsistent: the *στίχοι* are reckoned for the first table, but not for the second. Either table is useful taken by itself, but the table of No. ix. gives more information than that of No. v.: its black numeration being continuous throughout the Epistles, it enables the reader to see at a glance the total amount of use which St. Paul's writings make of any particular OT book. Which of the two is the table promised in the prologue, is a question we need not yet finally answer; but we shall hardly be wrong in supposing that they represent different strata in the development of the collection, and the natural hypothesis to start from will be that the fuller and more elaborate one is the later.

* See, further, for the meaning of *στίχος*, p. 527[b], below.

† But in the case of the prologue and the *Martyrium* the *στίχοι* are not given in all of Zacagni's MSS.

* Zacagni inserts a third numeration, which he admits is not in the MSS; he has misunderstood, as Robinson (*Euthaliana*, p. 19) points out, the language of the *πρόγραμμα*.

(x.) p. 569. List of the 14 epistles of St. Paul; probably connected with what follows.

(xi.) p. 570. 'Why the epistles of Paul are called 14?' This is taken from the same source as the next piece.

(xii.) p. 570: *ὑπόθεσις πρώτης πρὸς Ῥωμαίους ἐπιστολῆς* (*incipit* *ταύτην ἐπιστέλλει ἀπὸ Κορίνθου*, *explicit* *τελειοῖ τὴν ἐπιστολήν*). This and the preceding come, as Matthæi and von Dobschütz have pointed out, from the pseudo-Athanasian *Synopsis sacræ scripturæ*. But now that Euthalius is transferred to the 7th cent., there is no reason why matter which 'Euthalian' MSS have borrowed from the *Synopsis* should not have been borrowed by Euthalius himself. These pieces cannot have belonged to the collection in its original, or what we may without prejudice call the Evagrian, form: that they came to it through Euthalius himself is probable enough, but is one of the many things that cannot be decisively asserted until we have more knowledge of the MSS. None of the last three pieces are reckoned by *στίχοι*.

(xiii.) p. 573: *ἔκθεσις κεφαλαίων καθολικῶν καθ' ἑκάστην ἐπιστολὴν τοῦ Ἀποστόλου, ἐχόντων τινῶν καὶ μερικὰς ὑποδιαιρέσεις τὰς διὰ τοῦ κινναβάρεως*. 'List of all the chapters in each epistle of the Apostle, some chapters having also subdivisions; and such subdivisions are marked in red.' Nothing follows this title in Zacagni's edition; and it is on the whole probable that nothing was meant to follow, but that the title serves as a general introduction to the chapter-lists which precede each individual epistle. That for the Romans immediately follows.

(xiv.) p. 573: *κεφάλαια τῆς πρὸς Ῥωμαίους ἐπιστολῆς ιθ'* (37 *στίχοι*). In the list which follows, one chapter, the 17th, has subdivisions: in other epistles—their *κεφάλαια* (together with the pseudo-Athanasian *argumenta*) are given later on in Zacagni—subdivisions are rather more frequent. There can be no doubt that these chapter-lists correspond exactly with the scheme outlined under No. xiii.

(xv.) p. 576: *variæ lectiones* to the Epistles.—What ought to have appeared here is the text of the Epistles as contained in the Euthalian MSS: but, in order no doubt to save space, Zacagni only collated them with J. Morin's Paris NT (A.D. 1628). This list of various readings does not concern us, save in so far as we may note that every 50th *στίχος* is marked in the margin (Ro $1^{24}$ *στίχοι ν'*, $2^{14}$ *στίχοι ρ'*, and so on), and that each epistle has a subscription signifying (*a*) its place of writing —cf. No. vi. above,—and (*b*) the number of *στίχοι* contained in it;* generally also (*c*) its bearer. Thus for 1 Corinthians, *Πρὸς Κορινθίους α' ἐγράφη ἀπὸ Φιλίππων διὰ Στεφανᾶ καὶ Φορτουνάτου καὶ Ἀχαϊκοῦ καὶ Τιμοθέου· στίχοι ωο'* (870): for Titus, *Πρὸς Τίτον τῆς Κρητῶν ἐκκλησίας πρῶτον ἐπίσκοπον χειροτονηθέντα ἐγράφη ἀπὸ Νικοπόλεως τῆς Μακεδονίας· στίχοι ρζ'* (107).

2. *SOURCES EARLIER THAN THE SEVENTH CENTURY WHICH INCLUDE ANY EUTHALIAN MATTER.*—To show how much of all this matter is earlier than Euthalius we have the direct evidence of the fragmentary 6th century MS of the Pauline epistles known as H, reinforced up to a certain point by the Naples codex, and the less direct evidence of various Syriac MSS of the Epistles written between 400 and 625 A.D., as well as the dates contained in the *Martyrium Pauli*.

(*a*) Codex H was once a complete MS of the epistles of St. Paul, and belonged apparently before the end of the 10th cent. to the monastery of Athanasius on Mount Athos, where it was taken to pieces, and the leaves, or many of them, were employed in the binding of other MSS. The leaves thus distributed accompanied of course the MSS with which they had been incorporated, and are now dispersed throughout Europe: of the 41 leaves known to exist, 8 are still at Athos, 22 are at Paris, 2 at Turin, and the remaining 9 in various Russian libraries. Portions of nine epistles are preserved, the only ones unrepresented being Romans, Ephesians, Philippians, 2 Thessalonians, Philemon. The signatures *μϛ'* and *μθ'* (46 and 49) have been deciphered at He $12^{12}$ and 1 Ti $6^{11}$ respectively: from which it may be reckoned that each gathering contained nearly three pages of Westcott and Hort's smaller edition; and that, as the whole matter down to He $12^{12}$ occupies about 122 pages in that edition, while 46 gatherings would be equivalent to 130 pages, the MS must have originally contained enough in the way of additional or prefatory matter, other than *κεφάλαια*,* to account for the balance between the two figures. A complete transcription of all the 41 leaves was published in 1889 by M. Henri Omont (*Notices et Extraits*, xxxiii. 1); Dr. Robinson in his *Euthaliana*, pp. 48–69, added parts of 16 more pages, which he restored from the 'set-off' or traces which these pages, before they were lost, had left of their text on the pages that were originally next to them. From these two sources, combined with Dr. Ehrhard's paper, it results that codex H is distinguished by the following characteristics:—

*a.* The manuscript is written in 'sense lines.' At a time when manuscripts were written without anything like a developed system of punctuation, some imitation of the arrangement that already existed for the poetical books of the OT was one obvious means of filling the gap; the end of each *στίχος*, or 'verse,' was made to correspond to some sort of break in the sense, and, so far, was more or less equivalent to a comma. But as the original *στίχος* was the hexameter line, and this always remained the standard by which in ordinary cases the size of books or chapters was calculated, the sense *στίχος* naturally aimed at something like the same average length, and was therefore often a good deal shorter than the modern interval between comma and comma. Conversely, it was much longer than the actual line of a MS written, as so many uncial MSS were written, in narrow columns. In codex H itself (to judge from Dr. Robinson's transcriptions) the line in the literal sense never contains more than 21 letters, and the *στίχος*—which is distinguished by beginning further out to the left than the lines in the middle of a *στίχος* do—covers one, two, three, or sometimes even four, lines: the average is a little over two lines, and apparently about 37 letters.

*β.* To each epistle of which the commencement is extant is prefixed a table of *κεφάλαια*: the whole of that for 1 Timothy (*α'–ιη'*), and part of those for Galatians (*ι'–ιβ'*), Hebrews (*ζ'–ια'*), and Titus (*β'–ϛ'*), are preserved. In two instances, chapters *ζ'* and *θ'* of Hebrews, subdivisions are also marked, *α' β' γ'* in the first case, *β'* only in the second: these subdivisions are marked in red (Robinson, p. 66). Thus we have here substantial equivalence between codex H and Zacagni, Nos. xiii., xiv.

*γ.* At Col $2^{1}$ and $3^{5}$ the letters *ϛ'* and *θ'*, at 2 Ti $2^{4}$ and $2^{8}$ † the letters *γ'* and *δ'*, at Tit $2^{2}$ the letter *γ'*, are legible in the margin, indicating the commencement in the text of the chapters marked by the corresponding numbers in the list. It does not appear that Zacagni's apparatus anywhere

* The following is the Euthalian stichometry for the text of the Epistles, as collected out of Zacagni: Romans, 920; 1 Corinthians, 870; 2 Corinthians, 690; Galatians, 293; Ephesians, 312; Philippians, 208; Colossians, 208; 1 Thessalonians, 193; 2 Thessalonians, 106; Hebrews, 703; 1 Timothy, 230; 2 Timothy, 172; Titus, 107 [but codex H gives 97]; Philemon, 47.

* The *κεφάλαια* are included in the reckoning just made, since the three gatherings on which that reckoning is based contain the *κεφάλαια* for 1 Timothy, reckoned at 22 *στίχοι*.

† See the supplementary notes to M. Omont's transcript in Robinson, p. 68.

definitely promises that the chapters should be marked in the body of the text; but the analogy of the procedure with regard to the OT citations demands it; and the fact that Zacagni, in his Latin translations of the chapter-tables, inserts throughout the references to our own chapters and verses, seems to show that his MSS do actually mark the commencements in question.

δ. The OT quotations in the text are noted in the margin, and are clearly intended to be numbered through for each epistle. Thus at 1 Co $10^{26}$ we have *ιαʹ ψαλμ. κγʹ* (*i.e.* Ps 23, eleventh quotation in the epistle), and at He $2^{12}$ *θʹ ψαλμ. καʹ*, $2^{13}$ *ιʹ Ἠσαΐου*, $2^{16}$ *ιαʹ Ἠσαΐου* (*i.e.* Ps 21 supplies the ninth, Isaiah the tenth and eleventh quotations for the epistle); if at He $1^{5.\,6.\,7.\,8}$ we have only Βασιλ., *Δευτερονομ.*, *ψαλμ.*, *ψαλμ. μδʹ*, this shows that the system is not systematically carried out, and confirms what other indications suggest, namely, that codex H is not an original, but a copy, and not always an accurate copy. To which of Zacagni's two tables of OT quotations—Nos. iv., v., or Nos. viii., ix. --these marginal annotations correspond, there is so far nothing to decide.

ε. The number of *στίχοι* is noted at the end of each chapter-table, and at the end of the text of each epistle. Thus the *κεφάλαια* for 1 Timothy are 22 *στίχοι*, for Titus 8; the text of Hebrews contains 703, that of Titus 97. That every 50th *στίχος* was also noted in the margin our authorities do not apparently say; but the Naples codex (see immediately below) proves that Evagrius included that method in his system, and codex H is through its subscription connected clearly enough with Evagrius. In the case of the chapter-tables, as also of all documents such as the prologue, the *Martyrium*, and the like, there can be no doubt that the *στίχος* was the line of hexameter length (reckoned equivalent to 16 syllables or 36 letters): but it is possible that for the text of the epistles, arranged as it was in sense *στίχοι*, these latter were themselves taken as the basis of calculation. The practical difference would not be great, for we have seen (p. 527[b], above) that the sense *στίχος* in codex H averaged about 37 letters.

ζ. The subscriptions to the individual epistles contain, besides the number of *στίχοι*, similar historical data to those given in Zacagni. Thus for Titus: *Παύλου ἀποστόλου ἐπιστολὴ πρὸς Τῖτον τῆς Κρητῶν ἐκκλησίας πρῶτον ἐπίσκοπον χειροτονηθέντα ἐγράφη ἀπὸ Νικοπόλεως τῆς Μακεδονίας*, as in Zacagni (p. 527[a], above).

η. The subscription to the whole MS records that 'I [Evagrius *] wrote for public use this volume of Paul the Apostle in *στίχοι* to the best of my ability, with a view to making reading easier for our brethren . . . and the book was compared with the copy at Cæsarea in the library, written by the hand of the holy Pamphilus.'

(*b*) We have seen that codex H, to judge from its size, must in all probability have contained prefatory matter before the text and *κεφάλαια* of the Epistles; and some light is thrown upon this question of the apparatus of Evagrian MSS by the only other MS yet known which contains Evagrius' name, Naples II. a 7; though, as the MS is of later date than Euthalius, it must not be too hastily assumed that all its contents are Evagrian rather than Euthalian. Unfortunately, our knowledge of the details of its text is not yet complete; but the old Naples catalogue of 1826 (*Codices græci MSS regiæ bibliothecæ Borbonici descripti atque illustrati a Salvatore Cyrillo*, pp. 13–24) enumerates the following contents:—Fol. 1, prologue of Euthalius to the Acts, but without his name; fol. 3, second prologue to the Acts *πάλαι καὶ προπάλαι . . . πεποίηται ταύτην*—this has now been published in the *American Journal of Theology* (ii. [1898] 353–387) by Dr. E. von Dobschütz, who assigns it, apparently on good grounds, to Theodore of Mopsuestia's commentary; fol. 7, list of chapters, and summary of OT citations, in Acts; fol. 11, text of Acts; fol. 41, [Euthalian] prologue to the Catholic epistles; fol. 42, *argumenta*, lists of chapters, and text of the Catholic epistles; fol. 56, [Euthalian] prologue to the Pauline epistles, followed by the summary of lections (Zacagni, Nos. i. and iii.); fol. 66, *argumenta*, lists of chapters (Zacagni, Nos. xii. and xiv.), and text of the Pauline epistles, followed by the *Martyrium Pauli* (Zacagni, No. ii.) and the note Εὐάγριος ἔγραψα (as in codex H, save that the *Navigatio Pauli*, ἑκατόνταρχος . . . ἀνηνέχθησαν, is intercalated into the middle of it); fol. 122, the opening chapters of the Apocalypse. Thus the name Euthalius seems not to appear anywhere in the MS, while the name Evagrius appears in the note which concludes the Pauline matter. But we further learn from other sources (see Robinson, p. 6) that yet a second note contains the name Evagrius, namely, that which is appended to the summary of lections: in Zacagni, p. 541, this is in the first person, but anonymous; in the Naples MS it runs, 'I, Evagrius, have distinguished the lections, and have made an accurate stichometry for the whole book of the Apostle by marking every 50th *στίχος*, and have set out the chapters of each lection and the citations contained in it, and also the number of *στίχοι* in the lection.'

Thus the testimony of the Naples MS, late as it is, definitely vindicates for Evagrius, and therefore for the pre-Euthalian edition of St. Paul, something more than codex H in its mutilated condition was able to do, namely Zacagni's No. iii. Putting the evidence of the two MSS together, we see that before the year 600—and if we are right in treating codex H as already a rather corrupt exemplar of the edition, we might say before the year 500—a certain Evagrius published an edition of the Pauline epistles, with the text arranged 'colometrically' in sense lines; with OT references marked in the margin, and numbered through for each epistle; with an elaborate arrangement of chapters and subdivisions of chapters in black and red; with calculation of the stichometry, not only of the text itself of the Epistles (guaranteed by a mark at every 50th *στίχος*), but even of the editor's chapter headings; with a subscription to each epistle giving geographical and personal information; and, finally, with some prefatory matter, including at least a continuous table of 'lections' for the whole series of Epistles, in which the number of chapters, citations, and *στίχοι* contained in each lection was separately enumerated.

(*c*) In attempting to fix with more precision the date of the edition of Evagrius, the evidence of the early Syriac MSS of the Pauline epistles will have to be taken into account. Wright's British Museum catalogue comprises several MSS anterior to the time of Euthalius, and three or four of them may possibly contain Euthalian matter. Cod. cxxxiii. (Add. 14476), sæc. v.–vi., divides Romans into 21 sections by Greek letters, and has a further mark, found occasionally throughout the Epistles, consisting of a single Syriac letter; but no details are given which would make it possible to say whether or no these are Euthalian (Evagrian) chapters. Cod. cxxxiv. (Add. 14480), sæc. v.–vi., has the same place-colophons as Evagrius,—including 1 Corinthians 'from Philippi of Macedonia,' and 1 Timothy 'from Laodicea,'—and also a reckoning of the *στίχοι* for each epistle. In cod. cxxxviii. (Add. 14477), sæc. vi.–vii., the colophons give not only the place of writing and the number of *στίχοι*, but also in each case the bearers of the

* As restored by Ehrhard, see above, p. 525[a].

epistle; * and for 2 Timothy, Titus, and Philemon the same personal details as in Zacagni's text (and therefore in the case of Titus, see p. 528b, above, the same as in codex H). On the other hand, the stichometry of these MSS does not appear to coincide with that of Euthalius. Finally, cod. cxli. (Add. 14478), A.D. 622, has marginal notes, indicating the sources of the Apostle's quotations, which would seem to be of 'Euthalian' (Evagrian) origin. Further investigation of this line of inquiry, which promises to be not without fruit, must be left to Syriac scholars; but even without Syriac evidence there is ground enough on the Greek side to push back the Evagrian nucleus of the Euthalian edition into the 5th century.

(*d*) This being so, the witness of the *Martyrium Pauli* to a precise dating at the end of the 4th cent. acquires enhanced importance. It has been seen that that document (Zacagni's No. ii.) is dated by its writer in 396, while one branch of the MS tradition adds the supplementary date of a redactor in 458. The document is so brief that it hardly seems likely to have been borrowed, rather than composed, for the edition of the Epistles; and if it was composed for it, the whole Evagrian edition is naturally brought into immediate connexion with that year. But, again, an Evagrius who was writing in 396 could surely be no other than the well-known theologian and writer who was trained by Basil and his brother Gregory, who, after varied experiences in Cappadocia, Constantinople, and Jerusalem, sought refuge among the ascetics of Nitria and Scetis, where he numbered Rufinus and Palladius among his pupils, and where he poured out book after book, for the benefit of his fellow ascetics, till his death in 398 or 399. One phrase in the Evagrian colophon of codex H, τῶν καθ' ἡμᾶς ἀδελφῶν, suggests that the writer was living the monastic life, and so far would bear out the hypothesis; but it remains a hypothesis still, and nothing is more necessary in threading our way through the mazes of the Euthalian labyrinth than to keep clear the distinction between hypothesis and ascertained fact. The value of such a hypothesis at this stage is rather to suggest lines of inquiry, and to give point and direction to the further investigation of manuscripts which must precede final judgment.

We have now enough material at our disposal to turn back to the list of Zacagni's Euthalian matter (p. 526a), and to distinguish roughly how much of it is Evagrian, or, at any rate, pre-Euthalian. The true authorship of the first piece, the prologue, is the most difficult, as well as the most important, problem left for discussion, and cannot be settled off-hand. But for the rest a rapid summary will suffice. No. ii. is dated at 396 (458) A.D., and is therefore pre-Euthalian, whether or no it is Evagrian. No. iii. is vindicated for Evagrius by the Naples MS. Nos. iv. and v. go together, as do Nos. viii. and ix.: these two pairs of documents are alternative to one another, and therefore of different authorship; the probabilities are that the one pair is Evagrian, the other Euthalian, and, if so, the simpler method and briefer statement of Nos. iv. and v. indicate the earlier editor. Nos. vi. and vii. may be Evagrian, but are in any case less important. Nos. viii and ix. are probably, as has just been said, Euthalius' development of Nos. iv. and v. Nos. x., xi., xii. are not Evagrian, and indeed are inconsistent with Evagrius: their source is in the pseudo-Athanasian synopsis: but if we regard Euthalius as a compiler, there is no reason why it should not have been he who engrafted upon the Evagrian stock material borrowed from pseudo-Athanasius. Nos. xiii. and xiv. are again Evagrian, and so is the apparatus to the text in No. xv.

The time has perhaps hardly come for expressing even a hypothetical view about the authorship of the prologue. If it proceeds from Euthalius, then the 'Father' from whom the system of chapter divisions was taken over (p. 526a, above) was no doubt Evagrius; if Evagrius himself wrote in these terms, the Father to whom he acknowledged himself indebted may well have been Pamphilus. If Euthalius was the author, then the ἀναγνώσεων τομαί will probably mean the colometrical arrangement of the text, since that is the sense of the parallel passages in the prologue to Acts; but if Evagrius, then the words most naturally refer to the arrangement by lections, summarized in Zacagni's No. iii., which, as we have seen, was certainly part of Evagrius' work. One would naturally prefer the alternative which would connect the prologue with the earlier Evagrian edition; but it is not impossible that it may prove to be of composite origin—an Evagrian nucleus worked up and developed by Euthalius.

Here, again, little advance can be made without more knowledge of MSS, and it is certainly strange that no attempt has been made to produce a more critical edition than Zacagni's of the Euthalian apparatus. This inquiry may therefore be fitly brought to a close by a tentative and doubtless very imperfect enumeration of early Euthalian MSS—

(1) *Oecumenian MSS with Euthalian apparatus* (see above, p. 485b)—

Milan Ambros. C 295 inf., sæc. x.

Paris coislin 27, sæc. x.; coislin 28, A.D. 1056; coislin 30, sæc. xi.; coislin 224, sæc. xi.; gr. 219, sæc. xi.; gr. 223, sæc. xi.; gr. 224, sæc. x.

Patmos ιε', sæc. xi.

Venice Marcianus 34, sæc. xi.

(2) *Non-Oecumenian MSS with Euthalian apparatus*—

Basle AN iii. 11, sæc. xi.; AN iv. 2, sæc. x.

London Brit. Mus. 28816, A.D. 1111.

Naples II a 7, sæc. xi.?; II a 8, sæc. x.–xi.

Oxford Christ Church Wake 12, sæc. xi.; Wake 38, sæc. xi.

Paris arm. 9 (Græco-Armenian), sæc. xi.; gr. 105 (fragmentary), sæc. x.

Rome Vatic. gr. 363, sæc. xi.; gr. 1650 (Zacagni's Cryptoferratensis), A.D. 1037; gr. 1761 (Zacagni's Lollinianus), sæc. xi.; Vat. Urbin. gr. 3, sæc. xi.; Vat. Reg. gr. 29, sæc. xi.; Vat. Reg. gr. 179 (Zacagni's Regio-Alexandrinus), sæc. xi.

## INDEX OF THE WRITERS, ETC., DEALT WITH ABOVE.



* Zacagni's text omits the bearers for Gal., 1 Thess., 2 Thess., 1 Tim., 2 Tim., Titus.

* Clarendon figures indicate that the passage referred to is devoted *wholly* to the subject in question.

LITERATURE.—Books dealing only with individual writers have been mentioned in the text of the article, and are not named again here. Those of wider scope may be classified as (1) books on Patristic literature in general, and (2) books on Patristic exegesis in particular.

(1) For the ante-Nicene writers: Harnack's *Geschichte der altchristlichen Litteratur bis Eusebius: Erster Theil, Die Ueberlieferung und der Bestand* (2 vols. Leipzig, 1893) is of course invaluable; the parts which touch most nearly the subject-matter of this article fell to the share of Harnack's assistant, Dr. E. Preuschen of Darmstadt. Smith and Wace's *Dictionary of Christian Biography* (4 vols. London, 1877–1887) has been of much service, though it is marred by some curious omissions and inequalities, and is often weakest just on the critical and bibliographical side; but the general level is high, and the articles on Origen and Theodore of Mopsuestia raise it higher still. Dr. O. Bardenhewer's *Patrologie* (ed. 2, Freiburg im Breisgau, 1901) is a most useful book: the reissue in a greatly enlarged form has not, unfortunately for the present purpose, advanced as yet beyond the second volume and the Council of Nicæa. Tillemont's *Mémoires pour servir à l'histoire ecclésiastique des six premiers siècles* (Paris, 1693–1712), two hundred years old as it is, has never been superseded for the post-Nicene period, and is still for many purposes the best authority.

(2) For the history of Patristic exegesis there is little to enumerate. The present writer is acquainted with nothing in English that goes further than the brief account appended by bishop Lightfoot to his commentary on the Galatians (ed. 5, pp. 227-236): in this, as in every contribution of Lightfoot's to Patristic studies, new ground was broken, but the material is more abundant now than when he wrote. Much more abundant, therefore, is it than it was when Richard Simon, priest of the Oratory and founder of the science of Biblical Criticism, gave to the world his *Histoire critique des principaux commentateurs du Nouveau Testament* (of which about half is devoted to the Patristic commentators, Greek and Latin), Rotterdam, 1693: nor is its age quite the only drawback to its usefulness, since its obvious interest in the Jansenist controversies of its day perhaps detracts something from its critical value. Yet it remains, and always must remain, worthy to be named with Tillemont's *Mémoires* as one of the noblest fruits of the rich harvest of French Patristic scholarship in the age of Louis the Great, and the present article owes not a little to its inspiration.

[Among the friends who have assisted him, the present writer renders his grateful thanks to Dr. Sanday, who has found time to read through the whole of the proofs; to Mr. E. W. Brooks, who has kindly verified several points in regard to Syriac MSS in the British Museum; and to the Rev. C. Jenkins, who has undertaken most of the thankless task of verifying references. He must make, however, further and special mention of his indebtedness to Dr. G. Mercati of the Vatican Library, to whom he owes not only more information about Vatican Catenæ than has yet appeared in print, but also a reference to the discovery of Oecumenius' commentary on the Apocalypse, which has an important bearing on the date of the Oecumenian Catena on St. Paul. The printing of the article had advanced too far for the new information about Oecumenius to be incorporated at its proper place; and to the same cause is due the insertion, on pp. 520, 521, of the section on Clement of Alexandria, it having been omitted by the writer's oversight on p. 489. For these and for any other unevennesses it is hoped that indulgence may be claimed in view of the difficulties attaching to labour in a field where the ground has been left so long untilled].

C. H. TURNER.

**CONCORDANCES.**—When the minute verbal comparison of one passage of Holy Scripture with another was felt to play a necessary part in arriving at the proportion of faith, and, in later times, at a proper critical treatment of the text, and especially when the Bible was treated more as a whole than as a collection of books of varying dates and composition, the need for more or less exhaustive Concordances was immediately felt, and it was not long before attempts were made to provide for the need. This was rendered the more easy by the printing of the text divided into verses as well as chapters. Alphabetical lists of words occurring in the sacred books were drawn up, as well as lists of the passages in which they occurred, with the salient words of the context, such as are given in Cruden's *Concordance* to the AV. These lists of words varied in their degree of completeness; but no Concordance can reasonably be expected to contain every quotation of every word; *e.g.* in an English Concordance such words as 'and,' 'the,' etc., are omitted. The interest taken in this accumulation of evidence about the occurrence of words and phrases is testified to by the fact that, for instance, in the case of Concordances to the LXX there are not only several which have been published, but there is certainly one unprinted in the Library of Trinity College, Dublin,* by Dr. Ambrose Aungier, Chancellor of St. Patrick's Cathedral. There is also in existence a MS Hebrew Concordance by Elias Levita, compiled in the 16th century.

For the purposes of the present volume it will be useful to supply a list of Hebrew, Greek, Latin, and English Concordances to the Bible, giving the titles of those now most constantly in use, and of some of the earliest ones that seem to have been published.

i. HEBREW.—*Concordantiæ sacrorum bibliorum Hebraicorum* . . . auctore Mario de Calasio (Rome, 1621) [this was based on Isaac Nathan's earlier work, which was first published at Venice in 1564, more than a hundred years after its compilation]; Fuerst, *Librorum Sacrorum Veteris Testamenti Concordantiæ Hebraicæ atque Chaldaicæ* (Leipzig, 1840); Davidson, *Concordance of the Hebrew and Chaldaic Scriptures* (Bagster: London, 1876); Mandelkern, *Veteris Testamenti Concordantiæ Hebraicæ atque Chaldaicæ* (Leipzig, 1896). A smaller edition of the last work, without quotations, was published at Leipzig in 1897.

* See *Expositor*, 5th series, vol. iii. (1896) p. 72.

ii. GREEK.—(1) *SEPTUAGINT.*—*Concordantiæ Veteris Testamenti Græcæ Hebræis vocibus respondentes* . . . auctore C. Kirchero (Frankfort, 1607); Trommius, *Concordantiæ Græcæ versionis . . . LXX Interpretum* (Amsterdam); *Handy Concordance of the Septuagint*, without quotations (Bagster, 1887). All these are now more or less superseded by Hatch and Redpath's *Concordance to the Septuagint, and other Greek Versions of the OT* (Clarendon Press, 1892-1897), with its two supplemental fasciculi, of which one, containing the proper names, is already published, and the second is on the eve of publication.

(2) *NEW TESTAMENT.*—*Novi Testamenti Concordantiæ Græcæ* . . . (Basle, 1546); Bruder, *Concordance* (2nd ed., Leipzig, 1853); Moulton and Geden, *Concordance to the Greek Testament*, according to the Texts of Westcott and Hort, Tischendorf and the English Revisers (Edinburgh, 1897).

iii. LATIN.—The Concordance of Hugo de Sancto Caro (1244; revised 1290); *Concordantie maiores biblie tam dictionū declinabiliū quam indeclinabilium* [by Sebastian Brant] (Basle, 1496); Dutripon, *Concordantiæ Bibliorum Sacrorum Vulgatæ Editionis* (Paris, 1838); Cooraert, *Concordantiæ librorum Veteris et Novi Testamenti . . . juxta Vulgatam Editionem* (Bruges, 1892).

iv. ENGLISH.—*A Concordance, that is to say, a work wherein by the order of the letters of the A. B. C. ye maie redely finde any word conteigned in the whole Bible* . . . [by J. Marbeck] [London] 1550; Cruden, *A Complete Concordance to the Holy Scriptures* (1st ed.), London, 1738. Upon this almost all later Concordances have been more or less based; T. Taylor, *A New Concordance to the Holy Scriptures* (1st ed., York, 1782); Eadie, *A New and Complete Concordance to the Holy Scriptures*, on the basis of Cruden's (1st ed., Glasgow, 1840); R. Young, *Analytical Concordance to the Bible . . . containing every word in alphabetical order, arranged under its Hebrew or Greek original* (Edinburgh, 1879 [-84]); Strong, *The Exhaustive Concordance of the Bible, together with a comparative Concordance of the AV and RV* (Hodder & Stoughton: London, 1894). In the *Comprehensive Concordance to the Holy Scriptures* (London, 1895) is to be found a 'Bibliography of Concordances,' by Dr. M. C. Hazard.

A *Concordance to the NT in English* was published by T. Gybson [London] in 1535. *A Complete Concordance to the Revised Version of the NT* . . . by J. A. Thoms, was issued by the S.P.C.K. (London) in 1884.

For a fuller account of Hebrew Concordances, see art. 'Concordance' in the *Jewish Encyclopedia*, to which the present writer is indebted for certain statements in this article. For further details concerning Greek Concordances, see *Expositor*, 5th series, vol. iii. (1896) p. 72; and for an account of Cruden and his labours, see the article 'Cruden' in the *Dictionary of National Biography*.

HENRY A. REDPATH.

**RELIGION OF BABYLONIA AND ASSYRIA.**—

At the outset of an account of the religion of Babylonia and Assyria one is impressed by the circumstance that, with the single exception of the religion of the ancient Hebrews, there is no one of the religions of antiquity known to us that enables us to trace more satisfactorily the growth of religious ideas among a people, from a crude polytheism based on nature worship and accompanied by primitive rites, to a striking approach towards a monotheistic conception of the Universe, with a highly complicated priestly organization, and an elaborated theological system. There is also no other ancient religion—not even that of Egypt—which may lay claim to having exercised so large a measure of influence over surrounding nations, shaping as it did the myths and legends of the Hebrews, Phœnicians, and Greeks alike, showing its traces also in the religion of Egypt, and contributing in various ways to the systems of religious thought produced in the ancient East and West. Hardly less remarkable is the antiquity of the religion of Babylonia and Assyria, which became an important factor in the religious history of mankind as early at least as the third millennium B.C., and practically finished its rôle before Hebrew monotheism asserted itself.

These considerations fully justify the efforts put forth by the past two generations of scholars and continued by the present generation in the task of recovering for science the long-lost and forgotten sources for the study of this religion. And while we are not yet in a position to follow in detail the history of the movement, in connexion with the general culture that took its rise in the Euphrates Valley and subsequently spread northwards to the district more properly known as Assyria, more than enough material is forthcoming to furnish the basis for a satisfactory account of the pantheon, of the doctrines and rites, and of the literary productions that are an outcome of the spirit pervading the religion itself. More than this, we can with measurable certainty distinguish between certain periods in the history of the religion, and can indicate political and intellectual factors that contributed to the gradual transformation of certain doctrines, while in a general way the literary process involved in the production of rituals, epics, myths, and legends can now be determined.

i. The Sources.—Until the middle of the 19th cent. our sources for the religion of Babylonia and Assyria were a few scattered notices in a number of classical and other authors, notably Herodotus, Eusebius, and Syncellus, and in the compilation of the Jewish Rabbis known as the Talmud, and some incidental though valuable allusions in the historical and prophetical portions of the Old Testament. Through the excavations so successfully conducted by French, English, American, and German explorers in the mounds scattered along the banks of the Tigris and in the Euphrates Valley,* since the year 1842, these notices and allusions have been relegated to the rank of secondary sources, and, instead, we have now, as primary sources, the unearthed temples and palaces of Babylonia and Assyria, with their statues, furnishings, and inscriptions, and, above all, the abundant literary archives found in the mounds. The royal library, more particularly, collected by king Assurbanipal (668–625 B.C.) in his palace at Nineveh and unearthed by Layard and Rassam (1849–1854),† contained thousands of tablets with contents of a directly religious character—incantations, omens, myths, legends, hymns, prayers, and entire rituals, while the affiliation existing in Babylonia and Assyria between religion on the one hand, and astronomy, medicine, and even law, on the other, also renders other portions of the library, which ranges over numerous branches of literary activity, valuable as sources for the study of the Babylono-Assyrian religion. The library at Nineveh, though dating—at least for the greater part—from the days of Assurbanipal, represents a considerably older literature; for, as the king frequently informs us in the subscriptions of the tablets, the collection was formed by having copies made through his scribes from originals that existed in Babylonian archives. This statement carries with it the important corollary that Assurbanipal's library represents the remains of a literature produced not in Assyria but in Babylonia; and, in confirmation of this, many tablets have been found in the course of excavations in mounds in Babylonia proper, which are either duplicates of those in the Nineveh collection, or supplement them. The character of the writing, apart from other evidence, on some of these Babylonian 'originals' would justify us in carrying the literary activity of the scribes of the south back to about two millenniums before the days of Assurbanipal, while the discovery‡ of extensive literary archives in connexion with the American excavations at Nippur, the tablets of which are all said to be earlier than the third millennium before our era, warrants an even earlier date for the beginnings of Babylonian literature.

* See the bibliographical references attached to articles Assyria and Babylonia in vol. i., to which must now be added (1) Rogers' *History of Babylonia and Assyria* (New York and London, 1900), which contains (vol. i. pp. 1–253) the best detailed account of the excavations; (2) Hilprecht's *Explorations in Bible Lands* (Phila. 1903), pp. 3–577, supplementing Rogers in some particulars, and containing a full though severely criticised account of the excavations at Nippur; and (3) the *Mittheilungen der Deutschen Orient. Gesellschaft* (1898 to date), furnishing regular reports of the German excavations in and around the city of Babylon, which are to be extended also to other mounds in Babylonia and Assyria.

† For an account of this library, see, *e.g.*, Kaulen, *Assyrien und Babylonien* (5th ed., Freiburg, 1899, ch. vii.); Menant, *La Bibliothèque du Palais de Ninive* (Paris, 1880); and, above all, Bezold's invaluable catalogue of the Cuneiform Tablets in the Kouyunjik Collection (London, 1889–99, 5 vols.).

‡ See Hilprecht's *Explorations in Bible Lands* (Philadelphia and Edinburgh, 1903), pp. 511–532.

Roughly speaking, all the more important literary productions in Assurbanipal's library were in existence before the year 2000 B.C., while many are no doubt considerably older.

In the south, where the religious literature grew up in connexion with the activity of the Babylonian temples, the latter formed the natural depositories for these collections, just as in the temples, as the courts of justice and as the centres of astronomical and medical science, the official legal archives and the extensive scientific collections were kept. It is characteristic of the general relationship of Assyria to Babylonian culture that the Assyrian monarch was not only obliged to import his literature from the south, but in doing so made the palace the depository for this foreign product instead of the temple. The zeal which animated him in sending his scribes to ransack the libraries of the south was neither literary nor religious, but due to a political and in part also to a personal ambition to emphasize, by a transfer thither of the culture of the south, the complete ascendency of Assyria as the dominant power, and as the legatee of the civilization that arose in Babylonia. Along with this civilization, the religion of the south was also carried to the north; and while, in so far as the pantheon is concerned, the Assyrians manifested a certain originality, and while the northern scribes also made contributions to the religious literature, in all but minor details the views and doctrines embodied in these productions are identical with those developed in the theological and religious centres of the south. Thus for all practical purposes the religion of Assyria may be regarded as identical with that of Babylonia. This identity extends to the cult, which naturally presented variations in each centre of both the south and the north, but which was everywhere based upon the same conceptions of the relationship between man and the higher Powers, and reflected the same general religious doctrines.

ii. Early History of Babylonia and Assyria.—As a preliminary to an understanding of the religion of Babylonia and Assyria, it is essential to have clearly before us the general course taken by the history of these two countries.

1. The striking feature in the earliest period to which we can trace it, is the frequent change in the position of the political centres. We see the Euphrates Valley at this time divided into a varying number of States or principalities, at rivalry with one another, now the one, now the other exercising a certain supremacy over the whole district, without, however, bringing it into real subjection; while, on the other hand, for indefinite periods several of these States occupy an equal position of importance and prominence side by side, and even enter into compacts with one another. The various States centre each around a city, and the growth of the State is essentially the extension of that city. The political importance thus given to the leading towns of ancient Babylonia is further enhanced by the religious significance which is in close union with their political advance; for the deity presiding over a place shares, in accordance with the general view prevailing in antiquity, the fortunes of his subjects. The god, the place of his worship, and his worshippers, are in inseparable contact.

This state of affairs can now be traced back, thanks chiefly to the results of the excavations at Telloh and Nippur, to about 3500 B.C., though it should be added that the chronology beyond 2500 B.C. is still quite uncertain. Hence we can only deal in round numbers for the earlier periods, and indeed, according to some scholars, we are not justified in passing much beyond 3000 B.C. for the date of the earliest inscriptions as yet found.* In this earliest period known to us we find Eridu, Shirpurla (or Sirgulla), Ur, Gishban, Nippur, Erech, Larsa, and Isin (or Nisin) among the cities of southern Babylonia occupying a prominent position. In the northern portion, again, lay Kish, Cuthah, Agade, Sippar, and, youngest of all, Babylon. From the testimony of the inscriptions no certain conclusions can be drawn as to the relative age of these centres, for naturally the oldest written document presupposes a long anterior political history as well as a history of civilization, during which period an important rôle may have been played by cities that had disappeared from the horizon before monumental evidence begins; while others that appear to occupy an inferior position may have enjoyed a high degree of supremacy at a time for which no material is as yet at our disposal. Thus we have every reason to believe that a town **Eridu**, which lay on the Persian Gulf, must at one time have had control over a considerable section of southern Babylonia, since the cult of the patron deity of that place—the god Ea—survives all the vicissitudes of political fortunes. Down to the latest period of the Babylonian religion, Ea retains in the pantheon a place that is unique and almost inexplicable, except on the supposition that the political importance of the place gave the god his impregnable position. Similarly, while there are other cities in the oldest period that appear to be politically more powerful than **Nippur**, the chief god of the latter yields to none in the honours accorded to him. He is not only invoked by the rulers of other centres, but becomes known as Bel, 'the lord' *par excellence*; and, long after Nippur has passed into the background of Babylonian history, the old Bel retains his place as the second member in a triad that summed up for Babylonian theologians the quintessence of Divine control of the Universe in the largest sense. Unless totally different conditions prevailed in the period which is still beyond our ken, from those which characterize the relationship between political position and religious supremacy during the entire period for which we now have direct sources at our command, a political predominance of Nippur must likewise have preceded the fame and rank acquired by its patron deity.

The precise order of supremacy exercised by the various political centres has not yet been determined with that degree of certainty which would enable one to speak with perfect definiteness. It is still a matter of doubt whether the seat of the oldest Babylonian ruler at present known to us, En-shag-kush-anna, was Erech or Shirpurla, though the probabilities are in favour of the latter. The few brief inscriptions that we have from him were found at Nippur, and give expression to the king's homage to En-lil or Bel, while his title 'lord of Kengi' points to control over a large district—perhaps the whole of southern Babylonia. The most serious rival to En-shag-kush-anna was the ruler of **Kish** in northern Babylonia, and it would appear that not long after the days of En-shag-kush-anna Shirpurla enters upon a period of dependency upon Kish; its rulers no longer call themselves kings, but *patesis*, *i.e.* 'governors.' With some interruptions, during which the former conditions are for a time restored, this state of things continues until Kish is obliged to yield its supremacy in turn to other places, first to a centre **Gishban**, situated not far from Shirpurla—one of whose rulers, Lugalzaggisi, calls himself 'king of the world,' and claims sovereignty from the Persian Gulf to the Mediter-

* See Winckler in Helmolt's *History of the World* (1903), vol. iii. pp. 8–10.

ranean. The glory of Gishban, however, appears to have been of short duration, and we next hear of the kings of **Agade,** to the north of Kish, extending their rule far into the south, and including in their domain both Nippur and Shirpurla in the south. The most famous of these rulers of Agade were Sargon and his son Naram-Sin, the fame of whose exploits, involving military expeditions to the distant West, survived to a late period, and, becoming enveloped in myth, gave to Sargon more particularly a semi-legendary character.

Of the oldest history of **Erech** we as yet know little. The names of a few of her rulers whose date falls about or before 3000 B.C. are known, and some of their exploits, which show that this centre succeeded in maintaining its independence, without, however, attaining, within the period for which material is available, to a position of supremacy, except possibly for a short time. On the other hand, the prominence belonging to the chief goddess of the place, Nanâ, who retains an independent position down to the latest Assyrian period (despite the general tendency in both Babylonia and Assyria to consolidate the various goddesses worshipped at different centres in one great goddess, who becomes known as Ishtar), is again an important testimony to the part that Erech as a centre must have played in the political life of southern Babylonia at an early period—perhaps earlier even, as in the case of Eridu and Nippur, than the date of our oldest sources.

Much more satisfactory is our knowledge of another important centre of southern Babylonia, **Ur,** whose existence can also be traced back to about 3000 B.C. Its kings about this time secured control over Shirpurla. While the kingdom of Ur, with a frequent change of dynasties, maintains itself down to *c.* 2600 B.C., it was obliged at times to yield in rank to other cities—at one period to **Isin,** probably to the north of Erech—some of whose rulers (*c.* 2700–2500 B.C.) claim control over Ur, Nippur, Eridu, and Erech, and later to a centre, **Larsa,** which, for a short time at least (*c.* 2300 B.C.), succeeds in bringing the kingdom of Ur under its immediate control.

2. A new era of Babylonian history opens with the rise of a dynasty in the city of **Babylon** itself, of which until *c.* 2300 B.C. we hear nothing at all. Its position in the north is significant as pointing to the gradual shifting of the real centre of the entire Euphrates district in this direction. The sixth member of this dynasty, **Ḫammurabi** (*c.* 2250 B.C.), succeeded in accomplishing the great task of uniting northern and southern Babylonia under one sovereignty, and it is only from his time onwards that we can properly speak of a Babylonian empire. True, efforts were made from time to time by the southern districts—comprised under the term *Chaldæa*—to secure their independence, and the New Babylonian empire, which represents the last, and in some respects the greatest, effort of the Euphrates Valley to rise to a position as a world-empire, was founded by Chaldæans; but, amidst all the vicissitudes of the seventeen centuries following Ḫammurabi, Babylon maintains its position as the capital of the country, while the old centres, Eridu, Nippur, Ur, Erech, Larsa, Sippar, retain their importance as religious centres merely, or, as in the case of Shirpurla, Kish, Gishban, Agade, and Isin, disappear from the foreground of history entirely. We are able to distinguish a large number of dynasties ruling with Babylon as a centre from *c.* 2400 to 539 B.C. Not all of these, however, are of Babylonian origin. Indeed, the very first dynasty to which the position of Babylon as the permanent centre of the Euphrates Valley is due, represents a foreign invasion of the country from the interior or the western coast of Arabia, and marks the triumph of a migratory movement from this direction that had probably been going on for some time before the *dénouement* is reached under Ḫammurabi, *c.* 2250 B.C. The successors of Ḫammurabi maintain their supremacy till *c.* 2100 B.C., when they are forced to yield to invaders who appear to have come likewise from the south.

3. About 400 years later, foreigners from the east, who call themselves Kassites, obtain possession of the Babylonian throne, and maintain their supremacy for a period of 576 years (*c.* 1730 to *c.* 1150 B.C.); and, although the Kassite rulers manifest particular devotion to Nippur and its deity, Babylon still remains the political centre and the seat of government. At last the Kassites are driven out, and native Babylonians, hailing, as it would seem, from the ancient centre of Isin, mount the throne.

4. From this time onwards internal disturbances and the pressure from the north (where meanwhile a powerful kingdom had established itself, with its centre alternately at Ashur, Calah, and finally Nineveh) are the two factors that determine the changes that the south undergoes in its rulers. About the middle of the 13th cent. the relationship with Assyria,—as this northern kingdom was called,—which had at first been on the whole of a peaceable character, became hostile, and it was soon apparent that the more vigorous northern kingdom seriously threatened the older culture of the south. The steady advance of the Assyrian power, despite periods of retrogression, goes *pari passu* with the decline of Babylonia, until at the close of the 12th cent. an Assyrian ruler, Tiglath-pileser I., reduces Babylonia for a time to the rank of an Assyrian vassal, though it is significant that southern Babylonia or Chaldæa does not come under Assyrian sway. On the contrary, this latter district—divided once more into a number of States, loosely united to one another—maintains a large measure of independence, and at most is forced to pay tribute to Assyria during certain periods. On the whole, however, the political star of the south sinks behind the horizon, and only as the glory of Assyria herself is eclipsed by temporary discomfitures to her military ambitions or by internal dissensions, does Babylonia regain a portion of her former rank. If, despite this general condition of dependence upon the north, Babylonia at least enjoyed the privilege of having native rulers on the throne—with some exceptional periods, when it became a prey to invaders from the south or east, or when the Assyrian kings forced their choice (some favourite general, or their sons or brothers) upon the Babylonians, or in some cases themselves assumed the reins of government,—this was due, in the first instance, to the intellectual and commercial superiority of the south, which could not be set aside by mere force of arms; and, secondly, to the respect inspired by the religious sanctuaries of the south, to which the Assyrians were as fervently attached as the Babylonians, if for no other reason than because of the disasters that they dreaded in case of any offence offered to the great gods of the south,—whose position had in the course of millenniums become independent of the political kaleidoscope.

5. The union of the Babylonian States had definitely secured for the patron deity of the city of Babylon—the god **Marduk**—his position as the head of the pantheon; and, though attempts were made at times to set Marduk aside in favour of some other god,—Nebo, the god of Borsippa (opposite Babylon), or the old Bel of Nippur, or Shamash, the sun-god of Sippar,—they did not succeed in doing more than temporarily eclipsing the glory of Marduk, who on the whole maintained his position down to the fall of the New Babylonian empire. It is signifi-

cant that, when Cyrus entered Babylon in triumph in the autumn of B.C. 539, the first act of the conqueror was to pay his devotion to Marduk, as whose deputy he claims to act. This commanding position of Marduk in the pantheon is the most notable feature, from the religious point of view, of the period following upon Ḫammurabi. It opens a new era in the religious history of Babylonia, and forms a convenient dividing line between the oldest and the second period in this history. That it was brought about through a political act, is an illustration of the close relationship in Babylonia and Assyria between political and religious conditions, upon which we have dwelt. With Marduk as the head of the pantheon, it was necessary to regulate the position of the other gods of the great religious centres towards him. The older attempts of the theologians to systematize the pantheon had to be re-shaped in accordance with the state of affairs created by the acknowledgment of Babylon as the centre of government for the entire Euphrates Valley. The old myths and legends, which even before Ḫammurabi's days had been reduced to writing, were re-shaped so as to accord to Marduk the glory and rank due to him. Older gods, of whom stories were related, had to make way for Marduk, and this was done even at the risk of interfering with the original meaning of the myths.

The subsequent degradation of Babylonia to a position of greater or lesser dependence upon Assyria did not affect the position of Marduk, or the theological system based upon it. The kings of Assyria, when they came to Babylon, paid their homage to Marduk; they made no effort to put their chief deity—Ashur—in Marduk's place, and at most ventured to place the former by the side of the latter in their invocations; and, when the New Babylonian empire was founded by Chaldæans, the rulers, though the two most important representatives of them bore names compounded with the god Nebo (Nabopolassar, Nebuchadreẓẓar), vied with their predecessors in manifestations of devotion to the great Marduk. The new city of Babylon reared by them was essentially Marduk's metropolis.

6. Turning to the north, we encounter the same close bearing of the political development upon the cult. The rulers of Assyria, the earliest of whom known to us may be placed *c.* 1800 B.C., set out as *patesis* or 'governors' of the city of Ashur, situated on the Tigris; and it is the god of this place—likewise known as **Ashur**—who advances in rank with the progress of Assyrian arms. But, while Marduk remains attached to the place where his cult originated, Ashur follows the shifting of the capital of Assyria; and, whether the seat of government is at Calah or at Nineveh, it is Ashur who continues in the new capital his abode, as well as his guidance of the kings and of their armies. Parallel, therefore, to the supremacy of Marduk in the south, we have Ashur standing at the head of the pantheon in the north, from the earliest period to which Assyrian history can be traced back * down to the fall of Nineveh in 606 B.C.; and just as in the south the position of the other gods is regulated with reference to Marduk, so in the north the priests of Ashur engage in a work of systematization which results in establishing a court of deities grouped around Ashur as their king and leader.

iii. RELATION OF THE CULTURE AND RELIGION OF ASSYRIA TO THOSE OF BABYLONIA.—It will have become clear from the above sketch, that, corresponding to the greater age of Babylonia as compared with Assyria, it was in the south that culture was first developed, and from the south was carried to the north. As a matter of fact, despite some contributions to architecture, art, science, and literature made by the Assyrians, the civilization of Assyria is a direct importation from Babylonia, and continues to bear the impress of its southern origin. The temples and palaces of Assyria were modelled upon those in Babylonia, with the important exception, however, that stone was far more liberally employed as a building material in place of clay—which remained the standard material in the south. In sculptural decorations and in statues, more originality was displayed by the Assyrians than in their building constructions, and, as a great military power, it was natural that Assyria should likewise have developed her own methods of attack and defence; but, in all that pertains to the cult and to general religious doctrines, the originality of the Assyrians manifests itself only in the adaptation to their own conditions, of the modes of worship, of the ritual, and of the theology that were the outcome of the activity of a long series of generations of priests serving in the temples of the great religious centres of the south. When Assurbanipal, probably in imitation of an earlier example, resolved to collect a library in his palace, he was obliged to send his scribes to the temples of the south, in the archives of which the literary productions of the past—epics, myths, legends, collections of omens, rituals and magical incantations, hymns and prayers, as well as medical and astronomical compilations — were kept; and it does not appear that either his scribes or those of earlier days added much to this literary legacy, though, naturally, the Assyrian temples had their own rituals, prayers, and oracles specially adapted to Assyrian political and social conditions.

The relationship between the religion of Babylonia and that of Assyria thus resolves itself into an adoption of doctrines, cult, and rites of the south by the north, with such modifications as were called for by the different conditions prevailing in the north, and which led, in the case of the pantheon, to the assignment to Ashur of the place and rank occupied in the south by Marduk after the union of the States of the Euphrates Valley in the days of Ḫammurabi. We might also express this relationship in terms of a general extension northward of the religion of Babylonia, as a part of the culture that originated in the Euphrates Valley.

iv. ORIGIN OF BABYLONIAN CULTURE.—A question that suggests itself at this point, and which must be considered before we advance to a consideration of some of the details of the religion of Babylonia and Assyria, involves the problem as to the origin of Babylonian culture. At the earliest period to which we can now trace back Babylonian history we already find this culture in an advanced state, and it is safe to assume that its beginnings must be placed as early at least as 4000 B.C.—and it may turn out to be even considerably older. Scholarship is still divided on the question whether the culture is of Semitic or non-Semitic origin. The majority of scholars hold that the earliest settlers in the Valley were non-Semites, to whom the beginnings of the culture, including the invention and development of the earliest script—an essentially hieroglyphic system—are to be attributed. To this people the name **Sumerian** (or Sumero-Akkadian) is given, and it is held that the Semites—the Babylonians in the later sense—upon entering the land from the south, adopted this culture, developed it still further, and adapted the script to the expression of ideas in their own Semitic

* The existence of a city and district, *A-usar*, identical with Ashur, which represents a later designation of the god as well as of the city and of the district, can now be traced back to the days of Ḫammurabi. See Scheil, 'Code de Hammourabi,' col. iv. 55-64 (*Délégation en Perse, Mémoires*, iv. [*Textes Élamites-Sémitiques*, ii.]).

tongue. This view, however, is opposed by a small but powerful minority, led by the distinguished Prof. Joseph Halévy of Paris, which contends for the Semitic origin of the entire Babylonian culture, including, therefore, the script. The controversy which has raged for many years cannot be regarded as definitely settled,* nor is it likely to be until ethnology is in a position to reinforce or to controvert the arguments drawn by either side from the evidence of language and archæology. Meanwhile, it may be said that while, on the one hand, it seems tolerably certain that the Euphrates Valley, admirably adapted as a meeting-ground for races of various origin, actually contained in early times a population of a mixed character; on the other hand, it is no less clear that the traits of the culture, including the religion, are essentially the same in the latest days as in the earliest of which we have cognizance. The gods in the earliest texts are the same as those found in the latest; nor do the methods of invoking them, or the conceptions formed of them, undergo any other changes than those due to natural development. Nowhere is there a *violent* break with the past, but only, and at the most, a gradual transition. If, therefore, the later culture is to be regarded as Semitic,—and on this point there is general agreement,—there is no substantial reason for denying this predicate to the earliest. Such a consideration naturally does not solve the question of origins, for it may properly be argued that the non-Semitic stratum was so thoroughly absorbed by the Semites at the period to which our material for the study of Babylonia belongs, as to obscure the original features. With this admission, those who occupy an intermediate position between the opposing camps are for the present content, since it justifies the contention that the Babylonian culture, so far as known to us, is of one cast, and that therefore, in a treatment of the Religion of Babylonia and Assyria it is neither necessary nor justifiable to separate Semitic from supposedly non-Semitic features. If, therefore, there is a non-Semitic stratum to the culture which we encounter in the earliest period of Babylonian history, it belongs to a period which is, for the present at least, beyond our historical ken, and as little affects our views as to the general Semitic character of the Babylono-Assyrian religion in its earliest and latest manifestations, as the probably non-Grecian elements existing in Greek culture affect the essential unity of what we have been taught to regard as Greek religion.

Moreover, the possibility of a non-Semitic stratum to Babylonian culture must not be confused with the question as to the existence of traces of a Sumerian language in the Babylonian script and literature. Granting the existence of such a language as Sumerian, the position to which the advocates of the Sumerian theory are led in order to account for the continued use of the 'Sumerian' method of writing thousands of years after a far more suitable one had been evolved by the Semitic or Semitized Babylonians, justifies an attitude of reserve towards the far-reaching conclusions that have been drawn from the supposed non-Semitic origin of the script employed by the Babylonians; and the fact that these conclusions are brought forward in a spirit of consistency, derived by logical processes from a certain starting-point, only accentuates the difficulty of accepting the correctness of that starting-point. Besides, the advocates of the Sumerian theory have not yet fulfilled the obligation which obviously rests upon them of defining the character of the Sumerian language in a manner acceptable to philologists, and of indicating its position in the group of languages to which it belongs.*

Under these circumstances, the attitude of reserve is still further justified on the part of those who are content to wait for 'more light' before committing themselves to a position which involves such far-reaching consequences as the acceptance of the Sumerian theory in its *present* form carries with it. Without, therefore, encroaching upon doubtful territory, we are entitled in the treatment of our theme to assume a continued development of a religion which is to be regarded in its earliest form as Semitic, provided it be admitted that in its latest form it may be given this title.

The sketch furnished at the outset of this article as to the general development of the Babylono-Assyrian religion, so far as the relationship between religion and the political history of the two countries is concerned, suggests a threefold division in the History of the Religion: the first extending from the earliest period known to us (*c.* 3500 B.C.) to the union of the Babylonian States under Ḫammurabi (*c.* 2250 B.C.); the second embracing the period down to the rise of the New Babylonian or Chaldæan empire under Nabopolassar (625 B.C.); the third covering the short existence of this empire down to the taking of Babylon by Cyrus in 539 B.C. The Assyrian religion, in so far as it entails a separate treatment, falls within the second period, although it extends into the third—from *c.* 1800 B.C. down to the fall of Nineveh, 606 B.C. A sharp separation is marked only between the first and second divisions, though the third division likewise shows traits of a special character.—The further division of the general subject into (*a*) the Pantheon, (*b*) the Religious Literature, and (*c*) the Cultus, results from the character of the material at our disposal for the study of the Babylono-Assyrian religion, which consists chiefly, as already intimated, of (1) the numerous historical and votive inscriptions of the rulers; (2) the extensive literary productions of Babylonia (as preserved chiefly in the copies of the royal library unearthed at Nineveh†); and (3) in the archæological results—still rather meagre—of the excavations of Babylonian and Assyrian sanctuaries.

v. THE BABYLONO-ASSYRIAN PANTHEON.—The religion of Babylonia in the earliest form known to us may be defined as a combination of local cults with animistic conceptions of the powers of nature, with which man was either brought into immediate contact, or which affected his aims and his welfare. Each centre had its special patron deity, and this deity—in most cases conceived as masculine—was brought into association with some natural phenomenon. The two powers most commonly chosen were the sun and the moon, and by the side of these we find streams and stones per-

* It will be sufficient to refer for details of this controversy to Weissbach's monograph, *Die Sumerische Frage* (Leipzig, 1898), admirable as a summary, but which leaves the question pretty much where it was.

* The view formerly held, that the Sumerian belongs to the Ural-Altaic group, has been emphatically set aside by Prof. O. Donner—an eminent authority on this group—in an appendix to Haupt's monograph, *Die Akkadische Sprache* (Berlin, 1881). It should also be stated that, since the appearance of Haupt's monograph, little has been done towards elucidating the character of the so-called Sumerian (or Sumero-Akkadian) speech. See Winckler's remarkable confession: 'All attempts to establish an affinity with any language of the ancient world, even with the various languages of the neighbouring nations or of those still living, must be abandoned' (in Helmolt's *History of the World* (1903), vol. iii. p. 5).

† The recent discovery by J. H. Haynes of an extensive literary archive at Nippur, justifies the hope that at no distant day we may be able to study the religious literature to a large extent from 'originals' instead of from the copies prepared by the scribes of Assurbanipal. See Hilprecht's account of the Nippur library in *Explorations in Bible Lands in the Nineteenth Century*, pp. 509–532.

sonified as gods. The independence of the States and, in still earlier days, no doubt, of the towns of the Euphrates Valley, is sufficient to account for the fact that there should thus arise a considerable number of sun- and moon-deities, and it was only as a result of political development that in time a sun-god worshipped in the most important centre came to be the sun-god *par excellence*, and, in the theological system, was regarded as having absorbed the attributes and prerogatives of his former associates or rivals. This process of concentration was not necessarily carried out with consistency; and when, as happened, two centres acquired equal significance and sanctity, the worship of the sun-god or of the moon-god was maintained in both, or a compromise was effected by distinguishing between the varying action of the sun at the different seasons of the year or in the division of the day, so that, in the developed theological system, we have one sun-deity particularly singled out as the sun of spring or of morning, and another as the midsummer or noonday sun. The former, as the conqueror of the winter storms, would be pictured as a beneficent element, a youthful hero displaying his strength; the latter, as bringing discomfort, drought, and disease, would be invested with violence and destructive force—a grim warrior in the thick of battle.

Such a division of functions, effected as a compromise between rival sun-deities, was the work of the priests and theologians rather than a popular process, and the example adduced will suffice for the present to illustrate the importance of what may be called the theoretical factor in the development of the Babylonian religion. One of the main problems involved in considering the functions and traits of any particular deity is thus to distinguish between original elements and such as have been imposed upon him (or her) by the attempts at systematization that begin at an early period, and that lead to the rise of various schools of theological thought, of which traces are revealed in a careful study of the religious literature. At times, naturally, it is not an easy task to differentiate the popular conceptions connected with a deity from those unfolded in the schools. So, when two gods are viewed as father and son—like Ea and Marduk—or as father and daughter—like Sin (the moon-god) and Ishtar—or as master and servant—like Shamash (the sun-god) and Ishum, or Marduk and Nusku (the fire-god)—the process involved is not the same in all. Such relationships, likewise, are expressive of compromises effected between rival deities; but in some instances, as in the case of Ea and Marduk, popular thought is involved in specifying the relationship between the two as that of father and son. In general, however, the traces of relationship between various gods indicate the absorption in some way or another by one god of the attributes of his former rivals, and may be regarded as the work of the schools in their endeavour to weave the manifold threads of the pantheon into a single pattern. While, therefore, in the development of the pantheon there may be noted a general tendency to reduce the number of deities by the recognition of those only who had acquired a relatively superior position, and which had its outcome in the Assyrian pantheon in fixing the number of really active deities at about eleven, the numerous local deities, ranging to hundreds, do not entirely disappear. They survive in invocations and incantations, the efficacy of which is supposed to be increased by the *number* of deities invoked: and also in proper names—particularly in Babylonia—where conservative influences, emanating from the popular phases of the religion, have freer play.

Turning by way of illustration to the historical and votive inscriptions of the oldest period, one cannot help being impressed by the circumstance that, while the number of deities that may be regarded as belonging to the really active pantheon is not extraordinarily large—between twenty and thirty,—if we add to these the deities paraded by rulers on occasions when they wish to emphasize the extent of their sway, or when they desire to assure themselves of the protection and favour of as large a number of Divine forces as possible, the number is more than doubled. If, again, we take into account deities entering as elements into proper names occurring in inscriptions belonging to this period, the list reaches close to one hundred. So in a text dating from the days of Manishtusu, a king of Kish, who appears to be as early as any ruler of southern Babylonia as yet known to us,* we encounter about fifty names of deities which enter as elements into the four hundred and more names of individuals enumerated. Comparing this list with the deities introduced into the historical and votive inscriptions, it will be found that, while the five or six most prominent gods of the period are represented,—notably Sin, Ea, Ishtar, En-lil, or Bel,—by far the larger majority are such as are not found in these inscriptions at all. This may be due in part to the still limited historical material that we possess for this earliest period; and it is also true that a number of the gods in this text of Manishtusu, which was found at Susa, are foreign deities—notably such as were worshipped in Elam. But, making due allowance for the possible increase of the active Babylonian pantheon of the oldest period by further discoveries, it is still safe to assume that most of the gods that appear as elements of proper names in the text in question belong to a different category, and will not, with some possible exceptions, be encountered in historical inscriptions proper. It seems certain that the deities whom we thus encounter in proper names are the old local gods, who naturally survive in the designations of individuals hailing from places where their cult was carried on; and it is equally natural that the rulers in their inscriptions should ignore all these local deities, except such as had acquired a superior rank, rendering them worthy to be invoked by a powerful chief.

If we now turn to the incantation texts, of which several series are known, we encounter the same preponderance in the number of deities invoked, over those that play a part in the active pantheon, as revealed by the historical inscriptions of any period. To be sure, our copies of these incantation series are very late; but it is quite safe to assume, as already pointed out, that the originals belong to the second millennium before our era, if not to the third; and the circumstance that many of the deities enumerated are to be found in proper names of the *earliest* period, is an evidence of the antiquity of the substantial elements of the texts themselves. In the 'Shurpu' series, as published by Prof. Zimmern, about 150 deities are introduced, as compared with 20 or 30 in historical texts of the first period; and not only are a number of these identical with those occurring in proper names of Manishtusu's obelisk, but, what is more, even the foreign gods in this text have also found their place in the incantations. These incantation rituals continue in use during the Assyrian period, when 11 great gods constitute practically the entire pantheon, and this makes the contrast to the conditions revealed by these rituals all the more striking. The explanation is again to be sought in the distinction between purely local cults and

* See the evidence on the basis of which Scheil (*Textes Élamites-Sémitiques*, i. p. 2) places this ruler before 4500 B.C.—a date which scholars like Winckler would now reduce by about one thousand years.

the gods who, in consequence of political and other factors, rise to a superior position. The conservatism attaching to religious texts, added to the natural desire in the case of incantations to appeal to as large a number of gods as possible, in the hope that one or the other will grant the desired help or relief, leads to the retention of the old local deities; and this is done without reference to the selective process that has led to singling out a small number only of these deities as powers of first-rate importance.

In proper names, accordingly, and in incantation rituals, there are revealed to us some of the popular phases of the Babylono-Assyrian religion, and, as elsewhere, these phases stand in a certain contrast to the attempts at systematization of the pantheon which are naturally the work of the priests and of the theologians. We are thus prepared, in the historical and votive inscriptions of the earliest period and of the succeeding ones, to distinguish, on the one hand, deities of merely local significance, and those added from the desire to parade a long list of protecting powers; and, on the other hand, the really active pantheon, produced by a process of selection due in part to the natural prominence acquired by certain gods and by certain sanctuaries over others, and in part due to the attempts at systematization of the pantheon, begun by the priests in their capacity as theologians at an early period, and continued as political and social circumstances demanded.

In time this systematization reacts on the popular beliefs, and modifies them considerably; but, for all that, the popular religion always lags more or less behind the 'official' form as revealed in the scientific literature, such as the astronomical and astrological texts, and in the official inscriptions of the rulers, which were naturally produced under the prevailing theological influences. It would be idle to discuss to which of these two phases of the religion the preference is to be given. Both must be studied if we would penetrate to the core of the religion, and in the case of the pantheon it is obvious that due consideration of its systematization by the priests must be our guide in an endeavour to obtain a clear view of its extent and of its general character.

(A) *THE CHIEF DEITIES.*—1. **Anu, Bel, and Ea.**—Perhaps the most striking feature of the theological system devised by the priests is the doctrine which places at the head of the pantheon a triad consisting of the god of heaven, the god of earth and of the atmosphere above the earth, and a god of the watery element. These three gods, corresponding to the three divisions of the Universe, thus cover the sum and substance of Divine government; and it is hardly necessary to advance further arguments for the view that such a triad does not represent a popular belief, but is the outcome of theological speculation. Of the three gods,—Anu representing heaven, Bel the earth, and Ea the water,—Bel and Ea we know were originally deities of a local character, whose worship was centred in a well-defined locality. Bel, written ideographically *En-lil*, was the chief god of Nippur in northern Babylonia, and the prominence at one time of Nippur is illustrated by the title *Bel, i.e.* 'lord,' which became the common designation of En-lil. Ea belongs to the extreme south of Babylonia, whose worship was originally centred in Eridu, an exceedingly old settlement that at one time lay at the mouth of the Persian Gulf. The name 'En-lil' merely describes the god as a powerful demon; but from other sources we know that he was conceived also as an atmospheric deity, who manifested himself in storms and other violent disturbances of nature. Ea, on the other hand, was a water spirit; and one can readily understand how the character of the large body of water—the Persian Gulf, which was sacred to him, and which led directly to the shoreless ocean—should have led to making Ea the symbol of the watery element in general. As for Anu, while we find even as late as the 12th cent. B.C. that his cult was specifically associated with a definite centre,* the process which resulted in making him the personification of heaven in general, appears to have been a purely scholastic one, and independent of any traits that may originally have been ascribed to him. His worship in the south was never carried on at any of the large political or religious centres, and, whatever local associations he may have had, disappeared as early at least as the 4th millennium before our era, when we already find Anu generally written without the usual sign before deities, and designated simply as the 'heavenly' or 'exalted' one.† One is inclined, in view of this great antiquity of the symbolization of Anu, to regard the name, together with the conceptions associated with it, as due to scholastic speculation, and to suppose that the association of a god Anu with any particular locality is of later origin, due to the reaction of theoretical speculation in practical forms of belief.

However this may be, the parcelling out of Divine manifestations among a triad representing heaven, earth, and water, belongs distinctly to a theological system—is part and parcel of a *Weltanschauung* which could have arisen only in the schools, and which from the schools may have made its way to the people. The important feature of the triad is the symbolization underlying it: the choice of Bel and Ea to symbolize earth and water is secondary, as is the choice of Anu to symbolize heaven, whatever the origin of the name may have been. The Bel of the triad has in reality nothing but the name in common with the chief god of Nippur, and, similarly, when Ea of the triad was invoked there could have been only a remote association in the minds of the Babylonians with the water deity of Eridu. Still, such is the force of old conceptions that even the theologians could not entirely keep the double character thus resulting for Bel and Ea apart, and, accordingly, in the earliest occurrence of the triad dating from the days of Gudea‡ (*c.* 3000 B.C.) we have Nin-kharsag, the consort of Bel or En-lil, inserted between the latter and Ea. *Nin-kharsag*§ is a title of Belit as the wife of the chief god of Nippur, and the insertion of the name in connexion with the triad shows that the Babylonian scribes could not free themselves from the association of Bel with his original home at Nippur. In later periods this is rarely done, and it is interesting to compare the arrangement of the triad in Gudea's inscription with the one on a boundary stone from the 11th cent., where the goddess corresponding to the old Nin-kharsag, Belit, appears as *Ninmakh*, 'the great lady'—dissociated from the Belit of Nippur—and assigned a place behind Ea. Between these two dates we have the inscription of Agumkakrime (*c.* 1650 B.C.), in which we find at the beginning the usual order Anu, Bel, Ea, whereas towards the close there is associated with each one of the three a consort, thus furnishing the series Anu and Antum, Bel and Belit, Ea and Damkina. Of these consorts, Belit and Damkina represent the wives of the Bel of Nippur and Ea

* Dêr—in southern Babylonia, Rawl. v. 55, col. i. 14.

† *An*='heaven' + the phonetic complement *na*. This is the usual form; but various others occur, *e.g. An* with the determinative for 'god,' and the phonetic writings *An-nu-um* with and without the determinative for 'god.' See Radau, *Creation Story of Genesis*, 17, note 2.

‡ Inscription B, col. viii. 45-48.

§ Signifying 'lady of the mountain.'

of Eridu respectively, whereas Antum is an artificial figure introduced into the pantheon under the influence of the doctrine which assigned to every male god a female companion. One must therefore pass down to a comparatively late period, before, in the invocation of the triad, all traces of the old association of Bel and Ea with local cults disappear, and in a certain sense the process was never entirely and consistently completed.

The assigning of the local deity of Nippur to a position in the triad served to maintain his cult long after Nippur had lost its political supremacy. His temple at Nippur, known as *E-kur*, 'the mountain house,' became a place of pilgrimage to which worshippers came from all sides. In a measure this was the case with the sanctuaries in all or in most of the places that once formed political centres, but there were certain features connected with the Bel cult of Nippur that lent to it an air of uniqueness. Invoked in one of the earliest inscriptions known to us, that of En-shag-kush-annu* (*c.* 3500 B.C.), En-lil, at this time already designated as 'king of the lands,' maintains his position as the head of the pantheon even in the case of a ruler like Lugalzaggisi, king of Erech (*c.* 3500 B.C.), whose capital is not at Nippur.† We do not encounter the triad at this early period, and it is all the more significant therefore to find the god of Nippur occupying a position which is not affected by the political status of the centre in which he was worshipped. Such a condition is an important step on the road towards the differentiation between the local storm-god and his symbolization as one of the three elements of the universe.† Even in those inscriptions of the first period of Babylonian history in which En-lil does not occupy the first place, as for example in the list found in an inscription of E-anna-tum,‡ and in one of Gudea,§ his supremacy is still implied, for the preference given in these inscriptions to a god Nin-girsu, who is mentioned before En-lil, is simply due to the fact that the inscriptions in question are dedicated to Nin-girsu as the chief deity of the centre to which the rulers in question belong. Similarly, the rulers of other centres, like Agade, Ur, and Kish, present offerings and pay devotion to the Bel of Nippur; and it is not until the union of the Euphrates States under a dynasty which established its capital in the city of Babylon (*c.* 2300 B.C.) that we encounter an attempt to dethrone En-lil from his pre-eminent position, in favour of the chief deity of the city of Babylon, Marduk. The political union naturally brought in its wake the assignment of Marduk to a position at the head of the pantheon, and this was emphasized by transferring to Marduk the title *Bel* or 'lord,' and the old legends and traditions were likewise transformed under the influence of the priests of Babylon with a view of securing for the 'Bel' of Babylon the functions and deeds that properly belong to the 'Bel' of Nippur. The attempt, however, was not altogether successful, and, when in the 18th cent. B.C. the control of Babylonia passed into the hands of a people coming from Elam to the east, and known as the Kassites, the cult of Bel of Nippur enjoyed a renaissance.‖

There are good reasons for believing that the Kassites made a deliberate effort to reinstate En-lil as the head of the pantheon. For five centuries the Kassites held sway; and, though at the end of this period the reaction begins, in the list of gods found in inscriptions of this period Marduk receives his place immediately behind the triad,* though not invariably so.†

The rise of a serious rival to Babylonia in the north, where shortly after the end of Kassite rule in the south the Assyrians acquired sufficient strength to threaten the independence of Babylonia, again leads to a shifting in the ranks of the gods. In the presence of a common foe, the union between the States in the south becomes closer, and this condition finds expression in a more loyal attachment to the patron deity of Babylon — Marduk, — who in virtue of this fact henceforward holds undisturbed sway as the head of the pantheon. No more attempts are made to shake his position by playing off other gods against him. His supremacy becomes so secure that it is not endangered by the devotion shown by the rulers of Babylonia to the cults of other gods, either in Babylon itself or in any one of the religious centres of the south. The temple of Bel of Nippur continued to be a goal of pilgrimage down to the latest days of the Babylonian empire, and the series of sacred edifices there were an object of care to Assyrian kings as well as to Babylonian rulers; but the reverence paid to Bel was merely that due to the local deity, who had, in consequence of the earlier phases of the development of the Babylonian religion, acquired a greater prominence than the other gods. At the same time, the position of Bel in the triad served as a factor in maintaining this reverence, and formed in a measure the justification for it, in the minds of those who had separated their conception of Bel almost entirely from his originally local limitations.

We know as yet too little of the earliest history of Eridu—the original seat of the Ea cult—to determine the course of development that led to Ea's being singled out from among other water gods that were worshipped in early days, to become the general symbol of the watery element in the distribution of the Universe among three chief deities or power. Analogy might suggest that Eridu,‡ at the time that it still lay directly at the head of the Persian Gulf, was once an important political centre like Nippur, and that its patron deity rose into prominence in connexion with the political fortunes of the place. There is, however, no evidence to justify the claim that Eridu ever occupied such a position; and, since our knowledge of the early history of Babylonia now goes back to a remote period, we ought at least to have encountered some traces of a once dominating State in the Euphrates Valley with Eridu as a centre. Such notices as we have in the old Babylonian inscriptions almost all point to the *religious*§ but not to the political significance of the place, and illustrate the devotion of the rulers to En-ki or Ea, who is called the king of Eridu.‖ In the religious literature, likewise, Eridu appears chiefly as a religious centre, though, culture and religious prominence proceeding hand in hand in ancient Babylonia, Eridu was no doubt one of the *oldest* of the cities of the south. To a late day the

* Hilprecht, *Old Babyl. Inscr.* i. 2, Nos. 90, 91.
† Hilprecht, *ib.* No. 87, col. i. 1.
‡ Gudea, galet A, col. i. 6.
§ Inscription D, col. i. 3.
‖ See the votive inscriptions of Kassite kings published by Hilprecht (*Old Babylonian Inscriptions*, i., Nos. 28–82), which with few exceptions are dedicated to En-lil or his consort Nin-lil or Belit. In the 'boundary' inscriptions dating from this period (see *Keilinschriftliche Bibliothek*, iv. pp. 56–63), it is also significant that Marduk is mentioned after Shamash, and even the god Adad in one instance is given the preference over him.

* So in the inscription of the days of Marduknadinakhe (*c.* 1100), Rawlinson, iii. 43, col. iii. 31.
† *e.g.* Rawlinson, iii. 41, col. ii. 25, Marduk occupies the fourth place after the triad, being preceded by Sin, Shamash, and Ishtar.
‡ Now represented by the mound *Abu-Shahrein*, situated at some distance from the mouth of the Euphrates.
§ Bur-Sin of the Isin dynasty, *e.g.* (*c.* 2500 B.C.), refers to the oracle-tree at Eridu (Hilprecht, *Old Babylonian Inscriptions*, i. 1, No. 19, 5), and among the titles of Ur-Ninib of the same dynasty we find one which designates him (*ib.* No. 18, 6–7) as 'fulfilling the commands of Eridu.'
‖ Inscription of Entemena (Thureau-Dangin in *Revue d'Assyriologie*, ii. p. 148, col. iv. 5–7).

tradition survived which attributed the beginnings of culture to the instruction furnished to mankind by the water deity * who personified the Persian Gulf; and since, as a matter of fact, the course of civilization in the Euphrates Valley is from south to north, we may conclude that the prominence in culture as well as the antiquity of Eridu were the factors which led to the sanctity of the place, and, along with this sanctity, to the prominent position attained by the chief god of the place, so that his worship spread far beyond its original confines.

There is no god who in certain portions of the religious literature of Babylonia—notably in the numerous incantation texts—plays a greater rôle than Ea. He is apt to be appealed to, first of all; and, where other deities fail, Ea by his superior wisdom, which is his most characteristic feature, is certain to succeed in discovering the cause of the disease that troubles a man, and in effecting a cure. He is essentially the god of mankind, who loves the children of men, who originally taught them wisdom, and who, according to at least one cosmological system current in Babylonia, was the creator of mankind. This prominence of Ea in portions of the religious literature suggests, indeed, that the compositions themselves originated at Eridu; and there is distinct evidence for this in the transformation which many of the incantation texts clearly underwent in order to adapt them to the standards of the priesthood of Babylon, which was naturally jealous of anything that seemed to affect the pre-eminence of Marduk. Just as the titles and attributes as well as the prerogatives of the old Bel of Nippur were transferred to Marduk, so the latter also assumed the rôle of Ea; but he is represented as doing this with the full consent of Ea, who became in the theological system of the Babylonian priesthood the father of Marduk, proud of the achievements of his son, and rejoicing in the latter's supremacy. Marduk's name is either associated in the religious texts with that of Ea, so that both are represented as performing in concert acts that were originally attributed to Ea alone; or Ea is depicted as asking his son to act for him. This re-editing and adaptation of the ancient literary productions of the Euphrates Valley thus furnishes a valuable aid in tracing the gradual development of a theological system. A reconciliation between the claims of Ea and Marduk, respectively, having thus been brought about, the cult of Ea could be carried on without endangering the position of Marduk, and a sanctuary to Ea was erected in the sacred area around Marduk's own temple in the city of Babylon.

Anu is practically entirely freed from local associations, and is viewed as a god for the gods rather than for men—a deity who exercises a general supervision over all the gods. In a sense, the conception of Anu represents the highest point reached in the spiritualization of the Babylonian religion. He is the 'lofty god,' and it is significant that as early as the days of Ḫammurabi † he is in fact designated simply *ilu* 'god.' At no subsequent period, either in Babylonian or Assyrian history, do we find a closer approach to a monotheistic belief than in this early conception of Anu, although it must be borne in mind that the actual step of regarding one god as embodying the essence of all others was not taken in Ḫammurabi's days, nor was it taken in later days despite certain appearances to the contrary.‡ While not entering to the same extent as did Bel and Ea into the popular religion, yet the conception of Anu as an outcome of the best speculative thought in Babylonia is a most important feature of the Babylonian religion, and must not be lost sight of in an estimate of the best that this religion stood for.

It will thus be seen that each one of the three gods embraced in the doctrine of the triad has his peculiar origin, and retains his peculiar place outside of the rank accorded to him in the triad itself. The local cult of Bel of Nippur proceeds undisturbed by the admission of Bel to the second place in the triad, while the transfer of Bel's attributes to Marduk marks the concession made to the new order of things which eventually gave the patron god of the city of Babylon his undisputed rank at the head of the active pantheon. Lastly, Ea, rising to a place of importance through the sacred associations connected with the old city of Eridu, is stripped of local limitations to a much greater extent than is the case with Bel, and outside of his rank as a third member of the triad is worshipped and appealed to throughout Babylonia as the god of humanity *par excellence*, whose chief trait is wisdom, and one of whose chief functions consists in his power of healing disease and of relieving suffering in general.

2. **Ishtar.**—We have already had occasion to point out that with the gods of the triad their consorts are occasionally associated, and that, even when this is not the case, the consort of En-lil or Bel, under the form of *Nin-kharsag*, appears occasionally as a fourth member associated with Anu, Bel, Ea. The association of consorts with the three gods is due merely to the influence of the general belief, which is a part both of the popular religion and of the system devised by the priests, according to which every male deity was supposed to have a partner—who, however, is generally merely his pale reflexion. The case is different, however, in the association of Nin-kharsag with the triad. Although bearing a name signifying 'lady of the mountain,' which belongs to the consort of En-lil, the chief god of Nippur, and whose chief sanctuary was known as *E-kur*, 'mountain-house,' the fact that this name is subsequently replaced by a more general one, *Nin-makh*, which has the force of 'great lady,' and is generally added as a fourth member of the triad after Ea, is sufficient to show that we are dealing here, not with the associate of a male deity, but with some more general principle recognized by the priests at least as a factor in the workings and divisions of the Universe. That factor may in a general way be defined as the life-producing power manifested in the world, without which heaven, earth, and water would be a desolate waste. The influence of this doctrine, which appears to have been formulated as early at least as the third millennium, leads to the phenomenon which, next to the constitution of the triad at the head of the pantheon, is the most characteristic feature of the Babylonian doctrine of the gods, according to which, from a certain time onwards, only *one* goddess occupying an independent position is recognized. The general name by which the goddess comes to be known is *Ishtar*. She is the great mother to whom vegetation, as well as fertility in the animal world, is due, and she is naturally viewed also as the mother of mankind. That in the triad she is designated as *Nin-kharsag*, may possibly point to the formulation of the doctrine at a time when the Bel cult of Nippur was still in the ascendency, and when naturally the consort of this god—who was called Belit, 'lady' *par excellence*, as En-lil was called Bel—had the distinction of representing the life-giving principle assigned to her. However this may be, the choice of the later and specific

* Called Oannes by Berosus in his account of this tradition (Cory, *Ancient Fragments* (2nd ed.), p. 57).

† 'Code de Hammourabi,' col. i. 45, etc. (ed. Scheil, *Textes Élamites-Sémitiques*, ii. p. 16).

‡ See below, p. 550[a], and Jastrow, *Die Religion Babyloniens und Assyriens*, p. 203, note 1.

designation *Ishtar*, as the name of the great goddess, is due to influences emanating again from the city of Babylon, for it is there that down to the latest days we find *Nin-makh* used as one of the designations of the chief goddess.*

That the name *Ishtar*—conveying in all probability the force of 'leading,' 'overseeing,' from a stem *aśâru*—also originated in the city of Babylon, cannot be definitely stated, but seems likely. The phonetic writing appears for the first time in the inscriptions of Ḫammurabi,† and it would be natural for the priests of Babylon to use the name of a goddess who was worshipped in the capital by the side of Marduk as the designation of the general life-producing power. That, at all events, they were anxious to regard the associate of Marduk as identical with Ishtar, follows from the etymology they proposed for the name of this consort, whose real name *Sarpanitum* (or *Sarpanit*), *i.e.*, probably, the 'shining one,' they converted into *Zêr-bânîtum*, 'the seed-producing' goddess.

Whatever the origin of Ishtar may have been, and wherever the cult of this goddess may originally have been centred, she gradually absorbs the rôles and the names of the other goddesses who as consorts of gods in important religious centres had acquired a certain, though restricted, importance. Thus at Erech, in the extreme south, there flourished the cult of a goddess known as *Nanâ*, who appears to have been conceived as a deity of a violent character, punishing severely those who disobey her—a war-goddess rather than a mother of life, but who in later texts is identified with Ishtar. Again, at another ancient centre, Shirpurla, we find the cult of a goddess *Ninâ*, who is regarded as the sister of the chief god of the place, Nin-girsu, and whose special function appears to have been the interpretation of dreams. She is called the great divining queen of the gods, and it is to her that Gudea, one of the most famous rulers of the place (*c.* 3000 B.C.), goes to ascertain the meaning of a dream which disturbs him.‡ Ishtar absorbs the rôle of both Nanâ and Ninâ, and hence, side by side with her character as the mother of all life, she is portrayed already in the inscriptions of Ḫammurabi as the great war-goddess who stands by the king's side in the midst of the fray, and to whose aid every victory is in a measure due. This phase of the character of the goddess is naturally emphasized even more prominently among a people like the Assyrians, whose thoughts and activities were so largely occupied with military pursuits, and among whom all gods take on a warlike and fierce character. While the conception of Ishtar as the great mother of mankind is also found among the Assyrians, the kings of the north more frequently speak of her as the companion of the chief god Ashur, and as co-operating with the latter to lead the Assyrian armies to victory. She is pictured as armed with bow and arrow, and it is likewise she who, like Ninâ, furnishes oracles and appears in dreams to encourage her favourites—the kings—by reassuring messages. Again, a goddess *Anunit*, who, as the name indicates, stood in some relationship to Anu, the god of heaven, becomes a form of Ishtar; and in the same way Ishtar absorbs the rôle of other of the chief goddesses of the religious and political centres of the ancient Babylonian cities, such as *Bau*, originally the consort of Nin-girsu, the chief deity of Shirpurla, who at one time acquired an independent position of great prominence.

The extent to which this process of concentration was carried is illustrated by the common use of the term *ishtar*, particularly in religious texts, in the sense of 'goddess'; and from it a plural *ishtarâte* is formed, with the signification 'goddesses.' While, therefore, the other goddesses who are merely the consorts of male deities—their pale reflexions—continue to preserve their identity, they are in reality merely so many Ishtars, with this distinction, however, that the name Ishtar as that of a specific deity is confined to the associate of the chief god—Marduk in the south and Ashur in the north.

A certain vagueness in the use of the name Ishtar, to be observed especially in Assyrian historical texts, followed from the attempt to concentrate the attributes of all the important goddesses—important by virtue of the part once played by the centres in which as consorts of male deities they were worshipped—in a single personage. Ishtar is not really the wife of Ashur, who indeed is essentially a god standing by himself without wife or offspring; but as the chief goddess she takes her place by the side of Ashur, just as she does by the side of Marduk, and hence she is addressed occasionally in terms which might be taken as representing the relationship of a wife to her husband. In the south, again, owing to Marduk's absorption of the rôle of the old Bel of Nippur, Ishtar naturally becomes the *Bêlit* of Babylonia, though Belit was originally the consort of the Nippurian Bel; and, in so far as she takes on the traits of the older Belit, she is associated with Marduk in the relationship of consort to the chief male deity. Yet the amalgamation is not complete until a relatively late period, and Marduk continues to have as a special consort *Sarpanit*, who is generally distinguished, albeit not sharply, from Ishtar. Confusing as this double character of Ishtar, as the one great mother-goddess, the source of life, and as the consort of the head of the pantheon, may appear to us, it probably occasioned no difficulty to the Babylonian theologians, to whom Ishtar was essentially the goddess of life and vegetation; nor to the Assyrian priests, among whom she took on the rôle of the great war-goddess, who in company with Ashur led the armies of the kings to victory.

3. **Sin.**—Next to the triad and the great mother-goddess, the worship of the two great orbs of light—the moon and the sun—is a feature of the Babylonian religion that clings to it from the earliest period of which we have any record, down to the latest. It is impossible to say definitely that the cult of the one is older than the other, but the greater prominence which, so far as the evidence goes, was enjoyed by the moon cult in the earliest forms of Semitic culture, justifies the preference given to it in the order of treatment. In a general way it may be said that the moon cult is coexistent with the nomadic grade of culture, while sun worship corresponds more to the frame of mind and to the conditions prevailing among a people that has reached the agricultural stage. This generalization, though open to the objections that attach to all generalizations, is nevertheless of value, provided it be not pushed to the extreme of denying the possibility of sun worship in the pre-agricultural period of the Semites. The movements of nomads in Arabia—the home *par excellence* of the Semites—taking place for a great part of the year at night, the moon naturally served as an important guide. The more regular changes in the orb of night and the briefer period in which these regular changes run their course, constituted further features that helped to emphasize the im-

* The temple erected in Babylon in honour of this goddess has recently been excavated by the German expedition. See *Mittheilungen der Deutschen Orient. Gesellschaft*, Nos. 4 and 5; and also Delitzsch, *Im Lande des einstigen Paradieses*, pp. 38, 39.

† See King, *Inscriptions of Hammurabi*, i., No. 34, 6. 9. 15. and 23, *ish-ta-ra-a-tim* already used in the general sense of 'goddesses.'

‡ See Thureau-Dangin's article, 'Le Songe de Goudéa' (*Comptes rendus de l'Académie d'Inscriptions*, 1901, pp. 112-128).

portance of the moon as a medium for the calculation of time. However this may be, two of the oldest religious centres in Babylonia were seats of moon worship—Ur and Ḥarran (or Ḥaran),—and the sanctuaries at both places retained their popularity until the days of the New Babylonian empire. Assyrian rulers vied with those in the south in paying homage to the god worshipped in these centres.

The common name given to the moon-god is *Sin*. The meaning and etymology of this name are not yet clear; but there were numerous epithets by which he was known. Among these is one *Nannar*, which, signifying 'the one who gives light' or 'place of light,'* appears to have been used at one time as a genuine name and not merely as an epithet. Possibly Nannar is even an older name than Sin, which appears to have originated at Ḥarran. Besides the two places named, there were, no doubt, other places in Babylonia where the moon cult flourished, and it was merely the religious prominence of Ur and Ḥarran that lent to their association with the moon-god a special significance. The moon-god is ordinarily designated ideographically *En-zu*, which describes him as the 'lord of wisdom,' and this attribute is perhaps the most important of the conceptions connected with him. This designation appears in one of the earliest inscriptions known to us. Lugalzaggisi† enumerates En-zu among the gods serving as his protectors, and from the sequence it is evident that this ruler has in mind the moon-god of the city of Ur. The cultivation of the science of astronomy by the Babylonian priests served to emphasize the association of wisdom with the moon, as the overseer of the starry heavens; and, since the motive predominating in the development of this science was the belief in the influence of the position and movements of the stars upon the fate of the individual, the wisdom of Sin was to a large extent coextensive with the giving of oracles and the interpretation of omens. Hence the prominence accorded to Sin in the omen literature. It is he who sends dreams. He is addressed as the lord of decisions, the god who gives counsel; and if in later times it is Shamash—the sun-god—rather than Sin who appears as the god of oracles, this is due to the greater prominence which Shamash acquired in the agricultural stage of culture, and which led to the relegating of Sin to a secondary position. Sin's traits as the illuminator likewise continue to be dwelt upon both in historical texts and in the hymns composed in his honour; and, with the tendency to lay stress on the ethical phase of the natures of the gods, the light diffused by Sin becomes a symbol of his function in revealing to men the snares that are laid for them in the dark. As a protection against the workings of the mischievous spirits who ply their trade generally at night, the appeal is frequently made in the incantations to the moon-god; but here, again, there are other tendencies at work in the Babylonian religion that prevent the fullest development of the traits of wisdom and of protection ascribed to Sin. In the later periods the element of wisdom is so prominently associated with another god—Ea, who through various causes becomes the god of humanity *par excellence*—as to set the moon cult almost aside, while the greater attachment felt towards the sun by an agricultural population, added to the much more powerful character of the sun's light, leads not only to Shamash becoming an oracle god in the place of Sin, but exalts the sun-god to the position of chief protector of mankind against injustice, the god who far above any other reveals wrongdoing and brings wickedness to light. Sin, in short, while his cult remains prominent, loses his touch, as it were, with his worshippers. The personal element is moved into the background. As he no longer entered into the daily life of a population that became agricultural and then commercial, the later hymns to him do not breathe that spirit of genuine attachment which characterizes the addresses to such gods as Shamash, Ea, and Marduk. He retains his supreme position among the gods; but, calm and cold as his light, he is not the deity to whom the people turn in their distress, and it was due chiefly to the reverence in which such ancient centres as Ur and Ḥarran were held by virtue of their great antiquity that he continued to be a member of a second great triad, consisting of Sin, Ishtar, and the sun-god.

* So Lehmann, *Zeitschrift für Assyriologie*, xvi. p. 405.

† Hilprecht, *Old Bab. Inscriptions*, i. 2, No. 87, col. i. 21–22.

4. **Shamash, Ninib, Nergal.**—We have indicated the main reason for the steadily growing popularity of the sun cult, which is a feature of the development both of the popular religion and of the system of theology established by the influence of the priests. While the worship of the sun-god, as one of the great powers of nature, is no doubt much earlier among all nations than the period when the agricultural stage was reached, it is among agricultural communities that such a cult acquires a popularity corresponding to the importance of the sun in the life of the people. Hence the phenomenon, which at first sight may seem strange, that the majority of the local gods worshipped in the cities of ancient Babylonia are solar deities. Besides the two chief centres of sun worship—Sippar in northern Babylonia and Larsa in the southern portion—the patron deity of Shirpurla (known as *Nin-girsu*) is a solar deity; a god *Nergal*, worshipped in another important centre—Cuthah—is likewise a sun-god; similarly, *Za-mal-mal*, who belongs to an important city—Kish; while Marduk, originally merely the god of the city of Babylon, but destined, with the growing dignity of the city as the capital of the united Babylonian States, to become the official head of the pantheon, is also distinctly a solar god.

Besides these, we have a host of other deities belonging to cities and towns of minor importance that are distinctly solar in character. With that same tendency towards the systematization of beliefs which led to the concentration of the goddesses of the more important centres in the person of a single goddess Ishtar, so in the course of time these various local sun-gods came to be looked upon as so many forms or manifestations of the one great orb, though the tendency never went so far as to concentrate all the solar deities into a single one. By the side of a god, symbolical of the sun in general, and who receives the name of Shamash, the official Babylonian pantheon continues to recognize two other solar deities—one whose name is provisionally read *Ninib*, and the other *Nergal*—exclusive of Marduk, who, although a sun-god, also acquires, as already intimated, a unique position. The real reason for the continued independent existence of Ninib and Nergal is, no doubt, to be sought again in the political and religious significance of the centres in which they were worshipped. That centre was, in the case of Nergal, the city of Cuthah, which is first referred to in an inscription of king Dungi of Ur (*c.* 2800 B.C.). As for Ninib, indications point to his identity with Nin-girsu, the chief god of Shirpurla, the capital of one of the oldest Babylonian States; though the origin of the writing *Nin-ib* and its precise relationship to the form *Nin-girsu* are as yet unknown to us. In the systematized Babylonian theology, however, the distinction between Shamash, Ninib, and

Nergal was interpreted in such a manner, that, while Shamash was regarded as the sun-god *par excellence* and in general, Ninib was looked upon as the personification of the morning and spring sun, and Nergal as the sun of noon and of the summer season.* This differentiation was suggested by the two aspects which the sun as a great power of nature presents in a climate like that of Babylonia. It is, on the one hand, a beneficent power which, in the spring, drives away the rain and storms, and restores the life and vegetation of nature; and, on the other hand, it is a destructive power which, during the hot season, by its too fierce and burning rays, brings about disease and suffering, and even causes ruin to the crops.

Confining ourselves for the moment to the personification of the sun in general, the name *Shamash*, having perhaps the force of 'servitor,' appears to go back to the very early period when the moon cult still enjoyed a supremacy over that of the sun. And if it be borne in mind that, both in the earlier and in the later inscriptions of Babylonia and Assyria,† the moon-god is, almost without exception, accorded the preference over Shamash in an enumeration of the pantheon, the conclusion appears to be warranted that the 'service' implied in the name had reference originally to the subservient relationship in which Shamash stood to Sin. We have, however, also had occasion to note the causes that led to the later predominance of the sun cult over that of the moon, at least in the popular phase of the religion, and the influence of this phase is to be seen in the absorption on the part of Shamash of attributes that once belonged to Sin.

The chief centres of the Babylonian Shamash cult were, as already indicated, Sippar and Larsa, both of them cities whose foundation reaches back to a high antiquity. Of the two, Larsa appears to have been politically the more important, whereas Sippar acquired greater religious sanctity, from which we may perhaps conclude that it was the older of the two. That there is some historical connexion between the two places, is indicated by the identity of the name borne by the chief temple in both Sippar and Larsa, viz. *E-barra* (or *E-babbara*), signifying 'resplendent house.' In the further development of the conceptions connected with Shamash it is important to note the introduction of ethical ideas. Represented ideographically as 'the god of day,' he is worshipped not merely as the symbol of light and as the beneficent power that drives away the winter storms and clothes the earth with verdure, but as the god who, among mankind, as in nature, brings about order and stability. As his light illumines all dark places, so he is regarded as the one who can drive evil, which was pictured as 'darkness,' out of the body of man. Shamash is therefore frequently appealed to in the incantation texts as the god who can provide healing, who can secure release from sufferings by driving away the demons and evil spirits. The symbolical rites prescribed in these texts to be carried out in connexion with the pronouncing of certain formulæ are generally to be performed at daybreak, when the rule of Shamash begins. But not only evil in the form of disease or bewitchment can be removed by Shamash, it is he likewise who brings hidden crimes to light, and it is he who punishes the evil-doer. His light thus becomes a symbol also of justice, and perhaps the most frequent epithet by which he is addressed both in hymns and in historical texts is that of 'judge of heaven and earth.' He is pictured as sitting on a throne in a court of justice, receiving the petitions of those who have been injured, and rendering a just verdict. It is significant that Ḫammurabi (*c.* 2250 B.C.) places at the head of his famous Code of laws* a picture of Shamash, and in the body of the text the god is frequently introduced as the one who inspired Ḫammurabi with the project of gathering together the laws of the country for the purpose of ensuring justice and security to all the inhabitants of the land. Among the titles that the king bestows on himself he takes special pride in designating himself the 'king of righteousness,' which is precisely the rôle in which Shamash himself appears in the religious literature.

By the side of Shamash we not only find his consort *Â* frequently referred to, but a group of minor deities (or spirits), who form, as it were, the court of the god. A god *Bunene* is pictured as his chariot driver, and *Kettu* ('Right') and *Mesharu* ('Justice') as his children who are in his service. It is likely that *Bunene* was originally the name of the sun-god in some locality, who was overshadowed by the great Shamash, and therefore accorded a place as an attendant; while *Kettu* and *Mesharu* are clearly designations of the sun-god as the lord of justice, that have been personified as independent beings.

*Ninib.*—As the sun-god associated more specifically with the spring and morning, it is natural to find Ninib regarded as essentially an agricultural deity, who presides over the fields, and who is appealed to, not merely to ensure fertility, but to protect the boundaries of the fields against unlawful invasion or wilful interference. A feature of Ninib which stands in close connexion with his position as an agricultural deity, is his absorption of the rôle of numerous other gods, who, originally local patrons of the fields, are viewed as merely so many manifestations of Ninib. Thus we find *Nin-gish-zida, Nin-shakh, Za-mal-mal, Dun-pa-uddu, Zizanu, Shedu*, all once worshipped as independent gods, assimilated to Ninib in accordance with the same tendency that led to a concentration of all the independent goddesses in the great Ishtar, and which led to making Shamash of Larsa and Sippar the representative of the sun-god in general, thus gradually obscuring the numerous local sun cults that must once have flourished. There is, however, another side to Ninib, due to his having been the chief deity in an important political centre — probably Shirpurla. As the patron of rulers whose position was due to their force of arms, Ninib (or Nin-girsu†) was naturally also a god of war, who appeared in the midst of the fray as a warrior fully armed. In hymns composed in his honour, Ninib is very frequently addressed as the god of battle, whose strength is irresistible, and who leads the armies of the king to victory.

This violent character of the god also leads to his being invoked by the Assyrian rulers as the one who, with Nergal, presides over the sports—hunting of lions, bulls, and stags—to which the Assyrians were devoted. Indeed, some of the Assyrian kings, notably Ashurnaṣirpal (B.C. 885–860),‡ are so devoted to Ninib that he becomes the god of war *par excellence*, and they fairly exhaust their vocabulary in extolling him as the strong

* See Jensen (*Kosmologie*, p. 457 f.), to whom the indication of this distinction is due, and whose views are more plausible than the opinion of Winckler (*Geschichte Israels*, ii. p. 79), who is inclined to look upon Ninib as the symbol of the summer season.

† An exception appears in the inscription of Lugalzaggisi (Hilprecht, *Old Bab. Inscr.* i. 2, No. 87, col. i. 20); but see the note on p. 67 of the present writer's *Religion Babyloniens und Assyriens*.

* English translation by Johns under the title, *The Oldest Code of Laws in the World* (Edinburgh, 1903).

† See above, p. 542b.

‡ See Rawlinson, i. 17, col. i. 1–17; Ninib as god of hunting with Nergal, Rawlinson, i. 28, col. i. 1.

and powerful hero who overthrows all opponents, whose victory is assured, who holds the sceptre in his hands; the lord of lords, who drives along like a raging storm. There is but little trace, in such a description, of the solar deity, though phrases are interspersed here and there which show the solar origin of the god in question. It is natural that among the warlike Assyrians, where all the gods assume a fierce and more violent aspect, this side of the deity should have been particularly emphasized; whereas, among the Babylonians, it is, on the whole, as an agricultural god that Ninib retains his position in the pantheon down to the latest period.*

The consort of Ninib is *Gula*, also designated as *Nin-karrak*, who, besides being very frequently associated with him, especially in the invocation of the gods at the close of the boundary inscriptions, appears in the magic tests chiefly as the 'great physician' who provides healing for the sick.

*Nergal.*—As the symbol of the great power of nature in its destructive phase, Nergal is consistently regarded as a violent deity, who alternately appears as a war-god and as a god of pestilence and fevers, dealing out death and suffering on every side. Dissociated from his originally local limitations as the god of Cuthah, he absorbs the rôle of other gods, who, likewise solar deities of the more violent type, were viewed as hostile to man. Such a figure was *Ira* (or *Gira*);† another was *Ishum*, more specifically a god of fire; a third was *Namtar*, the plague-god *par excellence*; though, instead of being directly identified with Nergal, the latter is regarded as his servitor, in which rôle Ira, also, appears at times.

We have seen that Nergal is also associated with Ninib as the god of war; but the most important function assigned to Nergal in the systematized pantheon is as the chief of the gods who preside over the world of the dead. The Babylonian priests, in further development of the current popular views in regard to the condition of the dead in the nether world (upon which we shall dwell in a subsequent section), set up two pantheons—one for the living, and one for the dead. In the course of time the differentiation between the two became so marked that it was commonly held that the gods, whom we have hitherto been considering, exercised control over the living only, who upon death passed out of their supervision. The dangers from hostile gods and demons, however, did not cease with the approach of death, and it was necessary to secure protection from the spirits that infested the graves, and that followed the dead to their abode in the subterranean cave in which they were popularly supposed to be housed. Such protection could be gained only by an appeal to deities more powerful than the demons; but the gods so addressed were quite different from those who protected the living. Nergal, as the god of fevers and pestilence—a prototype of the angel of death—was appropriately selected as the chief of this nether world pantheon. At his side was a consort, *Eresh-kigal* or *Allatu*. She is a kind of counterpart to Ishtar, and, originally ruling independently in the lower world, is represented as accepting Nergal as her mate.

Grouped around Nergal and Eresh-kigal are a series of gods forming the court of the Divine pair, who, besides doing their bidding, determine with them the condition of the dead. Besides Eresh-kigal, we encounter a consort, *Laz*, given to Nergal in his position as a member of the pantheon of the living; and just as Nergal belongs to both pantheons, so there are other deities, like *Nin-gish-zida*, whom we encounter in the pantheon both of the upper and of the lower regions. Remembering that this latter pantheon represents largely a doctrine of the schools, we need not be surprised to find gods who belong to both pantheons; and, though there is no direct evidence for the fact, it seems likely that, as among the Greeks, most of the gods of the lower world were regarded as having their sojourn in that region for a part of the year only. In short, the popular element in this doctrine of a lower world pantheon is represented by the nature myth, which symbolizes the change of seasons by transferring the abodes of certain gods—more particularly gods of vegetation and of life in general—to the nether world during the season of rain and storms, when Nature herself seems to have succumbed to the powerful Nergal and his consort.

5. **Adad.**—Shamash, Ninib, and Nergal, as we have seen, symbolize the sun in general, and in its twofold aspects as a beneficial and a harmful power. But, besides the destruction brought about by the fierce rays of the summer sun, Babylonia and Assyria suffered from the even greater havoc wrought by the rainstorms, accompanied by destructive winds, during the wintry season, which lasted for almost six months. The god who, in the systematized pantheon, personifies these winter storms is Adad, who was also known, in Assyria at least, as *Ramman*, *i.e.* 'the thunderer.' He bears some resemblance to the old Bel of Nippur, who, as the god of the earth and of the atmosphere immediately above it, has also the traits of a storm-god.

Besides Adad and Ramman, there are various other names by which the god is known (apart from numerous epithets), such as *Martu*, *Mer*, and *Bur*, which may be taken as indications that he likewise, just as Ishtar, Ninib, and Shamash, has absorbed the rôles of other local deities who personified the wind and storm. On seals and in sculptured scenes he is depicted as armed with the thunderbolt and lightning; and, since many of the myths of Babylonia deal with the conflict of the powers of nature, Adad is rarely absent in them, being generally, indeed, assigned a prominent rôle. But even the destructive winter rains and storms have their favourable aspects, since they are essential to the fructification of the earth; hence Adad is viewed also as a god who brings blessings to the fields. It was essential, therefore, to propitiate him in order to secure oneself against his too great violence, which would result in havoc instead of blessing. His curse was particularly powerful; and, accordingly, at the close of their inscriptions, Babylonian and Assyrian rulers alike are found invoking Adad to bring famine and devastation upon their enemies by a failure of the crops. Instead of bringing forth plants, he can cause weeds and thistles to spring up. Woe, therefore, to him whom Adad desires to punish! The ethical element is also introduced into the conceptions concerning Adad, and he is very often associated with Shamash as the god who punishes the wrong-doer and secures justice for one who has been injured. Shamash and Adad appear, indeed, so frequently in hymns and in oracles as 'the lords of justice,' the Divine judges, that one is justified in interpreting this association in terms of a doctrine forming part of the Babylonian theology, according to which the specifically beneficial and specifically violent manifestations of nature were combined to give expression to the view that good and evil, blessings and curses, are dealt out on the basis of justice.

* A temple to Ninib, dating from the days of the New Babylonian period, has been unearthed by the German expedition at Babylon (*Mittheil. d. Deutschen Orient. Ges.*, No. 10).

† The former reading, *Dibbarra*, is to be abandoned. Although the correct reading is still uncertain, the probabilities are in favour of *Ira*, which is adopted by Zimmern, *Keilinschriften u. d. Alte Testament*, p. 587.

The consort of Adad is *Shala*, who, however, is merely a pale reflexion of the male deity, and plays no independent part whatsoever. She is not even as frequently mentioned by the side of Adad as are the consorts of some of the other gods.

6. **Marduk.**—The political supremacy acquired by the city of Babylon *c.* 2250 B.C., and maintained with some interruptions, notably during the Kassite rule (*c.* 1730 to 1150 B.C.), when the attempt was made to reinstate Bel of Nippur as the head of the pantheon, brought about such important changes in the old Babylonian pantheon that one is tempted to divide the Babylonian religion into two periods—the one prior to the supremacy of Babylon, the other after this supremacy had been secured. With Babylon as the capital of the united States of the Euphrates Valley, the advance of the local deity, Marduk, to a position at the head of the pantheon naturally followed. Originally a solar deity, and symbolizing more specifically, like Ninib, the sun of the spring solstice, which triumphs over the storms of the winter season, Marduk becomes 'the lord' *par excellence*; and this supreme position is emphasized by his actually assuming the dignity and name of *Bel*—hitherto the designation of the chief deity of Nippur. Such a change involved a general shifting in the relationship of the gods of the old Babylonian pantheon to one another, with the result that under the influence of the priests of Babylon an entirely new theological system was evolved. Ancient myths were transformed so as to accord to Marduk the place due to him. Important acts, such as the regulation of the order of the Universe and the creation of mankind—hitherto ascribed to Bel of Nippur, to Ea of Eridu, or to a goddess Aruru—were transferred to Marduk. The incantation rituals were to a large extent altered with a view to establishing the position of Marduk as the ultimate source of healing, of protection, and of all blessings. The gods were represented as forming a court around their chief, hailing Marduk as their leader, and paying him homage. The hymns composed in his honour and the prayers addressed to him by the rulers embody sentiments that might be regarded as an index of a decided advance towards a monotheistic conception of the Universe, and unquestionably the steady growth of the Marduk cult had its outcome in giving to the Babylonian religion a far more spiritual character than it had hitherto acquired. While the cults of En-lil at Nippur, of Sin at Ur and Ḫarran, of Shamash at Sippar and Larsa, and of Ea at Eridu, were maintained, and these places continued to be regarded as religious centres of the first rank, the temple of Marduk at Babylon, known as *E-sagila*, *i.e.* 'the lofty house,' became the central sanctuary of the land, and around the sacred area in which it stood chapels and sanctuaries were erected, as formerly at Nippur, to all the chief gods, who could thus be worshipped in one place. True, certain concessions were made to the traditions of the past, such as making Ea the father of Marduk; but the dependence of Marduk upon Ea involved in such a relationship was cancelled by the readiness and zeal with which Ea acknowledged the superiority of his son.

The Babylonian creation story in the final form in which it has come down to us may be taken as the typical illustration of the transformation of doctrines brought about through Marduk's advance to the head of the pantheon. Several old nature myths have been combined in this story to form a great 'Marduk' epic—a grand pæan sung in his honour. The overthrow of Tiamat, the monster symbolical of the chaos that rules during the rainy season, was probably accomplished by Marduk, as the sun-god who drives away the storms. But there are evidences in the tale of the existence of a far more powerful being, *Apsu* ('the deep'), who has been conquered by Ea; and it was the latter, no doubt, to whom, in one form of the story, the creation of mankind was ascribed. So in other versions, originating in different centres, we find other gods invested with this distinction. But all rivals fall into the background by the side of Marduk, to whom everything is attributed; and the gods themselves bestow fifty glorious names upon him—and thus transfer their own attributes and powers to the chief god of the city of Babylon.* They resign, as it were, in his favour. Hence the interesting phenomenon that the originally solar character of the deity crops out only in the ideographic method of writing his name as 'child of the day,'† and in incidental references; whereas the side that is most strongly emphasized is his headship of the pantheon, concentrating in his person all the attributes and powers distributed among the gods.

His consort is generally *Sarpanit*—a name signifying originally the 'shining one,' but interpreted as though compounded of *zêr* 'seed' and *bânîtu* 'producing,' so as to admit of identifying her with the mother-goddess Ishtar. This is actually done in hymns,‡ though the process is not, as a rule, completely carried out. Sarpanit appears merely as an associate of the powerful Marduk, sharing in his glory without materially contributing to it.

7. **Nebo.**—Opposite Babylon lay a city, Borsippa, which there are good reasons for believing to have been older than Babylon itself. Such a supposition best accounts for the fact that the god of the place, Nebo, holds a prominent position in the pantheon by the side of Marduk. True, Borsippa becomes, in course of time, merely a suburb of Babylon, and this dependence finds expression in making Nebo the son of Marduk; but, on the other hand, on the great festival of Marduk, which was the New Year's Day, Nebo takes a part; and even Marduk pays homage to Nebo, his son, by accompanying the image of the latter part of the way back to the sanctuary at Borsippa, after the formal visit of the son to his father. Moreover, there is one attribute assigned to Nebo which signals him out even from Marduk. He is the representative of wisdom; and to him the art of writing is ascribed even by the priests of Babylon, who in their astronomical reports do not hesitate to mention Nebo before Marduk—a custom that was adopted by the Assyrian scholars. In this respect he bears an affinity to Ea; and, like the latter, he appears to have been originally a water deity—perhaps the god who had his seat in the Euphrates river, as Ea was supposed to dwell in the Persian Gulf.

There is, clearly, some connexion between the Ea and Nebo cults, though its precise nature is still unknown to us. Nebo appears under the form *Dumu-zi-zuab*, which designates him as a son of the 'deep,' here used for Ea. Berosus is in accord with the evidence derived from the Babylonian literature in representing Ea—whose name appears in Syncellus' extract from Berosus as *Oannes*§—as the god who instructs mankind in various arts, including writing. Ea retains to the latest period the general attribute of wisdom, besides being regarded as the general protector of mankind; but the specific trait of

* See King, *Seven Tablets of Creation*, i. pp. 94–111.
† Delitzsch, *Beiträge zur Assyr.* ii. 623.
‡ *e.g.* Craig, *Assyrian and Babylonian Religious Texts*, i., No. 1, lines 12–25.
§ Cory's *Ancient Fragments*, p. 57.

being the god of writing is transferred to Nebo, though this is done to a much more decided extent by the Assyrian scribes than by the Babylonians. One is inclined to conjecture that the northward course of culture, which led to the founding of the city Borsippa and to the establishment of an important school there, with a more special cultivation of astronomy than elsewhere, led to the investing of Nebo with Ea's attributes; and, as the intellectual centre shifted from Eridu to Borsippa, Nebo assumes, in a measure, the rôle formerly assigned to Ea, without, however, overshadowing the latter. The priests of Babylon seek to effect a compromise between the present and the past, by making Marduk the son of Ea, while Nebo in turn becomes the son of Marduk, so that the ultimate source of wisdom under this system is still the god of Eridu, even though his activity is transferred in such large measure to Marduk and Nebo. It is a feature of an established priesthood that it never breaks entirely with the past, and in the systematized Babylonian pantheon the honour of Ea is protected by making him a member of the great triad, whereas the real head of the pantheon is Marduk, to whom Nebo is given as a kind of messenger, entrusted with carrying out his dictates. In Assyria, where the connexion with the remote past was less keenly felt, this process is still further developed, and the Nebo cult is laid hold of as an offset to the predominance of Marduk, who was felt to be a rival to the patron god of Assyria—Ashur, naturally placed at the head of the pantheon by the Assyrian priests. Hence some of the Assyrian rulers, while not altogether ignoring Marduk, preferred to manifest their homage to the gods of the south by the glorification of Nebo. They erected sanctuaries to this god in their capital, and proclaimed their confidence in him. Assurbanipal, in collecting the literature produced in the south, ascribes the inspiration of this policy to Nebo and his consort Tashmit (or Tashmitum), who, as he tells us in the subscription frequently attached to the copies, 'opened his ears' and instructed him to make the wisdom of ancient times accessible to his subjects. As originally a water god, Nebo is also an agricultural deity, who opens the subterranean sources and irrigates the fields. In religious as well as in historical texts he is invoked as the one who causes the corn to grow. His consort, generally termed *Tashmit*, but also known as *Nanâ*, plays an independent part. The name Nanâ, properly belonging to the chief goddess of Erech, indicates that this consort was regarded merely as a form of Ishtar—at least in the later periods—while Tashmit is a purely artificial creation. The name signifies 'revelation'; and *Tashmit* appears to have been originally merely a designation of Nebo himself, who is, in fact, spoken of as *ilu tashmêti*, *i.e.* 'god of revelation.' Under the influence of the doctrine which assumed that every god must have a female consort, Tashmit became the associate of the god of Borsippa.

8. **Girru-Nusku.**—Another phase of solar worship in Babylonia is represented by the conception of a deity symbolizing the element of fire. In the Babylonian pantheon this fire-god commonly bears the name of *Girru** (formerly read *Gibil*), whereas in Assyria he is generally known as *Nusku*.† Though decidedly to be classed among the great gods of the pantheon, Girru plays a rôle in the incantation texts rather than in the historical inscriptions of Babylonia and Assyria. He is invoked in the incantation rituals compiled as a means of driving away the demons and evil spirits; and this is due to the prominence held by fire in the ritual. Images of the demons—in wood, wax, and other materials—were made, and burned to the accompaniment of incantations; and, as the images were consumed, it was believed that the demons themselves were destroyed. Night being a favourite time for the exorcizing rites, Nusku was brought into association with the moon-god; although the fire symbolized by Nusku is, without much question, the heat of the sun. On the other hand, the possibility of differentiating Nusku from Girru is furnished by the relationship which the former is made to bear to Nebo. Like Nebo, Nusku is called 'the bearer of the brilliant sceptre' and the 'wise god'; and, when ideographically written, the god is designated as 'the one wielding the sceptre and the stylus.' Girru, on the other hand, is brought into connexion with Anu, the god of heaven, and with Ea, the god of the deep,—with Anu by virtue of the belief which identified fire with the heat of the sun, with Ea because of the part that fire plays in the development of civilization, and particularly of the arts, of which Ea is the patron. While, therefore, in both instances the fire which they symbolize is associated with wisdom, in the case of Nusku this wisdom is specialized, as it were, while Girru is accorded more general and less definite traits. The ethical phases are also somewhat more emphasized in the case of Girru, though, as the conqueror of demons, both Nusku and Girru become forces that are hostile to wrong-doing and crime. While in this way we may still in a measure follow the process which led to the amalgamation of two fire-deities who once had an existence independent of one another, and belonged probably to two different localities, in the religious literature this process of amalgamation is complete. Nusku is viewed as the messenger of Marduk, who carries the words of Marduk to his father Ea, while Girru acts in a similar capacity in association with Marduk and Ea.

9. **Ashur.**—The dependency of Assyria upon Babylonian culture extends into the domain of religious doctrines and rites. The contributions of the Assyrian *literati* to the religious literature preserved in the brick library of Assurbanipal were limited in number and of a minor character. They represented the adaptation of Babylonian models to conditions prevailing in Assyria, rather than original contributions; and, similarly, in the rites observed in the temples of Assyria we have Babylonian rituals modified so far as was needed, and still further elaborated. It is natural, therefore, to find the Assyrian pantheon practically identical in character with the one produced in the south. To be sure, local cults continued to exist in large numbers both in Babylonia and Assyria; but the movement which, as a result of various factors, led to the singling out among the large number of local cults of the group of deities set forth above, who formed what may be called the active pantheon of Babylonia, was extended to Assyria. There we meet with the doctrine of the triad, involving the recognition of three great powers controlling the Universe, as well as with the singling out of the forces of nature such as Sin, Shamash, Ninib, Nergal, Adad, Nusku, who, together with Ishtar, the symbol of fertility and vegetation, constitute the great gods invoked by the Assyrian kings in their official inscriptions. That less attention was paid to Marduk in Assyria than in Babylonia, is not surprising; for, although recognized as the head of the Babylonian pantheon, to Assyrian rulers Marduk was also the patron deity of the city of Babylon, which was the natural rival of the centre chosen as the seat of Assyrian rule. It was chiefly when the Assyrian

* See Zimmern, *Keilinschriften u. das Alte Testament*, p. 417.

† With various by-forms like *Nashukh*, *Nashku*, etc. See Johns, *An Assyrian Doomsday Book*, pp. 12–14.

kings wished to emphasize their control over the affairs of Babylonia that they invoked the name of Marduk; and even in such a case they preferred the name of En-lil or Bel, which, though adopted as the designation of Marduk, disguised the close association of the god with the city of Babylon. In like manner, the consort of Marduk is generally called Nin-lil or Belit in the Assyrian inscriptions, instead of Sarpanit. There was less objection to paying homage to Nebo, and indeed there are indications that the Assyrian rulers at various periods endeavoured to play off Nebo against Marduk. It can hardly be accidental that one ruler Adad-nirari III. (812-783 B.C.) should go so far as to declare that Nebo is the only god whom mankind should trust; and one feels likewise that when Assurbanipal attributes his inspiration to collect the remains of Babylonian literature to Nebo and Tashmit, he is aiming a blow at the rival Marduk in thus implying that the wisdom of Babylonia is the work of the god of Borsippa and not of the god of Babylon.

Instead of Marduk, indeed, the Assyrians recognized as the practical head of their pantheon the deity who presided over the fortunes of the ancient city on the Tigris, known in earlier times as A-usar, and later on as Ashur; and the circumstance that in the north a powerful State developed by the extension of a city (precisely as in the south the Babylonian empire represented merely the extension of the city of Babylon) made it obligatory to assign to the god of A-usar the same position which was accorded in the south to the god of Babylon. We thus obtain one figure in the Assyrian pantheon who represents an original contribution, and who embodies, as it were, the genius of Assyria. That the Assyrians, in thus raising the god of A-usar to a position at the head of the pantheon, had in mind the creation of a rival to Marduk, is shown not only in their avoidance of the latter, as just pointed out, but in the choice of the name *Ashur*, a modification of *Ashir*,* which with the force of 'overseer' or 'protector' is one of the titles given to Marduk.† The assonance between *A-usar*, the name of the oldest capital of Assyria, and *Ashur*, helped to bring about the introduction of Ashur as the name of the patron deity of the place, and from the god the name was extended to the city and to the country; so that *A-usar* disappears almost completely, and we find in Assyrian inscriptions *Ashur* applied to the god, to the city, and to the country or district of Assyria alike and without distinction. The god Ashur becomes so thoroughly identified with the country of Assyria that the change of the capital from Ashur to Calah, and later to Nineveh, in no way affects the position of this deity, who sums up, as it were, the power and spirit of the Assyrian empire. The local deity of A-usar appears to have been originally regarded as a sun-god; but this phase is entirely obscured by the warlike traits given to Ashur in consequence of the prowess displayed by the Assyrian armies. War was the natural element of the Assyrians, who in this respect present a contrast to their more peacefully inclined cousins in the south; and to such an extent was this the case, that almost all the gods of the Assyrian pantheon take on a warlike aspect, becoming, as it were, minor Ashurs by the side of the great and chief god of war. It is Ashur who, surrounded by the other gods acting as his guards and attendants, leads the Assyrian armies to victory. Instead of erecting statues to him, the Assyrians represented him by a standard surrounded by a winged disc, to which a picture of a warrior in the act of discharging an arrow was attached. This standard was carried into the camp, and the god was literally present in the thick of battle, guiding and encouraging his favourites—the kings and their generals. To Ashur, accordingly, all victories were ascribed; and so secure was his position that it was possible for Assyrian kings to recognize by the side of Ashur a special patron god—one choosing Nebo, another Ninib, a third Shamash—on whom they could shower honours and glorifying epithets without arousing the suspicion of disloyalty to the head of the Assyrian pantheon.

* In one of the oldest of Assyrian inscriptions—that of Irishum (*c.* 1730 B.C.)—the god of A-usar is called *Ashir*. See Meissner, *Assyriologische Studien*, i. p. 17.

† *e.g.* Rawlinson, iv.[2] 57, obv. 32; Delitzsch, *Weltschöpfungsepos*, p. 155; K 2107, obv. 2. For the full proof of the views here advanced, see an article by the present writer, 'The god Ashur,' in the 24th vol. of the *Journal of the American Oriental Society*, pp. 282-311.

There was another aspect of Ashur which makes him the most characteristic figure in the Assyrian religion. He was not brought into direct association with any other god. Marduk, despite his position at the head of the Babylonian pantheon, had to yield to certain prerogatives possessed by Ea, as whose son therefore he was depicted. In turn he became the father of Nebo. Ashur, on the other hand, is childless, and acknowledges no other god as his father. What is even more noteworthy, although Ishtar is frequently named by the side of Ashur she is not his wife, and there is, in fact, no female reflexion or consort assigned to Ashur such as we find in the case of all other deities. He rules without a rival, and he stands virtually alone. Indeed, we gain the impression at times of his being the only god recognized by the Assyrians as exerting a real influence over his subjects. He reminds us in some respects of the national deity of the Hebrews, Jahweh, who without consort or offspring brooks no other god by His side. And just as in Babylonia the spiritualizing process, which accompanies the development of every religion, leads to the establishment of the doctrine of a *triad* of gods standing far above the gods of the active pantheon, so in Assyria this process has its outcome in the conception of a single deity who presides over the fate of the country, who marks the genius of the empire established by the Assyrian kings, and who seems to suffice for all the needs of his subjects. This unique position of Ashur was first recognized by Sayce,* who goes so far as to express the opinion that, under other circumstances, there might have developed as spiritualistic a faith as marked the growth in Israel of Jahweh from a national to a universal deity. However this may be, the conception of Ashur as expressed in the annals of Assyrian kings and in the hymns composed in his honour, represents the closest approach to a monotheistic conception of the Universe, despite certain well-marked limitations, to be found in the religion of ancient Mesopotamia.

(B) *MINOR DEITIES.*—Besides the chief deities to whom in a general sketch we must largely confine ourselves, the historical texts, the religious literature, and proper names, reveal the existence of a large number of gods that may in a general way be included under the term 'minor.' To a large extent, the cult of these deities is of a purely local character; and it is natural to find the names of these numerous local gods surviving in the thousands of proper names that we encounter in the legal and commercial documents from the age of Sargon I. to the end of the New Babylonian empire. In the historical texts, on the other

* Hibbert Lectures on *The Religion of the Babylonians and Assyrians*, p. 129; also Gifford Lectures on *The Religions of Egypt and Babylonia*, p. 346.

hand, gods of merely local significance are introduced only in special instances, and generally when the rulers wish to parade their own prominence by invoking as large a number of gods as possible, who are represented as combining to shower their favours on their royal minions. Similarly, in the religious literature, and more particularly in incantations, the natural desire to secure the assistance of as many deities as possible in the struggle against evil demons and the mischief wrought by sorcerers would lead to the introduction of many other gods besides those recognized in the official pantheon as belonging to the first rank. We have already had occasion to refer to some of these minor gods and goddesses, whose rôles were gradually absorbed by some important god to whom they bore a resemblance. Thus we have seen that solar cults centring around Nin-gish-zida, Ningirsu, Nin-shakh, Za-mal-mal, and others, are all represented in the official pantheon by Ninib. This, however, does not prevent the survival of these solar deities to a late period in proper names and in incantations. Again, as we have seen, Nanâ the goddess of Erech, Ninâ associated with a quarter of Shirpurla known as Ninâ, and Anunit connected with Agade, became in the course of time merely names of the great Ishtar, though surviving likewise in the religious literature in myths and legends, as well as in incantations.

Among other gods who in the old Babylonian texts still enjoy an independent existence are **Lugal-banda,** signifying 'mighty king,' and his consort **Nin-sun,** 'the destructive lady,' who were worshipped in Erech. The latter may be identical with Nanâ; the former is a solar deity of the violent type, and is absorbed by Nergal.—A distinctively local goddess is **Nin-mar,** the 'lady of Mar,' whose seat of worship lay in or near the Persian Gulf; and the name of her temple, *Ishgutur, i.e.* 'the court for all peoples,' testifies to the prominence given to her at one time by her worshippers.—A goddess of the agricultural type is **Nidaba,** invoked by several of the old Babylonian rulers, and her name survives to the days of Assurbanipal as a synonym of fertility.—Again, we encounter in the inscriptions of rulers, so far removed from one another as Gudea on the one side (*c.* 3000 B.C.) and Sennacherib on the other (B.C. 705–681), a god **Ka-di** (probably an ideographic designation), who appears to have been the patron of Dur-ilu, a town situated near the Elamitic frontier.

The consort of Nin-girsu, known as **Bau,** is one of the most prominent goddesses in the old Babylonian pantheon. She would have been included in the official pantheon as one of the great deities, but for the absorption of the rôle of Nin-girsu by Ninib, which led to the substitution of Gula for Bau. As Nin-girsu is more particularly connected with Girsu, one of the quarters of Shirpurla, so Bau belongs to another quarter of the town (or district) known as *Uru-azagga*, 'the glorious city,' where her temple stood. As the 'mother of Shirpurla' and 'the chief daughter of Anu,' she is pictured as presiding over the fates of her subjects. It is she who grants success to the labours of the tillers of the soil. The rulers of Shirpurla ascribe to Bau the power and glory that they command; and one of the oldest of the Babylonian festivals, *Zag-muk*, celebrated as the New Year's Day, was instituted in her honour. In the oldest period Bau already absorbs the rôle of another goddess Ga-tum-dug, from whom, however, she is still distinguished in the inscriptions of Gudea.

A god of the solar type, **Dumu-zi,** 'child of life,' appears in various of the inscriptions of the Old Babylonian period; and, besides continuing to play an important rôle in the eschatology of the Babylonians, survives in the name of the fourth Babylonian month.*

Owing to the peculiarity that in the Old Babylonian inscriptions and in the religious literature the names of the deities are written ideographically, we cannot be certain in all cases whether an ideographic form actually represents a new deity or is merely a designation of one already encountered; but the enumeration of lists of gods frequently attached by the rulers either at the beginning or at the end of their inscriptions, enables us to gather in a general way the extent of the pantheon in the various periods of Babylonian history; and the study of these lists justifies the distinction which we have emphasized between the period before Ḫammurabi and the period subsequent to this ruler, when, as we have seen, a shifting of the pantheon took place, and a new direction was given to the development of a theological system by the prominence assigned to Marduk as the chief god of the capital of the Babylonian empire. Two of the oldest lists are furnished by Lugalzaggisi, whose date may be as early as 3500 B.C., though according to other scholars we are not justified in going much beyond 3200 B.C., and by Gudea (*c.* 3000 B.C.). Lugalzaggisi † invokes the following ten deities: En-lil (Bel), Anu, Nidaba, Ea, Shamash, Sin, Innanna (or Ishtar), Nin-kharsag (or Belit), **Shid,** and **Nin-agid-khadu.** We have had occasion to refer to all of these except the two last named, who are both goddesses, and of whom nothing more can be said than that they belong to the immediate pantheon of Erech, and are probably purely local deities. Gudea's largest list ‡ embraces eighteen deities: Anu, En-lil, Nin-kharsag, Ea, Sin, Nin-girsu, Ninâ, Nin-dara, Ga-tum-dug, Bau, Innanna (or Ishtar), Shamash, Ishum, Gal-alim, Dun-shagga, Nin-mar, Dumu-zi-zuab, and Nin-gish-zida. Of those not as yet referred to, namely **Nin-dara, Ishum, Gal-alim, Dun-shagga,** and **Dumu-zi-zuab,** it is sufficient to remark that they are all deities of a purely local character. The first named is a solar deity, whose rôle appears to have been absorbed by Nin-girsu. The same appears to have been the case with Gal-alim and Dun-shagga. Ishum is merely another designation of the fire-god Girru, while Dumu-zi-zuab, *i.e.* 'child of life of the deep,' is a water deity, associated with Borsippa, and apparently merely an older designation of the god Nebo, though in later times identified with Marduk.

Altogether, we encounter about thirty distinct deities in the historical and votive inscriptions of the rulers before Ḫammurabi; but that this number is far from exhausting the minor deities worshipped by the side of those holding the front rank as the greater gods, is demonstrated by the circumstance that the names of more than fifty gods entering as elements into proper names occur in one of the oldest Babylonian inscriptions, that of Manishtusu,§ whose date is certainly before 3000 B.C., and perhaps as early as 3500 B.C.‖ Some of the gods thus utilized in the formation of proper names are of foreign origin—Elamitic and Kassitic; but abstracting these, we still obtain quite an addition to those directly invoked in the inscriptions of this period. The number is still further increased by a study of the proper names in legal and commercial documents of the Ḫammurabi period, which furnishes

* *i.e. Tammuz*, according to the Hebrew form of the name of the month.

† Hilprecht, *Old Babylonian Inscriptions*, i. 2, No. 87, col. i. 1–35.

‡ Inscription B, col. viii. and ix. (de Sarzec, *Découvertes en Chaldée*, pls. 16–19).

§ Published by Scheil in *Textes Élamites-Sémitiques*, i. pp. 6–39.

‖ Scheil places this ruler at 4500 B.C., which is, however, too early a date. See above, p. 537b.

more than seventy distinct deities;* and, when we turn to incantation texts and add the gods who are there invoked, the total ranges considerably over one hundred.

But even in this way we cannot be certain of obtaining even an approximate estimate of the minor deities worshipped in Babylonia and Assyria; and in view of the fact that our material is still scanty compared with the enormous extent of the Babylonian literature, taken together with the circumstance that almost every new publication of texts brings new gods to our notice, it is easier to err by too low than by too high an estimate.

More important, however, than the attempt to estimate the number of gods once worshipped in Babylonia, is the recognition of the distinction to be drawn in a study of the religion of Babylonia and Assyria between the popular phases of the religion as represented chiefly by the very numerous local cults, and the endeavours of the priests and theologians to systematize the current beliefs. The outcome of these endeavours was the distribution of the forces working in the Universe among a comparatively restricted number of deities, representing on the one hand the gods and goddesses worshipped in the chief religious centres of the Euphrates Valley and of Assyria, and, on the other, symbolizing the chief phenomena and great powers of nature—the whole being arranged according to certain guiding principles.

(C) *THE COMBINED INVOCATION OF DEITIES.*—To see these principles at their best, we must turn to the combined invocation of deities to be found in the inscriptions of the period subsequent to the days of Ḫammurabi. 1. For Babylonia, our best sources are the so-called boundary stones, which guarantee certain rights to owners of lands. These inscriptions almost invariably conclude with invoking the curse of the gods of the pantheon upon any who attempt to set aside these rights or to deface or destroy the monumental records on which they are inscribed. A sufficient number of such boundary stones—from the 14th to the 8th cents. B.C.—have now been found to enable us to draw definite conclusions.† The number of deities called upon varies from twelve to nineteen. The list usually begins with the triad Anu, Bel, and Ea, to which at times a female representative —Nin-makh or Nin-kharsag—is added; followed by the second group, consisting of Sin, Shamash, and Adad, or these three with Ishtar; followed by Ninib and Gula,—the latter also under the form Nin-karrak,—who, as the gods presiding over boundaries and boundary rights, are never wanting; but here the agreement among the monuments of this character ends. On many, but not on all, we find Marduk and Nebo. Occasionally Marduk occupies the first place, which of right belongs to him, but, inasmuch as many of these documents date from the Kassite period, when, as will be remembered, the attempt was made to reinstate Bel of Nippur in the rank formerly occupied by him, Marduk is more frequently placed after the second group of deities. Nergal is generally included, and also a serpent-god, Sir, who, besides being named, is invariably depicted among the symbols of the gods, which, in most cases, are attached to the inscription.‡ Girru and Nusku appear only in one instance, while the two chief Kassite deities, Shukamuna and Shumalia, corresponding to the Babylonian Ninib and Ishtar, are added on several of the monuments dating from the Kassite period. Lastly, a series of local gods —Za-mal-mal, the chief god of Kish, and Dun-pa-uddu (both absorbed by Ninib), Pap-nigin-garra (merely again another form of Ninib) and his consort Belit-ekalli ('lady of the palace,' which is another designation of Gula), Shubu and Belit of Akkad (described along with Sin as the gods of a district, Bit-khabban), and, finally, the goddesses Nanâ, Ishkhara, and Anunit (absorbed by the great Ishtar)—are in several instances introduced, as well as Sarpanit, the consort of Marduk, who in one instance, on an Assyrian boundary stone of Marduk-baliddin's days (721-709 B.C.), appears as Erua.* In all, therefore, we have only about twenty-five distinct deities introduced on some twenty of these monuments, or, abstracting the two Kassite deities, we find the Babylonian pantheon restricted to about twenty-three.

Of course it must be borne in mind again that in some cases the place where the monument is erected leads to the introduction of specifically local deities, who are designated as such; and, since it is a matter of chance *which* local deities are invoked in this way, we ought properly to remove these from the total. Similarly, a god like Sir is introduced by virtue of the character of the monuments in question. There remain the following thirteen, who may be regarded as constituting the official pantheon during the second period of Babylonian history: the triad Anu, Bel, and Ea; the group Sin, Shamash, Adad, and Ishtar; the pairs Ninib and Gula, and Marduk and Nebo respectively; Nergal and Girru-Nusku. If we add to these the consorts who play an active part in the religious life, Belit and Damkina, the consorts of Bel and Ea respectively; Nin-gal, A, and Shala, the consorts of Sin, Shamash, and Adad respectively; Sarpanit and Tashmit for Marduk and Nebo,—we have a total of twenty gods.

The general tendency to be observed in the invocation of deities on the boundary stones, as we pass from one century to another, is to reduce the number introduced; and this tendency is in accord with the general course taken by the development of the theological system as devised by the priests. In the days of the Assyrian empire the tendency becomes even more marked. So Assurbanipal (B.C. 668-626), who is fond of calling upon all the great gods, never extends the list beyond eleven, as follows: Ashur, Sin, Shamash, Adad, Bel (by whom he means Marduk), Nebo, the two Ishtars (the Ishtar of Nineveh and the Ishtar of Arbela), Ninib, Nergal, and Nusku. To these the triad, although less prominently dwelt upon in Assyrian inscriptions, is to be added, which again gives us fourteen: in adding the consorts of Bel, Ea, Sin, Shamash, Adad, Marduk, Nebo, and Ninib, we have twenty-two deities, the addition of two to the Babylonian pantheon being formed by the second Ishtar and by Ashur. In the New Babylonian period, so far as the testimony of the inscriptions goes, the actual cult is confined chiefly to Marduk, Nebo, Sin, Shamash, and Ishtar; and though kings like Nebuchadreẓẓar pride themselves upon erecting chapels and sanctuaries to many other deities, including some whose cult they appear to have revived, still these five deities receive such a large share of attention as to make the others quite subsidiary during the Assyrian period likewise, though in the earlier part of this period the cult of Anu is still prominent, and quite a number of other gods are occasionally introduced besides those that appear in Assurbanipal's ordinary list.†

* See Ranke's monograph, *Die Personennamen in den Urkunden der Hammurabidynastie* (München, 1902).

† See Peiser's collection of them in Schrader's *Keilinschriftliche Bibliothek*, vol. iv. pp. 56-104; and Scheil, *Textes Élamites-Sémitiques*, i. and ii.

‡ On the meaning of these symbols, see Jastrow, *Die Religion Babyloniens und Assyriens*, pp. 191, 192.

* Delitzsch in *Beiträge zur Assyriologie*, ii. p. 265 (col. v. 41-42).

† See, *e.g.*, two inscriptions of Sennacherib (Meissner-Rost, *Bauinschriften Sanheribs*, pp. 99-102), where we find lists of

The actual cult, nevertheless, centres so largely around Ashur, Ishtar, Sin, Shamash, Adad, and Nebo (to which number, perhaps, Marduk might be added), that these constitute for all practical purposes the active pantheon during the greater part of the existence of the Assyrian empire.

2. To what extent local cults continued to flourish during the second and third Babylonian periods, and in the Assyrian period, it is quite impossible to say. No doubt, the little sanctuaries scattered throughout the country retained some of their popularity, though even places removed from the great centres of religious life could hardly have escaped the influence of the system that was developed, and that identified the various moon-deities as forms of one and the same god, and similarly distinguished only a limited number of distinct solar deities, so that many of the old local deities would represent in the later periods a survival largely in name. On the other hand, the process of concentration did not extend further than above indicated. The active pantheon was limited to five or six deities; and though occasionally Ashur is celebrated in terms which might lead one to suppose that he was recognized as the only god actually controlling the fate of mankind; and though there are indications in the religious literature and even texts * which point to Marduk's having been represented as having the qualities of all the other great gods,—Ninib, Nergal, Bel, Sin, Shamash, and Adad,—we must not be misled by such phenomena into supposing that the conception which regarded the Universe as the emanation of a single Power or Spirit ever obtained a decided foothold in the Euphrates Valley. It may be that to a few choice minds this view presented itself, but there are no traces of it either in the historical inscriptions of any period or in the religious literature, which are sufficiently definite to warrant us in assuming this to have been the case. At all events, the view never entered to any degree—even the slightest—into the religious life of the people or of the priests; and it is the religious life as *actually* lived that forms the only safe criterion, when dealing with an ancient civilization, for determining the beliefs and doctrines that prevailed. The testimony of the entire Babylonian literature, as of the historical texts of Babylonia and Assyria, is unmistakable in this respect.

We may indeed distinguish, as we have endeavoured to do, several periods in the development of the religious doctrines. We observe clearly the tendency to concentrate the cult on a selection of the numerous deities once worshipped, and we can trace the leading principles which led to the belief in a triad standing above all the gods, and to a group of deities, varying from about thirty in the oldest period to some twenty at a later time, subsidiary to this triad; and we may furthermore note the tendency to reduce the active pantheon to a still smaller number of deities, who absorb the largest share of attention to such an extent as to obscure the others almost completely: but here the process ends. Ashur in Assyria reminds one of the national Jahweh; and Marduk in Babylonia is given certain attributes which are associated by Hebrew writers with Jahweh at the time that the latter is on the verge of becoming more than the god of a single people; but neither Ashur nor Marduk was ever conceived as a deity who brooks no others by his side, as a *logical* consequence of a belief that there can be only one Power presiding over the Universe, from whom all things emanate. That idea transcends the spiritual horizon of ancient Babylonia and Assyria, and was left to another people to evolve.

vi. THE RELIGIOUS LITERATURE OF BABYLONIA.—Corresponding to the long period covered by the history of Babylonia and Assyria, an exceedingly extensive and varied literature was produced in the Euphrates Valley, a great portion of which is distinctively religious in character, while the parts that cannot be so designated yet contain traces of the influence exerted both by the popular religion and by the theologians who systematized the popular doctrines. In Babylonia, perhaps more than in any other centre of ancient culture, religion was the mainspring of the intellectual activity that was developed. Not only are the religious divisions of the Babylonian literature its oldest constituents, but they represent likewise the most valuable contribution of Babylonia to posterity; and, apart from the value of this literature as a means of penetrating still closer to the core of the Babylono-Assyrian religion, it contains much that is worthy of notice, and some of its productions can be matched in ancient times only by some of the finest writings contained in the Old Testament.

1. To what age the origin of this literature is to be traced is a question that in the present state of our knowledge cannot be answered. While, as already indicated, the bulk of our knowledge of the ancient Babylonian literature—using this word in the stricter sense—is gained from the tablets in the library of Assurbanipal, these represent merely the copies made in the 7th cent. from the originals that existed in the temple archives of the south; and a sufficient number of these originals have now been found to warrant full confidence in the assertion of Assurbanipal, that he actually sent his scribes to the temples in the old religious centres of Babylonia, for the purpose of having copies made. The script in some of these originals, and above all the dating of a number of them, leave no substantial doubt that at the time of Ḫammurabi (*c.* 2250 B.C.) a considerable literature had been produced, and, what is more, such notable productions as the great epic of a hero named Gilgamesh * were already in existence, though perhaps this epic had not yet the form in which it has come down to us in the tablets of Assurbanipal's library. Again, the character of some of the oldest Babylonian inscriptions, and more particularly the diction of the prayers embodied in them, confirm the general impression that the age of Ḫammurabi represents the culmination of the first period of Babylonian literature, which may thus be safely dated beyond 2500 B.C., and probably will be found to extend to a date close to 3000 B.C. Still, it is advisable to bear in mind that we are as yet without sufficient data to speak with any degree of positiveness as to the beginnings or the early phases of Babylonian literature. We do know, however, that this literature, as was to be expected, is largely religious; and if we exclude the historical and votive inscriptions, which can scarcely be called literature, in its beginnings this literature is *entirely* religious. It centres around the ancient temples; and since the priests attached to the temples remained for

eighteen and twenty-five deities respectively; among them some like Gaga, Azag-shud, that occur again only in the religious literature; also the list of twelve and eleven deities respectively in inscriptions of Esarhaddon, dealing with building operations in Babylonia (Meissner-Rost in *Beiträge z. Assyr.* iii. pp. 228 and 260).

* *e.g.* the text just published by T. G. Pinches, *Transactions of the Victoria Institute*, xxvii. (1896) p. 8, which has recently been used by Frdr. Delitzsch as a proof of his thesis that monotheistic beliefs were developed in Babylonia. See Johns' translation of Delitzsch's two lectures, *Babel and Bible* (London, 1903), pp. 75 and 144.

* See, *e.g.*, the fragment of a Deluge narrative (published by Scheil in *Recueil de Travaux relatifs à la Phil. et Arch. Égypt. et Assyr.* xx. pp. 55–59; consult also Meissner, *Ein altbabylonisches Fragment des Gilgamos-Epos* (Berlin, 1902).

all times not only the scribes, but the authors of all literary productions, and the exponents of the entire intellectual life, the literature never lost its association with the religion. Again, we are safe in assuming that this oldest religious literature arose from utilitarian motives, or at all events pursued the practical purpose of providing a suitable ritual, that had stood the test of experience in effectually securing the desired ends. It is therefore to the cult that we must look for the key to an understanding of the Babylonian literature in its largest extent, and particularly in its oldest portions.

2. It is not necessary for the purpose of this sketch to determine how far the old Babylonian religion was based on animistic conceptions, or what other features entered into it, since we are unable to trace it further back than the literary evidence, the very existence of which betokens a comparatively advanced stage of thought — certainly a stage far removed from a primitive state of religion. It is sufficient to recognize that the gods, however the belief in them arose, were approached mainly for two purposes — to secure the fulfilment of certain requests or hopes, and to ward off actual or threatened misfortunes. These purposes cover alike the occasions when the ordinary individual saw fit to approach the god, and those when the rulers sought out the ancient shrines; and, whatever the cause that prompted the approach, the favourable answer was dependent upon a single factor—the disposition of the god or gods invoked. But the gods, though each was all-powerful within the jurisdiction assigned to him or to her, were not supposed to control all occurrences in the life of the individual. Their protection extended only—except when specially appealed to—to a general surveillance of the affairs of the individual. The smaller mishaps and accidents incident to daily life were ascribed to the mischievous influence of a lower order of beings, whom, for want of a better name, we may designate demons or evil spirits. The current views with regard to such beings do not appear at any time to have been very definite, and it is therefore difficult to gather from the religious literature any adequate description of them. The demons were supposed to lurk everywhere. They could make themselves invisible, and indeed they generally acted in so mysterious a manner that their presence was perceived only when the consequences of their activity became manifest. They assumed at times the forms of animals, and the strange movements of serpents—their sudden appearance as though coming up out of the ground, and their gliding away as noiselessly as they came — led to a preference being given to this species of animal life, as the mould in which demons took up their being; but, besides serpents, we also have demons in the shape of birds, and in sculptured representations the demons are sometimes given a human shape with grotesque features or with heads of fantastic animals of terror-inspiring aspect.* At no time was one safe from the attacks of evil spirits, who lurked in the streets, and who could pass through walls, chinks, and crevices into the house. Some were supposed to inhabit groves, others had their hiding-places in fields or in ruins. The tops of the mountains, the rivers and seas, and the wilderness, were alike infested with them. To these demons all manner of evil was ascribed: a fall, a headache, a quarrel, an explosion of temper, were all due to them, as well as the more serious diseases to which mankind is heir; and it was generally believed in these cases that some evil spirit had taken up its abode in the body of the afflicted individual, and was causing the pain or the wasting away from fever or the decay of a diseased organ.

* See, *e.g.*, the illustration in Thompson, *Devils and Evil Spirits of Babylonia* (1903), vol. i. pl. 2.

3. **Incantation rituals.** — Against the demons appeal was made to the gods, and, through the medium of priests acting as exorcizers, an endeavour was made to get rid of their pernicious influence, or to drive them forcibly out of the body. The power thus vested in the hands of the priests lay in the use of the proper words which would serve as a check on the actions of the demons, accompanied by certain symbolical rites, such as ablution and purification, which would complete the work of overpowering the hostile powers. Prayer thus takes its rise in Babylonia as the utterance of certain appeals to the gods; and it is natural to find in the earlier stages of religious thought as much and perhaps more stress laid upon the words so used as on the motive which prompted the direct appeal to the intervention of the gods. To the body of the people the favourable response to the appeal was at all times directly associated with the words employed, and up to a certain stage in the development of the religious beliefs this view was, no doubt, shared by the priests. As a consequence, the greatest possible importance was attached to the use of the proper words or formulas in seeking relief from the baneful spirits; and, when the exorcizing priests failed in their task, the failure was consistently ascribed to the use of a wrong or unfortunate formula that was not applicable to the case in question. There thus arose in the temple service, on the basis of actual experience, fixed formulas varying for different emergencies, the efficiency of which had been tested by a sufficiently large number of instances to warrant complete confidence in them. These formulas, handed down from one generation to another, were given a permanent form so as to ensure their preservation; and it was a further natural step to collect these formulas into a series of greater or shorter extent that could properly be designated as 'incantation rituals.' Quite a number of such series have been found among the tablets of Assurbanipal's library, and the names given to them are themselves indicative of the ideas underlying the collection. Thus we have a series which embraced at least sixteen tablets, each one of which bore a number designating it as a part of a ritual known as 'the Evil Demons.' Another series, consisting of at least nine tablets, was called the 'Head-sickness,'* because a goodly portion of it was devoted to formulas for ridding individuals of various diseases that had their seat in the head, and were due to some demon that had taken up its abode in the human body. Again, two series bear the names 'Maḳlu' and 'Shurpu' respectively, both terms having the sense of 'burning,' and owing their designation to the prominence assigned in them to the burning of effigies of the demons or of the witches who controlled the demons, as a means of getting rid of their baneful influence. Corresponding to the distribution of functions among the gods, the attempt was made to specialize the powers of the demons, though it is doubtful whether this process of differentiation was ever fully carried out. Thus there was a female demon, or rather a class, called *Labartu*, supposed to be specially dangerous to children and their mothers; and we have an incantation series which was known as 'Labartu,'† and which was

* These two series are published in *Cuneif. Texts from Tablets in the British Museum*, parts xvi. and xvii., and interpreted by Thompson, *Devils and Evil Spirits of Babylonia*, vols. i. and ii.

† See Myhrman, *Zeitschrift für Assyriologie*, xvi. pp. 141–200.

entirely taken up with formulas and directions against this special class of evil spirits.

These rituals thus form a distinct division of the religious literature, and we are probably justified in assuming that they represent the oldest division. In regard to their composition—more particularly as to time and place—we are dependent for the present on internal evidence alone, and that often of an unsatisfactory nature. The fact that the god Ea, as the protector of humanity, plays a prominent part in many of the series, taken in connexion with the sanctity that continued from the earliest to the latest days to be attached to Eridu, the seat of Ea worship, points to the temple of Eridu as one of the centres in which incantation rituals were compiled; and, on the other hand, the association of Marduk with Ea, introduced in some of the Ea rituals in a manner which betrays the intention of Marduk's priests to give their favourite a share in the privilege of driving off the evil spirits, is conclusive evidence that the older texts were subject to revision subsequent to the period when Marduk was recognized as standing at the head of the pantheon. Considerations such as these suggest that the rituals were subject to growth and modification. The priests in one religious centre would have no hesitation in embodying in their ritual formulas that had originated and that had been tested in another; but, in doing so, they would be led to introduce such modifications as were required to bring the latter into accord with other portions of the special ritual of the temple in question, and to combine them with formulas of their own. Even a superficial examination of the rituals reveals their composite character; and, upon closer investigation, it is possible to separate in many instances the older from the more recent parts. The mixture of primitive thought with utterances that belong to a much more advanced stage of religious belief is, in fact, a trait that marks all the rituals hitherto brought to light. The conservative instinct led to the retention of what is oldest in these texts, while the impressive hymns and the often strikingly beautiful prayers inserted amidst a jumble of incantation formulas, represent the attempt to give to the old beliefs a more spiritual interpretation.

Before entering upon a description of one of these rituals, which may serve as an example of this division of the religious literature of Babylonia, there is one feature connected with them that yet remains to be considered. Correlative to the belief in the power of the priest to exorcize the evil demons, we find among the Babylonians the belief in the power of certain individuals over the demons, with a view to bringing individuals under their influence; and, as among other nations, this power was more commonly ascribed to women than to men, though we find the belief in sorcerers prevalent as well as the belief in witches. The dividing line between the demons and spirits on the one hand and the witches and sorcerers on the other becomes at times faint; so that it would appear that the latter were also regarded as demons, and not merely as those who had control over them. Still, in general, it is possible to keep the two classes apart, except that, in course of time, the view which supposes the demons to be working at the instigation of the witches and sorcerers rather than independently becomes more marked. In the rituals themselves, however, both phases of the belief in question are found, now the one, now the other being more prominent; and, similarly, in the appeals to the gods, the petitioner sometimes asks relief from those who have bewitched him, as well as from the demons who have independently brought him into their power. Of the two phases, it is more natural to give the preference in point of primitiveness to the independent power of the demons, who, being naturally hostile to man, would feel prompted to make their attack whenever the opportunity offered. The strange and weird impression made by individuals of deformed stature, like dwarfs, or with unusual features, unusually large or unusually small eyes, or otherwise presenting a grotesque appearance, would prompt the conclusion that such persons possessed unusual powers and were capable of working mischief. Evil being associated with demons, it was a logical conclusion that these strange individuals were in league with the demons, or were actually evil spirits that had assumed human shape. Consistency in anything connected with popular beliefs is never to be expected, and hence we find in the rituals a constant vacillation between the attributing of accidents, misfortunes, and disease to the direct activity of witches and sorcerers, and the tracing back of the ills to which human flesh is heir, to the demons acting independently or at the instigation of certain individuals who exercised a direct or indirect control over them. In this respect, therefore, the incantation texts likewise betray their composite character; and, corresponding to the older and later components in the formulas prescribed for the various cases involved, we have the mixture of exorcizing rites aimed at witches and sorcerers, with such as are clearly employed against the demons and evil spirits directly.

The symbolical rites prescribed in connexion with the recital of the formulas, to which we have already referred, similarly presuppose both phases of demonic possession; but some are more applicable to witches and sorcerers than to the demons. Thus a very common practice prescribed in the texts was to make an image of the witch or sorcerer of wax, honey, clay, pitch, or of metal, and to burn such images, while pronouncing the sacred formulas. As the image was thus being consumed, the witch or sorcerer was supposed to suffer the tortures of the fire, and to be gradually annihilated. Instead of burning the image, the plan was sometimes to throw it into the water, or to bury it in the ground; and the symbolical rite being supposed to have an effect on the witch, her evil influence was thus disposed of. Again, one of the favourite means resorted to by a witch in order to secure a hold on her victim was the tying of knots—each fresh knot thus tied, to the accompaniment of a powerful formula, representing symbolically the binding of the unfortunate victim. Hence the exorcizing priest would, by a species of 'sympathetic magic,' endeavour to undo the evil by taking a knotted rope and untying the knots one by one, pronouncing at the same time the counter formulas, and in this way seek to bring about the relief of the sufferer. But images of the demons were also made, and similar ceremonies gone through with them; so that, in connexion with the rites likewise, the dividing line between demons and witches is not always kept in view.

Taking up now a series known as the 'Maḳlu,'* a brief analysis will show the method followed in the grouping of the formulas. It deals almost exclusively with methods for ridding oneself of the influence of witches and sorcerers, and derives its name, 'Burning,' from the prominent part played by the symbolical burning of the images of the witches. The opening incantation is an appeal of a general character to the gods, put into the mouth of the afflicted individual—

> 'Arise, ye great gods, hear my complaint;
> Grant me justice, take cognizance of my condition.

* Published by Tallqvist, *Die Assyrische Beschwörungsserie Maqlû* (Leipzig, 1895).

Not knowing whether the bewitchment is due to a sorcerer or a sorceress, the victim has made an image of each, and then, referring more particularly to the witch, he exclaims—

'May she die! Let me live!'

Cleansing potions concocted of various herbs are drunk by the victim, who hopes in this way to become 'as pure as water,' 'resplendent as fire.' As a specimen of a genuine incantation formula the following may serve—

> 'Earth, earth, earth!
> Gilgamesh* is the master of your witchcraft;
> What ye have done, I know;
> What I do, you know not;
> All the mischief wrought by my sorcerers is destroyed, dissolved—is gone.'

What is here expressed as a fact is intended as a hope to be realized after the accomplishment of the incantation rites. A variety of symbolical rites are then prescribed, such as depositing the image of the witch in a boat placed on the waters, and surrounded by an enclosure so as to prevent her escape; while, in connexion with the burning of the images, hymns, at times most impressive in diction, are addressed to the fire-god Nusku or Girru. The purpose of thus furnishing a variety of rites is to afford a chance to the exorcizer to select the one appropriate to the case with which he is asked to deal. No fewer than ten different kinds of material are prescribed for the making of the images—wax, earth, bronze, honey, clay, pitch, sesame flour, pitch with clay, and two varieties of wood.† For each material a special incantation is prescribed, though the formulas do not differ very materially from one another. The thought, both in the mind of the exorcizer in prescribing and of the victim in carrying out the burning rite, is clearly brought out in the words uttered as the images are consumed—

> 'On this day, arise‡ to my judgment;
> Suppress the mischief, overpower the evil.
> As these images tremble, dissolve, and melt away,
> So may the sorcerer and sorceress tremble, dissolve, and melt away.'

Just as the images of the sorcerer and the sorceress were made to be burnt in certain prescribed cases, so, in others, images of the demons were destroyed in a similar manner. An incantation in connexion with such a rite furnishes the names of the chief classes of demons—

> 'I raise the torch, their images I burn—
> Of the *utukku*, the *shedu*, the *rabisu*, the *ekimmu*,
> The *labartu*, the *labasu*, the *akhkhazu*.
> Of the *lilu*, *lilitu*, and *ardat lili*,
> And of every evil that seizes hold of men.
> Tremble, melt away and disappear!
> May your smoke rise to heaven!
> May Shamash destroy your limbs!
> May the son of Ea,§ the chief exorcizer, restrain your strength!'

Of these demons the two first appear to have been of a general character, both terms conveying the idea of strength. *Rabisu*, signifying 'the one who lies in wait,' is a demon who springs upon his victim unawares; *ekimmu*, also used to describe the 'ghost' of a man, represents the class of demons that infest the graves. *Labartu* is the demon who is particularly dangerous to women and children; of *labasu*, 'the one who throws down,' and *akhkhazu*, 'the seizer,' we only know that they have the power of securing their victims under their control; while *lilu* ('night'), *lilitu* (feminine form of *lilu*), and *ardat lili* ('maid of night') are mischievous spirits who ply their trade at night under cover of darkness.

* The semi-mythical hero whose deeds are celebrated in the Gilgamesh epic, upon which we shall touch later on.
† One of them cedar; the other, called *binu*, has not been identified.
‡ The address is 'to the fire-god.'
§ *i.e.* Marduk.

In regard to all these names, the remark applies that they represent general classes of demons rather than individual spirits, and that (excluding *shedu*) the first six named, moreover, are sometimes used to designate demons in general. Similarly, two other designations that frequently occur in the incantation texts—*alu*, signifying probably 'the strong one,' and *gallu*, 'the great one'—are used, though not always, in a very general way. This indicates that, if at one time a differentiation was attempted, that period was succeeded by one in which the various designations for demons represented, in the case of those most frequently used, merely the different forms of activity represented by the demons, and in the case of others the time and the various ways in which they attack and secure control of their victims.

Somewhat different is the use of the term *shedu*, which is applied both to a hostile demon and to the protecting spirit who stands by man's side and helps him in his endeavour to thwart the attack of the demons, or to rid himself of them. The latter use is the more usual, and in this sense the term is generally associated with *lamassu*, which likewise represents a protecting power. The two, *shedu and lamassu*, were symbolized by fantastic creatures—one with the features of a lion, the other with those of a bull—placed as guardians at the entrances of palace gates and doors. This symbolization, however, which is an outcome probably of the idea of strength connected with the demons, and recalled by the lion and the bull, appears to have belonged to a comparatively late period, for in the days of Ḫammurabi* we still find *lamassu* used to designate the chief protecting deity of a place. It is only, therefore, as the differentiation between god and spirit becomes sharply defined, that *lamassu*—represented ideographically by two signs with the force of 'strong god'—is confined in its application to a protecting and favourably inclined spirit or demon, while the double sense in which *shedu*, also embodying the idea of 'strength,' is used, testifies to the currency of the earlier conception whereby the demons were viewed as either favourable or unfavourable.

Corresponding to the tendency to differentiate gods from spirits, the view seems to have arisen that in general the gods were favourably inclined, or could be made so, by propitiation, appeals, and gifts; whereas the demons, as a rule, were hostile, and could be overcome only with the help of the gods. The *shedu* and *lamassu* were the exceptions, and could therefore be appealed to in the struggle against the hostile forces equally with the gods. Accordingly, we frequently find the hope expressed in the incantations that the bad demons may be driven out of the body, and that the *shedu* and *lamassu* may enter into the head or into the limbs of the unfortunate victim in place of the *utukku*, *gallu*, *alu*, etc., as the case may be.

Continuing our analysis of the 'Maḳlu' series, the third tablet is concerned largely with descriptions of the witches who, possessing the same power as the demons, have the additional quality of being able to select their victims, whereas the demons stumble upon them, as it were, and strike whomsoever they happen to encounter. The witches—and the same applies also to the male sorcerers—appear to have acted not only on their own initiative but when engaged by others to cast their spells on individuals against whom they harboured a grudge for some reason or other. In this connexion it is interesting to note that the laws of Ḫammurabi, in order to safeguard this means of punishing an enemy, provide that, if a spell be unjustly cast upon a man, the one who

* 'Code de Hammourabi' (ed. Scheil), obv. col. iv. 56.

induced the bewitchment shall be put to death.* The descriptions of the witches in the third tablet of the 'Maḳlu' series form an integral part of the incantations. Thus we read at the beginning of this tablet—

'The witch who goes about through the streets,
Enters into houses,
Glides into courts,
Treads the open places,
Turning forwards and backwards,
Plants herself in the streets and retraces her steps,†
Interposes herself on the highway,
Robs the good man of his strength,‡
Robs the good maid of her fruit.§
At her sight, desire seizes him:
She sees the man, and robs him of his strength;
She sees the maid, and robs her of her fruit.
With her witchcraft she barricaded the way;
With her spittle she blocked the road.
The witch saw me, and pursued me.'

But the sorceress is not always visible to her victim. She can work in silence and be unknown; and it would appear, indeed, that the invisible and unknown witch represents the more potent form of bewitchment. Hence the incantation is at times couched in the form of a question—

'Who art thou, witch,
Who carries the word of my misfortune in her heart,
Whose tongue brings about my destruction,
Through whose lips I am poisoned,
In whose footsteps death follows?
O witch, I seize thy mouth, I seize thy tongue,
I seize thy piercing eyes,
I seize thy restless feet,
I seize thy active knees,
I seize thy outstretched hands,
I tie thy hands behind thee.
May Sin‖ give thee a fatal blow!
May he cast thee into an abyss of water and fire!
O witch, like the setting of this seal ring,
May thy face glow and become pale!'¶

The witch has endless means at her disposal for securing control of the selected victim. Her spittle is poisonous, and can torture one on whom it falls or whoever treads on it; the words that she utters have a mystic power; and her eye is deadly, and can spellbind one on whom its glance is thrown. Ever active, moving about on the lookout for her victim, her hands can seize him at any time. Hence the victim, whether already caught, or in danger of falling into the witch's hands, is told to prepare an image of the sorceress, whoever she may be; and, suiting the action to the word, binds fast the mouth, tongue, lips, limbs, and hands of the image, and then casts the helpless figure into the fire; and, not satisfied with this, drowns it in water.

In other incantations in this tablet the witch is pictured as being imprisoned in a pit, and then drowned by having water poured over her; and, again, she is placed on a small ship and given over to the mercy of the elements. In all such cases we are justified in assuming that there was some symbolical act suited to the words, carried out in the hope that the symbol, fortified by the proper formulas, will be converted into a reality.

More common, however, appears to have been the burning of the images; and, in connexion therewith, we encounter a considerable number of addresses appropriately directed to the fire-god, Girru-Nusku, some of which merit the designation of hymns, embodying an imagery and conceptions that appear to transcend the intellectual horizon of belief in the efficacy of sacred formulas. As a specimen—and this is perhaps the finest of this series of addresses—we may choose the one with which the second tablet of the series opens—

'O Nusku, great god, chief of the great gods,
Guardian of the offerings of all the *Igigi*,*
Founder of cities, restorer of sanctuaries;
Brilliant day, whose command is supreme;
Messenger of Anu,† obedient to the decrees of Bel;
Mighty in battle, whose attack is powerful.
Nusku, glowing, overthrower of enemies,
Without thee no sacrificial feast is held in E-kur;‡
Without thee Shamash the judge does not execute
any judgment.'

Fire being an element common to heaven—as shown by the lightning—and to earth, the god Nusku is appropriately figured as the messenger of the god of heaven, and as obedient to the dictates of Bel, who here represents the god of earth. The presence of fire in the sanctuaries, and its use in the sanctification of the sacrifices brought by the worshippers, suggest the references in the second and eighth lines of this hymn, while its power as an indispensable factor in all forms of civilization and its destructive force in war emphasize two other phases of the god's nature. Up to this point we appear to have before us a hymn composed in honour of Nusku that might appropriately have been sung in connexion with a sacrificial ritual in a temple erected in honour of the god in question. The following lines, however, reveal the real purpose of the invocation. The victim, about to burn the images of the evil powers that have brought about his misfortune, is represented as saying—

'I, thy servant *So and So*,§ son of *So and So*,
Whose god is *So and So*,‖ whose goddess is *So and So*,
I turn to thee, I seek thee, I raise my hands, I prostrate
myself before thee:
Burn my sorcerer and my witch;
May the life of my sorcerer and my witch be taken hold
of and destroyed!
Let me live that I may praise thee, and in humility
extol thee.'

The images, as has already been pointed out, were made of various materials, and the second tablet of the 'Maḳlu' series contains no fewer than eight Nusku hymns, introduced as preludes to the formulas prescribed for the burning of the images of the sorcerers and witches. We are to assume, of course, that the officiating priest selects the one appropriate to the occasion and to the material employed for the making of the image, and gives the necessary instructions to the worshipper in regard to the ceremonies to be performed in connexion with the exorcizing rites. But the witch and the sorcerer also have recourse to making images of their proposed victims, and have the power of transferring to the individual the symbolical tortures and miseries that they inflict upon his counterpart. The fourth tablet of the series is largely taken up with a description of the various manipulations to which the witches submit the images as a means of adding to the tortures of those whom the images represent. To symbolize their victims and thus bring about their death, the witches place the images in coffins and bury them, or immure them, or conceal them under the thresholds of houses—both representing primitive modes of burial,—or they are thrown into wells, or placed on bridges where they would be exposed to being trampled upon, and more of the like. As a counter move, the same treatment was prescribed for the images of the witches, to which, likewise, poisonous plants would be symbolically adminis-

* Paragraph 1 of the 'Code de Hammourabi' (ed. Scheil), obv. col. v. 26–32, Johns' translation, *The Oldest Code of Laws in the World*, p. 1.
† *i.e.* moves in all directions, and passes to and fro.
‡ A reference apparently to sexual vigour.
§ *i.e.* prevents conception, or brings about a miscarriage.
‖ *i.e.* the moon-god.
¶ *i.e.* 'May thy face glow with the heat of the fire like the metallic setting of a stone seal cylinder, and then lose its colour—like the heated metal when thrown into the water.'

* A designation for the throng of heavenly deities or spirits.
† The god of heaven.
‡ Name of the temple of Bel in Nippur, which, however, has become a generic designation for a sanctuary, and also for the earth in general.
§ Here the name of the victim is to be inserted.
‖ Here the victim names the special patron god and goddess, whom each individual is supposed to possess. See Jastrow, *Religion Babyloniens und Assyriens*, p. 194 f.

tered in order to counteract the poison that the witches had, in some way, introduced into the bodies of their victims; and the attempt, it would seem, was also made to find the hidden images made of the victims, and thus to release the unfortunate ones from the ills with which they were afflicted. An incantation at the beginning of the fifth tablet, to be used in connexion with such rites, reads—

'The witch and the sorceress—
She sits in the shadow of the wall,
Sits and brings about my bewitchment, makes my images.*
I will send thee *khaltappan* plant and sesame,
To break up thy charm, to make thy words return to thee; †
The bewitchment prepared by thee,—may it be for thee!
The images that thou hast made,—may they represent thee!
The water that thou hast concealed,‡—may it be for thee!
May thy incantation not come nigh, may thy words have no effect!
By command of Ea, Shamash, Marduk, and the great mistress of the gods.' §

This fifth tablet illustrates also the faintness of the demarcation between witch and demon, to which attention has already been directed, ‖ for almost imperceptibly the incantations pass from denunciations of the witches to imprecations hurled against the demons. The last incantation of the tablet, applicable to the demons, furnishes a characteristic example of a direct formula intended to drive the demons out of a man's body—

'Away, away, far away, far away!
For shame, for shame, fly away, fly away!
Round about face, go away, far away!
Out of my body, away!
Out of my body, far away!
Out of my body, for shame!
Out of my body, fly away!
Out of my body, round about face!
Out of my body, go away!
Into my body do not return!
To my body draw not nigh!
To my body do not approach!
Into my body do not force your way!
My body torture not!
By Shamash, the mighty, be forsworn!
By Ea, the lord of everything, be forsworn!
By Marduk, the chief exorcizer of the gods, be forsworn!
From the fire-god, who consumes you, be forsworn!
From my body may you be restrained!'

The sixth tablet of the series is taken up with a series of addresses directed against the witches, and appeals to the fire-god, which furnish some further interesting portrayals of the partly hidden and wholly mischievous workings of the witches, without, however, adding anything of material value to our conception of these beings.

In the seventh tablet we pass from incantations used in connexion with the burning of images and with other treatment accorded to them, to the use of oil and water as means of purification. A reference in one of these incantations to the waters of Eridu, the old city sacred to Ea, at the head of the Persian Gulf, is a valuable indication of the place at which this part of the 'Maḳlu' ritual originated; and in general, when waters of purification are referred to in the incantation texts, the two chief streams of Babylonia—the Euphrates and the Tigris—both of which had a sacred character, are introduced or implied, though the conception of purification has, in the course of time, widened so as to include the efficacy of water in general as a symbol of purification. It will be sufficient to reproduce one of these incantations, which may serve as a specimen of their general character—

'I have washed my hands, cleansed my body,
With the pure waters of a source which arises in Eridu;
Whatever is evil, whatever is not good,
That is lodged in my body, in my flesh, in my limbs,—

* *i.e.* images of me.
† *i.e.* lose their power.
‡ *i.e.* gathered for the purpose of pouring over the image.
§ *i.e.* Nin-makh or Ishtar.
‖ See p. 552a.

The evil arising from bad dreams, omens, and unfavourable portents,
The evil of unfavourable omens for city and country,
. . . . . . . . . . . .
Which I see by day,
Trample on in the street, cast aside,—
The evil *shedu*, the evil *utukku*;
Sickness, Pestilence, Fever,
Distress, Pain, Complaint, Weakness, Groaning,
Woe and Ache, severe bodily affliction,
Terror and extreme Misery, etc. etc.'

—all manner of distress, it is hoped, may be effectually removed by the purifying power of the sacred element.

The addition of such incantations, in which water plays the chief part of the ritual, points to the composite character of the 'Maḳlu' series, which, from dealing exclusively with the burning of images and with appeals to the fire-god, is thus enlarged into a general incantation ritual, to serve as a guide for the exorcizing priest in picking out such portions as are applicable to the case brought before him. Further light is thrown on the principles underlying the combination of incantations into a fixed and elaborate ritual by the eighth and last tablet of the series, which furnishes a summary of all the incantations contained in the previous seven, by repeating their opening words or lines in uninterrupted succession. One is tempted to conjecture that this arrangement, which is also found at the close of another incantation series,* was intended to serve the purposes of an index or table of contents, to enable the officiating functionary of the temple to obtain a rapid survey of the incantations comprised in the ritual, and then to turn to those chosen by him. However this may be, the 'Maḳlu' series, like the various other ones that have been put together from the tablets of Assurbanipal's library,† clearly points to an elaborate process of composition and editing of the hundreds of formulas produced in the course of time for the purpose of relieving those attacked by the demons, or bewitched by the sorcerers and sorceresses.

Besides the incantation series in the proper sense, the priests also compiled for their own use handbooks to serve as guides in the performance of incantation rites, in which specific directions of all kinds are given, detailing the manner in which the images of protecting spirits are to be grouped around the couch on which the man stricken with disease lies, so as to guard him against further harm from the demons; what sacrifices are to be offered in connexion with the recital of the incantations, where they are to be offered, what prayers or formulas should be spoken in connexion with these sacrifices, and more of the like. In the subdivision of priestly functions which followed with the growth of the temples of Babylonia and Assyria, a special class of priests arose, known as the *âshipu*,‡ into whose hands the carrying out of exorcizing rites was entrusted; just as another class, known as the *bârû*, took charge of the omen rituals. Indeed we are justified in concluding from the elaborate character of the incantation texts and the incantation rituals, that, throughout the duration of the Babylono-Assyrian religion, the beliefs upon which

* The 'Labartu' series. See Myhrman, *Zeitschrift für Assyr.* xvi. p. 190 f.
† No fewer than six distinct series are now known, distinguished by the following names:—1. Maḳlu, edited by Knudtzon; 2. Shurpu, 'Burning,' ed. by Zimmern, *Beiträge zur Kenntnis der Babylonischen Religion*, i., Leipzig, 1896; 3. Labartu, ed. by Myhrman, *Ztschr. für Assyr.* xvi. 141–200; 4. Utukku limnuti, 'Evil Demons,' published in *Cuneiform Texts from Babylonian Tablets in the British Museum*, part xvi. with supplements in part xvii., London, 1903; 5. Ti'u, 'Head sickness'; and 6. Ashakku marsu, '*Ashakku* sickness.' The two last named are published in *Cuneiform Texts*, part xvii. The last three are transliterated and translated by Thompson in *Devils and Evil Spirits of Babylonia*, vols. i. and ii. (London, 1903).
‡ Cf. the equivalent Hebrew term *'ashshāp* (Dn 1[20] 2[2]).

the incantations rested, and the ceremonies connected with the incantations, continued to exercise a strong hold on the people, and constituted, in fact, one of the main factors of the religion itself, viewed from the side of religious practice.

4. **Omens and oracles.**—Inseparably linked to the beliefs on which the incantation texts and rituals rest, is a second branch of the religious literature of the Babylonians and Assyrians. While, as we have seen, the view gradually arose which attributed the small ills and minor worries and misfortunes of existence to the mischievous workings of evilly disposed demons, whereas the gods were regarded as, on the whole, favourably inclined, it was the gods with whom the control of the fate of the individual, as of the nation, in the final instance rested. To the gods, therefore, the appeal was made for relief from the sufferings caused by demons or witches; and it was of vital importance, even when the skies seemed serene, to retain the favour and goodwill of the gods, so as to be sure of their assistance when clouds appeared on the horizon. Moreover, the faith in the goodness of the gods was not so strong as to engender a feeling of absolute security in their worshippers. On the contrary, it was felt that their favour could easily be turned into hostility, and their favourable disposition towards man did not prevent them from manifesting their displeasure at any slight provocation. Failure to bring the proper homage, entering upon an important undertaking without assuring oneself of the support of the deity, or without making certain that it was begun at the proper moment, or even choosing the wrong formulas in an incantation ritual,—these and other errors might be fraught with disastrous consequences. Again, even after the incantation rites had been performed, the prayers recited, the sacrifices brought, the symbolical ceremonies carried out, it was necessary to know whether the hoped-for relief would be forthcoming.

To keep the gods favourably disposed, and to determine if possible what help they would grant, were two goals that the worshipper in Babylonia and Assyria was ever compelled to hold before him. Preventive measures were therefore called for, as well as remedial efforts. Punctiliousness in carrying out prescribed rites was an important element in such measures, but by no means the only one; it was equally important to ascertain in some direct way the will of the gods and their future intentions. If happily one could forestall the future, then all fears might be dissipated, and, at all events, one would not be overwhelmed by an unexpected check to one's endeavours. Naturally, the occasions when, through the mediation of the priests, oracles were sought, were chiefly such as concerned the general weal. The individual came in for his share, but that share, judging from the specimens of the oracle literature that have been preserved, was a small one in comparison with the part played by matters of public concern. Most notable among these specimens is a group of prayers addressed to the sun-god,* dating from the reigns of Esarhaddon and Assurbanipal. They have reference to expeditions undertaken against a group of nations to the north-east of Assyria known as the Kashtariti, who at various times, abetted by other tribes and peoples settled in their vicinity, appear to have given the Assyrians considerable trouble. The interesting feature of these prayers is the pattern according to which they are arranged—a pattern which points to the development of a fixed ritual prescribed for such occasions. Each prayer may be subdivided into five parts, consisting (1) of a question or a series of questions addressed to the sun-god; (2) an appeal to the god not to manifest anger, and to forgive errors unwittingly committed in the sacrificial rites that accompany the appeal; (3) a repetition of the question or questions, generally in a somewhat varying form; (4) a second appeal; and, finally, (5) an examination of the omens to be derived from the inspection of the sacrificed animals.

* Published by J. A. Knudtzon, *Assyrische Gebete an den Sonnengott* (Leipzig, 1893).

As in the case of the incantation rituals, the greatest possible care had to be observed in the performance of details. The sacrificial animal—generally a lamb—had to be guarded against all impurities. It must be physically sound, and before passing on to the inspection of the organs—upon the position, proportions, and character of which, together with any possible peculiarities, much depended—the priest was obliged to exercise almost innumerable precautions against interference with a trustworthy interpretation. He had to don the proper dress, guard himself against any kind of impurity; he had to assume the right position in making the inspection, which itself had to proceed in a certain order; he had to speak the proper words, and much more of the like. In the questions that he asks, likewise, all contingencies are to be taken into consideration, and the ritual indicates all the various marks and symptoms that should be sought for in the organs of the sacrificial animal. A few extracts from one of these prayers will serve as an illustration of the general character of these oracles. The priest, who throughout the ritual acts as mediator, addresses the sun-god—

> 'O Shamash, great lord, as I ask thee, do thou in thy mercy answer me.
>
> 'From this day, the 3rd day of this month of Iyyar (the 2nd month), to the 11th day of the month of Ab (the 5th month) of this year, a period of one hundred days and one hundred nights is the prescribed term for the oracular inquiry.'

The request is thus specified—for an oracle that should indicate what is to take place during the coming 100 days. The question itself, always unfolded in a most elaborate manner, concludes in one case as follows:—

> 'The capture of that city Kishassu, through any enemy whatsoever within the specified period—is it definitely ordained by thy great and divine will, O Shamash? Will it actually come to pass?'

The phrases used to prevent any interference with the correct and proper inspection of the animal are generally as follows:—

> 'Prevent anything unclean from defiling the place of inspection. Prevent the lamb of thy divinity which is to be inspected from being imperfect and unfit.
>
> 'Guard him who takes hold of the body of the lamb, who is clothed in the proper sacrificial dress, from having eaten, drunk, or handled anything unclean. Make his hand firm; guard the diviner, thy servant, from speaking a word hastily.'

After the inspection has been made and all the various points noted, the priest prays—

> 'By virtue of this sacrificial lamb, arise and grant true mercy, favourable conditions of the parts of the animal; may a declaration favourable and beneficial be ordained by thy great divinity; grant that this may come to pass! To thy great divinity, O Shamash, great lord, may it be pleasing, and may an oracle be sent as an answer!'

Following the same general model, a large number of questions regarding the outcome of military movements on the part of the Assyrian rulers are propounded through the priest, who, in his capacity as diviner, bears the specific designation of *bârû*.* Subjects of a more personal character, connected with the royal household, are likewise introduced. So in one instance an oracle is sought of Shamash to determine whether Nikâ, the mother of Esarhaddon, will recover from a

* *i.e.* 'the seer,' from *barû*, 'to see.'

sickness from which she is suffering; * and again, before giving his daughter in marriage to a foreigner, Bartatua, the king of Ishkuza,† Esarhaddon inquires whether he is to be trusted, 'whether he will fulfil the promises that he has made, and execute the decrees of the Assyrian king in good faith.' Another interesting illustration is furnished by an inquiry on the occasion when the same king proposes to associate his son with him in the affairs of government ‡—

'O Shamash, great lord, as I ask thee, do thou in good faith answer me. Esarhaddon, the king of Assyria, may his purpose be pleasing and meet with success! Siniddinapal his son, whose name is written on this tablet and placed before thy great divinity, is it pleasing to thy great divinity, that he should enter into the government,§ is it acceptable in thine eyes? Thy great divinity knows it. Is the entry of Siniddinapal the son of Esarhaddon, whose name is written on this tablet by command of thy great divinity, is it ordained and fixed, O Shamash, great lord! Will it actually come to pass?'

In the oracle texts of the class published by Knudtzon the answers to the questions are not given, the purpose of the texts being to furnish and preserve the rituals observed for the occasions referred to, so that these might serve as models for future days, just as these rituals, no doubt, followed models that had been preserved from earlier days, reverting, in all probability, to the usages developed in the temples of Shamash in Babylonia. Other texts, however, furnish the answers. So we have a series of eight oracles delivered to the same Esarhaddon by the goddess Ishtar of Arbela.‖ An interesting feature of these oracles is that, in most cases, the medium of communication is a priestess, which recalls the prominent part played by women as sorceresses in incantation texts. The female soothsayer forms the natural complement to the priestess; it is the attachment to the service of a deity that changes the priestess from a messenger of evil into one who can fathom the Divine intention. But both functions rest on the belief in the mysterious power of women—a belief which is widespread among ancient nations, and survives among people who are still in the primitive stage of culture. A reassuring message given to the king by a priestess Baya, a native of Arbela, and uttered by her in the name of Ishtar and Nebo, reads as follows: ¶—

'Fear not, Esarhaddon, I, the Lord,** speak to thee. The beams of thy heart I strengthen as thy mother who gave thee life. Sixty †† great gods are with me, drawn up to protect thee. The god Sin is on thy right side, Shamash on thy left. Sixty great gods are round about thee, drawn up in battle array in the centre of the citadel. On men do not rely. Lift up thine eyes and look to me. I am Ishtar of Arbela, who has made Ashur gracious to thee. Thy weakness I will change to strength. Fear not! Glorify me! Is not the enemy subdued who has been handed over to thee? I proclaim it aloud. The future I will make glorious, as [I did] the past. I am Nebo, the lord of the writing tablet. Glorify me!'

Of a more definite character is a message sent to Esarhaddon from Ashur, who is, like Nebo and Ishtar, represented as addressing the king directly ‡‡—

'As for those enemies that plot against thee, that force thee to march out, since thou didst open thy mouth [saying], "I implore Ashur!" I have heard thy cry. Out of the great gate of heaven I proclaim it aloud. Surely I will hasten to let fire devour them. Thou shalt stand among them. Before thee I shall appear. Into the mountains I shall bring them to rain down upon them stones of destruction. Thy foes I shall cut down, filling the river with their blood. Let them behold and glorify me, for Ashur the lord of gods am I.'

Accompanying this message are instructions to pour out precious oil, and to offer sacrifices with sweet-smelling incense. The oil and the sacrifices at the delivery of an oracle may properly be regarded as prompted by the desire to retain the favour of the gods, and as a manifestation of grateful homage; but oil and the offering of animals also play an important part in securing the oracle itself. In the series of prayers addressed to the sun-god, of which we have above given a brief account, there are included indications of the features in the animals, the position of the organs, special marks and peculiarities to which the attention of the officiating priests is directed. These indications are of primal significance, for on the results of the inspection the answer to the questions depended. One is probably safe in asserting that no oracle was furnished without the interpretation of omens, so that, even when no reference to omens is expressly made, we may feel certain that it is implied. Indeed the study and interpretation of omens appear to have formed in Babylonia and Assyria the basis of oracular utterances. In the prayers in question the priest is instructed to observe whether there is a slit at the nape of the neck on the left side, whether there is some peculiarity at the bottom of the bladder on the left side, whether the viscera are sound. The size of the limbs and organs of the animal were likewise of importance; and indeed there is no feature of any special character that could be overlooked, before, as a result of the most careful study, the priest was in a position to reveal from the various omens the intention of the gods. A special significance appears to have been attached to the *liver*, due, apparently, to an association of ideas—found among many nations of antiquity—between the liver and the general disposition and character. Among the tablets in the British Museum * there is an interesting diagram of the liver of a sheep, divided off into small sections, with explanatory notes, to serve as a guide for the priests in their inspection.

Not only the omens derived from sacrifices, but the appearance, position, number, and size of the bubbles formed by oil poured into a goblet or bowl of water, constituted a means of determining the will or purpose of the gods. Here was a phase of the 'oracle' ritual that lent itself to an almost more detailed development than even the inspection of sacrificial animals. There were innumerable possibilities to be considered, and we are fortunate in possessing some texts † which furnish the proof of the care expended in taking all imaginable contingencies into consideration. From these texts, which served as handbooks to the *bârû* priests, it appears that, according as the oil bubbles appeared to the left or the right side of the goblet or bowl, separated into smaller bubbles or united into larger ones, it portended good or evil. The size and also the colour of the oil bubbles had a significance, as well as the action of the bubbles after their appearance on the surface. In short, an elaborate science of divination grew up in the course of time in Babylonia and Assyria, which embraced many more elements than the inspection of sacrificial animals, and the action of oil when mixed with water.

Before turning to some of these other phases of

* See the text in Knudtzon, *ib.* No. 101.
† A district to the north-east of Assyria. See Knudtzon, No. 29.
‡ Knudtzon, No. 107.
§ Literally, *bît ridûti*, *i.e.* 'house of government.'
‖ Rawl. iv. pl. 61. See the translations of Banks, *American Journal of Semitic Languages*, xiv. 272 f., which, however, require correction at many points.
¶ Rawlinson, iv. 61; obv. col. ii. 16-39.
** *i.e.* Nebo.
†† The number 'sixty' is chosen as representative of all the gods, so that the phrase is equivalent to 'the entire pantheon.'
‡‡ Strong, *Beiträge z. Assyriologie*, ii. 628.

* *Cuneiform Texts from Babylonian Tablets, etc., in the British Museum*, pt. vi. pl. 1 (Bu. 89-4-28, 238). See Boissier, (*a*) 'Note sur un monument babylonien se rapportant à l'extispicine' (Geneva, 1899); and (*b*) 'Note sur un nouveau document babylonien se rapportant à l'extispicine' (Geneva, 1901).
† *Cuneiform Texts*, etc., pt. iii. pl. 2-4, and pt. v. pl. 4-7. See Hunger, *Becherwahrsagung bei den Babyloniern* (Leipzig, 1903)

the science, it is necessary to point out here the natural extension of oracles and omens from public affairs of the State, and from the semi-public interests of royalty to the affairs of the individual. The fact that, in such a large portion of the oracle and omen literature, the national welfare and conditions affecting the political situation form the subject, must not mislead us into under-estimating the share that the individual had in benefiting from the prerogatives enjoyed by the priests as the mediators between the gods and their worshippers. The preponderance of public affairs over the concerns of the individual which appears in these texts, is due in part to the circumstance that most of them were drawn up at the instigation of the rulers, and in part to the natural desire of the priests to provide, first of all, for proper guides in carrying out the demands made upon them by their royal masters. The example of Assurbanipal in ordering his scribes to provide him with copies of the literary productions of the country, was probably merely a continuation of a much older custom of Babylonian rulers in ordering the rituals required for the various purposes of official exigencies, and for the various occasions of the year, to be perpetuated in writing. Furthermore, the welfare of the country was a natural preliminary condition to the happiness of the individual; for, unless the gods showed a favourable attitude towards the country as a whole, it was not to be assumed that the individual could hope for Divine favour. Next to the attitude of the gods towards the State, their good-will towards the ruler was of primary importance, partly because of the close identification of the career of the ruler with the State, partly because of the continued strength of the belief that the ruler stood nearer to the gods than the ordinary individual, and that upon his conduct and upon the consequent disposition of the gods towards him a large share of the national welfare depended.* Hence even such an event as illness or misfortune in the royal family was of public significance, for it portended, or at all events might portend, that some deity was angry with the ruler himself, and had thus manifested his displeasure. The ordinary individual could hardly hope for consideration in approaching a deity who had plainly shown his ill-humour towards the most important personage in the land.

But such conditions represented, after all, the exceptional state of affairs. Unless the country was engaged in warfare, or unless some accident had befallen a member of the royal family, the supposition was that the gods were inclined to listen to petitions or to assist the individual in his appeals for help or advice; at all events, it was safe to make the attempt to approach the Divine throne through the mediation of the priests. Again, if some god had shown his anger by punishing an individual with sickness or by overwhelming him with disaster, it was perfectly reasonable to make the attempt to regain his goodwill, 'to set the deity's heart at rest,' as the religious phraseology expressed it.

The extension of the order of ideas which enabled the priests to ascertain the intention of the gods when affairs of State or of the royal household were in question, resulted in the preparation of more or less elaborate handbooks covering the interpretation of all unusual phenomena, whether occurring in the heavens or on earth. Eclipses, disturbances in the usual order of natural events, the movements of the moon and sun, as well as of the planets and stars, and the appearance of the clouds, represent some of the main incidents to which the attention of the priests was directed for the purpose of determining their bearing on the general welfare, as well as on the fate of individuals. Coming to such terrestrial phenomena as enter more particularly into the life of the individual, we find that dreams, for instance, or unusual signs in the case of newborn children,—abnormally large or abnormally small features, monstrosities of all kinds,—were regarded as revealing the intentions of the deities, or were looked upon as portents of future events. The movements of certain animals,—more particularly of dogs,—the flight of birds, the appearance of snakes or of certain insects in the highways or in houses, as well as monstrosities among animals, were fraught with meaning, and, in general, it may be said that every incident that had any unusual feature connected with it called for an interpretation. In this way the omen literature representing the record of past experience, and embodying the wisdom of the past in the interpretation of signs of all kinds, assumed in the course of time enormous dimensions—so large that it is quite difficult to obtain an accurate survey of the field covered by the omen texts. For the purposes of this sketch, however, it will be sufficient to characterize briefly some of the chief classes of this branch of the religious literature of Babylonia and Assyria.

Taking as our first illustration *unusual occurrences in the movements of the heavenly bodies*, it is natural to find special significance attached to *eclipses* of the sun and moon; and it is also obvious that such occasions were interpreted as having a bearing chiefly on public affairs or on the fate of the royal household, because of the close relations between the gods and earthly rulers—their representatives, in a measure—to which reference has already been made. Calendars were drawn up with indications of what the obscuring of the sun or moon, through eclipses or through the movements of clouds, on any particular day of the month portended. Arranged in the order of the months, the days of the month are entered on which, according to past experience, eclipses occurred, and also those on which, according to calculation, they might occur, and then the interpretation is set forth for each of the days enumerated. Interchanging with the references to actual eclipses, a record is also made of what the concealment of the sun behind clouds on certain days portended. Selecting from a long text of this nature, covering many tablets, the section devoted to the month of Tishri, the 7th month, we find the following entries* recorded :—

'If on the 1st day of the month of Tishri the sun is obscured, king against king will declare war.
If on the 9th day, Adad † will raise his cry.
If on the 11th day, a disaster will occur, the king of Mar dies.
If on the 13th day, the king of Akkad ‡ dies, and, in the case of an eclipse, [the same fate] is portended for the king of Akkad.
If on the 14th day there is an eclipse of the sun, there will be destructive rains, and the king of Amurru dies.
If on the 15th day, the wealth of the sea perishes.§
If on the 16th day, there will be food in plenty in the land, the canals will be full, or [it portends that] the *abkallu* will burst forth.‖
If on the 18th day, then will be peace for the king; Bel in the country [will proclaim ?] an oracle regarding the land of the enemy.
If on the 20th day, the country will be diminished, the throne o Elam will be overthrown.

* On the position of the king as standing closer to the gods, and as originally viewed as the representative or even incarnation of a deity, see Frazer, *The Golden Bough*[2], i. 142 ff., 232, etc.

* Craig, *Astrological-Astronomical Texts*, pl. 25, obv. 1–17.

† Adad is the god of storms. The phrase is therefore to be taken as an indication that storms will sweep the land.

‡ *i.e.* Babylonia.

§ An expression which apparently refers to the destruction of animal life in the waters.

‖ *Abkallu* is a title of a high officer. The sense of this prediction is obscure.

If on the 21st day, the obscuration portends destruction to the country.
If on the 28th day, Bel will cause destruction; the king of that land during that year will overrun the country or [it portends that] the king will be safe.
If on the 29th day, in that year the king will die, the country will suffer misfortune. . . .
If on the 30th day, the king will have a long reign . . . there will be food in plenty in the land.
If from the 1st to the 30th day the sun is obscured, the gods will overwhelm the whole country [with disaster].
If the day is dark, but the planets Dilbar * and Dapinu † are seen together, city, king, and people will be safe, canals will be full of water.
If, contrary to calculation, the sun is obscured, the king will be in distress . . .
If in the month of Tishri the sun is obscured, the king dies, the country will witness disaster or [it portends] joy.'

Obscure as some of the predictions are—due in part to the defective nature of the text—their general character is quite clear. The references to specific personages like the king of Amurru, of Elam, of Akkad, may be taken as indications that at some time or another the death of a ruler in one of these countries took place on the day in question, or that some disaster overtook him. This occurrence would then naturally be made the basis for determining the inauspicious character of the day. We are not therefore to suppose that the death of a particular ruler of the countries named is intended to be predicted; but, from the circumstance that a ruler died on that day in the past, the obscuration of the sun on such a day portends a misfortune for the country, or possibly for the ruler in question. Bearing in mind that these omen calendars are intended to serve as guides for the priests, one can also understand the contradictory notes recorded for one and the same day. Such statements must obviously be interpreted as embodying observations of various events that at some time in the past took place.

It is, accordingly, for the officiating priest to determine by additional resources—such, *e.g.*, as the inspection of sacrificial animals, or an oil and water test, or the like—whether the favourable or unfavourable omen is to be depended upon. That, in general, the disappearance of the sun owing to heavy clouds, or an actual eclipse, portends some evil, is a conclusion suggested by the natural association of ideas between darkness and misfortune. Hence, at the close of the preceding and of the following omens dealing with the other months, it is stated as a general conclusion that an obscuration of the sun portends evil to the king, being a prediction of his death, and also indicating disaster to the country. But the text adds the possible alternative that on certain days and under certain conditions the phenomenon indicates 'joy'—*i.e.* is to be regarded as a favourable omen. Here, again, when the indications for such days, based on past experience, are either favourable or unfavourable, it lies with the priest to determine by other means at his disposal which of the alternatives will be likely to occur.

The omens derived from the second great heavenly body—the moon—were in some respects of even greater importance, because of the more definite character of its movements; or, as we ought perhaps to put it, because of the greater ease with which these movements could be followed. Completing its course as it does in 29 or 30 days, the most obvious point to which the attention of observers would be directed would be the appearance of the new moon as the period marking the beginning of a new course. In the second place, note would be taken on what day—whether 12th, 13th, 14th, 15th, or 16th day—the *sun* was to be seen together with the *moon*; for upon this phenomenon, as was ascertained by experience, depended the day at the end of the month when the moon and the sun would again be in conjunction. Again, the varying appearance of the moon's horns, the character of the halo around the moon, and naturally such more extraordinary occurrences as the lunar eclipse, would serve as a basis for lunar omenology. Our knowledge of these omens is derived chiefly from reports from court astrologers to their royal masters.* These reports are at times brief, consisting of only a few lines, as, *e.g.*, the following connected with the appearance of the new moon on the 1st day of the calculated lunar month—that is, when the preceding month had its full 30 days †—

'If the moon is seen on the 1st day, [it portends that] the country will be favoured with tranquillity.‡ If the day according to its calculation is long, it portends a reign of long days.' [Report from Bullutu].

The same omen is furnished in the reports of quite a number of other astrologers that have been preserved to us, but in some cases further specifications are given. So in one report there is added that in the case of the months Nisan and Tishri—the 1st and 7th months—if the moon is full at the regular time, there will be good crops, and the king will be supreme.§ Somewhat different is a report from an astrologer Nebo-shum-ishkun, who announces ‖—

'If the moon appears covered with a headband,¶ the king will be supreme. If the moon is seen on the first day, the day being, in accordance with calculation, long, it portends a long rule. The month will have 30 days in full. If the moon appears on the first day, it is favourable to Akkad (*i.e.* Babylonia), unfavourable for Elam or Amurru. If this happens in the month of Ab, then for Akkad it portends something favourable to the king, my lord.'

Coming to reports that furnish omens according to the day on which the moon and sun are seen together, the following may serve as a specimen:**—

'If the moon appears out of season,†† traffic will be small; on the 12th day the moon was seen with the sun. If, contrary to calculation, the moon and sun are seen together, a powerful enemy will come to the land. The king of Akkad will defeat his enemy. On the 12th day the moon with the sun was seen. If the moon is seen on the 12th day, it portends evil for Akkad, good for Elam and Amurru, but is an unfavourable omen for Akkad.'

Comparing these two classes of reports, the guiding principle in both is apparent. A full month of 30 days suggests by association of ideas—fulness, plenty, and general success, while a premature conjunction of the sun with the moon, indicative of a curtailment of the moon's course, as against the calculated lunar month, portends shortness of crops, diminution of traffic, and loss of dominion. In accordance with this, the appearance of the moon and sun together on the 13th and on the 16th day of the month portends unfavourable events, while on the 14th and 15th days the indications, varying somewhat according to the months, are, on the whole, favourable. That the various reports do not always agree, and that even in one and the same report alternatives are offered, or an intentional ambiguity appears, are features that point to differences in the methods adopted by the astrologers, or to the natural differences in experience which enter so largely into the judgment of the foretellers of events. An evidence of the high antiquity of the custom of deriving

* Venus or Ishtar.

† Jupiter or Marduk.

* A large collection of these reports has been published and interpreted by R. C. Thompson in *The Reports of the Magicians and Astrologers of Nineveh and Babylon* (2 vols., London, 1900).

† Thompson, No. 1.

‡ Lit. 'closing of month'—*i.e.* silence, as Thompson renders the phrase; but it is to be understood in the sense of absence of disturbances, external or internal.

§ *asharidutu illak*, 'will proceed to supremacy'—apparently an idiomatic expression, to indicate that he will be successful in his endeavours. See Thompson, No. 9.

‖ Thompson, No. 17.

¶ *Agu*—also used to indicate the full moon, but here intended to designate some shadow on the moon.

** Thompson, No. 119.

†† At an unexpected time, or contrary to calculations.

omens from lunar phenomena is to be seen in the persistent use of the geographical terms so constantly recurring in the texts. Akkad is retained as the old designation of Babylonia; Amurru, later the designation of Northern Syria, is used, as in very ancient historical texts, for the West in general; while Elam, in a similar manner, is applied to the East in general. These same geographical designations occur in connexion with those most significant of all heavenly phenomena—the eclipses of the moon and sun; and it may be regarded as a noteworthy indication of the advance made in the interpretation of such phenomena, that under certain circumstances an eclipse which must have been startling to primitive nations, as a necessary omen of evil, might portend peace and prosperity. In a report from an astrologer,* the various sections of the moon are made to correspond to the chief districts—the right side being Akkad or Babylonia, the left Elam, the top Amurru, and the bottom Subartu; and according to the direction in which the shadow passes off from the moon is the eclipse to be interpreted. The moon drawing off from the shadow in a south-westerly direction portends evil for Elam and Amurru, while, if the eastern and northern parts are not affected by the eclipse but remain bright—the eclipse being therefore a partial one—it is a good sign for Subartu † and Akkad. In another report ‡ we encounter the following more specific indications:—

'When an eclipse happens during the morning watch § and is complete (?), it portends corpses,‖ and the ruler will also die. When an eclipse takes place in the morning watch and lasts through that watch, and a north wind comes, the sick in Akkad will recover. When an eclipse begins in the first section and remains in the second (*i.e.* is partial), it portends disaster for Elam. Guti ¶ will not approach Akkad. If the eclipse begins at the first section and the second remains bright (*i.e.* even more partial), it portends that disaster will overtake Elam but not reach Akkad. If the eclipse takes place and stands on the second side, it portends mercy to the country. If the moon is obscured in the month of Siwan,** Adad will inundate (the land) at the end of the year; if there is an eclipse in the month of Siwan, there will be a flood, and the product of the waters will be carried to the land.†† If an eclipse happens at the morning watch during the month of Siwan, it portends disaster to the temples of the land, and Shamash will be hostile.‡‡ If an eclipse takes place in Siwan on the 14th day, the king will complete the year and then die, and his son will strive for the rulership and seize the throne, and there will be hostility and corpses. If an eclipse happens in Siwan at any time from the 1st to the 30th day, it is an eclipse that portends something to the king of Akkad. There will be a general flood, and Adad will inundate the product of the land, and disaster will overtake a large army. . . . If an eclipse happens in Siwan out of the calculated time, the king of legions will die, and Adad will inundate; a flood will come, Adad will diminish the product of the land, and the leader of the army will encounter disaster.'

In general, as will be seen, the eclipse, by a natural association of ideas, reinforced by the survival of the primitive sense of terror at the startling phenomenon of the moon passing into a shadow, was generally regarded as an evil omen, and it was merely a question which quarter of the world was to be affected. The frequency of inundations in a land like the Euphrates Valley made it safe to hazard a prediction of an overflow of the Tigris and Euphrates; and a single coincidence of an eclipse in the spring, with particularly heavy floods during the rainy season, would be sufficient to establish in the minds of the people a connexion between the two events. Indeed, so unusual an occurrence as an eclipse would necessarily prompt a closer attention to events—such as poor crops, or the death of a king, or even a military expedition with its inevitable result of greater or lesser loss of life—that at other times would be taken for granted as perfectly normal occurrences, or, if not normal, at least not of an extraordinary character.

The principles underlying the omens derived from other conditions observed in connexion with the moon are of the same general character—natural association of ideas and conclusions drawn from past events coincident with the conditions in question. Thus, in an interesting series of reports regarding the significance of a halo around the moon, a favourable or unfavourable interpretation depends upon the character of the halo, whether bright or dark—the latter being regarded in general as an indication of rain—or whether the halo was continuous or interrupted, and what planets or stars were to be seen within the halo. One of these reports,* which begins with the omen to be derived from the conjunction of the moon and sun on the 16th day, passes on to halo omens, and furnishes the following data:—

'If the moon has a halo, and the sun † stands within the halo of the moon, throughout the land one will speak justice, the father with his son will speak justice, the hosts will be successful. If the moon has a halo, and Mars stands within it, there will be destruction of cattle throughout the land, the planting of dates will not prosper, or it portends that Amurru will be diminished. If the moon has a halo, and two stars stand within the moon's halo, it portends a long rule. If Mars and a planet stand facing each other [within it], it portends an attack on Elam. If Mars passes out (?) of the halo, the king of Elam will die.'

It thus appears that Mars, which bears a name (*Mushtabarru mutânu*, *i.e.* 'portending death') that suggests ill-luck, is an unfavourable planet, whereas the 'sun' planet, Saturn, carries with it associations of good fortune and prosperity. The presence of Mars with another planet suggests a conflict; while Mars leaving the halo, again by a natural association of ideas transfers the ill-omen to Elam, the hated rival of Babylonia. Likewise, from omens derived from observation of the movements of the planets, we learn that this distinction between favourable and unfavourable planets is maintained, though there are circumstances under which a favourable planet like Marduk-Jupiter may become a portender of evil, while Nergal-Mars may under certain conditions change his forbidding aspect to one of good fortune. Thus, when Marduk-Jupiter appears at the beginning of the year, it portends a good crop of corn; ‡ whereas, if the moon casts his shadow on Marduk,§ it means that a king will die in that year, or that an eclipse of the sun or moon will take place, and a 'great king' ‖ will die; and, again, it is interesting to observe the combination of favourable with unfavourable omens in the approach of a planet like Jupiter towards Mars, or in their position towards each other. We learn ¶ that when Marduk stands in front of Nergal there will be prosperous crops, but also that it portends a slaughter of men. The approach of Nergal to Marduk means devastation, death among cattle, or that the king of Akkad will die in that year; but at the same time it indicates plentiful crops. The evil suggested by Nergal is therefore compensated in a measure by the favourable indications associated under

* Thompson, No. 268.
† Here used apparently for Assyria.
‡ Thompson, No. 271.
§ The night and day were ordinarily divided into three watches of four hours each. See Delitzsch, *Zeitschr. für Assyr.* vol. iv. pp. 284–287.
‖ *i.e.* many will die.
¶ A country to the north-east of Babylonia. The omen means that Babylonia need not fear an attack from this region.
** The third month.
†† *i.e.* the country will be so deeply inundated that the fish will swim about in all directions.
‡‡ *i.e.* there will be failure of crops.

* Thompson, No. 99. See the general remarks on the halo of the moon, in the Introduction, vol. ii. pp. xxiv–xxvi.
† By sun is here meant the 'sun star' or the planet Saturn, as the text, No. 176, rev. 3–4, specifically states.
‡ Thompson, No. 184 § *Ib.* No. 192.
‖ The 'great king' in these reports means apparently the king of Babylonia, or perhaps also Assyria; whereas 'a king' means a ruler of some smaller country.
¶ Thompson, No. 195.

most circumstances with Marduk. Again, though the omens connected with Nergal-Mars are on the whole unfavourable, there are notable exceptions; as, *e.g.*, when a report* tells us that if Mars is visible in the month of Elul—the 6th month—the crops of the land will be plentiful, and everything in the land will be prosperous; but, on the other hand, if Nergal approaches the moon, the god Sin will cause evil to descend upon the land;† and in this report the 'unlucky' character associated with Mars compensates the generally favourable nature of the portents in the case of other stars being seen near the moon. After this omen with reference to Nergal and Sin, the report continues—

'If any [other] planet stands on the left horn of the moon, the king will be powerful; or if a star appears in front of the moon on the left side, the king will also be powerful. If a star stands behind the moon on the left side, the king of Akkad will be powerful. If the star Dilgan (*i.e.* Virgo) stands at the left horn, the crops in Akkad will be plentiful; or if Dilgan stands above the moon, the crops will be plentiful.'

The report continues in this way with a further series of omens derived from stars appearing on the left side, which, while portending evil because of the association between 'left' and 'unlucky,' yet are in so far favourable as the evil—loss of territory, or floods—is predicted for an enemy and his land, and not for the king of Assyria, to whom the report is furnished.

Wind and thunderstorms as well as earthquakes are included within the scope of the natural phenomena on which the astrologers of Babylonia and Assyria render reports to their royal masters. In regard to both wind and thunderstorms, the season of the year is naturally the prime factor in the decision whether the omen is to be interpreted as favourable or unfavourable. The storms and rains forming in a land like Mesopotamia a natural season, upon which the fertility of the soil is dependent, are, in fact, under ordinary circumstances regarded as signs of the favour of the gods; and we may well suppose that the Babylonians, like the ancient Hebrews, included in their ritual, at the approach of the rainy season, prayers that the gods might send the rains and also the storms—since the former never came without the latter—over the land. In accordance with this view, a storm is ordinarily an omen of prosperity; and it is only when the excessive severity of the rains causes a flood, or when the rain comes at the wrong time—in the spring instead of in the autumn and winter—that the omen is naturally unfavourable. A report from Asharidu, the servant of the king, reads ‡—

'If a rainstorm comes over the land, crops will flourish, prices will be steady. If a rainstorm continues in the land, there will be an increase of royal power. If a rainstorm bursts forth in Shebet,§ there will be a Kassite eclipse.‖

A storm still later in the season, in Adar ¶ (12th month), when the rains ordinarily have ceased, portends blighted crops; and as with rainstorms, so, up to a certain point in regard to thunderstorms, the season of the year determines whether the omen is to be regarded as favourable or unfavourable. But apparently a new factor enters into consideration here, for the voice of the god Adad himself is heard in the thunder; and it is this voice that the astrologers are called upon to interpret. In consequence, as the priests were guided necessarily by observation of events that in the past had followed upon the sound of thunder at a particular season of the year or time of the

* Thompson, No. 233. † *Ib.* No. 234. ‡ *Ib.* No. 250.
§ *i.e.* the 11th month, towards the spring, when the severe storms ought to be over.
‖ An eclipse portending some evil for the country north-east of Babylonia.
¶ *e.g.* Thompson, No. 252.



day, the reports manifest a greater degree of inconsistency than in the interpretation of omens from rainstorms, where normal conditions constituted a firm basis for calculations. Thus, in the case of several reports dealing with omens in regard to thunder in the month of Ab—the 5th month—one * informs us that the crops will be plentiful, while another † declares that the omen portends evil. A distinction is made between thunder accompanied by rain and thunder in a cloudless sky. The report says ‡—

'If Adad sends forth his voice in the month of Ab, on a dark day, with rain and lightning, waters will be poured forth in the canals. If on a cloudless day Adad roars, there will be distress or famine in the land.'

Or again §—

'If it lightens on a cloudless day, Adad will cause a flood.'

The association between a thunderstorm and a rainstorm out of season suggests the portent that ‖—

'If, in Tishri,¶ Adad sends forth his voice, there will be hostility in the land. If it rains in the month of Tishri, there will be disaster to the sick and to cattle, and disaster to the enemy.'

An earthquake naturally always portends some disaster, and the omens derived from this phenomenon appear in general to have reference to a national calamity. The trembling of the earth suggests invasion and ruin. We are told **—

'If the earth quakes all day, it portends destruction of the land; if it quakes continually, (?) there will be an invasion of the land.'

And again ††—

'If in the month of Tishri the earth quakes, the country will rebel against the king; if the earth quakes during the night, the land will incur disaster or devastation.'

At the same time the evil omen is at times compensated by the assurance that the misfortune will not affect the crops, for we are told ††—

'If the earth quakes in Tishri, the crops will be plentiful, though it portends hostility in the land.'

We have seen that in the case of various phenomena of the heavens and of nature, which form the basis of the official reports of the astrologers, the omens deal chiefly with three subjects—war, crops, and internal disturbances in the country—while the affairs of the individual play no part whatsoever. But besides these phenomena there is an almost infinite number of occurrences in the life of mankind that by their more or less unusual character call for an explanation; and in the explanation offered the individual is involved, even if not exclusively so. Monstrosities among human beings and animals, peculiar actions of animals, extraordinary occurrences in one's life, or even ordinary ones, like dreams, constitute some of the phenomena, to the study of which the priests were likewise obliged to devote themselves in order to answer inquiries as to their meaning. In the interpretations offered we may observe again the application of practically the same principles which guided the astrologers in their reports as to the meaning of phenomena in the heavens—association of ideas, and conclusions derived from observation and experience. For purposes of illustration, it will be sufficient to give some examples from what we may call birth portents, of which the tablets furnish a very large number.‡‡ In this division, even so common an occurrence as the birth of twins, merely because it deviates from

* Thompson, No. 256*d*. † *Ib.* No. 257.
‡ *Ib.* No. 257, lines 1–5. § *Ib.* No. 256*d*.
‖ *Ib.* No. 260. ¶ The 7th month.
** Thompson, No. 263*d*. †† *Ib.* No. 265*c*.
‡‡ See Bezold's Catalogue, etc., vol. v. Index, *sub* 'Omens,' p. 2181.

normal conditions, is subjected to an interpretation, and we are told *—

'If a woman gives birth to twins, one male and the other female, it is an unfavourable omen. The land is in favour, but the house † will be reduced.'

Here we have an example of a purely individual portent; but it is noticeable that the moment any unusual signs are observed in the case of the twins, they are interpreted as having a bearing on public affairs, though at times the family in which the occurrence has taken place is also involved. In accordance with this principle we are told that—

'If a woman gives birth to twins and both are brought forth alive, but neither of them have right hands, the produce of the land will be consumed by the enemy. . . . If a woman gives birth to twins and both are brought forth alive, but the right foot of one is missing, an enemy will for one year cause disturbances in the country.'

A monstrosity as such, however, does not portend evil, and distinctions are drawn, again based largely on association of ideas.

Thus, in the case of newborn babes with heads that suggest the features of certain animals, a lion's or a swine's head represents favourable omens, while a dog's or a bird's or a serpent's head portends some disaster to the country ‡—

'If a woman gives birth to a child with a lion's head,§ a powerful king will rule in the land. If a woman gives birth to a child with a dog's head, the city (where the child is born) will be in distress, and evil will be in the country. If a woman gives birth to a child with a swine's head, offspring and wealth will increase in that house. If a woman gives birth to a child with a bird's head, the land will be destroyed. If a woman gives birth to a child with a serpent's head, there will be famine in the land.'

The monstrosities taken up in this same series of tablets include such phenomena as a babe with two heads, or two mouths, or a double pair of eyes, or with misplaced eyes, or peculiarly shaped ears, or with an organ or a limb missing, and much more of the like. If among human beings monstrosities have a bearing on the public and general weal, it is natural to find this principle adopted in the case of monstrosities occurring among animals. The anomalies introduced are almost endless. Among the examples we find the following: ‖—

'If five young ones are born in the flock, one with a bull's head, one with a lion's head, one with a dog's head, one with a sheep's head, one with a swine's head, there will be a series of devastations in the land.

If in the flock young ones are born with five legs, it is a sign of distress for the country. The house of the man will perish, and his stalls will be swept away. If the young ones have six legs, the population will decrease, and devastation come over the land. . . . If the young one has its ears at its neck, the ruler will be without judgment.¶ If a young one has its ears below the neck, the strength of the land will be weakened. If the young one has no right ear, the rule of the king will come to an end, his palace will be uprooted, and the population of the city will be swept away; the king will be devoid of judgment, the produce of the country will be small, the enemy will cut off the supply of water. If the young one has no left ear, the deity will hear the king's prayer, the king will capture his enemy's land, and the enemy's palace will be destroyed. The enemy will be deprived of judgment, the produce of the enemy's land will be taken away, and everything will be captured. If the right ear of the young one falls off, the stall ** will be destroyed. If the left ear of the young one falls off, the stall will be increased, the stall of the enemy will be destroyed.'

In this enumeration it will be observed that a defect in regard to a 'right' limb or organ portends evil to the owner or the country, or both, while the defect in a 'left' limb or organ is an omen of disaster to the enemy, but not to the owner or his country—a reversal, though a perfectly logical one, of the usual association of ideas with reference to 'right' and 'left.' It is because 'right' is generally a good omen that the absence of a 'right' ear portends evil, whereas a defect in regard to a 'left' ear represents a bad sign for the 'other party.' The specific character of the omens may be taken as evidence that the tablets were drawn up on the basis of answers given in the past to inquiries made at a time when the monstrosities, or the unusual phenomena in question, actually occurred; though it also seems likely that these actual answers were supplemented by indications, furnished in accordance with the principle underlying the science of omen interpretation, in order to cover future and possible contingencies. The tablets themselves thus assume, in contradistinction to the astrological reports above discussed, the character of handbooks, and therefore resemble the incantation texts and rituals. Each large temple would be supplied with such a handbook, and it would be the natural endeavour of the priests of each generation to make additions to it, so as to be in a position to answer readily any question that might be put. As there were special omen collections for oxen, sheep, swine, colts, birds, insects, and the like, one can readily see how, in this way, the collections would in the course of time assume exceedingly large dimensions.*

It will also be clear that such collections could never be absolutely complete. Cases would arise not thought of or not provided for, and it would then devolve upon the priests to work out new decisions that might be depended upon as trustworthy. Besides monstrosities among animals, the actions of certain animals—dogs, oxen, ravens, and certain insects, etc.—were invested with significance; and the task of the priests would be increased by the endeavour to explain what it meant if one encountered a yellow, white, black, or speckled dog on the street; or if a dog entered a palace or temple or an ordinary house; or if a raven flew into a man's house; and even so trivial an occurrence as the dropping of a bit of meat into a man's house by a raven was regarded as fraught with some meaning. A tablet informs us that †—

'If a yellow dog enters a palace, it is a sign of an ominous fate for the palace. If a speckled dog enters the palace, the palace will secure peace from the enemy. If a dog enters the palace and some one kills him, the peace of the palace will be disturbed. If a dog enters a palace and crouches on a couch, no one will live in that palace in peace. If a dog enters a palace and crouches on the throne, the palace will encounter an ominous fate. If a dog enters a palace and lies on a bowl, the palace will secure peace from the enemy.'

As with dogs, so the appearance of locusts in a house was regarded as an omen of ill-luck; but here, again, distinctions were drawn according to the colour of the locusts, whether black, yellow, white, brown, or speckled. In short, these handbooks of omen interpretation endeavoured, though of course in vain, to cover all possible occurrences that in any way might arouse the attention of those who were directly or indirectly involved; and the task of the priests, constantly consulted as to the meaning of the purely trivial incidents which form a large proportion of the cases introduced, was no easy one. On the other hand, it was precisely their supposed power of being able to interpret 'signs,' and thus to aid the inquirers in preparing for the event prognosticated, and perhaps to forestall it, that enabled the priests to retain a firm hold on the people. It was of the utmost importance, therefore, for the priests to cultivate the science of omen interpretation, as representing, with the endeavour to free the subjects of the gods from ills and troubles, the practical side of

* Boissier, *Documents Assyriens relatifs aux présages*, p. 110 f.

† Wherein the child is born.

‡ Boissier, p. 11.

§ *i.e.* like a lion. The preposition 'like' is sometimes added, though generally omitted.

‖ Boissier, pp. 132, 143 f., 169, etc.

¶ Will become insane (?).

** *i.e.* the herd.

* The most complete collection as yet published, from which the above examples are taken, is that of Boissier, *Documents Assyriens relatifs aux présages*, Paris, 1894.

† Boissier, p. 104.

the prevailing religion; just as the doctrines represented the theoretical phase, and the cult the natural outcome of the desire to do homage to the gods, in order to retain the goodwill of the powers in whose hands the welfare of the country, the success of the rulers, and the fate of the individual lay. The large space occupied by the omen texts in the religious literature that was produced in Babylonia and Assyria, is a valuable testimony to the strength and persistence of the belief that the intention of the gods was revealed in the movements of the sun, moon, and planets, and the phenomena of heaven in general, or in the unusual happenings in nature, and in abnormal events among men and animals, as well as in all manner of incidents arousing special attention or calling for comment of whatever kind.

Before leaving this large subject, the importance of which for an understanding of the religion of Babylonia and Assyria justifies the rather elaborate treatment accorded to it here, it is necessary to consider briefly one more of its phases, which, because of its direct bearing on the fate of the individual, is of considerable importance. The mystery of *sleep*, with its most characteristic manifestation, the *dream*, profoundly impressed people in a primitive stage of culture, and continued to do so long after they had cast aside many of the beliefs belonging to the first attempts at the development of civilization. One could control, at least in large measure, one's thoughts and fancies while awake, but what one saw and heard while asleep appeared to be manifestations directly brought to one's attention through outside forces. The gods, who showed their power in storms and earthquakes, who made themselves heard in thunder, and who spoke indirectly to men by signs written in the heavens, gave a direct message in the dreams that they sent to those lying in the embrace of sleep. Every dream represented such a direct message; and, whether we turn to early Babylonian rulers like Gudea (*c.* 3000 B.C.), who receives instructions through a dream to build the temple E-ninnu to his favourite god Ninib,* or to a late Assyrian king like Assurbanipal, who is encouraged to go forth to battle by a vision at night of Ishtar clothed in battle array,† we find throughout the duration of the Babylonian-Assyrian religion the same profound significance attached to dreams.

Hence, in addition to the moon, sun, planet, and star portents, and handbooks for guidance in interpreting 'birth' and 'animal' portents, manuals were prepared that might serve the priests in interpreting for anxious inquirers the meaning of the visions that they saw during the hours of sleep. While here, again, the endeavour might be made to provide for all contingencies, the task would be even more hopeless than in the case of handbooks for 'birth' portents, and the priests would have to be content to collect as many instances as possible of dreams and the interpretations vouchsafed in the past, and to regard these as typical instances which might serve as guides for the new dreams that would constantly be brought to their notice. A careful study of these collections will enable us to understand the principles which in general controlled the interpretations; and, even though in many instances we shall fail to understand the basis for the interpretations, we gain the conviction that the dream interpreter proceeded in some methodical way, and did not follow caprice, or allow himself to be led by happy guesses. Thus, in the case of animals appearing to one in dreams, we note that certain animals portend misfortune, while others represent a favourable omen. A dog portends sorrow, a lion success, a goat indicates the death of a son, a stag the death of a daughter, a jackal Divine favour, a fish power, and so on. One can also see the natural association of ideas which suggested that a mountain appearing in a dream was an indication of unrivalled strength, and that salt meant protection; while, on the other hand, the connexion between a date and distress is less conspicuous; but what appears arbitrary to us may properly be attributed to our ignorance of the ideas that the Babylonians and Assyrians associated with the objects in question, and furthermore one must bear in mind that association of ideas formed only one factor in the science of dream interpretation. Past experience of the supposed connexion between some occurrence and a dream formed a second factor; and besides these two there must have been a variety of considerations that served as guides in the development of this science. Over and above this, no doubt, a certain scope was allowed to the judgment of the individual priest, who was obliged, however, to exercise due precaution to make sure that his judgment was based upon solid ground, derived from his experience, and from his study of the manuals that were produced in connexion with the temple organization. To a far greater degree than in the case of other branches of the omen literature which we have considered, the dreams of an individual had a bearing on his own fate. It was a message meant primarily for him; and only when he to whom the gods communicated their purpose was also the occupant of the throne or belonged to the royal household, did the dream assume a wide significance, involving the general welfare. The dream portents thus bring us still closer to the circle of the direct and personal influence exerted by the prevailing religion upon worshippers in their private capacity.

5. **Prayers and hymns.**—Recourse to incantations and omens, we have seen, was perfectly compatible with the development of advanced conceptions regarding the chief gods recognized in the systematized pantheon; and the prominent part played by incantation rituals and by omen collections in religious practice down to the latest days in no way hindered the growth of other branches of religious literature in Babylonia, and the extension of these branches to Assyria. The belief that the ills and misfortunes of life were due to the mischievous influence of demons and spirits, either acting independently or at the instigation of those who had the power to control their actions, was too deeply ingrained in the flesh and blood of the people to be seriously affected by the view that the gods, so much more powerful than demons or witches, were on the whole favourably inclined towards mankind, and inflicted punishment upon them only for sufficient cause, chief among which, to be sure, was the neglect of proper homage and devotion to them. The theological system devised by the schools was forced to take cognizance of the popular beliefs, and indeed strengthened them by thus emphasizing the contrast that existed between gods and demons.

As a consequence, higher speculations regarding the manner of the Divine government of the Universe could be introduced into the incantations themselves, without seriously affecting the much more primitive conceptions on which the incantations rested. The 'Maḳlu' series furnishes examples of compositions worthy of the term 'hymns,' which were introduced as preludes to the recital of a jumble of formulas, the power of which rested in the combination of words employed; and through-

* See Thureau-Dangin's essay, 'Le Songe de Goudéa' (*Comptes rendus de l'Académie d'Inscriptions*, 1900, pp. 112–122.

† See Schrader's *Keilinschriftliche Bibliothek*, vol. ii. p. 251.

out the other series known to us similar compositions addressed to various deities are scattered. Nor did the belief, also deeply ingrained, that the study of heavenly phenomena offered an opportunity of ascertaining the intention of the gods, check the religious development which ascribed ethical motives and considerations of right and wrong to the gods in their dealings with their subjects. It might be that, through the movements of the stars, or the birth of monstrosities among mankind or animals, or through a dream, the Divine anger against the country, the ruler, or the individual, was revealed, yet it was generally possible by prayer and by sacrifice to alter the Divine will, and to avert the threatened catastrophe by securing the goodwill of the angry god, or even by fortifying oneself through the protection of one's special Divine protector against some hostile power, just as one could invoke a god against the mischievous devices of a demon or a witch. Nay, even when the blow fell upon one, the hope of averting its full force still remained. Oppressed by the fear of demons lurking everywhere, by the dread of witches and sorcerers who prepared their attacks in secret, and hampered by the multitudinous occurrences that were so full of significance, the outlook for the individual would indeed have been hopeless but for the outlet afforded, through prayers and hymns, for a direct appeal to the Divine powers, irrespective of what the stars declared or what the demons purposed. The prayers and hymns thus reveal the brighter side of the religion of Babylonia and Assyria, as well as its more spiritual phase and its higher aspirations. They tell us of the hopes that filled the breasts of the worshippers, enabling them to overcome the gloom that must have resulted from reflecting on the dangers that beset them at every turn, and the evils that were constantly staring them in the face. Even though a great majority of this class of compositions that have been preserved for us are royal prayers and hymns, placed in the mouth of royal personages or having reference to public events, the spirit embodied in them reflects the popular conceptions formed of the gods, and in a large measure at least they embody aspirations and hopes shared by the people at large.

For the study of the prayers and hymns we have, besides the tablets in the library of Assurbanipal, the votive and historical inscriptions of the rulers of Babylonia and Assyria, in which prayers are frequently introduced. Such prayers, embodying requests for a long life, a prosperous rule, victory over enemies, and abundant offspring, are more frequently encountered in the inscriptions of the rulers of the south than in those of the north. The Assyrian rulers contented themselves with an invocation addressed to some god, or to the chief gods of the pantheon, at the beginning of their inscriptions, and with curses and threats hurled at those who should destroy or deface their monuments; but the historical inscriptions of Assyria furnish us also with some specimens of genuine prayers.

Taking up, first, the prayers introduced in the inscriptions of Babylonian rulers, one of the best examples, though not in the form of a direct address, is to be found in the inscription of Lugalzaggisi (*c.* 3500 B.C.). The king, after ascribing his success to the help of the gods, and more especially to Bel of Nippur, closes with a fervent appeal to Bel *—

'En-lil, king of the lords, my beloved father; may he grant me long life, and the land peace and tranquillity! May he cause the army to flourish, and guard the sanctuaries! May he regard the land with favour, and grant mercy to its inhabitants; and may I continue to rule as a powerful leader!'

* Hilprecht, *Old Babylonian Inscriptions*, i. 2, No. 87, col. i. 13-36.

Another southern ruler, Gudea (*c.* 3000 B.C.), wishing to assure himself of the support of Bau in his undertakings, addresses her as follows:—

'O my queen, lofty daughter of Anu,*
Who furnishes proper counsel, and holds the first rank among the gods.
Thou who grantest life to the land.

. . . . . . . .

Thou art the queen, the mother, who has founded Shirpurla.
The nation upon which thou lookest in mercy prospers.
Long life is vouchsafed to the hero on whom thou dost look with favour.
I have no mother—thou art my mother.
I have no father—thou art my father.'

The finest specimens of royal prayers, however, are to be found in the inscriptions of rulers of the New Babylonian period—Nabopolassar, Nebuchadreẓẓar, and Nabonidus.† Singling out those of Nebuchadreẓẓar as those possessing greater interest than the others, the prayer addressed to Marduk by the king upon his ascending the throne‡ may serve as a third example of this branch of religious literature—

'O eternal ruler, lord of everything, grant that the name of the king whom thou lovest, whose name thou hast proclaimed, may flourish, as seems pleasing to thee. Lead him in the right path. I am the prince who obeys thee, the creature of thy hand. Thou hast created me, and hast entrusted to me sovereignty over mankind. According to thy mercy, O lord, which thou bestowest upon all, may thy supreme rule be merciful! The fear of thy divinity implant in my heart! Grant me what seems good to thee, for thou art the one who hast given me my life.'

The prayer emphasizes in impressive diction the dignity which the ruler attaches to his royal post, and lays stress upon the responsibilities it involves rather than upon its pomp and glory. Hence the tone of humility which pervades the composition, and which is surprising in a ruler whom we have been accustomed to regard as representing the acme of mortal pride and arrogance. Still more impressive is the expressed hope and purpose to rule according to the dictates of justice and equity, embodied in a dedication prayer on the completion of the temple at Sippar in honour of Shamash, the Divine judge and oracle-god *par excellence* §—

'Shamash, great lord, on entering joyfully thy glorious temple E-barra, look with favour on my precious handiwork. May thy lips proclaim mercy for me! Through thy righteous order may I have abundant offspring! Long life and a firm throne grant me! May my rule ‖ be extended to eternity, with a righteous sceptre and beneficent authority. With a legitimate staff of authority bringing salvation to men adorn my kingdom for ever. With strong weapons protect my troops at the call of battle! O Shamash, through judicial decision and through dreams answer me aright. By thy lofty, unchangeable decree may my sharp weapons proceed to overthrow the weapons of the enemies!'

The repetition of such expressions as 'justice,' 'right,' 'legitimate,' is an interesting illustration of the emphasis which this king, contrary again to the current view, laid upon exalted principles in carrying out his policy, and of the high sense of duty by which he was swayed.

The occurrence in historical inscriptions of hymns giving expression to such worthy sentiments, furnishes the proof that the compositions found in the library of Assurbanipal are not to be regarded as literary exercises indicative of the intellectual ambitions cherished by the priests attached to the various temples, but as part of the ritual employed in obtaining oracles, in offering sacrifices,

* Cylinder B (ed. Price), col. ii. 27-iii. 4.
† For a translation of practically all the prayers in the Babylonian and Assyrian inscriptions, see Jastrow's *Religion Babyloniens und Assyriens*, pp. 394-418.
‡ Rawlinson, i. 53, col. i. 55-ii. 1.
§ Ball, *Proceedings of Society of Bibl. Archæology*, xi. p. 127 col. ii. 32-iii. 30.
‖ *i.e.* my dynasty.

and in praying for relief from sufferings and from the attacks of demons, witches, and sorcerers, or for averting impending disaster.

Although a large number of the hymns and prayers in this library—most of them, unfortunately, mere fragments—still await publication,* yet enough are at our disposal to enable us to judge of the general character of this division of the religious literature of Babylonia and Assyria. All the great gods, Marduk, Ishtar, Sarpanit, Tashmit, Shamash, Sin, Adad, Ninib, Nergal, as well as Ea, Bel of Nippur, and Ashur, are represented in the library by hymns of a more or less extensive character. On the whole, the traits assigned to the gods in those hymns are the same as we encounter in the votive and historical inscriptions, though frequently the devotion of the composers leads them to address some favourite god in terms which might lead one to believe that this god embodied all the traits possessed by his fellow-deities,—a phenomenon that finds an interesting parallel in the hymns of the Rigveda, where so often the god addressed has heaped upon him the attributes of all the gods.

Taking up hymns to the heads of the southern and the northern pantheon respectively, Marduk and Ashur, it will be interesting to compare, by an example, the spirit in which each is appealed to. One of the Marduk hymns reads as follows: †—

'O strong, exalted strength of the city of ‡ . . .
Supreme ruler, offspring of Ea,
Marduk, mighty one, chief of E-turra, §
Lord of E-sagila, the strength of Babylon, lover of E-zida;
Preserver of life, prince of E-makhtila, restorer of life,
Protector of the land, taking care of distant peoples.
Mighty sovereign over all sanctuaries,
Thy name is ever good in the mouth of men,
O Marduk, great lord . . .
By thy exalted command let me live in tranquillity,
Let me behold thy divinity!
What I purpose may I secure!
Place justice in my mouth,
Implant mercy in my heart.
May my god ‖ stand at my right side,
May my goddess stand on my left side,
May the god granting salvation stand firm at my side,
To be propitious, to hearken, and to be favourable!
Let the word that I speak be favourable as I speak it.
O Marduk, mighty ruler, command life, command my life!
Before thee have I most humbly bowed myself.
May Bel be thy light, Ea rejoice thee!
May the gods of the universe pay homage to thee!
May the great gods do what is pleasing to thee!'

While this hymn evidently forms part of an incantation text, or was originally composed as an incantation, yet it serves as a good example of the general character of the Babylonian hymns, and illustrates the current conceptions of Marduk as strong and mighty on the one hand, but also, on the other, as one who is inclined to listen to the appeals of sufferers, and from whom they may expect to receive new life.

Hymns to Ashur are not numerous, and the best specimen that has been found ¶ is of interest chiefly as showing how completely the *literati* of Assyria are under the influence of the intellectual life unfolded in Babylonia. The hymn in question is made up of phrases that can be matched in Babylonian hymns addressed to various gods, and only incidentally are the traits that distinguish the war-god of Assyria introduced. It begins as follows:—

'Mighty chief of the gods, omniscient;
Honoured, exalted lord of gods, fixer of destinies.
Ashur, mighty lord, omniscient;
Honoured, exalted lord of gods, fixer of destinies.
. . . Ashur, powerful chief of the gods, lord of countries.
[Let me proclaim] his greatness, celebrate his glory.
Ashur, let me glorify his being, exalt his name;
Dwelling in E-kharsag-gal-kur-kur-ra,* let me celebrate his glory.
[His strength] let me recall, his courage commemorate;
Dwelling in E-sherra, Ashur fixer of destinies.
. . . . . . . .
Forever let me exalt his power,
Mightily wise leader of the gods, illustrious.
Creator of Shamash, maker of mountains;
Creator of the gods, progenitor of Ishtar.
. . . . . . . .
. . . illustrious whose name is revered,
. . . Ashur whose command is extended,
[Firm?] like mountains whose base is not seen,
[Brilliant?] as the writing of the heavens,† of unlimited extent.
Let his name be celebrated, his command that stands firm.'

The frequent repetitions indicate that each two lines were to be sung or recited by a leader and a chorus respectively—an arrangement that we come across frequently in these compositions.

Decidedly superior in form, more particularly in tone, are the hymns to Shamash; and this may be accounted for through the influence of the conceptions of law and justice associated from early days with the sun-god. It is an image of Shamash that Ḫammurabi attaches as the headpiece to his famous Code,‡ as the symbol of the principles of justice on which he claims to base his ordinances. In almost all the Shamash hymns that we possess, whether forming part of incantations or representing independent compositions, this phase of his character as the protector of the oppressed, the liberator of those who dwell in gloom and darkness, and the destroyer of the wicked, is strongly emphasized. Taking, for example, a hymn intended for the morning service, Shamash is addressed as follows: §—

'O lord, illuminator of darkness, who reveals the face [of heaven?] . . .
Merciful god, who lifts up the lowly, protects the weak.
To thy light all the great gods look up.
All the Annunaki look up to thee.
All mankind thou guidest like a single being.
Expectantly with raised head they look up to the sunlight.
When thou dost appear, they rejoice and exult.
Thou art the light for the most distant ends of the heavens,
The standard for the wide earth.
The multitudes look up to thee with joy.'

The ethical traits of the god are even more effectively brought out in a section of one of the finest of the Shamash hymns, which is too long to be quoted in full ‖—

'Who plans evil—his horn then thou dost destroy,
Who in fixing boundaries annuls rights.
The unjust judge thou restraineth with force.
Who accepts a bribe, who does not judge justly—on him thou imposest sin.
But he who does not accept a bribe, who has a care for the oppressed,
To him Shamash is gracious, his life he prolongs.
The judge who renders a just decision
Shall end in a palace, the place of princes shall be his dwelling.
. . . . . . . .
The seed of those who act unjustly shall not flourish.
What their mouth declares in thy presence wilt thou destroy; what they purpose thou wilt annul.
Thou knowest their transgressions; the declaration of the wicked thou dost cast aside.
Every one wherever he may be is in thy care.
Thou directest their judgments, the imprisoned dost thou liberate.

* See the Index, *sub* 'Hymns' and 'Prayers,' of Bezold's Catalogue of the Tablets in the Kouyunjik Collection, vol. v.
† King, *Babylonian Magic and Sorcery*, No. 9.
‡ The name of the city is, according to King, Ashur, and the traces point to this reading. But if this be correct, then we must perforce assume that Assurbanipal's scribe intentionally substituted the capital of the northern kingdom for Babylon or some other southern town.
§ Temple at Eridu.
‖ The special protecting god and goddess of the individual are meant.
¶ Craig, *Assyrian and Babylonian Religious Texts*, i. pl. 32–37.

* 'Great mountain of countries'—name of temple to Ashur.
† A frequent expression designating the stars.
‡ See the illustration in Scheil, *Textes Élamites-Sémitiques*, ii., frontispiece.
§ Rawlinson, iv.² 19, No. 2.
‖ See C. D. Gray, *Shamash Religious Texts* (Chicago, 1901), pp. 17–19.

Thou hearest, O Shamash, petition, prayer, and appeal,
Humility, prostration, petitioning, and reverence.
With loud voice the unfortunate one cries to thee.
The weak, the exhausted, the oppressed, the lowly,
Mother, wife, maid, appeal to thee.
The one removed from his family, the one dwelling afar from his city.
The peasant when he gathers in his harvest appeals to thee.'

In this way the hymn proceeds to enumerate the various classes of society—the merchant, the hunter, the shepherd, the learned; and the various conditions under which the appeal for help or recognition of assistance is addressed to the great sun-god.

6. **Penitential Psalms.**—There is only one other subdivision of the religious literature of Babylonia and Assyria in which a still higher ethical and spiritual level is reached, in a series of compositions, also known to us chiefly from the library of Assurbanipal, in which the central idea is the consciousness of guilt, and in which, in connexion with a confession of sins, the fervent appeal is made to some god or goddess, or to the gods in general, for forgiveness. To these compositions, of which a considerable number have been published, and which appear to have been collected into a series, like the Incantation texts and the somewhat similar collection of the Prayers, the name 'Penitential Psalms'* has been given by scholars because of the striking resemblance in the general tone, and to a certain extent even in phraseology, to certain of the Biblical Psalms in which confession of sins and shortcomings constitutes the keynote. In a general way, of course, these 'Penitential Psalms' belong to the division of 'Hymns and Prayers'† which so often touch upon the question of guilt and sin; and it is often difficult to determine whether a composition, in which glorification of a deity's power, the appeal to his or her assistance, and the consciousness of sin are about equally distributed, is to be placed in the special category of 'Penitential Psalms.' Bearing in mind that sharp divisions do not exist here any more than between prayers and incantations, appeals or formulas, let us pass on to some specimens which will illustrate the general character of these compositions. The adaptation of these 'Psalms' for the ritual is indicated by the alternating utterances of the penitent and the priest acting as mediator between the worshipper and his deity.

As an example of the penitent's appeal—in this case to the goddess Ishtar—the following may serve:‡—

'I, thy servant, full of sighs, call upon thee.
The fervent prayer of him who has sinned dost thou accept.
If thou lookest upon a man, that man lives,
O powerful mistress of all mankind,
Merciful one to whom it is good to turn, who accepts sighs.'

The priest thereupon strengthens the appeal of the penitent—

'Since his god and his goddess § are angry with him, he calls upon thee.
[Turn thy face towards] him, take hold of his hand.'

The penitent—

'Besides thee, there is no guiding deity.
Look in mercy on me, accept my supplication,
Proclaim pacification, and let thy liver be appeased.
How long, O my mistress, till thy countenance be turned towards me?
Like doves I lament, I am satiated with sighs.'

The priest again appeals on behalf of the sinner—

'With distress and pain, his spirit is full of sighs;
Tears he weeps, [he pours forth] laments.'

Perhaps the finest specimen of these Penitential Psalms is one that has quite recently been published by Mr. L. W. King, and is likewise addressed to Ishtar.* Consisting of 106 lines with eight additional lines, containing ceremonial instructions, it is too long to quote in its entirety. It is pieced together, indeed, from three distinct hymns,† and the first two of these hymns may again be subdivided into two sections, namely the invocation, with the epithets of the goddess, followed by the appeal for appeasement of the goddess's anger. In the first hymn Ishtar is glorified under the names of *Irnina* ‡ and of *Gushea*, representing goddesses, whose attributes and rôle the 'great goddess' has absorbed. It begins as follows:—

'I pray to thee, lady of ladies, goddess of goddesses,
Ishtar, queen of all peoples, guide of mankind.
Irnini,‡ exalted art thou, lady of the Igigi;
Mighty and sovereign art thou, supreme is thy name,
The light of heaven and earth, valiant daughter of Sin art thou;
Bearer of weapons, arrayed for battle,
Controlling all laws, clothed with the crown of sovereignty.
O lady, exalted is thy rank, supreme over all the gods!
Thou causest lamentation, thou createst hostility among friendly brothers,
Thou givest strength.
Strong art thou, lady of victory, who dost overthrow those who oppose me.'

Addressing her as Gushea,§ the petitioner exclaims—

'Sacred chambers, shrines, temples, and sanctuaries look to thee.
Where is thy name not (pronounced)? Where is thy decree not (obeyed)?
Where are thine images not made? Where are thy sanctuaries not founded?
Where art thou not great? Where art thou not supreme?'

In the second hymn the appeal begins—

'O goddess of men, O goddess of women, whose way none can fathom!
Where thou lookest in mercy, the dead revives, the sick is healed;
The afflicted one is redeemed who looks on thy countenance.
I, in humiliation and sorrow, thy servant racked with pain, call on thee.
Look upon me, my lady, hear my supplication;
Look in mercy on me, hear my prayer;
Announce my release,|| and let thy liver be appeased,—
The release of my suffering body, which is full of distress and pain;
The release of my sick heart, full of tears and sorrow;
The release of my suffering entrails, full of distress and pain;
The release of my troubled house, shaken with grief;
The release of my liver,¶ which is satiated with tears and sorrow.'

In the third hymn the penitent inquires—

'What have I done, O my god and my goddess?
As though I did not reverence my god and my goddess, am I treated.
Sickness, disease,** ruin, and destruction have overwhelmed me;
Misfortune, turning away of countenance, and fulness of anger are my lot;

* See Reisner, *Sumerisch-Babylonische Hymnen* (Berlin, 1896), Introduction. In 1885 Zimmern published nine Penitential Psalms with full commentary, under the title *Babylonische Busspsalmen*. Further specimens are to be found in Craig, *Assyrian and Babylonian Religious Texts* (Leipzig, 1895–1897), and a particularly fine one is given in King's *Seven Creation Tablets*, vol. i. pp. 222–237. See also Zimmern, *Keilinschriften und Bibel*, pp. 35–38, for a German version.

† See the Introduction to King, *Babylonian Magic and Sorcery*, p. xv f.

‡ Rawlinson, iv.[2] 29*, No. 5; Zimmern, *Busspsalmen*, No. 1.

§ The special protecting god and goddess of the individual are meant. See above, p. 554b.

* King, *Creation Tablets*, i. 222–237 (transliteration and translation, ii. pl. 75–84 (text).

† (*a*) lines 1–34, (*b*) 35–50, (*c*) 51–106.

‡ In the incantation texts, *e.g.*, 'Labartu' series (Myhrman, *Zeitschr. f. Assyr.* xvi. p. 154), Ishtar is addressed as *Irnina*.

§ The name also occurs in incantation rituals, *e.g.* Zimmern, *Beiträge zur Kenntnis der Bab. Religion*, p. 130 (l. 73).

|| The word used here and in the following, *akhula(ia)*, signifying literally 'how long yet,' has become a conventional expression for the hoped-for release from suffering.

¶ *i.e.* spirit.

** Lit. 'head disease'—here a general term for lingering illness.

Anger, indignation, the fury of gods and men.
I behold, O my lady, days of affliction, months of distress, and years of misfortune;
I behold, O my mistress, slaughter, turmoil, and rebellion;
Death and misery have made an end of me.'

Ishtar is his only hope, and to her accordingly he prays—

'Dissolve my sin, my iniquity, my transgression and sin.
Forgive my transgression, accept my supplication.

. . . . . . . .

Guide my steps that I may walk gloriously among men.
Command, and at thy command may the angry god be appeased!
And may the angry goddess turn towards me!
May the dark smoking brazier flame up again!
My extinguished torch be relit!'

There are sufficient signs in this beautiful composition to indicate a royal personage as the one who thus pours out his soul before the Divine throne; and the same is the case in most of the other 'Penitential Psalms' that have been preserved. While this is due in large measure to the circumstance that the rulers could more readily have their supplications committed to writing, their position, as those upon whose relationship to the gods the general welfare of the country depended, is also to be taken into consideration to explain why the priests were zealous in giving a permanent form to the proper phrases and expressions to be used in times of general distress ascribed to the displeasure of some god or goddess with him in whose hands the affairs of State lay. Despite the advanced religious sentiments expressed in those prayers for forgiveness, they still rest upon the primitive belief that the ruler must have in some way provoked the anger of some deity—through insufficient reverence, or by an unintentional disobedience to his dictates. Hence the appeal was accompanied with rites of an expiatory character; and it seems a sharp descent from a lofty eminence when we find attached to this fervent supplication to Ishtar, directions for symbolical purification by sprinkling water on a green bough, for a fire-offering and a libation, and for a recital of the prayer three times 'without looking behind,' *—precisely as we find such directions in incantation texts proper. The link between the incantations and the hymns, despite the differences in religious conceptions, is illustrated by the retention of the term *shiptu*, *i.e.* 'incantation,' even to designate the finest and purest appeals for Divine grace and mercy. The 'Penitential Psalms'—the flowering of the religious spirit of Babylonia and Assyria—form no exception; and the hymn to Ishtar, of which extracts have been furnished, is designated both at the beginning and in the colophon as '*shiptu*.'

The continuity of the development of religious thought in the Euphrates Valley is thus preserved, and finds an expression even in its literature. The 'new' sprout is grafted on to the 'old' branch, and is nurtured by the same roots; but the example of the rulers in publicly acknowledging their dependence upon the gods was made all the more impressive by the bond thus maintained between the higher flights of religious spirit and the primitive rites, which, in the minds of the masses, must have continued to represent the essence of the religion itself.

7. **The Babylonian Cosmology.**—It is natural to find in a country which developed such a remarkable culture as that of Babylonia and Assyria, that the popular and more or less crude speculations regarding the beginnings of things should in the course of time have yielded to more consistent and systematic cosmological theories. Corresponding to the efforts of the priests attached to the temples in the great religious centres of Babylonia to systematize the pantheon, which, through the political supremacy acquired by the city of Babylon, led to making Marduk, the god of Babylon, the central figure of the Babylonian theology, we have a literary and intellectual process which had its outcome in the production of a poem or epic * of Creation, in which the chief rôle is assigned to this same god, Marduk. As constituting one of the main sources for our knowledge of Babylonian and Assyrian cosmology, it will be desirable to present an outline of this production, so far as the portions of it found in Assurbanipal's library and in New Babylonian copies from Babylonian temple archives enable us to do so. Although, since the discovery of the first fragments of the composition by George Smith in 1875, large portions of it have come to light, due chiefly to the activity and scholarship of Budge and King of the British Museum, even in the latest and most complete publication † there are many gaps which often seriously interfere with a satisfactory interpretation. We can also see in the composition itself evidences of considerable editing before it received its definite shape. Thus, while the poem embodies distinct traces of purely popular speculations and fancies which form, indeed, the basis upon which the main conceptions rest, an interpretation has been put upon these speculations and fancies that places them upon a much higher level of thought. What is, perhaps, even more significant, is the evidence which the composition affords of having been originally an 'epic' celebrating the deeds of En-lil or Bel—the god of Nippur—in his capacity as the creator, or, to speak more accurately, as the establisher of order and law in the Universe. We are thus led to Nippur as the source of the main features found in the composition, and it is furthermore safe to conclude that in connexion with the literary activity centring around the great temple E-kur, the seat of the worship of Bel, a Creation poem or epic arose which was remodelled by the priests of Marduk's temple E-sagila at Babylon. The rôle of Bel is transferred to Marduk, and additions were made to the old tale, partly intended to justify and illustrate this transfer, and in part prompted by the desire to glorify the chief god of Babylon, and to interpret old traditions in a manner in accordance with the theological system perfected in Babylon, and which became the dominant school of thought in the Euphrates Valley as well as in Assyria, albeit with certain modifications introduced by the Assyrian priests. The assigning of the chief rôle in the establishment of the Universe to En-lil or Bel, of course, reflects the attachment of the priests, and in a measure also of the populace of Nippur, to their own favourite deity; but from indications in the Creation poem itself, as well as from other sources, we know that traditions were also current in Babylonia which assigned the same rôle to Ea. Such a tradition would naturally arise in the ancient city

* The same direction is given, *e.g.*, in the 'Labartu' series (Myhrman, *Zeitschr. f. Assyr.* xvi. 160), and forms a parallel to similar directions among the Greeks in the case of offerings to Hecate, with whom Labartu has much in common, as Myhrman, *l.c.* p. 151 f., points out.

* Our justification for speaking of this Babylonian Creation story as a 'poem' rests upon the character of the composition itself, which is distinctly poetical in its form. See King, *Creation Tablets*, i. pp. cxxii–cxxiii, and more fully Delitzsch, *Das Babylonische Weltschöpfungsepos* (Leipzig, 1896), pp. 60–68, and the references to the opinions of Budge, Zimmern, and Gunkel; it partakes of the character of an epic by virtue of the prominence assigned in it to a single personage, Marduk, whose glorification constitutes the main purpose of the composition in its present form.

† *Cuneiform Texts from Babylonian Tablets, etc., in the British Museum*, pt. xiii. (1901), with a volume of supplementary texts and transliterations and translations of all the fragments known, by L. W. King, *The Seven Tablets of Creation; or the Babylonian and Assyrian Legends concerning the Creation of the World and of Mankind* (2 vols., London, 1902).

of Eridu, the main and oldest seat of Ea worship; and there are reasons for believing that in other religious centres Ishtar and, perhaps also, Anu were accorded the distinction of having brought the Universe into existence. At all events, it is certain that the Creation story which we are about to analyze represents one only of several versions produced in the Euphrates Valley; and, in extracting from it the cosmological theories upon which it rests, we must make due allowance for those features which reflect the attitude of a specific body of priests or a special school of thought towards a favourite deity.

Bearing in mind that in its present form the most complete Babylonian Creation story known to us has assumed the character of a pæan in honour of the chief god Marduk, we find that it consisted of seven tablets, and contained, according to King's calculation, about one thousand lines.* The story itself, known from its opening words as the *Enuma elish* or 'When above' series, may be divided into six sections, representing the chief steps in the establishment of the Universe: (1) the conflict of Apsu and Mummu with the gods, ending with the overthrow of Apsu and the capture of Mummu, brought about largely through the instrumentality of Ea; (2) the revolt of Tiamat and her consort Kingu and their followers against the gods, and the discomfiture of the rebellious host by Marduk, who is sent against Tiamat by Anshar with the approval of the gods; (3) the establishment of the order of the Universe, involving the spreading of an expanse underneath the heavens, the creation of the earth, the establishment of the planets and stars in their courses and place, and the regular change of seasons and of day and night, through the determination of the movements of the moon, and of her relationship to the sun; (4) the creation of man by Marduk; (5) the glorification of Marduk by the gods and mankind, ending with the entrusting to him of the 'tablets of fate' and the assignment to him of fifty 'glorious' names; the whole concluding with (6) an epilogue embodying good counsel to men, with instructions to recall the deeds of Marduk, and to pay proper homage to him.

The composite character of the story in its present form is revealed by the introduction, at the beginning, of two conflicts which both symbolize the same process. *Apsu*, signifying the 'deep,' is a symbol of primeval chaos, figured as a time when the waters covered everything, and were filled with monstrous beings subject to no laws. By the side of Apsu are two other beings—*Mummu*, an obscure word, but also conveying the general idea of chaos and confusion, and *Tiamat*, which, equivalent to the Hebrew word *tĕhôm* (תְּהוֹם), occurring in the Creation story of Gn 1, likewise embodies the idea of 'the great deep.' That all three beings are identified with the primeval waters, follows from the description furnished by the opening lines of the poem, where 'their waters' are spoken of as being 'mingled together.' The three terms thus prove to be practically synonymous, and the most probable explanation of the existence of all three terms is that they represent the 'survival' of varying traditions current in regard to the primeval chaos, which have been combined in the tale that became the standard account of how the Universe, with its laws and phenomena, came into being.† A factor that may also have been at work in leading to the retention of three terms for the primeval chaos is the desire to find, in primeval times, a triad corresponding to Anu, Bel, and Ea, who, in the later system of Babylonian theology, represent the quintessence of Divine control of the several divisions of the Universe. But however we are to account for the introduction of Apsu and Mummu by the side of Tiamat, the fact is clear that these beings, symbolizing the chaotic watery mass, were regarded as the original elements, the existence of which not only precedes that of heaven and earth, but which flourished before the gods were born. This theory is set forth at the beginning of the story—

> 'When above, the heavens were not named;*
> Below, the dry land did not bear a name.*
> Apsu, the primeval,† their progenitor,
> Mummu [and] Tiamat,‡ the mother of all of them,
> Their waters were mingled together.
> No field was marked off, no marsh was to be seen
> When none of the gods had yet been produced.
> No name was called, no fate decreed.
> Then the gods were created in the midst [of heaven?]
> Lakhmu and Lakhamu were produced.
> Time went by. . . .
> Anshar and Kishar were created [over them?]
> Days passed and there came forth . . .
> Anu their son. . . .'

In these lines the attempt is made to furnish a description of the time when 'nothing' was, with the inevitable result of such attempts, whether made in ancient times or in our own days, of involving us in a hopeless tangle of contradiction and obscurity. It is a gratuitous task to pick out the weak points in this endeavour to solve the hopeless but fascinating puzzle of beginnings; and it will be more useful to endeavour to grasp the theories embodied in it. The language is frequently obscure, due to the desire of the narrator to avoid definite terms that would be misleading by their very definiteness. He avoids the common word for earth, which is *irṣitum*, but uses instead a rare term, *ammatum*, with the purpose, as it would seem, of conveying the idea of a measured-out expanse of dry land. To convey more vividly the conception that nothing grew in the primeval waters, it is added that 'fields were not marked off, and no marsh was seen'—expressions suggested by the appearance of the land in the Euphrates Valley, where fields were marked off by boundary stones, and vegetation often appeared where, during the rainy season, there was nought but water. The narrative wishes to emphasize the fact that, in the primeval days, there was water but no vegetation. The grammatical construction warrants and justifies the conclusion that the narrator places at the beginning of things—before the existence of heaven and earth or the gods—the three beings symbolized by Apsu, Mummu, and Tiamat, even though the conception of the second being has already become so obscure that no further specification of it is attempted. Another illustration of the obscurity unavoidable in any attempt to picture primeval chaos is to be seen in the expressions 'their progenitor' and 'the mother of all of them.' The narrator anticipates the conception subsequently set forth, that both Apsu and Tiamat are surrounded by a brood of monsters, and he clearly has these beings in mind when speaking of 'their

* King says 'some nine hundred and ninety-four lines' (*Seven Tablets of Creation*, vol. i. pp. iv, xxv). Almost exactly one half of it is complete; and if we add to this the incomplete lines, we have recovered up to the present almost three-fourths of the text.

† *Tohu* and *bohu*, mentioned in Gn 1[2] in connexion with *tĕhôm*, are perhaps to be regarded as a faint trace of the primeval triad, Apsu, Mummu, and Tiamat.

* *i.e.* called into being.

† *Rishtu*, literally 'first,' which is added to distinguish this Apsu from the ordinary use of the word as 'the watery deep, which actually occurs in Tablet iv. line 142.

‡ It has been customary to regard *Mummu* here as an epithet of Tiamat in the sense of 'chaos,' 'raging,' and the like; but, since Mummu occurs in Tablet i. lines 30 and 31 as the 'messenger' of Apsu, it is clear that a separate personage is also intended in the opening lines. The omission of the conjunction is no objection, for the conjunction is omitted also between Apsu and Tiamat.

generator' and 'the mother of all of them.' The eighth line, with equal vagueness, dwells upon the fact that no name was called and no fate decided, to picture the time when nothing had as yet been created, since there were no gods. The first part of the line seems to be a reference to the animal world in general, the second part a more particular reference to man, whose fate is decreed by the gods. In a general way it is stated that the gods were created, though it is not said by whom, or how many there were. Along with the gods two beings, Lakhmu and Lakhamu, are specified as having been called into being;* and since, in the course of the narrative, they appear on the side of Tiamat, they are evidently introduced as types or symbols of the host of monsters in the wake of Apsu and Tiamat. It is difficult to know how the statement, that after the lapse of time the gods Anshar and Kishar were 'created,' is to be reconciled with the assertion in line 9, unless indeed we may fall back upon the hypothesis of a composite production, after the manner of the 'doublets' so frequently found in the composition of two versions of a story in the OT narratives. At all events, the Divine pair, Anshar and Kishar, represent, in the opinion of the Babylonian theologians, the oldest gods, from whom, indeed, by a doctrine closely akin to emanation, ten pairs of gods are descended.† These pairs are, with one exception, gods who do not play any part whatsoever in the active pantheon as we find it in the historical periods of Babylonia and Assyria; and since, furthermore, neither Anshar nor Kishar, the 'parents,' belong to the active pantheon, it is evident that, by the side of the gods actually worshipped and brought together into a system by the Babylonian theologians, we have a purely 'theoretical' pantheon devised in accordance with the theological speculations of the Babylonian schools of thought. Anshar, signifying the 'heavenly' (or upper) Universe (or 'totality'), and Kishar the earthly (or lower) Universe (or 'totality'), sum up the Divine power in control of all things; and one can follow the logical process which made them the progenitors of the various special powers into which this control was divided. In the Babylonian Creation story, as it lies before us, only two such special powers are introduced—Anu and Ea, the latter under the form Nudimmud; but since Anu and Ea represent two of the three personages constituting the triad which, according to a school of thought that became at one time the prevailing one, comprised the control of the Universe,‡ it is reasonable to suppose that in an older version the third figure, Bel, was also included. The omission of Bel, who in the narrative is identified with Marduk, is again an evidence of the transformation which the old traditions and speculations underwent in order to make them conform to the main purpose for which the entire tradition is preserved—the glorification of the favourite Marduk.

Anu, the god of heaven, and Nudimmud or Ea, who is described as without a rival in wisdom and strength, are the commanding figures in the conflict that now arises between the gods, as the representatives of order, and Apsu, Mummu, and Tiamat, as the representatives of chaos and chaotic anarchy, though the fragmentary state of the first tablet does not permit us to grasp clearly the part that Anu plays by the side of Ea, who is the principal contestant. The gods, it appears,

* The verbal form used (so also in line 7) of the creation of the gods is *shupû*, which conveys the idea of coming forth and streaming forth.

† See the lists in Rawlinson, ii. 54, Nos. 3 and 4; and iii. 69, No. 1, obv.; and Radau's valuable commentary, 'Bel, the Christ of Ancient Times' (*Monist*, vol. xiv. 81-87).

‡ See above, p. 538.

were unable for a long time to secure control of the three beings symbolical of primeval chaos. The latter, not content with a passive resistance, plot an attack upon the representatives of order. Apsu calls upon his 'messenger' Mummu for aid, and together they go to Tiamat to consult with her in regard to a plan for the destruction, or at all events for the crushing, of the independent spirit of the gods. From new fragments quite recently found* it is now certain that at this point of the narrative the gods are regarded as the offspring of Apsu and Tiamat. We may therefore, in view of this, venture to proceed a step further, and look upon Apsu and Tiamat as the 'male' and 'female' elements respectively of the primeval chaos, through whom not only Mummu and the brood of monsters, but also the gods, are produced. This, indeed, is implied, although not distinctly mentioned, in the opening lines of the first tablet above quoted. The Babylonian theologians would thus, with commendable consistency, trace both classes of beings—the monsters who form the army of Apsu and Tiamat as well as the 'great gods'—to primeval chaos. It is the gods, therefore, who organize a revolt against their progenitors, the purpose of which is to put an end to the chaos and confusion for which Apsu and Tiamat stand. Apsu presents his complaint against the gods to Tiamat. In rage he exclaims—

> 'By day I have no rest, at night I cannot lie down,
> I will surely destroy their course, surely overthrow them.'

Tiamat shares Apsu's anger—

> 'She plotted evil in her heart.†
> What shall we do? Let us indeed destroy.'

The text at this point becomes defective; but so much is clear that Ea, described as the 'one who knows everything,' takes up the conflict on behalf of the gods, and that Anu is in some way associated with him. It is also probable, though not certain, that the weapon with which Ea overcomes Apsu and his followers is the 'pure incantation,' which, presumably, he hurls against them. Such a procedure would be in perfect accord with the current conceptions about Ea, who is essentially a god acting by the power of the word.‡ At all events, Apsu is overthrown and Mummu is captured.

Thus ends the first episode in the symbolical conflict between chaos and order; and the second, which, as has been suggested, is merely a 'doublet,' or second version, is at once introduced.

Evidently, the version which assigned the conquest of Apsu and Mummu to Ea was the one which assigned to this god the distinction of having established the laws of the Universe. We may call it the 'Eridu' version of Creation; but, naturally, only so much of it could be introduced as would not interfere with Marduk's prerogatives. After the recital of Apsu's defeat, the 'Eridu' version disappears, and the 'Nippur' version, transformed by the substitution of Marduk for Bel into a 'Babylon' version, is taken up.

Tiamat, whose part in the Ea-Apsu conflict is not clearly defined, is represented as depressed; but her courage is revived by a deity called the 'bright god,' who is probably to be identified with Kingu,§ appointed by Tiamat to be the leader

* See King's *Seven Tablets of Creation*, i. pp. 183-184, settling the reading at the end of line 34 of the first tablet, 'the gods, their sons.'

† Literally, 'stomach.' See the restoration of these lines in King, vol. i. p. 184.

‡ Ea, it will be recalled, was one of the chief gods invoked in the incantation series, many of which originated at his seat of worship, Eridu. A special incantation known as the *Shipat Eridu*, 'Eridu incantation,' is frequently referred to, *e.g.* *Cuneiform Texts*, xvi. pl. 21, 205; 22, 250, etc.

§ See King, *Creation Tablets*, i. p. 14, n. 1.

of her hosts, and who occupies a position by the side of Tiamat somewhat similar to that of Mummu by the side of Apsu. Kingu urges Tiamat on to the fray, and encourages her to entrust the war of vengeance to be waged against the gods to her host of monsters, who, accordingly—

'Banded themselves together, advancing at the side of Tiamat;
Mighty in planning mischief night and day without respite,
They prepared for war, fuming and raging,
Uniting forces and preparing for the fray.'

Besides supplying her followers with invincible weapons, Tiamat gives birth to monster serpents, described in the following terms:—

'With sharp teeth and merciless fangs,
Their bodies filled with poison instead of blood;
Terrible dragons, clothed with terror,
Decked out with awful splendour, of lofty stature;
Whoever saw them was overcome with terror.
Their bodies rose up, and no one could resist their attack.
She * set up vipers and monster serpents and Lakhmu,
Hurricanes (?), raging hounds, scorpion-men,
Mighty tempests, fish-men, and rams,
Bearing merciless weapons, fearless in battle,
Mighty were her commands, irresistible.
In this fashion eleven huge monsters she made.
Since among the gods, her offspring, he had encouraged her,
She raised Kingu among them to power,
To march in front of the host, to lead the forces,
To seize the standard, to advance to the attack,
To direct the battle, to regulate the fight.'

Tiamat still claims control over the gods, and, in investing Kingu with supreme power, declares—

'I have uttered thy incantation. In the assembly of the gods have I raised thee to power;
The dominion over all the gods have I entrusted to him.
Be thou exalted, my chosen consort art thou.'

To further emphasize her control, she hands Kingu the 'tablets of fate' to be hung on his breast. The meaning of the elaborate description of the monsters and monstrosities forming the army of Tiamat is quite clear — it is to emphasize the reign of terror and confusion which preceded the control of the Universe by the gods. Tiamat, the symbol of chaos, can give birth only to creatures of terror and destruction, to monstrous dragons, and to the hybrid beings, half men and half animals, with which, probably, popular fancy conceived the Universe to have been populated in primeval days, and of which the sculptured representations of human-headed lions and bulls with enormous wings—placed as guardians against evil spirits at the entrances to palaces and temples—represent the survival in historical times. Nor is it difficult to see how this picture of chaos, which agrees substantially with the account of Berosus,† arose. The climatic conditions prevailing in ancient Babylonia suggest the obvious explanation based on the long season of rains and storms, when the elements of nature seem to be set loose without control, when wind and rain sweep over the land, everywhere causing inundations, which, before the perfection of the canal system, must have regularly placed entire districts of the Valley under water for a period each year. This annual chaos would be regarded as typical of a permanent condition before the great gods, identified with the powers of nature—the sun and moon—and associated with the starry firmament, introduced the orderly process of events, of which the regular movements of sun, moon, and planets, and the fixed position of the other stars, were the natural symbols. The subsequent course of the narrative bears out this interpretation, and shows that the Babylonian cosmology rests upon the principle of the substitution of order and law for chaos and lawlessness. The thought of a *creatio ex nihilo* lay beyond the mental horizon of

* Tiamat.
† In Eusebius, *Chronicle* (ed. Schoene), vol. i. pp. 14, 15. See Zimmern, *Keilinschriften und das Alte Testament*, pp. 488–490.

the Babylonian and Assyrian theologians; and it is to be observed that even in the Biblical account, where the Universe, with all it contains, is conceived as coming into existence by the decree of one supreme Power, the chaos, represented by 'darkness resting upon the deep,' is regarded as a real substance. In short, ancient man no less than his modern successor was unable to conceive of a *real* beginning of things, and it is merely a question as to where the boundary line representing the limitation of human logic or of human fancy is to be placed. Beyond that border line we pass into the domain of faith, or of mystic speculation.

The second and third tablets of the Creation story are taken up with the preparation and preliminary stages of the great conflict about to ensue between Tiamat and the gods. The connecting link between this conflict and the previous one between Apsu and Ea is revealed at the beginning of the second tablet, where it is said that Tiamat formulated her evil plans in order to avenge the discomfiture of Apsu. Ea, who, it will be recalled, appears in the first conflict as the 'one who knows everything,' is also in the second conflict the god through whom the gods learn of the designs of Tiamat. He comes to Anshar, 'the father who begat him,' and says—

'Our mother, Tiamat, is full of hate towards us;
With gathered forces she hath waxed furious,—
All the gods have turned to her,
Even those whom ye created * are at her side;
Banded together they advance at the side of Tiamat,
Mighty in planning mischief night and day without respite.'

It would appear, therefore, that not merely the offspring of Tiamat, but also some of those beings sprung from the gods, are on the side of 'chaos.' Ea, unfortunately, does not specify which gods he has in mind, but we may perhaps assume that the Babylonian theologians thought of such forces as Adad,† the god of storms *par excellence*; Nergal and Namtar, associated with destruction and pestilence, who must have been conceived as, apparently at least, abetting the cause of Tiamat.

Anshar appeals in turn to his sons, Ea and Anu, to lead the attack against Tiamat. The details of Ea's endeavours to either conquer or pacify Tiamat are, unfortunately, missing;‡ but from a subsequent reference§ it follows that Ea was 'afraid,' and obliged to 'turn back'; nor is Anu more successful. He is sent out by Anshar, in the hope that Tiamat may be appeased by hearing the 'word' of Anshar—

'Go and stand before Tiamat,
That her liver may be appeased, her heart pacified;
But if she will not hearken to thy word,
Then speak to her our word, that she may be appeased.'

But as Anu approaches, Tiamat growls,‖ and the god also turns back in terror. The third son is now appealed to by his father Anshar; and as one of many indications that by this son was originally meant the third member, Bel, of the triad Ea, Anu, and Bel, it is to be noted that he is referred to as *be-lum*, *i.e.* 'the lord,'¶ though subsequently the identification with Marduk is made without reservation by the writing *Amar-ud*,** the ordinary

* The plural is used because the address is evidently to Anshar and his consort Kishar, although only the former is specifically mentioned.
† Adad occurs, and apparently as one of the abettors of Tiamat, in a fragment (*Cuneiform Texts*, xiii. pl. 24, K 3445+Rm. 396, rev. v. 1) which represents a specifically 'Assyrian' version of Creation. See Zimmern, *l.c.* p. 496.
‡ The second tablet is very defective, though large portions may be restored through comparison with the third.
§ Tablet iii. 54. That Nudimmud or Ea was sent out first and Anu second, despite the fact that in the third tablet the order is reversed, has been shown by King, *Creation Tablets*, i. p. 188, n. 1.
‖ See King, *ib.* i. p. 12, n. 2. ¶ Tablet ii. 113, 131.
** *e.g.* Tablet iii. 55, 113, 138, and *passim* in Tablet iv., and in the Epilogue, Tablet vii. 139, though, l. 129, he is called *En-ul* (or *Bêl*) *ilâni*, Marduk.

designation of the chief god of Babylon. Bel turns out to be the real conqueror of Tiamat, and the introduction, therefore, of Ea and Anu is made partly with the intent to glorify the chief god of Nippur at the expense of his two companions, and partly as a consequence of the endeavour to combine in the story other existing versions, and to reconcile these various versions with one another. The Ea-Apsu conflict points clearly to the existence of an 'Eridu' version, which celebrated Ea as the creator of man and establisher of the laws of the Universe. In another centre Anu was accorded the distinction; and, when Nippur rose to political and religious supremacy, Bel was invested with the rôle of the conqueror of chaos. Our narrative, therefore, represents the 'Nippur' version; but, by the transfer of the title of Bel to Marduk, it was transformed into the 'Babylon' version, and there the process stopped, though we have traces, as already pointed out, of a distinctively 'Assyrian' version,* in which, by an identification of Anshar with Ashur, the chief god of the Assyrian pantheon, the step is taken which makes Anshar-Ashur the real creator. However, the version which, owing to the long-continued supremacy of Babylon as the centre of the empire, became the dominant—we might almost say 'orthodox'—one, was the narrative with which we are concerned. Anshar kisses Bel-Marduk, and thus dispels his fear. While still implying that Bel-Marduk is to pacify Tiamat by his pure incantation, as Ea overcame Apsu, this reference is merely introduced in order to show that Bel-Marduk possesses all the powers that may be ascribed to any other god. In reality, Bel-Marduk is a warrior, and Anshar also addresses him as such, urging him to proceed and 'trample the neck of Tiamat under foot.' Bel-Marduk accepts the challenge, but in a speech to Anshar, the lord of gods, who determines the destiny of the great gods, imposes the condition that, if he succeeds, he is to supplant Anshar as the chief of the gods—

'If I, your avenger,
Bind Tiamat and save your life,
Call an assembly, declare the pre-eminence of my fate.
In Upshukkinaku † gather together in joy,
Let my utterance, like yours, decree fates.
May whatever I do remain unalterable!
May my orders be unchangeable and irrevocable!'

In speeches like these the purpose of the priests of Nippur and Babylon to justify the position accorded in their system to Bel-Marduk as the decreer of fates is revealed.

The third tablet is taken up with the summoning of the gods by Gaga, the messenger of Anshar, in order to procure their consent to the condition exacted by Bel-Marduk. The vagueness and contradictions resulting from the attempt to combine in the narrative conflicting traditions are illustrated by the position accorded in this tablet to Lakhmu and Lakhamu as leaders of the hosts of gods sometimes referred to as Igigi, and again as Annunaki, though in the perfected theological system the former embody the group of 'heavenly' gods, while the Annunaki represent the group of 'earthly' or rather subterranean gods.‡ Elsewhere in the narrative Lakhamu is introduced along with the monsters who constitute the followers of Tiamat.§ The gods obey the summons, enter into the presence of Anshar, and sit down to a feast, in the course of which, as the narrative states, they fill themselves with wine, and then formally do homage to Bel-Marduk. The fourth tablet begins—

'They fitted out for him a lordly chamber,
Before his fathers to reign supreme.
Thou art the honoured one among the great gods.
Thy fate is unrivalled, thy utterance—supreme.*
O Marduk! thou art the honoured one among the great gods;
Thy fate is unrivalled, thy utterance—supreme.*
From this day onward, thy order shall be irrevocable.
Lifting up and abasing shall be in thy hand;
Thy utterance is fixed, thy command unalterable.
None among the gods shall transgress thy boundary.
. . . . . . . .
O Marduk, thou art our avenger.
We give thee sovereignty over the entire Universe.
Thou shalt preside in the assembly, thy word is supreme.
May thy weapon never become blunt; may it strike down thy foe!
O lord, spare the life of him who trusts in thee,
And pour out the life of the god who seized hold of evil.'

As a token of the power assigned to him, Marduk is asked to make a garment disappear and appear again by the mere force residing in his word—again an intimation that Marduk, like Ea, rules by the power of the word. Sceptre, throne, and ring are bestowed on him as symbols of royalty, and he is given the invincible weapon that strikes down the foe. They salute him, 'Marduk is king,' and encourage him for the attack—

'Go and cut off the life of Tiamat.
Let the wind carry her blood into secret places.'

An interesting description follows of the manner in which the god proceeds to equip himself for the fray. Bow, quiver, spear, and club are his weapons. He places the lightning in front of him, and fills his body with flaming fire. From his 'father Anu' he receives a net wherewith to entrap Tiamat. The four winds he assigns to their stations, so as to intercept the escape of Tiamat. Evil winds, tempests, and hurricanes are created by him—in all, seven kinds of winds—that follow behind his 'storm' chariot, on which, drawn by four swift and ferocious horses, he now mounts, brandishing the thunderbolt.

The picture thus drawn of the god making straight for Tiamat is most impressive, and admirably served the purpose of illustrating the terror which Bel-Marduk was supposed to inspire. The picture evidently fits an atmospheric 'storm' god, such as was the old En-lil of Nippur, but is hardly suitable for Marduk, who is distinctly a solar deity, though the transfer of Bel's rôle to Marduk appeared to be justified by the consideration that it is the sun which eventually triumphs over the storms of the rainy season, which, as we have seen, suggested the conceptions formed of Tiamat.

Kingu, the leader of the host of Tiamat, is utterly dumbfounded at the sight of the terrible Bel. His mental and physical paralysis is effectively portrayed, and his followers fall back in terror. Tiamat alone is not dismayed, and, enraged at the challenge—'Stand! I and thou, let us join battle'—which he utters, boldly meets Marduk. The narrative proceeds—

'When Tiamat heard those words,
She became like one possessed, bereft of reason.
Tiamat shrieked with piercing cries,
She trembled and shook to her very foundations.
She pronounced an incantation, she uttered her spell,
And the gods of the battle took to their weapons.
Then Tiamat and Marduk, the leader of the gods, stood up,
They advanced to the fray, drew nigh to the fight.
The lord spread out his net and caught her,
The evil wind behind him he let loose in her face.
As Tiamat opened her mouth to its full extent,
He drove in the evil wind before she closed her lips.
The mighty winds filled her stomach,
Her heart failed her, and she opened wide her mouth;

* See above, p. 567[b]; and, further, King, *Creation Tablets*, pp. 197–200, and the authorities there referred to.
† The sacred chamber in which the gods assemble, originally localized in Bel's temple E-kur in Nippur, and afterwards transferred to Marduk's temple E-sagila in Babylon.
‡ See Zimmern, *Keilinschriften u. d. Alte Testament*, p. 451 ff.
§ Tablet ii. 27, and parallel passages, iii. 31, 89.

* Literally, *Anu*.

He seized the spear and pierced her stomach,
He cut through her organs and slit open her heart.
He bound her and cut off her life.
He cast down her carcass and stood upon it.'

The followers of Tiamat, dismayed at the overthrow of their leader, take to flight; but Bel-Marduk surrounds them, and captures them all in the net. He takes from Kingu the 'tablets of fate' and hangs them around his own breast—thus establishing his prerogative as the decreer of destinies for all future times.

At this point the composite character of the narrative is again revealed, for Marduk is represented as returning to Tiamat to stand upon her, to smash her skull, and to drive her blood, carried away by the north wind to secret places, out of her body. It is evident that various traditions existed as to what Bel-Marduk did with Tiamat.

The close of the fourth tablet directs the current of the narrative into a new channel, and introduces us to Bel-Marduk as the creator of heaven, and as the establisher of law and order in the Universe. Out of one half of the carcass of Tiamat, flattened out by him 'like a flat fish,' he makes a covering for the heaven—a kind of door provided with a bolt—and with a watchman to stand guard against the pouring forth of the waters from above. Corresponding to the watchman placed over the waters of heaven, Nudimmud or Ea is assigned to the centre of 'Apsu'—here no longer used as 'chaos,' but as the watery deep, which is conceived as a structure, the limits of which are fixed by Bel-Marduk. Corresponding to this 'subterranean' mansion, a similar structure, which he calls E-sharra, is built in heaven, and Anu, Bel, and Ea are assigned to their respective districts.

The narrative thus leads us to the astrological system perfected by the Babylonian priests, and standing in close relation to their cosmology. According to this system, which rests on the identification of the gods with the sun, moon, and stars, the heavens constitute a structure provided for the gods. The regularity of the movements of the sun and moon and the course of the planets within defined limits, were accounted for by the theory which assigned to some god the distinction of having established the fixed order of events in the upper firmament. It is natural to suppose that Anshar should have been the one to do so; but, since he relinquishes his authority to Bel-Marduk, the latter is accorded the distinction; and, since Marduk is identified with the sun, a further change had to be introduced into the narrative by omitting all references to the creation of the sun. More important, however, than the assumption in the present form of the narrative, that it is the sun-god Marduk who creates the heavens and assigns to the gods their positions and functions, is the system itself, which is revealed at the close of the fourth tablet, and further developed at the beginning of the fifth tablet. The triad, Anu, Bel, and Ea, in this astrological system are not the old local deities who bear that name from the centres in which they were worshipped, nor do they sum up the control of the Universe, but they are simply certain sections of the ecliptic chosen as guides for determining the position and courses of the stars and planets respectively, Anu being the middle strip of the ecliptic, Bel the northern section, and Ea a star in the southern section.* With these as guiding points, the positions are assigned for the great gods; and the identification of the latter with the stars being specifically set forth, the seven *lumashi* stars or constellations of the zodiac are specially referred to, by means of which the divisions of the year are determined. At each end of the great structure E-sharra gates are placed, through which the sun passes in and out on his daily march across the expanse; and to the moon-god the control of the night is entrusted, by means of which the days are to be calculated. Further details as to the manner in which this calculation is to be made are given, so that incidentally the basis of the Babylonian calendar is furnished as another feature of the cosmology. Indeed, the entire theology enters into the narrative of the creation—(*a*) the systematized pantheon; (*b*) the astrological system upon which was built up the science of determining the intentions of the gods by observing their movements as represented in the planets and stars with which they were identified; (*c*) the lunar calendar.

Unfortunately, that part of the work of creation which would be of special interest to us—the formation of the earth, with its vegetation—is lacking, though it was, in all probability, contained in the fifth tablet, which, like the second, is very defective. Whether this part of creation was also attributed to Bel-Marduk alone, or to the gods in common, must for the present remain an open question. We have a fragmentary tablet* in which, incidental to a story assigning a prominent rôle to a god Nin-igi-azag, a reference is introduced to the creation of 'living creatures,' 'cattle of the field,' 'beasts of the field, creatures of the city,' which are described as having been produced by the gods in their assembly; but this may represent another version, whereas in the Creation narrative under discussion Marduk probably appeared as the creator of the earth,† just as in the sixth tablet the creation of man is assigned to him. The reason given for the creation of man is that the gods desired worshippers; and this view is ascribed in the narrative to none other than Marduk himself, who, in an address to Ea, says—

'My blood will I take, and bone ‡ . . .
I will set up man, that man . . .
I will create man to inhabit [the earth],
To establish the service of the gods, and that shrines [may be built].'

From the 'blood' of Marduk himself man is thus formed—a remarkable doctrine, which illustrates the high position accorded to man in the theological system of Babylonia. The introduction of Ea as a kind of associate to Marduk is, again, a trace of the composite character of the narrative, and points to a version in which the creation of man was assigned to Ea, who, in the Babylonian pantheon, is the god of mankind *par excellence*. From certain allusions in Marduk's address to Ea, and from Ea's reply, it would appear that the creation of man was opposed by the gods, who perhaps feared his power; and it is likely, though by no means certain, that, after creating man, Marduk gave him instructions,§ detailing religious and moral obligations.

The seventh tablet is taken up entirely with the glorification of Marduk by the gods and by mankind. First, the gods are represented as hailing him in their assembly as the avenger of their wrongs, and they bestow upon him fifty glorious names, enumerated in detail, emphasizing his power, his functions as the giver of life, the creator of vegetation, as the source of plenty; his righteousness, his mercy, his wisdom, his

* See Mahler, 'Die Wege des Anu, Bel, und Ea' (*Orientalistische Literaturzeitung*, vol. vi. No. 4 (pp. 155–160)).

* *Cuneiform Texts*, xiii. pl. 34; see King, *Creation Tablets*, i. pp. 122–125.

† See the reference, Tablet vii. 115, 'he (*i.e.* Marduk) created heaven and fashioned the earth.'

‡ King, *l.c.* i. p. 87, suggests the restoration, 'I will fashion.'

§ King has shown (*l.c.* i. p. 202 ff.) that the fragment which was supposed to contain the address does not belong to the series; but the possibility that Marduk gave some instructions to man must nevertheless be admitted.

power in removing evil, and more of the like. Mankind is called upon to join in paying homage to Marduk as the one who ordained the courses for the stars of heaven, shepherding the gods like a flock of sheep, as the conqueror of Tiamat, and as the creator of heaven and earth. Father Bel is represented as transferring to Marduk his own title, 'lord of the worlds,' and Ea declares that Marduk's name shall henceforth be Ea, as his own name. The epilogue to the narrative is an impressive appeal to the wise and the intelligent to ponder on Marduk's deeds, the memory of which the father should hand down to his son. All should rejoice in Marduk, from whom fertility and prosperity emanate, whose word is unchangeable, whose anger is irresistible, but who is merciful and compassionate to the repentant sinner.

There is little that need be added by way of comment to this analysis of this main narrative of Creation which has come down to us, and which may be taken as representing the matured cosmological theories of the Babylonians — the combination of primitive popular traditions with the scholastic astrological system, and the whole interpreted in accord with the theological doctrines developed in the schools of Babylonia. This main narrative, moreover, preserves traces of varying versions of Creation which were once current, but which differed chiefly in ascribing the work of creation to different deities, representing the gods worshipped in the various centres of religion in the Euphrates Valley. The principle underlying these versions, of which, outside of the traces in the main narrative, a number of fragments have been found,* is everywhere, so far as can be ascertained, the same—the overthrow of powers representing chaos and disorder by those standing for law and order. In place of a genuine theory of beginnings, the Babylonian and Assyrian cosmology thus furnishes a theory of emanation and of the evolution from chaos to order. Chaos is a primeval element, from which the gods emanate; the gods in turn produce gods, and, after the conquest of chaos, the laws of the Universe which the gods are forced to obey are imposed by the conquering god. The formation of 'deep' and the 'heavens' are the two chief factors in this work, to which, as a third factor, is added the earth proper, on which man is placed in order that he may pay the proper homage to the gods, and, above all, to Marduk.

8. **Life after death.**—Besides the Incantation texts, the Oracles, Omens, and Portents, the Hymns and Prayers, and the various versions of the Creation and unfolding of the Universe, we have quite a number of myths and legends in the literature of the Babylonians that bear more or less directly on the religion.

Among these, mention may be made (*a*) of a story of the ravages committed by a deity, Ira,† who is identified in the later literature with Nergal, the raging power of the summer solstice; (*b*) a series of myths, in which the solar deity, Ninib, plays the chief rôle;‡ (*c*) stories of the storm-bird, Zu,§ detailing an attempt of this bird, which symbolizes the clouds, to take away from En-lil or Bel, the conqueror of Tiamat, the 'tablets of fate,' which Bel himself had snatched away from Kingu, the chief of Tiamat's army. Zu succeeds, and flies away with the 'tablets of fate' to the mountains. As in the Creation story Anshar calls upon Anu, Ea, and Bel in turn to pacify Tiamat, so Anu, the god of heaven, calls upon Adad the storm-god, Ishtar, Bara, and Nin-igi-azag (Ea ?), to pursue Zu; but they are kept back through fear, and it is left for Marduk* to recapture the tablets, though it is likely that, in the present form of the narrative, Marduk takes the place of some other deity — possibly Shamash — to whom, as the conqueror of the storms, the feat appears to have been originally ascribed. (*d*) We have a story of a king of Cuthah,† narrating how the gods had delivered him and his land from monsters which remind us of those in the army of Tiamat.

Interesting as it would be to give an analysis of these and other tales,‡ we must pass them by, and take up three myths,§ which all touch upon one of the most important phases in every religion—the views held of life after death. These three myths are, (i.) the story of Adapa, (ii.) the story of Nergal and Eresh-kigal, and (iii.) the story of the Descent of Ishtar to the world of the dead.

(i.) The purpose of the story of Adapa appears to be to offer an explanation of how man, although the offspring of the gods,—Bel-Marduk, it will be recalled, forms him of his own blood,—does not share the distinguishing trait of the gods—immortality. The story belongs to the 'Ea' cycle of myths, and points to Eridu as its source. Ea appears here as the god of humanity, the protector, and, one is inclined to add, the creator of man. The principal personage, a semi-Divine being, Adapa, is a son of Ea, distinguished, like the latter, by wisdom, and serving as a kind of priest at the Eridu sanctuary, which he provides with 'bread and water.' One day, while fishing in the waters of Eridu, *i.e.* the Persian Gulf, his ship is seized by the south wind and sunk in the waters. In his rage Adapa breaks the wings of the south wind, so that for seven days it is unable to blow across the land. News of this occurrence reaches the gods, whose dwelling is placed in heaven, and Anu, the chief god, orders Adapa to be brought before him. Ea intervenes, and gives his favourite, Adapa, instructions how to conduct himself before Anu. In order to arouse the sympathy of the two watchmen at the gate of heaven, Tammuz and Gish-zida, he is to put on a mourning garb, and, in reply to the question as to the meaning of this garb, he is to state that the mourning is for two gods of the earth who have disappeared. Tammuz and Gish-zida, who will know that they are meant, will then intercede in Adapa's behalf before Anu. But Ea, furthermore, warns Adapa not to touch

* Thus we have (*a*) a version of the Tiamat myth, in which Marduk's name does not appear, but only that of Bel (King, *l.c.* i. p. 116 ff.); (*b*) a version in which the goddess Aruru is associated with Marduk in the creation of man and of animals and of vegetation, and in which the order of creation appears to be quite different from that found in the main narrative (King, *l.c.* 130 ff.). Moreover, from references to the conflict with Tiamat, and to other incidents of the cosmology introduced in incantations, astrological texts, hymns, legends, and myths, we see the numerous variations in details which marked the versions that were current.

† For the reading, see Zimmern, *Keilinschriften und das Alte Testament*, p. 587; for a recent translation, see Jensen, *Keilinschriftliche Bibliothek*, vi. 1, pp. 57–73.

‡ See Hrozny, *Sumerisch-babylonische Mythen von dem Gotte Ninrag (Ninib)*, Berlin, 1903.

§ Jensen, *l.c.* 47–57.

* In addition to the evidence for this view presented in the present writer's *Religion of Babylonia and Assyria*, p. 537 ff., see the passage in Craig's *Assyrian and Babylonian Religious Texts*, i. 29, obv. 15, where Marduk is referred to as the smiter of Zu.

† The latest translation by King, *Seven Tablets of Creation*, i. 140–155.

‡ A full analysis and discussion of these and other myths and legends will be found in the 24th chapter of the present writer's *Religion Babyloniens und Assyriens* (Giessen, 1904). The story of Etana (Jensen, *l.c.* 100–115), of Ea and Atarkhasis (Jensen, *l.c.* 274–291), and portions of the Gilgamesh epic (Jensen, *l.c.* 116–273; Jeremias, *Izdubar-Nimrod*, Leipzig, 1891; and Zimmern, *l.c.* 566–582), also have a bearing on the religious beliefs and conceptions, though of a more indirect character than the other three referred to in the text.

§ For the transliteration and German translation with commentary, see Jensen, *Keilinschriftl. Bibliothek*, vi. 1, pp. 92–101, 74–79, and 80–91 respectively; also Zimmern, *Keilinschriften und das Alte Testament*, pp. 520–527, 583–584, and 561–564; and for the text, E. J. Harper, 'Babylonische Legenden von Etana, Zu, Adapa, and Dibbarra' in *Beiträge zur Assyriologie*, ii. 390–521, and the references further on.

the food that Anu will place before him, nor to drink the water that will be offered—

'When thou steppest before Anu, they will offer thee food of death; do not eat! They will offer thee waters of death; do not drink! They will offer thee a garment; put it on! They will offer thee oil; anoint thyself! Carry out strictly the orders that I have given thee, cling to what I have commanded thee!'

It is evident from this speech, that Ea, who had given his favourite wisdom, but had not bestowed on him eternal life, presumably because it was not in his power, anticipates that Anu will punish Adapa with death; but the unexpected happened. At first Anu shows himself merciless, but the intercession of Tammuz and Gish-zida prompts him to reconsider his decision, and, instead of offering Adapa the food and water of death, he places before him the food and water of life—

'Fetch for him food of life, that he may eat thereof. They brought him food of life, but he did not eat. They brought him water of life, but he did not drink. They brought him a garment; he put it on. They brought him oil; he anointed himself therewith.'

Adapa, it will be observed, strictly carries out Ea's orders, and thus forfeits the boon of immortality, which was placed within his reach. The story presents parallels and contrasts with the Biblical story of the Fall. Adam's loss of immortality is due to *disobedience*; but in his case an *intentional* deception is practised on him by an evil spirit in the guise of a serpent, as against the unintentional deception of Adapa by Ea. It is evident that the story of Adapa is based on the common nature myth of the change of seasons, portrayed as a conflict between the storms of the rainy season and the vegetation symbolized by Adapa, who stands in some direct connexion with the solar deity, Marduk, the son of Ea. The story reflects the religious doctrine, developed in Babylonia, that man, though of Divine origin, does not share in the Divine trait of immortality, but the reference to the food and water of life may be taken as an indication that a contrary doctrine must also have had its advocates; and this view is confirmed by allusions to a 'life' plant and to 'life' waters in historical inscriptions and in literary productions. Marduk is addressed as the one who bestows this 'life' plant;* and if a king like Esarhaddon expresses the hope that his rule may be as beneficial as the 'life' plant,† it is evident that the conception of the existence of such a plant must have been a current one. So, again, whatever the purpose that Gilgamesh, the hero of the great Babylonian epic, has in mind in seeking for a plant bearing the remarkable name 'restorer of youth to old age,'‡ the incident would be unintelligible if it did not rest on the view that 'life' was a gift that could be given to man by the will of the gods, and that the life meant was not merely a limited existence but life without end. The same conclusion may be drawn from the occurrence of the phrase 'water of life' in the religious literature. In the story of Ishtar's descent to the lower world she is sprinkled with the 'waters of life' before she ascends to earth again,§ and on the idea that water is a symbol of life is based an entire series of rites practised in the Babylonian temples.‖

The doctrine, thus combined in the story of Adapa with an old nature myth, furnishes the proof of the deep interest which the problem of death awakened in the Babylonian schools. Along with the development of a systematized pantheon we find the attempt made to give some definite shape to the views regarding man's fate after death has touched his body. The mystery of death was deepened in the mind of primitive man by the difficulty of conceiving that life could come to an end; and the daily phenomenon of the awakening from sleep—which must have appeared to him as temporary death—strengthened in him the conviction that life does *not* come to an end, or perhaps it would be more correct to say, made it more difficult for him to persuade himself that death was equivalent to an annihilation of life. The problem that thus presented itself was how to reconcile the evident extinction of earthly activity in the case of death with the conviction or the instinct that life as such cannot come to an end. There thus arose, as a result of primitive and popular speculation on the mysterious theme, the idea that, corresponding to the surface of the earth as the scene of man's activity while life was in his body, there was an abode in which those whose earthly careers were over continued to enjoy the privilege of the spark of life. The prevailing custom of earth-burial, at least within the period for which historical documents are at our disposal, suggested, as a further natural conclusion, that the abode in question was situated below the surface of the earth. At this point, however, popular speculation appears to have stopped, and the theologians of the Euphrates Valley stepped in to develop the conception further, and to bring it into accord with the theological system devised by them. The sharp division between life and death led them to select out of the company of gods and goddesses a number that seemed fitted to be placed in control of the dead. A nether world pantheon thus, gradually, arose by the side of the group of great gods whose concern was with the living.

(ii.) A nature myth found among the Tel el-Amarna tablets,* based upon the phenomenon of the change of seasons, has been made the medium for giving expression to some of the doctrines of the priests regarding this pantheon for the dead. It appears from the story, that originally a goddess known as Eresh-kigal, signifying the 'lady of the nether world,' was placed at the head of this pantheon. Pictured as the sister of the gods, she is supposed to have her abode in the interior of the earth, and is the counterpart of the great goddess Ishtar, who, it will be recalled, is the great mother-goddess, the symbol of vegetation and fertility on the earth. The gods are represented as gathered together at a banquet, and they send a message to their sister Eresh-kigal, asking her, inasmuch as she cannot come up to the gods, whose seat, according to the astro-theology of the priests, is in heaven, at least to send a messenger to fetch some of the food for her. Eresh-kigal sends Namtar, the god of pestilence, who is welcomed by all the gods except Nergal. This god fails to pay proper respect to Eresh-kigal's messenger, and accordingly, on the demand of the 'lady of the lower world,' Nergal is handed over to her to receive the punishment of death. At this juncture Ea steps in, and reassures Nergal by giving him a bodyguard of fourteen demons, who will aid him in his encounter with Eresh-kigal. To judge from the names of these demons—Burning, Fever, Abyss, etc.—they seem to symbolize misfortunes, ills, and accidents, that bring death in their wake. Accompanied by these

* Craig, *Assyrian and Babylonian Religious Texts*, i. 59 (K 8961, 5).

† Meissner-Rost in *Beiträge zur Assyr*. iii. 255 (col. viii. 10–13).

‡ Tablet xi. l. 298. See Jensen, *Keilinschriftl. Bibliothek*, vi. 1, p. 252.

§ See below, p. 576a.

‖ See Zimmern's article, 'Lebensbrot u. Lebenswasser im Babylonischen und in der Bibel' in *Archiv f. Religionswissenschaft*, ii. 165–177.

* Published by Bezold, *Tell el-Amarna Tablets in the British Museum* (London, 1892), p. 141 (No. 82), and Winckler-Abel, *Thontafelfund von El-Amarna* (Berlin, 1889), pp. 164, 165. See Jensen, *Keilinschriftl. Bibl.* vi. 1, pp. 74–79.

demons, Nergal comes to the gates of the nether world. His presence is announced to his 'sister' Eresh-kigal. Placing his fourteen attendants at the various gates, he advances to Eresh-kigal, who is seated on her throne, seizes her, and pulls her to the ground. She appeals for mercy—

'Do not kill me, my brother. Let me speak to thee.'

Nergal, on hearing her, releases her. She weeps and cries—

'Thou shalt be my husband, and I will be thy wife;
Kingship over the wide earth I will bestow on thee;
The tablet of wisdom I will place in thy hand.
Thou shalt be lord; I will be lady.'

When Nergal heard these words, he took hold of her, kissed her, and wiped away her tears. The tablet, badly preserved at various points, breaks off with the beginning of Nergal's conciliatory reply. Whatever else the story may be intended to illustrate, it aims to account for the fact that at the head of the pantheon of the lower world stand two deities, Nergal and Eresh-kigal. The character of Nergal as the fierce and destructive power of the summer and the midday sun * made him the appropriate personage for this position, and, in accordance with the general principle pervading the theological system of Babylonia, it was proper that a male deity and not a goddess should be the supreme ruler. On the other hand, the story points to the existence of an earlier view—perhaps of popular origin—according to which a goddess occupies this position. The suggestion has already been thrown out, that Eresh-kigal, 'the lady of the nether world,' is the counterpart of Ishtar, 'the lady of the earth' as she is frequently termed. An element in the myth embodied in the story is therefore the view found among many nations, that the earth-goddess, during the period when vegetation ceases, has descended into the bowels of the earth—either voluntarily or carried off by force. At the time, however, that the myth received a definite literary form, the differentiation between the two Ishtars or the two aspects of the great goddess had taken place, and Eresh-kigal has become an independent figure, whose place is permanently fixed in the region below the surface of the earth.

(iii.) A more definite view of this region is furnished in another tale—likewise based on a myth symbolical of the change from the summer to the winter season, which incidentally strengthens the view here proposed that there were originally two forms of Ishtar, corresponding to the different aspects presented by the earth during the period of vegetation and during the equally long period of the year when nature seems to have perished. At the same time, the story, like that of Nergal and Eresh-kigal, already assumes the existence of an independent goddess ruling in the nether world, while antedating the association of a male deity at her side. Although the closing lines of the story, which probably indicated some occasion for which the composition was written, are very obscure, one of the purposes of the tale appears to have been to suggest the possibility of an escape from the region of the dead under certain conditions not easy of fulfilment. The more direct value of the story for us, however, lies in the picture it draws of the conditions prevailing in the place where the dead were supposed to be gathered together—a picture embodying in part popular conceptions, and in part the further elaboration of these conceptions by the theologians of Babylonia. The story opens as follows: †—

'To the land without return, the earth . . .
Ishtar, the daughter of Sin directed her mind.*
The daughter of Sin directed her mind,*
To the dark house, the dwelling of Irkalla,
To the house whence those who enter do not return,
To the road from which there is no path leading back,
To the house in which those who enter are deprived of light,
Where dust is their nourishment, clay their food.
They do not see light, they dwell in darkness,
Clothed like a bird, with wings as a covering;
On door and lock dust has settled.'

Ishtar arrives at the gate of the land without return, and demands admission of the watchman, threatening to break the threshold and the doors and lock, and to bring up the dead and restore them to life unless her request is granted. Ishtar's hostile spirit indicates that she has in mind an attack upon Eresh-kigal, very much of the same order which prompts Nergal to seek admission to the lady of the lower world. Both stories accordingly illustrate the hostility existing between the upper and the lower pantheon; but it may be questioned whether in an earlier form of the story this hostility was introduced. From subsequent references it would rather appear that Ishtar is forced to descend into the nether world, to dwell there for a certain time; but with the introduction of Eresh-kigal as an independent figure permanently in control of the lower world the old myth underwent a transformation, and Ishtar is now represented as planning an invasion of the region presided over by Eresh-kigal. The latter regards the visit in this light, for, when the presence of Ishtar at the gate is announced, she is both enraged and grieved. The departure of Ishtar from the upper world inaugurates a season of lamentation for the dead, and Eresh-kigal resents the presence in her realm of Ishtar, who will arouse the dead to a realization of their sad fate—

'What has prompted her, what has induced her spirit?
Should I indeed sit with her,
Eat clay instead of food, drink water instead of wine?
Should I weep over the husbands who left their wives?
Over the women who were snatched away from the embrace of their consorts?
Over the young taken before their time should I weep?'

A motive had to be found for the hostile attitude of the two sisters towards each other. In the case of Ishtar, it is anger with Eresh-kigal, who now controls those who once belonged to her as the mother of mankind. Ishtar loves mankind, and in another tale—that of the Deluge—she is portrayed as actually weeping over the destruction of her offspring. Popular fancy, reinforced by theological speculation, accordingly pictured Ishtar as proceeding to the lower world once a year, in order to sit with the dead, share their food, and weep over their inexorable fate. Hence her violent hatred of Eresh-kigal. The watchman is ordered to admit the goddess, and to treat her according to the existing laws. That the story has been transformed by the introduction of new motives rendered necessary by the differentiation of Ishtar from Eresh-kigal, is shown by the welcome which the watchman gives Ishtar, and which is in glaring contradiction to the threats which Ishtar has uttered—

'Enter, my lady, Cuthah † greets thee;
The palace of the land without return rejoices at thy presence.'

As she passes through the seven gates of the nether world the various articles of her apparel are taken away. At the first gate her crown is

* See above, p. 543a.

† The latest edition of the text is to be found in *Cuneiform Texts from Tablets in the British Museum*, etc., xv. pl. 45–47, corresponding to Rawlinson, iv.[2] pl. 31; recent translations by Jensen, *Keilinschriftl. Bibl.* vi. 1, pp. 80–91; and Jeremias in Roscher's *Lexikon der griech- und römischen Mythologie*, article 'Nergal.' See also Zimmern, *Keilinschriften u. d. Alte Testament*, pp. 561–563.

* Literally, 'placed her ear.'

† The name of an important centre in southern Babylonia which was the seat of Nergal worship, and hence becomes a poetical designation for the nether world.

removed, at the second her earrings, at the third her necklace, at the fourth her breastplate, at the fifth her studded girdle, at the sixth the ornaments on her hands and feet, and at the seventh, finally, her loincloth, so that, when she enters the presence of Eresh-kigal, she is quite naked.

The symbolical significance of this gradual stripping of the goddess is quite evident; it marks the gradual decay of vegetation at the approach of the rainy and winter season, and incidentally may have furnished the priests with a doctrinal explanation why the images of Ishtar, which the people placed in the temples as votive offerings, frequently portrayed her as naked.*

The naked Ishtar, thus forced to obey laws not of her making, is clearly a different figure from the one portrayed at the opening of the story, intent upon forcing an entrance to Eresh-kigal with some evil intent. To adapt the old myth to the later conception, Ishtar is described as rushing towards Eresh-kigal, but, without a struggle, is overpowered by Namtar, who, at the command of the lady of the nether world, smites Ishtar with sixty diseases affecting all her organs and limbs. The symbolism of the original myth is once more apparent in the description of what followed upon the imprisonment—for such it is—of Ishtar in 'the palace of the land without return.'

> 'When the lady Ishtar had descended to the land without return,
> The bull no longer mounted the cow, the ass did not mount the she-ass,
> The man did not go to the maid to lie with her.'

These lines evidently describe in naïve language the cessation of fertility on earth with the departure of the great mother-goddess. The gods, also, bewail the departure of Ishtar from their midst, and plan for her release from the nether world. Sin and Ea are appealed to, and Ea creates a mysterious being, Asushu-namir, whose name, signifying 'his going forth is brilliant,' points to a solar deity—perhaps the god of the spring sun—who brings back vegetation and fertility to nature. Asushu-namir forces his entrance into the nether world despite the opposition of Eresh-kigal, who is enraged also at this new intruder. He besprinkles Ishtar with the water of life and takes her with him. At each gate the articles taken away from her at her entrance are restored to her, until she emerges in all her glory. The story closes with references, which are not altogether clear, to a festival in honour of Tammuz, a solar deity, symbolizing the spring, who is designated as the youthful lover of Ishtar.

We see, then, that we are to distinguish in the story the following elements—(1) the old nature myth symbolical of the change of seasons, representing Ishtar as forced at a certain season of the year to leave the earth, followed by her release in the spring; (2) the combination of this myth with the later view, representing Eresh-kigal as an independent goddess, permanently established as ruler in the nether world; leading to (3) the hostility between the two goddesses. It will be observed that references to two festivals celebrated in Babylonia have been introduced into the story—a lamentation at the time of Ishtar's descent, and a rejoicing on her return. Further, the story has been made the medium for illustrating the current views regarding the abode of the dead, and the hope at least is suggested that, through the gods, a release from the control of Eresh-kigal is possible. Beyond this, however, the theologians did not venture to go, and such epithets as 'restorer of the dead,' occasionally given to certain gods, have reference to the power of the gods to save the desperately ill—those apparently already in the power of the gods of the nether world—from the dark abode; but they do not imply a real resurrection of the dead.

On the whole, the description given of 'the land without return,' at the opening of the story we have just considered, represents the prevailing doctrines in both Babylonia and Assyria. The name given to the abode of the dead is commonly *Aralû*, and the references to it in the religious literature show that it was pictured as a large dark cavern in the interior of the earth, with the entrance from the west, within which was situated the palace of Eresh-kigal. The approach to the great cavern is by means of a stream which must be crossed by the dead. Once in the great cavern, the dead are under the control of Nergal and Eresh-kigal, and around this pair we find a group of deities and demons who act as messengers and attendants, and constitute the pantheon of the nether world, which is almost as extensive in its scope as that which controls the world of the living. How far, according to the popular view, the dead were endowed with consciousness of their sad state, it is difficult to say. If the references to dust and earth as the food of the dead are more than poetical metaphors, they must have been conceived as being at least conscious of their misery; while references both in the historical and religious literature to libations and food-offerings for the dead and to the curse resulting from leaving the dead unburied, or from exposing them, after burial, to the sunlight, show that the dead were supposed to require the care and forethought of the survivors.* In this respect, a passage at the close of the Gilgamesh epic—perhaps the most notable literary achievement of Babylonia—is of significance. Eabani, housed in Aralû, appears to Gilgamesh at his solicitation, and reveals to him some of the secrets of the life in the dark abode†—

> 'He rests on a couch,
> Drinking pure water,
> Who died in battle, as you and I have seen.‡
> His father and mother support his head,
> His wife with him. . . .
> But he whose body is thrown in the field,
> As you and I have seen,
> The leavings of the pot, remains of food,
> What is thrown into the street, he eats.'

According to this passage, a distinction was made between the fate of those who died an honourable death, and by implication were properly taken care of, and those who were not accorded a fitting burial. Still, even the fate of those who were suitably provided for, to whom food and libation-offerings were regularly made, was sad enough; and Gilgamesh, in a lament over his dead friend Eabani, portrays with striking vividness the gloomy existence of those who are gathered together in Aralû.§ They lie there, inactive, deprived of the pleasures that this world offers, shorn of their strength and powers—prisoners without hope of release. Sadness is thus the prevailing note when the thoughts of the living turn to the fate in store for mankind after life has fled from the body. Only occasionally do we find the expression of a faint belief that all is not dark and gloomy for the dead, that at least some favoured individuals enjoy a better fortune. At one time the view appeared to have been held that the kings after their death were accorded a place among the gods.‖ Statues of the

* See, *e.g.*, the illustrations in Peters' *Nippur*, ii. p. 379, pl. ii.; Scheil, *Une Saison de Fouilles à Sippar* (Cairo, 1902), p. 81.

* See the collection of passages in A. Jeremias, *Die Babylonisch-Assyrischen Vorstellungen vom Leben nach dem Tode* (Leipzig, 1887), pp. 46–58.

† Tablet xii. col. vi. (ed. Haupt, *Beiträge z. Assyr.* i. p. 65). See Jensen, *Keilins. Bibl.* vi. 1, pp. 264, 265.

‡ *i.e.* as every one knows.

§ Tablet xii. col. i. (ed. Haupt, *Beit. z. Assyr.* i. p. 57).

‖ See the collection of references in Radau, *Early Babylonian History*, pp. 307–317.

rulers were placed in the temples and accorded Divine honours, and even temples were erected bearing their names. But though this view may have had a strong hold upon the masses at one time, in connexion with the belief that the rulers, as standing close to the gods, were in some way descended from them, it soon lost its hold, and we learn little about it after the days of Ḥammurabi.

In the Gilgamesh epic, likewise, which want of space forbids us to treat at length,* there is a most important hint of an escape from the ordinary fate of mortals through the intercession of the gods. Gilgamesh, in the course of his wanderings, comes to Ut-napishtim † to seek release from the disease with which he has been smitten. Although a mortal, Ut-napishtim is placed with the gods, after Bel, the instigator of a flood which has destroyed mankind, has become reconciled, through the intervention of Ea—the god of humanity—to the preservation of Ut-napishtim and his family from the general destruction. There are also some further references,‡ though all more or less obscure, which admit of an interpretation pointing to the possibility of a renewal of real life after death. But these, while foreshadowing the rise of a doctrine of resurrection as taken up by later Judaism and by Christianity, do not counterbalance the gloomy view of Aralû, which seems to have remained for all times the prevailing one. Had this not been the case, we should not have found, as late as the days of Nebuchadreẓẓar II., pictorial representations of the life after death, which could have aroused only feelings of terror and fear on the part of those who beheld them.§

vii. Temples and Cult.—The existence of numerous temples, particularly in Babylonia, but also, though to a lesser degree, in Assyria, may be taken as an index of the firm hold which the religion we have been describing had upon the people. The political centres during the various periods of Babylono-Assyrian history are also the religious centres, and the rulers of Babylonia and Assyria vie with one another in manifesting their devotion to the gods, by rebuilding, restoring, enlarging, and beautifying the sacred edifices. These temples, unaffected by the political vicissitudes of the cities in which they stood, gained in sanctity as the years and centuries rolled on. Whether we turn to some of the oldest rulers known to us, like Naram-Sin and Gudea, or to the members of the New Babylonian dynasty, one of their chief concerns was the care of the temples. Gudea tells us in great detail of a dream which was sent to him, and which is interpreted as the order of Ninib to build his temple E-ninnu at Shirpurla.‖ At the close of Babylonian history we find Nebuchadreẓẓar II. invariably adding to his titles 'the beautifier of E-sagila and E-zida,' the sacred edifices of Babylon and Borsippa respectively. Considerably over one hundred temples and sanctuaries are mentioned in the native and historical inscriptions known to us; and if we add to these the several hundred incidentally mentioned in the religious literature, in the commercial tablets, and those occurring as elements in proper names, and in lists or syllabaries, it becomes evident that the Euphrates Valley was fairly studded with edifices of one kind or another dedicated to the gods and goddesses of the pantheon.

The names of these temples are both interesting and instructive, as reflecting the ideals and hopes by which their builders were swayed. Marduk's main edifice at Babylon is called *E-sagila*, 'the lofty house'; the temple of Nebo at Borsippa is *E-zida*, 'the true *or* legitimate house'; the temple of the sun-god at Sippar and Larsa is appropriately called *E-barra*, 'the brilliant house'; and in the same spirit the temple of the moon-god at Ur was designated as *E-gish-shir-gal*, 'house of the great luminary'; while his sanctuary at Ḥarran was called *E-khul-khul*, 'the house of joys.' Bel's sanctuary at Nippur was known as *E-kur*, 'the mountain house'; Ishtar's temple at Erech as *E-anna*, 'house of heaven' or 'lofty house,' her sanctuary in Nineveh as *E-mash-mash*, signifying probably 'house of oracles'; a sanctuary of Nin-kharsag is known as *E-gal-makh*, 'the great palace.' Other names are *E-kharsag-kurkura*, 'the house of the mountain of all lands'; *E-kharsag-ella*, 'house of the shining mountain'; *E-dim-anna*, 'the house of heavenly construction'; *E-nun-makh*, 'house of the great lord'; *E-nin-makh*, 'house of the great lady'; *E-tila*, 'house of life,' and so on, *ad infinitum*. In the case of these names, it is to be observed that some of them designate a temple by an attribute or descriptive epithet of the god to whom it is dedicated, like *E-barra*, 'house of splendour,' for Shamash, or *E-nin-makh*, 'house of the great lady,' for Ishtar; others are expressive of a hope or ideal, as 'house of life,' or 'legitimate house.' Many of the names embody the idea of great height, as of a mountain. To this category belong not only those which contain the word 'mountain' as one of their parts, but such as convey the idea of reaching up to heaven. Such names are more than mere metaphors. They furnish, indeed, the keynote to the explanation of what is the most characteristic feature of sacred edifices in Babylonia. Besides the temple proper, in which the worshippers assembled, and in which there was an inner chamber for the reception of the sacred image of the god, every temple in an important centre had attached to it a tower, consisting of three to seven storeys, provided either with a sloping ascent leading around each storey till the top was reached, or having a staircase from one storey to another. The winding ascent described by Herodotus (i. 181) appears to have been the more characteristic form, and suggests a mountain road; while the main purpose served by these towers, namely, to erect something that would be impressive by its height, points likewise in the direction of their being, in fact, imitations of mountain peaks. To such towers the name *zikkurat*, signifying a 'high' place or edifice, was given. If it were certain that the *zikkurat* represented the oldest type of the Babylonian sanctuary, important conclusions might be drawn as to the origin of the race that laid the foundations of Babylonian culture. The proof, however, for such a view is not forthcoming, and all therefore that can be said is that the idea of erecting a sacred edifice in imitation of a mountain must have been introduced by some group which, before settling in the flat Euphrates Valley (which is absolutely devoid of hills, and where not even stone is found to serve as building material), must have lived in a mountainous country. One naturally thinks of Arabia, whence we know

* A full discussion of the various divisions of the epic, with an interpretation of its religious features, will be found in the 23rd chapter of the present writer's *Religion Babyloniens und Assyriens* (1905).

† The reading now adopted for the name of the hero of the Flood. See Zimmern, *Keilinschriften u. d. Alte Testament*, p. 545, n. 2.

‡ See Jensen, *Keilinschriftliche Bibl.* vi. 1, p. 480; Zimmern, *Keilinschriften und das Alte Testament*, i. pp. 638–639; Delitzsch, *Babel und Bibel* (Erster Vortrag), p. 38 ff.

§ See the illustration in *Mittheilungen d. Deutschen Orient. Gesellsch.* No. 9; Weissbach, *Babylonische Miscellen.* p. 42; and a similar tablet in Perrot and Chipiez, *History of Art in Chaldæa and Assyria*, vol. i. 350–351.

‖ Cylinder A, col. i.–vii. See Thureau-Dangin, 'Le Songe de Goudéa' (*Comptes rendus de l'Académie des Inscriptions*, 1901, pp. 112–128).

there was a steady stream of migration into the Euphrates Valley; and if it be borne in mind that among the ancient Arabs mountain tops were regarded as sacred, and that down to a very late date the favourite sanctuaries of the Semite population of Palestine and Syria were on eminences, we may perhaps go a step further, and regard the *zikkurat* as a distinctively Semitic product—an attempt on the part of the Semitic settlers in the Euphrates Valley to reproduce, by heaping up masses of clay (the only building material available), the mountain peaks, on the top of which they supposed their gods to dwell, and which their priests, acting as mediators, ascended when they wished to obtain an oracle or to secure aid from their gods.

The *zikkurats*, like the temples proper, have their names. These names, while frequently embodying the view that the *zikkurats* were intended to be built in imitation of mountains, are also of interest because of their testimony to the cosmological doctrines taught in the schools of Babylonian theology. Thus the *zikkurat* at Nippur bore the name *E-dur-an-ki*, 'the link of heaven and earth,' a name originally suggested by the ambition of the builders to raise the tower to a great height, but with which speculations were connected associating the *zikkurat* with the great mountain of the world where the gods dwell, which reaches from the confines of Apsu—'the deep,' as the seat of Ea—to the domain of Anu, 'the god of heaven.' The seven storeys, of which some of the most notable *zikkurats*—as, *e.g.*, those in Babylon, Borsippa, and Erech—consisted, were associated with the seven zones into which the earth was divided by the Babylonians, or with the seven planets. Accordingly, the *zikkurat* of Borsippa was called *E-ur-imin-an-ki*, 'house of the seven planets (literally 'governors') of heaven and earth,' while that at Erech was *E-gipar-ur*, 'house of seven zones.' Similarly, *E-temen-an-ki*, 'the foundation stone of heaven and earth,' the name of Marduk's *zikkurat* at Babylon, conveys a cosmological conception of a more specific character, while *E-pa*, 'the summit house,' the name of the *zikkurat* at Shirpurla, embodies merely the idea of great height, and *E-gubba-an-ki*, 'the point of heaven and earth,' the name of a *zikkurat* in Dilbat, combines again the original idea of great height with speculations regarding 'the mountain of the world.'

If, now, we find temples, pure and simple, bearing names connected with the idea of mountain heights, it is evident that such nomenclature is dependent upon the names given to the *zikkurats*, and that, even though temples may be as old in the Euphrates Valley as *zikkurats*, it is the *zikkurat* which acquires predominant significance as the characteristic sanctuary. Whether every sanctuary contained at the top a shrine where the image of the god was placed—as described by Herodotus—is a question that cannot be answered definitely. If there was an ascent leading to the top, it is natural to conclude that the ascent was made, and that some symbol of sanctity was to be found there. But the evidence is overwhelming, that in later times it was to the temples—the large structures with courts and halls for worshippers—that the people repaired, while the *zikkurat* survived as a religious symbol,—rather than as the active expression of the desire for communion with the gods. The interesting suggestion has recently been thrown out,* that around the base of the *zikkurats* the Babylonians were accustomed to bury their dead. But it could only have been the privileged few, as in the case of the 'pyramid' burials of Egypt, to whom such a sacred site was assigned as their last resting-place; and the custom could only have arisen at a time when the original purpose of the *zikkurats* was obscured by the greater and more active prominence assumed by the temples.

* Hilprecht, *Explorations in Bible Lands*, p. 465 f.

As yet the excavations conducted in Babylonia and Assyria have not succeeded in furnishing us with definite material for determining more than the general character of the Babylonian temples. In the case of large centres such as Nippur, Sippar, Babylon, and Nineveh, there developed an entire sacred area, or quarter, which took its name from the chief edifice. So at Nippur, *E-kur* is not merely the name for the temple of Bel or En-lil, but for a large quarter of the city, in which stood sanctuaries and chapels erected to various gods and goddesses. At Nippur and at Babylon all the great gods and goddesses were thus represented, forming, as it were, the court gathered around the chief deity. The sacred area of E-kur at Nippur is estimated to have covered eight acres, and that of E-sagila at Babylon, at which excavations are now being conducted, was probably much greater. Near the *zikkurat* stood the sanctuary of the chief god, surrounded by a large court, and, if one may draw a general conclusion from two small Assyrian temples excavated by Layard at Nimrod,* the main features of the temple proper were a long hall leading into a small room, and the 'holy of holies,' known as the *papakhu* or *parakku*, in which stood the image of the god or goddess, as the case might be. Into this sacred chamber none but the priests, or a worshipper accompanied by a priest, were permitted to enter.† In front of the image stood the altar to the god; but it is likely that in the larger room, as well as in the open court around the sanctuary, altars were also placed for the regular and ordinary sacrifices, the penetration into the 'holy of holies' being restricted to special occasions, and probably also to privileged individuals, besides the priests, and absolutely forbidden to the general masses. At Nippur two large divisions appear to have existed within the sacred area—one devoted perhaps to the chapels and sanctuaries of the deities (according to a tablet, no fewer than 24‡) that were worshipped in Nippur; the other reserved for the *zikkurat*, the temple of Bel proper, and possibly for the dwellings of the priests, the temple treasury, and the like.

Apart from this feature of the temples of Babylonia and Assyria in the large centres, which made them gathering-places for the worship of other deities besides the one to whom the entire area was sacred, the position of the priests as judges and scribes led to the extension of the temple area for other than strictly religious purposes. Not only were the courts of justice established within the sacred place, but commercial agreements were drawn up there in the presence of priests acting as scribes; and all transactions involving money matters, such as marriage-settlements, registering of wills, agreements between landlord and tenant, sale of slaves, houses, fields and crops, building contracts, hiring of ships, workmen, and the like, came before the priests, in whose presence, likewise, all legal disputes and lawsuits were adjudicated. Within the temple area the legal archives of the country were kept, and the public treasury was under the control of the representatives of religion. More than this, the temple organizations acquired large holdings of lands and property, and themselves engaged in commercial transactions on a large scale. The legal archives, found in such

* *Discoveries among the Ruins of Nineveh and Babylon* (London, 1857), plan 2.

† For a pictorial representation of a king being led into the presence of the sun-god by a priest, see Bezold, *Nineveh und Babylon* (Leipzig 1903), p. 87. On seal-cylinders similar scenes are frequently depicted.

‡ Hilprecht, *l.c.* 480.

centres as Sippar, Shirpurla, and Nippur, reveal indeed an astonishing activity of the temples in this direction. Large bodies of labourers were indentured to the temples, and slaves were owned or controlled by the priests acting as the accredited agents of some temple organization. These labourers and slaves were in turn hired out by the temples; banks were established in connexion with the temples, and hundreds of tablets have been found recording sums lent on interest, accounts of the temple in disposing of crops, in renting fields, selling and buying cattle, and dealing with all the branches of barter and exchange in which lay merchants were engaged.* Such a state of affairs aided materially, not only in promoting the importance of the temples, but in maintaining the influence of the priests, to whose more specifically religious functions we now turn.

The political growth of both Babylonia and Assyria contributed directly towards making the religious position of the priests more secure. Military enterprises were never undertaken without consulting the wish of the gods by means of omens and oracles. In like manner, the masses, imitating the example of their royal masters, repaired to the temples before setting out on a journey, or before building a house, or in order to secure relief from suffering, to avert impending disaster, or to seek for the interpretation of all strange and unusual occurrences. From being originally the guardians of small shrines and sanctuaries, erected as the dwelling-places of the gods represented by images placed in the most sacred part of the edifice, the priests thus became, and continued to be, the guides, physicians, and counsellors of the king and of his subjects.

The general term for 'priest' was *shangû*, the meaning of which is not certain,† but with the growth of the temples into large establishments a differentiation of priestly functions took place, and we can distinguish three chief classes: *bârû*, 'soothsayer *or* omen priest'; *âshipu*, 'exorcizer'; and *zammaru*, 'singer.' Each of these classes was probably further subdivided so as to provide for continuous attendance at the shrines. The special duties pertaining to each class are clearly indicated by their names, the *bârû* being the priest versed in the interpretation of omens, the *âshipu* the one by whom the demons and witches were exorcized, and the *zammaru* the designation for the body of priests who conducted the service proper at festivals and in connexion with the sacrifices. But besides these three general classes there must have been others to whom the other functions carried on by the priests were assigned. Such designations for 'priest,' as *munambû* = 'wailer,' *lallaru* = 'howler,' indicate that 'dirge-singers' formed a special subdivision, who chanted the lamentations for the dead.

The instruction of aspirants to the temple service was another important function. This led to the institution of schools, and the numerous tablets for exercise and practice, found in Assurbanipal's library, and in other collections of which fragments are now known to us, introduce us to the methods perfected in these schools. Beginning with the simple acquirements of reading and writing, the exercises led step by step to acquaintance with astrological, medical, and judicial lore, as well as to initiation into the interpretation of omens, methods of divination and exorcizing, sacrificial

* See Peiser's account of the financial side of the temple establishments, in the Introduction to his *Babylonische Verträge des Berliner Museums* (Berlin 1890), pp. xvii–xxix.

† Zimmern's suggestion (*Keilinschriften u. d. Alte Test.* p. 590, note 7) of 'the *raging* or *howling* one' is not plausible. More probable is Jensen's view (*Zeitschr. f. Assyr.* vii. 174) that it is a compound of *ša naḳî*, 'the one over the sacrifice'; but this theory also involves difficulties of a grammatical character.

details, the ritual to be observed on various occasions, and knowledge of the doctrines taught by the theologians.*

While as yet we know little of the details of the organization of the priesthood at the great temples, beyond the fact of its general divisions, and the existence of a 'high-priest' who exercised a measure of authority over all, it is interesting to note that, as among the Hebrews, certain qualifications were required on the part of those who wished to devote themselves to the priesthood. They had to be sound in mind and body, and well proportioned. The leper was excluded, as well as any one who had a bodily defect: a mutilated limb, defective eyesight, or even the lack of a full set of teeth, appears to have been sufficient to exclude one from the priesthood.† The chief classes among the priests formed a kind of guild composed of certain families. To this guild none but members of these families were admitted; but such restrictions do not seem to have applied to the large body of attendants who performed the menial duties in the great temples, or who were engaged in connexion with their business affairs.

A feature of the Babylonian priesthood which calls for some mention is the presence of women in the priestly service. Gudea refers to 'wailing women' in one of his inscriptions. We have had occasion to refer to oracles furnished by women,‡ and in historical and votive inscriptions of various periods women attached to the service of some god or other are not infrequently mentioned. While such priestesses are by no means limited to temples dedicated to goddesses, Shamash priestesses being particularly prominent, it would appear that as devotees to the service of the great goddess Ishtar in her temples in the south, as at Erech, Agade, and Babylon, as well as in the north, at Nineveh and Arbela, they retained positions of influence throughout all periods, though the general observation may be made, that this position is more prominent in the earlier than in the later periods. The names for 'priestesses' were: *Ḳadishtu*, 'holy one'; *kharimtu*, which embodies a similar idea of being 'set aside'; *shamkhatu*, 'pleasure maiden'; and *kizritu*, the meaning of which is not known.§ Priestesses appear also to have been employed in connexion with certain mysterious rites practised in the temples, to symbolize the fertility for which the goddess Ishtar stood, though it should be added that no references have as yet been found in the religious literature to justify Herodotus' statement (i. 199) that obscene rites formed part of the regular Ishtar cult.

Abundant as is the material now at our disposal for a study of the religious rites and ceremonies observed in Babylonia and Assyria, it is not sufficient to enable us to reconstruct in detail the ritual observed in the temples in connexion with the offering of sacrifices, the seeking of oracles, the interpretation of omens, and the homage to the gods on festive occasions. All that we can do at present is, by piecing together the references to the cult scattered through the historical literature, and by combining these references with data furnished by the religious texts, to present a general picture of the different phases of the cult carried on at the temples of Babylonia and Assyria.

As in other religions of antiquity which had

* See an article by the present writer, 'The Textbook Literature of the Babylonians' (*Biblical World*, 1897, pp. 248–268, and chap. 3 of Scheil's *Une Saison de Fouilles à Sippar*.

† See Zimmern's Introduction to part ii. of his *Beiträge zur Kenntnis der Babylonischen Religion*, p. 87.

‡ See above, p. 557a.

§ *Ḳadishtu* is of frequent occurrence; *kizritu* occurs as early as the days of Hammurabi (King, *Letters and Inscriptions of Hammurabi*, vol. i. No. 34); while the three last named in the list are found in the Gilgamesh epic (Tablet vi. ll. 184, 185).

reached an advanced stage of organization, sacrifices, both of animals and of vegetable products, played the most prominent part in the official cult. Gudea, in one of his inscriptions,* furnishes us with a long list of offerings made by him. These include oxen, sheep, goats, lambs, fish, birds (*e.g.* eagles, doves, etc.), and such products as dates, milk, and greens. From other sources we may add gazelles, wine, butter, honey, garlic, corn, herbs, oil, spices, and incense. The list itself shows that the conception of sacrifice had advanced from mere homage to the gods to providing an income for the needs of the temple service. While there are some traces in the Babylonian religion pointing to the existence, at one time, of the conception of sacrifice as a meal to be shared by the worshipper with his deity,† this stage had long been passed before the days of Gudea (*c.* 3000 B.C.). The organization of the priesthood, with the various functions of the priests above set forth, necessitated a system that might secure to the temples a regular income; and the frequent references to tithes in the tablets forming part of the temple archives, and even to monthly tributes, indicate a fixed system of taxes levied upon the people. The sacrifice, which invariably accompanies the act of consulting the priest for any particular purpose, falls likewise within the category of an assessment for the service rendered, and not a merely voluntary offering or a ritualistic observance, though such an observance is also a factor involved. The pure homage to the gods, by virtue of this development of the cult, was reserved largely for the priests, who, on their part, offered a daily sacrifice, as well as on stated occasions during the year, to ensure the goodwill of the gods in whose service they were. We have indeed reason to believe that, in the large temples, sacrifices of animals were brought twice every day —in the morning and in the evening; but in the case of these sacrifices, likewise, only certain portions were consumed on the altar, while the rest belonged to the priests.

Besides the tithes and the regular sacrifices, there were frequent occasions—as after a victory, or at the rebuilding of a sacred edifice, or the reinstitution of a temple cult, which, for some reason, had suffered interruption—when the rulers bestowed liberal gifts, or pledged themselves to a regular offering of animals, produce of the fields, garments, ornaments, and the like,—all of which helped to swell the income of the temples. Gifts of various kinds, and votive tablets of precious stone or of precious metals, are also frequently referred to as having been presented to the temples by State officials, and by individuals in their private capacity, so that the element of personal homage to the gods did not entirely disappear in the ever-increasing share taken by the official cult in the performance of religious rites.

There were also certain occasions of the year when the people repaired to the temples to join in the homage to be rendered to the gods. Indeed the religious calendars drawn up by the Babylonian priests‡ show that in the course of time every day of the year was invested with some significance; but, in addition to this, there were certain months and certain days set aside for special homage to some god or goddess. Thus the sixth and eleventh months — Elul and Shebat — appear to have been sacred to Ninib.§ This same sixth month was observed as a sacred period in honour of Ishtar. At the temple to Shamash in Sippar we learn of six days in the year*—the 7th day of Nisan (first month), 10th of Iyyar (second month), 3rd of Elul (sixth month), 7th of Tishri (seventh month), 15th of Arakhshamna (eighth month), and the 15th of Adar (twelfth month)— that were invested with a special significance. There are two festivals, however, that appear to have been particularly prominent from the oldest period down to the latest days — the New Year's festival, celebrated for a period of eleven days during the month of Nisan, which fell in the spring; and the festival of Tammuz, which occurred in the fourth month.

The New Year's Day, known as *Zagmuk*, is referred to in the inscriptions of Gudea, and is there declared to be in honour of the solar deity Nin-girsu and of his consort Bau, who occupies at this time, in the district controlled by Gudea, the position which afterwards was reserved for Ishtar. The spring, as the period when nature awakens to fresh life, when fertility, interrupted by the long season of rain and storms, once more manifests its power, would naturally be associated with a solar deity and with the mother-goddess; but when, at a subsequent period, Marduk was advanced to a position at the head of the pantheon, the honours of the New Year's celebration were transferred to him. The festival season in the month of Nisan was known as *Akîtu*, whereas the term *Zagmuk* proper is applicable only to the first day. Gifts to Bau marked the day in Gudea's time, whereas, in the days of Marduk's supremacy, a formal procession of the gods, headed by Marduk, along the sacred street of Babylon,† was one of the chief features. In accordance with the views developed in the schools of Babylon, Marduk was supposed to hold an assembly of the chief gods extending from the 8th to the 11th day of the sacred month, for the purpose of deciding the fate of individuals during the coming year. In this way a more distinctively religious character was given to an occasion which was originally an agricultural festival, marking the beginning of seed-time in the spring.

Likewise of popular origin was the festival of Tammuz, the youthful consort of Ishtar, who is slain by the goddess. The death of Tammuz symbolizes the approaching end of the summer season. Ishtar, though the producer of fertility, cannot maintain it beyond a certain period, and the change of seasons was popularly interpreted as due to the cruelty of the goddess, who deceives the youthful Tammuz—a solar deity, symbolizing more particularly the sun-god of spring-time—and, after gaining his love, destroys his life. Tammuz disappears in the fourth month of the year, and in his place comes Nergal, the violent and raging summer sun, which consumes everything with his fiercely burning rays, and in whose wake follow disease and pestilence. To this festival a more distinctively religious turn was likewise given by the Babylonian theologians, through making it a kind of 'All Souls' Day' for the commemoration of the dead. Dirges were sung by the wailing women, to the accompaniment of musical instruments, and offerings were made to the dead. This Tammuz festival appears to have been common to several branches of the Semites, though its spread and continuance throughout the Semitic world may have been due directly to Babylonian influences. The Tammuz cult was maintained till a late day by the Phœnicians, among whom the youthful god was known as *Adonis*; and there is an interesting reference in Ezekiel ($8^{14}$), showing that the Hebrews also continued to observe the Tammuz

* Inscription G, cols. iii.–vi. (de Sarzec, *Découvertes en Chaldée*, pl. 16.

† See W. Robertson Smith, *Religion of the Semites* (2nd ed. London, 1894), Lectures vi.–ix.

‡ See, *e.g.*, Rawlinson, iv.[2] pl. 32, 33; v. pl. 48, 49.

§ Rawlinson, i. 23, col. ii. 134.

* Rawlinson, v. 61, col. v. 51–vi. 8.

† Now excavated by the German expedition. See *Mittheilungen der Deutschen Orient. Gesellschaft*, No. 6.

festival, just as the Greek population of Asia Minor yielded to Semitic influences, and incorporated the Babylonian nature myth with their own mythology.

The frequent references to the sense of guilt, and the emphasis laid upon a penitent spirit, both in the Incantation texts and Hymns, and more particularly in that subdivision of the religious literature known as the Penitential Psalms,* show that the Babylono-Assyrian religion must have had its sombre aspects; and at times the impression is left, that constant fear of the gods and of the demons and evil spirits overshadowed confidence in the goodwill and favour of the superior powers. The chief festival of the year after the supremacy of Babylon as the capital of the country—the *Akîtu*—was of a decidedly serious character; and in a religious calendar,† setting forth in detail the specific character of each day, whether unfavourable or favourable, the unfavourable days on the whole predominate. All the festivals of the Babylonians and Assyrians, so far as our knowledge goes, partake, to a greater or less extent, of the nature of 'penitential' occasions, appropriate for securing, by the manifestation of a contrite spirit and by expiatory rites, the favour of the gods. Even in the joyful words of the hymns sung on these occasions in honour of the gods there is an undertone of sadness, occasioned by the dread lest at any moment the gods may change their favour into wrath.

In keeping with this general character of the religion, we find that, at least in two months—the 6th and 8th—of the year, no fewer than five days in each ‡—the 7th, 14th, 19th, 21st, and 28th—were set aside as 'evil days,' on which priests and rulers had to observe special precautions in order not to provoke the gods to anger. The priest was not to furnish oracles on those days, the physician (likewise a priest) was not to attempt a cure, while the ruler was not to put on his festive robes, nor to mount his chariot, nor to eat food prepared by fire, nor to announce any official decisions. Such days appear to have been known as 'days of pacification,'§ a designation expressing the hope of the worshippers rather than the real character of the occasions; and, while it is not certain that the term *shabattu* (or *shapattu*) was also applied to these days, it seems likely that this was the case.‖ At all events, we know that the Babylonians used the term *shabattu* to designate a 'day of pacification'; and there are good reasons for believing that the Sabbath of the Hebrews, which must stand in some relationship to the Babylonian rite, originally had a sombre and penitential character, and that it subsequently underwent a total transformation by making the *shabattu* in the literal sense 'a day of rest' for God, and then, in imitation of the Divine example, for mankind also.

Whether these same five days were observed in the other months of the Babylonian calendar, is again a question that cannot be answered definitely. It seems, likely, however, that such was the case, and, if not those days, there were at all events some days in each month that were designated as 'evil ones.'

Both for joyous and for sombre occasions sacrifices were enjoined, coupled with prayers, but the details as to the specific kind of sacrifices chosen for the various occasions are still unknown to us. Accompanying the sacrifice of animals there were libations and incense-offerings; and, from the numerous terms found in Babylonian conveying the idea of sacrifices of one kind or another, it is evident that there were a variety of classes of sacrifice which must have corresponded, in a general way, to the subdivisions enumerated in the religious codes of the Hebrews.*

*Summary and General Estimate.*—If we judge the Babylono-Assyrian religion from the point of view of the general character of the civilizations developed in ancient times, it may fairly be said that, with one exception, it represents on its best side the high-water mark of ancient thought. That exception is the Hebrew religion, which, by reason of the supreme emphasis which, as a consequence of the teachings of the pre-exilic and exilic prophets, was laid upon the ethical conception of the Divine government of the Universe, took an entirely unique direction. The religious literature produced in Babylonia transcends in variety, extent, and depth that which arose in Babylonia's great rival—Egypt. The influence of this literature may be measured by the traces of Babylonian conceptions, Babylonian myths, and Babylonian customs and rites to be found in the pages of the Old Testament. For, while a protest must be entered on purely scientific grounds against endeavours to carry back specifically Jewish ideas and institutions to Babylonian prototypes, merely because of resemblances that may in part be accidental; yet the general thesis may be maintained, that an understanding of the Hebrew religion is impossible without a constant consideration of the religion and culture that were developed in the Euphrates Valley. The stories in Genesis embodying traditions of the creation of the world and of the early fortunes of mankind, contain fragments of Babylonian myths, the specifically Hebrew contribution consisting in the interpretations put upon traditions which, largely through Babylonian influence, became current throughout the Semitic world, and from the Semites spread to other nations. Again, in the Hebrew codes, both as regards the purely legal portions and those sections dealing with religious ritual, Babylonian methods of legal procedure and the ritual developed in the Babylonian temples must be taken into consideration as determining factors.† And when we come to New Testament times we have not yet passed beyond the sphere of Babylonian influence,‡ though here likewise caution must be exercised lest we vitiate the results of a legitimate comparative method by straining it beyond proper bounds.

We have seen throughout this article that a distinction must be made between popular conceptions and the attempts of the priests to systematize these conceptions, leading to the establishment of a more or less fixed body of doctrines regarding the relationship of the gods to one another and to their worshippers. As a result of the influence exerted by the theologians upon popular beliefs, the local cults, both in the large centres and in the smaller places, gradually lost their distinctive character; and the numerous gods, who once enjoyed an independent and individual character, came to be regarded as aspects or forms or specific manifestations of one or another of the limited number of great gods, who as a whole represent the deities worshipped in sanctuaries which for political or

* See above, p. 566.
† Rawlinson, v. pl. 48 and 49.
‡ Rawlinson, iv.² pl. 32–33*.
§ Lit. 'days of rest for the heart.'
‖ See the recent discussion of the question by Zimmern, *Keilinschriften u. das Alte Test.* pp. 592–594.

* See, especially, Lv 1–7.
† For a sober and careful discussion of Babylonian influences in the legal portions of the Pentateuchal codes, S. A. Cook's *The Laws of Moses and the Code of Hammurabi* (London, 1903) is to be especially recommended.
‡ See, in connexion with this subject, an article by Gunkel, entitled 'Religio-Historical Interpretation of the New Testament' in the *Monist* for April 1903, also the same writer's *Schöpfung und Chaos* (Göttingen, 1895), pp. 379–398; Zimmern, *Keilinschriften u. d. Alte Testament*, especially pp. 377–395, and the same author's *Keilinschriften und Bibel* (Leipzig, 1903).

other reasons acquired great prominence. A movement of this kind led to the identification of practically all the goddesses (except those who were merely the consorts of male gods) as forms of one great goddess, Ishtar. This process likewise gave rise to a large number of names, all representing some phase of the solar deity, and paved the way for the grouping of those great gods as a kind of court around one who was regarded as presiding over the assembly. At an early period, lying as yet beyond our ken, Ea, the chief deity of Eridu, appears to have occupied this position. Within historic times, we know that En-lil or Bel, the 'lord' of Nippur, enjoyed this distinction at a time when his centre of worship was also the seat of a powerful succession of rulers, who controlled a large portion of the Euphrates Valley. From En-lil this supremacy appears to have been passed on to Ninib, but after the union of the Babylonian States, and the transfer of the political centre to the city of Babylon, the local deity Marduk usurped the place once occupied by Ea and Bel, and retained it, despite sporadic attempts to restore the old Bel to power, until the end of the New Babylonian empire.

More important, however, for its influence upon the development of religious thought than the question which deity was to be regarded as the head, was the establishment, among the masses, of the view that *one* particular deity deserved to be regarded as superior to the rest; and it is reasonable to suppose that in the course of time such a view would lead to considering Marduk as concentrating in his person the powers and attributes possessed by the members of his court. In Assyria, less influenced by persistent traditions than Babylonia, this view gave to the chief of the northern pantheon, Ashur, a position entirely unique; and, even to a larger degree than Marduk in the south, Ashur was regarded as the one god with whom practically the fate of the country and of individuals rested. Had the Babylonian and Assyrian theologians been able to conceive of the head of the pantheon as a distinctively ethical power, governing the Universe by laws based upon justice and profound distinctions of right,—nay, as the very source of righteousness and of the moral order of the Universe,—Ashur or Marduk might have developed, as did the national Jahweh of the Hebrews, into the one universal Power. That step, however, was not taken either in Babylonia or in Assyria. The limitation of the religious thought of the leaders and of the masses is marked by the circumstance that, while the attributes of the chief gods are concentrated in one, who thus becomes stronger, more powerful than the others, he is not invested with any traits of a more spiritual character. Ashur, indeed, becomes nothing more than a great war-lord of irresistible force, who protects his lands and subjects, but whose mercy and interest are not extended to nations that do not come within his sphere. Marduk, again, though showing milder traits, remains merely the greatest among the gods of Babylonia, and gradually disappears as his great sanctuary E-sagila crumbles to pieces. The God of the Hebrew prophets alone survives the decline and destruction of His central seat of worship.

But, while these limitations in the Babylono-Assyrian conception of Divine government are to be recognized, it must not be supposed that ethical traits were entirely wanting in the views formed of the gods, and more particularly of Marduk and Ashur. A great civilization can be produced only by a people imbued with an ethical as well as an intellectual spirit. It is no accidental circumstance that Ḫammurabi, the founder of the Babylonian empire in the full sense of the term, was also the one to gather the laws of the country into a great Code,* and he bases his claim to the gratitude of posterity upon his desire to diffuse righteousness throughout his land. This Code itself, dating from *c.* 2250 B.C., is the most striking evidence of the ethical soundness and moral aspirations of the Babylonians; and, if it be borne in mind that the predecessors of Ḫammurabi also emphasize their ambition to promote the happiness of their subjects, it will be apparent that we cannot form too high an estimate of the ethical spirit pervading the population of the Euphrates Valley from the earliest historical period known to us.

Taking Ḫammurabi's Code as a basis, it is important to observe that it provides for the rights of women as well as of men, that throughout it seeks to protect the weak against the tyranny of the strong, that it not only provides for punishment of crimes according to certain principles of equity (even though these are different from those which a modern nation would adopt), but takes into consideration the motives that prompt to acts in themselves illegal. Thus illegal claims are punished with a fine, but, if it can be proved that the claimant had the intention to defraud, a severer punishment, and, as a general rule, the death penalty, was imposed. The rights of the father over his wife and children, and of the master over his slave, are so regulated as to prevent tyranny and cruelty. The *lex talionis* is applied with a logical severity which does not stop short at apparently absurd conclusions,—as when it is provided that a physician, who instead of curing brings about the death of a patient or the loss of an organ, is held responsible for the result, and punished according to the position occupied by the victim of his lack of skill. The thousands of commercial and legal tablets found in the archives of Babylonian and Assyrian temples, and dating from the days of Sargon and Gudea down to the era of the Greek occupation, prove that the provisions of the legal codes, of which that of Ḫammurabi is only one instance of several that were compiled, were also carried out. Those tablets show the great care exercised in drawing up agreements between parties, and the endeavours of the judges to decide disputed cases brought before them by a careful sifting of the evidence and by strict standards of equity. In the religious literature, likewise, stress is laid upon right conduct as a preliminary to securing the favour and help of the gods, and the 'Penitential Psalms' furnish a further proof, if such were needed, of the intensity of the sense and consciousness of guilt.

Even among the Assyrians, despite the martial spirit shown by their kings and the cruelties practised by them in their incessant warfare, the ethical spirit was not lacking. Such kings as Sargon, Sennacherib, and Assurbanipal, who stand forth as the exponents of Assyria's ambition to extend her dominion by force of arms over distant lands, pride themselves upon having instituted righteous enactments, and claim to be the establishers of law, order, and justice; and, while the desire for self-glorification may have been one of the factors prompting Assurbanipal to gather within his palace walls copies of the literary productions of the south, the fact that he did this for the benefit of his subjects, as he expressly tells us,

* See art. CODE OF ḪAMMURABI in present vol. p. 584 ff.; and cf. Scheil, *Textes Élamites-Sémitiques*, ii. (Paris, 1902), with French translation: also in a revised edition, *La Loi de Hammourabi* (Paris, 1903); F. Mari, *Il Codice di Hammurabi e la Bibbia* (Rome, 1903); G. Cohn, *Die Gesetze Hammurabis* (Zürich, 1903); J. Jeremias, *Moses und Hammurabi* (Leipzig, 1903); Johns, *The Oldest Code of Laws in the World* (Edinburgh, 1903); R. F. Harper, *The Code of Ḫammurabi* (autograph text, transliteration, translation, glossary, etc.), 1904; and the German translations of Winckler, Peiser, and Müller, as well as Cook's discussion of the Code above referred to.

indicates that there were other factors at work of a higher order.

The Code of Ḫammurabi has its decided limitations. Many of its provisions are cruel, bordering almost upon barbarous viciousness. But it must be borne in mind that even the more humanitarian Pentateuchal codes are not free from enactments which, from the modern point of view, are reprehensible, as, *e.g.*, the putting to death of the woman suspected of witchcraft. Again, in the provisions made by the courts for the settlement of disputes, methods are followed which do not commend themselves to us. But, down to a late period in European countries, debtors had but little mercy shown them when brought into court, and miscarriages of justice occur frequently in our own day. Moreover, it can hardly be urged, in view of the elaborate and ever-growing provisions made by modern legislative bodies against all manner of crimes, frauds, and encroachments on the rights of others, that the necessity for regulating all legal and commercial transactions by formal contracts—which is a characteristic feature of Babylonian and Assyrian civilization—points to the laxity of the moral sense in these ancient centres.

On the whole, it will be found that the Babylono-Assyrian religion exercised a wholesome influence upon the people, who at all times showed a marked devotion to their gods. It is perfectly true that the practices of the cult were, down to the latest days, linked to beliefs of a crude and primitive character, of which the Incantation texts and the Omen literature represent the natural outcome; but the speculations of the theologians, and the cosmological and astrological system perfected by them, must be taken as an evidence of the higher possibilities of the religion. Religious practices in all religions are apt to lag behind doctrines and speculations, and the test by which a religion should be tried is not so much what it was or even what it is, as what it aimed to be, or under more favourable circumstances might have become. Applying this test, the religion of Babylonia and Assyria stands out among ancient religions as the one that approaches nearest to that phase from which there eventually came forth three of the most important Faiths of mankind—Judaism, Christianity, and Islam.

LITERATURE.—1. *GENERAL WORKS.*—The writer begs to explain that in mentioning his own work, *The Religion of Babylonia and Assyria* (Boston, 1898), first, he does so because it happens to be the only complete treatise on the subject that has as yet appeared. A German edition of this work, entirely revised, to a very large extent rewritten, and with copious additions and new translations of the religious literature, is now in course of publication under the title *Die Religion Babyloniens und Assyriens* (J. Ricker, Giessen). Up to the present (March 1904), six parts have been issued, and the work will be completed in about eleven parts, with an extra portfolio of appropriate illustrations. Professor Sayce's two works, *The Religion of the Ancient Babylonians* (Hibbert Lectures, London, 1887), and *The Religions of Ancient Egypt and Babylonia* (Gifford Lectures; Edinburgh, 1902), while containing many interesting suggestions, do not aim at covering the entire field. The former work, moreover, is now antiquated to a large extent, and the latter is concerned more with a speculative elucidation of the 'conception of the Divine' among the Babylonians than with the details of the religion. Among shorter sketches, those of C. P. Tiele, 'Die Religion in Babylonien und Assyrien' [being pages 127-216 of part i. of his *Geschichte der Religion im Alterthum* (Gotha, 1895), translated from the Dutch edition (Amsterdam, 1893)], and Friedrich Jeremias, 'Die Babylonier und Assyrier' in Chantepie de la Saussaye's *Lehrbuch der Religionsgeschichte* (2nd ed. Freiburg i. B. 1897), vol. i. pp. 163-221, are to be specially commended. Of a later date, and therefore replacing these earlier sketches to a certain extent, are L. W. King's little volume on *Babylonian Religion and Mythology* (London, 1899), and Domenico Bassi, *Mitologia Babilonese-Assira* (Milan, 1899). Alfred Jeremias' articles on the various gods of the Babylono-Assyrian Pantheon (Marduk, Ninib, Nergal, Ea (Oannes), Nusku, etc.) in Roscher's *Ausführliches Lexikon der Griechischen und Römischen Mythologie* are also to be highly recommended.

2. *RELIGIOUS TEXTS.*—Besides the collections of religious texts in the publications of the British Museum, more particularly in the fourth volume of *A Selection from the Miscellaneous Inscriptions of Western Asia*, ed. by H. C. Rawlinson (2nd ed. London, 1891), and in parts 13 to 17 (last issued) of *Cuneiform Texts from Babylonian Tablets, etc. in the British Museum*, under the general editorship of E. A. Wallis Budge (London, 1901-1903), and the invaluable Catalogue of the Cuneiform Tablets in the Kouyunjik Collection of the British Museum by Carl Bezold, 5 vols. (London, 1889-1899), the following publications merit special mention:—H. Zimmern, *Babylonische Busspsalmen* (Leipzig, 1885), same author's *Beiträge zur Kenntnis der Babylonischen Religion: (a) Beschwörungstafeln Shurpu, (b) Ritualtafeln für den Wahrsager, Beschwörer, und Sänger* (Leipzig, 1901; texts with translation and commentary); K. L. Tallqvist, *Die Assyrische Beschwörungsserie Maqlû* (Leipzig, 1895); J. A. Knudtzon, *Assyrische Gebete an den Sonnengott für Staat und königliches Haus aus der Zeit Asarhaddons und Assurbanipals* (2 vols. Leipzig, 1893); J. A. Craig, *Assyrian and Babylonian Religious Texts* (2 vols. Leipzig, 1895-1897), of which transliterations and translations into French are furnished by François Martin, *Textes Religieux Assyriens et Babyloniens* (two publications, (a) Paris, 1900, (b) Paris, 1903, both under the same title—the former covering vol. ii., the latter vol. i., of Craig's texts); Geo. Reisner, *Sumerisch-Babylonische Hymnen nach Thontafeln Griechischer Zeit* (Berlin, 1896); L. W. King, *Babylonian Magic and Sorcery* (London, 1896); R. C. Thompson, *The Devils and Evil Spirits of Babylonia* (2 vols. London, 1903-1904), translations of incantation series in parts 16 and 17 of *Cuneiform Texts*, etc.; C. Fossey, *La Magie Assyrienne* (Paris, 1902), embodying translations of the greater portion of the fourth volume of the Rawlinson series above referred to, and other texts; A. Boissier, *Documents Assyriens relatifs aux présages* (Paris, 1894-1897, in course of publication); J. A. Craig, *Astrological-Astronomical Texts* (Leipzig, 1899); Ch. Virolleaud, *L'Astrologie Chaldéene* (Paris, 1903, in course of publication); R. C. Thompson, *The Reports of the Magicians and Astrologers of Nineveh and Babylon* (2 vols. London, 1900).

3. *COSMOLOGY, LEGENDS, ETC.*—L. W. King, *The Seven Tablets of Creation, or the Babylonian and Assyrian Legends concerning the Creation of the World and of Mankind* (2 vols. London, 1902), latest and best translation based on the most complete collection of fragments of the various versions; translations of the Creation story, and of all the important legends, and of the Gilgamesh epic, are given in P. Jensen's 'Mythen und Epen' (Schrader's *Keilinschriftliche Bibliothek*, vol. vi. 1st part, Berlin, 1900; 2nd part not yet published). Of fundamental importance is the same author's *Kosmologie der Babylonier: Studien und Materialen* (Strassburg, 1890), which marked the beginning of the systematic study of Babylonian cosmology. Cf. Friedrich Delitzsch, *Das Babylonische Weltschöpfungsepos* (Leipzig, 1896); Paul Haupt, *Das Babylonische Nimrodepos* (2 vols. Leipzig, 1891); Edward T. Harper, 'Die Babylonische Legenden von Etana, Zu, Adapa, und Dibbarra' in *Beiträge zur Assyriologie*, Bd. ii. pp. 390-521. See also the translations of selected texts (including Creation story, legends, etc.) in *Assyrian and Babylonian Literature*, ed. by R. F. Harper (New York, 1901), pp. 282-444.

4. *LIFE AFTER DEATH.*—Besides the chapters in the general works on the Babylono-Assyrian religion, cf. Alfred Jeremias, *Die Babylonisch-Assyrischen Vorstellungen vom Leben nach dem Tode* (Leipzig, 1887, 2nd ed. announced); and the same author's 'Hölle und Paradies bei den Babyloniern' (*Der Alte Orient*, i. 3, Leipzig, 1900; 2nd ed. 1903).

5. *GENERAL CHARACTER AND BEARINGS ON THE OLD TESTAMENT.*—Out of the mass of literature on the subject, the following are intended to represent merely a selection that will serve as an introduction to the main phases of the subject and of the problems involved:—Schrader's *Keilinschriften und das Alte Testament*[2], 1883 [English translation by O. C. Whitehouse, *The Cuneiform Inscriptions and the Old Testament*, London, 1885-1888], is still of value as a collection of material, though superseded for the Creation story by King's work above referred to; the 3rd ed. of Schrader's work (Berlin, 1902-1903), by Hugo Winckler and H. Zimmern, is an entirely new work—the first part embodying Winckler's views of the bearings of Babylonian records on the Geography of Palestine and History of the Hebrews, which are based on theories and speculations that remain to be tested; the second part being a most careful and valuable survey of the material for the study of the Babylonian religion by H. Zimmern, with constant reference to the certain and possible bearings both on the Old and the New Testament. See also Zimmern's 'Babylonische und Biblische Urgeschichte' (*Der Alte Orient*, ii.[2] Leipzig, 3rd ed. 1903) [also in English translation, *The Babylonian and the Hebrew Genesis*, London, 1901]. In connexion with Professor Fried. Delitzsch's two lectures on *Babel und Bibel*, Leipzig, 1902-1903 [English translation by C. H. W. Johns, *Babel and Bible*, Edinburgh, 1903], cf. the monographs of Bezold, *Die Babylonisch-Assyrischen Keilinschriften und ihre Bedeutung für das Alte Testament* (Tübingen, 1904); Zimmern, *Keilinschriften und Bibel* (Berlin, 1903); C. F. Lehmann, *Babyloniens Kulturmission einst und jetzt* (Leipzig, 1903); Alfred Jeremias, *Im Kampfe um Babel und Bibel* (4th ed. Leipzig, 1903). For the Literature on the Excavations conducted in Babylonia and Assyria, and for general and special works on the History and general Culture, see the articles ASSYRIA and BABYLONIA in vol. i. of this Dictionary; to the references there given should now be added: R. W. Rogers, *History of Babylonia and Assyria* (New York, 1901), the most complete as yet published; the shorter history of Geo. S. Goodspeed, *History of Babylonia and Assyria* (New York, 1902); and Winckler's sketch in vol. iii. of Helmolt's *History of the World* [English translation, New York, 1902]. For a general

account of the Babylono-Assyrian culture, Bezold's admirably written and profusely illustrated work, *Ninive und Babylon* (2nd ed. Leipzig, 1903), is to be highly recommended as superseding Kaulen's *Assyrien und Babylonien*, the 5th edition of which (Freiburg, 1899) is not brought down to date, and is therefore of little use; while, for the general Babylono-Assyrian Literature, Teloni's manual, *Letteratura Assira* (Milan, 1903), may be mentioned as the latest survey of the field.

MORRIS JASTROW, Jr.

## CODE OF ḪAMMURABI.—

I. HISTORY AND ANALYSIS.
- i. *DISCOVERY OF THE CODE.*
- ii. *LITERATURE CALLED FORTH BY THE DISCOVERY.*
  1. *Editio princeps* of the Code.
  2. Versions and notices.
- iii. *IMPORTANCE OF THE INSCRIPTION.*
- iv. *ḪAMMURABI'S LIFE AND REIGN.*
  1. The sources.
  2. Ḫammurabi's genealogy.
  3. ,, nationality.
  4. ,, name.
  5. ,, date, and the date of the monument. Is Ḫammurabi the Amraphel of Gn 14?
  6. Principal events of Ḫammurabi's reign.
  7. Ḫammurabi's letters.
  8. Character of Ḫammurabi, and view of the monarchy disclosed in the Code and the letters.
  9. Extent of Ḫammurabi's empire.
- v. *SOCIAL GRADES RECOGNIZED IN THE CODE.*
  1. The aristocrat.
  2. The commoner.
  3. The slave.
- vi. *CLASS LEGISLATION A FEATURE OF THE CODE.*
  1. Feudal landowners: (*a*) 'levy-masters,' (*b*) 'constables,' (*c*) 'renters.'
  2. Votaries.
  3. Palace warders.
  4. Beer-sellers.
  5. Doctors, veterinary surgeons, branders.
  6. Builders and boatmen.
- vii. *AGRICULTURE.*
  1. Systems of land tenure.
  2. Agricultural loans.
  3. Irrigation.
  4. Wages and hire.
  5. Flocks and herds.
- viii. *SHIPPING, AND TRADE AND COMMERCE.*
  1. The shipping trade.
  2. Commerce.
  3. Interest.
  4. Debt and distraint.
  5. Sales.
  6. Hire.
- ix. *THE TEMPLE.*
- x. *JUSTICE.*
  1. Procedure.
  2. Judges.
  3. Witnesses.
  4. Parties.
  5. Penalties.
  6. Crimes and misdemeanours.
- xi. *MARRIAGE, AND FAMILY LIFE.*
  1. Marriage a contract. Rights and responsibilities of parties.
  2. Divorce.
  3. Monogamy presupposed in the Code.
  4. Votaries allowed to marry.
  5. Bars to marriage.
  6. Concubinage.
  7. Case of a free woman marrying a slave.
  8. Case of a girl vowed to a temple.
  9. Parents and children.
  10. Adoption.
  11. Law of inheritance.

II. THE CODE *in extenso*.

III. COMPARISON OF THE CODE OF ḪAMMURABI WITH THE EARLIEST HEBREW LEGISLATION.
- i. *THE QUESTION STATED, AND THE DATA AVAILABLE FOR ANSWERING IT.*
  1. What is involved in influence.
  2. Source of material.
  3. Alternative views of likeness.
  4. Common material: (*a*) customs, (*b*) enactments.
  5. 'Babylonian' influence progressive.
  6. Parallels in method of codification.
  7. Casuistic style.
  8. Adaptation.
  9. Primitive features in Hebrew law.
  10. Philological divergence not decisive.
  11. Order of clauses.
  12. Suggestions of conscious change: (*a*) selection, (*b*) revision, (*c*) amendment.
  13. Similarity to other ancient codes.
- ii. *VIEWS AS TO CHARACTER OF CONNEXION.*

### I. HISTORY AND ANALYSIS.

i. *DISCOVERY OF THE CODE.*—This body of ancient laws was first recovered to modern scholarship by the discovery, in December 1901 and January 1902, of three enormous fragments of a block of black diorite, which, when fitted together, formed a stele 2·25 metres high and tapering from 1·90 to 1·65 metres. At the upper end of the front side was a sculptured bas-relief representing the king Ḫammurabi receiving his Code of Laws from the seated sun-god Shamash. The discovery was made by J. de Morgan at the Acropolis of Susa, the ancient Persepolis, once capital of an independent Elamite monarchy.

This bas-relief measures ·65 metres in height and ·60 metres across. Immediately below it commences the longest Semitic inscription in cuneiform hitherto discovered. It is arranged in parallel columns, but each column is written belt-wise across the curved surface of the stele. Hence a reader must have turned his head on one side—to the left—to read the inscription. On the front side there are sixteen of these columns preserved. There were once five more, of which scarcely a trace is preserved, the inscription having been chiselled out and the stone repolished. On the reverse, twenty-eight columns are completely preserved, with one or two breaks due to the surface being destroyed. The whole inscription may therefore be estimated to have contained forty-nine columns, four thousand lines, and about eight thousand words.

ii. *LITERATURE CALLED FORTH BY THE DISCOVERY.*—1. The inscription is most beautifully cut in the well-known style characteristic of the Ḫammurabi period. Careful rubbings or 'squeezes' were taken and sent to France. V. Scheil, with remarkable promptitude, published the text by photogravure in the fourth volume of the *Mémoires de la Délégation en Perse* (Leroux, Paris), under the direction of the French Minister of Public Instruction. This *editio princeps* was accompanied by an excellent transliteration into Roman characters, a good first translation, with a few useful footnotes, and a recapitulation of the legal enactments. This superb volume, in quarto, appeared in October 1902.

2. It at once attracted attention. In October the present writer gave a full account of it in a paper read before the Cambridge Theological Society, an abstract of which appeared in the *Journal of Theological Studies*, January 1903. In November, H. Winckler published an independent version in German under the title of *Die Gesetze Hammurabis, Königs von Babylon um 2250 v. Chr.: Das älteste Gesetzbuch der Welt* (Hinrichs, Leipzig; second edition in March, third in November, 1903). This was in some respects an improvement on Scheil's translation, and was accompanied by some ingenious footnotes. About the same time R. Dareste gave a full account of the Code, comparing it with other ancient codes, in the *Journal des Savants* for October and November. In December the *New York Independent* began a series of articles by W. H. Ward, called 'The most ancient Civil Code' (December 11, 18, January 8, 15, 22). This closely followed Winckler's translation, but introduced some parallels from the laws of Moses. In February the present writer published a translation which aimed at being as literal as possible. This was accompanied by an exhaustive index, and appeared as the *Oldest Code of Laws in the World* (T. & T. Clark, Edinburgh). In March appeared an article entitled 'The recently discovered Civil Code of Hammurabi,' by C. F. Kent, in the *Biblical World*. This gave a very readable account of the whole subject, and pointed out many Mosaic parallels. The translation followed Winckler. In August, F. Mari issued an Italian translation, *Il Codice di Hammurabi e la Bibbia* (Desclée & Co., Rome). In November,

D. H. Müller gave, in the *X Jahresbericht der Israelitisch-Theologischen Lehranstalt in Wien*, a very full account of the Code under the title 'Die Gesetze Hammurabis und die mosaische Gesetzgebung' (A. Holder, Vienna). This is specially noticeable for a beautiful Hebrew rendering, as well as an improved transcription and German translation. It has a very full commentary. About the same time appeared the first volume of *Hammurabi's Gesetz*, by J. Kohler and F. E. Peiser (Pfeiffer, Leipzig). It contains a new translation, juristic version, and some good explanatory matter.

A number of books have been devoted to the comparison of this Code with other ancient legislations: S. Oettli, *Das Gesetz Hammurabis und die Thora Israels* (Deichert, Leipzig); J. Jeremias, *Moses und Hammurabi* (Hinrichs, Leipzig [first edition in March, second in November, 1903]); R. Dareste, 'Le Code Babylonien d'Hammourabi' (*Nouvelle Revue Historique de droit français et étranger*, xxvii. p. 5 f., Larose, Paris); C. Stooss, 'Das babylonische Strafrecht Hammurabis' (*Schweizerische Zeitschrift für Strafrecht*, xvi. p. 1 ff.); G. Cohn, *Die Gesetze Hammurabis*, a Rectorial address (Füssli, Zürich); H. Grimme, *Das Gesetz Chammurabis und Moses* (Bachem, Cologne); Père Lagrange, 'Le code de Hammourabi' (*Revue Biblique*, xii. p. 27, Lecoffre, Paris); S. A. Cook, *The Laws of Moses and the Code of Hammurabi* (A. & C. Black, London); W. St. C. Boscawen, *First of Empires* (Harper, London). Besides these, there have been a large number of reviews and notices. Most of the books just cited refer to other literature on cognate subjects. The comparisons with the Bible which they suggest will be given in square brackets at the end of the corresponding sections of the Code (below, p. 599[b] ff.).

iii. *IMPORTANCE OF THE INSCRIPTION.*—At Susa, where the monument was actually found, the French explorers have of late years been conducting a very scientific examination of the remains of the oldest strata. They have given to the world, along with many records of the native Elamite monarchs, a number of splendid monuments of Babylonian kings. These had been transported from Babylonia as trophies of conquest, as is shown by the fact that sundry specimens have had parts of their inscriptions erased, and replaced by the name and titles of some Elamite ruler. We can hardly doubt that this was to have been done in the space left vacant by the erased five columns of this stele, but the inscription was never cut in. Hence we do not know for certain when this monument was carried to Susa. That it was meant to be set up in Sippara is clear from the words *E-barra šuati*, 'this E-barra,' the name of the temple of Shamash at Sippara (line 76, rev. col. xxviii.).

The value of the inscription is enormously enhanced by its being the original autograph. Copies existed. There was found with it at Susa a large fragment of a duplicate. The scribes of Assurbanipal, king of Assyria (B.C. 668-626), made copies of it, or one of its duplicates, dividing the text into possibly fifteen books. They called the series, in their edition, *dinâni (ša) Ḫammurabi*, either 'the judgments of Ḫammurabi,' or perhaps 'the image of Ḫammurabi.' A number of fragments of this Assyrian edition, preserved in the British Museum, were copied and edited, with attempted translation and notes, by B. Meissner, under the title 'Altbabylonische Gesetze' (*Beiträge zur Assyriologie*, iii. pp. 493-523). A fragment or two had been already published, noticed under the title 'Code d'Asourbanipal.' But Meissner, who had edited a large number of contracts of the time of Ḫammurabi in his 'Das altbabylonische Privatrecht' (*Assyriolog. Bibliothek*, xi.), recognized forms of expression, measures of capacity and area, which showed that the Assyrian scribes had copied from some ancient document of that period. Frdr. Delitzsch, in his article 'Zur juristischen Litteratur Babyloniens' (*Beiträge zur Assyriologie*, iv. pp. 78-87), again went over Meissner's texts, and, giving an improved translation, definitely named them the 'Code Ḫammurabi.' This deduction was amply verified in a few months by the discovery at Susa. The Assyrian copies are wonderfully faithful, and the few variants which occur in them may be due to their having been copied, not from this stele but from a contemporary duplicate. The credit of recognizing these copies in Meissner's edition is due to Professor Scheil, who also pointed out that they actually restore parts of the erased five columns. T. G. Pinches, in a paper entitled 'Ḫammurabi's Code of Laws' (*Proceedings of the Society of Biblical Archæology*, 1902, p. 301 ff.), showed the existence of a further fragment, published in *Cuneiform Texts from Babylonian Tablets, etc., in the British Museum* (xiii. pls. 46, 47). H. Winckler, in a review of Scheil's edition (in the *Orientalische Litteraturzeitung*, January 1903), gives a long examination of these Assyrian copies. It is to be hoped that further fragments may now be recognized and published.

Not only did the Assyrian lawyers study this great Code, but the later Babylonians did the same. F. E. Peiser, in his *Jurisprudentiæ Babylonicæ quæ supersunt* (Cöthen, 1890), published the text of a number of fragments of late Babylonian copies preserved in the Berlin Museum (V.A.Th. 991, 1036). From these we learn that the scribes had edited the Code in a series of books, or tablets, under the title *Nînu ilu ṣîrum*, which are the first words of the Susa stele. As the seventh book ended with Scheil's § 154, we may fairly assume that this edition was in twelve books. It was the habit of the Assyrian and Babylonian scribes to write commentaries on the works they studied. Now that the text of the Code is known, we may expect that commentaries, like those published by L. W. King in his edition of the Creation Tablets, will be found and published.

The monument not only contains the Code, but Ḫammurabi devoted some seven hundred lines to a prologue and epilogue, which narrated his glory and that of the gods whom he worshipped, and blessed those who should respect his inscription, while they cursed the future vandals who should injure or deface it. This part of the inscription is either conventionally phrased or very difficult, and many editors have done wisely in ignoring it altogether. There are, however, several noteworthy points about these portions of the inscription which help to fix our views as to its date. We may first sketch briefly what is known as to the king's life and reign. Much fresh information has come to light since the article BABYLONIA (in vol. i.) was written.

iv. *ḪAMMURABI'S LIFE AND REIGN.*—1. The fresh sources for Ḫammurabi's reign are chiefly the *Letters and Inscriptions of Ḫammurabi*, published by L. W. King in three magnificent volumes (Luzac, London, 1898-1900). They consist of fifty-five letters written by Ḫammurabi to his vassal Sin-idinnam of Larsa; ten of his great inscriptions, besides a multitude of other letters and inscriptions relating to the other kings of his Dynasty. Most important of all is the Chronicle of the Kings of the First Dynasty of Babylon (pp. 212-252). In the *Cuneiform Texts from Babylonian Tablets, etc., in the British Museum* (vols. ii. iv. vi. viii.) were also published a large number of contracts, lists, and letters from the same period. They were copied by T. G. Pinches. Professor Scheil, in various numbers of the *Recueil de Travaux*, and more fully in *Une Saison de Fouilles à Sippar* (Cairo, 1902), has added many more contemporary documents (quoted as S). Dr. Pinches published a few in his *Babylonian Tablets in the possession of Sir H. Peck, Bart.* (London, 1888). Strassmaier had published a large collection of tablets, found by W. K. Loftus at Tell Sifr, in the *Verhandlungen des V internationalen Orientalisten Congresses* (Berlin, 1882) (quoted as B). Dr. Meissner in his 'Das altbabylonische Privatrecht' published the text of many more, chiefly from the collection brought home by E. A. W. Budge, and registered in the British Museum as Bu. 88–5–12 (quoted here as B[1]), and the collection of J. Simon in the Berlin Museum (quoted as V.A.Th. The collection made by Dr. Budge, registered in the British Museum as Bu. 91–5–9, is quoted as B[2]). Dr. E. Lindl in his article 'Die Datenliste der ersten Dynastie von Babylon' (*Beiträge zur Assyriologie*, iv. pp. 338–402), Dr. G. Nagel in 'Die Briefe Hammurabi's an Sinidinnam' (*Beiträge zur Assyriologie*, iv. pp. 434–483), with remarks by Professor Delitzsch (pp. 483–500), Dr. Mary W. Montgomery's *Briefe aus der Zeit des babylonischen Königs Ḫammurabi* (A. Pries, Leipzig), Dr. S. Daiches, *Altbabylonische Rechtsurkunden aus der Zeit der Ḫammurabi-Dynastie* (Hinrichs, Leipzig), all deal with the same period.

Important studies of the proper names of this period have been made by Hommel in *Ancient Hebrew Tradition*, and Ranke in *Die Personennamen in den Urkunden der Ḫammurabidynastie* (Franz, Munich, 1902). Other literature is quoted in these works. T. G. Pinches' *Old Testament in the light of the Historical Records of Assyria and Babylonia* (S.P.C.K., London) is a mine of information for the period. The second edition has a fresh translation of the Code.

It will be seen from the above that we are exceptionally well informed about the times of the First Dynasty of Babylon. These very numerous documents illustrate by actual practical examples the working of Ḫammurabi's laws. They furnish innumerable parallels for the rare words and expressions.

2. According to the Babylonian King-Lists A and B (see Rogers, *Hist. Bab. Assyr.* p. 312 f.), Ḫammurabi was the sixth king of the First Dynasty of Babylon, being son of Sin-muballiṭ, grandson of Apil-Sin, great-grandson of Zabum, who was son of Suma-lailu and grandson (?) of Sumu-abi, founder of the Dynasty. In the Susa inscription (col. iv. ll. 68–70) the king names himself 'Ḫammurabi, son of Sin-muballiṭ, descendant of Sumu-lailu.' There can therefore be no possible doubt as to his identity. His son Samsuiluna calls Sumu-lailu the 'fifth father of my father' (King, iii. p. 205). A later king (King, iii. p. 208), Ammiditana, calls himself 'descendant of Sumu-lailu,' so that it seems as if the family traced back descent only as far as Sumu-lailu. The King-Lists also do not say that Sumu-lailu was son of the founder Sumu-abi.

3. The nationality of the First Dynasty has been much discussed, and is of considerable importance in determining the origin of the Code itself; as, if the Dynasty was foreign, the Code may reflect non-Babylonian influence. There is no doubt that the names of the kings, except Apil-Sin and Sin-muballiṭ, are not of the usual Babylonian type; though Jensen (*Zeitschrift für Assyriologie*, x. p. 342) maintains that they are. They, and other names of this period, exhibit many peculiarities: such as *Samsu* instead of the usual Babylonian *Šamaš*; the enigmatic *Sumu* perhaps for *Sumu*; imperfects like *iamlik* in place of the Babylonian *imlik*; strange words like *zaduga*, *ditana*, *ammi* (if not a Divine name), *zimri*, besides strange gods like Elali, Wadd, 'Anat. But scholars are greatly divided as to the nationality indicated by such names. Hommel, Sayce, A. Jeremias, and Ranke favour Arabian, especially in its old forms as preserved in Minæan and Sabæan inscriptions. Winckler and Delitzsch call these names West Semitic or North Semitic, as belonging to the group of Canaanite dialects—Phœnician, Moabite, Hebrew, Aramæan. S. A. Cook, after reviewing opinions, wisely says that we know too little of the earlier history of the languages of Arabia and Canaan. We may content ourselves with saying that these people were a freshly arrived Semitic race who retained, in Babylonia, names and words which they brought from a former home. In the 7th cent. B.C. the Ḫarran census (*Assyriologische Bibliothek*, xvii.) shows many of these peculiarities in names borne by the serfs under Assyrian rule. They may, then, belong to a race recently transplanted by Assyrian conquests, or, if indigenous, may point to a nationality descended from those who raised the First Dynasty to empire. So far as cuneiform sources go, we find most affinity with the names of Canaanites in the time of the Tel el-Amarna tablets. But this distinctly foreign influence appears not only in names. The Code shows it in such words as *šittin* for 'two-thirds.'

4. The name Ḫammurabi has long been well known. In vol. i. of Rawlinson's *Cuneiform Inscriptions of Western Asia*, 1861 (p. 4, Nos. 1, 2, 3), three inscriptions of his were published. Inscriptions in the Louvre were given by Oppert in 1863 in his *Expédition scientifique en Mesopotamie*. The Babylonian scribes of a later period regarded the name as foreign, for they drew up a list of the names of the kings who reigned 'after the Flood,' with their explanations of those names. Some of the names are Sumerian, or Kassite; but among them is Ḫammurabi, whose name is translated *Kimtarapaštum*. Another is Ammizaduga, whose name is translated *Kimtum-kittum*. Hence they regarded *ḫammu* as the same word as *ammi*, and equivalent to *kimtu*, 'family.' The variants of Ḫammurabi's name, such as Ammi-rabi, Ammurapi (late Assyrian), Ḫammum-rabi, etc., show that they were partly right (King, iii. p. lxv, note 4). But it is doubtful if they were right in rendering it *kimtum*. *Ammu* or *Ḫammu* may well be the name of a god. In compounds like Sumu-ḫammu, Jasdi-ḫammu, Zimri-ḫammu, it can hardly mean 'family,' unless this was deified. The element *rabi* is so very common in Babylonian that we can hardly be wrong in rendering it 'is great.' The name is like Sin-rabi, Samaš-rabi, and may well mean 'Ammu is great.' The adjective *rapaštu*, applied to the feminine *kimtu*, is 'wide' or 'great' also; and in that the old grammarians were right.

5. The date to be assigned to the First Dynasty of Babylon has been much disputed. The King-Lists, if taken in their integrity, would put the beginning of the Dynasty at B.C. 2454, and Ḫammurabi's accession at B.C. 2342. But many doubts attach to these figures. Nabonidus puts Ḫammurabi seven hundred years before Burnaburiash, who cannot be much before B.C. 1400. Rost reduces the length of the Kassite Dynasty by a hundred and eighty years, and so places the beginning of the Dynasty in B.C. 2232, which agrees with Berosus as explained by Peiser, and with Simplicius on one reading. The whole question is well discussed by Rogers in his *History of Babylonia and Assyria*, ch. xii.; but no definite result can be expected from present materials. Even the lengths of the reigns are in doubt now.

The Babylonians at this period gave each year a name. The year-name recorded some prominent event—the building of a shrine, or an expedition, for example. Now the Chronicles published by King give the year-names for the reigns of the kings, and assign forty-three years to Ḫammurabi, while the King-Lists give him fifty-five. The difference may be accounted for by the proved fact that the same year had sometimes two separate names. The King-Lists may have counted all year-names, and so have made the reigns too long. But this is not always the case: thus, in the King-List, Samsu-iluna has only thirty-five years, while the Chronicle gives him thirty-eight. Here, again, we must await further evidence.

But we can place the monument approximately in the reign. For, when we recall what we know from various sources, we find that Rim-Sin was reigning in Larsa till the 30th year of Ḫammurabi's reign. Then Ḫammurabi defeated Elam and overthrew Rim-Sin. The following year he conquered Iamutbal, a province of Elam. Now, Ḫammurabi boasts in the prologue (col. ii. ll. 32–36) that he had 'avenged Larsa and renovated Ebabbar,' the temple of Shamash there. This he could hardly have done while Rim-Sin was still ruling. We may therefore date the stele after the thirtieth year of his reign.

Of some interest is the usually received identification of Ḫammurabi with the Amraphel of Gn 14. With this is bound up the question whether Arioch of Ellasar is Rim-Sin of Larsa. For this view, which has the support of most Assyriologists, see especially Pinches (*Old Testament*, etc., ch. vi.); on the other side, see King (i. pp. xxv f., xlix f.). An ingenious method of disposing of the superfluous final *l* in Amraphel has been suggested by Hüsing, who would join it to the next word, and read, 'And it came to pass in the days of Amraph, as Arioch king of Ellasar was over Shinar, that Chedorlaomer,' etc. But Arioch is nearly as difficult, and the whole incident is quite inconsistent, unless the configuration of the country has entirely changed since. The same uncertainties remain as to date on both chronologies.

6. The Chronicle gives us the following skeleton outline of the events of this reign, being the list of year-names. (1) *The year in which Ḫammurabi became king.* (2) *The year in which Ḫammurabi established the heart of the land in righteousness.* This has been taken to refer to the initiation of legal reforms; but the same formula is used of Sumu-lailu (B[2] 2177 A), and may only mean religious reform. The Code was probably not promulgated this year. (3) *The year in which the throne of Nannar was made.* Nannar was god of Erech, but this throne was made in Babylon. We cannot, therefore, conclude that Ḫammurabi was already ruler in Erech. (4) *The year in which the wall of Malgâ was destroyed.* Ḫammurabi also destroyed the fortress of Maer in this year. Malgâ is probably not the same place as the frequently named Malgia, which was close to Sippara. Maer was an important shipping town. Weissbach thinks both were on the Euphrates, near its junction with the Ḫabur (*Babylonische Miscellen*, p. 13). These fortresses were later repaired. The date of the fifth year is not preserved, but some god's temple was probably restored. The sixth year is noted for the restoration of some fortress. Some event at Isin marked the seventh year. (8) *The year in which . . . on the bank of the canal Nuḫuš-niši.* The meaning of the name is 'the abundance of the people.' An inscription in the Louvre is devoted to the record of the completion of this canal. Ḫammurabi built on the banks of it a lofty fortress, which he called after his father, Dûr-Sin-muballiṭ-abim-walidia, and the gap in the Chronicle here may have contained the name of this fortress. (9) *The year in which the canal Ḫammurabi was dug.* It is not clear whether this canal or the one called Tišid-Bêl was meant here. The latter ran from the Euphrates to Sippar. This event may have been used only to date Sippar documents. (10) *The year in which the . . . inhabitants of Malgi.* This probably refers to a reinstatement of the people, on the restoration, of Malgâ and Maer. Some event connected with a city dated the next year. (12) *The year in which the throne of Ṣarpanitum was made.* This goddess was the consort of Marduk. The date of the next year is not made out clearly. (14) *The year in which the throne of Ištar of Babylon was made.* (15) *The year in which the seven images were made.* (16) *The year in which the throne of Nabû was made.* Next year another image was made; the year following, something for Bêl. The next year something was said about 'the mountain'?. (20) *The year in which the throne of Adad was made.* (21) *The year in which the wall of Bazu was made.* The city *Bazu* was close to Sippara, and not far from Kish. Next year perhaps a canal was cut or an image of Ḫammurabi set up. Then something seems to have been done at Sippara. Then something was done for Bêl. (25) *The year in which the wall of Sippara was made.* It was the foundation that was laid this year, and it was 'the great wall,' probably an outer circle. The next year records a great flood. Then a great temple was built. (28) *The year in which the temple E-NAM-ḪE was built.* This was the temple called 'the house of abundance,' the temple of Adad at Babylon. (29) *The year in which the image of the goddess Šala was made.* Šala was the consort of Adad. (30) *The year in which the army of Elam was defeated.* (31) *The year in which the land of Iamutbal was annexed.* A fuller form of this date is, '*The year of Ḫammurabi the king, in which with the help of Anu and Bêl he established his good fortune, and his hand cast to the earth the lana of Iamutbal and Rim-Sin the king.*' A further conquest is recorded for the next year, perhaps of the land Dupliaš. (33) *The year in which the canal of Ḫammurabi . . .* This may refer to the completion of the work begun in the ninth year, or to a new canal whose name is not preserved. (34) *The year in which for Anu, Ištar, and Nanâ (the temple E-TUR-KALAMA was restored).* This date is restored from contemporary documents. The next year perhaps the great wall named Kara-Šamaš was built. The dates of the next two years are lost. (38) *The year in which the city of Dupliaš was destroyed by flood.* This date is restored from contemporary documents. An alternative date for this year is, *The year of Ḫammurabi the king in which the people of Turukku, Kakmum, and Subê. . . .* Whether they were destroyed by flood or conquered does not appear. The dates of the next five years are lost, but the Chronicle gives the total length of the reign as forty-three years. We know several other year-names for this reign, but are not able to place them yet. *The year in which Ibik-Adad captured the city of Rabiḳu.* Another date refers to the building of the walls of Rabiḳu and Kâr-Šamaš. The latter was built on the banks of the Tigris. *The year of Ḫammurabi the king in which the goddess Tašmêtum made favourable her word. The year of Ḫammurabi the king in which the temple E-ME-TE-UR-SAG was restored and the temple IGI-E-NIR-KIDUR-MAH was built for Zamama and Ninni, and its summit made high like the heavens.* (For further details, see King and Lindl).

7. This sketch we may fill out by the details

given in letters and contracts. There the king appears as an energetic benevolent ruler, who kept the chief business of importance under his own direction. Most of his letters are addressed to one Sin-idinnam, who, if not a vassal king of Larsa, was the governor of that city. If he was set in the place of Rim-Sin, who was independent king of Larsa for the first thirty years of Ḫammurabi's reign, we may suppose all these letters dated after that event. But, in any case, it is unlikely that Ḫammurabi could give such minute orders to Sin-idinnam as long as Rim-Sin reigned there. We find that Sin-idinnam exercised authority also over Erech and Ur. At one time Sin-idinnam had a military command, for the king ordered him to send certain Elamite goddesses, who had been captured, under escort to Babylon; and when the same goddesses were sent back to their temples, under the escort of Inuḫsamar and his troops, Sin-idinnam was told to attack the Elamites first, lest it might seem to be a confession of weakness. The earliest known reference to Assyria occurs in these letters, when 240 men of the 'King's company' are said to have left Assyria. The Code also names Ashur, the city, and Nineveh (col. iv. ll. 55–63); but last among the list of subject-towns. The name of the god Asur already occurs in the reign of Sin-muballiṭ ($B^1$ 3, $B^1$ 14).

8. The king's piety and care for the worship of the gods appear not only in the prologue to the Code, where he boasts of having built, restored, or adorned the temples of the chief cities of the empire, but also in the above list of year-names. Further, in his letters we find him directing the collection of temple revenues and superintending their shepherds and herdsmen. He postponed the hearing of a trial because one of the parties was on duty at a festival in Ur. He controlled the calendar, sending Sin-idinnam notice that the month now beginning was to be a second Elul. He is, however, careful to add that this must not be taken as an excuse for postponing payments for a month.

The king also gave directions as to the canals. We have seen that he constructed several. In one letter he orders the dwellers on the banks of a certain canal to clear it out. In another case a canal was so badly dredged that ships could not come to Erech. Ḫammurabi orders the work to be done 'in three days.' Even the Euphrates (?) stream had to be cleared.

But it is in the administration of justice that this king is seen in the most favourable light. Apparently, he was accessible to all. Bribery he dealt with promptly; he enforced a merchant's claim for a debt against a city governor; he sent instructions as to how cases were to be treated. Against money-lenders he was severe, and several letters deal with loans or debts. He orders the parties concerned to be sent to Babylon, and gives instructions for their being guarded.

The collection of revenue, the due care of the royal flocks and herds, the audit of accounts, the regulation of food supplies, shipping and other transport, labour on public works, and the proper exemptions from duty, are all frequently dealt with in the letters. For fuller details and the parallels from other reigns of the First Dynasty, see King's *Letters of Ḫammurabi.*

The period of Ḫammurabi's Dynasty was one of great literary activity. Many of the tablets in Assurbanipal's library are ascribed to this period by their characteristic forms of expression; but no works are definitely ascribed by the documents themselves to this king. Still, the view is general among Assyriologists that this period produced most of the masterpieces which later generations chiefly reproduced.

The picture of monarchy which these sources and the Code reveal is by no means unpleasing. Like all Oriental despotisms, it is ideally a strong, energetic, benevolent monarchy. In the words of Ḫammurabi, he was indeed 'a father of his people' (col. xxv. 21 f.) and 'the sun of Babylon' (col. v. 4). His Code amply justifies his boast, if it was carried out. That is rendered probable by the host of contemporary documents, not only for his reign, but for those of his predecessors and successors. So far as they refer to the class of cases considered in the Code, they confirm its working. Of course a large number of cases, especially criminal cases, were not the subject of written records. We have no records of trials for murder, rape, incest, or the like grievous wrongs. But we have not only contracts of marriage, partnership, loans and commissions, and other commercial business, but also a number of legal decisions. These mostly relate to property disputes, but a few touch crime as well. So far as they go, they prove that the Code was literally carried out. Further, they show that it was no new invention, but codified the customary law of the country.

The king was a *quasi*-Divine person. This is shown not only by the invocation of his name along with those of the gods in solemn oaths, but by such names as *Ḫammurabi-ilu*, 'Ḫammurabi is god'; *Ḫammurabi-šamšî*, 'Ḫammurabi is my sun.' Men swore by 'Šamaš, Aia (his consort), and Ḫammurabi the king,' as also by the name of Marduk or of Rim-Sin, other gods or other kings. See a list of these oaths in Kohler-Peiser, i. p. 107 f. The king was often accorded the title *i-lu* as a prefix to his name. This custom continued in use until late in the Kassite Dynasty. In the prologue to the Code (col. ii. 48), Ḫammurabi calls himself the 'Divine shelter,' *i-lu ṣululu*, of his land, (col. iii. 16) the 'Divine king of the city,' *i-lu šar ali*, (col. v. 4) the 'Divine sun' of Babylon, *i-lu Šamšu.*

As one consequence of this sacred majesty of the king, he does not directly appear as party to any commercial or business transaction. This was not so in early times. In one of the oldest monuments of Babylonia which we possess, the stele of Maništusu, king of Kish (*Mémoires de la Délégation en Perse*, tom. ii. p. 1 ff.), we find the king buying lands, like any other person, to make up an estate for his son Mesalim, afterwards king of Kish also. But in all later times the rule holds good. The king's stewards, shepherds, and other officials buy and sell, obviously for their master, but his name does not come into the transaction.

9. The extent of Ḫammurabi's empire can be gathered only partly from the Code. He names in the prologue the cities of Babylon, Sippara, Nippur, Dûrilu, Eridu, Ur, Larsa, Erech, Isin, Kish, Cuthah, Borsippa, Dilbat, Shirpurla, Ḫallab, Karkar, Maškan-šabri, Malkâ, Agade, Ashur, Nineveh, but only as having done benefits to the temples there. The list covers all Assyria and Babylonia. He is called king of Martu in an inscription set up in his honour, and that is usually taken to mean the Westland or Palestine (King, *Letters*, iii. p. 195 f.).

v. *SOCIAL GRADES RECOGNIZED IN THE CODE.*—The Code recognizes three grades of society: the *amêlu*, the *muškênu*, and the *ardu*.

1. The first grade were the men of gentle birth, men of family, and very likely were largely of the same race as the royal family. Winckler has compared them with the *amêlu* of the Tel el-Amarna tablets, where it is still a distinct title, and with early Arabic *'âlû, ulai* (*Altorientalische Forschungen*, ii. p. 313). The king himself seems to be addressed by the title *amêlu ša Marduk liballiṭsu*, 'the *amêlu* to whom may Marduk grant life.' He

thus held the position of the First Gentleman of Babylonia. In many passages *amêlu* is distinctly equivalent to 'officer.' By courtesy it was extended, like our 'Sir' or 'Esquire,' to mark every person of position not otherwise titled. Even in the Code it is usually applied to all free citizens, when no distinction from the *muškênu* is necessary. It is also used as a determinative before names of trades and occupations. Thus the potter, the tailor, the stone-cutter, carpenter, builder, and other artisans, who are paid a daily wage but may have belonged to old trade guilds, are *amêlê*; but not the doctor, the veterinary surgeon, or the brander. In some cases this may be accidental, but must be remembered in case further evidence should come to light. He was an officer when performing military service. His residence appears to be called an *êkallu*, which is best rendered 'mansion'; the usual rendering 'palace' is apt to suggest the royal residence. It seems probable that every town contained one or more such 'mansions.' They are named in contracts as being built for persons who were certainly not kings (B² 333, B² 381). Consequently the slave of the 'palace' is not necessarily a royal slave (§§ 175–176).

2. The *muškênu*, whose name passed into Hebrew as מִסְכֵּן (*miṣkēn*), Ital. *meschino*, *meschinello*, Portug. *mesquinho*, French *mesquin*, etc., occupies a lower rank. His penalties are less, but so are his compensations for injury. He is specially legislated for (§§ 8, 140, 198, 201, 204, 208, 211, 216, 219, 222). The rendering of the name is difficult. The translation 'poor man' is not very good. For he was no pauper, certainly not a beggar. He had slaves (§ 15) and goods. Müller calls him an *Armenstiftler*; but there is no evidence of his receiving any pension. Kohler and Peiser give *Ministerial*; but there is no evidence of his having any special association with the court, or any special duties. The name itself may be taken to mean a 'subject,' originally 'suppliant.' We take it he was a 'commoner,' one of the *plebs*, perhaps of the conquered race. At any rate he was free, but apparently subject to the *corvée*, perhaps obliged to serve in the ranks of the army. We find that his offering in the temple was allowed to be less than others (Meissner, *Beiträge zur Kenntnis der Babylonischen Religion*, p. 176 f.). In Assyrian times the Babylonians complained that they were being treated as *muškênu*, not so much 'poor men,' but subject to indignities. In the Tel el-Amarna tablets Amenophis quotes the letter of Kadašman-Bêl to him, inquiring after his daughter Ṣuḫarti. The Babylonian king says the Egyptian had his sister to wife; but no messenger of his had ever been able to see the princess, or know whether she was alive or dead. A certain lady they had seen, but *mindi martu išten muškênu*, 'whether she was the daughter of some *muškênu*,' they could not tell. In omen tablets it is a curse that a man *muškênûtu allak*, 'should come to poverty' (Bezold, *Catalogue*, p. 1566).

3. The slave (*ardu*) was treated very much as a chattel. He could be sold or pledged (§§ 118, 147); damage done to him had to be paid for, but the compensation went to his master (§§ 213, 214, 219, 220). A repudiation of servitude on his part was punished by mutilation (§ 282). The master is not said to have power of life and death; indeed his power seems expressly limited to mutilation. The slave could acquire wealth, and act in business as a free man, but his master had to be cognizant of his transactions. If he was living in his master's house he could not buy or sell, except by power of attorney, or written licence from his master (§ 7). But many slaves married and had homes of their own. Then the master acted as patron, and recovered their debts for them. A slave who married one of his master's slave girls was able to acquire wealth, but his master was his sole heir, and his children were slaves. On the other hand, a slave, at any rate if in the service of a 'great house,' or of a *muškênu*, could marry a free woman. In that case the children were free (§ 175), and the free woman's marriage portion remained hers, for her children, on her husband's death (§ 176). The property which the pair acquired after marriage was divided into two equal portions: the master, as his slave's heir, took one half, the wife and children the other half. A slave could buy his freedom with his savings. This must have been a free bargain between slave and master. The former had to choose between freedom and poverty on one side, and service and comfort on the other. The master accepted a present gain in lieu of a deferred reversion of the slave's property. The Code does not notice this point.

A female slave could become her master's concubine. Her children were free (§§ 170–171); and so was she, at her master's death. If her master chose he could acknowledge her children, and then they inherited equally with the children of his free wife; but these had first choice in the sharing of his property (§ 170). If she was the property of a free woman who was married, the slave girl might be given by her mistress to her husband to bear him children (§ 144). Her mistress retained the right to punish presumption and insolence by degradation to full slavery again; but the slave girl, if she had borne children to her master, could not be sold. At his death she was free (§§ 146, 147).

The slave was not always contented with his lot. He might run away. His captor was bound to bring him back to his master, and was then rewarded by statute with a payment of two shekels (§ 17). But if the captor kept him in his own house, and did not give him up on demand, he was punished with death (§ 19). So was any one who enticed a slave away from his master (§ 15). The slave seems to have had liberty to go about freely in the city where his master lived, but not to leave the city without his master's consent (§ 15). A slave usually had his owner's name, or some mark by which he could be recognized, branded or tattooed on his arm. If a captured fugitive slave would not name his owner, he had to be taken to the 'palace' or governor's residence, and there put to the question, and so restored to the owner (§ 18). We find from the letters that the officers over the levy claimed, for the *corvée*, unowned slaves (B² 419). The tattooing of the slave's mark was the business of the *gallabu*, who could also render it irrecognizable again. To do this without the consent of the owner, rendered the *gallabu* liable to have his hands cut off (§ 226). If he had been deceived into doing this by some one who was judged to have designs on that slave, the *gallabu* could swear to his innocence and be let off; but the fraudulent holder of the slave was treated as a slave stealer, and put to death (§ 227). To 'mark' a man was equivalent to reducing him to slavery. This might be done to a rebellious child by the Sumerian laws. Also it might be inflicted on a man for slander (§ 127), or on a rebellious or insolent slave (§ 146). A fugitive slave might be put in chains by his master. Harbouring a fugitive was punished with death (§ 16).

The slaves were probably recruited principally from captives taken in war. We see that certain persons might be bought abroad and brought back by merchants. These would, no doubt, be offered for sale as slaves. But, if they were natives of Babylonia, their relatives, their town temple, or, in the last resort, the State, would ransom them (§ 32). If they had been slaves before, in Babylonia, it seems that they had to be set at liberty on being brought back (§ 280). But the Code may only mean that they returned to their former condition. Foreigners, once slaves in Babylonia, captured thence in war, bought abroad by a merchant and again offered for sale by him in Babylonia, if recognized by a former master, might be re-bought by him at the price the merchant gave for them abroad (§ 281). The Code apparently aims at excluding a profit on the transaction, but leaves the price to be settled by the merchant's oath as to the money paid by him.

There is no trace in the Code, or contemporary documents, of serfs, or *glebæ adscripti*, such as were so common in Assyria and the district about Ḫarran in the 7th cent. B.C. (see 'Ḫarran census,' *Assyriologische Bibliothek*, xvii.). The serf seems to have held his lands by inheritance, and had property of his own. The class was largely recruited from slaves and town artisans. A serf's father is usually named. He was sold with the land, and subject apparently to military service. Many captives taken in war were settled as serfs, and the Assyrian kings usually assigned lands to the transported peoples.

The slave proper usually appears as fatherless; but a number of cases occur at all periods, when parents sell their children. Free men might be sold for debt, or reduced to slavery as punishment for crime. In the latter case they probably became public slaves. Slaves were subject to the *corvée*, as king's servants. Even female slaves owed service to the State—usually work, such as weaving or spinning. It was of great importance to a buyer of a slave whether this duty had been discharged, and he often demanded a guarantee that it was no longer due. It probably was confined to a number of years—six seems likely in the case of the Ḫarran serfs. A great many slaves were skilled workmen; they were often apprenticed to learn a trade. But in early times the trades were in the hands of free men.

Slaves might be adopted as children by free men and women, usually to care for the old age of one whose own family had already grown up and left the home. Such adopted children became free, and usually inherited their adoptive parents' property. Further details on the status of slaves, especially in later times, will be found in Meissner, *de Servitute*, Pries, Leipzig; and S. A. Cook, *The Laws of Moses*, etc., ch. vii.

The value of a slave varied much with age, accomplishments, sex, etc. The Code avoids the question by awarding 'slave for slave' (§§ 219, 231), 'half his price' (§§ 199, 220). A maidservant was worth twenty shekels of silver (§ 214), her unborn babe two shekels (§ 213). In contemporary documents a male slave sold for as little as six shekels or as much as twenty. A female slave might fetch as little as four and a half, or, with a babe, as much as ninety-four shekels.

The reward for restoring a fugitive to his master (§ 17), or for curing a slave (§§ 217, 223), was two shekels of silver, evidently calculated as one-tenth of the ordinary value. This value of twenty shekels remained constant as the average to the times of the Second Babylonian Empire.

vi. *CLASS LEGISLATION A FEATURE OF THE CODE.*—A distinctive feature of the Code is its class legislation. Not only are the aristocrat, the commoner, and the slave treated separately, but the Code legislates separately for certain classes of the community.

1. The first class are feudal landowners. They hold lands of the crown by service. Their names, *rid ṣâbê* and *bâ'iru*, are difficult to translate, because we have no modern officials whose functions exactly correspond to theirs. (*a*) For the first we propose 'levy-master.' The 'levy-master' was over the *corvée*. He had to make up the local quota for the army, or for forced labour. On the former side he might answer to the field-cornet, commandant, pressgang officer, *Feldwebel*, *Stattvertreter*; and, on the other, to the ganger on public works. He may have had other duties, such as the maintenance of local order, but these chiefly appear in the letters of the time (see King's *Letters of Ḫammurabi*, under '*ridû*,' iii. p. 290). To their gangs were condemned fugitive slaves, if unclaimed ($B^2$ 419).

The king in various letters orders the exemption of temple bakers, royal shepherds or herdsmen, and *patêsis* from the *ilku*, or 'duty,' of these officers. Further, it is certain that on some occasions this duty was military service, on others public works. It is not, however, clear that we have always a class exemption.

The Code fixes their status very clearly in some respects. They might be sent on 'the king's way,' perhaps a term for a military expedition, but probably including any royal business. It was a capital offence not to go. To send a hired substitute involved death, and the substitute took over the appointment (§ 26). For a magistrate to allow such personation was punished by death also (§ 33). If such an officer was captured abroad, and there was bought by a Babylonian slave-dealer, he had, on his return, to be ransomed from his own means, failing that, by the temple treasury of his town, failing that, by the State (§ 32). But his holding could not be sold for the purpose. It consisted of land, house, garden, and stock given him by the king, as well as a salary, and could not be sold, pledged, or exchanged (§ 34). The penalty for its alienation was that it had to be returned, and the buyer, lender, or exchanger lost what he had given for it. The officer could not be oppressed by the governor, neither robbed, defrauded of salary, let out on hire, nor wronged in court, on pain of death (§ 34). The officer could not leave his holding to his wife or daughter, nor any part of it (§ 38). He had, of course, full power over his own acquired property (§ 39). He could name his son as *locum tenens* in his absence, if capable of discharging the duties of his office, which therefore were not solely military. If his son could not take the duty, being a child, one-third of the estate was sequestered to the child's mother for his maintenance, and a *locum tenens* put in by royal authority. To secure the estate from dilapidation, the *locum tenens* acquired a prescriptive right to it, if the absentee was away three years or more. This held good only if the absentee had been a neglectful holder. In any case, one year's absence did not invalidate his claim to resume it on his return.

(*b*) In nearly every case the *bâ'iru* is associated with this officer. The term means simply 'catcher,' and is used of fishermen and hunters alike. In contemporary documents it seems always to be used of fishermen. Perhaps they, too, were a privileged class, as being necessary to the provision of food for the palace. It appears that they had their special fisheries reserved in each district, and were not allowed to poach on other fisheries (King, *Letters*, p. 121 f.). But it is not quite clear that the *bâ'iru*, or 'catcher,' may not have been, like the old 'catchpole,' a sort of constable. He could, like the 'levy-master,' be sent 'on the king's way,' might be captured abroad, held the same sort of estate, could make the same arrangements as to his son's taking his duty. He is not expressly exempted from the governor's oppressions, but surely was not meant to be at his mercy. This rather goes to prove that *bâ'iru* is almost a synonym for *rîd ṣâbê*.

(*c*) So far as inalienability of holding was concerned, the *nâš bilti*, or 'payer of tribute,' was in the same position as the *rîd ṣâbê* and the *bâ'iru*. It seems, therefore, that land was held of the crown, as in other Oriental countries — notably Morocco now—on two forms of tenure. One carried an obligation to personal service, the other only a rent or tribute. Both were thus inalienable, but might be hereditary. Land could also be held by others, who might alienate: votaries, merchants, and foreign residents are named (§ 40); but the duty, whatever it was, went with the land, and must be discharged by the buyer. Some land was freehold (*zakû*); and it is expressly laid down as a special privilege that the estates of a Marduk votary were thus exempt from the 'duty.' There is no express mention of tithe, but that probably grew out of the 'duty.'

2. The votary was also the subject of special legislation. She might be devoted to the service of a god (Šamaš and Marduk are named in the Code; Sin, Anunit, and others elsewhere) by her parents; or she might herself elect to become a votary. She thus became a 'bride' of the god, and might be dowered by her father as for marriage (§ 178). Her father could give her complete power over her property, or not. In any case, she had the life interest in it (§ 179). If not absolutely at her own disposal,—on her father's death, her brethren, who had the reversion of it, might assume possession and maintain her. If they did not do this to her satisfaction, she had the power to appoint a steward, who would administer it as she wished. In any such case it reverted at her death, unless her father had granted her the disposal of it by a special deed of gift. If he gave her no allowance of this sort, she did not forfeit her rights as a daughter in his estate, but came in for one-third of a son's share at his death (§ 180). To all appearances, the votary was vowed to perpetual virginity; but she might marry, and give her husband a maid to bear him children (§ 146). If she broke her vow and had children, they were not recognized as in her power; they could be adopted by any one without her having power to claim them back (§ 193). From contemporary documents we find that votaries often adopted children, mostly other votaries, doubtless to care for their old age. Normally, the votaries lived in a convent (§ 110), or common home, called 'the bride chamber.' It was a very large establishment, and is often named as a neighbour in sales of lands. If they did not live there, they were expected to be staid in their behaviour. They might not open a beer-shop, nor enter one, on pain of being burned (§ 110). They were highly respected. No one might slander them, on pain of being branded on the forehead (§ 127). We read of Iltâni, daughter of king Ammizaduga, as a votary (V.A.Th. 630). They had a common scribe ($B^2$ 2175 A) and a 'lady superior' ($B^1$ 61). The votary of Marduk had special treatment, as was natural for a king who had made Babylon the capital of his empire, and Marduk supreme, even over Šamaš in Sippara. She was, even if not dowered by her father, able to claim one-third of a son's share in his property at his death, and had full testamentary powers over it. She had no 'duty' to discharge (§ 182). We continually meet with votaries in contemporary documents, chiefly devoted to Šamaš. They were clearly a wealthy body, and carry on business freely. They agree with brothers about their estates, put in stewards, leave property, and carry on ordinary contracts. Many marry. Nowhere in the Code or elsewhere is there any trace of the evil reputation which Greek writers assign to these ladies, and the translations which make them prostitutes, or unchaste, are not to be accepted. Greek influence may later have corrupted their morals.

3. Men were also vowed to the service of a god, but the Code does not refer to them. The rather obscure *manzâz pâni*, who 'stood in the presence' of the king, were naturally celibates. Their wives could not be tolerated in the palace. Their children, if they had any, were treated as homeless (§ 192), and could be adopted by any one without the father's consent. There is no ground for assuming any vicious habits on their part, as the term included some of the highest officials of the State.

4. Special professions were also legislated for. The beer-shop was usually kept by women. Even as late as the Second Babylonian Empire we find a master setting up a female slave in a wine-shop. The price of beer was not to be dearer than corn, measure for measure (§ 108). Corn was legal tender, and silver was not to be demanded by the great weight. The beer-seller had to give information of all treasonable conspiracy she overheard in her shop (§ 109). She was severely dealt with: if she broke these rules, death was the penalty. There is no hint that her house was a brothel, though later custom suggests it.

5. The doctor does not seem to hold a high profession. He is not an *amêlu*. The fee for a successful operation, involving surgery (removal of a cataract with the bronze lancet is probably meant), is fixed and graded according to the position of the patient (§§ 215–217). An unsuccessful operation is penalized by loss of the hands, reparation, or a fine (§§ 218–220). A cure of an injured limb, or a rupture (?), is similarly treated (§§ 221–223). The veterinary surgeon is likewise dealt with (§§ 224, 225). The brander, who may also be a barber, and perhaps a shearer, naturally follows a surgeon. His special treatment concerns his attempting to efface a slave's tattooed mark. If he did this wittingly, he lost his hands. If he was deceived, he could get free on oath of innocence, but the procurer suffered death (§§ 226, 227).

6. Builders are treated much the same. The builder's fee is fixed according to the size of the house. His bad workmanship is punished if it leads to damage. He has to make good all loss, and repair at his own expense; and, further, suffer the same damage in his own person as he has brought on the house-owner (§§ 228–233). The boatman gets a fixed fee according to the size of the boat he builds. Damage due to bad workmanship appearing within a year's time has to be made good, or the boat replaced (§§ 234, 235). A boatman had to make good a boat lost through his carelessness, if hired to navigate it. He was responsible for the freight, if any. If he sank a boat, but raised it again, he paid half value. His hire was fixed (§§ 236–239).

vii. *AGRICULTURE*. — 1. Land was already private property, subject to its duty to the State. An impost was levied upon the crop, and was clearly proportional to its amount (*miksu*). How men came into possession of waste or unreclaimed land, which might be expected to be common, does not appear. The reclamation may have constituted a title. At any rate, the Code contemplates land being given to a farmer to reclaim (§ 44), and the contracts show the practice to have been common ($B^1$ 186, etc.). The unreclaimed land was usually taken along with arable land (double in amount), and without rent for a time. Then, say in the fourth year, fixed rent was expected from all—that from the virgin soil being threefold the ordinary. The landlord further made an allowance of provisions towards the farmer's keep. The penalty fixed by the Code for neglect to reclaim is that the farmer should leave it in good tilth, and pay a fair rent (§ 44). Ordinary arable land was let, usually at fixed rents, so much corn per acre, six *GUR* per *GAN* being very usual. A deposit was expected, and it was ordinary debt not to pay the rent. The Code only enacts that, if the rent had been paid, no rebate could be claimed if a storm destroyed the crop afterwards (§ 45). But if the rent was not paid, or if the land was let on the share-profit system, the damage done by storm was borne by landlord and tenant equally, or in proportion to their shares (§ 46). This system of produce-rent, or share-profit, was very common, the landlord taking half the crop, or two-thirds, according to agreement. In such a case the tenant's neglect to do the proper work prejudiced the landlord as well as himself; in this case the Code enacts that he shall pay an average rent, 'like his neighbours,' or 'like right and left of him' (§ 42, B² 1031). He had to leave it in proper tilth. An important measure of precaution, often stipulated for in the contracts (B² 361, 460), especially when the field lay some way from the town, was the erection of a farmer's cottage on the field. He had to be present, as an old work on agriculture, often compared to Hesiod's *Works and Days*, tells us, 'to scare the birds, capture antelopes or wild goats, collect locusts.' The landlord might have a cottage already there, and charge for it, stipulating that it be vacated with the field; or he might stipulate that the tenant should put it up, and leave it at the end of the lease. The Code contemplates the neglect to put up this cottage, and the tenant subletting the field, probably to one who lived nearer. The landlord could not object, if he had his proper rent at harvest, and if his field was duly cultivated by some one (§ 47).

An important form of tenure was the *metayer* system, where the landlord found seed, implements, and oxen, besides paying a wage to the farmer. Here the farmer might embezzle the seed, or the provender, for which the Code enacts that his hands be cut off (§ 253). He might take the corn and starve the oxen (it was furnished partly for their food), for which he must restore from what he planted (§ 254). He might hire out the oxen to another, stealing their provender and not producing a crop, for which he had to pay a heavy fine, sixty *GUR* per *GAN* (§ 255). If he could not pay, he was to be torn to pieces by the oxen on the field (§ 256).

Gardens or plantations were usually let, if already planted, at a rent of two-thirds produce, as fixed by the Code (§ 64). Neglect which would diminish the crop was guarded against by enacting that an average yield should be returned (§ 65). Land was given to be planted as a garden, the owner often stipulating as to what plants he wished for. The terms were that the gardener paid no rent for four years, and in the fifth year he and his landlord divided the land equally (§ 60). If he left part uncultivated, that was reckoned in his share (§ 61). If he had failed to carry out his work, he was bound to do so before giving it up, and further fined an average year's rent for the time he held it, if it was corn land (§ 62), or ten *GUR* of corn per *GAN* for each year, if it had been unreclaimed land (§ 63).

2. The Babylonian landowner was often in want of ready money despite his magnificent harvests, which often yielded a hundredfold. He had to employ extra labourers to get in his harvest, find seed at seedtime, and was liable to destructive floods. If he had borrowed money and a storm destroyed his crops, he might post-date the bond, and not pay interest on the loan that year (§ 48). He frequently pledged his field to a money-lender; but, whatever the terms of his offer, the Code enacted that he should always reap the crop himself, and from the produce pay off the loan, and the expenses of the lender, if he had to find a cultivator (§§ 49, 50). Speculation in 'futures' was forbidden to the money-lender. Further, this man could not demand money; corn or produce was legal tender in satisfaction of such loans (§ 51). It was a practice with money-lenders to stipulate for the return of a loan in the exact form in which it was borrowed. If the cultivator put in by the creditor does not produce a crop, as the owner had left the care of the field to the creditor, he must bear the loss; he can claim no rebate on that account (§ 52). Hence it was dangerous to mortgage for more than an average crop. Gardens or plantations were also protected from money-lenders' speculations in the same way (§ X). The owner, whatever his offer, must take the crop himself, and whatever is over and above his debt and interest is his. He was protected in other ways. No one could distrain upon a working ox, except under fine of one-third of a mina of silver (§ 241). The ox was not only used for ploughing, it was constantly employed to work the watering machines, which sometimes required as many as eight oxen. It was also needed for threshing.

3. Babylonian culture was dependent upon water supply. On the one side, floods were frequent, and had to be provided against by an elaborate system of ditches and canals; on the other, the summer heat turned all herbage to dust, unless watered. One chief claim to the gratitude of posterity on the part of kings and priests was the furnishing of new canals. Once made, these were expected to be kept in order by the riparian landowners. The work of repairs, dredging, and cleaning was always considerable, from the floods, silt, and rapid growth of water vegetation. Ḫammurabi's letters often deal with the needs of the canals (King, *Letters*, pp. 15, 16, 18, 64, lxiv f., xxxvi f.).

The ordinary repair of the bank was the duty of the man whose field adjoined it. If he neglected to strengthen it, a burst was likely. He was responsible for the damage done to the neighbours' crops (§ 53). He and all his possessions could be sold to pay the damage (§ 54). He had the right to open a runnel to water his field; but, if he left it running and swamped his neighbours' crops, he had to compensate (§ 55) according to the extent of the damage (§ 56). The theft of a watering machine, probably that consisting of a pole and bucket, was penalized by five shekels of silver. The bucket alone, or a harrow, was protected from theft by a fine of three shekels (§§ 259, 260).

4. Considerable attention is paid by the Code to fixing wages, or hire. The harvester had to be paid eight *GUR* of corn per year (§ 257). An ordinary labourer was paid six *ŠE* of silver per day for the first five months, five *ŠE* for the remaining seven (§ 273). This would be about twelve *GUR* of corn per year. A working ox could be hired for four *GUR* of corn per year (§ 242), a milch cow for three *GUR* (§ 243). An ox for threshing fetched twenty *ḲA* of corn per day, an ass ten *ḲA*, a calf 1 *ḲA* (§§ 268–270). A waggon, with its driver and oxen, cost one hundred and eighty *ḲA* of corn per day (§ 271). As the waggon alone cost forty *ḲA* (§ 272), and two oxen another forty *ḲA* (§ 268), we may take it that a man cost one hundred *ḲA* per day for carting. A cart might be hired for ten *ḲA* a day (S 572). An ox-driver had six *GUR* of corn per year as wages (§ 258).

The care of the hired animals was strictly guarded. A lion might kill ox or ass, and the owner had to bear the loss (§ 244). But neglect or ill-treatment had to be paid for (§§ 245, 246). Partial injury was assessed (§§ 247, 248). The hand of God was the owner's loss (§ 249). The responsibility for a savage bull was decided. If the animal suddenly got out of hand and killed a man, it was treated as an accident (§ 250). But if the animal was known to be vicious and his owner took no means to prevent his doing harm, the owner had to pay blood money (§§ 251, 252). The price of a three year old ox was twenty shekels (B[2] 448).

5. Vast herds and flocks were owned. Hundreds of sheep are named as under the care of one man. The king had occasion to call as many as forty-seven shepherds to account at one time (King, iii. p. 70). The sheep had to be taken some distance to pasture. The shepherd gave a receipt for the animals entrusted to him, and was bound to return them with reasonable increase in the amount by breeding. He was allowed to use a certain number for his keep and that of his underlings. He had to face perils from wild beasts and robbers. The Sutî nomads were specially feared. We find a Sutu hired to protect the flocks from his clansmen (B[1] 532). The shepherd or herdsman was paid eight *GUR* of corn per year (§ 261). He had to restore ox for ox, sheep for sheep (§ 263). He had to see that the flock did not waste or prove unprofitable, or else make good the deficiency (§ 264). Wilful embezzlement was to be repaid tenfold (§ 265). Loss by the hand of God or wild beasts was the owner's loss (§ 266). But carelessness was to be made good (§ 267). When the sheep were taken out or brought home, they had to traverse the meadows, and must be kept from eating the growing crops. To let his flock eat the corn in a field without consent of the owner of the field, was punished by a fine of twenty *GUR* of corn per *GAN*. This was when the crop was green and the owner might expect the corn to recover and bear a crop (§ 57). It was worse if the crop was nearly ripe and the sheep had already reached the common fold within the city, where they were fed on corn by the shepherd. If he then allowed them to stray in a standing field of corn, he had to take entire responsibility for the field, and make what he could of it, but had to pay sixty *GUR* of corn per *GAN* (§ 58).

viii. *Shipping, and Trade and Commerce.*—1. The shipping trade was considerable. We are not altogether in a position to say what the ships were like at this time, but freight boats of sixty *GUR* capacity were common, and one of seventy-five *GUR* is named (King, *Letters*, iii. p. 67). On the canals, at least, they seem to have been propelled with poles, which were also used to fasten them. They were numerous; as many as twenty-five together were anchored at the quay of Šamaš, in Sippara, at one time (S 160). At all times there is evidence of considerable activity in commerce and fishing along these waterways. (For later times, see Meissner and Knudtzon, *Vienna Oriental Journal*, iv. p. 129 f.; Pinches, *Sir H. Peck's Tablets*, p. 82 f.). The temple ships are named in § 8. The same word was used for boatbuilder and boatman. If he had completed (literally 'caulked,' 'closed') a ship of sixty *GUR* for a man, he was entitled to two shekels of silver as a fee; the owner probably found the materials (§ 234). He had to give a year's guarantee with it, replacing it with a sound ship if it showed faults within that time (§ 235). The boatman who navigated the ship was paid six *GUR* of corn per year (§ 239). The hired boatman was responsible for the care of the ship, restoring ship for ship if lost (§ 236); also for the cargo, if lost by his carelessness (§ 237). But if he refloated a ship he had sunk, and it was sound, he only paid half value (§ 238). A ship which ran down another at anchor was held responsible for the damage (§ 240). The hire of a passenger or fast boat was two and a half *ŠE* of silver per day (§ 276), that of a freight ship of sixty *GUR*, a sixth of a shekel of silver per day (§ 277), twelve times as much.



2. A great deal of business was done by ship, or caravan, with foreign countries. The Code contemplates captives in war carried away from Babylonia being bought abroad by slave-dealers and brought back (§§ 132, 280, 281). Slaves might be sold and transported abroad by merchants (§ 118). We read of a free man who had been sold as a slave to Dupliaš, perhaps for debt (B[2] 419). The Code legislates for the case of consignments of gold, silver, jewels, or portable treasures sent by a man resident abroad. The carrier was bound to deliver, or pay fivefold (§ 112). In this period Carchemish wares were already to be found in Babylonian homes (B[1] 19).

Business was done on the *Commenda* system, as later in Islam. The principal, called 'merchant' in the Code, entrusted money or goods to his agent, who gave a receipt for them, and went off to seek a market. On his return he had to repay his commission and give a fair profit, or share with his principal. This profit was agreed on as a matter of free contract. If he was unlucky in his transactions, he yet had to pay cent. per cent. as profit (§ 101). But the merchant might merely speculate and not bargain for profit on a fixed scale. The agent must at least return the capital (§ 102). The trader has his risks. In the Tel el-Amarna period we find the king complaining of caravans being robbed (*KIB* v. p. 25). The Code contemplates this, and allows the agent to clear his liability by oath that the enemy robbed him (§ 103). All was to be done by written contract (§ 104); money or goods not sealed for could not be claimed in the reckoning (§ 105). Disputes were punished. False claims on the part of the agent were to be repaid threefold, on the part of the principal sixfold (§§ 106, 107). The contemporary documents abound with cases of partnership. The usual method was for each partner to take back his capital and interest, and then the partners divided the profit equally. The common stock was divided into two classes—property 'in town' and property 'on the road.' The reckoning was made yearly, unless the absent agent was detained beyond the year. It took the form of a dissolution of partnership; all the common stock was inventoried and a settlement made, usually in the temple, upon oath, and each party entered into compact not to dispute the settlement. The partnership might then be renewed.

Warehousing and deposit were frequently resorted to. It had to be a matter of written contract, the goods being deposited before witnesses, otherwise no claim for return could be made. The warehouseman took all responsibility. If he denied the deposit, he had to repay double (§§ 122–125). The storage of corn is specially dealt with; the warehouseman took all responsibility, even for loss by theft from his store. If he falsified his liability, he had to pay double (§ 120). He charged a fee of one-sixtieth per year (§ 121). It was common to hire a granary. The granary was protected from a distraint (§ 113). False claims on a warehouseman had to be repaid twofold (§ 126). We have noted the shipping business and the beer-shop above.

3. There is much said of interest on money. We miss any regulation in the Code on the point, save that interest had to be returned with borrowed money (§§ 49, 50, 100, X). It was usually about 40 per cent. or 33⅓ per cent. on corn loans. In the lapse of time it grew less—25 per cent. in Assyria, 20 per cent. in the Second Babylonian Empire. But there was never any fixed rate, it was matter of free contract. Loans of corn at seedtime are very frequent; a poor man was then often without corn. They were usually repaid at harvest without interest; but interest was set down to be paid if

the loan was kept longer. Loans were also frequent at harvest time to pay the harvesters. With pledges of crops we have already dealt under 'Agriculture.' A debtor could pay in corn, or sesame, according to the royal standard exchange value (§§ 51, 111). At harvest time, when corn was dearest and drink most needed, the beer-seller sold cheap (§ 108), otherwise she might not make drink cheaper than corn. The creditor could not refuse to take goods in liquidation of a debt (§ 88). Debt might be discharged by a written order to a third party to pay ($B^2$ 315).

4. Debt might lead to distraint. The debtor could 'name' a surety or *mancipium*, who had to enter the creditor's house and there work off the debt. But the hostage was protected from blows or starvation; he was still the debtor's property, and the creditor must restore him, if a free man, wife, or child, of debtor, at the end of three years (§§ 115–117). A hostage slave might be sold if the creditor wished to leave the city (§ 118). But if the slave was a maid who had borne her master children, he was bound to redeem her (§ 119). As a creditor was bound to accept goods in payment, it is clear these distraints were a last resource. They could not be made on the creditor's own responsibility. If he distrains upon the debtor's corn without the debtor's consent, he has to pay back what he takes and lose all claim for his debt (§ 113). If he distrains without having a debt owing him, he pays a fine of one-third of a mina (§ 114). He might not distrain a working ox (§ 241), under the same penalty. In fact, 'self-help' is forbidden; the debtor must name 'his' hostage.

The hostage was an antichretic pledge. We find many examples of this in later times. Land and crops might be pledged, as above. Goods were also pledged, or assigned in lieu of debt. As a summary proceeding we may note that, if a man incurred a public debt and could not pay, he was sold with all his goods, and the claimants shared the proceeds (§ 54).

5. The Code does not deal with sale, which was a matter of free contract, except to forbid the sale of benefices (§ 35), or to allow sale of estate subject to territorial liability. Sales of all sorts of property, especially estate, are very common in contemporary documents. The prices varied, of course, according to circumstances, and there is nothing remarkable about them, as a rule. But the transfer of ownership appears to have been made by the handing over of a stake or rod. There were certain rights of pre-emption or redemption on the part of the seller's family. They could even buy back sold property. In Assyrian times the district governors, city magistrates, captains of the seller's 'hundred,' creditors with a mortgage on the property, had similar rights. The sale is always professedly made outright. No credit was given. The buyer might, however, borrow money to pay, even of the seller, and execute a bond for the debt, or pledge the property back to the seller for it. Slave sales are especially frequent. The buyer could, however, return his purchase, if disease showed itself in a month (later, 100 days), and female slaves were often bought on trial for one to three days. An undisclosed defect in the slave, or a claim upon him for State service not discharged, might be grounds for demanding back his price at any time (§§ 278, 279). The seller usually gave a guarantee against these contingencies, as also against vices, like a tendency to run away. In the case of other purchases, such as houses, stipulations were made that all was in good order, the door and the lock sound, beams and sills in position, etc., and all breaches made good.

Exchanges were often made, and the balance of value, if any, paid in money. These were free contracts. The Code refers to the practice (§ 41).

6. Hire is frequent. We have noticed estates and workmen. Houses were often hired. The term was generally for one year, but eight and even ten years are named. The usual stipulations as to sound condition are made. Further, the tenant binds himself to leave the house in good repair, and to vacate it at the end of the lease. Rent, of course, varies much. It is reckoned by the area occupied by the house, from one-third to two shekels per *SAR*. A *SAR* of house costs two shekels to build (§ 228). Rent was usually paid in advance, half-yearly. The lost part of the Code dealt with house leases, ordering that if a landlord turned out his tenant before the lease was out he should compensate him; but we do not know to what extent (§ Y). Many other buildings are named as hired, especially granaries.

ix. *THE TEMPLE.*—It is curious that the Code has so little to say of the temple. It was a very powerful factor in the life of the period. It possessed large estates, from which a constant revenue was derived. These were mostly endowments given by former kings, estates held on payment of certain dues. The temples and the administration of their revenues, herds and flocks, were a source of constant care to the king. Ḫammurabi's letters abound with references to them. There is no need to suppose that he derived any direct benefit from them. He had his own vast estates and property as well. The temples maintained a very large number of persons, wholly or in part. Many folk had the right of so many days' service there and the accruing profits. One of the most curious sorts of property consisted in these rights to so many days a year in a temple. The rights were hereditary, and could not be alienated; but were freely bought and sold, or pledged, subject to the reversions. The Code protects temple property (§§ 6, 8), putting it on a level with that of the 'palace.' The temple had its duties. It was bound to ransom its townsman, when captured in war (§ 32). To it men often went for loans, though at Ḫammurabi's time most of the money-lending was in the hands of so-called 'merchants.' These seem usually to have been foreigners. Later, most of the money-lending, at any rate when without interest, was done by the temple.

x. *JUSTICE.*—1. The temple was also the chief scene of justice. Here men went to take their oath, at the gate of the temple or before the censer. The object in dispute was taken there and resigned into the hands of the god, who was held to do judgment and restore it to the rightful owner. The judges were not necessarily priests, nor were they necessarily scribes. But the body of 'ancients,' who usually served as witnesses, and also assessors to the judge, were usually found there. Very little is expressly stated as to the procedure in the law courts. But we know that the pleas were conducted by the parties in person. They had to be put in writing. The judge 'saw' them, and, if there was a case, fixed a day for hearing. Then the parties had to bring their witnesses. The judge gave his decision, and it was embodied in an agreement to which both parties consented and swore to observe. This document was drawn up by the scribe and sealed by judge, witnesses, and parties concerned. It seems that in cases concerning money or goods a single judge might sit; the heavier cases were taken before a bench of judges. The first five sections of the Code deal with the process. The first two sections are peculiarly difficult. It seems that a man might accuse another of plotting his death, perhaps by magic spells; if he could prove this, the offender was put to death (§ 1).

But the sense of several words is doubtful, and we do not know either the nature of the spell, or the kind of evidence required. In the second case, the plaintiff appears to demand the ordeal from the defendant, throwing on him the burden of proof that he is not a wizard. The ordeal by water, in other cases known to us, demanded that the guilty should swim and the innocent sink, but be saved in time. This may be the meaning here also. In either case the guilty one was put to death, and his opponent took his estates. In the next two sections we have false witness dealt with. If it endangered the life of the accused, the penalty was death (§ 3). If it involved corn or money, the false witness had to bear the same injury as he sought to bring on the accused (§ 4). By 'slander' in the first case may be meant 'treason,' or such offence against the State as was capital. At any rate, it is the 'crime alleged.'

2. The judge is not very often named in the Code. If he had given a judgment and completed the business, it was irrevocable by him. He could not retry the case. Appeal to a higher court was allowed. If he retried the case, or altered his judgment, he was deposed from office, and had to repay twelvefold what he had given as the penalty of the case (§ 5). He had to examine into the depositions (§ 9), fix a time, within six months, for production of witnesses (§ 13), be present at the execution of sentences (§ 127), reconcile father and son (§ 168), inventory the property of a widow's children on her remarriage (§ 174), decide family quarrels (§ 172). But his presence and decision are elsewhere implied, and, from the numerous legal decisions preserved to us, we conclude that he was constantly employed.

He had a local jurisdiction. Suitors might be referred from one court to another, or summoned to a higher court. He was a professional man, keeping his title even when not acting in a judicial capacity. Most higher officials of the State act as judges on occasion, and cases were often referred on appeal to the king. No priest ever appears as holding the office; but that may be because 'judge' was the higher title. We often find several judges together on the bench, and the highest official in rank doubtless was 'chief judge' on that occasion. But there was an office of Chief Justice. There is no evidence that the judge had any fee. The king's judges are referred to, but it is not certain that the king appointed all. Certainly, the office was hereditary in some cases.

3. Witnesses played an important part in the law courts. The term applied to them, *šîbu*, really means 'grey-headed,' and they were probably, therefore, the elders of the city. As such, they were expected to know the rights of the case as well as its facts. But the term gradually extended its area. Those who know (*mûdu*) were not necessarily old, and they are called *šîbi* (§ 9). We may distinguish three classes of witnesses who all bear the same name: (i.) the 'elders,' who appear as assessors with the judge, and form a sort of jury; (ii.) the 'deponents' in a court, who were put on oath, and whose false evidence is penalized (§§ 1–4); (iii.) the attesting witnesses to a document. In the case of legal decisions these included the whole of (i.), but also interested persons; in ordinary contracts, relatives of the principal parties, neighbours whose estates adjoined, and often persons who seem to have been regularly available at the court. In later times this class were called the *mukinnê*, or 'confirmers.' The parties, especially the plaintiff, were often called upon to 'justify' their plea. This was done by witness. Cases had to be adjourned for the production of witnesses (§ 13). Purchase from a minor (§ 7), deposit (§ 122), and even sale (§ 9), were invalid without witnesses.

4. The plaintiff pleaded his own case. There were no professional advocates. As a rule, in disputes the parties agreed to submit the case to judges, and together 'captured' a judge, who gave them a decision. They mutually swore not to reopen the case. Many cases were, so to speak, settled out of court. The parties mutually agreed, got an agreement drawn up by a scribe, and swore to observe it. There is no mention of a judge in such cases, but the oath was taken in the temple.

5. The death penalty may be regarded as simple or specific. In most cases it is enacted in the words 'he shall be killed' (*iddak*). In these cases we are quite in the dark as to how it was inflicted, or what was its nature. It may be noted that the penalty is permissive, not imperative. The verb is imperfect, the 'shall' of the version is future. That this was the case, is seen by the fact that a clause was introduced in one case allowing the husband to pardon his wife and the king to reprieve his servant (§ 129). In another case death is only in default of multiple restitution (§ 8). We read of other cases where the plaintiff accepted a composition. In fact, the Code marks the transition from the period when blood-revenge ruled. There is no trace of this left. The Code, however, does not refer to deliberate murder at all. Whether, in that case, the avenger's right was too strong to be denied, or whether the law of retaliation was too well known, we cannot say. The Code does not regard the crime as one against the State, but against the individual, and he or his representatives plead for revenge rather than punishment. The Code, however, regulates this and assigns its bounds.

The unspecified death penalty is enacted against a man who alleges witchcraft, and so puts another in danger of death (§ 1) without justification: for endangering life by false witness in a capital suit (§ 3); for entry and theft from mansion or temple (§ 6); for kidnapping a free-born child (§ 14); for housebreaking (§ 21); for highway robbery (§ 22); for rape of a betrothed maiden living at home (§ 130); for building a house so badly as to bring about the death of its owner (§ 229); for striking a gentlewoman with child and causing her death (§ 209); certain forms of theft, taking on deposit or buying from a domestic inferior, without power of attorney on his part, or in secret (§ 7); receiving stolen goods (§ 6); appropriation of things found (§ 9); selling same (§ 10); vexatious claim of property (§ 11); procuring flight of slave (§ 15); harbouring fugitive slave (§ 16) or fugitive militiaman (§ 16); holding captured slave (§ 19); getting slave's brand erased (§ 227); neglect of duty on part of privileged classes, as a beer-seller who did not procure arrest of seditious brawlers (§ 109); evasion of service or substitution of hireling on part of levy-master or catchpole (§ 26),—were all punished in this way.

Death with specified accessories, or manner, is enacted thus: *burning*—for theft at a conflagration (§ 25); for votary, opening or entering beer-shop for drink (§ 110); for incest with mother (§ 157: cf. Gn $38^{24}$, Lv $20^{14}$ $21^{9}$, Jos $7^{15}$); *drowning*—for selling beer too cheap (§ 109); adultery (§ 129); being a bad wife (§ 143); incest with daughter-in-law (§ 155); deserting husband's house in his enforced absence, if provided with maintenance (§ 133); *impalement*—for procuring husband's death (§ 153, cf. Est $7^{9}$); *dismemberment*—for fraud uncompensated under the *metayer* system (§ 256). These special forms either make the punishment peculiarly appropriate to the deed, or perhaps embody ancient custom. The penalty in § 21 may perhaps imply that a man who tunnelled through the wall (built of sun-dried bricks) into his neighbour's house might be killed 'on the spot,' and buried in the tunnel he had made; or it may mean that he could be buried in the opening from which his tunnel started, in his own house, assuming him to be a neighbour, and so desecrate that house for ever. In the case of an adulterous pair, the Code enacts that they shall be 'bound' (together?) and drowned (§ 129). A man who committed incest with his daughter-in-law was to be 'bound,' and she was to be drowned (§ 155). Some think there is an error in the text, but it is possible that 'bound' really means 'strangled.' It is very unlikely that the man would be only 'bound.' The ordeal by water, to which a man accused of witchcraft, or a woman suspected by her husband of infidelity, had to submit, was likely to end in death (§§ 2, 132).

The working of § 2, which describes the ordeal, has been misunderstood. It is well known that a wizard or witch ought to float. The Code shows that if the river 'conquers' him he is guilty; while, if he is saved, he is innocent. It is difficult to see how 'conquering' can mean 'rejecting.' Hence this ordeal is not in harmony with the ordinary ideas of witchcraft.

Mutilation as a penalty comes into the Code in two ways. First, as a mere retaliation for a mutilation. Eye for eye (§ 196), tooth for tooth (§ 198), limb for limb (§ 197), are examples. Second, the mutilation is the punishment of the offending member. A surgeon who, through want of skill or care, causes the death of a patient under operation, has his hands cut off (§ 218). So has a brander who erases a slave's brand (§ 226), or a son who strikes his father (§ 195). A wet-nurse, for substituting a changeling for the child committed to her charge, has her breasts cut off (§ 194). An ungrateful adopted son, who spies out the disgraceful origin of his existence, has his eye torn out (§ 193). A slave who repudiates his master's authority, or smites a gentleman on the cheek, has his ear—the organ of hearing and understanding, therefore of obedience—cut off (§§ 282, 205). An adopted child who used his tongue to repudiate his adoptive parents, had it cut out (§ 192). A man who used his hands to steal instead of to work, had them cut off (§ 253).

Scourging is only once named — sixty strokes with a cow-hide whip, laid on in the assembly, for smiting the cheek of a superior (§ 202). Branding on the forehead was the punishment for slander of a votary or married woman (§ 127). It is disputed whether this may not mean cutting off the forelock, as the mark of a freeman. But it is expressed by the same verb as is used to denote the putting of a slave mark on a presumptuous slave girl (§ 146). This mark was usually on the arm, and was visible (B² 419), and it could be eradicated by a brander. In later times we know that slaves had their owner's name on their arms. This points to a tattoo. The sentence was, evidently, equivalent to degradation to slavery. The levy-masters claimed all slaves who were not owned privately (B² 419). Hence the sentence meant 'hard labour for life.' These slaves were clothed and fed at the public expense, but had no wages.

Banishment from the city was the penalty of incest with a daughter (§ 154). Disinheritance was rather a family affair than a punishment. Confiscation does not occur. When a man takes the house of one who has bewitched him or falsely accuses him of witchcraft (§ 2), he is merely compensated for vexatious disturbance. Failure to attend to a holding, benefice of an office, led to forfeiture of office and the benefice (§ 30). Certain unrighteous actions led to forfeiture: thus, if a man bought part of a benefice from an official, he had to return his purchase and forfeit the price (§ 37). The same penalty fell upon one who bought the property of wards in chancery (§ 177). If a man exchanged with an official part of his benefice, he had to restore it and lose his exchanged property (§ 41). If he lent corn and helped himself to his debtor's crop without the debtor's consent, he had to restore what he took, and lost all claim to repayment (§ 113).

Simple restitution occurs only when the holder came by the property innocently, as having bought property which the seller had no right to sell (§ 9). This is compensated for by the seller also returning the price.

Multiple restoration is very common. Fraudulent claim is punished by paying double. A warehouseman who falsifies the amount entrusted to him (§ 120), a receiver of deposit who denies it (§ 124), a man who takes presents from a suitor for his daughter and does not allow him to marry her (§§ 160, 161), pays double. The agent who did not succeed in business repaid the capital double (§ 101). If he cheated his principal, he paid threefold (§ 106); if the principal cheated his agent, he paid sixfold (§ 107). An innocent purchaser of goods illegally sold, having to give them up, could extract fivefold from the estate of the seller, if deceased (§ 12). A carrier who misappropriated goods entrusted to him to forward paid fivefold (§ 112). A judge who altered his judgment paid twelvefold what his sentence awarded (§ 5). A gentleman who stole from temple or mansion had to pay thirtyfold, a plebeian tenfold, or be put to death (§ 8).

Some of the penalties for breach of contract in agricultural matters have been misunderstood. They depend upon an estimate of average yield. The errors are due to misunderstanding of the scale of measures of area. G. Reisner long ago showed (*Sitzungsberichte der Berlin Akademie*, 1896, p. 417 f.) that the *GAN* contained 1800 *SAR*, the *SAR* had 60 *GIN*. Further, the *SAR* was equivalent in area to a square, each side being one *GAR*-(*DU*), while the *GAR* was 12 *U* long. Taking the *U* to be a cubit, this gives the *SAR* to be about 18 feet square. The area of a house was usually about 1 *SAR* (§ 228), and we find even as little as ⅓rd *SAR* in contemporary documents. Now, the average rent of corn land was 6 to 8 *GUR* per *GAN*; of freshly opened land about 18 *GUR* per *GAN*. The penalty in § 44 would be not heavy at 10 *GUR* per *GAN*. Kohler, Müller, Peiser, Winckler, Boscawen, and Pinches follow Scheil in making the penalty 10 *GUR* per 10 *GAN*, or 1 *GUR* per *GAN*—an absurdly small amount. Besides, if that was meant, why did not the scribe write '1 *GUR* per *GAN*'? So (in §§ 56, 57, 58, 63) they all make the penalty $\frac{1}{10}$th of the right amount. Further, in estimating other fines or wages it is well to remember that the *GUR* contained 300 *ḲA*, the *ḲA* had 60 *GIN*, and the *GIN* 180 *ŠE*. This *ŠE* must not be confounded with the *ŠE* of silver, of which 180 also went to the *GIN* or shekel, and 60 shekels to the mina. The *GUR* of corn was, from the time of Maništusu down to the 5th cent. B.C., reckoned as worth 1 shekel of silver. Of course the price of corn varied in times of scarcity or plenty, and even during the year.

We are nowhere told how the sentence of the law was executed. Perhaps the judge and the elders carried it out; perhaps the whole adult population had a hand in it. At any rate, the deposition of a judge and the scourging of one who assaulted his superior in rank were carried out 'in the assembly' (*ina puḫri*; §§ 5, 202). In contemporary documents the judges are said to 'assemble' the city (*daiane alum ipḫur*; B 74). The beer-seller was supposed to be able to hale brawlers and seditious persons to the palace

(§ 109). The highway robber might be arrested (§ 22). These references suppose a sort of police, perhaps the *bâ'iru* above.

6. We may now turn to the crimes or misdemeanours considered in the Code. Theft was held to be the unlawful possession of property. The worst kind was that which involved entry—it may be styled burglary. There is no need to suppose that sacrilege was involved, for it was hardly less sacrilegious to steal the property of a temple from the open field (§ 6). Receiving was as bad as stealing (§ 6). The 'goods' referred to are any portable furniture, and are not confined to 'treasure.' Theft in the open is less guilty as less deliberate (§ 8). A minor, or a slave, had of course great opportunity to steal. To assist by buying of such, or receiving from such, was very heinous (§ 7). But such were often empowered by deed to act for the householder; the Code insists on such power being duly witnessed. If a man found property anywhere, he took possession of it at great peril. If the loser recognized it in his possession, he might be condemned as a thief (§ 9). He could not sell it; if that were proved against him, he would have to restore the price and suffer as a thief. The only thing to do was to make known his discovery as widely as possible, and restore it to its owner. If he did this with a runaway slave whom he caught in the open field, he was entitled to a reward of about one-tenth of the restored property (§ 17). In this he would be guided by the slave's brand, and the slave himself might name his master. If not, he must take the slave to the palace, there to be examined, and so restored to his owner. To harbour a runaway or keep a recaptured fugitive for his own service, was treated as theft (§§ 16, 19). Kidnapping, or inducing a slave to leave his master's service, was theft (§§ 14, 15). Theft at a fire was peculiarly heinous as a breach of good faith (§ 25). Brigandage, or highway robbery, was a capital offence (§ 22).

Some offences against property were assessed at a fair value, and simple or multiple restitution enacted (§§ 57–59). Minor thefts were fined (§§ 259, 260).

It is evident that offences against the rights of property were most severely repressed, perhaps on account of their frequency; cf. Gn $31^{32}$ $44^{9}$.

Offences against the person were graded, according to the rank of the injured person relatively to the offender. Murder is not expressly dealt with; but that the penalty was death, may be assumed from the treatment of manslaughter in a quarrel (§ 206 f.). Here, if there was no malice, a payment of the doctor covered any wound, and death resulting involved a fine only. If a pregnant woman was struck and abortion caused, the child's life was estimated at a fine on a graduated scale. If the woman died, the compensation was also graduated according to the woman's rank (§§ 209–214). A rash or careless operation was penalized according to the rank of the sufferer (§§ 218–220).

Assaults are treated much the same way. To strike a parent was very heinous (§ 195). Injuries by one gentleman to another were punished by retaliation (§§ 196, 197),—to a poor man by fines (§§ 198–201), to a slave by lower fines (§ 199). To strike a superior on the cheek involved scourging (§ 202); an equal, a fine (§§ 203, 204). A slave who struck a superior on the cheek was mutilated (§ 205).

Offences against morality were mostly capital: adultery (§ 129); rape of a daughter-in-law (§ 130); bad conduct on a wife's part (§ 143); procuring a husband's death (§ 153); incest (§§ 154–158). However, seduction of a betrothed virgin involved only a fine (§ 155), and incest with a mother-in-law, outlawry (§ 158).

Desertion of a wife dissolved marriage (§ 136); persistent worthlessness of a wife justified divorce (§ 141); mutual aversion also (§ 142). Persistent unfilial conduct justified disinheritance (§ 169). Ingratitude on the part of adopted sons was punished according to the status of the son, apart from his adoption (§§ 192, 193). Presumption on the part of a maid against her mistress earned degradation to slavery (§ 146). A maid was not necessarily a slave.

The principle of retaliation was extended to the intention of a crime. To put a man in danger of a damage was punished by the infliction of that damage on the offender. This elucidates several points. To accuse a man wrongfully of witchcraft (black magic?) put the accused in danger of death, for it was punished by death (§ 1). Similarly, to accuse a man of magical arts subjected him to the risk of death (§ 2), and, if not proved by the result of ordeal, was punished by death. It is clear that the Code did not mean to let a witch live.

False witness was brought under this principle. If it imperilled life, it was punished by death (§ 3); if it endangered property, it was punished by equivalent loss (§ 4). False claim to property, involving peril of life to accused, was capital (§ 5).

Slander against a respectable woman (§ 127) was punished by degradation to slavery. Overreaching (§ 126), unjustifiable distraint (§§ 114, 241), fraudulent claim, undisclosed defects of sale (§ 278), were fined. 'Self-help' was forbidden, even when most reasonable (§§ 49, 113).

Breach of contract had to be made good (§§ 42, 43, 62, 65, 125), and was further often penalized (§§ 44, 124). Evasion or falsification was strictly forbidden (§ 52). Denial of deposit (§ 124); substitution of a changeling (§ 194); breach of trust (§§ 253–256); neglect of entrusted flocks or herds (§§ 263–267); bad workmanship in building a house or ship (§§ 229, 235); neglect of hired animals (§ 45 ff.),—were all penalized.

Neglect of duty was severely punished, due regard being had to the degree of responsibility of the offender. Levy-masters, constables, beer-sellers, governors, magistrates, were severely punished for breach of duty. Riparian owners were held responsible for repairs to canals and for all damage due to neglect. Neglect of reasonable precautions was penalized (§§ 251, 252).

Oppression, bribery, misappropriation of public property, were capital offences in governors and magistrates (§§ 33, 34). Cruelty to or neglect of a hostage for debt was punished (§ 116).

All disputed cases were left at the decision of the king, or decided according to statutory tariffs (§ 51). All contracts were to be duly drawn up and attested, or were invalid (§§ 105, 122).

Extenuating circumstances were admitted in some cases. A woman left without provision by her husband might remarry (§ 134). A man who could not hold the slave he had caught was free (§ 20). Desertion excused bigamy (§ 136). Bearing children to her master, so far excused a maid's insolence to her mistress that she could not be sold as a slave (§ 146). Refloating a ship partly excused sinking it (§ 238). Deception excused a brander's illegally rebranding a slave (§ 227).

Accident, the stroke of God, a thunderstorm, the attack of wild beasts, robbery by the enemy (§§ 45, 48, 103, 244, 249, 266), relieved a man of responsibility for damage to trust, or debt. A sudden charge on the part of an ox did not involve his owner (§ 250). The natural death in a creditor's employ of a hostage for debt did not render the creditor liable (§ 115). But a depositary was liable for damage done to goods deposited with him, even if he could not help it, because he was under contract, and charged a fee for safe keeping

(§§ 120, 125). Want of malice excused manslaughter, partly (§ 207).

Suspicion of evil was not enough. The Code continually insists that the criminal must be caught in the act. If accused of harbouring a slave, the slave must be seized in his possession (§ 19). The adulterer, ravisher, etc. (§§ 129, 130, 131), must be caught in the act.

An injured party could condone the offence in some cases. A man might save the life of an adulterous wife (§ 129).

xi. *MARRIAGE, AND FAMILY LIFE.* — 1. The laws dealing with the family are very numerous. For the most part, the Code keeps them together. The foundation of the family is marriage. This was a contract, first on the part of the parents of the man and wife who seem to have arranged marriages quite young. The Code, however, treats the man as a free suitor; he comes himself to the house of the bride's father and brings him presents. The maid does not seem to be free. Her father gives her in marriage, accepts or rejects the suitor. Women who had been married, or were seduced, were free to marry the man of their choice (§§ 137, 156, 172).

Besides the presents, the suitor gave a bride-price (*terḫatu*) to the father of the bride (*marḫitu*). This was usually a mina of silver (§ 139), though we find much less in contemporary documents: one shekel, four, five, or ten shekels. These irregularities may be due to special circumstances; but even a princess, daughter of Ammiditana (B$^1$ 193), had only four shekels given for her. It might not be given at all. The father often gave this to the bride. If a suitor now retreated, he had to relinquish the presents and bride-price paid. If the father refused the girl to the suitor, he had to return double what he had received (§§ 159, 160). If the marriage was childless, the *terḫatu* had to be returned to the husband on the wife's death, if it had not been returned before (§ 163; cf. Gn $24^{22}$ $29^{18f.}$ $31^{15}$ $34^{12}$, Ex $22^{16}$, Dt $22^{29}$, 1 S $18^{25}$).

The wife brought a dowry with her, the marriage portion (*šeriḳtu*), her share of her father's property. Though she brought this into her husband's house, it was tied to her for life. It had to be returned to her family, by her husband, if she died childless, but he might deduct the amount of the bride-price given by him, if this had not been paid back to him (§ 164). The *šeriḳtu* therefore was normally larger than the *terḫatu*. We have several contemporary lists of these dowries. They included gold, silver, jewels, garments, household furniture, slaves even, if not also estates (B$^1$ 10, B$^1$ 33, B$^1$ 163). If her husband died before her, though his property might be divided up, she retained her *šeriḳtu* (§§ 171, 172); and, after her death, it fell to be divided among her children (§§ 162, 167, 173, 174). If she had no children, it went back to her father's house (§§ 163, 164). Even if she were divorced, she kept her *šeriḳtu* (§§ 137, 138, 142, 149). She of course forfeited it if she were an adulteress, or reduced to slavery for misconduct (§§ 141, 143; cf. Gn $16^2$ $24^{59.61}$ $29^{24.29}$, Jos $15^{18}$, Jg $1^{14}$).

If the marriage was dissolved without her fault, she took a child's share when her husband's property was divided. If she had children, the father had to allow her the usufruct of his estates till the children were grown up (§ 137). She was free to marry again when the children were grown up, and apparently not till her husband was dead. If she had no children when the marriage was dissolved, she got back her marriage portion and either her *terḫatu*, or divorce price (*uzûbu*), of one mina, if her husband was a gentleman; or a third of a mina if he was a 'poor man' (§§ 138–140). When the husband died and she had a family, she had a right to a son's share (§ 172), unless her husband had given her a settlement (*nudunnû*) by deed of gift in his lifetime. She might have power given her to leave this as she liked among her sons, but not outside her husband's children. Her family could not disturb her possession of these benefits as long as she lived and remained a widow; but, if she remarried, she gave them up to her family, to whom they came at her death (§ 172). She had a right to live in her husband's house, and the family could not turn her out.

The married pair formed a unit. Each was responsible for the debts of the other, even prenuptial debts. This shows that they were not always children when married, and that unmarried women could contract debt. The Code allowed a woman to get her husband to give her a bond that she should not be held responsible for his prenuptial debts, in which case his creditors could not touch her (§ 151). But it enacted that this should also exempt him from responsibility for her prenuptial debts. Further, it enacted that both together should be responsible for all debts contracted after marriage. This was a heavy responsibility for the wife. For she could be assigned by her husband to work off his debts as a *mancipium* (§ 117). Her contracting debt was one of the offences which might lead to divorce, or even death (§ 141 f.).

Marriage was a contract. There had to be a marriage deed drawn up, sealed, and witnessed. Without such *riksati*, 'bonds' or 'marriage lines,' a woman was not a wife (§ 128). The marriage deed might contain some peculiar stipulations. Thus a man married a sister of his first wife, on condition that she was to be his wife, but wait on her sister, care for her, and carry her stool when she went to the temple of Marduk (B$^1$ 21, B$^2$ 2176 A). The children were to be reckoned children of the first wife, probably to inherit her property. Two contracts were drawn up—one between the husband and wife, one between the sisters. If the wife repudiated her husband, she was to be branded and sold as a slave. If the husband repudiated her, he was to pay her a mina of silver. In another case, a man marries a wife on condition that she treat his mother as mistress of the house, or be branded and sold for a slave. The mother then contracts to leave all her property to the pair, if they keep her as long as she lives (B$^2$ 707).

2. Divorce was allowed. The husband had it in his power to divorce his wife with the words, 'Thou art not my wife'; but he could not do so without a cause. He had to return what she brought with her, and either pay her a compensation or forfeit the bride-price he paid for her (§§ 137, 138; cf. Dt $24^1$ $22^{19.29}$, Hos $2^4$, Mt $5^{31}$ $19^7$). She retained custody of the children until they were of age, and he had to make them and her an allowance. But, if the wife had so misconducted herself as to merit divorce, she lost her property, or the husband could degrade her to slavery. In the former case she was homeless, unless her family would take her back, and also penniless. In the latter case she had at least home, food, and clothing. If the wife sought the divorce herself, she could get it if she could prove cruelty (§ 142). She then took her marriage portion and went back to her family, but forfeited her bride-price. On the other hand, if in this case the fault was on her side, she lost her life (§ 143). The wife who was childless could not oppose her husband's taking a concubine, unless she chose to give him a maid to bear him children. If she was seized with incurable disease, her husband could not divorce her on that ground, but might marry again (§ 148). He was bound to let her stay in his house, and to maintain her as long as she lived (§ 148). But she was not bound to stay; she might

take back her marriage portion and go back to her father's house (§ 149). Desertion on the man's part dissolved marriage (§ 136); but mere absence did not, if the wife was provided for (§§ 133, 134). Otherwise, she might remarry to get maintenance, but she was then bound to return to her husband if he came back (§ 135).

3. It is clear that the Babylonian was a monogamist: he could have only one proper wife. But he could have a concubine, if his wife were childless (§ 145). The children by a concubine were legitimate, the concubine a real wife. He could not put her away except on the same terms as the first wife (§ 137).

4. It was not forbidden to votaries to marry (§§ 144–146). As the contemporary documents show, they frequently did so. But it was evidently contemplated that they would not have children.

5. Bars to marriage are enacted: when a comrade slanders a suitor so that he is rejected, he may not marry the girl himself (§ 137); when a widow has young children, she may not marry except by the judge's permission (§ 177). This was granted only when the first husband's goods had been inventoried, and given in trust for the children to the widow and her new husband.

6. Connexion with a maid was not marriage. But the children were free, and so was the maid at her master's death. He could acknowledge the children as his (§ 170); then they shared equally with the other children. A maid given by her mistress to her master to bear him children was still in the power of her mistress, who could degrade her to slavery again for insolence; but, if she had fulfilled her function, she could not be sold.

7. Special cases arose when a free woman married a slave. The wife kept her marriage portion, if any; and she, with her children, had a right to half what her husband left (§ 176).

8. A girl might be vowed to a temple. In this case she became the bride of a god, and, as such, might have a marriage portion given her. Of this she had the enjoyment for life. But her brothers had the reversion of it on her death. She could alienate nothing from it. If she did not receive this marriage portion from her father, she had the right to receive one-third of a son's share at his death (§§ 180–182). The votaries of Marduk had, further, the free disposal of their property at death, and exemption from duty (§ 182). The ladies might hand over their property at once to their brothers to administer and maintain them, or they could appoint a steward to do so.

Sons were also vowed to temples (B² 2183, 2480).

9. The father had power over his children. He could pledge or sell them for his debts (§ 119). He sought wives for his sons, and provided them with a proper bride-price. This was so important a duty, that, if he had not performed it for all his children before his death, the brethren at the division of the property, at his death, had to set aside a bride-price for the unmarried sons, and get them married. The father gave his daughters in marriage. After his death the mother took his place. She usually acted in concert with the grown-up children. In default of both parents, the elder brother acted.

Children were often hired out by their parents to work. It seems that, as long as a son lived in his father's house, the father had a right to his work or earnings.

Sonship could be dissolved; but only on grave grounds. The judge had to consent, and was bound to try to reconcile the father first. Only on a repetition of the offence was disinheritance allowed (§§ 168, 169).

10. Adoption was very common. An adopted son was as difficult to disinherit as a real son. The adoption was usually made by contract; the father gave the son a 'deed of sonship' (*duppu aplûtišu*). This might lay down conditions. The most usual was that the adopted son should care for and maintain his adoptive father as long as he should live. Mothers often adopted daughters, to be cared for by them. The other members of the family were consenting parties. The arrangement disturbed their succession to their parents' property; but if married they might prefer, and even procure, this means of providing for old people.

Adoption could be rescinded for faults on either side. When an adopted child failed to keep his contract (§ 186), when the adopting parent did not treat the adopted child properly (§§ 189, 190), or when the adoptive parent chose to dissolve the contract (§ 191), it could be done. In the contracts, the right to break the bond was sometimes expressly reserved to both parties (B 27). Sometimes the right to dissolve the relation was reserved to the parents alone (B¹ 210). Sometimes it was laid down that, if they did that, they must give the child a son's share of the estate (B¹ 54).

In such cases we may regard the adopted child as a scion of a good family, whose real parents consented and saw after their child's interests. Such a consent was needed (§ 186). When a man adopted a foundling, or his own children by a maid, no one could make a stipulation (§§ 170, 185, 187). But, even when the real parents were alive, the adopted child might be severely punished for attempting to repudiate his adoptive parents. Usually he was to be made a slave, branded, and sold. The Code prescribes mutilation as punishment in specially ungrateful cases (§§ 192, 193). It is not unlikely that in these cases the real parents stipulated that they should not be known. We find that votaries often adopted daughters, and, whenever a child of a votary is named, this may be the explanation. Slaves were adopted (B¹ 322, V.A.Th. 847).

11. Sons inherited equally. Adopted sons were usually heirs to a residuary portion. A married and portioned daughter had no share. But if she was not portioned she had a share like a son (§ 180), but only a life interest in it. The brothers might give her a portion after her father's death (§ 184). When there were children of two mothers by the same father, they all shared equally in the father's property (§ 167); but each family shared only their own mother's portion.

On sharing, if there was an unmarried son, a bride-price had to be reserved for him over and above his share (§ 166). A girl's share was her *šeriḳtu*, or marriage portion. If she had had that, she had no other share; if not, she had it now. A father's free gift to a favourite son did not come into the division, nor was his share less on that account (§ 165). Daughters, of course, inherited in default of sons. The widow took one son's share (§ 171) and her own property. The contemporary documents often show divisions of inheritance, or lawsuits about them.

## II. The Code.

§ 1. If a man has accused a man and laid (a charge of ?) death [a deadly spell ?] upon him and has not justified it, he that accused him shall* be put to death.

§ 2. If a man has laid (a charge of ?) sorcery upon a man and has not justified it, he upon whom the sorcery is laid shall go to the holy river, he shall plunge into the holy river, and if the holy river overcome him, he who accused him shall take to himself his house. If the holy river has made out that man to be innocent and has saved him, he

* 'Shall' is future. In many cases it could be rendered 'may.' It fixes the extreme penalty.

who accused him shall be put to death. He who plunged into the holy river shall take to himself the house of him who wove the spell upon him. [Ex 22$^{18}$, Dt 18$^{10}$, Jer 27$^{9}$].

§ 3. If a man in a case (pending judgment), as witness to slander has lied and has not justified the word that he has spoken, if that case be a capital suit, that man shall be put to death. [Dt 19$^{16f.}$].

§ 4. If as witness to corn or money he has lied, he shall himself bear the sentence of that case. [Ex 23$^{8}$, Dt 16$^{19}$].

§ 5. If a judge has judged a judgment, decided a decision, granted a sealed sentence, and afterwards has altered his judgment, they shall call that judge to account for the alteration of the judgment that he judged, and he shall pay twelvefold the penalty which was in the said judgment. Further, in the assembly they shall expel him from his judgment seat, and he shall not return and with the judges at a judgment he shall not take his seat.

§ 6. If a man has stolen the goods of temple or palace, that man shall be put to death. Further, he who has received the stolen thing from his hand shall be put to death. [Gn 31$^{32}$, Jos 7$^{1f.}$].

§ 7. If a man has bought silver, gold, manservant or maidservant, ox or sheep or ass or anything whatever its name, from the hand of a man's son, or of a man's slave, without witness or power of attorney, or has received the same on deposit, that man has acted the thief, he shall be put to death. [Gn 23$^{10-18}$, Ru 4$^{2f.}$].

§ 8. If a man has stolen ox or sheep or ass or pig or ship, whether from the temple or the palace, he shall pay thirtyfold. If from a poor man, he shall render tenfold. If the thief has not wherewith to pay, he shall be put to death. [Gn 44$^{9}$, Ex 21$^{37}$ 22$^{1f. 9}$, 2 S 12$^{6}$].

§ 9. If a man who has lost something of his has seized something of his that was lost in the hand of a man, (while) the man in whose hand the lost thing has been seized has said, 'A giver gave it me,' or 'I bought it before witnesses'; and further, the owner of the thing that was lost has said, 'Verily, I will bring witnesses that know my lost property'; (if) the buyer has brought the giver who gave it him, or the witnesses before whom he bought it, and the owner of the lost property has brought the witnesses who know his lost property, the judge shall see their depositions, the witnesses before whom the purchase was made, and the witnesses knowing the lost property shall say out before God what they know; and if the giver has acted the thief he shall be put to death, the owner of the lost property shall take his lost property, the buyer shall take the money he paid from the house of the giver. ['to give' is often = 'to sell.']. [Ex 22$^{7-9}$, Lv 6$^{3}$].

§ 10. If the buyer has not brought the giver who gave it him or the witnesses before whom he bought, and the owner of the lost property has brought the witnesses knowing his lost property, the (professed) buyer has acted the thief, he shall be put to death. The owner of the lost property shall take his lost property.

§ 11. If the owner of the lost property has not brought witnesses knowing his lost property, he has slandered, he has stirred up strife, he shall be put to death. [Dt 19$^{16f.}$].

§ 12. If the seller has betaken himself to his fate (is dead), the buyer shall take from the house of the seller fivefold as the penalty of that case.

§ 13. If that man has not his witnesses near, the judge shall set him a fixed time, up to six months, and if within six months he has not brought in his witnesses, that man has slandered, he himself shall bear the penalty of that case.

§ 14. If a man has stolen the young son of a freeman, he shall be put to death. [Ex 21$^{16}$, Dt 24$^{7}$].

§ 15. If a man has caused either a palace slave or palace maid, or a slave of a poor man or a poor man's maid, to go out of the gate, he shall be put to death.

§ 16. If a man has harboured in his house a manservant or a maidservant, fugitive from the palace, or from a poor man, and has not produced them at the demand of the commandant, that householder shall be put to death. [Dt 23$^{15f.}$, 1 S 30$^{15}$].

§ 17. If a man has captured either a manservant or a maidservant, a fugitive, in the open country and has driven him back to his master, the owner of the slave shall pay him two shekels of silver. [Gn 16$^{7f.}$, Dt 23$^{16}$, 1 K 2$^{39}$].

§ 18. If that slave will not name his owner, he shall drive him to the palace, and one shall inquire into his past, and cause him to return to his owner.

§ 19. If he confine that slave in his house, and afterwards the slave has been seized in his hand, that man shall be put to death.

§ 20. If the slave has fled from the hand of his captor, that man shall swear by the name of God to the owner of the slave, and shall go free. [Ex 22$^{1-3}$, Jer 2$^{32}$, Mt 6$^{19f.}$].

§ 21. If a man has broken into a house one shall kill him before the breach, and bury him in it (?).

§ 22. If a man has carried on brigandage and has been captured, that man shall be put to death.

§ 23. If the brigand has not been caught, the man who has been despoiled shall recount before God what he has lost, and the city and governor in whose land and district the brigandage took place shall render back to him whatever of his was lost. [Dt 21$^{1f.}$].

§ 24. If it was life, the city and governor shall pay one mina of silver to his people. [Dt 21$^{1f.}$].

§ 25. If in a man's house a fire has been kindled, and a man who has come to extinguish the fire has lifted up his eyes to the property of the owner of the house, and has taken the property of the owner of the house, that man shall be thrown into that fire.

§ 26. If either a ganger or a constable, whose going on an errand of the king has been ordered, has not gone, or has hired a hireling and sent him in place of himself, that ganger or constable shall be put to death, his hireling shall take to himself his house. ['ganger' = 'levy-master'].

§ 27. If a ganger or a constable has been assigned to the fortresses of the king, and after him one has given his field and his garden to another who has carried on his duty, if he has returned and regained his city, his field and his garden shall be returned to him, and he shall carry on his duty himself.

§ 28. If when a ganger or a constable has been assigned to the fortresses of the king, his son be able to carry on the duty, one shall give him field and garden, and he shall carry on his father's duty.

§ 29. If his son is young, and is not able to carry on his father's duty, one-third of the field and garden shall be given to his mother, and his mother shall bring him up.

§ 30. If a ganger or a constable has neglected his field, his garden, and his house, from the beginning of his duty, and has caused it to be waste, and another after him has taken his field, his garden, and his house, and has gone about his duty for three years, if he has returned and regained his city, and would cultivate his field, his garden, and his house, one shall not give them to him; he who has taken them and carried on his duty shall carry it on.

§ 31. If it is one year only and he had let it go

waste, and he has returned, one shall give him his field, his garden, and his house, and he himself shall carry on his duty.

§ 32. If a ganger or a constable has been assigned on an errand of the king's, and a merchant has ransomed him and caused him to regain his city, if in his house there is means for his ransom, he shall ransom himself; if in his house there is no means for his ransom, he shall be ransomed from the temple of his city; if in the temple of his city there is not means for his ransom, the palace shall ransom him. His field, his garden, and his house shall not be given for his ransom.

§ 33. If either a governor or a magistrate has taken to himself the men of the levy, or has accepted and sent on the king's errand a hired substitute, that governor or magistrate shall be put to death.

§ 34. If either a governor or a magistrate has taken to himself the property of a ganger, has plundered a ganger, has given a ganger on hire, has defrauded a ganger in a judgment by high-handedness, has taken to himself the gift the king has given the ganger, that governor or magistrate shall be put to death. [Lk 12[38]].

§ 35. If a man has bought the cattle or sheep which the king has given to the ganger, at the hand of the ganger, he shall be deprived of his money.

§ 36. The field, garden, and house of a ganger, or constable, or a tributary, one shall not give for money.

§ 37. If a man has bought the field, garden, or house of a ganger, a constable, or a tributary, his tablet shall be broken, and he shall be deprived of his money. The field, garden, or house he shall return to its owner.

§ 38. The ganger, constable, or tributary shall not write off to his wife or his daughter, from the field, garden, or house of his benefice. Further, he shall not assign it for his debt.

§ 39. From the field, garden, and house which he has bought and acquired he may write off to his wife or his daughter, and give for his debt. [Ezk 46[18]].

§ 40. A votary, merchant, or foreign sojourner may sell his field, his garden, or his house; the buyer shall carry on the duty of the field, garden, or house which he has bought.

§ 41. If a man has bartered for the field, garden, or house of a ganger, constable, or tributary, and has given exchanges, the ganger, constable, or tributary shall return to his field, garden, or house, and further shall keep the exchanges given him.

§ 42. If a man has taken a field to cultivate and has not caused the corn to grow in the field and has not done the entrusted work on the field, they shall call him to account and he shall give a crop like its neighbour to the owner of the field.

§ 43. If he has not cultivated the field and has left it to itself, he shall give corn like its neighbour to the owner of the field. Further, the field he left he shall break up with hoes, and shall harrow it and return to the owner of the field.

§ 44. If a man has taken on hire an unreclaimed field for three years to open out, and has left it aside, has not opened the field, in the fourth year he shall break it up with hoes, he shall hoe it, and harrow it, and return to the owner of the field. Further, he shall measure out ten *GUR* of corn per *GAN*.

§ 45. If a man has given his field for produce to a cultivator, and has received the produce of his field, and afterwards a thunderstorm has ravaged the field or carried away the produce, the loss is the cultivator's.

§ 46. If he has not received the produce of his field, or has given the field either for one-half or for one-third of the corn that is in the field, the cultivator and the owner of the field shall share according to the tenour of their contract. [Gn 47[24]].

§ 47. If the cultivator, because in the former year he did not set up his dwelling, has assigned the field to cultivation, the owner of the field shall not interfere; he shall wait (?); his field has been cultivated, and at harvest time he shall take corn according to his bonds.

§ 48. If a man has a debt upon him and a thunderstorm ravaged his field or carried away the produce, or if the corn has not grown through lack of water, in that year he shall not return corn to the creditor, he shall alter (lit. moisten, so as to rewrite) his tablet. Further, he shall not give interest for that year.

§ 49. If a man has borrowed money from a merchant and has given to the merchant a field planted with corn or sesame, and said to him, 'Cultivate the field, reap and take for thyself the corn and sesame which there shall be,' if the cultivator has caused corn or sesame to grow in the field, at the time of harvest the owner of the field, forsooth, shall take the corn or sesame which is in the field, and shall give to the merchant corn for the money which he took from the merchant and for its interest and for the dwelling of the cultivator.

§ 50. If the field was cultivated or the field of sesame was cultivated when he gave it, the owner of the field, forsooth, shall take the corn or sesame which is in the field and shall return the money and its interest to the merchant.

§ 51. If he has not money to return, he shall give to the merchant the sesame, according to its market price, for the money and its interest which he took from the merchant, according to the standard fixed by the king.

§ 52. If the cultivator has not caused corn or sesame to grow in the field, his bonds shall not be altered.

§ 53. If a man has neglected to strengthen his bank of the canal, has not strengthened his bank, a breach has opened out itself in his bank, and the waters have carried away the meadow, the man in whose bank the breach has been opened shall render back the corn which he has caused to be lost.

§ 54. If he is not able to render back the corn, one shall give him and his goods for money, and the people of the meadow whose corn the water has carried away shall share it. [Ex 22[3], Lv 25[39f.]].

§ 55. If a man has opened his runnel to water and has neglected it, and the waters have carried away the field of his neighbour, he shall pay corn like his neighbour.

§ 56. If a man has opened the waters, and the waters have carried away the plants of the field of his neighbour, he shall pay ten *GUR* of corn per *GAN*.

§ 57. If a shepherd has caused the sheep to feed on the green corn, has not come to an agreement with the owner of the field, without the consent of the owner of the field has made the sheep feed off the field, the owner shall reap his fields, the shepherd who without consent of the owner of the field has fed off the field with sheep shall give over and above twenty *GUR* of corn per *GAN* to the owner of the field. [Ex 22[4f.]].

§ 58. If from the time that the sheep have gone up from the meadow, and the whole flock has passed through the gate, the shepherd has laid his sheep on the field and has caused the sheep to feed off the field, the shepherd who has made them feed off the field shall keep it, and at harvest time he shall measure out sixty *GUR* of corn per *GAN* to the owner of the field.

§ 59. If a man without the consent of the owner of the orchard has cut down a tree in a man's orchard, he shall pay half a mina of silver. [2 K 3[25]].

§ 60. If a man has given a field to a gardener to plant a garden, and the gardener has planted the garden, four years he shall rear the garden, in the fifth year the owner of the garden and the gardener shall share equally. The owner of the garden shall cut off his share and take it. [Lv 19[23-25]].

§ 61. If the gardener has not included all the field in the planting, has left a waste place, one shall set him the waste place in his share.

§ 62. If he has not planted the field which has been given him as a garden; if it was corn land, the gardener shall measure out to the owner of the field produce of the field, like its neighbour, for the years that are neglected. Further, he shall do the prescribed work on the field and return to the owner of the field.

§ 63. If the field was unreclaimed land, he shall do the prescribed work on the field and return it to the owner of the field. Further, he shall measure out ten *GUR* of corn per *GAN* for each year.

§ 64. If a man has given his garden to a gardener to farm, the gardener as long as he holds the garden shall give to the owner of the garden two-thirds from the produce of the garden, and he himself shall take one-third.

§ 65. If the gardener does not farm the garden and has diminished the yield, he shall measure out the yield of the garden like its neighbour.

Here five columns of the monument have been erased, only the commencing characters of column xvii. being visible. The subjects of this last part included the further enactments concerning the rights and duties of gardeners, the whole of the regulations concerning houses let to tenants, and the relationships of the merchant to his agents, which continue on the obverse of the monument. Scheil estimates the lost portion at 35 sections, and, following him, we recommence with—

§ 100. . . . the interests of the money, as much as he took, he shall write down, and when he has numbered his days he shall answer the merchant.

§ 101. If where he has gone he has not seen prosperity, the agent shall double the money he took and shall give to the merchant.

§ 102. If a merchant has given to the agent money as a favour, and where he has gone he has seen loss, the full amount of money he shall return to the merchant.

§ 103. If while he goes on his journey the enemy has made him quit whatever he was carrying, the agent shall swear by the name of God and shall go free.

§ 104. If the merchant has given to the agent corn, wool, oil, or any sort of goods, to traffic with, the agent shall write down the price and hand over to the merchant; the agent shall take a sealed memorandum of the price which he shall give to the merchant.

§ 105. If an agent has forgotten and has not taken a sealed memorandum of the money he has given to the merchant, money that is not sealed for he shall not put in his accounts.

§ 106. If an agent has taken money from a merchant, and has disputed with his merchant, that merchant shall put the agent to account before God and witnesses concerning the money taken, and the agent shall give to the merchant threefold the money he has taken.

§ 107. If a merchant has wronged an agent and the agent has returned to his merchant whatever the merchant gave him, but the merchant has disputed with the agent as to what the agent gave him, that agent shall put the merchant to account before God and witnesses, and the merchant because he disputed the agent shall give to the agent sixfold whatever he has taken.

§ 108. If a wine merchant has not received corn as the price of drink, has received silver by the great stone, further has made the price of drink less than the price of corn, that wine merchant one shall put to account and throw her into the water. [Jos 2[1f.]].

§ 109. If a wine merchant has collected a riotous assembly in her house, and has not seized those rioters and driven them to the palace, that wine merchant shall be put to death.

§ 110. If a votary, a lady, who is not living in the convent, has opened a wine-shop or has entered a wine-shop for drink, one shall burn that woman. [Gn 38[24], Lv 21[9]].

§ 111. If a wine merchant has given sixty *ḲA* of best beer at harvest time for thirst, she shall take fifty *ḲA* of corn.

§ 112. If a man stays away on a journey and has given silver, gold, precious stones, or portable treasures to a man, has caused him to take them for transport, and that man has not given whatever was given for transport, where he has transported it, but has taken it for himself, the owner of the transported object shall put that man to account concerning whatever he had to transport and gave not, and that man shall give to the owner of the transported object fivefold whatever was given him. [Ex 22[7f.], Lv 6[2-5]].

§ 113. If a man has corn or money upon a man, and without consent of the owner of the corn has taken corn from the heap or from the store, one shall call that man to account for taking of the corn without consent of the owner of the corn from the heap or from the store, and he shall return the corn as much as he has taken. Further, he shall lose all that he gave whatever it be. [Dt 24[18]].

§ 114. If a man has not corn or money upon a man but levies a distraint, for every single distraint he shall pay one-third of a mina.

§ 115. If a man has corn or money upon a man and has levied a distraint, and the distress in the house of his distrainer dies a natural death, no case lies.

§ 116. If the distress has died in the house of his distrainer, of blows or of want, the owner of his distress shall put his merchant to account, and if he be the son of a freeman (that has died), one shall kill his son; if the slave of a freeman, he shall pay one-third of a mina of silver. Further, he shall lose all that he gave whatever it be. [Mt 18[28f.]].

§ 117. If a debt has seized a man and he has given his wife, his son, or his daughter for the money, or has handed them over to work off the debt; for three years they shall work in the house of their buyer or exploiter, in the fourth year he shall set them at liberty. [Gn 31[41] 47[19], Ex 21[2. 7], Lv 25[39f.], Dt 15[12. 14. 18], 1 S 22[2], 2 K 4[1], Neh 5[5f.], Is 16[14] 21[16] 50[1], Jer 34[8], Am 2[6. 8], Mt 5[25] 18[28f.], Lk 12[58]].

§ 118. If he has handed over a manservant or a maidservant to work off a debt and the merchant shall go further and sell them for money, no one can object.

§ 119. If a debt has seized a man and he has handed over for the money a maidservant who has borne him children, the money the merchant paid him the owner of the maid shall repay, and he shall ransom his maid.

§ 120. If a man has heaped up his corn in a heap in the house of a man, and in the granary a disaster has taken place, or the owner of the house has opened the granary and taken the corn, or has disputed as to the total amount of the corn that was heaped up in his house, the owner of the corn shall estimate his corn before God, the owner of the house shall double the corn which he took and shall give to the owner of the corn. [Ex $22^{5-11}$].

§ 121. If a man has heaped up corn in the house of a man, he shall give as the price of storage five *ḲA* of corn per *GUR* of corn per year.

§ 122. If a man shall give silver, gold, or anything whatever to a man on deposit, all whatever he shall give he shall show to witnesses and fix bonds and shall give on deposit. [Ex $22^{7f.}$].

§ 123. If without witness and bonds he has given on deposit, and where he has deposited they keep disputing him, no case lies.

§ 124. If a man has given silver, gold, or anything whatever to a man on deposit before witnesses and he has disputed with him, one shall call that man to account, and whatever he has disputed he shall make up and shall give double.

§ 125. If a man has given anything of his on deposit, and where he gave it, either by house-breaking or by rebellion, something of his has been lost, along with something of the owner of the house who has defaulted, all that was given him on deposit and he has lost he shall make good and render to the owner of the goods. The owner of the house shall seek out whatever of his is lost and take it from the thief. [Ex $22^{7}$].

§ 126. If a man has lost nothing of his, but has said that something of his is lost, has estimated his loss; since nothing of his is lost, his loss he shall estimate before God, and whatever he has claimed he shall double and shall give as his loss.

§ 127. If a man has caused the finger to be pointed against a votary or a man's wife and has not justified himself, that man they shall throw down before the judge and brand his forehead.

§ 128. If a man has married a wife and has not laid down her bonds, that woman is no wife.

§ 129. If the wife of a man has been caught in lying with another male, one shall bind (strangle ?) them and throw them into the waters. If the owner of the wife would save his wife, the king may also save his servant. [Gn $38^{24}$, Lv $20^{10}$, Dt $22^{22-27}$].

§ 130. If a man has forced the wife of a man who has not known the male and is dwelling in the house of her father, and has lain in her bosom and one has caught him, that man shall be put to death; the woman herself shall go free. [Ex $22^{16}$, Dt $22^{23f.}$].

§ 131. If the wife of a man has been accused by her husband, and she has not been caught in lying with another male, she shall swear by God and shall return to her house.

§ 132. If a wife of a man on account of another male has had the finger pointed at her and has not been caught in lying with another male, for her husband's sake she shall plunge into the holy river. [Nu $5^{12f.}$].

§ 133. If a man has been taken captive and in his house there is maintenance, but his wife has gone out from her house and entered into the house of another; because that woman has not guarded her body and has entered into the house of another, one shall call that woman to account and throw her into the waters.

§ 134. If a man has been taken captive and in his house there is no maintenance, and his wife has entered into the house of another, that woman has no blame.

§ 135. If a man has been taken captive and in his house there is no maintenance before her, his wife has entered into the house of another and has borne children, afterwards her husband has returned and regained his city, that woman shall return to her bridegroom. The children shall go after their father.

§ 136. If a man has left his city and fled, and after his departure his wife has entered the house of another, if that man shall return and seize his wife; because he hated his city and fled, the wife of the truant shall not return to her husband.

§ 137. If a man has set his face to put away his concubine who has borne him children or his wife who has granted him children, to that woman he shall return her marriage portion. Further, he shall give her the usufruct of field, garden, and goods, and she shall bring up her children. From the time that her children are grown up, from whatever is given to her children, they shall give her a share like that of one son and she shall marry the husband of her choice.

§ 138. If a man has put away his bride who has not borne him children, he shall give her money as much as her bride-price. Further, he shall pay her the marriage portion which she brought from her father's house, and shall put her away. [Dt $24^{1}$, Mal $2^{16}$].

§ 139. If there was no bride-price he shall give one mina of silver for a divorce.

§ 140. If he is a poor man he shall give her one-third of a mina of silver.

§ 141. If the wife of a man who is living in the house of her husband has set her face to go out and has acted the fool, has wasted her house, has belittled her husband, one shall call her to account, and if her husband has said, 'I put her away,' he shall put her away and she shall go her way, he shall not give her anything for her divorce. If her husband has said, 'I will not put her away,' and her husband shall marry another woman, that woman as a maidservant shall dwell in the house of her husband.

§ 142. If a woman hates her husband and has said, 'Thou shalt not possess me,' one shall inquire into her past as to what is her lack, and if she has been economical and has no vice, while her husband has gone out and greatly belittled her, that woman has no blame, she shall take her marriage portion and go off to her father's house.

§ 143. If she has not been economical but a goer about, has wasted her house, has belittled her husband, one shall throw that woman into the waters.

§ 144. If a man has espoused a votary and that votary has given a maid to her husband and has brought up children, but that man has set his face to take a concubine, one shall not countenance that man, he shall not take a concubine. [Gn $16^{1f.}$ $21^{10f.}$ $30^{3f.\ 9f.}$].

§ 145. If a man has espoused a votary and she has not granted him children and he has set his face to take a concubine, that man shall take a concubine, he shall cause her to enter into his house. That concubine shall not put herself on an equality with the wife.

§ 146. If a man has espoused a votary and she has given a maid to her husband and the maid has borne children, and afterwards that maid has made herself equal with her mistress; because she has borne children her mistress shall not sell her for money, she shall put a mark upon her and count her among the maidservants. [Gn $16^{4f.}$ $21^{10}$, Dt $21^{14}$, 1 S $1^{1f.}$].

§ 147. If she has not borne children her mistress may sell her for money.

§ 148. If a man has married a wife and a sickness has seized her, and he has set his face to marry a second wife, he may marry her, but his wife whom the sickness has seized he shall not put away, in the home she shall dwell, and as long as she lives he shall sustain her.

§ 149. If that woman is not content to dwell in the house of her husband, he shall pay her her marriage portion which she brought from her father's house and she shall go off.

§ 150. If a man has presented to his wife field, garden, house, or goods, has left her a sealed deed, after her husband's death her children shall not dispute with her. The mother shall give after her to the child whom she loves. To brothers she shall not give.

§ 151. If a woman, who is dwelling in the house of a man, has bound her husband that she shall not be seized on account of a creditor of her husband's, has got a deed granted her; if that man before he married that woman had a debt upon him, his creditor shall not seize his wife. Further, if that woman before she entered the man's house had a debt upon her, her creditor shall not seize her husband.

§ 152. If from the time that that woman entered into the house of the man a debt has come upon them, both together they shall answer the merchant.

§ 153. If a man's wife on account of another male has caused her husband to be killed, that woman shall be impaled. [Dt 21[21-23]].

§ 154. If a man has known his daughter, that man one shall expel from the city.

§ 155. If a man has betrothed a bride to his son and his son has known her, and he afterwards has lain in her bosom and one has caught him, that man one shall bind (strangle?) and cast her into the waters. [Gn 24[4f.]].

§ 156. If a man has betrothed a bride to his son and his son has not known her, and he has lain in her bosom, he shall pay her half a mina of silver. Further, he shall pay to her whatever she brought from her father's house, and she shall marry the husband of her choice. [Ex 22[16], Lv 20[12], Dt 22[28]].

§ 157. If a man, after his father's death, has lain in the bosom of his mother, one shall burn them both together. [Lv 20[14]].

§ 158. If a man, after his father's death, has been caught in the bosom of his head wife who has borne children, that man shall be cut off from his father's house. [Lv 20[11], Dt 22[30]].

§ 159. If a man, who has brought in a present to the house of his (prospective) father-in-law, has given a bride-price, has looked upon another woman, and has said to his father-in-law, 'Thy daughter I will not marry,' the father of the girl shall take to himself all that he brought him. [Gn 24[53f.] 31[15]].

§ 160. If a man has brought in a present to the house of his father-in-law, has given a bride-price, and the father of the girl has said, 'My daughter I will not give thee,' he shall return double everything that he brought him.

§ 161. If a man has brought in a present to the house of his father-in-law, has given a bride-price, and a comrade of his has slandered him, (so that) his father-in-law has said to the claimant of the wife, 'My daughter thou shalt not espouse,' he shall return double all that he brought him. Further, his comrade shall not marry his wife.

§ 162. If a man has married a wife and she has borne him children and that woman has gone to her fate, her father shall have no claim on her marriage portion, her marriage portion is her children's forsooth. [Gn 31[16]].

§ 163. If a man has married a wife and she has not granted him children, (and) that woman has gone to her fate, if his father-in-law has returned him the bride-price that that man brought to the house of his father-in-law, her husband shall have no claim on the marriage portion of that woman, her marriage portion belongs to the house of her father forsooth.

§ 164. If his father-in-law has not returned to him the bride-price, he shall deduct all her bride-price from her marriage portion and shall return her marriage portion to the house of her father.

§ 165. If a man has apportioned to his son, the first in his eyes, field, garden, and house, has written him a sealed deed, after the father has gone to his fate, when the brothers divide, the present his father gave him he shall take and over and above he shall share equally in the goods of the father's house. [Gn 24[36] 25[5] 27[29. 37] 48[22], Lk 15[31]].

§ 166. If a man has taken wives for the sons whom he has possessed, but has not taken a wife for his young son, after the father has gone to his fate, when the brothers divide, from the goods of the father's house to their young brother who has not taken a wife, beside his share, they shall assign him money as a bride-price and shall cause him to take a wife.

§ 167. If a man has taken a wife and she has borne him sons, (and) that woman has gone to her fate, (and) after her he has taken to himself another woman and she has borne children, after the father has gone to his fate, the children shall not share according to their mothers, they shall take the marriage portions of their mothers and shall share the goods of their father's house equally. [Gn 31[16]].

§ 168. If a man has set his face to cut off his son, has said to the judge, 'I will cut off my son,' the judge shall inquire into his reasons, and if the son has not committed a heavy crime which cuts off from sonship, the father shall not cut off his son from sonship. [Dt 21[18f.]].

§ 169. If he has committed against his father a heavy crime which cuts off from sonship, for the first time the judge shall reconcile them; if he has committed a heavy crime for the second time, the father shall cut off his son from sonship. [Dt 21[21]].

§ 170. If there be a man, whose wife has borne him sons, and his maidservant has borne him sons, (and) the father in his lifetime has said to the sons which the maidservant has borne him 'my sons,' has numbered them with the sons of his wife, after the father has gone to his fate, the sons of the wife and the sons of the maidservant shall share equally in the goods of the father's house; the sons that are sons of the wife at the sharing shall choose and take. [Gn 16[15. 23. 26] 21[10] 25[6], Jg 11[27]].

§ 171. However, if the father in his lifetime, to the sons which the maidservant bore him has not said 'my sons,' after the father has gone to his fate, the sons of the maid shall not share with the sons of the wife in the goods of the father's house. One shall assign the maidservant and her sons freedom, the sons of the wife shall have no claim on the sons of the maidservant for service. The wife shall take her marriage portion and the settlement which her husband gave her and wrote in a deed for her and shall dwell in the dwelling of her husband; as long as she lives she shall enjoy it, for money she shall not give it, after her it is her sons' forsooth. [Gn 27[37] 31[16], Ex 21[10f.], Dt 21[16f.]].

§ 172. If her husband did not give her a settlement, one shall pay her her marriage portion, and from the goods of her husband's house she shall take a share like one son. If her sons worry her to leave the house, the judge shall inquire into her wishes and shall lay the blame on the sons; that woman shall not go out of her husband's house. If that woman has set her face to leave, the settlement which her husband gave her she shall leave to her sons, the marriage portion from her father's house she shall take and she shall marry the husband of her choice. [Ex 21[9]].

§ 173. If that woman where she has entered shall have borne children to her later husband, after that woman has died, the former and later sons shall share her marriage portion.

§ 174. If she has not borne children to her later

husband, the sons of her bridegroom shall take her marriage portion.

§ 175. If either a slave of the palace or a slave of a poor man has taken to wife the daughter of a gentleman and she has borne sons, the owner of the slave shall have no claim on the sons of the daughter of a gentleman for service. [2 K $22^{12}$ Jer $38^{7}$ $39^{16}$].

§ 176. However, if a slave of the palace or a slave of a poor man has taken to wife the daughter of a gentleman, and, when he married her, with a marriage portion from her father's house she entered into the house of the slave of the palace, or of the slave of the poor man, and from that time they started to keep house and acquired property, after either the slave of the palace or the slave of the poor man has gone to his fate, the daughter of the gentleman shall take her marriage portion, and whatever her husband and she had acquired from the time they started one shall divide in two parts, and the owner of the slave shall take one-half, the gentleman's daughter shall take one-half for her children. If the gentleman's daughter had no marriage portion, whatever her husband and she from the time they started have acquired one shall divide into two parts and the owner of the slave shall take half, the gentleman's daughter shall take half for her sons.

§ 177. If a widow whose children are young has set her face to enter into the house of another, without consent of a judge she shall not enter. When she enters into the house of another, the judge shall inquire into what is left of her former husband's house, and he shall entrust the house of her former husband to her later husband and that woman and cause them to receive a deed. They shall keep the house and rear the little ones. Not a utensil shall they give for money. The buyer that has bought a utensil of a widow's sons shall lose his money and shall return the property to its owners.

§ 178. If a lady, a votary, or a vowed woman whose father has granted her a marriage portion, has written her a deed, in the deed that he has written her has not, however, written for her 'after her wherever is good to her to give,' has not permitted her full choice, after the father has gone to his fate, her brothers shall take her field and her garden and according to the value of her share shall give her corn, oil, and wool, and shall content her heart. If her brothers have not given her corn, oil, and wool according to the value of her share, and have not contented her heart, she shall give her field or her garden to a cultivator, whoever pleases her, and her cultivator shall maintain her. The field, garden, or whatever her father has given her she shall enjoy as long as she lives, she shall not give it for money, she shall not answer with it to another. Her sonship is her brothers' forsooth. [Hos $2^{5f.}$].

§ 179. If a lady, a votary, or a vowed woman whose father has granted her a marriage portion, has written her a deed, in the deed he wrote her has written for her 'after her wherever is good to her to give,' has allowed to her all her choice, after the father has gone to his fate, after her she shall give wherever is good to her, her brothers have no claim on her.

§ 180. If a father to his daughter, a votary, bride, or vowed woman, has not granted a marriage portion, after the father has gone to his fate, she shall take in the goods of the father's house a share like one son, as long as she lives she shall enjoy it, after her it is her brothers' forsooth.

§ 181. If a father has vowed to God a votary, hierodule, or virgin, and has not granted her a marriage portion, after the father has gone to his fate, she shall take in the goods of the father's house one-third of a son's share and shall enjoy it as long as she lives, after her it is her brothers' forsooth.

§ 182. If a father, to his daughter, a votary of Marduk of Babylon, has not granted a marriage portion, has not written her a deed, after the father has gone to his fate, she shall share with her brothers in the goods of the father's house, one-third of a son's share, and shall pay no tax. A votary of Marduk, after her, shall give wherever it is good to her.

§ 183. If a father to his daughter by a concubine, has granted her a marriage portion, has given her to a husband, has written her a deed, after the father has gone to his fate, she shall not share in the goods of the father's house. [Gn $25^{6}$, Jg $11^{2}$].

§ 184. If a man to his daughter by a concubine has not granted a marriage portion, has not given her to a husband, after the father has gone to his fate, her brothers, according to the capacity of the father's house, shall grant her a marriage portion and shall give her to a husband. [Gn $25^{6}$, Dt $21^{15-17}$].

§ 185. If a man has taken a young child 'from his waters' to sonship and has reared him up, no one has any claim against that nursling. [Gn $48^{5}$].

§ 186. If a man has taken a young child to sonship, and when he took him his father and mother rebelled, that nursling shall return to his father's house.

§ 187. The son of a *NER-SE-GA*, a palace warder, or the son of a vowed woman no one has any claim upon.

§ 188. If an artisan has taken a son to bring up and has caused him to learn his handicraft, no one has any claim.

§ 189. If he has not caused him to learn his handicraft, that nursling shall return to his father's house.

§ 190. If a man has not numbered with his sons the child whom he took to his sonship and brought up, that nursling shall return to his father's house.

§ 191. If a man, after he has taken a young child to his sonship and brought him up, has made a house for himself and acquired children and has set his face to cut off the nursling, that child shall not go his way, the father that brought him up shall give to him from his goods one-third of his sonship and he shall go off; from field, garden, and house he shall not give him.

§ 192. If a son of a palace warder or of a vowed woman to the father that brought him up and the mother that brought him up has said, 'Thou art not my father, thou art not my mother,' one shall cut out his tongue.

§ 193. If a son of a palace warder or of a vowed woman has known his father's house, and has hated the father that brought him up or the mother that brought him up, and has gone off to the house of his father, one shall tear out his eye. [Pr $30^{17}$].

§ 194. If a man has given his son to a wet-nurse, (and) that son has died in the hand of the wet-nurse, (and) the wet-nurse without consent of his father and his mother has procured another child, one shall call her to account, and because without consent of his father and his mother she has procured another child, one shall cut off her breasts.

§ 195. If a man has struck his father, one shall cut off his hands. [Ex $21^{15. 17}$, Lv $20^{9}$, Dt $21^{18}$ $25^{12}$, Pr $30^{17}$].

§ 196. If a man has caused the loss of a gentleman's eye, one shall cause his eye to be lost. [Ex $21^{24f.}$, Lv $24^{19f.}$, Dt $19^{21}$, Mt $5^{38}$].

§ 197. If he has shattered a gentleman's limb, one shall shatter his limb.

§ 198. If he has caused a poor man to lose his

eye or shattered a poor man's limb, he shall pay one mina of silver.

§ 199. If he has caused the loss of the eye of a gentleman's servant or has shattered the limb of a gentleman's servant, he shall pay half his price. [Ex 21[26f.]].

§ 200. If a man has made the tooth of a man that is his equal to fall out, one shall make his tooth fall out. [Ex 21[24]].

§ 201. If he has made the tooth of a poor man to fall out, he shall pay one-third of a mina of silver.

§ 202. If a man has struck the cheek of a man who is his superior, he shall be struck in the assembly with sixty strokes of a cow-hide whip.

§ 203. If a man of gentle birth has struck the cheek of a man of gentle birth who is his equal, he shall pay one mina of silver. [Lv 24[17. 21]].

§ 204. If a poor man has struck the cheek of a poor man, he shall pay ten shekels of silver.

§ 205. If a gentleman's servant has struck the cheek of a freeman, one shall cut off his ear.

§ 206. If a man has struck a man in a quarrel and has caused him a wound, that man shall swear, 'I did not strike him knowingly,' and shall answer for the doctor. [Ex 21[18f.], Nu 35[16f.], Dt 19[4f.]].

§ 207. If he has died of his blows, he shall swear, and if he be of gentle birth he shall pay half a mina of silver. [Ex 21[20]].

§ 208. If he be the son of a poor man, he shall pay one-third of a mina of silver.

§ 209. If a man has struck a gentleman's daughter and caused her to drop what is in her womb, he shall pay ten shekels of silver for what was in her womb. [Ex 21[22. 27]].

§ 210. If that woman has died, one shall put to death his daughter. [Ex 21[23], Dt 24[16]].

§ 211. If through his blows he has caused the daughter of a poor man to drop that which is in her womb, he shall pay five shekels of silver.

§ 212. If that woman has died, he shall pay half a mina of silver.

§ 213. If he has struck a gentleman's maid-servant and caused her to drop that which is in her womb, he shall pay two shekels of silver. [Ex 21[20]].

§ 214. If that maid-servant has died, he shall pay one-third of a mina of silver. [Ex 21[22]].

§ 215. If a doctor has treated a gentleman for a severe wound with a bronze lancet and has cured the man, or has removed a cataract of the eye for a gentleman with the bronze lancet and has cured the eye of the gentleman, he shall take ten shekels of silver.

§ 216. If he (the patient) be the son of a poor man, he shall take five shekels of silver.

§ 217. If he be a gentleman's servant, the master of the servant shall give two shekels of silver to the doctor.

§ 218. If the doctor has treated a gentleman for a severe wound with a lancet of bronze and has caused the gentleman to die, or has removed a cataract of the eye for a gentleman with the bronze lancet and has caused the loss of the gentleman's eye, one shall cut off his hands.

§ 219. If a doctor has treated the severe wound of a slave of a poor man with a bronze lancet and has caused his death, he shall render slave for slave. [Ex 21[22]].

§ 220. If he has removed a cataract with a bronze lancet and has made him lose his eye, he shall pay in money half his price.

§ 221. If a doctor has cured the shattered limb of a gentleman, or has cured a diseased bowel, the patient shall give five shekels of silver to the doctor.

§ 222. If he is the son of a poor man, he shall give three shekels of silver.

§ 223. If a gentleman's servant, the master of the slave shall give two shekels of silver to the doctor.

§ 224. If a cow doctor or an ass doctor has treated a cow or an ass for a severe wound and cured it, the owner of the cow or ass shall give one-sixth of a shekel of silver to the doctor as his fee.

§ 225. If he has treated a cow or an ass for a severe wound and has caused it to die, he shall give a quarter of its price to the owner of the ox or ass. [Lv 21[6]].

§ 226. If a brander without consent of the owner of the slave has made a slave's mark irrecognizable, one shall cut off the hands of that brander.

§ 227. If a man has deceived the brander, and has caused him to make a slave's mark irrecognizable, that man one shall kill him and bury him in his house; the brander shall swear, 'Not knowing I branded him,' and shall go free.

§ 228. If a builder has built a house for a man and has completed it, he shall give him as his fee two shekels of silver per *SAR* of house.

§ 229. If a builder has built a house for a man and has not made strong his work and the house he built has fallen and he has caused the death of the owner of the house, that builder shall be put to death.

§ 230. If he has caused the son of the owner of the house to die, one shall put to death the son of that builder. [Dt 24[16]].

§ 231. If he has caused the slave of the owner of the house to die, he shall give slave for slave to the owner of the house.

§ 232. If he has caused the loss of goods, he shall render back whatever he has caused the loss of. Further, because he did not make strong the house he built and it fell, from his own goods he shall rebuild the house that fell.

§ 233. If a builder has built a house for a man and has not jointed his work and the wall has fallen, that builder at his own cost shall make good that wall.

§ 234. If a boatman has completed a ship of sixty *GUR* for a man, he shall give him two shekels of silver for his fee.

§ 235. If a boatman has completed a ship for a man and has not made his work trustworthy, and in that same year that he built that ship it has suffered an injury, the boatman shall exchange that ship or shall make it strong at his own expense and shall give a strong ship to the owner of the ship.

§ 236. If a man has given his ship to a boatman on hire, and the boatman has been careless, has grounded the ship, or has caused it to be lost, the boatman shall render ship for ship to the owner.

§ 237. If a man has hired a boatman and ship, and with corn, wool, oil, dates, or whatever it be as freight, has freighted her, (and) that boatman has been careless and grounded the ship, or has caused what is in her to be lost, the boatman shall render back the ship which he has grounded and whatever in her he has caused to be lost.

§ 238. If a boatman has grounded the ship of a man and has refloated her, he shall give money to half her price.

§ 239. If a man has hired a boatman, he shall give him six *GUR* of corn per year.

§ 240. If a ship that is going forward has struck a ship at anchor and has sunk her, the owner of the ship that has been sunk shall recount before God whatever he has lost in his ship, and that of the ship going forward which sunk the ship at anchor shall render to him his ship and whatever of his was lost.

§ 241. If a man has taken an ox on distraint, he

shall pay one-third of a mina of silver. [Ex $22^{25}$, Dt $24^{6.17}$].

§ 242. If a man has hired a working ox for one year, he shall pay four *GUR* of corn as its hire. [Ex $22^{14}$].

§ 243. If a milch cow, he shall give three *GUR* of corn to its owner. [Gn $31^{39}$, Ex $22^{13}$].

§ 244. If a man has hired an ox or ass, and a lion has killed it in the open field, that loss is for its owner forsooth.

§ 245. If a man has hired an ox and through neglect or by blows has caused it to die, ox for ox to the owner of the ox he shall render. [Ex $22^{10-15}$, Lv $24^{15.21}$].

§ 246. If a man has hired an ox and has crushed its foot or has cut its nape, ox for ox to the owner of the ox he shall render. [Ex $22^{10-15}$].

§ 247. If a man has hired an ox and has caused it to lose its eye, he shall pay half its price to the owner of the ox. [Ex $22^{10-15}$].

§ 248. If a man has hired an ox and has broken its horn, cut off its tail, or pierced its nostrils, he shall pay a quarter of its price. [Ex $22^{10-15}$].

§ 249. If a man has hired an ox and God has struck it and it has died, the man who has hired the ox shall swear before God and shall go free. [Ex $22^{10f.}$].

§ 250. If a savage bull in his charge has gored a man and caused him to die, that case has no remedy. [Ex $21^{28}$].

§ 251. If the ox has pushed a man, by pushing has made known his vice, and he has not blunted his horn, has not shut up his ox, and that ox has gored a man of gentle birth and caused him to die, he shall pay half a mina of silver. [Ex $21^{29}$].

§ 252. If a gentleman's servant, he shall pay one-third of a mina of silver. [Ex $21^{32}$].

§ 253. If a man has hired a man to reside in his field and has furnished him implements, has entrusted him oxen and furnished harness for them for cultivating the field, if that man has stolen the seed or provender and they have been seized in his hands, one shall cut off his hands.

§ 254. If he has taken the implements, starved the oxen, from the seed which he has hoed he shall restore.

§ 255. If he has hired out the man's oxen or has stolen the seed and has not caused it to grow in the field, one shall call that man to account and he shall measure out sixty *GUR* of corn per *GAN* of land.

§ 256. If he is not able to pay his compensation, one shall cause him to be torn in pieces by the oxen on that field.

§ 257. If a man has hired a harvester, he shall give him eight *GUR* of corn per year.

§ 258. If a man has hired an ox-driver, he shall give him six *GUR* of corn per year.

§ 259. If a man has stolen a watering machine from the meadow, he shall give five shekels of silver to the owner of the watering machine.

§ 260. If he has stolen a watering bucket or a harrow, he shall pay three shekels of silver.

§ 261. If a man has hired a herdsman for the cows or a shepherd for the sheep, he shall give him eight *GUR* of corn per year.

§ 262. If a man, ox, or sheep to [this section is defaced]. [Ex $22^{1}$].

§ 263. If he has caused an ox or sheep which was given him to be lost, ox for ox, sheep for sheep, he shall render to their owner. [Lv $24^{18.24}$].

§ 264. If a herdsman who has had cows or sheep given him to shepherd, has received his hire, whatever was agreed, and his heart has been contented, yet has diminished the cows, diminished the sheep, lessened the offspring, he shall give offspring and produce according to the tenour of his bonds.

§ 265. If a shepherd to whom cows and sheep have been given him to breed, has falsified and changed their price, or has sold them, one shall call him to account, and he shall render cows and sheep to their owner tenfold what he has stolen.

§ 266. If in a sheepfold a stroke of God has taken place or a lion has killed, the shepherd shall purge himself before God, and the owner of the fold shall face the accident to the fold. [Ex $22^{10f.}$, Jn $10^{12}$].

§ 267. If a shepherd has been careless and in a sheepfold caused a loss to take place, the shepherd shall make good the fault of the loss which he has caused to be in the fold and shall pay cows or sheep and shall give to their owner.

§ 268. If a man has hired an ox for threshing, twenty *ḲA* of corn is its hire.

§ 269. If he has hired an ass for threshing, ten *ḲA* of corn is its hire.

§ 270. If he has hired a calf (goat?) for threshing, one *ḲA* of corn is its hire.

§ 271. If a man has hired oxen, a waggon, and its driver, he shall give one hundred and eighty *ḲA* of corn per day.

§ 272. If a man has hired a waggon by itself, he shall give forty *ḲA* of corn per day.

§ 273. If a man has hired a labourer, from the beginning of the year till the fifth month, he shall give six *ŠE* of silver per day; from the sixth month to the end of the year he shall give five *ŠE* of silver per day.

§ 274. If a man shall hire an artisan—

| | | |
|---|---|---|
| (*a*) | the hire of a . . . . | five *ŠE* of silver |
| (*b*) | the hire of a brickmaker | five *ŠE* of silver |
| (*c*) | the hire of a tailor . . | five *ŠE* of silver |
| (*d*) | the hire of a stone-cutter . | *ŠE* of silver |
| (*e*) | the hire of a . . . . . | *ŠE* of silver |
| (*f*) | the hire of a . . . . . | *ŠE* of silver |
| (*g*) | the hire of a carpenter . | four *ŠE* of silver |
| (*h*) | the hire of a . . . | four *ŠE* of silver |
| (*i*) | the hire of a . . . . . | *ŠE* of silver |
| (*j*) | the hire of a builder . . | *ŠE* of silver |

per day he shall give.

§ 275. If a man has hired a (boat?) per day, her hire is three *ŠE* of silver.

§ 276. If a man has hired a fast ship, he shall give two and a half *ŠE* of silver per day as her hire.

§ 277. If a man has hired a ship of sixty *GUR*, he shall give one-sixth of a shekel of silver per day as her hire.

§ 278. If a man has bought a manservant or a maidservant, and he has not fulfilled his month and the *bennu* sickness has fallen upon him, he shall return him to the seller, and the buyer shall take the money he paid.

§ 279. If a man has bought a manservant or a maidservant and has a complaint, his seller shall answer the complaint.

§ 280. If a man has bought in a foreign land the manservant or the maidservant of a man, when he has come into the land and the owner of the manservant or the maidservant has recognized his manservant or his maidservant, if the manservant or maidservant are natives, without price he shall grant them their former condition. [Ex $21^{8}$].

§ 281. If they are natives of another land the buyer shall tell out before God the money he paid, and the owner of the manservant or the maidservant shall give to the merchant the money he paid, and shall recover his manservant or his maidservant.

§ 282. If a slave has said to his master, 'Thou art not my master,' as his slave one shall call him to account and his master shall cut off his ear.

The judgments of righteousness which Ḫammurabi the mighty king confirmed and caused the land to take a sure guidance and a gracious rule.

[There are three sections of the Code which have been recovered to us from the fragments of the copies made by Assyrian scribes. They were once to be found in the five columns which are now erased from the stele. They may be given here, for the sake of completeness.—

§ X. If a man has borrowed of a merchant and has assigned him a plantation of dates and said, 'Take the dates that are in my plantation for thy money,' the merchant shall not consent. The owner of the plantation shall take the dates that are in the plantation and he shall answer to the merchant for the loan and its interest according to the tenour of his bond. The dates that are over, which are produced in the plantation, the owner of the plantation shall take for himself.

§ Y. If a house tenant has paid the year's rent for the house in full to the landlord, but the landlord has ordered the tenant to go out before the time is up, the landlord because he has ordered the tenant to leave before his time is up, shall give back . . . of the rent.

§ Z. If a man has to pay, in money or corn, but has not the money or corn to pay with, but has goods, he shall give to the merchant whatever he has, before witnesses. The merchant shall not object, he shall receive it].

### III. Comparison of the Code with Early Hebrew Legislation.

The comparison of such a Code with the Mosaic Laws is not one to be dismissed in a few paragraphs. Its obvious likenesses are not more remarkable than the contrasts which exist. The whole question of common origin may depend on how these are regarded. In some cases a conscious deviation is as strong proof of influence as an agreement.

i. *THE QUESTION STATED, AND THE DATA AVAILABLE FOR ANSWERING IT.*—1. We may begin by stating, as concisely as may be, what we understand by the influence of the Code of Ḫammurabi on Mosaic legislation. There need be no discussion as to whether Moses knew cuneiform. Such a proposition could be maintained only by insisting, firstly, on the literal truth of the statement that Moses was learned in all the wisdom of the Egyptians (Ac $7^{22}$); secondly, that such learning must have included cuneiform. The latter proposition is not very safe. The evidence of the Tel el-Amarna tablets can only establish the existence of some scribes at the courts of Amenophis III. and IV. who could read and write Babylonian. The current opinion of critics does not ascribe much of the Hebrew Law to Moses. So his personality may be set aside.

Nor do we need to discuss exactly how far Babylonian influence had modified the life of the inhabitants of Palestine before the incursion of the Hebrews. Some men doubt whether that incursion did not find a widely spread Hebrew population already in possession. Whoever was in Palestine then, of whatever nationality, there is evidence that the chief rulers of the settled districts wrote in Babylonian to the kings of Egypt, and, presumably, also to the kings of Mitanni, Assyria, and Babylonia. Whether they used any other form of writing besides cuneiform we do not know. They did use words which were not pure Babylonian, but are at least Semitic, if not Hebrew. These words they glossed by a more or less accurate Babylonian. That the whole population of Palestine was Semitic or Hebrew, or read Babylonian literature at that time, are not propositions that we need trouble about. All that we need is that the people who drew up the Hebrew legislation, whenever that was done, should have embodied the laws observed in Palestine at their own date, and that those laws should have there remained unchanged from the time when they were the same as were to be found in Babylonia at the time when Ḫammurabi codified them. Indirect influence is then proved.

2. The laws may have once been common to all the Semitic races, or to the populations they displaced or overran. The greater part of the common ideas of the two legislations may be due to this source. It may not even be Semitic at all, only human, such as man, anywhere and everywhere, under similar conditions would and did agree upon. Such a common stock, including many most striking things, is no proof of Babylonian influence, either upon the Hebrews or upon the inhabitants of Palestine before the Exodus. Thus the principle of retaliation, the making a punishment as far as possible an exact reproduction of the injury, was a primitive view. It might well be Sumerian in Babylonia, and pre-Israelitish in Palestine. It omits the consideration that such a punishment only gratifies revenge, does not benefit either the offender or the injured. It is characteristic of very inadequate justice. Now, in the Code we find that already a system of compensation to the injured was growing up. But the aristocracy, the *amêlû*, would not accept money for their bodily injuries, they insisted upon the primitive 'eye for eye, tooth for tooth, limb for limb' (§§ 196, 200, 197), and so did the Hebrews (Ex $21^{24}$, etc.). If this had been a peculiar or abnormal form of carrying out the principle, we might argue for a racial connexion between the Babylonian aristocrats of Ḫammurabi's time and the Hebrews. This has been done on the ground of linguistic affinities. But there is no reason to doubt that if retaliation, pure and simple, were the rule anywhere, it would be expressed in this way. All we can say is, that, whether from pride, conservatism, or racial peculiarity, the aristocrat of Babylon clung to the primitive method of punishing bodily injuries. The acceptance by the commoner, or *muškênu*, of compensation may well point to a different race and a subject position. It would be interesting if we could show that the conquered races in Palestine used to accept compensation in a similar way.

Whatever view be taken of the similarities between the legislations, the greatest difficulty in asserting Babylonian influence is that the Israelitish law as we know it is a composite affair, of uncertain date, and combining new with old in a most perplexing manner. If we could be satisfied that the Mosaic Laws still existed in their original order, or that any one stratum of them had preserved its original features, we might better institute a comparison.

3. As it is, if any law should turn out to be very like the Babylonian, in wording or idea, it is open to say that it was foisted in after the Captivity, when the Jews had become acquainted with that law in Babylonia itself. On the other hand, it is open to say that Abraham became acquainted with it in Ur of the Chaldees, and its memory never died out. Others may maintain that it only embodies a common Semitic idea, which is thus proved to have the widest extent in place and time. Each of these views will continue to have its advocates, and there is no evidence to decide between them. To speak of Babylonian influence is not so to decide.

4. It may be well to set out first the material which seems to be equally conclusive for all views. (*a*) The following common practices or ideas are pointed out by S. A. Cook. The appeal to the decision of God, the resort to the gate of the city as a place of justice, the declaration on oath before God, the oath for purgation, warnings

against injustice, bribery, false witness, the need of witness for proof, are all common to the judicial systems of Ḫammurabi and Moses. In both, the woman was in the hand of her husband, who was her *bêl* or *ba'al*; marriage was arranged by parents, or relatives, on both sides, the girl's consent not being asked. A purchase price was paid for the wife (*terḫatu*, Heb. *mōhar*), returned in her dowry, and other marriage customs are similar. The customs as to divorce, concubines, and maidservants are in thorough harmony, allowing for the greater explicitness on one side or the other.

(*b*) The punishment for false witness, that the false witness should suffer what he had put the accused in danger of suffering, is the same in both (§§ 3, 4; Dt 19[19]). The punishments of slander (§ 127; Lv 19[16], Dt 22[13-21]), and accusation of infidelity, though unlike in details, both recognize the nature of the offence. Ordeal was the purgation for suspected wives (§ 132; Nu 5[11-31]). The regulations as to the shepherd's responsibility for his flock are similar (§ 266; Ex 22[10f.]). The eating of the fruit of newly planted land is deferred to the fifth year (§ 60; Lv 19[23f.]). Kidnapping was a capital offence in both legislations (§ 14; Ex 21[16]). Both contemplate the extirpation of wizards (§§ 1, 2; Ex 22[18]). Assaults upon a woman, leading to miscarriage and death (§§ 209–214), are similar to Ex 21[22f.], but with characteristic variations.

5. Supposing that there had been a knowledge of the Babylonian law and custom in Palestine, we should not expect that it would be adopted at once into the Code of Israel. The treatment of the slave in Dt 24[7] or Dt 23[16] is certainly a contrast to Ḫammurabi's law forbidding the harbouring of a slave (§ 17), and ordering his restoration to his owner. But we are not without indication that such was the custom, at any rate, among the Amalekites (1 S 30[15]). The older law in Palestine may not have been so considerate. Nor is it all pure humanity, later. Fugitive slaves from other lands may not have been an unwelcome addition to the population. The sentimental reason that Israel had once been a slave was in accordance with current ideas.

6. There is a close parallelism between the laws of deposit in §§ 124–126 and those in Ex 22[6-11] [Heb.]. Further, there is a striking similarity in the treatment of the three parties in Ex 22 and the three in §§ 9–11. We may here note a parallelism of method, which may once have characterized a great deal that did not survive in either code. Both make selections, sometimes fuller, sometimes less full, one than the other. We could suppose that in a common source both the cases of illegal holding or sale of lost property, or of treasure trove, and the fraudulent retention or loss by theft, of deposit, were treated exactly alike, viz. that the fraudulent person should restore twofold. Ḫammurabi leaves the full treatment as a norm in §§ 9–11, and later condenses his source, for deposit, assuming the method. The Exodus legislator gives a full abstract in Ex 22[6-11], and a condensed form in Ex 22[1]. The procedure in the cases differs, but only as a common source so treated might be expected to differ, under different social organizations.

7. Of considerable importance is it to notice that these ancient codes do not lay down general principles, but select cases which exemplify them. Thus, while Ḫammurabi (§§ 57, 58) takes only the cases where a shepherd feeds his flock off a field of corn, and Ex 22[5] deals with a field or vineyard, we may be sure that Ḫammurabi's Code would have been interpreted by the judges as applying to vineyards as well, if they came in question.*

* The vine was rare, if not quite unknown, in Babylonia.



8. In Exodus the transition to damage by fire is natural. In Babylonia, damage by careless management of water was more characteristic. It might have come next, only the order of ideas led to its being put first, as § 56. Here the differences of legislation are quite such as any legislator might introduce if he were using a foreign code as a source. The votary was forbidden to open a wine-shop (§ 110). At first sight there is nothing at all like this in the Hebrew legislation. But Lv 21[9] forbids the daughter of a priest to commit folly in Israel, on pain of being burnt. Josephus understands that to mean 'open a wine-shop.' The penalty is the same in both codes. It may well have been that one law was adapted from the other. So while a hostage for debt was freed after six years' service in Israel, but after only three in Babylonia, it has to be excused on the ground that such had already served a *double* term (Dt 15[18]). The custom was clearly to release at the end of three years—a custom which seemed hard to the recently settled Israelite; and so concession was made to his prejudices, fixing it at six years instead. Thus we may account for the absence of other humane laws in Hebrew codes. They were too advanced to adopt, unmodified. The fact, then, that more of the Babylonian Code does not find parallels in the Hebrew, even when its regulations would be quite acceptable, may be due to the fact that custom had already adopted them. Law is needed, not to enact custom, but to modify it. It may legalize it, but usually seeks either to unify varieties or to sanction growing changes, and so to decide between competing views of right. Ḫammurabi saw no cause to promulgate any law about murder; the Hebrew codes leave some other things unsettled. Some of these may have been settled by Ḫammurabi or his fore runners, and already been in force in Canaan. In many other cases we may plausibly argue that the legislations show a common source, treated differently in adoption.

9. The absence of law courts, the persistent blood-revenge, — though subjected to a series of regulations, — the severer treatment of some offences, the milder treatment of others, are held to be strong proofs of a more primitive state of civilization in Israel. The differences from the Code of Ḫammurabi are therefore important to notice. The treatment of theft is less severe in Hebrew than in Babylonian law, except perhaps in the case of the nocturnal burglar (§ 21; Ex 22[2]). The severer penalty against a son who struck his father (§ 195; Ex 21[15]), which Hebrew law also enacted for cursing parents (Ex 21[17] etc.), the treatment of the rebellious son (Dt 21[18-21]), are traces of a more primitive state. The rights of the firstborn, so marked in Hebrew, show no trace in the Code. They were earlier in Babylonia. The Code was much more favourable to widows than early Israelite custom; but the later law (in Israel) is more considerate. In Babylonia daughters had rights of inheritance, which appear only late in Israel. The position of the slave is quite distinct. The laws as to hired animals show no resemblance. The penalty for allowing a vicious ox to gore a man was death in the Hebrew Code, but a fine in Babylonia (§§ 251, 252; Ex 21[28f.]).

10. Of course, whole groups of laws in the Code concern matters which were purely Babylonian. The position of the feudal tenants, levy-masters, etc., and the regulations relating to shipping, caravans, the laws for the builders, doctors, surgeons, branders, artisans, etc., cannot be expected to reappear even in a copied legislation.

The names of the articles in use are often alike in Hebrew and Babylonian, but the technical terms differ. This would be very important, as showing an independent growth of similar institutions, but for one consideration. There is no ground to suppose that on either side the terms compared were the only terms in use. Thus, while the Babylonian verb 'to marry' is *aḫâzu*, and the Hebrew *lākah*, the Assyrian is *likû*. The Hebrew *'ēraś*, 'to betroth,' has a parallel in Babylonian *ērišu*, 'bridegroom.' The itinerant trader, *šamallū*, was explained by *ša nâš mašak ša abni*, 'he who carries the bag (*kîsu*) of weights'; compare the Hebrew *kîṣ* and *'ăbānîm*. In the directions as to the inquiry into the conduct of the alleged idolaters (Dt 13[14] and 17[4]) the same verb is used, *kûn*, as in the Code, for establishing an accusation, *uktin*; the *kussû daianuti* of § 5 is the *kiṣṣê dîn* of Pr 20[8]; the phrase 'to cause the finger to be pointed at' as a technical term for 'slander' is paralleled by Is 58[9] 'the putting forth of the finger.' The list of linguistic parallels could, doubtless, be much extended. There was, however, no reason why a Hebrew legislator, even if a copy of the Code lay before him in cuneiform, should transliterate its words. He might equally well translate them into his own language.

11. Of much more importance, as a proof of dependence, would be the preservation of the order of ideas, especially where this is not due merely to their logical sequence. Of such a transfer of arrangement we can hardly expect to find much trace. Whatever trace can be found is therefore all the more significant. A comparison of the order of the Book of the Covenant (vol. iii. p. 67) shows as much difference as likeness in the order. Yet who can say that the present order does not exhibit rearrangement and interpolation? For example, in ii. (*l.c.* p. 67[b]), why are § 7 and § 9 separated by § 8?

12. Some things are very suggestive of a deliberate change. The Code has a slanderer thrown down before the judge and branded. In Dt 25[2] we get directions for scourging. The judge shall cause him to lie down and be beaten before his face. The 'certain number' of stripes in Israel was not to exceed forty; Ḫammurabi ordered sixty for some cases. We are told that scourging was a late introduction into Israel. This may be true of the bastinado, but there seems no reason to regard scourging as a late form of punishment. It is curious that Dt 25[11], which may be a parallel to §§ 202–205, should come so close to the mention of scourging in Dt 25[2. 3], separated from it by clauses which seem to have no possible connexion with either. If v.[11] followed v.[3] in the source, that would seem to have been a distinct reminiscence of §§ 202-205. Authorities differ as to the sense of *lêtu*, usually 'strength'; some take it to mean 'head,' but the *genitalia* may be meant: compare *littûtu*, 'progeny.'

(*a*) A case that must have occurred to the mind of both lawgivers, though not perhaps very practical, was what should be done if a man had intercourse with mother and daughter, or a woman with father and son. The case where the daughter was his own child, or the son her own son, was especially bad. Now Ḫammurabi takes one case in § 157, and enacts that, if a man has intercourse with his own mother, both shall be burned. He does not touch the case of a woman and her mother with the same man. In Lv 20[14] that is taken as the test case, and both are to be burned. The Mosaic Law does not touch Ḫammurabi's case. It may well be that the actual text of the Code was known to the later legislator; and either to show the further application of the same principle, or because the former case was now so well known as to need no further legislation, he takes the new example. One can hardly suppose that in one society the one crime was known and the other unknown, while the reverse held in the other society. In both Codes the penalty for this sort of thing was burning. That is awarded only once again in either Code, and there also for what may well be the same crime in both, described in different terms. Of course we may refer both back to a common Semitic primitive law; but a younger lawgiver would naturally prefer to select a different example if he could. Taken in this way, we can arrange a very remarkable parallel, due to Müller—

| Ḫammurabi. | Leviticus 20. |
|---|---|
| Man with daughter-in-law (§ 155). | Man with daughter-in-law (v.[12]). |
| Man with father's wife (§ 158). | Man with father's wife (v.[11]). |
| Man and son with one woman (§ 157). | Mother and daughter with one man (v.[14]). |

(*b*) Again, we may note that Ḫammurabi (§ 210) ordains that if a man caused the death of a pregnant woman by his blows, then not he, but his daughter, should be put to death. Now this is retaliation pure and simple, and can only be meant as a limit to which the compensation might be pushed by a revengeful father. The accused might have no daughter at all; he might have several. The old discussions as to the relative value to the accused and accuser of the damage inflicted by exact retaliation must come up. Now Ex 21[23] solves this question by the phrase 'soul for soul.' That may be the result of reflexion on this very crude law. It is a convenient phrase for laying down, that as a woman's life was worth less than that of a man, the compensation exacted must not exceed the damage done.

(*c*) Further, when we read in Lv 24[22] that there shall be one law for 'foreigner and native' set at the end of a passage which otherwise literally repeats §§ 196–201, where careful distinction of rank is made in awarding penalties, one may well be tempted to suspect a reminiscence. That differences of treatment should be expressly excluded, surely points to knowledge that they existed somewhere. Where else was this than in the Code? The common Semitic source hardly had these gradations. That cattle are included in Lv 24[18. 21] may be due to a desire to get together all that fell under the same rule.

13. It is not a little instructive to notice that the Code of Ḫammurabi shows marked similarities to other ancient codes. Professor Müller has worked out a number of striking parallels with the Roman XII Tables. Professor Cohn compared the Laws of the West Goths. Incidental comparisons with the Laws of Manu are noted by Mr. Cook. The Code receives illustration from a variety of other sources in the books named above for the bibliography. Whether a knowledge of this Code can really have spread to Rome and India, depends upon the results of much further research than has yet been made.

ii. *VIEWS AS TO THE CHARACTER OF THE CONNEXION.*—Opinions are divided as to the reality of the connexion between the Code of Ḫammurabi and Mosaic legislation. The positive view has been well stated thus: 'The Babylonian and Mosaic Codes are conceived in the same literary form; they contain a considerable number of practically identical laws; they present not a few cases of actual verbal agreement, and both are designed for the regulation of a civilized community. The parallels are too close to be explained upon a somewhat vague theory of common tradition. . . . It has been shown that, in Palestine, Israel learned and appropriated the ancient Babylonian myths. Why should they not learn Babylonian law as well? . . . The foundation of the Babylonian law was the Code of Ḥammurabi, and thus the enactments of the old Babylonian king, formulated about B.C. 2250, passed more than a thousand years later into the Book of the Covenant, and so became the heritage of Israel and the world' (Professor C. Johnston, *Johns Hopkins University Circular*, June 1903).

Mr. Cook minimizes the extent to which Palestine was permeated by the other elements of Babylonian culture. The discovery of cuneiform tablets at Taanach by Professor Sellin may now be added to the evidence of the Tel el-Amarna letters. Documentary evidence may any day be found of the existence in Palestine of all sorts of Babylonian literature. That will not of itself prove that the Hebrew legislators read the Code in cuneiform. What is needed is proof from the Hebrew monuments of such similarities as can be explained only by a knowledge of the Code as we now know it. There is small likelihood of such a proof being found. For no one can suppose that any one of the documents into which the Hebrew law is resolved on critical grounds was put forward at any period as a complete code. We have fragments of several codes at different dates, but not one that can really be trusted for a comparison. Such fragments as are left are very valuable as showing what was at one time considered to be law in Israel, but after the composition they have undergone it is impossible to say whether they really are ancient or not. The words 'primitive' and 'ancient' are not synonymous in the history of law. Nor is it quite clear that 'savage' penalties are always more primitive. The Hebrew law treats unfilial conduct more severely than Ḥammurabi does. This is not a proof of age, nor of primitive ideas, for the normal Arabs show little trace of parental authority. The intrusion of priestly power into the law courts, while definitely dated as late, is a recrudescence under changed conditions of a state of things from which Hammurabi shows an emancipation nearly complete. If any signs of a Babylonian influence can be made out anywhere now, the presumption is that it was once enormously powerful. For the whole history of Israel appears to consist in reformation, a readjusting of old material in faith and practice to new conditions. The old Babylonian stuff must have taken a most powerful root to survive at all. Professor D. H. Müller has done great service in pointing out the significance of any traces of similarity of order which can be found. Professor Kohler insists on the presence or absence of the theocratic idea as a test of primitive stages. The Indian law is purely theocratic, making no distinction between right and morality. The Israelite laws vary; some are theocratic, and the prohibitive commands ancient in type. Ḥammurabi's Code is very modern, almost purely legal. This puts it on a level with the Gortyn Laws and the XII Tables, while it is even more advanced than they are. In Israel the religious idea received its highest development in pre-Christian times, and that dominated law, morals, and history alike. In Babylonia law reached its highest development, and largely in independence of religion. The common life was Semitic, the likenesses are due to racial affinity. The social order was widely different. There can be no question of actual borrowing, at any rate until post-exilic times.

This view leaves out of consideration the evident fact that the Code of Ḥammurabi does not reflect the result of any continuous evolution of law in a homogeneous and progressive people, but an adaptation of widely distinct systems. An aristocracy which clung to primitive ideas, presumably a recent infusion of a wilder Semitic race, amalgamated with a long settled, even if mixed and already partly Semitic, people. Some of its laws may be a recrudescence of primitive views already long modified among the Babylonians. The advent of the First Dynasty of Babylon had a close parallel in the settlement of Israel in Palestine. May not the settled population there have been in much the same stage of civilization as the native Babylonians, with local variations? May not the more primitive stamp of the Israelite laws as we have them be due to the greater predominance of the newcomers? Then the common features would be of two separate origins: one, the civilization that had once been common to Babylonia and Palestine, juristically the more advanced; the other, a system common to the two Semitic peoples, who in Babylonia conquered the land, founded the First Dynasty, formed the new aristocracy, or in Palestine conquered the land and are known to us as Israel. This would furnish the politically dominant, characteristically Semitic, primitive features. Which of the two systems should impose itself on the other, depended in either land on the relative power of the invaders and the invaded. This would be largely conditioned by the suitability of the competing races to the conditions of the country. In Babylonia the larger settled population, the necessary conditions of life, made the invaders rather become absorbed in the people they politically ruled. In Palestine the conditions worked in the opposite direction. Whether by greater preponderance of numbers, or less modifying power in their new environment, the invaders to a greater extent imposed themselves on the previous inhabitants. We need not speak of borrowing as an act on the part of the Israelite legislators. What they preserved of existing law was already centuries before influenced by Babylonia. What they imposed as their national contribution was common property with the legislators who imposed part of it on Babylonian law. That these did not make Babylonian law as primitive as the Book of the Covenant, was due to their more complete absorption by the settled civilization. Hammurabi's Code crystallized the law at a later stage of the process than did the Book of the Covenant. The process was more rapid there. Hence also the greater stability of his work. It lasted practically unchanged some fifteen hundred years. The subsequent developments in Israel show perpetual progress. The progress was on totally different lines, till Israel came once more in contact with Babylonian culture. Then it had made contributions of its own, some of which it modified, some it emphasized as a result of the contrast.

We may say that the Israelite legislation shows strong traces of Babylonian influence, and yet not destroy the independence of its origin. We cannot suppose that the author of any code set to work to draw up a comprehensive scheme of law. Each built upon the already prevailing custom. His attention would be directed chiefly to what was not matter of uniform treatment. The most characteristically Babylonian things in the current custom of the day in Israel may be just those which are not legislated for. The new legislation did not require to touch what was so firmly established. Other things of Babylonian origin may have been abrogated by the new laws—it would not be necessary to say what they had been, but merely by stating the new law to say they should be no longer. That any Israelite code shows marked differences from the Code of Ḥammurabi is enough to show an independent origin. The absence of any difference would show complete dependence. The coexisting likenesses and differences argue for an independent recension of ancient custom deeply influenced by Babylonian law. The actual Code of Ḥammurabi is a witness to what that influence might accomplish. It cannot be held to be a creative source. The Code may only be itself a proof of the same influences. These may be called Semitic in preference to Babylonian. But that view calls for overwhelming proof that there was any source of civilization powerful enough to have this influence on both Israel and Babylonia. The presumption that Babylonia had a prominent influence on Palestine long before Israelite codes were drawn up, is one that grows stronger as time goes on.

C. H. W. JOHNS.

**RELIGION OF ISRAEL.***—*Introduction.*—The origin of the religion of Israel is treated in greater or less detail by all the four sources—or, more correctly, strata of sources—of which the present Pentateuch is made up: the Jahwistic stratum (which originated between 900 and 700 B.C.), the Elohistic (between 750 and 650), the Deuteronomistic (650–550), and the Priestly (550–400). Their respective statements exhibit numerous differences, and even discrepancies. But on *one* point they are in absolute agreement: namely, that the founding of the religion of Israel was the work of Moses, of the tribe of Levi; that it took place in connexion with the leading of the people out of Egypt; and that it consisted pre-eminently in the proclamation of Jahweh as the national God of Israel. The strength and the uniformity of this tradition leave no doubt of its correctness, however much the details of the process may be the proper subject of criticism.

We are thus entitled to commence the history of the religion of Israel with Moses. It is another question whether we can also attain to any certainty regarding the religion of Israel, or, perhaps more correctly, of the Israelitish tribes in pre-Mosaic times. This question could at once be answered in the affirmative, if it were possible to regard the whole contents of the Book of Genesis as history in the strict sense of the term. According to this account, the self-revelation of the one true God began at the very outset, *i.e.* with the first human being created, and was then reproduced from generation to generation — always, indeed, only through the instrumentality of the firstborn of each family — until, finally, in the families of the three patriarchs proper, Abraham, Isaac, and Jacob, it developed into a religion which is hardly distinguished in any way from the future religion of the nation of Israel as this is presented to us in the earlier traditions. Abel and Cain already bring offerings to Jahweh—the one, of the firstlings of the flock and of their fat; the other, of the fruits of the field (Gn $4^{3ff.}$). Noah sacrifices to Jahweh upon an altar burnt-offerings of all clean beasts and all clean birds ($8^{20}$). In like manner we hear not infrequently of the patriarchs building altars and offering sacrifices, as well as of their calling upon Jahweh, especially at those spots where He had appeared to them, or which were hallowed by previous appearances of God ($12^{7}$ $13^{18}$ $22^{9}$ $26^{25}$ $35^{7}$). Further, the erection of monumental stones or pillars (*maẓẓēbôth*, $28^{18ff.}$ $33^{20}$ [where for *mizbēaḥ* 'altar' we should certainly read *maẓẓēbāh* 'pillar'] $35^{14.\,20}$) corresponds to a custom which was practised even by Moses (Ex $24^{4}$), and came only at the end of the pre-exilic period to be prohibited as heathenish. When, again, Rebeḳah goes to consult Jahweh, and actually obtains an oracle from Him (Gn $25^{22f.}$), this manifestly implies not only the existence of a sanctuary of Jahweh, but also the presence of priests or other mediums of the oracle. In short, the cult of Jahweh as practised by the people of Israel after their conquest of Canaan is presented to us as simply the continuation of the worship already rendered by the patriarchs to the same God, and, indeed, almost in every instance at the same sanctuaries. Israel, in other words, simply entered by the conquest of the land into the heritage of which they had been assured long ago by the promises of Jahweh to the patriarchs, and, above all, by the solemnly ratified 'covenant' of God with Abraham (Gn 15).

It must be confessed, however, that a proper critical examination of the religious history of Israel has shown incontrovertibly that the above view of the primeval and the patriarchal religion became possible only by carrying back unreservedly to the centuries prior to Moses, up to the very commencement of all, the conceptions and the conditions of the Jahweh religion as these present themselves somewhere about the 9th cent. B.C. The picture thus drawn of the early history is therefore an extremely valuable authority *for the period from which it emanates*; but for the pre-Mosaic period we can make use of it only with the utmost caution and with strict observance of complicated critical principles. We then discover that in various traditions found in Genesis as well as in those of many other books of the Bible a recollection has been preserved of the pre-Mosaic religious stage of Israel. It is true that this recollection is not infrequently so faint and so unintelligible to the narrators themselves that they take no offence at it, nay, believe it to be in perfect accord with the religion of Jahweh. In such instances the correct interpretation of the tradition may be confirmed or even discovered in two ways: (1) from other traces of the same tradition in the OT, even outside Genesis; (2) from the analogies found in other, especially Semitic, religions,* which will be found not infrequently to supply a surprising amount of information about ritual customs which are strange, and which were no longer understood by Israel itself. There is a repetition here of a phenomenon whose occurrence may be noted almost all over the world: namely, the tendency of religious usages to maintain themselves with the greatest tenacity even after they have come, in consequence of altered religious conceptions, to lose all real meaning. Their retention is generally justified by giving them some new interpretation which renders them tolerable to the new religion (so, for instance, with circumcision in Israel), or they may continue to be practised simply through force of habit, without any attempt at explanation at all. The latter principle may be found to hold good, for instance, of all or at least the majority of mourning usages. In all probability, the whole of these had their root in religious motives; but that this was understood we cannot assume except in those instances in which they were expressly prohibited by the Jahweh religion. For the most part they represent simply petrified custom, whose original meaning it is often very difficult to determine. At all events, the *symbolical* interpretations (for instance, that of the rending of the garments as an expression of utter indifference to one's outward appearance, or even as a symbol of the rending of the heart with grief), which we meet with fre-

* See 'Table of Contents' at end of article, p. 732 ff.

* On the subject of Semitic religion we possess such extremely valuable contributions as J. Wellhausen's *Reste arabischen Heidentums* (Berlin, 1887; 2nd ed. 1897), and W. Robertson Smith's *Lectures on the Religion of the Semites* (London, 1889; 2nd ed. 1894; Germ. tr. by R. Stübe, Freiburg i. B. 1899). Much valuable material is contained also in B. Stade's *Gesch. des Volkes Israel*, Berlin, 1887 (Buch 7: 'Israels Glaube und Sitte in vorprophetischer Zeit'), Bd. i. p. 358 ff. Cf. also Ch. Piepenbring, 'La religion primitive des Hébreux' (*Rev. de l'Hist. des Religions*, 1889, pp. 171–202); and C. G. Montefiore, *Lectures on the Origin and Growth of Religion as illustrated by the Religion of the ancient Hebrews*, London, 1892.

quently even in Christian exegesis and theology, are foredoomed to rejection.

### I. Traces of a pre-Mosaic Religion of Israel.

Before we attempt now to collect the possible traces of a pre-Mosaic religion of Israel, there are two points that we must emphasize very strongly: (1) that in almost every instance we have here to deal with hypotheses and not with facts, so that our task will be in reality to determine the greater or smaller degree of probability attaching to any hypothesis; (2) that everything which survived in Israel merely as a custom that was *not understood*, may claim an interest from the point of view of Archæology and the History of Religion in general, but has, strictly speaking, none so far as the Religion and Theology of the Bible are concerned. It appears to us that the effect is simply to lead one astray as to the correct understanding of the religion of Israel, when certain recent descriptions leave the reader in doubt whether all kinds of primeval customs were not practised in Israel with full consciousness of their original signification, and, when introduced into the framework of the Jahweh religion, so continued down to the latest times. The truth is that anything which was recognized by the Jahweh religion as of heathen origin, and whose meaning was understood by it, was declared unclean and accordingly prohibited absolutely, as, for instance, necromancy. Any one who notwithstanding addicted himself to such practices, set himself deliberately in opposition to the requirements of his religion. The fact that this happened again and again gives us no more right to saddle the religion of Israel with these derelictions than we have to hold Christianity responsible for all the heathen superstition which still continues to prevail even in Christian nations.

i. *CONCEPTION OF THE DEITY, ETC.*—The most important question which has to be dealt with by any one who undertakes to give an account of a particular stage of religion is that relating to *the nature of the god or gods recognized.*

1. Amongst the lowest forms of religious veneration, the more recent authorities on Comparative Religion reckon not only the common Fetishism (which elevates an arbitrarily chosen object to the rank of its gods, and again, it may be, deposes it), but also the so-called **Totemism.*** The following may suffice by way of definition of this widely diffused phenomenon. In the vocabulary of modern Comparative Religion the term *totem* † stands for some natural object—generally an animal—with which a tribe considers itself to have blood relationship, and which accordingly in the person of all its representatives is treated by the tribe with the utmost consideration and indulgence, or may actually receive Divine worship. Such Totemism may be recognized most frequently in the name by which the particular tribe is designated, although it may happen, indeed, that names long in existence come only subsequently to have a totemistic sense attached to them.

In searching for indications that Totemism once prevailed in Israel, we must leave out of consideration *one* practice, namely the worship of Jahweh in the form of a molten bull, as practised in the Northern kingdom from the time of Jeroboam I. onwards (1 K 12[28]). It is probable that, in this, Jeroboam simply revived a form of the Jahweh cult that had been long familiar; but it was beyond doubt of Canaanite origin, and had nothing to do with Totemism. The molten bull is nothing but a symbol of the strength and creative power of Jahweh, who in the earliest times—as far back as we can trace the matter—was never thought of as appearing on earth except in human form.

On the other hand, among the names of Israelitish tribes there are a few which, upon certain conditions, might testify that Totemism once prevailed: for instance SIMEON (שִׁמְעוֹן *Shim'ôn*), *if* this name, like the Arabic *sim'u*, stands for a hybrid of wolf and hyæna; LEAH, *if* this = 'wild cow'; and LEVI, *if* this is really a gentilic name from *Leah*; and, finally, RACHEL (= *rāḥēl*, 'ewe'). With reference to the two female names in this list, it is true also that it must first be proved that wives in the patriarchal narratives always stand for certain weaker tribes which became amalgamated with other stronger ones into a single whole. It is clear that here we have many difficulties in the way, and at most we can speak only of the possibility that Totemism once prevailed in particular tribes. Nor are we carried much further by another argument, to which it has been sought to attach the strongest evidential value. We refer to the so-called 'food taboos,' by which the flesh of certain animals is to be scrupulously avoided as unclean. It sounds very plausible, no doubt, to interpret this as meaning that each tribe regarded it as strictly forbidden to kill and eat the totem animal with which it believed itself to have blood affinity. When smaller tribes became amalgamated with larger, and when these finally combined to form one nation, the totems of all the different clans would be recognized by the whole body, and the eating of them avoided, and the Jahweh religion would sanction and retain this practice, only altering the motive for it. At the totemistic stage these animals were forbidden because they were *holy*; the Jahweh religion, on the other hand, declared them, as relics of a foreign cultus, *unclean*. Now, in reply to this it may be remarked that certainly the long list of unclean animals enumerated in Lv 11[4ff.] and Dt 14[3ff.] cannot possibly be all explained on the ground of a previous Totemism. On the contrary, it is quite clear in these passages that the prohibition of certain animals which were expressly regarded as unclean was afterwards extended to the whole class which exhibited the same characteristics. Thus originated that *system* of food taboos in virtue of which uncleanness attached to all four-footed animals which do not chew the cud and have not completely divided hoofs, and to all water-animals which have not fins and scales, as well as to all four-legged winged creatures. It is vain to seek to explain this supplementary schematizing by religious motives, as if, for instance, all creatures to which any imperfection attaches had been forbidden as food. All that it is correct to hold is that in very ancient times the eating of *particular* animals was disallowed on religious grounds. But it is quite another question whether these grounds were connected with Totemism. It is quite possible that when such customs arose the determining factors were wholly different forms of superstition, such in particular as some form of belief in demons (see below). In this way the impulse would be given less by religious veneration than by simple fear. Upon the whole we must conclude once more that,

* Out of the copious literature on this question the following may be noted as of importance for our present purpose: W. Robertson Smith, 'Animal Worship and Animal Tribes among the Arabs and in the Old Testament' in *Journal of Philology*, ix. (1880), cf. the same writer's *Kinship and Marriage in Early Arabia* [2] (1903), p. 217 ff.); J. G. Frazer, *Totemism*, Edinburgh, 1887; Jos. Jacobs, 'Are there Totem-clans in the Old Testament?' in *Archæol. Review*, iii. (1889) 3, p. 145 ff.; F. V. Zapletal, *Der Totemismus und die Religion Israels*, Freiburg i. B. 1901 [denies any existence of Totemism in Israel]; S. A. Cook, 'Israel and Totemism' in *JQR*. xiv. No. 55; L. Germain Lévy, 'Du totémisme chez les Hébreux' in *REJ* xliv. (1902), No. 89, p. 13 ff. [likewise with wholly negative results].

† This term, borrowed from the Ojibway Indians of N. America and brought into vogue especially by Lubbock, denotes originally the family or tribe itself.

while it is certainly possible that Totemism once prevailed in Israel, its prevalence cannot be proved; and, above all, we must hold that the religion of Israel as it presents itself in the OT has not retained the very slightest recollection of such a state of things.

2. It is different with another of the preliminary steps towards real religion which is still more widely illustrated amongst primitive peoples, namely **Animism.** In its pure form this is the belief in the activity of the spirits of recently deceased relatives. From the nature of the case, however, it is not always possible here to draw the lines sharply. Even those who have been long dead may appear to their surviving relatives in bodily form in dreams. Hence the animistic belief produces the conviction that the spirit of the dead man either still lingers in the neighbourhood, or may temporarily leave the place of sojourn of the dead (called by the Hebrews probably even in pre-Mosaic times *Shĕ'ōl*; see below). On the other hand, the appearances that present themselves in dreams are not confined to actual relatives; hence Animism readily includes all the members of the tribe, or creates a still wider realm. But it is always of the essence of original Animism that the activity of the spirits of the dead is thought of as ill-disposed, and even harmful, so that the survivors' interest is to keep them at as far a distance as possible, and to omit nothing that will conduce to the satisfying of their legitimate wishes, which have respect, above all, to the proper treatment and burial of the corpse.

It is evident that Animism of this kind cannot, strictly speaking, yet be called religion, but is at most only a preliminary step towards it. For it wants the element of *veneration* of powers regarded as superhuman. This comes to associate itself with Animism only when the latter concentrates its interest especially upon the spirits of ancestors, and passes into a formal veneration for them, when, in short, it becomes **Ancestor Worship.***

With reference to the pre-Mosaic religion of Israel, the question is generally raised in the form whether in the later religion traces are demonstrable of a former Animism *and* Ancestor Worship. At present it is the fashion to pronounce unhesitatingly in favour of the presence of both these elements. But in the opinion of the present writer, while there are undoubted traces that Animism once prevailed, the alleged indications of Ancestor Worship are all exposed to more or less serious objections.

As might have been expected, the traces of Animism are most marked in connexion with certain *mourning customs*. Not that *all* mourning customs can be explained, as has been attempted, from one and the same point of view; on the contrary, they clearly belong to different grades of religious thought, and some of them have hitherto defied all efforts at interpretation. Most of them, however, may be most simply explained as due to the naïve attempt, by means of a variety of bodily alterations (*e.g.* the cropping or shaving of the head and beard, the wounding of the body by bloody incisions, etc., the covering of the face, or at least of the hair on the upper lip), to render oneself *unrecognizable* by the spirit of the dead, and thus to escape its malign influence. Also the rending of the garments, like the going barefoot and other partial uncoverings of the person, is in all probability simply a relic of an entire laying aside of one's clothes; only that absolute nakedness already in very early times assumed the mitigated form of putting on sackcloth, which was originally a coarse cloth thrown around the loins. Such a complete alteration of the outward appearance seemed best fitted to deceive the spirit of the dead, and to divert its attention from the survivors. But the same purpose was already served by going about in a filthy condition, by neglecting all attention to the hair, and by sprinkling oneself with ashes; or, on the other hand, by sitting on the ground, in dust and ashes if possible—in the place, in short, where one does not usually sit, and hence is not likely to be looked for.

Part of these mourning practices were retained without scruple even within the pale of the Jahweh religion—a proof that their original intention was no longer understood. Others, like the cutting of a bald spot on the head, the disfiguring of the beard, and the wounding of the person, were strictly forbidden by the later legislation (Lv $19^{28}$ $21^{5}$). The circumstance that the Jahweh religion regarded all contact with a dead body, nay, even the proximity of one (Nu $19^{14}$), as defiling, is sufficiently explained by the consciousness that at least part of the mourning and burial customs had their root in another religion. At the same time, however, it is noteworthy that the Law itself still retains a manifest trace of animistic beliefs when it enacts (Nu $19^{15}$) that any open vessel without a cover fastened with a string is defiled by the proximity of a dead body. Here we have evidently the reminiscence of a very ancient practice whereby it was sought to prevent the spirit of the dead from taking up its quarters in the house—the practice, namely, before or at the moment of a death, of carefully closing all open vessels that happened to be in the neighbourhood.

The question whether Animism underwent in pre-Mosaic Israel, as in some other instances, the further development into Ancestor Worship, cannot be decided by such peremptory declarations as that Animism, in virtue of an inward necessity and hence *always*, is coupled with Ancestor Worship. Not theories but only facts must decide here; and it is simply not true that, thanks to invariable laws of evolution, the process of development has always, and in the case of all peoples, been from Animism to Ancestor Worship, and from the latter to Polytheism, and finally to Monotheism. Let us proceed now to examine the facts which have been held to prove that Ancestor Worship once prevailed among the Israelites.

Here, again, the principal rôle is played by *mourning customs*. Almost everything in this department is held to have the intention of declaring the mourner to be the slave of the deified ancestor. So, for instance, with the uncovering of the person,* the putting on of sackcloth as what was once the servile garb, and every other act by which expression is given to a humiliation of the person; and, finally, even the wounding of oneself by bodily incisions as a rite of dedication to the spirit of the dead. But these explanations

* Of the very extensive literature on Animism and Ancestor Worship (in addition to the works of Stade and W. R. Smith cited in note on p. 612[b]), the following may be noted: F. Schwally, *Das Leben nach dem Tode nach den Vorstellungen des alten Israel u. des Judenthums*, Giessen, 1892; J. Frey, *Tod, Seelenglaube und Seelenkult im alten Israel*, Leipzig, 1898 [denies spirit-worship, and explains mourning customs as due to fear of death or of its author]; K. Grüneisen, *Der Ahnenkultus und die Urreligion Israels*, Halle, 1899 [finds indubitable traces of Animism in the OT, but none that are positively convincing of Ancestor Worship; explains (with Frazer) mourning customs in great measure as *averruncatio*; cf. also the instructive review of Grüneisen's book by Wellhausen in the *Deutsche Literaturzeitung*, 1900, No. 20]; J. C. Matthes, 'Rouw en doodenvereering in Israël' in *Theol. Tijdschr.* 1900, pp. 97 ff., 193 ff. [especially directed against Frey's (see above) rejection of Ancestor Worship], also 'De doodenvereering bij Israël,' *ib.* 1901, p. 320 ff. [against Grüneisen].

* According to Büchler (art. 'Das Entblössen der Schulter und des Armes als Zeichen der Trauer' in *ZATW*, 1901, p. 81 ff.), by the practice in question the mourner submits himself to the dead, and declares himself his subject, by showing himself prepared to perform the hardest tasks on his behalf. The forced character of this explanation strikes one at once.

of the mourning customs appear to us far less natural than the above proposal to trace them back to an effort to render oneself unrecognizable by the spirit.

A stronger argument would be found in the custom of *funeral repasts*, if it were really beyond doubt that we have to do here with a sacrificial meal in honour of the dead. But the few passages to which appeal is made in this connexion prove no such thing. That 'mourning bread' (Hos 9[4]) is unclean is sufficiently explained by the circumstance that it is eaten by one who is defiled by a dead body. This is all that appears to be spoken of in Dt 26[14], and not the use of bread for a sacrificial offering to the dead. The latter might, indeed, seem to be alluded to in the addition 'nor have I given thereof for the dead.' But a funeral repast may very readily bear a different sense from one in honour of a now deified ancestor. It may be an expression of a determination to maintain with the deceased the same fellowship in worship that subsisted when he was alive, this purpose being indicated by holding a repast once more in presence of the corpse. Still more probable appears to us to be the other explanation, according to which the special object is to provide the spirit of the dead with what it requires during its journey to the realm of death. The same purpose (and not that of a sacrificial gift proper) might be served also by the placing of food on or in the grave, if it is this and not the use of bread at the funeral repast that is alluded to in Dt 26[14]. In the case of Jer 16[7], again, it is only by perfectly arbitrary alteration of the text that the passage can be converted into a testimony to sacrificial meals in honour of the dead. All that the prophet really says is that, after the coming of the Divine judgment, no one will seek to force men to take food to strengthen themselves, or to drink of the 'cup of consolation,' and thus bring the mourning fast to an end. As we see from 2 S 3[35] 12[17], it was the custom to employ pressure of this kind; but in this whole matter we have nothing to do with Ancestor Worship, especially as there is no question of ancestors in connexion with the mourning fasts in either of these two passages any more than in 1 S 31[13] or 2 S 1[12].

A further evidence that Ancestor Worship once prevailed in Israel has been discovered in the great importance attached to the mention of *tombs*. This, we are told, is explicable only on the ground that these graves were places of worship. Now it is a fact that the patriarchs' place of burial in a cave at Ḥebron is repeatedly mentioned. Abraham purchased it as a hereditary tomb from the Ḥittites (Gn 23[3ff.]); and he himself (25[9]) as well as Isaac (35[29]) and Jacob (cf. 49[29ff.], according to which it was the resting-place also of Rebeḳah and Leah, and 50[12f.]) were buried there. But all these passages (as well as in all probability the mention of the burial-place of Aaron in Dt 10[6]) belong to the so-called Priests' Code, which cannot surely be supposed in mentioning them to have had any thought of Ancestor Worship, but only to have intended to establish the title of the Israelites, when they returned from Egypt, to a portion of the soil of Canaan. According to the Jahwistic narrative, also, Jacob desires to be buried with his fathers (47[29f.]); but here it is not Ḥebron but Gōren-hā'āṭād, on the east side of Jordan (50[10ff.]), that is the burial-place. Besides, among the earlier sources E mentions the tomb of Deborah, Rebekah's nurse (35[8]), and J or E that of Rachel (35[19ff.]) and of Miriam, the sister of Moses (Nu 20[1]). But there is not a word anywhere of any of these tombs being a place of worship. For to attempt to discover such an allusion in the *maẓẓēbāh* set up on Rachel's tomb (Gn 35[20]) is to forget the fact that Ancestor Worship was paid only to *male* ancestors, rarely, if ever, to the mother of the tribe, not to speak of the impossibility of supposing the practice of Ancestor Worship at the tomb of the *nurse* of Rebeḳah. The object of the *maẓẓēbāh* on Rachel's grave must accordingly have been originally something other than to mark it as a place of worship.

Finally, on the theory we are discussing, it must strike us as very surprising that of all the sons of Jacob who, as ancestors of the various tribes, had the strongest claim to veneration, it is Joseph alone whose place of burial is mentioned (Jos 24[32]; cf. also Gn 50[25], Ex 13[19] [all E]). Now we do not mean to suggest any doubt that the tomb of Joseph at Shechem, that of Joshua at Timnath-seraḥ (Jos 24[30]), and no less those of Gideon (Jg 8[32]), Jephthaḥ (12[7]), Samson (16[31]), and the so-called 'minor judges' (10[2. 5] 12[10. 12. 15]), may have had the reputation of 'heroes' graves,' although we hear nothing of any cult being practised at them. But, even if Hero Worship could be proved, this would not necessarily be equivalent to Ancestor Worship. Even 1 S 20[29], where the practice of an (? annual) family sacrifice is presupposed, does not justify the conclusion that it was offered to ancestors.

Of all the arguments in favour of the former prevalence of Ancestor Worship, the most plausible is that based upon the injunction of the so-called *levirate marriage* (Dt 25[5ff.]). The original aim of this practice is held to have been to provide the childless deceased with a successor and thus with a cult, since the want of the latter was counted a serious misfortune. The custom in question is already presupposed in Gn 38[8ff.], where indeed it appears as unconditionally binding, whereas in Dt 25[7ff.] it has more the character of a simply moral obligation on the part of the surviving brother. But, even if levirate marriage had actually a connexion with Ancestor Worship, the Deuteronomist is certainly unconscious of this, and hence there is also little probability in the supposition that Lv 18[16] 20[21], in prohibiting marriage with a brother's wife, meant to raise a protest against Ancestor Worship.

A certain evidence of Ancestor Worship has been supposed to lie in 2 S 18[18]. This, however, is a mistake. For the meaning of the words there is not 'I have no son to invoke my name with veneration in the cult of the dead,' but simply 'I have no son to keep my name in remembrance,' as would be the case if there were any one who was called 'So and So, the son of Absalom.' In default of a son, the *maẓẓēbāh* must keep his name from being forgotten. Hence we are unable in this instance to discover the slightest trace of Ancestor Worship.

From 1 S 28[13], again, where the spirit of Samuel called up by the witch is called an *'ĕlōhîm, i.e.* a superhuman being, the most that can be inferred is that the spirits of the dead were one and all included in the category of *'ĕlōhîm* or *bĕnê 'ĕlōhîm*; there is no proof here of a worship of the dead, not to speak of a worship of ancestors.

To sum up the results of this whole discussion. If Ancestor Worship ever prevailed in the pre-Mosaic period—and it is psychologically quite conceivable that respect for the dead bodies and the tombs of parents inspired at least tendencies to a kind of Ancestor Worship,—no consciousness of this survived to historical times, and the whole question, as was remarked before, has at best an interest from the point of view of Archæology but not of Biblical Theology.

3. Real worship, however, was rendered by Israel in the pre-Mosaic period to the many **numina** (*'ēlîm* [sing. *'ēl*, 'deity,' 'god']), which were believed to be the inhabitants and possessors of certain places, and which were venerated as such. These make their appearance most frequently in

connexion with trees, stones, and springs, which thereby assume a sacred character. Whether there ever was a time when a local *numen* of this kind (answering to the *dryads, oreads, hyads* of the Greeks) was believed to be connected with every tree, is a question that cannot be decided.* We should probably, however, find a trace of *numina loci* in every instance where, in spite of what was for Jahwism a matter of course, namely, the identification of the *numen* with Jahweh, the original sacredness of the particular tree, etc., has survived. This comes out most distinctly in Gn 28[11ff.] (E, except vv.[13-16]), where Jacob sets up the *stone*, by which he had lain and had a remarkable dream, as a *mazzēbāh* and anoints it with oil, vowing at the same time that upon his return he will make this *mazzēbāh* a *bēth-'ēl* or 'god's house.' As a matter of fact, after his return and the erection of an altar, he calls the place *'Ēl-bēth-'ēl*, 'God of Bethel' (35[7] [also E]). It is plain that the anointing with oil (28[18]) was intended originally for the deity connected with the stone, and that the object of the whole narrative is to give a sanctity in the sense of Jahwism to the time-hallowed *mazzēbāh* of Bethel. A similar instance of Jahwism superseding an ancient view-point that had been taken over from the pre-Mosaic period, is present perhaps also in Jos 24[26] (E), where the setting up of the sacred stone under the oak in the sanctuary of Jahweh is attributed to Joshua, whereas, according to Gn 12[6], the sacred tree was in existence as early as the arrival of Abraham, appearing as 'the soothsayer's (*Mōreh*) terebinth'; that is to say, in all probability it was a spot where the *numen* connected with the tree gave oracles through a priest or prophet. But the sacred stone probably stood from the first in connexion with the tree, to which circumstance, no doubt, the designation of the latter as 'terebinth of the *mazzēbāh*' [read in Jg 9[6] *mazzēbāh* for *muzzāb*] is due. Pre-Jahwistic in all probability is also the sacred stone-circle near the Jordan at Jericho, from which a frequently named sanctuary (*hag-Gilgāl*, 'the [stone] circle') derives its name. According to Jos 4[2-8] and v.[20ff.] these stones, twelve in number after the number of the tribes, were set up by Joshua at Gilgal in memory of the miraculous passage through the dry bed of the Jordan; according to v.[9] (J), on the other hand, they were erected in the midst of the river itself. Both statements are manifestly attempts to give to the originally heathen character of this stone-circle a stamp that would be unobjectionable to Jahwism.—An ancient sanctuary is, doubtless, to be discovered also in 'the serpent's stone' (*'eben haz-zōheleth*) beside 'the fuller's spring' (*'Ên-rōgēl*) to the south of Jerusalem, for in 1 K 1[9] it serves as a place of sacrifice.—Of other sacred stones we hear nothing, there being no mention even of meteoric stones, although these played their part elsewhere on Semitic soil. The notion that the sacred Ark (see below, p. 628[b]) contained meteoric stones, rests upon pure conjecture. On the employment of *mazzēbōth* in the cult of Jahweh, see below, p. 620.

Amongst sacred *trees* we have already made mention of 'the soothsayer's terebinth' at Shechem, which is in all probability identical with the terebinth under which, according to Gn 35[4] (E), Jacob buried the foreign idols, as well as with 'the augurs' *or* prognosticators' (*Mĕ'ônĕnîm*) terebinth' of Jg 9[37]. To the same category belongs the 'terebinth of Mamre' at Hebron, which is constantly brought into connexion with Abraham (Gn 13[18] 14[13] 18[1]. The circumstance that in all these passages we find the plural, 'terebinths of Mamre,' is due to a correction made in dogmatic interests, namely, to get rid of the single sacred tree: this is clear from 18[4] as well as from the LXX, which has uniformly the singular). We may compare, further, the tamarisk of Abraham at Beersheba (Gn 21[33]); 'the oak of weeping' (*'allōn-Bāchûth*) named after Deborah at Bethel (35[8]); the palm of the female judge Deborah, between Ramah and Bethel (Jg 4[5]); the terebinth at Ophrah, beside which the angel of Jahweh appeared to Gideon (6[11]); the pomegranate (1 S 14[2]), and the tamarisk on the height of Gibeah (22[6]), under which Saul executed judgment; and, finally, the tamarisk [in 1 Ch 10[12] 'terebinth'] at Jabesh, beneath which the bones of Saul and his sons were interred.

In all the above instances we have to do presumably with trees which, as the abode of local *numina*, were already sacred to the Canaanites, and which for the same reason were so regarded by the Israelites as well, only that the process early began of bringing them into relation to the patriarchs, and thus to the cult of Jahweh, thereby removing all ground of offence connected with them. Nearly all of them now make their appearance as hallowed by the building of altars to Jahweh and by His worship in proximity to them. It is quite true that in the beliefs of the people the old conception of a special *'ēl* of the particular tree may have maintained itself tenaciously, even if without a clear consciousness, till far into the monarchical period.—Of the trees and tree-stumps or poles (*'ăshērîm*), which till towards the end of the pre-exilic period were reckoned amongst the necessary apparatus of a place for the worship of Jahweh, we shall have to speak later on (see p. 620).

Finally, in regard to sacred *springs*, we must first of all infer from the analogy of Semitism elsewhere, that in primitive times the most important, if not all, springs were regarded as the abode of a local *numen*. Express testimony to the sacredness of particular springs—whether on their own account or owing to a sanctuary erected near them—is forthcoming, indeed, in only a few instances. Thus, according to Gn 14[7], Ḳadesh (*i.e.* 'sanctuary') in the desert was known also as *'Ên-mishpāṭ*, 'spring of judgment.' This name might indeed have been bestowed upon it in allusion to the judicial decisions given by Moses at Ḳadesh during the wilderness wanderings, but it may also point, above all, to the presence of an oracle in the sanctuary by the sacred spring. In Gn 16[14] the (assuredly long established) sacredness of the spring *Laḥai-roi* in the desert is traced back to an appearance of Jahweh to Hagar; and in 21[29ff.] that of the spring at *Beersheba* to a compact by oath between Abraham and Abimelech. Adonijah, according to 1 K 1[9], holds a sacrificial meal at 'the serpent's stone' (see above) beside 'the fuller's spring' (the modern Job's Well); and v.[38] tells how Solomon was anointed king at Giḥon (the modern Virgin's Spring). The latter circumstance would be inexplicable unless a high degree of sanctity attached to Giḥon.

The above described preliminary step towards a religion, which consisted in the belief in numerous *'ēlîm*, and probably also in the presenting of offerings to them, has been designated **Polydemonism,** as distinguished from Polytheism. No exception need be taken to the name, provided it be understood that in this instance 'demon' stands for a Divine being of an inferior order and not simply for an evil spirit.

4. It is another question when we ask whether traces are to be discovered in Israel of a once prevailing **Polytheism** alongside of the traces of

* That this was the case with *'ēlāh* and *'ēlōn*, 'terebinth,' might be certainly assumed if these Hebrew names were really connected with *'ēl*, 'deity,' and did not rather mean 'the strong tree.'

Polydemonism. This question is generally answered in the negative by the adherents of the Ancestor Worship hypothesis. They tell us that Jahwism, with its toleration of the worship of *one* God only, had the effect of suddenly interrupting the natural transition from the Ancestor Worship of the family to Hero Worship as the cult of the progenitors of the tribe, and finally to Polytheism as the cult of tribal heroes exalted to Divine rank or of what were once merely local *numina*. Others, however, discover traces of actual gods, and thus of a once prevailing Polytheism in Israel.*

In dealing with this question we leave entirely out of account the numerous attempts to trace all the Scripture characters in primeval and patriarchal times to astral myths, or at all events to explain the majority of them (notably Abraham and Sarah, but also Isaac and Jacob, and, from the primeval period, at least the wives and the sons of Lamech [Gn 4[19ff.]], as well as Samson in the period of the Judges) as depotentiated forms of what once were gods. We fail to see in any of these attempts anything more than unprovable fancies. As little can we consent to regard the use of the plural form *'Ĕlōhîm* for 'God' as a relic of former Polytheism; it is much more likely that it is a so-called *pluralis majestatis.* At the very most it might be asked whether, perhaps, in certain tribal and personal names we have not a shortened form of originally theophorous names. Thus it has been proposed to find in *Gad* (Gn 30[11], Is 65[11]) a god of Fortune, and in *Asher* (Gn 30[13]) the male counterpart to the goddess Asherah. But, even supposing that *Gad* were shortened for *Obēd Gad*, 'worshipper of Gad,' or some similar form, the name of this mixed tribe (sprung from a concubine of Jacob) would prove nothing as to a specifically Israelitish god of Fortune. Moreover, if such an idea had been conveyed by the name, it is hardly likely that it would have been borne by a prophet of Jahweh living in the time of David (1 S 22[5] *et al.*). And as to *Asher* there is no trace elsewhere of a *god* of this name, while the explanation of the name as 'the happy one' is perfectly satisfactory. On the other hand, *'Anāth* in Jg 3[31] 5[6] should decidedly be regarded as abbreviated from *'Obēd 'Anāth*, 'worshipper of (the Canaanite goddess) 'Anāth.' But no one can prove that Shamgar the son of 'Anāth is rightly spoken of in the redactory gloss of Jg 3[31] as an Israelite. The name is there evidently borrowed from 5[6], where, according to Moore (*Journal of American Oriental Society*, XIX. ii. p. 159 f.), he is meant to be taken as the father of Sisera. In the opinion of the present writer, no weight at all can be attached to the somewhat numerous names from the periods of the Judges and the monarchy, compounded with *Ba'al*, 'lord,' or *Melekh*, 'king.' For in the most of these it is simply Jahweh Himself that is meant by *Ba'al* or *Melekh*. So it is, for instance, with *Jerubba'al* (*i.e.* 'he who contends for Ba'al,' notwithstanding the opposite interpretation of the name in Jg 6[32]); *'Eshba'al*, 'man of Ba'al,' the son of Saul (1 Ch 8[33] 9[39]); *Meriba'al*, 'man of Ba'al,' the son of Jonathan (8[34] 9[40]); *Be'eliada'*, 'Ba'al knoweth,' the son of David (14[7]). The preservation of the original form of the last three names only in Chronicles, *-ba'al* having its place taken in Samuel by *-bōsheth*, 'shame' (2 S 2[8. 10] *et al.*, 4[4] *et al.*; except that 2 S 5[16] substitutes *'Eliada'*, 'El knoweth,' for *Be'eliada'*), proves simply the eagerness of later generations to eliminate as far as possible the hated name of Ba'al, as is already enjoined in Hos 2[18]. But, granting that in certain names from that period it is actually the *heathen* Ba'al or Melekh that is meant, this would be simply an evidence of Israelitish *idolatry* due to foreign influences. That Israel had at all times tendencies to such idolatry has not as yet been disputed; but this cannot, of course, be counted amongst the relics of a once prevalent *Israelitish* Polytheism.

Further, if it should be objected that the OT tradition itself quite unambiguously attributes to the people in primitive times the worship of heathen gods, we reply that this is so, but that the passages in question are much in need of closer examination. Gn 31[30ff.] drops out of consideration. If Rachel stole the god (in v.[34f.] called *tĕrāphîm*) of her father Laban, this would at the most be an indication that the Teraphim cult was introduced from the Aramæan sphere, for Laban is regarded by the narrator as an Aramæan. We shall see afterwards, however, that upon *Hebrew* soil the Teraphim cannot have had the significance of a foreign god.—On the other hand, in Jos 24[2. 15] (E) it is really assumed that the forefathers of the Israelites on the other side of the Euphrates (*i.e.* before the time of Abraham) as well as in Egypt (v.[14]) served 'other gods.' That does not mean that from the first they had their own specifically Israelitish gods, but that they abandoned themselves to the worship of the foreign gods in whose country and sphere they sojourned. In this matter the narrator simply follows the theory to which even David gives drastic expression (1 S 26[19]) when he speaks of expulsion from Jahweh's own land as amounting to a compulsion to serve foreign gods.—But Am 5[26] cannot, in view of the whole context, be understood as alluding to idolatry on the part of Israel during the period of the wilderness wanderings, but only as containing a threat of something to come.—In Ezk 20[7f. 24] Israel is charged with having defiled itself with the idols of *Egypt*, and with refusing to abandon these even in the wilderness. Thus we have here again to do with *foreign* gods, and not with a native Israelitish Polytheism.

Finally, the possibility might remain that in certain beings of 'demon' order, occasionally mentioned, a reminiscence has survived of actual gods that were once worshipped. In favour of this view might be urged the analogy of other monotheistic religions, in which the gods of past heathen times are not straightway declared to be mere figments of the imagination, but (at least in the beliefs of the people) are degraded to 'demons' or spook forms. Thus lived on the once mighty gods of Greece among the early Christians; and so did the Arab tribal gods even after the conquest of Islam, just as the ancient German gods still survive in various superstitions that prevail amongst Christianized Germanic peoples. As a matter of fact, we find in some late passages of Scripture what may be pronounced certain, or at least very probable, examples of this depotentiating of former popular gods: *e.g.* Dt 32[17], where they are spoken of as *shēdîm*, 'demons,' to which at one time sacrifices were offered (cf. also Ps 106[37], where the once existing practice of offering children is thought of as having these 'demons' for its object); 2 Ch 11[15], where by the term שְׂעִירִים (*sĕ'îrîm*, 'goats' or 'goatlike forms'), the Chronicler evidently understands, above all, the heathen popular gods, for whom Jeroboam I. is said to have appointed priests. But in all these instances we have to do expressly with idolatrous worship of foreign gods, and not with relics of an Israelitish Polytheism. And when in Lv 17[7] it is forbidden to offer the usual sacrifices any more to the *sĕ'îrîm*, what comes here once more to the front is the belief in local *numina*, field spirits, with which there was an unwillingness, in spite of the uncontested

* Cf. the thorough discussion of all the controverted questions dealt with in what follows, in Baethgen's *Beiträge zur semit. Religionsgeschichte* (Berlin, 1888), p. 131 ff.

sole legitimacy of the Jahweh cult, to break completely, seeing that these beings could so readily injure man. But these field spirits are not, properly speaking, 'gods' any more than the spirits that make their abode in sacred trees and stones. Elsewhere, too, the *sĕʿîrîm* are nothing more than 'demon' forms, akin to the fauns and satyrs of classic mythology. In Is 13[21] they perform their dances in the destroyed palaces of Babylon, in 34[14] they hold their gatherings amongst the ruins of Edom.

Like the *sĕʿîrîm*, *Lilith* (*i.e.* 'the nightly one'), who, according to Is 34[14], dwells in the ruined palaces of Edom, belongs in all probability to the category of monstrosities to which the popular belief gave birth. The same is the case with the *Alûkāh* of Pr 30[15], the mention of whose two daughters is sufficient to show that it is not the common leech that is meant, but that the name, like the Arabic *'Alûk* or *'Aulak*, stands for a blood-sucking 'demon.' In another connexion we shall come upon still further remnants of a belief in and fear of 'demons.'* *'Azāzēl*, again, to whom on the Great Day of Atonement the goat laden with the sins of the people was sent forth (Lv 16[8. 10. 21ff.]), is evidently an unclean 'demon' who inhabits the desert. At the same time it is very questionable whether this figure can be regarded as a survival from the pre-Mosaic belief in 'demons,' and was not rather first borrowed from a foreign source during the Exile.—Of the *Cherubim* and *Seraphim* we shall not speak till later on, because these, although certainly a product of non-Israelite soil, attained to something of an independent significance in Jahwism. The *Saṭan*, on the contrary, viewed as an individual, is not met with till the post-exilic period.

ii. *Forms of Worship, and other Rites and Usages.*—The essential character of every ancient religion reveals itself pre-eminently in the *worship* it offers to the Deity. That such worship formed an element also in the pre-Mosaic stage of the religion of Israel is to be assumed, and various traces of it survived for long even in the cultus of Jahweh. These are recognizable by their great resemblance to, or even complete identity with, the ritual usages of the heathen Semites. As in the case of mourning customs, the original meaning, it is true, is often difficult to recognize, or the features of the custom have been so toned down or completely transformed as to make identification impossible.

1. By far the most important ritual transaction in the primitive stage of religion is **sacrifice.** To the later Israelitish conceptions this appeared almost exclusively from the point of view of a *gift*, and, above all, as an offering of food to the Deity; even fat and blood are expressly named in Ezk 44[7. 15] as food of Jahweh. It cannot be doubted that this aspect of the matter was not wholly wanting even in the pre-Mosaic period, and that offerings of fruit in particular were presented to the local *numina*, by being deposited within the sacred precincts (as was done afterwards with the shewbread), or being thrown into the sacred wells.

Also the ordinary burnt-offering, which was *all* assigned to the Deity (hence called also *kālîl*, 'whole-offering'), can scarcely be regarded otherwise than as an offering of food, *i.e.* as a gift. But, on the other hand, it is impossible to explain all sacrificial rites from this point of view. The extraordinary importance which is manifestly attributed to the blood of the sacrificial victim carries us forward to another idea, namely, that of the *sacramental communion* established between the god and his worshippers through their common eating of the (*eo ipso* sacred) body of the sacrificial victim. And, since from the earliest times the blood is regarded as pre-eminently the seat of the life, the sacramental communion was undoubtedly reached in the most primitive stage by drinking the sacrificial blood, the same blood as was assigned in some way (it might be by smearing the image or the altar, or by pouring out the blood within the sacred precincts) to the Deity. A clear trace of this notion—although in a form that has been very much toned down—has survived in Ex 24[5ff.]. When we read here of Moses sprinkling the altar with one portion of the blood and the people with the other, and thus sealing the covenant between Jahweh and the people, the main feature of the rite is the common share in the blood which establishes a communion, and which is hence called by Moses 'the blood of the covenant.'

It could not have been long till the advance of culture gave rise to repugnance to the drinking of blood. Hence arose naturally a partition of the sacred food; the portion of the Deity being the blood along with the fat (the latter in all probability on account of the facility with which it could be made over to the Deity by letting it go up in smoke), the portion of the worshippers being the flesh. The sacramental communion, however, finds expression in late as well as in early times in the consumption of the sacrificial meal at a sacred spot, in eating and drinking 'before Jahweh' (in early times, no doubt, in the actual presence of the image). That the flesh even in these so-called meal-offerings bore a sacred character, is evident from the circumstance that the mingling of sacred and common food in the body was sought to be avoided by fasting previous to the sacrificial meal. The record of this undoubtedly very ancient practice has come down to us only in connexion with war (Jg 20[26], 1 S 7[6]) and mourning (1 S 31[13], 2 S 3[35] [the case is different in 12[16]]). The strict command to avoid the use of blood for food, which was afterwards extended to the case of animals that could not be offered in sacrifice, may have been originally due not simply to the fact that the blood was reserved for the Deity, but also to the fear of absorbing a second soul along with the blood, the seat of life.

It cannot be determined whether, in addition to what were afterwards the usual victims, other animals were used for sacrifice by the tribes of Israel in pre-Mosaic times. On the other hand, it may be asserted with confidence that in special cases *human sacrifice* was practised in order to propitiate the Deity or gain His favour.* This is witnessed to by the persistency with which, down to the 7th cent. B.C., the sacrifice of the first-born is regarded as the highest act of service, in spite of the clear protest uttered against this notion in Gn 22 (E). The teaching of the latter narrative plainly is that Jahweh is satisfied with the disposition which is prepared to offer to Him one's dearest, and that He has appointed the substitutionary offering of an animal in place of the

* Cf. E. Ferrière, *Paganisme des Hébreux jusqu' à la captivité de Babylone*, Paris, 1884; C. H. Toy, 'Evil Spirits in the Bible' in *JBL* ix. pt. i. p. 17 ff.; J. van der Veen, 'Daemonologie van het Judaisme' in *Theol. Studiën*, 1890, p. 301 ff. There is the closest connexion between the belief in 'demons' (as also, indeed, the worship of local *numina*) and the great majority of the manifold forms of magic and soothsaying. Much of the latter may have been first taken over by Israel on Canaanite soil, but not a little must have belonged to the pre-Mosaic stage. Cf. on this point the classical article of W. R. Smith, 'On the Forms of Divination and Magic enumerated in Deut. xviii. 10 f.' in *Journal of Philology*, xiii. p. 273 ff., and xiv. p. 113 ff.; also T. W. Davies, *Magic, Divination, and Demonology among the Hebrews and their Neighbours*, etc., London, 1898 (also as Dissertation, Leipzig, 1901).

* Cf. on this point the exhaustive discussion of A. Kamphausen, *Das Verhältniss des Menschenopfers zur israelit. Religion*, Bonn, 1896.

actual sacrifice of a child. Nevertheless, Ahaz (2 K 16[3], very probably during the straits to which he was reduced by the attack of the allied Aramæans and Ephraimites) and Manasseh (21[6]) both caused a son to pass through the fire; and in Mic 6[7b] the question is evidently submitted to very serious consideration whether the sacrifice of the firstborn is not to be offered as the surest expiation of guilt.

From passages like Dt 12[31], 2 K 17[17] 23[10], Ezk 16[20f.] 20[31] 23[37ff.] (on Jer 19[5] see below) it would appear as if these burnt-offerings of human victims were presented not to Jahweh, but to Melekh (LXX Moloch), *i.e.* 'king [of heaven]' as a heathen god. Apart, however, from Gn 22, this is expressly opposed by Jg 11[30f. 36], according to which Jephthah, in terms of his vow, sacrificed his daughter to *Jahweh*. In 2 K 3[27] we read of how Mesha, king of Moab, offered his firstborn, naturally to Chemosh, the god of the land; but the now mutilated close of the narrative plainly shows that the writer was firmly convinced of the efficacy of such an offering, and would no doubt have expected that a similar sacrifice to Jahweh on Israelitish soil would be equally efficacious. Jer 7[31] 19[5] [delete in the latter the gloss 'as burnt-offerings to Baal,' which is wanting in the LXX] 32[35] plainly show that the sacrifice of children was popularly supposed to be well-pleasing to Jahweh. And even Ezekiel, to whom such offerings, like every other form of cultus in pre-exilic times, appear as simple idolatry, reckons the sacrifice of all the firstborn among the statutes 'that were not good' (20[25f.]), which Jahweh Himself gave to the people as a punishment for their backsliding. This strange assertion is in all probability to be understood as meaning that the command to offer the firstlings of cattle gave rise to the erroneous notion that human sacrifice was well-pleasing to God.

If human sacrifices were, in the nature of things, burnt-offerings or whole-offerings, thus constituting pre-eminently valuable *gifts*, yet in the earliest times the use made of the blood must have held an important place in the same connexion. And, seeing that in the case of the offering of children the blood in question was closely related to that of the offerer, this species of sacrifice also must unquestionably be regarded from the point of view of the establishing of a sacramental communion between the offerer and the Deity.

A somewhat different character belongs, on the other hand, to other two rites, which are certainly also pre-Mosaic, namely the ratifying of a covenant by cutting one or more animals in pieces, so that the contracting parties might pass between the pieces laid opposite one another; and the *ḥērem* or ban.

In Gn 15[9ff. 17] (J), in the case of the 'covenant' of Jahweh with Abraham, the first named of these rites is enjoined and performed by God alone; but here we have to do not with a covenant in the ordinary human sense, but with a *religious* '*bĕrîth*,' whose essence lies in the Divine institution, demand, and promise. God accommodates Himself here to human custom by passing between the pieces of the dismembered animal, just as in Jer 34[18f.] the contracting parties pass between the parts of the calf cut in twain. The whole transaction in so far resembles a sacrificial one, as the kinds of animals enumerated in Gn 15[9], as well as the calf of Jer 34[18], all belong to the class usually employed for sacrifice; nor is it impossible that the blood of these animals was in some way utilized as sacrificial blood. The kernel of the rite is manifestly the invoking of a curse upon oneself in case of a breach of the obligation undertaken.* This is clearly alluded to in 1 S 11[7] (as well as in the incident of Jg 19[29], which must be interpreted in the same way), only that the curse invoked must have originally concerned not the cattle, but the person of the man who was false to his obligation.

The **ban** (Heb. חֵרֶם) * was, without doubt, originally a war custom, and consists in the devoting † (even before the actual battle, Nu 21[2], Jos 6[17], 1 S 15[3ff.]) of the enemy and all their belongings to destruction—in Israel, in the post-Mosaic period, naturally in honour of Jahweh as the God of war. Schwally rightly denies that the *ḥērem* has the character of an offering or present. To 'ban' means to give over to destruction; the religious element is found in the complete renunciation of any profit from the victory, and this renunciation is an expression of gratitude for the fact that the war-God has delivered the enemy, who is His enemy also, and all his substance into the hands of the conqueror. The earliest practice appears to have required the massacre of everything living, whether man or beast, and the burning or destroying in some other way of houses and property; cf. Jos 6[21. 24] (after the capture of Jericho) 8[24ff. 28] 10[28], 1 S 15[8ff.] (where the sparing of the best of the cattle for a future offering, and the failure to put to death the Amalekite king Agag, are held up by Samuel as a transgression on the part of Saul) 22[19] (although in this instance the expression *ḥērem* is not employed); so in Mic 4[13] in an eschatological prophecy the 'devoting' of all the substance of the peoples that besiege Jerusalem is announced. The original rigour of the *ḥērem* appears in a somewhat milder form in Dt 2[34f.] 3[6f.], Jos 8[2. 27] 11[14], where human beings, indeed, are all to be put to death, but the cattle and other possessions of the enemy are to fall as spoil to the Israelites. According to Dt 20[16ff.] the ban is to be enforced with unsparing severity in the case of Canaanite cities, whereas, according to v.[13ff.], in far distant non-Canaanite cities only the males are to be slaughtered; the women and children, the cattle and other property, are to be regarded as spoil. This rule is followed in the case of the Midianites, according to Nu 31[7ff.], but Moses afterwards (v.[17f.]) demands the slaughter also of all the female prisoners except those that were still virgins. A further mitigation of the practice is found, finally, in the possibility of making some of the prisoners slaves of the sanctuary; cf. Jos 9[23] and the *Nĕthînîm* or 'given ones' amongst the *personnel* of the post-exilic temple.

The *ḥērem*, as a solemn devoting to destruction, might, however, include in its scope even Israelites, and not only individuals but communities. Thus Dt 13[16ff.] requires the putting to death of *all* the inhabitants of any Israelitish city that fell into idolatry, and the burning of *all* their property as 'a whole-offering to Jahweh.' ‡ According to Jg 20[48] all the members of the tribe of Benjamin were slaughtered and their cities burned on account of the outrage at Gibeah; according to 21[10ff.] the ban was executed on all the inhabitants of Jabesh-gilead with the exception of 400 virgins who were

* F. Schwally (*Semit. Kriegsaltertümer*, Heft 1, 'Der heilige Krieg im alten Israel,' Leipzig, 1901, p. 54) well describes the action of Saul in 1 S 11[7] as a 'Schwur- oder Bundesritus'; the dismembered bodies have in all the instances above cited the significance of an 'Eidopfer,' to which numerous analogies are found in other religions as well.

* Cf. Schwally, *l.c.* p. 29 ff.

† In Jer 12[3] the expression 'dedicate (lit. hallow) them for the day of slaughter' answers exactly to the elsewhere employed 'ban.'

‡ In view of what has been said above, this cannot be taken to mean that the destruction in consequence of the *ḥērem* actually represents a whole- or burnt-offering, but that it has this force *comparatively*, being as well-pleasing as a burnt-offering. Schwally very appropriately refers to the statement of Mesha on the Moabite Stone, l. 11 f.: 'and I slew all the people of the city, a pleasing spectacle for Chemosh and for Moab.' In the same way is explained why the touching of the 'devoted' thing roused the anger of the Deity (Jos 7[26]).

urgently required. That the man who stole anything of what had been 'devoted' came himself under the ban, because he had broken the 'taboo' caused by the *ḥērem*, is shown by the case of Achan (Jos 7[1ff.]). The 'holy indignation of Jahweh,' which burns at first against the whole people (v.[12ff.]), is appeased only when Achan is stoned to death (v.[26]). Nor is it easy to understand 1 S 14[45] except to mean that the curse resting upon Jonathan (cf. v.[24]), in which he had involved himself by disregard of Saul's prohibition, as of a kind of *ḥērem*, was removed by drawing lots for and putting to death a substitute. In 2 S 21[3ff.] Israel is delivered from the consequences of the curse of the Gibeonites by the giving up and putting to death of seven members of the family of Saul, whose action was responsible for the curse.

A unique character belongs to the case supposed in Lv 27[28ff.], that an Israelite might 'devote' any possession of his, including human beings (slaves or captives taken in war?) and cattle. Everything so 'devoted' is most holy to Jahweh: if human beings, they must be put to death.

The circumstance that in the earliest times there is no trace of drink-offerings of wine, is explicable very simply on the ground that these were possible only after Israel had become used to vine-culture in Canaan. On the other hand, the libations of water mentioned as prayer-offerings before battle (1 S 7[6], cf. also 2 S 23[15ff.]) are in all probability a survival from a time when water (in the desert) was considered an article of value. Extraordinary occasions such as war (see below) led to a revival of the primitive ritual practice.

Regarding the usual sacrificial transaction we have information in the very word for altar, namely *mizbēaḥ*, *i.e.* 'place of slaughter.' This shows that the victims, as is presupposed also in Gn 22[9], were slain upon the altar itself. The *horns* of the altar, which afterwards played a rôle in connexion with the application of the blood (Lv 4[7] *et al.*) and the function of the altar as an asylum (1 K 1[50f.] 2[28]), should in all probability be traced back to the custom of spreading the skin of the victim, horns and all, over the altar. This custom can be proved also in the case of heathen cults, and is thus presumably older than Jahwism. Apart from other considerations, the latter supposition is favoured by the circumstance that in the earliest times altars were composed either of large flat stones (Jg 6[20] 13[19], 1 S 6[14] 14[33ff.]) or of piles of turf or unhewn stones (Ex 20[24f.]). The introduction of *artificial* horns would follow after altars came to be constructed of different materials. The explanation of the horns as symbols of strength in connexion with the worship of Jahweh as a bull-God could thus, in any case, have been introduced only at a later period. The circumstance that the number of horns required by the Priests' Code (Ex 27[2], cf. Ezk 43[15. 20]), which no doubt embodies here a long-established usage, is four (one on each corner of the altar), proves nothing against the view that the horns were originally only two in number.

2. The *essentials of a place of worship* in the earliest times probably always included a *maẓẓēbāh* (מַצֵּבָה) and a sacred tree, or, in default of the latter, a sacred tree-stump or pole. It is true that Ex 23[24] 34[13] and Dt 7[5] 12[3] convey the impression that in Israel the *maẓẓēbāh* was first introduced in imitation of Canaanite modes of worship; but such a notion is contradicted by the prevailing belief (see above, p. 616[a]) that the *maẓẓēbāh* was the abode of the *numen loci*. This belief had its origin as far back as the period of Polydemonism, and Jahwism retained it to this extent, that even in this religion the *maẓẓēbāh* was viewed as the symbol and pledge of the nearness of Jahweh. It is thus all the more readily comprehensible that down even to the late monarchical period no offence was taken at the *maẓẓēbāh*. In Gn 31[45. 51f.] the *maẓẓēbāh* serves as a witness of the agreement between Jacob and Laban. Moses himself erects at Sinai not only an altar to Jahweh but twelve *maẓẓēbôth*, 'according to the number of the tribes of Israel' (Ex 24[4]). These stones cannot possibly have possessed for this narrator the same significance as the sacred stone of Bethel had for the narrator of Gn 28[17f.]. The two brazen pillars at the entrance to Solomon's temple (1 K 7[15ff.]) should also, no doubt, be regarded as representing a form of *maẓẓēbāh*. According to 2 K 12[10 (9)] [read, with the LXX, 'by the *maẓẓēbāh*' instead of 'by the altar'] a *maẓẓēbāh* stood in the forecourt of the temple; in Hos 3[4] the *maẓẓēbāh* is taken for granted as part of the *materia sacra* of the regular worship of Jahweh; and in Is 19[19] the *maẓẓēbāh* spoken of is not an obelisk, but a stone which serves along with the altar to mark a spot consecrated to the worship of Jahweh. We are told in 2 K 18[4] that the *maẓẓēbôth* had already been destroyed by Ḥezekiah, but this should probably be set down as an antedating of the cultus reform of Josiah (2 K 23[14]); for the first [unless Mic 5[12 (13)] is as early as the time of Manasseh] prohibition of the *maẓẓēbāh* appears in Deuteronomy (16[22]; cf. also Jer 2[27] [if the mockery of the prophet has for its objects *'ăshērîm* (see below) and *maẓẓēbôth*] and Lv 26[1]). As with the worship on high places, the erecting of *'ăshērîm* and *maẓẓēbôth* by the kings prior to Josiah is imputed to them as a fault by the Deuteronomistic redactors of the Book of Kings (1 K 14[23], 2 K 17[10]).

Like the *maẓẓēbāh*, the *'ăshērāh* (אֲשֵׁרָה, plur. אֲשֵׁרִים), *i.e.* the sacred tree-stump or pole, must also be reckoned among the survivals of the pre-Jahwistic cultus, although it likewise held its place for centuries unopposed beside the altars of Jahweh (as in Jg 6[25ff.] it appears beside an altar of Baal). It is, without doubt, a substitute for the sacred tree (see above), which was not available everywhere (especially, for instance, in the case of hastily erected altars in the desert). But, as the regular sanctuaries on the high places would always have green trees in their neighbourhood, there was less occasion for the mention of the *'ăshērîm* [in 1 K 14[23] and 2 K 17[10] they are a superfluity, due probably to the eagerness of the Deuteronomist to condemn alike the trees and the *'ăshērîm*]. That the *'ăshērāh* said to have been cut down by Hezekiah (2 K 18[4]) and restored by Manasseh (21[3]) stood in the temple down to the time of Josiah, is shown by its removal and burning in the Ḳidron Valley (2 K 23[6]). In like manner an *'ăshērāh* (according to 1 K 16[33], first set up by Ahab) stood in Samaria (2 K 13[6]; cf. also 1 K 14[15], 2 K 17[16]). The command to cut down (Ex 34[13], Dt 7[5]) or to burn (Dt 12[3]) heathen *'ăshērîm* implies at the same time, of course, a repudiation of their use in Israel. They are expressly forbidden in Dt 16[21] (cf. also Mic 5[13 (12)], where it is predicted that they are to be plucked up; Jer 17[2], Is 27[9], and the late addition to Is 17[8]). With the exception perhaps of Mic 5[13], none of these passages goes further back than the time of Josiah. There is, of course, a complete distinction between the *'ăshērāh* as the sacred pole, and the *goddess* Asherah, whose existence appears to be now placed beyond doubt by the Tel el-Amarna letters. Her worship (1 K 15[13], 2 K 21[7] 23[4]) wears the aspect of pure idolatry, and hence does not come under the category of the religion of Israel.

The use of other figures besides the *maẓẓēbāh* and the *'ăshērāh* to represent the nearness of the Deity cannot be proved, to say the least of it, for the pre-Mosaic period. In favour of such a view may be urged the tenacity with which the Jahweh cultus clung for a very long period to the use of images of Jahweh; and it is not impossible that in these the form of the *'ēlîm* that were once worshipped had been handed down. On the other hand, the notion cannot be admitted that any but images of Jahweh were ever tolerated within the pale of the Jahweh worship. This must hold good also of the *Tĕrāphîm*, even if these were originally derived from the realm of heathendom; and the whole question must accordingly be left for discussion in connexion with the pre-Prophetic cultus of Israel.

3. But, again, the worship of Jahweh retained a number of *ritual practices* which may be held with all the more certainty to have been derived from the pre-Mosaic period, since they one and all have their analogues in the practices of the heathen Semites. This category includes *walking barefoot in sacred places* (Ex $3^{5}$, Jos $5^{15}$; even the going barefoot in token of mourning, 2 S $15^{30}$, Is $20^{2ff.}$, like other forms of uncovering, has to be looked at, as explained above, from the religious point of view); *washing the person and the clothes* (Ex $19^{10}$ and often) *before approaching the presence of the Deity* (cf. the changing of the clothes, Gn $35^{2}$). When we find in the Priests' Code constant injunctions to wash the person and the clothes in order to recover lost Levitical purity, no doubt the primary intention of these is that outward physical purity is to be the symbol and representation of inward. But, all the same, there is here a relic of those conceptions which led to the attempt, by means of external cleansing, to escape direct injury from demons or even from an angry god. And if in Ex $28^{43}$ and Lv $6^{4\,(10)}$ $16^{23}$ the priests are enjoined to wear their official garments only when they are conducting Divine service, the older passage, Ezk $44^{19}$, shows that there was a further intention in this than simply to guard against a profanation of the holy garments. The danger was rather that by touching these garments the people would be 'hallowed,' *i.e.* become forfeit to the sanctuary, and thus require a ransom to be paid for them. Here, again, we make acquaintance with the primitive notion that all close contact with the Deity or with anything consecrated to Him was, if not fatal, at least dangerous. But amongst forms of close contact was included the act of *looking upon*; hence the covering of the head in presence of the Deity, as is done by Moses in Ex $3^{6}$ and Elijah in 1 K $19^{13}$. The same idea, that the beholding of the Deity is fatal, meets us in Gn $16^{13}$ $32^{30}$, Ex $19^{21}$ $33^{20}$. In all these instances it is true it is Jahweh that is in question, but it may be regarded as certain that the idea is an inheritance from the pre-Jahwistic era.

4. Of *priests* in pre-Jahwistic times no recollection has been preserved. In any case there was no need of their services for offering sacrifice, seeing that this office could be performed equally well, even in the worship of Jahweh, by any head of a household. The more menial services were discharged, as still continued to be the case under Moses (Ex $24^{5}$), by the young men. On the other hand, designations like 'Oracle-terebinth' (see above, p. $616^{a}$) point to the existence of Oracle priests at particular sanctuaries, just as Gn $25^{22}$ naïvely assumes the existence of a Jahweh-oracle in the time of Rebekah.

5. There are various passages from which (in combination with the hypothesis of Ancestor Worship) the inference has been drawn that at first only the family or the tribe was regarded as the *sacral body*. Thus in Ex $21^{6}$ the slave who does not wish to go free is to be pinned by the ear to the doorpost 'before God,' and thus incorporated with the sacral body belonging to this God. The Passover ceremony (see below) likewise assumes the family to be the sacral body. In 1 S $20^{6}$ we read of an annual offering by the family of David; but this does not prevent David's being at the same time missed at a sacrificial meal (for in ancient times this character belongs to all eating of the flesh of an animal that was lawful for sacrifice) at the New Moon; and there were many other occasions when the sacral fellowship could not possibly be confined to a family or even to a tribe. Thus in war, which from the ancient Semitic point of view always came under the category of religious transactions, it is evident that all comrades in arms formed *one* sacral fellowship, whose members collectively 'hallow the war,' *i.e.* consecrate themselves for battle by abstinence from sexual intercourse (cf. 1 S $21^{5}$, where David pretends to be on military duty; 2 S $11^{11}$), as well as by inaugural offerings (1 S $7^{9}$ $13^{12}$, where the sacrifices are intended to propitiate Jahweh), just as in Ex $19^{15}$ the people prepare themselves by continence for drawing near to God. Also the prescriptions of Dt $20^{5-7}$ $23^{10-14}$, so strange to our notions, are explicable as survivals from a time when certain bodily functions, and in particular sexual relations, were believed to involve danger from demons.*

6. Whether in pre-Mosaic times there was a sacrificial cultus practised at *fixed, frequently recurring periods*, cannot be determined. An observance of the Sabbath is extremely improbable, although its sacred character is carried back in Gn $2^{3}$ (P) to the very beginning of the world. More conceivable—and here again combined with the fear of demonic influences—is it that there should have been a celebration of the New Moon, seeing that there are the clearest traces of this (see below, p. $662^{a}$) till far down in the monarchical period, without any recognizable connexion with Jahwism. As to the later annual festivals, it is self-evident that those which depend upon agriculture and vine-growing cannot be taken into account for the nomad period of Israel's history; they are one and all of Canaanite origin. On the other hand, the ancient tradition clearly assumes that the **Passover** festival (of course with its original significance, and quite independent of the Feast of Unleavened Bread) was already kept in pre-Mosaic times. When Moses and Aaron (Ex $5^{3}$) make the demand of Pharaoh, 'Let us go three days' journey into the wilderness, to offer sacrifice to Jahweh, our God,' and repeat this demand before each plague ($7^{16}$ $8^{1}$ etc.), it is assumed that they wish to celebrate in the wilderness a long-established sacrificial festival. For Moses ($8^{26}$) assigns as motive for going outside the land of Egypt that they are accustomed to offer sacrifices that are an abomination to the Egyptians, and in $10^{9}$ he says expressly, 'We have to keep *the* feast of Jahweh.' Again in $12^{21}$ (J) the direction runs, 'Kill *the* Passover.' Here, too, accordingly, it is assumed (as even in $12^{11}$ [P] 'It is a Passover for Jahweh') as something that has been long familiar,—in opposition to the directions of v. $^{22ff.}$, which make the ritual to have first taken its

* Cf. the very instructive remarks of Schwally in the above-cited 'Der heilige Krieg im alten Israel,' esp. p. 45 ff., on the hallowing of war (Jos $3^{5}$, Mic $3^{5}$, Jer $6^{4}$ *et al.*) also by anointing the shield (2 S $1^{21}$) and consecrating the weapons (Jer $22^{7}$), as well as by burnt-offerings which in the earliest times represented also the most solemn form of guilt-offering (1 S $7^{9}$ $13^{9.\,12}$). Again, the allowing of the hair to grow long (if Jg $5^{2}$ is to be rendered 'with long streaming locks,' etc. [see Moore, *ad loc.*], and if this implies a general warlike custom) marked the warrior as *nāzîr* or 'consecrated.' Schwally appears to the present writer to go too far when (p. 74 ff.) he discovers the peril to the newly married man in the circumstance that by taking part in war he was guilty of turning aside to another cultus. The explanation rather commends itself that by such conduct he would expose himself to the curses of his wife, or that the consecration of a new house appeared indispensable for the expulsion of hostile demons.

rise upon the occasion of the Exodus, and to the derivation of the name *pesaḥ* (פֶּסַח) from *pāsaḥ* 'to pass over.' This explanation of the word from the sparing action of Jahweh in passing by the houses of the Israelites when He smote the firstborn of the Egyptians (so Ex $12^{27}$), cannot be reconciled with the circumstance that in the oldest usage of language *pesaḥ* appears to stand for the so-called Paschal lamb or (Dt $16^{2}$) other animals used for the sacrifice (cf. the expressions 'kill *or* burn *or* eat the Passover'). This fact shatters also the derivation of the name from *pāsaḥ*, 'to limp' * (cf. the limping of the prophets of Baal around the altar, 1 K $18^{26}$, and the limping—undoubtedly a custom derived from very early times—of the Mecca pilgrims around the sacred stone of the Ka'aba), although in itself it is favoured by the analogy of *ḥāgag*, prop. 'to dance *or* circle round,' then 'to celebrate a festival.' Even if the attempt to fix the etymology of the word must be given up, there are still sufficient starting-points to enable us to get at the original character of the Passover. † Ex $34^{19}$ shows that in the month Abib, in which the Exodus fell, the firstlings of cattle, or, more strictly, the first male offspring of sheep and cows, were offered. According to $5^{3}$ these sacrifices are to be offered in the wilderness, lest Jahweh visit the people with pestilence or the sword. That is to say, they are guilt- or propitiatory-offerings. But quite the same is the character of the Paschal meal, however later theological motives may have transformed its original meaning, or the Priests' Code have entirely given up its sacrificial character. ‡ The eating of the Paschal lamb (whether originally one of the firstlings used for this purpose, while the rest were sacrificed as burnt- or whole-offerings, or no) is, beyond question, a sacrificial meal celebrated by the family as the sacral body; for the flesh is holy, and none of it is to be left till the morning, while the blood is to be smeared on the lintel and the doorposts to guard those within from pestilence. From the later point of view this part of the ritual amounts to nothing more than a memorial of a former deliverance from a particular danger. But originally, as is shown by numerous primitive heathen analogies, it was sought by an annual smearing with blood to protect house and herd from demonic influences, in particular from the plague or other diseases.

The *Mazzôth* festival, which immediately followed the Passover, might be brought into close connexion with the latter, only if, with Beer (*Theol. Ltztg.* 1901, col. 588), following Holzinger, we could see in the *mazzôth* simply a memorial of the nomad period, during which Israel in Bedawîn fashion ate unleavened bread. When the nomad life was given up (Gn $4^{14}$), the *mazzôth*, on Beer's theory, became 'bread of affliction' (Dt $16^{3}$). The view that the *mazzôth* represented the bread baked from the new corn (and thus implied an agrarian festival) is held to be contradicted, especially by their use in connexion with sacrifices all the year through, and no less by their being used as common food. The only objection to Beer's explanation is the difficulty of supposing that the memory of an obsolete manner of life was solemnly celebrated by a return to it, and that for a period of six days. Moreover, the agrarian character of the spring festival appears to be assured by Dt $16^{9}$ and by the presentation of the so-called wave-sheaf (Lv $23^{10ff.}$).

The festal character of the *Sheep-shearing* is still witnessed to by 1 S $25^{11ff.}$ and 2 S $13^{23ff.}$ (cf. also Gn $31^{19}$ $38^{12f.}$). It is, however, quite intelligible that this festival, so important for nomads, afterwards fell more into the background as compared with the agrarian festivals that were celebrated in common.

7. As to the *course of procedure* at a festival we have information in Ex $32^{6}$ which no doubt applies also to the pre-Mosaic period: sacrifice, sacrificial meals, amusements (chiefly, in all probability, dancing). Many a practice, which afterwards aroused the righteous indignation of the prophets, may have had its roots in the ritual customs of pre-Mosaic times instead of being derived from the evil example of the Canaanites.

8. A religious character belongs, finally, to other two customs whose origin in like manner goes, without doubt, back to the pre-Mosaic era: circumcision and blood-revenge.

**Circumcision.*** — All attempts to explain this practice as due to purely sanitary considerations are now rightly regarded as exploded. As little weight can be attached to such explanations as that it is a milder symbolic form of the once prevalent sacrifice of children, or of self-emasculation in honour of a deity. On the contrary, circumcision has, amongst numerous (including Semitic) tribes, an evident connexion with a boy's reaching puberty; it is the sign of maturity, and thus of full admittance to the number of capable warriors of the tribe. But, since it has at the same time a religious meaning (for *'ārēl* 'uncircumcised' is equivalent to '[religiously] unclean,' and hence a strongly disparaging word), it can be viewed only as an act of consecration for the benefit of a tribal god or some particular demon. It thus serves at once as a tribal mark † and as a defence against the harmful influence of other demons. Even for Jahwism circumcision is primarily a sign that a man belongs to the people and the worship of Jahweh, although the specifically theological interpretation of it as a sign of the covenant (Gn $17^{10ff.}$) belongs only to the latest stage (P).

The oldest tradition as to the origin of child circumcision meets us in Ex $4^{24ff.}$ (J). In this now mutilated passage it is implied that Moses aroused the indignation of the Deity (here of course already Jahweh) because at the time of his marriage with Ẓipporah he was not circumcised as religious custom required (cf. also Gn $34^{22ff.}$ [J]). Ẓipporah

* Toy ('The Meaning of Pesach,' in *JBL*, 1898, p. 178 ff.) thinks otherwise, holding that the *pesaḥ* was originally a ritual dance, accompanied by the sacrifice of a lamb, and that it was only afterwards that the name was transferred to the sacrifice.

† Cf. on the most recent explanations of the term (including its comparison with the Assyr. *pašâḫu*, 'calm oneself,' so that *pesaḥ* would='calming *or* appeasing [the anger of the Deity])' Riedel in *ZATW*, 1900, p. 319 ff. He holds *pesaḥ* to be the Egyp. *pōseḫ*, 'harvest.' Schäfer, again (*Das Passah-Mazzoth-Fest nach seinem Ursprunge, seiner Bedeutung, und seiner innerpentateuchischen Entwickelung*, Gütersloh, 1900), holds the Passover to have been a purificatory offering of very early origin, common to all the Semites, and designed to appease the Deity. At the same time he denies the pre-Mosaic origin of the OT Passover, declaring it to have been, along with its pendant the *Mazzôth* feast (which was meant to recall the haste of the Exodus), from first to last a historic-theocratic festival. His argument is manifestly under the spell of tradition.

‡ The view that the Passover and the offering of firstlings were not originally connected (so Volz in *Theol. Ltztg.* 1901, col. 635 f.) appears to the present writer to be at least incapable of demonstration.

* Cf., on this subject, H. Ploss, 'Geschichtliches und Ethnologisches über Knabenbeschneidung' in *Deutsches Archiv für Geschichte der Medicin und medicinischen Geographie*, viii. 3, p. 312 ff.; P. Lafargue, 'La circoncision, sa signification sociale et religieuse' in *Bulletins de la soc. d'Anthropologie de Paris*, ser. iii. tome x. 3, p. 420 ff.; P. C. Remondino, *History of Circumcision from the Earliest Times to the Present*, Philadelphia, 1891; A. Glassberg, *Die Beschneidung*, etc., Berlin, 1896; S. Kohn, *Die Geschichte der Beschneidung bei den Juden von den ältesten Zeiten bis auf die Gegenwart*, Frankfurt a. M., 1902 (Hebrew).

† As such, it appears to go back to a time when the men still went naked; cf. Gunkel, 'Ueber die Beschneidung im AT' in *Archiv für Papyrusforschung*, ii. 1, p. 13 ff. (against Reitzenstein, *Zwei religionsgeschichtliche Fragen*, Strassburg, 1901, according to whom Israel borrowed circumcision from the priestly aristocracy of Egypt, whereas Gunkel holds correctly that *all* Egyptians were circumcised).

rescues him from the attack of Jahweh by circumcising her son with a (sharp) stone (cf. also the stone knives of Jos 5[3], a proof of the high antiquity of the practice), and touching the *pudenda* of Moses with the severed (and still bleeding) foreskin, while she exclaims, 'Thou art to me a bridegroom of blood.' This can mean only that she transfers the efficacy of the child's circumcision symbolically to the husband, and declares him to be what he ought to have been at marriage, namely a bridegroom consecrated by the blood of circumcision, and thus safe from the anger of the tribal god. Whether, perhaps in very early times, the blood shed in circumcision was employed in any other sacral transaction, is a question that must be left unsettled.

Another account of the origin of circumcision is found in the original text of Jos 5[2ff.], namely v.[2] without the harmonistic additions 'again' and 'the second time,' and vv.[3. 8. 9]. We are told that Joshua circumcised the Israelites with stone knives at the Hill of Foreskins, and that the place was hence called *Gilgal*, *i.e.* 'rolling away' of the reproach which arose from the impurity of the uncircumcised condition, and which called forth the contempt of the Egyptians. As Stade (*ZATW*, 1886, p. 132 ff.) has shown, we have here an etymological legend intended to explain the name Gilgal; in reality the 'Hill of Foreskins' derived its name from the circumstance that there, beside the ancient sanctuary of Gilgal, was the common place of circumcision for the neighbouring (Benjamite) youths, and that their foreskins were buried in that hill.

When, finally, the Priests' Code (Gn 17[10ff.]) makes the introduction of circumcision as a sign of the covenant rest upon a command of God to Abraham, an explanation is thus offered of the circumstance that all Abraham's descendants—the Arabs, Edomites, Moabites, and Ammonites—were circumcised (a condition of things that applied also, it is true, to the Egyptians and the Phœnicians, although not to the Philistines).

**Blood-revenge.**—That this custom, which is assumed in Gn 4[14. 23ff.] as already existing amongst the earliest generations of men, actually took its rise in the pre-Mosaic period, is proved by its wide diffusion also among the heathen Semites and elsewhere. The originally religious character of the practice is supported, apart from other considerations, by the extraordinary tenacity with which it maintained itself—a tenacity which would be scarcely conceivable without religious motives. It is true that the precise bond of connexion is not now discoverable. In view of the above-discussed narrative, 2 S 21[1ff.] (cf. esp. v.[9] 'before Jahweh'), it would appear as if the putting of the murderer to death was originally regarded as a sacrifice by which the anger of the tribal god was appeased. According to the earliest notions, this anger is due less to moral causes (as came afterwards to be the established view, cf. *e.g.* Gn 9[6]) than to the damage sustained by the god through the loss of a life belonging to him; and, as the members of the tribe, in the first instance the family, are responsible for preserving the lives that are the property of the god, blood-guiltiness attaches to them until the guilt is atoned for by the death of the murderer. The original absence of an ethical viewpoint is evident from the simple fact that no distinction is made between murder and unintentional manslaughter; even in Dt 4[41ff.] (a probable addition by P) and Nu 35[22ff.] the right of blood-revenge in the latter case is still ideally recognized, although care is taken to make this right ineffective by providing an asylum for the manslayer in one of the Cities of Refuge. Jahwism was thus able to give a milder form to this deeply-rooted custom, but not to abolish it entirely. From the narrative of 2 S 14[6ff.] (which is fictitious, indeed, but no doubt reflects the conditions of real life), where 'the whole family' demands that the fratricide be given up, we learn that occasionally the execution of blood-revenge might be prevented by the intervention of the king. At the same time, the language of the woman of Tekoa (v.[9]) contains the suggestion that by such intervention the king might bring guilt upon himself. Here, again, we see the mechanical way in which the matter was viewed by primitive rigid custom.

*Summary.*—Looking back now on the results which we have reached by examination of the pre-Mosaic period of the religion of Israel, we have been able in not a few instances to point to phenomena which contain the germ of similar appearances on the soil of Jahwism, and which are of the utmost importance for the understanding of the latter.

In the first place, as to the *notion of God* which prevailed in that period, it is only in a very restricted sense that we can speak of such a notion at all. The principal constituent of the yet rudimentary religious sense was fear of the constantly threatening but always incalculable influence of demonic powers. These powers are of very varied kinds, and it would be vain to try to reduce them to any system, or to assume that any reflexions regarding their nature and treatment passed through the minds of men in the state of nature that then prevailed. Men believed in them upon the ground of custom inherited from birth, and acted towards them according to the ancient sacred usage followed by all members of the family and the tribe. These 'demons' are partly spirits of the dead, and, above all, the spirits of the nearest kin of the family. Besides measures adopted to keep them off or to avert injury at their hands, there were acts prompted by dutiful affection towards them, but we have no perfectly clear traces that Animism in the narrower sense had already developed into Ancestor Worship.—A very important rôle is played, again, by all the local *numina* (*'ēlîm*), whose presence appears as attached to sacred trees, stones, and springs. They are not identical with the latter in such a sense that we could speak here of a deification of nature, but they are locally so inseparable from these objects that they can be found and worshipped only at the particular spots in question.—This 'Polydemonism' advances a stage when such a *numen loci* comes to be regarded as the tutelary god of a family or clan, or even of a whole tribe. In place of simple gifts of homage or for propitiation, rites are now introduced whose object is to witness or to establish a close connexion, nay a blood relationship, with the Deity. Even if *Totemism* cannot be proved to have once prevailed among the tribes of Israel, yet we certainly meet with a conception of sacrifice which regards sacramental communion between the Deity and the offerer as the principal feature—a communion which is established by their jointly partaking of the sacrificial blood (afterwards by the god receiving the blood and the fat, while the offerer has the flesh for his portion).

As to the manifold other rites and usages (mourning customs, the *ḥērem* and other warlike practices, human sacrifice, circumcision, celebration of festivals), the original motive has not always been discoverable with certainty; but in most instances the connexion with Animism or some other form of belief in demons is clear enough.

iii. *Moral Conditions.*—Not without interest, finally, is the question, What were the *moral con-*

*ditions* which Moses found amongst the Israelitish tribes of his time? It was long the fashion (especially as the result of Schiller's essay on 'Die Sendung Mose's') to represent the contemporaries of Moses as utterly uncivilized and at the same time—upon the ground of an Egyptian narrative handed down by Josephus (*c. Apion.* i. 26)—as a people quite permeated with leprosy. All the brighter was the halo of glory about the name of Moses, who was believed to have so quickly transformed this half-brutalized horde into a religious community that stood so high, both intellectually and morally. As a matter of fact, however, the moral conditions in Israel must have been quite the same as we still find existing among the genuine Bedawîn at the present day. There is no such thing as acting upon conscious moral principles; and hence there is no thought of *morality* properly so called, but *custom* exercises a powerful influence, which no one can disregard with impunity. 'No such thing is wont to be done in Israel' (2 S 13[12], cf. also Gn 20[9] 29[26] 34[7]),—this is the strongest condemnation of an act of wrong-doing. Custom allows even a married man the freest intercourse with concubines and female slaves, but it guards most strictly the honour of the virgin and the married woman; custom demands, unconditionally, the execution of blood-revenge, but (at least for a time) subordinates even this duty to the sacredness of a guest's rights; custom requires honesty and uprightness towards one's fellow-tribesmen, but has no scruple about allowing deceit and cheating to be practised on a stranger.—As in social life, so also in matters of cultus it is custom that is the ruling factor. Fear to violate custom, fear of the consequences of such violation—in particular, dread of ceremonial uncleanness,—all this is deeply ingrained; but of 'sin,' in the moral sense attached by us to the term, it is impossible to speak.

The condition of things above described was not all at once changed by the proclamation of Jahwism. The force of custom asserted itself even in retaining practices which could never be reconciled with any true morality, just as Islam has succeeded only to a very limited extent in transforming the character of the genuine Bedawîn. Nevertheless, it will be found that, at the very commencement of the religion of Israel, the fruitful germs must have been sown from which—although only very gradually, and at first only among a few—conscious morality sprang up. Without such a germinating power Israel's triumph over the undoubtedly superior culture of the Canaanites would be inconceivable.

## II. Founding of the Religion of Israel (Jahwism) by Moses at Sinai.

Regarding the work of Moses, and especially regarding the extent and content of the laws promulgated by him, we have very varied accounts in the different sources of the Pentateuch. But there are certain points which they all take for granted as firmly established by tradition: namely, that Moses, of the tribe of Levi, was the first to proclaim Jahweh as the God of the *whole* people of Israel, and as their Deliverer from the bondage of Egypt; that at Sinai he brought about the conclusion of a 'covenant' (see below) between Jahweh and Israel; that he at least laid the foundation of the judicial and ceremonial ordinances in Israel, and that he left behind him more or less copious notes on all this.

The supposition that the Pentateuch still contains passages from Moses' own hand is not to be unconditionally set aside. But its scientific proof is now absolutely impossible. Hence the only question can be, Is the correctness of the above propositions, which we noted as fixed elements of tradition, demonstrable by backward inferences from later historical facts? Our answer is that to a large extent—all hypercriticism notwithstanding—this proof is possible, and that especially in regard to the main points. Amongst the latter we include—

i. *The person of Moses as the founder of the Jahweh religion.*—1. All attempts to relegate the person of Moses to the realm of myth have quite properly been abandoned. It is another question how far the traditions concerning him rest on pure legend. As points that are quite beyond suspicion may be noted: his descent from the tribe of Levi; his name *Mosheh* (prob. = Egyp. *mesu* 'son,' possibly combined originally with the name of a god); his flight to Sinai on account of a homicide, and his marriage with a Midianite priest's daughter, Ẓipporah, who became the mother of two sons; his return to Egypt, and deliverance of the Israelite serfs from Pharaoh; further, his strife with his brother Aaron (whose historicity has been denied on insufficient grounds) and his sister Miriam on account of a Cushite woman; and, finally, his prolonged sojourn in Ḳadesh, and his death on the east side of Jordan. All these data are derived from the early sources, and their invention is either inconceivable or at least extremely improbable. On the other hand, the legend of his birth and exposure may have been woven about the (linguistically impossible) interpretation of his name in Ex 2[10]; the names of his parents, Amram and Jochebed, are first known to the Priests' Code. The assumption that he was 'instructed in all the wisdom of the Egyptians' (Ac 7[22]) is connected, of course, with his being brought up by Pharaoh's daughter, but it finds no real support in Ex 2[10]. In any case there is no justification for finding in Moses' acquaintance with Egyptian mysteries the explanation not only of his intellectual superiority to his fellow-countrymen, but even of the Divine name *Jahweh* and of certain institutions (for example, the sacred Ark) connected with worship, if not, indeed, of the whole activity of Moses as a founder of religion.* Such borrowing on his part is not only incapable of proof, it is extremely improbable; for it is not the way of one ancient people to adopt the gods of another, or even elements of their cultus, at a time when it sees this other people and its gods overcome by another god. Whether Moses was moved to his work by other influences, such as that of the Ḳenites about Mt. Sinai, will have to be afterwards considered. The ancient tradition of Israel knows of nothing except that he was directly called by Jahweh at Sinai, and, in spite of his refusal at first, sent to deliver his people. The work of Moses is thus traced to Divine revelation. *How* this produced its effect on the mind of Moses, remains a secret to us as much as in all similar cases when God reveals Himself to His chosen instruments. But the *fact* is not on that account any the less certain to us, for it is witnessed to by its results. However many of the features of that Pandemonism which was common to the Semites may have continued to adhere to the religion of Israel after the time of Moses, it exhibits, even as early as the period of the Judges, features which raise it far above the popular religions of the neighbouring peoples, and which can be explained only as due to the continued influence of a highly endowed spiritual personality.

* So esp. Schiller in his brilliant essay, 'Die Sendung Mose's' (first published in Heft 10 of *Thalia*). We leave quite out of account the fables cited by Josephus (*c. Apion.* i. 26, 28) from Manetho's *Egyptiaca* about the identity of Moses with the priest Osarsiph of Heliopolis.

It is true that elsewhere we frequently meet in history with similar instances where a far-reaching influence is very palpable, and yet we do not feel compelled on that account to postulate a special Divine revelation. But in the case of Moses it is the peculiar character of the new ideas promulgated by him that forbids us to derive these from his own reflexions or to ascribe them to shrewd calculations for selfish ends. Upon the foundation laid by him there has arisen in the course of three thousand years the building which includes also the Christian nations. But the laying of a foundation like this is beyond a man's power; the capacity must have been given him by God. And on this very account the importance of the personality of Moses can hardly be exaggerated. Such is the conviction of the Deuteronomistic author of Dt 34[10] when he remarks: 'There hath not arisen a prophet since in Israel like unto Moses, whom the LORD knew face to face.'

2. It is true, indeed, that it has been felt to be very surprising that in the Old Testament, and especially in the Prophets, the references to Moses are so few in number and so late in date. Apart from the interpolation added in Hos 12[14 (13)] ('By a prophet the LORD brought Israel up out of Egypt, and by a prophet was he preserved'), we find allusions to Moses and Aaron as the deliverers of the people in Mic 6[4] (along with Miriam; although, it is true, the attributing of this passage to Micah is strongly contested), 1 S 12[6. 8] (in a Deuteronomistic address), Ps 105[26] 106[16]. Moses alone as leader of the people is referred to in Is 63[12], Ps 106[32]; the power of his intercession with God is mentioned in Ps 106[23] and Jer 15[1]. The last-cited passage shows clearly in what light the importance of Moses appeared even to a Jeremiah, and that it is thus evidently a mere accident that he is not more frequently mentioned elsewhere.

It might appear even more strange that Moses as *the founder of a religion* appears to be practically unknown to the Prophets and the Psalms (apart from Ps 99[6], where Moses and Aaron are called 'priests,' and 103[7]). But over against this must be set the fact that throughout the OT *all* the various legislations (except, of course, that contained in the vision of Ezekiel, chs. 40–48) are said to have been introduced, and in part even written down, by him. This would be quite unintelligible unless there had been an indelible recollection which demanded his recognition as the real author of religious traditions and institutions, so that later codifications could obtain authority only if they were carried back to his weighty name. If any one feels compelled to call this last course of procedure by the name of *forgery* (and therefore to repudiate it with indignation), he is radically mistaken as to the notions that prevailed in ancient Israel with respect to literary property. So far from being looked upon as forgery, it was regarded as a sacred duty to give as Moses' own words anything that had to be promulgated for the good of the people in continuation of his work and in the sense and spirit of his laws (for instance, and very specially, the legislation of Deuteronomy). The idea of forgery, however natural it may be to *us*, is quite out of the question here.

ii. *JAHWEH PROCLAIMED BY MOSES AS THE GOD OF ISRAEL.** — 1. All the sources of the Pentateuch are at one in pointing out as the fundamental act of Moses his proclamation of Jahweh as the God of Israel, *i.e.* as the God who means certainly to deliver Israel from the slavery of Egypt, and who on that account has sole claim to the worship and obedience of this people. But this proclamation did not imply that Jahweh is to be regarded as the only God that has any real existence; such 'absolute monotheism' was undoubtedly as yet far below the horizon even of Moses as well as of all his contemporaries. Jahweh is one God among many, although mightier and more terrible than the rest. Upon the whole, however, there is not much consideration of what is His relation to other gods. The main thing from the very first is to know no other god besides Him, to worship none but this One whose name is Jahweh. The demand of Moses is thus not for real or absolute monotheism, but for '*henotheism*,' *i.e.* the recognition of only *one* God, or '*monolatry*,' the worship of one alone. But the more distinctly 'Jahweh' makes its appearance as a personal name (quite like 'Zeus,' 'Poseidon,' etc.), the more naturally does the question arise, Whence did Moses derive this name and proclaim it as that of Israel's God?*

2. The most natural course is to seek to explain the name 'Jahweh' (יהוה) from itself, that is, from the etymology underlying the form of the word. This seems all the more proper, because in at least one of the sources of the Pentateuch (E) we meet with an actual interpretation of the name (Ex 3[13ff.]). When Moses asks what name he is to give to the people as that of his Divine sender, God replies: '(Say) the I AM THAT I AM (or, again, the 'I AM') hath sent me unto you.' Here 'Jahweh' is plainly understood as the 3rd pers. sing. Imperf. of the old verb *hāwāh* 'to be.' But in Hebrew the Imperfect is the mood of continuance as well as of ever renewed activity. Upon this interpretation 'Jahweh' denotes at once the *Eternal* (the form in which modern Jews reproduce the name) and the One who ever remains the same, the *Constant*.

Against this explanation, however, the strongest objections have been brought. From the time of Ewald it has been set down as a mere attempt at an artificial interpretation of an ancient name whose meaning had been long forgotten. But the root-idea of this name, we are told, just because it is so ancient, must have been a *material* one, and cannot have been derived from abstract reflexion and metaphysical speculation. But this last objection, while it would apply to explanations which make *Jahweh*='the truly Existing' or 'the absolute Being,' etc., do not apply (or at least not to the same extent) to the simple view of the name as that of the Eternal and Constant,

* Cf. Hunnius, *Natur und Charakter Jahwehs nach den vordeuteronomischen Quellen der Bücher Genesis-Könige*, Strassburg, 1902.

* We take it for granted that our readers are aware that the form 'Jehovah,' which has the appearance of being handed down by tradition in the OT, is based upon a Christian misunderstanding, the vowels of the word *'Ădōnai* 'Lord' being taken (first in the year A.D. 1518) to be the real vowels of the Divine name, whereas they were attached by the Jews to the consonants *JHWH* (which are alone original) in order to warn the reader to avoid the actual pronunciation of the word and to substitute *'Ădōnai* for it. This treatment of the name 'Jahweh' as 'unutterable' sprang from an exaggerated dread of transgressing the commandment in Ex 20[7]. The traces of this aversion to the utterance of the name can be carried back to about B.C. 300, although its utterance was for long after that regarded as allowable in the sacred domain, *e.g.* in the mouth of priests pronouncing the benediction. Neither in the Septuagint (whether in the Canonical or in the Apocryphal books) nor in the whole of the NT is the name 'Jahweh' once used; it is always ὁ Κύριος 'the Lord.'

Of the four possible ways of pronouncing the consonants *JHWH* (the so-called Tetragrammaton), namely, *Jahweh* or *Jahăweh*, *Jahwāh*, or *Jahăwāh*, the form *Jahweh* has rightly come to be prevailingly accepted. The following considerations tell in its favour: (1) that, according to Epiphanius (*Hær.* I. iii. 20), a Jewish-Christian sect (according to Theodoret [*Quæst. 15 in Ex.*], the Samaritans) pronounced the name 'Ιαβέ; (2) that in Jewish-Samaritan poems the end-vowel of *JHWH* rhymes with *é*, not *ā*; (3) that the shortening of the Divine name to *Jĕhō* [*Jō*] and *Jāhū* in personal names like *Jĕhōnāthan* [*Jonathan*] and *Jĕshă'jāhū* [*Isaiah*] are linguistically explicable only by assuming as the basal form *Jahweh*. See, further, art. JEHOVAH in vol. ii.

the God whose living activity is always in exercise. Besides, the rejection of the interpretation offered in Ex $3^{15}$ involves the conclusion that even the early sources of the Pentateuch were in error as to the true meaning of the most important and most sacred Divine name in Israel. But can it be supposed that at the time of E (*c.* 750 B.C.) the living apprehension of the genius of the Hebrew language was no longer adequate to interpret correctly a name like 'Jahweh'? We cannot help thinking that this question has been answered in the affirmative far too hastily by those who follow the prevailing current of opinion on this subject. And we are only strengthened in our conviction when we note the extremely varied interpretations which have been proposed as substitutes for that adopted in Ex $3^{15}$.* These fall into two categories according as they start likewise from the verb *hāwāh* in the sense of 'to be,' or assume another meaning for this verb.

(*a*) The first of these two schools of interpreters takes 'Jahweh' to be the Imperfect of the Hiphil or Causative conjugation, and thus obtains the meaning 'He who causes to be,' 'the Creator.' But, apart from the circumstance that early Semitic languages want the Causative of the verb *hāwāh*, the idea of 'the Creator' is precisely what is quite foreign to the name 'Jahweh' as we find it employed. No doubt, in later times, after the triumph of absolute monotheism, Jahweh is naturally brought into connexion with the work of creation. But at first He has to do almost exclusively with the deeds and fortunes of the people of Israel. This flows from His nature as a national God, and it is plain that it was in this latter capacity and not as the Creator that Moses at first proclaimed Him.—Absolutely to be rejected is the theory of an interchange of sound between *hāyāh* (*hāwāh*) and *ḥāyāh* 'to live,' so that *Jahweh* (here again Causative) would be = 'He who gives life,' 'He who produces true (spiritual) life.' However attractive this interpretation may be for its contents, it is shattered by the laws of the interchange of sound. These laws forbid an exchange between *h* and *ḥ* at the *beginning* of a word.

(*b*) Among the explanations which start from a different meaning of the root *hāwāh*, special favour has been accorded to that which finds it in *hāwāh* 'to fall' (so esp. de Lagarde and Stade). Upon this view *Jahweh* may be explained either as = 'the falling One'; *i.e.* the name originally stood for a meteoric stone that fell from heaven and was hence the object of worship (a so-called βαιτύλιον; see below, in the discussion of the sacred Ark, p. 628); or, again Causative, as = 'He who fells *or* causes to fall (by lightning),' *i.e.* as the storm-God. This last explanation would seem to be favoured at least by a number of features which from the first appear to be bound up with the representation of Jahweh. It is, above all, as a God of the desert that Jahweh appears, for Moses is in the first instance to lead the people into the wilderness, there to serve God by offering sacrifice (Ex $3^{18}$ $5^{3}$ *et al.*). But it is in the desert that the most imposing effects are produced by storm; hence the natural abode of the storm-God is a desert range like Sinai with frequent lightning playing about its peaks. It may be added that thunder and lightning and storm-clouds play a prominent part not only at Jahweh's appearances in connexion with the giving of the Law at Sinai (Ex $19^{16\text{-}19}$ $20^{18}$ *et al.*), but upon the occasion of almost all the later theophanies, whether these present themselves as historical events (*e.g.* Jg $5^{4\text{f.}}$, 1 K $19^{11\text{ff.}}$), or as prophetic visions (*e.g.* Is $30^{27\text{f.}}$, Mic $1^{3\text{f.}}$, Nah $1^{3\text{ff.}}$, Hab $3^{3\text{ff.}}$), or merely as poetical descriptions (Ps $18^{8\text{ff.}}$ $77^{18\text{ff.}}$ $97^{2\text{ff.}}$). But these arguments are not sufficient to prove that Jahweh was originally thought of as the storm-God *only*. In all ages thunder and lightning have been regarded as the special accompaniments and principal marks of Divine majesty and glory, and nothing is more natural than that these should have been associated also with the God of Israel, especially upon occasions when He appeared for extraordinary ends, whether to fight with and chastise His people's enemies, or solemnly to conclude a covenant with the people themselves.

Upon the whole, then, the above attempts to find another explanation of the name 'Jahweh' than that offered in Ex $3^{15}$ must be regarded as doubtful. And the same remark also applies, in the judgment of the present writer, to the explanation of Wellhausen, who falls back upon the onomatopoetic root *hāwāh* 'to breathe,' and thus makes *Jahweh* = 'the Breather' (which comes again in the end to the same thing as the storm-God).

3. But, even if the attempt to arrive by the way of etymology at the original conception underlying the name 'Jahweh' must be abandoned, there may be another possibility, namely, to assign the *home* of the God proclaimed by Moses. Moses fled from Egypt to Sinai, where he became son-in-law to the *priest* of a Midianite (according to another, more specialized, tradition, a Ḳenite) tribe. There the God who dwelt enthroned on Sinai appeared to him and called him to be His instrument. Thither he led the rescued tribes of Israel, and there the will of the God of Sinai was solemnly announced to them and the covenant with Him concluded. What does all this mean, it is asked, but that Moses made acquaintance at Sinai with Jahweh, the god of the Ḳenites, and proclaimed him thenceforward as the God of Israel? As a matter of fact, Jahweh would thus have been a foreign god so far as Israel was concerned, and it is nothing but a naïve anachronism when the Jahwistic source employs the name 'Jahweh' even in its narrative of the Creation (Gn $2^{4\text{ff.}}$), and represents the worship of God under this name as beginning as early as the time of Enosh, the grandson of Adam.

This 'Ḳenite hypothesis,' since the example was set by Stade, has found favour with many, and it cannot be denied that it contains much that is worthy of notice. It appears to be supported, above all, by the circumstance that Sinai (evidently identical with the Ḥoreb of other sources)* is regarded as the proper dwelling-place of Jahweh not only at the time of the Exodus, but till far into the monarchical period (cf. Jg $5^{5}$, and the passages dependent upon it, namely Dt $33^{2\text{f.}}$, Hab $3^{3}$, Ps $68^{9\,(8)}$; and esp. 1 K $19^{8}$, where Elijah journeys to Ḥoreb to obtain an oracle from his God). But this was possible only on the ground of a general conviction of the people that He was enthroned there prior to the call of Moses. Then, again, very great stress is laid upon the narrative of Ex 18,† which is interpreted as describing the admittance of Israel to the Jahweh cult of the Ḳenites. Jethro rejoices (v.$^{9\text{ff.}}$) in the evidences of power displayed by *his* god, Jahweh, on behalf of Israel; he finds an evidence therein that this god of his is mightier than all gods;

* We purposely leave out of account the latest attempts to discover the name 'Jahweh' (as presumably introduced into Babylonia by Canaanites) in very ancient cuneiform texts (so, *e.g.*, Frdr. Delitzsch in his much discussed lecture *Babel und Bibel*, Leipzig, 1902, p. 46 f.), because the reading as well as the interpretation of the names in question still form the subject of controversy amongst Assyriologists.

* We here leave out of account, of course, the controversy as to whether in the *oldest* tradition Sinai and Ḥoreb were already identified, as well as the question where the Sinai or Horeb of our present narratives is to be found. See art. SINAI in vol. iv.

† So esp. Budde, *Die Religion des Volkes Israel*, Giessen, 1900, p. 17 ff.

whereupon he organizes a sacrificial meal in honour of him, and admits Aaron and all the nobles of Israel to take part in it. In other words, he, the Ḳenite priest, opens for them at Sinai, the dwelling-place of his god, an approach to the cult of the latter. And this is the very reason why the religion of Israel became, according to Budde,* an ethical one, because it was a religion adopted by choice and not a nature religion.

Now we do not mean to deny the *possibility* of such an order of events. Yet there is no lack of weighty considerations of an opposite kind. It is true, indeed, that the argument that Sinai is the proper dwelling-place of Jahweh is not weakened by the circumstance of His presence with the people in Egypt and during the Exodus (as also afterwards in the wilderness), since passing appearances for special ends are not inconsistent with the possession of a fixed abode. But might not Sinai (or Ḥoreb) have been for long the 'mount of God' also to certain Israelitish tribes, as appears to be implied in Ex $4^{27}$? This supposition would be all the more plausible if it is true, as many have recently come to hold, that the whole of the tribes of Israel did not undergo serfdom in Egypt, but that part of them led the life of nomads in the neighbourhood of Sinai, and had long continued to worship the god that was established there. The work of Moses would thus have consisted in proclaiming and securing recognition for the special god of certain tribes as the God of the whole nation. These are, indeed, mere conjectures, but they tally with a circumstance which appears to us to be far too readily ignored by the defenders of the Ḳenite hypothesis: this, namely, that even in the oldest sources of the Pentateuch it is always implied that Jahweh was not proclaimed to Israel as an absolutely new and therefore unknown god.

We have already remarked that the Jahwist uses the name 'Jahweh' from the first, and regards it as known and honoured by the ancestors of Moses and his contemporaries. On the other hand, E (Ex $3^{13ff.}$) and P ($6^{2ff.}$) assume that it was first revealed to Moses and through him to the people. At the same time it is not at all the idea of these sources that the God Himself was unknown to the people. We are not thinking of the frequent designation of Jahweh as the God of Abraham, Isaac, and Jacob (Ex $3^{6.\ 15f.}$ $4^{5}$), for such allusions to the God of the patriarchs might quite conceivably have been in every instance inserted in order afterwards to give to the Canaanite places of worship, supposed to have been taken over from the patriarchs, a legitimate standing as sanctuaries of the same God. But even the assumption of interpolation of this kind would not destroy the fact that even the early sources of the Pentateuch see in Jahweh the God of the ancestors of Israel. At the very first mention of Him (Ex $3^{6}$) He is called 'the God of thy (Moses') father'; He has seen the oppression of *His people* in Egypt, and means now to deliver them (v.$^{7ff.}$); face to face with Pharaoh the appeal of Moses is to be to 'the God of the Hebrews' (v.$^{18}$, cf. also $5^{3}$ $7^{16}$ $9^{1.\ 13}$ $10^{3}$). Even if the term 'Hebrews' here be an anachronism, in none of the passages cited is it implied that Jahweh first became 'the God of the Hebrews' after the call of Moses; on the contrary, He has long held this position. If, all the same, Moses is regarded as the *founder* of the Jahweh religion, this can be understood only in the sense that the god of one or more tribes, or perhaps the god of one particular family, was proclaimed by him as the God of the whole body. Jahweh would thus not have been an absolutely strange and new god, but one whose power and help had already been experienced by part of the confederated tribes; whereas, on the other hand, the proclamation of the yet untried god of the Ḳenites could hardly have met with such rapid acceptance. Beyond this we can fall back only upon conjectures. It will always remain the most plausible supposition that Jahweh had a connexion with Moses' own tribe, the tribe of Levi. This hypothesis has at least as good a claim as that which makes Him the god of the Rachel-tribes.

* *Op. cit.* p. 31.

As to the argument in support of the Ḳenite hypothesis drawn from Ex 18, we are at one with its defenders in holding that there we have a testimony to the community of worship of the Israelites and the Ḳenites. But this is quite different from 'the admittance of the Israelites to the Jahweh cult of the Ḳenites' (see above, p. $626^{b}$ f.). The community of worship of Israel and the Ḳenites was a fact; Ex 18 recounts its historical origin; but the question of the origin of Jahwism among the two peoples is not considered. The circumstance that it is Jethro who organizes the sacrificial meal is sufficiently accounted for by his residence on the spot, which imposes upon him the duty of showing hospitality to the strangers.

4. The beliefs cherished by Moses and his contemporaries regarding the mental and moral character of Jahweh will form the subject of discussion presently (see p. 629 ff.). But we must here say a word about the conceptions of His *bodily* personality. For there are quite a number of the strongest testimonies which place it beyond doubt that a bodily—and indeed a *human*—form was then and for centuries afterwards attributed to Him; and, even if in Ex $20^{4}$ and Dt $5^{8}$ the making of any figure representing Jahweh was forbidden, this would not amount to an absolute denial that He possessed the bodily form of a man. But in any case the making of images of Jahweh was regarded as unobjectionable till about the 8th cent. B.C., although in all probability a distinction was drawn between the images carved in wood and stone, which had come down from very early times, and molten images of metal. The latter were undoubtedly of Canaanitish origin, and hence were prohibited in the worship of Jahweh (Ex $34^{17}$; this certainly ancient passage has nothing to say against carved images).* And, although narratives like Gn $3^{8f.}$ and the older form of Gn 18 had not their origin till the settlement in Canaan, the human form of Jahweh is assumed by them as so much a matter of course that it is impossible to see here anything but the reflexion of a very widely diffused notion. Again, the numerous ascriptions of human organs (eyes, ears, nose, hands, feet, etc.) to Jahweh may have been in the latest times regarded as conscious anthropomorphisms, *i.e.* shifts to which language is reduced when it would describe the action of a purely spiritual personality; but at first they were certainly meant as the literal expression of the prevailing conception of the *bodily* personality of Jahweh.†

5. It is quite true that no notice has been preserved in the early sources of the Pentateuch of images of Jahweh in human form in the time of Moses; the mention even of the *ephod* (Jg $8^{26f.}$

* Ed. König in his art. 'Die Bildlosigkeit des legitimen Jahwehcultus' (*Ztschr. f. kirchl. Wissenschaft und kirchl. Leben*, 1886, Heft 5, 6; also publ. separately under the title *Beiträge zum positiven Aufbau der Religionsgeschichte Israels*, i., Leipzig, 1886) denies that images of Jahweh were at any period allowed in His legitimate worship; but this is opposed to facts, as has been shown above and will be further demonstrated presently.

† It is another question whether the *theologumenon* of the 'Angel of Jahweh' as a passing appearance of Jahweh is to be placed so early as the Mosaic period. This and other forms of manifestation of Jahweh (face, name, glory) will be discussed by us in connexion with the framework of Jahwism as we find it at the close of the time of the Judges and the commencement of the monarchical period. See p. 638 ff.

$17^{4f.}$ $18^{14. 17f. 20}$, 1 S $21^{9}$ etc.), which is most probably to be regarded as an image of Jahweh, does not occur till the following period. On the other hand, in 2 K $18^{4}$ there is the strange piece of information that Ḥezeḳiah broke in pieces a brazen serpent which was made by Moses, and to which up till then incense had been burnt by the Israelites, who called it *Nĕḥushtān* (*i.e.* 'the brazen one'). The language plainly implies the paying of Divine honours in the form of sacrifice. Was the *Nĕḥushtān*, then, an image of Jahweh? This is scarcely conceivable, and finds no analogy elsewhere. If, on the other hand, it represented some demon, how could its construction have been traced back to Moses, and how could it have received Divine worship down to the time of Ḥezekiah? The enigma is not solved by pointing to Nu $21^{8f.}$, for there can be little doubt that in this passage we have simply a later attempt to account for (and justify) the presence of the well-known brazen serpent in Jerusalem. It is most probable that the deriving of this idol from Moses is to be set down to some misunderstanding of the popular belief. See, further, art. NEHUSHTAN in vol. iii.

6. There are, however, the clearest traces of another visible representation of Jahweh, which goes back to the time of Moses—in connexion with the history of **the sacred Ark.** The ancient and original designation of this object is 'the Ark of Jahweh' or 'the Ark of God.' The Deuteronomistic writers are the first who know of the Ark as the receptacle of the two stone tables of the Law which Moses received from God at Ḥoreb; and on this account they call it 'the Ark with the Law of Jahweh' (Dt $10^{1ff.}$ $31^{26}$, 1 K $8^{9}$).* Wherever this designation occurs in ancient narratives (*e.g.* 1 S $4^{3-5}$, but not vv.$^{11. 17. 19. 22}$), *bĕrîth* is a later addition by Deuteronomistic hands; it is still unknown to the LXX in the passages cited.

Seeing that both the early sources of the Pentateuch in their account of the wilderness journeyings give prominence to the Ark as a most sacred object, they must have somewhere given an account of its origin. And indeed this narrative, which has now (on account of its proximity to the entirely different account given by P in Ex $25^{10ff.}$) dropped out, must have stood before Ex $33^{7ff.}$. Here we are told all at once about *the* tent which Moses regularly pitched before the camp and called 'the Tent of Meeting.' This is the same name as is applied (in a different sense, indeed) by the Priests' Code to the tent in which the sacred Ark was lodged. Prior to Ex $33^{7}$, then, it must have been told how Moses used the ornaments stripped off by the people at Ḥoreb (v.$^{6}$) for the construction of the Ark and the tent that sheltered it, the Ark (as must be inferred from v.$^{5}$) being intended as a substitute for the personal presence of Jahweh, which would have been fatal to so stiff-necked a people.

How this substitute for Jahweh's own presence is to be understood comes out unmistakably in two very ancient verses preserved in Nu $10^{35f.}$ (prob. J). There we read: 'When the ark [which, according to v.$^{33}$, went before the people to search out a camping-place for them] set forward, Moses said—

> Rise up, Jahweh, and let thine enemies be scattered;
> And let thine adversaries flee before thee!

And when it rested, he said—

> Return, Jahweh, to the myriads of the thousands of Israel!'

Jahweh and the Ark, that is to say, appear here as practically identical. Not as though this wooden chest represented Jahweh. But His presence appeared inseparably connected with the Ark; wherever it was seen there Jahweh was, and showed Himself active. This notion has frequent and express testimony borne to it down to the time of Solomon. In Nu $14^{42ff.}$ Israel's defeat by the Amalekites is explained by the absence of the Ark. According to 1 S $3^{3}$ the youthful Samuel slept in the temple of Jahweh at Shiloh where the Ark of God was, and this is used to account for the revelation given him by Jahweh at night. When the sons of Eli bring the Ark of Jahweh to the camp, 'that it may come among us and save us out of the hands of our enemies' (1 S $4^{3}$), the Philistines —quite in the spirit of the Hebrew narrator— exclaim, 'God is come into their camp . . . Who will deliver us out of the hand of this mighty God?' etc. (v.$^{7f.}$). With the Ark the 'glory,' *i.e.* the presence of Jahweh, is departed from Israel (v.$^{22}$). And, even when the Ark is captured, the Dagon of the Philistines falls upon his face before Jahweh the more powerful God present in it, and tumbles down as if dead when he is set up in his place again (1 S $5^{1ff.}$). The Ark of Jahweh brings pestilence upon the other cities of the Philistines (v.$^{9ff.}$) Nay, even the Israelites of Beth-shemesh look with fatal results upon the Ark when it is sent back by the Philistines ($6^{19f.}$), so that the survivors exclaim, 'Who is able to stand before Jahweh, this exalted God?' And when David went to bring up to Jerusalem 'the ark of God which is called by the name of Jahweh of hosts' (2 S $6^{1ff.}$), we read that he and all the house of Israel danced 'before Jahweh' (v.$^{5}$, cf. also vv.$^{14. 16. 21}$), but that Uzzah was struck dead on the spot by Jahweh for having, with the best of intentions, laid hold of the swaying Ark to steady it (v.$^{6}$).

It need hardly be remarked that all the above statements would be meaningless if the Ark had been simply the receptacle of the tables of the Law, and not a symbol and pledge of the presence of Jahweh. With all the more force does the question urge itself upon us, What can account for so high a place being assigned to the Ark? Unfortunately, we are here again thrown back upon mere conjectures. The most probable explanation, however, appears to be that the Ark of Israel, like the sacred arks of other religions,* contained stones—in point of fact, one or more meteoric stones (βαιτύλια); but it can hardly be supposed to have had in it a stone image of the Deity.† But,

* The usual translation 'Ark of the Covenant' fails to recognize that *bĕrîth* here cannot mean 'covenant,' but only the *Law* on which the covenant was based. Instead of *bĕrîth* the Priests' Code uses *'ēdûth* 'testimony' in the same sense (Ex $25^{16f.}$ and often).

* Cf. Schwally, *Semit. Kriegsaltertümer*, i. p. 9 ff.

† From the copious recent literature on the Ark we select the following as deserving of special notice: F. Seyring, 'Der alttest. Sprachgebrauch in betreff des Namens der sogen. "Bundeslade"' (*ZATW* xi. [1891] 114 ff.); L. Couard, 'Die religiös-nationale Bedeutung der Lade Jahwes (*ib.* xii. [1892] 53 ff.). According to the latter, the Ark contained stone fetishes in which Jahweh was believed to be present, whence the Ark and its contents were in the earliest times identified with Jahweh Himself. Kraetzschmar, again (*Die Bundesvorstellung im AT*, Marburg, 1896, p. 208 ff.), thinks that the Ark most likely contained the stones used in forming the alliance of the Rachel-tribes; while Budde ('Bücher Sam.' [in *Kurzer Hdcom.*] p. 31) makes these stones to have been taken from Sinai as a representation of this abode of Jahweh. W. Reichel (*Ueber vorhellenische Götterculte*, Vienna, 1897, p. 23 ff.) explains the Ark as a portable throne of Jahweh—a view opposed by Budde (*Expository Times*, ix. [1898] 398 f.) but strongly reaffirmed by Meinhold (*Die Lade Jahwehs*, Tübingen and Leipzig, 1900; cf. also the 'Nachtrag' to this in *SK*, 1901, p. 593 ff.). Meinhold holds that the Ark was originally the moving rocky throne of the god enthroned on Sinai, and that the charge of this one pre-Canaanite common sanctuary of the Hebrews became hereditary in the family of Moses. The view of Meinhold appears to be favoured by the circumstance that once (Jer $3^{17}$) the whole of Jerusalem takes the place of the Ark as the throne of Jahweh; while even the Priests' Code appears (*e.g.* in Nu $7^{89}$) to look upon the lid of the Ark as Jahweh's seat, from which He reveals Himself to Moses. But all this does not refute the argument reasserted by Budde (*ZATW*, 1901, p. 193 ff.), that the Heb. word *'ārōn* means nothing but a *box* or *chest*, and that

again, there are numerous indications that the Ark primarily represented Jahweh as *the war-God*. On the one hand, there is the fact that down to the time of David the Ark (cf. 2 S $7^{2.6}$) was as a rule kept in a tent, the natural place of abode in war [even in the temple at Shiloh it may have stood in a tent, as, according to 2 S $6^{17}$, it did in the citadel of David]; and, on the other hand, the fact that in the historical books it is brought with remarkable frequency into connexion with the name *Jahweh Ẓěbā'ôth*, the designation of the war-God (see the following section, p. 636 f.). Moreover, we have direct evidence of this sense being attributed to the Ark in Nu $10^{35f.}$ (see above, p. $628^{a}$) $14^{42ff.}$ (see above, p. $628^{b}$), Jos $6^{6ff.}$ (where the Ark brings about the downfall of the walls of Jericho), 1 S $4^{3ff.}$ (see above, p. $628^{b}$), 2 S $11^{11}$ (where the Ark has its place in the camp at Rabbath-ammon) $15^{24}$ (where the priests imagine that the presence of the Ark will ensure victory over Absalom).

It cannot be decided with certainty whether the Ark was from the first the sacred shrine of *all* the tribes, or only (so Stade, *Gesch. des Volkes Israel*, i. 458) the war *palladium* of the Josephites or the Josephite tribe of Ephraim [in 1 S 1 ff. we meet with it as giving its character to the tribal sanctuary of Shiloh]. Its original connexion with *all* the tribes is favoured, however, not only by its construction being attributed to Moses—a tradition which it is very difficult to set aside—but by the narrative of 1 S 4, and very specially by the evident importance which David attaches to the introduction of the Ark into his newly captured residence, Jerusalem (2 S 6). Had the Ark been the *palladium* of an alien tribe, would he not have been afraid of giving them the most serious offence by appropriating it? On the other hand, if the Ark was well known to have been the representative of the God of Israel in the 'wars of Jahweh,' it was pre-eminently suited to be established at the residence of the monarch as the symbol of the now closely united tribes.

It may be as well to note here once for all what is necessary regarding the subsequent fortunes of the Ark. After its transference to the dark inner sanctuary of Solomon's temple (1 K $8^{4.6ff.}$) there is no mention of its ever again leaving this place, down to the destruction of the temple in B.C. 586. [In Ps $24^{7ff.}$, then, where the doors of the temple are already addressed as 'primeval gates,' there must be preserved an allusion to the war-God *Jahweh Ẓěbā'ôth*, v.[10], returning in the company of the Ark from a campaign]. That the Ark even in Solomon's temple continued for a long time to be regarded as representing the presence of Jahweh, is shown not only by the ancient verses contained in 1 K $8^{12}$, which can refer only to the place of the Ark in the dark inner sanctuary of the temple, but by the Ark's being placed under the wings of two huge cherub forms (1 K $8^{6f.}$). Here, as elsewhere, the cherubim denote the near presence of Deity. But, as the conception of God came to be increasingly spiritualized in the Prophetic period, it became impossible to hold to the ancient, grossly material view of the Ark. In place of an actual representation of the presence of Jahweh it came to be a mere symbol of His presence. Nay, in the Deuteronomistic statements on the subject we see the Ark almost robbed of any special significance of its own. As the receptacle of the tables of the Law it is only a means to an end, and its place might have been taken equally well by any other vessel; for its only claim to veneration and sanctity rests upon its contents. The question may now be asked, Are we to assume that at some time or other the old stone fetishes, of which people were now ashamed, were really displaced by stone tables with a copy of the Decalogue? This would be conceivable only if we could assume that there was a periodical opening of the Ark: for instance, upon the occasion of a particular festival. But even Dt $31^{26}$ speaks merely of a depositing of the Book of the Law *beside* the Ark. Or, again, do the Deuteronomistic statements involve the recollection that, at any rate, stones were originally kept in the Ark? This is a question we cannot answer.

On the other hand, the closest attention is due to the circumstance that in the theories of the Priests' Code so important a rôle is assigned to the Ark both as a centre of revelation (Ex $25^{22}$, Lv $16^{2}$, Nu $7^{89}$) and in connexion with the process of sacrifice (Lv $16^{14ff.}$), although even according to this source (Ex $25^{16.21}$) the Ark is, properly speaking, nothing more than the receptacle of the 'testimony,' which means the tables of the Law. But, as in so many other instances, even the Priests' Code cannot shake off entirely the old conception of the Ark. It is no longer, indeed, identical with Jahweh, but it is a very holy centre of revelations from Him. This is still indicated by the cherub forms, only that these no longer stand, as in Solomon's temple, on each side of the Ark, but, made of pure gold, are placed (Ex $25^{17ff.}$) on the ends of the lid (the *kappōreth*). Here, according to Lev $16^{14f.}$, the blood of the most important guilt-offerings of the whole year had to be sprinkled in order to bring Jahweh as near as possible.

These statements and requirements of the Priests' Code are all the more surprising, as there can be no doubt that the Ark perished in the destruction of the temple in B.C. 586.* This agrees with the circumstance that Ezekiel, in his sketch of the new order of the theocracy, has no mention of the Ark, and the Holy of Holies of the second temple was, according to unimpeachable Jewish tradition, completely empty. Hence those expressions in the Priests' Code which take the Ark for granted must have emanated from priestly circles which looked upon its restoration as necessary, *but did not succeed in carrying out this aim*. To the eagerness with which at one time the restoration or non-restoration of the Ark was discussed we have an instructive witness in Jer $3^{16}$ (which is a later insertion in the Book of Jeremiah). Here we have the heart's desire of a man of the prophetic spirit; and it is to the effect that, when the exiles are brought home again and tended by shepherds after God's own heart, when Jerusalem has become a place of true worship even for the heathen, there shall be no need of an *outward* sign of the presence of Jahweh, and thus no need even of the Ark.

iii. *THE ESSENTIAL CHARACTER OF JAHWISM AS THE RELIGION OF ISRAEL.*—1. Ever since Josephus† defined the constitution of Israel as a

such a name would not have been given to a *throne*. Even Reichel's further exposition of his hypothesis (in *Theologische Arbeiten aus dem wissenschaftlichen Rheinischen Predigerverein*, Tübingen, 1902, p. 28 ff.) has made no difference on this point. On the other hand, the strict defence of the Deuteronomistic tradition by Lotz (*Die Bundeslade*, Erlangen and Leipzig, 1901 [from the 'Festschrift' for the 80th birthday of the Prince Regent of Bavaria]) is a piece of wasted labour.

* No importance attaches, of course, to the statements of 2 Mac $2^{5ff.}$ about Jeremiah's concealing of the Tabernacle (!), the Ark, and the Altar of Incense in a cave of Mt. Nebo.

† *c. Apion.* ii. 16 [Niese, *Fl. Josephi Opera*, v. p. 75, § 164 f.]: 'Some entrusted the government of the State to a single person, others to a few, others to the whole body of the people; whereas our lawgiver turned his thoughts to none of those methods, but, if we might use a somewhat bold expression, drew up a political constitution in the form of a *theocracy*, assigning the rule and power to God.' The whole manner of expression adopted by Josephus shows that in using the word 'theocracy' he is conscious of having coined a *new* term. See also art. THEOCRACY, above, p. 337.

**'theocracy,'** or 'rule by God,' this term has been repeated over and over, and its use has been extended even to the political and religious system introduced by Moses. As a 'theocracy' the religion founded by him has been represented as distinguished from all others; that is to say, the constitution was so arranged that all the organs of government were without any independent powers, and had simply to announce and to execute the will of God as declared by priests and prophets or reduced to writing as a code of Laws. This ideal was illustrated by the action of Gideon when (Jg $8^{22f.}$) he refused the monarchical dignity for himself and his son on the ground that 'Jahweh shall rule over you.' On the other hand, according to the view represented in 1 S $8^{10. 17ff.}$ and ch. 12, the people wickedly ignored the idea of the theocracy when they demanded a king from Samuel: 'It is not *thee* that they have rejected,' says God to Samuel (1 S $8^{7}$), 'but they have rejected *me*, that I should no longer be king over them.' Is there not here a perfectly serious claim put forward on behalf of the theocracy, and is not this form of government put forward as the only legitimate one? That is so. But this does not represent the view taken in the earlier monarchical period,—which sees in the monarchy a beneficent institution for the deliverance of the people (1 S $9^{16}$),—but that of the later centuries, after people had had unhappy experiences of the monarchy, and especially after they had come to lay upon it the blame for the religious and moral degeneration of the nation, even for the destruction of the State. But for the time of Moses the conception 'theocracy' cannot be taken account of, for the sufficient reason that at that time it is impossible to speak of any *constitution* at all as in existence. All through the period of the Judges, and in part even under Saul, the tribes lived each their own life; it was at most only for the settling of processes of law that they needed a kind of supreme authority, and this latter function was discharged by the heads of clans and families—of course not, however, upon the basis of written laws, but of usage and custom. It is true that common pressure by foes had at times the effect of bringing about a coalition, not perhaps of all, but of a number of tribes; but even then human leaders could not be dispensed with. That in all this an important rôle was played by religion we shall see presently (see p. $635^{b}$ f.). But for a 'theocracy' in the form defined by Josephus there is no room here. Scope was found for it only when, after the loss of political independence, national interests receded into the background and the interests of the cultus assumed on that account all the more prominence. So it was in the programme for the future sketched by Ezekiel (chs. 40–48), where the partition of the soil of the country is moulded upon the sacredness of the temple and its surroundings, and where the 'prince' (*nāsî*; not 'king') has scarcely any more important duty than to make careful provision for the public sacrifices. The complete realization of the 'theocracy' was next undertaken by the Priests' Code. Here everything, even civil and criminal law, is looked at from the *religious* standpoint. The outward sway is in the hands of the foreigner, but what is left of the ancient national life presents itself in the form of a priestly State; the insignia of royalty—diadem and purple—are now assigned to the spiritual head, the high priest.

In carrying back the theocracy to Moses, Josephus has accordingly been guilty of a glaring anachronism. But those go to the opposite extreme who admit that Moses proclaimed Jahweh as the God of Israel, but deny anything beyond this, and cast doubt in particular upon any fundamental act of his which could be spoken of as a real founding of the religion of Israel. Everything of this kind related in the middle books of the Pentateuch is regarded by them at best as a late theological misunderstanding of something quite different, but most frequently as pure invention in the interests of religious ideas which had not their development till centuries afterwards. Here, again, we shall do well first of all to look at the tradition itself.

2. In all the Pentateuchal sources, without exception, there is a uniform tradition to the effect that the central place amongst the incidents at Sinai is occupied by the concluding of a *bĕrîth* (בְּרִית, commonly rendered **'covenant'**). What this means may be readily learned from a brief examination of the usage of the word *bĕrîth*. After the thoroughgoing investigations of J. P. Valeton * and R. Kraetzschmar,† there can be no doubt that *bĕrîth* belongs primarily to the secular vocabulary, and means 'cutting in pieces,' namely, of one or more sacrificial victims (cf. Gn $15^{9ff.}$, where God, according to the narrative of the Jahwist in v.$^{17}$, accommodates Himself to this practice; and Jer $34^{18f.}$), that the parties to an agreement might pass between the pieces and invoke upon themselves the fate of the animals in the event of their being guilty of a breach of their oath. For every *bĕrîth* consisted partly of an oath which defined the obligation taken upon oneself, partly of a curse invoked on oneself as the penalty of violating this oath.‡

The religious is naturally distinguished from the secular use of the word *bĕrîth* by the fact that God cannot be thought of in the same way as a man who enters into an agreement or covenant with other men, the two parties having exactly the same standing, with their mutual rights and obligations strictly defined. Hence the religious *bĕrîth* always stands primarily for a Divine order or arrangement § which takes its rise without the co-operation of man or, to be more precise, of the people of Israel, and yet is unconditionally binding upon the latter. The duties of the people have, it is true, promises—that is, so to speak, a self-pledging of Himself by God—corresponding to them, and thus there exists so far a mutual relationship. But, however the statements contained in the different sources of the Pentateuch may vary in laying stress now upon the Divine promises and now upon the duties resting on men, it is always the will and determination of God that accounts for the origin and the character of the *bĕrîth*. Hence the usual rendering of *bĕrîth*, namely 'covenant,' ought to be avoided as incorrect and misleading.

It has already been remarked that *all* the sources of the Pentateuch assume that at Sinai a *bĕrîth* in the sense just described was solemnly enacted by God, and that henceforward it was upon this *bĕrîth* that the intimate relation between Jahweh, as the God of Israel, and His people was based. According to the Jahwist, the sacramental com-

* 'Bedeutung und Stellung des Wortes *bĕrîth* im Priestercodex' (*ZATW* xii. 1 ff.); 'in den jahwistischen und deuteronomistischen Stücken des Hexateuchs sowie in den verwandten historischen Büchern' (*ib.* 224 ff.); 'bei den Propheten und in den Ketubim' (*ib.* xiii. 245 ff.).

† *Die Bundesvorstellung im Alten Testament*, Marburg, 1896.

‡ Akin to this are the certainly ancient forms in which a curse is conditionally invoked, namely, by sending round pieces of a corpse (Jg $19^{29}$) or of some sacrificial animal (1 S $11^{7}$). In every instance these pieces have the significance of an 'oath-offering.' The formula 'so shall it be done to his cattle' in the latter passage is in all probability a toning down of an original 'so shall it be done to *him*.' Whether the blood of the animals in question was used for the performance of sacred rites on the occasion of concluding a *bĕrîth* (as, for instance, among the Arabs it is sprinkled on seven stones), is doubtful; it is expressly witnessed to only in Ex $24^{8}$.

§ The LXX gives proper expression to this condition of things by rendering the Heb. *bĕrîth* not by συνθήκη ('agreement,' 'covenant'), but by διαθήκη ('arrangement').

munion was established by sprinkling with blood both the altar and the people, the 'book of laws of the covenant' [this is the meaning here of *bĕrîth*] being read by Moses to the people between these two acts (Ex $24^{4-8}$). In v.$^{9ff.}$ there comes next an account [probably by E] of a meal* partaken of by the representatives of the people before God. This meal can be understood only as a sacrificial one, such as, for instance, we read of again in the case of Jacob and Laban (Gn $31^{54}$) after their compact at Mount Gilead. So also the Deuteronomist and the Priests' Code speak very frequently of the *bĕrîth* which God through Moses gave to the people at Ḥoreb (or Sinai). Even if they do not refer expressly to a covenantal ceremony, they certainly presuppose what is related in the older sources. It is an established fact for them that there was a solemn proclamation of the Divine will by God to Moses, and through him to the people.

Is all this now to be set down as fiction—a carrying back of much later theological conceptions and terminology to a time for which no real tradition was any longer extant? This is a view to which the present writer cannot assent, having regard to either external or internal evidence.

Under the head of *external* evidence we must reckon not only the strength and unanimity of the tradition, which it would need the very strongest reasons to set aside, but also the narrative of Ex $24^{4ff.}$. The deviation here from the traditional rites at sacrifices and covenants, which meet us elsewhere, testifies at least to the high antiquity of the record.

But, even if the attempt to prove its historicity should have to be abandoned, there remain weighty *internal* reasons for holding that it is impossible to set aside as pure fiction the assumption of a *bĕrîth* at Sinai as a historical incident.

It was undoubtedly with very heterogeneous elements that Moses had to set to work in accomplishing his mission. The familiar genealogy of the tribes of Israel makes an emphatic—no doubt, historically justified—distinction between tribes of full and of half blood, the latter being represented as descended from female slaves (Bilhah and Zilpah, Gn $30^{5ff.}$). Moreover, Ex $12^{38}$ (cf. also Nu $11^{4}$) speaks of a non-Israelite 'mixed multitude' which attached itself to Israel at the Exodus. Yet Moses must have succeeded in imparting a certain unity to all these diverse elements, in controlling them by his will, and in planting amongst them a variety of fruitful germs of religious and legal ordinances. And although even after the immigration into Canaan it is still far from possible (see above, p. $630^{a}$) to speak of an Israelitish *State*, yet a historical document of the first rank, like the Song of Deborah, shows how in the beginning of the period of the Judges the majority of the tribes were permeated with a strong feeling of their unity under the leadership of the God of Israel. Particularly worthy of notice is the express manner in which war (which, as was pointed out above [p. $621^{b}$], even in the pre-Mosaic stage of religion had the closest connexion with the cultus) is now placed in relation to Jahwism. After the defeat of the Amaleḳites, Moses is commanded to write down a formula expressive of the Divine curse on Amaleḳ (Ex $17^{14ff.}$ [E]). Thereupon he erects an altar and calls it *Jahweh-niṣṣi* ('Jahweh is my banner'), 'for Jahweh hath war with the Amaleḳites to all generations.' Primarily, then, this war is not the affair of the people but of their God. The battles which led to the conquest of Canaan (Nu $21^{14}$), like those which had still to be fought by David in the struggle which freed the land from the yoke of the Philistines (1 S $18^{17}$ $25^{28}$), are included under the title 'wars of Jahweh.' See vol. iv. p. $896^{b}$.

Would all this be conceivable if the proclamation of Jahweh as the God of Israel—the founding of the Jahweh religion—had taken place, so to speak, fortuitously, by the incidental passing of the name 'Jahweh' from mouth to mouth? Instead of anything of this kind, we get the strongest impression that the further development of the religion of Israel during the period of the Judges and of the monarchy was the result of some occurrence of a fundamental kind of whose solemnity and binding force and character the whole nation retained a lively recollection. And this occurrence can have been nothing but the solemn proclaiming of the God *who had just manifested Himself in wondrous wise as the Helper and Deliverer of the people* upon a definite occasion, and in the binding of the people to do His will and to worship Him alone. Every one of the numerous allusions (whether in the Pentateuchal sources, the Prophets, or the Psalms) to the mighty acts of Jahweh at the Exodus, how with a strong hand and a stretched-out arm He brought the hosts of Israel out of the house of bondage, held back the waves of the Red Sea from Israel but plunged the chariots and the horsemen of Pharaoh into the waters,—every one of these allusions is at the same time an allusion to the days of Sinai, when for the first time these mighty acts of Jahweh were brought to the consciousness of the people in their true greatness, and extolled accordingly, and made the occasion of a solemn confession of Jahweh as the God of Israel and a solemn binding of the people to do His will.*

The foregoing observations have at the same time furnished the answer to the question as to the essential character of *Jahwism* as a name for the special relation between Jahweh and Israel. If we had to do with nothing more than the mutual relations between a particular god and a particular people, we should be standing simply upon the soil of a national religion such as prevailed amongst heathen peoples as well. Moab is called 'the people of Chemosh' (Nu $21^{29}$) just as Israel is 'the people of Jahweh'; Moab likewise felt itself bound to the worship of this its national god, and expected powerful aid from Chemosh in return, particularly in matters of war. And if such aid was not rendered, this was ascribed not to inadequate power on the part of the god, but to the fact that 'Chemosh was angry with his land' (Mesha's inscription, l. 5 f.). The presuppositions appear thus to be precisely the same in Moab as in Israel. And yet is it possible to conceive of a Moabite reflecting on the origin of the worship of Chemosh or tracing it back to a *bĕrîth* between that god and the Moabites? On the contrary, none of them dreamt of anything but that the special relation between god and people had subsisted from the first, nor did any one doubt that between the two there was a blood relationship in virtue of which the god would as a matter of course take the part of his people, without any necessary regard to ethical considerations. He upon whom, according to

* It cannot, indeed, be denied that it is hard to think of 74 people sitting down to a meal on the top of the mountain, and that all difficulty is removed if we accept the suggestion of Riedel (*SK*, 1903, p. 161 ff.), that וַיִּשְׁתּוּ ('and they drank') is corrupted from וַיִּשְׁתַּחֲווּ ('and they cast themselves down'), and that וַיֹּאכְלוּ ('and they ate') was interpolated after וַיִּשְׁתּוּ had found its way into the text.

* Cf., on the above, the admirable discussion by F. Giesebrecht in *Die Geschichtlichkeit des Sinaibundes*, Königsberg, 1900; on 'Jahweh's relation to the people of Israel according to the ancient Israelitish conception' in general, see Sellin in the *Neue Kirchliche Zeitschrift*, 1894, pp. 316 ff., 376 ff. [also published separately under the title *Beiträge zur israel. und jüdischen Religionsgeschichte*, Heft 1, Leipzig, 1893]; Wildeboer, *Jahvedienst en Volksreligie in Israël*, Groningen, 1898 [German tr., Freiburg, 1899].

primitive Semitic notions, the duty of blood-revenge lay, did not first inquire whether the bloody expiation was justifiable on moral grounds as well. Blood demands blood: this principle held good for the god as much as for every individual among the people.

From all this it is clear that from the very first there was a far-reaching difference between the national religion of Israel and other national religions. At its very foundation the religion of Israel made a notable advance beyond the naïve, purely naturalistic basis which we have just noted in the religion of Moab. *It was not Israel that first chose Jahweh, but Jahweh that chose Israel.* Their mutual relation does not therefore rest upon blood relationship,—such a notion is sufficiently contradicted by the circumstance that at the time of the Exodus a community of the same blood, or a nation, was not yet in existence,—but upon the free determination of a mighty God. This determination, however, was no arbitrary one; it sprang from the fundamental attributes of this God, namely righteousness and mercy. He saw the misery of the people as they pined under cruel and yet wholly undeserved oppression, and was filled with compassion for them; He determined to deliver them, and with a strong hand He carried this purpose to a victorious issue. The religious ideas which flow from this did not first originate, as some in recent times never weary of asserting, as a product of the 'ethical monotheism' of the prophets; they already lay to hand for the Israel of Mosaic times. Righteousness and mercy are essentially moral qualities. If *they* were the motive for the choice and the deliverance of Israel, the religion derived from them bore from the first an ethical stamp in quite a different sense from anything that had ever been conceivable in a purely national religion. It is thoroughly appropriate that the Deuteronomist * in a number of passages should urge *gratitude* as the leading motive for love to God and obedience to His commandments. But this, again, is no naturalistic but a specifically ethical motive, and, as such, could be appreciated even by the contemporaries of Moses. —And, finally, it was self-evident that the God who in His very choice and deliverance of Israel had exhibited moral attributes, would require from the people the same qualities on which His relation to them was based. Hence we are quite entitled to claim—not ethical monotheism in the strict sense of the term, but—*ethical henotheism* for the time of Moses.

And so at last the way in which this God fulfils His promise, putting the mighty host of Egypt to shame before a petty people of shepherds, gave occasion for the triumphant question: 'Who is like thee, O Jahweh, among the gods; who is like thee, glorious in loftiness, fearful in praises, doing wonders?' But this power of His is not thought of as mere brute force arbitrarily exercised, but once more as serving moral ends. In this lies the pledge of its final triumph over all unrighteousness and impiety, whether within or outside the people of Israel. It may be that this idea was not yet realized with perfect clearness in the time of Moses, that all its consequences were not yet deduced. But in germ it was already there as certainly as faith in the power of right, or desire that it should always prevail, is implanted by nature in the hearts of men in general. The religion of Israel was able from the first to supply nourishment to this faith as no other national religion could. Those who deny this, and who recognize everywhere simply development in a straight line from crude or at least naïve naturalism to more and more purified moral conceptions, quite overlook the circumstance that their contention is opposed by demonstrably historical facts. Epoch-making religious ideas generally come upon the scene in full strength and purity; it is only in course of further development that these products of religious creative genius, or, better, of Divine impulse, are corrupted and disfigured by the intrusion of vulgar human ideas and selfish interests. Such was the fate of the religion of Jesus Christ in the Roman Church with its popes and monks; and the same thing happened to many of the great fundamental ideas of the Reformation at the hands of Protestant scholasticism. And we are quite safe to assume something of the same kind in the process of the development of Jahwism. The great fundamental ideas upon which its institution rests were often forced into the background during the wandering period of the people's history and in the time of endless struggles for national existence under the Judges. Besides, as was pointed out already (see p. 615 f.), these ideas still continued for long to be supplemented by powerful remnants of the Polydemonism common to the Semites. But they did not die out for all this, and, when in the 8th cent. B.C. they were put forward by Amos and others with the greatest clearness and precision and urged upon the conscience of the people, these prophets had a perfect right to claim that they were making no new and unheard-of demands, but only proclaiming what from Sinai downwards had been recognized as a fact: 'A God of right is Jahweh; blessed are all they that wait on him' (Is $30^{18}$).

We insist, then, upon a *bĕrîth* between Jahweh and the people of Israel as the starting-point of Jahwism, and at the same time as the source of its peculiar character. This of itself sets aside the view recently maintained * that there was actually a *bĕrîth* concluded at Sinai—not, however, between Jahweh and Israel, but between the various Israelitish tribes. It was only the later theologians, we are told, that misunderstood this, or arbitrarily transformed its meaning to suit their purposes. This hypothesis might perhaps be sufficient to account for the coalition of heterogeneous elements so as to form a nation. But it is wholly inadequate to explain how it came about that their common religion imparted to this new confederation a wholly peculiar stamp, so that this people of nomads afterwards completely absorbed the advanced civilization of Canaan, instead of being subdued by it.

iv. *THE STAMP OF JAHWISM ON OUTWARD ORDINANCES IN THE TIME OF MOSES.*—By 'outward ordinances' we understand not only usages connected with worship in the widest sense, but also the form given by religion to the life of the people in all its aspects. As to both these points, the materials for arriving at a certain conclusion are very meagre, since no account can be taken of the elaborate priestly and ritual enactments of the Priests' Code, which are merely the theories of later centuries.

1. Even the question whether Moses instituted

* So also Ezk $16^{5ff.}$ in a striking comparison.

* For instance by Schwally, who writes (*Semit. Kriegsaltertümer*, i. p. 2): 'Probably some Israelitish tribes entered into a covenant relation with Midian, in connexion with which the national god of the more powerful of the contracting parties was called to watch over the oath.' Afterwards, however, we are told (p. 3): 'The actual course of things faded gradually from men's memory, and the notion could establish itself that at Sinai what was concluded was not a covenant between Israel and Midian under the protection of Jahweh, but simply a covenant of Jahweh with His chosen people.'—Different, again, is the judgment of Eerdmans (in *Theol. Tijdschrift*, xxxvii. p. 19 ff.). According to him, the *bĕrîth* at Sinai consisted in the union of a number of nomadic clans into a tribal confederation, accompanied by the invoking of Jahweh as the god to whom part of those tribes considered that they owed their deliverance from Egypt.

a *priestly order* at all is one which cannot be answered offhand from the early sources. He himself exercises priestly functions on the occasion of the concluding of the *bĕrîth* (Ex $24^{4ff.}$), and as a medium of oracles in the Tent of Meeting ($33^{7ff.}$). This is in harmony with the general presupposition that the founder and mediator of the Sinai religion was the prototype of both of what were afterwards the most important organs of this religion—the priests and the prophets (cf., for the latter, Dt $18^{18}$ $34^{10}$ and Hos $12^{14(13)}$). Indeed it is only thus that the habit can be explained of tracing back to his personality *all* codifications of law, even those affecting the ritual. But the early sources know nothing of Moses having further entrusted to his brother Aaron alone the discharge of priestly functions.* Aaron is indeed called in Ex $4^{14}$ 'the Levite,' which means in all probability 'the priest' (for, so far as the *tribe* was concerned, Moses was also a 'Levite'), but it is extremely questionable whether this designation really emanates from an early source. In any case, nothing is there related of him except that he served Moses as speaker in dealing with the people and with Pharaoh (Ex $4^{14ff.\ 27.\ 30}$ $5^{1ff.}$ etc.), and that he supported him during the battle with the Amalekites ($17^{12ff.}$). Even in connexion with the idolatrous worship of the golden calf (Ex $32^{1ff.}$) there is no mention of priestly functions or prerogatives belonging to Aaron. On the contrary, the assistants of Moses at the covenantal sacrifices of Ex $24^{5}$ are simply young men of the children of Israel, while the guardian of the Tent of Meeting is the *Ephraimite* Joshua (Ex $33^{11}$), who frequently appears elsewhere also as servant and attendant of Moses.

Leaving Aaron, then, out of the question, we have still, indeed, one passage from E (Ex $32^{29}$) in which, although the text in its present form is plainly mutilated, it is related that Moses awarded the priesthood to *the tribe of Levi* in recognition of their fidelity on the occasion of a revolt of the people. But, seeing that in the same chapter we have a parallel narrative to quite a different effect from the pen of the Jahwist, it is impossible to say whether in Ex $32^{29}$ we have a strictly historical narrative or merely an attempt to supply a historical explanation of the origin of the Levitical priesthood.

The story of the covenantal sacrifices (Ex $24^{4ff.}$) quite gives the impression that Moses simply followed long-established usage. And this will be true to the condition of things then as well as during the whole of the subsequent period. Not legal prescriptions, but old familiar custom, decided the practice followed in matters affecting the cultus. Even in the monarchical period priests were still unneeded for the offering of sacrifice; the same usage as had been followed for other gods or 'demons' was equally capable of application to the cult of Jahweh. This does not forbid us to hold that certain ceremonial enactments emanated from Moses, and were orally handed down under his name. But what was their precise character we are unable to decide, any more than the question whether he is to be regarded as the originator of a particular form of oracular communication. At all events, it is worthy of note that in Am $5^{25}$ (perhaps also Jer $7^{22}$) the existence of the practice of sacrifice during the wilderness wanderings is flatly denied. This passage can hardly be explained, with Marti (*Gesch. der israel. Religion*⁴, p. 71), to mean that, while sacrifices to Jahweh were abandoned, those were perhaps offered which were peculiar to families and clans, but were not meant for the God of the whole body. Marti urges that the different tribes and clans might have retained their tribal and household gods without seeing in this any repudiation of the claims of Jahweh. But, while it is not impossible that a syncretism of this kind still continued to prevail for a considerable time, it must always have appeared to the chosen representatives of Jahwism as a culpable abuse.

* According to Stade and others, the figure of Aaron is utterly unknown to the older stratum of J.

2. As to religious *festivals*, the only one that can be taken into account for the Mosaic period is the Passover (see above, p. 621ᵇ f.). The other principal festivals, in the form in which we make their acquaintance in OT tradition, point by their agrarian character to a Canaanite origin.

3. As in the cultus of the Mosaic age, so also in the *social life* of Israel the controlling factor was not a body of definite prescriptions, but the power of custom—custom, it is true, upon which from the first an ever-increasing influence was exerted by the religious uniqueness of Jahwism. When any shameful act was condemned by the formula 'It is not wont so to be done' (Gn $34^{7}$, 2 S $13^{12}$), there was assuredly in the background the thought 'because it is unworthy of Israel and their God, because it is an abomination in the sight of Jahweh which He will not let go unpunished.' Here again the possibility must be recognized that Moses himself, in the course of his long-continued judicial activity (cf., on this point, the very instructive narrative of Ex $18^{13ff.}$ [E]), especially at Kadesh or 'Ên-mishpat, laid the foundation of many usages both in civil and criminal law, nay, that not a few of the enactments afterwards codified in the Book of the Covenant go back directly to him. But in this matter, again, we are without any precise knowledge of details.

4. There is *one* question, however, which we cannot pass by in silence. If none of the rest of the legal contents of the Pentateuch can be with certainty traced back to Moses, must not at least some form of **the Decalogue** be attributed to him —having regard to the strength and the unanimity of the tradition which require this assumption?

Now, the 'unanimity' of the tradition must be left out of the question so long as it is still disputed whether in addition to the two Elohistic [E] or, according to others, Deuteronomistic recensions of the Decalogue in Ex 20 and Dt 5, we have not a Jahwistic one in Ex $34^{14-26}$.* The greater antiquity of the latter appears to be supported by the fact that it contains almost exclusively ceremonial, not yet ethical enactments; these last, it is alleged, could not have originated in *this* form except as a deposit of the Prophetic current of ideas. But this Jahwistic Decalogue is perhaps nothing more than an appearance. If the Jahwist had essentially the same Decalogue as the Elohist, the redactor could not possibly, after it had been given in Ex 20, have introduced it once more in Ex 34, and so he filled up the consequent gap with ceremonial prescriptions which can be recognized at the first glance as parallels to the laws of the Book of the Covenant. Hence the question still remains whether some form of *the* Decalogue may not be traced back to Moses.

That this form was extremely brief and concise

* This, as is well known, was already maintained by Goethe in his essay 'Das Zweitafelgesetz' (1773), and is held at present by the majority of critics. Regarding the Decalogue of Ex 20 and Dt 5, the view has come to prevail, thanks to Kuenen, Stade, Cornill, etc., that it belonged to the Judæan recension of the Elohist [E²]; so also Staerk (*Das Deuteronomium*, Leipzig, 1894), who maintains, further, that the Decalogue of E¹ is dispersed throughout the so-called Book of the Covenant. On the other hand, according to Meisner (*Der Dekalog*, Halle, 1893) and Baentsch ('Exodus u. Leviticus' in Nowack's *Hdkom.*, Göttingen, 1900), the present form of the Decalogue emanates from the Deuteronomic pen (D), and was only subsequently transferred from Deuteronomy to Ex 20. Likewise Marti (*Gesch. der israel. Religion*⁴, p. 174) holds that the Decalogue was 'in any case drawn up in the 7th cent., perhaps in the circles influenced by Isaiah.'

may be at once assumed. This conclusion is favoured even by the very striking difference in extent between the two tables of the Law: the first (namely the five Commandments, according to the method of reckoning adopted by the Reformed Churches, down to and including that of respect to parents) containing 146 words, the second only 26. Accordingly, the whole of the reasons assigned for obedience in the first five Commandments may be pronounced later additions. In this way two very considerable difficulties are removed in a very simple fashion. These are (1) the great difference in regard to the motives urged for obedience to the Sabbath-command, and (2) the Deuteronomistic colouring which, as we have seen, has led many to ascribe the whole to the 7th century. For this colouring does not affect the brief enunciations, but, above all, the motives assigned.

But it may still be asked, Does not so fully-developed an ethical system underlie even the Commandments themselves that one must hesitate to give the Decalogue its place at the head of the whole development? We should allow full weight to this objection if the standpoint of the Ten Commandments were beyond doubt and exclusively an ethical one. That this is the case, appears self-evident to *us* who from our infancy are taught and accustomed to apply a purely ethical standard, and to discover in the Commandments a guide to true piety and morality. But it is not difficult to show that originally it was not the question of morals but of regard to *rights* that occupied the foreground.* *All* the Commandments may readily be subsumed under the prohibition: '*Thou shalt not do violence to* (1) what belongs to God (His sole right to worship, His superiority to any earthly form, His name, His day [as the type of all His other 'holy ordinances'], His representatives); (2) what belongs to thy neighbour (his life [as his most precious possession], his wife [as next in preciousness], his goods and chattels, his honour).' It is only in the last of the Commandments that another point of view makes its appearance, namely, in the prohibition to touch even in thought the property of one's neighbour. Thus the climax is reached of the ascending scale which presents itself in the arrangement of the Commandments of the second table—in the advance from sins of act to sins of word, and finally to sins of thought. The correctness of the view which emphasizes the non-ethical aspect of the Decalogue is specially evident in connexion with the prohibition of adultery. The object is not to keep the youth or the married man from immorality in general, as our catechisms are wont to explain the matter,† but to ward off attack from one of the most important of a neighbour's rights of property. It is only in this sense that the notion of adultery is known to the ancient Hebrew mind; while, on the other hand, no limits are placed upon a married man's sexual intercourse with female slaves. In like manner, the seduction or violation of a virgin was plainly regarded in the earliest times more as a damage to one's rights (notably, for instance, in the way of lowering the selling price of a daughter) than as a moral transgression.

In view of all this there would be no valid reason for refusing to attribute to Moses himself a primitive concise form of the Decalogue, were it not for the formidable difficulty presented by *the prohibition of the use of images*. Down to the 8th cent. no one appears to be acquainted with so categorical a command that images of Jahweh are not to be made. Are we to hold that originally another commandment stood in the place of this one, or that Moses promulgated not ten but seven Commandments? The latter position has recently been maintained by Eerdmans.* He refers the command against images to the 7th cent., but seven of the commands of the Decalogue to the time of Moses, the first of these being 'I, Jahweh, am your God.' We are largely in accord with Eerdmans when he discovers no such affinity between the Decalogue and the great Prophets that it *must* be regarded as a product of the current of ideas initiated by them; we are at one with him also in holding that the different commands and prohibitions have not an absolute but only a relative scope. In this last respect, however, he goes too far when he maintains that the *only* obligations meant to be enjoined (*e.g.* in the matter of the prohibition of killing) are towards fellow-countrymen, and when he transforms the 'coveting' of the tenth Commandment into appropriating of ownerless property, alleging that in the OT it is only the act and not the disposition that constitutes sin. It has been rightly urged by Wildeboer† against Eerdmans that in this way the deeper moral sense of the Decalogue is degraded, and the whole reduced to a mere scheme ministering to the utilitarian necessities of the common life of Bedawîn.

The result of the above discussion is that the Mosaic origin of some rudimentary form of the Decalogue (apart from the command against images) does not appear to be absolutely excluded, but that here again we must be content to refrain from pronouncing a more definite judgment. In any case, the religious and moral significance and the germinal power—we might almost say the power of expansion—of the ideas of the Decalogue are not lessened if we must place it, not at the first beginnings but in the later stages of development of the religion of Israel. Even then, in view of its aims, and above all in view of its structure, which in the first table shows an advance from the general and more spiritual to the more concrete and external duties, while in the second table the opposite course is followed, it remains a religious document which has a good title to be regarded, even by the Christian Church at the present day, as a kind of *Magna Charta* for the guidance of the religious life.

## III. The Religion of Israel in Canaan during the Pre-Prophetic Period.‡

i. *The Sources.*—For the periods with which we have hitherto been dealing we have had to content ourselves with backward inferences from later sources, but now we have at our command records of considerable compass, which enable us to take a reliable glance at the religious and moral conditions of the period of the judges and of the early monarchy. The circumstance is immaterial that the records in question, apart from the very ancient Song of Deborah, did not assume their present form till a considerable time after the events (somewhere from about the 10th to the middle of the 8th cent. B.C.). For, in the first

* Noteworthy indications pointing to this view are already supplied by A. Menzies (*Sermons on the Ten Commandments*, London, 1888), according to whom the Decalogue belongs to the age of the Prophets, and contains the fundamental principles of social life.

† So, *e.g.*, Luther: 'Wir sollen Gott fürchten und lieben, dass wir keusch und züchtig leben in Worten und Werken, und ein jeglicher sein Gemahl liebe und ehre' ('We are to fear and love God by living chaste and modest in words and deeds, and every man is to love and honour his wife').

* 'Oorsprong en beteekenis van de tien woorden' (in *Theol. Tijdschrift*, xxxvii. p. 18 ff.).

† 'De Dekalog' (in *Theol. Studiën*, 1903, p. 109 ff.).

‡ Cf. Ch. Piepenbring, 'La religion des Hébreux à l'époque des juges' in *Revue de l'Histoire des Religions*, t. xxvii. 1; F. Seyring, *Die altisrael. Religion in den 'Heldengeschichten' des Richterbuchs*, Hamburg, 1892; C. H. Toy, 'The pre-Prophetic Religion of Israel' in *New World*, 1896, p. 123 ff.

place, all the evidence is in favour of the supposition that during the whole of this period the moral and religious viewpoint was a fixed one; and, secondly, the date when the traditions were finally committed to writing must not be confounded with the date when the oral tradition became fixed. Thus the conditions underlying the patriarchal narratives as presented by the Jahwist cannot be brought down at latest beyond the time of Saul, even although the main part of the Jahwistic *written* source was not composed till about B.C. 850. The same remark applies to the so-called hero-narratives of the Book of Judges, which occupy themselves with the six 'great judges' (Ehud, Deborah, Barak, Gideon, Jephthah, Samson), and to the same category with which belong also the very ancient and important narratives contained in Jg 9 and in the Appendix, chs. 17–21 (although it is true that chs. 19–21 have been subjected to a very late revision). All these written sources—after various more recent components have been sifted out—give us a true picture of the conditions that prevailed during the period prior to the advent of written prophecy.

As a source of the first rank must be reckoned the ancient biography of Saul and David, which, now interwoven with many later—notably even Deuteronomistic—elements, is incorporated in the Books of Samuel. But what we have said is true in quite a special sense of the so-called 'Jerusalem source' in 2 S 9–20, which reveals so intimate an acquaintance with the course of events, and shows at the same time so delicate a psychological estimate of David, that in all probability it should be placed as early as the time of Solomon. So also the older components of the biography of Solomon in 1 K 1–11 contain a great variety of valuable material. And finally, from the earliest of the writing prophets, Amos and Hosea, important backward inferences may be drawn as to the conceptions that prevailed before their day.

ii. *THE CONCEPTION OF GOD.*—1. That even in this period we can speak at most of henotheism (see above, p. 625[b] f.) but not of absolute monotheism, would be sufficiently proved by the constant inclination of the people to Baal worship (on which see below, § iii.). This tendency assumes, of course, a belief in the existence of Baal (or the baals). If it should be contended that this belief ought to be treated as a delusion, not shared by the proper representatives of Jahwism, but at all times strenuously combated by them, this contention would be opposed to a number of clear statements. What was combated at all times was the *worship* of Baal and of other gods, but not the belief in their existence. When in Jg 11[24] Jephthah bids his messengers say to the king of the Ammonites, 'Wilt not thou possess that which Chemosh* thy god giveth thee to possess?' he only gives expression to a notion which was self-evident to his contemporaries and to the narrator. A similar notion underlies the language of 1 S 26[19], where David regards banishment from the ancestral domain of Jahweh as necessitating the worship of other gods. The idea of a national god involves that the sphere of influence as well as the sphere of worship of the particular god extends only to the land of his people. Outside this other gods rule, and the man who has been driven within their sphere does well to accommodate himself to their service.

It is true that the worship of a god upon foreign soil is not absolutely excluded. According to 1 K 11[7] Solomon erected upon the Mount of Olives a place of sacrifice for Chemosh, the god of the Moabites.* The narrative in its present form sees in this (v.[1ff.]) a lapse on the part of Solomon into idolatry, into which he was seduced by his heathen wives. But, in all probability, what is in view here is—what to the original narrator was quite an unobjectionable procedure—the erection by Solomon of a sanctuary for a Moabite wife, where even in the land of Judah she might render worship to her ancestral god. Such a desire on her part would appear to Solomon quite fair and reasonable, without its ever entering his mind to take part himself in this cult. Moreover, such an aberration on the part of the builder of a splendid temple for the God of the land would be absolutely inconceivable. In this connexion it may be remarked that there is scarcely room for doubt that even then a method had been discovered whereby the worship of a national god upon foreign soil was rendered possible. Earth was brought from *his* land to the foreign country, in order thus to be able to offer sacrifice to him on his own soil. Thus Naaman the Syrian (2 K 5[17]) asks from Elisha two mules' burden of (Israelitish) earth, because he is resolved henceforward to offer neither burnt-offering nor sacrifice to any other god but to Jahweh alone. It is quite clear that Naaman's idea was quite in harmony with the belief of the Israelitish narrator. But, on the other hand, the conviction that the power of a national god in his own land is irresistible when it has been properly invoked, has very drastic testimony borne to it in 2 K 3[27]. The 'fierce anger' which comes upon Israel after Mesha has sacrificed his firstborn son upon the wall (thus in the view of the besiegers) is the anger of the god of the land, Chemosh, who after such an offering cannot remain inactive, but drives the enemy out of his country. It is possible for *us* to explain this result very naturally on the ground that the besiegers lost all courage through fear of the supposed anger of Chemosh; but this is by no means the view of the narrator and his contemporaries.

2. But if, in view of all this, the question for this whole period is not whether Jahweh, the God of Israel, is the only God, the question arises all the more, what special significance He had for His people. As we have already (p. 631[b] f.) pointed out, the full meaning of the fundamental propositions, 'Jahweh is the God of Israel, and Israel is the people of Jahweh,' always comes out when we have to deal with action on the part of a number of the tribes, if not the whole of them.

(*a*) This is the case almost exclusively in *war*. There the name of Jahweh is the connecting link which brings the otherwise heterogeneous elements into the closest union with one another, inspires them with enthusiasm, and leads them to victory. He is the *war-God*, Jahweh, whose commander-in-chief appears to Joshua in Gilgal (Jos 5[13ff.]);† who, represented by the sacred Ark (see above, p. 628 f.), causes the walls of Jericho to fall down (Jos 6); and after the battle of Gibeon rains great stones upon the fleeing Canaanites (10[11]). With peculiar energy the joyful confidence in Jahweh as the real leader in battle meets us in the Song of Deborah. The whole Song is meant, above all, to celebrate the praises of Jahweh (Jg 5[2f. 9. 11]), who left His dwelling-place on Sinai to hasten by Mt. Seir to the battlefield. He was the true leader in the fight, for the inhabitants of Meroz are cursed 'because they came not to the help of Jahweh, to the help of Jahweh among the

* Probably, by a confusion, for *Milcom*, for everywhere else Chemosh appears as the god of the *Moabites*.

* This statement alone probably belongs to the original text; the rest here, as in 2 K 23[13], is Deuteronomistic or still later expansion. The LXX has in part a different text.

† The narrative now breaks off in the middle of a sentence. The close may have been deliberately suppressed because it contained a different explanation of the name 'Gilgal' from that given shortly before in 5[9].

heroes' (v.$^{23}$); on the other hand, 'from heaven fought the stars, in their courses they fought against Sisera' (v.$^{20}$). It is specially worth noting with what force expression is given also in other passages in the Song to the thought that on such an occasion it is the unconditional duty of the different tribes to take the field with Jahweh against the common foe. Hence the panegyric on the valiant tribes which showed their willingness for this service (vv.$^{13\text{-}15.\ 18}$); and, on the other hand, the bitter scorn poured upon the dilatory ones (vv.$^{15b\text{-}17}$). And the concluding verse once more lays the strongest emphasis upon the fact that the enemies of Israel are on that very account the enemies of Jahweh, but that glory and happiness attend on those who choose Him—

> 'So must all thine enemies perish, O Jahweh:
> But those that love him are as the rising of the sun in his strength.'

The belief in a personal presence of Jahweh in decisive battles does not present itself, however, merely in highly strung poetry like the Song of Deborah. Apart from passages according to which He accompanies Israel into battle in the train of the Ark (see above, p. 628 f.), David still declares, after his first decisive victory over the Philistines: 'Jahweh hath broken mine enemies before me as waters break through (the dam),' 2 S 5$^{20}$; and before the second battle he receives from Jahweh this oracle: 'When thou hearest the noise of marching in the tops of the *baka* trees, set out; for then is Jahweh gone forth to make a slaughter in the camp of the Philistines' (v.$^{24}$).

Even if many usages which Israel practised in war, and which gave to war the appearance of an uninterrupted exercise of a religious function, date from the times of Polydemonism, and were originally evoked by regard to the 'demons' (see above, p. 621$^{b}$), there is manifestly no longer any consciousness of this in the period with which we are now dealing. Israel's wars are the 'wars of Jahweh' (Nu 21$^{14}$). The acts of consecration and the restraints to which warriors submit themselves have regard to Jahweh. Very instructive from this point of view is the very ancient narrative of 1 S 21$^{4\text{ff.}}$. The priest is prepared to give the sacred bread (the so-called shewbread) to David only in case his pretended followers have kept themselves from women. David professes that it is so, and that his company set out with sacred 'vessels' (*i.e.*, probably, clothes and weapons). David thus puts aside the fear that he and his companions are wanting in the purity required *towards Jahweh.* It was to Him then expressly that the consecration of the warrior was due. Even in Deuteronomy (23$^{9\ (10)\ \text{ff.}}$) the prescriptions about maintaining cleanliness in the camp, which in all probability have a Polydemonist motive, are in v.$^{14.\ (15)}$ based simply on the ground that 'Jahweh thy God walketh in the midst of thy camp to deliver thee and to give up thine enemies before thee; therefore shall thy camp be holy.'

(*b*) Again, as regards the frequent mention of the execution of the 'ban' (cf. above, p. 619$^{b}$ f.), we find all through this period no other supposition than that the devoting of human beings and of spoil is purely for the honour of Jahweh. So in Jos 6$^{24}$ 7$^{11\text{ff.}\ 23}$, and especially 1 S 15$^{33}$ where Samuel in the sequel executed the 'ban' upon the Amalekite king Agag by hewing him to pieces 'before Jahweh' (as one devoted to Jahweh) in Gilgal.

(*c*) The circumstance that during this period the character of Jahweh as the war-God is so prominent a feature in the conception of God, explains why now, for the first time, we make acquaintance with a designation of Jahweh which, beyond doubt, is originally connected with this side of His character, namely *Jahweh Ẓĕbā'ôth* (צְבָאוֹת). That *Ẓĕbā'ôth* is the plural of *ẓābā*, 'host,' and thus signifies 'hosts' or 'armies,' is generally admitted. It is equally recognized that '*Jahweh Ẓĕbā'ôth*' is simply an abbreviation for the complete formula '*Jahweh 'Ělōhê Ẓĕbā'ôth*,' or, with the article, '*Jahweh 'Ělōhê haz-Ẓĕbā'ôth*,* *i.e.* **'Jahweh, the God of Hosts.'** † But now, what species of hosts is meant? Or, to be more accurate, let us ask, What was *originally* meant? For there is the strongest initial probability that this name of God assumed in the usage of the Prophets a more comprehensive sense than originally belonged to it. The controversy now turns upon the question whether the primary reference in the 'hosts' is to hosts of 'demons,' ‡ or to the heavenly hosts (*i.e.* the angels), § or, finally, to the earthly hosts of Israel. ‖

(*α*) It is probable enough, in the light of what has been formerly said, that even in the post-Mosaic period an important rôle was more or less consciously attributed to the 'demons' in war as well as elsewhere. But that, after the adoption of Jahwism, Jahweh should have been treated simply as the leader of the 'demons,' and that the title 'Jahweh of Hosts' in this sense should have been employed even by the prophets without scruple, nay, even by preference, is inconceivable. For genuine Jahwism occupies a position of natural opposition to the faith in 'demons,' and hence we have nowhere any certain trace of such a *quasi*-official recognition of the latter as would be implied if the explanation we are examining were correct.

(*β*) On the other hand, a number of witnesses, some of them ancient, can be called in favour of the conception of an angelic host surrounding Jahweh. In this category we must not, indeed, include passages like 1 K 22$^{19}$. For 'the whole host of heaven' which the prophet Micaiah beheld on the right and the left of Jahweh is no more a war host than is 'the host of the height' in the very late passage Is 24$^{21}$. But in Gn 32$^{3\ (2)}$ (E) the angels of God are probably thought of as belonging to a camp of war; the 'leader of Jahweh's host' in Jos 5$^{13\text{f.}}$ can only mean the leader of a host of angels; and the horses and chariots of fire round about Elisha (2 K 6$^{17}$) are plainly driven by warrior angels.

(*γ*) All this, however, does not weaken the force of the circumstance that the plural *ẓĕbā'ôth*, in all the 26 passages where it occurs outside the Divine title, never stands for the host of heaven, ¶ but always for the earthly battalions of Israel (Ex 7$^{4}$ 12$^{17.\ 41}$ etc., down to the late Ps 44$^{10\ (9)}$ 'Thou goest not forth with our armies'); and it would surely be strange if *ẓĕbā'ôth* had a different meaning only in the collocation '*Jahweh Ẓĕbā'ôth.*'

* Cf., on the different collocations of the word in the Divine name (including its reproductions in the LXX), the exhaustive synopsis of Löhr in his *Untersuchungen zum Buch Amos* (Giessen, 1901), p. 37 ff.

† Such a shortening must be assumed even if the fuller formula, as Löhr holds, took its rise only a short time before the Exile (upon the analogy of 'Jahweh, the God of Israel').

‡ So already Wellhausen ('Skizzen und Vorarbeiten,' v. 77) and recently again Schwally ('Der heilige Krieg im alten Israel,' p. 5), only that the latter will have it that the special reference is to the 'demons' of war (the 'wild host which rages in war along with Jahweh').

§ So most, following the example of Ewald (*Die Lehre der Bibel von Gott*, ii. 339), who supposed the new name to have been once proclaimed by a great prophet upon the battlefield after a sudden victory had been gained. The same interpretation has been recently upheld afresh by Borchert in *SK*, 1896, p. 619 ff.

‖ So already J. G. Herder (in *Geist der hebräischen Poesie*) and others; then, after the view which refers the expression to the hosts of angels had long been the prevailing one, E. Schrader in *Jahrbücher für prot. Theologie*, 1875, p. 316 ff.; and, recently, esp. Kautzsch in art. 'Ẓebaoth' in *PRE*$^{2}$ xvii. p. 423 ff., and in *ZATW*, 1886, p. 17 ff.

¶ This, on the contrary, is everywhere represented by the singular *ẓābā*; even in Ps 103$^{21}$ and 148$^{2}$ the plural form is demonstrably due to error.

But why—as Delitzsch asked years ago *—is it that the Divine name *Jahweh Ẓĕbā'ôth* is not found in the very period when we should most naturally look for it, namely, at the time of the Exodus and of the conflicts with the Canaanites? Instead of this, the title first meets us in 1 S 1³ as an appellation of the God who dwells in Shiloh! Now, it is quite true that the complete absence of the name in the Hexateuch and the Book of Judges would be very surprising. But Klostermann (*Geschichte Israels*, p. 76) has made it in the highest degree probable that the name *Jahweh Ẓĕbā'ôth* was, at least in the case of the Hexateuch, removed from the text by the hand of a late redactor (perhaps from the fear of its being misunderstood in the sense of the prohibited star-worship). Thus in Jos 3¹¹· ¹³, in place of the strange expression 'the ark with the law of the Lord of the whole earth,' surely there must have stood originally the usual formula 'the ark of Jahweh of Hosts'; and in 6¹⁷ the LXX (Κυρίῳ σαβαώθ) expressly witnesses to the reading *Jahweh Ẓĕbā'ôth*.

Another objection to our interpretation is raised by Borchert, who argues that all the passages in which *ẓĕbā'ôth* means the hosts of Israel belong to the latest elements in the Canon (20 of them to the latest source of the Pentateuch), and, moreover, that they speak, not of military hosts but of multitudes of people in general. But the latter assertion (even apart from 1 K 2⁵, where *ẓib'ôth* in the present Deuteronom. narrative belongs in all probability to an earlier source) is not to the point. For the latest source of the Pentateuch always thinks of the people as a military body, whether on the march or in camp, ranged in fixed order about the sanctuary (cf. especially Nu 2). And the circumstance that in the older linguistic usage the earthly army (like the heavenly, Jos 5¹⁴) is designated *ẓābā* in the singular, does not prevent the conclusion that the plural likewise served originally as a designation of *earthly* hosts. This view finds a very strong support in 1 S 17⁴⁵. When David there says to the Philistine giant, 'I come in the name of Jahweh of Hosts, the God of the armies of Israel,' he plainly intends by the latter addition to give his heathen opponent an authentic interpretation of the name *Jahweh Ẓĕbā'ôth*, which, without this, must have remained unintelligible to him.

But, if we abide accordingly by the interpretation of the title as referring to the hosts of Israel who are to put their trust in battle in Jahweh (as in Jg 5²³, 2 S 5²⁰· ²⁴) as their true leader and champion, an additional remark requires to be made. *Jahweh Ẓĕbā'ôth* is originally the war-God *as represented by the sacred Ark*.† That the ark itself was a warlike shrine was shown above (p. 628 f.). But now, when we find that, of the 11 passages in the Books of Samuel where the title *Jahweh Ẓĕbā'ôth* occurs, no fewer than 5 stand in a direct or indirect relation to the sacred Ark, this cannot be accidental. Cf. 1 S 1³· ¹¹ *Jahweh Ẓĕbā'ôth* at Shiloh, where the Ark was then located; 4⁴ 'the ark of *Jahweh Ẓĕbā'ôth*.' But one of the strongest evidences may be found in 2 S 6². It is true that the *original* text of this passage has suffered corruption, as is shown by the different form in the parallel 1 Ch 13⁶.‡ But to strike out the *whole* sentence after *Ẓĕbā'ôth* is quite an unjustifiably violent procedure. Rather may we conclude that here in any case it was stated that 'over the ark the name of Jahweh of Hosts was named,' *i.e.* that the Ark stood in the closest relation to Jahweh as *the war-God*, being the representation and the pledge of His presence. And when, in 2 S 6¹⁸, David blesses the people in the name of Jahweh of Hosts, this is the solemn termination of all the arrangements for the conveying of the sacred Ark to Zion, which had thus for their objective Jahweh of Hosts, the war-God. Again, in Ps 24¹⁰, the designation of God as 'Jahweh of Hosts' (‖ v.⁸, where He is called a mighty one and a war-hero) is most simply explained by supposing that in this Psalm-fragment the subject is the return of the Ark to the temple from a campaign.

(δ) While convinced that the above is the true interpretation of *Jahweh Ẓĕbā'ôth* as an original appellation of the war-God represented by the sacred Ark, we do not mean to deny that another conception gradually established itself in the linguistic usage, to such an extent that in many passages the original conception appears to be quite forgotten. This is shown even by the statistics of the employment of the expression. Of the 278 passages in which *Jahweh Ẓĕbā'ôth* (so 234 times) or another combination with *Ẓĕbā'ôth* occur, there are 19 in the Historical books (11 in Samuel, 5 in Kings, but only in the mouth of prophets; 3 in Chronicles in parallels to Samuel); 15 in the Psalms (in the first book only Ps 24¹⁰; 14 in the second and third books); while all the other instances are in the Prophetical books. Even if amongst the last named there are a few which *might* point to *Jahweh Ẓĕbā'ôth* as the war-God, such an interpretation is quite impossible in the vast majority of instances. On the contrary, the addition *Ẓĕbā'ôth* has plainly attached to it the notion of the *supramundane* power and glory of Jahweh. It is manifestly so in those passages in which this Divine name stands in parallelism with the notion of the 'holiness,' *i.e.* (in accordance with the Prophetic use of the term) the absolutely exalted being of Jahweh, as in Is 5¹⁶· ²⁴ 6³. How this change of signification is to be understood is not possible to say with certainty. Only so much is clear, that, after the permanent establishment of the Ark in the mysterious darkness of the *adytum* of the temple, its former connexion with the war-God, *Jahweh Ẓĕbā'ôth*, must have vanished from the popular consciousness, and that in place of this the awe-inspiring majesty of this God must have come into the foreground. It remains, however, the most plausible supposition that now the hosts of angels and perhaps also (at least in later times) of stars came involuntarily to be substituted for the earthly hosts, so that, finally, the idea of Ruler of the Universe connected itself *per se* with the title *Jahweh Ẓĕbā'ôth*. In this way we could explain most simply the surprising circumstance that there is no instance of the occurrence of *Jahweh Ẓĕbā'ôth* in the Book of Ezekiel, although it is met with very frequently in Jeremiah and immediately after the Exile. Ezekiel may have purposely avoided it because it was capable of being misinterpreted as a justification of star-worship.

3. Another weighty question connected with the conception of the Deity is this: Are there to be discovered, even in the pre-Prophetic period, tendencies towards overcoming the initial crass conception of the bodily form of God, or, in other words, a disposition to free the Divine being from the realm of the visible and sensible, and thus to spiritualize it? Now, it is an undeniable fact that the clothing of Jahweh with a body is a practice that still extends into this period. This is proved by the Jahwistic passages Gn 3⁸ᶠᶠ· and

* In Rudelbach's *Zeitschrift für die gesammte lutherische Theologie und Kirche*, 1874, p. 217 ff.

† This connexion was already suggested by Vuilleumier (art. 'Le nom de Dieu Jahvéh-çebaoth' in *Revue de Théol. et de Philos.*, April 1877, p. 302); it was established in detail by Kautzsch (*loc. cit.* above, p. 636ᵇ note ‖).

‡ On the difficulties presented by the present text, and the numerous attempts that have been made to emend it, cf. Giesebrecht, *Die alttest. Schätzung des Gottesnamens* (Königsberg, 1901), p. 132 ff.

18$^{1ff.}$ * Nevertheless, the answer to the above question must be a decided affirmative, and there are even various methods of distinguishing between the transcendent, unapproachable, real being of Jahweh and the passing appearances which do not completely exhaust His being.

(*a*) To this category certainly belongs the *mal'akh Jahweh* or **'angel of Jahweh'** † in the original sense of that term. This sense could never have been mistaken if men had not obstinately persisted in demanding that this *theologumenon* should have the same sense throughout the whole of the Old Testament—a course to which they were driven on the ground of a mechanical doctrine of inspiration. Since, now, in certain late passages the 'angel of Jahweh' is undoubtedly, as a creature angel, clearly distinguished from Jahweh, it was thought that he could be also so distinguished in all the earlier passages.‡ In reality the 'angel of Jahweh' is originally a *form of appearance* of Jahweh Himself, 'a temporary descent of the latter to visibility,' distinguishable from Himself only in so far as it does not represent the full and complete majesty of His being. The circumstance, which has been felt to be very strange, that the expression 'angel of Jahweh' is not infrequently suddenly exchanged for the simple 'Jahweh,' is very simply explained. The designation 'angel of Jahweh' is necessary wherever he comes (particularly in conversation) into direct contact with men, whereas the simple 'Jahweh' is sufficient when God is to be thought of as if by Himself, separate from men or at least unseen by them. Although in some passages this condition of things is obscured by touches of the redactor's hand, there are others where it is readily recognizable.§ So in Jg 5$^{23}$ 'Curse Meroz, said the angel of Jahweh [addressing Israel], because they came not to the help of [the invisibly present] Jahweh.' In like manner, in Gn 16$^{7ff.}$ the God who speaks to Hagar is always called *mal'akh Jahweh*, whereas, according to v.$^{11}$, Jahweh Himself has heard her affliction, this being a function for which He did not require a personal meeting with her. In any case, it is quite in the spirit of the narrator when in v.$^{13}$ Hagar discovers in Him who has spoken with her Jahweh Himself. Again, in Gn 21$^{17ff.}$ (the Elohistic parallel to the Jahwistic narrative of ch. 16) it is *God* that hears the voice of the lad, but the *angel of God* that calls to Hagar out of heaven, etc. And if in v.$^{19}$ it is *God* that opens her eyes, so that she sees the well of water, this required no *personal, mechanical* operation. On the contrary, it might be accomplished by an act of the Divine will working from afar, and this is plainly the meaning of the narrator. But it is to be observed how here in E a marked spiritualizing of the ancient *theologumenon* has already taken place. In J the angel of Jahweh evidently meets Hagar at the well personally and in human form; in E, on the other hand, he calls to her 'from heaven.' The thought of a human body pertaining to Jahweh is thus, if not exactly dropped, forced into the background. The same is true of Gn 22$^{11}$ [where *mal'akh Jahweh*, occurring in what is otherwise an uninterrupted Elohistic narrative, can be only a variant for *mal'akh 'Ĕlōhîm*, due to a redactor, and occasioned perhaps by the redactory addition in v.$^{15}$, which also speaks of the angel of Jahweh]. In Gn 31$^{11}$ (E) the angel of God calls to Jacob 'in a dream,' so that here too any allusion to direct personal intercourse is avoided. But the angel of Jahweh expressly identifies himself with the God of Bethel. In this instance, then, there is no possibility of denying a self-revelation of Jahweh in the form of the angel. In the story of Jacob's wrestling (32$^{25ff.}$) only a 'man' is spoken of; but the latter appears to be thought of also as *mal'akh Jahweh*, for he blesses Jacob, who declares (v.$^{31}$), 'God have I seen face to face, and yet have escaped with my life.'—We encounter the *mal'akh Jahweh* again in Ex 3$^{2}$. Here he *appears* to Moses as a flame of fire, and thus comes into the realm of the visible. Hence it must be due to a redactor that in v.$^{4b}$, the Elohistic addition to the Jahwistic v.$^{4a}$ ('Jahweh saw'—analogous to Gn 21$^{17}$ 'Jahweh heard'), it is God Himself and not the angel of God that calls to Moses from the bush. By the way, in the whole of the further transaction (v.$^{6ff.}$) there is not the slightest whisper of doubt that it is God Himself and not some messenger of God that speaks.

In precisely the same way as in Gn 16 and 21 may be explained the remarkable interchange of 'Jahweh' or 'God' and 'angel of Jahweh' in Nu 22$^{22-35}$. The latter opposes the progress of Balaam (vv.$^{22.24.26}$); he is seen by the ass (vv.$^{23.25.27}$), and at last by Balaam himself (v.$^{31}$); it is *he* that speaks to Balaam (vv.$^{32.35}$), and the latter replies to him (v.$^{34}$). On the other hand, 'Jahweh' gives the ass the faculty of speech (v.$^{28}$); He opens the eyes of Balaam (v.$^{30}$, cf. the precisely similar case in Gn 21$^{19}$)—both examples of far-working effects of the power of Jahweh.

In Jg 6$^{11ff.}$, again, we have, according to v.$^{14}$, a personal manifestation of Jahweh. This is called *mal'akh Jahweh* everywhere except in vv.$^{14.16.23}$; but even in vv.$^{14.16}$ the LXX read *mal'akh Jahweh*, and no doubt this was the original reading, and not an intentional change introduced for the sake of harmony with the text elsewhere. Finally, in Jg 13$^{3ff.}$ the angel of Jahweh, whom the parents of Samson took at first for a man of God, is intended to be an appearance of Jahweh Himself, as is shown not only by v.$^{18}$, but quite expressly by v.$^{22f.}$. The last passage to which we may claim to appeal in this connexion is Hos 12$^{4f.}$ 'Jacob contended with God, he contended against a Divine manifestation (*mal'akh*),' etc. The prophet evidently avoids naming Jahweh Himself, but his meaning is clearly the same as is intended in the passage which underlies his reference (see above). Other witnesses to this sense of the expression *mal'akh Jahweh* are to be found in the statements, summary as they are, of Gn 48$^{16}$ (E), Jg 2$^{1.4}$, 2 K 1$^{3.15}$, and in the mention of the angel of God (in E parallel with the pillar of cloud in J) in Ex 14$^{19}$. On Mal 3$^{1}$ see below.

It is intelligible how, as the conception of God grew more profound, the above described pale manifestation, although only temporary and not exhausting the complete being of Jahweh, must have given offence to the religious sense. But this offence was not summarily removed by transforming the *mal'akh Jahweh* into a created angel; on

* In Gn 18$^{1ff.}$ there are now, indeed, as has been shown by Kraetzschmar (*ZATW*, 1897, p. 81 ff.), two recensions of the same narrative combined. According to the earlier of these, Jahweh Himself appears, accompanied by two angels; according to the later (the 'plural source') three angels are sent by Jahweh, who Himself abides in heaven (cf. esp. 19$^{24}$).

† The E source of the Pentateuch remains even here true to its principle of avoiding the name 'Jahweh,' and says (but in quite the same sense) *mal'akh 'Ĕlōhîm* (Gn 21$^{17}$) or *mal'akh hā-'Ĕlōhîm*, 'angel of God' (Gn 31$^{11}$, Ex 14$^{19}$).

‡ The monographs on the *mal'akh Jahweh* from this standpoint have, of course, now ceased to possess interest. The correct view is represented especially by Kosters (art. 'De mal'ach Jahve' in *Theol. Tijdschrift*, 1875, p. 367 ff.). Only, he goes too far in seeking to explain *all* appearances of angels (even in the plural, as Gn 28$^{12}$ 32$^{2(1)}$) in pre-exilic passages as self-manifestations of God.

§ This frequent interchange of 'Jahweh' and '*mal'akh Jahweh*' shatters the (at first sight very plausible) theory that the motion of the '*angel* of Jahweh' is the necessary consequence of Jahweh *Himself* being supposed to have His dwelling-place at Sinai. Enthroned there, He might be supposed incapable of appearing elsewhere at the same time. But this is a false assumption. On the contrary, where the angel of Jahweh appears, there is Jahweh also active, but it is only His form of manifestation that is *visible* and *audible*.

the contrary, men still held fast to a representation of Jahweh, although with a stronger emphasis laid upon the distinction between this and Jahweh Himself. Under this head fall certain passages in which it is sometimes hard to say whether we are still to think of a *mal'akh Jahweh* in the form described above, or simply of a created angel. So in Ex $23^{20ff.}$ 'Truly I will send my* angel before thee, to keep thee by the way, and to bring thee into the place which I have prepared. Take ye heed of him, and hearken unto his voice; be not rebellious against him, for he will not forgive your transgression; *for my name is in him*.' This last expression means nothing else than 'for he is a representation of my being' (see below, p. $640^b$ f.), and is not to be weakened, with Ewald and others, as if it meant only that the angel represents God as the ambassador does the king, and has power to speak in His name; on the contrary, he is himself essentially Divine. We shall presently see, however, that the 'name' of God is not *so* directly identical with God as could be said of the *mal'akh Jahweh*. In the same sense as we have just established for $23^{20}$ we are to understand also $32^{34}$ and $33^2$ [read again, with Luc., '*my* angel']. For in $33^{3.5}$ it is said of God Himself that He cannot go up in the midst of the Israelites, for He should have to destroy such a stiff-necked people. Perhaps we ought, finally, to include in this category the passages where David is compared to *the* angel of God (2 S $14^{17.20}$ $19^{28}$; on the other hand, 1 S $29^9$ has 'like *an* angel of God'). The expression is too general to permit of a certain interpretation. But, seeing that the woman of Tekoa would hardly have ventured to treat David's wisdom as equal to the wisdom of God Himself, it is not unlikely that we are here also to think of a representation of Jahweh which is not absolutely identical with Him. On the other hand, 'the angel of Jahweh' in 2 S $24^{16}$ is a creature angel, for Jahweh commands him to leave off his work of destruction. The case is similar in 1 K $19^7$ (cf. v.$^5$) and 2 K $19^{35}$ (Is $37^{36}$). Finally, in Ps $34^{8(7)}$ $35^{5f.}$ we have perhaps simply the idea of a guardian angel (appointed by God).

The *theologumenon* of the 'angel of Jahweh' is wholly wanting in the pre-exilic prophets; and in Zec $1^{11ff.}$ $3^{1.5ff.}$, where it reappears after a long interval, there can be no doubt as to the creaturely character of this 'angel of Jahweh.' For he prays to Jahweh, and Jahweh answers him in comforting words. He delivers the Divine commission ($1^{14}$); he is met by 'another angel' ($2^{7(3)}$); and again in $3^2$ [where, in view of v.$^1$, read 'and the angel of Jahweh said'] he is once more expressly distinguished from Jahweh. In the considerably later passage, Zec $12^8$, 'the angel of Jahweh' stands in parallelism with *'Ělōhîm*; but the latter term is here manifestly not simply the equivalent of *Jahweh*, but stands for 'a supramundane, Divine being'; so that even here 'the angel of Jahweh' is kept quite distinct from Jahweh Himself. One might rather be tempted to think of a self-revelation of Jahweh in the 'angel of the covenant' of Mal $3^1$, seeing that he is named immediately after 'the Lord,' *i.e.* Jahweh. In reality, however, he is coupled with Jahweh only as His attendant and instrument, and thus at the same time distinguished from Him.

(*b*) Closely akin to the 'angel of Jahweh,' in its original sense, we have sometimes the **'face** (פָּנִים *pānîm* †) **of Jahweh,'** *i.e.* simply Jahweh Himself as personally present, although (like the *mal'akh Jahweh*) in a form of manifestation which does not exhaust His full being. Unfortunately, the principal passage which treats of this *theologumenon*, namely Ex 33, has not been preserved entire, and hence its interpretation is difficult. In the text (v.$^{3ff.}$), which is a combination of various sources and strata of sources, God declares that He cannot [personally] go up in the midst of the people, else He should have to consume them. Israel is much disturbed at this announcement; but at God's command the people put off their ornaments, while He announces His intention of considering how He may provide a substitute for His personal presence. After v.$^6$ there must have been (from the pen of E) an account of the constructing of the tent and the sacred Ark from the ornaments of the people, for the existence of the tent is all at once assumed in v.$^7$. The Ark, in fact, which represents Jahweh, is the substitute for His personal presence. When, now, in J's parallel (v.$^{12ff.}$) God, in answer to Moses' question whom He means to send with the people, replies (v.$^{14}$), 'My face shall go [with you],' this cannot, in flat opposition to E, mean 'I in my own person.' That is to say, J, as well as E, must have had in view something secondary, some *partial* representation of the full being of Jahweh, whether he, too, thought of the sacred Ark, or the self-manifestation of God in the form of the *mal'akh Jahweh* was before his mind's eye. It is to Ex $33^{14}$, beyond doubt, that allusion is made in Dt $4^{37}$ and Is $63^9$. In the latter passage the present text speaks of 'the angel of his face (*pānîm*).' That would mean the angel in whom His *pānîm*, the manifestation of His presence, was found. But we should certainly read, with the LXX, 'No messenger or angel [read צִיר וּמַלְאָךְ], but his face, saved them.' Here, plainly, *pānîm*, as the proper manifestation of Jahweh, is opposed to messengers and angels, who are quite distinct from Him. Yet even the author of Is $63^9$ cannot have regarded the *pānîm* of Jahweh as absolutely identical with Him, else he would surely have said simply 'Jahweh, *he* saved them,' and not 'his face saved them.' In three other passages the *pānîm* of Jahweh denotes His appearing to execute judgment upon the foes of Israel (Ps $21^{10(9)}$), or upon Israel itself (Ps $80^{17(16)}$, La $4^{16}$ 'The angry glance of Jahweh hath scattered them').

(*c*) To the category of forms of Divine manifestation belongs, further, the **'glory** (כָּבוֹד *kābôd*) **of Jahweh.'*** It is true that no perfectly certain evidence can be adduced of the currency of this *theologumenon* as early as the pre-Prophetic period. For in the very ancient passage, 1 S $4^{22}$, *kābôd* appears to be a designation of Jahweh who dwells in the sacred Ark, and hence belongs to quite a different category from the *kābôd* in all other pre-exilic passages. In the latter the *kābôd* is the manifestation-form in which Jahweh on solemn occasions shows Himself to Israel; it stands, above all, for the *brightness* which streams from the cloud surrounding Him. It may be that here, too, there was originally a connexion with the thought of the storm-God who appears in dark lightning-flashing clouds (so, probably, still in Ex $33^{18}$ and Dt $5^{21(-3)}$), but the *kābôd* may exhibit itself apart from storms (so especially in 1 K $8^{11}$ ∥ 2 Ch $7^1$, where the *kābôd* of Jahweh in the form of a [bright] cloud fills the newly built temple). On

* The Massoretic text has '*an* angel' (as in Nu $20^{16}$); but doubtless we should read, with the Samaritan text and Lucian's recension of the LXX, '*my* angel' (*mal'ākhî*). Cf. even the MT of v.$^{23}$ 'For *mine* angel shall go before thee,' etc.; and Gn $24^{7.40}$, where we already read, 'He shall send *his* angel before thee.'

† A remarkable light is thrown upon this peculiar designation by the circumstance that in Carthaginian inscriptions the goddess Tanit very frequently receives the honorific title 'Face of Baal' (*pĕnê Ba'al*), *i.e.* personal (as it were, incarnate) representation of the Deity in general.

* A very thorough examination of the history of this notion will be found in von Gall's *Die Herrlichkeit Gottes: eine biblisch-theologische Untersuchung ausgedehnt über das Alte Testament, die Targume, Apokryphen, Apokalypsen und das Neue Testament*, Giessen, 1900.

the other hand, in Is $6^{3}$ (and so also in Nu $14^{21f.}$, Hab $2^{14}$, and often in the Psalms, *e.g.* $19^{2(1)}$ $72^{19}$) *kābôd* appears to stand in a much wider sense for the manifestations of the Divine majesty and omnipotence which are displayed in all parts of the earth.

Quite a different sense attaches to the *kābôd* of Jahweh in Ezekiel as well as in Is 40–66 and in the so-called Priests' Code. Here it is plainly the form itself in which Jahweh becomes visible, and not simply the temporarily assumed veiling of His real being. This *kābôd* shines like *ḥashmal* * (Ezk $1^{27f.}$); it rises from its place with a noise like that of a great earthquake ($3^{12}$), leaves the cherubim-chariot, and approaches the threshold of the temple, so that the temple is filled with the cloud [which veils the *kābôd*], and the fore-court with the brightness of the *kābôd* of Jahweh ($9^{3}$ $10^{4}$). Then, once more mounting the chariot ($10^{18f.}$, cf. also $3^{23}$ $8^{4}$), it leaves the city and fixes its abode on the Mount of Olives during the period of judgment and desecration ($11^{22f.}$). Thence, when the day of deliverance dawns, it returns by the east door to the temple, and the latter as well as the whole land shines anew in its reflexion.

The same conception of the *kābôd* as a figure shooting out rays afar is found, although in a somewhat different form, in the Messianic glimpses of Is 40–66. According to $40^{5}$ it is to show itself as soon as the preparations for the return of the exiles are undertaken; here, in all probability, it is thought of as the guide at the head of the returning band. On the other hand, in $60^{1f.}$ the *kābôd* of Jahweh streams *over them* (thus apparently in heaven); in $59^{19}$ (∥ the 'name of Jahweh,' see below), again, and in $66^{18f.}$ *kābôd* may stand, as in Is $6^{3}$ etc., for the glorifying of the majesty and omnipotence of Jahweh, which is visible to the whole world.

The conception of the *kābôd* of Jahweh present in Ezk 1–11 and in ch. 43 recurs quite clearly in the Priests' Code, naturally without the connected notion of the cherubim-chariot. It is enthroned upon Sinai, enveloped in the cloud; but to the eyes of Israel it presents itself as devouring fire (Ex $24^{16f.}$; cf. also Lv $9^{23f.}$, Nu $14^{10}$ $16^{19}$ $20^{6.8}$). In Ex $40^{34f.}$ and Nu $17^{7}$ [$16^{42}$] the cloud appears, as it were, as the herald and signal of the *kābôd* of Jahweh which appears immediately after it, and fills the Tent of Meeting. Cf. also the discussion of the 'Glory of Jahweh' in vol. ii. p. 184 ff.

All the *theologumena* we have just described are attempts to bridge the gulf between the real being of Jahweh, which eludes human sight and comprehension, and the realm of the visible, which is alone accessible and intelligible to man. One perceives the inadequacy of all comparisons, and yet these cannot be dispensed with so long as the human mind cannot conceive of *personal* action and influence proceeding except from a bodily form (this bodily form, moreover, being always primarily human). Hence it marks a considerable advance on the old notion of the *mal'akh Jahweh* when in the *theologumena* of the *pānîm* and the *kābôd* of Jahweh the thought of a human form is kept as much as possible in the background. Even if Ezekiel ($1^{26f.}$) still ventures—in a supplementary sort of fashion—on a comparison of the *kābôd* of Jahweh with the human form ('a likeness as the appearance of a man,' v.$^{26}$; 'from that which appeared as his loins,' v.$^{27}$), in Deutero-Isaiah and the Priests' Code there is no allusion whatever to the form of a man. The only images that are considered worthy to represent the supramundane and mysterious being of God are fire (which is, as it were, the least material element) and the more than earthly brightness which proceeds from it, and which is rendered tolerable to the human eye only by an enveloping cloud.

(*d*) We have still, however, in this connexion, to speak of a *theologumenon*, which likewise aims at distinguishing between the immanent Jahweh and His manifestations and acts, avoiding at the same time all introduction of a bodily form. We refer to the remarkable expressions regarding the **'name of Jahweh.'** * The modern mind finds it hard to realize the profound meaning which a person's name possessed in the eyes of men, including the Israelites, in ancient times. Giesebrecht (*l.c.* p. 94) rightly defines a name as meaning, according to the ancient conception, 'a something parallel to the man, relatively independent of its bearer, but of great importance for his weal or his woe, a something which at once describes and influences its bearer.' He supports this definition (*ib.* p. 68 ff.) by very numerous and striking testimonies, derived from the conceptions of other peoples and religions. But what is true of a human name is true also, *mutatis mutandis*, of the Divine name. To know it is of vital importance, for this is the condition of being able to use it in invocation; and invocation has, according to primitive notions, a real efficacy, giving to the invoking party a kind of power over the name invoked, so that he can compel its aid. This explains why, in heathen cults, the name of a particular god was studiously kept secret, lest it might be abused through being invoked by an improper party.†

Now it is self-evident that in the OT, in the numerous passages, particularly in the Prophets, and the Psalms, where the 'name of Jahweh' is introduced in various connexions, such crass and superstitious notions as underlie heathen magical formulas are entirely absent. The conception of God found in the Prophets (including Deuteronomy, as the specifically Prophetical law-book) and the Psalms permits of no other view than that all those manifold expressions are used from a thoroughly purified religious and ethical standpoint. But, on the other hand, Giesebrecht is certainly right in declaring the (almost universally) current explanation of these expressions to be inadequate, and, in attributing to the 'name of Jahweh,' in at least a great number of instances, a far deeper meaning. Most are content to explain the 'name' as the expression of the character, the connotation of the Divine attributes, in so far as these have become known to the Israelites, or have manifested themselves for

* According to the LXX and the Vulgate, this word (חַשְׁמַל) stands for *electron*, that is, an amalgam of gold and silver.

* Cf. Giesebrecht's monograph, *Die alttest. Schätzung des Gottesnamens und ihre religionsgeschichtliche Grundlage* (Königsberg, 1901), which is at once thorough-going, and opens up a number of new points of view.

† A trace of this notion may be discovered with certainty in Gn $32^{30}$ and Jg $13^{18}$. In both passages the manifestation of Jahweh (for such is originally meant) declines to give its name, thus escaping, as it were, any further annoyance. It may be, again, that in the Decalogue the commandment not to take Jahweh's name 'in vain' meant originally that men were not to compel action on the part of the sacred name by invoking it. So, too, Am $6^{10}$ is best explained, with Giesebrecht (p. 128), as expressing a dread of provoking the fiercely enraged Deity still further by uttering His name (cf. also $8^{3}$). Consideration is due, finally, to the remark of Giesebrecht (*Friede für Babel und Bibel*, Königsberg, 1903, p. 41), that the abstract notion *'ēl*, 'deity,' is employed so frequently in personal names because, like the terms expressing relationship, this served as a protection to the Divine name, which might not be uttered. Cf. the numerous examples of such name-taboos collected from all quarters by Giesebrecht, *l.c.* p. 38, note 1; see also Frazer, *Golden Bough*², i. 403 ff.

With the magical and at the same time irresistible efficacy of the solemnly invoked Divine name is plainly connected the firm belief in the terrible power of the *curse*. Thus Abimelech succumbs to the curse of Jotham (Jg $9^{20.57b}$); Micah escapes the effects of his mother's curse by prompt restitution of the money he had stolen from her; and his mother at once removes the curse by pronouncing a formula of blessing, in which the name of Jahweh is invoked (Jg $17^{1ff.}$); the curse of Elisha 'in the name of Jahweh' brings summary destruction upon forty-two children (2 K $2^{24}$).

their protection or deliverance. In point of fact, a number of frequently employed expressions are more or less satisfactorily explained in this way (*e.g.* when we read of proclaiming, praising, celebrating, glorying in, the name of God); there are even others where the name appears to be intended only in the sense familiar to *us*—as a combination of particular sounds (so in all connexions where a pronouncing of the Divine name is spoken of, such as calling upon, profaning, blaspheming the name, or putting it [in blessing] upon any one, Nu $6^{27}$, Ps $129^{8}$). But there remains a very large number of passages in which these two methods of interpretation, so far from being satisfactory, yield no sense at all—passages in which the name, in short, appears to be identical with the person of God. This applies where such expressions as 'fear,' 'love,' 'honour,' 'confess,' 'trust in,' 'wait for,' are prefixed to the name of God. That a manifestation-form of Jahweh as *present to help* is here thought of, is evident from such instances as Ps $20^{2(1)}$ ('the name of the God of Jacob defend thee!') $44^{6(5)}$ ('through thy name we tread down our foes,' cf. $118^{10-12}$) $54^{3(1)}$ ('help me, O God, through thy name,' cf. $124^{8}$), Pr $18^{10}$ ('a strong tower is the name of Jahweh').*

If in the above passages the 'name' is really a personified 'power placed *side by side with* the proper person of Jahweh' (Giesebrecht, *l.c.* p. 66), this throws a clear light not only upon the above (p. $639^{a}$) cited passage Ex $23^{21}$ ('My name is in him'), but also upon the expressions just noticed, such as 'call upon, praise, thank, the name of Jahweh.' They refer not to the name 'Jahweh' as the pronunciation of certain sounds, but to the 'power' which has become hypostatized in it; otherwise, passages like Ps $54^{8(6)\,f.}$ ('I will declare to the praise of thy name, Jahweh, that it is good, that it hath delivered me out of all trouble') would be quite unintelligible.

All the more intelligible, on the other hand, become the very numerous passages which speak of a localizing of the name at particular sanctuaries, notably at the temple in Jerusalem. Favourite forms of expression with Deuteronomy and with the Deuteronomic redactors of the Historical books are, that Jahweh 'causes' His name 'to dwell' in the temple, or 'sets' it in the place chosen by Him, or that 'a house is built for his name,' so that now He is to dwell for ever at Jerusalem (2 K $23^{27}$, 2 Ch $33^{4}$). It might be supposed that this application of the 'name of Jahweh' took its rise in the age of Deuteronomy, perhaps because the purified Prophetical conception of God urgently demanded such a distinction between the unapproachable, immanent Jahweh and His earthly forms of manifestation. But that this was not so is shown by Ex $20^{24}$, which stands at the very head of the Book of the Covenant: 'In every spot [more exactly, 'at every place of worship'] where I will cause my name to be remembered [*i.e.* simply, 'where I will cause my "name" to be honoured as a manifestation of my being localized there'], will I come to thee and bless thee.' We are thus entitled not only to regard the *theologumenon* of the 'name of Jahweh' as one of the most significant attempts at distinguishing between the real essential being of Jahweh and His more or less perfect manifestation-forms—analogous to the angel, the face, and the glory, of Jahweh—but to carry it back even to the pre-Prophetic period of the religion of Israel. Nay, in this very period the belief in a *magical* efficacy of the name must have played a more important rôle than later, when men, while laying emphasis upon the 'name' in expressions that had become quite current, had no longer any clear consciousness of its once deeper signification.

4. All the above-described attempts to distinguish between the real being of Jahweh and His forms of manifestation * did not prevent men from seeking, even during this period, to realize a concrete presence of the God of Israel by having recourse to **images of Jahweh.** A proof of this lies in the circumstance that presenting oneself at the sanctuary is spoken of as 'beholding the face of Jahweh.' † Although this expression may have come afterwards to be employed in quite a weakened sense (as, for instance, in Is $1^{12}$), it certainly referred *originally* (like the extremely frequent 'before Jahweh') to looking upon the image of the Deity. Exactly in the same way the expression 'stroke the face of Jahweh *or* of God,' which had at first a literal sense, was afterwards weakened to the general meaning of 'propitiate God *or* beg His favour.' As images of God we must reckon not only the very ancient *peṣel* (פֶּסֶל) or carved image and the bull-figures (prohibited in Judah), but also the *'ēphôd* and the *tĕrāphîm*.

(*a*) The *peṣel* was a Divine figure, originally carved from wood or hewn in stone, for the most part probably in the form of a man, or at least with a human head. At first distinguished from the molten image (מַסֵּכָה *maṣṣēkhāh*), the word comes at last to be used also of the latter (Is $40^{19}$ $44^{10}$, etc.). Of course, for our present purpose, we leave out of account all those passages in which *peṣel* [*pĕṣîlîm*, with the same meaning, serves as plural] stands for the image of a heathen god (Nah $1^{14}$ *et al.*). There are many passages, however, in which *peṣel* means an image of Jahweh; and such a carved image appears to have been for long regarded as unobjectionable, whereas the molten image (probably with allusion to Israel's bull worship) is already prohibited in the Jahwistic section of which Ex $34^{17}$ forms a part. Even if the prohibition of the *peṣel* in the Decalogue (Ex $20^{4f.}$, Dt $5^{8}$) extends to images of Jahweh, this would be simply a proof that the Decalogue (or at least the prohibition of images) originated later than J—a conclusion which is favoured by the circumstance that there were also other species (see below) of images of Jahweh which, till far into the monarchical period, continued to be reverenced without opposition, or at least to be employed as a means of obtaining Divine oracles. No doubt, it is an image of Jahweh that we are to understand by the *peṣel* ‡ of Micah (Jg $17^{3f.}$), seeing that it was procured with a sum of money that had been dedicated to Jahweh. The original narrative is not intended to convey any censure of Micah's action, but simply to give an account of the origin of the cult of the Jahweh-image at Dan (cf. $18^{30f.}$).

(*b*) The *'ēphôd* (אֵפוֹד) appears exclusively as an image of Jahweh, and more than once is clearly connected with the obtaining of oracles. The word means primarily 'something *thrown over*' (as applied to a garment it answers to the German *Überwurf*

* The most striking instance of this usage would be found in Is $30^{27}$ ('The name of Jahweh cometh from afar, glowing is his anger,' etc.), if the text has come down to us correct.

* Among these may also be included in a certain sense the 'spirit of Jahweh *or* of God'; on which see below, pp. 653, $656^{b}$ f.

† It is simply a correction made in dogmatic interests (in view of Ex $33^{30}$), when already in the LXX, and consequently in the MT, by means of a pointing which is linguistically hardly conceivable, the beholding of the face of God is transformed into an 'appearing before the face of God.' In Ex $34^{23}$ and Dt $16^{16}$ (and hence also Ex $23^{17}$, where the Samaritan text still offers correctly the accusative sign אֶת־ instead of אֶל־) read יִרְאֶה ('let him behold') for יֵרָאֶה ('let him appear'); and in Ex $34^{24}$, Dt $31^{11}$, Is $1^{12}$ read לִרְאוֹת ('to behold') for לֵרָאוֹת ('to appear'). Even in Ex $23^{15}$ $34^{20}$, where the passive יֵרָאוּ (in the sense of 'my face shall not be seen') might be possible, we should probably read the active יִרְאוּ ('they shall behold').

‡ The 'molten image' named along with the *peṣel* is, in all probability, a mistaken addition, and so is the *tĕrāphîm* coupled with the *'ēphôd* in v.[5] (in the other recension of the narrative). In $18^{30f.}$ only *a peṣel* is spoken of.

or *Überzug*); coupled with *bad*, 'linen,' it stands for the 'waistcoat' (see vol. i. p. $725^{a}$) worn by the priests or by people in general on ritual occasions (1 S $2^{18}$ worn by the youthful Samuel, 2 S $6^{14}$ by David before the sacred Ark). In the Priests' Code, finally, the *'ēphôd* (without *bad*) is the ornamental 'waistcoat' of the high priest, in which is the pocket with the sacred lots, the Urim and Thummim (Ex $25^{7}$, and esp. $28^{4ff.}$). The attempt made, on the ground of these passages, to explain *'ēphôd* in every instance as = 'waistcoat' or the like, and thus to get over the mention of an image of God, is shattered by a number of ancient passages, about whose true meaning no doubt can arise. When Gideon, according to Jg $8^{26f.}$, expended 1700 shekels of gold on the making of an *'ēphôd*, and 'set' [it is the same word, הִצִּיג, that is used elsewhere of the erecting of *maṣṣēbôth* or monuments] it in Ophrah, it cannot be a 'waistcoat' that is in view; on the contrary, the writer means to record to the credit of Gideon how, out of the spoil, he had an image of Jahweh constructed. The redactor of the Book of Judges, it is true, views his conduct differently (v.$^{27b}$): 'All Israel went a whoring after it,' *i.e.* practised idolatry with it. But this very expression clearly indicates that the redactor, too, thinks of the *'ēphôd* as a Divine image, only that to him such an image is absolutely forbidden, under any circumstances, by the principles of the Deuteronomic legislation. Again, in Jg $17^{5}$ the *'ēphôd*, being parallel to the *pesel* of the other recension of the narrative (see above, p. $641^{b}$, note ‡), is nothing other than an image of Jahweh. The same holds good of 1 S $21^{10\,(9)}$, where everything becomes clear if we think of the sword of Goliath, wrapped in a garment 'behind the ephod,' as hanging upon the wall behind the image of Jahweh standing on a pedestal in the apse of the sanctuary. In like manner the *'ēphôd* of 1 S $2^{28}$ $14^{3.\,18}$ [here correcting the text by the LXX] $23^{6.\,9}$ $30^{7}$ is the *portable* image of Jahweh, which the priest brings forward at the command of Saul or of David, because it was required for the obtaining of an oracle from Jahweh. It is nowhere indicated that the *'ēphôd* itself contained any mechanism for casting lots. On the contrary, the lots would appear simply to have been cast in presence of the image, and thus as it were before the face of Jahweh, and the result was accordingly regarded as having His sanction. That such an employment of the image of Jahweh was still viewed as quite unobjectionable, is shown by Hos $3^{4}$, where the prophet simply means that Israel (in exile) will have to dispense with all the requisites for a normal political and religious life, including *'ēphôd* and *tĕrāphîm*.

Now, it may naturally be asked how the Divine image and the priestly 'waistcoat' could be designated by one and the same name.* The view that *'ēphôd* stands properly for the gold or silver overlaying or casing of an image of wood, clay, or even brass, can appeal for support to Is $30^{22}$, where the certainly equivalent feminine form *'ăphuddāh* stands parallel with *ẓippûi*, the metal casing of carved images. Yet it is a question whether *'ēphôd* did not primarily denote simply the garment used to clothe the Divine image (cf. Jer $10^{9}$, Ezk $16^{18}$). From this, as the most precious part and that which most struck the eye, the whole image might soon come to take its name. If we might assume that this ephod already had attached to it a pocket with the sacred lots, this would explain very simply how in the Priests' Code (Ex $28^{6ff.}$) the objectionable *'ēphôd* could be wholly ignored as an image of the Deity, but retained without prejudice in the form of a garment with the oracle-pocket.*

(*c*) Not only the *'ēphôd* but also the *tĕrāphîm* (תְּרָפִים) should doubtless be understood as images of the Deity—for the most part (see below), images of Jahweh. With the exception of 2 K $23^{24}$ and Zec $10^{2}$, the word *tĕrāphîm*, in spite of the plural form, should probably be everywhere (quite certainly so in 1 S $19^{13.\,16}$) taken as the designation of only *one* image; that is to say, it is an example of the so-called *pluralis majestatis*, as happens frequently with such words as *'ădōnîm*, *bĕ'ālîm*, and usually *'ĕlōhîm*. The etymology is still quite obscure. The connexion with the *rĕphā'îm*, or shades, favoured by many, is extremely improbable. All that is clear is that the *tĕrāphîm* is related to the *'ēphôd* in the same way as the image of a household god is to the more official image set up in a 'god's house' and attended to by a priest. That the *tĕrāphîm* is not necessarily an image of Jahweh is proved by the case of the *tĕrāphîm* stolen by Rachel from Laban (Gn $31^{19.\,34f.}$), which the latter calls 'my god' (vv.$^{30.\,32}$); and by Ezk $21^{26\,(21)}$, where the king of Babylon consults the *tĕrāphîm* at the crossing of the roads. In all other passages it is quite *possible* to understand *tĕrāphîm* to mean an image of Jahweh. So [probably, indeed, by a later and mistaken expansion], along with the *'ēphôd*, in Jg $17^{5}$ $18^{14.\,17f.\,20}$, 1 S $19^{13.\,16}$ (which passages speak plainly in favour of a human-like form), and Hos $3^{4}$ (again coupled with the *'ēphôd*; see above). The circumstance that in 1 S $15^{23}$, 2 K $23^{24}$, and Zec $10^{2}$ (where the *tĕrāphîm* appear just as in Ezk $21^{26}$, as giving oracles) the possession and use of a *tĕrāphîm* is branded as a species of idolatry, proves nothing against its character as an image of Jahweh. From the Prophetic point of view, which is that represented in all the above passages, there is little difference between *images* of Jahweh and images of actual *idols*. The hypothesis that the *tĕrāphîm* represented a survival of images of ancestors or stood for former tribal and family gods, would indeed suit well their character as household gods, but lacks all probability. Apart from the fact that no certain evidence can be adduced in favour of the prevalence of Ancestor Worship in Israel (see above, p. 614 ff.), it is hard to suppose that in the house of so zealous a Jahweh-worshipper as David there should have been found any image but one of Jahweh. Of the existence of the latter kind of image we have proof, above all, in Ex $21^{6}$. There we read that the slave who has no desire to go free in the seventh year is to be pinned by the ear to the doorpost before [the image of] God, which is evidently assumed as set up by the entrance. In view of the whole spirit and standpoint of the Book of the Covenant, this can refer only to an image of Jahweh as the witness of this symbolical transaction.† In like manner 'God' in $22^{7\,(8)}$

* Th. U. Foote, in what is in itself a very thorough and ingenious monograph, *The Ephod: its Form and Use* (Baltimore, 1902), denies that there is any distinction between *'ēphôd* and *'ēphôd bad*. The latter expression, since בַּד in the sense of 'linen' is unproved, he explains as = ''ēphôd partis [virilis],' and the *'ēphôd* itself as the container of the sacred lots, a kind of pocket which may have been developed from the primitive loin-cloth. Foote arrives at this result (although he himself recognizes *images* in the *tĕrāphîm* so often associated with the *'ēphôd*) by a quite artificial and untenable exegesis of Jg $8^{27}$, 1 S $21^{10}$, and other passages. Moreover, if the *'ēphôd* was nothing but a pocket for the sacred lots, whence its sharp condemnation in Jg $8^{27b}$, and the bold alteration of the text in 1 S $14^{18}$, where, in place of the objectionable *'ēphôd* [so still the LXX], the Ark—wholly impossible here—is inserted in the MT? The *only* explanation of this is that even at a very late date the true meaning of the *'ēphôd* in those passages was still well known, and on that account gave offence.

* Mention should be made here of the suggestion of Schwally (*Semit. Kriegsaltertümer*, i. 15) that the priest, when giving oracles, himself put on the *'ēphôd*, the clothing of the idol, that the knowledge of the god might thus be transmitted to him.

† That *'ĕlōhîm* in this passage cannot be understood, according to the usual interpretation, as meaning 'judges' (as representatives of God), is proved by Dt $15^{17}$, where, in the otherwise

might also be understood of a *tĕrāphîm*; but there, as well as in v.$^{8\ (9)}$, the reference is more likely to a Divine image in a public sanctuary.

From the above we conclude, then, that the *'ēphôd* and (at least from the monarchical period) the *tĕrāphîm* as well were images of Jahweh, which as such were regarded as quite unobjectionable in the pre-Prophetic period, nay, even as late as Hosea (3$^{4}$), until at last they were involved in the same condemnation as images of idols proper (cf. below, p. 679$^{b}$ ff.).

(*d*) Finally, the *golden bulls* set up by Jeroboam at Bethel and Dan were intended as images of Jahweh, and not as heathen images. It might appear otherwise from the language of the Chronicler (2 Ch 13$^{8}$ *et al.*), but the truth was still quite evident to the Deuteronomic redactor of the Books of Kings (cf. 1 K 12$^{28f.}$). In like manner the narrative of Ex 32$^{1ff.}$, which belongs to the older sources of the Pentateuch, is quite aware that Aaron meant to represent Jahweh by the golden calf which had brought Israel out of Egypt, for he makes him in v.$^{5}$ proclaim a feast to Jahweh. But even here the giving of this form to Jahweh is looked upon as a grievous offence on the part of Aaron; and the Deuteronomist is never weary in the Books of Kings of denouncing this cult as 'the sin of Jeroboam,' and of discovering in it one of the principal causes of the downfall of the Northern kingdom (cf. especially 2 K 17$^{21ff.}$).

The question whether in the pre-Prophetic period all those different kinds of images were actually identified with Jahweh, and were thus venerated as *fetishes*, cannot be answered right off by a Yes or a No. The plurality of images (so in particular also the *two* official bull-figures at Bethel and Dan) would naturally lead of itself to a distinguishing between Jahweh enthroned in heaven or upon Sinai and His numerous pictorial representations. But only too frequently, at least amongst the lower orders, there would be a tendency to fall into the error of confounding the Deity with His image, just as in the Roman Catholic Church distinctions are made by the people between different images of the Mother of God in regard to their miraculous virtues, although all these images are meant to represent one and the same person. The reproach so frequently addressed by the pre-exilic Prophets to their contemporaries, that they 'bowed down to the work of their hands,' must have been no less applicable in the pre-Prophetic period. Half unconsciously men changed, like the heathen (Ro 1$^{23}$), the glory of the immortal God into the image of perishable men and beasts.

5. Before closing our discussion of the conception of God, it may be fitting here to touch briefly upon the few passages that speak of *angels* as intermediate beings betwixt God and man, and of certain *half-mythological figures* which had already taken their place in Jahwism in the pre-Prophetic period.*

(*a*) The belief in supramundane and at the same time almost independent powers shows itself in the most surprising fashion in Gn 6$^{1-4}$, a passage with a strong mythological colouring, which belongs to the older stratum of J. The *bĕnê 'ĕlōhîm* [lit. 'sons of the gods,' but really a designation of those who belong to the category of *'ĕlōhîm* or *numina* (just as *bĕnê nĕbî'îm* does not mean 'sons of the prophets,' but members of the guild of *nĕbî'îm*)] appear here, if not as full-blooded popular gods in the sense of polytheism, yet as standing outside the realm of Jahwism as a kind of demi-gods. In all probability the original text meant simply to record that from their union with the daughters of men there sprang up on earth a hybrid race similar to the Titans and giants of Greek mythology. But it must be added that Gn 6$^{1ff.}$ is the only passage of this kind. The *bĕnê 'ĕlōhîm* are mentioned elsewhere only in Job 1$^{6}$ 2$^{1}$ 38$^{7}$, where they are simply angelic beings in the service and train of God.

A more frequent designation of these intermediate beings is *mal'ākh*, 'messenger,' 'angel.' Of course we here leave out of account the above (p. 638 f.) described *theologumenon* of the 'angel of Jahweh *or* of God.' To the category of creature angels serving or surrounding Jahweh may have belonged, according to the pre-Prophetic popular belief, the 'men' who accompany Jahweh on His visit to Abraham [in Gn 19$^{1.\ 15}$, after parting from Jahweh, they are first called 'angels'] and are entertained by the latter.* So also the guardian-angel sent by Jahweh in Gn 24$^{7.\ 40}$, Nu 20$^{16}$ (although in these passages the idea of the *mal'akh Jahweh* is not remote), and 1 K 19$^{5}$; further, the angels of Gn 28$^{12}$ (E) whom Jacob in a dream sees ascending and descending a ladder (namely, in order to facilitate communication between heaven and earth at Bethel, a principal centre of revelation [the mention of the ladder in this passage shows that angels are still thought of as unwinged]); and the troop of angels of God (Gn 32$^{3\ (2)}$ [E]) whose appearance led Jacob to give the city of *Maḥanaim* ('camp') its name. In the very doubtful text, Dt 33$^{2}$, the 'holy myriads' may probably refer originally to the attendants of God at theophanies. In addition to these few passages from the Pentateuch there are in the older strata of the Historical books: Jos 5$^{13}$ (J ?), where the leader of the [heavenly] army of Jahweh meets Joshua; and 2 K 6$^{17}$, where the fiery horses and chariots are to be thought of as driven by angels. The 'destroying angel' of 2 S 24$^{16}$, who at the command of Jahweh smites the people with pestilence, is evidently thought of, not as a professional 'executioner angel,' but as one appointed by God to carry out His judgment in this particular instance. In 1 K 22$^{19}$, again, in the vision of the prophet Micaiah the whole host of heaven on the right and the left of Jahweh represents a celestial deliberative assembly. Quite a peculiar position is occupied here by 'the spirit,' who, in the light of the whole context, can be only the personified spirit of prophecy. Nothing is said in any of these passages about the moral quality of the angels, for even in Dt 33$^{2}$ [if the text be correct] 'holiness' refers not to their moral perfection, but only to their exaltation above this world and their belonging to God. So also the comparison of David to an angel of God (1 S 29$^{9}$) has in view only the trust and reverence due to angels.—Our whole survey shows, however, that in early Israel statements about angels play only a subordinate part, and belong rather to the popular beliefs than to Jahwism proper. It is to be noted, moreover, that the most characteristic expressions are connected either with a dream (Gn 28$^{12}$) or a vision (1 K 22$^{19}$, 2 K 6$^{17}$ may also be included in this category).

(*b*) To the realm of angels belong, beyond doubt, the *sĕrāphîm* (שְׂרָפִים). Although mentioned only in

almost identical text, the reference to *'ĕlōhîm* is omitted. The Deuteronomist, in fact, quite correctly understood the reference to be to an image of Jahweh, and suppressed it on that account. Again, in Ex 22$^{8.\ 27\ (9.\ 28)}$ and 1 S 2$^{25}$ *'ĕlōhîm* has no other sense than that of 'Deity.'

* Cf. Kosters, art. 'Het onstaan en de entwikkeling der angelologie onder Israel' in *Theol. Tijdschr.* 1876, pp. 34 ff., 113 ff.; A. Aeberhard, art. 'Gottes Umgebung nach den vorexilischen Schriften' in *Schweizer Theol. Zeitschrift*, 1902, p. 193 ff.

* According to the oldest form of this narrative, as comes out plainly in 18$^{1.\ 3.\ 10-15}$, Jahweh alone appears to Abraham. Offence is naturally taken at this by a later recension, which is now skilfully interwoven with the earlier one, and which introduces three men or angels in place of Jahweh.

the vision of Isaiah ($6^{2}$), they appear there as well-known beings, so that the belief in them may certainly be assumed for the pre-Prophetic period. Furnished with six wings, they offer around God's throne antiphonal praise in the Trisagion; one of them purges the lips of the prophet, and announces to him the forgiveness of his sins. They are thus, in fact, intelligent beings, angels. Of the numerous explanations of the name, the only one that can be taken in earnest is that which traces it back to the singular *sārāph.* This word means properly 'serpent' (Nu $21^{8}$, Dt $8^{15}$), and the seraphim must accordingly have been originally serpent-formed creatures—embodiments, indeed, of the serpent-like lightning-flashes that play around Jahweh. But, in the case of the seraphim of Isaiah, the six wings may be regarded as all that has survived of this somewhat mythological form. Moreover (probably long before the time of Isaiah), they have assumed human form, as is evident not only from the song of praise (v.$^{3}$), which would be inconceivable in a serpent's mouth, but from the hand (v.$^{6}$) and the speech of the *sārāph* (v.$^{7}$). It may be noted, finally, that here again in Is 6 it is a vision that is recorded.

(*c*) Even more clearly than the seraphim, the *cherubim* (*kĕrûbîm,* כְּרֻבִים or כְּרוּבִים, sing. *kĕrûb*) belong originally to the realm of mythology.* The etymology of the word is still disputed. According to some, *kĕrûb* is from the same root (Sanskrit *gribh,* 'grip') as the Greek γρύψ, 'griffin'; according to others, it is due to a transposition of the consonants of *rĕkûb,* 'chariot' (cf. Ps $104^{3}$), from the root *rākab,* 'ride' or 'drive' (see below). The most probable derivation would be from the Assyr. *kurūbu* (plur. *kurūbi*), 'great,' 'strong,' if it could be proved with certainty that the winged bull-colossi with human heads, found at the entrance of Assyrian palaces, bore the name *kurūbi.*

All the various references to the cherubim have this in common, that they always imply the nearness of God, or at least indicate a sacred spot. But there are evidently two quite distinct underlying conceptions, which were only at a late period combined into one [hence even the name *kĕrûb* might have a double etymology]. According to Ps $18^{11}$ (cf. also Is $19^{1}$) the cherub is a pale form of the wind-driven storm-cloud which serves Jahweh as His chariot [or which, originally, He rides as a horse?].† The other sense of the word *kĕrûb* is that of a guardian of sacred spots. To this category belong the cherubim of Gn $3^{24}$, who, after the expulsion of our first parents, guard the entrance to the Garden of Eden [*i.e.* according to the original intention of the narrative, the dwelling-place of God]; and also the huge cherub forms, carved in olive wood, which Solomon set up in the temple to the right and the left of the sacred Ark, in such a way that with their outstretched wings they filled the whole space (1 K $6^{23ff.}$ $8^{6f.}$). So also the carved figures of cherubim on the walls and doors (1 K $6^{29.\ 32.\ 35}$) and vessels ($7^{29.\ 36}$) of the temple indicate the near presence of God. Hence they appear also in the visionary temple of Ezekiel (Ezk $41^{18ff.}$), as well as in the sanctuary which the Priests' Code assumes for the period of the wilderness wanderings. In the latter they present themselves, partly as worked on the curtains and the veil (Ex $26^{1.\ 31}$), partly as two golden figures, with their faces turned towards each other, placed on the lid of the sacred Ark ($25^{18ff.}$; cf. preced. col., note †).

It is hard to say what *form* we ought to attribute to the cherubim with which we are dealing. In Ex $25^{20}$ they have only *one* face each, whereas in Ezk $41^{18ff.}$ each has a man's and also a lion's face. Still more complicated is the description of them in the first vision of Ezekiel ($1^{5ff.}$). Here each of the four cherubim has four faces (a man's, a lion's, an ox's, and an eagle's) and four wings, besides human hands. Besides this, they are, according to $10^{12}$, quite covered with eyes, symbols of the Divine omniscience. That they are creatures endowed with reason might be inferred at least from $10^{7}$, if the cherub there belongs to the original text; but not from $3^{12}$, where for בָּרוּךְ we should read בְּרוּם ('when the glory of Jahweh lifted itself up'). A comparison of all the above data leads to the conclusion that the cherub was indeed thought of all along as a hybrid being, but originally as probably composed of only *two* different bodies.* At the same time it can hardly be doubted that the Biblical cherubim are of Babylono-Assyrian origin, although they need not have been first borrowed in the age of Solomon. But it is impossible to decide whether the ordinary cherub form corresponded to the Assyrian winged bulls or lions with a human head or the human forms with a bird's head. All that appears to be certain is that the complicated cherub forms in Ezk 1 and 10 (with all their additions) owed their initiation to the imagination of this prophet, only that he has perhaps united in one what the popular belief attributed to a number of hybrid beings. The most important point to notice is that Ezekiel, in his description, is the first to unite the conception of a griffin form with the other in which we found a pale form of the storm-cloud as the bearer of Jahweh. For the cherubim of Ezekiel, as is plain from $1^{22.\ 26ff.}$ $9^{3}$ (where the whole appearance is included in the singular 'cherub') $10^{4.\ 18f.}$, are the bearers of the crystal plane on which the throne of Jahweh rests; by means of the wheels, which are inseparable from them, they move the chariot-throne of Jahweh. Of quite a different kind is the cherub of Ezk $28^{13ff.}$, who, all covered with precious stones, walks upon the sacred mount of the gods amongst stones of fire. Here a direct borrowing from a *mythologumenon* of the East, as well as a partial affinity with Gn $3^{24}$, is unmistakable. It should be remarked, however, that this cherub serves only the purpose of comparison (with the king of Tyre), while the cherubim of chapters 1 and 10 belong simply to a vision, and those of the temple and the tabernacle are merely symbolical ornaments. Hence they can in no case be reckoned amongst the necessary elements of Jahwism.

### iii. *SYNCRETISM BETWEEN JAHWEH AND THE CANAANITE BAAL. DEFEAT OF BAAL THROUGH JAHWEH'S BEING FINALLY LOCALIZED IN*

* Cf., for the special literature, Kosters, art. 'De Cherubim' in *Theol. Tijdschr.* 1879, p. 445 ff.; Triebs, *Veteris Testamenti de Cherubim doctrina*, Berlin, 1888; J. Nikel, *Die Lehre des AT über die Cherubim und Seraphim* [Würzburg dissertation; full of dogmatic prejudices], Breslau, 1890; J. Petersen, *Cherubim*, Gütersloh, 1898 [account of the various interpretations from the time of Luther downwards].

† Instead of *one* cherub, a number of cherubim appear in 1 S $4^{4}$, 2 S $6^{2}$, 2 K $19^{15}$ as bearers of God or of the Divine throne. Of these passages the last cited can scarcely have any other meaning, especially as there Ḥezeḳiah prays for a judicial intervention of Jahweh against Assyria, and thus, as it were, for an appearance of Jahweh. In a similar connexion 'He that sitteth upon the cherubim' is still mentioned in such late passages as Ps $80^{2\,(1)}$ $99^{1}$. On the other hand, it is scarcely to be doubted that in 1 S $4^{4}$ and in 2 S $6^{2}$ the same expression is due to a subsequent interpolation, and is intended of the golden cherubim upon the lid of the sacred Ark, which are first mentioned in the Priests' Code (Ex $25^{18ff.}$). According to the latter (Nu $7^{89}$), Jahweh speaks to Moses from this lid, 'from between the two cherubim,' *i.e.* He has His proper dwelling-place there. The above interpolation was very natural on the part of a late redactor of 1 S $4^{4}$ and 2 S $6^{2}$, because in both these passages there is express mention of Jahweh's relation to the sacred Ark. It is impossible that any of the above passages can refer to the two great cherubim which Solomon (see text above) set up beside the sacred Ark.

* This conclusion is favoured also by the circumstance that they are compared by Philo and Josephus with the sphinxes.

*CANAAN AND COMING TO BE CONCEIVED OF AS GOD OF HEAVEN.*—1. Israel on entering Canaan found itself in presence of a pretty highly civilized people, which had long ago adopted the settled form of life, was skilled in agriculture, gardening, and vine-culture, and in consequence enjoyed great material prosperity. Nothing was more natural than that Israel should seek to compete with the Canaanites in the above-named industries. True, the transition from the purely nomadic to the agricultural state was accomplished but slowly. The patriarchal narratives, which may be regarded as a faithful picture of the conditions that prevailed during the earlier part of the period of the Judges, still exhibit a mingling of the settled with the nomadic life; and even in the so-called Book of the Covenant (Ex 21–23) the pasturing of flocks evidently still plays an important rôle along with the cultivating of the soil. The necessity of learning the finer arts of field- and vine-culture from the Canaanites—and that in constant association with them—would of itself suffice to explain numerous Canaanite influences upon the conduct and the habits of thought of the Israelites. But there are other two very powerful factors that come into view in this connexion.

(*a*) In the first place, the land into which Israel penetrated had belonged from times remote to another god who, in various forms, was worshipped at the different sanctuaries of the country, and whose rights as owner no one at first dreamt of contesting. To Israel, as to every other people of those days, it was self-evident that every nation and country had its own god. The latter may indeed be temporarily overcome by the more powerful god (or gods) of a foreign nation, but his existence is not therewith ended. The thought, however, of a defeat of Baal (or the baals) of Canaan could not take its rise among the Israelites so long as they were able only with difficulty (as is shown by Jg $1^{5}$ $18^{1\text{ff.}}$ etc.) to maintain their position in the land *side by side with* the Canaanites. In view of all this, it was *per se* self-evident that Baal, the god of the land, was to be regarded as the bestower of the fruits of the land, and was entitled to thanks accordingly. (*b*) But, in the second place, according to the conceptions of antiquity, agriculture itself was viewed as a branch of the cult of the god of the land, or at least as part of the religious customs and usages which are traced back to him, and on that account are observed and handed down with superstitious care. This view finds an instructive exposition in Is $28^{23\text{ff.}}$.

When we take all the above considerations into account, the conclusion we inevitably draw is that it was almost impossible that Israel should escape being involved in the cult of Baal if it desired to maintain its existence on *his* soil, in the midst of *his* people, who were ill affected towards Israel. The only question is whether this way of looking at the matter was—at least for a length of time—shared by all classes of the people without exception, or whether, at least amongst the intellectual and religious leaders there were those who even then put forward in downright earnest the supreme plea of the Sinai religion: 'Jahweh—and Jahweh alone—is the God of Israel.' We may infer that there were, judging from the energy with which the struggle against Baal was afterwards undertaken, and which implies a continuous maintenance of exclusive Jahwism. There are, however, no *direct* testimonies to a struggle maintained at every period with the worship of Baal. It might perhaps be supposed that a distinction should be drawn between the Canaanite Baal, who was quite early superseded, and of whom there is no further trace even in the *ancient* records of the opening monarchical period, and the Tyrian Baal imported by Jezebel and Athaliah, against whom a violent storm of opposition at once arose. But this would be to disregard a very trustworthy witness, whose testimony is to quite a different effect, namely Hos $2^{7\,(5)\,\text{ff.}}$. When the prophet here reproaches his countrymen with going after their lovers [the baals], who were supposed to have bestowed upon them bread and water, wool and flax, oil and 'drinks' (v.$^{14\,(12)}$ vines and fig-trees), he is thinking not of times long gone by, nor of the cult of the Tyrian Baal, but of an ineradicable delusion of the people which can be traced down to the time of Hosea—that is, till the closing days of the Northern kingdom: 'she knoweth not that it is *I* [Jahweh] who have bestowed upon her the corn and the must and the oil, and have given her silver and gold in abundance—upon Baal hath she expended it' (Hos $2^{10\,(8)}$). It may be that the complaint of Hosea applied in a much larger measure to the kingdom of Israel than to that of Judah. But, in any case, it furnishes a very notable testimony to the tenacity with which the belief in Baal as the god of the land and the dispenser of its fruits persisted amongst a portion of the people.*

2. From all the above considerations it follows that the picture which the Deuteronomic redactor of the Book of Judges (cf. esp. $2^{11\text{ff.}}$) sketches of the religious conditions of the period of the Judges is not true to the historical reality. To him—from the standpoint of the 7th or 6th cent. B.C.—no other view is possible except that any inclination to the cult of other gods is at the same time complete apostasy from Jahweh, the God of the fathers (Jg $2^{11}$). It is the anger of Jahweh, occasioned by their conduct, and the oppression at the hands of their foes to which He gives them over, that (according to this view) first bring Israel to reflexion and a return to Jahweh. But the truth is that in these early times men considered it quite an intelligible position that, on the one hand, they should hold fast to Jahweh in all matters affecting the people as a whole (so, for instance, especially in war; cf. above, p. 636a); while, on the other hand, they did not break with Baal, the god of the land and the bestower of fruits, but rendered to him the thanks and the offerings that were his due. Such conduct is not to be viewed as pure idolatry, and still less as polytheism; it is simply a species of syncretism which aims at satisfying, each in its own way, all the varieties of religious needs. In like manner, among the Arabs, long after the victory of Islam, the local cult of the pre-Islamic gods persisted, partly in the popular usages (forbidden by Islam), partly in some usages incorporated with Islam itself.

3. In the long run, however, this double cult of quite heterogeneous gods became impossible: one or other must yield. And, as a matter of fact, by aid of the ancient sources we can still trace pretty accurately the long process which led to the complete conquest and suppression of the

* Surviving traces of this notion are discovered by Schwally (*Semit. Kriegsaltertümer*, i. 81 ff.) in such legal prescriptions as that newly planted fruit trees were to be left untouched for three years, but in the fourth year their fruits were to be dedicated to Jahweh (Lv $19^{23\text{ff.}}$; cf. Dt $20^{6}$, where a similar rule is supposed to hold of vineyards); that a field was not to be reaped to its very edges (Lv $19^{9\text{ff.}}$); that a forgotten sheaf was not to be fetched from the field, and that in general all gleaning was to be dispensed with (Dt $24^{19\text{ff.}}$). In all these usages it is supposed that there was an intention of propitiating the 'demons' and baals (cf. what was said above, p. 617b f., about the sacrifices offered to the *sĕ'îrîm*). But here again, as elsewhere, it is very questionable whether Deuteronomy (not to speak of Leviticus) has still any consciousness of *this* meaning of customs inherited from olden times; at all events, the ancient custom is now grounded *only* on considerations of humanity (the care of widows, orphans, and *gērîm*).

baals by Jahweh, at least so far as the better portion of the people were concerned.

(*a*) One of the most essential factors in achieving this result was unquestionably *the localizing of Jahweh in Canaan*, especially at certain primeval and much frequented sanctuaries. Such a localizing process was by no means a matter of course from the most ancient point of view. True, even from the earliest times we hear of appearances of Jahweh on Canaanite soil in the form of the *mal'akh Jahweh* (see above, p. 638 ff.). But the latter came and went without its being possible to speak of any fixed dwelling-place. The sacred Ark, again, guaranteed, nay represented (cf. above, p. 628 f., the presence of Jahweh. But the Ark was, above all, the shrine of *Jahweh Zĕbā'ôth*, the war-God, who had nothing to do with the cultivating of the soil or the training of vines. The proper seat of Jahweh continued to be, as before, Sinai. It is from there that Jahweh comes to aid the tribes of Israel in their struggle with Sisera (Jg 5$^{4}$). We may perhaps leave out of account Dt 33$^{2f.}$, Hab 3$^{3}$, and Ps 68$^{8}$ as merely poetical reminiscences of Jg 5$^{4}$, while Dt 33$^{16}$ ('the dweller in the bush') suffers from uncertainty of interpretation. But there is still left 1 K 19$^{8ff.}$ as a positive proof that in the time of Elijah the seat of Jahweh was found at 'Ḥoreb the mount of God.'

But it cannot be pronounced that the above was the only way of looking at the matter that prevailed in the time of the Judges, not to speak of the monarchical period. The gradual subjugation of the Canaanites, which was completed by the entire subjection of their surviving representatives by Solomon, and the signal proof of the might of Jahweh afforded by David's victories, naturally involved a lowering of the prestige of Baal more and more—nay, in many places its complete annihilation. To this was added the erecting of new sanctuaries, dedicated to Jahweh exclusively: like that of Gideon at Ophrah (Jg 6$^{24}$ 8$^{27}$), the temple for the sacred Ark at Shiloh, then the tent for it in the city of David, and, above all, the temple of Solomon, which no doubt surpassed in splendour and in art all the hitherto existing sanctuaries of Canaan (with the possible exception of the Phœnician ones). All these spots, where Jahweh alone was venerated, could not fail to familiarize men's minds with the notion of His personal dwelling in Canaan. And thus it was only the last step towards the complete localizing of Him there, when even the former Canaanite sacred places, which, as such, had long given an advantage to the Baal worship, were expressly brought into relation with Jahweh. Jahweh thus becomes simply identified with Baal, steps into possession of all the property and functions of the latter. This could be done all the more readily that Baal is not, like Jahweh, a real proper name, but an appellative = 'lord' or 'owner,' so that it could serve equally well as a designation of Jahweh.

The surest evidence that Jahweh thus took the place of Baal is to be found in the employment of *Baal* in the composition of Israelitish personal names (possibly also in a number of place-names [so certainly in 2 S 5$^{20}$]) as quite the equivalent in meaning of *Jahweh*.* Thus we find *Jerubba'al* (the real name of Gideon), *Eshba'al*, *Meriba'al* (descendants of Saul), *Be'eliada'* (one of David's sons); cf. also 1 Ch 12$^{5}$ *Be'eliah*, 'Jah[weh] is Baal.'

With the transference of the cult of Jahweh to the spots where Baal worship had been practised is certainly connected a circumstance which by itself appears very strange to us, but which finds its analogies in all popular religions which have images of gods (or even of saints). The Canaanite Baal was originally *one* particular god; but, as his images became localized in different lands and sanctuaries, he was correspondingly broken up as it were into different deities. This is proved by the numerous discriminating appellations, where the name of a place is added to that of Baal (*e.g.* *Baal-Peor*, *Baal-Ḥermon*, etc.), or where we have some other distinguishing mark (*e.g.* *Baal-bĕrîth*, 'Baal of the covenant'; *Baal-zĕbūb*, 'the fly-Baal,' etc.). So also Milcom the god of the Ammonites, Chemosh the god of the Moabites, and Melkart the city-god of Tyre, are manifestly examples of such localizing of the *one* Canaanite Baal. It is thus intelligible that in Jg 2$^{11}$ 3$^{7}$ 10$^{6}$ etc., and even in Hos 2$^{15.19\,(13.17)}$ 11$^{2}$, a worship of 'the baals' is spoken of. But the same differentiating process was applied also to Jahweh when He (or His images) stepped into the place of Baal, or had even new places of worship assigned to Him. The proof of this is supplied once more by the special names given to particular altars or places of worship of Jahweh; this special name serving to distinguish, as it were, the local God of *this* place from other local gods. The Jahweh who was worshipped at the sacred tamarisk of Beersheba (Gn 21$^{33}$) is called *Jahweh 'Ēl 'ôlām* ('the God of primeval time'? or 'the eternal God'?); He who appears to Jacob at Luz is called *'Ēl Bēthēl*, 'the God of Bethel' (31$^{13}$ 35$^{7}$); the altar erected by Jacob at Shechem is called *'Ēl 'Ĕlōhê Israel*, 'El, God of Israel' (33$^{20}$); that which Jerubbaal built at Ophrah receives the name *Jahweh shālôm*, 'Jahweh is safety' (Jg 6$^{24}$). When, finally, Absalom declares (2 S 15$^{7f.}$) that he must go to Ḥebron to discharge a vow to Jahweh, he evidently means to distinguish the Jahweh of Ḥebron from the Jahweh of Jerusalem. Presumably, a sacrifice offered at the far older place of worship at Ḥebron was believed to have greater efficacy than one presented at the more recent sanctuary at Jerusalem.

The whole process of localizing Jahweh in Canaan, and the consequent destruction of the syncretism between Jahweh and Baal, presents itself to us as already accomplished in the patriarchal narratives of Gn 12 ff. These have not a word to say about any places of worship of Baal in the land; *all* the future Israelitish sanctuaries are already consecrated by the patriarchs (for the most part in consequence of manifestations of Jahweh) by the building of altars (Gn 12$^{7.8}$ 13$^{18}$ 26$^{25}$ 33$^{20}$) or the planting of a sacred tree (21$^{33}$). In two instances (12$^{6}$ 28$^{11ff.}$), indeed, there can still be clearly detected a recollection that the sacredness of these spots dates really from an earlier, Canaanite, period; but for Israel it dates from the occasion when Jahweh came upon the scene as the *numen loci*, and manifested Himself to Israel's ancestors.

(*b*) In all this we have not as yet mentioned one prime factor which explains very simply the permanent triumph of Jahweh over Baal in the

* Later generations were so unable to comprehend this that (probably with reference to Hos 2$^{17f.}$) for *Baal* they substituted either *Ēl*, 'God' (so in the family of David, 2 S 5$^{16}$, 1 Ch 3$^{8}$ *Eliada'* for *Be'eliada'* of 1 Ch 14$^{7}$), or *bōsheth*, 'shame.' So, in the family of Saul, *Eshba'al*, 'man of Baal' [so still in 1 Ch 8$^{33}$ 9$^{39}$], becomes *Ishbosheth* [2 S 2$^{8ff.}$]; *Mĕrîba'al*, 'man of Baal' [so still in 1 Ch 9$^{40}$, whereas in 1 Ch 8$^{34}$ the objection is removed by the form *Mĕribba'al*, 'opponent of Baal'], becomes *Mephibosheth*, (?) 'despiser of Baal' [2 S 4$^{4}$ 9$^{6ff.}$ 21$^{8}$]. On the other hand, *Jerubba'al* (prob. = 'he who contends for the lord' [*i.e.* Jahweh]) was retained unchanged, with the same signification as *Israel* [the very artificial interpretation in Jg 6$^{25ff.}$ takes it as a surname afterwards given to Gideon, whereas the probability is rather that it is the latter name itself that should be regarded as a surname], Jg 7$^{1}$ 8$^{29.35}$ 9$^{1ff.}$; but cf. also 2 S 11$^{21}$, where we have the form *Jerubbesheth* for Jerubbosheth. The LXX retains *Baal* in the text, but means this to be read *αἰσχύνη* (= *bōsheth*, 'shame'). In no other way can we explain the presence of the feminine article in τῇ Βάαλ of Ro 11$^{4}$ (= 1 K 19$^{18}$).

capacity of the latter as god of the land—namely, the introduction of the conception of Jahweh as a God enthroned *in heaven.* This implies of itself the idea of His supramundane elevation, not only above all earthly powers, but above all local divinities. From heaven Jahweh looks down and directs the actions and fortunes of men, or at least, in the first instance, of His people; from heaven He sends or withholds rain and dew and all the associated blessings of the soil; but from heaven also He rains down fire and brimstone upon Sodom and Gomorrah (Gn $19^{24}$), and thus shows Himself to be the almighty supramundane Lord over all the elements.

According to the view just presented, this conception of Jahweh did not make its way all at once, and still less did it penetrate the *whole body* of the people; side by side with it there continued to prevail for long an ill-defined mingling of the notions which localized Jahweh at Sinai (see above, p. $626^{b}$) or at Canaanite places of worship. But, on the other hand, traces of the conception of Jahweh as a God of heaven can be discovered comparatively early. We must not allow ourselves to be misled by passages where a different view appears to be presented, simply because the narrative form of the myth is adopted. In Gn $3^{8}$, for instance, the Garden of Eden is still God's dwelling-place, but, according to the same source (J), Jahweh comes down from heaven [the context permits of no other meaning] to see the Tower of Babel ($11^{5.7}$). He sends down destruction from heaven from Jahweh ($19^{24}$, see above); He is called 'the God of heaven' ($24^{7}$, v.$^{3}$ 'the God of heaven and earth'). In the E source the idea of Jahweh as the God of heaven has so completely gained the ascendency that even the *mal'akh 'Elōhîm* (cf. above, p. 638 ff.) calls from heaven ($21^{17}$ $22^{11}$, where 'Jahweh' instead of 'Elohim' is due to the redactor who inserted vv.$^{15-18}$). In $28^{12}$ (E) the ladder upon which the angels ascend and descend establishes the connexion between earth and heaven, the dwelling-place of God. Hence Jacob (v.$^{17}$) calls the place at once the house of God (corresponding to the earlier conception) and the gate of heaven.

4. The above assertion, that the cult of Baal was gradually superseded through the localizing of Jahweh at the Canaanite sanctuaries and the growing conception of Him as the God of heaven, appears at first to be violently contradicted by the circumstance that even in the reign of Ahab of Israel (*i.e.* in the first half of the 9th cent. B.C.) the worship of Baal comes upon the scene once more, and in such force that we almost receive the impression that Jahwism had then to engage in a life-and-death struggle, and was brought to the verge of extinction. Elijah complains (1 K $19^{14}$) that the altars of Jahweh had been thrown down and His prophets put to death, that he himself alone was left, and that they sought his life to destroy it. But apart from the answer of God (v.$^{18}$), that the number of those who had remained loyal to Jahweh amounted to 7000, there are other points on which our judgment must be considerably modified with respect to the degree and the universality of the apostasy from Jahweh, particularly so far as Ahab is concerned (1 K $16^{30ff.}$). The names of Ahab's children (Ahaziah, Joram, 'Athaliah) are one and all compounds with the name of Jahweh. The fact that he built for his Tyrian consort Jezebel a Baal temple and altar at Samaria may be explained in the same way as Solomon's building of a Chemosh sanctuary upon the Mount of Olives (see above, p. 635). The bloody persecution of the prophets of Jahweh is expressly (1 K $18^{4}$ $19^{2}$) laid to the charge of Jezebel alone; it is at *her* table that the 450 prophets of Baal * eat ($18^{19}$). Ahab chides Elijah as the author of a famine, but he does not seek his life. On the contrary, he did sincere penance ($21^{27ff.}$) when Jahweh's decree of rejection on account of the judicial murder of Naboth had been announced to him by Elijah. From 1 K $22^{6ff.}$ (the closing period of Ahab's reign) it is evident that a very large number of Jahweh's prophets as well as Micaiah ben-Imlah had been left unmolested. Noteworthy, further, is the judgment of Ahab put in the mouth of Jehu in 2 K $10^{18}$. All this, indeed, does not imply that Ahab was not seriously blameworthy in conniving too much at the conduct of his unscrupulous wife, but the principal guilt plainly lies at the door of Jezebel.

All the more on that account we must ask what was the real aim of Jezebel's conduct. In view of the complaint of Elijah ($19^{14}$) about the throwing down of Jahweh's altars, it looks as if she sought to destroy the cult of Jahweh root and branch and to put that of Baal in its place—in short, to introduce a change of religion. But this appears impossible in face of the attitude of Ahab to Elijah (see above), and especially in view of 2 K $10^{23}$. In the latter passage (in the last days of Jezebel) the presence of a very large number of Jahweh worshippers is assumed alongside of the worshippers of Baal, otherwise Jehu would have had to extirpate not only the dynasty but almost the whole nation. According to v.$^{21}$, however, the worshippers of Baal throughout the whole land were not more than could be assembled by Jehu in the temple of Baal at Samaria. Hence the bloody persecution of the prophets of Jahweh is doubtless to be explained on the ground that they, with Elijah at their head, offered the most violent opposition not only to the according to Baal of equal rights with Jahweh, but even to the introduction and spread of his cult at all. Their acting in this way is an evidence that, at least on the part of thinking representatives of Jahwism, the syncretism that formerly prevailed had been completely overcome, and that their conscience had been sufficiently quickened to apprehend the full meaning of the principle, 'Jahweh alone is the God of Israel.' And they rightly recognized, in *that* form in which syncretism was sought to be revived by Jezebel, a doubly serious danger. Now it was no longer a question of long-established local divinities, in whose place Jahweh could be put without difficulty, but of a foreign god—the same god who had made Tyre the proud mistress of the seas, and the possessor of dazzling wealth. The danger that thus threatened was not simply that Jahweh would be held in less esteem, but that He would be absolutely rejected as weak in comparison with *this* Baal. Jezebel herself doubtless wished devoutly for this consummation, and many a one, to gain her favour, or in dread of her wrath, may have displayed such an excess of zeal for Baal as to have gone the length of tearing down altars of Jahweh (1 K $18^{30}$ $19^{14}$). We shall have to show presently that Jehu's destruction of the work of Jezebel was actuated, if not exclusively, yet mainly by religious motives.

If Jezebel's zeal for the Tyrian Baal occasioned a serious danger and led to a bitter conflict in the Northern kingdom, the cult of Baal is only a quickly passing episode in the kingdom of Judah. From 2 K 11 we do not at all derive the impression that 'Athaliah, the daughter of Ahab and Jezebel, after her attempt to extirpate the Davidic dynasty, took any measures to prevent the continuance of the worship of Jahweh in Solomon's

* The 400 prophets of the *'ăshērāh* named along with them are a later (perhaps in allusion to the Deuteronom. note in $16^{30}$) addition to the text, as is plain from v.$^{40}$, where they could not possibly have failed to be mentioned.

temple. On the contrary, the high priest Joiada is so notable a personage that he has no difficulty in enlisting the royal bodyguard in a conspiracy against 'Athaliah. It is only at the close of the narrative (v.[18]) that we first learn that there was then, even in Jerusalem, a temple of Baal under the charge of a priest named Mattan. The zeal with which 'all the people of the land' tear down this temple, destroy Baal's altars and images, and slay the priest, proves how hateful to the Judahites was the cult imported by 'Athaliah.

iv. *THE ORGANS OF GENUINE JAHWISM: PRIESTS, PROPHETS, NAZIRITES AND RECHABITES, 'JUDGES' AND KINGS.*—In the foregoing section the conflict between Jahweh and Baal is described as primarily one of different religious ideas and needs. As a matter of fact, the latter may gather such strength that they lay hold of wide circles of people and make them their half-unconscious instruments. But this excludes the existence neither of regular, official representatives of particular religious interests, nor the appointment of extraordinary instruments called and equipped by God. Examples of both these are found in considerable numbers in Israel in the period prior to the rise of written prophecy. The official character belongs to priests and kings; the extraordinary mission is represented by the various species of prophets, in which category may be included also the Nazirites and Rechabites, and in a certain sense even the so-called 'judges.'

**1. Priests.**—1. We have already (p. 633[a]) pointed out how few and uncertain are the traditions of the Mosaic period regarding the founding of the Jahweh priesthood.* Even in the period with which we are now dealing, the stream of tradition is a tiny one. This is simply explained on the ground that priests were not required for the most important transaction of the cultus, namely sacrifice, but only for bearing the sacred Ark (so, according to J and E, Jos 3[3ff.] 4[9ff.] 6[6ff.]),† for taking charge of a 'God's house,' *i.e.* the container of an image of Jahweh, and for consulting the sacred lot, which was connected in some way with this image. In the whole Book of Judges there is no mention of priests except in the first appendix (chs. 17 and 18); but that narrative, when rightly interpreted, is extremely instructive in regard to the conditions prevailing under the Judges. The Ephraimite Micah constructs a 'God's house' containing a Divine image [on the plurality of images, which owe their origin to the welding together of two parallel accounts and to a process of glossing, see above, p. 641[b]], and appoints one of his sons to be priest. But when a young Levite, *i.e.* a member of the tribe of Levi, who has hitherto sojourned in Bethlehem-judah as a *gēr*, passes by, he engages him, for a yearly salary of ten shekels of silver and the cost of food and clothing, to serve as 'father' and priest; and he now feels sure that Jahweh will bless him because he has a Levite for priest. The very designation of a young man as 'father' (17[10] 18[19]) shows that this honorific title (used especially, no doubt, as a mode of address) was regularly given to priests as it was, according to 2 K 2[12] 6[21] 13[14], to prophets. A counterpart to this is found in Jg 5[7], where Deborah is called a 'mother in Israel.'

We see from the above, that, even for attending to a 'God's house' and an oracle-image, a Levite was not indispensable, but that particular value was attached to him when his services could be obtained. For, as a descendant of the tribe of Moses, he was supposed, on the ground of the family tradition, to have the best acquaintance with ritual affairs, and, above all, with the method of obtaining oracles. And Micah had all the more ground for this assumption, seeing that his Levite, as we first learn from 18[30], was a son of Gershom and a grandson of Moses,* named Jonathan. Thus there was a priesthood known then, which traced its origin direct to Moses, and there is no reason to doubt the historicity of the statement (18[30]) that in particular the priests of the oracle-image at Dan, which evidently stood in high repute down to B.C. 734, sprang from the family of the above-named Jonathan, and thus of Moses. The circumstance that the image, along with the priest, was originally stolen by the Danites (18[14ff.]), would certainly not damage its character in the least, from the naïve point of view of these early times.

2. It is not till the end of the period of the Judges that we encounter once more a priesthood in Israel, in the person of Eli, with his sons Hophni and Phinehas, in attendance on the sacred Ark at Shiloh (1 S 1[3. 9ff.] 2[12ff.] 4[4ff.]). According to the Deuteronomic addition, 2[27ff.], Eli and his sons are the descendants of a priestly family to whom, in Egypt, Jahweh had already entrusted all fire-offerings of the Israelites. By this is meant, of course, the priestly tribe of Levi, the 'chosen of all the tribes' (v.[28]). The earlier accounts of Eli and his family say nothing of their having belonged to Levi, and the indifference of the ancient sources to any such connexion is shown by the frank statement about the priestly functions discharged by the young Samuel, who was of the tribe of *Ephraim* (1 S 2[18] 3[1ff.], according to which he slept beside the Ark). The Deuteronom. prediction put in the mouth of an unnamed man of God (2[27ff.]) contains what might be called a programme of the subsequent history of the priesthood, the meaning of which is perfectly transparent to us. The destruction of the house of Eli with the sword (v.[33]) refers to Saul's massacre of the priests of Nob (22[18ff.]).† The transference of the sanctuary to Nob (without the Ark, which had been carried off by the Philistines, and was ultimately stationed at Ḳiriath-jearim, 4[11] 5[1]–7[1]) was, without doubt, due to the destruction of the Shiloh temple by the Philistines (cf. Jer 7[12ff.]), Ahimelech the son of Aḥiṭub, who, in Saul's time, officiated there as priest (1 S 21[2ff.]

* Cf. Baudissin's art. PRIESTS AND LEVITES in vol. iv. p. 67 ff., and the same author's *Geschichte des alttest. Priesterthums*, Leipzig, 1889. Unfortunately, this exhaustive monograph is not uninfluenced by the author's untenable hypothesis that the source P originated as early as the 7th cent. B.C., much about the same time as Deuteronomy.

† Everywhere in these passages only 'the priests' are spoken of except on the first mention of them in 3[3], where, in harmony with the usage of Deuteronomy, we have the addition 'the Levites,' the two designations combined being='the Levitical priests.' The glossator meant to leave no possibility of doubt that even then the only priests that could be held legitimate were those sprung from Levi.

* The subsequent correction of *Moses* to *Manasseh* by a superlinear *n* was due simply to a desire to save Moses the shame of having a descendant who held an illegitimate (because not derived from Aaron) priesthood, and, in addition, practised the worship of images. In the estimation of the original narrator, both these things were quite justifiable and praiseworthy.

† If 85 men 'who wore the linen ephod' (*i.e.* officiating priests) were slain by Doeg, this is a surprisingly large number. At Shiloh only three priests are mentioned; at Jerusalem under David, only two (apart from David's sons, 2 S 8[18], and 'Ira the Jairite, 20[26]), as was the case also under Solomon, according to the original text of 1 K 4[2-5] (Azariah the son of Ẓadok, and Zabud the son of Nathan). It is true that *hak-kōhēn* denotes 'the priest' κατ' ἐξοχήν, in olden times the chief priest (as is still the case in 2 K 11[9ff.], Is 8[2], and 2 K 22[4ff.] where Ḥilḳiah first becomes 'high priest,' thanks to a later redactor), so that the existence of other priests along with the above named is by no means excluded (cf. *e.g.* 2 K 12[5ff.]). But, while a considerable number is supposable in the case of the splendid temple of Solomon, it is not so with the more modest sanctuaries of the early monarchical period. Now, it is a possibility that in 1 S 22[18] the number 85 may originally have stood for the whole of Aḥimelech's descendants and relations (cf. v.[19]). But, seeing that the LXX gives 305 (Luc. 350) in place of 85, it is evident that the number was a later insertion, based upon diverse guesses. Is it accident that 85 is the numerical value of the consonants of '*kōhănê* [Jahweh]' in v.[17]?

etc.), was, according to 1 S 14³, a grandson of Eli. The sole survivor of the massacre at Nob was Abiathar the son of Aḥimelech (1 S 2³³ 22²⁰), who fled with the *'ēphôd* (see above) to David. The 'trustworthy priest,' however, for whom Jahweh, according to 2³⁵, is to build an enduring house, *i.e.* to whom He is to give an unbroken line of successors who shall go out and in continually before the anointed of Jahweh—the king—is Ẓadoḳ, who already, in the time of David, had been priest along with Abiathar (2 S 15²⁴· ²⁹ etc.). Under Solomon he continued alone in office when the curse on the house of Eli was fulfilled in the deposition of Abiathar (1 K 2-⁷). It is not stated that Ẓadoḳ was of Levitical descent; even the name of his father is not given.* Nevertheless, the prediction of the 'enduring house' was fulfilled. Towards the end of the pre-exilic period *all* priests at Jerusalem passed for 'sons of Ẓadoḳ,' and in the programme for the future sketched by Ezekiel (44¹⁵ᶠᶠ·) it is to them alone out of all the existing 'priests of Levi' that the priestly prerogatives are accorded. Deuteronomy had at least left open the possibility that the priests of the high places might discharge priestly functions at Jerusalem after the concentration of the cultus in the temple there. We see, however, from 1 S 2³⁶ that it was difficult for them to obtain this privilege. The man of God there predicts to Eli that his descendants (*i.e.* the priests of the high places in the time of Josiah and down to B.C. 586) would have to humble themselves very low before Ẓadoḳ (*i.e.* the legitimate priestly family at Jerusalem) and to beg from them the necessary maintenance.

3. Let us now ask,—and this is the main question,—What was the spiritual and religious significance of the priesthood during the whole period prior to the advent of written prophecy? Unfortunately, here again we have to rest content with very meagre sources of information. Essentially, all that we learn is that the priests guarded the Ark, and, if necessary, carried it. Moreover, it is no inferior priests or *Levites* † in the sense of P that carry it, but the priests proper, as is plain from 2 S 15²⁴· ²⁹ (and even from 1 S 4⁴). But there is specially frequent mention of a function of the priests which consisted in guarding or carrying and consulting the *'ēphôd* (see above): 1 S 14³ 21¹⁰ ⁽⁹⁾ 22¹⁵ [according to the LXX, also v.¹⁸] 23⁹ [where David asks Abiathar to produce the *'ēphôd* which he (v.⁶) had brought with him from Nob] 30⁷ [where, however, it is David himself that consults Jahweh]. Further, in 1 S 14¹⁸, we are to read, with the LXX, 'the *'ēphôd*' instead of 'the ark,' and then 'for he bore then the *'ēphôd*,' etc.‡ There is no mention of any participation of the priests in the offering of sacrifice. Even at the head sanctuary at Shiloh all that is presupposed in 1 S 2¹¹ᶠᶠ· is at most an ordinance hallowed by custom in connexion with the handing over of the sacrificial dues to the priests; the heinous sin of the sons of Eli consisted, not in their transgressing the requirements of a written law (such as that of P), but in treating with contempt the ancient hallowed sacrificial customs, and demanding their portion before the fat had been burned to Jahweh (v.¹⁶). But it is not clear whether the presenting of the fat was an act that could be performed by priests alone. And even if statements like those of 1 S 13⁹ᶠ·, 2 S 6¹³· ¹⁷ᶠ·, 1 K 3⁴ etc., might readily be interpreted as meaning that the kings offered sacrifice through the medium of the priests, on the other hand there are passages, such as 2 S 6¹⁸ and 1 K 8¹⁴, which show that in ancient times even a ritual act like blessing (which in Dt 10⁸ [probably from P] is reserved for the priests) could be performed without offence by the kings.

Of what, according to the statements of the prophets, was the most important official duty of the priests, namely, the giving of *tōrāh* or 'direction' in ritual and legal questions (even without the employment of the sacred lot), we do not hear till towards the close of our period, in the so-called Blessing of Moses (see below, p. 650ᵃ). For the earlier period it is significant that in the whole of the so-called Book of the Covenant, although it deals for the most part with questions of law, priests are not mentioned at all. This does not, indeed, prove that the above function was wholly wanting to them. When a fitting occasion arose, in the case of Eli we find indeed a kind of pastoral office discharged: 1 S 1⁹⁻¹⁸· ²⁶ᶠᶠ· 2²⁰ (towards Ḥannah and Elḳana) 2²²ᶠᶠ· (towards his own sons); but even this bears no specifically priestly character.

As to other, especially political, influence exercised by the priests, it was to all appearance small throughout this whole period. This admits of a simple explanation on the ground that there were as yet no priestly *guilds* to give support to the individual. As we saw above, connexion with the tribe of Levi was not as yet a condition of attaining the dignity of priest. The Deuteronomic redactor of the Books of Kings is the first to reckon it a sin on the part of Jeroboam that he appointed all and sundry, who were not descended from the tribe of Levi, to be priests of the high places (1 K 12³¹ 13³³ᵇ). How little advantage, however, even the Levitical priests had over the others, is sufficiently plain from the story of the wayfaring Levite, Jonathan (Jg 17⁷ᶠᶠ·), and in quite a special way from Gn 49⁷. Here (probably as late as the time of David) a curse is pronounced on the *tribe* of Levi, without any allusion to the prerogatives attributed and actually continued to that tribe owing to its connexion with Moses (cf. above, p. 648ᵇ). This shows clearly that these very prerogatives were, at least in the time of the poetical author of Gn 49⁷, very lightly esteemed. The tribe of Levi was accounted accursed; only a portion of its members, who had had the good fortune (Jg 17⁸), discharged priestly functions. But even in this instance the Levite with his family occupied an isolated position at some sanctuary, and enjoyed no special consideration there. But the same was the case also with the priests who were not of Levitical descent. It is true that as early as the end of the period of the Judges and the opening of the monarchical period we meet with a tendency towards a hereditary, settled, and therefore more respected, priesthood, in the family of Eli. The prestige he enjoyed is explicable, above all, from the circumstance that he attended to the sacred Ark in the temple at Shiloh, the sanctuary most highly esteemed by the people. His descendants continued to live upon this reputation, as we find them doing under Saul at Nob, evidently the principal sanctuary after the destruction of Shiloh (1 S 22¹⁹ 'the city of the priests'), and as Abiathar did at the court of David.

With all this, however, there is no word of any sovereignty exercised by the priests alongside that of the king. Aḥimelech assumes the attitude of an inferior towards even the subject of Saul (1 S 21²), and most unreservedly towards Saul

* It is true that in 2 S 8¹⁷ (1 Ch 18¹⁶ 24⁶· ³¹) Ẓadoḳ is called 'the son of Aḥiṭub.' But the MT here has certainly been corrected in dogmatic interests, with the object of inserting Ẓadoḳ in a genealogy and, at the same time, of setting aside Abiathar (in contradiction to 2 S 15²⁴ etc.) in advance. With Wellhausen and others we should read 'Ẓadoḳ and Abiathar, the son of Aḥimelech, the son of Aḥiṭub.'

† The mention of these in 1 S 6¹⁵, 2 S 15²⁴ (but not v.²⁹), and 1 K 8⁴ (contradicting v.³), is due to a late interpolation.

‡ It is doubtful, on the other hand, whether, with Thenius and others, we should substitute 'the *'ēphôd*' for 'the ark' also in 1 K 2²⁶.

himself ($22^{12ff.}$). The bodyguard of Saul hesitate, it is true, to slaughter the priests of Jahweh (v.[17]), plainly because the bloody command of the king appeared to them so unjust and monstrous; but no one interposed in defence of the priests when they and their families fell victims to the blind fury of the king, using as its instrument Doeg the Edomite. The sole survivor, Abiathar, was indeed taken by David under his protection (v.[23]), but only as a servant whom he could order about as he pleased; and the same position was held by Abiathar under David when the latter became king. In 2 S $8^{17}$ $20^{25f.}$, 1 K $4^{1.5}$, the priests are named amongst the principal officials in Judah, mostly, however, *after* these, or at least after a portion of them. The circumstance that the punishment inflicted by Solomon upon Abiathar for his participation in Adonijah's attempt was only banishment, was due not to his peculiar standing, but simply to the services he had personally rendered to David. It is quite intelligible that the settled priesthood at so splendid a sanctuary as Solomon's temple should have been the first to attain to wealth and higher culture, and on that account to great consideration, that at an early period these priests came even to form a species of temple aristocracy, united in a close society, and allied themselves in marriage with the most powerful families, even up to the royal house.* All the same, the chief priests are nothing but officials of the king, and the circumstances are quite exceptional that determine Joiada the priest (2 K $11^{4ff.}$) to play a great political part in the conspiracy against 'Athaliah. Moreover, his action was in favour of the only legitimate heir of the Davidic dynasty, and thus in the service of the same. But the regard which king Jehoash owed him in return did not prevent that monarch from showing towards him and the priests ($12^{7ff.}$) not merely annoyance but distrust, when he deprived them of the free control of the temple dues and handed this over to the Secretary of State.

We cannot wonder that in the Northern kingdom, where a central sanctuary was wanting, it took far longer than in Judah to form reputable and, in a certain measure, politically powerful priestly societies. But that this point was reached is testified to us by the saying regarding Levi in the (Ephraimite) Blessing of Moses, Dt $33^{8ff.}$ (probably dating from the time of Jeroboam II. or not much earlier). The interpretation of some expressions is not, indeed, without difficulty. According to Wellhausen and others, v.[9] alludes to those who, renouncing their tribe and their family, have attached themselves to a guild of Levites. But probably we should rather find an allusion to the narrative of Ex $32^{29}$ (cf. above, p. 633[a]), where the priesthood is assigned to the tribe of Levi as a recompense for the courageous way in which it stood up for Jahweh. With this accords the circumstance that the whole saying is spoken of Levi as of a *tribe* standing on the same footing as Benjamin, Joseph, etc. Here, then, the belonging to Levi is already a condition of priesthood, although this, of course, does not exclude isolated instances of members of other tribes (particularly, it may be presumed, those who had married the daughters of priests) obtaining the office. The whole saying betrays in lofty language a legitimate pride in the importance and the power of the priesthood, and an assured confidence (v.[11b]) that Jahweh will annihilate its foes, of whom there is no lack. Amongst its official functions the first place is still held by the manipulating of the sacred lot (Urim and Thummim), but in addition to this (v.[10]) the priests teach the people the statutes and the *tōrāh* of Jahweh and attend to the sacrificial service.

* Thus, according to the certainly historical note in 2 Ch $22^{11}$, Jehosheba, a sister of king Ahaziah, was wife of the chief priest Joiada. Except for this, even 2 K $11^{3}$ would be unintelligible.

Just as in the above passage the priests sprung from Levi appear as zealous upholders of the service of Jahweh, so it may have been true of the Jahweh priesthood in general in the Northern kingdom that its members were entitled to be counted among the organs of genuine Jahwism. It is surprising, indeed, that in the struggle against the Tyrian Baal we never hear of the priests, but only of the prophets, being persecuted for their fidelity to Jahweh. But, on the other hand, nowhere during this period are the priests reproached as favouring the service of Baal. An express reference, however, to priestly zeal for Jahweh is found nowhere but in the case of Eli. The latter feels it a grievous scandal that his sons give occasion to evil reports among 'the people of Jahweh'; he dreads the heavy judgment of Jahweh which tolerates no opposition; he submits most humbly to the sentence of rejection (1 S $3^{18}$ 'it is Jahweh, let him do what seemeth good to him'). And during the battle with the Philistines he trembles, above all, for the Ark of Jahweh ($4^{13}$); and it is when he hears that *it* is taken that he sinks down and dies (v.[18]). In like manner, the last thought of the dying wife of Phinehas is grief at the carrying away of the Ark, for 'the glory is departed from Israel' (v.[21]). All these are features which may lay claim to being historical. They prove that Jahwism, amidst all amalgamation with relics of ancient Semitic nature religions, was even then a power which struck deep into the life and thought of its adherents, and was capable of awakening in them genuine piety.

**2. Prophets.**—1. By far the most prominent place among the organs of genuine Jahwism is occupied by the prophets.* It is usual in this connexion, to bring together quite heterogeneous phenomena, and to couple the representatives of heathen Semitic mantic and sorcery with the genuine Hebrew prophetism which stood in the service of Jahwism. It cannot be denied that in the traditions of ancient Israel traces even of the former category are to be found, and such as plainly appear not to be inconsistent, in the mind of the narrators, with genuine Jahwism. This was rendered possible when the moving force was no longer found in demonic powers, but in Jahweh Himself. Thanks to the gifts with which Jahweh endows him, Moses surpasses the achievements of the Egyptian magicians (Ex $4^{2ff.}$ $7^{8ff.}$), making at the same time frequent use of his staff as of a magician's wand (Ex $7^{20}$ $9^{23}$ $17^{5.8ff.}$, Nu $20^{7ff.}$). The same efficacy that is attributed to the stretching forth of Moses' staff is produced by the spear stretched forth by Joshua (Jos $8^{18.26}$); it procures victory for Israel and the complete destruction of the inhabitants of Ai. Even in 2 K $13^{15ff.}$ a relic has been rightly discovered of the belief in divining by arrows.† It is not merely a symbolical action when king Joash, with his hands covered by the hands of Elisha, shoots an arrow in the direction of the Syrians, and then, at the prophet's command, smites with the arrows upon the ground. These actions are rather a curse, ex-

* Of monographs on Israelitish prophetism in general [see § IV. for the Literature on the writing prophets] we would note specially: A. Knobel, *Der Prophetismus der Hebräer*, 2 Theile, Breslau, 1837 [antiquated in many respects, but a thorough-going work, and one that is still useful]; A. Kuenen, *De profeten en de profetie onder Israel*, 2 vols., Leiden, 1875 [Eng. tr., London, 1877]; C. H. Cornill, *Der Israelitische Prophetismus: in 5 Vorträgen für gebildete Laien geschildert*, Strassburg, 1894 u. ö; R. Kraetzschmar, *Prophet und Seher im alten Israel*, Tübingen, 1901; cf. also A. B. Davidson's article PROPHECY AND PROPHETS in vol. iv., and his posthumous work, *Old Testament Prophecy*, Edinburgh, 1903.

† So Schwally, *Semit. Kriegsaltertümer*, i. 22.

pressed by deeds, which cannot fail to accomplish its purpose on the Syrians. Balaam, to whom (Nu 22[6]) the magical power of effectually blessing or cursing an entire nation is attributed, appears, nevertheless, in the whole passage (Nu 22–24) as a genuine prophet of Jahweh. All these are instances of the survival of a primitive system of magic, which, however, it was found possible to reconcile with Jahwism. So, according to Gn 44[5. 15], Joseph practised the so-called *hydromancy*, a method of divining by means of a liquid in a bowl; and in Nu 17[16 (1) ff.] we have simply a peculiar form of *rhabdomancy*, or divining by means of a number of rods. Other forms of magic, such as *necromancy*, the art of the *mĕʻōnĕnîm*,* etc., were at all times regarded by the representatives of genuine Jahwism as illegitimate.† But all the zeal of the prophets did not avail to prevent sorcery and divining from continuing in vogue down to the Exile and even beyond it, as outgrowths of superstition for which the Jahweh religion can no more be held responsible than can Christianity for the countless forms of superstition which continue to hold sway within its pale down to the present day.

The prophetism which is called up to us by names like Amos, Hosea, Isaiah, etc., has its roots in two altogether different phenomena, which finally became one, and consequently both received the same designation. On the one hand, there are the 'seers' of ancient times, on the other the ecstatic figures of the *nĕbî'îm*. The latter name became in the 8th cent. the collective title for the proper prophets of Jahweh; hence it is usual—although less appropriate—to render the word *nĕbî'îm*, when it occurs in the time of Samuel and Saul, by 'prophets.'

2. The 'seer' (רֹאֶה *rō'eh*, or חֹזֶה *ḥōzeh*) derives his name, not from *foreseeing* the future, although this is not, upon occasion, outside his rôle, but because, with spiritual eye opened for him by his God, he sees what is hidden, and is able to announce it. A condition of ecstasy is not necessary for this,—we never hear of such, for instance, in the case of Samuel,—but it may be connected with the act of vision. Thus Balaam, who is nowhere, indeed, called 'seer' or 'prophet,' but who belongs all the same to this category, speaks of himself as a man 'whose [outward] eye is closed,‡ who heareth the words of God, who seeth visions of the Almighty, sunk down and with unveiled eye' (Nu 24[3f. 15f.]). In the case of all in this period who are entitled to be regarded as 'seers' there is an unmistakable connexion with mantic and sorcery, and that in the belief not only of the people but of the ancient narrator. We have spoken of Moses as an expert in magic. True, he is never called 'seer,' while the name 'prophet' (in its later sense) is first given to him in Deuteronomy (18[15] 34[10]). The earlier view (Nu 12[6] [prob. E]) distinguishes him, as one with whom God speaks face to face, from prophets elsewhere, to whom God reveals Himself by visions and dreams. The people of Israel must, however, in all ages have seen in Moses not only the 'man of God,' the powerful instrument of Jahweh in the establishing of the covenant at Sinai, the leader filled with the spirit of Jahweh (Nu 11[17. 25]), but also the '*seer*' acquainted with the future. This is plain from the circumstance that two notable predictions of the future are put in his mouth: the Blessing of Moses, Dt 33 (see above, p. 650[a]), although in v.[4] it speaks of him in the third person; and the much later Song, Dt 32, although in v.[7] it looks back to the time of Moses as the days of old, and in v.[13ff.] describes the experiences of Israel in Palestine as historical facts that belong to a far distant past.

In the case of Balaam a mantic element emerges in so far as, while he repeatedly insists that he can speak only what Jahweh gives him to say (Nu 22[8. 18ff. 35. 38]), he yet has recourse to external measures (23[1ff.]), and actually goes out for a vision, *i.e.* a revelation of Jahweh by outward signs (23[3f.] [where in v.[4] after the word 'Balaam' a more precise statement about the kind of revelation has in all probability dropped out] [13ff. 27ff.]), until, finally, (24[1ff.]) he abandons the rôle of soothsayer, and utters his oracles simply at the impulse of the Divine spirit.

In the time of the Judges we should doubtless assign Deborah to the same category. She is called in Jg 4[4] 'a prophetess,' *i.e.*, in this instance, a woman capable of magical possession by the spirit of Jahweh, and able when in this condition to pronounce judicial decisions (v.[5]). The really original account of her may, however, be expected to have survived in the Song of Deborah, although the attributing of this song to herself (in spite of her being addressed in v.[12]) may be based on an erroneous interpretation of v.[7] (where we ought to render 'till thou didst arise,' etc.). She is called in v.[7] 'a mother in Israel.' This implies the possession of the dignity of a highly esteemed priestess (cf. above on Jg 17[10] 18[19]), who watches over the welfare of the people, and can in times of oppression indicate beforehand the way of escape and the successful issue (4[6ff.]). But, above all, it is true of her that (like the God-inspired battle maidens of Germanic antiquity) she can bewitch the people by her song, and inflame their courage to the highest degree. That the whole activity of Deborah is only in the spirit and service of Jahweh, is manifestly presupposed throughout its description. She rouses the wretchedly broken-up tribes to the consciousness that they form one body as the people of Jahweh, and inspires them with courage to fight, and confidence in the war-God who hastens from Sinai to their help.

Still more, however, does this rôle of an organ of Jahweh—nay, of a deliverer of the people from sore straits—belong to the man who for the first time expressly receives the honourable name of 'seer' (1 S 9[11. 18. 19]). In 9[9] a prefatory gloss explains that in ancient times those who are now called 'prophets' (*nĕbî'îm*) were called 'seers.' According to the narrative of 1 S 1[11. 27f.] 2[18ff.] 3[1ff.] (which is somewhat later than 1 S 9–10[16]), Samuel was even before his birth dedicated to Jahweh; at a tender age he was brought to Shiloh to enter upon Jahweh's service, and there also he was honoured with a nocturnal revelation from Jahweh. We thus meet here with the same combination of the functions of priest (cf. also 9[13]) and seer (or prophet in the later sense of the term) as in the case of Moses. It may be noted, however, that the different sources present quite different pictures of Samuel. According to the later ones (1 S 7. 8. 10[17ff.] 12. 13[8ff.] 15) he is the last 'judge,' which means here not only temporary leader in a struggle, as in the 'hero-stories' of the Book of Judges, but simply 'ruler,' one who wants only the title in order to be king. He recalls the people from idolatry (7[3ff.]), and procures for them, by prayer and sacrifice (v.[8ff.]), lasting victory over the Philistines. In his old age he appoints his sons to be judges, lays before Jahweh the people's demand

* That is, either 'cloud-gazers' (weather makers?) or those who deliver their oracles in a *nasal* or *murmuring* tone. In general, necromancers and other sorcerers have attributed to them a *whispering, chirping, sighing*, or *murmuring*.

† The *locus classicus* for the various forms of sorcery is Dt 18[10ff.], which is admirably expounded by W. Robertson Smith in his art. 'On the Forms of Divination and Magic enumerated in Deut. xviii. 10 f.' in *Journ. of Philol.* xiii. 273 ff., xiv. 113 ff. Cf. also T. Witton Davies, *Magic, Divination, and Demonology among the Hebrews and their Neighbours*, London, 1898.

‡ This meaning of the word is, indeed, uncertain; others prefer to interpret 'whose [spiritual] eye is opened.'

for a king ($8^{1ff.}$), calls together an assembly of the people at Mizpah, where Saul is chosen by lot out of all the tribes of Israel as king. This does not, however, prevent Samuel from continuing to act as before as the real ruler. He dismisses the people ($10^{25}$); on the occasion of another popular assembly, at the urgent request of the people he promises his powerful intercession, and that he will instruct them in the good and right way ($12^{19. 23ff.}$). But, above all, in the rejection of Saul ($13^{8ff.}$; far milder is his conduct in $15^{10ff.}$, a passage of a highly prophetic strain) he appears to display a caprice and a lust for rule which have long caused this passage to be regarded as containing the original type of hierarchical demands in opposition to the secular power.

A very different picture of Samuel is sketched for us in the far older source, 1 S 9–$10^{16}$. As he searches for the lost asses of his father, Saul with his servant passes by the house of Samuel. The servant draws Saul's attention to the presence of the 'man of God' in this city, $9^{6}$ 'The man is famous; all that he says comes to pass. Perhaps he may tell us the way by which we have come' [*not* 'the way we should go.' The servant means first to test Samuel's knowledge of their previous journey, and, if that proves correct, his further counsel may be trusted]. Their only difficulty is about the customary present to the man of God, for their bread is exhausted. Luckily, however, the servant has a quarter shekel, and this they propose to give him. Samuel brilliantly justifies their confidence in him. He knows that the asses are already found (v.$^{20}$). But he knows also something quite different regarding the high destiny of Saul, secretly anoints him king next morning, and gives him exact details of three experiences he is to have the same day; and all these turn out as he has said.

The high antiquity of this narrative as compared with that of the more recent sources strikes one at the first glance. The circumstance that the seer is applied to for information even in such secular and everyday matters as is the case here, betrays a very early date; and still more the circumstance that some bread or a quarter shekel should be considered sufficient remuneration for him. We see very clearly, further, that this function of seer is combined with mantic. Even the later source, no doubt, attributes to Samuel extraordinary powers, as when ($12^{17f.}$) in the time of the wheat harvest (and therefore contrary to the usual course of nature) he can cause Jahweh to send thunder and rain. Still this magical power of prayer is something different from the magical knowledge of the past and the future of which we are told in $9^{20}$ and $10^{2ff.}$.

If we were to be guided merely by appearances, we should have to conclude that in ch. 9, in the most glaring opposition to the later record, Samuel is represented as a personage of purely local importance, a something betwixt seer and priest, such as was probably to be found then in every country town of Israel. For Saul himself knows nothing of him, but needs to have his attention drawn to him by his servant. It can easily be shown, however, that such an impression is due to an illusion purposely created by the narrator in order to heighten the dramatic effect of his description. But all the while even he makes no concealment of the fact that Samuel is in quite a special manner the confidant and the instrument of Jahweh. The day before Saul's arrival Jahweh has already ($9^{15ff.}$) announced him to Samuel as His chosen deliverer of His people, and Samuel feels himself thus authorized to anoint Saul in the name of Jahweh to be prince over His people Israel. This last act, in particular, implies a very high sense of the importance of the man and his relation to Jahweh. Then, again, Saul's cousin ($10^{14ff.}$), at the mention of Samuel, who is evidently named here as a well-known personage, is at once curious to know what he said, which shows that Saul must have known him as well, so that a merely local importance of the man in his own place of abode is out of the question. Rather must we still admit that in the later narrative a correct estimate is given, not indeed of the political rôle of the seer, but of his high spiritual and religious importance. The latter he evidently possessed as the maintainer and protector of pure Jahwism against all attempts to seduce the people to idolatry or at least to syncretism. But pure Jahwism was in those days synonymous with patriotism, for it was only from their own national God that the people could look for deliverance from the cruel oppression of the Philistines. And so he was honoured by later generations not only as the man of action, who, to carry out the strict command of Jahweh, hewed the Amalekite king Agag to pieces with his own hand 'before Jahweh' (1 S $15^{32f.}$, an undoubtedly good historical narrative), but also as the man powerful in prayer, whose intercession for his people can be compared for efficacy to that of Moses (Jer $15^{1}$).*

The last † who in the early sources receives the designation 'seer' (*ḥōzeh*) is Gad, 'the prophet (*nābî'*), the seer of David' (2 S $24^{11}$). This is manifestly to be understood as meaning, on the one hand, that Gad is to be reckoned among the prophets (in the later sense; and so we find him giving counsel to David, 1 S $22^{5}$, and conveying to him an oracle from Jahweh, 2 S $24^{11ff.}$); and, on the other hand, that Gad filled the special office of 'seer' to David. In the latter capacity he would probably obtain oracles in the traditional fashion by mantic machinery. It is not difficult to understand why later generations, to whom this kind of official seership had a heathen smack about it, preferred to ignore it and to put in its place a prophetic activity, which appeared to them far more intelligible and—in the case of a David—far more fitting. For this very reason, however, 'the seer of David' may be considered to be an older and more correct designation of Gad than 'the prophet.'

3. We have learned from the above discussion that the seers and 'men of God' of ancient times —Moses, Deborah, Gad (partly)—received even at an early date the further designation of נָבִיא *nābî'*,‡

* It was customary at one time to infer from 1 S $19^{18ff.}$ that Samuel, especially in his capacity of head of a guild of prophets at Ramah, developed an activity which wrought in favour of the theocracy, and probably promoted also the growth of religious literature. But, apart from the fact that these *nĕbî'îm* (see below) are not to be offhand identified with the 'prophets' in the later sense of the term, there are the strongest objections to the historical character of this whole passage. The manifest contradiction with $15^{35a}$ is alone sufficient to show that in $19^{18ff.}$ we have to do with a very late *midrāsh*, after the manner of $16^{1ff.}$.

† We leave out of account the circumstance that the Chronicler is acquainted with a 'seer' named Je'do (2 Ch $9^{29}$) or 'Iddo ($12^{15}$) in the reigns of Solomon, Rehoboam, and Abijah, whereas in $13^{22}$ he is called 'prophet'; and with a 'seer' Jehu in the reign of Jehoshaphaṭ ($19^{2}$). When, again, the Chronicler gives the name of 'seer' even to the music masters of David, namely Asaph (2 Ch $29^{30}$), Heman (1 Ch $25^{5}$), Jeduthun (2 Ch $35^{15}$), he follows a usage of language unknown elsewhere.

‡ Here we may give all that is most essential regarding the etymology and the history of the usage of this term. The root *nābā'* has not survived in Hebrew, for the verbal forms *nibbā'* and *hithnabbē'* ('to show oneself a *nābî'*') are derived from the substantive *nābî'*. But the Arabic and the cognate Heb. roots *nābaḥ* ('bark') and *nāba'* ('bubble forth') show that *nābā'* means originally *to throw out* words or particular sounds *with violence*, as happens in mantic rapture or holy frenzy. (On the corresponding Assyr. root='to carry off,' 'to tear away violently' [carried away by a supernatural power], cf. J. Bewer, *Amer. Journ. of Semit. Lang. and Lit.* xviii. 2, p. 120). Hence the howling dervishes of Islam have been rightly compared with the *nĕbî'îm* of ancient Israel. *Nābî'* then denotes [actively] properly one who professionally [this is implied in the

'prophet' (or *nĕbî'āh*, 'prophetess'). This, however, may safely be pronounced an anachronism. In earlier times, down at least to the middle of the 9th cent. and even later, *nābî'* (plur. *nĕbî'îm*) meant something so different that this name could not have been given to Moses or Samuel. Hence, it may be added, the rendering of *nĕbî'îm* in the time of Samuel by 'prophets' is misleading, and had better be avoided. The descriptions contained in 1 S 10$^{5f. 10f.}$, taken along with the etymology of the word, show that we have to do with bands of enthusiasts, of whom the spirit of God has laid hold with overpowering force, and who, stimulated by loud music to greater frenzy, readily carry along others to participate in their conduct. This last feature is prominent not only in 1 S 10$^{6. 10}$, but in the late *midrāsh* 19$^{18ff.}$, and it reflects truly the character of such phenomena, as does also the statement that Saul stripped off his clothes, and lay naked for a day and a night in holy frenzy.*

Analogous phenomena are reported alike from the ancient religions, from the Christian Middle Ages, and from the sphere of heathen peoples at the present day; and it would be complete perversity to set them all down simply to deceit and hypocritical pretensions. The only question that arises for us is: What is the special significance of this phenomenon upon ancient Hebrew soil, and how far has it a *religious* significance in the realm of Jahwism? Unfortunately, owing to the scanty traditions at our disposal, we must here have recourse to pure conjectures. These, however, are such as may claim a high degree of probability. In the first place, it will not admit of doubt that these *nĕbî'îm* were originally a Canaanite growth, and were adopted by the Hebrews from that quarter. This conclusion is favoured by the fact that the other forms of mantic, possession, and sorcery, also took their rise in all probability upon Canaanite soil. But the 'spirit of God,' which, according to the word of Samuel, passes from the *nĕbî'îm* at Gibeah to Saul, is expressly called in 1 S 10$^{6}$ 'the spirit of Jahweh,' and nothing else could be thought of in view of the whole context. The moving cause, again, that led to whole companies being inflamed by the spirit of Jahweh to holy frenzy was doubtless the sore straits of the time, the heavy yoke of the Philistine domination. It can hardly be an accident that Saul (10$^{5}$) is seized with holy frenzy at the very spot where the pillar (נְצִיב), or, according to another interpretation, the administrator of the Philistines, was located. As in the Middle Ages the ravages of the plague gave rise to troops of flagellants, so, in the period of which we are speaking, subjection to a people hated and esteemed unclean produced a condition of great excitement, and led to frequent gatherings of those who were seized with a violent desire to procure the intervention of the national God of Israel, who was regarded, above all, as the war-God. This purpose was served chiefly by the ecstatic cries from which the *nĕbî'îm* originally derived their name. Hence Schwally (*Semit. Kriegsaltertümer*, i. 110) may be right in assigning a warlike origin to the whole appearance of these *nĕbî'îm* (as well as the Nazirites; see below). We are reminded how, in the case of Samson, his being seized with the spirit of Jahweh is repeatedly connected with acts of vengeance on the Philistines (Jg 14$^{19}$ 15$^{14ff.}$). In a certain sense, then, these *nĕbî'îm* may be regarded as organs of Jahweh; but they belonged to quite a different species, and followed a different calling from the so called organs of Jahweh of later times.

4. Notwithstanding, there was not wanting even at the court of David some representation of genuine prophetism in the later sense of the term. Apart from Gad, who announced to David a coming punishment at the hands of Jahweh (2 S 24$^{11ff.}$), we meet with a representative of it in the remarkable personality of Nathan. Nowhere, indeed, do we read of his special endowment with the spirit of Jahweh. After David's sin in the matter of Uriah, we read in 2 S 12$^{1}$ simply: 'And Jahweh sent Nathan to David.' But the combination of skill and courage in the way in which Nathan awakens the conscience of the king and pronounces the judgment of Jahweh upon him, and then follows this up by announcing the forgiveness of his sin, reminds us of the way in which Isaiah afterwards faced Aḥaz (Is 7) and Ḥezekiah (39). It is nowhere stated that Nathan held any official position, and the usual comparison with a court preacher has no support in the early source. The rôle, not quite free from danger, which he plays in 1 K 1 in the palace intrigue, in favour of Solomon and against Adonijah, is sufficiently explained by the position he had held as the tutor of Solomon (2 S 12$^{25}$). Besides, it may be questioned (as in the case of Gad) whether the title *nābî'* as applied to Nathan is as early as the time of David (which would contradict 1 S 9$^{9}$, where this signification of the word is plainly reserved for a much later date), or whether it is due to a readily intelligible expansion at a redactor's hand. In 7$^{2}$ it may belong to the Deuteronomic revision of the older narrative. Strangely enough, however, it is wanting in 12$^{1}$ in the MT on the occasion of the *first* mention of his name in the early source, and throughout the whole of this narrative. In 1 K 1 the title is almost always attached to the name, yet there are certain indications* that make it at least possible that its presence is due to a late insertion. If it is original, we must conclude that it stands for an official position, that indeed of a 'seer' like Gad, and in the interposition of Nathan in 2 S 12 we should have to see an unusual evidence of that position.

The same difficulty recurs in the case of Aḥijah of Shiloh (1 K 11$^{29ff.}$ 14$^{2. 18}$, but not 15$^{29}$). Aḥijah's symbolical action in tearing his mantle to pieces and giving ten of these to Jeroboam, as well as his conduct towards Jeroboam's wife and his utterances in the name of Jahweh, place him quite in line with the Jahweh prophets of the 8th cent.; but the question remains whether the title *nābî'* is not to be set down to the account of the Deuteronom. recension, in which the original story about Aḥijah is unquestionably now presented to us. The same remark applies to Jehu, the son

formation of the word] gives utterance to ecstatic cries, or exhibits other tokens of holy frenzy. True, this original sense of the word became more and more weakened. Even the *nĕbî'îm* of the time of Elijah and Elisha (see above) have already become only pale reflexions of the *nĕbî'îm* of Samuel's day. But when *nābî'* had been fully adopted as the honorific appellation of the true prophets of Jahweh (so already in Am 2$^{11}$, Is 8$^{3}$ [where the wife of Isaiah is called by himself, in conformity with his official name, 'the prophetess']), the recollection of its original meaning was all the more forgotten. Otherwise, Abraham could not have been in Gn 20$^{7}$ (E) called a *nābî'*, to whom one could look for effectual intercession. Nay, in Ps 105$^{15}$ the same title is given to the patriarchs in general, with their families. Evidently, all that still attaches to the word here is the notion of confidants and favourites of God.

* A trace of the bearing of these *nĕbî'îm* has very probably survived down to a late date in the verb הִטִּיף *hiṭṭîph*, 'prophesy,' which means primarily 'to let drop,' *sc.* slaver, as is usual with epileptics and madmen.

* In v.$^{10}$ the MT but not Luc. has the addition. In v.$^{34}$ the LXX has certainly preserved the original text ('and anoint him,' etc., without any subjects following); in the MT there has been inserted from v.$^{39}$ first 'Ẓadoḳ the priest' (hence 'shall [sing.] anoint him,' etc.), and then, further, 'Nathan the prophet.' In v.$^{45}$ Luc. still betrays the original text 'and there anointed [sing.] him the priest Ẓadoḳ'; yet here too, as we see in MT and LXX (both 'and there anointed' [plur.] etc.), there was inserted after 'Ẓadoḳ,' although this in contradiction of v.$^{34}$, 'Nathan the prophet.'

of Hanani, who announced an oracle of Jahweh against Baasha, king of Israel (1 K 16[1ff.]).

But, even if in all the above instances *nābî'* should be an anachronism, the important fact remains that at no period were there wanting in Israel suitable organs for giving expression at the Divine command to the pleasure and, in a remarkable degree, the displeasure of Jahweh. We are reminded of the old naïve seership of a Samuel, when the wife of Jeroboam I. goes to consult Aḥijah about the illness of her son, and proposes to recompense him with ten loaves and cakes and a jar of honey (1 K 14[3]). But, just as Samuel was informed beforehand of the coming of Saul (1 S 9[15]), the approach of Jeroboam's wife is made known to the blind Aḥijah. This serves also to authenticate him as an instrument of Jahweh; and the importance of his message to the whole Northern kingdom raises him (and Jehu) far above a 'seer' of the olden time, and gives him the appearance of a worthy forerunner of the true Jahweh prophets.

5. Of ecstatics such as meet us in 1 S 10[5ff.] 19[18ff.] we have encountered none since the time of Samuel; of 'seers' in the ancient sense only a few names have come under our notice. All the more is our interest aroused by the manifold and strong evidences of the presence of prophetism in the Northern kingdom in the 9th cent., from the time of Aḥab (*c.* 876 ff.) down to the death of Elisha under king Joash (2 K 13[14ff.]). For the copious stream of tradition regarding this period we are indebted to the circumstance that the compiler of the present Books of Kings has largely incorporated in his work the special (written) accounts of Elijah and Elisha, the so-called 'Mirror of the Prophets' (1 K 17-19. 21[1-20a] 27-29, 2 K 2-8[15] 9[1-13] 13[14-21]). It is true that even here we must be on our guard against understanding the narrative absolutely from the standpoint of a later age. Elijah and Elisha, like the *nĕbî'îm* who surround them, are not to be summarily identified with the Jahweh prophets of the following century. These *nĕbî'îm*, on the contrary, remind us in many respects of the *nĕbî'îm* of the time of Saul, except that their zeal for Jahweh is directed against a different foe.

(*a*) To begin with Elijah, it is noteworthy here once more that in the original text he is only once reckoned amongst the *nĕbî'îm*, namely in 1 K 18[22], in words put into his own mouth, but in a context where no other designation was possible. In 18[36], on the other hand, the original text, according to the LXX, was simply, 'And Elijah called to heaven and said,' etc. Now, it is surely no accident that the narrator himself avoids giving the name *nābî'* to Elijah, who, in spite of some cognate features (see below), is not to be placed on the same platform as the *nĕbî'îm* of his *entourage*, but holds a higher place than they. The widow of Zarephath (1 K 17[18. 24]) calls him (as the servant of Saul does Samuel in 1 S 9[6ff.]) a 'man of God' in whose mouth is the true word of Jahweh.*

The circumstance that the imposing figure of Elijah the Tishbite now (1 K 17[1]) steps quite abruptly upon the stage, may be due to the compiler of the present Books of Kings having suppressed something that went before. But elsewhere, too, the sudden appearances and disappearances of Elijah are remarkable (cf. 1 K 18[7ff.] and 2 K 2[16]). The very commencement of his activity exhibits him as quite an extraordinary personality. He does not announce it as a message from Jahweh that the next years shall see neither dew nor rain till he shall intimate the contrary, but swears by Jahweh, in whose service he is, that it shall be so. This conveys the impression that Jahweh has given him full powers over the forces of nature. Yet he himself (v.[14]) ascribes the miracle of the widow's cruse of oil to the command of Jahweh, and the return of the rain to His sending it. By his prayers he wins back from Jahweh the newly deceased son of the widow (v.[17ff.]), and shows himself, finally, at Jahweh's command, to Aḥab (18[1ff.]). Now at last, when we make acquaintance with 'Obadiah, Aḥab's *majordomo* (18[2ff.]), we learn what has been the real cause of the years of drought. These are manifestly traced to Jezebel's bloody persecution of the *nĕbî'îm* because they had opposed the spread of the cult of the Tyrian Baal (see above, p. 647[b]). 'Obadiah himself, in harmony with his name, a true 'worshipper of Jahweh,' had hid a hundred *nĕbî'îm* by fifties in a cave, and supplied them with food—a proof this of the bloody earnestness of the persecution. 'Obadiah shows such deference to Elijah (v.[7ff.]) that the impression of the latter as a magical personality is once more left upon us. Elijah, however, exhibits himself in his true greatness in his meeting with Aḥab on the occasion of the Divine judgment at Carmel (18[19ff.]), for which he compels the king to make the necessary preparations. There he stands alone, over against the 450 *nĕbî'îm* of Baal.* His words to the people (v.[21]) show that his aim is, at any cost, to put an end to the prevailing syncretism between Jahweh and Baal. The ridicule which he pours (v.[27]) upon the vain efforts of the prophets of Baal goes essentially beyond the sphere of mere henotheism, and is equivalent to a complete denial, not only of the power but of the very existence of Baal. And, when Jahweh by a heightened (v.[34f.]) miraculous display has brilliantly evinced His claim to be the true God, Elijah is content with no half measures. The complete reversal of the sentiments of the people leads them to consent, at his command, to slaughter the 450 prophets of Baal at the Kishon.

In the appendix to this narrative (18[41ff.]) we meet with several features which again remove Elijah from the purely spiritual sphere and set him—even physically—in a kind of magical light. He hears in advance the rushing of the rain. The whole of the strange attitude he assumes in v.[42] can scarcely be otherwise explained than as a performance (rain-charming?) borrowed from the sphere of magic. But in v.[46] the 'hand of Jahweh' (*i.e.*, in view of the linguistic usage elsewhere, an ecstatic condition produced by Jahweh) is expressly called in to account for Elijah's running before Aḥab's chariot from Carmel to Jezreel (at least a five hours' journey). To the same category belongs the statement of 19[5-8], that, in the strength of the food brought him by an angel, he was able to travel 40 days and 40 nights till he came to Ḥoreb, the mount of God.

It may be noted that even ch. 19 is still dominated by the *one* great idea at the root of Elijah's ministry, namely, his struggle on behalf of Jahweh against Baal. His complaint to Jahweh (v.[14]) relates to the fruitlessness of his zeal for Jahweh, the throwing down of His altars and the slaying of His prophets. In Jahweh's reply (v.[15ff.]) it is well worthy of note that Elijah receives commissions —the anointing of Ḥazael to be king of Syria, and Jehu to be king of Israel—which involve his taking part in a political upheaval, nay, in a rebellion against the regularly constituted ruler. The further 'Histories of the Prophets' know nothing of any executing of the latter commission by Elijah; at most it might be conjectured from

* 2 K 1[9f. 13], where likewise Elijah is called 'man of God,' is a late *midrāsh*. Again, 1 K 20[28], where one of the *nĕbî'îm* (cf. v.[22]) is spoken of as a 'man of God,' does not belong to the 'Histories of the Prophets.'

* On the 400 prophets of the *'ăshērāh* afterwards introduced into v.[19], see above, p. 647[b], note.

2 K $8^{12f.}$ and $9^{1ff.}$ that he handed over to Elisha those commissions which it was impracticable for himself to carry out. All that he attended to personally was the call of Elisha (1 K $19^{19f.}$) by casting his mantle over him. This might be interpreted as simply a symbolical transaction—an investiture with the prophetic office by means of what had become even then the usual official garb of the prophets, the mantle [of hair]. In reality, however, a feature of the ancient mantic once more presents itself here. As we see from 2 K $2^{8.\ 13ff.}$, miraculous virtues belong to this mantle: through its possession Elisha becomes heir also of the spirit of Elijah. It is in the light of this that we must understand 1 K $19^{19}$. The mantle of Elijah, cast upon Elisha, exerts a magical power over him, compelling him to attach himself to Elijah.

The ministry of Elijah finds a fitting conclusion in the courageous front he offers to Ahab on account of the judicial murder of Naboth (1 K $21^{17ff.}$). As Nathan had once done to David, and Ahijah to the wife of Jeroboam I., so here Elijah comes forward, at Jahweh's command, as the embodied conscience of the theocracy to face the king. And so overwhelming is the power of his word, that Ahab, although at first defiant (v.$^{20}$), ends by submitting as a humble penitent.

To sum up the results of our investigation, we gather, on the one hand, that the tradition regarding Elijah has not remained uninfluenced by legend; and, on the other hand, that prophetism even in his person still exhibits a connexion with various survivals of the most ancient conceptions—nay, even with magic. All this is said quite apart from his altogether extraordinary end—his translation to heaven in a fiery chariot with fiery horses. Whether this story (2 K 2) belongs to the original Elijah-narratives, or whether it has not rather displaced an older narrative of his end, is open to dispute. But, in any case, it is strong evidence of the estimate formed of the imposing figure of Elijah by his countrymen. Even if the legend of Elijah's translation be connected with the honorific appellation 'Israel's chariot and horsemen' (2 K $2^{12}$; used also of Elisha in $13^{14}$), *i.e.* equal in importance to, or taking the place of, chariots and horsemen to Israel, it remains true that such a legend could have taken its rise only about one whose activity could not be thought of but as enduring, and whose fellowship with his God was known to have been so close that its interruption seemed inconceivable. Viewed in this way, even the legend becomes a witness of the first rank to the fact that, in the times of greatest peril to the continuance of Jahwism, the God of Israel did not lack chosen vessels for His service—figures such as one would look for in vain in the whole realm of heathen religions.

(*b*) Elijah's servant and successor Elisha, who fell heir not only to his mantle but (according to 2 K $2^{9ff.}$) to a double portion of his spirit, is notably inferior in significance to him. This is partly explained by the circumstance that, after the bloody extirpation of the worship of Baal by Jehu, whose revolt against Jehoram was instigated by Elisha himself (2 K $9^{1ff.}$), there was no longer much occasion for vigorous activity in the *religious* sphere. Elisha's last interview with Joash ($13^{14ff.}$) shows clearly the high consideration which he received from the dynasty of Jehu. But even in the passages which record incidents in the reign of Jehoram, though Elisha expresses his strong disapproval of this king ($3^{13f.}$; $6^{32}$ probably has to do still with Ahab), we never (except in $9^{1ff.}$) hear of his bearding the monarch after the manner of Elijah. In the forefront of the Elisha-narratives stands the sore oppression of Israel by the Syrians, and here Elisha interposes actively more than once. By the way, these Elisha-narratives, when compared with those regarding Elijah, which are not indeed without *lacunæ*, but are far more of a unity, exhibit a somewhat motley mixture of separate anecdotes, as these were supplied by the varying popular tradition. It is a vain effort to seek for a chronological thread running through them. (The unnamed king of $6^{21ff.}$ evidently belongs to the dynasty of Jehu, whereas the 'son of a murderer' of v.$^{32}$ is in all probability Ahab). Some narratives may be plainly recognized as imitations of the stories about Elijah (so certainly 2 K $4^{2ff.}$ compared with 1 K $17^{14ff.}$, and 2 K $4^{32ff.}$ compared with 1 K $17^{19ff.}$), and thereby betray at the same time the secondary character of the whole figure of Elisha in comparison with that of Elijah. There prevails in the Elisha-narratives an unmistakable tendency to lay special emphasis not only on his wonder-working power, but also on his high prestige and the inviolability of his person (2 K $2^{23f.}$). A recommendation from him is of great weight with the king and the commander-in-chief (2 K $4^{13}$); the king readily follows his counsel and yields to his demand ($6^{21ff.}$ $13^{15ff.}$), and is anxious to hear from Elisha's servant Gehazi of the great deeds of his master ($8^{4}$). The fame of Elisha extends far beyond the borders of the Northern kingdom. Jehoshaphaṭ of Judah knows that the word of God is to be found with him ($3^{12}$). The Syrian king Benhadad has scarcely heard of his arrival in Damascus ($8^{7ff.}$) when he sends Ḥazael to consult him about the issue of his sickness; and Ḥazael takes with him 40 camels' burden of the precious things of Damascus as a present for Elisha. Elsewhere ($5^{16}$) the absolute disinterestedness of the prophet is emphasized, as are his magnanimity and mildness in $6^{22ff.}$.

In regard to the activity of Elisha it is noteworthy that, while he is called by preference (28 times) 'man of God,' he also appears in the Elisha-narratives as *nābî'*, and that in the later sense of the term. So in 1 K $19^{16}$, where Elijah is directed to anoint* him to be a *nābî*; 2 K $3^{11ff.}$, where Jehoshaphaṭ recognizes him as a true prophet, through whom Jahweh may be consulted; cf. also $5^{8}$, where Elisha classes himself amongst the *nĕbî'îm*. In the mouth of others he is called without qualification 'the prophet' ($5^{3}$ $9^{1}$), receiving this title even from heathen speakers ($5^{13}$ $6^{12}$).

The methods by which Elisha works are partly the usual ones, which are recorded also of Samuel and Elijah—namely, the proclaiming of a word that has come to him from Jahweh (2 K $3^{16ff.}$ $4^{43}$ $7^{1}$), and prayer ($4^{33}$ $6^{17f.}$). Along with these, however, we meet in his case again with a variety of features which have been already described in speaking of Elijah, and which recall the ecstatic conditions and magical methods of the ancient *nĕbî'îm*. He needs the services of a harper if 'the hand of Jahweh' (see above, on 1 K $18^{46}$) is to come upon him. Quite peculiar to him is the gift which we nowadays call telepathic sight and hearing (2 K $5^{26}$ $6^{12.\ 32}$ $7^{2}$ $8^{13}$; cf. also $6^{16ff.}$, where Elisha and, at his prayer, his servant also see the heavenly horses and fiery chariots on the mountain). But with special frequency miraculous acts are attributed to him. Even if stories like the purifying of the spring at Jericho by using salt ($2^{19ff.}$), the making of bitter fruits palatable through meal ($4^{38ff.}$), or the causing of the axe to spring to the surface of the water ($6^{6}$) are not

* Since we never hear elsewhere of prophets being anointed, and as it is not even performed by Elijah in this instance (cf. v.$^{19}$), 'anoint' must here be used in the weakened sense of 'install.'

meant to be taken as recording miracles, but merely prove what a fondness there was for handing down the memory even of less important incidents of his life, there remain a number of others which, to say the least, place him alongside of Elijah. The wonder wrought on the widow's cruse of oil (2 K $4^{2ff.}$) exhibits a heightened form as compared with the general promise of 1 K $17^{14ff.}$; and the same is the case with the raising from the dead recorded in 2 K $4^{29ff.}$, seeing that a much longer time had elapsed since the death than in 1 K $17^{19ff.}$. At the same time 2 K $4^{29ff.}$ expressly teaches that magical weapons are not efficacious in every hand: in vain Gehazi lays the staff of Elisha upon the face of the dead—it is only the prayer and the personal *physical* influence of the man of God that can call back to life. The fulfilment of Elisha's promise to the Shunammite ($4^{16}$) and of that to Naaman the leper (in the latter instance the promise being carried by a messenger) might also be attributed to the intercession of the prophet. In reality, however, the narrative may be intended to be understood to mean that the promise of the prophet is as certain to be inevitably fulfilled as was his curse ($2^{23f.}$). In $6^{18.\,20}$ it is the prayer of Elisha that strikes the Syrians blind and restores them to sight; and in both these cases (as already in $6^{17}$) the efficacy of the prayer is instantaneous. The feeding of 100 men with 20 barley loaves ($4^{42ff.}$) is the counterpart of the miracle of the widow's oil-cruse; the transferring of the leprosy of Naaman to Gehazi ($5^{27}$) corresponds to the instantaneous effect of the curse in $2^{24}$.

All this may be regarded as furnishing sufficient evidence that even Elisha is still closely allied to the *nĕbî'îm* in the old sense, but at the same time also that, like Elijah, he is distinguished from them, and forms along with him a connecting link between the old seers and the prophets proper. That his political activity, too, as exercised in the interest of pure Jahwism, was no slight one, would be sufficiently evidenced even by $9^{1ff.}$, and it is not without reason that he too received from king Joash the honourable appellation of 'chariot and horsemen of Israel.' Regarding what was perhaps his most important activity, the direction of the guilds of *nĕbî'îm*, we shall have to speak below.

(*c*) But we have still to notice one Israelitish prophet who in the reign of Ahab holds as peculiar a place as Elijah himself, namely Micaiah ben-Imlah, the subject of the narrative of 1 K $22^{8ff.}$. Ahab cannot endure him, because it is his wont always to prophesy evil to him. Jehoshaphat deprecates Ahab's remark; evidently he sees, in the very fact that Micaiah is mostly a prophet of ill, the evidence of true inspiration, whereas the unbroken harmony with which the numerous other prophets promise good fortune had awakened his distrust. In fact, Micaiah will speak only what Jahweh bids him (v.[14]). It is thus the intention of Jahweh that he, like the others, should at first hold out deceitful promises (v.[15]). Ahab, however, sees through this conduct, and Micaiah, when the king presses him, delivers Jahweh's message of woe, explaining at the same time, by relating his remarkable vision, why all the rest of the prophets had become victims of the 'lying spirit': Jahweh Himself has ordered it to be so. The circumstance that Micaiah himself does not share their fate, but is informed in his vision as to the real course of Jahweh's purpose, shows sufficiently the height at which he stands above the ordinary *nĕbî'îm*; and his threat against Ahab finds speedy realization at Ramoth-gilead. Hence we may say that Micaiah ben-Imlah is the first who bears all the marks of the true prophet of Jahweh, without anything to remind us of a connexion with the *nĕbî'îm* in the old sense.

6. With the *nĕbî'îm* of the latter class, as these belong to the time of Elijah and Elisha, we have still to occupy our attention here. Their affinity with the *nĕbî'îm* of the time of Saul consists, above all, in the circumstance that, like the latter, they make their appearance in whole groups—nay, in guilds. This is implied by the very designation so frequently applied to them—*bĕnê han-nĕbî'îm* (lit. 'sons of the prophets'). This does not mean 'pupils *or* disciples of the prophets,' but 'those who belong to the prophetic order'* (or, at times, evidently to prophetic guilds; so, *e.g.*, in 2 K $2^{3.\,5.\,7.\,15}$ $4^{1.\,38}$ $6^{1}$), and in so far they are the same as the simple *nĕbî'îm* (1 K $18^{4.\,13}$ $20^{41}$ $22^{6-13.\,22f.}$). An individual is called *nābî'* (1 K $20^{13.\,22.\,38}$) or 'one of the *bĕnê han-nĕbî'îm*' (v.[35]). The existence of a guild is pointed to also in $20^{41}$. This passage can be understood to mean only that the prophet there spoken of put the covering above his eyes to conceal a tattooing or some other characteristic mark † by which the *nĕbî'îm* in general were recognized as belonging to the service of Jahweh.

There are a number of passages which indicate that groups of these *nĕbî'îm* lived together: so at Bethel (2 K $2^{3}$) and at Jericho (v.[5]; $4^{38}$ 'in Gilgal'). Such a settlement is pointed to plainly by the story about an enlargement of a building ($6^{1ff.}$). That Elisha lived with them is nowhere said; even $4^{38}$ implies no more than that once, when on a visit to Gilgal, he set about providing a meal for them. But it is very noteworthy that we twice ($4^{38}$ and $6^{1}$) meet with an expression which supplies us with unexpected information regarding the nature of these guilds: 'they *sit before* Elisha.' This means not simply that they group themselves around him or rejoice in his company, but that (after the manner of the NT expression 'to sit at the feet of some one') they sit before him as disciples before the master or pupils before the teacher. It is true that even here the current term 'schools of the prophets' is justified only to a very limited extent. For, in the first place, according to $4^{1}$ there are amongst the *bĕnê han-nĕbî'îm* even married men; and, secondly, they already exercise to a large extent (see below) a public activity. Nor do we read anywhere of any founding of these 'schools' by Elijah or Elisha. Still it appears to admit of no doubt that in $4^{38}$ and $6^{1}$ we have to do with occasional instruction of the members by Elisha, or with didactic conversations with them; nay, even the idea of their occupying themselves with religious literature is not a far-fetched one, although there is no direct allusion to it. That the relation between them and Elisha was that of disciples to a master, is favoured by the affection and reverence so evidently shown by the *nĕbî'îm* in addressing him as 'man of God.'

It might appear from the majority of the Elisha-narratives as if the *nĕbî'îm*, with him at their head, led a life wholly retired and devoted to the worship of Jahweh; but there are other passages which testify to a public activity, and that—in harmony with the main postulate of genuine prophetism—at the impulse of the spirit of Jahweh. In 1 K $20^{35}$ one of the *bĕnê han-nĕbî'îm* asks his companion, *by the direction of Jahweh*, to wound him; and, when he refuses, he tells him that for disobedience to the command of Jahweh he shall be torn by a lion. His message to Ahab, again, he announces as a word from Jahweh (v.[42]), and so already in vv.[13.28] [where this prophet is even called a 'man of God']. And in $22^{5ff.}$ the spirit

* Cf. above, p. 643, regarding an analogous expression, *bĕnê hā-'ĕlōhîm*.

† So Kraetzschmar, *Prophet und Seher im alten Israel*, p. 9.

of Jahweh is expressly spoken of in connexion with the *nĕbî'îm*. The same Ẓedeḳiah, the son of Chenaanah, who in 1 K 22$^{11}$ supports his promise to Aḥab by the symbol of iron horns, asks (v.$^{24}$) Micaiah in anger: 'In what way is the spirit of Jahweh passed from me to speak with thee?' He cannot believe that he has now become the victim of a lying spirit when he knew himself formerly to be inspired by the true spirit of Jahweh. So also in 2 K 2$^{3.5}$ the question of the *bĕnê han-nĕbî'îm* to Elisha is to be understood as meaning that they too have had it revealed to them by the spirit that the translation of Elijah is impending.

Like the true Jahweh prophets, these *nĕbî'îm* sometimes answer inquiries (1 K 22$^{5ff.}$); at other times, acting on their own initiative, they proclaim the word of Jahweh in the public interest (20$^{13f. 28. 39ff.}$). In this connexion we are struck with their great numbers. 'Obadiah rescues 100 of them from the fury of Jezebel; some 400 are assembled by Aḥab (22$^{6}$); more than 50 live together at Gilgal (2 K 2$^{7. 16}$). These numbers are surely evidence of the intensity of the excitement and the zeal for the God of Israel when His worship appeared to be endangered by Baal (to whom, in 1 K 18$^{19}$, so many as 450 *nĕbî'îm* are attributed).

Now, it has been argued that none of the passages which speak of any public activity on the part of the *nĕbî'îm* belong to the Elijah- and Elisha-narratives, but to the very valuable ancient 'Aḥab-source' (1 K 20. 22). The latter, it is pointed out, knows nothing of guilds of *nĕbî'îm* or of their being directed by Elijah or Elisha, as, conversely, the Elisha-narratives know nothing of a public activity on the part of their *bĕnê han-nĕbî'îm*. The difference between the two sources must at once be acknowledged. But their accounts are not mutually exclusive, although their historical viewpoint is different, and the period involved in the Elisha-narratives is somewhat later than the other. A very notable evidence of the continuance of the old view of the *nĕbî'îm* is found in 2 K 9$^{11}$. The officers of Jehu roundly call Elisha's messenger, who in v.$^{1}$ is expressly reckoned among the *bĕnê han-nĕbî'îm*, a 'mad enthusiast' (מְשֻׁגָּע). This implies that there was expected of him, and certainly not of him alone but also of his comrades, an ecstatic condition, and even utterances due to a kind of possession; which shows that, in spite of the milder character of the later *nĕbî'îm*, there were still occasional outbursts of their old nature, as we make its acquaintance in 1 S 10$^{5ff.}$ and 19$^{19ff.}$.

7. A final trace of the old notion of the prophetic spirit as a mysterious agency which hurries a whole crowd along is found in the narrative of Nu 11$^{17. 25ff.}$. The latter belongs in all probability to the E source, and hence falls within the period with which we are dealing, namely, prior to the rise of written prophecy. A portion of the spirit of Jahweh, which rests upon Moses, suffices to throw 70 of the elders of Israel into a condition of rapture. Two who remained behind in the camp, Eldad and Medad, are seized even *there* by the spirit of Jahweh because they also are marked out as amongst those destined to share in the leadership of the people (cf. v.$^{17}$). This endowment with the spirit for more secular ends is indeed foreign to the oldest point of view; but, on the other hand, the seizure of whole groups by the spirit of Jahweh finds its only analogy in the old *nĕbî'îm*, so that we could not deal with this case except by way of appendix to our account of the latter.

**3. Nazirites.**—1. Amongst those who served as express organs of genuine Jahwism we must, further, include the Nazirites. The name (נָזִיר) is generally explained to mean 'the consecrated one.' But it is questionable if the verbal forms to which appeal is made in favour of this sense are not derived from the substantive *nāzîr*, and this again from *nēzer*, the [consecrated] head-ornament (frequently used of a diadem, but also of the unshorn hair of the head). In that case *nāzîr* would denote originally one whose head is graced with unshorn hair—a view which is supported by the circumstance that in Lv 25$^{5. 11}$ the unpruned vine, which is still decked with its full quota of leaves, is likewise called *nāzîr*. All the same, we do not mean to deny that the notion of 'consecrated' one came, at an early period, to be connected with *nāzîr*; so especially in the collocation 'a *nāzîr* of God,' Jg 13$^{5. 7}$ 16$^{17}$.

2. The few OT passages which inform us as to the Nazirate are all at one as to its being a condition of consecration to God which shows itself in submitting to certain restrictions. Three of these are specified: the leaving of the hair of the head unshorn, abstinence from wine and intoxicating drink, and the avoiding of defilement by a corpse. It is questionable, however, whether these restrictions were always in force at the same time, and especially is there doubt as to the relation between the obligation for life and the obligation for a fixed period. We must first, therefore, examine the various statements separately.

3. The only historical instance of a Nazirite is Samson. As to Samuel, who is also usually included among the Nazirites, all that is said in 1 S 1$^{11}$ is that his mother vowed before his birth to give him over to Jahweh for life, and that no razor was to come upon his head. But his not being shorn did not suffice to constitute him a Nazirite; according to Ezk 44$^{20}$ this was no unusual practice with priests, and it may have meant no more in the case of Samuel; at all events, he is never called a Nazirite.

The Nazirate of Samson is spoken of in Jg 13$^{4-14}$ and, indirectly, in 16$^{17ff.}$. According to ch. 13 he was, even before his birth, expressly marked out by the angel of Jahweh as 'consecrated to God.' At the same time his mother is bound over—evidently prior to, and during, pregnancy—to abstain from wine * and intoxicating drink, and from unclean food; while no razor is to come upon the head of her child, who, from his mother's womb down to the day of his death, is to be consecrated to God. Now, it is surely very surprising that the obligation to abstain from wine and what is unclean is imposed, not upon the son, for whom such abstinence would have been equally possible, but upon the mother. Everywhere else it is taken for granted that the Nazirite himself abstains from wine. Hence we are forced to the conclusion that the abstinence from wine enjoined upon the mother in vv.$^{4. 7. 13f.}$ was afterwards † inserted by some one who could not conceive of a Nazirate without any such prohibition. Seeing that, in the story of Samson (ch. 14 f.; cf. esp. 14$^{10. 12. 17}$) the practice of the hero himself gave no countenance to such a theory, recourse was had to the expedient adopted in ch. 13.

Accordingly, the Nazirate of Samson is based exclusively upon his unshorn hair, and, as a matter of fact, the greatest stress is laid upon the latter in 16$^{17ff.}$. His enormous strength is bound up with his hair remaining inviolate, and that simply because the presence of Jahweh is, in some mysterious way, connected with the hair. After the seven locks have been cut off his head, he becomes weaker and weaker (v.$^{19}$); he strives in vain to free

* In v.$^{14}$ the prohibition is extended to 'all that comes from the vine' (as in Nu 6$^{4}$); but this is probably a later addition, as is indicated even by its position, *before* the main prohibition.

† That it is so in v.$^{4}$ is clear from the fact that in v.$^{5a}$ the closing words of v.$^{3}$ are repeated.

himself, 'for he knew not that Jahweh was departed from him' (v.[20]). On the other hand, when his hair had grown again, he recovered the strength for his last achievement in the destruction of the Philistines.

All this shows that the Nazirate of Samson is a condition in which he is under the influence of the spirit of Jahweh, and that this condition is connected with the hair of his head being unshorn. The spirit appears, indeed, to be often latent, breaking into action only on special occasions (cf. Jg 13[25]). Violently seized by the spirit of Jahweh, he tears asunder the lion (14[6]), slaughters 30 Philistines at Ashkelon (v.[19]), bursts his bonds and kills 1000 Philistines with the jawbone of an ass (15[14ff.]). It is therefore, above all, displays of strength against the foes of his people for which the spirit of Jahweh endows him, and his Nazirate recalls certain phenomena that present themselves elsewhere, in which we have to do with vows and forms of abstinence for warlike ends.* An analogy is presented, in particular, by the Arab warriors, who vow to leave the hair of their head unshorn during the whole period of a war of revenge, and to make a fire-offering of it after revenge has been achieved. The only difference would be that in the case of Samson it was no vow for a fixed period, but a 'perpetual warlike consecration' (Schwally). For his proposal to enter into friendly relations with the Philistines by marriage (14[1ff.]) is expressly traced (v.[4]) to a providential dispensation of Jahweh, 'because he sought an occasion [for hostilities] against the Philistines.' This, his life-work, is pointed to from the first (v.[5b]). As a matter of fact, all that is related of him in ch. 15 resolves itself into a series of single combats with the Philistines. We have already noted that in this warlike Nazirate no regard is paid to abstinence from wine. And it is sufficiently evident from 14[8f.] that there can be as little question of avoiding unclean food.

4. We receive quite a different impression of the Nazirites from Am 2[11f.] 'And I raised up of your sons for prophets, and of your young men for Nazirites. . . . But ye gave the Nazirites wine to drink, and commanded the prophets, saying, Prophesy not.' Here it is evident that the Nazirate is based essentially upon the prohibition of wine, and it is not easy to hold that the prohibition of cutting the hair is passed over simply because it is taken for granted. We must conclude rather that in Amos we have to do with a different form of Nazirate, which reminds us strongly of the vow of the Rechabites (see below). Regarding the nature and aim of this Nazirate, we must indeed have recourse to pure conjecture. Only this much is clear from the words of Amos—since he places the Nazirites in parallelism with the prophets—that the Nazirate is a condition approved by Jahweh and consecrated to His service. To induce the Nazirite to break his vow to abstain from wine is as great a religious enormity as to prevent the prophet from delivering the message with which Jahweh has charged him. Further, the Nazirate here spoken of is probably thought of as life-long, as is the case with the prophetic office which appears in parallelism with it. As to the purpose, however, for which Nazirites were raised up we are quite in the dark. May it be that here again we are to think of unwearied service of Jahweh in war against the foes of His people (as, for instance, the Aramæans)? Or, was the abstaining from wine meant (as in the case of the Rechabites) to be a silent protest against the seductive products of the culture of Baal's land, and thus, at the same time, a standing allusion to Jahweh as the God of Israel?

* Cf., on this subject, above all, W. R. Smith, *RS*² 333 f., and Schwally, *Semit. Kriegsaltertümer.* i. 101 ff.

In any case, we must assume that the Nazirite, prior to and during the time of Amos, had certain positive services to render in order to justify his title of 'one consecrated to God.'

5. In connexion with these scanty testimonies to a historical Nazirate we must look also at the legal Nazirate of Nu 6. The oldest part* of this code (vv.[2-8]) requires, in the case of every man or woman who desires to pay the vow of a *nāzîr*, that there shall be, for the whole period of duration of the vow, a strict abstinence from wine and everything that comes from the vine, as well as a careful guarding against defilement by a corpse—even that of one's nearest relation. But, in addition to this, the Nazirite must, during the period of his vow, leave the hair of his head unshorn, for in this, above all, according to v.[7], is represented the consecration to his God. The difference between this Nazirate and that which meets us in history is at once apparent. The characteristics encountered separately in Jg 13 and Am 2[11] are here combined, and a new requirement is added, namely, that of avoiding defilement by a corpse. Another new and very surprising feature is the extending of the Nazirate to women, whereas elsewhere the only place allowed to women in the cultus appears to be participation in the sacrificial meals. But in every instance we have to do only with a temporary vow, not (as in the case of Samson and probably also Am 2[11]) with a life-long obligation.

About the significance of the Nazirate, so far as the Priests' Code is concerned, we are not left in doubt. The only other class that are commanded to avoid defilement by a corpse are the priests. But an exception is allowed, even in their case (Lv 21[2]), when it is the corpse of their nearest blood relation. On the other hand the prohibition is absolute for the high priest (v.[11]). Now, when the same demand is made on the Nazirites, a kind of enhanced priestly dignity is accorded them, a lay priesthood, indeed, and one without official functions (which would be *per se* inconceivable in the case of a woman), but yet allied to the actual priesthood as a condition of high consecration to God. In all probability, the Priests' Code has in this way discovered the desired expedient whereby the ancestral and highly esteemed institution of the Nazirate, which, as life-long, had no proper place in the priestly State, might yet be conserved and worthily incorporated among the institutions of the post-exilic theocracy. As always happens in such instances, everything is stripped off in this process which could possibly be regarded as a survival of ancient naturalistic or even heathen notions. The unshorn hair is no longer, as in the case of Samson, the medium of mysterious powers and a pledge of the immediate nearness of Jahweh. Rather is it inviolable because it forms part of the body which, as a whole, is consecrated to God, and the hair is a principal sign of this consecration. Again, the prohibition of wine, which, as we found above, had quite a peculiar significance for the ancient Nazirite, is probably, in Nu 6, to be thought of as finding its motive in the similar prohibition laid upon priests during the exercise of their official functions (Lv 10[9]).

Somewhat later than Nu 6[2-8] are the prescriptions in vv.[13-21] regarding the release of a Nazirite after the expiry of the period of his consecration. In addition to various animal offerings he has to take his hair, which has been cut off before the door of the sanctuary, and cast it into the fire which is under the peace-offering. This enactment is not, however, to lead us to see in the hair-offering the kernel and purpose of the Nazirate as a whole (as if, for instance, it were a symbolical offering of

* Cf., for the above analysis, Wurster in *ZATW* iv. (1884) p. 126.

the body in the form of the representative offering of a part of it). It is quite possible that the hair-offering elsewhere, especially on Semitic soil, has an independent significance of this kind. But it has certainly no such significance in Nu 6[13ff.]. Rather is the burning in the fire of the altar the simplest way of getting rid of what had once been consecrated to God, and hence could not be treated as a common thing. Similarly, the parts of the sin-offering victim which cannot be presented on the altar are required (Ex 29[14], Lv 4[11f. 21] 6[23]) to be burned elsewhere. The burning of the Nazirite's hair *in* the altar-fire may be a feature corresponding to the ancient usage, which was retained by the Priests' Code without the hair having on that account a sacrificial character conferred upon it. The latest component in Nu 6 is undoubtedly vv.[9-12], containing prescriptions for the case of a Nazirite who has been rendered Levitically unclean by a death occurring suddenly beside him. In that event the consecrated hair is to be cut off, and, after certain guilt-offerings have been presented, the period of consecration is to begin *de novo*.

**4. Rechabites.**—We have already called attention to the close affinity subsisting between the prohibition of wine to the Nazirites and the corresponding vow of the Rechabites.* But, even apart from this, the latter must be dealt with here, because their founding as a religious sect falls, at latest, in the time of Jehoram the son of Ahab, *i.e.* before B.C. 842.

1. We read in 2 K 10[15f.] that the usurper Jehu, while driving along the road from Jezreel to Samaria, met Jonadab the son [or descendant of the family] of Rechab, and gave him his hand in token of his regard, and took him up into his chariot that he might enjoy the spectacle of Jehu's zeal for Jahweh. From this summary notice we can only suppose that Jonadab was an influential man upon whose adherence Jehu must have laid weight, and that he was inspired with the same zeal for Jahweh as Jehu himself.

2. Fortunately, a much later passage, Jer 35, has preserved for us more exact details regarding the significance of this Jonadab. During the reign of Jehoiaḳim, after the Chaldæans had moved into Judah (*i.e.* in B.C. 602 or shortly thereafter), Jeremiah is directed by Jahweh to bring the guild of the Rechabites into a chamber of the temple and to set wine before them. But the Rechabites [whose names one and all end with *Jah* (Jahweh)] flatly refuse to drink wine, and appeal to the prohibition of their ancestor Jonadab the son of Rechab, who had enjoined them not only to abstain from the use of wine, but to neglect the building of houses and every species of agriculture. They had always remained true to this prohibition, and only the invasion of Nebuchadreẓẓar had compelled them to take refuge in Jerusalem. Thereupon Jeremiah reproaches the Judahites, pointing out how this example of fidelity to a human command puts to shame those who are constantly disobedient to their God. To the Rechabites, on the other hand, he announces as a recompense that they shall never want descendants in the service of Jahweh.

3. This last expression shows that their manner of life amounts to a kind of service of Jahweh. For it is a protest against the whole system of culture connected with the settled mode of life, with the tilling of the soil, and, above all, with vine-culture. The life of the nomads in the steppes knew nothing of all this; it was exclusively devoted to the service of Jahweh, the God of the desert, who manifested Himself, above all, in storm and in battle, against the foes of His people. But, since Israel had forsaken their tents and appropriated all the benefits of Canaanite culture, they had fallen a prey to the seductive influences which accompanied these, including not only luxury and intemperance, but even idolatry. The only way of escape from this lay in a resolute return to the pre-Canaanite manner, a renunciation of the false benefits of culture. And it cannot be doubted that this return was coupled at the same time with the rigid observance of the oldest ritual usages in the service of Jahweh, although, unfortunately, no information on this point has come down to us. In any case, this oldest type of anchoritism, on the part of a whole tribe, from religious motives, is something very peculiar, and demanding of appraisement: these Rechabites have as good a claim to be reckoned organs of genuine Jahwism as the *nĕbî'îm*. The explanation of the circumstance that it was *this* particular family that felt called on to protest against the cultivating of the fruit-land is perhaps to be found in 1 Ch 2[55], where Ḥammath, the [tribal] father of the house of Rechab, is reckoned among the Ḳenites. The latter are, according to Jg 4[11], the descendants of Ḥobab, the father-in-law of Moses. The Ḳenites who attached themselves to Israel at the Exodus (Jg 1[16]) continued even at a later period to live a nomadic life, partly in the Plain of Jezreel (Jg 5[24]), partly in the extreme south of the country among the Amaleḳites (1 S 15[6]). The action of Jonadab may thus have consisted in recalling to the ancient nomad life that portion of his tribe which had adopted settled habits. True, before accepting this explanation it must first be proved that by the 'house of Rechab' in 1 Ch 2[55] is meant exactly the same family as in Jer 35[2]. According to Neh 3[14] one Malchijah the son of Rechab helped to rebuild the walls of Jerusalem. This seems to prove the continued existence of the guild in post-exilic times. But how can this Malchijah be called at the same time 'the ruler of the district of Beth-haccherem,' if he adhered to the tent-life enjoined by Jonadab?

**5. 'Judges' and kings.**—If we include, finally, the 'judges' and kings of ancient Israel among the organs of genuine Jahwism, this is justifiable not only on the ground that all of them (down at least to David) were expressly chosen and called by Jahweh to be leaders and saviours of the people, but, above all, because they too were filled with the 'spirit of Jahweh' as a mysterious agency, and thereby were fitted for the performance of extraordinary deeds.

1. It is true that P is the first to tell us that Joshua, as a man in whom the spirit is, is consecrated by Moses to be his successor, by the laying on of his hands (Nu 27[18f.]). On the other hand, the early 'hero-narratives' (and not merely the author of the present scheme to which the book is adjusted, *e.g.* 3[10]) in the Book of Judges are already aware that the spirit of Jahweh was powerfully at work in those heroes: so in Gideon (6[34]), Jephthah (11[29]), and frequently Samson (see above, p. 657ᵇ f.).

2. In the case of the kings, however, the spirit is imparted by means of *anointing*.* This is expressly recorded for Saul (1 S 10[1]), David (2 S 2[4]; the story of the anointing of David by Samuel in 1 S 16[13] is a late *midrāsh*), Solomon (by Ẓadoḳ, 1 K 1[39]), and Jehu (2 K 9[6]). From the passage last cited, as well as from 1 S 10[1], it is evident that the anointing consisted of no mere smearing process, but of a pouring of oil upon the head. Of all the manifold interpretations of this symbolical action, that one has most in its favour which starts from the oil-libation. This, too, consisted in *pouring oil over* (*e.g.* the stone of Bethel, Gn 28[18] 31[13]), and

* Cf. L. Gautier's art. 'À propos des Récabites' in *Liberté Chrétienne*, 15th June 1901.

* Cf. on this subject Weinel's art. 'Mashaḥ [salben] und seine Derivate' in *ZATW* xviii. (1898) p. 1 ff.

imparted to the anointed object the character of something consecrated and sacrosanct. Both these features come out clearly in connexion with the anointing of kings. As one consecrated to Jahweh the king is called frequently 'my anointed,' or 'his [Jahweh's] anointed,' or even 'the anointed of Jahweh,' *i.e.* one who by anointing has been in a special manner assigned or consecrated to Him. On that very account the king is sacred, and hence it is a heinous sin 'to put forth one's hand on the anointed of Jahweh' (1 S 26$^{9. 11. 23}$ of Saul, 2 S 19$^{22 (21)}$ of David). A consecration rite, analogous to the oil-libation, is favoured, further, by the circumstance that the anointing is performed with 'holy' (*i.e.* used in the cultus for other purposes as well) oil; cf. *e.g.* Ps 89$^{21 (20)}$, with reference to David. Zadok in 1 K 1$^{39}$ takes not *a* but *the* oil-horn (filled with holy oil) out of the tent (of the sacred Ark) for the anointing of Solomon; and in 2 K 9$^{1}$ Elisha hands over a vessel of oil to the prophet who is to anoint Jehu, so that here again the use of any ordinary vessel appears to be excluded. In P, finally, the anointing of the sacred fittings and utensils (Ex 30$^{26ff.}$) is plainly an act of consecration, while in the case of the priests the terms 'anoint' and 'consecrate' frequently appear in parallelism (Lv 8$^{10f.}$ *et al.*).

The efficacy of the anointing of kings is not, however, exhausted by the notions of consecration and the imparting of a sacrosanct character. The spirit of Jahweh is also communicated. This is plain already from the story of the anointing of Saul. Directly after it had been performed, Samuel announced to Saul (1 S 10$^{5ff.}$) that, when he should meet with the *nĕbî'îm* at Gibeah, the spirit of Jahweh would come upon him, and he would be changed into another man. And, when this comes to pass, it is not merely that Saul is infected by the example of the *nĕbî'îm*; for the spirit of Jahweh has been in him ever since his anointing,* and only waits for an external occasion to reveal itself. In 11$^{6}$ the occasion is different, but the effect is the same. The melancholy of Saul is attributed in 16$^{14}$ to the spirit of Jahweh (which had been imparted to him at his anointing) having departed from him, and an 'evil spirit'—likewise proceeding from Jahweh—having come in its place to trouble him.

In favour of the great antiquity of anointing, and its having been taken over by Israel from the Canaanites, is its mention in the Tel el-Amarna letters.† But it is a question whether on the soil of Jahwism it did not assume another, deeper religious significance. It is true that even here the efficacy of the oil is still thought of as not merely symbolical, but direct and physical—nay, as establishing a sacramental fellowship between the Deity to whom the holy oil is consecrated and the man who is anointed with it.‡ This view of the matter may have been borrowed from the Canaanites, but a specifically Israelitish origin may be confidently claimed for the connecting of the anointing with the bestowal of the spirit of Jahweh. This answers best to the idea of the spirit of Jahweh as the principle which shows its creative activity on all sides, and which gives birth to special powers—an idea whose many-sided development and application we owe undoubtedly to Jahwism alone.

* The author of the *midrāsh* in 16$^{1ff.}$ understands this rightly when in v.$^{13}$ he makes the spirit of Jahweh come upon David 'from that day forward.'

† Cf. H. Winckler, *Die Thontafeln von Tell-el-Amarna*, Berlin, 1896, p. 99 (Letter 37 of Ramman-nirari to the Pharaoh), line 4: 'Behold, when Manahbi(r)ia, king of Egypt . . . installed my grandfather in Nuhašši as king, and poured oil upon his head,' etc.

‡ Weinel, *l.c.* p. 54: 'When the priest at the holy place pours consecrated oil on the king's head, he conveys the material and character of holiness to him, and makes him a participator in Jahweh's superior life.'

3. It is clear that such a conception and religious estimate of the anointing of the king could not have taken root unless—at least at the outset—the monarchy had been considered a blessing, a gracious gift of Jahweh.* And this is, in point of fact, the standpoint of the early sources. Even if the 'shout of a king' in Nu 23$^{21}$ should be referred rather to Jahweh than to the earthly king, there is still left the weighty testimony of 1 S 9$^{15f.}$. According to this passage, Jahweh Himself commanded Samuel to anoint Saul: 'he shall deliver my people from the power of the Philistines, for I have looked upon the oppression of my people, since their cry for help has reached me.' A long course of unhappy experiences of the monarchy must have intervened before this conception could be expelled by the wholly different one which meets us in the later source (1 S 8. 10$^{17ff.}$ 12). Here the earthly kingship is regarded as implying a denial of Jahweh, the true King—a falling away from the principle once laid down, according to Jg 8$^{22f.}$, by Gideon. It was said to have been with the utmost reluctance that Samuel at last yielded to the people's improper demand for a king. He did so at Jahweh's command, but not without warning the people that one day they would cry out in vain because of the king whom they had themselves chosen. The early conception knew of no such scruples. It was Jahweh Himself, according to it, that designed the monarchy; true, it was He also that brought about the unhappy disruption of the kingdom. For it was in His name that the prophet Ahijah of Shiloh foretold to Jeroboam I. the breaking off of the ten Northern tribes from Judah. Ahijah, as an Ephraimite, naturally represents here the standpoint which afterwards prevailed in the Northern kingdom: the real heir of the kingdom of David and Solomon is the kingdom of the Ten Tribes, which accordingly even retained the collective name 'Israel.' It is Judah that has broken off from *it*; hence the prayer in the Ephraimitic Blessing of Moses (Dt 33$^{7}$): 'Hear, O Jahweh, the cry of Judah, and bring him back to his people.' On the other hand, the Judahite view of the disruption of the kingdom is presented to us in Is 7$^{17}$: it was a misfortune, a time of sorest distress for Judah, 'when Ephraim *departed from* Judah.'

At the close of this survey of the organs of genuine Jahwism we have still to refer to a circumstance which establishes an essential difference between the religion of Israel—even at this stage—and the other popular religions so closely allied to it in many respects. Apart from the priests, of whose anointing and consequent filling with the spirit no evidence can be adduced for the pre-exilic period, all other organs of Jahweh are fitted for the exercise of their office by the inward working of His spirit. Such a working on seers and prophets, throwing them into an ecstatic condition, is known to heathenism as well. But it does not know *that* working of the spirit of God which impels the 'man of God' to present himself before kings unsummoned, and by sharp condemnation of their sins to obtain satisfaction for outraged justice and morality. In this way Nathan and Elijah become forerunners of the prophets proper, and, long before the day of the latter, prove that Jahweh is always and for all members of His people an absolutely moral Being. To recognize this truth and to impress it on all is the main task of those whom the spirit of Jahweh has constituted His organs. Once more we have to ask:

* Cf. J. Boehmer, *Gottesgedanken in Israels Königtum*, Gütersloh, 1902; K. Budde, *Die Schätzung des Königtums im AT*, Marburg, 1903.

Is anything like this even remotely conceivable in the religion of a Chemosh or a Milcom?

v. *CULTUS AND MANNERS.*—1. In the matter of the cultus, some changes from the state of things in the preceding period must have been introduced in consequence of the above-mentioned taking over of the ancient Canaanite sanctuaries. The places of worship (or, what is the same thing for this period, places of sacrifice) are **high places** (בָּמוֹת *bāmôth*),* that is, primarily, the hills and rising grounds in the neighbourhood of the particular localities (so, *e.g.*, 1 S 9[13] 10[5]), but afterwards standing also for places of sacrifice upon mountains, such as the Mount of Olives, Mt. Carmel, Mt. Tabor, all of which are mentioned upon occasion as places of worship. Hence the Syrians speak (1 K 20[23]) of Jahweh as 'a god of the mountains,' who can be combated with success only on the low ground (cf. also Gn 22[14], if the correct rendering there is 'Upon the mountain Jahweh appears'). It was evidently a pre-Canaanite custom to complete the apparatus of a place of worship by providing, in addition to the altar, a *mazzēbāh* and an *'ăshērāh* or sacred pole (see above, p. 620). Since the *mazzēbāh* was a pledge of the presence of the Deity, a *bēth 'ĕlōhîm* or shrine containing a Divine image was not indispensable. Such 'high place temples' appear, it is true, more frequently in later writers in the catalogue of Israel's sins (1 K 13[32], 2 K 17[29. 32] 23[19]), but in olden times (as the medium for obtaining oracles) they are mentioned even apart from any connexion with 'heights.' In 1 S 9[22], again, we read of a *lishkāh*, that is, a room at the place of sacrifice, in which the sacrificial meal was eaten. A further evidence that *bāmāh* might stand also for the sanctuary erected on the height is found in the frequent mention (1 K 11[7] 14[23] etc.) of building as well as (2 K 23[8]) pulling down the *bāmôth*. The last-cited passage shows, moreover, that a *bāmāh* might stand on quite a small (artificial) height, else *bāmôth* at the entrance of the door of Joshua the governor of the city could not be spoken of. On the other hand, 2 K 23[15] shows that the *bāmāh* is not identical with the altar. The latter, as we see from Ex 20[24ff.], might be built either of earth (*i.e.*, probably, sods) or of stones; but the latter, to avoid desecration, must not be dressed with iron tools. It was likewise forbidden to ascend the altar by steps, to prevent indecent exposure of one's person. Both these regulations are plainly intended by way of protest against innovations that had crept in, and in favour of the ancient simple ritual usages, which were as yet quite uninfluenced by art and higher culture. It may be added that Ex 20[24ff.] is irrefutable evidence that the author of the Book of the Covenant knew nothing of the requirement of *one* central sanctuary.†

2. The central feature of the cultus continued to be *sacrifice*. The original significance of the latter (cf. above, p. 618), as the sacral communion of the offerers with the Deity and with one another, still finds its only expression during this period in the form of the common sacrificial meals,‡ of which we have instructive instances in 1 S 1[4ff.] and 9[12ff.]. According to the latter passage, the guests at the meal number about 30 persons, specially invited; and, before they begin to eat, a blessing is pronounced (something after the manner of our saying of grace) by Samuel (v.[13]). According to 1 S 2[13f.], the offerer himself killed the victim and boiled its flesh; but even the portion for the priests could not be taken till the portion of Jahweh, namely the fat, had been burned [on the altar]. There is no mention in this passage of a sprinkling of blood on the altar, but this is no doubt taken for granted; at all events, the eating of the flesh *with* the blood is regarded in 1 S 14[32f.] as a heinous offence.

Like the fat and blood of the meal-offering, the burnt-offering or whole-offering also falls completely under the category of a cheering *gift*, the presenting of food. This comes out very clearly in the offering which Gideon presents to the angel of Jahweh (Jg 6[18ff.]). He calls it by the ancient name applied to every species of offering — מִנְחָה, 'gift' (cf. Gn 4[3ff.]). It consists of a kid of the goats and unleavened cakes of an ephah [about 8 gals.] of meal. The [boiled] flesh is put by Gideon in a basket, and the broth in a pot. Then, at the angel's bidding, he lays the flesh and the cakes upon a stone [which, as in 1 S 14[33], takes the place of the altar] and pours the broth over them. The meal is now ready, and is consumed by the fire that comes out of the rock. In like manner, Manoah (Jg 13[19]) offers to the angel of Jahweh a kid of the goats, with the proper accompaniments, upon the rock [in v.[20] it is called 'altar'], as a burnt-offering (v.[23]). Both offerings—that of Gideon and that of Manoah — would have been inconceivable to the ritual of P, and for that very reason they may be supposed to represent the sacrificial usages of the narrator's own time. It may be added that for the whole of this period burnt-offerings were the exception, although upon quite special occasions they might be presented in great numbers. Thus Solomon, at his accession, offered (1 K 3[4]) upon the 'great high place' at Gibeon 1000 burnt-offerings; and, at the dedication of the temple (8[64]), found it necessary to consecrate the middle portion of the forecourt [as a place of sacrifice], because the altar was unable to contain all the burnt-offerings and the fat of the meal-offerings.

During this period there is no mention of other species of offerings* (apart from the fruit-offerings, which were presented at all periods [Ex 23[19]], amongst which must be included the regularly renewed 'shewbread' of the sanctuary [1 S 21[5. 7]]). As is shown by Gn 8[20], the burnt-offering serves also as a thank-offering, just as in 1 S 7[9] (in the form of a sucking lamb) it is an offering with a propitiatory and intercessory aim. The same character belongs to the burnt-offerings presented by Saul (1 S 13[9f.] along with peace-offerings) as inaugural offerings before commencing his campaign against the Philistines, and David's offering at the threshing-floor of Araunah (2 S 24[22ff.]). On the other hand, more general names are used to designate propitiatory offerings (1 S 3[14] slaughter-offering and *minḥah*, 26[19] *minḥah*). Regarding human sacrifices during this period, see above, p. 618[b] f.; on the significance still retained throughout the whole period by the sacred Ark, see p. 628 ff.; and on the institution of the 'ban,' see p. 619[b].

* Cf. Piepenbring, art. 'Histoire des lieux de culte et du sacerdoce en Israel' in *Revue de l'Hist. des Religions*, Juill.-Août, 1891; v. Gall, *Altisrael. Cultstätten*, Giessen, 1898 [where 106 names are discussed].

† The obvious contradiction with the Deuteronomic legislation is sought to be removed in the MT of Ex 20[24] by the reading בְּכָל־הַמָּקוֹם ('in the whole place'), as if here too *one* central sanctuary were spoken of. But the whole context requires בְּכָל־מָקוֹם ('in every place'), and this was still read by the LXX (ἐν παντὶ τόπῳ).

‡ These are called sometimes simply זְבָחִים, *i.e.* 'slaughter-offerings' intended to be eaten (Ex 18[12], 2 S 15[12] *et al.*), or שְׁלָמִים (Ex 20[24], 1 S 11[15] *et al.*), but also, using the complete expression, *zĕbāḥîm shĕlāmîm*, *i.e.* 'slaughter-offerings in the form of *shĕlāmîm*-offerings' (Ex 24[5] *et al.*). The meaning of the latter term [sing. *shélem*, Am 5[22] only] is still disputed. The choice lies between 'peace [=safety]-offering,' *i.e.* in testimony of the peaceful relation with the Deity, and 'recompense- *or* thank-offering.'

* In 1 S 6[3] אָשָׁם is not a guilt-offering in P's sense, and in 2 K 12[17 (16)] it is not guilt- and sin-offerings in the proper sense that are spoken of, but money contributions which bear the names אָשָׁם and חַטָּאת.

3. There are extremely few notices of *festivals*—a proof that even in this sphere custom rather than legal prescription was the ruling principle. (*a*) It cannot, indeed, be doubted that even the oldest form of the Decalogue contained a command to rest on the **Sabbath** (cf. also Ex $34^{21}$, in the so-called Jahwistic Decalogue), but it is noteworthy that in the Book of the Covenant (Ex $23^{12}$, cf. also Dt $5^{12}$) it is enforced, not with religious but with humanitarian motives, such as care for the refreshing of cattle and ass, slave and *gēr*. In the same source ($23^{10f.}$) we find already an approach to the keeping of a Sabbatical year: every seven years the fields, the vineyards, and oliveyards are to lie fallow—evidently, however, not all at the same time, but each in its turn—that the [spontaneous] produce may be for the benefit of the poor and the beasts of the field. It will be observed that here again the motive is humanitarian, not religious.

(*b*) Along with the Sabbath a special festal significance belongs to the **New Moon** (and that far beyond our period). From 1 S $20^{5ff.\ 24ff.}$ we see that the New Moon festivities even lasted for two days, being made the occasion of a common [sacrificial] meal, and at the same time that it was a favourite practice to present the year's offerings of whole families at the New Moon. In 2 K $4^{23}$, again, it is assumed that the Sabbaths and New Moons (when riding-animals were available) were readily utilized for undertaking journeys to consult a 'man of God.' Further, Am $8^{5}$ shows that on Sabbaths and at New Moons there was a cessation, not only from field work but also from trade and the ordinary business of life.

(*c*) For the three regular annual festivals—apart, perhaps, from the Harvest festival—we have no real testimony for this period except the legal prescriptions in the Book of the Covenant (Ex $23^{14ff.}$) and the almost identical text of Ex $34^{18ff.}$. According to these, all males are to appear three times a year before Jahweh (*i.e.* at some sanctuary) with gifts. (α) The first of these is the **Feast of Unleavened Bread** (*Maẓẓôth*), which is to be held for seven days in the month Abib, the month when the grain passes into the ear. Here, then, the *Peṣaḥ* day is included in the *Maẓẓôth* festival (cf., on the original significance of each of these, above, p. $622^{a}$); but the prescription of $34^{19f.}$ regarding the presenting of the firstlings of cattle shows that in this code there must have been at one time mention of the *Peṣaḥ* as well.* The emphasis laid upon the month Abib as the month of the Exodus from Egypt is the first approach to a theocratic motive, *i.e.* one derived from the religious history of the people.—(β) The second occasion is the **Feast of Weeks** (*i.e.*, as follows from Dt $16^{9}$, seven weeks after the beginning of the [barley] harvest), as the feast of firstfruits of the wheat harvest.—(γ) Thirdly, there is the **Feast of Harvest,** of the fruit and vintage, at the close of the year.

The Feast of Weeks and that of Harvest, as being purely harvest-thanksgiving festivals, were not possible till after Israel's entrance into Canaan. A trace of their having been borrowed from the Canaanites is found in Jg $9^{27}$, where the vintage festival, under the name *hillûlîm* ('jubilant rejoicing') is celebrated by the [heathen] Shechemites. For Israel itself the Feast of Harvest is the only one for which we have historical testimony (Jg $21^{19ff.}$, where it is celebrated by the maidens of Shiloh with dances in the vineyards; and in all probability also 1 S $1^{3}$). Hence it is often called simply *the* Feast, and that not only in early passages like Jg $21^{19}$ and 1 K $8^{2.\ 65\ (?)}$, but even as late as Ezk $45^{25}$.

There is as yet no fixed date for the festivals (apart from the general assignment of the spring festival to the month Abib).* People were guided, as is natural in the case of harvest festivals, by considerations of weather and climate, and in consequence held the feasts at different dates in different places. This view is supported by the frequently recurring expression 'proclaim a feast,' *i.e.* invite to the keeping of it by intimating its date. The self-evident terms of Sabbath and New Moon needed no such intimation.

That the festivals in ancient times were, without exception, occasions of rejoicing is shown by a great many expressions: to celebrate a festival and to rejoice before Jahweh are practically identical notions. The suspicion of Eli (1 S $1^{13}$) and the stern denunciation of Isaiah (Is $28^{7f.}$) prove that the sacrificial meals which (along with the dances, Ex $32^{6}$, Jg $21^{21}$; the religious dance, with musical accompaniment, of 2 S $6^{5}$ belongs to a different category) formed the culminating point of the festival, readily led to excesses. It was a still worse feature that immoral ritual practices were taken over from the Canaanites. In Hos $4^{13f.}$ fornication and adultery are evidently connected with the sacrificial meals at the high place cult under every green tree; and Am $2^{7}$ (like Hos $4^{14}$) refers to the evil of the קְדֵשׁוֹת *ḳĕdēshôth*, or 'sacred [girls],' who, in accordance with a widespread practice of the heathen Semites, prostituted themselves in honour of the Deity. No less frequent is the mention of male *hierodouloi* (*ḳĕdēshîm*). It cannot, unfortunately, be denied that, in spite of the energetic protests of the prophets and the prohibitions of the Law, the notion that such practices were reconcilable even with Jahwism must have been pretty widely prevalent in Israel. It is indeed mentioned to the honour of king Asa (in 1 K $15^{12}$) that he expelled the *ḳĕdēshîm* (whose presence is witnessed to as early as the reign of Rehoboam, 1 K $14^{24}$) from Judah; yet not only do we hear of remnants of them under Jehoshaphaṭ (1 K $22^{46}$), but it is recorded of Josiah that (in the year B.C. 623) he broke down the houses of the *ḳĕdēshîm* which were situated by the temple of Jahweh (2 K $23^{7}$). The latter statement permits of no other explanation than that this abuse was connected with the cult of Jahweh. The prohibition contained in Dt $23^{18\ (17)}$ might, if need be, be referred to *ḳĕdēshîm* and *ḳĕdēshôth* in the service of a heathen deity, but v.$^{19\ (18)}$ shows clearly that it was nothing uncommon to bring the earnings of these male [here called 'dog'] and female *hierodouloi* as a votive offering into the temple of Jahweh. This would, however, be quite inconsistent if we were intended to think of them as in the service of another god.

4. Outside the cultus proper stands communion with the Deity by seeking and obtaining *oracles.* We have repeatedly spoken already (*e.g.* p. 641 ff.) of the connexion of Divine images such as the *'ēphôd* and *tĕrāphîm* with the consulting of oracles. It is a question whether there was even then an inseparable connexion between the *'ēphôd* and the **Urim and Thummim** (such as in Ex $28^{30}$, where the latter have their place in the oracle-pocket attached to the ephod of the high priest). The meaning of the names *'ûrîm* and *tummîm* (אוּרִים וְתֻמִּים) is as much disputed as the nature of the lots for which they stand. All that is

* There is a further interpolated mention of the *Peṣaḥ* in Ex $34^{25}$, in the direction that the Peṣaḥ offering is not to be kept till the following morning. It is not clear, however, whether this refers to the flesh of the Paschal lamb.

* In 1 K $12^{32}$ Jeroboam I. is charged with having instituted a feast on the 15th day of the 8th month after the manner of the feast in Judah, but it is disputed whether this means that at that time the Feast of Harvest was celebrated even in Judah in the 8th month (instead of the 7th, as was the later practice). The fixing upon the 15th day (as in P) may be due simply to the author of this note about Jeroboam.

certain is that even in early times *'ûrîm* and *tummîm* represented the sacred lot, which was handled only by priests: Dt 33[8], 1 S 14[36. 41] 28[6] [where *'ûrîm* is no doubt merely an abbreviation for the complete expression *'ûrîm wĕthummîm*, as in Nu 27[21] (P)]. The suggestion that *'ûrîm* expressed an affirmative (especially as to where guilt lay), *tummîm* a negative, answer to a question, is favoured by 1 S 14[41], where, in place of the corrupt MT, we are to read with the LXX: 'If this guilt be in me or my son Jonathan . . . let *'ûrîm* appear, but if it be in thy people Israel, let *tummîm* appear.' As to the nature of these lots, we should probably think of small stones (cf. *gôrāl*, 'lot'; but properly, as the Arabic shows, 'pebble,' 'small stone'), which were shaken in an urn till one 'came out' (Jos 19[1ff.]).

If an oracle was to be obtained, the applicant must be on good terms with the Deity. To one who is under the weight of guilt unatoned for, the oracle is silent. This happens even if it is not himself that has incurred the guilt (so in 1 S 14[37f.], where Saul obtains no response because of the offence of Jonathan; and 28[6], where Saul consulted Jahweh, but He answered him not, by dreams, nor by *'ûrîm*, nor by prophets). The man to whom guilt attaches is to all intents and purposes unclean, and, as such, is *ipso facto* excluded from any approach to God or handling of objects consecrated to Him. How far these prescriptions as to cleanness were carried (even without a written law), we see from the casual notice of 1 S 20[26], according to which a state of uncleanness excluded from participation in the sacrificial meal at the New Moon; and from 21[5ff.], where abstinence from sexual intercourse is the condition of being allowed to eat sacred bread.* How deeply such considerations, enforced by religious usage, had impressed themselves on the daily life, could find no better illustration than that usage of language whereby the male population is divided into those who are admissible to, and those who are excluded from, the cultus,† the mention of both serving to express the totality (1 K 14[10] 21[21], 2 K 9[8] 14[26], Dt 32[36]).

5. In regard to the morality of this period, we must refer once more to what was said above (pp. 624[a], 633) as to the power of *custom* in the earliest times. But, if it had to be assumed even there that custom was not altogether unconnected with religion, this holds in increased measure of the period preceding that of the writing prophets. It is very significant that in 2 S 12[14] Nathan, after he has acted as the mouthpiece of the outraged popular conscience in calling David to account for his crime, discovers the special guilt of the king in the circumstance that by his action he has shown contempt for Jahweh.‡ This requires the death of Bathsheba's child as an atonement, although David has already been assured of the forgiveness of his sin.

We have all the less right to judge of the general condition of morality from isolated deeds wrought in passion, seeing that these were almost always condemned by contemporary opinion. The outrage wrought by Amnon on Tamar (2 S 13) is to be viewed as an instance of rape rather than of incest. Tamar herself contemplates the possibility (v.[13]) of being given by the king to Amnon as his wife, although she is his half-sister; while in Gn 20[12] it appears to be no way repugnant to E that Abraham's wife should be his half-sister Sarah. But Amnon's act was avenged by his murder by Absalom, who must have considered it a heinous offence. He thus carried out a species of blood-revenge, but, at the same time, exceeded the bounds prescribed by custom (just as Joab did when he treacherously murdered Abner, 2 S 3[27ff.]), and had to expiate this by a lengthened term of banishment.

6. The truest reflexion of the manners and morals of our period is preserved, without doubt, in the stories of the patriarchs in Gn 12–50. In these figures we have a twofold presentation of types that are thoroughly true to life—in Abraham a kind of ideal of ancient Israelitish piety, in Jacob the empirical phenomenon of the ancient Israelite, with his virtues, but also with his shady side.* We may leave it an open question whether the Abraham-narratives in their present form were not developed a good deal later than those about Jacob-Israel, the type of the character of the people with the same name. In any case, both fall within the period with which we are dealing. Of both types it is pre-eminently true that their conduct is by no means actuated simply by custom, but quite expressly also by religious motives.

The whole life of Abraham, as related in both the ancient Pentateuchal sources, is viewed as a continued trial of his faith and obedience. With faith in the promise of Jahweh he leaves his fatherland and sets out for the unknown country afar; he acquiesces in the expulsion of Ishmael, and even shows himself willing to sacrifice his late-born only son. The latter narrative (Gn 22), even if it is based upon some cult-legend,† is, in its present form (cf. v.[1]), the record of the last and severest trial of his faith to which Abraham was subjected by God. The brilliant manner in which he sustained the test is reckoned to him (v.[12]) a proof of true fear of God. It is very remarkable that already in 15[6] it is not an act, but simply trustful confidence in Jahweh that is counted to Abraham for 'righteousness,' *i.e.* a display of genuine piety. The Apostle Paul (Ro 4[1ff.]) is perfectly entitled to find here the proof that the righteousness of Abraham is grounded, even in Genesis, in quite an evangelical fashion, upon no merit of works.

As in the case of Abraham, so in that of Jacob, in spite of his wholly different character, there are not wanting marks of that humility and resignation by which true piety and fear of God are characterized. So in the grand confession of Gn 32[11 (10)] (J): 'I am not worthy of all the mercies and all the faithfulness which thou hast shown unto thy servant'; the expression of resignation in 43[14], and the beautiful thanksgiving of 48[11. 15f.]. A counterpart is presented by the expression of profoundest resignation put in the mouth of David in 2 S 15[26f.] and 16[11f.]. Again, what a high level of moral appreciation of the actions and fortunes of men is found in the words of Joseph (Gn 50[20]), in

* Cf. J. C. Matthes, art. 'De begrippen rein en onrein in het OT' in *Theol. Tijdschr.* xxxiii. 293 ff. [these are, according to him, 'cultus notions,' an answer to the question, How am I fit to serve Jahweh?].

† This interpretation of עָצוּר וְעָזוּב (lit. 'restrained and left free'), which is that of W. Robertson Smith (*RS*[2] 456: 'he who is under taboo and he who is free'), is to be preferred absolutely to the interpretations formerly current (such as 'bond and free,' or 'minors and of age,' or 'tribesmen and of no family' [for which A. S. Jahuda contends with much learning in the *Ztschr. f. Assyr.* 1902, p. 240 ff.]). Cf. especially the expression used of Doeg '*nĕ'ẓār* before Jahweh,' *i.e.* 'restrained' [as it were, in confinement], 1 S 21[8 (7)]. So in all probability *'ăzārāh*, 'a festal gathering' (Am 5[21] *et al.*), means originally 'a state of being bound,' namely, by the obligation to certain forms of abstinence.

‡ So we should read with Lucian. The MT inserts 'the enemies [of Jahweh]' before 'Jahweh,' and the (linguistically objectionable) interpretation is usually offered: 'because thou hast given the enemies of Jahweh occasion to blaspheme.'

* We may leave Isaac out of account here, since, in comparison with Abraham and Jacob, he plays almost throughout a passive rôle.

† According to Gunkel (Com. on Genesis) it is the cult-legend of the place of sacrifice at Jeruel, and is intended simply to explain how the former practice of child sacrifice had been superseded by the offering only of rams.

which he, as it were, sums up his own and his father's fortunes: 'Ye, indeed, meant evil against me, but God has turned it to good, to . . . save much people alive.' To recognize that God makes even the sins of men serve His purposes, without thereby lessening in the least their moral responsibility, is the only solution that is worthy and satisfying, from the point of view of religion, of the seeming contradiction between the universal activity of God and the moral freedom of man; and it is not the smallest of the evidences of a Divine factor in the religion of Israel, that even at so early a period it had discovered this solution.

Other features that are honourable to Abraham, such as his ready hospitality (Gn $18^{1ff.}$; cf. its still more striking exhibition by Lot, $19^{1ff.}$), may be best put down to the credit of custom. On the other hand, we are certainly true to the intention of the narrator if we ascribe to religious principle his peaceable attitude and disinterestedness (Gn $13^{7ff.}$), as well as his unwearied intercession even for the wicked inhabitants of Sodom ($18^{23ff.}$).

7. All the above evidences of a high moral standpoint in the patriarchal narratives appear to be little in harmony with the serious moral defects and transgressions which are recorded without a word of censure. Abraham lies (Gn $12^{13}$ $20^{2}$; so also Isaac, $26^{7}$) in passing off his wife as his sister; Jacob artfully deceives his twin-brother Esau in order to obtain the blessing of the firstborn, and his uncle Laban in the matter of the increase of his herds. Does this not justify the conclusion that God has two standards of measurement; that the Israelite in dealing with the foreigner, the chosen of God in dealing with the rejected, may go any length without its being counted to him a sin?

(*a*) If the above question is to be correctly answered, two things must be taken into account. Firstly, as a matter of fact, it is one of the principles of ancient ethics, from which even Israel freed itself only with difficulty and slowly, that towards a stranger the same moral obligations do not hold that apply in dealing with a fellow-countryman. In particular, cunning and deceit in the former case are not liable to the same condemnation as in the latter. They appear rather in the light of a duty of self-defence, especially as one has to look for nothing but damage and defrauding at the hands of a stranger, whenever he has the power to inflict harm. But, again, the idea of the national god involves (at least for the older naïve conception) his taking the part of his own people against the foreigner, and protecting them without scruple not only in their rights, but wherever their interests are concerned. So Jahweh acts in relation to Pharaoh ($12^{17}$), and, according to $20^{17}$, towards Abimelech.

Secondly, however, and closely connected with the above, what we have really to do with, at least in the Jacob-narratives, are not the actions and experiences of individuals, but the relations of one people to another, namely, of Israel towards the Edomites (Esau) on the one hand, and the Aramæans (Laban) on the other. The Esau-narratives are the naïve deposit of the reflexions of very early times as to why the brother who was notoriously the firstborn, *i.e.* who attained to a settled life and to importance sooner than Israel, was yet surpassed by the younger. From the Aramæans, again, Israel had from olden times experienced so much hostility that we can readily understand how the cheating of the greedy Aramæan by Jacob should have been regarded as quite right and proper, and the exercise of this right have formed the subject of unmitigated rejoicing.

(*b*) Notwithstanding all this, however, we must still ask the final question, Is it really the case that the above-cited instances of morally objectionable actions are recorded without a word of censure or disapproval? First, then, it may be observed that in this matter the E source, in opposition to or at least deviating to some extent from J, repeatedly offers a narrative in which the cause of offence, if not wholly removed, is made as slight as possible. This is a proof that at least towards the end of our period a finer moral sensitiveness had come in to sit in judgment on those ancient narratives. Sarah is, according to E, really Abraham's sister on the father's side (Gn $20^{12}$), so that Abraham is cleared of the charge of lying. It is only with great reluctance, and not till he has received the express command of God, that Abraham consents to the expulsion of Hagar and Ishmael ($21^{11f.}$ [E]; contrast $16^{6}$ [J]). In the transactions of Laban and Jacob, it is not the latter, but Laban alone, that is guilty of deceit and violent dealing ($31^{4ff.}$).* Reuben advises, indeed, that Joseph be cast into the empty cistern, but it is with the intention of delivering him. Joseph's brothers did not sell him (as J records), but he was stolen out of the cistern by a passing company of Midianites ($37^{22. 23b-24. 28a c. 29f.}$ $40^{15a}$).

(*c*) But there is yet another fact to be taken into account. It has been rightly noticed that it is the peculiarity of a particular form of narration in the legendary history to avoid passing any direct judgment upon the transactions described, but to allow this judgment to be expressed indirectly by one of the parties concerned. Thus Abimelech in Gn $20^{9f.}$ (E) severely condemns the conduct of Abraham, and in $26^{9f.}$ (J) that of Isaac. In $27^{12}$ Jacob himself declares that by imposing upon his father he will exhibit himself in the light of one who mocks at sacred things, and who thus deserves a curse and not a blessing.

8. But, in addition to the narratives belonging to this period, the oldest codification of legal ordinances, the so-called Book of the Covenant, also contains notable evidences of a moral disposition, which could have grown up only upon the soil of a considerably elevated religious system. True reverence for parents regards it as an offence worthy of death to strike or to curse them (Ex $21^{15. 17}$). In dispensing justice the strictest rectitude and impartiality are to be observed ($23^{1f. 6f.}$). Mildness and pity are due to the poor ($22^{25a. 26f.}$), protection from harsh treatment and violence to the *gēr* ($22^{21}$ $23^{9}$) and even to the slave ($21^{20. 26f.}$); the latter is even to be let go free if his master have struck out a tooth. The Sabbath is to be pre-eminently a day of rest for cattle, menials, and *gērîm* (employed as hirelings). As to the command in $23^{4f.}$ to take back to an enemy his ox or ass when they have strayed, and to help him to raise up an ass that has sunk under its burden, this does not, indeed, as yet amount to the Christian command of love to one's enemy, but it is a first step towards it. For it demands a subduing of carnal hatred and malice, a self-denial of which the natural man and natural ethics know nothing, but which is required by that God who watches the conduct of His people and seeks to redress every species of wrong and oppression. For, evidently, it is not only of the poor that the saying ($22^{27}$) holds good: 'When he crieth unto me, I will hear him; for I am pitiful.'

Since the discovery of the diorite block with the code of the Babylonian king Ḫammurabi (see art. CODE OF ḪAMMURABI in present volume, p. 584 ff.), many hands have been busy seeking to demonstrate

* It was quite a perverse attempt that was made by the older harmonizers to remove the contradiction between $31^{4ff.}$ [E] and $30^{37ff.}$ [J] by assuming that in $31^{4ff.}$ Jacob tells a false story to his wives. The fact is that we have here E's account of things, which is meant to be taken seriously, and which completely clears Jacob of blame.

not only the considerable priority (*c.* 2300 B.C.) of this law-book to the oldest codification of laws in Israel, but even its higher standing in all matters of justice and social order. We readily admit that the laws of Ḫammurabi imply much more complicated conditions of society than the enactments of the Book of the Covenant, which are intended for a simple race of peasants, and that, consequently, the juridical technique of Ḫammurabi may frequently exhibit a higher level. A fair estimate of the two codes is reached, however, not by comparing the matter which they have in common, but by looking at the sayings where the Book of the Covenant has the advantage over the Babylonian code. But these are the sayings to which we have already adverted, regarding the poor, *gērîm*, slaves, and enemies, and for parallels to them we may search the 282 paragraphs of Ḫammurabi in vain, because such are impossible on the soil of natural religion.

vi. *ANTHROPOLOGY AND THEORY OF THE UNIVERSE* (*WELTANSCHAUUNG*).—Under this twofold heading we propose to treat of everything which, according to modern views, constitutes the scientific standpoint of a period, but which to ancient, and especially to Israelitish, notions is so closely connected with religion that it cannot be passed over in a history of religion. This means that we are concerned, on the one hand, with the anthropological or psychological notions of this period, including conceptions of the state after death; and, on the other hand, with the ideas that were cherished as to the origin and purpose of the universe, the relation of man to the brute world, the opening period of the world's history, and the future goal towards which the present course of things is moving. As elsewhere, the notions about all these things meet us, not in didactic statements but in the guise of narrative (so, especially, in the J portions of Gn 1–11), or in casual notices. The latter almost always take for granted that the notions in question are universally known, and hence refrain from fuller explanation or description. Unfortunately, this leads to our being left in the dark on many an important question.

1. The drawing of a distinction between two main constituents of the human *personality*—one bodily and one spiritual—must have set in as soon as men came to realize the fundamental difference between a living and a dead body. (*a*) The corporeal being, at least immediately after death, was quite the same as before. What had been the seat of the life which had now taken flight? The readiest reply was: the *breath*. Observation shows that, when the last breath has been drawn, the life disappears; while, conversely, the revivification of one that is dead is accomplished through the breath returning into him (1 K $17^{21f.}$).* Alongside of this we encounter another conception, which is also deeply rooted, namely, that the seat of life is to be found in the *blood*. It is true that express statements to this effect do not occur till much later (Dt $12^{23}$, Lv $17^{11}$); but the very ancient prohibition to eat blood (1 S $14^{32ff.}$) must have been due in ancient Israel, as elsewhere on heathen Semitic soil, chiefly to the fear of absorbing another life along with the blood. Under special circumstances, indeed (as, for instance, at the sacrificial meals of brotherhoods in pre-Mosaic times; cf. above, p. $618^{b}$), this result might be desired; but in the realm of Jahwism, as far back as we can trace the evidence, such a practice was excluded. It may be added that the conception of the blood as the seat of life must have rested on the observation that, as the blood pours from a wound, the powers of life sensibly diminish, and at last disappear entirely—an observation which could always be made afresh when animals were slaughtered. We shall have to speak afterwards of the importance for the theory of sacrifice which this view of the blood came to assume in the latest period of Israel's history.

(*b*) For the period with which we are dealing, another question seemed more important, namely, that as to the *origin* of the breath of life, upon whose presence or absence the life or death of the body depends. The answer which the Old Testament gives to this question, and which forms the basis of OT psychology, is connected most intimately with the religion of Jahwism, or, to be more precise, with its notion of God. But our discussion of this point must be preceded by a remark of a general character. Almost all the accounts of so-called Biblical Psychology * are vitiated by the introduction of dogmatic prejudices, and the attempt to read into Scripture a finished system of one's own, instead of closely studying the usage of language. Especially unfortunate has been the attempt to discover in both Testaments exactly the same point of view, whereas the psychology of the OT has for its basis a dichotomy, that of the NT for the most part a trichotomy.

Keeping now to the exact terms of the fundamental and principal passage, Gn $2^{7}$, we learn from this, in the form of narrative, that Jahweh at first formed a man [proleptically for 'a human body'] from clods [not 'dust'] of the field, and then breathed into his nostrils breath of life, so that man became a living being. In view of this, there can be no doubt that Gn $2^{7}$ assumes a dichotomy in man's personality. As far as concerns his bodily substance, man is earth, and must accordingly return at death to the earth ($3^{19}$). But his breath of life emanates directly from an inbreathing of that of God, and ceases at the man's death, when God calls back this His spirit of life to Himself. We must not, however, think of the 'return of the spirit to God who gave it' (Ec $12^{7}$) after the manner of the Christian hope of immortality, as if it meant a passing of the individual spirit to be with God, but only as a reabsorption in the creative Divine spirit which pervades the whole Universe. We should even be reminded here of the pantheistic doctrine of the world-soul, were it not that any such thought is excluded by the OT conception of God which lays such emphasis on His living *personality*.

* The clearest evidence of the identification of breath and life is found in the circumstance that in Hebrew, as in other languages (cf. Sansk. *ātman* = 'breath,' 'spirit,' 'soul'; Gr. πνεῦμα, orig. = 'breath,' 'blowing'; Lat. *animus* and *anima*, *spiritus*), the notions of 'breath,' 'wind,' 'soul,' 'spirit' are expressed by one and the same word. Thus רוּחַ is at once the name of the wind which dries up the waters of the Flood (Gn $8^{1}$), and of the Divine breath of life which, at the Creation, hovers over the waters ($1^{2}$), and of the breath of life within man. In like manner it is true of the Heb. נֶפֶשׁ that it may designate at one time the breath, at another the spirit of life within man, the soul and its functions (*e.g.* longing or eager desire for something); but it may also stand simply for life itself, and, finally, even for the living being or (in the case of men) the person; nay, by a loose kind of usage, it may mean even 'the person of one who is dead,' or, without the genitive, a 'corpse' (Lv $19^{28}$ $22^{4}$ *et al.*). It is, of course, a glaring error, but a deeply rooted one, to give to *nephesh*, in all these manifold senses, the one uniform rendering 'soul.'

* Of the special works on the subject, Beck's *Umriss der biblischen Seelenlehre* (Stuttgart, 1843, 3rd ed. 1871) is based partly on Roos' *Fundamenta Psychologiæ ex Sacra Scriptura collecta*, 1769 [Germ. tr. 1857, under title *Grundzüge der Seelenlehre aus der heiligen Schrift*]. Wörner in his *Bibl. Anthropologie* (Stuttgart, 1887) builds largely upon Beck. Franz Delitzsch's *System der bibl. Psychologie* (Leipzig, 1855, 2nd ed. 1861) is not without a certain mixture of theosophy. More impartial are the accounts of Wendt, *Die Begriffe Fleisch und Geist im biblischen Sprachgebrauch* (Gotha, 1878), and Westphal, *Chair et esprit* (Toulouse, 1885). J. Köberle's *Natur und Geist nach der Auffassung des AT: eine Untersuchung zur historischen Psychologie* (Munich, 1901) is a very thorough and valuable discussion of all questions relating to the conception of the external world and the life of the human soul, the attributing of a soul to nature, mythology, and the notion of the spiritual, together with the influence of religion upon all this.

(*c*) Not only human but also animal life in general depends upon the possession of the Divine breath of life. Passages like Ps 104[29f.] and Job 34[14f.] leave no doubt on this point: Jahweh is a 'God of the living spirits of all flesh' (Nu 16[22] 27[16]). Accordingly, the question presses itself upon our attention: What, then, is the precise difference which under all circumstances must be assumed to exist between man and beast? It is not in the manner of their origin that the difference lies, at least according to J. While P (Gn 1[20ff.]) makes water-animals and birds spring into being at the simple *fiat* of the Creator, and land-animals proceed from the earth, J (2[19]) records a forming process exactly as in the case of man (v.[7]), that is to say, an individual creation of the animals. In the case of the latter, however, he makes no mention of an animating by the in-breathing of the Divine breath of life, and in this alone—even if we must assume here the result of reflexion on this question—the distinction between man and beast may be seen: man received the breath of life immediately from God, and on that account he has a far more direct share in the Divine being and life than the animal, in whose case nothing more than a general animating (of the whole species) is assumed. By the theory that the man first formed was directly animated by God, expression was given to the perception which—although without a clearly defined philosophic terminology—had evidently established itself at an early date, that man alone possesses individuality, and is therefore a being capable of individual communion with God, whereas the animal always represents only an example of its species.—J, however, gives expression in another way to the notion of the inferiority of the animal world to man when (Gn 2[19f.]) he quite unambiguously describes animals as having been created on man's account and named by him, with the result, however, that there could be found among them none corresponding to man, and thus suitable to be a 'help' to him.

(*d*) From God's direct animating of the first created human being we are not, however, to infer that the same thing is presupposed for each particular human individual. The OT has been wrongly burdened with this so-called 'Creationism,' which supposes God to create a special soul for every newly begotten body, and to unite it about the 40th day with the embryo. On the contrary, the OT from first to last is based upon 'Traducianism': he who begets the body implants at the same time the germ of the life or the soul. Otherwise, the view would be impossible by which the OT is unquestionably dominated, that through the process of generation even moral weakness, the inclination to sin, passes as an inheritance from parents to children. This is not 'original sin' in the sense in which it is mostly taught in Protestant confessions, namely, as implying the imputing of the guilt of Adam to all his posterity, but original sin in the more general sense, according to which that term is applied to the strong and almost irresistible inclination to sin, which appears to be inseparably bound up with human nature as such, and consequently looks as if it were the result of descent from parents of like disposition. Thus it is intelligible why allusions to this hereditary sinful disposition are introduced for the most part as furnishing a motive for the forgiveness of sin. In view of the fact that 'the imagination of man's heart is evil from his youth' (Gn 8[21]), God cannot apply the strictest standard of judgment. In addition to Ps 51[7 (5)] ('Behold, in guilt was I born, and in sin did my mother conceive me'), the *locus classicus* for this doctrine of the *natal* quality of sin, we have to take specially into account for the same purpose Job 14[4] ('How could a clean come from an unclean? Not one.') 15[14] 25[4ff.]—late passages, but manifestly intending to express nothing more than is meant already by J in Gn 8[21].

In the last-cited passages from Job the question is put, 'How can one born of woman be pure [before God]?': this shows how the connexion between descent and sinfulness was more precisely thought of. The latter as moral weakness is the natural result of the *physical* weakness of the body. Man is in the narrower sense the offspring of woman, the weaker vessel and the one more exposed to physical hardships. From her, man inherits moral as well as physical (Job 14[1]) weakness.

(*e*) In view of all this, it might have seemed natural that the material substratum of human personality, the *flesh* or the *body* [the Heb. בָּשָׂר may stand for either], should be regarded as the seat of sin, just as the NT σάρξ undeniably has this collateral notion attached to it. But, in spite of appearances such as arise from Gn 6[3], it is wrong to conclude that such a view was held. It is true that the flesh or the body, in consequence of its origin from the earth, is a type of the decaying and transitory (cf. the characteristic contrast in Is 31[3] 'Their [the Egyptians'] horses are flesh, and not spirit'), and this thought attaches itself almost always to the very frequent expression 'all flesh' (*i.e.* either all men or all earthly living creatures). But the truth that the flesh, although an occasion also of moral weakness, is not thought of as *per se* sinful and therefore unclean, is unmistakably implied in the circumstance that in sacrifice it was used as a gift to God, and such a gift could never have been in itself *unclean*.

(*f*) The habit already mentioned of putting upon the OT a trichotomous view of human personality was due almost entirely to a false conception of the *nephesh* (נֶפֶשׁ commonly tr. 'soul'), and of its relation to the *rûaḥ* (רוּחַ commonly tr. 'spirit'). This distinction between soul and spirit naturally caused the actually existing dichotomy of body (or flesh) and spirit of life to be missed. The real state of things is as follows. As long as the Divine breath of life is outside man, it can never be called *nephesh* but only *rûaḥ* (more completely *rûaḥ ḥayyîm*, *i.e.* 'spirit *or* breath of life,' in which sense we find also *nishmath ḥayyîm* used [*e.g.* Gn 2[7]]). On the other hand, the breath of life which has entered man's body and manifests its presence there may be called either *rûaḥ* or *nephesh*. The two alternate in poetical parallelism in such a way that the same functions are attributed at one time to the *nephesh* and at another to the *rûaḥ*. This, indeed, has not prevented its coming about that in certain expressions usage has established only one of the terms, or has at least secured a preference for it. Further, it may be noted that both very frequently stand in parallelism with לֵב ('heart,' 'disposition,' also 'understanding *or* insight,' the heart and not the head being with the Hebrews the seat of intellect). But in no case should that use of *nephesh*, whereby it stands for particular functions of the soul or even for a complex of these, be confused with its signification of 'person *or* living being' (and even 'corpse'; cf. above, p. 665[a] n.). In this latter sense *nephesh* could never have its place taken by *rûaḥ* or *lêbh*.

The religious significance of the anthropological views represented by the above-described dichotomy is at once apparent. Everything which in any way can be recognized as spirit and life is brought into direct relation to God, and has its origin in Him, and Him *alone*. The Pauline saying, 'In him we live, and move, and have our being' (Ac 17[28]), corresponds exactly to the postulates of OT psychology. The latter proceeds so

shows, however, that the shades were thought of *in general* after the fashion in which their originals had been accustomed to appear on earth.

According to what is at present the prevailing opinion, the old conception of Shĕ'ōl survived down to the last in the express designation of the shadowy being as *nephesh.* If so, we should have to assume for this word not only the senses described above (namely, the spirit of life specialized in a human body, and hence = 'life,' and also 'person' or 'living being'), but a third wholly different meaning.* Very strong support appears to be given to this by the circumstance that even in late passages we hear expressly of a going down of the *nephesh* into Shĕ'ōl or of its sojourn there, or, finally, of its rescue from Shĕ'ōl (Ps $16^{10}$ $30^{4\,(3)}$ $49^{16\,(15)}$ $86^{13}$ $89^{49\,(48)}$, Pr $23^{14}$; cf. also Ps $94^{17}$, where instead of *Shĕ'ōl* we have the poetic *dûmāh*, 'silence'). But in all these passages *nephesh* may quite well be understood as equivalent to 'life' or (as happens frequently elsewhere) simply a circumlocution for the personal pronoun ('my soul' being = 'I' or 'me'). Thus in Ps $16^{10}$ the meaning is 'Thou wilt not give over my life (*or* me) to Shĕ'ōl,' *i.e.* 'Thou wilt not suffer me to die.' Ps $30^{4\,(3)}$ must, on Schwally's theory, mean: 'Thou causedst the phantom image of my person, which was already in Shĕ'ōl, to come up from it again.' But the speaker had not actually died, his life *only seemed* already a prey to Shĕ'ōl, but obtained a timely rescue from it. If the defenders of *nephesh mēth* or the bare *nephesh* as equivalent to 'soul of the dead' should appeal in support of it to the contrasted expression *nephesh ḥayyāh*, 'living soul' (Gn $2^{7}$ *et al.*), they would overlook the fact that *nephesh mēth* or (abbreviated) *nephesh* in the passages in question stands for neither more nor less than 'corpse'; and this, by the *touching* of which uncleanness is occasioned, is surely something quite different from the invisible phantom image of the living personality which goes straight to Shĕ'ōl. *Nephesh mēth* in the sense of 'corpse' is based simply upon the very frequent (cf. *e.g.* Lv $2^{1}$ 'if *any one* offereth to Jahweh,' etc., $5^{2}$ $7^{18}$ etc.) weakening of the meaning 'person' to the notion of 'some one'; and *nephesh ḥayyāh*, 'living being,' is not opposed to another form of being of the *nephesh*, but is a pleonasm intended to lay greater stress upon the main idea (cf. our own expression 'a living personality,' which would not suggest to any one the contrast of 'a dead personality'). An argument against Schwally's contention lies in the very circumstance that nowhere is the plural of *nephesh* used for *manes*, as we should then have certainly expected. From the time of the Exile (probably for the first time in Is $14^{9}$) they are called *rĕphā'îm*, *i.e.* probably 'flaccid ones,' but never *nĕphāshôth.*

For the truth mentioned above, that the whole conception of Shĕ'ōl lies outside genuine Jahwism, and was at all times a part, indeed, of the popular faith, but not of religion proper, there is evidence not only in the stern rejection of necromancy (as the appendage of another, heathen, religion), but, above all, in the denial of *any* relation between the inhabitants of Shĕ'ōl and the objects and arrangements of the upper world —in particular, those of the theocracy. Only the living are members of the latter, and have a share in its blessings; at death every connecting link with it is broken. In Shĕ'ōl there is no more giving of thanks or praise to God (Ps $6^{6\,(5)}$ $30^{10\,(9)}$ $115^{17}$, Is $38^{18ff.}$)—nay, God Himself does not remember the shades any more, or work wonders for those that dwell in 'the land of forgetfulness' (Ps $88^{6.\,11f.}$). The fortunes of their children do not concern them (Job $14^{21}$ $21^{21}$), 'for there is no work nor device nor knowledge nor wisdom in Shĕ'ōl, whither thou goest' (Ec $9^{10}$).* There is no contradiction between all this and the way in which, according to Pr $15^{11}$ and Job $26^{6}$, the omniscience, nay, according to Ps $139^{8}$, even the omnipresence of God, is extended even to Shĕ'ōl. This is the necessary consequence of the highest stage of the conception of God; but even here a direct relation of God to the inhabitants of Shĕ'ōl is not asserted.

In spite of its very loose connexion with genuine Jahwism, the conception of Shĕ'ōl—like the Hades-belief of the Greeks and all the cognate phenomena in other religions—contains an important religious feature. The tenacity with which it maintains itself all through the centuries, notwithstanding its irreconcilability with the prevailing anthropological presuppositions (see above), is a strong testimony to the fact that man's natural way of thinking revolts at the notion of a complete annihilation of the living personality, even if it has to content itself with a sorry substitute for a real continuation of life. Even in this there are fruitful germs of a later doctrine of immortality, and we shall afterwards see that these were not wanting also in the soil of Jahwism.

3. To the realm of notions which we have included in the title of the present section under the general term *Weltanschauung*, belong, in the first place, those relating to *the origin of the world.* (*a*) Unfortunately, our only source of information on this point for the present period is the Jahwistic record contained in Gn $2^{4ff.}$. It is very probable, however, that only a part of this (the story of the creation of men and animals) has been preserved; while the introduction, which also must surely have contained some more detailed account of the creation of heaven and earth,† has now been dropped, perhaps on account of its deviations from the immediately preceding cosmogony of P. But, even granting that J would have contented himself with a summary mention (in v.$^{4b}$) of the creation of the world by Jahweh, his narrative, with all its naïveness, remains a worthy and valuable counterpart to the preceding cosmogony. Like the latter, it avoids all intermixture of a mythological character—in particular, all thought of an evolution such as is usually bound up inseparably with the cosmogonies of ancient religions. Jahweh is always exalted above matter, sharply distinguished from it, and ruling over it. As in the case of every truly religious *Weltanschauung*, our

* So esp. Schwally, *Leben nach dem Tode*, p. 7 ff. (founding upon *nephesh mēth* of Lv $21^{11}$ and Nu $6^{6}$, which Schwally renders by 'Totenseele'), also in *Archiv für Relig.-Wissensch.* iv. 2, p. 181 ff.; Willy Staerk, art. 'Nephesh ḥajjā und nephesh mêt' in *SK*, 1903, p. 156 f. ('The *nephesh* does not die, but changes its form of existence').

* It may be that this conception of Shĕ'ōl first arose in the later period, which was influenced by Prophetism (so Charles, *Critical History*, etc., see above, p. 668[b], note §), whereas at an earlier time an influence of the spirits of the dead upon the upper world was held to be possible. True, we have no other evidence for the latter assumption than the existence of the practice of necromancy so peremptorily forbidden (cf. Is $8^{19}$) by the prophets. The further assumption of Charles, that the earlier conception grew out of Ancestor Worship, cannot, to say the least of it, be proved in face of what we have said already (p. 614 ff.). The same remark applies to Beer's theory ('Der biblische Hades,' p. 3 ff.), that the Shĕ'ōl-belief is a survival of the cult of subterranean gods and demons.

† When Stade (*ZATW*, 1903 p. 178) argues that the belief in Jahweh as the Creator could have taken its rise only as a result of the preaching of the prophets, this is certainly correct in so far as the idea of the creation and control of the *Universe* is concerned. For this idea is essentially irreconcilable with the recognition of foreign national gods, and becomes possible for the first time on the basis of a consistent monotheism. But this does not exclude naïve ideas about a creative activity on the part of the national god (*e.g.* a creation of man), as is shown by numerous analogies in popular and nature religions. Perhaps the very naïveness of the Jahwistic cosmogony supplied a motive for its suppression. Cf. the remarks of Gunkel in *Schöpfung und Chaos* (Göttingen, 1895, p. 159). He considers that, in early days, people, in speaking of the creation of 'the heavens and the earth,' probably thought primarily of the land of Canaan and the skies of Canaan.

record is thoroughly anthropocentric; and man is not only (as in Gn 1) the goal and crown of creation, but to such a degree is he its central point that the world of animals is created solely on his account, with the result that in no way do they come up to his dignity and exalted position. It requires a second, wondrous new creation to provide man with the 'help' who is bone of his bone and flesh of his flesh. God Himself brings her to him; so that upon His appointment rests that fellowship against which even the strongest ties of blood are not to prevail. If we note, further, that it is only upon the basis of monogamy that this whole description attains to its full meaning, all the more must we pronounce that we have here a view of the nature and the mystery of marriage as beautiful and worthy as could be conceived of. Here, again, the religion of Israel exercised a powerful influence on its estimate of earthly relationships and duties.

(*b*) If an underlying Babylonian source for Gn 2 can be proved only in part, and not at all for ch. 3 as yet, it is different with other components of the Hebrew primitive history. In these a far-reaching Babylonian influence has been assumed, and the traces of this have been sought almost everywhere in the OT down to the latest times. But it has become more and more evident that a strong scepticism is justified in face of the excessive zeal of the 'Panbabylonists.'* We are not, indeed, to be held as calling in question the possibility of an extensive influence of Babylonian culture and religious ideas upon Canaan. The cuneiform letters discovered in 1887 at Tel el-Amarna in Egypt, which were addressed about B.C. 1400 from the Euphrates lands to two Pharaohs, prove the existence of a very active intercourse between Babylon and Egypt *viâ* Canaan, and it is possible (though not strictly proved) that even then a footing had been gained in Canaan by the ancient Babylonian mythology, which was subsequently taken over by the Israelites when they entered the Promised Land. A great influx of Babylonian ideas has been claimed also for the time of world-wide intercourse in the reign of Solomon, not to speak of the numerous occasions of direct contact with Assyria from the middle of the 9th cent. B.C. downwards. Still the only instance where the dependence of the Biblical narrative upon a Babylonian archetype is absolutely unquestionable is (*a*) the story of the Deluge. And even here the dependence shows itself rather in subordinate points (like the repeated sending out of birds), and not in the main point—the cause of the judgment of the Flood. In the Biblical record this is always traced to moral causes: the Flood comes as a well-merited punishment on the wholly degenerate race of man; Noah only, on account of his righteousness, finds favour in God's sight. The mythological background, which presents itself sometimes in a very offensive way in the Babylonian narrative, wholly disappears in Genesis. Over against men responsible for their actions stands the righteous and almighty God alone.

(*β*) Of late, special emphasis has been laid on what are supposed to be a number of OT allusions to the Babylonian story of Creation, or, more precisely, to the victorious struggle of the god Marduk with the ocean, personified as a woman, Tiāmat (*i.e.*, as appellative, 'sea'), and the monsters that assist her. A large part of Gunkel's able and ingenious work (*Schöpfung und Chaos in Urzeit und Endzeit: eine religionsgeschichtliche Untersuchung über Gn 1 und Apoc. Joh. 12*, Göttingen, 1895) is devoted to an attempt to discover numerous traces of this myth in the OT. He rightly repels the objection that Gn 1 now forms a part of the latest Pentateuchal source, P. This circumstance does not exclude the possibility that this cosmogony, which in its present form is accommodated to the very highest conception of God, may be based upon a far older form of the myth. The points of contact between Gn 1 and the Tiāmat-myth are, however, few and uncertain. The Heb. *tĕhōm* (תְּהוֹם), over which darkness hangs (v.$^{2}$), is, it is true, the masculine corresponding to the Bab. *tiāmat*; but there is nothing to suggest any other meaning than the simple 'sea' or 'ocean.' As little can it be proved that the large water-animals of v.$^{21}$ are originally of a mythological cast.

But the recollection of the conflict of Marduk with the dragon is supposed to be preserved, above all, in certain mythological names—*Rahab*, *Leviathan*, *Behemoth*. The fact that all * the passages where these occur are very late (Ezekiel, Deutero-Isaiah, Job, late Psalms) might not count for much. It would be quite intelligible if the ancient *mythologumena* were again dragged to the light and utilized for poetical ends, when once the triumph of absolute monotheism appeared to have removed all danger of their being misunderstood or misapplied. A stronger objection is, that a considerable number of the alleged allusions can be referred only by very artificial methods to the conflict with Tiāmat. How, for instance, if the kernel of the Tiāmat-myth consists in the killing and *cutting in pieces* of Tiāmat, can the serpent at the bottom of the sea, which Jahweh commands to bite (Am $9^{3}$), possibly be Tiāmat? Of the *Rahab* passages, Is $51^{9}$, Ps $89^{10f.}$, Job $26^{12f.}$ and $9^{13}$ ('Rahab's helpers') should in all probability be referred to the defeat of Tiāmat, only that the conqueror is naturally not Marduk, but Jahweh. In Ps $87^{4}$ Rahab is a symbolical name of Egypt, while in Ps $40^{5\,(4)}$ the plural *rĕhābîm* is a designation of the false gods, but surely not in the sense of 'dragons of chaos.' Of the *Leviathan* passages, Ps $74^{13f.}$ should perhaps be interpreted mythologically. On the other hand, in Ps $104^{26}$ there is absolutely no necessity for such an interpretation. In Is $27^{1}$ Leviathan the fleeing serpent, and Leviathan the coiled serpent, coupled with the dragon in the sea (Egypt), are again nothing but symbolical designations of two world-powers. In Job $3^{8}$ it is much more natural to interpret Leviathan as a monster in the heavens which threatens to swallow up the sun. The poetical author of Job $40^{25ff.}$ ($41^{1ff.}$) certainly means by Leviathan nothing but the crocodile. And his *Behemoth* ($40^{15ff.}$) stands in the same way simply for the hippopotamus. As little are we compelled to explain Job $7^{12}$, Ps $44^{20\,(19)}$, Jer $51^{34.\,36.\,42}$ as allusions to the Tiāmat-myth; and even in Ezk $29^{3ff.}$ and $32^{2ff.}$ there is, at most, only a general comparison of the Pharaoh to a bound monster. In all the passages, finally, where Gunkel sees an allusion to the binding of the primeval ocean (Ps $104^{6f.}$, Job $38^{8ff.}$, Pr $8^{22ff.}$, Jer $5^{22}$ $31^{35}$, Ps $33^{7}$ $65^{8\,(7)}$), all that the present writer can discover is a reference to the omnipotence of Jahweh, who commands even the waves of the

* Amongst these the first place belongs to Frdr. Delitzsch, in view of his first two Berlin lectures on *Babel und Bibel* (Leipzig, 1902 and 1903), which have given birth to a violent controversy and an interminable literature. We content ourselves here with naming two of the most recent writings which treat soberly of the points in dispute: Zimmern, *Biblische und Babylonische Urgeschichte*³, Leipzig, 1903 [cf. also his *Keilinschriften und Bibel*, Berlin, 1903]; and Gunkel, *Israel und Babylonien: der Einfluss Babyloniens auf die israelitische Religion*, Göttingen, 1903.

* At most we should have to except only the serpent of Am $9^{3}$ (see above) and Rahab of Is $30^{7}$ (as a designation of Egypt). But not only is the authenticity of the last passage disputed, but the correctness of its text is very doubtful, and, finally, *rahab* may here be quite well an appellative 'raging' 'blustering'). Cf. vol. iv. p. 195[a].

sea, but nowhere any allusion to a conflict with the ocean as a mythological monster.

But, even if all the passages cited by Gunkel were coloured by such allusions, they would be still quite without relevancy as affecting our estimate of the religion of Israel for the period we are considering. For, apart from the fact that, in the few passages that are certainly entitled to be considered, Jahweh expressly takes the place of Marduk (*i.e.* there has been a complete transplanting of the myth to the soil of Jahwism), we must, further, note with emphasis that in every instance we have to do with the utilizing of those mythological reminiscences *in poetry*. Now, the freedom of which the Hebrew poets availed themselves in this matter is as far from supplying a standard whereby to judge of their religious beliefs as the mention of Scylla and Charybdis by a modern writer would be a fair test of his beliefs.

(γ) Finally, the attempts that have been made to give a mythological sense to the vessels of Solomon's temple appear to us to have failed completely: *e.g.* the supposition that the so-called brazen sea (1 K 7[23ff.]) represents the *tĕhōm* or primeval ocean, or that the oxen are symbols of Marduk.* On this question the present writer must express his full accord with Stade, who (*ZATW*, 1903, p. 179) sees in these vessels no evidence that at that time the myths possibly attached to them had been adopted by the Israelites, or that they were even known to them. 'It was not a religious need, but the needs of kingly pomp, that led to the introduction of a foreign institution into the temple. The Phœnician artist, who was called in to execute the work, wrought according to the fashions of style with which he was familiar, and turned out a product which could be transferred from a Phœnician temple to the temple of Jahweh.'

From all sides, then, it may be considered as established that the extent of Babylonian influence upon the religion of Israel—at least for the pre-exilic period—has been considerably overestimated. Examples of dependence and of allusions are not to be denied. But upon the soil of revelation the foreign material undergoes such transformation, and appears in such a new light, when viewed from an immeasurably higher moral and religious standpoint, that the question has not unreasonably been asked whether, in many passages, we should speak, not of dependence and imitation, but rather of a polemical intention towards the alleged source.

The further question, whether to this period religious *expectations as to the future* (connected with the *theologumenon* of the 'Day of the LORD') should be attributed, will have to be discussed in the following section.

## IV. The Period of the Writing Prophets, down to the Exile.

i. *The Sources.*—As sources for this period, which embraces some 180 years, we have to take account not only of the Prophetical writings, but also of portions of the Pentateuch and of the Historical literature. Thus in the Pentateuch there are the later and latest strata of J and E, and the Book of Deuteronomy; in the Historical books we have the prophetically influenced sections of Judges and Samuel (such as 1 S 1. 2[11-26] 3. 8. 10[17-24] 15), but, above all, the first Deuteronomic redaction of the Books of Kings (*c.* 600 B.C.). For our present purposes we can practically leave out of account the circumstance that the exact chronological position of the particular passages referred to is still the subject of much controversy. For there is practically complete agreement that they are dependent upon the preaching of the pre-exilic writing prophets, and that is the only point that concerns us. Besides, the whole of the historical literature of this period exhibits such a uniformity of ideas that the questions of analysis of sources and precise dating possess only a subordinate importance. For this reason we may leave open the complicated questions connected with the origin of Deuteronomy, namely, whether the law-book introduced by Josiah in 621 is to be regarded as the original Deuteronomy or was compiled from older codifications. So far as the description of the process of development of the OT religion is concerned, the present Book of Deuteronomy may quite properly be treated as a unity.

On the other hand, no little difficulty attaches to the questions of literary criticism affecting the main sources, namely, the Prophetical writings themselves. Here even the most cautious and conservative of critics have been compelled by the latest investigations to make such concessions as would have been considered impossible twenty years ago. Of course this is not the place to describe exhaustively either the process of literary criticism which has led to this, or the results of this criticism. But it may be as well to indicate clearly the general viewpoints which have forced themselves upon investigators in ever-growing measure, and without which a just judgment and a correct employment of the Prophetical writings are impossible.

There are two facts which must be kept steadily in view, because they suffice to explain all the phenomena in the Prophetical literature. (*a*) In the first place, it is, throughout, a *religious* literature; it does not profess to give anything, and we must accordingly not look to it for anything, that goes beyond religious purposes. (*b*) Secondly, Israel, to which we owe the Prophetical writings in their present form, had as yet no idea of what we call 'literary property.'* The question was not in what terms a prophet of Jahweh had spoken in former times, but whether those terms were still fitted to fulfil the religious purpose which he once meant to serve. If this did not appear to be the case, it was regarded as not only perfectly right, but as a sacred *duty*, to modify the original form of expression, to give a milder turn to what was too harsh and no longer applicable to a differently constituted age, to expand and state more clearly what was too concise or obscure, to introduce matter that was wanting in the original but indispensable for a later age. To this last category should be assigned a good part of the material on which at one time great stress—and that rightly—was laid, namely, so-called Messianic prophecy. When the threatenings of punishment uttered by the pre-exilic prophets had been fulfilled, when the people languished in exile, or after the Return dragged on a miserable existence under the oppression of the hostile world-power, it could not but seem a piece of cruelty to let words of threatening be the sole or even the predominating feature in the Prophetic oracles, at a time when the people were filled with burning zeal to secure by painful fulfilment of the Law that great change in their lot which had long been promised. We can understand how, under such circumstances, consolation and promise had an ever larger place given them within the framework of the traditional Prophetical writings — nay, how, for instance, the Book of Isaiah could come to assume the form of an an-

* So Kittel in his Com. on Kings (in Nowack's *Hdkom.*, Göttingen, 1900, p. 64), following Kosters (*Theol. Tijdschr.* 1879, p. 445 ff.). According to Gunkel (*l.c.* p. 153, cf. also 164 f.), the 12 oxen must rather have stood in some relation to the 12 signs of the zodiac.

* Cf. what was said above (p. 625[a]) on the custom of tracing back all the legislation to Moses.

thology of Prophetical oracles and be even understood and read by the people as such — oracles which in all probability embrace a period of well-nigh 500 years. In saying this we do not mean to give our assent to what an illegitimate hyper-criticism has exalted to a principle, that no word of comfort or of promise is to be allowed to the pre-exilic prophets. But we do mean to claim a perfect right to test fully the authenticity of the various Prophetical words. It is surely not the outcome of a frivolous and unbelieving spirit to seek an answer to the question whether Micah ($4^{10ff.}$) could have predicted in one and the same breath the carrying captive of Jerusalem to Babylon, and (v.$^{11}$) the miraculous deliverance of the city out of the power of its besiegers. Here sober criticism has a readily available resource, namely, to assign the prediction of the destruction of many peoples before the walls of Jerusalem to a much later date then the 8th cent. B.C. In cases where this resource is not available, such criticism will readily waive any decision. Fortunately, there remains enough that is certain and unassailable to enable us to understand and to depict the ways of God in Hebrew prophetism.

ii. *NAME AND CHARACTERISTICS OF THE WRITING PROPHETS.** — 1. In speaking of the *nĕbî'îm* (p. 650 ff.) we avoided as far as possible the name 'prophets,' so as not to obliterate the deep-seated distinction between them and the Jahweh prophets properly so called, the succession of whom begins with Amos. We found it necessary, indeed, to recognize even those *nĕbî'îm* who clustered about Elijah and Elisha, and especially the last named themselves, as organs of Jahweh, in whom 'the spirit of Jahweh' worked as a mysterious agency, and who could accordingly be rightly called 'men of God.' But on closer examination we discover such characteristic differences between the two kinds of prophets that we cannot, for instance, place even an Elijah upon the same footing as Amos.

The writing prophets † are essentially connected with the ancient seers (*rō'îm*), as is expressly testified in 1 S $9^{9}$ 'Those who are now called "prophets" (*nĕbî'îm*) were called in former times "seers."' The old names (*rō'îm* and *ḥōzîm*) in an honourable sense appear elsewhere only in Is $30^{10}$;

* Of the very extensive literature on the characteristics of prophetism and the theology of the writing prophets, we note, in addition to the works cited on p. 650ᵇ n., the following: B. Duhm, *Die Theologie der Propheten*, Bonn, 1875 [a work which already occupies the standpoint of the Reuss-Graf hypothesis, although on questions of literary criticism the author is still pretty conservative]; Ed. König, *Der Offenbarungsbegriff des AT*, Leipzig, 1882, 2 vols. [mainly an analysis of the self-consciousness of the prophets and of their leading statements based upon this, regarding (1) their miraculous powers, call, and endowment with the Spirit of God; (2) the manifestation and speaking of God as the source of the revealed message, König maintaining that in this matter the prophets see and hear with the bodily senses; (3) the fact that it is not their own heart that is the source of the prophets' predictions]; A. Kuenen, *De profeten en de profetie onder Israël: Histor.-dogmat. Studie*, 2 vols., Leiden, 1875 [Eng. tr. under title 'Prophets and Prophecy in Israel,' London, 1877]; W. Robertson Smith, *The Prophets of Israel and their place in History, to the close of the 8th cent. B.C.*, Edinburgh, 1882 [2nd ed., 1895, with Introduction and Additional Notes by T. K. Cheyne]; J. Darmesteter, *Les prophètes d'Israël*, Paris, 1892; A. F. Kirkpatrick, *The Doctrine of the Prophets* (Warburtonian Lectures for 1886–1890), London, 1892; P. Schwartzkopff, *Die prophetische Offenbarung nach Wesen, Inhalt und Grenzen*, Giessen, 1896; F. Giesebrecht, *Grundlinien für die Berufsbegabung der alttest. Propheten* (in 'Greifswalder Studien zu Ehren H. Cremers,' Gütersloh, 1895, pp. 37–81); Leitner, *Die prophetische Inspiration* (in Bardenhewer's 'Biblische Studien' [Rom. Catholic]), Freiburg i. B., 1896; Ed. König, *Das Berufungsbewusstsein der alttest. Propheten*, Barmen, 1900.

† The emphasis we lay on the word *writing* in this title is not intended to deny that there were true prophets of Jahweh in Israel besides these (cf. what was said above, p. 656ᵃ, about Micaiah ben-Imlah, and what is said in Jer $26^{20ff.}$ of Uriah ben-Shemaiah); but we can judge only of those about whose messages we have written evidence.

for in Mic $3^{7}$ the 'seers' (coupled with 'soothsayers') mean false prophets; in Is $29^{10}$ 'the prophets' and 'the seers' are wrong explanatory glosses; and, finally, in Am $7^{12}$ the term 'seer' (*ḥōzeh*), with which Amaziah the priest addresses Amos, has a flavour of contempt about it. But the reply of Amos (v.$^{14}$) must not be misunderstood, as if he absolutely repudiated any claim to be a 'prophet' (*nābî'*), because the word *nābî'* had questionable associations to him coming down from those *nĕbî'îm* of the time of Saul and of Aḥab. This is quite impossible simply on the ground of Am $2^{11}$ and $3^{7}$, where Amos himself speaks of the *nĕbî'îm* in the most honourable sense. Moreover, we read in $7^{15}$ that God charged him to 'go as a prophet' to His people Israel. The meaning of Amos in $7^{14}$ can only be, then, that he disclaims being a *professional* prophet, in the sense familiar to Amaziah, or a member of a prophetic guild. On the contrary, the call to be a prophet surprised him in the midst of occupations of a wholly different kind: Jahweh took him from the herd.*

2. Here we have already a very essential difference between the prophets of early times and the writing prophets. The latter are conscious of an express **call**, at a definite moment, by Jahweh to their office. We have not an actual account of this in the case of all of them; but its preciseness in the case of five justifies our assuming that from the time of Amos onwards a similar call was experienced by all true prophets of Jahweh. We have already spoken of *Amos'* own witness to his call. According to Hos $1^{2}$, the commencement of *Hosea's* prophetic ministry was contemporaneous with his recognition that Jahweh intended even the prophet's unhappy experiences in his married life to be a reflexion of Israel's relation to Himself. *Isaiah* records a vision he had in the year that king Uzziah died, when the Divine commission was given him to drive the people by his message into ever-increasing obduracy. Attempts have been made to explain this vision—the only one in Isaiah—as simply the literary garb invented for inward reflexions and conflicts, so that the prophet's own determination would take the place of an express Divine call. But all such attempts are shattered by the earnest terms of the narrative, which will not permit us to think but of a real occurrence. The very same is the impression we receive from *Jeremiah's* record of his call in the 13th year of Josiah. Quite remarkable here is the emphasis laid ($1^{5}$) on the choice and consecration of Jeremiah to the prophetic office even before his birth. How could any one invent a thing of this kind and proclaim it as a word addressed to him by God? But as little could he have added the supplementary invention that he tried to evade the Divine commission (v.$^{7}$) by pleading want of skill in speaking, and youth. Rather must we see here again an experience the prophet once had, which left an ineffaceable impression upon his memory. In the case of *Ezekiel*, his exact dating of his first vision ($1^{1f.}$) by year, month, and day, is the pledge that he too is conscious that his call to be a prophet ($2^{3ff.}$) was a definite occurrence.

As it is not in man's power of his own initiative to effect the call to be a prophet, or to complete it by his own determination, so, on the other hand, he has no power to evade it. Nay, as even the boldest will tremble involuntarily when the roar of a lion is heard in the neighbourhood, so the man to whom the word of Jahweh has come *must* prophesy (Am $3^{8}$). The most striking testimony to this is found in Jer $20^{7ff.}$. With an impatience

* The meaning of Amos becomes still clearer if, with Riedel (*SK*, 1903, p. 163 f.), we render 'I *was* no prophet,' etc.

bordering close on blasphemy, the prophet here reproaches Jahweh with having enticed him (by the call to be a prophet) and prevailed upon him, so that he has become a laughing-stock and an object of ridicule. But, he goes on, 'when I thought, I will not make mention of him nor speak any more in his name, then there was in mine heart as it were a burning fire shut up in my bones, I wearied myself with holding out, but I was unable.' It would be no easy task to weaken the convincing power and force of *this* testimony to the unique character of Hebrew prophetism, by pointing to any analogous phenomena elsewhere.

3. A characteristic of the *nĕbî'îm* in the old sense was a condition of **ecstasy,** occasionally rising to rapture and holy frenzy; and the first of these, namely ecstasy, we find witnessed to also in the case of the writing prophets. For, even apart from the vision, which likewise implies a condition of trance, there is repeated mention of 'the hand of Jahweh' being strong upon the prophet (Is $8^{11}$, Ezk $3^{14}$), or coming upon him (Ezk $1^3$ $3^{22}$ $37^1$ $40^1$), or falling upon him ($8^1$), or being over him ($33^{22}$, here with the more precise note that it was 'at evening'), and on account of which he sits solitary (Jer $15^{17}$). In all these passages 'the hand' is an expression for the Divine influence which lays irresistible hold upon the prophet, being almost the equivalent of 'the spirit of Jahweh,' which likewise 'falls' upon the prophet (Ezk $11^5$), and imparts to him special revelations from God. In the case of Ezekiel, the effect of the hand of Jahweh is almost always to induce a vision. Nevertheless, there is plainly a considerable difference between this kind of ecstasy and that of the ancient *nĕbî'îm.* It is true that under all forms the extraordinary influence of the spirit of God presents an unfathomable mystery. But on the part of the writing prophets we find no trace of their being plunged by this influence into a condition of *amentia* or unconscious rapture. They always retain a clear consciousness and a distinct recollection of what they saw in spirit and of what was said to them.* Otherwise it would be impossible for them to describe the vision or to announce the word of God that came to them in their ecstasy.

4. Now, it is quite true that in opposition to this it has been maintained (so, in great detail, by A. Klostermann in *SK*, 1877, p. 391 ff., and again recently by Duhm in his Commentary on Isaiah, p. 129) that, at least in the case of Ezekiel, by the prophet's own confession, cataleptic conditions, namely, temporary loss of the power of motion and speech, must be assumed, although this morbid condition did not exclude an exact recollection of the hallucinations of sight and hearing that were experienced during the catalepsy. In point of fact, Ezekiel tells us that, after his vision of the cherubim-chariot, he went *in bitterness* (מַר) in the heat of his spirit, and that he then sat stunned with astonishment (מַשְׁמִים) in the midst of his people for seven days ($3^{14f.}$). He speaks, further

* This simple fact refutes the ancient orthodox theories, such as that which goes back to Philo, that human reason left the prophet, to make room for the Divine spirit. Equally futile are all attempts to reduce the prophets to mere instruments of the Divine spirit, *devoid of will,* and comparable to a flute in the hand of the player or a pen in the hand of the scribe. Such attempts suffer shipwreck on the rock of what is an undeniable fact, that the individuality of the different prophets is very clearly revealed in their style and their manner of speech. Isaiah writes quite differently from Jeremiah, and the latter, again, quite differently from Ezekiel. Of course all this does not exclude the possibility of a heightening of the natural gifts and powers of the prophets by the influence of the Divine spirit. Such a process is evident, for instance, in the manner of speech of the herdsman Amos, which is as forcible as it is clear. Jerome's opinion regarding the 'rustic style' of Amos must be pronounced quite unproved and incorrect.



(v.$^{26f.}$), of a dumbness which God sends upon him, which can indeed be interrupted when it is the Divine will that he make prophetic announcements, but whose entire removal does not take place till the evening before the news comes of the capture of Jerusalem. All these phenomena agree remarkably with those observed in cataleptics. Duhm is inclined to reckon especially the vision in $8^1$–$11^{24}$ among the cases 'in which the body lies seemingly dead and the phantom (that has left it) represents the Ego.' On the other hand, Zechariah, with his 'angel that spake with me,' is included by Duhm among the instances 'in which consciousness remains in the body, and the phantom that comes forth is apparently unconscious.' But however much the assumption of cataleptic conditions on the part of Ezekiel may have in its favour, this does not yet amount to evidence of a relapse to the old form of mantic. Above all, there are two points not to be overlooked. In the first place, Ezekiel represents his bitterness of spirit and stunned condition, those alleged cataleptic phenomena ($3^{14f.}$), as the *result* of the vision of the cherubim-chariot; whereas he describes the vision itself with a preciseness which does not look like that of a man whose mental balance has been disturbed. Secondly, before and after the story of his being carried to Jerusalem ($8^{1ff.}$) and the lengthy account of his visions there, he says not a word about cataleptic conditions, and we have no right simply on the ground of $3^{14f.}$ to postulate them here also. But, above all, the whole nature and contents of the great vision in chapters 40–48 are very hard to reconcile with any notion of a morbid condition on the part of the prophet. Everything here breathes such an air of deliberation and purpose that only a small share in the inception of this lengthy programme for the future can be set down to the account of vision (see below, p. 676^b). Again, as to the 'double consciousness' of Zechariah, it is really only in $4^1$ that there is any indication of an abnormal condition of the prophet; and this is very far from justifying the assumption of actual cataleptic conditions. For, when we read that the angel who talked with him reawakened him as a man that is wakened out of his sleep, this means merely that the prophet, exhausted by the preceding visions, had fallen into a kind of sleep, and had now to be made capable of experiencing a new vision. But here, again, in the case of Zechariah, it will be found that his night-visions in their present form are to be in large measure set down to the account of the *littérateur* and not of the visionary.

5. Taking everything into account, the **vision** did not, upon the whole, play such a large rôle in prophetism as there has been a disposition to attribute to it. As for the classical examples, so to speak, of visions which we find on the part of Amos, Isaiah, and Jeremiah, the descriptions are almost all extremely meagre; nay, in some instances they contain nothing more than names of objects with which the utterance of religious truths and exhortations is connected. The more detailed the description (as, for instance, in Ezk $1^{4ff.}$), the more it contains not only framework and motive but exhibits deliberate purpose, the more is it deficient in specifically religious contents. In every instance the word spoken in the course of the vision or for the purpose of explaining it, is by far the most important part of the revelation communicated to the prophet.

6. Finally, it must be pronounced a gross exaggeration to think of *all* the activity of the prophets as carried on under ecstatic conditions. When a prophet begins his message with the expression 'Thus saith the LORD' (כֹּה אָמַר יהוה), or introduces into his address the very frequent

'word of the LORD' (נְאֻם יהוה), he means to claim that he does not speak a message of his own creation, like the false prophets: Jahweh must have spoken to him before he can proclaim the word of Jahweh. But this does not imply that the inspiration from Jahweh must in every instance be connected with the throwing of the prophet into the ecstatic condition. It may, further, be asked whether for every particular message of the prophets there was needed a special inspiration from Jahweh, or whether we should not rather hold that they always spoke in the power of the spirit of God, which was imparted to them at their call. The answer is, that both these possibilities are witnessed to in the Prophetical writings. (*a*) In the story of the call of Isaiah ($6^{9ff.}$), as well as in that of Jeremiah ($1^{9ff.}$) and of Ezekiel ($2^{3ff.}$ and $3^{17ff.}$), we hear of a general commission from God to these prophets, a kind of programme of their ministry, to which at all times they are to give heed in word and act.

(*b*) But, on the other hand, we possess also some notable evidences that the word of Jahweh may in a particular instance be at first withheld, and only communicated after a while.—(*α*) Thus the prophet Ḥabaḳḳuḳ can at first give no reply to the complaint which he has to make to Jahweh (in chapter 1). Nay, he resolves to take his stand upon his watch-tower* to look out and to learn what Jahweh has to say to him, and what reply He will make to his grievance. And, in fact, Jahweh answers him at once, and even commands him to write down the revelation he receives.

But there are two testimonies of Jeremiah which point still more clearly in the same direction.—(*β*) When the false prophet, Ḥananiah of Gibeon, in the presence of Jeremiah proclaims to priests and people as a word from Jahweh (Jer $28^{1ff.}$) that the yoke of Nebuchadreẓẓar is about to be broken, and the temple-vessels carried away under Jehoiakim to be brought back from Babylon, Jeremiah gives his Amen to this. He expresses, indeed, his suspicion at the suddenness of the change from the predictions of woe uttered by the old prophets to the opposite. But he allows Ḥananiah to take from his neck and break the yoke which he had worn for some time as a threatening allusion to the yoke of the Chaldæans. Straightway Jeremiah takes his departure. But soon thereafter the command comes to him from God to announce to Ḥananiah that Jahweh would put an iron yoke in place of the wooden one broken by him, and would bring all nations under the yoke of Nebuchadreẓẓar. Ḥananiah himself was further to be told that as a false prophet he was doomed to die the same year. And so it fell out in the seventh month of that year. In this whole transaction it is highly noteworthy that Jeremiah at first considers it possible that Ḥananiah has spoken a true message from Jahweh, because he himself has received none to a contrary effect, but that afterwards he has no hesitation in opposing his subsequent communication from Jahweh to Ḥananiah's lying word. Here, again, all notion of mere imagination or invention on the part of the prophet is absolutely excluded. What he speaks is based upon real, direct inspiration.

(*γ*) The other testimony, which is no less characteristic, is found in Jer $42^{1ff.}$. The remnant of the people, which had fled from Miẓpah after the murder of Gedaliah, beg the prophet to give them a message from Jahweh to indicate the right course for them to pursue, and assure him that, whatever be the instructions, they will carry them out. Jeremiah promises that he will pray to Jahweh for a message, and that he will not keep back a single word of it when he receives it. But ten days elapse before the Divine word comes to him, forbidding absolutely the migration to Egypt, and commanding the people to remain in their own land. The charges of falsehood and treachery which the spokesmen of the people then prefer against the prophet are such as no one will have any difficulty in attributing to the blind zeal of infatuated men. But it would be equally unjust to regard those ten days as simply a period of delay which the prophet took for calm consideration, and with a view to the allaying of excited feelings. Here, too, we must believe him when he tells us that he could not announce a 'word of Jahweh' until it had been given him.

7. In all that we have said hitherto in the way of characterizing the writing prophets, we have not, however, yet mentioned the most essential feature. This we find in the *subjects* of prophetic announcement, which are exclusively the affairs of the theocracy, not to say the kingdom of God in the wide sense of that expression. The prophecies are addressed to the whole body of the people, whether in Israel or Judah,—or at least relate to them; and in every instance the contents are exclusively moral and religious. The few exceptions, where a prophecy is addressed to individuals, are only apparent. When Isaiah ($7^{11}$) invites king Aḥaz to ask a sign from Jahweh, he is speaking to the man who had the control of, and the responsibility for, the fortunes of the people at a critical period. And when the same prophet (Is $22^{15ff.}$) announces to the king's *majordomo* his deposition and banishment, and the appointment of Eliaḳim in his place, the whole context shows that Shebna had brought this punishment upon himself by the harm he had done the theocracy, and by his oppression of the people; whereas it was to be expected of Eliaḳim, the servant of Jahweh, that he would be 'a father to the house of Judah.' In the same way, of course, we must interpret the minatory prophecies of Jeremiah addressed to individuals: for instance, that to Pashḥur ($20^{3ff.}$), whose ill-treatment of the prophet had proved him to be a rebel against Jahweh Himself; that to Ḥananiah ($28^{13ff.}$; see above); that to Shemaiah ($29^{24ff.}$); and, not less, the numerous prophetic addresses to various kings of Judah ($21^{3ff.}$ $22^{1ff.\ 10ff.}$ $27^{12ff.}$ $38^{14ff.}$). Again, the very frequent words of threatening uttered against whole classes, the nobles and judges of the people, the priests or the (false) prophets, have in view the members of these, not as individuals but as the holders of important offices, on whose conduct the weal and the woe of the whole body depend. The true prophet of Jahweh, on the other hand, holds an office only in so far as he is called *by God* to a definite activity, never for State reasons or by a king's commission. Accordingly, nothing could argue greater perversity than to represent Isaiah, when he announced to Shebna his deposition ($22^{15ff.}$), as acting in an official capacity and by the king's directions—something after the fashion of a court preacher!

8. It is quite in harmony with the position of the

* The much discussed passage, Is $21^{6ff.}$, belongs (if we adopt the present text) to a different category. We leave it an open question whether this oracle belongs to Isaiah (dating from *c.* 710 B.C.), or whether it should not rather be placed about the year 540. In v.[6] Jahweh bids the prophet set a watcher, who is to mount the tower and tell what he sees. This is generally explained as an embodiment of the fact that the prophet, under the influence of the Divine spirit, distinguishes in himself, as it were, two personalities. According to Duhm (Com. on Isaiah, p. 129), 'the meaning of the command is that the prophet is to yield himself to catalepsy (cf. above, p. 673[b]) and let loose from himself the angel, who, untrammelled by the bodily senses, can perceive supra-sensual things.' But it is hardly open to question that the present text of v.[6] is due to a misunderstanding of the Massorah, and ought, with Buhl (*ZATW*, 1888, p. 157 ff.) and Stade (*ib.* p. 165 ff.), to be emended so as to read as a command of Jahweh to the prophet to mount the tower. Thus the catalepsy alleged by Duhm falls away of itself, and Is $21^{6}$ becomes a simple parallel to Hab $2^{1}$.

prophets in the service of Jahweh that they perform their ministry without any claim to fee or reward—differing thus from the ancient seers, who received gifts in return for the answers they gave to inquirers (1 S 9[7f.], 1 K 14[3]). According to Mic 3[11], it is a sign of the false prophets that they divine for money—conduct which is pronounced equally disgraceful with that of judges who take gifts to give decisions, or of priests who impart *tōrāh* for a fee.

9. Once more, as to the numerous oracles and addresses spoken against *foreign peoples*: these fall in large measure within the sphere of prophetic activity, for the simple reason that their motive is the hostile attitude of these nations to the theocracy. They denounce the judgment of Jahweh upon those who in their blindness have abused His commission to chastise and have cruelly destroyed (Is 10[5ff.]); or who, like the Edomites, in Jerusalem's 'evil day,' exhibited a savage joy, and did their best to humiliate and destroy Judah (Ob [10ff.]). But even where such motives are not present, or at least not recognizable by us, the oracles against foreign nations occupy a high place in the prophetic addresses. For they are all testimonies that it is recognized that Jahweh alone, with almighty hand, guides the fortunes of the nations, near and remote; that He alone can reward and punish; and that He does both according to the unalterable standard of right and righteousness. It is no more the merely national god, who concerns himself about the course of the world only when his own people are assailed by another, and then—such was the popular belief—takes their part blindly; but One who avenges even the outrage perpetrated by the Moabites on the bones of the king of Edom (Am 2[1]). And thus it may well be said that in these very oracles against the nations clear and forcible expression is given to the universalism of the prophetic conception of God, the omnipotence, wisdom, and righteousness of Jahweh. There is nothing in them to invalidate the judgment expressed a little ago, that the activity of the writing prophets is always concerned with the interests and aims of the theocracy, the ways of God with the latter, and that the contents of their prophecies are uniformly of a moral and religious nature.

10. From this follows another result, which is not least in importance, namely, that the minatory prediction, however categorically it may be expressed, has always only a *conditional character*. Even Amos, whose denunciation of judgment sounds so irrevocable that he actually strikes up the funeral dirge (*ḳînāh*) over Israel (5[1]), does not abandon all hope, for immediately thereafter he utters the exhortation: 'Seek Jahweh, that ye may live' (vv.[4. 6]); 'Yea, if ye hate the evil and love the good, it may be that Jahweh, the God of Hosts, will be gracious unto the remnant of Joseph' (v.[15]). Isaiah, again, although expressly called (6[10f.]) to harden the people still more by his preaching of repentance, predicts (1[25ff.]) the coming of a time when Jerusalem shall once more be called a city of righteousness, a faithful city, after a portion of her inhabitants have been brought by purifying judgment to repentance. Similarly, in 38[3] Isaiah, by the instruction of Jahweh, announces to king Ḥezekiah his speedy end, but immediately thereafter tells him that, owing to his prayer and tears, his life is to be prolonged for fifteen years. Jeremiah announces as a message from Jahweh (26[3]) that the threatenings uttered against city and temple may perhaps have the effect of leading the people to hearken and turn from their ways, in which case Jahweh will repent Him of the evil which He thought to bring upon them because of the evil of their doings. In short, the prophetic word is not a *decretum absolutum*, which must work itself out after the manner of a blind natural force, an inexorable fate; it pursues moral aims; it is designed to bring about knowledge and repentance. Hence it is subject to recall, according to the conduct of the party threatened; just as the potter can transform the marred vessel as he pleases (Jer 18[1ff.]). For Jahweh has no pleasure in the death of the wicked, but in his turning from his evil way, that he may live (Ezk 18[23]). It was to emphasize this truth, and that even as extended to the heathen, that the little Book of Jonah was composed in the post-exilic period.

iii. *The Forms of Divine Revelation to the Prophets.*—1. The simplest form of communication from God to the prophets is the *word* which comes to them, and which is very frequently the equivalent of 'revelation.' According to Jer 18[18] it was a current saying of the time that *tōrāh* ('direction') could never be lacking to the priest, nor 'counsel' to the wise, nor the 'word' to the prophet. That the prophet, in virtue of his call, could speak in the name of Jahweh, without having in *every* instance received an extraordinary revelation, we have already (p. 674[a]) pointed out. On the other hand, the exact dating of particular Divine messages (particularly in Ezekiel, Haggai, and Zechariah, but occasionally also in Jeremiah) is an evidence that the prophet could be quite conscious of having received a special revelation.

The same is witnessed to by the expression (Is 22[14], cf. 5[9]) 'Jahweh revealed himself in my ears,' *i.e.* called to me audibly. It has been argued by Ed. König that a hearing with the *bodily* ear is what is thought of in this phrase; but that it is not so, is shown by the fact that elsewhere the Divine word is said to be *seen* by the prophet. But this seeing is with the eye of the spirit, like the beholding of the prophetic visions. Both kinds of seeing are designated by the same word in Hebrew (חָזוֹן *ḥāzôn*; cf., for instance, the expression 'Vision of Isaiah,' placed as a collective title at the head of the present Book of Isaiah). This is explicable only on the supposition that the boundary between the two—especially in early times—was a fluid one: even the receiving of a Divine message might readily be coupled with ecstatic visionary conditions.

2. Still we are entitled to speak of *visions* proper, *i.e.* of the beholding of concrete pictures and incidents, of which the prophet afterwards gives an account, and, if necessary, an interpretation. It is noteworthy that *this* seeing is almost everywhere (cf. Am 7[1. 4. 7] 8[1] 9[1], Is 6[1], Jer 1[11. 13], Ezk 1[1], Zec 1[8] 2[1] etc.) expressed by the verb רָאָה (*rā'āh*), which usually stands for bodily vision. Here, again, it cannot be inferred from this that we have to do with an unveiling of the invisible world to the bodily eye of the prophet, but rather that he with the spiritual eye beholds real pictures and incidents as at other times he does with the bodily eye. Of all the analogies which have been adduced to make the mystery of this kind of seeing (namely, the prophetic vision in the narrower sense) intelligible, that which deserves most attention is the largely attested 'artistic intuition.' In the latter, a work of art, which has been planned and perhaps long considered, may all at once present itself to the mind's eye of the artist in unthought-of finish and beauty, and that so clearly that he is able henceforth to retain it in his memory and carry it into execution. But, even with such an analogy as this, we must not overlook the considerable differences in kind between the two, artistic and prophetic inspiration,

and, above all, the difference in their subject-matter.

But, further, the visions present themselves to us in such multiplicity that we can readily understand how attempts have been made to distinguish between genuine vision and the purely literary garb given to prophetic ideas—not to speak of the attempt to reduce *all* visions to a mere literary device. To refute the latter notion, it is necessary only to point to (*a*) the single vision recorded by Isaiah (in ch. 6). It is inconceivable that he should have invented this incident, to which his solemn call to the prophetic office is attached, merely in order to present in this form certain thoughts of his own about the nature and the prospects of his prophetic calling. For any such purpose the labour spent on the description would be too great, and everything favours the assumption that the prophet on this *one* occasion actually beheld the supra-earthly pictures which he describes, experienced the atoning influence (v.[7]), and heard the Divine commission given him. And, in truth, the pictures are of sublime simplicity, while the succession of the incidents is clear and impressive (just as in the vision of Micaiah ben-Imlah, 1 K 22[19ff.])—both indications of a real inward experience.

(*b*) It is much more difficult to gain a harmonious conception of the first two visions of Amos (7[1ff.]). In the third of them (v.[7ff.]) it is to one object alone, the plumbline, that the Divine oracle attaches itself; while the object of the fourth, the basket of harvest fruits, serves merely as a symbol of the harvest which is to be sent to the people. The fifth vision (9[1ff.]) is the first to offer, although described with extreme brevity, an analogy to that of Isaiah. But, in the opinion of the present writer, it is possible to regard the others also, in spite of their peculiarities, as something more than merely the literary garb of prophetic ideas. This latter device makes its appearance only after the prophetic vision has had a considerable history, and the public ministry of the prophets has had to yield more and more to the activity of the pen. Moreover, the testimony to visions on the part of *pre-exilic* prophets is confined, apart from those of Amos and Isaiah, to those recounted in Jer 1[11. 13]. In both of the last two a single object (an almond-tree and a seething-pot) seen by the prophet furnishes the motive (and that in connexion with the immediately subsequent call of the prophet) for a prophetic announcement.

(*c*) In Ezekiel, on the other hand, the vision makes its appearance in a highly detailed and somewhat complicated form. As in the case of Isaiah and Jeremiah, the first vision (Ezk 1[1ff.]) ushers in the call of the prophet. Ezekiel relates at the outset how, after the heavens were opened (*i.e.* after he had received the faculty of beholding even the supra-earthly), he saw visions produced by God. Yet it is not from heaven, but from the north, that the theophany comes, in a storm-driven fiery cloud. This conceals the very minutely described cherubim (see above, p. 644[b]), and it is only at the close (v.[26ff.]) that we learn that they bear the platform on which the throne of God stands, with God seated upon it. The merely allusive way in which the prophet speaks of the form of Him who is thus enthroned is in accordance with the reverential reserve which we note also in Ex 24[10] and Is 6[1]. But the extraordinary circumstantiality of the preceding description, notwithstanding which it is impossible to form a clear conception of the objects, justifies the conclusion —not that the prophet simply coined the vision (whose exact date is given) but—that literary skill played a very considerable part in his description of it. The same remark applies to the explanation attached (2[9ff.]) to his eating of the book-roll which was inscribed with sighs and lamentations. Of course the eating of the roll, which is a materializing of the purely spiritual inspiration thought of elsewhere, likewise belongs to the realm of vision, for it is not till 3[12ff.] that the prophet hears behind him the noise of the cherubim-chariot which bears away again 'the glory' of Jahweh. On the appended description (3[14f.]) of the physical condition of the prophet, cf. above, p. 673. When the same theophany recurs in 3[22ff.] the prophet contents himself with a simple mention of it. On the other hand, there is a very detailed account (8[1ff.]) of the idolatrous horrors which he saw in the precincts of the temple, when he was carried by the spirit to Jerusalem. Then follow, in the same locality, the visions (chs. 9–11) which present to his view the destruction of the city and the temple, together with the threatening address to the heads of the people. From this point the vision does not recur till ch. 37—the reanimating of the dead bones, which symbolize Israel dead, as it were, in the Exile. Here, as in chs. 8–11, there is no reason to doubt that the prophet really saw what he asserts; but the individual descriptions and, in quite a special sense, the detailed interpretations and practical applications must certainly be once more set down to the account of a literary performance. The same is true in quite a peculiar measure of the great vision in the last part of the book (chs. 40–48), where the prophet sketches the future form of the temple and its cultus and of the land. Here the details are so multiplied and involved that it has been plausibly suggested that the prophet worked out his description with the aid of maps and plans. It is evident that the matter which could suggest such a method does not belong to the contents of the vision. Elsewhere the transition from the sphere of the vision to that of literature is betrayed by the elaborate justification of prescriptions which are to come into force only in the future; so, especially, the new regulation about the priesthood (44[9ff.]), and the distribution of the tribes (ch. 48). These prescriptions and much else are fitted into the framework of the vision only by being put in the mouth of the prophet's guide (cf. 40[3f.]), or even of Jahweh Himself.

(*d*) The latest* accounts of visions proper lie before us in the eight night-visions of Zechariah (1[8]–6[8]). We have already (p. 673[b]) pointed out that, apart from 4[1], there are no indications pointing to a cataleptic condition of the prophet when he had these visions. Hence it appeared to us quite improbable that 'the angel who talked with me' (1[9. 13] 2[3] etc.) is to be referred, with Duhm, to the seemingly double consciousness of a cataleptic. Rather might we perhaps say, with Baudissin (*Einleitung in die Bücher des AT*, Leipzig, 1901, p. 565): 'The introduction of this medium (the so-called *angelus interpres*) between God and the prophet changes the character of OT prophecy, which was based upon the notion that the prophet was *directly* filled with the Divine spirit.' This already implies that in these night-visions the great bulk of the matter is to be attributed to the prophet's own imagination and literary activity. On several occasions (so, quite especially, in 1[14ff.] 2[10ff.]) the description of the vision passes over into the usual tone of prophetic address.

iv. *The Forms of the Prophetic Message.* —1. Amongst the various ways in which the prophets communicated the revelations they received, by far the most important place, at least in the early period, is taken once more by the *word* or

* The visions of Daniel, which really belong to a different category—that of apocalyptic—will be dealt with later on (see p. 714).

the prophetic address, whether in the form of a brief oracle or of a somewhat longer, clearly connected discourse. But it is only with reservations that the view can be maintained that the extant oracles and discourses of the earlier prophets are practically, without exception, to be regarded as the (subsequent) written record of what were originally actual spoken addresses. To be sure, in every instance where the prophet himself gives place and time, and names ear-witnesses of his discourse (as, for instance, in Is $7^{1ff.}$), we must find the record of an actual address. But even such a case as this does not exclude the use of much freedom in regard to the form and the dimensions of what is committed to writing.

Here, once more, we have to keep in mind what holds good of the whole of the literature of the OT, namely, that it aims not at a diplomatically exact record of words and actions, but at exercising a religious influence, and hence that the prophet, when he became an author, must have reserved to himself full liberty as to the method by which he was to achieve this result. But, above all, must this liberty be postulated where it was not till years had elapsed that a prophet reproduced from memory a long series of addresses and dictated these to an amanuensis, as we are told Jeremiah did after twenty-three years of prophetic activity (Jer $36^{1ff.}$). In such a procedure it would be impossible for the earlier addresses to escape being influenced in a variety of ways by the later experiences and views of their author. And, when the roll written by Baruch was burned by king Jehoiakim, the greatest freedom was used once more in reproducing it: 'Then took Jeremiah another roll, and gave it to Baruch the scribe, the son of Neriah; who wrote therein from the mouth of Jeremiah all the words of the book which Jehoiakim king of Judah had burned in the fire; *and there were added besides unto them many like words*' (Jer $36^{32}$). But there are also other Prophetical books, like that of Amos, whose very dating ($1^{1}$ 'two years before the earthquake') shows it to have been composed later than the events, and no less those of Hosea and Isaiah, which bear such evident traces of the subsequent reduction to writing and of the polishing and expansion of the supposed spoken address, that it is scarcely possible anywhere to maintain the absolute identity of the address and its report. In saying this we are leaving entirely out of account the fact that in the end the Prophetical writings were subjected almost, without exception, to editing by other hands—a process which introduced changes not only in their dimensions, but in many instances even in their language. It is useless to seek to deny this. On the other hand, however, it is perverse to see in this a destroying of the character of revelation and of the high value in general which belongs to the word of the prophets. Whatever may have suffered from all those influences which are unavoidable in the course of human tradition, the genuine Divine word retains amidst it all a power and a majesty which even at the present day do not miss their effect.

2. The prophetic address occasionally avails itself, with a view to heightening the effect, of the *forms of poetical art*, such as the parable (Is $5^{1ff.}$ $28^{23ff.}$; even the 'riddle' [חִידָה, *ḥîdāh*] of Ezk $17^{1ff.}$ is there designated at the same time 'comparison,' 'parable' [מָשָׁל *māshāl*]), or plays upon words (*e.g.* Mic $1^{10ff.}$); nay, in the pre-exilic period, and repeatedly even in later times, it passes into poetic rhythms.* We must be content, however, with merely alluding to this, for it lies outside the scope of an article dealing with the history of religion.

3. Full notice must be taken, however, of the *symbolical actions* whereby the prophets gave, as it were, a concrete form to the truths they proclaimed. We meet with an example of this even in very early times, when Ahijah of Shiloh (1 K $11^{30f.}$) rent his new mantle into twelve pieces and gave Jeroboam ten of these. Here the interpretation follows straight upon the action, whereas in 1 K $22^{11}$ the latter comes after the prophetic oracle. With the writing prophets the state of things is the same with symbolical actions as with the vision. At first rare and simple, these actions occur in Ezekiel in considerable numbers, and at times in so complicated a form as to justify the question whether they are meant to be thought of as actually performed, and not simply as the literary garb given to prophetic ideas. In Amos, Hosea, Micah there are no examples.

(*a*) In Isaiah, as there is only one vision, so there is only one symbolical action (ch. 20). The prophet is to go about for three years naked (*i.e.* without his upper garment) and barefooted, and thus to furnish an impressive emblem of the condition of the Egyptians and Ethiopians going into captivity. But this action of his serves also, as v.[5] shows, a practical purpose of extreme importance, namely, to keep Judah from foolishly revolting from Assyria, through trust in the delusive aid of the Egyptians and the Ethiopians. The symbolical action then appears here in the direct service of the Divine guidance of the people by means of the prophet, and hence (like all the symbolical actions we meet with in the writing prophets) is directly commanded by God.

(*b*) After Is 20 the next instances of symbolical actions occur in the life of Jeremiah. In Jer 13 the prophet is told to buy a linen girdle, and first to put it upon his loins and then to hide it in a hole of a rock by the water.* The consequent destruction of the girdle is to symbolize the inevitable destruction of Judah and Jerusalem. With a like aim he goes to Topheth ($19^{1ff.}$), the place of child-sacrifice, and before the eyes of many witnesses breaks an earthen pitcher—an action whose significance is heightened by the scene where it takes place. According to $27^{1ff.}$, Jeremiah, in order to symbolize the necessity for Judah's submitting patiently to the yoke of Nebuchadreẓẓar, places bands and yoke-bars upon his own neck (cf. also $28^{10.13}$). It is noteworthy that the explanation of this symbolical action, along with a corresponding warning, is sent also to the kings of the surrounding peoples—a strong proof that the prophet felt that he spoke on behalf of the God who rules over all. It is a very crass misconception that sees here an unbecoming interference with foreign politics, or even an evidence that the prophet acted thus because he was in the pay of the Chaldæans. Finally, our present category includes in a certain sense also $43^{8ff.}$, where the prophet, by Jahweh's instructions, buries great stones in the clay-ground in front of the palace of the Pharaoh at Taḥpanḥes, as a testimony to the

* Thus, for instance, the so-called *ḳînāh* or 'mourning measure' (discovered by Ley and Budde), *i.e.* the bringing together of a longer and a shorter verse-member (generally 3 and 2 'rises'), plays a much larger rôle in the prophetical writings than used to be supposed; cf. *e.g.* Am $5^{2f.}$, Is $1^{2ff.}$ $2^{5ff.}$ $13^{2ff.}$ $14^{4ff.}$ $16^{2ff.}$ $22^{1b-4}$ $37^{22ff.}$ $47^{1ff.}$ $52^{7ff.}$ $57^{1ff.}$ $60^{10ff.}$, Jer $9^{20f.}$ $15^{8f.}$, Ezk $19^{1bff.}$ etc. Cf. art. POETRY in vol. iv.

* If by *Pĕrāth* (פְּרָת) of v.[4ff.] the river Euphrates must be understood, there is no alternative but to regard the account of the whole transaction as simply a literary device, or even (with Duhm in his Commentary on Jeremiah, p. 119) as the free invention of a late redactor. For Jeremiah cannot possibly have undertaken the long journey to the Euphrates twice over, merely to establish the fact that a linen girdle is ruined by damp. But now L. Gautier (cf. *Bote aus Zion*, July 1894, p. 62 f.) points to an *'Ain* ('fountain') *Fara* in the neighbourhood of Anathoth, the home of the prophet. Assuming this to be meant by *Pĕrāth*, all difficulty disappears (cf. *Enc. Bibl.* ii. 1429).

fact that Nebuchadrezzar would one day set up his throne over these stones, to execute grim judgment upon Egypt.

The above instances, however, exhaust the symbolical actions of Jeremiah; for his purchase, by Divine command, of a field, while he was in prison (32$^{7\text{ff.}}$), is a legal transaction, whose symbolical sense, as we learn from v.$^{25\text{f.}}$, was not evident to the prophet himself till afterwards. Moreover, all the above enumerated symbolical actions are as simple as they are impressive; they are easy to interpret and easy to remember.

(*c*) Much more circumstantial is even (*α*) the first of the emblematical transactions required of Ezekiel (4$^{1\text{ff.}}$). He is to draw upon a tile a plan of Jerusalem, to set in array various siege appliances, nay even whole armies, against the city, and, finally, to place an iron pan between himself (as God's representative) and the city. Still the direction to give the house of Israel a 'sign' in this way was quite capable of execution, whatever room there may be for difference of opinion as to the method by which the prophet depicted the besieging armies.—(*β*) But it is different with the case contemplated in 4$^{4\text{ff.}}$. Here Ezekiel is to lie upon one side, bound with cords to prevent his turning over on his other side, and first to bear for 190 * days the guilt of Israel, and then for other 40 days the guilt of Judah—these numbers corresponding to the number of years, respectively, of the captivity of the two kingdoms. No appeal to the prophet's alleged tendency to catalepsy will suffice to make a literal fulfilment of this command conceivable: for this reason, apart from any other, that such a prolonging of the symbolical transaction over nearly eight months would have tended to rob it of effect, or at least would have been quite unnecessary for the purpose in view. We must therefore assume that the symbolical action was indeed actually carried on by the prophet for a time, but that its prolongation to 190 + 40 days is merely part of his subsequent explanation of it.—It is only upon this assumption, again, that (*γ*) the prescription (4$^{9\text{ff.}}$) as to the stinted use of unclean food by the prophet while he was bound as above described,† can be conceived as capable of being obeyed. A daily allowance of 20 shekels [about 5 oz. avoir.] weight of the composite bread prescribed would scarcely have sufficed to support life for 230 (not to speak of 430) days. —(*δ*) Very graphic and impressive, on the other hand, is the fourth sign (5$^{1\text{ff.}}$). The prophet, having cut the hair of his head and beard, burns a third of the hair, smites about another third with a sword, scatters the other third to the winds, and finally burns some of the hairs that have been concealed in the skirt of his mantle—all this as a sign of the fate that was reserved for the people of Judah. Even if the use of a balance (v.$^{1}$) to apportion the hair suggests the somewhat mechanical fondness of Ezekiel for exact measures and numbers, the whole transaction is well fitted to make the most lasting impression; and one can well imagine the eager attention with which the onlookers watched the prophet at work, and listened to the explanations that followed.—(*ε*) No less impressive is the fashion in which he is told (12$^{1\text{ff.}}$) to give the people an emblematic representation of the cheerless departure into exile. He is to bring out his baggage by day in their sight, and in the evening is to make his way, with his face concealed, through a hole cut in the wall of the house.—(*ζ*) Again, 12$^{17\text{ff.}}$ is certainly to be understood in the sense that the prophet, as he eats and drinks, is to exhibit all the signs of terror, in order to portray to those about him the fear and horror of the besieged in Jerusalem.—(*η*) In 24$^{15\text{ff.}}$ the symbolism consists in the neglect of the mourning customs enjoined by usage.* The prophet himself testifies how much the curiosity of his countrymen was excited by this very strange neglect. All the more impressive on that account must have been the explanation he gave of it.

All the symbolical actions of Ezekiel as yet described had but one purpose: to exhibit the certainty and the terrors of the Divine judgment upon Judah. In opposition to these there is at least one action, of a very simple kind, whose interpretation issues in *a comforting promise.* We refer to the two staves, inscribed with the names of Judah and Joseph, which were to be joined together in one in the hand of the prophet, as a sign that the two separated and apparently ruined kingdoms of Israel were to be restored and united in the old home under *one* king.

The threatenings, which the previous symbolical actions of the prophet served to emphasize, were literally fulfilled; but the restoration, in spite of the very definite terms of Ezk 37$^{19\text{ff.}}$, included only Judah—an undeniable proof of the 'conditional' character of prophecy. The firm conviction of the prophet that at a given moment he was giving utterance to a genuine message from God, does not exclude the possibility of God's ways afterwards taking a different turn.

(*d*) Something similar applies to the solitary instance of a symbolical action (if this designation can be applied to it at all) in the post-exilic period, namely, the making of a costly crown † from the gifts sent by the Babylonian Jews (Zec 6$^{10\text{ff.}}$). If it is the case that in v.$^{11}$ the coronation of Zerubbabel is enjoined, the symbolical action consists in the anticipation and therewith the pre-announcement of a very important event. But it is the last action of its kind—a clear proof that Jahweh prophecy of the fashion inaugurated by Amos had come to an end. Along with a vivid consciousness of being the immediate recipients of a Divine revelation there disappears also any motive for seeking by accompanying action to give an impressive concrete form to the contents of the revelation.

v. *THE CONTENTS OF THE PROPHETIC MESSAGE.*—1. *The conception of God.*—To the writing prophets, as to the men of earlier days, Jahweh is primarily the God of Israel. To emphasize this was laid upon the prophets as their principal duty: to preach repentance to the people, to hold up to them their ingratitude towards the Creator of their national existence, their Deliverer from Egyptian bondage, their constant Benefactor for so many centuries. But, with all this, Jahweh is no longer simply the God of Israel in the old sense

* So, with most moderns, we should read (following the LXX) in place of 390. From the beginning of the exile of Israel to that of Judah there are reckoned in round numbers 150 years [in reality they amount to only about 130, or, counting from 734, to 142], which are followed by 40 years of joint exile. Nothing can be made of the number 390.

† That in v.$^{9}$ the '390 [LXX '190'] days' are an erroneous gloss, is evident from the simple fact that, in view of v.$^{5\text{f.}}$, it should be '430 [230] days.'

* The procedure described in v.$^{3\text{ff.}}$ is expressly stated (v.$^{3\text{a}}$) to be a 'parable' and not a symbolical action.

† The present text of Zec 6$^{11\text{ff.}}$ is undoubtedly corrupt, but its correct restoration is still a matter of dispute. On the ground of the plural 'crowns,' Ewald suggested as the original: 'Place [them] upon the head of Zerubbabel and Joshua,' etc. But the singular verb (תִּהְיֶה) in v.$^{14}$ shows incontrovertibly that only *one* crown was in view—that, namely, of the Messianic king. In this way Joshua disappears from v.$^{11}$, having been first introduced when, under the post-exilic theocracy, the high priest was actually at the head of the State. The question now is whether v.$^{11}$ read, 'and place it upon the head of Zerubbabel' [this is favoured by 'to *him*' of v.$^{12}$], or whether v.$^{11\text{b}}$ is to be struck out altogether [and then 'to *them*' to be read in v.$^{12\text{a}}$]. In any case, in view of 4$^{9}$, the crown is to be thought of as destined for Zerubbabel, even if the actual crowning is reserved for a later occasion, with a view to which the crown is directed (v.$^{14}$) to be laid up in the temple.

of the national God, whose sphere of power ends, strictly speaking, at the boundaries of His land. On the contrary, we note on the part of all the writing prophets a strong, and almost everywhere successful, effort to burst the barriers of the old particularist conception of God, and to lay prominent emphasis on the unconditioned superiority of Jahweh to every form of restriction by space or time, and especially to every restriction of His sphere of power. The old representation of the national God is still at work in so far as the manifestations of His omnipotence, in the world of nature as well as in dealing with the heathen world, are almost always connected with His purposes towards His people. Yet there are not wanting approaches to a *Weltanschauung* which brings even the heathen nations, and that on their own account, within the scope of the Divine rule of the world and plan of salvation.

(*a*) In seeking to establish these propositions in more detail, we may look first at what is said of the *Person of God*. It was an unavoidable necessity that even in this period the analogy of the *human* personality should still be used to give a clear, nay even an intelligible, idea of the nature and working of the Divine personality. Even we, who stand on Christian ground, must have recourse to the same analogy if we wish to set up the concept of a living, energetically active, Personality. Hence even the prophets resort not infrequently to anthropomorphisms and anthropopathisms, which, in early times (cf. above, p. 627[b]) owed their origin to the naïve belief in Jahweh's possession of a human bodily form. But there is not a single trace that they continued to share that naïve belief. When Isaiah, in the vision which marked his call to the prophetic office (6[1]), beholds Jahweh seated upon a throne high and lifted up, no doubt a human form is here thought of. But it must be remembered that this is a *vision*, a sight beheld with the spiritual eye of the prophet, and, moreover, he says nothing more about the figure on the throne than that it had a long flowing train. He does not thus go beyond the simple indication of a splendidly-clothed, majestically-enthroned, ruler.

We must by no means conclude from the above single instance of the localizing of Jahweh in the earthly temple [for nothing else can be thought of, in view of the 'house' of Is 6[4] and the altar of v.[6]], that during this period the notion was still retained that Jahweh dwelt in a grossly material fashion in the sanctuary. The temple, it is true, and Zion in general, is the spot where Jahweh manifests Himself: He has Himself founded it as a precious corner-stone of the theocracy (Is 28[16]), as a refuge for the afflicted of His people (14[32]); He roars from Zion, and causes His voice to be heard from Jerusalem (Am 1[2]); He dwells on Zion (Is 8[18]), where, in the form of the sacrificial hearth, he has His fire and His furnace (Is 31[9]; cf. also 29[1f.], where *'ărî'el* probably stands for 'hearth of God'). Hence, in praying, one readily turns towards the city and temple of Jahweh (1 K 8[38. 44. 48], but cf. also v.[22]). But numerous other passages leave no doubt that, notwithstanding all this, heaven was regarded as the proper dwelling-place of Jahweh, as had already been the case even in the preceding period (cf. above, p. 646[b] f.). What dwells on Zion is not the Person of Jahweh in the most real sense, but a more or less secondary representation of this, such as His 'glory' (cf. above, p. 639[b] f.) or His 'name' (cf. the references, especially those from Deuteronomy, p. 640[b] f.). He Himself is enthroned in heaven. From there He spoke already to the people at Sinai (Ex 20[22], Dt 4[36]); there is His holy dwelling-place (Is 31[4], Mic 1[2] [where the 'holy palace' must, in the light of v.[3], be understood of heaven], Dt 26[15], 1 K 8[30]); there He hears the prayers of His people (1 K 8[32. 34] etc.), when they spread forth their hands towards heaven (v.[22]). But it comes to be strongly felt that this localizing of Jahweh in heaven, if taken literally, amounts to an unworthy limitation of His boundless being. Hence it is more than once stated emphatically that not only the heaven to its utmost heights, but also the earth with all that it contains, belongs to Him (Dt 10[14]); that He alone is God in heaven above and on the earth below (Dt 4[39], Jos 2[11]). Nay, in 1 K 8[27], in the prayer of Solomon at the consecration of the temple, it is positively declared that heaven to its utmost bounds cannot contain Him, not to speak of the earthly house which Solomon has built for Him. When, again, in Jer 23[24] Jahweh asks, 'Do not I fill heaven and earth?', it is true that we must be careful not to give to this question anything of a pantheistic sense, for this would be in the sharpest conflict with the OT conception of God. But, on the other hand, the above question certainly contains a protest against the crass notion of Jahweh as the God of heaven, and at the same time shows an approximation to that conception which is so very difficult to the human mind—the conception of a purely spiritual being. A clear formula for the notion of pure spirituality, such as we find in Jn 4[24], was beyond the reach of the Old Testament. But when Isaiah (31[3]) exclaims, 'The Egyptians are men, not God; and their horses are flesh, not spirit,' he manifestly contrasts man and perishing flesh with God, who is spirit. In like manner, the analogy of the human personality in the matter of the so-called anthropopathisms is denied; *e.g.* Nu 23[19] (1 S 15[29]), where it is declared that 'God is not a man that he should lie, nor a son of man that he should repent' (cf. also Hos 11[9]).

The great advance in the spiritualizing of the notion of God shows itself clearly in two other points—

(*b*) The first of these is that nowhere in the pre-exilic prophets are *angels** spoken of as beings mediating between God and man. For the seraphim in the vision of Isaiah (see above, p. 644[a]), which might readily occur to one's mind, are really the retinue of Jahweh, not His messengers who are supposed to be at a distance from Him, and who perform His will. The latter notion is indeed contradictory of the idea of a living presence of God, and hence it is wanting in the prophets, however familiar they may be otherwise with the conception of angels.

(*c*) The other evidence of the spiritualizing of the notion of God is the unwearied polemic the prophets carry on against the *images* of Jahweh in both kingdoms. At one time it used to be assumed that this polemic was almost exclusively directed against the images of heathen gods, or, at most, against the golden bulls of the Northern kingdom, whose construction was viewed as a glaring violation of the Second Commandment in the Decalogue. But we found (see above, p. 641[b]) that the making of images of Jahweh must have been regarded, down to the 8th cent., and that in the most widely separated circles, as quite unobjectionable, and hence there is the greatest difficulty in holding that the prohibition of images was an original feature of the Decalogue. In the Elijah- and Elisha-narratives there is not a trace of any polemic against the bull worship of the Northern kingdom. All the more marked is the fashion in which the indignation of the writing prophets is roused when that God who in His majesty is exalted above

* On Hos 12[4f.] as an allusion to a manifestation of *God*, see above, p. 638[b].

everything earthly is brought down to the sphere of the visible and transitory—a process which only too readily leads also to a dishonouring of Him.*

The answer to the question whether *Amos* had already opened the polemic against the images of Jahweh, depends upon how we interpret Am $8^{14}$.† The 'sin of Samaria' may there refer to the golden bulls of Jeroboam I.; but the text is probably corrupt. As to *Hosea*, it cannot be proved from Hos $3^{4}$ that he expressly repudiated the ancestral representation of Jahweh in the form of the *'ēphôd* (see above, p. $641^{a}$) or the *tĕrāphîm* (see above, p. $642^{b}$), for his primary object in this passage is simply to affirm that Israel in exile will have to do without everything which at present it regards as indispensable. On the other hand, there are other passages which leave no doubt that, to the mind of Hosea, the Divine images of gold and silver, the work of men's hands, and the bull figures pre-eminently, were an abomination; cf. Hos $8^{4-6}$ (especially v.$^{5}$ 'thy bull, O Samaria, stinketh') $10^{5}$ $13^{2}$ $14^{3}$. The polemic of *Isaiah* against the אֱלִילִים (prob. originally 'gods,' but also the equivalent of 'nothings,' and hence to the prophets a welcome occasion for a play upon words) applies not only to the idols of the heathen (Is $10^{10}$ $19^{3}$) and the gods whom they represented ($19^{1}$), but to the images of Jahweh ($2^{8. 18. 20}$ $10^{11}$). Even the latter are only men's work, and on that account contemptible ($2^{8}$ $17^{8}$ [in the latter passage the 'altars' are to be struck out as an incorrect gloss] where the Divine images are called 'the work of your hands'; in Jer $1^{16}$ $25^{6}$ $32^{30}$ 'the work of their own hands' may refer to images of Jahweh, but perhaps includes also, as it certainly does in $44^{8}$, actual heathen idols). In Dt $4^{15f.}$ the representation of Jahweh by any figure is strictly forbidden, on the ground that Israel at Ḥoreb saw nothing of this kind; while in $27^{15}$ a curse is pronounced on the making of a carved or a molten image by the hands of an artist. Here, as in the Decalogue, the reference is to every species of Divine image, including those of Jahweh. The rigour of the Deuteronomist has all the less power to astonish us, seeing that he repudiates in express terms, not only the *'ăshērāh*, or sacred pole at places of sacrifice, but also (Dt $12^{3}$ $16^{22}$) the *maẓẓēbāh*, which, in earlier times, were regarded as quite unobjectionable (see above, p. 620).

(*d*) What we have said about the character of Jahweh as God of heaven, and the sharp rejection of all pictorial representations of the Deity, may seem to have already answered another question, namely, as to the *solity* of Jahweh, as contrasted with the mere henotheism (see above, pp. $625^{b}$, $635^{a}$) of earlier times. Now, it must indeed be remarked that it is still customary to cite, as proofs of the absolute monotheism of the Prophetic period, a number of passages which in truth are intended only to emphasize Israel's obligation to reverence Jahweh alone, and which thus amount simply to henotheism.‡ Such are, for instance, the very frequent cautions in Deuteronomy against other gods; in none of the passages containing these is there any expression of opinion as to the reality or non-reality of these 'other gods.' Even the famous 'Hear, O Israel' of Dt $6^{4}$, which the Jews and many Christian exegetes are wont to regard as the formulated fundamental confession of monotheism, signifies by itself no more than that Jahweh is the God of Israel, Jahweh alone,* and that hence the veneration of Israel is due to Him alone. The declaration is thus on a parallel with the First Commandment. Hos $13^{4}$, again, says only that Israel knows (or should know) no other God, and has experienced no other deliverer than Jahweh. Moses testifies in Dt $3^{24}$, as Solomon does in 1 K $8^{23}$, that Jahweh the God of Israel has no other god like Him, either in heaven above or on earth below. But here the existence of other gods seems to be yet always assumed, precisely as in the question of Ex $15^{11}$ 'Who is like thee, O Jahweh, among the gods?'; or in the designation of Jahweh as 'God of gods' and 'Lord of lords' (Dt $10^{17}$); or, finally, in the statement of the prophet: 'Before him (Jahweh) trembled the idols of Egypt' (Is $19^{1}$).

There can, however, be no doubt that the passages last cited are to be set down simply to the account of poetic colouring or of an involuntary accommodation to the still subsisting popular conceptions. The real belief of the leading circles of thought is presented to us—at least in the later Deuteronom. stratum—in the confession: 'Jahweh is the [true] God' (Dt $7^{9}$); 'Besides him there is none' ($4^{35. 39}$, 1 K $8^{60}$; cf. also Is $37^{16}$, 2 K $19^{15}$). But the same faith is held by the writing prophets, although it is never reduced to so precise a formula. Without it the conception of Jahweh as God of heaven could never have established itself in the shape above (p. 679) described. The God to whom 'belongeth the heaven to its utmost heights, the earth and all that is upon it' (Dt $10^{14}$), cannot possibly share this sovereignty of His with another god. It might indeed appear surprising that the allusions to the creative power of Jahweh, in which afterwards His uniqueness as God of the whole world comes into the sharpest prominence, are so scanty in the pre-exilic prophets. For, apart from the oft recurring Divine name *Jahweh Ẓĕbā'ôth*, which, in the mind of the writing prophets (see above, p. $637^{b}$), doubtless includes a confession of the supramundane power and glory of Jahweh, and leaving out of account occasional allusions to Jahweh as bestower of the rain (Am $4^{7}$, Jer $5^{24}$ $14^{22}$) and, conversely, as the author of drought and famine, all that we find is an express reference in Jer $27^{5}$ to Jahweh as the Creator of the earth, with man and beast, and an allusion (put in the mouth of Ḥezekiah in 2 K $19^{15}$ = Is $37^{16}$) to Him as the Creator of the heaven and the earth.†

But the scantiness of these allusions should not excite our wonder. It is richly counterbalanced by the abundance of other passages which witness to the solity, or at least the incomparable omnipotence, of Jahweh in *the world of nations*. It was not the function of the prophets to solve cosmic or purely metaphysical problems, but to hold up

* We see from Hos $13^{2}$ that in Hosea's time it was still customary to kiss the bull-images, and thus to put them (like the images of Baal in Elijah's time, 1 K $19^{18}$) on a footing of equality with the God whom they were meant to represent. Also the expression חִלָּה אֶת־פְּנֵי יהוה (Ex $32^{11}$, 1 S $13^{12}$, and often, in sense of 'propitiate Jahweh') originally means in all probability 'stroke the face of [the Divine image],' and points to a practice which must have been in vogue wherever images of Jahweh were worshipped.

† Am $2^{4}$, with its allusion to the (Judæan) כְּזָבִים, lit. 'lies,' [='idols'], is generally recognized to be a later interpolation.

‡ On the controversy as to the beginning of absolute monotheism, the reader may consult: A. Kuenen, art. 'Jahweh and the other gods' in *Theol. Review*, July 1876; Baudissin, *Studien zur semit. Religionsgeschichte*, i., Leipzig, 1876 [Studie 2 'Die Anschauung des AT von den Göttern des Heidenthums']; Baethgen, *Beiträge zur semit. Religionsgeschichte: der Gott Israels und die Götter der Heiden*, Berlin, 1880 [cf. esp. pp. 131–152 'Israels Verhältniss zum Polytheismus']; Ed. König, *Beiträge zum positiven Aufbau der Religionsgeschichte Israels*, ii.: 'Der Monotheismus der legitimen Religion Israels,' Leipzig, 1889.

* This interpretation of the words is claimed, in our opinion rightly, on the ground of the accentuation. The prevailing explanation, on the other hand, yields the sense: 'Jahweh our God is *one* Jahweh' (*i.e.* not broken up into a number of local deities; cf. Zec $14^{9}$). Even thus the question of the reality of the strange gods is still left quite out of account.

† So far as their contents are concerned, Am $4^{13}$ $5^{8f.}$ $9^{5f.}$ would also fall under this category; but these passages are now pretty generally regarded as late glosses. The same remark applies to Jer $10^{12f.}$ and $33^{25}$, where we read of a covenant of Jahweh with the day and the night, and of His appointing of the ordinances of heaven and earth.

to the eyes of their people the greatness of their responsibility and the dreadfulness of the God to whom they had to give account. Thus the judgments of God, present and future, supply a constant motive to portray Jahweh as the God who has at His command not only the resources and powers of the whole Universe, but, no less, the nations of the earth, when it is necessary to realize His purposes. When He commences a lawsuit with His people, heaven and earth have to listen in reverential silence (Is 1[2]; cf. also Mic 6[1f.], Hab 2[20]); and, when He comes to execute judgment, the whole course of nature reels (Mic 1[3ff.], Nah 1[3ff.]), and men hasten to hide themselves in terror of His majestic appearance (Is 2[10. 19. 21]). The mighty Assyria, with all its subject peoples, is like a lifeless instrument in His hands if He cares to employ it for the chastisement of Israel. He whistles for it from the end of the earth (Is 5[26]), much as the shepherd whistles to his dog, and it comes hurrying up. And if, in its haughty conceit, Assyria fancies that it has accomplished by its own strength what it has done only as the chastising rod in Jahweh's hand (Is 10[5ff.]), it has to listen to the crushing question: 'Does the axe boast itself against him that heweth therewith, or does the saw magnify itself against him that worketh it?' (v.[15]). Then by a fearful judgment is Assyria taught the truth of the all-superior might of Jahweh (vv.[16ff. 25ff.]). The rôle that Assyria plays in Isaiah is played in Jeremiah by 'all the families of the kingdoms of the north' (Jer 1[15]). These are called by Jahweh to execute judgment upon Jerusalem; He has given all lands into the power of Nebuchadreẓẓar (Jer 27[6]; cf. 28[14], Hab 1[12], also 2 K 15[37]). Jahweh's judgments upon foreign nations are for the most part occasioned by their hostility to Israel (so Am 1[3. 9. 11. 13], Is 14[24ff.] 17[12ff.] 18[3ff.], Nah 3[5ff.], Hab 2[16]). Yet passages are not wholly wanting which speak of an unlimited exercise of the Divine sway amongst the nations, even apart from any such motive. Jahweh punishes Moab for its outrage on the king of Edom (Am 2[1ff.]); it was Jahweh that brought the Philistines from Caphtor and the Aramæans from Ḳir (9[7]). He stirs up the Egyptians against one another, and gives them over into the hand of a cruel lord (Is 19[2. 4]); He produces in them a spirit of dizziness (v.[14]). He has determined upon the destruction of Tyre, 'to stain the pride of all glory, to bring into contempt all the honourable of the earth' (23[9], cf. also v.[11]). At His command, Jeremiah hands to all kings of the earth the intoxicating cup, and, whether they will or no, they *must* drink it (Jer 25[15f.]).

In view of all these testimonies to a lofty view of history and a conception of God which embraced the whole Universe, we can now see also the polemic against images in its true light. We perceive how to the prophets every attempt to give to this powerful, majestic God a petty visible form, must have been an abomination. But we understand also how, in the case of the heathen idols, they could recognize no reality except that of metal, wood, and stone. This is not yet (except perhaps in Hab 2[18f.], Jer 2[11] 16[19f.], and in the later Deuteronom. stratum, Dt 28[36. 64]) expressed so definitely as in the next period; but the above-described notion of God leaves no doubt that there is no room for real 'other gods' alongside of the one God who rules over the Universe and the world of men. A proof of this is found even in the numerous designations of the idols which lay stress either upon their repulsiveness or upon their utter nothingness (or unreality). Some at least of these designations are as early as the pre-exilic period. Evidently, there lies at the root of almost all of them the assumption that the gods whom they represent are nothing but vain imaginations of the heathen. To the first category, that of opprobrious epithets, belong the following terms: שִׁקּוּץ 'abomination' (Jer 4[1] 7[30]; and used repeatedly by the Deuteronom. redactors of the Books of Kings, 1 K 11[5], 2 K 23[13. 24]), and, with the same sense, תּוֹעֵבוֹת (2 K 23[13]); still later probably is גִּלּוּלִים, *i.e.* perhaps 'round blocks *or* dolls,' if not rather, 'excrements' (Dt 29[16 (17)] 'of wood and stone, of silver and gold,' 1 K 21[26], 2 K 17[12], and oft. in Ezekiel). To the second category, terms expressive of unreality, belong: הֶבֶל, lit. 'breath,' 'nothingness' (Jer 2[5], 1 K 16[13], 2 K 17[15]; in plur. Jer 8[19] 14[22]); and שָׁוְא 'vain,' 'null' (Jer 18[15]). Cf., finally, the threatening of Dt 4[28] (that is to say, within the later framework of Deut.) that Israel in exile will have to serve gods which are the work of men's hands [and nothing more], wood and stone, which can neither see nor hear nor eat nor smell.

(*e*) If, by way of supplement to this, we further ask in traditional fashion how the being of Jahweh reveals itself in the prophets in the way of special *attributes*, we must from the very first renounce all idea of discovering any didactic abstract statements or purely scholastic definitions. Here, again, it holds good that the mission of the prophets was primarily to preach repentance to their people. Hence they exhibit to them their God in a light corresponding to changing needs, now as the terrible avenger of their apostasy, now as the long-suffering and merciful One. Nay, these qualities always make their appearance first in the special bearing of Jahweh in concrete instances. It was not till the days of the late-Jewish theology that it became possible to draw up a 'doctrine of the attributes,' upon the basis of a scholastic analysis of the living being and acting of Jahweh, which to the prophets had been the object of direct vision.

(*a*) Under the heading of 'attributes' it has from the first been usual to discuss, above all, the **holiness** * of God, and to follow the definition, borrowed from dogmatics, according to which God is called holy because He loves only good and hates evil. But we shall find that this definition, however it may answer to the NT conception of holiness, is true only in a very limited measure to the OT conception.

We might have spoken of the latter conception, even in dealing with the earlier periods, for the terms קָדוֹשׁ 'holy,' קֹדֶשׁ 'holiness,' and קִדֵּשׁ 'to declare holy,' 'to consecrate,' are, beyond doubt, very ancient. But they occur primarily—and that as marking an attribute especially of things, rarely of (human) persons—in a ritual connexion, and, as is a matter of course in the case of things, without any ethical connotation. Anything is called קָדוֹשׁ † which is withdrawn from profane possession and use, nay even from profane touch, and in place of this is destined for the possession and service of the Deity. Thus the name 'holy' is given naturally to all the ritual apparatus, all the rooms which serve as the dwelling-place or the spot of worship of Jahweh, all the sacrificial gifts intended for Him. But the same name is given also to such things as have, for some special reason, been forfeited, not indeed to the service

* Cf. the very thorough discussion by Baudissin, 'Der Begriff der Heiligkeit im AT' (*Studien zur semit. Religionsgeschichte*, ii. pp. 1–142); R. Schröter, *Der Begriff der Heiligkeit im AT und NT*, Halle, 1892. See also art. HOLINESS (in OT) in vol. ii. of the present work.

† The etymology is disputed. There is still, however, most to be said in favour of tracing it to the root קדשׁ, in the sense of 'separate,' 'segregate.' At all events this answers admirably to the Hebrew usage, which is more than can be said of the proposal to trace it to the Heb. חָדָשׁ 'new,' and hence 'pure,' 'bright,' 'sparkling' (cf. also Assyr. *ḳuddushu*, 'shining,' 'pure').

of God, but so as to be His property and that of His sanctuary. Thus the censers of Ḳoraḥ and his company become 'holy' (Nu 17$^{3}$ [16$^{37}$]), and are accordingly to be employed to overlay the altar. In the same way, however, even a person by unauthorized touching of what is itself holy may 'become holy,' *i.e.* fall forfeit to the sanctuary, enter into a special relation to God: so, for instance, by touching the altar (Ex 29$^{37}$) or the sacred vessels (30$^{29}$, Hag 2$^{12}$ etc.). In such an event, special offerings and atonements are needed in order to remove the condition of 'being holy,' which presses upon the individual as a danger. The danger lies in the fact that, while he is in this condition, every species of defilement, whether due to his own fault or no, may readily prove fatal to him.

It cannot occasion us any surprise that *this* use of the concepts 'holy' and 'holiness' meets us most frequently in the latest stratum of the Pentateuch, the so-called Priests' Code, for the latter is concerned, above all, with ritual prescriptions. But in this matter it is plain that it simply follows a long-established usage of language, and that, too, even long after the notion of holiness had begun to assume a positive connotation.

At a very early period we already hear (1 S 21$^{5\,(4)}$) not only of 'holy' bread (*i.e.* bread consecrated to God and hence withdrawn from profane use), but also (v.$^{6\,(5)}$) of holy 'vessels,' *i.e.* clothes and weapons. The 'holiness' is here manifestly produced by special rites such as were customary at the beginning of a campaign. This is proved by the expression 'hallow a war *or* a festival,' *i.e.* prepare oneself for the conflict or the celebration of the festival by performing certain acts of consecration. There are quite a number of passages which show that this consecration, apart from certain forms of abstinence, consisted mainly in the washing and cleansing of the person and the clothes. Thus 'holy' and 'hallow oneself' come to be almost synonymous with 'clean' and 'cleanse oneself' (cf., for example, 1 S 20$^{26}$ where לֹא טָהוֹר 'not clean' stands for one who, in consequence of a nocturnal pollution, has been incapacitated for taking part in the sacrificial meal at the New Moon festival).

When the demand is made in Dt 7$^{6}$ 14$^{2}$ that Israel shall be a holy people to Jahweh its God, because He has chosen it out of all peoples to be the people of His own possession, the notion of holiness is not here restricted merely to the point that Israel has been separated from the peoples and appropriated by Jahweh to be His property alone. In that case the notion of 'holiness' would be concerned merely with a relation (as in the case of the sacred bread), and would not imply any alteration in the quality of the persons or things dedicated to God.* In reality, however, the 'holy' people means one that carefully guards against any defilement that would make it incapable of being called the people of this very God and of taking part in His worship. But here, again, it is far from being the case that moral defilement is primarily in view. What incapacitates for participating in the cultus is physical or so-called 'Levitical' uncleanness. To this category belongs every kind of contact with persons or things belonging to the realm of idol worship, as well as the touching (even unwittingly and unintentionally) of a corpse, the partaking of unclean food (Dt 14$^{21}$), and other acts of the same kind. Even in the so-called 'Law of Holiness' (Lv 17–26, cf. also 11$^{44\text{f.}}$), in spite of such general expressions

* How far removed any such implication was in the oldest linguistic usage, is best shown by the designations קְדֵשִׁים and קְדֵשׁוֹת, given to those who prostituted themselves in honour of a deity (cf. above, p. 662$^{b}$). Here, of course, any thought of a religious-moral quality is out of the question.

as are found in 19$^{2}$ 20$^{7\text{f.}}$, we have to do, not with a demand for absolute moral holiness, but with the same caution against every species of physical defilement. The circumstance that the latter may frequently include at the same time a religious offence is left at first out of view in applying the notions of clean or holy. Hence is to be explained the fact, which is so strange from *our* point of view, that outward, physical, and it may be even unwitting defilement involves guilt, and necessitates the same sacrifices and other means of atonement as actual moral defilement. This view, which characterizes the Priests' Code, presents itself to us most clearly in Ex 19$^{6}$, where the ideal goal of God's ways with Israel is set up as consisting in His making them a 'kingdom of priests,' a holy people, *i.e.* a people every member of which answers always to the conditions of perfect (Levitical) purity as these were binding at all times on the priests.

Still more marked is the filling of the concept 'holy' with moral contents, when it is transferred to God, and—what is very noteworthy—exclusively to the God of Israel. The earliest passage of this kind is probably 1 S 6$^{20}$, where the inhabitants of Bethshemesh, after the stroke which fell upon them for looking into the sacred Ark, ask in terror: 'Who can stand in presence of Jahweh, this holy God?' Here the word 'holy' manifestly contains the notion of terrible and unapproachable—nay, death-dealing; for there is a deep cleft between the imperishable being of the Deity and everything which is subject to decay and uncleanness. To say that Jahweh is a holy God means thus that He is *elevated* above all that is outside Him, that He holds a unique position over against all that is created. Hence it has been rightly said that the holiness of Jahweh is not a single attribute (such as 'moral perfection'), but a designation of His essential being, practically identical with the notion of being Divine (*Gottsein*). Hence Jahweh in Am 4$^{2}$ swears by His holiness, *i.e.*, as is seen from Gn 22$^{16}$ and Jer 22$^{5}$, by Himself.

It may be added that expressions about the holiness of God are at first very rare. Ex 15$^{11}$ ('Who is like thee, glorious in holiness, terrible in exploits, doing wonders?') should probably be assigned to the later Prophetical period. Jos 24$^{19}$ ('Ye cannot serve Jahweh, for he is a holy God'), from the pen of E, emphasizes, like 1 S 6$^{20}$, the terrible and unapproachable nature of Jahweh. All that occurs in Amos, apart from 4$^{2}$ (see above), is the reference in 2$^{7}$ to the dishonouring of the *holy name* of Jahweh by shameless immorality. In Hos 11$^{9}$ ('For I am God, and not man; as holy I dwell among you') 'holy' means raised above human passion and hasty anger.

It is in Isaiah that the notion of the holiness of God first comes to be frequently mentioned and is most sharply defined. Already in the vision that marked his prophetic call, he hears the antiphonal song of the seraphim that surround the throne of Jahweh—

> 'Holy, holy, holy is Jahweh of Hosts,
> The whole earth is full of his glory.'

These two parallel members contain two statements, which supplement one another, about the inmost being of Jahweh. The first concerns the *immanent* being—that elevation above everything earthly or creaturely which belongs in the highest degree* to Jahweh; the second, again, the *transcendent* being—the glory that manifests itself over the whole earth (cf. above, p. 639$^{b}$ f.). In so far, now, as absolute elevation above everything earthly includes, as a matter of course, superiority to all

* On the expression of the superlative by repetition of the adjective, see Gesenius, *Heb. Gram.*$^{27}$ § 133 *k*.

infirmity and sin, we may speak also of an ethical content of the notion of holiness. But even in Isaiah this does not yet make its appearance expressly or quite exclusively. The designation of Jahweh as 'the Holy One of Israel' (a favourite expression with Isaiah, $1^{4}$ $10^{20}$ $17^{7}$ etc.) implies that He is to be recognized and correspondingly venerated by Israel as the absolutely exalted and therefore terrible One, who is not to be provoked with impunity; for towards His despisers He shows Himself holy by His punitive justice ($5^{16}$).

The only pre-exilic prophet, besides Isaiah, who uses 'holy' as a predicate of Jahweh, is Ḥabakkuk ($1^{12}$). Here the ethical quality of the Divine holiness comes pretty clearly into the foreground. Immediately after the question, 'Art thou not from everlasting, Jahweh, my Holy One?' comes the statement, 'Thou art of purer eyes than to behold evil, and thou canst not look on perverseness' (v.$^{13}$).

We have already (p. $682^{a}$) pointed out that the holiness of God, which is so often urged in the 'Law of Holiness' as a motive why Israel should be holy, is, above all, the contrast to all Levitical impurity. This priestly notion of holiness is thus markedly inferior in depth and significance to Isaiah's conception. But the latter did not on that account disappear from the language of religion. We meet with it frequently in the exilic and post-exilic prophets (especially Deutero-Isaiah), and no less in the Psalms. And we may say that it is *the* essential designation of the God of Israel, laying the greatest stress, as it does, on His uniqueness and incomparable character, before which all gods recognized elsewhere shrink into their nothingness. Holy things and persons (*i.e.* set apart for the exclusive service of a deity) are known to other religions as well; but the holiness of its God is known to Israel only through the revelation given to it. Thus the application of the notion of holiness to Jahweh includes, when rightly understood, a kind of monotheistic confession, a far-reaching testimony to the surpassing greatness of the religion of Israel.

Although, as was remarked above, the idea of moral perfection and aversion to evil was not the primary one attaching to the notion of holiness, it is by no means strange to the Prophetical conception of God. This idea comes to light in the absolute truthfulness and fidelity of Jahweh, as well as in the unconditional character of the moral demands made on Israel; but, above all, in the attitude of Jahweh to heathen nations, for He avenges outrage and injustice everywhere on earth, even although these have not (as in Am $1^{3.\ 6.\ 9.\ 11}$) been inflicted on Israel. Thus He once punished Sodom and Gomorrah; thus, according to Am $2^{1}$, will He chastise Moab for their sacrilegious treatment of the bones of the king of Edom. The prophet thus takes it as self-evident that there are moral principles which are binding upon all peoples, and on whose observance Jahweh, as an absolutely moral Being, and at the same time Ruler and Judge of all, keeps strict watch. But, above all, Israel itself must be taught that Jahweh is a God of right * (Is $30^{18}$), and of right at any price. In another connexion we shall have to speak of how He causes it to triumph over wrong and sin, even if this involves the giving up and destruction of His own people. Here it may suffice to refer to one other illustration of how widely the genuine Prophetical judgment of things differs from that of the mass of the people of Israel. Jehu's extirpation of Baal worship in Israel was carried out with terrible bloodshed. The early narrative of 2 K 9. 10 evidently saw in this a laudable 'zeal for Jahweh' ($10^{16}$), and the Deuteronom. redactor, who on this point represents the general opinion of Israel in the supposed interest of the Jahweh religion, makes Jahweh Himself declare to Jehu (v.$^{30}$) that he has done what is well-pleasing in His eyes, and has treated the house of Ahab entirely after His mind. Quite different is the judgment of Hosea ($1^{4}$). To him it appears impossible that blood-guiltiness should not be called blood-guiltiness simply because it assumes the title of zeal for Jahweh. And so the prophet threatens that the blood-guiltiness of Jezreel shall be avenged on the house of Jehu, by the destruction of the kingdom of Israel and the shattering of her military power in the Plain of Jezreel.

($\beta$) As was remarked above (p. $681^{b}$), the conviction of the prophets regarding other attributes of God presents itself, not in express definitions, but rather (apart from certain Divine names) * in casual utterances about His activity and the occurrences which He brings about. Thus we have His absolute **omnipotence** (which is already, if only in a general way, presupposed in such early passages as Gn $18^{14}$, Nu $11^{23}$, 1 S $14^{6}$), which shows itself in His unconditioned supremacy over all, even the mightiest, peoples of earth (see above, p. $681^{a}$), but no less also in such remarkable passages as Is $7^{11}$. The whole context of this last passage permits of no other view than that Isaiah holds with unshaken confidence, that whatever Ahaz may demand from Jahweh as a confirmatory sign, be it as great a wonder as it may, Jahweh will bring it to pass. So firm a belief is with difficulty conceivable by us, because our judgment is influenced by all the dogmatic considerations about the possibility and the limits of miracles as a 'violation of the laws of nature'—laws which, however, are imposed by God Himself. Such considerations, it is plain, never crossed the prophets' minds. Of 'miracles' in the sense familiar to us they know nothing. They are acquainted with extraordinary occurrences and actions (נִפְלָאוֹת) which transcend the ordinary course of things, but to them nothing is so extraordinary as to be beyond the sphere of Jahweh's power (Jer $32^{27}$). This conviction is a self-evident result of their notion of God; the *idea* of the Divine omnipotence is a postulate of their faith long before language had coined a special term for this attribute. Such a term could be dispensed with all the more readily, seeing that allusions to the Divine omnipotence served not scholastic speculations, but prominent religious interests; they brought consolation to the godly, who could now unreservedly trust to the help of their God; they were meant to instil

* We may take this opportunity of pointing out that the Hebrew words which are commonly rendered 'righteous' (צַדִּיק) and 'righteousness' (צֶדֶק, צְדָקָה) have originally a different sense from that of forensic justice. צֶדֶק or צְדָקָה denotes a way of acting or a condition corresponding to a standard (so quite clearly in מֹאזְנֵי צֶדֶק 'correct scales,' אַבְנֵי צֶדֶק 'correct weights'). When used of men, it is mostly = 'righteousness' (δικαιοσύνη), 'piety'; used of God, it denotes the attitude corresponding to the norm of the Divine being. But to this norm belong not only strict justice, but also God's covenant faithfulness, coupled with long-suffering and grace; and hence צְדָקָה (esp. in Is 40–66) is used not infrequently of that aspect of Jahweh's activity which has for its object the salvation of His people. See, further, Kautzsch, *Ueber die Derivate des Stammes ẓādaq im alttest. Sprachgebrauch*, Tübingen, 1881; G. Martin, *La notion de la justice de Dieu dans l'ancien Testament*, Montauban, 1892; G. Dalman, *Die richterliche Gerechtigkeit im AT*, Berlin, 1897; Bouwman, *Het begrip gerechtigheid in het Oude Testament*, Kampen, 1899.

* On the title *Jahweh Ẓĕbā'ôth* as used by the prophets in allusion to the supramundane power and glory of Jahweh, cf. above, pp. $637^{b}$ and $680^{b}$. Cf., further, the designation of Jahweh as אֲבִיר יִשְׂרָאֵל 'the strong One of Israel' (Is $1^{24}$); and as צוּר 'rock' (Is $17^{10}$ $30^{29}$; elsewhere in the later passages, $26^{4}$ $44^{8}$, Dt $32^{4.\ 15.\ 18.\ 30.\ 31.\ 37}$, 1 S $2^{2}$, 2 S $22^{3.\ 32.\ 47}$ $23^{3}$, and 14 times in the Psalms; cf. Wiegand, 'Der Gottesname *ẓûr*,' etc. in *ZATW* x. [1890] 85 ff.; and art. Rock in vol. iv. of the present work).

terror into the hearts of sinners, whom nothing could deliver from this God's mighty arm.

(γ, δ) Precisely similar remarks apply to the occasional allusions to the **omnipresence** and **omniscience** of God. That the first named of these could be regarded only with reference to the Divine activity (*i.e.* God's cognition and Providential care) and not of the Divine substance, has been already remarked; and for the OT conception of God this is self-evident, in so far as any approach to pantheistic notions would destroy, or at least greatly endanger, the idea of the living Personality, which forms the inmost kernel of the conception in question. But this does not prevent His care from always following His people, or, on the other hand, His eye from penetrating all darkness, so that there is no secret corner where the workers of iniquity can remain unseen by Jahweh (Jer $23^{24}$). If in this last statement the idea of omnipresence already touches that of omniscience, still more is this the case with the declarations about Jahweh as One who can see into the most hidden depths of the human heart. He penetrates the secret plans of the Judæans with reference to an alliance with Egypt, however carefully they may seek in their folly to conceal these from Him (Is $29^{15}$); He it is that searches the heart, tries the reins, to recompense every man according to his works, according to the fruit of his deeds (Jer $17^{10}$). And this applies not only to Israel, but He alone knows the heart of *all* men. But the strongest evidence of the firmness of the belief in the omnipresence and omniscience of God, and at the same time the most significant fruit of this faith, is the conviction (already felt in the preceding period) that Jahweh hears, and for the most part also answers, the prayers of His people.* This conviction meets us everywhere in the Prophets, most markedly perhaps in Jeremiah's manifold communion in prayer with his God, but in every case as a conviction that is a matter of course. All the more on that account may it be reckoned among the evidences that the religion of Israel, at an early date and in quite a special way through the influence of the pre-exilic prophets, was filled with an imperious desire to burst the barriers of a merely national religion, and to pave the way to a worship of God in spirit and in truth, such as should satisfy the deepest longings of every individual soul that drew near to this God.

(ε) In view of the above-described strong emphasizing of the holiness of God as the absolute elevation and unapproachableness, nay the awfulness, of the Divine essence, and, in no less degree, owing to the circumstance that the preaching of repentance was the main task of the prophets, it is readily intelligible that expressions about the **love,** the **goodness,** and **mercy** of God should recede more into the background. The terms so frequently used of human love are transferred to God first by Hosea ($3^{1}$ $11^{9}$), more frequently by the Deuteronomist ($4^{37}$ $7^{8.13}$ $10^{15}$ $15^{16}$ $23^{5}$, cf. 1 K $10^{9}$), once also by Jeremiah ($31^{3}$). But, apart from Dt $10^{18}$ ('Jahweh loveth the *gēr*'), it is always God's love to the people of Israel that is spoken of; and, besides, the words used for 'love' (both noun and verb) have always attached to them the notion of choice, nay, of preference; the full unfolding of the idea of the Divine love is not yet reached. In like manner, the expressions for 'mercy,' 'grace,' 'compassion' are in later linguistic usage transferred to God, or at least somewhat frequently employed in making predications about Him. A collection of almost all the qualities of the love of God is brought together in Ex $34^{6}$ ('Jahweh, a God full of compassion and gracious, slow to anger, and plenteous in mercy and truth'), but this passage, too, is undoubtedly from the hand of a later redactor than the J *pericope* in which it is now inserted.

2. *The relation of Jahweh to Israel.*—That an intimate relation has subsisted from the first between Jahweh and Israel, is assumed in all the OT sources as a matter of course. They likewise hold that this relation is not based, as in the nature-religions, on some primeval and not to be explained condition of things, but upon a *bĕrîth* (cf. above, p. $630^{b}$), or solemn transaction, at Sinai, whereby the nation becomes the 'peculiar people' of Jahweh, who by mighty acts has delivered it from the bondage of Egypt.

(*a*) Already in Ex $4^{22}$ J speaks of the position of Israel as that of a firstborn son. This, in spite of Jer $3^{19}$, is not to be understood as if it meant to ascribe filial rights to all other peoples as well. The emphasis lies upon 'firstborn' in the sense that Israel alone possesses all the prerogatives which belong to the firstborn as the one who is loved and preferred before all others. These filial privileges, however, are predicated only of the people collectively, not of the individual Israelite. The latter, on the other hand, is a 'servant' of Jahweh (so in Nu $12^{7f.}$, and repeatedly, of Moses; in Is $20^{3}$ of Isaiah; in Jer $7^{25}$ of the prophets). Even the OT, it is true, is acquainted with the notion of individual sonship, but only* in the person of the theocratic king (2 S $7^{14}$, Ps $2^{7}$ $89^{27}$ [of David]), not yet in the NT sense of sonship for which all men are destined.

We meet with this same conception of the sonship of collective Israel not infrequently in the Prophetical period: Is $1^{2}$ $30^{1.9}$, Dt $14^{1}$ (where 'children' ‖ 'people holy to Jahweh,' v.[2]), Is $43^{6}$ (where sons and daughters are distinguished) $45^{11}$.† The necessary reverse side of this is the idea of the *Fatherhood of God.* Disregarding here passages where 'father' stands mainly for the physical Creator of the people (Dt $32^{6}$, Mal $2^{10}$), the fatherly relation is once more one that is sustained towards the nation collectively: so Jer $3^{4.19}$ $31^{9}$ (towards Ephraim as 'firstborn son'); cf. also Is $63^{16}$ (‖ 'redeemer'), Mal $1^{6}$.

(*b*) The foundation of this close relation is *the election of Israel.* Israel has been chosen out of all nations to be the people of God's own possession, *i.e.* a highly prized and therefore carefully guarded and cherished piece of property. Thus Amos ($3^{2}$) says, 'You only have I known [*i.e.* made the object of my intimate knowledge and close care] of all the peoples of the earth,' from which, indeed, he draws the inference, so startling to the popular view of the matter, that for that very reason Jahweh will visit upon them all their offences. The idea of a choice [verb בָּחַר] of Israel from amongst the numerous nations makes its appearance first in the vocabulary of the Deuteronomist: Dt $4^{37}$ $7^{6}$ $10^{15}$ $14^{2}$, 1 K $3^{8}$ $8^{53}$; cf. also Ps $33^{12}$ $47^{5\,(4)}$ $135^{4}$ etc., and numerous passages in Is 40–66. Quite a unique contrast is drawn in Dt $4^{20}$ between the choice of Israel and the fact that Jahweh has assigned to the other nations of the earth the stars as the object of their veneration.

The motive assigned for Israel's election is in 1 S $12^{22}$ the good pleasure of Jahweh, but repeatedly (so already in Hos $11^{1}$, Dt $4^{37}$ $10^{15}$) Jahweh's love to Israel (coupled in Dt $7^{8}$ with His oath to the patriarchs) is exhibited as the motive. A reason for this love itself is not stated. But

* Cf. Caldesaigues, *La prière dans la religion de Jéhovah*, etc., Cahors, 1899; Köberle, *Die Motive des Glaubens an die Gebetserhörung im AT*, Erlangen and Leipzig, 1901.

* In Ps $68^{6\,(5)}$ ('father of the orphans') 'father,' as the parallelism shows, is figurative = 'protector,' 'provider'; cf. P. Bauer, 'Gott als Vater im AT' in *SK*, 1899, p. 483 ff.

† In Hos $11^{1}$ (MT 'out of Egypt I called my son') we should probably read, with LXX and Targ., 'his sons' (לְבָנָיו).

the Book of Deuteronomy labours to impress it upon the people's minds that it was not on account of any greatness (Dt 7[7]) or any special righteousness of theirs that they were so highly favoured of God. On the contrary, Israel was the smallest of peoples, and a stiff-necked people to boot. All the more, it is urged, is Israel bound to show heartfelt gratitude to God.

(*c*) In the closest connexion with the idea of Israel's election stands the *theologumenon* of the 'jealousy of Jahweh.' The Heb. word (קִנְאָה) appears to stand originally for angry zeal in general (Zeph 1[18] 3[8], Dt 29[19 (20)], and very often in Ezekiel; cf. also קַנּוֹא 'jealous,' in Jos 24[19] and Nah 1[2]); more specially the zeal of God on behalf of Israel against the heathen, as manifested particularly in the exact fulfilment of His promises (Is 9[6], 2 K 19[31], and often in Ezekiel and Is 40–66). If קִנְאָה here already denotes God's jealous guarding of His honour, no less does the adjective קַנָּא import the 'jealous' God who vehemently asserts His sole right to the love and reverence of Israel, and hence tolerates no kind of idolatry: so in Ex 20[5] [Dt 5[9]] 34[14], Dt 4[24] 6[15], all of which passages are probably not earlier than the Deuteronom. stratum.

(*d*) Jahweh's special love to Israel, evinced in the choice of this people, shows itself, further, in the wise *guidance* and powerful *protection* He accorded them from the first and all through their history. This is a favourite theme of the prophets, and very specially of Deuteronomy, and it serves in almost every instance as a motive for strong denunciations of Israel's ingratitude. Thus Amos (2[9f.]) holds up to the people the powerful aid given by Jahweh in the extirpating of the Canaanites, His deliverance of them from Egypt, and His 40 years leading of them in the wilderness. Hosea (11[3ff.]) recalls how, in spite of their disloyalty, God taught Ephraim, like a child, to walk, took them in His arms, and bound them to Himself by cords of love. Isaiah (1[2]) begins his great arraignment of Israel with the words: 'I have nourished and brought up children, but they have rebelled against me.' Micah (6[4f.]), too, presses upon the people's notice the gracious acts of Jahweh after their deliverance from Egyptian bondage. In Jeremiah (2[2ff.]), again, Jahweh Himself recalls the time of the wilderness wandering as the glorious bridal era of the people's history; and speaks of His marvellous guidance of them through the terrible wilderness (v.[6]), and his settling of them in the fruitful land of Canaan. The transfigured light in which the initial stages of the national history appeared to a later age is witnessed to by the Deuteronom. speech of Joshua (Jos 23[9f.]). According to the latter, none could then stand against Israel: a single Israelite could chase a thousand foes, for Jahweh their God Himself fought for them. A glorious description of the blessings which Jahweh showered upon the people in the days of their youth is contained also in the (probably exilic) Song of Moses (Dt 32[8-14]).

(*e*) Such numerous and important benefits received from Jahweh demand, as a matter of course, Israel's gratitude and obedience to their God. This leads us now to ask, *What does Jahweh, according to the teaching of the prophets, require of the people?* In the first place, naturally, there must be abstinence from every species of idolatry and of image worship, the images of Jahweh included. This inexhaustible theme of the warnings and reproaches of Deuteronomy, as it had been already with the great prophets of the 8th cent., will have to be more fully discussed below (see p. 689 f.). On the repudiation of the images of Jahweh, see above, p. 679[a].

(*a*) Here the primary question that concerns us is this. When the prophets repudiate an external cultus, to which even the cult of Jahweh, with its intermixture of heathen ritual customs, belongs, do they at least demand a purified, God-pleasing cultus? This question, if it is *sacrifice*, the proper centre of ancient worship, that is in view, is to be answered with a flat negative, and this negative—in spite of appearances to the contrary—is to be extended even to Deuteronomy. It is true that the latter law-book imperatively requires (12[5ff.] etc.) all kinds of sacrifice to be brought to the *one* sanctuary chosen by Jahweh, and the offerers are to eat and drink and rejoice there before Jahweh. But, apart from such general prescriptions as 12[26f.], there is not a single trace of any importance being attached to the ritual at these sacrificial meals. All that the code is concerned about is that the latter, which are now ancestral, deeply-rooted practices, should be held at the *one* legitimate sanctuary * which Jahweh has chosen. Only thus is there any security that the cultus shall be so watched over that the relics of heathen ritual customs shall at length be combated successfully. Further, it is the case that Deuteronomy (26[1ff.])—no doubt, taking up a long-established custom—requires a basket of the firstfruits of the field to be handed to the priest. But it does not neglect to prescribe to the offerer (v.[5ff.]) a prayer (the only prayer for public worship, besides that of v.[13ff.], in the whole Pentateuch!) which gives the true meaning and sets in a clear light the deeper significance of the outward gift as a grateful testimony to Jahweh as the bestower of the fruits in question. With regard to the so-called 'poor's tithe,' again, the most important question for Deuteronomy, as 26[14] shows, is whether the gifts in question have been brought into connexion with practices which are to be regarded as a denial of the pure Jahweh-cult.

While Deuteronomy accommodates itself to prevailing customs, there are, on the other hand, sayings of the prophets proper which cannot be understood except as absolutely disclaiming any demand on God's part for sacrificial gifts—a proof, by the way, that these prophets, one and all, are as yet quite unacquainted with a law-book such as P, where sacrifice becomes a sacred duty. It is readily intelligible that for a long time there was a reluctance to admit this fact. Sacrifice appeared to form such an integral part of the religion of Israel that it was *a priori* declared to be impossible that the prophets could have carried on a polemic against it. And so it is a favourite subterfuge still to say that the prophets never polemize against the offerings *per se*, but only against offerings that are presented hypocritically, without repentance and a right disposition, with blood-stained hands; against the *opera operata* of the carnally-minded, half-heathen mass of the people. But such an interpretation is made possible only by doing violence to the clear language of the passages in question. When, in Am 5[25], Jahweh, after very warmly repudiating the offerings of Israel (v.[21ff.]), asks, 'Did ye bring unto me sacrifices and offerings in the wilderness forty years?' He evidently expects the answer, No. And the practical application is equally self-evident: if Jahweh could do without their offerings then, He does not need them now. In like manner, it is perfectly futile to read out of Hos 6[6] anything else than a categorical rejection of sacrifice: 'For I have pleasure in mercy and not in sacrifice, in the knowledge of

* That this did not imply such a mechanically conceived concentration of the sacrificial cultus as if only the *one* altar of burnt-offering could serve as a legitimate place of sacrifice, is shown by 1 K 8[64] (D), where we read that Solomon consecrated the whole of the middle court because the brazen altar was too small for the multitude of offerings at the dedication of the temple.

God and not in burnt-offerings!'* With regard to Is $1^{11\mathrm{f.}}$ it has been maintained with some appearance of plausibility that the flat rejection there of offerings and festivals is intended to apply only to the false worship, which is coupled with a sinful disposition. But any one who reads the whole passage carefully must pronounce it impossible that the prophet, after the burning words (v.$^{16\mathrm{f.}}$), in which he impresses upon his hearers what are the real demands of God, could still have left room for the exhortation: 'And then come and bring your offerings!' On the contrary, once they have cleansed themselves, once they have helped the widow and the orphan to their rights, *then* they have done what God asks of them, and there need be no word of sacrifice. The very same meaning attaches to the words of Micah ($6^{6-8}$). The people are still under the delusion that it may be possible by multiplying their offerings—in an extreme case by perhaps giving up even their firstborn son—to atone for their sin, and thus, as it were, compel the favour of Jahweh. But the prophet does not go on to answer the questions put by those who are so deluded. In this way he gives it to be clearly understood that they are questions that are not worth discussing. Instead he points them to the requirements of God which were made known to them long ago, and in which everything is comprehended that is well-pleasing to God—namely, to do justly, and to show love, and to walk humbly with their God. Alongside of this threefold command there is plainly no room for requiring any outward services. Much about the same time, if not somewhat later (for the *tĕrāphîm* are already reckoned among the apparatus of idolatry), we may place 1 S $15^{22\mathrm{f.}}$. It is true that here obedience is only declared to be better than sacrifice, and disobedience put on the same level as idolatry. But the whole tone of the statement leaves no doubt that we are listening to the words of a narrator who has penetrated deeply into the thoughts of the true prophets of Jahweh, and who shares their conviction of the utter worthlessness of outward offerings.

A final testimony, and that of the strongest kind, to this judgment of the sacrificial cultus is found in Jeremiah. Already in $6^{20\mathrm{f.}}$ the prophet combats the notion that Jahweh has any pleasure either in the incense of Saba and the costly cane from a distant land, or in the burnt-offerings and slain beasts of the people. Still his language here might be explained as amounting only to a rejection of sacrifice as a hypocritical *opus operatum.* But when, in $7^{21}$, Jahweh says, 'Add your burnt-offerings unto your sacrifices, and eat ye flesh,' this can mean only that it is to Him a matter of pure indifference whether they themselves eat not only the sacrificial meals but the burnt-offerings (which, according to very ancient custom, had to be wholly consumed by fire). And when He goes on (v.$^{22}$) to say, 'For I spake not unto your fathers, nor commanded them in the day that I brought them out of the land of Egypt [*i.e.* at the time when the foundation of the theocracy was laid], concerning burnt-offerings or sacrifices,' this is intended to show that it is a complete delusion to suppose that God requires any such offerings or makes His favour depend upon them. Not outward services, but *obedience* to His will is what He demands; in other words, a moral life, for this and nothing else is the meaning of the words (v.$^{23}$), 'Walk ye in all the way that I command you.'

This testimony of Jeremiah weighs all the more that he himself was a priest. His denial that God gave any commands as to sacrifice appeared so unheard of that men did not shrink from the most incredible exegetical operations in order to compel him to say something different from what he actually says. But no wresting of the text can alter the fact that Jeremiah is as little acquainted as the prophets before him with a law-book which issued in God's name statutes as to sacrifice. This does not mean that the Book of Deuteronomy was unknown to him. This book, however, as we saw a little ago, never sets itself to distinguish in principle the value and the necessity of sacrifice, but simply takes sacrifice for granted as a present fact, an old-established custom. And so the result of our whole inquiry is that no one has any right to depreciate the merit which belongs to the above-named prophets, of having discovered the ideal of true service of God in the worship of Him in spirit and in truth, without any outward ceremonies and performances.

We may anticipate a little by adding that this Prophetical conception was not so very quickly obliterated even in the post-exilic period, which is mostly thought of as the era of torpid, rigid legalism. Even Ps $40^{7\,(6)}$ roundly declares: 'Sacrifice and offering thou hast no delight in; ears hast thou opened [lit. digged] for me [namely, that I may hear and obey thy will]; burnt-offering and sin-offering thou requirest not.' In Ps $50^{8\mathrm{ff.}}$ the writer repels as a piece of childish imagination, not to say ridicules, the notion that the flesh of bulls and the blood of goats are to be offered as food to God, the Lord of the whole world of beasts. Ps $51^{18\,(16)}$ insists once more that God does not desire sacrificial victims and has no pleasure in burnt-offerings, but with the very weighty addition (v.$^{19\,(17)}$) that the true sacrifices of God are a broken spirit, a broken and contrite heart. We may compare, finally, Ps $69^{31\,(30)\,\mathrm{f.}}$, according to which Jahweh has more pleasure in grateful praise than in a young bullock with horns and hoofs.

We have not here to inquire how it was possible for these Psalms, with their very emphatic setting forth of the Prophetic view of sacrifice, to find their way into the 'song-book of the post-exilic congregation,' which was at all times profoundly penetrated with the notion of sacrifice as a sacred and quite indispensable duty. Was it that a forced interpretation was put upon the actual expressions so as to remove what was offensive to the later, priestly view of sacrifice? This would really appear to have been the case, in view of the present conclusion (v.$^{20\,(18)\,\mathrm{f.}}$) of Ps 51. Here the Prophetical view expressed in v.$^{18\,(16)\,\mathrm{f.}}$ has evidently *this* turn given to it: all this applies as long as Israel languishes under God's wrath; in this situation sacrifices are useless and displeasing to God. But once He has compassion again on Zion, and has built again the walls of Jerusalem,—a proof that the time of wrath is finally over, and the long-promised great restoration begun,—then once more will He take pleasure in right offerings, then shall bullocks be offered on His altar. The most recent commentators on the Psalms are in part disposed to regard this conclusion as original, and to find in it the simple solution of the problem how a Psalmist could have given utterance to such revolutionary sentiments. But the present writer agrees with Duhm in holding that it is quite impossible to remove the difficulty in *this* way.* It implies the doing of quite unseemly violence to the language of v.$^{19\,(17)}$. A saint, who had reached so

* The usual rendering, 'more than in burnt-offerings,' by which, after all, a recognition of sacrifice is introduced into the saying, would be in itself linguistically possible, but is absolutely excluded by the first half-verse; מֵעֹלוֹת means simply 'apart from (*or* to the exclusion of) burnt-offerings.'

* We are compelled to pronounce completely mistaken also the argument of Jacob (*ZATW* xvii. [1897] 265) and Matthes (*ib.* xxi. [1901] 73 ff.), according to which the meaning is that God asks for thank-offerings and votive offerings in preference to others (in which, however, He also takes pleasure, the teaching of the Psalms being uniformly favourable to sacrifice).

thoroughly purified and truly evangelical a conception of the proper service of God as we find in that verse, could never have sunk to such an appreciation of external sacrificial worship as manifestly underlies v.[21 (19)].

In view of all this, it cannot surprise us that, apart from sacrifice and from frequent denunciations of false worship, the Prophetical references to matters of the cultus are scanty, and are based, moreover, rather upon accommodation to the prevailing popular view than upon an independent appreciation of it. To the people, to be sure, it is a terrible threat that Jahweh is to put an end to all their festivals, new moons and sabbaths (Hos $2^{11}$); that in exile they shall be without king and ruler, without altar * and *maẓẓēbāh*, ephod and *tĕrāphîm* ($3^4$); that there, in an unclean land, where no cult of Jahweh is possible, they shall have to eat unclean food, and be unable to present offerings of any kind ($9^{3ff.}$). But all that the prophet is concerned about is simply to threaten something that shall sound terrible to his hearers, not to express approval or disapproval of the cultus and its necessary apparatus. Elsewhere, too (Am $8^5$, Is $29^1$ [Jer $17^{21ff.}$ is a later addition, probably from the time of Nehemiah]), it is only in a secondary way that the festivals, New Moons and Sabbaths, are mentioned. We have already explained the sense in which Deuteronomy commends the observance of the yearly festivals (ch. 16) and the use of the tenth for sacrificial meals ($14^{22ff.}$). Moreover, this book seizes every opportunity of substituting humanitarian for ritual motives, or at least of putting them alongside the latter: so, for instance, with the commandment to hallow the Sabbath ($5^{12ff.}$); the tithe every third year ($14^{28f.}$ $26^{12f.}$); the year of release ($15^{1ff.}$); and the letting go of a Hebrew slave in the seventh year ($15^{12ff.}$). And if Deuteronomy, as is only reasonable, requires the punctual fulfilment of vows once they have been taken ($23^{21}$), it does not omit to add that the man who forbears to vow is guilty of no sin (v.$^{22}$).

But the strongest evidence of the Prophetical spiritualizing of the old ritual customs is the turn now given to the very ancient and strictly observed requirement of *circumcision* (cf. above, p. $622^b$ f.), when in Jer $4^4$ (cf. also Dt $10^{16}$ $30^6$) the removal of the foreskin of the *heart* is called for. We shall not be wrong in assuming that the prophet here passes a judgment on the value of external circumcision similar to what he passed in $7^{21ff.}$ on the value of sacrifice. To him it is a symbol of the purifying of the heart, which is what God requires above all, and without which it has neither use nor value.

(*β*) In all other instances as well as in those we have considered, the actual demands of the prophets are of a specifically *religious* and, above all, specifically *moral* nature. But the latter are in no way separated from the former. Nothing would be more perverse than to represent the prophets as preachers of a bare moral religion simply because in their writings the inculcating of justice, honesty, and mercy, in relation to one's neighbour, always plays a most important part. Behind all this is the implication that the determining motive for such conduct is to be the revealed will of the God of Israel and the reverent fear of His displeasure [in Deuteronomy ($6^5$) hearty love to God]. It is in harmony with this that, as in the First Commandment, the demand for veneration of Jahweh alone precedes all others. It is indirectly expressed in the numerous denunciations of idolatry, but has also positive utterance given to it frequently (cf. *e.g.* Am $5^{4.6}$, Is $8^{12f.}$). The greatest zeal in this direction is displayed by Deuteronomy (cf. $4^{19}$, the reasoned exhortation against star worship; but, above all, $12^{1ff.}$). Any enticing to idolatry, even if it emanate from prophets or from one's nearest relations, is regarded by this book ($13^{2ff.}$ $17^{2ff.}$) as nothing less than a capital crime; and the penalty is to be executed on the guilty party without pity, even if this should involve the destruction of a whole city with all its inhabitants and all their property ($13^{13ff.}$).

Real reverence for Jahweh shows itself, above all, in unreserved confidence in His wise disposal of events and His help in time of need (Is $7^4$, and esp. v.$^{9b}$ 'if ye trust not, ye shall not stand'; cf. also the *locus classicus* Jer $17^{5ff.}$). This is at the root of the unvarying policy which the true prophets of Jahweh commend to their countrymen in relation to the world-powers. After Ahaz, against the earnest counsel of Isaiah, has called in the aid of the Assyrians and become their vassal, the prophet sees in this a Providential dispensation of Jahweh and a well-deserved punishment of Judah. And now what is required is to keep still under the salutary chastening rod ($28^{12}$ $30^{15}$ ['In turning away (from the wild struggles of the others) consists your safety, in quietness and confidence is your strength']), until the hour has come for Jahweh to interpose and to display His power on the defiant Assyria itself ($10^{16ff.\ 24ff.\ 33f.}$ $18^{4f.}$). Precisely the same standpoint is assumed by Jeremiah in reference to the Chaldæans. There is no resource for the nations subject to them (Jer $27^{2ff.}$), or for Ẓedeḳiah of Judah (v.$^{12ff.}$), but to put their neck under the yoke of Nebuchadreẓẓar (cf. also $38^{2f.\ 17ff.}$ $42^{10ff.}$). How little on this account Jeremiah despairs of the return of God's favour to the nation and their restoration, he proves by purchasing, although a prisoner, a field ($32^{6ff.}$), when already the embankments of the besiegers stretch up to the city.

The right knowledge of Jahweh issues likewise in due humility, such as love to one's neighbour (cf. the prophetic programme of true morality in Mic $6^8$). The latter shows itself primarily in striving after justice at any price, especially when protection and care for oppressed widows and orphans are concerned: Am $5^{12}$, Is $1^{17.23}$ $10^2$, Jer $7^{5ff.}$ $22^3$ (addressed to the king), Dt $10^{18}$ (coupled with the injunction to love the *gēr*) $24^{17ff.}$ $27^{19}$. In general, the whole legislation of Deuteronomy is permeated with a spirit of the most genuine humanity, and thus constitutes, as it were, a deposit of the ethical system of the prophets. It evidently discovers the main value of the sacrificial meals, as well as of the three years' tithe, in the provision for the Levites, the poor, the widow, and the orphan ($14^{29}$ and oft.); in face of an extremely powerful custom—that of blood-revenge—it provides for the deliverance of the unintentional manslayer ($19^{2ff.}$); it claims tender consideration for female prisoners of war ($21^{10ff.}$), and the less loved spouse (v.$^{15ff.}$), as well as for the poor when a pledge for a loan is taken from them ($24^{6.\ 10ff.}$). An escaped slave is not to be given up ($23^{16f.}$); a day-labourer is not to be oppressed, but to be paid his wages before sunset ($24^{14f.}$). Interest is to be taken only from foreigners, not from one's countrymen ($23^{20f.}$). The property of the latter is to be jealously safeguarded ($22^{1ff.}$); the danger of falling from a roof is to be averted by a railing ($22^8$).

But all this humanity and mildness in Deuteronomy goes hand in hand with an unbending strictness, not only against idolatry but against every form of lawlessness. The son who is hopelessly corrupt is, at the instance of his own parents, to be stoned to death ($21^{18ff.}$). In like manner, in the case of adultery ($22^{22}$), or of the seduction of a

* Since the LXX still retains 'altar' along with 'sacrifice' (οὐδὲ οὔσης θυσίας οὐδὲ ὄντος θυσιαστηρίου), we should probably read מִזְבֵּחַ for זֶבַח. 'Altar and *maẓẓēbāh*' forms a good collocation, not 'sacrifice and *maẓẓēbāh*.'

betrothed maiden within the city, the penalty of death is to be inflicted on both parties (22$^{23ff.}$). Seduction of a maiden who is not betrothed is punished by a money fine and the obligation to contract an indissoluble marriage with her (22$^{28}$). Shameless conduct on the part of a woman is avenged by her having her hand cut off (25$^{11f.}$). A newly married woman who proves to be not a virgin is to be stoned (22$^{20f.}$), while a false accusation on this score by the husband involves his paying of a considerable money fine and agreeing to hold his marriage with her indissoluble (22$^{13ff.}$). If a husband wishes to put away his wife 'because he has found some unseemly thing in her,' he is required to give her a bill of divorcement. To all appearance, dissolution of marriage was pretty frequent; it was only gradually that even the people of Israel shook itself free of the general Oriental conception of woman as a kind of chattel. Yet at least remarriage with a divorced wife who in the interval has been married to another man, is strictly forbidden as a defilement of the land (24$^{1ff.}$). Finally, a sort of compendium of the Deuteronomic ethics may be discovered also in the twelve curses of Dt 27$^{15ff.}$.

In all this, moreover, Deuteronomy implies that the demands put forward by it are not (with such exceptions as that relating to the concentration of the cultus) addressed to the people as something entirely new. Nay, Jahweh has from the first provided organs for the communication of His will, in the shape of priests and prophets. To the former of these the following functions are assigned in Deuteronomy: the decision of the more difficult law-cases (17$^{9-12}$ 19$^{17ff.}$ 21$^{5}$); the service of Jahweh in the sanctuary, which gives them a means of livelihood in the absence of a tribal portion of the land (18$^{1ff.}$ 26$^{3f.}$); the encouraging of warriors before battle (20$^{2ff.}$); and the supervision of leprosy (24$^{8f.}$). As regards the prophets, Deuteronomy finds itself involved in a certain measure of self-contradiction in so far as, upon the one hand, it emphasizes the pre-eminence, nay perfection, of the code it promulgates (4$^{8}$ 30$^{11ff.}$; cf. also Jos 1$^{8}$); while, on the other hand, it recognizes the importance of the Prophets, although these were, properly speaking, rendered superfluous by the written Law. This contradiction, however, is resolved by considering that Dt 18$^{15ff.}$ has manifestly in view only one particular function of the prophets—not the announcement of the Divine will in general, but the prediction of the future. Prophecy is Jahweh's substitute for the soothsaying and prognosticating of other nations (v.$^{14}$). Jahweh Himself sees to it that this substitute is always* present; but the only proof that a prophet has really spoken in the name of Jahweh is the fulfilment of his prediction (v.$^{21}$).

Of the prophets proper, Jeremiah indeed commends the observance of 'the words of *this* law' (11$^{2ff.}$),† by which only Deuteronomy can be meant. But he can never have been of opinion that true Jahweh prophecy, the living word of Jahweh, which is as a fire, and like a hammer breaking the rock in pieces (23$^{29}$), is ever to be rendered superfluous by a written Law. Jahweh still acts as He has done since the choice of Israel, sending without intermission His servants, the prophets, to announce His will (7$^{25}$ 25$^{4}$ 26$^{5}$ 29$^{19}$). And only this immediate *tōrāh* ('direction') of God offers a guarantee that it is a true Divine word—an assurance which cannot be unreservedly felt regarding a written Law. It is only in this way that we can explain the remarkable words of Jer 8$^{8}$ 'How can ye say, We are wise, and the *tōrāh* (here = the [written] Law) of Jahweh is with us? Nay, the lying pen of the scribe hath worked so as to deceive.'* If this is not exactly a repudiation of the law-book discovered and introduced in Josiah's reign, it is at least an allusion to the dangers which beset a written code; and hence the latter can never take the place of the living word communicated through the prophets.

Amongst the earlier prophets, Hosea (8$^{12}$) assumes the existence of a multitude of written *tōrôth*† ('directions'); but the context of the passage shows that these cannot be regulations for the cultus, but only guides to a moral life. In Is 8$^{16}$ the *tōrāh* that is to be laid up and sealed refers only to the immediately preceding predictions. Nowhere except in Jeremiah and Hosea do we find any allusion to a written Law. On the other hand, we encounter everywhere (cf. Am 2$^{11}$, Hos 6$^{5}$, Is 6$^{1ff.}$ 8$^{11}$, Mic 3$^{8}$, Hab 2$^{1ff.}$ etc.) the conviction of the Divine mission and the direct communion of the genuine Jahweh prophets with their God.

Since we have already (p. 672 ff.) discussed fully the nature and functions of these, we may here refer to other two points only. There is, first, the very definite way in which the prophets look for the fulfilment of their predictions (cf. esp. Is 8$^{1f.}$ 30$^{8}$, Hab 2$^{2}$, where the prediction is still further strengthened by being committed to writing; but also Is 20$^{1ff.}$, Jer 20$^{6}$ 21$^{7}$ 28$^{16f.}$). The other point is that the natural feelings of the prophet may readily come into conflict with the message he is commanded by God to utter, whether it be that he has a transitory fit of doubt as to the justice of the principles that govern the course of the world (Jer 12$^{1ff.}$), or that he despairs of any success to his mission (15$^{15ff.}$ 20$^{7ff.}$), or that he is unable to suppress a feeling of profound compassion for the objects of his threatening (Is 22$^{4}$, Mic 1$^{8}$, Jer 4$^{19}$ 8$^{18ff.}$). In the end, however, the conviction always triumphs which Jeremiah (12$^{1}$) prefixes to his complaint and reproaches: 'Thou remainest in the right, O Jahweh, if I think to strive with thee.' Nay, in God's sight all human wisdom and strength and all riches are as nothing (Jer 9$^{23}$).

Amongst other organs of Jahweh, Amos once (2$^{11}$) mentions the Nazirites (see above, p. 658$^{a}$); but of the priests, apart from the honourable reference to the chief priest Uriah in Is 8$^{2}$, all that we hear from the prophets are vehement denunciations for neglect of duty. Almost as frequent are serious complaints against the kings. Not, indeed, that the old conception (cf. above, p. 660$^{b}$), which saw in the monarchy a blessing from Jahweh, and in the king as well as in the priests and prophets an organ of the theocracy, is wholly denied. It meets us clearly in the present (Deuteronom.) form of 2 S 7; but experience of the monarchy in general —particularly in the Northern kingdom—as this is very clearly reflected in the so-called 'law of the kingship' (Dt 17$^{14ff.}$), must inevitably have led to a judgment almost entirely adverse.

(γ) There is still one question we must answer before passing from this division of our subject. Do the prophets consider that *perfect obedience* to

* The referring of 'the prophet' of v.$^{15}$ and v.$^{18}$ to a particular individual, namely the Messiah (on which the old dogmatic founded the *munus propheticum* of Christ), is at once seen to be mistaken, when one looks at v.$^{20}$ and v.$^{22}$.

† In this connexion we should not omit to say that the strong objections taken by Duhm (in his Commentary on Jeremiah) to Jeremiah's authorship of this passage, rest on what is by no means an airy foundation.

* The usual interpretation, 'the lying pen of the scribe hath made deceit of it,' would require the reading עָשָׂהוּ instead of עָשָׂה.

† Instead of the sing. תּוֹרָתִי, by which the MT means to suggest the *one* Law of Moses, read the plur. תּוֹרֹתַי. Only thus does 'the countless number' spoken of bear any sense.—On the usage of the word תּוֹרָה, cf. J. Valeton, art. 'Beteekenis en gebruik van het woord Thorâ in het Oude Testament' in *Theol. Studiën*, 1891, p. 101 ff.

the Divine will is possible, and do they measure each man's responsibility accordingly? The answer must be that the prophets know only too well the inborn sinfulness of man, which is connected with the weakness of the flesh. Even an Isaiah must lament (6⁵) that he is a man of unclean lips and dwells in the midst of a people of unclean lips. Jeremiah ($17^9$, cf. also $13^{23}$) pronounces that 'the heart is deceitful above all things and desperately sick: who can know it?' The Deuteronomist, again, makes Solomon declare (1 K $8^{46}$) at the dedication of the temple: 'There is not a man that sins not.' But, in spite of this general condition of sinfulness, the prophets know of a relative righteousness, a piety which honestly endeavours to satisfy the Divine claims. What it still lacks, owing to error, haste, and weakness, is made up to it by the sparing, pardoning grace of God. In this connexion it is noteworthy that, in all the numerous expressions for the forgiveness of sins, stress is laid, not upon a complete destroying of sin (as in the Catholic sense, without which there could be no 'saints'), but only upon an overlooking of it or rendering it invisible, so that it no more provokes the judicial eye of God to punish it. No doubt, we have figurative language here, but language answering to the true evangelical view, according to which the man remains as before a poor sinner, but is *declared* by God in His grace to be righteous, and accordingly free from condemnation. Propitiation* consists in a 'covering' (and thus making invisible) of guilt; and, according to the Prophetic usage of language, it is God Himself that covers the sin (Is $6^7$, Jer $18^{23}$ *et al.*). Other expressions for the forgiveness of sins are 'take away,' 'put aside,' 'let pass,' 'wash away,' 'wipe away,' 'heal'; God plunges sin into the depths of the sea (Mic $7^{19}$), or casts it behind His back (Is $38^{17}$)—all with the same result, that sin is now withdrawn from His view. In all this it is assumed as a matter of course that true contrition and repentance are present, and these can make sins that are blood-red to be white as snow, and make the purple-red to be like wool (Is $1^{18}$).

The proof that at least a *relative* righteousness is regarded by the prophets as attainable, is found, on the one hand, in allusions to such righteousness in past times (Is $1^{21f.\ 26}$); and, on the other hand, in the frequent promises attached to the honest fulfilment of the Divine will (Is $1^{19}$, and with special frequency and emphasis in Deuteronomy [$7^{12ff.}$ $11^{13ff.}$, and, with the corresponding threatenings against disobedience, $28^{1ff.}$ $30^{1ff.}$]). The question how such a doctrine of retribution, according to which a man's lot corresponds exactly to his conduct, is in harmony with the experiences of real life, is not yet raised. Pious faith holds simply to the postulate which must always be maintained by any truly religious *Weltanschauung*, that genuine godliness must find its reward, ungodliness its punishment. This postulate appeared to be justified all the more as it was applied, above all, to the conduct and the lot of the people as a whole, and less to those of the individual. And if, according to D (for to this stratum belongs, no doubt, the expansion of the Decalogue in Ex $20^{5b.\ 6}$), a continued influence of guilt upon the children, grandchildren, and great-grandchildren of the ungodly is taught, as conversely a continuance of the Divine favour, gained by godliness, till the thousandth generation, this is merely to affirm, in the sense of the Prophets, a truth which is frequently testified to elsewhere in Scripture and confirmed a thousand times over by experience. As the merits of David benefit the peoples for centuries long (1 K $11^{12f.\ 32}$ $15^4$, 2 K $8^{19}$), so, on the other hand, the sins of Manasseh inevitably bring about the destruction of the nation (Jer $15^4$, 2 K $24^3$). Deuteronomy, however, is far from inferring the false converse of this postulate that virtue is sure of reward, and wickedness of punishment; it does not assert, what was afterwards the popular opinion, that all human suffering is a consequence of sin, and that a very severe affliction must be due to a very heinous transgression. No less does the prophet Jeremiah ($31^{29f.}$) oppose the proverb (whose currency is witnessed to also by Ezk $18^2$) with which it was then customary to ridicule the misunderstood retribution doctrine of Ex $20^{5b}$ 'The fathers have eaten sour grapes, and the children's teeth are set on edge.' No, says the prophet, every man must pay the penalty of his own guilt (cf. also Dt $24^{16}$); no one can shirk the moral responsibility that rests upon him, and in this lies the proof that the fulfilment of Jahweh's demands is thought of as practicable.

Under all circumstances, however, rewards and punishments are thought of as bestowed in this present life; of any expectation of a continued life after death or of a resurrection there is not a trace in pre-exilic prophecy. On the contrary, so far as its view of the conditions after death is concerned, the latter evidently still occupies the position of the old popular belief in Shĕ'ōl (cf. above, p. 668 f.), although mention of the latter is only rare and incidental (Am $9^2$, Is $5^{14}$ $7^{11}$ $28^{15.\ 18}$, Hab $2^5$). The national religion, with which the pre-exilic prophets have mainly to do, had its interest simply in the continuance and, if necessary, the restoration of the earthly theocracy. Questions of immortality and resurrection concern the individual. We shall therefore first make acquaintance with these at a time when, after the political downfall of the nation, the interests of the religious unit as opposed to the mass obtained more and more recognition.

3. *The relation of the nation to Jahweh.*—How far now does the people chosen by Jahweh answer to the picture we have just sketched of God's demands by the mouth of the prophets? It is a very sorry view that is opened up to us in almost all the writings of the pre-exilic prophets; and one has no right to assert that, after the manner of preachers of repentance in all ages, the conditions are painted too black in order that denunciations and warnings may have more effect. On the contrary, the principle which underlies all these descriptions is that the high privilege accorded to Israel involved an equally high responsibility, but that this was precisely what the people refused to see. They were only too ready to hear of the privilege, 'You only have I chosen of all the nations of the earth' (Am $3^2$); but the conclusion, 'for that very reason I will visit upon you all your transgressions,' appeared to them incomprehensible. The words of Amos we have just quoted are addressed primarily to the inhabitants of the Northern kingdom, like the whole of Hosea's prophecies, and a variety of sayings elsewhere (*e.g.* Is $17^{3ff.}$ $28^{1ff.}$; cf. also Jer $31^{2ff.\ 15ff.}$, as well as the judgment expressed by $D^2$ in 2 K $13^5$ $14^{26f.}$, and the whole viewpoint of $17^{7ff.}$). In point of fact, the prophets show no difference in their judgment of the two kingdoms, in so far as Ephraim, even after the disruption, is still counted the people of Jahweh, and is consequently under precisely the same responsibility, and exposed therefore to the same condemnation for its apostasy and wickedness.*

In the forefront of all the charges against Israel stand those which concern the root of all their perverse conduct: denunciations of idolatry proper,

* Cf., on this subject, art. PROPITIATION in vol. iv.

* Cf. the elaborate discussions of O. Procksch, *Geschichtsbetrachtung und geschichtliche Ueberlieferung bei den vorexilischen Propheten*, Leipzig, 1902.

of false views of Jahweh and His will, and of the false service of Jahweh based thereupon.

(*a*) With reference to *idolatry*, we had occasion, in dealing with the preceding period (see above, p. 645), to show that what is in view is not a complete denial of Jahweh as the national God (not to speak of a denial of His existence), but simply an ineradicable attachment to a syncretism which will not break with Baal (or, more precisely, the baals, *i.e.* the various localized forms of Baal). This, which was the complaint of Elijah, is still heard with equal loudness from the lips of Hosea (2[7ff.]), that is, about 25 years before the downfall of the kingdom. However unobjectionable such conduct might appear to the people, the prophet brands it as adultery (1[2] 2[4ff.] and often; cf. also Jer 3[1ff.] 13[27]). We leave it an open question whether the comparison between Jahweh's relation to Israel and a married or betrothed relation was introduced by Hosea in allusion, first of all, to the unfaithfulness of his own wife, in which he saw a reflexion of the unfaithfulness of Israel to Jahweh. In any case this picture fulfilled the prophet's purpose, to portray to the common understanding the conduct of Israel as something shameful and worthy of the most unreserved condemnation.

In the category of idolatry, Hosea (4[12]) clearly includes also divining by means of small staves (the so-called rhabdomancy), as Isaiah (8[19]) includes necromancy and in general every form of divination and magic (2[6], cf. also 2 K 23[24]). The popular belief might imagine these things to be reconcilable with the worship of Jahweh. But, even apart from syncretism in the matter of the baals, there are not wanting allusions to idolatry in the proper sense: so, *e.g.*, Is 1[29], and very frequently in Jeremiah (1[16] 2[5ff. 13. 20ff.] 11[13]). After the middle of the 7th cent. B.C. the denunciations are directed especially against the worship of the host of heaven (Zeph 1[5], Jer 7[17ff.] 8[2] 19[13]; very characteristic are the words of the people in Jer 44[17ff.]; cf. also 2 K 23[11f.]), and against the sacrifice of children (Jer 7[30f.] 19[5], 2 K 23[10]). In this last case it is not indeed certain whether the מֶלֶךְ ('king'),* to whom these sacrifices were offered, is not meant to stand for a special form of Jahweh (cf. above, p. 646). A similar doubt arises, as we have already (p. 643[a]) explained, regarding the Divine images (Is 2[20], etc.), where in many instances it may be images of Jahweh that are in view.

Amongst the denunciations of idolatry it was formerly the custom to include numerous sayings which are meant in reality for the perverted, unthinking worship of Jahweh, with its strong admixture of Canaanite ritual practices. The sacrificial meals were frequently the occasion of excess (cf. esp. Is 28[7ff.]) and immorality. Thus already Amos (2[8]) complains: 'Beside every altar they stretch themselves on pledged garments, and drink penalty-wine † in the temple of their God.' According to Am 4[4f.], seeming zeal for the cultus at Bethel and Gilgal is coupled with disgraceful acts. To Hosea (4[13f.]) the sacrificial worship upon the high places, in the company of the *ḳĕdēshôth*, is no better than idolatry, and the offerings of the people are therefore valueless in the sight of Jahweh (5[6]). They may have erected numerous altars [to Jahweh], but these have become to them only an occasion of sin (8[11] 10[1], although the last passage might refer also to altars and *maẓẓēbôth* of Baal). On Isaiah's polemic against the multiplied but wholly useless *opera operata*, see above, p. 685[b] f. The people draw near, indeed, to Jahweh with their mouth, and honour Him with their lips, but their heart is far from Him, and their fear of God nothing but a commandment of men which they have learned by rote (Is 29[13], Jer 12[2]). Similar are the complaints of Micah and Jeremiah. But the strongest evidence of the radically perverted character of the cultus is found in the circumstance that such a shocking abuse as that of the presence of *ḳĕdēshîm* and *ḳĕdēshôth* (see above, p. 662[b]) in connexion with the cult of Jahweh (for this must be our inference from Dt 23[18f.] and 2 K 23[7]) was able to maintain its hold down to the reform of the cultus by Josiah.

(*b*) Both the above aberrations, idolatry and the perverted worship of Jahweh, spring from a common source: a complete *failure to recognize the true character of Jahweh.* Only this can explain the people's gross ingratitude to Him who has been their Benefactor and Guardian from the earliest times (Is 1[3] 5[1ff.]), and their false confidence in Jahweh as the national God, who, for the sake of His own credit, cannot finally abandon His people and temple to the heathen, but must at last overlook all their rebellions and sin (Jer 7[10] *et al.*). Very often this misplaced confidence is ascribed to the seductive words of false prophets, who still preach safety even when all the terrors of judgment present themselves vividly to the eyes of the true prophets of Jahweh (Mic 3[5. 11b], Jer 5[12. 31] 7[4] 14[14f.] 23[16-18] 27[9. 14ff.] 28[1ff.] 29[8f. 21-23. 31]).

This false trust in Jahweh is far, however, from preventing distrust of His power and aid—a distrust which shows itself in an eager striving after self-help and in the attaching of value to self-chosen carnal expedients. This is one of the principal sources of complaint on the part of the prophets, whether the subject of their censure be the people's trust in resources of their own (battle-chariots and warriors, gold and treasures: Hos 10[3b], Is 2[7] 22[8ff.] 30[16], Mic 5[9 (10)]); or alliances, now with Assyria, now with Egypt or with the neighbouring peoples as a defence against Assyria (Hos 5[13] 7[11] 8[9f.] 12[2 (1)] 14[4 (3)], all referring to the Northern kingdom; Is 28[14] 29[15f.] 30[1f.] 31[1f.], of Judah's alliance with Egypt).

The want of real belief and confidence in God, which reveals itself in such conduct, reaches a climax in open renunciation of Jahweh and frivolous mockery of His prophets and of the Divine oracles announced by them (Am 2[12], Hos 9[7f.], Is 1[4] 5[19] 11[18ff.] 12[6] 15[10. 15] 18[18-23] 2.)[7ff.] 22[11ff.] 28[9ff.] 30[9ff.]; Mic 2[6. 11], Jer 6[10]). Is 22[12ff.] in particular reminds us strongly of the 'sin against the Holy Ghost' (Mt 12[31f.]), which can never be forgiven.

(*c*) The character of the conception of God and the religious conditions find their natural reflexion in the *moral conditions* that prevailed in the nation. On this head we have endless complaints by the prophets, directed at times against the people as a whole, and at times against particular classes. Beginning with the latter, we find, at least in Hosea, no longer an echo of the ancient sentiment (cf. above, p. 660[b]) about the monarchy as a blessing bestowed by Jahweh. There is no bond of union between these later kings of Israel, who made their way to the throne largely by rebellion or even assassination, and the kingship in the sense and spirit of the theocracy (Hos 8[4] 13[10f.]).* Isaiah's opinion of Ahaz is presumably contained in the statement of 3[12], and the downfall of Judah is ultimately traced to the iniquities of Manasseh (2 K 23[26f.] 24[2-4]). Numerous, and at times very vehement, are the complaints against the heads of the people (Is 3[12ff.], Mic 3[11] 7[4]) as unfaithful shepherds (Jer 23[1ff.]); against the priests (Hos 4[4ff.],

* Cf. B. D. Eerdmans, *Melekdienst en vereering van hemellichamen in Israëls assyr. Periode*, Leiden, 1892.

† *i.e.* wine which they have exacted in lieu of a money fine.

* If Hos 9[9. 15] 10[9] really referred to the introduction of the monarchy, these passages (like 1 S 8[6ff.] 12[12]) would contain an absolute repudiation of it. But this interpretation is, to say the least of it, doubtful.

Mic 3[11], Zeph 3[4], Jer 2[8] 5[31] 6[13]), and against the false prophets (Zeph 3[4], Jer 2[8] 6[13] 23[9ff. 21. 25ff. 30ff.]). No wonder that under such guidance all kinds of vices flourished luxuriantly. Abundance of outward possessions gives birth to arrogance (Am 6[8. 13], Jer 13[9], Dt 8[12ff.]), luxury (Am 6[4ff.]), ostentation, especially on the part of women (Am 4[1], Is 3[16ff.]), and licentiousness (Am 2[7b]). But it is, above all, the oppression of the poor and needy, the turning aside of justice in the case of widows and orphans, that provokes the bitterest complaints (Am 2[6. 7a], Is 5[23] 10[1ff.], Mic 2[2] 3[1f.]). Finally, not only are the people charged with particular vices and offences, but there is attributed to them such a perversion of all moral ideas (Is 5[20]), such radical and general corruption, that any increase of it seems hardly possible. Hosea (4[1ff.]) is already constrained to lament that there is no fidelity, no love, no knowledge of God in the land: 'they curse and lie, they murder and steal and commit adultery, and one bloody deed treads upon the heels of another.' Is 3[8f.] refers to the shamelessness with which, in bold defiance of Jahweh, they proclaim their sins, like the Sodomites, without concealment. No less cheerless is the condemnatory verdict of Micah (7[1ff.]; cf. esp. v.[4] 'The best of them is as a brier, the most upright is as a thorn hedge') and of Jeremiah (5[1ff.] 6[13. 28] 9[1ff.]). Jeremiah declares the corruption to be so deeply rooted that the Ethiopian could more readily change his skin or the leopard his spots than the people their evil course of conduct (13[23]). Deceit and treachery are so general that they find their way into the closest friendship and the most sacred family connexions, so that it has become a rule that 'a man's foes are they of his own household' (Mic 7[5f.]).

4. *The attitude of the Prophets to the corrupt moral condition of the people.*—In view of the conditions above described, it might have been expected that the efforts of the prophets would be primarily directed towards preaching repentance and amendment, so as, if possible, to snatch the people from destruction even at the eleventh hour. And so in point of fact it was. The assertion so often repeated at the present day, that the writing prophets before the Exile announced judgment only, without any alleviation or any prospect of at least a partial deliverance and restoration, is *ab initio* psychologically unintelligible. A prophet who had a perfectly definite expectation of the destruction of the State and *all* the members of the nation, must have regarded it as quite purposeless to proclaim unceasingly nothing but this destruction, especially if his words met with no credit. The most natural course for him would have been to abandon the multitude to their fate, and in the company of those like himself to bewail their obduracy and the ruin of his nation. Instead of this we find that all these prophets, in proclaiming the word of Jahweh, display a burning zeal which finds its only explanation in the aim which they always set before them in the discharge of this duty. They seek to rescue what is still capable of being rescued, to open the eyes of at least a portion of their infatuated countrymen, and to bring them within the small remnant which has been chosen by God to survive the judgment. And so we have the following stages in the prophetic message: a simple call to repentance, coupled with the indication of a still possible escape; then the denunciation of judgment, so far as the godless majority of the people are concerned. This judgment assumes more and more of an inevitable aspect, and appears as a total destruction of the State and the hitherto existing nationality. But, notwithstanding all this, there is ever in the background the thought that for a portion of the people it will prove a purifying and not a destroying judgment. And across the terrors of the judgment there smiles an era of grace and Divine compassion, an era of renewal, when the remnant of the nation shall once more answer to the idea of a people of God, and reap the fruits of such a privilege. It is only natural that these various stages of the prophets' message should not be always found complete or in the same order. Special motives or differences in the audiences addressed might push sometimes one and sometimes another into the foreground, but none of the features above described will be found wanting, at least in the more considerable Prophetical writings. It must be admitted, indeed, that the difficulty of forming a conclusion is not seldom materially increased by what are undeniably later additions to the text (see above, p. 671[b] f.). In the following survey we shall limit ourselves to the rejection only of such passages as are generally admitted not to be genuine, and will reserve for separate treatment the phenomenon of so-called 'Messianic prophecy.'

(*a*) The above-mentioned assertion that the threatening of final judgment constitutes the sole contents of pre-exilic Prophetic preaching has most to say for itself in the case of *Amos*. In his message not the faintest glimmer of consolation seems to shine in the dark night whose advent he proclaims. For not only must we leave out of account the present conclusion of the book (9[8ff.]), but the repeated reference in the visions of 7[1ff.] to the long-suffering of God, who at the intercession of the prophet may be brought to repent of the evil intended, is designed only to prepare for the moment when God's long-suffering has an end, and there is scope left only for the execution of judgment (7[7ff.]). This accords also with the whole preceding message of Amos. He sees the judgment impending over the Northern kingdom in the form of a devastating horde of foreign enemies, whom none can escape either by strength or speed (2[14ff.] 3[11] 4[2f.] 5[3] 7[9] 9[1f.]; in 6[14] there is a pretty clear allusion to the Assyrians as the hostile power). There is no contradiction between this and the threat of exile (5[5. 27] 6[7] 7[11. 17] 9[4]) or even of a wasting pestilence (so, probably, 5[16] 6[9f.] 8[3. 10]). For pestilence and famine (8[13]) step in of themselves after the ravages of the sword. In view of all this, it appears to follow that the funeral dirge,* which Amos (5[1]) raises over the virgin of Israel, is the final word of his prophecy, especially as he has immediately before (4[6ff.]) been pointing to the utter fruitlessness of previous judgments.

The **'Day of the LORD'** is the term fixed for the execution of judgment. The prophet already alludes to it in 2[6], but a more detailed description of it is first found in 5[18ff.]. Here we learn that the expectation of the Day of Jahweh was already quite familiar to the hearers of the prophet, only that they manifestly attached to it quite a different sense from what he did. To them it is a day of Jahweh's vengeance on all the foes of His people, and hence a day of victory and glory for Israel—a day whose coming is heartily desired. To Amos, too, it is a day on which the justice of Jahweh is glorified, but—true to the principle expressed in 2[3]—the claims of this justice are directed against His own people. Hence the prophet is constrained to pronounce a woe upon those who long for the coming of this day of terror: 'What shall the day of Jahweh bring to you? It is darkness, not light'; and it is wholly vain to seek to escape it. Indirect allusions to this day of Jahweh's judgment alike upon Israel and Judah and upon the heathen nations underlie all those passages where a prophetic message is introduced with the formula

* Even the rhythm of the two *stichoi* of 5[1] is that of the so-called *ḳinâh*, or mourning refrain, with alternating longer and shorter verse-members. See art. POETRY in vol. iv. p. 5.

'upon that day.' Direct allusions are found, further, in Is $2^{12ff.}$ in the lengthy catalogue of all the objects that fall victims to that day which Jahweh has reserved, when all that is proud and lofty shall be brought low, when 'the loftiness of man shall be bowed down, and the haughtiness of men shall be brought low, and Jahweh alone shall be exalted on that day.' Finally, in Zeph $1^{7ff.}$ the Day of Jahweh, which is close at hand, is described under the figure of a great sacrificial feast, which Jahweh Himself has appointed, and for which He has sanctified His guests (*i.e.*, as in Is $13^3$, the heathen nations who are to be the instruments of His vengeance). Jerusalem falls before their storming attack, and so (v.$^{15}$) 'that day is a day of wrath, a day of trouble and distress, a day of wasteness and desolation, a day of darkness and gloominess, a day of clouds and thick darkness, a day of the trumpet and alarm.'

Turning again to Amos after this digression, we have to keep in mind two points in connexion with his seemingly unconditional threatenings of judgment. In the first place, these threatenings, if we leave out of account the manifest gloss $2^{4f.}$, are directed exclusively against the Northern kingdom, and they were fulfilled on it practically to the letter. But all this time the 'people of God' continued to exist in Judah as heir of the historical recollections, and as possessor of the hopes of a better future. Secondly, it is not the case that all thought of the possibility of a timely repentance and consequent escape of Israel is wholly wanting in Amos. For do we not read in $5^4$ the exhortation, 'Seek me that ye may live,' and in v.$^{14}$ 'Strive after the good and not the evil, that ye may live; for then will Jahweh the God of Hosts be with you, as ye have said. Hate the evil and love the good, and establish right in the gate: it may be that Jahweh the God of Hosts will be gracious unto the remnant of Joseph'? These last words suggest the question whether perhaps, after all, the closing part of the Book of Amos did not contain originally something of a consoling outlook for a remnant of the Northern kingdom, without prejudice to the condemnatory judgment passed on the mass of the people.

(*b*) Amos, at Jahweh's command, travelled from Judah to Bethel, and, when he had discharged his Divine commission, returned to his home. *Hosea*, on the other hand, was a citizen of the Northern kingdom, and hence could not but feel quite a personal interest, different from the herdsman of Teḳoa, in the Divine decree of condemnation on this kingdom. In fact we are face to face, on every page of Hosea, with the tragic lot of a man who is selected by God to proclaim to his own people and his native land the well-deserved and inevitable final catastrophe, and who, amidst all his acquiescence in the justice of the Divine judgment, is filled with bitter sorrow at their destruction. With him, too, the possibility of repentance and amendment on the part of the people before the judgment falls is not wholly excluded, as when he cries, in $10^{12f.}$ 'Sow in righteousness, and ye shall reap according to the measure of love; plough your fallow ground, for it is time to seek Jahweh, that he may come and teach you righteousness.' Still more express are the terms of this exhortation in $14^{2ff.}$, where, at the same time, a confession of sin is put in the mouth of the people, which straightway (v.$^{5ff.}$) calls forth a Divine promise of restoration. But this very fact shows that judgment is already executed, and that we are here listening to a later speaker, who believes that after wrath the time for pity is come again. Hosea himself looked for the outpouring of wrath as a thing of the future. Like Amos, he thinks of it as accomplished by means of a hostile invasion ($1^5$ $5^8$), which makes the land a desolation ($5^9$ $10^8$; also $2^{11ff.}$ should certainly be explained in the same sense), while the people themselves have to go into captivity to Egypt and Assyria ($8^{13}$ $9^{3.6}$ $11^5$). But, certain as all this is to happen, seeing that 'the iniquity of Ephraim is laid up and hidden [with God for future punishment],' $13^{12}$, it is ultimately only a purifying, not a destroying, judgment that God purposes with him. For He is God and not man, that He should be hurried away by fury to destroy Ephraim entirely ($11^9$). On the contrary, He means, as Hosea has already explained in another connexion ($2^{16ff.}$), by the wasting of the land and the exile of the people to bring about a salutary change: 'The valley of trouble shall be to her a door of hope, so that she shall there [in exile] be again submissive as in the days of her youth, when she went forth out of Egypt.' Then shall the names of the baals ($2^{19.\,(16)\,ff.}$) be no more on the lips of the people; everything that can harm shall be destroyed, the old intimate relation with Jahweh returns again to the basis of right and justice, kindness and love; nor are outward blessings—corn, must, and oil—wanting to complete this happy state of things.

Strong objection has recently* been taken to the genuineness of this whole passage (Hos $2^{16ff.}$). It has been proposed to set it down as one of those later additions whereby for after-generations (especially in Judah) the cheerlessness of an unpitying series of denunciations of judgment was sought to be alleviated. Only in that case we must go further, and (with Marti) pronounce chapter 3 also a later addition. For so long as the wife of $3^1$ is held—and this still appears to us the only natural view—to be Gomer bath-Diblayim, taken back by Hosea in spite of her unfaithfulness, the conduct of the prophet teaches quite expressly that this very wife of his is a type of the nation which, in spite of all its ingratitude and all its unfaithfulness, is not to be cut off from the pitying and pardoning love of Jahweh.

(*c*) The case of *Isaiah*, once more, gives much plausibility to the assertion that the pre-exilic prophets were messengers only of woe. At his very call the Divine commission is given him ($6^{9ff.}$) to produce in the people by his preaching the extreme of hardening, so that all understanding and repentance, nay more, all escape, may be rendered impossible for them. But here, again, we have to remark that an entirely literal interpretation of this Divine saying is neither psychologically conceivable nor reconcilable with the actual ministry of Isaiah. It is true that the mass of the people is hopelessly marked for judgment: with this terrible conviction the prophet is profoundly inspired. But this does not prevent a small band of faithful ones from grouping themselves around the prophet—a band which, when the judgment comes, is to remain under the protection of its God. These are the 'disciples' (Is $8^{16}$), among whom (or 'by whose help') the Divine revelation rejected by Aḥaz and the mass of the people is to be sealed; so, too, the 'sons' of v.$^{18}$ should perhaps be understood, not of the prophet's sons literally but of these same disciples. But, at all events, Isaiah gave to one of his own sons the name *Shĕ'ār-jāshûb*, 'a remnant shall return,' and thereby gave expression to his hope that the coming judgment did not signify the destruction of all.† Again, Isaiah, after his unfavourable verdict on the value of the people's offerings, exhorts them thus ($1^{16}$): 'Wash you, make you clean. Put away your evil deeds out of sight. Learn to do good, strive after right. Set violent doers in the

* Cf. esp. Marti, 'Dodekapropheton' (in *Kurzer Hdcom.*, Tübingen, 1903), p. 27 ff.

† On the 'holy seed' of $6^{13}$ see below, p. 696$^b$.

right way. Procure justice for the orphan, plead the cause of the widow.' These words surely indicate that he does not consider it an impossible supposition that at least some of his hearers may take his words to heart. Otherwise, there would be no meaning in his asserting immediately afterwards (v.$^{16ff.}$) the possibility of a complete forgiveness of sin, and in his giving the people the choice between obedience and blessing on the one side and stubbornness and destruction by the sword on the other. Even a man like Aḥaz has the words addressed to him ($7^{9}$), 'If ye believe not, ye shall not stand,' in which is implied, on the other hand, 'Whosoever believeth shall not be put to shame' ($28^{16}$). The judgment predicted then is, after all, a purifying one—a smelting process in which Jahweh Himself ($1^{25ff.}$) purges away all base metal, so that only the pure silver ('judges as of old and rulers as at the first') is left, while 'the rebellious and sinners shall be shattered one and all, and they that forsake Jahweh must perish.'

Like his predecessors, Isaiah thinks of the judgment as brought about by the destructive invasion of the then world-powers, Assyria ($5^{26ff.}$) and Egypt (the latter, however, only in $7^{18}$ and there coupled with Assyria). A complete devastation and desolation of the land is the result ($5^{5f.\ 10}$ $6^{11f.}$ $7^{18ff.}$ $8^{6ff.\ 21f.}$). All the men but a few perish in the conflict, until seven women press their suit upon *one* man, simply that they may escape the reproach of being unmarried ($3^{25}$ $4^{1}$; cf. also $5^{24f.}$). It is a question to what extent Isaiah contemplated the exile of the inhabitants of the land. As in the case of the Northern kingdom ($17^{4ff.}$), there appears, according to $5^{13}$ $6^{12f.}$ $10^{4}$ $30^{13f.\ 17}$, to be in prospect for Judah as well a complete destruction of the people by sword and exile; and even the tenth, which at first escapes the judgment, is to be sifted once more. On the other hand, in $3^{1ff.}$ what is contemplated is the exile only of all the leaders of the people (as in v.$^{24}$ it is the carrying away to slavery of the aristocratic ladies); among those that are left behind wild anarchy rages, and a war of one against another. The dignity of ruler becomes so cheap that no one cares for it. It is impossible to resist the impression that the prophet here beholds in spirit the conditions which, to a large extent, actually arose in Judah after the first deportation by the Chaldæans in 597.

But we have still to face the question, Did Isaiah at all times hold fast to these cheerless expectations, or is there not much in favour of the view that all the threatenings referred to belong to his first period (say down to the death of Aḥaz), whereas, under the righteous rule of the pious Ḥezekiah, he changed his tone, and, while still expecting a purifying judgment effected by the Assyrian invasion, felt assured of the deliverance of the city and the State at the moment of extreme peril, his idea being that the cruel sufferings and consequences of the war would suffice to appease the just anger of Jahweh, so that He could once more have compassion on His people before things came to the worst ($10^{24}$)?

The possibility of such change is not to be *ab initio* called in question. The notion that Assyria in its overweening pride has far exceeded the Divine commission, and thought to destroy Judah instead of merely chastising it, is so marked in Isaiah (and that too, as would appear, pretty early) that it connects itself of necessity with the threat of a thorough chastisement of Assyria. Only the most pitiful hypercriticism can deny to Isaiah such passages as Is $10^{16ff.\ 25ff.\ 33ff.}$ $14^{24ff.}$ $17^{12ff.}$ $18^{5f.}$. As soon as this is recognized, there is equally little difficulty about accepting the oracle $37^{22-29}$, and in that case the prophecy of Isaiah achieved in the destruction of Sennacherib's host ($37^{36f.}$) as brilliant a triumph as can be imagined. Thus was confirmed what Isaiah, in allusion to the successive actions of the husbandman ($28^{24ff.}$), emphasizes so strongly as a type of the conduct of the Divine wisdom: God's action is not like the working of a *blind* fate, but wisely accommodates itself to changing circumstances, times of severe chastisement being followed in turn by times of compassion and sparing grace. Nor is there any contradiction in the fact that, on the approach of the Assyrian peril after the death of Sargon (B.C. 705), Isaiah not only expressly condemns the arbitrary revolt of Ḥezeḳiah and the carnal measures adopted for defence, particularly the alliance with Egypt ($29^{15}$ $30^{1ff.}$ $31^{1ff.}$), but predicts the futility of such enterprises ($30^{3}$ $31^{2f.}$), the siege and the great anxiety of the city ($29^{1ff.}$), as well as the ravaging of the country ($32^{9-13}$). For the inevitable judgment upon the carnally secure and godless ($28^{13f.\ 17ff.}$) does not exclude the deliverance of the humble and penitent ($10^{24}$), even if this is preceded by a time of sore trouble.

We must still ask, however, whether Isaiah meant thus to recall all his earlier threatenings of a far-reaching judgment, and especially of a deportation of almost the whole nation. In face of Divine utterances like that in $6^{11f.}$ (addressed to the prophet on the occasion of his call), such a complete transformation of his expectations as to the future must be pronounced impossible. The original pitiless threatenings of his opening ministry may have, even for himself, receded into the background amidst the excitement of Sennacherib's invasion, but he certainly did not on that account lose his conviction that the incidents of the year 701 formed merely an episode in the general plan of Jahweh, and meant nothing more than a postponement of the final judgment. And if the oracle of $22^{1ff.}$ should be assigned to the period *after* the retreat of the Assyrians, the prophet must have returned only too soon to his former extremely gloomy view of the future. What hopes he cherished, nevertheless, of a restoration *after* the judgment, we shall have to consider elsewhere (see p. 695$^{b}$ f.).

(*d*) The question whether, in the case of *Micah*, the contemporary of Isaiah, the threatening of the total destruction not only of Samaria ($1^{6f.}$) but also of Jerusalem ($3^{12}$) was the final word of his prophecy, depends upon the other question, how much of Mic 4 ff. is from the pen of Micah himself. In any case we cannot regard as genuine such passages as $4^{11ff.}$, which anticipate a sudden deliverance of besieged Jerusalem; but it may be possible to reconcile $3^{12}$ with the prediction of exile and subsequent deliverance contained in $4^{9.\ 10.\ 14}$ [$5^{1}$] (on $5^{1\,(2)\,ff.}$ see below, p. 696$^{a}$) and $6^{13ff.}$.

(*e*) The greatest variety meets us, as might have been expected, in *Jeremiah's* expectations as to the future. He lived through the period not only of the decline but of the fall of the nation, with all the attendant terrors, and was a witness of all the vacillations between fear and hope, between unbelieving despair and foolish illusion—a witness, too, whose personal fortunes were very closely intertwined with all this. Considering the state of things, it is only natural that with this prophet, again, threatenings of judgment should occupy the foreground. Sword, famine, and pestilence are the means whereby Jahweh means to destroy the people ($14^{12.\ 18}$ $24^{10}$ $29^{18}$, and very often); the Chaldæan invasion introduces them into the land. The total destruction of the city ($9^{10}$), the deportation of all the inhabitants of Judah ($9^{15}$ $13^{19}$ $14^{18b}$ $16^{13}$ $17^{4}$; according to $25^{11}$, the exile will last 70 years), are beheld by the prophet in spirit, and in addition—and here is a new element in the prediction—the boundless mockery and scorn of the heathen towards the people abandoned by their God (18$^{16}$ 19$^{8}$ 25$^{9.\ 18}$ 26$^{6}$ 29$^{18}$).

But, in spite of all this, Jeremiah teaches his people (18$^{3ff.}$) that neither the threatenings nor the promises of God amount to a *decretum absolutum*.* Nay, as the potter can remodel the marred vessel after his pleasure, God can change His threatenings and His promises into their opposite, according to the conduct of a people in each case. Accordingly, Jeremiah too regards his exhortations to repentance, at least for a time, as not absolutely hopeless. By Jahweh's command (7$^{1ff.}$ and, quite similarly, 26$^{2f.}$) he takes his stand at one of the gates of the temple, and declares to those who pass through what are the conditions on which they may have a permanent place in the land. But, as time went on, the certainty was more and more borne in upon the prophet's mind, that all calls to repentance would fall unheeded upon the ears of the hardened people, as in former times all Jahweh's chastisements had proved ineffectual (5$^{3}$). Judgment has become an irrevocable necessity. To this conviction Jeremiah gives forcible expression in a variety of ways. There is, for instance, the symbolical action of the breaking of an earthen pitcher before the eyes of the chiefs of the people (19$^{1ff.}$); and, no less telling, there is the repeated declaration that any intercession for the people has been forbidden him by God as wholly useless (7$^{16}$ 11$^{14}$ 14$^{11}$). Yea, although Moses and Samuel—the most powerful intercessors and deliverers of the people—should present themselves before God on their behalf, His determination to cast off the people would remain unshaken (15$^{1}$). But the strongest evidence of the prophet's perfect certainty as to the Divine resolution is afforded by 37$^{3ff.}$. When the Chaldæans were compelled temporarily to raise the siege of Jerusalem owing to the advance of Pharaoh-hophra, all Judah broke into a frenzy of joy and imagined itself to be already delivered from all straits and danger. Jeremiah alone did not suffer himself to be deceived for a moment, but answered the inquiries of king Ẓedekiah in the words: 'Though ye had smitten the whole army of the Chaldæans that fight against you, and there remained but a few wounded men among them, yet should they rise up every man in his tent and burn this city with fire.'

The course of events showed the prophet to be right: all his threatenings were fulfilled in the horrors of the long siege, the terrible famine, and the slaughter wrought by the sword of the enemy. But all these judgments are not the concluding stage in God's ways with Israel. Jeremiah already beholds in spirit the time when Jahweh shall have gathered the dispersed from all lands and brought them back to the sacred soil, to dwell there under the charge of faithful shepherds, and to have henceforward no cause for fear or alarm (Jer 23$^{3f.}$ 30$^{9.\ 18ff.}$ 32$^{37ff.}$). And when the wounds of Judah have thus been healed (30$^{17}$), their plunderers and oppressors fall in turn a prey to plunder and exile (v.$^{16}$). Moreover, the return of Divine favour extends to all the tribes of Israel, and thus includes also the exiles of the Northern kingdom: 31$^{1ff.}$ (cf. esp. vv.$^{5.\ 9.\ 18ff.\ 27}$). In regard to the Judahites, a distinction is drawn between those already deported in the year 597 and those that remained in the land with Ẓedekiah (24$^{1ff.}$). The former are like the good figs which Jeremiah saw in a vision; to them belong all the comforting promises of return and repatriation (v.$^{5ff.}$). But the others, who correspond to the bad figs, are to fall a prey to the sword, the famine, and the pestilence, besides the cruel mockery of all peoples of the earth.

* Cf. above, p. 675$^{a}$.

5. *The so-called 'Messianic prophecy.'*—(*a*) So far as words are concerned, we have to deal here, properly speaking, only with such predictions as have for their subject the Messiah, the 'Anointed,'* *i.e.* the King of the house of David, who, after the purifying judgment is over, is to hold sway as an ideal ruler over the regenerate people. But it has long been customary to speak of 'Messianic prophecy' in a wider sense, to include such predictions as occupy themselves with the conditions of the Messianic era inaugurated by the Messiah. Nay, predictions are included which do not even mention the person of the Messiah at all, and of which it is even doubtful whether they look for any such personality. In what follows we purpose to deal also with those Messianic prophecies in the wider sense. But one reservation must be made. *Every* expectation of a restoration after the purifying judgment (as, for example, Is 1$^{26}$, Dt 30$^{3ff.}$) cannot be set down right off as a Messianic prediction.† On the contrary, it is essential to the latter that the transformation be brought about by an extraordinary interposition of Jahweh (for the most part accompanied also by violent natural phenomena), and, no less, that the new-created conditions represent not merely a copy of those that have been already experienced by the people (*e.g.* in the era of David and Solomon), but in some way transcend anything hitherto known. Apart from certain fundamental characteristics, the descriptions in question exhibit a very great variety. Moreover, the question has not infrequently to be asked how much the prophet means to be taken literally, and how much is to be set down simply to the account of poetical embellishments, and even of poetical hyperbole.

Owing to the extraordinary importance attached by the early Church to the OT predictions (which were viewed as much as possible in a magical light) about the Person and the Work of Christ, the literature on this subject has been all along very copious. We confine our attention here naturally to such works as have either actually advanced the knowledge of the subject, or exercised for a longer or a shorter period some considerable influence on the view taken of Messianic prophecy. The titles of the following works are arranged in three classes, and in chronological order; we leave out of account the relevant sections in works on Biblical Theology and articles in Dictionaries of the Bible.

I. The standpoint of the so-called mechanical theory of inspiration, or at least a specifically dogmatic point of view, is represented by: E. W. Hengstenberg, *Christologie des AT, und Commentar über die messianischen Weissagungen der Propheten*, Berlin, 1829–1835, 2nd ed. 1854–1857, 3 parts [according to Hengstenberg, the prophets always pronounce their oracles in the ecstatic condition, often without themselves understanding the contents and scope of their words, and, in virtue of Divine inspiration, thus anticipate the whole Christology of orthodox dogmatics]; Joh. Chr. von Hofmann, *Weissa-*

* Cf., on the history and meaning of the anointing of persons, above, p. 695$^{b}$ f. The term *Μεσσίας*, which is frequently used, is derived, as is well known, from the NT Μεσσίας or Μεσίας (so only in Jn 1$^{41}$ and 4$^{25}$; elsewhere, as in the LXX, ὁ Χριστός [so for the most part in the Gospels] or Χριστός [so generally in St. Paul])—a form which itself springs *not* from the Hebrew מָשִׁיחַ (*māshîaḥ*), but from the Aramaic form מְשִׁיחָא (*mĕshîḥā*, the so-called *status emphaticus*, with the determinative ending א ָ, which corresponds to the Hebrew article, so that the name = ὁ Χριστός). The written form Μεσσίας is after the same analogy as Γεσσούρ = גְּשׁוּר, or 'Ιεσσηνά = יְשָׁנָה, and does not justify the assertion of de Lagarde (*Bildung der Nomina*, Göttingen, 1889, p. 93 ff.) that Μεσσίας cannot go back except to a form מִשִּׁיחַ (*mishshîaḥ* = Arab. *missîḥ*) whose meaning would be 'oft anointing.'

† In the same way, of course, *every* threatening against the nations hostile to Israel is not to be summarily assigned to the realm of Messianic prophecy. Such threatenings may spring simply from a general faith in the righteous conduct of Jahweh as the Ruler of the world (so Am 1$^{3ff.}$) or from special faith in the righteousness of the God of Israel, who chastises the overweening pride of the world-power employed by Him as the rod of chastening (so with Isaiah's threatenings against Assyria [see above, p. 693], Naḥum's against Nineveh, Ḥabaḳḳuḳ's [2$^{3ff.}$] against the Chaldæans). The case is different, to be sure, where the threatening stands in connexion with an allusion to the personal Messiah or other indubitable characteristics of Messianic prophecy.

*gung und Erfüllung im AT und NT*, Nördlingen, 1841–1844, 2 parts [attempts to prove that the time and all the details of fulfilment were already predesignated in the *facts* of the OT history of salvation, the *word* of prophecy simply accompanying the facts by way of supplement and confirmation. The types of Christ which were supposed to be embodied in the history were arrived at by an extremely artificial system of exegesis, without any regard to literary criticism].

II. A scientific but critically conservative standpoint is occupied by: C. v. Orelli, *Die altest. Weissagung von der Vollendung des Gottesreiches in ihrer geschichtlichen Entwickelung dargestellt*, Wien, 1882, Eng. tr. 1885 [contains a number of specimens of translation and a commentary on the individual prophecies]; Ch. A. Briggs, *Messianic Prophecy*, New York, 1886; Franz Delitzsch, *Messianische Weissagungen in geschichtlicher Folge*, Leipzig, 1890, Eng. tr. 1891.

III. The following represent a free critical standpoint: Ferd. Hitzig, *Vorlesungen über die biblische Theologie und* [forming an independent 2nd part] *die messianischen Weissagungen des AT, herausgegeben von Kneucker*, Karlsruhe, 1880; Ed. Riehm, *Die messianische Weissagung*, Gotha, 1875, 2nd ed. 1885, Eng. ed. 1900; V. H. Stanton, *The Jewish and the Christian Messiah*, Edinburgh, 1886 [successfully maintains that the Jewish Messianic expectation had not yet attained to the full contents of the Christian idea of the Messiah, which was based upon a deeper knowledge of His nature and functions]; H. Hackmann, *Die Zukunftserwartung des Jesaja*, Göttingen, 1893; P. Volz, *Die vorexilische Jahweprophetie und der Messias*, Göttingen, 1897 [seeks, by the aid of very bold literary criticism, to prove that the Messianic idea is foreign to the character of pre-exilic prophecy, and makes its first appearance in Ezekiel. Even there it is held to be not a derivative of the spirit of pre-exilic prophecy, which was pre-eminently a preaching of judgment and a call to repentance, but a concession by Ezekiel to the national and particularistic sentiments of the Jewish popular mind—in opposition to his ordinary viewpoint]; H. Hühn, *Die Messianischen Weissagungen des israelitischen und jüdischen Volks bis zu den Targumen*, Freiburg i. B., part i., 1898 [a concise but very able handling of the subject; part ii., Tübingen, 1900, deals with the OT citations and allusions that occur in the NT]; G. Nowack, *Die Zukunftshoffnungen Israels in der assyrischen Zeit*, Tübingen, 1902; A. B. Davidson, *Old Testament Prophecy*, Edinburgh, 1903 [a posthumous work edited by J. A. Paterson].

One of the principal difficulties in this connexion is occasioned by questions of literary criticism. The authenticity of those prophecies, especially the Isaianic ones, in which a personal Messiah is spoken of, has recently been powerfully assailed by Hackmann (see above), Cheyne, and others; and, although the last word may not have been spoken on all the sections in question, there is scarcely a single passage which does not labour under serious difficulties in regard either to its contents or its language.

(*b*) In view of what has been said, it is only under reserve that we commence our examination of strictly Messianic prophecies with—

(*a*) Is $7^{14}$.—According to the presently prevailing opinion, indeed, this so-called Immanuel-prophecy would have to be left quite out of account in our discussion. The prophet, we are told, meant to say nothing more than that any boy born within a short time from then might receive from his mother the name 'God with us,' in allusion to the quickly following deliverance from the foes that were then threatening Judah. The 'sign' which Ahaz had disdained, and which the prophet now announces to him in the name of his God, is held to consist simply in the name 'Immanuel,' neither the person of the young woman (עַלְמָה) nor that of the boy being of any importance. We cannot help feeling, however, that this interpretation overlooks in its haste two serious objections. In the first place, is it possible that the confirmatory sign announced so solemnly by Isaiah should have consisted merely in affirming, by the name given to any boy, the deliverance of Judah? Would not the logic of this prophetical announcement simply come to this: 'The deliverance will take place as surely as it will take place'? Secondly, is it possible in Is $8^8$ to rest content with the explanation that the expression, 'thy land, O Immanuel,' is intended to refer to the home of that casual, purely *imaginary* boy, who may receive the name? But if, in view of these difficulties, the ancient Messianic interpretation of Is $7^{14}$ is still entitled to serious regard, a number of concessions must be made. First of all, it must be admitted that the prophet expected the advent of the Messiah, not merely within the period of Assyrian world-empire but in the immediate future; and consequently that he was mistaken on this point. Secondly, his announcement of Immanuel as the Messiah and as the Deliverer is intelligible only on the assumption that he could confidently take it for granted that his hearers were familiar with the *theologumenon* of the Messiah. Otherwise, his mode of expression would be so obscure and enigmatic that scarcely any one could have understood him. Now, it is quite conceivable that an ancient Divine oracle regarding the perpetual duration of the Davidic dynasty, such as doubtless underlies the present recension of 2 S 7 (cf. especially v.[14]), may have already become transformed in the popular belief into the expectation of *one* ideal ruler of David's family, and that this expectation always prevailed more powerfully when the nation saw itself menaced by any serious danger. The prophet could then without anything further count upon the intelligence of his hearers, if he simply alluded to that expectation. All this does not indeed answer the question how it comes to pass that the prophet never again recurs to this *theologumenon* of the Messiah, even in a case where (as amidst the sore distress caused by Assyria in the year 701) this procedure would have been most natural. Are we to hold with some that Isaiah afterwards abandoned his Messianic expectations and attributed to Jahweh alone all the functions of the Messiah; or even that, in the matter of his expectations as to the future, we must distinguish not two but three, or even four, periods?* Such a notion is contradicted by all that we are really able to learn of the personality of Isaiah. All the more weight, indeed, thus attaches to the circumstance that, subsequent to $8^{8.10}$, he never returns to the subject of Immanuel.

(*β*) Is $9^{1-6}$ and $11^{1-9}$.—The same difficulty arises, of course, in estimating the two great, undoubtedly Messianic prophecies, Is $9^{1-6}$ and $11^{1-9}$ [the secondary character of $11^{10ff.}$ is now pretty generally acknowledged]. It is no objection to Isaiah's authorship that in $9^1$ the circumstances of the Exile appear to be presupposed, and that in $11^1$ the stock of David seems to be reduced to a mere stump. For it lay quite within the range of true Jahweh prophetism that Isaiah should be transported by the spirit of God into these very future conditions—a result which would not at all impair his connexion with the present. Again, as regards the further features of the prediction of $9^{1ff.}$, namely, the hope of a brilliant victory, whereby *Jahweh* breaks the yoke of the enemy (v.[3]), the burning of all instruments of war (v.[4]), the righteous and peaceful rule of the descendant of David (for such is certainly intended) over the kingdom of David restored to its old extent,—all these are expectations which an Isaiah may quite well have cherished. Nor is any stumbling-block occasioned by the names by which God (v.[5]) calls the Messiah, provided one does not render אֵל גִּבּוֹר 'hero God,' but finds in it an epithet='god of a hero,' *i.e.* 'Godlike hero': an absolute predication of Godhead, even in the case of the Messiah, would be inconceivable in the OT.† But it *is* an undeniable difficulty that

* Two periods (the first from 736–724) are assumed by Guthe (*Das Zukunftsbild des Jesaja*, Leipzig, 1885); a 'threefold picture of the future' by Giesebrecht (*Beiträge zur Jesajakritik*, Göttingen, 1890, p. 70 ff.); a fourfold one by Meinhold (*Studien zur israel. Religionsgeschichte*: i. 'Der heilige Rest,' Bonn, 1903).

† Rabbinical exegesis, as is well known, gets over the difficulty by taking the first three (or at least two) titles as subjects, Divine names in apposition with the 'He' of 'and He calls,' so that only the last title (or at most the last two) belongs to the Messiah.

the announcement of the Messiah is conveyed by such enigmatic expressions as 'a child' or 'a son' without any more specific explanation—a manner of procedure which indeed reminds us of the purposely obscure manner of speech of the later prophecy, which is already on the point of passing into apocalyptic. The same cannot be said of 11$^{1ff.}$. The fresh shoot from the stump of Jesse could not be misunderstood by any one, and as little could this be the case with the beautiful description of the righteous sway that he is to exercise in virtue of his extraordinary endowment with the spirit of Jahweh, with its many-sided influences. The whole prediction is indeed dominated by religious points of view, but the ideal picture of the theocracy is yet far from that of a priestly State under the dominion of a written law. On the contrary, the expectation in question moves quite within the sphere of ideas that strike us as perfectly natural to a prophet of the 8th cent., looking to the historical experiences of the past and to the conditions of his own time. Even the appended description (v.$^{6ff.}$) of the paradisaic peace that reigns among wild animals could be pronounced Utopian and derived from the later apocalyptic only if in v.$^{9}$ the animals had attributed to them a share in the universal knowledge of God which marks the Messianic age. If this latter piece of (certainly unjustified) exegesis be rejected, all that remains is a highly poetical carrying out of the true Prophetical notion that even the external course of nature and the changes it undergoes stand in the closest connexion with the fortunes of the people of God, whether their fall or their rising again. In view of all this, it is quite intelligible that even so radical a critic as Duhm holds to the authenticity of 9$^{1-6}$ and 11$^{1-9}$; and we should readily subscribe unreservedly to this view, if the question were first answered how such express and strong expectations of a personal Messiah could possibly find no echo in the later oracles of Isaiah.

(γ) Mic 5$^{1ff.}$.—New difficulties are raised by the Messianic prophecy of Mic 5$^{1ff.}$. These do not lie in the seemingly magical prediction that Bethlehem is to be the place from which the Messiah is to come forth. For (as in Is 11$^{1}$) all that is meant by this is plainly nothing more than that the Davidic dynasty must first be reduced to the pre-Davidic conditions before the Messiah can make His appearance. Again, the reference to the remote antiquity * from which the origin of the Messiah dates, would tell against Micah's authorship only if the allusion were to the time when David first came upon the scene and not rather to the primeval resolution of Jahweh to send the Messiah. But our difficulties do begin with v.$^{2}$. Are we to hold that Micah, with an eye upon the prophecy (which he interpreted in a Messianic sense) of his contemporary Isaiah (Is 7$^{14}$), used the peculiarly veiled expression 'till the time when one who is to bear shall have brought forth'? When the hope is expressed of the return of the *residue* of his countrymen along with the Israelites (v.$^{3b}$), is not the return of a portion already presupposed (and thus not predicted)? And does not the announcement that the Messiah shall be great 'even to the ends of the earth' already recall the late *theologumenon* of the world-empire of Israel under the Messiah? All these are questions which still wait for a satisfying answer. But the main difficulty here, again, is that so sharply defined a Messianic expectation should apparently have passed again into oblivion both with Micah himself and with the prophets who succeeded him.

(δ) Jer 23$^{5ff.}$.—In view of all that has been said, it might not be an impossible supposition that the real starting-point of the expectation of a personal Messiah is to be found in Jer 23$^{5ff.}$, the prophecy of the 'righteous shoot' of David.* He is called the 'righteous shoot' because, unlike David's descendants in the time of Jeremiah, He will correspond to the ideal of a Davidic ruler. But the little that Jeremiah says about Him (that He will rule wisely and justly, that under Him Judah and Israel shall be saved and dwell secure) implies no very extraordinary fortunes or attributes of the subject of the prophecy; so that the question might almost be asked whether the concept of 'Messiah' is applicable at all to Jeremiah's 'righteous shoot.' Nor are we carried any further by the name given Him in v.$^{6}$ 'Jahweh is our righteousness,' especially as it is exegetically uncertain whether this name is intended for the Messiah and not rather for the land and the people: in the late imitation of our passage in 33$^{16}$ the same name is bestowed upon Jerusalem. But, even if Jeremiah means by the 'righteous shoot' the Messiah in the narrower sense, he by no means thinks of *a single* descendant of David who lives and reigns for ever. For already in v.$^{4}$ he promises *shepherds* to feed the people when they are collected again, that is to say, he expects a succession of righteous descendants of David, as the author of Jer 33$^{17}$ already understood him to do. This would not indeed exclude the supposition that the shoot of David who first arises and inaugurates the great revolution was thought of as the Messiah in the narrower sense; but a closer examination of the passage shows that the idea of the personal Messiah does not come so prominently forward as to be capable of being regarded as a landmark in the history of Messianic prophecy.

(*c*) The Messianic prophecies in the wider sense which are attributed to pre-exilic prophets, stand in urgent need of careful sifting. Many of them are encumbered with serious difficulties as to their authenticity, and hence had better be reserved for treatment at a later stage. Others are based upon the expectation of a *natural* course of things, and hence lack the marks of true Messianic prophecy mentioned above (p. 694$^{b}$). To this category belong—

(*α*) Is 7$^{3}$.—A certain expectation is here embodied in the name given by Isaiah to his son, *Shĕ'ār-jāshûb*, 'a remnant † shall return.' The underlying notion is that the impenitent mass of the people shall be involved in destruction on Jahweh's day of judgment, but that a small number of godly ones shall survive the judgment, and, under a regenerated political constitution, lead a life well-pleasing to God. So also the closing words of 6$^{13}$ 'and a holy seed shall be the stump [of the tenth that survives at the end of the first judgment],' ‡ may be understood to mean simply that the survivors are to form the stock of a population of Judah 'consecrated' to Jahweh, *i.e.* truly belonging to Him. The additional idea that their conversion and deliverance as well as the forming of the new political constitution are to be brought about by a miraculous interposition and extraordinary measures on the part of Jahweh, could be supplied from the above-noticed prophecies of a personal Messiah, only if the latter certainly emanated from Isaiah.

(*β*) Hos 2$^{20\,(18).\;23\,(21)\,f.}$.—Along with the promise of

* Dt 32$^{7}$ shows that *this* is the meaning of יְמֵי עוֹלָם (not 'days of eternity,' as if what were spoken of were the eternal pre-existence of the Messiah).

* The authenticity of this prophecy appears to us (against Duhm in his Commentary on Jeremiah) to be absolutely proved by Zec 3$^{8}$ and 6$^{12}$, where 'Shoot' (EV 'Branch') has already become (no doubt, on the authority of Jeremiah) a *nomen proprium* of the Messiah.

† On the 'holy remnant' see the above-cited studies of Meinhold (p. 695$^{b}$ note *).

‡ We do not forget that these words also [they are wanting in the LXX] are denied by many to Isaiah.

a community purified from sin and introduced into the closest fellowship with God we meet here with the promise of extraordinary outward blessings: protection from all harm from animals (as in Is $11^{6ff.}$), and the so-called 'Messianic fertility'—a theme which, in the later eschatological prophecies, is treated with special predilection and in language of the strongest hyperbole.

(γ) Zeph $3^{11-13}$.—From the period prior to Jeremiah, at most Zeph $3^{11-13}$ can be assigned to our present category. But even this passage speaks only of taking away the consciousness of guilt and preventing fresh guilt on the part of 'the humble and small people,' which, after the removal of the haughty ones, is to be left on the holy mountain, where henceforward it shall dwell in peace.

(δ) Jer $12^{14ff.}$.—In Jeremiah we encounter, perhaps for the first time,* the notion—still indeed expressed in a very limited fashion—that the Gentiles are to be partakers of the blessings of the theocracy. In $12^{14ff.}$ there is a promise that the heathen neighbours of Judah who have been carried captive shall be planted again, and shall flourish in the midst of Judah, provided they confess the name of Jahweh; otherwise, they are to be plucked up once more and completely destroyed. Beyond doubt, we must see in this oracle an approximation to the *theologumenon*, so important in after-times, of the conversion of the heathen and their reception into the kingdom of God—an expectation which witnesses to a profound insight into the Divine plan of salvation, and deserves more than any other the name of a truly Messianic hope of the future.

(ε) Jer $31^{31-34}$.—We do not find that Jeremiah follows out the above notion elsewhere. But in its place he offers in $31^{31-34}$ a prophecy regarding the condition of Judah after the purifying judgment, which goes far beyond the announcement of simple restoration and renewed prosperity. This is the famous prophecy of the 'new covenant' which Jahweh is yet to make with Israel [so that the long exiled Northern kingdom is included in the prophecy] and Judah. We pass over the fact that even in Jeremiah the word בְּרִית does not denote simply a 'covenant' or engagement entered into at will by two parties, and to be abandoned at pleasure, but, in accordance with the *religious* use of the term in the OT (cf. above, p. 630[b]), stands for an ordinance emanating from God and binding unconditionally upon Israel. But this is not inconsistent with what is a fact, that here a wholly new conception of the בְּרִית makes its appearance in history. The prophet himself emphasizes this in the words: 'not according to the covenant that I made with their fathers in the day that I took them by the hand to bring them out of the land of Egypt, which my covenant *they* broke.' And the continuation in v.[33] teaches plainly wherein the deep-seated difference between the two forms of בְּרִית consists. In the first instance, it was outward ordinances [the prophet is thinking in all probability of the law-book introduced by Josiah in the year 621] that were laid upon the whole body of the people, which always confronted them as external, *dead* statutes, incapable of penetrating to the heart and conscience of the individual, and producing there an enduring spiritual life. This is now to be quite different: Jahweh will put His law within them and write it in their heart; and *upon this* shall henceforward be based the truth, 'Jahweh the God of Israel, Israel the people of Jahweh.' Then no longer shall any one need (v.[34]) to be taught or exhorted to know Jahweh, for they shall all know Him from the least to the greatest, thanks to the enlightening that shall go forth from Him. For the latter they are prepared, moreover, by the guilt of their transgressions being removed, and their sins being no more remembered against them. True knowledge of God, as well as worship of Him in spirit and truth, can take root only in the soil of pure hearts.

The importance of this prophecy of Jeremiah's about the 'new covenant' cannot readily be exaggerated. It means nothing less than a distinct breaking with the conception of the religion of Israel as a merely national religion indissolubly connected with particular outward forms of the cultus, and, above all, with a particular land. The 'new covenant' can blossom and bear fruit wherever an Israelite looks up to his God with a grateful and trustful heart. In place of the general body of the people, which had hitherto constituted the 'subject of religion,' the individual * now comes forward with his claim to the most direct personal communion with his God. Thus the victory is finally won over those particularistic features, nay, features bordering upon nature-religion, which from early times had clung to the religion of Israel.

vi. *The External Course of Development of the Religion of Israel during the Period of Pre-exilic Prophecy.*—1. After the disruption under Rehoboam, the two kingdoms went each its own way in matters of religion, and, as time went on, these ways always deviated more and more. Not indeed that there was no longer a consciousness of what was common to all the tribes—the *one* God and His former mighty acts. That the opposite was the case is shown by the almost complete identity of the conceptions and the institutions found in the two kingdoms. Image worship and the localizing of Jahweh at different sanctuaries had the same vogue in Israel as in Judah, and, if Judah repudiated the bull worship, it sacrificed, down to the time of Ḥezekiah, to a brazen serpent, even if the latter had not its place in the temple. Both kingdoms are reproached with over-zealous—only, indeed, external—practice of the sacrificial cult (Am $5^{25ff.}$, Is $1^{11ff.}$). In both kingdoms priests and prophets of Jahweh are at work. The high appreciation of Israel for her priests is sufficiently attested by the eulogistic language of Dt $33^{8ff.}$, which shows that in their claims they were not a whit behind their brethren at Jerusalem. When, again, Jehoshaphaṭ (1 K $22^{7}$), dissatisfied with the bearing of the 400 prophets of Ahab, asks, 'Is there not yet a prophet of Jahweh here, whom we may consult?' he assumes that even in Israel there are genuine prophets of Jahweh, and his expectation is not disappointed. In short, Israel as well as Judah continues to be the people of Jahweh, and that in the estimation not merely of Hosea, who himself belonged to the Northern kingdom, but of Amos the Judahite (Am $7^{15}$), and of all the later prophets. Otherwise, it would be unintelligible that the expectation of a return of Israel from exile and of its reunion with Judah under *one* king should have persisted so tenaciously, and that far beyond the time of Ezekiel, whose strong emphasizing of

* The authenticity of Is $18^{7}$, and above all of $19^{18ff.}$, is encumbered (like that of Is $2^{2ff.}$ and Mic $4^{1ff.}$) with difficulties too serious to allow of the placing of these passages prior to Jeremiah. It may be added that Jer $12^{14ff.}$ is denied to Jeremiah by Stade and Duhm, but (with the exception of v.$^{14b}$ β) is held by Giesebrecht (with whom the present writer agrees) to be authentic.

* It would of course be a gross exaggeration to deny any individualistic traits to the religion of Israel prior to the time of Jeremiah. Such an assertion would be contradicted by such notices of individual prayer as we find in 1 S $1^{10ff.}$ etc. But, on the other hand, we are not entitled, with Sellin (*Beiträge zur israel. und jüd. Religionsgeschichte*: Heft 1, 'Jahwes Verhältnis zum israel. Volk und Individuum nach altisrael. Vorstellung,' Leipzig, 1896), to deny the profound difference between Jeremiah's position and that which was maintained prior to his time.

this expectation (37[15ff.]) is strange enough when we take into account his sternly condemnatory judgment of Samaria in chs. 16 and 23.

2. But, in spite of all this, it cannot be overlooked that a difference between the two kingdoms showed itself early and sank deep. The Northern kingdom had inherited, along with the name of Israel, the claim to represent the proper continuation of the Davidic-Solomonic empire—a claim which finds drastic expression in the words of king Joash in 2 K 14[9], as well as in Dt 33[7]. In the political sphere it might be to a large extent justified: the strength of the whole nation was, above all, represented by Israel, whereas Judah—notwithstanding the silence of its historians—was in all probability a vassal of Israel, not only in the time of Jehoshaphat, but on other occasions as well. But in the religious sphere it was only in a very precarious sense that Israel could be called the heir of the ancient traditions. Everything indicates that the religious conceptions as well as the cultus of the Northern kingdom were far more strongly permeated with relics of the once prevailing nature-religion than was the case in Judah. The syncretism between Baal and Jahweh, which Hosea still found it necessary to denounce so sharply, proves how far removed the people were (only a generation before the fall of Samaria!) from a consistent henotheism, not to speak of a real monotheism. We find also in Amos and Hosea abundant indications of the extent to which the ritual customs in Israel were full of imitations of Canaanite practices.

But yet another element entered into the situation. Israel was drawn earlier than Judah into the vortex of the great world of politics, which turned mainly on the question of Assyria's supremacy in Western Asia and its designs upon Egypt. Now, the tendency of political experience was to produce, not indeed leanings towards the gods of the world-powers as the stronger, but—as could hardly happen otherwise from the standpoint of a purely national religion—an involuntarily depreciatory judgment of the power of the God of the land, as compared with the immense superiority of Assyria, and a consequent depreciation of this God himself. However much in the narrower sphere men might still look to Him for all kinds of blessing and aid, His power appeared inadequate to meet the needs of the people at large, struggling for their existence, and it was thought necessary to look around for other resources and allies. We understand now why Hosea displays such holy zeal, above all, against his people's wooing the favour sometimes of Assyria, sometimes of Egypt: such conduct amounted to a flat denial of the God of Israel, even to a species of blasphemy. And it is easy to comprehend that a religion and a cultus with such a notion of God could be no source of moral renewal to the life of the people. One dynasty after another fell a prey to assassination and the bloody strife of factions; terrible corruption prevailed among the heads of the people and the priests; and even among the lower classes the last relic of loyalty and trust, reverence for any kind of authority, not to speak of regard for the holy will of God, had disappeared. We hear no longer of 7000 who had not bowed the knee to Baal (which is now the same thing as reposing fleshly confidence in worldly resources). The rottenness to which the body of the nation had fallen a prey wrought its effects without intermission. In 722 Israel, after a protracted struggle of despair, fell before the conquering might of Sargon. The circumstance that the name of not a single leader has come down to us from the period of the fall of the kingdom can be explained only on the ground that the religious factor was completely overshadowed at this crisis in Israel's history. Had it been otherwise, the Judahite historical narrative, which still shows a religious interest in the remnant of the inhabitants of Samaria (2 K 17[24ff.]), would surely have preserved for us one name.

3. As a matter of course, the fall of the Northern kingdom was bound to exercise a very powerful influence on the condition of things in Judah. The immediate result, indeed, was simply to strengthen the national religion. Samaria had fallen, Jerusalem remained. Consequently, it was felt, Jahweh had rejected the Northern kingdom, the apostate from Judah (Is 7[17]), whereas Judah was now 'the people of Jahweh,' the continuation of the totality of Israel, and henceforward it, too, came readily to be called 'Israel.' But, above all, the course of events raised the prestige of the temple in the eyes of the people. Although primarily only the palace-sanctuary of Solomon, the possession of the temple must have served, after the disruption of the kingdom, to give a great advantage to Judah, so that Jeroboam I. descried in the halo that surrounded it a danger to the permanence of his monarchy (1 K 12[27]). To the sacred Ark, which now stood in the temple in mysterious darkness, attached the most sacred recollections of the Heroic Age of the nation; while the proud building of Solomon, with its giant substructures, was associated with the most glorious recollections of the Golden Age of united Israel; and the Northern kingdom could only reflect with envy that it had no share left in this pride of the whole nation.

But was not this advantage of Judah, after all, only an outward, not to say a purely imaginary and unreal, one? And did not the prophets find it necessary, even in Judah, to complain bitterly of crass image worship, crude faith in *opera operata* in the cultus, disregard of justice, and carnal trust in outward politics? Such questions are justified, but equally justified is the assertion that in Judah things were different from what they were in Israel. In the first place, the continuity of the Davidic dynasty, the legitimate heir of the monarchy instituted by Jahweh Himself, was a powerful bulwark against political disorder. Once (2 K 14[15ff.]), indeed, we hear of a conspiracy against king Amaẓiah, which issued in his murder, without, however, the continuance of the dynasty being thereby affected. The extirpation of the family of David by 'Athaliah (2 K 11[1]) is the work of a foreigner, but the latter is overthrown with all possible speed by the chief priest Jehoiada, in favour of a prince of David's line. Similarly, in 2 K 21[23f.] the murder of Amon is quickly expiated by the putting to death of his assassins and the placing of Josiah on the throne. If, owing to the prestige of the dynasty, even worthless kings like Ahaz were tolerated, how much more must a distinct blessing have emanated from able and religiously well-disposed rulers like Amaẓiah, Uzziah, Jotham, and Ḥezeḳiah.

Again, the priesthood at the temple of Jerusalem must have ranked considerably higher than that at Bethel and Dan. Its hereditary character from early times, as well as the not infrequent marriages which there are various indications that it contracted with the royal family, gave it high standing and political influence; while the care of literary and, above all, of spiritual interests was, without doubt, almost exclusively in its hands.

4. In this way, by means of kings and priests, at least during certain considerable periods, all the conditions were present in Judah for implanting more deeply the ideas of the prophets concerning God and His true worship. And, what is the main point, despite the presence of many false prophets there were never wanting powerful repre-

sentatives of true Jahweh prophecy. It is true that outside the ranks of the writing prophets only a few isolated names have come down to us, but at least we have evidence in Is $8^{16ff.}$ of the existence of a band of disciples gathered about Isaiah; and to these, as guardians and champions of the thoughts of the master, we must ascribe a far-reaching influence on future times. This passage conveys the distinct impression that Isaiah at that time, despairing of any improvement in religious conditions under an Ahaz, resolved to retire completely into the inner circle of his disciples and give himself to esoteric teaching. It is accordingly not without reason that Robertson Smith* writes: 'The formation of this little community was a new thing in the history of religion. . . . It was the birth of a new era in the Old Testament religion, for it was the birth of the conception of the *Church*, the first step in the emancipation of spiritual religion from the forms of political life.' Still, even for Isaiah there was left in the times of Ḥezekiah occasion enough to make his influence felt in favour of a truly theocratic scheme of politics.

It is another question how far Isaiah succeeded in carrying through the Prophetic demands even in the matter of the cultus, and, above all, of the outward form in which the Jahweh religion expressed itself. According to the Deuteronomic narrative of 2 K $18^{4}$, Ḥezekiah had already entirely abolished the worship on the high places, shattered the *maṣṣēbôth*, and cut down the *'ăshērāh* (*i.e.* here the sacred pole beside the altar); and it is usual to trace this 'cultus reform of Ḥezekiah' in a general way to the influence of Isaiah. But the following period knows nothing of such reforms by Ḥezekiah.† This is explained, indeed, by a late gloss in 2 K $21^{3ff.}$ as due to the circumstance that Ḥezekiah's son, Manasseh, rebuilt the destroyed high places and set up a new *'ăshērāh*. But the whole description contained in 2 K 22 and 23 permits of no doubt that the state of things which was finally put an end to by Josiah's cultus reform had been for centuries regarded as quite unobjectionable, and had accordingly maintained itself without any opposition. Nay, as we see from 2 K $23^{13}$, this held good even of the 'high places,' *i.e.* places of sacrifice, which Solomon once erected on the Mount of Olives for the convenience of his heathen wives.

But if in this respect the influence of Isaiah upon Ḥezekiah cannot be maintained, especially as nowhere in Isaiah do we hear a word against the high places or the *maṣṣēbôth*, such influence is very probable in another direction. We have seen that Isaiah, owing to his conception of God, felt himself called to a fiery polemic against the images of Jahweh. And so it was he, doubtless, that inspired Ḥezekiah's destruction of the brazen serpent made by Moses (2 K $18^{4}$),‡ and brought about—at least in circles favourably disposed to the teaching of the prophets—a general abandonment of images of Jahweh. This supposition is favoured especially by the circumstance that in after-times Jeremiah found occasion, indeed, to inveigh vigorously against heathen idols, but not, to all appearance, against images of Jahweh.

In what has been said above we do not mean to affirm that the idea of centralizing the cultus, which was first realized in 621 through the law-book of Ḥilkiah, was wholly remote in the time of Isaiah, or altogether foreign to that prophet's own mind. Not that, after the fashion of the ancient national religion, he reposed a carnal confidence in the continuance of the temple, as a place which Jahweh could not under any circumstances give over to the enemies of His people. But the idea that Jahweh, or at least a form of manifestation of Jahweh, dwelt upon Ẓion, was familiar even to Isaiah. Even he sees in Ẓion—although in an infinitely deeper, spiritual sense—a bulwark of the theocracy ($28^{16}$), the dwelling-place and hearth of God ($8^{18}$ $29^{1f.}$ [if אֲרִיאֵל in the latter passage = 'hearth'] $31^{9}$). This idea of the 'house of Jahweh' was, however, clearly opposed to the partitioning of Jahweh among a number of sanctuaries; and, if Isaiah himself did not yet press for a concentration of the cultus, this may have been simply because he attached no importance at all to the external cultus, especially in the then prevailing forms. On the other hand, they may be right who discover in Isaiah's band of disciples the forces we have to thank for the first preliminary steps towards the law-book of Deuteronomy.

Meanwhile, however, things had taken quite a different course. After the death of Sargon (705), Ḥezekiah, manifestly with the strong disapproval of Isaiah, had allowed himself to be drawn into the vortex of the rebellion of Western Asia against Sennacherib. It is not improbable that the king himself would have preferred to listen to the counsels of the prophet, but that he was not strong enough to withstand the veritably intoxicated war-party. Isaiah (cf. especially $30^{1ff.}$ $31^{1ff.}$) declared with the utmost frankness how the alliance with Egypt against Assyria, which was promoted at first secretly and then openly, was to be judged from Jahweh's point of view. But when the catastrophe had befallen, when the land was frightfully ravaged by the Assyrians, and (as we now know from the cuneiform inscriptions) over 200,000 of the inhabitants had been carried captive, Isaiah comes forward to announce that Jahweh intends, not the destruction but the deliverance of the sorely beset capital. Without doubt, this change of opinion on the part of the prophet was due, above all, to the perfidy with which Sennacherib, in spite of the submission of Ḥezekiah and the payment of an enormous tribute by Judah (2 K $18^{14ff.}$), insisted upon the surrender of the city.

5. The incredible happened. The Assyrians were compelled by pestilence to beat a hasty retreat; Jerusalem saw itself saved in the course of a night. The prophetical insight of Isaiah had achieved a great triumph. But the practical application of these occurrences, which was made by popular opinion and, if not by Ḥezekiah himself, soon afterwards by his son Manasseh, was to the following effect. The deliverance was attributed, not to the God of the prophets, with His inexorable demands, but to the ancient national God of the land, Jahweh, who, from regard to His own honour, could never give over city and temple to the heathen, provided only that there was no lack of offerings—in extreme cases, even child-sacrifices—presented to Him. That this fancy as to the certain efficacy of child-sacrifice—a notion which was the offspring of a naturalistic conception of God—had not died out even in Judah, is proved by the unimpeachable note of 2 Ch $28^{3}$ regarding the offering of his own sons by Ahaz (in all probability in the year 735, during the stress of the Syro-Ephraimitic war). But what happened then as an isolated occurrence in the extremity of need, what was a relapse to a stage of religion that had been overcome through the prophets, became to all appearance the rule under Manasseh: the old naturalism revived, the whole life-work of

* *The Prophets of Israel*, Edinburgh, 1882, p. 274 f.

† The attempt of W. Erbt (*Die Sicherstellung des Monotheismus*, Göttingen, 1903), notwithstanding, to trace the concentration of the cultus to Ḥezekiah must be pronounced a failure.

‡ The note on this subject cannot, like the rest of the narrative, be the work of the Deuteronomist, but must have been taken from the so-called Great Book of Kings used by him as a source.

an Isaiah and a Micah seemed to have been in vain. Regarding the varied and gross idolatry of Manasseh, all that we can learn is on the authority of a late addition (2 K $21^{3-6}$) to the older narrative of the Deuteronomic writer. It is quite possible, however, that Manasseh did not shrink from an amalgamation of the cult of Jahweh with that of the host of heaven.* But the child-sacrifice with which he is charged, as well as the magic and sorcery and necromancy, and no less the *'ăshērāh* at which the Deuteronomic compiler takes such umbrage ($21^{7ff.}$), are certainly to be put down to the account, not of a disposition to idolatry but of a radically mistaken view of the kind of worship that was pleasing to God. When, again, the shedding of much innocent blood is attributed (v.$^{16}$) to him, this may refer to nothing more than outbreaks of hatred and cruelty in general. But we shall probably not be wrong in thinking, above all, of the blood of martyrs, of prophets, and prophets' disciples, who in holy indignation withstood the abominations that were creeping in, and who paid for their opposition with their life. As is well known, a tradition, which may be more than a pure legend, includes the aged Isaiah among the victims of the senseless fury of the king.

It is worthy of note that since the time of Micah, whose swan-song, full of the bitterest complaints, may be preserved in the fragment Mic $7^{1-6}$, the voice of Jahweh prophecy had been, so far as we know, completely hushed. The oracle of Naḥum against Nineveh (dating probably about 660), lies, in view of its contents, outside our sphere of consideration; while the next prophet, Zephaniah (*c.* 630), already belongs to the time of Josiah. This *lacuna* of some 60 years in the succession of prophets is surely not to be explained on the ground that cowardly fear of man closed the mouths of those who were raised up by God. Rather may we say, it was only natural that, in view of the cheerless condition of public religion and the complete purposelessness of any opposition, religious zeal concentrated itself above all on literary work, in order to prepare in this way the dawn of better days. We should probably assign to this period not only the preliminary steps towards Ḥilkiah's law-book (see above, p. 699$^{b}$), but in all probability also the combining of the early sources, J and E, of the Pentateuch—possibly also other fresh recensions of the earlier Historical books and Prophetical writings.

6. The language of Zeph 1 permits us to look far into the conditions that prevailed prior to Jeremiah's coming upon the scene. Zephaniah commences with the threat of an annihilating judgment, which is to sweep away man and beast. Judah and Jerusalem are to be affected by it because of their prevailing idolatry. But, alongside of the idolaters, Zephaniah ($1^{6.12}$) knows also of men who seek not after Jahweh because He can neither bestow happiness nor inflict harm. This conclusion is again characteristic of the standpoint of national religion; its adherents are completely mistaken as to the power of the God of Israel. Long experience has taught them that He is no match for the gods of the world-empires. It is not then by any means that they deny His existence, but they deny that there is any profit in serving Him. Of what use is a God who can render no help? The idea that the seeming inactivity of Jahweh is due to the fault of the people themselves is incomprehensible to them: 'they are settled upon their lees' (v.$^{12}$).

* The altars for the whole host of heaven, mentioned in 2 K $21^{5}$, are derived from $23^{12}$, but in the latter passage it may very well be Jahweh altars that are meant. Are we to hold, with Budde, that Manasseh regarded the Assyrian star-gods as vassals of Jahweh?

7. Jeremiah, who came upon the scene shortly after Zephaniah, had to combat first of all the carnal security with which the deluded people shut their eyes to the terrible seriousness of the situation. All signs of approaching ruin, all calls to repentance, were unheeded, thanks to the vain notion that, if it came to the worst, Jahweh *must* snatch the city and the temple out of the enemy's hands (cf., especially, $7^{4ff.\ 8ff.}$). In this delusion they were constantly encouraged by false prophets, who sought to heal the hurt of the people hastily, saying, 'Peace, peace,' when there was no peace ($8^{11}$). From these circles naturally emanated afterwards the encouragement to a senseless resistance of the Chaldæans, contrary to the unceasing exhortation of Jeremiah to patient submission, as what was alone in conformity with the purpose of Jahweh.

But once more it seemed as if that indispensable change in the religious sentiments of the people, for which the prophets had wrought in vain, was to be accomplished from another quarter. The contents of the law-book found by Ḥilkiah* had produced an immense impression, at least upon the pious king Josiah, and had led him to introduce this code, and, at a solemn gathering in the temple, to bind the whole people to observe it (2 K $23^{1ff.}$). The circumstance that before doing so he took counsel ($22^{12ff.}$), not with Jeremiah but with the prophetess Ḥuldah, can be explained only on the supposition that Jeremiah happened to be absent from Jerusalem at the time. For that Jeremiah himself placed great hopes on this law-book is evident from the fact that he still, about the year 605, utters very earnest exhortations to render obedience to it ($11^{1ff.}$). At a later period, indeed, the uselessness even of this last attempt appears to have become quite clear to him; for while he sharply denounces ($34^{12ff.}$), about the year 588, the neglect of a Deuteronomic command, he no longer mentions the law-book as a whole.

Ḥilkiah's law-book did not fail at first of outward results. Apart from the rigid concentration of the whole of the cultus at Jerusalem,† it led to a radical cultus reform in general. One is astounded in reading 2 K $23^{4ff.}$ to learn what, up till now, had been possible in and around Jerusalem, under the eyes of so pious a king as Josiah. But it would be wrong to represent the improvement of outward conditions as the only aim of the law-book in question. We have already (p. 687 f.) seen that the whole of Deuteronomy is inspired with the spirit of true Jahweh prophecy, that the service of God and the moral conduct it requires are based upon truly religious motives, namely, the humble recognition of one's own unworthiness, love to God, and hearty gratitude for His inexhaustible benefits. Josiah himself may have been deeply impressed and permeated with these ideas. But the reform which he based upon them remained for the mass of the people simply a royal decree which showed its effects in a variety of external matters,

* Regarding this law-book it must suffice here (cf. also above, p. 671$^{b}$) to remark that, although not wholly identical with our present Book of Deuteronomy, it must have had the closest affinity with the latter. Further, we have to confess ourselves convinced that the discovery of the book by Ḥilkiah was really accidental (on the occasion of repairs on the temple) and not due to some collusion between Shaphan and Ḥilkiah, with a view to imposing upon the king. The fruit of holy zeal in prophetical circles (see above, p. 699$^{b}$), the expression of a firm conviction that only by the centralizing of the cultus was deliverance still possible, the book may have been deposited in the temple in the time of Manasseh, in the hope of better days, and afterwards (perhaps on the death of the depositor) forgotten. Only thus is it explicable that 18 years of Josiah's reign had passed before it was discovered. What object could the authors of the alleged 'pious fraud' have had in waiting so long, when all the conditions were extremely favourable for its perpetration?

† The attempt of Fries (*Die Gesetzesschrift des Königs Josia*, Leipzig, 1903) to explain away the demand of Dt 12 for the concentration of the cultus is a complete failure.

but, so far as the inward disposition was concerned, left everything as before. Moreover, the new law-book produced one effect which can hardly have been intended by its authors, but which was inevitable all the same. The *written Law*, being apparently the exhaustive revelation of the Divine will, rendered the *living word* of the prophets really superfluous, in spite of the promise of Dt 18[18]. The supreme authority now rests with the letter of the Law. It is by this standard that the Deuteronomic redactors of the Books of Kings judge the theocratic quality of the different kings (cf. also Dt 17[18]). All that is really left to the prophets is the task of expounding and enforcing the Law.

The decisive proof that the effect of Josiah's reform was only an external one, is found in the treatment to which Jeremiah was constantly subjected on account of his calls to repentance and his threatenings of judgment (20[1ff.]). The old dogma of the inviolability of the city and the temple still persisted unweakened in the popular imagination. The people, it is true, are on one occasion (26[1ff.]) so overpowered by the greatness of the prophet that they shield him successfully from the fury of the priests and the false prophets, and even among the princes of Judah there were not wanting some that favoured Jeremiah (36[19. 25]); but all this could not check the infatuation of his enemies. Among the latter we have to reckon, above all, king Jehoiakim. With mingled defiance and fear he burned (36[21ff.]) the roll containing Jeremiah's messages from God, as if the final doom of Judah and Jerusalem could be averted by the destruction of the writing which announced it. And, even after a terrible warning had been furnished by the deportation (in 597) of Jehoiachin and the spiritual heads of the people, the activity of the false prophets continued (28[1ff.] 29[1ff.]). King Ẓedeḳiah vacillated continually between fear of the Divine word spoken by the prophet and of the threats of the war-party, until finally his dread of the latter gained the upper hand, and he abandoned the prophet to them (38[4ff.]). If evidence were still wanting that the Judah of those days was ripe for judgment, it would be supplied by the circumstance that it was a foreigner, an Ethiopian, who rescued the great sufferer from an ignominious death. But even the last drop in Jeremiah's bitter cup was not to be spared him, namely, to see that even the terrible Divine judgment which overtook Jerusalem in 586 had remained without effect on the remnant of the people that was left in the land. In 597 they had refused to believe in the real seriousness of the Divine judgment, but after the murder of Gedaliah at Miẓpah they are seized with mad terror, for now they entertain no doubt that Jahweh has for ever forsaken the land and abandoned His people. In Egypt, to which, in spite of all the efforts of the prophet to dissuade them, they fled, taking him along with them, thev commenced afresh the cult of the queen of heaven, and attributed all the disasters of recent times simply to the interruption of this cult (by the reforms of Josiah). No wonder that in the effrontery with which they proclaim these sentiments Jeremiah sees a self-condemnation which excluded all thought of repentance and forgiveness.

If, in spite of all his bitter disillusionings, Jeremiah still expected (see above, p. 697) the resettlement of the exiles in their native land, and the establishment of a 'new covenant,' based on the true knowledge of God, between God and Israel, this is a striking evidence of the unconquerable certainty with which he clung to the revelations of his God. He looked for the great transformation, consisting in a complete renewal of heart, to be yet wrought by God Himself (31[31ff.]). His younger contemporary, Ezekiel, sees in a somewhat different light the further course of God's ways with Israel. He, too, is aware that the rebellious disposition of the people can be overcome only by a new heart and spirit bestowed by God; but the way to this leads, according to him, through a school of iron discipline, which accustoms the people to quite new forms of worship, and leads to the final triumph of the idea that for all Israel's acquirements and actions there is but one supreme standard and one final goal—God's holiness.

### V. Ezekiel.

1. The great importance of Ezekiel for the further development of the religion of Israel, as we have sketched it at the close of the preceding section, could not be recognized until the dependence of the Priests' Code upon his programme for the future (Ezk 40–48) was placed beyond doubt. As long as it was held possible that he, the priest, occupied the leisure of the Exile in constructing fantastic variations on the priestly legislation which had already been long in existence, nothing could be made of his book, or at least of the closing parts of it. Nay, it was possible, as we see from the Talmud, even to dispute whether the Book of Ezekiel was entitled to a place at all in the canon of the Old Testament. But quite a different judgment has to be formed if Ezk 40–48 is to be regarded as a bold sketch of the future form of the State and the cultus. Then the 'priest in prophet's clothing' is all at once transformed into the pioneering genius, the real creator of Judaism in the narrower sense, the religion of the Law, which is the subsequent form of the religion of Israel. Not as if on that account the name of prophet is to be denied him altogether. On the contrary, we shall see immediately that in every particular he attaches himself to his predecessors—to Jeremiah in particular—and that he frequently assumes their ideas as self-evident. But with all this it remains true that, for the realizing of God's plans with Israel and of the demands and the promises of the earlier prophets, he looks to the establishment of a priestly State, whose chief aim shall be the conserving of the holiness of God This last idea is Ezekiel's own, and through it he acquired an extraordinary influence on succeeding ages.

2. The truth that Ezekiel simply takes for granted the religious notions of his predecessors, holds good in quite a remarkable way of his *conception of God*. The zeal with which he constantly insists upon his two main themes—the guilt of the people and the way to its removal—scarcely gives him any occasion for specific declarations regarding the being and attributes of God. Indeed, if one were to judge merely by appearances, Ezekiel's detailed description of the glory (כָּבוֹד) of Jahweh as His sensible form of manifestation (1[26ff.] 43[2f.], cf. above, p. 639[b] f.), and of the temple as the place of God's throne and the place of the soles of His feet (43[7]), might seem a return to long superseded material conceptions of the Godhead. But it is inconceivable that to Ezekiel the 'glory' of Jahweh which dwells in the temple should be wholly identical with His essential being. He himself inveighs (8[12]) against the silly delusion of those who had been left in Judah, that 'Jahweh sees us not, Jahweh hath forsaken the land.' But, above all, it is noteworthy how Ezekiel handles the attitude of Jahweh to the heathen peoples hostile to Israel. Scarcely anywhere * do we find an indication of the reasons for this attitude, or a rejection of false notions,

* It is, in any case, one of the very isolated exceptions, when in 29[16] it is put forward as one result of the judgment upon Egypt that this country shall be no more a source of confidence for Israel.

except the very frequently recurring formula, 'that they may know that I am Jahweh' (so four times over in the oracle against Edom in ch. 35). This is as much as to say, 'that My absolute omnipotence, My absolute sovereignty over all peoples of the earth, My inviolable holiness, may be brought to their consciousness.' Nay, in view of 36[20ff.], it looks quite as if Jahweh's only reason for resolving upon the restoration of Israel was that their continuing in exile gave occasion for blasphemies on the part of the heathen, and the consequent dishonouring of His holy name.

3. The thought of the election of the people and of the benefits bestowed upon them by Jahweh appears only in the striking allegory contained in 16[4ff. 10ff.], where there is clearly dependence upon the ideas of Deuteronomy, and the inference is silently implied of the immensity of the debt of gratitude which the Divine goodness imposes upon Israel. The ethical demands of Jahweh, collected in a sort of canon in Ezk 18[5ff.] (cf. also 22[6ff.]), partly agree *verbatim* with those of the pre-exilic prophets, but are partly intermingled already with allusions to specifically religious or, more precisely, ritual obligations (regard to what is sacred to Jahweh, Sabbath observance, refraining from sacrifice upon the high places, etc.). In his view of the moral responsibility of the individual, Ezekiel attaches himself entirely to the teaching of Jeremiah. Like the latter (cf. Jer 31[29f.]), he opposes the delusion that Jahweh makes the children suffer innocently for the sins of the fathers (18[2ff.]); on the contrary, 'he that sinneth, he shall die' (v.[20]). But the general rule expressed in this last saying does not exclude the efficacy of timely repentance: Jahweh wills not the death of the sinner, but that he should turn and live (v.[23] 33[11]). Therefore He takes measures even for the warning of the ungodly by the prophets, and the latter are held fully responsible if they neglect this duty (3[17ff.] 33).

4. The rarity with which the above ideas are touched upon in Ezekiel is plainly owing to the circumstance that he feels himself in the first instance far more impelled to give strong expression to his holy indignation at the sins and the consequently enormous guilt of his people. Hence his Divine commission has for its very starting-point that he is sent to 'the apostate ones, the house of rebellion' (2[3. 5] 5[5ff.] and often). And indeed it is always the same complaint that occupies the foreground in all his arraignments of the people, namely, that of gross apostasy from Jahweh—idolatry.

In order rightly to appreciate this charge, two things must be kept in view. (*a*) First of all, by idolatry Ezekiel understands not merely the actual worship of strange, heathen gods,* such as he once beheld (8[1ff.]) in a vision, when he saw carried on in the temple at Jerusalem the worship of the 'image of jealousy' (? an *'ăshērāh*) and of all kinds of creeping things, the lamenting for Tammuz, and the adoration of the sun. He includes in the term the whole of the Jahweh cult, in so far as it is combined with the use of images of Jahweh and sacrificial worship on the so-called 'high places.'

The Book of Deuteronomy makes no secret that the abolition of the high place worship is an innovation, which must be carried out with a certain measure of forbearance. For it really amounted to counting every spot outside Jerusalem profane—an intolerable idea to the ancient way of thinking. Consequently, Deuteronomy had conceded to the former priests of the high places at least the right of officiating in the temple, and at the same time commended them as far as possible to kindness at the hands of the people. An absolute condemnation of the high place worship as a heinous sin was thus far from its intention, although it held that subsequent to the time of Solomon the confining of the cultus to the temple had become a universal obligation. Quite different is the judgment of Ezekiel. The occurrences of the year 597, by which he had suffered so much personally, and the days that followed, had revealed to him that the roots of the evil lay too deep to be removed by the reforms of Josiah. Not only from the time of Solomon, but from the very first the worship of Israel, even when it had Jahweh for its object, had been pure idolatry, masquerading first in Egyptian (23[3. 8])* and afterwards in Canaanite dress. The latter is what is referred to by the prophet at the commencement of his great arraignment of Jerusalem in ch. 16: 'Thy birth and thy nativity are of the land of the Canaanites; thy father was an Amorite, and thy mother a Hittite.' Ezekiel's intention here is not to teach anything new about the earliest history of Israel, but simply to characterize in the strongest fashion the heathenish form of its worship. This comes out not only in the two great indictments of chs. 16 and 23, but also elsewhere (cf. *e.g.* 44[6ff.]). The heathen character of this worship is shown to consist not only in specifically heathen practices connected with the cultus, such as excess and immorality at the sacrificial meals, but in the utter lack of fine feeling for what is holy and worthy of the Deity. No wonder that Ezekiel regarded the transferring of *this* cultus to *one* sanctuary as only a half measure, which must now be energetically superseded by a whole one. For, even after the reforms of Josiah, the sanctuary had been further 'defiled'; in particular, images of Jahweh appear to have been afterwards reintroduced and to have played an important rôle (5[11] 6[4ff. 13] 7[20]).

(*b*) But, secondly, the charge of idolatry as adultery against Jahweh includes also courting the favour and aid of the heathen powers. This is clearly the case in 16[26ff.], probably also in 23[3. 8. 14f. 21]; elsewhere it is sometimes doubtful whether actual apostasy to heathen gods, as the result of political intercourse, is not intended. To Ezekiel, indeed, *all* contact with the sphere of heathendom causes outward and inward defilement.

5. In the view of Ezekiel, both kingdoms (Samaria in 23[4] under the name *'Oh̆ŏlāh*='her [own] tent,' and Jerusalem under the name *'Oh̆ŏlîbāh*='my tent is in her') are naturally in the same condemnation. Yet Judah's guilt is greater in so far as she has not only failed to take warning from the fate of Sodom and of Samaria, but has acted even more corruptly than these her sisters. Therefore the ill-fortune of the latter is to be reversed, that they may serve for the profound humiliation of Judah; for the latter has shown by her conduct, that, in comparison with herself, even Sodom and Samaria still deserved consideration (16[46ff.] 23[11]).

6. The special charges made by Ezekiel (esp. 22[6ff.]) against Jerusalem are concerned, above all, with the perverting of justice and the committing of deeds of violence, and remind us strongly of the ever recurring complaints of the earlier prophets. The only strange feature is the emphatic mention of incest (22[10ff.]), which it is impossible to understand in a figurative sense. Moreover, all classes share in the general corruption: the king (Ẓedeḳiah), who is to pay heavily for his perjury and

* There is no evidence for the view of Robertson Smith and Smend, that in Ezk 8 it is ancient Israelitish family or tribal gods that are in view.

* The picture of gross unchastity which the prophet draws in such realistic fashion in chs. 16 and 23 can only be intended, in accordance with a familiar usage of language, to stand for idolatry (a view which is confirmed by 20[8]); and thus the suggestion is very natural that Ezekiel was led to the above judgment by referring Am 5[26] to the Egyptian period of the people's history.

breach of treaty ($17^{12ff.}$); the princes, who are like wolves and worthless shepherds ($22^{27}$ $34^{1ff.}$); the priests, who are forgetful of their duties ($22^{26}$); the lying prophets ($13^{1ff.}$ $22^{28}$) and prophetesses ($13^{17ff.}$), who lull the people into false security.

All this guilt cries for vengeance. A feeling of pity for the perishing people is awakened, indeed, in the heart of Ezekiel by the view of the approaching terrible judgment, but the transgression is too great for pardon to be still possible ($9^{8}$ $11^{13}$ and often). Even such examples of piety as Noah, Daniel, and Job could now effect nothing by their intercession; at most they would be able to save only themselves ($14^{14ff.}$). The judgments that now threaten are only the close of those that have long—always, indeed, in vain—been impending over Israel. Quite peculiar in this connexion is the prophet's doctrine that Jahweh has punished the Israelites for their apostasy by giving them commandments that were not good, as, for instance, the order for child-sacrifice. Only in this sense can the language of $20^{25ff.}$ be understood, even if the prophet in $16^{20f.}$ and $23^{39}$ speaks of these sacrifices as offered to idols. But it is almost inconceivable that Ezekiel should have represented child-sacrifice as instituted by Jahweh Himself for the purpose of destroying Israel. Perhaps he speaks of the command of Ex $22^{28\,(29)\,b}$ as 'not good' simply because it gave occasion to the delusion that God demanded not only the dedication but the actual sacrifice of the first-born.

Ezekiel foresees with perfect clearness the approach of the Chaldæans ($21^{27ff.}$), the siege of the city, with all its horrors ($4^{1ff.\,16f.}$), as well as its burning to the ground ($10^{2}$). By symbolical actions he portrays the fate of the besieged, the fresh decimation of those who had apparently escaped ($5^{1ff.}$), and their departure to exile ($12^{3ff.}$). Sword, famine, and pestilence shall devour them without intermission; the land shall become a desolation and, along with its people, the subject of savage mockery by the heathen ($5^{14ff.}$ $33^{27ff.}$); the inhabitants themselves, carried into exile, shall have to eat unclean bread in the place of their captivity ($4^{9ff.}$).

7. But this casting off is not to be final. It would appear, indeed, from $21^{6ff.}$ as if the pious and the ungodly were alike to be overwhelmed by the judgment—a declaration to which Ezekiel evidently felt impelled for the time by the facts of the case; but at bottom the old Prophetic expectation abides, that a certain number, however few, shall escape sword and famine, wild beasts, and pestilence ($14^{21ff.}$). For Ezekiel beholds in spirit ($9^{4ff.}$) not only the fall of Jerusalem into the hands of the enemy, but also the mark put by the angel on the foreheads of those who are destined to escape. And, further, he sees in spirit ($37^{1ff.}$) the resurrection of the dead bones (*i.e.* the people sunk as it were into the grave in exile) by the breath of God, which awakens them to new life. Those who are brought back to the Holy Land shall henceforward, after the removal of all the former abominations, dwell there secure, and rejoice in rich blessings from Jahweh's hand ($11^{17f.}$ $28^{25f.}$ $34^{13ff.}$ $36^{8f.\,33ff.}$ $39^{25ff.}$). For He remembers His former promises, forgives Jerusalem all her sins, and concludes with her an ever enduring covenant ($16^{60ff.}$ $37^{26}$). He can no more hide His face from His people now that He has poured out His spirit upon them ($39^{29}$). And, as the result of this receiving of the spirit of God, it is promised that the old nature shall have its place taken by another spirit and a new heart,* that the stony heart shall be changed into a soft heart of flesh ($11^{19}$ $36^{26f.}$).

8. In so far as its fulfilment necessitates an extraordinary interposition of God, the last mentioned promise may already be included in the category of Messianic prophecies (in the wider sense). Such prophecies, even in the narrower sense, are found in Ezekiel, although sparingly and with no special emphasis. Thus the tender sprout taken from the top of the tall cedar, and planted on a high and lofty mountain (the temple hill), where it grows to be a majestic cedar ($17^{22ff.}$), can stand only for the Messianic king of David's race, under whom Israel is to dwell secure. By his exaltation shall the heathen kingdoms ('all the trees of the field') learn to know the power of Jahweh. There is no mention here then of the exercise of world-empire by the Messianic king. So also in $21^{32.\,(27)}$ it is said only that the State shall lie low until *he* comes to whom it [*sc.* the rule] belongs and to whom Jahweh gives it. A descendant of David is first expressly promised by Ezekiel in $34^{23f.}$; but even there not as the champion and saviour of the people, but only as the faithful shepherd, who shall feed the flock after Jahweh Himself (v.$^{1ff.}$, clearly dependent on Jer $23^{1ff.}$) has intervened on behalf of His sheep and even zealously discharged the shepherd's office for them (v.$^{11ff.}$). It is only after this that He is to set over them a single shepherd, namely His servant David. That this does not mean king David *redivivus*, but, as in the case of the 'righteous shoot' of David in Jer $23^{5}$, only one who rules in the spirit of David, is shown by the simple fact that he is not once called 'king'; on the contrary, it is said in v.$^{24}$ 'I, Jahweh, will be their God, and my servant David shall be *prince* (נָשִׂיא) in the midst of them.' But, beyond this, nothing is predicated of him. It is Jahweh alone that concludes a covenant of peace with the people (v.$^{25ff.}$), confers upon them security from wild beasts, as well as from oppression and mockery by their enemies, and imparts rich fertility to the land. The same prediction occurs in $37^{22ff.}$ in connexion with the symbolic action whereby two staves (Judah and Joseph) are to be joined together in the hand of Ezekiel. Even the long fallen Northern kingdom is to be reunited with Judah so as to form *one* kingdom under *one* king. But once more it is Jahweh Himself (v.$^{23}$) who delivers and purifies them, that they may become again His people. Now, it is true that in $37^{22ff.}$, as compared with $34^{23}$, there appears to be an advance in so far as $37^{24f.}$ declares not only 'and my servant David shall be *king* over them,' but (v.$^{25}$) 'my servant David shall rule over them *for ever*.' Can it be that the expectations of Ezekiel underwent such a transformation in the interval that he now looked for a king whose dominion should be unending? This is impossible, for it would completely contradict the rôle which the 'prince' (not the *king*) plays in the future programme of Ezk 40–48 (see below). But, even apart from that, in ch. 37 as in ch. 34 Jahweh appears so prominently as the real Ruler dwelling in His sanctuary in the midst of the people and exercising towards them the everlasting covenant of peace, that there is scarcely room left for the idea of the Messiah.

9. As elsewhere in the expectations of the prophets regarding the future, a pretty large space is occupied in Ezekiel with threatenings against foreign nations; nay, it would seem from $30^{2f.}$ as if the 'Day of the LORD,' which had been looked for from the time of Amos, was exclusively a day of judgment upon foreign peoples. The hostility of these peoples to Israel is also, it is true, specified as a ground of the Divine anger [thus we have the malicious joy and thirst for revenge of

* The call in $18^{31}$, in a somewhat different connexion, 'Make you a new heart and a new spirit,' does not invalidate the truth that the bestowal of the new spirit can come from God only.

the Ammonites, $25^{3}$; the Moabites, v.[8]; the Edomites, v.[12], and again in ch. 35; the Philistines, $25^{15}$; the Tyrians, $26^{2}$]; but the main point of view always is that all the splendour and proud display of the heathen is to be brought low, 'in order that they may know that I am Jahweh' ($25^{7.\ 11.\ 17}$ etc.). Hence the longest and the severest threatenings are directed against the haughtiest and most powerful peoples: against Tyre (chs. 26–28), because she has declared herself to be the perfection of beauty ($27^{3}$), and her king has claimed even to be a god ($28^{2}$); against the Egyptians (chs. 29–32), because the Pharaoh has boasted, 'mine is the Nile, I have made it' ($29^{3}$). God is going to punish this arrogance as He formerly punished that of the Assyrian warriors, whose graves (as those of the most heinous offenders) are 'set in the uttermost parts of the pit' ($32^{23}$, where by the way there is the first approximation to a distinction between inhabitants of the under world, and thus to the doctrine of the pains of hell).

10. A peculiarity of the eschatology of Ezekiel is his expectation of a hostile storm of great masses of people, led by Gog the prince of the land of Magog, against the resettled land of Israel, that is to say, *after* the dawn of the Messianic age (ch. 38 f.). Here too the essential point of view is that stated in $38^{16}$ 'that the nations may know me when I shall show myself holy before their eyes' (cf. also $39^{7}$). Neither here nor anywhere else in Ezekiel is there any hint that this knowledge is to lead further to these peoples attaching themselves to Jahweh and thus sharing in Israel's salvation. Gog is to fall upon the mountains of Israel; and so enormous shall be the number of his warriors, that for seven years on end their weapons shall serve for fuel, and seven years shall be required for the burying of their dead bodies.

When Ezekiel ($38^{17}$) appeals to the predictions of former prophets concerning Gog, it is impossible to say what utterances of theirs (provided they have come down to us at all) he may have had in view. But, in any case, his allusion to them is a proof that the pre-exilic prophecies had already become to him the object of reflexion. And this implies at the same time the consciousness that the old form of prophecy, as the product of a direct operation of the spirit of God, was practically extinct, and had essentially to be replaced by literary activity.

11. To this last domain belongs, beyond doubt, the whole section made up of chs. 40–48, which, as was pointed out above, proved of epoch-making importance for the form afterwards assumed by the religion of Israel, containing as it does a sketch of the new form to be given to the sanctuary and the cultus after the return of the people from exile.* Not that even in chs. 1–39 there are no hints at all pointing to this final aim of the Divine judgments, for we find such, for instance, in $20^{40\text{f.}}$ and $37^{26.\ 28}$. But in chs. 40–48 these interests—the reconstruction of the temple in all its details, the exact regulation of offerings and festivals, etc.—come so strongly into the foreground that everything else, *i.e.* all that does not belong to the cultus, looks like a mere appendage and scarcely worthy of mention.

(*a*) All the manifold and complicated regulations in chs. 40–48 have, strictly viewed, only *one* underlying idea—namely, the perfect representation and conservation of the holiness of God, in opposition to the endless detriment done to it in the pre-exilic period. This conservation, moreover, is to be effected by means of a great number of external institutions and ordinances. To be sure, these are at bottom only *symbolical* pictures of the Divine holiness and of the zeal directed towards its maintenance, but strict attention to them is absolutely indispensable instead of being (as the sacrifices were in the estimation of the earlier prophets) merely an expression, that might be dispensed with at need, of a pious frame of mind. Ezekiel is in fact the founder of *legal religion*, the Levitical system. It is, above all, characteristic of this standpoint that any wrong done to the holiness of God is estimated exclusively as an objective fact, without regard to the intention and motive of the author of the wrong. Unwitting Levitical defilement and knowing sin involve exactly the same degree of guilt.

(*b*) At the head of all the regulations in question naturally stand those about *holy ground*. The idea that now the whole land is sacred to Jahweh, finds its symbolical expression in the high degree of holiness which attaches not only to the temple, the dwelling-place of Jahweh, but to the whole quarter surrounding the temple, on the summit of the hill ($43^{12}$). For city and temple are henceforth to stand on a very lofty mountain ($40^{2}$), in token that they surpass in importance every other spot on earth. Any pollution of the sanctuary, such as was formerly occasioned by the close proximity of the royal graves to the temple ($43^{7}$), is now completely excluded. The holiness of the fore-court is constantly recalled by the keeping shut of the east door ($44^{1}$), by which Jahweh returned from the Mount of Olives to the sanctuary. But the whole of the sacred precincts, including the quarters of the priests and the Levites, is a *tĕrûmāh* of the land ($45^{1\text{ff.}}$ $48^{8\text{ff.}}$), a kind of oblation whereby all the rest of the land is likewise hallowed and made fit for use, as the fruits of the land are, through the rendering of the firstfruits to Jahweh. Directly adjoining the sacred precincts is the ground occupied by the city, and the land which appertains *ex officio* to the 'prince.' To the former of these a certain measure of holiness still belongs; in fact, according to $48^{35}$ (the closing word of the whole section), the city is to be called *Jahweh-shāmmāh*, 'Jahweh is there.' It belongs to no one tribe exclusively, but members of all the tribes are to people it ($48^{19}$).

(*c*) Suitably to its above significance, the city along with the sacred *tĕrûmāh* is the heart and almost the exact central point of the whole country; for to the north of it lie seven, and to the south five tribes, the latter—quite contrary to the former historical state of things—including even Issachar, Zebulun, and Gad. The district to the east of the Jordan had been probably for a long time too largely occupied by heathen for Ezekiel to count it as any longer belonging to the Holy Land. On the other hand, the strangers dwelling in the midst of Israel, who have begotten sons (*i.e.* who are permanently settled there), are to be on exactly the same footing as native-born Israelites, and are equally to receive a possession ($47^{22}$). The meaning of this at first sight strange prescription is simply that in the new State there can be only full-blooded members of the worshipping community, possessed of equal rights, but sharing also equal responsibilities.

(*d*) Finally, the idea that the land consecrated to Jahweh has His blessings showered upon it, finds very drastic expression in the prophecy of the temple spring ($47^{1\text{ff.}}$), which, taking its rise under the temple itself, is at first a tiny rill, but after a course of 4000 cubits has already become a mighty river, which causes the numerous trees on its banks to bear foliage that is ever green and fruits that never fail, which makes the waters of the Dead Sea wholesome and teeming with fish. The explanation offered for all this is that 'because the water proceeds from the sanctuary' it has a magical efficacy ($47^{12}$).

(*e*) The degree to which even the most subtle

* Cf. Bertholet, *Der Verfassungsentwurf des Ezechiel in seiner religionsgeschichtlichen Bedeutung*, Freiburg i. B., 1896.

prescriptions regarding points in the cultus are of importance in the eyes of Ezekiel, is shown by his regulations concerning the sacrificial tables ($40^{39ff.}$), the priests' cells ($42^{13f.}$), the sin-offering in connexion with the seven days' dedication of the altar ($43^{18ff.}$), the measures and weights to be used in the cultus ($45^{9ff.}$), the rules for festivals and sacrifices ($45^{18ff.}$; cf. also the complicated prescriptions as to the place and number of the sacrifices to be offered by the 'prince,' ch. 46). With reference to the festivals, it is noteworthy that, as is shown even by their exact dating, they have now lost their connexion with the course of nature [*sc.* as harvest festivals] and have become simply church festivals; for, apart from the prohibition of leaven at the time of the Passover, there is no mention of anything but the official offerings to be presented ($45^{21ff.}$). Very striking is the complete ignoring of the Feast of Weeks, which, on the ground of very ancient tradition, is retained even by P; and no less so is the fact that the two days of atonement, of which Ezekiel places one at the beginning of each half of the year ($45^{18ff.}$), do not represent days of humiliation on the part of the people, but contemplate an atonement for the sanctuary by means of external ceremonies 'on account of those who may have offended through error or ignorance.' The purifying of the temple building from Levitical defilement appears here as the main object to such a degree that the cleansing of the heart, which to the pre-exilic prophets was by far the most important matter, remains unmentioned.

(*f*) Much of what is ordained by Ezekiel may have been based upon ancient tradition, which was perhaps familiar to him in connexion with the exercise of his duties as *priest*. New, however, beyond doubt, and of great consequence is his distinction ($40^{46}$ and esp. $44^{6ff.}$) between those priests of Levi who are also descendants of Ẓadoḳ (*i.e.* who belong to the hereditary priesthood established at Jerusalem), and those other priests of Levi who have ministered to the people in the times of error (*i.e.* the former priests of the high places). The priesthood in future is to pertain to the Ẓadoḳites alone. The other class are 'to bear the consequences of their guilt' ($44^{10ff.}$), and are condemned to discharge all the menial offices of the cultus which were formerly attended to by uncircumcised ones (slaves and prisoners of war). Ezekiel in this way first paved the way for that distinction between priests and Levites which is so familiar to us in P and the Chronicler, that we can hardly conceive of the cultus of Israel without it from the time of Sinai downwards, although, as a matter of fact, it is still quite unknown even to the Book of Deuteronomy.

(*g*) When we turn to the special rules for the priests ($44^{17ff.}$), it is again noteworthy that at the head of their official duties (v.[23]) is the instruction of the people in the distinction between holy and common, clean and unclean; it is only after this that there is mention of their judicial functions.

(*h*) By the side of the priests the *nāsî* or 'prince' plays, as was remarked above, a somewhat colourless part. A head was necessary, and nothing was more natural than to form a connexion here with the historical tradition of many centuries, namely, the expectation of a political head belonging to the family of David. Surprise has been felt quite unnecessarily that Ezekiel does not assign to the priestly State a spiritual head—nay, that he is altogether silent about the 'high priest.' But in the pre-exilic period there had been no *high* priests at all, but at most at Jerusalem *chief* priests. The latter, moreover, were simply exalted officials of the king, and it may very well be that Ezekiel had good reasons for not wishing to see priestly officials of this kind reintroduced. It was quite outside the scope of his ideas that in the new Jerusalem the place of the national political head should be taken by a spiritual one—in fact, by a *high priest*. Ezekiel, then, retained a political head; but the latter is, strictly speaking, only the guarantor for the regular performance of the cultus. It is scarcely right to speak of a sovereign prince. If this *nāsî* has a tract of land assigned to him at the eastern and western ends of the *tĕrûmāh*, it is with the strangely distrustful remark added, 'that my princes may no more oppress my people, but give the land to the house of Israel according to their tribes' ($45^{8}$ $46^{18}$). The prince, indeed, receives a further *tĕrûmāh* from the people, levied on wheat, barley, oil, and sheep ($45^{13ff.}$); but in return he is to provide all the offerings for the congregation at the festivals, the new moons, and the Sabbaths, as well as the daily morning burnt-offering and meal-offering ($46^{13ff.}$). The one prerogative he enjoys is that of entering the vestibule of the east door (which is usually closed), that from its threshold he may behold the preparing of his sacrifices by the priests, and may stand there and pray ($44^{3}$ $46^{2}$). That Ezekiel does not think of this *nāsî* as the Messiah, is a fact that needs no proof.

(*i*) When we now ask, finally, What was Ezekiel's own view about the fulfilment of his programme for the future?, the answer must be to the following effect. A distinction must be drawn between expectations the fulfilment of which was in no man's power (such as the elevation of the temple hill, or the producing of the temple spring, or even the bringing back of the ten tribes), and expectations within the range of human effort. With these last Ezekiel was perfectly in earnest, and he was fully justified by the further course of events. In some instances, it is true, the force of ancient usage was stronger than the theory of the prophet, as, for example, in the case of the Feast of Weeks. Other prescriptions, such as the degrading of the former priests of the high places, evidently could be carried out only after severe conflicts and in a very much mitigated form. But, upon the whole, it remains true that we have now in P a rearrangement of the cultus approximating as nearly as possible to the prescriptions of Ezekiel. Particularly convincing is the evidence for this which is furnished by the parallels in P to the special rules for the priests contained in Ezk $44^{17ff.}$. To all appearance, the priestly circles—and that, too, at different centres—had already begun during the Exile to reduce the ideas of Ezekiel to a cultus law. The fruit of these labours—varied, yet all inspired with the same spirit—was the great priestly book of history and law, the introduction of which gave to post-exilic Judaism the final stamp which it bears, not only in New Testament times but down to the present day.

But here once more the truth is manifested that historical development is not always in a straight line. Right in the midst of the labours devoted to the codification of a priestly law in the spirit of Ezekiel we come once more upon a powerful exhibition of genuine Jahweh prophetism in the form of the so-called Deutero-Isaiah, to which we must next turn our attention.

## VI. The so-called Deutero-Isaiah.

1. It may now be regarded as finally established that with Is 40 an entirely new book commences, which nowhere makes any claim to be the work of Isaiah. The compass of this so-called Deutero-Isaiah is still, however, the subject of controversy. According to the view that at one time generally prevailed, it embraced chs. 40–66. But more and

more confirmation has been discovered for the proposition already propounded by Eichhorn and reaffirmed by Kuenen, that a portion of these chapters can have been composed only at Jerusalem after the return from the Exile.* At first it was thought sufficient to separate off chs. 63–66 as a later addition, but finally it has become almost the general fashion to distinguish between chs. 40–55 as Deutero-Isaiah, and chs. 56–66 as Trito-Isaiah. The present writer is among those to whom this view commends itself as the correct one. It may be remarked that Is 40–66 is a striking proof that questions of authenticity have little bearing upon the value of the religious and ethical contents—or, in short, upon the character as revelation—of an OT writing. The full meaning of the glorious book made up of Is 40–55 could be first appreciated and established only by those who taught men to understand it historically from the last years before the conquest of Babylon by Cyrus (538 B.C.) and the return of a portion of the exiles as authorized by him.

2. The book of the 'Great Unknown' would have had significance enough for his contemporaries even if it had been nothing more than a book of consolation for the exiles, assuring them of the end of the captivity, return to the Holy Land, and a renewed dispensation of Jahweh's grace. But it contains infinitely more than this. From an elevated prophetical viewpoint, which is scarcely reached again in the OT period, it brings the whole preceding history of Israel as well as its whole future under the scheme of an original, all-wise, saving purpose of Jahweh, which has for its object the whole world of nations. The barriers of national religion are here completely burst, and the foundation laid for a universal religion, and all this without the old Prophetic ideas of the election and pre-eminence of Israel being given up. How these two apparently heterogeneous notions could be united, will have to be shown afterwards. The whole, solitary glory of Deutero-Isaiah we shall best appreciate if we compare it with Ezekiel or the nearly contemporaneous passages Dt $4^{19f.}$ and $32^{8}$. In Ezekiel's future expectations there was no room for any share of the heathen in the salvation of Israel. In Dt $4^{19f.}$, again, the view is stated without any circumlocution that Jahweh has destined the heathen to serve the star-gods (*i.e.* practically condemned them to idolatry), whereas He has chosen Israel to be *His own* possession. Quite the same notion is expressed in Dt $32^{8}$ 'Jahweh fixed the bounds of the peoples according to the number of the gods' [בְּנֵי אֱלֹהִים, LXX ἀγγέλων θεοῦ, MT wrongly בְּנֵי יִשְׂרָאֵל], *i.e.* He assigned to each of the (subordinate) gods a particular people, whereas He declared Israel to be His own heritage.

3. We have just described Deutero-Isaiah's fundamental notion of a Divine purpose of salvation, which is at present becoming plain—a purpose which includes all nations, and which at the same time solves all the enigmas of Israel's history. It is primarily under this notion that we must subsume all the declarations from which our prophet's very lofty *conception of God* may be gathered. An absolutely harmonious plan of the Universe implies the solity of God. Absolute monotheism here reaches its clearest and sharpest expression ($43^{10f.}$ $44^{6.8}$ $45^{5f.14.18}$). The continuous fulfilment of the plan presupposes His eternity ($41^{4}$ $44^{6}$), unchangeableness ($41^{4}$ $43^{13}$), and always equally full power ($40^{28ff.}$). God's omnipotence is proved, above all, by His creative work: He alone has stretched forth the heavens and formed the earth ($40^{12.22ff.28}$ $42^{5}$ $44^{24}$ $45^{12.18}$) in the fulness of His omnipotence and the strength of His might ($40^{26}$); it needed but His call, and these things were there ($48^{13}$). He is the maker of all families of men from the beginning ($41^{4}$), and controls by His sovereign omnipotence the fortunes even of the greatest ($40^{23f.}$)—nay, the nations are before Him only as a drop on [the side of] the bucket or a speck of dust on the balance ($40^{15ff.}$). How shall the individual ever contend with Him, the potsherd with the potter ($45^{9}$)? As in the first Isaiah, so here God is frequently called 'the Holy One of Israel,' and that, in like manner, in the sense of His absolute elevation above everything creaturely and perishable, and hence, of course, above all stain and dishonour ($41^{14.16}$ $43^{3.14}$ etc.). The same attribute excludes absolutely any representation of God by images ($40^{18ff.}$), and, in general, our prophet cannot sufficiently emphasize the folly and senselessness of idol and image worship (cf. $41^{29}$, and very specially the almost humorous description in $44^{9ff.}$ $46^{6f.}$). The holiness of God requires also that all His actings should have for their deepest motive the honour of His name ($48^{9.11}$). He will not give His honour to another, nor His glory to idols ($42^{8}$), as if *they* had accomplished what was His work alone.

4. The scanty references to the means whereby God accomplishes His world-plan and saving purpose, make mention, above all, of the *prophetic word*. This has irresistible power ($55^{10f.}$) and eternal validity ($40^{8}$). In the exact pre-announcement of the wonderful events that are passing (the mission of Cyrus and the impending deliverance of Israel), our prophet sees one of the strongest evidences of the solity and omnipotence of the God of Israel ($41^{25ff.}$ $42^{9}$ $43^{10ff.}$ $44^{7f.26f.}$ $45^{21}$ $46^{10f.}$ $48^{3ff.14ff.}$); the idols, which are things of nought, can neither explain the past nor predict the future ($41^{21ff.}$).

5. Deutero-Isaiah, like the pre-exilic prophets and the Book of Deuteronomy, traces the preferential treatment of Israel to its election ($41^{8f.}$); but this last is ascribed not simply to God's love for Israel, as might appear from $43^{3f.}$, but to the special purposes which Jahweh wills to accomplish for the benefit of the whole world, by the instrumentality of Israel, His servant (see below). On this account He has carried them all along from their mother's womb ($46^{3}$); and, when by their sins they provoked His just anger, He gave them, indeed, into the hands of their enemies ($42^{23ff.}$ $50^{1}$ $51^{17}$); but it was not His intention that Babylon, the instrument of executing His vengeance, should show herself pitiless against Judah ($47^{6}$). All the more on that account God regards the old guilt of the people as atoned for—nay, as doubly expiated ($40^{2}$ $51^{19}$). All the same, the coming deliverance is nothing but the outcome of the free favour of God; it has been brought about neither by sacrifice nor any other merit on the part of Israel, which, on the contrary, has sinned from the time of its first father (Jacob) and deserved destruction in consequence ($43^{22ff.}$ $48^{1.4.8}$). But Jahweh blots out their transgressions as a cloud ($44^{22}$).

In view of all this, there is the less justification for Zion's discouragement, and her complaint that she is forsaken and forgotten by God ($40^{27}$ $49^{14}$). As little as a mother is forgetful of her sucking child has God forgotten the community of Israel ($49^{15}$). Nay, He is at once her creator and her

* The following have specially contributed to the elucidation of the controversy regarding Deutero- and Trito-Isaiah: Duhm, in his Commentary on Isaiah in the *Kurzer Hdcom.*, Göttingen, 1892, 2nd ed. 1902 [holds that Trito-Isaiah commences with ch. 56]; Cheyne, *Introduction to the Book of Isaiah*, London, 1895 [places $56^{1-8}$ 58. 59 under Artaxerxes II. or III.; $63^{7}$–$64^{12}$ about 350 B.C.; ch. 66 under Darius Ochus]; H. Gressmann, *Ueber die in Jes. cc. 56–66 vorausgesetzten zeitgeschichtlichen Verhältnisse*, Göttingen, 1899 [holds that chs. 56–66 are not a unity, but that they are all post-exilic and emanate from Judæa]; E. Littmann, *Ueber die Abfassungszeit des Tritojesaja*, Freiburg i. B., 1899 [Trito-Isaiah is held to embrace 56–$63^{6}$ (except $59^{5-8}$ and perhaps $56^{1-8}$) as well as chs. 65 and 66 (except $66^{23f.}$), and to emanate wholly from the period between 457 and 445, prior to the arrival of Nehemiah; on the other hand, $63^{7ff.}$ and 64 date from between 538 and 520].

husband, who can never cast off the wife of his youth ($54^{5ff.}$).

6. The instrument employed by Jahweh for the deliverance of His people and the further accomplishment of His saving purpose, is *Cyrus*, of whom and of whose Divine mission the prophet speaks in such honourable terms that it has been suggested that he actually saw in him the Messiah promised by the earlier prophets. Jahweh Himself speaks of Cyrus as His 'shepherd' ($44^{28}$), nay as His 'anointed,' whom He has taken by the right hand that He may cast down peoples before him, whom for Israel's sake He has called by name ($45^{1ff.}$), for whom He will make all his ways plain ($45^{13f.}$), as the man of His counsel ($46^{11}$), whom He loves ($48^{14}$).

If the victorious career of Cyrus is to be *thus* interpreted, Israel has no more occasion for anxious fears, but may with full complacency look for the manifestation of the glory of Jahweh ($40^5$ $41^{10ff.}$). God ensures to the exiles a secure return; He gathers them from all quarters ($43^{5ff.}$), and outdoes even His own former mighty acts when He brought His people forth from Egypt ($43^{16ff.}$). He fashions for them in the desert a road well constructed and free from danger ($40^3$ $42^{16}$ $43^2$ $49^{10f.}$), makes abundant provision of water and noble trees ($41^{18f.}$ $43^{18ff.}$ $48^{21}$), and Himself leads them like a loving shepherd ($40^{11}$ $52^{12}$). All nature accompanies these redemptive acts with a song of jubilation ($42^{10f.}$ $44^{23}$ $49^{13}$ $55^{12}$). The returned exiles shall be as a bridal ornament to Zion, the seemingly forsaken and sorely troubled, who shall now be astonished at the multitude of her children, and scarcely find room for them all ($49^{18ff.}$ $54^{1ff.}$). For along with Jacob (Judah) shall return also 'those who have been preserved of Israel' ($49^{5f.}$). Jahweh, moreover, shall once more reign as king over Zion ($52^{7f.}$), and all His gracious promises to David, the witness of His glory and the ruler of nations, shall be fulfilled to the whole people, who also shall draw to them foreign peoples—nay, peoples as yet unknown to them ($55^{3ff.}$). All these other nations are brought to recognize that Jahweh has called Cyrus, and crowned him with victory, and to give the glory to the God of Israel ($41^{1ff.}$). As for Israel itself, the outpouring of the spirit of God, which seals the truth that every individual is His special property ($44^{3ff.}$), and makes them all true disciples of Jahweh ($54^{13}$), brings about a wondrous renewing of the nation's youth ($40^{29ff.}$). Moreover, the duration of this renewed 'covenant' is to be unlimited; the brief period of God's anger is to be followed by a time of eternal favour and blessing ($45^{17}$ $54^{7ff.}$).

In the above orderly summary of the ideas of Deutero-Isaiah, which appear in the book itself, for the most part, in a scattered detached fashion, we have purposely passed over two statements, because they can in no way be brought into harmony with the other expectations of the prophet, and must accordingly be regarded as later additions—

(*a*) According to $41^{15f.}$, Israel is to become a new, sharp, many-toothed threshing-waggon, which goes so thoroughly to work that it crushes the very mountains and hills. This figure, of course, refers to the destruction of Israel's foes. Now, it is true that our prophet has a threat against Babylon ($47^{1ff.}$); she, the oppressor of Israel, has now in turn to take the 'intoxicating cup' which Jerusalem had formerly to drink ($51^{22f.}$). But there is no indication of anything except that Cyrus is to execute the judgment on Babylon, while the other peoples are called to share in Israel's salvation. Thus $41^{15f.}$ belongs to quite a different sphere of ideas—that, namely, of Ezk 38 f. and Mic $4^{11ff.}$.

(*b*) In $49^{22f.}$, instead of the return of the exiles through the wilderness under the leadership of Jahweh, we have a bringing of them back by the Gentiles acting under Jahweh's orders. It may be said that these two representations are not mutually exclusive. But in the statement that kings shall be the guardians of Israel and queens her nurses, nay, that they shall in humble obeisance lick the dust of her feet ($49^{23}$), we have the expression of expectations that belong, not to Deutero-Isaiah but to a considerably later phase of Judaism.

7. But all this does not exhaust the ideas contained in this unique book. The most wonderful thing in it is the idea of Israel as the 'Servant of Jahweh,' who, in accordance with His eternal purpose, which transcends all human comprehension, is destined to expiate, by his penal sufferings, not only Israel's own guilt, but also that of the heathen world, and then to exercise a great missionary vocation on the world of nations, that 'all ends of the earth may see the salvation of the God of Israel' ($52^{10}$).

Ever since Biblical study began, it has been felt to be a very difficult problem how the statements in which the Servant of Jahweh (עֶבֶד יהוה) is undoubtedly to be understood of the *people* of Israel ($41^{8f.}$ $42^{19}$ $43^{10}$ $44^{1f.\ 21}$ $45^4$ $48^{20}$, cf. also the 'servants of Jahweh' in $54^{17}$) are to be reconciled with those which, to all appearance, have an individual in view (thus in the so-called *'Ebed Jahweh Songs*: $42^{1-4}$ [according to others, $42^{1-7}$], $49^{1-6}$, $50^{4-9}$ [with v.$^{10}$], and $52^{13}$–$53^{12}$). Countless are the attempts which have been made to solve the problem in question.

After Duhm, in his Commentary on Isaiah (Göttingen, 1892), assigned the *'Ebed-Jahweh-Lieder* to a different and later hand than that of Deutero-Isaiah, and hence pronounced them a subsequent addition to the latter, explaining them, at the same time, in the individual sense (as perhaps referring to Jeremiah), there sprang up a crop of similar hypotheses. The individual interpretation of the *'Ebed-Jahweh-Lieder* is supported also by J. Ley (*Historische Erklärung des 2 Teils des Jesaja*, Marburg, 1893; art. 'Die Bedeutung des Ebed-Jahweh,' etc., in *SK*, 1899, p. 163 ff.) and L. Laue (*Die Ebed-Jahweh-Lieder im 2 Teil des Jesaja*, Wittenberg, 1898; also in *SK*, 1904, Heft 3). Both see in the Servant of Jahweh 'the Messiah of the future,' as does also G. Füllkrug (*Der Gottesknecht des Deuterojesaja*, Göttingen, 1899), only that he believes the *Lieder* to have been composed by Deutero-Isaiah himself. E. Sellin (*Serubbabel*, Leipzig, 1898) identified the Servant with Zerubbabel, who, he contended, actually assumed the crown, and in consequence suffered a terrible martyrdom at the hands of the Persians. In his *Studien zur Entstehungsgeschichte der jüdischen Gemeinde*, i. (Leipzig, 1901), Sellin substitutes for Zerubbabel some other descendant of David. Kittel (*Zur Theologie des AT*, ii., Leipzig, 1898) finds at least in ch. 53 the crucified Zerubbabel. Bertholet (*Zu Jesaja 53*, Freiburg i. B., 1899) refers $53^{1-11}$ to the sufferings and death of the ninety year old scribe Eleazar (cf. 2 Mac $6^{18ff.}$). The composition of $52^{13}$–$53^{12}$ by a different poet from the rest of the *'Ebed-Jahweh-Lieder* (whose authorship by Deutero-Isaiah is likewise denied) is maintained also by Laue (see above) and Schian (*Die Ebed-Jahweh-Lieder in Jes. 40–66*, Halle, 1895). It was the merit of K. Budde (art. 'The so-called Ebed Yahweh Songs and the Meaning of the term *Servant of Jahweh* in Is 40–55' in *Amer. Journal of Theology*, 1899, iii. p. 499 ff. [in German, *Die sogenannten Ebed-Jahweh-Lieder und die Bedeutung des Knechtes Jahwehs in Jes. 40–55*, Giessen, 1900]) and K. Marti (*Das Buch Jesaja*, Tübingen, 1900) to recall the exegesis of these passages from the forest of hypotheses to a more sober consideration of facts. Their argument was strengthened on all sides by the very thorough discussion of F. Giesebrecht (*Der Knecht Jahwes des Deuterojesaja*, Königsberg, 1902), and it may be considered as henceforward a position that is not likely to be shattered, that even the so-called 'Ebed-Jahweh Songs are the work of Deutero-Isaiah, and that their subject is Israel, with its call to serve a missionary function to the Gentiles.

On the present occasion we must be content to say that, in the violent controversy which has raged since the year 1892, the explanation of the Servant of Jahweh as referring to the people appears to us to have retained the victory. Once the fondness of Hebrew poetry and prophecy for far-reaching personifications of collective notions, and especially of bodies of people, is grasped, and $53^{1ff.}$ rightly understood as spoken by the Gentiles, *all* the declarations about the Servant combine into one perfectly intelligible whole. The question seems to us quite an idle one, whether Deutero-Isaiah meant the Servant of Jahweh to be understood of the whole nation or only of the truly godly kernel of it, the 'spiritual Israel,' which fully answered the idea of a people of God. When the prophet has to speak of the election of Israel and its destined mission in the world's history, his words naturally refer to the whole body of the nation, for it was this that was the object of election and of manifold guidance in the course of its history. But it is equally natural that, in the passages which have in view the representative suffering of the Servant and his missionary function, not those should be thought of who perish in the purifying judgment, but only the truly pious kernel of the people, who seek God and have penitent hearts. Nay, it is not an impossible position that the Servant, as a portion of the people, namely, that which is specially penitent and afflicted, should be opposed to the general body (49$^{5}$ 'Jahweh that formed me from the womb to be his servant, to bring Jacob again to him, and that Israel should be gathered unto him,' cf. also v.$^{6}$). But much more frequently and emphatically than this work on his fellow-countrymen is the missionary vocation exercised by the Servant towards the heathen world set forth. This is the central point of our prophet's whole world of ideas. It is only from this standpoint that the problem either of Israel's election or of her temporary rejection can be brought into harmony with the Divine plan of the world. The grievous sufferings of Israel were the indispensable condition of the salvation of the whole world.

That even the Gentiles are from the first destined to entrance into the kingdom of God, is shown by the Divine call (45$^{22ff.}$) to all the ends of the earth to turn to Him and let themselves be saved, as well as by God's oath that at last every knee shall bow to Him and every tongue swear by Him. But the instrument in proclaiming His salvation is His Servant, whom He has called from the mother's womb (*i.e.* from the beginning), that He may be glorified in him (49$^{1.3}$). God has put His spirit upon him (42$^{1}$), given him persuasive eloquence (49$^{2}$), the tongue of a proper disciple of Jahweh (50$^{4}$), that he may proclaim the true religion to the heathen (42$^{1}$), and thus become a light to the heathen (42$^{6}$ 49$^{6}$), the founder of a covenant (בְּרִית) between God and men (42$^{6}$ 49$^{8}$). And Israel is to await this call with all meekness and lowly submission (42$^{2ff.}$). True, there is not wanting a certain measure of preparedness of the heathen for the Servant's gospel of salvation. Already the isles wait for his instruction (42$^{4}$)—nay, the nations must themselves recognize that Jahweh alone could have accomplished the mighty transformation wrought through Cyrus (41$^{1ff.}$). But the decisive influence is brought to bear, finally, by the great sufferings of the Servant, and the patience with which he has submitted to every species of ill-treatment and mockery (50$^{6}$). To their own extreme astonishment, the perception dawns upon many peoples and kings that the Servant of Jahweh—marred almost beyond recognition as a man, utterly despised, and maltreated to the uttermost—has, through his voluntary, patient sufferings, borne the punishment of others as a guilt-offering, atoned for their sins, and procured salvation for them (52$^{13ff.}$).

This idea of a vicarious penal suffering of Israel for the Gentile world, in order to bring salvation to the latter, is so extraordinary and unique that one can easily understand how it has called forth all kinds of explanations, and that ever and anon voices are still raised in support of the contention that the direct reference of this passage to the vicarious suffering of Christ (cf. 1 P 2$^{22ff.}$) is the only one that meets the necessities of the case. And, as a matter of fact, the Church is entitled to see the complete fulfilment of this very remarkable prophecy only in the person of Christ. But nothing is taken from its significance in that direction through our interpreting the Servant of Jahweh, so far as the mind of the prophet was concerned, primarily of Israel. Only, we must be careful not to limit his meaning to the idea that the Gentiles, touched by the spectacle of the patience of Israel amidst all its sufferings, are moved to a ready acceptance of its message of salvation, and thus brought to adopt its religion; for the prophet expressly emphasizes the fact that the Servant of Jahweh has fulfilled his high calling by bearing the sins of many *and making intercession for the transgressors.* He speaks thus of a high-priestly intercession performed by Israel, in conjunction with its vicarious sufferings. In this way he gives his readers a view into the depths of the Divine counsel of salvation, such as is offered by scarcely any one of his fellow-prophets—a view of the truth that the seeming disturbance of God's saving purpose by man's sin, and the sufferings introduced in consequence, are really made to serve the end of realizing His saving purposes. But from the beginning all other purposes have been subordinated to *this* one: 'The heavens shall vanish away like smoke, and the earth shall fade like a garment . . . but my salvation shall be for ever' (51$^{6}$). Behind and above the temporary, perishing world there is another, which offers higher, eternal blessings. That the entrance to it should be open even to all the heathen, was a notion still beyond the horizon of any Israelitish mind of the time. But the prophet understood the word of his God: 'My thoughts are not your thoughts, neither are your ways my ways; but, as the heavens are higher than the earth, so are my ways higher than your ways, and my thoughts than your thoughts' (55$^{8f.}$).

## VII. Remaining exilic Prophecies, post-exilic Prophecy, and the beginnings of Apocalyptic.

i. *The Sources.*—To the time of the Exile may, further, be assigned with some confidence Is 21$^{1-10}$ and 13$^{1}$–14$^{23}$, and perhaps also chs. 34 and 35, which are closely akin to Deutero-Isaiah. On the other hand, it is difficult to decide whether a portion of the later additions (noted below) to pre-exilic Prophets are as early as the Exile. At all events, this view is not sufficiently proved by the (very frequent) allusions to the gathering and bringing back of the exiles. For, apart from the fact that such expectations are more than once put into the mouth of the earlier prophets from the standpoint of fulfilment, and indeed for the purpose of softening their denunciations, the number of Jews living in all quarters of the Diaspora even after 537 and 458 was still very great, and the expectation of their return might hence become very readily an indispensable element in the hopes of the future.

To the earliest post-exilic period belong: Ḥaggai (520), Zechariah (520–518), and the Book of Malachi (probably before 458), as well as Ob $^{10-21}$ and the so-called Trito-Isaiah (Is 56–66, probably about 440). To the beginning of the 4th cent. we assign Joel and Jonah; towards the end of the 4th, if not in the 3rd or even the 2nd cent., we would place the so-called Apocalypse of Isaiah (Is 24–27) and Zec 9–14. Of the additions to the older prophets which cannot be more precisely dated, a not inconsiderable portion may come down to the 4th and even the 3rd cent. B.C. Passing over some isolated verses, we give the following as almost universally acknowledged later additions:—

Is 2$^{2-4}$ (Mic 4$^{1-4}$) 4$^{2-6}$ 8$^{9f.}$ 10$^{20-23}$ 11$^{10}$–12$^{6}$ 13$^{1}$–14$^{23}$ (see above) 18$^{7}$ (?) 19$^{18-25}$ 21$^{1-10}$ (see above) 23$^{15-18}$ 29$^{5.7f.17-24}$ 30$^{18-26.27-33}$ (?) 31$^{5-8}$ 32. 33. 34 f. (see above).

Jer 3$^{14-18}$ 10$^{1-16}$ 16$^{18-21}$ 17$^{19-27}$ 29$^{16-20}$ 30$^{10f.}$ 31$^{10-14}$ (?) 31$^{38-40}$ 32$^{17-23}$ 33$^{14-26}$ chs. 46–49 (?) 50$^{1}$–51$^{58}$.

Hos 2$^{1-3}$ 3$^{5}$ (?; in any case, the words 'and David their king') 14$^{2-10}$ (?).

Am 9$^{8-15}$.

Mic 4$^{1-4.6-8.}$ (?) $^{11-13}$ 7$^{7-20}$.

Hab 3.

Zeph 2$^{4-15}$ 3$^{14-20}$.

ii. *Historical background.*—Deutero-Isaiah's prophecy of the freeing of the people by Cyrus had been fulfilled in 538 after the conquest of Babylon. The edict of Cyrus granted permission to the exiles to return, and about 50,000, under the leadership of Zerubbabel and Joshua the priest, availed themselves of it. But the condition of things in the home so eagerly longed for did not answer the high-flown expectations of the returned exiles. The foreign domination still continued, and all energy was paralyzed by poverty and failure of crops, as well as by the hostility of the Jewish - heathen mixed population, which had gradually spread over the land during the Exile. Even if the cultus was resumed, immediately after the Return, by the re - erection of the altar of burnt-offering (Ezr 3[2ff.]), it was not till the year 520 that, thanks to the energetic stimulation of Ḥaggai and Zechariah, the work of building the temple was taken in hand in earnest, and finished in 516. Evidently, these prophets expected the dawn of the Messianic age after the building was finished, and at the same time saw in Zerubbabel the 'shoot of David' promised by Jeremiah (Hag 2[6. 20ff.], Zec 3[8] 6[11f.], where in all probability there was originally mention only of a crowning of Zerubbabel). These hopes, too, were completely deceived. We possess, indeed, only very scanty traditions regarding the history of the post-exilic Jewish colony down to the time of Malachi (Ezr 4[6-23]), but the Book of Malachi itself shows that the conditions had rather changed for the worse since 516. The offerings naturally suffered from the continued poverty of the people (3[8ff.]), but no less from the unscrupulous character of the priests (1[6f.] 3[3f.]). The prophet also complains bitterly of the facile putting away of Jewish wives in order to contract new marriages with heathen women (2[10ff.]). But the worst feature was the resigned, not to say despairing, disposition which had taken possession of the people. This showed itself in such blasphemous judgments as that 'Every one that doeth evil is well pleasing to Jahweh, and in such he hath his delight, or where is the God of judgment?' (2[17], and still more fully in 3[14f.]). One can readily conceive how to the priestly circles in the Diaspora, which had been for long following in the footsteps of Ezekiel in laying down new regulations for the cultus (see below, § VIII.), it might seem that the time had come for them to step in. But even Ezra, the leader of a second band of exiles (B.C. 458), soon had the conviction forced upon him that it was necessary first to attend to other tasks than the introducing of the priestly legislation he had brought with him from Babylon. His Draconic zeal in dissolving the numerous mixed marriages so increased the hostility of the heathen and Jewish families thereby affected, that they obtained from Artaxerxes I. full powers to destroy the walls and gates of Jerusalem, which had been scarcely yet completed by Ezra. How thoroughly this process was carried out does not indeed appear from the timid allusion in Ezr 4[23], but is clear enough from the documentary report of Neḥemiah (1[3ff.] 2[12ff.] 3[1ff.]). The arrival of the latter at Jerusalem (445) had for its main result the solemn introduction of the priestly law - book (Neh 8, probably extracted in large part from the Memoirs of Ezra). Of the high significance of this act we shall have to speak in the next section. That all these occurrences, moreover, found an echo in prophecy is *a priori* probable, and is confirmed especially by the contents of Trito-Isaiah. In this way the enigma in which Is 66 was formerly involved is very simply cleared up, when it is recognized that there we have to do with a polemic against the Samaritans, belonging to the time of Ezra-Neḥemiah. From the second visit of Neḥemiah to Jerusalem (Neh 13[4ff.]) in 432 [according to others, not till 412] OT tradition is silent till we reach the commencement of the Maccabee wars, even if a considerable portion of the above-mentioned Prophetical literature may emanate from the intervening period.

iii. *Conception of God, and Ethics.*—The whole of the exilic and post-exilic literature with which we have here to do, bears almost without exception a secondary character, and—apart from the further colouring given to the hopes for the future—lives entirely upon the ideas of the older prophets, or simply takes these for granted. This comes out clearly in regard to the *conception of God.* The reason why the statements in this sphere are so scanty is that there was nothing to add to the message of the pre-exilic prophets. Belief in the solity and supramundane character of Jahweh is the common possession of the whole of this period. The apparent localizing of Him on Sinai (Hab 3[3]) can be regarded only as a poetical reminiscence of ancient descriptions, such as that of Jg 5[4]. His omnipotence and omniscience are revealed in the creation of heaven and earth (Jer 10[12ff.]); to Him nothing is impossible (32[17]). The mighty Babylon is simply a hammer in His hand (51[20ff.]). He chose Israel because He loved it, whereas He hated Israel's twin brother Esau (Mal 1[2f.]); here there seems to be no attempt to trace the election to an ethical motive, as in Deutero-Isaiah. Jahweh shows Himself to be the father and saviour of Israel in a far deeper sense than Abraham or Jacob could claim to be (Is 63[16] 64[7]). But the old conception of the national God, Jahweh, who has His eye upon Israel alone, has no longer any room left for it. Jahweh is great beyond the realm of Israel, His name is feared among the nations as that of a great king (Mal 1[5. 14], Jer 10[7]); nay, the incense-offerings and pure gifts, which from the rising to the setting of the sun are offered by the Gentiles, have Him, strictly speaking, for their object (Mal 1[11])—a remarkable witness to the far-reaching influence of Deutero-Isaiah's teaching! There is no longer any need for a polemic against the folly of image and idol worship; Is 57[3ff.] is in all probability addressed to the half-heathen mixed population in and about Judah, and Jer 10[1ff.] to the exiles who are endangered by their heathen environment.

The supramundane character of Jahweh is not impaired by the frequent emphasis laid upon His accompanying the exiles, or His dwelling upon Zion (see below); for in the latter instance what is in view is, as in the conception of God in the pre-exilic period, the indwelling of His 'glory' (*i.e.* a manifestation-form of His person), which is not absolutely identical with His full being. The 'angel of Jahweh,' in olden times (see above, p. 638[a] ff.) a form of appearance of Jahweh Himself, is in Zec 1[12ff.] (where he prays to Jahweh and is comforted by Him) clearly distinguished as a serving angel from Jahweh. In Zec 3[1] 'the Satan' makes his appearance for the first time, not as a mere appellative='adversary' (as in Nu 22[22. 32] [of the angel of Jahweh], 1 K 11[14. 23] *et al.* [of enemies in war]), but as a definite angelic being, who comes forward as the accuser of Joshua the high priest; but this is no proof of the rise of a dualistic conception of God. The Satan, who by the way cannot have been newly introduced by Zechariah, but is presupposed by him as long familiar to his readers, manifestly belongs (as he still does in Job 1[6f.]) to the category of serving angels, only that, in his zeal as Jahweh's prosecutor, he goes too far. Rather may we find in Is 24[21f.] an allusion to angelic feuds corresponding to those among the peoples of earth. But even in this very late *theologumenon*, with which we shall meet again when we come to speak of the Book of Daniel, the supremacy of Jahweh, who imprisons the rebellious ones, and only pardons them after a long interval, remains quite unaffected.

The consciousness that they lived in an age of *epigoni*, as compared with the creative times of prophecy, betrays itself clearly in the repressed tone of the post-exilic prophets, and their very frequent use of the formula 'thus saith Jahweh,' as well as in Zechariah's preference for the vision, the latter being no doubt in large measure simply to be regarded as a literary device. The same consciousness is manifested in the express appeals to earlier Prophetic oracles (Is 34[16], Jl 3[5] [2[32]]), and no less by the announcement of a messenger who is to prepare the way of Jahweh prior to the dawn of the day of judgment (Mal 3[1]; in v.[23] [4[5]] the prophet Elijah is named as this forerunner). There were even yet required energetic instruments of God to bring about the great transformation. Finally, again, in Zec 13[2ff.] the expectation is expressed that in the Messianic age the prophets and the unclean spirit shall be removed from the land, and that any one who yet ventures to come forward as a prophet shall be put to death by his own parents. Here, of course, it is false prophets that are in view, but the whole form of expression shows that it is not considered possible that any others shall then be found.

Like the conception of God, the *ethical demands* of the exilic and post-exilic prophets correspond exactly with those of their pre-exilic predecessors. At least in theory the justice of these demands is generally acknowledged, although the practice of the people still continues to supply occasion for bitter complaints (Is 56[9ff.] 58[1ff.] 59[2ff.]). As with Amos and Isaiah, the urgent call is to do right and justice and show pity to the poor, the widow, the orphan, and every class of afflicted ones (Zec 7[10f.] 8[16f.], Is 56[1] 58[6ff.], Mal 3[5ff.] [this last passage denouncing, however, also sorcerers, adulterers, and perjurers]). Moreover, it cannot be contested that even in the early post-exilic period a mechanical theory of retribution shows itself—the notion of a direct succession of sin and punishment, right conduct and outward blessing (Zec 8[12f.]). Thus the scanty harvest is, according to Hag 1[5f. 10f.], the direct penalty for the people's remissness in the work of rebuilding the temple; according to 2[14ff.] all offerings presented before the temple is finished count as unclean, and consequently inefficacious, but after that event all the richer an era of blessing shall set in.

iv. *THE CULTUS.*—The few utterances about the cultus—we here leave out of account those that belong to the realm of eschatology—show again a certain falling away from the height of the true prophetical point of view (cf. above, p. 685[a]). The law-book of Ḥilkiah, although marked by the prophetic spirit, had at the same time laid down such definite rules for the cultus that it was inevitable that a tendency should arise to attach value to the merely external performance of these. In addition to this, Ezekiel's conceptions, with his total rejection of the past and his sketch of a radically new constitution of the cultus, must have permeated all Jewish circles to such an extent that long before the introduction of the Priests' Code there had been produced a positively painful attention to matters connected with the cultus. It is true that even yet evidences are not lacking of a truly prophetical appreciation of ritual services. The description of the proper kind of fasting contained in Is 58[3bff.] might well have come from Isaiah ben-Amoz himself, while Joel's (2[13]) call, 'Rend your heart and not your garments,' recalls Jeremiah's demand for a circumcision of the heart. Similarly, the ideal of the duties and the significance of the priesthood set up in Mal 2[5ff.] must be pronounced a thoroughly worthy one. On the other hand, the way in which Ḥaggai and Zechariah make all blessing for Judah depend essentially upon the rebuilding of the temple (Hag 1[4ff.], Zec 8[9ff.]), the emphasis laid upon outward observance of the Sabbath (Jer 17[19ff.] [cf. especially the motive urged in v.[25]], Is 56[2], 58[13]), the extraordinary value attached to the regular food- and drink-offerings in the temple (Jl 1[9. 13. 16] 2[14]),—all this is hardly in accordance with the view of the cultus held by an Isaiah or a Jeremiah.

v. *ESCHATOLOGY.*—1. The edict of Cyrus had indeed brought freedom to a portion of the people, but had by no means introduced the great transformation of things contemplated by Deutero-Isaiah. On the contrary, the returned exiles had to struggle hard for their existence, and their lot could scarcely appear an enviable one to those who had remained behind in the land of their captivity. No wonder that men's minds turned with all the more longing to the future as that which should finally bring all their hopes to pass. With attention ever more tense they listened for the signs which were to herald a movement among the nations and the birth-pangs of the Messianic age. Zechariah, indeed, in the first of his night-visions learns (1[8ff.]) from the heavenly horsemen, who have reconnoitred the earth, that the whole world is still at rest and quiet. But, when the angel reminds Jahweh that the seventy years of anger have elapsed, comforting words, with the promise of happiness, are spoken to him. Ḥaggai announces as a message from Jahweh that within a short time He will make the earth tremble and throw all peoples into commotion (2[6. 21f.]). But even Trito-Isaiah has yet to complain (Is 59[9]) that Israel has always hitherto waited in vain for light, and he begs the heavenly 'watchers,' whom Jahweh has placed over the walls of Jerusalem, to give themselves and Jahweh no rest until He has established and glorified Jerusalem (62[6f.]).

2. The great transformation is brought about, according to the ancient expectation (see above, p. 691[b]), by the **'Day of the LORD,'** the day of judgment alike upon the sinners in Judah and upon the nations hostile to Israel. Properly speaking, it is only Malachi (3[2ff.]) that mentions the judgment upon Judah, when the angel of the covenant, like a refiner's fire and like fuller's lye, tries and purifies the Levites and the people; the 'great and dreadful day' (whose coming is preceded by the advent of Elijah to reconcile the fathers and the children, and so to avert the curse from the land, 4[5f.] [Heb 3[23f.]]) devours in its fury all the proud and all the workers of wickedness (4[1] [3[19]]), whereas upon those that fear God the sun of righteousness shall arise, and they shall come forth unharmed and tread down the wicked (4[2f.] [3[20f.]]). In Joel it looks at first as if in the devastating of the land by the locusts the precursors of the Day of Jahweh have appeared, 'a day of darkness and gloom, a day of clouds and thick darkness' for Judah (1[15] 2[1f.]); but in 3[1ff.] [2[28ff.]] the outpouring of the spirit on Judah precedes the advent of the 'great and terrible day.' That is to say, the judgment of that day overtakes only the heathen. The latter ('all nations') are again the only subject of judgment in the Valley of Jehoshaphat (3[4][1ff.]), where Jahweh calls them to account 'for his people and his heritage Israel.' So in Is 13[5ff.], although the avenging host is sent out by Jahweh to make the earth a desolation and to destroy the sinners upon it (v.[9]), the Day of the LORD affects mainly Babylon. [In 34[8ff.] it is a day of vengeance, a year of retribution for Zion against Edom; also in Ob [15ff.] all peoples, but especially Edom, are visited with vengeance on the Day of Jahweh. On the

other hand, in Zeph $2^{4-15}$ (a later addition to the threatening against Judah in vv.$^{1-3}$) the Day of Jahweh overtakes five different nations]. Finally, in Zec $14^{1ff.}$ the situation of Ezk 38 f. is implied, only that the onslaught of the heathen at first results in the capture and plunder of the city and the carrying captive of a portion of its inhabitants. But then Jahweh with all His holy ones [angels] fights from the Mount of Olives against those nations, while those who are destined for deliverance make their escape through a wide cleft in the same mount (v.$^{3ff.}$). For other features in this *fantastic* prophecy, which, after the fashion of the late eschatologies, mingles quite disparate elements, see below.

The ancient *theologumenon* of the interweaving of the world of nature with the fortunes of the people of God appears here also, in association with the Day of Jahweh, or in general as a mark of the Messianic last days, but in more striking forms. Thus we have allusions to strange, fear-compelling, natural phenomena such as the darkening of sun, moon, and stars (Is $13^{10}$, Jl $2^{10.\ 30f.}$ [$3^{3f.}$] 3[4]$^{15}$, Zec $14^{6f.}$ [according to which, on the Day of Jahweh it shall be neither day nor night, but at eventide it shall be bright]); earthquakes (Is $13^{13}$ $24^{18bff.}$)—nay, the dissolving of the host of heaven along with the heavens themselves (Is $34^{4}$). On the other hand, according to Is $30^{26}$, when the Messianic age comes, the light of the moon is to equal that of the sun, and that of the sun to be multiplied sevenfold.

3. Apart even from the occasions when it is brought into connexion with the Day of Jahweh, the idea of vengeance upon the heathen nations occupies the forefront of expectations as to the future. Those nations in particular are specified which either aided to the best of their ability in the destruction of Jerusalem, or at least indulged in savage mockery and malicious jubilation over it. Among these the pre-eminence belongs to Edom (Is $34^{5ff.}$, Ob $^{10ff.}$, Jer $49^{7ff.}$, Jl 4 [3]$^{19}$; also Am $1^{11f.}$ was in all probability added after the Exile). Jer 48 is directed against Moab; Is $13^{2ff.}$, and the whole series of threatenings contained in Jer 50 f., against Babylon; Jer 46 against the Egyptians; ch. 47 against the Philistines; $49^{1ff.}$ against the Ammonites; Zeph $2^{4ff.}$, Jl 4 (3)$^{1ff.}$, Zec $9^{1ff.}$ against almost all the neighbours of Israel. But no less frequent are the threatenings which are directed against the nations in general, and which contemplate the laying waste and depopulating of the whole earth (Mic $7^{13}$, Is $24^{1ff.}$)—nay, the trampling down of the nations by Jahweh Himself as one treads grapes (Is $63^{1ff.}$); or the burning of them to lime (Is $33^{12}$). Zechariah in the second of his night-visions sees four horns ($1^{18ff.}$ [$2^{1ff.}$]), which represent the hostile powers in all four quarters of heaven that have scattered Judah; but he beholds at the same time four smiths that are to cut off the horns. In his eighth vision, again, he sees ($6^{1ff.}$) the war-chariots which drive out in all directions to execute the judgment. And the reason why Jahweh is sore displeased against the nations is because, when He was a little displeased (with Judah), 'they of themselves helped forward the affliction' ($1^{15}$). Here the old conception that Jahweh employed the heathen as His rod of chastisement for Israel is almost forgotten, and we hear only of the offence of the heathen. In Mic $7^{9f.}$, indeed, the guilt of Judah is freely admitted, but this confession is at the same time coupled with the hope of revenge. Cf. also Is $8^{9f.}$, Jer $10^{25}$ $25^{30ff.}$. Nevertheless, all these threatenings do not prevent very different expectations regarding the Gentile nations from being expressed elsewhere.

In all the passages discussed above, judgment upon the heathen is the condition of the gathering together and reuniting of Israel in the Holy Land. From all sides they are to stream: neither floods nor deserts can check them, for Jahweh Himself prepares the way for them and leads them (Is $35^{1ff.}$ $11^{11ff.}$). According to Is $27^{12f.}$, they are gathered by Jahweh one by one from all quarters, and follow the call of the great trumpet that summons them home; cf. also Jer $30^{10f.}$ $46^{27f.}$, Zec $10^{8ff.}$. In a way altogether unique the deliverance of the captives is connected in Zec $9^{11ff.}$ $10^{5ff.}$ with victorious conflicts of Judah and Ephraim with the Ionians, *i.e.* the Greek world-power. As in Ezk $37^{15ff.}$, the expectation is firmly established that the exiles of the Northern kingdom as well are to return (cf. Hos $2^{2}$, Mic $2^{12}$, Jer $3^{18}$ $50^{4}$, Ob $^{18}$); of envy and jealousy betwixt Judah and Ephraim no more is heard (Is $11^{12}$).

A favourite expectation of the post-exilic period is evidently that the heathen themselves shall bring the exiles home, and thus play a very humiliating rôle. We already encountered this expectation in an addition to Deutero-Isaiah (Is $49^{22ff.}$, see above, p. 707$^{a}$, small type), cf. also Is $60^{4b}$ and v.$^{9f.}$. According to Is $66^{19ff.}$, certain of those who have escaped Jahweh's judgment upon the heathen are sent to the distant nations to bring reverently to Zion, as an offering to Jahweh, all yet banished Israelites. According to Is $60^{10}$, foreigners shall then build their walls for the Judahites, and kings shall minister to them; according to v.$^{14}$ (cf. also Mic $7^{16f.}$), the sons of their former oppressors shall pay them lowly homage. They themselves are to be as priests, *i.e.* free from all secular employment; for the foreigners shall be their shepherds, farmers, and vine-dressers (Is $61^{5f.}$). Of the same kind is the expectation expressed in Is $14^{1bf.}$, that the Israelites, after their arrival in the land of Jahweh, shall make slaves of the heathen that brought them home, and thus 'they shall take them captive whose captives they were, and they shall rule over their oppressors.' Elsewhere (Is $11^{14f.}$, Am $9^{12}$, Ob $^{19ff.}$) the subjugation of the former vassals of the Davidic kingdom is thought of as the work of the already returned exiles. To quite a different order of thought belongs the expectation (connecting itself with Ezk 38 f.) that the mass of heathen peoples, gathered before the walls of Jerusalem, which they already look upon as a certain prey, shall be speedily destroyed through the sudden intervention of Jahweh (cf. Is $29^{5.\ 7f.}$ $30^{27ff.}$ $33^{3f.\ 23b}$, Mic $4^{11ff.}$, Zec $12^{2ff.}$ [where also the princes of Judah co-operate in the destruction of the nations] $14^{12ff.}$ [where the terrible punishment inflicted on the assailants, and the immense booty that falls to Judah, are described]); on the different expectation expressed in Zec $14^{2ff.}$, see preceding column. If we are right in assigning these passages to the post-exilic period, they can have in view only one coming final attack by the heathen peoples on Jerusalem. The frequent vacillation and obscurity of statement is due to their eschatological character, which can tolerate the close conjunction of heterogeneous elements.

4. If, in all the above expectations hostile to the heathen, we meet with a particularism which can be regarded only as a denial of the message of Deutero-Isaiah, there are, fortunately, not wanting numerous witnesses that his work had not been by any means in vain. Zec $2^{15\,(11)}$ foresees many peoples attaching themselves to Jahweh, that they may belong to His people and dwell in Judah. According to $8^{20ff.}$, many peoples and nations shall come to seek Jahweh and entreat His favour; ten men of different languages shall lay hold of the skirt of *one* Jew, that they may go with them of whom they have heard that God is with them. But a merely external attachment is not all. The whole of the heathen are to stream to the moun-

tain of Jahweh, there to receive instruction as to the manner of conduct He requires, and to submit to His judicial decisions; universal peace among the nations shall be the result (Is $2^{2ff.}$, Mic $4^{1ff.}$, Zeph $3^{9}$, Is $60^{3}$). In like manner, the feast of fat things which Jahweh, according to Is $25^{6}$, will prepare on Ẓion for all peoples, must be understood as a sacrificial meal by which they are received into the fellowship of the people of God; v.$^{7}$ declares how at the same time the covering shall be destroyed which has hitherto been cast over all peoples, and has kept them from the joyful fulfilment of the will of God which is known even to them. According to Is $56^{3ff.}$, not only foreigners but even eunuchs who have attached themselves to Jahweh and keep His Sabbaths, may present to Him in Ẓion sacrifices that shall be well-pleasing in His eyes, for His house shall be called 'an house of prayer for all nations' (v.$^{7}$).

But the victory over particularism reaches its culminating point in the remarkable prophecy of Is $19^{19ff.}$, which contemplates the conversion of the Egyptians and their joining with Assyria and Judah in a common worship of the true God. It may be that Assyria is here only a symbolical name (for Syria), and that the special circumstances of a late period (the 3rd, if not the 2nd, cent. B.C.) supplied the motive for this prophecy. But, in any case, it is an important witness that all the particularism of the later post-exilic period had not been able to quench the spirit of Deutero-Isaiah. The same remark applies to the Book of Jonah. The simple teaching of this much misunderstood, and therefore inadequately appreciated, little book, is that God in His mercy desires not the death of sinners, even among the heathen, but that they should turn and live; and, further, that it is within His power to effect such a turning, in opposition to all human expectation. Hence it only shows a carnal disposition and a low desire for revenge, if Judah, instead of rejoicing in the conversion of the heathen, is filled with fury because vengeance has not yet overtaken Nineveh (which here probably stands for Babylon). Thus understood—and the closing words of the narrative imperatively demand this interpretation—this little book, too, represents the highest elevation reached by the point of view characteristic of Deutero-Isaiah.

5. In what precedes we have brought together all the expectations concerning the heathen world. But the centre round which the expectations of this period revolve is always Israel, the 'heritage' of Jahweh (Is $19^{25}$). It is for it, above all, that the joyful message is meant, which comforts the mourners of Ẓion (Is $61^{1}$); on it is accomplished the wondrous transformation, nay the conversion of all conditions into their opposite (Is $29^{17ff.}$), and therewith the triumph of the patient and the poor among men (v.$^{19}$).

The principal guarantee for all blessings of the Messianic age is found—as in the earlier prophecies—in the restored personal presence of Jahweh, or, to be more precise, in the indwelling of His 'glory' (Zec $2^{4.\ 6f.}$ $8^{3}$, Is $4^{5}$ [where cloud and shining flame, after the purifying judgment is over, are meant to recall the fiery cloud in which Jahweh once accompanied Israel on the wilderness march]). With His appearing upon Ẓion, He enters at the same time on the kingly rule over Israel, and judicial authority over all nations (Is $2^{4}$ $33^{22}$ $24^{23}$, Jer $10^{10}$, Ob $^{21}$, Zeph $3^{15}$, Zec $14^{9}$). Under His sway, the population (which in post-exilic times was long so small) is to multiply beyond measure (Zec $8^{5}$, Hos $2^{1}$ [$1^{10}$]); the walls of Jerusalem must stretch far out (Mic $7^{11}$, Jer $31^{38ff.}$), nay even be dispensed with altogether, on account of the multitude of men and cattle (Zec $2^{5ff.}$); for Jahweh Himself will be to them as a wall of fire (v.$^{9}$). Jerusalem is henceforward holy: foreigners shall no more pass through her (Jl 4 [3]$^{17}$), no oppressor shall again lord it over her, for Jahweh now with sleepless eye interposes Himself as the bulwark of His temple against all that comes and goes (Zec $9^{8}$; cf. also Is $60^{18}$). Nor is there any further need of the sun and the moon, for Jahweh is their unceasing light (Is $60^{19f.}$).

Corresponding to the glory of her king is the external glory, the renown and splendour of the new Jerusalem, and the happiness of her inhabitants. They are there as a boast and a praise among all the peoples of the earth (Zeph $3^{20}$); all nations shall praise their country as a delightsome land (Mal $3^{12}$), Jerusalem as the pride and joy of all future generations (Is $60^{15}$). Ẓion, the city of the festivals, shall be like a secure habitation, subject to no change (Is $33^{20}$; cf. also Am $9^{15}$, Jl 4 [3]$^{20}$); Israel shall be like splendidly blossoming plants (Hos $14^{6\,(5)\,ff.}$, Is $27^{6}$; according to many, also Is $4^{2}$). One and all, the inhabitants shall enjoy a long duration of life (Zec $8^{4}$, Is $65^{20.\ 22}$), surrounded by blessings, including fertility (Is $30^{23ff.}$, Jer $31^{11-14}$, Am $9^{13}$, Jl 4 (3)$^{18}$); for they are 'a family blessed by Jahweh' (Is $65^{23}$). In the profoundest peace they pass their days (Mic $4^{4}$, Is $60^{17bf.}$)—a peace which extends even to the wild animals (Is $65^{25}$).

But the heathen, above all, have to contribute to the splendour of Jerusalem. All their wealth is to flow to that city as a token of homage to the temple (Hag $2^{7}$, Is $11^{10}$ $18^{7}$ (?) $23^{18}$ $60^{5f.\ 11}$), their flocks are to be available for the sacrifices (Is $60^{7}$), and the glory of Lebanon for the beautifying of the sanctuary (v.$^{13}$). Thus then shall Israel 'suck the milk of the nations, and suck the breast of kings' (v.$^{16}$).

But it is not only upon endowment with the good things of earth that the happiness of the new Jerusalem shall rest. Prophecy does not forget higher, spiritual blessings, even if their limitation to Israel preponderates, showing here again a falling away from the height reached by Deutero-Isaiah's expectations. The most important point, because it is the prerequisite for all other blessing, is the complete atonement for all the past guilt of the people. From the way in which Zechariah in his fourth night-vision ($3^{1ff.}$) hears the Satan simply commanded to be silent when he charges the people in the person of the high priest Joshua with their old guilt, it might appear as if the past judgments had sufficed of themselves to constitute a full atonement. But this is not the meaning of the prophets. On the contrary, Jahweh (v.$^{4}$) must expressly forgive the people's sin. The clothing of the high priest in clean garments is a symbolical action, declaring him (and with him the people) justified, but of course with the implication of the presence of a penitent frame of mind, such as is well-pleasing to God. In reality it is the grace of God which brings about the atonement, as is expressly urged in Is $12^{1ff.}$ $33^{24}$ and, above all, Mic $7^{18f.}$. Thus Israel becomes a people who are all righteous (Is $60^{21}$), who are holy (Is $4^{3}$) to Jahweh (*i.e.* consecrated to Him as an inalienable possession)—nay, Jerusalem is to bear the honorific appellation, 'Jahweh is our righteousness' (Jer $33^{16}$). It is only occasionally that the religious and moral regeneration of the people is traced to the bestowal of the Divine spirit; cf. Is $32^{15ff.}$ $59^{21}$, Zec $12^{10}$, and especially Jl $3^{1ff.}$, although in this last passage the outpouring of God's spirit upon all branches of the people, even male and female slaves, refers mainly to the bestowal of the gift of prophecy. But the mental transformations described in Is $29^{24}$ $33^{5f.}$ are also, no doubt, thought of as due to the influence of the Divine spirit.

6. Amidst all this, however, it cannot be denied

that the 'legal' religion, for which the way was laid by Ezekiel, and which became an actual fact during the period with which we are dealing, casts its shadow even upon the expectations regarding the time of consummation. The very commanding part played by temple and cultus at present (see above, p. $710^{a}$) is to be retained even in the Messianic future. It is true that embodiments of the Divine presence such as the sacred Ark shall then be readily dispensed with, because the whole of Jerusalem shall be called the throne of Jahweh (Jer $3^{16f.}$). But the temple hill, as the holiest and most important, shall tower above all others (Is $2^{2}$, Mic $4^{1}$), whereas, according to Zec $14^{10}$, the whole of the rest of the country shall be changed into a plain. Ezekiel's prophecy (ch. 47) of the temple spring undergoes an advance in Zec $14^{8}$ in so far as the living waters, starting from Jerusalem, flow down to both seas, east and west, and thus fertilize the whole land. The importance attached, again, to the performance of the cultus is evidenced not only by the expectation of gifts of homage offered to the temple by the Gentiles (see above, p. $712^{b}$), but also by passages like Jer $33^{18.\ 21}$, in which the regular succession of Levitical priests is put on a level with the succession of the Davidic dynasty. According to Is $66^{21}$, however, the priesthood is to be open also to the returned exiles (not, presumably, to the Gentiles who bring them home). The religious festivals present themselves in a specially important light. The former fast-days shall indeed be transformed into days of rejoicing (Zec $8^{18ff.}$), but at every New Moon and at every Sabbath all flesh (in Israel) shall come to worship at Jerusalem and—here we have a strange expectation, due probably to a later insertion—to look upon the corpses of the apostate ones, 'whose worm dieth not and whose fire is not quenched' (Is $66^{23f.}$; on this passage see p. $714^{a}$). Zechariah ($14^{16ff.}$), on the other hand, looks at every Feast of Tabernacles for a pilgrimage of all nations to Jerusalem to pray before Jahweh and to join in the keeping of the festival: if any one neglects this, his land shall be punished with drought. The holiness belonging to the temple shall extend even to the bells of the horses in Jerusalem and the cooking-pots of the temple. It need not be pointed out that *this* notion of holiness cannot be explained from the usage of an Isaiah or a Deutero-Isaiah, but only from the mechanical and outward conception characteristic of the 'legal' religion.

7. We have purposely left out of account until now that branch of the expectations as to the future which, according to a still prevailing opinion, occupied the forefront of interest, namely, the hope of the appearing of the Messiah, the 'shoot of David,' predicted at the latest by Jeremiah (see above, p. $696^{b}$). Really, however, it cannot be said that this aspect of prophecy plays a prominent part in our period, unless the very important oracles contained in Is $9^{1-6}$ and $11^{1-9}$, as well as Mic $5^{1ff.}$ (cf. above, p. $696^{a}$), are to be assigned to the post-exilic period. Leaving these passages out of account, we find a direct allusion to Jeremiah's ($23^{5ff.}$) 'shoot of David' in Jer $33^{14ff.}$ (where, however, vv.$^{17.\ 21f.}$ show that it is not one particular ruler, but a continuous succession of rulers of David's line, that is thought of) and Zec $3^{8}$ $6^{12}$.* Here 'Shoot' has already become a proper name, but one has no longer to look for his coming, since he is present in the person of Zerubbabel. All that is now needed is the revelation of his dignity as a signet-ring chosen by Jahweh (Hag $2^{23}$), and his elevation to the throne of his fathers—an event which appears to be connected in Zec $6^{12}$ with the completion of the building of the temple. We have already (p. $678^{b}$) pointed out that the crowning there enjoined had in the original text not Joshua but Zerubbabel for its object. It is perfectly intelligible that, after the shattering of the hopes reposed on Zerubbabel, the high priest should have taken his place (v.$^{11}$), especially as in the fifth of Zechariah's night-visions ($4^{14}$) he is already reckoned as one of the two 'anointed' ones who stand before the Lord of the whole earth.

In Is $11^{10}$, which clearly looks back to v.$^{1}$, we hear of the 'shoot from the root of Jesse,' which is to be as an ensign to the nations (*i.e.* to indicate to them the way they are to go), who shall seek his favour and (by their gifts of homage, cf. above, p. $712^{b}$) enhance the splendour of his residence. In the whole of the following description, however, he is not mentioned again.

The expectation of a king of David's family is found also, beyond doubt, in the beautiful prophecy of Zec $9^{9f.}$, although he is there called simply 'king.' Jerusalem is to rejoice over him who returns home as a conqueror over all enemies, but mounted upon the animal ridden in times of peace, in token that henceforward he is to rule as a peaceful prince to the ends of the earth. The idea of the world-empire of the Messiah appears here with its final stamp, and indeed in a form which goes far beyond all prophecies uttered hitherto, and to which there is no parallel except in passages like Ps $2^{8}$.

Apart from the above prophecies, we meet only with quite general promises, such as that of the righteous rule of a king and his ministers (Is $32^{1f.}$), the choice of a common head over Judah and Israel at the advent of the Messianic age (Hos $2^{2}$ [$1^{11}$]); also the 'breaker' of Mic $2^{13}$ means the earthly leader, but the real king at the head of the returning people is Jahweh Himself), and the rearing up again of the fallen tabernacle of David (Am $9^{11}$). The last-named expectation might, however, refer simply to the re-establishing of the residence and kingdom of David; while in Zec $12^{8.\ 10}$ the 'house of David,' which (in the joy of victory) is to be like the angel of Jahweh, stands simply for the aristocracy of the nation. A closer examination of all these passages always yields the same result, namely, that during this period the person of the Messiah is either of only secondary importance, or, if this be not the case, the rôle it plays is far less religious than political.

8. Finally, we have still to mention some quite isolated expressions, which (like some even of those above mentioned) belong to the sphere of late apocalyptic expectations. We should hardly include in this category the promise of a new heaven and a new earth (Is $65^{17}$ $66^{22}$). For, although this promise plainly attaches itself to Is $51^{6}$ (the annihilation of heaven and earth), Trito-Isaiah, as the whole context shows, is thinking rather of the complete transformation of all conditions than of an actual new creation of the Universe. On the other hand, Is $25^{8}$ contains an apocalyptic feature in the announcement that death shall be destroyed for ever,* as does also $26^{19}$ in the hope expressed of the resurrection of the godly dead. In the latter case the form of expression appears to the present writer to exclude a symbolical explanation of this resurrection as referring to the return from exile (as in Ezk $37^{11ff.}$). 'They that lie in the dust' are those actually buried; the mysterious dew descending from the starry region causes the earth to send forth the shades again. The definiteness with which the

* We leave out of account Is $4^{2}$, because there 'shoot' or 'sprout' [better 'sprouting'] of Jahweh can only mean, in view of the parallelism, 'that which Jahweh causes to sprout.'

* We leave the question open whether this clause, which suits neither the rhythm nor the contents of the two following clauses, belonged from the first to Is $25^{8}$.

resurrection hope is here put forward can cause us all the less surprise, seeing that the so-called Apocalypse of Isaiah (chs. 24–27) appears to belong to a period from which we possess other witnesses to this expectation (see below, on Dn $12^{3}$). Elsewhere, throughout this period we find everywhere assumed the old conception of Shĕ'ôl (see above, p. $668^{a}$), the place whence no return is possible. Only, it is questionable whether the description in Is $14^{9ff.}$ of the conditions in the kingdom of the dead, after the analogy of the conditions that prevail in the upper world, is to be put to the account of bold poetical colouring or of a further development of the ancient and simpler conception. If the latter must be assumed, yet even in this passage (especially v.$^{15}$, cf. Ezk $32^{23}$) nothing more than an approach can be discovered to the doctrine of a separation between the good and the bad. On the enigmatic saying in Is $66^{24}$ (probably a later addition), cf. above, p. $713^{a}$. It would have to be regarded as a clear approach to the doctrine of the pains of hell if there were here any reference to the under world at all, and not rather to the corpses of apostates lying before the walls of Jerusalem.

9. In what precedes we have already had to notice a variety of passages which pass beyond merely eschatological expectations into the sphere of apocalyptic, in so far as their language is purposely obscure and veiled, nay enigmatic in form, partly perhaps with the well-founded intention of rendering it unintelligible to outsiders. But apocalyptic proper meets us in the extant literature for the first time in the *Book of Daniel* (*c.* 165 B.C.). Since this book has found entrance into the OT canon, we cannot pass it over entirely in our present exposition. In reality, however, it belongs to the category of post-canonical (apocryphal and apocalyptical) literature, and hence we refer for details to the article DEVELOPMENT OF DOCTRINE IN THE APOCRYPHAL PERIOD (above, p. 272 ff.); cf. also P. Volz, *Jüdische Eschatologie von Daniel bis Akiba*, Tübingen and Leipzig, 1903; W. Bousset, *Die jüdische Apokalyptik*, etc., Berlin, 1903; W. Baldensperger, *Die messianisch-apokalyptischen Hoffnungen des Judenthums*³, Strassburg, 1903.

The apocalyptic character of the Book of Daniel is already indicated by the command ($8^{26}$ $12^{4.9}$) to Daniel to keep the revelations made to him secret, and to seal the book till the time of the end. But it is seen most clearly of all in the contents of chs. 2. 7. 10 ff. Throughout these chapters events are *predicted*, some of which had happened within the author's own experience, while others had long been things of the past: in chs. 2 and 7 the world-empires that succeeded the empire of Babylon, along with the ten kings of the fourth kingdom; in 10 ff. the conflicts of the Ptolemies and the Seleucids, with numberless details; and, most of all, the terrible danger to the religion of Israel threatened by Antiochus IV. Epiphanes ($11^{36ff.}$). The purpose is everywhere the same: the author means to encourage his countrymen to unconquerable endurance amidst the severe persecution to which their faith and their fidelity to the Law were subjected. With this view he shows them, by the example of the young Daniel and his companions ($1^{8ff.}$), the blessing of unqualified obedience to the laws about food; by the example of the three men in the fiery furnace (ch. 3), and by the example of Daniel in the lions' den (ch. 6), he exhibits how for courageous confessors of the God of Israel wondrous deliverance is wrought, while punishment inevitably overtakes the despisers of this God ($3^{22f.}$ $4^{30ff.}$ $5^{30}$ $6^{25(24)}$). On the other side, the consolation he offers is based upon the prediction—veiled indeed in true apocalyptic fashion, yet on that account exact—of the end of the oppression. It is derived (ch. 9) from a mystical interpretation of Jeremiah's prophecy of a seventy years' period of rejection for Jerusalem, the years being explained as weeks of years. Even this instance of occupation with the long-canonized Sacred Writings, in order to discover a secret sense, is a characteristic mark of apocalyptic.

It would be doing the Book of Daniel serious injustice to deny it all claim to a truly religious tone, and to see in it merely an embodiment of rigid zeal for the Law. Even if the beautiful confession of sins contained in $9^{4-19}$ should have to be regarded, with many moderns, as a later addition, yet in $8^{19}$ and $11^{36}$ there is the implication that the advent of the final age is still kept back by the continuance of God's well-merited anger against Israel. But elsewhere, it cannot be denied, the strict observance of the outward demands of the Law, especially those relating to the cultus, occupies the forefront of interest. To our apocalyptist what appears to be the principal misfortune in the religious persecution under Antiochus Epiphanes, is plainly the abolition of the regular morning and evening burnt-offering ($8^{11.13}$ $11^{31}$ [coupled in the latter passage with the defilement of the sanctuary by a heathen image]), while its reintroduction is the subject of exact calculation ($8^{13f.}$ $12^{11f.}$).*

Considering the date of origin of the Book of Daniel, it is a matter of course that its conception of God should occupy the level reached by the writing prophets. It is remarkable, however, that here already there should be such striking traces of the effort, which afterwards reached a climax in the Rabbinical theology, to jealously guard the person of God from all direct contact with the visible world. This explains the great multiplying of comparatively independent intermediate beings, who hold converse with the apocalyptist, in order to give him information ($7^{16ff.}$ $8^{15ff.}$ $9^{21ff.}$, where, for the first time, we meet with the name of an angel, Gabriel; $10^{4ff.}$); or whom he beholds otherwise in his visions, such as the countless myriads of $7^{10}$ (cf. also $8^{13f.}$ $12^{5ff.}$, and the mention of guardian angels in $3^{25}$ $6^{23}$). In the story of the madness of Nebuchadreẓẓar ($4^{10ff.}$) it looks almost as if the rule of the world was left to the 'determination of the *watchers*' [certain superior angels] and the command of the 'holy ones'; it is not till v.$^{21(24)}$ that we hear of a 'determination of the Highest.' No less do the struggles of the nations appear to be decided simply by angelic princes (שָׂרִים) as the guardians and champions of the various peoples;† cf. $10^{4ff.}$, where probably we should see Gabriel in the fantastically described figure of the champion of Israel, who, with the aid of Michael,‡ one of the chief princes ($10^{13.21}$; in $12^{1}$ he is called 'the great prince who protects thy countrymen'), contends with the patron angels of the Persian empire and (v.$^{20}$) of Greece.

The above-described tendency to keep the person of God at a distance appears to be quite contradicted by the description in $7^{9ff.}$, where the 'ancient of days,' who takes his seat upon the throne to execute judgment, can be understood only of God. But apart from the fact that here we have to do with a mere vision, and that on the occasion in question personal action on the part of God was indispensable, the description is confined wholly to externals (clothing, hair of the head, dazzling throne, and myriads of attendant spirits), God is not once introduced as speaking. On the contrary, it appears as if the decision of the assessors of the court (v.$^{10b}$) were pronounced on the ground

* In $12^{11f.}$ there may be two later systems of reckoning, different from that of $8^{14}$.

† Cf. what was said above (p. $709^{b}$ f.) on Is $24^{21f.}$.

‡ Cf. the exhaustive monograph of W. Luecken, *Michael*. Göttingen, 1898.

of the 'books,' in which, presumably, the actions of the parties to be judged had been written down.

This judgment evidently enters as a principal component into the eschatological expectations of the apocalyptist. And its result is not merely to cast down the heathen world-empire personified in the God-blaspheming Antiochus Epiphanes, but to bestow the world-dominion for ever on the 'saints of the Most High,' *i.e.* on the people of Israel ($7^{13f. 21f. 27}$; cf., by the way, even $2^{44}$). In view of the express interpretation of the angel in $7^{27}$, the figure who, *like* a man, comes with the clouds of heaven, can be understood only of Israel, and not of a personal Messiah, of whom, strangely enough, the book contains no hint. On the other hand, it is the Book of Daniel ($12^{2}$) that contains the first undoubted * reference to the resurrection. Even here, however, what is looked for is not a general resurrection of *all* the dead, but only a resurrection of *many*, including both the godly (to everlasting life) and the ungodly (to shame and everlasting abhorrence). The number of the first naturally includes Daniel himself (v.$^{13}$).

That this last offshoot of prophecy should now exhibit only faint traces of the true prophetic spirit, and should move rather on the lines of 'legal' religion, is only natural in view of the fact that the latter had held almost unlimited sway for nearly 300 years at the date when the Book of Daniel was composed.

In speaking of the Book of Daniel, and even in dealing with a not inconsiderable portion of post-exilic prophecy, we have been compelled to anticipate the order of the stages of development of the religion of Israel. Our next task will be to seek to realize more fully the nature of the 'Priests' Code.'

### VIII. The Priests' Code (P).

i. *The Sources.* — Regarding the numerous questions connected with the literary criticism of the stratum usually known as P, we must here be content with a few remarks. It is generally admitted that not only the present Pentateuch but also its latest stratum, namely P, must be viewed as the fruit of a somewhat lengthy literary process. Nevertheless, the spirit and the diction of this whole stratum exhibit such unity, that, from the point of view of the history of the religion of Israel, it is a matter of only subordinate interest to determine the component elements more exactly. Thus we do not dispute the possibility that the so-called Law of Holiness (H) may include some pre-exilic passages, but we regard by far the most of H as having originated within the priestly circles of the Exile, and that by way of carrying out the programme sketched by Ezekiel (chs. 40–48). The same remark applies to the priestly law-book, which, according to the express statement of Ezr $7^{25}$ (cf. also Neh $8^{1f. 13}$), was first brought with him from Babylon by Ezra, and which, in view of Ezr $7^{12. 21}$ ('the *writer* of the law of the God of heaven'), must at least have been edited by him. Whether this law-book of Ezra was identical with that recension which embodied the cultus laws in the form of a cultus history (cf. *e.g.* Lv $10^{1ff.}$, Nu $15^{32ff.}$), and included also the historical parts of Genesis, Exodus, Numbers, and Joshua, we leave an open question. Only, we have no doubt on this point, that Ezra's law-book was identical neither with the whole of the present Pentateuch nor with the whole of the present P stratum. For, in the one case, the occasional glaring differences between the laws in D and in P would have occasioned serious confusion; while, on the other supposition, it would be quite impossible to account for the very frequent repetitions (for instance, the duplicate versions of the ordinances regarding the building and furnishing of the Tent of Meeting, Ex 25–31 and 35–40), as well as the partial divergences of the components of certain groups (for instance, in the so-called sacrificial *tôrāh* of Lv 1–7). On the contrary, we can only conclude that the code of Ezra, which was originally *harmonious*, was subsequently enlarged by the products of other priestly schemes, and so finally (probably still within the 5th cent. B.C.) united with the older sources (J, E, D) into a single whole.

ii. *The Conception of God.*—1. P's conception of God can, properly speaking, be gathered only from the Creation narrative of Gn 1. For, as almost his whole interest is fixed on the preparation for and the establishment of the Israelitish theocracy, little occasion presents itself elsewhere for descanting on the being of God. But in the story of Creation (cf. above, p. 666) we encounter such a transcendence of God in relation to matter, in opposition to all pantheistic intermixing of the two, and to every theory of evolution, that we may here pass by the much debated question of the dependence of the narrator on the Babylonian or the Phœnician cosmogony.* At most, a mythological echo has survived in the allusion to a chaos (v.$^{2}$) and the hovering (scarcely 'brooding') of the creative spirit of God over the primeval ocean. But, even if v.$^{2}$ should be urged in opposition to the assumption of a creation *ex nihilo*, there would still be left the making of light, of the firmament of heaven, and, above all, of the stars, which are evidently to be thought of not as formed from pre-existing material but as called immediately into being. The absolute omnipotence of the Creator results of itself from the fact that His word of command is all that is needed to bring things into being according to His pleasure; while His absolute wisdom is manifested in the progressive order of the creative work, culminating in man, the goal and the crown of creation; as well as by the testimony of the Creator Himself (v.$^{31}$) that all He had made was 'very good,' *i.e.* perfect.

2. This lofty conception of the living, personal, but at the same time purely spiritual, God—a product of perfected prophetism—shows itself elsewhere in P in his careful avoidance of all anthropomorphism. True, indeed, even he cannot entirely dispense with theophanies at specially important crises in the history of redemption; but he always contents himself with almost imperceptible allusions to the near presence of God (Gn $17^{22}$ $35^{13a}$), or to the appearing of the 'glory of Jahweh' (see above, p. $639^{b}$ f.) in the cloud (Ex $16^{10}$, Nu $9^{15ff.}$ $17^{7}$ [$16^{42}$]). This glory appears to the Israelites upon the top of Mount Sinai like devouring fire (Ex $24^{17}$); its reflexion causes the skin of Moses' face to shine, so that he has to cover his countenance with a veil (Ex $34^{29}$). But none of these passages venture on even a remote description of the being of God. Under these circumstances it is surely no accident, again, that in P we find no trace of intermediary beings between God and man, the sole medium of revelation being the word of God. Manifestly, the sending forth of angels, who had to be thought of all the same as wearing some bodily form, appeared to P as itself a degrading of the Divine sphere to the realm of the creaturely.

3. All the less can it be that, when man is said to have been created after the image of God and

* The above (p. $713^{b}$) cited passage, Is $26^{19}$, which, by the way, perhaps belongs to the same period as Daniel, is by not a few explained of the *political* resurrection of the people.

* The fullest treatment of these questions is by H. Gunkel, *Schöpfung und Chaos in Urzeit und Endzeit* (Göttingen, 1894); and Frdr. Delitzsch, *Das babylonische Weltschöpfungsepos* (Leipzig, 1896).

in His likeness (Gn $1^{27}$), there is any thought of a copying of the *bodily form* of God. Even if something of the kind may have been intended in the heathen source which is assumed by many to have been used by the narrator, he himself would have indignantly repelled any such conception. Man is the image of God in so far as he, in distinction from all other living creatures, belongs to the realm of rational and moral beings, whose supreme head is God Himself. The idea that this Divine image was lost by a fall into sin is quite unknown to P. On the contrary, he expressly notes (Gn $5^3$) that it was transmitted by Adam, through the process of generation, to Seth (and his further posterity); and, even after the Flood, murder is declared to be an act worthy of punishment by death ($9^6$), because it amounts to a destroying of the Divine image.

A result of the position of pre-eminence held by man as the bearer of the Divine image is the dominion accorded him by God over the earth, and in particular over the world of animals (Gn $1^{28}$). For the exercise of this dominion men are capacitated by becoming fruitful and multiplying in accordance with the so-called 'Creation-blessing.' At the same time, however, they are at first (v.$^{29}$) confined exclusively to a vegetable diet; permission to use animal food (but to the exclusion of eating blood) does not come till after the Flood (Gn $9^{3ff.}$), *i.e.* it is simply a concession to the corruption that has now set in, a perversion of the condition originally designed by God. In His perfect creation slaughter could not have held sway from the first.

iii. *THE REGULATIONS OF THE THEOCRACY.*—1. That interest in the regulations of the theocracy by which the whole of P is dominated, makes itself felt already in the Creation narrative, in so far as the latter represents the Sabbath as blessed and hallowed from the beginning as the day on which God rested from His six days' work (Gn $2^3$). The Flood is indeed, as in J, a judgment of God ($6^{11ff.}$) on a wholly corrupt humanity, but at the same time furnishes the occasion for concluding a *bĕrîth* (cf., on this so-called 'covenant,' above, p. $630^b$ f.) with the new race of men descended from Noaḥ. It consists in God's promise that mankind is in future to be safe from the recurrence of destruction by the waters of a flood, and in the binding of Noaḥ (and in him of all mankind) to abstain from eating blood and from murder. The covenantal sign confirmatory of the Divine promise is the rainbow ($9^{12ff.}$).

2. In the history of the patriarchs, which is dismissed by P in a few very brief notices, there emerges prominently once more the concluding of the *bĕrîth* with Abraham (Gn $17^{1ff.}$). The Divine promise in this instance has reference to the bestowing upon the patriarch of a very numerous posterity, which shall include even kings, and to the assigning of the land of Canaan to Abraham's seed as a permanent possession. On the other hand, Abraham is bound to an upright walk before God and to the adoption of circumcision as the outward sign of this second 'covenant.' It is clear that circumcision, which, as a very ancient practice of many nations surrounding Israel, must originally have rested upon other grounds (cf. above, p. $622^b$ f.), is here brought under a specifically religious point of view. Since an uncircumcised person is 'unclean,' circumcision, as the taking away of a portion of the uncleanness, is a symbolical act of purifying. But this negative sense is supplemented by a positive one—an act of consecration. Circumcision is the rite whereby a child is received into the fellowship of the pure God-consecrated people, and it includes at the same time the obligation to conform to all the Divine ordinances that are binding on this body. All these features (purification, consecration, engagement) impart to circumcision, as viewed by P, a sacramental character, which suggests comparison with Christian Baptism. The circumstance that, according to v.$^{12}$, circumcision is to be performed also on every class of slaves, appears at the first glance very strange, in view of the particularism with which P elsewhere insists on the sole claim of Israel to the name of a people of God. But it seems to him even more important that no unclean one shall be tolerated in the company of the clean, and hence he resorts more readily to the expedient of requiring that even foreigners who have come into external fellowship with Israel shall be bound to the Law by circumcision, and be thereby constituted full citizens of the Divine commonwealth.

3. Except for his detailed account of the purchase of the burial-place at Ḥebron (Gn 23), upon which he evidently means to base a claim on the part of Abraham's posterity to the land of Canaan, P hastens rapidly over the history preliminary to the Sinai covenant, that he may dwell all the more fully on this third *bĕrîth*, whose duration is to be eternal, and whose sign is the Sabbath (Ex $31^{13ff.}$). In the forefront stands (Ex $6^{2ff.}$) the solemn revelation of the name 'Jahweh' to Moses. This name is expressly said to have been then first communicated, God having revealed Himself to the fathers only as *El-shaddai* ('God almighty'). No explanation of the name 'Jahweh' is given. Doubtless, the explanation which underlies Ex $3^{15}$ is assumed as long familiar. But here already the promises of Jahweh are enumerated, upon which the *bĕrîth* at Sinai is to be founded: the deliverance from the bondage of Egypt, whereby at the same time Israel's election as the people of God's own possession is sealed, and the settlement of them in Canaan in fulfilment of the sworn promise to the patriarchs that this land was to be given to their descendants for a perpetual possession. The obligations, again, to which the people have to submit themselves, in order to prove themselves worthy of these Divine blessings and of the name 'people of Jahweh,' are laid down in the numerous ordinances which form the kernel of the so-called 'Priests' Code.' The latter name is not meant to imply that this code is concerned only with prescriptions for the priests—by way of opposition, for instance, to Deuteronomy as a law-book for the people. On the contrary, the majority of the laws contained in it assume the form of communications which Moses by God's command imparts to the people. But, as all strictly ritual acts can be performed only by priests, and the laws have reference very largely to the cultus, the designation of the whole as the 'Priests' Code' is perfectly justified. The realm of civil and criminal jurisprudence,* which plays by no means an unessential part in the 'Book of the Covenant,' comes into consideration in P only where specifically religious interests are involved.

4. The fundamental notions on which the so-called *Ceremonial Law*, in dependence on the legislative programme of Ezekiel, is based, are extremely simple. They amount essentially to the one idea that in the domain of Israel, Jahweh's own people, everything without exception belongs, and is thus consecrated, to Him alone. This holds good accordingly of all space and time, and of all pro-

* On this side of the legislation, which we pass by here, the reader may compare the following: W. Nowack, *Die socialen Probleme in Israel*, Strassburg, 1892; E. Schall, *Die Staatsverfassung der Juden*, Leipzig, 1896; F. Buhl, *Die socialen Verhältnisse der Israeliten*, Berlin, 1899; G. Förster, *Das mosaische Strafrecht in seiner geschichtlichen Entwickelung*, Leipzig, 1900.

perty and life. The full logical consequence of this now would be, properly speaking, that man would have to renounce all use of what is God's sole property—nay, that all life would have to be brought to Him in sacrifice. But this would make the continued existence of the God-consecrated people impossible. Hence God has so ordained it in His law that only a portion of the property in question is to be exclusively hallowed to Him and thus withdrawn from profane use. This due (*tĕrûmāh*), levied upon the whole, gives symbolical expression to the confession that Jahweh is incontrovertibly Lord of everything. With this admission He is graciously satisfied; and by the sacred *tĕrûmāh* all the rest is also hallowed and its safe use procured for Israel. But all the heavier is the vengeance that overtakes him who omits the prescribed hallowing and rendering of a portion to Jahweh, or lays his hands on what has already been hallowed. It will be our object in the following survey to show what was the special portion of Jahweh under all the categories above referred to.

(*a*) *Holy places.*—Jahweh is sole Lord of all space. But He contents Himself with requiring that a limited space be marked off and declared absolutely sacred. This space is the place where His 'glory' dwells, and thus at the same time supplies the condition of approach to Him and of all kinds of ritual proceedings. (*α*) The latter became possible for the first time after the construction of the *one* legitimate sanctuary, in the form of the 'Tent of Meeting' (commonly called 'the tabernacle,' German *Stiftshütte*) at Sinai. Hence P nowhere speaks of the erecting of altars or the offering of sacrifices by the patriarchs, but the constitution of the sanctuary is the first and very minutely handled subject of the Sinaitic legislation (Ex 25[1ff.] and 35[4ff.]). The concentration of the cultus at *one* legitimate sanctuary, which Deuteronomy (12[1ff.]) put forward as a new demand and which it carried through not without difficulty, appears in P as something that is self-evident and needs not to be specially enjoined. Nor does P, like Deuteronomy, regard the unification of the cultus as coming into force only after the termination of the conquest of Canaan [or, to be more precise, after the building of Solomon's temple], but as a principle that was valid from the very first. The tent-sanctuary erected at Sinai is indeed, in view of its whole character, nothing but the Jerusalem temple projected back into the time of the wilderness journeyings; but there are two considerations that forbid our speaking, in this connexion, of P's account as pure fiction. In the first place, even the ancient tradition (Ex 33[7ff.]) knows of a 'Tent of Meeting,' only that the latter is not a place of worship but simply the seat of an oracle, and that it stands not in the midst of but outside the camp. Secondly, the tent-sanctuary of P belongs to the numerous theories which owe their form, not to an actual tradition but to a religious postulate. Things must have been *so* ordered, it was argued, if they were to harmonize with the (much later, but) absolutely authoritative theories. Thus a delicate symbolical idea comes to be transformed into tangible history. Any one who straightway pronounces this a falsifying of history, shows that he has no notion of the peculiar character of the whole genus of literature known as the *midrāsh* (for it is to *this* realm that we must assign all this embodying of religious ideas in history, within the Ceremonial Law). See, further, art. TABERNACLE in vol. iv.

The setting up of the sacred tent in the midst of the camp of Israel naturally implies that Jahweh means to take up His abode amidst His people, if not in His real person, yet with a representation of His being (cf. above, p. 639[b] f., on the 'glory of Jahweh'). The special seat of His revealing presence, and consequently the most holy centre of the sacred spot, is the lid of the Ark of the Law in the dark *adytum* of the tent (Ex 25[22]). Next to this 'Holy of Holies,' which, it would appear from Lv 16, could be entered only by the high priest, and even by him only on the Great Day of Atonement,* comes the 'Holy Place,' which only the priests, not the Levites, might enter. These two spaces are surrounded by the fore-court, in which the priests, with the assistance of the Levites, attend to the sacrificial cultus. Between the fore-court, again, and the tribes of Israel which—three on each side—surround the court, the Levites are encamped. In virtue of the consecration which they have undergone, they are fitted to serve as a bulwark to the people against the Divine holiness, which threatens with destruction everything unclean that comes near it (Nu 1[53]).

(*β*) The idea of a *tĕrûmāh* of the land being due to Jahweh as an acknowledgment that one owes the whole to Him, finds a further expression in the command to set apart 13 priestly and 35 Levitical cities, each with a piece of pasture-land round about it (Nu 35, Jos 21). The circumstance that these cities and the pasturage pertaining to them are intended for the use of man, does not exclude the possibility of looking upon them as a due paid to Jahweh. For in other instances as well (*e.g.* the thigh in meal-offerings) the *tĕrûmāh* falls to the priests. This whole enactment, however, is intended simply to embody one of those theories spoken of above, without regard to the possibility of carrying it into practice. This is sufficiently proved by the single fact that the territory of the twelve tribes, in each of which, in proportion to their size, a certain number of cities are to be set apart (Nu 35[8]), had long ceased to be under the control of the people, and that it cannot be proved that in the post-exilic period such a law was carried out even in the case of Judah, although priests and Levites may have fixed their abode by preference in those particular cities of Judah and Benjamin. In favour of the view that we are here dealing with a mere theory, there is, finally, the further circumstance that several of the cities enumerated were situated so near to one another that the pasture-lands attached to them (extending each to a distance of 2000 cubits from the city wall) would in many instances have overlapped. The late date, however, at which this theory was constructed is evident from the way in which the Priests' Code proper repeatedly (Nu 18[20f.] 26[62]) insists that the tribe of Levi is to be compensated by the offerings of the people for having *waived its claim* to a share of the land: Jahweh is its portion.

(*γ*) A final embodiment of the idea of Jahweh as the sole owner of the land is found in a portion of the regulations about the *Sabbatical year* and the so-called great *year of jubile* (Lv 25). It is true that even the Book of the Covenant prescribes (Ex 23[10f.]) that the land is to be allowed to lie fallow once in seven years, for the good of the poor and the beasts of the field. The motive there, however, is a humanitarian, not a theocratic, one; and, moreover, the rule is certainly not meant to apply to all cultivated land in one and the same year. Deuteronomy prescribes (ch. 15) only a remission

* The opening part of Lv 16 contains, indeed, primarily only regulations as to the precautions to be taken by Aaron to ensure his being able to enter the sanctuary without danger, and thus manifestly assumes the possibility of repeated entrances. This introductory passage was afterwards amalgamated with the ritual of the Day of Atonement. Nu 18[7], again, implies that *all* priests may officiate in the Holy of Holies.

of debts for the seventh year, again on humanitarian grounds. On the other hand, Lv 25[3ff.] requires that every seven years *all* land shall enjoy absolute rest. There is no more word of humanitarian motives: the Sabbath of the land in the Sabbatical year denotes a consecration of the land just as the weekly Sabbath signifies the consecration of a specified shorter period of time. But this consecration implies once more the solemn acknowledgment that the people have received the land only on revocable lease from Jahweh, the sole feudal owner.

We have the express testimony of the history of the Maccabæan wars to the fact that the prescriptions regarding the Sabbatical year were carried into practice. On the other hand, Jewish tradition itself admits that the so-called great year of jubile, which fell every fiftieth year (after the complete lapse of seven Sabbatical-year weeks), was only counted but not actually observed. As a matter of fact, the carrying out of the prescriptions of Lv 25[13], so far as this was possible at all, would have led to a total want of certainty as to all matters of property and a consequent paralyzing of economic relations. But the consistent theory of P's legislation is indifferent to questions of practicability, and even to such considerations as that the year of jubile immediately follows a Sabbatical year and thus implies a second fallow year. All this appears to P insignificant compared with the principle which here (v.[23]) finds its most notable and clearest expression: the land (like every other possession), being the property of Jahweh, may not be sold. On the contrary, one man can sell to another only a certain number of harvests; the price is to be proportioned to the number of years which have yet to elapse before the next jubile year, when the property spontaneously falls back to the original usufructuary of it, the proper feudatory of Jahweh. It is significant that, according to v.[29ff.], the houses in a walled city do not pass back in the year of jubile into the hands of the seller. They are the handiwork of man, and, as such, do not belong to the feudal property of which Jahweh gives a lease. On the other hand, the houses in villages are, according to v.[31], a part of the landed property; hence they are redeemable at any time, and pass back in the year of jubile to their original owner.

(*b*) *Holy times.*—Jahweh is Lord also of all time. Hence the employing of time in any pursuit that brings profit amounts to an encroaching upon God's right of property. He permits, however, of such encroachment, upon condition that special portions of the whole time are set apart and 'hallowed,' *i.e.* withdrawn from profane use, as belonging to God. The essential point is thus abstention from work. It is only in a secondary way that P thinks of the spending of holy days in Divine worship or private meditation. On ordinary holy days it is only professional work that is forbidden (Lv 23[7f. 21. 25] etc.), but on the Sabbath and the Great Day of Atonement it is work *of every kind* (vv.[3 30]). The standpoint of P comes out, above all, in the motives he assigns for the festivals. The original agrarian character of these (cf. above, p. 662 ff.) still survives—apart from the dedication of the firstling sheaf at the *Mazzôth* festival, Lv 23[9ff.]—only in the Feast of Weeks, as the occasion when the firstling loaves are presented. On the other hand, the Passover, as an independent festival, precedes the seven (formerly six) days of Unleavened Bread. Already instituted in Egypt (Ex 12[1ff.]), it is meant for all time, in grateful remembrance of the sparing of Israel the night before the Exodus, when God smote all the firstborn of the Egyptians. The manifestly primitive form of the celebration (the eating of the lamb in the houses, and the besprinkling of the doorposts with its blood) could be retained by P only through giving up the sacrificial character of the festival; for otherwise it could not have been celebrated except (as in Dt 16[5f.]) at the central sanctuary. In the case of the *Mazzôth* festival it is repeatedly emphasized that the strict prohibition of leaven was given at the very Exodus itself, thereby conferring upon this festival also the character of a theocratic memorial ordinance. With the Feast of Tabernacles (now an eight days' instead of a seven days' festival), which was originally the joyous feast of the fruit- and wine-gathering, the same result was reached by giving to the ancient custom of dwelling in booths during the festival the stamp of a memorial of the wilderness journeyings. This giving up of the original motive of the festivals, namely, the course of the various harvests, permits also of an exact dating of them. Thus the Passover falls on the evening of the 14th Nisan, *Mazzôth* extends from the 15th to the 21st of the first month, Tabernacles from the 15th to the 22nd of the seventh month, while the Feast of Weeks falls on the fiftieth day after the offering of the firstling sheaf, which was always to be presented the day after the Sabbath of the *Mazzôth*-week. Of new festivals we have: the Feast of Trumpets at the new moon of the seventh month [otherwise the New Moon, to which such importance was attached in early times, is signalized in P only by a multiplication of the official offerings], and the Great Day of Atonement on the 10th day of the same month. Once more it is significant that the latter festival, which is undoubtedly of very late origin, and whose motives are purely theocratic, should have become the most important and the holiest of all. By the way, it is only in the case of seven of these days (the 1st and 7th days of *Mazzôth*; the Feast of Weeks; the 1st, 10th, 15th, and 22nd days of the seventh month [but, according to Lv 23[3], also every Sabbath]) that a 'holy convocation' of the whole people is required at the sanctuary—a demand which is intelligible only if one thinks of the people as living in the neighbourhood of the sanctuary, as was actually the case during the first period after the Return from the Exile.

All the festivals hitherto enumerated recurred every year. But the underlying idea of all the festal seasons made its way to a further realization in the setting apart, as hallowed to God, of seasons within larger divisions of time. This led to the expansion of the idea of the Sabbath by the separation and hallowing of every seventh year as the close of a year-week, and of the fiftieth year after the termination of a cycle of seven year-weeks. The celebration of these is based upon a renunciation of the use of the soil. Since in this instance the theory of sacred *time* is in the closest contact with that of sacred *space*, we have already (p. 717[b]) had to speak of the Sabbatical year and the great year of jubile.

(*c*) *The consecrated character of all members of the people; 'holy persons' in the narrower sense (Priests and Levites).*—(*a*) The fact that Jahweh by mighty acts 'redeemed' the people from the bondage of Egypt, constituted Israel the property of Jahweh alone (Lv 25[42. 55]); and henceforward it was to be a people consecrated to Him, and thus —in harmony with His superiority to every kind of stain—an absolutely pure people. This idea finds expression on the one hand in the purificatory act of circumcision, and on the other in the numerous regulations about cleanness (cf. especially Lv 11–15), which furnish instructions as to the precautions to be taken to avoid defilement, and as to the atoning acts necessary when Levitical purity has been lost. In so far as these acts consist of sacrificial transactions, we shall have to speak of them more fully below in connexion with the subject of sacrifice. But, besides these, we have to do here with the command to consecrate to God all the male firstborn (and therewith all the further offspring of the same womb), and, following out this idea, to redeem them by a prescribed performance from the condition of forfeiture to the Deity (Ex 13[1. 12ff.], Nu 18[16]). The same object is aimed at in the requirement of a poll-tax of half a shekel from every adult Israelite as a protective 'covering' of his life upon the occasion of the numbering of the people (Ex 30[11ff.]). For this last is, as it were, an encroaching upon Jahweh's sphere of sovereignty; hence an express acknowledgment of His sole claim to the life of all persons is necessary, and this takes the form of a poll-tax (Heb. כֹּפֶר 'covering,' 'atonement'), which is of the same amount for all. A natural result of the same assumption is found, finally, in the injunction (Lv 25[39ff.]) that Israelites, who from any cause have become bondmen, are not to be regarded and treated as real slaves, although in the Book of the Covenant (Ex 21[1ff.]) and even in Deuteronomy (15[12ff.]) this is treated as quite possible. On the contrary, P demands that, as really the property of Jahweh, they are to rank only as hirelings or *tôshābhîm* (Lv 25[40]), and in any case are to go free in the year of jubile.

(β) But, more clearly than in any way hitherto mentioned, the idea of a people consecrated to God finds expression in the *organization of the priesthood*. Properly speaking, all male Israelites ought to discharge priestly functions, and thereby testify their willing devotion to God. But for this an indispensable requisite is such a condition of purity as cannot possibly be maintained by every man amidst the duties of common life. Hence Jahweh has arranged for a permanent representation * of the people, in the form of the hereditary priesthood entrusted to Aaron and his sons. The restriction of the priesthood to the 'sons of Ẓadoḳ,' demanded by Ezekiel (see above, p. 705[a]), was impossible for P for the reason that his whole legislation dates from Moses, and thus long before the time of Ẓadoḳ. At the same time, moreover, the deriving of the priesthood from Aaron made it possible to recognize the priestly rights of certain non-Ẓadokite families.† But, in the main, P's 'sons of Aaron' are just the Ẓadokites.

In order to be able to approach God and present Israel's offerings to Him without danger, the priests have to guard carefully against all defilement. In particular, they are not to incur defilement from any dead body (Lv 21[1ff.]), except in unavoidable cases when the body was that of a parent, a brother, an unmarried sister, or one's own child. Any bodily defect serves of itself to exclude from priestly functions, for one thus affected would 'desecrate the sanctuaries of Jahweh' (v.[23]). But the highest requirements in the matter of outward purity apply to the high priest, in whose person the idea of a personal representation of the holy people reaches its climax. He may not defile himself with *any* dead body, even that of father or mother, and is not to leave the sanctuary at all, that he may not (by contact with what is profane) 'desecrate the sanctuary of his God.' Moreover, his very clothing shows (Ex 28[2ff.]) by various symbols that he represents not only the holiness of the priestly people but also their kingly dignity. He wears a robe of blue and red-purple, and a golden diadem inscribed 'Holy to Jahweh,' and upon his shoulder-piece and breastplate are the names of the twelve tribes engraved on precious stones. In short, in place of the pre-exilic chief priest, who is an official of the king, we have now the sovereign, hereditary high priest. At his death the claim of the avenger of blood upon the life of the manslayer lapses (Nu 35[25]). This means simply that with the supreme head of the State ends the period of political life which began with his entry upon office. In like manner the anointing of the high priest, at least according to the theory which represents him alone as anointed (Ex 29[7]; cf. Lv 4[3. 5. 16] 8[12] 'the anointed priest,'* Lv 21[12] 'the consecration of the anointing oil of his God rests upon him') is undoubtedly thought of as a parallel to the anointing of the king. In the other theory, which makes all priests anointed, the thought is probably the ancient one (cf. above, p. 659[b] f.) of an imparting of the spirit as the result of the anointing (Ex 40[15]; on the other hand, in 29[21] and 30[30] the sprinkling of the priests' garments with anointing oil seems to be distinguished from the pouring of oil upon the head of Aaron in 29[7]).

(γ) As to the *Levites*, it is a very general error to regard them as priests of a lower grade, the rank and file, as it were, of the 'priestly tribe' of Levi, from which the priests proper, with the high priest at their head, emerge as a special branch. But this is by no means the intention of P. The circumstance that it is from the tribe of Levi that the Levites are taken, is due to a Divine arrangement equally with the setting apart of the priests from Levi; it is not the consequence of the latter arrangement. On the contrary, the Levites are a selection *from the people* to represent them in connexion with the lower offices of the cultus. These offices ought to be discharged by the people themselves, or, to be more precise, by the firstborn who are consecrated to God. But here, again, the unavoidable absence of constant purity would have rendered such service impossible, seeing that the firstborn could not be kept from all contact with profane life. Hence, according to Nu 3[40ff.], each of the firstborn is to have his place taken by a Levite. Now, as there were only 22,000 Levites available, whereas the number of the firstborn was 22,273, the extra 273 of the latter had to be specially redeemed from their obligation by a further payment of five shekels each. In this requirement P's real view of the character of the Levites finds very clear expression. They are a 'gift' of the people to the priests (Nu 3[9] etc.), to minister to the latter. According to Nu 8[10ff.], they are, like all 'wave-offerings,' assigned to Jahweh through laying on of hands (see below) by the Israelites; they are 'waved' [*i.e.*, probably, led hither and thither, in place of being waved backwards and forwards in the hands, like other sacrificial gifts] by Aaron before Jahweh, and then fall, like all heave- and wave-offerings, to the priests as their property. Their installation is not spoken of, as in the case of the priests, as a consecration, but as an atonement and a purifying (Nu 8[5ff. 21]). In view of all this, we cannot speak of any *priestly service* rendered by the Levites. Nay, according to Nu

* It needs no argument to show that the parallel it was once customary to draw between the OT and the Catholic conception of the priesthood is quite a mistaken one. According to the latter, the priest acts the part of God over against the people, and hence in God's name gives absolution and imparts blessing. On the other hand, in P the high priest is nothing more than a representative—highly exalted and dignified, indeed—of the God-consecrated people. He represents it before God in every regard (see below). Any (ritual) shortcoming on his part involves the whole people in guilt. As to the blessing of Jahweh, again, the high priest, like the other priests, cannot impart this of himself, but must supplicate it of God (cf. Nu 6[23ff.], and especially v.[27]).

† These have their genealogy traced not to Eleazar but to Ithamar, another son of Aaron. It may be noted that only *one* head of a family is named in Ezr 8[2] as a descendant of Ithamar, namely Daniel.

* The title so familiar to us, 'high (lit. 'great,' גָּדוֹל) priest,' appears in Lv 21[10] in the form 'the priest who is greater than his brethren,' while in Ezr 7[5] we have 'the priest [who is] the head.'

$4^{15}$, they are not to touch the sacred vessels upon pain of death, but to carry them only after they have been carefully covered up by the priests. It is true, however, that their superior condition of purity enables them to come nearer to the sanctuary than the profane multitude can do, and to serve as a bulwark to the latter against the destroying holiness of God (cf. above, p. 717).

(δ) We have already (p. $658^{b}$ f.) noted how even P recognizes also a kind of lay priesthood in the shape of the *Nazirate* undertaken for a fixed period of time.

(*d*) *The hallowed character of all property.*—This principle finds expression partly in the ancestral custom of offering the firstfruits of barley, must, and oil (Nu $18^{12ff.}$), and partly in a number of sacrificial transactions. Every due paid from the products of the soil signifies that one owes the whole to Jahweh, and it is only when He has received His portion that the rest is hallowed and given over freely to the use of man. Amongst the regular ritual dues is included also the tenth paid in early times to the king, only that it is no longer, as in Deuteronomy ($14^{22ff.}$), eaten at the sanctuary and given every three years to the poor, but is assigned to the Levites as a recompense for the service which they render in the sanctuary as representatives of the people (Nu $18^{21ff.}$).

(*a*) But in P, as in the pre-Prophetic period, by far the most important place among gifts to God is held by the *sacrifices*. They, too, are in many instances the expression of the consciousness that man owes to God all blessings connected with his earthly possessions, and that he has solemnly to testify his gratitude for these. But this is not the only point of view. On the contrary, there were still at work here a number of motives, partly very ancient, whose presence in sacrificial transactions we have already had to note, although it is hard to say how far a consciousness of the original meaning of the ritual survives in the minds of the authors of P. The idea of the sacral communion (cf. above, p. 661 ff.) still continues to find expression in the employment of blood, as the most important part of all sacrificial transactions; and, indeed, the blood is brought always the nearer to God in proportion to the importance and holiness of the sacrifice. Thus the blood of the peace-offering and the burnt-offering is poured only round about the altar (Lv $1^{5.11}$ $3^{2}$); whereas of the blood of the sin-offering the priest has to sprinkle a portion before the curtain which separates the Holy Place from the Holy of Holies, to smear a portion on the horns of the altar of incense, and to pour the rest upon the ground beside the altar of burnt-offering (Lv $4^{6f.16f.25}$). On the Great Day of Atonement the blood of the guilt-offering is actually brought by the high priest into the Holy of Holies, and sprinkled upon and before the lid of the sacred Ark (Lv $16^{14f.}$). But even the idea of the offering of food still plays a part (although, no doubt, a less prominent one) in P, as is evident from such facts as that—apart of course from incense—it is only what may be eaten that is to be offered, and indeed—as befits the holiness of God—only clean and unblemished animals; that every sacrifice must be seasoned with salt (the meal-offering with oil); and, above all, that every complete sacrifice includes not only flesh but an additional dish in the form of a food-offering, and a portion of drink in the shape of a wine-libation.

But in all this we have not yet the answer to the most important question from the point of view of the history of religion, namely this: *Wherein consists, according to P, the efficacy of sacrifice?* Is it effectual simply *ex opere operato*, or do other, specifically religious, points of view come into consideration? The reply to this question depends upon a correct understanding of the force of the so-called *sĕmîkhāh* (סְמִיכָה) or laying on of hands, and of the significance of the blood in the sacrificial ritual.

In every species of bloody sacrifice the offerer has to take his stand before the door of the sanctuary and lay his hand upon the head of the victim (Lv $1^{4}$, here of the burnt-offering, with the addition 'so shall it be accepted for him and procure atonement for him'; $3^{2.8.13}$, of the peace-offering; $4^{4.15.24.29}$, of the sin-offering). What is the meaning of this ceremony of hand-imposition, upon which manifestly great weight is laid in the sacrificial ritual? It was natural to think of a transference of guilt, especially as this is expressly witnessed to in Lv $16^{21ff.}$. There the high priest lays both hands on the head of the so-called 'scape-goat' (see art. AZAZEL in vol. i.), confesses over him all the transgressions of Israel, and then sends him away, laden with the people's guilt, into the wilderness. Beyond doubt, the laying on of hands in this instance denotes a transference of guilt, but the 'scape-goat' is no *sacrificial victim*, and hence the whole parallel is unsuitable as an aid to explaining the ritual of *sacrifice*. Besides, the laying on of hands is practised also with peace- or thank-offerings, which are not presented for atoning purposes, as well as in connexion with the consecration of the Levites (Nu $8^{10}$). The latter ceremony, in particular, permits of no other explanation than that the laying on of hands is an act whereby a renunciation of personal possession and a giving over with a view to sacrifice [or, in the case of the Levites, with a view to perpetual service in the sanctuary] is accomplished. Hence the comparison with the *manumissio* of Roman law is quite appropriate.*

It is another question whether—quite apart from the meaning of the סְמִיכָה—there may not have been present, at least in the guilt-offering, the idea of a surrender of the life of the animal in place of the forfeited human life—in other words, the inflicting of a penalty upon the victim, and thereby accomplishing a *satisfactio vicaria*. This view has been maintained all the more positively, because in the New Testament the sacrificial death of Christ is undeniably at times looked at from this viewpoint. Further, in Lv $17^{11}$ it is expressly insisted that the seat of life is in the blood, and that God has ordained that blood be used at the altar to accomplish propitiation, for 'the blood atones through the life [contained in it].' Here, surely, it appears to be clearly declared that the life of the victim is a substitute for that of the sinner. But this conclusion is once more rendered impossible by the circumstance that then the sacrificial victim must have been regarded as laden with guilt and curse, and hence as unclean, whereas in reality it is

* Volz (art. 'Die Handauflegung beim Opfer' in *ZATW*, 1901, p. 93 ff.) protests against the idea of the *manumissio*, and refuses to separate the סְמִיכָה of sacrifice from that of blessing and of installation in office (Nu $27^{18.23}$, Dt $34^{9}$). What is in view, he holds, is the conveying of a substance from one party to another—in the case of the sin-offering, the conveying of sin, uncleanness, and curse to the sacrificial victim. But how then could the flesh of the sin-offering have been counted *most holy*, and been directed to be eaten by the priests in a holy place (Lv $6^{18f.}$)? Volz meets this objection by supposing that the sin-offering was meant originally not for Jahweh but for demons hostile to man, and that the סְמִיכָה was then transferred from the sin-offering to the other offerings as well. On the other hand, Matthes (art. 'Der Sühnegedanke bei den Sündopfern' in *ZATW*, 1903, p. 97 ff.) rightly contends, in opposition to Volz, for different kinds of hand-imposition. Bertholet's proposal (Com. on Lv $1^{4}$) to start from Lv $24^{14}$ and to explain the סְמִיכָה of sacrifice as the 'establishing of a solidarity between offerer and offering,' comes in the end to the same thing as the *manumissio* interpretation, only that, according to Bertholet, the fundamental notion of the *communio* is meant here again to find expression.

treated as most holy and serves as holy food for the priests.

In view of all this, in the mind of P there could be no other answer to the question as to the efficacy of sacrifice, but simply this: God has connected the accomplishment of atonement with the obedient discharge of the sacrificial prescriptions; whoever fulfils these and gets the priest to perform the atoning usages, is forgiven (Lv $4^{20. 26. 31. 35}$ and oft.). The ritual, especially the prescribed presenting of the blood, is accordingly the indispensable condition of atonement, but is not yet exactly synonymous with the latter. On the contrary, the forgiveness of sin flows from the grace of God exactly as in the Prophets, only that the latter regard the outward offering as a thing that may be dispensed with, provided the true penitent disposition is present, whereas, according to P, it is imperatively required that this disposition be accompanied by its outward manifestation in the shape of an offering. Even from the point of view of linguistic usage, the difference between the prophetical and the priestly view of atonement is characteristic. According to the prophets (cf. above, p. 689[a]), God Himself covers the sin, *i.e.* He declares it invisible, so that the sinner is safe from the wrath of God, whereas, according to P, the *priest* covers the *person* of the sinner by means of presenting the blood [only in exceptional cases also through an unbloody offering, Lv $5^{11ff.}$], so as to shield him from the destroying holiness of God.

The circumstance that the process of atonement is primarily connected with the presenting of the blood, explains itself naturally as a powerful after-influence of primitive sacrificial usages, in which the sprinkling of the blood had a different signification. The latter is no longer in the mind of P; for even the view is untenable, that the blood, being the seat of life, is regarded as the most precious gift which man can offer. At most, we might hold that P has still the idea of a symbolical (not real) *satisfactio*, or, in other words, the notion that, through the offering of the life of the animal, *symbolical* expression is given to the acknowledgment that, strictly speaking, the sinner's own life is forfeit to God. But the main idea continues to be, as already noted, this: 'thou shalt procure atonement in this and in no other way, because God has so commanded it.'

(β) The technical questions connected with the sacrifices may here be passed by. Their various degrees of value come out clearly in the order in which they have to be offered in all cases where a number of different kinds of sacrifice are combined. (i.) The first place is always held by the *propitiatory* offerings, which include two species: the *sin-offering* (חַטָּאת) and the *guilt-offering* (אָשָׁם). The difference between the two is not very easy to determine from the descriptions contained in Lv 4 f. Both are presented even in the case of unintentional and even unconscious offences; but the guilt-offering (Lv $5^{15ff.}$) has very largely to do with occasions when one has unconsciously (vv.$^{15. 17}$) or consciously (v.$^{20ff.}$ [$6^{1ff.}$]) interfered with the property of another, whether God or one's neighbour. The guilt-offering (in the shape of a ram without blemish) is always coupled with restitution of what has been wrongly taken, with an additional fifth of its value. Of sin-offerings the holiest and most important are naturally those presented on the Great Day of Atonement (Lv 16), when the blood of the victims is brought by the high priest into the Holy of Holies, and thus into the immediate presence of the Divine form of manifestation whose seat is the sacred Ark. It is quite a unique feature that in this instance P introduces, along with the customary atoning medium of sacrifice, another, perhaps very ancient, form of propitiation, namely, the loading of the 'goat for 'Azazel' with the sins of the people by the high priest, and the sending of this goat away to 'Azazel into the wilderness. The interpretation of the name '*Azazel* is disputed; it may mean either 'the apostate' or 'the one who takes away [sin].' Only, there can be no doubt of this, that a personal being must be intended, for in v.$^{8ff.}$ he is expressly opposed to Jahweh; and it is equally clear that he is thought of as an unclean demon dwelling in the desert (or as the prince of the demons that dwell there?). The sending away of the goat to him is simply an act symbolical of the cleansing of the sacred God-consecrated soil from sin and guilt (cf. the precisely similar example of a symbolical removal of uncleanness in Lv $14^{53}$); sin and guilt are sent off into the unclean wilderness to the demon with whose character they correspond. It would be quite wrong to discover in P's recognition of 'Azazel any tendency to dualistic conceptions. 'Azazel is not a power hostile to Jahweh, a power to be in any way compared with Him, but simply a demon, standing outside the theocracy, but none the less on that account subject to Jahweh, the almighty Creator and Ruler of the world (see, further, art. AZAZEL in vol. i.).

There is a widely diffused notion that P regards propitiatory offerings as effectual only in the case of unintentional or, at most, hastily committed sins. This view is based upon Nu $15^{22ff.}$, where in point of fact a distinction is expressly drawn between unwitting offences and those that are committed 'with a [defiant] high hand.' It is only for the first of these that the propitiatory usages have efficacy. The man who sins wilfully is guilty of blasphemy against Jahweh, and is to be cut off without pity (v.$^{30f.}$).

Such is indeed the theory of this passage (Nu $15^{22ff.}$), but it is impossible to regard it as the meaning of P everywhere.* How could it have failed to be seen that, if every wilful transgression was to be punished by cutting off the offender, the undeniably universal sinfulness of man would have speedily led to the extinction of the whole nation? But such a reflexion as this was unneeded. The offences enumerated in Lv $5^{20ff.}$ [Eng. $6^{1ff.}$] as calling for guilt-offerings (denial of a deposit, or of the finding of a lost article, perjury, extortion) surely do not belong to the category of unwitting or hastily committed sins. It may be added that the Psalms also furnish on almost every page evidence that even in the post-exilic theocracy the belief of the prophets in a grace of God which can take away even heinous guilt has not died out.

(ii.) A stage lower than the propitiatory offerings

* The result of such an assumption would be that the notion of atonement (and forgiveness of sins) is not really taken into consideration at all by P. This conclusion is drawn by A. Ritschl (*Lehre von der Rechtfertigung und Versöhnung*, ii.[3] [1889] 68 ff., 184 ff.), according to whom the 'covering' (*kappārā*) needed was not against the wrath of God on the sinner, but against the destroying majesty (holiness) of God, to which man, owing to his creaturely weakness, could not otherwise draw near. The procuring of the *kappārā* [Ritschl would prefer to see the term 'atonement' avoided here] is thus simply the condition of safely approaching God with an offering, and always implies the undisturbed continuance of the covenanted grace of God, without which no sacrifice is possible. But, quite apart from the oft-recurring (Lv $4^{20. 26}$ etc.) formula 'and he shall be forgiven [after the atoning acts have been performed],' the theory of Ritschl is shattered by the fact that the 'covering' of the man by the priest is, of course, only the later transformation given to the prophetic formula, according to which God covers the guilt. In both cases the point is that the *guilt* is to be declared powerless—in other words, it is an atoning act that is in view. Cf., further, on the whole question, A. Cave, *The Scriptural Doctrine of Sacrifice and Atonement*, Edinburgh, 1890; A. Schmoller, 'Das Wesen der Sühne in der alttest. Opferthora' (*SK*, 1891, p. 205 ff.). Stade's definition (*Geschichte Israels*, ii. 57), 'Atonement means reconsecration or restoring, by means of rites, a sacred character that has been lost,' while it is quite applicable to a great many cases, needs, in view of what is said above, to be enlarged.

stands the *burnt-offering* (עֹלָה) or whole-offering (כָּלִיל). But, as wholly belonging to Jahweh, it retains a higher significance than the meal-offering. At one time presented also as a propitiatory offering, it has in P the significance of a general 'adoration offering,' a testimony to the normal relation between Jahweh and the people. Hence it has its place after the propitiatory offerings, since the latter are appointed for the purpose of removing any disturbance of the normal relation. But, even unpreceded by propitiatory offerings, the burnt-offering may be presented as a dutiful expression of absolute dependence on the covenant God, and of the consciousness of owing all blessings to Him. Thus we find it especially in the form of the so-called תָּמִיד or 'continual' offering, *i.e.* the offering every morning and evening of a yearling lamb, along with food-offering and drink-offering (Ex 29[38ff.], Nu 28[3ff.]). On the Sabbath (v.[9f.]) and still more at the New Moon (v.[11ff.]) this regular offering undergoes material enlargement.

(iii.) A third species of offering meets us in the *meal-offerings* (שְׁלָמִים Lv 3. 7[29ff.]), of which the fat is burned, the blood sprinkled on the altar, the breast 'waved'* and given along with the right leg (as a so-called *tĕrûmāh*) to the priests, while the rest of the flesh is eaten by the offerers. A special branch of the *shĕlāmîm* is supplied by the 'thanksgiving offerings' of Lv 7[11ff.]. But to P all *shĕlāmîm*-offerings are only offerings of the second rank, since they are not appropriated by Jahweh (*i.e.* the priests) alone, but are meant to be consumed also by the laity—in other words, are destined for profane use. The small value attached to the meal-offering by P as compared with the place it still holds in Deuteronomy (cf. above, p. 661) is explained by the completely changed conception of the cultus which had already been produced by the programme of Ezekiel (45[17. 22] etc.). The private cultus that once prevailed, whose central point was the joyous sacrificial meal, has now been displaced by the official cult performed with scrupulous regularity by the priests † in the name (it might be without even the presence) of the theocratic community. It was quite in the spirit of the Priests' Code, that when the temple square was stormed by Pompey the priests continued unflinchingly the performance of their functions until they were cut down at the altar; and that during the siege by Titus the daily burnt-offering was continued morning and evening even after the city had long been brought to the extreme of famine.

We pass over all further prescriptions regarding festal offerings and freewill services, and content ourselves with noting the fact that *all* directions regarding holy places, times, persons, and actions have ever in view the *one* aim of realizing the idea of a God-consecrated people, the fact of its absolute dependence upon Him, and the necessity of ever renewed surrender to Him. It is quite possible that, in the working out of the system in detail, Babylonian ‡ influences may have co-operated; but in any case these are so incorporated with, nay even subordinated to, the theocratic fundamental ideas, that they are no longer felt to be a foreign element, hence requiring to be considered less from the standpoint of Biblical Theology than from that of the History of Religion in general.

5. On the other hand, we have still to answer another extremely important question, namely, as to the *ethical system* upon which P builds, and which he desires to see realized. What ideal of morality floats before his mental vision, and by what means does he aim at realizing it?

In dealing with these questions it is necessary at the very outset to repel a charge which, for reasons that are readily intelligible, is often brought against P, namely, that moral commands proper recede in his pages so far behind ritual ordinances that they seem to possess no importance at all. But we must not forget that P represents the close of a long development in the course of which the moral demands of the prophets, at least after the introduction of Deuteronomy, had long become flesh and blood in the case of the better portion of the people—certainly of all who accepted the future hope. It did not appear to P to be necessary to emphasize these demands afresh, seeing that in the form of the Decalogue they had long been a common possession of the people. Moreover, there is not wanting, at least in the Law of Holiness (Lv 19 and 20), a collection of a whole series of essentially moral commands, although these are for the most part amalgamated in a remarkable fashion with ritual prescriptions (cf. *e.g.* 19[5ff. 19. 21f. 23ff. 27f.]), and the way in which humanitarian prescriptions, like those contained in 19[10f. 13f.], are based upon the motive of the fear of God (see especially vv.[14. 32]) more than once vividly recalls Deuteronomy. The same remark applies to the exhortations to the strictest impartiality in judicial decisions (vv.[15. 35]), and to absolute honesty in business and uprightness of life (vv.[11. 13a. 36]). Besides, v.[33f.] contains not only a prohibition against oppressing the *gēr*,* but a command to love him as oneself. On the other hand, however, it cannot be disputed that the concept 'neighbour' in vv.[16. 18] is restricted solely to one's fellow-countrymen. Amongst other instances, this comes out clearly in the prohibition to treat Israelites as slaves: the heathen and even settlers in Israel may be purchased as slaves and bequeathed as such to one's children, but not so with Israelites (Lv 25[44f.]). Everything of heathen origin is *eo ipso* unclean, and hence so far beneath Israel that the latter recognizes no consideration or equal rights as belonging to it. Deutero-Isaiah's thought of Israel as having a missionary function to discharge to the heathen appears to be completely forgotten.

But, if we cannot thus speak of moral duties towards non-Israelites (with such exceptions as the general prohibition of murder, Gn 9[5f.], and the above-mentioned kindly recommendation of the *gērîm*, Lv 19[33f.]), it is true that otherwise the ethical system of the prophets may be regarded as binding for P. Only, in his estimation, the moral ideal is not exhausted in the fulfilment of specially *ethical* demands, but he places along with these, at least upon the same level, if not upon a higher one, regulations as to the cultus—nay, purely external, ritual requirements. Here, if anywhere, we see that P sets before him the realizing of the system sketched by Ezekiel. The aim to which every other interest must give way is the setting up of a pure God-consecrated people;

* This waving (lit. 'swinging') of the offering or part of it denotes, according to what is surely the right interpretation, a moving backwards and forwards in the hands, the priest making as if he would cast the offering into the altar flame, but ending by taking it back as food assigned by God to the priests. A different explanation is given by Philo (in a fragment of his treatise *de Victimis*, edited by Wendland in 1891), who holds that the waving of the offering consisted in holding it up towards heaven.

† According to the list of offerings in Nu 28 f., the number of *official* sacrifices amounts yearly to 115 young bullocks, 1100 lambs, 38 rams, and 32 goats, besides the food- and drink-offerings pertaining to them.

‡ On this point cf. especially P. Haupt, 'The Origin of the Mosaic Ceremonial' in *John Hopkins University Circular*, xix. No. 145 (Baltimore, 1900), in which a Babylonian origin is claimed even for קָרְבָּן, תּוֹרָה, בְּרִית, and כִּפֶּר; and the same author's art. 'Babylonian Elements in the Levitic Ritual' in *Journ. of Bibl. Lit.* xix. i. 55 ff.

* By the *gēr* here is evidently to be understood not a heathen but an Israelite of another tribe or family, or even a foreigner who has settled in Israel and become completely incorporated therewith; cf., on this controverted question, Bertholet, *Die Stellung der Israeliten und der Juden zu den Fremden*, Freiburg, 1896.

but this is achieved, not primarily, as in the view of the prophets, by circumcision of the heart, but by means of all the countless purifying and atoning acts prescribed by the Law for every conceivable case (cf. especially Lv 12 and 15). Neglect of these rules—even wholly unintentional and unconscious neglect—involves the same degree of culpability as a mortal sin does. The rigid consistency and outwardly mechanical character of this whole conception come out, above all, in the ritual of the Great Day of Atonement. The solemn propitiation made by Aaron with the goat of the people (Lv $16^{15ff.}$) is intended, properly speaking, not for the people themselves but (vv.$^{16. 20}$) for the inner sanctuary, the Tent of Meeting and the altar—in other words, for things without life. Atonement on behalf of these for all the ritual transgressions and omissions of the people thus appears as the most important feature in the ritual of the Great Day of Atonement.

It can occasion no surprise that very depreciatory judgments have often been passed on P alike for his exclusiveness towards foreigners and his placing of moral and physical (ritual) purity on precisely the same level. The gulf between the religion of the Prophets—above all, of Deutero-Isaiah—and that of the Priests' Code has been described as one that cannot be bridged. That there is, in fact, a deep gulf between the two, and that this shows itself in P in the shape of a falling away from the pure level reached by the Prophets, are truths that need be denied all the less, seeing that the teaching of Jesus certainly attached itself to the prophets, and would have the Law interpreted only in their sense and spirit. Yet, if we would do justice to P, there are two things that must not be forgotten. In the first place, even his system did not exclude the possibility of viewing the revelation of the Divine will as a guide to real inward piety and morality, and of thus finding in it a means of joy and edification.* Many passages in the Psalms ($1^2$ $19^{8ff.}$, and almost the whole of Ps 119) testify to this rejoicing of the heart in God's law. The period of *painful* attention to the observance of the Law first set in when the religion of Israel was seriously endangered by Antiochus Epiphanes. It was thought then that the anger of God could be appeased only by the strictest, most literal fulfilment of the Law, and the time of consummation be thus brought on. But the heavy burden of the Law was increased, above all, by the addition of the alleged oral tradition from Sinai downwards, the casuistry developed in Pharisaic circles, with its endless particular rules, which kept the Israelite who was loyal to the Law in momentary anxiety lest he had in any way incurred defilement and consequently heinous guilt.

But, secondly, it must not be forgotten that, in spite of its inferiority to the religion of the Prophets, the Law fulfilled an important mission in the course of the history of the religion of Israel as a whole. Experience had taught that the great mass of the people had proved themselves incapable of understanding and fruitfully assimilating the teaching of the prophets. Hence the latter had its place taken by another Divine pædagogic method—the discipline of the Law, with its ceaseless reminders of the immense distance between the holy God and the sinful uncleanness of everything creaturely, with its constant compelling of a lively sense of the need of forgiveness and atonement, and of the duty of a conscientious use of the prescribed means of propitiation. In short, the Law proved a παιδαγωγὸς εἰς Χριστόν (Gal $3^{24}$) not only in the sense that it forced the recognition of the impossibility of attaining to righteousness before God by the works of the Law, but also that it was a school which taught absolute submission to the will of God and therewith sincere piety. And what an intensely religious life might be developed alongside of and under the rule of the Law, is witnessed by the last two groups of literature we have yet to consider: the religious Lyric and Elegiac poetry, and the remnants of the so-called *Ḥokhmāh* or Wisdom literature.

* Cf. Gunkel, *Ausgewählte Psalmen*, Göttingen, 1904, p. 22 ff.

## IX. The religious Lyric and Elegiac poetry (Books of Psalms and Lamentations).

If, in addition to the Prophets, only the Law had come down to us, a wholly inadequate, nay partially wrong, idea of the power exercised by the Prophetic religion would have been inevitable. But, fortunately, more than one literary product has survived, and amongst these the Psalms are, above all, fitted to guide us to a profounder judgment. In them is exhibited such a wonderful variety and intensity of the genuinely religious life, that our verdict must be that there is practically no trace to be detected of the serious danger that was called up by the complete equalizing of ritual obligations with specially moral duties, of physical with moral purity; nay, testimonies are not wanting to an express repudiation of sacrifice (see above, p. $685^b$), *i.e.* of what is to P the most important element in the cultus.

The numerous critical questions connected with the Books of Psalms and Lamentations may here be entirely passed over (see article LAMENTATIONS in vol. iii., and PSALMS in vol. iv.). It may be that in the Psalms there still survive scattered relics of pre-exilic religious poetry, but in *that* form in which the book now lies before us it is a work of the post-exilic period* and may thus, in spite of all its variety of contents, be treated without hesitation as a harmonious whole, and a consistent witness to the faith and hopes of post-exilic Israel.

The question so much debated in recent times, who is to be regarded as the speaking subject ('*das betende Ich*') in the Psalms,† must undoubtedly, with Olshausen, Reuss, Cheyne, *et al.*, be answered very frequently in favour of the so-called *collective* subject, as against the almost uniformly *individual* interpretation of Ewald, Hupfeld, Duhm, *et al.* Reuss in particular has rightly argued that the endless complaints against cruel foes and persecutors can be felt to be intelligible and justified,

* What appears to the present writer the most probable view of the case is as follows. The oldest collection, Ps 3–41, was already formed in the time of Ezra; then, say towards the close of the Persian period, a second collection, made up of further (alleged) Davidic psalms (51–71), songs of contemporaries of David (42–49. 50. 72. 73–83), and a supplementary collection (84–89). The third collection (90–150) can scarcely have originated before the founding of the Hasmonæan dynasty by Simon (B.C. 142 ff.). Psalms 1 and 2 were probably first prefixed by the final redactor of the whole Psalter, as a very appropriate prologue.

As to the Book of Lamentations, it may suffice to remark that the oldest components (chs. 2 and 4) are based upon quite fresh recollections of the destruction of Jerusalem in 587, whereas ch. 5 may belong to the 6th cent., ch. 1 to the 5th, but ch. 3 as late as the 3rd cent. B.C.

† On this controverted question, cf. R. Smend, art. 'Ueber das Ich der Psalmen' in *ZATW*, 1888, p. 49 ff. [where the idea of the collective subject is almost consistently carried through]; J. Z. Schuurmans Stekhoven, *ZATW*, 1889, p. 131 ff. [a partial modification of Smend's view]; G. Beer, *Individual- und Gemeindepsalmen*, Marburg, 1894; F. Coblenz, *Ueber das betende Ich in den Psalmen*, Frankfurt, 1897; H. Roy, *Die Volksgemeinde und die Gemeinde der Frommen im Psalter*, Gnadenfeld, 1897; D. Leimdörfer, *Das Psalter-ego in den Ich-Psalmen*, 1897; Engert, *Der betende Gerechte der Psalmen*, Würzburg, 1902. The last six of these insist with more or less emphasis that it is not the actual people that is to be looked on as the '*betende Ich*,' but only the godly portion, which pines under the oppression of the enemy and prays and hopes for deliverance. They point out, further, that (altogether apart from psalms which are absolutely individual in their reference) even the psalms which represent the community, although spoken in the name of the latter, were primarily the work of a particular individual.

nay even touching, only if they are referred not to private affairs, but to the straits ever the same to which the godly community is reduced by heathen oppressors and by renegades within the nation itself. It would, however, be altogether an unjustifiable exaggeration to seek to refer practically all the Psalms to a collective subject—the godly community. On the contrary, for the proper appreciation of the Psalter, it is of the very highest importance to note that 'individualism' in religion, for which the way was paved especially by Jeremiah, already has clear expression given to it in many ways in this very book.* The numerous witnesses to the pining and striving of individual suppliants after living communion with their God, and to the blessed assurance of this communion, will alone explain how the Psalter has been able to serve even down to the present day as the prayer-book even of Christian nations.

1. *Conception of God.*—(*a*) As in exilic and post-exilic prophecy, the conception of God is seen in the Psalms occupying a height which could not be surpassed even on New Testament soil except in a few points. The solity of Jahweh (18$^{32}$), the impossibility of comparing Him with any other being, the utter nothingness of idols (115$^{4ff.}$), are to the psalmists axioms which need no proof. As Creator of the world (24$^{1ff.}$ 74$^{16f.}$ 95$^{4}$ 104$^{2ff.}$, and often), and that by the simple word of His power (33$^{6.\ 9}$), He is at the same time also the absolute Ruler of the whole (33$^{14f.}$ 46$^{7.\ 9ff.}$ 47$^{2ff.}$ 65$^{6ff.}$ 66$^{7}$ 82$^{8}$ 103$^{19}$ 113$^{4}$). He glorifies Himself continually in inanimate nature (8$^{4f.}$ 19$^{2ff.}$; in 29$^{3ff.}$ by the majesty of His thunder); hence it is summoned, as well as living creatures, to praise Him (148$^{3ff.}$). Above all, wonderful appears His condescension to man, who by himself is so weak; He has constituted him only a little short of the nature of Divine beings (8$^{6ff.}$, with a manifest allusion to Gn 1$^{27ff.}$). The care of God for His creatures is evidently not separated, after the manner of Christian dogmatics, from the work of creation and classed as a preserving and governing, or even thought of as a continued working of laws of nature once established; but consists in ever renewed, independent creative acts of an actively ruling God (65$^{10ff.}$ 104$^{13ff.\ 27f.}$ 145$^{15f.}$ 147$^{8f.}$).

(*b*) The solitary limitation of the being of God which in itself is absolutely without limits, which might be discovered, would be the frequent mention of His heavenly dwelling-place (11$^{4}$ 14$^{2}$ 20$^{7\,(6)}$, and very often). But this form of spatial limitation could not be dispensed with by the conception of God, even at its highest reach, if it was to escape the danger of being dissipated into pantheism. The no less frequent allusions to Zion as God's abode and the starting-point of His action (20$^{3\,(2)}$ 50$^{2}$ 68$^{17}$ etc.) does not, as we have already had occasion to explain, contradict in the least the idea of the God of heaven. Heaven is His throne, Zion the place of His revealed presence, which is not identical with His most essential being. The magnificent description of the theophany in Ps 18$^{8ff.}$, where God mounts the cherub and thus flies abroad, belongs to the domain of poetic licence, equally with His appearing from Sinai in 68$^{18}$.

(*c*) On the other hand, it might appear strange that we still meet in the Psalms with traces of a *theologumenon* with which we have already (above, p. 684$^{b}$) made acquaintance in Dt 4$^{19}$ as well as in Dn 10 (see above, p. 714$^{b}$). We refer to the idea of under-gods (*bĕnê 'ĕlōhîm* or, shortly, *'ĕlōhîm* or *'ēlîm* 'gods'; even *bĕnê 'ĕlōhîm* does not mean 'sons of gods,' but 'those who belong to the category of *'ĕlōhîm*'), who, either independently, although commissioned by Jahweh, rule over the heathen peoples (so with the star-gods in Dt 4$^{19}$ *), or under the ægis of Jahweh take their part as a kind of vassal kings in the government of the world. Only in this sense are we to explain not only the שָׂרִים or 'princes' of Dn 10, but also the אֵלִים [so read for the corrupt אֵלֶם] of Ps 58$^{2}$ and the אֱלֹהִים of 82$^{1.\ 6}$ [v.$^{6b}$ בְּנֵי עֶלְיוֹן 'sons of the highest']. In both passages the injustice and partiality of their rule are complained of,—alluding, of course, to the treatment of Israel by heathen peoples,—and in 82$^{7}$ they are even threatened with death after the manner of man, by way of punishment for their conduct. This last passage shatters all possibility of explaining these אֱלֹהִים as human judges; to 'die like men' is possible only to those who in themselves are immortal. Now, even although it cannot be denied that in the whole conception of these under-gods we have a manifest after-effect of the belief in the reality of the former gods of the nations, yet the idea is so incorporated with and subordinated to Jahwism that it is impossible to regard it as a survival of the once prevailing Henotheism or even of a former Polytheism. The same complete welding of originally heathen *mythologumena* with Jahwism is met with also in 74$^{13f.}$ and 104$^{26}$, with their allusions to the subduing of Leviathan; and in 89$^{11\,(10)}$, with its crushing of Rahab.†

These same under-gods of Ps 58 and 82 are, beyond doubt, intended also by the אֱלֹהִים of 86$^{8}$ 95$^{3}$ 96$^{4}$ 97$^{7.\ 9}$ 135$^{5}$ 138$^{1}$ and the בְּנֵי אֱלֹהִים of 29$^{1}$ and 89$^{7}$, over whom Jahweh is absolutely exalted. Distinguished from them, we have in 103$^{20f.}$ 148$^{2}$ the angels (מַלְאָכִים, lit. 'messengers'), who surround the throne of God offering praise, or, sent by Him, stand by the side of the godly to protect him (34$^{8}$ 35$^{5f.}$, both times 'the angel of Jahweh,' but certainly not now in the sense of a self-manifestation of Jahweh [cf. above, p. 639$^{a}$]; 91$^{11ff.}$). The idea of a heavenly council includes also 'the holy ones' (*i.e.*, as elsewhere, those who stand in the closest relation to God, not those who are morally perfect) of Ps 89$^{7f.}$. The angels, again, who bring misfortune (78$^{49}$), being sent *by God* to punish, are not morally wicked beings or even hostile to God, but are simply 'angels of evils' (מַלְאֲכֵי רָעִים), *i.e.* such as are sent by God to bring trouble upon sinners.

(*d*) The so-called *attributes of God*, or, to be more correct, the various sides on which His one being displays itself, are never with the Psalmists the subject of metaphysical speculation, but are always put forward only with a specifically religious interest—at one time for the warning, at another for the consolation, of the godly. The Eternity of God is the pledge that He can be a true refuge to His people (90$^{1f.\ 4}$). His Omnipotence has proved itself alike in creation and in the directing of history (115$^{3}$ 135$^{6}$). His Unchangeableness sets the nothingness of all created things in its true light: heaven and earth shall decay, and He shall change them like a garment, but He Himself remains unchangeably the same (102$^{26ff.}$). His Wisdom has manifested itself, above all, in the work of creation (104$^{24}$), but in other matters too the depth of His thoughts awakens wondering admiration (92$^{6\,(5)}$ 139$^{17f.}$). His Omniscience extends to every action, however trifling, and every thought of man (139$^{1ff.}$)—a salutary warning to him; for even the most secret depth of the heart is open to Him (7$^{10\,(9)}$ 44$^{22\,(21)}$). And when it is said in 139$^{5f.}$ that He takes cognizance even of the embryo in the womb, and that

* Cf. the articles of Sellin on 'Das Subject der altisraelitischen Religion' in *Neue kirchliche Zeitschrift*, iv. (1893) Heft 6, and v. (1895) Heft 4.

* The same idea is certainly present when we read of the fixing of the bounds of the peoples according to the number of the *bĕnê 'ĕlōhîm* (Dt 32$^{8}$, reading, with the LXX, בְּנֵי אֱלֹהִים for the בְּנֵי יִשְׂרָאֵל of MT).

† Cf. above, p. 670$^{b}$ f.

the span of life and perhaps also the fortunes of the individual in question are written in His book, this is certainly to be understood not in the sense of a rigid predestination, but only as implying that absolutely nothing can evade the knowledge or thwart the will of God. Similarly, His Omnipresence ($139^{7ff.}$) is described not (pantheistically) as that of His substance, but of His knowledge and His power, in order to check at the outset all thought of escape from Him. His moral Perfection comes to view in His horror of sin ($5^{5ff.}$), His Righteousness in His attitude not only to His own people ($7^{12}$ $11^{7}$ $33^{3}$ etc.) but to heathen nations as well ($9^{8}$). But, naturally, the largest space is occupied in the psalmists' descriptions by such attributes of God as His Love, by the praise of His inexhaustible Grace and Compassion, His Long-suffering and Truth ($86^{15}$ $103^{8ff.}$ $36^{6.8}$). In His Goodness all His creatures may take comfort ($33^{6(5)}$ $145^{8f.}$); but, above all, He shows Himself 'the Father of the orphan and the Provider of the widow' ($68^{6(5)}$ $146^{9}$). It is noteworthy that, apart from this application of the name 'Father,' the idea of the Fatherly love of God, which forms the central point of the NT conception of God, meets us only once more (Ps $103^{13}$), and there only in the form of a comparison, not to speak of its being manifestly restricted to Israel—another of the evidences that the OT conception of God was capable of enlargement in one very important direction.

2. *Anthropology outside the sphere of Jahwism proper.*—In the judgments passed in the Book of Psalms on the purely human, we find, side by side with panegyrics on the lofty pre-eminence of man in his lordship over creation ($8^{4ff.}$, see above, p. 724a), lamentations over the weakness and transitory nature of everything human ($33^{16f.}$ $62^{10}$ $103^{14ff.}$; $144^{4}$ 'Man is like a breath, his days are as a shadow that passeth away'). This lament applies to even the strongest ($146^{3f.}$). And when the life —all too short—comes to an end ($39^{5ff.}$ $90^{10.12}$), dark *Shĕ'ōl* (see above, p. 668 f.) awaits the departed, and cuts him off finally from all relation to the upper world, and above all from the blessings of the theocracy or the praise of God ($6^{6}$ $30^{10}$ $88^{11ff.}$ $115^{17}$). None can escape this fate ($89^{49}$). It is true that at times the sense of close fellowship with God (see below) reaches a height and a strength which seem to leave only a short step to the conviction that *true* fellowship with God must of necessity be enduring and extend beyond the present life;* but this step is never definitely taken. Only as a 'stranger and a sojourner' does man continue with God during his earthly walk ($39^{13(12)f.}$), at death the bond of connexion is severed for ever. In this matter, if anywhere, it is clear what a power and stimulus must have belonged to faith in the God of Israel, seeing that, even without the hope of immortality, it could produce fruits of such intense religiousness as we find in the Psalms (and Job). The question whether there are not really to be found in the Psalms traces of the hope of a continued existence, will have to be discussed when we come to speak of the eschatological expectations.

The physical weakness of man finds its analogue in his moral weakness. When in Ps $51^{7(5)}$ the latter is traced back to his generation and birth by sinful parents, this is not intended, of course, to mean that generation and birth are of themselves sinful.

* Thus R. H. Charles (in the second chapter of his *Critical History of the Doctrine of a Future Life in Israel, in Judaism, and in Christianity*, London and New York, 1899) discovers in Ps 49. 73, as well as in the Book of Job, approaches to an immortality doctrine—an individual eschatology which finally (according to ch. 3) combined with the popular eschatology to form the doctrine of the resurrection (cf. below, p. 728a note; and the later article of Charles, 'The Rise and Development in Israel of Belief in a Future Life,' *Expositor*, Jan. 1903, p. 49 ff.).

The whole statement amounts to a plea that God would judge leniently one who, as sprung from sinners, necessarily carries within him from the womb a sinful habit and sinful inclinations. It is only in the latter sense that the statement can be called a contribution to the doctrine of original sin. There is not the faintest reference to an imputation of Adam's guilt—the very kernel of the dogmatic doctrine of original sin.

3. *Nature and history of the Theocracy.*—The idea of an election of Israel to be God's own people is firmly held also by the Psalmists ($33^{12}$ $74^{2}$ $135^{4}$), and it cannot be doubted that here again this conviction carried with it the serious danger of national conceit and a mischievous disposition to look down on all other peoples—a danger which threatened to stifle completely the existence of those great thoughts of Deutero-Isaiah regarding a missionary vocation of Israel to all the heathen. It is true that this conceit was materially diminished by the honourable confession that Israel has almost always shown itself unworthy of the Divine choice and the great acts of Jahweh in connexion with the deliverance from Egyptian bondage ($77^{15ff.}$ $78^{4.11ff.}$ $106^{7ff.}$). It is the well-deserved anger of God that has given Israel over to the powerful oppression and the savage mockery of her enemies (La $2^{1f.21f.}$ $4^{11}$, Ps $22^{7ff.}$, and numerous other passages). Israel heeded not the threatenings of Jahweh repeated from the days of old (La $2^{17}$), but allowed herself to be deceived by false prophets and priests (La $2^{14}$ $4^{13}$). But in spite of all this the Divine covenant is assured for ever (Ps $105^{8}$ $111^{9}$); and thus to those who humbly submit themselves to Him the day must come when all the comforting promises of days gone by shall be fulfilled (La $3^{21ff.}$). The principal expectations attached to the theocracy of the future will come out in the section devoted to the Messianic hopes.

4. *The theocratic institutions.*—There are a great many passages in the Psalms, in which touching and powerful expression is given to high esteem for the temple as the place of Jahweh's gracious presence, and to longing after the beautiful service conducted there ($5^{8}$ $26^{8}$ $27^{4}$ $43^{3f.}$ $65^{5}$ $84^{2ff.11}$ $116^{18f.}$ $122^{1ff.}$). But it would certainly be an error to discover the principal motive of this longing in joy in the cultus in the narrower sense, *i.e.* in the sacrificial performances. Against such a supposition there is not only the fact that mention of sacrifice is extremely rare ($20^{4}$ $54^{8}$ $66^{13ff.}$; in $141^{2}$ it is only symbolical sacrifice that is in view), but it is well known that there are not wanting in the Psalms passages in which the necessity of sacrifice and its acceptableness to God are repudiated in the most unqualified terms, and not without a touch of sarcasm ($40^{7}$ $50^{8ff.}$ $51^{18}$ $69^{32}$; see more fully, above, p. 686b). We must hold then that the piety of the psalmists occupies in general a higher level than that of the framers of the Priests' Code. Their joy in the beautiful service of the temple was evidently derived primarily from what appealed to the heart and the feelings: the festal processions, the prayers and benedictions of the priests, and, not last, it may be presumed, the temple music and singing (to which last the greatest care seems from all accounts to have been given). All this is supported by the circumstance that the (not very frequent) praise of the Law ($1^{2}$ $19^{8(7)ff.}$) is probably everywhere intended for the specifically moral (so quite clearly in $19^{12f.}$) commands and not for the Ceremonial Law. Even the endless utterances—mostly of quite a general character—in Ps 119 as to the value and efficacy of the Divine commands show at times (so vv.$^{9.36.133}$) that what they have in view is the moral content of the Law.

5. *The character of the religion of the Psalms.*—If a *sine quâ non* of all true religion is a sincere

confession of sin, then the religion of the psalmists has undoubtedly a firm basis. In addition to the ready admission of the general guilt of the people, of which we have already spoken, there are not a few testimonies to the impossibility of all attempts of one's own to attain to a righteousness which can bear to be tested by the eye of a holy God (38[19] 51[3ff.] 130[1ff.] 143[2], La 1[5. 8. 14. 18. 22] 3[39ff.] 4[6] 5[16]), as well as evidences of a tenderness of conscience which feels concerned even about unconscious sins (Ps 19[13] 90[8]) and sins of youth (25[7]), and prays God to forgive them. It is only rarely that we still meet with outbursts of self-righteousness, showing itself in a disposition to boast of one's minute observance of the Law (17[5] 18[21ff.] 44[18ff.]), and even to complain that God, notwithstanding all this, delays to help His people (44[10ff.]). No less surprising, and quite opposed to the usual language of the Book of Lamentations, is the complaint of La 5[7] 'The fathers sinned, and we bear their guilt.'

More than once we meet with an almost evangelical perception in what is said about the forgiveness of sin. The Apostle Paul was thoroughly justified (Ro 4[6ff.]) in using Ps 32[1f.] as a Scripture proof that the blessedness of a conscience at peace with God is based not upon any merit of works, but upon the fact that God in His grace does not impute guilt (cf. also Ps 103[3ff.], esp. v.[8ff.]).

To those, again, who are ever mindful of their constant need of fresh grace, who are 'of a broken heart and contrite spirit,' Jahweh is near (34[19] 51[19]), and creates in them—for an actual new creation is needed—a clean heart and a new, right spirit (51[12]). He teaches them to recognize in God the highest, yea the only, good (16[2]), the source of all true spiritual life and all real light (36[10]); He awakens in them an inextinguishable longing for blessed peace in God and the closest fellowship with Him, and provides for the full satisfying of this longing. Sayings like those of 16[5. 8f.] 42[2f.] 63[2] 73[25f.] 143[6], and, above all, the noble words of 131[1f.], have found a perfect echo even in Christian hearts all through the centuries.

(*a*) A fruit of such fellowship with God is a life of *prayer* (supplication, thanksgiving and adoration) of inexhaustible variety and intimacy. Examples of this it is all the less necessary to quote, since the whole Psalter is *one* witness to this fact. A single remark may, however, be made. How petty and empty appear all those philosophical and theological discussions about prayer as an attempt to interfere with the unalterable predetermination of God, when compared with the grand simplicity and inward certainty of the praying psalmists! Their hearts have no room for such considerations. No doubt they, too, feel the manifold mysteries of the course of things in this world, and are plunged by them into doubt and unrest. Nor are they strangers to impatience, nay, at times, even displeasure, on account of the delay of Divine aid and the seeming silence of God in presence of violence and injustice. But in the end the certainty forces its way that the omnipotence, the wisdom, and the righteousness of God must triumph over all unreason and unrighteousness. And the conviction that prayer, the indispensable nourishment of the soul, is more precious than aught else (92[2ff.]), and that God is ever near to them that call upon Him (145[18f.]), is placed at last beyond the reach of doubt.

(*b*) A further fruit of this spiritual life in and with God shows itself in the disposition which recognizes all the actions and the whole lot of the godly to be absolutely dependent upon the wise and gracious will of God, and which is therefore prepared in all things to give the glory not to man but to God alone (115[1ff.]), and to expect all things from His blessing alone (127[1f.]). The Psalm passages, in which an inflexible confidence in the wise and loving guidance and protection of the godly finds touching and often typical expression (*e.g.* 3[4ff.] 5[12f.] 23[4] 27[1] 91[1ff.] 118[6ff.] 121[1ff.]), have in all ages retained their place even in Christian hearts as forms of prayer which possess inexhaustible living power.

6. *Morality*.—After what we have had to say about the attitude of the Psalmists to the cultus, and about the character of their religion, we could not but expect that their moral disposition would show itself in a corresponding form. The testimonies to this can hardly be called numerous, if we leave out of account the endless complaints against the heathen and against faithless fellow-countrymen [the latter being for the most part referred to in the term רְשָׁעִים or 'ungodly']. The contents of these complaints point of themselves to the opposite as constituting what is right and moral. Of more importance, however, are the passages in which we find positively, as it were, set up an ideal of the life that is truly moral and well-pleasing to God. It is noteworthy in this connexion that in almost all these passages (15[1ff.] 24[3f.] 34[13f.] 101[1ff.]; in a negative form in 50[16ff.]) the strongest emphasis is laid upon those requirements, inattention to which had furnished the main occasion for the denunciations and complaints of the prophets: honesty and truthfulness, above all in judicial cases which might issue in endangering the rights of the poor and the weak.

A dark shadow is undeniably cast on this attractive picture by those outbursts of sometimes passionate longing for revenge that are found in the so-called 'imprecatory psalms' (41[11] 58[11] 109[7ff.], and esp. 137[8ff.]; cf. also La 1[21f.] 3[64ff.] 4[21f.]). The expedient of declaring that the objects of hatred and revengeful longing in these passages are not persons but the cause they represent, their hostility to God and His kingdom, is utterly untenable in view, for example, of Ps 137[8ff.]. We have simply to acknowledge that there is not to be detected here the slightest breath of the spirit which inspires the words of Mt 5[44f.]. And, however readily we may concede that such utterances are partly intelligible as the cry of distress of a people long enslaved and maltreated, and that on that account they are in a measure excusable, they still continue to be at the same time instructive witnesses to the fact that in the OT, side by side with the word of God, the disposition and the voice of the natural man may still be remarked.

7. *The doctrine of retribution*.—The problem ever raised afresh by experience, namely, how the actions and the fortunes of men are related to one another, had already, as we saw above (p. 689), engaged the attention of the later Prophets, and had led first to the conclusion that no one has to pay the penalty of another's guilt, but only his own. But in proportion as the place of the old popular religion, which had regard almost exclusively to the nation as a whole, had its place taken by an interest in the religious individual, the question always became a more burning one,—in view of the complete absence of any hope of a compensatory process in the world beyond,—how the sufferings of the godly and the prosperity of the wicked were to be reconciled with faith in a Divine, and thus absolutely righteous, rule of the world. At first the Psalmists, too, abide by the simple postulate, which appears to be imperatively required by the conception of God, and which the very first psalm states in the sharp antithesis, 'Happiness to the righteous, woe to the wicked!' The description of the happiness of the godly (23[1ff.] 92[13ff.] 112[1ff.] 128[1ff.]) is presented in such beautiful pictures and with such definiteness that there appears to be no room left to raise the problem above referred to. But it was impossible

permanently to shut one's eyes to the glaring facts supplied by experience of real life. And so we find three psalms (the 37th, the 49th, and the 73rd; also the opening part of the 39th),* in which the problem of the prosperity of the ungodly is subjected to an examination which shows only too clearly how heavily this question pressed upon men's minds, and what a struggle was required to reach anything like a satisfying result. But this result is the same in all the three psalms named. The sufferings of the righteous and the prosperity of the wicked are both alike pronounced to be *always* only temporary, and hence to be merely a deceitful appearance. Soon and suddenly release comes to the one, shameful ruin to the other; and all the more are men to be warned not to fret on account of the prosperity of the wicked, instead of waiting calmly for God's judgment to fall.

Is this attempt at a theodicy to be called a satisfying one? We can only say that, while there is something extremely touching and edifying in the testimony of the author of Ps $37^{25}$ that up to his old age he had never seen the righteous forsaken or his seed begging bread, unfortunately every one is not in a position to testify to the same experience. On OT soil the solution of the problem was possible only in such a way as we find exhibited in the Book of Job. On this we shall have to speak below (p. $730^{b}$ f.).

8. *Messianic expectations.*—If it is the case, as is very frequently asserted, that the whole interest of the later post-exilic religion of Israel turns on the two great hinges of the Law and the Messianic hope, this assertion can be justified even in regard to the last point only to a very limited extent *from the Psalms*. Now that a sober exegesis has swept away a great number of supposed Messianic (or at least typically Messianic) psalms, there remain only three (if we leave out of account the brief promise of a victorious descendant of David, $132^{17f.}$) in which the expectation of a *personal* Messiah cannot well be disputed—the 2nd, the 72nd, and the 110th. Ps 2 might have been called forth by the victory of a Maccabæan prince, which moved the writer to recognize in him the long promised Messiah. Any other interpretation (such, for instance, as to assume that we have here the hyperbole of flattery) would in any case be shattered by v.$^{8f.}$, which contemplates that the king addressed is to exercise absolutely unlimited sway *over the world*. The only question is whether a definite historical occurrence was needed to lead to the utterance of such a prophecy. The simplest view will always continue to be that the poet is transported in spirit to the birth-pangs of the Messianic era, and from this standpoint describes the course of things.—Similarly, in Ps 72 it follows from v.$^{8}$ that we have to do with a purely future prophecy, a glance into the period when Jahweh has set up a king under whose powerful and just sway peace and abundant blessing are the lot of the people,—above all, of those hitherto oppressed, all poor and needy ones (vv.$^{4. 12ff.}$). From v.$^{5}$ it would appear as if eternal rule were contemplated for this king personally; but, since in v.$^{17}$ it is his *name* that has eternal continuance and eternal renown promised to it, we must think here, as elsewhere (cf. above, pp. $696^{b}$, $713^{a}$), of the permanence of the dynasty. It is not said that this ideal king is descended from David, but it may be presupposed all the same.—In Ps 110 we are compelled by v.$^{4}$ to hold that the person is a military commander (v.$^{3}$) who has received not only priestly but also kingly dignity (cf. v.$^{2}$ 'thy mighty sceptre'), and so can be compared with the priest-king Melchiẓedeḳ of Gn $14^{18ff.}$. All this is intelligible only if the subject addressed is a Maccabæan* priest-prince. That the writer believed the Messiah to have made his appearance in the person of this priest-prince can be inferred only from v.$^{1}$ (the seat of honour beside Jahweh) and at all events from v.$^{6}$ (provided that the judgment of the nations at the dawn of the Messianic age is what is meant): for the rest, it would be sufficient to understand the sovereign power and the career of victory as extending over only a smaller circle of peoples.

It is noteworthy that in all three psalms we hear only of the monarchical qualities of this ruler (in Ps 72 of monarchical virtues, in Ps 2 and 110 of warlike achievements), not of any spiritual activity on his part—again an evidence of how wide was the gulf between the picture of the Jewish Messiah and that of the actual Messiah of the New Testament.

But at certain times (especially those when Israel enjoyed outward prosperity, as happened, for instance, under the rule of the Ptolemies) or in certain circles the expectation of a personal Messiah fell quite out of sight. This is shown by certain passages in which (so also perhaps in Hab $3^{13}$) *the nation* is expressly called 'the anointed' of Jahweh: Ps $28^{8}$ $84^{10}$ (but hardly $89^{39. 52}$); in $105^{15}$ the patriarchs are spoken of as Jahweh's anointed ones. This usage could scarcely have established itself unless the thought of the 'anointed' in an individual sense had—at least at times—almost entirely faded away.

But the circumstance last alluded to by no means excludes the possibility that the expectation of a Messianic *time* always continued as a living and powerful force. It is the object of longing (Ps $14^{7}$) and of confident hope. With the cry of jubilation, 'Jahweh reigneth' ($47^{9f.}$ $93^{1f.}$ $97^{1ff.}$ $99^{1ff.}$),† the poet transports himself to the time when Jahweh has at last assumed kingly rule on Zion, and advances to execute judgment on Israel's foes, and showers upon Israel a superabundance of spiritual and temporal blessings.

As in the earlier Prophets, the heathen peoples play a prominent rôle again in the future expectations of the Psalmists. Only, it must be admitted at the outset that this rôle is almost uniformly accommodated to the particularistic assumptions which we have already encountered in the Psalms. The Messianic judgment is indeed, at the same time, what it is primarily to the earlier prophets, a purifying judgment for Israel itself, in which the ungodly perish ($1^{5}$; even in $7^{7ff.}$ and $94^{1ff.}$ Israel may be included); but, as a rule, it is meant for 'the peoples of the world' ($96^{13}$ $98^{9}$), and, amongst these, especially of course for the oppressors and enemies of Israel. The executing of the judgment is almost always looked for from Jahweh Himself. Only in $149^{6ff.}$ does the poet formally revel in the thought that the godly in Israel are to execute with their own hand the long predicted judgment on the heathen and their kings.

Considering the frequency of allusions to the relation of the heathen to the Messianic kingdom, one might expect also some words which, in the spirit of Deutero-Isaiah, should recognize that the heathen have a part in the kingdom of God. But, apart from Ps $22^{28ff.}$, where a conversion of the heathen to Jahweh is spoken of, no indubitable witness to such an expectation can be produced. For the very frequent calls to the heathen to praise Jahweh ($47^{2}$ $66^{1ff.}$ $67^{3ff.}$ $68^{33}$ $97^{2}$ $98^{4}$ $100^{1}$

* Cf. Couard, 'Die Behandlung und Lösung des Problems der Theodicee in den Psalmen 37. 39. 73' in *SK*, 1901, p. 110 ff.

* All doubt on this point would be dispelled if the acrostic discovered by G. Margoliouth in vv.$^{1-4}$ (שׁ in שֵׁב, מ in מַטֵּה, ע in עַמְּךָ, נ in נִשְׁבַּע; the whole yielding the name שִׁמְעֹן) is a real one. In the year 141 B.C. Simon became, by a popular resolution, hereditary high priest and prince of the people.

† On this interpretation of the psalms in question, cf. B. Stade, 'Die messianische Hoffnung im Psalter' in *Zeitschrift für Theologie und Kirche*, ii. (1892) 369 ff.

$117^{1}$ $138^{4f.}$ $148^{11}$) *may* quite well be understood in the sense of readily confessing the superior power of Jahweh and the consequent necessity of submitting themselves to serve Him. The same may be the meaning also of passages like $86^{9}$ $96^{7ff.}$ $102^{16.\,23}$, and certainly of $68^{30ff.}$ $72^{9ff.}$. The gifts brought to the temple by the kings of the heathen are simply the tribute offered by them in testimony of their subjection to the supreme God. In view of all this, it cannot be denied that here again we may mark a falling from the level of prophetism down to specifically Jewish particularism.

9. *The question of personal immortality.*—An old controverted question still remains to be dealt with: Are there to be found in the Psalter—in spite of what was said above about *Shĕʾōl*—passages in which expression is given to the hope of individual immortality? We here leave out of account passages like Ps $31^{6}$ or $49^{16}$, which are put out of court by a correct exegesis [in Ps 31 all that is needed to do this is v.[16]]. On the other hand, it deserves to be seriously considered whether $16^{10ff.}$ speaks only of preservation from sudden death and not rather from death altogether, namely, through living to see the Messianic time (cf., for this expectation expressed in Is $25^{8}$, above, p. $713^{b}$). And no less may it be considered whether in Ps $17^{15}$ we are not to think of an awakening in like manner to enter upon the enjoyment of the Messianic age (in the sense of Is $26^{19}$). In that case we should have a parallel to the resurrection hope expressed in Dn $12^{2}$ (see above, p. $715^{a}$).* But these two passages in the Psalms would thus stand so isolated, besides being of so doubtful interpretation, that we must be content, after all, to return on the question at issue a verdict of *non liquet.*

## X. The so-called Ḥokhmāh (Wisdom) Literature (Proverbs, Job, Ecclesiastes).

The earliest trace of the 'wise' as a separate professional class is found in Jer $18^{18}$, where they are placed side by side with the priests and prophets as possessors of 'counsel,' *i.e.* ability to select the best course in particular cases. They also appear frequently as a separate class in Proverbs ($1^{6}$ $13^{14}$ $22^{17}$ etc.; cf. also Ec $12^{11}$), above all as teachers of youth ($1^{4}$ $2^{1}$ $3^{1}$ $4^{1.\,10}$ etc.). This is quite compatible with the fact that they are likewise (in part, perhaps, exclusively) to be conceived as writers. And, since in the period to which the creations of the *Ḥokhmāh* (חָכְמָה) belong it is impossible to speak of authorship beyond the limits of the religion of the Law, the 'wise' ought in the main to be identified with the 'scribes'; only, they rather represent a particular side of the scribes' activity,—not the fixing of the letter of the Law, or instruction in its punctual observance (*e.g.* in matters of cultus),—but the useful application of the specifically ethical content of the Law and of Scripture generally—so far as Scripture existed—as the revelation of the will of God, which alone may determine human action. For 'wisdom,'* the unsurpassable worth of which is ceaselessly lauded in Proverbs, and the attainment of which at any cost is incessantly inculcated, is not the fruit of philosophic or religious speculation, or even an esoteric or secret doctrine; it is (as already in Jer $18^{18}$, see above) ability for the right conduct of life, or, in one word, *the practical wisdom of life.* One who possesses wisdom is capable of rightly judging every situation in which he may find himself, and of taking the best way to master it. Thus what distinguishes the wise from fools is, as it were, the art of taking a wide view of things. Now, if we consider that the political situation of the people under heathen rulers, and the increasing, and in part wealthy and influential, Jewish Diaspora in heathen lands, made ever greater demands for a prudent attitude towards foreigners, we can understand how it is that the doctrine of wisdom shows traces here and there of a certain cosmopolitanism, at all events the inculcation of prudent judgment of, and attitude towards, the king and heathen rulers. The tendency of wisdom to run out into the practical prudence of life is shown, above all, in the multiplicity of its principles and aims. It is astonishing to mark what a number of questions relating to the prudent conduct of life are canvassed in Proverbs: occupation, profit, business in general, intercourse with superiors and inferiors and with different classes of men generally, one's attitude to rulers, and numberless others. How far the specifically religious interest gets justice alongside of the thoroughly predominant practical interest, is a question to be investigated when we come to discuss the individual books.

1. *Proverbs.*—(*a*) Like the Psalms, Proverbs ought also for our purposes to be treated as a literary unity, in spite of the variety, and, it may well be, the divergence in age, of its component parts.† Between the Prologue (chs. 1–9) and the collections of proverbs proper the difference is at most this, that in the first we find not only numerous connected arguments, but also—at least on one point—attempts at religious speculation; while in the 'Proverbs of Solomon' and the collections which follow we encounter almost everywhere isolated proverbs, antithetic in form (so from the very first, $10^{1\text{-}17}$), in the most motley mixture, and only very seldom in connected groups. Besides, it has long been recognized that the number of proverbs which can be viewed as real proverbs, current on the lips of the people, is small. The majority obviously belong to artificial poetry both in contents and form.‡

* Cf. the literature cited on p. $668^{a}$, and add F. Schmidt, *Der Unsterblichkeits- und Auferstehungsglaube in der Bibel*, Brixen, 1902. We may take this opportunity of remarking that we do not consider that proof has been given of the influence of Parsism on the rise of the Jewish hope of the resurrection. Charles (in work cited on p. $725^{a}$ note) holds Mazdæan influences possible in Dn $12^{2}$, but sees in Is $26^{19}$ a product of purely Jewish thought. But the distance from Is $26^{19}$ to Dn $12^{2}$ is easily bridged. Cf., further, on the question of Parsi influences: J. H. Moulton's art. Zoroastrianism in vol. iv. of the present work; T. K. Cheyne, 'Possible Zoroastrian Influences on the Religion of Israel,' *Expos. Times*, Aug. 1891; E. Stave, *Ueber den Einfluss des Parsismus auf das Judentum*, Leipzig, 1898 [holds that the future expectations connected with this world emanated from Judaism, while those connected with the world beyond, particularly the (post-canonical) doctrine of a *general* resurrection, are traced to Parsism]; E. Böklen, *Die Verwandtschaft der jüdischchristlichen mit der parsischen Eschatologie*, 1902 [a careful collection of matter, the author's own intention being, above all, to provide material for arriving at a judgment; but his procedure in adducing Parsi parallels to OT passages is in not a few instances too artificial].

* Cf., for special literature on the *Ḥokhmāh*: T. K. Cheyne, *Job and Solomon, or the Wisdom of the Old Testament*, London, 1887 [an incisive critical, exegetical, and biblico-theological discussion of the Books of Job, Proverbs, Ecclesiastes, and Sirach]; H. Zschokke, *Der dogmatisch-ethische Lehrgehalt der alttest. Weisheitsbücher*, Wien, 1889; W. T. Davison, *The Wisdom Literature of the Old Testament*, London, 1894; K. Benkenstein, *Der Begriff der Chokhma in d. Hagiographen d. AT*, Nordhausen, 1895.

† The superscription מִשְׁלֵי שְׁלֹמֹה, which was later prefixed also to the Prologue ($1^{1}$), indicates that $10^{1}$–$22^{16}$ was the basis of the collection. Whether in $10^{1ff.}$ there are present any relics of a collection of proverbs attributed to Solomon (cf. the trace of such a collection in 1 K $5^{12}$) is a question on which we cannot even form an opinion; the present Book of Proverbs cannot have been put together before the post-exilic period. Two supplements were added to the original basis noted above ($22^{17}$–$24^{22}$), which are not attributed to Solomon. A second collection of 'Proverbs of Solomon' is given in $27^{1}$–$29^{27}$, with three supplements—the words of Agur (ch. 30), the words of king Lemuel ($31^{1\text{-}9}$), and the acrostic eulogy of the virtuous woman ($31^{10\text{-}31}$). It was only as a last step (and not before the middle of the 4th cent. B.C.) that the Prologue can have been prefixed to the whole.

‡ For special literature on Proverbs, cf. R. Pfeiffer, *Die religiös-sittliche Weltanschauung des Buches der Sprüche in*

(*b*) The approach to religious speculation, to which reference was made above, has to do with the personification of Wisdom in several passages of the Prologue. Here it is a question whether we have to do with a purely poetical manner of speech, or with a hypostatizing of Wisdom, that is, with the introducing of an intermediate being between God and matter. The descriptions in $1^{20f.}$ $8^{1ff.}$ and $9^{1ff.}$ can quite well be interpreted as purely poetical personifications, all the more that in $9^{13ff.}$ 'Madam Folly' is contrasted with Wisdom, and in this second case it is impossible to speak of hypostatization. The case, however, is different in $8^{22ff.}$. *The* Wisdom, whom Jahweh created of old as the first of His works, and set up of everlasting, who was there when He established the heavens, and *was by Him as a master-workman* 'daily his delight, rejoicing always before him, rejoicing in his habitable earth'—this Wisdom is no longer a merely poetical personification, but a being which has come forth from God, and works independently by His side, or, more accurately, with Him. And indeed we are probably not mistaken if we see in it a hypostatization of the creative ideas,—the passing into self-conscious personality of the system of archetypes, in accordance with which is determined the nature and measure of created things,—as it were, the fundamental principle of the Divine world-order. On this interpretation, a comparison with the 'Ideas' of Plato involuntarily suggests itself, but it is a further question whether we are to suppose that the influence of the Platonic philosophy was direct. Such a supposition is not absolutely necessary. On the other hand, it is hardly to be doubted that a causal connexion exists between the hypostatizing of Wisdom (Pr $8^{22ff.}$) and the Logos idea in the New Testament. This, however, is not the place to pursue this question further.

The interpretation of Pr $8^{22ff.}$ given above is considerably strengthened by Job $28^{1ff.}$. It is true, the hypostatization of Wisdom here is still in its rudimentary stage, and the passage is therefore certainly older than Pr $8^{22ff.}$. Job speaks at length ($28^{1-14. 21f.}$) of the complete unattainability and (v.$^{15ff.}$) of the incomparable worth of Wisdom, until finally (v.$^{23ff.}$) he gives the explanation : *God* understandeth the way thereof, and He knoweth the place thereof. At the settling of the laws of nature (v.$^{25f.}$) 'then did he see it, and declared it; he established it, yea, and searched it out.' Obviously, Wisdom is here something other than the 'master-workman' of Pr 8; it is rather a secret talisman, endowed with wondrous powers, and accessible to God alone; but it is also equally obvious that it is closely connected with God's works of creation, and so here again is equivalent to a system of types for the individual creatures.

(*c*) As to the further contents of the Book of Proverbs, their dependence on the specifically religious presuppositions of their age, as these were formed above all by the doctrine of the prophets, and preeminently by their conception of God, is a fact which needs no demonstration. There is more ground for saying that the specifically religious background and atmosphere of Proverbs has been at times far too much depreciated by modern writers, in view of its eudæmonistic and even utilitarian standpoint. It is indeed undeniable that a prominence which is often startling is given to considerations of the outward success of good and bad actions. The reader has not seldom an impression as though offences and even gross sins were to be avoided, not because to commit them is to forfeit the grace of God, heap guilt upon oneself, and burden one's conscience, but because by such actions one may all too easily incur disgrace, danger, and loss. (Cf. *e.g.* $6^{29}$ and $^{32ff.}$, also $5^{15ff.}$ $24^{17ff.}$; and the warnings against wine, $20^{1}$ $21^{17}$ $23^{20f.}$ and $^{29ff.}$; for more general expressions, $3^{9f.}$ $4^{10}$ $22^{4}$).*

In spite of this, however, it would be unjustifiable to regard Wisdom, in the form which it assumes in Proverbs, as *only* a means of attaining eudæmonistic ends—protection from everything that might disturb the quiet enjoyment of life. For not a few expressions reveal to us a far more intense religious life. Apart from $3^{9}$, exhortations and warnings throughout are concerned with the precepts of morality proper, not with duties of the cultus; in $21^{3}$, indeed, righteousness is declared better than sacrifice (quite in the spirit of Hos $6^{6}$, etc.). The warning against adultery and profligacy ($6^{24ff.}$ $7^{1ff.}$) is grounded beforehand in $6^{23}$ by reference to the command of God, as is the case just as often with exhortations to righteousness, integrity, and compassion ($3^{27ff.}$ $14^{34}$ and very specially $14^{31}$ $17^{5}$ $19^{17}$ $28^{8}$). But we can point further to altogether different evidences of a moral disposition based upon true piety. The fear of Jahweh, which according to $1^{7. 29}$ $9^{10}$ is the beginning of wisdom (or, more accurately perhaps, the most important thing in wisdom)—though represented, conversely, in $2^{3ff.}$ as the fruit of wisdom—is not identical with slavish fear of Jahweh's punishment and the loss it brings, but with the knowledge that what is needed is the unconditional surrender of body and soul to Him ($18^{10}$) who knows the most secret places of the heart ($15^{11}$ $17^{3}$ $24^{12}$), who rules all things, even the doings of kings, by His will ($16^{9. 33}$ $21^{1. 31}$), and on whose blessing everything depends ($10^{22}$). The wise man knows that the corruption of sin is universal ($20^{9}$); he understands the healing chastisement of Jahweh, which comes precisely on him whom He loves ($3^{12}$), and is aware that nothing but penitent confession can deliver out of the distress of sin ($28^{13}$). He mistrusts his own understanding ($3^{5}$ $28^{26}$), and exercises himself at all times in humility ($16^{19}$ $18^{12}$) and contentment ($15^{16f.}$ $16^{8}$ $30^{8b}$), as the best supports of the fear of God. If we add to this the estimate of woman and of marriage which is given in $17^{1}$ $31^{10ff.}$ (above all, in the noble saying of v.$^{30}$), the exhortation to compassion even towards animals ($12^{10}$), the warning against retaliation and vengeance ($20^{22}$ $24^{29}$), the exhortation to magnanimity towards a foe, which almost touches on love to enemies ($25^{21f.}$), and, finally, the reference to the love that covereth all transgressions ($10^{12}$),—we shall no longer doubt that the ethic of Proverbs stands in great measure on a far higher level than the catchword of eudæmonism and utilitarianism is willing to admit.

(*d*) As to the doctrine of retribution, we find Proverbs occupying exactly the same standpoint as the Psalmists (see above, p. 726^b), viz. founding on the postulate that virtue and ungodliness must receive on earth a precisely equivalent requital ($2^{21f.}$ $10^{25}$ $11^{21. 31}$ $13^{9. 21f.}$ $14^{11}$ $24^{20}$ etc.). Nowhere is there a trace to prove that the authors of Proverbs had felt the least difficulty in making this postulate. But that this very problem had exercised the devotees of *Ḥokhmāh* profoundly and persistently is shown by the book which must undoubtedly be described as the ripest fruit of this whole movement, as it is in general one of the sublimest monuments of the religion of Israel, and even of the pre-Christian literature of the world.

2. *The Book of Job.*—(*a*) Of the critical questions

*ihrem inneren Zusammenhange dargestellt*, München, 1896; O. Meusel, *Die Stellung der Sprüche Salomos in der israelitischen Litteratur und Religionsgeschichte*, Leipzig, 1900.

* To the same category of 'rules for life,' tinged with a utilitarian complexion, belongs the repeated and extremely insistent warning against becoming surety for others ($6^{1ff.}$ $17^{18}$ $20^{16}$ $22^{26f.}$), as also against sloth ($6^{6ff.}$ and frequently).

that gather round the Book of Job one only need be taken into account for our purposes—the question touching the genuineness of the speeches of Elihu (chs. 32–37), which break the connexion between ch. 31 and ch. 38 in an unintelligible fashion, and suddenly introduce a speaker who is quite unknown both to the Prologue and to the Epilogue of the poem. We shall have to state briefly at the close our reasons for holding his observations to be an incontestably later addition. The theory, at present well-nigh dominant (owing to the commentaries of Duhm and Budde), that in the Prologue and Epilogue we have an older popular writing, in which the author of the main part has inserted the speeches of Job, of his friends, and of Jahweh, is one to which the present writer is unable to subscribe, believing as he does that the Prologue and Epilogue were written by the same hand as the rest (though, of course, as Ezk $14^{14.\ 20}$ demands, in dependence on an old and familiar tradition).* As to the date of the book, not only its angelology, which presents similarities to that of Daniel, but also linguistic reasons, compel us to bring it down to the later post-exilic period. That its conception of God (especially in regard to the creation and government of the world, ch. 38 ff. and elsewhere) stands on the loftiest height of OT beliefs, needs no proof.† And as to its ethics, passages like $29^{12ff.}$, and, above all, $31^{1ff.}$, with their truly evangelical idea of morality, have hardly a parallel in the OT.

(*b*) As regards the angelology, the novel element lies less in the rôle played by the Satan ($1^{6ff.}$ $2^{1ff.}$) than in some other expressions. The Satan here is distinguishable from his counterpart in Zechariah (cf. above, p. $709^{b}$) at most by this, that, while not yet the calumniator of the pious man, he still excites suspicion against him. He still belongs to the *bĕnê 'Ĕlōhîm*, who stand around Jahweh as His servants ($1^{6}$ $2^{1}$; in $38^{7}$ they are named alongside of the morning-stars, which are to be conceived as personified), and he is absolutely bound to the will of God. But there is plainly in him a strain of malice, a joy in the fall of the godly. So far we have here a further development of the idea of the Satan as found in Zec $3^{1}$. 1 Ch $21^{1}$—an instructive parallel to 2 S $24^{1}$—is the first passage where the Satan has become a being dualistically hostile to God. The further expansion of the idea, as presupposed in NT, belongs to the department of the Apocrypha (cf., especially, Wis $2^{24}$).

Peculiar to the Book of Job is the idea of interceding angels ($5^{1}$ $33^{23}$), as also that of angels of death ($33^{22}$). The description of the angels as holy ($15^{15}$) is no more here than elsewhere meant to emphasize their moral perfection, as is clear from this very passage, which (like $4^{18}$) makes the angels subject to error and sin.

(*c*) In view of the ever renewed attempt to draw from $19^{25ff.}$ indications of the sudden flaming up of the hope of resurrection or immortality, emphasis must never cease to be laid on this fact: the view set forth in Job in regard to *Shĕ'ōl*—its cheerless darkness, the complete isolation of its inmates from the upper world, and the impossibility of return from it ($7^{9f.}$ $10^{21f.}$ $14^{10ff.\ 21f.}$ $16^{22}$ $21^{26}$ $30^{23}$)—is uniformly the same throughout the whole poem. With such an idea, however, the hope of immortality would be in insoluble contradiction. The expectation to which expression is given in Job $19^{25ff.}$, accordingly, relates to this life, and this is expressly confirmed by the clear reference back from $42^{5}$ to $19^{27}$.

* Cf. on this point Karl Kautzsch, *Das sogenannte Volksbuch von Hiob und der Ursprung von Hiob 1. 2. 41⁷-17*, Tübingen, 1900.

† Of the particular mythological allusions ($3^{8}$ to the Leviathan, $9^{13}$ to the helpers of Rahab, $26^{12}$ to Rahab, $29^{18}$ to the phœnix) the same view must be taken as of those in the Psalms.

(*d*) The problem to the solution of which this sublime poem is devoted is simply, How is the suffering, nay the sore and hopeless suffering, of a notoriously good man compatible with the justice of God?; and, conversely, How is it compatible with the justice of God that notoriously godless men enjoy to the end of life an absolutely untroubled happiness? These became burning questions once men had learned to distinguish the weal and woe of the individual from that of the nation, and to face the actual facts of the individual life.

The poet brings the problem before us in the Prologue in the guise of historical facts. Job has witness to his exemplary piety from God Himself ($1^{8}$ $2^{3}$). And yet measureless woe has fallen upon him. Why? The reader is told in the Prologue:—the torture of Job rests on the permission extended by Jahweh to the Satan, with the object of proving that there does exist a piety which no temptation can cause to waver. The suffering of Job, accordingly, is in no way a manifestation of God's anger, but rather of His love; it is a martyrdom for the honour of God and human fidelity towards God. The fact that the reader is put in possession of accurate knowledge on this point from the first, and therefore can quietly watch the controversy as from a watchtower, is one of the poet's finest strokes of art. The other *dramatis personæ*, however, know nothing of this solution of the problem, and are therefore groping in the darkness. They carry on the controversy only as human judgment and knowledge best can.

Job, with heroic devotion, offers a steadfast resistance to the repeated assaults of evil, in spite of his being sorely tempted by his own wife. But the mute reproach which he perceives in the silence of his friends, together with his awful, excruciating, and hopeless malady, finally breaks down the courage of his faith. With the monologue in which he curses the day of his birth (ch. 3), he opens the threefold cycle of speeches and counter-speeches, in which the problem, instead of drawing nearer to solution, becomes ever more complicated. The standpoint of the friends is that of the old doctrine of retribution—that false inversion of the fact declared in Ex $20^{5f.}$, that the fear of God brings a blessing, while sin brings ruin. The friends deny the existence of any problem at all: all suffering is punishment; monstrous suffering is punishment for monstrous, and very specially for secret, guilt. The happiness of the ungodly, however, is never more than apparent, and is destined to sudden destruction.

Job does not in the least deny ($14^{4}$ $19^{4}$) his participation in the universality of human sin as affirmed by the friends ($4^{17}$ $15^{14}$). But he repudiates in the strongest way any such guilt as would even come near explaining his fate. On the other hand, he is never weary of pointing to the facts of actual life (cf., especially, $21^{7ff.}$ and $24^{1ff.}$), the infinite enigmas created by the hopeless suffering of the godly, and the untroubled happiness of the wicked. This does not lead him, it is true, to doubt the omnipotence of God ($9^{5ff.}$ $12^{13ff.}$ $26^{5ff.}$ $26^{14}$), but he can recognize only its incalculable and destructive effects. He rejects, with justifiable indignation ($21^{19ff.}$), the expedient, which was plainly in high favour in his day, of saying that God lays up the punishment of the godless for their children. For this theory was in fact nothing but a desperate device, which overthrew the principle of the current doctrine of retribution—otherwise so eagerly defended—that each receives according to his deserts.

Still, his doubts regarding the justice of God (cf., especially, $9^{22ff.}$) are gradually overcome by his better faith. He begins to distinguish between the wise and righteous God, whose image lives on indelibly in his heart, and the enigmatical God of his trial, and appeals to the first for help against the second ($16^{18ff.}$). Nay, he has the adamantine assurance that God Himself will at the end arise for him, and bring his innocence to the light ($19^{25ff.}$). But, even though with all this he gradually silences the contradictions of the friends, he himself, in view of the enigmas that confront him, attains to no more than a painful renunciation of the hope of their solution. The moving delineation of his former happiness (ch. 29), of his present misery (ch. 30), and of his pious life (ch. 31), closes ($31^{35ff.}$) with the solemn demand addressed to God, to afford him the opportunity of defending his cause in a regular judicial trial.

And indeed Jahweh does appear ($38^{1ff.}$). But not, as Job had requested and hoped, to enter into a controversy with him, —anything of the kind had been utterly unworthy of Him,—but in order, by means of the tempest and with withering irony, to make him feel the absolute foolishness and childishness of what he expected from God. And the whole arrangement of the poem forbids us to doubt that only in these speeches of Jahweh (chs. 38–41), with their Divine irony, and nowhere else have we to seek the solution of the problem intended by the poet himself. In all conceivable simplicity it runs thus: God, who has made known His unfathomable omnipotence and wisdom in the multiform wonders of creation, and His goodness in His loving care for the animal world ($38^{41ff.}$), rules likewise over the fortunes of men, and here too all His action can flow only from wisdom and love, whether much or little of it be comprehensible by man.

It has been said that this is no solution of the problem, but a compulsory abandonment of it. But in both his answers ($40^{4f.}$ and $42^{3ff.}$) Job himself takes quite another view. He humbles himself to the very dust; not, however, in painful resignation, but in the elevating assurance that his God has acknowledged him, and that he must regard all the elements of his lot as evidences of an all-wise and loving will. While, then, the justification of Job as against the friends in the Epilogue, and the return of his prosperity, may only be meant to satisfy so-called 'poetic' justice, yet they were indispensable for the harmonious solution of all difficulties for the reader, who in the Prologue had been enlightened as to the innermost connexion of events.

All this of itself settles what we are to think of the Elihu-speeches. They are the work of a reader of the original poem, who felt dissatisfied that the speeches of Job, dubious in part, and almost bordering on blasphemy, should not have received a more stringent refutation. This lack the author of the Elihu-speeches seeks to supply, and does so by explaining the suffering of Job as *purificatory*, designed for the purging out of the sins of pride and self-righteousness which clung to him. In themselves many of this author's ideas are beautiful and good. But as a professed solution of the problem they are irreconcilably opposed to the presuppositions of the original poem.

3. *Ecclesiastes* (*the Preacher*).—(*a*) It is not without hesitation that we enumerate Ecclesiastes as one of the creations of the *Ḥokhmāh* literature; for it is only in a very relative sense that it can be treated in the same series as Proverbs and Job. The original portions of the book,* at all events, stand on the extreme periphery of OT faith; and of a hope for the future, be it for the nation or the individual, they exhibit not a trace. The Preacher shows himself to be dominated by a dark, almost pessimistic, tone of feeling. The history of his nation obviously appears to him like an extinct volcano. He does not touch upon it even in a single word; the cheerless conditions of the present alone occupy his mind, together with the prospect of the cheerless end, identical for all. The thesis of which he makes a headline—'vanity of vanities, all is vanity'—recurs again and again even in the course of his argument. Everywhere he sees things in restless revolution, ending in nothing profitable ($1^{4ff.}$); there is no new thing under the sun ($1^{9f.}$). Vain is the pursuit of riches and pleasure, even when it rests upon industrious labour ($2^{1ff.}$). But vain also is the pursuit of wisdom ($1^{13ff.}$ $6^{8ff.}$ $7^{23}$), for he that increaseth knowledge increaseth sorrow ($1^{18}$). Wise men and fools have ultimately the same destiny ($2^{14ff.}$ $9^{2f.}$). Nay, vain is even the pursuit of piety ($4^{17}$ [$5^{1}$] $7^{15}$ $8^{10.\,14}$); it does not change the fact that man and beast at last go to the one place ($3^{19ff.}$), to the joyless *Shĕ'ōl* and everlasting oblivion. The attempt by means of mistaken exegesis to foist upon the Preacher a hope of immortality has completely failed. Passages like $3^{20}$ $9^{4ff.\,10b}$, 'there is no work, nor device, nor knowledge, nor wisdom, in the grave, whither thou goest,' admit of no doubt as to his real opinion. Even in $3^{21}$ the sense of the doubting question * is not to ask whether the spirit of man as immortal returns to God, but whether a difference between the breath of man and of beast exists so far that the latter, it may be, goes downward to the earth, but the former upward—not in any sense as self-conscious spirit, but (exactly as in $12^{7}$) as once more re-entering the universal Divine life-spirit, from which it had once come forth. The expectation of a future judgment can at most be found in the closing verse ($12^{13f.}$), 'fear God, and keep His commandments: for this pertains to all men. For God shall bring every work into the judgment which tries every hidden thing, whether it be good or whether it be evil.' But it is certain that this epilogue (from v.$^{9}$ onwards) does not belong to the work of the original author. For the folly and injustice which manifest themselves everywhere in the course of the world ($3^{16}$ $4^{1ff.}$), that author knows no consolation other than the possibility of securing, by means of a rational enjoyment of life, the relatively best side of what is in every respect a mournful earthly existence. This is the counsel he is never weary of giving ($2^{24}$ $3^{12f.\,22}$ $5^{17}$ $8^{15}$ $9^{7ff.}$ $11^{8}$), not in the sense of vulgar Epicureanism, but still from the standpoint of a man who has made up his mind about the value of all other earthly goods and aims.

What preserved him from vulgar godless Epicureanism is the fact that even he had retained one important relic of the believing treasures of

* The very striking contradictions in the statements of the Preacher (cf. for example $7^{11ff.\,19}$ $8^{1}$ $9^{17f.}$ $10^{12}$, with expressions used elsewhere regarding the worth of wisdom $1^{13ff.\,18}$ $6^{8ff.}$ $7^{23}$; or again $5^{7\text{-}16}$ $7^{1ff.}$ with the opinions he expresses as to the injustice that dominates the course of the world $3^{16}$ $4^{1ff.}$; as also $8^{10.\,14}$ on the worth of piety with v.$^{11ff.}$) have long been noticed and explained, sometimes in mechanical fashion (by supposing a dialogue between the doubting scholar and the didactic master, or even by the hypothesis that parts of the MS have got out of order), sometimes from the character of a mind tossed hither and thither by doubt. The present writer, however, is now convinced that C. Siegfried was on the right track when (in his Commentary on Ecclesiastes, Göttingen, 1898) he argued in favour of a number of successive hands, which from very divergent standpoints sought to supplement, to correct, or even in many places expressly to refute, the judgments of their predecessors. Siegfried's analysis may in part be needlessly artificial, since he postulates first a pessimist (Q[oheleth] $^{1}$) infected with Greek philosophy, then an epicurean glossator belonging to Sadducean circles ($Q^{2}$), next a 'wise' man who defends wisdom ($Q^{3}$), and, finally, one of the 'pious' (*ḥāsîd*, $Q^{4}$), who defends the justice of the Divine government of the world, together with two further glossators—yet in the main his theory is a sound one.

* According to the correct text (הָעֹלָה and הַיֹּרֶדֶת; the MT has been corrected on dogmatic grounds, so as to express the hope of immortality).

his people, viz. the kernel of the OT conception of God. All his scepticism and all his pessimism had not impaired his faith in a personal God who is at the same time the God of the whole world.* He does not really doubt even the wisdom and justice of this God: 'He hath made everything beautiful in its time, yet so that man cannot find out the work that God hath done from the beginning to the end' ($3^{11.14}$ $8^{17}$). What pains the Preacher is this, that comforting insight into the enigmas of the world, for which in view of God's wisdom and justice there must be a solution, is for ever forbidden to man.

(*b*) We can well understand that the reception of Ecclesiastes into the canon should have awakened serious doubts, even as late as the 1st cent. A.D. Nevertheless, we have cause to thank the editors of the canon for having suppressed these doubts (perhaps on account of the conciliatory epilogue). By doing so they have bequeathed to us a priceless evidence that those of Israel who to this day believe that God's last word to humanity was spoken in the revelations and institutions of the Old Covenant, are in error. Having once perceived the insufficiency of all works of the Law and renounced belief in the trustworthiness of his own wisdom, the Preacher could find solace and support only in faith in redress beyond this life. But of such a faith, so far as the individual was concerned, the religion of his people knew nothing, and to be pointed to the Messianic future of the nation as a whole evidently appeared to him but a dubious substitute. In all this he affords a proof that this religion called for supplement and completion—a completion which came in the fulness of time through Christ, who is the end of the Law.

LITERATURE.—The older works on Biblical Theology and on the History of the Religion of Israel may be all the more readily passed over, since they are almost without exception based upon incorrect critical principles—a blemish which attaches, indeed, even to some of the more recent works cited below. The view which once held sway, namely, that the beginnings of the Religion of Israel as well as of its codification are to be sought in P, gives so completely false a picture of the development of this religion, that in such works it is at most only the treatment of neutral points (where the question of gradual development does not arise) that can have any value. The foundation of a true knowledge of the subject was laid by E. Reuss in 1833 (in theses for his students) and in 1850 (in his art. 'Judenthum' in the so-called *Hallesche Encyklopädie* of Ersch and Gruber); and, independently of Reuss, by W. Vatke in *Die biblische Theologie wissenschaftlich dargestellt*, vol. i. 'Die Religion des AT nach den canonischen Büchern entwickelt,' Berlin, 1835.—In what follows we distinguish the following branches of literature on our subject—

I. WORKS DEALING WITH THE HISTORY OF RELIGION IN GENERAL, IN WHICH THE TREATMENT OF THE RELIGION OF ISRAEL IS INCLUDED.—C. P. Tiele, *Vergelijkende Geschiedenis van den Godsdienst* [Dutch, 1876 (2nd ed. 1894), French, 1882], and the same author's *Geschiedenis van den Godsdienst en de Oudheit*, 2 vols. 1876 ff. [Germ. tr. by Gehrich, 1896–1903], and *Inleiding tot de Godsdienstwetenshap*, Amsterdam, 1897, 1899, 2 parts [German tr. by Gehrich, Gotha, 1899, 1901]; Chantepie de la Saussaye, *Lehrbuch der Religionsgeschichte*² [in collaboration with Buckley, Lange, Fr. Jeremias, Valeton (whose account of the Religion of Israel is amongst the best parts of the work), Houtsman, Lehmann], Freiburg i. B. 1897, 2 vols.; C. von Orelli, *Allgemeine Religionsgeschichte*, Bonn, 1899.

II. WORKS ON THE HISTORY OF SEMITIC RELIGION, WHICH TAKE ACCOUNT OF THE OT PARALLELS.—See above, p. $612^{b}$, and add: Père Lagrange, *Études sur les religions sémitiques*, Paris, 1903.

III. WORKS ON BIBLICAL THEOLOGY OR ON THE HISTORY OF THE RELIGION OF THE OT.—A. Kuenen, *De Godsdienst van Israël tot den ondergang van den Joodschen staat* [Dutch, Haarlem, 1869–1870, 2 vols.; Eng. tr. by May, London, 1874, 1875, 3 vols.]; H. Schultz, *Alttest. Theologie*, Braunschweig, 1869 [5th ed. Göttingen, 1896]; G. F. Oehler, *Theologie des AT, herausgegeben von Herm. Oehler*, Tübingen, 1873, 1874, 2 vols. [3rd ed. by Theodor Oehler, Stuttgart, 1891]; A. Kayser, *Die Theologie des AT in ihrer geschichtlichen Entwicklung, herausgegeben von E. Reuss*, Strassburg, 1886 [the 3rd edition of 1897 was completely revised by K. Marti and published as *Geschichte der israelitischen Religion* (4th edition 1903)]; Ch. Piepenbring, *Théologie de l'ancien Testament*, Paris, 1886 [intended also for educated laymen]; W. L. Alexander, *System of Biblical Theology*, Edinburgh, 1888, 2 vols.; Ed. Riehm, *Alttest. Theologie, herausgegeben von K. Pahncke*, Halle, 1889; K. Schlottmann, *Kompendium der bibl. Theologie des AT und NT, herausgegeben von E. Kühn*, Leipzig, 1889 [2nd ed. 1895]; R. Smend, *Lehrbuch der alttest. Religionsgeschichte*, Freiburg and Leipzig, 1893 [2nd ed. 1899]; A. Dillmann, *Handbuch der alttest. Theologie, aus dem Nachlass des Verfassers herausgegeben von R. Kittel*, Leipzig, 1895; W. H. Bennett, *The Theology of the OT*, London, 1896; T. K. Cheyne, *Jewish Religious Life after the Exile*, New York, 1898 [German tr., with the assistance throughout of the author, by H. Stocks, Giessen, 1899]; A. Duff, *OT Theology, or History of Hebrew Religion*, London, 1891, 2 vols., and the same author's *History and Ethics of the Hebrews*, London, 1902; A. B. Davidson, *The Theology of the OT* [posthumous work, ed. by S. D. F. Salmond], Edinburgh, 1904; K. Budde, *Religion of Israel to the Exile*, New York, 1899 [German edition under title 'Die Religion des Volkes Israel bis zur Verbannung,' Giessen, 1900]. This sketch of Budde's is designed for a wider circle of readers, and so is F. Giesebrecht's *Die Grundzüge der israelitischen Religionsgeschichte*, Leipzig and Berlin, 1904.

IV. THE MORE CONSIDERABLE MONOGRAPHS (supplementary of the literature cited in the footnotes at the commencement of different sections of the above article).—F. Baethgen, *Beiträge zur semitischen Religionsgeschichte* (i. 'Der Gott Israels und die Götter der Heiden,' Berlin, 1888); E. Sellin, *Beiträge zur israelitischen und jüdischen Religionsgeschichte* (i. 'Jahwes Verhältnis zum israelitischen Volk und Individuum nach altisraelitischer Vorstellung,' Leipzig, 1896; ii. 'Israels Güter und Ideale,' 1897); J. Köberle, *Natur und Geist nach der Auffassung des AT: eine Untersuchung zur historischen Psychologie*, München, 1901.

E. KAUTZSCH.

TABLE OF CONTENTS OF ABOVE ARTICLE.



* This faith is indicated by the very fact that the Divine name 'Jahweh' is consistently replaced by the appellative *'Ĕlōhîm* (as almost everywhere in the 2nd and 3rd books of the Psalter, very frequently in Chron., and generally in the latest Scriptures). It is true that the influence of awe at the use of the sacred name also had to do with this result; but, on the other hand, this complete equating of 'Jahweh' and *'Ĕlōhîm* affords a proof that the faith of Israel had now finally decided on the absolutely unique character of Jahweh.

# INDEXES

## TO THE COMPLETE WORK

### (INCLUDING THE EXTRA VOLUME)

# I. INDEX OF AUTHORS

## AUTHORS' NAMES, AND LIST OF THEIR PRINCIPAL ARTICLES.

[As a rule, only those articles which occupy at least a column are included in the following lists. Articles whose title is followed by '[Ext.]' will be found in the Extra Volume].

ABRAHAMS, ISRAEL, M.A., Editor of the *Jewish Quarterly Review*, and Reader in Talmudic in the University of Cambridge.
New Moon, Time, Trumpet.

ADAMSON, Rev. A., M.A., B.D., Dundee.
Reconciliation.

ADENEY, Rev. WALTER F., M.A., D.D., Professor of Theology and Principal of the Lancashire College, Manchester.
Augustus, Blessedness, Blessing, Cæsar, Cæsar's Household, Centurion, Contentment, Decision, Governor, Man, Martha, Mediator (Mediation), Offence, Preaching, Publican, Self-surrender, Teacher (Teaching), Temperance, Woman, Worship (in NT); besides some shorter articles.

AGLEN, Ven. A. S., M.A., D.D., Archdeacon of St. Andrews.
Beth-horon, Compassion (Pity), Friend, Hand, Lord, Rahab (the harlot), Shiloh (Gn $49^{10}$); and a few shorter articles.

ALLEN, Rev. WILLOUGHBY C., M.A., Chaplain, Fellow, and Lecturer in Theology and Hebrew, Exeter College, Oxford.
Asherah, Gershon, High Place, Kohath, Merari; besides some shorter articles.

BACHER, W., Ph.D., Professor of Biblical Studies in the Landes-Rabbinerschule, Budapest.
Sanhedrin, Synagogue.

BACON, Rev. BENJAMIN WISNER, M.A., D.D., Professor of New Testament Criticism and Interpretation in Yale University, New Haven.
Genealogy of Jesus Christ.

BANKS, Rev. JOHN S., D.D., Professor of Systematic Theology in the Headingley College, Leeds.
Conversion, Hardening, Hope, Jealousy, Joy, Justice, Liberty, Meekness, Perfection.

BARNES, Rev. W. EMERY, M.A., D.D., Fellow and Chaplain of Peterhouse, and Hulsean Professor of Divinity, Cambridge.
Armour, Army, Banner, Camp, Israel (History of), Judges (Period of), Legion, Shield, Sling, Spear, Sword, Tower, War; and a few shorter articles.

BARTLET, JAMES VERNON, M.A., D.D., Professor of Church History in Mansfield College, Oxford.
Didache [Ext.], Epistle, Helps, Matthew (Evangelist, and Gospel of), Regeneration, Saint, Sanctification.

BATTEN, Rev. L. W., M.A., Ph.D., Rector of St. Mark's Church, New York; formerly Professor of Hebrew in the Protestant Episcopal Divinity School, Philadelphia.
Ezra, Ezra-Nehemiah (Books of), Nehemiah.

BAUDISSIN, Graf WILHELM VON, Ph.D., Professor of Theology in the University of Berlin.
Priests and Levites.

BEBB, Rev. LLEWELLYN J. M., M.A., Principal of St. David's College, Lampeter; formerly Fellow and Tutor of Brasenose College, Oxford.
Continental Versions [Ext.], John the Baptist, Luke (Evangelist, and Gospel of), Versions (general Article), Versions (Georgian, Gothic, Slavonic).

BEECHER, Rev. WILLIS JUDSON, D.D., Professor of Hebrew Language and Literature in Auburn Theological Seminary, New York.
Dagon, Drunkenness, Emerods, Giant, Nephilim, Philistines, Rephaim; and some shorter articles.

BEET, Rev. JOSEPH AGAR, D.D., Professor of Systematic Theology in the Richmond Theological College.
Christology.

BENECKE, P. V. M., M.A., Fellow and Tutor of Magdalen College, Oxford.
Claudius, Claudius Lysias, Magi, Star.

BENNETT, Rev. WILLIAM HENRY, M.A., Litt.D., D.D., Professor of Old Testament Exegesis in Hackney and New Colleges, London; sometime Fellow of St. John's College, Cambridge.
Adam, Beriah, Cruelty, Debt, Family, Gad (person and tribe), Heir, Hunting, Irrigation, Jashar (Book of), Mercy, Moab (Moabites), Molech (Moloch), Moreh, Moses, Nebo (towns), Palace, Poverty, Prison, Queen of Heaven, Rechab (Rechabites), Reuben, Shuthelah, Trade and Commerce, Tribe, Usury, Wages [Ext.], Wealth, Widow, Zabad.

BERNARD, Rev. EDWARD RUSSELL, M.A., Chancellor and Canon of Salisbury Cathedral; formerly Fellow of Magdalen College, Oxford.
Citizenship, Conversation, Prayer, Resurrection, Sin.

BERNARD, Very Rev. JOHN HENRY, D.D., Dean of St. Patrick's, Fellow of Trinity College, and Archbishop King's Lecturer in Divinity in the University of Dublin.
Apollos, Fall, Heredity, Jael, Miracle, Natural, Nature, Nicodemus, Philemon (person, and Epistle to), Sign, Thomas.

BETHUNE-BAKER, Rev. J. F., M.A., Fellow and Dean of Pembroke College, Cambridge.
Forgiveness, Hatred.

BLISS, FREDERICK J., B.A., Ph.D., formerly Director of the Palestine Exploration Fund in Jerusalem.
Gilgal, Jericho, Lachish, Lebanon, Pottery.

BLOMFIELD, Rear-Admiral, R.M., C.M.G., Controller-General of Ports and Lighthouses.
Ships and Boats [Ext.].

BOYD, Rev. ROBERT MASSON, M.A., Glenbervie, Kincardineshire.
Achan, Achsah, Adoni-zedek, Amasa, Arpachshad, Arphaxad, Baasha, Basemath; and a few shorter articles, chiefly on Proper Names.

BROWN, Rev. FRANCIS, M.A., D.D., D.Litt., LL.D., Professor of Hebrew and Cognate Languages in Union Theological Seminary, New York.
Chronicles (I. and II.).

BROWN, Rev. W. ADAMS, M.A., Ph.D., Professor of Systematic Theology in Union Theological Seminary, New York.
Cross, Excommunication, Millennium, Obedience (Obey), Parousia, Peace, Ransom, Redeemer (Redemption), Salvation (Saviour).

BRUCE, the late Rev. ALEXANDER BALMAIN, M.A., D.D., Professor of Apologetics and New Testament Exegesis in the Free Church College, Glasgow.
Hebrews (Epistle to).

BUDDE, KARL, Ph.D., D.D., Professor of Theology in the University of Marburg.
Poetry, Samson.

BUHL, FRANTS, Ph.D., Professor of Semitic Languages in the University of Copenhagen.
New Testament Times [Ext.], Roads and Travel (in OT) [Ext.].

BURKITT, F. CRAWFORD, M.A., Trinity College, Cambridge.
Arabic Versions, Moses (Assumption of).

BURNEY, Rev. CHARLES FOX, M.A., Lecturer in Hebrew, and Fellow of St. John Baptist's College, Oxford.
Arcturus, Eliakim, Hazael, Hilkiah, Kings (I. and II.); and a number of shorter articles, chiefly on Proper Names.

BURROWS, Rev. WINFRID O., M.A., Vicar of St. Augustine's, Birmingham; formerly Principal of Leeds Clergy School.
Appeal, Captain, Fear, Humility.

CAMERON, Rev. GEORGE G., M.A., D.D., Professor of Hebrew in the United Free Church College, Aberdeen.
Joel.

CANDLISH, the late Rev. JAMES S., M.A., D.D., Professor of Systematic Theology in the Free Church College, Glasgow.
Adoption, God (Children of).

CARSLAW, Rev. WILLIAM, M.A., M.D., of the Lebanon Schools, Beyrout, Syria.
Hammer, Hinge, Key (Lock), Mattock, Mill (Millstone), Mortar, Saw, Shaving, Smith, Tools, Wheel.

CHAPMAN, Rev. ARTHUR THOMAS, M.A., Fellow, Tutor, and Hebrew Lecturer, Emmanuel College, Cambridge.
Exodus and Journey to Canaan [jointly with J. Rendel Harris], Heshbon, Hormah, Jabbok, Jahaz, Jeshimon, Libnah, Medeba, Meribah, Midian (Midianites), Mixed Multitude, Nebo (Mt.), Paran, Pisgah, Rephidim, Shittim, Sin (Wilderness of), Succoth, Tabernacles (Feast of), Zin, Zoan; besides a number of shorter articles, especially on the 'stations' of the Israelites.

CHARLES, Rev. ROBERT HENRY, D.D., Professor of Biblical Greek in the University of Dublin.
Alpha and Omega, Apocalyptic Literature, Baruch (Apocalypse of), Enoch (Ethiopic), Enoch (Book of Secrets of), Eschatology of the Apocrypha and Apocalyptic Literature, Ethiopic Version, Gehenna, Michael, Noah (Book of), Testaments of the Twelve Patriarchs.

CHASE, Rev. FREDERIC HENRY, M.A., D.D., Vice-Chancellor of the University, Norrisian Professor of Divinity, and President of Queens' College, Cambridge.
Babylon (in NT), Enoch (in NT), John (father of Simon Peter), Jude (Epistle of), Mark (John), Peter (Simon), Peter (I. and II.).

CONDER, Col. CLAUDE REIGNIER, R.E., LL.D., M.R.A.S.
Bethesda, Bethlehem, Bethpeor, Gethsemane, Hermon, Jerusalem, Kiriath-jearim, Palestine; besides a great many shorter articles (geographical).

CONYBEARE, FRED. C., M.A., formerly Fellow of University College, Oxford.
Areopagus, Armenian Version of Old Test., Armenian Version of New Test., Athens, Epicureans, Essenes, Greece (Hellenism), Patmos.

COOKE, Rev. G. A., M.A., Dalkeith; formerly Fellow of Magdalen College, Oxford.
Bethel, Deborah, Gaal, Gideon, Haggai, Jephthah, Jeroboam, Jotham, Levi, Maon, Shibboleth, Sisera, Zebah and Zalmunna, Zebul.

COWAN, Rev. HENRY, M.A., D.D., Professor of Church History in the University of Aberdeen.
Esau, Gallio, Joseph of Arimathæa, Manaen, Matthias, Nathanael, Nero, Nicolaitans, Nicolas, Philip (in NT), Silas.

CRUM, W. E., M.A., of the Egyptian Exploration Fund.
Egypt, Hophra, Neco, Nile.

CURTIS, Rev. EDWARD LEWIS, Ph.D., D.D., Professor of Hebrew Language and Literature in the Divinity School of Yale University, New Haven.
Chronology of the Old Testament, Daniel (persons, and Book of), Genealogy, Old Testament.

DAVIDSON, the late Rev. ANDREW BRUCE, D.D., LL.D., Litt.D., Professor of Hebrew and Oriental Languages in the New College, Edinburgh.
Angel, Covenant, Eschatology of the Old Testament, God (in OT), Hosea, Immanuel, Jeremiah, Prophecy and Prophets.

DAVIES, Rev. T. WITTON, B.A., Ph.D., M.R.A.S., Professor of Hebrew and Old Testament Literature in the Baptist College, Bangor, and Lecturer in Semitic Languages in University College, Bangor.
Arch, Boaz (pillar), Pinnacle, Porch, Sea (Brazen), Temple, Treasury (of Temple), Veil.

DAVISON, Rev. W. T., M.A., D.D., Professor of Systematic Theology in the Handsworth Theological College, Birmingham.
Job, Psalms; and a few short articles.

DENNEY, Rev. JAMES, M.A., D.D., Professor of New Testament Language, Literature, and Theology in the United Free Church College, Glasgow.
Adam (in NT), Ascension, Brotherly Love, Chastening, Creed, Curse, Forbearance (Long-suffering), Ignorance, Knowledge, Law (in NT), Priest (in NT), Promise, Reprobate.

DICKSON, the late Rev. W. P., D.D., LL.D., Professor of Divinity in the University of Glasgow.
Adria, Apollonius, Berœa, Colony, Euraquilo, Macedonia, Neapolis, Rulers of the City, Sosthenes, Thessalonica.

DOBSCHÜTZ, E. VON, Lic. Theol., Professor of Theology in the University of Jena.
Nicodemus (Gospel of).

DODS, Rev. MARCUS, M.A., D.D., Professor of Exegetical Theology in the New College, Edinburgh.
Galatians (Epistle to).

DRIVER, Rev. SAMUEL ROLLES, D.D., Litt.D., Canon of Christ Church, and Regius Professor of Hebrew in the University of Oxford.
Abomination, Abomination of Desolation, Argob, Ashtaroth, Ashtoreth, Atonement (Day of) [jointly with H. A. White], Azazel, Bezer, Creeping Things, Dizahab, Ephod, Gilead (Mt.), Habakkuk, Hazerim, Hazeroth, Hill (Hill-country), Hivites, Host of Heaven, Ir-ha-heres, Ishmael (Hagar's son), Jacob, Jah, Jebus (Jebusi, Jebusite), Jehovah-jireh, Joseph (the patriarch), Koa, Laban, Law (in OT), Lord of Hosts, Lot, Machir, Mamre, Manasseh (tribe), Massah, Meni, Moriah, Most High, Nahor, Naioth, Nob, North Country, Offer (Offering, Oblation), Parbar, Pethor, Plain, Poor, Potiphar, Propitiation, Rachel, Ramah (Nos. 5. 6), Rebekah, Riblah, Sabbath, Sarah, Shiloh, Shur, Siddim (Vale of), Son of Man, Tongues (Confusion of), Vale (Valley), Zamzummim, Zoar, Zuzim.

DRUMMOND, Rev. JAMES, M.A., LL.D., Litt.D., Principal of Manchester College, Oxford.
Philo [Ext.].

EATON, Rev. DAVID, M.A., D.D., Glasgow.
Herodians, Lawyer, Nazirite, Pharisees, Sadducees, Scribes.

EDDY, Rev. WILLIAM K., of the American Mission, Sidon, Syria.
Fishing; and a few shorter articles, illustrating Eastern occupations and customs.

EWING, Rev. WILLIAM, M.A., Stirling; formerly of Tiberias, Palestine.
Acco, Aphek, Asher, Bethsaida, Cæsarea Philippi, Cana, Capernaum, Damascus, Esdraelon, Garden, Hair, Hauran, Hospitality (Host), Inn, Jacob's Well, Jezreel, Kishon, Ladder of Tyre, Linen, Magadan, Merom (Waters of), Meroz, Mines (Mining), Modin, Naphtali, Peræa, Pharpar, Pit, Street, Tent, Village, Zebulun.

FAIRWEATHER, Rev. W., M.A., Kirkcaldy.
Maccabees (persons, and Books of), Development of Doctrine in the Apocryphal Period [Ext.].

FARNELL, LEWIS RICHARD, M.A., Litt.D., Fellow and Senior Tutor of Exeter College, Oxford.
The Section on 'Worship of Apollo' in Professor Ramsay's article 'Religion of Greece and Asia Minor' [Ext.].

FERRIES, Rev. GEORGE, M.A., D.D., Cluny, Aberdeenshire.
Good (chief), Heathen, Judgment, Kindness, Oath, Perseverance, Power.

FINDLAY, Rev. GEORGE G., B.A., D.D., Professor of Biblical Literature, Headingley College, Leeds.
Paul the Apostle.

FLINT, Rev. ROBERT, D.D., LL.D., Emeritus Professor of Divinity in the University of Edinburgh.
Solomon.

GARVIE, Rev. ALFRED ERNEST, M.A., D.D., Professor of Ethics, Theism, and Comparative Religion in New and Hackney Colleges, London.
Belial, Godliness, Providence, Revelation [Ext.], Shame, Slander, Vanity, Way; and a few shorter articles.

GAYFORD, Rev. SYDNEY C., M.A., Vice-Principal of Cuddesdon College, Oxford.
Christian, Church.

GIBB, Rev. JOHN, M.A., D.D., Professor of New Testament Exegesis in Westminster College, Cambridge.
Alexandria, Philippians (Epistle to); and a few shorter articles.

GRAY, G. BUCHANAN, M.A., D.D., Professor of Hebrew in Mansfield College, Oxford.
Glory (in OT), Name, Names (Proper); besides a number of shorter articles, especially on Proper Names.

GRIEVE, Rev. ALEXANDER, M.A., Ph.D., Glasgow.
Cornelius, Gabriel, Kiss, Stephen.

GRIFFITH, FRANCIS LLEWELLYN, M.A., F.S.A., Superintendent of the Archæological Survey of the Egypt Exploration Fund.
Goshen, Hanes, Migdol, No (No-amon), On (Heliopolis), Pharaoh, Pi-beseth, Seveneh, Shishak, Sin (city), So (king), Tahpanhes, Tahpenes, Zaphenath-paneah.

GWATKIN, Rev. HENRY MELVILL, M.A., D.D., Fellow of Emmanuel College, and Dixie Professor of Ecclesiastical History in the University of Cambridge.
Apostle, Bishop, Church Government in the Apostolic Age, Deacon, Ordination, Persecution, Prophet (in NT), Roman, Roman Empire.

GWILLIAM, Rev. S. T., F.R.G.S., Hampton Poyle Rectory, Reading.
Apple of the Eye.

HARDING, Rev. EDWIN ELMER, M.A., Principal of the Theological College, Lichfield.
Feasts and Fasts.

HARFORD, Rev. George, M.A., Balliol College, Oxford; Vicar of Mossley Hill, Liverpool.
Exodus, Laver, Leviticus, Numbers, Sabbatical Year; and a few shorter articles, chiefly on Proper Names.

HARRIS, J. RENDEL, M.A., Litt.D., Principal and Lecturer, Settlement for Social and Religious Study, Woodbrooke; late Fellow and Librarian of Clare College, Cambridge.
Exodus and Journey to Canaan [jointly with A. T. Chapman], Sibylline Oracles [Ext.], Sinai.

HASTINGS, Rev. JAMES, M.A., D.D., St. Cyrus, Kincardineshire; Editor of this *Dictionary of the Bible* and of the *Expository Times*.
Nearly all the articles on words in the English Versions which demand attention.

HEADLAM, Rev. ARTHUR CAYLEY, M.A., D.D., Principal of King's College, London; formerly Fellow of All Souls College, Oxford.
Acts of the Apostles, Gnosticism, Herod, Jubilees (Book of), Julius, Paulus (Sergius), Prisca or Priscilla, Province, Rufus, Sceva, Simon Magus, Tertullus, Theatre, Theudas, Tryphæna, Unknown God.

HENDERSON, Rev. ARCHIBALD, M.A., D.D., Crieff.
Akeldama, Dalmanutha; and a few other short geographical articles.

HOLMES, E. M., F.L.S., Curator of the Museum of the Pharmaceutical Society of Great Britain.
Censer [jointly with Professor A. R. S. Kennedy].

HOMMEL, FRITZ, Ph.D., LL.D., Professor of Semitic Languages in the University of Munich.
Assyria, Babel (City and Tower of), Babylonia.

HULL, EDWARD, M.A., LL.D., F.R.S., F.R.G.S., late Director of the Geological Survey of Ireland, and Professor of Geology in the Royal College of Science, Dublin.
Arabah, Beersheba, Brass, Brimstone, Brook, Cave, Clay, Dead Sea, Dew, Earthquake, Fountain, Gaza, Geology of Palestine, Great Sea, Haven, Hor (Mt.), Kadesh (Kadesh-barnea), Lake, Meadow, Mount (Mountain), Rain, Red Sea, Salt, Salt (City of), Sea, Sela, Ships and Boats, Tadmor, Well, Whirlwind [jointly with G. M. Mackie], Ziz.

JAMES, MONTAGUE RHODES, M.A., Litt.D., Fellow and Tutor of King's College, and Director of the Fitzwilliam Museum, Cambridge.
Andrew, Asenath, Man of Sin and Antichrist, Psalms of Solomon.

JASTROW, MORRIS, junr., Ph.D., Professor of Semitic Languages in the University of Pennsylvania, Philadelphia.
Races of the Old Testament [Ext.], Religion of Babylonia and Assyria [Ext.].

JEVONS, FRANK BYRON, M.A., Litt.D., Principal of Bishop Hatfield's Hall, and Sub-Warden of the University, Durham.
Dionysus, Divination, Dreams.

JOHNS, Rev. C. H. W., M.A., Fellow of Queens' College, Cambridge.
Code of Ḫammurabi [Ext.], Kir (of Moab), Kir-hareseth (Kir-heres), Lud (Ludim), Naphtuhim.

KAUTZSCH, E., Ph.D., Professor of Theology in the University of Halle.
Religion of Israel [Ext.].

KENNEDY, Rev. ARCHIBALD R. S., M.A., D.D., Professor of Hebrew and Semitic Languages in the University of Edinburgh.
Altar, Ark of the Covenant, Bason, Bath, Breastplate of the High Priest, Calf (Golden), Censer [jointly with E. M. Holmes], Cup, Curtain, Cuttings in the Flesh, Education, Fringes, Goel (Avenger of Blood), Harrow, Hearth, Kidneys, Knop, Lamb, Liver, Money, Money-changers, Nahum, Nehushtan, Ouches, Phylacteries (Frontlets), Red Heifer, Sackcloth, Sanctuary, Shewbread, Snuffers, Tabernacle, Urim and Thummim, Weights and Measures.

KENNEDY, Rev. H. A. A., M.A., D.Sc., Callander.
Latin Versions (The Old), Talitha-cumi.

KENNEDY, Rev. JAMES HOUGHTON, M.A., D.D., Rector of Stillorgan, and Canon of Christ Church Cathedral, Dublin.
Kidron (The Brook).

KENYON, FREDERIC G., M.A., D.Litt., Ph.D., of the Department of Manuscripts in the British Museum; late Fellow of Magdalen College, Oxford.
Papyri [Ext.], Writing.

KILPATRICK, Rev. Thomas, M.A., D.D., Professor of Systematic Theology and Apologetics in Manitoba College, Winnipeg, Canada.
Conscience, Philosophy.

KÖNIG, EDUARD, Ph.D., D.D., Professor of Old Testament Exegesis in the University of Bonn.
Jonah, Judges (Book of), Number, Parable (in OT), Proverb, Samaritan Pentateuch [Ext.], Style of the Bible [Ext.], Symbols and Symbolical Actions [Ext.].

LAIDLAW, Rev. JOHN, M.A., D.D., Emeritus Professor of Systematic Theology in the New College, Edinburgh.
Body, Flesh, Heart, Image (the Divine), Mind, Psychology, Soul, Spirit.

LOCK, Rev. WALTER, M.A., D.D., Warden of Keble College, and Dean Ireland's Professor of New Testament Exegesis in the University of Oxford.
Ephesians (Epistle to), Hymn, Kenosis, Love-feasts, Onesimus, Pleroma, Praise (in NT), Thessalonians (I. and II.), Timothy (person, and Epistles to), Titus (person, and Epistle to).

LUPTON, Rev. J. H., D.D., formerly Surmaster of St. Paul's School, London.
Versions (English) [Ext.].

MACALISTER, ALEXANDER, LL.D., M.D., D.Sc., F.R.S., F.S.A., Fellow of St. John's College, and Professor of Anatomy in the University of Cambridge.
Anointing, Baldness, Basket, Bread, Circumcision, Food, Hail, Leprosy, Manna, Meal, Medicine, Oil, Ointment, Perfume, Pestilence, Pitcher, Plague, Plagues of Egypt, Poison, Pottage, Table, Vinegar.

MACKIE, Rev. GEORGE M., M.A., D.D., Chaplain to the Church of Scotland at Beyrout, Syria.
Age, Amulets, Bag, Bit, Bonnet, Child, City, Cloud, Dress, Ear-ring, Ebal, Embroidery, Engraving, Eye, Foot, Gerizim, Gestures, Joppa, Lod (Lydda), Neighbour, New (Newness), Ornament, Picture, Ring, Rod, Salutation, Shoe, Tyre, Whirlwind [jointly with Professor Hull], Wind, Wool, Zarephath, Zidon; and a number of shorter articles, illustrative chiefly of Eastern manners and customs.

M'CLYMONT, Rev. J. A., M.A., D.D., Aberdeen.
Caiaphas, Esther (person, and Book of), Hezekiah, Naaman, New Testament, Purim; and a few shorter articles.

MCCURDY, J. FREDERIC, Ph.D., LL.D., Professor of Oriental Languages in the University of Toronto.
Semites [Ext.].

MACMILLAN, the late Rev. HUGH, M.A., D.D., LL.D., Greenock.
Nain, Ptolemais.

MACPHERSON, the late Rev. JOHN, M.A., Edinburgh.
Amalek, Ammon, Dedan, Hagrites, Kittim, Restoration, Seleucidæ, Seleucus (I.–IV.), Zacharias, Zechariah (persons, except the prophet), Zephaniah (persons, except the prophet); and a number of shorter articles.

MARGOLIOUTH, Rev. D. S., M.A., D.Litt., Fellow of New College, and Laudian Professor of Arabic in the University of Oxford.
Achmetha, Arabia, Arabian, Cush, Dumah, Ethiopia, Ethiopian Eunuch, Ethiopian Woman, Ham, Japheth, Javan (Ezk 27[19]), Joktan, Kedar, Language of the Old Testament, Language of the Apocrypha, Letushim, Massa, Medan, Mene Mene Tekel Upharsin, Meshech, Nebaioth, Seba, Sephar, Sheba, Uzal.

MARSHALL, Rev. JOHN TURNER, M.A., Principal of the Baptist College, Manchester.
Asmodæus, Baruch (exclusive of Apocalypse of), Bel and the Dragon, Corban, Jannes and Jambres, Jeremy (Epistle of), Pre-existence of Souls, Raphael, Shekinah, Susanna, Three Children (Song of the), Tobit, Uriel, Zephaniah (Apocalypse of).

MARTIN, Rev. ALEX., M.A., D.D., Professor of Apologetic Theology in the New College, Edinburgh.
Inheritance.

MARTIN, Rev. GEORGE CURRIE, M.A., D.D., Professor of New Testament Theology and Patristics in the United College, Bradford.
Life and Death.

MASON, Rev. ARTHUR JAMES, M.A., D.D., Master of Pembroke College, Cambridge.
Power of the Keys.

MASSIE, JOHN, M.A., formerly Yates Professor of New Testament Exegesis in Mansfield College, Oxford.
Allegory, Amen, Bar-jesus, Blasphemy, Disciple, Dominion, Element, Evangelist, Fable, Glory (in NT), Gospel, Happiness, Living Creature, Manger, Minister (Ministry), Officer, Perdition, Purity, Raca, Sabbath Day's Journey, Sea of Glass, Seal, Testament.

MAYOR, JOSEPH BICKERSTETH, M.A., Litt.D., Emeritus Professor of Classics in King's College, London; Honorary Fellow of St. John's College, Cambridge.
Brethren of the Lord, James (persons, and Epistle of), Mary.

MENZIES, Rev. ALLAN, D.D., Professor of Church History in the University of St. Andrews.
Hebrews (Gospel of) [Ext.].

MERRILL, Rev. SELAH, D.D., LL.D., U.S. Consul at Jerusalem.
Galilee, Galilee (Sea of), Gennesaret (Land of), Gilead, Golan, Jabesh-gilead, Jazer, Kedesh-naphtali, Peniel, Ramoth-gilead, Refuge (Cities of) Tiberias.

MILLAR, Rev. JAMES, M.A., B.D., New Cumnock.
Alliance, Dancing, Ephraim, Music.

MILLIGAN, Rev. GEORGE, M.A., D.D., Caputh, Perthshire.
Aquila, Barnabas, Hymenæus, Onesiphorus, Versions (English), Zebedee.

MORGAN, Rev. WILLIAM, M.A., Tarbolton.
Repentance, Trance, Vision; and several shorter articles.

MOSS, Rev. R. WADDY, D.D., Professor of Classics in the Didsbury College, Manchester.
Alcimus, Alexander the Great, Alexander Balas, Antiochus (I.–VII.), Demetrius (I.–III.), Jeremiah (except the prophet), Micah (except the prophet), Onias, Ptolemy (I.–VI.).

MOULTON, Rev. JAMES H., M.A., D.Lit., Professor of New Testament Language and Literature, Didsbury College, Manchester; sometime Fellow of King's College, Cambridge.
Zoroastrianism.

MOULTON, Rev. WARREN JOSEPH, M.A., B.D., Ph.D., Professor in the Biblical and Semitic Department of Yale University, New Haven.
Passover.

MUIR, Rev. WILLIAM, M.A., B.D., B.L., Blairgowrie.
Dalmanutha, Publius; and a few other short articles.

MÜLLER, W. MAX, Ph.D., LL.D., Professor of Archæology in the University of Pennsylvania, Philadelphia.
Gozan, Halah, Hara, Kir, Lehabim, Lubim, Memphis, Pathros, Put, Tarshish.

MURRAY, Rev. J. O. F., M.A., D.D., Principal of St. Augustine's College, Canterbury; late Fellow of Emmanuel College, Cambridge.
A (the MS), א (the MS), Atonement, B (the MS), C (the MS), Colossians (Epistle to), D (the MS), Election, Textual Criticism of the New Testament [Ext.].

MYRES, JOHN L., M.A., F.S.A., Student and Tutor of Christ Church, Oxford.
Cyprus, Paphos.

NESTLE, EBERHARD, Ph.D., D.D., Professor at Maulbronn.
Gabbatha, Har-magedon, L (the MS), Nasbas, Septuagint, Sirach, Syriac Versions, Text of the New Testament, Thaddæus, Timæus.

NICOL, Rev. THOMAS, M.A., D.D., Professor of Divinity and Biblical Criticism in the University of Aberdeen.
Burial, Games, Island, Mourning, Riddle, Sepulchre, Snow, Yoke, Zerah.

NOWACK, W., Ph.D., Professor of Theology in the University of Strassburg.
Micah (prophet, and Book of), Proverbs (Book of), Zechariah (Book of).

ORR, Rev. JAMES, M.A., D.D., Professor of Systematic Theology and Apologetics in the United Free Church College, Glasgow.
Anger (Wrath) of God, Kingdom of God (*or* of Heaven), Love.

OTTLEY, Rev. ROBERT LAWRENCE, M.A., Canon of Christ Church and Regius Professor of Pastoral Theology in the University of Oxford.
Incarnation.

PATERSON, JOHN WAUGH, B.Sc., Ph.D., Lecturer on Agricultural Chemistry in the Glasgow and West of Scotland Technical College.
Agriculture.

PATERSON, Rev. WILLIAM P., M.A., D.D., Professor of Divinity in the University of Edinburgh.
Cain, Decalogue, Harlot, Idolatry, Jonathan, Lie (Lying), Marriage, Sacrifice.

PATRICK, Rev. JAMES, M.A., B.D., B.Sc., Burntisland; Examiner for Degrees in the University of St. Andrews.
Coal, Fire, Flint, Glass, Iron, Lightning, Lime, Marble, Micaiah, Mirror, Nephthar, Night, Rainbow, Seed, Soap, Spain, Steel, Stone, Thunder, Tile, Water.

PATRICK, Rev. JOHN, M.A., D.D., Professor of Biblical Criticism and Biblical Antiquities in the University of Edinburgh.
Libertines, Rest, Rome [jointly with F. Relton], Simplicity, Word.

PEAKE, ARTHUR S., M.A., Professor of Biblical Exegesis in the University of Manchester; sometime Fellow of Merton and Lecturer in Mansfield College, Oxford.
Ahaz, Baal, Benjamin, Dan, Dionysia, Ecclesiastes, First Fruits, Issachar, Josiah, Judah (person and tribe), Manasseh (except the tribe), Unclean (Uncleanness), Vow.

PETRIE, W. M. FLINDERS, D.C.L., Litt.D., LL.D., Ph.D., F.R.S., Professor of Egyptology in University College, London.
Architecture, Art, Balance, Bell, Brick, Gold, Goldsmith, Lead, Stones (Precious), Tin.

PHILPS, Rev. GEORGE M., M.A., B.D., Glasgow.
Earnest.

PINCHES, I. A., Sippar House, London.
Darius the Mede, Erech, Girgashite, Hamath, Haran.

PINCHES, THEOPHILUS GOLDRIDGE, LL.D., M.R.A.S., of the Egyptian and Assyrian Department in the British Museum.
Astronomy and Astrology, Carchemish, Gad (god), Mazzaroth, Moon, Nebushazban, Nimrod, Nisroch, Parthians, Rab-mag, Rab-saris, Rab-shakeh, Rehoboth-ir, Rephan, Resen, Rezeph, Sarsechim, Shinar, Sun, Tartak, Tartan, Uphaz, Ur of the Chaldees, Uz.

PLUMMER, Rev. ALFRED, M.A., D.D., formerly Master of University College, Durham.
Baptism, Baptism for the Dead, Barabbas, Beatitude, Bride, Bridegroom, Bridegroom's Friend, Cremation, Hypocrite, Judas Iscariot, Lazarus (of Bethany), Lazarus and Dives, Lord's Prayer, Lord's Supper, Parable (in NT), Quirinius (Census of), Sacraments, Transfiguration.

bosheth, Jareb, Jeduthun, Jeshua, Jeshurun, Jethro, Jeruel, Jezebel, Joab, Keturah, Korah (Dathan, Abiram), Lamech, Lamentations (Book of), Lawgiver, Leah, Leg, Lilith, Man-stealing, Mantle, Mephibosheth, Metheg-ammah, Mizar, Nadab, Obadiah (persons, and Book of), Obed-edom, Oholah and Oholibah, Open Place, Othniel, Parlour, People, Pi-hahiroth, Pillow, Pledge, Potter, Praise (in OT), Prince, Quarry, Rahab (symbolical term), Rehoboth, River, Rock, Sceptre, Sea-monster, Seth, Shallum, Shalman, Sharon, Sheshach, Sheshbazzar, Shovel, Simeon, Simon (except Simon Magus), Speckled Bird, Suph, Synagogue (the Great), Table (Tablet), Terebinth, Testimony, Thigh, Threshold, Throne, Thumb, Treasure, Tribute (in OT), Tryphon, Tubal, Tubal-cain, Wars of the LORD (Book of), Wilderness (Desert), Witness, Xerxes, Zaanannim, Zachariah, Zaphon, Zarethan, Zelzah, Zephaniah (Book of), Zerubbabel, Zorah; besides many shorter signed articles, and a very large proportion of the unsigned.

SIEGFRIED, the late C., Ph.D., Geh. Kirchenrath and Professor of Theology in the University of Jena.
Wisdom (general subject, and Book of).

SIMON, Rev. DAVID W., M.A., D.D., Principal of the United College, Bradford.
Justification.

SKINNER, Rev. JOHN, M.A., D.D., Professor of Hebrew and Old Testament Exegesis in Westminster College, Cambridge.
Ezekiel, Holiness (in OT), Righteousness (in OT).

SMITH, Rev. GEORGE ADAM, M.A., D.D., LL.D., Professor of Hebrew in the United Free Church College, Glasgow.
Antioch (in Syria), Arbela, Bashan, Carmel, Isaiah, Ituræa, Joshua (person, and Book of), Trachonitis.

STANTON, Rev. VINCENT HENRY, M.A., D.D., Fellow of Trinity College, and Ely Professor of Divinity in the University of Cambridge.
Almsgiving, Canon, Fasting, Gospels, Messiah, New Testament Canon, Theocracy [Ext.], Truth, Will, World.

STENNING, JOHN F., M.A., Fellow and Lecturer in Hebrew and Theology, Wadham College, Oxford.
Diatessaron [Ext.], Eli, En-rogel, Geba, Gibeah, Gibeon, Hiram, Mahanaim, Millo, Rabbah, Rehob, Samuel (prophet, and Books of), Shammah, Shobach, Shobi, Zobah, Zoheleth; besides a number of shorter articles, chiefly on Proper Names.

STEVENS, Rev. GEORGE B., Ph.D., D.D., Dwight Professor of Systematic Theology in Yale University.
Holiness (in NT), Righteousness (in NT).

STEVENSON, Rev. W. B., M.A., B.D., Professor of Hebrew and Old Testament Introduction in the Theological College, Bala.
Old Prophet (The), Ophrah, Pedaiah, Sharezer, Shavsha, Shebna, Shunem; and a number of shorter articles, especially on Proper Names.

STEWART, Rev. ALEX., M.A., D.D., Principal of St. Mary's College, and Professor of Systematic Theology in the University of St. Andrews.
Adoration, Bible, Doctrine, Envy, Foreknowledge, Grace, Mystery.

STOCK, ST. GEORGE, M.A., Pembroke College, Oxford.
Stoics.

STRACHAN, Rev. JAMES, M.A., Belgrave Presbyterian Church, London.
Elijah, Elisha, Gehazi, Scourge, Seraphim, Zeruiah, Ziba; and a few shorter articles.

STRACK, HERMANN L., Ph.D., D.D., Professor of Theology in the University of Berlin.
Text of the Old Testament.

STRONG, Very Rev. THOMAS B., M.A., D.D., Dean of Christ Church, Oxford.
Ethics, John the Apostle (Life and Theology of).

SUFFRIN, Rev. AARON EMMANUEL, M.A., Curate of Sparsholt with Kingstone Lisle, Berks.
Nod, Nodab.

SWETE, Rev. HENRY BARCLAY, M.A., D.D., Litt.D., Regius Professor of Divinity, Cambridge.
Holy Spirit, Laying on of Hands.

TASKER, Rev. JOHN G., Professor of Biblical Literature and Exegesis in Handsworth College, Birmingham.
Apocryphal Gospels [Ext.].

TAYLOR, the late Rev. ISAAC, M.A., Litt.D., LL.D., Rector of Settrington, and Canon of York.
Alphabet.

TAYLOR, Rev. JOHN, M.A., D.Lit., Vicar of Winchcombe.
Amos, Chiun, Mahlah, Mauzzim, Melzar, Menahem, Nethinim, Onyx, Orion, Patriarchs, Pit (metaphorical), Pleiades, Rezin, Rezon, Ruby, Sapphire, Sardius, Sardonyx, Selah, Signet, Solomon's Servants, Tekoa, Topaz, Zadok; and a number of shorter articles.

THACKERAY, HENRY ST. JOHN, M.A., Examiner in the Board of Education, formerly Divinity Lecturer in Selwyn College, Cambridge.
Esdras (I. and II.), Josephus [Ext.]; and a number of short articles (for the most part unsigned) on the Proper Names in 1 and 2 Esdras.

THATCHER, Rev. G. W., M.A., B.D., Hebrew Tutor and Lecturer on Old Testament History and Literature in Mansfield College, Oxford.
Colours, Government, Judge (Judging), Nazarene, Nazareth, Phœnicia.

THAYER, the late Rev. JOSEPH HENRY, M.A., D.D., Litt.D., Bussey Professor of New Testament Criticism and Interpretation in the Divinity School of Harvard University.
Abba, Hosanna, Language of the New Testament, Maranatha.

TURNER, CUTHBERT HAMILTON, M.A., Fellow of Magdalen College, Oxford.
Chronology of the New Testament, Greek Patristic Commentaries [Ext.], Philippi.

VOS, Rev. GEERHARDUS, D.D., Professor of Biblical Theology in Princeton Theological Seminary, New Jersey.
Fool.

VOTAW, CLYDE WEBER, M.A., Ph.D., Assistant Professor of New Testament Literature in the University of Chicago.
Sermon on the Mount [Ext.].

WALKER, Rev. GEORGE, M.A., B.D., Aberdeen.
Eunuch; and a few other short articles.

WALKER, Rev. THOMAS, M.A., Professor of Hebrew in the Assembly's College, Belfast.
Targum.

WARFIELD, Rev. B. B., M.A., D.D., LL.D., Professor of Theology in Princeton Seminary.
Doubt, Faith, Predestination.

# II. INDEX OF SUBJECTS

# III. INDEX OF SCRIPTURE TEXTS AND OTHER REFERENCES

## *A.* Old Testament.

1 SAMUEL—*continued.*





1 SAMUEL—*continued.*



2 SAMUEL.



2 SAMUEL—*continued.*

2 KINGS—*continued.*



1 CHRONICLES.



1 CHRONICLES—*continued.*



2 CHRONICLES.

ISAIAH—*continued.*



ISAIAH—*continued.*



JEREMIAH.



JEREMIAH—*continued.*

## *B.* NEW TESTAMENT.

ACTS—*continued.*



ROMANS.

### 1 Timothy.



### 2 Timothy.



### 2 Timothy—*continued.*



### Titus.



### Philemon.



### Hebrews.



### Hebrews—*continued.*



### James.

## 1 PETER.



## 2 PETER.



## 1 JOHN.



## 2 JOHN.



## 3 JOHN.



## JUDE.



## REVELATION.



REVELATION—*continued.*

## *C.* Apocrypha.

## *D.* APOCALYPTIC AND OTHER LITERATURE.

# IV. INDEX OF HEBREW AND GREEK TERMS

## *A.* Hebrew.

## *B.* Greek.

# V. INDEX OF ILLUSTRATIONS

---

# VI. LIST OF MAPS



Coll of Pac 31